D0151213

# WEST'S
# BUSINESS LAW

Text
Cases
Legal, Ethical, Regulatory
and International Environment

SIXTH EDITION

# WEST'S BUSINESS LAW

Text
Cases
Legal, Ethical, Regulatory,
and International Environment

**SIXTH EDITION**

**KENNETH W. CLARKSON**
Director, Law and Economics Center
University of Miami

**ROGER LeROY MILLER**
School of Law
University of Miami

**GAYLORD A. JENTZ**
Herbert D. Kelleher
Professor in Business Law
MSIS Department
University of Texas at Austin

**FRANK B. CROSS**
MSIS Department
and
Associate Director, Center for Legal and Regulatory Studies
University of Texas at Austin

**WEST PUBLISHING COMPANY**
Minneapolis/St. Paul   New York   Los Angeles   San Francisco

## WEST'S COMMITMENT TO THE ENVIRONMENT

In 1906, West Publishing Company began recycling materials left over from the production of books. This began a tradition of efficient and responsible use of resources. Today, up to 95 percent of our legal books and 70 percent of our college texts are printed on recycled, acid-free stock. West also recycles nearly 22 million pounds of scrap paper annually—the equivalent of 181,717 trees. Since the 1960s, West has devised ways to capture and recycle waste inks, solvents, oils, and vapors created in the printing process. We also recycle plastics of all kinds, wood, glass, corrugated cardboard, and batteries, and have eliminated the use of styrofoam book packaging. We at West are proud of the longevity and the scope of our commitment to our environment.

Production, Prepress, Printing and Binding by West Publishing Company.

Two study guides have been developed to assist you in mastering the concepts in the text. Both workbooks are available from your local bookstore under the following titles:

- *Study Guide to Accompany West's Business Law* prepared by Barbara Behr, James A Bernstein and Susan Bernstein.

- *Study Guide/Outline to Accompany West's Business Law* prepared by Roger LeRoy Miller and Eric Hollowell.

For more information on the study guides, please see the preface of this text where they are explained in greater detail.

————————

The Uniform Commercial Code is reproduced with permission of the American Law Institute and the National Conference of Commissioners on Uniform State Laws. Copyright © 1994.

*Composition:* Parkwood Composition
*Copy Editing:* Beverly Peavler and Mary Berry

British Library Cataloguing-in-Publication Data. A catalogue record for this book is available from the British Library.

COPYRIGHT ©1980, 1983,
1986, 1989, 1992          By WEST PUBLISHING COMPANY
COPYRIGHT ©1995          By WEST PUBLISHING COMPANY
                          610 Opperman Drive
                          P.O. Box 64526
                          St. Paul, MN 55164-0526

All rights reserved

Printed in the United States of America

02 01 00 99 98 97 96 95          8 7 6 5 4 3 2 1

**Library of Congress Cataloging-in-Publication Data**

West's business law : text, cases, legal, regulatory, and
    international environment / Kenneth W. Clarkson . . . [et al.].—6th ed.
        p.    cm.
    Includes index.
    ISBN 0-314-04220-2 (hard)
    1. Commercial law—United States—Cases.  2. Business law—United
States.  I. Clarkson, Kenneth W.
KF888.C55    1995
346.73'07—dc20
[347.3067]
                                                94–22665
                                                CIP

 TEXT IS PRINTED ON 10% POST CONSUMER RECYCLED PAPER

 PRINTED WITH SOY INK

# CONTENTS IN BRIEF

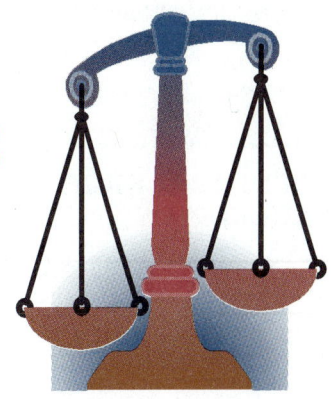

Preface    xx

## UNIT ONE

### THE LEGAL ENVIRONMENT OF BUSINESS    1

1   Introduction to Law and Legal
    Reasoning    2
2   Business Ethics    24
3   Courts and Alternative Dispute
    Resolution    41
4   Court Procedures    63
5   Constitutional Authority to Regulate
    Business    84
6   Torts and Strict Liability    105
7   Torts Related to Business    128
8   Intellectual Property and Computer
    Law    143
9   Criminal Law and Procedures    164
10  Comparative Law    189

FOCUS ON ETHICS: Ethics and Social
    Responsibility    208

## UNIT TWO

### CONTRACTS    213

11  Nature and Terminology    214
12  Agreement    230
13  Consideration    248
14  Capacity    261
15  Genuineness of Assent    275
16  Legality and the Statute of Frauds    291
17  Third Party Rights    313
18  Performance and Discharge    326

19  Breach of Contract and Remedies    340

FOCUS ON ETHICS: Contract Law and the
    Application of Ethics    357

## UNIT THREE

### DOMESTIC AND INTERNATIONAL SALES LAW    363

20  Introduction to Sales Contracts and Their
    Formation    364
21  Title, Risk, and Insurable Interest    395
22  Performance and Obligation    413
23  Remedies of the Buyer and Seller for
    Breach    429
24  Sales Warranties    444
25  Product Liability    463

FOCUS ON ETHICS: Domestic and
    International Sales Law    479

## UNIT FOUR

### COMMERCIAL PAPER AND BANKING    485

26  Basic Concepts, Negotiability, and
    Transferability    486
27  Holder in Due Course and Defenses    511
28  Liability and Discharge    529
29  Checks and the Banking System    547
30  Electronic Fund Transfers    569

FOCUS ON ETHICS: Commercial Paper and
    Banking    583

## Unit Five

### CREDITORS' RIGHTS AND BANKRUPTCY 587

31 Secured Transactions 588
32 Other Creditors' Remedies and Suretyship 615
33 Bankruptcy and Reorganization 631

FOCUS ON ETHICS: Creditors' Rights and Bankruptcy 653

## Unit Six

### AGENCY 657

34 Agency Formation and Duties 658
35 Liability to Third Parties and Termination 673

FOCUS ON ETHICS: Agency 697

## Unit Seven

### EMPLOYMENT AND LABOR RELATIONS 701

36 Employment and Labor Law 702
37 Employment Discrimination 721

FOCUS ON ETHICS: Employment and Labor Relations 741

## Unit Eight

### BUSINESS ORGANIZATIONS 747

38 Forms of Business Organizations and Private Franchises 748
39 Partnerships—Nature, Formation, and Operation 766
40 Partnerships—Termination and Limited Partnerships 786
41 Corporations—Formation and Financing 801
42 Corporations—Directors, Officers, and Shareholders 824
43 Corporations—Merger, Consolidation, and Termination 846

44 Corporations—Investor Protection 860

FOCUS ON ETHICS: Business Organizations 880

## Unit Nine

### GOVERNMENT REGULATION 885

45 Administrative Law 886
46 Consumer Law 906
47 Environmental Law 925
48 Antitrust Law 944

FOCUS ON ETHICS: Government Regulation 964

## Unit Ten

### PROPERTY 969

49 The Nature of Property and Personalty 970
50 Bailments 988
51 Real Property 1006
52 Landlord-Tenant Relationships 1026

FOCUS ON ETHICS: Property 1046

## Unit Eleven

### SPECIAL TOPICS 1051

53 Insurance 1052
54 Wills, Trusts, and Estates 1072
55 Liability of Accountants and Other Professionals 1095
56 The International Legal Environment 1113

FOCUS ON ETHICS: Special Topics 1130

### PERSONAL LAW HANDBOOK P-1

### APPENDICES
A How to Brief a Case and Selected Cases A-1
B The Constitution of the United States A-16
C The Uniform Commercial Code A-24
D The United Nations Convention on Contracts for the International Sale of Goods (Excerpts) A-179

E   The Uniform Partnership Act      A-183

F   The Revised Uniform Partnership Act
        (Excerpts)      A-191

G   The Revised Uniform Limited Partnership
        Act      A-195

H   The Revised Model Business Corporation
        Act      A-205

I   The Securities Act of 1933
        (Excerpts)      A-245

J   The Securities Exchange Act of 1934
        (Excerpts)      A-247

K   Title VII of the Civil Rights Act of 1964
        (Excerpts)      A-248

L   The Americans with Disabilities Act of 1990
        (Excerpts)      A-250

M   The Civil Rights Act of 1991
        (Excerpts)      A-252

N   The Administrative Procedure Act of 1946
        (Excerpts)      A-254

O   The General Agreement on Tariffs and Trade
        of 1994 (Excerpts)      A-256

P   The North American Free Trade Agreement of
        1993 (Excerpts)      A-259

Q   A Guide to Research in Business Law—
        Including Using the Internet      A-262

R   Spanish Equivalents for Important Legal
        Terms in English      A-268

Glossary      G-1

Table of Cases      TC-1

Index      I-1

# TABLE OF CONTENTS

Preface    xx

## UNIT ONE

### THE LEGAL ENVIRONMENT OF BUSINESS    1

**Chapter 1    Introduction to Law and Legal Reasoning    2**
What Is Law?    2
Schools of Jurisprudential Thought    3
The Common Law Tradition    4
Other Sources of American Law    7
Classifications of Law    9
Remedies at Law versus Remedies in Equity    10
How to Find Statutory and Administrative Law    13
How to Find Case Law    13
How to Analyze Case Law    16
Terms and Concepts to Review    22
Questions and Case Problems    23

**Chapter 2    Business Ethics    24**
The Nature of Business Ethics    24
Sources of Ethical Standards    26
Obstacles to Ethical Business Behavior    28
    CASE 2.1    *United States v. Schreier*    29
Ethical Issues in Business    30
    CASE 2.2    *United Automobile Workers v. Johnson Controls, Inc.*    31
    CASE 2.3    *Campbell v. Bic Corp.*    35
EMERGING TRENDS IN BUSINESS LAW: The Institutionalization of Ethics    36

The Ever-Changing Ethical Landscape    38
Terms and Concepts to Review    38
Questions and Case Problems    38

**Chapter 3    Courts and Alternative Dispute Resolution    41**
Jurisdiction    41
Venue    43
Standing    43
State Court Systems    44
The Federal Court System    46
Jurisdiction of the Federal Courts    47
How Cases Reach the Supreme Court    50
Judicial Review    51
Alternative Dispute Resolution    52
    CASE 3.1    *Shearson/American Express, Inc. v. McMahon*    54
    CASE 3.2    *Fletcher v. Kidder, Peabody & Co.*    56
    CASE 3.3    *State v. Council 4, AFSCME*    57
Terms and Concepts to Review    61
Questions and Case Problems    61

**Chapter 4    Court Procedures    63**
Procedural Rules    64
Consulting with an Attorney    65
Pretrial Procedures    66
    CASE 4.1    *Peoples Restaurant v. Sabo*    70
At the Trial    74
    CASE 4.2    *Ohio v. Lessin*    76
Posttrial Motions    77
    CASE 4.3    *Gainesville Radiology Group v. Hummel*    78
The Appeal    79

CASE 4.4   *Chabad House-Lubavitch of Palm Beach County, Inc. v. Banks    80*
Enforcing the Judgment    81
Terms and Concepts to Review    81
Questions and Case Problems    82

**Chapter 5   Constitutional Authority to Regulate Business    84**
The Constitutional Powers of Government    85
CASE 5.1   *Heart of Atlanta Motel v. United States    86*
CASE 5.2   *Chemical Waste Management, Inc. v. Hunt    87*
CASE 5.3   *Greenwood Trust Co. v. Commonwealth of Massachusetts    89*
Business and the Bill of Rights    91
CASE 5.4   *City of Cincinnati v. Discovery Network, Inc.    93*
CASE 5.5   *Austin v. Michigan Chamber of Commerce    95*
CASE 5.6   *Employment Division, Department of Human Resources of the State of Oregon v. Smith    97*
Other Constitutional Protections    99
CASE 5.7   *Robotham v. State    101*
Terms and Concepts to Review    102
Questions and Case Problems    102

**Chapter 6   Torts and Strict Liability    105**
The Basis of Tort Law    106
Intentional Torts against Persons    106
CASE 6.1   *Fudge v. Penthouse International, Ltd.    108*
CASE 6.2   *Staples v. Bangor Hydro-Electric Co.    110*
Intentional Torts against Property    112
Negligence    114
CASE 6.3   *Bray v. Kate    116*
CASE 6.4   *Palsgraf v. Long Island Railroad Co.    117*
CASE 6.5   *Schroyer v. McNeal    120*
Strict Liability    123
CASE 6.6   *Old Island Fumigation, Inc. v. Barbee    124*
Terms and Concepts to Review    125
Questions and Case Problems    125

**Chapter 7   Torts Related to Business    128**
Wrongful Interference    129
CASE 7.1   *Texaco, Inc. v. Pennzoil Co.    129*
Wrongful Entry into Business    132
CASE 7.2   *Tuttle v. Buck    132*
Appropriation    133
CASE 7.3   *White v. Samsung Electronics America, Inc.    133*
Defamation in the Business Context    134

CASE 7.4   *Cubby, Inc. v. Compuserve, Inc.    135*
Disparagement of Property    136
CASE 7.5   *Alpo Petfoods, Inc. v. Ralston Purina Co.    136*
CASE 7.6   *Dun & Bradstreet, Inc. v. Greenmoss Builders, Inc.    138*
RICO    139
CASE 7.7   *Quick v. Peoples Bank of Cullman County    140*
Terms and Concepts to Review    141
Questions and Case Problems    141

**Chapter 8   Intellectual Property and Computer Law    143**
Trademarks and Related Property    144
CASE 8.1   *The Coca-Cola Co. v. the Koke Co. of America    145*
CASE 8.2   *Vuitton et Fils, S.A. v. Crown Handbags    146*
Patents    148
Copyrights    149
CASE 8.3   *Bellsouth Advertising & Publishing Corp. v. Donnelley Information Publishing, Inc.    150*
CASE 8.4   *Sony Corp. v. Universal City Studios    151*
EMERGING TRENDS IN BUSINESS LAW: Copyright Infringement in the Electronic Age    154
Trade Secrets    156
CASE 8.5   *E. I. du Pont de Nemours & Co. v. Christopher    156*
Computer Crime    158
Privacy Rights and Computers    159
Terms and Concepts to Review    160
Questions and Case Problems    161

**Chapter 9   Criminal Law and Procedures    164**
The Nature of Criminal Law    164
Classification of Crimes    165
The Essentials of Criminal Liability    165
CASE 9.1   *Johnson v. State    166*
Crimes Affecting Business    167
CASE 9.2   *In the Matter of the Amended Administrative Penalty Order Issued to Paul S. Dougherty III    171*
EMERGING TRENDS IN BUSINESS LAW: Getting Tougher on Corporate Crime    174
Defenses to Criminal Liability    176
CASE 9.3   *Katco v. Briney    178*
CASE 9.4   *Jacobson v. United States    180*
Criminal Procedures    181
CASE 9.5   *Miranda v. Arizona    182*

Terms and Concepts to Review    186
Questions and Case Problems    187

**Chapter 10   Comparative Law    189**
Doing Business Abroad    189
Comparative Legal Systems    191
National Laws Compared    195
   CASE 10.1   *Re Product Liability (CASE VI ZR 103/89)    198*
   CASE 10.2   *Fong Fung-Ying and Attorney General    200*
   CASE 10.3   *Wineworths Group, Ltd. v. Comite Interprofessionel du Vin de Champagne    201*
The European Union    204
   CASE 10.4   *Alsatel-Société Alsacienne et Lorraine de Télécommunications et d'Electronique v. S.A. Novasam    204*
Expanding Overseas Business Opportunities    205
Terms and Concepts to Review    206
Questions and Case Problems    206

**FOCUS ON ETHICS: Ethics and Social Responsibility    208**

## UNIT TWO

## CONTRACTS    213

**Chapter 11   Nature and Terminology    214**
The Function of Contract Law    215
Definition of a Contract    216
   CASE 11.1   *Computer Network, Ltd. v. Purcell Tire & Rubber Co.    216*
Freedom of Contract and Freedom from Contract    217
   CASE 11.2   *Beasley v. Medin    218*
The Basic Requirements of a Contract    219
Types of Contracts    219
   CASE 11.3   *Weller v. Spring Creek Resort, Inc.    221*
   CASE 11.4   *Partipilo v. Hallman    222*
   CASE 11.5   *Industrial Lift Truck Service Corp. v. Mitsubishi International Corp.    224*
Interpretation of Contracts    226
Terms and Concepts to Review    227
Questions and Case Problems    228

**Chapter 12   Agreement    230**
Mutual Assent    230
Requirements of the Offer    231
   CASE 12.1   *Lefkowitz v. Great Minneapolis Surplus Store, Inc.    232*

   CASE 12.2   *Lawrence Paper Co. v. Rosen & Co.    234*
Termination of the Offer    236
Acceptance    239
   CASE 12.3   *Chosnyka v. Meyer    241*
   CASE 12.4   *Feist & Feist Realty Corp. v. Dockside Urban Renewal Corp.    242*
Terms and Concepts to Review    245
Questions and Case Problems    245

**Chapter 13   Consideration    248**
Legal Sufficiency of Consideration    249
   CASE 13.1   *Hamer v. Sidway    249*
Adequacy of Consideration    250
The Preexisting Duty Rule    251
Moral Obligations    252
Past Consideration    253
Problem Areas Concerning Consideration    253
   CASE 13.2   *Bennett v. Shinoda Floral, Inc.    254*
   CASE 13.3   *Hoffman v. Red Owl Stores, Inc.    256*
Terms and Concepts to Review    259
Questions and Case Problems    259

**Chapter 14   Capacity    261**
Minors    262
   CASE 14.1   *Dodson v. Shrader    263*
   CASE 14.2   *Haydocy Pontiac, Inc. v. Lee    265*
   CASE 14.3   *Bobby Floars Toyota, Inc. v. Smith    267*
Intoxicated Persons    269
   CASE 14.4   *Lucy v. Zehmer    270*
Mentally Incompetent Persons    271
Aliens    271
Terms and Concepts to Review    273
Questions and Case Problems    273

**Chapter 15   Genuineness of Assent    275**
Mistakes    275
   CASE 15.1   *Whitaker v. Associated Credit Services, Inc.    276*
   CASE 15.2   *Raffles v. Wichelhaus    278*
   CASE 15.3   *Wilkin v. 1st Source Bank    279*
Fraudulent Misrepresentation    280
   CASE 15.4   *Vokes v. Arthur Murray, Inc.    281*
Nonfraudulent Misrepresentation    284
Undue Influence    285
Duress    285
Adhesion Contracts and Unconscionability    286
   CASE 15.5   *Campbell Soup Co. v. Wentz    287*
Terms and Concepts to Review    288
Questions and Case Problems    289

**Chapter 16   Legality and the Statute of Frauds    291**
Legality    291
   CASE 16.1   *Metropolitan Creditors Service of Sacramento v. Sadri    292*
   CASE 16.2   *Baxter International, Inc. v. Morris    295*
   CASE 16.3   *Kotovsky v. Ski Liberty Operating Corp.    297*
Statute of Frauds    299
   CASE 16.4   *Wilson Floors Co. v. Sciota Park, Ltd.    304*
The Parol Evidence Rule    307
   CASE 16.5   *Chafetz v. United Parcel Service, Inc.    308*
Terms and Concepts to Review    310
Questions and Case Problems    310

**Chapter 17   Third Party Rights    313**
Assignments and Delegations    314
   CASE 17.1   *Smith v. Buege    316*
   CASE 17.2   *Rosenberg v. Son, Inc.    319*
Third Party Beneficiaries    320
   CASE 17.3   *Orr v. Orr    321*
Terms and Concepts to Review    324
Questions and Case Problems    324

**Chapter 18   Performance and Discharge    326**
Conditions    326
   CASE 18.1   *McLanahan v. Farmers Insurance Co. of Washington    327*
Discharge by Performance    329
   CASE 18.2   *Jacobs & Young, Inc. v. Kent    330*
Discharge by Agreement    333
Discharge by Operation of Law    334
   CASE 18.3   *Syrovy v. Alpine Resources, Inc.    335*
Terms and Concepts to Review    338
Questions and Case Problems    338

**Chapter 19   Breach of Contract and Remedies    340**
Damages    340
   CASE 19.1   *Hadley v. Baxendale    343*
   CASE 19.2   *Parker v. Twentieth Century-Fox Film Corp.    345*
   CASE 19.3   *Weber v. Rivera    347*
Rescission and Restitution    347
   CASE 19.4   *Racicky v. Simon    349*
Specific Performance    350
Reformation    351
Recovery Based on Quasi Contract    351
Election of Remedies    352

Waiver of Breach    353
Contract Provisions Limiting Remedies    353
Terms and Concepts to Review    354
Questions and Case Problems    354

**FOCUS ON ETHICS: Contract Law and the Application of Ethics    357**

**UNIT THREE**

**DOMESTIC AND INTERNATIONAL SALES LAW    363**

**Chapter 20   Introduction to Sales Contracts and Their Formation    364**
The Uniform Commercial Code    365
The Scope of Article 2—The Sale of Goods    365
   CASE 20.1   *Advent Systems, Ltd. v. Unisys Corp.    367*
   CASE 20.2   *Colorado-Kansas Grain Co. v. Reifschneider    368*
The Formation of a Sales Contract    369
   CASE 20.3   *Providence & Worcester Railroad Co. v. Sargent & Greenleaf, Inc.    372*
   CASE 20.4   *Dawkins and Co. v. L&L Planting Co.    378*
   CASE 20.5   *Heggblade-Marguleas-Tenneco, Inc. v. Sunshine Biscuit, Inc.    380*
   CASE 20.6   *Jones v. Star Credit Corp.    382*
Leases    383
Contracting for the International Sale of Goods    385
   CASE 20.7   *Filanto, S.P.A. v. Chilewich International Corp.    386*
Terms and Concepts to Review    392
Questions and Case Problems    392

**Chapter 21   Title, Risk, and Insurable Interest    395**
Identification    395
When Title Passes    396
Risk of Loss    397
   CASE 21.1   *Jason's Foods, Inc. v. Peter Eckrich & Sons, Inc.    401*
Insurable Interest    405
Bulk Transfers    405
Sales by Nonowners    406
   CASE 21.2   *Lane v. Honeycutt    406*
   CASE 21.3   *Executive Coach Builders v. Bush & Cook Leasing, Inc.    408*
Terms and Concepts to Review    410
Questions and Case Problems    410

## Chapter 22 Performance and Obligation 413

The Good Faith Requirement 413
Seller's Obligation—Tender of Delivery 414
   CASE 22.1 *BAII Banking Corp. v. UPG, Inc.* 418
Buyer's Obligations 419
   CASE 22.2 *Henery v. Robinson* 421
Anticipatory Repudiation 422
   CASE 22.3 *Neptune Research & Development, Inc. v. Teknics Industrial Systems, Inc.* 424
Dealing with International Contracts—The Letter of Credit 425
Terms and Concepts to Review 426
Questions and Case Problems 426

## Chapter 23 Remedies of the Buyer and Seller for Breach 429

Remedies of the Seller 429
   CASE 23.1 *Royal Jones & Associates, Inc. v. First Thermal Systems, Inc.* 432
Remedies of the Buyer 433
   CASE 23.2 *Tongish v. Thomas* 436
   CASE 23.3 *Hapag-Lloyd, A.G. v. Marine Indemnity Insurance Co. of America* 437
Contractual Provisions Affecting Remedies 439
Lemon Laws 440
Remedies for Breach of International Sales Contracts 440
Terms and Concepts to Review 442
Questions and Case Problems 442

## Chapter 24 Sales Warranties 444

Warranty of Title 445
Express Warranties 446
   CASE 24.1 *Sessa v. Riegle* 446
   CASE 24.2 *Martin Rispens & Son v. Hall Farms, Inc.* 448
Implied Warranties 450
   CASE 24.3 *Webster v. Blue Ship Tea Room, Inc.* 451
Overlapping Warranties 453
Warranties and Third Parties 453
   CASE 24.4 *Crews v. W. A. Brown & Son, Inc.* 454
Warranty Disclaimers 455
Statute of Limitations 456
   CASE 24.5 *Moore v. Puget Sound Plywood, Inc.* 457
Magnuson-Moss Warranty Act 459
Warranties under the CISG 459
Terms and Concepts to Review 460
Questions and Case Problems 460

## Chapter 25 Product Liability 463

Warranty Law 463
Negligence 464
   CASE 25.1 *MacPherson v. Buick Motor Co.* 464
Misrepresentation 466
Strict Liability 466
   CASE 25.2 *Greenman v. Yuba Power Products, Inc.* 467
   CASE 25.3 *Fitzpatrick v. Madonna* 469
EMERGING TRENDS IN BUSINESS LAW: Where Punitive Damages Are Headed 472
   CASE 25.4 *Embs v. Pepsi-Cola Bottling Co. of Lexington, Kentucky, Inc.* 474
Terms and Concepts to Review 477
Questions and Case Problems 477

FOCUS ON ETHICS: Domestic and International Sales Law 479

# UNIT FOUR

## COMMERCIAL PAPER AND BANKING 485

## Chapter 26 Basic Concepts, Negotiability, and Transferability 486

Article 3 and Its Revision 486
The Function of Instruments 487
Types of Negotiable Instruments 487
Requirements for Negotiability 491
   CASE 26.1 *Holly Hill Acres, Ltd. v. Charter Bank of Gainesville* 494
   CASE 26.2 *Goss v. Trinity Savings & Loan Association* 496
Factors Not Affecting Negotiability 500
Transfer by Assignment or Negotiation 500
Indorsements 502
   CASE 26.3 *General Motors Acceptance Corp. v. Abington Casualty Insurance Co.* 507
Terms and Concepts to Review 508
Questions and Case Problems 509

## Chapter 27 Holder in Due Course and Defenses 511

Holder versus Holder in Due Course 511
Requirements for HDC Status 512
   CASE 27.1 *In Re Joe Morgan, Inc.* 515
Holder through an HDC 518
Defenses 520
   CASE 27.2 *Federal Deposit Insurance Corp. v. Culver* 521

CASE 27.3   *New Jersey Mortgage & Investment Corp. v. Berenyi*   *524*
Federal Limitations on HDC Rights   526
Terms and Concepts to Review   527
Questions and Case Problems   527


**Chapter 28   Liability and Discharge   529**
Signature Liability   529
   CASE 28.1   *Husker News Co. v. South Ottumwa Savings Bank*   *535*
Warranty Liability   538
   CASE 28.2   *Steinroe Income Trust v. Continental Bank, N.A.*   *540*
Discharge   541
   CASE 28.3   *Firstier Bank, N.A. v. Triplett*   *542*
Terms and Concepts to Review   544
Questions and Case Problems   544


**Chapter 29   Checks and the Banking System   547**
Checks   547
The Bank-Customer Relationship   551
Honoring Checks   551
   CASE 29.1   *Kendall Yacht Corp. v. United California Bank*   *552*
   CASE 29.2   *First American Bank and Trust v. Rishoi*   *555*
   CASE 29.3   *Cumis Insurance Society, Inc. v. Girard Bank*   *556*
   CASE 29.4   *Knight Communications, Inc. v. Boatmen's National Bank of St. Louis*   *559*
Accepting Deposits   562
Terms and Concepts to Review   567
Questions and Case Problems   567


**Chapter 30   Electronic Fund Transfers   569**
Types of Electronic Transfers   570
Consumer Electronic Fund Transfers   571
   CASE 30.1   *Curde v. Tri-City Bank & Trust Co.*   *571*
   CASE 30.2   *Bisbey v. D.C. National Bank*   *575*
   CASE 30.3   *Kruser v. Bank of America NT & SA*   *577*
Commercial Fund Transfers   579
Terms and Concepts to Review   581
Questions and Case Problems   581


**FOCUS ON ETHICS: Commercial Paper and Banking   583**


## UNIT FIVE

## CREDITORS' RIGHTS AND BANKRUPTCY   587


**Chapter 31   Secured Transactions   588**
Article 9 of the UCC   589
Creating Security Interests   589
   CASE 31.1   *In re Ziluck*   *591*
Purchase-Money Security Interest   592
Perfecting a Security Interest   593
   CASE 31.2   *Banque Worms v. Davis Construction Co.*   *598*
The Scope of a Security Interest   599
Resolving Priority Disputes   601
   CASE 31.3   *Big Knob Volunteer Fire Co. v. Lowe & Moyer Garage, Inc.*   *603*
Rights and Duties of Debtor and Creditor   606
Default   607
   CASE 31.4   *In re Whatley*   *609*
Terms and Concepts to Review   612
Questions and Case Problems   612


**Chapter 32   Other Creditors' Remedies and Suretyship   615**
Laws Assisting Creditors   615
   CASE 32.1   *Midwest Environmental Consulting & Remediation Services, Inc. v. Peoples Bank of Bloomington*   *616*
   CASE 32.2   *Chrysler Credit Corp. v. Keeling*   *618*
   CASE 32.3   *Topjian Plumbing and Heating, Inc. v. Bruce Topjian, Inc.*   *620*
   CASE 32.4   *Johnson v. Town of Trail Creek*   *622*
Suretyship and Guaranty   624
   CASE 32.5   *General Motors Acceptance Corp. v. Daniels*   *626*
Protection for Debtors   628
Terms and Concepts to Review   629
Questions and Case Problems   629


**Chapter 33   Bankruptcy and Reorganization   631**
Types of Bankruptcy Relief   631
Liquidation Proceedings   632
   CASE 33.1   *In re Richmond*   *633*
   CASE 33.2   *In re Lazar*   *638*
   CASE 33.3   *In re Baker*   *641*
Reorganizations   643
   CASE 33.4   *In re Johns-Manville Corp.*   *643*

EMERGING TRENDS IN BUSINESS LAW:
Revising the Bankruptcy Code: Chapter 11 under
Attack     646
Additional Forms of Bankruptcy Relief     648
Terms and Concepts to Review     651
Questions and Case Problems     651

FOCUS ON ETHICS: Creditors' Rights and
Bankruptcy     653

## UNIT SIX

# AGENCY     657

Chapter 34     Agency Formation and
Duties     658
Agency Relationships     658
CASE 34.1     *Oestman v. National Farmers
Union Insurance Co.*     661
Formation of the Agency Relationship     662
CASE 34.2     *Wabash Independent Oil Co. v.
King & Wills Insurance Agency*     663
Duties of Agents and Principals     664
CASE 34.3     *Bias v. Advantage International,
Inc.*     666
Remedies and Rights of Agents and
Principals     668
CASE 34.4     *Ramsey v. Gordon*     669
Terms and Concepts to Review     671
Questions and Case Problems     671

Chapter 35     Liability to Third Parties and
Termination     673
Scope of Agent's Authority     673
CASE 35.1     *Bloom v. Weiser*     674
CASE 35.2     *Red River Commodities, Inc. v.
Eidsness*     677
CASE 35.3     *Theis v. duPont, Glore Forgan
Inc.*     679
Liability for Contracts     680
CASE 35.4     *Fairchild Publications Division of
Capital Cities Media, Inc. v. Rosston,
Kremer & Slawter, Inc.*     681
Liability for Agent's Torts     683
CASE 35.5     *Joel v. Morison*     686
Liability for Independent Contractor's Torts     688
CASE 35.6     *MBank of El Paso v.
Sanchez*     688
Liability for Agent's Crimes     690
Liability for Subagent's Acts     690
Termination of an Agency     690
Terms and Concepts to Review     694
Questions and Case Problems     694

FOCUS ON ETHICS: Agency     697

## UNIT SEVEN

# EMPLOYMENT AND LABOR RELATIONS     701

Chapter 36     Employment and Labor
Law     702
Employment at Will     703
Statutory Protection for Whistleblowers     704
CASE 36.1     *Texas Department of Human
Services v. Green*     705
Privacy Rights of Employees     706
CASE 36.2     *American Federation of
Government Employees, AFL-CIO, Local
2391 v. Martin*     707
CASE 36.3     *Soroka v. Dayton Hudson
Corp.*     709
Health and Safety Protection     711
CASE 36.4     *Marshall v. Barlow's, Inc.*     712
Retirement and Security Income     713
COBRA and Other Employment Laws     714
Unions and Collective Bargaining     716
CASE 36.5     *Kenrich Petrochemicals, Inc. v.
National Labor Relations Board*     717
Terms and Concepts to Review     719
Questions and Case Problems     719

Chapter 37     Employment
Discrimination     721
Title VII of the Civil Rights Act of 1964     722
CASE 37.1     *Harris v. Forklift Systems,
Inc.*     723
CASE 37.2     *Bradley v. Pizzaco of Nebraska,
Inc.*     726
Discrimination Based on Age     727
CASE 37.3     *Maresco v. Evans Chemetics,
Division of W. R. Grace & Co.*     728
Discrimination Based on Disability     729
CASE 37.4     *Harmer v. Virginia Electric and
Power Co.*     730
Affirmative Action     731
EMERGING TRENDS IN BUSINESS LAW:
Accommodating Workers with
Disabilities     732
Defenses to Claims of Employment
Discrimination     735
CASE 37.5     *McKennon v. Nashville Banner
Publishing Co.*     736
State Laws Prohibiting Employment
Discrimination     737
CASE 37.6     *Xieng v. Peoples National Bank of
Washington*     737
Terms and Concepts to Review     738
Questions and Case Problems     739

FOCUS ON ETHICS: Employment and Labor
Relations    741


UNIT EIGHT

## BUSINESS ORGANIZATIONS    747

### Chapter 38    Forms of Business Organizations and Private Franchises    748
Sole Proprietorships    748
Partnerships    749
Corporations    750
Major Business Forms Compared    750
Other Organizational Forms    753
   CASE 38.1    *Hill v. Zimmerer*    754
Private Franchises    756
EMERGING TRENDS IN BUSINESS LAW: Limited
   Liability Companies (LLCs)    758
   CASE 38.2    *Burger King Corp. v.*
    *Weaver*    760
   CASE 38.3    *Beck Oil Co. v. Texaco Refining &*
    *Marketing, Inc.*    762
Terms and Concepts to Review    763
Questions and Case Problems    764

### Chapter 39    Partnerships—Nature, Formation, and Operation    766
Definition of Partnership    767
The Nature of Partnerships    767
Partnership Formation    769
Partnership Operation    772
   CASE 39.1    *Lawson v. Rogers*    774
   CASE 39.2    *Cates v. International Telephone*
    *and Telegraph Corp.*    776
   CASE 39.3    *Estate of Witlin v. Rio Hondo*
    *Associates*    778
EMERGING TRENDS IN BUSINESS LAW: Limited
   Liability Partnerships (LLPs)    780
Terms and Concepts to Review    783
Questions and Case Problems    783

### Chapter 40    Partnerships—Termination and Limited Partnerships    786
Partnership Termination    786
   CASE 40.1    *Williams v. Burrus*    788
   CASE 40.2    *Felton Investment Group v.*
    *Taurman*    789
   CASE 40.3    *Lenkin v. Beckman*    791
   CASE 40.4    *Lowther v. Riggleman*    793
Limited Partnerships    794
   CASE 40.5    *Pitman v. Flanagan Lumber*
    *Co.*    797
Terms and Concepts to Review    798
Questions and Case Problems    799

### Chapter 41    Corporations—Formation and Financing    801
The Nature of the Corporation    802
Corporate Powers    803
Classification of Corporations    804
   CASE 41.1    *Loral Fairchild Corp. v. Victor*
    *Company of Japan, Ltd.*    805
   CASE 41.2    *Rosiny v. Schmidt*    808
   CASE 41.3    *Boyd, Payne, Gates & Farthing,*
    *P.C. v. Payne, Gates, Farthing & Radd,*
    *P.C.*    810
Corporate Formation    811
Improper Incorporation    815
Disregarding the Corporate Entity    816
   CASE 41.4    *Intertherm, Inc. v. Olympic Homes*
    *Systems, Inc.*    817
Corporate Financing    818
Terms and Concepts to Review    821
Questions and Case Problems    821

### Chapter 42    Corporations—Directors, Officers, and Shareholders    824
Role of Directors and Officers    824
   CASE 42.1    *Veco Corp. v. Babcock*    828
The Role of Shareholders    830
   CASE 42.2    *Amalgamated Clothing and Textile*
    *Workers Union v. Wal-Mart Stores,*
    *Inc.*    832
   CASE 42.3    *Compaq Computer Corp. v.*
    *Horton*    837
   CASE 42.4    *Glenn v. Hoteltron Systems,*
    *Inc.*    839
   CASE 42.5    *Pedro v. Pedro*    842
Terms and Concepts to Review    843
Questions and Case Problems    843

### Chapter 43    Corporations—Merger, Consolidation, and Termination    846
Merger and Consolidation    846
   CASE 43.1    *Spinnaker Software Corp. v.*
    *Nicholson*    849
   CASE 43.2    *Schwadel v. Uchitel*    850
Purchase of Assets    851
   CASE 43.3    *Davis v. Celotex Corp.*    852
Purchase of Stock    853
Termination    854
   CASE 43.4    *Balvik v. Sylvester*    856
Terms and Concepts to Review    858
Questions and Case Problems    858

### Chapter 44    Corporations—Investor Protection    860
The Securities and Exchange Commission    860
Securities Act of 1933    861
   CASE 44.1    *Escott v. BarChris Construction*
    *Corp.*    862

Securities Exchange Act of 1934    867
    CASE 44.2    *Diamond v. Oreamuno*    *869*
    CASE 44.3    *SEC v. Texas Gulf Sulphur*
        *Co.*    *870*
    CASE 44.4    *Dirks v. SEC*    *871*
    CASE 44.5    *United States v. Libera*    *874*
Regulation of Investment Companies    876
State Securities Laws    877
Terms and Concepts to Review    877
Questions and Case Problems    877

**FOCUS ON ETHICS: Business
    Organizations    880**

# UNIT NINE

## GOVERNMENT REGULATION    885

**Chapter 45    Administrative Law    886**
Agency Creation    886
Types of Agencies    887
Agency Powers and Functions    887
Rulemaking    890
Enforcement    893
    CASE 45.1    *Sandsend Financial Consultants,
        Ltd. v. Federal Home Loan Bank
        Board*    *894*
Adjudication    895
Judicial Review    896
    CASE 45.2    *American Dental Association v.
        Martin*    *897*
    CASE 45.3    *Marsh v. Oregon Natural Resources
        Council*    *899*
Other Controls over Administrative Agencies    900
Public Accountability    901
State Agencies    901
Terms and Concepts to Review    903
Questions and Case Problems    903

**Chapter 46    Consumer Law    906**
Advertising    906
    CASE 46.1    *In re Pfizer, Inc.*    *907*
    CASE 46.2    *Kraft, Inc. v. Federal Trade
        Commission*    *909*
Labeling and Packaging Laws    910
Sales    911
Credit Protection    913
    CASE 46.3    *Elsner v. Albrecht*    *914*
    CASE 46.4    *Stevenson v. TRW, Inc.*    *916*
    CASE 46.5    *Miller v. Payco–General American
        Credits, Inc.*    *918*
Consumer Health and Safety    920
State Consumer Protection Laws    921

    CASE 46.6    *Morris v. Mack's Used
        Cars*    *921*
Terms and Concepts to Review    923
Questions and Case Problems    923

**Chapter 47    Environmental Law    925**
Common Law Actions    925
    CASE 47.1    *Sterling v. Velsicol Chemical
        Corp.*    *926*
Federal Regulation    927
Air Pollution    929
Water Pollution    931
    CASE 47.2    *Hoffman Homes, Inc. v.
        Administrator, United States Environmental
        Protection Agency*    *931*
Noise Pollution    933
EMERGING TRENDS IN BUSINESS LAW:
    Expanding CERCLA Liability    934
Toxic Chemicals    936
    CASE 47.3    *Anspec Co. v. Johnson Controls,
        Inc.*    *937*
    CASE 47.4    *Phoenix v. Garbage Services
        Co.*    *939*
Radiation    940
State and Local Regulation    941
Terms and Concepts to Review    941
Questions and Case Problems    941

**Chapter 48    Antitrust Law    944**
The Sherman Antitrust Act    945
    CASE 48.1    *Summit Health, Ltd. v.
        Pinhas*    *946*
Section 1 of the Sherman Act    947
    CASE 48.2    *Wilk v. American Medical
        Association*    *949*
    CASE 48.3    *Continental T.V., Inc. v. GTE
        Sylvania, Inc.*    *951*
Section 2 of the Sherman Act    952
    CASE 48.4    *Spectrum Sports, Inc. v.
        McQuillan*    *954*
The Clayton Act    955
    CASE 48.5    *Federal Trade Commission v.
        Procter & Gamble Co.*    *958*
The Federal Trade Commission Act    959
Enforcement of Antitrust Laws    959
Exemptions from Antitrust Laws    960
Terms and Concepts to Review    961
Questions and Case Problems    961

**FOCUS ON ETHICS: Government
    Regulation    964**

# UNIT TEN

## PROPERTY    969

**Chapter 49   The Nature of Property and Personalty   970**
The Nature of Personal Property   971
The Nature of Real Property   971
   CASE 49.1   *City of North Charleston v. Claxton   973*
Property Ownership   973
   CASE 49.2   *Graves v. Kelley   974*
Acquiring Ownership of Personal Property   976
   CASE 49.3   *In re Estate of Piper   977*
   CASE 49.4   *Smart v. Woo   979*
Mislaid, Lost, or Abandoned Property   981
   CASE 49.5   *Michael v. First Chicago Corp.   983*
Terms and Concepts to Review   985
Questions and Case Problems   985

**Chapter 50   Bailments   988**
Elements of a Bailment   989
   CASE 50.1   *Liddle v. Salem School District No. 600   989*
Ordinary Bailments   991
Rights and Duties of the Bailee   991
   CASE 50.2   *Brockwell v. Lake Gaston Sales and Service   993*
   CASE 50.3   *Mueller v. Soffer   995*
Rights and Duties of the Bailor   996
   CASE 50.4   *Prince v. Atlanta Coca-Cola Bottling Co.   997*
Termination of Bailments   999
Special Features of Specific Bailments   999
   CASE 50.5   *Missouri Pacific Railway Co. v. Elmore & Stahl   1001*
Terms and Concepts to Review   1003
Questions and Case Problems   1003

**Chapter 51   Real Property   1006**
Ownership Interests in Real Property   1006
   CASE 51.1   *Wood v. Board of County Commissioners of Fremont County   1007*
Transfer of Ownership   1011
   CASE 51.2   *Klos v. Molenda   1016*
Limitations on the Rights of Property Owners   1017
   CASE 51.3   *Kirsch v. Prince George's County   1018*
   CASE 51.4   *Nollan v. California Coastal Commission   1020*
   CASE 51.5   *Breeling v. Churchill   1022*
Terms and Concepts to Review   1023
Questions and Case Problems   1023

**Chapter 52   Landlord-Tenant Relationships   1026**
Creation of the Landlord-Tenant Relationship: The Lease   1026

   CASE 52.1   *Walker v. Crigler   1027*
Parties' Rights and Duties   1028
   CASE 52.2   *SDR Associates v. ARG Enterprises, Inc.   1031*
   CASE 52.3   *Light v. Sheets   1032*
Liability for Injuries on the Premises   1035
   CASE 52.4   *Alabama Power Co. v. Dunaway   1037*
Transferring Rights to Leased Property   1039
EMERGING TRENDS IN BUSINESS LAW: The Limitation of Landlords' Liability for Crimes on Leased Premises   1040
Termination or Renewal of the Lease   1042
Terms and Concepts to Review   1043
Questions and Case Problems   1043

**FOCUS ON ETHICS: Property   1046**

**UNIT ELEVEN**

**SPECIAL TOPICS   1051**

**Chapter 53   Insurance   1052**
Insurance Concepts and Terminology   1052
   CASE 53.1   *Motorists Mutual Insurance Co. v. Richmond   1055*
The Insurance Contract   1056
   CASE 53.2   *Humana Health Care Plans v. Snyder-Gilbert   1057*
   CASE 53.3   *Clyburn v. Allstate Insurance Co.   1060*
   CASE 53.4   *New York Life Insurance Co. v. Johnson   1061*
   CASE 53.5   *Roberts v. National Liberty Group of Companies   1063*
Types of Insurance   1064
Terms and Concepts to Review   1069
Questions and Case Problems   1069

**Chapter 54   Wills, Trusts, and Estates   1072**
Wills   1072
   CASE 54.1   *Estate of Cancik   1073*
   CASE 54.2   *Bolan v. Bolan   1076*
   CASE 54.3   *In re Estate of Thompson   1080*
Intestacy Laws   1081
   CASE 54.4   *White v. Randolph   1083*
Trusts   1086
   CASE 54.5   *Zeigler v. Cardona   1087*
Estate Administration   1091
Estate Taxes   1092
Terms and Concepts to Review   1092
Questions and Case Problems   1092

**Chapter 55 Liability of Accountants and Other Professionals 1095**
Potential Common Law Liability to Clients 1095
   CASE 55.1 *Moores v. Greenberg 1097*
   CASE 55.2 *In re The Hawaii Corp. 1098*
Auditors' Liability to Third Parties 1100
   CASE 55.3 *First Florida Bank, N.A. v. Max Mitchell & Co. 1101*
Liability of Attorneys to Third Parties 1103
   CASE 55.4 *Central Bank Denver, N.A. v. Mehaffy, Rider, Windholz & Wilson 1103*
Potential Statutory Liability of Accountants 1104
   CASE 55.5 *Central Bank of Denver, N.A. v. First Interstate Bank of Denver, N.A. 1107*
Potential Criminal Liability 1108
Working Papers 1108
Confidentiality and Privilege 1110
Terms and Concepts to Review 1111
Questions and Case Problems 1111

**Chapter 56 The International Legal Environment 1113**
The Nature and Sources of International Law 1113
Legal Principles and Doctrines 1115
   CASE 56.1 *W. S. Kirkpatrick & Co. v. Environmental Tectonics Corp., International 1116*
   CASE 56.2 *Eckert International, Inc. v. Government of the Sovereign Democratic Republic of Fiji 1118*
Doing Business Internationally 1119
Regulation of Specific Business Activities 1120
U.S. Laws in a Global Context 1123
   CASE 56.3 *Matsushita Electric Industrial Co. v. Zenith Radio Corp. 1124*
   CASE 56.4 *Fortino v. Quasar Co., a Division of Matsushita Electric Corp. of America 1125*
Resolving International Contract Disputes 1126
Bribing Foreign Officials 1127
Terms and Concepts to Review 1128
Questions and Case Problems 1128

**FOCUS ON ETHICS: Special Topics 1130**

**PERSONAL LAW HANDBOOK P-1**

**APPENDICES**
A   How to Brief a Case and Selected Cases   A-1
B   The Constitution of the United States   A-16
C   The Uniform Commercial Code   A-24
D   The United Nations Convention on Contracts for the International Sale of Goods (Excerpts)   A-179
E   The Uniform Partnership Act   A-183
F   The Revised Uniform Partnership Act (Excerpts)   A-191
G   The Revised Uniform Limited Partnership Act   A-195
H   The Revised Model Business Corporation Act   A-205
I   The Securities Act of 1933 (Excerpts)   A-245
J   The Securities Exchange Act of 1934 (Excerpts)   A-247
K   Title VII of the Civil Rights Act of 1964 (Excerpts)   A-248
L   The Americans with Disabilities Act of 1990 (Excerpts)   A-250
M   The Civil Rights Act of 1991 (Excerpts)   A-252
N   The Administrative Procedure Act of 1946 (Excerpts)   A-254
O   The General Agreement on Tariffs and Trade of 1994 (Excerpts)   A-256
P   The North American Free Trade Agreement of 1993 (Excerpts)   A-259
Q   A Guide to Research in Business Law— Including Using the Internet   A-262
R   Spanish Equivalents for Important Legal Terms in English   A-268

**Glossary G-1**

**Table of Cases TC-1**

**Index I-1**

# CONCEPT SUMMARY LIST

**1.1** Sources of American Law    8

**3.1** Types of Courts    49

**3.2** Jurisdiction    51

**3.3** Alternative Dispute Resolution (ADR)    60

**4.1** Pretrial Procedures    73

**4.2** Trial Procedures    77

**4.3** Posttrial Options    81

**6.1** Intentional Torts    114

**6.2** Negligence    122

**9.1** Crimes Affecting Business    173

**11.1** Classification of Contracts    226

**12.1** Methods by Which an Offer Can Be Terminated    240

**12.2** Effective Time of Acceptance    245

**13.1** Consideration    258

**14.1** Legal Effect of Incapacity    272

**15.1** Genuineness of Assent    288

**16.1** Legality    300

**16.2** The Statute of Frauds    307

**18.1** Discharge of Contracts    337

**19.1** Damages    348

**19.2** Equitable Remedies    352

**20.1** The Formation of Sales Contracts    384

**21.1** Passage of Title and Risk of Loss Absent Agreement    403

**22.1** Performance and Obligation    423

**23.1** Remedies for Breach of Contract    441

**24.1** Warranties under the UCC    458

**25.1** Comparison of Negligence and Strict Liability in the Area of Product Liability    476

**26.1** Requirements for Negotiability    501

**26.2** Types of Indorsements and Their Consequences 506

**27.1** Rules and Requirements for HDC Status    519

**27.2** Valid Defenses against Holders of Negotiable Instruments    525

**28.1** Transfer Warranty Liability for Transferors Who Receive Consideration    539

**29.1** Honoring Checks    563

**30.1** Electronic Fund Transfer Act of 1978    580

**31.1** Priority of Claims to a Debtor's Collateral    605

**31.2** Remedies of the Secured Party upon the Debtor's Default    611

**32.1** Remedies Available to Creditors    624

**33.1** Forms of Bankruptcy Relief Compared    650

**34.1** Formation of Principal-Agent Relationship    665

**35.1** Requirements for Ratification    679

**35.2** Authority of Agent to Bind Principal and Third Party    684

**35.3** Termination of an Agency    693

**41.1** Classification of Corporations    812

**42.1** Role of Directors and Officers    831

**42.2** Role of Shareholders    841

**49.1** Personal Property    984

**50.1** Rights and Duties of the Bailee and Bailor    1003

**54.1** Wills    1082

**54.2** Trusts    1089

**55.1** Liability of Accountants and Other Professionals    1109

# PREFACE TO THE INSTRUCTOR

**B**usiness law and, more generally, the legal environment of business have universal applicability. A student entering virtually any field of business must have at least a passing understanding of business law in order to function in the real world. Additionally, students preparing for a career in accounting, government and political science, economics, and even medicine can fruitfully use much of the information they learn in a business law or legal environment course. Every individual throughout a lifetime can use knowledge of contracts, real property law, landlord-tenant relationships, and the like. Consequently, we have fashioned this text as a useful "tool for living" for all students (including those taking the CPA exam).

## KEY AREAS OF EMPHASIS

To make sure that instructors and students alike can rely on the coverage, accuracy, and applicability of *West's Business Law,* we emphasize the following throughout the text:

- **Comprehensiveness**—Virtually every important topic in business law and the legal environment is covered in this book. We have made the text extremely comprehensive to allow instructors complete flexibility in choosing those areas of the law and legal environment that they wish to emphasize.
- **Authoritativeness**—Virtually every aspect of business law and the legal environment has been fully researched for inclusion in this text. Instructors can rely on its accuracy and can find references to case and statutory law, as needed, for any needed external authority. Complete parallel citations are given throughout the text. An extensive set of appendices includes the latest revisions to the UCC and other uniform codes and statutes. Accuracy is the watchword of *West's Business Law.*
- **Ethics**—Because of the importance of ethics, there is an early chapter on the subject, with continuing references to ethics throughout.

- **International**—As the world gets smaller, a knowledge of the international and comparative aspects of the law must become part of any student's background. To this end, *West's Business Law* includes a full chapter on comparative law (Chapter 10); the integration of the United Nations Convention on Contracts for the International Sale of Goods (CISG) throughout all of the chapters on sales law; international considerations at the end of certain cases in every chapter; and finally, a full chapter on international law (Chapter 56).

- **AACSB Curriculum Requirements**—This text explicitly addresses the AACSB's broad array of curriculum requirements by focusing on the global, political, ethical, social, environmental, technological, and cultural-diversity context of many of the cases presented. Specifically, selected cases are preceded by a *Historical and [. . .] Setting,* which places the case in a particular political, ethical, social, or other setting. Additionally, *Company Profiles* precede many of the cases in this edition. Finally, the materials in Unit One (Chapters 1 through 10) explore virtually every facet of the AACSB's curriculum requirements. The AACSB's emphasis on the global and ethical context of the law is addressed throughout the rest of the text in the *International* and *Ethical Considerations* that follow many of the cases and in the *Focus on Ethics* section found at the end of each unit.

- **Personal Law**—To make sure that your students get a sense of how the law can affect them on a personal level, we have developed a *Personal Law Handbook,* which is placed just following Chapter 56.

- **Tomorrow's Technology Today**—Just as the content of *West's Business Law* is authoritative, accurate, and up to date, so is the manner in which the content can be accessed. Students have the option of using *The West's Business Law Interactive CD-ROM Edition* as either a substitute for the printed text or as a complement to the printed text.

## *WEST'S BUSINESS LAW* MAKES BUSINESS LAW COME ALIVE

Perhaps the most exciting aspect of the Sixth Edition of *West's Business Law* is that the subject matter comes alive for your students. Within the text itself, the *Company Profiles, Historical and Social [or other] Settings, International Considerations, Ethical Considerations,* and the extensive use of real-world examples throughout guarantee a high-interest level, even when the topic under study is somewhat technical.

But the text itself does not stand alone. Student users of this text have an impressive list of supplements that also make the study of business law and the legal environment come alive. These include audiocassettes of actual arguments before the Supreme Court; videos ranging from *Moot Court* (a simulated Supreme Court case in which Stephen Breyer—who has since been appointed to the Supreme Court bench—was one of the mock Supreme Court justices) to *The Making of a Case* (featuring Richard Dysart, star of "L.A. Law") to twenty original dramatizations (*The Drama of the Law, Parts I and II*) made specifically by the *West's Business Law* author/editorial team to demonstrate the application of legal principles to common business situations. Students can also further develop their understanding of the law and legal environment by using some of the extensive interactive software programs currently available with this text. And, of course, students with CD-ROM players can actively participate in the learning process by using *The West's Business Law Interactive CD-ROM Edition.*

## REVISED ARTICLES 3 AND 4 OF THE UNIFORM COMMERCIAL CODE

At the writing of this edition, thirty-six states have adopted revised Articles 3 and 4 of the UCC. In order to satisfy all users of *West's Business Law,* we have carefully revised all chapters covering Articles 3 and 4. Within the text itself, all explanations are now based on the revised articles. The formal UCC citations within the text and the exhibits, however, refer to the relevant sections in both the revised and the unrevised articles.

Additionally, whenever there has been a significant change from the unrevised articles, there is a full explanatory footnote.

Next, when appropriate, two answers are given to each of the end-of-chapter case problems involving the application of Articles 3 and 4 of the UCC: the answer under the unrevised UCC and the answer under the revised UCC.

Finally, the *Test Bank* includes a separate set of questions for both the unrevised Articles 3 and 4 and the revised Articles 3 and 4.

Hence, no matter what has happened in your state, you can use *West's Business Law,* Sixth Edition. Even if your state shifts from the unrevised to the revised articles during the life of this edition, you will have no problems with these materials.

# EMPHASIS ON THE INTERNATIONAL SIDE OF THE LAW

As already mentioned, because our world is becoming smaller, we feel that business law and legal environment students must have more than a passing understanding of the international aspects of the law. Consequently, we have emphasized international and comparative law throughout the book. Your students will find the following special features:

- **Comparative Law**—All of Chapter 10 at the end of Unit One is devoted to comparative law. There your students will see how different countries treat contract law, employment law, and the like.
- **International Considerations**—There are more than fifty *International Considerations* judiciously placed at the end of appropriate cases throughout the text. Your students can quickly learn how other countries treat similar legal issues.
- **International Sales Law**—At the end of virtually every chapter in Unit Three (Chapters 20 through 25), there is a section that shows how the CISG mirrors or is different from the UCC.
- **Special Appendices**—The appendices include excerpts from the CISG (in Appendix D), from the General Agreement on Tariffs and Trade (in Appendix O), and from the North American Free Trade Agreement (in Appendix P).

# OTHER SPECIAL FEATURES OF THIS TEXT

In addition to offering coverage of the topics of special concern discussed above, our text provides many other unique features for you and your students.

## CASES

Special attention is given in *West's Business Law* to case selection and presentation, as well as to simplifying the task of finding and analyzing case law.

**CLASSIC AND CONTEMPORARY CASES** You will find a diverse selection of case excerpts in the chapters. We have attempted to provide classic and landmark cases, as well as some of the most modern examples of business law. There are approximately one hundred cases in this edition from 1992, 1993, and 1994.

**AN EFFECTIVE STANDARD CASE FORMAT** Each case presented in *West's Business Law* follows a standard format:

- *Case Title and Full Case Citation*—The case title and full case citation (including all parallel citations) are presented in the margin at the beginning of each case.
- *Background and Facts*—This section contains a summary, in the authors' own words, of the events leading up to the lawsuit.
- *Case Excerpt*—Following the summary of the background of the case, an excerpt from the actual court opinion is presented—in a contrasting type size to differentiate it from the surrounding textual material. Whenever the court opinion contains a term or phrase that may be difficult for the student to understand, a brief explanation is provided in brackets. Important phrases and sentences are italicized, and a bracketed note clearly indicates that the emphasis was added by the authors, not by the court.
- *Decision and Remedy*—In this section, the authors summarize, in their own words, the outcome of the case.

**ADDITIONAL SECTIONS IN THE CASES** Many cases include additional sections, some of which have already been described.

- *Company Profiles*—Over fifty companies are profiled before appropriate cases. A history and makeup of the company involved in the particular case are presented to give your students the real-world background of these cases.
- *Historical and [. . .] Settings*—When appropriate, the global, political, ethical, social, envi-

ronmental, technological, or cultural-diversity context of a case is presented in one of these *Settings*.

- *Comments*—Sometimes a special clarifying comment is added by the authors following the *Decision and Remedy* section.
- *Ethical Considerations*—These sections discuss ethical aspects of the law or laws under consideration.
- *International Considerations*—As explained above, these sections let your students know how the particular issue at bar is treated in other countries.

## CASE CITATIONS FULLY EXPLAINED

In Chapter 1, we use a comprehensive format to explain case citations. In addition to our explanatory text, we offer an exhibit in four-color graphics to lead the student to a full understanding of how to read and understand case citations in this text and in other legal references.

## CASE BRIEFING ASSIGNMENTS

Some professors prefer to have their students brief a few cases. To make these assignments more manageable for both students and professors, we provide in Appendix A a short explanation of how to brief a case, followed by a briefed version of the sample court case presented in Chapter 1 and selected cases for briefing. Case briefing assignments, including questions that should be answered for each of the cases chosen for briefing, are found at the end of the problem sets in eleven of the chapters in the text (one for each unit). Sample answers to the questions listed in the case briefing assignments are found in the *Answers to Questions and Case Problems* manual.

## ETHICS

The teaching of ethics has become an integral part of every introductory course in business law and the legal and regulatory environment of business. To satisfy the increased interest in ethical questions, we have integrated ethics throughout this text.

### AN EARLY CHAPTER ON ETHICS

Chapter 2, which deals with business ethics, sets the tone for ethical analyses throughout the remainder of the text.

### CASE ETHICAL CONSIDERATIONS

As already mentioned, numerous cases contain special concluding sections called *Ethical Considerations*. These sections expose and define the ethical issues brought out in the cases.

### A QUESTION OF ETHICS

Twenty-seven chapters of *West's Business Law,* Sixth Edition, have a special problem at the end of the chapter entitled *A Question of Ethics*. A real-world case is summarized, and then questions about ethical aspects of the case are presented for the student to answer. Suggested answers to these questions are included in the *Answers to Questions and Case Problems*.

### FOCUS ON ETHICS

At the end of each of the eleven units in this text is a special section entitled *Focus on Ethics*. Each of these sections addresses ethical aspects of the law discussed in the preceding unit. While these sections are not intended to substitute for a course in ethics, each section is designed to elicit comments and discussion from the student-readers on ethical issues. For this reason, each *Focus* ends with a set of discussion questions. Brief suggested answers to these questions can be found in the *Instructor's Manual*. Further comments on, and references for, these sections are also given in the *Instructor's Manual*.

## EMERGING TRENDS IN BUSINESS LAW

A number of chapters include a feature entitled *Emerging Trends in Business Law*. These two-page spreads emphasize policy issues that have arisen, or will arise, with respect to certain aspects of business law and the legal environment. Each feature concludes with the following two sections:

- *Implications for the Businessperson*—A list of the steps that businesspersons might take to prevent legal problems in the particular area being discussed.
- *For Critical Analysis*—A set of two or three questions that require the student-reader to critically analyze aspects of the emerging trend discussed in the feature.

The following *Emerging Trends* are included in this edition:

- The Institutionalization of Ethics (Chapter 2)
- Copyright Infringement in the Electronic Age (Chapter 8)
- Getting Together on Corporate Crime (Chapter 9)

- Where Punitive Damages Are Headed (Chapter 25)
- Revising the Bankruptcy Code: Chapter 11 under Attack (Chapter 33)
- The Expanding Scope of the ADA (Chapter 37)
- Limited Liability Companies (LLCs) (Chapter 38)
- Limited Liability Partnerships (LLPs) (Chapter 39)
- Lender Liability under Superfund (Chapter 47)
- The Limitation of Landlords' Liability for Crimes on Leased Premises (Chapter 52)

## CONCEPT SUMMARIES

Whenever key areas of the law need additional emphasis, we provide a *Concept Summary*. These summaries have always been a popular pedagogical tool in this text. There are now fifty-one such summaries, including the following:

- Trial Procedures (Chapter 4)
- Intentional Torts (Chapter 6)
- The Statute of Frauds (Chapter 16)
- Warranties under the UCC (Chapter 24)
- Remedies of the Secured Party upon the Debtor's Default (Chapter 31)
- Forms of Bankruptcy Relief Compared (Chapter 33)
- Role of Directors and Officers (Chapter 42)
- Liability of Accountants and Other Professionals (Chapter 55)

## EXHIBITS

When appropriate, we have illustrated important aspects of the law in graphic or summary form in exhibits. In all, eighty-nine exhibits are now featured in *West's Business Law,* Sixth Edition, including the following:

- *Exhibit 1–6*—How to Read Case Citations
- *Exhibit 4–1*—Stages in a Typical Lawsuit
- *Exhibit 10–2*—The Legal Systems of Nations
- *Exhibit 19–1*—Measurement of Damages—Breach of Construction Contracts
- *Exhibit 22–1*—Letter-of-Credit Transaction
- *Exhibit 29–4*—A Stop-Payment Order
- *Exhibit 32–1*—Suretyship and Guaranty Parties
- *Exhibit 43–3*—The Terminology of Takeover Defenses
- *Exhibit 44–3*—Comparison of Coverage, Application, and Liabilities under Rule 10b-5 and Section 16(b)
- *Exhibit 50–1*—Degree of Care Required of a Bailee
- *Exhibit 56–1*—Multilateral International Organizations in Which the United States Participates

## VOCABULARY STRESSED

In addition to including bracketed explanations of difficult terms and phrases within the court opinions presented in the text, this edition has been completely edited to ensure that every important legal term used by the authors is fully defined when it is first introduced.

At the end of each chapter, all terms that were boldfaced within the chapter are listed in alphabetical order under the heading *Terms and Concepts to Review*. The page on which the term is defined is given after each term. Students can briefly examine the list to make sure that they understand all important terms introduced in the chapter and can immediately review terms that they do not completely understand by referring to the page number given. All boldfaced terms are listed and again defined in the *Glossary* at the end of the text.

## QUESTIONS AND CASE PROBLEMS

Every chapter of this text ends with ten to fourteen questions and case problems. The first three to six of these are hypothetical questions. The remainder are actual case problems, many of which (approximately 75 throughout the book) are from 1992, 1993, and 1994. Some of the case problems are based on cases that can be found in their entirety in the LEGAL CLERK Research Software System (discussed below). Complete answers are given in a separate manual for all questions and case problems in the text, including the ethical questions and case briefing assignments. The *Answers to Questions and Case Problems* is free to adopters and can be placed on reserve in the library, if desired.

## PERSONAL LAW HANDBOOK

At the end of the regular text, your students will find a *Personal Law Handbook*. We view this as a practical guide to applications of the law to personal, financial, business, and consumer problems. Under no circumstances do we ever suggest that the student act as his or her own attorney. Indeed, the maxim that "he who acts as his own attorney has a fool for a client'' is stressed at the beginning of the handbook. The topics we have chosen to cover in the *Personal Law Handbook* are as follows:

- Renting a Home
- Family Law (including divorce settlements)
- Consumer Law
- Employment Law
- Owning and Operating Motor Vehicles
- Criminal Law
- Jury Duty

## APPENDICES

Because the majority of students keep their business law texts as a reference source, we have included a full set of appendices. They are as follows:

A. How to Brief a Case and Selected Cases
B. The Constitution of the United States
C. The Uniform Commercial Code
D. The United Nations Convention on Contracts for the International Sale of Goods (Excerpts)
E. The Uniform Partnership Act
F. The Revised Uniform Partnership Act (Excerpts)
G. The Revised Uniform Limited Partnership Act
H. The Revised Model Business Corporation Act
I. The Securities Act of 1933 (Excerpts)
J. The Securities Exchange Act of 1934 (Excerpts)
K. Title VII of the Civil Rights Act of 1964 (Excerpts)
L. The Americans with Disabilities Act of 1990 (Excerpts)
M. The Civil Rights Act of 1991 (Excerpts)
N. The Administrative Procedure Act of 1946 (Excerpts)
O. The General Agreement on Tariffs and Trade (Excerpts)
P. The North American Free Trade Agreement (Excerpts)
Q. A Guide to Research in Business Law— Including Using the Internet
R. Spanish Equivalents for Important Legal Terms in English

## THE RESEARCH GUIDE AND USING THE INTERNET

You will notice that we have included an appendix (Appendix Q) on research in business law. For those instructors who require their students to do research projects covering legal topics, this is an invaluable research guide.

Additionally, your students can find out how to do legal research using the Internet. This unique section presents what is currently available on the ''electronic superhighway'' as it relates to business law and the legal environment.

## THE WEST'S BUSINESS LAW INTERACTIVE CD-ROM EDITION

Increasingly, students and instructors alike are turning to the CD-ROM format to obtain information and to study. Your students can now order *West's Business Law* in its entirety as an electronic book on CD-ROM. But simply transferring the text files of this book to a CD-ROM does little good. Consequently, West Publishing Company has developed the first truly interactive electronic book in business law and the legal environment. The CD-ROM Edition provides the following:

- Video segments
- Voice/audio accompaniment where appropriate (for example, excerpts of oral arguments before the United States Supreme Court)
- Biographical enrichment material of important jurists and others
- Advanced topics as enrichment materials
- The availability of full case presentation
- Appropriate statute excerpts corresponding to their particular references within the text
- A notebook function so that students can make their own notes
- A built-in study guide
- Selected supplements that accompany *West's Business Law*

The *West's Business Law Interactive CD-ROM Edition* can be ordered as a substitute for the printed text. Alternatively, your students can obtain it for an additional charge as a supplement to the printed text. In this way, they can use the printed text to read the assigned material and go to the electronic book to obtain enrichment videos, audios, and the like.

# THE COMPLETE SUPPLEMENTS PACKAGE

While some of the supplements, such as the CD-ROM Edition, have already been mentioned, there are numerous other supplements that make up the complete *West's Business Law,* Sixth Edition, teaching/learning package.

## A PLANNING GUIDE

To simplify and make more efficient the work effort of the instructor using *West's Business Law,* Sixth Edition, we offer a unique guide that integrates all of the printed, software, video, and CD-ROM supplements. For each chapter in *West's Business Law,* Sixth Edition, this guide will give you helpful suggestions on what parts of the complete learning/teaching package to use.

## PRINTED SUPPLEMENTS

The printed supplements for *West's Business Law,* including the *Planning Guide* just mentioned, have a single goal in mind: to make the task of teaching and the task of learning more enjoyable and more efficient.

**INSTRUCTOR'S MANUAL** The *Instructor's Manual* has been written by text author Roger LeRoy Miller, together with William Eric Hollowell. Having one of the authors of the main text write the *Instructor's Manual* has resulted in complete agreement between what is stressed in the text and what is fully outlined in the *Instructor's Manual.* A computerized version of the *Instructor's Manual* is also available. (This version is described below, under software supplements.)

**TWO STUDY GUIDES** You have the choice of ordering one of two available study guides. One guide has been prepared by Professor Barbara E. Behr, James A Bernstein and Susan Bernstein and is entitled *Study Guide to Accompany West's Business Law.*

The other study guide, entitled *Study Guide/ Outline to Accompany West's Business Law,* has been prepared by text author Roger LeRoy Miller, together with William Eric Hollowell.

A computerized version of the study guide by Barbara Behr—called *Microguide*—is also available. (See below, under software supplements.)

**CASE PRINTOUTS** Most of the cases in the main body of the text have been reprinted *in their entirety* and published in a separate booklet, called *Case Printouts to Accompany West's Business Law.* This supplement is available free to adopters.

**ANSWERS MANUAL** A complete answers manual entitled *Answers to Questions and Case Problems* is available to all adopters. Each answer is presented in a standard format:

- *Point of Law*—The point of law to which the problem relates is first stated in boldface.
- *Section Reference*—The point of law is followed by the chapter section number in which the point of law is discussed.
- *Answer*—The specific answer to the question or problem is then given.

*ADVANCED TOPICS AND CONTEMPORARY ISSUES: EXPANDED COVERAGE* A specially prepared paperback text entitled *Advanced Topics and Contemporary Issues: Expanded Coverage to Accompany West's Business Law* has been created by text author Frank B. Cross. The book is available to students at their instructor's option. *Advanced Topics* provides supplemental detailed coverage on the following topics:

1. Business Ethics
2. International Business Law
3. Individual Employee Rights
4. Employment Discrimination Law
5. Occupational Safety and Workers' Compensation
6. Accountant Liability
7. Securities Law and Regulation
8. Mergers and Acquisitions
9. Insurance Law
10. Real Estate Law
11. Banking Regulation and Liability
12. Unfair Competition
13. Advertising Law
14. Environmental Liability
15. Health Care Law
16. Sports and Entertainment Law
17. Hospitality Management Law
18. Communications Law
19. Government Contracts
20. Legal Representation of Business

Additionally, each chapter ends with *Ethical Perspectives* and *International Perspectives.*

**HANDBOOK OF SELECTED STATUTES** This supplement is available for your students upon request. It includes excerpts from the following statutes:

- The Federal Trade Commission Act of 1914
- The National Labor Relations Act of 1935
- The Occupational Safety and Health Act of 1970
- The Privacy Act of 1974
- The Foreign Corrupt Practices Act of 1977
- The Electronic Fund Transfer Act of 1978
- The Counterfeit Access Device and Computer Fraud and Abuse Act of 1984
- The Electronic Communications Privacy Act of 1986
- The False Claims Reform Act of 1986
- The Family and Medical Leave Act of 1993

**SELECTED STATE SUPPLEMENTS** For selected states, a state supplement will describe the differences between the law as presented in the text and the state's law for the court system, contracts, the UCC, and other selected topics.

**HANDBOOK ON CRITICAL THINKING AND WRITING** A booklet entitled *Introduction to Critical Thinking and Writing in Business Law* provides students with an overview of techniques used in critical thinking. It allows students to examine and analyze legal assumptions and arguments. Copies are available to adopters and their students when requested.

**A COMPREHENSIVE TEST BANK** To ensure consistency between the teaching materials and the text, one of the authors, Roger LeRoy Miller, has co-written the examination bank. There are approximately 2,500 multiple-choice questions with answers and over 1,600 true-false questions with answers. These questions are available in printed form or, as discussed below, on software.

**A SECOND TEST BANK** Approximately three thousand additional questions are available in this companion test bank.

**CITATION-AT-A-GLANCE** This handy reference card provides a quick, portable reference to the basic rules of citation for the most commonly cited legal sources, including judicial opinions, statutes, and second sources, such as legal encyclopedias and legal periodicals. *Citation-at-a-Glance* uses the rules set forth in *A Uniform System of Citation,* Fifteenth Edition (1991). Classroom quantities are available to qualified adopters.

**TRANSPARENCY ACETATES** The supplements package contains over one hundred transparency acetates for overhead projection in the classroom. Included in this package are actual key business forms.

**REGIONAL REPORTERS** West's regional reporters cover all state appellate court decisions. Qualified adopters may select from the following reporters: Pacific, North Western, South Western, North Eastern, Atlantic, South Eastern, and Southern.

## SOFTWARE SUPPLEMENTS

Software supplements represent an increasingly significant portion of the *West's Business Law* teaching/learning package.

**LEGAL CLERK SOFTWARE** The LEGAL CLERK Research Software System is an interactive software package that simultaneously introduces students to the rudiments of computer-aided legal research and reinforces the underlying concepts of business law and legal environment. LEGAL CLERK provides a valuable learning tool to help your school meet AACSB recommendations for using microcomputers in business law and legal environment courses.

LEGAL CLERK covers three subject areas of business law and the legal environment: (1) UCC/Article 2—Sales, (2) Government Regulation and the Legal Environment of Business, and (3) Contracts. Instructors may select one version or all three versions for their classes. Cases appearing in LEGAL CLERK are clearly identified in the text with a computer logo. The logos are color coded to help users easily identify which version of LEGAL CLERK contains specific cases.

 Uniform Commercial Code/Article 2—Sales (Version 1.0)

 Government Regulation and the Legal Environment of Business (Version 1.0)

 Contracts (Version 1.0)

Each version is accompanied by an *Instructor's Resource Guide* and, for student purchase, a *Student User's Guide.*

**LEGAL REVIEW SOFTWARE** This software allows students to review legal concepts found in all three LEGAL CLERK versions. A *LEGAL REVIEW Student User's Manual* can be purchased by the student.

**COMPUTERIZED INSTRUCTOR'S MANUAL** For those instructors who wish to modify the *Instructor's Manual* by adding their own notes or who wish to print out some of the class-enrichment materials, we provide a fully computerized version of the *Instructor's Manual.* You may order the manual in any popular format.

**COMPUTERIZED STUDY GUIDE—MICROGUIDE** The questions from the study guide by Barbara Behr, James A Bernstein and Susan Bernstein are on diskette, allowing your students to practice taking computerized tests. Multiple-choice, true-false, and fill-in test questions are included. *Microguide* runs on IBM PCs and compatible microcomputers or Macintosh microcomputers (with Hypercard).

**COMPUTERIZED TEST BANK—WESTEST** The test bank is available on the latest version of WESTEST, a highly acclaimed computerized testing system that is offered for IBM PCs and compatible microcomputers or the Macintosh family of microcomputers.

**INTERACTIVE SOFTWARE—CONTRACTS AND SALES** For those students who have their own computers or who have access to computers through friends, libraries, or learning labs, we have developed unique interactive programs for the teaching and learning of contracts and sales. These programs use HyperText and allow for flexibility in learning the subject matter based on each user's level of understanding.

**"YOU BE THE JUDGE"** This software provides case problems for ten topic areas. The user is supplied with the facts and is then asked how the issue should be decided. A word processor, integrated into the software, allows the user to key in his or her response and print it. A glossary of key legal terms is also included.

**CASE-PROBLEM CASES ON DISKETTE** Cases for virtually all of the case problems found at the ends of all chapters of the text are now available in ASCII format on diskette. These can be imported into any word-processing program, such as Microsoft Word or WordPerfect.

**WESTLAW** WESTLAW, the premiere computerized legal-research system, is renowned for its ability to help law professors, law students, attorneys, and paralegals do research in the law. Qualified adopters of *West's Business Law,* Sixth Edition, are allowed free hours of WESTLAW. Contact your West sales representative for more details.

**CD-ROM RESOURCES FOR BUSINESS LAW & LEGAL ENVIRONMENT** This CD-ROM was designed to aid in your class preparation by providing instant and easy access to important cases, key legislation and regulation, relevant articles of the UCC, and more. This CD-ROM includes West's PREMISE© software, which allows you to search for and retrieve specific items in a matter of seconds. Here are the six sections (or books) in this CD-ROM:

- Selected Congressional Acts
- Selected Constitutions
- Selected Federal Regulations
- Selected Uniform Laws
- Selected Business Law and Legal Environment Cases
- The North American Free Trade Agreement (NAFTA)

## WEST'S BUSINESS LAW AND LEGAL ENVIRONMENT AUDIOCASSETTE LIBRARY

Some instructors and students find it interesting to listen to actual arguments made before the Supreme Court. For adopters of *West's Business Law,* Sixth Edition, you can order any of the following audiocassettes.

- *Austin v. Michigan Chamber of Commerce*
- *Employment Division, Department of Human Resources of the State of Oregon v. Smith*
- *United Automobile Workers v. Johnson Controls, Inc.*

- *Shearson/American Express, Inc. v. McMahon*
- *Chemical Waste Management, Inc. v. Hunt*
- *Feist Publications, Inc. v. Rural Telephone Service Co.*
- *Sedima, S.P.R.L. v. Imrex Co.*
- *Jacobson v. United States*
- *Summit Health, Ltd. v. Pinhas*
- *Kirkpatrick & Co. v. Environmental Tectonics Corp., International*

## ENHANCING THE LEARNING EXPERIENCE: VIDEOCASSETTES AND VIDEODISC

No introductory business law and legal environment text would be complete without supplemental visual materials. We are proud to have an extensive videocassette library that is available for adopters of *West's Business Law,* Sixth Edition. These instructional videos can help you in the teaching of business law and legal environment in a variety of areas, including ethics and social responsibility, employment law, and others.

Technology has provided instructors of business law with yet another way to present teaching materials: the laser videodisc. We are making available for this edition a videodisc that provides you with the latest method for presenting important topics to your students.

For more information, contact your West sales representative.

# FOR USERS OF THE FIFTH EDITION

First of all, we want to thank you for helping make *West's Business Law* the best-selling business law text in America today. Second, we want to make you aware of the numerous additions and changes that we have made in this edition. The major additions and changes are summarized below.

## NEW CHAPTERS

To keep pace with current legal trends and developments, we have added new materials to each edition of *West's Business Law.* To ensure that the Sixth Edition is as up to date as possible, we have added the following new chapters on topics of special interest today:

- Chapter 4 (Court Procedures)
- Chapter 10 (Comparative Law)
- Chapter 37 (Employment Discrimination)

## CHAPTERS THAT HAVE BEEN EXTENSIVELY REVISED

- Chapter 5 (Constitutional Authority to Regulate Business) has been extensively revised. The chapter now offers more detail on the relative powers of the federal government and state governments under the commerce clause, and the concept of preemption is given fuller treatment. The section on freedom of speech has been expanded to present a fuller discussion of the types of speech that are (or are not) protected under the First Amendment. Additionally, the coverage of due process has been expanded, and a new section on the privileges and immunities clause has been added to the chapter.
- Chapter 6 (Torts and Strict Liability) now includes subsections on the duty of care as it applies to landowners and professionals, as well as an explanation of the general lack of a duty to rescue. The chapter also contains a new section on special negligence statutes and doctrines, including dram shop acts, Good Samaritan statutes, and negligence *per se.* The section on strict liability has also been expanded.
- Chapter 20 (Introduction to Sales Contracts and Their Formation) has been revised to include a discussion of international sales contracts and the United Nations Convention on Contracts for the International Sale of Goods (materials that were presented in Chapter 24 of the Fifth Edition).
- Chapter 26 (Basic Concepts, Negotiability, and Transferability), Chapter 27 (Holder in Due Course and Defenses), and Chapter 28 (Liability and Discharge) have all been rewritten as necessary to base the text of these chapters on the revised Articles 3 and 4 of the Uniform Commercial Code.
- Chapter 33 (Bankruptcy) now places less emphasis on Bankruptcy Code chapter numbers (such as Chapter 7) and more emphasis on the type of bankruptcy proceeding (such as liquidation proceedings). The concept of debtor in possession is treated more fully, and an

*Emerging Trends in Business Law* explores the controversy surrounding reorganizations under Chapter 11 of the Bankruptcy Code.

- Chapter 36 (Employment and Labor Relations) has been restructured consequent to the treatment of employment discrimination in the entirely new Chapter 37. Chapter 36 also presents new materials relating to statutory protection for whistleblowers, privacy rights, the requirements of the Occupational Safety and Health Administration, the Family and Medical Leave Act of 1993, the Immigration Act of 1990, and the Consolidated Omnibus Budget Reconciliation Act of 1985.
- Chapter 38 (Forms of Business Organizations and Private Franchises) contains a new discussion of the limited liability company, and an *Emerging Trends in Business Law* indicates the growing use of this new business organizational form within the business community. The discussion of joint ventures has been significantly expanded.
- Chapter 39 (Partnerships—Nature, Formation, and Operation) and Chapter 40 (Partnerships—Termination and Limited Partnerships) now include footnote references to the Revised Uniform Partnership Act (RUPA) whenever the RUPA significantly changes or modifies an aspect of the partnership law being discussed in the text.
- Chapter 41 (Corporations—Formation and Financing) now contains the section on corporate financing that was previously in the chapter on investor protection. The materials on corporate management have been moved to Chapter 42.
- Chapter 42 (Corporations—Directors, Officers, and Shareholders) offers a streamlined presentation, in one chapter, of the rights and duties of directors, officers, and shareholders, including the roles that directors and shareholders play in corporate management. The chapter also contains a new discussion of shareholder proposals in proxy materials.
- Chapter 44 (Corporations—Investor Protection) has been updated throughout, and the section on exemptions to registration requirements under the 1933 Securities Act has been rewritten to reflect current law.
- Chapter 45 (Administrative Law) has been reorganized and rewritten as necessary to make the discussion of administrative law and procedures more understandable for students. The chapter now contains an entirely new section on the delegation doctrine and a fuller description of the types of administrative agencies. Additionally, an exhibit has been added to clarify the structural relationship between administrative agencies and the federal government. The chapter also now contains a discussion of the relationship between federal and state administrative agencies.
- Chapter 46 (Consumer Law) has been significantly revised to reflect current consumer protection law. New sections have been added on fax and telephone advertising and the Consumer Leasing Act of 1988. The section on mail order merchandise now includes a discussion of the Federal Trade Commission's "Mail or Telephone Order Merchandise Rule" of 1993, and the section on credit protection has been modified as necessary to bring it up-to-date.
- Chapter 55 (Liability of Accountants and Other Professionals) contains a significantly revised section on the liability of accountants to third parties under the common law.
- Chapter 56 (The International Legal Environment) now contains sections on the regional trade agreements affecting the global business context, including the European Union, the General Agreement on Tariffs and Trade of 1994, and the North American Free Trade Agreement of 1993.

## NEW FEATURES AND SUPPLEMENTS

To make *West's Business Law* as useful as possible for both the instructor and the student, we have included in the Sixth Edition text a number of new pedagogical features and have expanded the supplements package. These new elements are listed below to give you a brief overview of what is new to this edition. Each item has been discussed in greater detail in the preceding sections of this preface.

**NEW *EMERGING TRENDS IN BUSINESS LAW*** There are now ten *Emerging Trends in Business Law,* all of which are either new or completely revised.

**NEW CONCEPT SUMMARIES** There are now fifty-one *Concept Summaries,* twelve more than in the last edition. Twenty-six of these concept summaries are new. The following *Concept Summaries* are new to the Sixth Edition:

- *Concept Summary 1.1*—Sources of American Law
- *Concept Summary 3.1*—Types of Courts
- *Concept Summary 3.2*—Jurisdiction
- *Concept Summary 3.3*—Alternative Dispute Resolution (ADR)
- *Concept Summary 4.1*—Pretrial Procedures
- *Concept Summary 4.2*—Trial Procedures
- *Concept Summary 4.3*—Posttrial Options
- *Concept Summary 6.1*—Intentional Torts
- *Concept Summary 6.2*—Negligence
- *Concept Summary 9.1*—Crimes Affecting Business
- *Concept Summary 13.1*—Consideration
- *Concept Summary 14.1*—Legal Effect of Incapacity
- *Concept Summary 15.1*—Genuineness of Assent
- *Concept Summary 16.1*—Legality
- *Concept Summary 16.2*—The Statute of Frauds
- *Concept Summary 19.1*—Damages
- *Concept Summary 19.2*—Equitable Remedies
- *Concept Summary 22.1*—Performance and Obligation
- *Concept Summary 29.1*—Honoring Checks
- *Concept Summary 31.2*—Remedies of the Secured Party upon the Debtor's Default
- *Concept Summary 41.1*—Classification of Corporations
- *Concept Summary 41.2*—Corporate Formation and Financing
- *Concept Summary 42.1*—Role of Directors and Officers
- *Concept Summary 42.2*—Role of Shareholders
- *Concept Summary 49.1*—Personal Property
- *Concept Summary 54.2*—Trusts

**NEW EXHIBITS**   There is a total of eighty-nine exhibits in this edition, seven more than in the last edition. Of those eighty-nine, seventeen are entirely new. They are the following:

- *Exhibit 9–2*—Major Steps in Processing a Criminal Case
- *Exhibit 10–1*—Excerpt from the Code Napoléon
- *Exhibit 10–2*—The Legal Systems of Nations

- *Exhibit 10–3*—Number of Lawyers per 100,000 Citizens
- *Exhibit 10–4*—Civil Code Tort Definitions
- *Exhibit 26–1*—Basic Types of Instruments
- *Exhibit 26–6*—Converting Order Paper to Bearer Paper and Vice Versa
- *Exhibit 27–1*—Taking for Value
- *Exhibit 32–1*—Suretyship and Guaranty Parties
- *Exhibit 34–1*—IRS Factors for Determining Employee Status
- *Exhibit 41–2*—Types of Corporate Bonds
- *Exhibit 44–2*—A Sample Restricted Stock Certificate
- *Exhibit 45–1*—Executive Departments and Important Subagencies
- *Exhibit 45–2*—Selected Independent Regulatory Agencies
- *Exhibit 45–3*—A Page from the *Federal Register*
- *Exhibit 45–4*—Sample Letter Requesting Information from an Executive Department or Agency
- *Exhibit 54–1*—A Sample Will

**NEW CASES**   Of the 242 in-text cases, 149 are new. Approximately 100 of the new cases are from 1992, 1993, and 1994.

**NEW CASE PROBLEMS**   Of the 362 case problems, 159 are new to this edition. Of the new case problems, 73 are from 1992, 1993, and 1994.

**NEW FEATURES IN SELECTED CASES**

- Company Profiles
- International Considerations

**PERSONAL LAW HANDBOOK**   This new handbook appears within the text, just following Chapter 56.

**NEW SUPPLEMENTS—PRINTED**

- *Instructor's Manual* to accompany *Drama of the Law, Part II*
- *Study Guide/Outline* to Accompany *West's Business Law,* Sixth Edition
- Handbook of Selected Statutes
- State supplements
- A second test bank
- Citation-at-a-Glance

## NEW SUPPLEMENTS—VIDEO

- *Drama of the Law, Part II* (ten videos)

## NEW SUPPLEMENTS—AUDIO

- West's Business Law and Legal Environment Audiocassette Library

## NEW SUPPLEMENTS—MULTIMEDIA

- *West's Business Law Interactive CD-ROM Edition*
- CD-ROM Resources for Business Law & Legal Environment
- Interactive Software—Sales

## NEW APPENDICES

**D.** The United Nations Convention on Contracts for the International Sale of Goods (Excerpts)
**F.** The Revised Uniform Partnership Act (Excerpts)
**G.** The Revised Uniform Limited Partnership Act
**I.** The Securities Act of 1933 (Excerpts)
**J.** The Securities Exchange Act of 1934 (Excerpts)
**K.** Title VII of the Civil Rights Act of 1964 (Excerpts)
**L.** The Americans with Disabilities Act of 1990 (Excerpts)
**M.** The Civil Rights Act of 1991 (Excerpts)
**N.** The Administrative Procedure Act of 1946 (Excerpts)
**O.** The General Agreement on Tariffs and Trade (Excerpts)
**P.** The North American Free Trade Agreement (Excerpts)

## USING THE INTERNET

- There is information on how to use the Internet to study law in Appendix Q (A Guide to Research in Business Law—Including Using the Internet).

# ACKNOWLEDGMENTS FOR THE FIRST EDITION

Barbara E. Behr, Bloomsburg University of Pennsylvania; Robert Staaf, Daniel E. Murray, Richard A. Hausler, Irwin Stotsky, and Patrick O. Gudridge, all of the University of Miami School of Law; William Auslen, San Francisco City College; Donald Cantwell, University of Texas at Arlington; Frank S. Forbes, University of Nebraska; Bob Garrett, American River College, California; Thomas Gossman, Western Michigan University; Charles Hartman, Wright State University, Ohio; Telford Hollman, University of Northern Iowa; Robert Jesperson, University of Houston; Susan Liebeler, Loyola University; Robert D. McNutt, California State University, Northridge; Roger E. Meiners, Texas A&M University; Gerald S. Meisel, Bergen Community College, New Jersey; James E. Moon, Meyer, Johnson & Moon, Minneapolis; Bob Morgan, Eastern Michigan University; Arthur Southwick, University of Michigan; Raymond Mason Taylor, North Carolina State; Edwin Tucker, University of Connecticut; Gary Victor, Eastern Michigan University; Gary Watson, California State University, Los Angeles.

# ACKNOWLEDGMENTS FOR THE SECOND EDITION

Robert Staaf, Kenneth Burns, Judith Kenney, and Thomas Crane, all of the University of Miami; Sylvia A. Spade, David A. Escamilla, Peyton J. Paxson, and JoAnn W. Hammer, all of the University of Texas at Austin.

Frank S. Forbes of the University of Nebraska, Omaha, Jeffrey E. Allen, University of Miami; Raymond August, Washington State University; David L. Baumer, North Carolina State; Barbara E. Behr, Bloomsburg University of Pennsylvania; William J. Burke, University of Lowell, Massachusetts; Robert Chatov, State University of New York, Buffalo; Larry R. Curtis, Iowa State University; Gerard Halpern, University of Arkansas; June A. Horrigan, California State University, Sacramento; John P. Huggard, North Carolina State University; John W. McGee, Southwest Texas State University; Robert D. McNutt, California State University, Northridge; Thomas E. Maher, California State University, Fullerton; David Minars, Brooklyn College, New York; Joan Ann Mrava, Los Angeles Southwest College; Thomas L. Palmer, Northern Arizona University; Charles M. Patten, University of Wisconsin, Oshkosh; Arthur D. Wolfe, Michigan State University.

# ACKNOWLEDGMENTS FOR THE THIRD EDITION

Kristi K. Brown, Kenneth S. Culotta, Michele A. Dunkerley, Karen Kay Matson, Melinda Ann Mora, Dana Blair Smith, Marshall Wilkerson, and Elizabeth Anene Wolfe, all of the University of Texas at Austin; Tamra Kempf, University of Miami; Janine S. Hiller, Virginia Polytechnic Institute and State College; Margaret Jones, Southwest Missouri State College; Carol D. Rasnic, Virginia Commonwealth University; Lorne H. Seidman, Larry Strate, and Cotton Meagher of the University of Nevada, Las Vegas; Thomas M. Apke, California State University, Fullerton; John J. Balek, Morton College, Illinois; Joseph E. Cantrell, DeAnza College, California; Frank S. Forbes, University of Nebraska, Omaha; Chris L. Hamilton, Golden West College, California; Woodrow J. Maxwell, Hudson Valley Community College, New York; David Minars, City University of New York, Brooklyn; Rick F. Orsinger, College of DuPage, Illinois; Ralph L. Quinones, University of Wisconsin, Oshkosh; Jesse C. Trentadue, University of North Dakota; Robert J. Walter, University of Texas, El Paso.

# ACKNOWLEDGMENTS FOR THE FOURTH EDITION

Lawrence J. Bradley, University of Notre Dame; Robert J. Enders, California State Polytechnic University, Pomona; Frank Forbes, University of Nebraska, Omaha; James M. Haine, University of Wisconsin, Stevens Point; Christopher L. Hamilton, Golden West College, California; Harry E. Hicks, Butler University, Indianapolis; Janine S. Hiller, Virginia Polytechnic Institute and State University; June A. Horrigan, California State University, Sacramento; Terry Hutchins, Pembroke State University, North Carolina; Carey Kirk, University of Northern Iowa; Nancy P. Klintworth, University of Central Florida; Kathleen M. Knutson, College of St. Catherine, St. Paul, Minnesota; Gene A. Marsh, University of Alabama; Richard Mills, Cypress College; Alan Moggio, Illinois Central College; Violet E. Molnar, Riverside City College; Dwight D. Murphey, Wichita State University; Paula C. Murray, University of Texas; John M. Norwood, University of Arkansas; Michael J. O'Hara, University of Nebraska, Omaha; Peyton Paxson, Mesa College; S. Alan Schlact, Kennesaw College, Georgia; Lorne H. Seidman, University of Nevada, Las Vegas; Bennett D. Shulman, Lansing Community College, Michigan; David Vyncke, Scott Community College.

# ACKNOWLEDGMENTS FOR THE FIFTH EDITION

Robert J. Cox, Salt Lake Community College; O. E. Elmore, Texas A & M University; Michael Engber, Ball State University; E. Clayton Hipp, Jr., Clemson University; Bryce J. Jones, Northeast Missouri State University; Gene A. Marsh, University of Alabama; George A. Nation, III, Lehigh University; Daniel J. O'Shea, Hillsborough Community College; Rudy Sandoval, University of Texas, San Antonio; Martha Sartoris, North Hennepin Community College; Barbara P. Scheller, Temple University; Brenda Steuer, North Harris Community College, South; H. Allan Tolbert, Central Texas College; John L. Weimer, Nicholls State University; Ronald C. Young, Kalamazoo Valley Community College.

# ACKNOWLEDGMENTS FOR THE SIXTH EDITION

The extensive revision of *West's Business Law* could never have been done without the extremely helpful criticisms, comments, and suggestions that we received from the following professors: Heidi Boerstler, University of Colorado at Denver; Richard Dalebout, Brigham Young University; Joe W. Fowler, Oklahoma State University; Anthony H. Holliday, Jr., Howard University; Sal Marchionna, Triton College; Bruce E. May, University of South Dakota; Caleb L. Nichols, Western Connecticut State University; Marvin H. Robertson, Harding University; William H. Walker, Indiana University–Purdue University, Fort Wayne; Daniel R. Wrentmore, Santa Barbara City College.

As in all past editions, we owe a debt of extreme gratitude to the numerous individuals who worked directly with us or at West Publishing Company. We especially wish to thank Lavina Leed Miller for her management of the entire project, as well as for the application of her superb editorial skills. William Eric Hollowell, who also coauthored the *Instructor's Manual, Study Guide/Outline,* and

*Test Bank,* helped with much of the research. Laura Anne Valade also provided expert research services. We were again fortunate enough to have the copy-editing services of Beverly Peavler and Mary Berry. Literally dozens of individuals helped proofread the galleys and pages of this edition over many, many months. They include Lavina Leed Miller, William Eric Hollowell, Marie-Christine Loiseau, Barbara Curtiss, and Suzie Franklin DeFazio.

Our appreciation also goes to Liz Morris for her tireless efforts in proofreading, editing, and assisting in the flow of manuscript, galleys, and page proofs through Austin, and to Sam Nielson for his meticulous proofreading.

We continue to be the fortunate recipients of an incredibly skilled and dedicated editorial, production, and printing and manufacturing team at West Publishing Company. In particular, we wish to thank our long-time editor, Clyde Perlee, Jr., for helping us devise a rigorous and complete revision program. Our long-time developmental editor, Jan Lamar, also helped us plan this project and made sure we addressed all reviewers' criticisms and suggestions. She additionally made sure that the preparation of supplements went smoothly and on time. For this edition, we must highlight our admiration to both Clyde and Jan as well as to C. J. Olsen and Stephanie Johnson, Steven Augustinack, Mark Jacobsen, Tom Hilt, and Kevin Stanek for making *West's Business Law Interactive CD-ROM Edition* become a reality. Also, we would like to thank the following content specialists: Kathleen M. Knutson (contributor), College of St. Catherine, and John T. Wendt (author of *Drama of the Law Interactivity*), University of St. Thomas. Their contributions are greatly appreciated.

Our faithful production manager and designer at West, John Orr, along with our production editor, Shannon Buckels, made sure that we came out with an error-free, visually appealing edition. We will always be in their debt.

All errors are solely our own responsibility. Through the years, we have enjoyed a continuing correspondence with many of you who have found points on which you wish to comment. We continue to welcome all comments and promise to respond promptly. By incorporating your ideas, we can continue to write a business law text that is best for you and best for your students.

# DEDICATION

RLM dedicates this edition to
Penny and Dick; may we forever
ski together.

Gaylord A. Jentz dedicates this
edition to his wife, JoAnn; his
children, Kathy, Gary, Lori,
and Rory; and his two
granddaughters, Erin Marie
and Megan Kathleen.

Frank B. Cross dedicates this
book to his parents and sisters.

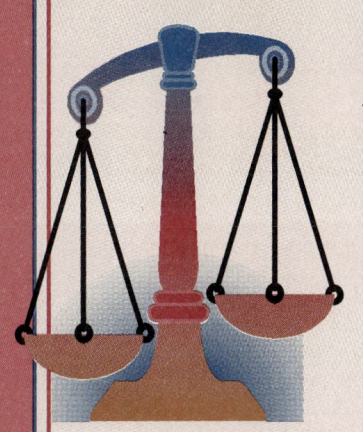

# UNIT ONE

# THE LEGAL ENVIRONMENT OF BUSINESS

### CONTENTS

1  Introduction to Law and Legal Reasoning

2  Business Ethics

3  Courts and Alternative Dispute Resolution

4  Court Procedures

5  Constitutional Authority to Regulate Business

6  Torts and Strict Liability

7  Torts Related to Business

8  Intellectual Property and Computer Law

9  Criminal Law and Procedures

10  Comparative Law

# CHAPTER 1

# INTRODUCTION TO LAW AND LEGAL REASONING

**C**ivilized societies require order and some degree of certainty. The law generates both. If any society is to survive, its citizens must be able to determine what is legally right and legally wrong. When citizens believe that a legal wrong has occurred, they must have some idea of how to seek redress. The law provides such a vehicle.

In this introductory chapter, we first look at the nature of law in general. We then look at the history and sources of American law. A major source of American law is the *common law* that originated in medieval England. Laws, or statutes, enacted by Congress and the state legislatures constitute another important source of American law, a source generally referred to as *statutory law*. Other sources of American law are *constitutional law,* which is based on the federal Constitution and state constitutions, and *administrative law*. The latter consists of the numerous regulations created by administrative agencies, such as the Food and Drug Administration. Each of these important sources of law will be described in the following pages. Next, because we cite statutes, regulations, and cases throughout this text, we explain how to read citations to these sources of law and how to find them. The chapter concludes with a section on how to read and understand case law, including an annotated sample court case.

## SECTION 1

## WHAT IS LAW?

There have been and will continue to be different definitions of law. The Greek philosopher Aristotle (384–322 B.C.) saw law as a ''pledge that citizens of a state will do justice to one another.'' Aristotle's mentor, Plato (427?–347 B.C.), believed law was a form of social control. The Roman philosopher

Cicero (106–43 B.C.) contended that law was the agreement of reason and nature, the distinction between the just and the unjust. The British jurist Sir William Blackstone (1723–1780) described law as "a rule of civil conduct prescribed by the supreme power in a state, commanding what is right, and prohibiting what is wrong." In America, the eminent jurist Oliver Wendell Holmes, Jr. (1841–1935), contended that law was a set of rules that allowed one to predict how a court would resolve a particular dispute—"the prophecies of what the courts will do in fact, and nothing more pretentious, are what I mean by the law."

Although these definitions vary in their particulars, they all are based on the following general observation concerning the nature of **law:** *Law consists of enforceable rules governing relationships among individuals and between individuals and their society.* In the study of law, often referred to as **jurisprudence,** this very broad statement concerning the nature of law is the point of departure for all legal scholars and philosophers.

## SECTION 2

# SCHOOLS OF JURISPRUDENTIAL THOUGHT

The court opinions in this book show that judges often refer to logic, history, custom, or philosophy in making their decisions. These opinions also show that when different judges—for example, a trial court judge and a reviewing court judge—examine the same case, they sometimes arrive at different conclusions about how the law should apply. That judges differ in their philosophies of law should come as no surprise to Americans. We frequently read or hear about the differences in legal philosophy among United States Supreme Court justices, especially when a significant, controversial case—such as one relating to abortion—is before the court. Part of the study of law, or jurisprudence, is discovering how different approaches to law affect judicial decision making.

Legal philosophers and scholars frequently disagree on what the proper function of law should be, and their disagreements have produced different schools of jurisprudence, or philosophies of

law. The three most influential schools of legal thought are described below.

## THE NATURAL LAW SCHOOL

The oldest and one of the most significant schools of jurisprudence is the **natural law school.** Those who adhere to the natural law school of thought believe that government and the legal system should reflect universal moral and ethical principles that are inherent in human nature.

Because natural law is universal, it takes on a higher order than positive, or conventional, law. It was this higher law to which the international tribunal of judges at Nuremburg appealed when convicting Nazi war criminals of "crimes against humanity" at the end of World War II. Although these "criminals" may not have disobeyed any positive law of their country and may have been merely following their government's (Hitler's) orders, they were deemed by the tribunal to have violated a natural law that transcends any particular country's written laws. The natural law school of thought encourages individuals to disobey conventional, or written, laws if those individuals believe that the laws are in conflict with natural law. Protesters who felt that America's involvement in Vietnam (1964–1973) was wrong, for example, used natural law as their reason to violate written laws when they protested America's war effort.

In essence, the natural law tradition presupposes that the legitimacy of conventional, or positive, law derives from natural law. Whenever it conflicts with natural law, conventional law loses its legitimacy and should be changed.

## THE POSITIVIST SCHOOL

At the other end of the spectrum is the **positivist school.** Those who adhere to this school believe that there can be no higher law than a nation's **positive law**—law created by a particular society at a particular point in time. In the positivist view, the significance and finality of positive law are greater than in the natural law tradition. Essentially, from the positivist perspective, the law is the law and must be obeyed. Whether a particular law is bad or good is irrelevant. The merits or demerits of a given law can be discussed, and laws can be changed—in an orderly manner through a legitimate lawmaking process—but as long as a law exists, it must be obeyed.

## THE LEGAL REALISTS

**Legal realism,** which was a popular school of legal thought in the 1920s and 1930s, left a strong imprint on American jurisprudence. The legal realists were in a sense rebels. They were rebelling against some of the common assumptions of the legal theorists and jurists of their time. One such assumption was that judges, at least ideally, apply the law impartially, logically, and uniformly. The legal realists believed that each judge is influenced by the beliefs and attitudes unique to his or her personality. They also believed that each case is attended by a unique set of circumstances. That is, no two cases, no matter how similar, are ever exactly the same. Therefore, judges should tailor their decisions to take account of the specific circumstances of each case, rather than rely on some abstract rule that may not relate to those particular circumstances. Judges should also consider extra-legal sources, such as economic and sociological data, in making decisions, to the extent that such sources illuminate the circumstances and issues involved in specific cases.

SECTION 3

# THE COMMON LAW TRADITION

Because of our colonial heritage, much of American law is based on the English legal system. A knowledge of this tradition is necessary to an understanding of the nature of our legal system today.

In 1066, the Normans conquered England, and William the Conqueror and his successors began the process of unifying the country under their rule. One of the means they used to this end was the establishment of the king's courts, or *curia regis.* Before the Norman Conquest, disputes had been settled according to the local legal customs and traditions in various regions of the country. The king's courts sought to establish a uniform set of customs for the country as a whole. What evolved in these courts was the beginning of the **common law**—a body of general rules that prescribed social conduct and applied throughout the entire English realm.

Courts developed the common law rules from the principles behind judges' decisions in actual legal controversies. Judges attempted to be consistent. When possible, they based their decisions on the principles suggested by earlier cases. They sought to decide similar cases in a similar way and considered new cases with care, because they knew that their decisions would make new law. Each interpretation became part of the law on the subject and served as a legal **precedent.** Later cases that involved similar legal principles or facts could be decided with reference to that precedent.

In the early years of the common law, there was no single place or publication in which legal opinions could be found. In the late thirteenth and early fourteenth centuries, however, decisions of each year were gathered together and recorded in *Year Books.* These books were informal, containing only notes of cases made by lawyers and law students, and were not organized according to different legal topics. They were not official reports, did not include every case, and sometimes did not report cases until two or three years after the cases had been decided. Nevertheless, the *Year Books* were useful to lawyers and judges. In the sixteenth century, the *Year Books* were discontinued, and other reports of cases became available.

## THE DOCTRINE OF *STARE DECISIS*

The practice of deciding new cases with reference to former decisions, or precedents, eventually became a cornerstone of the English and American judicial systems. It forms a doctrine called *stare decisis*[1] ("to stand on decided cases"). Under this doctrine, judges are obligated to follow the precedents established within their jurisdictions.

The doctrine of *stare decisis* performs many useful functions. It helps the courts to be more efficient, because if other courts have carefully reasoned through a similar case, their legal reasoning and opinions can serve as guides. *Stare decisis* also makes the law more stable and predictable, because if the law on a given subject is well settled, someone bringing a case to court can usually rely on the court to make a decision based on what the law has been.

**DEPARTURES FROM PRECEDENT**  Sometimes a court will depart from the rule of precedent if it decides that the precedent should no longer be followed. If a court decides that a ruling precedent is

---

1.  Pronounced *ster*-ay dih-*si*-ses.

simply incorrect or that technological or social changes have rendered the precedent inapplicable, the court might rule contrary to the precedent. Cases that overturn precedent often receive a great deal of publicity. For example, in *Brown v. Board of Education of Topeka*,[2] the United States Supreme Court expressly overturned precedent when it concluded that separate educational facilities for whites and African Americans, which had been upheld as constitutional in numerous previous cases,[3] were inherently unequal. The Supreme Court's departure from precedent in *Brown* received a tremendous amount of publicity as people began to realize the ramifications of this change in the law.

**CASES OF FIRST IMPRESSION** Sometimes, there is no precedent on which to base a decision. For example, in 1986, a New Jersey court had to decide whether a surrogate-parenting contract should be enforced against the wishes of the surrogate parent (the natural mother).[4] This was the first such case to reach the courts, and there was no precedent in any jurisdiction to which the court could look for guidance. When deciding such a case, called a "case of first impression," or when there are conflicting precedents, courts may consider a number of factors, including legal principles and policies underlying previous court decisions or existing statutes, fairness, social values and customs, public policy, and data and concepts drawn from the social sciences. Which of these sources is chosen or receives the greatest emphasis will depend on the nature of the case being considered and the particular judge hearing the case.

Although judges always strive to be free of subjectivity and personal bias in deciding cases, each judge has his or her own unique personality, set of values or philosophical leanings, and intellectual attributes—all of which necessarily frame the decision-making process.

## STARE DECISIS AND LEGAL REASONING

**Legal reasoning** is the reasoning process by which a judge harmonizes his or her decision with de-

cisions that have been made before. When applying, overruling, or creating precedent, judges use many forms of reasoning, including those discussed below.

**DEDUCTIVE REASONING** Generally, a judge writes an opinion in the form of **syllogism**—that is, deductive reasoning consisting of a major premise, a minor premise, and a conclusion. For example, a **plaintiff** (a suing party) comes before the court alleging *assault* (a wrongful and intentional action, or tort, in which one person makes another fearful of immediate physical harm). The plaintiff claims that the **defendant** (the party who is sued) threatened her while she was sleeping. Although the plaintiff was unaware that she was being threatened, her roommate heard the defendant make the threat. The judge might point out that "under the common law, an individual must be *aware* of a threat of danger for the threat to constitute civil assault" (major premise); "the plaintiff in this case was unaware of the threat at the time it occurred" (minor premise); and "therefore, the circumstances do not amount to a civil assault" (conclusion).

**LOGICAL THOUGHT PROGRESSION** A second important form of commonly employed legal reasoning might be thought of as a knotted rope, with each knot tying together separate pieces of rope to form a tight length. As a whole, the rope represents a logical progression of thought connecting various points, and the last knot represents the conclusion. For example, imagine that a tenant in an apartment building sues the landlord for damages for an injury resulting from an allegedly dimly lit stairway. The landlord, who was on the premises the evening the injury occurred, testifies that none of the other nine tenants who used the stairway that night complained about the lights. The court concludes that the tenant is not entitled to compensation on the basis of the stairway's lighting. The "pieces of rope" might be stated as follows:

1. The landlord testifies that none of the tenants who used the stairs on the evening in question complained about the lights.
2. The fact that none of the tenants complained is the same as if they had said the lighting was sufficient.
3. That there were no complaints does *not* prove that the lighting was sufficient but proves that

---

2. 347 U.S. 483, 74 S.Ct. 686, 98 L.Ed. 873 (1954). (Legal citations are explained later in this chapter.)
3. See *Plessy v. Ferguson*, 163 U.S. 537, 16 S.Ct. 1138, 41 L.Ed. 256 (1896).
4. *In re Baby M*, 217 N.J. Super. 313, 525 A.2d 1128 (1987).

the landlord had no reason to believe that it was not.

4. The landlord's belief was reasonable, because no one complained.

5. Therefore, the landlord acted reasonably and was not negligent in respect to the lighting in the stairway.

**REASONING BY ANALOGY** In the majority of cases, the two methods of legal reasoning discussed above predominate, and it is unnecessary to look beyond them. There is, however, another important form of reasoning that judges use in deciding cases: reasoning by *analogy.*

To reason by **analogy** is to compare the facts in the case at hand to the facts in other cases and, to the extent the *patterns* are similar, apply the same rule to the case at hand. To the extent the facts are unique, or "distinguishable," different rules may apply. For example, in case A, it is held that a driver who crosses a highway's center line is negligent. In case B, a driver crosses the line to avoid hitting a child. In determining whether case A's rule applies in case B, a judge would consider what the reasons were for the decision in A and whether B is sufficiently similar for those reasons to apply. If the judge holds that B's driver is not liable, that judge must pinpoint a policy and explain a rule that is not inconsistent with the rule underlying the decision in case A.

## THERE IS NO ONE "RIGHT" ANSWER

Many persons believe that there is one "right" answer to every legal question. The law is not an exact science, however, and in most situations involving a legal controversy, there is no single correct result. Good arguments can often be made to support either side of a legal controversy. Quite often a case does not present the situation of a "good" person suing a "bad" person. In many cases, both parties have acted in good faith in some measure or have acted in bad faith to some degree. Also, legal rules tend to be expressed in general terms, and this means that judges have some flexibility in interpreting and applying the law. Judges can sometimes be very creative in their legal reasoning in the interests of preventing injustice. As indicated above, each judge has his or her own personal beliefs and moral philosophy that shape, at least to some extent, the process of legal reasoning.

## THE COMMON LAW TODAY

The body of law that was first developed in England and that is still used today in the United States consists of the rules of law announced in court decisions. These rules of law include interpretations of constitutional provisions, of statutes enacted by legislatures, and of regulations created by administrative agencies. Today, this body of law is referred to variously as the common law, judge-made law, or **case law.**

The common law governs all areas not covered by *statutory law,* which, as will be discussed shortly, generally consists of those laws enacted by state legislatures and, at the federal level, by Congress. The body of statutory law has expanded greatly since the beginning of our nation, and this expansion has resulted in a proportionate reduction in the scope and applicability of the common law. Nonetheless, the common law remains a significant source of legal authority. Even when legislation has been substituted for common law principles, courts often rely on the common law as a guide to interpreting the legislation, on the theory that the people who drafted the statute intended to codify an existing common law rule.

## RESTATEMENTS OF THE LAW

To summarize and clarify common law rules and principles, the American Law Institute (ALI) drafted and published compilations of the common law called Restatements of the Law. The ALI, which was formed in the 1920s, consists of practicing attorneys, legal scholars, and judges. There are Restatements of the Law in the areas of contracts, torts, agency, trusts, property, restitution, security, judgments, and conflict of laws. Many of the Restatements are now in their second editions. The *Restatement of the Law of Contracts,* for example, was first published in 1932. Thirty years later, a second edition was undertaken. It was completed in 1979 and is referred to as the *Restatement (Second) of the Law of Contracts* or, more simply, as the *Restatement (Second) of Contracts.*

The Restatements, which generally summarize the common law rules followed by most states, do not in themselves have the force of law but are an important secondary source of legal analysis and opinion on which judges often rely in making their decisions. We refer to the Restatements frequently in subsequent chapters of this text.

# OTHER SOURCES OF AMERICAN LAW

In addition to the common law, or case law, the courts have numerous other sources of law to consider when making their decisions.

## CONSTITUTIONAL LAW

The federal government and the states have separate constitutions that set forth the general organization, powers, and limits of their respective governments. The U.S. Constitution is the supreme law of the land. A law in violation of the Constitution, no matter what its source, will be declared unconstitutional and will not be enforced. The Tenth Amendment to the U.S. Constitution, which defines the powers and limitations of the federal government, reserves all powers not granted to the federal government to the states. Unless they conflict with the U.S. Constitution, state constitutions are supreme within the states' respective borders.

The regulation of interstate commerce is one of the chief ways in which the U.S. Constitution affects business. The constitutional authority to regulate business and other aspects of constitutional law will be discussed in detail in Chapter 5. The complete text of the U.S. Constitution is presented in Appendix B.

Many state constitutions provide for referenda. A *referendum* asks the citizens of a state, or of a political subdivision of the state, to approve or reject a proposal for a new state constitution or amendments to the existing state constitution. Referenda may also ask the citizens to approve or reject a new law enacted by the state legislature.

## STATUTORY LAW

Laws passed by the federal Congress and the various state legislatures are called **statutes.** These statutes make up another source of law, which, as mentioned earlier, is generally referred to as **statutory law.** When a legislature passes a statute, that statute is ultimately included in the federal code of laws or the relevant state code of laws (these codes are discussed later in this chapter).

The "California Code," for example, refers to the statutory law of the state of California.

Statutory law also includes local ordinances. An **ordinance** is a statute (law, rule, or order) passed by a municipal or county governing unit to govern matters not covered by federal or state law. Ordinances commonly have to do with city or county land use (zoning ordinances), building and safety codes, and other matters affecting the local governing unit. Persons who violate ordinances may be fined or jailed, or both. No state statute or local ordinance can violate the U.S. Constitution or the relevant state constitution.

**UNIFORM LAWS**  No two states in the United States have identical statutes, constitutions, and case law. In other words, state laws differ from state to state. The differences among state laws were even more notable in the 1800s, when conflicting state statutes frequently made the rapidly developing trade and commerce among the states very difficult. To counter these problems, a group of legal scholars and lawyers formed the National Conference of Commissioners (NCC) on Uniform State Laws in 1892 to draft uniform statutes for adoption by the states. The NCC still exists today and continues to promulgate uniform statutes.

Adoption of a uniform law is a state matter, and a state legislature may reject all or part of the uniform law or rewrite it as the legislature wishes. Hence, even when a uniform law is said to have been adopted in many states, those states' laws may not be entirely "uniform." Once adopted by a state, a uniform act becomes a part of the statutory law of that state.

The earliest uniform law, the Uniform Negotiable Instruments Law, was completed by 1896 and was adopted in every state by the early 1920s (although not all states used exactly the same wording). Over the following decades, other acts were drawn up in a similar manner, including the Uniform Sales Act, the Uniform Warehouse Receipts Act, the Uniform Bills of Lading Act, the Uniform Partnership Act, the Model Business Corporation Act (drafted by the American Bar Association), the Uniform Stock Transfer Act, the Uniform Probate Code, and, more recently, the Uniform Status of Children of Assisted Conception Act (also known as the Uniform Surrogacy Act) and the Uniform Prenuptial Agreements Act. The most ambitious uniform act of all, however, was the Uniform Commercial Code.

■ CONCEPT SUMMARY 1.1 **Sources of American Law**

| SOURCE | DESCRIPTION |
|---|---|
| **The Common Law** | The common law originated in medieval England with the creation of the king's courts; consists of past judicial decisions and reasoning; and involves the application of the doctrine of *stare decisis*—the rule of precedent—in deciding cases. Common law governs all areas not covered by statutory law. |
| **Constitutional Law** | The law as expressed in the U.S. Constitution and the various state constitutions. The U.S. Constitution is the supreme law of the land. State constitutions are supreme within state borders to the extent that they do not violate a clause of the U.S. Constitution or a federal law. |
| **Statutory Law** | Laws (statutes and ordinances) created by federal, state, and local legislatures and governing bodies. None of these laws can violate the U.S. Constitution or the relevant state constitutions. Uniform statutes, when adopted by a state, become statutory law in that state. |
| **Administrative Law** | The branch of law concerned with the power and actions of administrative agencies at all levels of government. Federal administrative agencies are created by enabling legislation enacted by the U.S. Congress. Agency functions include rulemaking, investigation and enforcement, and adjudication. |

**THE UNIFORM COMMERCIAL CODE (UCC)**

The Uniform Commercial Code (UCC), which was created through the joint efforts of the NCC and the American Law Institute, was promulgated in 1952. The UCC, at least in part, has been adopted by all states, the District of Columbia, and the Virgin Islands. The UCC facilitates commerce among the states by providing a uniform, yet flexible, set of rules governing commercial transactions. The UCC assures businesspersons that their contracts, if validly entered into, will be enforced. Because of its importance in the area of commercial law, the UCC will be cited frequently in this text, particularly in Unit Three, which covers commercial transactions. The entire text of the latest version of the UCC is presented in Appendix C.

**ADMINISTRATIVE LAW**

**Administrative law** consists of the rules, orders, and decisions of **administrative agencies.** Federal administrative agencies are created by Congress through **enabling legislation,** which specifies the name, composition, and powers of the agency being created. For example, the Federal Trade Commission (FTC) was created in 1914 by the Federal Trade Commission Act.[5] The act prohibits unfair and deceptive trade practices. It also describes the procedures the agency must follow to charge persons or organizations with violations of the act, and it provides for judicial review (review by the courts) of agency orders.

Other portions of the act grant the agency powers to ''make rules and regulations for the purpose of carrying out the Act,'' to conduct investigations of business practices, to obtain reports from interstate corporations concerning their business practices, to investigate possible violations of the act, to publish findings of its investigations, and to recommend new legislation. The act also empowers the FTC to hold trial-like hearings and to adjudicate certain kinds of trade disputes that involve FTC regulations.

Although created by congressional legislation, most federal agencies, such as the Food and Drug Administration and the Environmental Protection Agency, are considered part of the executive branch of government. They are, therefore, under

---

5.   15 U.S.C. Sections 45 *et seq.* (Citations to statutes, such as the United States Code, will be discussed later in this chapter.)

the authority of (and accountable to) the president of the United States. Other agencies, called **independent regulatory agencies,** are not subject to presidential authority—they are independent, and their officials cannot be removed from office without *good cause* (sufficient reason). Because removal requires good cause, independent agency officials are not affected by political changes to the extent that regular agencies are. Their relative independence provides these agencies with some continuity from one presidential term to another. The Securities and Exchange Commission and the Federal Communications Commission are two examples of independent regulatory agencies.

Administrative agencies occupy an unusual niche in the American legal scheme, because they perform functions normally divided among all three branches of the government. Note that the FTC's grant of power incorporates functions associated with the legislative branch of government (rulemaking), the executive branch (investigation and enforcement), and the judicial branch (adjudication). Taken together, these functions constitute what has been termed **administrative process** (the administration of law by administrative agencies), in contrast to **judicial process** (the administration of law by the courts).

Administrative law and procedures, which will be examined in detail in Chapter 45, constitute a dominant element in the regulatory environment of business. Regulations issued by various administrative agencies affect virtually every aspect of a business's operation, including the firm's capital structure and financing, its hiring and firing procedures, its relations with employees and unions, and the way it manufactures and markets its products.

## SECTION 5

# CLASSIFICATIONS OF LAW

The body of law is huge. To study it, one must break it down by some means of classification. No single classification system can cover such a large mass of information; consequently, those systems that have been devised tend to overlap. Moreover, they are, of necessity, arbitrary in some respects. A discussion of the best-known classifications of law follows.

## SUBSTANTIVE VERSUS PROCEDURAL LAW

**Substantive law** includes all laws that define, describe, regulate, and create legal rights and obligations. For example, a rule stating that promises are enforced only when each party has received something of value from the other party is part of substantive law. So, too, is a rule stating that a person who has injured another through negligence must pay damages.

**Procedural law** establishes the methods of enforcing the rights established by substantive law. Questions about how a lawsuit should begin, what papers need to be filed, which court will hear the suit, which witnesses can be called, and so on are all questions of procedural law. In brief, substantive law tells us our rights; procedural law tells us how to exercise them.

Exhibit 1–1 classifies law in terms of its subject matter, dividing it into law covering substantive issues and law covering procedural issues. Most of this text concerns substantive law.

## PUBLIC VERSUS PRIVATE LAW

**Public law** addresses the relationship between persons and their government, whereas **private law** addresses direct dealings between persons. Criminal law and constitutional law, for example, are generally classified as public law, because they deal with persons and their relationships to government. Criminal acts, though they may involve only one victim, are seen as offenses against society as a whole and are prohibited by governments for the purpose of protecting the public. Constitutional law is frequently classified as public law, because it involves questions of whether the government—federal, state, or local—has the power to act in a particular fashion; often the issue is whether a law, duly passed, exceeds the limits set on the government.

When persons deal with or affect other persons, such as in a contractual relationship, the law governing these relationships is classified as private law. Exhibit 1–2 offers examples of private and public law.

## CIVIL VERSUS CRIMINAL LAW

**Civil law** is concerned with the duties that exist between persons or between citizens and their

■ **Exhibit 1–1  Subject Matter of Substantive and Procedural Law**

The importance of the distinction between substantive and procedural law is more than academic. The *result* of a case may well depend upon the determination that a rule is substantive rather than procedural.

| Substantive Law | Procedural Law |
|---|---|
| Administrative law | Administrative procedure |
| Agency | Appellate procedure |
| Bailments | Civil procedure |
| Commercial paper | Criminal procedure |
| Constitutional law | Evidence |
| Contracts | |
| Corporation law | |
| Criminal law | |
| Insurance | |
| Intellectual property | |
| Partnerships | |
| Personal property | |
| Real property | |
| Sales | |
| Sports and | |
|    entertainment law | |
| Taxation | |
| Torts | |
| Trusts and wills | |

■ **Exhibit 1–2  Examples of Public and Private Law**

Public law governs the relationship between persons and their government. Private law governs the relationships among individuals.

| Public Law | Private Law |
|---|---|
| Administrative law | Agency |
| Civil, criminal, and | Commercial paper |
|    appellate procedure | Contracts |
| Constitutional law | Corporation law |
| Criminal law | Partnerships |
| Evidence | Personal property |
| Taxation | Real property |
| | Sales |
| | Torts |
| | Trusts and wills |

governments, excluding the duty not to commit crimes. Contract law, for example, is part of civil law. The whole body of *tort law,* which has to do with the infringement by one person of the legally recognized rights of another, is an area of civil law. Tort law will be discussed in Chapter 7, as well as in Chapters 8 and 9.

**Criminal law,** in contrast to civil law, is concerned with wrongs committed against the public as a whole. Criminal acts are prohibited by local, state, or federal government statutes. Criminal law is always public law, whereas civil law is sometimes public and sometimes private. In a criminal case, the government seeks to impose a penalty on an allegedly guilty person. In a civil case, one party (sometimes the government) tries to make the other party comply with a duty or pay for the damage caused by failure to so comply. Criminal law is discussed in Chapter 9. Exhibit 1–3 lists some of the areas of law falling within each of these classifications.

SECTION 6

# REMEDIES AT LAW VERSUS REMEDIES IN EQUITY

In the early English king's courts, the kinds of **remedies** (the legal means to recover a right or redress a wrong) that the courts could grant were severely restricted. If one person wronged another in some way, the king's courts could award as compensation one or more of the following: (1) land, (2) items of value, or (3) money. The courts that awarded this compensation became known as **courts of law,** and the three remedies were called **remedies at law.** Even though the system introduced uniformity in the settling of disputes, when plaintiffs wanted a remedy other than economic compensation, the courts of law could do nothing, so "no remedy, no right."

When individuals could not obtain an adequate remedy in a court of law because of strict technicalities, they petitioned the king for relief. Most of these petitions were decided by an adviser to the king, called a **chancellor,** who was said to be the "keeper of the king's conscience." When the chancellor thought that the claim was a fair one, new and unique remedies were granted. In this way, a new body of rules and remedies came into being, and eventually formal courts of chancery, or **courts of equity,** were established.

■ **Exhibit 1–3 Criminal and Civil Law**

An important feature distinguishing criminal and civil law is the legal consequence for the wrongdoer. Violations of criminal laws may lead to fines or imprisonment, or both, whereas violations of civil laws usually involve compensating the person harmed by paying money damages.

| Criminal Law | Civil Law |
|---|---|
| Administrative law | Agency |
| Antitrust law | Bailments |
| Constitutional law | Bankruptcy |
| Criminal law | Business organizations |
| Environmental law | Commercial paper |
| Labor law | Contracts |
| Securities law | Insurance |
| | Property |
| | Sales |
| | Secured transactions |
| | Torts |
| | Trusts and wills |

## EQUITY COURTS

The distinction between law and equity courts is now primarily of historical interest, but it is still relevant to students of business law because legal and equitable remedies differ. To seek the proper remedy for a wrong, one must know what remedies are available.

Equity is that branch of law, founded on what might be described as notions of justice and fair dealing, that seeks to supply a remedy when there is no adequate remedy available at law. With the establishment of equity courts, two distinct court systems were created, each having a different set of judges. Two bodies of rules and remedies existed at the same time: remedies at law and **remedies in equity.** Plaintiffs had to specify whether they were bringing an ''action at law'' or an ''action in equity,'' and they chose their courts accordingly. Only one remedy could be granted for a particular wrong, and even in equity the wrong had to be of a type the court could recognize as remediable.

Courts of equity had the responsibility of using discretion in supplementing the common law. Even today, when the same court can award both legal and equitable remedies, such discretion is often guided by so-called **equitable maxims.** Equitable maxims are propositions or general statements of

rules of equity that courts often invoke. Listed below are a few of the maxims of equity.

1. *Whoever seeks equity must do equity.* (Anyone who wishes to be treated fairly must treat others fairly.)
2. *When there is equal equity, the law must prevail.* (The law will determine the outcome of a controversy in which the merits of both sides are equal.)
3. *One seeking the aid of an equity court must come to the court with clean hands.* (Plaintiffs must have acted fairly and honestly.)
4. *Equity will not suffer a right to exist without a remedy.* (Equitable relief will be awarded when there is a right to relief and there is no adequate remedy at law.)
5. *Equity regards substance rather than form.* (Equity is more concerned with fairness and justice than with legal technicalities.)
6. *Equity aids the vigilant, not those who rest on their rights.* (Equity will not help those who neglect their rights for an unreasonable period of time.)

The last maxim is worthy of discussion. It has become known as the equitable doctrine of **laches,** and it can be used as a **defense** (an argument raised by the defendant to defeat the plaintiff's cause of action or recovery). The doctrine arose to encourage people to bring lawsuits while the evidence was fresh. What constitutes a reasonable time, of course, varies according to the circumstances of the case. Time periods for different types of cases are now usually fixed by **statutes of limitations.** After the time allowed under a statute of limitations has expired, no action can be brought, no matter how strong the case was originally.

## EQUITABLE RELIEF

A number of equitable remedies are available. Three of them—specific performance, injunctions, and rescission—are briefly discussed here. These and other equitable remedies are discussed in more detail at appropriate points in the chapters that follow. As a general rule, courts today will not grant these equitable remedies unless the remedy at law (in the form of money **damages**) is inadequate.

**SPECIFIC PERFORMANCE**   When courts of law and equity were still separate, a plaintiff might come into a court of equity asking it to order a

■ **Exhibit 1–4  Procedural Differences between an Action at Law and an Action in Equity**

| Procedure | Action at Law | Action in Equity |
|---|---|---|
| Initiation of lawsuit | By filing a complaint | By filing a petition |
| Decision | By jury or judge | By judge (no jury) |
| Result | Judgment | Decree |
| Remedy | Monetary damages | Injunction, decree of specific performance, or rescission |

defendant to perform within the terms of a contract. A court of law could not issue such an order, because its remedies were limited to payment of money or property as compensation for damages. A court of equity, however, could issue a decree of **specific performance**—an order to perform what was promised in a contractual agreement. This remedy was, and still is, only available when the dispute before the court involves a *contractual* transaction.

A court today will usually grant the equitable remedy of specific performance when the remedy at law (money damages) is not an adequate remedy. For example, if a seller **breaches** (fails to perform as promised) a contract for the sale of a unique item—such as a work of art, a classic antique car, or a parcel of land—money damages may be inadequate. Because the buyer could not obtain that unique item anywhere else, the court may order the seller to perform the contract as promised.

**INJUNCTIONS**  If a person wanted to prevent the occurrence of a certain activity, he or she would have to go to the chancellor in equity and ask that the person doing the wrongful act be ordered to stop. The order is called an injunction. An **injunction** is usually an order to a specific person, directing that person to do or to refrain from doing a particular act.

For example, assume that your neighbor has several dogs that stay out in your neighbor's yard all night and bark ceaselessly. You have tried in vain to convince your neighbor to keep the dogs in at night or otherwise cure the noise problem. Finally, you petition the court for an injunction. In effect, you ask the court to *enjoin* your neighbor from letting the dogs stay out at night, thereby disrupting the peace by their barking.

**RESCISSION**  Sometimes the legal remedy of the payment of money for damages is unavailable or inadequate when disputes occur over agreements.

In such cases, the equitable remedy of rescission may be appropriate. **Rescission**[6] is an action to undo an agreement—to return the parties to their *status quo* prior to the agreement. If rescission is granted, all duties created by the agreement are abolished. If, for example, a person is fraudulently induced to enter into a contract and the fraud is discovered before any performance under the contract takes place, the innocent party might seek to rescind the agreement.

A contract might also be rescinded if the parties were mistaken as to the subject matter of the contract. For example, assume that Daron has two automobiles, one worth $5,000 and the other worth $10,000. Daron wants to sell the car worth $5,000 and tells his friend, ''I'll sell you my car for $7,000.'' The friend, believing that the contract is for the $10,000 car, agrees to purchase it for $7,000. Upon learning of the mistake, either party might seek to have the contract rescinded.

## THE MERGING OF LAW AND EQUITY

During the nineteenth century, most states adopted rules of procedure that resulted in combined courts of law and equity—although some states, such as Arkansas, still retain the distinction. Today, a plaintiff or a petitioner in equity (the person bringing the action) may request both legal and equitable remedies in the same action, and the trial court judge may grant either or both forms of relief.

Despite the merging of the courts, it is still important to distinguish between actions at law and actions in equity. As mentioned, the primary importance is in the remedy sought. Vestiges of the procedures used when the courts were separate still exist. Today, differences in procedure depend on whether the civil lawsuit involves an action in equity or an action at law. Exhibit 1–4 is illustrative and applies to most states.

---

6.  Pronounced reh-*sih*-zhen.

The major practical difference between law and equity today is the right to demand a jury trial in actions at law. In the old courts of equity, the chancellor heard both sides of an issue and decided what should be done. Juries were considered inappropriate. In actions at law, however, juries heard evidence and made determinations regarding questions of fact, including the amount of damages to be awarded. Today, in a case involving equitable rights, a judge may impanel a jury to serve in an advisory capacity.

## SECTION 7

# HOW TO FIND STATUTORY AND ADMINISTRATIVE LAW

This text includes numerous citations to federal and state laws and regulations. When Congress passes laws, they are collected in a publication titled *United States Statutes at Large.* When state legislatures pass laws, they are collected in similar state publications. Most frequently, however, laws are referred to in their codified form—that is, the form in which they appear in the federal and state codes.

In these codes, laws are compiled by subject. The *United States Code* (U.S.C.) arranges all existing federal laws of a public and permanent nature by subject. Each of the fifty subjects into which the U.S.C. arranges the laws is given a title and a title number. For example, laws relating to commerce and trade are collected in Title 15, which is titled "Commerce and Trade." Titles are subdivided by sections. A citation to the U.S.C. includes title and section numbers. Thus, a reference to "15 U.S.C. Section 1" means that the statute can be found in Section 1 of Title 15. ("Section" may also be designated by the symbol §, and "Sections," by §§.) Sometimes a citation includes the abbreviation *et seq.*—as in "15 U.S.C. Sections 1 *et seq.*" The term is an abbreviated form of *et sequitur,* which in Latin means "and the following"; when used in a citation, it refers to sections that concern the same subject as the numbered section and follow it in sequence.

State codes follow the U.S.C. pattern of arranging law by subject. They may be called codes, revisions, compilations, consolidations, general statutes, or statutes, depending on the preference of the states. In some codes, subjects are designated by number. In others, they are designated by name. For example, "13 Pennsylvania Consolidated Statutes Section 1101" means the statute can be found in Title 13, Section 1101, of the Pennsylvania code. "California Commercial Code Section 1101" means the statute can be found under the subject heading "Commercial Code" of the California code in Section 1101. Abbreviations may be used. For example, "13 Pennsylvania Consolidated Statutes Section 1101" may be abbreviated "13 Pa. C.S. § 1101," and "California Commercial Code Section 1101" may be abbreviated "Cal. Com. Code § 1101."

Rules and regulations adopted by federal administrative agencies are compiled in the *Code of Federal Regulations* (C.F.R.). Like the U.S.C., the C.F.R. is divided into fifty titles. Rules within each title are assigned section numbers. A full citation to the C.F.R. includes title and section numbers. For example, a reference to "17 C.F.R. Section 230.504" means that the rule can be found in Section 230.504 of Title 17.

Commercial publications of these laws and regulations are available and are widely used. For example, West Publishing Company publishes the *United States Code Annotated* (U.S.C.A.). The U.S.C.A. contains the complete text of laws included in the U.S.C., as well as notes of court decisions that interpret and apply specific sections of the statutes, plus the text of presidential proclamations and executive orders. The U.S.C.A. also includes research aids, such as cross-references to related statutes, historical notes, and library references. A citation to the U.S.C.A. is similar to a citation to the U.S.C.: "15 U.S.C.A. Section 1."

## SECTION 8

# HOW TO FIND CASE LAW

Laws pertaining to business consist of case law, as well as statutory law. A substantial number of cases are presented in this text to provide you with concise, real-life illustrations of the interpretation and application of the law by the courts. Many other court decisions have been referenced in footnotes throughout the text. Because of the importance of knowing how to find these and other court opinions, this section offers a brief introduction to the case reporting system and to the legal "shorthand" employed in referring to court cases.

First, though, we need to look briefly at the court system. As will be discussed in Chapter 3, there are two types of courts in the United States, federal courts and state courts. Both the federal and state court systems consist of several levels, or tiers, of courts. *Trial courts,* in which evidence is presented and testimony given, are on the bottom tier (which also includes lower courts handling specialized issues). Decisions from a trial court can be appealed to a higher court, which commonly would be an intermediate *court of appeals,* or an *appellate court.* Appellate courts are known as *reviewing courts,* because they do not hear evidence or testimony, as trial courts do; rather, an appellate court reviews all of the records relating to a case to determine whether the trial court's decision was correct. Decisions from these intermediate courts of appeals may be appealed to an even higher court, such as a state supreme court or the United States Supreme Court.

## STATE COURT DECISIONS

Most state trial court decisions are not published. Except in New York and a few other states that publish selected opinions of their trial courts, decisions from the state trial courts are merely filed in the office of the clerk of the court, where they are available for public inspection.

Written decisions of the appellate, or reviewing, courts are published and distributed. The reported appellate decisions are published in volumes called *Reports,* which are numbered consecutively. State appellate court decisions are found in the state reports of that particular state.

Additionally, state court opinions appear in regional units of the *National Reporter System,* published by West Publishing Company. Most lawyers and libraries have the West reporters because they report cases more quickly, and are distributed more widely, than the state-published reports. In fact, many states have eliminated their own reporters in favor of West's National Reporter System. The National Reporter System divides the states into the following geographical areas: *Atlantic* (A. or A.2d), *South Eastern* (S.E. or S.E.2d), *South Western* (S.W. or S.W.2d), *North Western* (N.W. or N.W.2d), *North Eastern* (N.E. or N.E.2d),

*Southern* (So. or So.2d), and *Pacific* (P. or P.2d). (The *2d* in the preceding abbreviations refers to *Second Series.*) The states included in each of these regional divisions are indicated in Exhibit 1–5, which illustrates West's National Reporter System.

After appellate decisions have been published, they are normally referred to (cited) by the name of the case (called the *style* of the case); the volume, name, and page of the state's official reporter (if different from West's National Reporter System); the volume, unit, and page number of the National Reporter; and the volume, name, and page number of any other selected reporter. This information is included in what is called the **citation.** (Citing a reporter by volume number, name, and page number, in that order, is common to all citations.) When more than one reporter is cited for the same case, each reference is called a *parallel citation.*

For example, consider the following case citation: *Leasefirst v. Hartford Rexall Drugs,* 168 Wis.2d 83, 483 N.W.2d 585 (1992). We see that the opinion in this case may be found in volume 168 of the official *Wisconsin Reports, Second Series,* on page 83. The parallel citation is to volume 483 of the *North Western Reporter, Second Series,* page 585. In reprinting appellate opinions in this text, in addition to the reporter, we give the name of the court hearing the case and the year of the court's decision.

A few of the states—including those with intermediate appellate courts, such as California, Illinois, and New York—have more than one reporter for opinions given by courts within their states. Sample citations from these courts, as well as others, are listed and explained in Exhibit 1–6.

## FEDERAL COURT DECISIONS

Federal trial court decisions are published unofficially in West's *Federal Supplement* (F.Supp.), and opinions from the circuit courts of appeals are reported unofficially in West's *Federal Reporter* (F. or F.2d or F.3d). Cases concerning federal bankruptcy law are published unofficially in West's *Bankruptcy Reporter* (Bankr.). Opinions from the United States Supreme Court are reported in the *United States Reports* (U.S.), West's *Supreme Court Reporter* (S.Ct.), the *Lawyers' Edition of the Supreme Court Reports* (L.Ed. or L.Ed.2d), and other publications.

The *United States Reports* is the official edition of all decisions of the United States Supreme Court

### ■ Exhibit 1–5 National Reporter System—Regional/Federal

| Regional Reporters | Coverage Beginning | Coverage |
|---|---|---|
| *Atlantic Reporter* (A. or A.2d) | 1885 | Connecticut, Delaware, Maine, Maryland, New Hampshire, New Jersey, Pennsylvania, Rhode Island, Vermont, and District of Columbia. |
| *North Eastern Reporter* (N.E. or N.E.2d) | 1885 | Illinois, Indiana, Massachusetts, New York, and Ohio. |
| *North Western Reporter* (N.W. or N.W.2d) | 1879 | Iowa, Michigan, Minnesota, Nebraska, North Dakota, South Dakota, and Wisconsin. |
| *Pacific Reporter* (P. or P.2d) | 1883 | Alaska, Arizona, California, Colorado, Hawaii, Idaho, Kansas, Montana, Nevada, New Mexico, Oklahoma, Oregon, Utah, Washington, and Wyoming. |
| *South Eastern Reporter* (S.E. or S.E.2d) | 1887 | Georgia, North Carolina, South Carolina, Virginia, and West Virginia. |
| *South Western Reporter* (S.W. or S.W.2d) | 1886 | Arkansas, Kentucky, Missouri, Tennessee, and Texas. |
| *Southern Reporter* (So. or So.2d) | 1887 | Alabama, Florida, Louisiana, and Mississippi. |

| Federal Reporters | | |
|---|---|---|
| *Federal Reporter* (F., F.2d, or F.3d) | 1880 | U.S. Circuit Court from 1880 to 1912; U.S. Commerce Court from 1911 to 1913; U.S. District Courts from 1880 to 1932; U.S. Court of Claims (now called U.S. Court of Federal Claims) from 1929 to 1932 and since 1960; U.S. Court of Appeals since 1891; U.S. Court of Customs and Patent Appeals since 1929; and U.S. Emergency Court of Appeals since 1943. |
| *Federal Supplement* (F.Supp.) | 1932 | U.S. Court of Claims from 1932 to 1960; U.S. District Courts since 1932; and U.S. Customs Court since 1956. |
| *Federal Rules Decisions* (F.R.D.) | 1939 | U.S. District Courts involving the Federal Rules of Civil Procedure since 1939 and Federal Rules of Criminal Procedure since 1946. |
| *Supreme Court Reporter* (S.Ct.) | 1882 | U.S. Supreme Court since the October term of 1882. |
| *Bankruptcy Reporter* (Bankr.) | 1980 | Bankruptcy decisions of U.S. Bankruptcy Courts, U.S. District Courts, U.S. Courts of Appeals, and U.S. Supreme Court. |
| *Military Justice Reporter* (M.J.) | 1978 | U.S. Court of Military Appeals and Courts of Military Review for the Army, Navy, Air Force, and Coast Guard. |

**NATIONAL REPORTER SYSTEM MAP**

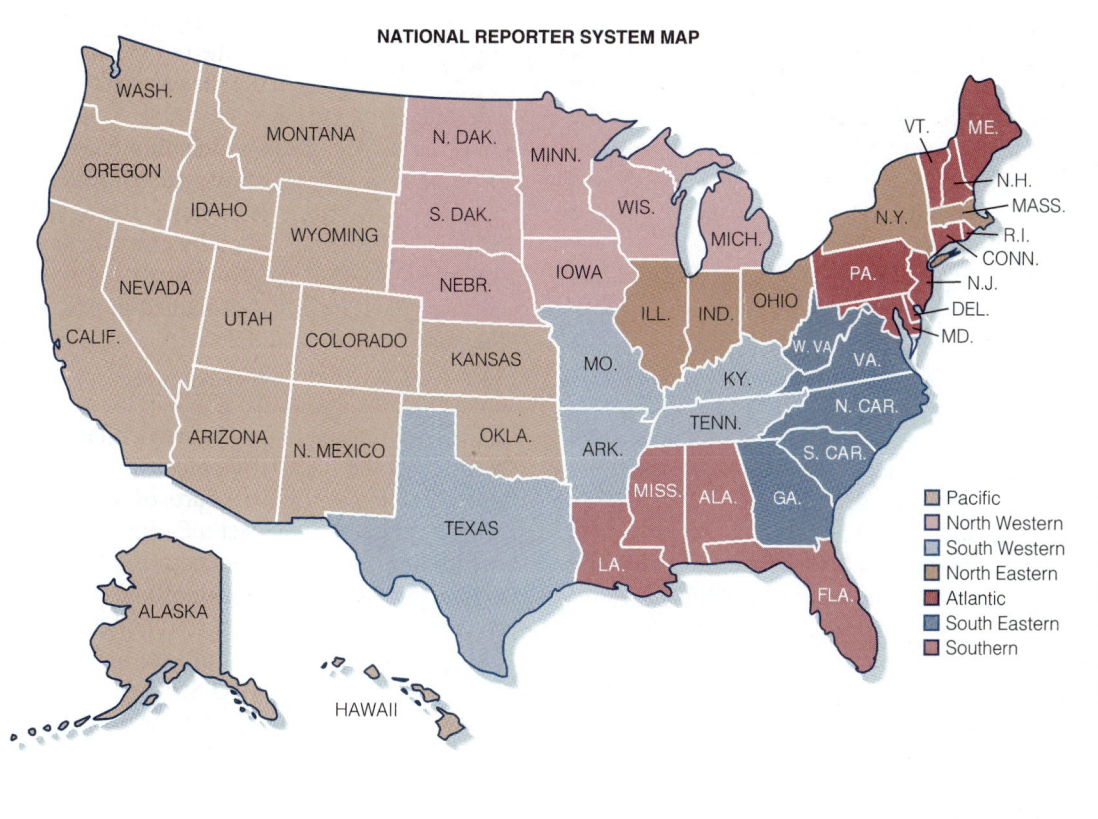

for which there are written opinions. Published by the federal government, the series includes reports of Supreme Court cases dating from the August term of 1791, although originally many of the decisions were not reported in the early volumes.

West's *Supreme Court Reporter* is an unofficial edition dating from the Court's term in October 1882. Preceding each of its case reports are a summary of the case and *headnotes* (brief editorial statements of the law involved in the case, numbered to correspond to numbers in the report). The headnotes are also given classification numbers that serve to cross-reference each headnote to other headnotes on similar points throughout the National Reporter System and other West publications. The numbers facilitate research of all relevant cases on a given point. This is important because, as may be evident from the discussion of *stare decisis,* a lawyer's goal in undertaking legal research is to find an authority that cannot be factually distinguished from his or her case.

The Lawyers Cooperative Publishing Company of Rochester, New York, publishes the *Lawyers' Edition of the Supreme Court Reports,* which is an unofficial edition of the entire series of the Supreme Court reports and contains many of the decisions not reported in the early official volumes. Also, among other editorial features, the *Lawyers' Edition,* in its second series, precedes the report of each case with a full summary, includes excerpts from the attorneys' notes on the cases, and discusses in detail selected cases of special interest to the legal profession.

Sample citations for federal court decisions are listed and explained in Exhibit 1–6.

## OLD CASE LAW

On a few occasions, this text cites opinions from old, classic cases dating to the nineteenth century or earlier; some of these are from the English courts. The citations to these cases appear not to conform to the descriptions given above, because the reporters in which they were published have since been replaced. A sample citation for an English reporter is included in Exhibit 1–6.

## CASE DIGESTS AND LEGAL ENCYCLOPEDIAS

The body of American case law consists of nearly five million decisions, to which more than forty

thousand decisions are added each year. Because judicial decisions are published in chronological order, finding relevant precedents would be a Herculean task if it were not for case digests, legal encyclopedias, and many other publications that classify decisions according to subject. These and other resources for the legal researcher are discussed in Appendix G at the end of this book.

**SECTION 9**

# HOW TO ANALYZE CASE LAW

Case law is critical to decision making in the business context because businesses must operate within the boundaries established by law. It is thus essential that businesspersons understand case law.

The cases in this text have been condensed from the full text of the courts' opinions. For those wishing to review court cases for future research projects or to gain additional legal information, the following sections will provide useful insights into how to read and understand case law.

## CASE TITLES

The title of a case, such as *Adams v. Jones,* indicates the names of the parties to the lawsuit. The *v.* in the case title stands for *versus,* which means ''against.'' In the trial court, Adams was the plaintiff—the person who filed the suit. Jones was the defendant. If the case is appealed, however, the appellate court will sometimes place the name of the party appealing the decision first, so that the case may be called *Jones v. Adams* if Jones is appealing. Because some appellate courts retain the trial court order of names, it is often impossible to distinguish the plaintiff from the defendant in the title of a reported appellate court decision. You must carefully read the facts of each case to identify each party. Otherwise, the discussion by the appellate court will be difficult to understand.

## TERMINOLOGY

The following terms, phrases, and abbreviations are frequently encountered in court opinions and legal publications. Because it is important to understand what is meant by these terms, phrases, and abbreviations, we define and discuss them here.

■ **Exhibit 1–6 How to Read Case Citations**

---

**State Courts**

242 Neb. 614, 497 N.W.2d 339 (1993)[a]

> *N.W.* is the abbreviation for West's publication of state court decisions rendered in the northwestern region of the National Reporter System. *2d* indicates that this case was included in the second series of those reports. The number 497 refers to the volume number of the reporter; the number 339 refers to the first page in that volume on which this case can be found.

> *Neb.* is an abbreviation for *Nebraska Reports,* Nebraska's official reports of the decisions of its highest court, the Nebraska Supreme Court.

6 Cal.4th 539, 25 Cal.Rptr.2d 97 (1993)

> *Cal.Rptr.* is the abbreviation for West's unofficial reports—titled *California Reporter*—of the decisions of California courts.

81 N.Y.2d 623, 619 N.E.2d 998, 601 N.Y.S.2d 686 (1993)

> *N.Y.S.* is the abbreviation for West's unofficial reports—titled *New York Supplement*—of the decisions of New York courts.

> *N.Y.* is the abbreviation for *New York Reports,* New York's official reports of the decisions of its court of appeals. The New York Court of Appeals is the state's highest court, analogous to other states' supreme courts. In New York, a supreme court is a trial court.

209 Ga.App. 853, 434 S.E.2d 769 (1993)

> *Ga.App.* is the abbreviation for *Georgia Appeals Reports,* Georgia's official reports of the decisions of its court of appeals.

---

**Federal Courts**

___ U.S. ___, 114 S.Ct. 1164, 127 L.Ed.2d 500 (1994)

> *L.Ed.* is an abbreviation for *Lawyers' Edition of the Supreme Court Reports,* an unofficial edition of decisions of the United States Supreme Court.

> *S.Ct.* is the abbreviation for West's unofficial reports—titled *Supreme Court Reporter*—of United States Supreme Court decisions.

> *U.S.* is the abbreviation for *United States Reports,* the official edition of the decisions of the United States Supreme Court. Volume and page numbers are not included in this citation because they have not yet been assigned.

---

a. The case names have been deleted from these citations to emphasize the publications. It should be kept in mind, however, that the name of a case is as important as the specific page numbers in the volumes in which it is found. If a citation is incorrect, the correct citation may be found in a publication's index of case names. The date of a case is also important because, in addition to providing a check on error in citations, the value of a recent case as an authority is likely to be greater than that of earlier cases.

■ **Exhibit 1–6 How to Read Case Citations (Continued)**

---

**Federal Courts (continued)**

12 F.3d 176 (10th Cir. 1994)

> *10th Cir.* is an abbreviation denoting that this case was decided in the United States Court of Appeals for the Tenth Circuit.

814 F.Supp. 564 (D.Ariz. 1993)

> *D.Ariz.* is an abbreviation indicating that the United States District Court for the Middle District of Arizona decided this case.

---

**English Courts**

9 Exch. 341, 156 Eng.Rep. 145 (1854)

> *Eng.Rep.* is an abbreviation for *English Reports, Full Reprint,* a series of reports containing selected decisions made in English courts between 1378 and 1865.

> *Exch.* is an abbreviation for *English Exchequer Reports,* which included the original reports of cases decided in England's Court of Exchequer.

---

**Statutory and Other Citations**

15 U.S.C. Section 1262(e)

> *U.S.C.* denotes *United States Code,* the codification of *United States Statutes at Large.* The number 15 refers to the statute's U.S.C. title number and 1262 to its section number within that title. The letter e refers to a subsection within the section.

UCC 2–206(1)(a)

> *UCC* is an abbreviation for *Uniform Commercial Code.* The first number 2 is a reference to an article of the UCC and 206 to a section within that article. The number 1 refers to a subsection within the section and the letter a to a subdivision within the subsection.

Restatement (Second) of Torts, Section 568

> *Restatement (Second) of Torts* refers to the second edition of the American Law Institute's *Restatement of the Law of Torts.* The number 568 refers to a specific section.

16 C.F.R. Section 453.2

> *C.F.R.* is an abbreviation for *Code of Federal Regulations,* a compilation of federal administrative regulations. The number 16 is a reference to the regulation's title number and 453.2 to a specific section within that title.

**PARTIES TO LAWSUITS** As mentioned previously, the party initiating a lawsuit is referred to as the *plaintiff,* and the party against whom a lawsuit is brought is the *defendant.* Lawsuits frequently involve more than one plaintiff and/or defendant. When a case is appealed from the court or jurisdiction in which the case was originally brought to another court or jurisdiction, the party appealing the case is called the **appellant.** The **appellee** is the party against whom the appeal is taken. Sometimes, an appellant that appeals a lower court's decision is referred to as the **petitioner,** and the appellee is referred to as the **respondent.**

**JUDGES AND JUSTICES** The terms *judge* and *justice* are usually synonymous and represent two designations given to judges in various courts. All members of the United States Supreme Court, for example, are referred to as *justices.* And *justice* is the formal title usually given to judges of appellate courts, although this is not always the case. In New York, a justice is a judge of the trial court (which is called the Supreme Court), and a member of the Court of Appeals (the state's highest court) is called a *judge.* The term *justice* is commonly abbreviated to J. and *justices,* to JJ. A Supreme Court case might refer to Justice Kennedy as Kennedy, J., or to Chief Justice Rehnquist as Rehnquist, C.J.

**DECISIONS AND OPINIONS** Most decisions reached by reviewing, or appellate, courts are explained in written **opinions.** The opinion contains the court's reasons for its decision, the rules of law that apply, and the judgment. There are four possible types of written opinions for any particular case decided by an appellate court. When all judges or justices unanimously agree on an opinion, the opinion is written for the entire court and can be deemed a *unanimous opinion.* When there is not a unanimous opinion, a *majority opinion* is written; it outlines the views of the majority of the judges or justices deciding the case. Often, a judge or justice who feels strongly about making or emphasizing a point that was not made or emphasized in the unanimous or majority opinion will write a *concurring opinion.* That means the judge or justice agrees (concurs) with the judgment given in the unanimous or majority opinion, but for different reasons. In other than unanimous opinions, a *dissenting opinion* is usually written by a judge or justice who does not agree with the majority. The dissenting opinion is important because it may

form the basis of the arguments used years later in overruling the precedential majority opinion.

**ABBREVIATIONS** In court opinions, as well as in other areas of this text, certain terms appearing in the names of firms or organizations will often be abbreviated. The terms *Company, Incorporated,* and *Limited,* for example, will frequently appear in their abbreviated forms as *Co., Inc.,* and *Ltd.,* respectively. Certain organizations and legislative acts are also frequently referred to by their initials or acronyms. In all such cases, to prevent confusion we will give the complete name of the organization or act when it is first mentioned in a given section of the text.

## A SAMPLE COURT CASE

Knowing how to read and analyze a court opinion is an essential step in undertaking accurate legal research. A further step involves ''briefing'' the case. Legal researchers routinely brief cases by summarizing and reducing the texts of the opinions to their essential elements. Instructions on how to brief a case are given in Appendix A, which also includes selected cases for briefing and a briefed version of the first case.

To illustrate how to read and analyze a court opinion, we have annotated an actual case that was heard by the United States Supreme Court in 1994. The lawsuit was initiated by Acuff-Rose Music, Inc., which held the copyright to a popular song entitled "Oh, Pretty Woman." 2 Live Crew, a musical group, authored and profited from a parody (satiric) rendition of the same song. As will be discussed in Chapter 8, federal copyright law allows writers, artists, and other authors of creative works to have the exclusive right to reproduce those works. Copyright *infringement* occurs when someone reproduces a copyrighted work without the author's permission to do so.

You will note that triple asterisks (\* \* \*) and quadruple asterisks (\* \* \* \*) frequently appear within the opinion. The triple asterisks indicate that we have deleted a few words or sentences from the opinion for the sake of readability or brevity. Quadruple asterisks mean that an entire paragraph (or more) has been omitted. Also, when the opinion cites another case or legal source, the citation to the referenced cases or sources has been omitted to save space and to improve the flow of the text. These editorial practices are continued in the other court opinions presented in this text. In addition, whenever a case opinion presented in this text includes a term or a phrase that may not be readily understandable, we have added a bracketed definition or paraphrase of the term or phrase. In the sample case below, important sections, terms, and phrases are defined or discussed in the margins.

## CAMPBELL v. ACUFF-ROSE MUSIC, INC.
Supreme Court of the United States, 1994.
____ U.S. ____ ,
114 S.Ct. 1164,
127 L.Ed.2d 500.

| | |
|---|---|
| This line gives the name of the justice who authored the opinion for the court. | Justice *SOUTER* delivered the opinion of the Court. |
| The first paragraph of this opinion states the issue to be decided by the Court. An *issue* is a disputed point of fact or law, such as a dispute over the interpretation or application of a statute. | We are called upon to decide whether 2 Live Crew's commercial parody of Roy Orbison's song, ''Oh, Pretty Woman,'' may be a fair use within the meaning of the Copyright Act of 1976. * * *<br><br>* * * * |

I

| | |
|---|---|
| These paragraphs describe the factual background of the case. | In 1964, Roy Orbison and William Dees wrote a rock ballad called ''Oh, Pretty Woman'' and assigned [transferred] their rights in it to respondent Acuff-Rose Music, Inc. Acuff-Rose registered the song for copyright protection. |
| Sent back to the trial court for further proceedings. | Petitioners Luther R. Campbell, Christopher Wongwon, Mark Ross, and David Hobbs, are collectively known as 2 Live Crew, a popular rap music group. * * * On July 5, 1989, 2 Live Crew's manager informed Acuff-Rose that 2 Live Crew had written a parody of ''Oh, Pretty Woman,'' that they would afford all credit for ownership and authorship of the original song to Acuff-Rose, Dees, and Orbison, and that they were willing to pay a fee for the use they wished to make of it. * * * Acuff-Rose's agent refused permission * * *. Nonetheless, in June or July 1989, 2 Live Crew released records, cassette tapes, and compact discs of ''Pretty Woman'' |
| A Latin term [pronounced sur-shee-uh-*rah*-ree] meaning that the United States Supreme Court ordered the appellate court to send it the record of the case for review. | * * *. |

Almost a year later, after nearly a quarter of a million copies of the recording had been sold, Acuff-Rose sued 2 Live Crew and its record company * * * for copyright infringement. The District Court * * * held that 2 Live Crew's song made fair use of Orbison's original.

The [federal Court of Appeals] reversed and **remanded,** * * *

We granted *certiorari* to determine whether 2 Live Crew's commercial parody could be a fair use.

* * * *

II

| | |
|---|---|
| This paragraph sets out the rule that governs the fair use of another's copyrighted work. Under the fair use provision of the statute, a copyrighted work may be reproduced without the copyright owner's permission for certain purposes, such as to criticize or comment on the original work. The statute requires the application of a four-factor test to determine whether an unauthorized reproduction constitutes a fair use. | [Section 107 of the Copyright Act of 1976 states that] ''the fair use of a copyrighted work * * * for purposes such as criticism, comment, news reporting, teaching * * *, scholarship, or research, is not an infringement of copyright. In determining whether the use * * * is a fair use the factors to be considered shall include [the four factors discussed below].'' |

* * * *

The Court begins its analysis with the first factor of the fair use test.

The first factor in a fair use enquiry is "the purpose and character of the use, including whether such use is of a commercial nature or is for nonprofit educational purposes." * * * The central purpose of this investigation is to see * * * whether the new work * * * adds something new, with a further purpose or different character, altering the first with new expression, meaning, or message; it asks, in other words, whether and to what extent the new work is "transformative." * * * [T]he more transformative the new work, the less will be the significance of other factors, like commercialism, that may weigh against a finding of fair use.

* * * [P]arody has an obvious claim to transformative value * * *, it can provide social benefit, by shedding light on an earlier work, and, in the process, creating a new one. [T]hus * * * parody, like other comment or criticism, may claim fair use under [Section] 107.

* * * *

The Court of Appeals * * * [confined] its treatment of the first factor essentially to * * * the commercial nature of the use. The court [stated] that "every commercial use of copyrighted material is presumptively . . . unfair. . . . [unfair until proved otherwise]" * * * [T]he Court of Appeals erred.

The Court's conclusion on the first factor of the test—the first step in resolving the issue.

The language of the statute makes clear that the commercial * * * purpose of a work is only one element of the first factor enquiry into its purpose and character. * * * Accordingly, the mere fact that a use is educational and not for profit does not insulate it from a finding of infringement, any more than the commercial character of a use bars a finding of fairness. * * *

* * * *

The Court lets stand the lower courts' resolution of the second factor of the fair use test.

The second statutory factor, "the nature of the copyrighted work," * * * calls for recognition that some works are closer to the core of intended copyright protection than others * * * We agree with both the District Court and the Court of Appeals that the Orbison original's creative expression for public dissemination falls within the core of the copyright's protective purposes. * * *

The Court begins its analysis of the third factor.

The third factor asks whether "the amount and substantiality of the portion used in relation to the copyrighted work as a whole," * * * are reasonable in relation to the purpose of the copying. * * *

The District Court considered the song's parodic purpose in finding that 2 Live Crew had not helped themselves overmuch. The Court of Appeals disagreed, stating that "[w]hile it may not be inappropriate to find that no more was taken than necessary, the copying was qualitatively substantial. . . . We conclude that taking the heart of the original and making it the heart of a new work was to purloin a substantial portion of the essence of the original."

* * * *

* * * [W]e part company with the court below[.] * * * When parody takes aim at a particular original work, the parody must be able to "conjure up" at least enough of that original to make the object of its critical wit recognizable. * * *

* * * 2 Live Crew copied the characteristic opening bass riff (or musical phrase) of the original, and * * * the words of the first line copy the Orbison

lyrics. But if quotation of the opening riff and the first line may be said to go to the "heart" of the original, the heart is also what most readily conjures up the song for parody, and it is the heart at which parody takes aim. *  *  *

*  *  *  *

**The Court's conclusion on the third factor.**

*  *  * [A]s to the lyrics, we think the Court of Appeals correctly suggested that "no more was taken than necessary," but just for that reason, we fail to see how the copying can be excessive in relation to its parodic purpose, even if the portion taken is the original's "heart." As to the music, we express no opinion whether repetition of the bass riff is excessive copying, and we remand to permit evaluation of the amount taken, in light of the song's parodic purpose and character, its transformative elements, and considerations of the potential for market substitution sketched more fully below.

**The Court begins its analysis of the fourth and final factor of the fair use test.**

The fourth fair use factor is "the effect of the use upon the **potential market** for or value of the copyrighted work," *  *  *

*  *  * In assessing the likelihood of significant market harm, the Court of Appeals [held] that "[i]f the intended use is for commercial gain, that likelihood may be presumed. *  *  * "

**Potential purchasers of the original version of "Oh, Pretty Woman."**

*  *  * [W]hen a commercial use amounts to mere duplication of the entirety of an original, it clearly *  *  * serves as a market replacement for it, making it likely that cognizable market harm to the original will occur. But when, on the contrary, the *  *  * use is transformative, *  *  * market harm may not be so readily inferred. Indeed, as to parody pure and simple, it is more likely that the new work will not affect the market for the original *  *  *. This is so because the parody and the original usually serve different market functions.

**The Court's conclusion on the fourth factor.**

*  *  *  *

### III

**The Court summarizes its conclusions and gives its order in the final portion of the opinion.**

It was error for the Court of Appeals to conclude that the commercial nature of 2 Live Crew's parody *  *  * rendered it presumptively unfair. *  *  * The court also erred in holding that 2 Live Crew had necessarily copied excessively from the Orbison original, considering the parodic purpose of the use. We therefore reverse the judgment of the Court of Appeals and remand for further proceedings consistent with this opinion.

It is so ordered.

---

## TERMS AND CONCEPTS TO REVIEW

| | | |
|---|---|---|
| administrative agency  8 | case law  6 | criminal law  10 |
| administrative law  8 | chancellor  10 | damages  11 |
| administrative process  9 | citation  14 | defendant  5 |
| analogy  6 | civil law  9 | defense  11 |
| appellant  19 | common law  4 | enabling legislation  8 |
| appellee  19 | court of equity  10 | equitable maxims  11 |
| breach  12 | court of law  10 | |

| | | |
|---|---|---|
| independent regulatory agency  9 | ordinance  7 | remedy in equity  11 |
| injunction  12 | petitioner  19 | rescission  12 |
| judicial process  9 | plaintiff  5 | respondent  19 |
| jurisprudence  3 | positive law  3 | specific performance  12 |
| laches  11 | positivist school  3 | *stare decisis*  4 |
| law  3 | precedent  4 | statute  7 |
| legal realism  4 | private law  9 | statute of limitations  11 |
| legal reasoning  5 | procedural law  9 | statutory law  7 |
| natural law school  3 | public law  9 | substantive law  9 |
| opinion  19 | remedy  10 | syllogism  5 |
| | remedy at law  10 | |

# QUESTIONS AND CASE PROBLEMS

**1–1. Philosophy of Law.** In the middle of the last century, the United States declared war on Mexico and levied taxes to support the war effort. Henry David Thoreau (author of *Walden*), who felt that the war was unjust, refused to pay taxes to support it and was subsequently imprisoned for violating the law. Thoreau maintained that obeying the law in these circumstances would be unethical. Which of the schools of legal philosophy discussed in this chapter would be the most sympathetic toward Thoreau's views on law? Explain.

**1–2. Statutory versus Common Law.** How does statutory law come into existence? How does it differ from the common law? If statutory law conflicts with the common law, which law will govern?

**1–3. Reading Citations.** Assume that you want to read the entire court opinion in the case of *Xieng v. Peoples National Bank of Washington,* 120 Wash.2d 512, 844 P.2d 389 (1993). The case deals with an employer's alleged discrimination against an Asian American. Explain specifically where you would find the court's opinion.

**1–4. Sources of American Law.** This chapter discussed a number of sources of American law. Which source of law takes priority in the following situations, and why?

(a) A federal statute conflicts with the U.S. Constitution.

(b) A federal statute conflicts with a state constitution.

(c) A state statute conflicts with the common law of that state.

(d) A state constitutional amendment conflicts with the U.S. Constitution.

**1–5. Stare Decisis.** In the text of this chapter, we stated that the doctrine of *stare decisis* "became a cornerstone of the English and American judicial systems." What does *stare decisis* mean, and why has this doctrine been so fundamental to the development of our legal tradition?

**1–6. Court Opinions.** What is the difference between a concurring opinion and a majority opinion? Between a concurring opinion and a dissenting opinion? Why do judges and justices write concurring and dissenting opinions, given the fact that these opinions will not affect the outcome of the case at hand, which has already been decided by majority vote?

**1–7. Common Law versus Statutory Law.** Courts are able to overturn precedents and thus can change the common law. Should judges have the same authority to overrule statutory law? Explain.

**1–8. Stare Decisis.** "The judge's role is not to make the law but to uphold and apply the law." Do you agree or disagree with this statement? Discuss fully the reasons for your answer.

**1–9. Remedies.** Arthur Rabe sued Xavier Sanchez for breaching a contract in which Sanchez promised to sell Rabe a Van Gogh painting for $150,000. What remedy would Rabe seek if he wanted Sanchez to perform the contract as promised? What remedy would Rabe seek if he wanted to cancel the contract because Sanchez fraudulently misrepresented the painting as an original Van Gogh when in fact it was a copy? Would the remedy Rabe seeks in either case be a remedy at law or a remedy in equity?

**1–10. Terminology.** In the Rabe-Sanchez lawsuit above, which party was the plaintiff? If Rabe loses in the trial court and appeals that court's decision, which party will be the appellant (or petitioner), and which party will be the appellee (or respondent)? Assume that one of the three appellate judges reviewing the case disagrees with the other two judges. What would you call the written opinion representing the decision of the court—a unanimous opinion, a concurring opinion, a majority opinion, or a dissenting opinion?

# CHAPTER 2

# BUSINESS ETHICS

**F**ew people today would claim that it is unethical to seek profits. In fact, successful businesspersons are often ranked among the most admired individuals in our society. But there has always been—and continues to be—an underlying tension between the pursuit of profits and the welfare of those groups affected by this pursuit, which may include employees, shareholders, consumers, creditors, the community, and the global society as a whole. When a business firm concentrates on the ''bottom line'' at the expense of one or more of these groups, that firm may end up being targeted by the press as unethical and subject to sanctions, such as boycotts. In the long run, the firm may lose customers, and therefore profits, because its behavior is perceived to be unethical. In sum, businesspersons have to walk a fine line to ensure that their profit-making activities do not exceed the ethical boundaries established by society.

In preparing for a career in business, you will therefore find that a background in business ethics and a commitment to ethical behavior are just as important as a knowledge of the specific laws that you will read about in this text. Furthermore, if you wish to truly understand the law, you need to be aware of the ethical framework within which it operates. In this chapter, we first examine the nature of business ethics and some of the sources of ethical standards that have guided others in their business decision making. We then look at some of the obstacles to ethical behavior faced by businesspersons. In the next section of the chapter, we examine some important ethical issues in today's business world.

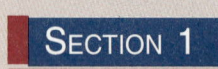

## THE NATURE OF BUSINESS ETHICS

Before we can talk about business ethics, we need to define what is meant by ethics generally. **Ethics** can be defined as the branch of philosophy that

24

focuses on morality (right and wrong behavior) and the way in which moral principles are applied to daily life. Ethics has to do with questions relating to the fairness, justness, rightness, or wrongness of an action. What is fair? What is just? What is the right thing to do in this situation? These are essentially ethical questions.

Although the concepts of ethics and ethical duties may seem abstract, in fact ethics plays an active role in our lives. Ethics affects and gives meaning to our everyday lives and the decisions we make. We constantly apply our values and moral convictions to our actions and decisions, frequently without even being aware that we are doing so. The clothes we buy, the music we prefer, the way we treat our friends and family, the books we choose to read—these and a thousand other everyday activities and decisions, if you analyze them carefully, ultimately relate to ethical values and goals.

## DEFINING BUSINESS ETHICS

**Business ethics** focuses on what constitutes right or wrong behavior in the world of business and on how moral principles are applied by businesspersons to situations that arise in their daily activities in the workplace. It is important to remember that business ethics is not a separate *kind* of ethics. That is, businesspersons do not necessarily adopt one set of ethical principles to guide them in their business decisions and another set to guide them in their personal lives. The ethical standards that guide our behavior as, say, mothers, fathers, or students apply equally well to our activities as businesspersons. Business activities are just one part of the human enterprise, and business ethics is a subset of ethics that relates specifically to the kinds of situations that arise in the everyday world of business.

## THE COMPLEXITY OF BUSINESS ETHICS

Ethical decision making in the business world is somewhat more complicated than it is in our personal lives, however. First of all, a businessperson rarely has complete control over the decision-making process. In the corporate setting, for example, the ultimate decision makers are the members of the board of directors, who must make decisions as a group. No one individual (normally) can dictate policy or decide corporate issues. Corporate officers and managers, of course, also make decisions that affect the corporation, but their decision-making authority is usually limited to their departments or particular spheres of activity. Furthermore, their decisions must harmonize with the policies and decisions made by the directors and top management. If you are an employee of a large company, you will find that the decision as to what is right or wrong for the company is not yours to make, although your input may weigh in the decision.

Decisions made by businesspersons also normally have wider effects than private decisions do. Indeed, one business decision can have repercussions throughout the entire society. Therefore, as a businessperson, you need to be prepared to justify—to your superiors, to your colleagues or employees, to corporate shareholders, or even in a court of law—whatever decisions you make. It is not enough to say, as we might in our private lives, "I felt that it was the best decision in the circumstances" or "It seemed like the right thing to do at the time." You will need to demonstrate the rational basis for your decision and explain why, given the alternatives facing you, you concluded that your decision was the right one. In the business context, ethical behavior requires that you decide ethical issues on the basis of clearly defined ethical standards.

## TRADE-OFFS AND BUSINESS ETHICS

Ideally, each decision you make as a businessperson would fall readily into the center area of the diagram shown in Exhibit 2–1. Frequently, however, to ensure that a decision or action is at once profitable, legal, and ethical, some profitability or some ethical considerations must be sacrificed, or traded off, in the decision-making process. A **trade-off** occurs when it becomes necessary to sacrifice one desired goal to obtain another.

It is important to realize that the ethical trade-offs normally faced by businesspersons are not clear-cut trade-offs between "good" and "bad" alternatives. By definition, ethical dilemmas only arise when two or more *ethical* goals come into conflict. For example, assume that a corporate executive has to decide whether to approve the sale of a new product that would be beneficial for most consumers but that might have undesirable side

■ **Exhibit 2–1 Ethical Decision Making**
This diagram illustrates how legality, profitability, and ethical factors interrelate in the ethical decision-making process in the business context. Ideally, business decisions will fall within the shaded area in which all circles overlap. If they do not, ethically responsible decision making requires that trade-offs be made so that all three criteria are satisfied.

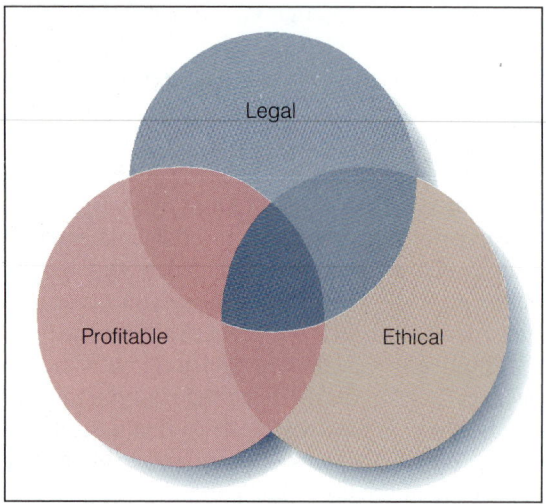

effects for a small percentage of its users. In this situation, the trade-off becomes relatively obvious: expose an unknown but extremely small number of individuals to possible harm while allowing all other consumers to enjoy the benefits of the new product (and in the process, probably make higher profits for the shareholders), or protect that small number of individuals from possible harm and not allow all other consumers to enjoy the benefits of the new product.

In statistics, this trade-off is known as a trade-off between *Type I* and *Type II errors*. A **Type I error** occurs because of the sin of *commission*. When a new product, such as a drug, is sold and there is an undesirable side effect—a customer becomes sick or is injured—this occurs because of the sin of commission. But if the product is not entered into the marketplace, a **Type II error** will occur. Type II errors result from the sin of *omission*. All of the benefits that people would have derived had the product been introduced do not exist if the product is not marketed.

# SOURCES OF ETHICAL STANDARDS

Despite our progressive and technologically advanced modern world, science and technology offer us little guidance when it comes to establishing ethical standards of behavior. In fact, science and technology sometimes create serious ethical dilemmas that did not exist previously. Medical technology is a good example. Organ transplants and life-sustaining medical equipment have created life-lengthening possibilities that did not even exist a decade or so ago. But these developments have also created difficult ethical issues, such as whether individuals should have the ''right to die'' and whether health care should be rationed. Technology cannot answer such questions, because such questions relate to human values and beliefs that cannot be measured quantitatively.

This is not to say that there are no resources to which we can turn for ethical guidance. One important guiding source is business law itself. Other sources of ethical standards include religious beliefs and philosophically derived ethical values.

## ETHICS AND THE LAW

In all societies, ethics and the law go hand in hand. Law can never operate in a vacuum. It cannot be a series of rules that are imposed on society from without; rather, the law must reflect a society's customs and values and reinforce principles of behavior that society deems right and just.

**BUSINESS LAW AS A GUIDE TO ETHICAL BEHAVIOR** Laws governing business all reflect, directly or indirectly, the moral assumption that businesspersons should act ethically in their dealings with one another. Business law requires that people in business honor their contractual commitments, cooperate with one another in the performance of contracts, act reasonably and in good faith, and exercise due care and consideration for others in their undertakings. When studying business law, in essence you are studying particular applications of general ethical precepts held by society and expressed through statutes and court decisions. Although a law may seem arbitrary at first glance, if you look closely, you will often find the connection between that particular law and the broad, underlying ethical premise on which it ultimately rests. Insofar as possible, we will help you see this connection by indicating, as we discuss particular laws in this text, how these laws relate to broad social policies and ethical principles.

## THE DISTINCTION BETWEEN ETHICS AND THE LAW

Because the law reflects and codifies a society's ethical values, many of our ethical decisions are made for us—by our laws. Nevertheless, simply obeying the law does not fulfill all ethical obligations. In the interest of preserving personal freedom, as well as for practical reasons, the law does not—and cannot—codify all ethical requirements. No law says, for example, that it is *illegal* to lie to one's family, but it may be *unethical* to do so. Likewise, in the business world, numerous actions might be unethical but not necessarily illegal. And even though it may be convenient for businesspersons to satisfy themselves by mere compliance with the law, such an approach may not always yield ethical outcomes.

Consider the following hypothetical example. The U.S. government has discovered that a child's toy is dangerous and has caused the deaths of some children. Consequently, the government has banned sales of the toy, leaving the manufacturer with a large unsold inventory. Although sales of the product are banned in the United States, it may be perfectly legal to export this toy to nations that have little consumer protection legislation. But would it be ethical to do so?

In short, the law has its limits—it cannot make all our ethical decisions for us. When it does not, ethical standards must guide the decision-making process.

## THE DERIVATION OF ETHICAL STANDARDS

Religious and philosophical inquiry into the nature of "the good" is an age-old pursuit. Broadly speaking, though, ethical reasoning relating to business has traditionally been characterized by two fundamental approaches. One approach defines ethical behavior in terms of *duty*. The other approach determines what is ethical in terms of the *consequences,* or outcome, of any given action. We examine each of these approaches in the following sections.

**DUTY-BASED ETHICS** In America, the dominant duty-based ethical standard derives from religious sources. Religious ethical standards are *absolute.* When an act is prohibited by religious teachings, it is unethical and should not be undertaken, regardless of its consequences. Religious ethical standards also involve an element of *compassion.* Therefore, even though it might be profitable for a firm to lay off a less productive employee, if that employee would find it difficult to find employment elsewhere and his or her family would suffer as a result, this potential suffering would be given substantial weight by the decision makers. Compassionate treatment of others is also mandated—to a certain extent, at least—by the Golden Rule of the ancients ("Do unto others as you would have them do unto you"), which has been adopted by most religions.

Ethical standards based on a concept of duty may also be derived solely from philosophical principles. Immanuel Kant (1724–1804), for example, identified some general guiding principles for moral behavior. Kantian ethics are based on what Kant believed to be the fundamental nature of human beings. Kant held that it is rational to assume that human beings are qualitatively different from other physical objects occupying space. Persons are *moral* agents; that is, they are endowed with moral integrity and the capacity to reason and conduct their affairs rationally. Therefore, their thoughts and actions should be respected. When human beings are treated merely as means, they are being treated as the equivalent of objects and are being denied their basic humanity.

A central postulate in Kantian ethics is that individuals should evaluate their actions in light of the consequences that would follow if *everyone* in society acted in the same way. This **categorical imperative** can be applied to any action. For example, say that you are deciding whether to cheat on an examination. If you have adopted Kant's categorical imperative, you will decide not to cheat because if everyone cheated, the examination would be meaningless. The categorical imperative also implies that when deciding whether to take a certain action, you should put yourself in the shoes of the person or persons who will be affected by the action. Would you be satisfied with the decision in that situation?

**OUTCOME-BASED ETHICS—UTILITARIANISM** "Thou shalt act so as to generate the greatest good for the greatest number." This is a paraphrase of the major premise of the utilitarian approach to ethics. **Utilitarianism** is a philosophical theory first developed by Jeremy Bentham (1748–1832) and then advanced, with some modifications, by John Stuart Mill (1806–1873)—both British philosophers. In contrast to duty-based ethics, utilitarianism is outcome oriented. It focuses on the consequences of an action, not on the nature of the action itself or on any set of preestablished moral values or religious beliefs.

Under a utilitarian model of ethics, an action is morally correct, or "right," when, among the people it affects, it produces the greatest amount of good for the greatest number. When an action affects the majority adversely, it is morally wrong. Applying the utilitarian theory thus requires (1) a determination of which individuals will be affected by the action in question; (2) an assessment, or **cost-benefit analysis,** of the negative and positive effects of alternative actions on these individuals; and (3) a choice among alternative actions that will produce maximum societal utility (the greatest positive benefits for the greatest number of individuals).

The utilitarian approach to decision making is commonly employed by businesses, as well as by individuals. Weighing the consequences of a decision in terms of its costs and benefits for everyone affected by the decision is a useful analytical tool in the decision-making process. As mentioned previously, businesses frequently must face ethical trade-offs, and utilitarian analysis helps to define the relative utility of the conflicting goals. At the same time, utilitarianism is often criticized because its objective, calculated approach to problems tends to reduce the welfare of human beings to plus and minus signs on a cost-benefit worksheet and to "justify" human costs that many find totally unacceptable.

# OBSTACLES TO ETHICAL BUSINESS BEHAVIOR

It cannot be denied that in the pursuit of self-interest, people sometimes behave unethically in the business context, just as they do in their private lives. Some businesspersons knowingly engage in unethical behavior because they think that they can "get away with it"—that no one will ever learn of their unethical actions. Examples of this kind of unethical behavior include padding expense accounts, casting doubts on the integrity of a rival co-worker to gain a job promotion, stealing company supplies or equipment, and so on. Obviously, these acts are unethical and, in many cases, illegal as well.

In other situations, the distinction between ethical and unethical (and legal and illegal) behavior is not quite so clear-cut. For example, what if you wanted to use your employer's computer system for private purposes? Clearly, it would be wrong to do so if your employer's interests would be harmed as a result. But would they be? After all, you would not be stealing anything in the sense of physically "taking away" your employer's property.

Similarly, would it be wrong to make a copy of your employer's software without permission? As in the previous example, the personal benefit is clear. You would avoid having to pay for the software. But would your employer suffer any detriment as a result of your actions? Would anyone suffer? (In the past decade or so, the laws governing the nature of ownership rights in technological and intellectual property have been expanded by statutes and court decisions, and new laws have been created to cover these kinds of situations, as you will see in Chapter 8. But because these laws are relatively new, many people are unaware of them.) The point is, in these kinds of situations, it is easy to rationalize by telling yourself that because your behavior will not harm another, it is ethical. Even if you conclude that such behavior is wrong and perhaps illegal, you may be tempted to go ahead with it under the assumption that nobody will ever discover what you have done.

In the following case, a travel agent took advantage of her position to transfer unclaimed mileage credits to herself to gain, ultimately, free airline tickets. She claimed that she had not harmed the interests of the airline and therefore had not committed any wrongful or illegal action.

**BACKGROUND AND FACTS**   *Gayle Schreier, who worked in a travel service office, had access to the American Airlines computer reservation system, which stores passengers' names and flight information. On a number of occasions, Schreier accessed the system to replace the names of passengers with "G. Johnson" (a fictitious person whom Schreier enrolled as a member of American's Frequent Flyer AAdvantage Program), as well as the names of other fictitious passengers. The fictitious passengers received mileage credits, for which American issued coupons that were used to acquire tickets for American flights. Irwin Schreier, Gayle's husband, set up a number of mail drops, the addresses of which were provided to American as the addresses of fictitious AAdvantage members like G. Johnson. The Schreiers were convicted in U.S. district court of wire fraud. On appeal, they argued that the proof against them was "fatally flawed" because it did not show that they had acquired property of American. The Schreiers contended that if the mileage they acquired was the property of anyone, it was the property of the passengers, none of whom complained.*

| |
|---|
| CASE 2.1 |

**UNITED STATES v. SCHREIER**

United States Court of Appeals,
Tenth Circuit, 1990.
908 F.2d 645.

*LOGAN,* Circuit Judge.

\*   \*   \*   \*

Mileage credited to AAdvantage members is considered a liability of the airline for accounting purposes. \*   \*   \*

The Schreiers' scheme involved the accumulation of mileage for which American would not otherwise be liable because it was not claimed by the passengers who actually flew. When liability is created on American's books, through a transfer of mileage \*   \*   \*, the victim is American, because that corporation thereby owes a liability that otherwise would not exist. By their device of replacing \*   \*   \* passengers' names in the computer with a fictional name and account number, the Schreiers have victimized American, by fraud, and through use of computer access, wire fraud. \*   \*   \*

We have examined the indictment; it is consistent with our analysis and is not fatally defective. In acquiring mileage the Schreiers created liability for the airline, and obtained property for themselves. The Supreme Court has recognized that the taking of intangible [nonphysical] property may be the basis of a wire fraud charge. We need not pursue a metaphysical argument regarding whether the "property" existed as such in the possession of American to conclude that the creation of a liability on the part of a corporation is no less the misappropriation of its property than would be the theft of an asset worth an equal amount.

*The U.S. Court of Appeals affirmed the convictions of the Schreiers for wire fraud.*

**DECISION AND REMEDY**

**International Computer-Related Theft**   *Computer-related theft crosses national boundaries and represents a growing global problem. Australia, Canada, Great Britain, and other nations have passed detailed statutes governing computer crime. In some respects, these statutes go beyond U.S. laws. There are no significant treaties, conventions, or United Nations resolutions on computer "hacking," however, and many countries lack any laws against computer fraud.*

**INTERNATIONAL CONSIDERATIONS**

## ETHICS AND THE CORPORATE STRUCTURE

To a certain extent, the corporate structure itself may promote unethical behavior, because it tends to shield corporate actors from personal responsibility for their actions. For example, if a corporation markets a product that results in a consumer's death, the corporate officer who made the decision to market the product may not be deemed a "murderer." Nor would that officer, in all likelihood, condone the killing of others.

In effect, corporate decision makers are protected from the consequences of their decisions by the corporate entity—that is, they do not witness or deal directly with the harm or injuries generated by their decisions. To a certain extent, they are also shielded from personal responsibility for their actions by the corporate collectivity. As mentioned earlier, normally, no one individual makes a corporate decision, and therefore no one individual ever has to assume total responsibility for a corporate action. In recent years, however, as will be discussed later in this text, the courts have been increasingly willing to look behind the "corporate veil" and hold individual corporate actors liable for actions resulting in harm to others.

## ETHICS AND MANAGEMENT

It is important to realize that much unethical business behavior occurs simply because it is not always clear what ethical standards and behaviors are appropriate or acceptable in a given business context. Although today, most firms issue ethical policies or codes of conduct, often these policies and codes are ineffective in indicating to employees what behavior is expected of them. Sometimes, the firm's ethical policies are not communicated clearly to employees or do not bear on the real ethical issues confronting decision makers. At other times, management may talk about ethics but in fact, by its own conduct, indicate that ethical considerations take second place.

Surveys of business executives indicate that management's behavior, more than anything else, sets the ethical tone of a firm. For example, if management makes no attempt to deter unethical behavior by reprimands or discharge, it will be clear to employees that management is not all that serious about ethics. Likewise, if a company rewards—for example, through promotions or salary increases—those who obviously engage in unethical tactics to increase the firm's profits, employees who do not resort to unethical tactics will be at a disadvantage.

Another deterrent to ethical behavior is created when management sets unrealistic production or marketing goals. If a sales quota, for example, can only be met through high-pressure, unethical sales tactics, employees trying to act "in the interest of the firm" may think that management is implicitly asking them to behave unethically.

## THE WHISTLEBLOWER'S DILEMMA

Of course, an even stronger deterrent to ethical behavior occurs when managers engage in blatantly unethical or illegal conduct and expect their employees to do likewise. Ethical employees may then have to face the most uncomfortable of all dilemmas: "blow the whistle" on the employer's unethical or illegal conduct and probably be fired as a result, or keep silent and suffer a bad conscience—and possibly criminal penalties—for participating in the illegal activity.

Employees who are required by their employers to participate in unethical or illegal practices face a particularly difficult ethical dilemma. The employee must weigh the duty of loyalty to the firm for which he or she works against the duty of loyalty to his or her conscience. If the employee's spouse, children, or both rely on the employee's income for essential expenses, this further complicates the issue.

SECTION 4

# ETHICAL ISSUES IN BUSINESS

It would be impossible to describe all of the different kinds of ethical issues that arise in the business world. As you will discover in reading through this text, ethics relates to all aspects of business activity. Broadly speaking, ethical issues can be categorized as internal issues or external issues. Ethical issues internal to the firm frequently concern the relationship between the firm and its employees. Ethical issues external to the firm predominantly relate to the products or services marketed by the firm and to how marketing decisions affect the welfare of the ultimate consumers of those products and services. We examine both of these types of issues in the following sections.

Note that external issues also involve a firm's relationship with its suppliers, its creditors, the surrounding community, and other external groups. In the *Focus on Ethics* after the end of Chapter 10, you will read further about both internal and external ethical issues in the context of corporate social responsibility.

## EMPLOYMENT RELATIONSHIPS

One of the primary concerns of every employer is the ability to control the workplace environment. After all, it is the employer who is responsible for making the business firm a success, and success requires qualified, competent, loyal employees and efficient operations. But employees also have concerns. They want to earn a fair wage; they want to work in an environment free of health-endangering hazards; they want to be treated fairly and equally by their employers; and, increasingly in recent years, they want employers to respect their personal integrity and privacy rights.

By law, employers are required to provide a safe workplace, to pay a minimum wage, and to provide equal employment opportunities for all potential and existing employees. But does an employer have ethical obligations to employees that go beyond those duties written into the law? And what if in fulfillment of one ethical (or legal) obligation, another duty must be violated? We discuss here some employment decisions facing employers in which various ethical or legal duties come into conflict.

**EMPLOYMENT DISCRIMINATION** As will be discussed in Chapter 37, by law employers must offer equal employment opportunities to all job applicants and employees. Today's employers are prohibited from discriminating against existing or potential employees on the basis of race, color, national origin, sex, pregnancy, religion, age, or disability. This means that employers must sometimes treat employees unfairly and unequally. For example, many companies have adopted *affirmative action* policies to make up for past discriminatory practices against protected classes, such as minority groups or women. These policies occasionally result in what has been termed ''reverse discrimination''—that is, discrimination against qualified members of the ''majority'' group.

Essentially, the ethical question here is whether it is fair to promote one employee to a position instead of an equally qualified employee simply to correct for past discrimination. Some would say yes; others, no. But the question indicates how employers who are trying to fulfill a perceived ethical obligation to treat employees fairly and equally can sometimes find themselves in a no-win situation.

The following case is illustrative. Even though the employer went substantially beyond minimum legal compliance in attempting to provide a safe workplace for employees, the firm was nonetheless charged by some of its employees with having violated another ethical (and legal) duty—that of providing equal employment opportunities for women.

---

**COMPANY PROFILE** *In 1880, janitors at a school in Whitewater, Wisconsin, wanted to regulate the temperature in the classrooms without disturbing the classes. Professor Warren Johnson developed a device using mercury and a heat element to control a circuit and thereby control the temperature. With this invention—the thermostat—Johnson and investor William Plankinton formed Johnson Electric Service Company in 1885. Johnson invented a number of other devices and also worked on tower clocks and steam-powered automobiles until his death in 1911. The company continued to improve its temperature control systems, to diversify, and to expand. Renamed Johnson Controls, Inc., in 1974, the company acquired Globe-Union (an automobile battery manufacturer) in 1978, Hoover Universal (an automobile seat and plastics manufacturer) in 1985, and other U.S. and international businesses in the 1980s and 1990s. Based in Milwaukee, Johnson Controls is the world's largest manufacturer of plastic*

**CASE 2.2**

**UNITED AUTOMOBILE WORKERS v. JOHNSON CONTROLS, INC.**

Supreme Court of the United States, 1991.
499 U.S. 187,
111 S.Ct. 1196,
113 L.Ed.2d 158.

*containers, North America's leading independent manufacturer of auto-
mobile seats, and the top U.S. manufacturer of automobile batteries. Most
of the batteries (85 percent) are marketed through retailers such as Sears
and Wal-Mart under their own brand names.*

**BACKGROUND AND FACTS** *Johnson Controls, Inc., created its Battery Division in 1978. In 1982, as part of an ongoing attempt to reduce
the health hazards that might result from lead exposure, Johnson adopted
a "fetal protection policy," under which women of childbearing age were
prohibited from working in the Battery Division. This decision was reached
after scientific studies indicated that a pregnant woman's exposure to high
lead levels could harm the fetus. Johnson adopted this mandatory policy
largely because its previous voluntary policy had failed to achieve the
desired purpose: protecting pregnant women and their unborn children
from dangerously high blood lead levels. Employees and their union,
United Auto Workers, brought a suit against Johnson, claiming that the
fetal protection policy violated Title VII of the Civil Rights Act of 1964,
which prohibits discrimination in employment on the basis of sex. The trial
court held for Johnson, and the unions and employees appealed. The appellate court affirmed the trial court's ruling. The case was then appealed
to the United States Supreme Court.*

JUSTICE *BLACKMUN* delivered the opinion of the Court.
    * * * *
Under * * * Title VII [of the Civil Rights Act of 1964], an employer may
discriminate on the basis of "religion, sex, or national origin in those certain instances
where religion, sex, or national origin is a bona fide occupational qualification [BFOQ]
reasonably necessary to the normal operation of that particular business or enterprise." We therefore turn to the question whether Johnson Controls' fetal-protection
policy is one of those "certain instances" that come within the BFOQ exception.
    * * * *
Johnson Controls argues that its fetal-protection policy falls within the so-called
safety exception to the BFOQ. * * *
    * * * *
Our case law * * * makes clear that the safety exception is limited to instances
in which sex or pregnancy actually interferes with the employee's ability to perform
the job. This approach is consistent with the language of the BFOQ provision itself,
for it suggests that permissible distinctions based on sex must relate to ability to
perform the duties of the job. Johnson Controls suggests, however, that we expand
the exception to allow fetal-protection policies that mandate particular standards for
pregnant or fertile women. We decline to do so. Such an expansion contradicts not
only the language of the BFOQ and the narrowness of its exception but the plain
language and history of the Pregnancy Discrimination Act [PDA].
    The PDA's amendment to Title VII contains a BFOQ standard of its own: unless
pregnant employees differ from others "in their ability or inability to work," they
must be "treated the same" as other employees "for all employment related purposes." * * * In other words, women as capable of doing their jobs as their male
counterparts may not be forced to choose between having a child and having a job.
    * * * *
We have no difficulty concluding that Johnson Controls cannot establish a BFOQ.
Fertile women, as far as appears in the record, participate in the manufacture of
batteries as efficiently as anyone else. * * * Title VII and the PDA simply do not
allow a woman's dismissal because of her failure to submit to sterilization.

*The Supreme Court reversed the judgment of the appellate court and re-manded the case for further proceedings. Johnson Controls' fetal protec-tion policy was discriminatory in violation of Title VII of the Civil Rights Act and the Pregnancy Discrimination Act.*

**DECISION AND REMEDY**

### "PRICE DISCRIMINATION" IN EMPLOYMENT

In recent years, some firms have been criticized for firing highly paid employees who have worked for—and received annual raises from—the firms for years and then replacing those employees with younger, less experienced persons who are happy to accept lower salaries. Such actions are not nec-essarily illegal. If the fired employee cannot prove that the employer has breached an employment contract or violated the Age Discrimination in Em-ployment Act (ADEA) of 1967, he or she will not have a **cause of action** (the right to seek legal redress or relief) against the employer. The ADEA prohibits discrimination against workers forty years old and older on the basis of age, but em-ployers can always say that lack of performance or ability, not age, was the deciding factor.

Increasingly, employers who want to shed older, highly paid employees are avoiding liability for age discrimination by offering the employees early retirement plans, financial incentives, and perhaps job-placement services—in return for a written **waiver** (or relinquishment) of the right to sue the firm for age discrimination. To ensure that employees are fully cognizant of the rights they are waiving, the Older Workers Benefit Protection Act, which went into effect in 1990, requires that employees be given forty-five days to consider the waiver agreement and seven days to revoke the waiver after signing it. But from an ethical view-point, is it fair to long-time, loyal employees to force them to make a choice between early retire-ment and continuing on the job when the latter choice may involve a lower salary, a demotion to a less desirable position, or even eventual dismissal on the ground of some "manufactured" reason other than age?

In deciding this issue, remember that if em-ployers fail to keep their eyes on their profit mar-gins, they may place in jeopardy the financial well-being of the firm. Why should a firm retain highly paid employees if it can obtain essentially the same work output for a lower price by hiring cheaper labor? Does an employer or manager have an ethical duty to employees who have served the firm loyally over a long period of time? Most peo-ple would say yes. Should this duty take precedence over, say, a corporate manager's duty to the firm's owners to maintain or increase the profitability of the firm? Would your answer be the same if the firm faced imminent bankruptcy if it could not lower its operational costs? What if long-time em-ployees were willing to take a slight reduction in pay to help the firm through its financial difficul-ties? What if they were not?

### SEXUAL HARASSMENT VERSUS WRONGFUL DISCHARGE

Another conflict of duties that sometimes faces employers poses the choice of being sued for sexual harassment against the choice of being sued for wrongful discharge. Lawsuits for *sexual harassment* in the workplace (discussed in Chapter 37) have climbed dramatically in number in the past decade. So have suits for *wrongful discharge*—firing an employee without good cause or for discriminatory reasons (see Chapters 36 and 37). And in some cases, those who have been fired for sexually harassing female co-workers have in turn claimed that they were wrongfully discharged—and won in court.

An obvious question presents itself: How can a court hold an employer liable for wrongful dis-charge when, in firing the employee, the employer was complying with a legal requirement? After all, federal law and the Equal Employment Opportu-nity Commission's guidelines require employers to take "immediate and appropriate corrective ac-tion" in response to an employee's complaint of sexual abuse. The answer to this question is that under some state laws and employment agree-ments, employers are prohibited from firing em-ployees without a "just cause." And particular incidents of sexual harassment may or may not constitute just cause for firing the harasser.

Such a predicament faced Chrysler Corpora-tion when one of its female employees informed management that she had been sexually assaulted by a male co-worker. Chrysler acted promptly. A brief investigation of the incident confirmed that Ronald Gallenbeck, a forklift operator, had indeed assaulted the woman. Gallenbeck had approached the woman from behind while she was inspecting a door panel; grabbed her breasts; returned to the phone conversation he was having; and said, "Yup, they're real." Chrysler summarily discharged Gallenbeck for his actions. Gallenbeck claimed that his employment had been wrongfully terminated.

In accordance with a collective bargaining agreement (an agreement between Chrysler and its employees' union representatives), the dispute was heard eventually by an arbitrator. (In arbitration proceedings, the dispute is heard by an impartial third party, the arbitrator, who decides the issue. The arbitrator's decision can be appealed to the courts, although courts, with few exceptions, defer to the arbitrator's decision—see Chapter 3.) The collective bargaining agreement also stipulated that employees could only be discharged for a "just cause." The arbitrator concluded that one incident of sexual assault did not qualify as a "just cause" for summary discharge and that severe discipline— short of discharge—would have been adequate to deter Gallenbeck from further misconduct. Although Chrysler presented evidence of at least four other incidents in which Gallenbeck had grabbed or pinched female employees, the arbitrator refused to consider these incidents because Chrysler had learned of them *after* Gallenbeck's discharge. The arbitrator directed Chrysler to reinstate Gallenbeck with back pay, following a thirty-day suspension. A federal district court affirmed the arbitrator's decision, as did the appellate court, when Chrysler appealed the case.[1]

Firms that fire employees for sexual harassment may find, as Chrysler did, that they have simply traded one set of problems for another. The question is, which set of problems is worse? The prevailing wisdom seems to be that risking a lawsuit for wrongful discharge may be the most reasonable course. This is because firing the harasser may prevent multiple sexual harassment lawsuits brought by other female employees who may be harassed by the same male worker.

1. *Chrysler Motors Corp. v. International Union, Allied Industrial Workers of America,* 959 F.2d 685 (7th Cir. 1992).

**EMPLOYEE PRIVACY RIGHTS** An increasingly significant ethical issue in the employment context concerns the privacy rights of employees. To what extent, for example, may employers engage in drug testing, integrity testing, performance monitoring, or other procedures without violating an employee's right to privacy? To what extent can employers base employment decisions on off-the-job employee habits—such as smoking or drinking—or other behavior? Do employers have the right to require potential employees to undergo psychological screening tests before they will be considered as job candidates? These and other employment-related questions involving an ethical dimension will be discussed in Chapters 36 and 37.

## CONSUMER WELFARE

To a certain extent, product liability laws and warranty laws (discussed in Chapters 24 and 25), as well as other laws protecting consumers, help to ensure that corporations will market only products that are safe to use or consume. But there is a large "gray area" in which marketing a certain product may be legal but would be considered unethical. For example, suppose a corporation produces a type of baby food that babies like and mothers buy but that is not nutritionally satisfactory for babies because of a high monosodium glutamate (MSG) or sugar content. It would not be *illegal* to market the food, although it might be *unethical* to do so.

Consider, for example, a situation that recently faced the H. B. Fuller Company, which markets its glues, sealants, paints, and other products worldwide. Fuller was presented with an ethical dilemma when it was learned that thousands of children in Guatemala, Brazil, and other Latin American countries inhaled Fuller glues, thus inviting future kidney disease and brain damage. In the spring of 1993, Minnesota activists (Fuller is headquartered in St. Paul, Minnesota) picketed outside the building in which Fuller's annual meeting was taking place, demanding that Fuller cease producing and marketing glues in Latin America and stop "putting profits before people." Although Fuller has since suspended sales of shoe glue in Guatemala and Honduras, many critics feel that the company should go further and suspend sales throughout Latin America.

Of course, product misuse can occur anywhere, including in the United States, and the central question raised in this section remains the same: If a consumer is harmed by a product because that consumer failed to exercise due care or did not use the product as directed by the manufacturer, who should bear the responsibility for that harm, the consumer or the manufacturer? The following case addresses this issue.

---

**CASE 2.3**

**CAMPBELL v. BIC CORP.**
Supreme Court, Fulton County, 1992.
154 Misc.2d 976,
586 N.Y.S.2d 871.

**BACKGROUND AND FACTS** *Terry Campbell, a six-year-old boy, placed a cigarette lighter under his shirt and lit the lighter. His shirt caught on fire, causing him to suffer severe burns. Terry's mother, Mary Campbell, sued Bic Corporation, the manufacturer of the lighter, for damages. Mary Campbell contended that the corporation had the capacity to produce cigarette lighters with child-resistant qualities and that its failure to do so was a design defect that made its lighters unreasonably dangerous. (Under strict product liability laws—discussed in Chapter 25—if a design defect makes a product unreasonably dangerous, the manufacturer and seller of the product may be held liable for any resulting injuries.) Bic sought to dismiss the complaint, claiming that it did not have a duty to design and manufacture child-resistant lighters because the lighters it manufactured were intended only for adult use.*

*WHITE,* Justice.

\* \* \* \*

Defendant contends that [the plaintiff's] allegations do not set forth a cognizable cause of action either in strict products liability or negligence as it did not have a duty to design and manufacture child resistant lighters since the lighters it manufactured were intended only for adult use. In support of its position it relies upon Section 402A of the Restatement (Second) of Torts and cases from other jurisdictions.

\* \* \* [The defendant] maintains that, under Section 402A, a manufacturer does not owe a plaintiff a duty of care unless its product was in a condition not reasonably contemplated by the ultimate consumer and was being used for the purposes and in the manner normally intended. Defendant contends that plaintiff cannot make this showing since the use of its lighter by a child is not a normally intended use and, since the risks associated with a lighter are open and obvious, plaintiff cannot argue that the lighter was in a condition not reasonably contemplated by the ultimate consumer.

The law in New York is broader than that set forth in the Restatement. In this State, in addition to having a duty to design a product so that it avoids an unreasonable risk of harm to anyone who is likely to be exposed to danger when the product is being used as intended, a manufacturer also has the duty to design its product so that it avoids an unreasonable risk of harm when it is being used for an unintended but foreseeable use. Because the lighters manufactured by defendant are commonly used and kept about the home, it is reasonably foreseeable that children will have access to them and will try to use them. Thus, the Court finds that defendant did owe plaintiff a duty of care. The law of the other jurisdictions cited by defendant does not affect this finding as it is not comparable to New York's. Nor does defendant's invocation of the ''open and obvious'' doctrine because in New York that is simply another factor that is considered in determining the reasonable care exercised by the parties.

*The court denied Bic's motion to dismiss the claim. Although Terry's use of the lighter was an unintended use, Bic should have known that harm caused by a child's use of its product was a foreseeable risk. Because Bic failed to design its product in such a way as to avoid this risk, it did not exercise reasonable care and was therefore liable for Terry's injuries.*

**DECISION AND REMEDY**

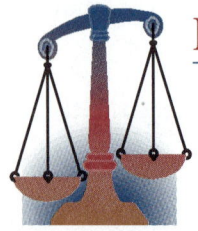

# EMERGING TRENDS IN BUSINESS LAW

# The Institutionalization of Ethics

The ethical dimension of business law has been receiving much wider attention by all groups in society—from business law professors who want to prepare their students for real-world ethical issues to members of the public concerned with protecting human rights and the environment. Business firms must pay special attention to the ethical ramifications of their decisions if they wish to maintain their integrity in the eyes of the public—and consequently, to thrive financially.

The widespread concern over ethical business behavior has led business firms to do what once only professional groups, such as attorneys and physicians, did: draft and implement codes of ethics to guide employee behavior. In a sense, these codes reflect an attempt to institutionalize ethics, or to incorporate ethics within an institutional framework.

## Ethical Codes within the Firm

One way that many firms make their employees aware of the ethical standards expected of them is through drafting and distributing to all employees a code of ethics. Such a code may be called a code of ethics, a code of conduct, a mission statement, a policy statement, or some other name. In general, ethical codes provide employees with the knowledge of what the firm expects in terms of their responsibilities and behavior. Relationships that are covered include employee-employee, employee-manager, employee-consumer, and employee-supplier relationships. Some ethical codes offer a lengthy and detailed set of guidelines for employees. Others are not really codes at all but summary statements of goals, policies, and priorities. Today, nearly all major U.S. firms have ethical codes and ethical training programs in place.

## The Effectiveness of Ethical Codes

To the extent that the codes and training programs address the real ethical concerns of a company and to the extent that management is fully committed to ethical behavior, these codes have proved to be effective. For example, the mission statement of the Johnson & Johnson Company (J&J) is a brief list of its ethical priorities, the first one reflecting its commitment to the safety of its customers. This statement helped J&J management deal promptly and effectively with the Tylenol crisis it faced in 1982.

The crisis arose when it was learned that some of J&J's Tylenol, a nonaspirin pain reliever, was "spiked" with cyanide, causing the deaths of several persons in Chicago. When top management was informed of the problem, it immediately formed a committee to handle the crisis. In accordance with the company's ethical guidelines, the company recalled Tylenol from the market until the company could develop tamper-resistant packaging for its product. The company also communicated with the public through numerous press releases, press conferences, and printed statements, as well as television and radio interviews.

In all, the swift and open actions taken by J&J management allowed the company to maintain its goodwill and reputation and to recover its dominance over the pain-reliever market, which many people felt it would never be able to do.

## Ethical Codes and Corporate Criminal Penalties

One of the benefits of having an ethical program in place is that it may result in fewer violations of criminal laws or less severe penalties for corporate crimes. Under the U.S. Sentencing Guidelines (discussed in Chapter 9), which provide standardized criminal sentences for federal crimes, corporate lawbreakers face sanctions and fines that can be as high as hundreds of millions of dollars. The guidelines allow judges to ease up on penalties, however, when companies have taken substantial steps to prevent, investigate, and punish wrongdoing by corporate employees.

## International Ethical Codes

International codes of ethics have also been drafted. In 1988, for example, to smooth out some of the ethical difficulties faced by multinational firms, the United Nations Economic and Social Council adopted an international code of conduct to regulate transnational corporations. More recently, in 1992, the International Franchise Association approved of a new ethical code to protect both franchisers and franchisees from mutual abuse.

The pros and cons of international ethical codes have been debated for decades. One of the difficulties in creating an effective international code of conduct is that it is hard to find consensus among different nations on what is appropriate conduct.

Nations have widely varying laws governing business transactions and generally what is or is not appropriate behavior in the business context. In many countries, for example, the giving of gifts and side payments in return for political or economic favors is a normal way of doing business. American businesspersons, however, are prohibited from bribing foreign officials to obtain contracts or other favorable treatment.

Also, in the Muslim world, the role of women in society is markedly different than in the United States. Therefore, Muslim countries would be reluctant to agree to an ethical code calling for the equal treatment of women in the employment context.

## ■ Implications for the Businessperson

1.   The old adage "If it's legal, it's okay" no longer justifies managerial decisions in today's business world. Today's businessperson benefits most by *preventive measures*—that is, by anticipating problems (including potential court judgments or legislative restraints) that could result from unethical business practices and by taking steps to prevent those problems. Paying attention to the "ethical credentials" of potential employees is one such preventive measure; training current employees in the goals and benefits of ethical behavior is another.

2.   Top management in any corporation is well advised to develop a meaningful and appropriate code of ethics, to have it printed, to give every employee a copy, and, especially, to explain to employees the importance of ethics and how the specific components of the code relate to the company's overall ethical goals and policies.

3.   Traditionally, business managers have framed their responsibilities in response to the demand for their firms' products and the actions of competitors in the marketplace. Today's

managers must also evaluate their decisions from the opposite perspective—that is, by looking at how the firm affects the environment in which it operates, including the global environment.

## ■ For Critical Analysis

1.   Because of the increasingly international scope of business transactions, many efforts have been directed toward the creation of an effective international code of business ethics. Do the differences in ethical standards among nations mean that a workable international code of business conduct is an impossible dream?

2.   To what extent do you believe that ethical codes are adopted simply to make firms look good in the eyes of their employees, shareholders, customers, and suppliers (and federal prosecutors)? Is it possible that even if an ethical code were adopted for such a reason, it would still be a step in the right direction?

3.   Analysts of ethical codes maintain that to be effective, an ethical code should relate to the specific business activities of the firm. But what about a huge conglomerate corporation that owns and ultimately directs the activities of numerous, completely diverse subsidiary companies? Is it possible to create a code of ethics that can apply to all employees in the conglomerate and yet be specific enough to offer practical and useful guidance to each employee?

## SECTION 5

# THE EVER-CHANGING ETHICAL LANDSCAPE

It is important to remember that our sense of what is ethical—what is fair or just or right in a given situation—changes over time. Conduct that might have been considered ethical ten years ago might be considered unethical today. For example, the commercial bribery of foreign government officials has characterized international business transactions for centuries. Not until 1977, however, did the bribery of foreign officials become an ethical issue. It took several scandals involving large pay-offs to bring this issue to the forefront. Because enough groups concluded that this type of behavior was unethical, Congress was induced to pass a law

prohibiting it (the Foreign Corrupt Practices Act of 1977—see Chapter 56). In short, the previous trade-off—looking the other way when it came to bribery of foreign officials in return for more profitable foreign contracts—was no longer acceptable to society.

Indeed, most of the ethical and social issues discussed in this chapter and elsewhere in this text either did not exist or were of little public concern at the turn of the century and, in some cases, even as recently as a decade ago. Technological innovations, the communications revolution, pressing environmental problems, and social movements resulting in greater rights for minorities, women, and consumers have all dramatically changed the society in which we live and, consequently, the business and ethical landscape of America.

## TERMS AND CONCEPTS TO REVIEW

| | | |
|---|---|---|
| business ethics 25 | ethics 24 | utilitarianism 28 |
| categorical imperative 27 | trade-off 25 | waiver 33 |
| cause of action 33 | Type I error 26 | |
| cost-benefit analysis 28 | Type II error 26 | |

# QUESTIONS AND CASE PROBLEMS

**2–1. Business Ethics.** Some business ethicists maintain that whereas personal ethics has to do with ''right'' or ''wrong'' behavior, business ethics is concerned with ''appropriate'' behavior. In other words, ethical behavior in business has less to do with moral principles than with what society deems to be appropriate behavior in the business context. Do you agree with this distinction? Do personal and business ethics ever overlap? Should personal ethics play any role in business ethical decision making?

**2–2. Ethical Decision Making.** Assume that you are a high-level manager for a shoe manufacturer. You know that your firm could increase its profit margin by producing shoes in Indonesia, where you could hire women for $40 a month to assemble them. You also know, however, that a competing shoe manufacturer recently was accused, by human-rights advocates, of engaging in exploitative labor practices because the manufacturer

sold shoes made by Indonesian women for similarly low wages. You personally do not believe that paying $40 a month to Indonesian women is unethical, because you know that in that impoverished country, $40 a month is a better-than-average wage rate. Assuming that the decision is yours to make, should you have the shoes manufactured in Indonesia and make higher profits for your company? Or should you avoid the risk of negative publicity and the consequences of that publicity for the firm's reputation and subsequent profits? Are there other alternatives? Discuss fully.

**2–3. Ethical Decision Making.** Susan Whitehead serves on the City Planning Commission. The city is planning to build a new subway system and is accepting bids on the proposal. Susan's brother-in-law, Jerry, who owns the Custom Transportation Co., has submitted the lowest bid for the system. The Transportation-We-Make-It Co. has submitted a slightly higher bid. Susan knows that Jerry could complete the job for the estimated amount, but she also knows that if Jerry gets and completes this job, he will have enough money to sell his company and quit working. Susan is concerned that

Custom Transportation's subsequent management might not be as easy to work with if revisions need to be made on the subway system after its completion. She is torn as to whether she should tell the city about the potential changes in Custom Transportation's management. If the city knew about the instability of Custom Transportation, it might prefer to give the contract to Transportation-We-Make-It, whose bid was higher than Custom Transportation's bid by only an insignificant amount. Does Susan have an ethical obligation to disclose the information about Jerry to the City Planning Commission? Discuss.

**2–4. Ethical Decision Making.** Shokun Steel Co. owns many steel plants. One of its plants is much older than the others. Equipment at the old plant is outdated and inefficient, and the costs of production at that plant are now twice what they are at any of Shokun's other plants. The price of steel cannot be increased because of competition, both domestic and international. The plant is located in Twin Firs, Pennsylvania, which has a population of about forty-five thousand and currently employs over a thousand workers. Shokun is contemplating whether to close the plant. What factors should the firm consider in making its decision? Will the firm violate any ethical duties if it closes the plant? Analyze these questions from the various perspectives on ethical reasoning discussed in this chapter.

**2–5. Whistleblowing.** George Geary was employed by the United States Steel Corp. to sell tubular products to the oil and gas industry. Geary believed that one of the company's new products, a tubular casing, had not been adequately tested and constituted a serious danger to anyone who used it. Even though Geary at all times performed his duties to the best of his ability, he continued to express his reservations with respect to the company's new product. Geary alleged that because of his complaints, he was summarily discharged without notice. Given these facts, and in view of the fact that Geary was not a safety expert and had bypassed ordinary company procedures in his complaints, address the following questions. [*Geary v. United States Steel Corp.,* 456 Pa. 171, 319 A.2d 174 (1974)]

   (a) Did the employer act wrongfully in discharging Geary?
   (b) Did Geary have an ethical duty to complain about the company's product?
   (c) Did the employer's need to maintain internal administrative order and harmony in the company outweigh its duty to do all it could to ensure product safety? Suppose that you were a manager and Geary raised the matter with you. How would you act, and what ethical factors would influence your decision?

**2–6. Consumer Welfare.** Two eight-year-old boys, Douglas Bratz and Bradley Baughn, were injured while riding a mini-trail bike manufactured by Honda Motor Co. Bratz, who was driving the bike while Baughn rode as a passenger behind him, ran three stop signs and then collided with a truck. Bratz did not see the truck because, at the time of the accident, he was looking behind him at a girl chasing them on another mini-trail bike. Bratz wore a helmet, but it flew off on impact because it was unfastened. Baughn was not wearing a helmet. The owner's manual for the mini-trail bike stated in bold print that the bike was intended for off-the-road use only and urged users to ''Always Wear a Helmet.'' A prominent label on the bike itself also warned that the bike was for off-the-road use only and that it should not be used on public streets or highways. In addition, Bratz's father had repeatedly told the boy not to ride the bike in the street. The parents of the injured boys filed suit against Honda, alleging that the mini-trail bike was unreasonably dangerous. Honda claimed it had sufficiently warned consumers of potential dangers that could result if the bike was not used as directed. Should Honda be held responsible for the boys' injuries? Why or why not? [*Baughn v. Honda Motor Co.,* 107 Wash.2d 127, 727 P.2d 655 (1986)]

**2–7. Employment Relationships.** In 1984, the General Telephone Co. of Illinois, Inc. (GTE), for reasons of efficiency, decided to consolidate its nationwide operations and eliminate unnecessary job positions. One of the positions eliminated was held by John Burnell, a fifty-two-year-old employee who had worked for GTE for thirty-four years and had always received ''above average'' performance ratings. GTE offered Burnell the choice of either accepting another position within the firm at the same salary or accepting early retirement with a salary continuation for a certain period of time. Burnell did not want to retire, but he was afraid that if he did accept the other position and if the other position was later eliminated, he might not then have the choice of early retirement with the same separation benefit. Because he received no assurances that the other job would be secure in the future, he accepted the early-retirement alternative. Burnell later alleged that he had been ''constructively discharged'' (forced to resign) because GTE had made his working conditions so intolerable that he was forced to resign. Had GTE constructively discharged Burnell? Can GTE's actions toward Burnell be justified from an ethical standpoint? Discuss. [*Burnell v. General Telephone Co. of Illinois, Inc.,* 181 Ill.App.3d 533, 536 N.E.2d 1387, 130 Ill.Dec. 176 (1989)]

**2–8. Consumer Welfare.** Beverly Landrine's infant daughter died after the baby swallowed a balloon while playing with a doll known as ''Bubble Yum Baby.'' When a balloon was inserted into the doll's mouth and the doll's arm was pumped, thereby inflating the balloon, the doll simulated the blowing of a bubble gum bubble. The balloon was made by Perfect Product Co. and distributed by Mego Corp. Landrine brought a suit against the manufacturer and distributor, alleging that the balloon was defectively made or inherently unsafe when used by children and that Perfect had failed to warn of the danger associated with the balloon's use. Discuss whether the producer and distributor of the balloon should be held liable for the harm caused by its product. [*Landrine v. Mego Corp.,* 95 A.D.2d 759, 464 N.Y.S.2d 516 (1983)]

**2–9. Consumer Welfare.** The Seven-Up Co., as part of a marketing scheme, placed two glass bottles of ''Like'' cola at the front entrance of the Gruenemeier residence. Russell Gruenemeier, a nine-year-old boy, began playing while holding one of the bottles. He tripped and fell, and the bottle broke, severely cutting his right eye and causing him to eventually lose the eye. Russell's mother brought an action against the Seven-Up Co. for damages, claiming that the cause of Russell's injury was Seven-Up's negligence. She claimed that the company was negligent because it placed potentially dangerous instrumentalities—glass bottles—within the reach of small children and that the firm should have used unbreakable bottles for its marketing scheme. Are glass bottles so potentially dangerous that the Seven-Up Co. should be held liable for the boy's harm? If you were the judge, how would you decide the issue? [*Gruenemeier v. Seven-Up Co.,* 229 Neb. 267, 426 N.W.2d 510 (1988)]

**2–10. Consumer Welfare.** The father of an eleven-year-old child sued the manufacturer of a jungle gym because the manufacturer had failed to warn users of the equipment that they might fall off the gym and get hurt, as the boy did in this case. The father also claimed that the jungle gym was ''unreasonably dangerous'' (a ground, or basis, for liability under product liability law) because, as his son began to fall and reached frantically for a bar to grasp, there was no bar within reach. The father based his argument in part on a previous case involving a plaintiff who was injured as a result of somersaulting off a trampoline. In that case [*Pell v. Victor J. Andrew High School,* 123 Ill.App.3d 423, 462 N.E.2d 858, 78 Ill.Dec. 739 (1984)], the court had held that the trampoline's manufacturer was liable for the plaintiff's injuries because it had failed to warn of the trampoline's propensity to cause severe spinal cord injuries if it was used for somersaulting. Should the court be convinced by the father's arguments? Why or why not? [*Cozzi v. North Palos Elementary School District No. 117,* 232 Ill.App.3d 379, 597 N.E.2d 683, 173 Ill.Dec. 709 (1992)]

**2–11. A Question of Ethics**

*Hazen Paper Co. manufactured coated, foil-laminated, and printed paper and paper-board for use in such products as cosmetic wrap, lottery tickets, and pressure-sensitive items. Walter Biggins, a chemist hired by Hazen in 1977, developed a water-based paper coating that was both environmentally safe and of superior quality. By the mid-1980s, the company's sales had increased dramatically as a result of its extensive use of ''Biggins Acrylic.'' Because of this, Biggins thought he deserved a substantial raise in salary, and from 1984 to 1986, Biggins's persistent requests for a raise became a bone of contention between him and his employers. Biggins ran a business on the side cleaning up hazardous wastes for various companies. Hazen told Biggins that unless he signed a ''confidentiality agreement'' promising to restrict his outside activities during the time he was employed by Hazen and for a limited time afterward, he would be fired. Biggins said he would sign the agreement only if Hazen raised his salary to $100,000. Hazen refused to do so, fired Biggins, and hired a younger man to replace him. At the time of his discharge in 1986, Biggins was sixty-two years old, had worked for the company nearly ten years, and was just a few weeks away from being entitled to pension rights worth about $93,000. In view of these circumstances, evaluate and answer the following questions. [Hazen Paper Co. v. Biggins, ____ U.S. ____ , 113 S.Ct. 1701, 123 L.Ed.2d 338 (1993)]*

1. Biggins sued Hazen for age discrimination in violation of the Age Discrimination in Employment Act of 1967. If you were the judge, would you hold for Biggins or Hazen? Discuss fully.

2. Did the company owe an ethical duty to Biggins to increase his salary, given the fact that its sales increased dramatically as a result of Biggins's efforts and ingenuity in developing the coating? If you were one of the company's owners, would you have raised Biggins's salary? Why or why not?

3. Generally, what public policies come into conflict in cases involving employers who, for reasons of cost and efficiency of operations, fire older, higher-paid workers and replace them with younger, lower-paid workers? If you were an employer facing the need to cut back on personnel to save costs, what would you do, and on what ethical premises would you justify your decision?

# CHAPTER 3

# COURTS AND ALTERNATIVE DISPUTE RESOLUTION

T oday in the United States there are fifty-two court systems—one for each of the fifty states, one for the District of Columbia, plus a federal system. Keep in mind that the federal courts are not superior to the state courts; they are simply an independent system of courts, which derives its authority from Article III, Section 2, of the U.S. Constitution. U.S. territorial courts are established by Congress, by its authority under Article I of the U.S. Constitution. Congress has extended the federal court system beyond the boundaries of the United States to U.S. territories such as Guam, the Virgin Islands, and Puerto Rico. (In Guam and the Virgin Islands, territorial courts serve as both federal courts and state courts, whereas in Puerto Rico, they serve only as federal courts.) As we shall see, the United States Supreme Court is the final controlling voice over all of these fifty-two systems, at least when questions of federal law are involved.

Because businesspersons will likely face either a potential or an actual lawsuit at some time in their careers, it is important for anyone involved in business to have an understanding of both American court systems and methods of dispute resolution that can be pursued outside the courts. This chapter first examines the state and federal court systems and then looks at alternative methods of resolving disputes. The next chapter explores in detail the judicial procedures that frame the litigation process.

Whenever a case is brought before a court, the first question raised is whether the court has the power and authority to decide the case—that is, whether the court has jurisdiction.

## SECTION 1

## JURISDICTION

In Latin, *juris* means ''law''; *diction* means ''to speak.'' Thus, ''the authority to speak the law'' is the literal meaning of the term **jurisdiction.**

Jurisdiction refers either to the geographical area within which a court has the right and power to decide cases or to the right and power of a court to adjudicate matters concerning certain persons, property, or subject matter.

## IN PERSONAM AND IN REM JURISDICTION

Before any court can hear a case, it must have jurisdiction over the person against whom the suit is brought or over the property involved in the suit and jurisdiction over the subject matter.

**IN PERSONAM JURISDICTION** A court's power is generally limited to the territorial boundaries of the state in which it is located. Thus, a court can exercise **in personam jurisdiction** (personal jurisdiction) over residents of the state and anyone who can be served with a *summons* (an order directing a party to a lawsuit to appear in court) within the state's boundaries. *In personam* jurisdiction is required before a court can enter a judgment against a party to the action. For example, if Santos, an Arkansas resident, is involved in an automobile accident in Missouri with Bud, a Missouri resident, Santos could sue Bud in Missouri for a claim arising from the accident. But Santos could not sue Bud in an Arkansas court, because the court could not exercise personal jurisdiction over Bud.

**IN REM JURISDICTION** A court can also exercise **in rem jurisdiction** (''jurisdiction over the thing'') over property located within its boundaries. In an *in rem* proceeding, a court may use property within a state to help satisfy a general debt. As an example of *in rem* jurisdiction, imagine that in the previous hypothetical example, Santos dies in Missouri from injuries suffered in the accident. Santos's heirs live in Texas. Santos's estate consists entirely of property located in Arkansas. Santos's heirs will bring an action in an Arkansas court to settle Santos's estate on the basis of the Arkansas court's jurisdiction over property.

**QUASI IN REM JURISDICTION** A third type of jurisdiction—**quasi in rem jurisdiction**—is based on a person's interest in property within the court's jurisdiction. In other words, *quasi in rem* jurisdiction allows a party to file an action against a nonresident personally in a court that can exercise jurisdiction over the nonresident's property. Be-

cause the action is brought against the party personally, it is not an *in rem* proceeding. This type of jurisdiction is used when *in personam* jurisdiction is not possible, but there must be a minimum connection between the property and the subject matter of the action for the court to use it.

For example, imagine that in the above hypothetical example, Santos is only injured in the accident and receives a judgment against Bud in a Missouri court. Bud has no insurance, but Bud does have a bank account in Iowa. Santos brings an action in Iowa against Bud and the bank to collect the judgment by garnishing the funds in Bud's bank account. (Garnishment proceeds to satisfy a debt are discussed in Chapter 32.) Santos can apply the balance in Bud's bank account to his recovery.

**LONG ARM STATUTES** In some cases, a court can exercise personal jurisdiction over nonresidents under the authority of a long arm statute. A **long arm statute** is a state law permitting courts to exercise jurisdiction over nonresident defendants. Before a court can exercise jurisdiction over a nonresident under a long arm statute, though, it must be demonstrated that the nonresident had sufficient contacts, or *minimum contacts,*[1] with the state to justify the jurisdiction.

For example, if an individual has committed a wrong within the state, such as selling defective goods within the state, a court can usually exercise jurisdiction even if the person or firm causing the harm is located in another state. Similarly, a state may exercise personal jurisdiction over a nonresident defendant who is sued for breaching a contract that was formed within the state. In regard to corporations, the minimum-contacts requirement is usually met if the corporation does business within the state or places goods within the ''stream of commerce'' with the expectation that the goods will be purchased by residents in the state.[2]

## SUBJECT MATTER JURISDICTION

*Subject matter jurisdiction* is a limitation on the types of cases a court can hear. The subject matter

---

1. The *minimum-contacts* requirement was established in the landmark case of *International Shoe Co. v. Washington,* 326 U.S. 310, 66 S.Ct. 154, 90 L.Ed. 95 (1945).
2. For a further discussion of the ''stream of commerce'' theory of minimum contacts, see *Loral Fairchild Corp. v. Victor Co. of Japan, Ltd.,* 803 F.Supp. 626 (E.D.N.Y. 1992). This case is presented as Case 41.1 in Chapter 41.

jurisdiction of a court is usually defined in the statute or constitution creating the court. The distinction between *courts of general jurisdiction* and *courts of limited jurisdiction* lies in the subject matter of cases heard. (Courts that have limited jurisdiction are sometimes said to have ''special'' jurisdiction.) A court of general jurisdiction can decide virtually any type of case, including some cases that involve matters of federal law. Every state has courts of general jurisdiction, which may be called county courts, circuit courts, district courts, or some other name.

At both the federal and state levels there are also courts of limited jurisdiction. **Probate courts**—state courts that handle only matters relating to wills and estates—are a common example of courts having limited subject matter jurisdiction. A court's subject matter jurisdiction can be limited not only by the subject of the lawsuit but also by the amount of money in controversy and by whether a case is civil or criminal.

## ORIGINAL AND APPELLATE JURISDICTION

Another distinction is between courts of original jurisdiction and courts of appellate jurisdiction. The difference normally lies in whether the case is being heard for the first time. Courts having *original jurisdiction* are courts of the first instance—that is, courts where the trial of a case begins. In contrast, courts having *appellate jurisdiction* act as reviewing courts. In general, cases can be brought to them only on appeal from an order or a judgment of a lower court (appellate courts will be discussed shortly).

## SECTION 2

# VENUE

Jurisdiction has to do with whether a court has authority to hear a case involving specific persons, property, or subject matter. Commonly, more than one court possesses potential jurisdiction over a case. **Venue**[3] is concerned with the most appropriate location for a trial. The question of venue arises after a determination of jurisdiction. A particular court may have jurisdiction but not venue.

The general federal venue statute[4] controls venue unless special venue requirements are fixed by other statutes or by case law. Basically, the concept of venue reflects the policy that a court trying a suit should be in the geographic neighborhood (usually the county) in which the incident leading to the suit occurred or in which the parties involved in the lawsuit reside. If venue requirements are not met, venue is said to be improper.

Improper venue does not necessarily deprive the court of power to hear a case, but a party can request a change of venue if the party deems that venue is not proper. Even if venue is proper, a change of venue may be permitted in the interests of justice or for the convenience of witnesses. Pretrial publicity, for example, may permit a change of venue to another community, especially in criminal cases in which the defendant's right to a fair and impartial jury is impaired. For instance, in 1992, when the four Los Angeles police officers accused of beating up Rodney King were brought to trial, the attorneys defending the police officers requested a change of venue from Los Angeles to Simi Valley, California. The attorneys argued that to try the case in a Los Angeles court would prejudice the police officers' right to a fair trial. The court agreed and granted the request. (The ''not guilty'' verdict entered by the Simi Valley jurors, however, was followed by several days of the most extensive and expensive inner-city rioting in the history of South Central Los Angeles—and of the United States.)

## SECTION 3

# STANDING

**Standing to sue** is a jurisdictional issue that affects the power of courts to hear and decide cases. A party who has *standing to sue* has a sufficient ''stake'' in a controversy to seek judicial resolution of it. In other words, a party must have a legally protected and tangible interest at stake in the litigation to have standing. The party must have been injured or have been threatened with injury by the action about which he or she is complaining.

The question is whether the **litigant**—an active party in a lawsuit—is the proper party to fight the suit, not whether the matter at issue is *justiciable*.

---

3. Pronounced *ven*-yoo.

4. 28 U.S.C. Section 1391.

(A **justiciable controversy** is real and substantial, as opposed to hypothetical or academic.) To illustrate: A conservation organization wanted to challenge a government agency's approval of locating a ski complex near a national wilderness area. Before the court would consider whether the challenge involved justiciable issues, the organization needed to show that it was a proper party to bring the suit. To show that it was a proper party—that is, to show that it had standing—the organization alleged that some of its members used, hiked in, and enjoyed the wilderness area that the development threatened. The organization also alleged that the ski complex compromised these members' enjoyment of the area.[5]

## SECTION 4

# STATE COURT SYSTEMS

As Exhibit 3–1 indicates, there are several levels, or tiers, of courts within state court systems: (1) state trial courts of limited jurisdiction, (2) state trial courts of general jurisdiction (and some courts of limited jurisdiction), and (3) appellate courts, which include state supreme courts. Any person who is a party to a lawsuit typically has the opportunity to plead the case before a trial court and then, if he or she loses, before at least one level of appellate courts. Finally, if a federal statute or constitutional issue is involved in the decision of the state supreme court, that decision may be further appealed to the United States Supreme Court.

## TRIAL COURTS

**Trial courts** are exactly what their name implies— courts in which trials are held and testimony is taken. Trial courts may be courts of record, in which case a written record is taken, or courts not of record. Today, most are courts of record. Every state has trial courts that have original jurisdiction. Most states have trial courts of both limited and general jurisdiction.

Trial courts that have *limited jurisdiction* as to subject matter are often called special trial courts or minor judiciary courts. **Small claims courts** are inferior trial courts that hear only civil cases in-

volving claims of less than a certain amount, usually $2,500.[6] Suits brought in small claims courts are generally conducted informally, and lawyers are not even allowed to represent people in small claims courts for most purposes. Decisions of small claims courts may be appealed to a state trial court of general jurisdiction. Other courts of limited jurisdiction include probate courts, as mentioned earlier; *domestic relations courts,* which handle only divorce actions and child custody cases; and local *municipal courts,* which handle mainly traffic cases. Typically, the minor judiciary courts do not keep complete written records of trial proceedings.

Trial courts that have *general jurisdiction* as to subject matter may be called county, district, superior, or circuit courts.[7] These courts of general jurisdiction may be supplemented by the courts of limited jurisdiction, or minor judiciary courts, discussed above. The jurisdiction of these courts of general and original jurisdiction is often determined by the size of the county in which the court sits. Many important cases involving businesses originate in these general trial courts.

## APPELLATE COURTS

Appellate courts, or courts of review, are not usually trial courts—although in some states trial courts of general jurisdiction also have limited jurisdiction to hear appeals from the minor judiciary (for example, small claims and traffic cases). Every state has at least one appellate court, or court of appeals, and many states have intermediate reviewing courts and one court at the highest level. The intermediate appellate court is often called the court of appeals. The highest court of the state is normally called the supreme court but may be called by some other name. For example, in both New York and Maryland, the highest state court is called the Court of Appeals.

The jurisdiction of these courts is substantially limited to hearing appeals. Appellate courts nor-

---

5. *Sierra Club v. Morton,* 348 F.Supp. 219 (N.D.Cal. 1972).

6. Some states have raised their thresholds for small claims to allow more people to take advantage of the benefits offered by small claims courts, in which disputes are usually resolved simply and quickly. Tennessee, for example, has a threshold of $10,000. Any claims below this amount can be handled in small claims court.

7. The name in Ohio is Court of Common Pleas; the name in New York is Supreme Court.

■ **Exhibit 3–1 State Court Systems***

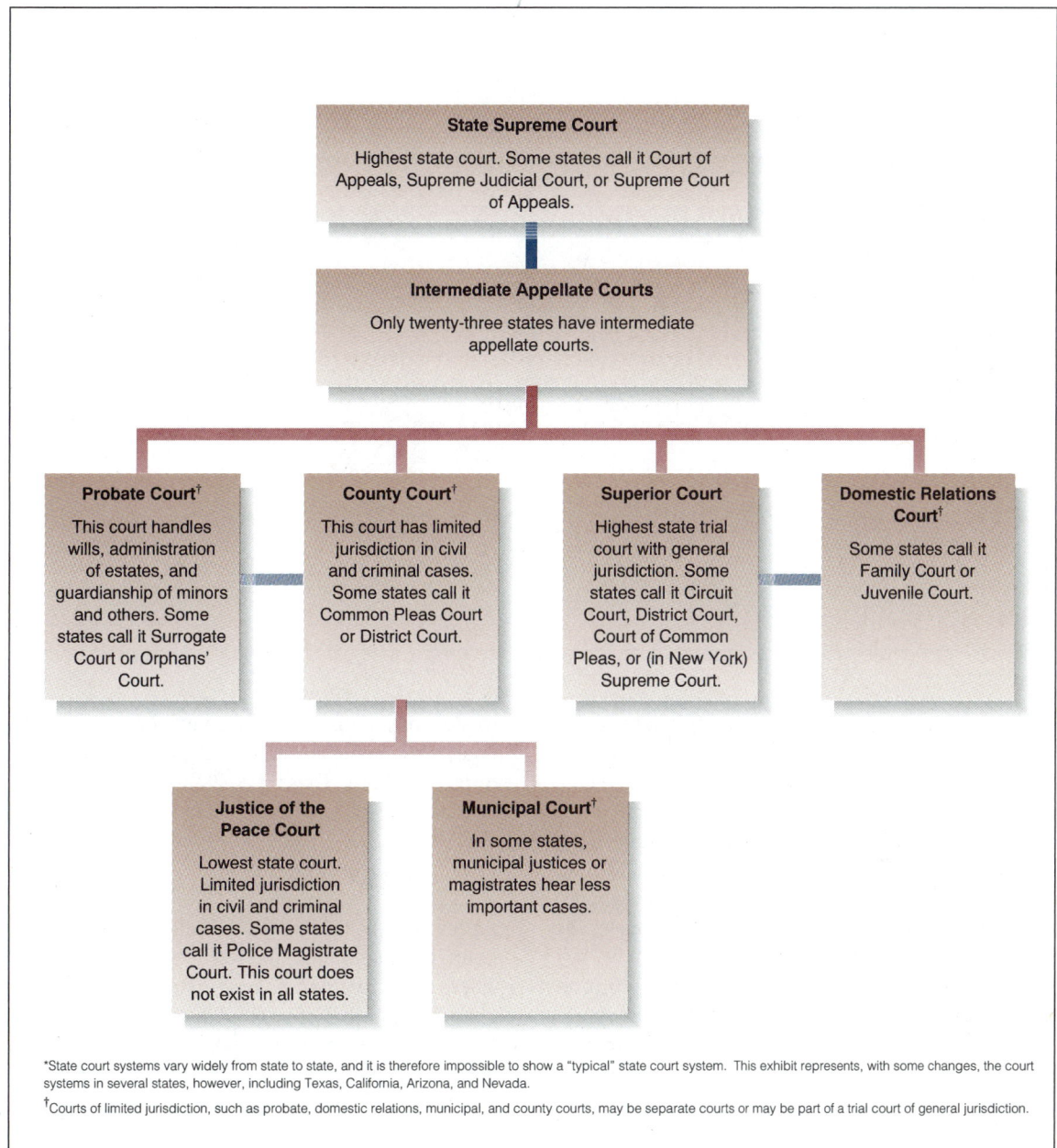

*State court systems vary widely from state to state, and it is therefore impossible to show a "typical" state court system. This exhibit represents, with some changes, the court systems in several states, however, including Texas, California, Arizona, and Nevada.

†Courts of limited jurisdiction, such as probate, domestic relations, municipal, and county courts, may be separate courts or may be part of a trial court of general jurisdiction.

mally examine the record of the case on appeal and determine whether the trial court committed an error. They look at **questions of law** (questions about the application or interpretation of the law) and procedure but usually not at **questions of fact** (questions about what really happened in regard to the dispute being tried). An appellate court will tamper with a trial court's finding of fact when the finding is clearly erroneous (that is, when it is con-

trary to the evidence presented at trial) or when there is no evidence to support the finding.

If the reviewing court believes that an error was committed during the trial or that the jury was improperly instructed, the judgment of the trial court will be *reversed*. Sometimes the case will be *remanded* (sent back to the court that originally heard the case) for a new trial. In most cases, the judgment of the lower court is *affirmed*, resulting

■ **Exhibit 3–2  The Federal Court System**

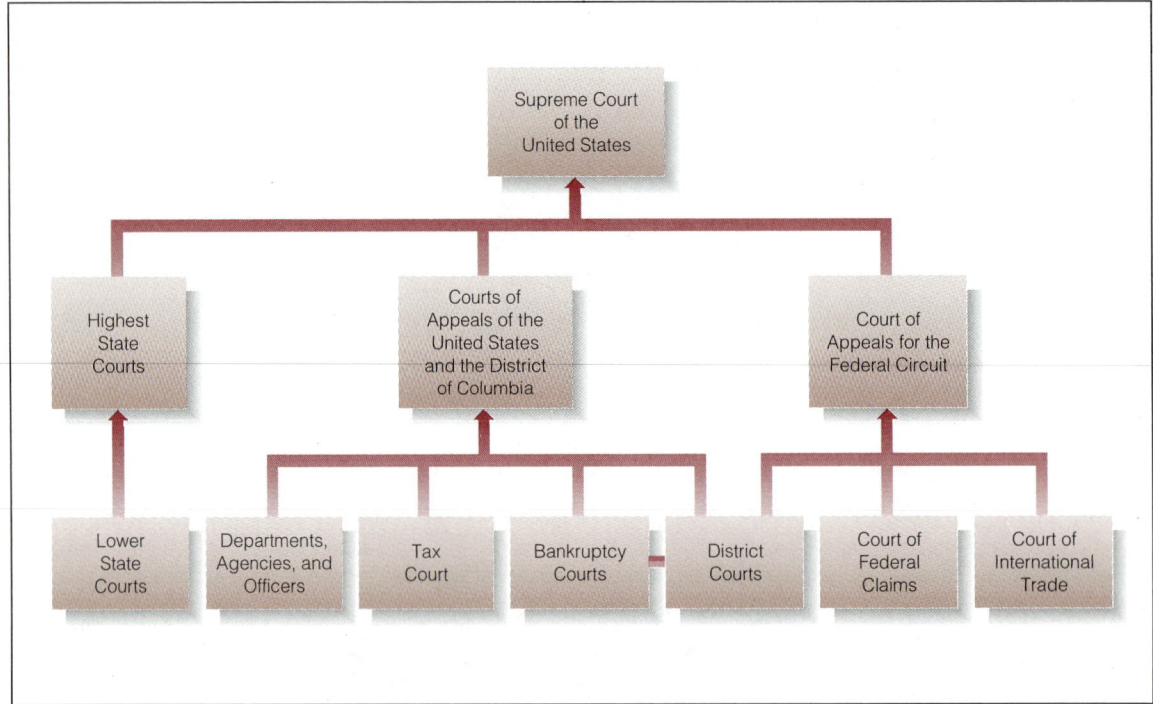

in the enforcement of the court's judgment or decree. The three options of the appellate court—to reverse, to remand, or to affirm a decision—may be combined. For example, an appellate court might affirm in "part" a lower court's judgment, while reversing another part of the decision. Should there be a tied decision, which can result when a judge is absent or has withdrawn from a case, the lower court's decision stands.

The decisions of each state's highest court on all questions of state law are final. Only when issues of federal law are involved can a party appeal a decision made by a state's highest court to the United States Supreme Court. (As will be discussed shortly, the latter court is not obligated to review appealed cases and usually hears only a fraction of them.)

<br>

# THE FEDERAL COURT SYSTEM

The federal court system is similar in many ways to most state court systems. It is a three-tiered

model consisting of (1) trial courts, (2) intermediate courts of appeals, and (3) the United States Supreme Court. Exhibit 3–2 shows the organization of the federal court system.

## U.S. DISTRICT COURTS

At the federal level, the equivalent of a state trial court of general jurisdiction is the district court. There is at least one federal district court in every state. The number of judicial districts can vary over time, primarily owing to population changes and corresponding caseloads. The law now provides for 179 circuit court judgeships within the 13 circuits (including the federal circuit) and 649 district court judgeships within the 96 judicial districts.[8]

U.S. district courts have original jurisdiction in federal matters. Federal cases originate in district courts. There are other trial courts with original, albeit special (or limited), jurisdiction, such as the U.S. Tax Court, the U.S. Bankruptcy Court, and the U.S. Court of Federal Claims.[9] Certain admin-

---

8.   See 28 U.S.C. Sections 44(a), 133.
9.   Formerly the U.S. Claims Court.

istrative agencies and departments with judicial power also have original jurisdiction.

## U.S. COURTS OF APPEALS

There are thirteen judicial circuits within the United States. The U.S. (circuit) courts of appeals for twelve of the circuits hear appeals from the federal district courts located within their respective judicial circuits. The court of appeals for the thirteenth circuit, called the federal circuit, has national jurisdiction over certain types of cases, such as those concerning customs law and patent law.

The decisions of the circuit courts of appeals are final in most cases, but appeal to the United States Supreme Court is possible. Appeals from federal administrative agencies, such as the Federal Trade Commission, are also made to the U.S. circuit courts of appeals. Judicial opinions on cases heard in one of the U.S. courts of appeals are binding on the federal courts within that jurisdiction, but they are not binding on courts in other circuits. Other circuits can use such opinions as precedents if they wish, but they are not legally bound to do so. See Exhibit 3–3 for the geographical boundaries of U.S. district courts and U.S. courts of appeals.

## THE UNITED STATES SUPREME COURT

The highest level of the three-tiered model of the federal court system is the United States Supreme Court. According to the language of Article III of the U.S. Constitution, there is only one national Supreme Court. All other courts in the federal system are considered "inferior." Congress is empowered to create other inferior courts as it deems necessary. The inferior courts that Congress has created include the second tier in our model—the U.S. circuit courts of appeals—as well as the district courts and any other courts of limited, or specialized, jurisdiction.

The United States Supreme Court consists of nine justices; these justices are nominated by the president of the United States and confirmed by the Senate. Like all federal district and courts of appeals judges, the Supreme Court justices receive lifetime appointments, because under Article III they "hold their offices during Good Behavior." Although the United States Supreme Court has original, or trial, jurisdiction in rare instances (set forth in Article III, Section 2), most of its work is as an appeals court. The Supreme Court can review

any case decided by any of the federal courts of appeals, and it also has appellate authority over some cases decided in the state courts.

SECTION 6

# JURISDICTION OF THE FEDERAL COURTS

Because the federal government is a government of limited powers, the jurisdiction of the federal courts is limited. Article III of the U.S. Constitution established the boundaries of federal judicial power. Section I of Article III states that "[t]he judicial Power of the United States shall be vested in one supreme Court and in such inferior Courts as the Congress may from time to time ordain and establish."

In line with the *checks and balances system* of the federal government (discussed in Chapter 5), Congress has the power to control the number and kind of inferior courts in the federal system. Except in those cases in which the Constitution gives the Supreme Court original jurisdiction (including cases involving ambassadors and controversies between states), Congress can also regulate the jurisdiction of the Supreme Court. Although the Constitution sets the outer limits of federal judicial power, Congress can set other limits on federal jurisdiction. Also, the courts themselves can promulgate rules that further narrow the types of cases they will hear.

## FEDERAL QUESTIONS

"The judicial Power shall extend to all cases . . . arising under this Constitution, the Laws of the United States and Treaties made . . . under their Authority." This statement from Article III, Section 2, of the Constitution defines a **federal question** as a cause of action based, at least in part, on the U.S. Constitution, a treaty, or a federal law. Such cases come under the judicial power of federal courts. Any lawsuit involving a federal question can originate in a federal court. People whose claims are based on rights granted by an act of Congress can sue in a federal court. People who claim that their constitutional rights have been violated can also begin their suits in a federal court.

■ Exhibit 3–3 U.S. Courts of Appeals and U.S. District Courts

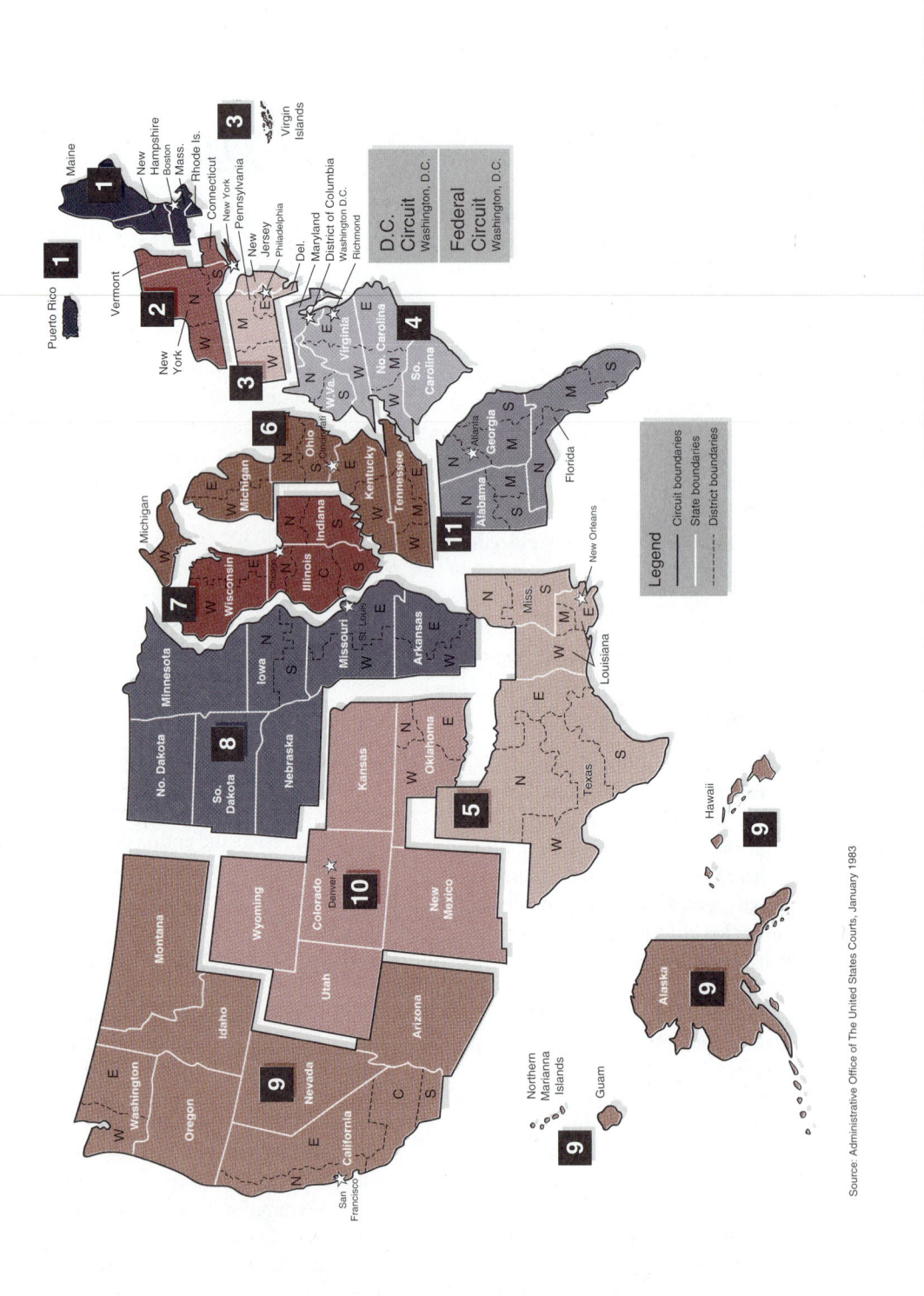

Source: Administrative Office of The United States Courts, January 1983

# ■ CONCEPT SUMMARY 3.1 Types of Courts

| COURT | DESCRIPTION |
|---|---|
| **Trial Courts** | Trial courts are courts of original jurisdiction in which actions are initiated. <br>1. *State courts*—Courts of general jurisdiction can hear any case that has not been specifically designated for another court; courts of limited jurisdiction include domestic relations courts, probate courts, municipal courts, small claims courts, and others. <br>2. *Federal courts*—The federal district court is the equivalent of the state trial court. Federal courts of limited jurisdiction include the U.S. Tax Court, the U.S. Bankruptcy Court, and the U.S. Court of Federal Claims. |
| **Intermediate Appellate Courts** | Courts of appeals are reviewing courts; generally, appellate courts do not have original jurisdiction. Many states have an intermediate appellate court; in the federal court system, the U.S. circuit courts of appeals are the intermediate appellate courts. |
| **Supreme Court** | The highest state court is that state's supreme court, although it may be called by some other name. Appeal from state supreme courts to the United States Supreme Court is only possible if a federal question is involved. The United States Supreme Court is the highest court in the federal court system and the final arbiter of the Constitution and federal law. |

For example, a woman who believes that her employer has discriminated against her in violation of a federal law may sue the employer in federal court.

## DIVERSITY OF CITIZENSHIP

Federal district court jurisdiction also extends to cases involving **diversity of citizenship.** Such cases may arise between (1) citizens of different states, (2) a foreign government and citizens of a state or of different states, or (3) citizens of a state and citizens or subjects of a foreign government. The amount in controversy must be more than $50,000 before a federal court can take jurisdiction in such cases. For purposes of diversity-of-citizenship jurisdiction, a corporation is a citizen of the state in which it is incorporated and of the state in which its principal place of business is located. A case involving diversity of citizenship can commence in the appropriate federal district court, or, if the case starts in a state court, it can sometimes be transferred.

Diversity jurisdiction originated in 1789. The authors of the Constitution felt that a state might be biased in favor of its own citizens. Hence, the option of using the federal courts provided by the principle of diversity of citizenship is a means of protecting the out-of-state party. A large percentage of the more than seventy thousand cases filed in federal courts each year are based on diversity of citizenship.

## CONCURRENT VERSUS EXCLUSIVE JURISDICTION

When both federal and state courts have the power to hear a case, as is true in suits involving diversity of citizenship, **concurrent jurisdiction** exists. When cases can be tried only in federal courts or only in state courts, **exclusive jurisdiction** exists. The concepts of concurrent and exclusive jurisdiction are illustrated in Exhibit 3–4.

Federal courts have exclusive jurisdiction in cases involving federal crimes, bankruptcy, patents, and copyrights; in suits against the United States; and in some areas of admiralty law. States also have exclusive jurisdiction in certain subject matters—for example, in divorce and adoptions.

These jurisdictional principles are rooted in the framework of federalism established by the U.S. Constitution, which provides for concurrent federal

■ **Exhibit 3–4  Exclusive and Concurrent Jurisdiction**

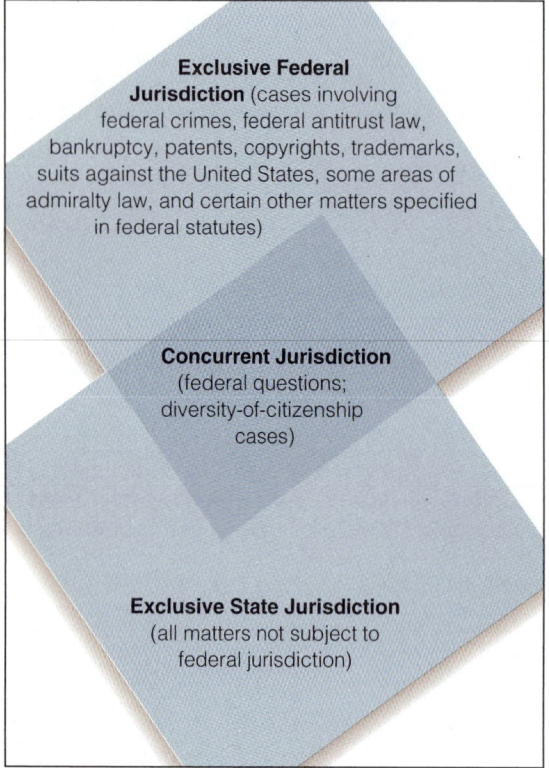

**Exclusive Federal Jurisdiction** (cases involving federal crimes, federal antitrust law, bankruptcy, patents, copyrights, trademarks, suits against the United States, some areas of admiralty law, and certain other matters specified in federal statutes)

**Concurrent Jurisdiction** (federal questions; diversity-of-citizenship cases)

**Exclusive State Jurisdiction** (all matters not subject to federal jurisdiction)

and state powers. For example, both the federal and state governments have the power to levy taxes, regulate highway systems, undertake environmental clean-up programs, and so on. Issues relating to concurrent powers, and therefore concurrent jurisdiction, will be discussed in more detail in Chapter 5 in the context of constitutional law.

## HOW CASES REACH THE SUPREME COURT

The Supreme Court is given original, or trial court, jurisdiction in a small number of situations. In all other cases, its jurisdiction is appellate "with such Exceptions, and under such Regulations as the Congress shall make." Many people are surprised to learn that there is no absolute right of appeal to the United States Supreme Court. Thousands of cases are filed with the Supreme Court each year,

yet it hears, on average, less than 100. To appeal a case to the Supreme Court, a party requests the Court to issue a writ of *certiorari.*

A **writ of *certiorari*** is an order issued by the Supreme Court to a lower court requiring the latter to send it the record of the case for review. Parties can petition the Supreme Court to issue a writ of *certiorari,* but whether the Court will issue one is entirely within its discretion. In no instance is the Court required to issue a writ of *certiorari.*[10]

Below are some of the situations in which the Supreme Court may issue a writ of *certiorari:*

1. When a state court has decided a substantial federal question that has not been determined by the Supreme Court or when a state court has decided such a question in a way that is probably in disagreement with the trend of the Supreme Court's decisions.
2. When two or more federal courts of appeals reach conflicting decisions on issues.
3. When a federal court of appeals has decided an important state question in conflict with state law, has decided an important federal question not yet addressed by the Court but that should be decided by the Court, has decided a federal question in conflict with applicable decisions of the Court, or has departed from the accepted and usual course of judicial proceedings.
4. When a federal court of appeals holds that a state statute is invalid because it violates federal law.
5. When the highest state court of appeals holds a federal law invalid or upholds a state law that has been challenged as violating federal law.
6. When a federal court holds an act of Congress unconstitutional and the federal government or one of its employees is a party.

Most petitions for writs of *certiorari* are denied. A denial is not a decision on the merits of a case, nor does it indicate agreement with the lower

---

10.  Between 1790 and 1891, Congress allowed the Supreme Court almost no discretion over which cases to decide. After 1925, the Court could choose in almost 95 percent of appealed cases whether to hear arguments and issue an opinion. Beginning with the term of October 1988, mandatory review was eliminated altogether.

## ■ CONCEPT SUMMARY 3.2 Jurisdiction

| TYPE OF JURISDICTION | DESCRIPTION |
| --- | --- |
| **Personal/Property** | Exists when a defendant or a defendant's property is located within the territorial boundaries within which a court has the right and power to decide cases. |
| **Subject Matter** | Limits the court's jurisdictional authority to particular types of cases.<br>a. Limited jurisdiction—Exists when a court is limited to a specific subject matter, such as probate or divorce.<br>b. General jurisdiction—Exists when a court can hear any kind of case. |
| **Original** | Exists with courts that have the authority to hear a case for the first time (trial courts). |
| **Appellate** | Exists with courts of appeal and review; generally, appellate courts do not have original jurisdiction. |
| **Federal** | Arises in the following situations:<br>a. In diversity-of-citizenship cases between (1) citizens of different states, (2) a foreign country and citizens of a state or of different states, or (3) citizens of a state and citizens or subjects of a foreign country. The amount in controversy must exceed $50,000.<br>b. When a federal question is involved (when the plaintiff's cause of action is based at least in part on the U.S. Constitution, a treaty, or a federal law). |
| **Concurrent** | Exists when two different courts have authority to hear the same case. |
| **Exclusive** | Exists when only a particular court or only state courts or only federal courts have authority to hear a case. |

court's opinion. Denial of the writ also has no value as a precedent.[11] The Court will not issue a writ unless at least four justices approve of it. This is called the "rule of four." Typically, the Court only grants petitions that raise the possibility of important constitutional questions.

## JUDICIAL REVIEW

The problem often arises as to whether a law is contrary to the mandates of the Constitution. **Judicial review** is the process for making such a determination. It is the judicial branch of the national government that has the authority and power to determine whether a particular law violates the Constitution. Thus, any court may refuse to enforce a statute that, in the court's view, violates the U.S. Constitution. Assuming that the jurisdictional criteria are satisfied, both state and federal courts may rule on the validity of state and federal statutes, as well as executive acts. Also, federal courts may rule that provisions of state constitutions are unconstitutional under the U.S. Constitution.

The power of judicial review was established in *Marbury v. Madison,* a case decided by the United States Supreme Court in 1803. In determining that the Court had the power to decide that a law passed by Congress violated the Constitution, the Court stated, "It is emphatically the province and duty of the Judicial Department to say what the law is. . . . If two laws conflict with each other, the courts must decide on the operation of

---

11. *Singleton v. Commissioner of Internal Revenue,* 439 U.S. 940, 899 S.Ct. 335, 58 L.Ed. 335 (1978).

each. . . . So if the law be in opposition to the Constitution . . . [t]he Court must determine which of these conflicting rules governs the case. This is the very essence of judicial duty.''[12]

In another famous case, *United States v. Nixon,*[13] the United States Supreme Court established its power over actions of the president. In 1974, a grand jury (discussed in Chapter 9) indicted seven individuals for obstruction of justice and conspiracy to defraud, among other things. President Richard Nixon was ordered by the special prosecutor to produce tapes, memoranda, papers, and transcripts. The president attempted to avoid the subpoena on the ground of ''executive privilege,'' but this ground was denied him by the district court.

The president's view of the privilege was broad, and he claimed the courts lacked the power to demand the records sought. The Supreme Court subsequently heard the case, denied the claim of executive privilege that was at the heart of the controversy, and affirmed the order of the district court. Among other things, the Court balanced the president's claim against the needs of the defendants and the courts to have the records.

## SECTION 9

# ALTERNATIVE DISPUTE RESOLUTION

Because the number of court cases filling the **dockets** (court schedules listing the cases to be tried) grows every year and the cost of litigation continues to increase, more and more businesspersons, consumers, and others are turning to **alternative dispute resolution (ADR)** as an alternative to civil lawsuits. Methods of ADR range from neighbors sitting down over a cup of coffee to work out their differences to huge multinational corporations agreeing to resolve a dispute through a formal hearing before a panel of experts. In what follows, we look at the numerous methods used for settling disputes outside the court system.

---

12.  5 U.S. (1 Cranch) 137, 2 L.Ed. 60 (1803).
13.  418 U.S. 683, 94 S.Ct. 3090, 41 L.Ed.2d 1039 (1974); *certiorari* denied 431 U.S. 933, 97 S.Ct. 2641, 53 L.Ed.2d 250 (1977); rehearing denied 433 U.S. 916, 97 S.Ct. 2992, 53 L.Ed.2d 1103 (1977).

## NEGOTIATION, CONCILIATION, AND MEDIATION

Negotiation, conciliation, and mediation are all forms of ADR that are nonadversarial in nature. In other words, the goal in these procedures is not to determine which side is more at fault or which side should win or lose but to search for common grounds for agreement.

**NEGOTIATION**  In the process of **negotiation,** the parties come together informally, with or without attorneys to represent them. Within this informal setting, the parties air their differences and try to reach a settlement or resolution without the involvement of independent third parties. Because no third parties are involved and because of the informal setting, negotiation is the simplest form of ADR. Even if a lawsuit has been initiated, the parties may continue to negotiate their differences at any time during the litigation process and settle their dispute. Less than 10 percent of all corporate lawsuits, for example, end up in trial—the rest are settled beforehand.

**CONCILIATION**  Disputes may also be resolved in a friendly, unantagonistic manner through **conciliation,** in which a third party assists the parties to a dispute in reconciling their differences. The conciliator helps to schedule negotiating sessions and carries offers back and forth between the parties when they refuse to face each other in direct negotiations. Technically, conciliators are not to recommend solutions. In practice, however, they often do. In contrast, a mediator is expected to propose solutions.

**MEDIATION**  In the **mediation** process, the parties themselves must reach an agreement, although the mediator may propose solutions for the parties to consider. The parties may select the mediator on the basis of expertise in a particular field or on the basis of the person's reputation for fairness and impartiality. The mediator may be a volunteer from the community and need not be a lawyer. Usually, a mediator will charge a fee for his or her services (which can be split between the parties).

In mediation, the mediator talks face to face with the parties and allows them to discuss their disagreement in an informal atmosphere, such as a community center, church, or neighbor's home. There are few procedural rules—certainly fewer than in a courtroom. In fact, most mediation programs discourage lawyers from participating, and thus legal terminology is frequently avoided.

Mediation often results in the quick settlement of disputes. Initial meetings between the parties and the mediator often occur within several weeks after a voluntary request to mediate has been made by one or both parties.

## ARBITRATION

A more formal method of alternative dispute resolution is **arbitration.** The key difference between arbitration and the forms of ADR just discussed is that in negotiation, conciliation, and mediation, the parties themselves settle their dispute, although a third party may assist them in doing so. In arbitration, the third party hearing the dispute decides the issue. Depending on the circumstances and the parties' wishes, the decision may be legally binding on the parties, or it may be nonbinding. In arbitration, the arbitrator becomes, in a sense, a private judge, even though the arbitrator does not have to be a lawyer. Frequently, a panel of experts arbitrates the dispute.

Virtually any commercial matter can be submitted to arbitration. When a dispute arises, the parties can agree to settle their differences through arbitration rather than through the court system. Frequently, however, disputes are arbitrated because of an arbitration clause in a contract entered into before the dispute arose. An **arbitration clause** provides that any disputes arising under the contract will be resolved by arbitration.

**THE ARBITRATION PROCESS** The arbitrator may be given power at the beginning of the arbitration process to establish rules that will govern the proceedings. Typically, these rules are much less restrictive than those governing formal litigation. Regardless of who establishes the rules, the arbitrator will apply them during the course of the *hearing.* In the typical hearing format, the parties begin as they would at a trial by presenting opening arguments to the arbitrator and stating what remedies should or should not be granted. After the opening statements have been made, evidence is presented. Witnesses may be called and examined by both sides. After all the evidence has been presented, the parties give their closing arguments. On completion of the closing arguments, the arbitrator closes the hearing.

After each side has had an opportunity to present evidence and to argue its case, the arbitrator will reach a decision. The final decision of the arbitrator is called an **award,** even if no money is conferred on a party as a result of the proceedings. Under most statutes, the arbitrator must render an award within thirty days of the close of the hearing.

**ARBITRATION STATUTES** Most states have statutes (often based in part on the Uniform Arbitration Act of 1955) under which arbitration clauses will be enforced. Some state statutes compel arbitration of certain types of disputes, such as those involving public employees.

At the federal level, the Federal Arbitration Act (FAA), enacted in 1925, enforces arbitration clauses in contracts involving maritime activity or interstate commerce, and the FAA can preempt state coverage in these areas in the event of conflict between a state statute and the federal act. Even business activities that have only remote or minimal effects on commerce between two or more states are regarded as interstate commerce. Thus, arbitration agreements involving transactions only slightly connected to the flow of interstate commerce may fall under the FAA.

The FAA does not establish a set arbitration procedure. The parties themselves must agree on the manner of resolving their disputes. The FAA provides the means for enforcing the arbitration procedure that the parties establish for themselves.

**THE ENFORCEMENT OF ARBITRATION AGREEMENTS** It is important to note that if parties enter into a contract containing an arbitration clause, it is likely that a state or federal statute will compel them to arbitrate any dispute arising under the contract—providing there are no reasons against arbitrating the dispute.

The role of the courts in the arbitration process is limited. One important role is played at the prearbitration stage. When a dispute arises as to whether or not the parties have agreed in an arbitration clause to submit a particular matter to arbitration, one party may file suit to compel arbitration. The court before which the suit is brought will not decide the basic controversy but must decide the issue of *arbitrability*—that is, whether the matter is one that must be resolved through arbitration. The arbitrability of a dispute is at issue in the following case.

**CASE 3.1**

**SHEARSON/ AMERICAN EXPRESS, INC. v. McMAHON**

Supreme Court of the
United States, 1987.
482 U.S. 220,
107 S.Ct. 2332,
96 L.Ed.2d 185.

**COMPANY PROFILE**   *The firm that came to be known in the 1980s as Shearson/American Express, Inc., began in 1960 as Carter, Berlind, Potoma & Weill, a Wall Street brokerage firm. By the end of the 1960s, the principals in the firm had changed, and the firm had changed its name: first to Carter, Berlind & Weill and then to Carter, Berlind, Weill & Levitt. Through the 1970s, the firm took over other Wall Street brokerage houses and renamed itself four times. The company ranked as Wall Street's tenth largest brokerage house in 1979. Two years later, American Express, Inc., bought the firm and changed the name to Shearson/American Express, Inc. Lehman Brothers Kuhn Loeb came aboard in 1984, and the firm became Shearson Lehman Brothers. During the rest of the decade, misfortune beset Shearson Lehman Brothers: the firm was indicted for money laundering, lost $140 million in a bad bank investment, and suffered a notable defeat in an attempt to take over RJR Nabisco. By the early 1990s, the firm had cost American Express more than $1.5 billion.*

**BACKGROUND AND FACTS**   *In October 1984, Eugene and Julia McMahon filed a complaint in a federal district court against Shearson/ American Express, Inc. (a brokerage firm registered with the Securities and Exchange Commission), and Mary Ann McNulty, the broker who handled the McMahons' account with Shearson. The complaint alleged, among other things, that with Shearson's knowledge McNulty had violated Section 10(b) of the Securities Exchange Act of 1934 by engaging in fraudulent excessive trading on the McMahons' accounts and by making false statements. Relying on two customer agreements signed by Julia McMahon that provided for the arbitration of any controversy relating to the McMahons' accounts with Shearson, McNulty and Shearson moved to compel arbitration of the McMahons' claim pursuant to the Federal Arbitration Act. The district court found that the McMahons' Section 10(b) claims were arbitrable under the terms of the agreement. The court of appeals reversed the decision. The United States Supreme Court granted* certiorari *to resolve the issue.*

*O'CONNOR,* Justice.

\*   \*   \*   \*

The Federal Arbitration Act provides the starting point for answering the questions raised in this case. \*   \*   \* The Arbitration Act provid[es] that arbitration agreements ''shall be valid, irrevocable, and enforceable, save upon such grounds as exist at law or in equity for the revocation of any contract.'' The Act also provides that a court must stay [suspend] its proceedings if it is satisfied that an issue before it is arbitrable under the agreement, and it authorizes a federal district court to issue an order compelling arbitration if there has been a ''failure, neglect, or refusal'' to comply with the arbitration agreement. \*   \*   \*

The Arbitration Act thus establishes a ''federal policy favoring arbitration.''
\*   \*   \*

The Arbitration Act mandates enforcement of agreements to arbitrate statutory claims. Like any statutory directive, the Arbitration Act's mandate may be overridden by a contrary congressional command. The burden is on the party opposing arbitration, however, to show that Congress intended to preclude a waiver of judicial remedies for the statutory rights at issue. \*   \*   \*

To defeat application of the Arbitration Act in this case, therefore, the McMahons must demonstrate that Congress intended to make an exception to the Arbitration Act for claims arising under * * * the Exchange Act, an intention discernible from the text, history, or purposes of the statute. * * *

* * * *

Congress did not intend * * * to bar enforcement of all predispute arbitration agreements. In this case, where the SEC has sufficient statutory authority to ensure that arbitration is adequate to vindicate Exchange Act rights, enforcement does not effect a waiver of "compliance with any provision" of the Exchange Act. * * * Accordingly, we hold the McMahons' agreements to arbitrate Exchange Act claims "enforce[able] * * * in accord with the explicit provisions of the Arbitration Act."

**DECISION AND REMEDY**

*The Supreme Court reversed the judgment of the court of appeals. The Court held that the Section 10(b) Securities Exchange Act claim should be sent to arbitration pursuant to the parties' agreement in their contract to have any disputes concerning the accounts arbitrated.*

**ARBITRABILITY AND PUBLIC POLICY** In the *Shearson* case just presented, the decision to compel arbitration was viewed by many as contradicting the public policy enunciated by the federal legislation passed to protect investors. But in making their decisions concerning the arbitrability of disputes, courts must weigh this policy against two other policies: (1) freedom of contract, which means that the courts are reluctant to interfere with contracts (and arbitration clauses contained therein) voluntarily formed, and (2) the policy favoring alternative methods of dispute settlement to reduce the heavy caseload of the courts.

Four years after the *Shearson* decision, the United States Supreme Court underscored its willingness to enforce arbitration clauses against persons falling within other classes that are protected under federal law. The case arose when Robert Gilmer, a financial manager for Interstate/Johnson Lane Corporation, sued his employer for age discrimination after being fired from his job. As a condition of his employment with Interstate, Johnson was required to register as a securities representative with the New York Stock Exchange. Gilmer's application for the securities registration contained an arbitration clause under which Gilmer agreed to the arbitration of any disputes between himself and his employer arising out of his employment. In his lawsuit against Interstate, Gilmer claimed that his termination violated the Age Discrimination in Employment Act (ADEA) of 1967,[14] a federal act passed specifically to prevent employers from discriminating against older employees. The employer filed a motion to compel arbitration, and the issue of arbitrability was ultimately decided by the United States Supreme Court. In its decision, the Court held that it could "find nothing in the text, legislative history, or underlying purposes of the ADEA indicating a congressional intent to preclude enforcement of arbitration agreements."[15]

In the following case, the New York Court of Appeals, that state's highest court, evaluates the arbitrability of a claim alleging racial discrimination in employment in light of the United States Supreme Court's ruling in *Gilmer.*

14. 29 U.S.C. Sections 621–634.
15. *Gilmer v. Interstate/Johnson Lane Corp.,* 500 U.S. 20, 111 S.Ct. 1647, 114 L.Ed.2d 26 (1991).

CASE 3.2

**FLETCHER v. KIDDER, PEABODY & CO.**
Court of Appeals of New York, 1993.
81 N.Y.2d 623,
619 N.E.2d 998,
601 N.Y.S.2d 686.

**BACKGROUND AND FACTS** *In November 1989, Kidder, Peabody & Company hired Alphonse Fletcher, an African American, to work as a trader analyst. Fletcher stated that his annual compensation was to be no less than 20 percent, and no more than 25 percent, of his trading profits and that his 1990 bonus payment was to be paid no later than early 1991. Fletcher contended that in 1990 he generated profits of over $25.5 million, entitling him to between $5 million and $6.5 million in compensation. Fletcher alleged that Kidder, Peabody concluded that "the amount it was obligated to pay Mr. Fletcher was simply too much money to pay a young black man." Thus, the company purportedly reneged on the agreement by withholding 50 percent of his bonus compensation, deferring payment for up to eighteen months, and requiring him to pay for trading losses on a dollar-for-dollar basis—all terms to which his white counterparts were not subjected. Fletcher also alleged that the firm's human resources and equal employment opportunity officer told him not to complain: he was "one of the highest paid black males" in the country. Fletcher resigned in March 1991 and filed a lawsuit against Kidder, Peabody, charging the firm with racial discrimination in violation of state law. Kidder, Peabody filed a motion asking the court to compel arbitration on the basis of an arbitration clause in the form that Fletcher had signed as part of his application for registration with the New York Stock Exchange and securities exchanges— Fletcher had to be registered with the securities exchanges as a condition of working for Kidder, Peabody as a trader analyst. The court denied the motion, and the firm appealed. The appellate court reversed this decision, and Fletcher appealed to the state's highest court.*

*TITONE, Judge.*

\* \* \* \*

Under [*Gilmer v. Interstate/Johnson Lane Corp.*], the party seeking to avoid enforcement of an arbitration clause governed by the [Federal Arbitration Act (FAA)] must demonstrate a congressional intent "to preclude a waiver of a judicial forum [regular court]" for disputes based on a particular statutory right. Where the right is predicated on a State or local statute rather than on a congressional enactment, \* \* \* the courts are obliged to draw an analogy to the equivalent Federal law, where possible, and to consider Congress' intentions with regard to the rights created by that law.

The closest Federal analog to [the state antidiscrimination law] under which [Fletcher's] claims arise, is title VII of the Civil Rights Act [of 1964]. Contrary to [Fletcher's] contentions, there is nothing in the legislative history of either that Federal statute itself or the recently adopted amendments to that statute [the Civil Rights Act of 1991] that would suggest the existence of a congressional intent to override the general rule that anticipatory contracts to arbitrate are enforceable under the FAA.

\* \* \* \*

\* \* \* [T]he issue before us is not whether discrimination is a social evil that should be eradicated with whatever tools we have. Rather, the issue is whether, under existing precedent, the important public policies underlying title VII of the Federal Civil Rights Act may be deemed to override the " 'emphatic' national policy favoring arbitration," as reflected in the FAA. The Supreme Court has already ruled \* \* \* that the proper question is \* \* \* whether Congress, in creating a statutory remedy, intended that arbitration of the statutorily established claim would be foreclosed.

*The New York Court of Appeals affirmed the decision of the intermediate appellate court, holding that an agreement to arbitrate a dispute involving a claim of unlawful discrimination is enforceable. Therefore, Fletcher was compelled to submit his claim for arbitration.*

**DECISION AND REMEDY**

**International Arbitration and Public Policy** *International standards for the recognition of arbitration agreements and awards were set by the 1958 United Nations Convention. Article V(2) of the Convention creates an exception to enforcement of arbitration clauses that are "contrary to the public policy" of the relevant country. While this is similar to the standard applied in the United States, the resolution of a case will depend on the strength of a public policy in a given country.*

**INTERNATIONAL CONSIDERATIONS**

**SETTING ASIDE AN AWARD** Courts also may play an important role at the postarbitration stage. If the arbitration has produced an award, one of the parties may appeal the award or may seek a court order compelling the other party to comply with the award. In determining whether an award should be enforced, a court conducts a review that is much more restricted in scope than an appellate court's review of a trial court decision. The general view is that because the parties were free to frame the issues and set the powers of the arbitrator at the outset, they cannot complain about the result.

An arbitration award may be set aside (nullified, or rendered ineffective), though, in certain circumstances. An arbitrator's award may be set aside if the award resulted from the arbitrator's misconduct or "bad faith." For example, if the arbitrator exhibited bias or corruption, refused to hear pertinent evidence, or acted in any way that substantially prejudiced the rights of one of the parties, the award may be set aside. Another basis for setting aside an award exists if the arbitrator exceeded his or her powers in arbitrating the dispute. An arbitrator is empowered to resolve only those issues that are covered by the agreement to submit to arbitration. As mentioned, if the arbitrability of a dispute is in question, the courts must decide that issue, not the arbitrator.

In keeping with contract law principles, no award will be enforced if compliance with the award would result in the commission of a crime or would conflict with some greater social policy mandated by statute. A court will not overturn an award, however, simply because the arbitrator was called on to resolve a dispute involving a matter of important public concern. For an award to be set aside, it must call for some action by the parties that would conflict with, or in some way undermine, public policy. In the following case, the court refused to enforce an arbitrator's award on the ground that its enforcement would be contrary to a significant and explicitly enunciated public policy.

**HISTORICAL AND SOCIAL SETTING** *Traditionally, in regard to employment contracts, the common law held that employment was "at will." Employers could discharge employees at any time for any reason. Today, employers' rights are much more restricted. In many states, the employment-at-will doctrine has been superseded by statutes governing employment relationships. Even in states in which the at-will doctrine still controls, employer-employee contracts or employer-union contracts may limit the conditions under which an employee may be fired. Federal laws regulating employment relationships further restrict an employer's ability to discharge employees.*

| CASE 3.3 |
| --- |

**STATE v. COUNCIL 4, AFSCME**
Appellate Court of Connecticut, 1992.
27 Conn.App. 635,
608 A.2d 718.

**BACKGROUND AND FACTS**  *Phillip Beaudry, who suffered from mental illness, worked in the department of income maintenance for the state of Connecticut. Between November 1989 and March 1990, Beaudry misappropriated approximately $1,640 in state funds, which was a ground for dismissal under state personnel regulations. After he was fired from his job, Beaudry filed a complaint with his union, Council 4 of the American Federation of State, County, and Municipal Employees. Eventually the dispute was submitted to an arbitrator. The arbitrator concluded that Beaudry had been dismissed without "just cause" because Beaudry's acts were caused by his mental illness and "were not willful or volitional or within his capacity to control." Because Beaudry was disabled, the employer was required, under state law, to transfer Beaudry to a position that he was competent to hold. The arbitrator awarded Beaudry reinstatement, back pay, seniority, and other benefits. The state appealed the decision to a state court, which vacated (cancelled or nullified) the award on the ground that it was contrary to the public policy of not rewarding state employees who knowingly misappropriate state funds. The union appealed.*

*HEIMAN*, Judge.
   *   *   *   *

A public policy challenge to an arbitration award is rooted in the principle that the parties cannot expect "conduct which is illegal or contrary to public policy to receive judicial endorsement any more than parties can expect a court to enforce such a contract between them." *   *   *

This state's compelling public policy of not tolerating the knowing misappropriation of state funds by state officials or employees cannot be disputed. General Statutes [Section] 53a-119(6), which explicitly proscribes such conduct, represents an unequivocal legislative articulation of this policy. The public policy of discouraging fraud generally is firmly rooted in our common law as well.

The trial court properly found that the arbitration award contravened Connecticut's public policy of not countenancing the knowing misappropriation of state moneys by state officials or employees. *   *   *
   *   *   *   *

The defendant contends initially that the trial court failed to consider the public policy of discouraging discrimination against the mentally ill. The trial court's memorandum makes clear, however, that it was well aware that the arbitrator determined that just cause to discharge Beaudry did not exist because Beaudry's psychiatric disorder rendered his acts of misconduct nonvolitional. The trial court nonetheless concluded that our state's policy of not tolerating embezzlement by state employees required it to vacate the arbitration award. We cannot say that the trial court's conclusion was unreasonable. Although the arbitrator found that Beaudry's mental illness caused him to misappropriate funds, it did not find that Beaudry's discharge was motivated by an intent to discriminate against the mentally ill.

**DECISION AND REMEDY**  *The appellate court affirmed the trial court's decision, holding that the arbitrator's award had been properly vacated on the ground that it was contrary to public policy.*

---

**ARBITRATION SERVICES**  Arbitration services are provided by government agencies and private organizations. The major source of arbitration services is the **American Arbitration Association** (**AAA**). Most of the largest law firms in the nation are members of this association. Founded in 1926, the AAA now settles more than sixty-two thousand disputes a year in its numerous offices around the country. Settlements usually are effected quickly and, at times, in informal settings, such as a conference room or even a hotel room. Cases brought before the AAA are heard by an expert or a panel of experts in the area relating to the dispute. Generally, about half of the panel members are lawyers. To cover its costs, the nonprofit organization charges a fee, which is paid by the party filing the claim. In addition, each party to the dispute pays a specified amount for each hearing day, as well as a special additional fee in cases involving personal injuries or property loss.

## COURT-MANDATED ADR

Increasingly, the courts are requiring that parties attempt to settle their differences through some form of ADR before proceeding to trial. Usually, the claims involved must fall under a certain threshold amount. In 1984, federal courts in several districts began to experiment with court-sponsored, nonbinding arbitration for cases involving up to $100,000. Because of the success of this program (less than 10 percent of the cases referred for arbitration go to trial), federal courts continued to refer cases for ADR. Today, nearly 40 percent of federal trial courts and nearly 50 percent of federal appellate courts have adopted formal rules regarding the use of ADR, and many other courts without such rules use ADR procedures.

State courts are also increasingly turning to ADR programs as a means of relieving their burgeoning caseloads. In California, for example, disputes involving claims of under $50,000 must be heard by an arbitrator before proceeding to a court trial. Hawaii has a program of mandatory, nonbinding arbitration for disputes involving less than $150,000, and numerous other states have implemented similar programs.

In the federal courts and in many state courts, when cases are referred for arbitration, the arbitrator's decision is not binding. If either party rejects the award, the case proceeds to trial, and the court reconsiders all of the evidence and legal questions pertaining to the dispute.

## OTHER FORMS OF ADR

A fairly recent development in the area of ADR is the use of mini-trials to facilitate dispute settlement. A **mini-trial** is a private proceeding in which each party's attorney briefly argues the party's case

before the other party. Often, a neutral third party, who acts as an adviser, is also present. If the parties fail to reach an agreement, the adviser renders an opinion as to how a court would likely decide the issue if the case went to trial.

A variant of the mini-trial that has been employed successfully in the federal system is the **summary jury trial (SJT).** The key difference between an SJT and a mini-trial is that in an SJT, a jury participates. The litigants present their arguments and evidence, and the jury then renders a verdict. The jury's verdict is not binding, but it does act as a guide to both sides in reaching an agreement during the mandatory negotiations that immediately follow the trial. Because no witnesses are called, an SJT is much speedier than a regular trial, and frequently the parties are able to settle their dispute without resorting to an actual trial. If no settlement is reached, both sides have the right to a full trial later.

Recently, the Sixth Circuit Court of Appeals faced the question as to whether SJTs can be mandatory. The court concluded that it would be unfair to litigants to force them to undergo SJTs before they are permitted to have their claims heard in a federal court.[16]

## THE PRIVATIZATION OF JUSTICE

Given the popularity of alternatives to traditional court proceedings, it is not surprising that the private enterprise system would respond to the growing demand for more efficient, less costly forums for settling disputes. One such response is the so-called rent-a-judge system. The rent-a-judge option began in 1976 in California, the state that still handles about half of the cases submitted to hired judges for decision. Under a California state statute,[17] litigants can bypass the formal court system by having their cases heard before former judges of the California courts. Under the statute, cases can be "tried before a referee selected and paid by the litigants and empowered by the statute to enter decisions having the finality of trial court judgments." In California, as well as in the dozen or so other states with similar statutes, jurors can be selected from the public jury rolls, and verdicts can

---

16. *In re NLO, Inc.,* 5 F.3d 154 (6th Cir. 1993).

17. California Civil Procedure Code Sections 638–645.

■ CONCEPT SUMMARY 3.3 **Alternative Dispute Resolution (ADR)**

| TYPE OF ADR | DESCRIPTION |
|---|---|
| **Negotiation** | The parties come together, with or without attorneys to represent them, and try to reach a settlement without the involvement of a third party. |
| **Conciliation** | A third party, called a conciliator, assists the parties to a dispute in reconciling their differences. |
| **Mediation** | The parties themselves reach an agreement with the help of a third party, called a mediator, who proposes solutions. |
| **Arbitration** | In this more formal method of ADR, the parties submit their dispute to a neutral third party, the arbitrator, who renders a decision. The decision may or may not be legally binding, depending on the circumstances. Some courts refer certain cases for arbitration before allowing the cases to proceed to trial; in most cases, this kind of arbitration is nonbinding on the parties. |
| **Mini-trial** | In a private proceeding, each party's attorney argues the party's case before the other party. Often, a neutral third party acts as an adviser and renders an opinion on how a court would likely decide the issue. |
| **Summary Jury Trial (SJT)** | Some federal courts employ a kind of trial in which litigants present their arguments and evidence, and the jury then renders a nonbinding verdict. This SJT acts as a guide to both parties in reaching an agreement during the mandatory negotiations that immediately follow the trial. |
| **Rent-a-Judge Courts** | The parties rent a judge to hear their case and render a verdict, to which the parties agree to be bound. Several firms now provide this kind of private justice. |

be appealed to a state appellate court. Private courts are a boon to those who do not wish to wait for years to go to trial. In Los Angeles County, for example, litigants must wait from three to eight years (the national average is eighteen months) to be heard in a public court.

The private system of justice spread quickly, and now hundreds of firms throughout the country offer dispute-resolution services by hired judges. The two leading firms in this new industry, Endispute and Judicial Arbitration and Mediation Services, recently merged. In 1994, their combined revenues were estimated to be $40 million. Procedures in these private courts are fashioned to meet the desires of the clients seeking their services. For example, the parties usually can decide on the date of the hearing, the presiding judge,

whether the judge's decision will be legally binding, and the site of the hearing—which could be a conference room, a law-school office, or a leased courtroom. The judges follow procedures similar to those of the federal courts and use similar rules. Normally, each party to the dispute pays a filing fee and a designated fee for a hearing session or conference. Although rent-a-judge courts first became popular in settling contract and employment disputes, in recent years they have been frequently used to settle disputes relating to family law and personal injuries as well.

Many are concerned, understandably, with the implications of the marketing of justice. Some observers feel, for example, that the rise of an alternative, private system of justice is making needed reforms of the public system less likely.

## TERMS AND CONCEPTS TO REVIEW

alternative dispute resolution (ADR) 52
American Arbitration Association (AAA) 58
arbitration 53
arbitration clause 53
award 53
conciliation 52
concurrent jurisdiction 49
diversity of citizenship 49
docket 52

exclusive jurisdiction 49
federal question 49
*in personam* jurisdiction 42
*in rem* jurisdiction 42
judicial review 51
jurisdiction 41
justiciable controversy 44
litigant 43
long arm statute 42
mediation 52
mini-trial 59

negotiation 52
probate court 43
*quasi in rem* jurisdiction 42
question of fact 45
question of law 45
small claims court 44
standing to sue 43
summary jury trial (SJT) 59
trial court 43
venue 43
writ of *certiorari* 50

## QUESTIONS AND CASE PROBLEMS

**3–1. Arbitration.** In an arbitration proceeding, the arbitrator need not be a judge or even a lawyer. How, then, can the arbitrator's decision have the force of law and be binding on the parties involved?

**3–2. Courts of Appeals.** Sometimes on appeal there are questions concerning whether the facts presented in the trial court support the conclusion reached by the judge or the jury. The appellate court will reverse a lower court's decision on the basis of the facts only when so little evidence was presented at trial that no reasonable person could have reached the conclusion that the judge or jury reached. Appellate courts normally defer to a judge's decision with regard to the facts. Can you see any reason for this?

**3–3. Courts of Appeals.** Appellate courts normally see only a written transcript of trial proceedings when they are reviewing cases. Today, in some states, videotapes are being used as the official trial reports. If the use of videotapes as official reports continues, will this alter the appellate process? Should it? Discuss fully.

**3–4. Jurisdiction.** Marya Callais, a citizen of Florida, was walking near a busy street in Tallahassee, Florida, one day when a large crate flew off a passing truck and hit her, resulting in numerous injuries. She incurred a great deal of pain and suffering, plus significant medical expenses, and she could not work for six months. She wanted to sue the trucking firm for $300,000 in damages. The firm's headquarters were in Georgia, although the company did business in Florida. In what court might Callais bring suit—a Florida state court, a Georgia state court, or a federal court? What factors might influence her decision?

**3–5. Jurisdiction.** Achim and Nadira Ulrik live in Massachusetts. One day they noticed in the *Boston Globe* an advertisement for vacationers that was sponsored by a national hotel chain: "Stay in Maximum Inns' beachfront hotel in Puerto Rico for one week for only $300; continental breakfast included." The Ulriks decided to accept the offer and spent a week at the Puerto Rico hotel. On the last day, Nadira fell on a wet floor in the hotel lobby and sustained multiple fractures to her left ankle and hip. Because of the injuries, which were subsequently complicated by infections, she was unable to work at her job as an airline flight attendant for ten months. The Maximum Inns chain has no hotels in Massachusetts and does not conduct business in that state. Nadira wants to bring a lawsuit against Maximum Inns in a Massachusetts state court. Can a Massachusetts court exercise jurisdiction over Maximum Inns? What factors should the court consider in deciding this jurisdictional issue?

**3–6. Arbitration.** Gates worked for Arizona Brewing Co. and was a member of the International Union of United Brewers, Flour, Cereal, and Soft Drink Workers of America. A contract between Gates's employer and the union stated that the employer and the union were to try to settle their differences, but if the parties could not reach a settlement, the matter was to be decided by arbitration. Claiming that the arbitration clause was void under an Arizona arbitration statute, Gates brought a lawsuit against Arizona Brewing Co. to recover wages. Gates had not made any attempt to submit the dispute between him and the employer to arbitration. The employer argued that Gates could not bring a lawsuit until after arbitration had occurred. A provision in the Arizona arbitration statute, which generally enforced arbitration clauses in contracts, stated that "this act shall not apply to collective contracts between employers and . . . associations of employ[ees]." Must Gates undergo arbitration before bringing a lawsuit? Explain. [*Gates v. Arizona Brewing Co.,* 54 Ariz. 266, 95 P.2d 49 (1939)]

**3–7. Arbitration.** Roger and Susan Faherty divorced, and entered into a property settlement agreement that was incorporated into the final divorce decree. The property settlement agreement contained a clause that mandated arbitration of any dispute arising out of the agreement. Roger failed to make several alimony and child-support payments, and Susan sought court enforcement of the property settlement agreement. Roger's consequent motion to have the court compel arbitration was granted by the court, and the dispute was arbitrated. The arbitrator's decision required Roger to pay Susan $37,648 for back alimony payments and $12,284 for overdue child support. Roger, although he had been the one to petition the court for arbitration, now challenged the validity of the arbitration clause in alimony and child-support matters. He claimed that as a matter of public policy, such matters should be settled by the courts, not by arbitration. Will the court agree with Roger? Discuss. [*Faherty v. Faherty,* 97 N.J. 99, 477 A.2d 1257 (1984)]

**3–8. Arbitration.** Colorado's Mandatory Arbitration Act required that all civil lawsuits involving damages of less than $50,000 be arbitrated rather than tried in court. The statutory scheme, which was a pilot project, affected eight judicial districts in the state. It provided for a court trial for any party dissatisfied with an arbitrator's decision. It also provided that if the trial did not result in an improvement of more than 10 percent in the position of the party who demanded the trial, that party had to pay the costs of the arbitration proceeding. The constitutionality of the act was challenged by a plaintiff who maintained in part that it violated litigants' rights of access to the courts and to trial by jury. What will the court decide? Explain your answer. [*Firelock, Inc. v. District Court, 20th Judicial District,* 776 P.2d 1090 (Colo. 1989)]

**3–9. Arbitration.** New York State revised its New Car Lemon Law to allow consumers who complained of purchasing a "lemon" to have their disputes arbitrated before a professional arbitrator appointed by the New York attorney general. Before it was revised, the Lemon Law allowed for the arbitration of disputes, but the forum in which arbitration took place was sponsored by trade associations within the automobile industry, and consumers often complained of unfair awards. The revised law also provided that consumers were not required to arbitrate but, if they wished, could sue a manufacturer in court. Manufacturers, however, were *compelled* to arbitrate claims if a consumer chose to do so and could not resort to the courts. Trade associations representing automobile manufacturers and importers brought an action seeking a declaration that the alternative arbitration mechanism of the Lemon Law was unconstitutional because it deprived them of their right to trial by jury. How will the court decide? Discuss. [*Motor Vehicle Manufacturers Association of the United States v. State,* 551 N.Y.S.2d 470, 550 N.E.2d 919, 75 N.Y.2d 175 (1990)]

**3–10. Jurisdiction.** Alex Sutton, a professional golfer living in Middleburg, Florida, entered into a sponsorship agreement with ARS & Associates, a Michigan partnership. Among other things, the agreement provided that (1) ARS would sponsor Sutton on a Professional Golfing Association (PGA) tour, (2) ARS would pay all of Sutton's expenses, (3) ARS and Sutton would split the proceeds (whatever remained after ARS had been reimbursed for expenses) fifty-fifty, and (4) ARS would provide health insurance for Sutton. Preliminary negotiations were carried out mostly over the phone. ARS drew up the agreement in Michigan and sent it to Sutton in Florida; Sutton signed and returned the contract to ARS. ARS then signed the agreement and sent a copy of it to Sutton. Sutton subsequently participated in several senior PGA events, including two tournaments in Florida. While playing golf in a senior PGA tournament in Palm Springs, California, Sutton suffered a heart attack and, as a result, later incurred costs of more than $100,000 for open-heart surgery and related medical expenses. Because ARS had not obtained health-insurance coverage for Sutton, Sutton sued ARS in a Florida state court for breach of the agreement. ARS moved to dismiss the action for lack of personal jurisdiction. Can the Florida court, under its long arm statute, exercise personal jurisdiction over the Michigan defendant in this case? Discuss. [*Sutton v. Smith,* 603 So.2d 693 (Fla.App. 1992)]

# CHAPTER 4

# COURT PROCEDURES

**A**merican and English courts follow the *adversarial system of justice.* Although clients are allowed to represent themselves in court (called *pro se* representation),[1] most parties to lawsuits hire attorneys to represent them. Each lawyer acts as his or her client's advocate, presenting the client's version of the facts in such a way as to convince the judge or the jury (or both) that this version is true.

The judge's role is viewed as nonbiased and mostly passive, but not entirely so. Judges are responsible for the appropriate application of the law. They do not have to accept the legal reasoning of the attorneys. They can base a ruling and a decision on a personal study of the law. Judges sometimes ask questions of witnesses, sometimes limit the amount of information that can be introduced about an expert witness's qualifications, and sometimes even suggest types of evidence to be presented. For example, if a defendant chooses to act as his or her own counsel, the judge will often play a role more like that of an advocate, intervening during the trial proceedings to help the defendant.

Most of the judicial procedures that you will read about in this chapter are rooted in the adversarial framework of the American legal system. The adversarial system also frames the ethical rules that govern the behavior of attorneys, who are key participants in the litigation process.

In this chapter, after a brief overview of judicial procedures, we illustrate the steps involved in a lawsuit with a hypothetical civil case (criminal procedures will be discussed in Chapter 9).

---

1.  This right was definitively established in *Faretta v. California,* 422 U.S. 806, 95 S.Ct. 2525, 45 L.Ed.2d 562 (1975).

■ **Exhibit 4–1  Stages in a Typical Lawsuit**

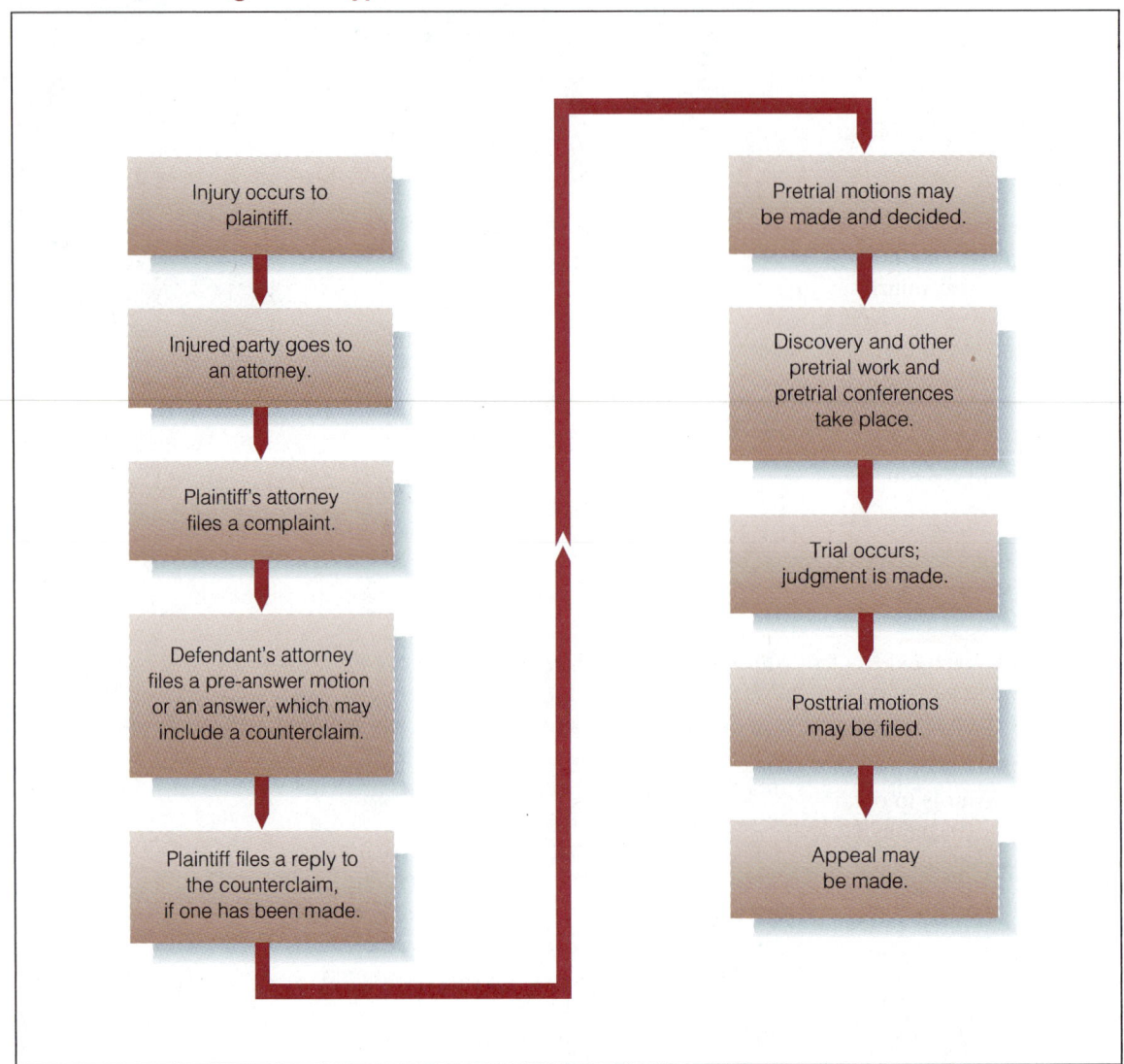

Injury occurs to plaintiff.

Injured party goes to an attorney.

Plaintiff's attorney files a complaint.

Defendant's attorney files a pre-answer motion or an answer, which may include a counterclaim.

Plaintiff files a reply to the counterclaim, if one has been made.

Pretrial motions may be made and decided.

Discovery and other pretrial work and pretrial conferences take place.

Trial occurs; judgment is made.

Posttrial motions may be filed.

Appeal may be made.

---

## SECTION 1

# PROCEDURAL RULES

Understanding and meeting procedural requirements are essential in the litigation process. All civil trials held in federal district courts are governed by the **Federal Rules of Civil Procedure (FRCP).**[2] Each state also has its rules of civil procedure that apply to all courts within that state. These rules specify what must be done, when, and

at which stage of the litigation process. In addition, each court has its own local rules of procedures that supplement the federal or state rules. At the outset of any lawsuit, the attorney may inform his or her client of the rules of procedure that apply to the particular court in which the trial will take place.

Although civil trials may vary greatly in terms of complexity, cost, and detail, they all share similar structural characteristics. Even though each case has its own particular set of facts to which specific laws apply, most civil lawsuits typically follow some version of the course charted in Exhibit 4–1. This exhibit shows that civil litigation typically progresses in very well-defined and

---

2. The United States Supreme Court's authority to promulgate these rules is set forth in 28 U.S.C. Sections 2071–2077.

discrete stages. Although it may take years for a case to wind its way through court, almost every case follows the same basic steps.

We now turn to our hypothetical case. The case arose from an automobile accident, which occurred when a car driven by Antonio Carvello, a resident of New Jersey, collided with a car driven by Jill Kirby, a resident of New York. The accident took place at an intersection in New York City. Kirby suffered personal injuries, incurring medical and hospital expenses, as well as lost wages for four months. In all, she calculated that the cost to her of the accident was $100,000. Carvello and Kirby are unable to agree on a settlement, and Kirby faces the decision of whether to sue Carvello for the $100,000 compensation that she feels she deserves.

## SECTION 2

# CONSULTING WITH AN ATTORNEY

The first step taken by virtually anyone contemplating a lawsuit is to obtain the advice of a qualified attorney. In the hypothetical Kirby-Carvello case, Kirby would consult with an attorney, who would advise her on what she might expect to gain from a lawsuit, her probability of success if she sued, what procedures would be involved, and how long it might take to resolve the issue through the judicial process. Depending on the court hearing the case, the time costs of the litigation may be enormous. Cases involving personal injuries usually take two to three years to resolve, and this is an important factor for Kirby to consider.

### LEGAL FEES

Another crucial factor that Kirby must consider is, of course, the cost of the attorney's time—the legal fees that she will have to pay to collect damages from the defendant, Carvello. Attorneys base their fees on such factors as the difficulty of a matter, the amount of time involved, the experience and skill of the attorney in the particular area of the law, and the cost of doing business. In the United States, legal fees range from $60 per hour to $450 per hour (the average fee per hour is between $140 and $160). Not included in attorneys' fees are such

expenses as court filing charges and other costs directly related to a case.

A particular legal matter may include one or a combination of several types of fees. *Fixed fees* may be charged for the performance of such services as drafting a simple will. *Hourly fees* may be computed for matters that involve an indeterminate period of time. Any case brought to trial, for example, may involve an expenditure of time that cannot be precisely estimated in advance. *Contingent fees* are fixed as a percentage (between 25 and 40 percent) of a client's recovery in certain types of lawsuits, such as personal injury. If the lawsuit is unsuccessful, the attorney receives no fee. If Kirby retains an attorney on a contingency-fee basis, she normally will not have to pay any fees unless she wins the case. She will, however, have to pay the court fees and any other expenses incurred by the attorney (such as travel expenses, copying expenses, and so on—often called out-of-pocket costs) on her behalf.

Many state and federal statutes allow for an award of attorneys' fees in certain legal actions, such as probate matters. In these cases, a judge sets the amount of the fee, based on such factors as the results obtained by the attorney and the fee customarily charged for similar services. In some cases, a client may receive an award of attorneys' fees as part of his or her recovery.

### SETTLEMENT CONSIDERATIONS

A client's decision as to how much money he or she can afford to invest in the resolution of a particular legal problem is frequently the most important factor in determining the extent to which an attorney will pursue a resolution. If a client decides that he or she can afford a lengthy trial and one or more appeals, an attorney may pursue those actions. Often, once a client learns the extent of the costs involved in litigating a claim, he or she will be more willing to settle the claim for a lower amount. For example, assume that Kirby is seeking damages of $100,000 in a lawsuit against Carvello and that the attorney's contingency fee is 30 percent. If Kirby is awarded $100,000, she will end up with only $70,000 (less filing fees and other expenses incurred by the attorney on her behalf). If Carvello offers her $75,000 to settle the claim without a trial, Kirby may want to consider settling the claim for this amount.

# PRETRIAL PROCEDURES

Assuming that Kirby decides to sue Carvello, the next step will be to retain the attorney with whom she consulted (or another attorney of her choice). This is usually accomplished by signing a *retainer agreement* and, if the attorney has not dealt with her previously, paying the attorney an advance (retainer) fee. Once Kirby has retained an attorney and indicated that she wants to initiate a lawsuit, the litigation process begins.

The pretrial litigation process involves the filing of pleadings, the gathering of evidence (called *discovery*), and other procedures, such as a pretrial conference or jury selection.

## THE PLEADINGS

The *complaint* and *answer* (and the *counterclaim* and *reply*)—all of which are discussed below—taken together are called the **pleadings.** The pleadings inform each party of the claims of the other and specify the issues (disputed questions) involved in the case. Pleadings remove the element of surprise from a case. They allow lawyers to gather the most persuasive evidence and to prepare better arguments, thus increasing the probability that a just and true result will be forthcoming from the trial.

**COMPLAINT AND SUMMONS** Kirby's suit, or action, against Carvello will commence when her lawyer files a **complaint** (sometimes called a petition or declaration) with the clerk of the trial court in the appropriate geographical area (the proper venue). In most states, it will be a court having general jurisdiction; in others, it may be a court having special jurisdiction with regard to subject matter. The complaint will contain (1) a statement alleging the facts necessary for the court to take jurisdiction, (2) a short statement of the facts necessary to show that the plaintiff is entitled to a remedy, and (3) a statement of the remedy the plaintiff is seeking. A typical complaint is shown in Exhibit 4–2.

The complaint will state that Kirby was driving her Ford Taurus through a green light at the specified intersection, exercising good driving habits and reasonable care, when Carvello negligently drove his Cadillac through a red light and into the intersection from a cross street, striking Kirby and causing serious personal injury and property damage. The complaint will go on to state that Kirby is entitled to $85,000 to cover medical bills, $10,000 to cover lost wages, and $5,000 to cover property damage to her car.

After the complaint has been filed, the sheriff or a deputy of the county or other *process server* (one who delivers a complaint and summons) will serve a **summons** and a copy of the complaint on the defendant, Carvello. The summons notifies Carvello that he is required to prepare an answer to the complaint and to file a copy of his answer with both the court and the plaintiff's attorney within a specified time period (usually twenty to thirty days after the summons has been served). The summons also informs Carvello that failure to answer will result in a **default judgment** for the plaintiff—in which case the plaintiff would be awarded the damages alleged in her complaint. A typical summons is shown in Exhibit 4–3.

Rules governing the service (delivery) of a summons vary, but usually service is made by handing the summons to the defendant personally or by leaving it at the defendant's residence or place of business. In a few states, a summons can be served by mail. When the defendant cannot be reached, special rules sometimes permit serving the summons by leaving it with a designated person, such as the secretary of state.

**CHOICES AVAILABLE AFTER RECEIPT OF THE SUMMONS AND COMPLAINT** Once the defendant has been served with a copy of the summons and complaint, the defendant must respond by filing either a *motion to dismiss* or an *answer*. If a defendant does not respond, either by choice or for some other reason, the court may enter a default judgment against him or her, as mentioned above.

*Motion to Dismiss.* If the defendant challenges the sufficiency of the plaintiff's complaint, the defendant can present to the court a **motion to dismiss** for failure to state a claim on which relief can be granted, or a *demurrer.* (The rules of civil procedure in many states do not use the term *demurrer;* they use only *motion to dismiss.*) The motion to dismiss for failure to state a claim on which relief can be granted is an allegation that,

■ **Exhibit 4–2  A Typical Complaint**

IN THE UNITED STATES DISTRICT COURT
FOR THE ___Southern___ DISTRICT OF ___New York___

CIVIL NO. _9-1047_

_____Jill Kirby_____
Plaintiff

vs.                                                    COMPLAINT

_____Antonio Carvello_____
Defendant.

Comes now the plaintiff and for his cause of action against the defendant alleges and states as follows:

1. This action is between plaintiff, who is a resident of the State of New York, and defendant, who is a resident of the State of New Jersey. There is diversity of citizenship between parties.
2. The amount in controversy, exclusive of interest and costs, exceeds the sum of $50,000.
3. On September 10th, 1995, plaintiff, Jill Kirby, was exercising good driving habits and reasonable care in driving her car through the intersection of Broadwalk and Pennsylvania Ave. when defendant, Antonio Carvello, negligently drove his vehicle through a red light at the intersection and collided with plaintiff's vehicle.
4. As a result of the collision plaintiff suffered severe physical injury, that prevented her from working, and property damage to her car. The cost she incurred included: $85,000 in medical bills, $10,000 in lost wages, $5,000 in automobile repairs.

WHEREFORE, plaintiff demands judgment against the defendant for the sum of $100,000 plus interest at the maximum legal rate and the costs of this action.

By ___Joseph Roe___
Joseph Roe
Attorney for Plaintiff
100 Main Street
New York, New York

1/2/96

■ **Exhibit 4–3 A Typical Summons**

SUMMONS IN A CIVIL ACTION

# United States District Court

FOR THE ___Southern___ DISTRICT OF: New York

CIVIL ACTION FILE NO. 9-1047

Jill Kirby

Plaintiff

v.

Antonio Carvello

Defendant

SUMMONS

To the above named Defendant:

You are hereby summoned and required to serve upon plaintiff's attorney, whose address is

Joseph Roe

100 Main Street

New York, New York

an answer to the complaint which is herewith served upon you, within 20 days after service of this summons upon you, exclusive of the day of service. If you fail to do so, judgment by default will be taken against you for the relief demanded in the complaint.

Samuel Raeburn
_____
*Clerk of Court*

Mary Doakes
_____
*Deputy Clerk.*

Date: 1/10/96

[Seal of Court]

NOTE:—This summons is issued pursuant to Rule 4 of the Federal Rules of Civil Procedure.

even if the facts presented in the complaint are true, their legal consequences are such that there is no reason to go further with the suit and no need for the defendant to present an answer. It is a contention that the defendant is not legally liable even if the facts are as the plaintiff alleges. If, for example, Kirby's complaint had alleged facts that excluded the possibility of negligence on Carvello's part, Carvello could move to dismiss, and he would not be required to answer if his motion were granted.

If the court denies the motion to dismiss, the judge is indicating that the plaintiff has stated a recognized cause of action. The defendant generally is given an extension of time to file a further pleading. If the defendant does not do so, a judgment will normally be entered for the plaintiff. If, however, the court grants the motion to dismiss for failure to state a claim on which relief can be granted, the judge is saying that the plaintiff has failed to state a recognized cause of action, and the defendant is not required to answer the complaint. The plaintiff generally is given time to file an amended complaint. If the plaintiff does not file this amended complaint, a judgment will be entered against the plaintiff solely on the basis of the pleadings, and the plaintiff will not be allowed to bring suit on the matter again.

In addition to a plaintiff's failure to state a claim on which relief can be granted, a defendant's pre-answer motion to dismiss may be based on the court's lack of subject matter, improper venue, insufficiency of process or service of process (delivery of the summons), and other specific reasons. The motion to dismiss is often used for purposes of delay.

If Kirby wishes to discontinue the suit because, for example, an out-of-court settlement has been reached, she can likewise move for dismissal. The court can also dismiss on its own motion.

*Answer.* If the defendant has not chosen to file a motion to dismiss or has filed a motion to dismiss that has been denied, then he or she must file an **answer** with the court. This document either admits the statements or allegations set out in the complaint or denies them and sets out any defenses that the defendant may have. If Carvello admits to all of Kirby's allegations in his answer, a judgment will be entered for Kirby. If Carvello denies Kirby's allegations, the matter will proceed to trial.

Carvello can deny Kirby's allegations and set forth his own claim that Kirby was in fact negligent and therefore owes Carvello money for damages

to the Cadillac. This is appropriately called a **counterclaim.** If Carvello files a counterclaim, Kirby will have to answer it with a pleading, normally called a **reply,** that has the same characteristics as an answer.

Carvello can also admit the truth of Kirby's complaint but raise new facts that will result in dismissal of the action. This is called raising an **affirmative defense.** For example, Carvello could admit that he was negligent but plead that the time period for raising the claim has passed and that Kirby's complaint must be dismissed because it is barred by the statute of limitations (a statutory limit on the time during which one can raise a claim). As will be discussed in subsequent chapters, there are affirmative defenses that can be raised by defendants in both civil and criminal cases. For example, a defendant accused of physically harming another might claim that he or she acted in self-defense. A defendant charged with breach of contract might defend on the ground (legal basis) of mistake or the fact that the contract was oral when it was required by law to be in writing.

## DISMISSALS AND JUDGMENTS BEFORE TRIAL

Many actions for which pleadings have been filed never come to trial. The parties may, for example, negotiate a settlement of the dispute at any stage of the litigation process. There are also numerous procedural avenues for disposing of a case without a trial. Many of them involve one or the other party's attempts to get the case dismissed through the use of **pretrial motions.** We have already mentioned the motion to dismiss. Another equally important motion is the motion for a judgment on the pleadings. Motions for summary judgment may also be used.

### MOTION FOR JUDGMENT ON THE PLEADINGS

After the pleadings are closed—after the complaint, answer, and any counterclaim and reply have been filed—either of the parties can file a **motion for judgment on the pleadings.** This motion may be used when no facts are disputed and, thus, only questions of law are at issue. For example, this motion would be appropriate if the facts as shown in the pleadings revealed that the time limit allowed for bringing the lawsuit has in fact expired. The difference between this motion and a motion for summary judgment, discussed below, is that the party requesting the motion may support a motion for summary judgment with sworn statements and other materials; on a motion for a judgment on the pleadings, however, a court may consider only those facts pleaded.

### MOTION FOR SUMMARY JUDGMENT

A lawsuit can be shortened or a trial can be avoided if there are no disagreements about the facts in a case and the only question is how the law applies to those facts. Both sides can agree to the facts and ask the judge to apply the law to them. In this situation, it is appropriate for either party to move for **summary judgment.** When the court considers a motion for summary judgment, it can take into account evidence outside the pleadings. The evidence may consist of sworn statements (affidavits) by parties or witnesses, as well as documents, such as a contract. The use of this additional evidence distinguishes the motion for summary judgment from the motion to dismiss and from the motion for judgment on the pleadings.

A motion for summary judgment will be granted only when there are no genuine *questions of fact* (which may be decided by a judge or jury), and the only question is a *question of law* (on which only a judge, not a jury, can rule). In the Kirby-Carvello accident, whether or not the light was red is a question of fact. During discovery (formal investigation prior to trial), Carvello obtained undisputable evidence that the stoplight was not working when Carvello drove through the intersection. Carvello files a motion for summary judgment on the ground that there is no evidence in the record to support Kirby's claim. The court will likely grant Carvello's motion, because there is no genuine factual dispute and Carvello is entitled to judgment as a matter of law.

Motions for summary judgment can be made before or during a trial, but they will be granted only if it is clear that there are no factual disputes. Judges sometimes disagree on what constitutes a question of fact and therefore on whether summary judgment is appropriate in a given case. The following case illustrates this point.

CASE 4.1

**PEOPLES RESTAURANT v. SABO**

Supreme Court of Florida, 1991.
591 So.2d 907.

**BACKGROUND AND FACTS**  *Mary Sabo suffered injuries in an automobile accident caused by Daniel Hoag, an intoxicated driver. Hoag had just left Peoples Restaurant after having consumed a large number of drinks. Sabo sued Peoples for damages, alleging that the restaurant had violated a state statute that provided that any person who "knowingly serves" an individual who is "habitually addicted" to alcohol may be held liable for any injuries or damages caused by the intoxication of that individual. In spite of evidence indicating that for the two years prior to the accident, Hoag had gone to Peoples twice a week and on each occasion had drunk liquor until he was intoxicated, the trial court granted Peoples' motion for summary judgment. The court held that Sabo had failed to show that Peoples had knowledge that Hoag was an alcoholic, and the bar had therefore not "knowingly" served an alcohol addict. Sabo appealed. The appellate court reversed the trial court's ruling, and Peoples appealed the case to the Supreme Court of Florida.*

*OVERTON, Justice.*
\* \* \* \*

\* \* \* Evidence in the summary judgment proceeding reflects that Hoag testified that he was an alcoholic at the time of the accident and that, for the two years prior to the accident, he regularly consumed a case of beer a day while on his construction job. Hoag also testified that, for the four months prior to the accident, he went to Peoples twice a week after work; that he would drink hard liquor each evening at Peoples or another bar near his residence until he became intoxicated; and that, even though he got drunk every time he went to Peoples, the bartenders never refused to serve him, despite his slurred speech, red eyes, and unsteady appearance. According to Hoag, the bartenders knew him well, frequently started pouring his favorite drink as soon as he came through the door, and, even though it was against Peoples' happy hour policy, always poured him doubles. Hoag testified that on the night of the accident he had been served the equivalent of twenty shots of hard liquor and was so intoxicated that he did not recall leaving the bar, eating dinner, whether he had had an argument with his girlfriend, or much about the accident itself.

Based on this record, the [appellate] court vacated the summary judgment, concluding that "there was sufficient evidence adduced to permit a jury to conclude that Hoag was habitually addicted to alcohol." *  *  * We agree *  *  * .

**DECISION AND REMEDY** *The Florida Supreme Court affirmed the appellate court's decision. The court ordered that the case proceed to trial.*

**INTERNATIONAL CONSIDERATIONS** **Findings of Fact and Civil Juries** *The Florida court found summary judgment inappropriate because disputed factual issues are for a jury to resolve, and the court concluded that the "evidence was sufficient to indicate" that whether the bar knew that Hoag was an alcoholic was a disputed factual issue. The principles of this case would be inapplicable in many foreign jurisdictions. Foreign nations typically do not employ juries in civil cases, which are tried before a judge. Even Canada makes little use of civil juries.*

## DISCOVERY

Before a trial begins, the parties can use a number of procedural devices to obtain information and gather evidence about the case. Kirby, for example, will want to know how fast Carvello was driving, whether he had been drinking or was under the influence of any medication, whether he was wearing corrective lenses if he was required by law to do so while driving, and so on. The process of obtaining information from the opposing party or from witnesses is known as **discovery.**

The Federal Rules of Civil Procedure and similar rules in the states set forth the guidelines for discovery activity. Discovery includes gaining access to witnesses, documents, records, and other types of evidence. The rules governing discovery are designed to make sure that a witness or a party is not unduly harassed, that privileged material is safeguarded, and that only matters relevant to the case at hand are discoverable.

Discovery prevents surprises by giving parties access to evidence that might otherwise be hidden. This allows both parties to learn as much as they can about what to expect at a trial before they reach the courtroom. Discovery also serves to narrow the issues so that trial time is spent on the main questions in the case. Currently, the trend is toward allowing more discovery and thus fewer surprises.[3]

**DEPOSITIONS AND INTERROGATORIES**   Discovery can involve the use of depositions, interrogatories, or both. **Depositions** are sworn testimony by a party to the lawsuit or any witness, recorded by an authorized court official. The person deposed gives sworn testimony under oath and answers questions asked by the attorneys from both sides. The questions and answers are taken down, sworn to, and signed. These answers, of course, will help the attorneys prepare their cases. They can also be used in court to impeach (challenge the credibility of) a party or a witness who changes testimony at the trial. In addition, they can be used as testimony if the witness is not available at trial. Lawyers from both sides can prepare for depositions with written questions ahead of time.

---

3.   This trend is particularly evident in the 1993 revision of the Federal Rules of Civil Procedure. The revised rules governing discovery require the parties and attorneys to meet shortly after a lawsuit is filed and voluntarily disclose certain information to each other.

**Interrogatories** are a series of written questions for which written answers are prepared and then signed under oath. The main difference between depositions with written questions and interrogatories is that the latter are directed to a party to the lawsuit (the plaintiff or the defendant), not to a witness, and the party can prepare answers with the aid of an attorney. Also, the scope of interrogatories is broader, because parties are obligated to answer questions, even if it means disclosing information from their records and files.

**REQUEST FOR ADMISSIONS** A party can serve a written request to the other party for an admission of the truth of matters relating to the trial. Any matter admitted under such a request is conclusively established as true for the trial. For example, Kirby can ask Carvello to admit that he was driving at a speed of forty-five miles an hour. A request for admission saves time at trial, because parties will not have to spend time proving facts on which they already agree.

**REQUEST FOR DOCUMENTS, OBJECTS, AND ENTRY UPON LAND** A party can gain access to documents and other items not in his or her possession in order to inspect and examine them. Likewise, a party can gain ''entry upon land'' to inspect the premises. Carvello, for example, can gain permission to inspect and duplicate Kirby's repair bills.

**REQUEST FOR EXAMINATIONS** When the physical or mental condition of one party is in question, the opposing party can ask the court to order a physical or mental examination. For example, to prepare for trial, Carvello would want to have his own medical professionals examine Kirby. If the court is willing to make the order, the opposing party can obtain the results of the examination. It is important to note that the court will make such an order only when the need for the information outweighs the right to privacy of the person to be examined.

## PRETRIAL CONFERENCE

After discovery has taken place and before the trial begins, the attorneys may meet with the trial judge in a **pretrial conference.** The purpose of this conference is to explore the possibility of resolving the case and, if a settlement is not possible at this time, at least to agree on the manner in which the trial will be conducted. In particular, the parties may attempt to clarify the issues in dispute and establish ground rules to restrict such things as the number of expert witnesses or the admissibility of certain types of evidence.

Once the pretrial conference concludes, both parties will have to turn their attention to the trial itself and, if the trial is to be a jury trial, to the selection of jurors who will hear the case.

## THE RIGHT TO A JURY TRIAL

A trial can be held with or without a jury. If there is no jury, the judge determines the truth of the facts alleged in the case. The Seventh Amendment to the U.S. Constitution guarantees the right to a jury trial for cases at law in federal courts when the amount in controversy exceeds $20. Most states have similar guarantees in their own constitutions, although many states put a higher minimum-dollar-amount restriction on the guarantee. For example, Iowa requires the dollar amount of damages to be at least $1,000 before there is a right to a jury trial. The right to a trial by jury does not have to be exercised, and many cases are tried without a jury. In most states and in federal courts, one of the parties must request a jury, or the right is presumed to be waived.

Although some types of trials require twelve-person juries, most civil matters can be heard by six-person juries. Note that there are two types of juries: the ordinary jury (*petit,* or small, *jury*), which may range in size from six to twelve persons and the *grand jury.* The latter is called ''grand'' because it consists of a greater number of jurors than the ordinary trial jury. A grand jury is called only in criminal cases and does not determine the guilt or innocence of a party. Rather, the grand jury determines whether there is sufficient evidence against the party that the case should go to trial (see Chapter 9).

## JURY SELECTION

Prior to the commencement of any jury trial, a panel of jurors must be assembled. The clerk of the court will usually notify local residents by mail that they have been selected for jury duty. The process of

# ■ CONCEPT SUMMARY 4.1 **Pretrial Procedures**

| PROCEDURE | DESCRIPTION |
|---|---|
| **Pleadings** | 1. *Complaint*—A statement of the cause of action and parties involved, filed with the court by the plaintiff's attorney. After the filing, a summons is served on the defendant.<br>2. *Motion to dismiss*—A motion made by the defendant, prior to filing an answer to the complaint, asking the court to dismiss the case because the complaint failed to state a claim for which relief can be granted.<br>3. *Answer*—Can take the form of (1) an admission; (2) an affirmative defense; (3) a counterclaim; or (4) an answer denying some or all of the allegations. |
| **Pretrial Motions** | 1. *Motion for judgment on the pleadings*—May be made by either party; will be granted if the pleadings show that no facts are in dispute and only questions of law are at issue.<br>2. *Motion for summary judgment*—May be made by either party; will be granted if the parties agree on the facts. The judge applies the law in rendering judgment. |
| **Discovery** | The process of gathering evidence concerning the case; involves (1) *depositions* (sworn testimony by either party or any witness); (2) *interrogatories* (in which parties to the action write answers to questions with the aid of their attorneys); and (3) requests for documents, examinations, or other information relating to the case. |
| **Pretrial Conference** | A pretrial hearing, at the request of either party or the court, to identify the matters in dispute after discovery has taken place, and to plan the course of the trial. |
| **Jury Selection** | The selection of members of the jury from a pool of prospective jurors. During a process known as *voir dire,* the attorneys for each side may challenge prospective jurors either for cause or peremptorily (for no cause). |

selecting the names of these prospective jurors varies, but often they are randomly selected by the court clerk from lists of registered voters and other records. These persons then report to the courthouse on the date specified in the notice. There they are gathered into a single pool of jurors, and the process of selecting those jurors who will actually hear the case begins.

The process by which the jury is selected is known as ***voir dire*** (a French phrase meaning ''to speak the truth''). In most jurisdictions, *voir dire* consists of oral questions that attorneys for the plaintiff and the defendant ask a group of prospective jurors (one at a time) to determine whether a potential juror is biased or has any connection with a party to the action or with a prospective witness. Usually, jurors are questioned one at a

time, although when large numbers of jurors are involved, the attorneys may direct their questions to groups of jurors instead to minimize the amount of time spent in jury selection. Some trial attorneys go so far as to use psychologists and other professionals to help them pick juries.

During *voir dire,* a party may challenge a certain number of prospective jurors *peremptorily*—that is, ask that an individual not be sworn in as a juror without providing any reason. The total number of peremptory challenges allowed each side is determined by statute or by the court. Alternatively, a party may challenge any juror *for cause*—that is, provide a reason why an individual should not be sworn in as a juror. If the judge grants the challenge, the individual is asked to step down. A prospective juror may not be excluded from participation in the trial process, however, with the use of discriminatory challenges, such as those based on racial criteria[4] or gender.[5]

After both sides have completed their challenges, those jurors who have been excused will be permitted to leave. The remaining jurors—those who have been found acceptable by both attorneys—will be seated in the jury box. Because unforeseeable circumstances or illness may necessitate that one or more of the sitting jurors be dismissed, the court, depending on the rules of the particular jurisdiction, might choose to have two or three alternate jurors present throughout the trial. If a juror has to be excused in the middle of the trial, then an alternate may take his or her place without disrupting the proceedings. Once the jury members are seated, the judge will swear in the jury members, and the trial itself can begin.

## SECTION 4

# AT THE TRIAL

Various rules and procedures govern the trial phase of the litigation process. There are rules governing what kind of evidence will or will not be admitted during the trial, as well as specific procedures that the participants to the lawsuit must follow.

### RULES OF EVIDENCE

Whether evidence will be admitted at court is determined by the **rules of evidence**—a series of rules that have been created by the courts to ensure that any evidence presented in court is fair and reliable. The Federal Rules of Evidence govern the admissibility of evidence in federal courts.

Evidence will not be admitted in court unless it is relevant to the matter in question. **Relevant evidence** is evidence that tends to prove or disprove a fact in question or to establish that a fact or action is more probable or less probable than it would be without the evidence. For example, evidence that a suspect's gun was in the home of another person when a victim was shot would be relevant—because it would tend to prove that the suspect did not shoot the victim.

Even relevant evidence may not be admitted in court if its probative (proving) value is substantially outweighed by other important considerations of the court. For example, even though evidence may be relevant, it might not be necessary—the fact at issue may have been already sufficiently proved or disproved by previous evidence, and the introduction of further evidence would be a waste of time and cause undue delay in the trial proceedings. Relevant evidence may also be excluded if it would tend to distract the jury from the main issues of the case, mislead the jury, or cause the jury to decide the issue on an emotional basis. A video or a photograph that shows in detail the severity of a victim's injuries, for example, would be relevant evidence, but the court might exclude the evidence on the ground that it would emotionally inflame the jurors.

Generally, hearsay is not admissible as evidence. **Hearsay** is defined as any testimony given in court about a statement made by someone else. Literally, it is what someone heard someone else say. For example, if a witness in the Kirby-Carvello case testifies in court what he or she *heard* another observer say about the accident, that testimony would be hearsay, because it is secondhand knowledge. Admitting hearsay into evidence carries many risks. For example, there is the risk that the listener incorrectly perceived the meaning of the statement that he or she heard someone else make, and without the opportunity of cross-examining the originator of the statement, the misperception cannot be challenged. Furthermore, there is the risk of faulty memory and the possibility that the statement was ambiguous or not made sincerely.

### OPENING STATEMENTS

At the commencement of the trial, both attorneys are allowed to make **opening statements** concerning the facts that they expect to prove during the trial, with the plaintiff's lawyer going first. The opening statement provides an opportunity for each lawyer to give a brief version of the facts and

---

4. *Batson v. Kentucky,* 476 U.S. 79, 106 S.Ct. 1712, 90 L.Ed.2d 69 (1986); *Holland v. Illinois,* 493 U.S. 474, 110 S.Ct. 803, 107 L.Ed.2d 905 (1990); *Powers v. Ohio,* 499 U.S. 400, 111 S.Ct. 1364, 113 L.Ed.2d 411 (1991).

5. *J.E.B. v. Alabama ex rel. T.B.,* _____ U.S. _____ , 114 S.Ct. 1419, 128 L.Ed.2d 89 (1994). (*Ex rel.* is Latin for *ex relatione.* The phrase refers to an action brought on behalf of the state, by the attorney general, at the instigation of an individual who has a private interest in the matter.)

the supporting evidence that will be used during the trial.

## EXAMINATION OF WITNESSES

Because Kirby is the plaintiff, she has the burden of proving that her claim is correct. Therefore, Kirby's attorney begins the presentation of Kirby's case by calling the first witness for the plaintiff and examining (questioning) the witness. (For both attorneys, the type of question and the manner of asking are governed by the rules of evidence.) This questioning is called **direct examination.** After Kirby's attorney is finished, the witness is subject to **cross-examination** by Carvello's attorney. Then Kirby's attorney has another opportunity to question the witness in *redirect examination,* and Carvello's attorney can follow with *recross-examination.* When both attorneys have finished with the first witness, Kirby's attorney calls the succeeding witnesses in the plaintiff's case, each of whom is subject to cross-examination (and redirect and recross, if necessary).

At the conclusion of the plaintiff's case, the defendant's attorney has the opportunity to ask the judge to direct a verdict for the defendant on the ground that the plaintiff has presented no evidence that would justify the granting of the plaintiff's remedy. This is called a **motion for a directed verdict** (federal courts use the term *judgment as a matter of law* instead of *directed verdict*). In considering the motion, the judge looks at the evidence in the light most favorable to the plaintiff and grants the motion only if there is insufficient evidence to raise an issue of fact. (Motions for directed verdicts at this stage of trial are seldom granted.)

The defendant's attorney then presents the evidence and witnesses for the defendant's case. Witnesses are called and examined (questioned) by the defendant's attorney. The plaintiff's attorney has the right to cross-examine them, and there is a redirect examination and a recross-examination, if necessary. At the end of the defendant's case, either attorney can move for a directed verdict, and the test again is whether the jury can, through any reasonable interpretation of the evidence, find for the party against whom the motion is made.

After the defendant's attorney has finished presenting evidence, the plaintiff's attorney can present a **rebuttal,** which includes additional evidence to refute the defendant's case. The defendant's attorney can refute that evidence in a **rejoinder.**

## CLOSING ARGUMENTS

After both sides have rested their cases, each attorney presents a **closing argument,** with the plaintiff's lawyer going first. In their closing arguments, each attorney summarizes the facts and evidence presented during the trial, indicates why the facts and evidence support the client's claim, reveals the shortcomings of the points made by the opposing party during the trial, and generally urges a verdict in favor of his or her client. Each attorney's comments must be relevant to the issues in dispute.

## THE BURDEN OF PROOF

In a civil case, the plaintiff—in this case, Kirby—must prove her case through a **preponderance of the evidence.** That is, she need not provide indisputable proof that she is entitled to a judgment. She need only show that her factual claim is more likely to be true than the defendant's. In contrast, in a criminal trial, the prosecution has a higher standard of proof to meet—it must prove its case *beyond a reasonable doubt* (see Chapter 9). Some civil claims must be proved by *clear and convincing evidence.* In these situations, the proof must show that the truth of the party's claim is highly probable. These situations include suits involving charges of fraud, suits to establish the terms of a lost will, some suits involving oral contracts, and other suits involving circumstances in which there is thought to be a particular danger of deception.

## JURY INSTRUCTIONS

The judge instructs the jury (assuming it is a jury trial) in the law that applies to the case. The instructions to the jury are often called *charges.* A charge is a document that includes statements of the applicable laws, as well as a review of the facts as they were presented during the case. Because the jury's role is to serve as the fact finder, the factual account contained in the charge is not binding upon them. Indeed, the jurors may disregard the facts as noted in the charge entirely. They are not free to ignore the statements of law, however. The charge will help to channel the jurors' deliberations, because the judge's request for findings of fact will typically be phrased in an "if, then" format.

To return to the Kirby-Carvello case, a request for a finding of fact might be as follows: "If you [the jurors] find that the plaintiff [Kirby] failed to yield to oncoming traffic, then you must find that the plaintiff was contributorily negligent." This instruction contains a statement of law that must be applied if the jury finds that a certain fact is true; it is left to the jury to decide whether to accept that fact as being true. Although the attorneys for both sides will draft the initial versions of the charges for the judge's consideration, the judge makes the final decision on what charges will be presented to the jury.

The importance of accuracy in jury instructions, in order to protect the rights of the accused, cannot be overstated. The reviewing court ordinarily remands, or sends back, the case for a new trial when the trial judge misstated the law in the jury instructions. The following case is illustrative.

---

| CASE 4.2 |
| :---: |
| **OHIO v. LESSIN** |
| Supreme Court of Ohio, 1993. |
| 67 Ohio St.3d 487. |
| 620 N.E.2d 72. |

**BACKGROUND AND FACTS**  *Cheryl Lessin, a member of the Revolutionary Communist Party, participated in a political demonstration over President George Bush's ordering of American troops to the Persian Gulf in 1990. Lessin made prepared political statements to the crowd; assisted in the burning of an American flag to illustrate her own and her party's disapproval of the president's decision; and then pushed, shoved, and punched her way through the crowd until she was arrested by police. In 1989, prior to Lessin's trial, the United States Supreme Court decided, in* Texas v. Johnson,[a] *that burning an American flag to convey a political message is protected speech under the First Amendment. The trial court, however, failed to instruct the jury on the law of* Johnson *and did not preclude the jury from considering the evidence of political speech, particularly flag burning, in their determination of Lessin's guilt. When Lessin appealed the court's guilty verdict, the court of appeals affirmed the trial court's decision. Lessin then appealed to the Ohio Supreme Court.*

*MOYER,* Chief Justice.
 \*   \*   \*   \*

The risk that a jury will premise its guilty verdict on constitutionally protected conduct is reduced, if not completely eliminated, by an accurate and thorough set of jury instructions which direct the jury to refrain from considering certain evidence as proof of guilt. In this case, the role of the jury instructions was critical in obviating [removing] the possibility that each juror would convict based on his or her personal prejudices against flag burners and Communists. \*   \*   \*
 \*   \*   \*   \*

We cannot uphold Lessin's conviction for the crime of inciting violence because it is impossible to say with any degree of certainty that her burning of the United States flag was disregarded by the jury in reaching its verdict. The trial court's instruction given to the jury on free speech did not serve to adequately protect the defendant's rights because it did not inform the jury that (1) flag burning in the absence of a call to violence is protected speech under the First Amendment and (2) the jury is not to consider the fact that Lessin burned the flag in determining whether she is guilty of inciting violence. The necessity of giving a more precise instruction is further underscored because of the \*   \*   \* exchange which occurred between defense counsel and the trial judge during *voir dire* [in which the trial judge told the defense counsel, "There has been no Supreme Court case, to my knowledge, that permits under any circumstances that it's okay to burn the flag"].

---

a.   491 U.S. 387, 109 S.Ct. 2533, 105 L.Ed.2d 342 (1989).

*The Ohio Supreme Court reversed the appellate court's decision. The case was sent back for a new trial in which jury instructions reflecting the United States Supreme Court's decision in* Johnson *would be given and Lessin's freedom of speech would be protected.*

**DECISION AND REMEDY**

## ■ CONCEPT SUMMARY 4.2 Trial Procedures

| PROCEDURE | DESCRIPTION |
|---|---|
| **Opening Statements** | Each party's attorney is allowed to present an opening statement indicating what the attorney will attempt to prove during the course of the trial. |
| **Examination of Witnesses** | 1. Plaintiff's introduction and direct examination of witnesses and cross-examination by defendant's attorney; possible redirect examination by plaintiff's attorney and recross-examination by defendant's attorney.<br>2. Defendant's introduction and direct examination of witnesses and cross-examination by plaintiff's attorney; possible redirect examination by defendant's attorney and recross-examination by plaintiff's attorney.<br>3. Possible rebuttal of defendant's argument by plaintiff's attorney, who presents more evidence.<br>4. Possible rejoinder by defendant's attorney to meet that evidence. |
| **Closing Arguments** | Arguments in favor of a verdict for their respective clients are made by the attorneys for both sides. |
| **Jury Instructions** | The judge instructs the jury as to how the law applies to the issues. |
| **Jury Verdict** | The jury renders its verdict, thus bringing the trial to an end. |

## THE JURY'S VERDICT

Following its receipt of the jury instructions, the jury retires to the jury room to deliberate a verdict. Once the jury has reached a decision, it may issue a **verdict** in favor of one party, which specifies the jury's factual findings and the amount of damages to be paid by the losing party. After the announcement of the verdict, which marks the end of the trial itself, the jurors will be discharged.

## SECTION 5

# POSTTRIAL MOTIONS

After the jury has rendered its verdict, either party may make a posttrial motion. The prevailing party usually files a motion for a judgment in accordance with the verdict. The nonprevailing party frequently files one of the motions discussed below.

## MOTION FOR A NEW TRIAL

At the end of the trial, a motion can be made to set aside an adverse verdict and any judgment and to hold a new trial. The motion will be granted if the judge is convinced, after looking at all the evidence, that the jury was in error but the judge does not feel it is appropriate to grant judgment for the other side. This will usually occur when the jury verdict is the obvious result of a misapplication of the law or a misunderstanding of the evidence. A new trial can also be granted on the grounds of newly discovered evidence, misconduct by the participants (such as the attorneys or the jury)[6] during the trial, or error by the judge.

---

6. Recently, the loser in a medical malpractice suit filed a motion for a new trial on the ground that jurors were improperly influenced by an episode of the television show "L.A. Law" that aired the day before the jury decided the case.

If a motion for a new trial is denied, the judge's denial may be appealed to a higher court. In the following case, a plaintiff who lost a trial made a motion for a new trial on the ground of juror misconduct. The issue concerns whether a juror's inattentiveness during *voir dire* constituted juror misconduct sufficient to justify a new trial.

---

### CASE 4.3

**GAINESVILLE RADIOLOGY GROUP v. HUMMEL**

Supreme Court of Georgia, 1993.

428 S.E.2d 786.

**BACKGROUND AND FACTS**   *Ms. Hummel sued Dr. James Strittmatter and his professional corporation, the Gainesville Radiology Group, P.C. ("the Group"), for medical malpractice. Hummel alleged that the Group was negligent in failing to diagnose her breast cancer in a timely manner after a mammographic examination. During* voir dire, *jurors were asked if any of them had family members who had been diagnosed with breast cancer or other forms of cancer, how the cancer had been diagnosed, and whether there had been any recurrence. One juror made no response, but it was later discovered that the juror's wife had died of breast cancer some years before. When the trial court jury returned a verdict for the Group, Hummel moved for a new trial on the ground that the juror had violated his oath and failed to disclose pertinent information during* voir dire. *In opposing the motion, the Group submitted an affidavit signed by the juror in which the juror averred that he had not answered the question because he had not heard it and that the cause of his wife's death had not influenced his judgment in the case. The trial court denied the motion, holding that the juror's "inadvertent" failure to respond to a question during* voir dire *did not "rise to the level of juror misconduct which would require the grant of a new trial." Hummel appealed. The appellate court reversed, holding that the juror's silence was tantamount to giving an untruthful answer and could not be construed as a harmless error. The Group appealed to the Supreme Court of Georgia.*

HUNSTEIN, Justice.
    \* \* \* \*
    \* \* \* The trial court noted that prior to *voir dire*, the jurors completed questionnaires. The questionnaire of juror Griffin, together with his demeanor, revealed that he was very possibly inattentive. Nevertheless, [the attorney for] Hummel did not request his individual examination. Moreover, as further noted by the trial court, Hummel did not strike from the panel a number of jurors who answered the *voir dire* cancer questions affirmatively. \* \* \*
    \* \* \* \*
    In the present case Hummel has failed to demonstrate any bias or prejudice resulting from juror Griffin's failure to respond in that there was no showing that a truthful response from the offending juror would have caused Hummel to strike him from the jury \* \* \*. [W]here the failure of a juror to respond is the result of an honest mistake, the denial of a litigant's opportunity to have exercised a peremptory strike is not, without more, a deprivation sufficient to invalidate the private and social investment in a trial and a new trial should not be granted merely to accord a renewed opportunity to exercise those strikes solely because certain information was not obtained on *voir dire*. Accordingly, we hold that new trials will not be granted unless the movant can demonstrate that: "a juror failed to answer \* \* \* honestly a

material question on *voir dire,* and then further show that a correct response would have provided a valid basis for a challenge for cause.''

*The Supreme Court of Georgia reversed the appellate court's judgment. The trial court did not err when it denied Hummel's motion for a new trial.*

**DECISION AND REMEDY**

**Jury Selection in Other Countries** *The facts of this case would be unlikely to arise in a foreign nation. Most countries do not use civil juries, so juror misconduct during* voir dire *is not an issue. England uses civil juries in some cases but has no* voir dire *process. Canada occasionally uses civil juries, but* voir dire *is limited and conducted by the judge.*

**INTERNATIONAL CONSIDERATIONS**

## MOTION FOR JUDGMENT *N.O.V.*

If Kirby wins, and if Carvello's attorney has previously moved for a directed verdict, Carvello's attorney can now make a motion for a **judgment n.o.v.** (from the Latin *non obstante veredicto,* ''notwithstanding the verdict''; federal courts use the term *judgment as a matter of law* instead of *judgment n.o.v.*). The standards for granting a judgment *n.o.v.* are the same as those for granting a motion to dismiss or a motion for a directed verdict. Carvello can state that even if the evidence is viewed in the light most favorable to Kirby, a reasonable jury should not have found in Kirby's favor. If the judge finds this contention to be correct or decides that the law requires the opposite result, the motion will be granted.

Assume here that this motion is denied. Carvello may then appeal the case. (If Kirby wins at trial but receives a smaller money award than she sought, she can appeal also.) Note, however, that very few trial court decisions are reversed on appeal. In most appealed cases (approximately 97 percent), the trial court's decision is affirmed and thus becomes final.

## SECTION 6

# THE APPEAL

If Carvello decides to appeal the decision, then his attorney must file a *notice of appeal* with the clerk of the trial court within a prescribed period of time. Carvello then becomes the *appellant,* or *petitioner.* His attorney files in the reviewing court (usually an intermediate court of appeals) the rec-

ord on appeal, which contains the following: (1) the pleadings, (2) a transcript of the trial testimony and copies of the exhibits, (3) the judge's rulings on motions made by the parties, (4) the arguments of counsel, (5) the instructions to the jury, (6) the verdict, (7) the posttrial motions, and (8) the judgment order from which the appeal is taken. Carvello may also be required to post a bond for the appeal.

Carvello's attorney is required to prepare a condensation of the record, known as an *abstract.* The abstract and the **brief** are filed with the reviewing court. The brief contains (1) a short statement of the facts; (2) a statement of the issues; (3) the rulings by the trial court that Carvello contends are erroneous and prejudicial (biased in favor of one of the parties); (4) the grounds for reversal of the judgment; (5) a statement of the applicable law; and (6) arguments on Carvello's behalf, citing applicable statutes and relevant cases as precedents. The attorney for the *appellee,* or *respondent,* Kirby, usually files an answering brief. Carvello's attorney can file a reply, although it is not required. The reviewing court then considers the case.

## NO EVIDENCE HEARD

A court of appeals does not hear any evidence. Its decision concerning a case is based on the abstracts, the record, and the briefs. The attorneys can present oral arguments, after which the case is taken under advisement. In general, the appellate courts do not reverse findings of fact unless the findings are unsupported or contradicted by the evidence. As mentioned in the previous chapter, an appellate court has basically three options: it can *affirm* the trial court's decision; it can *reverse* the trial court's judgment if it concludes that the trial court erred or that the jury did not receive proper instructions; or it can *remand* (send back) the case to the trial court for further proceedings consistent with its opinion on the matter.

In the following case, the appellant claimed as grounds for appeal that the jury had returned an inconsistent verdict and that the judge had im-properly submitted equitable issues to the jury. Recall from Chapter 1 that when a plaintiff seeks a remedy in equity, such as specific perfor-mance or rescission (cancellation) of a contract, a judge—not a jury—decides whether the remedy should be granted.

---

CASE 4.4

**CHABAD HOUSE-LUBAVITCH OF PALM BEACH COUNTY, INC. v. BANKS**

District Court of Appeal of Florida,
Fourth District, 1992.
602 So.2d 670.

**BACKGROUND AND FACTS** *Chabad House-Lubavitch of Palm Beach County, Inc. (the buyer-appellant), and Vannoy and Christian Banks (the seller-appellee) entered into a contract for the purchase of real property located in West Palm Beach, Florida. A dispute arose over mistaken as-sumptions about the nature of performance under the contract. The Bankses eventually sued Chabad House, claiming that Chabad House had breached the contract (not performed the contract as promised). The charges given to the jury at the end of the trial consisted of a number of questions that they were to answer. Essentially, the questions put to the jury were as follows: First, did either party breach the contract, and if so, what amount of damages should be awarded to the nonbreaching party? Second, if neither party breached an essential term of the contract, should the contract be rescinded (canceled) on the basis of mistake? In responding to these questions, the jury first decided that the buyer (Chabad House) had breached the contract, and it awarded the seller (the Bankses) $17,000 in damages. The jury also found that the contract was rescinded, or can-celed, on the basis of mistake. (In effect, the jury found that the buyer had breached a contract that was canceled!) The trial court entered a final judgment in favor of the Bankses, and Chabad House appealed.*

*WALDEN,* James H., Senior Judge.
\* \* \* \*

Appellant first argues that the jury verdict and final judgment entered thereon should be set aside due to a fundamental inconsistency in the verdict. We agree.
\* \* \*

\* \* \* We also reverse based upon the trial court's error in submitting equitable issues to the jury. The instant case presented both legal and equitable claims, including breach of contract, damages, specific performance, and rescission. Appellant re-quested a jury trial on the issue of damages, whereas appellees demanded no jury trial on any of their claims. The record indicates that appellant was concerned about equitable issues being determined by the jury. The record further indicates that the jury did, in fact, decide an equitable issue, i.e., whether the contract was cancelled due to mistake, which is "traditionally within the province of the equity court to determine."

We briefly note appellant's other points on appeal only so as to inform the parties not to repeat, on remand, the errors set forth in these points. [The court goes on to summarize other errors made by the trial court, including the admission of prior settlement negotiations and hearsay as evidence.] \* \* \*

**DECISION AND REMEDY** *The appellate court reversed the trial court's judgment and remanded the case for further proceedings.*

## ■ CONCEPT SUMMARY 4.3 **Posttrial Options**

| PROCEDURE | DESCRIPTION |
|---|---|
| **Posttrial Motions** | 1. *Motion for judgment in accordance with the jury's verdict.*<br>2. *Motion for a new trial*—If the judge is convinced that the jury was in error, the motion will be granted.<br>3. *Motion for judgment n.o.v. ("notwithstanding the verdict)"*—The party making the motion must have filed a motion for a directed verdict at the close of all the evidence during the trial; the motion will be granted and the jury's verdict overturned if the judge is convinced that the jury was in error. |
| **Appeal** | Either party can appeal the trial court's judgment to an appropriate court of appeals. After the posting of bond(s), briefs are filed, the appellate court hears oral arguments, and the court renders a written opinion. |

### HIGHER APPEALS COURTS

If the reviewing court is an intermediate appellate court, the losing party normally may appeal to the state supreme court. Such a petition corresponds to a petition for a writ of *certiorari* in the United States Supreme Court. If the petition is granted, new briefs must be filed before the state supreme court, and the attorneys may be allowed or requested to present oral arguments. Like the intermediate appellate courts, the supreme court may reverse or affirm the appellate court's decision or remand the case. At this point, unless a federal question is at issue, the case has reached its end. If a federal question is involved, the losing party (or the winning party, if that party is dissatisfied with the relief obtained) may appeal the decision to the United States Supreme Court by petitioning the Court for a writ of *certiorari*. (As discussed in Chapter 3, the Supreme Court may or may not grant the writ, depending on the type or significance of the issue in dispute.)

### ■ SECTION 7

# ENFORCING THE JUDGMENT

The uncertainties of the litigation process are compounded by the lack of guarantees that any judgment will be enforceable. The problem is more pronounced when a party is seeking to satisfy a judgment against a defendant who has few or no assets than it is with a deep-pockets defendant such as a major corporation with assets that can be easily located. In either case, the court may order the sheriff to seize nonexempt property owned by the defendant and hold that property until the defendant pays the judgment owed to the plaintiff. If the defendant fails to pay the judgment, then the defendant's property may be sold at a public auction and the proceeds given to the plaintiff. Or, the property itself may be transferred to the plaintiff in lieu of an outright payment. (Creditors' remedies, including those of judgment creditors, will be discussed in more detail in Chapter 32.)

## ■ TERMS AND CONCEPTS TO REVIEW

**affirmative defense** 69
**answer** 69
**brief** 79
**closing argument** 75
**complaint** 66

**counterclaim** 69
**cross-examination** 75
**default judgment** 66
**deposition** 71
**direct examination** 75

**discovery** 71
**Federal Rules of Civil Procedure (FRCP)** 64
**hearsay** 74
**interrogatories** 72

judgment *n.o.v.* 79
motion for a directed
   verdict 75
motion for judgment on the
   pleadings 69
motion to dismiss 66
opening statement 74

pleadings 66
preponderance of the
   evidence 75
pretrial conference 72
pretrial motion 69
rebuttal 75
rejoinder 75

relevant evidence 74
reply 69
rules of evidence 74
summary judgment 70
summons 66
verdict 77
*voir dire* 73

# QUESTIONS AND CASE PROBLEMS

**4–1. Appellate Process.** If a judge enters a judgment on the pleadings, the losing party can usually appeal but cannot present evidence to the appellate court. Does this seem fair? Explain.

**4–2. Adversarial Justice.** American courts are forums for adversarial justice, in which attorneys defend the interests of their respective clients before the court. This means that an attorney may end up claiming before a court that his or her client is innocent, even though the attorney knows that the client acted wrongfully. Is it ethical for attorneys to try to ''deceive'' the court in these situations? Can the adversarial system of justice really lead to ''truth''?

**4–3. Attorneys' Fees.** Attorneys in personal-injury and other tort lawsuits (see Chapter 6) frequently charge clients on a contingency-fee basis. That is, a lawyer will agree to take on a client's case in return for, say, 30 percent of whatever damages are recovered. What are some of the social benefits and costs of the contingency-fee system? In your opinion, do the benefits outweigh the costs?

**4–4. Discovery.** In the past, the rules of discovery were very formal, and trials often turned on elements of surprise. For example, a plaintiff would not necessarily know until the trial what the defendant's defense was going to be. Within the last twenty-five years, however, new rules of discovery have substantially changed all this. Now each attorney can discover practically all the evidence that the other will be presenting at trial, with the exception of certain information—namely, the opposing attorney's work product. *Work product* is not a clear concept. Basically, it includes all the attorney's thoughts on the case. Can you see any reason why such information should not be made available to the opposing attorney? Discuss fully.

**4–5. Motions.** When and for what purpose are each of the following motions made? Which of them would be appropriate if a defendant claimed that the only issue between the parties was a question of law and that the law was favorable to the defendant's position?

  (a) A motion for judgment on the pleadings.

  (b) A motion for a directed verdict.

  (c) A motion for summary judgment.

  (d) A motion for judgment *n.o.v.*

**4–6. Peremptory Challenges.** During *voir dire,* the parties or their attorneys select those persons who will serve as jurors during the trial. The parties are prohibited, however, from excluding potential jurors on the basis of race or other discriminatory criteria. An issue concerns whether the prohibition against jury discrimination extends to potential jurors who are physically or mentally handicapped. Federal law prohibits discrimination based on an individual's handicap or disability in many circumstances when that person could be accommodated without too much difficulty. Should this law also apply to the jury selection process? For example, should parties be prohibited from excluding blind persons, through peremptory challenges, from serving on juries? Discuss.

**4–7. Motion to Dismiss.** Martin brought a civil rights action against his employer, the New York Department of Mental Hygiene, when it failed to promote him on several occasions. His complaint stated only that the defendant had discriminated against him on the basis of race by denying him ''the authority, salary, and privileges commensurate with this position.'' The employer made a motion to dismiss the claim for failure to state a cause of action. Discuss whether the employer could be successful. [*Martin v. New York State Department of Mental Hygiene,* 588 F.2d 371 (2d Cir. 1978)]

**4–8. Jury Trials.** On June 16, 1986, the director of the Administrative Office of the U.S. Courts notified all federal district courts that no civil jury trials could be initiated until the end of the fiscal year (September 30) due to lack of funds with which to pay the jurors. The petitioners in this case (Armster) claimed that the consequent delay (of three and a half months) in scheduling a jury trial violated the Seventh Amendment right to a civil jury trial. The Justice Department maintained that unlike the Sixth Amendment, which guarantees a speedy *criminal* jury trial, the Seventh Amendment does not guarantee a speedy *civil* jury trial. The Justice Department further noted that district courts have postponed civil jury trials before, although for other reasons—such as court-calendar congestion, lack of sufficient number of judges, and the priority accorded to trying criminal cases before civil actions. Discuss whether the suspension of civil jury trials for a period of three and a half months due to lack of funds to pay jurors violates the constitutional right to a trial by jury. Are people always entitled to a jury trial in civil lawsuits? [*Armster v. United States District Court for the Central District of California,* 792 F.2d 1423 (9th Cir. 1986)]

**4–9. Jury Selection.** Benjamin Omoruyi was convicted in a federal district court for the possession of counterfeit securities in violation of federal law. Omoruyi appealed his conviction to the U.S. Court of Appeals for the Ninth Circuit, arguing that the district court erred by permitting the government to peremptorily challenge female prospective jurors on the basis of gender. (In a previous case decided by the Ninth Circuit, that court had held that equal-protection principles prohibit striking potential jurors on the basis of gender.) The first government peremptory challenge was exercised against an unmarried white woman, and the second was exercised against an unmarried black woman. Omoruyi objected to the second challenge on the basis that it was racially discriminatory. In response to the district court's request to explain the challenge, the government counsel responded: "Because she was a single female and my concern, frankly, is that she, like the other juror I struck, is single and given defendant's good looks would be attracted to the defendant." The district court denied Omoruyi's motion for a new jury. In response to Omoruyi's allegations on appeal, the government argued that the peremptory strikes were based on marital status, not gender. How should the court decide? Discuss fully. [*United States v. Omoruyi,* 7 F.3d 880 (9th Cir. 1993)]

### 4–10. A Question of Ethics

*The state of Alabama, on behalf of a mother (T.B.), brought a paternity suit against the alleged father (J.E.B.) of T.B.'s child. During jury selection, the state, through peremptory challenges, removed nine of the ten prospective male jurors. J.E.B.'s attorney struck the final male from the jury pool. As a result of these peremptory strikes, the final jury consisted of twelve women. When the jury returned a verdict in favor of the mother, the father appealed, asserting that the trial court erred in overruling his objection to the state's removal of potential male jurors through the use of its peremptory challenges. The father argued that the use of peremptory challenges to eliminate men from the jury constituted gender discrimination and violated his rights to equal protection and due process of law. The father requested the court to extend the principle enunciated in* Batson v. Kentucky *(cited in footnote 4 of this chapter), which prohibited peremptory strikes based solely on race, to include gender-based strikes. The appellate court, following a precedent established by the state's supreme court, refused to do so and affirmed the lower court's decision that J.E.B. was the child's father and had to pay child support. [J.E.B. v. Alabama ex rel. T.B., ____ U.S. ____, 114 S.Ct. 1419, 128 L.Ed.2d 89 (1994)]*

1. Do you agree with J.E.B. that the state's exercise of its peremptory challenges violated his right to equal protection and due process? Why or why not?
2. If you were the judge, how would you rule on this issue?
3. The late Supreme Court Justice Thurgood Marshall urged, when the Court was reviewing the *Batson* case, that peremptory challenges be banned entirely. Do you agree with this proposal? Discuss fully.

# CHAPTER 5

# CONSTITUTIONAL AUTHORITY TO REGULATE BUSINESS

**T**he U.S. Constitution is the supreme law in this country.[1] Neither Congress nor any state may pass a law that conflicts with the Constitution. Laws that govern business have their origin in the lawmaking authority granted by this document.

Before the Constitution was written, a *confederal* form of government existed. The Articles of Confederation, which went into effect in 1781, established a confederation of independent states and a central government of very limited powers. The central government could handle only those matters of common concern expressly delegated to it by the member states, and the national congress had no ability to make laws directly applicable to individuals unless the member states explicitly supported such laws. In short, the *sovereign power* to govern rested essentially with the states.[2] The Articles of Confederation clearly reflected the central tenet of the American Revolution—that a government should not have unlimited power.

After the Revolutionary War, however, the states began to pass laws that hampered national commerce and foreign trade by preventing the free movement of goods and services. Consequently, in 1787, the Constitutional Convention convened to **amend** the Articles of Confederation. Instead, the Convention created the Constitution and a completely new type of federal government, which it believed was much better equipped than its predecessor to resolve the problems of the nation.

---

1. The U.S. Constitution has been included as Appendix B in this text.
2. *Sovereign power* refers to that supreme power to which no other person or authority is superior or equal.

# THE CONSTITUTIONAL POWERS OF GOVERNMENT

The federal form of government established by the Constitution reflects the compromise made between those delegates to the Constitutional Convention who desired a strong national government and those delegates who believed that the states should hold sovereign power. A federal form of government is one in which the states form a union and the sovereign power is divided between a central governing authority and the member states.

The Constitution delegates certain powers to the national government, and the states retain all other powers. The relationship between the national government and the state governments is a partnership—neither partner is superior to the other except within the particular area of exclusive authority granted to it under the Constitution. Hence, the concept of **federalism** recognizes that society may be best served by a distribution of functions among state (and local) governments and the national government on the basis of which government is better equipped to perform those functions.

## SEPARATION OF POWERS

To prevent any one person or group from exercising the whole power of government, the Constitution provides for three branches of government, each of which performs a different government function. The legislative branch makes the laws; the executive branch enforces the laws; and the judicial branch interprets the laws. Each branch performs a separate function, and no branch may exercise the authority of another branch. Each branch, however, has some power to limit the actions of the other two branches, thereby establishing a system of **checks and balances.**

Congress, for example, has the power to tax the citizenry, but the president can veto that legislation. The executive branch is responsible for foreign affairs, but treaties with foreign governments require the advice and consent of members of the Senate. Although Congress determines the jurisdiction of the federal courts, the United States Supreme Court has the power to hold acts of the other branches of the federal government unconstitutional, as discussed in Chapter 3.[3] Thus, with this system of checks and balances, no one branch of government can accumulate too much power.

## THE COMMERCE CLAUSE

Article I, Section 8, of the United States Constitution expressly permits Congress ''[t]o regulate Commerce with foreign Nations, and among the several States, and with the Indian tribes.'' This clause, referred to as the **commerce clause,** has had a greater impact on business than any other provision in the Constitution. This power was delegated to the federal government to ensure the uniformity of rules governing the movement of goods through the states.

**REGULATORY POWER OF THE NATIONAL GOVERNMENT** For some time, the commerce power was interpreted as being limited to *interstate* commerce and not applicable to *intrastate* commerce. In 1824, however, the United States Supreme Court held that commerce within states could also be regulated by the national government as long as the commerce concerned more than one state.[4] Over time, the Supreme Court further extended the power of the national government to regulate commerce. In a 1942 case,[5] for example, the Court held that wheat production of an individual farmer intended wholly for consumption on his own farm was subject to federal regulation. The Court reasoned that the home consumption of wheat reduced the demand for wheat and thus could have a substantial effect on interstate commerce.

In a 1980 case, *McLain v. Real Estate Board of New Orleans, Inc.,* the Supreme Court acknowledged that the commerce clause had ''long been interpreted to extend beyond activities actually in interstate commerce to reach other activities, while wholly local in nature, which nevertheless substantially affect interstate commerce.''[6] Today, at least theoretically, the power over commerce authorizes the national government to regulate every commercial enterprise in the United States.

---

3. See *Marbury v. Madison,* 5 U.S. (1 Cranch) 137, 2 L.Ed. 60 (1803).
4. *Gibbons v. Ogden,* 22 U.S. (9 Wheat.) 1, 6 L.Ed. 23 (1824).
5. *Wickard v. Filburn,* 317 U.S. 111, 63 S.Ct. 82, 87 L.Ed. 122 (1942).
6. 444 U.S. 232, 100 S.Ct. 502, 62 L.Ed.2d 441 (1980).

The breadth of the commerce clause permits the national government to legislate in areas in which there is no explicit grant of power to Congress. The following case is illustrative. The case specifically demonstrates the United States Supreme Court's use of the commerce clause to affirm the power of Congress to pass the Civil Rights Act of 1964.

**CASE 5.1**

**HEART OF ATLANTA MOTEL v. UNITED STATES**

Supreme Court of the United States, 1964.
379 U.S. 241,
85 S.Ct. 348,
13 L.Ed. 2d 258.

**HISTORICAL AND SOCIAL SETTING**   *In the first half of the twentieth century, state governments sanctioned segregation on the basis of race. In 1954, the United States Supreme Court decided that racially segregated school systems violated the Constitution. In the following decade, the Court ordered an end to racial segregation imposed by the states in other public facilities, such as beaches, golf courses, buses, parks, auditoriums, and courtroom seating. Privately owned facilities that excluded or segregated African Americans and others on the basis of race were not subject to the same constitutional restrictions, however. Congress passed the Civil Rights Act of 1964 to prohibit racial discrimination in "establishments affecting interstate commerce." These facilities included "places of public accommodation."*

**BACKGROUND AND FACTS**   *The owner of the Heart of Atlanta Motel refused, in violation of the Civil Rights Act of 1964, to rent rooms to African Americans. The motel owner brought an action to have the act declared unconstitutional. The owner alleged that Congress had exceeded its power to regulate commerce by enacting the 1964 act. The owner argued that his motel was not engaged in interstate commerce but was "of a purely local character." The motel, however, was accessible to state and interstate highways. The owner advertised nationally, maintained billboards throughout the state, and accepted convention trade from outside the state (75 percent of the guests were residents of other states). The court sustained the constitutionality of the act and enjoined (prohibited) the owner from discriminating on the basis of race. The owner appealed. The case ultimately went to the United States Supreme Court.*

Mr. Justice *CLARK* delivered the opinion of the Court.
\* \* \* \*

While the [Civil Rights Act of 1964] as adopted carried no congressional findings, the record of its passage through each house is replete with evidence of the burdens that discrimination by race or color places upon interstate commerce \* \* \*. This testimony included the fact that our people have become increasingly mobile with millions of all races traveling from State to State; that Negroes in particular have been the subject of discrimination in transient accommodations, having to travel great distances to secure the same; that often they have been unable to obtain accommodations and have had to call upon friends to put them up overnight. \* \* \* These exclusionary practices were found to be nationwide, the Under Secretary of Commerce testifying that there is "no question that this discrimination in the North still exists to a large degree" and in the West and Midwest as well \* \* \*. This testimony indicated a qualitative as well as quantitative effect on interstate travel by Negroes. The former was the obvious impairment of the Negro traveler's pleasure and convenience that resulted when he continually was uncertain of finding lodging. As for the latter, there was evidence that this uncertainty stemming from racial discrimination had the effect of discouraging travel on the part of a substantial portion of the Negro community \* \* \*. We shall not burden this opinion with further details since the voluminous testimony presents overwhelming evidence that discrimination by hotels and motels impedes interstate travel.

&ast;   &ast;   &ast;   &ast;

It is said that the operation of the motel here is of a purely local character. But, assuming this to be true, ''if it is interstate commerce that feels the pinch, it does not matter how local the operation that applies the squeeze.'' &ast;   &ast;   &ast; Thus the power of Congress to promote interstate commerce also includes the power to regulate the local incidents thereof, including local activities in both the States of origin and destination, which might have a substantial and harmful effect upon that commerce.

| | |
|---|---|
| *The United States Supreme Court upheld the constitutionality of the Civil Rights Act of 1964. The power of Congress to regulate interstate commerce permitted the enactment of legislation that could halt local discriminatory practices.* | **DECISION AND REMEDY** |

## REGULATORY POWERS OF THE STATES

A problem that frequently arises under the commerce clause concerns a state's ability to regulate matters within its own borders.

The U.S. Constitution does not expressly exclude state regulation of commerce, and there is no doubt that states have a strong interest in regulating activities within their borders. As part of their inherent sovereignty, states possess **police powers.** The term does not relate solely to criminal law enforcement but also to the right of state governments to regulate private activities to protect or promote the public order, health, safety, morals, and general welfare. Fire and building codes, antidiscrimination laws, parking regulations, zoning restrictions, licensing requirements, and thousands of other state statutes covering virtually every aspect of life have been enacted under the state police power.

When state regulations impinge on interstate commerce, courts must balance the state's interest in the merits and purposes of the regulation against the burden placed on interstate commerce. Generally, state laws enacted pursuant to a state's police powers carry a strong presumption of validity. But if state laws substantially interfere with interstate commerce, they will be held to violate the commerce clause of the U.S. Constitution. In *Raymond Motor Transportation, Inc. v. Rice,* for example, the United States Supreme Court invalidated Wisconsin administrative regulations limiting the length of trucks traveling on its highways. The Court weighed the burden on interstate commerce against the benefits of the regulations and concluded that the challenged regulations ''place a substantial burden on interstate commerce and they cannot be said to make more than the most speculative contribution to highway safety.''[7]

Because courts balance the interests involved, it is extremely difficult to predict the outcome in a particular case. The following case concerns an issue that has elicited much controversy in recent years: whether states have the power to discriminate against shipments of out-of-state waste to intrastate disposal facilities.

_____

7. 434 U.S. 429, 98 S.Ct. 787, 54 L.Ed.2d 664 (1978).

---

| | |
|---|---|
| **COMPANY PROFILE** *Founded in 1894 as Chicago's first waste management company, Ace Scavenger Service was owned and operated by the Huizenga family. When the head of Ace, Elizabeth Huizenga's father, died in 1956, Elizabeth's husband, Dean Buntrock, took over the company. During the 1960s, as concern with air quality prompted restrictions on the burning of wastes, Ace grew rapidly. In 1971, the firm merged with a Florida company owned by Elizabeth's cousin, Wayne Huizenga (who would later control Blockbuster Entertainment Corporation, which includes the largest video rental chain in the United States) and became Waste Management, Inc. The new company expanded across the United* | **CASE 5.2**<br><br>**CHEMICAL WASTE MANAGEMENT, INC. v. HUNT**<br>Supreme Court of the United States, 1992.<br>____U.S.____,<br>112 S.Ct. 2009,<br>119 L.Ed.2d 121. |

*States during the 1970s. Simultaneously, the firm won contracts in a number of countries in Latin America and Europe. In 1975, the firm established a subsidiary, Chemical Waste Management, Inc., to handle hazardous waste. Through its own divisions, Chemical Waste Management offers hazardous waste site clean-up services and handles low-level nuclear waste.*

**BACKGROUND AND FACTS** *Chemical Waste Management, Inc., operates the hazardous waste disposal facility in Emelle, Alabama. The facility receives waste from sources in Alabama and from sources outside the state. Concerned about the volume of waste entering the facility and its effect on the environment and on the public's health and safety, Alabama imposed a fee on all of the waste that the facility received, with a higher fee imposed on waste that was generated outside the state. Chemical Waste filed a suit against the state in an Alabama court, seeking an injunction against enforcement of the higher fee. The court declared that the higher fee violated the commerce clause, and the state appealed. The Alabama Supreme Court reversed the decision of the trial court. Chemical Waste appealed to the United States Supreme Court.*

Justice *WHITE* delivered the opinion of the Court.

\* \* \* \*

No State may attempt to isolate itself from a problem common to the several States by raising barriers to the free flow of interstate trade. \* \* \*

[Alabama's] additional fee facially [on its face] discriminates against hazardous waste generated in States other than Alabama, and the [statute] has plainly discouraged the full operation of petitioner's Emelle facility. Such burdensome taxes imposed on interstate commerce alone are generally forbidden \* \* \* . Once a state tax is found to discriminate against out-of-state commerce, it is typically struck down without further inquiry.

The State, however, argues that the additional fee imposed on out-of-state hazardous waste serves legitimate local purposes related to its citizens' health and safety.

\* \* \*

\* \* \* \*

\* \* \* [T]he State's concern focuses on the volume of the waste entering the Emelle facility. Less discriminatory alternatives, however, are available to alleviate this concern, not the least of which are a generally applicable per-ton additional fee on all hazardous waste disposed of within Alabama, or a per-mile tax on all vehicles transporting hazardous waste across Alabama roads, or an evenhanded cap on the total tonnage landfilled at Emelle, which would curtail volume from all sources. To the extent Alabama's concern touches environmental conservation and the health and safety of its citizens, such concern does not vary with the point of origin of the waste \* \* \* . In sum, we find the additional fee to be "an obvious effort to saddle those outside the State" with most of the burden of slowing the flow of waste into the Emelle facility. "That legislative effort is clearly impermissible under the Commerce Clause of the Constitution."

**DECISION AND REMEDY** *The United States Supreme Court reversed the decision of the Alabama Supreme Court and remanded the case for consideration of the appropriate relief.*

## THE SUPREMACY CLAUSE

Article VI of the Constitution provides that the Constitution, laws, and treaties of the United States are "the supreme Law of the Land." This article, commonly referred to as the **supremacy clause,** is important in the ordering of state and federal relationships. When there is a direct conflict between a federal law and a state law, the state law is rendered invalid. But because some powers are concurrent—that is, they are shared by the federal government and the states—it is necessary to determine which law governs in a particular circumstance.

When Congress chooses to act exclusively in a concurrent area, it is said to have *preempted* the area. In this circumstance, a valid federal statute or regulation will take precedence over a conflicting state or local law or regulation on the same general subject. Congress, however, rarely makes clear its intent to preempt an entire subject area against state regulation; consequently, the courts must determine whether Congress intended to exercise exclusive dominion over a given area. Consideration of **preemption** often occurs in the commerce clause context.

No single factor is decisive as to whether a court will find preemption. Generally, congressional intent to preempt will be found if the federal law is so pervasive, comprehensive, or detailed that the states have no room to supplement it. Also, when a federal statute creates an agency—such as the National Labor Relations Board—to enforce the law, matters that may come within the agency's jurisdiction will likely preempt state laws.

In a widely publicized case decided by the United States Supreme Court in 1992, *Cipollone v. Liggett Group, Inc.,*[8] Antonio Cipollone sought to have a tobacco manufacturer held liable for the death of his wife, Rose, who died from lung cancer at the age of fifty-eight after having smoked cigarettes for forty-two years. Among other things, Cipollone contended that the cigarette manufacturer had not adequately warned consumers of the dangers associated with smoking cigarettes (warning consumers of potential product dangers is a requirement under product liability laws—see Chapter 25).

At issue in the case was whether the federal law mandating warnings on cigarette packages (the Federal Cigarette Labeling and Advertising Act of 1965,[9] as amended in 1969) preempted relevant state laws. The Court held that it did. Plaintiffs were therefore precluded from recovery under state laws requiring cigarette manufacturers to sufficiently warn consumers of the potential dangers associated with cigarette smoking. The Court stated, however, that a plaintiff may bring an action against a cigarette manufacturer under state laws that fall outside the scope of the federal law, such as laws governing fraudulent misrepresentation or conspiracy.

In the following case, the court had to determine whether a federal law regulating banking institutions preempted a state consumer protection statute.

---

8.  ____ U.S. ____ , 112 S.Ct. 2608, 120 L.Ed.2d 407 (1992).
9.  15 U.S.C. Sections 1331–1341.

---

**BACKGROUND AND FACTS**   *Greenwood Trust Company is a banking corporation chartered in Delaware. Greenwood offers a credit card (the Discover Card) to customers nationwide. Under the terms of the Discover Card, a late charge may be imposed for failing to make a minimum monthly payment on or before a designated due date. More than 100,000 cardholders live in Massachusetts. In 1989, the Commonwealth of Massachusetts advised Greenwood that its imposition of late charges violated state law. Massachusetts threatened to take legal action. Greenwood filed a complaint in the United States District Court for the District of Massachusetts, claiming that the federal Depository Institutions Deregulation and Monetary Control Act (DIDMA) of 1980 preempted the state prohibition against the imposition of late fees. The court held that Greenwood could not charge its Massachusetts customers late fees. Greenwood appealed.*

| CASE 5.3 |
| --- |
| **GREENWOOD TRUST CO. v. COMMONWEALTH OF MASSACHUSETTS** |
| United States Court of Appeals, First Circuit, 1992. 971 F.2d 818. |

*SELYA,* Circuit Judge.

This train wreck of a case arises out of a headlong collision between a state consumer-protection law and a federal banking law. It * * * present[s] a novel legal question: can a * * * bank, chartered in Delaware, charge its Massachusetts credit-card customers a late fee on delinquent accounts, notwithstanding a Massachusetts statute explicitly prohibiting the practice? * * *

* * * *

The Massachusetts statute is straightforward. It provides that: ''No creditor shall impose a delinquency charge, late charge, or similar charge on loans made pursuant to . . . [a credit-card] credit plan.''

On the other hand, section 521 [of the DIDMA] is equally uncompromising: ''* * * State bank[s] may, notwithstanding any State constitution or statute which is hereby preempted for the purposes of this section, * * * charge on any loan or discount made, * * * [late fees] allowed by the laws of the State, territory, or district where the bank is located * * * .''

* * * *

* * * [Under Section 521] a bank may continue to use the favorable * * * laws of its home state in certain transactions with out-of-state borrowers. To the extent that a law or regulation enacted in the borrower's home state purposes to inhibit the bank's choice of [a] term under section 521, [the DIDMA] expressly preempts the state law's operation.

* * * *

Delaware law explicitly * * * allows lenders to assess [late] fees against credit-card customers. * * *

* * * *

* * * [I]t is patent that the [Massachusetts] statute is on a collision course *vis-à-vis* section 521. Given the imperatives of the Supremacy Clause, the whistle sounds loud and clear. [The Massachusetts statute] must yield. It is preempted.

**DECISION AND REMEDY** *The U.S. Court of Appeals reversed the decision of the district court and held that the state statute was preempted by federal law.*

**INTERNATIONAL CONSIDERATIONS** **Preemption of Local Regulations in Canada** *The preemption issue is only relevant in countries with federal systems. Canada has a federal system, and the Canadian Constitution has a preemption provision similar to that of the United States. The preemption issue is less significant in Canada, however, because that country's national regulatory power is more circumscribed than the regulatory power of the U.S. government. The national government in Canada has less power over trade and commerce and cannot, for example, regulate the quality of goods sold at retail.*

## THE TAXING POWER

Article I, Section 8, of the Constitution provides that Congress has the ''power to lay and collect Taxes, Duties, Imposts, and Excises * * *; but all Duties, Imposts and Excises shall be uniform throughout the United States.'' The requirement of uniformity refers to uniformity among the states, and thus Congress may not tax residents and businesses in some states while exempting others.

Traditionally, in reviewing cases related to the taxing power, the courts examined whether Congress was actually attempting to regulate indirectly, by taxation, an area in which it had no authority to regulate directly. If the regulatory effect could have been achieved directly by Congress, then the tax would not be stricken as an invalid, disguised regulation. If Congress was attempting to regulate an area over which it had no authority, however, the tax would be invalidated.

Over time, the United States Supreme Court has come to focus less on the motives of Congress and more on whether the tax can be sustained as a valid exercise of federal regulation. The Court has upheld taxes on dealers in firearms,[10] on the transfer of marijuana,[11] and on persons engaged in the business of accepting wagers.[12] If Congress does not have the power to regulate the activity being taxed, the tax will still be upheld if it is a valid revenue-raising measure. If a tax measure bears some reasonable relationship to revenue production, it is generally held to be within the national taxing power. Moreover, the expansive interpretation of the commerce clause almost always provides a basis for sustaining a federal tax.

## THE SPENDING POWER

Under Article I, Section 8, Congress has the power "to pay the Debts and provide for the common Defense and general welfare of the United States." Through the spending power, Congress disposes of the revenues accumulated from the taxing power, and thus this power necessarily involves policy choices, with which taxpayers may disagree.

The requirement of *standing to sue* makes it difficult for taxpayers to use the judicial system to object to government spending. Consequently, the spending power is seldom challenged. As discussed in Chapter 3, the doctrine of standing to sue requires that a litigant must have a sufficient stake in a controversy before the litigant can bring a lawsuit. The plaintiff must demonstrate that he or she has suffered *a direct and immediate personal injury* caused by the challenged action. Thus, a litigant must show that the injury suffered can be fairly traced to the challenged action and will be redressed by the judicial relief sought.[13] Communicating directly with members of Congress has proved to be a more efficient way of influencing congressional spending decisions than litigation.

Congress can spend revenues not only to carry out its enumerated powers but also to promote any objective it deems worthwhile, so long as it does not violate the Bill of Rights. For example, Congress could not condition welfare payments on the recipients' agreements to be uncritical of government policies.

## SECTION 2

# BUSINESS AND THE BILL OF RIGHTS

The importance of having a written declaration of the rights of individuals eventually caused the first Congress of the United States to submit twelve amendments to the Constitution to the states for approval. Ten of these amendments, commonly known as the **Bill of Rights,** were adopted in 1791 and embody a series of protections for the individual against various types of interference by the federal government.[14] Some constitutional protections apply to business entities as well. For example, corporations exist as separate legal entities, or *legal persons,* and enjoy many of the same rights and privileges as *natural persons* do (see Chapter 41). Summarized in Exhibit 5–1 are the protections guaranteed by these ten amendments.[15] The *due process clause* of the Fourteenth Amendment (discussed later in this chapter) applies many of the rights guaranteed by these first ten amendments to the states.

Also held to be so fundamental as to be applicable at both the state and the federal level is a personal right to privacy. Although there is no specific guarantee of a right to privacy in the Constitution, such a right has been derived from guarantees found in the First, Third, Fourth, Fifth, and Ninth Amendments. Invasion of another's privacy is also a civil wrong (see Chapter 6), and over the last several decades, legislation has been passed at the federal level to protect the privacy of individuals in several areas of concern (see Chapter 8). Privacy rights in the employment context are examined in Chapter 36.

It is important to realize that the rights secured by the Bill of Rights are not absolute. The

---

10. *Sonzinsky v. United States,* 300 U.S. 506, 57 S.Ct. 554, 81 L.Ed. 772 (1937).

11. *United States v. Sanchez,* 340 U.S. 42, 71 S.Ct. 108, 95 L.Ed. 47 (1950).

12. *United States v. Kahriger,* 345 U.S. 22, 73 S.Ct. 510, 97 L.Ed. 754 (1953).

13. *Sierra Club v. Morton,* 405 U.S. 727, 92 S.Ct. 1361, 31 L.Ed.2d 636 (1972).

14. One of these proposed amendments was ratified 203 years later (in 1992) and became the Twenty-seventh Amendment to the Constitution. See Appendix B.

15. See the Constitution in Appendix B for the complete text of each amendment.

■ **Exhibit 5–1 Protections Guaranteed by the Bill of Rights**

| | |
|---|---|
| **First Amendment:** guarantees the freedoms of religion, speech, and the press and the rights to assemble peaceably and to petition the government. | **Sixth Amendment:** guarantees the accused in a criminal case the right to a speedy and public trial by an impartial jury and with counsel. The accused has the right to cross-examine witnesses against him or her and to solicit testimony from witnesses in his or her favor. |
| **Second Amendment:** guarantees the right to keep and bear arms. | |
| **Third Amendment:** prohibits, in peacetime, the lodging of soldiers in any house without the owner's consent. | **Seventh Amendment:** guarantees the right to a trial by jury in a civil case involving at least twenty dollars.[a] |
| | **Eighth Amendment:** prohibits excessive bail and fines, as well as cruel and unusual punishment. |
| **Fourth Amendment:** prohibits unreasonable searches and seizures of persons or property. | **Ninth Amendment:** establishes that the people have rights in addition to those specified in the Constitution. |
| **Fifth Amendment:** guarantees the rights to indictment by grand jury, to due process of law, and to fair payment when private property is taken for public use. The Fifth Amendment also prohibits compulsory self-incrimination and double jeopardy (trial for the same crime twice). | **Tenth Amendment:** establishes that those powers neither delegated to the federal government nor denied to the states are reserved for the states. |

a.   Twenty dollars was forty days' pay for the average person when the Bill of Rights was written.

principles enunciated in the Constitution are given form and substance by the government. Ultimately, it is the United States Supreme Court, as the interpreter of the Constitution, that both gives meaning to these constitutional rights and determines their boundaries.

## FREEDOM OF SPEECH

The First Amendment freedoms of religion, speech, press, assembly, and petition have all been applied to the states through the due process clause of the Fourteenth Amendment (discussed later in this chapter). As mentioned, however, none of these freedoms confers an absolute right.

**UNPROTECTED SPEECH** In interpreting the meaning of the First Amendment's guarantee of free speech, the United States Supreme Court has made it clear that certain types of speech will not be protected. Speech that harms the good reputation of another, for example, will not be protected under the First Amendment. Such speech can take the form of *libel* (if it is in writing) or *slander* (if it is oral). Libel and slander are both forms of *defamatory* speech, which is discussed in Chapter 6.

Lewd and obscene speech is another class of speech that is unprotected by the Constitution. Numerous state and federal statutes make it a crime to disseminate obscene materials. The United States Supreme Court has grappled from time to time with the problem of trying to establish an operationally effective definition of obscene speech, but frequently this determination is left to state and local authorities. Generally, obscenity is still a constitutionally unsettled area, whether it deals with speech or printed or filmed materials. In the interest of protecting against the abuse of children, however, the Supreme Court has upheld state laws prohibiting the sale and possession of child pornography;[16] also, in the interest of protecting women against sexual harassment in the workplace, at least one court has banned lewd speech and pornographic pinups in the workplace.[17] In recent years, obscenity issues have also arisen in relation to television shows, movies, the lyrics of musical recordings, and the content of monologues by ''shock'' comedians. The Wash-

16.   See *Osborne v. Ohio,* 495 U.S. 103, 110 S.Ct. 1691, 109 L.Ed.2d 98 (1990).
17.   *Robinson v. Jacksonville Shipyards, Inc.,* 760 F.Supp. 1486 (M.D.Fla. 1991).

ington Supreme Court recently held that a state law restricting minors' exposure to ''erotic'' rap and rock music did not violate the First Amendment.[18]

Other unprotected speech includes ''fighting words,'' or words that are likely to incite others to respond violently. Many people think that the hateful words (''hate speech'') exchanged between members of different groups on college campuses should be included in the category of ''fighting words.'' Courts, however, have been reluctant to uphold university ''hate speech codes'' that ban such speech. In a recent case, for example, a federal court enjoined (prohibited) the University of Wisconsin from enforcing its hate speech code. The court held that the code was unconstitutional because it went too far in restricting the free speech of students.[19]

**SYMBOLIC SPEECH** Not all expression is in words or in writing. Nonverbal expressions—such as gestures, movements, articles of clothing, and so on—may, under certain circumstances, be considered **symbolic speech.** Such speech is given substantial protection today by our courts. For example, in 1969, the United States Supreme Court held that an Iowa school district's regulation prohibiting students from wearing black arm bands to school, as a gesture of protest against the Vietnam War (1964–1973), violated the First Amendment.[20] In 1989, in *Texas v. Johnson,* the Supreme Court ruled that state laws that prohibited the burning of the American flag as part of a peaceful protest also violated the freedom of expression protected by the First Amendment.[21] More recently, the Supreme Court ruled that a city statute banning bias-motivated disorderly conduct (including, in this case, the placing of a burning cross in another's front yard as a gesture of hate) was an unconstitutional restriction of speech.[22]

**COMMERCIAL SPEECH—ADVERTISING** A distinction is often made between ''normal'' speech and ''commercial'' speech. Commercial speech consists of advertising and the like. Although commercial speech is protected by the First Amendment, its protection is not as extensive as that afforded to normal (noncommercial) speech. A state may restrict certain kinds of advertising, for example, in the interest of protecting consumers from being misled by the advertising. States also generally have a legitimate interest in the beautification of roadsides, and this interest allows states to place restraints on billboard advertising. Generally, a restriction on commercial speech will be considered valid as long as it (1) seeks to implement a substantial government interest, (2) directly advances that interest, and (3) goes no further than necessary to accomplish its objective.

There must be a ''reasonable fit'' between the government interest and the restriction chosen to accomplish the objective.[23] The case below involved the ''fit'' between a city's interest in safety and aesthetics and its decision to ban selective newsracks as the means to serve those interests.

---

18. *Soundgarden v. Eikenberry,* 871 P.2d 1050 (Wash. 1994).
19. *The UWM Post v. Board of Regents of the University of Wisconsin System,* 774 F.Supp. 1163 (E.D.Wis. 1991).
20. *Tinker v. Des Moines School District,* 393 U.S. 503, 89 S.Ct. 733, 21 L.Ed.2d 731 (1969).

21. 491 U.S. 397, 109 S.Ct. 2533, 105 L.Ed.2d 89 (1989).
22. *R.A.V. v. City of St. Paul, Minnesota,* ____ U.S. ____, 112 S.Ct. 2538, 120 L.Ed.2d 305 (1992).
23. *Board of Trustees of State University of New York v. Fox,* 492 U.S. 469, 109 S.Ct. 3028, 106 L.Ed.2d 388 (1989); *Central Hudson Gas & Electric Corp. v. Public Service Commission of New York,* 447 U.S. 557, 100 S.Ct. 2343, 65 L.Ed.2d 341 (1980).

---

**BACKGROUND AND FACTS** *Discovery Network, Inc., publishes a free magazine that consists primarily of Discovery's advertising but that also includes information about current events of general interest. Some of the magazines are distributed through thirty-eight newsracks that the city of Cincinnati authorized Discovery to place on public property in 1989. Harmony Publishing Company publishes and distributes a free magazine that contains information concerning real estate for sale in the Cincinnati area. In 1989, the city permitted Harmony to install twenty-four newsracks at approved locations. In March 1990, the city revoked the two publishers' permits and ordered the newsracks removed, under a city ordinance that*

| CASE 5.4 |
| --- |
| **CITY OF CINCINNATI v. DISCOVERY NETWORK, INC.** |
| Supreme Court of the United States, 1993. |
| ____ U.S. ____, 113 S.Ct. 1505, 123 L.Ed.2d 99. |

*prohibits the distribution of commercial handbills on public property because it detracts from the safety and attractive appearance of the city's streets and sidewalks. Cincinnati placed no restriction on other publishers' newsracks, including those used by local and national newspapers. Discovery and Harmony filed an action in federal district court, seeking to enjoin the city from enforcing the ordinance, on the ground that enforcement in their case violated the First Amendment. When the trial and appellate courts ruled in favor of Discovery and Harmony, Cincinnati appealed to the United States Supreme Court.*

Justice *STEVENS* delivered the opinion of the Court.

\* \* \* \*

There is ample support in the record for the conclusion that the city did not "establish the reasonable fit we require." The ordinance on which it relied was an outdated prohibition against the distribution of any commercial handbills on public property. \* \* \* The fact that the city failed to address its recently developed concern about newsracks by regulating their size, shape, appearance, or number indicates that it has not "carefully calculated" the costs and benefits associated with the burden on speech imposed by its prohibition. \* \* \*

\* \* \* \*

The city argues that there is a close fit between its ban on newsracks dispensing "commercial handbills" and its interest in safety and esthetics because every decrease in the number of such dispensing devices necessarily effects an increase in safety and an improvement in the attractiveness of the cityscape. In the city's view, the prohibition is thus *entirely* related to its legitimate interests in safety and esthetics.

\* \* \* \*

\* \* \* We \* \* \* agree with the Court of Appeals that Cincinnati's actions in this case run afoul of the First Amendment. Not only does Cincinnati's categorical ban on commercial newsracks place too much importance on the distinction between commercial and noncommercial speech, but in this case, the distinction bears no relationship *whatsoever* to the particular interests that the city has asserted.

**DECISION AND REMEDY**  *The United States Supreme Court affirmed the judgment of the appellate court. The Supreme Court held that the lesser status of commercial speech is relevant only when its regulation is designed "either to prevent false or misleading advertising, or to alleviate distinctive adverse effects of the specific speech at issue."*

---

**POLITICAL SPEECH** Speech that otherwise would be within the protection of the First Amendment does not lose that protection simply because its source is a corporation. For example, in *First National Bank of Boston v. Bellotti,*[24] national banking associations and business corporations sought United States Supreme Court review of a Massachusetts statute that prohibited corporations from making political contributions or expenditures that individuals were permitted to make. The Court ruled that the Massachusetts law was unconstitutional because it violated the right of corporations to freedom of speech. Similarly, the Court has held that a law forbidding a corporation from using bill inserts to express its views on controversial issues also violates the First Amendment.[25]

In the following case, decided by a more conservative Supreme Court, this trend was reversed.

---

24. 435 U.S. 765, 98 S.Ct. 1407, 55 L.Ed.2d 707 (1978).

25. *Consolidated Edison Co. v. Public Service Commission,* 447 U.S. 550, 100 S.Ct. 2326, 65 L.Ed.2d 319 (1980).

**BACKGROUND AND FACTS** *In June 1985, Michigan scheduled a special election to fill a vacancy in the state house of representatives. The Michigan State Chamber of Commerce, a Michigan corporation, sought to use its general corporate funds to place a newspaper advertisement supporting a specific candidate. Under the Michigan Campaign Finance Act, this is a felony. The act prohibits corporations from using general corporate funds for independent expenditures in state political campaigns. The act allows corporations to make expenditures through separate funds used solely for political purposes. The chamber filed a suit against the state in federal district court for an injunction against enforcement of the act, arguing in part that this restriction on expenditures is unconstitutional because it violates the First Amendment. The district court upheld the statute, and the chamber appealed. The court of appeals reversed the decision, reasoning that the act violated the First Amendment. The state, through Richard Austin, Michigan's secretary of state, appealed to the United States Supreme Court.*

CASE 5.5

**AUSTIN v. MICHIGAN CHAMBER OF COMMERCE**

Supreme Court of the United States, 1990.
494 U.S. 652,
110 S.Ct. 1391,
108 L.Ed.2d 652.

Justice *MARSHALL* delivered the opinion of the Court.

\* \* \* \*

To determine whether Michigan's restrictions on corporate political expenditures may constitutionally be applied to the Chamber, we must ascertain whether they burden the exercise of political speech and, if they do, whether they are narrowly tailored to serve a compelling state interest. Certainly, the use of funds to support a political candidate is "speech"; independent campaign expenditures constitute "political expression 'at the core of our electoral process and of the First Amendment freedoms.' " \* \* \*

\* \* \* \*

\* \* \* State law grants corporations special advantages—such as limited liability, perpetual life, and favorable treatment of the accumulation and distribution of assets—that enhance their ability to attract capital and to deploy their resources in ways that maximize the return on their shareholders' investments. These state-created advantages \* \* \* permit [corporations] to use "resources amassed in the economic marketplace" to obtain "an unfair advantage in the political marketplace." \* \* \*

\* \* \* Corporate wealth can unfairly influence elections when it is deployed in the form of independent expenditures, just as it can when it assumes the guise of political contributions. We therefore hold that the State has articulated a sufficiently compelling rationale to support its restriction on independent expenditures by corporations.

We next turn to the question whether the Act is sufficiently narrowly tailored to achieve its goal. We find that the Act is precisely targeted to eliminate the distortion caused by corporate spending while also allowing corporations to express their political views.\* \* \* [T]he Act does not impose an absolute ban on all forms of corporate political spending but permits corporations to make independent political expenditures through separate segregated funds.

*The Supreme Court reversed the decision of the court of appeals.*

**DECISION AND REMEDY**

**Political Contributions Abroad** *The American company's right to make campaign contributions does not extend overseas. Election laws in nations such as France, Taiwan, and the Philippines prohibit all foreign campaign*

**INTERNATIONAL CONSIDERATIONS**

*contributions. Israeli law permits contributions from foreign individuals but not foreign corporations. These restrictions are often circumvented through a local subsidiary, however.*

## FREEDOM OF RELIGION

The First Amendment states that the government may neither establish any religion nor prohibit the free exercise of religious practices. This constitutional provision is referred to as either the **establishment clause** or the **free exercise clause.** Government action, both federal and state, must be consistent with this constitutional mandate.

Federal or state regulation that does not promote or place a significant burden on religion is constitutional even if it has some impact on religion. "Sunday closing laws," for example, make the performance of some commercial activities on Sunday illegal. These statutes, also known as "blue laws," have been upheld on the ground that it is a legitimate function of government to provide a day of rest. The United States Supreme Court has held that the Sunday closing laws, although originally of a religious character, have taken on the secular purpose of promoting the health and welfare of workers.[26] Even though closing laws admittedly make it easier for Christians to attend religious services, the Court has viewed this effect as an incidental, not a primary, purpose of Sunday closing laws.

The First Amendment does not require a complete separation of church and state. On the contrary, it affirmatively mandates *accommodation* of all religions and forbids hostility toward any.[27] The courts do not have an easy task in determining the extent to which governments can accommodate a religion without appearing to promote that religion and thus violate the establishment clause. For example, the United States Supreme Court held in *Lynch v. Donnelly* that a municipality could include religious symbols, such as a Nativity scene, or crèche, in its annual Christmas display, as long

as the religious symbols constituted just one part of a holiday display in which other, nonreligious symbols (such as reindeer and candy-striped poles) were also featured.[28] The Court has applied this same reasoning in subsequent cases, and federal courts continue to face such issues.[29]

For business firms, an important issue involves the accommodation that businesses must make for the religious beliefs of their employees. Title VII of the Civil Rights Act of 1964 prohibits government employers, private employers, and unions from discriminating against persons on the basis of religion. The Equal Employment Opportunity Commission—the regulatory agency that interprets and applies Title VII—has required that private employers "reasonably accommodate" the religious practices of their employees, unless to do so would cause undue hardship to the employer's business. For example, if an employee's religion prohibits him or her from working on a certain day of the week or at a certain type of job, the employer must make a reasonable attempt to accommodate these religious requirements. Employers must reasonably accommodate an employee's religious belief even if the belief is not based on the tenets or dogma of a particular church, sect, or denomination. The only requirement is that the belief be sincerely held by the employee.[30]

In the following case, the sacramental use of peyote by two employees violated both an employment policy and a state law. When the employees were discharged for "misconduct," the state refused to grant them unemployment benefits. Ultimately, the United States Supreme Court had

---

26. *McGowan v. Maryland,* 366 U.S. 420, 81 S.Ct. 1101, 6 L.Ed.2d 393 (1961).

27. *Zorach v. Clauson,* 343 U.S. 306, 72 S.Ct. 679, 96 L.Ed. 954 (1952).

28. 465 U.S. 668, 104 S.Ct. 1355, 79 L.Ed.2d 604 (1984).

29. See, for example, *County of Allegheny v. American Civil Liberties Union,* 492 U.S. 573, 109 S.Ct. 3086, 106 L.Ed.2d 472 (1989); *Harris v. City of Zion, Lake County, Illinois,* 927 F.2d 1401 (7th Cir.1991); and *Congregation Lubavitch v. City of Cincinnati,* 807 F.Supp. 1353 (S.D. Ohio 1992).

30. *Frazee v. Illinois Department of Employment Security,* 489 U.S. 829, 109 S.Ct. 1514, 103 L.Ed.2d 914 (1989).

to determine whether a state law prohibiting the use of peyote violated the religious rights of members of the Native American Church whose religion required the sacramental use of this drug.

---

**BACKGROUND AND FACTS**  *Smith and Black, both members of the Native American Church, worked as drug and alcohol abuse rehabilitation counselors. They were discharged by their employer for ingesting peyote, a hallucinogenic drug, for sacramental purposes during a religious ceremony of the Native American Church. When Smith and Black applied for state unemployment compensation, their applications were denied under an Oregon statute disqualifying employees who were discharged for work-connected misconduct. Smith and Black appealed the Employment Division's decision to the courts, claiming that the sacramental use of peyote did not constitute ''misconduct'' and that the state's denial of unemployment benefits violated their religious rights under the free exercise clause of the First Amendment. The Supreme Court of Oregon ruled in their favor, notwithstanding the fact that the use of peyote was illegal under Oregon law. According to the Supreme Court of Oregon, the law prohibiting the sacramental use of peyote was itself in violation of the First Amendment. The United States Supreme Court then addressed the issue of the statute's constitutionality.*

CASE 5.6

**EMPLOYMENT DIVISION, DEPARTMENT OF HUMAN RESOURCES OF THE STATE OF OREGON v. SMITH**
Supreme Court of the United States, 1990.
494 U.S. 872,
110 S.Ct. 1595,
108 L.Ed.2d 876.

Justice *SCALIA* delivered the opinion of the Court.

\* \* \* \*

\* \* \* We have never held that an individual's religious beliefs excuse him from compliance with an otherwise valid law prohibiting conduct that the State is free to regulate. On the contrary, the record of more than a century of our free exercise jurisprudence contradicts that proposition. \* \* \*

\* \* \* \*

\* \* \* The government's ability to enforce generally applicable prohibitions of socially harmful conduct, like its ability to carry out other aspects of public policy, ''cannot depend on measuring the effects of a governmental action on a religious objector's spiritual development.'' To make an individual's obligation to obey such a law contingent upon the law's coincidence with his religious beliefs, \* \* \* —permitting him, by virtue of his beliefs, ''to become a law unto himself''— contradicts both constitutional tradition and common sense.

\* \* \* \*

\* \* \* It may fairly be said that leaving accommodation to the political process will place at a relative disadvantage those religious practices that are not widely engaged in; but that unavoidable consequence of democratic government must be preferred to a system in which each conscience is a law unto itself or in which judges weigh the social importance of all laws against the centrality of all religious beliefs.

---

*The United States Supreme Court reversed the Oregon court's ruling. The Oregon statute prohibiting the ingestion of peyote was constitutional, and denial of unemployment benefits to Smith and Black—whose employment dismissal resulted from the use of this drug—did not violate their rights under the free exercise clause.*

**DECISION AND REMEDY**

## THE PRIVILEGE AGAINST SELF-INCRIMINATION

The Fifth Amendment guarantees that no person ''shall be compelled in any criminal case to be a witness against himself.'' Thus, in any federal proceeding, an accused person cannot be compelled to give testimony that might subject him or her to any criminal prosecution. An accused person cannot be forced to testify against himself or herself in state courts either, because the due process clause of the Fourteenth Amendment incorporates the Fifth Amendment provision against self-incrimination.

The Fifth Amendment's guarantee against self-incrimination extends only to natural persons. Because a corporation is a legal entity and not a natural person, the privilege against self-incrimination is inapplicable to it. Similarly, the business records of a partnership do not receive Fifth Amendment protection.[31] When it is required that records of such organizations be produced, the information must be given even if it incriminates the persons who constitute the business entity.

Sole proprietors and sole practitioners (those who fully own their businesses) who have not incorporated cannot be compelled to produce their business records. These individuals have full protection against self-incrimination because they function in only one capacity: there is no separate business entity.[32]

## SEARCHES AND SEIZURES

The Fourth Amendment protects the ''right of the people to be secure in their persons, houses, papers, and effects.'' Generally, federal, state, and local government officers must obtain **search warrants** before searching or seizing private property. As discussed in Chapter 9, to obtain a warrant, law enforcement officers must convince a judge that they have reasonable grounds, or **probable cause,** to believe a search will reveal a specific illegality. Probable cause requires law enforcement officials to have trustworthy evidence that would convince a reasonable person that the proposed search or seizure is more likely justified than not. Furthermore, the Fourth Amendment prohibits *general* warrants. It requires a particular description of that which is to be searched or seized. General searches through a person's belongings are impermissible. The search cannot extend beyond what is described in the warrant.

There are exceptions to the requirement of a search warrant, as when it is likely that the items sought will be removed before a warrant can be obtained. For example, if a police officer has probable cause to believe an automobile contains evidence of a crime, and it is likely that the vehicle will be unavailable by the time a warrant is obtained, the officer can search the vehicle without a warrant.

Constitutional protection against unreasonable searches and seizures is important to businesses and professionals. As federal and state regulation of commercial activities increased, frequent and unannounced government inspections were conducted to ensure compliance with the regulations. Such inspections were at times extremely disruptive. In *Marshall v. Barlow's, Inc.,*[33] the United States Supreme Court held that government inspectors do not have the right to enter business premises without a warrant, although the standard of probable cause is not the same as that required in nonbusiness contexts.

The existence of a general and neutral enforcement plan will justify issuance of the warrant. Lawyers and accountants frequently possess the business records of their clients, and inspecting these documents while they are out of the hands of their true owners also requires a warrant. No warrant is required, however, for seizures of spoiled or contaminated food. Nor are warrants required for searches of businesses in such highly regulated industries as liquor, guns, and strip mining. General manufacturing is not considered to be one of these highly regulated industries.

Of increasing concern to many employers is how to maintain a safe and efficient workplace without jeopardizing the Fourth Amendment rights of employees ''to be secure in their persons.'' Requiring employees to undergo random drug tests, for example, may be held to violate the Fourth Amendment. Fourth Amendment issues in the em-

---

31. The privilege has been applied to some small family partnerships. See *United States v. Slutsky,* 352 F.Supp. 1005 (S.D.N.Y. 1972).

32. A sole proprietor can be compelled to produce tax, employment, and other records required to be kept by state and federal laws, however.

---

33. 436 U.S. 307, 98 S.Ct. 1816, 56 L.Ed.2d 305 (1978).

ployment context, as well as employee privacy rights generally, are discussed in Chapter 36.

SECTION 3

# OTHER CONSTITUTIONAL PROTECTIONS

Three other constitutional guarantees of great significance to Americans are mandated by the *privileges and immunities clause* of Article IV, Section 2, of the U.S. Constitution and the Fourteenth Amendment, the *due process clauses* of the Fifth and Fourteenth Amendments, and the *equal protection clause* of the Fourteenth Amendment.

## THE PRIVILEGES AND IMMUNITIES CLAUSE

Article IV, Section 2, of the Constitution provides that "[t]he Citizens of each State shall be entitled to all Privileges and Immunities of Citizens in the several States." This clause provides substantial protection and is often referred to as the interstate **privileges and immunities clause.**[34] When a citizen of one state engages in *basic and essential* activities in another state (the "foreign state"), such as transferring property, seeking employment, or accessing the court system, the foreign state must have a *substantial reason* for treating nonresidents differently from its own residents. The foreign state must also establish that its reason for the discrimination is substantially related to its ultimate purpose in adopting the legislation or activity.[35]

Charging nonresidents $2,500 for a shrimp-fishing license, for example, while residents are charged only $25 for the same license, may be considered unconstitutional discrimination against nonresidents who are pursuing the essential activity of making a living.[36] Similarly, attempting to limit the practice of law to residents only (on the premise that it would help reduce the state's unemployment rate) may unconstitutionally restrict the nonresident's professional pursuit without substantial justification.[37]

The Fourteenth Amendment provides that "[n]o State shall make or enforce any law which shall abridge the privileges or immunities of citizens of the United States." This clause also protects all individuals, as citizens of the United States, from state action that might infringe such privileges or immunities as the right to travel from state to state or to peaceably assemble.[38]

## DUE PROCESS

Both the Fifth and the Fourteenth Amendments provide that no person shall be deprived "of life, liberty, or property, without due process of law."[39] Through the **due process clause,** these constitutional amendments establish two significant protections against government attempts to overreach its authority. One protection is substantive, and the other is procedural.

**SUBSTANTIVE DUE PROCESS** *Substantive* due process focuses on the content, or substance, of legislation or government actions. When a statute is constitutionally challenged as violating the due process clause, the court reviewing the case first determines which type of legislation is involved and then decides which standard for review, or test, for the case is applicable. If economic legislation is involved, such as restrictions on business activities, the court applies a "rational-basis" test, which requires only that the legislation relate rationally to a legitimate government purpose. This is an easy test to satisfy, and governments enjoy wide latitude in creating and enforcing economic legislation. Under this test, virtually any business regulation may be upheld as rational, including insurance regulations, wage and price controls, banking controls, and laws prohibiting unfair competition and trade practices. The United States

---

34. The terms *privilege* and *immunity* are commonly used synonymously with regard to the interpretation of this clause. Generally the terms refer to certain rights, benefits, or advantages enjoyed by individuals.

35. *Supreme Court of New Hampshire v. Piper,* 470 U.S. 274, 105 S.Ct. 1272, 84 L.Ed.2d 205 (1985).

36. *Toomer v. Witsell,* 334 U.S. 385, 68 S.Ct. 1156, 92 L.Ed. 1460 (1948).

37. *Hicklin v. Orbeck,* 437 U.S. 518, 98 S.Ct. 2482, 57 L.Ed.2d 397 (1978).

38. Unlike the due process and equal protection clauses (to be discussed shortly), the privilege and immunities clause of the Fourteenth Amendment does not apply to the individual rights found in the Bill of Rights.

39. The Fifth Amendment applies to the federal government, whereas the Fourteenth Amendment applies to state governments.

Supreme Court has held that actions such as these do not violate substantive due process.

In contrast, a court will closely scrutinize a government statute or action that restricts an individual's *fundamental right* (such as the right to travel, as well as all First Amendment rights), because such rights are considered to be vitally important to our society. If a law or other governmental action limits a fundamental right, it will be held to violate substantive due process unless it promotes a *compelling* or *overriding interest*. State laws designating speed limits, for example, may be upheld by the court even though the laws affect interstate travel, a fundamental right, because the government has an overriding, compelling interest in protecting public safety.[40]

**PROCEDURAL DUE PROCESS** *Procedural* due process requires that any government decision to take away the life, liberty, or property interest of an individual be accompanied by strict procedural safeguards to ensure fairness. When the government proposes a taking of property for public use, for example, it must provide the owner with adequate notice of the taking, an opportunity to object to the proposed action, and an adversarial hearing before a fair and neutral decision maker (who need not be a judge).

Government action may simultaneously violate both procedural and substantive aspects of constitutional due process. Consider, for example, the following hypothetical law:

> It shall be a misdemeanor for any resident of this state to travel outside the state for a period of or exceeding sixty consecutive days in any year and attempt to vote in a state election in that same year. Sentencing shall be automatic and without review, requiring imprisonment in the county jail for a period of ninety days.

The law violates substantive due process, because it abridges the resident's fundamental right to travel. The law also violates procedural due process, because it unfairly imposes a penalty—incarceration—without giving the resident an opportunity to defend his or her actions.

---

40. Of course, if a state law designates a speed limit that conflicts with a federal law on speed limits, the state law will not be upheld. See the discussion of the supremacy clause earlier in this chapter.

## EQUAL PROTECTION

Under the Fourteenth Amendment, a state may not "deny to any person within its jurisdiction the equal protection of the laws." The United States Supreme Court has used the due process clause of the Fifth Amendment to make the **equal protection clause** applicable to the federal government. Equal protection means that the government must treat similarly situated individuals in a similar manner.

Both substantive due process and equal protection require review of the substance of the law or other governmental action rather than review of the procedures used. When a law or action limits the liberty of all persons to do something, it may violate substantive due process; when a law or action limits the liberty of some persons but not others, it may violate the equal protection clause. Thus, for example, if a law prohibits all persons from buying contraceptive devices, it raises a substantive due process question; if it prohibits only unmarried persons from buying the same devices, it raises an equal protection issue.

Basically, in determining whether a law or action violates the equal protection clause, a court will consider questions similar to those previously noted as applicable in a substantive due process review. Under an equal protection inquiry, when a law or action distinguishes between or among individuals, the basis for the distinction—that is, the *classification*—is examined. In matters of economic or social welfare, the classification will be considered valid if there is any conceivable *rational basis* on which the classification might relate to any legitimate government interest. It is almost impossible for a law or action to fail the rational-basis test.

Thus, for example, a city ordinance that in effect prohibits all pushcart vendors except a specific few from operating in a particular area of the city will be upheld if the city proffers a rational basis—perhaps regulation and reduction of traffic in the particular area—for the ordinance. Some laws, of course, do fail the rational-basis test. For example, a law that provides unemployment benefits only to people over six feet tall would violate the guarantee of equal protection. There is no rational basis for determining the distribution of unemployment compensation on the basis of height. Such a distinction could not further any legitimate government objective.

In contrast, if the challenged law or government action inhibits some persons' exercise of a fundamental right, the classification must be necessary to promote a compelling state interest. Also, if the classification is based on a *suspect* trait—such as race, national origin, or citizenship status—the classification must be necessary to promote a compelling state interest. Compelling state interests include remedying past unconstitutional or illegal discrimination but do not include correcting the general effects of "society's" discrimination. Thus, for example, if a city gives preference to minority applicants in hiring firefighters, the city must have a "strong basis in evidence" of past unconstitutional or illegal discrimination against minorities in the fire department that it is attempting to correct.[41]

Laws using these classifications based on gender or legitimacy, however, must be *substantially related to important government objectives.* For example, an important government objective is preventing illegitimate teenage pregnancies. Because males and females are not similarly situated in this circumstance—only females can become pregnant—a law that punishes men but not women for statutory rape will be upheld. But a state law requiring illegitimate children to bring paternity suits within six years after they are born will be struck down if legitimate children are allowed to seek support from their parents at any time. An important objective behind statutes of limitations is to prevent persons from bringing stale or fraudulent claims, but distinguishing between support claims on the basis of legitimacy has no relation to this objective.

The following case illustrates a court's application of the rational-basis test in determining the validity of a state statute requiring motorcyclists to wear helmets.

---

41. See, for example, *Ensley Branch, N.A.A.C.P. v. City of Birmingham,* 20 F.3d. 1489 (11th Cir. 1994).

---

**BACKGROUND AND FACTS** *In 1988, the Nebraska Legislature enacted a statute that requires any motorcycle operator or passenger on Nebraska's highways to wear a "protective helmet." Eugene Robotham, a licensed motorcycle operator, sued the state of Nebraska to block enforcement of the law. Robotham asserted, among other things, that the statute violated the equal protection clause because it placed requirements on motorcyclists that were not imposed on other motorists. The court concluded that the law was constitutional. Robotham appealed.*

CASE 5.7

**ROBOTHAM v. STATE**
Supreme Court of Nebraska, 1992.
241 Neb. 379,
488 N.W.2d 533.

*HASTINGS,* Chief Justice.
\* \* \* \*
Motorcycle ridership is not a classification of race, alienage, or national origin. \* \* \* Nor is motorcycle ridership a classification based upon gender or illegitimacy. \* \* \* Therefore, "the Equal Protection Clause requires only a rational means to serve a legitimate end."
\* \* \* The statement of purpose in [the statute] makes clear the ends the Legislature sought to achieve:

> The Legislature hereby finds and declares that head injuries that occur to motorcyclists and moped operators which could be prevented or lessened by the wearing of helmets are a societal problem and that the financial and emotional costs of such injuries cannot be viewed solely on a personal level. It is the intent of the Legislature to prevent injuries and fatalities which occur due to motorcycle and moped accidents and to prevent the subsequent damage to society which results due to the cost of caring for injured people, the pain and suffering which accompanies such injuries and fatalities, and the loss of productive members of society from such injuries.

\* \* \*

\* \* \* \*

The protection of motorcycle riders from serious injury and the concomitant protection of society from the repercussions of such injuries is a legitimate legislative aim. The sole question remaining is whether the helmet law is rationally related to these aims.

\* \* \* [In several cases, the United States Supreme Court] found that a mandatory helmet law is a reasonable exercise of legislative power \* \* \* .

The ends of protecting society from the extra economic costs incurred because of injuries to motorcycle riders, and of preventing the other impacts on society of unnecessarily severe motorcycle accidents, are permissible goals for legislation. The helmet law is a rational means to those ends. Therefore, the helmet law [does not violate] \* \* \* equal protection under \* \* \* the federal Constitution.

**DECISION AND REMEDY**   *The Nebraska Supreme Court affirmed the lower court's decision regarding Robotham's equal-protection challenge to the state's mandatory helmet law.*

## TERMS AND CONCEPTS TO REVIEW

| | | |
|---|---|---|
| amend  84 | establishment clause  96 | privileges and immunities |
| Bill of Rights  91 | federalism  85 | clause  99 |
| checks and balances  85 | free exercise clause  96 | probable cause  98 |
| commerce clause  85 | police powers  87 | search warrant  98 |
| due process clause  99 | preemption  89 | supremacy clause  89 |
| equal protection clause  100 | | symbolic speech  93 |

## QUESTIONS AND CASE PROBLEMS

**5–1. Commerce Clause.** A Georgia statute requires the use of contoured rear-fender mudguards on trucks and trailers operating within Georgia state lines. The statute further makes it illegal for trucks and trailers to use straight mudguards. In approximately thirty-five other states, straight mudguards are legal. Moreover, in Florida, straight mudguards are explicitly required by law. There is some evidence that suggests that contoured mudguards might be a little safer than straight mudguards. Discuss whether this Georgia statute violates any constitutional provisions.

**5–2. Commercial Speech.** A mayoral election is about to be held in a large U.S. city. One of the candidates is Luis Delgado, and his campaign supporters wish to post campaign signs on lampposts and utility posts throughout the city. A city ordinance, however, prohibits the posting of any signs on public property. Delgado's supporters contend that the city ordinance is unconstitutional because it violates their right to free speech. Do you agree? In your answer, discuss what factors a court might consider in determining the constitutionality of the ordinance.

**5–3. Freedom of Religion.** A business has a backlog of orders, and to meet its deadlines, management decides to run the firm seven days a week, eight hours a day. One of the employees, Abus Placer, refuses to work on Saturday on religious grounds. His refusal to work means that the firm may not meet its production deadlines and may therefore suffer a loss of future business. The firm fires Placer and replaces him with an employee who is willing to work seven days a week. Placer claims that his employer, in terminating his employment, violated his constitutional right to the free exercise of his religion. Do you agree? Why or why not?

**5–4. Government Powers.** The framers of the Constitution feared the twin evils of tyranny and anarchy. Discuss how specific provisions of the Constitution and the Bill of Rights reflect these fears and protect against both of these extremes.

**5–5. Freedom of Religion.** Thomas worked in the nonmilitary operations of a large firm that produced both military and nonmilitary goods. When the company discontinued the production of nonmilitary goods, Thomas was transferred to a plant producing war materials. Thomas left his job, claiming that it violated his religious principles to participate in the manufacture of materials to be used in destroying life. In effect, he argued, the transfer to the war-materials plant forced him to quit his job. He was denied unemployment compensation by the state because he had not been effectively "discharged" by the employer but had voluntarily terminated his employment. Does the state's denial of unemployment benefits to Thomas violate the free exercise clause of the First Amendment? Explain. [*Thomas v. Review Board of the Indiana Employment Security Division,* 450 U.S. 707, 101 S.Ct. 1425, 67 L.Ed.2d 624 (1981)]

**5–6. Freedom of Religion.** A 1988 Minnesota statute required all operators of slow-moving vehicles to display on their vehicles a fluorescent orange-red triangular emblem or, as an alternative, a dull black triangle with a white reflective border, plus seventy-two square inches of permanent red reflective tape. A vehicle operator who chose the alternate emblem still had to carry a regular orange-red emblem in the vehicle and display it externally during times of darkness or low visibility. The state brought charges against Hershberger and other members of the Amish religion (the defendants) because they refused to comply with the statute. The defendants claimed that the statute violated their freedom of religion under the First Amendment because displaying the "loud" colors and "worldly symbols" on their slow-moving vehicles (black, boxlike buggies) compromised their religious belief that they should remain separate and apart from the modern world. The defendants stated that they would not object to displaying a sign similar to the alternate symbol if they could use silver, instead of red, reflective tape, and if they did not have to display the "regular" emblem at night. The state argued that although the silver tape was as effective as the red in terms of visibility, vehicles, and therefore the Amish, should comply with the statute as written. What will the court hold? Discuss. [*State v. Hershberger,* 444 N.W.2d 282 (Minn. 1989)]

**5–7. Commercial Speech.** In 1982, Philip Zauderer, an attorney practicing in Columbus, Ohio, placed a series of newspaper ads directed at women who had used the Dalkon Shield intrauterine device (IUD). In his ads, Zauderer included a drawing of the Dalkon Shield and informed women that they could still sue for any injuries or other harm to their health sustained by its use, even though the IUD was no longer being marketed. As a result of these ads, Zauderer filed lawsuits for 106 women. The Ohio Supreme Court deemed such advertisements unethical, and Zauderer was reprimanded by the court for his actions. He was further reprimanded for not having disclosed in his ads that, although his clients would owe no legal fees if they lost, they might still be faced with other costs involved in litigation. Zauderer appealed, claiming the ads were protected under the First Amend-

ment as commercial speech and that failure to disclose other costs was not deceptive. Discuss the probable success of Zauderer's appeal. [*Zauderer v. Office of Disciplinary Counsel,* 471 U.S. 626, 105 S.Ct. 2265, 85 L.Ed.2d 652 (1985)]

**5–8. Commercial Speech.** In 1983, Gary Peel, an Illinois attorney, began placing on his letterhead the following statement: "Certified Civil Trial Specialist/ By the National Board of Trial Advocacy." In so doing, Peel violated Rule 2–105(a) of the Illinois Code of Professional Responsibility, which prohibits lawyers from holding themselves out as "certified" or "specialists" in fields other than admiralty, trademark, and patent law. The Attorney Registration and Disciplinary Commission (ARDC) censured Peel for the violation. The ARDC claimed that Peel's letterhead was misleading because it implied that Peel had special qualifications as an attorney, although in fact no such thing as a civil trial specialty existed in Illinois; because the word *certified* might be interpreted to mean "licensed," and the National Board of Trial Advocacy (NBTA) did not have the authority to license lawyers; and because, given the fact that not all attorneys licensed to practice in Illinois are certified by the NBTA, Peel's assertion might erroneously be construed by some readers to mean that those who are certified by that board are superior to those who are not. Peel argued that Rule 2–105(a) violated his constitutional right to free speech and appealed the ARDC's decision to the United State Supreme Court. What will the Court decide? Discuss. [*Peel v. Attorney Registration and Disciplinary Commission,* 496 U.S. 91, 110 S.Ct. 2281, 110 L.Ed.2d 83 (1990)]

**5–9. Commerce Clause.** Taylor owned a bait business in Maine and arranged to have live baitfish imported into the state. The importation of the baitfish violated a Maine statute. Taylor was indicted under a federal statute that makes it a federal crime to transport fish in interstate commerce in violation of state law. Taylor moved to dismiss the indictment on the ground that the Maine statute unconstitutionally burdened interstate commerce. Maine intervened to defend the validity of its statute, arguing that the law legitimately protected the state's fisheries from parasites and nonnative species that might be included in shipments of live baitfish. Were Maine's interests in protecting its fisheries from parasites and nonnative species sufficient to justify the burden placed on interstate commerce by the Maine statute? Discuss. [*Maine v. Taylor,* 477 U.S. 131, 106 S.Ct. 2440, 91 L.Ed.2d 110 (1986)]

**5–10. Commerce Clause.** In 1957, Rhodes and several other Georgia landowners entered into a sixty-five-year timber purchase contract with Inland-Rome, Inc. Thereafter, Inland-Rome cut timber from the landowners' land and then removed it for processing in certain Georgia facilities, after which it was shipped as lumber products to points throughout the country. In 1986, the landowners claimed that Inland-Rome had breached the contract, and they filed suit. Inland-Rome moved to compel arbitration because the parties had agreed, in their contract, to arbitrate any disputes arising thereunder. Georgia law enforces arbitration clauses only if they are contained in construction contracts. Arbitration clauses are enforceable under the Federal Arbitration Act only if the contracts in which they appear affect interstate commerce. Inland-Rome contended that because lumber products from the cut timber were shipped throughout the nation, the contract related to interstate commerce, and therefore the Federal Arbitration Act should apply. Will the court agree? Discuss. [*Rhodes v. Inland-Rome, Inc.*, 195 Ga.App. 39, 392 S.E.2d 270 (1990)]

**5–11. Equal Protection.** In response to rapidly rising property taxes, California voters approved a statewide ballot initiative, Proposition 13, that added Article XIIIA to the state constitution. Among other things, Article XIIIA embodied an "acquisition value" system of taxation, whereby property was reassessed up to the current appraised value on new construction or at the time of a change in ownership. Exemptions from the reassessment existed for two types of transfers: (1) exchanges of principal residences by persons over the age of fifty-five and (2) transfers between parents and children. Over time, the acquisition-value system created dramatic disparities in the taxes paid by persons owning similar parcels of property. Long-term owners paid lower taxes reflecting historic property values, whereas new owners paid higher taxes reflecting more recent values. Faced with such a disparity, Stephanie Nordlinger, who had recently bought a house in Los Angeles County, sued the county and Kenneth Hahn, the county tax assessor, claiming that Article XIIIA's reassessment scheme violated the equal protection clause. The complaint was dismissed, and ultimately Nordlinger appealed to the United States Supreme Court. Will the Court hold that the California property tax system violates the equal protection clause? [*Nordlinger v. Hahn*, ___U.S. ___, 112 S.Ct. 2326, 120 L.Ed.2d 1 (1992)]

**5–12. Case Briefing Assignment**

*Examine Case A.1 [Austin v. Berryman, 878 F.2d 786 (4th Cir. 1989)] in Appendix A. The case has been excerpted there in great detail. Review and then brief the case, making sure that you include answers to the following questions in your brief.*

1. Who were the plaintiff and defendant in this action?
2. Why did Austin claim that she had been forced to leave her job?
3. Why was she refused state unemployment benefits?
4. Did the state's refusal to give her unemployment compensation violate her rights under the free exercise clause of the First Amendment?
5. What logic or reasoning did the court employ in arriving at its conclusion?

**5–13. A Question of Ethics**

*Agnes and John Donahue refused to rent an apartment to an unmarried couple, Verna Terry and Robert Wilder. The Donahues were devout Roman Catholics and firmly believed, in accordance with the church's teachings, that engaging in sexual relations outside of marriage was a mortal sin. Agnes Donahue also believed that it would be sinful for her to aid another person in the commission of a sin. Renting an apartment to an unmarried couple would, in Agnes Donahue's mind, be aiding the couple in the commission of a sin, and therefore she refused to rent the apartment to Terry and Wilder. Terry and Wilder filed a complaint with the California Fair Employment and Housing Commission, alleging that the Donahues' refusal to rent them an apartment violated a state statute prohibiting discrimination on the basis of marital status. Eventually, the case was heard by a California appellate court. The question before the court was whether the state's interest in prohibiting discrimination based on marital status outweighed the Donahues' constitutional right to the free exercise of their religion. [Donahue v. Fair Employment and Housing Commission, 7 Cal.App.4th 1498, 2 Cal.Rptr.2d 32 (1991)]*

1. In your opinion, should the court make an exception to the state statute's applicability in the Donahues' case? Why or why not?
2. Review Case 5.6, which involved a conflict between a state statute and the federal constitutional right to the free exercise of religion. How did the court decide the issue in that case? Should the same principle be applied to the Donahues' actions?

# CHAPTER 6

# TORTS AND
# STRICT LIABILITY

**P**art of doing business today and, indeed, part of everyday life is the
risk of being involved in a lawsuit. A normal and ever-increasing
business operating cost is that of liability insurance to protect against
lawsuits. The list of circumstances in which businesspersons can be sued is
long and varied. An employee injured on the job may attempt to sue the
employer because of an unsafe working environment. The consumer who is
injured while using a product may attempt to sue the manufacturer because
of a defect in the product. At issue in these examples is alleged wrongful
conduct by one person that causes injury to another. Such wrongful conduct
is covered by the law of **torts** (the word *tort* is French for ''wrong'').

Tort law covers a wide variety of injuries. Society recognizes an interest
in personal physical safety, and tort law provides remedies for acts that cause
physical injury or that interfere with physical security and freedom of movement. Society recognizes an interest in protecting personal property, and tort
law provides remedies for acts that cause destruction or damage to property.
Society also recognizes an interest in protecting certain intangible interests,
such as personal privacy, family relations, reputation, and dignity, and tort
law provides remedies for invasion of these *protected interests*.

In this chapter, after a brief discussion of the basis of tort law, we examine
two broad categories of torts: intentional torts and torts committed through
negligence. In addition to liability for intentional torts or torts resulting from
negligence, businesspersons and others are also subject to potential *strict
liability* (liability without fault) when engaging in certain types of activities.
The principle of strict liability will be discussed in the final section of this
chapter. Torts that normally occur only within the business context will be
treated in detail in Chapter 7.

# THE BASIS OF TORT LAW

Two notions serve as the basis of all torts: wrongs and compensation. Tort law recognizes that some acts are wrong because they cause injuries to others. Of course, a tort is not the only type of wrong that exists in the law; crimes also involve wrongs. A crime, however, is an act so reprehensible that it is considered a wrong against the state or against society as a whole, as well as against the individual victim. Therefore, the *state* prosecutes a person committing a criminal act. A tort action, however, is a *civil* action in which one person brings a personal suit against another.

In some cases, such as *assault and battery* (explained in the next section), a basis could exist for a criminal prosecution, as well as a tort action. For example, Jonas is walking down the street, minding his own business, when suddenly he is attacked by someone. In the ensuing struggle, Jonas falls and breaks his leg. The wrongdoer is restrained and arrested by a police officer. In this situation, the attacker may be subject both to criminal prosecution by the state and to a tort lawsuit brought by Jonas for **damages** (money to compensate him for injuries incurred in the fall).

# INTENTIONAL TORTS AGAINST PERSONS

An **intentional tort,** as the term implies, requires *intent.* The **tortfeasor** (the one committing the tort) must intend to commit an act, the consequences of which interfere with the personal or business interests of another in a way not permitted by law. An evil or harmful motive is not required—in fact, the actor may even have a beneficial motive for committing what turns out to be a tortious act. In tort law, intent only means that the actor intended the consequences of his or her act or knew with substantial certainty that certain consequences would result from the act. The law generally assumes that individuals intend the *normal* consequences of their actions. Thus, forcefully pushing another—even if done in jest and without any evil

motive—is an intentional tort (if injury results), because the object of a strong push can ordinarily be expected to go flying. A light pat on the shoulder, in contrast, is not an intentional tort, even though, in drawing away suddenly, the person touched may be injured.

This section discusses intentional torts against persons. These include assault and battery, false imprisonment, intentional infliction of emotional distress, defamation, invasion of the right to privacy, and fraudulent misrepresentation.

## ASSAULT AND BATTERY

Any intentional, unexcused act that creates in another person a reasonable apprehension or fear of immediate harmful or offensive contact is an **assault.** Note that apprehension is not the same as fear. If a contact is such that a reasonable person would want to avoid it, and if there is a reasonable basis for believing that the contact will occur, then the plaintiff suffers apprehension whether or not he or she is afraid. The interest protected by tort law concerning assault is the freedom from having to expect harmful or offensive contact. The arousal of apprehension is enough to justify compensation.

The *completion* of the act that caused the apprehension, if it results in harm to the plaintiff, is a **battery,** which is defined as an unexcused and harmful or offensive physical contact *intentionally* performed. For example, Ivan threatens Jean with a gun, then shoots her. The pointing of the gun at Jean is an assault; the firing of the gun (if the bullet hits Jean) is a battery. The interest protected by tort law concerning battery is the right to personal security and safety. The contact can be harmful, or it can be merely offensive (such as an unwelcome kiss). Physical injury need not occur. The contact can involve any part of the body or anything attached to it—for example, a hat or other item of clothing, a purse, or a chair or an automobile in which one is sitting. Whether the contact is offensive or not is determined by the *reasonable person* standard.[1] The contact can be made by the defen-

---

1. The reasonable person standard is an objective test of how a reasonable person would have acted under the same circumstances. See ''The Duty of Care and Its Breach'' later in this chapter.

dant or by some force the defendant sets in motion—for example, a rock thrown, food poisoned, or a stick swung.

A number of legally recognized **defenses** can be raised by a defendant who is sued for assault, battery, or both:

1. *Consent.* When a person consents to the act that damages him or her, there is generally no liability for the damage done.
2. *Self-defense.* An individual who is defending his or her life or physical well-being can claim self-defense. In situations of both *real* and *apparent* danger, a person may normally use whatever force is *reasonably* necessary to prevent harmful contact (see Chapter 9 for a more detailed discussion of self-defense).
3. *Defense of others.* An individual can act in a reasonable manner to protect others who are in real or apparent danger.
4. *Defense of property.* Reasonable force may be used in attempting to remove intruders from one's home, although force that is likely to cause death or great bodily injury normally can never be used just to protect property.

## FALSE IMPRISONMENT

*False imprisonment* is defined as the intentional confinement or restraint of another person's activities without justification. It involves interference with the freedom to move without restraint. The confinement can be accomplished through the use of physical barriers, physical restraint, or threats of physical force. Moral pressure or future threats do not constitute false imprisonment. It is essential that the person being restrained not comply with the restraint willingly. In other words, the person being restrained must not agree to the restraint.

Businesspersons are often confronted with suits for false imprisonment after they have attempted to confine a suspected shoplifter for questioning. Under the privilege to detain granted to merchants in some states, a merchant can use the defense of *probable cause* to justify delaying a suspected shoplifter. Probable cause exists when the evidence to support the belief that a person is guilty outweighs the evidence against that belief. The detention, however, must be conducted in a *reasonable* manner and for only a *reasonable* length of time.

## INTENTIONAL INFLICTION OF EMOTIONAL DISTRESS

The tort of *intentional infliction of emotional distress* can be defined as an intentional act that amounts to extreme and outrageous conduct resulting in severe emotional distress to another.[2] For example, a prankster telephones an individual and says that the individual's spouse has just been in a horrible accident. As a result, the individual suffers intense mental pain or anxiety. The caller's behavior is deemed to be extreme and outrageous conduct that exceeds the bounds of decency accepted by society and is therefore **actionable** (capable of serving as the ground for a lawsuit).

As the intentional infliction of emotional distress is a relatively new tort, it poses some problems. One major problem is that emotional distress claims must be subject to some limitation, or they could flood the courts with lawsuits. A society in which individuals are rewarded if they are unable to endure the normal emotional stresses of day-to-day living is obviously undesirable. Therefore, the law usually focuses on the nature of the acts that come under this tort. Indignity or annoyance alone is usually not enough to support a lawsuit based on intentional infliction of emotional distress.

Many times, however, repeated annoyances, coupled with threats, are enough. In a business context, for example, the repeated use of extreme methods to collect a delinquent account may be actionable. Also, an unusually severe emotional reaction, such as the extreme distress of a woman incorrectly informed that her husband and two sons have been killed, may be actionable. Because it is difficult to prove the existence of emotional suffering, a court may require that the emotional distress be evidenced by some physical symptom or illness or some emotional disturbance that can be documented by a psychiatric consultant or other medical professional.

In recent years, some courts have permitted emotional distress lawsuits for psychic damage if the emotional trauma suffered was sufficiently severe. In some cases, emotional distress actions have

---

2. Restatement (Second) of Torts, Section 46, Comment d. The Restatement (Second) of Torts is a compilation of the law of torts by the American Law Institute.

been allowed to those who suffer emotionally and psychologically just from having witnessed a horrible accident. For example, in 1990, a California court allowed parties to bring an emotional distress lawsuit after they witnessed the traumatic death of a passenger—a total stranger to the plaintiffs—on a Palm Springs tramway car in which the plaintiffs were riding. The accident occurred when a part of

the tramway car broke loose, crashed through the overhead window, and killed the passenger.[3]

In the following case, the court looks at some of the requirements that plaintiffs must meet in establishing an emotional distress claim.

---

3.  *Ballinger v. Palm Springs Aerial Tramway,* 220 Cal.App.3d 581, 269 Cal.Rptr. 583 (Cal.App. 1990).

---

| CASE 6.1 |
| --- |
| **FUDGE v. PENTHOUSE INTERNATIONAL, LTD.** |
| United States Court of Appeals, First Circuit, 1988. 840 F.2d 1012. |

**BACKGROUND AND FACTS**   *Leslie Fudge was a student at the Oakland Beach Elementary School in Warwick, Rhode Island. In the fall of 1985, because of apparent conflicts between some of the school's male and female students, the school's principal decided to segregate the sexes during recess periods. A Providence, Rhode Island, newspaper ran an item on the story, along with a photograph showing Leslie Fudge and other girls giving the thumbs-down sign to show their disapproval of the principal's decision.* Penthouse *magazine eventually printed a one-paragraph story about the girls, along with a slightly cropped version of the photograph that had appeared in the Providence newspaper. The* Penthouse *story was headlined "Little Amazons Attack Boys" and appeared in a section of the magazine entitled "Hard Times: A Compendium of Bizarre, Idiotic, Lurid, and Ofttimes Witless Driblets of Information Culled from the Nation's Press." The brief item told how the Warwick school had segregated the sexes to protect the boys from the girls who "kick them in the shins, pull their hair, and kick them . . . well, in various painful places." The item concluded, "In the battle of the sexes, we'd certainly score this round for the girls." Four of the girls in the picture and their parents brought an action against the owners of* Penthouse *magazine, Penthouse International, Ltd., alleging, among other things, that the publication of the photograph of the girls in a sexually explicit men's magazine constituted the intentional infliction of emotional distress. Penthouse moved for summary judgment, which the district court granted. The plaintiffs—the girls and their parents—appealed.*

*COFFIN, Circuit Judge.*
\*   \*   \*   \*

The Rhode Island Supreme Court, in developing the law governing claims for intentional infliction of emotional distress, has relied heavily on the principles stated in Restatement (Second) of Torts section 46 (1964) and the comments thereto. We assume, therefore, that Rhode Island would follow the rule stated in comment h to that section:

> It is for the court to determine, in the first instance, whether the defendant's conduct may reasonably be regarded as so extreme and outrageous as to permit recovery \*   \*   \*. Where reasonable men [or women] may differ, it is for the jury, subject to the control of the court, to determine whether, in the particular case, the conduct has been sufficiently extreme and outrageous to result in liability.

\*   \*   \*

The "extreme and outrageous" standard is a difficult one to meet. "Liability has been found only where the conduct has been so outrageous in character, and so extreme in degree, as to go beyond all possible bounds of decency, and to be regarded as atrocious, and utterly intolerable in a civilized community." \*   \*   \*

Accepting as true all of the factual allegations of plaintiffs' complaint, we conclude that those facts do not allege conduct that is sufficiently extreme and outrageous to warrant the imposition of liability. The essence of plaintiffs' complaint is that the mere publication of a photograph of the girls in a sexually explicit magazine was extreme and outrageous. There is nothing false, misleading, suggestive, or inherently offensive or shocking about the photograph itself; plaintiffs merely object to the material that appeared in the neighboring pages. Magazines such as *Penthouse* are sufficiently a part of the contemporary scene that their reprinting of relatively innocuous news items or photographs that have already appeared in other media simply cannot be characterized as exceeding all possible bounds of decency, atrocious, or utterly intolerable in a civilized society.

**DECISION AND REMEDY**

*The appellate court agreed with the district court that the plaintiffs failed to state an emotional distress claim. The decision to grant Penthouse's motion for summary judgment against the plaintiffs was affirmed.*

**INTERNATIONAL CONSIDERATIONS**

**Emotional Distress Damages in New Zealand** *An interesting case arose in New Zealand when a horror film set in a cemetery displayed a tombstone, and relatives of the deceased sued for the intentional infliction of emotional distress. The Wellington High Court rejected this claim, holding that severe emotional distress was insufficient and the plaintiff had to show more than transient physical effects to recover.*[a]

a. *Bradley v. Wingnut Films, Ltd.,* 1 N.Z.L.R. 415 (1992).

## DEFAMATION

As discussed in Chapter 5, the freedom of speech guaranteed by the First Amendment is not absolute. In interpreting the First Amendment, the courts must balance the vital guarantee of free speech against another pervasive and strong social interest—preventing and redressing attacks on reputation. When one wrongfully hurts another's good reputation, the tort of **defamation** results.

Tort law has imposed a general duty on all persons to refrain from making false, defamatory statements about others. Breaching this duty orally involves the tort of *slander;* breaching it in writing or in any form of communication that has "the potentially harmful qualities characteristic of written or printed words"[4] involves the tort of *libel.* Courts have held that the forms of libelous communication include pictures, signs, statues, and films. (The tort of defamation also arises when a false statement is made about a person's product, business, or title to property. These torts are dealt with in the following chapter.)

The common law defines four types of false utterances that are considered torts *per se* (in themselves), meaning that no proof of damages is required before these false utterances become actionable:

1. *A statement that another has a loathsome communicable disease.* Courts have generally limited this tort to imputations that an individual has a venereal disease—although a statement that a person had AIDS has been held to be slanderous *per se.*[5]

2. *A statement that another has committed improprieties while engaging in a profession or trade.* For example, it is actionable to say of an attorney that he or she is unethical, of a merchant that his or her credit is bad, or of a person holding public office that he or she has accepted a bribe.[6] But statements alleging that

5. See *McCune v. Neitzel,* 235 Neb. 754, 457 N.W.2d 803 (1990).

6. Stating in a book review that a journalist's work is "sloppy," however, is not a ground for a defamation suit if the statement is a supportable interpretation of the journalist's work. See *Moldea v. New York Times Co.,* 22 F.3d 310 (D.C. Cir. 1994).

4. Restatement (Second) of Torts, Section 568.

a clerk has consorted with prostitutes or is a homosexual, that a physician has committed adultery, or that a stenographer's credit is bad have not been held to be actionable—because the clerk, the physician, and the stenographer may still be competent at their work.

3. *A statement that another has committed or has been imprisoned for a serious crime.* Courts generally agree that the crime referred to in the statement must involve "moral turpitude," which has been defined as "inherent baseness or vileness of principle in the human heart." Beating children, for example, involves moral turpitude, while other forms of battery may not.

4. *A statement that an unmarried woman is unchaste.*

**THE PUBLICATION REQUIREMENT**   The basis of the tort of defamation is the *publication* of a statement or statements that hold an individual up to contempt, ridicule, or hatred. *Publication* here means that the defamatory statements are com-municated to third parties (persons other than the defamed party). If Thompson writes Andrews a private letter accusing him of embezzling funds, the action does not constitute libel. If Peters calls Gelden dishonest, unattractive, and incompetent when no one else is around, the action does not constitute slander. In neither case was the message communicated to a third party. The courts have generally held that even dictating a letter to a sec-retary constitutes publication, although the publi-cation may be *privileged* (as explained in the following section). Moreover, if a third party over-hears defamatory statements by chance, the courts usually hold that this also constitutes publication. Note further that any individual who republishes or repeats defamatory statements is liable, even if that person reveals the source of such statements.

In the following case, an employer asserted that statements made about one employee's alleged wrongdoing to other employees of the same firm did not constitute publication to "third parties," and therefore the employer could not be liable for defamation.

---

**CASE 6.2**

**STAPLES v. BANGOR HYDRO-ELECTRIC CO.**

Supreme Judicial Court of Maine, 1993.
629 A.2d 601.

**BACKGROUND AND FACTS**   *Richard Staples was employed as a microcomputer specialist for Bangor Hydro-Electric Company. Avery Caldwell was the director of Staples's department. In February 1986, Staples expressed to Bangor Hydro's vice president and general counsel his dissatisfaction with the way Caldwell managed the department. Staples was told to put his concerns in writing, so he circulated to several employees an unsigned memo regarding the operation of the department. When Caldwell learned of the memo and that Staples had written it, their relationship deteriorated quickly. In April, Caldwell demoted Staples. In May, Caldwell became convinced that computer files had been erased and that Staples was responsible. Caldwell discussed this with a number of Bangor Hydro employees, including computer operators, administrative staff members, the director of personnel, and the vice president. Staples was discharged, and he brought an action for defamation, among other things. The trial court held for Staples, and Bangor Hydro appealed.*

*ROBERTS, Justice.*
　　　*　*　*　*

Bangor Hydro * * * contends that statements among its own employees cannot be considered a publication to a third party * * * . [W]e disagree. * * *

We recognize that a substantial number of jurisdictions follow the reasoning * * * that a corporation acting through one of its agents [employees or others working on behalf of the corporation] to send a defamatory communication to another of its agents is simply communicating with itself. We think the better reasoning, however, is * * * that damage to one's reputation within the corporate community may be as devastating as that outside * * * .

*The Supreme Judicial Court of Maine affirmed the lower court's judgment in Staples's favor.*

**DECISION AND REMEDY**

**DEFENSES TO DEFAMATION**   Truth is normally an *absolute* defense against a defamation charge. But the statement at issue must be true in whole, not in part, and if the statement is specific, the truth must also be specific. For instance, if the accusation is that Tony stole a stereo from Sara, it is insufficient to show that Tony is known as a bad character or that Tony stole stereos from Ruth. In contrast, if the statement is substantially true, it is not necessary to prove every detail. For example, saying a politician has wasted $80,000 of the taxpayers' money has been held justified when it was proved that he only wasted $17,500.

Other defenses to defamation may exist if the speech concerns a public figure or if the speech is privileged.

*Public Figures.*   **Public figures** include public officials and employees who exercise substantial governmental power, and generally any persons in the public limelight. Statements made about public figures, especially when they are made via a public medium, are usually related to matters of general public interest; they are made about people who substantially affect all of us. Furthermore, public figures generally have some access to a public medium for answering disparaging falsehoods about themselves; private individuals do not. For these reasons, public figures have a greater burden of proof in defamation cases than do private individuals. In *New York Times Co. v. Sullivan,* the United States Supreme Court held that to recover damages, a public figure must prove that a defamatory statement was made with **actual malice**— that is, *with either knowledge of its falsity or a reckless disregard of the truth.*[7]

*Privileged Speech.*   In some circumstances, a person will not be liable for defamatory statements because he or she enjoys a **privilege,** or immunity. Privileged communications are of two types: *absolute* and *qualified.* Only in limited cases, such as in judicial proceedings and legislative proceedings, is absolute privilege granted. For example,

statements made by attorneys and judges during a trial are absolutely privileged and therefore cannot be the basis for a defamation charge. Members of Congress making statements on the floor of Congress have an absolute privilege. Legislators have complete immunity from liability for false statements made in debate, even if they make such statements maliciously—that is, knowing them to be untrue. This absolute immunity is granted because judicial and legislative personnel deal with matters that are so much in the public interest that the parties involved should be able to speak out fully and freely and without restriction.

In other situations, a person will not be liable for defamatory statements because he or she has a *qualified* privilege. Qualified, or conditional, privilege is a common law concept based on the philosophy that the right to know or speak is of equal importance with the right not to be defamed. For example, a qualified privilege exists when there is a common interest between the person who makes the statement and the one who receives it. Thus, a statement concerning corporate business made by one corporate director to another is qualifiedly, or conditionally, privileged. If a communication is conditionally privileged, to recover damages, the plaintiff must show that the privilege was abused.

Another example of a qualified privilege is found in letters of recommendation and in written evaluations of employees. This privilege allows some latitude for making mistakes in the communication without defamation liability. Generally, if the communicated statements are made in good faith and the publication is limited to those who have a legitimate interest in the communication, the statements fall within the area of qualified privilege.

## INVASION OF THE RIGHT TO PRIVACY

A person has a right to solitude and freedom from prying public eyes—in other words, to privacy. Invasion of that privacy may constitute a tort. Four acts qualify as an invasion of privacy:

1.  *The use of a person's name, picture, or other likeness for commercial purposes without*

---

7.  *New York Times Co. v. Sullivan,* 376 U.S. 254, 84 S.Ct. 710, 11 L.Ed.2d 686 (1964).

*permission.* For example, using without permission someone's picture to advertise a product or someone's name to enhance a company name invades the person's privacy.

2. *Intrusion on an individual's affairs or seclusion.* For example, invading someone's home or illegally searching someone's briefcase is an invasion of privacy. This tort has been held to extend to eavesdropping by wiretap, unauthorized scanning of a bank account, compulsory blood testing, and window peeping.

3. *Publication of information that places a person in a false light.* This could be a story attributing to a person ideas not held or actions not taken by that person. (The publication of such a story could involve the tort of defamation as well.)

4. *Public disclosure of private facts about an individual that an ordinary person would find objectionable.* A newspaper account of a private citizen's sex life could be an actionable invasion of privacy. An example of what would *not* constitute this form of invasion of privacy is an article publicizing what a one-time child star is doing today, as long as nothing is revealed that the community would regard as highly objectionable (unless the objectionable information is truthful and contained in official records that are open to public inspection).

### FRAUDULENT MISREPRESENTATION

The tort of *fraudulent misrepresentation,* or **fraud,** involves the use of misrepresentation and deceit for personal gain. It includes several elements:

1. Misrepresentation of material facts or conditions with knowledge that they are false or with reckless disregard for the truth.
2. Intent to induce another to rely on the misrepresentation.
3. Justifiable reliance by the deceived party.
4. Damages suffered as a result of reliance.
5. Causal connection between the misrepresentation and the injury suffered.

A misrepresentation leads another to believe in a condition that is different from the one that actually exists. This is often accomplished through a false or an incorrect statement. Misrepresentations may be innocently made by someone who is unaware of the existing facts, but a misrepresentation

is fraudulent when it is made by a person who knows the facts to be false and intends to mislead another.

For fraud to occur, more than mere **puffery,** or *seller's talk,* must be involved. Fraud exists only when a person represents as a fact something he or she knows is untrue. For example, it is fraud to claim that the roof of a building does not leak when one knows it does. Facts are objectively ascertainable, whereas seller's talk is not. ''I am the best lawyer in town'' is seller's talk. The speaker is not trying to represent something as fact, because the term *best* is a subjective, not an objective, term.

Normally, the tort of fraudulent misrepresentation only occurs when there is reliance upon a *statement of fact.* Sometimes, however, reliance on a *statement of opinion* may involve the tort of fraudulent misrepresentation if the individual making the statement of opinion has a superior knowledge of the subject matter. For example, when a lawyer makes a statement of opinion about the law, a court would construe reliance on such a statement to be equivalent to reliance on a statement of fact. Fraudulent and nonfraudulent misrepresentation will be examined further in Chapter 15, in the context of contract law.

SECTION 3

# INTENTIONAL TORTS AGAINST PROPERTY

Intentional torts against property include (1) trespass to land and (2) trespass to personal property and conversion. Here, the wrong is committed against the individual who has legally recognized rights with regard to land or personal property. The law distinguishes real property from personal property (see Chapter 49). *Real property* is land and things ''permanently'' attached thereto. *Personal property* consists of all other items, which are basically movable. Thus, a house and lot are real property, whereas the furniture inside a house is personal property. Money and securities are also personal property.

### TRESPASS TO LAND

The tort of **trespass to land** occurs any time a person, without permission, enters onto, above, or below the surface of land that is owned by another;

causes anything to enter onto the land; or remains on the land or permits anything to remain on it. Note that actual harm to the land is not an essential element of this tort, because the tort is designed to protect the right of an owner to exclusive possession. Common types of trespass to land include walking or driving on the land; shooting a gun over the land; throwing rocks or spraying water on a building that belongs to someone else; building a dam across a river, thus causing water to back up on someone else's land; and placing part of one's building on an adjoining landowner's property.

In the past, the right to land gave exclusive possession of a space that extended from ''the center of the earth to the heavens,'' but this rule has been relaxed. Today, reasonable intrusions are permitted. Thus, aircraft can normally fly over privately owned land. The temporary invasion of the airspace over such land is, in effect, considered privileged as to the aircraft owner. Society's interest in air transportation preempts the individual's interest in the airspace.

Before a person can be a trespasser, the real property owner (or other person in actual and exclusive possession of the property) must establish that person as a trespasser. For example, ''posted'' trespass signs expressly establish as a trespasser a person who ignores these signs and enters onto the property. A guest in your home is not a trespasser—unless he or she has been asked to leave but refuses. Any person who enters onto your property to commit an illegal act (such as a thief entering a lumberyard at night to steal lumber) is established impliedly as a trespasser, without posted signs.

At common law, a trespasser is liable for damages caused to the property and generally cannot hold the owner liable for injuries that the trespasser sustained on the premises. This common law rule is being abandoned in many jurisdictions in favor of a ''reasonable duty'' rule that varies depending on the status of the parties; for example, a landowner may have a duty to post a notice that the property is patrolled by guard dogs. Also, under the ''attractive nuisance'' doctrine, young children do not assume the risks of the premises if they are attracted to the premises by some object, such as a swimming pool or an abandoned building. An owner can remove a trespasser from the premises through the use of reasonable force without being liable for assault and battery.

Trespass to land involves wrongful interference with another person's real property rights. But if it can be shown that the trespass was warranted, as when a trespasser enters to assist someone in danger, a defense exists. Another defense is to show that the purported owner did not actually have the right to possess the land in question.

## TRESPASS TO PERSONAL PROPERTY

Whenever any individual unlawfully harms the personal property of another or otherwise interferes with the personal property owner's right to exclusive possession and enjoyment of that property, **trespass to personal property**—also called *trespass to personalty*—occurs. Trespass to personal property involves intentional meddling. If a student takes another student's business law book as a practical joke and hides it so that the owner is unable to find it for several days prior to a final examination, the first student has engaged in a trespass to personal property.

If it can be shown that trespass to personal property was warranted, then a complete defense exists. Most states, for example, allow automobile repair shops to hold a customer's car (under what is called an *artisan's lien,* discussed in Chapter 32) when the customer refuses to pay for repairs already completed.

## CONVERSION

**Conversion** is defined as any act that deprives an owner of personal property without that owner's permission and without just cause and that places the property in the service of the trespasser or other person. Conversion is the civil side of crimes related to theft. A store clerk who steals merchandise from the store commits a crime and engages in the tort of conversion at the same time. When conversion occurs, the lesser offense of trespass to personal property usually occurs as well. If the initial taking of the property was unlawful, there is trespass; retention of that property is conversion. If the initial taking of the property was permitted by the owner or for some other reason is not a trespass, failure to return it may still be conversion.

Even if a person mistakenly believed that he or she was entitled to the goods, a tort of conversion may still occur. In other words, good intentions are not a defense against conversion; in fact, conversion can be an entirely innocent act. Someone who buys stolen goods, for example, is guilty of conversion even if he or she did not know the goods were stolen.

## ■ CONCEPT SUMMARY 6.1 **Intentional Torts**

| CATEGORY | NAME OF TORT |
|---|---|
| **Intentional Torts against Persons** | 1. *Assault and battery*—An unexcused and intentional act that causes another person to be apprehensive of immediate harm is assault. Assault resulting in physical contact is battery.<br>2. *False imprisonment*—Intentional confinement or restraint of another person's movement without justification.<br>3. *Infliction of emotional distress*—An intentional act that amounts to extreme and outrageous conduct resulting in severe emotional distress to another.<br>4. *Defamation (libel or slander)*—A false statement of fact, not made under privilege, that is communicated to a third person and that causes damage to a person's reputation. For public figures, the plaintiff must also prove malice.<br>5. *Invasion of the right to privacy*—Use of a person's name or likeness for commercial purposes without permission, wrongful intrusion into a person's private activities, publication of information that places a person in a false light, or disclosure of private facts that an ordinary person would find objectionable.<br>6. *Fraudulent misrepresentation (deceit)*—A false representation made by one party, through misstatement of facts or through conduct with the intention of deceiving another and on which the other reasonably relies to his or her detriment. |
| **Intentional Torts against Property** | 1. *Trespass to land*—Invasion of another's real property without consent or privilege. Specific rights and duties apply once a person is expressly or impliedly established as a trespasser.<br>2. *Trespass to personal property*—Unlawfully damaging or interfering with the owner's right to use, possess, or enjoy his or her personal property.<br>3. *Conversion*—A wrongful act in which personal property is taken from its rightful owner or possessor and placed in the service of another. |

A successful defense against the charge of conversion is that the purported owner does not in fact own the property or does not have a right to possess it that is superior to the right of the holder. Necessity is another possible defense against conversion. If Abrams takes Mendoza's cat, Abrams is guilty of conversion. If Mendoza sues Abrams, Abrams must return the cat or pay damages. If, however, the cat has rabies and Abrams took the cat to protect the public, Abrams has a valid defense—necessity (and perhaps even self-defense, if he can prove that he was in danger because of the cat).

## ■ SECTION 4

# NEGLIGENCE

In contrast to intentional torts, in torts involving **negligence,** the tortfeasor neither wishes to bring about the consequences of the act nor believes that they will occur. The actor's conduct merely creates a *risk* of such consequences. If no risk is created, there is no negligence. Moreover, the risk must be foreseeable; that is, it must be such that a reasonable person engaging in the same activity would anticipate the risk and guard against it. In determining what is reasonable conduct, courts consider the nature of the possible harm. A very slight risk of a dangerous explosion might be unreasonable, whereas a distinct possibility of burning one's fingers on a stove might be reasonable.

The tort of negligence occurs when someone suffers injury because of another's failure to live up to a required *duty of care*. In examining a question of negligence, one should ask four questions:

1. Did the defendant owe a duty of care to the plaintiff?
2. Did the defendant breach that duty?
3. Did the defendant's breach cause the plaintiff's injury?

4. Did the plaintiff suffer a legally recognizable injury as a result of the defendant's breach of the duty of care?

Each of these elements of neligence is discussed below.

## THE DUTY OF CARE AND ITS BREACH

The concept of a **duty of care** arises from the notion that if we are to live in society with other people, some actions can be tolerated and some cannot; some actions are right and some are wrong; and some actions are reasonable and some are not. The basic principle underlying the duty of care is that people are free to act as they please so long as their actions do not infringe on the interests of others.

When someone fails to comply with the duty of exercising reasonable care, a potentially tortious act may have been committed. Failure to live up to a standard of care may be an act (the improper storage of gasoline resulting in a fire) or an omission (failure to warn of a fire hazard). It may be an intentional act, a careless act, or a carefully performed but nevertheless dangerous act that results in injury. Courts consider the nature of the act (whether it is outrageous or commonplace), the manner in which the act is performed (cautiously versus heedlessly), and the nature of the injury (whether it is serious or slight) in determining whether the duty of care has been breached.

**THE REASONABLE PERSON STANDARD**    Tort law measures duty by the **reasonable person standard.** In determining whether a duty of care has been breached, the courts ask how a reasonable person would have acted in the same circumstances. The reasonable person standard is said to be (though in an absolute sense it cannot be) objective. It is not necessarily how a particular person would act. It is society's judgment on how people should act. If the so-called reasonable person existed, he or she would be careful, conscientious, even tempered, and honest. This hypothetical "reasonable person" is frequently used by the courts in decisions relating to other areas of law as well.

That individuals are required to exercise a reasonable standard of care in their activities is a pervasive concept in business law, and many of the issues dealt with in subsequent chapters of this text have to do with this duty. A court will decide what constitutes reasonable care based on the circumstances of the case.

**DUTY OF LANDOWNERS**    Landowners are expected to exercise reasonable care to protect from harm individuals coming onto their property . As mentioned earlier, in some jurisdictions, landowners are held to owe a duty to protect even trespassers against certain risks. Landowners who rent or lease premises to tenants are expected to exercise reasonable care to ensure that the tenants and their guests are not harmed in common areas, such as stairways, entryways, laundry rooms, and the like (see Chapter 52).

Retailers and other firms that explicitly or implicitly invite persons to come onto their premises are usually charged with a duty to exercise reasonable care to protect these **business invitees.** For example, if you entered a supermarket, slipped on a wet floor, and sustained injuries as a result, the owner of the supermarket would be liable for damages if, when you slipped, there was no sign warning that the floor was wet. A court would hold that the business owner was negligent because the owner failed to exercise a reasonable degree of care in protecting the store's customers against foreseeable risks that the owner knew or *should have known* about. That a patron might slip on the wet floor and be injured as a result was a foreseeable risk, and the owner should have taken care to avoid this risk or warn the customer of it.[8]

Some risks, of course, are so obvious that an owner need not warn of them. For example, a business owner does not need to warn customers to open a door before attempting to walk through it. But other risks, even though they may seem obvious to a business owner, may not be so in the eyes of another, such as a child. For example, a hardware store owner may not think it is necessary to warn customers that, if pulled, a stepladder leaning against the back wall of the store could fall down and harm them. Yet it is possible that a child could tip the ladder over and be hurt as a result and that the store could be held liable.

In the following case, the court has to decide whether a restaurant owner should be held liable for a customer's injuries on the premises.

---

8.    A business owner can warn of a risk by placing a sign, traffic cone, sawhorse, board, or any number of other things near, for example, a hole at the bottom of which is a water meter cover. See *Hartman v. Walkertown Shopping Center, Inc.,* 113 N.C.App. 632, 439 S.E.2d 787 (1994).

CASE 6.3

**BRAY v. KATE**

Supreme Court of Nebraska,
1990.
235 Neb. 315,
454 N.W.2d 698.

**BACKGROUND AND FACTS**   *Lowell Bray was about to open the door of a restaurant owned by Kate, Inc., when he slipped on some ice and fell, injuring his shoulder. He stated that he could not see the ice but felt it when he slipped. Bray sued Kate, Inc., for damages, alleging that Kate, Inc., by failing to remove the ice from in front of its restaurant door, had breached its duty of care to Bray and was thus negligent. The trial court held for Bray, and Kate, Inc., appealed.*

WHITE, Justice.
  *   *   *   *

  Summarized, defendant [Kate, Inc.] contends on appeal that the trial court erred *   *   * because the evidence showed that, as a matter of law, defendant owed no duty to plaintiff. *   *   *

  In its brief, defendant urges this court to adopt a possessor's duty of care other than the duty which is now required under Nebraska law. We decline to do so. *   *   *

  In view of this court's decisions [in previous cases], the correct statement of Nebraska law is: A possessor of land is subject to liability for injury caused to a business invitee by a condition on the land if (1) the possessor defendant either created the condition, knew of the condition, or by the exercise of reasonable care would have discovered the condition; (2) the defendant should have realized the condition involved an unreasonable risk of harm to a business invitee; (3) the defendant should have expected that a business invitee such as the plaintiff, either (a) would not discover or realize the danger, or (b) would fail to protect himself or herself against the danger; (4) the defendant failed to use reasonable care to protect the plaintiff invitee against the danger; and (5) the condition was a proximate cause of damage to the plaintiff.
  *   *   *   *

  As to the existence of a duty to the invitee *   *   * , a clear factual issue was presented and resolved by the jury verdict.

**DECISION AND REMEDY**   *The Supreme Court of Nebraska affirmed the lower court's judgment for Bray. Kate, Inc., owed a duty to its patron, Bray, and because it had breached that duty, was liable to Bray for damages.*

**ETHICAL CONSIDERATIONS**   *It is not uncommon for a court to hold a business owner liable when a customer is harmed by what may seem to be an obvious risk. To a certain extent, such decisions rest on the public policy that business owners are in a better position both to protect against the risks and to bear the costs associated with customers' injuries. Many, however, question whether it is fair to hold businesspersons responsible in these situations. (See the* Question of Ethics *at the end of this chapter for a further inquiry into this issue.)*

**DUTY OF PROFESSIONALS**   If an individual has knowledge, skill, or intelligence superior to that of an ordinary person, the individual's conduct must be consistent with that status. Professionals—including doctors, dentists, psychiatrists, architects, engineers, accountants, lawyers, and others—are required to have a standard minimum level of special knowledge and ability. Therefore, in determining what constitutes reasonable care in the case of professionals, their training and expertise is taken into account. In other words, an accountant cannot defend against a lawsuit for negligence by stating, "But I was not familiar with that principle of accounting."

  If a professional violates his or her duty of care toward a client, the professional may be sued for

**malpractice.** For example, a patient might sue a physician for *medical malpractice*. A client might sue an attorney for *legal malpractice*. The liability of professionals will be examined further in Chapter 55.

**NO DUTY TO RESCUE** Although the law requires individuals to act reasonably and responsibly in their relations with others, if a person fails to come to the aid of a stranger in peril, that person will not be considered negligent under tort law. For example, assume that you are walking down a city street and notice that a pedestrian is about to step directly in front of an oncoming bus. You realize that the person has not seen the bus and is unaware of the danger. Do you have a legal duty to warn that individual? No. Although most people would probably concede that in this situation, the observer has an *ethical* duty to warn the other, tort law does not impose a general duty to rescue others in peril. Duties may be imposed in regard to certain types of perils, however. For example, most states require a motorist involved in an automobile accident to stop and render aid. Failure to do so is both a tort and a crime.

When discussing the distinction between legal and ethical duties in Chapter 2, we pointed out that ethical duties exist beyond the scope of the law. In regard to the duty to rescue, the distinction is clearly evident. Although the law might not require a passerby to save a drowning toddler in a wading pool, society expects that people will aid others who are in danger and cannot help themselves.

## CAUSATION

Another element necessary to a tort is *causation.* If a person fails in a duty of care and someone suffers injury, the wrongful activity must have caused the harm for a tort to have been committed.

**CAUSATION IN FACT AND PROXIMATE CAUSE** In deciding whether there is causation, the court must address two questions:

1. Is there **causation in fact?** Did the injury occur because of the defendant's act, or would it have occurred anyway? If an injury would not have occurred without the defendant's act, then there is causation in fact. Causation in fact can usually be determined by the use of the *but for* test: "but for" the wrongful act, the injury would not have occurred.

2. Was the act the **proximate cause** of the injury? How far should a defendant's liability extend for a wrongful act that was a substantial factor in causing injury? For example: Ackerman carelessly leaves a campfire burning. The fire not only burns down the forest but also sets off an explosion in a nearby chemical plant that spills chemicals into a river, killing all the fish for a hundred miles downstream and ruining the economy of a tourist resort. Should Ackerman be liable to the resort owners? To the tourists whose vacations were ruined? These are questions of proximate cause (sometimes called legal cause). Proximate cause is not a question of fact but a question of law and policy. The question is whether the connection between an act and an injury is strong enough to justify imposing liability.

Probably the most cited case on proximate cause is the *Palsgraf* case. The question before the court was as follows: Does the defendant's duty of care extend only to those who may be injured as a result of a foreseeable risk, or does it extend also to a person whose injury could not reasonably be foreseen?

**BACKGROUND AND FACTS** *The plaintiff, Palsgraf, was waiting for a train on a station platform. A man carrying a package was rushing to catch a train that was moving away from a platform across the tracks from Palsgraf. As the man attempted to jump aboard the moving train, he seemed unsteady and about to fall. A railroad guard on the car reached forward to grab him, and another guard on the platform pushed him from behind to help him board the train. In the process, the man's package fell on the railroad tracks and exploded, because it contained fireworks. There was nothing about the package to indicate its contents. The repercussions of the explosion caused scales at the other end of the train platform to fall on Palsgraf, causing injuries for which she sued the railroad company. At*

| CASE 6.4 |
| --- |

**PALSGRAF v. LONG ISLAND RAILROAD CO.**

Court of Appeals of New York, 1928.

248 N.Y. 339,
162 N.E. 99.

*the trial, the jury found that the railroad guards were negligent in their conduct. The railroad company appealed. The appellate court affirmed the trial court's judgment, and the railroad company appealed to New York's highest state court.*

*CARDOZO*, C. J. [Chief Justice].
\* \* \* \*

The conduct of the defendant's guard, if a wrong in its relation to the holder of the package, was not a wrong in its relation to the plaintiff, standing far away. Relatively to her it was not negligence at all. \* \* \*
\* \* \* \*

\* \* \* What the plaintiff must show is ''a wrong'' to herself; i.e., a violation of her own right, and not merely a wrong to someone else, nor conduct ''wrongful'' because unsocial, but not ''a wrong'' to any one. \* \* \* The risk reasonably to be perceived defines the duty to be obeyed[.] \* \* \* Here, by concession, there was nothing in the situation to suggest to the most cautious mind that the parcel wrapped in newspaper would spread wreckage through the station. If the guard had thrown it down knowingly and willfully, he would not have threatened the plaintiff's safety, so far as appearances could warn him. His conduct would not have involved, even then, an unreasonable probability of invasion of her bodily security. Liability can be no greater where the act is inadvertent.

\* \* \* One who seeks redress at law does not make out a cause of action by showing without more that there has been damage to his person. If the harm was not willful, he must show that the act as to him had possibilities of danger so many and apparent as to entitle him to be protected against the doing of it though the harm was unintended. \* \* \* The victim does not sue derivatively \* \* \* to vindicate an interest invaded in the person of another. \* \* \* He sues for breach of a duty owing to himself.

\* \* \* [To rule otherwise] would entail liability for any and all consequences, however novel or extraordinary.

**DECISION AND REMEDY**

*Palsgraf's complaint was dismissed. The railroad was not negligent toward her, because injury to her was not foreseeable. Had the owner of the fireworks been harmed, there could well have been a different result if he had filed suit.*

**INTERNATIONAL CONSIDERATIONS**

**Differing Standards of Proximate Cause** *The concept of proximate cause is common among countries of the globe, but its application differs from country to country. French law uses the phrase ''adequate cause.'' An event breaks the chain of adequate cause if the event is both unforeseeable and irresistible. England has a ''nearest cause'' rule that attributes liability based on which event was nearest in time and space. Mexico bases proximate cause on the foreseeability of the harm but does not require that an event be reasonably foreseeable.*

**FORESEEABILITY** Since the *Palsgraf* case, the courts have used *foreseeability* as the test for proximate cause. The railroad guards were negligent, but the railroad's duty of care did not extend to Palsgraf, because she was an unforeseeable plaintiff. If the consequences of the harm done or the victim of the harm is unforeseeable, there is no proximate cause. Of course, it is foreseeable that people will stand on railroad platforms and that objects attached to the platforms will fall as the result of explosions nearby—however, this is not a chain of events against which a reasonable person would usually guard. It is difficult to predict when a court will say that something is foreseeable and when it will say that something is not. How far a court stretches foreseeability is determined in part by the extent to which the court is willing to stretch the defendant's duty of care.

**SUPERSEDING INTERVENING FORCE**  A superseding intervening force may break the connection between a wrongful act and an injury to another. If so, it cancels out the wrongful act. For example, keeping a can of gasoline in the trunk of one's car creates a foreseeable risk and is thus a negligent act. If lightning strikes the car and the car's gas tank *and* the can of gas explode, thereby injuring passing pedestrians, the lightning supersedes the original negligence as a cause of the damage, because it was not foreseeable.

In negligence cases, the negligent party will often attempt to show that some act has intervened after his or her action and that this second act was the proximate cause of injury. Typically, in cases in which an individual takes a defensive action—such as swerving to avoid an oncoming car—the original wrongdoer will not be relieved of liability even if the injury actually resulted from the attempt to escape harm. The same is true under the ''danger invites rescue'' doctrine. Under this doctrine, if Ludlam commits an act that endangers Schwaller, and Yokem sustains an injury trying to protect Schwaller, then Ludlam will be liable for Yokem's injury, as well as for any injuries Schwaller may sustain. Rescuers can injure themselves, or the person rescued, or even a stranger, but the original wrongdoer will still be liable.

## THE INJURY REQUIREMENT AND DAMAGES

For a tort to have been committed, the plaintiff must have suffered a *legally recognizable* injury. To recover damages (receive compensation), the plaintiff must have suffered some loss, harm, wrong, or invasion of a protected interest. Essen-

tially, the purpose of tort law is to compensate for legally recognized injuries resulting from wrongful acts. If no harm or injury results from a given negligent action, there is nothing to compensate—and no tort exists. For example, if you carelessly bump into a passerby, who stumbles and falls as a result, you may be liable in tort if the passerby is injured in the fall. If the person is unharmed, however, there normally could be no suit for damages, because no injury was suffered.

## DEFENSES TO NEGLIGENCE

The basic defenses in negligence cases are (1) assumption of risk, (2) contributory negligence, and (3) comparative negligence.

**ASSUMPTION OF RISK**  A plaintiff who voluntarily enters into a risky situation, knowing the risk involved, will not be allowed to recover. This is the defense of **assumption of risk.** For example, a driver entering an automobile race knows there is a risk of being killed or injured in a crash. The driver has assumed the risk of injury. The requirements of this defense are (1) knowledge of the risk and (2) voluntary assumption of the risk.

The risk can be assumed by express agreement, or the assumption of risk can be implied by the plaintiff's knowledge of the risk and subsequent conduct. Of course, the plaintiff does not assume a risk different from or greater than the risk normally carried by the activity. In our example, the race driver assumes the risk of being injured in the race but not the risk that the banking in the curves of the racetrack will give way during the race because of a construction defect.

Risks are not deemed to be assumed in situations involving emergencies. Neither are they assumed when a statute protects a class of people from harm and a member of the class is injured by the harm. For example, courts have generally held that an employee cannot assume the risk of an employer's violation of safety statutes passed for the benefit of employees.

In the following case, the defendant successfully asserted the defense of assumption of risk in defending against a lawsuit for negligence.

**CASE 6.5**

**SCHROYER v. McNEAL**
Court of Appeals of Maryland,
1991.
323 Md. 275,
592 A.2d 1119.

**COMPANY PROFILE**  *In 1952, Kemmons Wilson opened the first Holiday Inn (named after the hotel in the movie* Holiday Inn, *in which Bing Crosby sang ''White Christmas''). Within a year, there were four identical Holiday Inns in Memphis, and in 1954, Wilson decided to franchise. Known as Holiday Inns of America, the franchisor became the world leader in its market. In the 1980s, the company changed its name to Holiday Corporation and diversified its tourist accommodations by opening Embassy Suites, Homewood Suites, and Hampton Inns. Fighting a takeover attempt by Donald Trump, Holiday Corporation borrowed money from Bass PLC (Great Britain's leading brewer), which eventually bought the North American Holiday Inns (then numbering 1,400) from Holiday Corporation in 1990.*

**BACKGROUND AND FACTS**  *Shortly after checking in at a Holiday Inn in Maryland, Frances McNeal slipped and fell on some ice in the hotel parking area. McNeal had requested a room near an entrance because she had a great deal of luggage. To accommodate McNeal's request, she was given a room near the west entrance, in spite of the hotel's policy of not assigning rooms near that entrance in inclement weather. Also contrary to policy, McNeal was not advised that she should not use the west entrance, and no warnings were posted by that door. McNeal noticed that the parking lot and the sidewalk by the west entrance were covered with snow and ice and were slippery. She made one trip into the hotel without mishap, walking carefully because of the hazardous conditions, but she fell on the second trip. McNeal sustained a broken ankle in the incident and subsequently sued Thomas and Patricia Schroyer, the hotel owners, for negligence. McNeal alleged that the Schroyers had failed to maintain the parking lot, to warn guests of the slippery conditions, and to post warning signs. The jury found in McNeal's favor, and the Schroyers appealed. The appellate court affirmed the trial court's judgment, and the case was appealed to Maryland's highest court.*

*ROBERT M. BELL, Judge.*

     *    *    *    *

     *    *    * ''The defense of assumption of risk rests upon the plaintiff's consent to relieve the defendant of an obligation of conduct toward him, and to take his chances of harm from a particular risk. Such consent may be found: *    *    * by implication from the conduct of the parties. When the plaintiff enters voluntarily into a relation or situation involving obvious danger, he may be taken to assume the risk, and to relieve the defendant of responsibility. Such implied assumption of risk requires knowledge and appreciation of the risk, and a voluntary choice to encounter it.''
*    *    *

     *    *    *    *

     *    *    * The record reflects *    *    * that McNeal was fully aware of the dangerous condition of the premises. She knew that the area was ice and snow covered and that the ice and snow were slippery. Nevertheless, she parked in the area and, notwithstanding, according to her testimony, that she proceeded carefully, she took a chance and walked over the ice and snow covered parking lot and sidewalk because she did not think it was ''that'' slippery. It is clear, on this record, that McNeal took an informed chance. *    *    * [I]t cannot be gainsaid [denied] that she intentionally exposed herself to a known risk. With full knowledge that the parking lot and sidewalk were ice and snow covered and aware that the ice and snow were slippery, McNeal

voluntarily chose to park on the parking lot and to walk across it and the sidewalk, thus indicating her willingness to accept the risk and relieving the Schroyers of responsibility for her safety.

*The Court of Appeals of Maryland reversed the judgment of the lower court. The court of appeals held that McNeal was fully aware of the risk that she was taking and voluntarily assumed it.*

**DECISION AND REMEDY**

**CONTRIBUTORY NEGLIGENCE** All individuals are expected to exercise a reasonable degree of care in looking out for themselves. In some jurisdictions, a plaintiff cannot recover for an injury resulting from negligence if both parties have been negligent and their negligence has combined to cause the injury. When one party sues the other in tort for damages for negligence, the defendant can claim **contributory negligence,** which is a complete defense under common law rules. (Contributory negligence is not, however, a defense to intentional torts or to suits based on strict liability, a topic that will be covered later.)

In some jurisdictions, the *last clear chance* doctrine can excuse the effect of a plaintiff's contributory negligence. If applicable, the last clear chance rule allows the plaintiff to recover full damages despite failure to exercise care. This rule operates when, through his or her own negligence, the plaintiff is endangered (or his or her property is endangered) by a defendant who has an opportunity to avoid causing damage. For example, if Murphy walks across the street against the light, and Lewis, a motorist, sees her in time to avoid hitting her but hits her anyway, Lewis (the defendant) is not permitted to use Murphy's (the plaintiff's) prior negligence as a defense. The defendant negligently missed the opportunity to avoid injuring the plaintiff.

**COMPARATIVE NEGLIGENCE** Today, in most states, the adoption of the comparative negligence rule has effectively abolished both contributory negligence and last clear chance as defenses to negligence. Instead of allowing contributory negligence to negate a cause of action completely, a majority of states allow recovery based on the doctrine of **comparative negligence.** This doctrine enables both the plaintiff's and the defendant's negligence to be computed and the liability for damages distributed accordingly. Some jurisdictions have adopted a "pure" form of comparative negligence that allows the plaintiff to recover, even if the extent of his or her fault is greater than that of the defendant. For example, if the plaintiff was 80 percent at fault and the defendant was 20 percent at fault, the plaintiff may recover 20 percent of his or her damages. Many states' comparative negligence statutes, however, contain a "50 percent" rule, under which the plaintiff recovers nothing if he or she was more than 50 percent at fault.

## SPECIAL NEGLIGENCE DOCTRINES AND STATUTES

There are a number of special doctrines and statutes relating to negligence that are important. We examine a few of them here.

**RES IPSA LOQUITUR** Generally, in lawsuits involving negligence, the plaintiff has the burden of proving that the defendant was negligent. In certain situations, when negligence is very difficult or impossible to prove, the courts may infer that negligence has occurred, in which case the burden of proof rests on the defendant—to prove he or she was *not* negligent. The inference of the defendant's negligence is known as the doctrine of *res ipsa loquitur,* which translates as "the facts speak for themselves." This doctrine is applied only when the event creating the damage or injury is one that ordinarily does not occur in the absence of negligence.

*Res ipsa loquitur* has been applied to such events as trains derailing, wheels falling off moving vehicles, elevators falling, and bricks or windowpanes falling from a defendant's premises. For the doctrine to apply, the event must have been caused by an agency or instrumentality within the exclusive control of the defendant, and it must not have

## ■ CONCEPT SUMMARY 6.2 Negligence

| Definition | The careless performance of a legally required duty or the failure to perform a legally required act. |
| --- | --- |
| Elements of Negligence | 1. The defendant owed a duty of care to the plaintiff.<br>2. The defendant breached that duty.<br>3. The defendant's breach caused the plaintiff's injury.<br>4. The plaintiff suffered a legally recognizable injury as a result of the defendant's breach of the duty of care. |
| Defenses to Negligence | 1. Assumption of risk.<br>2. Contributory negligence.<br>3. Comparative negligence. |
| Special Negligence Doctrines and Statutes | 1. *Res ipsa loquitur*—A doctrine under which a plaintiff need not prove negligence on the part of the defendant because "the facts speak for themselves." *Res ipsa loquitur* has been applied to such events as trains derailing, wheels falling off moving vehicles, and elevators falling.<br>2. *Negligence* per se—A type of negligence that may occur if a person violates a statute or an ordinance providing for a criminal penalty and the violation causes another to be injured.<br>3. *Special negligence statutes*—State statutes that prescribe duties and responsibilities in certain circumstances. Dram shop acts and Good Samaritan statutes are examples of special negligence statutes. |

been due to any voluntary action or contribution on the part of the plaintiff. Some courts will add still another condition—that the evidence available to explain the event be more accessible to the defendant than to the plaintiff.

**NEGLIGENCE *PER SE*** Certain conduct, whether it consists of an action or a failure to act, may be treated as **negligence *per se*** (''in or of itself''). Negligence *per se* may occur if an individual violates a statute or an ordinance providing for a criminal penalty and that violation causes another to be injured. The injured person must prove (1) that the statute clearly sets out what standard of conduct is expected, when and where it is expected, and of whom it is expected; (2) that he or she is in the class intended to be protected by the statute; and (3) that the statute was designed to prevent the type of injury that he or she suffered. The standard of conduct required by the statute is the duty that the defendant owes to the plaintiff, and a violation of the statute is the breach of that duty.

**SPECIAL NEGLIGENCE STATUTES** A number of states have enacted statutes prescribing duties

and responsibilities in certain circumstances, the violation of which will impose civil liability. For example, many states have passed **dram shop acts.** These acts, or statutes, impose a duty on tavern owners or bartenders not to serve drinks to patrons who are intoxicated or who may become intoxicated. If this duty is breached, liability may be extended to the tavern owner or bartender for injuries caused by a person who became intoxicated while drinking at the bar or who was already intoxicated when served by the bartender. In some states, statutes impose liability on *social hosts* (persons hosting parties) for injuries caused by guests who became intoxicated at the hosts' homes.[9]

Most states now also have what are called **Good Samaritan statutes.** Under these statutes, persons who are aided voluntarily by others cannot

___
9. Under some circumstances, even in the absence of a statute, an employer may be held liable for injuries caused by employees who became intoxicated at a social gathering related to their work. See, for example, *Carroll Air Systems, Inc. v. Greenbaum,* 629 So.2d 914 (Fla.Dist.App. 1993).

turn around and sue the "Good Samaritans" for negligence. These laws were passed largely to protect physicians and medical personnel who voluntarily render their services in emergency situations to those in need, such as individuals hurt in car accidents.

---

## SECTION 5

# STRICT LIABILITY

Another category of torts is called **strict liability,** or *liability without fault.* Intentional torts and torts of negligence involve acts that depart from a reasonable standard of care and cause injuries. Under the doctrine of strict liability, liability for injury is imposed for reasons other than fault.

### THE ORIGINS OF STRICT LIABILITY

The modern concept of strict liability traces its origins, in part, to the English case of *Rylands v. Fletcher* of 1868. In the coal-mining area of Lancashire, England, the Rylands, who were mill owners, had constructed a reservoir on their land. Water from the reservoir broke through a filled-in shaft of an abandoned coal mine nearby and flooded the connecting passageways in an active coal mine owned by Fletcher. Fletcher sued the Rylands, and the court held that the defendants (the Rylands) were liable, even though the circumstances did not fit within existing tort liability theories. In justifying its decision, the court compared the situation to the trespass of dangerous animals: "the true rule of law is, that the person who for his own purposes brings on his land and collects and keeps there anything likely to do mischief if it escapes, must keep it at his peril, and, if he does not do so, is *prima facie* answerable for all the damage which is the natural consequence of its escape."[10]

The Rylands appealed to the House of Lords. The House of Lords had to decide whether one is responsible for the consequences of any extraordinary or dangerous process, even if one is as careful as possible—that is, as careful as "the

reasonable person." The House of Lords affirmed the ruling of the lower reviewing court but limited the ruling to apply only to the "nonnatural" use of the defendants' land.[11] In this case, the emphasis was placed on the abnormal and inappropriate character of a reservoir in coal-mining country, rather than on the mere tendency of water to "escape."

The doctrine that emerged from *Rylands v. Fletcher* was liberally applied by British courts, with some important exceptions. Initially, few U.S. courts accepted the doctrine, presumably because the courts were worried about the doctrine's effect on the expansion of American businesses. Today, however, the doctrine of strict liability is the norm rather than the exception.

### ABNORMALLY DANGEROUS ACTIVITIES

The rule from *Rylands v. Fletcher* can be seen in the strict liability rule for abnormally dangerous activities, which is one application of the strict liability doctrine. Abnormally dangerous activities have three characteristics:

1.  The activity involves potential harm, of a serious nature, to persons or property.
2.  The activity involves a high degree of risk that cannot be completely guarded against by the exercise of reasonable care.
3.  The activity is not commonly performed in the community or area.

Clearly, the primary basis of liability is the creation of an extraordinary risk. For example, even if blasting with dynamite is performed with all reasonable care, there is still a risk of injury. Balancing that risk against the potential for harm, it is fair to ask the person engaged in the activity to pay for injury caused by that activity. Although there is no fault, there is still responsibility because of the dangerous nature of the undertaking. In other words, it is reasonable to require the person engaged in the activity to stand prepared to compensate anyone who suffers as a result of the activity.

The following case illustrates an application of the doctrine of strict liability to an alleged ultrahazardous activity.

---

10.  *Fletcher v. Rylands,* L.R. 1 Ex. 265 (1866).

11.  *Rylands v. Fletcher,* L.R. 3 H.L. 330 (1868).

**CASE 6.6**

**OLD ISLAND FUMIGATION, INC. v. BARBEE**

District Court of Appeal of Florida,
Third District, 1992.
604 So.2d 1246.

**HISTORICAL AND SOCIAL SETTING**  *The early law of torts was not primarily concerned with whether a wrongdoer was at fault. It was concerned primarily with keeping the peace—with providing a remedy in lieu of private vengeance. A person who hurt another by accident, or even in self-defense, was required to pay for the injury or damage. The rule was "he who breaks must pay." Gradually, the law came to recognize fault as the basis for imposing liability, and it was suggested that there should be no liability without fault. In the late nineteenth century, however, the law began to accept that in some cases, a defendant may be liable not only in the absence of fault but even if he or she has followed a standard of reasonable care. In the context of abnormally dangerous activities, the courts recognized a new doctrine: in the event of harm for which no one is at fault, the party who can best bear the loss will be held liable.*

**BACKGROUND AND FACTS**  *Old Island Fumigation, Inc., fumigated buildings A and B of a condominium complex. Residents in buildings A and B were evacuated during the procedure, but occupants of building C were not. Shortly after the fumigation, which involved the use of Vikane gas, several residents of building C became ill and were treated for sulfuryl fluoride poisoning. Sulfuryl fluoride is the active ingredient of Vikane gas. Several months later, an architect discovered that the fire wall between buildings B and C was defective and contained a four-foot-by-eighteen-inch open space, through which the gas had entered building C. The defect was only visible from within the crawl space, and thus it had been missed by various building inspectors, as well as by the fumigating company. Residents of building C sued Old Island, alleging that fumigation was an ultrahazardous activity and that Old Island was therefore strictly liable for their injuries. The company asserted that it should not be responsible for injuries caused by the negligence of others—the original architect and contractors for the condominiums who had failed to note and repair the defect in the fire wall. The trial court granted the plaintiffs' motion for summary judgment against Old Island, and Old Island appealed.*

*PER CURIAM* [by the entire court].
\* \* \* \*

Old Island Fumigation, Inc., is strictly liable for damages caused to the plaintiffs by its fumigation of the condominium complex. Fumigation is an ultrahazardous activity as it "necessarily involves a risk of serious harm \* \* \* which cannot be eliminated by the exercise of the utmost care, and is not a matter of common usage." [F]actors to be considered in determining whether [the] activity is [an] ultrahazardous activity are: whether [the] activity involves [a] high degree of risk of harm to property of others; whether [the] potential harm is likely to be great; whether [the] risk can be eliminated by exercise of reasonable care; whether [the] activity is [a] matter of common usage; whether [the] activity is appropriate to [the] place where [the activity is] conducted; [and] whether [the] activity has substantial value to [the] community. Old Island Fumigation is thus liable regardless of the level of care exercised in carrying out this activity.

Any alleged negligence by a third party does not free the fumigation company from liability.

**DECISION AND REMEDY**  *The appellate court affirmed the trial court's judgment.*

## OTHER APPLICATIONS OF STRICT LIABILITY

Persons who keep wild animals are strictly liable for any harm inflicted by the animals. The basis for applying strict liability is the fact that wild animals, should they escape from confinement, pose a serious risk of harm to persons in the vicinity. An owner of domestic animals (such as dogs, cats, cows, or sheep) may be strictly liable for harms caused by those animals if the owner knew, or should have known, that the animals were dangerous or had a propensity to harm others.

A significant application of strict liability is in the area of *product liability*—liability of manufacturers and sellers for harmful or defective products. Liability here is a matter of social policy and is based on two factors: (1) the manufacturing company can better bear the cost of injury, because it can spread the cost throughout society by increasing prices of goods and services, and (2) the manufacturing company is making a profit from its activities and therefore should bear the cost of injury as an operating expense. Product liability will be discussed in detail in Chapter 25. Strict liability is also applied in certain types of *bailments* (a bailment exists when goods are transferred temporarily into the care of another—see Chapter 50).

## TERMS AND CONCEPTS TO REVIEW

actionable **107**
actual malice **111**
assault **106**
assumption of risk **119**
battery **106**
business invitee **115**
causation in fact **117**
comparative negligence **121**
contributory negligence **121**
conversion **113**
damages **106**
defamation **109**

defense **107**
dram shop act **122**
duty of care **115**
fraud **112**
Good Samaritan statute **123**
intentional tort **106**
malpractice **117**
negligence **114**
negligence *per se* **122**
privilege **111**
proximate cause **117**
public figure **111**

puffery **112**
reasonable person
    standard **115**
*res ipsa loquitur* **121**
strict liability **123**
tort **105**
tortfeasor **106**
trespass to land **112**
trespass to personal
    property **113**

## QUESTIONS AND CASE PROBLEMS

**6–1. Defamation.** Kendro is an employee of the Dun Construction Corp. While delivering materials to a construction site, he carelessly runs Dun's truck into a passenger vehicle driven by Lowenstein. This is Kendro's second accident in six months. When Dun learns of this latest accident, a heated discussion ensues, and Dun fires Kendro. Dun is so angry at Kendro that he immediately writes a letter to the union of which Kendro is a member and to all other construction outfits in the community, stating that Kendro is the ''worst driver in the city'' and that ''anyone who hires him is asking for legal liability.'' Kendro files suit against Dun, alleging libel on the basis of the statements made in the letter. Discuss the results.

**6–2. Defenses to Negligence.** Corinna was riding her bike on a city street. While she was riding, she frequently looked behind her to verify that the books that she had fastened to the rear part of her bike were still attached. On one occasion while she was looking behind her, she failed to notice a car that was entering an intersection just as she was crossing it. The car hit her, causing her to sustain numerous injuries. Three eye witnesses stated that the driver of the car had failed to stop at the stop sign before entering the intersection. Corinna sued the driver of the car for negligence. What defenses might the defendant driver raise in this lawsuit? Discuss fully.

**6–3. Negligence.** In which of the following situations will the acting party be liable for the tort of negligence? Explain fully.

    (a) Shannon goes to the golf course on Sunday morning, eager to try out a new set of golf clubs she has just purchased. As she tees off on the first hole, the head of her club flies off and injures a nearby golfer.

(b) Shannon goes to the golf course on Sunday morning. While she is teeing off at the eleventh hole, her golf ball veers off toward a roadway to the right of the golf course and shatters the windshield of a car.

(c) Shannon's doctor gives her some pain medication and tells her not to drive after she takes it, as the medication induces drowsiness. In spite of the doctor's warning, Shannon decides to drive to the store while on the medication. Owing to her lack of alertness, she fails to stop at a traffic light and crashes into another vehicle, in which a passenger is injured.

**6–4. Causation.** Ruth carelessly parks her car on a steep hill, leaving the car in neutral and failing to engage the parking brake. The car rolls down the hill, knocking down an electric line. The sparks from the broken line ignite a grass fire. The fire spreads until it reaches a barn one mile away. The barn houses dynamite, and the burning barn explodes, causing part of the roof to fall on and injure a passing motorist, Jim. Can Jim recover from Ruth? Why or why not?

**6–5. Trespass to Land.** Theo is a former employee of ABC Auto Repair Co. He enters the property of ABC, claiming that the company owes him $1,000 in back wages. An argument ensues, and the ABC general manager, Steward, orders Theo off the property. Theo refuses to leave, and Steward orders two mechanics to throw him off the property, which they do. Theo sues the mechanics, Steward, and ABC for assault and battery. Will Theo succeed in his claim? Explain.

**6–6. Emotional Distress.** Jim Meads had a VISA credit-card account with Citibank, a subsidiary of Citicorp. Meads fell behind in his payments on the $5,000 owing on the account, and in July 1986 Citibank closed Meads's account and notified him that the account would be referred to the Collection Group of Citicorp Credit Services, Inc. (CCSI), for collection. Thereafter, Meads wrote to CCSI, explaining that because of medical problems and related medical expenses, he was unable to meet the minimum-payment requirements but would make partial payments on the account. Meads's attorney also wrote to CCSI, requesting that CCSI not contact Meads again about the account and instead direct all future inquiries to the attorney's office. Nevertheless, CCSI continued to contact Meads, by telephone and letter, at frequent intervals (at times more often than once per week) over a four-month period. Calls were made not only to Meads's home but also to his place of work. Meads alleged that the callers were so abusive as to reduce his wife to tears. Meads finally sued CCSI for intentional infliction of emotional distress. Although Meads did not deny the validity of his debt to Citicorp, he felt that the collection attempts were abusive and stated that both he and his wife had suffered verifiable

emotional and physical complaints as a direct result of the actions of CCSI. Was CCSI's conduct sufficiently outrageous to warrant an emotional distress claim? [*Meads v. Citicorp Credit Services, Inc.,* 686 F.Supp. 330 (S.D.Ga. 1988)]

**6–7. Tort Theories.** The Yommers operated a gasoline station. In December 1967 their neighbors, the McKenzies, noticed a smell in their well water, which proved to be caused by gasoline in the water. McKenzie complained to the Yommers, who arranged to have one of their underground storage tanks replaced. Nevertheless, the McKenzies were unable to use their water for cooking or bathing until they had a filter and water softener installed. At the time of the trial, in December 1968, they were still bringing in drinking water from an outside source. The McKenzies sued the Yommers for damages. The Yommers claimed that the McKenzies had not proved that there was any intentional wrongdoing or negligence on their part and that therefore they should not be held liable. Under what theory might the McKenzies recover damages even in the absence of any negligence on the Yommers' part? Explain. [*Yommer v. McKenzie,* 255 Md. 220, 257 A.2d 138 (1969)]

**6–8. Contributory Negligence.** George Giles was staying at a Detroit hotel owned by the Pick Hotels Corp. While a hotel employee was removing luggage from the back seat of Giles's car, Giles reached into the front seat to remove his briefcase. As he did so, he supported himself by placing his left hand on the center pillar to which the rear door was hinged, with his fingers in a position to be injured if the rear door was closed. The hotel employee closed the rear door, and a part of Giles's left index finger was amputated. Giles sued the hotel for damages. The hotel claimed that it was not liable because Giles, by placing his hand on the car as he did, contributed to the injury. (Under state law, contributory negligence was an absolute defense to liability.) Discuss whether the hotel will succeed in its defense. [*Giles v. Pick Hotels Corp.,* 232 F.2d 887 (6th Cir. 1956)]

**6–9. Liability to Business Invitees.** While Charles and Esther Kveragas were in a rented motel room at the Scottish Inns, Inc., in Knoxville, Tennessee, three intruders kicked open the door, shot Charles, and injured Esther. The intruders also took $3,000 belonging to the Kveragases. The Kveragases brought an action against the motel owners, claiming that the owners had been negligent in failing to provide adequately for the safety of the motel's guests. At trial, the evidence showed that the door had a hollow core and that it fit poorly into the door frame. There was no deadbolt lock on the door, although such locks were easily available and commonly used in motels. The only lock on the door was one fitted into the door handle, which was described as a grade three lock, although a security chain was attached to the door. The Kveragases had both locked and chained the door, but still, a single kick on the part of the intruders was all that was necessary to open it. Evidence at trial also indicated that a deadbolt lock would have withstood the force that was applied to the door. Did the motel owners have a duty to protect their guests from criminal acts on the motel premises, and if so, did the owners breach that duty of care by failing to provide more secure locks on the doors of the motel rooms? [*Kveragas v. Scottish Inns, Inc.,* 733 F.2d 409 (6th Cir. 1984)]

**6–10. Strict Liability.** Danny and Marion Klein were injured when an aerial shell at a public fireworks exhibit went astray and exploded near them. They sued Pyrodyne Corp., the pyrotechnic company that was hired to set up and discharge the fireworks, alleging, among other things, that the company should be strictly liable for damages caused by the fireworks display. Will the court agree with the Kleins? What factors will the court consider in making its decision? Discuss fully. [*Klein v. Pyrodyne Corp.,* 117 Wash.2d 1, 810 P.2d 917 (1991)]

**6–11. Duty to Business Invitees.** George Ward entered a K–Mart department store in Champaign, Illinois, through a service entrance near the home improvements department. After purchasing a large mirror, Ward left the store through the same door. On his way out the door, carrying the large mirror in front and somewhat to the side of him, he collided with a concrete pole located just outside the door about a foot and a half from the outside wall. The mirror broke, and the broken glass cut his right cheek and eye, resulting in reduced vision in that eye. He later stated that he had not seen the pole, had not realized what was happening, and only knew that he felt "a bad pain, and then saw stars." Ward sued K–Mart Corp. for damages, alleging that the store was negligent. The issue before the court is whether the store should have foreseen the risk to its customers posed by the poles and guarded against it. What should the court decide? Discuss fully. [*Ward v. K–Mart Corp.,* 136 Ill.2d 132, 554 N.E.2d 223, 143 Ill.Dec. 288 (1990)]

**6–12. A Question of Ethics**

*Ernesto Parra choked to death on a piece of food while eating at a restaurant. The administrator of Parra's estate sued the restaurant, claiming, among other things, that the restaurant breached its duty to rescue Parra while he was choking. The court stressed that under the common law, there is no general duty to aid a person in peril: "A mere bystander incurs no liability where he fails to take any action, however negligently or even intentionally[,] to rescue another in distress." If Parra had been injured by a dangerous condition in the restaurant, such as a slippery floor, then the restaurant would have had a duty to come to Parra's assistance and ensure that he received any medical treatment necessary. But in the circumstances of the case before the court, the restaurant had not been responsible for placing Parra in danger; the fact that Parra choked was totally personal to Parra. According to the court, "As a general rule, a restaurateur is not an insurer of his customers' safety against all personal injuries. He has no duty as to 'conditions or risks which are ordinary and are, or should be, known or obvious to the patrons.'" [Parra v. Tarasco, Inc., 230 Ill.App.3d 819, 595 N.E.2d 1186, 172 Ill.Dec. 516 (1992)]*

1. Do you agree with the court's decision that the restaurant had no duty to rescue Parra? Why or why not?
2. Do you think that the law should impose a duty on all persons to rescue others in distress? What would be some of the implications of such a law for society? Discuss fully.

# CHAPTER 7

# TORTS RELATED TO BUSINESS

**O**ur economic system of free enterprise is predicated on the ability of persons, acting either as individuals or as business firms, to compete for customers and for sales. Unfettered competitive behavior has been shown to lead to economic efficiency and economic progress. Businesses may, generally speaking, engage in whatever is *reasonably* necessary to obtain a fair share of a market or to recapture a share that has been lost. But they are not allowed to use the motive of completely eliminating competition to justify certain business activities. Thus, an entire area of what is called business torts has arisen. Remember that a tort is a breach of a duty owed to an individual or to a group. **Business torts** are defined as wrongful interferences with others' business rights. Included in business torts are such vaguely worded concepts as *unfair competition* and *wrongfully interfering with the business relations of others*.

Because the area of business torts is so broad, we restrict our discussion in this chapter to the following causes of action:

1. Wrongful interference with contractual or business relationships.
2. Wrongful entry into business.
3. Appropriation of another's name or likeness without permission.
4. Defamation in the business context.
5. Disparagement of business property or reputation.

Following our discussion of these torts, we consider the application of the Racketeer Influenced and Corrupt Organizations Act (known more popularly as RICO) to fraudulent business activities.

# WRONGFUL INTERFERENCE

Torts involving wrongful interference with another's business rights generally fall into two categories—interference with a contractual relationship and interference with a business relationship. These two torts and the defenses that can be raised against them are discussed below.

## WRONGFUL INTERFERENCE WITH A CONTRACTUAL RELATIONSHIP

The body of tort law relating to *intentional interference with a contractual relationship* has increased greatly in recent years. A landmark case in this area involved an opera singer, Joanna Wagner, who was under contract to sing for a man named Lumley for a specified period of years.[1] A man named Gye, who knew of this contract, nonetheless "enticed" Wagner to refuse to carry out the agreement, and Wagner began to sing for Gye. Gye's action constituted a tort, because it interfered with the contractual relationship between Wagner and Lumley. (Wagner's refusal to carry out the agreement also entitled Lumley to sue for breach of contract.)

In principle, any lawful contract can be the basis for an action of this type. The plaintiff must prove that the defendant actually knew of the contract's existence and *induced* the breach of a contractual relationship, not merely that the defendant reaped the benefits of a broken contract. For example, suppose that Kharkhin has a contract with Sutton that calls for Sutton to do gardening work on Kharkhin's large estate every week for fifty-two

weeks at a specified price per week. Minnick, who needs gardening services, contacts Sutton and offers to pay Sutton a wage that is substantially higher than that offered by Kharkhin—although Minnick knows nothing about the Sutton-Kharkhin contract. Sutton breaches his contract with Kharkhin so that he can work for Minnick. Kharkhin cannot sue Minnick, because Minnick knew nothing of the Sutton-Kharkhin contract and was totally unaware that the higher wage he offered induced Sutton to breach that contract.

Three basic elements are necessary to the existence of wrongful interference with a contractual relationship:

1. A valid, enforceable contract must exist between two parties.
2. A third party must *know* that this contract exists.
3. This third party must *intentionally* cause either of the two parties to the contract to break the contract. Whether this third party acts in bad faith or with malice (the intention to harm another) is immaterial to establishing this tort, even though in most cases bad faith or malice is in evidence. The interference, however, must be for the purpose of advancing the economic interest of the inducer.

The contract may be between a firm and its employees or a firm and its customers, suppliers, competitors, or other parties. Sometimes a competitor of a firm may attempt to draw away a key employee, even to the extent of paying damages for wrongful interference with a contractual relationship. If the original employer can show that the competitor induced the breach—that is, that the employee would not normally have broken the contract—damages can be recovered.

The following highly publicized case illustrates the requirements for the tort of wrongful interference with a contractual relationship.

---

1. *Lumley v. Gye,* 118 Eng.Rep. 749 (1853).

---

**BACKGROUND AND FACTS**  *Pennzoil made an offer to buy control of Getty Oil and negotiated the offer with the major stockholders, Gordon Getty and the Getty Museum. A Memorandum of Agreement was made subject to the agreement of Getty's board of directors. The board declined to approve the arrangement and made a counteroffer; the board also began looking for other potential bidders. Although some details of the agreement remained unsettled, Pennzoil eventually accepted one of Getty's counter-*

CASE 7.1

**TEXACO, INC. v. PENNZOIL CO.**

Court of Appeals of Texas—Houston (First District), 1987.
729 S.W.2d 768.

*offers. The news was announced by both companies and reported widely in newspapers, including the* Wall Street Journal, *on January 5, 1984. While the lawyers from each company were negotiating a formal and specific written document, Getty's investment banker continued to look for another bidder. Texaco made a bid that Getty's board promptly accepted on January 6. Pennzoil subsequently sued Texaco, alleging tortious interference with its contract with Getty Oil. The trial court jury found that (1) Getty had agreed to Pennzoil's offer to purchase its stock; (2) Texaco knowingly interfered with this agreement; (3) as a result of Texaco's interference, Pennzoil suffered damages of $7.53 billion; (4) Texaco's actions were intentional, willful, and in wanton disregard of Pennzoil's rights; and (5) Pennzoil was entitled to punitive damages of $3 billion. Texaco appealed.*

WARREN, Justice.
       * * * *

Texaco contends that under controlling principles of * * * law, there was insufficient evidence to support the jury's finding that at the end of the Getty Oil board meeting * * * , the Getty entities intended to bind themselves to an agreement with Pennzoil.
       * * * *

Under [applicable principles of] law, if * * * there is no understanding that a signed writing is necessary before the parties will be bound, and the parties have agreed upon all substantial terms, then an informal agreement can be binding, even though the parties contemplate evidencing their agreement in a formal document later.
       * * * *

The record as a whole demonstrates that there was legally and factually sufficient evidence to support the jury's finding * * * that [Gordon Getty], the Museum, and the Company intended to bind themselves to an agreement with Pennzoil at the end of the Getty Oil board meeting * * * .
       * * * *

* * * Texaco [also] contends that the evidence is legally and factually insufficient to show that Texaco had actual knowledge of any agreement, [and] that it actively induced breach of the alleged contract * * * .
       * * * *

Pennzoil responds that * * * the jury could reasonably infer that Texaco knew about the Pennzoil deal from the evidence of (1) how Texaco carefully mapped its strategy to defeat Pennzoil's deal by acting to "stop the train" or "stop the signing"; (2) the notice of a contract given by a January 5 *Wall Street Journal* article reporting on the Pennzoil agreement—an article that Texaco denied anyone at Texaco had seen; (3) the knowledge of an agreement that would arise from comparing the Memorandum of Agreement with the Getty press release; (4) the demands made by the Museum and [Gordon Getty] for full indemnity from Texaco against any claims by Pennzoil arising out of the Memorandum of Agreement; and (5) the Museum's demand that, even if the Texaco deal fell through, the Museum would be guaranteed the price Pennzoil had agreed to pay for the Museum's shares. * * *
       * * * *

The jury was not required to accept Texaco's version of events in this case, and this Court may not substitute its own interpretation of the evidence for the decision of the trier of fact. There was legally and factually sufficient evidence to support an inference by the jury that Texaco had the required knowledge of an agreement.
       * * *
       * * * *

* * * It is necessary that there be some act of interference or of persuading a party to breach, for example by offering better terms or other incentives, for tort

liability to arise. The issue of whether a defendant affirmatively took steps to induce the breach of an existing contract is a question of fact for the jury.

\* \* \* Texaco argues that it merely responded to a campaign of active solicitation by Getty Oil and the Museum, who were dissatisfied by the terms of Pennzoil's offer.

\* \* \* \*

Texaco argues that its testimony shows that Getty Oil and the Museum were the real moving forces that eventually led to the Texaco contract. However, we find that there is legally and factually sufficient evidence in the record to support the jury's finding that Texaco actively induced the breach of the Getty entities' agreement with Pennzoil.

**DECISION AND REMEDY**

*The appellate court accepted the findings of the jury and affirmed the lower court's decision. The Supreme Court of Texas later found no reversible errors in this decision. Other issues in the case were appealed as high as the United States Supreme Court. In 1988, the case was settled for $3 billion. On the day of the payment, Texaco completed its reorganization and emerged from twelve months in bankruptcy proceedings.*

**INTERNATIONAL CONSIDERATIONS**

**Wrongful Interference with a Contractual Relationship in France** *Although not expressly recognized in France's civil law code (discussed in Chapter 10), that nation's judges have created an action for wrongful interference with a contractual relationship. The formal elements of the French action are virtually identical to those required under U.S. law, but there are differences in application. For example, French law does not apply the tort to letters of intention. France also does not recognize punitive damages in such an action.*

## WRONGFUL INTERFERENCE WITH A BUSINESS RELATIONSHIP

Individuals devise countless schemes to attract business, but they are forbidden by the courts to interfere unreasonably with another's business in their attempts to gain a share of the market. There is a difference between *competition* and *predatory behavior*. The distinction usually depends on whether a business is attempting to attract customers in general or to solicit only those customers who have already shown an interest in the similar product or service of a specific competitor. If a shopping center contains two shoe stores, an employee of Store A cannot be positioned at the entrance of Store B for the purpose of diverting customers to Store A. This type of activity constitutes the tort of wrongful interference with a business relationship, often referred to as interference with a prospective (economic) advantage, and it is commonly considered to be an unfair trade practice. If this type of activity were permitted, Store A would reap the benefits of Store B's advertising.

## DEFENSES TO WRONGFUL INTERFERENCE

A person will not be liable for the tort of wrongful interference with a contractual or business relationship if it can be shown that the interference was *justified,* or *permissible.* For example, *bona fide* competitive behavior is a privileged (justifiable, permissible) interference even if it results in the breaking of a contract. If Jerrod's Meats advertises so effectively that it induces Sam's Restaurant to break its contract with Burke's Meat Company, Burke's Meat Company will be unable to recover against Jerrod's Meats on a wrongful interference theory. After all, the public policy that favors free competition in advertising definitely outweighs any possible instability that such competitive activity might cause in contractual relations. Therefore, although luring customers away from a competitor through aggressive marketing and advertising strategies obviously interferes with the competitor's relationship with his or her customers, such activity is permitted by the courts.

Also, so long as there is no associated *illegal* activity, a businessperson normally will not incur tort liability for negotiating secretly behind a rival's back, refusing to do business with a competitor, or refusing to deal with third parties until they stop doing business with a rival.

# SECTION 2

# WRONGFUL ENTRY INTO BUSINESS

In a freely competitive society, it is usually true that any person can enter into any business to compete for the customers of existing businesses. Two situations in which this notion of free competition does not hold, however, are (1) when entering into business is a violation of the law and (2) when competitive behavior is predatory.

Any business or profession not subject to regulatory agencies or occupational licensing standards is open to an individual. No one can open a business for the sole purpose of driving another firm out of business, however; such a predatory motive is considered to be *simulated competition.* What the courts consider normal competitive activity is not always easy to ascertain—where does the normal desire to compete and obtain profits end and the tortious action begin? The following landmark case illustrates how a Minnesota court grappled with the question of malicious injury to business.

### CASE 7.2

### TUTTLE v. BUCK

Supreme Court of Minnesota,
1909.
107 Minn. 145,
119 N.W. 946.

**BACKGROUND AND FACTS**  *The plaintiff, Edward Tuttle, filed suit against the defendant, Cassius Buck, for malicious interference with his barbershop in the small village of Howard Lake, Minnesota. The plaintiff had owned and operated the shop for the previous ten years and had been able to maintain himself and his family comfortably from the income of the business. The defendant was a banker in the same community who "maliciously" established a competitive barbershop. The defendant employed a barber to carry on the business and used his personal influence to attract customers from the plaintiff's barbershop. Apparently, the defendant circulated false and malicious reports and accusations about the plaintiff and personally solicited and persuaded many of the plaintiff's patrons to stop using the plaintiff's services; indeed, the defendant used his personal power as the town's banker to threaten some customers in order to force them to use the defendant's shop instead. The plaintiff charged that the defendant undertook this entire plan with the sole design of injuring the plaintiff and destroying his business, not for serving any legitimate business interest. The trial court's decision for the plaintiff was affirmed by the appellate court, and the defendant appealed.*

*ELLIOTT, Justice.*
 \*  \*  \*  \*
 \*  \*  \* It is not at all correct to say that the motive with which an act is done is always immaterial, providing the act itself is not unlawful. \*  \*  \*
 \*  \*  \* [T]he principle that man may use his own property according to his own needs and desires, while true in the abstract, is subject to many limitations in the concrete. Men cannot always, in civilized society, be allowed to use their own property as their interests or desires may dictate without reference to the fact that they have neighbors whose rights are as sacred as their own. The existence and well-being of society requires that each and every person shall conduct himself consistently with the fact that he is a social and reasonable person. \*  \*  \*

\* \* \* To divert to one's self the customers of a business rival by the offer of goods at lower prices is in general a legitimate mode of serving one's own interest, and justifiable as fair competition. But when a man starts an opposition place of business, not for the make of profit to himself, but regardless of loss to himself, and for the sole purpose of driving his competitor out of business, and with the intention of himself retiring upon the accomplishment of his malevolent purpose, he is guilty of a wanton wrong and an actionable tort. In such a case he would not be exercising his legal right, or doing an act which can be judged separately from the motive which actuated him. To call such conduct competition is a perversion of terms. It is simply the application of force without legal justification, which in its moral quality may be no better than highway robbery.

*The plaintiff's cause of action was recognized under Minnesota law. The Supreme Court of Minnesota concluded that modern business requires certain protection against abusive business practices.*

**DECISION AND REMEDY**

## SECTION 3

# APPROPRIATION

The use of one person's name or likeness by another, without permission and for the benefit of the user, constitutes the tort of **appropriation.** Under the law, an individual's right to privacy includes the right to the exclusive use of his or her identity. A number of cases have arisen concerning the use of a famous person's name for the benefit of the user. One case involved the use of "Here's Johnny," which was the opening line of Johnny Carson's television show. A Michigan corporation that rented and sold portable toilets advertised them as "Here's Johnny" toilets. Carson brought suit, claiming that the Michigan corporation had violated his right to privacy by publicly appropriating his celebrity status for the corporation's commercial benefit. Even though the corporation had not used Carson's name or picture, the court held that the use of "Here's Johnny" was an appropriation of Carson's identity because the phrase was so strongly associated with Carson's public personality.[2]

Other cases have involved the unauthorized use of former world heavyweight boxing champion Muhammad Ali's appellation "The Greatest" to describe a nude male model[3] and the use of professional football wide receiver Elroy Hirsch's moniker "Crazylegs" as the name of a shaving gel.[4] In the following case, Vanna White sued a company for appropriating her celebrity status in one of its advertisements.

---

2. *Carson v. Here's Johnny Portable Toilets,* 698 F.2d 831 (6th Cir. 1983).
3. *Ali v. Playgirl, Inc.,* 447 F.Supp. 723 (S.D.N.Y. 1978).
4. *Hirsch v. S. C. Johnson & Son, Inc.,* 90 Wis.2d 379, 280 N.W.2d 129 (1979).

---

**BACKGROUND AND FACTS** *Vanna White is the hostess of "Wheel of Fortune," one of the most popular game shows in the history of television. Without White's permission, Samsung Electronics America, Inc., in an advertisement for Samsung videocassette recorders (VCRs), depicted a robot dressed in a wig, gown, and jewelry and posed next to a game board that resembled the "Wheel of Fortune" set, in a stance for which White is famous. The robot's hair, dress, and accessories were selected to resemble White's. White sued Samsung in federal district court, alleging, among other things, that Samsung had appropriated her celebrity status. The district court granted a motion for summary judgment against White, reason-*

**CASE 7.3**

**WHITE v. SAMSUNG ELECTRONICS AMERICA, INC.**

United States Court of Appeals,
Ninth Circuit, 1992.
971 F.2d 1395.

*ing in part that because the robot ad did not use White's name or likeness, Samsung had not appropriated her celebrity status. White appealed.*

*GOODWIN,* Senior Circuit Judge:

\* \* \* \*

[Previous] cases teach not only that the common law right of publicity reaches means of appropriation other than name or likeness, but that the specific means of appropriation are relevant only for determining whether the defendant has in fact appropriated the plaintiff's identity. \* \* \*

\* \* \* As [one] court explained: "[t]he right of publicity has developed to protect the commercial interest of celebrities in their identities. The theory of the right is that a celebrity's identity can be valuable in the promotion of products, and the celebrity has an interest that may be protected from the unauthorized commercial exploitation of that identity. . . . If the celebrity's identity is commercially exploited, there has been an invasion of his right whether or not his 'name or likeness' is used." \* \* \*

\* \* \* \*

Viewed separately, the individual aspects of the advertisement in the present case say little. Viewed together, they leave little doubt about the celebrity the ad is meant to depict. \* \* \*

Television and other media create marketable celebrity identity value. Considerable energy and ingenuity are expended by those who have achieved celebrity value to exploit it for profit. The law protects the celebrity's sole right to exploit this value \* \* \*.

**DECISION AND REMEDY** *The appellate court concluded that a jury should consider White's appropriation claim. The court reversed the part of the district court's decision that had held otherwise and remanded the case for further proceedings.*

**INTERNATIONAL CONSIDERATIONS** **Celebrity Appropriation in France** *French law, like that of many European nations, recognizes the "moral rights" of performers. This protection extends to appropriations of celebrities' likenesses and in many respects goes beyond U.S. law. When a shoe company advertisement imitated the voice of a famous French comedian, the comedian sued the company. The court held that the comedian had a moral right to control the commercial use of the sound of his voice.*

---

## SECTION 4

# DEFAMATION IN THE BUSINESS CONTEXT

As we stated in Chapter 6, the tort of *defamation* occurs when an individual makes a false statement that injures another's reputation. We also divided defamation into its component parts of libel (defamatory statements in written or printed form) and slander (defamatory statements made orally). Defamation becomes a business tort when the defam-atory matter injures someone in a profession, business, or trade or when it adversely affects a business entity in its credit rating and other dealings. When erroneous information from a computer about a person's credit standing or business reputation impairs that person's ability to obtain further credit, *defamation by computer* results.

In some cases, questions have arisen about the potential liability of on-line computer information services, such as CompuServe and PRODIGY, for defamatory statements made in sources included in their databases. The following case addresses this issue.

**HISTORICAL AND SOCIAL SETTING**  *Traditional notions of freedom of expression have always conflicted with the law of defamation. Following the oppression of political publications on grounds of defamation in the seventeenth and eighteenth centuries, a tide of sentiment in favor of freedom of speech and of the press led to cases in which liability for defamation was limited. Among those who came to be protected by the First Amendment's guaranties of freedom of speech and of the press were libraries, bookstores, newsstands, and other distributors of books and periodicals. The courts ruled that a distributor has no duty to monitor, for example, each issue of every periodical it distributes. As the United States Supreme Court has held, this would be an unreasonable demand on the seller and a restriction on the public's access to reading matter.[a] If the contents of bookstores and newsstands were restricted to materials that the proprietors had read, bookstores and newsstands might be nearly empty.*

| CASE 7.4 |
| --- |

**CUBBY, INC. v. COMPUSERVE, INC.**
United States District Court, Southern District of New York, 1991.
776 F.Supp. 135.

**BACKGROUND AND FACTS**  *CompuServe, Inc., offers subscribers CompuServe Information Service (CIS), to which access is gained through the use of phone lines, modems, and computers. Among CIS's thousands of information sources, which include electronic bulletin boards and topical databases, is the Journalism Forum, which is controlled by Cameron Communications, Inc., an organization independent of CompuServe. The Journalism Forum includes* Rumorville USA, *a newsletter that reports on the broadcast journalism industry. CompuServe has no opportunity to review* Rumorville's *contents before it is uploaded into CIS, from which it is immediately available to subscribers. In 1990, Cubby, Inc., and Robert Blanchard developed Skuttlebut, a computer database designed to focus on news and gossip in the television news and radio industries. In April 1990,* Rumorville *suggested that Skuttlebut gained access to information first published in* Rumorville *"through some back door," stated that Blanchard had been "bounced" from his previous employment, and described Skuttlebut as a "new start-up scam." Cubby and Blanchard filed suit against CompuServe in federal district court, alleging in part libel based on these statements. CompuServe filed a motion for summary judgment, denying that it knew or had reason to know of the statements.*

*LEISURE,* District Judge:

  \*  \*  \*  \*

Ordinarily, "one who repeats or otherwise republishes defamatory matter is subject to liability as if he had originally published it." With respect to entities such as news vendors, book stores, and libraries, however, "New York courts have long held that vendors and distributors of defamatory publications are not liable if they neither know nor have reason to know of the defamation."

  \*  \*  \*  \*

Technology is rapidly transforming the information industry. A computerized database is the functional equivalent of a more traditional news vendor, and the inconsistent application of a [different] standard of liability to an electronic news distributor such as CompuServe than that which is applied to a public library, book store, or newsstand would impose an undue burden on the free flow of information. Given the relevant First Amendment considerations, the appropriate standard of

a.  *Smith v. California,* 361 U.S. 147, 80 S.Ct. 215, 4 L.Ed.2d 205 (1959).

liability to be applied to CompuServe is whether it knew or had reason to know of the allegedly defamatory *Rumorville* statements.

\* \* \* \*

Plaintiffs have not set forth any specific facts showing that there is a genuine issue as to whether CompuServe knew or had reason to know of *Rumorville*'s contents. \* \* \* CompuServe, as a news distributor, may not be held liable if it neither knew nor had reason to know of the allegedly defamatory *Rumorville* statements \* \* \*.

**DECISION AND REMEDY**  *The court granted CompuServe's motion for summary judgment.*

---

# DISPARAGEMENT OF PROPERTY

**Disparagement of property** occurs when economically injurious falsehoods are made not about another's reputation but about another's *product* or *property*. Disparagement of property is a general term for torts that can be more specifically referred to as *slander of quality* or *slander of title*.

## SLANDER OF QUALITY

Publication of false information about another's product, alleging it is not what its seller claims, constitutes a tort of **slander of quality.** This tort has also been given the name **trade libel.** The plaintiff must prove that actual damages proximately resulted from the slander of quality. That is, it must be shown not only that a third person refrained from dealing with the plaintiff because of the improper publication but also that the plaintiff suffered damages because the third person refrained from dealing with him or her as a result of the improper publication. The economic calculation of such damages—they are, after all, conjectural—is often extremely difficult.

It is possible for an improper publication to be both a slander of quality and a defamation. For example, a statement that disparages the quality of a product may also, by implication, disparage the character of the person who would sell such a product. In one case, for instance, claiming that a product that was marketed as a sleeping aid contained "habit-forming drugs" was held to constitute defamation.[5]

The law of trademarks (to be discussed in Chapter 8) has, to some extent, made it easier for companies to sue other companies on the basis of purported false advertising. In the past, courts often ruled that companies could only be liable for false advertising when they misrepresented their own products. It mattered little what such companies claimed about their competitors' brands, particularly in so-called comparative advertisements. Today, false or misleading statements about another firm's products are actionable.

In the following case, the court evaluates the advertising claims made by the two leading competitors in the U.S. puppy food market.

---

5. *Harwood Pharmacal Co. v. National Broadcasting Co.,* 9 N.Y.2d 460, 174 N.E.2d 602, 214 N.Y.S.2d 725 (1961).

---

| CASE 7.5 |
| --- |
| **ALPO PETFOODS, INC. v. RALSTON PURINA CO.** |
| United States District Court, District of Columbia, 1989. |
| 720 F.Supp. 194. |

**BACKGROUND AND FACTS**  *From October 1985 through September 1986, Alpo Petfoods, Inc., and Ralston Purina Company both conducted extensive advertising campaigns for their puppy food products. Ralston claimed in its advertising that its Puppy Chow products helped reduce the incidence of canine hip dysplasia (CHD), a degenerative joint disease. This was a spectacular claim for dog owners and breeders, because CHD is one of the most feared dog diseases—it is incurable; difficult to treat; and in its advanced stages, very painful. Because of Ralston's status as the* *leading puppy food seller in the United States, the claim had a high degree of credibility. Alpo Petfoods, the second largest seller of puppy food in the United States, claimed in its advertising that, based on a survey it had conducted, veterinarians preferred the ''formula'' in Alpo Puppy Food ''2 to 1'' over the ''leading puppy food'' (Ralston's Puppy Chow). In October 1986, Alpo sued Ralston, alleging that Ralston's advertising claims were false, misleading, and deceptive, and thus were in violation of both the Lanham Act (a federal statute that prohibits false descriptions or false representations of goods) and common law. Ralston filed a counterclaim, alleging that Alpo's claims that veterinarians preferred Alpo's puppy food over Ralston's were false, misleading, and deceptive, and thus in violation of both the Lanham Act and common law. Ralston further claimed that statements made by Alpo to veterinarians and news media regarding Ralston's CHD claims constituted unfair competition, deceptive trade practices, and defamation. Both parties sought damages and permanent injunctions prohibiting the other party from further publication of the false claims.*

*SPORKIN,* District Judge.

\*    \*    \*    \*

\*    \*    \* [B]oth parties have made false, deceptive and misleading claims which are actionable. In this respect, both parties are entitled to relief, the extent to which is set out later in this opinion. Because liability has been found and relief has been granted under the Lanham Act, this court does not reach the question of whether the parties' actions constitute common law false advertising or unfair competition. The parties' respective claims, to the extent this court finds the conduct of the parties actionable, can be fully vindicated under the Lanham Act.

The court also finds that Alpo's statements to the media and the public regarding the challenged CHD claims are not defamatory and do not constitute unfair competition or deceptive trade practices.

\*    \*    \*    \*

\*    \*    \* The overwhelming weight of scientific authority indicates CHD is a hereditary disease and there is no reliable evidence that nutritional balance in a puppy's diet affects hip joint laxity, hip joint fit, CHD or degenerative joint disease. Ralston's research does not show that its puppy food reduces hip joint laxity. As a result, Ralston's CHD claims are false.

\*    \*    \*    \*

Considering Alpo's veterinarian preference claim against the undisputed fact that veterinarians overwhelmingly preferred Purina Puppy Chow, this court finds that Alpo's veterinarian preference claim was deceptive and misleading.

\*    \*    \*    \*

The court is particularly disturbed by its finding that the two leading manufacturers and distributors of dog food in the United States have engaged in serious, deceptive advertising practices. Because of the seriousness of these practices, the court has decided to enjoin both parties from engaging in such practices in the future.

**DECISION AND REMEDY**

*The court entered judgment for Alpo. Ralston was not awarded damages for Alpo's false advertising because of the ''magnitude of Ralston's misconduct'' compared with that of Alpo. Both parties were enjoined from further publication of their respective false claims, and both were ordered to issue corrective releases to those who had received the false information.*[a]

a.    On appeal, the judgment for Alpo was affirmed, but the amount of damages awarded to Alpo was reduced. See *Alpo Petfoods, Inc. v. Ralston Purina Co.,* 997 F.2d 949 (D.C.Cir. 1993).

## SLANDER OF TITLE

When a publication denies or casts doubt upon another's legal ownership of any property, and when this results in financial loss to that property's owner, the tort of **slander of title** may exist. Usually this is an intentional tort in which someone knowingly publishes an untrue statement about property with the intent of discouraging a third person from dealing with the person slandered. For example, it would be difficult for a car dealer to attract customers after competitors published a notice that the dealer's stock consisted of stolen autos.

The following case originated with untrue statements about "property" (a business firm's financial condition) in a credit report. The statements were clearly damaging to the firm's reputation.

---

| CASE 7.6 |
| :---: |

**DUN & BRADSTREET, INC. v. GREENMOSS BUILDERS, INC.**

Supreme Court of the United States, 1985.
472 U.S. 749,
105 S.Ct. 2939,
86 L.Ed.2d 593.

**COMPANY PROFILE** *One of the first commercial credit reporting agencies, Lewis Tappan's Mercantile Agency, was established in 1841 in New York City. In the 1850s, the firm expanded into Canada and Great Britain, and in 1859, Robert Dun took over the agency, changing its name to R. G. Dun & Company. The first edition of* Dun's Reference Book *included information on more than twenty thousand businesses; within twenty-five years, the number had increased to more than one million. In 1933, the John M. Bradstreet Company merged with Dun, and the company became Dun & Bradstreet, Inc., in 1939. In the 1960s, the firm acquired Moody's Investors Service and the Reuben H. Donnelly Corporation, publisher of the Yellow Pages.[a] Dun & Bradstreet owns the largest private database in the world. By repackaging this data in different formats, the firm doubled its sales between 1975 and 1980. With information on more than twenty million businesses, Dun & Bradstreet is the world's leading supplier of marketing and business information, the world's largest marketing research firm, and the world's largest credit reporting agency.*

**BACKGROUND AND FACTS** *Dun & Bradstreet, Inc., included false information concerning Greenmoss Builders, Inc., in a computerized letter sent to several of its subscribers. The false information was that Greenmoss had filed for bankruptcy, when, in fact, it had not. One of Greenmoss's employees had filed for bankruptcy, and a young, temporary employee of Dun & Bradstreet erroneously concluded that the firm itself had filed for bankruptcy. The inaccurate report resulted in a loss of business and income for Greenmoss, and because of these damages, Greenmoss sued Dun & Bradstreet for defamation. The trial court held for Greenmoss and awarded $50,000 in compensatory damages and $300,000 in punitive damages to Greenmoss. Dun & Bradstreet appealed, claiming that it was a public figure and its credit report was a form of speech protected by the First Amendment. Therefore, to recover damages for defamation, Greenmoss would have to prove that Dun & Bradstreet acted with "actual malice." The case was ultimately reviewed by the United States Supreme Court.*

Justice *POWELL* delivered the opinion of the Court.

&ast; &ast; &ast; &ast;

&ast; &ast; &ast; "Whether . . . speech addresses a matter of public concern must be determined by [the expression's] content, form, and context . . . as revealed by the whole record." These factors indicate that petitioner's credit report concerns no

---

a. For a case involving the Reuben H. Donnelly Corporation, see Case 8.3.

public issue. It was speech solely in the individual interest of the speaker and its specific business audience. This particular interest warrants no special protection when—as in this case—the speech is wholly false and clearly damaging to the victim's business reputation. Moreover, since the credit report was made available to only five subscribers, who, under the terms of the subscription agreement, could not disseminate it further, it cannot be said that the report involves any ''strong interest in the free flow of commercial information.'' There is simply no credible argument that this type of credit reporting requires special protection to ensure that ''debate on public issues [will] be uninhibited, robust, and wide-open.''

\* \* \* \*

We conclude that permitting recovery of presumed and punitive damages in defamation cases absent a showing of ''actual malice'' does not violate the First Amendment when the defamatory statements do not involve matters of public concern. \* \* \*

*The United States Supreme Court held for Greenmoss. Greenmoss was entitled to the damages awarded by the trial court.*

**DECISION AND REMEDY**

---

## SECTION 6

# RICO

Increasingly in recent years, businesses have been sued for fraudulent or other tortious activities under the Racketeer Influenced and Corrupt Organizations Act.[6] The act, which is commonly known as RICO, was passed by Congress in 1970 as part of the Organized Crime Control Act. The purpose of the act was to curb the apparently increasing entry of organized crime into the legitimate business world.

## ACTIVITIES PROHIBITED BY RICO

Under RICO, it is a federal crime (1) to use income obtained from racketeering activity to purchase any interest in an enterprise, (2) to acquire or maintain an interest in an enterprise through racketeering activity, (3) to conduct or participate in the affairs of an enterprise through racketeering activity, or (4) to conspire to do any of the preceding.

Racketeering activity is not a new type of substantive crime created by RICO; rather, RICO incorporates by reference twenty-six separate types of federal crimes and nine types of state felonies[7] and states that if a person commits two of these

offenses, he or she is guilty of ''racketeering activity.'' Recently, the statute has been rigorously enforced, and the penalties for violations are harsh. The act provides for both criminal liability (to be discussed in Chapter 9) and civil liability.

## CIVIL LIABILITY UNDER RICO

In the event of a violation, the RICO statute permits the government to seek civil penalties, including the divestiture of a defendant's interest in a business (called forfeiture—discussed in Chapter 9) or the dissolution of the business. Perhaps the most controversial aspect of RICO is that, in some cases, private individuals are allowed to recover three times their actual losses (treble damages), plus attorneys' fees, for business injuries caused by a violation of the statute.

The broad language of RICO has allowed it to be applied in cases that have little or nothing to do with organized crime, and an aggressive attorney may attempt to show that any business fraud constitutes ''racketeering activity.'' Plaintiffs have used the RICO statute in numerous commercial fraud cases because of the inviting prospect of being awarded triple damages if they win. The most frequent targets of civil RICO lawsuits are insurance companies, employment agencies, commercial banks, and stock-brokerage firms.

In one case, a business firm filed a lawsuit against a rival firm, claiming that the latter's fraudulent business activities violated RICO. The rival

---

6.  18 U.S.C. Sections 1961–1968.
7.  See 18 U.S.C. Section 1961(1)(A).

argued that it had been convicted of no crime. On appeal, the United States Supreme Court held that a party does not need to have been convicted of a criminal violation of RICO to be held liable in a civil RICO suit. The Court also held that a plaintiff does not have to show a separate racketeering injury to recover treble damages under the statute.[8]

Since that decision, the Court has continued to interpret RICO broadly. In one case, for example, the Court ruled that civil RICO suits may be brought in state courts or federal courts.[9] In another lawsuit, brought by the National Organization for

Women and two health clinics against antiabortion protesters, the protesters argued that to be held liable under RICO, there must be an economic motive to the acts that are alleged to constitute racketeering activity. The United States Supreme Court disagreed with the protesters, holding that an economic motive is not a requirement for liability under RICO.[10]

In the following case, a bank argued that it should not be held liable for a violation of RICO on the part of one of its assistant vice presidents.

---

8.  *Sedima, S.P.R.L. v. Imrex Co.*, 473 U.S. 479, 105 S.Ct. 3275, 87 L.Ed.2d 346 (1985).
9.  *Tafflin v. Levitt*, 493 U.S. 455, 110 S.Ct. 792, 107 L.Ed.2d 887 (1990).

10.  The Court acknowledged that in this case, the racketeering activities ''may not benefit the protesters financially, but they still may drain money from the economy by harming businesses such as the clinics.'' *National Organization for Women, Inc. v. Joseph Scheidler,* ____U.S. ____, 114 S.Ct. 798, 127 L.Ed.2d 99 (1994).

---

| CASE 7.7 |
| --- |

**QUICK v. PEOPLES BANK OF CULLMAN COUNTY**

United States Court of Appeals, Eleventh Circuit, 1993. 993 F.2d 793.

**BACKGROUND AND FACTS**   *Jimmy and Wanda Quick own and operate Quick Motors, which purchases vehicles at auction and refurbishes and resells them. James Buckelew, a loan officer at the Peoples Bank of Cullman County, asked the Quicks to move all of their banking business to the Peoples Bank. The Quicks did so, borrowing from the bank to finance their business. Among other things, Buckelew insisted that deposits and loan payments be made in cash, for which he refused to give receipts, and told the Quicks not to keep any records concerning the transactions. Meanwhile, Buckelew failed to forward the Quicks' deposits and loan payments to the appropriate accounts, which meant that the Quicks continued to incur more debt. As a result, the bank earned additional interest. After Buckelew was promoted to assistant vice president, the Quicks notified the bank of Buckelew's activities. The bank took no action for more than a year. Finally, Robin Cummings, the bank's president, and Candice Nails, one of the bank's vice presidents, met with the Quicks, asked them not to say anything about Buckelew, and told them the bank would help. Cummings and Nails presented the Quicks with a note that consolidated all of their debts to the bank. The Quicks disputed the amount but signed the note, because they could not obtain financing elsewhere (all of their assets were tied up as collateral by the bank). Following the meeting, Cummings asked Buckelew to resign. The Quicks brought a lawsuit against Buckelew and the bank under RICO. The jury returned a verdict for $15,000 in favor of the Quicks under the doctrine of* respondeat superior, *which provides that an employer may be held liable for harm caused by an employee within the scope of employment.[a] The court trebled the damages, entering a judgment against the bank and Buckelew for $45,000. The bank appealed.*

---

a.   The doctrine of *respondeat superior* is discussed in more detail in Chapter 35.

*ESCHBACH,* Senior Circuit Judge:

\* \* \* \*

\* \* \* The [U.S. Court of Appeals for the] Seventh Circuit, which has developed the most extensive jurisprudence extant [in existence] on this issue, has recognized that care must be taken not to impose *respondeat superior* liability on enterprises that are the victims of RICO violations perpetrated by their employees while at the same time imposing liability on enterprises that have benefitted from these activities. Because of this concern, the Seventh Circuit holds that *respondeat superior* liability may be applied in the context of [RICO's civil provisions] only when an enterprise has derived some benefit from the RICO violation. We agree with this holding.

\* \* \* \*

\* \* \* Buckelew's intervention prevented many of the Quicks' deposits and loan payments from being forwarded to the appropriate accounts. Therefore, the Quicks incurred more debt than would otherwise have been necessary. The presence of this additional debt benefitted the Bank through the resulting additional earned interest. Though the Bank might have been initially unaware of the accrual of these ill-gotten benefits, it ultimately accepted them when it requested that Jimmy Quick sign a consolidation note including them. The acceptance of these benefits suffice[s] to make the Bank subject to liability under [RICO's civil provisions] through the application of *respondeat superior.*

*The appellate court affirmed the trial court's judgment.*

**DECISION
AND REMEDY**

## TERMS AND CONCEPTS TO REVIEW

| | | |
|---|---|---|
| appropriation  133 | disparagement of property  136 | slander of title  138 |
| business tort  128 | slander of quality  136 | trade libel  136 |

# QUESTIONS AND CASE PROBLEMS

**7–1. Wrongful Interference.** Lothar owns a bakery. He has been trying to obtain a long-term contract with the owner of Martha's Tea Salons for some time. Lothar starts a local advertising campaign on radio and television and in the newspaper. This advertising campaign is so persuasive that Martha decides to break the contract she has had with Harley's Bakery so that she can patronize Lothar's bakery. Is Lothar liable to Harley's Bakery for the tort of wrongful interference with contractual relations? Is Martha liable for this tort? For anything?

**7–2. Wrongful Interference.** Katrina was stranded in Alaska as the result of a union strike against the airline. She had purchased a round-trip ticket before leaving her home in Dallas. She was forced to return to Dallas on another airline and incurred additional expense for her return ticket. She sued the union for tortious interference

with her contract with the airline and sought to recover the additional expense. Should the union be liable to Katrina for damages? Why or why not?

**7–3. Business Tort Theories.** After a careful study and analysis, Green Top Airlines decides to expand its operations into Harbor City. Green Top acquires the necessary regulatory authorizations and licenses, negotiates a lease at the airport terminal, and makes substantial capital expenditures renovating airport gates. Immediately thereafter, Red Stripe Airlines, Green Top's major competitor, also undertakes operations in Harbor City, even though (1) Harbor City is nowhere near any of Red Stripe's major existing routes and (2) Red Stripe will lose money by servicing Harbor City. Green Top claims that Red Stripe's entry into Harbor City constitutes a tort. Discuss fully Green Top's claim.

**7–4. Business Tort Theories.** Assume that Red Stripe Airlines (in Problem 7–3) negotiates a lease at the airport for gates on the same concourse as Green Top Airlines. In fact, for passengers to get to Green Top's gates, they must walk past Red Stripe's gates. Red Stripe puts up a large sign that states, ''Passengers of other airlines—turn in your tickets or cancel your reservations, and we will give you 25 percent off the price of your trip if you fly on Red Stripe Airlines.'' In addition, Red Stripe's ticket agents solicit business from travelers on their way to Green Top's gates. At this time, only Red Stripe and Green Top have operative gates on the concourse. Discuss fully any business tort theories under which Green Top can recover against Red Stripe for the latter's actions. (Remember: A ticket is a contract.)

**7–5. Business Tort Theories.** Luigi owns and operates a famous Italian restaurant in New York City. Luigi hires chef Toni to prepare the pasta and other dishes on his menu. Toni also contributes a column to *Gourmet Eating* magazine in which he discusses Italian food and restaurants in the area and rates all restaurants with stars. The ratings range from one star (the lowest rating) to five stars (the highest rating). Toni is prohibited from discussing or rating Luigi's restaurant in his column as long as he is employed by Luigi. One day, Luigi and Toni have a dispute over Toni's salary, and Toni, in front of a substantial number of regular customers who are well known in New York society, accuses Luigi of watering his house wine and of not making his own pasta. Luigi has on occasion purchased some pasta from a pasta shop in the neighborhood, but he has never watered his wine. Toni quits on the spot and later, in *Gourmet Eating,* rates Luigi's restaurant with only one star, adding a notation that Luigi's wine and pasta are inferior to the wine and pasta offered by other restaurants. Under what tort theories, if any, can Luigi file suit against Toni? Discuss fully.

**7–6. Wrongful Interference.** Duggin entered into a contract to purchase certain land from Williams. The contract specified that if the property was not rezoned by June 15, 1981, either party could cancel. Duggin invested a great deal of time and money for engineering studies and surveys that increased the value of the property. Before the June 15 rezoning deadline, Duggin made an agreement to assign the contract to Centennial Development Corp. at a profit. The land was not rezoned as of June 15, but Centennial was prepared to purchase the land without the rezoning. Williams's attorney, Adams, learned of Duggin's deal and convinced Williams to cancel on July 30, 1981, in accordance with the provision in the agreement. Adams also convinced Williams to transfer the property to Adams, after which he sold the land to Centennial. Adams claimed that he was merely working on behalf of his client, Williams. Does Duggin have a claim against Adams for wrongful interference with contract rights even though Williams had the right to terminate the contract at will? Explain your answer. [*Duggin v. Adams,* 234 Va. 221, 360 S.E.2d 832 (1987)]

**7–7. Wrongful Interference.** Lehigh Corp., a developer of real estate, obtained a restraining order (which is similar to an injunction) against one of its former sales representatives, Leroy Azar. Lehigh brought prospective customers to its development, Lehigh Acres, and provided accommodations at its company-owned motel. Azar pursued a practice of following Lehigh purchasers as they entered the motel and persuading them to rescind (cancel) their contracts with Lehigh and purchase less expensive property from him. Lehigh sued Azar, asserting that Azar was tortiously interfering with the advantageous business relationship between Lehigh and its customers. Azar contended that Lehigh's customers had a right under federal law to rescind their contracts within three days and that he was merely providing them with an opportunity to be relieved of their contracts and to obtain comparable property for lower prices. What should the court decide? Discuss fully. [*Azar v. Lehigh Corp.,* 364 So.2d 860 (Fla.App.2d 1978)]

**7–8. RICO.** Dierdorff was the president of Sun Savings and Loan Association (Sun). Sun claimed that over a period of time, Dierdorff had received kickbacks from several of Sun's larger loan customers. In relation to the fraudulent kickback scheme, Dierdorff had written letters to four entities—the Internal Revenue Service, the Federal Home Loan Bank Board, the California Savings and Loan commissioner, and the accounting firm of Arthur Young. Sun filed a civil suit alleging that Dierdorff had violated the federal Racketeering Influenced and Corrupt Organizations Act (RICO). The federal district court decided in favor of Dierdorff, holding that the plaintiff, Sun, had failed to allege a ''pattern of racketeering activity'' and that the acts had not been conducted by an ''enterprise.'' On appeal, how should the appellate court rule on the decision of the district court? Discuss. [*Sun Savings and Loan Association v. Dierdorff,* 825 F.2d 187 (9th Cir. 1987)]

**7–9. Wrongful Interference.** DBI Services, Inc., provided oil-field trucking services, brine water, and drilling mud to oil producers in the Seminole area of Texas. From 1983 to 1986, the major oil producer in the area, Amerada Hess Corp. (AH), regularly contracted with DBI for its services. AH learned in a 1986 audit of its contractors that DBI had engaged in lavish entertainment of certain AH employees who were responsible for awarding job contracts. Disturbed by this discovery, AH thereafter refused to deal with DBI. AH also refused to accept contract bids from any firms that planned to subcontract work out to DBI, even if the firms had submitted the lowest bids for the contracts. DBI sued AH for tortious interference with its contractual relationships with these other firms. AH claimed that it was not obligated to accept the lowest bids for contracts and that it had a right to determine with whom it would do business. How will the court decide the issue? Discuss. [*DBI Services, Inc. v. Amerada Hess Corp.,* 907 F.2d 506 (5th Cir. 1990)]

# CHAPTER 8

# INTELLECTUAL PROPERTY AND COMPUTER LAW

**M**ost people think of wealth in terms of houses, land, cars, stocks, and bonds. But wealth also includes **intellectual property,** which consists of the products of individuals' minds—products that result from intellectual, creative processes. Although it is an abstract term for an abstract concept, *intellectual property* is nonetheless wholly familiar to virtually everyone. *Trademarks, service marks, copyrights,* and *patents* are all forms of intellectual property. The book you are reading is copyrighted. Undoubtedly, the personal computer you use at home is trademarked. Some of the resident software within that computer might be copyrighted. You see advertisements for trademarked items every day—items marketed by Xerox, IBM, and the like. The study of intellectual property law is valuable because intellectual property has taken on an increasing importance, not only within the United States but globally as well. Much of what is sold abroad—including popular American television series, computer programs, and blockbuster films—consists of intellectual property.

The need to protect creative works was voiced by the framers of the U.S. Constitution over two hundred years ago: Article I, Section 8, of the Constitution authorized Congress "[t]o promote the Progress of Science and useful Arts, by securing for limited Times to Authors and Inventors the exclusive Right to their respective Writings and Discoveries." Laws protecting patents, trademarks, and copyrights are explicitly designed to protect and reward inventive and artistic creativity. For example, trademark law provides incentives to companies to invest in the development of goodwill by ensuring that others will not steal and profit from their trade symbols. Although intellectual property law limits the economic freedom of some individuals, it does so to protect the freedom of others to enjoy the fruits of their labors—in the form of profits.

In the last decade, computers have become dominant in the business world, and they are becoming increasingly familiar in every household in

America. But the many and diverse advantages brought about by the computer revolution have not been risk free. Not surprisingly, issues relating to unfair trade practice arise constantly in this growth industry. The protection of intellectual property relating to computers—such as computer software—has posed difficulties for legislatures and the courts, because computers were not envisioned by the legislators who drafted the previous patent, trademark, and copyright laws. Therefore, previous laws have had to be amended, or new laws created, to serve the needs of a computer generation. In the sections below on trademark, patent, and copyright laws, we discuss how these laws have been applied to computer software. In a later section of this chapter, we address another legal challenge presented by computers—the problem of computer crime.

## SECTION 1

# TRADEMARKS AND RELATED PROPERTY

A **trademark** is a distinctive mark, motto, device, or emblem that a manufacturer stamps, prints, or otherwise affixes to the goods it produces, so that they can be distinguished from the goods of other manufacturers and merchants. Bestowing an exclusive trademark right on the originator of a mark yields several benefits, some of which were mentioned at the beginning of this chapter. First, exclusive trademark protection creates incentives for merchants to invest in product development and improvement. Second, trademark law permits consumers to be certain that they are obtaining the same product from the same manufacturer every time they return to the marketplace. Trademark law therefore reduces "search costs" for consumers and prevents the confusion that would result in the marketplace if trademarks were not protected. Finally, trademark law prevents unjust enrichment by prohibiting unscrupulous merchants from selling inferior imitations under the same trademark as the original.

## DISTINCTIVENESS OF MARK

Generally, the more distinctive a trademark is, the less likely it is that it will be confused with other trademarks. Therefore, the extent to which the law protects a trademark is normally determined by how distinctive the trademark is. A very distinctive trademark is considered to be strong, and a much less distinctive trademark is considered to be weak. A strong trademark cannot be appropriated easily, while a weak trademark is more susceptible to use by others.

Fanciful, arbitrary, or suggestive trademarks are generally considered to be the most distinctive (strongest) trademarks, because they are normally taken from outside the context of the particular product and thus provide the best means of distinguishing one product from another. Fanciful trademarks include invented words, such as Xerox for one manufacturer's copiers and Kodak for another company's photographic products. Arbitrary trademarks include actual words used with products that have no literal connection to the words, such as "English Leather" used as a name for an aftershave lotion (and not for leather processed in England). Suggestive trademarks are those that suggest something about a product without describing the product directly. For example, "Dairy Queen" suggests an association between its products and milk, but it does not directly describe ice cream.

Descriptive terms, geographic terms, and personal names are not inherently distinctive and do not receive protection under the law until they acquire a secondary meaning. A secondary meaning may arise when customers begin to associate a specific trademark with the source of the trademarked product. For example, the name Calvin Klein is a strong trademark, because consumers associate that name with goods marketed by Calvin Klein or licensed distributors of Calvin Klein products. Whether a secondary meaning becomes attached to a term or name usually depends on how extensively the product is advertised, the market for the product, the number of sales, and other factors. Once a secondary meaning is attached to a term or name, a trademark is considered distinctive and is protected. Of course, geographic terms and personal names used in fanciful or arbitrary ways are inherently distinctive.

Trademark protection may also extend to a specific shade of color when the color meets all of the requirements for that protection, including acquiring a secondary meaning. Pink, for example, is so strongly associated with a particular brand of fiberglass insulation that competitors are barred from using it.[1] Recently, a court held that blue may be so strongly associated with a particular brand of photo splicing tape that it may also be protected under the trademark laws.[2] The United States Supreme Court has held that a product's color alone may be registered as a trademark.[3]

Generic terms, such as *bicycle* or *computer,* receive no protection, even if they acquire secondary meaning. A particularly thorny problem arises when a trademark acquires generic use. For example, *aspirin, thermos, escalator, trampoline, raisin bran, dry ice, cube steak, linoleum, nylon, kerosene,* and *cornflakes* originally were used only as trademarks, but they are now used to refer to those products generically. Even so, the courts will not allow other firms to use those names in such a way as to deceive a potential consumer.

In the following case concerning Coca-Cola, the defendants argued that the Coca-Cola trademark was entitled to no protection under the law, because the term did not accurately represent the product.

---

1.  *In re Owens-Corning Fiberglas Corp.,* 774 F.2d 1116 (Fed.Cir. 1985).
2.  *Master Distributors Inc. v. Pako Corp.,* 986 F.2d 219 (8th Cir. 1993).
3.  *Qualitex Co. v. Jacobson Products Co.,* _____ U.S. _____ , _____ S.Ct. _____ , _____ L.Ed.2d _____ (1995). This decision can be found on WESTLAW at 1995 W.L. 128239.

---

**BACKGROUND AND FACTS**  *The plaintiff, the Coca-Cola Company, sought to enjoin (prevent) the Koke Company of America and other beverage companies from, among other things, using the word "Koke" for their products. The defendants, the Koke Company of America and other beverage companies, contended that the Coca-Cola trademark was a fraudulent representation and that Coca-Cola was therefore not entitled to any help from the courts. The defendants alleged that the Coca-Cola Company, by its use of the Coca-Cola name, represented that the beverage contained cocaine (from coca leaves). The trial court granted the injunction against the Koke Company, but the appellate court reversed the lower court's ruling. Coca-Cola then appealed to the United States Supreme Court.*

| CASE 8.1 |
| :--- |
| **THE COCA-COLA CO. v. THE KOKE CO. OF AMERICA** |
| Supreme Court of the United States, 1920. |
| 254 U.S. 143, |
| 41 S.Ct. 113, |
| 65 L.Ed. 189. |

Mr. Justice *HOLMES* delivered the opinion of the Court.

\* \* \* \*

\* \* \* Before 1900 the beginning of [Coca-Cola's] good will was more or less helped by the presence of cocaine, a drug that, like alcohol or caffeine or opium, may be described as a deadly poison or as a valuable item of the pharmacopeia according to the rhetorical purposes in view. The amount seems to have been very small,[a] but it may have been enough to begin a bad habit and after the Food and Drug Act of June 30, 1906, if not earlier, long before this suit was brought, it was eliminated from the plaintiff's compound. \* \* \*

\* \* \* Since 1900 the sales have increased at a very great rate corresponding to a like increase in advertising. The name now characterizes a beverage to be had at almost any soda fountain. It means a single thing coming from a single source, and well known to the community. It hardly would be too much to say that the drink characterizes the name as much as the name the drink. In other words Coca-Cola probably means to most persons the plaintiff's familiar product to be had everywhere rather than a compound of particular substances. \* \* \* [B]efore this suit was brought the plaintiff had advertised to the public that it must not expect and would not find cocaine, and had eliminated everything tending to suggest cocaine effects

---

a.  In reality, until 1903 the amount of active cocaine in each bottle of Coke was equivalent to one "line" of cocaine.

except the name and the picture of [coca] leaves and nuts, which probably conveyed little or nothing to most who saw it. It appears to us that it would be going too far to deny the plaintiff relief against a palpable fraud because possibly here and there an ignorant person might call for the drink with the hope for incipient cocaine intoxication. The plaintiff's position must be judged by the facts as they were when the suit was begun, not by the facts of a different condition and an earlier time.

**DECISION AND REMEDY**    *The district court's injunction was allowed to stand. The competing beverage companies were enjoined from calling their products ''Koke.''*

## TRADEMARK INFRINGEMENT

Trademarks may be registered with the state or with the federal government. Once a trademark has been registered, a firm is entitled to its exclusive use for marketing purposes. Whenever that trademark is copied to a substantial degree or used in its entirety by another, intentionally or unintentionally, the trademark has been infringed.

The owner of the trademark need not register it with the state or with the federal government to obtain protection from the tort of trademark infringement, but registration does furnish proof of the date of inception of its use. Moreover, registration may prolong the life of the trademark. Registration is renewable between the fifth and sixth years after the initial registration and every twenty years thereafter, as long as the mark remains distinctive and is used.

The defendant firm in the following case was liable for trademark infringement.

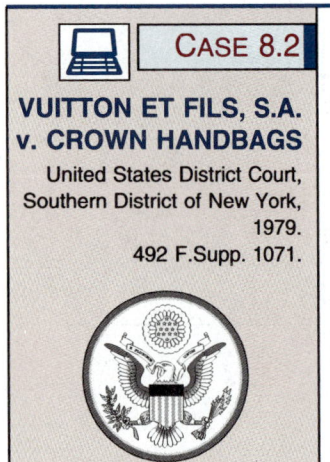

**CASE 8.2**

**VUITTON ET FILS, S.A. v. CROWN HANDBAGS**
United States District Court, Southern District of New York, 1979.
492 F.Supp. 1071.

**COMPANY PROFILE**    *Louis Vuitton opened his first store in Paris in 1854 to sell luggage and trunks. Thirty-eight years later, the company began to use the monogram LV that still appears on most of its products. The company sold primarily at wholesale until 1977, when it entered the retail market under the leadership of Henry Racamier, a steel executive who had married into the Vuitton family. Over the next decade, sales revenues increased from $20 million to nearly $1 billion. In 1987, Louis Vuitton merged with Moët Hennessy (a producer of champagne, wine, cognac, and perfume), and the company was renamed LVMH Moët Hennessy Louis Vuitton. After a battle for the control of LVMH between Racamier and others, Racamier left the company.*

**BACKGROUND AND FACTS**    *The plaintiff, Vuitton et Fils, S.A., is a French corporation that manufactures expensive handbags and distributes them through an exclusive retail network in the United States. (S.A. stands for société anonyme, which is the French equivalent of a corporation.) The handbags are of high quality and bear the Vuitton registered trademark, the firm's initials and a fleur-de-lis. Robert Cullen was employed by Vuitton as a private investigator and by chance passed the defendant's window display, which featured two handbags bearing the Vuitton trademark. The defendant, Crown Handbags, was not a retail outlet for Vuitton handbags. The defendant offered to sell Cullen six handbags in a bulk transaction. At the trial, the handbags were shown to be cheap imitations of Vuitton's product. Vuitton sued Crown Handbags for infringement of its registered trademark.*

*BRIEANT,* District Judge.

    \*   \*   \*   \*

[When] an alleged infringing mark is used in connection with the sale of similar goods, the long standing rule in this Circuit has been that the second comer to the marketplace ''has a duty to so name and dress his product as to avoid all likelihood of consumers confusing it with the product of the first comer.'' The second comer has no right to trade upon the good will of the first comer developed over a period of time and at considerable expense. \*   \*   \*

The great weight of the evidence in the case leads to the conclusion that the Vuitton trademark is a strong mark, and as such is entitled to broad protection. The strength of the mark stems from its conspicuously distinctive nature. It is unique in its design and color, and during the more than 46 years of its continuous use in this country it has come to represent a source of product of perceived quality and prestige. \*   \*   \*

    \*   \*   \*   \*

Both Vuitton and consumers in general would suffer by the purchase of counterfeit bags of inferior quality. Vuitton would soon lose its reputation for quality and exclusivity, and consumers would be deceived into believing they were getting something they were not.

---

*Vuitton was granted permanent injunctive relief from Crown Handbag's commercial practices that violated Vuitton's trademark rights. Crown had to pay damages amounting to the sales price of the six handbags offered to Vuitton's investigator. Crown also had to pay Vuitton's attorneys' fees.*

**DECISION AND REMEDY**

---

## THE TRADEMARK REVISION ACT

In 1988, the Trademark Revision Act was passed by Congress. This act, which took effect on November 16, 1989, significantly altered the prior registration scheme. That scheme required that the mark be used before an application could be filed. The 1988 act, in contrast, allows an applicant to file on the basis either of use or of the *bona fide* intention to use the mark in commerce. This is the so-called *intent to use* provision, which requires that the mark be put into commerce within six months after filing with the federal Patent and Trademark Office. At the end of the six months, the applicant must provide proof that the mark was put into commerce and that the application was not opposed.

Under extenuating circumstances, the six-month period can be extended by thirty months, giving the applicant a total of three years from the date of notice of trademark approval to make use of the mark and file the required use statement. Registration under the 1988 act is postponed until actual use of the mark. Nonetheless, during this waiting period, any applicant can legally protect his or her trademark against a third party who has neither used the mark nor filed an application for it. The 1988 act has considerably cut the costs in developing and marketing new products. It has particularly benefited small companies.

## SERVICE, CERTIFICATION, AND COLLECTIVE MARKS

A **service mark** is similar to a trademark but is used to distinguish the services of one person or company from those of another. For example, each airline has a particular mark or symbol associated with its name. Character names used in radio, films, and television are frequently registered as service marks. Service marks are registered in the same manner as trademarks.

Other marks protected by law include certification and collective marks. A **certification mark** is used by one or more persons, other than the owner, to certify the region, materials, mode of manufacture, quality, or accuracy of the owner's goods or services. When used by members of a cooperative, association, or other organization, such a mark is referred to as a **collective mark.** Examples of certification marks are the ''Good Housekeeping Seal of Approval'' and ''UL Tested.'' Collective marks appear at the ends of the credits of movies to indicate the various associations and organizations that participated in the making of the movies. The union marks found on the tags of certain products are also collective marks. The same policies and restrictions that apply to trademarks and service marks normally apply to certification and collective marks.

## TRADE NAMES

Trademarks apply to products. The term **trade name** is used to indicate part or all of a business's name, whether that business be a sole proprietorship, a partnership, or a corporation. Generally, a trade name is directly related to a business and to its goodwill. Trade names may be protected as trademarks or service marks if they are used as trademarks or service marks—for example, Apple Computer, Inc., uses the trade name ''Apple'' as a trademark, and McDonald's Corporation uses ''McDonald's'' as a service mark. Otherwise, a trade name cannot be registered with the federal government. Trade names are protected under the common law, however. As with trademarks, words must be unusual or fancifully used to be protected as trade names. The word ''Safeway,'' for example, was held by the courts to be sufficiently fanciful to obtain protection as a trade name for a foodstore chain.[4]

---

## SECTION 2

# PATENTS

A **patent** is a grant from the federal government that conveys and secures to an inventor the exclusive right to make, use, and sell an invention for a period of seventeen years. Patents for a lesser period are given for designs, as opposed to inventions. For either a regular patent or a design patent, the applicant must demonstrate to the satisfaction of the patent office that the invention, discovery, or design is genuine, novel, useful, and not obvious in the light of the technology of the time. A patent holder gives notice to all that an article or design is patented by placing on it the word *Patent* or *Pat.,* plus the patent number.

## PATENT INFRINGEMENT

If a firm makes, uses, or sells another's patented design, product, or process without the patent owner's permission, the tort of patent infringement exists. Patent infringement may exist even though not all features or parts of an invention are copied. (With respect to a patented process, however, all steps or their equivalent must be copied in order for infringement to exist.) Often, litigation for patent infringement is so costly that the patent holder will instead offer to sell to the infringer a license to use the patented design, product, or process. Indeed, in many cases the costs of detection, prosecution, and monitoring are so high that patents are valueless to their owners, because the owners cannot afford to protect them.

## PATENTS FOR COMPUTER SOFTWARE

At one time, it was difficult for developers and manufacturers of software to obtain patent protection, because many software products simply automate procedures that can be performed manually. In other words, the computer programs do not meet the ''novel'' and ''not obvious'' requirements previously mentioned. Also, the basis for software is often a mathematical equation or formula, which is not patentable. In 1981, the United States Supreme Court held that it is possible, however, to obtain a patent for a *process* that incorporates a computer program—providing, of course, that the process itself is patentable.[5] Subsequently, many patents have been issued for software-related inventions. Some critics believe that patents are being issued too readily for software that is not novel or that represents merely an obvious change of another's computer program.

Another obstacle to obtaining patent protection for software is the procedure of obtaining patents. The process can be expensive and slow. The time element is a particularly important consideration for someone wishing to obtain a patent on software: in light of the rapid changes and improvements in computer technology, the delay could undercut the product's success in the marketplace.

Despite these difficulties, patent protection is increasingly being used in the computer industry.

---

4. *Safeway Stores v. Suburban Foods,* 130 F.Supp. 249 (E.D.Va. 1955).

5. See *Diamond v. Diehr and Lutton,* 450 U.S. 175, 101 S.Ct. 1048, 67 L.Ed.2d 155 (1981).

If a patent is infringed, the patent holder may sue for an injunction, damages, and the destruction of all infringing copies, as well as attorneys' fees and court costs.

## INTERNATIONAL PATENT ISSUES

The scope of manufacturing and distribution is now very much international. Consequently, inventors often file for patent protection in many countries simultaneously. The international patent protection afforded a U.S. party is normally governed by the patent laws in each country in which the American inventor seeks protection. Additionally, the United States may have a treaty with another country, and the treaty may govern patents.

Patent law in most countries differs from patent law in the United States. In the United States, subject to certain exceptions, patents are granted only to the first inventor. In most other countries, patents are granted to the first party to file a patent application directed to an invention, with no regard to the question of whether the applicant was the first party to invent.

Patent policies and procedures in other countries also differ from those in the United States. For example, it took Texas Instruments thirty years to obtain a patent in Japan. Political and economic issues obviously were at play here, for the delay allowed the Japanese computer chip industry to flourish. In the United States, Texas Instruments was granted patent protection for the same invention within four years of the patent application.

The nature of the product for which a patent will be granted differs dramatically from country to country. A number of countries, for example, do not permit invention patents for pharmaceuticals (although some protection may be obtained by a process patent).

## SECTION 3

# COPYRIGHTS

A **copyright** is an intangible right granted by statute to the author or originator of certain literary or artistic productions. Works created after January 1, 1978, are automatically given statutory copyright protection for the life of the author plus fifty years. Copyrights owned by publishing houses expire seventy-five years from the date of publication or a hundred years from the date of creation, whichever is first. For works by one or more authors, the copyright expires fifty years after the death of the last surviving author. A copyright owner no longer needs to place a © or R on the work to have the work protected against infringement. Chances are that if somebody created it, somebody owns it.

## WHAT IS PROTECTED EXPRESSION?

Works that are copyrightable include books, records, films, works of art, architectural plans, menus, music videos, and product packaging. To obtain protection under the Copyright Act, a work must be original and fall into one of the following categories: (1) literary works; (2) musical works; (3) dramatic works; (4) pantomimes and choreographic works; (5) pictorial, graphic, and sculptural works; (6) films and other audiovisual works; and (7) sound recordings. In recent years, the Copyright Act has been amended to include protection for computer software and architectural plans. To be protected, a work must be "fixed in a durable medium" from which it can be perceived, reproduced, or communicated. Protection is automatic. Registration is not required.

Section 102 of the Copyright Act specifically excludes copyright protection for any "idea, procedure, process, system, method of operation, concept, principle or discovery, regardless of the form in which it is described, explained, illustrated, or embodied." Note that it is not possible to copyright an *idea*. The underlying ideas embodied in a work may be freely used by others. What is copyrightable is the particular way in which an idea is *expressed*. Whenever an idea and an expression are inseparable, the expression cannot be copyrighted.

Generally, anything that is not an original expression will not qualify for copyright protection. Facts widely known to the public are not copyrightable. Page numbers are not copyrightable, because they follow a sequence known to everyone. Mathematical calculations are not copyrightable. *Compilations* of facts, however, are copyrightable. Section 103 of the Copyright Act defines a compilation as "a work formed by the collection and assembling of preexisting materials or data that are selected, coordinated, or arranged in such a way that the resulting work as a whole constitutes an original work of authorship."

The key requirement to the copyrightability of a compilation is originality. Thus, the white pages of a telephone directory do not qualify for copyright protection when the information that makes up the directory is not selected, coordinated, or arranged in an original way. Names, addresses, and telephone numbers are "uncopyrightable facts," and there is nothing original or "remotely creative about arranging names alphabetically in a white pages directory." [6] Does the compilation of names, addresses, telephone numbers, and advertising in the yellow pages of a telephone directory qualify for copyright protection? This issue arose in the following case.

---

6.  *Feist Publications, Inc. v. Rural Telephone Service Co.,* 499 U.S. 340, 111 S.Ct. 1282, 113 L.Ed.2d 358 (1991).

---

CASE 8.3

**BELLSOUTH ADVERTISING & PUBLISHING CORP. v. DONNELLEY INFORMATION PUBLISHING, INC.**
United States Court of Appeals, Eleventh Circuit, 1993. 999 F.2d 1436.

**BACKGROUND AND FACTS**  *BellSouth Advertising & Publishing Corporation (BAPCO) publishes a yellow-pages advertising directory for the Greater Miami area. The listings in the directory are organized into alphabetized business classifications. Businesses can purchase cross listings under different classifications and advertisements to accompany each listing. In 1985, Donnelley Information Publishing, Inc., and Reuben H. Donnelley Corporation began selling space in a competitive yellow-pages directory. To generate a list of potential customers, Donnelley used the listings in BAPCO's directory. Each BAPCO listing was coded to indicate the size and type of advertisement and the type of business represented by the heading under which the listing appeared. These codes and the names, addresses, and telephone numbers of the businesses were entered into a computer database from which the Donnelley companies printed sales lead sheets. When the Donnelley directory was published, BAPCO sued in federal district court for, among other things, copyright infringement. BAPCO filed a motion for summary judgment, which the court granted. Donnelley appealed.*

*BIRCH,* Circuit Judge:
\* \* \* \*
\* \* \* Drawing upon the requirement of originality and the definition of "compilation" in the Copyright Act, the [United States Supreme] Court held [in *Feist Publications, Inc. v. Rural Telephone Service Co.*] that a compiler's selection, arrangement and coordination, if original, are the only protectable elements of a factual compilation.
\* \* \* \*
The district court found that BAPCO engaged in a number of acts of selection in compiling its listings. For example, BAPCO determined the geographic scope of its directory and the closing date after which no changes in listings would be included. The district court erred, however, in implicitly determining that these selective acts were sufficiently original to merit copyright protection. \* \* \* [A]ny collection of facts "fixed in any tangible medium of expression" will by necessity have a closing date and, where applicable, a geographic limit selected by the compiler. \* \* \* The district court also focused on a number of marketing techniques employed by BAPCO to generate its listings \* \* \*.
\* \* \* [T]hese acts are not acts of authorship, but techniques for the discovery of facts. \* \* \* Just as the Copyright Act does not protect "industrious collection," it affords no shelter to the resourceful, efficient, or creative collector. \* \* \*
In addition to these acts of selection, the district court found that BAPCO engaged in feats of coordination and arrangement \* \* \*. BAPCO's arrangement and coordination is "entirely typical" for a business directory. With respect to business

telephone directories, such an arrangement "is not only unoriginal, it is practically inevitable."

*The appellate court reversed the judgment of the district court and granted summary judgment for the Donnelley companies on BAPCO's claim of copyright infringement.*   **DECISION AND REMEDY**

## COPYRIGHT INFRINGEMENT

Whenever the form or expression of an idea is copied, an infringement of copyright has occurred. The reproduction does not have to be exactly the same as the original; nor does it have to reproduce the original in its entirety. If a substantial part of the original is reproduced, a copyright infringement exists.

Penalties or remedies can be imposed on those who infringe copyrights. These range from actual damages (damages based on the actual harm caused to the copyright holder by the infringement) or statutory damages (damages provided for under the Copyright Act, not to exceed $100,000), imposed at the court's discretion, to criminal proceedings for willful violations (which may result in fines and/or imprisonment).

An exception to liability for copyright infringement is made under the "fair use" doctrine. In certain circumstances, a person or organization can reproduce copyrighted material without paying royalties (fees paid to the copyright holder for the privilege of reproducing the copyrighted material). Section 107 of the Copyright Act provides as follows:

[T]he fair use of a copyrighted work, including such use by reproduction in copies or phonorecords or by any other means specified by [Section 106 of the Copyright Act], for purposes such as criticism, comment, news reporting, teaching (including multiple copies for classroom use), scholarship, or research, is not an infringement of copyright. In determining whether the use made of a work in any particular case is a fair use the factors to be considered shall include—

(1) the purpose and character of the use, including whether such use is of a commercial nature or is for nonprofit educational purposes;
(2) the nature of the copyrighted work;
(3) the amount and substantiality of the portion used in relation to the copyrighted work as a whole; and
(4) the effect of the use upon the potential market for or value of the copyrighted work.

Because these guidelines are very broad, the courts determine whether a particular use is fair on a case-by-case basis. Thus, anyone reproducing copyrighted material may still be subject to a violation. The following case discusses whether recording television broadcasts on home videotape recorders constitutes a copyright infringement.

**BACKGROUND AND FACTS**   *Universal City Studios, the respondent, owns the copyrights on some of the television programs broadcast on the public airwaves. Sony Corporation, the petitioner, manufactures and sells home videocassette recorders (VCRs, originally videotape recorders, or VTRs). Universal alleged that members of the general public used Betamax VTRs to record some broadcasts of Universal's copyrighted works, thereby infringing Universal's copyrights. Universal then maintained that Sony was liable for these copyright infringements because Sony marketed the Betamax VTRs. Universal sought money damages, an accounting for profits, and an injunction against the manufacture and marketing of Betamax VTRs. The district court denied Universal any relief, but the court of*

**CASE 8.4**

**SONY CORP. v. UNIVERSAL CITY STUDIOS**
Supreme Court of the United States, 1984.
467 U.S. 417,
104 S.Ct. 774,
78 L.Ed.2d 574.

*appeals held Sony liable for contributory infringement. The United States Supreme Court took up the case.*

*Justice STEVENS delivered the opinion of the Court.*

&ast;   &ast;   &ast;   &ast;

&ast;   &ast;   &ast; [T]he sale of copying equipment, like the sale of other articles of commerce, does not constitute contributory infringement if the product is widely used for legitimate, unobjectionable purposes. Indeed, it need merely be capable of substantial noninfringing uses.

&ast;   &ast;   &ast;   &ast;

Even unauthorized uses of a copyrighted work are not necessarily infringing. An unlicensed use of the copyright is not an infringement unless it conflicts with one of the specific exclusive rights conferred by the copyright statute. &ast;   &ast;   &ast; The most pertinent [section of the copyright statute] in this case is [Section] 107, the legislative endorsement of the doctrine of ''fair use.''

&ast;   &ast;   &ast;   &ast;

&ast;   &ast;   &ast; A challenge to a noncommercial use of a copyrighted work [requires] proof either that the particular use is harmful, or that if it should become widespread, it would adversely affect the potential market for the copyrighted work.

**DECISION AND REMEDY**

*The Supreme Court concluded (1) that a substantial number of television broadcast copyright holders would not object to having their broadcasts recorded and (2) that Universal had failed to demonstrate that the recordings would cause more than minimal harm to the market for, or value of, their copyrighted works. Therefore, the Betamax VTR is capable of noninfringing uses, and Sony was not liable for contributory infringement.*

**COMMENT**

*In the last few years, digital audiotape (DAT) and DAT recorders have come on the market. The owners of material that can be copied by DAT recorders have expressed some of the same fears as did the owners of copyrighted material that can be copied by VCRs, as discussed in the* Sony *case. The Copyright Act, as amended in 1992, allows home audio recording on DAT recorders but requires the recorders to be equipped to prevent copying from a copy. The act also requires royalties to be paid to the U.S. Copyright Office for every DAT recorder sold in, or imported into, the United States. The royalties are distributed to copyright holders whose material was available in digital format during the period in which the DAT recorders were sold.[a]*

a. 17 U.S.C. Section 1003.

## COPYRIGHT PROTECTION FOR COMPUTER SOFTWARE

In 1980, Congress passed the Computer Software Copyright Act, which amended the Copyright Act of 1976 to include computer programs in the list of creative works protected by federal copyright law. The 1980 statute defines a computer program as a ''set of statements or instructions to be used directly or indirectly in a computer in order to bring about a certain result.'' Because of the unique nature of computer programs, the courts have had many problems in applying and interpreting the 1980 act.

**THE LANGUAGE PROBLEM** Traditionally, copyright protection was extended only to literary works that were perceptible to humans—that is, to things written or printed in intelligible notation. But computer programs, which are classified as "literary works" under the 1980 act, are expressed in a language "readable" by machines. Should copyright protection be limited to those parts of a computer program that can be read by humans, such as the "high-level" language of a source code? Or should protection also extend to the binary-language object code of a computer program, which is readable only by the computer?

In a 1982 case, a program's source code was held to be copyrightable.[7] In an important 1983 decision, *Apple Computer, Inc. v. Franklin Computer Corp.*, copyright protection was extended to include both the binary object code and the source code of a computer program.[8]

**PROGRAM STRUCTURE, SEQUENCE, AND ORGANIZATION PROTECTION** By 1983, it was fairly well established—particularly by the *Apple Computer* decision just mentioned—that a program's computer codes were copyrightable. But should copyright protection cover other elements of computer software, such as the overall structure, sequence, and organization of a program? This issue was addressed in a significant 1986 case, *Whelan Associates, Inc. v. Jaslow Dental Laboratory, Inc.*[9] In *Whelan,* the court noted that copyrights of literary works can be infringed upon even when there is no substantial similarity between the works' literal elements. The copyright of a play or a book, for example, can be infringed upon if its plot or plot devices are copied. The court applied the same principle to computer programs, which are classified as "literary works" under the 1980 act, and held that the structure, sequence, and organization of computer programs were copyrightable.

**"LOOK AND FEEL" PROTECTION** An issue addressed in *Whelan* has evolved into what is now generally called program "look and feel" protection. Should the "look and feel"—the general appearance, command structure, video images, menus, windows, and other screen displays—of computer programs also be protected by copyright? This question has been at issue in several cases,

and the answer is not yet entirely clear. In a case brought by Lotus Development Corporation against Paperback Software International, Ltd., and its Canadian development partner, Stephenson Software, Ltd.,[10] Lotus claimed that Paperback Software had infringed its copyright by adapting its Lotus 1–2–3 spreadsheet format design and the keystroke sequences used in manipulating information. The court held that Lotus's menu command structure—including the choice of command terms, the structure and order of those terms, their presentation on the screen, and the long prompts—was copyrightable and that Paperback Software had infringed Lotus's copyright.

Recently, however, it would seem that the courts are narrowing their view of what software elements are protectable. For example, a federal district court in 1992 held that the user interface of Apple's Macintosh computer is not protectable under a "look and feel" theory and that Apple's use of windows, icons, and menus, and generally the series of images that Apple calls a "desktop metaphor," are unprotectable "ideas."[11] This decision concluded Apple's four-year-long legal struggle with Microsoft Corporation and the Hewlett Packard Company. Apple had claimed that the other two firms had imitated the "look and feel" of the Macintosh user interface.

In another 1992 decision that many feel is significant for the software industry, *Computer Associates International v. Altai, Inc.,*[12] the Court of Appeals for the Second Circuit adopted a test to be used in determining copyright infringement issues relating to computer programs. The test requires a court to divide a program into its component parts and then determine whether each individual component is (1) protectable as an expression of an idea or (2) unprotectable because it is an idea or a technique dictated by utilitarian considerations.

## INTERNATIONAL COPYRIGHT ISSUES

The United States is a party to a number of international copyright treaties, including the Berne

7. *Stern Electronics, Inc. v. Kaufman,* 669 F.2d 852 (2d Cir. 1982).

8. 714 F.2d 1240 (3d Cir. 1983).

9. 797 F.2d 1222 (3d Cir. 1986).

10. *Lotus Development Corp. v. Paperback Software International, Ltd.,* 740 F.Supp. 37 (D.Mass. 1990).

11. *Apple Computer, Inc. v. Microsoft Corp.,* 799 F.Supp. 1006 (N.D.Cal. 1992).

12. 982 F.2d 693 (2d Cir. 1992).

# EMERGING TRENDS IN BUSINESS LAW

## Copyright Infringement in the Electronic Age

I t would be hard to imagine life without photocopiers. Pages of textbooks, articles from journals, memos, and an endless variety of textual and illustrative material can be copied quickly and at relatively low cost for a myriad of purposes. The ease and low cost of making photocopies may be a boon for those making and using the photocopies, but publishers whose copyrighted works are copied lose millions of dollars in revenues.

In the world of electronic databases that contain literally billions of documents, many of which are copyrighted, the ease with which such material can be passed on to unauthorized users has created serious problems for owners of such materials. Because of this, some publishers have recently taken aim at those who make copies of their copyright-protected works without permission.

### Photocopies and Copyright Law

In 1989, for example, Basic Books and seven other major New York publishers sued Kinko's, the national chain of copy stores, for violating copyright laws by producing unauthorized course anthologies for students. For many years, professors on college campuses have assembled excerpts from relevant articles or textbooks into a packet, which would then be copied and bound by a local copy shop and sold to students at modest prices. The problem is that few professors and even fewer copy shops ever bothered to contact the copyright holders of the excerpted pages from copyrighted works to secure permission to reproduce the materials.

In defending against the publishers' claim of copyright infringement, Kinko's admitted that it had not obtained permission from the copyright holders but argued that its anthologies were protected under the "fair use" doctrine because the materials were for educational use.

The court thought otherwise. Noting that the profit motive for producing the anthologies was of primary importance to Kinko's, the court ordered Kinko's to pay the publishers over one million dollars in damages and legal expenses.[a] The court's decision has convinced copy shops to begin demanding proof of authorization before

agreeing to reproduce anthologies for university courses.

Other cases have been brought by publishers of journals or newsletters against clients who make multiple copies of journal articles or newsletters for purposes of internal circulation without the publishers' permission and without paying additional fees to the publishers. In 1991, for example, Washington Business Information, Inc. (WBII), the publisher of a product liability safety newsletter, settled a dispute with the Washington, D.C., law firm of Coller, Shannon, and Scott regarding the firm's allegedly unauthorized duplication of its newsletter. According to David Swit, the head of WBII, the law firm made the copies to avoid paying $590 for two additional subscriptions. The *New York Times* reported that this practice may have ended up costing the law firm an estimated one million dollars in legal fees.[b]

In a similar case, a U.S. District Court held that Texaco, Inc., infringed on the copyrights held by a number of publishers of scientific journals by allowing its employees to make photocopies of scientific

---

a. *Basic Books, Inc. v. Kinko's Graphics Corp.,* 758 F.Supp. 1522 (S.D.N.Y. 1991).

---

b. December 6, 1991, p. B10.

journals to which Texaco subscribed. Texaco argued that the unauthorized photocopying constituted a fair use because it was necessary for the advancement of scientific research. According to the court, however, profit-making companies, such as Texaco, cannot make copies of copyrighted journal articles without obtaining permission from and compensating the copyright holders.[c]

## Electronic Copying

Today, electronic copying has become a further problem for copyright holders. Newsletters, for example, can be scanned using optical character recognition (OCR) programs and relatively low-priced computerized scanning machines. Once a newsletter has been scanned into a computer, it can become part of a company's database and be distributed electronically either through diskette copies, or as is increasingly the case, through local area networks or more sophisticated local area computer networks. Indeed, it is even possible to transmit such newsletters via electronic mail (E-mail) through a telecommunications network that forms a part of today's growing "information highway."

Nonetheless, such high-tech copying still violates copyright law, as officials at Atlas Telecom, Inc., found out after admitting that it had electronically distributed a dozen telecommunication newsletters from Phillips

Business Information, Inc. Apparently, for over two years, Atlas Telecom had been making hundreds of copies of each newsletter by putting them on its in-house database. Atlas settled for $100,000 without going to trial.[d]

## The Digitized World

As more and more of the publishing world becomes digitized (puts letters and images into digital format), the issue of copyright protection will become even more thorny. It is now possible, for example, to digitize photographs of original art inexpensively. Such digitized reproductions can then be passed around to literally millions of individuals via electronic networks throughout the world. Furthermore, the increasing sophistication, speed, and memory capabilities of today's computers will guarantee that what exists on paper today will likely exist electronically tomorrow.

## ■ Implications for the Businessperson

1.  The decisions in the cases cited above should caution company managers not to make copies of published materials for internal distribution without first obtaining the permission of the copyright holders. Although securing permission may be inconvenient, it is bound to be much less costly than an adverse court ruling.

2.  In firms that subscribe to newsletters and other periodical publications, management should make sure that all employees know about copyright law and how costly a copyright-infringement action against the firm can be.
3.  While electronic copying and distribution of data may be a boon for certain sectors of the economy, this boon is not without costs. For publishers, today's "information highway" clearly makes it easier for their copyright-protected works to be copied by others without permission. Publishers will clearly have to devise means of protecting their works against infringing uses, and these means will no doubt be costly.

## ■ For Critical Analysis

1.  What two public policies must the courts balance when deciding cases involving the copying of copyrighted materials for educational or research purposes? Do you think that the courts, in the rulings discussed above, struck a fair balance between these two policies?
2.  Do you think that the copying of copyrighted works for educational or research purposes should be deemed a "fair use," even if the copying is done by a commercial enterprise?
3.  If you were a decision maker in a company publishing newsletters, how much copyright-infringement litigation should you undertake? On what criteria would you base your decision?

c. *American Geophysical Union v. Texaco, Inc.*, 802 F.Supp. 1 (S.D.N.Y. 1992).

d. Junda Woo, "Electronic Copying May Bring Lawsuits," *The Wall Street Journal*, October 6, 1993, p. B4.

Convention and the Universal Copyright Convention. Under the Berne Convention, if an American writes a book, his or her copyright in the book must be recognized by every country that has signed the convention. Also, if a citizen of a country that has not signed the convention first publishes a book in a country that has signed, all other countries that have signed the convention must recognize that author's copyright. Copyright notice is not needed to gain protection under the Berne Convention for works published after March 1, 1989.

## SECTION 4

# TRADE SECRETS

Some business processes and information that are not, or cannot be, patented, copyrighted, or trademarked are nevertheless protected against appropriation by a competitor as **trade secrets.** Customer lists, plans, research and development, pricing information, marketing techniques, production techniques, and generally anything that makes an individual company unique and that would have value to a competitor constitute trade secrets. The most widely used definition of a trade secret is found in the Restatement of Torts, Section 757(b):

> A trade secret may consist of any formula, pattern, device, or compilation of information which is used in one's business, and which gives him an opportunity to obtain an advantage over competitors who do not know or use it. It may be a formula for a chemical compound, a process of manufacturing, treating or preserving materials, . . . or a list of customers.

Virtually all law with respect to trade secrets is common law. Identical types of information reviewed by different courts in similar factual settings have been classified differently. In an effort to reduce the unpredictability of common law with respect to trade secrets, a model act, the Uniform Trade Secrets Act, was presented to the states in 1979 for adoption. Parts of it have been adopted in over twenty states. Typically, a state that has adopted parts of the act has only adopted those parts that encompass its own existing common law.

Unlike copyright and trademark protection, protection of trade secrets extends both to ideas and to their expression. (For this reason, and because a trade secret involves no registration or filing requirements, trade secret protection may be well suited for software.) Of course, the secret formula, method, or other information must be disclosed to some persons, particularly to key employees. Businesses generally attempt to protect their trade secrets by having all employees who use the process or information agree in their contracts never to divulge it. Thus, if a salesperson tries to solicit the company's customers for noncompany business, or if an employee copies the employer's unique method of manufacture, he or she has appropriated a trade secret and has also broken a contract—two separate wrongs. Theft of confidential business data by industrial espionage, as when a business taps into a competitor's computer, is a theft of trade secrets without any contractual violation and is actionable in itself.

Under Section 757 of the Restatement of Torts, "One who discloses or uses another's trade secret, without a privilege to do so, is liable to the other if (1) he discovered the secret by improper means, or (b) his disclosure or use constitutes a breach of confidence reposed in him by the other in disclosing the secret to him." In the following case, the court had to decide whether aerial photography was an "improper means" of discovering another's trade secret.

---

| CASE 8.5 |
| :--- |
| **E. I. du PONT de NEMOURS & CO. v. CHRISTOPHER** |
| United States Court of Appeals, Fifth Circuit, 1970. 431 F.2d 1012. |

**BACKGROUND AND FACTS** *In 1969, Rolfe and Gary Christopher, at the request of an unknown third party, took sixteen aerial photographs of a new plant being constructed by E. I. du Pont de Nemours & Company (DuPont) in Beaumont, Texas. Because the plant construction had not yet been completed, a process for making methanol, which DuPont was trying to keep secret, was not yet covered by a roof and so was visible from the air. DuPont, concerned about the airplane circling over the plant, conducted an investigation and learned that photographs had been taken and that the Christophers were the photographers. The Christophers refused to* *tell DuPont the name of the person or corporation requesting the photographs, stating that their client wished to remain anonymous. Having reached a dead end in the investigation, DuPont subsequently filed suit against the Christophers, alleging that they had wrongfully obtained photographs revealing DuPont's trade secrets. The Christophers argued that they had committed no "actionable wrong" in photographing the DuPont facility because "they conducted all of their activities in public airspace, violated no government aviation standards, did not breach any confidential relation, and did not engage in any fraudulent or illegal conduct." The trial court held that DuPont's claim was actionable, and the Christophers appealed.*

*GOLDBERG*, Circuit Judge.

\* \* \* \*

\* \* \* [T]he Texas rule is clear. One may use his competitor's secret process if he discovers the process by reverse engineering[a] applied to the finished product; one may use a competitor's process if he discovers it by his own independent research; but one may not avoid these labors by taking the process from the discoverer without his permission at a time when he is taking reasonable precautions to maintain its secrecy.

\* \* \* \*

In the instant case DuPont was in the midst of constructing a plant. Although after construction the finished plant would have protected much of the process from view, during the period of construction the trade secret was exposed to view from the air. To require DuPont to put a roof over the unfinished plant to guard its secret would impose an enormous expense \* \* \* . We should not require a person or corporation to take unreasonable precautions to prevent another from doing that which he ought not do in the first place.

**DECISION AND REMEDY**

*The appellate court affirmed the trial court's holding that DuPont had stated a cause of action and remanded the case to the trial court for further proceedings.*

**ETHICAL CONSIDERATIONS**

*The decision in this case illustrates a trade-off between the policy of promoting free competition and the policy of protecting the spirit of inventiveness. A free market requires competitiveness, and being competitive requires an awareness of what the competition is doing. Being competitive also requires inventiveness in the development of new products and processes—and protecting against the attempts of competitors to learn of those new products or processes. The trade-off occurs at the point when, in the words of the court, "the protections required to prevent another's spying cost so much that the spirit of inventiveness is dampened."*

a. Reverse engineering is a technique in which a process or secret formula is learned by analysis of the product that results from the process or secret formula.

# COMPUTER CRIME

The American Bar Association defines **computer crime** as any act that is directed against computers and computer parts, that uses computers as instruments of crime, or that involves computers and constitutes abuse. Generally, computer crimes are classified as white-collar crimes, because ordinarily they do not involve physical violence. Recall from the discussion earlier in this chapter the difficulties faced by the courts in applying conventional copyright law to computer software. Similar difficulties exist in attempting to apply traditional criminal law to computer crimes. In some cases, existing laws have been extended—either by amendment or through judicial interpretation—to include computer crimes. In other cases, new legislation has been enacted to specifically address crimes unique to the computer age.

## TYPES OF COMPUTER CRIME

Crimes committed with or against computers generally fall into five broad categories: financial crimes, software piracy (the unauthorized copying of another's computer program), theft of computer equipment, vandalism and destructive programming, and theft or unauthorized use of data or services.

**FINANCIAL CRIMES** Many computer crimes fall into the broad category of financial crimes. In addition to using computers for information storage and retrieval, businesses increasingly use computers to conduct financial transactions. This is equally true of the government, which handles many of its transactions by computer. These circumstances provide opportunities for employees and others to commit crimes that can involve serious economic losses. For example, employees of accounting and computer departments can, with little effort and without the risk involved in transactions evidenced by paperwork, transfer monies among accounts. The potential for crime in the area of financial transactions is great, and it is in this category of computer crime that most monetary losses are suffered.

**SOFTWARE PIRACY** In most states, the theft of software is classified as a crime. At the federal level, laws protecting intellectual property (such as patent and copyright laws) have been amended in recent years to extend coverage to computer programs—as was discussed earlier in this chapter. In 1990, in an attempt to control further the unauthorized copying of computer programs, the federal government passed a law that prohibits, with some exceptions, the rental, leasing, or lending of computer software without the express permission of the copyright holder.

**PROPERTY THEFT** Computer crimes can also involve property theft. The theft of computer equipment (hardware) has become easier and more commonplace as computer components have become smaller and thus more readily transportable. Computer-related theft also may involve goods that are controlled and accounted for by means of a computer applications program. For example, an employee in a company's accounting department could manipulate inventory records to conceal unauthorized shipments of goods. The theft of computer equipment and the theft of goods with the aid of computers are subject to the same criminal and tort laws as thefts of other property are (see Chapters 6, 7, and 9).

**VANDALISM AND DESTRUCTIVE PROGRAMMING** On occasion, political activists, terrorists, and disgruntled employees have physically damaged computer hardware or ruined computer software. These acts have included such conduct as smashing computer equipment with a crowbar, shooting it with a pistol, and—in an attempt to make a political point—pouring blood over a computer. In one instance, to erase a company's records, an individual merely walked past computer storage banks with a large electromagnet.

Other destructive acts have required greater technical awareness and facility. A knowledgeable individual can do a considerable amount of damage. For example, a computer program can be designed to rearrange, replace, or even destroy data. Activating a program's existing commands to tell the program to turn itself off, thereby shutting down a company's computerized telephone system, has also been held to constitute a computer crime.[13]

---

13. *People v. Versaggi,* 83 N.Y.2d 123, 629 N.E.2d 1034, 608 N.Y.S.2d 155 (1994).

**THEFT OF DATA OR SERVICES** Most people would agree that when an individual uses another's computer or computer information system without authorization, the individual is stealing. For example, an employee who used a computer system or data stored in a computer system for private gain and without the employer's authorization would likely be considered a thief, as would a politician who used a government computer to send out campaign brochures. Under an increasing number of revised criminal codes or broad judicial interpretations of existing statutes, the unauthorized use of computer data or services is considered larceny (a form of theft—see Chapter 9).

Particularly vulnerable to the theft of data or services are systems to which more than one party has access. Even systems accessible only through *passwords* (codes designed to prohibit access to all but authorized users) are often used illegally, especially when the codes are not changed for long periods of time. Breaking a computer's security code or device and perusing the information in the system's records is commonly known as *hacking*. Some instances of hacking have generated considerable alarm. For example, hackers have cracked computers' secret codes and gained access to businesses' telephone systems. Once a hacker breaks into a company's system, calls can be made to any location in the world with the charges billed to the company. The activities of these thieves and other computer hackers have brought to the public's attention the alarming vulnerability of computer systems—and the businesses and government agencies that rely on them.

## DETECTING AND PROSECUTING COMPUTER CRIME

One of the challenges presented by computer crime is its relative invisibility. Computer crime is often difficult to detect, and if the crime is cleverly executed, it may go undetected for some time. In some cases, victimized companies, and even the government, have discovered multimillion-dollar thefts only after a considerable lapse of time. Even when it is apparent that a computer crime has occurred, tracing the crime to the individual who committed it can be very difficult, because the individual's identity is "hidden," as it were, by the anonymous nature of the computer system.

In attempting to control computer crime, governmental bodies at both the federal and state levels have undertaken protective measures. At the federal level, the Counterfeit Access Device and Computer Fraud and Abuse Act of 1984 prohibits the unauthorized access to, or use of, certain types of information, including restricted government information, information contained in a financial institution's financial records, and information in a consumer reporting agency's files on consumers. Penalties for violations include up to five years' imprisonment and a fine of up to $250,000 or twice the amount that was gained or lost as a result of the crime. In addition, several states have also passed legislation specifically addressing the problem of computer crime.

## SECTION 6

# PRIVACY RIGHTS AND COMPUTERS

As mentioned in previous chapters, an individual's right to privacy is protected under tort law and, to a certain extent, under the U.S. Constitution. In situations involving computers, tort damages may be awarded for unauthorized intrusion into another's private records or unauthorized examination of another's bank account. But how does one demonstrate that private records have been invaded when there has been no physical intrusion into one's home or place of business? In such a situation, there is no "evidence" of the invasion of privacy.

In response to society's concern over the potential abuse of personal information collected by the government and other institutions, Congress has enacted several laws (see Exhibit 8–1). In addition, many of the laws that states have enacted to address computer crime are also necessarily concerned to some extent with the issue of privacy. The Privacy Act of 1974 has served as a model for many of the state laws regulating government records and recording practices. Although this legislation has helped to control the collection and dispersal of information contained in computer files, information in computer files is still to a great extent unprotected by rules, laws, or codes of ethics. In general, how to control computer use and abuse remains a significant legal challenge of our time.

■ **Exhibit 8–1 Federal Legislation Relating to Privacy**

| Title | Provisions Concerning Privacy |
|---|---|
| Freedom of Information Act (1966) | Provides that individuals have a right to obtain access to information about them collected in government files. |
| Fair Credit Reporting Act (1970) | Provides that consumers have the right to be informed of the nature and scope of a credit investigation, the kind of information that is being compiled, and the names of the firms or individuals who will be receiving the report. |
| Crime Control Act (1973) | Safeguards the confidentiality of information amassed for certain state criminal systems. |
| Family Educational Rights and Privacy Act (1974) | Limits access to computer-stored records of education-related evaluations and grades in private and public colleges and universities. |
| Privacy Act (1974) | Protects the privacy of individuals about whom the federal government has information. Specifically, the act provides the following: 1. Agencies originating, using, disclosing, or otherwise manipulating personal information must ensure the reliability of the information and provide safeguards against its misuse. 2. Information compiled for one purpose cannot be used for another without the concerned individual's permission. 3. Individuals must be able to find out what data concerning them are being compiled and how the data will be used. 4. Individuals must be given a means through which to correct inaccurate data. |
| Tax Reform Act (1976) | Preserves the privacy of personal financial information. |
| Right to Financial Privacy Act (1978) | Prohibits financial institutions from providing the federal government with access to a customer's records unless the customer authorizes the disclosure. |
| Electronic Fund Transfer Act (1978) | Requires financial institutions to notify an individual if a third party gains access to the individual's account. |
| Counterfeit Access Device and Computer Fraud and Abuse Act (1984) | Prohibits the use of a computer without authorization to retrieve data in a financial institution's or consumer reporting agency's files. |
| Cable Communications Policy Act (1984) | Regulates access to information collected by cable service operators on subscribers to cable services. |
| Electronic Communications Privacy Act (1986) | Prohibits the interception of information communicated by electronic means. |

# TERMS AND CONCEPTS TO REVIEW

certification mark  147
collective mark  147
computer crime  158
copyright  149

intellectual property  143
patent  148
service mark  147

trade name  148
trade secret  156
trademark  144

# QUESTIONS AND CASE PROBLEMS

**8–1. Fair Use Doctrine.** Professor Wise is teaching a summer seminar in business torts at State University. Several times during the course, he makes copies of relevant sections from business law texts and distributes them to his students. Wise does not realize that the daughter of one of the textbook authors is a member of his seminar. She tells her father about Wise's copying activities, which have been done without her father's or his publisher's permission. Her father sues Wise for copyright infringement. Wise claims protection under the "fair use" doctrine. Who will prevail? Explain.

**8–2. Computer Crime.** Adams, who owns and operates a restaurant, has had an account with Uptown Bank for over twenty years. All of Uptown's banking records are computerized. Greed, one of Adams's competitors, pays a sum of money to a disgruntled Uptown employee to access Uptown's computer system and provide Greed with information on Adams's financial position and activities. In addition to giving Greed this information, the employee gives one of Adams's creditors the access code of Uptown's computer system. The creditor, using its own computer, then gathers financial information on Adams. Uptown Bank learns of these activities and discharges the employee. Discuss whether any of the federal laws mentioned in this chapter are specifically applicable to these facts.

**8–3. Copyright Infringement.** In which of the following situations would a court likely hold Ursula liable for copyright infringement?

(a) From a scholarly journal at the library, Ursula photocopies ten pages relating to a topic on which she is writing a term paper.

(b) Ursula makes blouses, dresses, and other clothes and sells them in her small shop. She advertises some of the outfits as "Guest" items, hoping that customers might mistakenly assume that they were made by Guess, the well-known maker of clothing.

(c) Ursula owns a video store. She purchases the latest videos from various video manufacturers but buys only one copy of each video. Then, using blank videotapes, she makes copies to rent or sell to her customers.

(d) Ursula teaches Latin American history at a small university. She has a VCR and frequently tapes television programs relating to Latin America. She then takes the videos to her classroom so that her students can watch them.

**8–4. Copyright Protection.** One day during algebra class, Diedra, an enterprising fourteen-year-old student, began drawing designs on her shoelaces. By the end of the class, Diedra had decorated her shoelaces with the name of the school, "Broadson Junior High," written in blue and red (the school colors) and with pictures of bears, the school's mascot. After class, Mrs. Laxton, Diedra's teacher, reprimanded Diedra for not paying attention in class and asked Diedra what she had been doing during the lecture. Diedra showed Mrs. Laxton her shoelaces. When Diedra got home that night, she wrote about the day's events in her diary. She also drew her shoelace design in the diary. Mrs. Laxton had been trying to think of how she could build up the school spirit. She thought about Diedra's shoelaces and decided to go into business for herself. She called her business "Spirited Shoelaces" and designed shoelaces for each of the local schools, decorating the shoelaces in each case with the school's name, mascot, and colors. The business became tremendously profitable. Even though Diedra never registered her idea with the patent or copyright office, does she nonetheless have intellectual property rights in the shoelace design? Will her diary account be sufficient proof that she created the idea? Discuss fully.

**8–5. Fair Use Doctrine.** Original Appalachian Artworks, Inc. (OAA), makes and distributes the very successful product called Cabbage Patch Kids—soft, sculptured dolls that were in great demand in the early 1980s. The dolls are unique in appearance, and the name is registered as a trademark to OAA. The design, too, is protected under a copyright registration. In 1986 Topps Chewing Gum, Inc., had an artist copy many of the features of the dolls for Topps's new product—stickers that depicted obnoxious cartoon characters called Garbage Pail Kids. The stickers, along with another product line that Topps developed, proved very lucrative; in fact, Topps expanded the product line to include T-shirts, balloons, and school notebooks. Topps claimed that its product was actually a satire of (critical comment on) OAA's product and therefore a fair use of a protected work. Did Topps's use of OAA's product constitute a fair use of the product, or did it constitute trademark and copyright infringement? [*Original Appalachian Artworks, Inc. v. Topps Chewing Gum, Inc.,* 642 F.Supp. 1031 (N.D.Ga. 1986)]

**8–6. Trademark Infringement.** Nike, Inc., manufactures and markets footwear, apparel, and related accessories. To identify its products, Nike uses the word "Nike" and/or a "swoosh" design as its trademarks. From 1977 through 1992, Nike spent more than $320 million advertising the trademarks. Since 1971, sales revenues for items bearing the trademarks have exceeded $10 billion. Nike began using the phrase "Just Do It" in 1989 as a slogan for its sweatshirts, T-shirts, caps, and other accessories. "Nike," the swoosh design, and "Just Do It" have gained widespread public acceptance and recognition. Michael Stanard is an award-winning commercial artist whose works include, among others, the trademark "Louisville Slugger" printed on baseball bats. As a summer project, he and his daughter decided to market his first name, Mike, as a takeoff on the Nike logo. They named their project "Just Did It" Enterprises and concentrated on marketing T-shirts and sweatshirts to members of the general public with the given (first) name of Michael. They also mailed brochures to college athletes and celebrities named Michael. Sales were entirely by mail order. Approximately two-thirds of those purchasing the shirts were named Mike. Stanard believed that the other third probably bought a T-shirt for a friend, relative, or loved one named Mike. Ultimately, the project lost money. Nike sued Stanard for trademark infringement. Stanard argued that the word play was humorous and constituted a fair use of the trademarks as a parody. Should the court rule that Nike's trademark had been infringed? Explain. [*Nike, Inc. v. "Just Did It" Enterprises,* 6 F.3d 1225 (7th Cir. 1993)]

**8–7. Trademark Infringement.** On September 21, 1987, Quality Inns International, Inc., announced a new chain of economy hotels to be marketed under the name "McSleep Inns." The response of the owners of McDonald's Corp., the fast-food chain, was immediate. McDonald's wrote Quality Inns a letter stating that the use of "McSleep Inns" infringed upon the McDonald's family of marks characterized by the prefix "Mc" attached to a generic term. Five days later, Quality Inns filed an action seeking a declaratory judgment from the court that the mark "McSleep Inns" did not infringe on McDonald's federally registered trademarks or common law rights to its marks and would not constitute an unfair trade practice. McDonald's counterclaimed, alleging trademark infringement and unfair competition. McDonald's argued that the use of the name "McSleep Inns" by Quality Inns would confuse and mislead the public and allow Quality Inns to trade on the goodwill and reputation of McDonald's. Quality Inns claimed that "Mc" had come into generic use as a prefix and that therefore McDonald's had no trademark rights to the prefix itself. Quality Inns further claimed that its use of the prefix for lodging accommodations would not be confusing to the public, because McDonald's products were fast foods. Does the use of the prefix "Mc" by Quality Inns for its new "McSleep" chain of economy motels infringe on McDonald's trademarks? Explain. [*Quality Inns International, Inc. v. McDonald's Corp.,* 695 F.Supp. 198 (D.Md. 1988)]

**8–8. Fair Use Doctrine.** Jonathan Caven-Atack had been a member of the Church of Scientology for nine years when he decided that the church was a dangerous cult and its leader, L. Ron Hubbard, a vindictive and profoundly disturbed man. Caven-Atack spent the next several years investigating, and then writing a book about, Hubbard and the church. Caven-Atack's purpose was to expose what he believed was the pernicious nature of the church and the deceit upon which its teachings were based. Approximately 3 percent of Caven-Atack's book consisted of quotations from Hubbard's published works. When New Era Publications International, which held exclusive copyright rights in all of Hubbard's works, learned that the Carol Publishing Group planned to publish Caven-Atack's book, it sued Carol Publishing

for copyright infringement. Carol Publishing claimed that Caven-Atack's use of Hubbard's works was a "fair use" of the copyrighted materials. What factors must the court consider in making its decision? What will its decision be? Discuss. [*New Era Publications International, ApS v. Carol Publishing Group,* 904 F.2d 152 (2d Cir. 1990)]

**8–9. Copyright Infringement.** Nintendo of America, Inc., manufactures a home video game system, the Nintendo Entertainment System (NES). Nintendo designed the NES to prevent it from accepting unauthorized video game cartridges. Microprocessor chips in the NES consoles were coded to accept only Nintendo cartridges. Atari Games Corp. wanted to sell video game cartridges that could be used in the NES consoles. Atari attempted to analyze the NES lockout program through reverse engineering. Unable to do so successfully, Atari obtained a copy of the human-readable source code of the NES program from the U.S. Copyright Office by means of false representations. Atari was then able to decode the NES lockout program through reverse engineering and develop a program to place in its cartridges to allow its games to be played on the NES. Nintendo filed a lawsuit against Atari, alleging that Atari had infringed Nintendo's copyright in the NES program when it made copies of the program code during the course of its reverse engineering. Atari argued that copying for the purposes of reverse engineering is a fair use. What will result in court? Discuss. [*Atari Games Corp. v. Nintendo of America, Inc.,* 975 F.2d 832 (Fed. Cir. 1992)]

**8–10. Copyright Infringement.** Sega Enterprises, Ltd., develops and markets video entertainment systems, including the "Genesis" console and video game cartridges. Accolade, Inc., is an independent developer, manufacturer, and marketer of computer entertainment software, including game cartridges that are compatible with Genesis and other computer systems. Sega licenses its copyrighted computer code and its trademark to developers of Genesis-compatible games in competition with Sega. Accolade chose not to purchase a license from Sega, however, but to reverse-engineer Sega's games to discover the requirements of the code that would make Accolade's games compatible with Genesis. As part of the reverse engineering, Accolade transformed the machine-readable object code contained in Sega's game cartridges into human-readable source code using a process called "disassembly." At the end of the process, Accolade created a manual that incorporated the information it had discovered about the requirements for a Genesis-compatible game. The manual did not include any of Sega's code. With the manual, Accolade created a new computer code; with this code, Accolade developed Genesis-compatible games. Sega sued Accolade, claiming, among other things, that Accolade's disassembly of its computer program constituted copyright infringement. Accolade contended that its disassembly of the code was a fair use. How should the court rule? Discuss fully. [*Sega Enterprises, Ltd. v. Accolade, Inc.,* 977 F.2d 1510 (9th Cir. 1992)]

### 8–11. A Question of Ethics

*Peter Bonyhard, a physicist, had developed disk-drive heads for International Business Machines Corp. (IBM) for five years when he was hired away from IBM by Seagate Technology, Inc. Bonyhard's assignment was to develop at Seagate the same new type of disk-drive head, called a magnetoresistive (MR) head, that he had been working on for IBM. IBM sued Seagate and Bonyhard, alleging that Seagate had hired Bonyhard for the purpose of stealing IBM's secret formula for the MR heads. IBM, without any evidence that Bonyhard had actually disclosed any trade secrets, sought to have the court enjoin Bonyhard from working for Seagate on the ground that it would be simply impossible for Bonyhard to work for Seagate without disclosing IBM information. A district court granted the injunction, but on appeal, the injunction was vacated [nullified]. The appellate court held that the terms of the injunction were too vague and not based on any specific evidence that what IBM claimed were confidential information and trade secrets were so in fact.* [Seagate Technology, Inc. v. International Business Machines Corp., *962 F.2d 12 (8th Cir. 1992)*]

1. Do you agree with IBM that it would be simply impossible for Bonyhard to work for Seagate without disclosing IBM trade secrets? If so, do you agree with the district court that Bonyhard should be enjoined from continuing to work for Seagate? Why or why not?

2. The issue raised in this case is a significant one for high-tech industries that capitalize on state-of-the-art technology in producing and distributing new electronic products. Talented employees who are well versed in certain technology, as Bonyhard was in this case, are frequently sought after by competing firms. What two broad public policies, or ethical precepts, are at issue in this kind of situation?

3. Many firms require employees to sign "covenants not to compete" as a way to protect their interests and trade secrets. Covenants not to compete, agreements in which the employees promise not to work for any competitor of the firm in a given geographic area for a given period of time, are discussed in Chapter 16. But courts scrutinize such agreements closely and are often reluctant to enforce them. Can you think of alternative ways in which employers might protect themselves against the divulgence of their trade secrets by former employees?

4. Assuming that an employee is violating no law when he or she responds to an enticing offer from another firm, is it ethical for that employee to use his or her skills and talents to the detriment of a former employer?

# CHAPTER 9

# CRIMINAL LAW AND PROCEDURES

V arious sanctions are used to bring about a society in which individuals engaging in business can compete and flourish. These sanctions include those imposed by the civil law, such as damages for various types of tortious conduct (as discussed in the preceding chapter) and damages for breach of contract (to be discussed in Chapter 19). Chapter 1 also pointed out that the courts of equity may restrain certain types of unlawful conduct or require that things having certain unlawful effects be undone by issuing injunctions.

These remedies have not been sufficient deterrents in some instances. Consequently, additional sanctions have been developed for particular undesirable activities. As a result, a *criminal law element* exists within the legal environment of business. The prerequisites of *fault* or *guilt* in this area are different from those in the civil law, as are the sanctions and penalties.

## SECTION 1

## THE NATURE OF CRIMINAL LAW

*Civil law* spells out the duties that exist between persons or between citizens and their governments, excluding the duty not to commit crimes. Contract law, for example, is part of civil law. The whole body of tort law, which deals with the infringement by one person on the legally recognized rights of another, is also an area of civil law.

*Criminal law* has to do with crimes, which are different from other wrongful acts (such as torts) in a number of ways:

1. Crimes are *offenses against society as a whole* and thus are prosecuted by public officials, not by victims.

2. Those who commit crimes are punished. Tort remedies—remedies for civil wrongs—usually compensate the injured (except when punitive damages are assessed), whereas criminal law punishes (and, ideally, rehabilitates) the wrongdoer.

3. The source of criminal law is now primarily statutory, although common law was once the main body of criminal law.

Both crimes and punishments are very specifically set out in statutes. A **crime** can thus be defined as a wrong against society proclaimed in a statute and, if intentionally committed, punishable by society.

SECTION 2

# CLASSIFICATION OF CRIMES

Crimes are classified as either felonies or misdemeanors. Criminal statutes generally do not state whether the crimes they describe are felonies or misdemeanors. The distinction between the two classifications is found in the type of punishment that might be levied against the perpetrator if he or she is found guilty of the crime charged.

Serious crimes that are punishable by death or by imprisonment in a federal or state penitentiary for more than a year are **felonies.** The Model Penal Code[1] provides for four degrees of felony: (1) capital offenses, for which the maximum penalty is death; (2) first-degree felonies, punishable by a maximum penalty of life imprisonment; (3) second-degree felonies, punishable by a maximum of ten years' imprisonment; and (4) third-degree felonies, punishable by up to five years' imprisonment.

Under federal law and in most states, any crime that is not a felony is considered a **misdemeanor.** Misdemeanors are crimes punishable by a fine or by confinement for up to a year. If incarcerated (imprisoned), the guilty party goes to a local jail instead of a penitentiary. Disorderly conduct and trespass are common misdemeanors. Some states have different classes of misdemeanors. For example, in Illinois, misdemeanors are either Class A (confinement for up to a year), Class B (confinement for not more than six months), or Class C (confinement for not more than thirty days).

Whether a crime is a felony or a misdemeanor can also determine whether the case is tried in a magistrate's court (for example, by a justice of the peace), a county court, or a general trial court. In most jurisdictions, **petty offenses** are considered to be a subset of misdemeanors. Petty offenses are minor violations, such as violations of building codes. Even for petty offenses, however, a guilty party can be put in jail for a few days, fined, or both, depending on state law.

SECTION 3

# THE ESSENTIALS OF CRIMINAL LIABILITY

Two elements must exist simultaneously for a person to be convicted of a crime: (1) the performance of a prohibited act and (2) a specified state of mind, or intent, on the part of the actor. Even if both elements exist, there are defenses that the law deems sufficient to excuse such actions. These defenses will be discussed later in the chapter.

## THE CRIMINAL ACT

Every criminal statute prohibits certain behavior. Most crimes require an act of *commission;* that is, a person must *do* something in order to be accused of a crime. In criminal law, a prohibited act is referred to as the ***actus reus,***[2] or guilty act. In some cases an act of *omission* can be a crime, but only when a person has a legal duty to perform the omitted act. Failure to file a tax return is an example of an omission that is a crime.

The *guilty act* requirement is based on one of the premises of criminal law—that a person is punished for *harm done* to society. Thinking about killing someone or about stealing a car may be wrong, but the thoughts do no harm until they are translated into action. Of course, a person can be punished for attempting murder or robbery, but

---

1. The American Law Institute issued the Official Draft of the Model Penal Code in 1962. The Model Penal Code is not a uniform code. The Model Penal Code contains four parts: (1) general provisions, (2) definitions of special crimes, (3) provisions concerning treatment and corrections, and (4) provisions on the organization of correction.

---

2. Pronounced *ak*-tuhs *ray*-uhs.

only if substantial steps toward the criminal objective have been taken.

## STATE OF MIND

A wrongful mental state (**mens rea**)[3] is as necessary as a wrongful act in establishing guilt. The mental state required to establish guilt of a crime is indicated in the applicable statute or law. Murder, for example, involves the guilty act of killing another human being, and the guilty mental state is the desire, or intent, to take another's life. For theft, the guilty act is the taking of another person's property, and the mental state involves both the awareness that the property belongs to another and the desire to deprive the owner of it. There are several criminal mental states that, when coupled with a criminal act, may result in the defendant's conviction. The common forms of *mens rea* required to establish a guilty mental state, often referred to as the requisite *intent,* include purpose, knowledge, negligence, and recklessness.

**CRIMINAL PURPOSE AND KNOWLEDGE** A defendant is said to have *purposefully* committed

a criminal act when he or she desires to engage in certain criminal conduct or to cause a certain criminal result. If the government prosecutor, for example, accuses Shannon of burglary, then the prosecutor must prove that Shannon purposefully committed the crime. The crime of burglary requires two levels of *mens rea:* the desire to wrongfully break into a building and the desire to commit a felony once inside, such as larceny or arson.

For a defendant to have *knowingly* committed an illegal act, he or she must be aware of the illegality, must believe that the illegality exists, or must correctly suspect that the illegality exists but not do anything to dispel (or confirm) his or her belief. For example, if Striggels is accused of knowingly importing marijuana into the United States by car, the prosecutor must prove that Striggels put the marijuana in the automobile, saw others do so, or suspected that drugs were in the car but refused to inspect the vehicle to find out. Although drugs may have been in the automobile that Striggels drove across the border, she would not normally be found guilty of knowingly importing a controlled substance if she lacked the requisite mental state—knowledge that she was committing a crime.

In the following case, the issue is whether a defendant could be held liable for the theft of a firearm when he did not realize that the purse he snatched from an automobile contained the firearm.

---

3.    Pronounced mehns *ray-uh.*

---

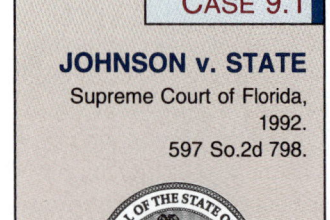

| CASE 9.1 |
| :---: |

**JOHNSON v. STATE**
Supreme Court of Florida,
1992.
597 So.2d 798.

**BACKGROUND AND FACTS** *Raymond Johnson allegedly snatched a purse left in an unattended car at a gas station. Because the purse contained both money and a firearm, among other items, the trial court convicted and sentenced Johnson for burglary of a conveyance (vehicle), grand theft of property (cash and payroll checks), and grand theft of a firearm. On appeal, Johnson claimed that he could not be guilty of grand theft of a firearm because he did not know that the purse contained a firearm. In other words, intent to commit the latter crime was lacking, and therefore that crime had not been committed.*

*PER CURIAM.*
   \*   \*   \*   \*

May a defendant be separately convicted and sentenced for grand theft of cash and grand theft of a firearm accomplished by means of snatching a purse that contained both cash and a firearm when the defendant did not know the nature of the purse's contents?

   \*   \*   \* We answer the \*   \*   \* question in the negative and remand for further proceedings.

   \*   \*   \*   \*

The theft occurred when Johnson wrongfully took the property of another. He did this in one swift motion. * * * A separate crime occurs only when there are separate distinct acts of seizing the property of another.

* * * In this case there was one intent and one act of taking the handbag. * * * Accordingly, there could be only one theft conviction in this case.

*The court held that Johnson could not be separately convicted for grand theft of cash and grand theft of a firearm accomplished by the single act of snatching a purse when he did not know the contents of the purse. The court remanded the case.*

**DECISION AND REMEDY**

## CRIMINAL NEGLIGENCE AND RECKLESSNESS

Criminal *negligence* involves the mental state in which the defendant grossly deviates from the standard of care that a reasonable person would use under the same circumstances. The defendant is accused of taking an unjustified, substantial, and foreseeable risk that resulted in harm. If Thebo is accused of vehicular homicide, having killed a pedestrian, the prosecutor would have to prove that Thebo deviated substantially from the standard that a reasonable driver would have used. If a reasonable driver would have stopped at a yellow light, but Thebo accelerated and hit the pedestrian, then Thebo may be guilty of negligent homicide.

The defendant who commits an act *recklessly* is more blameworthy than one who is criminally negligent. The Model Penal Code defines criminal recklessness as ''consciously disregard[ing] a substantial and unjustifiable risk.''[4] Some courts, such as those adhering to the Model Penal Code, require that a defendant must have been subjectively aware of the risk when he or she acted to find criminal recklessness. Other courts view the circumstances objectively and may find that a defendant acted with criminal recklessness even though he or she was unaware of the risk involved in the wrongful conduct. In a 1944 Massachusetts case,[5] for example, many patrons and employees of a nightclub were unable to leave the building when it caught on fire because several emergency exit doors were locked. The club's owner was found guilty of manslaughter even though he was away from the nightclub at the time of the fire and was unaware of the

risk of harm to the people inside. The owner's lack of awareness of the danger that inadequate fire exits posed for a busy nightclub was irrelevant.

SECTION 4

# CRIMES AFFECTING BUSINESS

Crimes occur in the business world, just as they do elsewhere. In this section, we focus on some of the important crimes affecting business. Many of the crimes discussed in the following pages are popularly referred to as **white-collar crimes.** Although there is no official definition of white-collar crime, the term is popularly used to mean an illegal act or series of acts committed by an individual or business entity using some nonviolent means to obtain a personal or business advantage. Usually, this kind of crime is committed in the course of a legitimate occupation. So-called white-collar crimes cost the public billions of dollars each year. Many white-collar crimes are committed via computer systems (discussed in Chapter 8).

## FORGERY

The fraudulent making or altering of any writing in a way that changes the legal rights and liabilities of another is **forgery.** If, without authorization, Pollocka signs Bennett's name to the back of a check made out to Bennett, Pollocka is committing forgery. Forgery also includes changing trademarks, falsifying public records, counterfeiting, and altering a legal document.

---

4. Model Penal Code Section 2.02(2)(c).

5. *Commonwealth v. Welansky*, 316 Mass. 383, 55 N.E.2d 902 (1944).

## ROBBERY

At common law, **robbery** was defined as forcefully and unlawfully taking personal property of any value from another. The use of force or intimidation is usually necessary for an act of theft to be considered a robbery. Thus, picking pockets is not robbery, because the action is unknown to the victim. Typically, states have more severe penalties for *aggravated* robbery—robbery with the use of a deadly weapon.

## BURGLARY

At common law, **burglary** was defined as breaking and entering the dwelling of another at night with the intent to commit a felony. Originally, the definition was aimed at protecting an individual's home and its occupants. Most state statutes have eliminated some of the requirements found in the common law definition. The time at which the breaking and entering occurs, for example, is usually immaterial. State statutes frequently omit the element of breaking, and some states do not require that the building be a dwelling. Aggravated burglary—which is defined as burglary with the use of a deadly weapon, burglary of a dwelling, or both—incurs a greater penalty.

## LARCENY

Any person who wrongfully or fraudulently takes and carries away another person's personal property, with the intent of depriving the owner permanently of the property, is guilty of **larceny.** Many business-related crimes involve larceny. Whereas robbery involves force or fear, larceny does not. Therefore, picking pockets is larceny, not robbery.

As society becomes more complex, the question often arises as to what is property. In most states, the definition of property that is subject to larceny statutes has expanded. Stealing computer programs may constitute larceny even though the "property" consists of magnetic impulses. Stealing computer time can also constitute larceny. Trade secrets can be subject to larceny statutes. Stealing the use of telephone wires through the device known as a blue box is subject to larceny statutes. So, too, is the theft of natural gas. These types of larceny are covered by "theft of services" statutes in many jurisdictions.

The common law distinction between grand and petit larceny depends on the value of the property taken. Many states have abolished this distinction, but in those that have not, grand larceny is a felony and petit larceny, a misdemeanor.

## OBTAINING GOODS BY FALSE PRETENSES

It is a criminal act to obtain goods by means of false pretenses (through fraud or deceit)—for example, buying groceries with a check, knowing that one has insufficient funds to cover it. Statutes dealing with such illegal activities vary widely from state to state.

## RECEIVING STOLEN GOODS

It is a crime to receive stolen goods. The recipient of such goods need not know the true identity of the owner or the thief. All that is necessary is that the recipient knows or should have known that the goods are stolen, which implies an intent to deprive the owner of those goods.

## EMBEZZLEMENT

When a person entrusted with another person's property or money fraudulently appropriates it, **embezzlement** occurs. Typically, embezzlement involves an employee who steals money. Banks face this problem, and so do a number of businesses in which corporate officers or accountants "juggle" the books to cover up the fraudulent conversion of money for their own benefit. Embezzlement is not larceny, because the wrongdoer does not physically take the property from the possession of another, and it is not robbery, because force or fear is not used.

Ordinarily, an embezzler who returns what has been taken will not be prosecuted, because the owner usually will not take the time to make a complaint, give depositions, and appear in court. That the accused intended eventually to return the embezzled property does not constitute a sufficient defense to the crime of embezzlement.

## ARSON

The willful and malicious burning of a building (and in some states, personal property) owned by another is the crime of **arson.** At common law, arson applied only to burning down another person's house. The law was designed to protect human life. Today, arson statutes have been extended to cover the destruction of any building, regardless of ownership, by fire or explosion.

Every state has a special statute that covers a person's burning a building for the purpose of collecting insurance. If Shaw owns an insured apartment building that is falling apart and sets fire to it himself or pays someone else to do so, he is guilty not only of arson but also of defrauding insurers, which is an attempted larceny. Of course, the insurer need not pay the claim when insurance fraud is proved.

## MAIL FRAUD

One of the most potent weapons against white-collar criminals is the Wire and Mail Fraud Act of 1988 (WMFA).[6] Under this act, it is a federal crime to use the mails to defraud the public. Illegal use of the mails must involve (1) mailing or causing someone else to mail a writing—something written, printed, or photocopied—for the purpose of executing a scheme to defraud and (2) a contemplated or an organized scheme to defraud by false pretenses. If, for example, Johnson advertises by mail the sale of a cure for cancer that he knows to be fraudulent because it has no medical validity, he can be prosecuted for fraudulent use of the mails. Violators may be fined up to $1,000, imprisoned for up to five years, or both. If the violation affects a financial institution, the fine may be up to $1 million, the imprisonment up to twenty years, or both.

Unlike the crime of obtaining goods by false pretenses, the crime of mail fraud does not require that the scheme succeed in defrauding anyone. The crime is committed when a person devises a scheme involving the making of a false promise and uses the mails to carry it out.

## BRIBERY

Basically, three types of bribery are considered crimes: bribery of public officials, commercial bribery, and bribery of foreign officials. The attempt to influence a public official to act in a way that serves a private interest is a crime. As an el-

ement of this crime, intent must be present and proved. The bribe can be anything the recipient considers to be valuable. It is important to realize that *the commission of the crime of bribery occurs when the bribe is offered.* The recipient does not have to agree to perform whatever action is desired by the person offering the bribe, nor does the recipient have to accept the bribe, for the crime of bribery to occur.

Typically, people make commercial bribes to obtain proprietary information, cover up an inferior product, or secure new business. Industrial espionage sometimes involves commercial bribes. For example, a person in one firm may offer an employee in a competing firm some type of payoff in exchange for trade secrets and pricing schedules. So-called kickbacks or payoffs for special favors or services are a form of commercial bribery in some situations.

Bribing foreign officials to obtain favorable business contracts is a crime. This crime and the Foreign Corrupt Practices Act of 1977, which was passed to curb the practice of bribery by American businesspersons to secure favorable foreign contracts, are discussed in detail in Chapter 56 in the context of international law.

## BANKRUPTCY FRAUD

Numerous white-collar crimes may be committed during the many phases of a bankruptcy proceeding. A creditor, for example, may file a false claim against the debtor, which is a crime. Also, a debtor may fraudulently transfer assets to favored parties before or after the petition for bankruptcy is filed. For example, a company-owned automobile may be "sold" at a bargain price to a trusted friend or relative. Closely related to the crime of fraudulent transfer of property is the crime of fraudulent concealment of property, such as hiding gold coins.

## MONEY LAUNDERING

The profits from illegal activities amount to billions of dollars a year, particularly the profits from illegal drug transactions and, to a lesser extent, from racketeering, prostitution, and gambling. Under federal law, banks, savings and loan associations, and other financial institutions are required to report currency transactions of over $10,000. Consequently, those who engage in illegal activities face difficulties in placing their cash profits from illegal transactions.

---

6.   18 U.S.C. Section 1341.

As an alternative to simply placing cash from illegal transactions in bank deposits, wrongdoers and racketeers have invented ways to launder "dirty" money to make it "clean." This **money laundering** is done through legitimate businesses. For example, a successful drug dealer might become partners with a restaurateur. As a shareholder or partner in the restaurant, the wrongdoer is able to report the income from the illegal activity as "profits" of the restaurant—seemingly legitimate income. The wrongdoer can then spend those monies without worrying about whether his or her lifestyle exceeds the level possible with his or her reported income.

## INSIDER TRADING

An individual who obtains "inside information" about the plans of large corporations can often make staggering profits by using that information to guide decisions relating to the purchase or sale of corporate securities. An *insider* is an individual who has inside information—that is, information not available to the general public—about a publicly traded corporation. **Insider trading** is a violation of securities law (discussed in Chapter 44). At this point, it may be said that one who possesses inside information and who has a duty not to disclose it to outsiders may not profit from the purchase or sale of securities based on that information until the information is available to the public.

## CORPORATE CRIME

As will be discussed in Chapter 41, a corporation is a legal entity created under the laws of a state. It is not a living person and therefore must act through human beings. Hence, any crime committed in the corporate name must be committed by a person or persons in control of the corporation's affairs or in the employment of the corporation. Both the corporation as an entity and the individual directors and officers of the corporation are potentially subject to liability for criminal acts.

**LIABILITY OF THE CORPORATE ENTITY** A criminal act requires a wrongful state of mind. Therefore, common law thinking was that a corporation, because it had no mind of its own, could not be guilty of a crime. Today, the common law view does not prevail. Corporations may be charged with many types of crimes. (They cannot be charged with all types of crimes—for example, a corporation cannot be charged with rape.) Crimes for which corporations have been indicted or convicted include manslaughter, homicide, arson, and grand theft.

The Model Penal Code provides that a corporation may be convicted of a crime in the following situations:

1. The criminal act by the corporation's agent or employee is within the scope of his or her employment, and the purpose of the statute defining the act as a crime is to impose liability on corporations.
2. The crime consists of a failure to perform a specific affirmative duty imposed on corporations by law.
3. The crime was authorized, requested, commanded, committed, or recklessly tolerated by one of the corporation's high managerial agents.

As implied by the first statement in the above list, corporate criminal liability is vicarious—the corporation as an entity may be liable for the criminal acts of its employees when the acts are committed within the scope of employment. Thus, the corporation that is found to be criminally responsible for an act committed by an employee can be fined for that offense. Through the fine, stockholders and other employees suffer because of the vicarious liability of the corporation. The justification for such criminal liability involves a showing that the corporation could have precluded the act or that there was authorization, consent, or knowledge of the act by persons in supervisory positions within the corporation.[7]

**LIABILITY OF CORPORATE OFFICERS AND DIRECTORS** Traditionally, corporate officers could be held personally liable for the crimes of their employees only if the officers directly participated in the crimes or directed employees to commit the wrongful acts. Today, as indicated below, that is no longer the case.

*"Responsible Corporate Officer" Doctrine.* Under what has become known as the "responsible

---

7. Section 2.07 of the Model Penal Code: "Liability of corporations, unincorporated associations, and persons acting, or under a duty to act, in their behalf."

corporate officer'' doctrine, a court may impose criminal liability on a corporate officer regardless of whether he or she participated in, directed, or even knew about a given criminal violation.

In *United States v. Park,*[8] for example, the chief executive officer of a national supermarket chain was held personally liable for sanitation violations in corporate warehouses in which food was exposed to contamination by rodents. The officer admitted that as president, he was responsible for the entire operation of the company, including providing sanitary conditions. He testified that he had no choice, however, but to delegate duties, including sanitation, to subordinates. He said that he had no reason to suspect that these subordinates were violating the law and that when violations came to light, he—acting through those subordinates—did everything possible to correct them. Evidence of earlier violations at another warehouse was introduced, however, to show that the officer was on

notice that he could not rely on those subordinates to prevent or correct unsanitary conditions. The court concluded that he was not justified in relying on the subordinates to handle sanitation matters. On appeal, the United States Supreme Court upheld the conviction.

Note that in *Park,* the court imposed personal liability on the corporate officer not because he intended the crime[9] or even knew about it. Rather, liability was imposed because the officer was in a ''responsible relationship'' to the corporation and had the power to prevent the violation. Since the *Park* decision, other courts have held corporate officers liable for their employees' statutory violations under the ''responsible corporate officer'' doctrine. The following case illustrates an application of this doctrine.

---

8. 421 U.S. 658, 95 S.Ct. 1903, 44 L.Ed.2d 489 (1975).

9. Recall from the discussion of criminal liability earlier in this chapter that two elements must be present for a crime to exist: a criminal act and criminal intent (a wrongful state of mind). In *Park,* the court dispensed with the latter requirement.

---

**BACKGROUND AND FACTS**   *Paul S. Dougherty III was the president and principal shareholder of MCM Industries, Inc., which operated a metal galvanizing business in Minneapolis. As part of its operations, MCM galvanized steel with zinc, a process involving the use of large quantities of sulfuric acid. The company also used hazardous materials in conducting a commercial painting operation. Dougherty was ultimately in charge of all operations at the facility. In 1990, the Minnesota Pollution Control Agency (MCPA) issued an order stating that MCM and Dougherty had violated Minnesota statutes regulating hazardous waste disposal. Pools of sulfuric acid accumulated on the floor of one of the rooms in the plant, and this acid was routinely swept outside by employees. Other violations included the failure to label a hazardous waste container and the failure to update a hazardous waste emergency contingency plan. The MCPA imposed a $10,000 penalty, which was later reduced to $7,075, on MCM and Dougherty. Dougherty sought court review of the decision.*

| CASE 9.2 |
| --- |
| **IN THE MATTER OF THE AMENDED ADMINISTRATIVE PENALTY ORDER ISSUED TO PAUL S. DOUGHERTY III** |
| Court of Appeals of Minnesota, 1992. |
| 482 N.W.2d 485. |

*CRIPPEN,* Judge.
\*    \*    \*    \*

While there is ample evidence to establish that Dougherty personally participated in corporate affairs, the record does not contain sufficient evidence to conclude that Dougherty directed other employees to sweep hazardous materials outside the building or ignore environmental regulations. There is no evidence Dougherty personally placed hazardous materials into the environment. The Commissioner's finding that Dougherty personally participated in the violations was erroneous.

However, Dougherty's personal liability is not premised solely on his personal participation in the violations. The Commissioner contends that even if Dougherty did not participate directly in the violations, he is liable under the ''responsible corporate officer'' doctrine. This doctrine imposes liability on parties due to their responsible relationship to a violation.

\* \* \* \*

Three essential elements must be satisfied before liability will be imposed upon a corporate officer under the responsible corporate officer doctrine: (1) the individual must be in a position of responsibility which allows the person to influence corporate policies or activities; (2) there must be a nexus between the individual's position and the violation in question such that the individual could have influenced the corporate actions which constituted the violations; and (3) the individual's actions or inactions facilitated the violations.

\* \* \* \*

\* \* \* Dougherty is personally liable because he satisfied all three elements of the doctrine, not merely because he is president of MCM.

**DECISION AND REMEDY**    *The court affirmed the agency's order and held that Dougherty could be held personally liable, as a responsible corporate officer, for failure to supervise adequately the actions of his employees.*

**ETHICAL CONSIDERATIONS**    *Some statutes impose criminal liability for what is termed ''public welfare'' offenses. A public welfare offense occurs under a statute that is intended to improve the public welfare. A violation of such a statute does not require intent; rather, strict liability is imposed. Environmental statutes, particularly hazardous waste laws, have been held to constitute public welfare statutes. Hazardous waste laws regulate activities that threaten human health and safety, as well as the environment, and violations often do not require ''wilfulness'' or ''intent.''* [a] *The court emphasized that imposing liability under the ''responsible corporate officer'' doctrine is particularly appropriate in the context of environmental laws, because ''[i]mposing liability upon only the corporation, but not those corporate officers and employees who actually make corporate decisions, would be inconsistent with [the legislature's] intent to impose liability upon the persons who are involved in the handling and disposal of hazardous substances.''*

a.   *United States v. Hayes International Corp.,* 786 F.2d 1499 (11th Cir. 1986); *United States v. Liviola,* 605 F.Supp. 96 (N.D. Ohio 1985).

*Pervasiveness of Control.* In *United States v. Cusack,*[10] a court enunciated yet another basis for imposing personal liability on a corporate officer. In that case, the court held that a corporate officer's control over corporate operations was so pervasive that, in effect, the officer was not only a corporate employee but also an employer. The defendant in the case, John Cusack, was the president and only officer of Quality Steel, Inc., and one of its two directors. The other director had supplied the capital for the small corporation but played no role in corporate management. Cusack alone was in charge of all corporate operations. He made all company decisions, had unlimited access to corporate funds, hired and fired all employees, determined their salaries as well as his own, made all the bids for construction jobs, directed all work activities, and generally had unrestricted discretion to run the company as he saw fit.

At one point, while constructing a warehouse, Cusack, who supervised the operation, allegedly violated safety standards required by the Occupational Safety and Health Act of 1970[11] relating

10.   806 F.Supp. 47 (D.N.J. 1992).

11.   29 U.S.C. Sections 553, 651–678. See Chapter 36 for a more detailed discussion of this act.

## ■ CONCEPT SUMMARY 9.1 Crimes Affecting Business

| CRIME | DESCRIPTION |
|---|---|
| Forgery | The fraudulent making or altering of any writing in a way that changes the legal rights and liabilities of another. |
| Robbery | The forceful and unlawful taking of personal property of any value from another. |
| Burglary | At common law, defined as breaking and entering the dwelling of another at night with the intent to commit a felony. State statutes now vary their definitions of burglary. |
| Larceny | The wrongful or fraudulent taking and carrying away of another's personal property with the intent to deprive the owner permanently of the property. |
| Obtaining Goods by False Pretenses | Obtaining goods through fraud or deceit, such as by cashing a check, knowing that there are insufficient funds in the bank to cover it. |
| Receiving Stolen Goods | A crime if the recipient knew or should have known that the goods were stolen. |
| Embezzlement | The fraudulent appropriation of another person's property or money by a person to whom the property or money was entrusted. |
| Arson | The willful and malicious burning of a building or (in some states) personal property owned by another. |
| Mail Fraud | Using the mails to defraud the public. |
| Bribery | Includes bribery of public officials, commercial bribery, and bribery of foreign officials. The crime of bribery is committed when the bribe is tendered. |
| Bankruptcy Fraud | Includes false claims of creditors, the fraudulent transfer of assets by the debtor before or after the bankruptcy petition is filed, and other actions that are planned and carried out for the purpose of defrauding creditors. |
| Money Laundering | Transferring the profits of illegal activities to or through legitimate enterprises. |
| Insider Trading | The buying or selling of corporate securities by a person in possession of material nonpublic information in violation of securities laws. |
| Corporate Crime | Crimes committed by corporations or by corporate officers. Both the corporation as an entity and individual corporate actors are subject to potential liability for criminal violations. |
| Criminal RICO Violations | The use of legitimate business enterprises to shield racketeering activity, such as securites fraud and mail fraud. |

to the installation of steel joists. As a result, the building collapsed and caused the death of an employee. Cusack was indicted for knowingly and willfully violating Section 666(e) of the act. That section provides that an "employer" convicted of a willful violation of standards required under the act that results in an employee's death may be fined up to $10,000, imprisoned for up to six months, or both. Cusack moved to dismiss the indictment on the ground that Section 666(e) imposes liability only on employers and he, as a corporate officer, was an employee and not an employer. The court

# EMERGING TRENDS IN BUSINESS LAW

# Getting Tougher on Corporate Crime

Traditionally, persons committing the same crime might have received very different sentences depending on the judge hearing the case, the jurisdiction in which it was heard, and many other factors. Many critics of this disparity in sentencing became quite vocal in the early 1980s, and in response to this criticism, Congress created in 1984 a seven-member U.S. Sentencing Commission. The commission was charged with the task of standardizing sentences for federal crimes. The argument in favor of such standardization was that if individuals have an idea of the penalties they will receive if convicted of a particular crime, it will help deter criminal acts.

The commission fulfilled its task of creating uniform sentences for federal crimes, but it also went further: it formulated specific guidelines for the punishment of crimes committed by corporate employees. It is clear that the new federal sentencing guidelines for corporate crimes have changed the way corporations will deal with potential wrongdoing for years to come.

## Tougher Sentences for Corporate Employees
The commission established sentencing guidelines for thirty-two levels of offenses. The punishment for each offense depends on such things as the seriousness of the charge, the amount of money involved, and the extent to which top company executives are involved. Under these new sentencing guidelines, corporate lawbreakers face sanctions and fines that can be as high as hundreds of millions of dollars.

But the guidelines allow judges to ease up on penalties when companies have taken substantial steps to prevent, investigate, and punish wrongdoing. Additionally, if companies cooperate with government investigators, the sentences may be less severe. Nonetheless, the net effect of the guidelines in the last few years has been a fivefold to tenfold increase in criminal penalties for crimes committed by corporate employees.

The new guidelines cover violations of federal laws in the following areas:

- Antitrust (see Chapter 48).
- Securities (see Chapter 44).
- Employment laws (see Chapters 36 and 37).
- Mail and wire fraud.
- Commercial bribery.
- Kickbacks and money laundering.

Thousands of businesses are therefore covered by the federal sentencing guidelines. These include brokerage houses, law firms, banks, and a host of large and small businesses.

## Businesses Can Prevent or Reduce Criminal Sanctions
The corporate sentencing guidelines present judges with a complicated formula for sentencing businesses based on the seriousness of the offense and the degree of the company's guilt. The so-called *culpability score* of a company depends on what role senior management had in the alleged wrongdoing, as well as the company's history of past violations and the extent of management's cooperation with federal investigators. Additionally, the effectiveness of the company's compliance program is important. Firms can establish "credits" against potential penalties if they have undertaken the measures listed below:

- The firm must establish and put in writing corporate crime-prevention standards and procedures for all employees and agents, and these standards must be communicated to all employees and agents in writing and/or during training programs.
- The standards must be enforced by high-level employees.
- When an employee demonstrates an apparent propensity to engage in criminal activities, the company must prevent that

employee from exercising discretionary authority.
- All anticrime standards of the company must include methods of detecting, as well as preventing, crimes.
- Whistleblowers must be protected from reprisals.

### ■ Implications for the Businessperson

**1.** Clearly, the new sentencing guidelines increase the need to pay serious attention to the allegations of whistleblowers—those who "blow the whistle" on their employers' illegal actions. A company that fails to investigate a whistleblower's allegations will incur a higher culpability score. Furthermore, the company's failure to investigate a whistleblower's allegations can allow the

government prosecutor to exercise a tremendous amount of discretion in recommending criminal rather than civil penalties. Failure to investigate whistleblowers' allegations in some cases may also constitute a breach of the duty of care, in which case the corporation could also be liable for punitive damages.

**2.** As mentioned in the *Emerging Trends* in Chapter 2, even if a company does not have a compliance program in place, if the firm has made obvious attempts to prevent or curb wrongful behavior in the workplace, the prosecutor may recommend lighter penalties for criminal violations. Business firms therefore have an incentive to create ethical codes and implement ongoing ethical committees and training programs.

### ■ For Critical Analysis

**1.** Given the fact that every case that comes before the courts involves unique circumstances, is it fair to defendants to base their sentences on a uniform set of guidelines? Should federal judges have more discretion in sentencing?

**2.** What are some of the costs and benefits of the corporate sentencing guidelines for corporations? For American society generally?

**3.** How do these guidelines affect the way in which senior management operates corporations today compared to, say, fifty years ago?

---

held otherwise, stating that "an officer's or director's role in a corporate entity (particularly a small one) may be so pervasive and total that the officer or director is in fact the corporation and is therefore an employer under [Section] 666(e)."

## CRIMINAL RICO VIOLATIONS

The Racketeer Influenced and Corrupt Organizations Act (RICO)[12] was passed by Congress in 1970 in an attempt to prevent the use of legitimate business enterprises as shields for racketeering and to prohibit the purchase of any legitimate business interest with illegally obtained funds. RICO provides for both civil and criminal liability. Civil liability under RICO was discussed in Chapter 7. We now look at criminal RICO.

**THE SCOPE OF CRIMINAL RICO**  Many criminal RICO offenses, such as gambling, arson, and extortion, have little, if anything, to do with normal

business activities. But securities fraud (involving the sale of stocks and bonds) and mail fraud also may constitute criminal RICO violations, and RICO has become an effective tool in attacking these white-collar crimes in recent years. RICO has also been applied to more unusual circumstances. Under criminal provisions of RICO, any individual found guilty of a violation is subject to a fine of up to $25,000 per violation, imprisonment for up to twenty years, or both.

**FORFEITURE**  Individuals found guilty in a criminal proceeding under RICO can be ordered to forfeit any interest gained in any enterprise as a result of the violation. As a forfeiture law, RICO is thought by many to be exceedingly harsh. The statute gives the prosecutor the power to have property seized before the accused is granted a hearing. The prosecutor need only establish that he or she has probable cause to believe that the property was acquired through illegal racketeering—a RICO violation. As will be discussed later in this chapter, *probable cause* means that there is a substantial

---

12.  18 U.S.C. Sections 1961–1968.

likelihood, not a mere probability, that the person has committed or is about to commit a crime. The confiscated property, such as an automobile, might be valued in the thousands of dollars and may be seized by authorities before the alleged perpetrator is convicted of a crime.

The United States Supreme Court has imposed an additional requirement when the property to be seized is real estate. Before real property linked to illegal drug trafficking can be seized by federal prosecutors, the owner of the property must be given the benefit of a court hearing. The Court held that the constitutional guarantee of due process (discussed in Chapter 5) obligated the government, before seizing real property, to notify the defendant of the seizure and to allow the defendant to oppose the seizure in court.[13]

Determining the rights of innocent people sharing ownership in the seized property has been largely left to the courts. The Court of Appeals for the Eleventh Circuit recently ruled that a bank that gave a home mortgage to drug dealers was an ''innocent owner.'' The mortgage could not be invalidated (seized along with the real estate) unless the prosecutor proved that the bank actually knew that the drug dealer was engaged in illicit activity; simply proving that a bank should know when drug money is laundered through a real estate transaction is insufficient.[14] Returning the property when no conviction results or when innocent people share ownership in the seized property may also be problematic and may take as long as five years.

# DEFENSES TO CRIMINAL LIABILITY

The law recognizes certain conditions that relieve a defendant of criminal liability. These conditions are called **defenses,** and among the important ones are infancy, intoxication, insanity, mistake, con-

■ **Exhibit 9–1 Responsibility of Infants for Criminal Acts under the Common Law**

| Age 0–7 | Absolute presumption of incompetence. |
|---|---|
| Age 7–14 | Presumption of incompetence, but government may oppose. |
| Age 14 + | Presumption of competence, but infant may oppose. |

sent, duress, justifiable use of force, entrapment, and the statute of limitations.

## INFANCY

The term *infant,* as used in the law, refers to any person who has not yet reached the age of majority (see Chapter 14). Under the common law, children up to age seven were considered incapable of committing a crime, because they did not have the moral sense to understand that they were doing wrong. Children between the ages of seven and fourteen were presumed to be incapable of committing a crime, but this presumption could be rebutted if it could be shown that the child understood the wrongful nature of the act (see Exhibit 9–1).

In all states, specialized courts handle cases involving children who are alleged to have violated the law. In some states, juvenile courts handle children's cases exclusively. In most states, however, courts that handle children's cases also have jurisdiction over other matters, such as traffic offenses. Originally, juvenile court hearings were informal, and lawyers were rarely present. Since 1967, when the United States Supreme Court ordered that a child charged with delinquency must be allowed to consult with an attorney before being committed to a state institution,[15] juvenile court hearings have become more formal. In some states, a child will be treated as an adult and tried in a regular court if he or she is above a certain age (usually fourteen) and is guilty of a felony such as rape or murder.

## INTOXICATION

The law recognizes two types of intoxication, whether from drugs or from alcohol: *involuntary*

---

13. *United States v. James Daniel Good Real Property,* ___U.S. ___, 113 S.Ct. 1576, 123 L.Ed.2d 145 (1993).
14. *United States v. Republic National Bank of Miami,* 995 F.2d 1558 (11th Cir. 1993).

15. *In re Gault,* 387 U.S. 1, 87 S.Ct. 1428, 18 L.Ed.2d 527 (1967).

and *voluntary.* Involuntary intoxication occurs when a person either is physically forced to ingest or inject an intoxicating substance or is unaware that a substance contains drugs or alcohol. Involuntary intoxication is a defense to a crime if its effect was to make a person incapable of understanding that the act committed was wrong or incapable of obeying the law.

Using voluntary drug or alcohol intoxication as a defense is based on the theory that extreme levels of intoxication may negate the state of mind that a crime requires. Many courts are reluctant to allow voluntary intoxication as a defense to a crime, however. After all, the defendant, by definition, voluntarily chose to put himself or herself into an intoxicated state. Voluntary intoxication as a defense may be effective in cases in which the defendant was *extremely* intoxicated when committing the wrong.

## INSANITY

Just as a child is often judged incapable of the state of mind required to commit a crime, so also may be someone suffering from a mental illness. When a person's mental illness or defect rises to the level of legal insanity, the defendant has a defense to a criminal charge. The courts have had difficulty deciding what the test for legal insanity should be, and psychiatrists as well as lawyers are critical of the tests used. Almost all federal courts and some states use the relatively liberal standard set forth in the Model Penal Code:

> A person is not responsible for criminal conduct if at the time of such conduct as a result of mental disease or defect he lacks substantial capacity either to appreciate the wrongfulness of his conduct or to conform his conduct to the requirements of the law.

Some states use the *M'Naghten* test,[16] under which a criminal defendant is not responsible if, at the time of the offense, he or she did not know the nature and quality of the act or did not know that the act was wrong. Other states use the irresistible-impulse test. A person operating under an irresistible impulse may know an act is wrong but cannot refrain from doing it.

In some states, a defendant found not guilty by reason of insanity is automatically committed to a mental institution. As the United States Supreme Court has stated, the defendant "whose mental illness was sufficient to lead him to commit a criminal act is likely to remain ill and in need of treatment."[17]

## MISTAKE

Everyone has heard the saying, "Ignorance of the law is no excuse." Ordinarily, ignorance of the law or a mistaken idea about what the law requires is not a valid defense. In some states, however, that rule has been modified. A person who claims that he or she honestly did not know that a law was being broken may have a valid defense if (1) the law was not published or reasonably made known to the public or (2) the person relied on an official statement of the law that was erroneous.

A *mistake of fact,* as opposed to a *mistake of law,* operates as a defense if it negates the mental state necessary to commit a crime. If, for example, Tai Lin mistakenly drives off in Rusty's car because Tai thinks it is his, there is no theft. Theft requires knowledge that the property belongs to another.

## CONSENT

What if a victim consents to a crime or even encourages the person intending a criminal act to commit it? The law allows **consent** as a defense if the consent cancels the harm that the law is designed to prevent. In each case, the question is whether the law forbids an act that was committed against the victim's will or forbids the act without regard to the victim's wish. The law forbids murder, prostitution, and drug use whether the victim consents to it or not. Also, if the act causes harm to a third person who has not consented, there is no escape from criminal liability. Consent or forgiveness given after a crime has been committed is not really a defense, though it can affect the likelihood of prosecution. Consent operates as a defense most successfully in crimes against property.

---

16. A rule derived from *M'Naghten's Case,* 8 Eng. Rep. 718 (1843).

17. *Jones v. United States,* 463 U.S. 354, 103 S.Ct. 3043, 77 L.Ed.2d 694 (1983).

## DURESS

**Duress** exists when the *wrongful threat* of one person induces another person to perform an act that he or she would not otherwise perform. In such a situation, duress is said to negate the mental state necessary to commit a crime. For duress to qualify as a defense, the following requirements must be met:

1. The threat must be of serious bodily harm or death.
2. The harm threatened must be greater than the harm caused by the crime.
3. The threat must be immediate and inescapable.
4. The defendant must have been involved in the situation through no fault of his or her own.

One crime that cannot be excused by duress is murder. It is difficult to justify taking a life of another person even if one's own life is threatened by a third party.

## JUSTIFIABLE USE OF FORCE

Probably the most well-known defense to criminal liability is **self-defense,** the right to protect oneself or one's property against injury by another. But there are other situations that justify the use of force: the defense of one's dwelling, the defense of other property, and the prevention of a crime. In all of these situations, it is important to distinguish between the use of deadly force and the use of nondeadly force. Deadly force is likely to result in death or serious bodily harm. Nondeadly force is force that reasonably appears necessary to prevent the imminent use of criminal force.

Generally speaking, people can use the amount of nondeadly force that seems necessary to protect themselves, their dwellings, or other property or to prevent the commission of a crime. Deadly force can be used in self-defense if there is a *reasonable belief* that imminent death or grievous bodily harm will otherwise result, if the attacker is using unlawful force (an example of lawful force is that exerted by a police officer), and if the defender has not initiated or provoked the attack. Deadly force can never be justified to combat nondeadly force. Deadly force can be used to defend a dwelling only if the unlawful entry is violent and the person believes deadly force is necessary to prevent imminent death or great bodily harm or—in some jurisdictions—if the person believes deadly force is necessary to prevent the commission of a felony in the dwelling.

What if deadly force results from a mechanical device, such as a spring gun rigged to go off when a trespasser enters through a doorway? A leading case on this issue is *Katco v. Briney,* presented below.

---

| CASE 9.3 |
| :---: |

**KATCO v. BRINEY**
Supreme Court of Iowa, 1971.
183 N.W.2d 657.

**BACKGROUND AND FACTS**    *In 1957, Bertha Briney inherited her parents' farm. Over the next ten years, the unoccupied farmhouse was broken into a number of times, resulting in the loss of some household items, in broken windows, and in the "messing up of the property in general." In June 1967, the Brineys set a shotgun trap in one of the bedrooms. Wire was rigged from the gun's trigger to the doorknob so that the gun would fire when the door was opened. On the night of July 16, Marvin Katco and Marvin McDonough broke into the house looking for antique bottles and jars. When Katco opened the bedroom door, he detonated the shotgun and was hit in the right leg above the ankle bone. Much of his leg, including part of the tibia, was blown away. He spent forty days in the hospital, a year on crutches, and a year in a special brace. He pleaded guilty to criminal charges of larceny, paid a $50 fine, and was paroled for good behavior from a sixty-day jail sentence. Katco sued the Brineys for damages. The trial court instructed the jury that "one may use reasonable force in the protection of his property, but * * * one may not use such means of force as will take human life or inflict great bodily injury." The jury returned a verdict for Katco for $30,000. The Brineys appealed.*

*MOORE,* Chief Justice.

\* \* \* \*

The overwhelming weight of authority, both textbook and case law, supports the trial court's statement of the applicable principles of law.

\* \* \* \*

Restatement of Torts, [S]ection 85, states: "The value of human life and limb, not only to the individual concerned but also to society, so outweighs the interest of a possessor of land in excluding from it those whom he is not willing to admit thereto that a possessor of land has \* \* \* no privilege to use force intended or likely to cause death or serious harm against another whom the possessor sees about to enter his premises or meddle with his [property], unless the intrusion threatens death or serious bodily harm to the occupiers or users of the premises. \* \* \* A possessor of land cannot do indirectly and by a mechanical device that which, were he present, he could not do immediately and in person. \* \* \* "

\* \* \* \*

In *Hooker v. Miller,* we held [a] defendant vineyard owner liable for damages resulting from a spring gun shot although plaintiff was a trespasser and there to steal grapes. [In the opinion] this statement is made: "This court has held that a mere trespass against property \* \* \* is not a sufficient justification to authorize the use of a deadly weapon by the owner in its defense; and that if death results in such a case it will be murder, though the killing be actually necessary to prevent the trespass." \* \* \*

\* \* \* \*

In addition to civil liability many jurisdictions hold a land owner criminally liable for serious injuries or homicide caused by spring guns or other set devices.

**DECISION AND REMEDY**

*The supreme court affirmed the trial court's decision.*

**ETHICAL CONSIDERATIONS**

*In the nineteenth century, some courts reasoned that the defense of a home was as important as the defense of a life. These courts permitted a homeowner to use deadly force if it reasonably appeared necessary to prevent forcible entry against the owner's will after a warning had been issued to the intruder not to enter and not to use force. In the twentieth century, this view was generally rejected as being too broad. Today, the states have different answers to the question of when deadly force may be used in the defense of property against a trespasser or a thief. The Model Penal Code takes the view that a deadly trap is never justifiable as a protection against trespass or theft. Under the Model Penal Code, to protect property, an owner may use nondeadly devices, such as spiked fences.*

## ENTRAPMENT

As a defense, **entrapment** is designed to prevent police officers or other government agents from encouraging crimes in order to apprehend persons wanted for criminal acts. In the typical entrapment case, an undercover agent *suggests* that a crime be committed and somehow pressures or induces an individual to commit it. The agent then arrests the individual for the crime. For entrapment to be considered a defense, both the suggestion and the inducement must take place. The defense is intended not to prevent the police from setting a trap for an unwary criminal but rather to prevent the police from pushing the individual into it. The crucial issue is whether a person who committed a crime was predisposed to commit the crime or did so because the agent induced it. The following case is illustrative in this respect.

CASE 9.4

**JACOBSON v. UNITED STATES**

Supreme Court of the
United States, 1992.
_____ U.S. _____,
112 S.Ct. 1535,
118 L.Ed.2d 174.

**BACKGROUND AND FACTS**   *Prior to the passage of the Child Protection Act of 1984, which makes it a crime to receive knowingly through the mails sexually explicit depictions of children, Keith Jacobson had ordered and received from a bookstore two* Bare Boys *magazines containing photographs of nude preteen and teenage boys. After the 1984 act was passed, government agents found Jacobson's name on the bookstore's mailing list. To test Jacobson's willingness to break the law, government agencies sent mail to him through five fictitious organizations and a bogus pen pal. Many of these "organizations" claimed that they had been founded to protect and promote sexual freedom and freedom of choice and that they promoted lobbying efforts through catalogue sales and other publications. The agencies continued to send mailings to Jacobson for two and a half years. Jacobson responded to some of the correspondence and finally, in response to a letter decrying international censorship, ordered a magazine. He testified at trial that he ordered the magazine because he was curious about "all the trouble and the hysteria over pornography and I wanted to see what the material was." When the magazine was delivered, Jacobson was arrested and subsequently convicted of violating the 1984 act. He appealed, claiming entrapment. The appellate court upheld the conviction, and Jacobson appealed to the United States Supreme Court.*

Justice *WHITE* delivered the opinion of the Court.
   *   *   *   *
   *   *   * [T]here can be no dispute that the Government may use undercover agents to enforce the law.

   In their zeal to enforce the law, however, Government agents may not originate a criminal design, implant in an innocent person's mind the disposition to commit a criminal act, and then induce commission of the crime so that the Government may prosecute. Where the Government has induced an individual to break the law and the defense of entrapment is at issue, as it was in this case, the prosecution must prove beyond reasonable doubt that the defendant was disposed to commit the criminal act prior to first being approached by Government agents.
   *   *   *   *

   *   *   * By the time [Jacobson] finally placed his order, he had already been the target of 26 months of repeated mailings and communications from Government agents and fictitious organizations. Therefore, although he had become predisposed to break the law by May 1987, it is our view that the Government did not prove that this predisposition was independent and not the product of the attention that the Government had directed at [him] since January 1985.

**DECISION AND REMEDY**   *The United States Supreme Court held that the government failed to prove that Jacobson, if left to his own devices, would have broken the law. The Supreme Court reversed the appellate court's decision.*

**INTERNATIONAL CONSIDERATIONS**   **The Entrapment Defense in Israel** *Israel's criminal justice system historically provided extensive rights to defendants, including their right to raise entrapment as a defense. With the growth of organized crime and terrorism, however, the entrapment defense has been largely eliminated—although entrapment is still a factor that will be considered by an Israeli court when passing sentence on a convicted defendant.*

## STATUTE OF LIMITATIONS

An individual can be excused from criminal liability by a **statute of limitations.** Such a statute provides that the state has only a certain amount of time—which varies from state to state and from crime to crime—within which to prosecute a crime. If the state does not prosecute within the allotted time, it loses its opportunity, and the suspect is free from prosecution. The idea behind such statutes is that people should not have to live under the threat of criminal prosecution indefinitely. Also, if prosecution is delayed too long, it becomes difficult to discover the truth, because witnesses die or disappear and evidence is destroyed. Most statutes of limitations do not apply to murder and do not run while the defendant is out of the jurisdiction or in hiding.

## IMMUNITY

At times, the state may wish to obtain information from a person accused of a crime. Accused persons are understandably reluctant to give information if it will be used to prosecute them, however, and they cannot be forced to do so. The privilege against self-incrimination is granted by the Fifth Amendment to the Constitution, which reads, in part, ''nor shall [any person] be compelled in any criminal case to be a witness against himself.'' In cases in which the state wishes to obtain information from a person accused of a crime, the state can grant *immunity* from prosecution or agree to prosecute for a less serious offense in exchange for the information.

Once immunity is given, the person can no longer refuse to testify on Fifth Amendment grounds, because he or she now has an absolute privilege against self-incrimination. Often a grant of immunity from prosecution for a serious crime is part of the **plea bargaining** between the defending and prosecuting attorneys. A plea bargain is a prosecutor's promise to make concessions (or seek concessions) in exchange for a suspect's guilty plea. Concessions may include a reduced charge or a lesser sentence.

## SECTION 6

# CRIMINAL PROCEDURES

Our criminal justice system operates on the premise that it is far worse for an innocent person to be punished than for a guilty person to go free. A person is innocent until proved guilty, and guilt must be proved *beyond a reasonable doubt.* The procedure of the criminal legal system is designed to protect the rights of the individual and to preserve the presumption of innocence.

## CONSTITUTIONAL SAFEGUARDS

Criminal law brings the force of the state, with all its resources, to bear against the individual. Specific safeguards are provided in the Constitution for those accused of crimes. The United States Supreme Court has ruled that most of these safeguards apply not only in federal but also in state courts by virtue of the due process clause of the Fourteenth Amendment. The safeguards include the following:

1. The Fourth Amendment protection from unreasonable searches and seizures.
2. The Fourth Amendment requirement that no warrants for a search or an arrest can be issued without probable cause.
3. The Fifth Amendment requirement that no one can be deprived of ''life, liberty, or property without due process of law.''
4. The Fifth Amendment prohibition against **double jeopardy** (trying someone twice for the same criminal offense).
5. The Sixth Amendment guarantees of a speedy trial, trial by jury, a public trial, the right to confront witnesses, and the right to a lawyer at various stages in some proceedings.
6. The Eighth Amendment prohibitions against excessive bails and fines and against cruel and unusual punishment.

THE EXCLUSIONARY RULE   Under what is known as the **exclusionary rule,** all evidence obtained in violation of the constitutional rights spelled out in the Fourth, Fifth, and Sixth Amendments must be excluded, as well as all evidence derived from the illegally obtained evidence. Illegally obtained evidence is known as the ''fruit of the poisonous tree.'' For example, if a confession is obtained after an illegal arrest, the arrest would be ''the poisonous tree,'' and the confession, if ''tainted'' by the arrest, would be the ''fruit.''

THE *MIRANDA* RULE   In regard to criminal procedure, one of the questions that had been facing many courts in the 1950s and 1960s was not whether suspects had constitutional rights—that was not in doubt—but how and when those rights could be exercised. For example, the Fifth Amendment to the Constitution guarantees the privilege against compulsory self-incrimination. But could this right be exercised during pretrial interrogation proceedings, or only during the trial? Were confessions obtained from suspects admissible in court if the suspects had not been advised of their right to remain silent and other constitutional rights? To clarify these issues, the United States Supreme Court issued a landmark decision in 1966 in *Miranda v. Arizona,* presented below.

CASE 9.5

**MIRANDA v. ARIZONA**

Supreme Court of the
United States, 1966.
384 U.S. 436,
86 S.Ct. 1602,
16 L.Ed.2d 694.

**BACKGROUND AND FACTS**   *On March 13, 1963, Ernesto Miranda, a man described by the court as "a seriously disturbed individual with pronounced sexual fantasies," was arrested at his home for the kidnapping and rape of an eighteen-year-old woman. Miranda was taken to a Phoenix, Arizona, police station and questioned by two officers. Two hours later, the officers emerged from the interrogation room with a written confession signed by Miranda. A paragraph at the top of the confession stated that the confession had been made voluntarily, without threats or promises of immunity, and "with full knowledge of my legal rights, understanding any statement I make may be used against me." Miranda was at no time advised that he had a right to remain silent and a right to have a lawyer present. The confession was admitted into evidence at the trial, and Miranda was convicted and sentenced to prison for twenty to thirty years. Miranda appealed the decision, claiming that he had not been informed of his constitutional rights. The Supreme Court of Arizona held that Miranda's constitutional rights had not been violated and affirmed his conviction. The Miranda case was subsequently consolidated with three other cases involving similar issues and reviewed by the United States Supreme Court.*

Mr. Chief Justice *WARREN* delivered the opinion of the Court.

The cases before us raise questions which go to the roots of our concepts of American criminal jurisprudence; the restraints society must observe consistent with the Federal Constitution in prosecuting individuals for crime. *   *   *
*   *   *   *

At the outset, if a person in custody is to be subjected to interrogation, he must first be informed in clear and unequivocal terms that he has the right to remain silent.
*   *   *
    *   *   *   *

The warning of the right to remain silent must be accompanied by the explanation that anything said can and will be used against the individual in court. This warning is needed in order to make him aware not only of the privilege, but also of the consequences of forgoing it. *   *   *

The circumstances surrounding in-custody interrogation can operate very quickly to overbear the will of one merely made aware of his privilege by his interrogators. Therefore the right to have counsel present at the interrogation is indispensable to the protection of the Fifth Amendment privilege under the system we delineate today.
    *   *   *   *

In order fully to apprise a person interrogated of the extent of his rights under this system then, it is necessary to warn him not only that he has the right to consult with an attorney, but also that if he is indigent [without funds] a lawyer will be appointed to represent him. *   *   * The warning of a right to counsel would be hollow if not couched in terms that would convey to the indigent—the person most often subjected to interrogation—the knowledge that he too has a right to have counsel present.

*The Supreme Court held that Miranda could not be convicted of the crime on the basis of his confession because his confession was inadmissible as evidence. For any statement made by a defendant to be admissible, the defendant must be informed of certain constitutional rights prior to police interrogation. If the accused waives his or her rights to remain silent and to have counsel present, the government must demonstrate that the waiver was made knowingly and intelligently.*

**DECISION AND REMEDY**

**THE EROSION OF THE *MIRANDA* RULE**  The Supreme Court and lower courts have enforced the *Miranda* rule hundreds of times since the *Miranda* decision. Today, both on television and in the real world, police officers routinely advise suspects of their "*Miranda* rights" upon arrest. When Ernesto Miranda himself was later murdered, the suspected murderer was "read his *Miranda* rights."

The *Miranda* rights have been gradually eroded, however. Congress in 1968 passed the Omnibus Crime Control and Safe Streets Act, which provided—among other things—that in federal cases a voluntary confession could be used in evidence even if the accused was not informed of his or her rights. In 1971, the United States Supreme Court allowed the prosecution to use an out-of-court statement, elicited in violation of *Miranda*, to impeach (discredit) the accused's in-court statement.[18] In 1984, the Court recognized a "public safety" exception to the *Miranda* rule.[19] The need to protect the public warranted the admissibility of statements made by the defendant (in this case indicating where he placed the gun) as evidence in a trial, even when the defendant had not been informed of his *Miranda* rights.

In 1990, the Court recognized "routine booking questions" as an exception to *Miranda*.[20] The statements made by the defendant to the police in answer to questions regarding biographical data necessary to complete booking (to be discussed shortly) or pretrial services were exempted from

*Miranda*. Today, juries can even accept confessions without being convinced of their voluntariness. In cases that are not tried in federal court, confessions made by criminal suspects who have not been completely informed of their legal rights may be taken into consideration.

The protection afforded accused persons by the *Miranda* case was strengthened in 1990, however. In *Minnick v. Mississippi*,[21] the Supreme Court held that once a defendant has requested counsel, the defendant cannot be questioned by police unless the defendant's attorney is present.

## CRIMINAL PROCESS

A criminal prosecution differs significantly from a civil case in several respects. These differences reflect the desire to safeguard the rights of the individual against the state. Exhibit 9–2 summarizes the major procedural steps in a criminal case. Each step is discussed below in more detail.

**ARREST**  Before a warrant for someone's arrest can be issued, the officer seeking the warrant must establish probable cause for believing that the individual in question has committed a crime. **Probable cause** can be defined as a substantial likelihood that the person has committed, or is about to commit, a crime—the mere possibility of criminal activity is not enough. Some exceptions to the warrant requirement of the Fourth Amendment do exist (such as when police are in hot pursuit of a suspected felon or in other exigent circumstances), but the arresting officer must still establish that he or she had probable cause to make the arrest.

---

18.  *Harris v. New York,* 401 U.S. 222, 91 S.Ct. 643, 28 L.Ed.2d 1 (1971).

19.  *New York v. Quarles,* 467 U.S. 649, 104 S.Ct. 2626, 81 L.Ed.2d 550 (1984).

20.  *Pennsylvania v. Muniz,* 496 U.S. 582, 110 S.Ct. 2638, 110 L.Ed.2d 528 (1990).

21.   498 U.S. 146, 111 S.Ct. 486, 112 L.Ed.2d 489 (1990).

■ **Exhibit 9–2 Major Steps in Processing a Criminal Case**

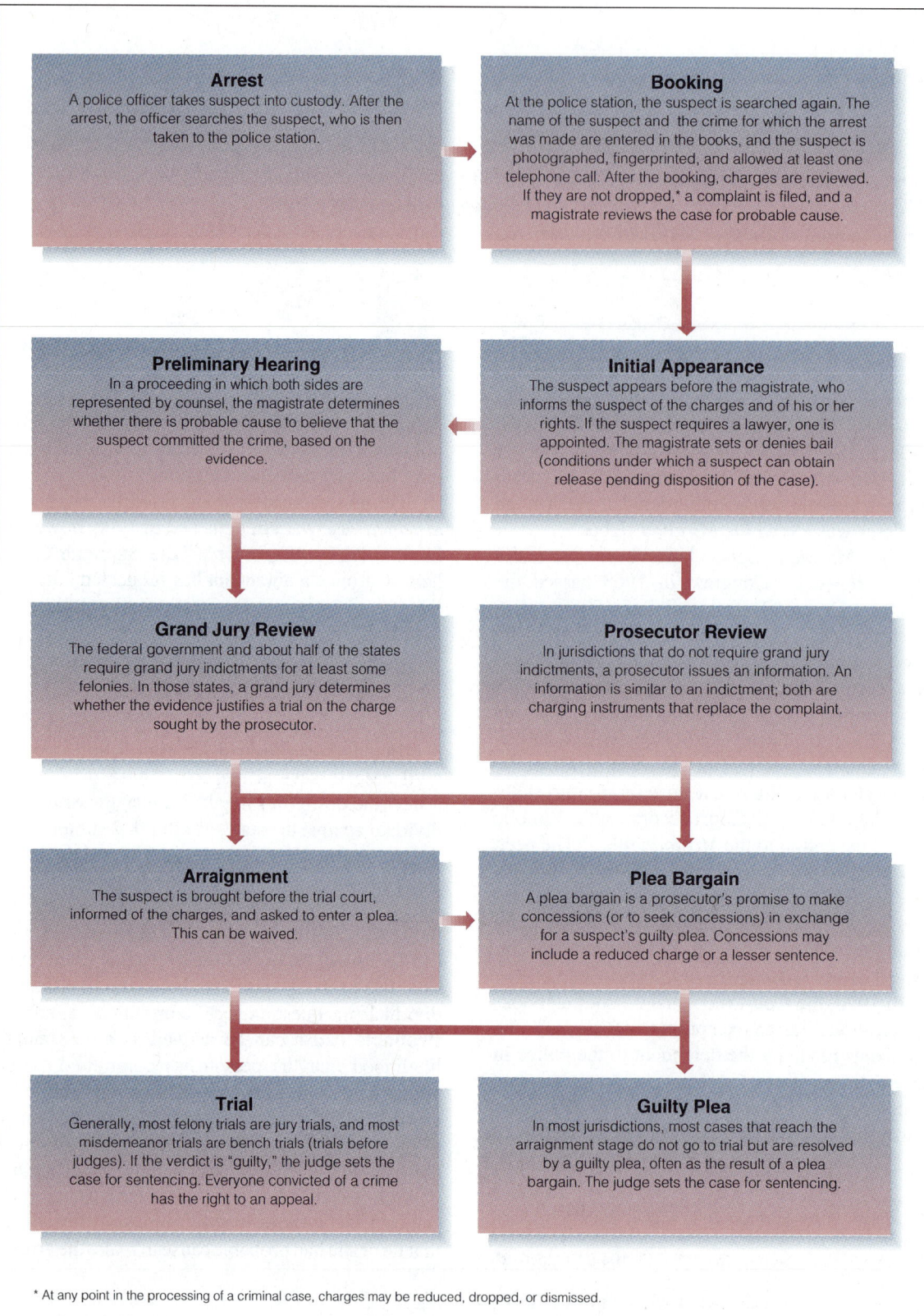

**Arrest**
A police officer takes suspect into custody. After the arrest, the officer searches the suspect, who is then taken to the police station.

**Booking**
At the police station, the suspect is searched again. The name of the suspect and the crime for which the arrest was made are entered in the books, and the suspect is photographed, fingerprinted, and allowed at least one telephone call. After the booking, charges are reviewed. If they are not dropped,* a complaint is filed, and a magistrate reviews the case for probable cause.

**Preliminary Hearing**
In a proceeding in which both sides are represented by counsel, the magistrate determines whether there is probable cause to believe that the suspect committed the crime, based on the evidence.

**Initial Appearance**
The suspect appears before the magistrate, who informs the suspect of the charges and of his or her rights. If the suspect requires a lawyer, one is appointed. The magistrate sets or denies bail (conditions under which a suspect can obtain release pending disposition of the case).

**Grand Jury Review**
The federal government and about half of the states require grand jury indictments for at least some felonies. In those states, a grand jury determines whether the evidence justifies a trial on the charge sought by the prosecutor.

**Prosecutor Review**
In jurisdictions that do not require grand jury indictments, a prosecutor issues an information. An information is similar to an indictment; both are charging instruments that replace the complaint.

**Arraignment**
The suspect is brought before the trial court, informed of the charges, and asked to enter a plea. This can be waived.

**Plea Bargain**
A plea bargain is a prosecutor's promise to make concessions (or to seek concessions) in exchange for a suspect's guilty plea. Concessions may include a reduced charge or a lesser sentence.

**Trial**
Generally, most felony trials are jury trials, and most misdemeanor trials are bench trials (trials before judges). If the verdict is "guilty," the judge sets the case for sentencing. Everyone convicted of a crime has the right to an appeal.

**Guilty Plea**
In most jurisdictions, most cases that reach the arraignment stage do not go to trial but are resolved by a guilty plea, often as the result of a plea bargain. The judge sets the case for sentencing.

* At any point in the processing of a criminal case, charges may be reduced, dropped, or dismissed.

Probable cause is also required to obtain a search warrant, which authorizes the police officer or other criminal investigator to search specifically named persons or property to obtain evidence or information in furtherance of the investigation.

**PRETRIAL PROSECUTION**  The prosecution of a criminal case begins when the police inform the **public prosecutor** (the government's attorney) of the alleged crime, provide the reports written by the arresting and investigating officers, and turn over evidence about the matter. The prosecutor then decides whether to prosecute the case or dismiss it and hence release the suspect. Most prosecutors will not go forward with a case unless they think that they have a strong chance of proving the charges against the suspect in court. If the decision is to prosecute the case, then a complaint, which includes a statement of the charges that are being brought against the suspect, will be filed with the **magistrate's court**—a court of limited jurisdiction presided over by a *magistrate,* a public official vested with judicial authority.

At this point in the process, the suspect becomes a criminal defendant. Because the defendant is now in the court system, prosecutors must show that they have legal grounds to proceed. They must show probable cause that a crime was committed and that the defendant committed the crime.

*Initial Appearance.*  The *initial appearance* is usually a brief proceeding before a magistrate. In most jurisdictions, defendants are taken before a magistrate within hours of arrest (usually within twenty-four hours). The magistrate makes sure that the person presented is the person named in the complaint, informs the defendant of the charge or charges made in the complaint, and explains to the defendant his or her rights—particularly, the right to remain silent and the right to be represented by counsel. If the defendant cannot afford to hire a private attorney, a public defender is usually appointed. But in some cases, private counsel is hired by the state to represent the defendant.

The magistrate also sets **bail**—the conditions required for release from jail pending further legal proceedings. In most cases, when bail is set, the defendant must post the amount of the bail in cash or property, or post 10 percent of the bail in cash with a private bail bondsman, who then pays the bail for the defendant. If no bail is set, the defendant may be released on his or her promise (called a personal recognizance) to appear in court when called.

*The Preliminary Hearing.*  If the defendant intends to plead guilty, he or she will usually waive the right to a **preliminary hearing** to help expedite the proceedings. In many jurisdictions, the preliminary hearing is not a common occurrence; it is only required in certain felony cases. At a preliminary hearing, a magistrate determines whether the evidence presented is sufficient to establish probable cause to believe that the defendant committed the crime for which he or she is charged.

*Indictment and Information.*  Individuals must be formally charged with having committed specific crimes before they can be brought to trial. This charge is called an **indictment** if issued by a grand jury and an **information** if issued by a public prosecutor. Before a charge can be issued, the grand jury or the public prosecutor must determine that there is sufficient evidence to justify bringing the individual to trial.

*Arraignment.*  Based on the information or the indictment filed, the prosecutor will submit a motion to the court to order the defendant to appear before the trial court for **arraignment.** At the arraignment, the defendant is informed of the charges against him or her, and is asked to respond to the charges by pleading not guilty or guilty. In some cases, a defendant may plead *nolo contendere,* which means that the defendant does not admit or deny the charges but will not contest the charges brought by the prosecutor.

At the arraignment, the defendant can move to have the charges dismissed, which happens in a fair number of cases for a variety of reasons. Most frequently, however, the defendant pleads guilty to the charge or to a lesser charge that has been agreed on through plea bargaining between the prosecutor and defendant. When the defendant pleads guilty, no trial is necessary, and the defendant is sentenced based on the plea.

**THE CRIMINAL TRIAL**  Criminal trial procedures are similar to those of a civil trial in many ways. Courts have complex rules about what types of evidence may be presented and how the evidence may be brought out, especially in jury trials. These rules are designed to ensure that evidence in trials is relevant, reliable, and not prejudicial against the defendant. The defense attorney cross-examines the witnesses who present evidence against his or her client and attempts to show that the witnesses' evidence is not reliable. The state may cross-examine any witnesses presented by the defendant.

At the trial, the accused person does not have to prove anything; the entire burden of proof is on the prosecutor (the government). Guilt must be established **beyond a reasonable doubt.** The prosecution must show that, based on all the evidence, the defendant's guilt is established beyond all reasonable doubt.

In all felony cases, the defendant has a constitutional right to a jury trial.[22] Of the criminal cases that go to trial, a majority are tried by a jury. If the right to a jury trial is waived by the defendant, the case will be decided by the judge. The jury is traditionally composed of twelve persons, but many states have reduced the size of juries to six persons for lesser offenses. In most jurisdictions, jury verdicts must be *unanimous* for **acquittal** (released from criminal liability) or **conviction** (deemed guilty of the crime). If the jury cannot obtain unanimous agreement on whether to acquit or convict the defendant, the result is a **hung jury,** and the judge may order a new trial.

SENTENCING    Whenever a defendant pleads guilty to a crime or is found guilty by a trial court, the judge will pronounce a **sentence,** which is the penalty imposed on anyone convicted of a crime. According to the punishment prescribed by law for the crime involved, which frequently involves minimum and maximum penalties, the judge may sentence the defendant to one or more of the following:

1. Death.
2. Imprisonment in a jail (for less serious crimes involving short sentences) or in a state or federal penitentiary (for serious crimes involving long sentences).
3. Probation, house arrest, or other form of supervised release.
4. Financial penalties, including fines, making restitution to victims, and payment of litigation costs.

In determining what penalty should be imposed, judges are guided by criminal sentencing guidelines (see this chapter's *Emerging Trends in Business Law*), juries' recommendations, their personal evaluation of the defendant's actions, recommendations from the prosecuting attorney and other court aides, recommendations from social service administrators, and state laws.

APPEAL    When the defendant is convicted of a crime, he or she has the right to appeal the conviction to a higher court. Death penalties (sentences) are automatically appealed. Because the Fifth Amendment prohibits double jeopardy,[23] or being tried twice for the same crime, if a conviction is overturned on appeal, the case has come to an end; the defendant is released.

---

22.   In some states, juries may also be requested for misdemeanor cases.

23.   ''No person . . . shall . . . be subject for the same offense to be twice put in jeopardy of life or limb.''

---

# TERMS AND CONCEPTS TO REVIEW

| | | |
|---|---|---|
| acquittal  186 | conviction  186 | forgery  167 |
| *actus reus*  165 | crime  165 | hung jury  186 |
| arraignment  185 | defense  176 | indictment  185 |
| arson  168 | double jeopardy  181 | information  185 |
| bail  185 | duress  178 | insider trading  170 |
| beyond a reasonable doubt  186 | embezzlement  168 | larceny  168 |
| burglary  168 | entrapment  179 | magistrate's court  185 |
| consent  177 | exclusionary rule  181 | *mens rea*  166 |
| | felony  165 | misdemeanor  165 |

money laundering  170
*nolo contendere*  185
petty offense  165
plea bargaining  181

preliminary hearing  185
probable cause  183
public prosecutor  185
robbery  168

self-defense  178
sentence  186
statute of limitations  181
white-collar crime  167

# QUESTIONS AND CASE PROBLEMS

**9–1. Criminal versus Civil Trials.** In criminal trials, the defendant must be proved guilty beyond a reasonable doubt, whereas in civil trials, the defendant need only be proved guilty by a preponderance of the evidence. Discuss why a higher standard of proof is required in criminal trials.

**9–2. Elements of a Crime.** Two basic elements are needed for a person to be convicted of a crime. The first element is called *actus reus,* and the second is called *mens rea.* Explain what these terms mean, and discuss how each is applied to the following:
 (a) Murder or manslaughter.
 (b) Forgery.
 (c) Arson.

**9–3. Types of Crimes.** The following situations are similar to one another (in all of them, Juanita's television set is stolen), yet three different crimes are described. Identify the three crimes, noting the differences among them.
 (a) While passing Juanita's house one night, Sarah sees a portable television set left unattended on Juanita's lawn. Sarah takes the television set, carries it home, and tells everyone she owns it.
 (b) While passing Juanita's house one night, Sarah sees Juanita outside with a portable television set. Holding Juanita at gunpoint, Sarah forces her to give up the set. Then Sarah runs away with it.
 (c) While passing Juanita's house one night, Sarah sees a portable television set in a window. Sarah breaks the front-door lock, enters, and leaves with the set.

**9–4. Types of Crimes.** Crimes are classified as either felonies or misdemeanors. Determine from the facts below what type of crime has been committed and whether the crime is a felony or a misdemeanor.
 (a) Jen and Gilda become involved in a shouting argument. Jen knocks Gilda down, causing a serious head injury to Gilda.
 (b) Darrell continually crosses Maria's backyard without permission, despite Maria's notice to Darrell to get off her land.
 (c) Hurto walks into a camera shop. Without force and without the owner's noticing, Hurto walks out of the store with a camera.

**9–5. Entrapment.** Makoto, an undercover police officer, stops Paulo on a busy street and offers to sell him an expensive wristwatch for a fraction of its value. After some questioning, Makoto admits that the watch is stolen property, although he says that he was not the thief. Paulo pays for and receives the wristwatch and is immediately arrested by Makoto for receiving stolen property. At trial, Paulo contends he was a victim of entrapment. What should be the result of the trial? Discuss.

**9–6. Criminal Intent.** In 1965, Rybicki failed to pay the federal government the total amount of income tax he owed. Attempts by the Internal Revenue Service (IRS) to collect the tax proved fruitless. Therefore, the IRS obtained (through lawful means) a tax lien on Rybicki's personal property, which included his truck. In February 1967, Rybicki's wife, upon hearing the truck's motor, awakened her sleeping husband. Wielding a shotgun, Rybicki went to his front door and told the two men who were attempting to take his truck to stop. Rybicki claimed that he did not know the two men were IRS agents. Subsequently, the federal government indicted Rybicki for obstructing justice. Can Rybicki be held criminally liable if he did not know that the men were IRS agents performing their duty? [*United States v. Rybicki,* 403 F.2d 599 (6th Cir. 1968)]

**9–7. Criminal Act.** Khoury went to a department store, spent some time shopping, and eventually filled a large, empty chandelier box with approximately $900 worth of tools. When he went to the check-out counter, the cashier indicated that she wanted to look inside the box before accepting Khoury's payment for the chandelier. Khoury then pushed the cart back into the store and departed from the premises. Khoury was convicted of grand larceny by the trial court. On appeal, Khoury alleged that because he had not actually removed any goods from the store, he had not committed larceny. Is Khoury correct? [*People v. Khoury,* 108 Cal.App.3d, 166 Cal.Rptr. 705 (1980)]

**9–8. Entrapment.** Gomez, an informant for the police who was posing as an ex-convict, urged Saldana on several occasions to sell cocaine to make money. But Saldana, although he used cocaine, did not wish to sell any. Finally, to get Gomez to stop pestering him, Saldana agreed to sell some cocaine to Castello, who turned out to be a police officer. May Saldana successfully claim an entrapment defense? Discuss. [*Saldana v. State,* 732 S.W.2d 701 (Tex.App.–Corpus Christi 1987)]

**9–9. Criminal Intent.** While at a grocery store, Moses Racquemore stuffed two packages of meat into his pants and was just pulling his shirt down over them when he noticed that the store manager and a security guard were watching him. He returned the meat to the counter, but he was arrested for shoplifting anyway. Had Racquemore committed a criminal act? Were Racquemore's actions in the store sufficient to prove the element of intent? Discuss. [*Racquemore v. State,* 204 Ga.App. 88, 418 S.E.2d 448 (1992)]

**9–10. Self-defense.** Britt was convicted of second degree homicide for the shooting death of his neighbor, Cavell. The victim was killed by a .44 caliber revolver that was part of a trap set by Britt to prevent forcible entry into his home from the back door. The booby trap was set to discharge if the door was opened a distance of two to four inches. The relevant Louisiana law reads as follows: ''A homicide is justifiable . . . when committed by a person lawfully inside a dwelling against a person who is attempting to make an unlawful entry into the dwelling or who has made an unlawful entry into the dwelling and the person committing the homicide reasonably believes that the use of deadly force is necessary to prevent the entry or to compel the intruder to leave the premises. The homicide shall be justifiable even though the person committing the homicide does not retreat from the encounter.'' Britt argued on appeal that the shooting of Cavell was justified because, had Britt been present, he would have been authorized to use deadly force and to use a mechanical contrivance. Will Britt's appeal be successful? Explain. [*State v. Britt,* 510 So.2d 670 (La.App. 1st Cir. 1987)]

**9–11. Criminal Liability.** In January 1988, David Ludvigson was hired as chief executive officer of Leopard Enterprises, a group of companies that owned funeral homes and cemeteries in Iowa and sold ''pre-need'' funeral contracts. Under Iowa law, 80 percent of the monies obtained under such a contract must be set aside in trust until the death of the person for whose benefit the funds were paid. Shortly after Ludvigson was hired, the firm began having financial difficulties. Ludvigson used money from these contracts to pay operating expenses until the company went bankrupt and was placed in receivership. Ludvigson was charged and found guilty on five counts of second degree theft stemming from the misappropriation of these funds. He appealed, alleging, among other things, that he was not guilty of any crime, because he had not intended to permanently deprive any of the clients of their trust funds. Furthermore, because none of the victims whose trust funds were used to cover operating expenses was denied services, no injury was done. Will the court agree with Ludvigson? Explain. [*State v. Ludvigson,* 482 N.W.2d 419 (Iowa 1992)]

### 9–12. A Question of Ethics

 *A troublesome issue concerning the constitutional privilege against self-incrimination has to do with ''jail plants''—that is, undercover police officers placed in cells with criminal suspects to gain information from the suspects. For example, in one case, the police placed an undercover agent, Parisi, in a jail cell block with Lloyd Perkins, who had been imprisoned on charges unrelated to the murder that Parisi was investigating. When Parisi asked Perkins if he had ever killed anyone, Perkins made statements implicating himself in the murder. Perkins was then charged with the murder. [Illinois v. Perkins, 496 U.S. 292, 110 S.Ct. 2394, 110 L.Ed.2d 243 (1990)]*

1. Review the discussion and case presentation of *Miranda v. Arizona* (Case 9.5). Should Perkins's statements be suppressed—that is, not be treated as admissible evidence at trial—because he was not ''read his rights'' (as required by the *Miranda* decision) prior to making his self-incriminating statements? Does *Miranda* apply to Perkins's situation?

2. Do you think that it is fair for the police to resort to trickery and deception to bring those who have committed crimes to justice? Why or why not? What rights or public policies must be balanced in deciding this issue?

# CHAPTER 10

# COMPARATIVE LAW

W hen doing business abroad, a company needs to be aware of how both international law and national law will affect its business activities. *International law* is that body of law that governs relations among or between nations. International customs, treaties, and organizations are all part of the international legal environment of business, which will be discussed in Chapter 56. **National law,** in contrast, is the law of a particular nation, such as the United States, Japan, Germany, or Brazil.

In this chapter, we examine and compare the traditions and legal systems of various nations, as well as specific legal concepts and principles relating to contracts, torts, employment relationships, and other areas of substantive law. While it is obviously impossible to discuss here all of the laws of every nation, the following pages will indicate how a variety of nations deal with some of the more important issues facing U.S. businesspersons doing business overseas or conducting business transactions with foreign enterprises.

## SECTION 1

## DOING BUSINESS ABROAD

The ability to conduct business successfully in a foreign nation requires not only a knowledge of that nation's laws but also some familiarity with its cultural system, economy, and business climate. In this section, we look at some of the ways in which cultural and structural differences can affect transnational business operations.

Many Americans find it difficult to understand and adapt to these differences and, as a consequence, do not conduct business as productively in an overseas setting. Research by the Washington International Center reports, for example, that only 20 percent of Americans who are sent abroad do well, while 40 to 60 percent quit early or function far below their abilities.[1]

## LANGUAGE AND COMMUNICATION

A crucial part of doing business abroad is understanding the local culture and how it differs from that of the United States. One obvious cultural difference among nations is language. Language differences have occasionally confounded efforts to do business abroad. The following is a list of just a few problems that American businesses have suffered because of language problems:

- Parker Pen's motto, ''Prevent embarassment, use Parker Ink,'' was an embarrassment because the Spanish word *embarazo* is translated as ''pregnancy.''
- Rolls-Royce changed the name of its ''Silver Mist'' in Germany, because in that country, *mist* translates as ''manure.''
- In Japan, Esso had difficulty selling gasoline in part because *Esso* sounds like the Japanese word for stalled car.
- Pepsi's ''Come Alive with Pepsi'' campaign was translated in Taiwan as ''Pepsi brings your ancestors back from the grave.''
- An airline in Brazil advertised plush ''rendez-vous lounges'' on jets; in Brazil, *rendezvous* implies a special room for making love.
- The Chevy Nova did not go over very well in Spanish-speaking countries because in Spanish *no va* means ''it does not go'' or ''it will not go.''

The meaning of nonverbal language (body movements, gestures, facial expressions, and the like) also varies from culture to culture. In the United States, for example, a nod of the head indicates ''yes,'' while in some countries, such as Greece, the same gesture means ''no.'' Similarly, Americans usually indicate ''no'' by moving the head from side to side, while in India, for example, the same movement means ''I'm listening. Please continue.''

## COLORS

Colors also are associated with different meanings in different countries. For example, green is the national color of Egypt, but in Malaysia, green is associated with disease. The same is true for numbers. For example, the number 4 represents bad luck in Japan and Korea.

## PERCEPTIONS OF TIME

A frequent source of cultural clashes abroad involves time. For many Americans, punctuality is crucial. In some foreign countries, businesspersons have a more flexible attitude toward time, and Americans seem excessively hurried. Northern Europeans tend to regard time in the same way as U.S. citizens do, but in Latin America, the Middle East, and parts of Asia, meetings may start late and last a long time.

## MANAGEMENT STYLES

Researchers have identified certain differences in management style across the continents. The American manager employs a direct, pragmatic, and competitive style. The Latin American manager is more humanistic and indirect, even though Latin American business firms are generally more hierarchical and authoritarian than firms in the United States. The Asian manager is more like the Latin American manager in that Asian management techniques are more indirect and designed to avoid confrontation. The European manager is more like the American, although there are substantial differences in management style between Northern European and Mediterranean nations, with the latter being somewhat less competitive and more family oriented.[2]

## ETHICS

Given the varied cultures and religions of the world's nations, one might expect frequent conflicts in ethics between foreign and United States businesspersons. In fact, many of the most important ethical precepts are common to virtually all countries. There are some important ethical differences, however. In Islamic countries, for example, the consumption of alcohol and certain foods is forbidden by the Koran (the sayings of the prophet Mohammad, which lie at the heart of Islam and Islamic law). It would be thoughtless and imprudent to invite a Saudi Arabian business contact

---

1.   Lennie Copeland and Lewis Griggs, *Going International* (New York: Random House, 1985), p. xix.

2.   Roger Axtell, *The Do's and Taboos of Hosting International Visitors* (New York: John Wiley & Sons, 1990), p. 89.

out for a drink. Two notable differences in regard to ethics involve the legitimacy of certain side payments, or gift giving, and the role of women.

**GIFT GIVING OR BRIBERY?**  In many foreign nations, gift giving is a common practice among contracting companies or between companies and government. To Americans, such gift giving may look suspiciously like an unethical (and possibly illegal) bribe. This has been an important source of friction in international business, particularly after the U.S. Congress passed the Foreign Corrupt Practices Act (FCPA)[3] in 1977 (discussed in Chapter 56). The act prohibits American business firms from offering side payments to foreign officials to secure favorable contracts. Payments to minor government officials—to facilitate necessary paperwork relating to a transaction, for example—are not prohibited by the FCPA.

Often, government workers in other countries are paid very little, and the government assumes that these workers will obtain extra income by receiving "grease payments" (to grease the wheels of the bureaucratic machine). Before an American company makes any kind of side payment, it should be sure that it understands local practice. Even when some payment is expected, the form or amount of the payment (if it is too excessive, for example) may violate the ethical rules of the foreign nation itself.

When a businessperson is presented with a gift in his or her official position as a corporate officer, the businessperson may face a dilemma. The company may itself prohibit the receipt of such gifts, for fear of being charged with favoritism by its other employees, yet rejecting the gift may seriously offend the giver. There may be some alternative, though, such as accepting the gift and quietly turning it over to the company or a charity.

**WOMEN IN BUSINESS**  The role played by women in other countries may present some difficult ethical problems for firms doing business internationally. Equal employment opportunity is a fundamental public policy in the United States, and Title VII of the Civil Rights Act of 1964[4] prohibits discrimination against women in the employment context (see Chapter 37). Some other countries, however, largely reject any role for women professionals, which may cause difficulties for American women conducting business transactions in those countries.

For example, when the World Bank sent a delegation including women to negotiate with the Central Bank of Korea, the Koreans were surprised and offended. They thought that the presence of women meant that the Koreans were not being taken seriously. (This problem might have been cured simply by some advance communication.) In Islamic nations, women are expected to avoid exposing their arms or legs in public. While American women may find it difficult to respect this custom, it may be necessary for them to do so if they wish to succeed in business transactions conducted in those nations.

Many companies are reluctant to assign women to work overseas because of these differences. A study of 686 companies found that none of them had sent a woman to work abroad alone and that women constituted only 3 percent of management personnel overseas. Note, however, that if the presence of a businesswoman is unusual in negotiations, that fact may not always work to her detriment. It might also work to her benefit.

---

## SECTION 2

# COMPARATIVE LEGAL SYSTEMS

When doing business abroad, a company generally subjects itself to the jurisdiction and laws of the foreign nation. Therefore, a wise businessperson will be familiar with the legal systems in foreign nations in which he or she conducts commercial transactions. The legal systems of foreign nations differ, in widely varying degrees, from that of the United States.

## CONSTITUTIONAL FOUNDATIONS

The foundation of a country's legal system is set forth in a governing document that is usually referred to as the nation's constitution. Most nations have several branches of government to exercise legislative, executive, and judicial powers. These systems can differ considerably. For example, Taiwan has five independent branches of government. Some nations have **federal systems,** in

---

3.  15 U.S.C. Sections 78m–78ff.
4.  42 U.S.C. Sections 2000e–2000e-17.

which government powers are divided between national and provincial governments, while other nations have centralized governments, called **unitary systems,** in which there are no independent local governing units.

In the United States, the Constitution is a single document setting forth powers and rights. The United Kingdom has no single document but refers to its constitution as a series of fundamental documents, including the Magna Carta, the Bill of Rights of 1689, and others. One important resulting difference is that British courts have no power to strike down a law as unconstitutional. In the United States, if the United States Supreme Court finds that an act of Congress violates the Constitution, the act will be declared illegal (see the section on judicial review in Chapter 3). In the United Kingdom, however, courts cannot invalidate laws passed by Parliament. French courts also lack the power of judicial review of legislative action, although a special constitutional council can invalidate laws. In Germany, laws can be reviewed for constitutionality but only in a special court, and the cases can only be brought by a government body, not individuals. India's constitution is a single document that grants to the courts the power of judicial review over statutory enactments. India also has a supreme court but lacks a fully independent judiciary.

Unlike the United States, some nations have specialized commercial law courts to deal with business disputes. France established such courts in 1807, and most nations with commercial codes have done likewise. Although England is a common law nation (discussed below), the United Kingdom also has special commercial courts overseen by judges with expertise in business law.

## COMMON LAW AND CIVIL LAW SYSTEMS

Legal systems around the globe are generally divided into *common law* and *civil law* systems. As discussed in Chapter 1, in the common law system, the courts independently develop the rules governing certain areas of law, such as torts and contracts. This judge-made law exists in addition to the laws passed by a legislature. Although the common law doctrine of *stare decisis* obligates judges to follow precedential decisions in their jurisdictions, courts may modify or even overturn precedents when deemed necessary. Also, if there is no

case law to guide a court, the court may create a new rule of law. Common law systems exist today in countries that were once a part of the British Empire (such as Australia, India, and the United States).

In contrast to Great Britain and the other common law countries, most of the European nations base their legal systems on Roman civil law, or ''code law.'' The term *civil law,* as used here, refers not to civil as opposed to criminal law but to *codified* law—an ordered grouping of legal principles enacted into law by a legislature or governing body. In a **civil law system,** the only official source of law is a statutory code. Courts are required to interpret the code and apply the rules to individual cases, but courts may not depart from the code and develop their own laws. In theory, the law code will set forth all the principles needed for the legal system. The best-known example of civil law is the French Napoleonic Code, or *Code Napoléon,* some provisions of which are presented in Exhibit 10–1. This legal system was developed in 1804 by Napoléon Bonaparte, after he became emperor of France. The Napoleonic Code survives to this day, although it has been amended by subsequent French governments. Other significant early law codes are the Spanish Commercial Code of 1885, the Japanese Commercial Code of 1890, and the German Commercial Code of 1900.

Today, the civil law system is followed in most of the continental European countries, as well as in the Latin American, African, and Asian countries that were once colonies of the continental European nations. Japan and South Africa also have civil law systems. Ingredients of the civil law system are found in the Islamic courts of predominantly Muslim countries. In the United States, the state of Louisiana, because of its historical ties to France, has, in part, a civil law system. The legal systems of Puerto Rico, Quebec, and Scotland are similarly characterized as having elements of the civil law system. Exhibit 10–2 lists some of the nations that use common law or civil law systems.

Common law and civil law systems are not wholly distinct. For example, although the United States has a common law system, criminal law is statutory law. Crimes are defined by statute as in civil law systems. Civil law systems also may allow considerable room for judges to develop law. Civil law codes cannot be so precise as to address *every* contested issue, so the judiciary must interpret the codes.

■ **Exhibit 10–1 Excerpts from the *Code Napoléon***

*Code Napoléon*

TITLE III.

OF CONTRACTS OR CONVENTIONAL OBLIGATIONS
IN GENERAL

*Decreed the 7th of February 1804. Promulgated the
17th of the same Month.*

CHAPTER I.

*Preliminary Regulations.*

1101.

A contract is an agreement that binds one or more persons, towards another or several others, to give, to do, or not to do something.

\*   \*   \*   \*

CHAPTER II.

*Of Conditions essential to the Validity of Agreements.*

1108.

Four conditions are essential to the validity of an agreement:
    The consent of the party who binds himself;
    His capacity to contract;
    A certain object forming the matter of the contract;
    A lawful cause in the bond.

Section I.

*Of Consent.*

1109.

There can be no valid consent if such consent has been given by mistake, or has been extorted through violence or surreptitiously obtained by fraud.

1110.

Mistake is not a cause for annulling the agreement except when it occurs in the very substance of the thing which is the object thereof.

It is not a cause for nullity when it occurs only in the person with whom it is intended to contract, unless the consideration of such person were the principal cause of the agreement.

SOURCE: *The French Civil Code* (Baton Rouge, La.: Claitor's Book Store, 1960 [Reprint]), pp. 302–305.

■ **Exhibit 10–2 The Legal Systems of Nations**

| Civil Law | Common Law |
|---|---|
| Argentina | Australia |
| Austria | Bangladesh |
| Brazil | Canada |
| Chile | Ghana |
| China | India |
| Egypt | Israel |
| Finland | Jamaica |
| France | Kenya |
| Germany | Malaysia |
| Greece | Nigeria |
| Indonesia | Singapore |
| Iran | United Kingdom |
| Italy | United States |
| Japan | Zambia |
| Mexico | |
| Poland | |
| South Korea | |
| Sweden | |
| Tunisia | |
| Venezuela | |

There are also significant differences among common law countries. The judges of different common law nations have produced differing common law principles. Thus, although the United States and India both derived their legal traditions from England, the common law principles governing contract law differ in some respects between the two countries. Similarly, the laws of nations that have civil law systems vary considerably. For example, the French code tends to set forth general principles of law, while the German code is far more specific and runs to thousands of sections. In the French code, there are no specific sections dealing with contract formation (discussed in a later section), so these concepts have been defined largely by case law and are similar to the doctrines developed in the United States. In some Middle Eastern countries, the code is grounded in religious, Islamic directives, known as **shari'a.** The religious basis of this code makes it far more difficult to alter.

## JUDGES AND PROCEDURES

Judges play a similar role in virtually all countries: their primary function is the resolution of litigation. The characteristics and qualifications of judges, which are typically set forth in the nation's con-

stitution, can vary widely, however. The U.S. judge normally does not actively participate in a trial, but many foreign judges involve themselves closely in the proceedings, such as by questioning witnesses. Because U.S. federal judges serve for life and cannot be removed by impeachment except in extreme cases (such as accepting bribes), their decisions are less likely to be influenced by politics than may be the case in other countries. In India, for example, judges issuing rulings contrary to the prime minister have been transferred or demoted on occasion.

The procedures employed in resolving cases also vary substantially from country to country. A knowledge of a nation's legal procedures is important for a person conducting business transactions in that nation. For example, an American businessperson was on trial in Saudi Arabia for assaulting and slandering a co-worker, an offense for which he might have been jailed or deported. He initially was required to present two witnesses to his version of events, but he had only one. Fortunately, he became aware that he could "demand the oath." In this procedure, he swore before God that he did not kick nor slander the complainant. After taking the oath, he was promptly adjudged not guilty, as lying under oath is one of the most serious sins under Islamic law. Had he failed to demand the oath, he almost certainly would have been found guilty.[5]

## LAWYERS AND LITIGATION

The role of lawyers, too, differs from country to country. In the United States, an attorney is required by state law to serve as an advocate of his or her client's interests. In contrast, Chinese lawyers in the People's Republic are obligated first to further the interests of the government and not necessarily the interests of their clients. Attitudes regarding the function of lawyers also vary. For example, while it is not unusual for American businesspersons to include lawyers and accountants on their negotiating teams, in foreign settings, the presence of these professionals may imply that one is planning some deception.[6]

Tort litigation tends to be more extensive and significant in common law systems. Indeed, some

---

5. J. Brand, "Aspects of Saudi Arabian Law and Practice," *Boston College International and Comparative Law Review,* Vol. 1, No. 9 (1986), pp. 9–10.

6. Copeland and Griggs, *Going International,* p. 81.

■ **Exhibit 10–3 Number of Lawyers per 100,000 Citizens**

| | | | |
|---|---|---|---|
| Iceland | 400 | Singapore | 74 |
| United States | 311 | Sweden | 29 |
| Israel | 295 | Guyana | 17 |
| Venezuela | 254 | Japan | 12 |
| Mexico | 153 | Kenya | 7 |
| England | 145 | Iran | 4 |
| Germany | 103 | Indonesia | 3 |

SOURCE: Based on information from Euromoney Publications, *The International Financial Law Review 1000*, 1993.

have blamed America's alleged litigiousness in part on our common law system. Of course, many other factors, such as cultural and business traditions, also affect the legal climate for business. For example, in some nations, such as Japan, citizens and businesses are less disposed to go to court than they are in the United States. The total number of lawyers in a country undoubtedly has some effect on litigation, though the vast majority of lawyers do not work directly on lawsuits and do not even appear in court. It is widely believed that the United States has more lawyers (as a percentage of the population) than any other country in the world with the exception of Iceland. Comparisons are difficult, however, because there is no uniform global definition of *lawyer*. In Sweden, virtually anyone may serve as a lawyer, without meeting state-mandated educational and other requirements. Exhibit 10–3 shows the relative number of lawyers in various nations as a percentage of population (lawyers per 100,000 citizens).

**SECTION 3**

# NATIONAL LAWS COMPARED

Certain legal principles are essential to a complex society, and virtually all nations have laws governing contracts, torts, patents, and other areas. Even when the basic principles are fundamentally similar (as in contract law), there are significant variations in the practical application and effect of these laws. This section summarizes the laws of

representative nations in several areas of interest to firms doing business abroad.[7]

## CONTRACT LAW

To a degree, contract law has been internationalized through the United Nations Convention on Contracts for the International Sale of Goods (CISG), which was mentioned in Chapter 1 and described in detail in Chapter 20. As of 1994, thirty-eight countries had ratified the CISG, including the United States, Canada, Mexico, some Central and South American countries, and most of the European nations.

For many transactions, however, the CISG may not apply. For one thing, the CISG applies only to transactions involving firms in countries that have signed the convention, or agreement, or parties (in nonsignatory nations) who have stipulated in their contract that the CISG will govern any dispute. When transactions involve firms in countries that are not signatory to the CISG, the contract parties need to determine which nation's law will govern any disputes that may arise under the contract. Also, even when the CISG would apply, *it applies only if the parties have not agreed otherwise in their contract.* For example, parties may agree in their contract that German law or U.S. law or some other nation's law will govern any contract dispute that arises. For these reasons, the contract laws of

---

7. A more detailed discussion of each nation's law can be found in a valuable series published by Price Waterhouse and entitled *Doing Business in [name of country]*. These booklets describe the law of many nations across the world, such as France, Nigeria, Taiwan, Australia, Mexico, and Jamaica. They are updated periodically, as necessary.

individual nations remain important to international businesspersons.

There are some important similarities in the contract laws of all nations. The requirements of offer and acceptance are common, although what is considered an offer varies by jurisdiction. (As will be discussed in Chapters 12 and 20, for legal purposes, contract formation is usually divided into two separate events: the making of a contractual *offer* by one person and the *acceptance* of that offer by another.) Many nations require that an offer, once made, must remain open for acceptance for some minimum period of time. Rules for damages for breach of contract (failure to perform the contract as promised) and the availability of other remedies also vary widely throughout the world. Other principles of contract law, such as those relating to fraud, illegality, and oral contracts, are relatively common around the globe.

**GERMANY** The German Civil Code has detailed provisions governing offer and acceptance. Unlike contract law in the United States, German contract law requires that a written contractual offer must be held open for a reasonable time, unless the offer specifically states otherwise. Oral contractual offers (those made in person or by telephone) must be accepted immediately or they expire. Like most civil law countries, Germany does not require the exchange of consideration (such as money or goods or something else of value—see Chapter 13) for a contract to be legally binding. Agreements to make gifts may thus be enforceable by the donee (the gift's recipient). In the United States, consideration is a required element for a valid contract, and promises to make gifts are normally not enforceable (because the donee does not give consideration for the gift).

German contract law also differs from that of the United States in regard to contractual performance and remedies. A special doctrine provides that if there is an unforeseeable change in the basis of the contract, German courts may reform (revise) the contract to address the changes. Germany's typical remedy for a breach of contract is specific performance, which means that the party must go forward and perform the contract. Damages are available only after notice and other procedures have been employed to seek performance. Recall from Chapter 1 that in the United States, the equitable remedy of specific performance will usually not be granted unless the remedy at law (money

damages) is inadequate and the subject matter of the contract is unique.

**SAUDI ARABIA** Saudi Arabian contract law requires an offer, acceptance, and consideration, as in America. The Saudis have strict requirements about a contract's definiteness of terms. In the United States, a contract's terms must be sufficiently definite that the parties (and a court) can determine whether the contract has been formed or not (see Chapter 12). For contracts for the sale of goods, however, which are governed by the Uniform Commercial Code (UCC), the common law requirements in respect to definiteness of contract terms are relaxed substantially (see Chapter 20).

Saudi Arabia does not absolutely require that contracts be in writing, but this is strongly encouraged by the law, and writings should be formally witnessed by two males or a male and a female. Contracts for goods forbidden in the Koran are illegal and unenforceable. Such goods include alcohol and pork products.

**CHINA** Mainland China's free enterprise system is yet emerging, and its contract law is still somewhat unclear. The basic structure of Chinese contract law is similar to that of the United States, and Chinese law provides for a number of common defenses to contract formation, such as fraud and duress. Some types of contracts require formal approval by the central government or the relevant provincial government. Failure to obtain such approval will void, or nullify, the contract.

**INDIA** In India, the traditional common law of contracts has been codified. Much of India's contract law is borrowed from the English tradition, though differences do exist. Some contracts are lawful in the absence of consideration, such as promises in exchange for a past act. (In the United States, "past consideration" is no consideration—see Chapter 13.) Contracts with consideration may be invalidated if they are considered immoral or contrary to public policy. Indian courts look to the adequacy of consideration (how much value, or money, is given in return for a contractual promise) when considering whether the parties' assent to the contract was truly genuine and therefore whether the contract should be enforced. In the United States, courts rarely inquire into the adequacy of consideration. Normally, only in cases in which the consideration is so grossly inadequate as to "shock the conscience of the court" will a court refuse to enforce a contract.

**MEXICO**   Mexico has some special rules for offer and acceptance that can be important. If a time for acceptance is not stated in an offer, the offer is deemed to be held open for three days, plus whatever time is necessary for the offer and acceptance to be sent through the mails. If acceptance is desired sooner, the offeror (the person making the offer) must state the time for acceptance in the offer. Mexico has adopted a commercial code, which, like the UCC, liberalizes the traditional requirements of definiteness and contractual formalities in mercantile transactions.

## TORT LAW

Tort law, which provides the ability to recover damages for harms or injuries caused by another's negligent or intentional wrongful actions, can vary widely among the nations. Common law nations have developed court-made law regarding what kinds of actions constitute negligence or some other tort that permits recovery. Civil law nations must authorize such recovery in their codes. Exhibit 10–4 shows how the civil law codes of different nations define what constitutes a tort.

Even when the statutory language is similar, the application of tort law varies among nations. One significant difference involves liability for omissions, or failures to act. Tort law in the United States generally holds that there is no "duty to rescue," and a person is normally not liable for failing to rescue another person in distress. German law is basically similar. As Exhibit 10–4 makes clear, some nations provide explicit liability for negligent omissions. Likewise, traditional Islamic law provides that a "keeper who, seeing an animal destroying the property of another, does not check it, is liable to compensate for the damage."

There are many other differences among national tort laws and many different approaches to the calculation of damages. For example, Swiss and Turkish law permit a court to reduce damages if an award of full damages would cause undue hardship to a party who was found negligent. Also, in some nations of northern Africa, different amounts of damages are awarded depending on the type of tortious action committed. In the United States, however, actual damages do not depend on whether the tort was negligent or intentional.

■ **Exhibit 10–4  Civil Code Tort Definitions**

**Brazil:** He who, by a voluntary act or omission, by negligence or carelessness, violates another's right, or causes him harm, is bound to compensate for the damage.

**Egypt:** Every culpable act that causes damage to another obliges the person who did it to compensate for it.

**The Netherlands:** Every unlawful act by which damage is caused to another obliges the person by whose fault the damage occurred to compensate for it.

**Spain:** He who by act or omission causes damage to another, either by fault or negligence, is obliged to compensate for the damage caused.

**Tunisia:** Every act a person does without lawful justification that causes willful and voluntary damage—material or moral—to another obliges the person who did it to compensate for the aforesaid damage, when it is shown that the act is the direct cause.

**Uruguay:** Every unlawful act a person does which causes damage to another imposes on the person whose malice, fault, or negligence brought it about the obligation to compensate for it. When the unlawful act was done maliciously, i.e., with the intention of causing harm—it amounts to a delict [an intentional tort, discussed in Chapter 6, or a crime], when the intention to cause harm is not present, the unlawful act amounts to a quasi-delict (a tort or a crime caused by negligence). In either case, the unlawful act can be negative or positive according to whether the breach of duty consists of an act or omission.

SOURCE: Andre Tunc, *International Encyclopedia of Comparative Law,* Vol. XI, Chapter 2, pp. 5–6.

Statutes of limitations (deadlines for filing a lawsuit) in other countries also vary and tend to be longer than in the United States. For example, in Italy the plaintiff must sue within five years of the tort's commission, and the general French limitations period is ten years. Which party has the burden of proof in a tort lawsuit also differs among countries. In the United States, the burden of proof is on the plaintiff. In Russia, the defendant has the burden of proving that he or she was not at fault.

A growing area of the law in many nations is product liability (liability for selling defective products—see Chapter 25). In the United States, strict liability principles are commonly applied in product liability lawsuits. The following case illustrates how the German Federal Supreme Court decided a product liability suit brought by a plaintiff who had been injured while using exercise equipment.

---

**CASE 10.1**

**RE PRODUCT LIABILITY (Case VI ZR 103/89)**

*Bundesgerichtshof* [German Federal Supreme Court], 1991. [1991] ECC 204. [Translated from the German.]

**BACKGROUND AND FACTS** *The plaintiff purchased an exerciser called the "Souplex-Expander" from a retail store. The exerciser was manufactured by one company (K-AG), but another company (K-KG) had supplied plastic handle moulds for the machine. While the plaintiff was exercising, one of the handles broke, and the expander flew upward, striking the plaintiff in the eye and causing her to lose all sight in that eye. The trial court held that K-KG was liable for damages, including damages for pain and suffering, but found that K-AG was not liable. On appeal, the court reversed and held that K-AG was also liable for these damages. K-AG appealed to the German Federal Supreme Court.*

*DECISION*
\* \* \* \*

(a) The appeal[s] court made no findings to the effect that the defendant [K-AG] was aware of the dangerous nature of the handle. It evidently proceeded on the basis that the defendant was in a position to find out about the matter, since it explained that the defendant, because of its special knowledge in the field of processing plastics, was not entitled to rely on the moulds supplied to it by K-KG being suitable for producing safe and unbreakable handles. This Court cannot agree with that conclusion to such a degree of generality. The [appeals court] is right in objecting that none of the parties to the case has made any submissions to the effect that the defendant had a special knowledge of the weak points in synthetic components under stress. \* \* \*

(b) In the present case the defendant also had no special cause to scrutinize the design of the expander handles inasmuch as the authorized testing office of the Rh-Technical Standards Association had tested the equipment, including the handle produced by the defendant, in accordance with section 3(4) of the Technical Equipment (Safety) Act and granted it the "GS" ("Safety Test") mark, and the B-Technical Standards association had assessed it as "good" after testing it. It is true that a manufacturer who designs his products himself is not exempted from liability for design faults therein solely because a testing institution has examined it and not found defects of the relevant sort. But the position is different for other enterprises that are brought in at various stages of the production process or of the distribution of industrial products; they have lower duties of care in relation to design risks than the actual manufacturer and designer of the product.

**DECISION AND REMEDY** *The court reversed the appellate court and reinstated the verdict in favor of K-AG.*

---

## EMPLOYMENT LAW

Employment law is particularly important in many foreign nations. The United States traditionally left the details of the employment relationship to a negotiation between the employer and the employee. Under the *employment-at-will* doctrine (discussed in Chapter 36), employers were free to hire and fire employees "at will"—that is, for any reason or no reason at all. Although in the United States an employer's ability to terminate employees at will is becoming more and more restricted, other nations have even more requirements that employers must meet before employees can be discharged.

**FRANCE** The concept of employment at will can be traced back to the original Napoleonic Code of France. Over the years, the French have modified this doctrine considerably. French courts developed the doctrine of *abus de droit* (abuse of rights), which prohibited employers from firing workers for illness, pregnancy, unionization, political beliefs, the exercise of certain rights, or even personal dislike. French courts also began requiring employers to follow customary procedures before terminating workers.

French employee-discharge laws were codified in the Dismissal Law of 1973. If an employment contract is for an indefinite term, the employer can fire a worker only for genuine and serious cause or for economic factors. The law also establishes procedural requirements. Before terminating a worker for cause, the employer must undertake a conciliatory session with labor court mediators. The employer has the burden of proof in labor court to demonstrate that the cause of the dismissal was serious. French courts have permitted dismissal for a wide variety of reasons. In one case, the court upheld the termination of a ship painter who was discharged for refusing to perform additional, temporary, off-site work.

**EGYPT** In Egypt, employers commonly use fixed-period employment contracts, which are automatically terminated at the end of the contract period. Under employment contracts with indefinite terms, however, it is difficult to discharge employees. The employee must first commit a serious offense, whereupon the employer must submit a proposal for termination to a committee consisting of representatives of the union, the employer, and the government. Employees may appeal adverse decisions received from this committee. Some employers get around these difficult termination procedures by making generous severance-pay offers to induce voluntary resignation.

**TAIWAN** Taiwanese law places clear restrictions on the termination of workers. An employer must provide a reason for terminating an employee. An employer may discharge an employee with advance notice and severance pay for a number of economic reasons or if the worker is incapable of performing the assigned work. The amount of notice and severance pay depends on the worker's tenure with the company. Employers may fire employees without notice or severance pay only for causes such as violence, imprisonment, extensive absenteeism, or lying on a job application should the lie cause the employer to suffer actual harm.

**POLAND** Under the Polish labor code, employment is predominantly "at will." Either party may terminate the employment relationship at any time, but advance notice is generally required. Notice requirements vary, depending on the length of the worker's tenure with the employer. An employer may terminate an employee immediately and without notice if the worker has committed a criminal offense, lost a license or other employment qualification, seriously breached his or her duties, or failed to appear regularly at the job site. An employer cannot immediately discharge an employee for the last reason if the employee's absence was due to child-care needs, infectious disease, or entitled sick leave.

**MEXICO** In addition to discharge rules, foreign nations place on employers a variety of requirements not found in the United States. In Mexico, for example, workers have a right to an annual bonus, equal to fifteen days' salary and paid at the end of the year. Mexican law requires a minimum amount of paid vacation time (six days in the first year of employment) and also requires that companies give workers a 25 percent bonus above their ordinary pay rates during those vacations. For example, if their ordinary pay is $200 per week, the vacation pay is $250 per week. Mexican employers also must periodically give training courses to workers.

**HONG KONG** Many nations have some form of workers' compensation laws, much like state workers' compensation laws in the United States (discussed in Chapter 36). These laws compensate employees who are injured on the job. As in the United States, these countries have rules defining the nature and scope of workers' compensation and limiting it to work-related injuries. In the following case, the issue before the Hong Kong court was whether a worker's death occurred in the course of employment.

| CASE 10.2 | **BACKGROUND AND FACTS** *A worker agreed to pick up some of his oxyacetylene welding and cutting equipment at the office of his supervisor at around 8 A.M. When his colleagues did not arrive, the worker and his supervisor went to a restaurant and drank wine until 8:50 A.M. The worker left the restaurant and went to a public lavatory in the same block as his office. He was stabbed and killed in the lavatory. His heirs sought to recover for his death under workers' compensation laws. The lower court held that the heirs could not recover under these laws because at the time of his death the worker was not acting in the course of employment. The heirs appealed.* |
|---|---|
| **FONG FUNG-YING AND ATTORNEY GENERAL** Hong Kong Court of Appeal, 1984. Civil Appeal No. 111 of 1984. | |

Sir Alan *HUGGINS,* V.P.

\* \* \* \*

Obviously it cannot be right to say that, because a visit to the lavatory might in some circumstances be incidental to the deceased's employment, the deceased was in the course of his employment on every occasion on which he went to that lavatory during working hours. There are two matters to be considered[:] (1) the purpose for which he went there and (2) the circumstances in which he went there. He might have gone there to place a bet with a book-maker, or merely to avoid working, and that would clearly not have been "in the course of" the employment. Of course, one could conceive of numerous possible alternative purposes, and if he went there on another frolic of his own he would have been no more in the course of his employment than he was during his visit to the restaurant. Is it a reasonable and proper assumption on the balance of probabilities that he went there to relieve himself, or was it for the claimant to adduce some evidence to show that that was his intention?

\* \* \*

It now being accepted that on the day in question the deceased's visit to the restaurant was not incidental to his employment, it follows that if he had gone from the restaurant to the lavatory with the intention of returning thereafter to the restaurant to continue his unauthorized break, that would equally not have been in the course of his employment.

**DECISION AND REMEDY** *The court concluded that the survivors bore the burden of proving that the deceased was acting in the course of his employment. Because they were unable to meet this burden, the court dismissed their appeal.*

## INTELLECTUAL PROPERTY

Protection of intellectual property is of critical importance in doing business overseas. Stolen, or "pirated," intellectual property, be it compact discs or computer software, represents a major loss to American business. Worldwide losses have been estimated to be $50 billion annually. While there is some international protection for some forms of intellectual property, business remains largely dependent on local protection of copyrights, patents, trademarks and related property, and trade secrets. The degree of protection varies widely, according to the culture, law, and history of a nation.

**JAPAN** Some of Japan's early economic growth was due to the use of imported U.S. intellectual property that could not be protected under Japanese law. At the time, this did not seem so serious, but the subsequent economic growth of Japan has made intellectual property protection a major economic and diplomatic issue. Japan now provides strong formal protection for patents, trademarks, and other forms of intellectual property.

Japan's legal structure for intellectual property protection has some shortcomings, however. The Japanese Patent Office (JPO) is understaffed, and some American companies have been forced to wait ten years for formal patent protection, although the Japanese government promises to improve this situation. Enforcement against patent infringement is more difficult, because Japanese courts lack authority to rule on the validity of a patent and must refer these issues back to the JPO. Trademark registration is also slow and takes, on average, four years to complete.

**MEXICO**  Mexico has extensive formal protection for intellectual property, much of it based on recently enacted laws. A 1991 law revised patent protection, which extends for twenty years in Mexico. Patent protection can be lost by lack of exploitation (lack of use) in Mexico or by failure to pay annual fees required by the nation. Registered trademarks are protected for ten years and may be renewed. Registration of the mark is denied if the mark has already been used in Mexico or in another country by another person. As discussed in Chapter 56, the North American Free Trade Agreement (NAFTA) has expanded Mexican intellectual property protection and brought Mexico's law closer to that of the United States. (Excerpts from the NAFTA are presented in Appendix P.)

**GULF COOPERATION COUNCIL**  The Gulf Cooperation Council was formed in 1981 by Saudi Arabia, Kuwait, Bahrain, Qatar, the United Arab Emirates, and Oman to jointly address certain trade issues. The United Arab Emirates, Qatar, and Oman have no patent law protection; Oman, Kuwait, and Qatar have no copyright laws. As a consequence, virtually all video, audio, and computer products sold in these nations are pirated copies. Kuwait has a patent law, but it is seldom enforced. Saudi Arabia tends to offer greater intellectual property protection, but even that nation has an unusually short term for copyright protection (twenty-five years).

**BRAZIL**  Brazilian law provides substantial protection for intellectual property, but there are some exceptions. For example, Brazil provides little patent protection for chemical compounds, pharmaceuticals, and some other substances. In addition, Brazil requires the active use of patented products, which limits the utility of obtaining an advance precautionary patent before entering the Brazilian market. In 1987, Brazil extended formal copyright protection to software. As in many nations, enforcement of the Brazilian laws is a problem, and pirating remains widespread. To protect a trademark in Brazil, a company must register with the National Institute for Industrial Property.

**EUROPE**  The nations of Western Europe have formed the European Union (discussed later in this chapter) in an effort to consolidate their economies and break down trade barriers. Intellectual property law remains inconsistent, however. For example, it is more difficult to copyright computer software in Germany than in other nations. Some European nations, such as France, recognize artists' ''moral rights'' in creative products. Even if an artist has sold his or her copyright in the product to a company, the remaining moral rights of the artist prevent the company from modifying the work, such as through colorization of a black-and-white film. Most civil law systems have similar concepts in regard to authors' rights.

Nations use intellectual property law to protect their leading industries. A classic example is the protection given to the word *champagne* in France. French law restricts the use of the word to wines from a specific region. French law even precluded Yves Saint Laurent from using *Champagne* as the name for his new perfume. French producers have sought to protect their trade names in other countries, as illustrated by the following action.

---

**BACKGROUND AND FACTS**  *Wineworths Group, Ltd.,*[a] *was an Australian company seeking to import Australian-made ''champagne'' into New Zealand. The French-based* Comité Interprofessionel du Vin de Champagne *filed suit under New Zealand's Fair Trading Act to prohibit the Australians from referring to their sparkling wine as ''champagne,'' even though Australian wines had been sold under this name in Australia for many years. The trial court held that the French company was entitled to a permanent injunction against the selling, in New Zealand, of Australian products as champagne, and the defendants appealed.*

CASE 10.3

**WINEWORTHS GROUP, LTD. v. COMITE INTERPROFESSIONEL du VIN de CHAMPAGNE**

Court of Appeal, Wellington (New Zealand), 1991.
2 N.Z.L.R. 327.

a.  *Ltd.* means ''limited,'' referring to limited liability, and is similar to our *Inc.*

*COOKE* (P).

\* \* \* \*

\* \* \* The attention, very large by New Zealand standards, which has been devoted in this case to the right to use the word [*champagne*] in New Zealand is in itself cogent proof of the value of the description in this country. The more one studied the written submissions of learned counsel for the appellant, Mr. Williams, and the longer one listened to his replies to questions from the Bench, the more it became manifest that ''champagne'' is a very valuable trade description indeed. Mr. Miles for the respondent spoke of Champagne as one of the great marks of the world, perhaps comparable in eminence only to Rolls-Royce.

\* \* \* \*

\* \* \* The more Seqview Australian Champagne were to penetrate the New Zealand market, the more it would inevitably dilute or erode the distinctiveness and consequent goodwill at present attaching in this country to the trade name ''Champagne,'' which is the name of the wine of the true producers thereof in France. Unless the injunction stands it is highly likely that a substantial portion of the New Zealand public, particularly those less well informed about wine, will be misled into thinking that there is no significant difference between the French and Australian products.

**DECISION AND REMEDY**   *The court upheld the permanent injunction against referring to Australian wines as "champagne." But Australian winemakers could use the word* champagne *within Australia, because they had used the word for so long that its meaning had become "debased" in that country alone.*

## CORPORATE LAW

A key to doing business overseas is understanding national corporate law. While virtually all nations have some form of limited-liability corporation for doing business, the names of such entities can differ considerably. (Limited liability in this context means that the liability of the corporate owners, or shareholders, is limited to the amount of their investment—see Chapter 38.)[8] Laws governing procedures for incorporation and corporate requirements also vary widely among the world's states. Failure to discern and abide by local law may subject an entity to considerable liability.

**NIGERIA**   Nigerian law prohibits a foreign company from operating a branch in that nation—the corporation must independently incorporate in Nigeria. It must first notify the Registrar of Company in writing and follow the procedures to secure ''approved status'' from the Ministry of Finance. The foreign entity may then obtain a *certificate of incorporation* from the Registrar of Company. The corporate formalities in Nigeria are roughly similar to those of the United States in many re-

spects, such as notice requirements for directors' and shareholders' meetings, eligibility of directors, and so on. Nigerian shareholders are known as ''members.''

The Nigerian Enterprises Promotion Act of 1977 contains important provisions for all limited-liability companies. Each firm is required to establish a trust for the benefit of its employees and pay into that trust at least 5 percent of the after-tax profits of the company. The law also requires substantial ownership by Nigerian nationals. There are several classes of limited-liability enterprises; they require different levels of local ownership but generally demand that at least 40 percent of the equity (ownership rights) be held by Nigerians. Certain types of companies can be 100 percent foreign owned, but a few other businesses are reserved for Nigerian ownership. In addition, corporations are expected to provide at least 10 percent of their equity shares for their employees. Nigerian law, however, is evolving toward greater encouragement of foreign investment.

**ARGENTINA**   A company may conduct business in Argentina as either an incorporated entity (a *sociedad anónima,* or S.A.), a partnership, a sole proprietorship, or a branch of a foreign corporation (see Chapter 38 for a description of these business

---

8.   See also Chapters 41–44 for a discussion of corporate law in the United States.

forms). In each situation, the company must file a registration with the state Public Registry of Commerce. Argentinian corporate law is similar to that of the United States and the rest of the world, with a few differences. Corporations are required to accumulate a legal reserve equal to 20 percent of their capital. Large corporations are required to appoint a committee to audit corporate accounts and monitor legal compliance at periodic intervals.

**KOREA** The most common form of business enterprise in Korea is a large limited-liability company known as a *Chusik Hoesa*. Seven or more promoters (those who undertake the initial tasks relating to corporate formation—see Chapter 41) must gain approval from the Ministry of Finance to form a company. Gaining approval takes about six months. Stock is then sold to individual or corporate shareholders, who assume ownership of the company. A *Chusik Hoesa* must employ a statutory auditor to examine corporate accounts and operations and report to the shareholders. Required corporate formalities are typical, including notice requirements relating to directors' and shareholders' meetings.

## GOVERNMENT REGULATION

Numerous rules apply to U.S. firms doing business in other countries. These rules govern such areas as environmental protection, securities regulation, product safety, business combinations, and a host of other topics.

**TAIWAN** Taiwan encourages free competition, and many regulatory controls have been relaxed in recent years. The Price Control Commission of the Taiwanese Ministry of Economic Affairs controls the prices that can be charged for some basic living commodities. Taiwan has strengthened its securities regulations and environmental protection rules.

Taiwan's Fair Trade Law contains antitrust provisions to prevent harmful monopolization of markets. (Antitrust laws promote competition in the marketplace by prohibiting firms from engaging in certain types of activities, such as monopolization, that result in too much control over a given market—see Chapter 48.) Any merger (the legal union of two firms) must receive government approval if the market share of one of the companies is as much as a quarter of the total market or if the market share of the combined companies would equal or exceed one-third of the total market. Businesses may collude on prices or markets, but only with the permission of the government and only for the purpose of lowering the cost of goods, improving their quality, enhancing exports, limiting production during a recession, or a few other reasons.

**INDIA** While India is moving in a deregulatory direction, there remain many government rules restricting business. For example, a company may not close an industrial plant in India without government permission, which may be difficult to obtain. Prices of necessary goods, raw materials, and some intermediate products are regulated by the Indian government, though these rules are being relaxed. The Monopolies and Restrictive Trade Practices Act regulates any company that has a market share in excess of 25 percent and may bar mergers and other practices that are deemed contrary to the public interest. India has special courts with broad powers to rule on consumer complaints.

**GERMANY** Germany has an extensive body of antitrust law to promote competition. A company with more than 20 percent of a major market segment must inform the Federal Cartels Office of this fact. The Cartels Office can prohibit acquisitions or mergers that would cause undesirable market concentration. A merger may be justified if it prevents unemployment, however. Mergers of particularly large companies are also subject to regulations issued by the European Union. German environmental regulations tend to be especially stringent. German laws against unfair competition establish consumer protection rules, and these rules effectively void (render legally ineffective) any "fine print" in consumer contracts. Germany also has a particularly extensive set of regulations on advertising.

**EGYPT** Egyptian national regulation is not particularly extensive. The majority of investments in the nation are still in publicly owned industries. Private firms are generally not subject to price controls, antitrust restrictions on mergers and acquisitions, or consumer protection laws. While Egypt has relatively little environmental regulation, the nation does have strict controls on herbicides, and Egyptian law imposes potentially severe penalties (such as plant closures) for violations of the rather vague environmental laws that do exist. The

Egyptian private sector is growing rapidly, and increased regulation of this sector can be anticipated.

**MEXICO**   The Mexican constitution prohibits monopolies and certain agreements that restrain trade. Mexican laws are similar in this respect to U.S. antitrust laws. Unlike the United States, Mexico in practice permits market concentration out of some concern that restrained competition can jeopardize total employment. Mexican law also permits the president to impose price controls on many products. The president may also place restraints on the production or consumption of products to correct for surpluses or shortages. With Mexico's new commitment to free enterprise, however, these presidential powers are not so frequently used.

**SECTION 4**

# THE EUROPEAN UNION

The European Union (EU) arose out of the 1957 Treaty of Rome, which created the Common Market among Belgium, France, West Germany, Italy, the Netherlands, and Luxembourg. Since 1957, more nations have been added to this free trade zone, and the powers of the EU have grown. The EU has added Spain, the United Kingdom, Denmark, Greece, Ireland, and Portugal to the original Common Market countries. Austria, Finland, Norway, and Sweden may have been added by the time you read this. Eastern European nations are applying for membership. Some believe that the result will eventually be a "United States of Europe."

The EU has its own governing authorities. One is the Council of Ministers, which coordinates economic policies, and includes one representative from each nation. The EU also has a commission that proposes regulations to the Council and an elected assembly, which oversees the commission. The community has its own court, the European Court of Justice, which can review each nation's court decisions and is the ultimate authority on EU law.

Some of Europe's efforts at harmonization have been confounded by national independence. For example, the effort to replace the member countries' currencies (lira, pounds, francs, and so on) with a common currency has been frustrated. On less public issues, the EU has gone far toward creating a new law to govern all of the member nations. The council and the commission issue regulations or directives that define the EU law in various areas, and these requirements are binding on member states.

EU directives govern such issues as environmental law, antitrust law, corporate structure, and securities law. The EU directive on product liability, for example, states that a "producer of an article shall be liable for damage caused by a defect in the article, whether or not he knew or could have known of the defect." Liability extends to anyone who puts a trademark or other identifying feature on the article, and liability may not be excluded, even by contract.

Development of the EU has complicated European business law. A company now must consider international regulations, as well as the rules of the country of operation. This effect is illustrated by the following case.

| CASE 10.4 | |
|---|---|
| **ALSATEL - SOCIETE ALSACIENNE et LORRAINE de TELE-COMMUNICATIONS et D'ELECTRONIQUE v. S.A. NOVASAM**  Court of Justice of the European Communities, 1988. Eur. Comm. Rep. 5987. [Translated from the French.] | **BACKGROUND AND FACTS**   Alsatel - Société Alsacienne et Lorraine de Télécommunications et d'Electronique *brought this claim against* S.A. Novasam, *a temporary employment agency.* Novasam *had terminated three contracts for the rental of telephone installations. A fifteen-year contract with* Alsatel *had bound* Novasam *to deal exclusively with* Alsatel *for any changes in service, extension of service, additional lines, or other modifications of the installation. The price of such modifications was to be set by* Alsatel. Novasam's *termination breached this contract under traditional contract law principles, but* Novasam *claimed that the contract was invalid under Article 86 of the EU treaty, which prohibits a company from abusing its dominant position or market power. The national court in France submitted the issue to the European Court of Justice for clarification.* |

*JUDGMENT:*
    \*   \*   \*   \*

Although the obligation imposed on customers to deal exclusively with the installer as regards any modification of the installation may be justified by the fact that the equipment remains the property of the installer, the fact that the price of the supplements to the contract entailed by those modifications is not determined but is unilaterally fixed by the installer and the automatic renewal of the contract for a 15-year term if as a result of those modifications the rental is increased by more than 25% may constitute unfair trading conditions prohibited as abusive practices by Article 86 of the treaty if all the conditions for the application of that provision are met.

The first condition for the application of that provision is that trade between member states must be affected. \*   \*   \* That condition would be satisfied, in particular, if the contractual clauses referred to above had the effect of restricting imports of telephone equipment from other member states, thereby partitioning the market. There is nothing in the documents before the court which suggests that such is the case. However, it is for the national court to make the necessary findings of fact in that regard.

The second condition laid down by Article 86 is that there must be a dominant position within the common market or in a substantial part of it. The court has defined such a dominant position (see the Judgment of 9 November 1983 in case 322/81 *Michelin v. Commission* [1983] ECR 3461) as a position of economic strength enjoyed by an undertaking which enables it to hinder the maintenance of effective competition on the relevant market by allowing it to behave to an appreciable extent independently of its competitors and customers.
    \*   \*   \*   \*

There is nothing in the documents before the court that suggests that plaintiff enjoys a dominant position throughout France. The only fact \*   \*   \* with regard to the plaintiff's economic strength is the large share it holds of the regional market.

A finding of that kind is insufficient to establish that the undertaking in question occupies a dominant position.

*The court formally ruled that "Article 86 of the [EU] treaty must be interpreted as meaning that contractual practices, even if abusive ones, on the part of an undertaking supplying telephone installations which has a large share of a regional market in a member state do not fall within the prohibition in that article where that undertaking does not occupy a dominant position in the relevant market, in this case the domestic market in telephone installations."*

**DECISION
AND REMEDY**

---

## SECTION 5

# EXPANDING OVERSEAS BUSINESS OPPORTUNITIES

International business transactions have always been attended by more risk than is normally involved in domestic transactions. Since the end of the Cold War, though, the economic climate for business has improved around the globe. In the past, businesses involved in overseas investments and operations faced the risk that a socialist government might come into power and nationalize their company, with or without compensation. While the risk of nationalization is still present today, the danger is far less. Also, in the past some countries restricted the ability of U.S. companies to repatriate their profits (take the profits back to the United States), but these restrictions are also disappearing.

Conversely, many countries are now privatizing companies that had been nationalized and run by the government. **Privatization** occurs when a company purchases an entire business that has been operated by the government or moves into competition in a field previously monopolized by the government. For example, Argentina is privatizing its mineral-extractive industries, communications industry, transportation industry, and energy industry. Argentina also has eliminated most of the restrictions that it had placed on foreign investment and is eliminating most price controls.

The movement toward privatization is at different stages in other nations. France temporarily suspended its denationalization program. India is still relatively socialized and requires government approval for much foreign investment. Government approval has become much easier to obtain, however. Egypt offers many investment incentives unavailable elsewhere.

The trend toward privatization has created significant opportunities for businesspersons. It has also created new opportunities for contracting on the basis of price, rather than politics. Other developments that have expanded international business opportunities will be examined in Chapter 56, in the context of the international legal environment of business.

# TERMS AND CONCEPTS TO REVIEW

| | | |
|---|---|---|
| *abus de droit* 199 | national law 189 | *shari'a* 194 |
| civil law system 192 | privatization 205 | unitary system 192 |
| federal system 191 | | |

# QUESTIONS AND CASE PROBLEMS

**10–1. Ethical Codes of Conduct.** A considerable ethical controversy surrounds multinational enterprises (''MNEs''), which are often beyond the reach of national laws. For ethical or public relations purposes, these MNEs have established internal codes of conduct to govern their behavior toward customers and other populations. Suppose that you were called upon to draft such a code for an MNE. What provisions would you include?

**10–2. Comparative Employment Laws.** Assume that you are president of a manufacturing company that intends to expand overseas. Shipping costs and tariffs for your product are uniformly low. Your manufacturing process, however, is highly labor intensive. How would the employment laws of various nations influence your decision on where to situate a new manufacturing plant?

**10–3. Women and Business.** Joe Henderson is the president of an Asian branch of a U.S. bank. His top vice president is a woman, Betty Carter. He would like to take her with him to an important meeting at which he will undertake loan negotiations with a huge company. He was advised, however, that he would lose respect in the eyes of the overseas company—and perhaps the company's business—if she accompanies him. He talks with her, and she informs him that she does not mind deferring to men at social activities, if local customs demand such deference, but that at the business meetings, she will expect business as usual and will not alter her behavior simply because she is a woman. What should Henderson do? Discuss.

**10–4. Government Regulation.** BPB Industries is an English company that controls about half of the entire European Union (EU) market for plasterboard. BPB began giving preferential deals to Irish customers who agreed to purchase exclusively from BPB. Customers who dealt with BPB's competitors faced delays in shipment and other inconveniences. The EU brought an antitrust claim against BPB. How should the court rule?

**10–5. Legal Systems.** As China and other formerly communist nations move toward free enterprise, they must develop a new set of business laws. If you could start from scratch, what kind of business law system would you adopt, a civil law system or a common law system? What kind of business regulations would you impose?

**10–6. Ethics and Exporting.** AgriChem is a U.S. firm that manufactures pesticides. AgriChem's main product is an effective insecticide called Rodeo. The U.S. Environmental Protection Agency banned Rodeo because it has the potential to cause cancer. AgriChem has huge inventories of Rodeo that no longer can be sold in the United States. There is a substantial market for Rodeo in many Latin American countries, however, and American law permits the pesticide's export. Moreover, the Latin American countries permit its sale. Should AgriChem export Rodeo for sale in these countries?

**10–7. Bribery of Foreign Officials.** The Foreign Corrupt Practices Act prohibits any U.S. corporation from paying foreign government officials to gain favorable business contracts. UsOil seeks to drill and produce oil and natural gas from a new field found in a foreign nation. The Minister of the Interior in that nation makes it clear, however, that he will consider the grant of drilling rights only to companies that make a major contribution to his family-run "charity." Should UsOil make this payment in order to obtain access to the market?

**10–8. Government Regulation.** The Armstrong Co. is a textile manufacturer that has identified a large potential market for its products in Nigeria. Armstrong must now decide how to sell in Nigeria. Two obvious options are (1) exporting its textiles from its United States produc-

tion facilities or (2) establishing a Nigerian corporation to produce textiles within that nation. What legal factors would be relevant to the choice between these two options?

**10–9. Doing Business Abroad.** You are the human resources director for a major American conglomerate. Your company decides that it wants to expand its international presence considerably and asks you to develop a training program for managers. The aim of this training program is to develop managers who can operate more effectively in foreign nations. What components would you include in such a program?

## FOCUS ON ETHICS

# Ethics and Social Responsibility

**B**usiness ethics and social responsibility are closely intertwined concepts, but they are not exactly the same thing. *Business ethics* involves the application of ethical standards to business activities. *Social responsibility* involves the fulfillment of social expectations concerning the relationship between business and all individuals—within or outside the firm—who are affected by business actions.

What is deemed to be socially responsible business activity varies from culture to culture, from time period to time period within a given culture, and from group to group at any moment in time. No one can tell you here what business actions will receive an "A plus" in terms of social responsibility, because there is no one definition of the term. It means different things to different people at different times.

### A Host of Duties

Business firms face a host of ethical (and legal) duties. Some of these duties, including a firm's duty to its employees and to the consumers of its products, have already been discussed in Chapter 2. Here we look at some other ethical obligations facing business firms.

### Duty to Shareholders

Traditionally in capitalist theory, profit-making

activities—insofar as they provided desired goods and services to society and violated no laws—were *per se* socially responsible. Profit making was and continues to be an essential goal of any business, and business decision makers must take profitability into account when determining what actions are in the firm's best interests.

Because the owners of any corporate business firm are the shareholders, corporate directors and officers have a duty to act in the shareholders' interest. Corporate directors and decision makers are regarded as trustees of the shareholders' funds. Because of the nature of the relationship between corporate directors and officers and the shareholder-owners, the law holds directors and officers to a high standard of care in business decision making (see Chapter 42).

Traditionally, this duty to shareholders appeared to take precedence over all other corporate duties. The primary goal of corporations remained profit maximization. Today, some observers claim that maximizing profits for the shareholders continues to be the corporation's primary duty. Milton Friedman, the Nobel–Prize–winning economist, effectively phrases this view:

In a free enterprise, private property system, a corporate

executive is an employee of the owners of the business [shareholders]. He [or she] has a direct responsibility to his [or her] employers. That responsibility is to conduct the business in accordance with their desires, which generally will be to make as much money as possible while conforming to the basic rules of society, both those embodied in law and those embodied in ethical custom.[1]

Those arguing for profit maximization as a corporate goal also point out that it would be inappropriate to use the power of the corporate business world to fashion society's goals. Determinations as to what exactly is in society's best interest are essentially political decisions, and therefore the political process—not the corporate boardroom—is the appropriate forum for such decision making.

### Duty to Stakeholders

Increasingly, the traditional duty to shareholders is being balanced against a corporation's duty to other groups affected by corporate decisions. In the last decade or so, for example, about half of the states have enacted

---

1. Milton Friedman, "Does Business Have Social Responsibility?" *Bank Administration,* April 1971, pp. 13–14.

statutes that allow corporate decision makers to take into consideration not only the welfare of shareholders but also the welfare of *stakeholders*—employees, customers, suppliers, communities, and any group that has a stake in the corporation. Some of the statutes, such as those of Indiana and Pennsylvania, allow corporate management to place the interests of stakeholders above those of shareholders.

The reasoning behind these statutes—and behind what has come to be called "the stakeholder view of corporate social responsibility"—is that in some circumstances, other groups may have a greater stake in company decisions than the shareholders do. Consider an example. A heavily indebted corporation is facing imminent bankruptcy. The shareholder-investors have little to lose in this situation, because their stock is already next to worthless. The corporation's creditors will be first in line for any corporate assets remaining. Because in this situation it is the creditors who have the greatest "stake" in the corporation, under the stakeholder view, corporate directors and officers should give greater weight to the creditors' interests than to those of the shareholders.

### Duty to the Community
In some circumstances, the community in which a business enterprise is located is a substantial stakeholder in the firm. Assume, for example, that a company employs two

thousand workers at one of its plants. If the company decides that it would be profitable to close the plant or move it to another location, the employees—and the community—would suffer as a result. What is the firm's social responsibility in this situation? Traditionally, companies have had the right to move freely. If a corporation wanted to move its operations from one community to another, the decision was solely that of the corporation to make. Of course, in making the decision, a socially responsible corporation would take community needs into consideration.

For example, the company might help to alleviate the situation by giving sufficient notice of the closing so that the workers would have more time to find work elsewhere. The firm might also help relocate workers to the best of its ability. But the community could not force the corporation to keep open a plant against the wishes of corporate management and the best interests of shareholders.

Today, the issue is not so clear-cut, as General Motors Corporation (GM) learned when it sought to move its Willow Run plant from the township of Ypsilanti, in Michigan, to another location. The township petitioned a Michigan court to estop (bar) GM from moving its plant on the ground that allowing GM to relocate its plant would be unjust, because GM had enjoyed the benefits of reduced taxes granted by the township to the company. The trial court entered a judgment

in favor of the township (although that decision was reversed on appeal).[2]

### Duty to Society
Many Americans believe that because so much of the wealth and power of this country is controlled by business, business in turn has a responsibility to society to use that wealth and power in socially beneficial ways. From this perspective, corporations are in a sense trustees or caretakers of society. Since the nineteenth century and the emergence of large business enterprises in America, corporations have generally recognized, at least implicitly, that they have an obligation to society to use some of their wealth to aid others. Corporations have generally been very responsive to social needs. Today, corporations routinely donate to hospitals, medical research, the arts, universities, and programs that benefit society.

For example, the Coca-Cola Company established the National Hispanic Business Agenda—a major program to expand ties with the Hispanic-American community. More recently, that firm contributed $50 million to support educational institutions and programs throughout the United States. As one of its many philanthropic projects, Levi Strauss & Company established an "AIDS

---

2. See *Charter Township of Ypsilanti v. General Motors Corp.*, 201 Mich.App. 128, 506 N.W.2d 556 (1993).

Initiatives" program to fund public educational programs concerning acquired immune deficiency syndrome (AIDS) and care for the victims of that disease. Indeed, today nearly every major corporation has a corporate department or foundation that has been established specifically to screen charitable requests and to decide on and manage corporate charitable contributions and programs.

### Global Responsibilities

Corporations also are charged with a host of other duties, many of which transcend national boundaries. To be perceived as socially responsible, at least in the eyes of many Americans, a corporation should not do business in countries that condone oppression or violate human rights. Additionally, in recent years the scope of the corporation's duties has expanded to embrace not only the actions of its own employees but those of its suppliers as well. For example, in late 1992, Wal-Mart became the target of negative publicity when it was accused by children's rights advocates of purchasing clothes, for distribution in its U.S. stores, that were made by nine-year-old children in Bangladesh.

A basic question raised by these types of charges is whether it is fair to demand suppliers in other countries to conform to U.S. standards of conduct. Do Americans have the right to decide, for example, at what age children in Bangladesh should be allowed to work? Regardless of how you answer this question, the fact that some groups believe that Americans do have such a right has caused many corporations to look seriously at the practices of its suppliers from those groups' point of view. Dow Chemical Company, for example, requests its foreign suppliers to abide by U.S. pollution and safety standards, even though they are stricter than those in the suppliers' countries. Levi Strauss & Company recently inspected each of its 600 suppliers, located around the world, and decided *not* to do business with 30 of them for ethical reasons. The company also requested that 120 of the suppliers reform their practices.

### The Corporate Balancing Act

Clearly, it is impossible for corporations to be all things to all people at all times. Each corporate board of directors has to make numerous trade-offs in determining corporate goals. Directors do have an ethical duty to shareholders, because they control the shareholders' wealth. They also have duties to numerous other groups, including employees, consumers, the community, and society at large. But deciding how to best fulfill each of these duties, and how to balance the duties against one another, is rarely easy.

In part, the difficulty arises because corporate ethical decision making is complicated by the fact that while the short-run results of a given action are usually fairly predictable, the action's long-run effects are less so. For example, many American firms import products manufactured in developing countries to save on production costs—because labor costs are substantially lower in those countries. Another alternative is to establish manufacturing operations abroad to take advantage of both lower labor costs and less restrictive government regulations affecting the workplace. In the short run, these actions will be beneficial for the firm's shareholders. They may also be profitable for the workers in those other countries, if the American firm pays higher wages than the prevailing rate in those countries.

Yet, as indicated above, while these actions may be profitable to the firm in the short run, if they cause the firm to suffer negative publicity, the firm's prosperity may suffer in the long run. Similarly, corporate philanthropic activities that receive wide publicity may benefit shareholders in the long run—if the public image of the firm entices more consumers to purchase its products—but such long-run possible benefits are difficult to calculate.

### Evaluating Social Responsibility

Now you can see why it is difficult to evaluate corporate social responsibility. First of all, because we live in a world of imperfect information, it is not always possible to acquire a sufficient amount of information about a given business firm's activities to make an informed decision as to whether that firm is acting in a socially responsible manner. We might read in the newspaper, for example, that a certain firm has made generous contributions toward a worthy social cause, and therefore we might assume that the corporation has socially responsible goals. What we might not know, however, is that the same corporation is marketing a product that some corporate officers have reason to suspect may be harmful to many of those who purchase it.

Second, social responsibility means different things to different persons, depending on their economic and moral convictions. What might be perceived as socially responsible behavior by one group might not be considered so by another. For example, a firm that makes a charitable contribution to an organization such as Planned Parenthood comes under fire from those groups opposed to that organization's goals and actions. Yet if the firm fails to make the contribution, or if it withdraws a pledge of support, it is attacked by supporters of Planned Parenthood.

Corporations and other business firms that strive to behave ethically face social mandates that are sometimes contradictory and sometimes representative of the interests of only a small, but intensely committed and politically active, interest group. Nonetheless, firms that fail to respond to these mandates often become targets of various sanctions, including adverse publicity, that can affect their profit margins.

## Competition and Social Responsibility

Today's business firms face a changed marketplace from that of two decades ago. For one thing, the public is more aware of the effect of ethical (or unethical) business behavior on the environment. Also, consumers are increasingly concerned about how a firm's activities affect the welfare and safety of those who produce and use the firm's products. In view of the economic pressures that consumers can bring to bear on business firms, many companies have decided that it pays to be ethical.

For example, consider the case of McDonald's Corporation. For years, McDonald's used Styrofoam containers for its Big Macs and other products. Styrofoam is inexpensive and a good insulator for keeping food products warm. But ozone-depleting chlorofluorocarbons are a necessary component in Styrofoam. Also, there has been the perception that Styrofoam does not decompose readily, thereby adding to our nation's landfill problems.[3] In the 1980s, some of McDonald's competitors were able to promote their use of paper containers in contrast to McDonald's Styrofoam containers. The market forced McDonald's to switch from Styrofoam to paper containers. To the extent that today's consumers are more aware of

environmental issues, corporations in search of greater profits will ultimately be forced to "do the right thing." Some have called this the power of the market to enforce good corporate citizenship.

Ben & Jerry's Homemade, Inc., the fanciful high-end ice-cream manufacturer in Vermont, has successfully used environmental issues to increase its market share in a highly competitive sector of the economy. It has chosen to name many of its products after environmentally sound causes to which it donates money (for example, "Rain Forest Crunch" ice cream and "Peace Pops"). That corporation has also supported groups that seek to help disadvantaged persons.

Finally, Ben & Jerry's has sought to use only ethical suppliers—for example, it purchases brownies for its "Chocolate Fudge Brownie" ice cream from a New York bakery staffed by homeless persons. All of this corporate generosity adds to the cost of Ben & Jerry's ice cream. In spite of its higher-than-competitive prices, however, it has remained a profitable corporation.

Businesses that continue to engage in perceived unethical or environmentally threatening practices may find themselves the target of consumer boycotts or the withdrawal of investors from the enterprise.

### Consumer Boycotts

Hundreds of consumer campaigns have been waged against business firms that are deemed to be acting unethically. Indeed, some

---

3. There is some evidence, however, that paper containers take just as long to decompose as Styrofoam containers do.

companies have become boycott veterans. Consider, for example, the boycott history of just one U.S. firm, Procter and Gamble (P&G). In the 1980s, in a rather bizarre controversy, P&G was boycotted by consumers who felt that its moon-and-stars logo was a satanic symbol. To end the controversy, P&G eventually redesigned its logo.

In 1990, P&G was again boycotted when it was learned that the coffee beans in P&G's Folgers coffee came from El Salvador. A peace organization ran a commercial in which coffee cups were shown to be oozing with blood. The message was that P&G was "brewing misery and death" by purchasing coffee beans from a country torn by "death squads." More recently, P&G again became the recipient of consumer hostility when a number of ethically conscious consumers discovered that the company used animals in the testing of household products.

### Ethical Investing

Refusing to invest in corporations that are perceived to act unethically is yet another sanction that society can impose. In the last decade or so, several ethical investment funds have been established that allow individuals to make their investment decisions on the basis of corporate conduct. These funds evaluate how ethical a firm is according to any number of criteria, such as whether the firm uses animals in product research or testing, does business in or with countries whose governments are oppressive, produces environmentally safe products or has environmentally sound policies, has a specified percentage of women and minorities on its board of directors, participates in the construction or maintenance of nuclear plants, and so on. Some funds, such as Green Century Funds, invest only in companies that meet clearly stated environmental rules and goals for environmental improvement. For business firms, the message is becoming increasingly clear: it pays to act ethically and to support socially desirable goals.

### ■ Discussion Questions

**1.** At the beginning of this *Focus on Ethics,* we stated that business ethics and social responsibility are distinct concepts, even though they are closely intertwined. Can you think of a situation in which a business firm may be acting ethically but not in a socially responsible manner? Explain.

**2.** Why are consumers and the public generally more concerned with ethical and socially responsible business behavior today than they were, say, fifty years ago?

**3.** The perception of what constitutes socially responsible business behavior in the United States may vary widely from that in other countries, particularly in developing countries. Discuss some of the ethical implications of these differing perceptions of social responsibility for American firms that do business abroad.

**4.** Should business firms *ever* manufacture products that have deleterious effects on the environment? How do you weigh the benefits of a product (such as automobiles) against the negative environmental effects (such as smog) caused by the product? Should these kinds of decisions be made by the business sector, or should political bodies be left to determine such policies?

# UNIT TWO

# CONTRACTS

### CONTENTS

**11** Nature and Terminology

**12** Agreement

**13** Consideration

**14** Capacity

**15** Genuineness of Assent

**16** Legality and the Statute of Frauds

**17** Third Party Rights

**18** Performance and Discharge

**19** Breach of Contract and Remedies

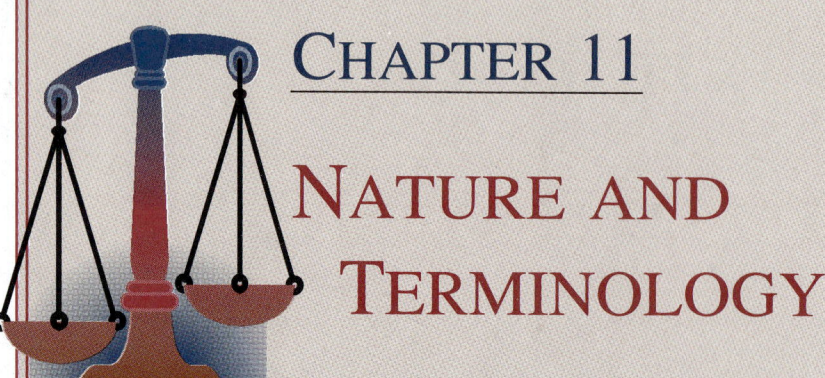

# CHAPTER 11

# NATURE AND TERMINOLOGY

**T**he noted legal scholar Roscoe Pound once said that "[t]he social order rests upon the stability and predictability of conduct, of which keeping promises is a large item."[1] Contract law deals with, among other things, the formation and keeping of promises (in Latin, *pacta sunt servanda*—"agreements shall be kept"). The law encourages competent parties to form contracts for lawful objectives. No aspect of modern life is entirely free of contractual relationships. Indeed, even the ordinary consumer in his or her daily activities acquires rights and obligations based on contract law. You acquire rights and obligations, for example, when you borrow money to make a purchase or when you buy a stereo or a house. Contract law is designed to provide stability and predictability, as well as certainty, for both buyers and sellers in the marketplace.

Like other types of law, contract law reflects our social values, interests, and expectations at a given point in time. It shows, for example, to what extent our society allows people to make promises or commitments that are legally binding. It shows what excuses our society accepts for breaking such promises. And it shows what promises are considered to be contrary to public policy and therefore legally void. If a promise goes against the interests of society as a whole, it will be invalidated. Also, if it was made by a child or a mentally incompetent person, or on the basis of false information, a question will arise as to whether the promise should be enforced. Resolving such questions is the essence of contract law.

In the legal environment of business, questions and disputes concerning contracts arise daily. Although aspects of contract law vary from state to state, much of it is based on common law. In 1932, the American Law Institute compiled the Restatement of the Law of Contracts. This work is a nonstatutory, authoritative exposition of the present law on contracts. The Restatement is presently in its second edition (although a third edition is being

---

1.    R. Pound, *Jurisprudence,* Vol. 3 (St. Paul: West Publishing Co., 1959), p. 162.

### ■ Exhibit 11–1 The Law Governing Contracts

This exhibit illustrates the relationship between general contract law and the law governing sales contracts. Sales contracts are not governed exclusively by Article 2 of the Uniform Commercial Code but are also governed by general contract law whenever it is relevant and has not been modified by the UCC.

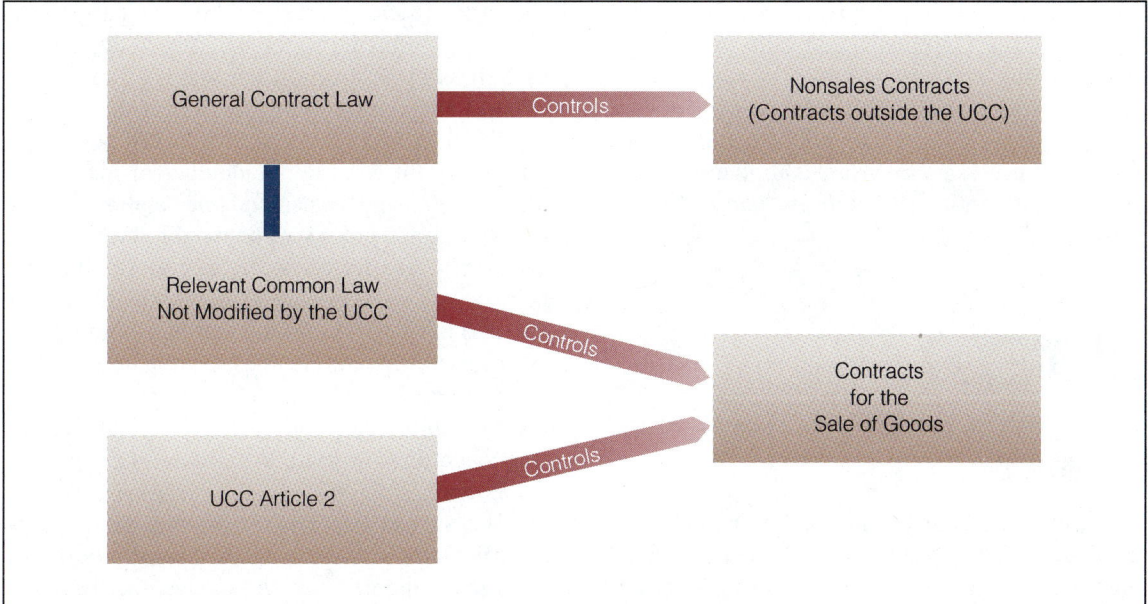

drafted) and will be referred to throughout the following contract chapters.

The common law governs all contracts except when the common law of contracts has been modified or replaced by statutory law or administrative agency regulations. Contracts relating to services, real estate, employment, insurance, and so on generally are governed by the general common law of contracts. All contracts for the sale of *goods,* however, are governed by statutory law—particularly by the Uniform Commercial Code (UCC)[2]—to the extent that statutory law has modified or replaced general contract law. The relationship between general contract law and the law governing sales of goods is illustrated in Exhibit 11–1. In the discussion of general contract law in this unit, we indicate in footnotes the areas in which the UCC has significantly altered common law contract principles.

---

2.   See Chapter 1 and Chapter 20 for further discussions of the significance and coverage of the Uniform Commercial Code. The UCC is presented in its entirety in Appendix C at the end of this book.

### SECTION 1

# THE FUNCTION OF CONTRACT LAW

Contract law assures the parties to private agreements that the promises they make will be enforceable. A **promise** is a declaration that something either will or will not happen in the future. Sometimes the promises exchanged create *moral* rather than *legal* obligations. Failure to perform a moral obligation, such as an agreement to take a friend to lunch, does not usually create a legal liability. Some promises may create both a moral and a legal obligation, such as a father's promise to pay for his daughter's college education.

Clearly, many promises are kept because of a sense of duty or because keeping them is in the mutual self-interest of the parties involved, not because the **promisor** (the person making the promise) or the **promisee** (the person to whom the promise is made) is conscious of the rules of contract law. Nevertheless, the rules of contract law are often followed in business agreements to avoid potential problems.

By supplying procedures for enforcing private agreements, contract law provides an essential condition for the existence of a market economy. Without a legal framework of reasonably assured expectations within which to plan and venture, businesspersons would be able to rely only on the good faith of others. Duty and good faith are usually sufficient, but when price changes or adverse economic factors make it costly to comply with a promise, these elements may not be enough. Contract law is necessary to ensure compliance with a promise or to entitle the innocent party to some form of relief.

## SECTION 2

# DEFINITION OF A CONTRACT

A **contract** is an agreement that can be enforced in a court of law or equity. It is formed by two or more parties who promise to perform or refrain from performing some act now or in the future. Generally, contract disputes arise when there is a promise of future performance. If the contractual promise is not fulfilled, the party who made it is subject to the sanctions of a court of law or equity (see Chapter 19). That party may be required to pay money damages for failing to perform; in limited instances, the party may be required to perform the promised act.

In determining whether a contract has been formed, the element of intent is of prime importance. In contract law, intent is determined by what is called the **objective theory of contracts,** not by the personal or subjective intent, or belief, of a party. The theory is that intention to enter into a contract is judged by outward, objective facts as interpreted by a *reasonable* person, rather than by the party's own secret, subjective intentions. Objective facts include (1) what the party said when entering into the contract, (2) how the party acted or appeared (intent may be manifested by conduct as well as by oral or written words), and (3) the circumstances surrounding the transaction.

Consider an example. Jaffe has just purchased a new car for $28,000. A number of his neighbors are admiring his car, and one neighbor in particular, Logan, states that he would like to own a car exactly like Jaffe's. Jaffe, in front of all of his neighbors, says to Logan, "I'll sell you this car for $20,000 in cash." Jaffe said that he would put his offer in writing, and he does so. Logan writes on the written offer the words "I accept" and signs his name. Jaffe immediately tells everyone his offer was made only in jest. Do Jaffe and Logan have a contract?

The answer depends on whether the circumstances (Jaffe's just having purchased a new car, the price of the new car, and the fact that Jaffe put his offer in writing) and Jaffe's words would, to a reasonable person, constitute an offer, which Logan then accepted. It is not Jaffe's inner belief or intent to make a joke that determines the answer. If a person in Logan's position could reasonably believe that an offer had been made, under the objective theory of contracts, Logan's acceptance would bind Jaffe in contract, and Jaffe would be legally required to sell the car to Logan.

The following case illustrates a court's use of the objective theory of contracts to review the conduct and circumstances surrounding a transaction to determine whether a contract exists and, if so, what its terms might be.

---

CASE 11.1

**COMPUTER NETWORK, LTD. v. PURCELL TIRE & RUBBER CO.**

Missouri Court of Appeals, Eastern District, Division Five, 1988.
747 S.W.2d 669.

**BACKGROUND AND FACTS** *Purcell Tire and Rubber Company operated fifteen motor-vehicle stores in Missouri. In 1983, Purcell discussed purchasing personal computers through Computer Network, Ltd. (CN), the plaintiff. On February 23, Harry Chapman, an agent of Purcell, signed a memo prepared by CN verifying some of the information that had been discussed in a prior meeting. The memo referred to twenty-one personal computers, described the equipment, and stated what its price would be. In 1984, nine computers were delivered to Purcell. Purcell paid for them but refused to accept any more. Chapman claimed that the memorandum did not constitute a contract and that "there had only been conversations regarding the possible transactions." He also stated at trial that he had only wanted to verify a price-and-equipment configuration and that he had* *intended eventually to purchase only fifteen personal computers, one for each store. CN claimed that the memo signed by Chapman was a contract and filed suit. The trial court gave a judgment for CN, and Purcell appealed.*

*SIMEONE,* Senior Judge.

\* \* \* \*

"For at least a century the objective theory of contracts has been dominant." The "subjective" theory of intent is now regarded as irrelevant. "The objective theory lays stress on the outward manifestation of assent made to the other party in contrast to the older idea that a contract was a true meeting of the minds." What a person may have intended subjectively is not controlling. \* \* \*

\* \* \* "The intent with which we are concerned is the objective manifestation of intent by the parties, that is, what a reasonably prudent person would be led to believe from the actions and words of the parties. This is a question to be resolved by the [trier of fact]."

\* \* \* \*

Tested by these principles, there was, under the circumstances here, "mutual assent" to purchase twenty-one computers. Regardless of Chapman's intent to purchase a lesser number, the letter of February 23 explicitly contained that number. \* \* \* Chapman acknowledged that he signed the letter containing that number; presumably he must have read the letter when it was presented to him. Having signed the letter, he is charged with knowledge of its contents. He admitted he signed the letter; he admitted that he could have changed the letter if he desired to do so but did not. A mere change could have effected a lesser number.

[The essentials] to formation of a contract may not be found or determined on the undisclosed assumption or secret surmise of either party but must be gathered from the intention of the parties as expressed or manifested by their words or acts.

Under these circumstances, the objective manifestation of mutual assent is present; the trial court so concluded and in this respect the court did not err.

**DECISION AND REMEDY** *The court of appeals affirmed the lower court's decision that a contract existed.*

**INTERNATIONAL CONSIDERATIONS** **The Objective Theory of Contracts in France** *Under French law, when there is a conflict between the objective and a subjective construction in a contract, the French civil law code prefers the subjective construction. Other nations that have civil law codes take this same approach. French courts, however, will look to writings and other objective evidence to determine a party's subjective intent. In operation, the difference between the French and U.S. approaches is therefore perhaps not that significant.*

---

## SECTION 3

# FREEDOM OF CONTRACT AND FREEDOM FROM CONTRACT

As a general rule, the law recognizes everyone's ability to enter freely into contractual arrangements. This recognition is called *freedom of contract,* a freedom protected by the U.S. Constitution in Article I, Section 10.

Because freedom of contract is a strongly held public policy, courts rarely interfere with contracts that have been voluntarily made. Of course, as in other areas of the law, there are many exceptions to the general rule that contracts voluntarily negotiated will be enforced. For example, illegal bargains, agreements unreasonably in restraint of trade, and certain unfair contracts made between one party with a great amount of bargaining power and another with little power are generally not enforced. In addition, certain contracts with consumers, as well as certain clauses within those contracts, may not be enforceable if they are contrary to public policy, fairness, and justice (see Chapter 16 for a discussion of contracts contrary to public policy). These exceptions provide *freedom from contract* for persons who may have been forced into making contracts unfavorable to themselves.

Despite these and other exceptions, however, freedom of contract is a highly valued principle in American law. In accordance with this principle, the failure to read a contract is not *normally* a defense to the contract's enforcement. Similarly, the failure to investigate the possible ramifications of a contract will not normally relieve parties of their contractual obligations—as the following case emphasizes.

CASE 11.2

**BEASLEY v. MEDIN**
Minnesota Court of Appeals,
1992.
479 N.W.2d 95.

**BACKGROUND AND FACTS**  *John Beasley and Laverne Kintop purchased $33,333 worth of stock in Medin Graphics (MGI), a small corporation, from Leone Medin, the company's president and sole shareholder. Beasley and Kintop based their decision to purchase the stock on Medin's oral representations of MGI's worth and a one-page tax return. Beasley and Kintop later discovered that MGI owed a number of debts, including back taxes, of which they had been unaware. They further learned that a bookkeeper had embezzled approximately $40,000 from the corporation. In short, they had entered into a bargain that was not what it seemed to be. Among other things, Beasley and Kintop brought suit to have the contract rescinded (canceled). The trial court found in their favor and ordered that the contract be rescinded on the ground of a mutual mistake. Medin appealed the rescission.*

*FORSBERG,* Justice.
\* \* \* \*

Medin argues rescission on the basis of mutual mistake is improper because Beasley and Kintop failed to make a reasonable investigation to discover readily available facts. Beasley had a college degree in business and Kintop's financial advisor told her that he needed more information to advise her on the propriety of the stock purchase. Furthermore, they both had the opportunity to question MGI's accountant. Prior to the stock purchase, MGI's books and records contained evidence of its poor financial condition and the embezzlement of which Beasley and Kintop subsequently complained.
\* \* \* \*

Beasley and Kintop claim that they requested financial information from Medin and MGI's accountant, that Medin represented to them that MGI had a value of $150,000 to $200,000, and that they trusted her statements. Because of Medin's knowledge of MGI's financial condition, and their relationship with her prior to the sale, Beasley and Kintop insist their investigation of MGI's financial condition was reasonable.

\* \* \* The trial court in this case determined Beasley and Kintop did not request nor were they denied access to MGI's complete financial records. Under these circumstances, we do not believe Beasley and Kintop's review of a one-page tax return and their reliance on Medin's representation constitute a ''reasonable inquiry'' sufficient to justify rescission for mutual mistake of material facts. \* \* \* [R]escission is inappropriate in the absence of a reasonable investigation of the facts
\* \* \* .

*The appellate court, concluding that Beasley and Kintop were both educated persons who should have had the foresight to investigate MGI's accounts and finances, reversed the trial court's order to rescind the contract. The stock purchase agreement was binding.*

**DECISION AND REMEDY**

---

## SECTION 4

# THE BASIC REQUIREMENTS OF A CONTRACT

The many topics that will be discussed in the following chapters on contract law require an understanding of the basic requirements of a contract and the way in which a contract is created. The following list briefly describes the basic requirements of a contract. Each requirement will be explained more fully in subsequent chapters.

1. *Agreement.* An agreement includes an *offer* and an *acceptance*. One party must offer to enter into a legal agreement, and another party must accept the terms of the offer.
2. *Consideration.* Any promises made by parties must be supported by legally sufficient and bargained-for *consideration* (something of value received or promised, such as money, to convince a person to make a deal).
3. *Contractual capacity.* Both parties entering into the contract must have the contractual *capacity* to do so; the law must recognize them as possessing characteristics that qualify them as competent parties.
4. *Legality.* The contract's purpose must be to accomplish some goal that is *legal* and not against public policy.

These four requirements constitute what are normally known as the elements of a contract. Also important are possible *defenses* to the formation or enforcement of a contract. These include the following:

1. *Genuineness of Assent.* The apparent consent of both parties must be genuine.
2. *Form.* The contract must be in whatever form the law requires; for example, some contracts must be in writing to be enforceable.

## SECTION 5

# TYPES OF CONTRACTS

There are many types of contracts. The categories into which contracts are placed involve legal distinctions as to formation, enforceability, or performance. The best method of explaining each type is to compare one type with another.

### BILATERAL VERSUS UNILATERAL CONTRACTS

Every contract involves at least two parties. The **offeror** is the party making the offer. The **offeree** is the party to whom the offer is made. The offeror always promises to do or not to do something and thus is also a promisor. Whether the contract is classified as *unilateral* or *bilateral* depends on what the offeree must do to accept the offer and to bind the offeror to a contract.

If to accept the offer the offeree must only *promise* to perform, the contract is a **bilateral contract.** Hence, a bilateral contract is a "promise for a promise." No performance, such as payment of money or delivery of goods, need take place for a bilateral contract to be formed. The contract comes into existence at the moment the promises are exchanged. In contrast, if the offer is phrased so that the offeree can accept only by completing the contract performance, the contract is a **unilateral contract.** Hence, a unilateral contract is a "promise for an act."[3]

A classic example of a unilateral contract is as follows: O'Searo says to Parker, "If you carry this

---

3. Clearly, a contract cannot be "one sided," because, by definition, an "agreement" implies the existence of two or more parties. Therefore, the phrase *unilateral contract,* if read literally, is a contradiction in terms. As traditionally used in contract law, however, the phrase refers to the kind of contract that results when there is only one promise being made (the promise made by the offeror in return for the offeree's performance).

package across the Brooklyn Bridge, I'll give you $10.'' O'Searo promises to pay only if Parker walks the entire span of the bridge with the package. Only upon Parker's complete crossing with the package does she fully accept O'Searo's offer to pay $10. If she chooses not to undertake the walk, there are no legal consequences. Contests, lotteries, and other prize-winning competitions are also examples of offers for unilateral contracts. If a person complies with the rules of the contest— such as by submitting the right lottery number at the right place and time—a unilateral contract is formed, binding the organization offering the prize to a contract to perform as promised in the offer.

A problem arises in unilateral contracts when the promisor attempts to *revoke* (cancel) the offer after the promisee has begun performance but before the act has been completed. The promisee can accept the offer only upon full performance, and offers are normally *revocable* (capable of being taken back, or canceled) until accepted. The modern-day view, however, is that the offer becomes irrevocable once performance has begun. Thus, even though the offer has not yet been accepted, the offeror is prohibited from revoking it for a reasonable time period.

Suppose that Sikora offers to buy Gil's sailboat, moored in San Francisco, upon delivery of the boat to Sikora's dock in Newport Beach, three hundred miles south of San Francisco. Gil rigs the boat and sets sail. Shortly before his arrival at Newport Beach, Gil receives a radio message from Sikora withdrawing her offer. Sikora's offer is part of a unilateral contract, and only Gil's delivery of the sailboat at her dock is an acceptance. Ordinarily, her revocation would terminate the offer, but because Gil had undertaken performance and sailed almost three hundred miles, under the modern-day view her offer is irrevocable. Gil can deliver the boat and bind Sikora to the contract.

## EXPRESS VERSUS IMPLIED CONTRACTS

An **express contract** is one in which the terms of the agreement are fully and explicitly stated in words, oral or written. A signed lease for an apartment or a house is an express written contract. If a classmate calls you on the phone and agrees to buy your textbooks from last semester for $50, an express oral contract has been made.

A contract that is implied from the conduct of the parties is called an **implied-in-fact contract** or an implied contract. This type of contract differs from an express contract in that the *conduct* of the parties, rather than their words, creates and defines the terms of the contract. For example, suppose you need a tax consultant or an accountant to fill out your tax return this year. You look through the Yellow Pages and find both an accountant and a tax consultant at an office in your neighborhood, so you drop by to see them.

You go into the office and explain your problem, and they tell you what their fees are. The next day you return, giving the secretary all the necessary information and documents—canceled checks, W-2 forms, and so on. You say nothing expressly to the secretary; rather, you walk out the door. Nonetheless, you have entered into an implied-in-fact contract to pay the tax consultant and accountant the usual and reasonable fees for their services. The contract is implied by your conduct and by their conduct. They expect to be paid for completing your tax return. By bringing in the records they will need to do the work, you have implied an intent to pay them.

The following three steps establish an implied-in-fact contract:

1. The plaintiff furnished some service or property.
2. The plaintiff expected to be paid for that service or property, and the defendant knew or should have known that payment was expected (by using the objective-theory-of-contracts test, discussed previously).
3. The defendant had a chance to reject the services or property and did not.

Assume that on a Monday morning in New York City, Morrissey is driving his automobile to work. He gets caught in the usual traffic jam in that area of the city, and while the car is motionless, he waves at Hart, who is standing on the sidewalk. Hart runs up to Morrissey's car, sprays the windshield, rear window, and all of the side windows with glass cleaner, and wipes them clean. Hart then holds out her hand for payment. Is Morrissey obliged to pay? If Morrissey waved at Hart to come over and clean the windows of his car, just as he has done every Monday on his way to work, then an implied-in-fact contract exists and Hart should be paid for the service she provided. If, however, Morrissey waved at Hart, mistaking her for someone else, and then shook his head from side to side when she started washing the car windows, no contract exists. By these actions (shaking his head from side to side), Morrissey rejected Hart's services, and he was under no obligation to pay her.

The court emphasizes in the following case that a contract can be implied by conduct as well as by express agreement.

**HISTORICAL AND SOCIAL SETTING** *At one time, when a plaintiff wanted to sue, he or she had to phrase the complaint very carefully, because if the facts as alleged did not fit a particular predefined cause of action, the case would be thrown out of court. (A cause of action is a situation or state of facts that entitles a party to judicial relief.) Sometimes, this strict requirement kept a plaintiff from obtaining any relief at all. Over time, however, the old causes of action were changed, and new causes of action were developed, to provide avenues for such plaintiffs to obtain relief. For example, in the early seventeenth century, when a buyer, at his or her request, received goods or services without expressly agreeing to the price, and he or she did not pay for the goods, there was no cause of action into which the seller could fit a complaint. A remedy for this problem developed later in the century when courts began to imply in these circumstances a promise to pay a reasonable price. This implied promise came to be known as a contract implied in fact.*

| CASE 11.3 |
| --- |
| **WELLER v. SPRING CREEK RESORT, INC.** |
| Supreme Court of South Dakota, 1991. |
| 477 N.W.2d 839. |

**BACKGROUND AND FACTS** *Richard and Darolyn Weller leased a marina mooring space for their houseboat at the Spring Creek Resort in 1988 and again in 1989, in which year Weller made improvements to the space. At the end of the 1989 season, Weller informed John Brakss, manager of Spring Creek Resort, that he wished to reserve the same mooring space for 1990. In January 1990, Weller learned that others who leased mooring spaces at Spring Creek had been informed that rent for the 1990 season should be paid by February 1, 1990. Weller then sent a check for the full amount of the rent to Brakss, who returned the check approximately two months later with the explanation that low water levels made it impossible to accommodate the Wellers' boat in 1990. The Wellers sued for damages, alleging, among other things, that Spring Creek Resort had breached an implied contract. The trial court dismissed the Wellers' complaint, on the ground that they had failed to state a claim. The Wellers appealed.*

*AMUNDSON,* Justice.
\* \* \* \*

In this jurisdiction, a contract can be either express or implied. It is express if the terms are stated in words, oral or written. \* \* \* An implied contract is one, the existence and terms of which are manifested by conduct. "Conduct" can be both acts and words. By its very nature, an implicit agreement is not as detailed as a written agreement formally negotiated. \* \* \* A contract is implied in fact where the intention as to it is not manifested by direct or explicit words by the parties, but is to be gathered by implication or proper deduction from the conduct of the parties, language used, or acts done by them, or other pertinent circumstances attending the transaction.
\* \* \* \*

\* \* \* [The Wellers'] complaint can only be construed as containing allegations of conduct on the part of Brakss which could serve as the basis for a determination that an implied contract existed or was created for the 1990 season. * * * Although the question of whether particular conduct is sufficient to support a finding that an implied contract exists is generally submitted to a trier of fact, the question may be resolved by summary judgment if reasonable minds could not differ.

**DECISION AND REMEDY**    *The appellate court concluded that the trial court erred in dismissing the Wellers' claim for breach of an implied contract. The appellate court remanded the case for a resolution of the claim at a trial or by summary judgment.*

## QUASI CONTRACTS— CONTRACTS IMPLIED IN LAW

**Quasi contracts,** or contracts *implied in law,* are wholly different from actual contracts. Express contracts and implied-in-fact contracts are actual, or true, contracts. Quasi contracts, as their name suggests, are not true contracts. They do not arise from any agreement, express or implied, between the parties themselves. Rather, quasi contracts are fictional contracts imposed on parties by courts in the interests of fairness and justice. Quasi contracts are therefore equitable, rather than contractual, in nature. Usually, quasi contracts are imposed to avoid the *unjust enrichment* of one party at the expense of another. The doctrine under which the court implies such a contract is called **quantum meruit,**[4] an expression that means "as much as he deserves." *Quantum meruit* essentially describes the extent of compensation owed under a contract implied in law.

**EXAMPLES OF QUASI CONTRACTS**    Suppose Tamas enters into a contract with Rex, agreeing to work for Rex for one year. At the end of the year, Tamas is to be paid $18,000. Tamas works for ten months and then leaves voluntarily, without cause. Rex refuses to pay her for the ten months she worked, so Tamas sues in quasi contract for the value of services rendered. Will the court allow Tamas to recover her salary for the ten months worked? Very likely, yes—minus any damages caused to Rex by her early departure.[5]

In another example, a vacationing doctor is driving down the highway and comes upon Dotterweich lying unconscious on the side of the road. The doctor renders medical aid that saves Dotterweich's life. Although the injured, unconscious Dotterweich did not solicit the medical aid and was not aware that the aid had been rendered, Dotterweich received a valuable benefit, and the requirements for a quasi contract were fulfilled. In such a situation, the law will impose a quasi contract, and Dotterweich normally will have to pay the doctor for the reasonable value of the medical services rendered.

In the following case, the defendant was totally unaware that a benefit had been bestowed on him by a neighbor who, because of a tax assessor's mistake, paid real estate taxes that should have been paid by the defendant. Furthermore, the defendant was not in any way at fault.

---

4. Pronounced *kwahn*-tuhm *mehr*-oo-whut.

5. *Britton v. Turner,* 6 N.H. 481 (1834).

---

| CASE 11.4 | |
|---|---|
| **PARTIPILO v. HALLMAN**<br>Appellate Court of Illinois,<br>First District, Fourth Division,<br>1987.<br>156 Ill.App.3d 806,<br>510 N.E.2d 8,<br>109 Ill.Dec. 387. | **BACKGROUND AND FACTS**    *Frank Partipilo and Elmer Hallman were neighbors. Hallman had made improvements on his property, but the county tax assessor's office mistakenly concluded that the improvements had been made on Partipilo's property instead. For the tax years 1977, 1978, and 1979, Partipilo paid nearly $26,500 in real estate taxes that should have been assessed against Hallman. (Real estate taxes will generally be increased whenever new buildings or other improvements are added to the real property.) When Partipilo discovered the error, he brought an action against Hallman to recover the extra taxes he had paid on the theory of unjust enrichment. The trial court ruled in favor of* |

*Partipilo. Hallman appealed, contending, among other things, that the theory of unjust enrichment did not support recovery in this case.*

Justice *JIGANTI* delivered the opinion of the court.
\* \* \* \*

In arguing that he had a right to recover the amount of the overassessment, Partipilo relies upon the general proposition that a person shall not enrich himself at another's expense. \* \* \*
\* \* \* \*

Hallman [suggests] that the plaintiff was at fault and that there was no fault on the part of Hallman. *A cause of action based on unjust enrichment, however, does not require fault on the part of the defendant.* [Emphasis added.] Instead the essence of the cause of action is that one party is enriched and it would be unjust for that party to retain the enrichment.
\* \* \* \*

Hallman further \* \* \* argues that he neither took nor received any benefit from Partipilo. Obviously, Hallman received a benefit in the form of lower taxes. His innocence in receiving the benefit does not mean that his retention of that benefit without payment is just.

**DECISION AND REMEDY**

*The appellate court held that Partipilo was entitled to recover in quasi contract the extra real estate taxes paid. Because the five-year statute of limitations[a] had run for the tax years 1977 and 1978, however, Partipilo could not recover the additional taxes paid for those years.*

**ETHICAL CONSIDERATIONS**

*The doctrine of unjust enrichment, which arose centuries ago in England, reflects the ethical conviction that justice should be done, even in the absence of a contractual cause of action. Although quasi-contractual recovery is a remedy at law, in which the relief is a money judgment, it is often mistakenly thought of as an equitable remedy because it has to do with fundamental issues of fairness and justice.*

a.   A statute of limitations prevents a party from suing on a contract after a certain period of time—in this case, five years—has elapsed.

**A LIMITATION ON QUASI CONTRACTS** Although quasi contracts exist to prevent unjust enrichment, the party obtaining the unjust enrichment is not liable in some situations. Basically, the quasi-contractual principle cannot be invoked by a party who has conferred a benefit on someone else unnecessarily or as a result of misconduct or negligence. Consider the following example. You take your car to the local car wash and ask to have it run through the washer and to have the gas tank filled. While it is being washed, you go to a nearby shopping center for two hours. In the meantime, one of the workers at the car wash has mistakenly believed that your car is the one that he is supposed to hand wax. When you come back, you are presented with a bill for a full tank of gas, a wash job, and a hand wax. Clearly, a benefit has been conferred on you. But this benefit has been conferred because of a mistake by the car-wash employee. You have not been *unjustly* enriched under these circumstances. People cannot normally be forced to pay for benefits "thrust" upon them.

In addition, the doctrine of quasi contract generally cannot be used when there is an actual contract that covers the area in controversy. For example, Bateman contracts with Camodeca to deliver a furnace to a building project owned by Jones. Bateman delivers the furnace, but Camodeca never pays Bateman. Jones has been unjustly enriched in this situation, to be sure. But Bateman cannot collect from Jones in quasi contract, because Bateman had an existing contract with Camodeca.

Bateman already has a remedy—he can sue for breach of contract to recover the price of the furnace from Camodeca. No quasi contract need be imposed by the court in this instance to achieve justice.

In the following case, the court refused to allow recovery in quasi contract because an express contract covering the area in controversy already existed.

## CASE 11.5

### INDUSTRIAL LIFT TRUCK SERVICE CORP. v. MITSUBISHI INTERNATIONAL CORP.

Appellate Court of Illinois, First District, Fourth Division, 1982.
104 Ill.App.3d 357,
432 N.E.2d 999,
60 Ill.Dec. 100.

**COMPANY PROFILE**   *The Mitsubishi Group is one of Japan's leading industrial groups and the fourth largest diversified service company in the world, with sales of nearly $150 billion. At the middle of the group of 160 companies are The Mitsubishi Bank, Ltd. (Japan's fourth largest city bank), Mitsubishi Heavy Industries, Ltd. (Japan's largest heavy machinery manufacturer), and Mitsubishi Corporation. Another important company in the group is Mitsubishi Electric Corporation, which oversees the production of satellite technology and consumer electronics, including large-screen televisions, and sells IBM computers in Japan under the Mitsubishi name. Another is Mitsubishi Motors Corporation, which produces the Diamante, among other vehicles, and manufactures cars in Illinois as Diamond-Star Motors. Founded in 1870 by Yataro Iwasaki, Mitsubishi diversified over the next thirty years into mining, banking, shipbuilding, railroads, and Japanese real estate. In 1918, the Mitsubishi conglomerate set up Mitsubishi Trading Corporation as the purchasing, sales, and management arm of the group. Thirty-six years later, Mitsubishi Trading established Mitsubishi International Corporation, which has become the leading exporter of U.S. goods into Japan. Mitsubishi Trading was renamed Mitsubishi Corporation in 1971.*

**BACKGROUND AND FACTS**   *In 1973 and again in 1976, an agreement was executed between Industrial Lift Truck Service Corporation (IL) and Mitsubishi International Corporation calling for IL to purchase forklift trucks from Mitsubishi and to use its best efforts to service and sell the trucks. The agreement also allowed Mitsubishi to terminate the agreement without just cause by giving ninety days' notice. From 1973 to 1977, IL allegedly became the nation's largest dealer of Mitsubishi forklift trucks. During this period, IL made design changes in the trucks to better suit the American market, design changes that Mitsubishi did not request but later incorporated into the trucks it sold to other dealers. In 1978, Mitsubishi terminated the agreement. IL sued under quasi-contractual principles to recover the benefits conferred on Mitsubishi by the design changes. The suit was dismissed, and IL appealed.*

*LINN,* Justice.
\*   \*   \*   \*

   In the present case, plaintiff obviously made the design changes with a view to being compensated pursuant to the contract terms. By its own admission, the design changes allowed plaintiff to become one of the nation's largest dealers in defendant's product. When the changes were made, plaintiff knew the risk involved. It knew the contract could be terminated as it was terminated, and thus knew when it made the changes that it might not be compensated under the contract to the extent it hoped to be compensated. Now that a situation plaintiff knew could occur has occurred, plaintiff seeks to shift a risk it assumed in light of the contract to defendant. In essence, plaintiff is seeking to use quasi-contract as a means to circumvent the realities of a contract freely entered into.

\* \* \* \*

The contract defined the entire relationship of the parties with respect to its general subject matter—the sale and servicing of defendant's products. Plaintiff's attempt here to bring a quasi-contract action is nothing more than an attempt to unilaterally amend the agreement in a manner prohibited by the agreement. In such circumstances, the benefit received by defendant can hardly be considered unjust. \* \* \* Defendant had a right to assume that the contract defined the entire relationship of the parties with respect to all matters related to defendant's product. Defendant had a right to assume, absent a valid amendment to the agreement, that it should not have to compensate plaintiff for any acts done in relation to the subject matter of the contract except pursuant to the contract terms.

*The existence of the specific contract barred the plaintiff's action in quasi contract, and the reviewing court held that the plaintiff's action in quasi contract was properly dismissed.*   **DECISION AND REMEDY**

## FORMAL VERSUS INFORMAL CONTRACTS

**Formal contracts** are contracts that require a special form or method of creation (formation) to be enforceable. One type of formal contract is the **contract under seal,** a formalized writing with a special seal attached. The seal may be actual (made of wax or some other durable substance) or impressed on the paper or indicated simply by the word *seal* or the letters *L.S.* at the end of the document. *L.S.* stands for *locus sigilli* and means ''the place for the seal.''[6]

A written contract may be considered sealed if the promisor *adopts* a seal already on it. A standard form contract purchased at the local office supply store, for example, may have the word *seal* (or something else that qualifies as a seal) printed next to the blanks intended for the signatures. Unless the parties who sign the form indicate a contrary intention, when they sign the form, they adopt the seal.

**Informal contracts** include all other contracts. Such contracts are also called *simple contracts*. No special form is required (except for certain types of contracts that must be in writing), as the contracts are usually based on their substance rather than their form.

## EXECUTED VERSUS EXECUTORY CONTRACTS

Contracts are also classified according to the degree to which they have been performed. A contract that has been fully performed on both sides is called an **executed contract.** A contract that has not been fully performed on either side is called an **executory contract.** If one party has fully performed but the other has not, the contract is said to be executed on the one side and executory on the other, but the contract is still classified as executory. For example, assume you agree to buy ten tons of coal from the Northern Coal Company. Further assume that Northern has delivered the coal to your steel mill, where it is now being burned. At this point, the contract is executed on the part of Northern and executory on your part. After you pay Northern for the coal, the contract will be executed on both sides.

## VALID, VOID, VOIDABLE, AND UNENFORCEABLE CONTRACTS

A **valid contract** has the elements necessary to entitle at least one of the parties to enforce it in court. Those elements, as mentioned earlier, consist of (1) an offer and an acceptance, (2) supported by legally sufficient consideration, (3) made by

---

6.    The contract under seal has been almost entirely abolished under such provisions as UCC 2–203 (Section 2–203 of the Uniform Commercial Code). In sales of real estate, however, it is still common to use a seal (or an acceptable substitute).

# ■ CONCEPT SUMMARY 11.1 Classification of Contracts

| Formation | 1. *Bilateral*—A promise for a promise. |
|---|---|
| | 2. *Unilateral*—A promise for an act (acceptance is the completed performance of the act). |
| | 3. *Express*—Formed by words (oral, written, or a combination). |
| | 4. *Implied in fact*—Formed by the conduct of the parties. |
| | 5. *Quasi contract* (implied in law)—Imposed by law to prevent unjust enrichment. |
| | 6. *Formal*—Requires a special form for creation. |
| | 7. *Informal*—Requires no special form for creation. |
| Performance | 1. *Executed*—A fully performed contract. |
| | 2. *Executory*—A contract not fully performed. |
| Enforceability | 1. *Valid*—The contract has the necessary contractual elements of agreement (offer and acceptance), consideration, parties with legal capacity, and a legal purpose. |
| | 2. *Void*—No contract exists, or there is a contract without legal obligations. |
| | 3. *Voidable*—One party has the option of avoiding or enforcing the contractual obligation. |
| | 4. *Unenforceable*—A contract exists, but it cannot be enforced because of a legal defense. |

parties who have the legal capacity to enter into the contract, and (4) for a legal purpose.

A **void contract** is no contract at all. The terms *void* and *contract* are contradictory. A void contract produces no legal obligations on the part of any of the parties. For example, a contract can be void because one of the parties was adjudged by a court to be legally insane or because the purpose of the contract was illegal.

A **voidable contract** is a valid contract but one that can be avoided at the option of one or both of the parties. The party having the option can elect either to avoid any duty to perform or to *ratify* (make valid) the contract. If the contract is avoided, both parties are released from it. If it is ratified, both parties must fully perform their respective legal obligations.

As a general rule, but subject to exceptions, contracts made by minors are voidable at the option of the minor (see Chapter 14). Contracts entered into under fraudulent conditions are voidable at the option of the defrauded party. In addition, contracts entered into under duress or undue influence are voidable (see Chapter 15).

An **unenforceable contract** is one that cannot be enforced because of certain legal defenses against it. It is not unenforceable because a party failed to satisfy a legal requirement of the contract; rather, it is a valid contract rendered unenforceable by some statute or law. For example, certain contracts must be in writing (see Chapter 16), and if they are not, they will not be enforceable except in certain exceptional circumstances.

## SECTION 6

# INTERPRETATION OF CONTRACTS

Common law rules of contract interpretation have evolved over time to provide the courts with guidelines for determining the meaning of, and giving effect to, contracts.

### THE PLAIN MEANING RULE

When the writing is clear and unequivocal, a court will enforce it according to its plain terms. There is no need for the court to interpret the language of the contract. The meaning of the terms must be determined from *the face of the instrument*—from the written document alone. This is sometimes referred to as the *plain meaning rule.* Under this rule, if a contract's words appear to be clear and unambiguous, a court cannot consider *extrinsic evidence,* which is any evidence not contained in the document itself. Admissibility of such evidence can significantly affect how a court may interpret ambiguous contractual provisions and thus the outcome of litigation.

## OTHER RULES OF INTERPRETATION

When the writing contains ambiguous or unclear terms, a court will interpret the language to give effect to the parties' intent *as expressed in their contract.* This is the primary purpose of the rules of interpretation—to determine the parties' intent from the language used in their agreement and to give effect to that intent. Usually, a court will not make or remake a contract, nor will it interpret the language according to what the parties *claim* their intent was when they made it. The following rules are used by the courts in interpreting ambiguous contractual terms:

1. Insofar as possible, a reasonable, lawful, and effective meaning will be given to all of a contract's terms.
2. A contract will be interpreted as a whole; individual, specific clauses will be considered subordinate to the contract's general intent. All writings that are a part of the same transaction will be interpreted together.
3. Terms that were the subject of separate ne-gotiation will be given greater consideration than standardized terms and terms that were not negotiated separately.
4. A word will be given its ordinary, commonly accepted meaning, and a technical word or term will be given its technical meaning, unless the parties clearly intended something else.
5. Specific and exact wording will be given greater consideration than general language.
6. Written or typewritten terms prevail over pre-printed ones.
7. Because a contract should be drafted in clear and unambiguous language, a party who uses ambiguous expressions is held to be responsible for the ambiguities. Thus, when the language has more than one meaning, it will be interpreted against the party who drafted the contract.
8. Evidence of trade usage, prior dealing, and course of performance may be admitted to clarify the meaning of an ambiguously worded contract. (These terms are defined and discussed in Chapter 20.) In such cases, what each of the parties does in pursuance of the contract will be interpreted as consistent with what the other does and with any relevant usage of trade and course of dealing or performance. In these circumstances, express terms are given the greatest weight, followed by course of performance, course of dealing, and usage of trade—in that order. When considering custom and usage, a court will look at the trade customs and usage common to the particular business or industry and to the locale in which the contract was made or is to be performed.

## TERMS AND CONCEPTS TO REVIEW

bilateral contract 219
contract 216
contract under seal 225
executed contract 225
executory contract 225
express contract 220
formal contract 225
implied-in-fact contract 220

informal contract 225
objective theory of
  contracts 216
offeree 219
offeror 219
promise 215
promisee 215
promisor 215

*quantum meruit* 222
quasi contract 222
unenforceable contract 226
unilateral contract 219
valid contract 225
void contract 226
voidable contract 226

# QUESTIONS AND CASE PROBLEMS

**11–1. Types of Contracts.** Suppose McCleskey, a local businessperson, is a good friend of Miller, the owner of a local candy store. Every day at his lunch hour McCleskey goes into Miller's candy store and spends about five minutes looking at the candy. After examining Miller's candy and talking with Miller, McCleskey usually buys one or two candy bars. One afternoon, McCleskey goes into Miller's candy shop, looks at the candy, and picks up a $1 candy bar. Seeing that Miller is very busy, he waves the candy bar at Miller without saying a word and walks out. Is there a contract? If so, classify it within the categories presented in this chapter.

**11–2. Types of Contracts.** Janine was hospitalized with severe abdominal pain and placed in an intensive care unit. Her doctor told the hospital personnel to order around-the-clock nursing care for Janine. At the hospital's request, a nursing services firm, Nursing Services Unlimited, provided two weeks of in-hospital care and, after Janine was sent home, an additional two weeks of at-home care. During the at-home period of care, Janine was fully aware that she was receiving the benefit of the nursing services. Nursing Services later billed Janine $4,000 for the nursing care, but Janine refused to pay on the ground that she had never contracted for the services, either orally or in writing. In view of the fact that no express contract was ever formed, can Nursing Services recover the $4,000 from Janine? If so, under what legal theory? Discuss.

**11–3. Bilateral versus Unilateral Contracts.** Atencio is confined to his bed. He calls a friend who lives across the street and offers to sell her his watch next week for $100. If his friend wishes to accept, she is to put a red piece of paper in her front window. The next morning, she places a red piece of paper in her front window. Is the contract formed bilateral or unilateral? Explain.

**11–4. Types of Contracts.** Burger Baby restaurants engaged Air Advertising to fly an advertisement above the Connecticut beaches. The advertisement offered $1,000 to any person who could swim from the Connecticut beaches to Long Island across Long Island Sound in less than a day. On Saturday, October 10, at 10:00 A.M., Air Advertising's pilot flew a sign above the Connecticut beaches that read: "Swim across the Sound and Burger Baby pays $1,000." Upon seeing the sign, Davison dived in. About four hours later, when he was about halfway across the Sound, Air Advertising flew another sign over the Sound that read: "Burger Baby revokes." Davison completed the swim in another six hours. Is there a contract between Davison and Burger Baby? Can Davison recover anything?

**11–5. Bilateral versus Unilateral Contracts.** Zdanis contacts Joe and makes the following offer: "When you finish mowing my yard, I'll pay you $25." Joe responds by saying, "I accept your offer." Is there a contract? Is this an offer to form a bilateral or a unilateral contract? What is the legal significance of the distinction?

**11–6. Enforceable versus Unenforceable Contracts.** Financial & Real Estate Consulting Co. (Financial) contracted with Regional Properties, Inc. (Regional), to sell to investors limited partnership interests (ownership interests) in some ventures being undertaken by Regional. Regional promised to pay Financial for its brokerage services. Financial sold a number of partnership interests and had been paid the stipulated fee for some (but not all) of the sales. Regional later discovered that Financial was not registered with the Securities and Exchange Commission as a broker-dealer, as required by law. Regional brought an action before the court to rescind (cancel) the contract with Financial. Financial counterclaimed for the unpaid fees. Is the contract between Financial and Regional enforceable? Why or why not? [*Regional Properties, Inc. v. Financial & Real Estate Consulting Co.*, 678 F.2d 552 (5th Cir. 1982)]

**11–7. Equitable Doctrines.** Ashton Co., which was engaged in a construction project, leased a crane from Artukovich & Sons, Inc., and hired the Reliance Truck Co. to deliver the crane to the construction site. Reliance, while the crane was in its possession and without permission from either Ashton or Artukovich, used the crane to install a transformer for a utility company, which paid Reliance for the job. Reliance then delivered the crane to the Ashton construction site at the appointed time of delivery. When Artukovich learned of the unauthorized use of the crane by Reliance, it sued Reliance for damages. What equitable doctrine could be used as a basis for awarding damages to Artukovich? [*Artukovich & Sons, Inc. v. Reliance Truck Co.,* 126 Ariz. 246, 614 P.2d 327 (1980)]

**11–8. Recovery for Services Rendered.** Sosa Crisan, an eighty-seven-year-old widow, collapsed while shopping at a local grocery store. The Detroit police took her to the Detroit city hospital by ambulance. She was admitted, and she remained there fourteen days. Then she was transferred to another hospital, at which she died some eleven months later. Crisan had never regained consciousness after her collapse at the grocery store. After she died, the city of Detroit sued her estate to recover the expenses of both the ambulance that took her to the Detroit city hospital and the expenses of her Detroit city hospital stay. Is there a contract between Sosa Crisan and the Detroit city hospital? If so, how much can the Detroit hospital recover? [*In re Estate of Crisan,* 362 Mich. 569, 107 N.W.2d 907 (1961)]

**11–9. Bilateral versus Unilateral Contracts.** Nichols is the principal owner of Samuel Nichols, Inc., a real estate firm. Nichols signed an exclusive brokerage agreement with Molway to find a purchaser for Molway's property within ninety days. This type of agreement entitles the broker to a commission if the property is sold to any purchaser to whom it is shown during the ninety-day period. Molway tried to cancel the brokerage agreement before the ninety-day term had expired. Nichols had already advertised the property, put up a ''for sale'' sign, and shown the property to prospective buyers. Molway claimed that the brokerage contract was unilateral and that she could cancel at any time before Nichols found a buyer. Nichols claimed that the contract was bilateral and that Molway's cancellation breached the contract. Discuss who should prevail at trial. [*Samuel Nichols, Inc. v. Molway,* 25 Mass.App. 913, 515 N.E.2d 598 (1987)]

**11–10. Implied Contracts.** Weichert Co. Realtors sought damages from Thomas Ryan and his partner because they refused to pay a commission to William Tackaberry, one of Weichert's agents, for work done on a sale of property. Tackaberry had contacted Ryan about the property and subsequently met with him to discuss the sale. At that time and during subsequent discussions, Tackaberry informed Ryan that his commission was to be 10 percent of the purchase price of the property, payable at closing. Despite Tackaberry's continued efforts to get Ryan to sign a letter that spelled out the terms of the commission, Ryan refused to sign it. Ryan offered several times to negotiate with Tackaberry the amount and terms of the commission, but Tackaberry insisted that his commission must be 10 percent of the final price and that it was due at closing. When the deal was finalized, Weichert sent Ryan and his partner a bill for Tackaberry's commission. When the bill remained unpaid, Weichert filed suit for breach of an implied-in-fact contract or, failing that, for quasi-contractual recovery. Did an implied-in-fact (implied) contract exist between Tackaberry and Ryan? If not, could Weichert recover in quasi contract for the value of Tackaberry's services? What should the court decide? [*Weichert v. Ryan,* 128 N.J. 427, 608 A.2d 280 (1992)]

**11–11. Recovery for Services Rendered.** Garris Briggs died on October 11, 1990, leaving $782 in unpaid medical bills. Following his death, insurance checks in the amount of $676.72, payable to Briggs, were sent to his widow, Beatrice Briggs. The Briggses had been living apart for the previous five years and during that time had not had any financial connections. Under state law, a surviving spouse, upon the execution of an affidavit before the appropriate county official, was entitled to all of the estate's assets without administration, and the assets of the estate up to $5,000 were free from all debts of the decedent (the one who died). Garris Briggs's estate was worth less than $5,000, so Beatrice Briggs signed the necessary affidavit, cashed the checks, and deposited the funds. The physicians who had provided medical services for Garris Briggs sued the widow to recover the insurance proceeds. The widow claimed that because she had not lived with her husband for five years, she should not be liable for his debts. Should the physicians be allowed to recover the insurance proceeds from Beatrice Briggs? Discuss fully. [*Drs. Laves, Sarewitz and Walko v. Briggs,* 259 N.J.Super. 368, 613 A.2d 506 (1992)]

**11–12. A Question of Ethics**

 *In 1982, in the closing days of Minnesota's gubernatorial campaign, Dan Cohen offered a reporter from the* Minneapolis Star and Tribune *some ''documents which may or may not relate to a candidate in the upcoming election.'' Cohen, who was actively promoting one of the gubernatorial candidates, agreed to give the reporter the documents—copies of two public court records of a rival party's candidate for lieutenant governor—if the reporter promised not to reveal the source of the information. The reporter promised to keep the source confidential. The editor of the* Tribune, *however, in spite of the reporter's objections, decided to name Cohen as the source of the information so as not to mislead the public into thinking that the information came from an unbiased source. On the day the newspaper article was published, Cohen was fired by his employer. Cohen sued the newspaper's owner, Cowles Media Co., for breach of contract. Given these facts, discuss the following questions.* [Cohen v. Cowles Media Co., *501 U.S. 663, 111 S.Ct. 2513, 115 L.Ed.2d 586 (1991)]*

1. Do you think that the editor's ethical duty to provide the reading public with unbiased news coverage should have overridden the editor's ethical duty to honor the reporter's promise to Cohen?

2. Did the reporter's promise to keep Cohen's identity confidential create solely an ethical obligation or a contract enforceable in a court of law?

3. If the court decides that an enforceable contract was formed between Cohen and the reporter, would the decision be counter to society's valuation—as expressed in the First Amendment to the Constitution—that freedom of the press should not be constrained?

# CHAPTER 12

# AGREEMENT

**E**ssential to any contract is an **agreement.** The agreement does not necessarily have to be in writing. Both parties, however, must manifest their assent to the same bargain. Once an agreement is reached, if the other elements of a contract are present (consideration, capacity, and legality—discussed in subsequent chapters), a valid contract is formed, generally creating enforceable rights and duties between the parties.

A contract normally must contain reasonably definite terms; otherwise, it would be impossible for a court to enforce the contract. What specific terms are required depends, of course, on the type of contract. Generally, a contract must include the following terms, either expressed in the contract or capable of being reasonably inferred from it:

1. The identification of the parties.
2. The identification of the object or subject matter of the contract (also quantity, when appropriate), including the work to be performed, with specific identification of such items as goods, services, and land.
3. The consideration to be paid.
4. The time of payment, delivery, or performance.

If these terms are expressly stated in the agreement, the contract is definite. Although terms and intent are equally important in both the offer and the acceptance, for simplicity's sake we will discuss the relevant laws only in terms of the offer.

## SECTION 1

## MUTUAL ASSENT

Ordinarily, mutual assent is evidenced by a contractual offer and acceptance. One party offers a certain bargain to another party, who then accepts that bargain. The parties are required to manifest to each other their **mutual assent** to the same bargain.[1] Because words often fail to convey the precise meaning intended, the law of contracts generally adheres to the objective theory of contracts, as discussed in Chapter 11. Under this theory, a party's words and conduct are held to mean whatever a reasonable person in the offeree's position would think they meant. The court will give words their usual meaning even if "it were proved by twenty bishops that [the] party . . . intended something else."[2]

## SECTION 2

# REQUIREMENTS OF THE OFFER

The parties to a contract are the *offeror*, the one who makes an offer or proposal to another party, and the *offeree*, the one to whom the offer or proposal is made. An **offer** is a promise or commitment to do or refrain from doing some specified thing in the future. Under the common law, three elements are necessary for an offer to be effective:

1. The offeror must have a *serious intention* to become bound by the offer.
2. The terms of the offer must be reasonably *certain*, or *definite*, so that the parties and the court can ascertain the terms of the contract.
3. The offer must be communicated by the offeror to the offeree, resulting in the offeree's knowledge of the offer.

Once an effective offer has been made, the offeree has the power to accept the offer. If the offeree accepts, an agreement is formed (and thus a contract, if other essential elements are present).

## INTENTION

The first requirement for an effective offer to exist is a serious intent on the part of the offeror. But serious intent is not determined by the *subjective* intentions, beliefs, and assumptions of the offeror. It is determined by what a reasonable person in the offeree's position would conclude the offeror's words and actions meant. Offers made in obvious anger, jest, or undue excitement do not meet the intent test. Because these offers are not effective, an offeree's acceptance does not create an agreement. For example, suppose you and three classmates ride to school each day in Davina's new automobile, which has a market value of $12,000. One cold morning, the four of you get into the car, but Davina cannot get the car started. She yells in anger, "I'll sell this car to anyone for $500!" You drop $500 in her lap. Given these facts, a reasonable person, taking into consideration Davina's frustration and the obvious difference in value between the market value of the car and the proposed purchase price, would declare that her offer was not made with serious intent and that you did not have an agreement.

The concept of intention can be further clarified by distinguishing between offers and various kinds of nonoffers.

**EXPRESSIONS OF OPINION** An expression of opinion is not an offer. It does not evidence an intention to enter into a binding agreement. Hawkins took his son to McGee, a doctor, and asked McGee to operate on the son's hand. McGee said the boy would be in the hospital three or four days and that the hand would *probably* heal a few days later. The son's hand did not heal for a month, but the father did not win a suit for breach of contract. The court held that McGee did not make an offer to heal the son's hand in three or four days. He merely expressed an opinion as to when the hand would heal.[3]

**STATEMENTS OF INTENTION** If Arif says "I *plan* to sell my stock in Novation, Inc., for $150 per share," a contract is not created if John "accepts" and tenders the $150 per share for the stock. Arif has merely expressed his intention to enter into a future contract for the sale of the stock. If John accepts and tenders the $150 per share, no contract is formed, because a reasonable person would conclude that Arif was only *thinking about* selling his stock, not promising to sell.

---

1. Restatement (Second) of Contracts, Section 22.
2. Learned Hand in *Hotchkiss v. National City Bank of New York*, 200 F. 287 (2d Cir. 1911), aff'd 231 U.S. 50, 34 S.Ct. 20, 58 L.Ed. 115 (1913). The term *aff'd* is an abbreviation for *affirmed;* an appellate court can affirm a lower court's judgment, decree, or order, thereby declaring that it is proper and must stand as rendered.

---

3. *Hawkins v. McGee*, 84 N.H. 114, 146 A. 641 (1929).

**PRELIMINARY NEGOTIATIONS**    A request or invitation to negotiate is not an offer. It only expresses a willingness to discuss the possibility of entering into a contract. Included are statements such as "Will you sell Blythe Estate?" or "I wouldn't sell my car for less than $1,000." A reasonable person in the offeree's position would not conclude that these statements evidenced an intention to enter into a binding obligation. Likewise, when construction work is done for the government and private firms, contractors are invited to submit bids. The *invitation* to submit bids is not an offer, and a contractor does not bind the government or private firm by submitting a bid. (The bids that the contractors submit *are* offers, however, and the government or private firm can bind the contractor by accepting the bid.)

**ADVERTISEMENTS, CATALOGUES, PRICE LISTS, AND CIRCULARS**    In general, advertisements, mail order catalogues, price lists, and circular letters are treated not as *offers* to contract but as *invitations to negotiate.* Suppose that Loeser advertises a used paving machine. The ad is mailed to hundreds of firms and reads, "Used Loeser Construction Co. paving machine. Builds curbs and finishes cement work all in one process. Price $21,250." If Star Paving calls Loeser and says, "We accept your offer," no contract is formed. Any reasonable person would conclude that Loeser was not promising to sell the paving machine but rather was soliciting offers to buy it. If such an ad were held to constitute a legal offer, and fifty people accepted the offer, there is no way that Loeser could perform all fifty of the resulting contracts. He would have to breach forty-nine contracts. Obviously, the law seeks to avoid such unfairness.

Price lists are another form of invitation to negotiate or trade. A seller's price list is not an offer to sell at that price; it merely invites the buyer to offer to buy at that price. In fact, the seller usually puts "prices subject to change" on the price list. Only in rare circumstances will a price quotation be construed as an offer.[4]

Although most advertisements and the like are treated as invitations to negotiate, this does not mean that an advertisement can never be an offer. *If the advertisement makes a promise so definite in character that it is apparent that the offeror is binding himself or herself to the conditions stated, the advertisement is treated as an offer.* In the following case, the court had to decide whether a newspaper advertisement announcing a "special sale" in a department store should be construed as an offer, the acceptance of which would complete a contract. (Today, the Federal Trade Commission has a set of rules governing such ads.)

---

4. See, for example, *Fairmount Glass Works v. Grunden-Martin Woodenware Co.,* 106 Ky. 659, 51 S.W. 196 (1899).

CASE 12.1

**LEFKOWITZ v. GREAT MINNEAPOLIS SURPLUS STORE, INC.**

Supreme Court of Minnesota, 1957.
251 Minn. 188,
86 N.W.2d 689.

**BACKGROUND AND FACTS**    *Plaintiff Lefkowitz read a newspaper advertisement offering certain items of merchandise for sale on a first-come, first-served basis. Plaintiff went to the store twice and was the first person to demand the merchandise and indicate a readiness to pay the sale price. On both occasions, the defendant department store refused to sell the merchandise to the plaintiff, saying that the offer was intended for women only, even though the advertisement was directed to the general public. The plaintiff sued the store for breach of contract, and the trial court awarded him damages.*

*MURPHY,* Justice.
\* \* \* \*

This case grows out of the alleged refusal of the defendant to sell to the plaintiff a certain fur piece which it had offered for sale in a newspaper advertisement. It appears from the record that on April 6, 1956, the defendant published the following advertisement in a Minneapolis newspaper:

"Saturday 9 A.M. Sharp
3 Brand New

Fur
Coats
Worth to $100.00
First Come
First Served
$1 Each''

On April 13, the defendant again published an advertisement in the same newspaper as follows:

''Saturday 9 A.M.
2 Brand New Pastel
Mink 3-Skin Scarfs
Selling for $89.50
Out they go
Saturday. Each . . . $1.00
1 Black Lapin Stole
Beautiful,
worth $139.50 . . . $1.00
First Come
First Served''

The record supports the findings of the court that on each of the Saturdays following the publication of the above-described ads the plaintiff was the first to present himself at the appropriate counter in the defendant's store and on each occasion demanded the coat and the stole so advertised and indicated his readiness to pay the sale price of $1. On both occasions, the defendant refused to sell the merchandise to the plaintiff, stating on the first occasion that by a ''house rule'' the offer was intended for women only and sales would not be made to men, and on the second visit that plaintiff knew defendant's house rules.

\* \* \* \*

The test of whether a binding obligation may originate in advertisements addressed to the general public is ''whether the facts show that some performance was promised in positive terms in return for something requested.''

\* \* \* \*

Whether in any individual instance a newspaper advertisement is an offer rather than an invitation to make an offer depends on the legal intention of the parties and the surrounding circumstances. We are of the view on the facts before us that the offer by the defendant \* \* \* was clear, definite, and explicit, and left nothing open for negotiation. The plaintiff having successfully managed to be the first one to appear at the seller's place of business to be served, as requested by the advertisement, and having offered the stated purchase price of the article, he was entitled to performance on the part of the defendant. We think the trial court was correct in holding that there was in the conduct of the parties a sufficient mutuality of obligation to constitute a contract of sale.

The defendant contends that the offer was modified by a ''house rule'' to the effect that only women were qualified to receive the bargains advertised. The advertisement contained no such restriction. This objection may be disposed of briefly by stating that, while an advertiser has the right at any time before acceptance to modify his offer, he does not have the right, after acceptance, to impose new or arbitrary conditions not contained in the published offer.

**DECISION AND REMEDY**

*The Supreme Court of Minnesota affirmed the trial court's judgment, awarding the plaintiff damages for the defendant's breach of contract.*

**ETHICAL CONSIDERATIONS**

*Although Lefkowitz recovered for his visit in response to the second advertisement (April 13), he did not recover for the earlier visit. The trial* *court disallowed the plaintiff's claim for the value of the fur coats in the first ad, because the value of those articles ("worth to $100.00") was speculative and too indefinite to serve as a basis for recovery. Retailers are frequently required to determine whether an advertised price should be treated legally as an invitation to trade or ethically as an offer to sell at the advertised price.*

**OTHER NONOFFER SITUATIONS** Sometimes what appears to be an offer is not sufficient to serve as the basis for formation of a contract. Particularly problematic in this respect are "offers" to sell goods at auctions and agreements to agree.

*Auctions.* In an auction, a seller "offers" goods for sale through an auctioneer. This is not, however, a *contractual* offer. Instead, the seller is only expressing a willingness to sell. Unless the terms of the auction are explicitly stated to be *without reserve,* the seller (through the auctioneer) may withdraw the goods at any time before the sale is closed by announcement or by fall of the auctioneer's hammer. The seller's right to withdraw goods characterizes an auction *with reserve;* all auctions are assumed to be of this type unless a clear statement to the contrary is made.[5] At auctions "without reserve," the goods cannot be withdrawn and must be sold to the highest bidder.

In an auction with reserve, there is no obligation to sell, and the seller may refuse the highest bid. The bidder is actually the offeror. Before the auctioneer strikes the hammer, which constitutes acceptance of the bid, a bidder may revoke his or her bid, or the auctioneer may reject that bid or all bids. Typically, an auctioneer will reject a bid that is below the price the seller is willing to accept. When the auctioneer accepts a higher bid, he or she rejects all previous bids. Because rejection terminates an offer (as pointed out below), if the highest bidder withdraws his or her bid before the hammer falls, none of the previous bids are reinstated. If the bid is not withdrawn or rejected, the contract is formed when the auctioneer announces, "Going once, going twice, sold" (or something similar) and lets the hammer fall.

In auctions with reserve, the seller may reserve the right to confirm or reject the sale even after the "hammer has fallen." In this situation, the seller is obligated to notify those attending the auction that sales of goods made during the auction are not final until confirmed by the seller. The following case illustrates this point.

5.  See UCC 2–328.

**CASE 12.2**

**LAWRENCE PAPER CO. v. ROSEN & CO.**
United States Court of Appeals, Sixth Circuit, 1991.
939 F.2d 376.

**HISTORICAL AND SOCIAL SETTING** *More than two hundred years ago, it was established at common law that when an auctioneer says, "What am I bid?" the auctioneer is not making an offer to sell but is inviting offers to buy that he or she is free to accept or reject. More than one hundred years ago, it was established in some cases that even if an auctioneer announces, "I will sell to the highest bidder," the statement does not constitute an offer. Of course, as noted above, an auction "without reserve" is a different situation. These common law rules governing auctions were adopted by the Uniform Commercial Code, which has covered most sales of goods for more than twenty-five years. It is also generally held that when a seller reserves the right to refuse a bid, a binding sale is not made until the seller accepts the bid.*

**BACKGROUND AND FACTS** *This dispute arose from an auction of equipment used to make corrugated cardboard boxes. The equipment, which had served as collateral for a loan obtained by North Coast Corrugator Company from Ameritrust Company, was to be sold at auction* *to satisfy the debt, in accordance with a court judgment. Ameritrust Company employed Rosen & Company to conduct the sale. Included in Rosen's extensive advertisements of the sale was the announcement that the sale was subject to confirmation by Ameritrust. The auctioneer made a similar announcement at the time of the sale. Sixty bidders attended the auction, including Alpine Company (a defendant), Lawrence Paper Company (a plaintiff), and American Corrugated Machine Corporation (ACMC) (a plaintiff). The auctioneer first offered the equipment in bulk, but only one bid—from Alpine for $50,000—was received. Then the equipment was offered piecemeal, and total bids of $139,000 were received. Two bids from Lawrence and ACMC were accepted, and both companies submitted checks for 25 percent of their bid totals, as requested. Subsequent to the auction, Alpine offered $175,000 for the equipment, and Ameritrust sold the entire lot to Alpine. Lawrence and ACMC sued for breach of contract. The trial judge dismissed the suit, and the plaintiffs appealed.*

*BERTELSMAN, District Judge:*

\* \* \* \*

\* \* \* Rosen & Company advertised the sale extensively in newspapers, trade journals, and a catalog which was prepared especially for the sale. On the cover page of the mail catalog, the terms of this particular auction were printed and included: "\* \* \* Sale subject to confirmation of the Secured Party [Ameritrust]." \* \* \* Terms and conditions that were announced [orally at the auction] and are relevant to the instant case include the following: "Be advised any and all sales are subject to confirmation by the Secured Party \* \* \*."

\* \* \* \*

[The trial court judge] based his dismissal of the complaint on his finding that the auction sale was "clearly with reserve" and that the sale was, as a matter of law, "subject to \* \* \* the confirmation of the secured party \* \* \*." In his view, there was no acceptance of the bid, because the sale was not confirmed by the secured party. Therefore, he held there was no binding contract and the sellers were free to accept the subsequent offer. We agree and affirm.

\* \* \* \*

\* \* \* [W]here a sale is with reserve and subject to "confirmation" by the seller, the bids are subject to rejection after the sale, even though accepted by the auctioneer.

**DECISION AND REMEDY**  *The appellate court affirmed the trial court's decision. No contract existed between the plaintiffs and Rosen as a result of the auctioneer's acceptance of the plaintiffs' bids, because the seller had notified the plaintiffs that no sale was final until confirmed by the seller.*

*Agreements to Agree.* Traditionally, agreements to agree—that is, agreements to agree to a material term of a contract at some future date—were not considered to be binding contracts. More recent cases illustrate the view that agreements to agree serve valid commercial purposes and can be enforced if the parties clearly intended to be bound by such agreements. For example, suppose Zahn Consulting leases office space from Leon Properties, Inc. Their lease agreement includes a clause permitting Zahn to extend the lease at an amount of rent to be agreed on when the lease is extended. Under the traditional rule, because the amount of rent was not specified in the lease clause itself, the clause would be too indefinite in its terms to enforce. Under the modern view, a court could hold that the parties intended the future rent to be a reasonable amount and could enforce the clause.[6]

In other words, under the modern view, the emphasis is on the parties' intent rather than on form. For example, when the Pennzoil Company discussed with the Getty Oil Company the possible purchase of Getty's stock, a ''Memorandum of Agreement'' was drafted to reflect the terms of the conversations. After more negotiations over the price, both companies issued press releases announcing an agreement in principle on the terms of the memorandum. The next day, Texaco, Inc., offered to buy all of Getty's stock at a higher price. The day after that, Getty's board of directors voted to accept Texaco's offer, and Texaco and Getty signed a merger agreement. When Pennzoil sued Texaco for tortious interference with its ''contractual'' relationship with Getty, a jury concluded that Getty and Pennzoil had intended a binding contract before Texaco made its offer, with only the details left to be worked out. Texaco was held liable for interfering with this contract.[7]

## DEFINITENESS

The second requirement for an effective offer involves the definiteness of its terms. An offer must have reasonably definite terms so that a court can determine if a breach has occurred and can provide an appropriate remedy.[8] Courts are sometimes willing to supply a missing term in a contract when the parties have clearly manifested an intent to form a contract. If, in contrast, the parties have attempted to deal with a particular term of the contract but their expression of intent is too vague or uncertain to be given any precise meaning, the court will not supply a ''reasonable'' term, because to do so might conflict with the intent of the parties. In other words, the court will not rewrite the contract.[9]

Article 2 of the UCC has different rules relating to the definiteness of terms used in a contract for the sale of goods. In essence, Article 2 modifies general contract law by requiring less specificity.

## COMMUNICATION

A third requirement for an effective offer is communication of the offer to the offeree, resulting in the offeree's knowledge of the offer. Ordinarily, one cannot agree to a bargain without knowing that it exists. Suppose that Estrich advertises a reward for the return of his lost dog. Hoban, not knowing of the reward, finds the dog and returns it to Estrich. Hoban cannot recover the reward, because she did not know it had been offered.[10]

# TERMINATION OF THE OFFER

The communication of an effective offer to an offeree gives the offeree the power to transform the offer into a binding, legal obligation (a contract) by an acceptance. This power of acceptance, however, does not continue forever. It can be terminated either by the action of the parties or by operation of law.

## TERMINATION BY ACTION OF THE PARTIES

An offer can be terminated by the action of the parties in any of three ways: by revocation, by rejection, or by counteroffer.

**REVOCATION OF THE OFFER BY THE OFFEROR** The offeror's act of withdrawing an offer is called **revocation.** Unless an offer is irrevocable, the offeror usually can revoke the offer (even if he or she has promised to keep it open), as long as the revocation is communicated to the offeree before the offeree accepts. Revocation may

---

6. Restatement (Second) of Contracts, Section 33. See also UCC 2–204, 2–305.

7. *Texaco, Inc. v. Pennzoil Co.*, 729 S.W.2d 768 (Tex.App—Houston [1st Dist.] 1987, writ ref'd n.r.e.). (Generally, a complete Texas Court of Appeals citation includes the writ-of-error history showing the Texas Supreme Court's disposition of the case. In this case, ''writ ref'd n.r.e.'' is an abbreviation for ''writ refused, no reversible error,'' which means that Texas's highest court refused to grant the appellant's request to review the case, because the court did not consider there to be any reversible error. ) The *Texaco* case was presented in Chapter 7 as Case 7.1.

8. Restatement (Second) of Contracts, Section 33.

9. See Chapter 20 and UCC 2–204.

---

10. A few states allow recovery of the reward but not on contract principles. Because Estrich wanted his dog to be returned, and Hoban returned it, these few states would allow Hoban to recover on the basis that it would be unfair to deny her the reward just because she did not know it had been offered.

be accomplished by express repudiation of the offer (for example, with a statement such as ''I withdraw my previous offer of October 17'' ) or by performance of acts inconsistent with the existence of the offer, which are made known to the offeree.

The general rule followed by most states is that a revocation becomes effective when the offeree or offeree's agent (a person acting on behalf of the offeree) actually receives it. Therefore, a letter of revocation mailed on April 1 and delivered at the offeree's residence or place of business on April 3 becomes effective on April 3.

An offer made to the general public can be revoked in the same manner the offer was originally communicated. Suppose that a department store offers a $10,000 reward to anyone giving information leading to the apprehension of the persons who burglarized the store's downtown branch. The offer is published in three local papers and four papers in neighboring communities. To revoke the offer, the store must publish the revocation in all seven papers for the same number of days it published the offer. The revocation is then accessible to the general public, even if some particular offeree does not know about it.

**IRREVOCABLE OFFERS**  Although most offers are revocable, certain offers can be made irrevocable. One type of irrevocable offer involves the option contract. Increasingly, courts also refuse to allow an offeror to revoke an offer when the offeree has changed position because of justifiable reliance on the offer. (In some circumstances, an offer for the sale of goods made by a merchant may also be considered irrevocable—see the discussion of the ''merchant's firm offer'' in Chapter 20.)

*Option Contract.*  An **option contract** is created when an offeror promises to hold an offer open for a specified period of time in return for a payment (consideration) given by the offeree. An option contract is a *separate* contract that takes away the offeror's power to revoke the offer during the period of time specified in the option. If no time is specified, then a reasonable period of time is implied.

Assume that you are in the business of writing movie scripts. Your agent contacts the head of development at Wide Angle Cinema and offers to sell Wide Angle your new script. Wide Angle likes your script and agrees to pay you $5,000 for a six-

month option. In this situation, you (through your agent) are the offeror, and Wide Angle is the offeree. You cannot revoke your offer to sell Wide Angle your script for the next six months. If after six months Wide Angle has not accepted your offer, however, Wide Angle loses the $5,000, and you are free to sell the script to another firm.

Generally, the death or incompetence of either party does not terminate a valid executory contract or an irrevocable offer; thus, the death of the offeror or offeree does not terminate an option contract.[11] Assume, for example, that Korell executes an option to Acoba entitling Acoba to purchase Korell's two-hundred-acre pineapple farm in Hawaii. Acoba pays $750 for the option, but before he can exercise it, Korell dies. Acoba can still exercise the option and accept Korell's offer, thus binding Korell's estate to the contract.

*Detrimental Reliance.*  When the offeree justifiably relies on an offer to his or her detriment, the court may hold that this *detrimental reliance* makes the offer irrevocable. For example, assume that Arenella has rented commercial property from Jake for the past thirty-three years under a series of five-year leases. Under business conditions existing as their seventh lease nears its end, the rental property market is more favorable for tenants than landlords. Arenella tells Jake that she is going to look at other, less expensive properties as possible sites for her business. Wanting Arenella to remain a tenant, Jake promises to reduce the rent in their next lease. In reliance on the promise, Arenella does not look at other sites but continues to occupy and do business on Jake's property. When they sit down to negotiate a new lease, however, Jake says he has changed his mind and will increase the rent. Can he effectively revoke his promise?

Normally, he cannot, because Arenella has been relying on his promise to reduce the rent. Had the promise not been made, she would have relocated her business. This is a case of detrimental reliance on a promise, which therefore cannot be revoked. The situation is normally called **promissory estoppel.** To **estop** means to bar, impede, or preclude from doing something. Thus, promissory estoppel means that the promisor (the offeror) is barred from revoking the offer, in this case because the offeree has already changed her

---

11.  Restatement (Second) of Contracts, Section 37.

actions in reliance on the offer. We look again at the doctrine of promissory estoppel in Chapter 13, in the context of consideration.

Detrimental reliance on the part of the offeree can also involve partial performance by the offeree in response to an offer looking toward formulation of a unilateral contract. As discussed in Chapter 11, the offer to form a unilateral contract invites acceptance only by full performance; merely promising to perform does not constitute acceptance. Injustice can result if an offeree expends time and money in partial performance, and then the offeror revokes the offer before performance can be completed. Many courts will not allow the offeror to revoke the offer after the offeree has performed some substantial part of his or her duties.[12] In effect, partial performance renders the offer irrevocable, giving the original offeree reasonable time to complete performance. Of course, once the performance is complete, a unilateral contract exists.

### REJECTION OF THE OFFER BY THE OFFEREE

The offer may be rejected by the offeree, in which case the offer is terminated. Any subsequent attempt by the offeree to accept will be construed as a new offer, giving the original offeror (now the offeree) the power of acceptance. A rejection is ordinarily accomplished by words or conduct evidencing an intent not to accept the offer. As with revocation, rejection of an offer is effective only when it is actually received by the offeror or the offeror's agent.

Merely inquiring about an offer does not constitute rejection. Suppose that a friend offers to buy your bicycle for $75, and you respond, "Is that your best offer?" or "Will you pay me $100 for it?" A reasonable person would conclude that you had not rejected the offer but that you had merely made an inquiry for further consideration of the offer. You can still accept and bind your friend to the $75 purchase price. When the offeree merely inquires as to the firmness of the offer, there is no reason to presume that he or she intends to reject it.

Some responses are borderline in nature, however. For example, suppose you respond to your friend's offer with, "The price seems low. I'll bet you can do better than that." It could be argued that you are merely inquiring about the offer,

but it could also be argued that you are rejecting the offer.

**COUNTEROFFER BY THE OFFEREE**   A rejection of the original offer and the simultaneous making of a new offer is called a **counteroffer.** Suppose Duffy offers to sell her home to Wong for $120,000. Wong responds, "Your price is too high. I'll offer to purchase your house for $100,000." Wong's response is a counteroffer, because it terminates Duffy's offer to sell at $120,000 and creates a new offer by Wong to purchase at $100,000.

At common law, the **mirror image rule** requires the offeree's acceptance to match the offeror's offer exactly—to mirror the offer. Any material change in, or addition to, the terms of the original offer automatically terminates that offer and substitutes the counteroffer. The counteroffer, of course, need not be accepted; but if the original offeror does accept the terms of the counteroffer, a valid contract is created.[13]

It is possible for an offeree to make a new offer without intending to reject the original offer. In such a case, two offers exist, each capable of being accepted. To illustrate, suppose Weinberg offers to sell her bicycle for $125. Dorazy's response is, "I do not have $125 now, but I will try to raise that sum. I do have $100 and offer to purchase your bicycle for that price." Since Dorazy, the offeree, did not reject the $125 offer, that offer remains alive. But Dorazy's offer to purchase the bicycle for only $100 has not been rejected. Therefore two offers exist simultaneously, and the first to be accepted will bind the parties to a contract for that amount.

### TERMINATION BY OPERATION OF LAW

The power of the offeree to transform the offer into a binding, legal obligation can be terminated by operation of the law through the occurrence of the following events:

1.   Lapse of time.
2.   Destruction of the subject matter of the offer.

---

12.   Restatement (Second) of Contracts, Section 25.

13.   The mirror image rule has been greatly modified in regard to sales contracts. Section 2–207 of the UCC provides that a contract is formed if the offeree makes a definite expression of acceptance (such as signing the form in the appropriate location), even though the terms of the acceptance modify or add to the terms of the original offer (see Chapter 20).

**3.** Death or incompetence of the offeror or the offeree.

**4.** Supervening illegality of the proposed contract.

**LAPSE OF TIME**  An offer terminates automatically by law when the period of time specified in the offer has passed. For example, suppose Alejandro offers to sell her camper to Kelly if he accepts within twenty days. Kelly must accept within the twenty-day period, or the offer will lapse (terminate). The time period specified in an offer normally begins to run when the offer is actually received by the offeree, not when it is sent or drawn up. When the offer is delayed (through the misdelivery of mail, for example), the period begins to run from the date the offeree would have received the offer, but only if the offeree knows or should know that the offer is delayed.[14]

If no time for acceptance is specified in the offer, the offer terminates at the end of a *reasonable* period of time. What constitutes a reasonable period of time depends on the subject matter of the contract, business and market conditions, and other relevant circumstances. An offer to sell farm produce, for example, will terminate sooner than an offer to sell farm equipment because farm produce is perishable and subject to greater fluctuations in market value.

**DESTRUCTION OF THE SUBJECT MATTER**  An offer is automatically terminated if the specific subject matter of the offer is destroyed before the offer is accepted.[15] If Johnson offers to sell his prize greyhound to Rizzo, for example, but the dog dies before Rizzo can accept, the offer is automatically terminated. Johnson does not have to tell Rizzo that the animal has died for the offer to terminate.

**DEATH OR INCOMPETENCE OF THE OFFEROR OR OFFEREE**  An offeree's power of acceptance is terminated when the offeror or offeree dies or is deprived of legal capacity to enter into the proposed contract.[16] An offer is personal to both parties and cannot pass to the decedent's heirs, guardian, or estate. Furthermore, this rule applies whether or not the other party had notice of the death or incompetence.

There are exceptions to the rule that the death of either the offeror or the offeree before acceptance terminates an offer. For example, an irrevocable offer, such as an option contract, cannot legally be withdrawn by the offeror once made. Also, if the offer is such that it can be accepted by the performance of a series of acts, and those acts began before the offeror died, the offeree's power of acceptance is not terminated.

**SUPERVENING ILLEGALITY OF THE PROPOSED CONTRACT**  When a statute or court decision makes an offer illegal, the offer is automatically terminated.[17] For example, Enker offers to loan Falcone $10,000 at an annual interest rate of 12 percent. Before Falcone can accept the offer, a law is enacted which prohibits interest rates higher than 8 percent. Enker's offer is automatically terminated. If the law had been passed after Falcone accepted the offer, a valid contract would have been formed, because the offer would still have been legal when it was accepted. In some circumstances, such a contract might be unenforceable, however, as when a statute or law is retroactively applied.

## SECTION 4

# ACCEPTANCE

**Acceptance** is a voluntary act (either words or conduct) by the offeree that shows assent (agreement) to the terms of an offer. The acceptance must be unequivocal and communicated to the offeror.

## UNEQUIVOCAL ACCEPTANCE

To exercise the power of acceptance effectively, the offeree must accept unequivocally. This is the *mirror image rule* previously discussed. If the acceptance is subject to new conditions or if the terms of the acceptance materially change the original offer, the acceptance may be deemed a counteroffer that implicitly rejects the original offer. An acceptance may be unequivocal even though the offeree expresses dissatisfaction with the contract. For example, ''I accept the offer, but I wish I could have gotten a better price'' is an effective acceptance.

---

14. Restatement (Second) of Contracts, Section 49.
15. Restatement (Second) of Contracts, Section 36.
16. Restatement (Second) of Contracts, Section 48.
17. Restatement (Second) of Contracts, Section 36.

# ■ CONCEPT SUMMARY 12.1 **Methods by Which an Offer Can Be Terminated**

| METHODS OF TERMINATION | BASIC RULES |
|---|---|
| **BY ACTS OF THE PARTIES** | |
| Revocation | 1. An offer can be revoked at any time before acceptance without liability unless the offer is irrevocable. |
| | 2. Option contracts, merchants' firm offers, and, in some circumstances, the promissory estoppel theory render offers irrevocable. |
| | 3. Except for public offers, revocation is not effective until received by the offeree or the offeree's authorized agent. |
| Rejection | 1. Rejection of an offer is accomplished by words or actions that demonstrate a clear intent not to accept or consider the offer further. Inquiries about an offer do not constitute a rejection. |
| | 2. A rejection is not effective until received by the offeror or an authorized agent of the offeror. |
| Counteroffer | A counteroffer is a rejection of the original offer and the making of a new offer. Inquiries are not rejections. |
| **BY OPERATION OF LAW** | |
| Lapse of Time | 1. If a time period for acceptance is stated in the offer, the offer ends at the stated time. |
| | 2. If no time period for acceptance is stated, the offer terminates at the end of a reasonable period. |
| Destruction | Destruction of the specific subject matter of the offer terminates the offer. |
| Death or Incompetence | Death or incompetence of either the offeror or offeree terminates an offer, unless the offer is irrevocable. |
| Illegality | Supervening illegality terminates an offer. |

So, too, is "I accept, but can you shave the price?" In contrast, the statement "I accept the offer but only if I can pay on ninety days' credit" is not an unequivocal acceptance and operates as a counteroffer, rejecting the original offer.

Certain terms when added to an acceptance will not qualify the acceptance sufficiently to constitute rejection of the offer. Suppose that in response to a person offering to sell a piano, the offeree replies, "I accept; please send written contract." The offeree is requesting a written contract but is not making it a condition for acceptance. Therefore, the acceptance is effective without the written contract. If the offeree replies, "I accept if you send a written contract," however, the acceptance is expressly conditioned on the request for a writing,

and the statement is not an acceptance but a counteroffer. (Notice how important each word is!)[18]

In the following case, the offeree accepted an offer but also returned to the offeror a separate document entitled "Acceptance and Counteroffer" that stipulated certain conditions of sale not contained in the offeror's offer. In this situation, has the offeree accepted the offer or made a counteroffer?

---

18. As noted in footnote 13, in regard to sales contracts, the UCC provides that an acceptance may still be valid even if some terms are added. The new terms are simply treated as proposals for addition to the contract.

**BACKGROUND AND FACTS** *Dominic Meyer, after seeing a "For Sale" sign on the plaintiffs' property and conducting a title search, offered to buy the property for $250,000. Meyer's offer read, in part, as follows: "Seller has ten (10) days from the date hereof to accept the offer." The plaintiffs (including the estate of Bernice Chosnyka) returned a signed copy of the agreement to Meyer the next day. Along with the signed offer, they returned to Meyer a document entitled "Acceptance and Counteroffer," which stated that their acceptance included these conditions: (1) the closing date was to be no later than sixty days from the date of acceptance, and (2) although the legal description of the property was accurate, the true number of acres had not been ascertained. Partly because the land was not warranted to be exactly ninety-five acres (the "For Sale" sign stated that "ninety-five acres" were for sale), Meyer told the real estate broker that he was withdrawing his offer. The plaintiffs, alleging that a contract of sale had been formed between them and Meyer, sued Meyer for $50,000 in damages, the difference between the contract price and the eventual selling price of the property. The trial court found for the plaintiffs, and Meyer appealed.*

**CASE 12.3**

**CHOSNYKA v. MEYER**
Appellate Court of Illinois,
Fifth District, 1992.
223 Ill.App.3d 493,
585 N.E.2d 204,
165 Ill.Dec. 808.

Justice *HOWERTON* delivered the opinion of the court:
\* \* \* \*

Defendant's first claim on appeal is that the document entitled "Acceptance and Counteroffer" was not a valid acceptance but a counteroffer that he never accepted.
\* \* \* We hold \* \* \* that plaintiffs' "Acceptance and Counteroffer" had, as a matter of law, no effect on the terms of the contract. It had no effect precisely because plaintiffs had accepted defendant's offer by signing and returning it to defendant within 10 days as dictated by the offer.
\* \* \* \*

Defendant argues secondly that since the acreage to be conveyed was not warranted to be 95 acres, mutual assent was destroyed. We disagree.
\* \* \* \*

In Illinois, the established rule "is that where a tract of land is conveyed by proper description, the boundaries thus included will control as to the quantity of acres \* \* \*. The mention of acres, in such a case, has no legal effect." \* \* \*
\* \* \* Unless the discrepancy in acreage is significant to its use and its potential, therefore, the law will find a meeting of the minds and will grant no remedy. Here, the acreage discrepancy is small and does not interfere with defendant's planned use as a mobile home park. Therefore, the discrepancy does not destroy mutual assent.

*The appellate court affirmed the trial court's ruling. A valid contract existed between Meyer and the sellers.*

**DECISION
AND REMEDY**

**Qualified Acceptance in France** *French law permits an acceptance to depart somewhat from the offer, without destroying the existence of a contract. France looks to whether the new or different terms are "nonessential." If so, a contract is still formed, and the courts resolve what terms are included. This approach is formally different from that used in the* Chosnyka *case but substantively very similar.*

**INTERNATIONAL
CONSIDERATIONS**

## SILENCE AS ACCEPTANCE

Ordinarily, silence cannot constitute acceptance, even if the offeror states, ''By your silence and inaction you will be deemed to have accepted this offer.'' This general rule applies because an offeree should not be obligated to act affirmatively to reject an offer when no consideration has passed to the offeree to impose such a duty.

In some instances, however, the offeree does have a duty to speak, in which case his or her silence or inaction will operate as an acceptance. For example, silence may be an acceptance when an offeree takes the benefit of offered services even though he or she had an opportunity to reject them and knew that they were offered with the expectation of compensation. Suppose that Sayre watches while a stranger rakes his leaves, even though the stranger has not been asked to rake the yard. Sayre knows the stranger expects to be paid and does nothing to stop her. Here, his silence con-

stitutes an acceptance, and an implied-in-fact contract is created. He is bound to pay a reasonable value for the stranger's work. This rule normally applies only when the offeree has received a benefit from the goods or services rendered.

Silence can also operate as acceptance when the offeree has had prior dealings with the offeror. Suppose that a merchant routinely receives shipments from a certain supplier and always notifies the supplier when defective goods are rejected. In this situation, silence regarding a shipment will constitute acceptance. Also, if a person solicits an offer specifying that certain terms and conditions are acceptable, and the offeror makes the offer in response to the solicitation, the offeree has a duty to reject—that is, a duty to tell the offeror that the offer is not acceptable. Failure to reject (silence) operates as an acceptance. The following case illustrates a situation in which the silence of the offeree operated as an acceptance.

---

| CASE 12.4 |
| :---: |

### FEIST & FEIST REALTY CORP. v. DOCKSIDE URBAN RENEWAL CORP.

Superior Court of New Jersey, 1992.
255 N.J.Super. 100, 604 A.2d 653.

**COMPANY PROFILE**   *In 1959, Sol Ganz founded the New York Bronze Powder Company in a Brooklyn garage with an investment of $2,500. Over the next twenty-five years, the company became a developer of spray paint and expanded to employ more than 350 people at factories and distribution centers in New Jersey, Pennsylvania, Texas, Illinois, and California. In 1983, New York Bronze was bought by Novo Corporation, which was involved primarily in the distribution of motion pictures and television programs, satellite communications, computer data management, and energy conservation. By 1985, Novo had become a leading manufacturer of home improvement and do-it-yourself products. On the night of February 21, 1985, in a three-block-long warehouse in Elizabeth, New Jersey, where New York Bronze stored aerosol paint cans, a power surge in a circuit breaker box sparked a fire. As the blaze intensified, the warehouse exploded, and multicolored fireballs shot 1,000 feet into the air. Newark International Airport and the New Jersey Turnpike were temporarily closed, residents were evacuated, and fire boats cruised nearby to protect passing ships. It took firefighters fourteen hours to control the fire, which continued to smolder for four days. Eventually, the fire would lead to the then-largest single-site fire damage settlement in history. In 1985, however, New York Bronze was concerned with finding another location in the area from which to continue its business.*

**BACKGROUND AND FACTS**   *Feist & Feist Realty Corporation sought rental premises for a tenant, the New York Bronze Powder Company. Feist introduced New York Bronze to a location in Newark owned by Dockside Urban Renewal Corporation. After showing the premises to New York Bronze, Feist sent the owner of Dockside a letter on December 18, by certified mail, advising the owner that if Dockside succeeded in leasing its property to New York Bronze, Feist would be entitled to a commission* *equal to 5 percent of the gross rental. Dockside acknowledged the receipt of the letter on December 19, 1985, and began negotiating with New York Bronze. A lease was formed between Dockside and New York Bronze on April 28, 1986. The total amount of the rent was $12,941,250 for a ten-year period, and the lease acknowledged that Feist had been "instrumental in consummating this lease." The lease further stated that Dockside would "satisfy any commissions due to Feist & Feist by a separate agreement." After the lease was signed, Feist demanded payment of its commission of $647,062 (5 percent of $12,941,250). When Dockside failed to respond to this letter and subsequent demands for payment, Feist sued. Dockside claimed that it had never contracted with Feist to pay Feist a commission.*

*FUENTES*, J.S.C. [Judge of the Superior Court]
\* \* \* \*

Defendant's claim that there was no agreement as to the specific commission and that the amount was to be resolved by "separate agreement" is \* \* \* unconvincing. First, it is significant to note that the lease itself recognizes that Feist was "instrumental in consummating" the lease. Thus, Dockside specifically acknowledged the broker's role in procuring the tenant. Further, I find, the phrase "by separate agreement" in the lease in fact refers to the broker's certified letter which presented the tenant in consideration of the commission. \* \* \* Dockside acknowledged receipt of the letter and accepted the tenant under the conditions stated. At no time did Dockside terminate the broker's involvement or repudiate the terms of the agreement. \* \* \* In fact, defendant had a period of just over four months in which to repudiate the agreement prior to negotiating the lease.

Several authorities [including the Restatement (Second) of Contracts, Section 69(1)] make it clear that where a party fails to repudiate an offer or remains silent and then accepts the benefit of the offer, the party may be deemed to have accepted the contract terms.

*The court held that a contract had been formed and Dockside was obligated to pay Feist the commission.*

**DECISION AND REMEDY**

## COMMUNICATION OF ACCEPTANCE

Whether the offeror must be notified of the acceptance depends on the nature of the contract. In a bilateral contract, communication of acceptance is necessary because acceptance is in the form of a promise (not performance) and the contract is formed when the promise is made (rather than when the act is performed). The offeree must communicate the acceptance to the offeror. Communication of acceptance is not necessary, however, if the offer dispenses with the requirement. Also, if the offer can be accepted by silence, no communication is necessary.

Because in a unilateral contract the full performance of some act is called for, acceptance is usually evident, and notification is therefore unnecessary. Exceptions do exist, however. When the offeror requests notice of acceptance or has no ad-

equate means of determining whether the requested act has been performed, or when the law requires notice of acceptance, then notice is necessary.[19]

## MODE AND TIMELINESS OF ACCEPTANCE IN BILATERAL CONTRACTS

Acceptance in bilateral contracts must be timely. The general rule is that acceptance in a bilateral

---

19. Under UCC 2–206(1)(b), an order or other offer to buy goods for prompt shipment may be treated as an offer contemplating either a bilateral or a unilateral contract and may be accepted by either a promise to ship or actual shipment. If the offer is accepted by actual shipment of the goods, the offeror must be notified of the acceptance within a reasonable period of time or the offeror may treat the offer as having lapsed before acceptance [UCC 2–206(2)]. See also Chapter 20.

contract is timely if it is made before the offer is terminated.

Problems arise, however, when the parties involved are not dealing face to face. In such cases, the offeree may use an authorized mode of communication. Acceptance takes effect, thus completing formation of the contract, at the time the communication is sent via the mode expressly or impliedly authorized by the offeror. This is the so-called **mailbox rule,** also called the ''deposited acceptance rule,'' which the majority of courts uphold. Under this rule, if the authorized mode of communication is the mail, then an acceptance becomes valid when it is dispatched (even if it is never received by the offeror).

Thus, whereas a revocation becomes effective only when it is *received* by the offeree, an acceptance becomes effective upon *dispatch*, providing that *authorized* means of communication are used. Authorized means of communication may be either expressly authorized—that is, expressly stipulated in the offer—or impliedly authorized by facts or law.

**AUTHORIZED MEANS OF ACCEPTANCE**   When an offeror specifies how acceptance should be made (for example, by overnight delivery), *express authorization* is said to exist, and the contract is not formed unless the offeree uses that specified mode of acceptance. Moreover, both offeror and offeree are bound in contract the moment such means of acceptance are employed. If overnight delivery is expressly authorized as the only means of acceptance, a contract is created as soon as the offeree delivers the message to the express delivery company. The contract would still exist even if the delivery company failed to deliver the message.

Most offerors, for one reason or another, do not indicate their preferred method of acceptance. When the offeror does not specify expressly that the offeree is to accept by a certain means, or that the acceptance will be effective only when received, acceptance of an offer may be made by any medium that is *reasonable under the circumstances*.[20] When two parties are at a distance, for example, mailing is impliedly authorized because it is a customary mode of dispatch.[21] Several factors determine whether the acceptance was reasonable: the nature of the circumstances as they existed at the time the offer was made, the means used by the offeror to transmit the offer to the offeree, and the reliability of the offer's delivery. If, for example, an offer was sent by Federal Express overnight delivery because an acceptance was required urgently, then the offeree's attempt to accept via first-class mail (which may take three days or more to deliver) might not be deemed reasonable.[22]

An acceptance sent by means not expressly or impliedly authorized is normally not effective until it is received by the offeror. If an acceptance is timely sent and timely received, however, despite the means by which it is sent, it is considered to have been effective on its dispatch.[23] If, in the previous example, the acceptance that was sent by first-class mail was actually delivered to the offeror the next day (the same as Federal Express overnight delivery), then the court would recognize the acceptance as operative.

**EXCEPTIONS**   There are three basic exceptions to the rule that a contract is formed when acceptance is sent by authorized means:

1.  If the acceptance is not properly dispatched by the offeree (if it was sent to an incorrect address, for example), in most states it will not be effective until it is received by the offeror.[24] For example, if mail is the authorized means for acceptance, the offeree's letter must be properly addressed and have the correct postage. If acceptance is timely sent and timely received, however, despite carelessness in sending it, it is considered to have been effective on dispatch.[25]

2.  The offeror can stipulate in the offer that an acceptance will not be effective until it is received by the offeror.

3.  Sometimes an offeree sends a rejection first, then later changes his or her mind and sends an acceptance. Obviously, this chain of events

---

20.  Restatement (Second) of Contracts, Section 30. This is also the rule under UCC 2–206(1)(a).

21.  *Adams v. Lindsell,* 106 Eng.Rep. 250 (K.B. 1818); Restatement (Second) of Contracts, Section 65, Comment c.

22.  See, for example, *Defeo v. Amfarms Associates,* 161 A.D.2d 904, 557 N.Y.2d 469 (1990).

23.  Restatement (Second) of Contracts, Section 67.

24.  Restatement (Second) of Contracts, Section 66.

25.  Restatement (Second) of Contracts, Section 67.

# ■ CONCEPT SUMMARY 12.2 **Effective Time of Acceptance**

| ACCEPTANCE | TIME EFFECTIVE |
|---|---|
| **By Authorized Means of Communication** | Effective at the time communication is sent via the mode expressly or impliedly authorized by the offeror (mailbox rule).<br>*Exceptions:*<br>1. If the acceptance is not properly dispatched.<br>2. If the offeror specifically conditioned offer on receipt of acceptance.<br>3. If acceptance is sent after rejection, whichever is received first is given effect. |
| **By Unauthorized Means of Communication** | Effective upon receipt of acceptance by the offeror (if timely received, it is considered to have been effective on dispatch). |

could cause confusion and even detriment to the offeror, depending on whether the rejection or the acceptance arrived first. Because of this, the law cancels the rule of acceptance upon dispatch in such situations, and the *first* communication to be received by the offeror determines whether a contract is formed. If the rejection is received first, there is no contract.[26]

---

26.  Restatement (Second) of Contracts, Section 40.

■

# TERMS AND CONCEPTS TO REVIEW

acceptance **239**                mailbox rule **244**            option contract **237**
agreement **230**                 mirror image rule **238**       promissory estoppel **237**
counteroffer **238**              mutual assent **231**           revocation **236**
estop **237**                     offer **231**

■

# QUESTIONS AND CASE PROBLEMS

**12–1. Offer and Acceptance.** Ball writes Sullivan and inquires how much Sullivan is asking for a specific forty-acre tract of land Sullivan owns. In a letter received by Ball, Sullivan states, "I will not take less than $60,000 for the forty-acre tract as specified." Ball immediately sends Sullivan a telegram stating, "I accept your offer for $60,000." Discuss whether Ball can hold Sullivan to a contract for sale of the land.

**12–2. Acceptance.** Sachs, operating a sole proprietorship, has a large piece of used farm equipment for sale. He offers to sell the equipment to Barry for $10,000. Discuss the legal effects of the following events on the offer.

(a) Sachs dies prior to Barry's acceptance, and at the time he accepts, Barry is unaware of Sachs's death.

(b) The night before Barry accepts, fire destroys the equipment.

(c) Barry pays $100 for a thirty-day option to purchase the equipment. During this period Sachs dies, and later Barry accepts the offer, knowing of Sachs's death.

(d) Barry pays $100 for a thirty-day option to purchase the equipment. During this period Barry dies, and Barry's estate accepts Sachs's offer within the stipulated time period.

**12–3. Offer and Acceptance.** Perez sees an advertisement in the newspaper that the ABC Corp. has for sale a two-volume set of books, *How to Make Repairs around the House,* for $22.95. All Perez has to do is send in a card requesting delivery of the books for a thirty-day trial period of examination. If he does not ship the books back within thirty days of delivery, ABC will bill him for $22.95. Discuss whether or not Perez and ABC have a contract under either of the following circumstances.

(a) Perez sends in the card and receives the books in the U.S. mail. He uses the books to make repairs and fails to return them within thirty days.

(b) Perez does not send in the card, but ABC sends him the books anyway through the U.S. mail. Perez uses the books and fails to return them within thirty days.

**12–4. Revocation.** On Thursday, Dennis mailed Tanya a letter offering to sell his car to her for $3,000. On Saturday, having changed his mind, Dennis sent a fax to Tanya's office revoking his offer. Tanya did not go to her office over the weekend and thus did not learn about the revocation until Monday morning, just a few minutes after she had mailed a letter of acceptance to Dennis. When Tanya demanded that Dennis sell his car to her as promised, Dennis claimed that no contract existed because he had revoked his offer prior to Tanya's acceptance. Is Dennis correct? Explain.

**12–5. Revocation.** Dodds signed and delivered to Dickinson the following memorandum on Wednesday, June 10:

I hereby agree to sell to Mr. George Dickinson the whole of the dwelling-houses, garden ground, stabling, and outbuildings thereto belonging, situated at Croft, belonging to me, for the sum of £800 [£ is the symbol for British pounds]. As witness my hand this tenth day of June, 1874.

£800 [signed] John Dodds.

P.S. This offer to be left over until Friday, 9 o'clock A.M. (the twelfth) 12th June, 1874
[Signed] J. Dodds.

The next afternoon (Thursday), Dickinson's agent told Dickinson that Dodds had decided to sell the property to a man named Allan and was negotiating with Allan for that purpose. That evening, Dickinson went to the house of Dodds's mother-in-law and left her a written acceptance. This document never reached Dodds. The next morning, at 7 A.M., Dickinson's agent gave Dodds a copy of the acceptance. Dodds replied that it was too late, as he had already sold the property. Did Dickinson's knowledge that Dodds was negotiating to sell the property to Allan revoke Dodds's offer to Dickinson? Explain. [*Dickinson v. Dodds,* 2 Ch.D. 463 (1876)]

**12–6. Offer and Acceptance.** Central Properties entered into a contract with Robbinson and Westside (Westside), a real estate development company, whereby Central Properties purchased sixty acres of land. The contract included a "right of first refusal" to purchase the water and sewage system on the remaining property of Westside. Westside wanted to sell the sewage system and over the course of three months exchanged letters with Central asking whether it wished to exercise its "right." Central Properties never affirmatively accepted in any of its responses but requested different terms, prices, and so on. Central now wishes to hold Westside to a contract for the system. Westside states that no contract was formed. Discuss who is right. [*Central Properties, Inc. v. Robbinson,* 450 So.2d 277 (Fla.App. 1st Dist. 1984)]

**12–7. Intent of Offeror.** Treece, a vice president of Vend-A-Win, Inc., was testifying before the Washington State Gambling Commission concerning an application his firm had made for a temporary license to distribute punchboards (gambling devices). The Gambling Commission was conducting an investigation into gambling practices, and Treece's testimony was given during a televised hearing. Treece made the following statement at the hearing: "I'll pay $100,000 to anyone to find a crooked board. If they find it, I'll pay it." The audience laughed, and Treece thought no more about the offer until he received a telephone call from Barnes. Barnes had watched Treece's television appearance and later read about Treece's statement in a newspaper. Barnes asked Treece if Treece had been serious when he made the statement, and Treece affirmed that he had been serious. Barnes then brought a crooked board into Vend-A-Win's offices and delivered another crooked board to the Gambling Commission. When Vend-A-Win and Treece refused to pay Barnes $100,000, Barnes sued them for the promised amount, claiming that Treece had made an offer for a unilateral contract. What will the court decide? Explain. [*Barnes v. Treece,* 15 Wash.App. 437, 549 P.2d 1152 (1976)]

**12–8. Offer and Acceptance.** James sent invitations to a number of potential buyers to submit bids for some timber he wanted to sell. Two bids were received as a result; the higher bid was submitted by Eames. James changed his mind about selling the timber, however, and did not accept Eames's bid. Eames claimed that a contract for sale existed and sued James for breach. Did a contract exist? Discuss. [*Eames v. James,* 452 So.2d 384 (La.App. 3d Cir. 1984)]

**12–9. Advertisements as Offers.** On July 31, 1966, Lee Calan Imports (the defendant) advertised a 1964 Volvo station wagon for sale in the Chicago *Sun Times.* The defendant had instructed the newspaper to advertise the price of the automobile at $1,795. Through an error of the newspaper, however, and without fault on the part of the defendant, the newspaper inserted a price of $1,095 for the automobile in the advertisement. Christopher O'Brien (the plaintiff) visited the defendant's place of business, examined the automobile, and stated that he wished to purchase it for $1,095. One of the defendant's sales agents at first agreed, but then refused to sell the car for the erroneous price listed in the advertisement. O'Brien sued Lee Calan Imports for breach of contract, claiming the ad constituted an offer that had been accepted by O'Brien. O'Brien died before the trial, and his administrator (O'Keefe) continued the suit. Discuss whether there is a contract. [*O'Keefe v. Lee Calan Imports, Inc.,* 128 Ill.App.2d 410, 262 N.E.2d 758 (1970)]

**12–10. Mode and Timeliness of Acceptance.** In August 1984, James and Barbara Gibbs submitted an offer of $180,000 to American Savings & Loan Association to purchase a house. The Gibbses submitted another offer on March 27, 1985, after learning from an American Savings employee, Dorothy Folkman, that their original offer had been lost. On the morning of June 6, 1985, the Gibbses received a counteroffer from American Savings containing several additional terms and conditions, but nothing was mentioned about the purchase price. Barbara Gibbs later claimed that she and her husband immediately signed the counteroffer—which American Savings had requested her to do if she wished to accept it—and at 10 A.M. on that same day handed an envelope containing the signed counteroffer to the mail clerk at her office, with instructions to mail it for her. (The mail clerk was not an employee of the U.S. Postal Service but an employee of Barbara's firm who handled the firm's mail.) An hour later, at 11 A.M., Barbara had a telephone conversation with Dorothy Folkman in which Folkman said that the counteroffer was in error, because American Savings had intended to increase the sales price to $198,000. Folkman said that because of this error the counteroffer was revoked. The Gibbses insisted that they had accepted the counteroffer before it was revoked. The trial court held that no contract had been formed because the actual postmark on the envelope was not June 6 but June 7. The Gibbses appealed, contending that they had placed the acceptance in the "course of transmission" at 10 A.M. on June 6 when Barbara handed the letter to the mail clerk in her office. Does handing the counteroffer to the mail clerk in her office constitute dispatch by mail in this case? Discuss. [*Gibbs v. American Savings & Loan Association,* 217 Cal.App.3d 1372, 266 Cal.Rptr. 517 (1990)]

**12–11. Offers versus Nonoffers.** Chia and Shin Chang read First Colonial Bank's advertisement about the bank's saving certificates, which stated that a depositor could deposit $14,000, receive a gift immediately, and collect $20,136.12 in three and a half years when the certificate matured. The Changs, in reliance on the ad, deposited $14,000 at First Colonial and received a color television and a certificate of deposit. When they cashed in the certificate upon its maturity, however, they received only $18,823.93 instead of the promised $20,136.12. First Colonial informed the Changs that the advertisement had contained a typographical error and that they would have had to deposit $15,000, not $14,000, to receive $20,136.12. The Changs filed suit to recover $1,312.19, the difference between the amount they received and the amount they had expected. Did the newspaper advertisement constitute an offer that, when accepted, created a legally enforceable contract? Explain. [*Chang v. First Colonial Savings Bank,* 242 Va. 388, 410 S.E.2d 928 (1991)]

# CHAPTER 13

# CONSIDERATION

The fact that a promise has been made does not mean the promise can or will be enforced. Under Roman law, a promise was not enforceable without some sort of *causa*—that is, a reason for making the promise that was also deemed to be a sufficient reason for enforcing it. Since the beginning of the common law tradition in England, good reasons for enforcing informal promises have been held to include something given as an agreed exchange, a benefit that the promisor received, and a detriment that the promisee incurred. Over time, these reasons came to be referred to legally as ''consideration.''

Thus, for centuries, it has been said that no informal promise is enforceable without consideration. **Consideration** is usually defined as the value (such as money) given in return for a promise (such as the promise to sell a stereo upon receipt of payment). Often, consideration is broken down into two parts: (1) something of *legal value* must be given in exchange for the promise, and (2) there must be a *bargained-for* exchange. The ''something of legal value'' may consist of a return promise that is bargained for. If it consists of performance, that performance may be (1) an act (other than a promise); (2) a forbearance (a refraining from action); or (3) the creation, modification, or destruction of a legal relation.[1]

For example, Anita says to her son, ''When you finish painting the garage, I will pay you $100.'' Anita's son paints the garage. The act of painting the garage is the consideration that creates the contractual obligation of Anita to pay her son $100. Suppose, however, that Anita says to her son, ''In consideration of the fact that you are not as wealthy as your brothers, I will pay you $500.'' This promise is not enforceable, because Anita's son has not given any consideration for the $500 promised.[2] Anita has simply stated her motive for giving her son a gift. The fact that the word *consideration* is used does not, alone, mean that consideration has been given.

---

1. Restatement (Second) of Contracts, Section 71.
2. See *Fink v. Cox,* 18 Johns. 145, 9 Am.Dec. 191 (N.Y. 1820).

# LEGAL SUFFICIENCY OF CONSIDERATION

To create a binding contract, consideration must be legally sufficient. To be *legally sufficient,* consideration for a promise must be either *legally detrimental to the promisee* (the one receiving the promise) or *legally beneficial to the promisor* (the one making the promise). Note that legal detriment is not synonymous with actual (economic) detriment. A person can incur legal detriment in either of two ways: (1) by doing or promising to do something that he or she had no prior legal duty to do or (2) by refraining from or promising to refrain from doing something that he or she had no prior legal duty to refrain from doing (that is, by forbearance).

Suppose that Santana owns the right to use the name ''The Brickhouse Restaurant.'' Katz offers Santana $5,000 to stop using the name for her restaurant, and Santana agrees. The consideration flowing from Santana to Katz is a promise to refrain from doing something that Santana is legally entitled to do—that is, use the name ''The Brickhouse Restaurant'' for her restaurant. The consideration flowing from Katz to Santana is the promise to pay a sum of money that need not otherwise be paid.

The following types of promises are normally unenforceable because they lack sufficient consideration:

1. A promise to perform a preexisting duty (to do something that one already has a duty to do).
2. A promise based on a moral obligation.
3. A promise to perform an act that has already been performed (past consideration).

We discuss each of these types of promises in later sections of this chapter.

In the following case, one of the classics of contract law, the court found that refraining from certain behavior at the request of another was sufficient consideration to support a promise to pay a sum of money.

---

**BACKGROUND AND FACTS** *William E. Story, Sr., was the uncle of William E. Story II. In the presence of family members and guests invited to a family gathering, the elder Story promised to pay his nephew $5,000 if he would refrain from drinking, using tobacco, swearing, and playing cards or billiards for money until he reached the age of twenty-one. (Note that in 1869, when this contract was formed, it was legal in New York to drink and play cards for money prior to the age of twenty-one.) The nephew agreed and fully performed his part of the bargain. When he reached the age of twenty-one, he wrote and told his uncle that he had kept his part of the agreement and was therefore entitled to $5,000. The uncle replied that he was pleased with his nephew's performance, writing, ''I have no doubt but you have, for which you shall have five thousand dollars, as I promised you. I had the money in the bank the day you was twenty-one years old that I intend for you, and you shall have the money certain. . . . P.S. You can consider this money on interest.'' The nephew received his uncle's letter and thereafter consented that the money should remain with his uncle according to the terms and conditions of the letter. The uncle died about twelve years later without having paid his nephew any part of the $5,000 and interest. The executor of the uncle's estate (Sidway, the defendant in this action) did not want to pay the $5,000 (with interest) to Hamer, a third party to whom the nephew had transferred his rights in the note, claiming that there had been no valid consideration for the promise. The court disagreed with the executor and reviewed the doctrine of detriment and benefit as valid consideration under the law.*

**CASE 13.1**

**HAMER v. SIDWAY**
Court of Appeals of New York,
Second Division, 1891.
124 N.Y. 538,
27 N.E. 256.

*PARKER,* J. [Justice]

\*   \*   \*   \*

The defendant contends that the contract was without consideration to support it, and therefore invalid. He asserts that the promisee, by refraining from the use of liquor and tobacco, was not harmed, but benefited; that which he did was best for him to do, independently of his uncle's promise,—and insists that it follows that, unless the promisor was benefited, the contract was without consideration,—a contention which, if well founded, would seem to leave open for controversy in many cases whether that which the promisee did or omitted to do was in fact of such benefit to him as to leave no consideration to support the enforcement of the promisor's agreement. Such a rule could not be tolerated and is without foundation in the law. \*   \*   \* Courts "will not ask whether the thing which forms the consideration does in fact benefit the promisee or a third party, or is of any substantial value to any one. It is enough that something is promised, done, forborne, or suffered by the party to whom the promise is made as consideration for the promise made to him. In general a waiver of any legal right at the request of another party is a sufficient consideration for a promise. Any damage, or suspension, or forbearance of a right will be sufficient to sustain a promise." \*   \*   \* Now, applying this rule to the facts before us, the promisee used tobacco, occasionally drank liquor, and he had a legal right to do so. That right he abandoned for a period of years upon the strength of the promise of the testator that for such forbearance he would give him $5,000. We need not speculate on the effort which may have been required to give up the use of those stimulants. It is sufficient that he restricted his lawful freedom of action within certain prescribed limits upon the faith of his uncle's agreement, and now, having fully performed the conditions imposed, it is of no moment whether such performance actually proved a benefit to the promisor, and the court will not inquire into it; but, were it a proper subject of inquiry, we see nothing in this record that would permit a determination that the uncle was not benefited in a legal sense.

**DECISION AND REMEDY**   *The court ruled that the nephew had provided legally sufficient consideration by giving up smoking, drinking, swearing, and playing cards or billiards for money until he reached the age of twenty-one and was therefore entitled to the money.*

**COMMENTS**   *The* Hamer v. Sidway *case is a good illustration of the distinction between benefits to the promisor and detriment to the promisee. Here the court did not inquire as to whether a benefit had flowed to the promisor but required only that there had been a legally sufficient detriment to the promisee.*

## SECTION 2

# ADEQUACY OF CONSIDERATION

Adequacy of consideration refers to the fairness of the bargain. In general, a court will not question the adequacy of consideration if the consideration is legally sufficient. Under the doctrine of freedom of contract, parties are normally free to bargain as they wish. If people could sue merely because they had entered into an unwise contract, the courts would be overloaded with frivolous suits. In extreme cases, a court of law may consider the adequacy of consideration in terms of its amount or worth because inadequate consideration may indicate fraud, duress, undue influence, or a lack of bargained-for exchange. It may also reflect a party's incompetence (for example, an individual might have been too intoxicated or simply too young to make a contract). Suppose Dylan has a house worth $100,000 and he sells it for $50,000. A $50,000 sale could indicate that the buyer unduly pressured Dylan into selling or that Dylan was defrauded into selling the house at far below market value. (It might also indicate that Dylan was in a hurry to sell.)

In an equity suit, courts will more likely question the adequacy of consideration. (Remember from Chapter 1 that actions at law allow for remedies that consist of some form of compensation. Actions in equity allow for such remedies as specific performance, injunction, and rescission.) In an equity suit, the defendant must show that the transaction was not **unconscionable**[3]—that is, generally speaking, so one sided under the circumstances as to be unfair—and that consideration was exchanged. *Adhesion contracts,* for example, may be held unconscionable. As will be discussed in Chapter 15, these contracts are written for the benefit of one of the contracting parties only—the dominant party. The adhesion contract (ordinarily a form contract) is presented to the other party, who must either agree to the dominant party's terms or put aside the deal. The adhesion contract is characterized by little, if any, actual bargaining between the parties.

As a general principle of contract law, the courts will not attempt to evaluate the adequacy of the consideration in an agreed-upon exchange, unless the consideration is so grossly inadequate as to "shock the conscience" of the court.

SECTION 3

# THE PREEXISTING DUTY RULE

Under most circumstances, a promise to do what one already has a legal duty to do does not constitute legally sufficient consideration, because no legal detriment or benefit has been incurred.[4] The preexisting legal duty may be imposed by law or may arise out of a previous contract. A sheriff, for example, cannot collect a reward for information

leading to the capture of a criminal if the sheriff already has a legal duty to capture the criminal.

Likewise, if a party is already bound by contract to perform a certain duty, that duty cannot serve as consideration for a second contract. For example, suppose that Holcomb Construction, Inc., begins construction on a seven-story office building and after three months demands an extra $80,000 on its contract. If the extra $80,000 is not paid, it will stop working. The owner of the land, having no one else to complete construction, agrees to pay the extra $80,000. The agreement is not enforceable, because it is not supported by legally sufficient consideration; Holcomb Construction was under a preexisting legal duty to complete the building.

## UNFORESEEN DIFFICULTIES

The rule regarding preexisting duty is meant to prevent extortion and the so-called hold-up game. But what happens when an honest contractor runs into extraordinary difficulties that were totally unforeseen at the time the contract was formed?

In the interests of fairness and equity, the courts sometimes allow exceptions to the preexisting duty rule. For example, assume that you hire Carvelli to sink a new well for your rural home. Carvelli estimates that he will have to drill 150 feet down to reach water (the same depth as all of your neighbors' wells) and contracts with you for a price of $1,800. Because of an unusual underground rock formation, however, Carvelli does not reach water until he has drilled 300 feet down, and he seeks an additional $1,200. You agree to the modification of the original contract. Because it was unforeseeable that Carvelli would have to dig so deep to reach water on your property, a court may refrain from applying the preexisting duty rule and enforce the agreement to modify the contract price.

When the "unforeseen difficulties" that give rise to a contract modification are the types of risks ordinarily assumed in business, however, the courts will usually apply the preexisting duty rule. In the above example, a court might conclude that Carvelli, at the time the contract was formed, should have known that he might have to drill more than 150 feet down to reach water and therefore assumed the risk of this possibility.

Cases involving unforeseen difficulties frequently arise under construction contracts and relate particularly to soil conditions. For instance,

---

3. Pronounced un-*kon*-shun-uh-bul.
4. See *Foakes v. Beer,* 9 App.Cas. 605 (1884).

there have been cases in which additional amounts were held payable under contracts to build (1) a drive-in theatre and drainage ditch, when it was discovered that a large amount of fill would have to be purchased elsewhere;[5] (2) a prefabricated building, when it was discovered that different construction materials would have to be used than had originally been contracted for;[6] (3) an embankment at an airstrip, when it was discovered that the soil subsidence was not what had been expected;[7] (4) concrete ramps, when it was discovered that twice as much dirt would have to be moved as had been expected;[8] and (5) a shipping channel, when it was discovered that more dredging would be necessary than had been contemplated.[9]

## RESCISSION AND NEW CONTRACT

The law recognizes that two parties can mutually agree to rescind, or nullify, their contract, at least to the extent that it is executory (still to be carried out). Suppose, for example, that Leon contracts with Anna to purchase Anna's watch for $100. Later, Leon tells Anna that he would prefer not to purchase the watch. As it happens, Anna no longer desires to sell it, so they call off the deal. This is called **rescission,** defined as the unmaking of a contract, in which the parties to it are returned to the positions they occupied before the contract was made.

Now suppose that one day later, Leon decides he really wants the watch and offers to purchase it once again. Anna is willing to sell, but this time for a price of $125. Leon agrees, and a new contract is formed. Similarly, in the Carvelli example above, the landowner and the well digger could arrange to rescind the first contract and agree to a new one that includes the increased payment. Note that in each of these situations there are three separate agreements—the initial agreement, the rescission agreement, and the later agreement. At the time of the later agreement, there are no preexisting duties, because they were discharged by the rescission agreement.

When rescission and the making of a new contract take place at the same time, some courts hold that the new agreement is unenforceable on the ground of insufficient consideration. Other courts consider the timing unimportant, as long as the rescission is express, and hold that the new promises furnish consideration for each other.[10] Still other courts hold that the original consideration carries over into the new agreement.[11] The UCC has resolved the issue by enforcing modifications to contracts for the sale of goods if the modifications were made in good faith.[12]

# MORAL OBLIGATIONS

Promises based on a moral duty or obligation are not enforceable, because a moral obligation does not constitute legally sufficient consideration. Suppose that your friend is injured in a distant city and a grocer takes care of him during his recovery. Thereafter, feeling a moral obligation to help your friend and aid the grocer, you promise the grocer to pay for your friend's expenses. The promise is unenforceable because it is supported only by your moral obligation—you have received no material benefit that would support an action by the grocer to recover from you his expenses in caring for your friend. (The grocer might recover from your friend the reasonable value of his services in *quantum meruit,* however—see Chapter 11.)

Another example of a promise made out of a moral obligation is a promise to pay the debts of one's parents or a promise to pay for the care rendered to relatives one was under no duty to support. A minority of states enforce such promises supported only by a moral obligation—but only to the extent of the actual obligation or of the services or care rendered.[13]

---

5. *Evergreen Amusement Corp. v. Milstead,* 206 Md. 610, 112 A.2d 901 (1955).
6. *Lange v. United States,* 120 F.2d 886 (4th Cir. 1941).
7. *Healy v. Brewster,* 251 Cal.App.2d 541, 59 Cal.Rptr. 752 (1967).
8. *Pittsburgh Testing Laboratory v. Farnsworth & Chambers, Inc.,* 251 F.2d 77 (10th Cir. 1958).
9. *Guilford Yacht Association, Inc. v. Northeast Dredging, Inc.,* 438 A.2d 478 (Me. 1981).

10. See, for example, *Schwartzreich v. Bauman-Basch, Inc.,* 231 N.Y. 196, 131 N.E. 887 (1921).
11. See, for example, *Holly v. First National Bank,* 218 Wis. 259, 260 N.W. 429 (1935).
12. The UCC deals with the problem of preexisting duty or modification of an existing contract very simply. UCC 2–209(1) simply states that "an agreement modifying a contract within this Article needs no consideration to be binding." See Chapter 20.
13. For an example, see California Civil Code Section 1606.

SECTION 5

# PAST CONSIDERATION

Promises made with respect to events that have already taken place are unenforceable. Because the element of bargained-for exchange is missing, these promises lack legal consideration. In short, you can bargain for something to take place now or in the future, but not for something that has already taken place. Therefore, **past consideration** is no consideration.

Suppose that an employer tells a retiring employee, ''In consideration of your forty years of faithful service, you will be paid a pension of $500 per month.'' The promise relates to an event that has already taken place, the many years of faithful service, so it is an unenforceable promise. Suppose instead that an employer tells newly hired employees, ''On retirement, in consideration of your years of faithful service from now until retirement age, you will be paid a pension of $500 per month.'' Here, there is a bargained-for exchange with legally sufficient consideration, so the employer normally is bound to pay.

SECTION 6

# PROBLEM AREAS CONCERNING CONSIDERATION

Problems concerning consideration usually fall into one of the following categories:

1. Promises exchanged when total performance by the parties is uncertain.
2. Settlement of claims.
3. Promises that are enforceable without consideration.

The courts' solutions to these types of problems can give you insight into how the law views the complex concept of consideration.

## UNCERTAIN PERFORMANCE

If the terms of the contract express such uncertainty of performance that the promisor has not definitely promised to do anything, the promise is said to be *illusory*—without consideration and unenforceable. For example, suppose that the president of Tuscan Corporation says to her employees, ''All of you have worked hard, and if profits continue to remain high, a 10 percent bonus at the end of the year will be given—if management thinks it is warranted.'' The employees continue to work hard, and profits remain high, but no bonus is given. This is an *illusory promise*, or no promise at all, because performance depends solely on the discretion of the president (the management). There is no bargained-for consideration. The statement declares merely that the management may or may not do something in the future. The president is not obligated (incurs no detriment) now or in the future.

Option-to-cancel clauses in contracts sometimes present problems in regard to consideration. For example, suppose that I contract to hire you for one year at $5,000 per month, reserving the right to cancel the contract at any time. On close examination of these words, you can see that I have not actually agreed to hire you, as I could cancel without liability before you started performance. I have not given up the opportunity of hiring someone else. This contract is therefore illusory.

## SETTLEMENT OF CLAIMS

There are several ways in which businesspersons or others can settle legal claims, and it is important to understand the nature of consideration given in these kinds of settlement agreements, or contracts. A common means of settling a claim is through an *accord and satisfaction,* in which a debtor offers to pay a lesser amount than the creditor purports to be owed. Other methods that are commonly used to settle claims include the *release* and the *covenant not to sue.*

**ACCORD AND SATISFACTION**   The concept of **accord and satisfaction** deals with a debtor's offer of payment and a creditor's acceptance of a lesser amount than the creditor originally purported to be owed. The *accord* is defined as the agreement under which one of the parties undertakes to give or perform, and the other to accept, in satisfaction of a claim, something other than that which was originally agreed on. *Satisfaction* takes place when the accord is executed. Accord and satisfaction deal with an attempt by the obligor to extinguish an obligation. A basic rule is that there can be no satisfaction unless there is first an accord.

For accord and satisfaction to occur, the amount of the debt *must be in dispute.* If a debt is *liquidated,* accord and satisfaction cannot take place. A liquidated debt is one whose amount has been ascertained, fixed, agreed on, settled, or exactly determined. For example, if Baker signs an installment loan contract with her banker in which she agrees to pay a specified rate of interest on a specified sum of borrowed money at monthly intervals for two years, that is a liquidated debt. The amount owing is precisely known to both of the parties, and reasonable persons will not differ over the amount owed. Suppose that Baker misses her last two payments on the loan and the creditor demands that she pay the overdue debt. Baker makes a partial payment and states that she believes that is all that she should have to pay and that, if the creditor accepts the payment, the debt will be satisfied, or discharged. In the majority of states, acceptance of a lesser sum than the entire amount of a liquidated debt is not satisfaction, and the balance of the debt is still legally owed. The rationale for this rule is that no consideration is given by the debtor to satisfy the obligation of paying the balance to the creditor—because the debtor has a preexisting legal obligation to pay the entire debt.

An *unliquidated debt* is the opposite of a liquidated debt. Here, reasonable persons may differ over the amount owed. It is not settled, fixed, agreed on, ascertained, or determined. In these circumstances, acceptance of payment of the lesser sum can operate as a satisfaction, or discharge, of the debt. For example, suppose that Devereaux goes to the dentist's office. The dentist tells him that he needs three special types of gold inlays. The price is not discussed, and there is no standard fee for this type of work. Devereaux leaves the office. At the end of the month, the dentist sends him a bill for $3,000. Devereaux, believing that this amount is grossly out of proportion with what a reasonable person would believe to be the debt

owed, sends a check for $2,000. On the back of the check he writes "payment in full for three gold inlays." The dentist cashes the check. Because we are dealing with an unliquidated debt—the amount has not been agreed on—payment accepted by the dentist normally will eradicate the debt. One argument to support this rule is that the parties give up a legal right to contest the amount in dispute, and thus consideration is given.

**RELEASE** A **release** bars any further recovery beyond the terms stated in the release. Assume that you are involved in an automobile accident caused by Donovan's negligence. Donovan offers to give you $1,000 if you will release him from further liability resulting from the accident. You believe that this amount will cover your damages, so you agree to the release. Later you discover that it will cost $1,200 to repair your car. Can you collect the balance from Donovan? The answer is normally no; you are limited to the $1,000 specified in the release because a valid contract existed. You and Donovan both assented to the bargain (hence, agreement existed), and sufficient consideration was present. The consideration was the legal detriment you suffered (by releasing Donovan from liability, you forfeited your right to sue to recover damages, should they be more than $1,000).

Clearly, you are better off if you know the extent of your injuries or damages before signing a release. Releases will generally be binding if they are (1) given in good faith, (2) stated in a signed writing (which is required in many states), and (3) accompanied by consideration.[14] The following case illustrates how important it is to know the extent of injuries or damages before signing a release.

---

14. Under the UCC, a written, signed waiver or renunciation by an aggrieved party discharges any further liability for a breach, even without consideration.

---

| CASE 13.2 | **BACKGROUND AND FACTS** *In August 1982, James Bennett was driving his automobile when it was struck from behind by a Shinoda Floral, Inc., truck driven by George Wasilche in the course of his employment. Following the collision, Bennett was told by his physician that he had incurred a lumbosacral and dorsal sprain, which would only temporarily disable him; eventually he would be able to return to his job. Aetna Casualty and Surety Company, Shinoda Floral's insurance company, paid Bennett's medical expenses and lost wages until December 1982, at which* |
|---|---|
| **BENNETT v. SHINODA FLORAL, INC.** Supreme Court of Washington, 1987. 108 Wash.2d 386, 739 P.2d 648. | |

*time Aetna offered Bennett $5,000 to settle his claim, stating that this was all Aetna would pay. Bennett accepted the offer and signed a release "of all claims of every nature and kind whatsoever . . . that are known and unknown, suspected and unsuspected." Later, Bennett's back condition worsened, and medical examinations revealed a herniated intravertebral disc in Bennett's lower back—a much more serious condition than the sprain that was originally diagnosed. The examining physicians concluded that Bennett was permanently and totally disabled. Bennett brought an action for damages against Wasilche and Shinoda Floral, the defendants. The defendants asserted the release as a defense to liability, and the trial court granted their motion for summary judgment. The appellate court reversed the decision. The case was consolidated with a similar case, and the consolidated appeals were heard by the Supreme Court of Washington.*

*DURHAM,* Justice.
     \*    \*    \*    \*

When a person signs a release of all claims and has no knowledge that he has any personal injury, \*   \*   \* it is supportable to permit avoidance of the release once it is found that the release was not executed fairly and knowingly. \*   \*   \* [I]n such a case the policy favoring just compensation of accident victims outweighs the policy favoring finality of private settlements. Because the plaintiff is unaware of any personal injury at the time he signs the release, it is unjust to hold him to the release where it is clear that he did not contemplate the possibility that an injury would arise in the future.

In contrast, when a person signs a release knowing that he has been injured, he assumes some risk that his condition may worsen. \*   \*   \* By signing a release when he knows he is injured, a person is aware that there is a chance that he could be left insufficiently compensated if the prognosis changes. He knowingly takes a gamble in agreeing to a settlement. \*   \*   \*

If we allowed a challenge to the validity of the releases in these cases, we would severely impair the policy favoring private settlements and promoting their finality. In every case where the known circumstances of the injury changed after settlement, the validity of the release would be open to question.

\*   \*   \* The absence of finality would greatly reduce the incentive to settle personal injury claims, thus impeding timely compensation to injury victims and adding to the congestion crisis in our courts.

**DECISION AND REMEDY**

*The Supreme Court of Washington held that Bennett was bound by the release that he had signed. The trial court's decision was affirmed.*

**ETHICAL CONSIDERATIONS**

*The law assumes that individuals will look after their own interests and, in the case of releases, not sign away rights without first exploring the possible consequences of such an action. Ethical questions arise, however, when an insurance company "pressures" an individual to sign a release. Certainly, the injured party should be allowed to make such a decision freely after having first been given all relevant information about the true options available.*

**COVENANT NOT TO SUE** A **covenant not to sue,** unlike a release, does not always bar further recovery. The parties simply substitute a contractual obligation for some other type of legal action based on a valid claim. Suppose (following the earlier example) that you agree with Donovan not to sue for damages in a tort action if he will pay for the damage to your car. If Donovan fails to pay, you can bring an action against him for breach of contract.

## PROMISES ENFORCEABLE WITHOUT CONSIDERATION

There are exceptions to the rule that only promises supported by consideration are enforceable. Circumstances in which promises will be enforced despite the lack of what one normally considers legal consideration are as follows:

1. Promises to pay debts barred by a statute of limitations.
2. Detrimental reliance, or promissory estoppel.
3. Charitable subscriptions.

**PROMISES TO PAY DEBTS BARRED BY A STATUTE OF LIMITATIONS**   Statutes of limitations in all states require a creditor to sue within a specified period to recover debts. If the creditor fails to sue in time, recovery of the debt is barred by the statute of limitations. A debtor who promises to pay a previous debt barred by the statute of limitations makes an enforceable promise. *The promise needs no consideration.* (Some states, however, require that it be in writing.) In effect, the promise extends the limitations period, and the creditor can sue to recover the entire debt, or at least the amount promised. The promise can be implied if the debtor acknowledges the barred debt by making a partial payment.

**DETRIMENTAL RELIANCE, OR PROMISSORY ESTOPPEL**   As discussed in Chapter 12 in the context of irrevocable offers, the doctrine of *detrimental reliance,* or *promissory estoppel,* involves a promise given by one party that induces another party to rely on that promise to his or her detriment. When the promisor can reasonably have expected the promisee to act on the promise, and injustice cannot be avoided any other way, the promise will be enforced.[15] Additionally, the promisee must have acted with justifiable reliance on the promise—that is, must have been justified in relying on it—and in most instances the act must have been of a substantial nature.

The promise is enforced by a refusal to allow the promisor to set up the defense of lack of consideration. That is, the promisor is *estopped* (prevented) from asserting the lack of consideration as a defense. The estoppel arises from the promise, and hence *promissory estoppel* is the term used. Imagine that your grandfather tells you, ''I'll pay you $350 per week so you won't have to work anymore.'' Then you quit your job, and your grandfather refuses to pay. You may be able to enforce the promise, because you have justifiably relied on it to your detriment.[16]

Promissory estoppel does not mean that each and every gratuitous promise will be binding merely because the promisee has changed position. Liability is created only when there is *justifiable* reliance on the promise. The promisor must have known or had reason to believe that the promisee would likely be induced to change position as a result of the promise. The following classic case illustrates this point.

---

15.   Restatement (Second) of Contracts, Section 90, provides as follows: ''A promise which the promisor should reasonably expect to induce action or forbearance on the part of the promisee or a third person and which does induce such action or forbearance is binding if injustice can be avoided only by enforcement of the promise.'' Note that the doctrine of promissory estoppel is not used in some jurisdictions.
16.   *Ricketts v. Scothorn,* 57 Neb. 51, 77 N.W. 365 (1898).

---

**CASE 13.3**

**HOFFMAN v. RED OWL STORES, INC.**
Supreme Court of Wisconsin, 1965.
26 Wis.2d 683,
133 N.W.2d 267.

**COMPANY PROFILE**   *In 1922, the St. Anthony and Dakota Elevator Company opened a grocery store in Rochester, Minnesota. By the end of the year, the company owned a chain of eleven grocery stores with headquarters in Minneapolis, Minnesota. By 1928, there were 141 stores incorporated as Red Owl Stores, Inc., which grew to 500 outlets in nine states by the late 1950s. Red Owl expanded beyond foods in 1962 when it acquired the Snyder's Drug Stores chain. In 1967, Red Owl was acquired by Gamble-Skogmo, Inc., another Minnesota firm. In 1979 Gamble-Skogmo was bought by Wickes Companies, Inc. Wickes filed for bankruptcy in 1982, and Red Owl became a locally owned and operated independent company.*

*In 1988, Super Valu Stores, Inc., bought Red Owl's warehouse and distribution facilities, leaving Red Owl with less than three dozen stores.*

**BACKGROUND AND FACTS**   *Red Owl Stores, Inc., induced the Hoffmans to give up their current business and run a Red Owl franchise. The Hoffmans relied on the representations of Red Owl, and when the deal ultimately fell through because of Red Owl's failure to keep its promise concerning the operation of the franchise agency store, the Hoffmans brought suit to recover their losses. The trial court found in their favor, and Red Owl appealed.*

*CURRIE,* Chief Justice.
\* \* \* \*

The record here discloses a number of promises and assurances given to Hoffman by Lukowitz in behalf of Red Owl upon which plaintiffs relied and acted upon to their detriment.

Foremost were the promises that for the sum of $18,000 Red Owl would establish Hoffman in a store. After Hoffman had sold his grocery store and paid the $1,000 on the Chilton lot, the $18,000 figure was changed to $24,100. Then in November, 1961, Hoffman was assured that if the $24,100 figure were increased by $2,000 the deal would go through. Hoffman was induced to sell his grocery store fixtures and inventory in June, 1961, on the promise that he would be in his new store by fall. In November, plaintiffs sold their bakery building on the urging of defendants and on the assurance that this was the last step necessary to have the deal with Red Owl go through.

We determine that there was ample evidence to sustain the answers of the jury to the questions of the verdict with respect to the promissory representations made by Red Owl, Hoffman's reliance thereon in the exercise of ordinary care, and his fulfillment of the conditions required of him by the terms of the negotiations [he] had with Red Owl.

**DECISION AND REMEDY**

*The trial court's judgment was affirmed. Hoffman was entitled to damages, the exact amount to be determined when the case was returned to the trial court.*

**INTERNATIONAL CONSIDERATIONS**

**Promissory Estoppel in France**  *A French court hearing a case similar to that of Red Owl would probably arrive at the same result but on the basis of different legal principles. In one French case, for example, a company led another party to believe that a contract would be forthcoming. In reliance on the anticipated contract, the party made large expenditures. Then the company abruptly broke off negotiations. Rather than relying on a theory of promissory estoppel, the French court held the company liable for "an abusive breaking off of negotiations."*

**CHARITABLE SUBSCRIPTIONS**   Subscriptions to religious, educational, and charitable institutions are promises to make gifts and are unenforceable on traditional contract grounds because they are not supported by legally sufficient consideration. A gift, after all, is the opposite of bargained-for consideration.

There have been cases in which it was held that a promise to give money to a charity was supported by consideration. For example, the promisor may have bargained for and received a promise from the charity that the gift would be used in a specific way or that it would be memorialized with the promisor's name. The modern view, however, is

## ■ CONCEPT SUMMARY 13.1 **Consideration**

| CONCEPT | DESCRIPTION |
|---|---|
| **Definition of Consideration** | Consideration is the value given in exchange for a promise. A contract cannot be formed without sufficient consideration. Consideration consists of three elements:<br>1. *Legal value*—Something of legal value must be given in exchange for a promise. In addition to money, value may be an act, a forbearance, a change in a legal relation, or a promise.<br>2. *Bargained-for exchange*—The value must be for something to take place in the present or in the future.<br>3. *Legal sufficiency*—Consideration must result in a legal detriment to the promisee or a legal benefit to the promisor. |
| **Legal Sufficiency of Consideration** | To be legally sufficient, consideration must be either legally detrimental to the promisee (the one to whom the promise is made) or legally beneficial to the promisor (the one making the promise). Doing something, promising to do something, forbearing from doing something, or promising to forbear from doing something that one is otherwise entitled to do is legally sufficient consideration to bind another's promise. The following types of promises normally are not enforceable because they lack sufficient consideration:<br>1. A promise to perform a preexisting duty.<br>2. A promise based on a moral obligation.<br>3. A promise to perform an act that has already been performed (past consideration). |
| **Adequacy of Consideration** | Adequacy of consideration relates to how much consideration is given and whether a fair bargain was reached. Courts will inquire into the adequacy of consideration (if the consideration is legally sufficient) only when fraud, undue influence, duress, or unconscionability may be involved. |
| **Problem Areas Concerning Consideration** | 1. *Uncertain performance*—When the nature or extent of performance is too uncertain, the promise is rendered illusory and unenforceable.<br>2. *Settlement of claims*—<br>  a. Accord and satisfaction—A debtor's offer of payment and a creditor's acceptance of a lesser amount than the creditor originally purported to be owed.<br>  b. Release—An agreement by which, for consideration, a party is barred from further recovery beyond the terms specified in the release.<br>  c. Covenant not to sue—An agreement not to sue on a present, valid claim.<br>3. *Promises enforceable without consideration*—<br>  a. Promises to pay debts barred by a statute of limitations.<br>  b. Detrimental reliance, or promissory estoppel.<br>  c. Charitable subscriptions. |

to enforce these promises under the doctrine of promissory estoppel or to find consideration simply as a matter of public policy.

The premise for enforcement is that a promise is made and an institution changes its position be-cause of reliance on that promise. For example, suppose a church solicits and receives donative subscriptions to erect a new church building. On the basis of these pledges, the church purchases land, employs architects, and makes other contracts that change its position. Courts may enforce the pledges under promissory estoppel. Alternatively, they may find consideration in the fact that each promise was made in reliance on the other promises of support or that the trustees, by accepting the subscriptions, impliedly promised to complete the proposed undertaking. Such cases represent exceptions to the general rule that consideration must exist for a contract to be formed. These exceptions come about as a result of public policy.

## TERMS AND CONCEPTS TO REVIEW

| | | |
|---|---|---|
| accord and satisfaction 253 | past consideration 253 | unconscionable 251 |
| consideration 248 | release 254 | |
| covenant not to sue 255 | rescission 252 | |

## QUESTIONS AND CASE PROBLEMS

**13–1. Contract Modification.** Tabor is the buyer of widgets manufactured by Martin. Martin's contract with Tabor calls for delivery of 10,000 widgets at $1 per widget in ten equal installments. After delivery of two installments, Martin informs Tabor that because of inflation, Martin is losing money and will promise to deliver the remaining 8,000 widgets only if Tabor will pay $1.20 per widget. Tabor agrees in writing. Discuss whether Martin can legally collect the additional $200 upon delivery to Tabor of the next installment of 1,000 widgets.

**13–2. Contract Modification.** Bernstein owns a lot and wants to build a house according to a specific set of plans and specifications. She solicits bids from building contractors and receives three bids: one from Carlton for $60,000, one from Friend for $58,000, and one from Shade for $53,000. She accepts Shade's bid. One month after construction of the house has begun, Shade contacts Bernstein and informs her that because of inflation and a recent price hike in materials, he will not finish the house unless Bernstein agrees to pay an extra $3,000. Bernstein reluctantly agrees to pay the additional sum. After the house is finished, however, Bernstein refuses to pay the additional $3,000. Discuss whether Bernstein is legally required to pay this additional amount.

**13–3. Payment for Services to Another.** Daniel, a recent college graduate, is on his way home for the Christmas holidays from his new job. Daniel gets caught in a snowstorm and is taken in by an elderly couple, who provide him with food and shelter. After the snowplows have cleared the road, Daniel proceeds home. Daniel's father, Fred, is most appreciative of the elderly couple's action and in a letter promises to pay them $500. The elderly couple, in need of money, accepts Fred's offer. Then, because of a dispute between Daniel and

Fred, Fred refuses to pay the elderly couple the $500. Discuss whether they can hold Fred in contract for the services rendered to Daniel.

**13–4. Consideration.** Costello hired Sagan to drive his racing car in a race. Sagan's friend Gideon promised to pay Sagan $3,000 if she won the race. Sagan won the race, but Gideon refused to pay the $3,000. Gideon contended that no legally binding contract had been formed because he had received no consideration from Sagan in exchange for his promise to pay the $3,000. Sagan sued Gideon for breach of contract, arguing that winning the race was the consideration given in exchange for Gideon's promise to pay the $3,000. What rule of law discussed in this chapter supports Gideon's claim?

**13–5. Consideration.** Martino was a police officer in Atlantic City. Gray, who lost a significant amount of her jewelry during a burglary of her home, offered a reward for the recovery of the property. Incident to his job, Martino possessed certain knowledge concerning the theft of Gray's jewelry. When Martino informed Gray of his knowledge of the theft, Gray offered Martino $500 to help her recover her jewelry. As a result of Martino's police work, the jewelry was recovered and returned to Gray. Martino sued Gray for the reward he claimed she promised him. Was there a valid contract between Gray and Martino? [*Gray v. Martino,* 91 N.J.L. 462, 103 A. 24 (1918)]

**13–6. Adequacy of Consideration.** In 1972, Thomas L. Weinsaft signed a written agreement with his son, Nicholas L. Weinsaft. Thomas agreed that during his lifetime he would not transfer any interest in his 765 shares of stock of Crane Manufacturing Co. unless he first gave Nicholas an opportunity to purchase it, and upon Thomas's death, Nicholas would have the "option and right to purchase all of the stock" from the estate. The agreement stated that it was entered into "In consideration of $10.00 and other good and valuable consideration, including the inducement of Second Party [Nicholas] to remain the chief executive officer of said company.'' Thomas died in 1980. Nicholas gave notice that he intended to buy the stock, but one of the beneficiaries under Thomas's will objected, contending that there was no consideration for Thomas's promises. Nicholas sued to force the estate to transfer the shares. Discuss whether this contract is supported by consideration. [*In re Estate of Weinsaft,* 647 S.W.2d 179 (Mo.App. 1983)]

**13–7. Reliance.** Gordon Hayes and Winslow Construction Co. (Hayes) promised to hire Kathleen Hunter as a flag person on a construction job beginning June 14, 1971. Relying on the offer, Hunter left her position with the telephone company, as Hayes had asked her to do. When Hayes failed to hire her, she was unemployed for two months—in spite of her efforts to find another job. Hunter sued Hayes for damages in the amount of $700, which she would have earned during the two months had she not left the telephone company (she had been earning $350 a month). The trial court ruled for Hunter, awarding her $700 in damages. Hayes appealed, contending that it should not be liable because no valid employment contract existed between the plaintiff and the defendant. Discuss whether Hunter should be allowed to recover damages incurred by her reliance on Hayes's offer of employment, even in the absence of a valid employment contract. [*Hunter v. Hayes,* 533 P.2d 952 (Colo.App. 1975)]

**13–8. Contract Modification.** Ellen and Gabriel Fineman held MasterCards issued by Citibank. Holders of these cards paid an annual $15 fee. The issuance and use of the cards were governed by a retail installment credit agreement, which contained the following statement: ''We can change this Agreement including the *finance charge* and the *annual percentage rate* at any time.'' The agreement did provide for thirty days' notice of any such changes, and the cardholder had a right to reject the changes in writing and return the credit card. Two months before the expiration of the Finemans' cards, Citibank notified them that it was increasing its annual fee to $20; however, Citibank was also providing its cardholders with extra services and benefits, such as ''$100,000 common carrier travel insurance.'' The Finemans did not object in writing, nor did they return the cards. Citibank added 83 cents to the Finemans' next bill, the prorated portion of the increase for the two months remaining on their cards. The Finemans filed suit (a class-action lawsuit on behalf of all cardholders) to recover the increased charges. Among other claims, the Finemans argued that the modification failed because the travel insurance was not adequate consideration for the modification, because they never received any benefits from the insurance, and because

its cost to Citibank was negligible. Was there adequate and legally sufficient consideration for Citibank's modification of the annual credit card fee? [*Fineman v. Citicorp USA, Inc.,* 137 Ill.App.3d 1055, 485 N.E.2d 591, 92 Ill.Dec. 780 (1985)]

**13–9. Promissory Estoppel.** An article written by Claudia Dreifus and published in *Glamour Magazine* discussed therapists who sexually exploit their patients. Jill Ruzicka had told Dreifus that she (Ruzicka) had been sexually abused as a child by her father and later by her therapist. Dreifus had promised to withhold Ruzicka's identity from the article, and the published article identified Ruzicka by a fictitious name (''Lundquist''). In the article, Dreifus stated that ''Lundquist'' was an attorney who had served on the Minnesota Task Force against Sexual Abuse. Ruzicka claimed that this detail revealed her true identity because she was, in fact, the only woman on that task force. Ruzicka asserted that she had relied to her detriment on Dreifus's promise and sued Dreifus to recover damages under, among other theories, a theory of promissory estoppel. Under the relevant state law, to support a promissory estoppel theory the plaintiff must prove (1) that the promise was clear and definite, (2) that the promisor intended to induce reliance on the part of the promisee and such reliance occurred to the promisee's detriment, and (3) that the promise must be enforced to prevent injustice. What should the court decide? Discuss fully. [*Ruzicka v. Conde Nast Publications, Inc.,* 999 F.2d 1319 (8th Cir. 1993)]

**13–10. Past Consideration.** Rivendell Forest Products, Ltd., had a computer program—the *Quote Screen* system—that allowed it to quote prices to its customers many times faster than its competitors. To keep the *Quote Screen* system a secret, Rivendell insisted that all of its employees, including Timothy Cornwell, sign a confidentiality agreement in 1988. Cornwell was employed by Rivendell from 1987 to 1990, when he left Rivendell to work as a marketing manager for the Georgia-Pacific Corp., a competitor of Rivendell. Cornwell introduced Georgia-Pacific to Rivendell's *Quote Screen* system. Rivendell sued Cornwell for, among other things, breach of the confidentiality agreement. The trial court held that the confidentiality agreement was not a valid contract because Rivendell had failed to provide consideration, such as a salary increase or a promotion, in exchange for Cornwell's promise to keep the *Quote Screen* system a secret. If Cornwell had signed the confidentiality agreement when he was first hired, would the result have been the same? Explain. [*Rivendell Forest Products, Ltd. v. Georgia-Pacific Corp.,* 824 F.Supp. 961 (D.Colo. 1993)]

# CHAPTER 14

# CAPACITY

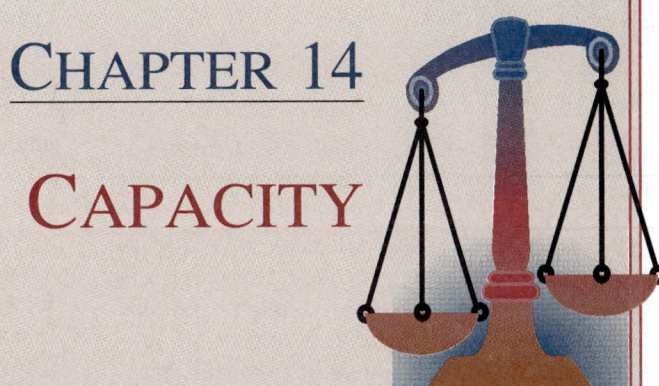

**A**lthough the parties to a contract must assume certain risks, the law indicates that neither party should be allowed to benefit from the other party's lack of **contractual capacity**—the legal ability to enter into a contractual relationship. Courts generally presume the existence of contractual capacity, but there are some situations in which capacity is lacking or may be questionable. In many situations, a party may have the capacity to enter into a valid contract but also have the right to avoid liability under it. For example, minors usually are not legally bound by contracts. Therefore, certain contracts are *voidable*. A *voidable contract* may be either validated or avoided (canceled) at the option of the incapable or wronged party. Other contracts may be *void*. A *void contract* lacks an essential element for the formation of a legal contract, and thus either party may ignore it.

Historically, the law has concerned itself with the relative strength of the bargaining power of each contracting party. Thus, special protection is afforded those who bargain with the inexperience of youth or those who lack the degree of mental competence required by law. *Full competence* exists when both parties have full legal capacity to enter into a contract and to have the contract enforced against them. *No competence* exists when one or both of the parties have been adjudged by a court to be mentally incompetent and therefore have no legal capacity to contract. In this event, an essential element for a valid contract is missing, and the contract is void. *Limited competence* exists when one or both of the parties are minors, intoxicated, or mentally incompetent but not yet adjudicated officially as such. These parties have full and legal capacity to enter into a contract; but if they wish, they can normally avoid liability under the contract, which is said to be voidable. The *Concept Summary* at the end of this chapter summarizes the legal effect of contracts entered into by minors, intoxicated persons, and mentally incompetent persons.

# MINORS

Under the common law, a minor was defined as a male who had not attained the age of twenty-one or a female who had not attained the age of eighteen. Today, in most states, the **age of majority** (when a person is no longer a minor) for contractual purposes has been changed by statute to eighteen years for both sexes.[1] In addition, some states provide for the termination of minority upon marriage. Subject to certain exceptions, the contracts entered into by a minor are voidable at the option of that minor. The minor has the option of *disaffirming* (renouncing) the contract and setting aside the contract and all legal obligations arising from it. An adult who enters into a contract with a minor, however, cannot avoid his or her contractual duties on the ground that the minor can do so. Unless the minor exercises the option to disaffirm the contract (to be discussed shortly), the adult party is bound by it.

## MINOR'S RIGHT TO DISAFFIRM

The general rule is that a minor can enter into any contract that an adult can enter into, provided that the contract is not one prohibited by law for minors (for example, the sale of alcoholic beverages). Although minors have the right to disaffirm their contracts, there are exceptions (to be discussed later).

**DISAFFIRMANCE IN GENERAL**    For a minor to exercise the option to avoid a contract, he or she need only manifest an intention not to be bound by it. The minor avoids the contract by disaffirming it. The technical definition of **disaffirmance** is the legal avoidance, or setting aside, of a contractual obligation. Words or conduct may serve to express this intent. Suppose that Jan Orozco, a seventeen-year-old, enters into a contract to sell her car to Burt Mincey, an adult. Orozco can avoid the contract and avoid her legal duty to deliver possession of the car to Mincey either by telling Mincey that she refuses to abide by the contract or by selling the car to a third person. In other words, Orozco

can disaffirm the contract by expressing her intention in words or by acting inconsistently with her duties under the contract.

The contract can ordinarily be disaffirmed at any time during minority or for a reasonable time after the minor comes of age. In some states, however, a minor's disaffirmance of certain contracts is prohibited by statute. The rule in most states, for example, is that a minor can disaffirm a contract for the sale of land only after attaining his or her majority. Other statutes completely prohibit minors from avoiding contracts for student loans, contracts for medical care, contracts for insurance, and contracts that the minor makes pursuant to running a business. On the basis of public policy, other promises of a minor may be enforced, particularly when they entail something that the law would compel anyway, such as financial support of an illegitimate child.

If a minor fails to disaffirm a contract within a reasonable time after reaching the age of majority, then the court must determine whether the conduct constitutes *ratification,* which binds the minor to the contract, or *disaffirmance,* which allows the minor to avoid the contract. Generally, a contract that is fully performed (executed) by both parties is presumed to be ratified. A contract that is still executory (not yet fully performed by both parties) is considered to be disaffirmed.

For example, assume that the age of majority in your state is eighteen. Your sister, age seventeen, contracts to purchase a bicycle from an adult for $125. Your sister then turns eighteen. If she has not taken possession of the bicycle or paid the $125 purchase price, then the contract is still executory. If she fails to take possession of and pay for the bicycle within a reasonable time after her eighteenth birthday, most courts would hold her conduct to be an act of disaffirmance. If she has taken possession of the bicycle and paid the purchase price, however, an executed contract exists. Most courts would hold her failure to actively disaffirm within a reasonable time after her eighteenth birthday to be an act of ratification. A minor must disaffirm the entire contract, not merely a portion of it. For example, the minor cannot decide to keep part of the goods and return the remainder.

**DUTY OF RESTITUTION**    When a contract has been executed, the general rule is that minors cannot disaffirm without returning whatever goods they may have received or paying for their rea-

---

1.   Although the age of majority applicable in contracts has been changed to eighteen in many states, it may still be twenty-one for some purposes, including the purchase and consumption of alcohol.

sonable value. Under the majority view, the minor need only return the goods (or other consideration), provided the goods are in the minor's possession or control. Even if the goods have been used, damaged, or ruined, the minor's right to disaffirm the contract remains. Suppose that Rodriguez, a seventeen-year-old, purchases a used car from Van Duyn, who is an adult. Rodriguez is a bad driver and negligently runs the car into a telephone pole. The next day he returns the car to Van Duyn and disaffirms the contract. Under the majority view, this return fulfills Rodriguez's duty, even though the auto is now wrecked. This rule protects minors from reckless commitments by discouraging adults from dealing with them.

A few states, either by statute or by court decision, have placed an additional duty on the minor—the *duty of restitution*. This duty accords with the maxim that one's youth may be used as a shield but not as a sword; the adult should be returned to his or her position before the contract was made.[2]

This rule recognizes the legitimate interests of those adults who deal with minors. The duty of restitution would require Rodriguez to pay Van Duyn for the damage done to the car in addition to returning it. Some states, however, do not require full restitution. A minor must pay only a "reasonable" amount to compensate the adult.

When a minor disaffirms, all property that he or she has transferred to the adult as consideration may be recovered. Sometimes, this rule applies even if the property is in the hands of a third party.[3] If the property itself cannot be returned, the adult must pay the minor its value.

In the following case, the Tennessee Supreme Court squarely faces the issue of whether a minor should be held responsible for damage, ordinary wear and tear, and depreciation of goods used by the minor prior to the minor's disaffirmation of the contract. The case illustrates the trend among today's courts in regard to this issue.

---

2. Sometimes, the term *restitution* is used interchangeably with the term *restoration*. At other times, restitution means returning the value of the goods, while restoration means returning only the goods.

3. UCC 2–403(1) allows an exception if the third party is a "good faith purchaser for value." See Chapter 21 for a further discussion of what requirements must be met to acquire the status of a good faith purchaser.

---

**BACKGROUND AND FACTS**  *Joseph Dodson, when he was sixteen years old, bought a used pickup truck from Shrader's Auto, which was owned by Burns and Mary Shrader. Nine months later, the truck developed mechanical problems. A mechanic informed Dodson that the problem might be a burnt valve. Without having the truck repaired, Dodson continued to drive it. One month later, the truck's engine "blew up," and the truck was rendered inoperable. Dodson disaffirmed the contract and sought to return the truck to the Shraders and obtain a full refund of the purchase price. The Shraders refused to refund the purchase price and would not accept possession of the truck. Later, the pickup was hit by an unknown driver while parked in the Dodsons' front yard. Dodson filed suit against the Shraders to compel a refund of the purchase price. Although the Shraders claimed that the truck's value was reduced to $500, the trial court granted rescission and ordered the Shraders to refund the full $4,900 purchase price to Dodson upon Dodson's delivery of the truck to them. The Shraders appealed.*

CASE 14.1

**DODSON v. SHRADER**
Supreme Court of Tennessee, 1992.
824 S.W.2d 545.

*O'BRIEN,* Justice.

\*  \*  \*  \*

\*  \*  \*If the minor has not been overreached [taken advantage of] in any way, and there has been no undue influence, and the contract is a fair and reasonable one, and the minor has actually paid money on the purchase price, and taken and used the article purchased, [then] he ought not to be permitted to recover the amount actually paid, without allowing the vendor of the goods reasonable compensation for the use of, depreciation, and willful or negligent damage to the article purchased, while in his hands. * * *

* * * Minors are permitted to, and do in fact, transact a great deal of business for themselves, long before they have reached the age of legal majority. * * * Further, it does not appear consistent with * * * proper moral influence upon young people * * * if they are taught that they can make purchases with their own money, for their own benefit, and after paying for them, and using them until they are worn out and destroyed, go back and compel the vendor to return to them what they have paid upon the purchase price. Such a doctrine can only lead to the corruption of principles and encourage young people in habits of trickery and dishonesty.

**DECISION AND REMEDY** *The Tennessee Supreme Court remanded the case to the trial court for a factual determination of the fairness of the contract and the fair market value of the truck.*

**INTERNATIONAL CONSIDERATIONS** **Minors' Contracts in Great Britain** *As in the United States, courts in Great Britain may permit minors' contracts to be voided on the ground that minors lack contractual capacity. Great Britain, however, has no single, fixed age limit for lack of capacity. British courts deal with contracts on a case-by-case basis and take into consideration the nature of the item contracted for and the relative maturity of the minor.*

**MISREPRESENTATION OF AGE**   Suppose a minor tells a seller that she is twenty-one years old when she is actually only seventeen. The majority view is that the minor can disaffirm the contract even though she has misrepresented her age. Moreover, in certain jurisdictions, a minor will not be held liable under the tort theory of deceit for misrepresenting his or her age, because indirectly such a judgment might force the minor to perform the contract.

Many jurisdictions, however, do find circumstances under which a minor can be bound by a contract when age has been misrepresented. First, several states have enacted statutes for precisely this purpose. In these states, misrepresentation of age is enough to prohibit disaffirmance.[4] Other statutes prohibit disaffirmance by a minor who has engaged in business as an adult.[5]

Second, some courts refuse to allow minors to disaffirm executed (fully performed) contracts un-

less they can return the consideration that they received. The combination of the minors' misrepresentation and their unjust enrichment has persuaded these courts, for purposes of equity, to *estop* (prevent) minors from asserting contractual incapacity. The estoppel approach is the minority view, although it is encouraged by the Restatement (Second) of Contracts.[6]

Third, some courts will allow a misrepresenting minor to disaffirm a contract but will hold the minor liable for damages in tort; the defrauded party may sue the minor for misrepresentation or fraud. A split of authority exists on this point because some courts, as previously pointed out, recognize that allowing a suit in tort is equivalent to indirectly enforcing the minor's contract.

In the following case, an Ohio appellate court had to deal with the problem of a minor's false representation of her age as the inducement to a contract. At the time this case was decided, the age of majority in Ohio was twenty-one.

---

4. See, for example, Revised Code of Washington 26.28.040.
5. See, for example, Iowa Code Section 599.3, Kansas Statutes Section 38–103, and Utah Code Section 15–2–3.

---

6. See Restatement (Second) of Contracts, Section 14, Comment c.

**COMPANY PROFILE**   *In the early twentieth century, the automobile industry consisted of hundreds of firms, each of which made and sold only a few models. William Durant, a one-time buggymaker who became president of Buick Motors, formed General Motors Corporation (GMC) in 1908 to acquire other auto makers. Before 1920, Durant brought more than two dozen companies into the GMC fold, including parts manufacturers and auto makers such as Oldsmobile, Cadillac, Chevrolet, and Pontiac (named for an Ottawa chief who laid siege to Detroit in 1763). One auto company that Durant had not acquired was the Willys-Overland Company in Toledo, Ohio. Walter Chrysler started as Durant's Buick plant manager and rose to head all of GMC's manufacturing operations. Dissatisfied with the way that Durant ran GMC, however, Chrysler left in 1920 to revitalize Willys-Overland and later to take over the Maxwell Motor Company. Chrysler renamed Maxwell Motor after himself. By 1935, Chrysler's sales were second only to those of GMC. Chrysler's brand names include Plymouth.*

CASE 14.2

**HAYDOCY PONTIAC, INC. v. LEE**

Court of Appeals of Ohio, Franklin County, 1969.
19 Ohio App.2d 217,
250 N.E.2d 898.

**BACKGROUND AND FACTS**   *The plaintiff is Haydocy Pontiac, Inc., a seller of automobiles. The defendant, Jennifer Lee, was twenty years of age when she contracted to purchase a 1964 Plymouth Fury from Haydocy, but she represented to the plaintiff that she was twenty-one years old. Lee purchased the car by making a trade-in and financing the rest of the purchase price. She executed a note for the unpaid purchase price, including financing charges and insurance charges. The total amount of the note was approximately $2,000. Immediately following delivery of the automobile, Lee turned the car over to a third person. She never at any time thereafter had possession of the automobile. Lee made no further attempt to make payment on the contract and attempted to disaffirm the contract. She did not return the automobile to the plaintiff, nor did she offer to return it. She merely announced that she had been a minor at the time of purchase, that she had not ratified the agreement to purchase the car, and that she was repudiating her contract and would not be bound by it. The trial court applied the general rule of law permitting a minor to avoid a transaction without being required to restore the consideration received. Haydocy Pontiac appealed.*

**STRAUSBAUGH,** Judge.
\* \* \* \*

To allow infants [minors] to avoid a transaction without being required to restore the consideration received where the infant has used or otherwise disposed of it causes hardship on the other party. We hold that where the consideration received by the infant cannot be returned upon disaffirmance of the contract because it has been disposed of the infant must account for the value of it, not in excess of the purchase price, where the other party is free from any fraud or bad faith and where the contract has been induced by a false representation of the age of the infant. *Under this factual situation the infant is estopped from pleading infancy as a defense where the contract has been induced by a false representation that the infant was of age.* [Emphasis added.]

The necessity of returning the consideration as a prerequisite to obtaining equitable relief is still clearer where the infant misrepresents age and perpetrated an actual fraud on the other party. The disaffirmance of an infant's contract is to be determined by equitable principles, whether sought in a proceeding in equity or a case at law.

The common law has bestowed upon the infant the privilege of disaffirming his contracts in conservation of his rights and interests. Where the infant, 20 years of age, through falsehood and deceit enters into a contract with another who enters therein in honesty and good faith and, thereafter, the infant seeks to disaffirm the contract without tendering back the consideration, no right or interest of the infant exists which needs protection. The privilege given the infant thereupon becomes a weapon of injustice.

**DECISION AND REMEDY**  *The judgment of the trial court was reversed. The Ohio appellate court allowed the seller, Haydocy Pontiac, Inc., to recover the fair market value of the automobile from the defendant, Lee. The only restriction imposed by the court was that the fair market value could not be in excess of the original purchase price of the automobile.*

**EMANCIPATION**  Emancipation is the release of a minor by his or her parents. It involves completely relinquishing the parental right to the minor's control, care, custody, and earnings. It is a repudiation of parental obligations. Emancipation may be express or implied, absolute or conditional, total or partial. Several jurisdictions permit minors to petition for emancipation themselves. In those states, a grant of emancipation may also remove a minor's lack of capacity to contract.

**LIABILITY FOR NECESSARIES**  A minor who enters into a contract for **necessaries,** such as food, clothing, and shelter, may disaffirm the contract but remains liable for the reasonable value of the goods. The legal duty to pay a reasonable value does not arise from the contract itself but is imposed by law under a theory of quasi contract. One approach is that the minor should not be unjustly enriched and should therefore be liable for purchases that fulfill basic needs. Another approach is that the minor's right to disaffirm a contract has economic ramifications in that a seller is likely to refuse to deal with minors because of it. If minors can at least be held liable for the reasonable value of the goods, a seller's reluctance to enter into contracts with minors may be offset. The courts narrow the subject matter to necessaries because without such a rule, minors might be denied the opportunity to purchase necessary goods.

There is no universally accepted definition of necessaries. Minimally, necessaries include food, clothing, shelter, medicine, and hospital care. In some cases, however, courts have not limited necessaries to items required for physical existence but have interpreted the term to include whatever is believed to be necessary to maintain a person's financial and social status. Thus, what will be considered a necessary for one person may be an extravagance for another. Moreover, necessaries have been held to include education as well as services that are reasonably necessary to enable a minor to earn a living.

If the minor's parent or guardian is able to provide the minor with necessaries, but fails to do so, the parent or guardian will be liable to the seller or provider of the necessaries for the reasonable value of the goods (such as clothing) that the minor has purchased. The rationale is that the seller or provider can hold the parent or guardian liable for these contracted-for necessaries and therefore the minor should be allowed to disaffirm the contracts rather than be held liable for the reasonable value of the goods or services.

**INSURANCE AND LOANS**  Traditionally, insurance has not been viewed as a necessary, so minors can ordinarily disaffirm their insurance contracts and recover all premiums paid. Some jurisdictions, however, prohibit the right to disaffirm—for example, when minors contract for life or medical insurance. Other jurisdictions allow a minor to disaffirm but limit recovery to the value of premiums paid, less the insurance company's actual cost of protecting the minor under the policy. Suppose Bob Berzak, a minor, takes out an automobile insurance policy and pays $1,000 in premiums. Bob has an accident for which his insurance company, State

Farm, pays a claim of $700. In states following the traditional rule, Bob's recovery upon disaffirmance will be $1,000, the full value of the premiums. In states limiting his recovery, Bob can recover only $300, the excess of the value of the premiums over State Farm's actual cost under the policy.

A financial loan is seldom viewed as a necessary, even if the minor spends the money on necessaries. If the lender makes a loan for the express purpose of enabling the minor to purchase necessaries, however, and the lender personally makes sure the money is so spent, then the minor is normally obligated to repay the loan.

## RATIFICATION

In contract law, **ratification** is the act of accepting and giving legal force to an obligation that previously was not enforceable. In relation to minors' contracts, ratification may be defined as an act or an expression in words by which a person, upon or after reaching majority, indicates an *intention* to become bound by a contract made as a minor. Ratification must occur, if at all, after the individual comes of age because any attempt to become legally bound prior to majority is no more effective than the original contractual promise. This protects the minor and is consistent with the theory that the contracts of a minor are voidable at his or her option.

**EXPRESS RATIFICATION**  An *express* ratification takes place when the individual, upon reaching the age of majority, states orally or in writing that he or she intends to be bound by the contract. Suppose Humphrey enters into a contract to sell a stereo to Lombard. At the time the contract is made, Lombard is a minor. Naturally, Lombard can avoid her legal duty to pay for the stereo by disaffirming the contract. Imagine that instead Lombard reaches majority and writes a letter to Humphrey stating that she still agrees to buy the stereo. Lombard thus ratifies the contract and is now legally bound. Humphrey can sue for breach of contract if Lombard refuses to perform her part of the bargain.

**IMPLIED RATIFICATION**  The contract can also be ratified by conduct. Suppose Lombard takes possession of the stereo as a minor and continues to use it after reaching the age of majority. This conduct evidences an intent to abide by the contract and is a form of *implied* ratification. Again, Lombard is legally bound, and Humphrey can sue her for breach of contract if she fails to perform her duty to pay the purchase price. When an individual, after reaching majority, continues to use and make payments on property purchased as a minor, the continued use and payment are inconsistent with disaffirmance and implicitly indicate an intention to be bound by the contract.

In general, any act or conduct showing an intention to affirm the contract will be deemed to be ratification. As previously suggested, however, silence after reaching the age of majority does not in and of itself constitute ratification of an executory contract in most situations. If Lombard had said nothing to Humphrey and had not taken possession or made payment, she would not have ratified the contract, because she would have expressed no intention to abide by it. There may be a duty to speak in some circumstances, however. Suppose that after coming of age, a former minor seller fails to disaffirm, knowing that the purchaser is making costly improvements on the property sold. In this case, the seller cannot disaffirm the contract.

In the following case, a person attempted to disaffirm a contract ten months after reaching the age of majority. The essential issue before the court is whether the ten months was a "reasonable time," after reaching the age of majority, within which to disaffirm a contract.

---

**BACKGROUND AND FACTS**  *Charles Edward Smith, Jr., purchased a car on credit from Bobby Floars Toyota, Inc., a month before his eighteenth birthday. Smith made regular monthly payments for eleven months but then returned the car to the dealer and made no further payments on it. The dealer sold the car and sued Smith to recover the difference between the amount obtained from the sale of the car and the money Smith still owed to the dealer. Smith refused to pay on the grounds that he had been a minor at the time of purchase and had disaffirmed the contract after he had reached the age of majority. The trial court ruled that Smith had*

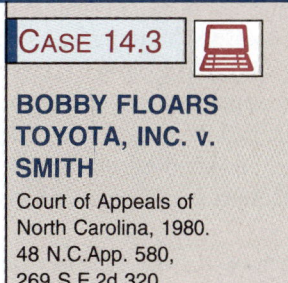

CASE 14.3

**BOBBY FLOARS TOYOTA, INC. v. SMITH**

Court of Appeals of North Carolina, 1980.
48 N.C.App. 580,
269 S.E.2d 320.

properly *"disaffirmed the contractual obligation"* by relinquishing the car ten months after attaining his majority, holding that ten months was a *"reasonable time within which to disaffirm his contractual obligations under the circumstances of this case."* The car dealer appealed.

*MORRIS,* Chief Judge.

\* \* \* \*

\* \* \* In the instant case, we believe that ten months is an unreasonable time within which to elect between disaffirmance and ratification, in that this case involves an automobile, an item of personal property which is constantly depreciating in value. Modern commercial transactions require that both buyers and sellers be responsible and prompt.

\* \* \* \*

In the present case, it is clear that defendant Smith recognized as binding the installment note evidencing the debt owed from his purchase of an automobile. It is undisputed that he continued to possess and operate the automobile after his eighteenth birthday, and he continued to make monthly payments as required by the note for ten months after becoming eighteen. \* \* \* There is no evidence to indicate that defendant ever made a demand for rescission [cancellation] of the contract because of his infancy [minority] or that he ever had any intention of doing so. We hold, therefore, that defendant's acceptance of the benefits and continuance of payments under the contract constituted a ratification of the contract, precluding subsequent disaffirmance.

**DECISION AND REMEDY**   *The appellate court reversed the decision of the trial court and remanded the case for further proceedings consistent with the appellate court's opinion.*

## NONVOIDABLE CONTRACTS

Many states have passed statutes restricting the ability of minors to avoid certain contracts. For example, as previously discussed, some states prohibit minors from disaffirming certain insurance contracts. Other states hold that loans for education or medical care received by minors create binding legal duties that they cannot avoid.[7]

In addition, certain statutes specifically require minors to perform legal duties. Suppose James Dornan, a minor, wants to legally seize the property of Davis Snowden for default of a loan. In some states, Dornan is required to file a bond before the legal seizure (called attachment) can occur. After filing the bond, Dornan cannot avoid the obligations of the bonding agreement, because the bond is a legal duty imposed by state statute. In such situations, a minor cannot rely on the common law rule that the contract is voidable. Similar legal duties are imposed on minors with respect to bank accounts and transfers of stock.

Some contracts cannot be avoided; they are enforced simply as a matter of law, on the grounds of public policy. For example, marriage contracts and contracts to enlist in the armed services fall into this category.

## LIABILITY FOR TORTS

Generally, minors are liable for their torts. Courts do, however, weigh the factors of age, mental capacity, and maturity before determining a minor's liability. As has been pointed out, a breach of contract is normally not treated as a tort for which the minor is liable. When the tort is more than simply the improper execution of some lawful act in the performance of a contract, however, and when it is independent of the contract, the court may rule against the minor. The test of whether an action can be brought against the minor is whether a basis for establishing liability exists apart from the contract.

For example, suppose a minor rents a boat. The rental agreement provides that the minor will use due care to prevent damage to the boat. Nonethe-

---

7. New York Education Law Section 281; California Civil Code, Section 36.

less, the minor's careless use of the boat damages it. Will a court uphold an action in tort for negligence? The answer to this question depends on whether the court interprets imposing tort liability on the minor as directly or indirectly enforcing the minor's promise, which, because of a lack of contractual capacity, is voidable. The minor may be held liable, however, to any third parties injured by the minor's negligence.

## PARENTS' LIABILITY

As a general rule, parents are not liable for contracts made by minor children acting on their own. This is why businesses ordinarily require parents to sign any contract made with a minor. The parents then become personally obligated under the contract to perform the conditions of the contract, even if their child avoids liability.

In some states, a parent may be liable if he or she failed to exercise proper parental control over the minor child and knew, or should have known, from the minor's habits and tendencies, that failure to exercise control posed an unreasonable risk of harm to others. Other states have enacted statutes imposing on parents legal responsibility for the consequences of the tortious acts of their children. These statutes vary. For example, in some states, liability will be imposed on parents only for the willful, malicious, or wanton acts of their minor children. In other states, liability will be imposed on parents for their children's negligent acts that result from the parents' negligence as well as for their children's willful and malicious acts.[8]

## SECTION 2

# INTOXICATED PERSONS

Intoxication is a condition in which a person's normal capacity to act or think is inhibited by alcohol or some other drug.[9] A contract entered into by an intoxicated person can be either voidable or valid.

If the person was sufficiently intoxicated to lack mental capacity, then the transaction is voidable at the option of the intoxicated person even if the intoxication was purely voluntary. For the contract to be voidable, it must be proved that the intoxicated person's judgment and ability to reason were impaired to such an extent that he or she did not comprehend the legal consequences of entering into the contract. If, despite intoxication, the person understands these legal consequences, the contract will be enforceable. Simply because the terms of the contract are foolish or obviously favor the other party does not mean that the contract is voidable (unless the other party *fraudulently* induced the person to become intoxicated). Problems often arise in determining whether a party was intoxicated enough to avoid legal duties. Rather than inquire into the intoxicated person's mental state, many courts prefer to look at objective indications to determine whether the contract is voidable owing to intoxication.

If a contract is voidable because of a person's intoxication, that person has the option of disaffirming it—the same option available to a minor. The vast majority of courts, however, require that the intoxicated person make full restitution (fully return any consideration received) as a condition of disaffirmance, except in cases involving necessaries (as explained below). For example, suppose Brinegar, who is intoxicated, contracts to purchase a set of encyclopedias from Stevens. If the books are delivered, Brinegar can disaffirm the executed contract and recover the payment made to Stevens only by returning the encyclopedias.

An intoxicated person, after becoming sober, may ratify a contract expressly or implicitly, just as a minor may do upon reaching majority. Implied ratification occurs when a person enters into a contract while intoxicated and fails to disaffirm the contract within a *reasonable* time after becoming sober. Acts or conduct inconsistent with an intent to disaffirm—such as the continued use of property purchased under a voidable contract—will also ratify the contract. In addition, contracts for necessaries are voidable, but the intoxicated person is liable in quasi contract for the reasonable value of the consideration received.

The following case shows an unusual business transaction in which boasts, brags, and dares "after a few drinks" resulted in a binding sale and purchase transaction. It should be noted that avoidance due to intoxication is very rare.

---

8. See, for example, the Texas Family Code, Section 33.02.
9. The lack of contractual capacity of a person intoxicated while the contract is being made must be distinguished from the contractual capacity of an alcoholic. If an alcoholic makes a contract while sober, there is no lack of capacity. See *Olsen v. Hawkins,* 90 Idaho 28, 408 P.2d 462 (1965).

**CASE 14.4**

**LUCY v. ZEHMER**

Supreme Court of Appeals of
Virginia, 1954.
196 Va. 493,
84 S.E.2d 516.

**BACKGROUND AND FACTS**   *W. O. Lucy and J. C. Lucy, the plaintiffs, filed suit against A. H. Zehmer and Ida Zehmer, the defendants, to compel the Zehmers to convey title of their property, known as the Ferguson Farm, to the Lucys for $50,000, as allegedly the Zehmers had agreed to do. Lucy had known Zehmer for fifteen or twenty years and for the last eight years or so had been anxious to buy the Ferguson Farm from Zehmer. One night, Lucy stopped in to visit the Zehmers in the combination restaurant, filling station, and motor court they operated. While there, Lucy tried to buy the Ferguson Farm once again. This time he tried a new approach. According to the trial court transcript, Lucy said to Zehmer, "I bet you wouldn't take $50,000 for that place." Zehmer replied, "Yes, I would too; you wouldn't give fifty." Throughout the evening, the conversation returned to the sale of the Ferguson Farm for $50,000. At the same time, the parties continued to drink whiskey and engage in light conversation. Eventually, Lucy enticed Zehmer to write up an agreement to the effect that Zehmer would sell to Lucy the Ferguson Farm for $50,000 complete. Later, Lucy sued Zehmer to go through with the sale. Zehmer argued that he had been drunk and that the offer had been made in jest and hence was unenforceable. The trial court agreed with Zehmer, and Lucy appealed.*

BUCHANAN, J. [Justice] delivered the opinion of the court.

\*   \*   \*   \*

In his testimony, Zehmer claimed that he "was high as a Georgia pine," and that the transaction "was just a bunch of two doggoned drunks bluffing to see who could talk the biggest and say the most." That claim is inconsistent with his attempt to testify in great detail as to what was said and what was done. \*   \*   \* The record is convincing that Zehmer was not intoxicated to the extent of being unable to comprehend the nature and consequences of the instrument he executed, and hence that instrument is not to be invalidated on that ground. \*   \*   \*

\*   \*   \*   \*

The appearance of the contract, the fact that it was under discussion for forty minutes or more before it was signed; Lucy's objection to the first draft because it was written in the singular, and he wanted Mrs. Zehmer to sign it also; the rewriting to meet that objection and the signing by Mrs. Zehmer; the discussion of what was to be included in the sale, the provision for the examination of the title, the completeness of the instrument that was executed, the taking possession of it by Lucy with no request or suggestion by either of the defendants that he give it back, are facts which furnish persuasive evidence that the execution of the contract was a serious business transaction rather than a casual, jesting matter as defendants now contend.

\*   \*   \*   \*

Not only did Lucy actually believe, but the evidence shows he was warranted in believing, that the contract represented a serious business transaction and a good faith sale and purchase of the farm.

In the field of contracts, as generally elsewhere, "*We must look to the outward expression of a person as manifesting his intention rather than to his secret and unexpressed intention.* [Emphasis added.] 'The law imputes to a person an intention corresponding to the reasonable meaning of his words and acts.' "

\*   \*   \*   \*

Whether the writing signed by the defendants and now sought to be enforced by the complainants was the result of a serious offer by Lucy and a serious acceptance by the defendants, or was a serious offer by Lucy and an acceptance in secret jest by the defendants, in either event it constituted a binding contract of sale between the parties.

*The Supreme Court of Virginia determined that the writing was an en-forceable contract and reversed the ruling of the lower court. The Zehmers were required by court order to carry through with the sale of the Ferguson Farm to the Lucys.*

**DECISION
AND REMEDY**

---

## SECTION 3

# MENTALLY INCOMPETENT PERSONS

Contracts made by mentally incompetent persons can be either void, voidable, or valid. If a person has been adjudged mentally incompetent by a court of law and a guardian has been appointed, any contract made by the mentally incompetent person is void—no contract exists. Only the guardian can enter into binding legal duties on the incompetent person's behalf.

If a mentally incompetent person not previously so adjudged by a court enters into a contract, the contract may be voidable if the person does not know he or she is entering into the contract or lacks the mental capacity to comprehend its nature, purpose, and consequences. In such a situation, the contract is voidable at the option of the mentally incompetent person but not the other party. Whenever there is no prior adjudication of mental incompetence, most courts examine whether the party was able to understand the nature, purpose, and consequences of his or her act at the time of the transaction. The contract may then be disaffirmed or ratified. Ratification must occur after the person is mentally competent or after a guardian is appointed and ratifies the contract. Like minors and intoxicated persons, mentally incompetent persons are liable (in quasi contract) for the reasonable value of any necessaries they receive.

A contract entered into by a mentally incompetent person may also be valid. A person may be able to understand the nature and effect of entering into a certain contract, yet simultaneously lack ca-pacity to engage in other activities. In such cases, the contract will be valid, because the person is not legally mentally incompetent for contractual purposes.[10] Similarly, an otherwise mentally incompetent person may have a *lucid interval*—a temporary restoration of sufficient intelligence, judgment, and will to enter into contracts without disqualification—during which he or she will be considered to have full legal capacity.

## SECTION 4

# ALIENS

An alien is a citizen of another country who resides in this country. Aliens who are legally in this country generally have the same contractual rights as U.S. citizens. They may be sued and they may sue in the courts to enforce their contractual rights. Some states restrict the right of an alien to own real property. In virtually all cases, an *enemy alien* (a citizen of a country with which we are at war) will not be able to enforce a contract, although the contract can be held in abeyance (temporarily set aside) until the war is over.

---

10. Modern courts no longer require a person to be completely irrational to disaffirm contracts on the basis of mental incompetence. A contract may be voidable if, by reason of a mental illness or defect, an individual was unable to act reasonably with respect to the transaction and the other party had reason to know of the condition. See *Ortelere v. Teachers' Retirement Board,* 25 N.Y.2d 196, 250 N.E.2d 460, 303 N.Y.S.2d 362 (1969).

# ■ CONCEPT SUMMARY 14.1 Legal Effect of Incapacity

| | MINORITY | INTOXICATION | MENTAL INCOMPETENCE |
|---|---|---|---|
| **General Rule** | Contracts entered into by minors are VOIDABLE at the option of the minor. | If an intoxicated person lacks the mental capacity to comprehend the legal consequences of entering into the contract, the contract is VOIDABLE at the option of the intoxicated person. | 1. Contracts made by a person adjudged to be mentally incompetent by a court of law and for whom a guardian has been appointed are VOID.<br>2. Contracts made by persons who lack the mental capacity to comprehend the subject matter, nature, and consequences of their actions, but who have not been adjudged by a court to be mentally incompetent, are VOIDABLE.<br>3. Contracts made by persons who understand the nature and effect of entering into a contract, even if the persons lack capacity to engage in other activities, are VALID. |
| **Rules of Disaffirmance** | A minor may disaffirm the contract at any time while still a minor and within a reasonable time after reaching the age of majority. Most states do not require restitution. | An intoxicated person may disaffirm the contract at any time while intoxicated and for a reasonable time after becoming sober, but must make full restitution. | A mentally incompetent person may disaffirm a voidable contract at any time while mentally incompetent and for a reasonable time after regaining mental competence, but must make full restitution. |
| **Exceptions to Basic Rules of Disaffirmance** | 1. *Necessaries* Liable for the reasonable value of the necessaries.<br>2. *Ratification* After reaching the age of majority, a person can ratify a contract he or she made as a minor, becoming fully liable thereon.<br>3. *Fraud or Misrepresentation* Misrepresentation of age in many jurisdictions prohibits the right of disaffirmance. | 1. *Necessaries* Liable for the reasonable value of the necessaries.<br>2. *Ratification* After becoming sober, a person can ratify a contract he or she made while intoxicated, becoming fully liable thereon. | 1. *Necessaries* Liable for the reasonable value of the necessaries.<br>2. *Ratification* After regaining mental competence, an individual can ratify the voidable contract, becoming fully liable thereon. |

## TERMS AND CONCEPTS TO REVIEW

age of majority 262
contractual capacity 261

disaffirmance 262
necessaries 266

ratification 267

# QUESTIONS AND CASE PROBLEMS

**14–1. Contracts by Minors.** Gonzalez is a seventeen-year-old minor who has just graduated from high school. She is attending a university two hundred miles from home and has contracted to rent an apartment near the university for one year at $450 per month. She is working at a convenience store to earn enough money to be self-supporting. She moves into the apartment and has paid rent for four months when a dispute arises between her and the landlord. Gonzalez, still a minor, moves out and returns the key to the landlord. The landlord wants to hold Gonzalez liable for the balance of the lease. Discuss fully Gonzalez's liability on the lease.

**14–2. Intoxication.** After Kira had several drinks one night, she sold Charlotte a valuable fur stole for one hundred dollars. The next day, Kira offered the one hundred dollars to Charlotte and requested the return of her stole. Charlotte refused to accept the one hundred dollars or return the stole, claiming that they had a valid contract of sale. Kira explained that she was intoxicated at the time the bargain was made and thus the contract is voidable at her option. Is Kira correct? Explain.

**14–3. Contracts by Minors.** Stewart, who was sixteen years old, purchased a used car at Harry Krank's Auto Lot for $300. At the time of the sale, Krank knew that Stewart was a minor. Stewart drove the car several times during the following week and discovered that the main bearing was burned out. He took the car back to the auto lot and was told by Krank that it would cost between $200 and $225 to repair the vehicle. Stewart refused to pay for any repairs, left the car on the lot, and later disaffirmed the contract and requested the return of the purchase price. Krank alleged that because Stewart's aunt had paid Krank $240 toward the purchase price of the car, she, and not Stewart, was the owner of the vehicle—notwithstanding the fact that Krank had made out the sales receipt in Stewart's name alone. Assuming the car is not a necessity for Stewart, how will the court rule? Discuss.

**14–4. Mental Incompetence.** Two physicians, Devito and Burke, leased an office suite for five years and agreed to share the rent payments equally—even if one of them moved out or was unable to occupy his part of the premises as a result of disability or for any other reason. Two weeks later, Devito consulted a neurologist about his increasing absent-mindedness and forgetfulness and dis-cussed the possibility of giving up his practice. A few months later, Devito was diagnosed as suffering from presenile dementia (premature deterioration of the brain). The condition had been developing slowly for a matter of years, resulting in the progressive loss of memory and other mental abilities. The following year, Devito was so impaired mentally that he had to close his practice and retire. Burke later sued Devito for his share of the remaining rent under the lease. Devito claimed that he had been mentally incompetent at the time he signed the agreement to share the rent and hence the agreement was voidable at his option. Will Devito prevail in court? Discuss.

**14–5. Mental Incompetence.** Allen Apfelblat began suffering from mental illness in the summer of 1983. In November of that same year, he executed three notes to his bank to purchase three automobiles. On January 6, 1984, Apfelblat was involuntarily committed to a psychiatric hospital, where he was successfully treated. Upon Apfelblat's release, the bank threatened to pursue legal recourse if Apfelblat did not pay on the notes. In response, Apfelblat agreed, at the insistence of the bank, to execute new notes to cover the accrued debts and to make several interest payments that were in arrears. Apfelblat later filed an action to discharge the notes due because of lack of capacity at the time the original notes were executed. Apfelblat also claimed that he did not intend to legally ratify the contract or to accept liability from a voidable contract when he did not have to do so. Discuss whether Apfelblat's contract is enforceable by the bank. [*Apfelblat v. National Bank of Wyandotte-Taylor,* 158 Mich.App. 258, 404 N.W.2d 725 (1987)]

**14–6. Contracts by Minors.** In 1973, James Halbman, Jr., a minor, entered into an agreement to buy a 1968 Oldsmobile from Michael Lemke for $1,250. He made a $1,000 down payment and took possession of the automobile immediately. After experiencing problems with the car, Halbman took it to a garage for repairs. When he failed to pay the garage bill of $637, the garage removed the vehicle's engine and transmission. Halbman subsequently disaffirmed the sales contract with Lemke and returned the title to the Oldsmobile. Halbman also successfully sued to obtain the return of the money that he had paid to Lemke. Can Lemke countersue for restitution of the amount by which the automobile has declined in value because of the removal of the auto parts? Why or why not? [*Halbman v. Lemke,* 99 Wis.2d 241, 298 N.W.2d 562 (1980)]

**14–7. Contracts by Minors.** Sheehan Buick, Inc., sold a 1965 Buick Riviera to Rose, a minor, for $5,176. While still a minor, Rose elected to disaffirm the purchase and notified Sheehan of his intention, offering to return the vehicle for a full refund. Sheehan refused, claiming that Rose appeared to be an adult and acted and negotiated like an adult. In addition, Sheehan claimed that the vehicle was a necessary item for Rose because it was used to carry on his school, business, and social activities. Discuss whether Rose can disaffirm the sale and, if so, whether Sheehan is entitled to an offsetting amount for depreciation in the automobile's value. [*Rose v. Sheehan Buick, Inc.,* 204 So.2d 903 (Fla.App. 1967)]

**14–8. Contracts by Minors.** Carol Ann White, a nineteen-year-old minor, went to Dr. Demetrios Cidis and asked him to furnish her with contact lenses. They agreed on a price of $225, and Carol gave Cidis her personal check for $100. The doctor examined Carol on Thursday evening, ordered the lenses on Friday, and received them on Saturday. The cost to the doctor for the lenses was $110. On Monday, at the insistence of her father, Carol called and canceled the contract and stopped payment on the check. At the time, Carol lived at home, had a full-time job, and paid her parents a sum each month for room and board. The lenses could be used by no one but Carol and thus had no market value. Dr. Cidis brought suit, claiming that the lenses were a necessary. Carol claimed her minority as a defense to any liability. Discuss whether contact lenses are necessaries. [*Cidis v. White,* 71 Misc.2d 481, 336 N.Y.S.2d 362 (1972)]

**14–9. Contracts by Minors.** April Iverson's uncle, John Polachek, obtained a life insurance policy through his employer, Scholl, Inc. The policy, issued by Bankers Life and Casualty, named April as the sole beneficiary. April, the plaintiff, was eleven years old when her uncle died and when Bankers mailed the $10,000 death-benefit check to her. The check was made out in her name because Scholl had not informed Bankers that April was a minor. Subsequently, April's father misappropriated the funds by having April sign (endorse) the check. Later, April sued Bankers and Scholl for the $10,000. Bankers claimed that her endorsement discharged its obligation to her. She claimed that as a minor she did not have the capacity to discharge this contractual obligation. Who will prevail in court? Discuss. [*Iverson v. Scholl, Inc.,* 136 Ill.App.3d 962, 483 N.E.2d 893, 91 Ill.Dec. 407 (1985)]

**14–10. Contracts by Minors.** In 1982, Webster Street Partnership, Ltd. (Webster), entered into a lease agreement with Matthew Sheridan and Pat Wilwerding. Webster was aware that both Sheridan and Wilwerding were minors. Both tenants were living away from home, apparently with the understanding that they could return home at any time. Sheridan and Wilwerding paid the first month's rent but then failed to pay the rent for the next month and vacated the apartment. Webster sued them for breach of contract. They claimed that the lease agreement was voidable because they were minors. Who will win, and why? [*Webster Street Partnership, Ltd. v. Sheridan,* 220 Neb. 9, 368 N.W.2d 439 (1985)]

**14–11. A Question of Ethics**

*Kevin Green, a sixteen-year-old minor, entered into a sales agreement to purchase a Camaro from Star Chevrolet Co. for $4,642.50. The title for the car was drawn up in Kevin's name, and the money came from Kevin's personal bank account. The question of Kevin's age was not raised by him or the car dealership. He used the car daily to drive six miles to school and back and to drive about one mile to his place of part-time work. Kevin brought the car back several times for repairs, and he later discovered that the size and power of the engine were not what they were supposed to be. Finally, when the main head gasket blew, Kevin's attorney informed Star Chevrolet that Kevin was disaffirming the contract. Kevin repaired the gasket and continued to use the car until an accident destroyed the car more than a year after the purchase. He then returned the Camaro and sought a refund of the full purchase price of the car. In the lawsuit that followed, the car was not deemed a necessary by the court, and the dealer was required to refund the full purchase price of the car to Kevin.* [Star Chevrolet Co. v. Green, *473 So.2d 157 (Miss. 1985)]*

1. Do you think that the law has achieved a "fair" balance between the policy of protecting minors and the policy of protecting innocent parties who are harmed by the failure of others to keep their contractual promises? In other words, does the law favor minors to an unfair extent?

2. If the car had been deemed a necessary in this case, the outcome would have been different—Kevin would not have been able to avoid the contract. What ethical principle underlies the doctrine that minors cannot avoid contracts for necessaries?

# CHAPTER 15

# GENUINENESS
# OF ASSENT

A contract has been entered into for a legal purpose between two parties, each with full legal capacity to form a contract. The contract is also supported by consideration. Nonetheless, the contract may be unenforceable if the parties have not genuinely assented to its terms. **Genuineness of assent** may be lacking because of mistakes, misrepresentation, undue influence, or duress (in other words, because there is no true ''meeting of the minds''). If the law were to enforce contracts not genuinely assented to by the contracting parties, injustice would result. In this chapter, we examine problems relating to genuineness of assent.

## SECTION 1

## MISTAKES

We all make mistakes, and it is therefore not surprising that mistakes are made when contracts are formed. It is important to distinguish between mistakes made *in judgment as to value or quality* and mistakes made *as to facts.* Only the latter have legal significance. Suppose Wong Sun plans to buy ten acres of land in Montana. If he believes the land is worth $100,000, and it is worth only $40,000, his mistake is one of value or quality. If he believes, however, that the land is the ten acres owned by the Boyds, and it is actually the ten acres owned by the Deweys, his mistake is one of fact. Only a mistake as to fact allows a contract to be avoided.

Mistakes occur in two forms—*unilateral* and *mutual (bilateral).* A unilateral mistake is made by only one of the contracting parties; a mutual, or bilateral, mistake is made by both.

### UNILATERAL MISTAKES

A unilateral mistake occurs when one contracting party makes a mistake as to some *material fact*—that is, a fact important to the subject matter of the contract. In general, a unilateral mistake does not afford the mistaken party any right to relief from the contract.[1] For example, DeVinck intends to sell his stereo for $550. He learns that Benson is interested in buying a used stereo. DeVinck writes a letter to Benson offering to sell his stereo, but he mistakenly types in the price of $500. Benson immediately writes back, accepting DeVinck's offer. Even though DeVinck intended to sell his stereo for $550, his unilateral mistake falls on him. He is bound in contract to sell the stereo to Benson for $500.

There are at least two exceptions. The contract may not be enforceable (1) if the *other* party to the contract knows or should have known that a mistake was made or (2) if the error was due to a mathematical mistake in addition, subtraction, division, or multiplication and was done inadvertently and without gross negligence (a mistake of this nature is sometimes referred to as a *scrivener's error*—meaning a writer's, or scribe's, error). Of course, the mistake must still involve some material fact.

Consider the following situation. Chimel Construction Company made a bid to install the plumbing in an apartment building. When Hector Chimel, the president, summarized his costs, he unintentionally omitted the figures for the pipe fittings. Because of the omission, Chimel's bid was $6,500 below that of the other bidders. The general contractor, Northern Industrial Development, Inc., accepted and relied on Chimel's bid. If Northern was not aware of Chimel's mistake and could not reasonably have been aware of it, the contract will be enforceable; Chimel will be required to install the plumbing at the bid price. If, however, it can be shown that Chimel's assistant mentioned his error to Northern, or that Chimel's bid was so far below the others that Northern should reasonably have known the bid was a mistake, the contract may be rescinded. Because the law of contracts only protects reasonable expectations, Northern would not be allowed to accept the offer knowing that it was made mistakenly.[2]

In the following case, a unilateral mistake was made when a typist erroneously transformed $500 to $500,000 in a settlement offer.

---

1. Restatement (Second) of Contracts, Section 153, liberalizes this rule to take into account the modern trend of allowing avoidance even though only one party has been mistaken.

2. *Peerless Glass Co. v. Pacific Crockery Co.*, 121 Cal. 641, 54 P. 101 (1898).

---

| CASE 15.1 |
| --- |

**WHITAKER v. ASSOCIATED CREDIT SERVICES, INC.**

United States Court of Appeals, Sixth Circuit, 1991. 946 F.2d 1222.

**BACKGROUND AND FACTS** *Kenneth and Linda Whitaker had filed an action against Trans Union Corporation and others, alleging violations of the Fair Credit Reporting Act. The lawyer for Trans Union drafted an offer of settlement and presented it to the Whitakers' attorney. The amount of the settlement was supposed to be $500, but the first draft contained a typographical error showing the amount as $500,000. The error went undetected, and the $500,000 figure was typed into the second draft, which was forwarded to Linda Gosnell, Trans Union's attorney, who also did not detect the mistake. Gosnell filed the offer with the clerk of court and mailed a copy to the Whitakers' lawyer. The Whitakers filed an acceptance of the settlement and forwarded it to Gosnell, who at that time noticed the typing error. The Whitakers refused a substitute offer, and Trans Union filed a motion to set aside the judgment. The district court found for Trans Union, and the Whitakers appealed.*

*MILBURN,* Circuit Judge.

\* \* \* \*

In this case, it is undisputed that there has been a clerical error resulting from a mistake and inadvertence which resulted in an erroneous judgment. \* \* \*

\* \* \* \*

* * * As the district court found, "this mistake is just too big to ignore." Plaintiffs' attorney himself characterized the offer of $500,000 as "outrageous," and admitted he was "shocked" by the offer when he received it. Moreover, we believe that any reasonable person would have been shocked by the offer in light of the circumstances of this case, *viz.,* the fact that before they filed their action, plaintiffs had made no demands for monetary damages; that while plaintiffs had requested $1 million in punitive damages on the underlying claim in their complaint, Trans Union was only one of six defendants named in the complaint; that plaintiffs in their complaint specified only $3,600 in actual damages caused by Trans Union's conduct; and that the purported $500,000 offer was the first offer of any kind that plaintiffs had received from defendants.

* * * If the $500,000 judgment were enforced, it would result in not only a windfall but unjust enrichment.

* * * *

* * * While plaintiffs contend that defendants manifested to them an offer of $500,000 to which they assented, there was in fact no meeting of the minds because plaintiffs were aware that such an offer was "outrageous."

*The court of appeals affirmed the district court's ruling. The judgment was properly set aside on the basis of mistake.*

**DECISION AND REMEDY**

*We all know that typographical and clerical errors can happen and that occasionally they result in grossly disproportionate benefits to one of the parties. For example, the Internal Revenue Service might send a tax refund for $50,000 when in fact the refund should have been only $5,000. There is a tendency to think that if the government or some "big business" firm has made a mistake, it is okay to retain the benefits. As some beneficiaries have proclaimed, it's like "winning the lottery." Little need be said about the ethics of these assumptions, just as little need be said about the ethics of the Whitakers, who tried to enforce an agreement under which they would have benefited from a gross error of which they were obviously aware.*

**ETHICAL CONSIDERATIONS**

## MUTUAL MISTAKES OF MATERIAL FACT

When both parties are mistaken about the same material fact, the contract can be rescinded by either party.[3] As with a unilateral mistake, the mistake must be about a material fact—a fact that is important to the subject matter of the contract. If, instead, a mutual mistake concerns the future market value or quality of the object of the contract, the contract normally can be enforced by either party.

To illustrate: Assume that at Umberto's art gallery, Keeley buys a painting of a landscape. Both Umberto and Keeley believe that the painting is by the artist Van Gogh. Later, Keeley discovers that the painting is a very clever fake. Because neither Umberto nor Keeley was aware of this material fact when they made their deal, Keeley can rescind the contract and recover the purchase price of the painting.

A word or term in a contract may be subject to more than one reasonable interpretation. In that situation, if the parties to the contract attach materially different meanings to the term, their mutual misunderstanding may allow the contract to be rescinded. The classic case on mutual misunderstanding involved a ship named Peerless that was to sail from Bombay with certain cotton goods on board. More than one ship named Peerless sailed from Bombay that winter, however.

---

3.  Restatement (Second) of Contracts, Section 152.

CASE 15.2

**RAFFLES v.
WICHELHAUS**
Court of Exchequer, England,
1864.
159 Eng.Rep. 375.

**BACKGROUND AND FACTS** *The defendant, Wichelhaus, purchased a shipment of Surat cotton from the plaintiff, Raffles, "to arrive 'Peerless' from Bombay." The defendant expected the goods to be shipped on the Peerless sailing from Bombay in October. The plaintiff expected to ship the goods on a different Peerless, which sailed from Bombay in December. By the time the goods arrived and the plaintiff tried to deliver them, the defendant was no longer willing to accept them.*

*PER CURIAM* [an opinion by the entire court].
\* \* \* \*

[The defendants asserted that the] ship mentioned in the \* \* \* agreement was meant and intended by the defendants to be the ship called the "Peerless," which sailed from Bombay \* \* \* in October; and that the plaintiff was not ready and willing and did not offer to deliver to the defendants any bales of cotton which arrived by the last mentioned ship, but instead thereof was only ready and willing and offered to deliver to the defendants 125 bales of Surat cotton which arrived by another and different ship, which was also called the "Peerless," and which sailed from Bombay \* \* \* in December.
\* \* \* \*

There is nothing on the face of the contract to show that any particular ship called the "Peerless" was meant; but the moment it appears that two ships called the "Peerless" were about to sail from Bombay there is latent ambiguity, and parol evidence[a] may be given for the purpose of shewing that the defendant meant one "Peerless" and the plaintiff another. That being so, there was no consensus ad idem [on the point], and therefore no contract.

**DECISION
AND REMEDY**

*The judgment was for the defendant, Wichelhaus. The court held that no mutual assent existed, because the parties attached materially different meanings to an essential term of the written contract (the ship that was to transport the goods). This being so, oral testimony would have been needed to determine whether the parties had actually meant the same ship. If both had meant the same ship, then the contract would have been enforceable.*

a. With respect to contracts, *parol evidence* is evidence that the document itself does not furnish but that other sources (such as, in this case, oral testimony) provide. See Chapter 16.

## MUTUAL MISTAKES IN VALUE

Value is variable. Depending on the time, place, and other circumstances, the same item may be worth considerably different amounts. When parties contract, their agreement establishes the value of the object of their transaction—for the moment. At the next moment, the value may change. Either party may be mistaken as to the shape that change will take, but a mistake as to value will almost never justify voiding a contract. Each party is considered to have assumed the risk that the value will change or prove to be different from what he or she thought. Without this rule, almost any party

who did not receive what he or she considered a fair bargain could argue mistake.

Suppose Yu Chin, after seeing Bev Weiler's violin, buys it for $250. Although both parties know that it is very old, neither party believes that it is extremely valuable. An antique dealer later informs the parties, however, that old violins in good condition, such as this one, are rare and worth thousands of dollars. Although Weiler may claim that a mutual mistake has been made, the mistake is not one that warrants contract rescission (cancellation). Both Chin and Weiler mistook the value of that particular violin. Therefore, the contract cannot be rescinded.

As pointed out previously, if the parties are mistaken as to some fact that is material to their transaction, the transaction may be avoided. This rule applies when the fact affects the value of the subject matter of the parties' deal. For example, an early Michigan case, *Sherwood v. Walker*,[4] involved two farmers who entered into a contract for the purchase of a cow. The owner told the purchaser that the cow was barren (incapable of breeding and producing calves). Based on this belief, the parties negotiated a price several hundred dollars less than it would have been had the cow been capable of breeding. Just before delivery, the owner discovered the cow had conceived a calf, and he refused to deliver the much more valuable cow to the purchaser. In a split decision, the court held that "a barren cow is substantially a different creature than a breeding one," and the transaction was avoided.

The following case illustrates a situation in which the parties were mutually mistaken as to the value of the personal property being transferred. In discussing the issue, the court compares the circumstances with those in *Sherwood v. Walker.*

---

4.  66 Mich. 568, 33 N.W. 919 (1887).

---

**BACKGROUND AND FACTS**  *At the time of her death in 1984, Olga Mestrovic owned a large number of works of art created by her husband, Ivan Mestrovic, an internationally known sculptor and artist who had died in 1962. By the terms of Olga's will, all of these works of art not otherwise disposed of by her will were to be sold and the proceeds distributed to members of the Mestrovic family. Also included in Olga's estate was certain real estate. In 1985, 1st Source Bank—which had been appointed by Olga in her will to handle all matters relating to her estate upon her death—sold the real estate to Terrence and Antoinette Wilkin. When the Wilkins complained that the premises had been left in a cluttered condition, the bank and the Wilkins agreed that the Wilkins would clean the premises themselves and keep any items of personal property that they wanted. At the time of this agreement, neither the bank nor the Wilkins suspected that any works of art remained on the property. During their clean-up efforts, the Wilkins found eight drawings and a plaster sculpture that had apparently been created by Ivan Mestrovic. The probate court held that the works of art belonged to Mestrovic's estate. The Wilkins appealed, claiming ownership of the works of art based on their agreement with the bank.*

**CASE 15.3**

**WILKIN v. 1ST SOURCE BANK**
Court of Appeals of Indiana, Third District, 1990.
548 N.E.2d 170.

*HOFFMAN,* Judge.

\*  \*  \*  \*

Mutual assent is a prerequisite to the creation of a contract. Where both parties share a common assumption about a vital fact upon which they based their bargain, and that assumption is false, the transaction may be avoided if[,] because of the mistake[,] a quite different exchange of values occurs from the exchange of values contemplated by the parties. There is no contract because the minds of the parties have in fact never met.

The necessity of mutual assent, or "meeting of the minds," is illustrated in the classic case of *Sherwood v. Walker* \*  \*  \* .

Like the parties in *Sherwood*, the parties in the instant case shared a common presupposition as to the existence of certain facts which proved false. The bank and the Wilkins considered the real estate which the Wilkins had purchased to be cluttered with items of personal property variously characterized as "junk," "stuff," or "trash." Neither party suspected that works of art created by Ivan Mestrovic remained on the premises.

\*  \*  \*  \*

The following commentary on *Sherwood* is equally applicable to the case at bar: "Here the buyer sought to retain a gain that was produced, not by a subsequent change in circumstances, nor by the favorable resolution of known uncertainties when the contract was made, but by the presence of facts quite different from those on which the parties based their bargain."

The probate court properly concluded that there was no agreement for the purchase, sale, or other disposition of the eight drawings and plaster sculpture, because there was no meeting of the minds.

**DECISION AND REMEDY**   *The probate court's decision was affirmed. The works of art belonged to Olga Mestrovic's estate.*

SECTION 2

# FRAUDULENT MISREPRESENTATION

Although **fraud** is a tort, it also affects the genuineness of the innocent party's consent to the contract. Thus, the transaction is not voluntary in the sense of involving "mutual assent." When an innocent party is fraudulently induced to enter into a contract, the contract normally can be avoided because that party has not *voluntarily* consented to its terms.[5] Normally, the innocent party can either rescind the contract and be restored to his or her original position or enforce the contract and seek damages for any injuries resulting from the fraud.

The word *fraudulent* means many things in the law. Generally, fraudulent misrepresentation refers only to misrepresentation that is consciously false and is intended to mislead another. The perpetrator of the fraudulent misrepresentation knows or believes that the assertion is false or knows that he or she does not have a basis (stated or implied) for the assertion.[6]

What is at issue is whether the defendant believed that the plaintiff was substantially certain to be misled as a result of the misrepresentation. Dantzler, for example, makes a statement to the ABC Credit Rating Company about his financial condition that he knows is untrue. Dantzler realizes that ABC will publish this information for its subscribers. Marchetti, a subscriber, receives the published information. Relying on that information, Marchetti is induced to make a contract to lend money to Dantzler. Dantzler's statement is a fraudulent misrepresentation, and the contract is voidable by Marchetti.

Typically, fraud consists of the following elements:

1. A misrepresentation of a material fact must occur.
2. There must be an intent to deceive.
3. The innocent party must justifiably rely on the misrepresentation.

To collect damages, a party must also have been injured. To obtain rescission of a contract, or to defend against the enforcement of a contract on the basis of fraudulent misrepresentation, in most states a party need not have suffered an injury.

## MISREPRESENTATION HAS OCCURRED

The first element of proving fraud is to show that misrepresentation of a material fact has occurred. This misrepresentation can be in words or actions. For example, the statement "This sculpture was created by Michelangelo" is an express misrepresentation of fact if the statue was sculpted by another artist. The misrepresentation as to the identity of the artist would certainly be a material fact in the formation of a contract.

Misrepresentation can also take place through the conduct of a party, such as concealment. Concealment involves preventing the other party from learning of a material fact.[7] Suppose, for example, that Rakas contracts to buy a new car from Bustamonte, a dealer in new automobiles. The car has been used as a demonstration model for prospective customers to test-drive, but Bustamonte has

---

5. Restatement (Second) of Contracts, Sections 163 and 164.
6. Restatement (Second) of Contracts, Section 162.

---

7. Restatement (Second) of Contracts, Section 160.

turned back the odometer. Rakas cannot tell from the odometer reading that the car has been driven nearly five hundred miles, and Bustamonte does not tell Rakas the distance the car has actually been driven. The concealment constitutes fraud because of Bustamonte's conduct. Likewise, if a salesperson shows a sample from the top of a large box but does not show the samples at the bottom, a misrepresentation by conduct has occurred if there is a marked difference in quality between the top and bottom merchandise and the salesperson knows of the difference.

Representations of future facts (predictions) or statements of opinion are generally not subject to claims of fraud. Every person is expected to exercise care and judgment when entering into contracts, and the law will not come to the aid of one who simply makes an unwise bargain. Statements such as ''This land will be worth twice as much next year'' or ''This car will last for years and years,'' for example, are statements of opinion, not fact. Contracting parties should recognize them as such and not rely on them. An opinion is usually subject to contrary or conflicting views; a fact is objective and verifiable. A seller of goods, then, is allowed to use *puffery* to sell his or her wares without liability for fraud.

In certain cases, however, particularly when a naïve purchaser relies on a so-called expert's opinion, the innocent party may be entitled to rescission or reformation. This occurred in the following case.

---

**COMPANY PROFILE**  *Arthur Murray began teaching people how to dance in 1919. At the time, dancing was becoming increasingly popular, in part because so many adults were shocked by the new ''jazz dancing.'' Across America, young people wanted to learn the new steps—the turkey trot, the fox trot, the kangaroo dip, the chicken scratch, the bunny hug, the grizzly bear, and others. Murray began selling lessons through the mail by sending customers projectors that flipped cards to show how a dance step was done. When the projectors proved unreliable, Murray designed silhouettes of shoeprints to place on a floor in a pattern corresponding to the steps of a dance. By the 1930s, Murray's instructors were giving lessons on cruise ships, in tourist hotels, and to the employees of New York stores during the employees' lunch breaks. In 1937, Murray popularized an African-American dance known as the Big Apple and, as an offshoot of this success, founded the Arthur Murray Studios, a chain of franchised dance schools. During the 1950s, Murray sponsored a television show— The Arthur Murray Party—to attract students to the schools. Murray retired in 1964, estimating that he had taught more than twenty million people how to dance.*

CASE 15.4

**VOKES v. ARTHUR MURRAY, INC.**

District Court of Appeal of Florida, Second District, 1968. 212 So.2d 906.

**BACKGROUND AND FACTS**  *The defendant, Arthur Murray, Inc., operated dancing schools throughout the nation through local, franchised operators, one of whom was the defendant. The plaintiff, Audrey E. Vokes, a widow without family, wished to become ''an accomplished dancer'' and to find ''a new interest in life.'' In 1961 she was invited to attend a ''dance party'' at J. P. Davenport's ''School of Dancing.'' Vokes went to the school and received elaborate praise from her instructor for her grace, poise, and potential as ''an excellent dancer.'' The instructor sold her eight half-hour dance lessons for $14.50 each, to be utilized within one calendar month. Subsequently, over a period of less than sixteen months, Vokes bought a total of fourteen dance courses, which amounted to 2,302 hours of dancing lessons for a total cash outlay of $31,090.45, all at Davenport's school. When it became clear to Vokes that she did not, in fact, have the potential to be an excellent dancer, she filed suit against the* *school, alleging fraudulent misrepresentation. When the trial court dismissed her complaint, she appealed.*

*PIERCE,* Judge.

\* \* \* \*

[The dance contracts] were procured by defendant Davenport and Arthur Murray, Inc., by false representations to her that she was improving in her dancing ability, that she had excellent potential, that she was responding to instructions in dancing grace, and that they were developing her into a beautiful dancer, whereas in truth and in fact she did not develop in her dancing ability, she had no "dance aptitude," and in fact had difficulty in "hearing the musical beat." \* \* \*

\* \* \* \*

It is true that "generally a misrepresentation, to be actionable, must be one of fact rather than of opinion." \* \* \* "A statement of a party having \* \* \* superior knowledge may be regarded as a statement of fact although it would be considered as opinion if the parties were dealing on equal terms."

It could be reasonably supposed here that defendants had "superior knowledge" as to whether plaintiff had "dance potential" and as to whether she was noticeably improving in the art of terpsichore [dancing]. And it would be a reasonable inference from the undenied averments of the complaint that the flowery eulogiums heaped upon her by defendants \* \* \* proceeded as much or more from the urge to "ring the cash register" as from any honest or realistic appraisal of her dancing prowess or a factual representation of her progress.

\* \* \* \*

\* \* \* "[W]hat is plainly injurious to good faith ought to be considered as a fraud sufficient to impeach a contract," and \* \* \* an improvident agreement may be avoided "because of surprise, or mistake, *want of freedom, undue influence, the suggestion of falsehood, or the suppression of truth.*" [Emphasis added.]

**DECISION AND REMEDY**   *Vokes's complaint was reinstated, and the case was returned to the trial court to allow Vokes to prove her case.*

---

**MISREPRESENTATION OF LAW**   Misrepresentation of law does not *ordinarily* entitle a party to relief from a contract. For example, Camara has a parcel of property that she is trying to sell to Pye. Camara knows that a local ordinance prohibits building anything on the property higher than three stories. Nonetheless, she tells Pye, "You can build a condominium fifty stories high if you want to." Pye buys the land and later discovers that Camara's statement is false. Normally, Pye cannot avoid the contract, because at common law people are assumed to know state and local laws. Additionally, a layperson should not rely on a statement made by a nonlawyer about a point of law.

Exceptions to this rule occur, however, when the misrepresenting party is in a profession that is known to require greater knowledge of the law than the average citizen possesses. The courts are recognizing an increasing number of such professions. For example, the courts recognize that real estate brokers are expected by their clients to know the law governing real estate sales, land use, and so on. If Camara, in the preceding example, were a lawyer or a real estate broker, her misrepresentation of the area's zoning status would probably constitute fraud.[8]

**SILENCE**   Ordinarily, neither party to a contract has a duty to come forward and disclose facts. Therefore, a contract cannot be set aside because certain pertinent information is not volunteered.

For example, suppose you have an accident that requires extensive body work on one side of your car. After the repair, the car's appearance and operation are the same as they were before the accident. One year later you decide to sell your car. Do you have a duty to volunteer the information about the

---

8.   Restatement (Second) of Contracts, Section 170.

accident to the seller? The answer is no. In this case, silence does not constitute misrepresentation. In contrast, if the purchaser asks you if the car has had extensive body work and you lie, you have committed a fraudulent misrepresentation.

Some exceptions to this rule exist. Generally, if a *serious* defect or a *serious* potential problem is known to the seller but could not reasonably be suspected by the buyer, the seller may have a duty to speak. For example, if a city fails to disclose to bidders subsoil conditions that will cause great expense in constructing a sewer, the city is guilty of fraud.[9]

Another example involved a woman, Judy Khan, who agreed to have a Bjork-Shiley mechanical valve implanted in her heart. Although Khan had been advised of the risks generally associated with mechanical heart valves (blood clotting, rejection of the valve by the body, the permanent need to take blood-thinner medication, and so on), she was not told of the risk that the valve might fracture. About two years after the valve was implanted, she learned from her surgeon that the Bjork-Shiley heart valve was one of a group of valves being recalled because of defects and malfunctions. But the risk of open-heart surgery to remove the valve was even greater than the risk of a valve malfunction. In Khan's lawsuit against the valve's manufacturer, Shiley, Inc., and its parent company, Pfizer, Inc., the court found that she had no cause of action under warranty or product liability theories (see Chapters 24 and 25), because the valve had not yet fractured or caused her physical injury. She did, however, have a cause of action for fraud because the manufacturer had not disclosed the risks attending the use of its heart valve, of which it was well aware.[10]

Failure to disclose important facts also constitutes fraud if the parties have a relationship of trust and confidence, called a **fiduciary relationship.** In such a relationship, if one party knows any facts that materially affect the other's interests, they must be disclosed. An attorney, for example, has a duty to disclose material facts to a client. Other such relationships include those between partners in a partnership, directors of corporations and shareholders, and guardians and wards.[11]

A seller's silence, coupled with active concealment, constitutes misrepresentation. In the Bustamonte-Rakas example discussed previously, for example, Bustamonte not only failed to disclose the true mileage to Rakas but concealed the true mileage by turning back the odometer. Disclosing some, but not all, of the facts can be equally deceitful. Such would be the case if Bustamonte had mentioned that the car actually had ''a few more miles on it'' than shown by the odometer—which registered three miles. In addition, if circumstances change so that what once was true is now false, the party knowing of the change has a duty to inform the other.

Statutes provide other exceptions to the general rule of nondisclosure. The Truth-in-Lending Act, for example, requires disclosure of certain facts (see Chapter 46). Statutes may even specify the typeface size to be used in the document providing the information.

## INTENT TO DECEIVE

The second element of fraud is knowledge on the part of the misrepresenting party that facts have been falsely represented. This element, normally called *scienter,*[12] or ''guilty knowledge,'' signifies that there was an *intent to deceive. Scienter* clearly exists if a party knows a fact is not as stated. *Scienter* also exists if a party makes a statement that he or she believes not to be true or makes a statement recklessly, without regard to whether it is true or false. Finally, this element is met if a party says or implies that a statement is made on some basis such as personal knowledge or personal investigation when it is not.

For example, assume that Meese, a securities broker, offers to sell BIM stock to Packer. Meese assures Packer that BIM stocks are blue-chip

---

9.   *City of Salinas v. Souza & McCue Construction Co.,* 66 Cal. 2d 217, 424 P.2d 921, 57 Cal.Rptr. 337 (1967). Normally, the seller must disclose only ''latent'' defects—that is, defects that would not readily be discovered even by an expert. Thus, termites in a house would not be a latent defect, because an expert could normally discover their presence.

10.   *Khan v. Shiley, Inc.,* 217 Cal.App.3d 848, 266 Cal.Rptr. 106 (1990). The valve's manufacturer, Shiley, Inc., and its parent company, Pfizer, Inc., have since been sued by hundreds of individuals in whom the defective valves are implanted. In 1992, Pfizer agreed to settle a class-action suit that had been brought by plaintiff-users of the valve.

11.   Restatement (Second) of Contracts, Sections 161 and 173.
12.   Pronounced sy-*en*-ter.

securities—that is, they are stable, are limited in risk, and yield a high return on investment over time. Meese, however, knows nothing about the quality of the BIM stock and does not believe the truth of what he is saying. Meese's statement is a misrepresentation because Meese does not believe the truth of what he told Packer and because he knows that he does not have any basis for making such a statement. Therefore, normally Packer can avoid his obligations under the contract, which was induced by Meese's intentional misrepresentation of a material fact.

In many cases involving a seller's misrepresentation, courts have held that proving fault is unnecessary. That is, a buyer need prove only that the seller's representation was false, without regard to the seller's state of mind. In those cases—often involving sales of land or stock—the courts reason that it is the seller's duty to know the truth of what he or she says.

## RELIANCE ON THE MISREPRESENTATION

The third element of fraud is reasonably *justifiable reliance* on the misrepresentation of fact. The deceived party must have a justifiable reason for relying on the misrepresentation, and the misrepresentation must be an important factor (but not necessarily the sole factor) in inducing that party to enter the contract.

Reliance is not justified if the innocent party knows the true facts or relies on obviously extravagant statements. Suppose a used-car dealer tells you, "This old Cadillac will get fifty miles to the gallon." You would not normally be justified in relying on the statement. Or suppose that Kovich, a bank director, induces Mallory, a co-director, to sign a guaranty that the bank's assets will satisfy its liabilities, stating, "We have plenty of assets to satisfy our creditors." If Mallory knows the true facts, he will not be justified in relying on Kovich's statement. If, however, Mallory does not know the true facts *and has no way of finding them out*, he normally will be justified in relying on the statement. The same rule applies to defects in property sold. If the defects are of the kind that would be obvious on inspection, the buyer cannot justifiably rely on the seller's representations. If the defects are hidden or latent (that is, not apparent on the surface), the buyer is justified in relying on the seller's statements.

## INJURY TO THE INNOCENT PARTY

Most courts do not require a showing of injury when the action is to *rescind* (cancel) the contract. These courts hold that because rescission returns the parties to the positions they held before the contract was made, a showing of injury to the innocent party is unnecessary.[13]

For a person to recover damages caused by fraud, proof of an injury is universally required. The measure of damages is ordinarily equal to the property's value had it been delivered as represented, less the actual price paid for the property. In actions based on fraud, courts often award **punitive damages,** or *exemplary damages,* which are granted to a plaintiff over and above the proved, actual compensation for the loss. Punitive damages are based on the public-policy consideration of punishing the defendant or setting an example to deter similar wrongdoing by others.

| SECTION 3 |

# NONFRAUDULENT MISREPRESENTATION

If a plaintiff seeks to rescind a contract because of *fraudulent* misrepresentation, the plaintiff must prove that the defendant had the intent to deceive. Most courts also allow rescission in cases involving *nonfraudulent* misrepresentation—that is, innocent or negligent misrepresentation—if all of the other elements of misrepresentation exist.

## INNOCENT MISREPRESENTATION

If a person makes a statement that he or she believes to be true but that actually misrepresents material facts, the person is guilty only of an **innocent misrepresentation,** not of fraud. If an innocent misrepresentation occurs, the aggrieved party can rescind the contract but usually cannot seek damages. For example, Parris tells Roberta that a tract contains 250 acres. Parris is mistaken—the tract contains only 215 acres—but Parris does not know that. Roberta is induced by the statement to make a contract to buy the land. Even though the misrepresentation is innocent, Roberta can avoid the contract if the misrepresentation is material.

---

13. See, for example, *Kaufman v. Jaffe,* 244 App.Div. 344, 279 N.Y.S. 392 (1935).

## NEGLIGENT MISREPRESENTATION

Sometimes a party will make a misrepresentation through carelessness, believing the statement is true. This misrepresentation is negligent if he or she fails to exercise reasonable care in uncovering or disclosing the facts or does not use the skill and competence that his or her business or profession requires. For example, an operator of a weight scale certifies the weight of Sneed's commodity, even though the scale's accuracy has not been checked in more than a year. In virtually all states, such **negligent misrepresentation** is equal to *scienter,* or to knowingly making a misrepresentation. In effect, negligent misrepresentation is treated as fraudulent misrepresentation, even though the misrepresentation was not purposeful. In negligent misrepresentation, culpable ignorance of the truth supplies the intention to mislead, even if the defendant can claim, "I didn't know."

---

## SECTION 4

# UNDUE INFLUENCE

Undue influence arises from special kinds of relationships in which one party can greatly influence another party, thus overcoming that party's free will. Minors and elderly people, for example, are often under the influence of guardians. If the guardian induces a young or elderly ward to enter into a contract that benefits the guardian, undue influence may have been exerted. Undue influence can arise from a number of confidential or fiduciary relationships: attorney-client, doctor-patient, guardian-ward, parent-child, husband-wife, or trustee-beneficiary. The essential feature of undue influence is that the party being taken advantage of does not, in reality, exercise free will in entering into a contract. A contract entered into under excessive or undue influence lacks genuine assent and is therefore voidable.[14]

To determine whether undue influence has been exerted, a court must ask, "To what extent was the transaction induced by domination of the mind or emotions of the person in question?" It follows, then, that the mental state of the person in question will often show to what extent the persuasion from the outside influence was "unfair."

When a contract enriches a party at the expense of another who is in a relationship of trust and confidence with, or who is dominated by, the enriched party, the court will often *presume* that the contract was made under undue influence. For example, if a ward challenges a contract made by his or her guardian, the presumption will normally be that the guardian has taken advantage of the ward. To rebut this presumption successfully, the guardian has to show that *full disclosure* was made to the ward, that consideration was adequate, and that the ward received, if available, independent and competent advice before completing the transaction.

In a relationship of trust and confidence, such as between an attorney and a client, the dominant party (the attorney) is held to extreme or utmost good faith in dealing with the subservient party. Suppose that a long-time attorney for an elderly man induces him to sign a contract for the sale of some of his assets to a friend of the attorney at below-market prices. It is presumed that the attorney has not upheld good faith in dealing with the man. Unless this presumption can be rebutted, the contract will be voidable.

---

## SECTION 5

# DURESS

Undue influence involves conduct of a *persuasive* nature; **duress** involves conduct of a *coercive* nature. That is, assent to the terms of a contract is not genuine if one of the parties is *forced* into agreement. Recognizing this, the courts allow that party to rescind the contract. Forcing a party to enter into a contract by threatening the party with a wrongful act is legally defined as *duress.* For example, if Piranha Loan Company threatens to harm you or your family unless you sign a promissory note for the money that you owe, Piranha is guilty of duress. In addition, threatening blackmail or extortion to induce consent to a contract constitutes duress. Duress is both a defense to the enforcement of a contract and a ground for rescission. Therefore, the party upon whom the duress is exerted can choose to carry out the contract or to avoid the entire transaction. (This is true in most cases in which assent is not real.)

Generally, the threatened act must be wrongful or illegal. Threatening to exercise a legal right is not ordinarily illegal and usually does not

---

14. Restatement (Second) of Contracts, Section 177.

constitute duress. Suppose that Donovan injures Jaworski in an auto accident. The police are not called. Donovan has no automobile insurance, but she has substantial assets. Jaworski is willing to settle the potential claim out of court for $3,000. Donovan refuses. After much arguing, Jaworski loses her patience and says, "If you don't pay me $3,000 right now, I'm going to sue you for $35,000." Donovan is frightened and gives Jaworski a check for $3,000. Later in the day, she stops payment on the check. Jaworski comes back to sue her for the $3,000. Although Donovan argues that she was the victim of duress, the threat of a *civil* suit is normally not duress.

Economic need is generally not sufficient to constitute duress, even when one party exacts a very high price for an item that the other party needs. If the party exacting the price also creates the need, however, *economic duress* may be found. The Internal Revenue Service, for example, assessed a large tax and penalty against Weller. Weller retained Eyman, the accountant who had filed the tax returns on which the assessment was based, to resist the assessment. Two days before the deadline for filing a reply with the Internal Revenue Service, Eyman declined to represent Weller unless he signed a very high contingency fee agreement for his services. The agreement was unenforceable.[15] Although Eyman had threatened only to withdraw his services, something that he was legally entitled to do, he was responsible for delaying the withdrawal until the last days. Because it would have been impossible at that late date to obtain adequate representation elsewhere, Weller was forced either to sign the contract or lose his right to challenge the IRS assessment.

## SECTION 6

# ADHESION CONTRACTS AND UNCONSCIONABILITY

Questions concerning genuineness of assent may arise when the terms of a contract are dictated by a party with overwhelming bargaining power and the signer must agree to those terms or go without

---

15. *Thompson Crane & Trucking Co. v. Eyman,* 123 Cal.App.2d 904, 267 P.2d 1043 (1954).

the commodity or service in question. Such contracts are often referred to as **adhesion contracts.** An adhesion contract is written *exclusively* by one party (the dominant party, usually the seller or creditor) and presented to the other party (the adhering party, usually the buyer or borrower), who has no opportunity to negotiate. Adhesion contracts usually contain copious amounts of fine print disclaiming the maker's liability for everything imaginable. Many automobile retailers have used contracts containing several pages of fine print when selling cars. In the past, nearly every automobile company excluded liability for personal injuries suffered as a result of using the product. The average consumer buying a car was in no position to bargain for personal injury coverage. The consumer could either go without an automobile or buy the auto, risking personal injury for which he or she could not hold the auto manufacturer liable.

Standard form contracts often contain fine-print provisions that shift a risk naturally borne by one party to the other. Such contracts are used by a variety of businesses and include life insurance policies, residential leases, loan agreements, and employment agency contracts. To avoid enforcement of the contract or of a particular clause, the aggrieved party must show that the parties had substantially unequal bargaining positions and show that enforcement would be manifestly unfair or oppressive. If the required showing is made, the contract or particular term is deemed *unconscionable* and not enforced. Technically, unconscionability under Section 2–302 of the UCC applies only to contracts for the sale of goods. Many courts, however, have broadened the concept and applied it in other situations.

Although unconscionability will be discussed in the next chapter, it is important to note here that the great degree of discretion permitted a court to invalidate or strike down a contract or clause as being unconscionable has met with resistance. As a result, some states have not adopted Section 2–302 of the UCC. In those states, the legislature and the courts prefer to rely on traditional notions of fraud, undue influence, and duress. On the one hand, this gives certainty to contractual relationships, because parties know they will be held to the exact terms of their contracts. But on the other hand, public policy does require that there be some limit on the power of individuals and businesses to dictate the terms of contracts. The following classic case is illustrative.

**BACKGROUND AND FACTS** *In June 1947, the Campbell Soup Company entered into a written contract with George and Harry Wentz for delivery by the Wentzes to Campbell of all the Chantenay red-cored carrots to be grown on fifteen acres of the Wentz farm during the 1947 season. The prices specified in the contract ranged from $23 to $30 per ton according to the time of delivery. The contract price for January 1948 was $30 per ton. In January of 1948, the Wentzes told a Campbell representative that they would not deliver their carrots at the contract price. The market price had risen to at least $90 per ton. Chantenay red-cored carrots were virtually unobtainable. The Wentzes harvested 100 tons of Chantenay red-cored carrots, sold 62 tons of the carrots to a neighboring farmer, Lojeski, and Lojeski sold approximately half of these carrots to Campbell on the open market. Campbell, suspecting that it was purchasing its "contract carrots" from Lojeski, refused to buy any more and brought suit against the Wentzes and Lojeski to enjoin further sale of the contract carrots to others and to compel specific performance of the contract. The trial court denied Campbell's petition, and Campbell appealed.*

CASE 15.5

**CAMPBELL SOUP CO. v. WENTZ**
United States Court of Appeals, Third Circuit, 1949.
172 F.2d 80.

*GOODRICH,* Circuit Judge.

\* \* \* \*

The reason that we shall affirm instead of reversing with an order for specific performance is found in the contract itself. We think it is too hard a bargain and too one-sided an agreement to entitle the plaintiff to relief in a court of conscience. For each individual grower the agreement is made by filling in names and quantity and price on a printed form furnished by the buyer. This form has quite obviously been drawn by skillful draftsmen with the buyer's interests in mind.

\* \* \* \*

\* \* \* Paragraph 10 provides liquidated damages to the extent of $50 per acre for any breach by the grower. There is no provision for liquidated or any other damages for breach of contract by Campbell.

The provision of the contract which we think is the hardest is paragraph 9, \* \* \* . It will be noted that Campbell is excused from accepting carrots under certain circumstances. But even under such circumstances the grower, while he cannot say Campbell is liable for failure to take the carrots, is not permitted to sell them elsewhere unless Campbell agrees. This is the kind of provision which the late Francis H. Bohlen would call "carrying a good joke too far." \* \* \*

We are not suggesting that the contract is illegal. Nor are we suggesting any excuse for the grower in this case who has deliberately broken an agreement entered into with Campbell. We do think, however, that a party who has offered and succeeded in getting an agreement as tough as this one is should not come to a chancellor and ask court help in the enforcement of its term. That equity does not enforce unconscionable bargains is too well established to require elaborate citation.

*The trial court's ruling was affirmed because the contract was unconscionable and therefore did not merit enforcement by a court of equity.*

**DECISION AND REMEDY**

**Unconscionability in Germany** *Section 138(2) of the German civil law code voids a legal transaction when "a person exploiting the need, carelessness or inexperience of another" contracts for "pecuniary [monetary] advantages [that] are in obvious disproportion to the performance." German courts closely scrutinize standardized contract provisions for unfairness and might well have voided a contract such as the one in the* Campbell *case.*

**INTERNATIONAL CONSIDERATIONS**

## ■ CONCEPT SUMMARY 15.1 Genuineness of Assent

| PROBLEMS OF ASSENT | RULE |
|---|---|
| **Mistakes** | 1. *Unilateral*—Generally, the mistaken party is bound by the contract, *unless* (1) the other party knows or should have known of the mistake or (2) in some states, the mistake is an inadvertent mathematical error in addition, subtraction, etc., that is committed without gross negligence.<br>2. *Bilateral (mutual)*—If both parties are mistaken about a material fact, such as the identity of the subject matter, either party can avoid the contract. If the mistake relates to the value or quality of the subject matter, either party can enforce the contract. |
| **Fraudulent Misrepresentation** | Three elements are necessary to establish fraudulent misrepresentation:<br>1. A misrepresentation of a material fact has occurred.<br>2. There exists an intent to deceive.<br>3. The innocent party has justifiably relied on the misrepresentation. |
| **Nonfraudulent Misrepresentation** | 1. *Innocent misrepresentation*—Occurs when a person makes a statement that he or she believes to be true but that actually misrepresents material facts. The aggrieved party can rescind the contract but usually cannot seek damages.<br>2. *Negligent misrepresentation*—Occurs when a person makes an untrue statement but, through carelessness, believes the statement to be true. Negligent misrepresentation has the same legal effect as fraudulent misrepresentation in virtually all states. |
| **Undue Influence/ Duress** | 1. *Undue influence*—Arises from special relationships, such as fiduciary relationships, in which one party's free will has been overcome by the undue influence of another. Usually, the contract is avoidable.<br>2. *Duress*—Defined as forcing a party to enter into a contract under the fear of threat—for example, the threat of violence or economic pressure. The party forced to enter the contract can rescind the contract. |
| **Unconscionability** | Concerned with one-sided bargains in which one party has substantially superior bargaining power and can dictate the terms of a contract. Unconscionability typically occurs as a result of the following:<br>1. "Standard form" contracts in which a fine-print provision purports to shift a risk normally borne by one party to the other (for example, a liability disclaimer).<br>2. "Take it or leave it" adhesion contracts in which the buyer has no choice but to agree to the seller's dictated terms if the buyer is to procure certain goods or services. |

## TERMS AND CONCEPTS TO REVIEW

| | | |
|---|---|---|
| adhesion contract 286 | fraud 280 | negligent misrepresentation 285 |
| duress 285 | genuineness of assent 275 | punitive damages 284 |
| fiduciary relationship 283 | innocent misrepresentation 284 | *scienter* 283 |

# QUESTIONS AND CASE PROBLEMS

**15–1. Assent.** Juan is an elderly man who lives with his nephew, Samuel. Juan is totally dependent on Samuel's support. Samuel tells Juan that unless he transfers a tract of land he owns to Samuel for a price 15 percent below market value, Samuel will no longer support and take care of him. Juan enters into the contract. Discuss fully whether Juan can set aside this contract.

**15–2. Assent.** Grano owns a forty-room motel on Highway 100. Tanner is interested in purchasing the motel. During the course of negotiations, Grano tells Tanner that the motel netted $30,000 last year and that it will net at least $45,000 next year. The motel books, which Grano turns over to Tanner before the purchase, clearly show that Grano's motel netted only $15,000 last year. Also, Grano fails to tell Tanner that a bypass to Highway 100 is being planned that will redirect most traffic away from the front of the motel. Tanner purchases the motel. During the first year under Tanner's operation, the motel nets only $18,000. It is at this time that Tanner learns of the previous low profitability of the motel and the planned bypass. Tanner wants his money back from Grano. Discuss fully Tanner's probable success in getting his money back.

**15–3. Assent.** Discuss whether either of the following contracts will be unenforceable on the ground that genuineness of assent is lacking.

    (a) Simmons finds a stone in his pasture that he believes to be quartz. Jenson, who also believes that the stone is quartz, contracts to purchase it for $10. Just before delivery, the stone is discovered to be a diamond worth $1,000.

    (b) Jacoby's barn is burned to the ground. He accuses Goldman's son of arson and threatens to bring criminal action unless Goldman agrees to pay him $5,000. Goldman agrees to pay.

**15–4. Fraudulent Misrepresentation.** Lund offered to sell Steck his car and told Steck that the car had been driven only 25,000 miles and had never been in an accident. Steck hired Carvallo, a mechanic, to appraise the condition of the car, and Carvallo said that the car probably had at least 50,000 miles on it and probably had been in an accident. In spite of this information, Steck still thought the car would be a good buy for the price, so he purchased it. Later, when the car developed numerous mechanical problems, Steck sought to rescind the contract on the basis of Lund's fraudulent misrepresentation of the auto's condition. Will Steck be able to rescind his contract? Explain.

**15–5. Mistake.** Steven Lanci was involved in an automobile accident with an uninsured motorist. Lanci was insured with Metropolitan Insurance Co., although he did not have a copy of the insurance policy. Lanci and Metropolitan entered settlement negotiations, during which Lanci told Metropolitan that he did not have a copy of his policy. Ultimately, Lanci agreed to settle all

claims for $15,000, noting in a letter to Metropolitan that $15,000 was the ''sum you have represented to be the . . . policy limits applicable to this claim.'' After signing a release, Lanci learned that the policy limits were actually $250,000, and he refused to accept the settlement proceeds. When Metropolitan sued to enforce the settlement agreement, Lanci argued that the release had been signed as the result of a mistake and was void. Should the court enforce the contract or void it? Explain. [*Lanci v. Metropolitan Insurance Co.,* 388 Pa.Super. 1, 564 A.2d 972 (1989)]

**15–6. Duress.** In 1982, William Schmalz was hired by the Hardy Salt Co. under an employment contract that stated that he was entitled to six months' severance pay in the event that he was laid off. The company would not have to pay in the event of any voluntary separation or involuntary termination for other reasons, such as for poor performance or for cause. In mid-1983, Schmalz was asked to resign after having an affair with the chairman's executive secretary. Schmalz was told that if he did not resign he would be fired but that if he did resign the company would keep him on the payroll for another six weeks. Schmalz resigned and signed an agreement releasing Hardy Salt from any liability for breach of the employment contract. Schmalz later claimed that he had signed the release under duress and sued Hardy Salt for the six months' severance pay under his employment contract. Discuss whether Schmalz's claim for duress should succeed. [*Schmalz v. Hardy Salt Co.,* 739 S.W.2d 765 (Mo.App. 1987)]

**15–7. Fraud and Duress.** William and Lilly Adams obtained a divorce in 1985 and began the process of dividing their property. They inventoried their worldly possessions and decided that certain property would go to Mrs. Adams and the remainder, along with the debts on their jointly owned property, would remain with Mr. Adams. Later, Mrs. Adams claimed that she had signed the agreement under duress and because of fraudulent misrepresentation. Mrs. Adams testified in legal proceedings that Mr. Adams had consistently told her that she must take the property as offered and agree not to seek alimony, that Mr. Adams had threatened to declare bankruptcy and force her to accept the responsibility for her share of the community debts if she did not agree, and that Mr. Adams had frequently cursed her but had not in any way threatened physical harm. Mrs. Adams also testified that she had examined the subsequent formal community property settlement and that she had basically understood it. At that time, she had casually spoken to two different attorneys about the settlement contract, but because both attorneys said that they would need time to investigate before giving advice, she went ahead and signed it. Discuss whether Mrs. Adams can rescind the settlement contract on the grounds of duress and fraudulent misrepresentation. [*Adams v. Adams,* 503 So.2d 1052 (La.App. 2 Cir. 1987)]

**15–8. Duress.** In July 1965, Loral Corp. was awarded a $6 million contract to produce radar sets for the Navy. For this contract Loral needed to purchase forty precision gear parts. Loral awarded to Austin Instrument, Inc., a subcontract to supply twenty-three of the forty gear parts. In May of 1966 Loral was awarded a second contract to produce more radar sets. Loral solicited bids for forty more gear parts. Austin submitted a bid for all forty but was told by Loral that the subcontract would be awarded only for items for which Austin was the lowest bidder. Austin's president told Loral that it would not accept an order for less than forty gear parts and, one day later, told Loral that Austin would cease deliveries on the existing contract unless (1) Loral awarded Austin a contract for all forty gear part units and (2) Loral consented to substantial increases for the prices of all gear parts under the existing contract. Ten days later Austin ceased making deliveries. Loral tried to find other suppliers to furnish the gear parts, but none were available. Because of deadlines and liquidated damage clauses (clauses providing for money damages to be paid in the event of delays) in the Navy contract, plus the possible loss of reputation by Loral with the government, Loral agreed to Austin's terms. After Austin's last delivery, Loral filed suit to recover the increased prices Austin had charged on the ground that the agreement to pay these prices was based on duress. Discuss Loral's claim. [*Austin Instrument, Inc. v. Loral Corp.*, 29 N.Y.2d 124, 272 N.E.2d 533, 324 N.Y.S.2d 22 (1971)]

**15–9. Unilateral Mistake.** Robert and Wendy Pfister held a hundred shares of Tracor Computing Corp. stock. The stock was no longer being traded on the New York Stock Exchange, and they thought their shares were of little value. They asked a stock brokerage firm, Foster & Marshall, Inc., to evaluate the shares for them. The brokerage firm advised the Pfisters that Tracor Computing had changed its name to Continuum Company, Inc., and that its stock was worth $49.50 a share; thus, the Pfisters' holdings were valued at $4,950. Robert Pfister suspected there might be an error in the valuation and asked Foster & Marshall to recheck the value, which was done. The Pfisters sold their shares to Foster & Marshall, which paid them the $4,950 for the hundred shares. Later, the brokerage firm discovered that the Tracor Computing stock had been exchanged for Continuum stock at a ten-to-one ratio, which meant that the Pfisters had owned only ten shares. The Pfisters refused to return the $4,455 overpayment they had received from the brokerage firm. Can Foster & Marshall recover the overpayment it made to the Pfisters resulting from its own unilateral mistake of fact? Discuss. [*Foster & Marshall, Inc. v. Pfister,* 66 Or.App. 685, 674 P.2d 1215 (1984)]

**15–10. Fraudulent Misrepresentation.** Nosrat, a citizen of Iran, owned a hardware store with his brother-in-law, Edwin. Edwin induced Nosrat to sign a promissory note for $11,400, payable to a third party, telling Nosrat that the document was a credit application for the hardware store. Although Nosrat could read and write English, he failed to read the note or to notice that the document was clearly entitled ''PROMISSORY NOTE (SECURED) and Security Agreement.'' The money received from the third party in exchange for the note was spent by Edwin and others. When the third party sued for payment, Nosrat sought to void the note on the basis of Edwin's fraudulent inducement. Will Nosrat succeed in his attempt? Discuss. [*Waldrep v. Nosrat,* 426 So.2d 822 (Ala. 1983)]

### 15–11. A Question of Ethics

*Mark and Kathryn Van Wagoner attended a real estate "open house" that was held by Carol Klas, who was selling the property for her former husband, John Klas. Mark Van Wagoner, an attorney experienced in real estate transactions, subsequently prepared and delivered to Carol Klas a written offer to purchase the property for $175,000. John Klas accepted the offer, and the Van Wagoners signed the agreement on August 11, 1987. Prior to signing the agreement, the Van Wagoners asked Carol Klas if there had been any appraisals of the property. She replied that there had been several appraisals, ranging from $175,000 to $192,000. At trial, Carol claimed that she understood the term "appraisal" to mean any opinion as to the market value of the house. The Van Wagoners did not request a written appraisal of the property until after signing the agreement. Carol Klas then provided them with a written appraisal, older than the others referred to by her, that listed the house's value as $165,000. The Van Wagoners subsequently refused to purchase the house, and John Klas brought suit to recover the difference between the agreement price and the price at which the house was later sold. In view of these facts, answer the following questions. [Klas v. Van Wagoner, 829 P.2d 135 (Utah App. 1992)]*

1. The Van Wagoners claimed that the contract should be rescinded on the basis of their mistaken assumption as to the value of the house. What kind of mistake was made in this situation (bilateral or unilateral, mistake of value or mistake of fact)? How should the court rule on this issue?

2. Mark Van Wagoner was an attorney experienced in real estate transactions. Should the court take this fact into consideration when making its decision? If this had been the Van Wagoners' first experience in purchasing real estate, would the legal result be any different? Should it?

3. Generally, what ethical principles, as expressed in public policies, are in conflict here and in similar situations in which parties enter into a contract with mistaken assumptions?

# CHAPTER 16

# LEGALITY AND THE STATUTE OF FRAUDS

A contract, to be enforced in court, must not call for the performance of an illegal act—that is, any act that is criminal, tortious, or otherwise opposed to public policy. The first part of this chapter considers what makes a bargain illegal—being contrary to state or federal statutes or to public policy—and the effects of an illegal bargain. Such contracts are normally void—that is, they really are not contracts.

A contract that is otherwise valid may still be unenforceable if it is not in the proper form. For example, certain types of contracts are required to be in writing. If a contract is required by law to be in writing and there is no written evidence of the contract, it may not be enforceable. In the second part of this chapter, we examine the kinds of contracts that require a writing under what is called the *Statute of Frauds.* The chapter concludes with a discussion of the *parol evidence rule,* under which courts determine the admissibility at trial of evidence extraneous, or external, to written contracts.

## SECTION 1

## LEGALITY

A contract to do something that is prohibited by federal or state statutory law is illegal and, as such, void from the outset and thus unenforceable. Also, a contract that is tortious or calls for an action contrary to public policy is illegal and unenforceable. It is important to note that a contract or a clause in a contract may be illegal even in the absence of a specific statute prohibiting the action promised by the contract.

### CONTRACTS CONTRARY TO STATUTE

Statutes often prescribe the terms of contracts. In some instances, the laws are specific, even providing for the inclusion of certain clauses and their wording. Other statutes prohibit certain contracts on the basis of their subject matter, the time at which they are entered into, or the status of the contracting parties. We now examine several ways in which contracts may be contrary to statute and thus illegal.

USURY   All states have statutes that set the maximum rates of interest that can be charged for different types of transactions, including ordinary loans. A lender who makes a loan at an interest rate above the lawful maximum is guilty of **usury.** The maximum rate of interest varies from state to state.

The maximum rate of interest should not be confused with either the **legal rate of interest** or the **judgment rate of interest.** The legal rate of interest is a rate fixed by statute when the parties to a contract intend an interest rate to be paid but do not fix the rate in the contract. This rate is frequently the same as the maximum rate of interest permitted by statute. A judgment rate of interest is a rate fixed by statute that is applied to a monetary judgment from the moment the judgment is awarded by a court until the judgment is paid. In some states, the legal rate is also the *prejudgment rate.* That is, it is the rate of interest that accrues on the amount of a judgment from the time of the filing of the suit to the issuance of the judgment.

Although usury statutes place a ceiling on allowable rates of interest, exceptions have been made to facilitate business transactions. For example, many states exempt corporate loans from their usury laws. In addition, almost all states have adopted special statutes allowing much higher interest rates on small loans to help those borrowers who are in need of money but simply cannot get loans at interest rates at or below the normal lawful maximum.

The effects of a usurious loan differ from state to state. A number of states allow the lender to recover only the principal of a loan along with interest up to the legal maximum. In effect, the lender is denied recovery of the excess interest. In other states, the lender can recover the principal amount of the loan but not the interest. In a few states, a usurious loan is a void transaction, and the lender cannot recover either the principal or the interest.

GAMBLING   In general, wagers and games of chance are illegal. All states have statutes that regulate gambling—defined as any scheme for the distribution of property by chance among persons who have paid a valuable consideration for the opportunity to receive the property.[1] Gambling is the creation of risk for the purpose of assuming it. In other words, a person making a bet creates the risk that he or she may lose the bet on the happening of an uncertain event in which he or she otherwise has no interest.

An increasing number of states do permit gambling. In certain states, such as Nevada and New Jersey, casino gambling is legal. In other states, certain forms of gambling are legal. California, for example, has not defined draw poker as a crime, although criminal statutes prohibit numerous other types of gambling games. Several states allow horse racing, and over half of the states have recognized the substantial revenues that can be obtained from gambling and have legalized state-operated lotteries and lotteries (such as bingo) arranged for charitable purposes.

The following case illustrates the general problem posed by differing state statutes on gambling, as well as how people from one state (where gambling debts are unenforceable) can avoid responsibility for gambling debts if they incur them in another state (where gambling debts are enforceable).

---

1. See *Wishing Well Club, Inc. v. Akron,* 66 Ohio L.Abs. 406, 112 N.E.2d 41 (Ohio Com. Pl. 1951).

---

| CASE 16.1 | **BACKGROUND AND FACTS**   *Soheil Sadri, a California resident, incurred debts totaling $22,000 over a two-day period in 1991 while gambling at Caesar's Tahoe casino in Nevada. On January 13 and 14, he wrote the casino two personal checks for $2,000 and $10,000. On January 14, he executed two memoranda of indebtedness for $5,000 each. In exchange for the checks and memoranda, Sadri received chips, which he lost playing the game of baccarat. Sadri subsequently stopped payment on the checks and memoranda, which were drawn on his account at a California bank. Caesar's Tahoe transferred its rights in the checks and memoranda to Metropolitan Creditors Service of Sacramento (MCS) for* |
|---|---|
| **METROPOLITAN CREDITORS SERVICE OF SACRAMENTO v. SADRI** | |
| California Court of Appeal, First District, 1993. | |
| 15 Cal.App.4th 1821, | |
| 19 Cal.Rptr.2d 646. | |

*collection, and MCS sued Sadri in California. The court issued a judgment in favor of Sadri, ruling that his gambling debts were unenforceable in California. MCS appealed.*

KING, Associate Justice.
   \*   \*   \*   \*

California has always had a strong public policy against judicial enforcement of gambling debts, going back virtually to the inception of statehood. \*   \*   \*
   \*   \*   \*   \*

The \*   \*   \* court [in *Hamilton v. Abadjian,* an earlier California case] stated the anti-enforcement rule within a context \*   \*   \* specific to the facts of \*   \*   \* the present case: ''The owner of a gambling house who honors a check for the purpose of providing a prospective customer with funds with which to gamble and who then participates in the transaction thus promoted by his act cannot recover on the check.''
   \*   \*   \*   \*

The *Hamilton* rule is on all fours [the facts are similar and the same questions of law are involved] with the present case. Caesar's Tahoe honored Sadri's checks and memoranda of indebtedness for the purpose of providing him with funds with which to gamble, and then participated in the game. \*   \*   \* [This rule] precludes judicial enforcement of Sadri's gambling debts in California state courts; \*   \*   \* the contracts underlying the debts are against public policy \*   \*   \* and thus the contracts are unlawful and the debts unenforceable.

*The appellate court affirmed the lower court's refusal to enforce the debts, on the ground that the enforcement of gambling debts incurred on credit violates California's public policy.*

**DECISION AND REMEDY**

---

**SABBATH LAWS** Statutes called Sabbath (Sunday) laws prohibit the formation or performance of certain contracts on a Sunday. Under the common law, such contracts are legal in the absence of this statutory prohibition. Under a few state statutes, all contracts entered into on a Sunday are illegal. Statutes in other states prohibit only the sale of certain types of merchandise, particularly alcoholic beverages, on a Sunday. These statutes, which date back to colonial times, are often called **blue laws.** Blue laws get their name from the blue paper on which New Haven, Connecticut, printed its new town ordinance in 1781. The ordinance prohibited all work on Sunday and required all shops to close on the ''Lord's Day.'' A number of states enacted laws forbidding the carrying on of ''all secular labor and business on The Lord's Day.'' Exceptions to Sunday laws permit contracts for necessities (such as food or drugs) and works of charity. A fully performed (executed) contract that was entered into on a Sunday cannot be rescinded (canceled).

Many states either have limited or do not enforce Sunday laws. Some of these laws have been held to be unconstitutional on the ground that they are contrary to the freedom of religion.

**LICENSING STATUTES** All states require that members of certain professions or callings obtain licenses allowing them to practice. Doctors, lawyers, real estate brokers, architects, electricians, and stockbrokers are but a few of the people who must be licensed. Some licenses are obtained only after extensive schooling and examinations, which indicate to the public that a special skill has been acquired. Others require only that the particular person be of good moral character.

Generally, business licenses provide a means of regulating and taxing certain businesses and protecting the public against actions that could threaten the general welfare. For example, in nearly all states, a stockbroker must be licensed and must file a bond with the state to protect the public from fraudulent transactions in stock. Similarly, a plumber must be licensed and bonded to protect the public against incompetent plumbers and to protect the public health. Only persons or businesses possessing the qualifications and complying with the conditions required by statute are entitled to licenses. Sometimes, for example, an owner of a saloon or tavern is required to sell food as a condition to obtaining a license to sell liquor for consumption on the premises.

When a person enters into a contract with an unlicensed individual, the contract may still be enforceable depending on the nature of the licensing statute. Some states expressly provide that the lack of a license in certain occupations bars the enforcement of work-related contracts. If the statute does not expressly state this, one must look to the underlying purpose of the licensing requirements for a particular occupation. If the purpose is to protect the public from unauthorized practitioners, a contract involving an unlicensed individual normally is illegal and unenforceable. If, however, the underlying purpose of the statute is to raise government revenues, a contract entered into with an unlicensed practitioner generally is enforceable—although the unlicensed person is usually fined.

### CONTRACTS TO COMMIT A CRIME

Any contract to commit a crime is a contract in violation of a statute.[2] Thus, a contract to sell an illegal drug (the sale of which is prohibited by statute) is not enforceable. Should the object or performance of the contract be rendered illegal by statute *after* the contract has been entered into, the contract is said to be discharged by law. (See the discussion under "Impossibility of Performance" in Chapter 18.)

## CONTRACTS CONTRARY TO PUBLIC POLICY

Although contracts are entered into by private parties, some are not enforceable because of the negative impact they would have on society. These contracts are said to be *contrary to public policy.* Numerous examples exist. Any contract to commit an immoral act falls in this category. Contracts that prohibit marriage have been held to be illegal on this basis. Suppose that Dangerfield promises a young man $500 if he will refrain from marrying Dangerfield's daughter. If the young man accepts, the resulting contract is void. Thus, if he married Dangerfield's daughter, Dangerfield could not sue him for breach of contract. Contracts that provide

for "surrogate-parenting" arrangements have also been deemed contrary to the public policy against "baby selling."[3] Very few states have laws governing surrogate-parenting contracts, and those that do either prohibit such contracts or refuse to enforce them.[4]

### COVENANTS NOT TO COMPETE

Contracts in restraint of trade (anticompetitive agreements) usually adversely affect the public (which favors competition in the economy) and typically violate one or more federal or state statutes.[5] An exception is recognized when the restraint is reasonable and an ancillary clause in a contract. Many such exceptions involve a type of restraint called a **covenant not to compete,** or a restrictive covenant.

Covenants (promises) not to compete are often contained as ancillary clauses in contracts concerning the sale of an ongoing business. A covenant not to compete is created when a seller agrees not to open a new store in a certain geographical area surrounding the old store. Such agreements enable the seller to sell, and the purchaser to buy, the "goodwill" and "reputation" of an ongoing business. If, for example, a well-known merchant sells his or her store and opens a competing business a block away, many of the merchant's customers will likely do business at the new store. This, in turn, renders valueless the good name and reputation sold to the new merchant for a price. If a covenant not to compete was not ancillary to a sales agreement, however, it would be void, because it unreasonably restrains trade and is contrary to public policy.

Agreements not to compete can also be contained in employment contracts. It is common for many people in middle-level and upper-level management positions to agree not to work for competitors or not to start a competing business for a specified period of time after terminating employment. Such agreements are legal so long as the specified period of time (of restraint) is not excessive in duration and the geographical restriction is reasonable.

---

2. See, for example, *McConnell v. Commonwealth Pictures Corp.*, 7 N.Y.2d 465, 166 N.E.2d 494, 199 N.Y.S.2d 483 (1960).

3. See, for example, *In re Baby M*, 217 N.J.Super. 313, 525 A.2d 1128 (1987).

4. The California Supreme Court, however, in a landmark 1993 decision, held that surrogate-parenting contracts are valid. See *Johnson v. Calvert,* 5 Cal.4th 84, 851 P.2d 776, 19 Cal.Rptr.2d 494 (1993).

5. Such as the Sherman Antitrust Act, the Clayton Act, and the Federal Trade Commission Act (see Chapter 48).

Basically, the restriction on competition must be reasonable—that is, not any greater than necessary to protect a legitimate business interest. The following case illustrates this point.

---

**HISTORICAL AND SOCIAL SETTING**    *At one time, if a court concluded that a covenant not to compete was unreasonable, the court would cut the entire covenant from the contract. Over time, courts adopted the "blue pencil" rule. Under this rule, a court would cut only those words from the covenant that made it unreasonable. For example, when an employee agreed not to compete against a former employer in forty-six specific counties, the court concluded that this was unreasonable and reduced the list of counties to thirty-one. More recently, courts have become more flexible. If a court concludes that a covenant is too broad, regardless of what cutting is grammatically possible, the court may issue an injunction that limits the restrictions of the covenant to make it reasonable. A court also has the option of holding that a covenant is unenforceable if there is no protection for the interests of the employee.*

**BACKGROUND AND FACTS**    *In 1988, Dr. Roger Morris, a research scientist holding a Ph.D. in physical biochemistry, signed an employment contract with Microscan, a subsidiary of Baxter International, Inc. The contract indicated that Microscan would be entrusting Morris, as an employee, with confidential information, and it included a covenant not to compete that read as follows: "I [Morris] will not render services, directly or indirectly, for a period of one year after the termination of my employment with [Baxter] to any Competing Organization in connection with any Competing Product within such geographic limits as [Baxter] and said Competing Organization are, or would be, in actual competition." In January 1992, Morris resigned his employment with Microscan and accepted a position with bioMerieux Vitek, Inc. (Vitek), which was essentially Microscan's only competitor in the research, development, manufacture, and sale of diagnostic equipment for use in microbiological laboratories. Baxter brought suit against Morris to enforce the clause containing the covenant not to compete. The district court entered a judgment restraining Morris from revealing trade secrets for a period of one year but refused to enforce the covenant not to compete. Baxter appealed.*

**CASE 16.2**

**BAXTER INTERNATIONAL, INC. v. MORRIS**

United States Court of Appeals, Eighth Circuit, 1992.
976 F.2d 1189.

*BEAM*, Circuit Judge.
\*    \*    \*    \*

\*    \*    \* [E]vidence at trial indicated that Vitek does not intend to elicit trade secrets from Morris, and in fact that Vitek has no need for that information. \*    \*    \*

\*    \*    \* [E]ven if Microscan compensated Morris during his restraint from employment with Vitek, a protracted absence could alienate Morris's new employer. \*    \*    \*

\*    \*    \*    \*

\*    \*    \* [R]estrictive covenants in employment agreements are enforceable only if reasonably necessary to protect a legitimate business interest of the employer. A restrictive covenant's reasonableness is measured by its impact on the parties, including its hardship on the employee. \*    \*    \*

In the present case, the employment agreement indicates that protection of trade secrets is the goal of the noncompete covenant. \*    \*    \* [T]he district court found that Morris is able to work at Vitek without disclosing Microscan's trade secrets. The court also found that even if Microscan paid Morris's salary for the year he would be forbidden to work by the covenant, Morris would suffer undue hardship. * * * We find that the district court's order enjoining Morris from the use or disclosure of confidential information he acquired at Microscan provides Baxter with adequate protection. The one-year noncompete covenant contained in Morris's employment agreement with Baxter is overbroad, unreasonably burdensome, and unnecessary for Baxter's protection.

**DECISION AND REMEDY** *The appellate court concluded that the noncompete covenant was unenforceable and affirmed the lower court's ruling.*

EXCULPATORY CLAUSES Ordinarily, a court does not look at the fairness or equity of a contract. That is, the courts generally do not inquire into the adequacy of consideration (see Chapter 13). Persons are assumed to be reasonably intelligent, and the courts will not come to their aid just because they have made an unwise or foolish bargain. In certain circumstances, however, bargains are so oppressive that the courts relieve innocent parties of part or all of their duties. As discussed in Chapter 15, such bargains are called *unconscionable* because they are so unscrupulous or grossly unfair as to be "void of conscience."

Contracts attempting to absolve parties of negligence or other wrongs are often held to be unconscionable. For example, suppose Jones and Laughlin Steel Company hires a laborer and has him sign a contract stating

> Said employee hereby agrees with employer, in consideration of such employment, that he will take upon himself all risks incident to his position and will in no case hold the company liable for any injury or damage he may sustain, in his person or otherwise, by accidents or injuries in the factory, or which may result from defective machinery or carelessness or misconduct of himself or any other employee in service of the employer.

This contract provision attempts to remove Jones and Laughlin's potential liability for injuries to the employee, and it is usually contrary to public policy.[6] Such clauses are called **exculpatory clauses,** which for our purposes may be defined as

clauses that purport to release a party from all liability for property damage or personal injury arising within contexts related to the subject matter of the contract.

Exculpatory clauses are also sometimes found in rental agreements, ordinary sales agreements, and commercial and residential property leases. In the majority of cases involving leases for commercial property, these clauses are held to be contrary to public policy. Additionally, they are almost universally held to be illegal and unenforceable when they are included in residential property leases. Generally, an exculpatory clause is not enforced if the party seeking its enforcement is involved in a business that is important to the public as a matter of practical necessity. These businesses include public utilities, common carriers, banks, and automobile repair shops. Because of the essential nature of these services, the companies offering them have an advantage in bargaining strength and could insist that anyone contracting for their services agree not to hold them liable. This would tend to relax their carefulness and increase the number of injuries.

An exculpatory clause may be enforced if it relates to harm occurring outside the party's ordinary course of business or harm caused by circumstances outside the party's control. For example, a school district might include an exculpatory clause in a parents' permission form to avoid being held liable for injuries to students on a field trip as a result of the negligence of someone outside the district's control. Also, a clause limiting liability—for example, in a common carrier's shipping agreement—may be enforced.

Exculpatory clauses have also been enforced when the parties seeking their enforcement were not involved in businesses considered important to the public interest. These businesses have included

---

6. For a case with similar facts, see *Little Rock & Fort Smith Railway Co. v. Eubanks,* 48 Ark. 460, 3 S.W. 808 (1887). In such a case, the clause may also be illegal on the basis of a violation of the state workers' compensation law.

health clubs, amusement parks, horse-rental concessions, golf-cart concessions, and skydiving organizations. Because these services are not essential, the firms offering them are sometimes considered to have no relative advantage in bargaining strength, and anyone contracting for their services is considered to do so voluntarily. The following case is illustrative.

---

**BACKGROUND AND FACTS**  *Karl Kotovsky signed an exculpatory agreement with the Ski Liberty Operating Corporation. Each skier who wanted to participate in a downhill ski race on Ski Liberty's slope had to sign the agreement. The agreement released Ski Liberty from any and all liability should Kotovsky be injured during the race. By signing the agreement, Kotovsky assumed all risk of injury, even if the injury resulted from the ''negligence or carelessness'' of Ski Liberty, the event's promoters, the equipment sponsors, and so on. During the race, Kotovsky ''collided with a wooden fence post,'' seriously injuring himself. He and his wife sued Ski Liberty for negligently failing to pad the fence post. The trial court upheld the exculpatory agreement. The Kotovskys appealed.*

**CASE 16.3**

**KOTOVSKY v. SKI LIBERTY OPERATING CORP.**
Superior Court of Pennsylvania, 1991.
412 Pa.Super. 442,
603 A.2d 663.

**WIEAND**, Judge.
* * * *
Downhill skiing is a dangerous activity. Downhill racing is even more dangerous.
* * *
* * * [Kotovsky] was an experienced skier, who was well acquainted with the hazards of downhill racing. Indeed, he had previously skied on the same slope on which he received his injuries. Despite this knowledge, he expressly agreed to assume the risk of injury and released the owner and operator of the slope from all liability, even that which might result from negligence. * * *
* * * [Kotovsky] was not required to enter the contract, but did so voluntarily in order to participate in a downhill ski race. This activity was not essential to [his] personal or economic well-being; it was purely a recreational activity.
The releases also did not contravene public policy. They were contracts between private parties and pertained only to the parties' private rights. They did not in any way affect the rights of the public. * * *
The exculpatory agreement and release in this case demonstrated clearly and unequivocally the intent of the parties. Its purpose, as stated expressly therein, was to release the ''ski area'' from all liability for injury to [Kotovsky] caused by natural or man-made obstacles on the slope, including hazards resulting from negligence by the owner.

---

*The appellate court affirmed the trial court's decision, holding that the exculpatory agreement releasing Ski Liberty from liability was enforceable. The Kotovskys were thus barred from recovery.*

**DECISION AND REMEDY**

---

**ADHESION CONTRACTS AND UNCONSCIONABILITY**  Contracts entered into because of one party's vastly superior bargaining power may also be deemed unconscionable. For example, if every auto manufacturer inserted an exculpatory clause in contracts for the sale of autos, consumers presumably would have no chance to bargain for the elimination of the clause from a given contract. Such contracts are called *adhesion contracts,* as discussed in Chapter 15. Essentially, the consumer's choice would be to take a contract or leave it. To combat such clauses, courts have held them to be unconscionable. The consumer has no choice, so the contract is contrary to public policy.

Another example of an unconscionable contract is a contract in which the terms of the agreement "shock the conscience" of the court. Suppose a welfare recipient with a fourth-grade education agrees to purchase a refrigerator for a price of $2,000, signing a two-year, nonusurious installment contract. The same type of refrigerator usually sells for $400 on the market. Some courts have held this type of contract unconscionable despite the general rule that the courts will not inquire into the adequacy of consideration.[7] Typically, the cases have involved consumer transactions in which the buyer was not aware of the actual price he or she was agreeing to pay.

Both the Uniform Commercial Code (UCC) and the Uniform Consumer Credit Code (UCCC) embody the unconscionability concept—the former with regard to the sale of goods[8] and the latter with regard to consumer loans and the waiver of rights.[9]

**DISCRIMINATORY CONTRACTS** Contracts in which a party promises to discriminate in terms of color, race, religion, national origin, or sex are contrary to statute and contrary to public policy.[10] For example, if a property owner promises in a contract not to sell the property to a member of a particular race, the contract is unenforceable. The public policy underlying these prohibitions is very strong, and the courts are quick to invalidate discriminatory contracts. Thus, the law attempts to ensure that people will be treated equally.

**CONTRACTS FOR THE COMMISSION OF A TORT** Contracts that require a party to commit a civil wrong, or a tort, have been held to be contrary to public policy. Remember that a *tort* is an act that is wrongful to another individual in a private sense, even though it may not necessarily be criminal in nature (an act against society).

**CONTRACTS INJURING PUBLIC SERVICE** Contracts that interfere with a public officer's duties are contrary to public policy. Agreements that involve a *conflict of interest* are also often illegal.

Public officers cannot enter into contracts that cause conflict between their official duties as representatives of the people and their private interests. Statutes require many public officers to liquidate their interests in private businesses before serving as elected representatives. Other statutes merely require that while they are in office, they take no part in the operation of, or decisions concerning, any business in which they have an interest, so that private and public responsibilities remain separate.

**AGREEMENTS OBSTRUCTING THE LEGAL PROCESS** Any agreement that is intended to delay, prevent, or obstruct the legal process is illegal. For example, an agreement to pay some specified amount if a criminal prosecution is terminated is illegal. Likewise, agreements to suppress evidence in a legal proceeding or to commit fraud upon a court are illegal. Tampering with a jury by offering jurors money in exchange for their votes is illegal.

A promise to refrain from prosecuting a criminal offense in return for a reward is void because it is against public policy. A reward given under the threat of arrest or prosecution is also void.

## EFFECT OF ILLEGALITY

In general, an illegal contract is void. That is, the contract is deemed never to have existed, and the courts will not aid either party. In most illegal contracts, both parties are considered to be *in pari delicto* (equally at fault).[11] In such cases the contract is void. If the contract is executory, neither party can enforce it. If it has been executed, there can be neither contractual nor quasi-contractual recovery.

That one wrongdoer who is a party to an illegal contract is unjustly enriched at the expense of the other is of no concern to the law—except under certain special circumstances that will be discussed below. The major justification for this hands-off attitude is that it is improper to place the machinery of justice at the disposal of a plaintiff who has broken the law by entering into an illegal bargain. Another justification is the hoped-for deterrent effect of this general "hands-off" rule. A plaintiff who suffers loss because of an illegal bargain

---

7. *Jones v. Star Credit Corp.*, 59 Misc.2d 189, 298 N.Y.S.2d 264 (1969).

8. See, for example, UCC 2–302 and 2–719.

9. See, for example, UCCC 5.108 and 1.107.

10. Civil Rights Act of 1964, 42 U.S.C. Sections 2000e–2000e-17.

11. Pronounced in *paa*-ree deh-*lick*-tow.

should presumably be deterred from entering into similar illegal bargains.

**EXCEPTIONS TO THE GENERAL RULE**   There are some exceptions to the general rule that neither party to an illegal bargain can sue for breach and that neither party can recover for performance rendered.

*Justifiable Ignorance of the Facts.*   When one of the parties is relatively innocent, that party can often recover any benefits conferred in a partially executed contract. In this case, the courts will not enforce the contract but will allow the parties to return to their original positions. It is also possible for an innocent party who has fully performed under the contract to enforce the contract against the guilty party. For example, a trucking company contracts with Gillespie to carry goods to a specific destination for a normal fee of $500. The trucker delivers the goods and later finds out that the contents of the shipped crates were illegal. Although the law specifies that the shipment, use, and sale of the goods were illegal, the trucker, being an innocent party, can still legally collect the $500 from Gillespie.

*Members of Protected Classes.*   When a statute is clearly designed to protect a certain class of people, a member of that class can enforce a contract in violation of the statute even though the other party cannot. A statute that prohibits employees from working more than a specified number of hours per month is designed to protect those employees. An employee who works more than the maximum can recover for those extra hours of service. Flight attendants are subject to a federal statute that prohibits them from flying more than a certain number of hours every month. If an attendant exceeds the maximum, the airline must nonetheless pay for those extra hours of service.

*Withdrawal from an Illegal Agreement.*   If an agreement has been only partly performed and the illegal part of the bargain has not yet been performed, the party rendering performance can withdraw from the bargain and recover the performance or its value. For example, Sam and Jim decide to wager (illegally) on the outcome of a boxing match. Each deposits money with a stakeholder, who agrees to pay the winner of the bet. At this point, each party has performed part of the agreement, but the illegal part of the agreement will not occur until the money is paid to the winner. Before such payment occurs, either party is entitled to withdraw from the agreement by giving notice of repudiation to the stakeholder.

*Contract Illegal through Fraud, Duress, or Undue Influence.*   Often, illegal contracts involve two blameworthy parties, but one party is more at fault than the other. When a party has been induced to enter into an illegal bargain by fraud, duress, or undue influence from the other party to the agreement, that party will be allowed to recover for the performance or its value.

**SEVERABLE, OR DIVISIBLE, CONTRACTS**   A *severable,* or divisible, contract consists of distinct parts that can be performed separately, with separate consideration provided for each part. An *indivisible* contract, in contrast, exists when the parties intended that complete performance by each party would be essential, even if the contract contains a number of seemingly separate provisions.

If a contract is divisible into legal and illegal portions, a court may enforce the legal portion but not the illegal portion, so long as the illegal portion does not affect the essence of the bargain. This approach of the courts is consistent with the basic policy of enforcing the legal intentions of the contracting parties whenever possible. For example, a covenant not to compete was drafted into an employment contract, but the covenant was overly broad and illegal (as it would be, for example, if it stated that ''the undersigned employee will be *forever* precluded from competing with his or her employer while *anywhere* in the United States''). The court then might allow the employment contract to be enforceable but *reform* the unreasonably broad covenant by converting its terms into reasonable ones. Alternatively, the court could declare the covenant illegal (and thus void) and enforce the remaining employment terms.

**SECTION 2**

# STATUTE OF FRAUDS

At early common law, parties to a contract were not allowed to testify. This led to the practice of hiring third party witnesses. As early as the

# ■ CONCEPT SUMMARY 16.1 Legality

| TYPES OF CONTRACTS | APPLICATIONS |
|---|---|
| **Contracts Contrary to Statute** | 1. *Usury*—The effects of a usurious loan (a loan made for interest rates that exceed the maximum legal rate of interest) vary from state to state. In a few states, the loan is a void transaction; in other states, the lender may recover up to the legal maximum rate of interest; in still other states, the lender cannot recover any interest.<br>2. *Gambling*—Gambling contracts that contravene (go against) state statutes are deemed illegal and thus are void.<br>3. *Sabbath (Sunday) laws*—Laws prohibiting the formation or the performance of certain contracts on Sunday vary widely from state to state, and many states do not enforce them.<br>4. *Licensing statutes*—Contracts entered into by persons who do not have a license, when one is required by state law, may not be enforceable, depending on the nature of the statute.<br>5. *Contracts to commit a crime*—All contracts to commit crimes violate statutes and are thus illegal and unenforceable. |
| **Contracts Contrary to Public Policy** | 1. *Covenants not to compete*—Restrictive covenants may be enforced by the courts if the terms are ancillary to a contract for the sale of a business or to an employment contract and the terms are reasonable as to time and area of restraint. If the terms are unreasonable as to time and area of restraint, the court may reform the covenant to make the restraints reasonable or declare the covenant illegal.<br>2. *Unconscionable contracts and clauses*—When a contract or contract clause is so unfair that it is oppressive to one party or "shocks the conscience" of the court, the court may deem the contract or clause unconscionable; as such, it is illegal and cannot be enforced.<br>3. *Exculpatory clauses*—Clauses that exempt one of the parties from all liability for property damage or personal injury arising from the subject matter of the contract are scrutinized closely by the courts and may be deemed unconscionable and thus unenforceable.<br>4. *Adhesion contracts*—Contracts that are entered into because of one party's vastly superior bargaining power may be unconscionable and unenforceable.<br>5. *Discriminatory contracts*—Contracts in which a party agrees to discriminate against another on the basis of color, race, religion, national origin, or sex are both contrary to public policy and contrary to statute.<br>6. *Contracts for the commission of a tort*—Contracts that require a party to commit a tort against another are unenforceable.<br>7. *Contracts injuring public service*—Contracts that impede a public official's duties, such as contracting to pay a legislator to vote a certain way, are unenforceable.<br>8. *Agreements to obstruct the legal process*—Contracts to delay, prevent, or obstruct the legal process are illegal and unenforceable. |
| **Effect of Illegality** | 1. In general, an illegal contract is void, and the courts will aid neither party when both parties are considered to be equally at fault. If the contract is executory, neither party can enforce it. If the contract is executed, there can be neither contractual nor quasi-contractual recovery. |

## ■ CONCEPT SUMMARY 16.1 Legality *(continued)*

| TYPES OF CONTRACTS | APPLICATIONS |
|---|---|
| **Effect of Illegality** **(continued)** | 2. Illegal contracts may be enforced in the following situations:<br>   a. When one party to the contract is relatively innocent.<br>   b. When one party to the contract is a member of a group of persons protected by statute.<br>   c. When one party was induced to enter into an illegal bargain through fraud, duress, or undue influence. |

seventeenth century, the English recognized the many problems presented by this practice and enacted a statute to help deal with it. The statute, passed by the English Parliament in 1677, was known as "An Act for the Prevention of Frauds and Perjuries." The act required that certain types of contracts, to be enforceable, had to be evidenced by a writing and signed by the party against whom enforcement was sought.

Today almost every state has a statute, modeled after the English act, that stipulates what types of contracts must be in writing. In this text, we refer to these statutes—even if a particular state has more than one statute relating to the topic—as the **Statute of Frauds.** The actual name of the Statute of Frauds is misleading because it neither applies to fraud nor invalidates any type of contract. Rather, it denies *enforceability* to certain contracts that do not comply with its requirements. The primary purpose of the act is *evidentiary*—to provide reliable evidence of the existence and terms of certain classes of contracts deemed historically to be important or complex. Although the statutes vary slightly from state to state, all states require certain types of contracts to be in writing or evidenced by a written memorandum signed by the party against whom enforcement is sought, unless certain exceptions apply. (These exceptions will be discussed later in this chapter.) The following types of contracts are said to fall "under" or "within" the Statute of Frauds and therefore require a writing:

1. Contracts involving interests in land.
2. Contracts that cannot *by their terms* be performed within one year from the date of formation.
3. Collateral, or secondary, contracts, such as promises to answer for the debt or duty of another and promises by the administrator or executor of an estate personally to pay a

debt of the estate—that is, out of his or her own pocket.
4. Promises made in consideration of marriage.
5. Under the UCC, contracts for the sale of goods priced at $500 or more.

## CONTRACTS INVOLVING INTERESTS IN LAND

Under the Statute of Frauds, a contract involving an interest in land must be attested to by a writing to be enforceable. Certain exceptions to this general rule are made in some circumstances, however, as will be discussed later in the chapter.

A contract calling for the sale of land is not enforceable unless it is in writing or evidenced by a written memorandum. Land is real property and includes all physical objects that are permanently attached to the soil, such as buildings, fences, trees, and the soil itself. The Statute of Frauds operates as a *defense* to the enforcement of an oral contract for the sale of land. Therefore, even if both parties acknowledge the existence of an oral contract for the sale of land, under most circumstances the contract will still not be enforced. If Sam contracts orally to sell Blackacre to Betty but later decides not to sell, under most circumstances Betty cannot enforce the contract. Likewise, if Betty refuses to close the deal, Sam cannot enforce the contract.

The Statute of Frauds requires contracts for the transfer of other interests in land, such as mortgages, easements, and leases, to be in writing, although most state statutes provide for the enforcement of short-term leases. These other interests will be described in detail in Chapters 49 through 52.

## THE ONE-YEAR RULE

A contract that cannot, *by its own terms,* be performed within one year from the date it was formed must be in writing to be enforceable.[12] Because disputes over such contracts are unlikely to occur until some time after the contracts have been made, resolution of these disputes is difficult unless the contract terms have been put in writing. For a particular contract to fall under the one-year rule of the Statute of Frauds, contract performance within a year from the date of contract formation must be objectively impossible.

The one-year period begins to run *the day after the contract is made.* Suppose you graduate from college on June 1. An employer orally contracts to hire you immediately (June 1) for one year at $2,000 per month. This contract is not subject to the Statute of Frauds (and thus need not be in writing to be enforceable) because the one-year period to measure performance begins on June 2. Because your performance of one year can begin immediately, it would take you exactly one year from the date of entering the contract to perform.

Suppose, however, that the oral contract had been formed on March 1 for the year's work that is to begin on June 1. Does this contract have to be in writing to be enforceable? The answer is yes. The one-year period used to measure whether performance by contract terms is possible begins on March 2. Because the twelve-month contract could not begin until June 1 and would end on May 31 of the next year, the contract performance period exceeds the one-year measurement period by three months. Thus, this contract is within the Statute of Frauds.

Even if performance within one year is improbable, if the contract, by its terms, makes complete performance within the year *possible,* the contract is not covered by the Statute of Frauds and need not be in writing. For example, suppose that Bankers Life orally contracts to loan $40,000 to Janet Lawrence "as long as Lawrence and Associates operates its financial consulting firm in Omaha, Nebraska." The contract is not within the Statute of Frauds—no writing is required—because Lawrence and Associates could go out of business in one year or less. In this event, the contract would be fully performed within one year. Although this occurrence is unlikely, it is nevertheless possible, and that possibility removes the contract from the province of the Statute of Frauds.[13]

12.   Restatement (Second) of Contracts, Section 130.
13.   See *Warner v. Texas & Pacific Railroad Co.,* 164 U.S. 418, 17 S.Ct. 147, 41 L.Ed. 195 (1896).

In summary, the test to determine whether an oral contract is enforceable under the one-year rule of the Statute of Frauds is not whether an agreement is *likely* to be performed within a year from the date of making the contract. Rather, the question revolves around whether performance within a year is *possible.* Even if performance takes place more than one year after the date of contract formation, an oral contract is binding as long as performance was possible in less than a year. Exhibit 16–1 illustrates graphically the application of the one-year rule.

## COLLATERAL PROMISES

A **collateral promise,** or secondary promise, is one that is ancillary to a principal transaction or primary contractual relationship. In other words, a collateral promise is one made by a third party to assume the debts or obligations of a primary party to a contract if that party does not perform. Any collateral promise of this nature falls under the Statute of Frauds and therefore must be in writing to be enforceable. To understand this concept, it is important to distinguish between primary and secondary promises and obligations.

**OBLIGATION MUST BE SECONDARY**   Suppose that Bancroft orally contracts with Harmony's Floral Boutique to send his mother a dozen roses for Mother's Day. Bancroft's oral contract with Harmony's Floral Boutique provides that he will pay for the roses when he receives the bill for the flowers. Bancroft is a direct party to this contract and has incurred a *primary* obligation under the contract. Because he is a party to the contract and has a primary obligation to Harmony's Floral Boutique, this contract does *not* fall under the Statute of Frauds and does not have to be in writing to be enforceable. If Bancroft fails to pay the florist and the florist sues him for payment, Bancroft cannot raise the Statute of Frauds as a defense. He cannot claim that the contract is unenforceable because it was not in writing.

Now suppose that Bancroft's mother borrows $1,000 from the International Trust Company on a promissory note payable six months later. Bancroft promises the bank officer handling the loan that he will pay the $1,000 *if his mother does not pay the loan on time.* Bancroft, in this situation, becomes what is known as a *guarantor* on the loan. That is, he is guaranteeing to the bank that he will

### ■ Exhibit 16–1 The One-Year Rule

Under the Statute of Frauds, contracts that by their terms are impossible to perform within one year from the date of contract formation must be in writing to be enforceable. Put another way, if it is at all possible to perform an oral contract within one year after the contract is made, the contract will fall outside the Statute of Frauds and be enforceable.

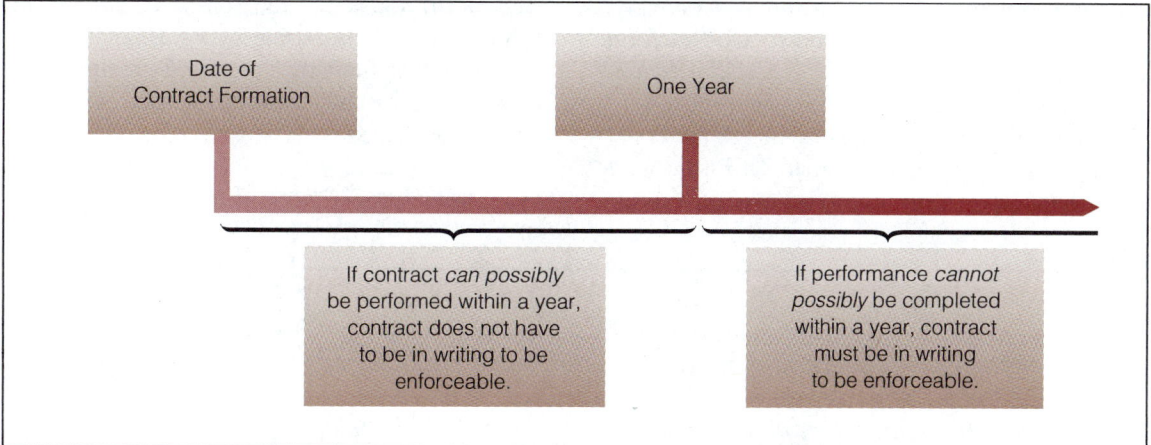

### ■ Exhibit 16–2 Collateral Promises

A collateral (secondary) promise is one made by a third party (C, in this exhibit) to a creditor (B, in this exhibit) to pay the debt of another (A, in this exhibit), who is primarily obligated to pay the debt. Under the Statute of Frauds, collateral promises must be in writing to be enforceable.

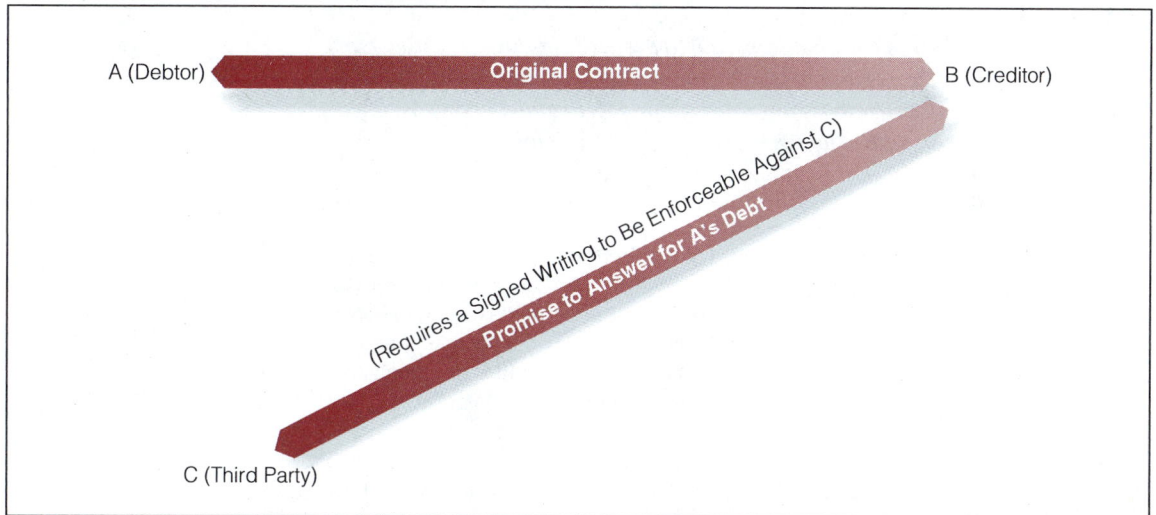

pay back the loan if his mother fails to do so. This kind of collateral promise, in which the guarantor states that he or she will become responsible *only* if the primary party does not perform, must be in writing to be enforceable. Exhibit 16–2 illustrates graphically the concept of a collateral promise.

We will return to the concept of guaranty and the distinction between primary and secondary obligations in Chapter 32, in the context of creditors' rights.

**"MAIN PURPOSE RULE" EXCEPTION** An oral promise to answer for the debt of another is covered by the Statute of Frauds *unless* the guarantor's main purpose in accepting secondary liability is to secure a personal benefit. This type of contract need not be in writing.[14] The assumption is that a court can infer from the circumstances of a case whether the "leading objective" of the

---

14.  Restatement (Second) of Contracts, Section 116.

promisor was to secure a personal benefit and thus, in effect, to answer for his or her own debt.

Consider an example. Braswell contracts with Custom Manufacturing Company to have some machines custom-made for Braswell's factory. She promises Newform Materials Supply Company, Custom Manufacturing's supplier, that if Newform continues to deliver materials to Custom Manufacturing, she will guarantee payment. This promise need not be in writing, even though the effect may be to pay the debt of another. This is because Braswell's main purpose in forming the contract is to secure a benefit for herself.[15]

Another typical application of the so-called main purpose doctrine is the situation in which one creditor guarantees the debtor's debt to another creditor to forestall litigation. This allows the debtor to remain in business long enough to generate profits sufficient to pay *both* creditors. The following case illustrates an application of the main purpose doctrine.

---

15. See *Kampman v. Pittsburgh Contracting and Engineering Co.*, 316 Pa. 502, 175 A. 396 (1934).

---

**BACKGROUND AND FACTS** *Wilson Floors Company contracted to provide flooring materials for a residential and commercial development known as "The Cliffs," which was owned by the defendant bank, Sciota Park, Ltd. When the general contractor for Sciota fell behind in payments to Wilson, Wilson stopped work on the project. Sciota assured Wilson that he would be paid if he returned to work. After Wilson's final bill was not paid, Wilson proceeded with this action against Sciota. The trial court held that the bank's assurances to Wilson that he would be paid did not fall under the Statute of Frauds because the bank assumed a "direct undertaking"—not a secondary obligation—when it guaranteed payment to Wilson. Therefore, the promise was enforceable, as it did not fall under the Statute of Frauds. The appellate court reversed, finding that the bank became only secondarily liable to Wilson when it guaranteed payment. Therefore, the contract fell under the Statute of Frauds and was unenforceable. Wilson appealed to the Supreme Court of Ohio.*

CASE 16.4

**WILSON FLOORS CO. v. SCIOTA PARK, LTD.**
Supreme Court of Ohio, 1978.
54 Ohio St.2d 451,
377 N.E.2d 514.

SWEENEY, Justice.
\* \* \* \*
\* \* \* [I]n a determination of whether an oral promise is enforceable to pay the debt of another, the court may employ one of two tests. The court may inquire as to whether the promisor becomes primarily liable on the debt owed by another to a third party. \* \* \* If it is found that the promisor does not become primarily liable for payment of the debt, the court may inquire as to whether the promisor's leading object was to subserve [serve] his own business or pecuniary interest. \* \* \*
\* \* \* \*
Because it is unquestioned that the bank in the instant cause [case] did not become primarily liable when it guaranteed the subcontractors that they would be paid the court must apply the second test \* \* \* to determine the enforceability of the verbal agreement.

Under the second test, it is of no consequence that when such promise is made, the original obligor remains primarily liable or that the third party continues to look to the original obligor for payment. So long as the promisor undertakes to pay the subcontractor whatever his services are worth irrespective of what he may owe the general contractor, and so long as the main purpose of the promisor is to further his own business or pecuniary interest, the promise is enforceable. Thus, under this test it is not required to show as a condition precedent [a condition that must be fulfilled] for enforceability of the oral contract that the original debt is extinguished.
\* \* \* \*
The facts in the instant cause reflect that the bank made its guarantee to Wilson to subserve its own business interest of reducing costs to complete the project. Clearly,

the bank induced Wilson to remain on the job and rely on its credit for future payments. To apply the statute of frauds and hold that the bank had no contractual duty to Wilson despite its oral guarantees would not prevent the wrong which the statute's enactment was to prevent, but would in reality effectuate a wrong.

*Judgment was entered in favor of Wilson Floors Co. The bank's main purpose (leading object) was to derive a benefit for itself. Therefore, the promise to pay the general contractor's debts was not within the Statute of Frauds and was enforceable.*

**DECISION
AND REMEDY**

**ESTATE DEBTS** The administrator (or executor) of an estate has the duty of paying the debts of the deceased and distributing any remainder to the deceased's heirs. The administrator can contract orally on behalf of the estate. Under the Statute of Frauds, promises made by the administrator or executor of an estate to pay *personally* the debts of the estate must be in writing to be enforceable, even though the nature of the promise is to assume a primary obligation to pay the creditor.

## PROMISES MADE IN CONSIDERATION OF MARRIAGE

Generally, courts tend to give more credence to prenuptial agreements that are accompanied by consideration. For example, assume that Miranda, who has little money, marries Elson, who has a net worth of $300 million. Elson has several children, and he wants them to receive most of his wealth upon his death. Prior to their marriage, Miranda and Elson draft and sign a prenuptial agreement in which Elson promises to give Miranda $200,000 per year for the rest of her life should they divorce. As consideration for her consenting to this amount, Elson offers Miranda $500,000. If Miranda consents to the agreement and accepts the $500,000, very likely a court would hold this to be a valid prenuptial agreement should the agreement ever be contested. To add certainty to the enforceability of prenuptial agreements, the Uniform Prenuptial Agreements Act (UPAA) of 1983 provides that prenuptial agreements must be in writing to be enforceable and that the agreements become effective when the parties marry.

## CONTRACTS FOR THE SALE OF GOODS

The Uniform Commercial Code (UCC) contains several Statute of Frauds provisions that require written evidence of a contract. Section 2–201 contains the major provision, which generally requires a writing or memorandum for the sale of goods priced at $500 or more. A writing that will satisfy the UCC requirement need only state the quantity term; other terms agreed upon need not be stated "accurately" in the writing, as long as they adequately reflect both parties' intentions. The contract will not be enforceable, however, for any quantity greater than that set forth in the writing. In addition, the writing must be signed by the person to be charged—that is, by the person who refuses to perform or the one being sued. Beyond these two requirements, the writing need not designate the buyer or the seller, the terms of payment, or the price. The UCC Statute of Frauds provisions will be examined in greater detail in Chapter 20.

## EXCEPTIONS TO THE STATUTE OF FRAUDS

Exceptions to the applicability of the Statute of Frauds are made in the following situations.

**PARTIAL PERFORMANCE** In cases involving contracts relating to the transfer of interests in land, if the purchaser has paid part of the price, taken possession, and made permanent improvements to the property and the parties cannot be returned to their pre-contract *status quo,* a court may grant *specific performance* (performance of the contract according to its precise terms). Whether the courts will enforce an oral contract for an interest in land when partial performance has taken place is usually determined by the degree of injury that would be suffered if the court chose not to enforce the oral contract. In some states, mere reliance on an oral contract is enough to remove it from the Statute of Frauds.

Under the UCC, an oral contract is enforceable to the extent that a seller accepts payment or a buyer accepts delivery of the goods.[16] For example, if XYZ Corporation ordered by telephone twenty personal computers from Com Best, Inc., and repudiated the contract after ten personal computers had been delivered and accepted, Com Best could enforce the contract to the extent of the ten personal computers accepted by XYZ.

**ADMISSIONS**   In some states, if a party against whom enforcement of an oral contract is sought ''admits'' in pleadings, testimony, or otherwise in court that a contract for sale was made, the contract will be enforceable.[17] A contract subject to the UCC will be enforceable, but only to the extent of the quantity admitted.[18] Thus, if the president of XYZ Corporation admits under oath that an oral agreement was made with Com Best, Inc., for twenty personal computers, the agreement will be enforceable to that extent.

**PROMISSORY ESTOPPEL**   In some states, an oral contract that would otherwise be unenforceable under the Statute of Frauds may be enforced under the doctrine of promissory estoppel, or detrimental reliance. Recall from Chapter 13 that if a promisor makes a promise on which the promisee justifiably relies to his or her detriment, a court may *estop* (prevent) the promisor from denying that a contract exists. Section 139 of the Restatement (Second) of Contracts provides that in these circumstances, an oral promise can be enforceable notwithstanding the Statute of Frauds if the reliance was foreseeable to the person making the promise and if injustice can be avoided only by enforcing the promise. Using promissory estoppel in these circumstances is intended to prevent the Statute of Frauds—which was created to prevent injustice—from being used to promote injustice. Nevertheless, this use of the doctrine of promissory estoppel is controversial. Enforcing an oral contract on the basis of a party's reliance arguably undercuts the essence of the statute.

**SPECIAL EXCEPTIONS UNDER THE UCC**   Special exceptions to the applicability of the Statute of Frauds apply to sales contracts. Oral contracts for customized goods may be enforced in certain circumstances. Another exception has to do with oral contracts *between merchants* that have been confirmed in writing. These exceptions will be examined in detail in the discussion of the UCC provisions regarding the Statute of Frauds in Chapter 20.

## SUFFICIENCY OF THE WRITING

To be safe, all contract terms should be fully set forth in a writing signed by all the parties. This assures that if any problems arise concerning performance of the contract, a written agreement can be introduced into court. The Statute of Frauds and the UCC require either a written contract or a written memorandum *signed by the party against whom enforcement is sought,* except when there is a legally recognized exception, such as partial performance. The signature need not be placed at the end of the document but can be anywhere in the writing. It can even be an initial rather than the full name. Note, however, that even if the Statute of Frauds is satisfied, the *terms* of the oral contract must be proved in court.

A memorandum evidencing the oral contract need only contain the essential terms of the contract. Under the UCC, for contracts evidencing sales of goods, the writing need only name the quantity term and be signed by the party to be charged. Any confirmation, invoice, sales slip, check, or telegram can constitute a writing sufficient to satisfy the Statute of Frauds. Under most other provisions of the Statute of Frauds, for contracts evidencing transactions other than sales of goods, the writing must also name the parties, the subject matter, the consideration, and the essential terms with reasonable certainty. In some states, contracts for the sale of land must state the price and describe the property with sufficient clarity to allow them to be determined without reference to outside sources.[19]

---

16.   UCC 2–201(3)(c).
17.   Restatement (Second) of Contracts, Section 133.
18.   UCC 2–201(3)(b).
19.   *Rhodes v. Wilkins,* 83 N.M. 782, 498 P.2d 311 (1972).

# ■ CONCEPT SUMMARY 16.2 **The Statute of Frauds**

| CONCEPT | DESCRIPTION |
|---|---|
| **Applicability of the Statute** | The following types of contracts fall under the Statute of Frauds and must be in writing to be enforceable:<br>1. *Contracts involving interests in land*—The statute applies to any contract for an interest in realty, such as a sale, a lease, an easement, or a mortgage.<br>2. *Contracts whose terms cannot be performed within one year*—The statute applies only to contracts objectively impossible to perform fully within one year from (the day after) the contract's formation.<br>3. *Collateral promises*—The statute applies only to express contracts made between the guarantor and the creditor whose terms make the guarantor secondarily liable. Exception: main purpose rule.<br>4. *Promises made in consideration of marriage*—The statute applies to promises to pay money or give property in consideration of a promise to marry and to prenuptial agreements made in consideration of marriage.<br>5. *Contracts for the sale of goods priced at $500 or more*—Under the UCC's Statute of Frauds provision in UCC 2–201(1). |
| **Exceptions** | 1. *Partial performance*—Applies to contracts for the sale of land, as well as to the sale of goods.<br>2. *Admissions*—Admission under oath, by the party against whom enforcement is being sought, that a contract exists.<br>3. *Promissory estoppel*—To prevent the injustice that might otherwise occur if an oral contract is not enforced. |
| **Sufficiency of the Writing** | To constitute an enforceable contract under the Statute of Frauds, a writing must be signed by the party against whom enforcement is sought, must name the parties, must identify the subject matter, and must state with reasonable certainty the essential terms. In a sale of land, the price and a description of the property may need to be stated with sufficient clarity to be determined without reference to outside sources. Under the UCC, a contract for a sale of goods is not enforceable beyond the quantity of goods shown. |

Many courts have addressed the question of whether a facsimile (fax) copy of a document is sufficient to satisfy the writing requirement of the Statute of Frauds. The general trend is toward accepting a fax as the equivalent of an original writing for Statute of Frauds purposes. A "mailgram," for example, sent to confirm a real estate transaction, was sufficient as a signed writing,[20] and a purchase order sent by "telecopier" was sufficient to satisfy the UCC's Statute of Frauds requirements governing contracts for the sale of goods.[21]

---

20. *Hessenthaler v. Farzin,* 388 Pa.Super. 37, 564 A.2d 990 (1989).
21. *Bazak International Corp. v. Mast Industries,* 73 N.Y.2d 113, 535 N.E.2d 633, 538 N.Y.S.2d 503 (1989).

## ■ SECTION 3

# THE PAROL EVIDENCE RULE

The **parol evidence rule** prohibits the introduction at trial of evidence of the parties' prior negotiations, prior agreements, or contemporaneous oral agreements that contradicts or varies the terms of their written contract.[22] The written contract is ordinarily assumed to be the complete embodiment of the parties' agreement. Because of the rigidity of the parol evidence rule, however, courts make several exceptions:

---

22. Restatement (Second) of Contracts, Section 213.

1. *Contracts subsequently modified.* Evidence of *subsequent modification* (oral or written) of a written contract can be introduced into court. Keep in mind that the oral modifications may not be enforceable if they come under the Statute of Frauds—for example, if they increase the price of the goods for sale to $500 or more or increase the term for performance to more than one year. Also, oral modifications will not be enforceable if the original contract provides that any modification must be in writing.[23]

2. *Voidable or void contracts.* Oral evidence can be introduced in all cases to show that the contract was voidable or void (for example, induced by mistake, fraud, or misrepresentation). In this case, if deception led one of the parties to agree to the terms of a written contract, oral evidence attesting to fraud should not be excluded. Courts frown upon bad faith and are quick to allow such evidence when it establishes fraud.

3. *Contracts containing ambiguous terms.* When the terms of a written contract are ambiguous, evidence is admissible to show the meaning of the terms.

4. *Incomplete contracts.* Evidence is admissible when the written contract is incomplete in that it lacks one or more of the essential terms. The courts allow evidence to "fill in the gaps."

5. *Prior dealing, course of performance, or usage of trade.* Under the UCC, evidence can be introduced to explain or supplement a written contract by showing a prior dealing, course of performance, or usage of trade.[24] These terms will be discussed in further detail in Chapter 20, in the context of sales contracts. Here, it is sufficient to say that when buyers and sellers deal with each other over extended periods of time, certain customary practices develop. These practices are often overlooked in the writing of the contract, so courts allow the introduction of evidence to show how the parties have acted in the past.

6. *Contracts subject to orally agreed-upon conditions.* The parol evidence rule does not apply if the existence of the entire written contract is subject to an orally agreed-upon condition. Proof of the condition does not *alter* or *modify* the written terms but involves the *enforceability* of the written contract. A leading case concerning this exception is *Pym v. Campbell,* in which the court stated that "evidence to vary the terms of an agreement in writing is not admissible, but evidence to show that there is not an agreement at all is admissible."[25]

7. *Contracts with an obvious or gross clerical (or typographic) error that clearly would not represent the agreement of the parties.* Parol evidence is admissible to correct an obvious typographic error.

The key in determining whether evidence will be allowed basically depends on whether the written contract is intended to be a complete and final embodiment of the terms of the agreement. If it is so intended, it is referred to as an **integrated contract,** and extraneous evidence is excluded. If it is only partially integrated, evidence of consistent additional terms is admissible to supplement the written agreement.[26]

In the following case, a shipper claimed that an oral understanding as to the insurance value placed upon shipped goods superseded a written contract.

---

23. UCC 2–209(2), (3).
24. UCC 1–205, 2–202.

25. 6 Ellis and Blackburn Reports 370 (Q.B. [Queen's Bench] 1856).
26. Restatement (Second) of Contracts, Section 216.

---

| CASE 16.5 | |
|---|---|
| **CHAFETZ v. UNITED PARCEL SERVICE, INC.** Massachusetts Appellate Division, District Court, 1991. 1992 Mass.App.Div. 67. | **COMPANY PROFILE** *In 1907, when Jim Casey and Claude Ryan were teenagers, they founded the American Messenger Company in Seattle, Washington, with six messengers, two bicycles, and one telephone. Soon they were delivering packages for local stores with seven motorcycles and a refitted Model T Ford, and in 1913, they changed the name of their company to Merchants Parcel Delivery. Within two years, the firm had a staff of twenty and was using the color brown to identify company vehicles. By 1930, the firm was renamed United Parcel Service (UPS) and had* |

*expanded to California, New York, New Jersey, and Connecticut. Over the next fifty years, UPS expanded its small-package delivery service across the rest of the continental United States and into western Europe. By 1982, UPS was guaranteeing delivery anywhere in the continental United States and Hawaii within forty-eight hours. In less than three years, the company was providing overnight delivery to the same locations, as well as to Puerto Rico. In 1990, UPS expanded into eastern Europe and Russia and formed a joint venture with a Japanese firm to deliver packages and other freight in Japan.[a] UPS service is now available in most of the world. With more than 300 aircraft and 129,000 delivery vehicles, UPS delivers more than 600,000 parcels and documents each day.*

**BACKGROUND AND FACTS**   *On November 11, 1988, Roberta Chafetz telephoned a UPS office to inquire about shipping two packages containing diamonds from her home to New York City. She told the UPS representative that each package would need to be insured for $25,000. Arrangements were made to pick up the packages, and three days later, a UPS driver called at Chafetz's home, presented her with the standard "pick-up record" form, and requested payment of $6.65. Chafetz paid the charge and signed the pick-up agreement form without reading it and without filling in the blank on the form that provided for extra insurance coverage. Subsequently, one of the two packages was lost or stolen during shipment. UPS claimed its liability was limited to $100—the standard package insurance specified on the shipping agreement that Chafetz signed. The trial court found for Chafetz, and UPS appealed.*

*FURNARI*, Justice.
   \*   \*   \*   \*
   \*   \*   \* "One who signs a contract in the absence of fraud or deceit cannot avoid it on the grounds that he did not read it or that he took someone else's word as to what it contained." \*   \*   \* The parol evidence rule \*   \*   \* precludes the admission of prior, extrinsic oral statements to vary the terms of an unambiguous shipping receipt or contract.
   Implicit in the trial court's finding in this case is that parol evidence of prior oral statements between the parties was admissible to vary the terms of the pick-up record because of fraud [or] deceit \*   \*   \* in the formation of the contract limiting UPS's liability for shipment loss. \*   \*   \* The reported evidence is, however, wholly insufficient to support findings in this case of requisite elements of fraud, including an intent to deceive by UPS and any reasonable reliance by Chafetz on alleged misrepresentations. At the time of shipment, UPS presented to Chafetz an unambiguous written pick-up record which fully disclosed shipment terms, including valuation and liability limitation. UPS was under no obligation to insure that Chafetz read the bill of lading, and in no way endeavored to prevent or discourage her from doing so.
   Conversely, Chafetz chose to ignore the only written receipt evidencing her delivery of what she alleges was $50,000.00 worth of diamonds to a common carrier. She paid without question or comment a mere $6.65 in total UPS charges which necessarily and obviously included at least a pick-up charge and interstate shipping costs for two packages. The minimal amount of such charges was sufficient to alert an ordinarily prudent person to the possibility that the shipment was not fully insured or accurately valued.

---

a.   Joint ventures are discussed in Chapter 38.

| DECISION AND REMEDY | *The appellate court held that Chafetz could not vary the written shipping agreement with UPS on the basis of prior oral statements.* |
|---|---|
| INTERNATIONAL CONSIDERATIONS | **Parol Evidence in International Contracts** *The Convention on Contracts for the International Sale of Goods (CISG) is far more open to parol evidence than is U.S. law. The CISG allows the introduction of parol evidence relating to "all relevant circumstances of the case, including the negotiations." Even under the CISG, however, a court may be reluctant to find that an oral arrangement should override an express written provision in a final contract.* |

## TERMS AND CONCEPTS TO REVIEW

| | | |
|---|---|---|
| blue law 293 | *in pari delicto* 298 | parol evidence rule 307 |
| collateral promise 302 | integrated contract 308 | Statute of Frauds 301 |
| covenant not to compete 294 | judgment rate of interest 292 | usury 292 |
| exculpatory clause 296 | legal rate of interest 292 | |

## QUESTIONS AND CASE PROBLEMS

**16–1. Covenant Not to Compete.** A famous New York City hotel, Hotel Lux, is noted for its food as well as its luxury accommodations. Hotel Lux contracts with a famous chef, Chef Perlee, to become its head chef at $6,000 per month. The contract states that should Perlee leave the employment of Hotel Lux for any reason, he will not work as a chef for any hotel or restaurant in the states of New York, New Jersey, or Pennsylvania for a period of one year. During the first six months of the contract, Hotel Lux substantially advertises Perlee as its head chef, and business at the hotel is excellent. Then a dispute arises between the hotel management and Perlee, and Perlee terminates his employment. One month later, he is hired by a famous New Jersey restaurant just across the New York state line. Hotel Lux learns of Perlee's employment through a large advertisement in a New York City newspaper. It seeks to enjoin Perlee from working in that restaurant as a chef for one year. Discuss how successful Hotel Lux will be in its action.

**16–2. Licensing Statutes.** In State X, persons must be at least eighteen years old before they can purchase alcoholic beverages. The state also has passed a law requiring that persons who prepare and serve liquor in the form of drinks in commercial establishments be licensed. The only requirement for obtaining a yearly license is that the person be at least eighteen years old. Moffitt, age thirty-five, is hired as a bartender for the Lone Star Restaurant. Ake, a staunch alumnus of a nearby university, brings twenty of his friends to the restaurant to celebrate a football victory. Ake has ordered four rounds of drinks, and the bar bill exceeds $150. Ake learns that Moffitt has failed to renew his bartender's license, and Ake refuses to pay, claiming the contract is unenforceable. Discuss whether Ake is correct.

**16–3. Statute of Frauds.** On May 1, by telephone, Yu offers to hire Benson to perform personal services. On May 5, Benson returns Yu's call and accepts the offer. Discuss fully whether this contract falls under the Statute of Frauds under the following circumstances:

 (a) The contract calls for Benson to be employed for one year, with the right to begin performance immediately.

 (b) The contract calls for Benson to be employed for nine months, with performance of services to begin on September 1.

 (c) The contract calls for Benson to submit a written research report, with a deadline of two years for submission.

**16–4. Statute of Frauds.** William Rowe, suffering from the effects of a severe gastric hemorrhage, was admitted to General Hospital. On the day Rowe was admitted, Rowe's son told the doctor, "We want you to do everything you can to save his life, and we don't want you to spare any expense. Whatever he needs, Doctor, you go ahead and get it, and I will pay you." After Rowe was discharged from the hospital, his son refused to pay the medical bills. Can the hospital enforce the son's oral promise? Discuss fully.

**16–5. Statute of Frauds.** Fernandez orally promised Pando that if Pando helped her win the New York state lottery, she would share the proceeds equally with him. Pando agreed to purchase the tickets in Fernandez's name, select the lottery numbers, and pray for divine intervention from a saint to help them win. Fernandez won $2.8 million in the lottery, which was to be paid over a ten-year period. When Fernandez failed to share the winnings equally, Pando sued for breach of her contractual obligation. Fernandez countered that the contract was unenforceable under the Statute of Frauds because the contract could not be performed within one year. Could the contract be performed within a year? Explain. [*Pando by Pando v. Fernandez*, 127 Misc.2d 224, 485 N.Y.S.2d 162 (1984)]

**16–6. Statute of Frauds.** Samuel DaGrossa and others were planning to open a restaurant. At some point prior to August 1985, DaGrossa orally agreed with Philippe LaJaunie that LaJaunie, in exchange for his contribution in designing, renovating, and managing the restaurant, could purchase a one-third interest in the restaurant's stock if the restaurant was profitable in its first year of operations. The restaurant opened in March 1986, and a few weeks later, LaJaunie's employment was terminated. LaJaunie brought an action to enforce the stock-purchase agreement. Is the agreement enforceable? Why or why not? [*LaJaunie v. DaGrossa*, 159 A.D.2d 349, 552 N.Y.S.2d 628 (1990)]

**16–7. Statute of Frauds.** Carol Mann and Gerald Harris worked for Helmsley-Spear, Inc. (HSI), as account managers for various HSI properties. In 1983, each received a bonus of $50,000 for their work in converting an HSI apartment complex, known as Windsor Park, into a cooperative housing unit. The conversion had taken several years to complete. After they had finished the Windsor Park conversion, they were asked to work on another cooperative conversion of two HSI apartment buildings known as Park West Village. Mann and Harris were orally promised compensation, over and above their base salaries, on the basis of a formula similar to the one that had been orally agreed upon with regard to the Windsor Park conversion. In 1987, after they had completed the conversion of Park West Village, they were fired, and HSI refused to pay them the additional compensation. Among other things, HSI contended that their oral agreement concerning the extra compensation was unenforceable under the Statute of Frauds. How should the court rule on this issue, and why? [*Mann v. Helmsley-Spear, Inc.*, 177 A.D.2d 147, 581 N.Y.S.2d 16 (1992)]

**16–8. Parol Evidence.** A 1965 bargaining agreement between employees and Wheelabrator Corp. clearly stated that the company would pay the cost of health insurance for employees who had retired prior to 1959. Later bargaining agreements (the last of which expired in 1988 when the plant at which the employees worked was closed) also indicated that once employees reached the age of sixty-five, Wheelabrator would pay for their health insurance, and that when they died, their spouses would continue to receive supplemental health benefits at the company's cost. Wheelabrator withdrew the health benefits of retired employees in 1988, when it closed its plant and the last agreement expired. Kenneth Bidlack and other retired employees sued the company to have their health benefits reinstated. The employees asserted that the agreements meant that they would be granted benefits for life. Wheelabrator contended that the agreements granted benefits only for the duration of the agreements. The court was left to decide whether extrinsic evidence (including letters from the company to retirees indicating that the company would pay the cost of the health insurance throughout the retirees' lives) was admissible to clarify terms of the contract. Should the court allow the employees to introduce extrinsic evidence to justify their claim? Discuss fully. [*Bidlack v. Wheelabrator Corp.*, 993 F.2d 603 (7th Cir. 1993)]

**16–9. Gambling Debts.** George Aubin, the ex-president of a failed bank and a resident of Texas (where gambling debts are unenforceable), traveled to the Bahamas (where gambling debts are enforceable) to gamble at the Cable Beach Hotel and Casino, owned by Carnival Leisure Industries, Ltd. Aubin took more than $2,000, which he lost at blackjack. The casino then approved credit of up to $25,000 for Aubin, if he chose to take advantage of it. In less than two days, Aubin gambled away the entire $25,000, issued to him in exchange for drafts (instruments similar to checks that ordered Aubin's bank in Texas to pay a certain sum of money to the casino). On each draft was printed "I represent that I have received cash for the above amount and that said amount is on deposit in said financial entity in my name, is free and clear of claim and is subject to this check and is hereby assigned to payee, and I guarantee payment with exchange and costs in collecting." Aubin returned to Texas. Over the next six weeks, Carnival sent Aubin letters asking him to pay the $25,000. When Aubin did not respond, Carnival presented the drafts to Aubin's bank for payment. Aubin had already directed his bank to stop payment. Carnival sued Aubin for the $25,000, on the ground of fraud, among other things. Aubin claimed that he had signed only markers (IOUs), not drafts, and that he had had no intention of honoring any drafts. How should the court rule? Discuss. [*Carnival Leisure Industries, Ltd. v. Aubin*, 830 F.Supp. 371 (S.D.Tex. 1993)]

**16–10. A Question of Ethics**

 *Michael Niemiec and Judith Polek (the plaintiffs) joined a buyers' club after they had been invited via telephone to visit the club's premises. A club salesperson told them that in exchange for a $1,160 membership fee, members would receive access to a number of catalogues from which they could order merchandise at supposedly low*

*prices. The plaintiffs were told that they either had to sign the contract then and there or forgo the ''once in a lifetime opportunity'' to join the club. They signed the contract. Three days later, having some misgivings about what they had done, they sought to cancel the contract but learned that they could not do so. The contract specified that no dues were refundable, even on a member's death. The contract also stated that a membership could not be transferred for any reason, merchandise could not be returned once accepted (members were warned in bold type not to accept merchandise until after they had examined it), and orders for merchandise could not be canceled even prior to shipment. Further, although members were to rely on warranties of the supplier for all merchandise, they were forbidden to make any ''contact with the suppliers of merchandise.'' The plaintiffs then sought re-lief in court. The court held that the contract was unconscionable. [Niemiec v. Kellmark Corp., 581 N.Y.S.2d 569 (1992)]*

1. Courts will sometimes hold contracts unconscionable because of gross inadequacy of consideration. Is that a possibility here? What, for example, did the club offer as consideration for the contract?

2. What might be some other possible reasons for the court's conclusion that this contract was unconscionable?

3. The defendant club argued that the plaintiffs in this case were neither poor (they earned over $50,000 a year and owned their own home) nor illiterate. Therefore, the club argued, they should be held to their bargain even if they found it unsatisfactory. Do you agree with this reasoning? Why or why not?

# CHAPTER 17

# THIRD PARTY RIGHTS

O nce it has been determined that a valid and legally enforceable contract exists, attention can turn to the rights and duties of the parties to the contract. Because a contract is a private agreement between the parties who have entered into it, it is fitting that these parties alone should have rights and liabilities under the contract. This is referred to as **privity of contract,** and it establishes the basic concept that third parties have no rights in contracts to which they are not parties.

Suppose that I offer to sell you my watch for $100, and you accept. Later, I refuse to deliver the watch to you, even though you present me with the $100. You decide to overlook my breach, but your close friend, Marie, is unhappy with my action and files suit. Can she receive a judgment? The answer is no, because she was not a party to the contract. You, as a party, have rights under the contract and could file a successful suit, but Marie has no *standing* (right) to sue.

There are two exceptions to the rule of privity of contract. One exception allows a party to a contract to transfer the rights arising from the contract to another or to free himself or herself from the duties of a contract by having another person perform them. Legally, the first of these actions is referred to as an *assignment of rights,* and the second, as a *delegation of duties.* A second exception to the rule of privity of contract involves a *third party beneficiary* contract. Here, the rights of a third party against the promisor arise from the original contract, as the parties to the original contract normally make it with the intent to benefit the third party. In this chapter, we first look at the law relating to assignments and delegations, and then examine how third party beneficiaries may acquire enforceable rights in contracts.

# ASSIGNMENTS AND DELEGATIONS

When third parties acquire rights or assume duties arising from contracts to which they were not parties, the rights are transferred to them by *assignment,* and the duties are transferred by *delegation.* Assignment and delegation occur *after* the original contract is made, when one of the parties transfers to another party an interest or duty in the contract.

## ASSIGNMENTS

In a bilateral contract, the two parties have corresponding rights and duties. One party has a *right* to require the other to perform some task, and the other has a *duty* to perform it. The transfer of *rights* to a third person is known as an **assignment.** When rights under a contract are assigned unconditionally, the *rights* of the *assignor* (the party making the assignment) are extinguished.[1] The third party (the *assignee,* or party receiving the assignment) has a right to demand performance from the other original party to the contract (the *obligor*).

For example, suppose Brower owes Horton $50, and Horton assigns to Kuhn the right to receive the $50. Here, a valid assignment of a debt exists. Kuhn is entitled to enforce payment in a court of law if Brower does not pay her the $50.

The assignee takes only those rights that the assignor originally had. Furthermore, the assignee's rights are subject to the defenses that the obligor has against the assignor. Suppose that Brower leases her apartment to Horton for one year. The lease provides that the monthly rent payment is $400 and that if Horton fails to pay the rent, she can be evicted. After Horton has lived in the apartment for six months, she gives Brower a worthless check for the seventh month's rent. The next day, Horton assigns her rights under the lease contract to Kuhn. On discovering the worthlessness of the check, Brower has a legal right to enforce the lease and evict Horton. Because Kuhn's (the assignee's) rights are subject to this same defense, Kuhn may

also be evicted, even though she is an innocent party to these events.

**HOW ASSIGNMENTS FUNCTION** Assignments are important because they are involved in much business financing. Probably the most common contractual right that is assigned is the right to the payment of money. For example, Kerr is in the business of selling video equipment—camcorders, VCRs, and television sets. To prepare for the holiday sales season, Kerr needs to buy more inventory. Because he sells on credit to most of his customers (who make small monthly payments), he does not have enough funds on hand, but he does have the *right* to receive the monthly payments from his customers. To obtain funds, Kerr assigns the rights to those payments to a financing agency, which then gives him cash. The agency may purchase those rights or only lend money to Kerr based on the accounts. The agency may insist that Kerr's customers make their payments directly to the agency, or it may have nothing to do with the accounts unless Kerr fails to repay.

Similarly, banks frequently assign the rights to receive payments under their loan contracts to other firms, which pay for those rights. For example, if you obtain a student loan from your local bank, you might later receive in the mail a notice from your bank stating that it has transferred (assigned) its rights to receive payments on the loan to another firm and that, when the time comes to repay your loan, you must make the payments to that other firm. Banks that make *mortgage loans* to allow prospective home buyers to purchase a house (see Chapter 51) often assign their rights to collect the mortgage payments to a third party, and the home buyers are notified that they must in the future make payments not to the bank that loaned them the funds but to the third party. Millions of dollars change hands daily in the business world in the form of assignments of rights in contracts. If it were not possible to transfer (assign) contractual rights, many businesses could not continue to operate.

**FORM OF THE ASSIGNMENT** In general, an assignment can take any form, oral or written. Naturally, it is more difficult to prove the occurrence of an oral assignment, so it is practical to put all assignments in writing.

Of course, assignments covered by the Statute of Frauds must be in writing to be enforceable. For

---

1. Restatement (Second) of Contracts, Section 317.

example, an assignment of an interest in land must be in writing to be enforceable. In addition, most states require contracts for the assignment of wages to be in writing.[2]

**CONSIDERATION**   An assignment need *not* be supported by legally sufficient consideration to be effective. A gratuitous assignment (one not made for money or other consideration) is just as effective as an assignment made for money. The absence of consideration becomes significant, however, when the assignor wants to revoke the assignment. If the assignment was made for consideration, the assignor normally cannot revoke it. If no consideration is involved, the assignor can revoke, thereby canceling the right of the third party to demand performance or to sue for failure to render that performance.[3] Gratuitous assignments can be revoked by

1. The subsequent assignment of the same right to another third party.
2. The death of the assignor.
3. The bankruptcy of the assignor.
4. A notice of revocation given to the assignee.

**RIGHTS THAT CANNOT BE ASSIGNED**   As a general rule, all rights can be assigned, except in the following special circumstances:

1. If a statute expressly prohibits assignment, the particular right in question cannot be assigned. Suppose that Quincy is a new employee of Specialty Computer, Inc. Specialty Computer is an employer under workers' compensation statutes in this state, and thus Quincy is a covered employee. Quincy has a relatively high-risk job. In need of a loan, Quincy borrows some money from Draper, assigning to Draper all workers' compensation benefits due her should she be injured on the job. The assignment of *future* workers' compensation benefits is prohibited by state statute, and thus such rights cannot be assigned.
2. When a contract is *personal* in nature, the rights under the contract cannot be assigned

unless all that remains is a money payment.[4] Suppose that Brower signs a contract to be a tutor for Horton's children. Horton then attempts to assign to Kuhn her right to Brower's services. Kuhn cannot enforce the contract against Brower. Kuhn's children may be more difficult to tutor than Horton's; thus, if Horton could assign her rights to Brower's services to Kuhn, it would change the nature of Brower's obligation. Because personal services are unique to the person rendering them, rights to receive personal services are likewise unique and cannot be assigned.

3. A right cannot be assigned if assignment will materially increase or alter the risk or duties of the obligor.[5] Assume that Horton has a hotel, and to insure it, she takes out a policy with Southeast Insurance. The policy insures against fire, theft, floods, and vandalism. Horton attempts to assign the insurance policy to Kuhn, who also owns a hotel. The assignment is ineffective, because it substantially alters Southeast Insurance's *duty of performance.* An insurance company evaluates the particular risk of a certain party and tailors its policy to fit that risk. If the policy is assigned to a third party, the insurance risk is materially altered. Therefore, the assignment will not operate to give Kuhn any rights against Southeast Insurance.
4. If a contract stipulates that the right cannot be assigned, then *ordinarily* it cannot be assigned, as discussed in the next section.

**ANTI-ASSIGNMENT CLAUSES**   Anti-assignment clauses in contracts are increasing in both number and importance. If the promisor makes it clear that a right is *not* to be assignable, generally no subsequent assignment will be effective. Whether an anti-assignment clause is effective depends in part on how it is phrased. A contract that states that any assignment is ''void'' effectively prohibits any assignment. Note that restraints on the power to assign operate only against the parties themselves. They do not effectively prohibit an assignment by operation of law, such as an assignment pursuant to bankruptcy or death.

---

2. See, for example, California Labor Code Section 300. There are other assignments that must be in writing as well.
3. Restatement (Second) of Contracts, Section 332.

4. Restatement (Second) of Contracts, Sections 317 and 318.
5. UCC 2–210(2).

There are several exceptions to the rule that a contract can, by its terms, prohibit any assignment of the contract. First, a contract cannot prevent an assignment of the right to receive money. This exception exists to encourage the free flow of money and credit in modern business settings. Second, the assignment of rights in real estate often cannot be prohibited, because such a prohibition is contrary to public policy. Prohibitions of this kind are called restraints against *alienation* (transfer of land ownership). Third, the assignment of *negotiable instruments* (see Chapter 26) cannot be prohibited. Fourth, in a contract for the sale of goods, the right to receive damages for breach of contract or for payment of an account owed may be assigned even though the sales contract prohibits such assignment.[6]

Anti-assignment clauses have appeared in leases for many years. Now they are being used more frequently in other types of contracts as well. Recently, they have appeared in mortgage contracts and represent attempts by the mortgagee (the lending person or institution in a mortgage contract) to restrict the assumption of mortgages by new owners of real property. The typical lease or mortgage today cannot be assigned without the landlord's or mortgagee's consent.

In the following case, the court discussed whether an assignment of proceeds payable under an insurance policy constituted an assignment of the personal contract represented by the policy.

---

6. UCC 2–210(2).

---

**CASE 17.1**

**SMITH v. BUEGE**
Supreme Court of Appeals of West Virginia, 1989.
387 S.E.2d 109.

**BACKGROUND AND FACTS**   *Thomas Smith agreed to buy a house from James, Jackie, Terrie, and Chong Buege. The contract provided that if fire damaged the property before the sale had been completed, Smith could either cancel the contract or accept the property as damaged and receive the insurance proceeds. Before the sale had been completed, fire damaged the house. The Bueges notified their insurer, Prudential Insurance Company, of the contract with Smith. Smith notified the Bueges and Prudential that he still wanted the property and that he was opting to receive the insurance proceeds. Prudential sent the Bueges a check. When Smith filed suit against the Bueges and Prudential to recover the insurance proceeds, Prudential moved to dismiss the suit against it on the grounds that it was not a party to the contract and had met its obligations under the policy by paying the Bueges. The trial court granted the motion, and Smith appealed. Smith contended that his claim against Prudential had been improperly dismissed because the contract included an assignment of the proceeds and therefore Prudential should have paid Smith, not the Bueges.*

*McHUGH,* Justice:
        *   *   *   *
        *   *   * Assignment, after loss, of the proceeds of insurance does not constitute an assignment of the personal contract represented by the policy, but only of a claim or right of action on the policy. Moreover, the recognized reason for the prohibition of assignments without the consent of the insurer, specifically, to protect the insurer against an increased risk resulting from the assignment, is not applicable after a loss because the liability of the insurer was already fixed by the loss prior to the effective date of the assignment, and *   *   * such liability is assignable regardless of the conditions of the policy in question.
        *   *   *   *
    In the case now before us there was an agreement to assign the fire insurance proceeds which was not effective as an assignment until after the loss when the

appellant-assignee decided to accept the damaged dwelling and the fire insurance proceeds, rather than rescinding the contract. Prudential Insurance had written notice of this post-fire assignment of the fire insurance proceeds prior to remitting the same to the Bueges, the assignors. Therefore, under [West Virginia law], Prudential was required to remit the fire insurance proceeds to the appellant-assignee *  *  * .

*The appellate court reversed the trial court's decision, holding that the trial court had improperly dismissed Smith's claim against Prudential. Smith was entitled to the fire insurance proceeds.*

**DECISION AND REMEDY**

**Contract Assignment in Germany** *German law was derived from Roman law, which had no provision relating to the assignment of contracts. The German civil code was amended to provide for assignment, but section 399 of the code provides that a right cannot be transferred "if such assignment has been precluded by an agreement with the debtor." Strict application of this rule would have precluded the assignment in the case presented above.*

**INTERNATIONAL CONSIDERATIONS**

---

**NOTICE OF ASSIGNMENT**   Once a valid assignment of rights has been made to a third party, the third party should notify the obligor of the assignment. Giving notice is not legally necessary to establish the validity of the assignment, because an assignment is effective immediately, whether or not notice is given. Two major problems arise, however, when notice of the assignment is not given to the obligor:

1.  If the assignor assigns the same right to two different persons, the question arises as to which one has priority—that is, which one has the right to the performance by the obligor. Although the rule most often observed in the United States is that the first assignment in time is the first in right, some states follow the English rule, which basically gives priority to the first assignee who gives notice.

2.  Until the obligor has notice of assignment, the obligor can discharge his or her obligation by performance to the assignor, and performance by the obligor to the assignor constitutes a discharge to the assignee. Once the obligor receives proper notice, only performance to the assignee can discharge the obligor's obligations. To illustrate, suppose that Brower owes Horton $1,000 on a contractual obligation. Horton assigns this monetary claim to Kuhn. No notice of assignment is given to Brower. Brower pays Horton the $1,000. Although the assignment was valid, Brower's payment to Horton was a discharge of the debt, and Kuhn's

failure to give notice to Brower of the assignment caused Kuhn to lose the right to collect the money from Brower. If Kuhn had given Brower notice of the assignment, Brower's payment to Horton would not have discharged the debt, and Kuhn would have had a legal right to require payment from Brower.

## DELEGATIONS

Just as a party can transfer rights through an assignment, a party can also transfer duties. Duties are not assigned, however; they are *delegated*. Normally, a **delegation** of duties does not relieve the party making the delegation (the *delegator*) of the obligation to perform in the event that the party to whom the duty has been delegated (the *delegatee*) fails to perform. No special form is required to create a valid delegation of duties. As long as the delegator expresses an intention to make the delegation, it is effective; the delegator need not even use the word *delegate*.

**DUTIES THAT CANNOT BE DELEGATED**   As a general rule, any duty can be delegated. There are, however, some exceptions to this rule. Delegation is prohibited in the following circumstances:

1.  When performance depends on the *personal skill or talents* of the obligor.
2.  When special trust has been placed in the obligor.
3.  When performance by a third party will vary materially from that expected by the obligee

(the one to whom performance is owed) under the contract.

4. When the contract expressly prohibits delegation.

Suppose that Brower contracts with Horton to tutor Horton in the various aspects of financial underwriting and investment banking. Brower, an experienced businessperson known for her expertise in finance, wants to delegate her duties to a third party, Kuhn. This delegation is ineffective because Brower contracted to render a service that is founded on Brower's *expertise*. The delegation would change Horton's expectations under the contract. Therefore, Kuhn cannot perform Brower's duties.

Suppose that Brower, the son of Horton's neighbor, contracts with Horton to *personally* mow Horton's lawn during June, July, and August. Then Brower decides that he would rather spend the summer at the beach. Brower delegates his lawn-mowing duties to Kuhn, who is in the business of mowing lawns and doing other landscaping work to earn money to pay for college. The delegation is not effective, no matter how competent Kuhn is, without Horton's consent. The contract was for *personal* performance.

Assume that Brower contracts with Horton to pick up and deliver heavy construction machinery to Horton's property. Brower delegates this duty to Kuhn, who is in the business of delivering heavy machinery. This delegation is effective. The performance required is of a *routine* and *nonpersonal* nature, and the delegation does not change Horton's expectations under the contract.

**EFFECT OF A DELEGATION**  If a delegation of duties is enforceable, the *obligee* (the one to whom performance is owed) must accept performance from the delegatee. The obligee can legally refuse performance from the delegatee only if the duty is one that cannot be delegated. A valid delegation of duties does not relieve the delegator of obligations under the contract.[7] If the delegatee fails to perform, the delegator is still liable to the obligee.

**LIABILITY OF THE DELEGATEE**  If the delegatee fails to perform, whether the obligee can hold the delegatee liable comes into issue. If the delegatee has made a promise of performance that will directly benefit the obligee, there is an "assumption of duty." Breach of this duty makes the delegatee liable to the obligee.

Suppose, for example, that Brower contracts to build Horton a house according to Horton's blueprint. Brower becomes seriously ill and contracts to have Kuhn build the house for Horton (the obligee). Kuhn fails to build the house. Because the delegatee, Kuhn, contracted with Brower (the obligor) to build the house for the benefit of Horton (the obligee), Horton can sue Brower, Kuhn, or both. Although there are many exceptions, the general rule today is that the obligee can sue both the delegatee and the obligor-delegator.

## ASSIGNMENT OF "ALL RIGHTS"

When a contract provides for an "assignment of all rights," this wording may also be treated as a delegation of duties.[8] Therefore, when general words are used (for example, "I assign the contract" or "I assign all my rights under the contract"), the contract is construed as implying both an assignment of rights and a delegation of duties.

Questions sometimes arise as to how an assignment of a contract in the sense just mentioned differs from a novation. As will be discussed in Chapter 18 in the context of how contractual obligations can be discharged, a **novation** occurs when both of the parties to the original contract agree to substitute a third party for one of the original parties. For example, suppose that Union Corporation contracts to sell its pharmaceutical division to British Pharmaceuticals, Ltd. Before the transfer is completed, Union, British Pharmaceuticals, and a third company, Otis Chemicals, execute a new agreement to transfer all of British Pharmaceutical's rights and duties in the transaction to Otis Chemicals. As long as the new contract is supported by consideration, the novation will discharge the original contract (between Union and British Pharmaceuticals) and replace it with the new contract (between Union and Otis Chemicals).

The key difference between an assignment and a novation is that in the former, the original party

---

7. *Crane Ice Cream Co. v. Terminal Freezing & Heating Co.*, 147 Md. 588, 128 A. 280 (1925).

8. Restatement (Second) of Contracts, Section 328; UCC 2–210(1), (4).

to the contract (the assignor) remains liable under the original contract, while in a novation, the original party's obligations are completely discharged. The following case illustrates this distinction.

---

**COMPANY PROFILE** *In 1938, J. F. McCullough, owner of the Homemade Ice Cream Company in Green River, Illinois, developed a new frozen dessert: soft ice cream. Harry Oltz developed a freezer to keep the ice cream at a constant temperature to maintain its soft consistency. In 1939, McCullough and his son, with Oltz, began a new company named Dairy Queen in honor of McCullough's cow. Dairy Queen sold franchisees the right to use its freezers in return for royalties on the amount of ice cream produced. The first Dairy Queen franchise opened in Joliet, Illinois, in 1940. By the end of the decade, there were 1,156 Dairy Queens. By 1960, there were 3,000 Dairy Queens in twelve countries. Two years later, some of the franchisees formed International Dairy Queen (IDQ) as a central authority for dealing with the problems of menu standardization and product uniformity. Today, IDQ franchises more than 6,000 Dairy Queens, Karmelkorn Shoppes (popcorn), Orange Julius stores (fruit drinks), and Golden Skillets (fried chicken).*

**CASE 17.2**

**ROSENBERG v. SON, INC.**
Supreme Court of North Dakota, 1992.
491 N.W.2d 71.

**BACKGROUND AND FACTS** *Mary Pratt contracted to buy Harold and Gladys Rosenberg's Dairy Queen on February 8, 1980. The purchase price for the "franchise, inventory, and equipment" was $62,000, with payments to be made over a fifteen-year period. In 1982, Pratt assigned her rights in the contract to Son, Inc. The Rosenbergs signed a "Consent to Assignment" clause at that time. Pratt then moved to Arizona and had nothing more to do with the Dairy Queen business. In 1984, Son assigned the contract to the Merit Corporation. The assignment did not contain a consent clause for the Rosenbergs to sign, but they were aware of the transaction and accepted Merit's payment on the balance. Merit took out a bank loan, using the equipment and inventory as security, or collateral, for the loan. After June 1988, Merit ceased making payments to the Rosenbergs. Merit filed for bankruptcy, and the bank repossessed the collateral. The Rosenbergs sued Son and Pratt for payment of the balance due ($17,326.24) under the original contract for the sale of the Dairy Queen. The trial court dismissed the Rosenbergs' claims, finding that Pratt was a guarantor and that the second assignment to Merit, Merit's pledging of the business assets as collateral for a loan, and other actions accomplished without Pratt's knowledge were sufficient alterations to the original contract to exonerate her.[a] The Rosenbergs appealed.*

*ERICKSTAD,* Chief Justice.
\* \* \* \*
\* \* \* [A] contracting party cannot escape its liability on the contract by merely assigning its duties and rights under the contract to a third party. \* \* \* "In spite of such an 'assignment,' the debtor's duty remains absolutely unchanged. The performance required by a duty can often be delegated; but by such a delegation the duty itself is not escaped."
\* \* \* \*

---

a. One who acts as a guarantor on a contract is no longer liable if the contract terms are substantially altered without the guarantor's knowledge. See the discussion of guaranty in Chapter 32.

* * * [A] contracting party * * * may seek the approval of the other original party for release, and substitute a new party in its place. In such an instance, the transaction is * * * called a novation. If a novation occurs in this manner, it must be clear from the terms of the agreement that a novation is intended by all parties involved. * * *

* * * *

* * * [T]he Rosenbergs did sign a consent * * * . However, by merely consenting to the assignment, the Rosenbergs did not consent to a discharge of the principal obligor—Pratt. * * * ''Where the obligee consents to the delegation, the consent itself does not release the obligor from liability for breach of contract. * * * For the obligor to be released from liability, the obligee must agree to the release. If there is an agreement between the obligor, obligee and a third party by which the third party agrees to be substituted for the obligor and the obligee assents thereto[,] the obligor is released from liability and the third person takes the place of the obligor.'' * * *

* * * *

* * * Pursuant to guaranty law, the trial court released Pratt from any liability on the contract due to the changes or alterations which took place following her assignment to Son, Inc. * * * [A]n assignor occupies a much different position from that of a guarantor; not every type of alteration is sufficient to warrant discharge of the assignor. * * * ''[U]nless the other contracting party has consented to release him, the assignor remains bound by his obligation under the contract and is liable to the other party if the assignee defaults, . . . However, the assignor is responsible only for the obligation which he originally contracted to assume, and the assignee cannot, without the assignor's knowledge, increase the burden.''

**DECISION AND REMEDY**
*The appellate court held that the trial court erred by applying guaranty law to the dispute. The court remanded the case to the trial court for further fact finding to determine whether the Pratt-Son agreement constituted a novation or an assignment of the contract. If it was a novation, Pratt would not be liable to the Rosenbergs. If it was an assignment, Pratt would be liable to the Rosenbergs for the balance due under the original contract.*

---

## SECTION 2

# THIRD PARTY BENEFICIARIES

To have contractual rights, a person normally must be a party to the contract. As mentioned earlier in this chapter, an exception exists when the original parties to the contract intend at the time of contracting that the contract performance directly benefit a third person. In this situation, the third person becomes a *beneficiary* of the contract and has legal rights.

The law distinguishes between two types of **third party beneficiaries:** *intended* beneficiaries and *incidental* beneficiaries. It is important to re-alize that only intended beneficiaries acquire legal rights in a contract.

## INTENDED BENEFICIARIES

An **intended beneficiary** is one for whose benefit the contract was made and who can thus sue the promisor directly for breach of the contract. But who is the promisor? In bilateral contracts, both parties to the contract are promisors, because they both make promises that can be enforced. In third party beneficiary contracts, courts will determine the identity of the promisor by asking which party made the promise that benefits the third party—that person is the promisor. Allowing a third party to sue the promisor directly in effect circumvents the ''middle person'' (the promisee) and thus reduces the burden on the courts. Otherwise, a third party would sue the promisee, who would then sue the promisor.

## TYPES OF INTENDED BENEFICIARIES

At one time, third party beneficiaries had no legal rights in contracts. Over time, however, the concept developed that a third party for whose benefit a contract was formed could sue the promisor to have the contract enforced. In a classic case decided in 1859, *Lawrence v. Fox,*[9] the court permitted a third party beneficiary to bring suit directly against a promisor. This case established the rule that a *creditor beneficiary*—one who benefits from a contract in which one party (the promisor) promises another party (the promisee) to pay a debt that party owes to a third party (the creditor beneficiary)—can sue the promisor directly. The creditor beneficiary, although not a party to the contract between the debtor and the other person, becomes the intended beneficiary and can thus enforce the promisor's promise to pay the debt.

Another landmark case, decided in 1918, established the rule that when a contract is made for the express purpose of giving a *gift* to a third party, the third party can sue the promisor directly to enforce the promise.[10] In this situation, the third

party is called a *donee beneficiary.* A donee beneficiary can enforce the promise of a promisor just as a creditor beneficiary can. Suppose Horton goes to her attorney, Brower, and enters into a contract in which Brower promises to draft a will naming Horton's son, Duncan, as an heir. Duncan is a donee beneficiary, and if Brower does not prepare the will properly, Duncan can sue Brower.[11] Or suppose Horton offers to put in a swimming pool in Brower's backyard if Brower pays $2,000 to Duncan, Horton's son. Horton wants to give the money to Duncan as a gift. Duncan is a donee beneficiary and, once Horton has put in the pool, can enforce Brower's promise to pay the $2,000.

As the law concerning third party beneficiaries evolved, numerous cases arose in which the third party beneficiary did not fit readily into either category—creditor beneficiary or donee beneficiary. Thus the modern view, and the one adopted by the Restatement (Second) of Contracts, distinguishes only between intended beneficiaries (who can sue to enforce contracts made for their benefit) and incidental beneficiaries (who cannot sue, as will be discussed in a later section).

In the following case, the issue before the court was whether an adult child was an intended beneficiary under her parents' divorce agreement.

---

9.   20 N.Y. 268 (1859).

10.  *Seaver v. Ransom,* 224 N.Y. 233, 120 N.E. 639 (1918).

11.  *Lucas v. Hamm,* 56 Cal.2d 583, 364 P.2d 685, 15 Cal.Rptr. 821 (1961).

---

**BACKGROUND AND FACTS**  *When Charles and Judy Orr were divorced in 1970, their divorce agreement included a provision that Charles would pay for the college or professional school education of the couple's two children, then minors. In 1990, Jennifer Orr, the Orrs' daughter, filed a petition to compel her father to pay her college expenses. The trial court dismissed the action on the ground that Jennifer, as an adult child of the involved parties, did not have standing to seek the relief asked for in the petition because she was not a party to her parents' divorce agreement. Jennifer appealed the ruling.*

**CASE 17.3**

**ORR v. ORR**

Appellate Court of Illinois, First District, 1992.
228 Ill.App.3d 234,
592 N.E.2d 553,
170 Ill.Dec. 117.

Presiding Justice *McNULTY* delivered the opinion of the court:
\*   \*   \*   \*

\*   \*   \* In the [Illinois] case *Miller v. Miller,* a child of divorced parents brought suit against his father to enforce a settlement agreement incorporated into the divorce decree which obligated the father to pay the child's college expenses. \*   \*   \* In reaching the decision that the child [could enforce the agreement] as a third-party beneficiary, the court found the following three factors controlling: (1) it must be clear from the contract that the parties to the contract intended the third party to benefit; (2) the benefit to the agreement is direct to the third party and the liability of the promisor affirmatively appears from the language of the agreement; and (3) the third party must have relied on the father's promise in the agreement to pay his college expenses. *   *   *

*   *   *   *

*   *   * "The rule is well established that where a person makes a promise to another, based upon a valid consideration, for the benefit of a third person, such third person may maintain an action on the contract." Moreover, children who are beneficiaries under a contract entered into by their parents [can] bring suit against their father to compel his compliance with the contract terms.

*   *   * We *   *   * find that because plaintiff is the child of the divorced parents and is seeking to enforce benefits conferred upon her directly by the settlement agreement, she is a direct beneficiary of her parent's divorce agreement. Finally, the record provides us with enough evidence from which to conclude that plaintiff relied upon the benefits of the settlement agreement by enrolling in college.

**DECISION AND REMEDY**    *The appellate court reversed the trial court's decision and remanded the case for further proceedings.*

**ETHICAL CONSIDERATIONS**    *The parent taking custody of a child after a divorce frequently bears the burden of paying for the child's college educational expenses. Even if the noncustodial parent agreed, during divorce proceedings, to help cover these expenses, by the time the child is grown, the noncustodial parent may have changed his or her mind and may try to avoid performance under the agreement, or contract. Allowing children to sue as third party beneficiaries increases the chances that such agreements will be enforced.*

---

**THE VESTING OF AN INTENDED BENEFICIARY'S RIGHTS**    An intended third party beneficiary cannot enforce a contract against the original parties until the rights of the third party have *vested,* which means the rights have taken effect and cannot be taken away. Until these rights have vested, the original parties to the contract—the promisor and the promisee—can modify or rescind the contract without the consent of the third party. When do the rights of third parties vest? Generally, the rights of an intended beneficiary vest when either of the following occurs:

1. When the third party demonstrates *manifest assent* to the contract, such as sending a letter or note acknowledging awareness of, and consent to, a contract formed for his or her benefit.
2. When the third party materially alters his or her position in *detrimental reliance* on the contract.

If the contract expressly reserves to the contracting parties the right to cancel, rescind, or modify the contract, the rights of the third party beneficiary are subject to any changes that result.

In such a case, the vesting of the third party's rights does not terminate the power of the original contracting parties to alter their legal relationships.[12] This is particularly true in most life insurance contracts, in which the right to change the beneficiary is reserved to the policyowner.

Exhibit 17–1 summarizes third party rights in contracts generally, including when the rights of an intended third party beneficiary vest.

## INCIDENTAL BENEFICIARIES

The benefit that an **incidental beneficiary** receives from a contract between two parties is unintentional. Therefore, an incidental beneficiary cannot enforce a contract to which he or she is not a party. In determining whether a third party beneficiary is an intended or an incidental beneficiary, the courts generally use the *reasonable person* test. That is, a beneficiary will be considered an intended beneficiary if a reasonable person in the position of

---

12. Defenses that may be raised against third party beneficiaries are given in Restatement (Second) of Contracts, Section 309.

■ **Exhibit 17–1 Third Party Rights in Contracts**

| | **Third Party Beneficiary Contract** | **Assignment** | **Delegation** |
|---|---|---|---|
| How are third party rights created? | Purpose of original contract is to benefit third party. If purpose is: 1. To discharge a duty or debt owed, third party is *creditor* beneficiary. 2. To confer a gift, third party is *donee* beneficiary. | After contract formation, rights are assigned to third party. | After contract formation, duties are delegated to third party. |
| Is the third party beneficiary contract, assignment, or delegation effective? | For a third party beneficiary contract to be effective, rights under the contract must vest by: 1. Third party's manifesting assent to the contract. 2. Third party's materially altering position in detrimental reliance. | To be effective, an assignment cannot involve: 1. Rights that a statute expressly prohibits from being assigned. 2. Rights to performance by personal service. 3. Rights the assignment of which will materially increase or alter the obligor's duties. 4. Rights that the contract stipulates cannot be assigned, except: a. Rights to receive money. b. Rights in real property (see Chapter 51). c. Rights to negotiable instruments (see Chapter 26). d. Rights to damages for breach of contract or for payment of an account. | To be effective, a delegation cannot involve: 1. Duties that depend on personal skill or talent of the obligor. 2. Duties that involve special trust placed in the obligor. 3. Duties the delegation of which will materially increase or alter the performance expected by the obligee. 4. Duties that the contract stipulates cannot be delegated. |

the third party beneficiary would believe that the promisee *intended* to confer upon the beneficiary the right to bring suit to enforce the contract. Several other factors must also be examined to determine whether a party is an intended or an incidental beneficiary. The presence of one or more of the following factors strongly indicates an *intended* (rather than an incidental) benefit to a third party:

1. Performance is rendered directly to the third party.
2. The third party has the right to control the details of performance.
3. The third party is expressly designated as the beneficiary in the contract.

In contrast, the following are examples of *incidental* beneficiaries. The third party has no rights in the contract and cannot enforce it against the promisor.

1. Escobedo contracts with Monell to build a cottage on Monell's land. Escobedo's plans specify that All-Weather Insulation Company's insulation materials must be used in constructing the house. All-Weather is an incidental beneficiary and cannot enforce the contract against Escobedo by attempting to require that Escobedo purchase its insulation materials.
2. Berkemer contracts with Coolidge to build a recreational facility on Coolidge's land. Once

the facility is constructed, it will greatly enhance the property values in the neighborhood. If Berkemer subsequently refuses to build the facility, Tien, Coolidge's neighbor, cannot enforce the contract against Berkemer because Tien is an incidental beneficiary.

Government contracts often benefit the public, but individual members of the public are treated as incidental beneficiaries, unless the contract provides otherwise. For example, Benningson contracts with the federal government to carry mail over a certain route. Cagney is a member of the public whose mail is to be carried over the route. Benningson fails to perform. Benningson is under no contractual duty to Cagney individually, and thus Cagney is treated as an incidental beneficiary and cannot enforce the contract.

## TERMS AND CONCEPTS TO REVIEW

| | | |
|---|---|---|
| assignment 314 | intended beneficiary 320 | third party beneficiary 320 |
| delegation 317 | novation 318 | |
| incidental beneficiary 322 | privity of contract 313 | |

# QUESTIONS AND CASE PROBLEMS

**17–1. Third Party Beneficiary.** Alexander has been accepted as a freshman at a college two hundred miles from his home for the fall semester. Alexander's rich uncle, Michael, decides to give Alexander a car for Christmas. In November, Michael makes a contract with Jackson Auto Sales to purchase a new car for $10,000 to be delivered to Alexander just before the Christmas holidays, in mid-December. The title to the car is to be in Alexander's name. Michael pays the full purchase price, calls Alexander and tells him about the gift, and takes off for a six-month vacation in Europe. Jackson never delivers the car, and Alexander files an action against Jackson. Discuss fully whether Alexander can recover for Jackson's breach of contract. What if Michael had agreed with Jackson to make installment payments on the car and then failed to make the payments? Could Alexander have sued his uncle for breach of the contract? Discuss.

**17–2. Assignment.** Five years ago, Hensley purchased a house. At that time, being unable to pay the full purchase price, she borrowed money from Thrift Savings and Loan, which in turn took a 9.5 percent mortgage on the house. The mortgage contract did not prohibit the assignment of the mortgage. Then Hensley secured a new job in another city and sold the house to Sylvia. The purchase price included payment to Hensley of the value of her equity and the assumption of the mortgage held by Thrift. At the time the contract was made, Thrift did not know about, or consent to, the sale. On the basis of these facts, if Sylvia defaults in making the house payments to Thrift, what are Thrift's rights? Discuss.

**17–3. Assignment.** Marsala is a student attending college. He signs a one-year lease agreement that runs from September 1 to August 31. The lease agreement specifies that the lease cannot be assigned without the landlord's consent. In late May, Marsala decides not to go to summer school and assigns the balance of the lease (three months) to a close friend, Fred. The landlord objects to the assignment and denies Fred access to the apartment. Marsala claims Fred is financially sound and should be allowed the full rights and privileges of an assignee. Discuss fully whether the landlord or Marsala is correct.

**17–4. Delegation.** Inez has a specific set of plans to build a sailboat. The plans are detailed in nature, and any boatbuilder can build the boat. Inez secures bids, and the low bid is made by the Whale of a Boat Corp. Inez contracts with Whale to build the boat for $4,000. Whale then receives unexpected business from elsewhere. To meet the delivery date in the contract with Inez, Whale delegates its obligation to build the boat, without Inez's consent, to Quick Brothers, a reputable boatbuilder. When the boat is ready for delivery, Inez learns of the delegation and refuses to accept delivery, even though the boat is built to specifications. Discuss fully whether Inez is obligated to accept and pay for the boat. Would your answer be any different if Inez had not had a specific set of plans but had instead contracted with Whale to design and build a sailboat for $4,000? Explain.

**17–5. Third Party Beneficiary.** Lo-Ji Creations, Inc., wrote a letter to Dixie Clothing Co., claiming that Dixie owed Lo-Ji $3,000 for the shipment of string bikinis that it had sent Dixie three months before. Dixie wrote back, saying that the bikinis were defective and that it therefore refused to pay. Lo-Ji responded that its lawyer had advised the company that it was questionable whether

Dixie had informed it of the defect in time and that Lo-Ji might have a valid claim for the purchase price of $3,000 despite any defects. About a month later, Dixie wrote to Lo-Ji, informing Lo-Ji that Jannel Retailers, Ltd., which owed Dixie $3,000 from a previous contract, had agreed with Dixie to make the payment to Lo-Ji. Thereafter, Jannel failed to make the payment to Lo-Ji. Can Lo-Ji sue Jannel for the payment? Discuss.

**17–6. Third Party Beneficiary.** Owens, a federal prisoner, was transferred from federal prison to the Nassau County Jail pursuant to a contract between the U.S. Bureau of Prisons and the county. The contract included a policy statement that required the receiving prison to provide for the safekeeping and protection of transferred federal prisoners. While in the Nassau County Jail, Owens was beaten severely by prison officials and suffered lacerations, bruises, and a lasting impairment that caused blackouts. Can Owens, as a third party beneficiary, sue the county for breach of its agreement with the U.S. Bureau of Prisons? Discuss fully. [*Owens v. Haas*, 601 F.2d 1242 (2d Cir. 1979)]

**17–7. Assignment.** Clement was seriously injured in a car accident with King. Clement sued King. King retained Prestwich as her attorney. Because of the alleged negligence of Prestwich, Clement was able to obtain a $21,000 judgment on her claim against King. Clement received from King a purported written assignment of King's malpractice claim against Prestwich as settlement for the judgment against her. Can King assign her cause of action against Prestwich to Clement? Explain. [*Clement v. Prestwich*, 114 Ill.App.3d 479, 448 N.E.2d 1039, 70 Ill.Dec. 161 (1983)]

**17–8. Assignment.** Fox Brothers Enterprises, Inc., agreed to convey to Canfield a lot, Lot 23, in a subdivision known as Fox Estates, together with a one-year option to purchase Lot 24. The agreement did not contain any prohibitions, restrictions, or limitations against assignments. Canfield paid the price of $20,000 and took title to Lot 23. Thereafter, Canfield assigned his option right in Lot 24 to the Scotts. When the Scotts tried to exercise their right to the option, Fox Brothers refused to convey the property to them. The Scotts then brought suit for specific performance. What was the result? [*Scott v. Fox Brothers Enterprises, Inc.*, 667 P.2d 773 (Colo.App. 1983)]

**17–9. Third Party Beneficiary.** Rensselaer Water Co. was under contract to the city of Rensselaer, New York, to provide water to the city, including water at fire hydrants. A warehouse owned by H. R. Moch Co. was totally destroyed by a fire, which could not be extinguished because of inadequate water pressure at the fire hydrants. Moch brought suit against Rensselaer Water for damages, claiming that Moch was a third party beneficiary to the city's contract with the water company. Will Moch be able to recover damages from the water company on the basis that the water company breached its contract with the city? Explain. [*H. R. Moch Co. v. Rensselaer Water Co.*, 247 N.Y. 160, 159 N.E. 896 (1928)]

**17–10. Assignment.** Abby's Cakes on Dixie, Inc., agreed in a lease contract to lease space in a shopping center from Colonial Palms Plaza, Ltd. The contract included a provision in which Colonial agreed to pay Abby's a construction allowance of up to $11,250 after Abby's had satisfactorily completed certain improvements to the rented premises. The contract also contained a clause stating that Abby's agreed "not to assign, mortgage, pledge, or encumber this Lease" without first obtaining the written consent of Colonial and that any such "assignment, encumbrance or subletting without such consent shall be void." Prior to the completion of the improvements, Abby's assigned its right to receive the first $8,000 of the construction allowance to Robert Aldana (without first obtaining Colonial's consent). In return, Aldana loaned Abby's $8,000 to finance the construction. Aldana notified Colonial of the assignment by certified mail. After Abby's had completed the improvements to the rented premises, Colonial ignored the assignment and paid Abby's the construction allowance. In Aldana's suit against Colonial for the $8,000 due him pursuant to the assignment, Colonial claimed that the assignment was prohibited by the contract provision and therefore void. Who will win, and why? [*Aldana v. Colonial Palms Plaza, Ltd.*, 591 So.2d 953 (Fla.App. 1992)]

# CHAPTER 18

# PERFORMANCE AND DISCHARGE

The **discharge** (termination) of a contract is ordinarily accomplished when both of the parties perform those acts promised in the contract. For example, a buyer and seller have a contract for the sale of a bicycle for $50. This contract will be discharged upon the buyer's payment of $50 to the seller and the seller's transfer of possession of the bicycle to the buyer.

Although a contract is ordinarily discharged by the parties' performance of their contractual duties, discharge can also occur in other ways. In this chapter, we will discuss some of the more important ways in which contracts can be discharged. Broadly speaking, contracts can be discharged by the following:

1. The occurrence or failure of a *condition* upon which a contract is based.
2. *Performance* (or breach of contract, in which case the nonbreaching party is discharged from the duty of performance).
3. *Agreement of the parties* (through rescission, novation, or accord and satisfaction).
4. *Operation of law* (resulting from material alteration of the contract, the statute of limitations, bankruptcy, or impossibility or commercial impracticability of performance).

## SECTION 1

## CONDITIONS

Normally, promises must be performed, or the party promising the act will be in breach of contract. For example, I promise to pay you $100 for your watch on September 1. The promise is unconditional. If I do not pay you the $100, I am in breach of contract.

In some cases, however, performance is contingent on the occurrence or nonoccurrence of a certain event. Therefore, a *condition* is inserted into the contract, either expressly by the parties or impliedly by courts. If this condition is not satisfied, the obligations of the parties are discharged. Thus, a **condition** is a possible future event, the occurrence or nonoccurrence of which will trigger the performance of a legal obligation or terminate an existing obligation under a contract.[1]

For example, suppose that I offer to purchase a tract of your land on the condition that your neighbor to the south agrees to sell me her land. You accept my offer. Our obligations (promises) are conditioned on your neighbor's willingness to sell her land. Should this condition not be satisfied (for example, if your neighbor refuses to sell), our obligations to each other are discharged and cannot be enforced.

Three types of conditions can be present in contracts—conditions *precedent,* conditions *subsequent,* and *concurrent* conditions. Conditions are also classified as *express* or *implied.*

## CONDITIONS PRECEDENT

A condition that must be fulfilled before a party's performance can be required is called a **condition precedent.** The condition precedes the absolute duty to perform. Real estate contracts frequently are conditioned on the buyer's ability to obtain financing. For example, Fisher promises to buy Calvin's house if Salvation Bank approves Fisher's mortgage application. The Fisher-Calvin contract is therefore subject to a condition precedent—the bank's approval of Fisher's mortgage application. If the bank does not approve the application, the contract will fail because the condition precedent was not met.

Insurance contracts frequently specify that certain conditions must be met before the insurance company will be obligated to perform under the contract. The following case is illustrative.

---

1. Restatement (Second) of Contracts, Section 224, defines a condition as ''an event, not certain to occur, which must occur, unless its nonoccurrence is excused, before performance under a contract becomes due.''

---

**COMPANY PROFILE**   *The British-American Tobacco Company was created in 1902 to end a cigarette price war in Great Britain between the Imperial Tobacco Company and the American Tobacco Company. An agreement between the companies granted Imperial the British market, American the U.S. market, and the jointly owned British-American the rest of the world. In 1911, the United States Supreme Court forced American to sell its interest in British-American and opened the U.S. market to British-American.[a] British-American's share of the U.S. market continued to grow until the 1960s.[b] As public concern over smoking mounted, the company began acquiring nontobacco businesses and changed its name to B.A.T Industries PLC in 1976. Through its American subsidiary BATUS Inc., B.A.T attempted a hostile takeover in 1988 of the Farmers Group, America's third largest auto and homeowners insurer. Among the Farmers Group companies is the Farmers Insurance Company of Washington, which was founded in 1983. Initially, the state of Washington opposed the takeover in part because of concern about jeopardizing nonsmoker discounts offered on auto and homeowners' insurance. BATUS made the Farmers Group's shareholders an offer that they could not refuse, however, and the Farmers Group companies joined BATUS in 1989.*

| CASE 18.1 |
| --- |

**McLANAHAN v. FARMERS INSURANCE CO. OF WASHINGTON**
Court of Appeals of Washington, 1992.
66 Wash.App. 36,
831 P.2d 160.

**BACKGROUND AND FACTS**   *Larry McLanahan's 1985 Lamborghini was stolen, and by the time McLanahan recovered the car, it had been*

---

a.   *United States v. American Tobacco Co.*, 221 U.S. 106, 31 S.Ct. 632, 55 L.Ed. 663 (1911).
b.   In 1994, American sold its interest to the British corporation for $1 billion.

*extensively damaged. The car was insured by Farmers Insurance Company of Washington under a policy providing comprehensive coverage, including theft. A provision in the policy stated that the coverage for theft damages was subject to certain terms and conditions, including the condition that any person claiming coverage under the policy must allow Farmers "to inspect and appraise the damaged vehicle before its repair or disposal." Farmers agreed to pay for damages resulting from the theft and requested that McLanahan make the car available to certain mechanics for inspection and appraisal. McLanahan, however, without notifying Farmers and without giving Farmers an opportunity to inspect the vehicle, sold the car to a wholesale car dealer. Farmers then denied coverage, and McLanahan brought suit to recover for the damages caused to his car by the theft. The trial court dismissed McLanahan's claim, and he appealed.*

*SHIELDS,* Chief Judge.

\* \* \* \*

The unchallenged findings, which are verities [truths] on appeal, establish that Mr. McLanahan knew of, and agreed to abide by, the requirement under the policy that Farmers be allowed to inspect the damaged Lamborghini as a condition precedent to recovery for damage due to theft. Instead, he sold the vehicle. Accordingly, the court's findings support its conclusion that Mr. McLanahan breached the contract, thus relieving Farmers of any obligation to pay.

**DECISION AND REMEDY** *The appellate court affirmed the trial court's decision.*

## CONDITIONS SUBSEQUENT

When a condition operates to terminate a party's absolute promise to perform, it is called a **condition subsequent.** The condition follows, or is subsequent to, the absolute duty to perform. If the condition occurs, the party need not perform any further. For example, imagine that a law firm hires Schuller, a recent law school graduate and a newly licensed attorney. Their contract provides that the firm's obligation to continue employing Schuller is discharged if Schuller fails to maintain her license to practice law. This is a condition subsequent, because a failure to maintain the license would discharge a duty that has already arisen.

Generally, conditions precedent are common; conditions subsequent are rare. The Restatement (Second) of Contracts deletes the terms *condition subsequent* and *condition precedent* and refers to both simply as "conditions."[2]

## CONCURRENT CONDITIONS

When each party's absolute duty to perform is conditioned on the other party's absolute duty to perform, there are **concurrent conditions.** Concurrent conditions occur only when the parties expressly or impliedly are to perform their respective duties *simultaneously.* For example, if a buyer promises to pay for goods when they are delivered by the seller, each party's absolute duty to perform is conditioned on the other party's absolute duty to perform. The buyer's duty to pay for the goods does not become absolute until the seller either delivers or tenders the goods. Likewise, the seller's duty to deliver the goods does not become absolute until the buyer tenders or actually makes payment. Therefore, neither can recover from the other for breach unless he or she first tenders his or her own performance.

## EXPRESS AND IMPLIED CONDITIONS

Conditions can also be classified as (1) express, (2) implied in fact, or (3) implied in law.

---

2. Restatement (Second) of Contracts, Section 224.

*Express conditions* are provided for by the parties' agreement. An express condition is usually prefaced by the word *if, provided, after,* or *when.*

Conditions *implied in fact* are similar to express conditions because they are understood to be part of the agreement, but they are not expressly found in the language of the agreement. The court infers them from the promises. For example, Wellbuilt Construction Company builds a house for Kirby, including in the contract a one-year warranty against defects in materials and construction—that is, Wellbuilt promises to fix or replace anything attributable to Wellbuilt's work that goes wrong within a year. That Kirby must notify Wellbuilt of any defects is an implied-in-fact condition of Wellbuilt's duty to correct the defects.

Finally, *implied-in-law,* or *constructive,* conditions are imposed by the law to achieve justice and fairness. They are not contained in the language of the contract or even necessarily implied.[3] Assume, for example, that Kirby contracts to pay Truly Green Landscaping $5,000 for landscaping the lawn surrounding Kirby's new house. If Truly Green fails to do the work but nonetheless sues Kirby for the $5,000 payment, a court would rule that Kirby was not obligated to pay Truly Green until the work was completed. In that situation, Truly Green's performance would be a constructive condition to Kirby's obligation to pay for the landscaping—the owner should not be compelled to perform unless the landscaper has performed.

# DISCHARGE BY PERFORMANCE

The great majority of contracts are discharged by performance. The contract comes to an end when both parties fulfill their respective duties by performing the acts they have promised. Performance can also be accomplished by tender. **Tender** is an unconditional offer to perform by one who is ready, willing, and able to do so. Therefore, a seller who places goods at the disposal of a buyer has tendered delivery and can demand payment. A buyer who offers to pay for goods has tendered payment and can demand delivery of the goods. Once perfor-

mance has been tendered, the party making the tender has done everything possible to carry out the terms of the contract. If the other party then refuses to perform, the party making the tender can sue for breach of contract.

## DEGREE OF PERFORMANCE REQUIRED

It is important to distinguish between *complete performance* and *substantial performance.* Courts typically use a *reasonable expectations test* for determining which of these categories a performance fits. Complete performance occurs when performance is within the bounds of reasonable expectations. Substantial performance occurs when performance is slightly below reasonable expectations. (As will be discussed in the next section, performance far below reasonable expectations constitutes a *material* breach of contract.)

A contract may stipulate that performance must meet the personal satisfaction of either the contracting party or a third party. Such a provision will also affect the degree of performance required under the contract.

**COMPLETE PERFORMANCE** Normally, conditions expressly stated in the contract must fully occur in all aspects for complete, or strict, performance to take place. Any deviation operates as a discharge. For example, a home building contract expressly states that *only* Fuller brand plasterboard is to be used for the walls, and no substitute brand is to be used without the owner's express permission. Suppose that the builder cannot secure the Fuller brand and, without obtaining the owner's permission, installs Honeyrock brand instead. Even though Honeyrock brand may be equivalent in quality to Fuller brand and all other aspects of construction conform to the contract, the failure of the contractor to meet the express contractual condition is a failure to comply strictly with the contract. A court could hold that this discharges the owner from his or her contractual obligation to pay for the house on completion.

**SUBSTANTIAL PERFORMANCE** Human nature dictates that performance will not always fully satisfy the parties. Therefore, for the sake of justice and fairness, the courts hold that a party must fulfill his or her obligation to perform as long as the other party has fulfilled the terms of the contract with

_____
3.   Restatement (Second) of Contracts, Section 226.

*substantial performance.* To qualify as substantial, the performance must not vary greatly from the performance promised in the contract. If performance is substantial, the other party's duty to perform remains absolute, less damages (if any) for the minor deviations. For instance, in the example given above, a court would most likely hold that the builder had substantially performed his end of the bargain and that the owner was therefore obligated to pay the builder.

Although substantial performance does not prevent discharge, a breach of contract—however slight—has occurred. If the plasterboard substituted for Fuller brand had been of a somewhat lower quality than Fuller, reducing the value of the house by $3,000, the contractor would still be allowed to recover the price agreed on in the contract, less that $3,000. Remedies will be discussed in detail in the next chapter.

The following classic case on substantial performance emphasizes that there is no exact formula for deciding when a contract has been substantially performed. The case also indicates some of the factors that courts will consider in deciding the issue.

---

| CASE 18.2 |
| --- |

**JACOBS & YOUNG, INC. v. KENT**

Court of Appeals of New York, 1921.
230 N.Y. 239,
129 N.E. 889.

**BACKGROUND AND FACTS** *The plaintiff, Jacobs & Young, Inc., was a builder who had contracted with the defendant, George Kent, to construct a country residence for the defendant. A specification in the building contract required that "[a]ll wrought-iron pipe must be well galvanized, lap welded pipe of the grade known as 'standard pipe' of Reading manufacture." The plaintiff installed substantially similar pipe that was not of Reading manufacture. When the defendant became aware of the difference, he ordered the plaintiff to remove all of the plumbing and replace it with the Reading type. To do so would require removing finished walls that encased the plumbing—an expensive and difficult task. The plaintiff explained that the plumbing was of the same quality, appearance, value, and cost as Reading pipe. When the defendant refused to pay the plaintiff the $3,483.46 still owed for his work, the plaintiff sued to compel payment. The trial court excluded evidence on the similarity of the installed pipe to that of the Reading type and held for the defendant. The plaintiff appealed, and the appellate court reversed the trial court's decision. The defendant then appealed to the Court of Appeals of New York, the state's highest court.*

*CARDOZO, Justice.*
\* \* \* \*

\* \* \* The courts never say that one who makes a contract fills the measure of his duty by less than full performance. They do say, however, that an omission, both trivial and innocent, will sometimes be atoned for by allowance of the resulting damage, and will not always be the breach of a condition[.] \* \* \*

\* \* \* Where the line is to be drawn between the important and the trivial cannot be settled by a formula. \* \* \* The same omission may take on one aspect or another according to its setting. Substitution of equivalents may not have the same significance in fields of art on the one side and in those of mere utility on the other. Nowhere will change be tolerated, however, if it is so dominant or pervasive as in any real or substantial measure to frustrate the purpose of the contract. There is no general license to install whatever, in the builder's judgment, may be regarded as "just as good." The question is one of degree, to be answered, if there is doubt, by the triers of the facts, and, if the inferences are certain, by the judges of the law. We must weigh the purpose to be served, the desire to be gratified, the excuse for deviation from the letter, [and] the cruelty of enforced adherence. Then only can we tell whether literal fulfillment is to be implied by law as a condition. \* \* \*

\* \* \* [W]e think the measure of the allowance is not the cost of replacement, which would be great, but the difference in value, which would be either nominal or nothing. Some of the exposed sections might perhaps have been replaced at moderate expense. The defendant did not limit his demand to them, but treated the plumbing as a unit to be corrected from cellar to roof. * * * The owner is entitled to the money which will permit him to complete, unless the cost of completion is grossly and unfairly out of proportion to the good to be attained. * * * The measure of allowance is not the cost of reconstruction. * * * "There may be omissions of that which could not afterwards be supplied exactly as called for by the contract without taking down the building to its foundations and at the same time the omission may not affect the value of the building for use or otherwise, except so slightly as to be hardly appreciable."

*The Court of Appeals of New York, holding that the plaintiff had substantially performed the contract, affirmed the appellate court's decision.*

**DECISION
AND REMEDY**

### PERFORMANCE TO THE SATISFACTION OF ANOTHER

Contracts often state that completed work must personally satisfy one of the parties or a third person. The question then arises whether this satisfaction becomes a condition precedent, requiring actual personal satisfaction or approval for discharge, or whether the test of satisfaction is an absolute promise requiring such performance as would satisfy a "reasonable person" (substantial performance).

When the subject matter of the contract is personal, a contract to be performed to the satisfaction of one of the parties is conditioned, and performance must actually satisfy that party. For example, contracts for portraits, works of art, medical or dental work, and tailoring are considered personal. Therefore, only the personal satisfaction of the party will be sufficient to fulfill the condition. Suppose Williams agrees to paint a portrait of Hirshon's daughter for $750. The contract provides that Hirshon must be satisfied with the portrait. If Hirshon is not, she will not be required to pay for it. The only requirement imposed on Hirshon is that she act honestly and in good faith. If she expresses dissatisfaction only to avoid paying for the portrait, the condition of satisfaction is excused, and her duty to pay becomes absolute. (Of course, the jury, or the judge acting as a jury, will have to decide whether she is acting honestly.)[4]

Contracts that involve mechanical fitness, utility, or marketability need only be performed to the satisfaction of a reasonable person. For example, construction contracts or manufacturing contracts are usually *not* considered to be personal, so the party's personal satisfaction is normally irrelevant. As long as the performance will satisfy a reasonable person, the contract is fulfilled.[5]

At times, contracts also require performance to the satisfaction of a third party (not a party to the contract). For example, assume you contract to pave several city streets. The contract provides that the work will be done "to the satisfaction of Phil Hopper, the supervising engineer." In this situation, the courts are divided. A few courts require the personal satisfaction of the third party, here Phil Hopper. If Hopper is not satisfied, you will not be paid, even if a reasonable person would be satisfied. Again, the personal judgment must be made honestly, or the condition will be excused. A majority of courts require the work to be satisfactory to a reasonable person. So even if Hopper was dissatisfied with the paving work, you would be paid, as long as a qualified supervising engineer would have been satisfied. All of the above examples demonstrate the necessity for *clear, specific wording in contracts*.

### MATERIAL BREACH OF CONTRACT

A **breach of contract** is the nonperformance of a contractual duty. The breach is *material*[6] when performance is not at least substantial—in other words, when there has been a failure of consideration. In such cases, the nonbreaching party is

---

4. For a classic case illustrating this principle, see *Gibson v. Cranage,* 39 Mich. 49 (1878).

5. If, however, the contract specifically states that it is to be fulfilled to the "personal" satisfaction of one or more of the parties, and the parties so intended, the outcome will probably be different.

6. Restatement (Second) of Contracts, Section 241.

excused from the performance of contractual duties and has a cause of action to sue for damages caused by the breach. If the breach is *minor* (not material), the nonbreaching party's duty to perform can sometimes be suspended until the breach has been remedied, but the duty to perform is not entirely excused. Once the minor breach has been cured, the nonbreaching party must resume performance of the contractual obligations undertaken.

Any breach entitles the nonbreaching party to sue for damages, but only a material breach discharges the nonbreaching party from the contract. The policy underlying these rules allows contracts to go forward when only minor problems occur but allows them to be terminated if major problems occur.

## ANTICIPATORY REPUDIATION OF CONTRACT

Before either party to a contract has a duty to perform, one of the parties may refuse to perform his or her contractual obligations. This is called **anticipatory repudiation**[7] of the contract and can discharge the nonbreaching party from performance. For example, De La Tour made a contract with Hochster in March to employ Hochster as a courier for three months—June, July, and August. On May 11, De La Tour wrote to Hochster, "I am going abroad this summer and will not need a courier." This is an anticipatory breach of the employment contract. Because De La Tour repudiated the contract, Hochster could treat the act as a present, material breach. Furthermore, he could sue to recover damages *immediately*, without having to wait until June 1 to sue.[8]

There are two reasons for treating an anticipatory repudiation as a present, material breach:

1.  The nonbreaching party should not be required to remain ready and willing to perform when the other party has already repudiated the contract.

2.  The nonbreaching party should have the opportunity to seek a similar contract elsewhere.

Thus, Hochster should not be required to remain ready to serve as De La Tour's courier until June 1, because that would be a waste of time. In the meantime, Hochster could be working elsewhere.

It is important to note that until the nonbreaching party treats an early repudiation as a breach, the repudiating party can retract his or her anticipatory repudiation by proper notice and restore the parties to their original obligations.[9]

Quite often an anticipatory repudiation occurs when performance of the contract would be extremely unfavorable to one of the parties because of a sharp fluctuation in market prices. For example, Martin Corporation contracts to manufacture and sell ten thousand personal computers to Com-age, a retailer of computer equipment that has five hundred outlet stores. Delivery is to be made six months from the date of the contract. The contract price is based on the seller's present costs of purchasing inventory parts from others. One month later, three inventory suppliers raise their prices to Martin. Based on these prices, if Martin manufactures and sells the personal computers to Com-age at the contract price, it stands to lose $500,000. Martin immediately writes Com-age that it cannot deliver the ten thousand computers at the contract price. Martin's letter is an anticipatory repudiation of the contract that allows Com-age the option to treat the repudiation as a material breach and to proceed immediately to pursue remedies, even though the actual contract delivery date is still five months away.[10]

## TIME FOR PERFORMANCE

If no time for performance is stated in the contract, a *reasonable time* is implied.[11] If a specific time is stated, the parties must usually perform by that time. Unless time is expressly stated to be vital, however, a delay in performance will not destroy the performing party's right to payment. When time is expressly stated to be vital, or when it is construed to be "of the essence," the time for per-

---

7.   Restatement (Second) of Contracts, Section 253, and UCC 2–610.

8.   The doctrine of anticipatory breach first arose in this landmark case [*Hochster v. De La Tour,* 2 Ellis and Blackburn Reports 678 (1853)], when the English court recognized the delay and expense inherent in a rule requiring a nonbreaching party to wait until the time for performance to sue on an anticipatory breach.

---

9.   See UCC 2–611.

10.   See *Reliance Cooperage Corp. v. Treat,* 195 F.2d 977 (8th Cir. 1952), as a further illustration.

11.   See UCC 1–204.

formance must usually be strictly complied with. The time element becomes a condition.

# SECTION 3

# DISCHARGE BY AGREEMENT

Any contract can be discharged by agreement of the parties. The agreement can be contained in the original contract, or the parties can form a new contract for the express purpose of discharging the original contract.

## DISCHARGE BY RESCISSION

*Rescission* is the process by which a contract is canceled or terminated and the parties are returned to the positions they occupied prior to forming it. For **mutual rescission** to take place, the parties must make another agreement, which must also satisfy the legal requirements for a contract. There must be an *offer,* an *acceptance,* and *consideration.* Ordinarily, in an executory contract in which neither party has yet performed, if the parties agree to rescind the original contract, their promises not to perform those acts promised in the original contract will be legal consideration for the second contract.

The rescission agreement is generally enforceable even if made orally. This applies even if the original agreement was in writing except when the new agreement falls within the Statute of Frauds (discussed in Chapter 16). Another exception applies to agreements rescinding a contract for the sale of goods regardless of price under the UCC when the contract requires written rescission.[12]

When one party has fully performed, however, an agreement to call off the original contract will not normally be enforceable. Because the performing party has received no consideration for the promise to call off the original bargain, additional consideration will be necessary.

In sum, contracts that are *executory on both sides* (contracts on which neither party has performed) can be rescinded solely by agreement.[13]

But contracts that are *executed on one side* (contracts on which one party has performed) can be rescinded only if the party who has performed receives consideration for the promise to call off the deal.

## DISCHARGE BY SUBSTITUTED AGREEMENT

As discussed in the previous chapter, the process of *novation* substitutes a new party for one of the original parties. Essentially, the parties to the original contract and one or more new parties get together and agree to substitute the new party for one of the original parties. The requirements of a novation are as follows:

1. A previous valid obligation.
2. An agreement of all the parties to a new contract.
3. The extinguishment of the old obligation (discharge of the prior party).
4. A new contract that is valid.

*Substitution* of a new contract between the same parties expressly or impliedly revokes and discharges a prior contract.[14] The parties involved may simply want a new agreement with somewhat different terms, so they expressly state in a new contract that the old contract is now discharged. They can also make the new contract without expressly stating that the old contract is discharged. If the parties do not expressly discharge the old contract, it will be *impliedly* discharged because of the change or because of the new contract's different terms, which are inconsistent with the old contract's terms.

A *compromise,* or settlement agreement, that arises out of a genuine dispute over the obligations under an existing contract will be recognized at law. Such an agreement will be substituted as a new contract, and it will either expressly or impliedly revoke and discharge the obligations under any prior contract.

## DISCHARGE BY ACCORD AND SATISFACTION

For a contract to be discharged by accord and satisfaction, the parties must agree to accept

---

12. UCC 2–209(2), (4).
13. Certain sales made to consumers at their homes can be rescinded by the consumer within three days for no reason at all. This three-day "cooling-off" period is designed to aid consumers who are susceptible to high-pressure door-to-door sales tactics. See Chapter 46 and 15 U.S.C. Section 1635(a).

14. It is this immediate discharge of the prior contract that distinguishes a substituting contract from accord and satisfaction, discussed in the next section.

performance that is different from the performance originally promised. As discussed in Chapter 13, an *accord* is defined as an executory contract to perform some act to satisfy an existing contractual duty.[15] The duty has not yet been discharged. A *satisfaction* is the performance of the accord agreement. An accord and its satisfaction discharge the original contractual obligation.

Once the accord has been made, the original obligation is merely suspended. (This differs from a novation, which, as pointed out above, operates to discharge the original obligation.) The obligor can discharge the obligation by performing the obligation agreed to in the accord (or the original obligation). If the obligor refuses to perform the accord, the obligee can bring action on the original obligation or seek a decree for specific performance on the accord.

SECTION 4

# DISCHARGE BY OPERATION OF LAW

Under certain circumstances, contractual duties may be discharged by operation of law. These circumstances include material alteration of the contract, the running of the statute of limitations, bankruptcy, and the impossibility or impracticability of performance.

## ALTERATION OF THE CONTRACT

To discourage parties from altering written contracts, the law operates to allow an innocent party to be discharged when the other party has materially altered a written contract without consent. For example, contract terms such as quantity or price might be changed without the knowledge or consent of all parties. If so, the party who was unaware of the alteration can treat the contract as discharged or terminated.[16]

## STATUTES OF LIMITATIONS

Statutes of limitations limit the period during which a party can sue on a particular cause of action. (A cause of action is the basis or reason for suing or bringing an action.) After the applicable limitations period has passed, a suit can no longer be brought in a court of law or equity. For example, the limitations period for bringing suits for breach of oral contracts is usually two to three years; for written contracts, four to five years; and for recovery of amounts awarded in judgment, ten to twenty years, depending on state law.

Section 2–725 of the UCC deals with the statute of limitations applicable to contracts for the sale of goods. For purposes of applying this section, the UCC does not distinguish between oral and written contracts. Section 2–725 provides that an action for the breach of any contract for sale must be commenced within four years after the cause of that action has accrued. The cause of action accrues when the breach occurs, regardless of the aggrieved party's lack of knowledge of the breach. By original agreement, the parties can reduce this four-year period to a one-year period. They cannot, however, extend it beyond the four-year limitation period.

Technically, the running of a statute of limitations bars access only to *judicial* remedies; it does not extinguish the debt or the underlying obligation. The statute precludes access to the courts for collection. But if the party who owes the debt or obligation agrees to perform (that is, makes a new promise to perform), the cause of action barred by the statute of limitations will be revived. For the old agreement to be revived by a new promise in this manner, many states require that the promise be in writing or that there be evidence of partial performance.

## BANKRUPTCY

A proceeding in bankruptcy attempts to allocate the assets the debtor owns at bankruptcy to the creditors in a fair and equitable fashion. Once the assets have been allocated, the debtor receives a **discharge in bankruptcy.** A discharge in bankruptcy will ordinarily bar enforcement of most of a debtor's contracts by the creditors. Partial payment of a debt *after* discharge in bankruptcy will not revive the debt. (Bankruptcy is fully discussed in Chapter 33.)

---

15. Restatement (Second) of Contracts, Section 281.

16. The contract is voidable, and the innocent party can also treat the contract as in effect, either on the original terms or on the terms as altered. A buyer who discovers that a seller altered the quantity of goods in a sales contract from 100 to 1,000 by secretly inserting a zero can purchase either 100 or 1,000 of the items.

## IMPOSSIBILITY OR IMPRACTICABILITY OF PERFORMANCE

After a contract has been made, performance may become impossible in an objective sense. This is known as *objective impossibility of performance,* or simply as *impossibility of performance,* and may discharge a contract.[17] Occasionally, if circumstances arise after the contract has been formed that make performance *extremely* difficult or costly, courts may allow the contract to be discharged under the doctrine of *commercial impracticability* or a closely related theory, *frustration of purpose.* These legal excuses from performance under a contract are discussed below.

**IMPOSSIBILITY OF PERFORMANCE** Certain basic types of situations generally qualify to discharge contractual obligations under the doctrine of **impossibility of performance:**

1. One of the essential parties to a personal contract *dies or becomes incapacitated* prior to performance.[18] To illustrate this type of impossibility, suppose Jane, a famous actress, contracts to play the leading role in a movie. Before the picture starts, she becomes ill and dies. Her personal performance was essential to the completion of the contract. Thus, her death discharges the contract and her estate's liability for her nonperformance.
2. The *specific* subject matter of the contract is destroyed.[19] For example, Pappagoras contracts to sell ten thousand bushels of apples to be harvested "from his Green Valley apple orchard in the state of Illinois." Flooding from the Mississippi River destroys his apples. Because the contracted-for apples were to come specifically from his Green Valley orchard, his performance has been rendered impossible by the flooding of the Mississippi River. Thus, this contract is discharged. Similarly, a contract to lease a building cannot be executed if the building is destroyed by fire, and a contract to sell oil from a particular well cannot be executed if the well goes dry.
3. A change in *law* renders performance illegal.[20] An example is a contract to build an apartment building, when the zoning laws are changed to prohibit the construction of residential rental property at this location. This change renders the contract impossible to perform.

**COMMERCIAL IMPRACTICABILITY** Courts will at times excuse performance under a contract when the performance becomes much more difficult or expensive than originally contemplated at the time the contract was formed. For someone to invoke successfully the doctrine of **commercial impracticability,** however, the anticipated performance must become *extremely* difficult or costly.[21] For example, in one case, a court held that a contract was discharged because a party would have had to pay ten times more than the original estimate to excavate a certain amount of gravel.[22] Caution should be used when invoking commercial impracticability. The added burden of performing must be *extreme* and, more important, must *not* have been within the cognizance of the parties when the contract was made.

The element of foreseeability is emphasized in the following case.

17. Restatement (Second) of Contracts, Section 261.
18. Restatement (Second) of Contracts, Section 262.
19. Restatement (Second) of Contracts, Section 263.
20. Restatement (Second) of Contracts, Section 264.
21. Restatement (Second) of Contracts, Sections 265 and 266; UCC 2–615.
22. *Mineral Park Land Co. v. Howard,* 172 Cal. 289, 156 P. 458 (1916).

**BACKGROUND AND FACTS** *The George Syrovy Trust (Syrovy) agreed to sell Alpine Resources, Inc., all of the timber from Syrovy's property that Alpine could harvest over a two-year period for $140,000. Over the next two years, Alpine harvested some timber and paid Syrovy $50,000. When Syrovy sued for the contract balance of $90,000, Alpine claimed that it should be released from its obligation to pay the remainder of the contract price on the ground of commercial impracticability. Alpine claimed*

CASE 18.3

**SYROVY v. ALPINE RESOURCES, INC.**
Court of Appeals of Washington, 1992.
841 P.2d 1279.

*that bad weather conditions during both winters and the fact that Alpine could not engage in logging operations during the hunting season made it impossible to harvest the quantity of timber it had planned to harvest when the contract was formed. The trial court granted Syrovy's motion for summary judgment, and Alpine appealed.*

*SWEENEY*, Judge.
     \*    \*    \*    \*

    \*    \*    \* [Under the defense of impracticability] performance is excused if events occur that are not foreseen or anticipated—a ''wholly unexpected contingency.'' Difficulties that are assumed by a party, at the time of contracting, cannot form the basis of an impracticability defense.

    Alpine argues that the winters of 1988 and 1989 were so severe that harvesting became impossible. However, Mr. Reoh [who negotiated the contract for Alpine] is a logger with considerable experience in purchasing timber. It would be unreasonable to suggest that weather conditions were an unforeseeable event. Also, there is no evidence to support the assertion that the weather was so remarkable that contract performance was impossible.

    Alpine also argues that it did not have access to the property during hunting season. \*    \*    \* Access problems were foreseeable and the risk was allocated in the contract. The problems cannot be asserted as a basis for an impracticability defense.

**DECISION AND REMEDY**

*The trial court's decision was affirmed.*

**INTERNATIONAL CONSIDERATIONS**

**Impossibility of Performance in Germany** *In the United States, when a party alleges that a contract is impossible or impracticable to perform due to circumstances unforeseen at the time the contract was formed, a court will either discharge the party's contractual obligations under the contract or hold the party to the contract. Under German law, however, a court may adjust the terms of a contract in light of economic developments. If an unforeseen event affects the foundation of the agreement, the court can compensate for the disruption in expectations and make the contract fair to the parties.*

---

**FRUSTRATION OF PURPOSE** A theory closely allied to the doctrine of commercial impracticability is the doctrine of **frustration of purpose.** In principle, a contract will be discharged if supervening circumstances make it impossible to attain the purpose both parties had in mind when making the contract.

The origins of the doctrine lie in the old English ''coronation cases.'' A coronation procession was planned for Edward VII when he became king of England following the death of his mother, Queen Victoria. Hotel rooms along the coronation route were rented at exorbitant prices for that day. When the king became ill and the procession was canceled, the purpose of the room contracts was ''frustrated.'' A flurry of lawsuits resulted. Hotel and building owners sought to enforce the room-rent bills against would-be parade observers, and would-be parade observers sought to be reimbursed for rental monies paid in advance on the rooms. Would-be parade observers were excused from their duty of payment. It was from this situation that the court developed its theory of recovery known as *frustration of purpose.*

**TEMPORARY IMPOSSIBILITY** An occurrence or event that makes it temporarily impossible to perform the act for which a party has contracted will operate to *suspend* performance until the impossibility ceases. Then, ordinarily, the parties

## ■ CONCEPT SUMMARY 18.1 **Discharge of Contracts**

| METHOD | TYPES AND BASIC RULES |
|---|---|
| **Discharge by Occurrence or Failure of a Condition** | 1. *Failure of a condition precedent*—Duty to perform does not become absolute absent fulfillment of condition precedent.<br>2. *Occurrence of a condition subsequent*—A condition that follows an absolute duty to perform, which, if it occurs, excuses a party's performance. |
| **Discharge by Performance (or Breach of Contract)** | 1. *Performance*—Complete or substantial.<br>2. *Breach*—Material nonperformance discharges the nonbreaching party. |
| **Discharge by Agreement** | 1. *Mutual rescission*—An enforceable agreement to restore parties to their precontract positions.<br>2. *Novation*—By valid contract, a new party is substituted for an original party, thereby terminating the old contract.<br>3. *Accord and satisfaction*—An agreement under which the original contract can be discharged by a different performance. |
| **Discharge by Operation of Law** | 1. *Alteration*—An innocent party is discharged by material alteration of the contract without consent.<br>2. *Statute of limitations*—The plaintiff's delay in filing suit bars availability of judicial remedies, thus discharging the defendant's duty to perform.<br>3. *Bankruptcy*—The decree discharges most of the debtor's contractual obligations.<br>4. *Impossibility or impracticability of performance*—<br>  a. A person whose performance is essential to completion of the contract dies or is incapacitated.<br>  b. The specific subject matter of the contract is destroyed prior to transfer.<br>  c. Performance is declared illegal.<br>  d. Performance becomes commercially impracticable.<br>  e. If performance is temporarily suspended because of events or occurrences (such as war), and subsequent circumstances make the contract substantially more difficult to perform, the parties may be discharged. |

must perform the contract as originally planned. If the lapse of time and the change in circumstances surrounding the contract make it substantially more burdensome to perform the promised acts, however, the parties will be discharged.

The leading case on this subject, *Autry v. Republic Productions,*[23] involved an actor who was drafted into the army in 1942. Being drafted rendered his contract temporarily impossible to perform, and it was suspended until the end of the war.[24] When the actor got out of the army, the value of the dollar had so changed that performance of the contract would have been substantially burdensome for him. Therefore, the contract was discharged.

---

23.  30 Cal.2d 144, 180 P.2d 888 (1947).

24.  Under the Soldiers' and Sailors' Civil Relief Act of 1940 (50 U.S.C. Sections 501–591), individuals serving in military service are assured of being informed of civil proceedings against them and of having the opportunity and sufficient time to appear and defend themselves.

## TERMS AND CONCEPTS TO REVIEW

anticipatory repudiation 332
breach of contract 331
commercial
   impracticability 335
concurrent conditions 328

condition 327
condition precedent 327
condition subsequent 328
discharge 326
discharge in bankruptcy 334

frustration of purpose 336
impossibility of
   performance 335
mutual rescission 333
tender 329

## QUESTIONS AND CASE PROBLEMS

**18–1. Performance.** The Caplans own a real estate lot, and they contract with Faithful Construction, Inc., to build a house on it for $60,000. The specifications list "all plumbing bowls and fixtures . . . to be Crane brand." The Caplans leave on vacation, and during their absence Faithful is unable to buy and install Crane plumbing fixtures. Instead, Faithful installs Kohler brand fixtures, an equivalent in the industry. Upon completion of the building contract, the Caplans, on inspection, discover the substitution and refuse to accept the house, claiming Faithful has breached the conditions set forth in the specifications. Discuss fully the Caplans' claim.

**18–2. Discharge.** Junior owes creditor Iba $1,000, which is due and payable on June 1. Junior has been in a car accident, has missed a great deal of work, and consequently will not have the money on June 1. Junior's father, Fred, offers to pay Iba $1,100 in four equal installments if Iba will discharge Junior from any further liability on the debt. Iba accepts. Discuss the following.

(a) Is the transaction a novation, or is it accord and satisfaction? Explain.
(b) Does the contract between Fred and Iba have to be in writing to be enforceable? (Review the discussion of the Statute of Frauds in Chapter 16.) Explain.

**18–3. Breach.** ABC Clothiers, Inc., has a contract with retailer Taylor & Sons to deliver 1,000 summer suits to Taylor's place of business on or before May 1. On April 1, Taylor senior receives a letter from ABC informing him that ABC will not be able to make the delivery as scheduled. Taylor is very upset, as he had planned a big ad sale campaign. He wants to file suit against ABC immediately (April 2). Taylor's son, Tom, tells his father that a lawsuit is not proper until ABC actually fails to deliver the suits on May 1. Discuss fully who is correct (Taylor or his son Tom).

**18–4. Impossibility of Performance.** The following events take place after the formation of the contracts. Discuss which of these contracts are discharged because the events render the contracts impossible to perform.

(a) Jimenez, a famous singer, contracts to perform in your nightclub. He dies prior to performance.
(b) Raglione contracts to sell you her land. Just before title is to be transferred, she dies.
(c) Oppenheim contracts to sell you one thousand bushels of apples from her orchard in the state of Washington. Because of a severe frost, she is unable to deliver the apples.
(d) Maxwell contracts to lease a service station for ten years. His principal income is from the sale of gasoline. Because of an oil embargo by foreign oil-producing nations, gasoline is rationed, cutting sharply into Maxwell's gasoline sales. He cannot make his lease payments.

**18–5. Time for Performance.** Murphy contracts to purchase from Lone Star Liquors six cases of French champagne for $1,200. The contract states that delivery is to be made at the Murphy residence "on or before June 1, to be used for daughter's wedding reception on June 2." The champagne is carried regularly in Lone Star's stock. On June 1, Lone Star's delivery van is involved in an accident, and the champagne is not delivered that day. On the morning of June 2, Murphy discovers the nondelivery. Unable to reach Lone Star because its line is busy, Murphy purchases the champagne from another dealer. That afternoon, just before the wedding reception, Lone Star tenders delivery of the champagne at Murphy's residence. Murphy refuses tender, and Lone Star sues for breach of contract. Discuss fully the result.

**18–6. Impracticability of Performance.** Sun Maid Raisin Growers signed a contract to buy 1,800 tons of raisins from Victor Packing Co. in 1976. Victor planned to supply the raisins by purchasing them in the market very late in the year in order to get a good price. It waited too long. Because of heavy, "disastrous" rains that year, 50 percent of the crop was destroyed, and the price of raisins skyrocketed from $860 per ton to $1,600 per ton. Victor Packing could not meet Sun Maid's contract demand without sustaining equally "disastrous" losses, and it notified Sun Maid that it was repudiating the contract. Sun Maid sued for damages for breach of contract, and Victor Packing claimed, among other things, that performance was impracticable. Discuss whether Victor

Packing's defense should succeed. [*Sun Maid Raisin Growers v. Victor Packing Co.,* 146 Cal.App.3d 787, 194 Cal.Rptr. 612 (5 Dist. 1983)]

**18–7. Substantial Performance.** Grane, a homeowner, contracted with Butkovich & Sons, Inc., to enlarge Grane's basement and build a new room over the new basement area. Butkovich was also to lay a new garage floor and construct a patio area. The parties agreed to a price of $19,290 for the work. When the construction was completed, Grane refused to pay the contractor the $9,290 balance he still owed, claiming that Butkovich had failed to install water stops and reinforcing wire in one concrete floor, in accordance with Grane's specifications, and that the main floor of the addition was 8⅞ inches lower than the plans had called for. Butkovich sued Grane for recovery of the $9,290. As a mortgage holder on the property, the State Bank of St. Charles was named co-defendant by Butkovich, because its interests would be affected by a judgment against Grane if the latter could not pay. Butkovich claimed that it had substantially performed the contract. Grane claimed that performance was of poor quality and that failure to follow contract specifications constituted a material breach. Discuss who should win. [*Butkovich & Sons, Inc. v. State Bank of St. Charles,* 62 Ill.App.3d 810, 379 N.E.2d 837, 20 Ill.Dec. 4 (1978)]

**18–8. Anticipatory Repudiation.** Larry Allen signed a contract with Weyerhaeuser, Inc., to work as a truck driver to haul timber. The contract provided the following: "Contractor agrees to comply with all operational safety and conservation rules and regulations promulgated by Weyerhaeuser." Billy Corey, the company's supervisor in charge of contract trucking, was responsible for informing contractors of safety regulations and ensuring that drivers complied with them. Before Allen signed the contract, Corey told him that Weyerhaeuser required its contract truckers to operate their trucks with headlights on while they were on the road. Initially, Allen complied. Occasionally, however, Corey had to remind him to turn on his lights. Allen's noncompliance became more frequent, even though Corey explained to him on several occasions that he had to comply with company policy. Finally, Allen told Corey that "he [wasn't] going to run with his lights on; that he was tired of it anyway and if [Corey] would fire him it would do him a favor." Weyerhaeuser terminated Allen's contract. Allen sued, claiming that the contract was wrongfully terminated. The trial court granted Weyerhaeuser a directed verdict in Weyerhaeuser's favor, and Allen appealed. Discuss whether Allen's conduct constituted an anticipatory repudiation of his contract. [*Allen v. Weyerhaeuser, Inc.,* 95 N.C.App. 205, 381 S.E.2d 824 (1989)]

**18–9. Frustration of Purpose.** Coker International, Inc., entered into a contract with Burlington Industries, Inc., under which Coker agreed to purchase 221 used textile looms from Burlington for a total price of $1,021,000. Under the contract, Coker was required to pay a 10 percent down payment, with the balance to be paid prior to the removal of the looms. Coker planned to resell the looms to a customer in Peru, but the contract was not conditioned on any resale of the looms by Coker. Because of actions of the Peruvian government, Coker's plan to resell the equipment to the Peruvian buyer fell through. Coker sought to rescind the contract with Burlington and recover its down payment, asserting that it should be excused from performance under the doctrine of frustration of purpose. Discuss fully whether Coker can be excused from performance of the contract under this doctrine. [*Coker International, Inc. v. Burlington Industries, Inc.,* 747 F.Supp. 1168 (D.S.C. 1990)]

**18–10. Conditions Precedent.** Edgar and Peggy Stacy owned a 588-acre farm in Mississippi County, Arkansas. In June 1985, the Williams family agreed to purchase the Stacys' farm for $882,000. The Stacys' real estate agent inserted into a preprinted contract (just after the provision stating the purchase price) the following typewritten statement: "Buyers to pledge approximately 900 acres of land in Tallahatchie County in Mississippi together with lands herein described for loan to pay purchase price." The Williams family failed to obtain financing for the property, in part because the farm in Tallahatchie County was subject to a long-term lease and because the value of the lands they held turned out to be less than they had assumed. The Williams family notified the Stacys' real estate broker of these facts, and the family also wrote a letter to Edgar Stacy stating that they wanted to rescind the contract for these reasons. Several months later, the Stacys sold the farm to another party for $630,000 and sued the Williams family for breach of contract, seeking $252,000, which represented the difference between the $882,000 purchase price offered by the Williams family and the $630,000 paid by the purchaser of the property. The issue before the court is whether the ability of the Williamses to obtain financing was a condition precedent to the Williamses' obligation to perform under the contract. Assuming that parol evidence is admissible (you may want to review the parol evidence rule, discussed in Chapter 16), how should the court rule? Discuss. [*Stacy v. Williams,* 38 Ark.App. 192, 834 S.W.2d 156 (1992)]

# CHAPTER 19

# BREACH OF CONTRACT AND REMEDIES

**W**henever a party fails to perform part or all of the duties under a contract, that party is in breach of contract. *Breach of contract* is the failure to perform what a party is under a duty to perform.[1] Once a party has failed to perform or has performed inadequately, the other party—the non-breaching party—can choose one or more of several remedies. A *remedy* is the relief provided for an innocent party when the other party has breached the contract. It is the means employed to enforce a right or to redress an injury.

The most common remedies available to a nonbreaching party include damages, rescission and restitution, specific performance, and reformation. As discussed in Chapter 1, a distinction is made between *remedies at law* and *remedies in equity*. Today, the remedy at law is normally money damages, which are discussed in the first part of this chapter. Equitable remedies include rescission and restitution, specific performance, and reformation, all of which will be examined later in the chapter. Usually, a court will not award an equitable remedy unless the remedy at law is inadequate. Special legal doctrines and concepts relating to remedies will be discussed in the final pages of this chapter.

## SECTION 1

## DAMAGES

A breach of contract entitles the nonbreaching party to sue for money (damages). Damages are designed to compensate the nonbreaching party for the loss of the bargain. When a party loses the benefit of the bargain or contract, the breaching party must make up this loss to the nonbreaching party. Often, courts say that innocent parties are to be placed in the position they would

---

1. Restatement (Second) of Contracts, Section 235(2).

have occupied had the contract been fully performed.[2] For example, in the famous case of the "hairy hand," a doctor promised to make a boy's scarred hand "a hundred percent perfect." Skin was taken from the boy's chest and grafted onto his thumb and fingers. The hand became infected, and the boy was hospitalized for three months. Use of the hand was greatly restricted, and hair grew out of the grafted skin. In hearing a suit against the doctor, the court explained that the amount of damages was to be determined by the difference between the value to the boy of the "perfect" hand that the doctor had promised and the value of the hand in its condition after the operation.[3]

## TYPES OF DAMAGES

There are basically four broad categories of damages:

1. Compensatory (to cover direct losses and costs).
2. Consequential (to cover indirect and foreseeable losses).
3. Punitive (to punish and deter wrongdoing).
4. Nominal (to recognize wrongdoing when no monetary loss is shown).

**COMPENSATORY DAMAGES** Damages compensating the nonbreaching party for the *loss of the bargain* are known as **compensatory damages.** These damages compensate the injured party only for damages actually sustained and proved to have arisen directly from the loss of the bargain caused by the breach of contract. They simply replace what was lost because of the wrong or damage. To illustrate, Wilcox contracts to perform certain services exclusively for Hernandez during the month of March for $2,000. Hernandez cancels the contract and is in breach. Wilcox is able to find another job during the month of March, but can only earn $1,000. He can sue Hernandez for breach and recover $1,000 as compensatory damages. Wilcox can also recover from Hernandez the amount that he spent to find the other job.[4] Expenses that are caused directly by a breach of contract—such as

those incurred to obtain performance from another source—are known as *incidental damages.*

The measurement of compensatory damages varies by type of contract. Certain types of contracts deserve special mention. They are contracts for the sale of goods, land contracts, and construction contracts.

*Sale of Goods.*    In a contract for the sale of goods, the usual measure of compensatory damages is an amount equal to the difference between the contract price and the market price.[5] For example, suppose that Chrysler Corporation contracts to buy ten model UTS 400 network servers from an XEXO Corporation dealer for $8,000 apiece. The dealer, however, fails to deliver the ten servers to Chrysler. The market price of the servers at the time the buyer learned of the breach is $8,150. Chrysler's measure of damages is therefore $1,500 (10 x $150) plus at least any incidental damages (expenses) caused by the breach. In a situation in which the buyer breaches and the seller has not yet produced the goods, compensatory damages normally equal lost profits on the sale, not the difference between the contract price and the market price.

*Sale of Land.*    Ordinarily, because each parcel of land is unique, the remedy for a seller's breach of a contract for a sale of real estate is *specific performance* (that is, the buyer is awarded the piece of property he or she bargained for). When this remedy, which is discussed more fully later in this chapter, is unavailable (for example, when the seller has sold the property to someone else), or when the breach is on the part of the buyer, the measure of damages is ordinarily the same as in contracts for the sale of goods—that is, the difference between the contract price and the market price of the land. The majority of states follow this rule. A minority of states, however, follow a different rule when the seller breaches the contract and the breach is not deliberate.[6] In such a case,

---

2. Restatement (Second) of Contracts, Section 347, and UCC 1–106(1).
3. *Hawkins v. McGee,* 84 N.H. 114, 146 A. 641 (1929).
4. It is one thing to have a court award damages; it is another to collect a judgment. See Chapter 4.

5. That is, the difference between the contract price and the market price at the time and place at which the goods were to be delivered or tendered. See UCC 2–708 and UCC 2–713.
6. "Deliberate" breaches include the seller's failure to convey the land because the market price has gone up. "Nondeliberate" breaches include the seller's failure to convey the land because an unknown easement (another's right of use over the property) has rendered title unmarketable. See Chapter 51.

### ■ Exhibit 19–1 Measurement of Damages—Breach of Construction Contracts

| Party in Breach | Time of Breach | Measurement of Damages |
| --- | --- | --- |
| Owner | Before construction has begun | Profits (contract price less cost of materials and labor) |
| Owner | During construction | Profits plus costs incurred up to time of breach |
| Owner | After construction is completed | Contract price plus interest |
| Contractor | Before construction is completed | Generally, all costs incurred by owner to complete construction |

these states allow the prospective purchaser to recover any down payment plus any expenses incurred (such as fees for title searches, attorneys, and escrows). This minority rule effectively places purchasers in the position they occupied prior to the sale.

*Construction Contracts.*  The measure of damages in a building or construction contract varies depending on which party breaches and when the breach occurs. The owner can breach at three different stages of the construction:

1. Before performance has begun.
2. During performance.
3. After performance has been completed.

If the owner breaches *before performance has begun,* the contractor can recover only the profits that would have been made on the contract (that is, the total contract price less the cost of materials and labor). If the owner breaches *during performance,* the contractor can recover the profits plus the costs incurred in partially constructing the building. If the owner breaches *after the construction has been completed,* the contractor can recover the entire contract price,[7] plus interest.

When the *construction contractor breaches the contract* by stopping part of the way through the project, the measure of damages is the cost of completion, which includes reasonable compensation for any delay in performance. If the contractor finishes late, the measure of damages will be the loss of use. If the contractor substan-

tially performs, the courts may use the cost-of-completion formula, but only if there is no substantial economic waste in requiring completion. Economic waste occurs when the cost of additional resources to finish the project exceeds any conceivable value placed on the additional work done. For example, if a contractor discovers that it will cost $10,000 to move a large coral rock eleven inches as specified in the contract, and the change in the rock's position will alter the appearance of the project only a trifle, full completion will involve an economic waste. These rules concerning the measurement of damages in breached construction contracts are summarized in Exhibit 19–1.

**CONSEQUENTIAL DAMAGES**  Foreseeable damages that result from a party's breach of contract are called **consequential damages,** or *special damages.* They differ from compensatory damages in that they are caused by special circumstances beyond the contract itself. They flow from the consequences, or results, of a breach.

For example, if a seller fails to deliver goods, and the seller knows that a buyer is planning to resell these goods immediately, consequential damages will be awarded for the loss of profit from the planned resale. The buyer will also recover compensatory damages for the difference between the contract price and the market price of the goods.

To recover consequential damages, the breaching party must know (or have reason to know) that special circumstances will cause the nonbreaching party to suffer an additional loss. This requirement is illustrated in the classic case of *Hadley v. Baxendale,* which is presented below. The case was decided in England in 1854 and involved a crankshaft used in a mill operation. In the mid-1800s, it was very common for large mills, such

---

7.  Actually, this is true for most contracts; the nonbreaching party is normally owed the contract profit plus the cost of performance.

as the one the plaintiffs operated, to have more than one crankshaft in the event that the main one broke and had to be repaired, as it did in this case. This case established the rule that when damages are awarded, compensation is given only for those injuries that the defendant could *reasonably* have foreseen as a probable result of the usual course of events following a breach.

---

**BACKGROUND AND FACTS**   *The Hadleys (the plaintiffs) ran a flour mill in Gloucester. The crankshaft attached to the steam engine in the mill broke, causing the mill to shut down. The shaft had to be sent to a foundry located in Greenwich so that the new shaft could be made to fit the other parts of the engine. Baxendale, the defendant, was a common carrier who transported the shaft from Gloucester to Greenwich. The Hadleys claimed that they had informed Baxendale that the mill was stopped and that the shaft must be sent immediately. The freight charges were collected in advance, and Baxendale promised to deliver the shaft the following day. It was not delivered for several days, however. As a consequence, the mill was closed for several days. The Hadleys sued to recover the profits lost during that time. Baxendale denied that the Hadleys had informed it that the mill was inoperative and contended that the loss of profits was "too remote." The court held for the plaintiffs, and the jury was allowed to take into consideration the lost profits. The defendant appealed.*

| CASE 19.1 |
| --- |
| **HADLEY v. BAXENDALE** |
| Court of Exchequer, 1854. |
| 156 Eng.Rep. 145. |

*ALDERSON*, B.
\* \* \* \*

   \* \* \* Where two parties have made a contract which one of them has broken, the damages which the other party ought to receive in respect of such breach of contract should be such as may fairly and reasonably be considered either arising naturally, i.e., according to the usual course of things, from such breach of contract itself, or such as may reasonably be supposed to have been in the contemplation of both parties, at the time they made the contract, as the probable result of the breach of it. Now, if the special circumstances under which the contract was actually made were communicated by the plaintiffs to the defendants, and thus known to both parties, the damages resulting from the breach of such a contract, which they would reasonably contemplate, would be the amount of injury which would ordinarily follow from a breach of contract under these special circumstances so known and communicated. \* \* \* Now, in the present case, if we are to apply the principles above laid down, we find that the only circumstances here communicated by the plaintiffs to the defendants at the time the contract was made, were, that the article to be carried was the broken shaft of a mill, and that the plaintiffs were the millers of that mill. But how do these circumstances show reasonably that the profits of the mill must be stopped by an unreasonable delay in the delivery of the broken shaft by the carrier to the third person? Suppose the plaintiffs had another shaft in their possession put up or putting up at the time, and that they only wished to send back the broken shaft to the engineer who made it; it is clear that this would be quite consistent with the above circumstances, and yet the unreasonable delay in the delivery would have no effect upon the intermediate profits of the mill. Or, again, suppose that, at the time of the delivery to the carrier, the machinery of the mill had been in other respects defective, then, also, the same results would follow. Here it is true that the shaft was actually sent back to serve as a model for a new one, and that the want of a new one was the only cause of the stoppage of the mill, and that the loss of profits really arose from not sending down the new shaft in proper time, and that this arose from the delay in delivering the broken one to serve as a model. But it is obvious that, in the great multitude of cases of millers sending off broken shafts to third persons by a carrier under ordinary circumstances, such consequences would not, in all probability, have occurred; and these special circumstances were here never communicated by the plaintiffs to the defendants. It follows, therefore, that the loss of profits here cannot reasonably be considered such a consequence of the breach of contract as could have been fairly and reasonably contemplated by both the parties when they made this contract.

**DECISION AND REMEDY**  *The Court of Exchequer ordered a new trial. According to the court, the plaintiffs would have to have given express notice of special circumstances that caused the loss of profits to collect consequential damages.*

**PUNITIVE DAMAGES**  Punitive, or exemplary, damages are generally not awarded in a breach of contract action. Punitive damages are designed to punish a guilty party and to make an example of the party to deter similar conduct in the future. Such damages have no legitimate place in contract law because they are, in essence, penalties, and a breach of contract is not unlawful in a criminal or societal sense. A contract is simply a civil relationship between the parties. The law may compensate one party for the loss of the bargain, no more and no less.

In a few situations, a person's actions can cause both a breach of contract and a tort. For example, the parties can establish by contract a certain reasonable standard or duty of care. Failure to live up to that standard is a breach of contract, and the act itself may constitute negligence.

A careful review of Chapters 6 and 7, which deal with torts, will indicate that some intentional torts may also be tied to a breach of the terms of a contract. In such cases it is possible for the non-breaching party to recover punitive damages for the commission of the tort, in addition to compensatory and consequential damages for breach of contract. Also, some jurisdictions—California, for instance—recognize that a breach of the implied covenant (promise) of good faith and fair dealing is actionable as a tort and may warrant an award of punitive damages.

**NOMINAL DAMAGES**  When no actual damages result from a breach of contract and only a technical injury is involved, the court may award **nominal damages,** a trivial amount, to the innocent party. Awards of nominal damages are often trifling, such as a dollar, but they do establish that the defendant acted wrongfully. For example, suppose that Jackson contracts to buy potatoes from Stanley at fifty cents a pound. Stanley breaches the contract and does not deliver the potatoes. In the meantime, the price of potatoes has fallen. Jackson is able to buy them in the open market at half the price he contracted for with Stanley. He is clearly better off because of Stanley's breach. Thus, in a breach of contract suit, Jackson may be awarded only nominal damages for the technical injury he sustained, because no monetary loss was involved. Most lawsuits for nominal damages are brought as a matter of principle under the theory that a breach has occurred and some damages must be imposed regardless of actual loss.

## MITIGATION OF DAMAGES

In most situations, when a breach of contract occurs, the innocent injured party is held to a duty to mitigate, or reduce, the damages that he or she suffers. Under this **mitigation of damages** doctrine, the duty owed depends on the nature of the contract. For example, some states require the lessor to use reasonable means to find a new tenant if the lessee abandons the premises and fails to pay rent. If an acceptable tenant becomes available, the landlord is required to lease the premises to this tenant to mitigate the damages recoverable from the former lessee. The former lessee is still liable for the difference between the amount of the rent under the original lease and the rent received from the new lessee. If the lessor has not taken the reasonable means necessary to find a new tenant, presumably a court can reduce the award made by the amount of rent he or she could have received had such reasonable means been taken.

In the majority of states, persons whose employment has been wrongfully terminated owe the duty to mitigate damages suffered by their employers' breach. The damages they receive are their salaries less the incomes they would have received in similar jobs that they could have obtained by reasonable means. The employer must prove both the existence of such a job and that the employee could have been hired. As the following case illustrates, however, the employee is under no duty to take a job that is not of the same type and rank.

**COMPANY PROFILE**   *Daryl Zanuck formed the Twentieth Century Company in 1933 with Joseph Schenk. Two years later, they merged with the Fox Film Company, which had been founded by William Fox, and became Twentieth Century-Fox Film Corporation. In the 1930s and 1940s, the number of movie tickets sold per year (four billion) was relatively stable. With the advent of television in the late 1940s, ticket sales dropped to one billion a year. Movies are expensive to produce and whether a picture is made can often depend on the success or failure of a film whose only connection is that it is produced by the same studio. Thus, a studio must often count on a few box-office successes to sustain it through many failures. In the 1960s,* The Sound of Music *sustained Twentieth Century-Fox. In the 1970s and 1980s, the studio was buoyed by receipts from the* Star Wars *trilogy, the* Porky's *films, the* Die Hard *series,* Working Girl, *and* Wall Street. *In the 1990s, the studio produced the* Home Alone *pictures. Twentieth Century-Fox also produces television shows, including ''L.A. Law,'' ''Beverly Hills 90210,'' and ''The Simpsons.'' The studio is currently owned by the News Corporation, Limited, which is headquartered in Australia.*

| CASE 19.2 |
| --- |

**PARKER v. TWENTIETH CENTURY-FOX FILM CORP.**
Supreme Court of California, 1970.
3 Cal.3d 176,
474 P.2d 689,
89 Cal.Rptr. 737.

**BACKGROUND AND FACTS**   *Twentieth Century-Fox Film Corporation planned to produce a musical,* Bloomer Girl, *and contracted with Shirley MacLaine Parker to play the leading female role. According to the contract, Fox was to pay Parker $53,571.42 per week for fourteen weeks, for a total of $750,000. Fox later decided not to produce* Bloomer Girl *and tried to substitute for the existing contract another contract under which Parker would play the leading role in* Big Country, *a Western movie, for the same amount of money guaranteed by the first contract. Fox gave Parker one week in which to accept the new contract. Parker filed suit against Fox to recover the amount of compensation guaranteed in the first contract because, she maintained, the two roles were not at all equivalent. The* Bloomer Girl *production was a musical, to be filmed in California, and could not be compared with a ''Western type'' production that was, according to tentative plans, to be produced in Australia. When the trial court held for Parker, Fox appealed.*

*BURKE*, Justice.
\*   \*   \*   \*

   \*   \*   \* [D]efendant's [Fox's] sole defense to this action which resulted from its deliberate breach of contract is that in rejecting defendant's substitute offer of employment plaintiff unreasonably refused to mitigate damages.

   The general rule is that the measure of recovery by a wrongfully discharged employee is the amount of salary agreed upon for the period of service, less the amount which the employer affirmatively proves the employee has earned or with reasonable effort might have earned from other employment. However, before projected earnings from other employment opportunities not sought or accepted by the discharged employee can be applied in mitigation, the employer must show that the other employment was comparable, or substantially similar, to that of which the employee has been deprived; the employee's rejection of or failure to seek other available employment of a different or inferior kind may not be resorted to in order to mitigate damages.

\* \* \* \*

\* \* \* [I]t is clear that the trial court correctly ruled that plaintiff's failure to accept defendant's tendered substitute employment could not be applied in mitigation of damages because the offer of the "Big Country" lead was of employment both different and inferior, and that no factual dispute was presented on that issue. The mere circumstance that "Bloomer Girl" was to be a musical review calling upon plaintiff's talents as a dancer as well as an actress, and was to be produced in the City of Los Angeles, whereas "Big Country" was a straight dramatic role in a "Western Type" story taking place in an opal mine in Australia, demonstrates the difference in kind between the two employments; the female lead as a dramatic actress in a western style motion picture can by no stretch of imagination be considered the equivalent of or substantially similar to the lead in a song-and-dance production.

**DECISION AND REMEDY**   *The Supreme Court of California affirmed the trial court's ruling. Parker could not be required to accept Fox's offer of the Western-movie contract to mitigate the damages she incurred as a result of the breach of contract.*

**INTERNATIONAL CONSIDERATIONS**   **Mitigation of Damages in France** *Many legal systems, including that of France, have no clear requirement that damages must be mitigated. For example, the French civil law code has no provision stating that an employee must make reasonable efforts to secure comparable employment.*

## LIQUIDATED DAMAGES VERSUS PENALTIES

Unliquidated damages are damages that have not been calculated or determined. For example, in a lawsuit, after Jane has proved her right to recover from Sam for his breach of their contract but before she has proved the amount she is entitled to recover, the damages are unliquidated. **Liquidated damages** are damages that are certain in amount. A liquidated damages provision in a contract specifies a certain amount to be paid in the event of a *future* default or breach of contract. For example, a provision requiring a construction contractor to pay $100 for every day he or she is late in completing the construction is a liquidated damages provision. Liquidated damages differ from penalties. **Penalties** specify a certain amount to be paid in the event of a default or breach of contract and are designed to *penalize* the breaching party. Liquidated damages provisions are enforceable; penalty provisions are not.

To determine if a particular provision is for liquidated damages or for a penalty, two questions must be answered. First, when the contract was entered into, was it apparent that damages would be difficult to estimate in the event of a breach? Second, was the amount set as damages a reasonable estimate and not excessive?[8] If both answers are yes, the provision will be enforced. If either answer is no, the provision will not be enforced. Section 2–718(1) of the UCC specifically permits the inclusion of liquidated damages clauses in contracts for the sale of goods as long as both of these tests are met. In construction contracts, it is difficult to estimate the amount of damages caused by a delay in completing construction, so liquidated damages clauses are often used.

One of the most contested areas in contract law involves the distinction between liquidated damages and penalties. Only the former are enforceable, as illustrated in the following case.

---

8.   Restatement (Second) of Contracts, Section 356(1).

**BACKGROUND AND FACTS**  *When Mary and George Rivera signed a standard-form, conditional real estate sales contract for some ranch property in Montana, the contract contained a liquidated damages clause. The clause stated that if either party failed to complete the transaction, that party would be required to pay the other party 10 percent of the purchase price—in this case, that 10 percent amounted to $43,000. The Riveras had a water test done, and the results showed that the water was contaminated. Consequently, they failed to close on the contract on the specified date. The owners of the ranch, Brien and Gayle Weber, sued the Riveras for breach of contract and sought to enforce the liquidated damages clause. The Riveras argued that the clause was actually a penalty clause and thus void. The trial court found in favor of the Webers, and the Riveras appealed.*

CASE 19.3

**WEBER v. RIVERA**
Supreme Court of Montana,
1992.
841 P.2d 534.

*HUNT*, Justice.
\* \* \* \*

\* \* \* As set out in the statute, a contractual provision in Montana purporting to set out in advance the amount of damages payable upon a breach of the contract is void. However, an exception is provided for situations in which the parties have agreed in advance on an amount of damages because it would be impracticable or extremely difficult to fix the actual damages. This Court has previously explained in interpreting this statute that: ''Whether the forfeiture provision imposed a penalty, or provided for liquidated damages, is to be determined from the language and subject matter of the contract, the evident intent of the parties and all the facts and circumstances under which the contract was made. The most important facts to be considered are whether the damages were difficult to ascertain, and whether the stipulated amount is a reasonable estimate of probable damages or is reasonably proportionate to the actual damages sustained at the time of the breach.''

In this case, the provision for liquidated damages was contained in a form contract prepared and required by United National Real Estate. There was absolutely no attempt on the part of the parties prior to entering the contract to reasonably estimate what the damages might be in the event of a breach. Both the Webers and the sales representative testified that they had no idea how the amount in the provision was even chosen. Pursuant to the provision, the Webers were entitled to $43,000 regardless of whether they were able to resell the property the next week, the next month, or the next year. They would have been entitled to the $43,000 even if they found a subsequent purchaser willing to pay more than the Riveras. In short, the provision provided for a set amount of damages without any regard for or attempt to determine what the actual damages might be.

*The Supreme Court of Montana held the contract provision to be a penalty clause and thus void. The court remanded the case to the trial court to make a factual determination of the amount of ''actual damages suffered by the Webers'' because the liquidated damages clause was unenforceable.*

**DECISION
AND REMEDY**

# SECTION 2

# RESCISSION AND RESTITUTION

**Rescission** is essentially an action to undo, or terminate, a contract—to return the contracting par-

ties to the positions they occupied prior to the transaction.[9] When fraud, a mistake, duress, undue

---

9.  The rescission discussed here is *unilateral* rescission, in which only one party wants to undo the contract. In mutual rescission, both parties agree to undo the contract (see Chapter 18). Mutual rescission discharges the contract; unilateral rescission is generally available as a remedy for breach of contract.

## ■ CONCEPT SUMMARY 19.1 Damages

| REMEDY | AVAILABILITY | RESULT |
|---|---|---|
| **Compensatory Damages** | A party sustains and proves an injury arising directly from the loss of the bargain. | The injured party is compensated for the *loss* of the bargain. |
| **Consequential Damages** | Special circumstances, of which the breaching party is aware or should be aware, cause the injured party additional loss. | The injured party is given the entire *benefit* of the bargain. |
| **Punitive Damages** | Damages are normally available only when a tort is also involved. | The wrongdoer is punished, and others are deterred from committing similar acts. |
| **Nominal Damages** | There is no financial loss. | Wrongdoing is established without actual damages being suffered. The plaintiff is awarded a nominal amount (such as $1) in damages. |
| **Liquidated Damages** | A contract provides a specific amount to be paid as damages in the event that the contract is breached. | The nonbreaching party is paid the amount stipulated in the contract for the breach. |

influence, misrepresentation, or lack of capacity to contract is present, unilateral rescission is available. Rescission may also be made available by statute.[10] The failure of one party to perform entitles the other party to rescind the contract. The rescinding party must give prompt notice to the breaching party. Generally, to rescind a contract, both parties must make **restitution** to each other by returning goods, property, or money previously conveyed.[11] If the goods or property received can be restored *in specie*—that is, if the actual goods or property can be returned—they must be. If the goods or property has been consumed, restitution must be made in an equivalent amount of money.

Essentially, *restitution* refers to the plaintiff's recapture of a benefit conferred on the defendant through which the defendant has been unjustly enriched. For example, Katchen pays $10,000 to Bob in return for Bob's promise to design a house for her. The next day Bob calls Katchen and tells her that he has taken a position with a large architectural firm in another state and cannot design the house. Katchen decides to hire another architect that afternoon. Katchen can obtain restitution of the $10,000.

Restitution may be appropriate when a contract is rescinded, but the right to restitution is not limited to rescission cases. Restitution may be sought in other breach-of-contract actions, tort actions, and other actions at law or in equity. Sometimes, restitution of money or property transferred by mistake or because of fraud can be awarded. An award in a case may include restitution of money or property obtained through embezzlement, conversion, theft, copyright infringement, or misconduct by a party in a confidential or other special relationship. The following case illustrates a situation in which the equitable remedy of rescission and restitution was deemed an appropriate remedy by the court.

---

10. The Federal Trade Commission and many states have rules or statutes allowing consumers to unilaterally rescind contracts made at home with door-to-door salespersons. Rescission is allowed within three days for any reason or for no reason at all. See, for example, California Civil Code Section 1689.5.

11. Restatement (Second) of Contracts, Section 370.

**HISTORICAL AND SOCIAL SETTING**  *When a seller breaches a contract to transfer land and it is impossible for the seller to perform, the buyer's normal remedy at law is damages consisting of the amount of the loss of the bargain, plus incidental damages. Usually, the amount awarded as damages for the loss of the bargain is the difference between the contract price and the market value of the land on the date of the breach. But suppose the seller's breach is unintentional (as it would be if, for example, it turned out that someone else had certain rights in the property that were unknown to the seller at the time the contract was formed). In that case, in some states, the buyer can recover only the amount paid on the purchase price. This rule, which is sometimes called the "restitutionary" rule, originated in 1776 in the English case of* Flureau v. Thornhill.[a] *Imagine that you sign a contract to buy some land and make payments on the price. Before the sale is complete, it becomes impossible for the seller to perform. Meanwhile, the market value of the land has decreased. Would you prefer to recover money damages in the amount of the loss of the bargain (which in this case would be a* net loss*), or would you prefer to have the contract rescinded and recover the amount that you paid toward the purchase price?*

**CASE 19.4**

**RACICKY v. SIMON**
Supreme Court of Wyoming,
1992.
831 P.2d 241.

**BACKGROUND AND FACTS**  *In January 1980, Bud Racicky entered into a contract to sell 320 acres of land to Dorothy Simon for $144,000, to be paid in three installments. Simon made the payments on time, and the contract price was fully paid by January 30, 1982. At the time the contract was formed, Racicky was in the process of buying from another party the land he was going to convey to Simon. In the fall of 1985 and before he completed the contract with the other party, Racicky sought bankruptcy relief. As a consequence of these events, it was impossible for Racicky to perform his contract with Simon. Simon died, and her personal representative brought an action against Racicky, seeking rescission of the contract and restitution of the full amount of the payments that Simon had made to Racicky. The trial court ordered rescission of the contract and restitution in the amount of the payments received, together with interest at 10 percent, which was calculated from the time that Racicky's performance became impossible. The total restitution awarded was $212,267.33. Racicky appealed the decision, contending that money damages (of a much lower amount) constituted an adequate remedy at law for his breach of contract.*

*THOMAS, Justice.*
   * * * *

   We recognize that the payment of money damages generally is considered an adequate remedy for a breach of contract, but this general rule does not control a situation in which the contract is one for the sale of land. In the instance of a contract for the sale of land, the legal presumption is that equitable concepts will control the resolution of the dispute. The rationale underlying this presumption is that the unique character of each individual parcel of land renders the remedy of money damages inadequate. * * * Obviously, the parties could not be returned to the status quo at the time the contract was made by invoking the remedy of money damages. * * *
   * * * *

a.  96 Eng.Rep. 635 (C.P. 1776).

In summary, we hold that the remedy of rescission was available to Simon under the contract for the sale of real property when Racicky was unable to convey the property described in the contract. * * * In an instance such as this, an award of money damages rather than restitution is neither required nor is it the preferred remedy.

**DECISION AND REMEDY**  *The trial court's decision was affirmed. The state supreme court held that the equitable remedy of rescission and restitution, instead of money damages, was proper.*

## SECTION 3

# SPECIFIC PERFORMANCE

The equitable remedy of **specific performance** calls for the performance of the act promised in the contract. This remedy is quite attractive to the nonbreaching party, because it provides the exact bargain promised in the contract. It also avoids some of the problems inherent in a suit for money damages.

There are three basic reasons for the attractiveness of the remedy of specific performance. First, the nonbreaching party need not worry about collecting the money damages awarded by a court. Second, the nonbreaching party need not look around for another contract. Third, the performance is more valuable than the money damages.

Although the equitable remedy of specific performance is often preferable to other remedies, specific performance will not be granted unless the party's legal remedy (money damages) is inadequate.[12] For example, contracts for the sale of goods rarely qualify for specific performance. The legal remedy, money damages, is ordinarily adequate in such situations, because substantially identical goods can be bought or sold in the market. If the goods are unique, however, a court of equity will decree specific performance. For example, paintings, sculptures, or rare books or coins are so unique that money damages will not enable a buyer to obtain substantially identical substitutes in the market.

### SALE OF LAND

Specific performance is granted to a buyer in a contract for the sale of land. The legal remedy for breach of a land sales contract is inadequate, because every parcel of land is considered to be unique. Money damages will not compensate a buyer adequately, because the same land in the same location obviously cannot be obtained elsewhere. Only when specific performance is unavailable (for example, when the seller has sold the property to someone else) will money damages be awarded instead.

### CONTRACTS FOR PERSONAL SERVICES

Personal service contracts require one party to work personally for another party. Courts of equity normally refuse to grant specific performance of personal service contracts. If the contract is not deemed personal, the remedy at law may be adequate if substantially identical service (for example, lawn mowing) is available from other persons.

In individually tailored personal service contracts, courts will not order specific performance by the party who was to be employed because public policy strongly discourages involuntary servitude.[13] Moreover, the courts do not want to have to monitor a continuing service contract if supervision would be difficult—as it would be if the contract required the exercise of personal judgment or talent. For example, if you contracted with a brain surgeon to perform brain surgery on you, and the surgeon refused to perform, the court would not compel (and you certainly would not want) the surgeon to perform under those circumstances. A court cannot assure meaningful performance in such a situation.[14]

---

12.   Restatement (Second) of Contracts, Section 359.

13.   The Thirteenth Amendment to the U.S. Constitution prohibits involuntary servitude, but *negative* injunctions (that is, injunctions prohibiting rather than ordering certain conduct) are possible. Thus, whereas you may not be able to compel a person to perform under a personal service contract, you may be able to restrain that person from engaging in similar contracts for a period of time.

14.   Similarly, courts often refuse to order specific performance of construction contracts because courts are not set up to operate as construction supervisors or engineers.

# REFORMATION

**Reformation** is an equitable remedy used when the parties have *imperfectly* expressed their agreement in writing. Reformation allows the contract to be rewritten to reflect the parties' true intentions. It applies most often when fraud or mutual mistake (for example, a clerical error) is present. Reformation is almost always sought so that some other remedy may then be pursued.

For example, if Gilge contracts to buy a certain parcel of land from Cavendish, but their contract mistakenly refers to a parcel of land different from the one being sold, the contract does not reflect the parties' intentions. Accordingly, a court of equity can reform the contract so that it conforms to the parties' intentions and accurately refers to the parcel of land being sold. Gilge can then, if necessary, show that Cavendish has breached the contract as reformed. She can then request an order for specific performance.

Two other examples deserve mention. The first involves two parties who have made a binding oral contract. They further agree to reduce the oral contract to writing, but in doing so, they make an error in stating the terms. Universally, the courts will allow into evidence the correct terms of the oral contract, thereby reforming the written contract.

The second example deals with written agreements (covenants) not to compete (see Chapter 16). If the covenant is for a valid and legitimate purpose (such as the sale of a business) but the area or time restraints of the covenant are unreasonable, some courts will reform the restraints by making them reasonable and will enforce the entire contract as reformed. Other courts, however, will throw out the entire restrictive covenant as illegal.

# RECOVERY BASED ON QUASI CONTRACT

As stated in Chapter 11, quasi contract is a legal theory under which an obligation is imposed in the absence of an agreement. The courts use this theory to prevent unjust enrichment. Hence, quasi contract provides a basis for relief when no enforceable contract exists. The legal obligation arises because the law considers that a promise to pay for benefits received is implied by the party accepting the benefits. Generally, when one party has conferred a benefit on another party, justice requires the party receiving the benefit to pay the reasonable value for it. The party conferring the benefit can recover *in quantum meruit,* which means ''as much as he deserves'' (see Chapter 11).

Quasi-contractual recovery is useful when one party has partially performed under a contract that is unenforceable. It can be used as an alternative to a suit for damages and will allow the party to recover the reasonable value of the partial performance, measured in some cases according to the benefit received and in others according to the detriment suffered.

To recover on a quasi contract, the party seeking recovery must show the following:

1. He or she has conferred a benefit on the other party.
2. He or she conferred the benefit with the reasonable expectation of being paid.
3. He or she did not act as a volunteer in conferring the benefit.
4. The party receiving the benefit would be unjustly enriched by retaining the benefit without making payment.

For example, suppose Watson contracts to build two oil derricks for Energy Industries. The derricks are to be built over a period of three years, but the parties do not make a written contract. Enforcement of the contract will therefore be barred by the Statute of Frauds.[15] Watson completes one derrick, and then Energy Industries informs him that it will not pay for the derrick. Watson can sue in quasi contract because (1) a benefit has been conferred on Energy Industries, because one oil derrick has been built; (2) Watson built the derrick (conferred the benefit) with the expectation of being paid; (3) Watson did not volunteer to build the derrick but built it under an unenforceable oral contract; and (4) allowing Energy Industries to retain the derrick without paying would enrich the company unjustly. Therefore, Watson should be able to recover the reasonable value of the oil derrick (under the theory of *quantum meruit*). The

---

15. Contracts that by their terms cannot be performed within one year must be in writing to be enforceable. See Chapter 16.

## ■ CONCEPT SUMMARY 19.2 Equitable Remedies

| REMEDY | AVAILABILITY | RESULT |
|---|---|---|
| **Rescission and Restitution** | The injured party is entitled to recapture a benefit conferred. | The contract is terminated. The parties are returned to the positions they occupied before the contract was made. |
| **Specific Performance** | The subject matter of the contract is unique. (The legal remedy, money damages, is inadequate.) | The injured party gets the bargain promised in the contract. |
| **Reformation** | The written contract imperfectly expresses the parties' agreement. | The contract is rewritten to reflect the parties' true intention. |
| **Quasi-contractual Recovery** | The parties have no contract, but unjust enrichment cannot otherwise be avoided. | The party who conferred the benefit gets the reasonable value of the benefit conferred. |

reasonable value is ordinarily equal to the fair market value.

## SECTION 6

# ELECTION OF REMEDIES

In many cases, a nonbreaching party has several remedies available. The party must choose which remedy to pursue. The purpose of the *election of remedies* doctrine is to prevent double recovery. Suppose McCarthy agrees in writing to sell his land to Tally. Then McCarthy changes his mind and repudiates the contract. Tally can sue for compensatory damages or for specific performance. If she receives damages, she should not be able to get specific performance of the sales contract, because failure to deliver title to the land was the cause of the injury for which she received damages. If Tally could seek compensatory damages in addition to specific performance, she would recover twice for the same breach of contract. The doctrine of election of remedies requires Tally to choose the remedy she wants, and it eliminates any possibility of double recovery. In other words, the election doctrine represents the legal embodiment of the adage "You can't have your cake and eat it, too."

The doctrine has often been applied in a rigid and technical manner, leading to some harsh results. For example, in a Wisconsin case,[16] Carpenter was fraudulently induced to buy a piece of land for $100. He spent an additional $140 moving onto the land and then discovered the fraud. Instead of suing for damages, Carpenter sued to rescind the contract. The court allowed Carpenter to recover only the purchase price of $100. The court denied recovery of the additional $140 because the seller, Mason, did not receive the $140 and was therefore not required to reimburse Carpenter for his moving expenses. So Carpenter suffered a net loss of $140 on the transaction. If Carpenter had elected to sue for damages instead of seeking the remedy of rescission and restitution, he could have recovered the $140 as well as the $100.

Because of such problems, the doctrine of election of remedies has been eliminated in contracts for the sale of goods. The UCC expressly rejects the doctrine. (See UCC 2–703 and UCC 2–711.) Remedies under the UCC are not exclusive but cumulative in nature and include all the available remedies for breach of contract. Thus, for example, under UCC 2–721, in a suit based on fraud, the defrauded party may obtain rescission of the contract, restitution of the benefits conferred, and any damages due to the fraud. Even though the UCC rejects the doctrine of election of remedies, parties may still not recover twice for the same harm by

---

16. *Carpenter v. Mason,* 181 Wis. 114, 193 N.W. 973 (1923).

seeking, for example, specific performance *and* damages at the same time.

## SECTION 7

# WAIVER OF BREACH

Under certain circumstances, a nonbreaching party may be willing to accept a defective performance of the contract. This knowing relinquishment of a legal right (that is, the right to require satisfactory and full performance) is called a **waiver.**[17] When a waiver of a breach of contract occurs, the party waiving the breach cannot take any later action on the theory that the contract was broken. In effect, the waiver erases the past breach; the contract continues as if the breach had never occurred. Of course, the waiver of breach of contract extends only to the matter waived and not to the whole contract. Businesspersons often waive breaches of contract to get whatever benefit possible out of the contract.

For example, a seller contracts with a buyer to deliver to the buyer ten thousand tons of coal on or before November 1. The contract calls for the buyer's payment to be made by November 10 for coal delivered. Because of a coal miners' strike, coal is scarce. The seller breaches the contract by not tendering delivery until November 5. The buyer may be well advised to waive the seller's breach, accept delivery of the coal, and pay as contracted.

Ordinarily, the waiver by a contracting party will not operate to waive subsequent, additional, or future breaches of contract. This is always true when the subsequent breaches are unrelated to the first breach. For example, an owner who waives the right to sue for late completion of a stage of construction does not waive the right to sue for failure to comply with engineering specifications on the same job.

A waiver will be extended to subsequent defective performance if a reasonable person would conclude that similar defective performance in the future will be acceptable. Therefore, a *pattern of conduct* that waives a number of successive breaches will operate as a continued waiver. To change this result, the nonbreaching party should give notice to the breaching party that full performance will be required in the future.

The party who has rendered defective or less-than-full performance remains liable for the damages caused by the breach of contract. In effect, the waiver operates to keep the contract going. The waiver prevents the nonbreaching party from calling the contract to an end or rescinding the contract. The contract continues, but the nonbreaching party can recover damages caused by defective or less-than-full performance.

## SECTION 8

# CONTRACT PROVISIONS LIMITING REMEDIES

A contract may include provisions stating that no damages can be recovered for certain types of breaches or that damages must be limited to a maximum amount. The contract may also provide that the only remedy for breach is replacement, repair, or refund of the purchase price. Provisions stating that no damages can be recovered are called *exculpatory clauses* (see Chapter 16). Provisions that affect the availability of certain remedies are called *limitation-of-liability clauses.*

Whether these contract provisions and clauses will be enforced depends on the type of breach that is excused by the provision. For example, a provision excluding liability for fraudulent or intentional injury will not be enforced. Likewise, a clause excluding liability for illegal acts or violations of law will not be enforced. A clause excluding liability for negligence may be enforced in appropriate cases, however. When an exculpatory clause for negligence is contained in a contract made between parties who have roughly equal bargaining positions, the clause usually will be enforced.

The UCC provides that in a contract for the sale of goods, remedies can be limited. We will examine the UCC provisions on limited remedies in Chapter 23, in the context of the remedies available upon the breach of a sales contract.

---

17.   Restatement (Second) of Contracts, Sections 84, 246, and 247. The Restatement uses the term *promise* rather than *waiver.*

# TERMS AND CONCEPTS TO REVIEW

compensatory damages 341
consequential damages 342
liquidated damages 346
mitigation of damages 344

nominal damages 344
penalty 346
reformation 351
rescission 347

restitution 348
specific performance 350
waiver 353

# QUESTIONS AND CASE PROBLEMS

**19–1. Liquidated Damages.** Cohen contracts to sell his house and lot to Windsor for $100,000. The terms of the contract call for Windsor to pay 10 percent of the purchase price as a deposit toward the purchase price, or as a down payment. The terms further stipulate that should the buyer breach the contract, the deposit will be retained by Cohen as liquidated damages. Windsor pays the deposit, but because her expected financing of the $90,000 balance falls through, she breaches the contract. Two weeks later Cohen sells the house and lot to Ballard for $105,000. Windsor demands her $10,000 back, but Cohen refuses, claiming that Windsor's breach and the contract terms entitle him to keep the deposit. Discuss who is correct.

**19–2. Specific Performance.** In which of the following breach-of-contract situations would specific performance be an appropriate remedy? Discuss fully.

(a) Thompson contracts to sell her house and lot to Cousteau. Then, upon finding another buyer willing to pay a higher purchase price, she refuses to deed the property to Cousteau.

(b) Amy contracts to sing and dance in Fred's nightclub for one month, beginning May 1. She then refuses to perform.

(c) Hoffman contracts to purchase a rare coin owned by Erikson, as Erikson is breaking up his coin collection. At the last minute Erikson decides to keep his coin collection intact and refuses to deliver the coin to Hoffman.

(d) There are three shareholders of the ABC Corp.: Panozzo, who owns 48 percent of the stock; Chang, who owns another 48 percent; and Ryan, who owns 4 percent. Ryan contracts to sell her 4 percent to Chang. Later, Ryan refuses to transfer the shares to Chang.

**19–3. Damages.** Ken owns and operates a famous candy store and makes most of the candy sold in the store. Business is particularly heavy during the Christmas season. Ken contracts with Sweet, Inc., to purchase ten thousand pounds of sugar to be delivered on or before November 15. Ken has informed Sweet that this particular order is to be used for the Christmas season business. Because of production problems, the sugar is not tendered to Ken until December 10, at which time Ken refuses it as being too late. Ken has been unable to purchase the quantity of sugar needed to meet the Christmas orders and has had to turn down numerous regular customers, some of whom have indicated that they will purchase candy elsewhere in the future. What sugar Ken has been able to purchase has cost him 10 cents per pound above the price contracted for with Sweet. Ken sues Sweet for breach of contract, claiming as damages the higher price paid for sugar from others, lost profits from this year's lost Christmas sales, future lost profits from customers who have indicated that they will discontinue doing business with him, and punitive damages for failure to meet the contracted delivery date. Sweet claims Ken is limited to compensatory damages only. Discuss who is correct.

**19–4. Breach.** Wallechinsky purchases an automobile from Anderson Motors, paying $1,000 down and agreeing to pay off the balance in thirty-six monthly payments of $200 each. The terms of the agreement call for Wallechinsky to make a payment on or before the first of each month. During the first six months, Anderson receives a $200 payment before the first of each month. During the next six months, Wallechinsky's payment is never made until the fifth of the month. Anderson accepts and cashes the payment check each time. When Wallechinsky tenders the thirteenth payment on the fifth of the next month, Anderson refuses to accept the check, claiming that Wallechinsky is in breach of contract. Anderson demands the entire balance owed. Wallechinsky claims that Anderson cannot hold her in breach. Discuss the result fully.

**19–5. Remedies.** Putnam contracts to buy a new Oldsmobile from Old Century Motors, paying $2,000 down and agreeing to make twenty-four monthly payments of $350 each. He takes the car home and, after making one payment, learns that his Oldsmobile has a Chevrolet engine in it rather than the famous Olds Super V-8 engine. Old Century never informed Putnam of this fact. Putnam immediately notifies Old Century of his dissatisfaction and tenders back the car to Old Century. Old Century accepts the car and returns to Putnam the $2,000 down payment plus the one $350 payment. Two weeks later Putnam, without a car and feeling angry, files a suit against Old Century, seeking damages for breach of warranty and fraud. Discuss the effect of Putnam's actions.

**19–6. Damages.** Kerr Steamship Co. delivered to Radio Corp. of America (RCA) a twenty-nine-word coded message to be sent to Kerr's agent in Manila. The message included instructions on loading cargo onto one of Kerr's vessels. Kerr's profits on the carriage of the cargo were to be about $6,600. RCA mislaid the coded message, and it was never sent. Kerr sued RCA for the $6,600 in profits that it lost because RCA never sent the message. Can Kerr recover? Explain. [*Kerr Steamship Co. v. Radio Corp. of America*, 245 N.Y. 284, 157 N.E. 140 (1927)]

**19–7. Recovery.** Southwestern Bell Telephone Co. executed a license agreement that gave United Video Cablevision of St. Louis, Inc., authority to construct and operate a cable television system using poles and conduits owned by Bell. The agreement specified that United Video would make a down payment for rent and telephone wire service. By law, Bell was required to locate and mark underground facilities, upon request, before any excavation so that no disruption of the telephone lines would take place. Bell had provided this service free of charge for many years, and it performed the service for United Video before United Video installed its lines. After United Video had substantially completed its installation, Bell notified the company of its intention to charge for the locating and marking service. The charge was not a part of the oral or written contract, and United Video refused to pay. Bell sought to recover based on *quantum meruit*. Discuss whether Bell should succeed in its claim. [*Southwestern Bell Telephone Co. v. United Video Cablevision of St. Louis, Inc.*, 737 S.W.2d 474 (Mo.App. 1987)]

**19–8. Waiver of Breach.** W. A. and Lola Dunn were payees of several installment promissory notes issued by General Equities of Iowa, Ltd. Each note contained an acceleration clause that permitted the holder of the note to accelerate and demand full payment of the note should any installment not be paid when due. Over a period of time the Dunns accepted late installment payments from General Equities without invoking the acceleration clause. General Equities made a further late payment. The Dunns returned the General Equities check and demanded payment of the entire balance, with interest, in accordance with the acceleration clause. General Equities claimed that the acceptance of the previous late payments constituted a waiver of the Dunns' right to invoke the acceleration clause. Discuss whether General Equities was correct. [*Dunn v. General Equities of Iowa, Ltd.*, 319 N.W.2d 515 (Iowa 1982)]

**19–9. Rescission.** Jeffrey Stambovsky was a resident of New York City. While looking at houses in the village of Nyack, New York, Stambovsky had come across a riverfront Victorian house that he liked. He purchased it, only to discover later that the house had a local reputation for being haunted. The seller, Helen Ackley, had promoted this reputation herself by reporting to the *Reader's Digest* in 1977 and to the local press in 1982 that the house was haunted. By 1989, the house was included in a five-home walking tour of Nyack because of the purported presence of ghosts in the house. There was even a newspaper article describing it as "a riverfront Victorian (with ghost)." Stambovsky brought an action to rescind the contract, contending that the house's reputation for being haunted impaired the value of the property. What will the court decide? Discuss fully. [*Stambovsky v. Ackley*, 169 A.D.2d 254, 572 N.Y.S.2d 672 (1991)]

**19–10. Limitation of Liability.** Patricia Elsken leased an apartment in a large apartment complex. She signed a "Residential Alarm Security Agreement" in which she agreed to have security services provided by Network Multi-Family Security Corp. The contract contained a clause limiting Network's liability to $250 for any injury or damage caused by a failure of the alarm service or by Network's negligent performance. The agreement stated, in all-capital letters, that Network was not an insurer and that "resident assumes all responsibility for obtaining insurance to cover losses of all types." The agreement also provided that "Resident may obtain from Network increased liability by paying an additional charge directly to Network." Network received an alarm signal indicating intrusion into Elsken's apartment at 10:33 A.M. on April 11, 1988. Network called Elsken's apartment and, receiving no answer, called the apartment manager instead of going to Elsken's apartment. The manager told Network to disregard the alarm. Later that day, Elsken was found dead in her apartment, the victim of an apparent homicide. The administrator of Elsken's estate brought an action for damages against Network, alleging negligence. Will the court hold that the contractual limitation of liability for personal injury is valid and enforceable? Discuss. [*Elsken v. Network Multi-Family Security Corp.*, 838 P.2d 1007 (Okla. 1992)]

**19–11. A Question of Ethics**

 *Robert Ryan, a widower with a ninth-grade education, fell behind in his mortgage payments and in April 1984 faced foreclosure. In May 1984, Norman Weiner, whom Ryan had never met, called on Ryan at his home and told Ryan that he could loan him money to help him keep his house if Ryan signed over the deed to the house as "security" for the loan. When Weiner left, he took Ryan's deed to the property with him for "safekeeping." The next day, Weiner drove Ryan to a lawyer's office, where Ryan signed several papers. Ryan signed the papers without reading them, believing that he was signing loan documents, because he trusted Weiner. In fact, he had signed documents that conveyed ownership of his house to Weiner. Weiner brought the mortgage payments up to date and continued to make the*

*payments on the house. Weiner also paid for electricity and other utilities and services necessary to maintain the house. Ryan continued to live in the house and made monthly payments to Weiner. The payments steadily increased from $100 to $310 a month. During that time, the mortgage payments increased also, from $93 in 1984 to $120 in 1991. In May 1991, Ryan concluded that he had paid off his mortgage and also his "loan" from Weiner and refused to make further payments. When Weiner initiated legal proceedings to evict Ryan, Ryan sought to rescind his transfer of the deed to Weiner. Based on these facts, answer the following questions. [Ryan v. Weiner, 610 A.2d 1377 (Del. 1992)]*

1. In view of the fact that Ryan voluntarily signed a document (contract) conveying his property to Weiner, should he be allowed to rescind that contract? What public policies are in conflict here?

2. When the equitable remedy of rescission and restitution is granted, the parties are restored to their status quo prior to the contract's formation. Is it possible to restore the parties to their status quo as of May 1984 in this case? Discuss.

### 19–12. Case Briefing Assignment

 *Examine Case A.2 [Potter v. Oster, 426 N.W.2d 148 (Iowa 1988)] in Appendix A. The case has been excerpted there in great detail. Review and then brief the case, making sure that you include answers to the following questions in your brief.*

1. Why was the plaintiff appealing the trial court's decision?

2. Why did the plaintiff assert that allowing the remedy of rescission and restitution in this case would lead to an inequitable result?

3. According to the court, what three requirements must be met before rescission will be granted?

4. Did the defendant meet these three requirements and, if so, why?

5. What reasons did the court give for its conclusion that remedies at law were inadequate in this case?

6. Why are remedies at law presumed inadequate for breach of real estate contracts?

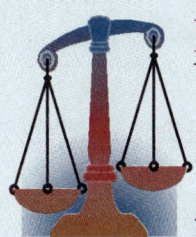

# FOCUS ON ETHICS

## Contract Law and the Application of Ethics

### Ethics and Freedom of Contract

In Chapter 2, we pointed out that in general, the responsible business manager will evaluate a business transaction on the basis of three criteria—legality, profitability, and ethics. But what does acting ethically mean in the area of contracts? If an individual with whom you enter into a contract fails to look after his or her own interests, is that your fault, and should you therefore be doing something about it? If the contract happens to be to your advantage and therefore to the other party's detriment, do you have a responsibility to correct the situation?

For example, assume that a neighbor whom you rarely see places a "for sale" sign on her car, offering to sell it for $3,000. You learn that she is moving to another state and needs the extra cash to help finance the move. You know that she could easily get $6,000 for the car, and you congratulate yourself on your good fortune. Even if you do not need a car, you can purchase it and then sell it at a profit. But you also learn that your neighbor has failed to do the preliminary research— checking *Blue Book* prices and so on—that most reasonable individuals would undertake when selling a car, and therefore she is unaware that the car is underpriced.

Are you obligated to tell her that she is essentially giving away $3,000 if she sells you the car for only $3,000? Do you have an ethical responsibility toward this woman—whom you will probably never see again— simply because she failed to look after her own interests? This kind of situation, transplanted into the world of commercial transactions, raises an obvious question: At what point should the savvy businessperson cease looking after his or her own economic welfare and become "his brother's keeper," so to speak?

The answer to this question is not simple. On the one hand, a common ethical assumption in our society is that individuals should be held responsible for the consequences of their own actions, including their contractual promises. This principle is expressed in the legal concept of freedom of contract, a topic discussed in Chapter 11. Applying this ethical precept to the above example, you could justify not saying anything about the true value of the car to your neighbor by stating that you were upholding the principle of freedom of contract.

On the other hand, a common assumption in our society is that individuals should not harm one another by their actions. This is the basis of both tort law and criminal law. If you applied this ethical yardstick to the above example, would you be obligated not to harm your neighbor's interests by taking advantage of her offer? How would you balance these two ethical principles?

In the area of contract law, ethical behavior often involves just such a "balancing act." In the above example, if you purchased the car and the neighbor later learned its true value and sued you for the difference, very likely no court of law would agree that the contract should be rescinded. In other words, the law would not "answer" your ethical question in this case. The court probably would not come to the aid of the neighbor, because she could easily have prevented the injustice by learning, as a "reasonable person" would have, the market price of the car. There are times, however, when courts will hold that the principle of freedom of contract should give way to the principle that people should not be harmed by the actions of others. We look below at some examples of how parties to contracts may be excused from performance under their contracts if that is the only way injustice can be prevented.

### Impossibility of Performance

The doctrine of impossibility of performance is based to some extent on the ethical question of whether one party should suffer economic loss when it is impossible to perform a contract. The rule that one is "bound by his or her contracts" is not followed when performance is made impossible. The doctrine of impossibility of performance is applied to relieve a contracting party of liability for failure to perform. This doctrine, however, is applied only when the parties themselves did not consciously assume the risk of the events that rendered performance impossible. Furthermore, this doctrine rests on the assumption that the party claiming the defense of impossibility has acted ethically. In other words, a party cannot arrange events intentionally to make performance impossible.

A contract is discharged, for example, if performance of the contract calls for the delivery of a particular car, and through no fault of either party this car is stolen and completely demolished in an accident. Yet the doctrine of impossibility of performance is not available if the party agreeing to sell his or her car either crashed the car to avoid performance of the contract or caused the car's destruction by his or her negligence. The well-known English case of *Taylor v. Caldwell* is also illustrative of the doctrine of impossibility of performance.[1] In *Taylor,* the plaintiff entered into a contract with the defendant to rent the defendant's music hall for a series of concerts. Before the first concert, but after the contract had been entered into, the music hall was destroyed by fire. The court held that the defendant was discharged from performing. Furthermore, because performance was impossible, his failure to perform was not a breach of contract.

Prior to the late nineteenth century, courts were reluctant to discharge a contract even when it appeared that performance was literally impossible. Just as society's ethics change with the passage of time, however, the law also makes a transition to reflect society's new perceptions of ethical behavior. Today, courts are much more willing to discharge a contract when its performance has become literally impossible. Holding a party in breach of contract, when performance has become literally impossible through no fault of the party claiming the defense of impossibility, no longer coincides with society's notions of fairness.

### Mistake

The notion that mistake in contracts should release the contracting parties from their obligations has gained strength as the ethics of society have changed. If one were to study the cases of several hundred years ago, one would find much less acceptance of mistake as an excuse to avoid a contractual obligation than exists today.

Mistakes can arise in numerous contexts surrounding the making of a contract. A mistake may be unilateral in that it is made by only one party. In a case tried early in this century, *Steinmeyer* v. *Schroeppel,*[2] a bidder on a construction project incorrectly calculated his costs and therefore submitted an offer that was substantially lower than it would have been if he had correctly calculated his costs. The Illinois court held that the bidder was not entitled to rescind the contract. The court further stated that rescission based on a unilateral mistake could not be obtained when the mistake resulted from a failure to exercise reasonable care and diligence.

More recent court decisions, however, appear to be less harsh. Some courts have concluded that rescission on the basis of computation errors is permissible when the only injury to the other party is the loss of the expectancy engendered by a favorably low bid. Thus, ideas of fairness to each of the contracting parties change over time.

### Unconscionability

The doctrine of

1. 122 Eng.Rep. 309 (K.B. 1863).

2. 226 Ill. 9, 80 N.E. 564 (1907).

unconscionability represents a good example of how the law attempts to enforce ethical behavior. This doctrine suggests that some contracts may be so unfair to one party as to be unenforceable, even though that party originally agreed to the contract's terms. Section 2–302 of the UCC provides that a court will consider the fairness of contracts and may consider a contract or any clause of a contract to have been unconscionable at the time it was made. If so, the court may refuse to enforce the contract, it may enforce the contract without the unconscionable clause, or it may limit the application of the clause so as to avoid an unconscionable result.

The UCC does not define the term *unconscionability*. The drafters of the UCC, however, have added explanatory comments to the relevant sections of the UCC, and these comments serve as guidelines to the UCC's application. Comment 1 to Section 2–302 suggests that the basic test for unconscionability is whether, under the circumstances existing at the time of the making of the contract, the clause in question was so one sided as to be unconscionable. This test is to be applied against the general commercial background of the contract. For example, a contract with a marginally literate consumer might be seen as unfair and unenforceable, whereas the same contract with a major business firm would be upheld by the courts. The doctrine of

unconscionability could be used broadly to ensure that all contracts appeared perfectly ethical, but the courts have not used it in this way. Only contracts that are so extremely one sided as to "shock the conscience" of the court have been found to be unconscionable.

A classic case dealing with unconscionability is *Williams v. Walker-Thomas Furniture Co.*[3] This case involved a consumer who purchased over several years, with an installment contract, various items of furniture from a furniture company. Under the terms of the contract, each time a new item of furniture was purchased, that item, in addition to all of the furniture purchased previously, would be used as collateral (property securing the debt).

In 1962, the consumer, Williams, bought a stereo set, on which she soon stopped making payments. The furniture company wanted to repossess all of the items that she had purchased from it since 1957. Both the trial court and the intermediate appellate court, even though they felt that the contract was unconscionable, nonetheless held for the furniture company. Because the UCC had not yet been adopted by the District of Columbia (the jurisdiction in which this suit was brought), there was no legal basis upon which to find the contract unenforceable.

Upon review, however, the District of Columbia Circuit Court of Appeals held that

_____

3. 350 F.2d 445 (D.C. Cir. 1965).

there was no reason why the lower courts could not, under the common law, apply the concept of unconscionability to contracts. The appellate court then remanded the case to the trial court for an examination of whether the terms of the contract were so extreme as to be unconscionable according to business customs and practices.

## Problems with Oral Contracts

Oral contracts are made every day. Many—if not most—of them are carried out, and no problems arise. Occasionally, however, oral contracts are not performed, and one party wishes to sue the other. Sometimes it is possible for one party to hide behind a technical defense to prevent the enforcement of a promise that he or she genuinely made to the other party. One of these technical defenses is the Statute of Frauds.

### Statute of Frauds

As you learned in Chapter 16, the Statute of Frauds was originally instituted in 1677 in England to prevent harm to innocent parties by requiring written evidence of agreements concerning important transactions. The British act was created specifically to prevent further perpetration of the many frauds caused by witnesses giving perjured testimony in cases involving breached oral agreements for which no written evidence existed.

The British courts, until the Statute of Frauds was passed, had enforced oral contracts on the strength of oral testimony by witnesses. It was not too difficult, therefore, to evade justice by alleging that a contract had been created and then breached by procuring "convincing" witnesses to support the claim. The possibility of fraud in such actions was enhanced by the fact that in seventeenth-century England, courts did not allow oral testimony to be given by the parties to a lawsuit—or by any parties with an interest in the litigation, such as husbands or wives. Defense against breach of contract actions was thus limited to written evidence or the testimony given by third parties.

Under the Statute of Frauds, if a contract is oral when it is required to be in writing, it will not, as a rule, be enforced by the courts. Since its inception over three hundred years ago, the statute has been heavily criticized. Critics attack the fact that although the statute was created to protect the innocent, it can also be used as a technical defense by a party breaching a genuine oral contract. Some legal scholars have suggested that the Statute of Frauds has actually caused more fraud than it has prevented. Because the statute limits the kinds of contracts that will be enforceable and because it is frequently used as a technical defense only, it generally renders commercial transactions more cumbersome.

But does this mean that the statute should be abandoned? In the interest of promoting commerce, many nations have

repealed similar statutes. Even England, the country that created the original Statute of Frauds, has repealed it. Following the lead of other nations, in 1988 the United States agreed (in the United Nations Convention on Contracts for the International Sale of Goods—see Chapter 20) that the Statute of Frauds would not apply to contracts between U.S. firms and firms in other nations. Nonetheless, it is still the law of the land for those doing business within U.S. borders. The retention of the statute in this country suggests that we are willing to accept the trade-off that it represents. Even though the statute may be used to perpetrate injustice and even though it encumbers commercial transactions, it also serves to protect innocent parties from being held to oral contracts that they did not in fact make.

Additionally, the statute accords with a basic ethical precept that pervades the common law of contracts—that individuals are expected to look after their own interests. Courts often stress that businesspersons who rely solely on oral promises, or the proverbial "handshake," do so at their own risk. The court emphasized this point in a case in which the plaintiff, Action Printing Company, sought to recover a debt from the defendant, Fred Beede. According to the manager and co-owner of Action Printing, Beede orally promised to pay personally for materials and services supplied by the printing company if his company was unable to meet

its obligations. Action Printing claimed that in reliance on this promise, it continued to supply services and materials to Beede's company.

When Action Printing sued Beede to recover the outstanding debt, Beede claimed, among other things, that the promise was unenforceable under the Statute of Frauds. Eventually, the case reached a Wisconsin appellate court, which held for Beede on the Statute of Frauds issue. The court concluded its opinion with the following statement: "We do not denigrate Action Printing for wishing to take a man at his word. We simply state that it is not the role of the courts to step in and remedy what reasonable caution might have prevented."[4]

### Promissory Estoppel

You learned in Chapter 13 that under the doctrine of promissory estoppel, a person who has reasonably relied on the promise of another can often obtain some measure of recovery. Ethical standards are certainly at issue here. It just does not seem fair that one party, in reliance on another's promise, should perform when the other party does not. As individuals, we face the problem of detrimental reliance all of the time.

Suppose, for example, that you are engaged in an important research project. Your roommate agrees to pick up a book that is being held

---

4. *Action Printing Co. v. Beede*, 170 Wis.2d 734, 492 N.W.2d 191 (1992).

for you at the library. You need it to finish your research report. Your roommate fails to pick up the book, and when you go to the library the next day to obtain it, you find that it has been released to another student and will not be returned until after your report is due. You relied on your roommate to your detriment. Had your roommate indicated that he or she would not be able to get the book, you would have gone yourself to ensure that you had it in time. In this particular situation, the doctrine of promissory estoppel would probably not allow you to recover anything from your roommate, except perhaps a statement of "I'm sorry."

In the business world, however, a person who relies to his or her detriment on the promise of another can often recover damages, particularly when justice is better served by estopping the other party from denying that a contractual promise was made. For example, in *Bower v. AT&T Technologies, Inc.,*[5] a number of AT&T repairpersons were laid off by AT&T when that company closed one of its Missouri plants to convert the plant into office space. AT&T promised the laid-off employees that as soon as the renovation of the plant building was completed, they would be rehired as clerical workers at a specified wage rate. AT&T also promised that the employees' seniority would be "bridged" and that their pension benefits would remain intact.

_____

5.  852 F.2d 361 (8th Cir. 1988).

For nearly five months, the workers continued to contact AT&T frequently and were always assured that as soon as AT&T began hiring clerical workers for the new plant, the laid-off employees would be notified. Relying on these assurances, the former employees refused other job offers and delayed their searches for other jobs. When the former employees learned that AT&T was hiring clerical workers and in fact did not intend to hire the laid-off workers for clerical positions in the new plant, the workers brought suit against AT&T for damages caused by their detrimental reliance on AT&T's promises. Although the trial court held for AT&T, the appellate court, on reviewing the issue, ruled that the employees had a right to recover damages sustained in their reliance on the "clear and unambiguous promise" that AT&T had made and broken.

## Quasi Contract

Quasi contracts, often referred to as contracts implied in law, arise to establish justice and fairness. The term *quasi contract* is misleading, because a quasi contract is not really a contract at all. It does not arise from any agreement between two individuals. Rather, a court imposes a quasi contract on the parties when justice requires it. Quasi contracts are used to prevent unjust enrichment. The doctrine of unjust enrichment is based on the theory that individuals should not be allowed to profit or enrich themselves inequitably at the expense of

others. This belief is fundamental in our society and is clearly inspired by ethical considerations.

A typical situation in which a court, as a matter of judicial policy, may impose a quasi contract on the parties arises when one person renders emergency services to another person without first entering into a contract. In these circumstances, courts generally allow the person who renders the emergency services to recover in quasi contract the reasonable fee for those services. This recovery is allowed irrespective of the fact that the parties never entered into a contract.

Obviously, by imposing contractual obligations on persons who did not freely enter into those obligations, the government, by way of the courts, is interfering with the personal freedom of individuals to contract as they wish and to be responsible for only those obligations they freely undertake. To a certain extent, when quasi-contractual remedies are granted, this freedom is sacrificed to attain greater justice and fairness by preventing the unjust enrichment of one person at the expense of others.

### ■ Discussion Questions

1.  Although minors have the power to avoid contracts, the adults with whom the minors contract do not. Because of this one-sided power, some observers have suggested that the law confers on minors a privilege and that it is thus inaccurate to speak of the

"limited" capacity of minors. But there is another side to consider. Adults often refuse to contract with minors because minors cannot provide legal assurance that they will not disaffirm. From this point of view, minors are under a legal and practical disability, and their right of disaffirmance may work against their own best interests. As is often the case, the protection of the law limits the liberty of the protected person. Is the price of this protection too high? Would governments best serve the interests of minors by granting them full freedom of contract?

Or should the law strike a different balance—perhaps by instituting a younger age of majority or permitting minors to avoid only those contracts that are not beneficial to them?

**2.** Suppose that you contract to purchase steel at a fixed price per ton. There is a lengthy steelworkers' strike, which causes the price of steel to triple from the price specified in the contract. If you demand that the supplier fulfill the contract, the supplier will go out of business. What are your ethical obligations in this situation? What are your legal rights?

**3.** People rely to their

detriment on others' promises in everyday life. Yet the doctrine of promissory estoppel is rarely, if ever, applied in these situations to enable the party who suffered a detriment to recover damages. Would society benefit if courts allowed all persons who suffered from detrimental reliance on others' promises to recover damages incurred by that reliance? If so, in what way? What would be the cost to society if such actions were permitted?

# UNIT THREE

# DOMESTIC AND INTERNATIONAL SALES LAW

## CONTENTS

**20** Introduction to Sales Contracts and Their Formation

**21** Title, Risk, and Insurable Interest

**22** Performance and Obligation

**23** Remedies of the Buyer and Seller for Breach

**24** Sales Warranties

**25** Product Liability

# CHAPTER 20

# INTRODUCTION TO SALES CONTRACTS AND THEIR FORMATION

**T**oday's law of sales originated centuries ago in the customs and traditions of merchants and traders. The *Lex Mercatoria* (Law Merchant) was a system of rules, customs, and usages self-imposed by early commercial traders and merchants to settle disputes and to enforce obligations among themselves. These rules were established at "fairs," at which merchants met to exchange goods and settle differences through "fair courts" established and operated by the merchants themselves.

By the end of the seventeenth century, the principles of the Law Merchant had become widely accepted. Quite naturally, they became part of the common law. From that time on, judges, not merchants, refined the principles of mercantile law into the modern commercial law of sales.

In the United States, sales law varied from state to state, and this made multistate sales contracts difficult. The difficulties became especially troublesome in the late nineteenth century as multistate contracts became the norm. For this reason, numerous attempts were made to produce a uniform body of laws relating to commercial transactions. Two major proposals, the Uniform Negotiable Instruments Law (1896) and the Uniform Sales Act (1906), were widely adopted by the states. Several other proposed "uniform acts" followed, although most were not widely adopted.

In the 1940s the need to integrate the half-dozen or so uniform acts covering commercial transactions into a single, comprehensive body of statutory law was recognized. Accordingly, the National Conference of Commissioners on Uniform State Laws developed the Uniform Commercial Code (UCC) to serve that purpose.

# THE UNIFORM COMMERCIAL CODE

It is important to note that when we focus on sales contracts, the subject of this chapter, we move away to some extent from common law principles and into a body of statutory law. The UCC is the statutory framework we will use, because it has been adopted as law by all states (with the exception of Louisiana, which has not adopted it in its entirety). Relevant sections of the UCC are noted in the following discussion of sales contracts. You should refer to Appendix C in the back of the book while examining these notations. Many similarities to the contract law discussed in Chapters 11 through 19 will be apparent. Indeed, such similarities should be expected, because the UCC represents the codification of much of the existing common law of contracts.

The UCC is the single most comprehensive codification of the broad spectrum of laws involved in a total commercial transaction. The UCC views the entire "commercial transaction for the sale of and payment for goods" as a single legal occurrence having numerous facets.

As an example, first look at the titles of the articles of the UCC in Appendix C. Now consider a consumer who buys a refrigerator from an appliance store and agrees to pay for it on an installment plan. Several articles of the UCC can be applied to this single commercial transaction. Because there is a contract for the sale of goods, Article 2 will apply. If a check is given as the down payment on the purchase price, it will be negotiated and ultimately passed through one or more banks for collection. This process is the subject matter of Article 3, Negotiable Instruments, and Article 4, Bank Deposits and Collections. If the appliance store extends credit to the consumer through the installment plan, and if it retains a right in the refrigerator (the collateral), then Article 9, Secured Transactions, will be applicable.

Suppose, in addition, the appliance company must first obtain the refrigerator from its manufacturer's warehouse, after which it is to be delivered by common carrier to the consumer. The storage and shipment of goods is the subject matter of Article 7, Documents of Title. If the appliance company arranges to pay the manufacturer, located in another state, for the refrigerator supplied, a letter of credit, which is the subject matter of Article 5, may be used. Thus, the UCC attempts to provide a consistent and integrated framework of rules to deal with all the phases *ordinarily arising* in a commercial sales transaction from start to finish.[1]

# THE SCOPE OF ARTICLE 2— THE SALE OF GOODS

No body of law operates in a vacuum removed from other principles of jurisprudence. A sales contract is governed by the same common law principles applicable to all contracts—offer, acceptance, consideration, capacity, and legality—and these principles should be reexamined when sales are studied. In regard to sales contracts, it is important to remember that when the UCC speaks, its principles will apply; when the UCC is silent on a given issue, then other state statutes and the common law of contracts will apply. The law of sales, found in Article 2 of the UCC, is a part of the law of contracts.

Two other things should be kept in mind. First, Article 2 deals with the sale of *goods,* not real property (real estate), services, or intangible property such as stocks and bonds. Second, in some cases, the rules may vary quite a bit, depending on whether the buyer or seller is a *merchant.* It is always a good idea to note the subject matter of a dispute and the kind of people involved. If the subject is goods, then the UCC will govern. If

---

1.   Two articles of the UCC seem not to apply to the "ordinary" commercial sales transaction. Article 6, Bulk Transfers, involves merchants who sell off the major part of their inventory (sometimes pocketing the money and disappearing, leaving creditors unpaid). Because bulk sales do not ordinarily arise in a commercial sales transaction, they are treated separately. Article 8, Investment Securities, deals with transactions involving certain negotiable securities (stocks and bonds), transactions that do not involve a sale of, or payment for, *goods.* The subject matter of Articles 6 and 8, however, was considered by the UCC's drafters to be related *sufficiently* to commercial transactions to warrant inclusion in the UCC.

it is real estate or services, then the common law will apply.

At present, a revision of Article 2, on sales transactions, is being drafted. Since its promulgation as part of the UCC over three decades ago, Article 2 has remained virtually unchanged. Yet business practices have not—electronic communications systems[2] and new forms of goods, such as computer software, have significantly changed commercial practices in regard to sales transactions. The revised Article 2 will clarify the law in regard to these new business practices.

## WHAT IS A SALE?

Section 2–102 of the UCC states that Article 2 "applies to transactions in goods." This implies a broad scope for this article, covering gifts, purchases of goods, and bailments. (A bailment involves delivery of personal property without title for a specific purpose, as when, for example, an individual drops off his or her clothes to be dry-cleaned. Bailments are discussed more fully in Chapter 50.) Article 2 is applicable only to an actual sale. A **sale** is officially defined "as the passing of *title* from the seller to the buyer for a *price*" [UCC 2–106(1), emphasis added]. The price may be payable in money or in other goods, services, or realty (real estate).

## WHAT ARE GOODS?

To be characterized as a *good,* an item must be *tangible,* and it must be *movable.* A tangible item has physical existence—it can be touched or seen, as can a horse, a car, or a chair. Intangible property, such as corporate stocks and bonds, promissory notes, bank accounts, patents and copyrights, and ordinary contract rights, have only conceptual existence and do not come under Article 2. A *movable* item can be carried from place to place. Hence, real estate is excluded from Article 2.

Two basic areas of dispute arise in determining whether the object of the contract is goods and thus whether Article 2 is applicable. One dispute concerns *goods associated with realty,* such as crops

and timber, and the other concerns contracts involving a combination of *goods and services.*

**GOODS VERSUS REALTY** Goods associated with real estate fall under Article 2. Section 2–107 provides the following rules:

1. A contract for the sale of minerals or the like (including oil and gas) or of a structure (such as a building) is a contract for the sale of goods *if severance, or removal, is to be made by the seller.* If the buyer is to sever the subject of the contract from the land, the contract is considered a sale of real estate governed by the principles of real property law, not the UCC.
2. A sale of growing crops or timber to be cut is a sale of goods *regardless of who severs them.*
3. Other "things attached" to realty but capable of severance without *material harm* to the land are considered goods regardless of who severs them.[3]

**GOODS VERSUS SERVICES** When goods and services are combined, courts have disagreed over whether a particular transaction involves the sale of goods or the rendering of a service. For example, is the blood furnished to a patient during an operation a sale of goods or the performance of a medical service? Some courts say a good; some say a service. The same kind of "mixed transaction" problem is encountered when a beautician applies hair dye to a customer in a beauty shop. The UCC does not provide the answer, and court decisions are in conflict. Whether the transaction in question involves the sale of goods or of services is important, because the majority of courts treat services as being excluded by the UCC. In discussing their decisions, the courts try to determine which factor is predominant—the good or the service.

The UCC states that the serving of food or drink to be consumed either on or off restaurant premises involves a sale of goods, at least for the purpose of an *implied warranty of merchantability*[4] [UCC

---

2. In *American Dredging Co. v. Plaza Petroleum Inc.,* 799 F.Supp. 1335 (E.D.N.Y. 1992), the court found that a telex "was a valid contract: it contains the names of the parties, the price, and quantity of goods to be sold and identifies that it is a contract for the sale of goods" [UCC 1–201(39)].

3. The UCC avoids using the term *fixtures* here because of the numerous definitions of the term. See Chapter 49.
4. Every merchant who deals in goods of the kind sold warrants that the goods are merchantable—that is, "reasonably fit for the ordinary purposes for which such goods are used." Implied warranties are examined in Chapter 24.

2–314(1)]. Also, a contract for specially manufactured goods is one for goods, not services [UCC 2–105(1)]. Several other types of sold items are explicitly characterized as goods by the UCC, including unborn animals and forms of money as a commodity (such as rare coins). In the following case, the key issue before the court was whether computer programs should be classified as goods or services.

---

**COMPANY PROFILE**  *In 1885, William Burroughs filed for a patent on an adding machine. To perfect his invention, he had worked day and night, at one point tossing fifty imperfect machines, one by one, out of a second-story window. With an eye towards selling adding machines to every bank in the United States, Burroughs founded the American Arithmometer Company in St. Louis, Missouri, in 1886. The company became the Burroughs Adding Machine Company and moved to Detroit, Michigan, in 1905. In 1953, the firm became the Burroughs Corporation and three years later entered the data-processing field by buying Electrodata. By the early 1980s, Burroughs was manufacturing and selling mainframe computers in competition with IBM, Inc. Another IBM competitor was Sperry Corporation. Sperry had begun as the result of a merger in 1955 of Sperry Gyroscope, an electronics company founded in 1910, and Remington Rand, a typewriter manufacturer and maker of the first commercially viable computer, the UNIVAC. In 1986, Burroughs and Sperry merged (in a take-over of Sperry by Burroughs) to become Unisys Corporation.*

CASE 20.1

**ADVENT SYSTEMS, LTD. v. UNISYS CORP.**

United States Court of Appeals, Third Circuit, 1991. 925 F.2d 670.

**BACKGROUND AND FACTS**  *Advent Systems, Ltd., a software producer, developed an electronic document management system through which engineering drawings and similar documents could be transformed into a computer database. In June 1987, Unisys Corporation agreed with Advent to market the document system in the United States. The agreement, which was to continue for two years, provided that Advent would supply sales and marketing material and personnel, as well as technical personnel to work with Unisys employees in building and installing the document systems. In December 1987, Unisys changed its plans and told Advent that their arrangement had ended. Advent filed a complaint against Unisys, alleging, among other things, breach of contract. As part of its defense, Unisys contended that the agreement involved primarily a sale of goods. Advent argued that software is not a good and that thus the contract was primarily one for services. The trial court agreed with Advent on this issue. Because the court found for Unisys on another issue, both parties appealed.*

*WEIS,* Circuit Judge.
\*  \*  \*  \*

Computer programs are the product of an intellectual process, but once implanted in a medium are widely distributed to computer owners. An analogy can be drawn to a compact disc recording of an orchestral rendition. The music is produced by the artistry of musicians and in itself is not a ''good,'' but when transferred to a laser-readable disc becomes a readily merchantable commodity. \*  \*  \*

That a computer program may be copyrightable as intellectual property does not alter the fact that once in the form of a floppy disc or other medium, the program is tangible, moveable and available in the marketplace. \*  \*  \*
\*  \*  \*  \*

Applying the U.C.C. to computer software transactions offers substantial benefits to litigants and the courts. *   *   *

The importance of software to the commercial world *   *   * [is a] strong policy [argument] favoring inclusion. *   *   * [W]e hold that software is a "good" within the definition in the Code.

**DECISION AND REMEDY**  *The appellate court ruled that software was a "good" within the meaning of the UCC. The judgment in favor of Advent was reversed, and the case was remanded for a new trial.*

## WHO IS A MERCHANT?

Article 2 governs the sale of goods in general. It applies to sales transactions between all buyers and sellers. In a limited number of instances, however, the UCC presumes that in certain phases of sales transactions involving professional merchants, special business standards ought to be imposed because of the merchants' degree of commercial expertise.[5] Such standards do not apply to the casual or inexperienced seller or buyer. Section 2–104 defines three ways in which merchant status can be determined:

1. A merchant is a person who *deals in goods of the kind* involved in the sales contract. Thus, a retailer, a wholesaler, or a manufacturer is a merchant of those goods sold in the business. A merchant for one type of goods is not necessarily a merchant for any other type. For example, a sporting equipment retailer is a

merchant when buying tennis equipment but not when buying stereo equipment.

2. A merchant is a person who, by occupation, *holds himself or herself out as having knowledge and skill peculiar to the practices or goods involved in the transaction.* This is a broad definition that can include banks or universities as merchants.

3. A person who *employs a merchant as a broker, agent, or other intermediary* has the status of merchant in that transaction. Hence, if a "gentleman farmer" who ordinarily does not run the farm hires a broker to purchase livestock, the farmer is considered a merchant in the livestock transaction.

In summary, a person is a merchant when that person, acting in a mercantile capacity, possesses or uses an expertise specifically related to the goods being sold. This basic distinction, however, is not always clear-cut. For example, disagreement has arisen over whether a farmer is a merchant. The answer depends on the particular goods involved; the transaction; and whether, in the particular situation, the farmer has special knowledge concerning the goods involved in the transaction. The following case is illustrative.

---

5. The provisions that apply only to merchants deal principally with the Statute of Frauds, firm offers, confirmatory memoranda, warranties, and contract modification. These special rules reflect expedient business practices commonly known to merchants in the commercial setting. They will be discussed later in this chapter.

---

| CASE 20.2 | **BACKGROUND AND FACTS**  *Albert Reifschneider was raised on a farm and had been in the business of selling corn and in the business of* |
| --- | --- |
| **COLORADO-KANSAS GRAIN CO. v. REIFSCHNEIDER** Colorado Court of Appeals, 1991. 817 P.2d 637. | *selling other crops under futures contracts (contracts for goods to be harvested in the future) for twenty years. In April 1988, Reifschneider orally agreed to sell 12,500 bushels of corn to Colorado-Kansas Grain Company after the harvest in the fall. The company sent Reifschneider a written confirmation of the agreement with instructions to sign it and return it. In June, Reifschneider told the company that he would not sign the confirmation and that no contract existed between the parties. The company demanded that Reifschneider deliver the corn, but the demand was to* |

*no avail. The company sued Reifschneider for breach of contract. The trial court held for the company, based in part on the court's conclusion that Reifschneider was a "merchant" within the meaning of the UCC. Reifschneider appealed.*

Opinion by Judge *JONES.*
    \*　\*　\*　\*

The courts among those states which have dealt with this issue are almost evenly split on whether a farmer can be a merchant. \*　\*　\*
    \*　\*　\*　\*

In considering the question at issue, we note that the cases which hold that farmers may be merchants reflect on the fact that today's farmer is involved in far more than simply planting and harvesting crops. Indeed, many farmers possess an extensive knowledge and sophistication regarding the purchase and sale of crops on the various agricultural markets. Often, they are more aptly described as agri-businessmen.

Thus, we conclude that \*　\*　\* a farmer may be a merchant.
    \*　\*　\*　\*

Still remaining, however, is the question of whether defendant was a merchant. \*　\*　\*
    \*　\*　\*　\*

Here, defendant's twenty years of experience in selling corn establishes that he is a "person who deals in goods of the kind." Moreover, defendant's extensive experience in selling corn, when coupled with his familiarity with futures contracts, supports the trial court's determination that he "by his occupation [held] himself out as having knowledge or skill peculiar to the practices or goods involved in the transaction."

*The appellate court affirmed the trial court's decision that Reifschneider was a merchant.*　　**DECISION AND REMEDY**

---

## SECTION 3

# THE FORMATION OF A SALES CONTRACT

The policy of the UCC is to recognize that the law of sales is part of the general law of contracts. The UCC often restates general principles or is silent on certain subjects. In those situations, the common law of contracts and applicable state statutes govern. The following sections summarize how UCC provisions *change* the effect of the general law of contracts.

## OFFER

In general contract law, the moment a definite offer is met by an unqualified acceptance, a binding contract is formed. In commercial sales transactions, the verbal exchanges, the correspondence, and the actions of the parties may not reveal exactly when a binding contractual obligation arises. The UCC states that an agreement sufficient to constitute a contract can exist even if the moment of its making is undetermined [UCC 2–204(2)].

**OPEN TERMS**　According to contract law, an offer must be definite enough for the parties (and the courts) to ascertain its essential terms when it is accepted. The UCC states that a sales contract will not fail for indefiniteness even if one or more terms are left open, as long as (1) the parties intended to make a contract and (2) there is a reasonably certain basis for the court to grant an appropriate remedy [UCC 2–204(3)].

The UCC has lessened the requirements for definiteness of essentials in contracts for sale, but it has not removed the common law requirement that the contract be at least definite enough for the court to identify the agreement so as to enforce it or award appropriate damages on its breach. Two factors should be kept in mind. First, the more terms that are left open, the less likely the courts will find that the parties intended to form a contract. Second, as a general rule, if the *quantity* term is left open, the courts will have no basis for determining a remedy, and the sales contract will fail unless it is either an output or a requirements contract [UCC 2–306]. (Output and requirements contracts will be discussed shortly.) The quantity need not be accurately stated, but a contract will not be enforced beyond the amount stated in the writing.

*Open Price Term.*   If the parties have not agreed on a price, the court will determine ''a reasonable price *at the time for delivery*'' [UCC 2–305(1)]. If either the buyer or the seller is to determine the price, the price is to be fixed in good faith [UCC 2–305(2)].

Sometimes the price fails to be fixed through the fault of one of the parties. In that case, the other party can treat the contract as canceled or fix a reasonable price. For example, Axel and Beatty enter into a contract for the sale of goods and agree that Axel will fix the price. Axel, however, refuses to fix the price. Beatty can either treat the contract as canceled or can set a reasonable price [UCC 2–305(3)].

*Open Payment Term.*   When parties do not specify payment terms, payment is due at the time and place at which the buyer is to receive the goods [UCC 2–310(a)]. Generally, credit is not used when payment terms are unspecified. The buyer can tender payment in cash or a commercially acceptable substitute, such as a check or a credit card. If the seller demands payment in actual cash, the buyer must be given a reasonable time to obtain it [UCC 2–511(2)]. This is especially important when a definite and final time for performance is stated in the contract.

*Open Delivery Term.*   When no delivery terms are specified, the buyer normally takes delivery at the seller's place of business [UCC 2–308(a)]. If the seller has no place of business, then the seller's residence is used. When goods are located in some other place and both parties know it, then delivery is made there. When the time for shipment or delivery has not been clearly specified in the sales contract, the court will infer a ''reasonable'' time under the circumstances for performance [UCC 2–309(1)].

*Duration of an Ongoing Contract.*   A single contract may specify successive performances but may not indicate how long the parties are required to deal with each other. Although either party may terminate the ongoing contractual relationship, principles of good faith and sound commercial practice call for reasonable notification before termination so as to give the other party reasonable time to seek a substitute arrangement [UCC 2–309(2), (3)].

*Options and Cooperation Regarding Performance.*   When no specific shipping arrangements have been made but the contract contemplates shipment of the goods, the *seller* has the right to make these arrangements in good faith, using commercial reasonableness in the situation [UCC 2–311]. (The obligations of good faith and commercial reasonableness in sales contracts will be discussed in detail in Chapter 22.)

When terms relating to the assortment of goods are omitted from a sales contract, the *buyer* can specify the assortment. For example, Harley and Babcock contract for the sale of one thousand pens. The pens come in a variety of colors, but the contract is silent on which colors are ordered. Babcock, the buyer, has the right to take whatever colors he wishes. Babcock, however, must make the selection in good faith and must use commercial reasonableness [UCC 2–311].

### REQUIREMENTS AND OUTPUT CONTRACTS

In a **requirements contract,** the buyer agrees to purchase and the seller agrees to sell all or up to a stated amount of what the buyer *needs* or *requires.* There is implicit consideration in a requirements contract, for the buyer gives up the right to buy from any other seller, and this forfeited right creates a legal detriment. Requirements contracts are common in the business world and are normally enforceable. If, however, the buyer promises to purchase only if the buyer *wishes* to do so, or if the buyer reserves the right to buy the goods from someone other than the seller, the promise is illusory (without consideration), and the promise is unenforceable by either party.

In an **output contract,** the seller agrees to sell and the buyer agrees to buy all or up to a stated amount of what the seller *produces.* Again, because the seller essentially forfeits the right to sell goods to another buyer, there is implicit consideration in an output contract.

The UCC imposes a *good faith limitation* on requirements and output contracts. The quantity under such contracts is the amount of requirements or the amount of output that occurs during a *normal* production year. The actual quantity purchased or sold cannot be unreasonably disproportionate to normal or comparable prior requirements or output [UCC 2–306].

**MERCHANT'S FIRM OFFER** Under common law contract principles, an offer can be revoked any time before acceptance. The major common law exception is an option contract, in which the offeree pays consideration for the offeror's irrevocable promise to keep the offer open for a stated period of time. The UCC creates a second exception that applies only to **firm offers** for the sale of goods made *by a merchant* (regardless of whether or not the offeree is a merchant). If the merchant gives *assurances* in a *signed writing* that the offer will remain open, the merchant's firm offer is irrevocable, without consideration[6] for the stated period of time, or if no definite period is specified, for a reasonable period (neither period to exceed three months) [UCC 2–205].

When a firm offer is contained in a form contract prepared by the offeree, a *separate* firm offer assurance must be signed as well. The purpose of the merchant's firm offer rule is to give effect to a merchant's deliberate intent to be bound to a firm offer. If the firm offer is buried in one of the pages of the offeree's form contract, the offeror might inadvertently sign the contract without realizing that the firm offer is included, thus defeating the purpose of the rule.

## ACCEPTANCE

Generally, acceptance of an offer to buy or sell goods may be made in any reasonable manner and by any reasonable means. If the response indicates a definite acceptance of the offer, a contract is formed, even if the response includes additional or different terms—so long as acceptance is not made expressly conditional on the offeror's assent to the new terms. An offeree's additional terms are considered proposals, and the contract is formed on

the offeror's terms, unless the parties are both merchants. These points are examined in the following sections.

**MEANS OF ACCEPTANCE** The general common law rule is that an offeror can specify or authorize a particular means of acceptance, making that means the only one effective for the contract. The common law rule has been altered recently, however, so that even unauthorized means of communication are effective as long as the acceptance is received by the specified deadline. For example, suppose the offer states, "Answer by fax within five days." If the offeree sends a letter, and it is received by the offeror within five days, a valid contract is formed.

When the offeror does not specify a means of acceptance, the UCC provides that acceptance can be made by any means of communication reasonable under the circumstances [UCC 2–206(1)(a)]. For example, Alpha Corporation writes Beta Corporation a letter offering to sell Beta $1,000 worth of goods. The offer states that Alpha will keep the offer open for only ten days from the date of the letter. Three days before the end of the ten-day period, Beta sends Alpha an acceptance, via an express-delivery courier, to be delivered to Alpha the next morning before 10:30 A.M. If the courier misplaces the packet and the acceptance does not reach Alpha until after the deadline, is a valid contract formed? The answer is yes, because express delivery appears to be a commercially reasonable medium of acceptance under the circumstances. Acceptance would be effective upon Beta's delivery of the message to the courier, which occurred before the offer lapsed.

**PROMISE TO SHIP OR PROMPT SHIPMENT** The UCC permits acceptance of an offer to buy goods for current or prompt shipment by either a *promise* to ship or *prompt shipment* of the goods to the buyer [UCC 2–206(1)(b)]. This provision of the UCC retains the common law means of acceptance of an offer (performance by delivery of conforming goods—that is, goods that are in accordance with the contract terms—to the carrier) and adds as another means of acceptance the commercial practice of sellers who send promises to ship conforming goods. These promises are effective when sent, if they meet the test of being sent by a medium that is commercially reasonable under the circumstances, as discussed above.

---

6. If the offeree pays consideration, then an *option contract* rather than a *merchant's firm offer* is formed.

The UCC goes one step further and provides that if the seller does not promise to ship conforming goods but instead ships (in response to the order) *nonconforming goods,* this shipment constitutes both an *acceptance* and a *breach.* This rule does not apply if the seller seasonably (within the time agreed on or within a reasonable time) notifies the buyer that the nonconforming shipment is offered only as an *accommodation.* The notice of accommodation must clearly indicate to the buyer that the shipment does not constitute an acceptance.

For example, Barrymore orders one thousand *blue* widgets from Stroh. Stroh ships one thousand *black* widgets to Barrymore, notifying Barrymore that because Stroh has only black widgets in stock, these are sent as an accommodation. The shipment of black widgets is not an acceptance but a counteroffer, and a contract will be formed only if Barrymore accepts the black widgets.

If, however, Stroh ships one thousand black widgets instead of blue without notifying Barrymore that the goods are being shipped *as an accommodation,* Stroh's shipment acts as both an acceptance of Barrymore's offer and a *breach* of the resulting contract. Barrymore may sue Stroh for any appropriate damages.

**COMMUNICATION OF ACCEPTANCE**   At common law, because a unilateral offer invites acceptance by a performance, the offeree need not notify the offeror of performance unless the offeror would not otherwise know about it. The UCC is more stringent than common law, stating that "[w]here the beginning of requested performance is a reasonable mode of acceptance an offeror who is not notified of acceptance within a reasonable time may treat the offer as having lapsed before acceptance" [UCC 2–206(2)].

To illustrate: On Monday, Johnson writes the Scroll Bookstore, "Please send me a copy of *West's Business Law* for $65, C.O.D.," signed "Johnson." Scroll receives the request on Tuesday. Scroll immediately prepares the book for shipment but does not ship it for four weeks. Upon its arrival, Johnson rejects the shipment, claiming that the book has arrived too late to be of value. In this case, because Johnson heard nothing from Scroll for a month, he was justified in assuming that the offer had lapsed.

**ADDITIONAL TERMS**   Under traditional common law, if Yakim makes an offer to Patrick, and Patrick in turn accepts but adds some slight qualification, there is no contract. This is known as the *mirror image rule* and requires that the acceptance exactly mirror the offer (see Chapter 12). Under this rule, Patrick's action would constitute a rejection of, and a counteroffer to, Yakim's offer.

The UCC generally takes the position that if the offeree's response indicates a *definite* acceptance of the offer, a contract is formed, even if the acceptance includes terms in addition to, or different from, the original offer [UCC 2–207(1)]. The UCC, however, provides that the offeree's expression cannot be construed as an acceptance if the modifications are subject to (conditional on) the offeror's assent.

For example, Trevor offers to sell Pentara five hundred pounds of chicken breasts at a specified price and on specified delivery terms. Pentara responds, "I accept your offer for five hundred pounds of chicken breasts, and I want that evidenced by a city scale weight certificate." Pentara's response constitutes a contract. If, however, Pentara says, "I accept your offer on the condition that the weight be evidenced by a city scale weight certificate," there will be no contract unless Trevor so agrees. The following case illustrates this point.

---

| CASE 20.3 | **BACKGROUND AND FACTS**   *The Providence & Worcester Railroad* |
| :--- | :--- |

**PROVIDENCE & WORCESTER RAILROAD CO. v. SARGENT & GREENLEAF, INC.**

United States District Court, District of Rhode Island, 1992.
802 F.Supp. 680.

*Company (P&W), by a printed form purchase order dated November 1986, purchased 198 switchlocks from Sargent & Greenleaf, Inc. (S&G). The front side of S&G's acknowledgment form contained the printed words "acceptance subject to terms and revisions on reverse side." On the reverse side, listed under the title "CONDITIONS GOVERNING THE ACCEPTANCE OF ALL ORDERS," were a number of provisions, including one disclaiming all warranties and limiting the buyer's remedies to the repair, replacement, or repayment of the purchase price of defective goods. In 1990, a vandal picked one of the S&G locks in less than two minutes* *and "threw" the switch secured by it, which resulted in the derailment of a freight train the next day. Although no persons were injured, the derailment caused nearly $1 million in property damage. In making the initial decision to purchase the S&G switchlocks, P&W had relied on statements made in various S&G advertising materials, including a statement that even after ten thousand operating cycles, an S&G switchlock could not be picked by an amateur in less than four minutes. P&W sued S&G for, among other things, breach of the express warranties made by S&G in its advertising materials. S&G claimed that it was not liable because it had specifically disclaimed all warranties on its acceptance (acknowledgment form).*

*LAGUEUX,* District Judge.

    \*   \*   \*   \*

    \*   \*   \* Under [UCC] 2–207(1), a form acknowledgement is ordinarily considered an acceptance of the order, even if it states different or additional terms. \*   \*   \*

    However, [UCC] 2–207(1) provides an exception to the acceptance rule where "acceptance is expressly made conditional on assent to the additional or different terms." \*   \*   \*

    \*   \*   \*   \*

    \*   \*   \* Sargent & Greenleaf's acknowledgement and invoice forms conditioned its participation in the agreement on Providence & Worcester's acceptance of those terms. Stated succinctly, Sargent & Greenleaf's response to Providence & Worcester's order became a counteroffer. Providence & Worcester had the opportunity to accept or reject this counteroffer or make its own counteroffer. Providence & Worcester chose to accept Sargent & Greenleaf's counteroffer by accepting the locks, paying for the locks and using the locks without objection to the additional terms. Performance of the contract became the acceptance. Thus, the warranty disclaimers, remedy limitations and [other provisions] became part of the contract \*   \*   \* .

    \*   \*   \*   \*

    Sargent & Greenleaf argues that \*   \*   \* Providence & Worcester's recovery is limited by the contractual provision stating: Seller shall not be liable for special, indirect, incidental or consequential damages. Seller's liability and Buyer's exclusive remedy is expressly limited, at Seller's option, to repair of defective goods or the replacement thereof with conforming goods . . . or the repayment of the purchase price. \*   \*   \*

    \*   \*   \* In the context of this transaction such a limitation is perfectly fair and equitable. \*   \*   \*

**DECISION AND REMEDY** *The court held that S&G's form, because it expressly conditioned its acceptance on the offeror's agreement to its terms, was not an acceptance but a counteroffer. P&W's recovery was limited to repair, replacement, or repayment of the purchase price of the lock that failed.*

**INTERNATIONAL CONSIDERATIONS** **Acceptance in International Contracts** *The United Nations Convention on Contracts for the International Sale of Goods (CISG) rejected the approach of UCC 2–207 and opted for a rule that is closer to the mirror image rule required under the common law. The CISG does permit an effective acceptance to contain additional terms but only insignificant terms that do not alter the terms of the offer. Any significant new terms would transform an acceptance into a counteroffer under the rules of the CISG. (See the discussion of the CISG later in this chapter.)*

*The "Battle of the Forms."* Once it has been determined that a contract exists, the next issue to be determined is whether performance will be measured under the offeror's terms or the offeree's terms (which include modifications). The UCC addresses this issue in an attempt to solve the so-called battle of the forms between commercial buyers and sellers. *Battle of the forms* is an informal term describing the effect of buyers' and sellers' use of standard purchase or sales forms. If the buyer, for example, uses its standard purchase form to accept an offer contained in the seller's form, the variance in the terms of the two forms results in the problem of determining whose terms form the contract [see UCC 2–207(2)].

Exhibit 20–1 is an example of a purchase order. The front of the form is the actual order for particular goods. The back contains standard contract clauses and terms governing the sale. These clauses are sometimes modified to meet a particular purchase requirement. The clauses will have even more meaning as you read the following materials on sales.

### Rules When the Seller or the Buyer Is a Non-merchant.

When either the seller or the buyer is a nonmerchant, or when both are nonmerchants, the additional terms are construed as mere proposals, and do not become part of the contract. Thus, the contract is formed on the offeror's terms [UCC 2–207(2)].

For example, O'Hare offers to sell his *personal* car to Golachev for $1,000. Golachev replies, "I accept your offer to purchase your car for $1,000. I would like a new spare tire to be included as part of the purchase price." Golachev has given O'Hare a definite expression of acceptance, creating a contract, even though Golachev's acceptance also suggests an added term for the offer. Because O'Hare is not a merchant, the additional term is merely a proposal, and O'Hare is not legally obligated to comply. In contrast, if Golachev made the spare tire a *condition* of acceptance, then Golachev would be making a counteroffer and rejecting the original offer.

### Rules between Merchants.

The UCC rule for additional terms in the acceptance is a little different when both buyer and seller are merchants. In a transaction between merchants, the additional proposed terms *automatically* become part of the contract unless

1. They materially alter the original contract.
2. The offer expressly states that no terms other than those in the offer will be accepted.
3. The offeror objects to the modified terms in a timely fashion [UCC 2–207(2)].

Suppose Vinson and Brady are merchants. Vinson offers to sell Brady one thousand pen-and-pencil sets at $10 per set *plus* freight. Brady responds, "I accept your offer. Price is $10.01 per set, *including* freight." There is a contract between Vinson and Brady, because Brady made a definite expression of acceptance. Unless Vinson objects to the modification within a reasonable time after receiving notice of the change, Vinson is bound to the $10.01 price per set, including freight. Such is not the case, however, if the modification is one that materially alters the contract. What constitutes a material alteration is frequently a question of fact that only a court can decide. Generally, if the modification involves no unreasonable element of surprise or hardship for the offeror, the court will hold that the modification did not materially alter the contract.

Now suppose that Vinson's offer states, "One thousand pen-and-pencil sets at a price of $10 per set plus freight. Your acceptance on these terms and these terms only." Brady's definite expression of acceptance with the modified freight terms still constitutes a contract. Because Vinson's offer specifically restricts his obligations to the terms of the offer, however, the contract is formed on Vinson's terms of "$10 per set plus freight."

## CONSIDERATION

The UCC radically changes the common law rule that contract modification must be supported by new consideration. Section 2–209(1) states that "an agreement modifying a contract needs no consideration to be binding." Of course, contract modification must be sought in good faith [UCC 1–203]. Modifications *extorted* from the other party are in bad faith and therefore unenforceable.

For example, Hal agrees to manufacture certain goods and sell them to Betty for a stated price. Subsequently, a sudden shift in the market makes it difficult for Hal to sell the items to Betty at the given price without suffering a loss. Hal tells Betty

## Exhibit 20–1 An Example of a Purchase Order (Front)

IBM

**Purchase Order**

NUMBER DATE

IBM DATA

| SUPPLIER | MACH | U/M | OC | SUC | PP | REC | EXP | COMMODITY | MM | DEPT. ORDER | ALT | JOB NO. | DEPT. CHG. | APPROP. | CC | PR ORIG. | CHG. RN |
|---|---|---|---|---|---|---|---|---|---|---|---|---|---|---|---|---|---|

| REC. NO. | B.J. S.O. OR REF. NO. | ACCOUNT NO. | COMMITMENT |
|---|---|---|---|

REMIT TO→

NOTIFY BUYER IMMEDIATELY IF REMIT TO ADDRESS IS DIFFERENT ON INVOICE.

SHIP TO: IBM 11400 BURNET ROAD AUSTIN, TEXAS 78758 BLDG.

OTHER THAN ABOVE

CODE | TAXES
DO NOT CHARGE TEXAS SALES USE TAX SINCE WE PAY DIRECT
OUR DIRECT PAY AUTHORIZATION NUMBER IS:
3-000001-7281-4

SPECIFICATION CODE
1. Print Attached.
2. Specifications Attached.
3. Sample Attached.
4. Print in Your Possession.
5. Specification in Your Possession.
6. Sample in Your Possession.

SEE CODE BELOW | SHIP VIA | IBM DATA | F.O.B. SHIP POINT | DESTINATION | IBM DATA | YOUR TERMS OF PAYMENT

TRANSPORTATION ROUTING GUIDELINES
*(DO NOT INSURE OR DECLARE VALUE)*

0-99 (45kg.) United Parcel Service, if available. If not,
0-40 (18kg.) Parcel Post *(Zones 1-8)* up to $1000 value.
All other Ship as indicated in "ship via" block.

IMPORTANT
1. SHOW OUR COMPLETE ORDER NUMBER, ITEM NUMBER AND IBM PART NUMBER (IF ANY) ON ALL INVOICES, SHIPPING CONTAINERS, PACKING LISTS AND CORRESPONDENCE.
2. SECURELY ATTACH PACKING SLIP TO OUTSIDE OF CARTON.
3. PACKAGES WEIGHING OVER 75 LBS MUST BE PACKAGED FOR HANDLING WITH A MECHANICAL DEVICE.

| ITEM | PART NUMBER | | E/C LEVEL | SHIP TO ARRIVE | QUANTITY | U/M | UNIT PRICE | U/M |
|---|---|---|---|---|---|---|---|---|
| | | | | | | | | |

*TOTAL QUANTITY OF ITEM ORDERED

**"SUBJECT TO THE TERMS AND CONDITIONS ON THE BACK HEREOF WHICH ARE INCORPORATED AND MADE A PART HEREOF"**

ADDRESS ALL INVOICES TO:
INTERNATIONAL BUSINESS MACHINES CORP.
Attn: Accounts Payable
P. O. Box 9928
Austin, Texas 78766

AUTHORIZED SIGNATURE 512-838-3300 EXT.

942-0262-4

■ **Exhibit 20–1 (Continued) An Example of a Purchase Order (Back)**

## STANDARD TERMS AND CONDITIONS

IBM EXPRESSLY LIMITS ACCEPTANCE TO THE TERMS SET FORTH ON THE FACE AND REVERSE SIDE OF THIS PURCHASE ORDER AND ANY ATTACHMENTS HERETO:

**PURCHASE ORDER CONSTITUTES COMPLETE AGREEMENT**
This Purchase order, including the terms and conditions on the face and reverse side hereof and any attachments hereto, contains the complete and final agreement between International Business Machines Corporation (IBM) and Seller. Reference to Seller's bids or proposals, if noted on this order, shall not affect terms and conditions hereof, unless specifically provided to the contrary herein, and no other agreement or quotation in any way modifying any of said terms and conditions will be binding upon IBM unless made in writing and signed by IBM's authorized representative.

**ADVERTISING**
Seller shall not, without first obtaining the written consent of IBM, in any manner advertise, publish or otherwise disclose the fact that Seller has furnished, or contracted to furnish to IBM, the material and/or services ordered hereunder.

**APPLICABLE LAW**
The agreement arising pursuant to this order shall be governed by the laws of the State of New York. No rights, remedies and warranties available to IBM under this contract or by operation of law are waived or modified unless expressly waived or modified by IBM in writing.

**CASH DISCOUNT OR NET PAYMENT PERIOD**
Calculations will be from the date an acceptable invoice is received by IBM. Any other arrangements agreed upon must appear on this order and on the invoice.

**CONFIDENTIAL INFORMATION**
Seller shall not disclose to any person outside of its employ, or use for any purpose other than to fulfill its obligations under this order, any information received from IBM pursuant to this order, which has been disclosed to Seller by IBM in confidence, except such information which is otherwise publicly available or is publicly disclosed by IBM subsequent to Seller's receipt of such information or is rightfully received by Seller from a third party. Upon termination of this order, Seller shall return to IBM upon request all drawings, blueprints, descriptions or other material received from IBM and all materials containing said confidential information. Also, Seller shall not disclose to IBM any information which Seller deems to be confidential, and it is understood that any information received by IBM, including all manuals, drawings and documents will not be of a confidential nature or restrict, in any manner, the use of such information by IBM. Seller agrees that any legend or other notice on any information supplied by Seller, which is inconsistent with the provisions of this article, does not create any obligation on the part of IBM.

**GIFTS**
Seller shall not make or offer gifts or gratuities of any type to IBM employees or members of their families. Such gifts or offerings may be construed as Seller's attempt to improperly influence our relationship.

**IBM PARTS**
All parts and components bailed by IBM to Seller for incorporation in work being performed for IBM shall be used solely for such purposes.

**OFF-SPECIFICATION**
Seller shall obtain from IBM written approval of all off-specification work.

**PACKAGES**
Packages must bear IBM's order number and show gross, tare and net weights and/or quantity.

**PATENTS**
Seller will settle or defend, at Seller's expense (and pay any damages, costs or fines resulting from), all proceedings or claims against IBM, its subsidiaries and affiliates and their respective customers, for infringement, or alleged infringement, by the goods furnished under this order, or any part or use thereof of patents (including utility models and registered designs) now or hereafter granted in the United States or in any country where Seller, its subsidiaries or affiliates, heretofore has furnished similar goods. Seller will, at IBM's request, identify the countries in which Seller, its subsidiaries or affiliates, heretofore has furnished similar goods.

**PRICE**
If price is not stated on this order, Seller shall invoice at lowest prevailing market price.

**QUALITY**
Material is subject to IBM's inspection and approval within a reasonable time after delivery. If specifications are not met, material may be returned at Seller's expense and risk for all damages incidental to the rejection. Payment shall not constitute an acceptance of the material nor impair IBM's right to inspect or any of its remedies.

**SHIPMENT**
Shipment must be made within the time stated on this order, failing which IBM reserves the right to purchase elsewhere and charges Seller with any loss incurred, unless delay in making shipment is due to unforeseeable causes beyond the control and without the fault or negligence of Seller.

**SUBCONTRACTS**
Seller shall not subcontract or delegate its obligations under this order without the written consent of IBM. Purchases of parts and materials normally purchased by Seller or required by this order shall not be construed as subcontracts or delegations.

**(NON-U.S. LOCATIONS ONLY)**
Seller further agrees that during the process of bidding or production of goods and services hereunder, it will not re-export or divert to others any IBM specification, drawing or other data, or any product of such data.

**TAXES**
Unless otherwise directed, Seller shall pay all sales and use taxes imposed by law upon or on account of this order. Where appropriate, IBM will reimburse Seller for this expense.

**TOOLS**
IBM owned tools held by Seller are to be used only for making parts for IBM. Tools of any kind held by Seller for making IBM's parts must be repaired and renewed by Seller at Seller's expense.

**TRANSPORTATION**
Routing—As indicated in transportation routing guidelines on face of this order.
F.O.B.—Unless otherwise specified, ship collect, F.O.B. origin.
Prepaid Transportation (when specified)—Charges must be supported by a paid freight bill or equivalent.
Cartage ) No charge allowed
Premium Transportation ) unless authorized
Insurance ) by IBM.
Consolidation—Unless otherwise instructed, consolidate all daily shipments to one destination on one bill of lading.

**COMPLIANCE WITH LAWS AND REGULATIONS**
Seller shall at all times comply with all applicable Federal, State and local laws, rules and regulations.

**EQUAL EMPLOYMENT OPPORTUNITY**
There are incorporated in this order the provisions of Executive Order 11246 (as amended) of the President of the United States on Equal Employment Opportunity and the rules and regulations issued pursuant thereto with which the Seller represents that he will comply, unless exempt.

**EMPLOYMENT AND PROCUREMENT PROGRAMS**
There are incorporated in this order the following provisions as they apply to performing work under Government procurement contracts: Utilization of Small Business Concerns (if in excess of $10,000) (Federal Procurement Regulation (FPR) 1-1.710-3(a)); Small Business Subcontracting Program (if in excess of $500,000) (FPR 1-1.710-3 (b)); Utilization of Labor Surplus Area Concerns (if in excess of $10,000) (FPR 1-1.805-3(a)); Labor Surplus Area Subcontracting Program (if in excess of $500,000) (FPR 1-1.805-3 (b)); Utilization of Minority Enterprises (if in excess of $10,000) (FPR 1-1.1310-2 (a)); Minority Business Enterprises Subcontracting Program (if in excess of $50,000) (FPR 1-1.1310-2(b)); Affirmative Action for Handicapped Workers (if $2,500 or more) (41 CFR 60-741.4); Affirmative Action for Disabled Veterans and Veterans of the Vietnam Era (if $10,000 or more) (41 CFR 60-250.4); Utilization of Small Business Concerns and Small Business Concerns Owned and Controlled by Socially and Economically Disadvantaged Individuals (if in excess of $10,000) (44 Fed. Reg. 23610 (April 20, 1979)); Small Business and Small Disadvantaged Business Subcontracting Plan (if in excess of $500,000) (44 Fed. Reg. 23610 (April 20, 1979)).

**WAGES AND HOURS**
Seller warrants that in the performance of this order Seller has complied with all of the provisions of the Fair Labor Standards Act of 1938 of the United States as amended.

**WORKERS' COMPENSATION, EMPLOYERS' LIABILITY INSURANCE**
If Seller does not have Workers' Compensation or Employer's Liability Insurance, Seller shall indemnify IBM against all damages sustained by IBM resulting from Seller's failure to have such insurance.

of the situation, and Betty agrees to pay an additional sum for the goods. Later, Betty reconsiders and refuses to pay more than the original price. Under Section 2–209(1) of the UCC, Betty's promise to modify the contract needs no consideration to be binding. Hence, Betty is bound by the modified contract.

In the example above, a shift in the market provides an example of a *good faith* reason for contract modification. Section 1–203 states: "Every contract or duty within this act imposes an obligation of good faith in its performance or enforcement." Good faith in a merchant is defined to mean honesty in fact and the observance of reasonable commercial standards of fair dealing in the trade [UCC 2–103(1)(b)]. But what if there really was no shift in the market, and Hal knew that Betty needed the goods immediately but refused to deliver unless Betty agreed to pay an additional sum of money? This sort of extortion of a contract modification without a legitimate commercial reason would be ineffective, because it would violate the duty of good faith. Hal would not be permitted to enforce the higher price.

There are situations in which modification without consideration must be written to be enforceable. For example, the contract itself may prohibit its modification or rescission except by signed writing. Therefore, only those changes agreed to in the signed writing are enforceable [UCC 2–209(2)]. If a consumer (nonmerchant buyer) is dealing with a merchant, and the merchant supplies the form that contains the prohibition against oral modification, the consumer must sign a separate acknowledgment of the clause.

Also, any modification that brings the contract under the Statute of Frauds must usually be in writing to be enforceable.

## STATUTE OF FRAUDS

Section 2–201(1) of the UCC contains a Statute of Frauds provision that applies to contracts for the sale of goods. The provision requires a writing for the contract to be enforceable when the price of the goods is $500 or more. The parties can have an initial oral agreement, however, and satisfy the Statute of Frauds by having a subsequent written memorandum of their oral agreement. In each case

the writing must have been signed by the party against whom enforcement is sought.

**WRITTEN CONFIRMATION BETWEEN MERCHANTS** Once again the UCC provides a special rule for contracts for the sale of goods between merchants. In transactions between merchants, the requirements of a writing for the Statute of Frauds are satisfied if, after the parties have agreed orally, one of the merchants sends a signed written confirmation to the other merchant. The communication must indicate the terms of the agreement, and the merchant receiving the confirmation must have reason to know of its contents. Unless the merchant who receives the confirmation gives *written* notice of objection to its contents within ten days after receipt, the writing will be sufficient against this merchant even though he or she has not signed anything.

For example, Jonas is a Miami merchant buyer. He contracts over the telephone to purchase $5,000 worth of goods from Sarah, a New York City merchant seller. Two days later Sarah sends written confirmation detailing the terms of the oral contract, which Jonas later receives. If Jonas wishes to use the Statute of Frauds as a defense against enforcement of the contract against him, he must give Sarah written notice of objection to the contents of the written confirmation within ten days of receipt.

**RELAXED REQUIREMENTS** The UCC has greatly relaxed the requirements for the sufficiency of a writing to satisfy the Statute of Frauds. A written contract or a memorandum will be sufficient as long as it indicates that a sales contract was intended and, with the exception of contracts between merchants mentioned above, as long as it is signed by the party against whom enforcement is sought. Except in the case of output and requirements contracts, a contract is not enforceable beyond the quantity of goods shown in the writing. Other terms, such as price and delivery terms, can be proved in court by oral testimony. Often, terms that are not agreed on can be supplied by the open term provisions of Article 2 itself.

What if a confirmatory letter is written on a business letterhead but is not manually signed by the sender? Will this letter constitute a "signed written confirmation" of an oral contract? This issue is addressed in the following case.

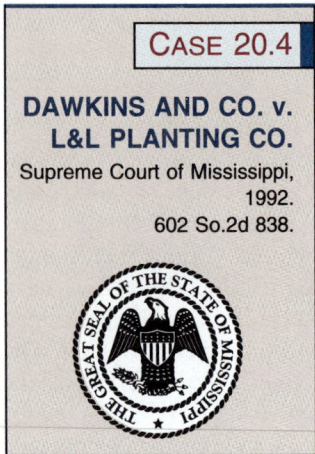

**CASE 20.4**

**DAWKINS AND CO. v.
L&L PLANTING CO.**

Supreme Court of Mississippi,
1992.
602 So.2d 838.

**BACKGROUND AND FACTS**  *On August 22, 1986, Dawkins and Company contracted orally, via telephone, with J. P. Love, a partner of L&L Planting Company (L&L), for the purchase of all of L&L's 1986 cotton crop. Dawkins followed up on the oral agreement with a contract sent to Love for his signature. Love did not sign the written contract. Dawkins then sent a copy of the contract by messenger to L&L, but Love's son (J. P. Love, Jr.), another partner of L&L Planting, orally repudiated the contract and refused to sign it. On September 3, 1986, Dawkins sent a letter on the Dawkins and Company stationery to L&L. The letter mentioned the unsigned contract and urged Love's son to sign it. When L&L failed to deliver the cotton as agreed, Dawkins sued to enforce the contract. The trial court granted summary judgment for L&L, holding that the oral contract was unenforceable under the Statute of Frauds. Dawkins appealed, arguing, among other things, that the trial court erred by not applying the UCC's "between merchants" exception.*

*Dan M. LEE, Presiding Justice, for the Court:*
* * * *

L&L * * * insists that the record fails to show the writing was * * * sufficient to bind the sender. L&L does not overlook the fact that Dawkins' letter of September 3 properly referred to the contract but asserts that (a) the September 3 letter was written subsequent to the date Love, Jr. effectively rejected the proposed contract and (b) the letter was not manually signed and therefore was not "sufficient against the sender." We disagree.

If the other provisions of the merchant's exception [UCC 2–201(2)] are met, and Dawkins, by writing "sufficient against the sender," confirmed the contract, then the statutory bar is removed unless L&L gave written notice of objection to its contents within ten days after receipt. L&L concedes it did not give written notice of objection within the prescribed time. * * * [T]he act of Love, Jr. on August 25, in orally rejecting the alleged contract could not suspend or negate subsequent application of [UCC 2–201(2)] if its prerequisites are otherwise satisfied.

The added assertion by L&L that the confirmatory writing be manually signed is without legal foundation. [UCC 1–201(46)] provides: "Written" or writing includes printing, typewriting, or any other intentional reduction to tangible form. [UCC 1–201(39)] provides: "Signed" includes any symbol extended or adopted by a party with present intent to authenticate a writing.

We have not previously considered what constitutes "signed" under the Uniform Commercial Code, but have little trouble concluding that the letter of September 3 on Dawkins' letterhead, bearing his address, which referred to and recited the contract terms, requested execution of the previously delivered forward contract, and included the typewritten name of the sender on the line where a manual signature is usually made, was a sufficient "writing in confirmation of the contract and sufficient against the sender."

**DECISION
AND REMEDY**  *The court held that the September 3 letter constituted a sufficient confirmatory writing under the UCC. The court thus reversed the trial court's decision and remanded the case for further proceedings, particularly for determination of whether the September 3 letter had actually been received by L&L.*

■ **Exhibit 20–2  Major Differences between Contract Law and Sales Law**

|  | **Contract Law** | **Sales Law** |
|---|---|---|
| Contract Terms | Contract must contain all material terms. | Open terms are acceptable, if parties intended to form a contract, but contract is not enforceable beyond quantity term. |
| Acceptance | Mirror image rule applies. If additional terms are added in acceptance, counteroffer is created. | Additional terms will not negate acceptance unless acceptance is made expressly conditional on assent to the additional terms. |
| Contract Modification | Modification requires consideration. | Modification does not require consideration. |
| Irrevocable Offers | Option contracts (with consideration). | Merchants' firm offers (without consideration). |
| Statute of Frauds Requirements | All material terms must be included in the writing. | Writing is required only for sale of goods of $500 or more, but contract is not enforceable beyond quantity specified. *Exceptions:* 1. Contracts for specially manufactured goods. 2. Contracts admitted to under oath by party against whom enforcement is sought. 3. Contracts will be enforced to extent goods are delivered or paid for. 4. Confirmatory memorandum (between merchants): Contract is enforceable if merchant fails to object in writing to confirming memorandum within ten days. |

**EXCEPTIONS**  Section 2–201 defines three exceptions to the Statute of Frauds requirement [UCC 2–201(3)]. A contract, if proved to exist, will be enforceable despite the absence of a writing, even if it involves a sale of goods for the price of $500 or more, under the circumstances indicated below. These exceptions and other ways in which sales law differs from general contract law are summarized in Exhibit 20–2.

*Specially Manufactured Goods.*  An oral contract for goods specially manufactured for a buyer is enforceable if the seller has made a substantial start on the manufacture of the goods or has made commitments for the manufacture of the goods and the goods are not suitable for resale to others in the ordinary course of the seller's business. In this situation, once the seller has taken action, the buyer cannot repudiate the agreement claiming the Statute of Frauds as a defense.

*Admissions.*  An oral contract may be enforceable when the party against whom enforcement of a contract is sought admits in pleadings (the complaint, the answer, the counterclaim, and the reply in a lawsuit), testimony, or other court proceedings that a contract for sale was made. Enforceability, however, is limited to the quantity of goods admitted.

*Partial Performance.*  Another exception exists when some payment has been made and accepted or some goods have been received and accepted. This ''partial performance'' exception to the Statute of Frauds renders the oral contract enforceable to the extent of the amount of performance that *actually* took place.

## PAROL EVIDENCE

If the parties to a contract set forth its terms in a confirmatory memorandum (a writing expressing offer and acceptance of the deal) or in a writing intended as their final expression, the terms of the contract cannot be contradicted by evidence of any prior negotiations or agreements or evidence of contemporaneous oral agreements. The terms of the contract can be explained or supplemented by consistent additional terms, however, or by *course of dealing, usage of trade,* or *course of performance* [UCC 2–202].

**CONSISTENT ADDITIONAL TERMS**  If the court finds an ambiguity in a writing that is supposed to be a complete and exclusive statement of the agreement between the parties, it may accept evidence of consistent additional terms to clarify or remove the ambiguity. The court will not, however, accept evidence of contradictory terms. This is the rule under both the UCC and the common law of contracts.

**COURSE OF DEALING AND USAGE OF TRADE**
In construing a commercial agreement, the court will assume that the course of dealing between the parties and the usage of trade were taken into account when the agreement was phrased [UCC 2–202; UCC 1–201(3)]. The UCC states, "A course of dealing between the parties and any usage of trade in the vocation or trade in which they are engaged or of which they are or should be aware give particular meaning to [the terms of an agreement] and supplement or qualify the terms of [the] agreement" [UCC 1–205(3)]. The UCC has determined, then, that the meaning of any agreement, evidenced by the language of the parties and by their actions, must be interpreted in light of commercial practices and other surrounding circumstances.

A **course of dealing** is a sequence of previous conduct between the parties to a particular transaction that establishes a common basis for their understanding [UCC 1–205(1)]. Course of dealing is restricted, literally, to the sequence of conduct between the parties that has occurred prior to the agreement in question. **Usage of trade** is defined as any practice or method of dealing having such regularity of observance in a place, vocation, or trade as to justify an expectation that it will be observed with respect to the transaction in question [UCC 1–205(2)]. The expressed terms of an agreement and an applicable course of dealing or usage of trade will be construed to be consistent with each other whenever reasonable. When such construction is *unreasonable,* however, the expressed terms in the agreement will prevail [UCC 1–205(4)].

Parol evidence of a course of dealing or usage of trade that is not inconsistent with the terms of the written agreement can be introduced in situations in which both parties knew, or should have known, of the existence of the particular custom or usage in that industry in that locality. Such evidence is supplemental to the contract and shows the meaning that the parties attach to the particular language. The evidence does not alter the contract terms. Just as a previous course of dealing between parties can be regarded as establishing a common basis for interpreting their expressions and conduct [UCC 1–205(1)], so, too, can a usage of trade establish a common basis for interpreting expressions or conduct [UCC 1–205(2)]. In the following case, the court permitted the introduction of evidence of usage and custom in the trade to explain the meaning of quantity figures that the parties took for granted when the contract was formed.

---

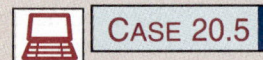 CASE 20.5

**HEGGBLADE-
MARGULEAS-
TENNECO, INC. v.
SUNSHINE BISCUIT,
INC.**

Court of Appeal of California,
Fifth District, 1976.
59 Cal.App.3d 948,
131 Cal.Rptr. 183.

**BACKGROUND AND FACTS**  *Heggblade-Marguleas-Tenneco, Inc. (HMT), contracted with Sunshine Biscuit, Inc., to supply potatoes to be used in the production of potato-snack foods. HMT had never marketed processing potatoes before. Heinie Hoffman, who had more than twenty years' experience in the potato-processing industry, was hired by HMT on October 1, 1970, to obtain more marketing contracts for its potatoes and to assist in selling the potatoes HMT was planning to grow. Hoffman signed formal contracts with Sunshine Biscuit for HMT on October 15, 1970. The quantity mentioned in the contract negotiations was 100,000 sacks of potatoes. It was agreed that the amount of potatoes to be supplied would vary somewhat with Sunshine Biscuit's needs. Subsequently, a decline in demand for Sunshine Biscuit's products severely reduced its need for potatoes, and it prorated the reduced demand among its suppliers, including HMT, as fairly as possible. Sunshine Biscuit was able to take* *only 60,105 sacks out of the 100,000 previously estimated. In HMT's suit for breach of contract, Sunshine Biscuit attempted to introduce evidence that it is customary in the potato-processing industry for the number of potatoes specified in sales contracts to be reasonable estimates rather than exact numbers that a buyer intends to purchase. The trial court held for Sunshine Biscuit. HMT appealed.*

*FRANSON,* Acting Presiding Justice.

\* \* \* \*

\* \* \* Since the contracts in question are silent about the applicability of the usage and custom, evidence of such usage and custom was admissible to explain the meaning of the quantity figures.

\* \* \* \*

Appellant's [HMT's] argument that the evidence of custom should not have been considered by the jury in interpreting the contracts because the officers of HMT were inexperienced in the marketing of processing potatoes and lacked knowledge of the custom is \* \* \* without merit. Mr. Hoffman was knowledgeable in the processing potato business and was aware of the trade custom. Since appellant pleaded that the contracts had been entered into on October 15, 1970, and Hoffman had been employed by HMT on October 1, 1970, his knowledge was imputed to HMT.

Moreover, persons carrying on a particular trade are deemed to be aware of prominent trade customs applicable to their industry. The knowledge may be actual or constructive, and it is constructive if the custom is of such general and universal application that the party must be presumed to know of it.

\* \* \* Because potatoes are a perishable commodity and their demand is dependent upon a fluctuating market, and because the marketing contracts are signed eight or nine months in advance of the harvest season, common sense dictates that the quantity would be estimated by both the grower and processor. Thus, it cannot be said as a matter of law that HMT was ignorant of the trade custom.

We conclude that the trial court properly admitted the evidence of usage and custom to explain the meaning of the quantity figures in the contracts.

**DECISION AND REMEDY**

*The trial court's judgment was affirmed. Sunshine Biscuit did not have to pay HMT for the difference between the 100,000 sacks of potatoes it estimated it would need and the 60,105 sacks of potatoes it actually purchased.*

---

**COURSE OF PERFORMANCE** A **course of performance** is the conduct that occurs under the terms of a particular agreement. The course of performance actually undertaken is the best indication of what the parties to an agreement intended it to mean, because presumably the parties themselves know best what they meant by their words [UCC 2–208].

To illustrate: Akron Lumber Company contracts with Blauveldt to sell Blauveldt a specified number of "2 by 4s." Akron agrees to deliver the lumber in five separate deliveries. Blauveldt accepts the first three deliveries but rejects the fourth, claiming that Akron has breached the contract by delivering lumber measuring 1⅞ inches by 3¾

inches rather than 2 inches by 4 inches. Akron can argue that in the trade (usage of trade), 2 by 4s are commonly 1⅞ inches by 3¾ inches and that Blauveldt, by accepting the lumber without objection in the three previous deliveries under the agreement (course of performance), attested to his understanding that "2 by 4" actually means "1⅞ by 3¾."

**RULES OF CONSTRUCTION**   The UCC provides *rules of construction* for the interpretation of contracts. Express terms, course of performance, course of dealing, and usage of trade are to be construed together when they do not contradict one another. When such construction is unreasonable, however, the following order of priority controls:

(1) express terms, (2) course of performance, (3) course of dealing, and (4) usage of trade [UCC 1–205(4); UCC 2–208(2)].

## UNCONSCIONABILITY

An unconscionable contract is one that is so unfair and one sided that enforcing it would be unreasonable. Section 2–302 allows the court to evaluate a contract or any clause in a contract. If the court deems the contract or clause to be unconscionable *at the time it was made,* the court can (1) refuse to enforce the contract, or (2) enforce the remainder of the contract without the unconscionable clause, or (3) limit the application of any unconscionable clauses to avoid an unconscionable result.

The court, in determining whether a contract or clause is unconscionable, must decide whether, in light of general commercial practice and the commercial needs of the particular trade involved, the contract or clause is so one sided as to be unconscionable under the circumstances at the time the contract was made. In this day of consumer law, more and more consumer sales contracts are being attacked as unconscionable. Typical cases involve high-pressure salespersons and uneducated consumers who contract away their basic rights. In general, the courts have concluded that unequal bargaining power, coupled with unscrupulous dealings by one party, will result in an unenforceable, unconscionable contract.

It is noteworthy that the doctrine of unconscionability expressed explicitly in Section 2–302 is a codification of a pre-UCC notion. The right of the courts to refuse to enforce all of the terms agreed to by the parties to a contract has been recognized for centuries. Equity courts have refused to grant performance of a contract deemed unfair (unconscionable). One of the leading cases involved Campbell Soup Company.[7] The form contract prepared by Campbell Soup contained a clause that excused the company from accepting goods under certain circumstances. Additionally, the clause prohibited the seller of the goods from selling them elsewhere without Campbell's written consent. The court refused to grant specific performance in this classic case on the basis that this clause was unconscionable.

The inclusion of Section 2–302 in the UCC reflects an increased sensitivity to certain realities of modern commercial activities. Classical contract theory holds that a contract is a bargain in which the terms have been worked out *freely* between parties that are equals. In many modern commercial transactions, this premise is invalid. Standard form contracts are often signed by consumer-buyers who understand few of the terms used and who often do not even read them. Virtually all of the terms are advantageous to the parties supplying the standard form contract. With Section 2–302, the courts have a powerful weapon for policing such transactions, as the next case illustrates.

---

7.   *Campbell Soup Co. v. Wentz,* 172 F.2d 80 (3d Cir. 1948). This case is presented in Chapter 15 as Case 15.5.

---

**CASE 20.6**

**JONES v. STAR CREDIT CORP.**

Supreme Court of New York, Nassau County, 1969.
59 Misc.2d 189,
298 N.Y.S.2d 264.

**BACKGROUND AND FACTS**   *The Joneses (the plaintiffs), who were welfare recipients, agreed to purchase a freezer for $900 as the result of a salesperson's visit to their home. Sales taxes and financing charges raised the total price to $1,439.69. At trial, the freezer was found to have a maximum retail value of approximately $300. After paying more than $600 toward the purchase of the freezer, the plaintiffs sued to have the purchase contract declared unconscionable under the UCC.*

*Sol M. WACHTLER,* Justice.
\* \* \* \*

Concededly, deciding [this case] is substantially easier than explaining it. No doubt, the mathematical disparity between $300, which presumably includes a reasonable profit margin, and $900, which is exorbitant on its face, carries the greatest weight. Credit charges alone exceed by more than $100 the retail value of the freezer. These alone may be sufficient to sustain the decision. Yet, a caveat is warranted lest we reduce the import of Section 2–302 solely to a mathematical ratio formula. It may, at times, be that; yet it may also be much more. The very limited financial resources of the purchaser, known to the sellers at the time of the sale, is entitled to weight in the balance. Indeed, the value disparity itself leads inevitably to the felt conclusion that knowing advantage was taken of the plaintiffs. In addition, the meaningfulness of choice essential to the making of a contract, can be negated by a gross inequality of bargaining power.

There is no question about the necessity and even the desirability of instalment sales and the extension of credit. Indeed, there are many, including welfare recipients, who would be deprived of even the most basic conveniences without the use of these devices. Similarly, the retail merchant selling on instalment or extending credit is expected to establish a pricing factor which will afford a degree of protection commensurate with the risk of selling to those who might be default prone. However, neither of these accepted premises can clothe the sale of this freezer with respectability.

| | |
|---|---|
| *Judgment was entered for the plaintiffs. The contract was reformed so that they were required to make no further payments.* | **DECISION AND REMEDY** |
| *A court may be reluctant to find a contract unconscionable if the retail price and the total installment-payment purchase price differ by a reasonable amount or if credit charges are reasonable in light of current interest rates. Generally, the court has to balance two ethical premises, and the public policies based on them, in determining whether a contract is unconscionable. On the one hand, the law seeks to preserve the integrity of contracts and allow people to deal and bargain as they will. On the other hand, the law seeks to protect individuals from becoming victimized by— in this court's words—the "exploitive" and "callous" practices of those with grossly superior bargaining power.* | **ETHICAL CONSIDERATIONS** |

## SECTION 4

# LEASES

The UCC also now applies to leases of goods under a separate section, Article 2A. Article 2A covers any transaction that creates a lease and includes subleases of goods [UCC 2A–102; UCC 2A–103(k)]. The article defines a **lease agreement** as the lessor and lessee's bargain, as found in their language and as implied by other circumstances, including course of dealing and usage of trade or course of performance [UCC 2A–103(k)]. A **lessor** is one who sells the right to possession and use of goods under a lease [UCC 2A–103(p)]. A **lessee** is one who acquires the right to possession and use of goods under a lease [UCC 2A–103(o)].

In short, Article 2A is a repetition of Article 2, except that it applies to leases, instead of sales, of goods and thus varies to reflect differences between sale and lease transactions. Differences between

the provisions of Article 2 and Article 2A include the following.

Article 2A does not provide for acceptance by shipment of goods or for additional terms in an acceptance or confirmation [UCC 2A–206]. Under Article 2, an oral contract is enforceable if the price of goods is less than $500 [UCC 2–201]. Under Article 2A, an oral lease is enforceable if the lease payments are less than $1,000 [UCC 2A–201]. Unlike Article 2, Article 2A does not say whether a lease as modified needs to satisfy the Statute of Frauds.

Article 2A replaces Article 2's implied warranty of title (discussed in Chapter 24) with an implied warranty of quiet possession. This is "a warranty that for the lease term no person holds a claim or interest in the goods that arose from an act or omission of the lessor . . . which will interfere with the lessee's enjoyment of its leasehold interest" [UCC 2A–211(1)].

## ■ CONCEPT SUMMARY 20.1 The Formation of Sales Contracts

| | |
|---|---|
| **Offer and Acceptance** | 1. The acceptance of unilateral offers can be made by a promise to ship or by shipment itself [UCC 2–206(1)(b)]. <br> 2. Not all terms have to be included for a contract to result [UCC 2–204]. <br> 3. Particulars of performance can be left open [UCC 2–204(3); UCC 2–311(1)]. <br> 4. A firm written offer made by a *merchant,* the duration of which is three months or less, cannot be revoked [UCC 2–205]. <br> 5. Acceptance by performance requires notice within a reasonable time; otherwise, the offer can be treated as lapsed [UCC 2–206(2)]. <br> 6. The price does not have to be included for a contract to be formed [UCC 2–305]. <br> 7. Variations in terms between the offer and the acceptance are not a rejection if there is a definite expression of acceptance [UCC 2–207(1)]. <br> 8. Acceptance of a bilateral offer may be made by any reasonable means of communication; it is effective when dispatched [UCC 2–206(1)(a)]. |
| **Consideration** | 1. Contract modification does not require consideration [UCC 2–209(1)]. |
| **Requirements under the Statute of Frauds** | 1. All contracts for the sale of goods priced at $500 or more must be in writing. A writing is sufficient as long as it evidences a contract between the parties and it has been signed by the party against whom enforcement is sought. A contract is not enforceable beyond the quantity shown in the writing. <br> 2. Exceptions to the requirement of a writing exist in the following situations: <br>   a. When written confirmation of an oral contract *between merchants* is not objected to in writing by the receiver within ten days [UCC 2–201(2)]. <br>   b. When the oral contract is for specially manufactured goods not suitable for resale to others, and the seller had substantially started to manufacture the goods [UCC 2–201(3)(a)]. <br>   c. When the defendant admits in pleadings, testimony, or other court proceedings that an oral contract for the sale of goods was made. In this case the contract will be enforceable to the extent of the quantity of goods admitted [UCC 2–201(3)(b)]. <br>   d. When payment has been made and accepted or possession has been taken under the terms of an oral contract. The oral agreement will be enforceable to the extent that such payment had been received and accepted or to the extent that goods had been received and accepted [UCC 2–201(3)(c)]. |
| **Parol Evidence** | 1. The terms of a clearly and completely worded written contract cannot be contradicted by evidence of prior negotiations or agreements or evidence of contemporaneous oral agreements [UCC 2–202]. <br> 2. Evidence is admissible to clarify the terms of a writing: <br>   a. If the contract terms are ambiguous [UCC 2–202]. <br>   b. If evidence of *course of dealing, usage of trade,* or *course of performance* is necessary to learn or to clarify the intentions of the parties to the contract [UCC 2–202(a)]. |

## ■ CONCEPT SUMMARY 20.1 *(continued)*

| Unconscionability | An unconscionable contract is one that is so unfair and one sided that it would be unreasonable to enforce it. If the court deems a contract or a clause within the contract to be unconscionable at the time the contract was made, the court can (1) refuse to enforce the contract; (2) refuse to enforce the unconscionable clauses of the contract; or (3) limit the application of any unconscionable clauses to avoid an unconscionable result [UCC 2–302]. |
| --- | --- |

Article 2A extends Article 2's protection against unconscionability to leases and expands it in cases concerning consumer leases. A consumer lease involves a lessor who regularly engages in the business of leasing or selling, a lessee (except an organization) who leases the goods "primarily for a personal, family, or household purpose," and total lease payments that are less than $25,000 [UCC 2A–103(1)(e)]. If unconscionable conduct induced the consumer to enter the lease or occurred in the collection of a claim under it, courts can grant relief, even if the lease itself is not unconscionable [UCC 2A–108(2)]. In cases involving consumer leases, courts can also award attorneys' fees [UCC 2A–108(4)].

One type of nonconsumer lease is a commercial finance lease. A finance lease—commercial or otherwise—involves a lessor, a lessee, and a third party: a financer who buys or leases goods from a supplier and leases or subleases them to the lessee [UCC 2A–103(g)]. The supplier manufactures or supplies the goods according to the lessee's specifications, the financer acquires the goods or the right to their possession and use in connection with the lease, and the lessee looks almost entirely to the supplier for warranties and so on. Article 2A, unlike ordinary contract law, makes the lessee's obligations under a commercial finance lease irrevocable and independent from the financer's [UCC 2A–407]. That is, the lessee must perform whether or not the financer performs.

Many leasing transactions are based on the parties' ability to provide for the measure of damages if there is a default or other act or omission. Article 2A allows greater flexibility in liquidation of damages with respect to leases than Article 2 does with respect to sales [UCC 2A–504].

Article 2A is included in the full text of the UCC in Appendix C of this book.

## ■ SECTION 5

# CONTRACTING FOR THE INTERNATIONAL SALE OF GOODS

Contracts for the international sale of goods between firms or individuals located in different countries are governed by the 1980 United Nations Convention on Contracts for the International Sale of Goods (CISG)—if the countries of the parties to the contract have ratified the CISG (and if the parties have not agreed that some other law will govern their contract). Essentially, the CISG is to international sales contracts what Article 2 of the UCC is to domestic sales contracts. In the following pages, we discuss the creation of the CISG and compare its provisions to parallel provisions of the UCC. We also look at some special provisions that are commonly included in international sales contracts.

### THE CISG

Although international trade has taken place since at least the beginning of recorded history, the emergence of multinational and global business enterprises is a twentieth-century phenomenon. As early as the 1930s, a number of nations saw the need for, and began to develop, uniform laws to cover contracts for the international sale of goods to facilitate international transactions. The end result of this important legal development was the CISG, which applies to all contracts between firms located in the countries that have adopted the convention (agreement). As of 1994, thirty-eight countries had ratified the CISG, including the United States, Canada, Mexico, some Central and South American countries, and most of the European nations.

**WHEN THE CISG APPLIES**   Recall that in domestic transactions the UCC applies when the parties to a contract for a sale of goods have failed to specify in writing some important term concerning price, delivery, or the like. Similarly, whenever the parties to international transactions have failed to specify in writing the precise terms of a contract, the CISG will be applied. In other words, any U.S. company dealing with a firm located in a signatory country can, by contractual agreement, provide that another law, and not the CISG, will apply. The specific language used in such a provision would have to be as follows:

The provisions of the Uniform Commercial Code as adopted by the state of [say] California, and *not* the Convention for the International Sale of Goods, apply.

The CISG does not apply to domestic sales or noncommercial sales—that is, it does not apply to consumer sales of goods bought for family, household, or personal use. Nor does it apply to the sale of services. In situations in which the contract calls for both services and goods, if the sale of goods outweighs the sale of services, then the CISG will apply. In these respects, the CISG is very similar to the UCC. The following case illustrates an application of the CISG.

---

| CASE 20.7 |
| --- |

**FILANTO, S.P.A. v. CHILEWICH INTERNATIONAL CORP.**

United States District Court, Southern District of New York, 1992. 789 F.Supp. 1229.

**BACKGROUND AND FACTS**   *Chilewich International Corporation is an export-import firm incorporated in New York. On February 28, 1989, Chilewich contracted with Raznoexport, the Soviet Foreign Economic Association, to supply boots to Raznoexport in what is now the Republic of Russia. The contract required all disputes to be settled by arbitration at the Russian Chamber of Commerce and Industry in Moscow. On July 27, Chilewich sent Filanto, S.P.A., an Italian footwear manufacturer with whom Chilewich had several ongoing contracts, a contract to purchase boots subject to "the standard contract in effect with the Soviet buyers." On March 13, 1990, Chilewich sent Filanto a memorandum confirming that Filanto would deliver 100,000 pairs of boots to Chilewich at the Italian/Yugoslav border on September 15, with 50,000 additional pairs to be delivered on November 1. Chilewich agreed to arrange for partial payment before each delivery date. The memorandum referred to Chilewich's contract with Raznoexport and stated that "any arbitration shall be in accordance with that Contract." Nearly five months later, on August 7, Filanto returned the memorandum with a letter purporting to exclude the arbitration clause. Filanto delivered the first shipment of boots on September 15 and accepted Chilewich's payment. Ultimately, however, Chilewich accepted only 60,000 pairs of boots. When Chilewich complained that some of the boots were defective, Filanto wrote a letter stating, among other things, that their contract was governed by Chilewich's contract with the Russians. Filanto filed a lawsuit against Chilewich for the rest of the contract price. Chilewich contended that their dispute should be arbitrated in Moscow.*

BRIEANT, Chief Judge.
      *   *   *   *

      *   *   * [The law] to be applied in this case is found in the United Nations Convention on Contracts for the International Sale of Goods [CISG].   *   *   * [A]bsent a choice-of-law provision,   *   *   * the Convention governs all contracts between parties with places of business in different nations, so long as both nations are signatories to the Convention. Since   *   *   * both the United States and Italy

are signatories to the Convention, the Court will [apply] * * * the substantive international law of contracts embodied in the Sale of Goods Convention.

* * * *

There is simply no satisfactory explanation as to why Filanto failed to object to the incorporation by reference of the Russian Contract in a timely fashion. * * * Chilewich had * * * commenced its performance under the [March 13 memorandum] * * * . An offeree who, knowing that the offeror has commenced performance, fails to notify the offeror of its objection to the terms of the contract within a reasonable time will, under certain circumstances, be deemed to have assented to those terms. The Sale of Goods Convention [CISG] itself recognizes this rule: Article 18(1) provides that "A statement made by or other conduct of the offeree indicating assent to an offer is an acceptance." Although mere "silence or inactivity" does not constitute acceptance, the Court may consider previous relations between the parties in assessing whether a party's conduct constituted acceptance. In this case, in light of the extensive course of prior dealing between these parties, Filanto was certainly under a duty to alert Chilewich in timely fashion to its objections to the terms of the March 13 Memorandum * * * .

* * * *

* * * [Filanto's] letter, which responds to claims by [Chilewich] that some of the boots that were supplied were defective, expressly relies on * * * the Russian Contract * * * . The Sale of Goods Convention [CISG] specifically directs that "[i]n determining the intent of a party . . . due consideration is to be given to . . . any subsequent conduct of the parties." In this case, as the letter post-dates the partial performance of the contract, it is particularly strong evidence that Filanto recognized itself to be bound by all the terms of the Russian Contract.

*The court held that the parties must arbitrate their dispute in Moscow.*

**DECISION AND REMEDY**

---

**A COMPARISON OF CISG AND UCC PROVISIONS**  The provisions of the CISG, although similar for the most part to those of the UCC, differ from them in some respects. In the event that the CISG and the UCC are in conflict, the CISG applies (because it is a treaty of the national government and therefore is supreme—see the discussion of the supremacy clause of the U.S. Constitution in Chapter 5).

The major differences between the CISG and the UCC in regard to contract formation concern the following:

1. The mirror image rule.
2. Irrevocable offers.
3. The Statute of Frauds.
4. The price term.
5. The time of contract formation.

CISG provisions relating to risk of loss, performance, remedies, and warranties will be discussed in the following chapters as those topics are examined.

*The Mirror Image Rule.*  As discussed earlier in this chapter, the UCC relaxed substantially the rules governing contractual agreement. Under the UCC, an acceptance that contains additional terms can still result in the formation of a contract, unless the additional terms constitute a material alteration of the contract.

Article 19 of the CISG provides the rules governing additional terms in international sales contracts. Article 19(1) states that if the terms of the acceptance vary from those of the offer, there is no contract: "A reply to an offer which purports to be an acceptance, but contains additions, limitations, or other modifications is a rejection of the offer and constitutes a counter-offer." But Article 19(2) then stipulates that an acceptance containing additional terms may still bind the offeror in contract:

However, a reply to an offer which purports to be an acceptance but contains additional or different terms *which do not materially alter* the terms of the offer constitutes an acceptance, unless the offeror, without undue delay, objects *orally* to the discrepancy or dispatches a notice to that effect. If he does not so object, the terms of the contract are the terms of the offer with the modifications contained in the acceptance. [Emphasis added.]

Do not get the mistaken impression, however, that Article 19(2) of the CISG is the same in effect as UCC 2–207(2). The definition of a "material alteration" under the CISG involves virtually any differences in the terms relating to payment, quality, quantity, price, time and place of delivery, extent of one party's liability to the other, or how disputes under the contract will be settled. In effect, then, Article 19 requires that the terms of the acceptance mirror those of the offer. As a practical matter, businesspersons undertaking international sales transactions therefore should not use the sale or purchase forms that they customarily use for transactions within the United States. Although the sample form shown in Exhibit 20–3 illustrates the typical terms and conditions that might be contained in an international purchase order, it is important to remember that international purchase and sale forms need to be specially drafted to suit the needs of the specific transaction.

*Irrevocable Offers.*   UCC 2–205 requires that an irrevocable offer without consideration must be in writing. In contrast, Article 16(2) of the CISG provides that an offer will be irrevocable if the offeror simply states orally that the offer is irrevocable or if the offeree reasonably relies on the offer as being irrevocable. In both of these situations, the offer will be irrevocable even without a writing and without consideration.

*Statute of Frauds.*   As mentioned previously, the UCC states that contracts for the sale of goods priced at $500 or more must be in writing [UCC 2–201]. The writing must be signed by the party against whom enforcement is sought and must be sufficient to show that a contract has been made. Article 11 of the CISG, however, does not include the formal requirements imposed by the Statute of Frauds:

> A contract of sale need not be concluded in or evidenced by writing and is not subject to any other requirements as to form. It may be proved by any means, including witnesses.

The difference between the UCC and the CISG in respect to writing requirements should not be

overstated, however. The UCC allows for many exceptions to the Statute of Frauds requirements, and as a result, oral contracts are often enforceable. In particular, whenever partial or complete performance has occurred, the plaintiff to a dispute need not produce a writing to demonstrate that a contract was made. Because the majority of contractual disputes occur after some degree of performance, the difference between the UCC and the CISG with respect to writing requirements may seem more significant than it actually is.

Article 11 of the CISG accords with the legal customs of most nations, in which contracts no longer need to meet certain formal or writing requirements to be enforceable. Ironically, even England, the nation that created the original Statute of Frauds in 1677, has repealed all of it except the provisions relating to collateral promises and to transfers of interests in land. Many other countries that once had such a statute have also repealed all or parts of it. Civil law countries, such as France, never had a writing requirement.

*The Necessity of a Price Term.*   Under the UCC, if the parties to a contract have not agreed on a price, the contract will not fail if the parties intended to form a contract (had a "meeting of the minds"). If the price term is left open, the court will determine "a reasonable price at the time for delivery" [UCC 2–305(1)]. Under the CISG, however, the price term must be specified, or at least provisions for its specification must be included in the agreement; otherwise, normally no contract will exist.

The CISG does not specifically require that the exact price be calculated in the offer, but the contract must include an *express* provision that allows for an exact determination of the price. For example, if the contract states that the price of wheat to be delivered in two months will be its price at the Chicago Board of Trade on that day, that is a sufficient price term under the CISG.

*Time of Contract Formation.*   Under the common law of contracts, an acceptance is effective on dispatch, and thus a contract is created when the acceptance is transmitted. The UCC does not alter this so-called mailbox rule. Under the CISG, however, a contract is created not at the time the acceptance is transmitted but only upon its *receipt* by the offeror. (The offer becomes *irrevocable,* however, when the acceptance is sent.) Article

■ **Exhibit 20–3 Sample International Purchase Order Form (Front)**

**Caution:** This form contains a typical set of terms written from the buyer's point of view, but it is not applicable to all factual situations and the laws of all states. Terms and conditions of sale or purchase must be custom drafted to be appropriate to the type of business and type of goods involved.

---

## Sample International Purchase Order Terms & Conditions*
### The _____ Company, Inc.
### International Terms and Conditions of Purchase

1. *Acceptance.* Acceptance of this order is expressly limited to the terms and conditions contained herein, including all terms and conditions set forth on the face hereof. Acceptance of this order by Seller may be made by signing and returning the attached acknowledgement copy hereof, by other express acceptance, or by shipment of goods hereunder. If Seller uses its own order acknowledgement or other form to accept this order, it is understood that said form shall be used for convenience only and any terms or conditions contained therein inconsistent with or in addition to those contained herein shall be of no force or effect whatsoever between the parties hereto.

2. *Warranty.* Seller warrants the goods covered by this Agreement and their packaging and labelling shall be in merchantable condition and shall be free from defects in workmanship and materials and shall be in conformity with the specifications, drawings, samples and descriptions attached hereto or referred to on the face hereof, if any. Seller warrants that the goods covered by this Agreement shall be fit for such particular purposes and uses, if any, as specified by BUYER or otherwise known to Seller. Seller warrants that the goods shall be free and clear of any lien or other adverse claim against title, and to the extent not manufactured to detailed designs furnished by BUYER shall be free from defects in design. All warranties contained herein shall survive inspection, test and acceptance by BUYER. Seller agrees, at its own costs and expense, to defend and hold BUYER harmless from and against any and all claims made against BUYER based upon, relating to, or arising out of any claimed defects in the goods or services ordered hereunder. Seller's warranties (and any consumer warranties, service policies, or similar undertakings of Seller) shall be enforceable by BUYER'S customers and any subsequent owner or operator of the goods as well as by BUYER.

3. *Shipping Instructions.* No charge shall be made to BUYER for draying and packaging unless authorized by BUYER. Merchandise shipped by freight or express shall be packed, marked and described and the carrier shall be selected, so as to obtain the lowest rate possible under freight or express classifications or regulations except when otherwise specified by BUYER, and penalties or increased charges due to failure so to do will be charged to Seller. The foregoing notwithstanding, Seller shall comply with all instructions of BUYER as to packaging, marking, shipping and insurance. Prior to passage of title to BUYER the goods shall be held by Seller without risk or expense to BUYER.

4. *Invoices, Other Documents and Charges.* Seller shall invoice in duplicate. Originals of all invoices, government and commercial bills of lading and air express receipts shall be air mailed to the Purchasing Department of BUYER when goods are shipped. Packing slips must accompany item number, and a complete description of its contents. Except as otherwise provided on the face hereof, the contract price includes all costs and charges to be paid or reimbursed to Seller by BUYER, including without limitation, all applicable taxes and duties and all charges for packing, loading and transportation. Transportation charges and taxes and duties, when applicable, and when agreed on the face hereof to be borne by BUYER shall be billed as separate items on Seller's invoices.

5. *Inspection—Nonconformity.* BUYER may inspect the goods and, with respect to nonconforming goods, may return them or hold them at the Seller's risk and expense, and may in either event charge the Seller with cost of transportation, shipping, unpacking, examining, repacking, reshipping, and other like expense. Promptly upon BUYER's written request, and without expense to BUYER, Seller agrees to replace or correct defects of any rejected goods or other goods not conforming to the warranty set forth above. In the event of failure of Seller to replace or correct defects in nonconforming goods promptly, BUYER after reasonable notice to Seller, may make such corrections or replace such goods and charge Seller for the costs incurred by BUYER in doing so. Time is of the essence in this transaction. In addition to its remedies for breach of contract, BUYER reserves the right to return any or all goods in unopened original packing to Seller if delivered to BUYER more than five (5) days after the delivery date shown in shipping instructions. If the delivery date shown in shipping instructions is revised by BUYER by notification to Seller, then such five (5) day period shall not commence to run until such revised delivery date. Also, BUYER reserves the right to refuse goods delivered contrary to instructions or not in recognized standard containers. BUYER shall be under no duty to inspect goods prior to BUYER's use or resale, and neither retention, use nor resale of such goods shall be construed to constitute an acceptance of goods not in compliance with the requirements of this order.

6. *Changes.* Unless agreed in writing by BUYER, Seller shall not purchase materials, or make material commitments, or production arrangements, in excess of the amount, or in advance of the time necessary to meet BUYER'S delivery schedule. BUYER shall have the right at any time to make changes in drawings, designs, specifications, materials, packaging, time and place of delivery and method of transportation. If any such changes cause an increase or decrease in the cost, or the time required for the performance, an equitable adjustment shall be made and this agreement shall be modified in writing accordingly. Seller agrees to accept any such changes subject to this paragraph. This right to an adjustment shall be deemed waived unless asserted within thirty (30) days after the change is ordered. BUYER reserves the right to terminate this order or any part hereof for its sole convenience. In the event of such termination, Seller shall immediately stop all work hereunder, and shall immediately cause any of its suppliers or subcontractors to cease such work. Seller shall be paid a reasonable termination charge consisting of a percentage of the order price reflecting the percentage of the work performed prior to the notice of termination. Such charge shall be Seller's only remedy for such termination. Seller shall not be paid for any work done after receipt of the notice of termination nor for any work done by Seller's suppliers or subcontractors which Seller could reasonably have avoided.

7. *Default.* BUYER may also terminate this order or any part hereof for cause in the event of any default by the Seller or if the Seller fails to comply with any of the terms and conditions of this offer. Late deliveries, deliveries of goods which are defective or which do not conform to this order, and failure to provide BUYER, upon request, reasonable assurances of future performance shall all be causes allowing BUYER to terminate this order for cause. In the event of termination for cause, BUYER shall not be liable to Seller for any amount and Seller shall be liable to BUYER for any and all damage sustained by reason of the default which gave rise to the termination.

---

*Copyright 1988, Barry A. Sanders. All rights reserved. Reprinted with permission. These sample terms and conditions were used in connection with a presentation with the 21st Annual Uniform Commercial Code Institute. Mr. Sanders is with Latham & Watkins in Los Angeles, CA.

■ **Exhibit 20–3 (Continued) Sample International Purchase Order Form (Back)**

8. *Indemnity.* Seller will defend and indemnify BUYER, upon demand, against all claims, actions, liability, damage, loss and expense (including investigative expense and attorney's fees incurred in litigation or because of threatened litigation) as the result of BUYER'S purchase and/or use of the goods and arising or alleged to arise from patent, trademark or copyright infringement; unfair competition; the failure or alleged failure of the goods to comply with specifications or with any express or implied warranties of Seller; the alleged violation by such goods or in its manufacture or sale of any statute, ordinance, or administrative order, rule or regulation; defects, whether latent or patent, in material or workmanship; defective design; defective warnings or instructions; or Seller's negligence.

9. *Price Reductions.* Seller will give BUYER the benefit of any price reductions occurring before the specified shipping date or to actual time of shipment, whichever is later. Likewise, if Seller accepts this order as a commission merchant, Seller shall obtain for BUYER from the manufacturer of such goods the benefit of price reductions to the specified date or to actual time of shipment, whichever is later. Seller warrants that the price for the articles sold BUYER hereunder are not less favorable than those currently extended to any other customer for the same or similar articles in similar quantities.

10. *Information.* Seller shall consider all information furnished by BUYER to be confidential and shall not disclose any such information to any other person, or use such information itself for any purpose other than performing this order unless Seller obtains written permission from BUYER to do so. This confidential requirement shall also apply to drawings, specifications, or other documents prepared by Seller for BUYER in connection with this order. Seller shall provide confidential information only to those of its agents, servants and employees who have been informed of the requirements of this paragraph and have agreed to be bound by them. Upon completion or termination of this order, Seller shall make such disposition of all such information and items as may be directed by BUYER. Seller shall not advertise or publish the fact that BUYER has ordered goods from Seller nor shall any information relating to this order be disclosed without BUYER'S written permission. Unless otherwise agreed in writing, no commercial, financial or technical information disclosed in any manner or at any time by Seller to BUYER shall be deemed secret or confidential and Seller shall have no rights against BUYER with respect thereto except such rights as may exist under patent laws.

11. *Tools, Dies, Etc.* Seller agrees that the information, tools, jigs, dies, etc., drawings, patterns and specifications supplied or paid for by BUYER shall be and remain BUYER'S property, shall be used only on BUYER'S orders, and shall be held by Seller for BUYER unless directed otherwise. Seller will account for such items and keep them in good working condition and fully covered by insurance at all times without expense to BUYER. In the event Seller devises and incorporates any new features design into any goods made under this order, Seller grants to BUYER the right of reproduction of such goods, together with a royalty-free, nonexclusive, irrevocable license to use such new features of design.

12. *General Provisions.*

(a) Seller and BUYER shall be independent contractors. This transaction does not create a principal-agent or partnership relationship between them, and neither one may legally commit the other in any matter.

(b) BUYER may deduct from any payment due to Seller or set-off against any claim by Seller any amount which is due to BUYER by Seller for any reason, including, among other reasons, any excess transportation charges caused by deviations from BUYER'S shipping instructions or the shipping of partial shipments.

(c) Seller shall comply with all laws, regulations and policies applicable to it by any jurisdiction and shall obtain all permits needed to complete this transaction under the laws of the country from which the shipment is made, including among other things, any required export permits and Central Bank approvals.

(d) All billings and payments shall be made in U.S. Dollars.

(e) In the event the importation of the goods results in the assessment of a countervailing duty on BUYER as the importer, Seller shall reimburse such countervailing duty to BUYER, provided such reimbursement is permitted under U.S. laws and regulations,

(f) Goods ordered hereunder to be made with use of BUYER'S confidential information, BUYER'S designs, BUYER'S trademarks or tradenames or BUYER'S customer's trademarks or tradenames shall be furnished by Seller exclusively to BUYER. Any excess of such inventory shall be destroyed by Seller at its own expense.

(g) Seller warrants that it has accepted no gratuities of any kind from any employee of BUYER in connection with placement of this order.

(h) Seller shall cooperate fully with BUYER at Seller's expense in obtaining approvals of the goods requested by BUYER from certifying organizations such as Underwriters Laboratories.

(i) Any goods that are hazardous will be packaged, marked and shipped by Seller to comply with all U.S. federal, state and local regulations and will further comply with all special BUYER requirements. Seller shall furnish BUYER a Material Hazard Data Sheet covering all such goods.

(j) BUYER shall not be liable to Seller for any loss incurred by Seller due to strikes, riots, storms, fires, explosions, acts of God, war, embargo, government boycott or other governmental action or any other causes similar thereto beyond the reasonable control of BUYER. Any failure or delay in performance of any of the foregoing shall not be a default hereunder.

(k) BUYER may waive performance of any condition, but waiver by BUYER of a condition shall not be considered a waiver of that condition for succeeding performance. None of BUYER'S remedies hereunder shall exclude its pursuit of its other legal remedies.

(l) This document and any other documents mentioned on the face hereof, constitute the entire agreement between the parties on this subject. All prior representations, negotiations or arrangements on this subject matter are superseded by these terms and shall not form a basis for interpretation of these terms. All amendments to these terms must be agreed to in writing by BUYER.

(m) If any manufacturer's excise tax, value added tax or other tax measured by selling price is included in or added to the price of the goods paid by BUYER, then, in the event all or any part of that tax shall be refunded to Seller, Seller shall promptly remit such refund in full to BUYER.

(n) This order is nonassignable. Any attempt to assign without BUYER'S written consent is void.

(o) This transaction and all its terms shall be construed in accordance with and all disputes shall be governed by the laws of the State of _____ , U.S.A., specifically including the provisions of the Uniform Commercial Code, as adopted by that state, and excluding the provisions of the Convention on the International Sale of Goods. Seller submits to the jurisdiction of the courts located in the State of _____ in the event of any proceedings therein in connection herewith.

(p) Any and all disputes arising between BUYER and Seller in connection with this transaction (other than actions for contribution or indemnity with respect to court actions involving third parties) shall be exclusively and finally decided by arbitration in _____ under the rules of the American Arbitration Association. The arbitration award shall be final and nonappealable. There shall be three arbitrators, one chosen by each party and the third chosen by the first two, or in the event of their failure to agree, by the _____ state court of general jurisdiction. The arbitrators shall reach their decision, and state it in writing with reason for it, within twelve months after the appointment of the third arbitrator.

(q) This order shall expire in thirty (30) days from the date of issuance by BUYER, unless earlier revoked by BUYER or accepted by Seller. ■

18(2) states that an acceptance by return promise "becomes effective at the moment the indication of assent reaches the offeror." Under Article 18(3), the offeree may also bind the offeror by performance even without giving any notice to the offeror. The acceptance becomes effective "at the moment the act is performed." The rule is therefore that it is the offeree's reliance, rather than the communication of acceptance to the offeror, that creates the contract.

## SPECIAL PROVISIONS IN INTERNATIONAL CONTRACTS

Language and legal differences among nations can create special problems for parties to international contracts when disputes arise. It is possible to avoid these problems by including in a contract special provisions designating the official language of the contract, the legal **forum** (place, or court) in which disputes under the contract will be settled, the substantive law that will be applied in settling any disputes, and the types of circumstances that will allow the parties to avoid performance obligations under the contract.

**CHOICE OF LANGUAGE** A deal struck between a U.S. company and a company in another country normally involves two languages. The complex contractual terms involved may not be understood by one party in the other party's language. Typically, many phrases in one language are not readily translatable into another. To make sure that no disputes arise out of this language problem, an international sales contract should have a **choice-of-language clause** designating the official language by which the contract will be interpreted in the event of disagreement. Such a clause might state that the agreement is being written in English, which is to be regarded as the authoritative and official language of the contract's text. The clause may further allow that the agreement is to be translated into, say, Spanish; that the translation is to be ratified by both parties; and that the foreign company can rely on the translation. If arbitration is anticipated, an additional clause must be added to indicate that the arbitration will be in, say, English, Spanish, or French—or whatever the case may be.

**CHOICE OF FORUM** In international contracts, it is especially important to include a **forum-selection clause.** When several countries are involved, litigation may be sought in courts in different nations. There are no universally accepted rules regarding the jurisdiction of a particular court over subject matter or parties to a dispute. Consequently, parties to an international transaction should always include in the contract a forum-selection clause designating the forum in which a dispute will be litigated. A forum-selection clause should specifically indicate the court that will have jurisdiction. The forum does not necessarily have to be within the geographical boundaries of either of the parties' nations.

Under certain circumstances, a forum-selection clause will not be valid. Specifically, if the clause denies one party an effective remedy, is the product of fraud or unconscionable conduct, causes substantial inconvenience to one of the parties to the contract, or violates public policy, the clause will not be enforced.

**CHOICE OF LAW** A contractual provision designating the applicable law, called a **choice-of-law clause,** is typically included in every international contract. At common law (and in European civil law systems—discussed in Chapter 10), parties are allowed to choose the law that will govern their contractual relationship, provided that the law chosen is the law of a jurisdiction that has a substantial relationship to the parties and to the international business transaction. Under Section 1–105 of the UCC, parties may choose the law that will govern the contract as long as the choice is "reasonable." Article 6 of the CISG, however, imposes no limitation on the parties in their choice of what law will govern the contract, and the 1986 Hague Convention on the Law Applicable to Contracts for the International Sale of Goods—often referred to as the "Choice-of-Law Convention"[8]—allows unlimited autonomy in the choice of law. Whenever a choice of law is not specified in a contract, the Hague Convention indicates that the governing law is that of the country in which the *seller's* place of business is located.

**FORCE MAJEURE** Every contract, and particularly those involving international transactions, should have a *force majeure* **clause.** The definition of the French term *force majeure* is

---

8.  See 24 International Legal Materials 1575 (1985).

"impossible or irresistible force"—which sometimes is loosely identified as "an act of God." *Force majeure* clauses commonly stipulate that in addition to acts of God, a number of other eventualities (such as governmental orders or regulations, embargoes, or shortages of materials) may excuse a party from liability for nonperformance.

## TERMS AND CONCEPTS TO REVIEW

| | | |
|---|---|---|
| choice-of-language clause 391 | *force majeure* clause 391 | lessor 383 |
| choice-of-law clause 391 | forum 391 | output contract 370 |
| course of dealing 380 | forum-selection clause 391 | requirements contract 370 |
| course of performance 381 | lease agreement 383 | sale 366 |
| firm offer 371 | lessee 383 | usage of trade 380 |

## QUESTIONS AND CASE PROBLEMS

**20–1. Offers between Merchants.** A. B. Zook, Inc., is a manufacturer of washing machines. Over the telephone, Zook offers to sell Radar Appliances one hundred Model Z washers at a price of $150 per unit. Zook agrees to keep this offer open for ninety days. Radar tells Zook that the offer appears to be a good one and that it will let Zook know of its acceptance within the next two to three weeks. One week later, Zook sends and Radar receives notice that Zook has withdrawn its offer. Radar immediately thereafter telephones Zook and accepts the $150-per-unit offer. Zook claims, first, that no sales contract was ever formed between it and Radar and, second, that if there is a contract, the contract is unenforceable. Discuss Zook's contentions.

**20–2. Accommodation Shipments.** Flint, a retail seller of television sets, orders one hundred Model Color-X sets from manufacturer Martin. The order specifies the price and that the television sets are to be *shipped* by Humming Bird Express on or before October 30. The order is received by Martin on October 5. On October 8, Martin writes Flint a letter indicating that the order was received and that the sets will be shipped as directed, at the specified price. This letter is received by Flint on October 10. On October 28, Martin, in preparing the shipment, discovers it has only ninety Color-X sets in stock. Martin ships the ninety Color-X sets and ten television sets of a different model, stating clearly on the invoice that the ten are being shipped only as an accommodation. Flint claims Martin is in breach of contract. Martin claims the shipment was not an acceptance, and therefore no contract was formed. Explain who is correct and why.

**20–3. Contract Modification.** Shane has a requirements contract with Sky that obligates Sky to supply Shane with all the gasoline Shane needs for his delivery trucks for one year at $1.10 per gallon. A clause inserted in small print in the contract by Shane, and not noticed by Sky, states, "The buyer reserves the right to reject any shipment for any reason without liability." For six months Shane orders and Sky delivers under the contract without any controversy. Then, because of a war in the Middle East, the price of gasoline to Sky increases substantially. Sky contacts Shane and tells Shane he cannot possibly fulfill the requirements contract unless Shane agrees to pay $1.30 per gallon. Shane, in need of the gasoline, agrees in writing to modify the contract. Later that month, Shane learns he can buy gasoline at $1.20 per gallon from Collins. Shane refuses delivery of his most recent order to Sky, claiming, first, that the contract allows him to do so without liability and, second, that he is required to pay only $1.10 per gallon if he accepts the delivery. Discuss fully Shane's contentions.

**20–4. Applicability of the UCC.** Hatter owns 360 acres of land in Bear County. Hatter makes three separate contracts, in writing, with Bean concerning the land. First, Hatter contracts to sell Bean five hundred tons of gravel from a quarry located on the land for a stated price. The contract calls for Bean to remove the gravel. The second contract sells to Bean all the wheat presently growing on a forty-acre tract. Hatter is obligated under the contract to harvest and deliver the wheat to Bean. The third contract is for the sale of the northeast ninety acres with all corn standing. Discuss fully which of these contracts, if any, fall under the UCC.

**20–5. Contract Formation.** Strike offers to sell Bailey one thousand shirts for a stated price. The offer states that shipment will be made by the Dependable Truck Line. Bailey replies, "I accept your offer for one thousand shirts at the price quoted. Delivery to be by Yellow Express Truck Line." Both Strike and Bailey are merchants. Three weeks later, Strike ships the shirts by the Dependable Truck Line, and Bailey refuses shipment.

Strike sues for breach of contract. Bailey claims, first, that there never was a contract, because the modification of carriers did not constitute an acceptance, and, second, that even if there were a contract, Strike would have been in breach by shipping the shirts by Dependable contrary to the contract terms. Discuss fully Bailey's claims.

**20–6. Goods versus Services.** Fred and Zuma Palermo contacted Colorado Carpet Installation, Inc., for a price quotation on providing and installing new carpeting and tiling in their home. In response, Colorado Carpet submitted a written proposal to provide and install the carpet at a certain price per square foot of material, *including* labor. The total was in excess of $500. The proposal was never accepted in writing by the Palermos, and the parties disagreed over how much of the proposal had been agreed to orally. After the installation of the carpet and tiling had begun, Mrs. Palermo became dissatisfied and sought the services of another contractor. Colorado Carpet then sued the Palermos for breach of the oral contract. The trial court held that the contract was one for services and was thus enforceable (that is, it did not fall under the Statute of Frauds [UCC 2–201], which requires contracts for the sale of *goods* for the price of $500 or more to be in writing to be enforceable). Discuss fully whether the contract between the Palermos and Colorado Carpet was primarily for the sale of goods or the sale of services. [*Colorado Carpet Installation, Inc. v. Palermo,* 668 P.2d 1384 (Colo. 1983)]

**20–7. Oral Agreements.** Loeb & Co. entered into an oral agreement with Schreiner, a farmer, whereby Schreiner was to sell Loeb 150 bales of cotton, each weighing 480 pounds. Shortly thereafter, Loeb sent Schreiner a letter confirming the terms of the oral contract. Schreiner neither acknowledged receipt of the letter nor objected to its terms. When delivery came due, Schreiner ignored the oral agreement and sold his cotton on the open market, because the price of cotton had more than doubled (from 37 cents to 80 cents per pound) since the oral agreement had been made. In a lawsuit by Loeb & Co. against Schreiner, can Loeb & Co. recover? Explain. [*Loeb & Co. v. Schreiner,* 294 Ala. 722, 321 So.2d 199 (1975)]

**20–8. Goods versus Services.** Helvey received electricity from the Wabash County REMC, the county electrical utility. A mistake in the voltage delivered over the electrical line resulted in damage to Helvey's household appliances; households require only 110 volts, and Wabash delivered 135 volts or more. Some years later, Helvey sued Wabash County for breach of express and implied contractual warranties. Wabash County claimed that under UCC 2–725, a four-year statute of limitations existed and that Helvey had no claim because more than four years had elapsed since the accident. State law provided for a shorter statute of limitations period for sales of goods than for service contracts, however. Helvey claimed that the UCC provision did not apply because electricity is a service and not a good. Discuss whether the UCC should be applied in this case. [*Helvey v. Wabash County REMC,* 151 Ind.App. 176, 278 N.E.2d 608 (1972)]

**20–9. Statute of Frauds.** R-P Packaging, Inc., is a manufacturer of cellophane wrapping material. The plant manager for Flowers Baking Co. decided to improve the company's packaging of cookies. The plant manager contacted R-P Packaging regarding the possible purchase of cellophane wrap imprinted with designed "artwork." R-P took measurements to determine the appropriate size of the wrap and submitted to Flowers a sample of wrap conforming to the measurements, along with a sample of the artwork to be imprinted. After agreeing that the artwork was satisfactory, Flowers gave a verbal order to R-P for the designed cellophane wrap at a price of $13,000. When the wrap was tendered, although it conformed to the measurements and design, Flowers complained that the wrap was too short and the design off center. Flowers rejected the shipment. R-P sued. Flowers contended that the oral contract was unenforceable under the Statute of Frauds. Discuss this contention. [*Flowers Baking Co. v. R-P Packaging, Inc.,* 229 Va. 370, 329 S.E.2d 462 (1985)]

**20–10. Statute of Frauds.** Peggy Holloway, a real estate broker, guaranteed payment for a shipment of over $11,000 worth of mozzarella cheese sold by Cudahy Foods Co. to Pizza Pride in Jamestown, North Carolina. The entire arrangement was made orally. Cudahy mailed to Holloway an invoice for the order, and Holloway did not object in writing to the invoice within ten days of receipt. Later, when Cudahy demanded payment from Holloway, Holloway denied having guaranteed payment for the cheese and raised the Statute of Frauds as an affirmative defense. Cudahy claimed that the Statute of Frauds could not be used as a defense, as both Cudahy and Holloway were merchants and Holloway had failed to object in writing within ten days to Cudahy's invoice. Discuss Cudahy's argument. [*Cudahy Foods Co. v. Holloway,* 286 S.E.2d 606 (N.C.App. 1982)]

**20–11. Forum-Selection Clause.** Royal Bed and Spring Co., a Puerto Rican distributor of furniture products, entered into an exclusive distributorship agreement with Famossul Industria e Comercio de Moveis Ltda., a Brazilian manufacturer of furniture products. Under the terms of the contract, Royal Bed was to distribute in Puerto Rico the furniture products manufactured in Brazil by Famossul. The contract contained forum-selection and choice-of-law clauses, which designated the judicial district of Curitiba, state of Paraná, Brazil, as the judicial forum and the Brazilian Civil Code as the law to be applied in the event of any dispute. Famossul terminated the exclusive distributorship and suspended the shipment of goods without just cause. Puerto Rican law refuses to enforce forum-selection clauses providing for foreign venues as a matter of public policy. In what jurisdiction should Royal Bed bring suit? Discuss fully. [*Royal Bed and Spring Co. v. Famossul Industria e Comercio de Moveis Ltda.,* 906 F.2d 45 (5th Cir. 1990)]

**20–12. Statute of Frauds.** Monetti, S.P.A., is an Italian firm that makes decorative plastic trays and related products for the food services industry. In 1981, Monetti set up a wholly owned subsidiary, Melform U.S.A., to market its products in the United States. In 1984, after orally agreeing with Anchor Hocking Corp. (Anchor) that Anchor would become the exclusive U.S. distributor of Monetti products, Monetti terminated all of Melform's current distributors and informed all of Melform's customers that Anchor would be the exclusive distributor of its products in the future. Relations between Monetti and Anchor deteriorated over the next several months, and eventually Monetti sued for breach of contract. Anchor contended that their contract was unenforceable under the Statute of Frauds. Although their agreement had never been reduced to a writing, at one point Raymond Davis, the marketing director of Anchor, summarized the terms of the agreement in a memorandum on Anchor's letterhead that was sent to Anchor's law department. The memo included some handwritten notes by Davis, which, Davis stated, represented ''more clearly our current position regarding the agreement.'' Will the memorandum signed by Davis constitute a sufficient writing under the UCC Statute of Frauds provisions? Discuss. [*Monetti, S.P.A. v. Anchor Hocking Corp.,* 931 F.2d 1178 (7th Cir. 1991)]

**20–13. Forum-Selection Clause.** Ronald Riley, an American citizen, wanted to underwrite some insurance policies issued by the Society and Council of Lloyd's, a British insurance corporation with its principal place of business in London. In 1980, Riley and Lloyd's entered into an agreement that allowed Riley to underwrite insurance through Lloyd's and provided that if any dispute arose between Lloyd's and Riley, the courts of England would have exclusive jurisdiction and the laws of England would apply. Over the next decade, some of the parties insured under policies that Riley underwrote experienced large losses, for which they filed claims. Instead of paying his share of the claims, Riley filed a lawsuit in a U.S. district court, seeking, among other things, rescission of his agreement with Lloyd's. The defendants included Lloyd's and those among its managers and directors—all British citizens or entities—with whom Riley had dealt when he began his association with Lloyd's. Riley alleged that the defendants had violated the Securities Act of 1933, the Securities Exchange Act of 1934, and Rule 10b-5. The defendants asked the court to enforce the forum-selection clause in the agreement. Riley argued that if the clause was enforced, he would be deprived of his rights under the U.S. securities laws. The court ruled that the clause was enforceable, and Riley appealed. What will the appellate court decide? Discuss. [*Riley v. Kingsley Underwriting Agencies, Ltd.,* 969 F.2d 953 (10th Cir. 1992)]

**20–14. Contract Modification.** Ritz-Craft Corp. contracted with the Stanford Management Group (SMG) to ''manufacture and install prefabricated multi-family housing units'' for SMG. Ritz-Craft was also to set the units on the foundations constructed by SMG, as well as provide some connective work for electricity, plumbing, and so on. The original contract price for forty-nine units was $1,613,500, but a subsequent modification to the contract due to unforeseen circumstances raised the price an additional $45,000. SMG refused to pay the additional $45,000, arguing that the modification was not enforceable because it had not been accompanied by consideration. Ritz-Craft sued for breach of contract. If no consideration was given, is the agreement to modify the original contract binding? Does the manufacture and installation of modular homes involve goods or services? Discuss fully how the court should rule on each of these issues. [*Ritz-Craft Corp. v. Stanford Management Group,* 800 F.Supp. 1312 (D.Md. 1992)]

### 20–15. A Question of Ethics

 *Gordonsville Industries, Inc., located in Virginia, entered into a contract with American Artos Corp., a North Carolina corporation, for the design, construction, and installation of a textile-drying system. Artos, in turn, contracted with GEA Luftkuhlergesellschaft, a German firm, for the design of a hot-oil boiler, one of the system's integral parts. GEA subcontracted the actual construction of the boiler to Industrial Boiler Co., a Georgia corporation. A forum-selection clause in the Artos-GEA contract specified that in the event of a lawsuit, ''it is agreed that the place for litigation shall be the Amtsgericht [civil court] in Bochum, Germany.'' Later, Gordonsville Industries, unhappy with the performance of the textile-drying system, filed suit in a U.S. federal court against Artos to recover damages. Artos then filed a complaint, essentially seeking indemnification (reimbursement), against GEA. GEA moved to dismiss the complaint on the ground that under the forum-selection clause in the Artos-GEA contract, the dispute should be heard in the specified German court. Artos contended that the clause should not be enforced, because the construction of the boiler had taken place in the United States, and all of the relevant records and witnesses were located in the United States, not Germany.* [Gordonsville Industries, Inc. v. American Artos Corp., 549 F.Supp. 200 (W.D.Va. 1982)]

1. Discuss whether the circumstances of this case would justify permitting the case to proceed in the U.S. courts.
2. What arguments might Artos raise against having the dispute heard in the German courts?
3. How would you evaluate the argument that strict enforcement of the forum-selection clause is necessary to promote certainty in international commercial transactions?

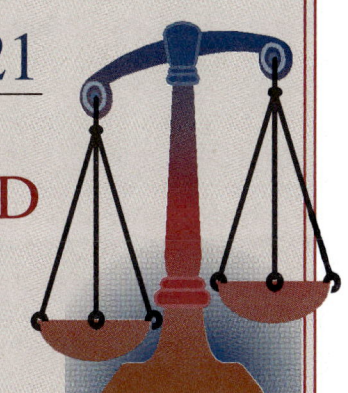

# CHAPTER 21

# TITLE, RISK, AND INSURABLE INTEREST

B efore the creation of the Uniform Commercial Code (UCC), *title*—right of ownership—was the central concept in sales law, controlling all issues of rights and remedies of the parties to a sales contract. Frequently, however, it was difficult to determine when title actually passed from seller to buyer, and therefore it was also difficult to predict which party a court would decide had title at the time of a loss. Because of such problems, the UCC divorced the question of title as completely as possible from the question of the rights and obligations of buyers, sellers, and third persons (such as subsequent purchasers and creditors).

In some situations, title is still relevant under the UCC, and the UCC has special rules for locating title. These rules will be discussed in the materials that follow. In most situations, however, the UCC replaces the concept of title with three other concepts: (1) identification, (2) risk of loss, and (3) insurable interest.

## SECTION 1

## IDENTIFICATION

Before any interest in specific goods can pass from the seller to the buyer, two conditions must prevail: (1) the goods must be in existence, and (2) they must be identified to the contract. If either condition is lacking, only a *contract to sell* (not a sale) exists [UCC 2–105(2)]. Goods that are not both existing and identified to the contract are called *future goods*. For example, a contract to purchase next year's crop of hay is a contract for future goods, a crop yet to be grown.

For passage of title, the goods must be identified in a way that will distinguish the particular goods to be delivered under the sales contract from all other similar goods.[1] **Identification** is a designation of goods as the subject matter of the sales contract.

In many cases, identification is simply a matter of specific designation. For example, you contract to purchase a fleet of five cars by the serial numbers listed for the cars, or you agree to purchase all the wheat in a specific bin at a stated price per bushel. Problems usually occur only when a quantity of goods is purchased from a larger mass, such as one thousand cases of peas from a ten-thousand-case lot.

There is a general rule that when a purchaser buys a quantity of goods to be taken from a larger mass, identification can be made only by separation of the contracted goods from the mass. Therefore, until the seller separates the one thousand cases of peas from the ten-thousand-case lot, title and risk of loss remain with the seller.

There are a few exceptions to this general rule. For example, a seller owns approximately five thousand chickens (hens and roosters). A buyer agrees to purchase all the hen chickens at a stated price. Most courts would hold that "all the hen chickens" is a sufficient identification, and title and risk can pass to the buyer without the goods identified in the contract being physically separated from the other goods (the hens from the roosters). The reasoning is that the contract identification serves as sufficient separation.

The most common exception deals with **fungible goods** [UCC 1–201(17)]. Fungible goods are goods that are alike by physical nature, by agreement, or by trade usage. Typical examples are wheat, oil, and wine. If these goods are held or intended to be held by owners in common (owners that have undifferentiated shares of the entire mass), an owner can pass title and risk of loss to a buyer without an actual separation. The buyer replaces the seller as an owner in common [UCC 2–105(4)].

For example, Ashworth, Bazelon, and Carroll are farmers. They deposit, respectively, 5,000 bushels, 3,000 bushels, and 2,000 bushels of the same grade of grain in a bin. The three become owners in common, with Ashworth owning 50 percent of the 10,000 bushels; Bazelon, 30 percent; and Carroll, 20 percent. Ashworth could contract to sell 5,000 bushels of grain to Tyson and, because the goods are fungible, pass title and risk of loss to Tyson without physically separating 5,000 bushels. Tyson now becomes an owner in common with Bazelon and Carroll.

Identification is significant because it gives the buyer the right to obtain insurance on the goods and the right to recover from third parties who damage the goods. In certain circumstances, identification allows the buyer to take the goods from the seller. In other words, the concept of identification is easier to understand if one looks at its consequences.

Parties can agree on whether identification will take place in their contract; but if they do not so specify, in addition to the preceding rules, the following rules apply [UCC 2–501(1)]:

1. Identification takes place at the time the contract is made *if the contract calls for the sale of specific and ascertained goods already existing.*
2. If the sale involves unborn animals that will be born within twelve months from the time of the contract, identification will take place when the young are conceived. If it involves crops to be harvested within twelve months (or during the next harvest season occurring after contracting, whichever is further in the future), identification will take place when the crops are planted or begin to grow.
3. In other cases, identification takes place when the goods are marked, shipped, or somehow designated by the seller as the particular goods to pass under the contract. The seller can delegate the right to identify goods to the buyer.

---

1. According to UCC 2–401, each provision of Article 2 "with respect to the rights, obligations, and remedies of the seller, the buyer, purchasers or other third parties applies irrespective of title to the goods except where the provisions refer to such title." These provisions referring to title include the following: UCC 2–312, warranty of title by seller; UCC 2–326(3), consignment sales; UCC 2–327(1)(a), sale on approval and "risk of loss"; UCC 2–403(1), entrustment; UCC 2–501(2), insurable interest in goods; and UCC 2–722, who can sue third parties for injury to goods.

## SECTION 2

# WHEN TITLE PASSES

Once goods exist and have been identified, the provisions of UCC 2–401 apply to the passage of title. Parties can expressly agree to when and under what conditions title will pass to the buyer. In virtually all subsections of UCC 2–401, the words ''unless otherwise explicitly agreed'' appear, meaning that any explicit understanding between the buyer and the seller will determine when title passes.

Unless an agreement is explicitly made, title passes to the buyer at the time and place at which the seller performs the physical delivery of the goods [UCC 2–401(2)]. The delivery terms determine when this occurs, as discussed below.

## SHIPMENT CONTRACTS

Under shipment contracts, the seller is required or authorized to ship goods by carrier. Here, the seller is required only to deliver the goods into the hands of a carrier (such as a trucking company), and title passes to the buyer at the time and place of shipment [UCC 2–401(2)(a)].

## DESTINATION CONTRACTS

With destination contracts, the seller is required to deliver the goods to a particular destination, usually directly to the buyer but sometimes to another destination designated by the buyer. Title passes to the buyer when the goods are tendered at that destination [UCC 2–401(2)(b)].

## DELIVERY WITHOUT MOVEMENT OF THE GOODS

When the contract of sale does not call for the seller's shipment or delivery (when the buyer is to pick up the goods), the passage of title depends on whether the seller must deliver a document of title, such as a bill of lading or a warehouse receipt, to the buyer. A **bill of lading** is a receipt for goods that is signed by a carrier and that serves as a contract for the transportation of the goods. A **warehouse receipt** is a receipt issued by a warehouser for goods stored in his or her warehouse. (See Exhibits 21–1 and 21–2.) When a document of title is required, title passes to the buyer *when and where the document is delivered*. Thus, if the goods are stored in a warehouse, title passes to the buyer when the appropriate documents are delivered to the buyer. The goods need not move. In fact, the buyer can choose to leave the goods at the same warehouse for a period of time, and the buyer's title to those goods will be unaffected.

When no documents of title are required, and delivery is made without the goods being moved,

title passes at the time and place the sales contract was made, if the goods have already been identified. If the goods have not been identified, then title does not pass until identification occurs. Consider an example: Fein sells lumber to Ozo. It is agreed that Ozo will pick up the lumber at the yard. If the lumber has been identified (segregated, marked, or in any other way distinguished from all other lumber), title will pass to Ozo when the contract is signed. If the lumber is still in storage bins at the mill, however, title will not pass to Ozo until the particular pieces of lumber to be sold under this contract are identified [UCC 2–401(3)].

---

## SECTION 3

# RISK OF LOSS

Under the UCC, risk of loss does not necessarily pass with title. The question of who suffers a financial risk if goods are damaged, destroyed, or lost is resolved primarily under Sections 2–509 and 2–319. Several factors determine when risk of loss passes from the seller to the buyer. We look at those factors below, as well as the effect of a breach of contract on risk of loss.

### PASSAGE OF RISK OF LOSS ABSENT A BREACH OF CONTRACT

Risk of loss can be assigned through an agreement by the parties, preferably in writing. Therefore, the parties can generally control the exact moment risk of loss passes from the seller to the buyer. Of course, at the agreed-on time, the goods must be in existence and identified to the contract for this contract provision to be enforceable. In the absence of agreement, risk of loss generally passes to the buyer when the seller delivers, or tenders delivery of, the goods to the buyer. We now discuss the basic rules governing passage of risk of loss when there has been no express agreement on the subject and no breach of contract.

**CARRIER CASES** Assuming that there is no specification in the agreement, the following rules apply to carrier cases (cases in which the goods are delivered by railroad, truck, airplane, ship, or other mode of paid transport).

*Contract Terms.* Certain specific terms in the contract, normally used in sales price quotations,

■ **Exhibit 21–1 A Sample Negotiable Bill of Lading**

1st Sheet

UNIFORM MOTOR CARRIER ORDER BILL OF LADING

Shipper's No._____

*Original—Domestic*

Agent's No._____

# CENTRAL FREIGHT LINES INC.

RECEIVED, subject to the classifications and tariffs in effect on the date of the issue of this Bill of Lading,

From _____ , Date _____ 19__

At _____ Street, _____ City, _____ County, _____ State

the property described below, in apparent good order, except as noted (contents and condition of contents of packages unknown) marked, consigned and destined as shown below, which said company (the word company being understood throughout this contract as meaning any person or corporation in possession of the property under the contract) agrees to carry to its usual place of delivery at said destination, if within the scope of its lawful operations, otherwise to deliver to another carrier on the route to said destination. It is mutually agreed, as to each carrier of all or any of said property over all or any portion of said route to destination, and as to each party at any time interested in all or any of said property, that every service to be performed hereunder shall be subject to all the conditions not prohibited by law, whether printed or written, herein contained, including the conditions on back hereof, which are hereby agreed to by the shipper and accepted for himself and his assigns.

The surrender of this Original ORDER Bill of Lading properly indorsed shall be required before the delivery of the property. Inspection of property covered by this bill of lading will not be permitted unless provided by law or unless permission is indorsed on this original Bill of lading or given in writing by the shipper.

**Consigned to Order of** _____

**Destination** _____ Street, _____ City, _____ County, _____ State

**Notify** _____

**At** _____ Street, _____ City, _____ County, _____ State

**I. C. C. No.** _____ **Vehicle No.** _____

**Routing** _____

| No. Pack-ages | Description of Articles, Special Marks, and Exceptions | *Weight (Subject to Correction) | Class or Rate | Check Column | Subject to Section 7 of Conditions, if this shipment is to be delivered to the consignee without recourse on the consignor, the consignor shall sign the following statement: |
|---|---|---|---|---|---|
| | | | | | The carrier shall not make delivery of this shipment without payment of freight and all other lawful charges. |
| | | | | | |
| | | | | | (Signature of consignor.) |
| | | | | | If charges are to be prepaid write or stamp here, "To be Prepaid." |
| | | | | | Received $_____ to apply in prepayment of the charges on the property described hereon. |
| | | | | | Agent or Cashier. |
| | | | | | Per_____ (The signature here acknowledges only the amount prepaid.) |

SAMPLE

*If the shipment moves between two ports by a carrier by water, the law requires that the bill of lading shall state whether it is "carrier's or shipper's weight."

Note—Where the rate is dependent on value, shippers are required to state specifically in writing the agreed or declared value of the property.

The agreed or declared value of the property is hereby specifically stated by the shipper to be not exceeding

_____ per _____

Charges advanced:

$_____

Shipper _____ Agent _____

Per _____ Per _____

Permanent address of Shipper _____ Street, _____ City, _____ State

MOORE BUSINESS FORMS, INC., WACO, TEX. M

Source: Reprinted with permission of Central Freight Lines Inc. © 1985 Central Freight Lines, Inc.
Note: This form is printed in yellow to warn holders that it is an order bill of lading. The back of the form permits negotiation by indorsement.

■ **Exhibit 21–2  A Sample Nonnegotiable Warehouse Receipt**

## Warehouse Receipt—Not Negotiable

HART

Agreement No. _____    Vault No. _____  _____  _____  _____  _____  _____

Service Order _____  _____  _____  _____  _____  _____  _____

Receipt and
Lot Number _____    Date of Issue _____ 19 _____

Received for the account of and deliverable to • _____

whose latest known address is _____

SAMPLE

_____ the goods enumerated on the inside or attached schedule to be

stored in Company warehouse, located at _____
which goods are accepted only upon the following conditions set forth below:

READ CAREFULLY➤ That the value of all goods stored, including the contents of any container, and all goods hereafter stored for Depositor's account to be not over $ _____ per pound † per article unless a higher value is noted in the schedule, for which an additional monthly storage charge of _____ ¢ on each $ _____ valuation in excess of $ _____ per pound † per article or fraction thereof will be made.

If there are any items enumerated in this receipt valued in excess of the above limitations per pound per article and not so noted in the schedule, return this receipt within 10 days with proper values so indicated in writing in order that the receipt may be re-issued and proper higher storage rates assessed.

OWNERSHIP. The Customer, Shipper, Depositor, or Agent represents and warrants that he is lawfully possessed of goods to be stored and/or has the authority to store or ship said goods. (If the goods are mortgaged, notify the Company the name and address of the mortgagee.)

PAYMENT OF CHARGES. Storage bills are payable monthly in advance for each month's storage or fraction thereof. Labor charges, cartage and other services rendered are payable upon completion of work. All charges shall be paid at the warehouse location shown hereon, and if delinquent, shall incur interest monthly at the rate of _____ per cent ( ) per year. The Depositor will pay reasonable attorney's fee incurred by The Company in collecting delinquent accounts.

LIABILITY OF COMPANY. The company shall be liable for any loss or injury to the goods caused by its failure to exercise such care as a reasonably careful man would exercise under like circumstances. The company will not be liable for loss or damage to fragile articles not packed, or articles packed or unpacked by other than employees of this company. Depositor specifically agrees that the warehouse will not be liable for contamination of or for insect damage to articles placed in drawers of furniture by the depositor. Periodic spraying of the warehouse premises shall constitute ordinary and proper care, unless the depositor requests in writing and pays for anti-infestation treatment of articles in drawers and compartments of stored furniture.

CHANGE OF ADDRESS. Notice of change of address must be given the Company in writing, and acknowledged in writing by the Company.

TRANSFER OR WITHDRAWAL OF GOODS. The warehouse receipt is not negotiable and shall be produced and all charges must be paid before delivery to the Depositor, or transfer of goods to another person; however, a written direction to the Company to transfer the goods to another person or deliver the goods may be accepted by the Company at its option without requiring tender of the warehouse receipt.

ACCESS TO STORAGE, PARTIAL WITHDRAWAL. A signed order from the person in whose name the receipt is issued is required to enable others to remove or have access to goods. A charge is made for stacking and unstacking, and for access to stored goods.

BUILDING—FIRE—WATCHMAN. The Company does not represent or warrant that its building cannot be destroyed by fire or that the contents of said buildings including the said property cannot be destroyed by fire. The Company shall not be required to maintain a watchman or sprinkler system and its failure to do so shall not constitute negligence.

CLAIMS OR ERRORS. All claims for non-delivery of any article or articles and for damage, breakage, etc., must be made in writing within ninety (90) days from delivery of goods stored or they are waived. Failure to return the warehouse receipt for correction within ( ) days after receipt thereof by the depositor will be conclusive that it is correct and delivery will be made only in accordance therewith.

FUTURE SERVICE. This Contract shall extend and apply to future services rendered to the Depositor by the Company and to any additional goods deposited with the Company by the Depositor.

WAREHOUSEMAN'S LIEN. The Company reserves the right to sell the goods stored, in accordance with the provisions of the Uniform Commercial Code (Business and Commerce Code if stored in Texas), for all lawful charges in arrears.

TERMINATION OF STORAGE. The Company reserves the right to terminate the storage of the goods at any time by giving to the Depositor thirty (30) days' written notice of its intention so to do, and, unless the Depositor removes such goods within that period, the Company is hereby empowered to have the same removed at the cost and expense of the Depositor, or the Company may sell them at auction in accordance with state law.

DEPOSITOR WILL PAY REASONABLE LEGAL FEES INCURRED BY WAREHOUSE IN COLLECTING DELINQUENT CHARGES.

THIS DOCUMENT CONTAINS THE WHOLE CONTRACT BETWEEN THE PARTIES AND THERE ARE NO OTHER TERMS, WARRANTIES, REPRESENTATIONS, OR AGREEMENTS OF EITHER DEPOSITOR OR COMPANY NOT HEREIN CONTAINED.

| | |
|---|---|
| Storage per month or fraction thereof . . . . | $ _____ |
| Warehouse labor . . . . . | $ _____ |
| Cartage . . . . . . | $ _____ |
| Packing at residence . . | $ _____ |
| Wrapping and preparing for storage . . . . . | $ _____ |
| Charges advanced . . . . | $ _____ |
| _____ | $ _____ |
| _____ | $ _____ |

By _____

*Insert "Mr. and/or Mrs." or, if military personnel, appropriate rank or grade.
†Delete the words "per pound" if the declared value is per article.
For goods stored for military personnel under PL 245, the contractor's liability for care of goods is as provided in Basic Agreement with U.S. Government.

THIS PROPERTY HAS NOT BEEN INSURED BY THIS COMPANY FOR FIRE OR ANY OTHER CASUALTY
SCHEDULE OF GOODS ON FOLLOWING PAGE OR ATTACHED

H-1 (9N1) Approved by SH H T4 ©          Re-order from Hart Graphics, Austin, Texas

Source: Reprinted with permission of Hart Graphics, Inc., of Austin, Texas. © 1985 Hart Graphics, Inc.

assist in determining when risk of loss passes to the buyer. Four such terms should be noted:

1. *F.O.B.* (free on board) means that delivery is at the seller's expense to a specific location. The parties can agree that delivery be either at the place of shipment (for example, the seller's city or place of business) or at the place of destination (for example, the buyer's city or place of business). Absent a contrary agreement, when the term is F.O.B. the place of shipment, the risk of loss passes when the seller puts the goods into the carrier's possession. When the term is F.O.B. the place of destination, the risk of loss passes when the seller tenders delivery [UCC 2–319(1)].

2. *F.A.S.* (free alongside) requires the seller, at his or her own expense and risk, to deliver the goods alongside the ship that will transport the goods, at which point risk passes to the buyer [UCC 2–319(2)].

3. *C.I.F.* or *C.&F.* (cost, insurance, and freight, or just cost and freight) requires, among other things, that the seller ''put the goods in possession of a carrier'' before risk can pass to the buyer [UCC 2–320(2)].

4. *Delivery ex-ship* (from the carrying vessel) means that risk of loss does not pass to the buyer until the goods leave the ship or are otherwise properly unloaded [UCC 2–322].

***Shipment Contracts.*** In a **shipment contract,** the seller is required or authorized to ship goods by carrier (that is, not required to deliver them to a particular destination). Risk of loss in shipment contracts passes to the buyer when the goods are duly delivered to the carrier [UCC 2–509(1)(a)].[2]

For example, a seller in New York sells ten thousand tons of sheet metal to a buyer in California, F.O.B. New York (free on board in New York—that is, the buyer pays the transportation charges from New York). The contract authorizes a shipment by carrier; it does not require the seller to tender the metal in California. Risk passes to the buyer when the conforming goods are properly placed in the possession of the carrier. If the goods are damaged in transit, the loss falls on the buyer. (For this reason, buyers may want to insure the goods from the time they leave the seller.) Gen-

erally, all contracts are assumed to be shipment contracts if nothing to the contrary is stated in the contract.

***Destination Contracts.*** A **destination contract** requires the seller to deliver the goods to a particular destination. The risk of loss in destination contracts passes to the buyer when the goods are tendered to the buyer at that destination. In the preceding example, if the contract had been F.O.B. California, risk of loss during transit to California would have fallen on the seller.

**DELIVERY WITHOUT MOVEMENT OF THE GOODS** Frequently, the goods are to be picked up from the seller by the buyer. In the absence of agreement, if the seller is a merchant, risk of loss passes to the buyer only on the buyer's taking physical possession of the goods. If the seller is a nonmerchant, risk passes to the buyer on the seller's tender of delivery [UCC 2–509(3)]. To illustrate: Mellor buys a stereo from Circuit Electronics on Tuesday and tells Circuit that she will pick it up on Thursday. On Wednesday, the electronics store burns down, and the stereo is lost. Because Circuit is a merchant and Mellor had not yet taken possession of the stereo, the loss falls on Circuit. If Mellor had bought the stereo from her neighbor, with Mellor agreeing to pick up the stereo at any time within the next two days, and the neighbor's house had burned down before Mellor picked up the stereo, the loss would fall on Mellor—because her neighbor is a nonmerchant.

When a bailee[3] is holding goods for a person who has contracted to sell them and the goods are to be delivered without being moved, the risk of loss passes to the buyer when (1) the buyer receives a negotiable (transferable by indorsement or delivery)[4] document of title for the goods, (2) the bailee acknowledges the buyer's right to possess the goods, or (3) the buyer receives a nonnegotiable document of title *and* has had a *reasonable time* to present the document to the bailee and demand

---

2. Assuming that the carrier is an independent carrier—that is, that the seller does not own and control the carrier.

3. Under the UCC, a bailee is a party who by bill of lading, warehouse receipt, or other document of title acknowledges possession of goods and contracts to deliver them [UCC 7–102(1)(a)]. A warehousing company, for example, or a trucking company that normally issues documents of title for goods it receives is a bailee. Bailments are the subject of Chapter 50.
4. UCC 7–104 states what constitutes negotiable and nonnegotiable documents of title. See Chapter 50.

the goods. Obviously, if the bailee refuses to honor the document, the risk of loss remains with the seller [UCC 2–509(2); UCC 2–503(4)(b)]. (See Exhibit 21–1 for a sample negotiable bill of lading and Exhibit 21–2 for a sample nonnegotiable warehouse receipt.)

To illustrate: McKee stores goods in Hardy's warehouse and takes a negotiable warehouse receipt for them. On the following day, McKee indorses the receipt (in this instance, signs his name on the document) and sells it to Byne, for cash. The day after that, Hardy's warehouse burns down, and the goods are completely destroyed. The risk of loss is on Byne, because it accompanied the negotiable warehouse receipt that gave him title to the goods.

In the following case, goods stored in a warehouse were destroyed by fire just a few days after they had been sold. The court had little difficulty in determining that title to the goods had passed from seller to buyer at the time the transfer was entered on the warehouse books—before the fire occurred. Because the goods were uninsured at the time of the fire, the significant issue for the parties involved was whether risk of loss had also passed to the buyer prior to the fire.

---

**BACKGROUND AND FACTS** *In December 1982, Peter Eckrich & Sons, Inc., contracted to buy from Jason's Foods, Inc., 38,000 pounds of "St. Louis style" pork ribs. It was arranged that the ribs would be transferred from Jason's account in an independent warehouse to Eckrich's account in the same warehouse, without any actual movement of the ribs. In its confirmation of the agreement, Jason's notified Eckrich that the transfer would be effected between January 10 and January 14. On January 13, Jason's telephoned the warehouse and requested that the transfer be made. The transfer was entered on the warehouse books immediately, but no warehouse receipt was sent to Eckrich until January 17 or 18, and Eckrich did not receive the receipt—and thus did not know the transfer had occurred—until January 24. The warehouse burned down on January 17, and Jason's subsequently sued Eckrich to recover the contract price. The trial court held that Eckrich was not liable, because risk of loss had not passed to Eckrich prior to the fire. The trial court judge granted summary judgment for Eckrich, and Jason's appealed.*

CASE 21.1

**JASON'S FOODS, INC. v. PETER ECKRICH & SONS, INC.**
United States Court of Appeals, Seventh Circuit, 1985. 774 F.2d 214.

*POSNER,* Circuit Judge.

\*   \*   \*   \*

\*   \*   \* Section 2–509(2) separates title from risk of loss. Title to the ribs passed to Eckrich when the warehouse made the transfer on its books from Jason's' account to Eckrich's, but the risk of loss did not pass until the transfer was "acknowledged."

\*   \*   \*   \*

A related section of the Uniform Commercial Code, section 2–503(4)(a) makes acknowledgment by the bailee (the warehouse here) a method of tendering goods that are sold without being physically moved; but, like section 2–509(2)(b), it does not indicate to whom acknowledgment must be made. The official comments on this section, however, indicate that it was not intended to change the corresponding section of the Uniform Sales Act, section 43(3). And section 43(3) had expressly required acknowledgment to the buyer. \*   \*   \* The acknowledgment need not, by the way, be in writing, so far as we are aware. Jason's could have instructed the warehouse to call Eckrich when the transfer was complete on the warehouse's books. \*   \*   \*

\*   \*   \*   \*

\*   \*   \* Does "acknowledgment" mean receipt, as in the surrounding subsections of 2–509(2), or mailing? Since the evidence was in conflict over whether the acknowledgment was mailed on January 17 (and at what hour), which was the day of the fire, or on January 18, this could be an important question—but in another case. Jason's waived it. The only theory it tendered to the district court, or briefed and argued in this court, was that the risk of loss passed either on January 13, when the transfer of title was made on the books of the warehouse, or at the latest on January 14, because Eckrich knew the ribs would be transferred at the warehouse sometime between January 10 and 14. We have discussed the immateriality of the passage of title on January 13; we add that the alternative argument, that Eckrich knew by January 14 that it owned the ribs, exaggerates what Eckrich knew. By the close of business on January 14 Eckrich had a well-founded expectation that the ribs had been transferred to its account; but considering the many slips that are possible between cup and lips, we do not think that this expectation should fix the point at which the risk shifts.

**DECISION AND REMEDY**  *The court of appeals, affirming the decision of the trial court, held that the risk of loss passes when there is "acknowledgment" to the buyer that the goods have been transferred to its account. Jason's could have instructed the warehouse supervisor to call Eckrich and acknowledge the transfer as soon as the transfer had been completed on the books. Because Jason's chose not to give these instructions, "acknowledgment" took place when Eckrich received the receipt on January 24. Thus, when the warehouse burned down on January 17, the risk of loss had not yet been transferred to Eckrich.*

## SALE ON APPROVAL AND SALE OR RETURN CONTRACTS

A **sale on approval** is not a sale until the buyer accepts (approves) the offer. A **sale or return** is a sale that can be rescinded by the buyer without liability. In each case, passage of title and risk of loss depend on the conditional event's happening or not happening, because these transactions are conditional by their very nature.

**SALE ON APPROVAL**  When a seller offers to sell goods to a buyer and permits the buyer to take the goods on a trial basis, a sale on approval is made. The term *sale* here is a misnomer, because only an *offer* to sell has been made, along with a bailment (the holding or storage of another's personal property—see Chapter 50) created by the buyer's possession.

Therefore, title and risk of loss (from causes beyond the buyer's control) remain with the seller until the buyer accepts the offer. Acceptance can be made expressly, by any act inconsistent with the *trial* purpose or seller's ownership, or by the buyer's election not to return the goods within the trial period. If the buyer does not wish to accept, the buyer may notify the seller of that fact within the trial period, and the return is at the seller's expense and risk [UCC 2–327(1)]. Goods held on approval are not subject to the claims of the buyer's creditors until acceptance.

To imagine a sale on approval, suppose that East Side Motors, a Nissan dealership, agrees to let Elena take a new 300SX home to drive for a day to see whether she wants to buy it. Under these circumstances, if Elena drives the 300SX for a day and then tells East Side Motors that she does not want to buy the car, she will be considered not to have accepted the car. If she takes the car for a week's drive along the coast, however, she will be considered to have accepted the car, because she used it in a manner inconsistent with the trial purpose—that is, she used it as if she were the car's owner.

**SALE OR RETURN**  The sale or return (sometimes called *sale and return*) is a species of contract by which the seller delivers a quantity of goods to the buyer with the understanding that if the buyer wishes to retain any portion of those goods (for use or resale), the buyer will consider the portion retained as having been sold to him or her and will pay accordingly. The balance will be returned to the seller or will be held by the buyer as a bailee subject to the seller's order. When the buyer receives possession, the title and risk of loss pass to

## ■ CONCEPT SUMMARY 21.1 Passage of Title and Risk of Loss Absent Agreement

| SITUATION | BASIC RULES |
|---|---|
| Contract terms call for goods to be *shipped* (i.e., F.O.B. seller's location). | 1. Title and risk pass upon seller's delivery of conforming goods to the carrier [UCC 2–401(2)(a), UCC 2–509(1)(a)]. |
| Contract terms call for goods to be delivered at *destination* (i.e., F.O.B. buyer's location). | 1. Title and risk pass upon seller's *tender* of delivery of conforming goods to the buyer at the point of destination [UCC 2–401(2)(b), UCC 2–509(1)(b)]. |
| Contract terms call for goods to be delivered *without physical movement* (i.e., the buyer must pick up the goods). | 1. If the goods are not represented by a document of title— <br> a. Title passes upon the formation of the contract [UCC 2–401(3)(b)]. <br> b. Risk passes to the buyer, if seller is a merchant, upon buyer's *receipt* of the goods or, if seller is a nonmerchant, upon seller's *tender* of delivery of the goods [UCC 2–509(3)]. <br> 2. If the goods are represented by a document of title— <br> a. If the document is negotiable, and the goods are held by a bailee, title and risk pass upon the buyer's *receipt* of the document [UCC 2–401(3)(a), UCC 2–509(2)(a)]. <br> b. If the document is nonnegotiable, and the goods are held by a bailee, title passes upon the buyer's receipt of the document, but risk does *not* pass until the buyer, after receipt of the document, has had reasonable time to present the document to demand the goods [UCC 2–401(3)(a), UCC 2–509(2)(c), UCC 2–503(4)(b)]. <br> 3. If the goods are held by a bailee and no document of title is transferred, risk passes to the buyer when the bailee acknowledges the buyer's right to the possession of the goods [UCC 2–509(2)(b)]. |

the buyer. Both remain with the buyer until the buyer returns the goods to the seller within the time period specified. If the buyer fails to return the goods within this time period, the sale is finalized. The return of the goods is at the buyer's risk and expense. The goods held on a sale or return contract are subject to the claims of the buyer's creditors while they are in the buyer's possession.

To illustrate: If Sapor, a diamond wholesaler, delivers diamonds to Brande Gems, a retailer, to resell on the understanding that Brande may return any unsold diamonds at the end of six months, the transaction is a sale or return. The risk of loss falls on Brande. If none of the diamonds is returned—because Brande has resold them (or even lost them)—Brande is responsible to Sapor for their price. Brande is also responsible for the expense of transporting whatever diamonds are returned. If Brande goes bankrupt, the diamonds will be subject to the claims of Brande's creditors.

It is often difficult to determine from a particular transaction which exists—a sale on approval or a contract for sale or return. The UCC states that (unless otherwise agreed) if the goods are primarily for the buyer to use, the transaction is a sale on approval; if the goods are primarily for the buyer to resell, the transaction is a sale or return [UCC 2–326(1)].

The UCC treats a **consignment** as a sale or return. Under a consignment, the owner of goods (the *consignor*) delivers them to another (the *consignee*) for the consignee to sell. If the consignee sells the goods, he or she must pay the consignor for them. If the goods are not sold, they may simply be returned to the consignor. While the goods are in the possession of the consignee, the consignee holds title to them, and creditors of the consignee will prevail over the consignor in any action to repossess the goods. The UCC does make an exception to this rule governing consignments if the person making delivery (the consignor) does one of the following:

1. Complies with an applicable law providing for a consignor's interest or the like to be evidenced by a sign.
2. Establishes that the person conducting the business (the consignee) is generally known by his or her creditors to be substantially engaged in selling the goods of others.
3. Complies with the filing provisions of Article 9 (to be discussed in Chapter 31) [UCC 2–326(3)].

For example, suppose that Buendia operates a retail furniture store under the name of Affordable Furniture. Lindo Outdoor Furniture Company delivers some patio sets to Buendia on consignment. Lindo is the consignor, and Buendia is the consignee. If (1) no sign is posted evidencing Lindo's interest, (2) Buendia is not generally known to sell from a consigned inventory, and (3) Lindo does not comply with the filing provisions of Article 9, the patio sets are subject to the claims of Buendia's creditors.

## RISK OF LOSS IN A BREACHED SALES CONTRACT

There are many ways to breach a sales contract. The transfer of risk operates differently depending on whether the seller or the buyer breaches. Generally, the party in breach bears the risk of loss.

**SELLER'S BREACH**  If the goods are so nonconforming that the buyer has the right to reject them, the risk of loss will not pass to the buyer until the defects are cured or until the buyer accepts the goods in spite of their defects (thus waiving the right to reject). For example, a buyer orders blue widgets from a seller, F.O.B. seller's plant. The seller ships black widgets, giving the buyer the right to reject. The widgets are damaged in transit. The risk of loss falls on the seller (although the risk would have been on the buyer if blue widgets had been shipped) [UCC 2–510].

If a buyer accepts a shipment of goods and later discovers a latent defect (a defect not immediately apparent), acceptance can be revoked. Revocation allows the buyer to pass the risk of loss back to the seller, at least to the extent that the buyer's insurance does not cover the loss [UCC 2–510(2)].

**BUYER'S BREACH**  The general rule is that when a buyer breaches a contract, the risk of loss *immediately* shifts to the buyer. There are three important limitations to this rule:

1. The seller must already have identified the goods under the contract.
2. The buyer will bear the risk for only a *commercially reasonable time* after the seller learns of the breach.
3. The buyer will be liable only to the extent of any *deficiency* in the seller's insurance coverage [UCC 2–510(3)].

## INTERNATIONAL SALES CONTRACTS AND RISK OF LOSS

As indicated in the preceding sections, there is always a possibility that goods will be lost or damaged in transit or at some time before the buyer takes possession of the goods. This possibility is enhanced when goods are shipped great distances, as is normally the situation with international sales contracts.

Recall from Chapter 20 that the United Nations Convention for the International Sale of Goods (CISG) applies to international sales contracts, providing that the countries involved are signatories to the agreement. As with the UCC, the CISG applies only when the parties have failed to specify some important term in their contract.

In regard to risk of loss, Article 67 of the CISG provides that unless the contract requires the seller to hand the goods over at a particular place, "the risk passes to the buyer when the goods are handed over to the first carrier for transmission to the buyer in accordance with the contract of sale." In no circumstances, however, will risk pass to the buyer until the goods are clearly identified to the contract. In regard to goods sold in transit, Article 68 provides that risk of loss "passes to the buyer from the time of the conclusion of the contract." Article 68 makes an exception to this rule in some circumstances. For example, if the seller knew or should have known that the contract goods were lost or damaged and failed to disclose this to the buyer, then the seller bears the risk.

Unlike the UCC, the CISG does not define the shipping terms (such as C.I.F., F.O.B., or F.A.S.) that normally have the effect of establishing when risk of loss passes. The CISG apparently assumes that parties to international sales contracts will follow the customary practice of including "incoterms" in their contracts. **Incoterms** are a series of twenty or so trade terms (including C.I.F., F.O.B., and F.A.S.) that are widely used in international commercial transactions and that serve to indicate, among other things, when risk of loss passes from the seller to the buyer.

# INSURABLE INTEREST

Any party purchasing insurance must have a "sufficient interest" in the insured item to obtain a valid policy. Insurance laws—not the UCC—determine sufficiency (see Chapter 53). The UCC is helpful, however, because it contains certain rules regarding a buyer's and a seller's **insurable interest** in goods on a sales contract.

Buyers have an insurable interest in *identified* goods. The moment the goods are identified to the contract by the seller, the buyer has this special property interest, which allows the buyer to obtain necessary insurance coverage for the goods even before the risk of loss has passed [UCC 2–501(1)].

Sellers have an insurable interest in goods as long as they retain title to the goods. Even after title has passed to a buyer, however, a seller who has a "security interest" in the goods (a right to secure payment) still has an insurable interest and so can insure the goods [UCC 2–501(2)].

Hence, both a buyer and a seller can have an insurable interest in identical goods at the same time. In all cases, one must sustain an actual loss to have the right to recover from an insurance company.

# BULK TRANSFERS

Special problems arise when a major portion of a business's assets are transferred. This is the subject matter of UCC Article 6, on bulk transfers. A *bulk transfer* is defined as any transfer of a major part of the transferor's material, supplies, merchandise, or other inventory *not made in the ordinary course of the transferor's business* [UCC 6–102(1)]. Difficulties may occur, for example, when a business that owes debts to nu-

merous creditors sells a substantial part of its equipment and inventories to a buyer. The business should use the proceeds to pay off the debts. But what if the merchant instead spends the money on a trip, leaving the creditors without payment? Can the creditors lay any claim to the goods that were transferred in bulk to the buyer?

To prevent this situation, UCC 6–104 and 6–105 establish certain requirements for bulk transfers. All four of the following steps must be undertaken in order for the statutory requirements to be met:

1. The seller must furnish to the buyer a sworn list of his or her existing creditors. The list must include those whose claims are disputed and must state names, business addresses, and amounts due.

2. The buyer and the seller must prepare a schedule of the property to be transferred.

3. The buyer must preserve the list of creditors and the schedule of property for six months and permit inspection of the list by any creditor of the seller or must file the list and the schedule of property in a designated public office.

4. The seller or buyer must give notice of the proposed bulk transfer to each of the seller's creditors at least ten days before the buyer takes possession of the goods or makes payments for them, whichever happens first.

If these requirements are met, the buyer acquires title to the goods free of all claims by the seller's creditors. If the requirements are not met, goods in the possession of the buyer continue to be subject to the claims of the unpaid creditors of the seller for six months [UCC 6–111].

The National Conference of Commissioners on Uniform State Laws recently recommended that those states that have adopted Article 6 repeal it, because changes in the business and legal contexts in which bulk sales are conducted have made their regulation unnecessary. For states disinclined to repeal Article 6, the article has been revised to provide creditors with better protection while reducing the burden imposed on purchasers.

The revised Article 6 limits its application to bulk sales by sellers whose principal business is the sale of inventory from bulk stock. It does not apply to transactions involving property valued at less than $10,000 or more than $25 million. If a seller has more than two hundred creditors, rather than send individual notice of the proposed bulk transfer to each creditor, a buyer can give notice by public filing (for example, in the office of a state's secretary of state). The notice period is increased from ten to forty-five days. The statute of limitations is extended from six months to one year. The text of the revised article—"Alternative B"—is included in Appendix C.

## SECTION 6

# SALES BY NONOWNERS

Special problems arise when persons who acquire goods with imperfect titles attempt to resell them. UCC 2–402 and UCC 2–403 deal with the rights of two parties who lay claim to the same goods, sold with imperfect titles.

Sometimes a seller of goods does not possess full ownership rights (good title) to the goods being sold. This can happen, for example, if the seller has stolen the goods or obtained them fraudulently. In such situations, does the buyer acquire title to the goods? The answer to this question depends on the circumstances. Generally, a buyer acquires at least whatever title the seller has to the goods sold.

### VOID TITLE

A buyer may unknowingly purchase goods from a seller who is not the owner of the goods. If the seller is a thief, the seller's title is *void*—legally, no title exists. Thus, the buyer acquires no title, and the real owner can reclaim the goods from the buyer.

For example, if Tarlow steals goods owned by Carl, Tarlow has *void title* (no legally recognized title) to those goods. If Tarlow sells the goods to Benson, Carl can reclaim them from Benson even though Benson acted in good faith and honestly had no knowledge that the goods were stolen.

### VOIDABLE TITLE

A seller has a *voidable title* if the goods that he or she is selling were obtained by fraud; paid for with a check that is later dishonored; purchased on credit, when the seller was insolvent; or purchased from a minor. Purchasers of goods acquire all title that their transferors either had or had the power to transfer. A purchaser of a limited interest acquires rights only to the extent of the interest purchased. A seller with voidable title has the power, nonetheless, to transfer a good title to a good faith purchaser.

A **good faith purchaser** is one who buys goods without knowledge of circumstances that would make a person of ordinary prudence inquire about the seller's title to the goods. In other words, such circumstances may exist, but the purchaser is unaware of them. The real owner cannot recover goods from a good faith purchaser for value (a good faith purchaser who gives value for the goods) [UCC 2–403(1)]. If the buyer of the goods is not a good faith purchaser for value, then the actual owner of the goods can reclaim them from the buyer (or from the seller, if the goods are still in the seller's possession).

To illustrate: Martin sells his bicycle to Denzer, who pays for the bicycle with a check that is later dishonored by the bank because of insufficient funds in Denzer's account. Before Martin can retrieve the bicycle from Denzer, Denzer sells it to Orne. Orne, who has no knowledge that Denzer has only voidable title to the bicycle, pays Denzer with a check that is honored by the bank. Martin cannot recover his bicycle from Orne, because Orne is a good faith purchaser. Orne has good title to the bicycle, and Martin's only recourse is to sue Denzer for the price of the bike—if Denzer is anywhere to be found.

The defendant in the following case had some warning that there was something suspicious about the transaction in which he was participating.

**CASE 21.2**

**LANE v. HONEYCUTT**

Court of Appeals of North Carolina, 1972.
14 N.C.App. 436,
188 S.E.2d 604.

**BACKGROUND AND FACTS** *Fred H. Lane (the plaintiff) was the owner of Lane's Outboard, and he was engaged in the business of selling boats, motors, and trailers. He sold a new boat, motor, and trailer to a person who called himself John W. Willis. Willis took possession of the goods and paid for them with a check for $6,285. The check was later dishonored. About six months later, the defendant, Jimmy Honeycutt, bought the boat, motor, and trailer for $2,500 from a man identified as "Garrett," who was renting a summer beach house to the defendant that* *year. The defendant had known Garrett for several years. The plaintiff sought to recover the boat, motor, and trailer from the defendant. The defendant's sole defense was that he was a good faith purchaser, and therefore the plaintiff should not be able to recover from him. The trial court held for the plaintiff, and the defendant appealed.*

*VAUGHN,* Judge.

\* \* \* \*

Garrett told defendant that he would let defendant have the boat for $2500. Defendant then paid Garrett a deposit of $100. Garrett had nothing to indicate that he was the owner of the boat, motor or trailer. Garrett told defendant he was selling the boat for someone else. "This guy comes down, you know, and does some fishing."

Two weeks later defendant returned to Garden City, South Carolina, with $2400, the balance due (on a boat, and trailer which had been sold new less than six months earlier for $6,285.00). On this occasion,

"Mr. Garrett had told me \* \* \* 'this guy does a lot of fishing around here but I can't seem to get ahold of him.' He said, 'I've called him, but I can't get ahold of him, so since you have the money and you're here after the boat[,] \* \* \* I don't believe he would object, so I'll just go ahead and sign this title for you so you can go on and get everything made out to you.' He then signed the purported owner's name on the documents and he signed the title over to me then."

The so-called "document" and "title," introduced as defendant's exhibit No. 8, was nothing more than the "certificate of number" required by G.S. [Section] 75A-5 and issued by the North Carolina Wildlife Resources Commission. This "certificate of number" is not a "certificate of title" to be compared with that required by G.S. [Section] 20–50 for vehicles intended to be operated on the highways of this State. Upon the change of ownership of a motor boat, G.S. [Section] 75A-5(c) authorizes the issuance of a new "certificate of number" to the transferee upon proper application. The application for transfer of the number, among other things, requires the seller's *signature.* A signature is "the name of a person written with his own hand." Defendant observed Garrett counterfeit the signature of the purported owner, John P. Patterson, on the exhibit. Following the falsified signature on defendant's exhibit No. 8, the "date sold" is set out as "June 12, 1970" and the buyer's "signature" is set out as "George (illegible) Williams." There was no testimony as to who affixed the "signature" of the purported buyer, George Williams, and there is no further reference to him in the record.

\* \* \* We hold that the evidence was sufficient to support the court's finding that defendant was not a good faith purchaser.

*The trial court's ruling was affirmed. The defendant was not a good faith purchaser. The plaintiff was determined to be the owner and to be entitled to immediate possession of the boat, motor, and trailer. The plaintiff was also awarded damages against the defendant for wrongful detention of the property.*

**DECISION AND REMEDY**

**Good Faith Purchasers in the International Art World** *The rights of good faith purchasers are particularly important in regard to international transactions for the purchase and sale of artwork. Many art treasures have passed from country to country in ways that cloud ownership rights. For example, national governments have claimed that precious works of art have been stolen by archaeologists or by looting armies. Ownership of certain art objects may thus be contested for these or other reasons. The*

**INTERNATIONAL CONSIDERATIONS**

*law generally protects the ownership interests of a good faith purchaser of an artwork but only if that person has undertaken reasonable inquiries into the title to the work to ensure that it was not stolen.*

## THE ENTRUSTMENT RULE

According to Section 2–403(2), entrusting goods to a merchant *who deals in goods of that kind* gives the merchant the power to transfer all rights to a *buyer in the ordinary course of business.* **Entrustment** includes both delivering the goods to the merchant and leaving the purchased goods with the merchant for later delivery or pickup [UCC 2–403(3)]. A ''buyer in the ordinary course'' is a person who buys in good faith from a person who deals in goods of that kind. The buyer cannot have knowledge that the sale violates the ownership rights of a third person.

For example, Sasha leaves her watch with a jeweler to be repaired. The jeweler sells both new and used watches. The jeweler sells Sasha's watch to Ann, a customer, who does not know that the jeweler has no right to sell it. Ann gets *good title* against Sasha's claim of ownership. Sasha's only recourse in this situation is to sue the merchant for wrongfully selling her watch to Ann.

The good faith buyer, however, obtains only those rights held by the person who entrusted the goods. For example, Sasha's watch is stolen by Thomas. Thomas leaves the watch with a jeweler for repairs. The jeweler sells the watch to Betty, who does not know that the jeweler has no right to sell it. Betty gets good title against Thomas, the entrustor, but not against Sasha, who neither entrusted the watch to Thomas nor authorized Thomas to entrust it.

The following case involves a situation in which the merchant to whom goods were allegedly entrusted never took actual possession of the goods. The issue before the court is whether the entrustment rule should apply.

---

### CASE 21.3

**EXECUTIVE COACH BUILDERS v. BUSH & COOK LEASING, INC.**

Court of Appeals of Ohio, 1992. 612 N.E.2d 408.

**COMPANY PROFILE**   *Executive Coach Builders was started in Springfield, Missouri, when John Bumgarner, a one-time farmer, mechanic, used-car salesman, and operator of a new-car dealership, bought a stretch limousine and made a profitable return on his investment. Bumgarner began making stretch limousines in 1977, with three employees. Within four years, Bumgarner had fifty-six employees and was building twelve cars a month. In 1981, Bumgarner sold the company to M. J. Rosenthal & Associates and Merrill Lynch Interfunding, Inc. Executive Coach Builders sells approximately 25 percent of its limousines—with such features as color televisions, VCRs, electrically retractable beds, and gold-plated telephones—to private and corporate accounts, which include movie and rock stars, business executives, and oil barons, but about 75 percent of the cars are sold to limousine services.*

**BACKGROUND AND FACTS**   *Gold Key Limousine, Inc., contracted with Bush & Cook Leasing, Inc., to have a limousine manufactured for Bush & Cook. Bush & Cook agreed to pay $57,645 for the vehicle. Executive Coach Builders agreed with Gold Key to manufacture the limousine at a cost of $39,200, and it was arranged that when the limousine was completed, Bush & Cook's agent, Royce Mason, would pick up the vehicle at Executive's facility. When Mason picked up the limousine, Bush & Cook paid Gold Key the $57,645 due under their contract. Gold Key, however, failed to pay Executive the $39,200 that it owed Executive for the vehicle. Executive, in an effort to get the limousine back from Mason, refused to relinquish the manufacturer's statement of origin. The statement* *of origin is required under the Ohio Certificate of Motor Vehicle Title Act to transfer title and to use the limousine as a leasing vehicle, as Bush & Cook intended.*[a] *Executive brought suit against Bush & Cook to get the limousine back. Bush & Cook sought to have Executive release the statement of origin. A key issue before the court was whether the entrustment rule applied to the transaction, given the fact that Executive's contract was with Gold Key, and Gold Key had never had actual possession of the limousine. The trial court held that the entrustment rule did apply and ordered Executive to deliver the statement of origin to Bush & Cook. Executive appealed.*

*WILLIAM W. YOUNG, Judge.*
        \*   \*   \*   \*

Entrustment should be given liberal reading. \*   \*   \* The general thrust of the cases involving entrustment of goods to a dealer is aimed at the protection of the purchaser, where the latter acts in ''good faith'' and the owner takes the risk by placing or leaving the good with a merchant of his own choosing who could convert or otherwise misdeal it.

Here, the core issue is whether a merchant must receive actual physical possession of the good to gain ''entrustee'' status. \*   \*   \* [I]n determining whether there is possession for the purpose of entrustment, a court should look to the merchant's appearance of control over the goods.
        \*   \*   \*   \*

Under the ''appearance of control'' test, we find that Gold Key had possession of the limousine for entrustment purposes. Even though the merchant here did not have actual physical possession of the limousine at the time of the sale to appellee [Bush & Cook], Gold Key nevertheless manifested its ability to control and dispose of the limousine as if it was in its inventory. The facts indicate that Gold Key informed appellee that the limousine would be delivered to it at appellant's [Executive's] place of business in Springfield, Missouri. The vehicle was subsequently picked up by Mason, appellee's agent. *Thus, focusing on Gold Key's appearance of control over the limousine, we find that Gold Key had possession, albeit constructive [symbolic] possession, of the vehicle.* [Emphasis added.]

*The Court of Appeals held that Executive had effectively entrusted the limousine to Gold Key. Gold Key had the power to transfer the ownership interest in the vehicle to Bush & Cook because Gold Key appeared to control the goods, which was sufficient to satisfy the requirements of the UCC's entrustment rule.*

**DECISION AND REMEDY**

a.   The relevant provision of the Ohio act reads as follows: ''No person acquiring a motor vehicle from its owner, whether the owner is a manufacturer, importer, dealer, or any other person, shall acquire any right, title, claim, or interest in or to the motor vehicle until such person has had issued to him a certificate of title to the motor vehicle, or delivered to him a manufacturer's or importer's certificate for it \*   \*   \* .''

## SELLER'S RETENTION OF SOLD GOODS

Ordinarily, sellers do not retain goods in their possession or use after the goods have been sold. A seller who retained goods after they had been sold could mislead creditors into believing that the seller's assets were more substantial than they really were.

Retention of the goods, and particularly their use by the seller, is basic evidence of an intent to defraud creditors. If a creditor can prove that the retention is in fact fraud, or if the state has a statute providing that such retention creates a presumption of fraud (and if the presumption is unrebutted), the creditor can set aside the sale to the buyer.

UCC 2–402(2), however, recognizes that it is not necessarily a fraud upon creditors if a *merchant* seller retains possession in good faith for a "commercially reasonable time" to accomplish some legitimate purpose (for example, to make repairs or adjustments).

A seller can defraud creditors by selling items at something substantially less than "fair consideration," thereby depleting the seller's assets. This is fraud on the seller's creditors if the seller is insolvent at the time of the sale, is made insolvent by the sale, or actually intended to defraud or delay actions by the creditors. Assets sold at less than fair consideration often are sold to a friend or relative of the seller. Such sales are considered **sham transactions** used to conceal assets.

For example, suppose that FL Boat Company is on the verge of bankruptcy. To obtain loans for the company, FL's owner agreed to be personally liable if FL did not pay off the loans. Knowing that FL's creditors can go after his personal assets to recover what FL owes them, FL's owner sells several expensive cars to his father for only $3,000 apiece, and he sells his personal yacht to his brother-in-law for $10,000 (although it is worth $110,000). He has an implicit understanding with his father and his brother-in-law that he will retain control over these assets but that they will have title. If the creditors find out about the sham transactions, they can void the sales.

This result is also possible under the Uniform Fraudulent Transfer Act (UFTA),[5] which has been adopted in a majority of the states. Under the UFTA, fraudulent transfers include preferential transfers by an insolvent insider, such as FL's owner, to creditors who had reasonable cause to believe that the debtor was insolvent. The UCC defines an *insolvent* person as one "who has either ceased to pay his debts in the ordinary course of business or cannot pay his debts as they become due or is insolvent within the meaning of federal bankruptcy law [UCC 1–201(23)]. Insolvency is defined in the Bankruptcy Code[6] as a financial condition in which an entity's debts exceed that entity's property (insolvency is presumed when failure to pay debts as they come due is established). Under the Bankruptcy Code, an *insider*[7] is defined in terms of a person's relationship with a debtor and includes a relative, an officer or director of a corporate debtor, a partner, or a person in control of a debtor.

---

5.   The Uniform Fraudulent Transfer Act was approved by the National Conference of Commissioners on Uniform State Laws in 1984.
6.   11 U.S.C. Section 101(32).
7.   11 U.S.C. Section 101(31).

---

# TERMS AND CONCEPTS TO REVIEW

| | | |
|---|---|---|
| bill of lading  397 | good faith purchaser  406 | sale or return  402 |
| consignment  403 | identification  396 | sham transaction  410 |
| destination contract  400 | incoterms  405 | shipment contract  400 |
| entrustment  408 | insurable interest  405 | warehouse receipt  397 |
| fungible goods  396 | sale on approval  402 | |

---

# QUESTIONS AND CASE PROBLEMS

**21–1. Risk of Loss.** Mackey orders from Pride one thousand cases of Greenie brand peas from Lot A at list price to be shipped F.O.B. Pride's city via Fast Freight Lines. Pride receives the order and immediately sends Mackey an acceptance of the order with a promise to ship promptly. Pride later separates the one thousand cases of Greenie peas and prints Mackey's name and address on each case. The peas are placed on Pride's dock, and Fast Freight is notified to pick up the shipment. The night before the pickup by Fast Freight, through no fault of Pride's, a fire destroys the one thousand cases of peas. Pride claims that title passed to Mackey at the time the contract was made and that risk of loss passed to Mackey when the goods were marked with Mackey's name and address. Discuss Pride's contentions.

**21–2. Risk of Loss.** On May 1, Sikora goes into Carson's retail clothing store to purchase a suit. Sikora finds a suit he likes for $190 and buys it. The suit needs alteration. Sikora is to pick up the altered suit at Carson's store on May 10. Consider the following separate sets of circumstances:

(a) One of Carson's major creditors obtains a judgment on the debt Carson owes and has the court issue a writ of execution (a court order to seize a debtor's property to satisfy a debt) to collect on that judgment all clothing in Carson's possession. Discuss Sikora's rights in the suit in these circumstances.

(b) On May 9, through no fault of Carson's, his store burns down, and all contents are a total loss. Between Carson and Sikora, who suffers the loss of the suit destroyed by fire? Explain.

**21–3. Conditional Sales.** Zeke, who sells lawn mowers, tells Stasio, a regular customer, about a special promotional campaign. On receipt of a $50 down payment, Zeke will sell Stasio a new Universal lawn mower for $200, even though it normally sells for $350. Zeke further states to Stasio that if Stasio does not like the performance of the lawn mower, he can return it within thirty days, and Zeke will refund the $50 down payment. Stasio pays the $50 and takes the mower. On the tenth day, the lawn mower is stolen through no fault of Stasio's. Stasio calls Zeke and demands the return of his $50. Zeke claims that Stasio should suffer the risk of loss and that he still owes Zeke the remainder of the purchase price, $150. Discuss whether Stasio or Zeke is correct.

**21–4. Sales by Nonowners.** In the following situations, two parties lay claim to the same goods sold. Discuss which of the parties would prevail in each situation.

(a) Toscano steals Dean's television set and sells the set to Bosky, an innocent purchaser, for value. Dean learns Bosky has the set and demands its return.

(b) Kerr takes her television set for repair to Unger, a merchant who sells new and used television sets. By accident, one of Unger's employees sells the set to Gale, an innocent purchaser-customer, who takes possession. Kerr wants her set back from Gale.

**21–5. Risk of Loss.** Benes contracts to purchase from Glover one hundred cases of Knee High Corn to be shipped F.O.B. Glover's warehouse by Reliant Truck Lines. Glover, by mistake, delivers one hundred cases of Green Valley Corn to Reliant Truck Lines. While in transit, the Green Valley Corn is stolen. Between Benes and Glover, who suffers the loss?

**21–6. Risk of Loss.** Harold Shook agreed with Graybar Electric Co. to purchase three reels of burial cable for use in Shook's construction work. When the reels were delivered, each carton was marked ''burial

cable,'' although two of the reels were in fact aerial cable. Shook accepted the conforming reel of cable and notified Graybar that he was rejecting the two reels of aerial cable. Because of a trucker's strike, Shook was unsuccessful in arranging for the return of the reels to Graybar. He stored the reels in a well-lighted space near a grocery store owner's dwelling, which was close to his work site. About four months later, he noticed that one of the reels had been stolen. On the following day he notified Graybar of the loss and, worried about the safety of the second reel, arranged to have it transported to a garage for storage. Before the second reel could be transferred, however, it was also stolen, and Shook notified Graybar of the second theft. Graybar sued Shook for the purchase price, claiming that Shook had agreed to return to Graybar the nonconforming reels and had failed to do so. Shook contended that he had agreed only to contact a trucking company to return the reels and that, because he had contacted three trucking firms to no avail (owing to the strike), his obligation had been fulfilled. Discuss who bears the risk of loss for the stolen reels. [*Graybar Electric Co. v. Shook,* 283 N.C. 213, 195 S.E.2d 514 (1973)]

**21–7. Conditional Sales.** Hargo Woolen Mills had purchased bales of card waste, used in Hargo's manufacture of woolen cloth, from Shabry Trading Co. for many years. On this occasion, however, Shabry shipped twenty-four bales to Hargo without an order. Rather than pay for reshipment, both parties decided that Hargo would retain possession of the bales and pay for what it used. Hargo kept the bales separate inside its warehouse and eventually used, and was billed for, eight bales. The remaining sixteen bales were still kept separate by Hargo. Hargo went bankrupt, and everything in its warehouse was taken by the receiver, Meinhard-Commercial Corp. Shabry claimed that it was the owner and title holder of the bales and requested their return, but Meinhard refused. Discuss fully whether Shabry will be able to retake possession of the bales. [*Meinhard-Commercial Corp. v. Hargo Woolen Mills,* 112 N.H. 500, 300 A.2d 321 (1972)]

**21–8. Sales by Nonowners.** A new car owned by a New Jersey car rental agency was stolen in 1967. The agency collected the full price of the car from its insurance company, Home Indemnity Co., and assigned all its interest in the automobile to the insurer. Subsequently, a thief sold the car to an automobile wholesaler, who in turn sold it to a retail car dealer. Schrier purchased the automobile from the car dealer without knowledge of the theft. Home Indemnity sued Schrier to recover the car. Can Home Indemnity recover? Discuss. [*Schrier v. Home Indemnity Co.,* 273 A.2d 248 (D.C.App. 1971)]

**21–9. Risk of Loss.** Kumar Corp. agreed to sell seven hundred television sets to Nava, a Venezuelan wholesaler. Kumar and Nava expressly agreed that Nava would not pay for the television sets until it received and actually sold the merchandise in Venezuela. Kumar loaded the goods from its Miami warehouse into a trailer and delivered the trailer to the freight handler but failed to procure insurance. The shipping documents reflected that the goods were sold by Kumar to Nava for $144,417, C.I.F. Venezuela. Several days later, the trailer was discovered missing and was subsequently found abandoned and empty. Kumar sued the carrier. The carrier challenged Kumar's standing (right) to sue on the ground that the term C.I.F. (or its equivalent) required Kumar, the seller, to perform certain obligations with respect to the goods—including placing the goods in possession of the carrier—and that when these obligations had been properly performed, the risk of loss or damage to the goods passed to Nava, the buyer. Because Nava suffered the loss, only Nava had standing to sue. Discuss whether this argument is persuasive in light of all of the terms of the contract. [*Kumar Corp. v. Nopal Lines, Ltd.*, 462 So.2d 1178 (Fla.App. 1985)]

**21–10. Entrustment Rule.** Bobby Locke, the principal stockholder and chief executive officer (CEO) of Worthco Farm Center, Inc., hired Mr. Hobby as the company's manager. Subsequently, it was discovered that during the approximately thirteen months of Locke's tenure as CEO, Hobby had sold corn stored with Worthco to Arabi Grain & Elevator Co. and pocketed the proceeds. When Locke brought an action against Arabi to recover the corn, Arabi alleged, among other things, that Locke had entrusted the corn to Hobby and that because Arabi was a purchaser in the ordinary course of business, Hobby had transferred ownership rights in the corn to Arabi. Assuming that Arabi was a buyer in the ordinary course of business, how should the court rule? Discuss. [*Locke v. Arabi Grain & Elevator Co.*, 197 Ga.App. 854, 399 S.E.2d 705 (1991)]

**21–11. Entrustment Rule.** Perez-Medina met Julio Lara at an auction at which they both bid on the same tractor. Perez-Medina purchased the tractor for $66,500. At a second auction, at which Lara was again present, Perez-Medina purchased equipment for installation on the tractor. Lara and Perez-Medina agreed that Lara would install the equipment for Perez-Medina at Lara's place of business, and the tractor was moved to Lara's shop. About four months later, Perez-Medina paid Lara $10,000 to make the installation. At that time, Perez-Medina thought Lara's business was a repair shop and not a "business dealing in heavy equipment." Lara, however, often purchased and sold heavy equipment at auction, and many people knew that Lara was a dealer. Lara sold the tractor to First Team Auction, Inc., for $54,000, representing to First Team that he was the tractor's true owner. Perez-Medina had no knowledge of the sale and received no payment from the transaction. First Team then sold the tractor to a dealer, who in turn sold it to a consumer. When the truth of Lara's actions became known, the dealer and consumer rescinded their contracts with First Team. Should First Team be required to return possession of the tractor to Perez-Medina? If Lara was a "merchant" and First Team a "buyer in the

ordinary course of business," would your answer differ? Explain. [*Perez-Medina v. First Team Auction, Inc.*, 426 S.E.2d 397 (Ga.App. 1992)]

### 21–12. A Question of Ethics

 *Toby and Rita Kahr donated some used clothing to Goodwill Industries, Inc. They were not aware that a small bag containing their sterling silver had been accidentally included within one of the bags of donated clothing. The silverware, which was valued at over $3,500, had been given to them twenty-seven years earlier by Rita's father as a wedding present and had great sentimental value for them. The Kahrs realized what had happened shortly after Toby returned from Goodwill, but when Toby called Goodwill, he was told that the silver had immediately been sold to a customer, Karon Markland, for $15. Although Goodwill called Markland and asked her to return the silver, Markland refused to return it. The Kahrs then brought an action against Markland to regain the silver, claiming that Markland did not have good title to it. In view of these circumstances, discuss the following issues. [Kahr v. Markland, 187 Ill.App.3d 603, 543 N.E.2d 579, 135 Ill.Dec. 196 (1989)]*

1. The basic issue in this case is whether the silver was "lost property" (defined as property unintentionally separated from its owner) or property entrusted to a merchant, Goodwill Industries. If the court decides that the silver was lost, this will mean that the party in possession of the property will have good title against all parties except the true owner—in which case, the Kahrs will be able to recover the silver from Markland. If the court decides that the Kahrs entrusted the silver to Goodwill, then the entrustment rule will be applied—in which case, the Kahrs will be unable to recover the silver from Markland, a good faith purchaser. If you were the judge, how would you decide the issue? Why?

2. The entrustment rule can sometimes result in unfair treatment of the entrustor, because the entrustor cannot recover the property from a good faith purchaser (although the entrustor can recover the *value* of the property from the merchant who wrongfully sold the entrusted property). Given this potential for unfair treatment, how can the entrustment rule be justified from an ethical point of view?

3. Did Karon Markland act wrongfully in any way by not returning the silver to Goodwill when requested to do so? What would you have done in her position?

4. Goodwill argued that the entrustment rule should apply. Is this ethical behavior on the part of Goodwill? Why or why not? How might Goodwill justify its argument from an ethical point of view?

# CHAPTER 22

# PERFORMANCE
# AND OBLIGATION

**T**o understand the *performance* that is required of a seller and of a buyer under a sales contract, it is necessary to know the duties and obligations each party has assumed under the terms of the contract. Keep in mind that "duties and obligations" under the terms of the contract include those specified by the agreement, by custom, and by the UCC.

In the **performance** of a sales contract, a seller has the basic obligation to *transfer and deliver conforming goods,* and the buyer has the basic obligation to *accept and pay for conforming goods* in accordance with the contract [UCC 2–301]. Overall performance of a sales contract is controlled by the agreement between the buyer and the seller. When the contract is unclear, or when terms are indefinite in certain respects and disputes arise, the UCC provides built-in standards and rules for interpreting the agreement.

In this chapter, after first looking at the general requirement of good faith, we will examine the basic performance obligations of the seller and the buyer under a sales contract.

**SECTION 1**

## THE GOOD FAITH REQUIREMENT

The obligations of "good faith" and "commercial reasonableness" underlie every sales contract within the UCC. These obligations can form the basis for a breach of contract suit later on. The UCC's good faith provision, which can never be disclaimed, reads as follows: "Every contract or duty within this Act imposes an obligation of good faith in its performance or enforcement" [UCC 1–203]. Good faith means honesty in fact. In the case of a merchant, it means honesty in fact *and* the observance of reasonable commercial standards of fair dealing in the trade [UCC 2–103(1)(b)]. In other words, merchants are held to a higher standard of performance or duty than nonmerchants are.

**413**

Good faith can mean that one party must not take advantage of another party by manipulating contract terms. Good faith applies to both parties, even the nonbreaching party. The principle of good faith applies through both the performance and the enforcement of all agreements or duties within a contract. Good faith is a question of fact for the jury.

The standards of good faith and commercial reasonableness are read into every contract, and they provide a framework in which the parties can specify particulars of performance. If a sales contract leaves open some particulars of performance and permits one of the parties to specify them, ''[a]ny such specification must be made in good faith and within limits set by commercial reasonableness'' [UCC 2–311(1)]. Thus, when one party delays specifying particulars of performance for an unreasonable period of time or fails to cooperate with the other party, the innocent party is excused from any resulting delay in performance. In addition, the innocent party can proceed to perform in any reasonable manner.



SECTION 2

## SELLER'S OBLIGATION— TENDER OF DELIVERY

**Tender** of delivery requires that the seller have and hold **conforming goods** (goods that conform exactly to the description of the goods in the contract) at the buyer's disposal and give the buyer whatever notification is reasonably necessary to enable the buyer to take delivery [UCC 2–503(1)]. Tender must occur at a *reasonable hour* and in a *reasonable manner*. What is reasonable depends in part on the subject matter of the contract. In most cases, a seller cannot call the buyer at 2:00 A.M. and say, ''The goods are ready. I'll give you twenty minutes to get them.'' Unless the parties have agreed otherwise, the goods must be tendered for delivery at a reasonable time and must be kept available for a reasonable period of time to enable the buyer to take possession of them [UCC 2–503(1)(a)].

All goods called for by a contract must be tendered in a single delivery unless the parties agree otherwise [UCC 2–612] or the circumstances are such that either party can rightfully request delivery in lots [UCC 2–307]. Hence, an order for one thou-

sand shirts cannot be delivered two shirts at a time. If seller and buyer contemplate, though, that the shirts will be delivered in four orders of 250 each as they are produced for summer, winter, fall, and spring stock and the price can be apportioned accordingly, it may be commercially reasonable to follow this course.

## PLACE OF DELIVERY

The UCC provides for the place of delivery pursuant to a contract if the contract does not mention delivery terms. Of course, the parties may agree on a particular destination, or their contract's terms or the circumstances may indicate the place.

**NONCARRIER CASES**    When no carrier is specified or implied, if the contract does not designate the place at which the goods will be delivered, the place of delivery is the *seller's place of business* or, if the seller has no place of business, the *seller's residence* [UCC 2–308]. If the contract involves the sale of *identified goods* (see Chapter 21 for a discussion of such goods) and the parties know when they enter into the contract that these goods are located somewhere other than at the seller's place of business (such as at a warehouse or in the possession of a bailee), then the *location of the goods* is the place for their delivery [UCC 2–308].

For example, Laval and Boyd live in San Francisco. In San Francisco, Laval contracts to sell to Boyd five used railroad dining cars, which both parties know are located in Atlanta. If nothing more is specified in the contract, the place of delivery for the railroad cars is Atlanta.

Suppose that the railroad cars are stored in a warehouse and that Boyd will need some type of document to show the warehouse (bailee) in Atlanta that he is entitled to take possession of the five dining cars. The seller tenders delivery without moving the goods. The seller may deliver either by giving the buyer a *negotiable document of title* or by obtaining the *bailee's* (warehouse's) *acknowledgment* that the buyer is entitled to possession.[1]

---

1.   If the seller delivers a nonnegotiable document of title or merely writes instructions to the bailee to release the goods to the buyer without the bailee's *acknowledgment* of the buyer's rights, this will also be a sufficient tender, unless the buyer objects [UCC 2–503(4)]. But risk of loss will not pass until the buyer has had a reasonable time to present the document or the instructions.

**CARRIER CASES** In many instances, resulting either from attendant circumstances or from delivery terms contained in the contract, it is apparent that the parties intend that a carrier be used to move the goods. There are two ways a seller can complete performance of the obligation to deliver the goods—through a shipment contract or a destination contract.

*Shipment Contracts.* A shipment contract requires or authorizes the seller to ship goods by an independent carrier. The contract does not require the seller to deliver the goods at a particular destination [UCC 2–509; UCC 2–319]. Unless otherwise agreed, the seller must do the following [UCC 2–504]:

1. Put the goods into the hands of the independent carrier.
2. Make a contract for the transportation of the goods that is reasonable according to the nature of the goods and their value. (For example, certain types of goods need refrigeration in transit.)
3. Obtain and promptly deliver or tender to the buyer any documents necessary to enable the buyer to obtain possession of the goods from the carrier.
4. Promptly notify the buyer that shipment has been made.

If the seller fails to notify the buyer that shipment has been made or fails to make a proper contract for transportation, and a *material loss* of the goods or a *delay* results, the buyer can reject the shipment.

*Destination Contracts.* Under destination contracts, the seller agrees to ensure that the goods will be duly tendered to the buyer at a particular destination. Once the goods arrive, the seller must tender the goods at a reasonable hour and hold conforming goods at the buyer's disposal for a reasonable length of time, giving appropriate notice. The seller must also provide the buyer with any documents of title necessary to enable the buyer to obtain delivery from the carrier.

## THE PERFECT TENDER RULE

As previously noted, the seller has an obligation to ship or tender *conforming goods,* and this entitles the seller to acceptance by and payment from the buyer according to the terms of the contract. At common law the seller was obligated to deliver goods in conformity with the terms of the contract in every detail. This was called the **perfect tender rule.** The UCC, in Section 2–601, preserves the perfect tender rule by providing that "if goods or tender of delivery fail *in any respect* to conform to the contract" (emphasis added), the buyer has the right to accept the goods, reject the entire shipment, or accept part and reject part.

## EXCEPTIONS TO THE PERFECT TENDER RULE

Because of the rigidity of the perfect tender rule, several exceptions have been created, some of which are discussed here.

**AGREEMENT OF THE PARTIES** Parties can agree, in their contract, that the perfect tender rule will not apply. If the parties have agreed, for example, that defective goods or parts will not be rejected if the seller is able to repair or replace them within a reasonable time, then the perfect tender rule does not apply.

**CURE** The term **cure** is not specifically defined in the UCC, but it refers to the seller's right to repair, adjust, or replace defective or nonconforming goods [UCC 2–508]. When any tender or delivery is rejected because of nonconforming goods and the time for performance has not yet expired, the seller can notify the buyer promptly of the intention to cure and can then do so *within the contract time for performance* [UCC 2–508(1)]. Even after the time for performance under the contract has expired, the seller can still exercise the right to cure if the seller had *reasonable grounds to believe that the nonconforming tender would be acceptable to the buyer.* Frequently the seller tenders nonconforming goods with some type of price allowance, but he or she may still have a reasonable belief that the goods will be accepted by the buyer for other reasons.[2]

When the seller offers a price allowance with the tender of nonconforming goods, this allowance

---

2. It has been held that UCC 2–508 does not apply to artwork. Thus, if a print turns out to bear a forged signature and the buyer revokes acceptance within a reasonable time, the seller has no right to substitute another print from the same series. See *David Tunick, Inc. v. Kornfeld,* 838 F.Supp. 848 (S.D.N.Y. 1993).

frequently creates a presumption that a buyer will accept the fortuitous offer. Suppose that a buyer contracts to purchase one hundred Model Z hand-held calculators at a price of $20 each from a seller, to be delivered on or before October 1. The seller cannot deliver one hundred Model Z calculators but tenders a hundred new, more sophisticated, more expensive Model A-1 calculators at the same price as the hundred Model Z calculators contracted for on October 1. The buyer rejects the delivery. If the seller *notifies* the buyer of intent to cure, the seller has a *reasonable time* (after October 1) to substitute a conforming tender of Model Z calculators.

The seller's right to cure substantially restricts the buyer's right to reject. If the buyer refuses a tender of goods as nonconforming but does not disclose the nature of the defect to the seller, the buyer cannot later assert the defect as a defense if the defect is one that the seller could have cured. The buyer must act in good faith and state specific reasons for refusing to accept the goods [UCC 2–605].

**SUBSTITUTION OF CARRIERS**    When an agreed-on manner of delivery (such as particular loading or unloading facilities) becomes impracticable or unavailable through no fault of either party, but a commercially reasonable substitute is available, this substitute must be used and is sufficient tender to the buyer [UCC 2–614(1)]. For example, a sales contract calls for the delivery of a large piece of machinery to be shipped by ABC Truck Lines on or before June 1. The contract terms clearly state the importance of the delivery date. The employees of ABC Truck Lines go on strike. The seller will be required to make a reasonable substitute tender, if available, perhaps by rail. Note that the seller here is responsible for any additional shipping costs, unless contrary arrangements have been made in the sales contract.

**INSTALLMENT CONTRACTS**    An **installment contract** is a single contract that requires or authorizes delivery in two or more separate lots to be accepted and paid for separately. In an installment contract, a buyer can reject an installment *only if the nonconformity substantially impairs the value of the installment* and cannot be cured [UCC 2–612(2); UCC 2–307]. Notice how this is a substantial limitation on the perfect tender rule.

The entire installment contract is breached only when one or more nonconforming installments *substantially* impair the value of the *whole contract*. If the buyer, after such a breach has occurred, accepts a nonconforming installment and fails to notify the seller of cancellation, then the contract is reinstated, however. Also, if the buyer brings an action with respect only to past installments or demands performance as to future installments, the aggrieved party has reinstated the contract [UCC 2–612(3)].

A major issue to be determined is what constitutes *substantial* impairment of the "value of the whole." For example, consider an installment contract for the sale of twenty carloads of plywood. The first carload does not conform to the contract, because 9 percent of the plywood in the car deviates from the thickness specifications. The buyer cancels the contract, and immediately thereafter the second and third carloads of plywood arrive at the buyer's place of business. The court would have to grapple with the question of whether the 9 percent of nonconforming plywood substantially impaired the value of the whole.[3]

A more clear-cut example is an installment contract that involves parts of a machine. Suppose that the first part is delivered and is irreparably defective but is necessary for the operation of the machine. The failure of this first installment will be a breach of the whole contract. Even when the defect in the first shipment is such that it gives the buyer only a "reasonable apprehension" about the ability or willingness of the seller to complete the other installments properly, the breach on the first installment may be regarded as a breach of the whole.

The point to remember is that, in the absence of agreement, the UCC substantially alters the right of a buyer to reject the entire contract in installment sales contracts. Such contracts are broadly defined in the UCC, which strictly limits rejection to cases of substantial nonconformity.

**COMMERCIAL IMPRACTICABILITY**    Whenever performance becomes commercially impracticable due to occurrences unforeseen by either party when

---

3.   *Continental Forest Products v. White Lumber Sales, Inc.,* 256 Or. 466, 474 P.2d 1 (1970). The court held that the deviation did not substantially impair the value of the whole contract. Additionally, the court stated that the nonconformity could be cured by an adjustment in the price.

the contract was made, the rule of perfect tender no longer holds. According to UCC 2–615(a), delay in delivery or nondelivery in whole or in part is not a breach when performance has been made impracticable "by the occurrence of a contingency the nonoccurrence of which was a basic assumption on which the contract was made." The seller, however, must notify the buyer as soon as it is practicable to do so that there will be a delay or nondelivery.

The concept of **commercial impracticability** is closely allied with contract law theories of impossibility of performance and frustration of purpose (see Chapter 18). Increased costs resulting from inflation do not in and of themselves excuse performance. This is the kind of risk ordinarily assumed by a seller conducting business. The unforeseen contingency must alter the essential nature of the performance, such as would occur with a sudden, severe shortage of raw materials.

For example, a major oil company that receives its supplies from the Middle East has a contract to supply a buyer with 100,000 gallons of oil. Because of an oil embargo by the Organization of Petroleum Exporting Countries (OPEC), the seller is prevented from securing oil supplies to meet the terms of this contract. Because of the same embargo, the seller cannot secure oil from any other source. This situation comes under the commercial impracticability exception to the perfect tender doctrine.

Sometimes the unforeseen event only *partially* affects the seller's capacity to perform. As a result, the seller is able to fulfill the contract partially but cannot tender total performance. In this event, the seller is required to allocate in a fair and reasonable manner any remaining production and deliveries among his or her contracted and regular customers. The buyer must receive notice of the allocation, with the obvious right to accept or reject it [UCC 2–615(b), (c)].

For example, a grower of cranberries in the state of Washington, Cran Plan, has contracted to sell this season's production to a number of customers, including the G & G grocery chain. G & G has contracted to purchase two thousand crates of cranberries. Cran Plan has sprayed some of its bogs of cranberries with a chemical called Green. The Department of Agriculture discovers that persons who eat products sprayed with Green may develop cancer. An order prohibiting the sale of these products is effected. Cran Plan has har-

vested all the bogs not sprayed with Green but cannot fully meet all contract deliveries. In this case, Cran Plan is required to allocate fairly its production, notifying G & G of the amount it is able to deliver.

**DESTRUCTION OF IDENTIFIED GOODS** The UCC provides that when a casualty occurs that totally destroys *identified goods* under a sales contract (through no fault of either party) *before risk passes to the buyer,* the seller and buyer are excused from performance [UCC 2–613(a)]. If the goods are only partially destroyed, however, the buyer can inspect them and either treat the contract as void or accept the damaged goods with an allowance off the contract price.

**ASSURANCE AND COOPERATION** Two other exceptions to the perfect tender doctrine apply equally to the seller and buyer: the right of assurance and the right to cooperation.

The right of assurance—the right to obtain objective indications that performance will occur—stems from the concept that the essential purpose of a contract is performance by both parties, and thus when one party has reason to believe the other party will not perform, forcing the first party to perform creates an undue hardship. The UCC provides that should a seller (or buyer) have "reasonable grounds" to believe the buyer (or seller) will not perform as contracted, he or she may "in writing demand adequate assurance of due performance" from the other party; until such assurance is received, he or she may "suspend" further performance without liability. The grounds for such belief and action must be reasonable. Between merchants, the grounds are determined by commercial standards [UCC 2–609]. The assurances requested also must be reasonable. If such assurances are not forthcoming within a reasonable time (not to exceed thirty days), the failure to respond may be treated as a *repudiation* of the contract.

For example, Zytka has contracted to ship Jenkins 100 dozen shirts on or before October 1, with Jenkins's payment due within thirty days of delivery. Zytka has made two previous shipments, neither of which has been paid for by Jenkins. On September 20, Zytka demands in writing certain assurances of payment (such as payment of the last two orders to bring the account up to date) before she will ship the 100 dozen shirts.

If these desired assurances are reasonable, Zytka can suspend shipment of the shirts without liability pending Jenkins's compliance. If Jenkins does not provide the assurances within a reasonable time (no longer than thirty days), Zytka can hold Jenkins in breach of contract without having made the contracted shipment.

Sometimes the performance of one party depends on the cooperation of the other. The UCC provides that when such cooperation is not forthcoming, the other party can suspend his or her own performance without liability and hold the uncooperative party in breach or proceed to perform the contract in any reasonable manner [see UCC 2–311(3)(b)].

For example, Amati is required by contract to deliver 1,200 Model Z washing machines to locations in the state of California to be specified later by Farrell. Deliveries are to be made on or before October 1. Amati has repeatedly requested the delivery locations, and Farrell has not responded. The 1,200 Model Z machines are ready for shipment on October 1, but Farrell still refuses to give Amati delivery locations. Amati does not ship on October 1. Can Amati be held liable? The answer is no. Amati is excused for any resulting delay of performance because of Farrell's failure to cooperate.

The assurances requested under UCC 2–609 must be reasonable. A request is not considered reasonable if it represents an attempt to avoid contractual performance that may be unprofitable. In the following case, the court considered whether the assurances requested by one merchant from another were reasonable.

### CASE 22.1

### BAII BANKING CORP. v. UPG, INC.
United States Court of Appeals, Second Circuit, 1993. 985 F.2d 685.

**COMPANY PROFILE** *Northern Natural Gas was organized in 1930 in Omaha, Nebraska, as a gas pipeline company. By 1950, Northern had doubled its capacity and in 1960 started processing and transporting natural gas liquids. The company changed its name to InterNorth in 1980. In 1983, it bought Belco Petroleum. The same year, the company participated in the building of the Northern Border Pipeline to link Canadian natural gas fields to American markets. Houston Natural Gas (HNG) was formed in 1925 in Texas as a natural gas distributor, serving more than 55,000 customers by the early 1940s. HNG started developing oil and gas properties in 1953. HNG bought the Houston Pipe Line Company in 1956, the Valley Gas Production Company in 1963, and the Bammel Gas Storage Field in 1965. In the 1970s, HNG started developing offshore natural gas fields in the Gulf of Mexico. In the early 1980s, HNG acquired Transwestern Pipeline of California and Florida Gas Transmission and became the operator of the only transcontinental gas pipeline. In 1985, InterNorth bought HNG for $2.4 billion, creating the longest natural gas pipeline system—38,000 miles—in the United States. InterNorth renamed itself Enron and moved its headquarters to Houston. In early 1986, Enron was more than $3 billion in debt, most of it related to the HNG acquisition. One of Enron's subsidiaries is UPG, Inc.*

**BACKGROUND AND FACTS** *Will Petroleum, Inc., was a small oil trading company. UPG Falco, a division of UPG, Inc., transports and markets oil products. In December 1985 and January 1986, Will Petroleum and Falco entered into agreements involving the sale of Rumanian blend-stock gasoline from Will Petroleum to Falco. BAII Banking Corporation provided financing to Will Petroleum for the agreements, which were to be performed before the end of January. During December and January, gasoline prices declined, and Falco determined that it would lose nearly*

*$1.5 million if the agreements were performed. In mid-January, rumors circulated that Will Petroleum might be filing for bankruptcy. When the* Konpolis, *one of the ships carrying the gasoline, arrived ahead of schedule at 2:30 P.M. on January 23, Falco refused it permission to dock. Ninety minutes later, Falco sent a telex to Will Petroleum requesting adequate assurances within twenty-three hours that Will Petroleum could perform the agreements. There was no immediate response. The next evening, Falco sent Will Petroleum a telex stating that it considered the agreements re-pudiated. On January 28, Will Petroleum told Falco to contact BAII re-garding any insecurity (any reason to believe that a party will not perform his or her obligations under a contract) related to Will Petroleum's ability to perform. Falco responded that it had already bought other gas in substitution for the gas due under the agreements. The next day, Will Petroleum filed a petition for bankruptcy. The gasoline was sold for approximately $5.5 million less than the contract prices. BAII and others filed a lawsuit against Falco and others. Falco contended, among other things, that Will Petroleum had repudiated the agreements by failing to provide adequate assurances under UCC 2–609. The district court ruled in favor of Falco. BAII appealed.*

*PIERCE*, Circuit Judge:
\* \* \* \*

Based upon [the] evidence, \* \* \* no reasonable fact-finder could have found that [UPG] Falco had ''reasonable grounds for insecurity,'' within the meaning of [UCC 2–609]. \* \* \* This evidence negates Falco's claim that as of 4:00 P.M. on January 23, it had reason to feel insecure as to whether Will would perform the \* \* \* [a]greement. Falco cannot rely upon its own conduct in not permitting the *Konpolis* to berth and discharge its cargo as a basis for a claim of its own insecurity. Nor can Falco validly assert that its purported insecurity arose from Will's failure to provide oral assurances before Falco sent the repudiation telex. *A party does not contract for oral assurances of performance, but for performance of the contract.* Will's actions in having the *Konpolis* arrive with cargo before the end of the delivery period provided for in the \* \* \* [a]greement spoke louder than any oral assurances Will could have provided. \* \* \* [Emphasis added.]

\* \* \* We note also that Falco's potential gain from the avoidance of the agreements at issue provided an incentive to avoid performance of the agreements.

*The court held that Falco did not have reasonable grounds on which to demand assurances under UCC 2–609. The court reversed the judgment of the district court and remanded the case for further proceedings.*

**DECISION AND REMEDY**

---

## BUYER'S OBLIGATIONS

Once the seller has adequately tendered delivery, the buyer is obligated to accept the goods and pay for them according to the terms of the contract. In the absence of any specific agreements to the contrary, the buyer must do the following:

1. Furnish facilities reasonably suited for receipt of the goods [UCC 2–503(1)(b)].
2. Make payment at the time and place the buyer *receives* the goods, even if the place of shipment is the place of delivery [UCC 2–310(a)].

## PAYMENT

When a sale is made on credit, the buyer is obliged to pay according to credit terms (for example, in 60, 90, or 120 days), *not* when the goods are received. The credit period usually begins on the *date of shipment* [UCC 2–310(d)].

Payment can be made by any means agreed on between the parties. Cash can be used, but the buyer can also use any other method generally acceptable in the commercial world. If the seller demands cash when the buyer offers a check, credit card, or the like, then the seller must permit the buyer reasonable time to obtain legal tender [UCC 2–511].

## RIGHT OF INSPECTION

Unless otherwise agreed or for C.O.D. (collect on delivery) goods, the buyer's right to inspect the goods is absolute. This right allows the buyer to verify, before making payment, that the goods tendered or delivered are what were contracted for or ordered. If the goods are not what the buyer ordered, there is no duty to pay. *An opportunity for inspection is therefore a condition precedent to the seller's right to enforce payment* [UCC 2–513(1)].

Unless otherwise agreed, inspection can take place at any reasonable place and time and in any reasonable manner. Generally, what is reasonable is determined by custom of the trade, past practices of the parties, and the like. The UCC also provides for inspection after arrival when goods are to be shipped. Costs of inspecting conforming goods are borne by the buyer unless agreed otherwise [UCC 2–513(2)].

**C.O.D. SHIPMENTS**  If a seller ships goods to a buyer C.O.D. (or under similar terms), the buyer can rightfully *reject* them (unless the contract expressly provides for a C.O.D. shipment). This is because C.O.D. does not permit inspection before payment, and the effect is a denial of the buyer's right of inspection. But when the buyer has agreed to a C.O.D. shipment in the contract or has agreed to pay for the goods on the presentation of a bill of lading, no right of inspection exists, because it was negated by the agreement [UCC 2–513(3)].

**PAYMENT DUE—DOCUMENTS OF TITLE**  Under certain contracts, payment is due on the receipt of the required documents of title, even though the goods themselves may not have arrived at their destination. With C.I.F. and C.&F. contracts, payment is required on receipt of the documents unless the parties have agreed otherwise. Thus, payment may be required *prior* to inspection, and if so, it must be made unless the buyer knows that the goods are nonconforming [UCC 2–310(b); UCC 2–513(3)].

## ACCEPTANCE

The buyer can manifest acceptance of the delivered goods in several different ways:

1.  The buyer can expressly accept the shipment by words or conduct. For example, there is an acceptance if the buyer, after having had a reasonable opportunity to inspect, signifies agreement to the seller that either the goods are conforming or they are acceptable despite their nonconformity [UCC 2–606(1)(a)].
2.  Acceptance will be presumed if the buyer has had a reasonable opportunity to inspect the goods and has failed to reject them within a reasonable period of time [UCC 2–606(1)(b); UCC 2–602(1)].
3.  The buyer can accept the goods by performing any act inconsistent with the seller's ownership. For example, any use or resale of the goods will generally constitute an acceptance. Limited use for the sole purpose of testing or inspecting the goods is not an acceptance, however [UCC 2–606(1)(c)].

## REVOCATION OF ACCEPTANCE

Acceptance does not in and of itself impair the right of the buyer to pursue remedies, although it does preclude the buyer from exercising the right of rejection. Also, if the buyer accepts nonconforming goods and fails to notify the seller of the breach when it is discovered (or when it should have been discovered), then the buyer is barred from pursuing any remedy against the seller. What is at issue here is the necessity for the buyer to notify the seller of the breach within a reasonable time [UCC 2–607(3)].

After a buyer accepts a lot or a *commercial unit*,[4] acceptance can be revoked if nonconformity *substantially* impairs the value of the unit or lot and if one of the following factors also is present:

1. Acceptance was predicated on the reasonable assumption that the nonconformity would be cured, and it has not been seasonably cured (cured within a reasonable time) [UCC 2–608(1)(a)].

2. The buyer does not discover the nonconformity, and his or her acceptance was reasonably induced by the difficulty of discovery before acceptance or by the seller's assurances that the goods conform [UCC 2–608(1)(b)].[5]

In the following case, the court considered whether five months was sufficient time within which to cure defects that substantially impaired the value of the goods—a mobile home.

---

4. A commercial unit is a unit of goods that, by commercial usage, is viewed as a single whole for purposes of sale and that cannot be divided without materially impairing the character of the unit, its market value, or its use [UCC 2–105]. A commercial unit can be a single article (such as a machine), a set of articles (such as a suite of furniture or an assortment of sizes), a quantity (such as a bale, gross, or carload), or any other unit treated in the trade as a single whole.

5. Prior to the passage of state lemon laws, purchasers of automobiles that turned out to be ''lemons'' frequently had no other recourse than to revoke acceptance and request the return of the purchase price. Because of limitations on the seller's liability and the fact that an attempted revocation often led to costly litigation, consumers found it difficult to prevail against the automobile dealer in such disputes. Lemon laws, discussed in the next chapter, have to a great extent eased this problem.

---

**BACKGROUND AND FACTS**  *In August 1987, David and Catherine Henery purchased a Liberty Homes mobile home from Gary and Ray Robinson, doing business as Ideal Trailer Village in The Dalles, Oregon. Ideal delivered the home to the Henerys' trailer court in Carson, Washington, on September 28. The Henerys immediately discovered numerous defects. Among other problems, the floor sloped down around the front door and had a give to it as if it were not supported. The Henerys were assured that Liberty would cure the defects. In spite of their disappointment in the overall quality of the home, the Henerys accepted delivery. Over the next five months, Liberty's attempts to fix the defects were generally unsuccessful. In some instances, they only made the situation worse. When workers attempted to fix the floor around the front door, for example, they dislodged the door frame, which prevented the door from closing properly and left a gap between the frame and the door. At the end of February, a representative of the Washington State Department of Labor and Industries inspected the home and found thirty-two violations. In March, the Henerys refused to schedule further repairs. The Henerys filed a lawsuit against the Robinsons, Liberty, and others, seeking, among other things, rescission of the contract. The trial court issued a judgment in favor of the Henerys. Liberty appealed.*

**CASE 22.2**

**HENERY v. ROBINSON**
Court of Appeals of Washington, 1992.
67 Wash.App. 277,
834 P.2d 1091.

*SEINFELD,* Judge.
\* \* \* \*

[UCC 2–608] provides in part: (1) The buyer may revoke his acceptance of a . . . commercial unit whose non-conformity substantially impairs its value to him if he has accepted it (a) on the reasonable assumption that its non-conformity would be cured and it has not been seasonably cured; . . . The UCC defines the term ''seasonably'' in [UCC 1–204] as [an action] taken at or within \* \* \* a reasonable time.
\* \* \* \*

Here, the record shows that the Henerys gave the seller and manufacturer over five months to repair the mobile home, that defendants' efforts were sporadic and unsuccessful, and that the Henerys eventually became frustrated and denied defendants further opportunities to cure the defects. From these facts, the trial court was entitled to find that the defects were not seasonably cured and that revocation of acceptance was, therefore, appropriate.

**DECISION AND REMEDY**    *The appellate court affirmed the trial court's order rescinding the contract of sale between the Henerys and Liberty.*

**INTERNATIONAL CONSIDERATIONS**    **Revocation of Acceptance in International Contracts** *Provisions of the United Nations Convention on Contracts for the International Sale of Goods (CISG) similarly allow buyers to rescind their contracts after goods have been accepted. The CISG, however, takes a somewhat different, and more direct, approach to the problem. Circumstances that would permit a buyer to revoke acceptance under the UCC would, under the CISG, allow the buyer to simply declare that the seller has fundamentally breached the contract. Article 25 of the CISG states that a ''breach of contract committed by one of the parties is fundamental if it results in such detriment to the other party as substantially to deprive him of what he is entitled to expect under the contract.''*

**NOTICE OF REVOCATION REQUIRED**    Revocation of acceptance will not be effective until notice is given to the seller, and that must occur within a reasonable time after the buyer either discovers or should have discovered the grounds for revocation. Also, revocation must occur before the goods have undergone any substantial change that was not caused by their own defects (such as spoilage) [UCC 2–608(2)].

**PARTIAL ACCEPTANCE**    If some of the goods delivered do not conform to the contract and the seller has failed to cure, the buyer can make a *partial* acceptance [UCC 2–601(c)]. A buyer cannot accept less than a single commercial unit, however.

## SECTION 4

# ANTICIPATORY REPUDIATION

What if, before the time for either party's performance, one party clearly communicates to the other the intention not to perform? Such an action is a breach of the contract by *anticipatory repudiation.*

When this occurs, the aggrieved party can, according to UCC 2–610, do the following:

1. For a commercially reasonable time await performance by the repudiating party.
2. Resort to any remedy for breach (see Chapter 23), even if the aggrieved party has notified the repudiating party that he or she awaits the latter's performance and has urged retraction.
3. In either case, *suspend performance* or proceed in accordance with the provisions of UCC 2–704 on the seller's right to identify goods notwithstanding breach or to salvage unfinished goods (see Chapter 23).

The key to anticipatory repudiation is that the repudiation takes place before the time that the party is required under contract to tender performance. The nonrepudiating party has a choice of two responses. He or she can treat the repudiation as a final breach by pursuing a remedy, or he or she can wait, hoping that the repudiating party will decide to honor the obligations required by the contract despite the avowed intention to renege. Should the latter course be pursued, the UCC permits the repudiating party (subject to some limitations) to ''retract'' his or her repudiation. The retraction can be made by any method that clearly indicates an

## ■ CONCEPT SUMMARY 22.1 **Performance and Obligation**

| Seller's Obligations | 1. The seller must ship or tender *conforming* goods to the buyer. Tender must take place at a *reasonable hour* and in a *reasonable manner.* Under the perfect tender doctrine, the seller must tender goods that exactly conform to the terms of the contract [UCC 2–301; UCC 2–503(1); UCC 2–601]. <br> 2. If the seller tenders nonconforming goods and the buyer rejects them, the seller may *cure* (repair or replace the goods) within the contract time for performance [UCC 2–508(1)]. <br> 3. If the seller tenders nonconforming goods, but the seller has reasonable grounds to believe the buyer would accept them, upon the buyer's rejection the seller has a reasonable time to substitute conforming goods without liability [UCC 2–508(2)]. <br> 4. If the agreed means of delivery becomes impracticable or unavailable, the seller must substitute an alternative means (such as a different carrier) if such is available [UCC 2–614(1)]. <br> 5. If a seller tenders nonconforming goods in any one installment under an installment contract, the buyer may reject the installment only if its value is substantially impaired and cannot be cured. The entire installment contract is breached when one or more installments *substantially* impair the value of the *whole* contract [UCC 2–612]. <br> 6. When performance becomes commercially impracticable owing to circumstances unforeseen when the contract was formed, the perfect tender rule no longer holds [UCC 2–615(a)]. |
|---|---|
| Buyer's Obligations | 1. Upon tender of delivery by the seller, the buyer must furnish facilities reasonably suited for receipt of the goods [UCC 2–503(1)(b)]. <br> 2. The buyer must pay for the goods at the time and place the buyer *receives* the goods, even if the place of shipment is the place of delivery, unless the sale is made on credit. Payment may be made by any method generally acceptable in the commercial world [UCC 2–310; UCC 2–511]. <br> 3. Unless otherwise agreed, the buyer has an absolute right to inspect the goods before acceptance [UCC 2–513(1)]. <br> 4. The buyer can manifest acceptance of delivered goods expressly in words or by conduct; by failing to reject the goods after a reasonable period of time following inspection or after having had a reasonable opportunity to inspect them; or by performing any act inconsistent with the seller's ownership [UCC 2–606(1)]. <br> 5. Following acceptance of delivered goods, the buyer may revoke acceptance only if the nonconformity *substantially* impairs the value of the unit or lot and if one of the following factors is present: <br> a. Acceptance was predicated on the reasonable assumption that the nonconformity would be cured, and it was not cured within a reasonable time [UCC 2–608(1)(a)]. <br> b. The buyer did not discover the nonconformity before acceptance, either because it was difficult to discover before acceptance or because the seller's assurance that the goods were conforming resulted in the buyer's decision not to inspect the goods [UCC 2–608(1)(b)]. |

intent to perform. Once retraction has been made, the rights of the repudiating party under the contract are reinstated [UCC 2–611]. The concept of anticipatory repudiation is illustrated in the following case.

**CASE 22.3**

**NEPTUNE RESEARCH & DEVELOPMENT, INC. v. TEKNICS INDUSTRIAL SYSTEMS, INC.**

Superior Court of New Jersey, 1989.
235 N.J.Super. 522,
563 A.2d 465.

**BACKGROUND AND FACTS**   *Neptune Research & Development, Inc., contracted to purchase a high-precision drilling machine for approximately $55,000 from Teknics Industrial Systems, Inc. Although the contract specified a mid-June delivery date, nothing was included in the contract about time being of the essence. In addition, one of the paragraphs within the standard terms and conditions stated that shipping dates were approximate. By late August, the machine still had not been delivered, and Neptune desperately needed it. Contact with Teknics on August 29 resulted in both parties' agreeing to a September 5 delivery date, and Robertson, a Teknics representative, promised to call Neptune on September 3 so that delivery arrangements could be made. Robertson did not call Neptune on September 3. On September 4, Neptune's representative called Robertson, who allegedly said that under "no circumstances" would Teknics be able to have the machine ready for pickup until, at the earliest, September 9. As a result of this telephone conversation, Neptune canceled the contract on that same day. Later on September 4, Teknics informed Neptune that the machine could in fact be ready for pickup on September 5, but Neptune refused to go through with the transaction and instead filed suit against Teknics a few weeks later to recover the $3,000 deposit it had paid toward the price of the machine. The trial court held for Neptune, concluding that Teknics had anticipatorily breached the contract on September 4, giving Neptune the right to cancel the contract. Teknics appealed.*

*KING*, P.J.A.D. [Presiding Judge, Appellate Division]
\* \* \* \*

What we \* \* \* have is a repudiation by seller that allegedly amounted to an anticipatory breach, followed by a retraction. \* \* \*

Until the repudiating party's next performance is due he can retract his repudiation unless the aggrieved party has since the repudiation cancelled or materially changed his position or otherwise indicated that he considers the repudiation final.
\* \* \* \*

We think under the circumstances here one could reasonably find that the seller's repudiation went to the essence of the contract. Defendant [Teknics] had agreed to a mid-June delivery. Throughout the summer it not only failed to deliver, but it refused to explain its reasons for non-delivery or to give plaintiff adequate assurances that the machine would be delivered soon. By late August buyer \* \* \* was in desperate need of the machine. \* \* \* We conclude that buyer readily could have cancelled [on August 29] but it did not. Rather, [buyer] agreed to accept the \* \* \* machine but only on the express condition that seller have the product available by September 5.

While [buyer] did not expressly state to any of seller's representatives that time had now become of the essence, we conclude this condition can fairly be implied, from the surrounding circumstances. \* \* \* Robertson's unequivocal statement on September 4, that under no circumstances would the machine be ready by the promised delivery date, September 5, was a repudiation going to the essence of the contract.

**DECISION AND REMEDY**   *The appellate court affirmed the trial court's ruling. The seller's statement on September 4 that it could not deliver the machine by September 5 constituted an anticipatory repudiation of the contract, justifying the buyer's cancellation of the contract. The seller's "retraction" of the repudiation was ineffective, because the buyer had already treated the breach as final and canceled the contract prior to the retraction.*

■ **Exhibit 22–1 Letter-of-Credit Transaction**

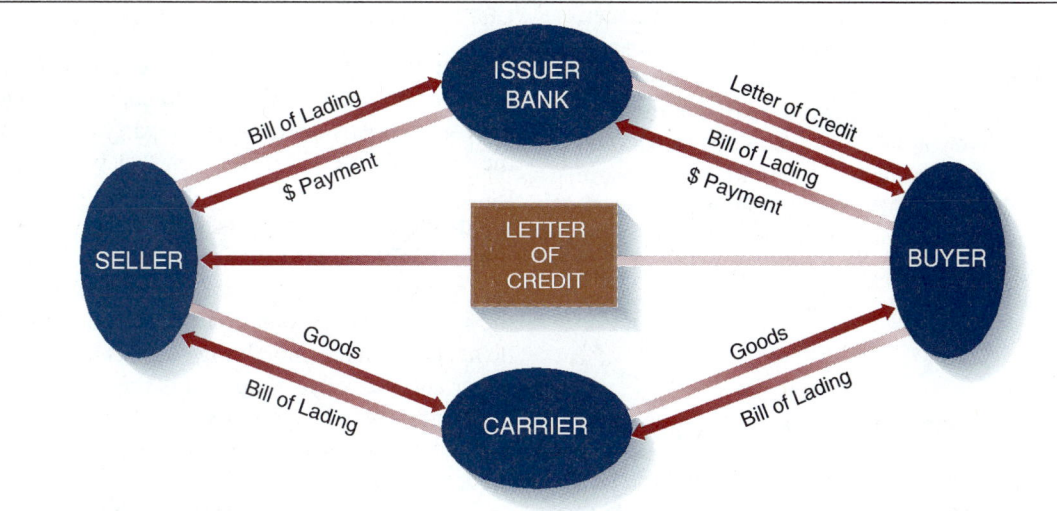

**CHRONOLOGY OF EVENTS**

1. Buyer contracts with issuer bank to issue a letter of credit; this sets forth the bank's obligation to pay on the letter of credit and buyer's obligation to pay the bank.

2. Letter of credit is sent to seller informing seller that upon compliance with the terms of the letter of credit (such as presentment of necessary documents—for example, a bill of lading), the bank will issue a payment for the goods.

3. Seller delivers goods to carrier and receives a bill of lading.

4. Seller delivers the bill of lading to issuer bank and, if the document is proper, receives payment.

5. Issuer bank delivers the bill of lading to buyer.

6. Buyer delivers the bill of lading to carrier.

7. Carrier delivers the goods to buyer.

8. Buyer settles with issuer bank.

SECTION 5

# DEALING WITH INTERNATIONAL CONTRACTS— THE LETTER OF CREDIT

Because buyers and sellers engaged in international business transactions are often separated by thousands of miles, special precautions are often taken to ensure performance under the contract. Sellers want to avoid delivering goods for which they might not be paid. Buyers desire the assurance that sellers will not be paid until there is evidence

that the goods have been shipped. Thus, **letters of credit** are frequently used to facilitate international business transactions. In a simple letter-of-credit transaction, the *issuer* (a bank) agrees to issue a letter of credit and to ascertain whether the *beneficiary* (seller) performs certain acts. In return, the *account party* (buyer) promises to reimburse the issuer for the amount paid to the beneficiary. There may also be an *advising bank* that transmits information, and a *paying bank* may be involved to expedite payment under the letter of credit. See Exhibit 22–1 for an illustration of the letter-of-credit transaction.

Under a letter of credit, the issuer is bound to pay the beneficiary (seller) when the beneficiary has complied with the terms and conditions of the letter of credit. The beneficiary looks to the issuer, not to the account party (buyer), when it presents the documents required by the letter of credit. Typically, the letter of credit will require that the beneficiary deliver a *bill of lading* to prove that shipment has been made. Letters of credit assure beneficiaries (sellers) of payment while at the same time assuring account parties (buyers) that payment will not be made until the beneficiaries have complied with the terms and conditions of the letter of credit.

## THE VALUE OF A LETTER OF CREDIT

The basic principle behind letters of credit is that payment is made against the documents presented by the beneficiary and not against the facts that the documents purport to reflect. Thus, in a letter-of-credit transaction, the issuer does not police the underlying contract; a letter of credit is independent of the underlying contract between the buyer and the seller. Eliminating the need for banks (issuers) to inquire into whether or not actual conditions have been satisfied greatly reduces the costs of letters of credit. Moreover, the use of a letter of credit protects both buyers and sellers.

## COMPLIANCE WITH A LETTER OF CREDIT

In a letter-of-credit transaction, generally at least three separate and distinct contracts are involved: the contract between the account party (buyer) and the beneficiary (seller), the contract between the issuer (bank) and the account party (buyer), and finally the letter of credit itself, which involves the issuer (bank) and the beneficiary (seller). As noted, given that these contracts are separate and distinct, the issuer's obligations under the letter of credit do not concern the underlying contract between the buyer and the seller. Rather, it is the issuer's duty to ascertain whether the documents presented by the beneficiary (seller) comply with the terms of the letter of credit.

If the documents presented by the beneficiary (seller) comply with the terms of the letter of credit, the issuer (bank) must honor the letter of credit. Sometimes, however, it is difficult to determine exactly what a letter of credit requires. Moreover, the courts are divided as to whether *strict* or *substantial* compliance with the terms of the letter of credit is required. Traditionally, courts required strict compliance with the terms of a letter of credit, but in recent years, some courts have moved to a standard of *reasonable* compliance.

## TERMS AND CONCEPTS TO REVIEW

| | | |
|---|---|---|
| commercial | cure 415 | perfect tender rule 415 |
| impracticability 417 | installment contract 416 | performance 413 |
| conforming goods 414 | letter of credit 425 | tender 414 |

## QUESTIONS AND CASE PROBLEMS

**22–1. Nonconforming Tender.** Ames contracts to ship to Curley one hundred Model Z television sets. The terms of delivery are F.O.B. Ames's city, by Green Truck Lines, with delivery on or before April 30. On April 15, Ames discovers that because of an error in inventory control, all Model Z sets have been sold, and the stock has not been replenished. Ames has Model X, a similar but slightly more expensive unit, in stock. On April 16, Ames ships one hundred Model X sets, with notice that Curley will be charged the Model Z price. Curley (in a proper manner) rejects the Model X sets tendered on April 18. Ames does not wish to be held in breach of contract, even though he has tendered nonconforming goods. Discuss Ames's options.

**22–2. Nonperformance.** Thal contracts to deliver to Hurwitz one thousand bushels of corn at market price. Delivery and payment are to be made on October 1. On

September 10, Hurwitz informs Thal that because of financial reverses, she cannot pay on October 1. Thal immediately notifies Hurwitz that he is holding her in breach of contract. On September 15, Thal files suit for breach of contract. On October 3, Hurwitz files an answer to Thal's lawsuit. Hurwitz claims that had Thal tendered delivery on October 1, she would have paid for the corn. Because no delivery was tendered, Hurwitz claims she cannot be held liable. Discuss whether Thal can hold Hurwitz liable for breach.

**22–3. Failure to Tender Delivery.** Kirk has contracted to deliver to Doolittle one thousand cases of Wonder brand beans on or before October 1. Doolittle is to specify the means of transportation twenty days prior to the date of shipment. Payment for the beans is to be made by Doolittle on tender of delivery. On September 10, Kirk prepares the one thousand cases for shipment. Kirk asks Doolittle how he would like the goods to be shipped, but Doolittle does not respond. On September 21, Kirk demands in writing assurance that Doolittle will be able to pay on tender of the beans. Kirk's demand is that the money be placed in escrow prior to October 1 in a bank in Doolittle's city named by Kirk. Doolittle does not respond to any of the requests made by Kirk, but on October 5 he wants to file suit against Kirk for breach of contract for failure to deliver the beans as contracted. Discuss Kirk's liability for failure to tender delivery on October 1.

**22–4. Buyer's Obligations.** Gibson contracts to deliver one hundred Model X color television sets to a new retail customer, Beaver, on May 1, with payment to be made on delivery. Gibson tenders delivery in her own truck. Gibson notices that one or two cartons have scrape marks on them. Beaver inquires of Gibson whether the sets might have been damaged as they were being loaded. Gibson assures Beaver that the sets are in perfect condition. Beaver tenders Gibson a check, but Gibson refuses the check, claiming that the first delivery to new customers is always for cash. Beaver promises to have the cash within two days. Gibson leaves the sets with Beaver, who stores them in a warehouse pending an ''opening sale'' date. Two days later, Beaver opens some of the cartons and discovers that a number of the televisions are damaged beyond ordinary repair. Gibson claims Beaver has accepted the sets and is in breach by not paying on delivery. Discuss fully Gibson's claims.

**22–5. Revocation of Acceptance.** Leemar Steel Co. manufactured counterweight inserts for CMI Corp. according to blueprints from CMI and shipped them to CMI. CMI prepared an internal memo rejecting the shipment for nonconformance two days after it was received. CMI did not send the rejection notice to Leemar. Instead, a few weeks later, it notified Leemar by phone that there was a ''problem with the inserts.'' CMI paid for the inserts and attempted, with Leemar's aid, to have the inserts ground to the correct tolerances during the next few months. Because this could not be accomplished,

CMI filed suit to cancel the contract and to recover the money that it had paid Leemar pursuant to the contract. Discuss whether CMI had accepted the goods. Could it still revoke its acceptance and get its money back? [*CMI Corp. v. Leemar Steel Co.,* 733 F.2d 1410 (10th Cir. 1984)]

**22–6. Anticipatory Repudiation.** Bryant Lewis contracted to sell Ross Cattle Co. four hundred head of cattle at $47.50 per hundredweight. Ross made an $8,000 down payment. Before delivery, Lewis heard a rumor that Ross was in poor financial condition, and Lewis demanded that he receive full payment before delivering the animals. Ross told Lewis the balance would be paid on delivery, based on the weight of the cattle delivered. Lewis refused to deliver the cattle and sold them to a third party. Ross filed suit. Lewis claimed that the refusal of Ross to pay was an anticipatory repudiation of the contract. Discuss whether Lewis was correct and what action Lewis could have taken on the basis of the rumor. [*Ross Cattle Co. v. Lewis,* 415 So.2d 1029 (Miss. 1982)]

**22–7. Tender of Delivery.** Rheinberg-Kellerei GMBH, a German wine producer and export seller, sold 1,245 cases of wine to Vineyard Wine Co., a U.S. company. The contract did not specify delivery to any particular destination, and Rheinberg, through its agent, selected the port of Wilmington for the port of entry. Rheinberg delivered the wine to the boat carrier in early December 1978. On or about January 24, 1979, Vineyard learned that the wine had been lost in the North Atlantic sometime between December 12 and December 22, when the boat sank with all hands aboard. Vineyard refused to pay Rheinberg. Rheinberg filed an action for the purchase price, claiming that risk of loss had passed to the buyer, Vineyard, on delivery of the wine to the carrier. Vineyard claimed that because of Rheinberg's failure to give prompt notice of shipment (notice had not been given until after the ship was lost at sea), risk of loss had not passed to the buyer. Discuss fully who is correct. [*Rheinberg-Kellerei GMBH v. Vineyard Wine Co.,* 281 S.E.2d 425 (N.C.App. 1981)]

**22–8. Revocation of Acceptance.** In September 1982, Kathleen Inniss purchased a 1982 Buick Skylark from Methot Buick-Opel, Inc. The car, which was a demonstrator, had nearly six thousand miles on it but was accompanied by a new-car, twelve-month or twelve-thousand-mile warranty. It also had a history of significant mechanical and electrical problems, which Methot failed to mention to Inniss. Shortly after Inniss took possession, she experienced problems with the car. Between September and December 1982, she took the car back to Methot eight times for repairs. The horn, rear window defogger, throttle, and brakes were repaired, but by the end of the warranty period, several other problems still had not been fixed. The temperature gauge continued to malfunction, intermittently the car would not start, it vibrated in the front end, and the directional indicators intermittently flashed incorrectly when in use. In addition, although the purchase agreement had provided that the car would be rustproofed, much of it had not been. Before the twelve-month warranty had lapsed, Innis sought to revoke her acceptance of the contract and asked for her money back. (The state of Maine did not have a lemon law at the time this case was brought.) Discuss fully whether Inniss could revoke her acceptance of the purchase contract and recover the purchase price of the automobile. [*Inniss v. Methot Buick-Opel, Inc.,* 506 A.2d 212 (Me. 1986)]

**22–9. Letters of Credit.** The Swiss Credit Bank issued a letter of credit in favor of Antex Industries to cover the sale of 92,000 electronic integrated circuits manufactured by Electronic Arrays. The letter of credit specified that the chips would be transported to Tokyo by ship. Antex shipped the circuits by air. Payment on the letter of credit was dishonored because the shipment by air did not fulfill the precise terms of the letter of credit. Should a court compel payment? Explain. [*Board of Trade of San Francisco v. Swiss Credit Bank,* 728 F.2d 1241 (9th Cir. 1984)]

# CHAPTER 23

# REMEDIES OF THE BUYER AND SELLER FOR BREACH

When a sales contract is breached, the aggrieved party may have a number of remedies from which to choose [UCC 2–703; UCC 2–711]. These remedies range from retaining the goods to requiring the breaching party's performance under the contract. The general purpose of these remedies is to put the aggrieved party ''in as good a position as if the other party had fully performed.'' It is important not only that the nonbreaching party know what remedies are available but also that he or she know which remedy is most appropriate for a given situation [UCC 1–106(1)].

## SECTION 1

## REMEDIES OF THE SELLER

The remedies available to a seller when the buyer is in breach under the UCC include the following:

1. The right to withhold delivery of the goods.
2. The right to stop a carrier or bailee from delivering the goods.
3. A limited right to reclaim goods in the possession of an insolvent buyer.
4. The right to identify and/or resell goods identified to the contract.
5. The right to recover the purchase price plus incidental damages in certain situations.
6. The right to recover damages for the buyer's wrongful repudiation or wrongful rejection of the goods.
7. The right to cancel the sales contract.

### THE RIGHT TO WITHHOLD DELIVERY

In general, sellers can withhold delivery of contract goods in their possession or discontinue performance of their obligations under a sales contract when buyers are in breach. If the breach is due to the buyer's insolvency,

**429**

the seller can refuse to deliver the goods unless the buyer pays in cash [UCC 2–702(1)]. A person is **insolvent** under the UCC when that person ceases to pay "his debts in the ordinary course of business or cannot pay his debts as they become due or is insolvent within the meaning of the federal bankruptcy law" [UCC 1–201(23)].

If a buyer has wrongfully rejected or revoked acceptance of the goods, failed to make proper and timely payment, or repudiated a part of the contract, the seller can withhold delivery of the goods in question (if the seller has possession or regains possession of the goods). Furthermore, the seller can withhold the entire undelivered balance of the goods if the buyer's breach is material [UCC 2–703]. (Recall that a material breach is one that substantially impairs the value of the entire contract.)

## THE RIGHT TO STOP DELIVERY OF GOODS IN TRANSIT

If the seller has delivered the goods to a carrier or a bailee but the buyer has not yet received them, the goods are said to be *in transit*. If the seller learns of the buyer's insolvency while the goods are in transit, the seller can stop the carrier or bailee from delivering the goods to the buyer on the basis of the buyer's insolvency, regardless of the quantity shipped. If the buyer is not insolvent but repudiates the contract or gives the seller some other right to withhold or reclaim the goods, the seller can stop the goods in transit only if the quantity shipped is at least a carload, a truckload, a planeload, or a larger shipment[1] [UCC 2–705(1)].

To stop delivery, the seller must *timely notify* the carrier or other bailee that the goods are to be returned or held for the seller. If the carrier has sufficient time to stop delivery, then the goods must be held and delivered according to the instructions of the seller, who is liable to the carrier for any additional costs incurred. If the carrier fails to act properly, it will be liable to the seller for any loss [UCC 2–705(3)]. The right of the seller to stop delivery is lost when one of the following events occurs:

1. The buyer obtains possession of the goods.

2. The carrier acknowledges the buyer's rights by reshipping or storing the goods for the buyer.
3. A bailee of the goods other than a carrier acknowledges that he or she is holding the goods for the buyer.
4. A negotiable document of title covering the goods has been negotiated to the buyer [UCC 2–705(2)].

Under general contract law, circumstances that make it unlikely that a party will be able to fulfill his or her contract may sometimes be treated as an anticipatory breach. As discussed in Chapter 22, under the UCC, circumstances that increase the risk of nonperformance but that do not clearly indicate that performance will not be forthcoming may not be treated as repudiation immediately. A seller may withhold performance—which includes stopping delivery—pending the buyer's assurances that performance will be forthcoming at the proper time. *If adequate assurances are not given within a reasonable time (thirty days), the seller may treat the contract as repudiated.* What is adequate, of course, depends on the circumstances [UCC 2–609].

## THE RIGHT TO RECLAIM THE GOODS

When a seller discovers that a buyer has received goods on credit while insolvent, the seller can demand return of the goods if the demand is made within ten days of the buyer's receipt of the goods. The seller can demand and reclaim the goods at any time if the buyer misrepresented his or her solvency in writing within three months prior to the delivery of the goods [UCC 2–702(2)].

The seller's right to reclaim, however, is subject to the rights of a good faith purchaser or other buyer who, in the ordinary course of business, purchases goods from the buyer before the seller reclaims. A *buyer in the ordinary course of business* is a person who, in good faith and without knowledge that the sale violates the ownership rights or security interest of a third party, purchases goods from a person (other than a pawnbroker) in the business of selling goods of that kind [UCC 1–201(9)].

It is obvious that the seller who successfully reclaims goods under the UCC receives preferential treatment over the buyer's other creditors. Because of this, the UCC provides that reclamation

---

1. This limitation of stoppage to larger shipments when the stoppage is due to reasons other than insolvency recognizes the burden that stoppage represents to carriers [UCC 2–705, Comment 1].

bars the seller from pursuing any other remedy as to these goods [UCC 2–702(3)].

## THE RIGHT TO RESELL THE GOODS

Sometimes a buyer breaches or repudiates a sales contract while the seller is still in possession of finished or partially manufactured goods. In this event, the seller can identify to the contract the conforming goods that are still in his or her possession or control, even if they were not identified at the time of the breach. Then the seller can resell the goods and seek to recover damages from the breaching party [UCC 2–704; UCC 2–706]. Alternatively, as will be discussed later, if the seller is unable to resell the goods, he or she can bring a legal action against the buyer for the price of the goods to recoup the value to the seller of the contract [UCC 2–709].

When the goods contracted for are unfinished at the time of breach, the seller can treat the unfinished goods in two ways. First, the seller can cease manufacturing the goods and resell them for scrap or salvage value. Second, the seller can complete the manufacture, identify the goods to the contract, and resell them. In choosing between these two alternatives, the seller must exercise reasonable commercial judgment to mitigate the loss and realize maximum value from the unfinished goods [UCC 2–704(2)].

When a seller possesses or controls the conforming goods at the time of the buyer's breach (because of the buyer's wrongful rejection or revocation of acceptance of the goods, failure to pay, or repudiation of the contract) or when the seller rightfully reacquires the goods by stopping them in transit, then the seller has the right to resell the goods. The resale must be made in good faith and in a commercially reasonable manner. The seller can recover any deficiency between the resale price and the contract price, along with **incidental damages**—defined as those costs to the seller resulting from stopping delivery of and transporting, caring for, and reselling the goods and other similar actions undertaken because of the breach [UCC 2–706(1); UCC 2–710]. The seller is *not liable to the buyer* for any profits made on the resale [UCC 2–706(6)].

The resale can be private or public, and the goods can be sold as a unit or in parcels. The seller must give the original buyer reasonable notice of the resale, unless the goods are perishable or will rapidly decline in value [UCC 2–706(2), (3)]. In the latter case, the seller has a duty to resell the goods as rapidly as possible to mitigate damages. A good faith purchaser in a resale takes the goods free of any of the rights of the original buyer, even if the seller fails to comply with the resale requirements just described [UCC 2–706(5)].

Consider an example. Cohen contracts on Monday to sell four thousand heads of romaine lettuce to Leuhrs for 30 cents per head, with delivery and payment due on Friday. On Wednesday, Cohen has fourteen thousand heads of romaine lettuce in his inventory, but he has not yet identified the four thousand he intends to sell to Leuhrs. On that day, Leuhrs telephones Cohen to inform him that he will not accept or pay for the lettuce. Leuhrs claims that because the four thousand heads of romaine lettuce for his contract have not yet been identified, Cohen cannot resell and recover damages from him. Leuhrs is incorrect here. Cohen has the right to identify the four thousand heads of lettuce for Leuhrs's contract and the right to resell the lettuce. Cohen can recover the difference between the resale price received and the contract price of 30 cents per head, plus any incidental damages [UCC 2–704(1); UCC 2–706(1); UCC 2–710].

## THE RIGHT TO RECOVER THE PURCHASE PRICE

Before the UCC was adopted, a seller could not sue for the purchase price of the goods unless title had passed to the buyer. Under the UCC, an unpaid seller can bring an action to recover the purchase price and incidental damages, but only under one of the following circumstances:

1. When the buyer has accepted the goods and has not revoked acceptance, in which case title would have passed to the buyer.
2. When conforming goods have been lost or damaged after the risk of loss has passed to the buyer.
3. When the buyer has breached after the goods have been identified to the contract and the seller is unable to resell the goods [UCC 2–709(1)].

If a seller sues for the contract price of goods that he or she has been unable to resell, the goods must be held for the buyer. The seller can resell at any time prior to the collection of the judgment from the buyer, but the net proceeds from the sale must be credited to the buyer. This is an example of the duty to mitigate damages.

To illustrate: Suppose Loomis has contracted to sell Yowell two hundred tablecloths with the name of Yowell's restaurant inscribed on them. Loomis delivers the two hundred tablecloths to Yowell, but Yowell refuses to pay. Or suppose Loomis tenders the two hundred tablecloths to Yowell, but Yowell refuses to accept them. In either case, Loomis has, as a proper remedy, an action for the purchase price.

In the first situation, Yowell accepted conforming goods, but he is in breach by failure to pay. In the second situation, the goods have been identified to the contract, and it is obvious that Loomis could not sell tablecloths inscribed with the name of Yowell's restaurant to anyone else. Thus, both situations fall under UCC 2–709.

In the following case, the court had to determine whether a seller was entitled to recover the purchase price of specially manufactured goods after the buyer had breached the sales contract.

---

| CASE 23.1 |
| :--: |

**ROYAL JONES & ASSOCIATES, INC. v. FIRST THERMAL SYSTEMS, INC.**

District Court of Appeal of Florida, 1990.
566 So.2d 853.

**BACKGROUND AND FACTS**  *Royal Jones & Associates, Inc., ordered three steel rendering tanks from First Thermal Systems, Inc., for use in its business of constructing rendering plants. The contract provided that First Thermal would manufacture the tanks according to Royal Jones's specifications for a price of $64,350. When the manufacture of the tanks was completed, Royal Jones refused to accept the tanks and refused to pay the contract price. First Thermal brought an action for the contract price of the tanks. The trial court, finding that Royal Jones had breached the contract and that the specially manufactured goods were not suitable for sale in the ordinary course of First Thermal's business, awarded First Thermal the full contract price as damages. Royal Jones appealed.*

*ZEHMER, Judge.*
\* \* \* \*

Applying the constructions given to section 2–709 in [previous] cases, we hold that the trial court did not err in awarding First Thermal the full contract price as damages, because the evidence presented at trial by First Thermal was sufficient to meet its burden of proving that the circumstances reasonably indicated that any effort to resell the tanks would have been unavailing. \* \* \* First Thermal proved that any effort at resale would have been unavailing because these were the only rendering tanks First Thermal ever made, the tanks were manufactured according to Royal Jones's specifications, First Thermal had no other customers to which it could resell the tanks, and it was unaware how the tanks could have been marketed for resale. Also, the tanks were built without needed internal components and to a special size in accordance with Royal Jones's specifications and could not be used as rendering tanks without special engineering to which First Thermal had no access. Finally, there was testimony that the tanks had only scrap value to First Thermal of about $700 if they were processed for a scrap dealer. This evidence was sufficient to shift the burden to Royal Jones to show that any effort at resale would not have been unavailing, or that the tanks had some potential market value beyond the salvage value claimed by First Thermal. However, Royal Jones presented no evidence to the contrary at trial, and the lower court did not err in awarding First Thermal the full contract price pursuant to section [2–709].

**DECISION AND REMEDY**  *The appellate court affirmed the trial court's ruling: First Thermal was entitled to the full contract price of the specially manufactured tanks as damages because the evidence showed that efforts to resell the tanks would be useless.*

## THE RIGHT TO RECOVER DAMAGES

If a buyer repudiates a contract or wrongfully refuses to accept the goods, a seller can maintain an action to recover damages. The seller may recover the difference between the contract price and the market price (at the time and place of tender of the goods), plus incidental damages [UCC 2–708(1)]. The time and place of tender are frequently given by such terms as F.O.B., F.A.S., C.I.F., and the like, which determine whether there is a shipment or destination contract. If the market price is less than the contract price, the proper measure of damages includes the seller's lost profits [UCC 2–708(2)].

## THE RIGHT TO CANCEL THE SALES CONTRACT

A seller can cancel a contract if the buyer wrongfully rejects or revokes acceptance of conforming goods, fails to make proper payment, or repudiates the contract in part or in whole. The contract can be canceled with respect to the goods directly involved, or the entire contract can be canceled if the breach is material [UCC 2–703].

The seller must *notify* the buyer of the cancellation, and at that point all remaining obligations of the seller are discharged. The buyer is not discharged from all remaining obligations but is in breach and can be sued under any of the subsections mentioned in UCC 2–703 and UCC 2–106(4). If the seller's cancellation is not justified, then the seller is in breach of the contract, and the buyer can sue for appropriate damages.

## SELLER'S LIEN

Under certain circumstances, a seller's rights go beyond the remedies provided for under the UCC. One such right is a seller's common law lien in the goods being sold. A **lien** is an interest in property to secure payment of a debt or performance of an obligation. Technically, a lien is a right that is incidental to the sale rather than a remedy for breach of contract. A seller's lien enables the seller to retain possession of the goods until the buyer pays for them.

The seller's lien can be waived or lost through (1) express agreement, (2) acts inconsistent with the lien's existence, (3) payment or tender of payment by the buyer, or (4) voluntary and unconditional delivery of the goods to a carrier or other bailee or to the buyer or an authorized agent of the buyer.

If the sales agreement provides for an extension of credit to the buyer, the seller normally has no lien on the goods, because the act of extending credit is inconsistent with the existence of the lien. The seller will have a lien on the goods, however, if the buyer becomes insolvent or if the credit period expires while the goods are still in the seller's possession.

The tender of payment or the actual payment of the debt that the lien secures will ordinarily discharge the lien. This occurs when the buyer pays the full price for the goods and the seller gives up possession. When the buyer gives a promissory note, the lien ordinarily will *not* be discharged until the note is paid, even if the seller relinquishes possession of the goods.

Finally, sellers lose their liens when they voluntarily deliver possession of the goods to the buyer or to an authorized agent of the buyer. The lien is not lost, though, when delivery is qualified—that is, when the seller reserves his or her rights to the lien—or when the buyer obtains possession fraudulently.

## SECTION 2

# REMEDIES OF THE BUYER

Under the UCC, the remedies available to the buyer include the following:

1. The right to reject nonconforming or improperly delivered goods.
2. The right, upon prepayment, to recover identified goods upon the seller's insolvency.
3. The right to obtain specific performance.
4. The right to replevy the goods.
5. The right to retain the goods and enforce a security interest in them.
6. The right to cancel the contract.
7. The right of cover.
8. The right to recover damages for nondelivery or repudiation by the seller.
9. The right to recover damages for breach in regard to accepted goods.

## THE RIGHT OF REJECTION

If the seller's tender of the goods fails to conform to the contract *in any respect,* the buyer can reject the goods. If some of the goods conform to the contract, the buyer can keep the conforming goods and reject the rest [UCC 2–601].

Goods must be rejected within a reasonable time, and the seller must be seasonably notified [UCC 2–602]. Recall that notification is seasonable if it occurs before there is any substantial change in the goods not caused by their own defects—for example, before perishable goods perish. Furthermore, the buyer must designate particular defects that are ascertainable by reasonable inspection. Failure to do so precludes the buyer from using such defects to justify rejection or to establish breach when the seller could have cured the defects if they had been stated seasonably [UCC 2–605]. After rejecting the goods, the buyer cannot exercise any right of ownership over them. If the buyer acts inconsistently with the seller's ownership rights, the buyer will be deemed to have accepted the goods [UCC 2–606].

If a *merchant buyer* rightfully rejects goods, and the seller has no agent or business at the place of rejection, the buyer is required to follow any reasonable instructions received from the seller with respect to the goods controlled by the buyer. The buyer is entitled to reimbursement for the care and cost entailed in following the instructions [UCC 2–603]. The same requirement holds if the buyer rightfully revokes acceptance [UCC 2–608(3)].

If no instructions are forthcoming and the goods are perishable or threaten to decline in value quickly, the buyer can resell the goods in good faith, taking the appropriate reimbursement from the proceeds; the buyer also is entitled under the UCC to a commission for selling the goods [UCC 2–603(1), (2)]. If the goods are not perishable, the buyer may store them for the seller's account or reship them to the seller at the seller's expense [UCC 2–604].

## THE RIGHT TO RECOVER IDENTIFIED GOODS

If a buyer has made a partial or a full payment for goods that remain in the possession of the seller, the buyer can recover the goods if the seller is insolvent or becomes insolvent within ten days after receiving the first payment and if the goods are identified to the contract. To exercise this right, the buyer must tender to the seller any unpaid balance of the purchase price [UCC 2–502].

## THE RIGHT TO OBTAIN SPECIFIC PERFORMANCE

Under UCC 2–716(1), a buyer can obtain specific performance when the goods are unique or in other proper circumstances. Although it is not stated in this section of the UCC, an award of specific performance is usually considered inappropriate unless the buyer's remedy at law is inadequate. Ordinarily, a suit for money damages will be sufficient to place a buyer in the position he or she would have occupied if the seller had fully performed. When the contract is for the purchase of a particular work of art, patent, copyright, or similarly unique item, however, money damages may not be sufficient. Under these circumstances, equity will require the seller to perform exactly by delivering the unique goods (a remedy of specific performance).

## THE RIGHT TO REPLEVY THE GOODS

Closely associated with a buyer's right to obtain specific performance is a buyer's right of replevin. Outside the UCC, the term **replevin** refers to a prejudgment process that permits the seizure of specific personal property in which a party claims an interest or to which a party has a right. For example, when a *buyer* defaults on installment payments under a contract for the purchase of an automobile, the seller might make use of replevin. Under the UCC, replevin is an action to recover goods that are identified to the contract and that are in the hands of a breaching *seller.* The buyer can use replevin if the seller has repudiated or breached the contract. Additionally, buyers must show that they were *unable to effect cover* [UCC 2–716(3)]. As will be discussed below, *cover* is the right of a buyer, after the seller's breach, to purchase goods in substitution for those due under the contract; the purchase, however, must be made in good faith and without unreasonable delay.

Consider the following example. On July 1, Salvador contracts to sell her tomato crop to Bryan, with delivery and payment due on August 10. By August 1, it is clear that the local tomato crop will be bad and that the price of tomatoes is going to rise. Salvador contracts to sell her tomato crop to Green for a higher price and then informs Bryan that she will not deliver on August 10 as agreed. Bryan indicates that cover is unavailable and that he is therefore going to bring a replevin action against Salvador to force her to deliver her tomatoes to him on August 10.

This replevin action will normally succeed. Although a tomato crop is not unique, a buyer of goods identified to the contract for which no cover is available has a right to replevin. In a normal tomato year, cover would probably have been available, and Bryan would have been limited to an action for damages.

## THE RIGHT TO RETAIN AND ENFORCE A SECURITY INTEREST IN THE GOODS

Buyers who rightfully reject goods or who justifiably revoke acceptance of goods that remain in their possession or control have a security interest in the goods (basically, a lien to recover expenses, costs, and the like). The security interest encompasses any payments the buyer has made for the goods, as well as any expenses incurred with regard to inspection, receipt, transportation, care, and custody of the goods [UCC 2–711(3)]. A buyer with a security interest in the goods is a ''person in the position of a seller.'' This gives the buyer the same rights as an unpaid seller. Thus, the buyer can resell, withhold delivery, or stop delivery of the goods. A buyer who chooses to resell must account to the seller for any amounts received in excess of the amount of the security interest [UCC 2–711(3); UCC 2–706(6)].

## THE RIGHT TO CANCEL THE CONTRACT

When a seller fails to make proper delivery or repudiates the contract, or the buyer has the right to reject or revoke acceptance of the goods, the buyer can cancel, or rescind, the contract. Under these circumstances, the buyer can cancel, or rescind, that portion of the contract directly involved in the breach. If the seller's breach is material and substantially impairs the value of the whole contract, the buyer can cancel, or rescind, the whole contract. Upon notice of cancellation, the buyer is relieved of any further obligations under the contract but still retains all remedy rights that can be assessed against the seller.

## THE RIGHT OF COVER

In certain situations, buyers can protect themselves by obtaining **cover** (by purchasing goods in substitution for those due under the contract). This option is available to a buyer who has rightfully rejected goods or revoked acceptance. It is also available when the seller repudiates the contract or fails to deliver the goods. In obtaining cover, the buyer must act in good faith without unreasonable delay [UCC 2–712].

After purchasing substitute goods, the buyer can recover from the seller the difference between the cost of cover and the contract price, plus incidental and consequential damages less the expenses (such as delivery costs) that were saved as a result of the seller's breach [UCC 2–712; UCC 2–715]. Consequential damages include (1) any loss suffered by the buyer that the seller could have foreseen at the time of contract and (2) any injury to the buyer's person or property proximately resulting from a breach of warranty[2] [UCC 2–715(2)].

Buyers are not required to cover, and failure to cover will not bar them from using any other remedies that are available under the UCC [UCC 2–712(3)]. But a buyer who fails to cover when it is reasonably possible to do so may *not* be able to collect consequential damages that he or she could have avoided by purchasing acceptable substitute goods [UCC 2–715(2)(a)]. Thus, the UCC encourages buyers to cover to mitigate damages. For example, if a wholesaler is supposed to supply a grocer with eggs for resale and the wholesaler is unable to deliver them, the grocer has the option of covering. If the grocer covers, he or she can recover any lost profits resulting from the wholesaler's breach of the contract. If the grocer does not cover and has no eggs to sell, he or she cannot recover lost profits to the extent that appropriate cover could have reasonably prevented their loss.

## THE RIGHT TO RECOVER DAMAGES FOR NONDELIVERY OR REPUDIATION

If a seller repudiates the sales contract or fails to deliver the goods, the buyer can sue for damages.

---

2. *Warranties,* which are discussed more fully in Chapter 24, may be defined generally as sellers' statements or representations referring to the character, quality, or title of their goods and constituting part of the contracts of sale. Under the UCC, certain warranties are implied in a sale of goods.

The measure of recovery is the difference between the contract price and the market price of the goods at the time that the buyer *learned* of the breach. The market price is determined at the place at which the seller was supposed to deliver the goods. In some cases, the buyer can also recover incidental and consequential damages less the expenses that were saved as a result of the seller's breach [UCC 2–713]. Note that the damages here are based on the time and place a buyer would normally obtain cover.

In the following case, the question at issue was whether the measure of a buyer's damages in a contract breached by the seller should be the buyer's actual losses caused by the breach (as suggested by UCC 1–106) or the difference between the contract price and the market price of the goods at the time the buyer learned of the breach (as provided by UCC 2–713).

---

| CASE 23.2 |

**TONGISH v. THOMAS**
Supreme Court of Kansas,
1992.
251 Kan. 728,
840 P.2d 471.

**BACKGROUND AND FACTS**    *In April 1988, Denis Tongish agreed to sell sunflower seeds grown on certain acres to the Decatur Cooperative Association (the co-op). One-third of the seeds were to be delivered by December 31, 1988, one-third on March 31, 1988, and one-third on May 31, 1989. The co-op then entered into a contract to sell the seeds, when they had been delivered by Tongish, to Bambino Bean & Seed, Inc., for the same price plus a handling charge of 55 cents per hundredweight. Tongish delivered seeds to the co-op in October and November 1988. A smaller-than-normal crop, bad weather, and other factors caused the market price of sunflower seeds to double that winter from what it had been in April, and in January 1989, Tongish notified the co-op that he would not deliver any more seeds. Tongish then sold 82,820 pounds of sunflower seeds to Danny Thomas for $14,714.89, which was $5,153.13 more than the co-op contract price. Thomas failed to pay the entire purchase price of the seeds, and Tongish sued him. The co-op intervened in the action, seeking damages for Tongish's breach of their contract. The district court, finding that Tongish had breached the contract, awarded damages to the co-op in the amount of $455.51—the co-op's actual losses (the handling charges) resulting from the breach. The co-op appealed, contending that the damage award should have been the difference between the contract price of the seeds and the market price of the seeds at the time of the contract's breach. The appellate court agreed with the co-op and reversed the trial court's decision. Ultimately, the case was reviewed by the Supreme Court of Kansas.*

*McFARLAND*, Justice:
\* \* \* \*

The measure of damages in this action involves two sections of the Uniform Commercial Code: K.S.A. [Kansas Statutes Annotated] 84–1–106 and K.S.A. 84–2–713. The issue to be determined is which statute governs the measure of damages. \* \* \*
\* \* \* \*
\* \* \* K.S.A. 84–1–106(1) states:
"The remedies provided by this act shall be liberally administered to the end that the aggrieved party may be put in as good a position as if the other party had fully performed but neither consequential or special nor penal damages may be had except as specifically provided in this act or by other rule of law."
\* \* \* K.S.A. 84–2–713(1) \* \* \* provides:
"\* \* \* [T]he measure of damages for nondelivery or repudiation by the seller is the difference between the market price at the time when the buyer learned of

the breach and the contract price together with any incidental and consequential damages provided in this article * * * .''

* * * *

* * * K.S.A. 84–1–106 offers a general guide of how remedies of the UCC should be applied, whereas K.S.A. 84–2–713 specifically describes a damage remedy that gives the buyer certain damages when the seller breaches a contract for the sale of goods.

* * * General and special statutes should be read together and harmonized whenever possible, but to the extent a conflict between them exists, the special statute will prevail * * * .

*The Supreme Court of Kansas affirmed the appellate court's decision. The appropriate remedy for the co-op for Tongish's breach was the difference between the contract price of the seeds and the market price of the seeds at the time of breach.*

**DECISION AND REMEDY**

---

## THE RIGHT TO RECOVER DAMAGES FOR BREACH IN REGARD TO ACCEPTED GOODS

A buyer who has accepted nonconforming goods must notify the seller of the breach within a reasonable time after the defect was or should have been discovered. Otherwise, the buyer is precluded from pursuing any remedies [UCC 2–607(3)]. In addition, the parties to a sales contract can insert a provision requiring the buyer to give notice of any defects in the goods within a certain prescribed period. Such a requirement is ordinarily binding on the parties.

The requirement that a buyer who has accepted nonconforming goods must notify the seller of the breach within a reasonable time after the breach was discovered is emphasized in the following case.

---

**COMPANY PROFILE**  *Hapag-Lloyd, A.G.,*[a] *was formed in 1970 in a merger between two German corporations: the 123-year-old Hamburg-Amerikanische Packetfahrt, A.G., and the 113-year-old Norddeutscher Lloyd. Before World War I, Albert Ballin built Hamburg-Amerikanische Packetfahrt into the world's largest shipping company, with a fleet of more than 200 ships. With headquarters in Hamburg, Germany, and central offices in New York and Singapore, Hapag-Lloyd's activities are concentrated mainly in shipping and tourism, although it also has interests in port and coastal services, freight forwarding, and the insurance business. The company's shipping division includes support services to sea transport, freight brokers and other agents facilitating sea transport, and a fleet of worldwide oceangoing vessels. The company owns 95 percent of its own ships—the highest proportion in the shipping industry. The tourism division includes Hapag-Lloyd Reiseburo, one of Germany's largest travel agencies; Hapag-Lloyd Flug, a charter airline with a fleet of twenty-one Boeings and Airbuses; and a cruise operation with the* Europa *as its flagship and the* Frontier Spirit, *based in Fort Lauderdale, Florida.*

| **CASE 23.3** |
| --- |

**HAPAG–LLOYD, A.G. v. MARINE INDEMNITY INSURANCE CO. OF AMERICA**

District Court of Appeal of Florida, Third-District, 1991. 576 So.2d 1330.

**BACKGROUND AND FACTS**  *Marine Indemnity Insurance Company of America purchased a ''toploader'' (a piece of ship-loading equipment)*

---

a.   A.G. is an abbreviation for *Aktiengesellschaft,* the German equivalent of a publicly held corporation.

*from Hapag-Lloyd, A.G. Marine Indemnity was aware of the fact that the wiring in the toploader's engine was defective but nevertheless used the equipment in its defective state without notifying the seller. After Marine Indemnity had used the toploader for about four weeks, the wiring caused an explosion in the engine, which severely damaged the equipment. After the accident, Marine Indemnity brought an action against Hapag-Lloyd for breach of express warranty.[b] The trial court held for Marine Indemnity. Hapag-Lloyd appealed, contending that Marine Indemnity's failure to give timely notice of the breach barred it from pursuing any remedy.*

*SCHWARTZ*, Chief Judge.
\* \* \* \*

In these circumstances, we find as a matter of law that the buyer did not give the notice to the seller of the alleged breach "within a reasonable time after [it] discover[ed] or should have discovered any breach," as is required to permit a recovery for breach of warranty under section 672.607(3)(a), Florida Statutes [Florida's equivalent of UCC 2–607(3)(a)]. It is obvious that the failure to afford the seller reasonable notice of an already-discovered defect until after the loss caused by the breach of warranty had already occurred—when, as clearly appears, the seller could have remedied the defect and prevented the loss—requires a conclusion that, as the statute provides, the buyer is "barred from any remedy."

**DECISION AND REMEDY** *The trial court's judgment was reversed.*

**INTERNATIONAL CONSIDERATIONS** **Notice of Claims under International Law** *The United Nations Convention on Contracts for the International Sale of Goods (CISG) establishes notice requirements for international sales transactions. At the behest of developing nations, the CISG imposes weaker notice requirements on buyers. The CISG requires notice by the buyer only when the seller has no knowledge or is reasonably unaware that the goods that were shipped did not conform to the contract promises. Thus, lack of prompt notice of nonconformity need not defeat a buyer's claim.*

b.   An express warranty is a seller's oral or written promise to the buyer that assures the quality, description, or performance of the goods being sold—see Chapter 24.

## DAMAGES FOR BREACH OF WARRANTY

When the seller breaches a warranty, the measure of damages equals the difference between the value of the goods as accepted and their value if they had been as warranted [UCC 2–714(a)]. For example, suppose that a law firm purchased a computer for $30,000. As warranted, the computer was worth $40,000. As delivered, however, the computer was worth only $20,000 because of defects. Unless special circumstances would show proximate damages of a different amount, the measure of damages is the difference between the value as warranted ($40,000) and the value as delivered ($20,000), or $20,000.

## SUIT BY A BUYER'S CUSTOMER FOR BREACH OF WARRANTY

When a buyer resells defective goods that were originally sold by a breaching seller, the buyer's customer can sue the buyer. Under these circumstances the buyer has two alternatives:

1.   The buyer can notify the seller of the pending litigation. The notice should state that the seller can become a party in the customer's action against the buyer and defend. The notice should also point out that if, after seasonable receipt of the notice, the seller does not come in, the seller may nevertheless be bound by

determinations of fact in the customer's action against the buyer. If the buyer brings a subsequent action against the seller, the seller cannot relitigate factual issues that are common to both the buyer's action against the seller and the buyer's customer's action against the buyer and that were determined in the customer's action [UCC 2–607(5)(a)].

2. The buyer can also defend against the customer's suit and later bring an action against the original seller. This situation arises most frequently when there is a manufacturer-dealer arrangement; for example, when a car dealer sells a defective automobile, and the customer sues the dealer but not the manufacturer.

**OTHER MEASURES OF DAMAGES** The UCC also allows for two additional remedies for damages in accepted goods. Both can also be applied when there has been a breach of warranty.

The first applies when the buyer has accepted nonconforming goods. The buyer is entitled to recover for any loss "resulting in the ordinary course of events . . . as determined in any manner which is reasonable." Thus, this remedy is available for both a breach of warranty situation and any other failure of the seller to perform according to the contractual obligations [UCC 2–714(1)].

The second remedy is extremely important to a buyer, as the buyer not only has possession of the goods but also determines the amount of damages. The UCC permits the buyer, with proper notice to the seller, to deduct all or any part of the damages from the price still due and payable to the seller [UCC 2–717].

SECTION 3

# CONTRACTUAL PROVISIONS AFFECTING REMEDIES

The parties to a sales contract can vary their respective rights and obligations by contractual agreement. Certain restrictions are placed on the ability of parties to contract to limit their rights and remedies under the UCC, but provisions that the parties frequently include relate to the limitation of damages, the limitation of remedies, and the waiver of defenses.

## LIMITATION OF DAMAGES

The parties can provide in the sales contract that a specified amount of damages will be paid in the event that either party breaches. These damages, called *liquidated damages,* must be reasonable in amount in view of the anticipated or actual loss caused by the breach, the difficulties of proof of loss, and the inconvenience or nonfeasibility of otherwise obtaining an adequate remedy. If the provision is valid, the aggrieved party is limited to recovering the amount of agreed-on damages. If the amount of liquidated damages is unreasonably large, the provision is void, because it imposes a penalty. In this situation, the court will determine the appropriate amount of damages [UCC 2–718].

A buyer often makes a down payment when a contract is executed. If the buyer defaults and the contract contains a liquidated damages provision, the seller retains the down payment as damages, and the buyer can recover only the part of the down payment that exceeds the amount specified as liquidated damages. The buyer is entitled to this sum as restitution. If the contract contains no provision for liquidated damages, the seller's damages are deemed to be 20 percent of the purchase price or $500, whichever is less [UCC 2–718(2)(b)]. The amount by which the buyer's down payment exceeds this sum must be returned to the buyer. If the seller can prove that his or her actual damages are higher, the buyer can recover only the excess over the seller's actual damages.

## LIMITATION OF REMEDIES

The parties to a sales contract can vary their respective rights and obligations by contractual agreement. For example, a seller and a buyer can expressly provide for remedies in addition to those provided in the UCC. They can also provide for remedies in lieu of those provided in the UCC, or they can change the measure of damages. The seller can provide that the buyer's only remedy on breach of warranty will be repair or replacement of the item, or the seller can limit the buyer's remedy to return of the goods and refund of the purchase price. An agreed-on remedy is available in addition to remedies provided in the UCC unless the parties expressly agree that the remedy is exclusive of all others [UCC 2–719(1)].

If the parties state that a remedy is exclusive of all other remedies, then it is the sole remedy.

But when circumstances cause an exclusive remedy to fail in its essential purpose, the remedy will no longer be exclusive [UCC 2–719(2)]. Of course, any clause limiting remedies in an unconscionable manner is void.

Suppose that Helio buys a motorcycle from merchant Eccles. The sales contract is accompanied by an express warranty stating that the exclusive remedy is repair or replacement of defective parts. Helio discovers numerous defects in her motorcycle after only a few days' use. After discovering each defect, she returns the motorcycle for repairs. Some of the parts are out of stock and will not arrive at Eccles's repair station for months. Helio sues Eccles. A trier of fact in this situation may return a verdict for Helio in an amount far exceeding the cost of repairs. The reason is that the exclusive remedy of repair or replacement of defective parts fails in its essential purpose, because the motorcycle cannot be repaired to make it operate as it should, free of defects.

A contract can limit or exclude consequential damages provided the limitation is not unconscionable. When the buyer is a consumer, the limitation of consequential damages for personal injuries resulting from a breach of warranty is *prima facie* (on its face) unconscionable. The limitation of consequential damages is not necessarily unconscionable when the loss is commercial in nature—for example, lost profits and property damage [UCC 2–719(3)].

### WAIVER OF DEFENSES

A buyer can be precluded from objecting to a breach of warranty by a seller in certain situations. For example, when a buyer purchases on credit, the seller usually assigns the note or account to a financial institution to obtain ready cash. To facilitate the assignment of these notes or accounts, the seller will include a clause in the sales contract stating that the buyer agrees not to assert against the assignee defenses that may apply to the seller. In essence, the buyer must complain directly to the seller, and the buyer cannot withhold payment for breach of warranty.

In such situations, buyers are in the same position as if they had signed a waiver. Because of this, many states, including those that have adopted the Uniform Consumer Credit Code, have invalidated such clauses in sales contracts for consumer

goods. In addition, the Federal Trade Commission has adopted a special rule that applies to *consumer credit* sales transactions that are evidenced by negotiable instruments (promissory notes). The rule states that any defense of the buyer against the seller is also a defense against any other party to whom the note is negotiated (transferred). This rule will be discussed more fully in Chapter 27.

### SECTION 4

# LEMON LAWS

Some purchasers of defective automobiles—called "lemons"—found that the remedies provided by the UCC, after limitations had been imposed by the seller, were inadequate. In response to the frustrations of these buyers, the majority of states have enacted *lemon laws*. Basically, lemon laws provide that if an automobile under warranty possesses a defect that significantly affects the vehicle's value or use, and the defect has not been remedied by the seller within a specified number of opportunities (usually four), the buyer is entitled to a new car, replacement of defective parts, or return of all consideration paid.

In most states, lemon laws require an aggrieved new-car owner to notify the dealer or manufacturer of the problem and provide the dealer or manufacturer with an opportunity to solve it. If the problem remains, the owner must then submit complaints to the arbitration program specified in the manufacturer's warranty before taking the case to court. Decisions by arbitration panels are binding on the manufacturer (that is, cannot be appealed by the manufacturer to the courts) but are not usually binding on the purchaser.

### SECTION 5

# REMEDIES FOR BREACH OF INTERNATIONAL SALES CONTRACTS

The United Nations Convention on Contracts for the International Sale of Goods (CISG) provides international sellers and buyers with remedies very similar to those available under the UCC. Article

# ■ CONCEPT SUMMARY 23.1 **Remedies for Breach of Contract**

| | |
|---|---|
| **Seller's Remedies for Buyer's Breach** | 1. If the goods are in the seller's possession, the seller may do the following:<br>  a. Withhold delivery [UCC 2–703(a)].<br>  b. Identify goods to the contract [UCC 2–704].<br>  c. Resell the goods [UCC 2–706].<br>  d. Sue for breach of contract [UCC 2–708].<br>  e. Cancel (rescind) the contract [UCC 2–703].<br>2. If the goods are in transit, the seller may stop the carrier or bailee from delivering the goods [UCC 2–705].<br>3. If the goods are in the buyer's possession, the seller may do the following:<br>  a. Sue for the purchase price [UCC 2–709].<br>  b. Reclaim goods received by an insolvent buyer if the demand is made within ten days of receipt (excludes all other remedies on reclamation) [UCC 2–702]. |
| **Buyer's Remedies for Seller's Breach** | 1. If the seller refuses to deliver the contract goods or the seller tenders nonconforming goods and the buyer rejects them, the buyer may do the following:<br>  a. Cancel (rescind), with notice [UCC 2–711].<br>  b. Cover [UCC 2–712].<br>  c. Sue for breach of contract [UCC 2–713].<br>2. If the seller tenders nonconforming goods and the buyer accepts them, the buyer, with notice, may do the following:<br>  a. Sue for ordinary damages [UCC 2–714(1)].<br>  b. Sue for breach of warranty [UCC 2–714(2)].<br>  c. Deduct damages from the price of the goods [UCC 2–717].<br>3. If the seller refuses delivery and the buyer wants the goods, the buyer may do the following:<br>  a. Sue for specific performance [UCC 2–716(1)].<br>  b. Replevy the goods [UCC 2–716(3)].<br>  c. Recover the goods from the seller, if the buyer has paid part or all of the purchase price and the seller is insolvent or becomes insolvent within ten days after receiving the first payment [UCC 2–502]. |

74 of the CISG provides for money damages, including *foreseeable* consequential damages, on a contract's breach. As under the UCC, the measure of damages is normally the difference between the contract price and the market price of the goods. Under Article 49, the buyer is permitted to avoid obligations under the contract if the seller breaches the contract or fails to deliver the goods during the time specified in the agreement or later agreed upon by the parties. Similarly, under Article 64, the seller can avoid obligations under the contract if the buyer breaches the contract, fails to accept delivery of the goods, or fails to pay for the goods.

The CISG also allows for specific performance as a remedy under Article 28, which provides that "one party is entitled to require performance of any obligation by the other party." This statement is then qualified, however. Article 28 goes on to state that a court may only grant specific performance as a remedy if it would do so "under its own law in respect of similar contracts of sale not governed by this Convention." As already discussed, in the United States the equitable remedy of specific performance normally will only be granted if there is no adequate remedy at law (money damages) available and the goods are unique in nature. In other countries, however, such as Germany (see Chapter 10), specific performance is a commonly granted remedy for breach of contract.

## TERMS AND CONCEPTS TO REVIEW

| | | |
|---|---|---|
| cover 435 | insolvent 430 | replevin 434 |
| incidental damages 431 | lien 433 | |

## QUESTIONS AND CASE PROBLEMS

**23–1. Remedies of the Seller.** Klink contracts to ship Albright via Quickway Truck Line one hundred cases of Knee High brand corn, F.O.B. Albright's city, at $6.50 per case. Albright is to make a 10 percent down payment. The payment is to be received at Klink's place of business before shipment occurs. Klink ships the corn as contracted, although he has not yet received the down payment, and the goods arrive in Albright's city. There they remain in the delivery van. Because Albright has failed to make the down payment, Klink orders Quickway not to make the delivery to Albright's warehouse. Albright claims that the transit has ended and that Klink has no right to stop the delivery of the corn. Discuss the validity of Albright's claim and Klink's action.

**23–2. Remedies of the Seller.** Topken has contracted to sell Lorwin five hundred washing machines of a certain model at list price. Topken is to ship the goods on or before December 1. Topken produces one thousand washing machines of this model but has not yet prepared Lorwin's shipment. On November 1, Lorwin repudiates the contract. Discuss the remedies available to Topken.

**23–3. Remedies of the Buyer.** Roy has contracted with Schnee for the purchase and delivery of one hundred Model Z dryers. At the time for the contracted tender, Schnee does not have a hundred Model Z dryers in stock and does not expect to acquire any for at least three months. Schnee tenders eighty Model Z dryers and twenty Model X dryers. Roy wants one hundred Model Z dryers or none at all. Discuss the remedies available to Roy under these circumstances.

**23–4. Remedies of the Buyer.** McDonald has contracted to purchase five hundred pairs of shoes from Vetter. Vetter manufactures the shoes and tenders delivery to McDonald. McDonald accepts the shipment. Later, on inspection, McDonald discovers that ten pairs of the shoes are poorly made and will have to be sold to customers as seconds. If McDonald decides to keep all five hundred pairs of shoes, what remedies are available to her? Discuss.

**23–5. Remedies of the Buyer.** Lehor is an antique car collector. He contracts to purchase spare parts for a 1938 engine from Beem. These parts are not made anymore and are scarce. To get the contract with Beem, Lehor agrees to pay 50 percent of the purchase price in advance.

On May 1, Lehor sends the payment, which is received on May 2. On May 3, Beem, having found another buyer willing to pay substantially more for the parts, informs Lehor that he will not deliver as contracted. That same day, Lehor learns that Beem is insolvent. Discuss fully any possible remedies available to Lehor to take possession of these parts.

**23–6. Remedies of the Seller.** Lupofresh, Inc., contracted to sell a quantity of hops to the defendant, Pabst Brewing Co. Lupofresh processed the hops and notified Pabst that the hops were ready for shipment. Pabst responded with a letter indicating acceptance of the hops but later refused to issue shipping orders, claiming that the price determination violated antitrust laws. Lupofresh sued for the full purchase price under UCC 2–709(1)(a). Pabst claimed that the goods had not been accepted but merely identified to the contract and that Lupofresh was required to attempt to resell the hops before it was entitled to recover the purchase price. Discuss fully which party was correct. [*Lupofresh, Inc. v. Pabst Brewing Co.,* 505 A.2d 37 (Super.Del. 1985)]

**23–7. Remedies of the Buyer.** Engineering Measurements Co. (EMCO) agreed to manufacture and deliver to International Technical Instruments, Inc. (ITI), a specified number of optical communication links (devices that allow wireless communication between two points). The links were to be delivered in stated installments. During a seven-month period, ITI continually complained that EMCO had failed to meet delivery schedules and had delivered some defective units. ITI did not refuse any shipment during this period. Eventually, ITI filed suit, claiming EMCO had breached its contract by failing to meet its delivery schedules and by delivering defective units. EMCO argued that ITI had accepted the goods and that by failing to revoke its acceptance and give notice, ITI was precluded from any remedy under UCC 2–607(3)(a). Discuss fully whether ITI was able to recover under its suit for breach of contract. [*International Technical Instruments, Inc. v. Engineering Measurements Co.,* 678 P.2d 558 (Colo.App. 1983)]

**23–8. Remedies of the Seller.** Servbest Foods, Inc., had a contract with Emessee Industries, Inc., under which Emessee was to purchase 200,000 pounds of beef trimmings from Servbest at 52.5 cents per pound. Servbest delivered to Emessee the warehouse receipts and invoices for the beef trimmings. The price of beef trimmings then fell significantly, and Emessee returned the documents to Servbest and canceled the contract.

Servbest then sold the beef trimmings for 20.25 cents per pound and sued Emessee for damages (the difference between the contract price and the market price at which it had been forced to sell the trimmings) for breach of contract, plus incidental damages. Discuss whether Servbest Foods exercised a proper remedy and was entitled to the damages alleged in its lawsuit. [*Servbest Foods, Inc. v. Emessee Industries, Inc.*, 82 Ill.App.3d 662, 403 N.E.2d 1, 37 Ill.Dec. 945 (1980)]

 **23–9. Measure of Damages.** Bigelow-Sanford, Inc., entered into a contract to buy 100,000 yards of jute at $0.64 per yard from Gunny Corp. Gunny delivered 22,228 yards to Bigelow but informed the company that no more would be delivered. Several other suppliers to Bigelow defaulted, and Bigelow was forced to go into the market one month later to purchase a total of 164,503 yards of jute for $1.21 per yard. Bigelow sued Gunny for the difference between the market price and the contract price of the amount of jute that Gunny had not delivered. Discuss whether Bigelow could recover this amount from Gunny. [*Bigelow-Sanford, Inc. v. Gunny Corp.*, 649 F.2d 1060 (5th Cir. 1981)]

### 23–10. A Question of Ethics

*In March 1985, Bruce Young purchased from Hessel Tractor & Equipment Co., a John Deere equipment dealer, a feller-buncher to shear trees in his logging business. The only warranty in the contract was a one-year warranty against defects in the equipment with an exclusive remedy of repair and replacement for any defect in material or assembly. All other warranties were expressly and conspicuously disclaimed. Young began to have serious problems with the equipment after less than a month of use. After over a year of continuing unsuccessful attempts at repair and after the one-year warranty had expired, Hessel, the seller, stopped repairing the machine. Given these facts, consider the following questions. [Young v. Hessel Tractor & Equipment Co., 782 P.2d 164 (Or.App. 1989)]*

1. Do you think that it is fair for a seller to limit available remedies under a sales contract to just one, exclusive remedy—such as repair and replacement of parts? Is there anything unethical about this practice?

2. When an exclusive remedy leads to unfair results, as in this case, what, if anything, can be done about it?

3. What UCC provisions might Young cite to persuade the court that he is entitled to revoke his acceptance of the machine and recover the purchase price? How do these provisions reflect the UCC's attempt to balance freedom of contract against the need for fairness and justice in commercial transactions?

# CHAPTER 24

# SALES WARRANTIES

I n the past, *caveat emptor*—let the buyer beware—was the prevailing philosophy in sales law. This may not have been an unrealistic approach when buyers and sellers were more or less equally capable of judging the quality (or lack of it) of the goods that were the subjects of their bargains. In twentieth-century America, however, it is unlikely that any buyer will comprehend the workings of any but a few of the goods he or she purchases, much less grasp all of the risks and be able to assume them intelligently and pay for any resulting injuries or damage. Thus, *caveat emptor* has given way to a consumer-oriented approach. Today, most goods are covered by some type of warranty designed to protect consumers. This change, of course, has not been without cost to consumers, who generally pay higher prices imposed by sellers and their insurers to cover their increased costs.

The concept of *warranty* is based on the seller's assurance to the buyer that the goods will meet certain standards. The UCC designates five types of warranties that can arise in a sales contract:

1. Warranty of title [UCC 2–312].
2. Express warranty [UCC 2–313].
3. Implied warranty of merchantability [UCC 2–314(1), (2)].
4. Implied warranty of fitness for a particular purpose [UCC 2–315].
5. Implied warranty arising from the course of dealing or trade usage [UCC 2–314(3)].

In the law of sales, because a warranty imposes a duty on the seller, a breach of warranty is a breach of the seller's promise. If the parties have not agreed to limit or modify the remedies available to the buyer on the seller's breach of warranty, the buyer can sue to recover damages against the seller. Under some circumstances, a breach can allow the buyer to rescind (cancel) the agreement.[1]

---

1. Rescission restores the parties to the positions they were in before the contract was made.

# WARRANTY OF TITLE

Title warranty arises automatically in most sales contracts. UCC 2–312 imposes the three types of warranties of title discussed below.

## GOOD TITLE

In most cases, sellers warrant that they have good and valid title to the goods sold and that transfer of the title is rightful [UCC 2–312(1)(a)]. For example, Alice steals goods from Henry and sells them to Ona, who does not know that they are stolen. If Henry discovers that Ona has the goods, then Henry has the right to reclaim them from Ona. Under this UCC provision, however, Ona can then sue Alice for breach of warranty, because a thief has no title to stolen goods and thus cannot give good title in a subsequent sale. When Alice sold Ona the goods, Alice *automatically* warranted to Ona that the title conveyed was valid and that its transfer was rightful. Because this was not in fact the case, Alice breached the warranty of title imposed by UCC 2–312(1)(a) and became liable to the buyer for appropriate damages. (See Chapter 21 for a detailed discussion of sales by nonowners.)

## NO LIENS

A second warranty of title provided by the UCC protects buyers who are *unaware* of any encumbrances (claims or liens) against goods at the time the contract is formed [UCC 2–312(1)(b)]. This warranty protects buyers who, for example, unknowingly purchase goods that are subject to a creditor's security interest (an interest in property that secures payment to the creditor—see Chapter 31). If a creditor legally repossesses the goods from a buyer who *had no actual knowledge of the security interest,* then the buyer can recover from the seller for a breach of warranty. (The buyer who has *actual knowledge* of a security interest has no recourse against a seller.)

To illustrate: Henderson buys a used boat from Loring for cash. A month later, Barish repossesses the boat from Henderson, having proved that she, Barish, has a valid security interest in the boat and that Loring is in default, having missed five payments. Henderson demands his money back from Loring. Under Section 2–312(1)(b), Henderson has

legal grounds to recover, because the seller of goods warrants that the goods shall be delivered free from any security interest or other lien of which the buyer has no knowledge.

## NO INFRINGEMENTS

A third category of title warranty is the warranty against infringement. A merchant is deemed to warrant that the goods delivered are free from any patent, trademark, or copyright claims of a third person[2] [UCC 2–312(3)]. If this warranty is breached and the buyer is sued by the claim holder, the buyer *must notify the seller* of litigation within a reasonable time to enable the seller to decide whether to defend the lawsuit. If the seller states in writing that he or she has decided to defend and agrees to bear all expenses, including that of an adverse judgment, then the buyer must let the seller undertake litigation; otherwise the buyer loses all rights against the seller if any infringement liability is established [UCC 2–607(3)(b), (5)(b)]. If the seller refuses to defend, the buyer can do so and then, in turn, sue the seller.

This infringement warranty does not apply to buyers who furnish specifications for goods to be made in a particular way. In fact, it is the buyer who must ultimately bear the responsibility for any third person's claims of infringement arising out of goods manufactured to the buyer's specifications [UCC 2–312(3)]. Under these circumstances, the requirements of notice described above apply to a seller who is sued for breach of an infringement warranty [UCC 2–607(6)].

## DISCLAIMER OF TITLE WARRANTY

In an ordinary sales transaction, the title warranty can be disclaimed or modified only by *specific language* in a contract. For example, sellers may assert that they are transferring only such rights, title, and interest as they have in the goods.

In certain cases, the circumstances of the sale are sufficient to indicate clearly to a buyer that no assurances as to title are being made. The classic example is a sheriff's sale, when buyers know that

---

2.   Recall from Chapter 20 that a *merchant* is defined in UCC 2–104(1) as a person who deals in goods of the kind involved in the sales contract or who, by occupation, presents himself or herself as having knowledge or skill peculiar to the goods involved in the transaction.

the goods have been seized to satisfy debts, and it is apparent that the goods are not the property of the person selling them [UCC 2–312(2)].

# SECTION 2

# EXPRESS WARRANTIES

A seller can create an **express warranty** by making representations concerning the quality, condition, description, or performance potential of the goods. Under UCC 2–313, express warranties arise when a seller indicates any of the following:

1. The goods will conform to any *affirmation* or *promise* of fact that the seller makes to the buyer about the goods. Such affirmations or promises are usually made during the bargaining process. Statements such as "These drill bits will *easily* penetrate stainless steel—and without dulling" constitute express warranties.
2. The goods will conform to any *description* of them—for example, a label that states that a "crate contains one 150-horsepower diesel engine" or a contract that calls for delivery of a "camel's hair coat" creates an express warranty that the goods delivered will conform to the description given on the label or in the contract.
3. The goods will conform to any *sample* or *model.* For example, an express warranty arises when a buyer is shown a swatch of cloth, and based on this sample, the buyer orders one hundred bolts of cloth.

Express warranties can be found in a seller's advertisement, brochure, or promotional materials, in addition to being made orally or in an express warranty provision in a sales contract. If an express warranty is not intended, the marketing agent or salesperson should not promise too much. According to Section 2–313(2), "It is not necessary to the creation of an express warranty that the seller use formal words such as 'warrant' or 'guarantee' or that [the seller] have a specific intention to make a warranty." It is necessary only that a reasonable buyer would regard the representation as part of the basis of the bargain.

## BASIS OF THE BARGAIN

The UCC requires that for any express warranty to be created, the affirmation, promise, description, or sample must become part of the "basis of the bargain." To become part of the basis of the bargain, an affirmation, promise, description, or sample must come at such a time that the buyer could have relied on it when he or she agreed to the contract. The buyer does not have to prove that he or she actually did rely on it, but the seller can nullify the warranty if the seller can prove that the buyer did not rely on it. It does not matter whether the seller intended the statement, sample, or model to create a warranty. Each case presents a question of fact as to whether a representation came at such a time and in such a way that it induced the buyer to enter the contract.

Are certain telephone statements affirmations of fact and part of the basis of the bargain? That is the question addressed in the following case.

| CASE 24.1 | **BACKGROUND AND FACTS**  *Riegle sold a racehorse to Sessa for $25,000. Prior to the sale, Sessa sent a friend, Maloney, to examine the horse. Maloney reported that he "liked him." Additionally, during a telephone conversation, Riegle stated to Sessa that Sessa would like the horse and that he was a "good one" and "sound." After the sale had been completed and after delivery, the horse almost immediately went lame in the hind legs. Experts were unable to identify the cause. They could not establish whether the condition had been present before Riegle shipped the horse. Even though the horse—Tarport Conaway—was later able to race, Sessa sued for damages.* |
|---|---|
| **SESSA v. RIEGLE** United States District Court, Eastern District of Pennsylvania, 1977. 427 F.Supp. 760. | |

*HANNUM,* District Judge.

\* \* \* \*

In deciding whether statements by a seller constitute express warranties, the court must look to UCC [Section] 2–313 which presents three fundamental issues. First, the court must determine whether the seller's statement constitutes an ''affirmation of fact or promise'' or ''description of the goods'' under [Section] 2–313(1)(a) or (b) or whether it is rather ''merely the seller's opinion or commendation of the goods'' under [Section] 2–313(2). Second, assuming the court finds the language used susceptible to creation of a warranty, it must then be determined whether the statement was ''part of the basis of the bargain.'' If it was, an express warranty exists and, as the third issue, the court must determine whether the warranty was breached.

With respect to the first issue, the court finds that in the circumstances of this case, words to the effect that ''The horse is sound'' spoken during the telephone conversation between Sessa and Riegle constitute an opinion or commendation rather than express warranty. This determination is a question for the trier of fact. \*   \*   \* Whether use of that language constitutes warranty, or mere opinion or commendation depends on the circumstances of the sale and the type of goods sold. While [Section] 2–313 makes it clear that no specific words need be used and no specific intent need be present, not every statement by a seller is an express warranty.

\* \* \* \*

Even assuming that Riegle's statements could be express warranties, it is not at all clear that they were ''part of the basis of the bargain,'' the second requisite of [Section] 2–313. This is essentially a reliance requirement and is inextricably intertwined with the initial determination as to whether given language may constitute an express warranty since affirmations, promises, and descriptions tend to become part of the basis of the bargain. It was the intention of the drafters of the U.C.C. not to require a strong showing of reliance. In fact, they envisioned that all statements of the seller became part of the basis of the bargain unless clear affirmative proof is shown to the contrary.

It is Sessa's contention that his conversation with Riegle was the principal factor inducing him to enter the bargain. He would have the court believe that Maloney was merely a messenger to deliver the check. The evidence shows, however, that Sessa was relying primarily on Maloney to advise him in connection with the sale. Maloney testified that he had talked to Sessa about the horse on several occasions and expressed the opinion that he was convinced ''beyond the shadow of a doubt'' that he was a good buy. \*   \*   \*

\* \* \* \*

The Court believes that Maloney's opinion was the principal, if not the only, factor which motivated Sessa to purchase the horse. The conversation with Riegle played a negligible role in his decision.

*The court decided that no express warranty had been made. The court further concluded that even if the defendant's statements gave rise to an express warranty, those statements were not relied on as part of the bargain.*

**DECISION AND REMEDY**

## STATEMENTS OF OPINION AND VALUE

As stated above, according to Section 2–313(2), it is not necessary that a seller use formal words such as *warrant* or *guarantee* to make an express warranty. It is necessary only that a reasonable buyer would regard the representation as part of the basis of the bargain.

In contrast, if the seller merely makes a statement that relates to the value or worth of the goods or makes a statement of opinion or recommendation about the goods, the seller is not creating an express warranty [UCC 2–313(2)]. For example, a seller claims, ''This is the best used car to come along in years; it has four new tires and a 200-horsepower engine just rebuilt this year.'' The seller has made several *affirmations of fact* that can create a warranty: the automobile has an engine; it is a 200-horsepower engine; it was rebuilt this year; there are four tires on the automobile; the tires are new. But the seller's *opinion* that it is "the best used car to come along in years" is known as *puffing* and creates no warranty. (Puffing is the expression of an opinion by a seller that is not made as a representation of fact.) A statement relating to the value of the goods, such as "It's worth a fortune" or "Anywhere else you'd pay $10,000 for it," will not normally create a warranty.

The ordinary seller can give an opinion that is not a warranty. If the seller is an expert and gives an opinion as an expert, however, then a warranty can be created. For example, Saul is an art dealer and an expert in seventeenth-century paintings. If Saul states to Lauren, a purchaser, that in his opinion a particular painting is a Rembrandt, Saul has warranted the accuracy of his opinion.

The question of what constitutes an express warranty and what constitutes puffing is not easy to resolve. Merely recognizing that some statements are not warranties does not tell us where one should draw the line between puffs and warranties. The reasonableness of the buyer's reliance appears to be the controlling criterion in many cases. For example, a salesperson's statements that a ladder "will never break" and will "last a lifetime" are so clearly improbable that no reasonable buyer should rely on them. Also, the context within which a statement is made might be relevant in determining the reasonableness of the buyer's reliance. For example, any statement made in a written advertisement is more likely to be relied on by a reasonable person than a statement made orally by a salesperson. Another factor is the specificity of the statements made. The following case illustrates a court's consideration of phrases that were claimed to be express warranties.

---

| CASE 24.2 |
| --- |

**MARTIN RISPENS & SON v. HALL FARMS, INC.**

Supreme Court of Indiana, 1993.
621 N.E.2d 1078.

**COMPANY PROFILE** *Howard Peto and Vic Hollar began producing tomato seeds in Ventura, California, in 1950 as the Petoseed Company. Selling exclusively to commercial farmers and other seed companies, Petoseed began developing hybrid cantaloupes, cucumbers, eggplants, peppers, pumpkins, tomatoes, and watermelons. When Peto and Hollar split in 1953, Peto, who held a Ph.D. in agronomy, kept Petoseed. Five years later, Peto moved the company to Saticoy, California. In 1967, Petoseed was acquired by George J. Ball, Inc. Ball also owns the W. Atlee Burpee Company, the nation's largest marketer of seeds to home gardeners, and the Pan-American Seed Company, a flower seed concern. Ball is the dominant force in the U.S. vegetable and flower seed industry. Among companies that breed and produce hybrid vegetable seeds, Petoseed is considered the leader in this country and among the top five in the world. Petoseed has developed a cornucopia of disease-resistant hybrids, including tomato varieties resistant to five major diseases and cucumber hybrids resistant to four major viruses. In the early 1990s, Petoseed established Peto Europe to oversee a network of seed distribution and test stations in Europe, the Middle East, and Africa. Petoseed has also set up operations in Taiwan, Thailand, Japan, and Indonesia. Currently, Petoseed is marketing seeds or developing new plant varieties in more than one hundred countries.*

**BACKGROUND AND FACTS** *Hall Farms, Inc., in Knox County, Indiana, produces a variety of crops, including watermelons. In August 1988, Hall Farms ordered forty pounds of the Prince Charles variety of watermelon seeds from Martin Rispens & Son. At the top of Rispens' purchase order was the phrase "strictly high grade seeds." Rispens obtained the seeds from Petoseed and delivered them in February 1989, packaged in* *sealed one-pound cans. The label on the cans stated that they were "top quality seeds." Hall Farms stored the unopened cans until early April, when the seeds were germinated in two greenhouses. On April 25, Mark Hall, the owner of Hall Farms, noted that about fifteen seedlings were spotted with small yellow lesions. The lesions did not affect the plants' growth, however, and no plants died. The seedlings were transplanted to the fields in May. Hall monitored the plants every three or four days for the next several weeks. In early July, Hall spotted a watermelon blemished by a small purple blotch. By mid-July, the blotch had spread to other plants, and by harvest time ten days later, a significant portion of the watermelon crop had been ruined. Hall Farms sued Rispens and Petoseed, arguing, in part, that the phrases on Rispens's purchase order and Petoseed's cans constituted express warranties, which they breached. When Petoseed and Rispens were granted a summary judgment, Hall Farms appealed.*

*KRAHULIK, Justice.*

\*   \*   \*   \*

\*   \*   \* The label on the Petoseed cans \*   \*   \* is the sole basis for Hall Farms' express warranty claims against Petoseed.

\*   \*   \* The phrase ["top quality seeds"] contains no definitive statement as to how the product is warranted or any assertion of fact concerning the product, but is merely the opinion of Petoseed that the seeds are "top quality." The [lower court] correctly concluded that the statement "top quality seeds" is a "classic example of puffery."

\*   \*   \*   \*

Hall Farms also argues that the phrase, "strictly high grade seeds," which appeared at the top of the purchase order, created an express warranty. The [lower court] held that this language may have constituted an express warranty, but Hall Farms failed to meet its burden of proof by presenting evidence about the meaning of this phrase, so Rispens was entitled to summary judgment. Whether Rispens gave an express warranty which was breached encompasses a question of fact: in the seed industry, does "high grade" connote some promise that the seeds will be free from disease or is it mere puffing[?] However, it is Rispens' burden \*   \*   \* to show the absence of material fact. Having failed to do so, Rispens is not entitled to summary judgment on the express warranty claim.

**DECISION AND REMEDY**

*On the express warranty claims of Hall Farms, the court upheld part of the summary judgment, reversed part, and remanded the case for further proceedings in accordance with its opinion.*

**INTERNATIONAL CONSIDERATIONS**

**Warranties and Puffing in the United Kingdom** *The law of the United Kingdom (UK) tends to be somewhat stricter in regard to holding sellers to their words. Certain kinds of general promises that in the United States would probably be considered as seller's puffery may be construed as warranties by courts in the UK. In one case, for example, a seller described a bungalow as "nice, cosy and comfortable" when in fact it was a converted wooden chapel that turned out to be cold, damp, and overrun with rats and mice. The plaintiff was unable to view the house before the purchase. The court found that words such as "cosy" and "comfortable" constituted a warranty and were not merely "puff."*

# IMPLIED WARRANTIES

An **implied warranty** is one that *the law derives* by implication or inference from the nature of the transaction or the relative situations or circumstances of the parties. For example, Kaplan buys an axe at Enrique's Hardware Store. No express warranties are made. The first time she chops wood with it, the axe handle breaks, and Kaplan is injured. She immediately notifies Enrique. Examination shows that the wood in the handle was rotten but that the rottenness could not have been noticed by either Enrique or Kaplan. Nonetheless, Kaplan notifies Enrique that she will hold him responsible for the medical bills. Enrique is responsible, because a merchant seller of goods warrants that the goods he or she sells are fit for the ordinary purposes for which such goods are used. This axe was obviously not fit for those purposes.

Under the UCC, merchants impliedly warrant that the goods they sell are merchantable and, in certain circumstances, fit for a particular purpose. In addition, an implied warranty may arise from a course of dealing or usage of trade. We examine these three types of implied warranties in the following subsections.

## IMPLIED WARRANTY OF MERCHANTABILITY

An **implied warranty of merchantability** automatically arises in every sale of goods made *by a merchant* who deals in such goods [UCC 2–314(1)]. Thus, a retailer of ski equipment makes an implied warranty of merchantability every time the retailer sells a pair of skis, but a neighbor selling skis at a garage sale does not.

Goods that are *merchantable* are ''reasonably fit for the ordinary purposes for which such goods are used'' [UCC 2–314(2)]. They must at least

1. Be of average, fair, or medium-grade quality.
2. Pass without objection in the trade or market for goods of the same description.
3. Be adequately packaged and labeled as provided by the agreement.
4. Conform to the promises or affirmations of fact made on the container or label.
5. Be of an even quality and quantity in each unit and among all units.

Some examples of nonmerchantable goods include light bulbs that explode when switched on, pajamas that burst into flames on slight contact with the heating elements of an electric room heater, high heels that break off shoes under normal use, and shotgun shells that explode prematurely. It makes no difference whether the merchant knew of, or could have discovered, a defect that makes the product unsafe. (Of course, merchants are not absolute insurers against *all* accidents arising in connection with the goods. For example, a bar of soap is not unmerchantable merely because a user can slip and fall by stepping on it.) In an action based on breach of warranty, it is necessary to show that an implied warranty existed, that the warranty was broken, and that the breach of warranty was the proximate cause of the damage sustained.

The serving of food or drink to be consumed on or off the premises is recognized as a sale of goods subject to the warranty of merchantability [UCC 2–314(1)]. Merchantable food means food that is fit to eat. What is food that is fit to eat? It might be argued that a food containing cholesterol is nonmerchantable because cholesterol may cause heart disease. But if that food is exactly like all other food of the particular brand and virtually the same as other brands on the market, it is unlikely that a court would agree. In such cases, consumers can reasonably expect the product to contain cholesterol.

Similarly, the courts assume that consumers should reasonably expect to find, on occasion, bones in fish fillets, cherry pits in cherry pies, nutshells in packages of shelled nuts, and so on—because such substances are natural incidents of the food. Cases in which courts have found breaches of the implied warranty of merchantability have involved food containing substances that consumers would not reasonably expect to find there, such as an inchworm in a can of peas or a piece of glass in a soft drink.

The following classic case gives a court's interpretation of whether a fish bone in fish chowder is a foreign substance rendering the chowder unwholesome or not fit to be eaten.

**BACKGROUND AND FACTS** *Webster brought the following action against the Blue Ship Tea Room for personal injuries she sustained when consuming a bowl of its fish chowder. Her theory was breach of implied warranty of merchantability. A jury rendered a verdict for the plaintiff. The defendant appealed.*

CASE 24.3

**WEBSTER v. BLUE SHIP TEA ROOM, INC.**
Supreme Judicial Court of Massachusetts, 1964.
347 Mass. 421,
198 N.E.2d 309.

REARDON, Justice.

[The plaintiff] ordered a cup of fish chowder. Presently, there was set before her "a small bowl of fish chowder." * * * After 3 or 4 [spoonfuls] she was aware that something had lodged in her throat because she couldn't swallow and couldn't clear her throat by gulping and she could feel it." This misadventure led to two esophagoscopies at the Massachusetts General Hospital, in the second of which, on April 27, 1959, a fish bone was found and removed. The sequence of events produced injury to the plaintiff which was not insubstantial.

We must decide whether a fish bone lurking in a fish chowder, about the ingredients of which there is no other complaint, constitutes a breach of implied warranty under applicable provisions of the Uniform Commercial Code * * * . As the judge put it in his charge, "Was the fish chowder fit to be eaten and wholesome? * * * [N]obody is claiming that the fish itself wasn't wholesome. * * * But the bone of contention here—I don't mean that for a pun—but was this fish bone a foreign substance that made the fish chowder unwholesome or not fit to be eaten?"

* * * *

[We think that it] is not too much to say that a person sitting down in New England to consume a good New England fish chowder embarks on a gustatory [taste-related] adventure which may entail the removal of some fish bones from his bowl as he proceeds. We are not inclined to tamper with age old recipes by any amendment reflecting the plaintiff's view of the effect of the Uniform Commercial Code upon them. We are aware of the heavy body of case law involving foreign substances in food, but we sense a strong distinction between them and those relative to unwholesomeness of the food itself, e.g., tainted mackerel, and a fish bone in a fish chowder. Certain Massachusetts cooks might cavil at [object to] the ingredients contained in the chowder in this case in that it lacked the heartening lift of salt pork. In any event, we consider that the joys of life in New England include the ready availability of fresh fish chowder. We should be prepared to cope with the hazards of fish bones, the occasional presence of which in chowders is, it seems to us, to be anticipated, and which, in the light of a hallowed tradition, do not impair their fitness or merchantability.

**DECISION AND REMEDY** *The court "sympathized with a plaintiff who has suffered a peculiarly New England injury," but entered a judgment for the defendant, Blue Ship Tea Room.*

**COMMENTS** *The distinction between "natural" and "foreign" substances in food continues to plague the courts. The California Supreme Court established some guidelines to help clarify the foreign-natural distinction in a case concerning a bone in a chicken enchilada,* Mexicali Rose v. Superior Court.[a] *The court decided that if the injury-causing substance is "natural" to the food product, the food is considered merchantable, and a consumer does not have a cause of action for breach of the implied warranty of merchantability. The consumer can, however, pursue an action for negligence*

a. 1 Cal.4th 617, 4 Cal.Rptr.2d 145, 822 P.2d 1292 (1992).

*in food preparation. If the injury-causing substance is "foreign" to the food product, then a consumer can bring an action for breach of the implied warranty of merchantability. The court stated that "natural refers to bones and other substances natural to the product served, and does not encompass substances such as mold, botulinus bacteria or other substances (like rat flesh or cow eyes) not natural to the preparation of the product served." If a consumer is injured by a substance that is natural to the product, it is up to the jury to decide whether a consumer would reasonably expect to find the substance in the food and whether the substance rendered the food unfit or defective.*

## IMPLIED WARRANTY OF FITNESS FOR A PARTICULAR PURPOSE

The **implied warranty of fitness for a particular purpose** arises when *any seller* (merchant or non-merchant) knows the particular purpose for which a buyer will use the goods *and* knows that the buyer is relying on the seller's skill and judgment to select suitable goods [UCC 2–315].

A "particular purpose of the buyer" differs from the "ordinary purpose for which goods are used." Goods can be merchantable—suitable for the use to which such goods are ordinarily put—but still not fit for the buyer's particular purpose. For example, house paints suitable for painting ordinary interior walls are not suitable for painting exterior stucco walls.

A contract can include both an implied warranty of merchantability and an implied warranty of fitness for a particular purpose, which relates to a specific use or to a special situation in which a buyer intends to use the goods. For example, a seller recommends a particular pair of shoes, *knowing* that a customer is looking for mountain climbing shoes. The buyer purchases the shoes *relying* on the seller's judgment. If the shoes are found to be not only improperly made but suitable only for walking, not for mountain climbing, the seller has breached both the warranty of merchantability and the warranty of fitness for a particular purpose.

A seller does not need "actual knowledge" of the buyer's particular purpose. It is sufficient if a seller "has reason to know" the purpose. The buyer must have relied on the seller's skill or judgment in selecting or furnishing suitable goods for an implied warranty of fitness to be created, however.

For example, Kimbro buys a shortwave radio from Hi-Tech Electronics, telling the salesperson that she wants a set strong enough to pick up Radio Luxembourg, which is eight thousand miles away. Hi-Tech Electronics sells Kimbro a Model XYZ set. The set works, but it will not pick up Radio Luxembourg. Kimbro wants her money back. Here, because Hi-Tech Electronics is liable for a breach of implied warranty of fitness for the buyer's particular purpose, Kimbro will be able to recover. The salesperson knew specifically that she wanted a set that would pick up Radio Luxembourg. Furthermore, Kimbro relied on the salesperson to furnish a radio that would fulfill this purpose. Because the salesperson did not do so, the warranty was breached.

## IMPLIED WARRANTY ARISING FROM COURSE OF DEALING OR TRADE USAGE

The UCC recognizes in Section 2–314(3) that implied warranties can arise from a course of dealing, course of performance, or usage of trade. In the absence of evidence to the contrary, when both parties to a sales contract have knowledge of a well-recognized trade custom, the courts will infer that they both intended that custom to apply to their contract. For example, in the sale of a new car, when the industry-wide custom includes lubricating the car before delivery, a seller who fails to do so can be held liable to a buyer for resulting damages for breach of implied warranty. This failure, of course, also constitutes negligence on the part of the dealer.

## SECTION 4

# OVERLAPPING WARRANTIES

Sometimes two or more warranties are made in a single transaction. An implied warranty of merchantability or of fitness for a particular purpose, or both, can exist in addition to an express warranty. For example, when a sales contract for a new car states that "this car engine is warranted to be free from defects for 12,000 miles or twelve months, whichever comes first," there is an express warranty against all defects and an implied warranty that the car will be fit for normal use.

The rule of UCC 2–317 is that express and implied warranties are construed as cumulative if they are consistent with one another. If the warranties are inconsistent, the courts will usually hold as follows:

1. Express warranties displace inconsistent implied warranties except implied warranties of fitness for a particular purpose.
2. Samples take precedence over inconsistent general descriptions.
3. Technical specifications displace inconsistent samples or general descriptions.

Suppose that when Kimbro buys a shortwave radio at Hi-Tech Electronics, the contract expressly warrants that the radio will receive radio waves transmitted from as far as four thousand miles away. She tries to pick up Radio Luxembourg—the stated purpose of her purchase—which is eight thousand miles away. The set cannot perform that well. Kimbro claims that Hi-Tech Electronics is liable for breach of warranty of fitness. The express warranty takes precedence over any implied warranty of merchantability (that a shortwave set should pick up any station anywhere in the world). Kimbro does have a good claim for breach of implied warranty of fitness for a particular purpose, however, because she made it clear that she was buying the set to pick up Radio Luxembourg. In cases of inconsistency between an express warranty and a warranty of fitness for a buyer's particular purpose, the warranty of fitness for the buyer's particular purpose normally prevails [UCC 2–317(c)].

## SECTION 5

# WARRANTIES AND THIRD PARTIES

One of the general principles of contract law is that a person who is not one of the parties to a contract has no rights under the contract. As discussed in Chapter 17, the connection that exists between the contracting parties is called *privity of contract.* It was established at common law that privity must exist between a plaintiff and a defendant for any action based on a contract to be maintained. (Notable exceptions to the rule of privity include assignments and third party beneficiary contracts—see Chapter 17.)

For example, I purchase a ham from retailer Bollinger. I invite you to my house that evening. I prepare the ham properly. You are served first, because you are my guest, and you become severely ill because the ham is spoiled. Can you sue retailer Bollinger for breach of the implied warranty of merchantability? Because warranty is based on a contract for the sale of goods, under the common law you would normally have warranty rights only if you were a party to the purchase of the ham. Therefore, the warranty would extend only to me, the purchaser.

In the past, this hardship was sometimes resolved by court decisions removing privity as a requirement to hold manufacturers and sellers liable for certain defective products (notably food, drugs, and cosmetics) that were sold. The UCC, reflecting some of these decisions, has addressed the problem of privity, at least to the extent of including three optional, alternative provisions eliminating privity in various circumstances. All three alternatives are intended to eliminate the privity requirement with respect to certain enumerated types of injuries (personal versus property) for certain beneficiaries (for example, household members versus bystanders). Each state may adopt one of these three alternatives [UCC 2–318].

The following case involves a third party who suffered injuries as a result of a faulty lock on the door of a walk-in freezer, which was located in a church. The issue is whether the seller's express and implied warranties extended to the third party.

CASE 24.4

**CREWS v. W. A. BROWN & SON, INC.**
Court of Appeals of North Carolina, 1992.
106 N.C.App. 324,
416 S.E.2d 924.

**BACKGROUND AND FACTS** *Thirteen-year-old Vickie Crews was working as a volunteer at Calvary Baptist Church in Winston-Salem, North Carolina, on the evening of July 2, 1985. At about 8:45 P.M., Crews went to the church's kitchen and thought she heard a noise in the walk-in freezer. Crews, barefoot and wearing shorts, stepped inside the freezer, and the door closed behind her. She pushed the red emergency release button on the inside of the door, but the door did not open. At approximately 10:00 P.M., someone discovered Crews, and she was taken to a hospital and treated for severe frostbite. During the next two months, she endured five separate operations and the amputation of most of her toes. Crews and her mother (the plaintiffs) sued W. A. Brown & Son, Inc. (the manufacturer of the freezer), Foodcraft Equipment Company (the firm that had assembled and installed the freezer and sold it to the church), and the church. The plaintiffs alleged, among other things, breach of express and implied warranties. The court granted Foodcraft's motion for summary judgment, holding that the plaintiffs' claims were barred by a lack of privity with Foodcraft. The plaintiffs appealed.*

*GREENE,* Judge.
  \*    \*    \*    \*

Where \*    \*    \* [a] products liability action is brought against the seller for breach of either express or implied warranty, the privity barrier has been removed legislatively to the same extent as it has been removed in actions against manufacturers for breach of express warranty. Accordingly, assuming the existence of express and implied warranties, N.C.G.S. [North Carolina General Statutes Section] 25–2–318 [North Carolina's version of UCC 2–318] extends those warranties beyond the buyer but only to natural persons suffering personal injury who are in the buyer's family or household or who are guests in the buyer's home and only if it is reasonable to expect such persons may use, consume, or be affected by the goods. The statute does not extend warranty coverage to persons beyond those specifically enumerated.
\*    \*    \*
  \*    \*    \*    \*

Assuming the existence of express and implied warranties, however, those warranties do not extend to the plaintiffs. Because a church does not have a "family" or a "household" in the ordinary meanings of those terms, Crews cannot be classified as a member of Church's "family" or "household" under N.C.G.S. [Section] 25–2–318. Because a church is not a "home" within the ordinary meaning of that term, Church cannot be classified as a "home." Accordingly, because Crews was not in the buyer's "family" or "household," and because she was not a guest in the buyer's "home," N.C.G.S. [Section] 25–2–318 does not extend the coverage of Foodcraft's warranties to the plaintiffs.

**DECISION AND REMEDY**    *The appellate court affirmed the trial court's grant of summary judgment to Foodcraft.*

**ETHICAL CONSIDERATIONS**    *One could argue that the court applied the letter of the North Carolina statute too rigorously to the circumstances of this case. The case pointedly illustrates what is traded off in protecting sellers against unlimited warranty liability—namely, the rights of certain third parties, such as Vickie Crews, to recover for injuries caused by faulty products.*

# WARRANTY DISCLAIMERS

Courts view warranty disclaimers with disfavor, especially when consumers are involved. As discussed below, even when sellers have adhered exactly to the methods of disclaimer specified by the UCC, courts have sometimes held that the disclaimers are unconscionable. Also, there are other federal and state statutes (for example, the Magnuson-Moss Warranty Act, which is considered later in the chapter) that may make disclaimers of a particular warranty unenforceable. A buyer prevented from claiming breach of warranty may be able to sue successfully on a theory of negligence or strict liability (each of which is discussed in more detail in Chapter 25).

Obviously, then, the seller's best protection from being held accountable for affirmations of fact or promises is not to make them in the first place. Of course, a contract normally involves a sale of something describable and described. A clause purporting to disclaim all warranties cannot negate the seller's obligation with respect to this description [UCC 2–313, Comment 4]. Thus, the manner in which a seller can disclaim or qualify any warranty varies with the way the warranty is created. For example, a seller's description of his or her merchandise as an "automobile" creates an express warranty that what will be delivered to a buyer is an automobile. Stating that goods are being sold "as is" cannot disclaim this warranty; thus, a seller cannot deliver a car without wheels or without a motor and avoid liability.

## EXPRESS WARRANTIES

Any affirmation of fact or promise, description of the goods, or use of samples or models by a seller creates an express warranty. Obviously, then, a seller can avoid making express warranties by carefully refraining from making any promise or affirmation of fact relating to the goods, or describing the goods, or selling by means of a sample or model [UCC 2–313].

The parol evidence rule protects the seller from a buyer's false claims that an oral warranty was created. Under this rule, if the parties intended the written contract to be the complete expression of their agreement, the buyer cannot offer evidence of an oral warranty. Nevertheless, a court may conclude that the contract was not a complete expression of the parties' intentions and permit proof of oral terms.

The UCC does permit express warranties to be negated or limited by specific and unambiguous language, provided this is done in a manner that protects the buyer from surprise. Therefore, a written disclaimer in language that is clear and conspicuous, and called to a buyer's attention, could negate all oral express warranties not included in the written sales contract [UCC 2–316(1)].

## IMPLIED WARRANTIES

Generally speaking, and unless circumstances indicate otherwise, implied warranties (of merchantability and fitness for a particular purpose) are disclaimed by the expression "as is," "with all faults," or some other similar phrase that in common understanding for *both* parties calls the buyer's attention to the fact that there are no implied warranties [UCC 2–316(3)(a)].

The UCC also permits a seller to disclaim specifically the implied warranty either of fitness for a particular purpose or of merchantability [UCC 2–316(2)]. To disclaim the implied warranty of fitness for a particular purpose, the disclaimer *must* be in writing and be conspicuous. The word *fitness* does not have to be mentioned in the writing; it is sufficient, for example, for the disclaimer to state: "There are no warranties that extend beyond the description on the face hereof."

A merchantability disclaimer must be more specific; it must mention *merchantability*. It need not be written; but if it is, the writing must be conspicuous. According to UCC 1–201(10),

A term or clause is conspicuous when it is so written that a reasonable person against whom it is to operate ought to have noticed it. A printed heading in capitals . . . is conspicuous. Language in the body of a form is "conspicuous" if it is in larger or other contrasting type or color.

To illustrate: Merchant Urbain sells Breen a particular lawn mower selected by Urbain with the characteristics clearly requested by Breen. At the time of the sale, Urbain says to Breen, "I cannot warrant the merchantability of this mower because it is an outdated model and is no longer manufactured." Later, Breen discovers that the mower is defective and does not cut grass. Did Urbain breach either the implied warranty of merchantability or the implied warranty of fitness for a particular purpose?

Urbain breached the warranty of fitness for a particular purpose, but he did not breach the warranty of merchantability. Urbain's oral disclaimer, in which he used the word *merchantability,* was a proper disclaimer under the UCC. For Urbain to disclaim the implied warranty of fitness for a particular purpose, however, a conspicuous writing was required. Because no written disclaimer was made, Urbain can be held liable for the breach of warranty of fitness for a particular purpose.

## BUYER'S EXAMINATION OF THE GOODS

If the buyer refuses to examine the goods or if the buyer actually examines the goods (or a sample or model) as fully as desired before entering a contract, *there is no implied warranty with respect to defects that a reasonable examination will reveal* [UCC 2–316(3)(b)].

Failure to examine the goods is not refusal to examine them; it is not enough that the goods were available for inspection and the buyer failed to examine them. A refusal can occur only when the seller *demands* that the buyer examine the goods. Of course, the seller always remains liable for latent (hidden) defects that ordinary inspection would not reveal. What the examination ought to reveal depends on a particular buyer's skill and method of examination. Therefore, an auto mechanic purchasing a car should be responsible for the discovery of some defects that a nonexpert would not be expected to find. The circumstances of each case determine what defects a so-called reasonable inspection should reveal.

## UNCONSCIONABILITY

The UCC sections dealing with warranty disclaimers do not refer specifically to unconscionability. Eventually, however, the courts will test warranty disclaimers with reference to the unconscionability standards of Section 2–302. Such things as lack of bargaining position, "take it or leave it" choices, and failure of a buyer to understand or know of a warranty disclaimer provision will become relevant to the issue of unconscionability.

# STATUTE OF LIMITATIONS

An action brought by a buyer or seller for breach of contract must be commenced under the UCC *within four years after the cause of action accrues.* In addition to filing suit within the four-year period, an aggrieved party who has accepted nonconforming goods must ordinarily notify the breaching party of a defect within a reasonable time [UCC 2–607(3)(a)]. By agreement in the contract, the parties can reduce this period to not less than one year, but they cannot extend the period beyond the stated four years [UCC 2–725(1)].

A cause of action accrues for breach of warranty when the seller makes *tender* of delivery. This is the rule even if the aggrieved party is unaware that the cause of action has accrued [UCC 2–725(2)]. Remember, tender of delivery takes place under a shipment contract on delivery of the goods to the carrier and under a destination contract on tender of the goods at the specified destination delivery location. The statute of limitations in these cases may have a tremendous impact if the goods purchased are going to be stored primarily for future use. To avoid this impact, the UCC provides that when a warranty explicitly extends to future performance and discovery of its breach must await the time of that performance, the statute of limitations also begins to run at that time [UCC 2–725(2)].

For example, Hoover purchases a central air-conditioning unit for his restaurant. The unit is warranted to keep the temperature below a certain level during the summer months. The unit is installed in the winter, but when summer comes, the restaurant does not stay cool. Therefore, discovery of the warranty's breach is made in the summer and not when the unit was delivered in the winter. The statute of limitations does not begin to run until the summer.

When a buyer or seller brings suit on a legal theory unrelated to the UCC, the limitations periods specified above do not apply, even though the claim relates to goods. For example, Cane buys tires for his automobile. The tires prove to have an inherently dangerous defect. Four years and one month after purchasing the tires, Cane loses control of the car and injures several passengers, as well as himself. Cane can bring a suit against the tire manufacturer based on strict liability in tort (see Chapter 25). The suit will not be governed by the UCC's statute of limitations but rather by the state's tort statute of limitations.

The following case illustrates how the expectation of the parties extends the time of warranty performance to a future date for statute of limitation purposes.

**CASE 24.5**

**MOORE v. PUGET SOUND PLYWOOD, INC.**

Supreme Court of Nebraska, 1983.
214 Neb. 14,
332 N.W.2d 212.

**BACKGROUND AND FACTS**  *Puget Sound Plywood, Inc., manufactured certain lauan siding that Dennis and Lois Moore purchased during the construction of their house from 1970 to 1971. By October 1977, the Moores had noticed some "problems" with the appearance of the siding. The problem, delamination, resulted because the particular species of lauan tree used in making the siding was not susceptible to being glued with the resin that Puget Sound used. The Moores began investigating a remedy for the situation in 1979, but they had difficulty determining who had manufactured the siding. An action was filed in April 1981. The Moores alleged damages of $4,550, but two lower courts dismissed their case, holding that the statute of limitations had run. The Moores appealed.*

*CAPORALE*, Justice.
\*  \*  \*  \*

This analysis is required by reason of the operation of Neb. U.C.C. [Section] 2–313(1)(b) as delineated in *England v. Leithoff*, decided after the municipal court trials herein. That opinion foreshadows the outcome of this case. We held therein that an oral representation concerning the origin of goods, made in the course of a sale, constitutes an express warranty under [Section] 2–313(1)(b), which provides, among other things, that any description of goods which becomes a part of the basis of the bargain creates an express warranty that the goods shall conform to the description. According to the parties, the description of the goods as "siding" carried with it the representation that it would last the lifetime of the house. Therefore, the requisite elements of [Section] 2–313(1)(b) are present; that is, the description of the goods became a part of the bargain and created in the minds of the parties the expectation that the siding would last the lifetime of the house. Section 2–725(2) provides in part: "A breach of warranty occurs when tender of delivery is made, except that where a warranty explicitly extends to future performance of the goods and discovery of the breach must await the time of such performance the cause of action accrues when the breach is or should have been discovered." The instant breach did not occur upon tender of delivery since, in light of the expectations of the parties, the warranty herein necessarily extended explicitly to future performance.

The case \*  \*  \* relied upon by Puget Sound is not factually apposite [appropriate] here. Therein, discovery could, and in fact did, occur shortly after completion of the construction project; that is, the plaintiff knew about the defect prior to the tolling of the period of limitations but failed to act until after it had tolled [expired]. In this case, discovery could occur at any time between installation and the "life" of the house. The Moores acted within a reasonable period of time after they discovered the latent defect.

*The Supreme Court of Nebraska agreed with the Moores that the two lower courts were in error. The court remanded the case with instructions that a judgment be entered in favor of the Moores in the sum of $4,550.*

**DECISION AND REMEDY**

## ■ CONCEPT SUMMARY 24.1 Warranties under the UCC

| TYPE OF WARRANTY | HOW CREATED | POSSIBLE DEFENSES |
|---|---|---|
| **Warranty of Title** [UCC 2–312] | Upon transfer of title, the seller warrants<br>1. That he or she has the right to pass good and rightful title.<br>2. That the goods are free from unstated liens or encumbrances.<br>3. When the seller is a merchant, that the goods are free from infringement claims. | Specific language or circumstances excluded or modified the warranty [UCC 2–312(2)]. |
| **Express Warranty** [UCC 2–313] | As part of a sale or bargain, a seller may create an express warranty by<br>1. An affirmation of fact or promise.<br>2. A sale by description.<br>3. A sample shown as conforming to bulk. | 1. Statement that is purported to create the warranty was an opinion.<br>2. Specific language or conduct negated or limited the warranty [UCC 2–316(1)]. |
| **Implied Warranty of Merchantability** [UCC 2–314] | This warranty arises when the seller is a merchant who deals in goods of the kind sold. | 1. Warranty was specifically disclaimed (disclaimer can be oral or in writing, but must mention *merchantability* and, if in writing, must be conspicuous) [UCC 2–316(2)].<br>2. Sale was stated to be "as is" or "with all faults" [UCC 2–316(3)(a)].<br>3. The buyer examined the goods and is therefore bound by all defects that were found or should have been found. If the buyer refused or failed to examine, the buyer is bound by obvious defects [UCC 2–316(3)(b)].<br>4. Course of dealing, performance, or usage of trade [UCC 2–316(3)(c)]. |
| **Implied Warranty of Fitness for a Particular Purpose** [UCC 2–315] | This warranty arises when<br>1. The buyer's purpose or use is known or should be known by the seller, and<br>2. The buyer purchases in reliance on the seller's selection. | 1. Specific disclaimer excluded or modified warranty (disclaimer must be in writing and be conspicuous: "There are no warranties which extend beyond the description on the face hereof.") [UCC 2–316(2)].<br>2. Same as items 2–4 under merchantability, above. |
| **Implied Warranty Arising from Course of Dealing or Trade Usage** [UCC 2–314(3)] | This warranty is created by prior dealings and/or custom of trade. | Warranty was excluded by specific language or as provided under UCC 2–316. |

# MAGNUSON-MOSS WARRANTY ACT

The Magnuson-Moss Warranty Act[3] (enacted in 1975) was designed to prevent deception in warranties by making them easier to understand. The act is mainly enforced by the Federal Trade Commission (FTC). Additionally, the attorney general or a consumer who has been injured can enforce the act if informal procedures for settling disputes prove to be ineffective. The Magnuson-Moss Warranty Act modifies UCC warranty rules to some extent when *consumer* sales transactions are involved. The UCC, however, remains the primary codification of warranty rules for industrial and commercial transactions.

No seller is *required* to give a written warranty for consumer goods sold under the Warranty Act. But if a seller chooses to make an express written warranty and the cost of the consumer goods is more than $10, the warranty must be labeled as either full or limited. In addition, if the cost of the goods is more than $15 (by FTC regulation), the warrantor is required to make certain disclosures fully and conspicuously in a single document in "readily understood language." This disclosure states the names and addresses of the warrantors, what specifically is warranted, procedures for enforcement of the warranty, any limitations on warranty relief, and that the buyer has legal rights.

Although a *full warranty* may not cover every aspect of the consumer product sold, what it covers ensures some type of buyer satisfaction in case the product is defective. Full warranty requires free repair or replacement of any defective part; if it cannot be repaired within a reasonable time, the consumer has the choice of either a refund or a replacement without charge. The full warranty frequently does not have a time limit. Any limitation on consequential damages must be *conspicuously* stated. Also, the warrantor need not perform warranty services if the problem with the product was caused by unreasonable use or damage by the consumer.

A *limited warranty* arises when the written warranty fails to meet one of the minimum requirements for a full warranty. The fact that a seller is giving only a limited warranty must be conspicuously designated. If only a time limitation would distinguish a limited warranty from a full warranty, then the Warranty Act allows the seller to designate the warranty as full by such language as "full twelve-month warranty."

Although, under the UCC, express warranties can be created by description, sample, or model, only written promises or affirmations of fact are covered by the Magnuson-Moss Warranty Act. Thus, for purposes of the Warranty Act,

1. An express warranty is *any written promise* or *affirmation of fact* made by the seller to a consumer indicating the quality or performance of the product and affirming or promising that the product is either free of defects or will meet a specific level of performance over a period of time—for example, "this watch will not lose more than one second a year."
2. An express warranty is a written agreement to refund, repair, or replace the product if it fails to meet written specifications. This is typically a service contract.

The Magnuson-Moss Warranty Act does not deal with implied warranties. They continue to be created according to the UCC provisions. When an express warranty is made in a sales contract or a combined sales and service contract (when the service contract is undertaken within ninety days of the sale), the Magnuson-Moss Warranty Act prevents sellers from disclaiming or modifying the implied warranties of merchantability and fitness for a particular purpose. Sellers can impose a time limit on the duration of an implied warranty, but the time limit has to correspond to the duration of the express warranty.[4]

# WARRANTIES UNDER THE CISG

The United Nations Convention on Contracts for the International Sale of Goods (CISG) does not

---

3. 15 U.S.C. Sections 2301–2312.

4. The time limit on an implied warranty occurring by virtue of the seller's express warranty must, of course, be reasonable, conscionable, and set forth in clear and conspicuous language on the face of the warranty.

use the term *warranty* in regard to the rights and obligations of parties to international sales contracts. Instead, the CISG prefers to phrase the concept of warranty in terms of "conformity of the goods." Although the CISG uses different language, in effect, it provides for warranty protection similar to that available under the UCC. Article 35 of the CISG states that the seller "must deliver goods which are of the quantity, quality and description required by the contract and which are contained or packaged in the manner required by the contract." Other provisions of Article 35 are, in effect, equivalent to the UCC express and implied warranties.

## TERMS AND CONCEPTS TO REVIEW

| | | |
|---|---|---|
| express warranty  446 | implied warranty of fitness | implied warranty of |
| implied warranty  450 | for a particular | merchantability  450 |
| | purpose  452 | |

## QUESTIONS AND CASE PROBLEMS

**24–1. Express Warranties.** Shillitani contracted to purchase a used car from Johnson's Quality Used Cars. During the oral negotiations for the sale, Johnson told Shillitani that this used car was in "A-1 condition" and would get sixteen miles to the gallon. Shillitani asked if the car used a lot of oil. Johnson replied that he had personally checked the car, and in his opinion the car did not use a lot of oil. Since delivery, Shillitani has used the car for one month (four hundred miles of driving) and is unhappy with it. The car needs numerous repairs, does not get sixteen miles to the gallon, and has used two quarts of oil. Shillitani claims Johnson is in breach of express warranties as to the condition of the car, gas mileage, and oil use. Johnson claims no express warranties were made. Discuss who is correct.

**24–2. Implied Warranties.** Moon is a farmer who needs to place a two-thousand-pound piece of equipment in his barn. This will require lifting the equipment thirty feet up into a hayloft. Moon goes to Davidson Hardware and tells Davidson that he needs some heavy-duty rope to be used on his farm. Davidson recommends a one-inch-thick nylon rope, and Moon purchases two hundred feet of the rope. Moon ties the rope around the piece of equipment; puts it through a pulley; and, with a tractor, lifts the equipment off the ground. Suddenly the rope breaks. In the crash to the ground the equipment is severely damaged. Moon files suit against Davidson for breach of implied warranty of fitness for a particular purpose. Discuss how successful Moon will be in his suit.

**24–3. Warranty Disclaimers.** Darrow purchases a new car from Slippery Motors. The retail installment contract states immediately above the buyer's signature in large, bold type: "There are no warranties that extend beyond the description on the face hereof" and "There are no express warranties that accompany this sale unless expressly written in this contract." Before purchasing the car, Darrow specifically informed Slippery's salesperson that he wanted a car that could be driven in a dusty area without needing mechanical repairs. Slippery's salesperson said to Darrow, "Nothing will go wrong with this car, but if it does, return it to us, and we will repair it without cost to you." Neither this statement nor any similar statement appears in the retail sales contract. Darrow drives the car into a dust storm. The air filter gets plugged up and the car engine overheats, causing motor damage. Slippery Motors refuses to repair the engine under any warranty. Darrow claims that Slippery is liable for breach of the implied warranty of fitness for a particular purpose, that the Magnuson-Moss Warranty Act prohibits disclaiming this implied warranty, and that the salesperson's express warranty has also been breached. Discuss Darrow's claims.

**24–4. Implied Warranties.** Olivo has a used television set that she wishes to sell. Howard contracts to purchase the set. At the time of the making of the contract, Olivo demands that Howard inspect the set to be sure it is exactly what he wants. Howard tells Olivo that he does not have the time to do so. The set is delivered and paid for. Howard, on using the set, discovers that the picture has a tendency to "jump" and that the vertical control does not always correct that tendency. The cost to repair the set is $50. Howard claims that the set is neither merchantable nor fit for its purpose. Olivo claims she has no liability. Discuss who is correct.

**24–5. Warranty of Title.** Dlugash buys a one-karat diamond ring from Shady Sallor for $500. Dlugash is assured by Shady that the ring belonged to his deceased mother and that the only reason the price is so low is that he is behind in making payments on his car. Dlugash has no reason to believe differently. Bekins, a neighbor, admires the ring and offers to purchase it for $1,000. Dlugash agrees to sell the ring to Bekins, stating that he is transferring only such rights as he has in the ring. Two months later, the police confiscate the ring as property stolen in a burglary of Owen's home. Bekins seeks to hold Dlugash liable. Discuss Bekins's action under warranty laws.

**24–6. Express Warranties.** Vertis Smith was considering buying a used car from Fitzner Pontiac-Buick-Cadillac, Inc. He particularly liked a 1982 Olds Cutlass on the lot and took it for a test drive. Smith then told Fitzner's sales representative that if Fitzner would fix a rattle he had heard and paint the car, he would purchase it for $7,475. The salesperson agreed to have these things done and assured Smith that when the car was delivered, it would be in "first class shape." Fitzner performed as agreed, and the car was delivered shortly thereafter to Smith. During the next few months, Smith had to install a new intake gasket, a new transmission, and a new radiator—repairs that were made by others, not Fitzner. Fitzner repaired a broken taillight and adjusted a window mechanism. In addition, Smith claimed that the car stalled frequently in traffic and got only eleven miles per gallon of gas. Nine months after he had purchased the car, Smith returned it to Fitzner and requested a refund of the purchase price plus the cost of the repairs, alleging, among other things, that Fitzner had breached an express warranty. Discuss fully whether Fitzner's statement that the car would be delivered in "first class shape" constituted an express warranty. [*Fitzner Pontiac-Buick-Cadillac, Inc. v. Smith*, 523 So.2d 324 (Miss. 1988)]

**24–7. Express Warranties.** Myrtle Carpenter purchased hair dye from a drugstore. The use of the dye caused an adverse skin reaction. She sued the local drugstore and the manufacturer of the dye, Alberto Culver Co. Carpenter claimed that a salesclerk had indicated that several of Carpenter's friends used the product and that their hair came out "very nice." The clerk purportedly also told Carpenter that she would get very fine results. On the package, there were cautionary instructions telling the user to make a preliminary skin test to determine if the user was sensitive in any unusual way to the product. Carpenter stated that she had not made the preliminary skin test. Did the seller make an express warranty about the hair dye? Explain. [*Carpenter v. Alberto Culver Co.*, 28 Mich.App. 399, 184 N.W.2d 547 (1970)]

**24–8. Express Warranties.** In 1984, the Lindemann farm's cotton crop fared poorly because of lack of weed control. That year, and every year since the early 1960s, the Lindemanns (the plaintiffs) had used Treflan, an herbicide manufactured by the defendants, Eli Lilly and Co. The label specifically stated that Treflan would control weeds when used according to label instructions. The Treflan label recommended that the herbicide be incorporated into the soil twice after it had been sprayed. The

purpose of the double incorporation was to provide greater uniformity in the herbicide's distribution. The Lindemanns, in an effort to create still greater uniformity in the distribution of the Treflan, made an application by spraying half the amount of a normal application in one direction and half in the opposite direction. Each spraying was incorporated into the soil after it had been applied. If the directions did not contain a specific directive calling for a single application, could the Lindemanns recover for breach of express warranty of the herbicide to control weeds? Discuss. [*Lindemann v. Eli Lilly and Co.*, 816 F.2d 199 (5th Cir. 1987)]

**24–9. Express Warranties.** On December 22, 1980, Jack M. Crothers purchased a used 1970 Dodge from Maurice Boyd, a sales agent employed by Norman Cohen, the owner of Norm's Auto Sales. On December 23, 1980, Crothers was seriously injured when the Dodge he had just purchased went out of control and crashed into a tree. Crothers filed suit, asserting breach of an express warranty based on Boyd's representation to Crothers that the 1970 Dodge had a rebuilt carburetor and was a "good runner." Did Boyd's representations amount to an express warranty? [*Crothers by Crothers v. Cohen*, 384 N.W.2d 562 (Minn.App. 1986)]

**24–10. Express Warranties.** On March 13, 1980, Judith Roth went to the hairdresser she had been using for the last seven years to have her hair bleached. The hair stylist used a new bleaching product, manufactured by Roux Laboratories, on Roth's hair. Although other Roux products had been used previously with excellent results, the use of the new product resulted in damage to Roth's hair that caused her embarrassment and anguish for the next several months as her hair grew back. The product's label had guaranteed it would not cause damage to a user's hair. Roth sued Ray-Stel's Hair Stylists, Inc., and Roux Laboratories, Inc., alleging, among other claims, breach of express warranty resulting in personal injuries to her. Discuss whether there was a breach of express warranty. [*Roth v. Ray-Stel's Hair Stylists, Inc.*, 18 Mass.App. 975, 470 N.E.2d 137 (1984)]

**24–11. Implied Warranties.** While passing by the American Kennels pet store, owned by defendant George Rosenthal, Ruby Dempsey, the plaintiff, decided to purchase a pedigreed white poodle. Dempsey told the salesperson that she wanted a dog suitable for breeding purposes. She purchased the poodle, whom she named Mr. Dunphy. Five days later, the dog was examined by a veterinarian and was discovered to have a congenital defect. Dempsey returned to the store and demanded a refund of the purchase price. The store refused, and Dempsey filed suit. Dempsey claimed that the defendant was liable for breach of the implied warranties of merchantability and fitness for a particular purpose. The defendant claimed that the poodle was still capable of breeding and thus no warranties had been breached. Discuss fully whether Dempsey was successful. [*Dempsey v. Rosenthal*, 121 Misc.2d 612, 468 N.Y.S.2d 441 (1983)]

**24–12. Implied Warranties.** Robert Levondosky was a patron at Harrah's Marina Hotel Casino, an Atlantic City casino owned by Marina Associates. While playing at one of the casino's tables, he ordered a cocktail, which was served free of charge—it was the casino's custom to give complimentary drinks to patrons at the gambling tables. Levondosky alleged that he swallowed a few thin chips of glass from the rim of the glass in which the drink was served and, as a result, suffered internal injuries. Levondosky sued the casino, contending that the casino had breached an implied warranty of merchantability. In evaluating this claim, the court had to determine (1) whether a "sale" had in fact occurred, which is prerequisite to the creation of an implied warranty of merchantability, and (2) whether the casino gave an implied warranty as to the glass as well as to the drink within it. Review UCC 2–314, and discuss how the court should rule on both issues. [*Levondosky v. Marina Associates,* 731 F.Supp. 1210 (D.N.J. 1990)]

**24–13. Implied Warranties.** In March 1986, Donald Laird discussed the purchase of corn with the manager of Scribner Cooperative, Inc., Gary Ruwe, whom Laird had trained for his job as manager. Ruwe told Laird that the co-op was having some heating problems in its corn storage bins, but Laird said that he would take four loads (about 1,300 bushels) of corn if Ruwe would "pull out the center and pull out all the damaged corn and get the fines [the fine bits of corn kernel knocked off during handling of the grain] out of the center." On inspecting the corn after it was delivered, Laird noticed damaged corn and a silage odor (which is the result of a fermentation process caused by heating). Although Laird was dissatisfied with the corn, he did not reject it. After Laird began feeding his hogs the corn, the hogs became ill. Eventually, it was concluded that the problem might be in the corn. In October 1986, Laird asked the University of Nebraska to test the corn, and traces of a toxic substance called vomitoxin were found in the corn. The veterinarian tending Laird's hogs testified that their symptoms were the direct result of feed containing vomitoxin. Laird sued the co-op for breach of the implied warranties of merchantability and fitness for a particular purpose. How should the court rule? Discuss. [*Laird v. Scribner Cooperative, Inc.,* 237 Neb. 532, 466 N.W. 2d 798 (1991)]

**24–14. Warranty Disclaimers.** Khalid Ismael purchased a used 1985 Ford Tempo automobile from Goodman Toyota for $5,054 "as is," along with a Vehicle Service Agreement for $695. The service agreement was to cover repairs occurring during the first 24 months or first 24,000 miles, whichever came first. When Ismael test-drove the car prior to the purchase, it shook. Goodman's salesperson assured Ismael that the Tempo "probably just needed a tune-up and that Goodman would repair anything that was found wrong with the car at no charge." Ismael purchased the Tempo based on Goodman's assurances and the service agreement. During the first four months, Ismael was able to use the car for less than two weeks, and during the first six months the Tempo was in for repair six times. Having given up on Goodman's ability to repair the car, Ismael took it to a Ford dealer, who said the car was beyond repair due to "sludge in the engine." Ismael sued Goodman, asserting that Goodman had breached the implied warranty of merchantability. Goodman claimed that it should not be held liable, because the sale of the car "as is" effectively disclaimed the implied warranty of merchantability. Who will win in court, and why? Discuss fully. [*Ismael v. Goodman Toyota,* 106 N.C.App. 421, 417 S.E.2d 290 (1992)]

**24–15. A Question of Ethics**

*Arvo Lake, a retired seventy-one-year-old man, bought an air conditioner in May 1986. The unit was installed and operated according to the manufacturer's instructions. Un-* beknownst to Lake, the unit contained a hole in the refrigeration system that allowed Freon, the coolant, to escape from the unit. By August, the unit had ceased cooling, and Lake's residence reached a temperature of at least ninety-six degrees Fahrenheit. The heat caused Lake to suffer from hyperthermia, which caused circulatory failure and death. The executor of Lake's estate, David Garavalia, sued the manufacturer of the air conditioner for damages. The circuit court dismissed the suit, and Garavalia appealed. The appellate court found for the plaintiff, alleging that the risk of death from an air conditioner that failed to operate properly was foreseeable, given Lake's age and the climate in southern Illinois in the summer. [Garavalia v. Heat Controller, Inc., 212 Ill.App.3d 380, 570 N.E.2d 1227, 156 Ill.Dec. 505 (1991)]

1. For a manufacturer to be liable for consequential damages caused by a breach of warranty, the consequential damages must be foreseeable to the manufacturer. Do you agree with the court that Lake's death was a foreseeable consequence of the air conditioner's failure to operate properly?

2. In determining whether Lake's death was a foreseeable result of the malfunctioning air conditioner, the court considered such circumstances as the heat of the Illinois summer, Lake's age, and the high crime rate in Lake's neighborhood. Should these factors have any bearing on whether the manufacturer should be held liable for Lake's death? Why or why not?

3. One of the judges in this case dissented, stating that "[f]oreseeability means that which is objectively reasonable to expect, not merely what might conceivably occur." He went on to state that an air conditioner is "a rather benign machine" and that the manufacturer of such an appliance could not *reasonably* foresee that an air conditioner's failure to cool would result in death. Do you agree with this analysis? Discuss.

# CHAPTER 25

# PRODUCT LIABILITY

O ften retailers serve simply as go-betweens, selling manufacturers' goods to consumers in prepackaged, sealed containers. Even so, retailers may be liable to purchasers on express or implied warranties despite the fact that they cannot always examine the goods prior to resale. In the past, courts frequently addressed the question of whether the injured party should recover from the manufacturer, the processor, or the retailer for damages caused by the manufacture and marketing of a defective product. Today, liability has been extended to manufacturers and processors through the application of new and old principles of the law.

Manufacturers and sellers of goods can be held liable to consumers, users, and bystanders (people in the vicinity of the product) for physical harm or property damage that is caused by the goods. This is called **product liability,** and it encompasses the contract theory of *warranty* and tort theories of *negligence, misrepresentation,* and *strict liability.*

## WARRANTY LAW

Today, warranty law is an important part of the entire spectrum of laws relating to product liability. Consumers, purchasers, and even users of goods can recover *from any seller* for losses resulting from breach of implied and express warranties. A manufacturer is a *seller.* Therefore, a person who purchases goods from a retailer can recover from the retailer or the manufacturer if the goods are not merchantable, because in most states *privity of contract* (the connection that exists between contracting parties) is no longer a prerequisite for breach-of-warranty recovery for personal injuries. That is, a product purchaser may sue not only the firm from which he or she purchased a product but also a third party—the manufacturer of the product—in product liability.

Because warranty laws were discussed in Chapter 24, the balance of this chapter will deal with the tort theories of recovery for damages and injuries caused by defective products.

# SECTION 2

# NEGLIGENCE

*Negligence* is generally defined as the failure to use that degree of care that a reasonable, prudent person would have used under the circumstances. Recall from Chapter 6 that an action in negligence requires the plaintiff to prove that (1) a duty of care existed, (2) this duty was breached, (3) the plaintiff suffered a legally recognizable injury, and (4) the injury was proximately caused by the breach of due care.

If the failure to exercise reasonable care in the creation or marketing of a product causes an injury, the basis of product liability is negligence. Thus, the manufacturer of a product must exercise ''due care'' to make that product safe to be used as intended. Due care must be exercised in designing the product, in selecting the materials, in using the appropriate production process, in assembling and testing the product, and in placing adequate warnings on the label informing the user of dangers of which an ordinary person might not be aware. The duty of care extends to the inspection and testing of products purchased by the manufacturer for use in the final product. The failure to exercise due care is negligence. Failure to exercise due care must be proved in actions based on the theory of negligence—in contrast to actions based on the doctrine of strict liability (discussed below), in which liability does not depend on proof of negligence.

## PRIVITY OF CONTRACT NOT REQUIRED

An action based on negligence does not require privity of contract between the injured plaintiff and the negligent defendant-manufacturer. Section 395 of the Restatement (Second) of Torts states:

> A manufacturer who fails to exercise reasonable care in the manufacture of a chattel [movable good] which, unless carefully made, he should recognize as involving an unreasonable risk of causing physical harm to those who lawfully use it for a purpose for which the manufacturer should expect it to be used and to those whom he should expect to be endangered by its probable use, is subject to liability for physical harm caused to them by its lawful use in a manner and for a purpose for which it is supplied.

Simply stated, a manufacturer is liable for its failure to exercise due care to any person who sustains an injury proximately caused by a negligently made (defective) product. (The analysis of whether a product is so defective as to be *unreasonably dangerous* applies equally to actions based on strict tort liability and is discussed below.)

In the following landmark case, the New York court dealt with the liability of a manufacturer that failed to exercise reasonable care in manufacturing a finished product. The *MacPherson* case is the classic negligence case in which privity of contract was not required between the plaintiff and the defendant to establish liability. This is a forerunner to strict product liability, although it does not use product liability theory. Its subject matter, defectively manufactured wooden wheels for automobiles, is dated, but the principles involved are not.

---

 **CASE 25.1**

**MacPHERSON v.
BUICK MOTOR CO.**

Court of Appeals of New York,
1916.
217 N.Y. 382,
111 N.E. 1050.

**BACKGROUND AND FACTS**   *The defendant, Buick Motor Company, was sued by Donald C. MacPherson, the plaintiff, who suffered injuries while riding in a Buick automobile that suddenly collapsed because one of the wheels was made of defective wood. The spokes crumbled into fragments, throwing MacPherson out of the vehicle and injuring him. The wheel itself had not been made by Buick Motor Company; it had been bought from another manufacturer. There was evidence, however, that the defects could have been discovered by reasonable inspection and that no such inspection had taken place. Although there was no charge that Buick knew of the defect and willfully concealed it, MacPherson charged Buick with negligence for putting a human life in imminent danger. Keep in mind* *that MacPherson sued the automobile manufacturer directly, despite the fact that the automobile was purchased from a retail Buick dealer. The trial court held for MacPherson, and Buick Motor Company appealed.*

*CARDOZO,* Justice.

\*    \*    \*    \*

\*    \*    \* If the nature of a thing is such that it is reasonably certain to place life and limb in peril when negligently made, it is then a thing of danger. Its nature gives warning of the consequences to be expected. If to the element of danger there is added knowledge that the thing will be used by persons other than the purchaser, and used without new tests, then, irrespective of contract, the manufacturer of this thing of danger is under a duty to make it carefully. \*    \*    \* It is possible to use almost anything in a way that will make it dangerous if defective. That is not enough to charge the manufacturer with a duty independent of his contract. \*    \*    \* There must also be knowledge that in the usual course of events the danger will be shared by others than the buyer. Such knowledge may often be inferred from the nature of the transaction. But it is possible that even knowledge of the danger and of the use will not always be enough. The proximity or remoteness of the relation is a factor to be considered. We are dealing now with the liability of the manufacturer of the finished product, who puts it on the market to be used without inspection by his customers. If he is negligent, where danger is to be foreseen, a liability will follow.

We are not required, at this time, to say that it is legitimate to go back of the manufacturer of the finished product and hold [liable] the manufacturers of the component parts. To make their negligence a cause of imminent danger, an independent cause must often intervene; *the manufacturer of the finished product must also fail in his duty of inspection.* It may be that in those circumstances the negligence of the earlier members of the series is too remote to constitute, as to the ultimate user, an actionable wrong. \*    \*    \* There is here no break in the chain of cause and effect. In such circumstances, the presence of a known danger, attendant upon a known use, makes vigilance a duty. \*    \*    \* [Emphasis added.]

\*    \*    \*    \*

We think the defendant was not absolved from a duty of inspection because it bought the wheels from a reputable manufacturer. It was not merely a dealer in automobiles. It was a manufacturer of automobiles. It was responsible for the finished product. It was not at liberty to put the finished product on the market without subjecting the component parts to ordinary and simple tests. \*    \*    \* The obligation to inspect must vary with the nature of the thing to be inspected. The more probable the danger the greater the need of caution.

**DECISION AND REMEDY**

*The Court of Appeals of New York, the highest court in the New York state system, affirmed the judgment of the original trial court and the intermediate review court that the defendant, Buick Motor Company, was liable to Donald C. MacPherson for the injuries he sustained when he was thrown from the vehicle.*

**COMMENTS**

*This case has been interpreted to cover all articles that imperil life when negligently made. Prior to* MacPherson, *manufacturers escaped liability to consumers when their contractual dealings were with distributors or retailers. Since* MacPherson, *that has no longer been possible.*

## Violation of Statutory Duty

Numerous federal and state laws impose duties on manufacturers of cosmetics, drugs, foods, toxic substances, and flammable materials. These duties involve appropriate description of contents, labeling, branding, advertising, and selling. For example, federal statutes include the Flammable Fabrics Act; the Federal Food, Drug and Cosmetic Act; and the Hazardous Substances Labeling Act. In a tort action for damages, a violation of statutory duty is often held to constitute *negligence per se* (negligence in itself, or inherently).

## Defenses to Negligence

Any manufacturer, seller, or processor who can prove that due care was used in the manufacture of its product has an appropriate defense against a negligence suit, because failure to exercise due care is one of the major elements of negligence. As mentioned earlier, due care includes warning the products' potential users of possible side effects or of the consequences of foreseeable product misuses. Another defense that can be raised by a defendant is that the plaintiff failed to establish *causation*—that is, that the plaintiff's injury was caused by the defendant's acts (see Chapter 6).

Two other defenses are contributory negligence and, when recognized, assumption of risk. (Both of these defenses were discussed in Chapter 6.) Any time a plaintiff misuses a product or fails to make a reasonable effort at preserving his or her own welfare, the manufacturer or seller will claim that the plaintiff contributed to causing the injuries. The claim is that the plaintiff's negligence offsets the negligence of the manufacturer or seller. In some states, the contributory negligence of the plaintiff is an absolute defense for the defendant-manufacturer or seller. In many others, the negligence of both these parties is compared (under the theory of comparative negligence), and damages are based on the proportion of negligence attributed to the defendant.

## Section 3

# MISREPRESENTATION

When a fraudulent misrepresentation has been made to a user or consumer and that misrepresentation ultimately results in an injury, the basis of liability may be the tort of fraud. In this case, the misrepresentation must have been made knowingly or with reckless disregard for the facts. An example is the intentional concealment of a product's defects.

Nonfraudulent misrepresentation, which occurs when a merchant *innocently* misrepresents the character or quality of goods, can also provide a basis of liability. In this situation, it does not have to be proved that the misrepresentation was made knowingly. A famous example involved a drug manufacturer and a victim of addiction to a prescription medicine called Talwin. The manufacturer, Winthrop Laboratories, a division of Sterling Drug, Inc., innocently indicated to the medical profession that the drug was not physically addictive. Using this information, a physician prescribed the drug for his patient, who developed an addiction that turned out to be fatal. Even though the addiction was a highly uncommon reaction resulting from the victim's unusual susceptibility to this product, the drug company was still held liable.[1]

Whether fraudulent or nonfraudulent, the misrepresentation must be of a material fact (a fact concerning the quality, nature, or appropriate use of the product on which a normal buyer may be expected to rely). There must also have been an intent to induce the buyer's reliance. Misrepresentation on a label or advertisement is enough to show an intent to induce the reliance of anyone who may use the product. The buyer must rely on the misrepresentation—if the buyer is not aware of it or if it does not influence the transaction, there is no liability.

In contrast to actions based on negligence and strict liability, in a suit based on fraudulent misrepresentation, the plaintiff does not have to show that the product was defective or malfunctioned in any way.[2]

## Section 4

# STRICT LIABILITY

Recall from Chapter 6 that under the doctrine of *strict liability,* people may be held liable for the

---

1. *Crocker v. Winthrop Laboratories, Division of Sterling Drug, Inc.,* 514 S.W.2d 429 (Tex. 1974).
2. See, for example, the discussion in Chapter 15 of *Khan v. Shiley, Inc.,* 217 Cal.App.3d 848, 266 Cal.Rptr. 106 (1990).

results of their acts regardless of their intentions or their exercise of reasonable care. For example, a company that uses dynamite in constructing a road is strictly liable for any damages that it causes, even if it takes reasonable and prudent precautions to prevent such damages. In essence, the blasting company becomes liable for any personal injuries it causes and thus is an absolute insurer—that is, the company is liable for damages regardless of fault.

In several landmark cases involving manufactured goods in the 1960s, courts applied the doctrine, and strict liability has since become a common method of holding manufacturers liable. Section 402A of the Restatement (Second) of Torts, promulgated in 1965 and now adopted by most of the states, clearly espouses the doctrine of strict liability in tort.

## THE RESTATEMENT OF TORTS

The Restatement (Second) of Torts designates how the doctrine of strict product liability should be applied. It is a precise and widely accepted statement of the liabilities of sellers of goods (including manufacturers, processors, assemblers, packagers, bottlers, wholesalers, distributors, and retailers) and deserves close attention. Section 402A of the Restatement (Second) of Torts states:

(1) One who sells any product in a defective condition unreasonably dangerous to the user or consumer or to his property is subject to liability for physical harm thereby caused to the ultimate user or consumer or to his property, if
   (a) the seller is engaged in the business of selling such a product, and
   (b) it is expected to and does reach the user or consumer without substantial change in the condition in which it is sold.

(2) The rule stated in Subsection (1) applies although
   (a) the seller has exercised all possible care in the preparation and sale of his product, and
   (b) the user or consumer has not bought the product from or entered into any contractual relation with the seller.

Under this doctrine, liability does not depend on privity of contract. The injured party does not have to be the buyer or a third party beneficiary, as required under contract warranty theory [UCC 2–318]. Indeed, this type of liability in law is not governed by the provisions of the UCC. Under this doctrine, a plaintiff does not have to prove that there was a failure to exercise due care, as he or she does in an action based on negligence. If certain requirements (discussed below) are met, the seller's liability to an injured party may be virtually unlimited.

Strict liability is imposed by law as a matter of public policy. This public policy rests on the three-fold assumption that (1) consumers should be protected against unsafe products, (2) manufacturers and distributors should not escape liability for faulty products simply because they are not in privity of contract with the ultimate users of those products, and (3) manufacturers and sellers of products are in a better position to bear the costs associated with injuries caused by their products—costs that they can ultimately pass on to all consumers in the form of higher prices.

California was the first state to impose strict liability in tort on manufacturers. In the landmark decision that follows, the Supreme Court of California sets out the reasons for applying tort law rather than contract law to cases in which consumers are injured by defective products.

---

**BACKGROUND AND FACTS** *The plaintiff, William Greenman, wanted a Shopsmith (a combination power tool that could be used as a saw, drill, and wood lathe) after having seen the tool demonstrated by a retailer and having studied a brochure prepared by the manufacturer. The plaintiff's wife bought him one for Christmas. More than a year later, a piece of wood flew out of the lathe attachment of the Shopsmith while the plaintiff was using it, inflicting serious injuries on him. About ten and a half months later, the plaintiff sued both the retailer and the manufacturer for breach of warranties and negligence. The jury found for the plaintiff, and the defendants appealed.*

CASE 25.2

**GREENMAN v. YUBA POWER PRODUCTS, INC.**

Supreme Court of California, 1962.
59 Cal.2d 57,
377 P.2d 897,
27 Cal.Rptr. 697.

*TRAYNOR, Justice.*

\* \* \* \*

\* \* \* [The] theory of an express or implied warranty running from the manufacturer to the plaintiff, the abandonment of the requirement of a contract between them, the recognition that the liability is not assumed by agreement but imposed by law, and the refusal to permit the manufacturer to define the scope of its own responsibility for defective products make clear that the liability is not one governed by the law of contract warranties but by the law of strict liability in tort. Accordingly, rules defining and governing warranties that were developed to meet the needs of commercial transactions cannot properly be invoked to govern the manufacturer's liability to those injured by their defective products unless those rules also serve the purposes for which such liability is imposed.

\* \* \* The purpose of such liability is to insure that the costs of injuries resulting from defective products are borne by the manufacturers that put such products on the market rather than by the injured persons who are powerless to protect themselves. Sales warranties serve this purpose fitfully at best. In the present case, for example, plaintiff was able to plead and prove an express warranty only because he read and relied on the representations of the Shopsmith's ruggedness contained in the manufacturer's brochure. Implicit in the machine's presence on the market, however, was a representation that it would safely do the jobs for which it was built. Under these circumstances, it should not be controlling whether plaintiff selected the machine because of the statements in the brochure, or because of the machine's own appearance of excellence that belied the defect lurking beneath the surface, or because he merely assumed that it would safely do the jobs it was built to do. It should not be controlling whether the details of the sales from manufacturer to retailer and from retailer to plaintiff's wife were such that one or more of the implied warranties of the sales act arose. ''The remedies of injured consumers ought not to be made to depend upon the intricacies of the law of sales.'' To establish the manufacturer's liability it was sufficient that plaintiff proved that he was injured while using the Shopsmith in a way it was intended to be used as a result of a defect in design and manufacture of which plaintiff was not aware that made the Shopsmith unsafe for its intended use.

**DECISION AND REMEDY**    *The jury verdict for the plaintiff was upheld. The manufacturer was held strictly liable in tort for the harm caused by its unsafe product.*

---

## REQUIREMENTS OF STRICT PRODUCT LIABILITY

Just because a person is injured by a product does not mean he or she will have a cause of action against the manufacturer of the product. A cause of action will exist only if the following six basic requirements of strict product liability are met:

1.  The product must be in a defective condition when the defendant sells it.
2.  The defendant must normally be engaged in the business of selling that product.
3.  The product must be unreasonably dangerous to the user or consumer because of its defective condition.[3]

4.  The plaintiff must incur physical harm to self or property by use or consumption of the product.
5.  The defective condition must be the proximate cause of the injury or damage.
6.  The goods must not have been substantially changed from the time the product was sold to the time the injury was sustained.

Thus, in any action against a manufacturer or seller, the plaintiff does not have to show why or in what manner the product became defective. The plaintiff does, however, have to show that at the time the injury was sustained, the condition of the product was essentially the same as when it left the hands of the defendant manufacturer or seller.

The plaintiff normally must also show that the product was so defective as to be an **unreasonably**

---

3.  This element is no longer required in some states—for example, California.

**dangerous product.** A court may consider a product so defective as to be unreasonably dangerous if either (1) the product was dangerous beyond the expectation of the ordinary consumer or (2) a less dangerous alternative was economically feasible for the manufacturer, but the manufacturer failed to produce it.

Under the feasible-alternative approach, courts will consider a product's utility and desirability; the availability of other, safer products; the dangers that have been identified prior to an injured user's suit; the dangers' obviousness; the normal expectation of danger, particularly for established products; the probability of injury and its likely seriousness; the avoidability of injury by care in the product's use, including the contribution of instructions and warnings; and the viability of eliminating the danger without appreciably impairing the product's function or making the product too expensive. For example, people often cut themselves on knives, but a court would consider that knives are very useful. Reasoning that there is no way to avoid injuries without making the product useless and that the danger is obvious to users, a court normally would not find a knife to be unreasonably dangerous and would not hold a supplier of knives liable.

At the same time, a court may consider a snowblower without a safety guard over the opening through which the snow is blown to be in a condition that is unreasonably dangerous, even if the snowblower carries warnings to stay clear of the opening. The danger may be within the user's expectations, but the court will also consider the likelihood of injury and its probable seriousness, as well as the cost of putting a guard over the opening and the guard's effect on the blower's operation.

Some products are safe when used as their manufacturers and distributors intend but not safe when used in other ways. Suppliers are generally required to expect reasonably foreseeable misuses and to design products that are either safe when misused or marketed with some protective device—for example, a childproof cap. Whether a manufacturer should have placed a protective device over a propeller on an outboard motor is at issue in the following case.

---

**COMPANY PROFILE**  *Ole Evinrude helped William Harley and the Davidson brothers design the carburetor for the first Harley-Davidson motorcycles sold in 1903. Evinrude's later design for an outboard motor provided a product for the Evinrude Motor Company (EMC), which he formed in Milwaukee, Wisconsin, in 1907. In 1929, EMC was bought by Briggs & Stratton cofounder Stephen Briggs, who formed a syndicate with Ole Evinrude called the Outboard Motors Corporation (OMC). OMC introduced electric-starting outboard motors in 1930 and fully enclosed engines, which were safer and quieter, in 1934. A year later, OMC bought Johnson Motors Corporation, maker of Sea Horse outboard motors. OMC's foreign sales tripled between 1949 and 1956, the year the company changed its name to Outboard Marine Corporation. Outboard Marine introduced in the 1950s the first mass-produced, diecast, aluminum V-engine and a decade later an all-electronic outboard ignition, now the industry standard. Outboard Marine continued to expand, introducing the first V-8 outboard engine in 1985 and acquiring, among other companies, fifteen boat manufacturers (including boat builders in Canada, Australia, and France) between 1986 and 1990.*

**CASE 25.3**

**FITZPATRICK v. MADONNA**

Superior Court of Pennsylvania, 1993.
623 A.2d 322.

**BACKGROUND AND FACTS**  *On August 10, 1980, while swimming with his sister and friends in a cove near Ocean City, New Jersey, sixteen-year-old Kevin Fitzpatrick was struck and killed by a motorboat operated by Michael Madonna. Fitzpatrick's mother brought a wrongful-death action against Madonna and Outboard Marine Corporation (OMC), the manufacturer of the 1978 outboard motor used to propel the boat through the*

*water. The trial court held that both Madonna and OMC were negligent in contributing to Fitzpatrick's death and that OMC was also strictly liable for a defectively designed outboard motor. The court held that the motor was defective because the propeller blades were not encased in a protective guard. OMC appealed.*

*WIEAND,* Judge.

\* \* \* \*

An outboard motor is designed to move a boat through water. It has not been designed to allow motorboats to move among swimmers. The risk inherent in such movement is readily apparent. Moreover, it cannot be said with any degree of certainty that the risk of injury will be reduced by a safety guard, for the presence of a shroud over the propeller presents its own risks to swimmers. For example, a shroud creates a larger target area. In addition, the possibility exists that human limbs may become wedged between a shroud and the propeller, exposing a swimmer to even greater injury. From recreation to transportation, the open screw propeller has proven its utility for its intended purpose, i.e., powering a boat through the water. When used for its intended purpose, the open screw propeller functions safely and well. It must be conceded, nevertheless, that open screw propellers possess inherently dangerous qualities. The public, however, is aware of those qualities. A competent person knows that he or she must stay clear of the churning blades of an outboard motor in the same way as a person avoids airplane propellers, chain saw teeth, and lawn mower blades. Some products, by their nature, (or, in modern parlance, by their conscious design), place both users and bystanders in some measure of danger. A knife or an axe may cut persons, as well as their intended targets. Fish hooks can wound; saws can maim, and revolving propellers can cause fearful damage. When a boat powered by an outboard motor is handled in a common sense manner, the likelihood that bystanders will be injured by the rotating blades of the motor is not great.

\* \* \* \*

The plaintiff-appellee urges, however, that if technology existed in 1978 from which her expert could envision the development of a practical propeller guard, we should hold OMC strictly liable in order to encourage manufacturers to design safe outboard motors. We decline to do so. As a matter of policy there is no good reason for imposing strict liability on OMC merely because, at the time of manufacturing the motor in this case, OMC did not encase the propeller in a protective device. No practical devices were then available, and none had been developed which would have improved the safe operation of the boat in the instant case. In 1978, an outboard motor was not defectively designed merely because the propeller was not enshrouded in a protective device.

**DECISION AND REMEDY**   *The appellate court reversed the trial court's judgment. OMC could not be held liable for Kevin Fitzpatrick's death, because its motor was not defective.*

**INTERNATIONAL CONSIDERATIONS**   **Product Liability in the European Union** *The European Community (now the European Union) issued a final "Directive on Product Liability" in 1985. The directive provides for strict liability. Article 5 of the directive provides for a state-of-the-art defense to strict liability by stating that a "product will not be considered defective for the sole reason that a better product is subsequently put in circulation." If the technology for improvement were unavailable at the time of the initial sale, the manufacturer is not liable.*

## LIABILITY SHARING

As with other theories of product liability, a plaintiff using a theory of strict liability in tort has been required to prove that the defective product that caused his or her injury was the product of a specific defendant. In recent years, however, in cases in which plaintiffs could not prove which of many distributors of a harmful product supplied the particular product that caused the plaintiffs' injuries, some courts have dropped this requirement. This has occurred primarily with cases involving DES (diethylstilbestrol), a drug administered prior to the late 1970s to prevent miscarriages. DES's harmful character was not realized until, a generation later, daughters of the women who had taken DES developed health problems, including vaginal carcinoma, that were linked to the drug. Partly because of the passage of time, a plaintiff-daughter often could not prove which pharmaceutical company—of as many as three hundred firms—had marketed the DES her mother ingested.

In the DES cases, some courts have held that all firms that manufactured and distributed DES during the period in question were liable for the plaintiffs' injuries in proportion to the firms' respective shares of the market. This theory of **market-share liability** was first set out by the California Supreme Court in a 1980 case, *Sindell v. Abbott Laboratories*.[4] Although some states have adopted the theory,[5] many states have not.[6] When recovery is possible under a market-share theory of liability, the plaintiff is normally required to establish the following elements:

1. That the product alleged to be the source of the plaintiff's injury is *fungible* (identical in design and defect to products manufactured and marketed by several firms).
2. That the inability to prove the cause of the harm is not the plaintiff's fault.
3. That the manufacturer that produced the particular product is unidentifiable.

To date, courts have generally been reluctant to apply market-share liability to manufacturers of products other than DES.[7] An interesting exception was made by a Hawaii court in 1991, however, when the court applied market-share liability to the manufacturers of a blood protein, AHF (antihemophilic factor concentrate). A hemophiliac patient who had received AHF injections later tested positive for the AIDS (acquired immune deficiency syndrome) virus. He alleged that he had been exposed to the virus through the AHF injections. Because it was not known which manufacturer was responsible for the particular AHF received by the plaintiff, the court held that all of the manufacturers of AHF could be held liable. In justifying its decision to apply the market-share theory, the court stated that "the problem calls for adopting new rules of causation, for otherwise innocent plaintiffs would be left without a remedy."[8]

## LIMITATIONS ON RECOVERY

Some courts have limited the application of the strict liability doctrine to cases in which personal injuries have occurred. Thus, when a defective product causes only *property damage,* depending on the law of the particular jurisdiction, the seller may not be liable under a theory of strict liability. In addition, until recently, recovery for *economic loss* was not available in an action based on strict liability (and even today it is rarely available). Note, however, that recovery for *breach of warranty* may be available, depending on the type of injury and which alternative section of UCC 2–318 is in effect.

*Statutes of limitations* restrict the time within which an action may be brought. A typical statute of limitations provides that an action must be brought within a specified period of time after the cause of action accrues. Generally, a cause of action is held to accrue when some damage occurs. Sometimes the running of the prescribed period is tolled (that is, suspended) until the party

4. 26 Cal.3d 588, 607 P.2d 924, 163 Cal.Rptr. 132 (1980).
5. Including Florida, Washington, New York, Wisconsin, and Hawaii. Most cases in which the market-share liability theory has been applied involved DES.
6. Including Missouri, Illinois, Rhode Island, and Iowa. These states do not apply market-share liability even in DES cases.

7. See, for example, *Pennfield Corp. v. Meadow Valley Electric, Inc.,* 604 A.2d 1082 (Pa.Super. 1992); *Swartzbauer v. Lead Industry Association,* 794 F.Supp. 142 (E.D.Pa. 1992); *Santiago v. Sherwin-Williams Co.,* 782 F.Supp. 186 (D.Mass. 1992); and *Jackson v. Anchor Packing Co.,* 994 F.2d 1295 (8th Cir. 1993).
8. *Smith v. Cutter Biological, Inc.,* 72 Haw. 416, 823 P.2d 717 (1991).

# EMERGING TRENDS IN BUSINESS LAW

## Where Punitive Damages Are Headed

In recent years tort litigation has often resulted in large awards for damages, particularly for punitive damages. *Punitive damages,* which are awarded in civil cases as a means of deterring the defendant's actions, are assessed in addition to *compensatory damages.* Large punitive-damages awards, which in some cases have been more than one hundred times the compensatory damages awarded to the plaintiff, have led some defendants to claim that these awards violate the Eighth Amendment's prohibition against excessive fines or their constitutional rights to due process.

### The Supreme Court's Response

To date, the United States Supreme Court has not held that excessively high punitive damages awards are unconstitutional.[a] In a 1991

case,[b] however, the Court stated that a ratio of more than four to one between actual and punitive damages "may be close to the line" in terms of constitutionality and suggested that punitive damages awards should bear an "understandable relationship to compensatory damages." The Court declined, however, to draw "a mathematical bright line between the constitutionally acceptable and the constitutionally unacceptable" in regard to punitive-damages awards, and many courts have since held that excessively high punitive damages do not violate defendants' constitutional rights.[c] The Supreme Court went further in 1993 when it approved a $10 million punitive-damages award in *TXO Production Corp. v. The Alliance Resources Corp.*[d] The amount

of punitive damages in that case was 526 times the $19,000 awarded as compensatory damages.

Many defendants' attorneys have argued in favor of some type of objective criteria for assessing the constitutionality of large damage awards. In the *TXO* case, the lower court—the West Virginia Supreme Court of Appeals—enunciated a standard, but that standard will not satisfy most defendants' attorneys. The Virginia court stated that virtually any punitive-damages award would be appropriate if the defendant had been "really stupid" (extremely careless and thereby creating a likelihood of harm) or "really mean" (intentionally committing harmful acts).

In response to the *Haslip, TXO,* and other cases, many states have instituted tort reform measures.

### State Tort Reform Measures

Some states have legislated tort reform measures that have, in essence, rendered moot the effect of the several Supreme Court decisions mentioned above. Professors Michael Rustad and Thomas Koenig have supplied the following information about the tort reforms of various states:

a. See, for example, *Browning-Ferris Industries of Vermont, Inc. v. Kelco Disposal, Inc.,* 492 U.S. 257, 109 S.Ct. 2909, 106 L.Ed.2d 219 (1989), in which the Supreme Court held that the excessive-fines clause of the Eighth Amendment does not apply to awards of punitive damages in cases between private parties.

b. *Pacific Mutual Life Insurance Co. v. Haslip,* 499 U.S. 1, 111 S.Ct. 1032, 113 L.Ed.2d 1 (1991).
c. See, for example, *Southern Life and Health Insurance Co. v. Turner,* 586 So.2d 854 (Ala. 1991), a case decided five months after *Haslip,* in which the plaintiff was awarded punitive damages 499 times the amount of compensatory damages awarded.
d. ___ U.S. ___, 113 S.Ct. 2711, 125 L.Ed.2d 366 (1993).

- Eight states (Alabama, Colorado, Connecticut, Florida, Kansas, Oklahoma, Texas, and Virginia) have placed caps on punitive damages.
- Five states do not allow any punitive damages to be awarded in product liability cases. Numerous other states are currently taking steps to reduce the size and frequency of such awards. Georgia, for example, limits such awards to one per defendant and requires that 75 percent of each such award be paid to the state.
- Twenty-five states require plaintiffs to prove punitive damages using the standard of "clear and convincing" evidence.
- Seven states (Florida, Illinois, Iowa, Mississippi, New York, Oregon, and Utah) require that part of punitive-damages awards go for public purposes.[e]

## Pending Federal Reform Legislation

For many years, Senator Robert W. Kasten, Jr., of Wisconsin sponsored a product liability reform act, which was reintroduced on several occasions in Congress. That act, which would have superseded state law on virtually all established issues, was never passed. Other acts have been proposed in the 1990s. The most recent one is the Product Liability Fairness Act, which would establish specified statutes of repose and limitations, as well as bar joint liability for noneconomic

e. As cited in Debra C. Moss, "The Punitive Thunderbolt," *ABA Journal,* May 1993, pp. 88–92.

damages. The act would also require clear and convincing evidence to support a punitive-damages award.

Additionally, the act would penalize plaintiffs who reject a reasonable pretrial settlement offer. An early 1994 version of the act exempts from liability for punitive damages the makers of drugs and medical devices that are approved by the Food and Drug Administration (FDA). If, however, a manufacturer withheld or misrepresented data submitted to the FDA, that manufacturer would not obtain such an exemption.

Any type of federal tort reform legislation, if passed, would probably reduce punitive-damages awards, on average. In particular, if such legislation contained the requirement of clear and convincing evidence to support such awards, this requirement would definitely make it more difficult for jurors to award punitive damages.

## ■ Implications for the Businessperson:

1. If the continuing trend toward capping punitive damages continues, liability insurance rates will likely fall. This will have a beneficial effect on business firms.
2. So long as the Supreme Court does not establish an objective test on which to judge the constitutionality of punitive-damages awards, firms doing business in those states that do not bar or cap punitive damages will continue to run the risk of high punitive-damages awards.
3. If the Product Liability Fairness Act passes in its

current form, businesses may still face punitive damages in product liability suits. Such damages, though, will be harder for plaintiffs to obtain and will be automatically limited for products tested and approved by the FDA.

## ■ For Critical Analysis

1. One study of punitive-damages awards found that the "median" punitive-damages award in San Francisco County over a four-year period was $43,000, while the "average" punitive-damages award in that same county for that same period was $729,000. How do you account for this difference between the median and average amounts? What are the implications of these figures for the debate over "skyrocketing" punitive damages?
2. In another study, which evaluated 355 punitive-damages awards over a twenty-five-year period, the researcher found that the median punitive-damages award was $625,000, while the median compensatory-damages award was $500,100. Do you think that a median punitive-damages award of $625,000 is unacceptably high?
3. Do you think that the constitutionality of punitive-damages awards should be determined by the ratio of punitive damages to compensatory damages? Is it possible to establish an objective test of when punitive damages become so excessive as to violate due process rights or the constitutional protection against excessive fines?

suffering an injury has discovered it (or should have discovered it).

Many states have passed laws placing outer time limits on some claims so that the defendant will not be left vulnerable to lawsuits indefinitely. These **statutes of repose** may limit the time within which a plaintiff can file a product liability suit. Typically, a statute of repose begins to run at an earlier date and runs for a longer time than a statute of limitations. For example, a statute of repose may proscribe any claims not brought within twelve years from the date of *sale* or *manufacture* of the defective product. Therefore, it is immaterial that the product is defective or causes an injury if the injury occurs after this statutory period has lapsed. In addition, some of these legislative enactments have limited the application of the doctrine of strict liability to new goods.

Some states—for example, Massachusetts— have refused to recognize strict product liability.

In these states, recovery is gained mainly through breach of warranty or negligence theory.

## STRICT LIABILITY TO BYSTANDERS

All courts extend the strict liability of manufacturers and other sellers to injured **bystanders,** although the drafters of Restatement (Second) of Torts, Section 402A, did not take a position on bystanders. For example, the manufacturer of an automobile was held liable for injuries caused by the explosion of the car's motor while the car was in traffic. A cloud of steam that resulted from the explosion caused multiple collisions, because it kept other drivers from seeing well.[9] In the following case, the court extends the protections of Section 402A to bystanders whose injuries from defective products are reasonably foreseeable.

---

9.  *Giberson v. Ford Motor Co.,* 504 S.W.2d 8 (Mo. 1974).

---

**CASE 25.4**

**EMBS v. PEPSI-COLA BOTTLING CO. OF LEXINGTON, KENTUCKY, INC.**

Court of Appeals of Kentucky, 1975.
528 S.W.2d 703.

**BACKGROUND AND FACTS**   *The plaintiff, Janice Embs, was buying some groceries at Stamper's Cash Market. Unnoticed by her, a carton of 7-Up was sitting on the floor at the edge of the produce counter about one foot from where she was standing. Several of the 7-Up bottles exploded. Embs's leg was injured severely enough that Embs had to be taken to the hospital by a managing agent of the store. Embs brought an action against the manufacturer, but the trial court dismissed her claim. Embs appealed.*

*JUKOWSKY,* Judge.
　　　* * * *
    Our expressed public policy will be furthered if we minimize the risk of personal injury and property damage by charging the costs of injuries against the manufacturer who can procure liability insurance and distribute its expense among the public as a cost of doing business; and since the risk of harm from defective products exists for mere bystanders and passersby as well as for the purchaser or user, there is no substantial reason for protecting one class of persons and not the other. The same policy requires us to maximize protection for the injured third party and promote the public interest in discouraging the marketing of products having defects that are a menace to the public by imposing strict liability upon retailers and wholesalers in the distributive chain responsible for marketing the defective product which injures the bystander. *The imposition of strict liability places no unreasonable burden upon sellers because they can adjust the cost of insurance protection among themselves in the course of their continuing business relationship.* [Emphasis added.]
    We must not shirk from extending the rule to the manufacturer for fear that the retailer or middleman will be impaled on the sword of liability without regard to fault. Their liability was already established under Section 402A of the Restatement of Torts 2d. As a matter of public policy the retailer or middleman as well as the manufacturer should be liable since the loss for injuries resulting from defective products should be placed on those members of the marketing chain best able to pay

the loss, who can then distribute such risk among themselves by means of insurance and indemnity agreements. * * *

The result which we reach does not give the bystander a "free ride." When products and consumers are considered in the aggregate, bystanders, as a class, purchase most of the same products to which they are exposed as bystanders. Thus, as a class, they indirectly subsidize the liability of the manufacturer, middleman and retailer and in this sense do pay for the insurance policy tied to the product.

Public policy is adequately served if parameters are placed upon the extension of the rule so that it is limited to bystanders whose injury from the defect is reasonably foreseeable.

For the sake of clarity we restate the extension of the rule. The protections of Section 402A of the Restatement of Torts 2d extend to bystanders whose injury from the defective product is reasonably foreseeable.

**DECISION AND REMEDY**

*The appellate court reversed the trial court's directed verdict that dismissed Embs's claim. The case was remanded to the lower court for a new trial.*

## CRASHWORTHINESS DOCTRINE

Certain courts have adopted the **crashworthiness doctrine,** which imposes liability for defects in the design or construction of motor vehicles that increase the extent of injuries to passengers if an accident occurs. The doctrine holds even when the defects do not actually cause the accident.[10] By accepting the crashworthiness doctrine, the courts reject the argument of automobile manufacturers that involving a car in a collision does not constitute "ordinary use" of the car. There are, however, strong differences of opinion among the courts on this issue.

## OTHER APPLICATIONS OF STRICT LIABILITY

Under the rule of strict liability in tort, the basis of liability has been expanded to include suppliers of component parts and lessors of movable goods. Thus, if General Motors buys brake pads from a subcontractor and puts them in Chevrolets without changing their composition, and if those pads are defective, both the supplier of the brake pads and General Motors will be held strictly liable for the damages caused by the defects.

Liability for personal injuries caused by defective goods extends to those who lease such goods. Section 408 of the Restatement (Second) of Torts states that

> One who leases a chattel as safe for immediate use is subject to liability to those whom he should expect to use the chattel, or to be endangered by its probable use, for physical harm caused by its use in a manner for which, and by a person for whose use, it is leased, if the lessor fails to exercise reasonable care to make it safe for such use or to disclose its actual condition to those who may be expected to use it.

Some courts have held that a leasing agreement gives rise to a contractual *implied warranty* that the leased goods will be fit for the duration of the lease. Under this view, if Hertz Rent-a-Car leases a Chevrolet that has been improperly maintained, and a passenger in the Chevrolet is injured in an accident, the passenger can sue Hertz. (Liability here is based on the contract theory of warranty, not tort.)

## DEFENSES TO STRICT LIABILITY

Frequently, negligent misconduct or misuse of the product by the harmed person or a third party, coupled with the product's defect, causes damage or injury. If the misconduct or misuse can be charged to a claimant, it may be a defense to reduce the claimant's recovery or bar it altogether. Sometimes, if a buyer fails to heed a product-recall notice and thereafter is injured by the defect that led to the recall, the buyer will be deemed to have assumed the risk of injury.

---

10. *Turner v. General Motors Corp.,* 514 S.W.2d 497 (Tex. Civ.App. 1974).

■ CONCEPT SUMMARY 25.1 Comparison of Negligence and Strict Liability in the Area of Product Liability

| | NEGLIGENCE | STRICT LIABILITY |
|---|---|---|
| **Applicability** | All products. | Products dangerously defective in design or manufacture. |
| **Basic Test** | Considering all of the circumstances, was reasonable care exercised? | Is there a defect making the product unreasonably dangerous?[a] |
| **Elements** | 1. Duty of care exists.<br>2. Breach of the duty exists.<br>3. Breach causes injury or damage. | 1. Unreasonably dangerous defect exists.<br>2. Defect causes[b] injury or damage.[c] |
| **Defenses** | 1. Reasonable care was exercised.<br>2. Intervening or superseding event caused injury or damage.<br>3. Claimant unreasonably assumed risk.<br>4. Claimant was also negligent:<br>   a. Contributory-negligence jurisdiction—absolute defense.<br>   b. Comparative-negligence jurisdiction—damages apportioned. | 1. Defect did not exist when product was in defendant's hands.<br>2. Claimant misused product in an unforeseeable way.<br>3. Claimant unreasonably assumed risk.<br>4. Claimant was also negligent:[d]<br>   a. Contributory-negligence jurisdiction—absolute defense.<br>   b. Comparative-negligence jurisdiction—damages apportioned. |

a.   As mentioned, some jurisdictions do not require that a defect render a product unreasonably dangerous.
b.   In a few jurisdictions, under the crashworthiness doctrine, the defect need not have caused the accident that resulted in an injury. It need only have increased the extent of the injury.
c.   Some jurisdictions limit awards to cases involving personal injuries. A few jurisdictions permit recovery of economic losses.
d.   This defense is available in only a few states.

**ASSUMPTION OF RISK**    In some states, assumption of risk is a defense in an action based on strict liability in tort. For such a defense to be established, the defendant must show the following basic elements:

1. That the plaintiff voluntarily engaged in the risk while realizing the potential danger.
2. That the plaintiff knew and appreciated the risk created by the defect.
3. That the plaintiff's decision to undertake the known risk was unreasonable.

**MISUSE OF THE PRODUCT**    Similar to the defense of voluntary assumption of risk is that of **product misuse.** Here the injured party did not know that the product was dangerous for a particular use, but the use was not the one for which the product was designed. (Contrast this with assumption of risk.) This defense has been severely limited by the courts, however. If the misuse is reasonably

foreseeable, the seller must take measures to guard against it.

**COMPARATIVE FAULT**    As pointed out in Chapter 6, at common law, in any action based on negligence, contributory negligence of the injured party either completely barred recovery or reduced the amount of recovery under the rule of comparative negligence. In principle, contributory negligence is immaterial in any action based on the theory of strict liability in tort and in fact has been abolished as a defense by most courts.

Recent developments in the area of comparative negligence are affecting the doctrine of strict liability. Whereas previously the plaintiff's conduct was not a defense to strict liability, today a growing number of jurisdictions consider the negligent or intentional actions of the plaintiff in the apportionment of liability and damages. This "comparing" of the plaintiff's conduct to the defendant's strict liability results in an application of the doctrine of comparative negligence. Thus, for example, failure to take precaution against a known defect will reduce a plaintiff's recovery. The majority of states have adopted this doctrine, either legislatively or through court decisions. Its recent growth may have a pervasive effect on strict liability as well.

---

# TERMS AND CONCEPTS TO REVIEW

| | | |
|---|---|---|
| bystander **474** | product liability **463** | unreasonably dangerous |
| crashworthiness doctrine **475** | product misuse **476** | product **468–469** |
| market-share liability **471** | statute of repose **474** | |

---

# QUESTIONS AND CASE PROBLEMS

**25–1. Theories of Liability.** Chen buys a television set manufactured by Quality TV Appliance, Inc. She is going on vacation, so she takes the set to her mother's house for her mother to use. Because the set is defective, it explodes, causing considerable damage to her mother's house. Chen's mother sues Quality for the damages to her house. Discuss the theories under which Chen's mother can recover from Quality.

**25–2. Negligence.** Perfect Drug Co. manufactures and has placed on the market a drug for airsickness. Boro purchases the drug from Alban's Drug Store. Boro is going on a trip and takes two of the tablets as directed. Boro loses consciousness because of the side effects of the drug, and he falls down a flight of stairs at the airport, breaking an arm and a leg. Perfect Drug knew of the possible side effects but did not place any warning on the label. Also, it is learned that Perfect Drug failed to meet minimum federal drug standards in the manufacture of the drug—standards that would have reduced the side effects. Boro wants to file an action based on Perfect's negligence.

   (a) Discuss Boro's burden of proof.

   (b) Discuss how the situation would be different if a warning had been placed on the package and minimum standards had been met.

**25–3. Liability in Tort.** Colt manufactures a new pistol. Firing of the pistol is dependent on an enclosed high-pressure device. The pistol has been thoroughly tested in two laboratories in the Midwest, and it has been designed and manufactured according to current technology. Wayne purchases one of the new pistols from Hardy's Gun and Rifle Emporium. When he uses the pistol in the high altitude of the Rockies, the difference in pressure causes the pistol to misfire, resulting in serious injury to Wayne. Colt can prove that all due care was used in the manufacturing process, and it refuses to pay for Wayne's injuries. Discuss Colt's liability in tort.

**25–4. Liability to Third Parties.** Baxter manufactures electric hair dryers. Julie purchases a Baxter dryer from her local Ace Drug Store. Cox, a friend and guest in Julie's home, has taken a shower and wants to dry her hair. Julie tells Cox to use the new Baxter hair dryer that she has just purchased. As Cox plugs in the dryer, sparks fly out from the motor and continue to do so as she operates it. Despite this, Cox begins drying her hair. Suddenly, the entire dryer ignites into flames, severely burning Cox's scalp. Cox sues Baxter on the basis of the torts of negligence and strict liability. Baxter admits the dryer was defective but denies liability, particularly because Cox did not purchase the dryer. Discuss the validity of any defense claimed by Baxter.

**25–5. Strict Liability.** Gina is standing on a street corner waiting for a ride to work. Gomez has just purchased a new car manufactured by Optimal Motors. Gomez is driving down the street when suddenly the steering mechanism breaks, causing him to run over Gina. Gina suffers permanent injuries. Gomez's total income per year has never exceeded $15,000. Gina files suit against Optimal under the theory of strict liability in tort. Optimal pleads no liability because (1) due care was used in the manufacture of the car, (2) Optimal is not the manufacturer of the steering mechanism (Smith is), and (3) the Restatement governing strict liability applies only to users or consumers, and Gina is neither. Discuss the validity of the defenses claimed by Optimal.

**25–6. Negligence.** A two-year-old child lost his leg when he became entangled in a grain auger on his grandfather's farm. The auger had a safety guard that prevented any item larger than 4⅝ inches from coming into contact with the machine's moving parts. The child's foot was smaller than the openings in the safety guard. Was such an injury reasonably foreseeable? Discuss. [*Richelman v. Kewanee Machinery & Conveyor Co.,* 59 Ill.App.3d 578, 375 N.E.2d 885, 16 Ill.Dec. 778 (1978)]

**25–7. Duty to Warn.** During the 1960s, Aluminum Co. of America (Alcoa) designed, patented, manufactured, and marketed a closure system for applying aluminum caps to carbonated soft-drink bottles. In 1969, Alcoa sold a capping machine to Houston 7-Up Bottling Co. On June 3, 1976, James Alm suffered a severe eye injury when an aluminum bottle cap exploded off a thirty-two-ounce bottle of 7-Up that had come from the Houston 7-Up Bottling Co. Alm sued Alcoa, alleging that, as the manufacturer, Alcoa had a duty to warn consumers of the dangers of a possible bottle-cap explosion. Alcoa argued that it had not had a duty to warn Alm, because it had not manufactured or sold any component part or the final product that injured Alm. Alcoa had mentioned possible cap explosions in the machine user's manual, wall charts, and technical information that it had provided to the Houston 7-Up Bottling Co. Which allegation is correct? Explain. [*Alm v. Aluminum Co. of America,* 717 S.W.2d 588 (Tex. 1986)]

**25–8. Theories of Liability.** Frances Ontai entered the Straub Clinic and Hospital to have an X-ray examination of the colon. Ontai was placed in a vertical position on a table manufactured by General Electric. The footrest on the table broke, and Ontai fell to the floor of the examination room, suffering injuries. Ontai filed suit against Straub and General Electric. Ontai's suit against General Electric was based on strict liability in tort, negligence, and implied warranties. Discuss briefly each of these theories of liability. [*Ontai v. Straub Clinic and Hospital, Inc.,* 66 Hawaii 237, 659 P.2d 734 (1983)]

**25–9. Liability.** James Patterson, who worked as a clerk in a convenience store in Dallas, was shot and killed during a robbery of the store in 1980. The revolver used by the robber was a .38 caliber "Saturday Night Special" manufactured by a West German company, Rohm Gesellschaft. Patterson's mother brought a product liability action against Rohm and the Florida distributor of the handgun, claiming that the handgun was "defective and unreasonably dangerous" in design because its potential for injury and death far outweighs any social utility it may have. The defendant moved for summary judgment, contending that it could not be liable for Patterson's death because the handgun was not defective—the gun did not malfunction, nor did it lack any essential safety features. What will result? Discuss fully. [*Patterson v. Rohm Gesellschaft,* 608 F.Supp. 1206 (N.D.Tex.—Dallas Div. 1985)]

**25–10. Duty to Warn.** William Mackowick, who had worked as an electrician for thirty years, was installing high-voltage capacitors in a switchgear room in a hospital when he noticed that a fellow electrician had removed the cover from an existing capacitor manufactured by Westinghouse Electric Corp. Westing-

house had placed a warning label inside the cover of the metal box containing the capacitor on which users were instructed to ground the electricity before handling. Nothing was said on the label about the propensity of electricity to "arc." (Arcing occurs when electricity grounds itself by "jumping" to a nearby object or instrument.) Mackowick walked over to warn the other electrician of the danger associated with the exposed capacitor, and while talking, pointed his screwdriver toward the capacitor box. The electricity flowing through the fuses arced to the screwdriver and sent a high-voltage electric current through Mackowick's body. As a result, he sustained severe burns and was unable to return to work for three months. Should Westinghouse be held liable because it failed to warn users of arcing—a principle of electricity? Discuss. [*Mackowick v. Westinghouse Electric Corp.,* 575 A.2d 100 (Pa. 1990)]

**25–11. Strict Liability.** On February 16, 1986, David Jordon, a ten-year-old boy, lost control of his sled, hit a tree, and was injured. The sled was a plastic toboggan-like sled that had been purchased from K-Mart. David's parents brought suit against K-Mart, alleging that the sled was defective and unreasonably dangerous because (1) the sled contained design defects (the molded runners on the sled rendered the sled unsteerable, and the sled lacked any independent steering or braking mechanisms), and (2) there were no warnings of the dangers inherent in the use of the sled. K-Mart moved for summary judgment. Should the court grant K-Mart's motion? Discuss fully. [*Jordon v. K-Mart Corp.,* 611 A.2d 1328 (Pa.Sup. 1992)]

**25–12. Case Briefing Assignment**

*Examine Case A.3 [*Bernal v. Richard Wolf Medical Instruments Corp., *221 Cal.App.3d 1326, 272 Cal.Rptr. 41 (1990)] in Appendix A. The case has been excerpted there in great detail. Review and then brief the case, making sure that you include answers to the following questions in your brief.*

1. What product malfunction brought about this product liability suit?
2. What instructions did the trial court judge give the jury on the design-defect issue, and why did these instructions become the central issue on appeal?
3. According to the appellate court, which party bore the burden of proving that a safer alternative design was feasible, the plaintiff or the defendant?
4. Why did the appellate court state that it "would not hesitate to affirm the jury's verdict" if correct instructions had been given to the jury?

FOCUS ON ETHICS

# Domestic and International Sales Law

Transactions involving the sale of goods constitute a major portion of business activity in the commercial and manufacturing sectors of this economy. Since the 1960s, the sale of goods has been governed by the Uniform Commercial Code (UCC) in virtually every state. Many of the UCC provisions express our ethical standards.

## Good Faith and Commercial Reasonableness

"Good faith" and "commercial reasonableness" are two key concepts that permeate the UCC and help to prevent the success of unethical behavior by businesspersons. These two concepts are read into every contract and impose certain duties on all parties. Section 2–311(1) indicates that when parties leave the particulars of performance to be specified by one of the parties, "[a]ny such specification must be made in good faith and within limits set by commercial reasonableness."

The requirement of commercial reasonableness means that the term subsequently supplied by one party should not come as a surprise to the other. The party filling in the missing term may not take advantage of the opportunity to add a contractual term that will be beneficial to himself or herself (and detrimental to the other party) and then demand contractual performance of the other party that was totally unanticipated. Under the UCC, the party filling in the missing term may not deviate from what is commercially reasonable in the context of the transaction. Courts frequently look to course of dealing, usage of trade, and the surrounding circumstances in determining what is commercially reasonable in a given situation.

### Good Faith
The obligation of good faith is particularly important in so-called output and requirements contracts. UCC 2–306 states that "quantity" in these contracts "means such actual output or requirements as may occur in good faith."

For example, if General Motors contracts with Jalin's Fuel Injectors to purchase all of Jalin's output, Jalin's cannot then increase its production from one eight-hour shift per day to three eight-hour shifts per day to make greater profits under the contract. As another example, assume that Mandrow's Machines has fifty employees assembling IBM clones. Mandrow has a requirements contract with Advanced Tech Circuit Boards under which Advanced Tech is to supply Mandrow with all of the circuit boards it needs. If all of a sudden Mandrow quadruples the size of its business, it cannot insist that Advanced Tech supply it with all of its requirements as per the original contract.

In many situations, parties may find it advantageous (profitable) to avoid a legal obligation. Without the counterobligation of good faith, the potential for abuse in the area of sales contracts exists. Suppose, for example, that the market price of the good subject to a requirements contract rises rapidly and dramatically because of a shortage of materials necessary to its production. The buyer could claim that his or her needs are equivalent to the entire output of the seller. Then, after buying all of the seller's output at the contract price, which is substantially below the market price, the buyer could turn around and sell the goods that he or she does not need at the higher market price. Under the UCC, this type of unethical behavior is prohibited—even though the buyer in this instance has not technically breached the contract.

## Commercial Reasonableness

Under the UCC, the concept of good faith is closely linked to commercial reasonableness. All commercial actions—including the performance and enforcement of contract obligations—must exhibit commercial reasonableness. A merchant is expected to act in a reasonable manner according to reasonable commercial customs. Indeed, the words *reasonable* and *reasonableness* appear again and again in the UCC.

The concept of commercial reasonableness is clearly expressed in the doctrine of commercial impracticability. Under this doctrine, which is related to the common law doctrine of impossibility, a party's nonperformance of a contractual obligation may be excused when, because of unforeseen circumstances, performance of the contract becomes impracticable. But the courts make it clear that before performance will be excused under this doctrine, a contractual party must have made every reasonable effort to fulfill performance obligations.

Consider, for example, the actions of Medcon Enterprises, Inc., when President George Bush imposed a freeze on all Iraqi assets in the United States in the fall of 1990. Medcon had contracted with Engel Industries, Inc., to purchase from Engel certain heavy machinery, which Medcon would then sell to a purchaser in Iraq. The financing was to be handled through First American Bank, which would pay Engel the contract price when Engel

submitted documents proving that the machinery was crated, labeled, and ready for shipment to Iraq, which was to be no later than August 24, 1990. On August 2, however, the president ordered a freeze on all Iraqi assets in the United States. Shortly thereafter, Medcon wrote Engel a letter stating that because of the president's order, Medcon was terminating its purchase order for the machinery. First American also wrote Engel a letter stating that it was prohibited by the president's order from making payment.

Engel, however, had already substantially completed its performance under the contract. In an effort to mitigate its damages, Engel sold some of the machinery over the next few months but was unable to recoup its losses, which totaled $148,000. Eventually, Engel sued Medcon and First American. The issue before the court was whether the president's order had in fact rendered it impossible (illegal) for Medcon and First American to perform their obligations. The court held that it did not. In forming its conclusion, the court relied on an opinion it had requested from the federal Office of Foreign Assets Control (OFAC) regarding the legal effect of the freeze on contracts, specifically the Medcon-Engel contract. According to the court, OFAC stated that the freeze did not prevent the bank's payment to Engel, because the bank always retained the option of applying for a specific license from OFAC so that it could pay Engel. Accepting OFAC's

opinion, the court found that both Medcon and First American had anticipatorily repudiated the contract, and therefore Engel was entitled to damages.[1]

Implicit in the court's judgment in this case is that, upon learning of the president's order, Medcon and the bank could reasonably be expected to do as the court itself did: request information from an appropriate government agency on how the freeze would affect their contractual obligations.

## The Concept of the Good Faith Purchaser

The UCC defines a good faith purchaser as a person who buys without knowledge of circumstances that would cause a person of ordinary prudence to inquire about the seller's title to the goods. That means that even though such circumstances may exist, the purchaser must be unaware of them if he or she is to acquire the status of a good faith purchaser. The real owner cannot recover goods from a good faith purchaser who has given value for the goods [UCC 2–403(1)].

Here we see the UCC's emphasis on protecting innocent parties. If you innocently and in good faith purchase a boat, for example, from someone who appears to have good title and who demands and receives from you a fair market price, then

---

1. *Engel Industries, Inc. v. First American Bank, N.A.,* 798 F.Supp. 9 (D.C. 1992).

the UCC believes that you should be protected from the possibility that the real owner—from whom the seller may have fraudulently obtained the boat—may later appear and demand his or her boat back. (Nothing, however, prevents the true owner from bringing suit against the party who defrauded him or her.)

Ethical questions arise in situations in which the purchaser has reason to suspect that the seller may not have good title to the goods being sold but nonetheless lets the transaction go forward because it is a "good deal." At what point does the buyer, in such a situation, cross over the boundary that separates the good faith purchaser from one who purchases in bad faith? This boundary is a significant one in the law of sales, because the UCC will not be a refuge for those who purchase in bad faith. The term *good faith purchaser* means just that—one who enters into a contract for the purchase of goods without knowing, or having any reason to know, that there is anything shady or illegal about the deal.

## Unconscionability
The UCC's provisions on unconscionability clearly are based on ethical premises. Before the creation and adoption of the UCC, a court of law sometimes refused to enforce a contract on the ground that it was an agreement that no one in their "senses and not under delusion" would make and no honest and fair person would accept. The drafters of the UCC similarly allow courts to refuse to enforce a contract or

a clause in a contract if the court deems that the contract or clause is so one sided or unfair as to be deemed unconscionable.

The primary beneficiaries of the unconscionability provisions of the UCC have been consumers. Generally, the UCC assumes that merchant sellers and buyers have, or should have, a degree of expertise in the requirements and consequences of sales contracts. Therefore, as discussed in the preceding chapters, the UCC has some provisions that apply only to merchants. Consumers, in contrast, are more likely to fall victim to the sales tactics of experienced sellers and therefore receive greater protection under the law generally. This is particularly true when it comes to unconscionable contracts or clauses.

As an example, consider the situation in which Roger Brown found himself when he entered a contest to win a "house full of windows." As a result, sales representatives of Sho-Pro of Indiana, Inc., visited Brown at his home. After a sales pitch of more than four hours, the representatives caused Brown to sign a number of documents, which he did not read before signing. Three days later, Sho-Pro told Brown that he had bought four replacement windows for his home for $4,322. Brown protested that he had not bought any windows, that he could not afford to pay the $4,322, and that he did not even own the house in which he lived. No windows were

ever delivered. Sho-Pro sued Brown to collect the $4,322, plus attorneys' fees and interest.

During the trial, it was revealed that the windows cost Sho-Pro $1,080.50. The rest of the contract price represented "lead costs" of $432.20, "sales management costs" of $600.61, "administrative costs" of $379.99, sales commissions of $648.30, profit of $648.30, and $532.10 to cover installation costs. The court, stating that a contract may be declared unconscionable when there is "a great disparity in bargaining power which leads the party with the lesser power to sign a contract unwillingly or unaware of its terms," deemed that Sho-Pro's contract with Brown was unconscionable at the time it was formed and refused to enforce it.[2]

## Warranties
A seller has not only a legal obligation to provide safe products but also an ethical one. When faced with the possibility of providing additional safety at no extra cost, every ethical businessperson will indeed opt for a safer product. An ethical issue arises, however, when the production of a safer product means higher costs and therefore higher consumer prices. Also at issue is the extent to which manufacturers should be responsible for repairing products that fail or that are broken in the course of normal use.

To some extent, our warranty laws have been

2. *Sho-Pro of Indiana, Inc. v. Brown,* 585 N.E.2d 1357 (Ind.App.3d Dist. 1992).

deemed necessary to protect consumers from sellers who choose, perhaps, to neglect ethical concerns if what they are doing is both legal and profitable. We see, for example, that the use of the term *warranty* in the UCC reflects a promise or a guarantee made by a seller of goods that the goods will have certain characteristics.

### Express and Implied Warranties

Both express and implied warranties are recognized by the UCC. Under UCC 2–314(2), goods sold by a merchant must be fit for the ordinary purposes for which such goods are used, be of proper quality, and be properly labeled and packaged. A description of goods is an express warranty, and hence a seller of goods may be held to have breached a contract if the goods fail to conform to the seller's description. The UCC injects greater fairness into contractual situations by recognizing descriptions as express warranties. The UCC acknowledges the fact that a buyer may often reasonably believe that a seller is warranting his or her product, even though the seller may not use formal words such as *warrant or guarantee*. Thus, the law imposes an ethical obligation on merchants in a statutory form.

### Warranty Disclaimers

The UCC requirement that warranty disclaimers must be sufficiently conspicuous to catch the eye of a reasonable purchaser is based on the ethical premise that sellers of goods should not take advantage of unwary consumers who may not—in the excitement of making a new purchase—always read the "fine print" on standard purchase order forms. As discussed in Chapter 24, if a seller, when attempting to disclaim warranties, fails to meet the specific requirements imposed by the UCC, the warranties will not effectively be disclaimed.

The ethical significance of the UCC rules on warranty disclaimers can best be illustrated by looking at the situation that existed prior to the implementation of the UCC. Before the UCC was adopted by the states, purchasers of automobiles, for example, frequently signed standard-form purchase agreements, drafted by the auto manufacturer, without learning until later what all the fine print meant.

*Henningsen v. Bloomfield Motors, Inc.*,[3] a case decided in New Jersey before the UCC was in effect in that state, involves just such a situation. Henningsen had purchased a new Chrysler from Bloomfield Motors for his wife. Subsequently, his wife suffered severe injuries as a result of an apparent defect in the steering wheel mechanism. The standard-form purchase order used in the transaction contained an express ninety-day/four-thousand-mile warranty and, in fine print, a disclaimer of any and all other express or implied warranties. Thus, Bloomfield Motors and Chrysler Corporation refused to pay for Mrs. Henningsen's

_____

3. 32 N.J. 358, 161 A.2d 69 (1960).

injuries, asserting that the sales contract, which warranted that Bloomfield Motors would repair defects at no charge, disclaimed warranty liabilities for injuries suffered.

The case was eventually heard by the Supreme Court of New Jersey, which expressed outrage at the fact that the automobile manufacturer had used its grossly disproportionate bargaining power, as well as the unfair surprise of fine print, to relieve itself from liability and to impose on the buyer, who in effect had no real freedom of choice, the grave danger of injury that is posed by a defectively made automobile. In a landmark decision, the court held that the disclaimer was unconscionable and allowed the Henningsens to recover from the auto dealer and manufacturer.

Although freedom of contract reflects a basic ethical principle in our society, courts—including the New Jersey court mentioned above—have made it clear that when such freedom leads to gross unfairness, it should be curbed. (Several examples of the kinds of exceptions to freedom of contract that courts will make were offered in the *Focus on Ethics* at the end of Unit Two.) But in regard to warranty disclaimers in fine print or otherwise "hidden" in a standard purchase form, a court, before the UCC was in effect, would not intervene unless, as in the Henningsen case, the resulting unfairness "shocked the conscience" of the court. By obligating merchants to meet specific requirements when disclaiming warranties, the UCC has made dealing fairly with buyers—an already ethical obligation of all sellers of goods—a legal obligation as well.

Today, if a warranty disclaimer unfairly "surprises" a purchaser, chances are that the disclaimer was not sufficiently conspicuous, and the unfairness of the bargain will not have to be so great as to shock the court's conscience before a remedy will be granted.

## Ethics and "Puffing"

As explained in Chapter 24, *puffing* is defined as a salesperson's exaggerated claims concerning the quality of goods offered for sale. Puffing is considered a statement of opinion and not a statement of fact, and therefore it does not constitute an express warranty. The law assumes that most buyers know, or should know, that sellers traditionally have engaged in "huffing and puffing" their wares, and reasonable buyers will not be "taken" by this sort of seller's talk. Nonetheless, in some instances, buyers may rely on a seller's statements of opinion when deciding whether to purchase a particular product.

Consider, for example, what might happen when a salesperson deals with a customer who does not have complete command of the English language. A fast-talking sales representative may engage in a sufficient amount of puffing to convince a customer who does not speak English very well that the product the customer is buying is of much higher quality than it really is.

The line between statements that amount to puffery and statements that constitute express warranties is not always clear. Nor is the line between puffery and fraudulent misrepresentation always clearly discernible. For example, in one case, a sales representative for a Mazda dealer was trying to sell a used Mazda to Kevin Garrett. The salesperson said that although the car had nearly 15,000 miles on it, the salesperson himself had used the car as a demonstrator and for his personal use and had "babied it to death." In fact, the car had been stolen from the dealer and driven 10,000 miles, and prior to the theft, the dealer had had to replace the engine after the car had been driven only approximately 3,000 miles.

Were the salesperson's statements in this situation mere puffery? Did the salesperson have a duty to disclose the fact that the car had been stolen? When Garrett later experienced numerous problems with the car and eventually sued the dealer, the court held that the theft of the car was a material fact, and the salesperson had a duty to disclose this fact. In addition, according to the court, the statements made by the salesperson crossed over the line between puffing, or "seller's talk," and misrepresentation.[4]

## Product Liability

Ethical questions abound in the area of product liability. As the courts have imposed higher and higher damages on manufacturers in product liability lawsuits, so, it would seem, are more consumers bringing lawsuits to obtain damages when they are harmed by a product. In some cases, lawsuits are brought even though it is essentially the consumer who is at fault—if anyone is—and not the manufacturer. Such litigation raises an obvious ethical question: Is it fair that consumers should recover damages for harm caused by their own carelessness or product misuse or for simple accidents for which no one is really at fault?

Consider, for example, the case of *Kemp v. Beneke,* a 1990 Nevada district court case[5] that involved a nine-month-old child, Ryan Kemp, who fell through a toilet seat and suffocated in the water. The Kemp family sued the toilet-seat manufacturer, arguing that a warning sticker should have been placed on the toilet-seat lid to tell parents to take protective measures, such as buying a so-called "potty lock" to attach to the lid or installing self-closing hinges on the bathroom door. Should the toilet-seat manufacturer be required to warn against the obvious? Although in this case the manufacturer agreed to pay $90,000 to the Kemps, many persons might question the ethics of requiring a manufacturer to warn parents

---

4. *Garrett v. Mazda Motors of America,* 844 S.W.2d 178 (Tenn.App. 1992).

---

5. No. A 267563 (Clark Co.).

of such an obvious house-hold danger.

At the other end of the spectrum is the need to impose strict liability standards on manufacturers to ensure that they will do all they can, within reason, to prevent unsafe products from entering the marketplace. There is a fine line, however, between protecting and *over*protecting consumers—in the sense that strict liability opens the door to the possibility that consumers may recover damages that are essentially incurred by their own carelessness or product misuse.

## ■ Discussion Questions

**1.** Review the UCC provisions applying to the topics discussed in Chapters 20 through 25. How do various UCC provisions, excluding the provisions discussed above, reflect American social values and ethical standards? Discuss.

**2.** To what extent should economic considerations be taken into account in the determination of product safety standards? For example, suppose that a proposed regulation requires all commercial airlines to use aircraft that have two additional emergency exit doors. Given the average number of airline crashes per year and the average number of individuals injured or killed in such crashes, it is estimated that the new safety standard will save an additional ten lives per year. But the total cost of implementing the new regulation will be $50 million. This means that it will cost an estimated $5 million to save one life per year. Is this too much to pay for one human life? Too little? What if it would cost $300 million to implement the regulation? The point is, can a human life be subjected to a cost-benefit analysis by having a "price tag" attached to it? If not, how can it be determined whether a product

safety standard is "reasonable" or "unreasonable"?

**3.** Although the UCC good faith provisions hold merchants to a standard of honesty in fact, such honesty is weighed in the context of commercial customs and habitual practices—course of dealing, usage of trade, commercial reasonableness, and so on. Puffing is a case in point. Merchants may "huff and puff" their wares as they traditionally have and still—in most instances—not violate their duty of dealing honestly and in good faith with the buyers of their products. Do you think that the customary practice of puffing is a fundamentally dishonest practice that should be abandoned? Is there anything the law can, or should, do to ensure that buyers will not be taken in by sellers' statements of opinion?

# UNIT FOUR

# COMMERCIAL PAPER AND BANKING

## CONTENTS

**26** Basic Concepts, Negotiability, and Transferability

**27** Holder in Due Course and Defenses

**28** Liability and Discharge

**29** Checks and the Banking System

**30** Electronic Fund Transfers

# CHAPTER 26

# BASIC CONCEPTS, NEGOTIABILITY, AND TRANSFERABILITY

T he vast number of commercial transactions that take place daily in the modern business world would be inconceivable without commercial paper. **Commercial paper** is any written promise or order to pay a sum of money. Drafts, checks, and promissory notes are typical examples. Commercial paper is transferred more readily than ordinary contract rights, and persons who acquire it are normally subject to less risk than the ordinary assignee of a contract right.

The law governing commercial paper grew out of commercial necessity. As early as the thirteenth century, merchants dealing in foreign trade were using commercial paper to finance and conduct their affairs. Problems in transportation and in the safekeeping of gold or coins had prompted this practice. Because the king's courts of those times did not recognize the validity of commercial paper, the merchants had to develop their own rules governing its use, and these rules were enforced by ''fair'' or ''borough'' courts. Eventually, these decisions became a distinct set of laws known as the *Lex Mercatoria* (Law Merchant).

By the end of the seventeenth century, the principles of the Law Merchant were widely accepted and quite naturally became a part of common law. Later, the Law Merchant was codified in England in the Bills of Exchange Act of 1882. In 1896, in the United States, the National Conference of Commissioners on Uniform State Laws drafted the Uniform Negotiable Instruments Law. This law was reviewed by the states, and by 1920 all the states had adopted it. The Uniform Negotiable Instruments Law was the forerunner of Article 3 of the Uniform Commercial Code (UCC).

## SECTION 1

## ARTICLE 3 AND ITS REVISION

Both Article 3 and Article 4 of the UCC apply to transactions involving commercial paper, or instruments. In 1990, a revised version of the UCC's

Article 3 was promulgated for adoption by the states. As of this writing, the majority of the states have adopted the revised article. Many of the changes to Article 3 simply clarify old sections, whereas some significantly alter the existing UCC Article 3 provisions. Throughout this chapter, citations are made to the revised Article 3. Citations to the revised article are indicated by the letter *R* preceding the article number. For example, a citation to the revised version of UCC 3–104 would appear as UCC R3–104. *When the original and revised sections have the same number, only the revised citation is given.* When the numbers of the sections in the revised Article 3 are different from the comparable provisions of the earlier Article 3, citations to both versions are included. Where the revised Article 3 has made important changes in the law, the previous law is discussed in footnotes.

Article 4 of the UCC governs bank deposits and collections. Article 4 was also revised in 1990, in part to reflect changes in the revised Article 3 that affect Article 4 provisions. Both the unrevised and the revised versions of Articles 3 and 4 are included in Appendix C of this text, which contains the entire text of the UCC.

To understand the significance of Article 3, it is necessary to distinguish between *negotiable* and *nonnegotiable* instruments. To qualify as a **negotiable instrument,** commercial paper must meet special requirements relating to form and content. These requirements, which are imposed by UCC R3–104, will be discussed at length in this chapter. When an instrument is negotiable, its transfer from one person to another is governed by Article 3 of the UCC. Indeed, UCC R3–104(b) [UCC 3–102(e)] defines *instrument* to mean a "negotiable instrument." For that reason, whenever the term *instrument* is used in this book, it refers to negotiable commercial paper. Transfers of nonnegotiable instruments are governed by rules of assignment of contract rights that were discussed in Chapter 17.

## SECTION 2

## THE FUNCTION OF INSTRUMENTS

Instruments function in two ways—as a substitute for money and as a credit device. Debtors sometimes use currency, but for convenience and safety they often use instruments instead. For example, an instrument is being used when a debt is paid by check. The substitute-for-money function of instruments developed in the Middle Ages. Merchants deposited their precious metals with goldsmiths (''bankers'') to avoid the dangers of loss or theft. When they needed funds to pay for the goods they were buying, they gave the seller a written order addressed to the "bank." This authorized the bank to deliver part (or all) of the precious metals to the seller. These orders, called *bills of exchange,* were sometimes used as a substitute for money. Today people use checks and other types of instruments in the same way.

Instruments may represent an extension of credit. When a buyer gives a seller a promissory note, the terms of which provide that it is payable within sixty days, the seller has essentially extended sixty days of credit to the buyer. The credit aspect of instruments was developed in the Middle Ages soon after bills of exchange began to be used as substitutes for money. Merchant buyers were able to give to sellers bills of exchange that were not payable until a future date. Because the seller would wait until a maturity date to collect, this was a form of extending credit to the buyer.

For an instrument to operate *practically* as either a substitute for money, a credit device, or both, it is essential that the paper be easily transferable without danger of being uncollectible. This is the function that characterizes *negotiable* instruments. Each rule described in the following pages can be examined in light of this function.

## SECTION 3

## TYPES OF NEGOTIABLE INSTRUMENTS

The UCC specifies four types of negotiable instruments: *drafts, checks, notes,* and *certificates of deposit (CDs).* These instruments are frequently divided into the two classifications that we will discuss in the following sections: *orders to pay* (drafts and checks) and *promises to pay* (promissory notes and CDs). These instruments are summarized briefly in Exhibit 26–1.

Negotiable instruments may also be classified as either *demand instruments* or *time instruments.*

■ **Exhibit 26–1 Basic Types of Instruments**

| Instruments | Characteristics | Parties |
|---|---|---|
| **Orders to Pay**<br>Draft | An order by one person to another person or to bearer [UCC R3–104(e); UCC 3–104(2)(a)]. | Drawer—the person who signs or makes the order to pay [UCC R3–103(a)(3)]. |
| Check | A draft drawn on a bank and payable on demand [UCC R3–104(f); UCC 3–104(2)(b)].[a]<br>Checks include:<br>a. Cashier's check—a draft in which the drawer and drawee are the same bank or branches of the same bank [UCC R3–104(g)].<br>b. Teller's check—a draft drawn by a bank on another bank or payable at or through another bank [UCC R3–104(h)].<br>c. Traveler's check—an instrument drawn or payable at or through a bank that requires, as a condition to payment, a countersignature by a person whose signature appears on the instrument [UCC R3–104(i)]. | Drawee—the person to whom the order to pay is made [UCC R3–103(a)(2)].<br>Payee—the person to whom payment is ordered. |
| **Promises to Pay**<br>Note | A promise by one party to pay money to another party or to bearer [UCC R3–104(e); UCC 3–104(2)(d)]. | Maker—the person who promises to pay [UCC R3–103(a)(5)].<br>Payee—the person to whom the promise is made. |
| Certificate of deposit | A note made by a bank acknowledging a deposit of funds made payable to the holder of the note [UCC R3–104(j); UCC 3–104(2)(c)]. | |
| a. Under UCC R4–105(1), "banks" include savings banks, savings and loan associations, credit unions, and trust companies. | | |

A demand instrument is payable on demand. "A promise or order is 'payable on demand' if it (i) states that it is payable on demand or at sight, or otherwise indicates that it is payable at the will of the holder, or (ii) does not state any time of payment" [UCC R3–108(a)]. All checks are demand instruments, because by definition, they must be payable on demand. Therefore, checking accounts are sometimes called **demand deposits.** A demand instrument is payable immediately after it is *issued.* **Issue** is "the first delivery of an instrument by the maker or drawer, whether to a holder or nonholder [usually to the payee], for the purpose of giving rights on the instrument to any person" [UCC

R3–105].[1] Time instruments are payable at a future date.

## DRAFTS AND CHECKS (ORDERS TO PAY)

A **draft** is an unconditional written order that involves *three parties.* The party creating it (the **drawer**) orders another party (the **drawee**) to pay money, usually to a third party (the **payee**). Exhibit 26–2 shows a typical draft. The drawee must be

---

1. Under the unrevised UCC 3–102(1)(a), *issue* was limited to "the first delivery of an instrument to a holder or remitter."

■ **Exhibit 26–2  A Typical Time Draft—A Bill of Exchange**

Payee

Whiteacre, Minnesota

**January 16** 19 **96**

$ **1,000.00**

**Ninety days after above date**

DRAFT

PAY TO THE ORDER OF

**THE FIRST NATIONAL BANK OF WHITEACRE, MINNESOTA**

**One thousand and no/100** ———————————————————— DOLLARS

VALUE RECEIVED AND CHARGE THE SAME TO ACCOUNT OF

To _____ **Bank of Ourtown**

*Stephen L. Eastman*

**Ourtown, Michigan**

**Stephen L. Eastman**

Drawee

Drawer

---

obligated to the drawer either by agreement or through a debtor-creditor relationship for the drawee to be obligated to the drawer to honor the order. A *time draft* is payable at a definite future time. A *sight* draft or demand draft is payable on sight, that is, when it is presented for payment.[2] A draft drawn by one bank on another bank is referred to as a ''teller's check'' [UCC R3–104(h)].[3] A draft can be both a time and a sight draft; such a draft is one payable at a stated time after sight.

A **trade acceptance** is a draft frequently used in the sale of goods. The seller of the goods is both the drawer and the payee on this draft. Essentially, the draft orders the buyer to pay a specified sum of money to the seller, usually at a stated time in the future. For example, Midwestern Style Fabrics sells $50,000 worth of fabric to D & F Clothiers, Inc., each fall on terms requiring payment to be made in ninety days. One year Midwestern Style needs cash, so it draws a *trade acceptance* that orders D & F to pay $50,000 to the order of Midwestern Style Fabrics ninety days hence.

Midwestern Style presents the paper to D & F. D & F *accepts* by signing the face of the paper and returns it to Midwestern Style Fabrics. D & F's acceptance creates an enforceable promise to pay the draft when it comes due in ninety days. Midwestern Style can sell the trade acceptance in the commercial money market more easily than it can assign the $50,000 account receivable. Trade acceptances are the standard credit instruments in sales transactions (see Exhibit 26–3).

A **banker's acceptance** is a draft commonly used by persons or businesses involved in international trade. A banker's acceptance is drawn by a creditor against his or her debtor, who must pay the draft at maturity. Typically, the term is short.

The most commonly used type of draft is a **check.** The writer of the check is the drawer, the bank upon which the check is drawn is the drawee, and the person to whom the check is payable is the payee. As mentioned earlier, checks, because they are payable on demand, are demand instruments.

Checks will be discussed more fully in Chapter 29, but it should be noted here that with certain types of checks, such as *cashier's checks,* the bank is both the drawer and the drawee. The bank customer purchases a cashier's check from the bank— that is, pays the bank the amount of the check— and indicates to whom the check should be made payable. The bank, not the customer, is the drawer of the check (as well as the drawee).

---

2.  A sight draft may be payable on acceptance. Acceptance is the drawee's written promise to pay the draft when it comes due. The usual manner of accepting is by writing the word *accepted* across the face of the instrument, followed by the date of acceptance and the signature of the drawee.

3.  Referred to as a *bank draft* under the unrevised Article 3. See, for example, *Fulton National Bank v. Delco Corp.,* 128 Ga.App. 16, 195 S.E.2d 455 (1973).

■ **Exhibit 26–3  A Typical Trade Acceptance**

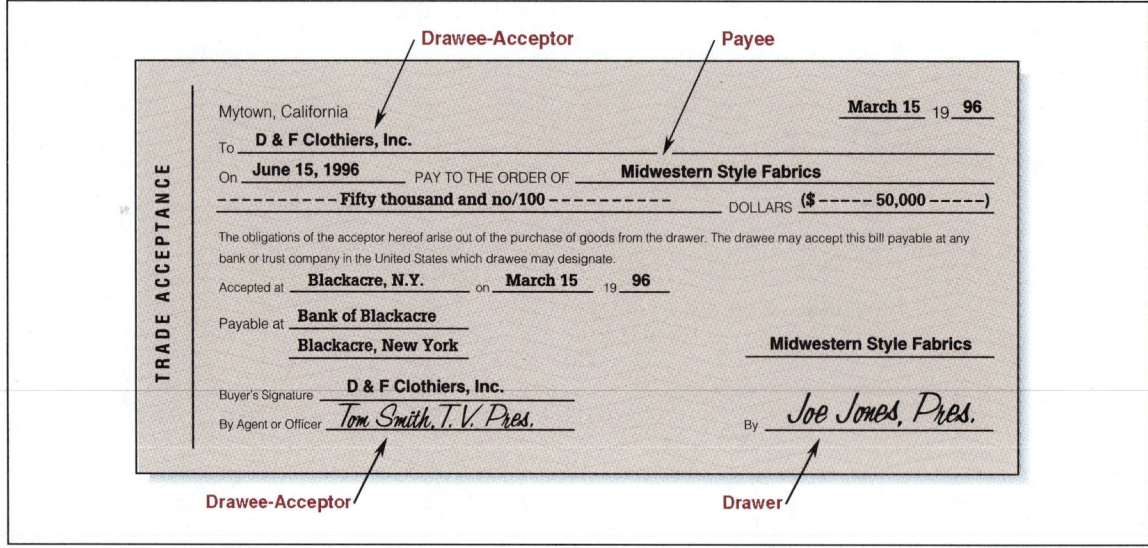

■ **Exhibit 26–4  A Typical Promissory Note**

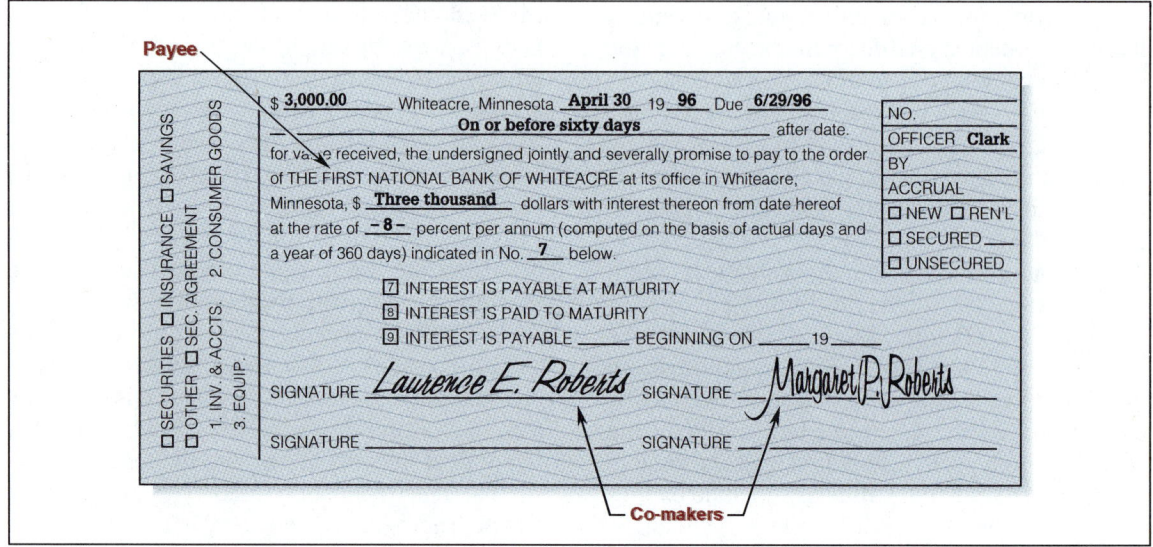

When *traveler's checks* are drawn on a bank, they are checks, but they require the purchaser's authorized signature before becoming payable.[4] A negotiable instrument may be a check even though it states that it is something else—a *money order,* for example [UCC R3–104(f)].

## PROMISSORY NOTES AND CDs (PROMISES TO PAY)

The **promissory note** is a written promise between *two parties.* One party is the **maker** of the promise to pay, and the other is the payee, or the one to whom the promise is made. A promissory note, which is often referred to simply as a *note,* can be made payable at a definite time or on demand. It can name a specific payee or merely be payable to bearer. A typical promissory note is shown in Exhibit 26–4.

---

4.  Technically, most traveler's checks are not checks but drafts, because the drawee—for example, American Express—is ordinarily not a bank.

■ **Exhibit 26–5 A Typical Small CD**

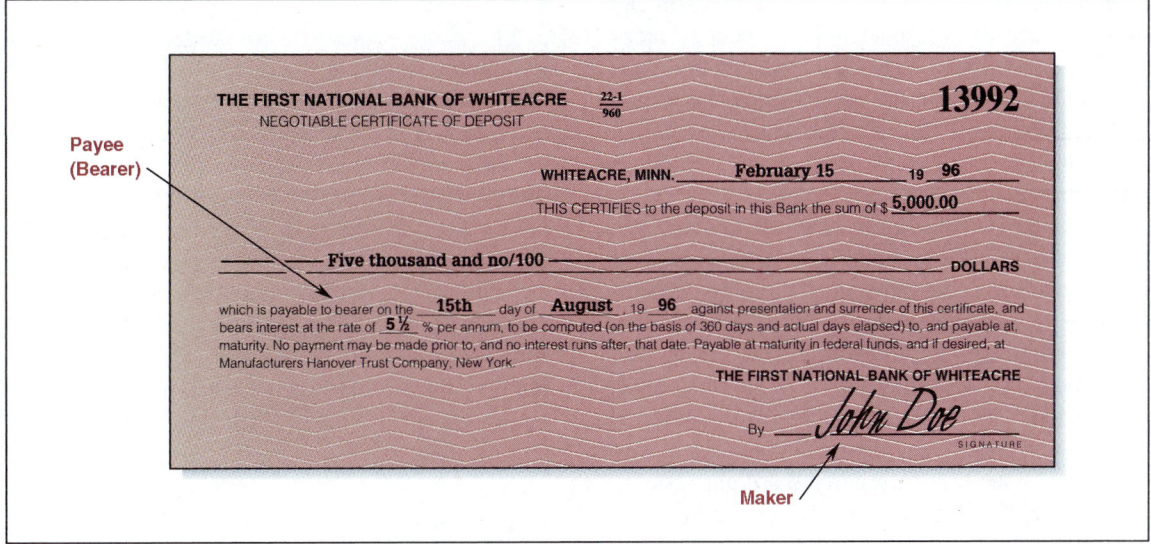

Notes are used in a variety of credit transactions and often carry the name of the transaction involved. For example, in real estate transactions, a promissory note for the unpaid balance on a house, secured by a mortgage on the property, is called a *mortgage note*. A note that is secured by personal property is called a *collateral note,* because the property pledged as security for the satisfaction of the debt is called *collateral*.[5] And a note payable in installments, such as for payment for a television set over a twelve-month period, is called an *installment note.*

A **certificate of deposit (CD)** is the bank's note. It is an acknowledgment by a bank that it has received a certain sum of money and that it promises to repay it [UCC R3–104(j); UCC 3–104(2)(c)]. Certificates of deposit in small denominations are often sold by savings and loan associations, savings banks, and commercial banks. They are called small CDs and are for amounts up to $100,000. Certificates of deposit for amounts over $100,000 are called large (or jumbo) CDs. Exhibit 26–5 shows a typical small CD.

5. To minimize the risk of loss when lending money, a creditor often requires the debtor to provide some collateral, or security, beyond a promise that the debt will be repaid. When this security takes the form of personal property (such as a motor vehicle), the creditor has an interest in the property known as a *security interest*. Security interests are discussed in more detail in Chapter 31.

## SECTION 4

# REQUIREMENTS FOR NEGOTIABILITY

For an instrument to be negotiable, it must meet the following requirements:

1. Be in writing.
2. Be signed by the maker or the drawer.
3. Be an unconditional promise or order to pay.
4. State a fixed amount of money.
5. Be payable on demand or at a definite time.
6. Be payable to order or to bearer, unless it is a check.

### WRITTEN FORM

Negotiable instruments must be in written form [UCC R3–103(a)(6), (9); UCC 3–104(1)].[6] Clearly, an oral promise can create the danger of fraud or make it difficult to determine liability. Negotiable instruments must possess the quality of certainty that only formal, written expression can give.

There are certain practical limitations concerning the writing and the substance on which it is placed. The writing must be on material that lends itself to *permanence*. Instruments carved in blocks of ice or recorded on other impermanent surfaces would not qualify as negotiable instruments. Suppose Shanda writes in the sand, "I promise to pay $500 to the order of Jason." This is not a negotiable instrument, because, although it is in writing, it lacks permanence.

Also, the writing must have *portability*. Although this is not a spelled-out legal requirement, if an instrument is not movable, it obviously cannot meet the requirement that it be freely transferable. For example, Cullen writes on the side of a cow, "I, Cullen, promise to pay Merrill or her order $500 on demand." Technically, this meets the requirements of a negotiable instrument, but as a cow cannot easily be transferred in the ordinary course of business, the "instrument" is nonnegotiable.

## SIGNATURES

For an instrument to be negotiable, it must be signed by (1) the maker if it is a note or a certificate of deposit or (2) the drawer if it is a draft or a check [UCC R3–103(a)(3), (5); UCC 3–104(1)(a)]. If a person signs an instrument as the *agent* for the maker or drawer, the maker or drawer has effectively signed the instrument, provided the agent has the appropriate authority. (Agents' signatures will be discussed in Chapter 28.)

Extreme latitude is granted in determining what constitutes a **signature.** The word *signed* "includes any symbol executed or adopted by a party with present intention to authenticate a writing" [UCC 1–201(39)]. A "signature may be made (i) manually or by means of a device or machine, and (ii) by the use of any name, including a trade or assumed name, or by a word, mark, or symbol executed or adopted by a person with present intention to authenticate a writing" [UCC R3–401(b); UCC 3–401(2)]. Thus, initials, an *X,* or a thumbprint will suffice. A trade name or an assumed name is sufficient. A so-called rubber stamp bearing a person's signature is permitted and frequently used in the business world. If necessary, parol evidence (discussed in Chapter 16) is admissible in identifying the signer. When the signer is identified, the signature becomes effective.

The location of the signature on the document is unimportant, though the usual place is the lower right-hand corner. A *handwritten* statement on the body of the instrument, such as "I, Kammie Orlik,

promise to pay Janel Tan," is sufficient to act as a signature.

There are virtually no limitations on the manner in which a signature can be made, but one should be careful about receiving an instrument that has been signed in an unusual way. Furthermore, an unusual signature clearly decreases the *marketability* of an instrument, because it creates uncertainty. One should also be careful when issuing instruments containing signatures created by automated means, such as with a check-writing machine. UCC R3–110(b) provides that the payee of such instruments is not determined by the "signer" but "by the intent of the person who supplied the name or identification of the payee, whether or not authorized to do so."

## UNCONDITIONAL PROMISE OR ORDER TO PAY

The terms of the promise or order must be included in the writing on the face of a negotiable instrument. These terms must not be conditioned on the occurrence or nonoccurrence of some other event or agreement [UCC R3–104(a); UCC 3–104(1)(b)].

**PROMISE OR ORDER**  For an instrument to be negotiable, it must contain an express order or promise to pay. A mere acknowledgment of the debt, which might logically *imply* a promise, is not sufficient under the UCC because the promise must be an *affirmative,* written undertaking [UCC R3–103(a)(9); UCC 3–102(1)(c)]. For example, the traditional I.O.U. is only an acknowledgment of indebtedness. Although the I.O.U. might logically imply a promise, it is not a negotiable instrument because it does not contain an express promise to repay the debt. But if such words as "to be paid on demand" or "due on demand" are added, the need for an affirmative promise is satisfied. For example, if a buyer executes a promissory note using the words "I promise to pay $1,000 to the order of the seller for the purchase of good X," then the requirement for a negotiable instrument is satisfied.

A certificate of deposit is different. Here, the requisite promise is satisfied because the bank's acknowledgment of the deposit and the other terms of the instrument clearly indicate a promise by the bank to repay the sum of money [UCC R3–104(j); UCC 3–104(2)(c)].

An *order* is associated with three-party instruments, such as trade acceptances, checks, and drafts. An **order instrument** orders, or directs, a third party to pay the instrument as drawn. In the typical check, for example, the word *pay* (to the order of a payee) is a command to the drawee bank to pay the check when presented, and thus it is an order. The order is mandatory even if it is written in a courteous form with words like ''Please pay'' or ''Kindly pay.'' Generally, precise language must be used. An order stating ''I wish you would pay'' does not fulfill the requirement of precision.

An order may also be addressed to more than one person, either jointly or alternatively [UCC R3–103(a)(6); UCC 3–102(1)(b)]. A jointly addressed order, for example, might be used by an insurance company when issuing a check to the insured party and a third party, such as a creditor or repairperson.

## UNCONDITIONALITY OF PROMISE OR ORDER

A negotiable instrument's utility as a substitute for money or as a credit device would be dramatically reduced if it had conditional promises attached to it. It would be expensive and time consuming to investigate conditional promises, and therefore the transferability of the negotiable instrument would be greatly restricted. Substantial administrative costs also would be required to process conditional promises. Furthermore, the payee or any **holder** of the instrument would risk the possibility that the condition would not occur. (The term *holder* includes any person in the possession of an instrument drawn, issued, or indorsed to him or her or to his or her order or to bearer or in blank [see UCC 1–201(20)]. The terms *indorse, bearer,* and *in blank* will be explained later in this chapter.)

Suppose Granados promises in a note to pay McGraw $10,000 only if a certain ship reaches port. No one could safely purchase the promissory note without first investigating whether the ship had arrived. Even then, the facts disclosed by the investigation might be incorrect. To avoid such problems, the UCC provides that only unconditional promises or orders can be negotiable [UCC R3–104(a); UCC 3–104(1)(b)].

UCC 3–105(2) and UCC R3–106(a) specify what constitutes an unconditional instrument. UCC R3–106(a) reads as follows:

[A] promise or order is unconditional [and negotiable] unless it states (i) an express condition to pay-

ment, (ii) that the promise or order is subject to or governed by another writing, or (iii) that rights or obligations with respect to the promise or order are stated in another writing. A reference to another writing does not of itself make the promise or order conditional.

The UCC expands the definition of *unconditional,* however, to prevent certain necessary conditions commonly used in business transactions, such as those discussed next, from rendering an otherwise negotiable instrument nonnegotiable.

*Statements of Consideration.*   Many instruments state the terms of the underlying agreement or refer to the consideration paid for the investment as a matter of standard business practice. Because the policy of the UCC is to integrate standard trade usages into its provisions, such statements are not considered conditions and do not affect negotiability. For example, the words ''as per contract'' or ''this debt arises from the sale of goods X and Y'' do not render an instrument nonnegotiable [UCC R3–106, Comment 1; UCC 3–105(1)(b)].

*References to Other Agreements.*   The UCC provides that mere reference to another agreement does not affect negotiability. If, however, the instrument is made subject to the other agreement, it is rendered nonnegotiable [UCC R3–106(a)(ii); UCC 3–105(2)(a)]. A reference to another agreement is normally inserted for the purpose of keeping a record or giving information to anyone who may be interested. Notes frequently refer to separate agreements that give special rights to a creditor for an acceleration of payment or to a debtor for prepayment. References to these rights do not destroy the negotiability of the instrument.

For example, an instrument states, ''On January 23, 1996, I promise to pay to the order of Koo Ryan $1,000, this note being secured under a security agreement and lien upon my 1995 Chevy Caprice, noted upon the title certificate thereof, [signed] Henry Winn.'' This instrument is negotiable. A statement that an instrument's payment is secured by collateral will not render an otherwise negotiable instrument nonnegotiable [UCC R3–104(a)(3)(i); UCC R3–106(b)(i); UCC 3–112(1)(b)]. In fact, this statement adds to the salability and marketability of the instrument.

Federal Trade Commission Rule 433 requires a statement in a consumer credit note to the effect that a holder or transferee of the note takes it subject to whatever claims or defenses the consumer can assert against the original payee.[7] UCC R3–106(d) provides that such a statement does not make a note conditional, and thus the note is negotiable. (Such a statement does make it impossible, however, for there to be a *holder in due course* of the note [UCC R3–106(d); see also UCC R3–302(g)]. A holder in due course is a holder who acquires special status. Holders in due course and this rule are discussed more fully in Chapter 27.)

*Payments out of a Particular Fund.* UCC R3–106(b)(ii) states that if the terms of an instrument provide that payment can be made only out of a particular fund or source, such terms will not render the instrument conditional—it remains negotiable.[8] Revised Article 3 allows market forces

_____

7.  16 C.F.R. Section 433.2.
8.  Under UCC 3–105(2)(b), the opposite was true. An instrument with a term providing that payment could be made only out of a particular fund or source rendered the instrument nonnegotiable.

to determine whether the instrument will be marketable. A note dated March 3, 1995, for example, reads, "Gilbert Corporation promises to pay to the order of the *Miami Herald* $1,500 on demand; payment of said obligation is restricted to payment from accounts receivable." In this case, payment is restricted to one particular source—accounts receivable. Although the instrument is negotiable, the *Miami Herald* may find it commercially unacceptable, in which case the *Herald* should refuse to take the note.

*Secured by a Mortgage.* A simple statement in an otherwise negotiable note indicating that the note is secured by a mortgage does not destroy its negotiability [UCC R3–106(b)(i); UCC 3–105(1)(c)]. Actually, such a statement might make the note even more acceptable in commerce. Realize, though, that the statement that a note is secured by a mortgage must not stipulate that the maker's promise to pay is *subject* to the terms and conditions of the mortgage [UCC R3–106(a)(ii); UCC 3–105(2)(a)]. The following case illustrates this point.

---

| | |
|---|---|
| **CASE 26.1**<br><br>**HOLLY HILL ACRES,<br>LTD. v. CHARTER<br>BANK OF<br>GAINESVILLE**<br><br>District Court of Appeal of<br>Florida, Second District, 1975.<br>314 So.2d 209.<br><br> | **BACKGROUND AND FACTS**   *Holly Hill Acres, Ltd., was the maker of a promissory note that named Rogers and Blythe as payees. Holly Hill Acres gave the note to Rogers and Blythe as payment for certain property, and Rogers and Blythe retained a mortgage (lien) on the property. [This type of mortgage is known as a* purchase money mortgage.*] The note stated in part: "This note is secured by a mortgage on real estate. \* \* \* The terms of said mortgage are by this reference made part hereof." Subsequently, Rogers and Blythe assigned the promissory note and the mortgage to Charter Bank of Gainesville. Holly Hill Acres defaulted on the note, and when the bank sued to recover, Holly Hill Acres claimed that Rogers and Blythe had fraudulently induced the company to purchase the land. Holly Hill Acres refused to pay on the note. The bank argued that it was a special type of assignee called a holder in due course[a] because the promissory note was a negotiable instrument. This being so, the bank claimed an unhampered right to recover on the note despite any underlying disputes between Holly Hill Acres and Rogers and Blythe. (A holder in due course takes a negotiable instrument free of most defenses to payment on it. This is the rule only when a negotiable instrument is involved.) The trial court held that the promissory note was negotiable and that the bank, as a holder in due course, could recover. Holly Hill Acres appealed, claiming that because the note was made subject to the mortgage agreement, the note was rendered nonnegotiable.* |

a.   A holder in due course is a holder who acquires special status by taking an instrument in good faith, among other things. See Chapter 27.

*SCHEB,* Judge.

\* \* \* \*

The note having incorporated the terms of the purchase money mortgage was not negotiable. The appellee Bank was not a holder in due course, therefore, the appellant was entitled to raise against the appellee any defenses which could be raised between the appellant and Rogers and Blythe. Since appellant asserted an affirmative defense of fraud, it was incumbent on the appellee to establish the non-existence of any genuine issue of any material fact or the legal insufficiency of appellant's affirmative defense. Having failed to do so, appellee was not entitled to a judgment as a matter of law; hence, we reverse.

\* \* \* \*

\* \* \* Mere reference to a note being secured by a mortgage is a common commercial practice and such reference in itself does not impede the negotiability of the note. There is, however, a significant difference in a note stating that it is "secured by a mortgage" from one which provides, "the terms of said mortgage are by this reference made a part hereof." In the former instance the note merely refers to a separate agreement which does not impede its negotiability, *while in the latter instance the note is rendered non-negotiable* [emphasis added].

*The appellate court reversed the trial court's decision and held the note to be nonnegotiable. The case was remanded for trial.*

**DECISION AND REMEDY**

## A FIXED AMOUNT OF MONEY

Negotiable instruments must state with certainty a fixed amount of money to be paid at any time the instrument is payable, a requirement that promises clarity and certainty in determining the value of the instrument [UCC R3–104(a); UCC 3–104(1)(b)].[9] Any promise to pay an amount to be determined in the future is risky, because the value of money (purchasing power) fluctuates. The present value, however, of such an instrument can be estimated with a reasonable degree of accuracy by financial experts. Also, if the instrument's value were stated in terms of goods or services, it would be too difficult to ascertain the market value of those goods and services at the time the instrument was to be paid.

The UCC mandates that negotiable instruments be paid wholly in money. A promissory note that provides for payment in diamonds, or in one thousand hours of services, would not be payable in money and thus would be nonnegotiable.

**FIXED AMOUNT**  The term *fixed amount* means an amount that is ascertainable from the instrument. A demand note payable with 12 percent interest,

for example, meets the requirement of fixed amount because its amount can be determined at the time it is payable [UCC R3–104(a); UCC 3–106(1)]. The amount or rate of interest may be determined with reference to information that is not contained in the instrument but that is readily ascertainable by reference to a formula or a source described in the instrument [UCC R3–112(b)].[10] For example, when an instrument is payable at the *legal rate of interest* (a rate of interest fixed by statute), at a *judgment rate of interest* (a rate of interest fixed by statute that is applied to a monetary judgment awarded by a court until the judgment is paid or terminated), or as fixed by state law, the instrument is negotiable.

Mortgage notes tied to a variable rate of interest (fluctuating as a result of market conditions) have become popular because lenders are protected when rates rise and borrowers benefit when rates decline. Under the revised Article 3, a variable-rate note can be negotiable. The requirement that to be negotiable a writing must contain a promise or order to pay a fixed amount applies only to the principal [UCC R3–104; UCC 3–112]. The interest, however, may be stated as a variable amount [UCC

---

9.  Under UCC 3–104(1)(b), the amount to be paid was called a *sum certain.*

10.  This was not possible under UCC 3–106, which required that an amount or rate of interest could be determined only from the instrument without reference to any outside source.

R3–112(b)].[11] In the following case, which was decided before the widespread adoption of the 1990 revision of Article 3, the court discusses the reasons for accepting variable-rate notes as negotiable.

---

11. Under UCC 3–106(1), the sum was not rendered uncertain if it was to be paid: "(a) with stated interest or by stated installments; or (b) with stated different rates of interests before and after default or a specified date; or (c) with a stated discount or addition if paid before or after the date fixed for payment; or (d) with exchange or less exchange, whether at a fixed rate or at the current rate; or (e) with costs of collections or an attorney's fee or both upon default."

---

CASE 26.2

**GOSS v. TRINITY SAVINGS & LOAN ASSOCIATION**

Supreme Court of Oklahoma, 1991.
813 P.2d 492.

**BACKGROUND AND FACTS**   *In May 1982, Earl and Cheryl Goss obtained a loan from Trinity Savings & Loan Association to purchase a new home. The loan was an adjustable-rate mortgage with the interest rate tied to an outside source (the rate of interest on U.S. Treasury securities). Under the note, monthly payments were payable at one interest rate while the loan accrued at another rate, with the difference being made up in graduated payments over the life of the loan. When Trinity attempted to sell the note to the Federal National Mortgage Association (FNMA), the note showed the accrual rate of interest as 12.5 percent. Trinity claimed that "12.5" was a mistake—that the Gosses had actually agreed to 16.5 percent. The note was changed, and the FNMA bought it. When the Gosses learned that the note had been changed, they filed a lawsuit against Trinity and the FNMA, claiming that they had not authorized the change. The trial court ruled in the Gosses' favor, the appellate court affirmed the ruling, and the FNMA and Trinity appealed to the state's highest court. One of the issues was whether the note was a negotiable instrument in light of the fact that its interest rate was tied to the Treasury securities' interest rate.*

*LAVENDER, Justice.*
        *    *    *    *

        *    *    * [UCC] 1–102   *    *    * provides in part that:
        (1) This act shall be liberally construed and applied to promote its underlying purposes and policies. (2) Underlying purposes and policies of this act are *    *    * to permit the continued expansion of commercial practices through custom, usage and agreement of the parties *    *    *.

        If the intent of the Code was to aid in the continued expansion of commercial practices, then common sense would tell us that when faced with a widespread commercial practice, such as in the present case, this court should acknowledge it. The rule requiring certainty in commercial paper was a rule of commerce before it was a rule of law. It requires commercial, not mathematical, certainty. *An uncertainty which does not impair the function of negotiable instruments in the judgment of business men ought not to be regarded by the courts* *    *    * [emphasis added].

        Adjustable interest rates are being routinely used in the commercial marketplace. "Since 1980, VRN's [variable-rate notes] have become increasingly popular. For example, in 1984 approximately 80 percent of new mortgages and 60 percent of all mortgages had variable rates." *    *    *

        *    *    * Any stranger to the transaction under the present set of facts would not have been disadvantaged by the terms of the note, since the rate on the note could easily have been determined by making a simple phone call to check on the [Treasury securities' interest] rate or [by referring] to a published listing.

**DECISION AND REMEDY**   *The Supreme Court of Oklahoma concluded that a note is negotiable when the interest rate is readily obtainable from a published source.*

**International Law for Negotiable Instruments** *There is an ongoing effort to make international law consistent for negotiable instruments. This effort has led to the rules of the United Nations Convention on International Bills of Exchange and International Promissory Notes (CIBN). Application of the CIBN gives assurances about negotiability. Unlike most national laws, the CIBN considers an instrument with a variable interest rate to be negotiable.*

**INTERNATIONAL CONSIDERATIONS**

**PAYABLE IN MONEY** A fixed amount is to be payable in money [UCC R3–104(a)(3); UCC 3–104(1)(b)]. The UCC defines money as "a medium of exchange authorized or adopted by a domestic or foreign government as a part of its currency" [UCC 1–201(24)].

Suppose that the maker of a note promises "to pay on demand $1,000 in U.S. gold." Because gold is not a medium of exchange adopted by the U.S. government, the note is not payable in money. The same result would occur if the maker promises "to pay $1,000 and fifty liters of 1964 Chateau Lafite-Rothschild wine," as the instrument is not payable *entirely* in money.

The statement "Payable in $1,000 U.S. currency or an equivalent value in gold" would render the instrument nonnegotiable if the maker reserved the option of paying in money or gold. If the option were left to the payee, some legal scholars argue that the instrument would be negotiable.

If an instrument is payable in a foreign currency, the revised UCC has a special provision. Any instrument payable in the United States with a face amount stated in a foreign currency can be paid in the equivalent in U.S. dollars "calculated by using the current bank-offered spot rate at the place of payment for the purchase of dollars on the day on which the instrument is paid" or be paid in the foreign money [UCC R3–107].

To summarize, only instruments payable in money are negotiable. An instrument payable in government bonds or in shares of Microsoft stock is not negotiable, because neither is a medium of exchange recognized by the U.S. government.

## PAYABLE ON DEMAND OR AT A DEFINITE TIME

A negotiable instrument must "be payable on demand or at a definite time" [UCC R3–104(a)(2); UCC 3–104(1)(c)]. Clearly, to ascertain the value of a negotiable instrument, it is necessary to know when the maker, drawee, or acceptor is required to pay. It is also necessary to know when the obligations of secondary parties will arise. Furthermore, it is necessary to know when an instrument is due in order to calculate when the statute of limitations may apply [UCC R3–118(a)]. Finally, with an interest-bearing instrument, it is necessary to know the exact interval during which the interest will accrue to determine the present value of the instrument.

**PAYABLE ON DEMAND** Instruments that are payable on demand include those that contain the words "Payable at sight" or "Payable upon demand" and those that say nothing about when payment is due. The very nature of the instrument may indicate that it is payable on demand. For example, a check, by definition, is payable on demand [UCC R3–104(f); UCC 3–104(2)(b)]. If no time for payment is specified, and if the person responsible for payment must pay when the instrument is presented (for example, when the holder of a check asks the drawee bank to cash it), then the instrument is payable on demand [UCC R3–108(a); UCC 3–108].

**PAYABLE AT A DEFINITE TIME** If an instrument is not payable on demand, to be negotiable it must be payable at a definite time specified on the face of the instrument. The maker or drawee is under no obligation to pay until the specified time. A "promise or order is 'payable at a definite time' if it is payable on elapse of a definite period of time after sight or acceptance or at a fixed date or dates or at a time or times readily ascertainable at the time the promise or order is issued, subject to rights of (i) prepayment, (ii) acceleration, (iii) extension at the option of the holder, or (iv) extension to a further definite time at the option of the maker or acceptor or automatically upon or after a specified act or event" [UCC R3–108(b); UCC 3–109].

An instrument dated February 1, 1995, states, "One year after the death of my grandfather, James Ezersky, I promise to pay to the order of Henry

Ling $500. [Signed] Mary Ezersky." This instrument is nonnegotiable. Because the date of the grandfather's death is uncertain, the maturity date is uncertain, even though the event is bound to occur. Even if the grandfather has already died, the note does not specify the time for payment.

When an instrument is payable on or before a stated date, it is clearly payable at a definite time, although the maker has the option of paying before the stated maturity date. This uncertainty does not violate the definite time requirement. Suppose Juan gives Ernesto an instrument dated February 1, 1995, that indicates on its face that it is payable on or before February 1, 1996. This instrument satisfies the requirement. In contrast, an instrument that is undated and made payable "one month after date" is clearly nonnegotiable. There is no way to determine the maturity date from the face of the instrument.

Drafts stating that they are payable within a fixed period after sight are considered payable at a definite time [UCC R3–108(b); UCC 3–109(1)(b)]. The term *sight* means the moment that the draft is presented by the holder for payment or for acceptance by the drawee. The UCC further states that instruments may be required to be presented for acceptance to the drawee to determine the maturity date [UCC R3–501(a); UCC 3–501(1)(a)]. Presenting an instrument to the drawee for acceptance establishes the sight and the time period, which run from the date the instrument is presented.

ACCELERATION CLAUSE   An **acceleration clause** allows a payee or other holder of a time instrument to demand payment of the entire amount due, with interest, if a certain event occurs, such as a default in payment of an installment when due. There must be, of course, a good faith belief that payment will not be made for an acceleration clause to be invoked.

Under the UCC, instruments that include acceleration clauses are negotiable because (1) the exact value of the instrument can be ascertained and (2) the instrument will be payable on a fixed date if the event allowing acceleration does not occur [UCC R3–108(b)(ii); UCC 3–109(1)(c)]. Thus, the fixed date is the outside limit used to determine the value of the instrument.

Furthermore, the payee or holder cannot accelerate the instrument even if it contains an ac-

celeration clause unless it is done in good faith. UCC 1–208 indicates that the acceleration clause "shall be construed to mean that [the holder of the instrument] shall have power to [accelerate] only if he [or she] in good faith believes that the prospect of payment or performance is impaired." But the burden of proving a *lack* of good faith is on the borrower—the maker of the note.

EXTENSION CLAUSE   The reverse of an acceleration clause is an **extension clause,** which allows the date of maturity to be extended into the future [UCC R3–108(b)(iii), (iv); UCC 3–109(1)(d)]. To keep the instrument negotiable, the interval of the extension must be specified if the right to extend is given to the maker of the instrument. If, however, the holder of the instrument can extend it, the maturity date does not have to be specified.

Suppose a note reads, "The maker [obligor] has the right to postpone the time of payment of this note beyond its definite maturity date of January 1, 1997. This extension, however, shall be for no more than a reasonable time." A note with this language is not negotiable, because it does not satisfy the definite-time requirement. The right to extend is the maker's, and the maker has not indicated when the note will become due after the extension.

In contrast, if a note reads, "The holder of this note at the date of maturity, January 1, 1997, can extend the time of payment indefinitely," it is a negotiable instrument. The length of the extension does not have to be specified, because the option to extend is solely that of the holder. After January 1, 1997, the note is, in effect, a demand instrument.

## PAYABLE TO ORDER OR TO BEARER

Because one of the functions of a negotiable instrument is to serve as a substitute for money, freedom to transfer is an essential requirement. To assure a proper transfer, the instrument must be "payable to order or to bearer" at the time it is issued or first comes into the possession of the holder [UCC R3–104(a)(1); UCC 3–104(1)(d)]. These words indicate that at the time of issuance, it is expected that future unknown persons—not just the immediate party—will eventually be the owners. If an instrument is neither order nor bearer paper, the instrument is nonnegotiable and therefore only assignable and governed by contract law. Under the revised Article 3, however, a check that meets all other requirements for negotiability is a negotiable instrument even if the words "to the order of" or "bearer" are missing [UCC R3–104(c)].

### ORDER INSTRUMENTS

An instrument that is a "promise or order that is not payable to bearer is payable to order if it is payable (i) to the order of an identified person or (ii) to *an identified person or order*" [emphasis added] [UCC R3–109(b); UCC 3–110(1)].

The purpose of order paper is to allow the maker or drawer to transfer the instrument to a specific, identified person.[12] The identified person is the one "to whom the instrument is initially payable [as] determined by the intent" of the maker or drawer [UCC R3–110(a)].[13] This in turn allows that person to transfer the instrument to whomever he or she wishes. Thus, the maker or drawer is agreeing to pay either the person specified or whomever that person might designate. In this way, the instrument retains its transferability.

Suppose an instrument states, "Payable to the order of James Jarrot" or "Pay to James Jarrot or order." Clearly, the maker or drawer has indicated that a payment will be made to Jarrot or to whomever Jarrot designates. The instrument is negotiable. If, however, the instrument states, "Payable to James Jarrot" or "Pay to James Jarrot only," the instrument loses its negotiability. The maker or drawer indicates that only Jarrot will be paid. (An instrument that is *indorsed* in such a manner, however, does not lose its negotiability, as will be discussed later in this chapter.)

In addition, except for bearer paper (explained in the following paragraph), the person specified must be identified with certainty, because the transfer of an order instrument requires an **indorsement** [UCC R3–201(b)].[14] (An indorsement is a signature placed on an instrument, such as on the back of a check, for the purpose of transferring one's ownership rights in the instrument.) If an instrument states, "Payable to the order of my kissing cousin," the instrument is nonnegotiable, as a holder could not be sure which cousin was intended to indorse and properly transfer the instrument.

### BEARER INSTRUMENTS

A **bearer instrument** is an instrument that does not designate a specific payee [UCC R3–109(a); UCC 3–111]. The term **bearer** refers to a person in possession of an instrument that is payable to bearer, is not payable to an identified person, does not state a payee, or is indorsed in blank (with a signature only, as will be discussed shortly) [UCC 1–201(5); UCC R3–109(a), (c)]. The maker or drawer of a bearer instrument agrees to pay anyone who presents the instrument for payment, and complete transferability is implied.

Any instrument containing the following terms is a bearer instrument:

- "Payable to the order of bearer."
- "Payable to James Jarrot or bearer."
- "Payable to bearer."
- "Pay cash."
- "Pay to the order of cash."

When an instrument "indicates that it is not payable to an identified person," it is bearer paper [UCC R3–109(a)(3)].[15] Thus, an instrument that is "payable to X" can be negotiated as bearer paper, as though it were payable to cash. An instrument "payable to the order of the Multimedia Company," however, when no such company exists, would not be bearer paper, because the UCC does not accept an instrument issued to a nonexistent organization as payable to bearer [UCC R3–109, Comment 3].

Suppose an instrument is made payable both to order and to bearer. If the bearer words are handwritten or typewritten, the instrument is a bearer instrument. But if the bearer words are in a preprinted form, it is an order instrument [UCC R3–114; UCC 3–110(3)].

---

12. "An instrument payable to bearer may become payable to an identified person if it is specially indorsed pursuant to [UCC R3–205(a)]. An instrument payable to an identified person may become payable to bearer if it is indorsed in blank [specifies no particular indorsee, as is discussed later in this chapter] pursuant to [UCC R3–205(b)]" [UCC R3–109(c)].
13. The name indicated on the instrument need not be the actual name of the person signing, as long as the person signing the instrument was the one intended by the maker.
14. Because the UCC uses the spelling *indorse* (*indorsement*, etc.), rather than *endorse* (and so on), we adopt that spelling here and in other chapters in the text.

---

15. UCC 3–111(c) includes "any other indication which does not purport to designate a specific payee."

# FACTORS NOT AFFECTING NEGOTIABILITY

Certain ambiguities or omissions will not affect the negotiability of an instrument. Article 3 provides rules for clearing up ambiguous terms. Some of these rules follow:

1. The promise or power to maintain or protect collateral or to give additional collateral will not affect negotiability [UCC R3–104(a)(3)(i); UCC R3–106(b)(i); UCC 3–112(c)].

2. Unless the date of an instrument is necessary to determine a definite time for payment, the fact that an instrument is undated does not affect its negotiability. A typical example is an undated check [UCC R3–113(b); UCC 3–114(1)].

3. Postdating or antedating an instrument does not affect negotiability [UCC R3–113(a); UCC 3–114(1)].

4. When there is no place of payment indicated on the instrument, it is payable at the address of the drawee or the maker stated in the instrument. If there is no address stated, then it is payable at the drawee's or maker's place of business. If the drawee or maker has no place of business, then it is payable at the drawee's or maker's residence [UCC R3–111].

5. Words that are typewritten prevail over those that are printed (forms), whereas handwritten words prevail over both [UCC R3–114; UCC 3–118(b)]. For example, if your check is printed (form), "Pay to the order of," and in handwriting you insert in the blank, "Susan Goetz or bearer," the check is a bearer instrument. An instrument reading "Pay to the order of Susan Goetz or bearer" is payable to order if it is entirely typewritten. If the "or bearer" segment is handwritten, however, the paper is a bearer instrument.

6. When interpreting an instrument with contradictory language as to the amount to be paid, the amount stated by words prevails over contradictory numbers. This is important when the numerical amount and written amount on a check differ [UCC R3–114].[16]

7. When a particular interest rate is intended to be paid but is not specified, such as when the instrument simply states "with interest," the interest rate is the judgment rate of interest (a rate provided by law to be paid on a judgment until the judgment is paid) [UCC R3–112(b); UCC 3–118(d)].

8. A notation on a check that it is "nonnegotiable" or "not governed by Article 3" has no effect on a check's negotiability. Any other instrument, however, even if it meets all of the requirements of negotiability, can be made nonnegotiable by the maker's or drawer's conspicuously noting on it that it is "nonnegotiable" or "not governed by Article 3" [UCC R3–104(d)].[17]

# TRANSFER BY ASSIGNMENT OR NEGOTIATION

Once issued, a negotiable instrument can be transferred by *assignment* or by *negotiation.*

## TRANSFER BY ASSIGNMENT

Recall from Chapter 17 that an assignment is a transfer of rights under a contract. Under general contract principles, a transfer by assignment to an assignee gives the assignee only those rights that the assignor possessed [UCC R3–203(b); UCC 3–201(1)]. Any defenses that can be raised against an assignor can normally be raised against the assignee. Article 3 applies only to negotiable instruments; obviously, there can be no negotiation of a nonnegotiable instrument. Furthermore, when a transfer fails to qualify as a negotiation, it becomes an assignment. The transferee is then an *assignee* rather than a *holder.*

## TRANSFER BY NEGOTIATION

**Negotiation** is the transfer of an instrument in such form that the transferee (the person to whom the instrument is transferred) becomes a holder [UCC R3–201(a); UCC 3–202(1)]. Under UCC principles, a transfer by negotiation creates a holder who,

---

16. UCC 3–118(c) states that words outweigh figures unless the words are "ambiguous."

17. This is not true under the unrevised Article 3.

# ■ CONCEPT SUMMARY 26.1 Requirements for Negotiability

| REQUIREMENTS | BASIC RULES |
|---|---|
| **Must Be in Writing[a]**<br>UCC R3–103(6), (9) | 1. A writing can be on anything that is readily transferable and that has a degree of permanence. [See also UCC 1–201(46).] |
| **Must Be Signed by the Maker or Drawer[b]**<br>UCC R3–103(a)(3), (5)<br>UCC R3–401(b)<br>UCC 1–201(39)<br>UCC R3–402 | 1. The signature can be any place on the instrument.<br>2. It can be in any form (such as a word, mark, or rubber stamp) that purports to be a signature and authenticates the writing.<br>3. It can be signed in a representative capacity. |
| **Must Be a Definite Promise or Order[c]**<br>UCC R3–104(a) | 1. A promise must be more than a mere acknowledgment of a debt.<br>2. The words "I/We promise" or "Pay" meet this criterion. |
| **Must Be Unconditional[d]**<br>UCC R3–106<br>UCC R3–103(a)(6), (9) | 1. Payment cannot be expressly conditional on the occurrence of an event.<br>2. Payment cannot be made subject to or governed by another agreement. |
| **Must Be an Order or Promise to Pay a Fixed Amount[e]**<br>UCC R3–104(a)<br>UCC R3–112(b) | 1. An instrument may state a fixed sum even if payable in installments, with fixed or variable rates of interest, at a stated discount, or at an exchange rate. |
| **Must Be Payable in Money[f]**<br>UCC R3–104(a)(3)<br>UCC R3–107 | 1. Any medium of exchange recognized as the currency of a government is money.<br>2. The maker or drawer cannot retain the option to pay the instrument in money *or* something else. |
| **Must Be Payable on Demand or at a Definite Time[g]**<br>UCC R3–104(a)(2)<br>UCC R3–108(a), (b) | 1. Any instrument that is payable on sight, presentation, or issue or that does not state any time for payment is a demand instrument.<br>2. An instrument is still payable at a definite time, even though it is payable on or before a stated date or within a fixed period after sight, or the drawer or maker has an option to extend time for a definite period.<br>3. Acceleration clauses, even if unenforceable, do not affect the negotiability of the instrument. |
| **Must Be Payable to Order or Bearer[h]**<br>UCC R3–104(c)<br>UCC R3–109<br>UCC R3–110(a) | 1. An order instrument must identify the payee with reasonable certainty.<br>2. An instrument whose terms intend payment to no particular person is payable to bearer.<br>3. Not a requirement for checks. |

a. UCC 3–104(1).
b. UCC 3–104(1)(a); UCC 3–401(2); UCC 3–403(1).
c. UCC 3–104(1)(b).
d. UCC 3–104(1)(b); UCC 3–105.

e. UCC 3–104(1)(b); UCC 3–106(1).
f. UCC 3–104(1)(b); UCC 3–107.
g. UCC 3–104(1)(c); UCC 3–108; UCC 3–109.
h. UCC 3–104(1)(d); UCC 3–110; UCC 3–111.

at the very least, receives the rights of the previous possessor [UCC R3–105(a); UCC 3–201(1)]. Unlike an assignment, a transfer by negotiation can make it possible for a holder to receive more rights in the instrument than the prior possessor had [UCC R3–203(b); UCC R3–305; UCC R3–306; UCC 3–305; UCC 3–306]. (A holder who receives greater rights is known as a *holder in due course,* discussed in Chapter 27.) There are two methods of negotiating an instrument so that the receiver becomes a holder. The method used depends on whether the instrument is order paper or bearer paper.

**NEGOTIATING ORDER PAPER** *Order paper* contains the name of a payee capable of indorsing, as in ''Pay to the order of Elliot Goodseal.'' Order paper is also paper that has as its last or only indorsement a *special* indorsement, as in ''Pay to Goodseal. [Signed] Johnson.'' (Special indorsements are discussed in more detail later in this chapter.) If the instrument is order paper, it is negotiated by delivery with any necessary indorsements. For example, the Carrington Corporation issues a payroll check ''to the order of Elliot Goodseal.'' Goodseal takes the check to the supermarket, signs his name on the back (an indorsement), gives it to the cashier (a delivery), and receives cash. Goodseal has negotiated the check to the supermarket [UCC R3–201(b); UCC 3–202(1)].

**NEGOTIATING BEARER PAPER** If an instrument is payable to bearer, it is negotiated by delivery—that is, by transfer into another person's possession. Indorsement is not necessary [UCC R3–201(b); UCC 3–202(1)]. The use of *bearer paper* involves more risk through loss or theft than the use of order paper.

Assume Alan Tyson writes a check ''Payable to cash'' and hands it to Blaine Parrington (a delivery). Tyson has issued the check (a bearer instrument) to Parrington. Parrington places the check in his wallet, which is subsequently stolen. The thief has possession of the check. At this point negotiation has not occurred, because delivery must be voluntary on the part of the transferor. If the thief ''delivers'' the check to an innocent third person, however, negotiation will be complete. All rights to the check will be passed *absolutely* to that third person, and Parrrington will lose all right to recover the proceeds of the check from that person [UCC R3–306; UCC 3–306]. Of course, Parrington can recover his money from the thief if the thief can be found.

**CONVERTING ORDER PAPER TO BEARER PAPER AND VICE VERSA** The method used for negotiation depends on the character of the instrument at the time the negotiation takes place. For example, a check originally payable to ''cash'' but subsequently indorsed with the words ''Pay to Ernestine'' must be negotiated as order paper (by indorsement and delivery) even though it was previously bearer paper [UCC R3–205(a); UCC 3–204(1)].

An instrument payable to the order of a named payee and indorsed in blank (by the holder's signature only, as will be discussed subsequently) becomes a bearer instrument [UCC R3–205(b); UCC 3–204(2)]. To illustrate, a check made payable to the order of Ernestine Parish is issued to Ernestine, and Ernestine indorses it by signing her name on the back. The instrument can now be negotiated by delivery without indorsement. Ernestine can negotiate the check to whomever she wishes by delivery, and that person in turn can negotiate by delivery without indorsement.

How indorsements can convert order paper to bearer paper and vice versa is illustrated in Exhibit 26–6.

## SECTION 7

# INDORSEMENTS

Indorsements are required whenever the instrument being negotiated is classified as an order instrument. (Many transferees of bearer paper require indorsement for identification purposes, even though the UCC does not require it.) An *indorsement* is a signature with or without additional words or statements. It is most often written on the back of the instrument itself. If there is no room on the instrument, indorsements can be written on a separate piece of paper called an **allonge.** The allonge must be ''affixed to the instrument'' to become a ''part of the instrument'' [UCC R3–204(a); UCC 3–202(2)]. Pins or paper clips will not suffice. Some courts hold that staples are sufficient.

A person who transfers a note or a draft by signing (indorsing) it and delivering it to another person is an **indorser.** For example, Tsing receives a graduation check for $100. She can transfer the check to her mother (or to anyone) by signing it on the back. Tsing is an indorser. If Tsing indorses the check by writing ''Pay to Aretha Parks,'' Aretha Parks is the **indorsee.**

One purpose of an indorsement is to effect the negotiation of order paper. Sometimes the transferee of bearer paper will request the holder-transferor to indorse the instrument. This is done to impose liability on the indorser. The liability of indorsers will be discussed in Chapter 28.

■ **Exhibit 26–6 Converting Order Paper to Bearer Paper and Vice Versa**

A check made payable to the order of Ernestine Parish is issued to Ernestine, who indorses it by signing her name on the back. This indorsement converts the check from order paper to bearer paper. The check is negotiated by delivery to Linda Cunningham, who negotiates it with a special indorsement. This indorsement converts the check back into order paper.

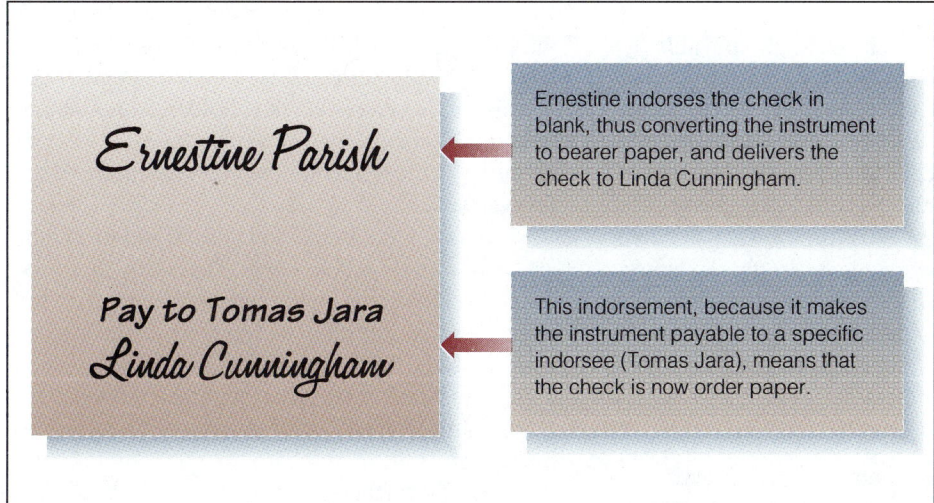

> *Ernestine Parish*
>
> Ernestine indorses the check in blank, thus converting the instrument to bearer paper, and delivers the check to Linda Cunningham.
>
> *Pay to Tomas Jara*
> *Linda Cunningham*
>
> This indorsement, because it makes the instrument payable to a specific indorsee (Tomas Jara), means that the check is now order paper.

Once an instrument qualifies as a negotiable instrument, the form of indorsement will have no effect on the character of the underlying instrument. Indorsement relates to the right of the holder to negotiate the paper and the manner in which it must be done.

## TYPES OF INDORSEMENTS

We will examine four categories of indorsements: blank, special, qualified, and restrictive.

**BLANK INDORSEMENTS** A **blank indorsement** specifies no particular indorsee and can consist of a mere signature [UCC R3–205(b); UCC 3–204(2)]. Hence, a check payable "to the order of Mark Deitsch" can be indorsed in blank simply by having Deitsch's signature written on the back of the check. Exhibit 26–7 shows a blank indorsement.

■ **Exhibit 26–7 A Blank Indorsement**

> *Mark Deitsch*

An instrument payable to order and indorsed in blank becomes payable to bearer and can be negotiated by delivery alone [UCC R3–205(b); UCC 3–204(2)]. In other words, a blank indorsement converts an order instrument to a bearer instrument, which anybody can cash. If Rita Chou indorses in blank a check payable to her order and then loses it on the street, Coker can find it and sell it to Duncan for value without indorsing it. This constitutes a negotiation, because Coker has made delivery of a bearer instrument (which was an order instrument until it was indorsed in blank).

**SPECIAL INDORSEMENTS** A **special indorsement** indicates the identified person to whom the indorser intends to make the instrument payable; that is, it names the indorsee [UCC R3–205(a); UCC 3–204(1)]. No special words of negotiation are needed. Words such as "Pay to the order of Clay" or "Pay to Clay" followed by the signature of the indorser are sufficient. When an instrument is indorsed in this way, it is order paper. Had the words "Pay to Clay" been used on the face of the instrument to indicate the payee, the instrument would not have been negotiable.

One may convert a blank indorsement to a special indorsement to avoid the risk of loss from theft.

This changes the bearer paper back to order paper. A holder may "convert a blank indorsement that consists only of a signature into a special indorsement by writing, above the signature of the indorser, words identifying the person to whom the instrument is made payable" [UCC R3–205(c); UCC 3–204(2)].

For example, a check is made payable to Jefferson Jones. He indorses his name by blank indorsement on the back of the check and negotiates the check to William Hsu. William, not wishing to cash the check immediately, wants to avoid any risk should he lose the check. He therefore writes "Pay to William Hsu" above Jefferson's blank indorsement. In this manner, William has converted Jefferson's blank indorsement into a special indorsement. Further negotiation now requires William Hsu's indorsement plus delivery. (See Exhibit 26–8.)

■ **Exhibit 26–8 A Special Indorsement**

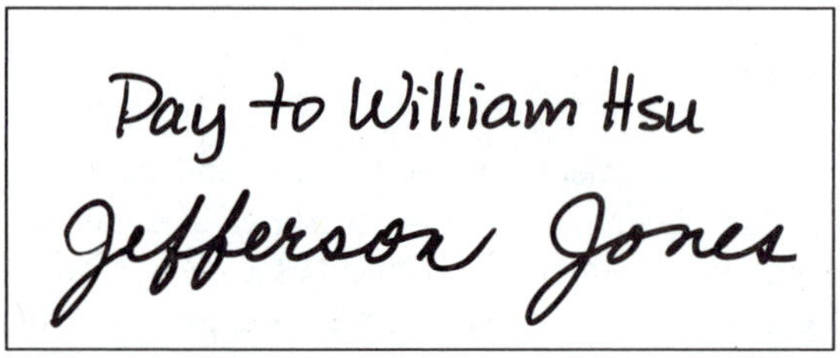

*Pay to William Hsu*

*Jefferson Jones*

**QUALIFIED INDORSEMENTS** Generally, an indorser, *merely by indorsing,* impliedly promises to pay the holder, or any subsequent indorser, the amount of the instrument in the event that the drawer or maker defaults on the payment [UCC R3–415(b); UCC 3–414(1)]. A **qualified indorsement** is used by an indorser to disclaim or limit this contract liability on the instrument. In this form of indorsement, the notation "without recourse" is commonly used. A sample of such an indorsement is shown in Exhibit 26–9.

■ **Exhibit 26–9 A Qualified Indorsement**

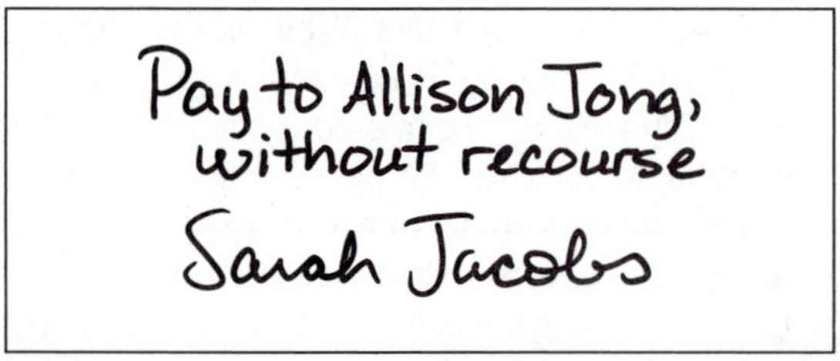

*Pay to Allison Jong, without recourse*

*Sarah Jacobs*

Qualified indorsements are often used by persons acting in a representative capacity. For instance, insurance agents sometimes receive checks payable to them that are really intended as payment to the insurance company. The agent is merely indorsing the payment through to the insurance company and should not be required to make good on the check if it is later dishonored. The "without recourse" indorsement absolves the agent. If the instrument is dishonored, the holder cannot obtain recovery from the agent who indorsed "without recourse" unless the indorser has breached a transfer warranty.[18]

Usually, then, blank and special indorsements are *unqualified indorsements.* That is, the blank or special indorser is guaranteeing payment of the instrument in addition to transferring title to it. The qualified indorser is not guaranteeing such payment. Nonetheless, the qualified indorsement ("without recourse") still transfers title to the indorsee; an instrument bearing a qualified indorsement can be further negotiated.

A qualified indorsement is accompanied by either a special or a blank indorsement that determines further negotiation. Accordingly, a special qualified indorsement makes the instrument an order instrument, and it requires an indorsement plus delivery for negotiation. A blank qualified indorsement makes the instrument a bearer instrument, and only delivery is required for negotiation.

Assume that a check is made payable to the order of Sarah Jacobs and that Sarah wants to negotiate the check specifically to Allison Jong with a qualified indorsement. Sarah would indorse the check as follows: "Pay to Allison Jong, without recourse. [Signed] Sarah Jacobs." For Allison to negotiate the check further to Frederick Lee, Allison would have to indorse and deliver the check to Frederick.

**RESTRICTIVE INDORSEMENTS** A **restrictive indorsement** does not prohibit the further negotiation of an instrument. Article 3 provides as follows: "An indorsement limiting payment to a particular person or otherwise prohibiting further transfer or negotiation of the instrument is not

---

18. Transfer warranties apply to all indorsers and nonindorsers [UCC R3–416; UCC 3–417(2), (3)]. These warranties, discussed in Chapter 28, relate to good title, authorized signature, no material alteration, and so forth.

effective to prevent further transfer or negotiation of the instrument'' [UCC R3–206(a); UCC 3–206(1)]. Restrictive indorsements come in many forms. The UCC describes four separate categories, which are discussed here.

*Indorsements Prohibiting Further Indorsement.* An indorsement such as ''Pay to Julie Thrush only. [Signed] Thomas Fasulo'' does not destroy negotiability. Thrush can negotiate the paper to a holder just as if it had read ''Pay to Julie Thrush. [Signed] Thomas Fasulo'' [UCC R3–206(a); UCC 3–206(1)]. This type of restrictive indorsement, which is rarely used, has the same legal effect as a special indorsement, except that Thrush must receive payment before she can be held liable on her indorsement, and a purchaser of the instrument can become a holder in due course.

*Conditional Indorsements.* When payment depends on the occurrence of some event specified in the indorsement (for example, ''Pay to Ernie Smoke if he completes the renovation of my kitchen by June 1, 1997'' ), the instrument has a conditional indorsement. Article 3 states that an indorsement conditioning the right to receive payment ''does not affect the right of the indorsee to enforce the instrument.'' A person paying or taking for value an instrument can disregard the condition without liability [UCC R3–206(b)].[19]

*Indorsements for Deposit or Collection.* A common type of restrictive indorsement is one that makes the indorsee (almost always a bank) a collecting *agent* of the indorser [UCC R3–206(c); UCC 3–206(3)]. Exhibit 26–10 illustrates this type of indorsement on a check payable and issued to Aimee St. Amant. In particular, a ''Pay any bank or banker'' or ''For deposit only'' indorsement has the effect of locking the instrument into the bank collection process. Only a bank can acquire the rights of a holder following this indorsement until the item has been specially indorsed by a bank to a person who is not a bank [UCC R3–206(c); UCC R4–201(b); UCC 3–206(3); UCC 4–201(2)]. A bank's liability for payment of an instrument with

a restrictive indorsement of this kind is discussed in Chapter 29.

■ **Exhibit 26–10 For Deposit/ For Collection Indorsement**

For deposit only
Aimee St. Amant

or

For collection only
Aimee St. Amant

*Trust Indorsements.* Indorsements by persons who are to hold or use the funds for the benefit of the indorser or a third party are called **trust indorsements** (also known as agency indorsements). For example, assume that Ralph Zimmer asks his accountant, Stephanie Contento, to pay some bills for him while he is out of the country. He indorses a check to Stephanie Contento ''as agent for Ralph Zimmer.'' This agency indorsement obligates Contento to use the funds only for the benefit of Zimmer [UCC R3–206(d), (e); UCC 3–206(4)]. Sample trust (agency) indorsements are shown in Exhibit 26–11.

■ **Exhibit 26–11 Trust Indorsements**

Pay to Stephanie Contento
in trust for Roger Zimmer

Ralph Zimmer

or

Pay to Stephanie Contento
as Agent for Ralph Zimmer

Ralph Zimmer

---

19. Under UCC 3–206(3), the indorsement was enforceable (except against intermediary banks, defined in Chapter 29), and neither the indorsee nor any subsequent holder had the right to enforce payment against that indorser on the instrument before the condition was met.

■ CONCEPT SUMMARY 26.2 **Types of Indorsements and Their Consequences**

| WORDS CONSTITUTING THE INDORSEMENT | TYPE OF INDORSEMENT | INDORSER'S SIGNATURE LIABILITY[a] |
|---|---|---|
| "Mark Deitsch" | Blank | Unqualifed signature liability on proper presentment and notice of dishonor.[b] |
| "Pay to William Hsu, Jefferson Jones" | Special | Unqualified signature liability on proper presentment and notice of dishonor. |
| "Without recourse, Sarah Jacobs" | Qualified (blank for further negotiation) | No signature liability. Transfer warranty liability if breach occurs.[c] |
| "Pay to Allison Jong, without recourse, Sarah Jacobs" | Qualified (special for further negotiation) | No signature liability. Transfer warranty liability if breach occurs. |
| "Pay to Julie Thrush only, Thomas Fasulo" | Restrictive—prohibitive (special for further negotiation) | Signature liability only on Julie Thrush's receiving payment. If Thrush receives payment, signature liability on proper presentment and notice of dishonor. |
| "Pay to Ernie Smoke if he completes the renovation of my kitchen by June 1, 1996, Becky Arnold" | Restrictive—conditional (special for further negotiation) | Signature liability, regardless of whether condition is met, on proper presentment and notice of dishonor. |
| "For deposit, Aimee St. Amant" | Restrictive—for deposit (blank for further negotiation) | Signature liability only on St. Amant's having amount deposited in her account. If deposit is made, signature liability on proper presentment and notice of dishonor. |
| "Pay to Stephanie Contento in trust for Roger Zimmer" | Restrictive—trust (special for further negotiation) | Signature liability to original indorsee only on payment to Stephanie Contento for Roger Zimmer's benefit. Regardless of whether restriction is met, signature liability to subsequent indorsers on proper presentment and notice of dishonor. |

a.  Signature liability refers to the liability of a party who signs an instrument. The basic questions include whether there is any liability and, if so, whether it is unqualified or restricted. Signature liability is discussed in more detail in Chapter 28.

b.  When an instrument is dishonored—that is, when, for example, a drawer's bank refuses to cash the drawer's check on proper presentment—an indorser of the check may be liable on it if he or she is given proper notice of dishonor. Dishonor and notice of dishonor are discussed in Chapter 28.

c.  The transferor of an instrument makes certain warranties to the transferee and subsequent holders, and thus, even if the transferor's signature does not render him or her liable on the instrument, he or she may be liable for breach of a transfer warranty. Transfer warranties are discussed in Chapter 28. See also UCC R3–416; UCC 3–417.

The result of a trust indorsement is that legal rights in the instrument are transferred to the original indorsee. To the extent that the original indorsee pays or applies the proceeds consistently with the indorsement (for example, "In trust for Roger Zimmer"), the indorsee is a holder and can

become a holder in due course (described in Chapter 27).

The fiduciary restrictions (restrictions mandated by a relationship involving trust and loyalty) on the instrument do not reach beyond the original indorsee [UCC R3–206(d), (e)]. Any subsequent purchaser can qualify as a holder in due course unless he or she has actual notice that the instrument was negotiated in breach of a fiduciary duty.[20] (Negotiation can be effective even if it is obtained as part of an illegal transaction, but it may be rescinded against a party who does not qualify as a holder in due course [UCC R3–202].)

## MISCELLANEOUS INDORSEMENT PROBLEMS

Of course, a significant problem in relation to indorsements occurs when an indorsement is forged or unauthorized. The UCC rules concerning unauthorized or forged signatures and indorsements will be discussed in Chapter 28 in the context of signature liability and again in Chapter 29 in the context of the bank's liability for payment of an instrument over an unauthorized signature. Here we look at two other problems that may arise with indorsements.

**CORRECTION OF NAME** An indorsement should be identical to the name that appears on the instrument. The payee or indorsee whose name is misspelled can indorse with the misspelled name,

the correct name, or both [UCC R3–204(d); UCC 3–203]. For example, if Marie Ellison receives a check payable to the order of Mary Ellison, she can indorse the check either ''Marie Ellison'' or ''Mary Ellison.'' The usual practice is to indorse the name as it appears on the instrument and follow it by the correct name.[21]

**MULTIPLE PAYEES** An instrument payable to two or more persons *in the alternative* (for example, ''Pay to the order of Ying or Mifflin'') requires the indorsement of only one of the payees [UCC R3–110(d); UCC 3–116(a)]. If, however, an instrument is made payable to two or more persons *jointly* (for example, ''Pay to the order of Bridgette and Tony VanHorn'' or ''Pay to the order of Bridgette VanHorn, Tony VanHorn''), all of the payees' indorsements are necessary for negotiation. If an instrument payable to two or more persons does not clearly indicate whether it is payable in the alternative or payable jointly, then ''the instrument is payable to the persons alternatively'' [UCC R3–110(d)].

The following case raises some interesting questions concerning checks payable to two persons jointly.

---

20. See *In re Quantum Development Corp.,* 397 F.Supp. 329 (D.Virgin Islands 1975).

21. *Watertown Federal Savings and Loan v. Spanks,* 346 Mass. 398, 193 N.E.2d 333 (1963).

---

**COMPANY PROFILE** *One of the major divisions of the General Motors Corporation is the General Motors Acceptance Corporation (GMAC). Created by William Durant, the founder of General Motors (GM) and president of GM before he resigned in 1920, GMAC originally lent money only to buyers of GM vehicles. Over time, however, GMAC became the second largest mortgage banker in the United States. In the 1980s, GMAC was sometimes more profitable than the GM automotive divisions. In 1994, GMAC held outstanding loans worth more than $95 billion. This was more than was held by any commercial bank in the United States except Citicorp.*

**BACKGROUND AND FACTS** *Abington Casualty Insurance Company issued an insurance policy to Robert Azevedo to cover Azevedo's 1984 Jeep. General Motors Acceptance Corporation (GMAC) held a security interest in the vehicle, and the insurance policy named GMAC as the beneficiary. In other words, if the Jeep was damaged and a claim submitted, Abington was to pay GMAC for the amount of appraised damages. The Jeep was later damaged, and Abington appraised the loss and issued a check payable jointly ''to the order of Robert A. Azevedo and G.M.A.C.'' The check was delivered to Azevedo, who then indorsed the check and*

| CASE 26.3 |
| --- |

**GENERAL MOTORS ACCEPTANCE CORP. v. ABINGTON CASUALTY INSURANCE CO.**

Supreme Judicial Court of Massachusetts, 1992. 413 Mass. 583, 602 N.E.2d 1085.

*presented it to the bank. The bank accepted the check, which had not been indorsed by GMAC, and Azevedo received full payment. GMAC never received the funds. GMAC sued the drawer of the check, Abington, to recover the insurance payment it should have received. The trial court dismissed the action, and GMAC appealed.*

NOLAN, Justice.
    \*   \*   \*   \*

Although the issue has never been addressed in Massachusetts, other States have held that the delivery of a negotiable instrument to one joint payee constitutes delivery to all joint payees. \*  \*  \* [S]ince under Massachusetts law a person must seek the endorsements of every payee to negotiate, transfer, or discharge a negotiable instrument, delivery of the instrument to one payee does not jeopardize the rights of other payees. We hold, therefore, that Abington's delivery of the check to only one joint payee, Azevedo, nevertheless constitutes delivery to the remaining joint payee, GMAC.
    \*   \*   \*   \*

\*  \*  \* However, \*  \*  \* where there are copayees \*  \*  \*, a negotiable instrument cannot be discharged by the actions of only one payee. Section 3–116(b) [UCC R3–110(d)] expressly prohibits the discharge of an instrument except by all the payees. \*  \*  \* Without this rule, there would be no assurance that all the joint payees would receive payment and that the drawer's underlying obligation would be fully discharged.

**DECISION AND REMEDY**   *The court held that GMAC presented a claim on which relief could be granted and reversed the lower court's dismissal of GMAC's complaint. The case was remanded to the trial court.*

**AGENTS OR OFFICERS**  A negotiable instrument can be drawn payable to a legal entity such as an estate, a partnership, or an organization. For example, a check may read ''Pay to the order of the Red Cross.'' An authorized representative of the Red Cross can negotiate this check.

Similarly, negotiable paper can be payable to a public officer. For example, checks reading ''Pay to the order of the County Tax Collector'' or ''Pay to the order of Larry White, Receiver of Taxes'' can be negotiated by whoever holds the office [UCC R3–110(c); UCC 3–110(1)(f)].

# TERMS AND CONCEPTS TO REVIEW

| | | |
|---|---|---|
| acceleration clause 498 | draft 488 | negotiation 500 |
| allonge 502 | drawee 488 | order instrument 493 |
| banker's acceptance 489 | drawer 488 | payee 488 |
| bearer 499 | extension clause 498 | promissory note 490 |
| bearer instrument 499 | holder 493 | qualified indorsement 504 |
| blank indorsement 503 | indorsee 502 | restrictive indorsement 504 |
| certificate of deposit | indorsement 499 | signature 492 |
|   (CD) 491 | indorser 502 | special indorsement 503 |
| check 489 | issue 488 | trade acceptance 489 |
| commercial paper 486 | maker 490 | trust indorsement 505 |
| demand deposit 488 | negotiable instrument 487 | |

# QUESTIONS AND CASE PROBLEMS

**26–1. Parties to Negotiable Instruments.** Maynard Keynes, a college student, wished to purchase a new component stereo system from Friedman Stereo, Inc. Because Keynes did not have the cash to pay for the entire stereo system, he offered to sign a note promising to pay $150 per month for the next six months. Friedman Stereo, anxious to sell the system to Keynes, agreed to accept the promissory note as long as Keynes had one of his professors sign it. Keynes did this and tendered a note to Friedman Stereo that stated, ''I, Maynard Keynes, promise to pay Friedman Stereo or its order the sum of $150 per month for the next six months.'' The note was signed by Maynard Keynes and his business law professor. About a week later, Friedman Stereo, which was badly in need of cash, signed the back of the note and sold it to the First National Bank of Halston. Give the specific designation of each of the four parties on this note.

**26–2. Requirements for Negotiation.** The following note is written by Juan Sanchez on the back of an envelope: ''I, Juan Sanchez, promise to pay Kathy Martin or bearer $100 on demand.'' Is this a negotiable instrument? Discuss fully.

**26–3. Requirements for Negotiation.** The following instrument was written on a sheet of paper by Sabrina Runyan: ''I, the undersigned, do hereby acknowledge that I owe Leo Woo one thousand dollars, with interest, payable out of the proceeds of the sale of my horse, Lightning, next month. Payment is to be made on or before six months from date.'' Discuss specifically why this instrument is nonnegotiable.

**26–4. Indorsements.** A check drawn by Cullen for $500 is made payable to the order of Jordan and issued to Jordan. Jordan owes his landlord $500 in rent and transfers the check to his landlord with the following indorsement: ''For rent paid. [Signed] Jordan.'' Jordan's landlord has contracted to have Casassa do some landscaping on the property. When Casassa insists on immediate payment, the landlord transfers the check to Casassa without indorsement. Later, to pay for some palm trees purchased from Better-Garden Nursery, Casassa transfers the check with the following indorsement: ''Pay to Better-Garden Nursery, without recourse. [Signed] Casassa.'' Better-Garden Nursery sends the check to its bank indorsed ''For Deposit only. [Signed] Better-Garden Nursery.''

(a) Classify each of these indorsements.

(b) Was the transfer from Jordan's landlord to Casassa, without indorsement, an assignment or a negotiation? Explain.

**26–5. Negotiable versus Nonnegotiable Instruments.** Jeremy Perka needs a loan. He borrows $500 from his friend Erin Murphy, signing a promissory note. Two clauses in the note are as follows:

(a) ''On or before July 1, 1995, I promise to pay to Erin Murphy or bearer $550 in cash or title to my 1982 car, at the holder's option.''

(b) ''The maker thereof reserves the right to extend the time of payment of said note for six months; however, the holder reserves the right to extend the time of payment indefinitely.''

Explain whether either clause or both clauses render Perka's note nonnegotiable.

**26–6. Negotiable versus Nonnegotiable Instruments.** Briggs signed a note that read in part as follows: ''Ninety days after date, I, we, or either of us, promise to pay to the order of Three Thousand Four Hundred Ninety-Eight and 45/100——Dollars.'' The words and symbols underlined were typed, and the remainder of the words in this quotation were preprinted. No blanks had been left on the face of the instrument; any unused space had been filled in with hyphens. The note contained several clauses that permitted acceleration in the event the holder deemed itself insecure. When the note was not paid at maturity, Broadway Management Corp. brought suit on the note for full payment, claiming that it (Broadway) was a holder. Is this order or bearer paper? What changes, if any, would have to be made on the note for it to be a negotiable instrument? [*Broadway Management Corp. v. Briggs*, 30 Ill.App.3d 403, 332 N.E.2d 131 (1975)]

**26–7. Requirements for Negotiation.** Dynamics Corp. and Marine Midland Bank had a long-standing agreement under which Marine Midland received checks payable to Dynamics and indorsed and deposited them into the Dynamics account. Dynamics never saw the checks. They were made out to the order of Dynamics and delivered directly to Marine Midland. Marine Midland stamped the backs of the checks with the Dynamics name and insignia and transferred them. Within the meaning of the UCC, is the act of sending checks to Marine Midland Bank a negotiation? If Marine Midland transfers the checks to other parties, is this a negotiation? [*Marine Midland Bank–New York v. Graybar Electric Co.*, 41 N.Y.2d 703, 363 N.E.2d 1139, 395 N.Y.S.2d 403 (1977)]

**26–8. Bearer Instruments.** Gilbert Ramirez claimed that he had purchased a winning lottery ticket, the prize for which was approximately $1.5 million. Unfortunately, Ramirez had lost the ticket itself and therefore could not claim the prize. Even though the evidence indicated that he very likely was indeed the purchaser of the winning ticket, under the state lottery rules, he could not claim the prize unless he produced the winning ticket. In a legal action brought by Ramirez against the state lottery bureau, Ramirez claimed, among other things, that the lottery ticket was a negotiable instrument because on the back of each lottery ticket were the following words: ''THIS TICKET IS A BEARER

INSTRUMENT SO TREAT IT AS IF IT WERE CASH.'' Because under UCC 3–804 the owner of a lost negotiable instrument can collect on the instrument if certain requirements are met—such as establishing proof of ownership, the terms of the instrument, and so on— Ramirez argued that he should be allowed to claim the prize if he could meet these requirements. Discuss fully whether Ramirez will succeed in his claim that the lottery ticket was a negotiable instrument. [*Ramirez v. Bureau of State Lottery,* 186 Mich.App. 275, 463 N.W.2d 245 (1990)]

**29–9. Words versus Figures.** Eugene Kindy, a seller of diesel engine parts, agreed to buy four diesel engines from Tony Hicks for $13,000. Kindy transferred $6,500 by wire and issued a check for the remainder. Kindy placed two different amounts on the check, because he did not want the check honored until Hicks had delivered the engine parts. Using a check-imprinting machine, Kindy imprinted $5,500 on the check in the space where the dollar amount is normally written in words, but he wrote $6,500 in figures in the box usually reserved for numbers. An employee of Galatia Community State Bank, noticing the discrepancy, altered the figures to read "$5,500," initialed the change, and accepted the check. The check was returned to Galatia by First National Bank at Kindy's request because Hicks had not delivered the engine parts. In the litigation that followed, a key issue was whether the machine-imprinted figure took precedence over the handwritten figure. What should the court decide on this issue? Discuss. [*Galatia Community State Bank v. Kindy,* 807 Ark. 467, 821 S.W.2d 765 (1991)]

**26–10. Requirements for Negotiation.** 1601 Partners, Ltd., executed a promissory note in the amount of $1,650,000 and delivered the note to Southmark Corp. As collateral for the loan represented by the note, 1601 Partners executed a deed of trust (a mortgage) for certain property owned by 1601 Partners. The note stated that "the terms, agreements and conditions of [the deed of trust] are by reference made part of the note." Southmark subsequently assigned the note to San Jacinto Savings Association, Federal Association (SJSA). When 1601 Partners failed to make the payments due under the note, SJSA sold the collateral property for $1,050,000. SJSA subsequently failed, and the Resolution Trust Corp. (RTC) took over its accounts. To recover the deficiency between the amount of the loan and the price for which the collateral was sold, the RTC filed a lawsuit against 1601 Partners and others. One of the issues before the court was whether the note was negotiable. The defendants argued that it was not, because it incorporated the terms of the deed of trust. How should the court rule on this issue? Discuss. [*Resolution Trust Corporation v. 1601 Partners, Ltd.,* 796 F.Supp. 238 (N.D.Tex. 1992)]

**26–11. Requirements for Negotiation.** Emil Amberboy and others invested in oil and gas partnerships formed by Vanguard Group International, Inc. Each investor made a down payment in cash and signed a promissory note payable to the partnership for the balance of the investment. Each note stated that its interest rate was to be determined by reference to a certain bank's published prime rate. Several months later, Vanguard sold the notes to Société de Banque Privée. Suspecting that the investments were being handled fraudulently, Amberboy and the other investors stopped making payments on the notes and filed a lawsuit against Société de Banque Privée and others. One of the issues before the court was whether the notes were negotiable. The plaintiffs contended that because the interest rate on the notes could be calculated only by reference to a source outside the notes, the notes could not be negotiable instruments. How should the court rule? [*Amberboy v. Société de Banque Privée,* 831 S.W.2d 793 (Tex. 1992)]

**26–12. A Question of Ethics**

*Richard Caliendo, an accountant, prepared tax returns for various clients. To satisfy their tax liabilities, the clients issued checks payable to various state taxing entities and gave them to Caliendo. Between 1977 and 1979, Caliendo forged indorsements on these checks, deposited them in his own bank account, and subsequently withdrew the proceeds. In 1983, after learning of these events and after Caliendo's death, the state brought an action against Barclays Bank of New York, N.A., the successor to Caliendo's bank, to recover the amount of the checks. Barclays moved for dismissal on the ground that because the checks had never been delivered to the state, the state never acquired the status of holder and therefore never acquired any rights in the instruments. The trial court held for the state, but the appellate court reversed. The state then appealed the case to the state's highest court. That court ruled that the state could not recover the amount of the checks from the bank because, although it was the named payee on the checks, the checks had never been delivered to the payee. [State v. Barclays Bank of New York, N.A., 561 N.Y.2d 533, 563 N.E.2d 11, 561 N.Y.S.2d 697 (1990)]*

1. If you were deciding this case, would you make an exception to the rule and let the state collect the funds from Barclays Bank? Why or why not? What ethical trade-offs are involved in this situation?

2. Under agency law, which will be discussed in Chapters 34 and 35, delivery to the agent of a given individual or entity constitutes delivery to that person or entity. The court deemed that Caliendo was not an agent of the state, but an agent of the taxpayers. Does it matter that the taxpayers may not have known this principle of agency law and might have thought that, by delivering their checks to Caliendo, they were delivering them to the state?

# CHAPTER 27

# HOLDER IN DUE COURSE AND DEFENSES

**N**egotiable instruments are not money; rather, they are instruments that are payable in money. The body of rules contained in Article 3 of the Uniform Commercial Code (UCC) governs a party's right to payment of a check, draft, note, or certificate of deposit.[1] Problems arise when a holder seeking payment of a negotiable instrument learns that a defense to payment exists or that another party has a prior claim to the instrument. In such situations, for the person seeking payment, it becomes important to have the rights of a *holder in due course (HDC).* As mentioned in Chapter 26, an HDC takes a negotiable instrument free of all claims and most defenses of other parties. Of course, the maker or drawer of the instrument might prefer that an instrument not be negotiable if he or she has a defense to payment on it that would not be good against an HDC.

We open this chapter by distinguishing between an ordinary holder and an HDC. We then examine the requirements for HDC status and look at the two types of defenses to payment that can be raised against holders of negotiable instruments. These defenses fall into two categories: *universal defenses* and *personal defenses.* Universal defenses, also referred to as *real defenses,* defeat payments to all holders, including HDCs. Personal defenses (which are sometimes referred to as *limited* defenses) can only be successfully asserted against ordinary holders.

## SECTION 1

## HOLDER VERSUS HOLDER IN DUE COURSE

As pointed out in Chapter 26, the UCC defines a *holder* as a person who possesses a negotiable instrument "if the instrument is payable to bearer or,

---

1. The rights and liabilities on checks, drafts, notes, and certificates of deposit are determined under Article 3 of the UCC. Other kinds of commercial paper, such as stock certificates, bills of lading, and other documents of title, meet the requirements of negotiable instruments, but the rights and liabilities of the parties on these documents are covered by Articles 7 and 8 of the UCC. See Chapter 50, on bailments, for information on Article 7.

in the case of an instrument payable to an identified person, if the identified person is in possession'' [UCC 1–201(20)]. In other words, the holder is the person who, by the terms of the instrument, is legally entitled to payment. The holder of an instrument need not be its owner to enforce payment of it in his or her own name [UCC R3–301].[2]

A holder has the status of an assignee of a contract right. A transferee of a negotiable instrument who is characterized merely as a holder obtains only those rights that the predecessor-transferor had in the instrument [UCC R3–203(b); UCC 3–201(1)]. In the event that there is a conflicting, superior claim to or defense against the instrument, an ordinary holder will not be able to collect payment [UCC R3–306; UCC 3–306(a)].

In contrast, a **holder in due course (HDC)** is a special-status transferee of a negotiable instrument who, by meeting certain acquisition requirements, takes the instrument *free* of most defenses and all claims to it [UCC R3–305(b); UCC R3–306; UCC 3–305(1), (2)]. Stated another way, an HDC can normally acquire a higher level of immunity than an ordinary holder in regard to defenses against payment on the instrument and claims of ownership to the instrument by other parties.

---

| SECTION 2 |

# REQUIREMENTS FOR HDC STATUS

The basic requirements for attaining HDC status are set forth in UCC R3–302. An HDC must first be a holder of a negotiable instrument and must take the instrument (1) for value; (2) in good faith; and (3) without notice that it is overdue, that it has been dishonored, that any person has a defense against it or a claim to it, or that the instrument contains unauthorized signatures, alterations, or is so irregular or incomplete as to call into question its authenticity.

The underlying requirement of ''due course'' status is that a person must first be a holder on that instrument. Regardless of other circumstances surrounding acquisition, only a holder has a chance to become an HDC.

## TAKING FOR VALUE

An HDC must have given *value* for the instrument [UCC R3–302(a)(2)(i); UCC R3–303]. A person who receives an instrument as a gift or who inherits it has *not* met the requirement of value. In these situations, the person becomes an ordinary holder and does not possess the rights of an HDC.[3]

The concept of *value* in the law of negotiable instruments is not the same as the concept of *consideration* in the law of contracts. An *executory promise* (a promise to give value in the future) is clearly valid consideration to support a contract [UCC 1–201(44)]. It does not, however, normally constitute value sufficient to make one an HDC. UCC R3–303(a)(1) provides that a holder takes the instrument for value only to the extent that the promise has been performed.[4] Therefore, if the holder plans to pay for the instrument later or plans to perform the required services at some future date, the holder has not yet given value. In that case, the holder is not yet a holder in due course. To the extent that the holder has paid for the instrument or performed the promise, however, the holder is an HDC [UCC R3–302(d)].

Suppose Marcia Morrison issues a $500 note payable to Reinhold Niebuhr in payment for goods. Niebuhr negotiates the note to Judy Larson, who promises to pay Niebuhr for it in thirty days. During the next month, Larson learns that Niebuhr has breached the contract by delivering defective goods and that Morrison will not honor the $500 note. Niebuhr has left town. Whether Larson can hold

---

2.   UCC 3–301 states that ''whether or not he is the owner,'' the holder may transfer, negotiate, enforce, or discharge an instrument.

3.   There is one way an ordinary holder who fails to meet the value requirement can have the rights of a holder in due course. The *shelter provision* of the UCC allows an ordinary holder to succeed to HDC status if any prior holder was an HDC. This exception is discussed later in the chapter [UCC R3–203(b); UCC 3–201(1)].

4.   UCC 3–303(a) provides that a holder takes an instrument for value only to the extent that the *agreed consideration* had been performed.

### ■ Exhibit 27–1 Taking for Value

By exchanging defective goods for the note, Niebuhr breached his contract with Morrison. Morrison could assert this defense if Niebuhr presented the note to her for payment. Niebuhr exchanged the note for Larson's promise to pay in thirty days, however. Because Larson did not take the note for value (as defined in UCC R3–303), she is not a holder in due course. Thus, Morrison can assert the defense of Niebuhr's breach against Larson when Larson submits the note to Morrison for payment. If Larson had taken the note for value, Morrison could not assert that defense and would be liable to pay the note.

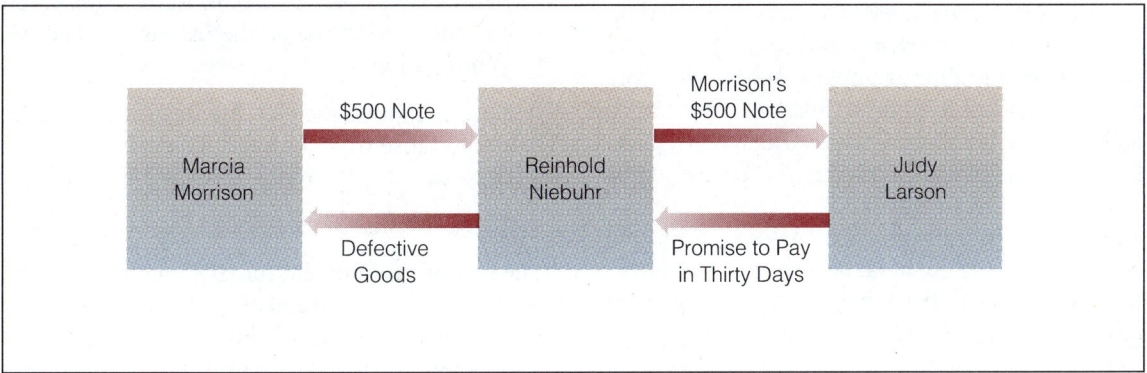

Morrison liable on the note will depend on whether Larson is a holder in due course.

Because Larson had not yet given value at the time that she learned of Morrison's defense to payment of the note (breach of contract), Larson is a mere holder, not a holder in due course. Thus, Morrison's defense is valid not only against Niebuhr but also against Larson. If Larson had paid Niebuhr for the note at the time of transfer (which would mean the promise had been performed), she would be a holder in due course and could hold Morrison liable on the note even though Morrison has a valid defense against Niebuhr on the basis of breach of contract or breach of warranty. Exhibit 27–1 illustrates these concepts.

Under UCC R3–303(a), a holder can take an instrument for value in one of five ways:

1. By performing the promise for which the instrument was issued or transferred.
2. By acquiring a security interest or other lien in the instrument (other than a lien obtained by a judicial proceeding).[5]
3. By taking an instrument in payment of, or as security for, an antecedent debt.
4. By giving a negotiable instrument as payment.
5. By giving an irrevocable commitment as payment.

**ANTECEDENT CLAIM**  When an instrument is given in payment of (or as security for) an **antecedent claim** (a preexisting claim), the value requirement is met [UCC R3–303(a)(3); UCC 3–303(b)]. Here again, commercial law and contract law produce different results. An antecedent claim is not valid consideration under general contract law, but it does constitute value sufficient to satisfy the requirement for HDC status in commercial law.

Assume Cary owes Dwyer $2,000 on a past-due account. If Cary negotiates a $2,000 note signed by Gordon to Dwyer and Dwyer accepts it to discharge the overdue account balance, Dwyer has given value for the instrument.

**NEGOTIABLE INSTRUMENT AS VALUE**
R3–303(a)(4) provides that a holder takes the instrument for value if "the instrument is issued or transferred in exchange for a negotiable instrument."

To illustrate: Martin has issued a $500 negotiable promissory note to Paula. The note is due

---

5. Security interests are discussed in Chapter 31. Other liens are discussed in Chapter 32.

six months from the date issued. Paula's financial circumstances are such that she does not want to wait for the maturity date to collect. Therefore, she negotiates the note to her friend Susan, who pays her $200 in cash and writes her a negotiable check for the balance of $300. Susan has given full value for the note by paying $200 in cash and issuing Paula the check for $300.

*A negotiable instrument has value when issued, not when the underlying obligation is finally paid.* In the preceding example, assume that before Paula cashes Susan's check, Susan learns that the maker of the note has a personal defense against Paula. In this event, Susan has the protection of HDC status. Practicality requires this rule because a negotiable instrument, by its nature, carries the possibility that it might be negotiated to an HDC. If it is, the party that issued it generally cannot refuse to pay [UCC R3–303; UCC 3–303].

**CHECK DEPOSITS AND WITHDRAWALS** Occasionally, a commercial bank can become an HDC when honoring other banks' checks for its own customers. In this situation, the bank becomes an ''involuntary'' HDC, in that at the time of giving value, the bank has no intention of becoming an HDC.

Assume that on Monday morning at the end of the month, Pat Stevens has $400 in her checking account at the First National Bank. That morning Stevens deposits her payroll check for $300, drawn by her employer on the Second Interstate Bank. During her lunch hour she issues a check to her landlord for $425. The landlord cashes the check at the First National Bank. Later, the Second Interstate Bank returns the payroll check marked ''insufficient funds.'' In most cases, First National would charge this check against Stevens's account. If that cannot be done, however, is the First National Bank an HDC of the employer's check? The answer is yes. According to what is referred to as the *first-money-in, first-money-out rule,* First National Bank has paid to the landlord $25 of its own funds [UCC R4–210(b); UCC 4–208(2)]. Therefore, First National is an HDC to the extent it has given value—$25—and to that extent, the bank can seek recovery of $25 from the employer (the drawer of the check).

**SPECIAL CASES** In a few exceptional circumstances, a holder can take an instrument for value but still not be accorded HDC status. UCC

R3–302(c) and UCC 3–302(3) specify the following situations:

1. Purchase at a judicial sale (for example, a bankruptcy sale) or by taking under legal process.
2. Acquisition when taking over an estate (as administrator).
3. Purchase as part of a bulk transfer (as when a corporation buys the assets of another corporation).

In these situations, the UCC limits the rights of the holder to those of an ordinary holder.

## TAKING IN GOOD FAITH

The second requirement for HDC status is that the holder take the instrument in *good faith* [UCC R3–302(a)(2)(ii); UCC 3–302(1)(b)]. This means that the purchaser-holder must have acted honestly in the process of acquiring the instrument. *Good faith* is defined for purposes of revised Article 3 as ''honesty in fact and the observance of reasonable commercial standards of fair dealing'' [UCC R3–103(a)(4)].[6] The good faith requirement *applies only to the holder.* It is immaterial whether the transferor acted in good faith. Thus, a person who in good faith takes a negotiable instrument from a thief may become an HDC.

Because of the good faith requirement, one must ask whether the purchaser, when acquiring the instrument, honestly believed that the instrument was not defective. One must also ask whether the purchaser, when taking the instrument, observed reasonable commercial standards (that is, conformed with what others might have done). If a person purchases a $10,000 note for $200 from a stranger on a street corner, the issue of good faith can be raised on the grounds of the suspicious circumstances *as well as* the grossly inadequate consideration. The UCC does not provide clear guidelines to determine good faith, so each situation must be examined separately.

In the following case, the court concluded that a party clearly met the subjective aspect of the good faith requirement for HDC status. At issue was whether the party also satisfied the *objective* aspect of the requirement.

---

6. Before the revision of Article 3, the applicable definition of good faith was ''honesty in fact in the conduct or transaction concerned'' [UCC 1–201(19)].

**BACKGROUND AND FACTS** *Joe Morgan, Inc. (JMI), was in the telephone-utility contracting business in Alabama. JMI owed to AmSouth Bank money secured by JMI's accounts receivable.[a] In September 1988, JMI obtained from Sunburst Bank loans also secured by JMI's accounts receivable. (Under the UCC, AmSouth and Sunburst were required to file certain documents in the office of the secretary of state to put all others on notice of their interests in JMI's accounts.) Utility Contractors Financial Services (UCON) was in the business of factoring (purchasing) accounts receivable from telephone-utility contractors. UCON factored a customer's receivable at a discount of the face value of the account and then collected the account from the account debtor. UCON began factoring JMI's accounts in the winter of 1989. JMI's customers always paid UCON with checks. UCON was, however, new to the factoring business and was at first unaware of the need to check for UCC filings with the secretary of state. Also, although UCON occasionally ran credit checks on its customers, it did not do so with JMI, despite doubts about JMI's financial health. UCON soon learned of AmSouth's interest in JMI's accounts but did not contact AmSouth or investigate further into the matter. UCON and Sunburst learned of each other's interests at a meeting on July 17. Two months later, when JMI filed for bankruptcy, UCON initiated proceedings to determine whether it or Sunburst was entitled to the proceeds from the accounts factored before July 17. (No one disputed that AmSouth was to be paid first.) The court held that UCON qualified as an HDC of the checks it had received in payment on those accounts and was therefore entitled to those proceeds. Sunburst appealed. One of the issues on appeal was whether UCON satisfied the objective standard for the good faith requirement for HDC status.*

CASE 27.1

**IN RE JOE MORGAN, INC.**
United States Court of Appeals, Eleventh Circuit, 1993.
985 F.2d 1554.

*CARNES,* Circuit Judge:

\* \* \* \*

The [lower] court clearly applied the \* \* \* subjective test in reaching the following conclusions: Knowledge [that] would lead a reasonable person to inquire about and discover facts of another's claim is not bad faith; instead, the holder must subjectively act in good faith, no matter how negligent he may be in overlooking important facts. There are no facts establishing that UCON acted in bad faith when it factored JMI's accounts. \* \* \*

\* \* \* \*

While UCON does meet the subjective good faith component, *we hold that [UCON] has failed to satisfy the objective component.* The record \* \* \* adequately supports our conclusion that UCON was "possessed of facts, sufficient to impute" knowledge to UCON that another lender had a prior \* \* \* interest in the accounts. [Emphasis added.]

\* \* \* \*

\* \* \* In light of the facts known to UCON and reflected in the record, a "reasonable" receivables factoring company would have investigated the state filing records before undertaking to factor the receivables of a company in JMI's financial condition. We concur with the \* \* \* conclusions that the record reflects that UCON acted with subjective good faith, i.e., "an empty head, but a white heart." Unfortunately for UCON, Alabama law incorporates the objective good faith

---

a. *Secured* means that the loan was backed by the accounts as collateral—if JMI failed to repay the loan, AmSouth could use the accounts to obtain payment.

requirement which does not countenance turning a blind eye, however empty the head and white the heart.

*The appellate court reversed the judgment of the lower court and remanded the case for further proceedings.*

**International Holders in Due Course** *Under the United Nations Convention on International Bills of Exchange and International Promissory Notes (CIBN), the equivalent of a holder in due course is known as a ''protected holder.'' As under the UCC, the protected holder is afforded greater protection than a simple ''holder.'' Unlike the UCC, however, the CIBN has no clear, objective standard for good faith. The CIBN qualifies someone as a protected holder if he or she was ''without knowledge'' of a fraud or other defense against the instrument.*

## TAKING WITHOUT NOTICE

The final requirement for HDC status involves *notice* [UCC R3–302; UCC 3–304]. A person will not be afforded HDC protection if he or she acquires an instrument knowing, or having reason to know, that it is defective in any one of the following ways [UCC R3–302(a)(1), (2)(iii), (iv), (v), (vi)]:

1. It is overdue.
2. It has been dishonored.
3. There is an uncured (uncorrected) default with respect to another instrument issued as part of the same series.
4. The instrument contains an unauthorized signature or has been altered.
5. There is a defense against the instrument, or claim to the instrument.
6. The instrument is so irregular or incomplete as to call into question its authenticity.[7]

**WHAT CONSTITUTES NOTICE?** Notice of a defective instrument is given whenever the holder has (1) actual knowledge of the defect; (2) receipt of a notice about a defect; or (3) reason to know that a defect exists, given all the facts and circumstances known at the time in question [UCC 1–201(25)]. The holder must also have received

the notice ''at a time and in a manner that gives a reasonable opportunity to act on it'' [UCC R3–302(f)]. Certain facts that a purchaser might know about an instrument, such as insolvency proceedings against the maker or drawer, do not constitute notice that the instrument is defective [see UCC R3–302(b); UCC 3–304(4)].

**OVERDUE INSTRUMENTS** Any negotiable instrument is either payable at a definite time (*time instrument*) or payable on demand (*demand instrument*). What constitutes notice that an instrument is overdue will vary depending on whether it is a time or a demand instrument.

*Time Instruments.* A holder of a time instrument who takes the paper the day after its expressed due date is *on notice* that it is overdue. Nonpayment by the due date should indicate to any purchaser who is obligated to pay that the primary party has a defense to payment [UCC R3–304(b)(2)]. Thus, a promissory note due on May 15 must be acquired before midnight on May 15. If it is purchased on May 16, the purchaser will be an ordinary holder, not an HDC. Sometimes instruments read, ''Payable in thirty days.'' A note dated December 1 that is payable in thirty days is due by midnight on December 31. If the payment date falls on a Sunday or holiday, the instrument is payable on the next business day.

In the case of an installment note, notice that the maker has defaulted on any installment of principal payments will prevent a purchaser from becoming an HDC [UCC R3–304(b)(1); UCC

---

7. UCC 3–302(1)(c) provided that HDC protection is lost if a holder has notice that an instrument is overdue or has been dishonored, or if there is a claim to or defense against it.

3–304(3)(a)].[8] Also, when a series of notes, each with successive maturity dates, is issued at the same time for a single indebtedness, a default on any one note of the series will constitute overdue notice for the entire series. In this way, prospective purchasers know that they cannot qualify as HDCs [UCC R3–302(a)(2)(iii); UCC 3–304(3)(a)].

Suppose that a note reads, "Payable May 15, but may be accelerated if the holder feels insecure." A purchaser, unaware that a prior holder has elected to accelerate the due date on the instrument, buys the instrument before May 15. UCC R3–304(b)(3) provides that an instrument becomes overdue on the day after the accelerated due date. A purchaser may still qualify as an HDC, however, if he or she has no reason to know that acceleration has occurred [UCC R3–302(a)(2)(iii); UCC 3–304(3)(b)].

*Demand Instruments.* A purchaser has notice that a demand instrument is overdue if he or she takes the instrument knowing that demand has been made the day before [UCC R3–304(a)(1)].[9] A purchaser has notice if he or she takes a demand instrument that has been outstanding for an unreasonable period of time after its date [UCC R3–304(a)(3)].[10] A reasonable time for a check is ninety days [UCC R3–304(a)(2)].[11] A reasonable time for other demand instruments depends on the circumstances [UCC R3–304(a)(3)].

**DISHONORED INSTRUMENTS** Actual knowledge that an instrument has been dishonored or knowledge of facts that would lead a holder to suspect that an instrument has been dishonored puts a holder on notice [UCC R3–302(a)(2)(iii); UCC 3–302(1)(c)]. Thus, a person who takes a check

clearly stamped "insufficient funds" is put on notice. No notice exists without this knowledge. For example, Schultz holds a demand note dated September 1 on Apfel, Inc., a local business firm. On September 17, she demands payment, and Apfel refuses (that is, dishonors the instrument). On September 22, Schultz negotiates the note to Braun, a purchaser who lives in another state. Braun does not know, and has no reason to know, that the note has been dishonored, so Braun is *not* put on notice and can therefore become an HDC.

**DEFENSES AGAINST OR CLAIMS TO AN INSTRUMENT** A holder cannot become an HDC if he or she has notice of any claim to the instrument or defense against it [UCC R3–302(a)(2)(v), (vi); UCC 3–302(1)(c)]. Knowledge of claims or defenses can be imputed to the purchaser if these claims or defenses are apparent on the face of the instrument—if the instrument is incomplete or irregular in any way, for example—or if the purchaser otherwise had reason to know of them from facts surrounding the transaction.[12]

*Incomplete Instruments.* A purchaser cannot expect to become an HDC of an instrument so incomplete on its face as to call into question its authenticity (for example, the amount is not filled in) [UCC R3–302(a)(1); UCC 3–304(1)(a)]. Minor omissions are permissible, because these do not call into question the validity of the instrument. For example, omission of connective words, such as the "or" in "Pay to Johnson or order," does not affect negotiability, and neither does omission of the date from a check that has the month and year [UCC R3–113(b); UCC 3–114(1)].

Similarly, when a person accepts an instrument that has been completed without knowing that it was incomplete when issued, the person can take it as an HDC [UCC R3–115(b); UCC R3–302(a)(1); UCC 3–115(a); UCC 3–304(4)(d)]. To illustrate: Cosford asks Brittany to buy a textbook for him when she goes to the campus bookstore. Cosford writes a check payable to the campus

---

8. An instrument does not become overdue if there is a default on a payment of interest only [UCC R3–304(c); UCC 3–304(4)(f)]. Most installment notes provide that any payment by the maker shall be applied first to interest and the balance to the principal. This serves as notice that any installment payment for less than the full amount results in a default on an installment payment toward the principal.

9. Under UCC 3–304(3)(c), a purchaser has notice that a demand instrument is overdue if he or she takes it *anytime* after demand was made.

10. UCC 3–304(3)(c) defines notice according to the reasonableness of the length of time after a demand instrument's *issue.*

11. A reasonable time for a domestic check under UCC 3–304(3)(c) is *thirty* days.

---

12. If an instrument contains a statement required by a statute or an administrative rule to the effect that the rights of a holder or transferee are subject to the claims or defenses that the issuer could assert against the original payee, the instrument is negotiable, but there cannot be an HDC of the instrument. See UCC R3–106(d) and the discussion of federal limitations on HDC rights later in this chapter.

store, leaves the amount blank, and tells Brittany to fill in the price of the textbook. The cost of the textbook is $35.00. If Brittany fills in the check for $75.00 before she gets to the bookstore, the bookstore cashier sees only a properly completed instrument. Therefore, he or she will take the check as an HDC, and the store can enforce it for the full $75.00. The unauthorized completion is not a sufficient defense against the store in this situation [UCC R3–115(b); UCC R3–302(a)(2)(iv); UCC R3–407(c); UCC 3–115; UCC 3–407].

If an instrument is originally incomplete and later completed in an unauthorized manner, however, the unauthorized completion is not a good defense against an HDC, who can enforce the instrument as completed [UCC R3–407(c); UCC 3–407(2), (3)]. (Such material alterations are discussed more fully later in this chapter.)

*Irregular Instruments.* Any irregularity on the face of an instrument that calls into question its validity or terms of ownership, or creates an ambiguity as to the party to pay, will bar HDC status [UCC R3–302(a)(1); UCC 3–304(1)(a)].

A difference between the handwriting used in the body of a check and that used in the signature will not in and of itself make an instrument irregular. Postdating or antedating a check or stating the amount in digits but failing to write out the numbers will not make a check irregular [UCC R3–113(a); UCC 3–114(1), (2)].

Visible evidence of forgery of a maker's or drawer's signature or alterations to material elements of negotiable paper will disqualify a purchaser from HDC status. Conversely, a careful forgery of a maker's or drawer's signature or a careful alteration can go undetected by reasonable examination; therefore, the purchaser can qualify as an HDC [UCC R3–302(a)(1); UCC 3–304(1)(a)]. Losses that result from careful forgeries, however, usually fall on the party to whom the forger transferred the instrument (assuming, of course, that the forger cannot be found). Also, a forged indorsement (see Chapter 28) does not transfer title, and thus a person obtaining an instrument that has a forged indorsement of a name necessary to good title cannot normally become a holder or an HDC.

*Voidable Obligations.* It stands to reason that a purchaser who knows that a party to an instrument has a defense that entitles that party to avoid the obligation cannot be an HDC. At the very least, good faith requires *honesty in fact and the observance of reasonable commercial standards* of the purchaser in a transaction. For example, a potential purchaser who knows that the maker of a note has breached the underlying contract with the payee cannot thereafter purchase the note as an HDC.

Knowledge of one defense precludes a holder from asserting HDC status in regard to all other defenses. For example, Litvov, knowing that the note he has taken has a forged indorsement, presents it to the maker for payment. The maker refuses to pay on the grounds of breach of the underlying contract. The maker can assert this defense against Litvov even though Litvov had no knowledge of the breach, because Litvov's knowledge of the forgery alone prevents him from being an HDC in *all* circumstances.

Knowledge that a fiduciary has wrongfully negotiated an instrument is sufficient notice of a claim against the instrument to preclude HDC status. Suppose O'Banion, a trustee of a university, improperly writes a check on the university trust account to pay a personal debt. Lewis knows that the check has been improperly drawn on university funds, but she accepts it anyway. Lewis cannot claim to be an HDC. When a purchaser knows that a fiduciary is acting in breach of trust, HDC status is denied [UCC R3–307(b); UCC 3–304(2)].

# HOLDER THROUGH AN HDC

A person who does not qualify as an HDC but who derives his or her title through an HDC can acquire the rights and privileges of an HDC. According to UCC R3–203(b),

> Transfer of an instrument, whether or not the transfer is a negotiation, vests in the transferee any right of the transferor to enforce the instrument, including any right as a holder in due course, but the transferee cannot acquire rights of a holder in due course by a transfer, directly or indirectly, from a holder in due course if the transferee engaged in fraud or illegality affecting the instrument.[13]

---

13.   UCC 3–201(1).

# ■ CONCEPT SUMMARY 27.1 **Rules and Requirements for HDC Status**

| BASIC REQUIREMENTS | RULES |
|---|---|
| **1. Must Be a *Holder*** | A *holder* is a person who possesses a negotiable instrument "if the instrument is payable to bearer or, in the case of an instrument payable to an identified person, if the identified person is in possession" [UCC 1–201(20)]. |
| **2. Must Take for *Value*** | A holder gives *value:*<br>a. By performing the promise for which the instrument was issued or transferred.<br>b. By acquiring a security interest or other lien in the instrument (other than a lien obtained by a judicial proceeding).<br>c. By taking an instrument in payment of, or as security for, an antecedent debt.<br>d. By giving a negotiable instrument as payment.<br>e. By giving an irrevocable commitment as payment [UCC R3–303]. |
| **3. Must Take in *Good Faith*** | *Good faith* is defined for purposes of revised Article 3 as "honesty in fact and the observance of reasonable commercial standards of fair dealing" [UCC R3–103(a)(4)]. |
| **4. Must Take without *Notice***<br>a. That the instrument is *overdue* | 1. Time instruments are overdue if they are not paid by their due dates.<br>2. Demand instruments are overdue if they have been outstanding for an unreasonable period of time after their dates.<br>3. Checks are overdue ninety days after their dates.<br>4. A note is overdue if any part of the principal is not paid when due.<br>5. If any acceleration of a time instrument has occurred, the instrument is overdue on the day after the accelerated due date [UCC R3–304(a), (b)]. |
| b. That the Instrument has been *dishonored* | 1. Actual knowledge or knowledge of facts that would lead a person to suspect that an instrument has been dishonored is notice of dishonor [UCC R3–302(a)(2)(iii)]. |
| c. That a *claim* or *defense* exists | 1. Notice exists if a person has actual knowledge of a claim to or defense against an instrument.<br>2. Notice exists if an instrument is so incomplete, bears such visible evidence of forgery or alteration, or is so irregular that a reasonable person would be put on notice from examination or from facts surrounding the transaction [UCC R3–302(a)(2)(iv), (v), (vi)]. |
| SPECIAL SITUATIONS | RULES |
| **1. Shelter Principle—Holder through a Holder in Due Course** | A holder who cannot qualify as a holder in due course has the rights of a holder in due course if he or she derives title through a holder in due course [UCC R3–203(b)]. |
| **2. Purchasers Not Holders in Due Course** | The following acquisitions cannot result in a holder having HDC status:<br>a. Purchase at a judicial sale.<br>b. Acquisition as part of an estate.<br>c. Purchase as part of a bulk transfer [UCC R3–302(c)]. |

This rule, sometimes called the **shelter principle,** seems counter to the basic HDC philosophy. It is, however, in line with the concept of marketability and free transferability of commercial paper, as well as with contract law, which provides that assignees acquire the rights of assignors. The shelter principle extends the HDC benefits, and it is designed to aid the HDC in readily disposing of the instrument.

Anyone, no matter how far removed from an HDC, who can trace his or her title ultimately back to an HDC comes within the shelter principle. Normally, a person who acquires an instrument from an HDC or from someone with HDC rights receives HDC rights on the legal theory that the transferee of an instrument receives at least the rights that the transferor had.

There are, however, limitations on the shelter principle. Certain persons who formerly held instruments cannot improve their positions by later reacquiring them from HDCs [UCC R3–203(b); UCC 3–201(1)]. Thus, if a holder was a party to fraud or illegality affecting the instrument or if, as a prior holder, he or she had notice of a claim or defense against an instrument, that holder is not allowed to improve his or her status by repurchasing from a later HDC. In other words, a person is not allowed to ''launder'' the paper by passing it into the hands of an HDC and then buying it back.

Suppose Matthew and Carla collaborate to defraud Lorena. Lorena is induced to give Carla a negotiable note payable to Carla's order. Carla then specially indorses the note for value to Larry, an HDC. Matthew and Carla split the proceeds. Larry negotiates the note to Stuart, another HDC. Stuart then negotiates the note for value to Matthew. Matthew, even though he obtained the note through an HDC, is not a holder through an HDC, for he participated in the original fraud and can never acquire HDC rights in this note.

## SECTION 4

# DEFENSES

Depending on whether a holder or an HDC (or a holder through an HDC) makes the demand for payment, certain defenses can bar collection from persons who would otherwise be primarily or secondarily liable on the instrument. There are two general categories of defenses—*universal defenses* and *personal defenses.*

## UNIVERSAL DEFENSES

**Universal defenses** (also called real defenses) are valid against all holders, including HDCs or holders who take through an HDC. Universal defenses include those described in the following subsections.

**FORGERY**  Forgery of a maker's or drawer's signature cannot bind the person whose name is used (unless that person ratifies the signature or is precluded from denying it) [UCC R3–401(a); UCC R3–403(a); UCC 3–401; UCC 3–404(1), (2)]. Thus, when a person forges an instrument, the person whose name is used has no liability to pay any holder or any HDC the value of the forged instrument. In addition, a principal can assert the defense of unauthorized signature against any holder or HDC when an agent exceeds his or her authority to sign negotiable paper on behalf of the principal [UCC R3–403; UCC 3–404].

**FRAUD IN THE EXECUTION**  If a person is deceived into signing a negotiable instrument, believing that he or she is signing something other than a negotiable instrument (such as a receipt), *fraud in the execution,* or inception, is committed against the signer. For example, a consumer unfamiliar with the English language signs a paper presented by a salesperson. The salesperson says the paper is a request for an estimate, but in fact it is a promissory note. Even if the note is negotiated to an HDC, the consumer has a valid defense against payment [UCC R3–305(a)(1)(iii); UCC 3–305(2)(c)]. This defense cannot be raised, however, if a reasonable inquiry would have revealed the nature and terms of the instrument.[14] Thus, the signer's age, experience, and intelligence are relevant, because they frequently determine whether the signer should have known the nature of the transaction before signing.

The following case concerns a farmer who signed a negotiable instrument under the mistaken assumption that he was signing a receipt for funds received. As you read the case, try to determine what the outcome might have been had the plaintiff been an ordinary holder instead of an HDC.

---

14. *Burchett v. Allied Concord Financial Corp.,* 74 N.M. 575, 396 P.2d 186 (1964).

**COMPANY PROFILE** *At the end of 1983, Rexford State Bank in Rexford, Kansas, had a strong primary-capital-to-asset ratio of 9.37 percent, low loan charge-offs (uncollectible debts) of 0.07 percent of all loans, and net income of $36,000. In early 1984, Texas businessman Nasib Ed Kalliel approached the Rexford Bank with what he represented as a plan to rescue farmers who were seeking to avoid financial disaster and possible bankruptcy. If the bank would loan the funds to keep the farmers in operation, Kalliel would guarantee repayment through one of his companies, the First Financial Guaranty Corporation. The bank did not have a sufficient deposit base to loan $2 million to the forty farmers in nine states that Kalliel eventually brought to the bank, however. For this reason, in June 1984 the bank agreed to accept deposits from the First United Fund, Ltd., an investment firm in Garden City, New York, with the understanding that the receipt of the deposits would be tied to the loans to the farmers. Known as* linked financing, *the deposits were made in the form of high-yield, jumbo ($100,000) certificates of deposit. By October, the Rexford Bank's assets included about $5.3 million in deposit accounts, including $2.4 million (45 percent) in the accounts tied to the farmers' loans.*[a] *Not all of the loan proceeds went to the borrowers. Kalliel diverted about $536,000 of the proceeds to himself, First Financial, and the Urethane Toy Company, another of his companies.*

**BACKGROUND AND FACTS** *Gary Culver, a Missouri farmer, made a business arrangement in 1984 with Nasib Ed Kalliel. Kalliel was to manage the business end of the farming enterprise while Culver did the actual farming. Culver was to receive a salary and a percentage of the profits. In the summer of 1984, Culver notified Kalliel that he urgently needed money to prevent foreclosure. One week later Culver received $30,000 from the Rexford State Bank of Rexford, Kansas. Culver thought that the money had come from Kalliel and that Kalliel was responsible for repayment. About a week later, a representative from the Rexford Bank, Jerry Gilbert, approached Culver and requested Culver's signature on a blank promissory note form, stating that "Rexford State Bank wanted to know where the $30,000.00 went, * * * for their records." Apparently, Gilbert led Culver to believe that the document was merely a receipt for the $30,000. The maturity date, interest rate, and amount of the promissory note were later filled in, but the amount read $50,000 instead of $30,000. It was later verified that $50,000 had been deposited into Kalliel's Rexford Bank account, from which the $30,000 sent to Culver had been drawn. Subsequent to these events, the Rexford Bank became insolvent, and the Federal Deposit Insurance Corporation (FDIC) purchased the bank's outstanding notes, including the one signed by Culver. The FDIC sought recovery on the note because the note had matured and no money had ever been paid on it, and the FDIC moved for summary judgment against Culver. Culver claimed that he should not be liable on the note because Gilbert's misrepresentations of the nature of the note constituted fraud in the execution.*

| CASE 27.2 |
| --- |

**FEDERAL DEPOSIT INSURANCE CORP. v. CULVER**

United States District Court, District of Kansas, 1986. 640 F.Supp. 725.

---

a.  At the time, federal bank regulators believed that a bank should have no more than 5 percent of its assets in such accounts.

*EARL E. O'CONNOR,* Chief Judge.

\* \* \* \*

\* \* \* K.S.A. [Kansas Statutes Annotated] 84–3–305(2)(c) [Kansas's version of UCC 3–305(2)(c)],[b] which provides as follows:

Rights of a holder in due course. To the extent that a holder is a holder in due course he takes the instrument free from

(2) all defenses of any party to the instrument with whom the holder has not dealt except

(c) such misrepresentation as has induced the party to sign the instrument with *neither knowledge nor reasonable opportunity to obtain knowledge of its character or its essential terms.* [Emphasis added.] \* \* \*

\* \* \* \*

It is obvious from reading defendant's deposition that he is able to read and understand the English language. Thus, \* \* \* defendant was negligent in relying on Gilbert's assurance that the note was only a receipt. \* \* \* [We] conclude as a matter of law that defendant had a "reasonable opportunity to obtain knowledge of [the document's] character" before he signed it.

Defendant's second argument \* \* \* is that he had no such opportunity to learn of the note's "essential terms." \* \* \*

\* \* \* Because defendant claims not to have authorized anyone to complete the note as it now reads, we are referred \* \* \* to K.S.A. 84–3–407. The latter statute provides, in part, as follows:

(3) A subsequent holder in due course may in all cases enforce the instrument according to its original tenor [intent, meaning, and contents], and when an incomplete instrument has been completed, he may enforce it as completed. \* \* \*

\* \* \* In other words, one who signs an instrument before all essential terms have been completed creates a "blank check" that may be enforced by a subsequent holder in due course according to any terms that are completed by an intervening holder.

**DECISION AND REMEDY**    *The court granted the FDIC's request for summary judgment against Culver.*

b.    Section 3–305(a)(l)(iii) in the revised Article 3 sets out these rights in slightly different language, but with the same basic meaning.

---

**MATERIAL ALTERATION**    An alteration is material if it changes the contract terms between any two parties in any way. Examples of material alterations include completing an instrument, adding words or numbers, or making any other change in an unauthorized manner that relates to the obligation of a party [UCC R3–407(a); UCC 3–407(1)].

Thus, cutting off part of the paper of a negotiable instrument, adding clauses, or making any change in the amount, the date, or the rate of interest—even if the change is only one penny, one day, or 1 percent—is material. But it is not a material alteration to correct the maker's address, to have a red line drawn across the instrument to indicate that an auditor has checked it, or to correct the total final payment due when a mathematical error is discovered in the original computation. If the alteration is not material, any holder is entitled to enforce the instrument according to its original terms.

Material alteration is a *complete defense* against an ordinary holder. An ordinary holder can recover nothing on an instrument if it has been materially altered [UCC R3–407(b); UCC 3–407(2)]. Material alteration may be at best, however, only a *partial defense* against an HDC. When the holder is an HDC and an original term, such as the monetary amount payable, has been altered, the HDC can enforce the instrument against the maker or drawer according to the original terms but not for the altered amount.

If the instrument was originally incomplete and was later completed in an unauthorized manner, alteration no longer can be claimed as a defense against an HDC, and the HDC can enforce the instrument as completed [UCC R3–407(b), (c); UCC 3–407(2), (3)]. This is because the drawer or maker of the instrument, by issuing an incomplete instrument, will normally be held responsible for the alteration, which could have been avoided by the exercise of greater care. If the alteration is readily apparent, then obviously the holder has notice of some defect or defense and therefore cannot be an HDC [UCC R3–302(a)(1), (2)(iv); UCC 3–302(1)(c); UCC 3–304(1)(a)].

**DISCHARGE IN BANKRUPTCY** Discharge in bankruptcy is an absolute defense on any instrument regardless of the status of the holder, because the purpose of bankruptcy is to settle finally all of the insolvent party's debts [UCC R3–305(a)(1)(iv); UCC 3–305(2)(d)].

**MINORITY** Minority, or infancy, is a universal defense only to the extent that state law recognizes it as a defense to a simple contract. Because state laws on minority vary, so do determinations of whether minority is a universal defense against an HDC [UCC R3–305(a)(1)(i); UCC 3–305(2)(a)]. See Chapter 14 for a further discussion of the contractual liability of minors.

**ILLEGALITY** When the law declares that an instrument is void because it has been executed in connection with illegal conduct, then the defense is universal—that is, absolute against both an ordinary holder and an HDC. If the law merely makes the instrument voidable—as in the personal (rather than the universal) defense of illegality, discussed later—then it is still a defense against a holder, but not against an HDC. The courts are sometimes prone to treat the word *void* in a statute as meaning *voidable* to protect a holder in due course [UCC R3–305(a)(1)(ii); UCC 3–305(2)(b)].

**MENTAL INCAPACITY** If a person is adjudicated mentally incompetent by state proceedings, then any instrument issued by that person thereafter is null and void. The instrument is *void ab initio* (from the beginning) and unenforceable by any holder or any HDC [UCC R3–305(a)(1)(ii); UCC 3–305(2)(b)]. (If a person has not been adjudicated mentally incompetent by state proceedings, mental incapacity is a personal, not a universal, defense.)

**EXTREME DURESS** When a person signs and issues a negotiable instrument under such extreme duress as an immediate threat of force or violence (for example, at gunpoint), the instrument is void and unenforceable by any holder or HDC [UCC R3–305(a)(1)(ii); UCC 3–305(2)(b)]. (Ordinary duress is a personal, not a universal, defense.)

## PERSONAL DEFENSES

**Personal defenses,** such as those described here, are used to avoid payment to an ordinary holder of a negotiable instrument.

**BREACH OF CONTRACT OR BREACH OF WARRANTY** When there is a breach of the underlying contract for which the negotiable instrument was issued, the maker of a note can refuse to pay it, or the drawer of a check can stop payment. Breach of warranty can also be claimed as a defense to liability on the instrument. For example, Elias purchases a dozen pairs of athletic shoes from De Soto. The shoes are to be delivered in six weeks. Elias gives De Soto a promissory note for $1,000, which is the price of the shoes. The shoes arrive, but many of the shoes are stained, and the soles of several pairs are coming apart. Elias refuses to pay the note on the basis of breach of contract and breach of warranty. (Under sales law, a seller impliedly promises that the goods are at least merchantable; see Chapter 24.) If the note is no longer in the hands of the payee-seller but is presented for payment by an HDC, the maker-buyer will not be able to plead breach of contract or warranty as a defense against liability on the note.

**LACK OR FAILURE OF CONSIDERATION** The absence of consideration may be a successful defense in instances involving commercial paper [UCC R3–303(b); UCC R3–305(a)(2); UCC 3–306(c); UCC 3–408]. For example, Tony gives Cleo, as a gift, a note that states ''I promise to pay you $100,000,'' and Cleo accepts the note; there is no consideration for Tony's promise, and a court will not enforce the promise.

Similarly, if delivery of goods becomes impossible, a party who has agreed to issue or has issued a draft or note under the contract has a defense for not issuing the note or for not paying the note if it has been issued. Thus, in the hypothetical athletic-shoe transaction described above, if delivery of the shoes became impossible due to their loss in an accident, De Soto could not subsequently sue successfully to enforce Elias's promise to pay the $1,000 promissory note. If the note is in the hands of an HDC, however, Elias's defense is not available against the HDC.

### FRAUD IN THE INDUCEMENT (ORDINARY FRAUD)

A person who issues a negotiable instrument based on false statements by the other party will be able to avoid payment on that instrument, unless the holder is an HDC. To illustrate, Gerhard agrees to purchase Carla's used tractor for $26,500. Carla, knowing her statements to be false, tells Gerhard that the tractor is in good working order and that it has been used for only one harvest. In addition, she tells Gerhard that she owns the tractor free and clear of all claims. Gerhard pays Carla $4,500 in cash and issues a negotiable promissory note for the balance. As it turns out, Carla still owes the original seller $10,000 on the purchase of the tractor, and the tractor is subject to a filed security interest (discussed in Chapter 31). In addition, the tractor is three years old and has been used in three harvests. Gerhard can refuse to pay the note if it is held by an ordinary holder, but if Carla has negotiated the note to an HDC, Gerhard must pay the HDC. Of course, Gerhard can then sue Carla.

### ILLEGALITY

Certain types of illegality constitute personal defenses. Other types, as mentioned, constitute universal defenses. The difference lies in the state statutes or ordinances that make the transactions illegal. If a statute provides that an illegal transaction is voidable, the defense is personal. If a statute makes an illegal transaction void, the defense is universal and can be successfully asserted against an HDC. For example, a state may make gambling contracts illegal and void but be silent on payments of gambling debts. Thus, the payment of a gambling debt becomes voidable and is the source of a personal defense. Whether a contract and the negotiable instrument paid under the contract are void is at issue in the following case.

---

**CASE 27.3**

**NEW JERSEY MORTGAGE & INVESTMENT CORP. v. BERENYI**

Superior Court of New Jersey, Appellate Division, 1976.
140 N.J.Super 406,
356 A.2d 421.

**BACKGROUND AND FACTS**   *On May 25, 1964, Kroyden Industries, Inc., a New Jersey corporation, was prohibited by court order from making certain representations to its customers in connection with the sale of carpeting. In August 1964, in violation of this order, one of Kroyden's employees offered to give Anna Berenyi and her husband carpeting free of charge if they referred prospective buyers to Kroyden Industries. Mr. and Mrs. Berenyi agreed to this condition, and relying upon the employee's offer, Anna Berenyi signed a promissory note for $1,521, from which "finder's fees" would be deducted when prospective buyers were referred to Kroyden Industries. Kroyden subsequently negotiated the note to the plaintiff in this case, New Jersey Mortgage & Investment Corporation. When Berenyi refused to pay the note, the plaintiff brought this legal action against her to recover the debt. Berenyi claimed that she was not liable on the note because the contract with Kroyden was illegal, having been prohibited by court order. The trial court held for the plaintiff, and Berenyi appealed.*

*PER CURIAM* [by the whole court].
\* \* \* \*

The controlling issue presented is whether the defense here asserted is a ["universal"] defense or a "personal" defense. [Universal] defenses are available against even a holder in due course of a negotiable instrument; personal defenses are not available against such a holder. \* \* \*
\* \* \* \*

\* \* \* In New Jersey, a holder in due course takes free and clear of the defense of illegality, unless the statute which declares the act illegal also indicates that payment thereunder is void. \* \* \*

There being no statute ordaining that a note obtained in violation of an injunction is void and unenforceable, the illegality involved is not a [universal] defense; the note is enforceable in the hands of a holder in due course who had no knowledge or notice of the injunction.

*The appellate court affirmed the trial court's judgment.*

**DECISION AND REMEDY**

**MENTAL INCAPACITY**  There are various types and degrees of mental incapacity. Ordinarily, it is only a personal defense; but if a maker or drawer is so extremely incapacitated that the transaction becomes a nullity (is void), then the instrument is void. In that case, the defense becomes universal, and it is good against an HDC as well as an ordinary holder [UCC R3–305(a)(1)(ii); UCC 3–305(2)(b)].

If the maker drafts a negotiable instrument while mentally incompetent but before a formal court hearing has declared (adjudicated) him or her to be so, many courts declare the obligation on the instrument to be voidable. If, however, the maker has been declared by a court to be mentally incompetent and a guardian has been appointed be-

fore the note is written, many courts will hold the obligation to be void.

**OTHER PERSONAL DEFENSES**  A number of other personal defenses can be used to avoid payment to an ordinary holder, but not an HDC, of a negotiable instrument, including the following:

1. Discharge by payment or cancellation [UCC R3–601(b); UCC R3–602(a); UCC R3–603; UCC R3–604; UCC 3–601(1)(a); UCC 3–602; UCC 3–604].
2. Unauthorized completion of an incomplete instrument [UCC R3–115; UCC R3–302; UCC R3–407; UCC R4–401(d)(2); UCC 3–115;

■ **CONCEPT SUMMARY 27.2 Valid Defenses against Holders of Negotiable Instruments**

| DEFENSES | TYPES |
|---|---|
| **Universal (real) Defenses**<br><br>Valid against all holders, including holders in due course and holders with the rights of holders in due course (through the shelter principle).<br><br>UCC R3–305; UCC R3–401; UCC R3–403; UCC R3–407<br><br>[UCC 3–305; UCC 3–401; UCC 3–404; UCC 3–407] | 1. Forgery.<br>2. Fraud in the execution.<br>3. Material alteration.<br>4. Discharge in bankruptcy.<br>5. Minority, if the contract is voidable.<br>6. Illegality, incapacity, or duress, if the contract is void under state law. |
| **Personal Defenses**<br><br>Valid against ordinary holders but not against holders in due course or holders with the rights of holders in due course.<br><br>UCC R3–105; UCC R3–115; UCC R3–302; UCC R3–305; UCC R3–306; UCC R3–407; UCC R3–601; UCC R3–602; UCC R3–603; UCC R3–604; UCC R4–401<br><br>[UCC 1–201; UCC 3–115; UCC 3–304; UCC 3–305; UCC 3–306; UCC 3–407; UCC 3–601; UCC 3–602; UCC 3–604; UCC 4–401] | 1. Breach of contract (including breach of contract warranties).<br>2. Lack or failure of consideration.<br>3. Fraud in the inducement.<br>4. Illegality, incapacity (other than minority), or duress, if the contract is voidable.<br>5. Previous payment or cancellation of the instrument.<br>6. Unauthorized completion of an incomplete instrument.<br>7. Nondelivery of the instrument. |

UCC 3–304(4)(d); UCC 3–407; UCC 4–401(2)(b)].

3. Nondelivery of the instrument [UCC R3–105(b); UCC R3–305(a)(2); UCC 1–201(14); UCC 3–305; UCC 3–306(c)].

4. Ordinary duress or undue influence rendering the contract voidable [UCC R3–305(a)(1)(ii); UCC 3–305(2)(b)].

## SECTION 5

# FEDERAL LIMITATIONS ON HDC RIGHTS

The HDC doctrine has been abused in consumer transactions. For example, a consumer purchases a stereo system under express warranty from a sound equipment dealer, paying $500 down and signing a promissory note to the dealer for the remaining $1,500 due on the system. The dealer then sells the bank this promissory note, which is a negotiable instrument, and the bank then becomes the creditor and an HDC, to whom the consumer makes payments. The stereo system does not perform as warranted, and the consumer returns it, requesting return of the down payment and cancellation of the contract. Even if the dealer did refund the $500, however, under the traditional HDC rule, the consumer would normally still owe the remaining $1,500, because the consumer's claim of breach of warranty is a personal defense, and the bank is a holder in due course. Thus, the traditional HDC rule leaves consumers who have purchased defective products liable to the holder for the debt.

To protect consumers, the Federal Trade Commission (FTC) issued Rule 433,[15] which effectively abolished the HDC doctrine in consumer transactions. Rule 433 limits the rights of an HDC in an instrument that evidences a debt arising out of a *consumer credit* transaction. Rule 433, entitled ''Preservation of Consumers' Claims and Defenses,'' attempts to prevent a situation in which a consumer is required to make payment for a defective product to a third party (the bank, in the previous example) who is an HDC of a promissory note that formed part of the contract with the dealer who sold the defective good.

FTC Rule 433 applies to any seller or lessor of goods or services who takes or receives a consumer credit contract. The rule also applies to a seller or lessor who accepts as full or partial payment for a sale or lease the proceeds of any purchase-money loan made in connection with any consumer credit contract. Under the rule, these parties must include in the consumer credit contract the following provision:

NOTICE

ANY HOLDER OF THIS CONSUMER CREDIT CONTRACT IS SUBJECT TO ALL CLAIMS AND DEFENSES WHICH THE DEBTOR COULD ASSERT AGAINST THE SELLER OF GOODS OR SERVICES OBTAINED PURSUANT HERETO OR WITH THE PROCEEDS HEREOF. RECOVERY HEREUNDER BY THE DEBTOR SHALL NOT EXCEED AMOUNTS PAID BY THE DEBTOR HEREUNDER.

A consumer who is party to a consumer credit transaction can bring any defense he or she has against the seller of a product against a subsequent holder as well. In essence, FTC Rule 433 places an HDC of the instrument in the position of a contract assignee. The rule makes the buyer's duty to pay conditional on the seller's full performance of the contract. Both the seller and the creditor are responsible for the seller's misconduct. The rule also clearly reduces the degree of transferability of negotiable instruments resulting from consumer credit contracts. An instrument that contains this notice or a similar statement required by law may remain negotiable, but there cannot be an HDC of such an instrument [UCC R3–106(d)].

Problems can arise, however, if the seller fails, for whatever reason, to include the notice in a promissory note and then sells the note to a third party, such as a bank. The seller has violated the rule, but the bank has not. The FTC rule does not prohibit third parties from purchasing notes or credit contracts that do *not* contain the required notice. Therefore, if the notice is not contained in the note, the bank does not become subject to the buyer's defenses against the seller. Some consumers have suffered as a result.[16] The FTC apparently

---

15. 16 C.F.R. Section 433.2. The rule was enacted in 1976 pursuant to the FTC's authority under the Federal Trade Commission Act, 15 U.S.C. Sections 41–58.

16. See, for example, *Blackmon v. Hindrew,* 824 S.W.2d 85 (Mo.App. 1992).

recognized this problem and proposed an amendment that would have protected consumers even

without the required notice. The proposed amendment was never promulgated, however.

---

# TERMS AND CONCEPTS TO REVIEW

antecedent claim   513

holder in due course   512

personal defense   523

shelter principle   520

universal defense   520

---

# QUESTIONS AND CASE PROBLEMS

**27–1. Requirements for HDC Status.** What are the requirements for attaining HDC status besides the requirement of being a holder? How can a person who does not qualify as an HDC acquire the rights and privileges of an HDC?

**27–2. Requirements for HDC Status.** Celine issues a ninety-day negotiable promissory note payable to the order of Hayden. The amount of the note is left blank, pending a determination of the amount of money Hayden will need to purchase a bull for Celine. Celine authorizes any amount not to exceed $2,000. Hayden, without authority, fills in the note in the amount of $5,000 and thirty days later sells the note to the First National Bank of Oklahoma for $4,500. Hayden does not buy the bull and leaves the state. The First National Bank has no knowledge that the instrument was incomplete when issued or that Hayden had no authority to complete the instrument in the amount of $5,000.

  (a) Does the bank qualify as a holder in due course? If so, for what amount? Explain.
  (b) If Hayden had sold the note to a stranger in a bar for $500, would the stranger qualify as a holder in due course? Explain.

**27–3. Requirements for HDC Status.** Luther Martin is a recent college graduate. A stranger comes to his door with a package. The stranger tells Luther that the package is a gift from an anonymous friend and asks Luther to sign a delivery receipt. Luther, without reading what he is signing, signs at the place designated by the stranger and marked with an *X*. Luther opens the package, and inside are two new compact discs. Luther does not give the incident a second thought until six months later, when an HDC demands $1,000 from Luther. Luther now learns that he signed a six-month, negotiable promissory note instead of a delivery receipt. He is the victim of fraud. Discuss fully whether Luther is obligated to pay $1,000 to the HDC.

**27–4. Requirements for HDC. Status.** Emilio has received from dishonest payees through negotiation two checks with the following histories:

  (a) The drawer issued a check to the payee for $9. The payee cleverly altered the numeral on the check from $9 to $90 and the written word from *nine* to *ninety*.
  (b) The drawer issued a check to the payee without filling in the amount. The drawer authorized the payee to fill in the amount for no more than $90. The payee filled in the amount of $900.

Discuss whether Emilio, by giving value to the payees, can qualify as a holder in due course of these checks.

**27–5. Defenses.** Niles sold Kennedy a small motorboat for $1,500, maintaining to Kennedy that the boat was in excellent condition. Kennedy gave Niles a check for $1,500, which Niles indorsed and gave to Frazier for value. When Kennedy took the boat for a trial run, she discovered that the boat leaked, needed to be painted, and needed a new motor. Kennedy stopped payment on her check, which had not yet been cashed. Niles has disappeared. Can Frazier recover from Kennedy as a holder in due course? Discuss.

**27–6. Defenses.** Metzger purchased a used car from Stein for $1,000. Metzger paid for the car with a check, written in pencil, payable to Stein for $1,000. Stein, through careful erasures and alterations, changed the amount on the check to read $10,000 and negotiated the check to Boz. Boz took the check for value, in good faith, and without notice of the alteration and thus met the UCC requirements for holder-in-due-course status. Can Metzger successfully raise the real defense of material alteration to avoid payment on the check? Explain.

**27–7. Requirements for HDC Status.** An employee of Epicycle Corp. cashed a payroll check at Money Mart Check Cashing Center, Inc. Money Mart deposited the check, with others, into its bank account. When the check was returned marked "Payment stopped," Money Mart sought to recover from Epicycle for the value of the check. Money Mart claimed that it was a holder in due course on the instrument because it had accepted the check for value, in good faith, and without notice that a stop-payment order had been made. Epicycle argued that Money Mart was not a holder in due course because it had failed to verify that the check was good before it cashed the check. Did Money Mart's failure to inquire into the validity of the check preclude it from being a holder in due course? Explain. [*Money Mart Check Cashing Center, Inc. v. Epicycle Corp.,* 667 P.2d 1372 (Colo. 1983)]

**27–8. Defenses.** James Balkus died without leaving a will. A few days later, Ann Vesely, his sister, discovered in his personal effects two promissory notes made payable to her in the amount of $6,000. She presented the notes to the Security First National Bank of Sheboygan Trust Department, the personal representative for the estate of Balkus, for payment. The personal representative refused to pay the notes, claiming that Vesely was not a holder in due course and that nondelivery of the notes to her was a proper defense. The trial court upheld the personal representative's claim, and Vesely appealed. Discuss whether nondelivery is a proper defense against Vesely. [*Vesely v. Security First National Bank of Sheboygan Trust Department,* 128 Wis.2d 246, 381 N.W.2d 593 (1985)]

**27–9. Requirements for HDC Status.** Pamela Haas, an employee of Trail Leasing, Inc., had access to her employer's blank checks. Over a period of about two and a half years, Haas used the firm's checks to fraudulently obtain cash from the firm's bank, Drovers First American Bank. She carried out her scheme by writing checks payable to Drovers First, having the checks signed by an authorized officer of Trail Leasing, and then taking the checks to the bank. There she would fill out a ''change order form''—a form used by bank customers to specify the coins and bill denominations in which they wished to take cash for business operations—and pocket the cash that she received. By the time the scheme was discovered (through a discrepancy in one of the change orders), Haas had negotiated fifty-five checks for a total of nearly $40,000. Trail Leasing sued the bank to recover the funds paid to Haas without its authorization, and the issue turned on whether the bank was a holder in due course of the checks delivered to it by Haas. The court had no trouble deciding that the bank took the checks in good faith and without notice of any claim. The issue thus became whether the bank met the remaining requirement for HDC status—taking for value. Trail Leasing argued that because the bank essentially paid Haas from Trail Leasing's funds (by debiting Trail Leasing's bank account), the bank had not given value for the instruments and therefore could not be an HDC. Will the court concur in this argument? Discuss. [*Trail Leasing, Inc. v. Drovers First American Bank,* 447 N.W.2d 190 (Minn. 1989)]

**27–10. A Question of Ethics**

 *Kirkman was involved in the horse business. He formed a business arrangement with an acquaintance, John Roundtree, who worked as a loan officer for American Federal Bank.*

*Under the arrangement, Kirkman would locate buyers for horses, and the buyers could seek financing from American Federal. Roundtree gave Kirkman blank promissory notes and security agreements from American Federal, and Kirkman was to locate potential purchasers, take care of the paperwork, and bring the documents to the bank for approval of the purchaser's loan. Eventually, Kirkman entered into a purchase agreement with Gene Parker, a horse dealer. Parker agreed with Kirkman that they would jointly purchase a certain horse for $35,000. Parker signed a blank American Federal promissory note, with the understanding that Kirkman would cosign the note and complete the details of the transaction with the bank. Parker also signed a form authorizing the bank to release the funds to the seller of the collateral (the horse). Kirkman did not cosign the note and completed it for $85,000 instead of $35,000. He then took the note and authorization form to Roundtree, told Roundtree that he was the seller, and received from Roundtree checks totaling $85,000. After paying the actual seller of the horse the agreed-on $35,000 and seeing to it that Parker received the horse, Kirkman skipped town with the remaining $50,000. Parker paid American Federal $35,000 but refused to pay any more, claiming that he had agreed to pay only $35,000 and that the other $50,000 was unauthorized by him. In the subsequent action brought by the bank to collect the $50,000, the bank prevailed. The court found that the bank was a holder in due course of the promissory note and had not been negligent in the way it handled the transaction.* [American Federal Bank, FSB v. Parker, *392 S.E.2d 798 (S.C. 1990)*]

1. Parker contended that the bank was negligent because it did not contact him to make sure that everything was correct before disbursing the proceeds of the loan to Kirkman. Do you agree with the court's finding that the bank was not negligent in this regard? Even if the bank had been negligent, would its negligence have outweighed Parker's negligence in signing a blank promissory note?

2. Because the bank was deemed a holder in due course and Parker had signed an incomplete instrument, Parker was prohibited under UCC 3–407(3) from asserting successfully the universal defense of material alteration. What ehtical premise underlies this rule?

3. Overall, from an ethical point of view, do you think that the court's holding in this case was fair? Would it have been fairer to hold the bank liable for the loss instead of Parker? If you were the judge, how would you decide the issue?

# CHAPTER 28

# LIABILITY AND DISCHARGE

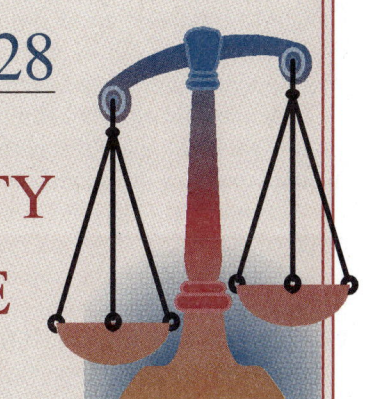

T wo kinds of liability are associated with negotiable instruments: signature liability and warranty liability. *Signature liability* relates to signatures on instruments. Those who sign commercial paper are potentially liable for payment of the amount stated on the instrument. *Warranty liability*, in contrast, extends to both signers and nonsigners. A breach of warranty can occur when the instrument is transferred or presented for payment.

The following sections cover the liability of the parties who sign the instrument—for example, drawers of drafts and checks, makers of notes and certificates of deposit, and indorsers. They also cover the liability of accommodation parties and the warranty liability of those who transfer instruments and present instruments for payment. The final section in the chapter looks at some of the ways in which parties can be *discharged* from liability on negotiable instruments.

Note that the focus is on liability *on the instrument itself or on warranties connected with transfer or presentment of the instrument* as opposed to liability on any underlying contract. Suppose, for example, that Donald agrees to buy one thousand compact discs from Luis and issues a check to Luis in payment. The liability discussed in this chapter does not directly relate to liability arising in connection with the contract (for instance, whether the compact discs are fit for the purpose for which they are intended). The liability discussed here relates to liability arising in connection with the *check* (for instance, what recourse the parties have if Donald's bank refuses to cash it).

## SECTION 1

## SIGNATURE LIABILITY

The key to liability on a negotiable instrument is a *signature*. The parties to a negotiable instrument are bound by all of the terms implied by their signatures by operation of law. Once it is established that a party signed an instrument (or that it was signed by the party's authorized agent), the UCC defines the party's liability. The liability is contractual in the sense that each party voluntarily incurs it and thus can modify it.

A **signature** is "any name, including a trade or assumed name," or "a word, mark, or symbol executed or adopted by a person with the present intention to authenticate a writing" [UCC 1–209(39); UCC R3–401(b); UCC 3–401(2)]. A signature can be handwritten, typed, or printed; it also can be made by mark, by thumbprint, by machine, or in virtually any other manner.

The requirement of a signature is based on the need to know whose obligation the instrument represents. The critical element with any signature is a "present intention to authenticate a writing." Parol evidence can be used to identify the signer, and once that person is identified, the signature is effective against him or her no matter how it is made. The general rule follows: "A person is not liable on an instrument unless (i) the person signed the instrument, or (ii) the person is represented by an agent or representative who signed the instrument and the signature is binding on the represented person" [UCC R3–401(a); UCC 3–401(1)]. The following subsections discuss the types of liability that exist in relation to negotiable instruments and the conditions that must be met before liability can arise.

## PRIMARY AND SECONDARY LIABILITY

Every party, except a qualified indorser,[1] who signs a negotiable instrument is either primarily or secondarily liable for payment of that instrument when it comes due.

**PRIMARY LIABILITY**   A person who is primarily liable on a negotiable instrument is absolutely required to pay the instrument, subject to certain defenses [UCC R3–305]. Primary liability is unconditional. The primary party's liability is immediate when the instrument is signed or issued and effective when the instrument becomes due.

No action by the holder of the instrument is required. *Makers* and *acceptors* are primarily liable [UCC R3–412; UCC R3–413; UCC 3–413(1)]. (Recall from Chapter 26 that one who signs a promissory note is called a *maker,* whereas one who signs a check or draft is referred to as a *drawer.*)

Also primarily liable is the issuer of a cashier's check or other draft drawn on the drawer [UCC R3–412].[2] (Any "draft drawn on the drawer" would be similar to a cashier's check, on which there are really only two parties—the first party is the payee, and the second party is a bank, which is both the drawer and the drawee. Of course, there is a third party—the person who pays the money to the bank for the check—but he or she is not a party to the instrument. Some courts view a bank money order as a "draft drawn on the drawer.")

The maker of a promissory note promises to pay the note. It is the maker's promise to pay that renders the note a negotiable instrument. The words "I promise to pay" embody the maker's obligation to pay the instrument according to the terms as written at the time of the signing or issue. If the instrument is incomplete when the maker signs it, then the maker's obligation is to pay it according to the terms written when it is completed as authorized or, if completion is unauthorized, as completed to a holder in due course [UCC R3–115; UCC 3–407(a), (c); UCC R3–412; UCC 3–407(3); UCC 3–413(1)].

The drawee-acceptor of a draft or check is in virtually the same position as the maker of a promissory note [UCC R3–413; UCC 3–413(1)]. A drawee's acceptance of a draft, which it makes by signing the draft, guarantees that the drawee will pay the draft when it is presented later for payment [UCC R3–409(a); UCC 3–410(1)].[3] When a drawee accepts a draft, the drawee becomes an **acceptor** and is primarily liable to all subsequent holders.

---

1.   A qualified indorser—one who indorses "without recourse"—undertakes no obligation to pay [UCC R3–415(b); UCC 3–414(1)]. A qualified indorser merely assumes warranty liability, which is discussed later in this chapter.

2.   Under UCC 3–118(a) and 3–413(1), a draft drawn on the drawer is "effective as a note," thus making the drawer liable as a maker.

3.   When a draft's payment date depends on presentment—for example, when the draft is payable thirty days after sight—a holder must present the draft for acceptance [UCC R3–502(b)(3), (4); UCC 3–501(1)(a)]. There are two other situations specified in UCC 3–501(1)(a) in which a holder has to present a draft to a drawee for acceptance: when the draft requires it and when the draft is payable at an address different from that of the drawee.

Imagine, for example, that Jones Outfitters, Inc., contracts to buy five thousand pairs of imported jeans from Worldwide Importers. The terms of the contract require Jones to issue to Worldwide a *trade acceptance* (see Chapter 26), payable ninety days after the date that the jeans are shipped. When the jeans are shipped, Worldwide can draw a draft on Jones in the amount of the price, payable in ninety days, and forward the draft to Jones. When Jones signs it, Jones accepts it, guaranteeing that Jones will pay it when it is presented later for payment. The draft becomes a trade acceptance, which Worldwide can negotiate further. (In this example, Worldwide is the drawer of the draft and Jones is the drawee.)

A drawee that refuses to accept a draft that requires the drawee's acceptance has dishonored the instrument. When a drawee has a contractual duty to accept or pay a draft but refuses to do so, the drawee is liable to the drawer but has no liability to either the payee or any holder [UCC R3–408; UCC 3–409].

A check is a special type of draft that is drawn on a bank and is payable on demand. Voluntary acceptance of a check by the bank is called *certification* (discussed in Chapter 29). Certification is not necessary on checks, and a bank is under no obligation to certify. Upon certification, however, the drawee-bank occupies the position of an acceptor and is primarily liable on the check to holders [UCC R3–409(d); UCC 3–411(1)].

**SECONDARY LIABILITY**   Secondary liability on a negotiable instrument is similar to that of a guarantor in a simple contract (described in Chapter 17). Drawers and indorsers have secondary liability, except that a drawer is not secondarily liable but primarily liable on a cashier's check or any other draft on which the drawer is also the drawee [UCC R3–412; UCC R3–414(a)]. Secondary liability is *contingent liability*. In the case of notes, an indorser's secondary liability does not arise until the maker, who is primarily liable, has defaulted on the instrument [UCC R3–412; UCC R3–415; UCC 3–413(1); UCC 3–414].

With regard to drafts and checks, a drawer's secondary liability does not arise until the drawee fails to pay or to accept the instrument, whichever is required.[4] Note, however, that the drawee is not

primarily liable. Makers of notes promise to pay, but drawees are ordered to pay. Therefore, drawees are not primarily liable unless they promise to pay—for example, by certifying a check. Nor are drawees even secondarily liable on an instrument. "A check or other draft does not of itself operate as an assignment of any funds in the hands of the drawee available for its payment" [UCC R3–408; UCC 3–409(1)]. Thus, unless a drawee *accepts*,[5] the drawee's only obligation is to honor the drawer's orders.

Dishonor of an instrument triggers the liability of parties who are secondarily liable on the instrument—that is, the drawer and *unqualified* indorsers. Parties who are secondarily liable on a negotiable instrument promise to pay on that instrument only if the following events occur:[6]

1. The instrument is properly and timely presented.
2. The instrument is dishonored.
3. Timely notice of dishonor is given.[7]

These requirements are necessary for a secondarily liable party to have signature liability on a negotiable instrument, but they are not necessary for a secondarily liable party to have warranty liability (to be discussed later).

"If an unaccepted draft is dishonored, the drawer is obligated to pay the draft * * *. The obligation is owed to a person entitled to enforce the draft or to an indorser who paid the draft" [UCC R3–414(b); UCC 3–413(2)]. For example, Lo An writes a check on her account at Universal Bank payable to the order of Val Carerra. If Universal Bank does not pay the check when Carerra presents it for payment, then Lo An is liable to Carerra on the basis of her secondary liability. A drawer is secondarily liable on a draft unless the liability is disclaimed by, for example, drawing the instrument "without recourse" (unless the draft is a check, in which case a drawer cannot disclaim liability) [UCC R3–414(e)].[8]

---

4.  If a bank accepts a draft, the drawer is discharged [UCC R3–414(c)].

5.  To accept a draft, the drawee must place his or her signature on it [UCC R3–409(a); UCC 3–410(1)].

6.  An instrument can be drafted to provide a waiver of the presentment and notice of dishonor requirements [UCC R3–504; UCC 3–511]. Presume, for simplicity's sake, that such waivers have *not* been incorporated into the instruments described in this chapter.

7.  These events are also required under the unrevised Article 3 to hold parties secondarily liable [UCC 3–502(2)(a), (b)].

Because drawers are secondarily liable, their liability does not arise until presentment and notice of dishonor have been made *properly* and in a *timely* way. If a draft (or check) is payable at a bank, improper presentment or notice relieves the drawer from secondary liability only when the drawee-bank is insolvent [UCC R3–414(f); UCC 3–502(1)(b)].

An unqualified indorser promises that in the event of presentment, dishonor, and timely notice of dishonor, the indorser will pay the instrument. (For example, if a check is made out to you and upon presentment to the drawer's bank it is dishonored, you must timely notify any unqualified indorsers to hold them liable.) Thus, the liability of an unqualified indorser is much like that of a drawer, with one major exception: unqualified indorsers are relieved of their contractual liability to the holder of the instrument by (1) improper (late) presentment or (2) late notice or failure to notify of dishonor [UCC R3–415(c), (e); UCC 3–414; UCC 3–501(1)(b); UCC 3–502(1)(a)].

When an indorser has actively caused an instrument to be dishonored or the drawer or indorser to be charged has so waived, the requirements of presentment and notice of dishonor are excused [UCC R3–504; UCC 3–511(2)]. Any delay in giving notice of dishonor is excused if the delay is due to circumstances beyond the control of the person giving the notice, and the person exercises reasonable diligence after the cause "cease[s] to operate" [UCC R3–504(c)].

## PROPER PRESENTMENT

The UCC spells out what constitutes a proper presentment. Basically, presentment by a holder must be made to the proper person, must be made in a proper manner, and must be timely [UCC R3–414(f); UCC R3–415(e); UCC R3–501; UCC 3–503; UCC 3–504].

The party to whom the instrument must be presented depends on what type of instrument is involved. A note or certificate of deposit (CD) must be presented to the maker for payment. A draft is presented by the holder to the drawee for acceptance, payment, or both, whichever is required. A check is presented to the drawee-bank for payment [UCC R3–501(a); UCC R3–502(b); UCC 3–504].

Presentment can be properly made in any of the following ways, depending on the type of instrument involved [UCC R3–501(b); UCC 3–504(2)]:

1. By any commercially reasonable means, including oral, written, or electronic communication (but presentment is not effective until the demand for payment or acceptance is received).
2. Through a clearinghouse procedure used by banks, such as for deposited checks.
3. At the place specified in the instrument for acceptance or payment.

One of the most crucial criteria for proper presentment is timeliness [UCC R3–414(f); UCC R3–415(e); UCC R3–501(b)(4); UCC 3–503]. Failure to present on time is the most prevalent reason for improper presentment and consequent discharge of unqualified indorsers from secondary liability. For example, for domestic checks, the holder must present the check for payment or collection within thirty days of its date to hold the drawer secondarily liable and within thirty days after an indorsement to hold the indorser secondarily liable [UCC R3–414(f); UCC R3–415(e)].[9]

## DISHONOR

An instrument is dishonored when presentment is properly and timely made and required acceptance or payment is refused or cannot be obtained within the prescribed time, or when required presentment is excused and the instrument is not properly accepted or paid [UCC R3–502(e); UCC 3–507(1)]. Payment can be postponed without dishonor if presentment is made after an established cut-off hour (not earlier than 2 P.M.), but not beyond the close of the next business day after the day of presentment [UCC R3–501(b)(4); UCC 3–506(1)]. In addition, the party to whom presentment is made may refuse payment without dishonor if the holder refuses to exhibit the instrument, to give reasonable identification and/or authority to receive payment,

---

8. Drawing without recourse is effective to disclaim the liability of the drawer even if the draft is a check, under UCC 3–413(2).

9. UCC 3–503(2) *presumes* these periods to be thirty days after the date or issue of the instrument with respect to a drawer's liability and seven days after indorsement for an indorser's liability.

or to sign on the instrument as a receipt for any payment made [UCC R3–501(b)(2); UCC 3–505]. Returning an instrument because it lacks a proper indorsement is not dishonor [UCC R3–501(b)(3)(i); UCC 3–507(3)].

## PROPER NOTICE

Once an instrument has been dishonored, proper notice must be given for secondary parties to be held liable. The rules of proper notice are basically as follows [UCC R3–503; UCC 3–508]:

1.  Notice operates for the benefit of all parties who have rights in an instrument against the party notified [UCC R3–503(b); UCC 3–508(8)]. For example, assume that there are four indorsers on a note that its maker dishonors, and the holder gives timely notice to indorsers 1 and 4. If the holder collects payment from indorser 4, indorser 4 does not have to give notice to indorser 1 again to collect from indorser 1. (Indorsers 2 and 3 are not liable to indorser 4, because they were not given timely notice.) It is important to remember that if more than one indorsement appears on an instrument, each indorser is liable for the full amount to any subsequent indorser or to any holder.
2.  Except for dishonor of foreign drafts, notice may be given in any reasonable manner. This includes oral notice, written notice, or electronic notice (notice by fax, modem, E-mail, and the like) and notice written or stamped on the instrument itself [UCC R3–503(b); UCC 3–508(3)]. To give notice of dishonor of a foreign draft (a draft drawn in one country and payable in another country), a formal notice called a *protest* is required [UCC R3–505(b); UCC 3–509].
3.  Any necessary notice must be given by a bank before its midnight deadline (midnight of the next banking day after receipt) [UCC R3–503(c); UCC 4–104(10); UCC 4–104(1)(h)]. Notice by any party other than a bank must be given within thirty days following the day on which the person receives notice of dishonor [UCC R3–503(c); UCC 3–508(2)].[10]

---

10. Under UCC 3–508(2), notice by a person other than a bank has to be given "before midnight of the third business day after dishonor or receipt of notice of dishonor."

## ACCOMMODATION PARTIES

An **accommodation party** is one who signs an instrument for the purpose of lending his or her name as credit to another party on the instrument [UCC R3–419(a); UCC 3–415(1)]. Accommodation parties are one form of security against nonpayment on a negotiable instrument. For example, a bank about to lend money, a seller taking a large order for goods, or a creditor about to extend credit to a prospective debtor all want some reasonable assurance that the debts will be paid. A party's uncertain financial condition or the fact that the parties to a transaction are complete strangers can make a creditor reluctant to rely solely on the prospective debtor's ability to pay. To reduce the risk of nonpayment, the creditor can require the joining of a third person as an accommodation party on the instrument.

If the accommodation party signs on behalf of the *maker,* he or she is an *accommodation maker* and is primarily liable on the instrument. If the accommodation party signs on behalf of a *payee or other holder* (usually to make the instrument more marketable), he or she is an *accommodation indorser* and is secondarily liable. Any indorsement not in the ordinary chain of title gives notice of its accommodation character [UCC R3–419(a), (b), (c); UCC 3–415(2), (4)]. For example, a signature that appears on an instrument above that of the payee, who would normally be the first indorser, is outside the chain of title. An accommodation party is never, however, liable to the party accommodated, and if the accommodation party pays the instrument, he or she has a right of recourse against the party accommodated [UCC R3–419(e); UCC 3–415(5)].

## AGENTS' SIGNATURES

The general law of agency, covered in Chapters 34 and 35, applies to negotiable instruments. An **agent** is a person who agrees to represent or act for another, called the **principal.** Agents can sign negotiable instruments and thereby bind their principals [UCC R3–401(a)(ii); UCC R3–402(a); UCC 3–403(1)]. Without such a rule, all corporate commercial business would stop—as every corporation can and must act through its agents. Because of the critical function the signature plays in determining liability on a negotiable instrument, this chapter will go into some detail concerning the potential problems of agents' signatures.

**AUTHORIZED AGENT**   Generally, an authorized agent binds a principal on an instrument if the agent *clearly names* the principal in his or her signature (by writing, mark, or some symbol).[11] The agent may or may not add his or her own name, but if the signature shows clearly that it is made on behalf of the principal, the agent is not liable on the instrument [UCC R3–402(b)(1); UCC 3–403(2)]. For example, suppose that Sandra Binney is an agent for Bob Apple. Binney would bind Apple on an instrument by signing "Apple, by Binney, agent," or simply "Apple."

If an authorized agent signs just his or her own name on the instrument ("Binney"), the agent is personally liable to a holder in due course who has no notice that the agent was not intended to be liable. For others, the agent can escape liability if the agent proves that the original parties did not intend the agent to be liable on the instrument [UCC R3–402(a), (b)(2)].[12] In either case, the principal is bound if the party entitled to enforce the instrument can prove the agency relationship. The parol evidence rule (discussed in Chapter 16) precludes the introduction of extrinsic evidence to establish that the signature was made for a principal.

The same rules apply (1) when an instrument is signed in both the agent's name and the principal's name ("Sandra Binney, Bob Apple" or "Apple, Binney") but nothing on the instrument indicates the agency relationship (so the agent cannot be distinguished from the principal); and (2) when an agent indicates agency status in signing a negotiable instrument but fails to name the principal ("Sandra Binney, agent") [UCC R3–402(b)(2); UCC 3–403(2)(b)]. Because these forms of signing are ambiguous, however, parol evidence is admissible *as between the original parties* (between the agent signing the instrument and the payee of the instrument) to prove the agency relationship.

When a negotiable instrument is signed in the name of an organization, and the organization's name is preceded or followed by the name and office of an authorized individual, the organization is bound; the individual who has signed the instrument in the representative capacity is not bound [UCC R3–402(b)(1), (c); UCC 3–403(3)].

**UNAUTHORIZED AGENT**   If the agent had no authority to sign the principal's name, the "unauthorized signature is ineffective except as the signature of the unauthorized signer" [UCC R3–403(a); UCC 3–404(1)]. Assume that Maya Campbell is the principal and Lena Chev is her agent. Chev, without authority, signs a promissory note as follows: "Maya Campbell, by Lena Chev, agent." Because Maya Campbell's "signature" is unauthorized, she cannot be held liable, but Chev is liable to a holder of the note. This would be true even if Chev had merely signed the note "Maya Campbell," without indicating any agency. In either case, the unauthorized signer, Chev, is liable on the instrument.

## UNAUTHORIZED SIGNATURES

People are not normally liable to pay on negotiable instruments unless their signatures appear on the instruments. The general rule is that an unauthorized signature is wholly inoperative and will not bind the person whose name is forged.[13] Assume, for example, that Pablo finds Veronica's checkbook lying on the street, writes out a check to himself, and forges Veronica's signature. If a bank fails to ascertain that Veronica's signature is not genuine and cashes the check for Pablo, the bank will generally be liable to Veronica for the amount. (The liability of banks for paying instruments on which there are forged signatures is discussed further in Chapter 29.) There are two exceptions to this rule:

1. Any unauthorized signature is wholly inoperative unless the person whose name is signed ratifies (affirms) it or is precluded from denying it [UCC R3–403(a); UCC 3–404(1)]. For example, a signature made by an agent exceeding the scope of the agent's authority can be ratified by the principal. A principal may ratify an unauthorized signature by failing

---

11.   If the agent signs the principal's name, the UCC presumes that the signature is authorized and genuine [UCC R3–308(a); UCC 3–307(1)(b)].

12.   See UCC R3–402, Comment 1. Under UCC 3–401(1), the principal is not liable on an instrument unless his or her signature appears on it, even if the parties are aware of the agency relationship.

13.   In contrast, a drawee (such as the drawer's bank) is charged with knowledge of the drawer's signature. The drawee cannot recover money it pays out to a holder in due course on a negotiable instrument bearing a forged drawer's signature. See UCC R3–418(c); UCC 3–418.

to repudiate it. Thus, Richard Eustler was held to have ratified his brother's forgery of Richard's signature on checks cashed at a bank when Richard asked the bank not to prosecute his brother for the forgery; agreed to a repayment schedule from his brother; and did not sue the bank until six months later, when his brother disappeared.[14]

Moreover, a person who writes and signs a check, leaves blank the amount and the name of the payee, and then leaves the check in a place available to the public can be estopped (prevented), on the basis of negligence, from denying liability for its payment [UCC R3–115; UCC R3–406; UCC R4–401(d)(2); UCC 3–115; UCC 3–406; UCC 4–401(2)(b)]. Whatever loss occurs may be allocated, however, between certain parties on the basis of comparative negligence [UCC R3–406(b)].[15] Suppose, for example, that a bank raises the negligence of the drawer who left the signed check available to the public as a defense to

the bank's payment of the check. If the drawer can prove that the bank failed to exercise ordinary care in the payment of this check and that this failure substantially contributed to whatever loss occurred, the loss may be allocated between the two parties on a comparative negligence basis.

2. An unauthorized signature operates as the signature of the unauthorized signer in favor of an HDC [UCC R3–403(a); UCC 3–404(1)]. For example, if Michel Vuillard signs ''Paul Richaud'' without Richaud's authorization, Vuillard is personally liable just as if he had signed his own name. Vuillard's liability is limited, however, to persons who take or pay the instrument in good faith. One who knew the signature was unauthorized would not qualify as an HDC and thus could not recover from Vuillard on the instrument.

In the following case, an employee, without authorization, indorsed checks payable to his employer and deposited them into his personal bank account. The question before the court is whether the employer's negligence should preclude liability on the part of the banks for paying the checks over an unauthorized indorsement.

---

14. *Eustler v. First National Bank, Pawhuska,* 639 P.2d 1245 (Okla. 1982).
15. UCC 3–406 does not provide for an allocation of such a loss on a comparative negligence basis.

---

**BACKGROUND AND FACTS** *Husker News Company, a wholesale distributor of magazines and books, employed Walter Hopf to deliver magazines and books to retail stores. Hopf's duties included delivering the magazines to Husker's customers, returning magazines not sold by the customers to Husker for credit on the customers' accounts, delivering bills to Husker's customers, and collecting payments on those bills. Husker allowed Hopf to deposit customers'* cash payments *into his personal bank account and to reimburse Husker for the cash deposited by writing personal checks to Husker. All checks received by Hopf, however, were to be delivered by Hopf to Husker. Hopf developed elaborate plots to appropriate funds from his customers' accounts. Among other things, he deposited checks payable to Husker into his personal account. Hopf indorsed the checks ''Husker News by Walter Hopf'' and told the bank teller at his bank that he was authorized to indorse the checks. The bank then stamped ''P.E.G.'' (prior endorsement guaranteed) onto the checks. Between 1982 and 1988, several customers notified Husker of possible wrongdoings by Hopf, but Husker never did anything about the situation. Finally, in 1988, Husker fired Hopf. Husker then sued its bank and the customers' banks, which had paid the checks over Hopf's unauthorized indorsements, to recover the funds. The trial court found for the defendant banks. Husker appealed.*

**CASE 28.1**

**HUSKER NEWS CO. v. SOUTH OTTUMWA SAVINGS BANK**

Supreme Court of Iowa, 1992. 482 N.W.2d 404.

*HARRIS*, Justice.

\* \* \* \*

Husker is correct in asserting that an unauthorized signature generally will prevent subsequent takers of an instrument from being holders, and therefore holders in due course. This is because a forger's signature does not constitute an endorsement, a requirement to qualify as a holder in due course.

\* \* \* \*

\* \* \* [T]he banks point out that they are entitled to dismissal under Iowa Code [Section] 554.3406 [Iowa's version of the unrevised UCC 3–406] which provides: Any person whose negligence substantially contributes to . . . the making of an unauthorized signature is precluded from asserting the . . . lack of authority . . . against a drawee or other payor who pays the instrument in good faith and in accordance with the reasonable commercial standards of the drawee's or the payor's business. \* \* \*

\* \* \* \*

\* \* \* [We] find \* \* \* negligence on Husker's part \* \* \* substantially contributed to Hopf's false signatures on the checks.

The banks also established they acted in good faith and in accordance with reasonable business procedures. \* \* \*

\* \* \* The checks, when presented, were examined for an endorsement which was compared with the named payee on the front of the check. The evidence was that there was no practical way to check further, and it was therefore necessary to rely on the P.E.G. stamp. The procedure was eminently reasonable in view of the obvious fact that Husker acquiesced in it for a period of years.

**DECISION AND REMEDY**  *The Supreme Court of Iowa held that Husker was precluded from denying Hopf's authority to indorse the checks. Under Iowa law, Husker was therefore barred from recovery, and the claims were dismissed.*

**ETHICAL CONSIDERATIONS**  *Did the customers serviced by Hopf have an obligation to do more to prevent Hopf's misconduct? The law does not recognize a Good Samaritan obligation to prevent the perpetration of a tort by another on a third party. The general common law rule is that a person has no duty to prevent a third party from causing harm to another. Thus, there is no legal reason to impose a duty on an outsider to protect an employer from its own employee. It might be argued, however, that the customers had an ethical duty to monitor Hopf, once they suspected misconduct, to prevent as much of his wrongdoing as arose from their dealings with him.*

## SPECIAL RULES FOR UNAUTHORIZED INDORSEMENTS

Generally, when there is a forged or unauthorized indorsement, the burden of loss falls on the first party to take the instrument with such an indorsement. Two situations are possible, however, in which the loss falls on the maker or drawer:

1. When an imposter induces the maker or drawer of an instrument to issue it to the imposter [UCC R3–404(a)].
2. When a person signs as or on behalf of a maker or drawer, intending that the payee will have no interest in the instrument, or when an agent or employee of the maker or drawer has supplied him or her with the name of the payee, also intending the payee to have no such interest [UCC R3–404(b); UCC R3–405; UCC 3–405(1)]. Such a situation often involves an employee who wishes to swindle an employer by padding bills or payrolls.

**IMPOSTERS**  An **imposter** is one who, by use of the mails, telephone, facsimile (fax) machine, or personal appearance, induces a maker or drawer to issue an instrument in the name of an impersonated payee. If the maker or drawer believes the imposter to be the named payee at the time of issue, the indorsement by the imposter is not treated as unauthorized when the instrument is transferred to an innocent party. This is because the maker or drawer intended the imposter to receive the instrument.

In these situations, the unauthorized indorsement of a payee's name can be as effective as if the real payee had signed. The *imposter rule* provides that an imposter's indorsement will be effective—that is, not a forgery—insofar as the drawer goes [UCC R3–404(a); UCC 3–405(1)(a)].

For example, a man walks into Ned March's sportswear store and purports to be Jerry Lewis soliciting contributions for his annual fund-raising for muscular dystrophy. March has heard of the Lewis Telethon but has never met or seen Jerry Lewis. Wishing to support a worthy cause, March writes out a check for $250 payable to Jerry Lewis and hands it to the imposter. The imposter indorses the check in the name of Jerry Lewis and negotiates the check to a Stop and Shop convenience store. March discovers the fraud and stops payment on the check, claiming that the payee's signature is forged. Because the imposter rule is in effect, March cannot claim a forgery against Stop and Shop but must seek redress from the imposter instead. If March had sent the check to the real Jerry Lewis, but the check had been stolen and negotiated to the store on a forged indorsement, the imposter rule would *not* apply, and Stop and Shop would have to seek redress against the forger.

The comparative negligence standard mentioned in connection with the liability of banks paying over forged signatures in the preceding section also applies in cases involving imposters [UCC R3–404(d)].[16] If, for example, a bank fails to exercise ordinary care in cashing a check made out to an imposter—for example, if the bank fails to check the identity of the holder-payee and this failure substantially contributes to the drawer's loss, the drawer may have a cause of action against the bank.

**FICTITIOUS PAYEES** The so-called **fictitious payee** rule deals with the intent of the maker or drawer to issue an instrument to a payee who has no interest in the instrument. This most often takes place when (1) a dishonest employee deceives the employer into signing an instrument payable to a party with no right to receive the instrument or (2) a dishonest employee or agent has the authority to issue an instrument on behalf of the employer. In these situations, the payee's indorsement is not treated as a forgery, and the employer can be held liable on the instrument by an innocent holder.

Assume that Goldstar Aviation, Inc., gives its bookkeeper, Leslie Rose, general authority to issue checks in the company name drawn on First State Bank so that Rose can pay employees' wages and other corporate bills. Rose decides to cheat Goldstar out of $10,000 by issuing a check payable to the Del Rey Company, a supplier of aircraft parts. Rose does not intend Del Rey to receive any of the money nor is Del Rey entitled to the payment. Rose indorses the check in Del Rey's name and deposits the check in an account that she opened in West National Bank in the name ''Del Rey Co.'' with her authority to draw on the account. West National Bank accepts the check and collects payment from the drawee-bank, First State Bank. First State Bank charges Goldstar's account $10,000. Rose transfers $10,000 out of the Del Rey account and closes the account. Goldstar discovers the fraud and demands that the account be recredited.

Who bears the loss? Because Rose's indorsement in the name of a payee with no interest in the instrument is ''effective,'' there is no ''forgery'' [UCC R3–404(b)(2); UCC 3–405(1)(b)]. Under this provision, West National Bank is protected in paying on the check, and the drawee-bank is protected in charging Goldstar's account. Thus, it is the employer-drawer, Goldstar, who will bear the loss.[17] Of course, Goldstar has recourse against Rose, who has, however, most likely spent the money or absconded with it.

Under some circumstances, Goldstar may also have recourse against West National Bank. The comparative negligence standard mentioned in connection with the liability of banks paying over forged signatures and in cases involving imposters also applies in cases involving fictitious payees [UCC R3–404(d)]. In addition, UCC R3–405(b) states, ''If a person paying the instrument or taking it for value or for collection fails to exercise ordinary care in paying or taking the instrument and

---

16. UCC 3–405 does not provide for an allocation of such a loss on a comparative negligence basis.

17. *K & M Contracting, Inc. v. Citizens National Bank,* 89 Ohio App.3d 157, 623 N.E.2d 1247 (Ohio App. 3 Dist. 1993).

that failure substantially contributes to loss resulting from the fraud, the person bearing the loss may recover from the person failing to exercise ordinary care to the extent the failure to exercise ordinary care contributed to the loss.''

Thus, West National Bank could be liable if it failed to exercise ordinary care when it allowed Rose to open an account in the name ''Del Rey Co.,'' to deposit the check payable to Del Rey in the account, or to withdraw from the account funds that were proceeds of the check payable to Del Rey. A failure to exercise ordinary care is determined in light of all the circumstances relating to the bank's conduct with respect to the bank's collection of the check, and the failure must contribute substantially to the loss. The bank may be liable to the extent that the failure contributes to the loss.

Suppose, for example, that Del Rey is a famous national corporation, and West National opened the Del Rey account for Rose without requiring Rose to provide any proof that she was authorized to act for Del Rey. Imagine further that after receiving payment on the check, West National allowed Rose to transfer the funds to an account in a bank in Switzerland. A court could find in those circumstances that West National did not exercise ordinary care, that the failure contributed to Goldstar's loss, and that Goldstar could recover part or all of its loss from West National.

Whether a dishonest employee actually signs the check or merely supplies his or her employer with names of fictitious creditors (or with true names of creditors having fictitious debts), the UCC makes no distinction in result. Assume that Dan Symes draws up the payroll list from which employees' salary checks are written. He fraudulently adds the name Penny Trip (a friend not entitled to payment) to the payroll, thus causing checks to be issued to her. Trip cashes the checks and shares the proceeds with Symes. Again, it is the employer-drawer who bears the loss.

## SECTION 2

# WARRANTY LIABILITY

In addition to the signature liability discussed in the preceding section, transferors make certain implied warranties regarding the instruments that they are negotiating. Liability under these warranties is not subject to the conditions of proper presentment, dishonor, and notice of dishonor. These warranties arise even when a transferor does not indorse the instrument (as in delivery of bearer paper) [UCC R3–416; UCC R3–417; UCC 3–417]. Transfer warranties are particularly important when a holder cannot hold a party liable on his or her signature. Warranties fall into two categories: those that arise from the *transfer* of a negotiable instrument and those that arise upon *presentment.*

## TRANSFER WARRANTIES

There are five **transfer warranties** [UCC R3–416; UCC 3–417(2)]. Any person who transfers an instrument *for consideration* warrants to the transferee and, if the transfer is by *indorsement,* to all subsequent transferees and holders who take the instrument in good faith:

1. The transferor is entitled to enforce the instrument.
2. All signatures are authentic and authorized.
3. The instrument has not been altered.
4. The instrument is not subject to a defense or claim of any party that can be asserted against the transferor.[18]
5. The transferor has no knowledge of any insolvency proceedings against the maker, the acceptor, or the drawer of an instrument.

If the person who transfers an instrument receives consideration, the manner of transfer and the negotiation that is used determine how far and to whom a transfer warranty will run. Transfer by indorsement and delivery of order paper extends warranty liability to any subsequent holder who takes the instrument in good faith. The warranties of a person who transfers without indorsement (by delivery of bearer paper), however, will extend only to the immediate transferee [UCC R3–416(a); UCC 3–417(2)].

Suppose that Wylie forges Kim's name as a maker of a promissory note. The note is made payable to Wylie. Wylie indorses the note in blank, negotiates it to Bret, and then leaves the country. Bret, without indorsement, delivers the note to

---

18. Under UCC 3–417(3), a qualified indorser who indorses an instrument ''without recourse'' limits this warranty to a warranty that he or she has ''no knowledge'' of such a defense rather than that there is no defense. This limitation does not apply under the revised Article 3.

## ■ CONCEPT SUMMARY 28.1 Transfer Warranty Liability for Transferors Who Receive Consideration

| TRANSFERORS | TO WHOM WARRANTIES EXTEND IF CONSIDERATION IS RECEIVED |
|---|---|
| **Indorsers** | Five transfer warranties extend to *all* subsequent holders: <br> 1. The transferor is entitled to enforce the instrument. <br> 2. All signatures are authentic and authorized. <br> 3. The instrument has not been altered. <br> 4. The instrument is not subject to a defense or claim of any party that can be asserted against the transferor. <br> 5. The transferor has no knowledge of insolvency proceedings against the maker, acceptor, or drawer of an instrument. |
| **Nonindorsers** | Same as for indorsers, but warranties extend *only* to the *immediate transferee*. |

Fern. Fern, in turn without indorsement, delivers the note to Rick. On Rick's presentment of the note to Kim, the forgery is discovered. Rick can hold Fern (the immediate transferor) liable for breach of warranty that all signatures are genuine. Rick cannot hold Bret liable, because Bret is not Rick's immediate transferor but is a prior nonindorsing transferor. This example shows the importance of the distinction between (1) transfer by indorsement and delivery of order paper and (2) transfer by delivery of bearer paper without indorsement.

A transferee or holder who takes an instrument in good faith can sue on the basis of a breach of a warranty as soon as he or she has reason to know of the breach [UCC R3–416(d)]. Notice of a claim for breach of warranty must be given to the warrantor within thirty days after the transferee or holder has reason to know of the breach and the identity of the warrantor, or the warrantor is not liable for any loss caused by a delay [UCC R3–416(c)]. The transferee or holder can recover damages for the breach in an amount equal to the loss suffered (but not more than the amount of the instrument), plus expenses and any loss of interest caused by the breach [UCC R3–416(b)].

These warranties can be disclaimed with respect to any instrument except a check [UCC R3–416(c)]. In the check collection process, banks rely on these warranties. In the case of all other instruments, the immediate parties can agree to a disclaimer, and an indorser can disclaim by including in the indorsement such words as "without warranties."

## PRESENTMENT WARRANTIES

Any person who obtains payment or acceptance of an instrument warrants to any other person who in good faith pays or accepts the instrument that

1. The person obtaining payment or acceptance is entitled to enforce the instrument or is authorized to obtain payment or acceptance on behalf of a person who is entitled to enforce the instrument. (This is in effect a warranty that there are no missing or unauthorized indorsements.)
2. The instrument has not been altered.
3. The person obtaining payment or acceptance has <u>no knowledge</u> that the signature of the drawer of the instrument is unauthorized [UCC R3–417(a), (d); UCC 3–417(1)].

These warranties are often referred to as **presentment warranties** because they protect the person to whom the instrument is presented. These warranties cannot be disclaimed with respect to checks, and a claim for breach must be given to the warrantor within thirty days after the claimant knows, or has reason to know, of the breach and the identity of the warrantor [UCC R3–417(e)].

The second and third warranties do not apply in certain cases (to certain persons) in which the presenter is a holder in due course. It is assumed, for example, that a drawer or a maker will recognize his or her own signature and that a maker or an acceptor will recognize whether an instrument has been materially altered.

Both transfer and presentment warranties attempt to shift liability back to a wrongdoer or to the person who dealt face to face with the wrongdoer and thus was in the best position to prevent the wrongdoing.

Under the unrevised UCC 3–417, it was sometimes held that presentment warranties were made to the drawer of a check when the check was presented to the drawee-bank for payment. UCC R3–417 rejects the holdings in these cases, thereby allowing certain presentment warranties to a drawer *only* in the case of a *dishonored* draft. The following case illustrates the effect of this change and indicates how a court might reconcile conflicting case law on the issue.

---

### CASE 28.2

**STEINROE INCOME TRUST v. CONTINENTAL BANK, N.A.**

Appellate Court of Illinois, First District, Fifth Division, 1992.
238 Ill.App.3d 660,
606 N.E.2d 503,
179 Ill.Dec. 671.

**COMPANY PROFILE**   *In 1924, three Chicago banks—Merchants' Loan and Trust, Illinois Trust and Savings, and Corn Exchange National Bank—merged to become Illinois Merchants' Trust. Illinois Merchants' Trust joined with Continental Bank and Commercial Bank in 1928 to become Continental Illinois Bank and Trust. In 1932, as part of the New Deal, the federal government loaned $50 million to Continental, which was suffering from the Great Depression. Walter Cummings, an officer in the new Federal Deposit Insurance Corporation, became chairman of Continental. Cummings believed in investing only in low-risk government securities and loaning only to the most solid customers. These policies enabled Continental to repay the government by 1939. In 1959, Cummings retired, and his successors pursued more aggressive lending policies. In the 1970s, Continental became Chicago's largest bank. Some of its growth came from loans purchased from Penn Square, a bank in Oklahoma City. Penn Square failed in 1982, leaving Continental with $1 billion in bad loans. Large depositors tried to withdraw their money, and in 1984, Continental collapsed in the largest banking collapse at that time in the history of the United States. Again, the federal government bailed out Continental, with $4.5 billion in guarantees. In 1988, Continental dropped ''Illinois'' from its name as it repositioned itself to focus on national corporate accounts. Three years later, the bank was free of its obligation to the government.*

**BACKGROUND AND FACTS**   *After the death of her husband, Mary Dybas filed a claim on his life insurance policy. In early 1987, the insurance company sent Dybas a check for approximately $100,000. Before the check reached Dybas, however, an unidentified culprit stole it. The culprit assumed the identity of ''Howard Brest'' and used the check to open an account with the Steinroe Income Trust, an investment company. Although the only payee on the check was Dybas, the account was opened as a joint account in the names of Dybas and Brest. The indorsements on the back of the check in the names of Dybas and Brest were unauthorized. Three days after opening the account, the culprit learned that the check had cleared. The next day, the culprit asked Steinroe for a check drawn on $87,500 of the amount in the account. This new check (the redemption check) was made payable to Dybas and Brest. The culprit opened an account with Continental Bank, N.A., in the name of Howard Brest and deposited the redemption check—again with false indorsements—into this account. Continental cashed the redemption check at Steinroe's bank. The culprit absconded with the proceeds. The insurance company eventually issued a new check to Mary Dybas, and Steinroe Income Trust reimbursed the insurance company for the amount of the first check. When Steinroe's* *bank refused to recredit its account for the amount of the redemption check, Steinroe filed a lawsuit against Continental for the loss. Steinroe argued that Continental had breached the presentment warranties when it presented the redemption check to Steinroe's bank for payment. Continental countered that it did not make the presentment warranties to Steinroe, the drawer of the redemption check, and that thus Steinroe did not have standing (that is, Steinroe was not the proper party) to enforce those warranties. When the trial court ruled in Steinroe's favor, Continental appealed.*

Justice *LORENZ* delivered the opinion of the court:

\* \* \* \*

\* \* \* According to the express language of the [unrevised UCC 3–417 and 4–207], a party had standing to enforce the presentment warranties only if it could be deemed the "payor bank" or "other payor" who pays or accepts. \* \* \*

It is clear that Steinroe did not have standing as a "payor bank." [Steinroe's bank], not Steinroe, was the "payor bank" on the redemption check.

However, at the time of the [trial court proceedings], it was somewhat unclear whether Steinroe, as the drawer of the redemption check, could be deemed an "other payor" and thereby satisfy the standing requirements. In fact, the parties set forth case law from across the country which presented a majority and minority view on this question. The majority view provided that the language "other payor" required a narrow construction which excluded the drawer of a check. Continental Bank argued that the court should apply this majority view \* \* \* . The minority view provided that the language "other payor" required a broad construction which included the drawer of a check. Steinroe argued that the court should apply this minority view and cited the leading case in support thereof, *Sun 'N Sand, Inc. v. United California Bank.*

We note that, after the parties filed their briefs, [unrevised UCC] 3–417 and 4–207 were amended [as part of the revisions to Article 3]. The Comments to [UCC R3–417] addressed the question concerning application of the majority and minority view: "In *Sun 'N Sand, Inc. v. United California Bank,* the court held that under former section 3–417(1) a warranty was made to the drawer of a check when the check was presented to the drawee for payment. The result in that case is rejected." Therefore, we also reject Steinroe's argument for application of the minority view \* \* \* .

*The appellate court held that Steinroe, as the drawer of the redemption check, did not have standing to enforce the presentment warranties. The court reversed the judgment of the trial court. Steinroe, who had arguably been in the best position to prevent the wrongdoing, thus suffered the loss of the funds.*

**DECISION AND REMEDY**

## SECTION 3

# DISCHARGE

Discharge from liability on an instrument can come from payment, cancellation, or, as previously discussed, material alteration. Discharge can also occur if a party reacquires an instrument, if a holder impairs another party's right of recourse, or if a holder surrenders collateral without consent.

## DISCHARGE BY PAYMENT OR TENDER OF PAYMENT

All parties to a negotiable instrument will be discharged when the party primarily liable on it pays to a holder the amount due in full [UCC R3–602; UCC R3–603; UCC 3–601; UCC 3–603].[19] The same is true if the drawee of an unaccepted draft or check makes payment in good faith to the holder. In these situations, all parties on the instruments are usually discharged. By contrast, such payment made by any other party (for example, an indorser,) will discharge only the indorser and subsequent parties on the instrument. The party making such a payment still has the right to recover on the instrument from any prior parties.

A party will not be discharged when paying in bad faith to a holder who acquired the instrument by theft or who obtained the instrument from someone else who acquired it by theft (unless, of course, the person has the rights of a holder in due course) [UCC R3–602(b)(2); UCC 3–603(1)(a)].

If a tender of payment of an obligation to pay an instrument is made to a person entitled to enforce the instrument and the tender is refused, indorsers and accommodation parties with a right of recourse against the party making the tender are discharged to the extent of the amount of the tender [UCC R3–603(b)]. If a tender of payment of an amount due on an instrument is made to a person entitled

to enforce the instrument, the obligor's obligation to pay interest after the due date on the amount tendered is discharged [UCC R3–603(c)].

## DISCHARGE BY CANCELLATION

The holder of a negotiable instrument can discharge any party to the instrument by cancellation. "A person entitled to enforce an instrument, with or without consideration, may discharge the obligation of a party to pay the instrument * * * by an intentional voluntary act, such as surrender of the instrument to the party, destruction, mutilation, or cancellation of the instrument, cancellation or striking out of the party's signature, or the addition of words to the instrument indicating discharge" [UCC R3–604(a)(i)]. For example, writing the word "Paid" across the face of an instrument constitutes cancellation. Tearing up a negotiable instrument cancels the instrument. Crossing out a party's indorsement cancels that party's liability and the liability of subsequent indorsers who have already indorsed the instrument, but not the liability of any prior parties.

Destruction or mutilation of a negotiable instrument is considered cancellation only if it is done with the intention of eliminating obligation on the instrument [UCC R3–604(a)(i); UCC 3–605(1)(a)]. Thus, if destruction or mutilation occurs by accident, the instrument is not discharged, and the original terms can be established by parol evidence [UCC R3–309; UCC 3–804]. The requirement of intent is considered in the following case.

---

19.   This is true even if the payment is made "with knowledge of a claim to the instrument * * * by another person" unless the payor knows that "payment is prohibited by injunction or similar process of a court of competent jurisdiction" or, in most cases, "the party making payment accepted, from a person having a claim to the instrument, indemnity against loss resulting from refusal to pay the person entitled to enforce the instrument" [UCC R3–602(a), (b)(1); UCC 3–603(1)].

---

| CASE 28.3 | **BACKGROUND AND FACTS** *Richard and Coralea Triplett executed* |
|---|---|

**FIRSTIER BANK, N.A. v. TRIPLETT**

Supreme Court of Nebraska, 1993.
242 Neb. 614,
497 N.W.2d 339.

**BACKGROUND AND FACTS**  *Richard and Coralea Triplett executed two promissory notes in favor of FirsTier Bank, N.A. (N.A. stands for National Association). The first note, dated April 17, 1986, was for $14,000. The second note, dated June 16, 1987, was for $3,500. On July 6, 1987, Richard Triplett tendered to FirsTier a check for $7,200 as a payment on the notes. At the time, the balances were $10,498.79 on the first note and $2,418.73 on the second note. A loan service clerk pulled the Tripletts' notes from the files and divided the $7,200 payment to pay the second note in full and to reduce the amount owed on the first note. The clerk then incorrectly stamped the first note "PAID," signed it, and mailed it to the Tripletts. In November, a different clerk stamped the second note "PAID," signed it, and returned it to the Tripletts. More than a year later, FirsTier notified the Tripletts that they still owed money on the first note. When the bank demanded payment, Richard Triplett indicated that "the loan was paid up." FirsTier sued the Tripletts. At the trial, the*

*Tripletts admitted that they knew their $7,200 payment was not enough to pay both notes in full but asserted that the bank had stamped "PAID" on the notes and returned them. The bank contended that it had not intended to release both notes and explained that the return of the first note was an error by a clerk who did not have the authority or power to authorize the release of promissory notes without payment in full. The court entered a judgment in favor of FirsTier. The Tripletts appealed.*

*FAHRNBRUCH,* Justice.

\* \* \* \*

Whether a promissory note is discharged pursuant to the Uniform Commercial Code when it is marked "paid" and surrendered to the maker is a question of first impression in Nebraska.[a] \* \* \*

\* \* \* \*

\* \* \* Courts that have considered discharge of a promissory note \* \* \* have held that cancellation must be accompanied by an intent to discharge the maker. \* \* \*

Although [the unrevised UCC] did not specifically state that surrender of an instrument must be intentional in order to effect a discharge, "[t]he courts have glossed this section by requiring that surrender of the instrument be accompanied by an intent to discharge the party." This is consistent with the Legislature's latest revision of Nebraska's Uniform Commercial Code. Discharge by cancellation or renunciation is now governed by [UCC R3–604] \* \* \* . Section [R3–604(a)] provides that "[a] person entitled to enforce an instrument . . . may discharge the obligation of a party to pay the instrument (i) by an intentional voluntary act, such as surrender of the instrument to the party . . . or cancellation of the instrument . . . ." This language requires that discharge be intentional, whether by cancellation or surrender.

All jurisdictions that have considered the issue have concluded that clerical error does not have the legal effect of canceling an existing debt or discharging an instrument. This is simply an application of the general rule that cancellation or surrender of an instrument has no effect when done by a person without authority from the holder of the instrument.

*The appellate court affirmed the trial court's judgment. The appellate court held that the unintentional cancellation and surrender of a promissory note through a clerical error does not discharge the maker of the note.*

**DECISION AND REMEDY**

a. A question of law is said to be "of first impression" when it is an entirely new question for the decision of the court and is not governed by an existing precedent.

## DISCHARGE BY REACQUISITION

A person who reacquires an instrument that he or she held previously discharges all intervening indorsers against subsequent holders who do not qualify as holders in due course [UCC R3–207; UCC 3–208; UCC 3–601(3)(a)]. Of course, the person reacquiring the instrument may be liable to subsequent holders.

## DISCHARGE BY IMPAIRMENT OF RECOURSE OR OF COLLATERAL

Discharge can also occur when a party's right of recourse is impaired [UCC R3–605; UCC 3–606]. A right of recourse is a right to seek reimbursement. Ordinarily, when a holder collects the amount of an instrument from an indorser, the indorser has a right of recourse against prior indorsers, the maker or drawer, and accommodation parties. If the holder has adversely affected the indorser's right to seek reimbursement from these other parties, however, the indorser is not liable on the instrument (to the extent that the indorser's right of recourse is impaired). This occurs when, for example, the holder releases or agrees not to sue a party against whom the indorser has a right of recourse. This also occurs when a holder agrees to an extension of the instrument's due date or to some other material modification that results in a loss to the indorser with respect to the right of recourse [UCC R3–605(c), (d)].

Sometimes a party to an instrument gives collateral to secure that his or her performance will occur. When a holder "impairs the value" of that collateral without the consent of the parties who would benefit from the collateral in the event of nonpayment, those parties to the instrument are discharged to the extent of the impairment [UCC R3–605(e), (f); UCC 3–606(1)(b)].[20]

For example, suppose that Jerome and Donna sign a note as co-makers, putting up Jerome's property as collateral. The note is payable to Mitsui. Mitsui is required by law to file a financing statement with the state to put others on notice of Mitsui's interest in Jerome's property as collateral for the note. If Mitsui fails to file the statement and Jerome goes through bankruptcy—which results in Jerome's property being sold to pay other debts and leaves him unable to pay anything on the note—Mitsui has impaired the value of the collateral to Donna, who is discharged to the extent of that impairment.[21]

---

20. Impairing the value of an interest in collateral includes "(i) failure to obtain or maintain perfection or recordation of the interest in collateral, (ii) release of collateral without substitution of collateral of equal value, (iii) failure to perform a duty to preserve the value of collateral owed, under Article 9 or other law, to a debtor or surety or other person secondarily liable, or (iv) failure to comply with applicable law in disposing of collateral" [UCC R3–605(g)].

21. Mitsui's failure to file the statement prevented Mitsui, when Jerome went through bankruptcy, from taking possession of the collateral, selling it, and crediting the amount owed on the note. Donna, as co-maker, would then have been responsible only for any remaining indebtedness, instead of the entire unpaid balance. Thus, Donna is discharged to the extent that the proceeds from the sale of the collateral would have discharged her liability on the note.

---

## TERMS AND CONCEPTS TO REVIEW

| | | |
|---|---|---|
| acceptor 530 | fictitious payee 537 | principal 533 |
| accommodation party 533 | imposter 536 | signature 530 |
| agent 533 | presentment warranty 539 | transfer warranty 538 |

# QUESTIONS AND CASE PROBLEMS

**28–1. Unauthorized Indorsements.** What are the exceptions to the rule that a bank will be liable for paying a check over an unauthorized indorsement?

**28–2. Liability on Negotiable Instruments.** Waldo makes out a negotiable promissory note payable to the order of Grace. Grace indorses the note by writing "without recourse, Grace," and transfers the note for value to Adam. Adam, in need of cash, negotiates the note to Keith by indorsing it with the words "Pay to Keith, Adam." On the due date, Keith presents the note to Waldo for payment, only to learn that Waldo has filed for bankruptcy and will have all debts (including the note) discharged in bankruptcy. Discuss fully whether Keith can hold Waldo, Grace, or Adam liable on the note.

**28–3. Discharge.** Gil makes out a $900 negotiable promissory note payable to Ben. By special indorsement, Ben transfers the note for value to Jess. By blank indorsement, Jess transfers the note for value to Pam. By special indorsement, Pam transfers the note for value to

Adrien. In need of cash, Adrien transfers the instrument for value by blank indorsement *back* to Jess. When told that Ben has left the country, Jess strikes out Ben's indorsement. Later she learns that Ben is a wealthy restaurant owner in Baltimore and that Gil is financially unable to pay the note. Jess contends she can hold Ben, Pam, or Adrien liable on the note as an HDC. Discuss fully Jess's contentions.

**28–4. Agents' Signatures.** Paris Lee is a purchasing agent for Ontario Products, Inc., a manufacturer of sports equipment. Paris has authority to sign checks in payment of purchases made by Ontario. Paris makes out three checks to suppliers and signs each one differently, as follows:

(a) Ontario Products, Inc., by Paris Lee, purchasing agent.

(b) Paris Lee, purchasing agent.

(c) Paris Lee.

Discuss briefly whether Paris is personally liable on each signature and whether parol evidence is admissible to hold Ontario Products, Inc., liable.

**28–5. Unauthorized Indorsements.** Douglas Law, an accountant, has worked for Liz Stein for five years. During that time, Stein has relied more and more on Law to prepare payment checks for suppliers, payroll checks, and the like. Unknown to Stein, Law is a compulsive gambler and is deeply in debt. To obtain funds to leave town and avoid paying the debt, Law prepares two checks payable to nonexistent suppliers. Stein signs both checks without knowledge of these events. Law indorses both suppliers' names and adds "Pay to Douglas Law" above both names. Law takes the checks and deposits them at his bank without indorsement. Later, he withdraws the funds from his bank. His bank sends the checks through the collection process. The checks are paid by Stein's bank, the drawee. Stein discovers Law's action after Law has left town. Stein claims that Law's indorsement of the suppliers' names constituted a forgery, that Law's bank did not have Law's indorsement, and that the bank must therefore recredit her account. Discuss Stein's contentions.

**28–6. Unauthorized Indorsements.** F. Mitchell, assistant treasurer of Travco Corp., caused two checks payable to a fictitious company, L. and B. Distributors, to be drawn on the corporation's account. Mitchell took both checks to his personal bank, indorsed them "F. Mitchell," and gave them to the teller. The teller cashed them. When Travco learned of the embezzlement, it demanded reimbursement from the bank. The bank contended that under the rule concerning fictitious payees and imposters, Mitchell's indorsement was valid and that therefore the bank should be allowed to collect. Discuss whether the bank's contention is true. [*Travco Corp. v. Citizens Federal Savings & Loan Association,* 42 Mich.App. 291, 201 N.W.2d 675 (1972)]

**28–7. Unauthorized Indorsements.** First National Bank collected debts owed to Rock Island Bedding Co. and Berry Industries, Inc., and in turn paid those two

firms the amounts collected by remitting checks to them drawn on First National Bank. On several occasions, Johns, an employee of First National, asked the bank's accounting department to prepare cashier's checks payable to Rock Island Bedding Co. and to Berry Industries, Inc. The requests did not appear to be irregular, because the bank had been making regular payments to the two firms. Johns, however, forged the payees' indorsements on eighteen of the checks so issued and deposited them into an account at First City Bank of Dallas. Johns fraudulently obtained $903,300 in this way. First City indorsed the checks "P.I.G." (prior indorsements guaranteed) and presented them to First National for payment. First National paid the checks and later recovered from its insurer, Fidelity & Casualty Co. Fidelity sought recovery from First City, claiming that Johns's forged indorsements did not authorize First City to pay the checks and that First City should bear the loss. Do you agree? Why or why not? [*Fidelity & Casualty Co. v. First City Bank of Dallas,* 675 S.W.2d 316 (Tex.App.—Dallas 1984, no writ.)]

**28–8. Unauthorized Indorsements.** Mowatt worked as a bookkeeper for the law firm of McCarthy, Kenney & Reidy, P.C., which had several branch offices in the Boston area. Part of Mowatt's job involved preparing checks payable to the partners in other offices for the authorized signature of a partner of the firm. On numerous occasions, Mowatt wrote such checks with no intention of transmitting them to the payee-partners. Instead, after they had been signed by an authorized partner, Mowatt forged indorsements on the checks and then either cashed them or deposited them in one of three bank accounts that he had opened for this purpose. The fraudulent scheme went on for a year and a half, and when the forgeries were finally discovered, the law firm demanded that the bank credit its account with the full amount of loss that it had sustained as a result of the forgeries. The bank refused to do so, and the law firm brought an action against the bank. Which party had to bear the loss arising from the forgeries, the law firm or the drawee-bank? Discuss. [*McCarthy, Kenney & Reidy, P.C. v. First National Bank of Boston,* 402 Mass. 630, 524 N.E.2d 390 (1988)]

**28–9. Unauthorized Indorsements.** James Liddell, the president of JHL & Associates, Inc., persuaded Clifford Marston and his wife to invest in Fidelity, a company that Liddell said he represented. To execute the transaction, Liddell had the Marstons issue a check for $15,000 payable to Seattle-First National Bank (Sea-First) for the purpose of obtaining cashier's checks, which would then be sent to Fidelity. Liddell, in Clifford Marston's presence, obtained three cashier's checks payable to "JHL & Associates, Trust." Liddell did not send the checks to Fidelity but rather indorsed them to different individuals as part of a fraudulent Ponzi scheme (a scheme in which the perpetrator uses funds of recent investors to pay previous investors— often referred to as pyramiding), signing the indorsements "JHL & Associates." Eventually, the Marstons sued Sea-First to recover their money, alleging that the bank was liable for the loss because the checks were indorsed by entities other than the named payee (JHL & Associates, Trust). Discuss fully whether Liddell's indorsements were ineffective and whether the bank should be liable to the Marstons. [*Marston Enterprises, Inc. v. Seattle-First National Bank*, 57 Wash.App. 662, 789 P.2d 784 (1990)]

**28–10. Unauthorized Signatures.** Peter Sather owned Kid Gloves, Inc. Larry Andrews introduced himself to Sather as an ex-officer of a bank that Sather had been using and expressed an interest in buying Kid Gloves. To become more familiar with the business, Andrews began working for Sather. Sather and Andrews went to the First National Bank of Jefferson Parish on May 20, 1988, to open a commercial checking account. Sather introduced Andrews to the bank's officer as "chief financial officer" of Kid Gloves. Sather and Andrews agreed that the signatures of both were to be required

on all corporate checks, and the signature card on file at the bank was stamped, "Two or more signatures required." According to bank procedures, when two signatures were required, only one signer had to be present to cash a check, but the bank manager had to approve any check for more than $2,500. Less than a month later, on June 17, Andrews cashed a check payable to "Cash" for $1,000, and five days later, he cashed a check payable to "Lawrence E. Andrews" for $4,500. The bank manager approved the second check. Both checks appeared to include Sather's signature. When Sather received notice of an overdraft and a monthly bank statement with the two canceled checks, he sought to have the account credited for the $5,500. The bank refused to credit the account. Meanwhile, Andrews had disappeared. Kid Gloves filed a lawsuit against the bank. How should the court rule? Discuss fully. [*Kid Gloves, Inc. v. First National Bank of Jefferson Parish*, 600 So.2d 779 (La.App. 1992)]

# CHAPTER 29

# CHECKS AND THE BANKING SYSTEM

C hecks are the most common kind of negotiable instruments regulated by the Uniform Commercial Code (UCC). Checks, credit cards, and charge accounts are rapidly replacing currency as a means of payment in almost all transactions for goods and services. It is estimated that sixty billion personal and commercial checks are written each year in the United States. Checks are more than a daily convenience—they are an integral part of the economic system.

This chapter identifies the legal characteristics of checks and the legal duties and liabilities that arise when a check is issued. Then it considers the check deposit-and-collection process—that is, the actual procedure by which checks move through banking channels, causing the underlying cash dollars to be shifted from one bank account to another.

Checks are governed by both Article 3 and Article 4 of the UCC. The extent to which any party is either charged with or discharged from liability on a check is established according to the provisions of Article 3. Article 4 is a statement of the principles and rules of modern bank deposit-and-collection procedures. It governs the relationship of banks with one another as they process checks for payment, and it establishes a framework for deposit and checking agreements between a bank and its customers. A check can therefore fall within the scope of Article 3 and yet be subject to the provisions of Article 4 while it is in the course of collection. In the case of a conflict between Articles 3 and 4, Article 4 controls [UCC R4–102(a); UCC 4–102(1)].

## SECTION 1

## CHECKS

Recall from Chapter 26 that a **check** is a special type of draft that is drawn on a bank, ordering it to pay a sum of money on demand [UCC R3–104(f);

**547**

UCC 3–104(2)(b)]. A *bank* is "a person engaged in the business of banking, including a savings bank, savings and loan association, credit union or trust company" [UCC R4–105(1)].[1] If any other institution handles a check for payment or collection, the check is not covered by revised Article 4.

The person who writes the check is called the *drawer* and is usually a depositor in the bank on which the check is drawn. The person to whom the check is payable is the *payee*. The bank or financial institution on which the check is drawn is the *drawee*. If Anne Gordon writes a check from her checking account to pay her school tuition, she is the drawer, her bank is the drawee, and her school is the payee.

The payee can indorse the check to another person, thereby making that receiver a holder. Recall that a holder is a person in possession of an instrument when the instrument is payable to bearer or, if the instrument is payable to an identified person, when the identified person is in possession [UCC R1–201(20)].[2] The *payee as a holder* of a check has the right to transfer or negotiate it or to demand its payment in his or her own name, *as does any subsequent holder.*

A check does not, in and of itself, operate as an assignment of funds [UCC R3–408; UCC 3–409(1)]. It does not show an intention to make immediate transfer of the right to the specified sum. Thus, the drawee-bank is not liable to a payee or holder who presents the check for payment, even though the drawer has sufficient funds to pay the check. The payee's, or holder's, only recourse is against the drawer. (The drawer, however, may subsequently hold the bank liable for its wrongful refusal to pay.)

Between the time a check is drawn and the time it reaches the drawee, the effectiveness of the check may be altered by some event—for example, the drawer may die or order payment not to be made, or the account on which the check is drawn may be depleted. To avoid this problem, a payee may insist on payment by an instrument that has already been accepted by the drawee. Such an instrument may be a cashier's check, a traveler's check, or a certified check.

## CASHIER'S CHECK

Checks are usually three-party instruments, but on certain types of checks, the bank can serve as both the drawer and the drawee. For example, when a bank draws a check upon itself, the check is called a **cashier's check** and is a negotiable instrument upon issue (see Exhibit 29–1) [UCC R3–104(g)]. In effect, with a cashier's check, the bank lends its credit to the check's purchaser (the **remitter**), thus making it available for immediate use in banking circles. A cashier's check is therefore an acknowledgment of a debt drawn by the bank upon itself.

Suppose, for example, that Sonya is moving from Kansas City to Lawrence to attend the University of Kansas. Sonya may close her bank account in Kansas City, take a cashier's check payable to herself as payment of the amount, and use the check to open a new account in Lawrence. After opening the new account and depositing the check, Sonya might buy a cashier's check from her new bank to pay her tuition to the university. In that circumstance, the check would likely be payable to the University of Kansas.

## TELLER'S CHECK

**Teller's checks** are drafts drawn by a bank on another bank or payable at or through a bank [UCC R3–104(h)]. Similar to cashier's checks, teller's checks are not drawn on a customer's account. A teller's check is usually drawn on a bank. In some cases, however, a teller's check is drawn on a party or an institution that does not fall within the UCC R4–105 definition of *bank*. In any case, both types of teller's checks are included in the definition of *check* in UCC R3–104(f) and are subject to Article 3.

## TRAVELER'S CHECK

A **traveler's check** is payable on demand; is drawn on or payable through a bank; is designated by the term "traveler's check" or some substantially similar term; and requires, as a condition to payment,

---

1. Under the unrevised Article 4, the term *bank* is not defined, except to distinguish among banks that deposit, collect, and pay instruments. The term is generally considered to include only commercial banks, which at the time the unrevised Article 4 was written were the only banks that could offer checking accounts. Revised Article 4's definition makes it clear that other depository institutions now have the authority to issue and otherwise deal with checks.
2. Under UCC 1–201(20), the term *holder* is defined in slightly different language, but the meaning is essentially the same.

■ **Exhibit 29–1  A Cashier's Check**

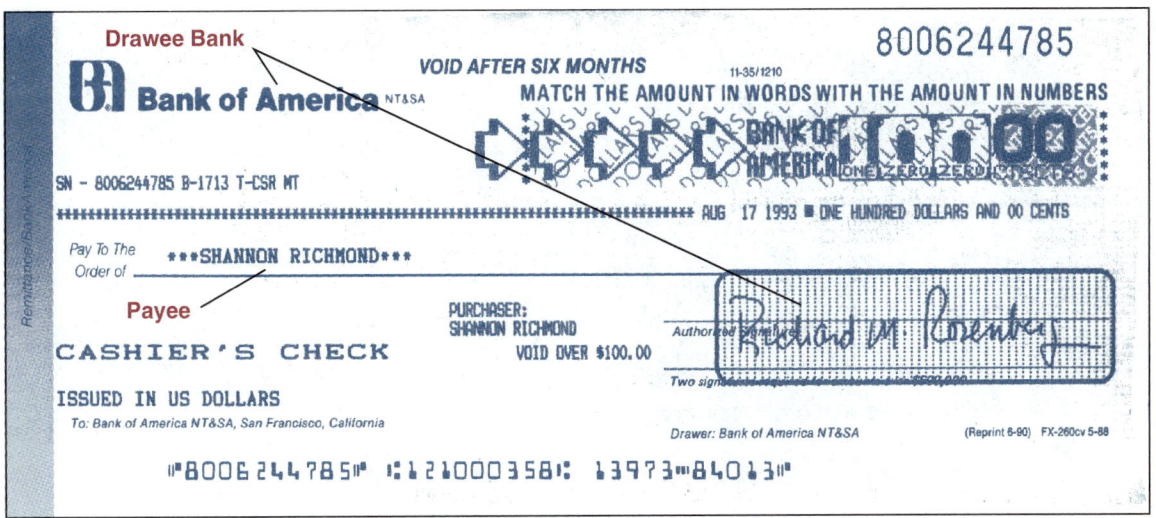

a countersignature by the person whose signature appears on the instrument [UCC R3–104(i)]. In other words, the purchaser of a traveler's check is required to sign the check at the time it is bought and again at the time it is used. Exhibit 29–2 shows an example of a traveler's check.

## CERTIFIED CHECK

A **certified check** is a check accepted by the bank on which it is drawn [UCC R3–409(d); UCC 3–411(1)]. When a drawee-bank agrees to certify a check, it immediately charges the drawer's ac-count with the amount of the check and transfers those funds to its own certified check account. In effect, the bank is agreeing in advance to accept that check when it is presented for payment and to make payment from those funds reserved in the certified check account. Essentially, certification prevents the bank from denying liability. It is a promise that sufficient funds are on deposit and *have been set aside* to cover the check. A certified check ensures against dishonor for insufficient funds. Sometimes, certified checks (or cashier's checks) are the required form of payment under state law—for example, in purchases at a sheriff's

■ **Exhibit 29–2  A Traveler's Check**

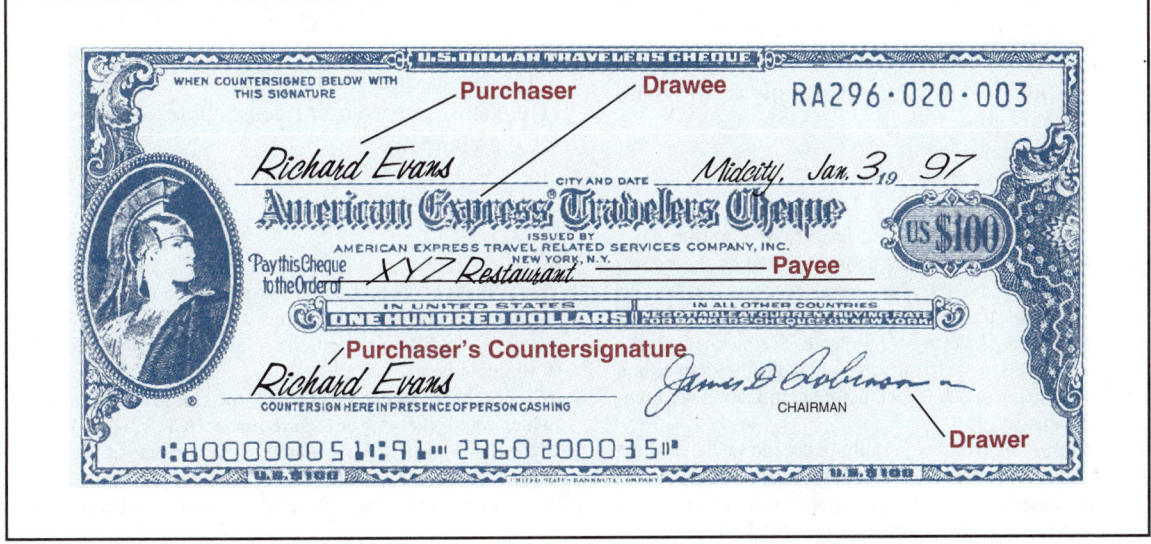

■ **Exhibit 29–3  A Certified Check**

sale. Exhibit 29–3 illustrates a sample certified check.

A drawee-bank is not obligated to certify a check, and failure to do so is not a dishonor of the check [UCC R3–409(d); UCC 3–411(2)]. If a bank does certify a check, however, the bank should write on the check the amount that it will pay. If the certification does not state an amount, and the amount is later increased and the instrument negotiated to a holder in due course (HDC), the obligation of the certifying bank is the amount of the instrument when it was taken by the HDC [UCC R3–413(b)].

Certification can be requested by a holder, as well as by the drawer. In either circumstance, on certification the drawer and any prior indorsers are completely discharged [UCC R3–414(c); UCC R3–415(d)].[3] A request for certification can be viewed as a choice of the bank's promise to pay over the drawer's and any indorser's promises. In this situation, a holder can look only to the bank for payment.[4]

## LOST, DESTROYED, OR STOLEN CASHIER'S, TELLER'S, AND CERTIFIED CHECKS

Suppose that Richie decides to move from Wichita, Kansas, to Dodge City. Richie closes his bank account in Wichita and takes a cashier's check payable to himself in the amount of the closed account. He plans to use the check to open a new account in Dodge City. After opening the new account and depositing the check, Richie plans to obtain a cashier's check to pay his initial month's rent, making the check payable to his new landlord, DC Apartments.

What happens if Richie loses either of the checks or if DC Apartments loses the check on which it is the payee? Under UCC R3–312,[5] the remitter or payee of a cashier's check or a teller's check—and the drawer of a certified check—can get a refund of the amount of the check from the bank by asking for it before the check is paid. The bank may require reasonable identification of the claimant.[6]

---

3. Under UCC 3–411, the legal liability of a drawer varies according to whether certification is requested by the drawer or a holder. The drawer who obtains certification remains *secondarily liable* on the instrument if the certifying bank does not honor the check when it is presented for payment. If the check is certified at the request of a holder, the drawer and anyone who indorses the check before certification are completely discharged.

4. If a certifying bank wrongfully refuses to pay a certified check, "the person asserting the right to enforce the check is entitled to compensation for expenses and loss of interest" and may also recover consequential damages [UCC R3–411(b)].

---

5. Although this section was promulgated after the revised Article 4, it has been recommended for enactment in all of the states by the National Conference of Commissioners of Uniform State Laws.

6. The bank cannot require that the claimant post a bond, which could otherwise be required under UCC R3–309. Posting a bond—depositing funds equal to the amount of the check with, for example, a court—gives the bank protection against a loss that might occur if there is a claim by another person to enforce the check.

The claim becomes enforceable ninety days after the date of the check [UCC R3–312(b)(1)]. Without regard to the claim, if a person entitled to enforce the check presents it for payment within that ninety days and the bank pays, the bank is discharged [UCC R3–312(b)(2)]. If the claim becomes enforceable and no one entitled to enforce the check has presented it for payment, the bank's refund to the claimant discharges the bank—even if the claim was false [UCC R3–312(b)(4)]. (This is because a person who asks for a refund warrants to the bank, and to anybody else who might have a right to enforce the check, that the check was in fact lost, stolen, or destroyed. If it was not lost, stolen, or destroyed, a holder who cannot obtain payment on the check can sue the claimant for breach of warranty.)

SECTION 2

# THE BANK-CUSTOMER RELATIONSHIP

The bank-customer relationship begins when the customer opens a checking account and deposits money that will be used to pay for checks written. The rights and duties of the bank and the customer are contractual and depend upon the nature of the transaction.

A creditor-debtor relationship is created between a customer and a bank when, for example, the customer makes cash deposits into a checking account or when final payment is received for checks drawn on other banks.

An agency relationship underlies the check-collection process. A check does not operate as an immediate legal assignment of funds between the drawer and the payee [UCC R3–408; UCC 3–409]. The money in the bank represented by that check does not immediately move from the drawer's account to the payee's account; nor is any underlying debt discharged until the drawee-bank honors the check and makes final payment. To transfer checkbook dollars among different banks, each bank acts as the agent of collection for its customer [UCC R4–201(a); UCC 4–201(1)].

Whenever a bank-customer relationship is established, certain rights and duties arise. The respective rights and duties of banks and their customers are discussed in detail in the following sections.

SECTION 3

# HONORING CHECKS

When a depositary institution provides checking services, it agrees to honor the checks written by its customers with the usual stipulation that there be sufficient funds available in the account to pay each check. When a drawee-bank *wrongfully* fails to honor a check, it is liable to its customer for damages resulting from its refusal to pay. The UCC does not attempt to specify the theory under which the customer may recover for wrongful dishonor; it merely states that the drawee is liable. Thus, the drawer-customer does not have to prove that the drawee-bank breached its contractual commitment, slandered the customer's credit, or was negligent [UCC R4–402(b); UCC 4–402]. When the bank properly dishonors a check for insufficient funds, it has no liability to the customer.

The customer's agreement with the bank includes a general obligation to keep sufficient money on deposit to cover all checks written. The customer is liable to the payee or to the holder of a check in a civil suit if a check is not honored. If intent to defraud can be proved, the customer can also be subject to criminal prosecution for writing a bad check.

## OVERDRAFTS

When the bank receives an item properly payable from its customer's checking account, but there are insufficient funds in the account to cover the amount of the check, the bank can either dishonor the item or it can pay the item and charge the customer's account, creating an **overdraft** if the customer has authorized the payment and the payment does not violate any bank-customer agreement [UCC R4–401(a); UCC 4–401(1)]. The bank can subtract the difference from the customer's next deposit, because the check carries with it an enforceable implied promise to reimburse the bank. If there is a joint account, the bank cannot hold any joint-account customer liable for payment of an overdraft, however, unless the customer has signed the item or has benefited from the proceeds of the item [UCC R4–401(b)].

When a check "bounces," a holder can resubmit the check, hoping that at a later date sufficient funds will be available to pay it. The holder must timely notify any indorsers on the check of the first dishonor; otherwise, they will be discharged from their signature liability.

Once a bank makes special arrangements with its customer to accept overdrafts on an account, the drawee-bank can become liable to its customer for damages proximately caused by its wrongful dishonor of overdrafts [UCC R4–402(a), (b); UCC 4–402]. The following case illustrates that when a bank agrees with a customer to pay overdrafts, the bank's refusal to honor checks on an overdrawn account is a wrongful dishonor.

---

### CASE 29.1

**KENDALL YACHT CORP. v. UNITED CALIFORNIA BANK**

Court of Appeal of California, Fourth District, Division 2, 1975.
50 Cal.App.3d 949, 123 Cal.Rptr. 848.

**COMPANY PROFILE** *Amadeo Giannini, the son of an Italian immigrant, had earned enough money by the age of thirty-one to retire. Instead, he dreamed of founding a national bank chain and began the Bank of Italy in San Francisco in 1904. Giannini formed Transamerica in 1928 as an umbrella company over the Bank of Italy and Los Angeles's Bank of America. During the next decade, Transamerica bought other banks in other states. In 1956, however, the federal government forced Transamerica to divorce its California banks (then known as Bank of America) from its other banks, which were organized as Firstamerica. Firstamerica returned to California in 1959, buying California Bank and merging it with the First Western Bank and Trust in 1961 to create United California Bank. Today Firstamerica—known as First Interstate Bancorp—ranks among the top fifteen U.S. banks.*

**BACKGROUND AND FACTS** *Lawrence and Linda Kendall were officers and the principal shareholders of Kendall Yacht Corporation, a corporation formed to build yachts on special order from customers. The corporation had never issued stock and was in need of operating funds. The corporation had a payroll checking account and a general business checking account with United California Bank. When the corporation ran into financial problems, Mr. Kendall spoke with Ron Lamperts, a loan officer at the bank, in an effort to obtain financing. The bank agreed to honor overdrafts on the corporate account until such time as the corporation was financially more stable. The Kendalls continued to write checks for supplies, payroll, and other corporate operating expenses from about mid-October through December. The corporate bank account was by then badly overdrawn, and a number of the checks had been dishonored by the bank. The Kendalls' business failed, and they later brought a lawsuit against United California Bank, charging that its wrongful dishonor of checks that it had initially agreed to accept as overdrafts had damaged the Kendalls' personal and credit reputation. The trial court held for the Kendalls, and the bank appealed.*

*McDANIEL, Associate Justice.*
\*   \*   \*   \*

The Bank contends first that under [California] Commercial Code section 4402 the wrongful dishonor of a check of a *corporation* does not give a cause of action for damages to individual officers and shareholders of the corporation. [California] Commercial Code section 4402, which represents [unrevised] section 4–402 of the Uniform Commercial Code, reads as follows: ''A payor bank is liable to its customer for damages proximately caused by the wrongful dishonor of an item. \*   \*   \*   ''

[It] was entirely foreseeable that the dishonoring of the Corporation's checks would reflect directly on the personal credit and reputation of the Kendalls and that they would suffer the adverse personal consequences which resulted when the Bank reneged on its commitments.

    *   *   *   *

[It] has been held in this state that a cause of action for wrongful dishonor of a check sounds in tort[a] as well as in contract, and ''if the conduct is tortious, damages for emotional distress may be recovered despite the fact that the conduct also involves a breach of contract.''

*The appellate court confirmed the trial court's ruling. The Kendalls were* **DECISION** *awarded $26,000 each as compensatory damages for the bank's wrongful* **AND REMEDY** *dishonor of the checks.*

a.   An action is technically said to *sound in tort* when it is brought for damages only and not for the specific recovery of a thing.

## POSTDATED CHECKS

A bank may also charge against a customer's account a postdated check, unless the customer notifies the bank of the postdating in time to allow the bank to act on the notice before the bank commits itself to pay on the check [UCC R4–401(c)]. If the bank fails to act on the customer's notice and charges the customer's account before the date on the postdated check, the bank may be liable for any damages incurred by the customer. Damages include those that result from the dishonor of checks that are subsequently presented for payment and are dishonored for insufficient funds.[7]

## STALE CHECKS

The bank's responsibility to honor its customers' checks is not absolute. A bank is not obliged to pay an uncertified check presented for payment more than six months after its date [UCC R4–404]. Commercial banking practice regards a check outstanding for longer than six months as a **stale check.** UCC R4–404 gives a bank the option of paying or not paying on such a check without liability. The usual banking practice is to consult the customer, and give the customer the option of issuing a stop-payment order. If a bank pays in good

faith without consulting the customer, however, it has the right to charge the customer's account for the amount of the check.

## DEATH OR INCOMPETENCE OF A CUSTOMER

UCC R4–405 provides that if, at the time a check is issued or its collection has been undertaken, a bank does not know of an adjudication of incompetence, an item can be paid and the bank will not incur liability. Neither death nor incompetence revokes the bank's authority to pay an item until the bank knows of the situation and has had reasonable time to act on such notice. Even when a bank knows of the death of its customer, for ten days after the date of death, it can pay or certify checks drawn on or before the date of death—unless a person claiming an interest in that account, such as an heir or an executor of the estate, orders the bank to stop payment. Without this provision, banks would constantly be required to verify the continued life and competence of their drawers.

## STOP-PAYMENT ORDERS

Only a customer or ''any person authorized to draw on the account'' can order payment of a check (or any item payable by the bank) to be stopped [UCC R4–403(a)]. This right does not extend to holders—that is, payees or indorsees—because the drawee-bank's contract is not with them, but only with its drawers.[8] A customer has no right to stop

---

7.   Under the unrevised UCC, postdating does not affect the negotiability of a check. Instead of treating postdated checks as checks payable on demand, however, many courts treat them as time drafts. Thus, a bank could not charge a customer's account for a postdated check, whether or not the customer notified the bank of the postdating, without potential liability for the payment of later checks. Under the automated check-collection system in use today, however, the check is usually paid without respect to its date.

8.   The only exception to this rule is in UCC R4–405(b) [UCC 4–405(2)], under which, if a customer is deceased, any person claiming an interest in the account can stop payment.

■ **Exhibit 29–4 A Stop-Payment Order**

**Bank of America**

Bank of America

Checking Account
Stop-Payment Order

To: Bank of America NT&SA
I want to stop payment on the following check(s).

ACCOUNT NUMBER: ☐☐☐☐☐☐☐ – ☐☐☐☐☐☐

**SPECIFIC STOP**

*ENTER DOLLAR AMOUNT: _____

*CHECK NUMBER: _____

THE CHECK WAS SIGNED BY: _____

THE CHECK IS PAYABLE TO: _____

THE REASON FOR THIS STOP PAYMENT IS: _____

**STOP RANGE** (Use for lost or stolen check(s) only.)

DOLLAR AMOUNT: 000

*ENTER STARTING CHECK NUMBER: _____

*END CHECK NUMBER: _____

THE REASON FOR THIS STOP PAYMENT IS: _____

**BANK USE ONLY**

**TRANCODE:**
☐ 21—ENTER STOP PAYMENT
(SEE OTHER SIDE TO REMOVE)

NON READS: _____
UNPROC. STMT HIST: _____
PRIOR STMT CYCLE: _____
HOLDS ON COOLS: _____
REJECTED CHKS: _____
LARGE ITEMS: _____
FEE COLLECTED: _____
DATE ACCEPTED: _____
TIME ACCEPTED: _____

I agree that this order (1) is effective only if the above check(s) has (have) not yet been cashed or paid against my account, (2) will end six months from the date it is delivered to you unless I renew it in writing, and (3) is not valid if the check(s) was (were) accepted on the strength of my Bank of America courtesy-check guarantee card by a merchant participating in that program. I also agree (1) to notify you immediately to cancel this order if the reason for the stop payment no longer exists or (2) that closing the account on which the check(s) is (are) drawn automatically cancels this order.

IF ANOTHER BRANCH OF THIS BANK OR ANOTHER PERSON OR ENTITY BECOMES A "HOLDER IN DUE COURSE" OF THE ABOVE CHECK, I UNDERSTAND THAT PAYMENT MAY BE ENFORCED AGAINST THE CHECK'S MAKER (SIGNER).

*I CERTIFY THE AMOUNT AND CHECK NUMBER(S) ABOVE ARE CORRECT.
☐ I have written a replacement check (number and date of check).

(Optional—please circle one: Mr., Ms., Mrs., Miss) CUSTOMER'S SIGNATURE X _____ DATE _____

payment on a check that has been certified or accepted by a bank, however. Also, a **stop-payment order** must be received within a reasonable time and in a reasonable manner to permit the bank to act on it [UCC R4–403(a); UCC 4–403(1)].

Although a stop-payment order can be given orally, usually by phone, it is binding on the bank for only fourteen calendar days unless confirmed in writing.[9] A written stop-payment order (see Exhibit 29–4) or an oral order confirmed in writing is effective for six months, at which time it must be renewed in writing [UCC R4–403(b); UCC 4–403(2)]. If the stop-payment order is not renewed, the check can be paid by the bank, as a stale check, without liability.

## BANK'S LIABILITY FOR WRONGFUL PAYMENT

Should the drawee-bank pay the check over the customer's properly instituted stop-payment order, the bank will be obligated to recredit the account of the drawer-customer for no more than the actual loss suffered by the drawer because of such wrongful payment. This loss may include damages for the dishonor of subsequent items (that is, items that would have been paid if the stop-payment order had been honored) [UCC R4–403(c); UCC 4–403(3)].

Assume that Toshio Murano orders one hundred cellular telephones from Advanced Communications, Inc., at $50 each. Murano pays in advance for the phones with a check for $5,000. Later that day, Advanced Communications tells Murano that it will not deliver the phones as arranged. Murano immediately calls the bank and stops payment on the check. Two days later, in spite of this stop-payment order, the bank inadvertently honors Murano's check to Advanced Communications for the undelivered phones. The bank will be liable to Murano for the full $5,000.

The result would be different if Advanced Communications had delivered and Murano had accepted ninety-nine phones. Because Murano would have owed Advanced Communications $4,950 for the goods delivered, Murano would have been able to establish actual losses of probably only $50 resulting from the bank's payment over the stop-payment order. Consequently, the bank would be liable to Murano for only $50.

## CUSTOMER'S LIABILITY FOR WRONGFUL STOP-PAYMENT ORDER

A stop-payment order has its risks for a customer. The drawer must have a *valid legal ground* for issuing such an order; otherwise, the holder can sue the drawer for payment. Moreover, defenses sufficient to refuse payment against a payee may not be valid grounds to prevent payment against a subsequent holder in due

---

9. Some states do not recognize oral stop-payment orders; they must be in writing.

course [UCC R3–305; UCC R3–306; UCC 3–305]. A person who wrongfully stops payment on a check will not only be liable to the payee for the amount of the check but might also be liable for special damages resulting from the wrongful order. These special damages must be separately pleaded and proved at trial.

### CASHIER'S CHECKS AND TELLER'S CHECKS

Cashier's checks and teller's checks, both of which were defined earlier in this chapter, are sometimes used in the business community as nearly the equivalent of cash. Except in very limited circumstances, payment will not be stopped by the drawer bank on a cashier's check or a teller's check. Once

it has been issued by a bank, the bank must honor it when it is presented for payment. If the bank issuing a cashier's check or a teller's check wrongfully refuses to pay it (whether as an accommodation to its customer or for other reasons), ''the person asserting the right to enforce the check is entitled to compensation for expenses and loss of interest'' as well as consequential damages [UCC R3–411(b)].

But what if, after issuing a cashier's check, the bank learns that the check was procured from the purchaser through fraud? May the bank stop payment on its check, as an accommodation to its customer, in such circumstances? This is the issue before the court in the following case.

---

**BACKGROUND AND FACTS**  *Clara Lamstein was the owner of a business firm, the primary ''business'' of which was an illegal pyramid scheme (in which payments made by current investors are used to pay off previous investors, and no* bona fide *business exists). The business was closed down by the state of Florida and placed in the hands of a receiver (a person appointed by a court to wind up the affairs of a business), William Rishoi. When the business was closed down, Lamstein had in her possession $100,000 in uncashed cashier's checks, which had been delivered to Lamstein by the Crosbys—who had been fraudulently induced by Lamstein to make a number of investments. The Crosbys requested the issuing bank, First American Bank and Trust, to stop payment on the outstanding cashier's checks, and the bank subsequently refused to honor the checks when they were presented for payment by Rishoi. Rishoi sued First American, claiming that the bank had improperly refused to honor the cashier's checks. The trial court granted summary judgment in favor of Rishoi, and First American appealed.*

**CASE 29.2**

### FIRST AMERICAN BANK AND TRUST v. RISHOI

District Court of Appeal of Florida, Fifth District, 1990. 553 So.2d 1387.

*DANIEL,* Chief Judge.
\* \* \* \*

On appeal, the bank argues that Rishoi is not a holder in due course and therefore it was justified in refusing to honor the cashier's checks. \* \* \* The bank further asserts that a person who is not a holder in due course takes an instrument subject to all valid claims to it on the part of any person. The bank's position is that Rishoi did not take the cashier's checks for value or without notice of any defenses or claims and therefore the bank may rely on the Crosby's defenses in refusing to pay the checks \* \* \* .
\* \* \* \*

\* \* \* [T]he Florida Supreme Court recently held that, in accordance with common commercial practice and the use of a cashier's check as a cash substitute, any defenses which a bank may assert to avoid payment must be narrowly limited. The court concluded that, upon presentment for payment by a holder, a bank may only assert its real and personal defenses in order to refuse payment on a cashier's check issued by the bank. The bank may not, however, rely on a third party's defenses to refuse payment. The only inquiry a bank may make on presentment of a cashier's check is whether the payee or endorsee is in fact a legitimate holder, that is, whether the cashier's check is being presented by a thief or one who simply found a lost check, or whether the check has been materially altered. The court concluded that this approach maintains the validity and use of cashier's checks yet acknowledges the valid concerns of banks.

In the present case, the receiver was a legitimate holder and the bank had no real or personal defenses to assert against his claim for payment. Thus, the bank wrongfully dishonored its own obligation and is liable for payment.

**DECISION AND REMEDY**
*The trial court's ruling was affirmed. The bank could not stop payment on the previously issued cashier's checks on the basis of the Crosbys' defenses. The bank was liable to the receiver, Rishoi, for the amount of the checks.*

**ETHICAL CONSIDERATIONS**
*The issue raised by this case is an ethically perplexing one, because it brings into conflict two fundamental ethical principles underlying commercial paper law—to protect against fraud on the one hand and to encourage the free flow of commerce on the other. The bank argued in this case that, on public policy grounds, it should be able to assist its customer by stopping payment on a cashier's check that had been obtained from the customer by a criminal act. A minority of courts would agree, on the theory that a cashier's check (because the bank draws it on itself) is a note and should thus be treated just like any other negotiable instrument and be afforded the same defenses to payment. The court in the case above represents the majority view—that cashier's checks, as the next best thing to cash, play a significant role in the business community by furthering certainty in commercial transactions. To preserve their cash-equivalent function, cashier's checks should be considered analogous to certified checks and be dishonored only in extremely limited circumstances.*

## PAYMENT ON A FORGED SIGNATURE OF THE DRAWER

When a bank pays a check on which the drawer's signature is forged, generally the bank suffers the loss.[10] A bank may be able to recover at least some of the amount of the loss, however, from a customer whose negligence contributed to the forgery, from the forger of the check, or from a holder who cashes the check.

**THE GENERAL RULE** A forged signature on a check has no legal effect as the signature of a drawer [UCC R3–403(a); UCC 3–404(1)]. For this reason, banks require signature cards from each customer who opens a checking account so the bank can determine whether the signature on a customer's check is genuine. The general rule, illustrated in the following case, is that the bank must recredit the customer's account when it pays on a forged signature.

---

10. Each year, check fraud costs banks many billions of dollars—more than combined losses from credit-card fraud, theft from automatic teller machines, and armed robberies.

---

| CASE 29.3 | **BACKGROUND AND FACTS** *Frankford Arsenal Employees Federal* |
|---|---|

**CUMIS INSURANCE SOCIETY, INC. v. GIRARD BANK**
United States District Court, Eastern District of Pennsylvania, 1981. 522 F.Supp. 414.

*Credit Union No. 1664 opened an account with Girard Bank in October 1977. Before opening the account, the bank required the credit union to agree to a resolution authorizing the bank to honor checks ''bearing or purporting to bear the facsimile signature or any signature or signatures resembling the facsimile specimens'' of credit-union manager Edward Colgan. The resolution also stated that the credit union agreed to ''hold harmless'' the bank from any damage for honoring those checks. In 1979, between September 14 and October 5, five checks allegedly drawn by the* *credit union were presented at various banks in Puerto Rico, Miami, and Dallas. Each check bore an unauthorized, facsimile signature resembling the facsimile signature of Edward Colgan, and each was made out for the amount of $20,000. Girard Bank paid the five checks and credited $100,000 against the credit union's account. On November 8, a bank employee discovered the checks and notified the credit union. The next day, Colgan asked the bank to recredit the credit union's account. When the bank refused to do so, the credit union's insurance company, Cumis Insurance Society, Inc., reimbursed the credit union for its loss. Cumis then sued the bank. The defendant bank asserted that the claim was barred by its agreement with the credit union to "hold harmless" the bank for honoring checks bearing Colgan's facsimile signature. Cumis filed a motion for summary judgment.*

*JOHN MORGAN DAVIS,* Senior District Judge.
   \*   \*   \*   \*
   \*   \*   \* [T]he payment on a forged drawer's signature violates the duty of the bank to charge its customers' accounts for only properly payable items. Because of this strict liability under the [Uniform Commercial] Code as between a drawee bank and a drawer customer, the loss must be assumed by the bank. Thus, the defendant bank is liable for the wrongful payments under its contract with the depositor, the Credit Union, absent special circumstances. \*   \*   \* [D]efendant asserts that the Resolution provides it with a complete defense for a loss arising from the instant forgeries. \*   \*   \* [T]he court disagrees.
   \*   \*   \*   \*
   \*   \*   \* Under the Code, the interest in finality of commercial transactions dictates that the risk of loss in forged check cases be placed on the drawee. The harshness of this rule of strict liability is mitigated by the Code's negligence provisions which shift the risk of loss based on fault. This scheme of \*   \*   \* liability appropriately provides the bank with a statutory vehicle to shift the loss herein if the Credit Union failed to exercise ordinary care by misuse of the facsimile machine. The defendant \*   \*   \* seeks to further insure against Code liability by contractually prescribing that the mere use of the facsimile machine is essentially negligence *per se* which absolves the bank notwithstanding its own lack of care. \*   \*   \* [S]uch a resolution \*   \*   \* is merely an attempted exculpation [removal, release] from all liability. And to the extent that such an agreement renders the Code provisions for liability in forged signature cases a nullity [void], it conflicts with the policy set by the legislature of the Commonwealth.

*The court granted Cumis's motion for summary judgment.*

**DECISION AND REMEDY**

**Forgery in Different Legal Systems** *Attempts by the United Nations to form an international law for negotiable instruments has proved to be complicated because different legal traditions handle liability for forged instruments differently. In common law systems, such as that of the United States, the person who takes an instrument from a forger assumes liability for the forgery. In civil law systems, such as that of France, a bona fide taker of a forged instrument is protected by the rule that the person whose signature is forged is liable on the instrument.*

**INTERNATIONAL CONSIDERATIONS**

**CUSTOMER NEGLIGENCE** When the customer's negligence substantially contributes to the forgery, the bank will not normally be obliged to recredit the customer's account for the amount of the check [UCC R3–406(a)]. Suppose that Compu-Net, Inc., uses a check-writing machine to write its payroll and business checks. A Compu-Net employee—Mac Malto—uses the machine to write himself a check for $10,000, and Compu-Net's bank subsequently honors it. Compu-Net requests the bank to recredit $10,000 to its account for incorrectly paying on a forged check. If the bank can show that Compu-Net failed to take reasonable care in controlling access to the check-writing equipment, Compu-Net cannot require the bank to recredit its account for the amount of the forged check.

A customer's liability may be reduced, however, by the amount of a loss caused by negligence on the part of a bank (or other "person") paying the instrument or taking it for value or for collection if the negligence substantially contributes to the loss [UCC R3–406(b)].[11] Thus, in the preceding example, if Compu-Net can show that the bank should have been alerted to possible fraud, the loss may be allocated between Compu-Net and the bank.

***Timely Examination Required.*** A bank can either return canceled checks to the customer or provide the customer with information to reasonably identify the checks paid (number, amount, and date of payment) and maintain the ability to furnish legible copies of the checks on the request of the customer for a period of seven years [UCC R4–406(a), (b)]. This provision recognizes that automated check-clearing procedures involve "truncation" (presentment by electronic means), which reduces check-collection costs. The check-collection process is discussed in more detail later in this chapter.

A customer has an *affirmative duty* to examine monthly statements and canceled checks promptly and with reasonable care and to report any forged signatures promptly [UCC R4–406(c); UCC 4–406(1)]. This includes forged signatures of indorsers, to be discussed later. Failure to examine and report, or any carelessness by the customer

that results in a loss to the bank, makes the customer liable for the loss [UCC R4–406(d); UCC 4–406(2)(a)]. Even if the customer can prove that reasonable care was taken against forgeries, the UCC provides that discovery of such forgeries and notice to the bank must take place within specific time frames for the customer to require the bank to recredit his or her account.

When a series of forgeries by the same wrongdoer has taken place, the UCC provides that the customer, to recover for all the forged items, must have discovered and reported the first forged check to the bank within thirty calendar days of the receipt of the bank statement and canceled checks [UCC R4–406(d)(2); UCC R4–406(2)(b)].[12] Failure to notify the bank within this period of time discharges the bank's liability for all similar forged checks that it pays prior to notification.

For example, First Merchants Bank sends out monthly statements and canceled checks on the last day of each month. Ira Gomez, the owner of a small restaurant, unknowingly has had a number of his blank checks stolen by employee Manny. On March 20, Manny forges Gomez's signature and cashes check #1. On March 22, Manny forges and cashes check #2. The checks canceled in March (including the forged ones) and the March statement from the First Merchants Bank are received by Gomez on April 1. Gomez sets aside the statement and does not reconcile his checking account. On April 20, Manny forges check #3. The checks canceled in April and the April statement are received by Gomez on May 1. On May 5, Gomez examines both statements, discovers the forgeries, and reports them to the bank. On May 7, Manny forges and cashes check #4.

Can Gomez demand that the bank recredit his account for all forged checks? The answer is no (unless Gomez can prove that the bank was *also* negligent, as will be discussed shortly). A series of forgeries by the same wrongdoer has been committed. Gomez is liable for the first three checks, because he failed to notify the bank of the March forgeries promptly (within the thirty-day period following the receipt of the bank statement and canceled checks). The bank is liable for the fourth check, because it paid the check after Gomez notified it of the forgeries.

---

11. The unrevised Article 4 does not include a similar provision.

12. The unrevised Article 4 limits the period for examining and reporting to *fourteen* days.

Had Gomez examined his March statement immediately upon receipt and reported the two March forgeries, the bank would have been obligated to recredit Gomez's account in full. If the bank could have proved that Gomez's carelessness in permitting the blank checks to be stolen substantially contributed to the forgery, however, Gomez would have been liable to the extent that such negligence contributed to the loss [UCC R3–406].

**When the Bank Is Also Negligent.** There is one situation in which a bank customer can escape liability for failing to notify the bank of forged or altered checks within the thirty-day period. If the customer can prove that the bank was also negligent, then the bank will also be liable, and an allocation of the loss between the bank and the customer will be made on the basis of comparative negligence [UCC R4–406(e)].[13] In other words, even though a customer may have been negligent, the bank may have to recredit the customer's account for a portion of the loss if the bank also failed to exercise ordinary care.

Does a bank fail to exercise ordinary care if it fails to examine every signature on every check? This question has posed a challenge for the courts. Because of the large volume of checks processed by banks, it is customary in the banking industry to manually examine signatures only on those checks written for amounts over a certain threshold, such as $1,000. The rationale behind this practice is that the time and money that banks save by so doing outweigh the liability that banks might have for paying checks in smaller amounts that have forged signatures or indorsements.

To resolve the question, UCC R3–103(a)(7) defines *ordinary care* to mean the "observance of reasonable commercial standards, prevailing in the area in which [a] person is located, with respect to the business in which that person is engaged."[14] Thus, in the case of a bank, reasonable commercial standards do not require the bank to examine all customers' checks if the failure to examine does not violate the bank's prescribed procedures and the procedures do not vary unreasonably from general banking usage.

Regardless of the degree of care exercised by the customer or the bank, the UCC has placed an absolute time limit on the liability of a bank for forged customer signatures. A customer who fails to report his or her forged signature within one year from the date that the statement and canceled checks were made available for inspection loses the legal right to have the bank recredit his or her account [UCC R4–406(f); UCC 4–406(4)]. The following case illustrates this requirement.

---

13. Under UCC 4–406(3), if both parties are negligent, the bank is wholly liable.

14. The unrevised Article 4 does not include similar provisions.

---

**BACKGROUND AND FACTS** *Two couples, the Browns and the Knights, formed Knight Communications, Inc., in late 1985 or early 1986. The Browns provided a capital contribution of about $50,000, and the Knights operated the company. An agreement between the corporation and Boatmen's National Bank of St. Louis specified that all corporate checks had to have two signatures: one from either of the Browns and one from either of the Knights. In February 1986, the bank began honoring checks with only one signature—that of either Mr. or Mrs. Knight. In August 1986, the Brown-Knight enterprise ended, and Mr. Brown received the corporation's books. He then telephoned the bank about some checks that had been signed by only one of the Knights, but he did not specify the amounts, dates, numbers, or payees of the checks. Late in 1988, Mr. Brown learned that Mr. Knight had given Mr. Brown's attorney more checks that lacked a Brown signature. Of the 502 checks issued by the corporation between February and May 1986, 105 checks lacked a Brown signature. Many of the checks lacking a Brown signature were for legitimate business expenses, but some were not. In September 1988, Knight Communications filed suit against the bank, alleging that the bank had wrongfully paid the*

**CASE 29.4**

**KNIGHT COMMUNICATIONS, INC. v. BOATMEN'S NATIONAL BANK OF ST. LOUIS**

Missouri Court of Appeals, Eastern District, Division Four, 1991.
805 S.W.2d 199.

*checks that lacked a Brown signature. The trial court found for Knight Communications. The bank appealed, contending that it was not liable, because it had not been notified by the customer of the wrongfully paid checks within the one-year period required under the UCC. Mr. Brown argued that his call to the bank in August 1986 constituted notification.*

*CARL R. GAERTNER,* Judge.
\* \* \* \*

The contract between the corporation and the bank authorized payment of a check containing two signatures. \* \* \* We hold that a missing but necessary drawer signature constitutes an "unauthorized signature" within the meaning of [Missouri Revised Statutes Section] 400.4–406(4) [Missouri's version of UCC 4–406(4)].[a]
\* \* \* \*

\* \* \* By sending the statements and cancelled checks each month, the bank triggered the duty of its customer, Knight Communications, to discover and report to the bank any item containing an unauthorized signature within one year.
\* \* \* \*

\* \* \* Mr. Brown's testimony fails to identify which of the 105 checks he discovered within one year after the receipt of the statements and which of them he first discovered after that time. \* \* \* [T]he claim involving unauthorized signature checks Mr. Brown discovered and "reported" at that time [of the telephone conversation] would not be barred by virtue of [Section] 400.4–406. A claim based upon the balance of the 105 checks would be barred because of his failure either to discover or to report them. Under the evidence it is impossible to determine which checks fall in one category and which fall into the other.
\* \* \* \*

Additionally, the evidence fails to establish with any specificity whatsoever what damages may have been sustained by Knight Communications by reason of the bank's honoring unauthorized signature checks. Mr. Brown admitted that some of the improperly signed checks were paid to corporation employees or suppliers of equipment.

**DECISION AND REMEDY** *The appeals court reversed the trial court's judgment. The bank was not liable, because it had not been properly notified of the unauthorized signature checks within the one-year period.*

a. UCC R4–406(f).

**OTHER PARTIES FROM WHOM THE BANK MAY RECOVER** As noted above, a forged signature on a check has no legal effect as the signature of a drawer; a forged signature, however, is effective as the signature of the unauthorized signer [UCC R3–403(a); UCC 3–404(1)]. Thus, when a bank pays a check on which the drawer's signature is forged, the bank has a right to recover from the party who forged the signature.

The bank may also have a right to recover from the person (its customer or a collecting bank) who transfers a check bearing a forged drawer's signature and receives a settlement. A customer or collecting bank guarantees that "all signatures on the item are authentic and authorized" [UCC R4–207(a)(2)]. If a drawee-bank pays or accepts a check on the mistaken belief that the drawer's signature was authorized, the bank may recover the amount of the check from "the person to whom or for whose benefit payment was made" [UCC R3–418(a)(ii)].

This right is limited, however. A drawee-bank cannot recover from "a person who took the instrument in good faith and for value or who in good faith changed position in reliance on the payment or acceptance" [UCC R3–418(c)]. This means that in most cases, a drawee-bank will not recover from the person paid, because usually there is a person who took the check in good faith and for value or who in good faith changed position in reliance on the payment or acceptance.

## PAYMENT ON A FORGED INDORSEMENT

A bank that pays a customer's check bearing a forged indorsement must recredit the customer's account or be liable to the customer-drawer for breach of contract. Suppose that Carlo issues a $50 check "to the order of Sophia." Marcello steals the check, forges Sophia's indorsement, and cashes the check. When the check reaches Carlo's bank, the bank pays it and debits Carlo's account. The bank must recredit Carlo's account $50, because it failed to carry out Carlo's order to pay "to the order of Sophia" [UCC R4–401(a); UCC 4–401]. (Carlo's bank will in turn recover—under breach of warranty principles—from the bank that cashed the check [UCC R4–207(a)(2); UCC 4–207(1)(a)].)

Eventually, the loss usually falls on the first party to take the instrument bearing the forged indorsement, because, as discussed in Chapter 28, a forged indorsement does not transfer title. Thus, whoever takes an instrument with a forged indorsement cannot become a holder.

The customer, in any case, has a duty to examine the returned checks and statements received from the bank and to report forged indorsements promptly upon discovery or notice. Failure to report forged indorsements within a three-year period after the forged items had been made available to the customer relieves the bank of liability [UCC R4–111; UCC 4–406(4)].[15]

## PAYMENT ON AN ALTERED CHECK

The customer's instruction to the bank is to pay the exact amount on the face of the check to the holder. The bank must examine each check before making final payment. If it fails to detect an alteration, it is liable to its customer for the loss, because it did not pay as the customer ordered. The loss is the difference between the original amount of the check and the amount actually paid. Suppose that a check written for $11 is raised to $111. The customer's account will be charged $11 (the amount the customer ordered the bank to pay). The bank will normally be responsible for the $100 [UCC R4–401(d)(1); UCC 4–401(2)(a)].

**CUSTOMER'S NEGLIGENCE** As in a case involving a forged drawer's signature, a customer's negligence can shift the loss when payment is made on an altered check. A common example occurs when a person carelessly writes a check, leaving large gaps around the numbers and words so that additional numbers and words can be inserted (see Exhibit 29–5).

Similarly, a person who signs a check and leaves the dollar amount for someone else to fill in is barred from protesting when the bank unknowingly and in good faith pays whatever amount is shown [UCC R4–401(d)(2); UCC 4–401(2)(b)]. Finally, if the bank can trace its loss on successive altered checks to the customer's failure to discover the initial alteration, then the bank can reduce its liability for reimbursing the customer's account [UCC R4–406].[16] The law governing the customer's duty to examine monthly statements and canceled checks, and to discover and report alterations to the drawee-bank, is the same as that applied to a forged drawer's signature.

In every situation involving a forged drawer's signature or alteration, a bank must observe reasonable commercial standards of care in paying on a customer's checks [UCC R4–406(e); UCC 4–406(3)]. The customer's contributory negligence can be asserted only if the bank has exercised ordinary care.

**OTHER PARTIES FROM WHOM THE BANK MAY RECOVER** The bank is entitled to recover the amount of loss (including expenses and any loss of interest) from the transferor who, by

---

15. The unrevised Article 4 limits this three-year period to the reporting of unauthorized indorsements. The revised Article 4 expands this limitation to cover any "action to enforce an obligation, duty, or right arising under this Article" [UCC R4–111]. In other words, under the revised Article 4, this is a general statute of limitations providing that any lawsuit must be begun within three years of the time that the cause of action occurs.

16. The bank's defense is the same whether the successive payments were made on a forged drawer's signature or on altered checks. The bank must prove that prompt notice would have prevented its loss. For example, notification might have alerted the bank not to pay further items or might have enabled it to catch the forger.

**■ Exhibit 29–5  A Poorly Filled-Out Check**

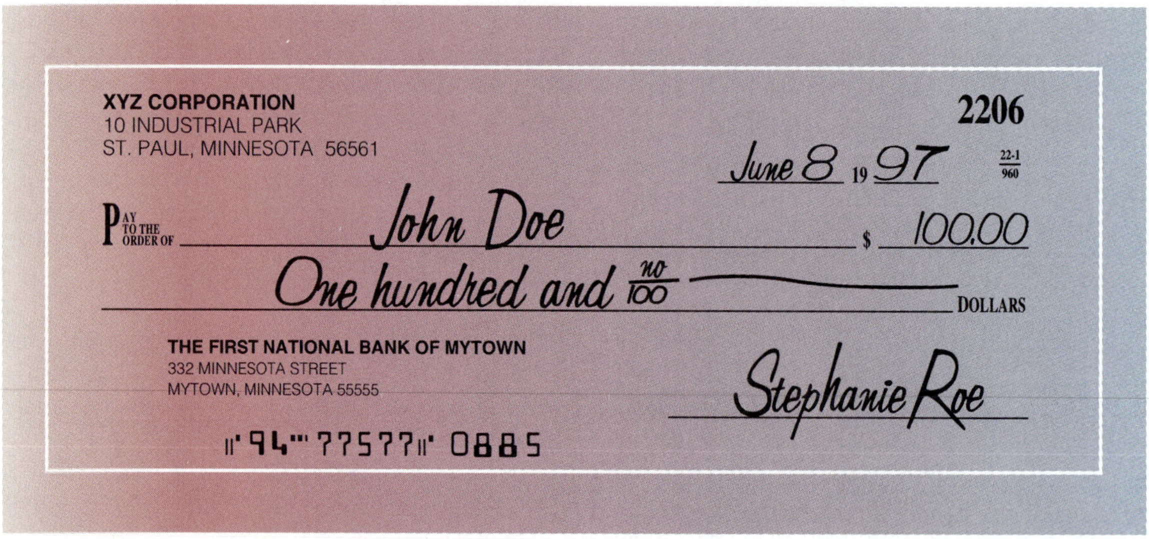

XYZ CORPORATION
10 INDUSTRIAL PARK
ST. PAUL, MINNESOTA 56561

2206

June 8 19 97      22-1/960

PAY TO THE ORDER OF    *John Doe*    $ 100.00

*One hundred and no/100*    DOLLARS

THE FIRST NATIONAL BANK OF MYTOWN
332 MINNESOTA STREET
MYTOWN, MINNESOTA 55555

*Stephanie Roe*

⑨⑤⑦⑦⑤⑦⑦  0885

presenting the check for payment, warrants that the check has not been altered.[17]

There are two exceptions dealing with accepted drafts, however. If the bank is the drawer (as it is on a cashier's check and a teller's check), it cannot recover on this ground from the presenting party if the party is an HDC acting in good faith [UCC R3–417(a)(2); UCC R4–208(a)(2); UCC 3–417(1)(c); UCC 4–207(1)(c)]. The reason is that an instrument's drawer is in a better position than an HDC to know whether the instrument has been altered.

Similarly, an HDC, acting in good faith in presenting a certified check for payment, does not warrant to the check's certifier that the check was not altered before the HDC acquired it [UCC R3–417(a)(2); UCC R4–208(a)(2); UCC 3–417(1)(c); UCC 4–207(1)(c)]. For example, Akio, the drawer, draws a check for $500 payable to Price, the payee. Price alters the amount to $5,000. The National City Bank, the drawee, certifies the check for $5,000. Price negotiates the check to Don, an HDC. The drawee-bank pays Don $5,000. On discovering the mistake, the bank cannot recover from Don the $4,500 paid by mistake,

even though the bank was not in a superior position to detect the alteration. This is in accord with the purpose of certification, which is to obtain the definite obligation of a bank to honor a definite instrument.

## SECTION 4

## ACCEPTING DEPOSITS

A second fundamental service a bank provides for its checking-account customers is that of accepting deposits of cash and checks. Cash deposits made in U.S. currency are received into the customer's account without being subject to further collection procedures. As a matter of routine, banks provisionally credit a customer's account for an item when it is first deposited. More than 99 percent of these items are paid, and the credits become final. In cases in which items are not finally paid, banks are allowed to charge back to customers' accounts the amounts that were provisionally paid [UCC R4–214; UCC 4–212].

This section focuses on the check after it has been deposited. In most cases, deposited checks involve parties who do business at different banks, but sometimes checks are written between customers of the same bank. Either situation brings into play the bank collection process as it operates within the statutory framework of Article 4 of the UCC.

---

17. Usually, the party presenting an instrument for payment is the payee, a holder, a bank customer, or a collecting bank. A bank's customers include its account holders, which may include other banks [UCC R4–104(a)(5); UCC 4–104(1)(e)]. A collecting bank is any bank handling an item for collection except the bank on which the check is drawn [UCC R4–105(5); UCC 4–105(d)].

# ■ CONCEPT SUMMARY 29.1 **Honoring Checks**

| SITUATION | BASIC RULES |
|---|---|
| **Wrongful Dishonor** [UCC R4–402] | The bank is liable to its customer for wrongful dishonor due to mistake for actual damages proved. Damages can include those proximately caused by subsequent arrest or prosecution of the drawer, as well as other consequential damages. |
| **Overdraft** [UCC R4–401] | The bank has a right to charge a customer's account for any item properly payable, even if the charge results in an overdraft. |
| **Postdated Check** [UCC R4–401] | A bank may charge against a customer's account a postdated check, unless the customer notifies the bank of the postdating in time to allow the bank to act on the notice before the bank commits itself to pay on the check. |
| **Stale Check** [UCC R4–404] | The bank is not obligated to pay an uncertified check presented more than six months after its date, but it may do so in good faith without liability. |
| **Death or Incompetence of a Customer** [UCC R4–405] | As long as the bank does not know of the death or incompetence of a customer, the bank can pay an item without liability. Even with knowledge of a customer's death, a bank can honor or certify checks (in the absence of a stop-payment order) for ten days after the date of the customer's death. |
| **Stop-Payment Order** [UCC R4–403] | The customer (or "any person authorized to draw on the account") must make a stop-payment order in time for the bank to have a reasonable opportunity to act. Oral orders are binding for only fourteen days unless they are confirmed in writing. Written orders are effective for only six months, unless renewed in writing. The bank is liable for wrongful payment over a timely stop-payment order to the extent that the customer suffers a loss. Except in very limited circumstances, payment will not be stopped on a cashier's check or a teller's check. |
| **Unauthorized Signature or Alteration** [UCC R4–406] | The customer has a duty to examine account statements with reasonable care on receipt and to notify the bank promptly of any unauthorized signatures or alterations. On a series of unauthorized signatures or alterations by the same wrongdoer, examination and report must be given within thirty calendar days of receipt of the statement. Failure to comply releases the bank from liability unless the bank failed to exercise reasonable care, in which case liability may be apportioned according to a comparative negligence standard. Regardless of care or lack of care, the customer is estopped from holding the bank liable after one year for unauthorized customer signatures or alterations and after three years for unauthorized indorsements. |

## THE COLLECTION PROCESS

The first bank to receive a check for payment is the **depositary bank**.[18] For example, when a person deposits an IRS tax-refund check into a personal checking account at the local bank, that bank is the depositary bank. The bank on which a check is drawn (the drawee-bank) is called the **payor bank.** Any bank except the payor bank that handles a check during some phase of the collection process is a **collecting bank.** Any bank except the payor bank or the depositary bank to which an item is transferred in the course of this collection process is called an **intermediary bank.**

During the collection process, any bank can take on one or more of the various roles of depositary, payor, collecting, and intermediary bank. To illustrate, a buyer in New York writes a check on her New York bank and sends it to a seller in San Francisco. The seller deposits the check in her San Francisco bank account. The seller's bank is both

---

18. All definitions in this section are found in UCC R4–105. The terms *depositary* and *depository* have a different meaning in the banking context. A depository bank refers to a physical place (a bank or other institution) in which deposits or funds are held or stored.

a *depositary bank* and a *collecting bank*. The buyer's bank in New York is the *payor bank*. As the check travels from San Francisco to New York, any collecting bank handling the item in the collection process (other than the ones already acting as depositary bank and payor bank) is also called an *intermediary bank*.

### BANK'S LIABILITY FOR RESTRICTIVE INDORSEMENTS

Only the first bank to which the item is presented for collection must pay in a manner consistent with any restrictive indorsement [UCC R3–206(c); UCC 3–206(3)]. To illustrate, Charles writes a check on his San Francisco bank account and sends it to Leota. Leota indorses the check with a restrictive indorsement that reads, ''For deposit into Account #4012 only.'' A Dallas bank is the first bank to which this check is presented for payment (the depositary bank), and it must act consistently with the terms of the restrictive indorsement. Therefore, it must credit account #4012 with the money or be liable to Leota for the tort of conversion (wrongfully taking another's property—see Chapter 6). Charles's check leaves the Dallas bank indorsed, ''For collection.'' As the check moves through the collection network of intermediary banks to Charles's San Francisco bank for payment, each intermediary bank is bound only by the preceding bank's indorsement to collect.

The division of responsibility between types of banks is necessary. Collecting banks process huge numbers of commercial instruments, and there is no practical way for them to examine and comply with the effect of each restrictive indorsement. Therefore, the only reasonable alternative is to charge the depositary bank with the responsibility of examining and complying with any restrictive indorsements.

### CHECK COLLECTION BETWEEN CUSTOMERS OF THE SAME BANK

An item that is payable by the depositary bank (also the payor bank) that receives it is called an ''on-us item.'' If the bank does not dishonor the check by the opening of the second banking day following its receipt, it is considered paid [UCC R4–215(e)(2); UCC 4–213(4)(b)]. For example, Otterley and Merkowitz both have checking accounts at First State Bank. On Monday morning, Merkowitz deposits into his own checking account a $300 check from Otterley. That same day, the bank issues Merkowitz a ''provisional credit'' for $300.

When the bank opens on Wednesday, Otterley's check is considered honored, and Merkowitz's provisional credit becomes a final payment.

### CHECK COLLECTION BETWEEN CUSTOMERS OF DIFFERENT BANKS

Millions of checks circulate throughout the United States each day, and every check must be physically transported to its payor bank before final payment is made. Once a depositary bank receives a check, it must arrange to present it either directly or through intermediary banks to the appropriate payor bank. Each bank in the collection chain must pass the check on before midnight of the next banking day following its receipt [UCC R4–202(b); UCC 4–202(2)].[19] Thus, for example, a collecting bank that receives a check on Monday must forward it to the next collecting bank before midnight on Tuesday. Unless the payor bank dishonors the check or returns it by midnight on the next banking day following receipt, the payor bank is accountable for the face amount of the check [UCC R4–302].[20]

Because of this and because of banks' need to maintain an even work flow in the many items they handle daily, the UCC permits what is called *deferred posting*, or delayed return, in which the posting (entering on the bank's records) of checks received after a certain time (say, 2:00 P.M.) can be deferred until the next day. Thus, a check received by a payor bank at 3:00 P.M. on Monday would be deferred for posting until Tuesday. In this case, the payor bank's deadline would be midnight Wednesday [UCC R4–108; UCC 4–107].

### HOW THE FEDERAL RESERVE SYSTEM CLEARS CHECKS

The **Federal Reserve System** has greatly simplified the clearing of checks—that is, the method by which checks deposited in one bank are transferred to the banks on which they were written. Suppose that Pamela Moy of Philadelphia writes a check to Jeanne Sutton in San Francisco.

---

19.   The bank may take a ''reasonably longer time,'' such as when the bank's computer system is down due to a power failure, but the bank must show that it is still timely [UCC R4–202(b)].

20.   Most checks are cleared by a computerized process, and communication and computer facilities may fail due to weather, equipment malfunction, or other conditions. If such conditions arise and a bank fails to meet its midnight deadline, the bank is ''excused'' from liability if the bank has exercised ''such diligence as the circumstances require'' [UCC R4–109(b); UCC 4–108].

■ **Exhibit 29–6  How a Check Is Cleared**

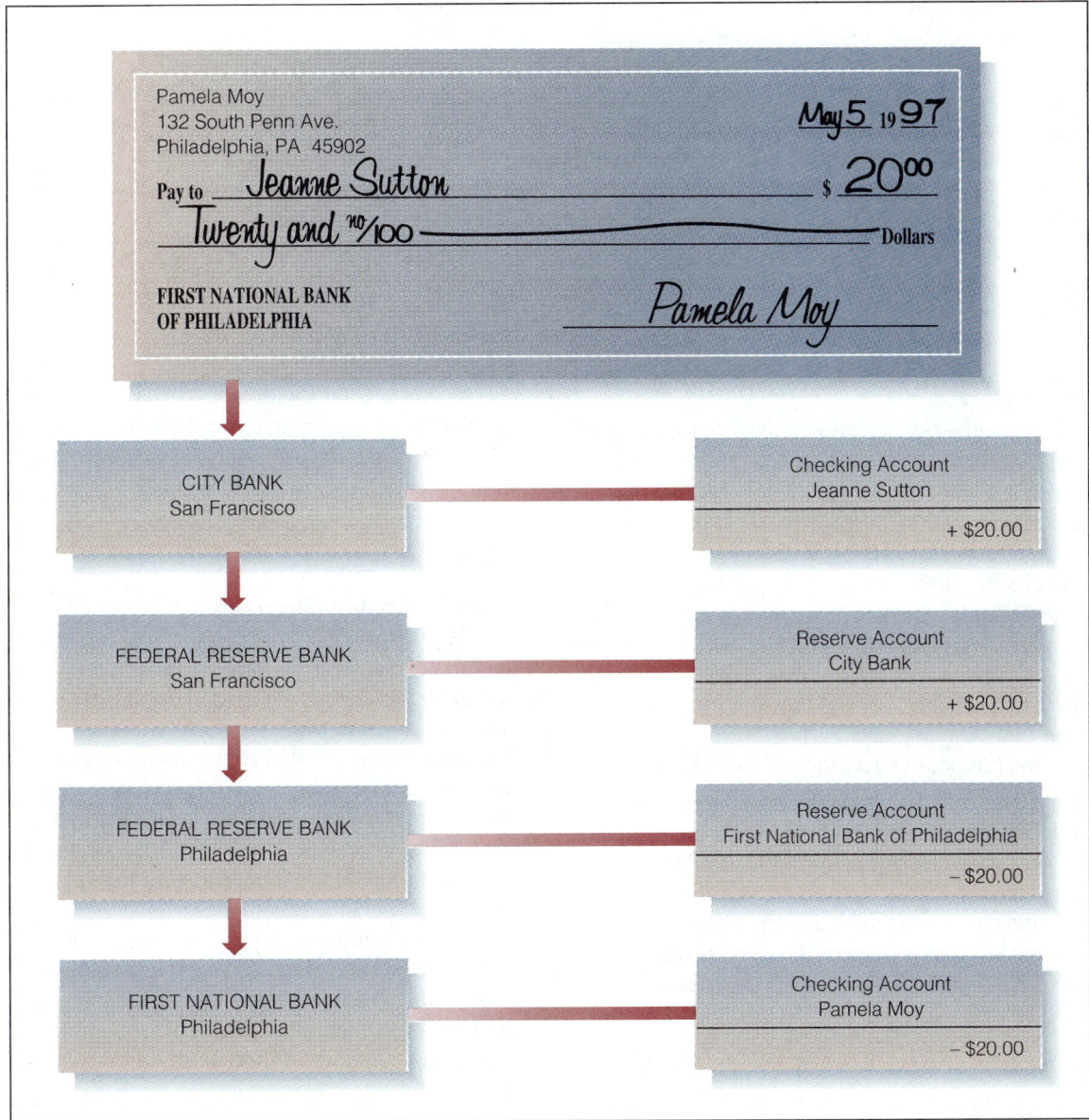

When Jeanne receives the check in the mail, she deposits it in her bank. Her bank then deposits the check in the Federal Reserve Bank of San Francisco, which transfers it to the Federal Reserve Bank of Philadelphia. That Federal Reserve bank then sends the check to Moy's bank, which deducts the amount of the check from Moy's account. Exhibit 29–6 illustrates this process.

**ENCODING AND RETENTION WARRANTIES**
At the time that the unrevised Article 4 was issued

and adopted, most checks were processed manually—the employees of each bank in the collection chain would physically handle each check that passed through the bank for collection or payment. By the time of the revised Article 4, however, most checks were being processed electronically. As part of this process, items may be encoded with information (such as the amount of the check) that is read and processed by other banks' computers. In some situations, a check may be retained at its place of deposit, and only its image or information describing it is presented for payment under a Federal Reserve agreement, clearinghouse rule, or truncation agreement [UCC R4–110].[21]

Under UCC R4–209, any person who encodes information on an item, or with respect to an item, after the item has been issued warrants to any subsequent bank or payor that the encoded information is correct. This is also true for any person who retains an item while transmitting its image or information describing it as presentation for payment. This person warrants that the retention and presentment of the item complies with the Federal Reserve or other agreement.

## EXPEDITED FUNDS AVAILABILITY ACT

The Expedited Funds Availability Act of 1987[22] and Regulation CC[23] require that any local check deposited must be available for withdrawal by check or as cash within one business day from the date of deposit. The Federal Reserve Board of Governors has designated check-processing regions, and if the depositary and payor banks are located in the same region, the check is classified as a local check. For nonlocal checks, the funds must be available for withdrawal within not more than five business days.

In addition, the act requires the following:

1. That funds be available on the *next business day* for cash deposits and wire transfers, government checks, the first $100 of a day's check deposits, cashier's checks, certified checks, and checks for which the depositary and payor banks are branches of the same institution.

2. That the first $100 of any deposit be available for cash withdrawal on the opening of the next business day after deposit. If a local check is deposited, the next $400 is to be available for withdrawal by no later than 5:00 P.M. the next business day. If, for example, you deposit a local check for $500 on Monday, at a minimum, you can withdraw $100 in cash at the opening of the business day on Tuesday, and an additional $400 must be available for withdrawal by no later than 5:00 P.M. on Wednesday.

A different availability schedule applies to deposits made at *nonproprietary* automated teller machines (ATMs). These are ATMs that are not owned or operated by the depositary institution. Basically, a five-day hold is permitted on all deposits, including cash deposits, made at nonproprietary ATMs.

Other exceptions also exist. A depositary institution has eight days to make funds available in new accounts (those open less than thirty days). It has an extra four days on deposits over $5,000 (except deposits of government and cashier's checks), on accounts with repeated overdrafts, and on checks of questionable collectibility (if the institution tells the depositor it suspects fraud or insolvency).

## TRUTH-IN-SAVINGS ACT

Under the Truth-in-Savings Act (TISA) of 1991[24] and Regulation DD,[25] banks must pay interest on the full balance of a customer's account each day. For example, Francisco has an interest-bearing checking account with the First National Bank. Francisco keeps a $500 balance in the account for most of the month but withdraws all but $50 the day before the bank posts the interest. The bank cannot pay interest on only the $50. The interest must be prorated to account for all of the days that Francisco's balance was higher.

Before opening a deposit account, new customers must be given certain information in a brochure, pamphlet, or other handout. The information, which must also appear in all advertisements, includes the following:

1. The minimum balance required to open an account and to be paid interest.
2. The interest, stated in terms of the annual percentage yield on the account.
3. Whether interest is calculated daily.
4. Any fees, charges, and penalties, and how they are calculated.

Also, under the TISA and Regulation DD, a customer's monthly statement must declare the interest earned on the account, any fees that were charged, how the fees were calculated, and the number of days that the statement covers.

---

21. The term *truncation* refers to presentment by notice rather than by delivery. Electronic check presentment—sending the number of the bank and the account number at the bottom of a check to the payor bank—can be done on the day of deposit. Before the banks open the next day, they know whether to put a hold on the check. In contrast, manual check processing can take days. This acceleration of information is a key to stopping check fraud.
22. 12 U.S.C. Sections 4001–4010.
23. 12 C.F.R. Sections 229.1–229.42.

24. 12 U.S.C. Sections 4301–4313.
25. 12 C.F.R. Sections 230.1–230.9.

## TERMS AND CONCEPTS TO REVIEW

cashier's check 548
certified check 549
check 547
collecting bank 563
depositary bank 563

Federal Reserve System 564
intermediary bank 563
overdraft 551
payor bank 563
remitter 548

stale check 553
stop-payment order 554
teller's check 548
traveler's check 548

## QUESTIONS AND CASE PROBLEMS

**29–1. Types of Checks.** Checks are usually three-party instruments. On what type of check, however, does a bank serve as both the drawer and the drawee? What type of check does a bank agree in advance to accept when the check is presented for payment?

**29–2. Forged Signatures.** Gary goes grocery shopping and carelessly leaves his checkbook in his shopping cart. His checkbook, with two blank checks remaining, is stolen by Dolores. On May 5, Dolores forges Gary's name on a check for $10 and cashes the check at Gary's bank, Citizens Bank of Middletown. Gary has not reported the theft of his blank checks to his bank. On June 1, Gary receives his monthly bank statement and canceled checks from Citizens Bank, including the forged check, but he does not examine the canceled checks. On June 20, Dolores forges Gary's last check. This check is for $1,000 and is cashed at Eastern City Bank, a bank with which Dolores has previously done business. Eastern City Bank puts the check through the collection process, and Citizens Bank honors it. On July 1, upon receipt of his bank statement and canceled checks, Gary discovers both forgeries and immediately notifies Citizens Bank. Dolores cannot be found. Gary claims that Citizens Bank must recredit his account for both checks, as his signature was forged. Discuss fully Gary's claim.

**29–3. Death of Bank Customer/Stale Checks.** On January 5, Brian drafts a check for $3,000 drawn on the Southern Marine Bank and payable to his assistant, Shanta. Brian puts last year's date on the check by mistake. On January 7, before Shanta has had a chance to go to the bank, Brian is killed in an automobile accident. The Southern Marine Bank is aware of Brian's death. On January 10, Shanta presents the check to the bank, and the bank honors the check by payment to Shanta. Brian's widow, Joyce, claims that the bank wrongfully paid Shanta, because it knew of Brian's death and also paid a check that was by date over one year old. Joyce, as executor of Brian's estate and sole heir by his will, demands that Southern Marine Bank recredit Brian's estate for the check paid to Shanta. Discuss

fully Southern Marine's liability in light of Joyce's demand.

**29–4. Overdrafts.** In September 1976, Edward and Christine McSweeney opened a joint checking account with the United States Trust Co. of New York. Between April 1978 and July 1978, 195 checks totaling $99,063 were written. In July 1978, activity in the account ceased. Ninety-five of the 195 checks, totaling $16,811, were written by Christine, and the rest of the checks were written by Edward. After deposits were credited for that period, the checks created a cumulative overdraft of $75,983. Can a bank knowingly honor a check when payment creates an overdraft, or must the bank dishonor the check? If the bank pays a check and thereby creates an overdraft, can the bank collect the amount of the overdraft from its customer? [*United States Trust Co. of New York v. McSweeney,* 91 A.D.2d 7, 457 N.Y.S.2d 276 (1982)]

**29–5. Unauthorized Indorsements.** Frank Quinn drew a check for $30,000 payable to Limetree Beach Associates, Ltd., a limited partnership formed for the purpose of investing in real estate. The check was delivered to Dan Wey, who served as the only general partner for the firm (in a limited partnership, general partners manage the firm, and those who invest in the firm are called limited partners). Wey was listed as an authorized signer for the partnership on its checking account with the American State Bank. Wey indorsed the check in his own name for deposit to his own personal account, which was also at American State. American State sent the check for collection to the drawee-bank, National Bank, which paid the check. Quinn subsequently demanded that National Bank recredit his account for the amount of the check because the check had been improperly paid under UCC 4–401(1). Will the court agree with Quinn? [*National Bank v. Quinn,* 126 Ill.2d 129, 533 N.E.2d 846, 127 Ill.Dec. 764 (1988)]

**29–6. Monthly Statements.** Steven Gerber had a joint checking account with his mother at City National Bank of Florida. Between January and May 1990, a number of checks were allegedly forged on the account. Gerber asked City National to recredit the account for the amount of the checks, but the bank refused. In March 1992, Gerber filed a lawsuit against the bank. City

National filed a motion to dismiss, claiming that the suit was barred because Gerber did not file it within a year of City National's making available to Gerber the bank statements that reflected the forged checks. Gerber argued that the only requirement was that he notify the bank of any unauthorized signatures within a year. How should the court rule? [*Gerber v. City National Bank of Florida*, 619 So.2d 328 (Fla.App. 1993)]

**29–7. Unauthorized Signatures.** In July 1979, Read & Read, Inc., a corporation owned by Thomas and Emerson Read, hired Judy Bode as a sales secretary. She was promoted to executive secretary shortly thereafter and worked primarily for Emerson Read. Bode eventually assumed responsibility for overseeing nearly all of Read's checking accounts, including his personal account. She also reviewed the bank statements for each account and reconciled them to the corresponding checkbooks. As a result of a hunting accident, Emerson Read lost his hand; to facilitate check signing, he had a rubber signature stamp made. Bode had easy access to the stamp. From September 1980 until January 1981, Bode used the rubber stamp to forge a total of fourteen checks for her own purposes on Read's accounts, including one check for over $8,000. Read, who did not review any bank statements during this entire period of time, was unaware of the forgeries. When the forgeries were discovered in January 1981, Read sued his bank, the South Carolina National Bank, to recover the amount of the forged checks that he alleged had been wrongfully honored by the bank. The trial court held for the bank, and Read appealed. Can Read recover from the bank the funds lost as a result of Bode's forgeries? Discuss. [*Read v. South Carolina National Bank*, 286 S.C. 534, 335 S.E.2d 359 (1985)]

**29–8. Missing Indorsements.** Mrs. Barber signed a blank check and gave it to her housekeeper with instructions to fill in the rest of the check as necessary to cover a medical bill for approximately $50. The housekeeper, however, made out the check for $7,300, payable to her husband, and using one of her husband's deposit slips, deposited the check into her husband's checking account at First Interstate Bank. She did not indorse the check at all. The only statement provided by the bank on the back of the check was as follows: "Pay any bank— P.E.G." The letters *P.E.G.* stand for "prior endorsements guaranteed." First Interstate sent the check for collection to the drawee-bank, United States National Bank, which paid the check. Mrs. Barber demanded that the bank recredit her account for the amount of the check. She argued that the check had not been properly paid under UCC 4–401(1), because it lacked any proper indorsement. The bank argued that First Interstate's statement, "Pay any bank—P.E.G," was sufficient under the statute to supply the missing indorsement. Who will win in court, and why? [*Barber v. United States National Bank*, 90 Or.App. 68, 750 P.2d 1183 (1988)]

**29–9. Wrongfully Dishonored Checks.** Robert Parrett was the principal shareholder, president, and chief operating officer of P & P Machinery, Inc., a farm machinery business located in Nebraska. On March 1, 1984, Parrett signed and delivered a check from P & P Machinery to a South Dakota firm. The check was dishonored by the bank even though P & P Machinery had sufficient funds in its account to cover the check. In addition, Parrett had a long-standing relationship with the bank as personal guarantor of corporate obligations to the bank and had never had any previous problems with the bank. As a result of the dishonored check, Parrett was charged with felony theft in South Dakota and extradited for trial in South Dakota. On learning that the bank had dishonored the check erroneously, the trial court dismissed the charge against Parrett. Parrett sued the bank for damages. The trial court held that Parrett had no standing to sue the bank because he was not the bank's "customer"—the corporation was. Will the appellate court agree that Parrett lacked standing to sue the bank? Discuss fully. [*Parrett v. Platte Valley State Bank & Trust Co.*, 236 Neb. 139, 459 N.W.2d 371 (1990)]

# CHAPTER 30

# ELECTRONIC FUND TRANSFERS

**T**he application of computer technology to banking, in the form of **electronic fund transfer systems (EFTS),** is helping to relieve banking institutions of the burden of having to move mountains of paperwork to process fund transfers. An **electronic fund transfer (EFT)** is a transfer of money made by the use of an electronic terminal, a telephone, a computer, or magnetic tape. Automatic payments, direct deposits, and other fund transfers are now made electronically; no physical transfers of cash, checks, or other negotiable instruments are involved. Through the use of EFTS, transactions that would otherwise take days can now be completed in seconds. For example, Hannah in New York can pay a debt to Chi in Los Angeles by entering into a computer a bank order to pay it. Chase Manhattan, the drawee bank, can instantly debit Hannah's account and transfer the credit to the Bank of America, Chi's bank, which can immediately credit her account. EFT transactions eliminate the **float time** that the drawer of a check currently enjoys. A drawer uses float time by retaining the use of the funds on which the check is written during the period between the check's issuance and final payment.

*Commercial* fund transfers, including electronic fund transfers, are now governed by Article 4A of the Uniform Commercial Code, which has been adopted by the majority of states. In those states that have not yet adopted Article 4A, commercial fund transfers continue to be governed by contract law and tort law. *Consumer* fund transfers using EFTS are subject to the Electronic Fund Transfer Act (EFTA)[1] of 1978, which is Title IX of the Consumer Credit Protection Act.

---

1. 15 U.S.C. Sections 1693 *et seq.*

# TYPES OF ELECTRONIC TRANSFERS

There are four principal types of EFTS in use: (1) automated teller machines, (2) point-of-sale systems, (3) systems handling direct deposits and withdrawals of funds, and (4) pay-by-telephone systems. To initiate a transaction on one of the machines involved, a consumer often uses a card that provides access to the computer system. Each card has an accompanying **personal identification number (PIN)** that is given only to the account holder—a number that is meant to be kept secret so as to inhibit others' use of the card.

## AUTOMATED TELLER MACHINES

Many electronic fund transfers involve **automated teller machines (ATMs).** ATMs, also referred to as customer bank communications terminals or remote service units, are located either on the bank's premises or at convenient locations such as supermarkets, drugstores and other stores, airports, and shopping centers. Automated teller machines receive deposits, dispense funds from checking or savings accounts, make credit-card advances, and receive payments. The devices are connected on-line to the bank's computers. Customers usually have a *debit card,* or *access card,* which is a plastic card that allows a customer to use a computer banking system. To make a withdrawal from an ATM, the customer uses his or her access card in addition to punching in a PIN. The PIN protects the customer from someone else's use of a lost or stolen access card.

## POINT-OF-SALE SYSTEMS

**Point-of-sale systems** allow consumers to transfer funds to merchants to pay for purchases. On-line terminals are located at checkout counters in, for example, grocery stores. Instead of receiving cash or a check from the customer, the checkout person inserts the customer's card into a terminal, which reads the data encoded on the card. The computer at the customer's bank verifies that the card and identification code are valid and that there are enough funds in the customer's account to cover the purchase. After the payment is made, the customer's account is debited for the amount of the purchase.

For the merchant, direct payment from customers by means of point-of-sale systems involves, under current law, less risk of nonpayment or "bounced" checks. For the customer, the electronic transfer makes bills and check writing unnecessary.

## DIRECT DEPOSITS AND WITHDRAWALS

Automated clearinghouses are similar to the ordinary clearinghouses in which checks are cleared between banks. The main difference is that entries are made in the form of electronic signals; no checks are used. Thus, these systems do not further automate the handling of checks; they replace checks. This type of EFTS allows a bank to complete a transaction for less than the cost of clearing a check.

A direct deposit may be made to a customer's account through an electronic terminal when the customer has authorized the deposit in advance. The federal government often uses this EFTS to deposit Social Security payments directly into beneficiaries' accounts. Similarly, an employer may agree to make payroll and pension payments directly into an employee's account at specified intervals.

A customer may also authorize a bank (or other financial institution at which the customer's funds are on deposit) to make automatic payments at regular, recurrent intervals to a third party. For example, insurance premiums, utility bills, and home mortgage and automobile installment loan payments may sometimes be made automatically. Additionally, a customer may authorize his or her bank to make a payment or payments to the Internal Revenue Service for taxes due.

## PAY-BY-TELEPHONE SYSTEMS

When it is undesirable to arrange in advance for an automatic payment—as, for example, when the amount of a periodic payment varies—some financial institutions permit their customers to pay bills through a pay-by-telephone system. This allows the customer to access the institution's computer system by telephone and direct a transfer of funds. Utility bills sometimes are paid directly by customers using pay-by-telephone systems. Customers may also be permitted to transfer funds between accounts—for example, to withdraw funds from a savings account and make a deposit in a checking account—in this way.

# CONSUMER ELECTRONIC FUND TRANSFERS

As mentioned previously, consumer electronic fund transfers are governed by the Electronic Fund Transfer Act (EFTA), which provides a ''basic framework establishing the rights, liabilities, and responsibilities of participants in electronic fund transfers.'' The EFTA is essentially a disclosure law designed to benefit consumers; it requires financial institutions to inform consumers of their rights with respect to EFTS.

Under the EFTA, the Federal Reserve System's board of governors is authorized to administer the act and to promulgate regulations to carry out the purposes of the act. The board of governors has issued a set of rules, called **Regulation E,** to protect users of EFTS; this regulation should be consulted for a complete understanding of the EFTA. Also, the board has drafted model clauses for financial institutions to use in disclosing information about their electronic systems.

## INSTITUTIONS AND TRANSACTIONS COVERED

The EFTA governs financial institutions that offer electronic fund transfers involving customer accounts. The EFTA defines **financial institutions** to include banks, savings and loan institutions, credit unions, and any other business entities that directly or indirectly hold accounts belonging to consumers. Thus, securities brokerage houses that permit consumers to make electronic transfers to and from money market fund accounts are included.

The types of accounts covered by the EFTA include demand accounts; savings accounts; and other asset accounts established for personal, family, or household purposes. All electronic fund transfers involving such accounts are covered by the EFTA. Note that although telephone transfers are included in the definition of an electronic fund transfer, they are covered by the EFTA only if they are made *pursuant to a prearranged plan under which periodic or recurring transfers are contemplated.* In the following case, the court had to determine whether an attempted ATM transaction qualified as an electronic fund transfer covered by the EFTA.

**BACKGROUND AND FACTS** *Melanie Curde went to the ATM at her bank, Tri-City Bank & Trust Company, checked her account balance, withdrew some funds, and attempted to deposit a $200 check that she had received. She inserted the check and a deposit slip into the ATM slot labeled ''Deposit.'' She later testified that the check and deposit slip disappeared into the slot and were not seen again. Several months later, when the front cover of the ATM was removed for servicing, Curde's check and deposit slip were found between the cover and the machine itself, in an area near the bottom of the machine away from the deposit slot. The bank's ATM tape for that day reflected that Curde had indeed checked her account balance, withdrawn funds, and attempted a third transaction (her deposit) that resulted in an error and was canceled by the customer. Curde filed suit against the bank for damages, alleging, in part, that the bank had violated the EFTA. The bank claimed that it could not be liable under the act because the act governs only when electronic fund transfers are made, and in this case no actual transfer of funds had ever taken place. The trial court, finding that the canceled deposit and the attempted deposit were both electronic fund transfers and therefore covered by the EFTA, granted summary judgment for Curde. The appellate court reversed the trial court's decision, holding that the EFTA was not applicable. Curde then appealed to the Supreme Court of Tennessee.*

**CASE 30.1**

**CURDE v. TRI-CITY BANK & TRUST CO.**

Supreme Court of Tennessee, 1992.

826 S.W.2d 911.

*DROWOTA,* Justice.

\* \* \* \*

The pivotal question presented here is whether a check deposit via an ATM is an "electronic fund transfer." \* \* \*

\* \* \* \*

\* \* \* Because we find the statutory language unclear as to whether the Act applies to check deposits via an ATM, we proceed to consider the related legislative history, Federal Reserve Board regulations, and case law.

\* \* \* \*

There was no personal contact between Ms. Curde and the Bank respecting her attempted deposit of the check. The absence of human contact between the parties was a major factor motivating Congress to pass the Act.

Another factor motivating passage of the Act was that consumers utilizing electronic transfers do not receive traditional written records of their transactions. Because of the "faceless" transaction with the ATM, a consumer does not, at the time of the deposit, receive the same receipt she would when dealing with a human teller. That a check deposit to an ATM is an impersonal transaction which does not supply the consumer with a traditional bank receipt weighs toward a finding that Congress intended these transactions to be within the scope of the Act.

\* \* \* \*

\* \* \* [A] completed transfer of funds is not a necessary prerequisite for a transaction to be an electronic fund transfer under the Act; if it were, a mistake by a financial institution that prevented actual transfer would remove the attempted transaction from the scope of the Act, thereby defeating the Act's purpose in "establishing the rights, liabilities, and responsibilities of participants in electronic fund transfer systems." \* \* \*

\* \* \* \*

\* \* \* Therefore, we find that an attempted check deposit to [an] ATM is an "electronic fund transfer" covered by the Act. Here, Ms. Curde had a dispute with Tri-City Bank & Trust over whether a deposit had been made to her account. Imposing a duty on a bank to investigate and report disputed transactions at faceless automated teller machines is precisely the kind of consumer protection the Act is meant to afford.

However, because \* \* \* Ms. Curde admitted (via stipulation) that she cancelled the attempted deposit (transfer of funds), we hold that the Act does not apply. Once the consumer, by her own action, cancels a transaction, she has prevented the automatic teller transaction from becoming an electronic fund transfer under the Act. In order to come within the Act, the automatic teller transaction must "order, instruct, or authorize a financial institution to debit or credit an account." Once the transaction was cancelled by Ms. Curde, the financial institution was no longer instructed to credit her account; it therefore was not an electronic fund transfer under the Act.

**DECISION AND REMEDY**  *The Supreme Court of Tennessee held that the trial court erred when it granted summary judgment for Curde. The appellate court's decision was affirmed, but on different grounds, and the case was remanded for further proceedings.*

## DISCLOSURE OF TERMS AND CONDITIONS

The EFTA requires that the terms and conditions of electronic fund transfers involving a customer's account must be disclosed in readily understandable language at the time the customer contracts for the services. Included among the required disclosures are the following:

1. The customer's liability for unauthorized transfers resulting from the loss or theft of the card, code, or other access device.

2. Whom and what phone number to call to report a theft or loss.
3. The charges for using the EFTS.
4. What systems are available and the limits on frequency of use and dollar amounts.
5. The customer's right to see evidence of transactions in writing.
6. How errors can be corrected.
7. The customer's right to stop payments.
8. The financial institution's liability to the customer.
9. Rules concerning disclosure of account information to third parties.

Exhibit 30–1 shows a disclosure form containing the requisite information.

## DOCUMENTATION REGARDING TRANSACTIONS

The EFTA considerably reduces the amount of paper used in transferring funds. Financial institutions are required to provide the customer with written documentation—a receipt—of each transfer made from an electronic terminal at the time of the transfer. (Receipts are not required for telephone transfers, even when a telephone transfer is otherwise subject to the EFTA.) The receipt must clearly state the date, the type of transfer, the amount, the identity of the customer's account, the identity of any third party involved (such as a merchant accepting the customer's card as a means of paying for purchased goods), and the location of the terminal involved.

In addition, financial institutions must give customers periodic statements describing types, amounts, dates, transferees, and locations of transfers for each account through which an EFTS provides access. The type of account and the frequency with which the customer uses it determine the timing of the statements. Monthly statements are required for every month in which there is an electronic transfer of funds. Otherwise, statements must be provided quarterly.

The statement must show the amount and date of the transfer, the fees charged, the location or identification of the terminal, and the name of the retailer or third party, if any, involved. Also, the statement must provide an address and phone number for inquiries and error notices.

Financial institutions must also notify customers if an automatic deposit is not made as scheduled. This helps customers avoid overdrawing their accounts.

## PREAUTHORIZED TRANSFERS

A **preauthorized transfer** is a transaction authorized in advance to recur at regular intervals. For example, an employee may be able to arrange with an employer and a bank for the direct deposit of payroll checks into his or her checking account. Similarly, an individual might authorize a monthly transfer from his or her account to pay insurance premiums or installments on a home mortgage or automobile loan.

A situation in which a credit to a customer's account from the same payor is made at least once in each successive sixty-day period requires the financial institution to notify the customer when the credit is made, if the payor does not make the notification. As mentioned in the preceding section, the financial institution must also notify the customer if the deposit is not made as scheduled. The parties can agree on the manner of notice when the service is contracted for. In other words, if an employee has arranged with his or her employer for the direct deposit of weekly payroll checks, the bank handling the receipt of the checks must notify the employee weekly, if the employer does not, whether a check has been deposited as arranged.

As its name implies, a preauthorized transfer must be authorized by the customer in advance. The authorization must be in writing, and a copy of it must be provided to the customer when it is made. To stop payment of a preauthorized EFT, a customer may notify the financial institution orally or in writing at any time up to three business days before the scheduled date of the transfer. The institution may require the customer to provide written confirmation within fourteen days of an oral notification. For example, suppose Temple has arranged with his bank, Manufacturers Hanover Trust, to have the bank make automatic payments on his automobile installment loan. If Temple wishes to make a given payment on the loan personally, he must order the bank more than three days before the automatic payment is scheduled to be made not to make the payment.

## STOPPING PAYMENT AND REVERSIBILITY

Under the EFTA, then, a customer may cancel a *preauthorized* transfer before the transfer is made,

**■ Exhibit 30–1 A Sample Form Disclosing Terms and Conditions Required under the EFTA**

## ELECTRONIC FUND TRANSFER AGREEMENT
(Automated Teller Machine and Point-of-Sale Transactions)

**Your Card cannot be used at electronic terminals without a Personal Identification Number ("PIN"). If you recently applied for automated teller machine or point-of-sale service, you will receive your PIN in the mail soon. If you did not apply for the service and do not want to use your Card, you can destroy your Card by cutting it in half. You may wish to retain the Card, however, if it contains our check guarantee. If you request a PIN, your Card and PIN will be subject to the following agreement, as amended from time to time.**

By retaining or using the Card(s) or PIN, you agree to the terms and conditions of this Agreement. This Agreement sets forth the terms and conditions governing the use of your First Interstate Red or Gold Bancard or Preferred Gold Bancard ("Card") at automated teller machines (ATMs) and point-of-sale terminals (collectively referred to as "Terminals"). It also governs the use of your Card in connection with point-of-sale transactions which do not involve a Terminal.

### 1. Services Available.

Depending on the accounts and services associated with your Card, you may be able to perform the following transactions:

(a) Withdraw cash from your checking or savings account;
(b) Make deposits to your checking or savings account;
(c) Transfer funds between your checking and savings account;
(d) Make payments to others from your checking account.

*Note:* Market Interest customers and customers who only have savings accounts linked to their Red Bancards may not use their Cards for point-of-sale transactions;

* (e) Make payments on a First Interstate Personal or Business Loan or to your Balance Plus® account; and
* (f) Obtain account balance information. (Note: The balance figure may not reflect recent transactions, and may include funds which are not subject to immediate withdrawal.)

Some of these services may not be available at all Terminals or at ATMs operated by other institutions.

All payments and deposits are subject to later verification by us.

*These particular transactions are not covered by the error resolution or liability section of this Agreement.

Deposits and payments must be accompanied by your personalized deposit slip or payment coupon. Failure to do so may result in a loss or delay in processing your transaction.

### 2. Limitations.

With a Red Bancard, you may withdraw up to $300 in cash from ATMs each day. With a Gold Bancard, you may withdraw up to $500 in cash from ATMs each day. With a Preferred Gold Bancard, you may withdraw up to $1,000 in cash from ATMs each day. You cannot make payments or deposits at ATMs operated by other institutions, including First Interstate banks outside California. Additional limitations may exist for ATMs operated by other institutions. Since point-of-sale transactions are guaranteed at the time you initiate payment, you may not stop payment on a point-of-sale transaction. We may place a $700 daily limit on point-of-sale (Interlink) and VISA® merchants transactions completed with a Red, Gold, VISA Check Card, or Preferred Gold Bancard at this time.

*Note:* You may not use your Card or PIN in systems or networks not authorized by us. Before signing an agreement with a third party to accept your Card or PIN which will access your account(s), you must verify that we have approved the use of your Card or access to your account(s) through that third party.

### 3. Charges.

Regular Savings account customers may make up to three withdrawals in a quarter (by teller, ATM or transfer) without charge, regardless of account balance. If the minimum quarterly balance is $300 or more, there is no limit to the number of withdrawals that may be made without charge. If the minimum quarterly balance is below $300 in any quarter, then a fee of $1.00 will be charged to the account in that quarter for every withdrawal beyond the first three.

All accounts are assessed a $2.00 service charge for cash withdrawals at ATMs that are not First Interstate Day & Night ATMs. A $.10 charge is imposed for each completed merchant point-of-sale transaction (e.g., at VISA and Interlink merchants, Mobile, Arco, or Vons), whether completed with an access device issued by us or by the merchant, when your account is debited for the transaction electronically or through an automated clearing house.

### 4. Foreign Transactions.

If you effect a transaction in a foreign currency, the charge will be converted into U.S. dollars by MasterCard® International and/or Visa International. Currently the conversion rate used to determine the transaction amount in U.S. dollars is generally either a government-mandated rate or the wholesale market rate in effect one day prior to the transaction processing date, increased by one percent. Since conversion may occur after the date of a transaction, the conversion rate may be different from the rate in effect at the time of the transaction. You agree to pay us the transaction amount converted by MasterCard International/Visa International.

### 5. Business Days.

Our business days are Monday through Friday, excluding weekends and holidays.

*Note:* If you perform a transaction on a non-business day or after 2:00 P.M. on a banking day, we may treat it as if we had received it on the next business day.

### 6. How to Notify Us of an Unauthorized Transaction.

If you believe that someone has transferred or may transfer money from your account without your permission, call us at 1-800-626-3400 or write First Interstate Bank, Consumer Affairs Dept. W35-13, P.O. Box 3666, Los Angeles, CA 90051.

### 7. How to Notify Us of a Lost or Stolen Card or Personal Identification Number.

If you believe your Card or Personal Identification Number (PIN) has been lost or stolen, call us at **1-800-955-5678**, or write First Interstate Bank, Bancard Division, Security Dept., P.O. Box 9700, Simi Valley, CA 93097-0016.

### 8. Business or Trust Accounts.

The error resolution and liability sections of this Agreement (Sections 9, 10, and 17), as well as those indicated on the back of the Periodic Statements, do not apply to Business or Trust Accounts. In no event shall the Bank be liable for any special or consequential damages. The business entity or trust for which a Card was issued shall assume the sole responsibility for any unauthorized use of its cards, and shall indemnify and hold the Bank harmless from any claims, losses and damages related to unauthorized transactions.

### 9. Your Liability.

Tell us AT ONCE if you believe your Card or PIN has been lost or stolen. Telephoning is the best way of keeping your possible losses down. You could lose all the money in your account (plus your maximum overdraft line of credit). If you tell us within 2 business days, you can lose no more than $50 if we determine that someone used your Card or PIN without your permission.

If you do NOT tell us within 2 business days after you learn of the loss or theft of your Card or PIN, and we can prove we could have stopped someone from using your Card or PIN without your permission if you had told us, you could lose as much as $500.

Also, if your statement shows transactions that you did not make, tell us at once. If you do not tell us within 60 days after the statement was mailed to you, you may not get back any money you lost after the 60 days if we can prove that we could have stopped someone from taking the money if you had told us in time.

If a good reason (such as a long trip or a hospital stay) kept you from telling us, we will extend the time periods.

### 10. First Interstate's Liability.

If we do not complete a transaction to or from your checking or savings account on time or, in the correct amount according to this agreement, we will be liable for your losses or damages. There are some exceptions, however. We will not be liable, for instance, if

(a) Through no fault of ours, your account does not contain sufficient available funds to make the transaction;
(b) The transaction would go over the credit limit on your overdraft line;
(c) The ATM where you are making the transaction does not have enough cash, or cash in the denominations you request;
(d) The Terminal is not in service;
(e) The Terminal is not working properly and you know about the breakdown when you start the transaction;
(f) Circumstances beyond our control (such as fire, flood or a mechanical or electrical failure) prevent the transaction and we have taken reasonable precautions to avoid those circumstances;
(g) The money in your account is subject to an uncollected funds hold, legal process, dispute or any other encumbrance or agreement restricting transfers; or
(h) The transaction information supplied to us by you or by third parties (e.g., Terminal owners) is incorrect, incomplete or untimely.

There may be other exceptions not specifically mentioned above.

### 11. Documentation.

You will get a receipt at the time you make any transaction at a Terminal. You will also get a monthly account statement unless there are no electronic fund transactions in a particular month. In any case, you will get a statement at least quarterly.

*Note:* This section does not apply to transactions occurring outside the United States.

just as a drawer—the person who signs a check—may stop payment on a check before it is paid. For other EFT transactions, however, the EFTA does not provide for the reversal of an electronic transfer of funds, once it has occurred. This is because the uniquely instantaneous nature of an electronic transfer of funds provides no float time during which an effective reversal of an order to pay can be made.

## MISTAKES AND CORRECTIONS

Under the EFTA, a customer has a duty to examine the periodic—monthly or quarterly—statements provided by the financial institution handling his or her account or accounts. Within sixty days after the institution has sent a statement, the customer must notify the institution of any errors that appear on it. Whether oral or written, the notice must contain the following information:

1. The customer's name and account number.
2. A sentence stating that an error has been made and its alleged amount.

3. Why the customer believes an error has been made.

The institution is required to investigate and report the results within ten business days. If the institution needs more than ten days, it may take up to forty-five, but it must recredit the customer's account for the amount alleged to be in error until the problem is resolved. If the institution determines that an error did occur, it has one business day to adjust the customer's account. Even if no mistake has been made, the institution has to give the customer a full written report with conclusions. Failure to investigate in good faith makes the institution liable to the customer for **treble damages**—three times the amount of provable damages.

Banks are held to strict compliance with the terms of the EFTA, and if they fail to adhere to the letter of the law of the EFTA they will be held liable for violation. This point is illustrated by the following case.

---

**BACKGROUND AND FACTS** *Bisbey (the plaintiff) opened a checking account with the District of Columbia National Bank (the defendant) in January 1981. Subsequently, she authorized the bank to debit her checking account for fund transfer directives that were submitted monthly by the New York Life Insurance Company (NYLIC) for payment of her insurance premiums. In September 1981, Bisbey's account lacked sufficient funds to cover the insurance directive, and no transfer was made. NYLIC resubmitted the September directive in October, along with the October monthly directive. Bisbey's funds were insufficient to satisfy either submission, but the bank covered the premiums. As a result, two overdraft notices were sent to Bisbey, each in the amount of her monthly insurance premium. Bisbey informed a customer representative of the bank that she believed that an error had occurred with regard to the preauthorized transfers. Approximately ten days later, an official of the bank telephoned Bisbey and explained that there had been no improper duplication of her insurance premiums. Bisbey, however, still considered the matter unresolved, and she filed suit under the EFTA, claiming that the bank had unlawfully failed to properly advise her about the result of its investigation. Under the EFTA, a bank's notification to a customer that no error has been made must be in writing. The trial court ruled in favor of the bank, and Bisbey appealed.*

CASE 30.2

**BISBEY v. D.C. NATIONAL BANK**

United States Court of Appeals, District of Columbia Circuit, 1986. 793 F.2d 315.

---

*Harry T. EDWARDS,* Circuit Judge:
\* \* \* \*

\* \* \* [Section 908(d) of the Electronic Fund Transfer Act] imposed a duty upon the Bank to ''deliver or mail'' the results of its investigation to Ms. Bisbey and to advise her of her right to request reproductions of all documents which it relied upon to conclude that no error occurred. The oral notice given to appellant was insufficient with respect to the [statute's] required "explanation," and it did not even purport to give "notice of the right to request reproductions" as required by the statute.

The Bank's foregoing failures to comply with the statute give rise to civil liability under section 915 of the Act. That section provides that "any person who fails to comply with any provision of [the Act] with respect to any consumer, except for an error resolved in accordance with section 908, is liable to such consumer" for actual damages or for a symbolic award. Thus, under the plain terms of the Act, civil liability attaches to *all* failures of compliance with respect to *any* provision of the Act, including section 908.

\* \* \* \*

It may seem odd that the Bank is held liable for a transaction that benefited the plaintiff. Ms. Bisbey's account contained insufficient funds to cover either of the premium requests submitted by NYLIC. Though she had no overdraft agreement, the Bank did not charge an overdraft fee. Thus, the effect of the Bank's payments was to provide her, at no cost, with insurance coverage she would not have had otherwise. Upon Bisbey's inquiry, the Bank gave her a correct report but neglected to send it in writing, as the statute requires. Ms. Bisbey conceded below that she had suffered no damage and the District Court's surmise that she may have been benefited seems correct. Despite this, the litigation has continued for nearly three years, and the statute compels a finding that the Bank is liable. \* \* \*

\* \* \* \*

The "fail[ure]s to comply" with the EFTA in the instant case are plain; moreover, they are failures to which civil liability attaches for they have not been resolved in accordance with section 908.

**DECISION AND REMEDY** *The court of appeals reversed the trial court's decision and remanded the case to the lower court for determination of the amount of an award of damages and attorneys' fees.*

**INTERNATIONAL CONSIDERATIONS** **International Law and EFTS** *Electronic fund transfers are particularly useful in the international business context. The expanded use of EFTS, though, depends on legal protections. The United Nations Commission on International Trade Law has developed a Model Law on International Credit Transfers, which was approved in 1992 for adoption by various countries. The model law, which is similar to U.S. laws in respect to fund transfers, spells out the rights and remedies of the parties involved in international EFTS. Although the model law has not yet been widely adopted, to the extent that nations adopt the law in the future, it will greatly facilitate international electronic fund transfers.*

## UNAUTHORIZED TRANSFERS

Unauthorized transfers of funds by means of EFTS are one of the hazards of electronic banking. A paper check leaves visible evidence of a transaction, and a customer can easily detect a forgery or an altered check with ordinary vigilance. But the evidence of an electronic transfer is in many cases only an entry in a computer printout of the various debits and credits made to a particular account during a specified time period.

Because of the vulnerability of EFTS systems to fraudulent activities, the EFTA clearly defined what constitutes an unauthorized transfer. Under the act, a transfer is unauthorized if (1) it is initiated by a person other than the consumer who has no actual authority to initiate the transfer; (2) the consumer receives no benefit from it; and (3) the consumer did not furnish the person "with the card, code, or other means of access" to his or her account. The unauthorized use of EFTS access devices constitutes a federal felony, and unauthorized users of EFTS are subject to criminal sanctions, including a $10,000 fine and ten years' imprisonment.

## CUSTOMER LIABILITY FOR UNAUTHORIZED TRANSFERS

Under the EFTA, before a customer can be held liable for any unauthorized transfer, it must be established that the transfer resulted from the use of an accepted means of access and that the customer had been provided with a means of identifying himself or herself to that means of access. For example, a bank's customer will not be held liable for unauthorized withdrawals from the customer's checking account unless the bank has provided the customer with an access card and a secret number for access to the bank's EFTS.

In the event that the access card or other device is lost, stolen, or misplaced, the EFTA limits the customer's liability for any unauthorized transfers of funds to $50 if the customer notifies the financial institution within two business days of learning of the loss or theft. If the customer does not inform the institution until after the second day, his or her liability is $500. The customer's liability may be unlimited if notification does not occur within sixty days of the customer's receipt of a periodic statement that reflects an unauthorized transfer.

In any action involving a customer's liability for an unauthorized transfer, the institution must prove (1) that the customer and the institution had an agreement under which the customer agreed to this liability and (2) that the customer knew that the access device had been lost, stolen, or misplaced. When an unauthorized transfer has appeared on a statement, the institution must show that any loss of funds due to the unauthorized transfer would not have occurred but for the customer's failure to report the unauthorized transfer's appearance on the statement within sixty days of the statement's transmittal. The importance of complying with the sixty-day requirement is illustrated in the following case.

---

**CASE 30.3**

**KRUSER v. BANK OF AMERICA NT & SA[a]**

California Court of Appeal, Fifth District, 1991.
230 Cal.App.3d 741,
281 Cal.Rptr. 463.

**COMPANY PROFILE** *In 1904, Amadeo Giannini founded the Bank of Italy in the North Beach section of San Francisco. Two years later, Giannini personally salvaged over $1 million in gold, cash, and other items from the bank as the fire caused by the 1906 earthquake engulfed neighborhoods less than three blocks away. This quick action allowed the bank to reopen in a temporary location on the waterfront to loan funds for the city's reconstruction while larger banks could not gain access to their vaults. In 1921, Giannini acquired the Bank of America of Los Angeles. By the end of the 1920s, the banks were operating as Bank of America, which, near the end of World War II, became the largest U.S. bank. In 1958, the company introduced the BankAmericard, which became the VISA credit card in 1977. By that time, Bank of America had more assets, more deposits, and higher profits than any bank in the world. Earnings and assets fell off in the early 1980s, when the prices of energy and commodities declined. In 1985, losses forced Bank of America to lay off employees for the first time, but the bank became profitable again in 1988. Today, through subsidiaries, Bank of America has a presence in all fifty states and serves almost half of the households in Washington and California.*

**BACKGROUND AND FACTS** *Lawrence and Georgene Kruser maintained a joint checking account with the Bank of America. The bank issued to each of them a "Versatel" card and separate personal identification*

---

a.   "NT & SA" stands for National Trust & Savings Association.

*numbers so that they could access funds in their account from ATMs. The Krusers believed that Mr. Kruser's card had been destroyed in September 1986. The December 1986 account statement mailed to the Krusers by the bank, however, reflected a $20 withdrawal of funds by someone using Mr. Kruser's card at an ATM. Mrs. Kruser underwent surgery in December 1986 and was in the hospital for eleven days. She spent the following months recuperating from the surgery. She therefore failed to examine the December bank statement promptly and did not discover the unauthorized December withdrawal until August or September 1987, at which time she reported it to the bank. In September 1987, the Krusers received bank statements for July and August 1987, which reflected forty-seven unauthorized withdrawals, totaling $9,020, made from an ATM by someone using Mr. Kruser's card. They notified the bank of these withdrawals within a few days of receiving the statements. When the bank refused to credit the Kruser's account for the amount of the unauthorized withdrawals, the Krusers sued. The trial court granted the bank's motion for summary judgment, holding that the bank was not liable for the unauthorized transfers because the Krusers had failed to notify the bank of the $20 unauthorized transfer within sixty days after receiving the statement, as required under the EFTA. The Krusers appealed.*

STONE (WM. A.), Associate Justice.

   \*   \*   \*   \*

Appellants [the Krusers] contend the December withdrawal of $20 was so isolated in time and minimal in amount that it cannot be considered in connection with the July and August withdrawals. \* \* \* They argue that if a consumer receives a bank statement which reflects an unauthorized minimal electronic transfer and fails to report the transaction to the bank within 60 days of transmission of the bank statement, unauthorized transfers many years later, perhaps totaling thousands of dollars, would remain the responsibility of the consumer.

The result appellants fear is avoided by the requirement that the bank establish the subsequent unauthorized transfers could have been prevented had the consumer notified the bank of the first unauthorized transfer. Here, although the unauthorized transfer of $20 occurred approximately seven months before the unauthorized transfers totaling $9,020, it is undisputed that all transfers were made by someone using Mr. Kruser's card[,] which the Krusers believed had been destroyed prior to December 1986. According to the declaration of Yvonne Maloon, the Bank's Versatel risk manager, the Bank could have and would have canceled Mr. Kruser's card had it been timely notified of the December unauthorized transfer. In that event[,] Mr. Kruser's card could not have been used to accomplish the unauthorized transactions in July and August. \* \* \*

In the alternative, appellants contend the facts establish that Mrs. Kruser, who was solely responsible for reconciling the bank statements, was severely ill and was also caring for a terminally ill relative when the December withdrawal occurred. Therefore they claim they were entitled to an extension of time within which to notify the bank.    \*   \*   \*

   \*   \*   \*   \*

[N]othing in the record reflects any extenuating circumstances which would have prevented Mr. Kruser from reviewing the bank statements. \* \* \*

   \*   \*   \*   \*

Appellants cite no authority which supports their claim [that] the consumer must not only receive the statement provided by the bank, but must acquire actual knowledge of an unauthorized transfer from the statement. Such a construction of the law would reward consumers who choose to remain ignorant of the nature of transactions on their account by purposely failing to review periodic statements. *Consumers must play an active and responsible role in protecting against losses which might result from unauthorized transfers.* A banking institution cannot know of an unauthorized electronic transfer unless the consumer reports it. [Emphasis added.]

*The appellate court affirmed the trial court's decision. The bank was not liable for the unauthorized transfers and was entitled to judgment as a matter of law.*

**DECISION AND REMEDY**

## LIABILITY OF THE FINANCIAL INSTITUTION

A financial institution is liable to a customer for all damages *proximately caused* by its failure to make an electronic fund transfer according to the terms and conditions of an account, in the correct amount, or in a timely manner when the customer properly instructs it to do so.

There are exceptions. The institution will not be liable in the following situations:

1. The customer's account has insufficient funds through no fault of the financial institution.
2. The funds are subject to legal process, such as attachment (see Chapter 32).
3. The transfer would exceed an established credit limit.
4. An ATM has insufficient cash.
5. Circumstances beyond the institution's control prevent the transfer.

The institution is also liable for failure to stop payment of a preauthorized transfer from a customer's account when instructed to do so under the account's terms and conditions.

For an institution's violation of EFTA, a consumer may recover actual damages, as well as punitive damages of not more than $1,000 or less than $100. (Unlike actual damages, punitive damages are assessed to punish a defendant or to set an example for similar wrongdoers.) In a class-action suit, the punitive-damage limit is the lesser of $500,000 or 1 percent of the institution's net worth.

It is a federal misdemeanor to violate the EFTA. Criminal sanctions for violations of the EFTA by banking institutions may subject an institution or its officials to a $5,000 fine and up to one year's imprisonment.

## SECTION 3

# COMMERCIAL FUND TRANSFERS

The transfer of funds "by wire" between commercial parties is another way in which funds are transferred electronically. In fact, the dollar volume of payments made via wire transfers is more than $1 trillion a day—an amount that far exceeds the dollar volume of payments made by other means. The two major wire payment systems are the Federal Reserve wire transfer network (Fedwire) and the New York Clearing House Interbank Payments Systems (CHIPS).

Unauthorized wire transfers are obviously possible and, indeed, can pose significant problems. If an imposter, for example, succeeds in having funds wired from another's account, the other party will bear the loss (unless he or she can recover from the imposter). In the past, any disputes arising as a result of unauthorized or incorrectly made transfers were settled by the courts under the common law principles of tort law or contract law. To clarify the rights and liabilities of parties involved in fund transfers not subject to the EFTA or other federal or state statutes, Article 4A of the UCC was promulgated in 1989. Most states have adopted this article.

The type of fund transfer covered by Article 4A is illustrated in the following example. American Industries, Inc., owes $5 million to Chandler Corporation. Instead of sending Chandler a check or some other instrument that would enable Chandler to obtain payment, American Industries tells its bank, North Bank, to credit $5 million to Chandler's account in South Bank. North Bank instructs South Bank to credit $5

## ■ CONCEPT SUMMARY 30.1 Electronic Fund Transfer Act of 1978

| AREA OF COVERAGE | ESSENTIAL PROVISIONS |
|---|---|
| **Disclosure** | Terms and conditions must be disclosed in readily understandable language. |
| **Documentation** | 1. The customer must be provided with a written receipt for each transfer made from an electronic terminal at the time of the transfer.<br>2. Financial institutions must provide customers with periodic statements of each account to which an electronic fund transfer system provides access. |
| **Preauthorized Transfers** | *Deposits*—Banks must notify the customer when the account is credited if the payor does not notify the customer or if the credit is not made as scheduled.<br>*Transfers*—Authorization must be in writing; three business days' notice is required to stop a preauthorized transfer. |
| **Mistakes and Corrections** | 1. The customer must notify the institution of a mistake within sixty days after the statement has been mailed.<br>2. The institution is required to investigate and report the results within ten business days; it can have up to forty-five days but must recredit the customer's account until the problem has been resolved.<br>3. The institution must give the customer a full written report, even if no mistake occurred. |
| **Customer Liability for Unauthorized Transfers** | 1. Liability is limited to $50 if the customer notifies the financial institution within two business days of learning of loss or theft of access card or device.<br>2. Liability limit is $500 if the customer fails to notify the institution within two business days but notifies within sixty days.<br>3. Liability may be unlimited if the customer fails to notify the bank within sixty days of receipt of the bank statement reflecting an unauthorized transfer. |
| **Liability of Financial Institution** | 1. The institution is liable for all damages proximately caused by its failure to make electronic fund transfers according to the terms and conditions of an account. Punitive damages may be assessed against the institution.<br>2. The institution is liable for failure to stop payment of a preauthorized transfer when instructed to do so under the terms and conditions of the EFTA.<br>3. Violation of the EFTA constitutes a federal misdemeanor. |

million to Chandler's account. In more complex transactions, additional banks would be involved.

In these and similar circumstances, ordinarily a financial institution's instruction is transmitted electronically. Any means may be used, however, including first-class mail. To reflect this fact,

Article 4A uses the term *funds transfer* rather than *wire transfer* to describe the overall payment transaction. The full text of Article 4A is presented in Appendix C, following revised Article 4 of the Uniform Commercial Code.

## TERMS AND CONCEPTS TO REVIEW

automated teller machine
 (ATM) 570
electronic fund transfer
 (EFT) 569
electronic fund transfer
 system (EFTS) 569

financial institution 571
float time 569
personal identification
 number (PIN) 570
point-of-sale system 570
preauthorized transfer 573

Regulation E 571
treble damages 575

## QUESTIONS AND CASE PROBLEMS

**30–1. Direct Deposits.** Kim has a checking account at First National Bank. She has had this bank account for over five years and has never had a check returned for insufficient funds. Kim works at Monmouth Medical Center and has arranged with her employer for direct deposit of her monthly paycheck into her checking account at First National. For an unexplained reason, Kim's July 1 paycheck is not deposited in her checking account. On July 15, Kim receives four notices from the bank stating that four of her checks have not been honored because her account is overdrawn. She incurs late charges from her creditors and charges from the bank for the overdrawn checks. Kim files suit against her bank. Can she recover any money from the bank? If so, under what theory, and how much?

**30–2. Error Resolution.** Yannuzzi has a checking account at Texas Bank. She frequently uses her access card to obtain money from the automatic teller machines. She always withdraws $50 when she makes a withdrawal, but she never withdraws more than $50 in any one day. When she received the April statement on her account, she noticed that on April 13 two withdrawals for $50 each had been made from the account. Believing this to be a mistake, she went to her bank on May 10 to inform the bank of the error. A bank officer told her that the bank would investigate and inform her of the result. On May 26, the bank officer called her and said that bank personnel were having trouble locating the error but would continue to try to find it. On June 20, the bank sent her a full written report advising her that no error had been made. Yannuzzi, unhappy with the bank's explanation, filed suit against the bank, alleging that it had violated the Electronic Fund Transfer Act. What was the outcome of the suit? Would it matter if the bank could show that on the day in question it had deducted $50 from Yannuzzi's account to cover a check that Yannuzzi had written to a local department store and that had cleared the bank on that day?

**30–3. Error Resolution.** On August 23, 1983, Robert Porter tried to withdraw $100 from his checking account at an automated teller machine. When no money was dispensed from the machine after Porter had pushed the necessary buttons, he reported the incident to a bank official. A few weeks later, on September 5, Porter tried to withdraw $200. When no money appeared after two tries, he again reported the problem to a bank official. As a result of these two incidents, Porter's next bank statement showed one withdrawal of $100 and two of $200 each (for a total of $500). Porter filed suit against the bank to recover the $500 debit on his checking account for money he never received. Discuss whether Porter was able to recover the $500. [*Porter v. Citibank, N.A.,* 123 Misc.2d 28, 472 N.Y.S.2d 582 (1984)]

**30–4. Unauthorized Transfers.** Parviz Haghighi Abyaneh and Iran Haghighi were co-owners of a savings account at First State Bank. On May 23, 1984, a person identifying himself as Abyaneh entered the Raleigh, North Carolina, office of Citizens Savings and Loan Association of Rocky Mount and opened a savings account. He then called the First State Bank and asked a bank employee to transfer funds from Abyaneh's First State account into the newly created account. As a result, $53,825.66 was transferred to the new account, and subsequently, the funds were withdrawn. When the true owners of the First State Bank account learned of the transfer, they filed suit against Merchants Bank, North, successor by merger to First State Bank, for violating the Electronic Fund Transfer Act. Discuss whether Abyaneh will be able to recover the $53,825.66. [*Abyaneh v. Merchants Bank, North,* 670 F.Supp. 1298 (M.D.Pa. 1987)]

**30–5. Consumer versus Commercial Transfers.** Shawmut Worcester County Bank, a Massachusetts bank, transferred $10,000 to First American Bank & Trust of Palm Beach, Florida, through Fedwire. Shawmut's payment order stated that the beneficiary of the transfer was Fernando Degan and that First American should credit account # 100 205 001 633. It turned out that the First American account under that number was held jointly by Degan and Joseph Merle. When Shawmut discovered its error 106 days after the mistaken transfer, it credited the account of its customer who had requested the transfer with the $10,000 and then asked First American to "reverse" the transfer. First American asked Merle, its customer, if he would authorize the reversal. Merle refused. Accordingly, First American told Shawmut it would not reverse the transfer. Shawmut then sued First American to recover the $10,000, alleging, among other claims, that the transaction fell under the EFTA, which prescribes specific requirements that must be followed in the event of error in an electronic fund transfer. Is Shawmut a consumer within the meaning of the EFTA? How should the court rule? [*Shawmut Worcester County Bank v. First American Bank & Trust,* 731 F.Supp. 57 (D.Mass. 1990)]

**30–6. Wire Transfers.** Dr. As'ad M. Masri and his wife borrowed $150,000 from First Virginia Bank–Colonial (FVBC). Masri then signed a wire-transfer request directing FVBC to transfer the funds to the Amro Bank in Amsterdam. The request also stated that the funds were to be deposited to the Lenex Corporation's account in that bank. FVBC transferred the funds to the Bank of Nova Scotia, an intermediary bank, and sent disbursal instructions directly to Amro. The following day, the funds were credited to the Lenex account at the Amro Bank. They were withdrawn, however, by someone other than the person intended by Masri to do so. When the Masris later defaulted on the loan, FVBC sought full repayment. The Masris claimed that FVBC breached the wire-transfer agreement. Has FVBC breached the transfer agreement? Where does FVBC's responsibility end? Discuss fully. [*First Virginia Bank–Colonial v. Masri, M.D.,* 245 Va. 461, 428 S.E.2d 903 (1993)]

**30–7. Error Resolution.** On August 16, 1981, Frederick Ognibene stopped at a Citibank automated teller machine located outside the bank to make a $20 withdrawal from his checking account. There were two ATMs located close together, and in between them was a customer service telephone. While Ognibene made his withdrawal, a man was talking on the phone and appeared to be telling the bank's customer service department that one of the machines was not working. The man, who Ognibene assumed was a bank employee, then turned to Ognibene and said that the bank's customer

service department had asked if he might try Ognibene's card in the malfunctioning machine to see if it would activate it. Ognibene complied with the request and watched the man insert his card in the ATM in question. The man then punched in a personal identification number (Ognibene's own PIN, which the other man had observed when Ognibene made his $20 withdrawal a few seconds earlier) and continued talking on the telephone. The man reinserted Ognibene's card and reported to the fictitious person on the other end of the phone line that the machine was now functioning. He then hung up, thanked Ognibene, took his cash, and left. Later, when Ognibene realized that $400 had been withdrawn from his account at that same time of that same day, he brought an action against the bank to recover the $400. Ognibene argued that he in no way had authorized the stranger to use his card. The bank contended that by his negligent actions, Ognibene had given that authority. What should the court decide? Explain. [*Ognibene v. Citibank, N.A.,* 112 Misc.2d 219, 446 N.Y.S.2d 845 (1981)]

**30–8. Case Briefing Assignment**

 *Examine Case A.4 [Mellon Bank, N.A. v. Securities Settlement Corp., 710 F.Supp. 991 (D.N.J. 1989)] in Appendix A. The case has been excerpted there in great detail. Review and then brief the case, making sure that you include answers to the following questions in your brief.*

1. Who brought this lawsuit, and why?
2. What was the threshold issue in this case, according to the court?
3. What did the court mean by its statement that it ''must sail between the Scylla of common law and the Charybdis of statute in an attempt to predict what Pennsylvania's highest court would do if confronted with this situation''?
4. What law governed the resolution of this case? Did the provisions of the UCC play a significant role in the court's reasoning?
5. What law or legal duty had Mellon violated?

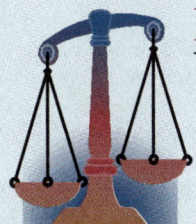

# FOCUS ON ETHICS

# Commercial Paper and Banking

**A**rticles 3 and 4 of the Uniform Commercial Code (UCC), which deal with negotiable instruments, constitute an important part of the law governing commercial transactions. These articles reflect several fundamental ethical principles. One principle is that individuals should be protected against harm caused by the misuse of negotiable instruments. Another basic principle—and one that underlies the entire concept of negotiable instruments—is that the free flow of commerce should be encouraged by practical and reasonable laws governing the use of negotiable instruments.

In the following pages, we first look at some of the ethical implications of the holder-in-due-course (HDC) concept and then at some other ethical issues that frequently arise in relation to negotiable instruments.

## Good Faith and the HDC Concept

The drafters of Article 3 did not create out of thin air the HDC concept. Indeed, under the common law, courts had often restricted the extent to which defenses could successfully be raised against a good faith holder of a negotiable instrument. As an example, consider the classic 1884 case, *Ort v. Fowler.*[1]

In this case, Ort, a farmer who was working alone in his field one day, was approached by a stranger who claimed to be the state agent for a manufacturer of iron posts and wire fence. The two men conversed for some time, and eventually the stranger persuaded the farmer to act as an area representative for the manufacturer. The stranger then completed two documents for Ort to sign, telling Ort that they were identical copies of an agreement in which Ort agreed to represent the manufacturer.

Because the farmer did not have his glasses with him and could read only with great difficulty, he asked the stranger to read what the document said. The stranger then purported to read the document to Ort, not mentioning that it was a promissory note. Both men signed each document. The stranger later negotiated the promissory note he had fraudulently obtained from Ort to an HDC. When the HDC brought suit against the farmer, the farmer attempted to defend on the basis of fraud in the execution.

The Kansas court deciding the issue entertained three possible views. One was that because Ort never *intended* to execute a note, he should not be held liable for the act. A second view was that the jury should decide, as a question of fact, whether Ort was guilty of negligence under the circumstances. The third view was that because Ort possessed all of his faculties and was able to read the English language, signing a promissory note solely in reliance on a stranger's assurances that it was a different instrument constituted negligence.

This third view was the one adopted by the court in 1884. The court held that Ort's negligence had contributed to the fraud and that such negligence precluded Ort from raising fraud as a defense against payment on the note. Today, the UCC expresses essentially the same reasoning: fraud is only a defense against an HDC if the injured party signed the instrument "with neither knowledge nor a reasonable opportunity to learn of its character or its essential terms" [UCC R3–305(a)(1)(iii)].[2]

Although it may not seem fair that an innocent victim

---

1. 31 Kan. 478, 2 P. 580 (1884).

2. UCC 3–305(2)(c).

should have to suffer the consequences of another's fraudulent act, the UCC assumes that it would be even less fair if an HDC could not collect payment. The reasoning behind this assumption is that an HDC, as a third party, is less likely to have been responsible for—or to have had an opportunity to protect against—the fraud in the underlying transaction.

In general, the HDC doctrine, like other sections of the UCC, reflects the philosophy that when two or more innocent parties are at risk, the burden should fall on the party that was in the best position to prevent the loss. For businesspersons, the HDC doctrine means that caution must be exercised in the issuance and acceptance of commercial paper to protect against the risk of loss through fraud.

## Efficiency versus Due Care
A major problem faced by today's banking institutions is how to verify customer signatures on the billions of checks that are processed through the banking system each month. If a bank fails to verify a signature on a check it receives for payment and the check turns out to be forged, the bank will normally be held liable to its customer for the amount paid. But how can banks possibly examine, item by item, each signature on every check that they pay?

The banks' solution to this problem is simply not to examine all signatures. Instead, computers are programmed to verify all signatures only on checks exceeding a certain threshold

amount, such as $1,000 or $2,500 or perhaps some higher amount. Checks for less than the threshold amount are selected for signature verification only on a random basis. In other words, serious attention is restricted to serious matters. The result is that many checks, if not most, are paid without signature verification. This practice, which has become an acceptable standard within the banking industry of today, is economically efficient for banks: even though liability costs are sometimes incurred—when forged checks are paid—the costs involved in verifying the authenticity of each and every signature would be far higher.

Some people have alleged that banks using such procedures are not exercising due care in the handling of the customers' accounts. Under the UCC, banks are held to a standard of "ordinary care." At one time in the banking industry, ordinary care normally was interpreted to mean that a bank had a duty to inspect *all* signatures on checks. The question is, what constitutes ordinary care in the context of today's world? Does a bank exercise ordinary care if it follows the prevailing industry practice of examining signatures on only a few, randomly selected checks under a certain amount? Or does ordinary care still mean that a bank should examine each signature?

Under the unrevised Article 3, a number of courts have held that banks do not breach their duty of care by establishing and adhering to a practice that is cost effective and customary within the

industry. Other courts, however, have reasoned that banks are supposed to verify all signatures on all checks, and thus banks are not exercising ordinary care when they fail to do so. The revised Article 3 specifically addressed this problem in UCC R3–103(a)(7). That section states that "[i]n the case of a bank that takes an instrument for processing for collection or payment by automated means, reasonable commercial standards do not require the bank to examine the instrument if failure to examine does not violate the bank's prescribed procedures and the bank's procedures do not vary unreasonably from the general banking usage."

## Agents' Signatures
Corporate officers and other agents are often authorized to sign negotiable instruments on behalf of their firms. As long as an agent indicates on the instrument that he or she is signing in a representative capacity and the principal is disclosed, the agent will not be personally liable for the instrument's payment. If the agent fails to indicate that he or she is signing in a representative capacity or the principal is only partially disclosed, however, the agent can be held liable to a holder in due course. Troublesome issues sometimes arise in respect to the signature liability of agents because it is not always too clear to an agent just how specifically the agent must spell out—on the instrument itself—the fact that he or she is signing in a representative capacity.

For example, in one case, Donald Galt, the president of

Woodside Construction, Inc., signed a promissory note for $912,000. Galt signed the note in two places. Beneath the first signature was typed "Woodside Construction, Inc." Below that line, Galt signed his name again. The second signature was followed by the typed words "Donald A. Galt, President." When Woodside defaulted on its payments, the Federal Deposit Insurance Corporation, as receiver for the bank that lent Woodside Construction the $912,000, sued Galt personally to collect on the note.

Galt contended that he could not be held personally liable on the note because the two signatures, taken together, clearly indicated that he had signed in a representative capacity. The court, however, viewed the situation differently. The court held that "the first signature above the principal designation fails to indicate the representative capacity, and the second signature above the representative capacity designation fails to indicate the principal." Because neither signature indicated both elements—Galt's representative capacity and the name of his principal—Galt was held personally liable on the note.[3]

The court's decision in Galt's case, albeit a harsh one, underscores one of the basic principles underlying the concept of negotiable instruments—that of encouraging trade and commerce. For a negotiable

---

3. *Federal Deposit Insurance Corp. v. Woodside Construction, Inc.,* 979 F.2d 172 (9th Cir. 1992).

---

instrument to serve as a substitute for money, the instrument must indicate, on its face, who will be liable for the instrument's payment. Although an instrument, such as a check, may be issued to a party who knows the agent-signer of the check and knows that the agent is authorized to sign for the principal, a third party to whom the instrument is negotiated will not necessarily have this knowledge. The UCC's provisions concerning agents' signatures, by protecting HDCs, thus encourage the ready acceptability of negotiable instruments in the marketplace.

## Electronic Fund Transfers

Electronic fund transfer systems have posed legal—and ethical—problems, just as computerized transactions have created problems in other areas of the law, such as torts and crimes. The major problem is that electronic fund transfers leave no "paper trail." For example, assume that you want to obtain $500 from your checking account. If you write a $500 check payable to "cash" and take it to your bank, you will obtain the cash and also have evidence of the transaction—the canceled check itself.

If you obtain the cash via an automated teller machine (ATM), however, the only evidence of the transaction is the ATM receipt that you receive and the bank's computerized record of the transaction. There is nothing on the ATM receipt or in the bank's computer files to indicate that you authorized

the transaction. If someone else used your personal identification number (PIN) and withdrew the cash from your account—or if a withdrawal from your account was simply due to a computer error—there would be no paper trail, no signatures, and so on that could be used as proof.

Although the Electronic Fund Transfer Act (EFTA) addressed many of the issues that involve the customer's liability with respect to electronic fund transfers and the bank's duty of care to the customer, not all issues have been resolved—particularly those that involve disagreement between the customer and the bank's computer. Consider the following situation.

Mrs. Judd and her husband had a joint checking account at a Citibank branch in New York. They also had Citicards that gave them access to the computer via the bank's ATMs located throughout the city. Each card, before it could access the computer, had to be first "validated" by the bank. Although Mrs. Judd had gone into the bank to receive her PIN and have her card validated, her husband had not yet done so. Thus, only Mrs. Judd's card could be used to obtain cash or to make any other transaction via the ATM, and then only if the user knew her PIN—which she said she had given to no one and which she had not even written down, but instead had memorized.

The Judds were thus stunned to learn that $800 had been charged to their checking account as a result of two transactions, one made on February 26, 1980, between

2:13 and 2:14 P.M., and the other on March 28, 1980, between 2:30 and 2:32 P.M. The bank maintained that there was no way the funds could have been withdrawn without the use of Mrs. Judd's card and PIN. But Mrs. Judd was convinced the bank had made an error—or, rather, that the computer had. She could not have withdrawn the funds at those times, she contended, because she had been at work on both days at those times; a letter from her employer confirmed her statement.

Eventually, the case came before the Civil Court of New York City, and Judge John Marmarellis was faced with the problem of deciding the issue. Whom was he to believe? Mrs. Judd, whom he described as a "credible witness"? Or the bank's computer printout, which, as "translated" by the bank's manager, verified that the amounts could have been withdrawn from her account only by the use of her card and PIN? The judge opted to believe Mrs. Judd and awarded her $800 plus interest and disbursements, having stated in his opinion the following: "It is too commonplace in our society that when faced with the choice of man or machine, we readily accept the 'word' of the machine every time. This, despite the tales of computer malfunctions that we hear daily."[4]

_____

4. *Judd v. Citibank*, 107 Misc.2d 526, 435 N.Y.S.2d 210 (1980).

Stories similar to that of the Judds do not always have happy endings, but courts recognize that machines can err and have shown a willingness, as in the Judds' case, to take the word of a credible witness over that of a computer. Nonetheless, in the absence of paper evidence of fund transactions, there is no foolproof guaranty that truth and fair play will win out in these kinds of situations. For example, what if Mrs. Judd had no witnesses to testify that she was somewhere else at the time of the ATM transactions? Without any testimony to corroborate her statement, would the court have found in her favor? Should it have found in her favor? After all, although it is natural to sympathize with a person who loses money at the hands of an erring and uncaring machine, banks can also be victimized by unethical individuals who falsely, but convincingly, allege computer mistakes and seek recovery from the bank.

### ■ Discussion Questions

1.  Because the UCC offers special protection to HDCs, innocent makers of notes or drawers of checks to fraudulent transactions often have no legal recourse. From an ethical standpoint, how could you justify to the "losers" in such situations the provisions of the UCC that fail to protect them? How would

you explain the trade-offs involved? Can you think of a way in which such problems could be handled more fairly or ethically than they are under the UCC?

2.  What do you think would result if a change in the law allowed personal defenses to be successfully raised against HDCs? Who would lose, and who would gain? What would happen to economic efficiency?

3.  Under the revised Article 4, banks are allowed to send their customers only a monthly itemized checking-account statement containing the check numbers, amounts, dates, and so on. Banks may include the canceled checks, but if the checks are not sent to the customer, the banks must have them available for a period of seven years should a customer wish to examine them [UCC R4–406(a), (b)]. What implications does this provision have for bank customers in terms of liability for unauthorized signatures and indorsements?

4.  Do you think that the UCC's provisions are weighted too heavily in favor of banks? How do the revised and unrevised Articles 3 and 4 compare in this regard?

# UNIT FIVE

# CREDITORS' RIGHTS AND BANKRUPTCY

## CONTENTS

**31** Secured Transactions

**32** Other Creditors' Remedies and Suretyship

**33** Bankruptcy and Reorganization

# CHAPTER 31

# SECURED TRANSACTIONS

The term *secured transaction* may seem somewhat daunting because it is not a term used (by most people) in everyday conversation. Yet the concept represented by the term is one that anybody can readily comprehend: the need for creditors to have some assurance that debtors will repay their loans. For example, if you were to finance the purchase of a new car with a loan from a bank or from the car dealer's credit department, the lender would want to have some guarantee (besides your word) that you would make the promised payments. Normally, a bank or other lender would loan you the purchase price only on the condition that if you failed to make the payments, the lender could repossess the car to satisfy, at least in part, the debt.

Your transaction with the lender in this situation qualifies as a **secured transaction,** which occurs whenever the payment of a debt is guaranteed, or *secured,* by personal property owned by the debtor or in which the debtor has a legal interest. The concept of the secured transaction is as basic to modern business practice as the concept of credit. Few purchasers (manufacturers, wholesalers, retailers, or consumers) have the resources to pay cash for all goods being purchased, yet lenders are reluctant to lend money to someone solely on that person's promise to repay the debt. Logically, lenders or sellers extending credit to buyers want some guarantee that the promise of payment will be fulfilled.

The importance of being a secured creditor cannot be overemphasized. Secured creditors are generally not hampered by state laws favorable to debtors, and they have a favored position should the debtor become bankrupt.

Article 9 of the UCC governs secured transactions. This chapter first presents the basic concept and terminology of a secured transaction and then discusses how the rights and duties of creditors and debtors are created and enforced.

## SECTION 1

# ARTICLE 9 OF THE UCC

Article 9 of the UCC applies to any transaction that is intended to create a security interest in personal property, accounts, chattel paper, and fixtures. (See Exhibit 31–4 on pages 596–597 for definitions of these terms.) Debtor-creditor transactions that are not covered under Article 9 are discussed in the next chapter.

As will become evident, the law of secured transactions tends to favor the rights of creditors. To a lesser extent, however, it also offers debtors some protection.

The UCC's terminology is now uniformly adopted in all documents used in situations involving secured transactions. A brief summary of the UCC's definitions of terms relating to secured transactions follows.

1. A **security interest** is any interest ''in personal property or fixtures which secures payment or performance of an obligation'' [UCC 1–201(37)].
2. A **secured party** is a lender, a seller, or any person in whose favor there is a security interest, including a person to whom accounts or **chattel paper** (any writing evidencing a debt secured by personal property) have been sold [UCC 9–105(1)(m)]. The terms *secured party* and *secured creditor* are used interchangeably.
3. A **debtor** is the party who owes payment or performance of the secured obligation, whether or not that party actually owns or has rights in the collateral (defined below). When the debtor and the owner of collateral are not the same person, the term *debtor* may refer to the actual owner of the collateral, the person responsible for the obligation, or both, depending on the context in which the term is used [UCC 9–105(1)(d)].
4. A **security agreement** is the agreement that creates or provides for a security interest between the debtor and a secured party [UCC 9–105(1)(ℓ)].
5. **Collateral** is the property subject to a security interest, including accounts and chattel paper that have been sold [UCC 9–105(1)(c)].

These basic definitions form the concept under which a debtor-creditor relationship becomes a secured transaction relationship (see Exhibit 31–1).

## SECTION 2

# CREATING SECURITY INTERESTS

Before a creditor can become a secured party, the creditor must have a security interest in the

■ **Exhibit 31–1 Secured Transactions—Concept and Terminology**

In a security agreement, a debtor and creditor agree that the creditor will have a security interest in collateral in which the debtor has rights. In essence, the collateral secures the loan and ensures the creditor of payment should the debtor default.

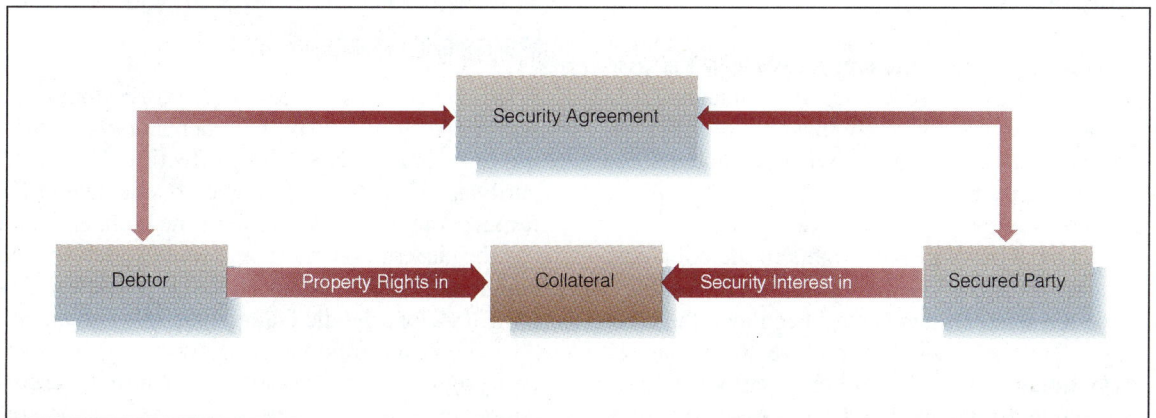

■ **Exhibit 31–2  A Sample Security Agreement**

---

_____

Date

_____

Name          No. and Street          City          County          State

(hereinafter called "Debtor") hereby grants to _____

Name

_____

No. and Street          City          County          State

(hereinafter called "Secured Party") a security interest in the following property (hereinafter called the "Collateral"): _____

_____

_____

_____

to secure payment and performance of obligations identified or set out as follows (hereinafter called the "Obligations"): _____

_____

_____

_____

Default in payment or performance of any of the Obligations or default under any
agreement evidencing any of the Obligations is a default under this agreement. Upon
such default Secured Party may declare all Obligations immediately due and payable
and shall have the remedies of a secured party under the _____ Uniform Commercial Code.

Signed in (duplicate) triplicate.

_____          _____

Debtor                                     Secured Party

By _____               By _____

---

collateral of the debtor. Three requirements must be met for a creditor to have an enforceable security interest:

1. Either (a) the collateral must be in the possession of the secured party pursuant to an agreement, or (b) there must be a written security agreement describing the collateral and signed by the debtor.
2. The secured party must give value.
3. The debtor must have rights in the collateral.

Once these requirements have been met, the creditor's rights are said to *attach* to the collateral. **Attachment** gives the creditor an enforceable security interest against the debtor. Attachment en-sures that the security interest between the debtor and the secured party is effective [UCC 9–203].

## WRITTEN AGREEMENT

When the collateral is not in the possession of the secured party, a security agreement must be in writing to be enforceable. To be effective, (1) the security agreement must be signed by the debtor, (2) it must contain a description of the collateral, and (3) the description must reasonably identify the collateral [UCC 9–203(1); UCC 9–110]. See Exhibit 31–2 for a detailed sample security agreement. At issue in the following case was whether a security agreement had reasonably identified the collateral and had, in fact, been signed by the debtor.

**COMPANY PROFILE**  *In Fort Worth, Texas, in 1899, the Tandy family opened a small leather store. During the 1950s, Charles Tandy expanded the business into a national chain of leathercraft and hobby stores. In the 1960s, Tandy Corporation expanded into other retail areas, buying, among other businesses, Radio Shack, which was an electronic parts supplier with a mail-order business and nine stores in the Boston area. Stocking the stores with quick turnover items and spending nearly 10 percent of the sales revenues on advertising caused Radio Shack's earnings to soar. By 1973, Radio Shack had grown to 3,000 stores, providing more than 50 percent of Tandy's sales and 80 percent of its earnings. The company sold off its other businesses to reposition itself as a consumer electronics business. In 1976 alone, Tandy opened an additional 1,200 Radio Shack stores. The next year, Tandy sold the first mass-marketed personal computer (PC) and, in 1984, the first IBM-compatible PC priced under $1,000. By the 1990s, Tandy believed that Radio Shack had exhausted its expansion possibilities and began to focus on other retail outlets, such as Computer City, a computer warehouse store. In 1992, Tandy, which had become the world's largest retailer of consumer electronics, opened its first Incredible Universe—a gigantic electronics superstore with a sales floor as large as three football fields.*

**BACKGROUND AND FACTS**  *David Ziluck applied for a Radio Shack credit card. The front of the application contained blanks for various personal and employment information and a space for the applicant to sign. Above the signature line was the following statement: "I have read the Radio Shack Credit Account and Security Agreement, including the notice provision in the last paragraph thereof, and it contains no blanks or blank spaces. I agree to the terms of the Agreement and acknowledge receipt of a copy of the agreement." The back of the application contained a "Radio Shack Credit Account and Security Agreement," which stated in part, "We retain a security interest under the Uniform Commercial Code in all merchandise charged to your Account. If you do not make payments on your Account as agreed, the security interest allows us to repossess only the merchandise that has not been paid in full." When Ziluck later filed for bankruptcy protection, the bankruptcy court had to decide whether the application form constituted a valid security agreement. The court concluded that it did* not *for two reasons. First, Ziluck's signature was not effective, because it was not on the back side of the form, which stated the terms of the security agreement. Second, the security agreement's description of the collateral ("all merchandise charged to your Account") was not sufficiently descriptive. The bankruptcy court's decision was appealed.*

*GONZALEZ*, District Judge.
\*    \*    \*    \*

Turning first to the signature issue, the Court finds that Ziluck did in fact sign the security agreement. \*   \*   \* The Court believes that Ziluck's signature on the

| |
|---|
| CASE 31.1 |

**IN RE ZILUCK**[a]
United States District Court, Southern District of Florida, 1992.
139 Bankr. 44.

---

a.  *In re* means in the matter of, concerning, or regarding. The use of *in re* is the usual method of entitling a judicial proceeding on some matter in which judicial action is to be taken, such as a debtor's estate in bankruptcy, in which there are no adversarial parties. *In re, Matter of,* and *Estate of,* or some combination of these phrases (such as *In re Estate of*) are all commonly used in the titles of cases involving such actions.

front of the credit card application * * * was sufficient to comply with Fla. Stat. [Section] 679.203(1)(a) [Florida's version of UCC 9–203(1)(a)]. The bankruptcy court's contrary finding was in error.

The Court also finds that the bankruptcy court erred in finding that the description of the collateral in the security agreement was insufficient. Florida Statute [Section] 679.110 provides that "any description of personal property . . . is sufficient whether or not it is specific if it reasonably identifies what is described." The Court believes that the language in * * * the security agreement, " * * * all merchandise charged to your account," reasonably identifies the property subject to the security interest—namely any property purchased with the subject credit card. Accordingly, the Court finds that the security agreement contains a sufficient description of the collateral as required by Fla. Stat. [Section] 679.203(1)(a).

**DECISION AND REMEDY** *The appellate court reversed the bankruptcy court's decision and remanded the case.*

## SECURED PARTY MUST GIVE VALUE

The secured party must give value, which, according to UCC 1–201(44), is any consideration that supports a simple contract. In addition, value can be security given for a preexisting (antecedent) obligation or any binding commitment to extend credit. Normally, the value given by a secured party is in the form of a direct loan, or it involves a commitment to sell goods on credit.

## DEBTOR MUST HAVE RIGHTS IN THE COLLATERAL

The debtor must have rights in the collateral; that is, the debtor must have some ownership interest or right to obtain possession of that collateral. The debtor's rights can represent either a current or a future legal interest in the property. For example, a retail seller-debtor can give a secured party a security interest not only in existing inventory owned by the retailer but also in future inventory to be acquired by the retailer.

## SECTION 3

# PURCHASE-MONEY SECURITY INTEREST

Often sellers of consumer durable goods, such as computers and television sets, agree to extend credit for part or all of the purchase price of those goods. Also, lenders not necessarily in the business of selling such goods often agree to lend much of the purchase price for them. There is a special name for the security interest that the seller or the lender obtains when such a transaction occurs. It is called a **purchase-money security interest (PMSI).** Formally, such an interest exists when one or the other of the following conditions arises:

1. A security interest is retained in, or taken by the seller of, the collateral to secure part or all of its price.
2. A security interest is taken by a person who, by making advances or incurring an obligation, gives something of value that enables the debtor to acquire rights in the collateral or to use it [UCC 9–107].

In either case, a lender or seller has essentially provided a buyer with the "purchase money" to buy goods. Suppose Benjamin wants to purchase an entertainment center from USA Appliances. The purchase price is $900. Not being able to pay cash, Benjamin signs a purchase agreement to pay $100 down and $50 per month until the balance plus interest is fully paid. USA Appliances is to retain a security interest in the purchased goods until full payment has been made. Because the security interest was created as part of the purchase agreement, it is a PMSI.

The same result will occur if Benjamin goes to Statewide Bank and borrows the $900 to buy the entertainment center from USA Appliances. After Benjamin has signed a loan agreement with

Statewide Bank, with the to-be-purchased goods as collateral, Statewide Bank has a PMSI the moment the goods are purchased from the appliance store. Obviously, if Benjamin uses the money for other purposes, Statewide Bank will not have a security interest. For this reason, Statewide Bank might arrange to pay the $900 directly to USA Appliances.

SECTION 4

# PERFECTING A SECURITY INTEREST

A creditor has two main concerns if the debtor **defaults** (fails to pay the debt as promised): (1) satisfaction of the debt through possession of the collateral and (2) priority over any other creditors and purchasers who may have rights in the same collateral. The concept of *attachment,* which establishes the criteria for creating an enforceable security interest, deals with the former concern; the concept of *perfection* deals with the latter.

Even though a security interest has attached, the secured party must nevertheless take steps to protect its claim to the collateral over claims that third parties may have. Third parties may be other secured creditors, nonsecured creditors, trustees in bankruptcy, or purchasers of the collateral that is the subject matter of the security agreement. **Perfection** represents the legal process by which secured parties protect themselves against the claims of third parties who may wish to have their debts satisfied out of the same collateral.

In some circumstances, a security interest becomes perfected without the filing of a financing statement. Usually, however, perfection is accomplished by the filing of a financing statement with the appropriate government official.

## PERFECTION WITHOUT FILING

In two types of situations, security interests can be perfected without filing a financing statement. First, when the collateral is transferred into the possession of the creditor, the creditor's security interest in the collateral is perfected. Second, a PMSI in consumer goods is perfected automatically. These two situations are discussed below. Note, however, that UCC 9–302(1) mentions other security interests that can be perfected without filing a financing statement, including a security interest created by an assignment of a beneficial interest in a trust or decedent's estate.

**PERFECTION BY POSSESSION**  Certain items, such as stocks, bonds, and jewelry, are commonly transferred into the creditor's possession when they are used as collateral for loans. This transfer is known as a **pledge.** (When the debt is paid, the collateral is returned to the debtor.) One of the benefits for creditors of having possession of the collateral is that the security agreement is perfected in these circumstances without filing. For most collateral, however, possession by the secured party is impractical, because it denies the debtor the right to use or derive income from the property to pay off the debt. For example, if a farmer took out a loan to finance the purchase of a piece of heavy farm equipment, using the equipment as collateral, the purpose of the purchase would be defeated if the farmer transferred the collateral into the creditor's possession. Note that with respect to negotiable instruments, nonnegotiable transferable instruments, and certain securities (such as stocks and bonds), with a few exceptions, the *only* way to perfect a security interest properly is through possession by the secured party. Remember, a security agreement need not be in writing to create a security interest [UCC 9–203(1)]. Thus you can create and perfect a security interest at the same time by possession of the collateral.

**PURCHASE-MONEY SECURITY INTEREST**  In certain circumstances, a security interest in tangible collateral can be perfected automatically at the time of a credit sale—that is, at the time that a PMSI is created under a written security agreement. Note that this automatic-perfection rule with regard to PMSIs applies only when the goods are consumer goods (defined as goods bought or used by the debtor primarily for personal, family, or household purposes). The seller in this situation need do nothing more to protect his or her interest. There are exceptions to this rule, however, that cover security interests in fixtures and in motor vehicles [UCC 9–302(1)(d)]. In states that have not adopted the 1972 UCC amendments[1] or that have decided to retain certain pre-1972 sections, a PMSI in farm equipment under a certain statutory value is also automatically perfected by attachment.

---

1. Vermont is the only state that has not adopted the 1972 amendments.

■ **Exhibit 31–3 A Sample Financing Statement**

This FINANCING STATEMENT is presented for filing pursuant to the California Uniform Commercial Code.

| 1. DEBTOR (LAST NAME FIRST—IF AN INDIVIDUAL) | | 1A. SOCIAL SECURITY OR FEDERAL TAX NO. |
|---|---|---|
| 1B. MAILING ADDRESS | 1C. CITY, STATE | 1D. ZIP CODE |
| 2. ADDITIONAL DEBTOR (IF ANY) (LAST NAME FIRST—IF AN INDIVIDUAL) | | 2A. SOCIAL SECURITY OR FEDERAL TAX NO. |
| 2B. MAILING ADDRESS | 2C. CITY, STATE | 2D. ZIP CODE |
| 3. DEBTOR'S TRADE NAMES OR STYLES (IF ANY) | | 3A. FEDERAL TAX NUMBER |

4. SECURED PARTY

NAME

MAILING ADDRESS

CITY          STATE          ZIP CODE

4A. SOCIAL SECURITY NO., FEDERAL TAX NO. OR BANK TRANSIT AND A.B.A. NO.

5. ASSIGNEE OF SECURED PARTY (IF ANY)

NAME

MAILING ADDRESS

CITY          STATE          ZIP CODE

5A. SOCIAL SECURITY NO., FEDERAL TAX NO. OR BANK TRANSIT AND A.B.A. NO.

6. This FINANCING STATEMENT covers the following types or items of property **(include description of real property on which located and owner of record when required by Instruction 4).**

As security for and in consideration of all present and any future advances or other obligations debtor hereby grants United California Bank a security interest in all of the following types or items of property ("Collateral" herein) in which the debtor now has or hereafter acquires any right, title, or interest, or rights present and future, wheresoever located and whether in the possession of the debtor, a warehouseman, bailee, trustee or any other person, and all increases, therein and replacements, products, and proceeds thereof. Proceeds include but are not limited to inventory, returned merchandise, accounts, chattel paper, general intangibles, insurance proceeds, documents, money, goods, equipment, instruments, and any other tangible or intangible property arising under the sale, lease or other disposition of collateral:

7. CHECK [X] IF APPLICABLE

7A. [ ] PRODUCTS OF COLLATERAL ARE ALSO COVERED

7B. DEBTOR(S) SIGNATURE NOT REQUIRED IN ACCORDANCE WITH INSTRUCTION 5(c) ITEM:
[ ] (1)  [ ] (2)  [ ] (3)  [ ] (4)

8. CHECK [X] IF APPLICABLE

[ ] DEBTOR IS A "TRANSMITTING UTILITY" IN ACCORDANCE WITH UCC § 9105 (1) (n)

9.

▶ SIGNATURE(S) of DEBTOR(S)

DATE:

TYPE OR PRINT NAME(S) OF DEBTOR(S)

▶ SIGNATURE(S) OF SECURED PARTY(IES)

TYPE OR PRINT NAME(S) OF SECURED PARTY(IES)

11. *Return copy to:*

NAME

ADDRESS

CITY

STATE

ZIP CODE

CODE

E
1
2
3
4
5
6
7
8
9
0

10. THIS SPACE FOR USE OF FILING OFFICER (DATE, TIME, FILE NUMBER AND FILING OFFICER)

*(1) FILING OFFICER COPY*          FORM UCC-1—FILING FEE $3.00
*Approved by the Secretary of State*

MS-336 10-78

## PERFECTION BY FILING

A creditor whose security interest is not automatically perfected can perfect the security interest by filing a **financing statement** with the appropriate state or local official. A sample financing statement is shown in Exhibit 31–3. The UCC requires a financing statement to contain (1) the signature of the debtor, (2) the names and addresses of both the debtor and the creditor, and (3) a description of the collateral by type or item [UCC 9–402(1)].[2] Filing is the most common method of perfecting a security interest under Article 9.

### THE DEBTOR'S NAME
The UCC requires that a financing statement be filed under the name of the debtor [UCC 9–402(1)]. If the debtor is an individual, the financing statement must be filed in the name of the individual, but if the debtor is a partnership or corporation, the financing statement must be filed under the partnership or corporate name [UCC 9–402(7)]. If a financing statement identifies the debtor by an incorrect name, the statement may be ineffective to perfect a security interest.

What happens to the perfected secured party's interest when the debtor changes its name, as might happen as a result of a business reorganization? In this situation, if the name change causes the financing statement to become *seriously misleading,* "the filing is not effective to perfect a security interest in collateral acquired by the debtor more than four months after the change, unless a new appropriate financing statement is filed before the expiration of that time" [UCC 9–402(7)]. To accomplish the change, the secured party merely files a new financing statement signed by the secured party instead of the debtor [UCC 9–402(2)(d)].

Assume that a debtor, Thomas T. Dibello, borrows money from a Pennsylvania bank, which in turn takes a security interest in Dibello's store inventory. The bank properly files a financing statement that lists "Thomas T. Dibello" as the debtor's name. Shortly thereafter, Dibello incorporates his business and changes the name of the business to "Just for Kids, Inc." The bank will continue to be protected as to the existing collateral and as to the new collateral acquired by the debtor during the four months following the name change, even if the bank fails to refile. At the end of the four-month period, however, unless the bank refiles under the new business name of the debtor, its security interest in any collateral acquired thereafter will be unperfected.[3]

### DESCRIPTION OF THE COLLATERAL
Both the security agreement and the financing statement must contain a description of the collateral in which the secured party has a security interest. The UCC requires that the security agreement include a description of the collateral, because no security interest in goods can exist unless the parties agree on which goods are subject to the security interest and then describe these goods in writing. The purpose of describing collateral in the financing statement is for the benefit of persons who might later wish to lend to the debtor or purchase the collateral; the description puts these persons on notice that certain goods in the debtor's possession are already subject to a security interest.

Sometimes, the descriptions in the security agreement and the financing statement vary, with the description in the security agreement being more precise and the description in the financing statement more general. For example, a security agreement for a commercial loan to a manufacturer may list all the manufacturer's equipment subject to the loan by serial number, whereas the financing statement may simply state "all equipment owned or hereafter acquired."

To avoid problems arising from such variations in descriptions, a secured party may repeat exactly the security agreement's description in the financing statement or file the security agreement itself as a financing statement (assuming the security agreement meets the previously discussed criteria). Alternatively, where permitted, the creditor might file a combination security agreement–financing statement form. If the financing statement is too general or vague, a court may find it insufficient to perfect a security interest.

### WHERE TO FILE
Depending on the classification of collateral, filing is done either centrally with the secretary of state, locally with the county clerk or other official, or both, according to state law.

---

2. Certain types of collateral—crops, timber to be cut, minerals, accounts, or goods that are to become fixtures—require more than mere description; a description of the real estate concerned may also be required [UCC 9–402(1), (5); UCC 9–103(5); UCC 9–313].

---

3. *In re Just for Kids, Inc.,* 150 Bankr. 123 (M.D.Pa. 1992).

■ **Exhibit 31–4 Types of Collateral and Methods of Perfection**

| Type of Collateral | Definition | Perfection Method | UCC Sections |
|---|---|---|---|
| **Intangible** | Nonphysical property that exists only in connection with something else. | | |
| 1. Chattel paper | Any writing that evidences both a *monetary obligation and a security interest*—for example, a thirty-six-month-payment retail security agreement signed by a buyer to purchase a car [UCC 9–105(1)(b)]. | Filing or possession by secured party. | 9–304(1); 9–305 |
| 2. Documents of title | Papers that entitle the person in possession to hold, receive, or dispose of the paper or goods the documents cover—for example, bills of lading, warehouse receipts, and dock warrants [UCC 9–105(1)(f); UCC 1–201(15); UCC 7–201]. | Filing or possession by secured party. | 9–304(1), (3); 9–305 |
| 3. Instruments | Writings that evidence rights to payment of money that are not security agreements or leases, and negotiable instruments or certificated securities (securities evidenced by a stock certificate—see Chapter 41) that in the ordinary course of business are transferred by delivery with any necessary indorsements or assignments—for example, promissory notes and certificates of deposit [UCC 9–105(1)(i); UCC 3–104; UCC 8–102(1)(a)]. | Except for temporary perfected status, possession only. | 9–304(1), (4), (5); 9–305 |
| 4. Accounts | Rights to payments for goods sold or leased or services rendered that are not evidenced by instruments or chattel paper—for example, accounts receivable and rights to payment under construction contracts [UCC 9–106]. | Filing required (with exceptions). | 9–302(1)(e), (g) |
| 5. General intangibles | Any personal property other than that defined above—for example, a patent, a copyright, goodwill, or a trademark [UCC 9–106]. | Filing only. | 9–302(1) |

According to UCC 9–401, a state may choose one of three alternatives.[4] In general, financing statements for consumer goods should be filed with the county clerk.[5] Other kinds of collateral require filing with the secretary of state [UCC 9–401]. An improper filing reduces a secured party's claim in bankruptcy to that of an unsecured creditor. The classification of collateral is also important in de-

termining whether filing is necessary. Exhibit 31–4 summarizes the various classifications of collateral and the methods of perfecting a security interest in them.

## EXCEPTIONS TO PERFECTION

There are sources of law other than UCC Article 9 that deal with the perfection of security interests. The three most important sources are federal law, such as the Federal Aviation Act; UCC Article 8, which deals with investment securities; and state certificate of title laws that deal with motor vehicles.

Most states require a certificate of title for any motor vehicle, boat, or motor home. The normal methods described above for perfection of a security interest typically do not apply to such ve-

---

4. At one time, most states required local filing for perfection of security interests in farm-related collateral. See UCC 9–401 in Appendix C for these three alternatives. Approximately half the states have adopted the second alternative. Filing fees range from as low as $3 to as high as $25.

5. On December 23, 1985, Congress passed the Food Security Act. In this act are provisions that protect a purchaser in the ordinary course of business of farm products from a prior perfected security interest, unless the secured party has perfected centrally and/or the buyer has received proper notice.

■ **Exhibit 31–4 Types of Collateral and Methods of Perfection—Continued**

| Type of Collateral | Definition | Perfection Method | UCC Sections |
|---|---|---|---|
| Tangible | All things that are *movable* at the time the security interest attaches or that are *fixtures* [UCC 9–105(1)(h)]. This includes timber to be cut, growing crops, and unborn animals. | | |
| 1. Consumer goods | Goods used or bought primarily for personal, family, or household purposes—for example, household furniture [UCC 9–109(1)]. | For purchase-money security interest, attachment is sufficient; for boats, motor vehicles, and trailers, there is a requirement of filing or compliance with a certificate of title statute; for other consumer goods, general rules of filing or possession apply. | 9–302(1)(d), (3), (4); 9–305 |
| 2. Equipment | Goods bought for, or used primarily in, business—for example, a delivery truck [UCC 9–109(2)]. | Filing or possession by secured party. | 9–302(1); 9–305 |
| 3. Farm products | Crops, livestock, and supplies used or produced in a farming operation in the possession of a farmer-debtor. This includes products of crops or livestock—for example, milk, eggs, maple syrup, and ginned cotton [UCC 9–109(3)]. | Filing or possession by secured party. | 9–302(1); 9–305 |
| 4. Inventory | Goods held for sale or lease and materials used or consumed in the course of business—for example, raw materials or floor stock of a retailer [UCC 9–109(4)]. | Filing or possession by secured party. | 9–302(1); 9–305 |
| 5. Fixtures | Goods that become so affixed to realty that an interest in them arises under real estate law—for example, a central air-conditioning unit [UCC 9–313(1)(a)]. | Filing only. | 9–313(1) |

hicles. Rather, perfection of a security interest only occurs when a notation of such an interest appears on the certificate of title that covers the vehicle.

As an example, suppose that your commercial bank lends you 80 percent of the money necessary to purchase a new car. You live in a state that requires certificates of title for all automobiles. If your bank fails to have its security interest noted on the certificate of title, its interest is not perfected. That means that a good faith purchaser of your car would take it free of the bank's interest. In most states, purchasers of motor vehicles can either buy or extend credit on those vehicles with the confi-

dence that no security interest exists that is not disclosed on the certificate of title.[6]

## COLLATERAL MOVED TO ANOTHER JURISDICTION

Obviously, collateral may be moved by the debtor from one jurisdiction (state) to another. In general, a properly perfected security interest in collateral

---

6. In the few states that do not require title registration of motor vehicles, one must examine the appropriate statutes to determine the priority of conflicting security interests.

moved into a new jurisdiction continues to be perfected in the new jurisdiction for a period of up to four months from the date it was moved into the new jurisdiction or for the period of time remaining under the perfection in the original jurisdiction, whichever expires first [UCC 9–103(1)(d); UCC 9–103(3)(e)]. Collateral moved from county to county within a state (if local filing is required), rather than from one state to another, however, may not have a four-month limitation [UCC 9–403(3)].

To illustrate, suppose that on January 1, Smith secures a loan from a Nebraska bank by putting up all his wheat-threshing equipment as security. The Nebraska bank files the security interest centrally with the secretary of state. In June, Smith has an opportunity to harvest wheat crops in South Dakota and moves his equipment into that state on June 15. The law just mentioned means that the Nebraska bank's perfection remains effective in South Dakota for a period of four months from June 15. If the Nebraska bank wishes to retain its perfection priority, the bank must perfect properly in South Dakota, the jurisdiction in which the machine is located, during this four-month period. Should the bank fail to do so, its perfection would be lost after four months, and subsequent perfected security interests in the same collateral in South Dakota would prevail.

Among mobile goods, automobiles pose one of the biggest problems. If the original jurisdiction does not require a certificate of title as part of its perfection process for an automobile, perfection automatically ends four months after the automobile is moved into another jurisdiction. When a security interest exists on an automobile in a state in which title registration is required, and when the security interest is noted on the certificate of title, the perfection of the security interest continues after the automobile is moved to another state requiring a certificate of title until the automobile is registered in the new state [UCC 9–103(2)]. This rule protects the secured party against anyone purchasing the car in the new state prior to the new registration. Moreover, because each title state requires that the old certificate of title be surrendered to obtain a new one, and because the secured party typically holds the certificate, the secured party usually is able to ensure that the security interest is noted on the new certificate of title.

## EFFECTIVE TIME OF PERFECTION

A financing statement is effective for five years from the date of filing [UCC 9–403(2)]. If a **continuation statement** is filed *within six months* prior to the expiration date, the effectiveness of the original statement is continued for another five years, starting with the expiration date of the first five-year period [UCC 9–403(3)]. The effectiveness of the statement can be continued in the same manner indefinitely.

In the following case, a perfected secured creditor filed a continuation statement two days early—that is, six months and two days before the expiration date of the original filing.

---

**CASE 31.2**

**BANQUE WORMS v. DAVIS CONSTRUCTION CO.**

Court of Appeals of Kentucky, 1992.
831 S.W.2d 921.

**BACKGROUND AND FACTS** *A New York bank, Banque Worms, provided the Big Oak Coal Company and the Dollar Branch Coal Corporation with an $11,750,000 loan. As collateral for the loan, the mining companies granted Banque Worms a security interest in a "Euclid R-25 rock truck," as well as other mining equipment. Banque Worms properly perfected its security interest in the equipment by filing a financing statement, effective for five years, on October 12, 1982. Banque Worms later filed a continuation statement on April 10, 1987, to maintain its priority status as a perfected secured party. Later that year, on November 23, the mining companies sold the rock truck to the Davis Construction Company to satisfy a $36,192 debt. Davis filed suit to clear title to the rock truck once it became aware of Banque Worms's security interest. The trial court, holding in favor of Davis, found that Banque Worms had failed to comply with UCC 9–403, because the bank had submitted its continuation statement two days before the six-month period in which such statements may be effectively filed. Banque Worms appealed.*

*GUDGEL,* Judge:

\* \* \* \*

Here, it is uncontroverted that [Banque Worms's] continuation statement was filed with the clerk on April 10, 1987, which was six months and two days before the expiration of the financing statement's five-year effective period. Because the continuation statement was not filed within six months prior to the lapse of the financing statement's effective period, [Banque Worms's] security interest in the rock truck became unperfected on October 12, 1987, which was five years after the date on which the financing statement was filed. [Banque Worms] argues, however, that [UCC 1–102] requires us to construe the provisions of the code liberally and in a manner which promotes its underlying policies and purposes, including those of protecting secured creditors from unauthorized transfers of collateral and providing appropriate remedies when such transfers occur. According to [Banque Worms], the literal application of the provisions of [UCC 9–403(3)] in a case such as this defeats this purpose. \* \* \*

\* \* \* \*

\* \* \* [A]lthough [UCC 1–102(1)] requires the code to be construed liberally, *the statute cannot be employed to overlook and defeat the clear and unambiguous statutory requirement as to timely filing which is imposed by [UCC 9–403(3)].* \* \* \* [T]his court interprets the language to be mandatory and finds that a filing of a continuation statement outside the last six months of life of a financing statement causes the perfection of a security interest to lapse. [Emphasis added.]

*The appellate court affirmed the trial court's decision. Banque Worms's interest in the rock truck was subordinate to Davis Construction's interest [UCC 9–301(1)(c)].*

**DECISION AND REMEDY**

---

## SECTION 5

# THE SCOPE OF A SECURITY INTEREST

A security agreement can cover various types of property in addition to collateral already in the debtor's possession—the proceeds of the sale of collateral, after-acquired property, and future advances.

### PROCEEDS

**Proceeds** include whatever is received when collateral is sold, exchanged, collected, or disposed of. A secured party has an interest in the proceeds of the sale of collateral. For example, suppose a bank has a perfected security interest in the inventory of a retail seller of heavy farm machinery. The retailer sells a tractor out of this inventory to a farmer, a buyer in the ordinary course of business. The farmer agrees, in a retail security agreement, to pay monthly payments for a period of twenty-four months. If the retailer should go into default on the loan from the bank, the bank is entitled to

the remaining payments the farmer owes to the retailer as proceeds.

A security interest in proceeds perfects automatically upon perfection of the secured party's security interest and remains perfected for ten days after receipt of the proceeds by the debtor. One way to extend the ten-day automatic period is to provide for such extended coverage in the original security agreement. This is typically done when the collateral is the type that is likely to be sold, such as a retailer's inventory.

The UCC provides that in the following circumstances the security interest in proceeds remains perfected for longer than ten days after the receipt of the proceeds by the debtor:

1. When a filed financing statement covers the original collateral and the proceeds are collateral in which a security interest may be perfected by a filing in the office or offices with which the financing statement has been filed. Furthermore, a secured creditor's interest automatically perfects in property that the debtor acquires with cash proceeds, if the original filing would have been effective as to that

property and the financing statement indicates that type of property [UCC 9–306(3)(a)]. Thus, in the farm-equipment example above, if the retailer used the farmer's monthly payments to acquire additional inventory, the bank would be entitled to that inventory, providing that the bank's original filing was effective as to that property and the financing statement indicated that type of property.

2. Whenever there is a filed financing statement that covers the original collateral and the proceeds are identifiable cash proceeds [UCC 9–306(3)(b)].

3. Whenever the security interest in the proceeds is perfected before the expiration of the ten-day period [UCC 9–306(3)(c)].

## AFTER-ACQUIRED PROPERTY

**After-acquired property** is collateral that is acquired by the debtor after the execution of the security agreement. The after-acquired property may consist of inventory, equipment, farm animals, or virtually any other kind of property, except for consumer goods acquired more than ten days "after the secured party gives value" [UCC 9–204(2)]. The security agreement itself may provide for coverage of after-acquired property [UCC 9–204(1)]. This is particularly useful for firms that want to obtain financing for the purchase of inventory (products to be sold in the ordinary course of the firm's business). A secured party whose security interest is in existing inventory knows that the debtor will replace that inventory, thereby reducing the collateral subject to the security interest.

Generally, the debtor will purchase new inventory to replace the inventory that is sold. The secured party wants this newly acquired inventory to be subject to the original security interest. Thus, the after-acquired property clause continues the secured party's claim to any inventory acquired thereafter. This is not to say that such original security interest will be superior to the rights of all other creditors with regard to this after-acquired inventory, as will be discussed later.

Consider a typical example. Liberta buys factory equipment from Stedler on credit, giving as security an interest in all of her equipment—both what she is buying and what she already owns. The security interest with Stedler contains an after-acquired property clause. Six months later, Liberta pays cash to another seller for additional equip-

ment. Six months after that, Liberta goes out of business before she has paid off her debt to Stedler. Stedler has a security interest in all of Liberta's equipment, even the equipment bought from the other seller.

## FUTURE ADVANCES

Often, a debtor will arrange with a bank to have a continuing *line of credit* under which the debtor can borrow funds intermittently. Advances against lines of credit can be subject to a properly perfected security interest in certain collateral. The security agreement may provide that any future advances made against that line of credit are also subject to the security interest in the same collateral. For example, Holtzman is the owner of a small manufacturing plant with equipment valued at $1 million. He has an immediate need for $50,000 of working capital, so he secures a loan from Northeastern Bank and signs a security agreement, putting up all his equipment as security. The security agreement provides that Holtzman can borrow up to $500,000 in the future, using the same equipment as collateral for any future advances. In such cases, it is not necessary to execute a new security agreement and perfect a security interest in the collateral each time an advance is made to the debtor [UCC 9–204(3)].

## THE FLOATING-LIEN CONCEPT

A security agreement may provide for the creation of a security interest in proceeds of the sale of the collateral that was the subject matter of the secured transaction—after-acquired property, future advances, or both. Such an agreement is referred to as a **floating lien.** Floating liens commonly arise in the financing of inventories. A creditor is not interested in specific pieces of inventory, because they are constantly changing, so the lien "floats" from one item to another as the inventory changes.

For example, suppose that Ski Paradise, Inc., a cross-country ski dealer, has a line of credit with New England Community Bank to finance an inventory of cross-country skis. Ski Paradise and New England Community enter into a security agreement that provides for coverage of proceeds, after-acquired inventory, present inventory, and future advances. This security interest in inventory is perfected by filing centrally (with the secretary of state). One day, Ski Paradise sells a new pair of the latest cross-country skis, for which it receives a used pair in trade. That same day, it purchases two new pairs of skis from a local manufacturer with an additional amount of money obtained from New England Community. New England Community gets a perfected security interest in the used pair of skis under the proceeds clause, has a perfected security interest in the two new pairs of skis purchased from the local manufacturer under the after-acquired property clause, and has all of these skis and those in present inventory for the new amount of money advanced to Ski Paradise secured by the future-advance clause.

All of this is accomplished under the original perfected security agreement. The various items in the inventory have changed, but New England Community still has a perfected security interest in Ski Paradise's inventory, and hence it has a floating lien on the inventory.

The concept of the floating lien can also apply to a shifting stock of goods. Under Section 9–205, the lien can start with raw materials and follow them as they become finished goods and inventories and as they are sold, turning into accounts receivable, chattel paper, or cash.

## SECTION 6

# RESOLVING PRIORITY DISPUTES

What happens when several creditors claim a security interest in the same collateral of a debtor? This important issue is addressed by the UCC with a set of rules for determining which of the conflicting security interests has priority—or the best claim to the collateral—when the debtor goes into default. The question of priority is particularly important when the debtor is in bankruptcy. In this situation, only the perfected secured party will recover, and other creditors may end up with little or nothing.

## SECURED VERSUS UNSECURED PARTIES

In general, secured creditors prevail over unsecured creditors and over creditors who have obtained judgments against the debtor but who have not begun the legal process to collect on those judgments [UCC 9–301]. In other words, once a security interest attaches, it has priority over the

claims of other creditors who do not have a security interest. This priority does not depend on whether the security interest has been perfected.

## SECURED PARTY VERSUS LIEN CREDITOR

A **lien creditor** is one who has a lien on the property because of a judgment.[7] Any security interest that is *perfected* has priority over lien creditors who acquired their liens after perfection. In contrast, a lien creditor has priority over a security interest that has not yet been perfected. A so-called ten-day exception to this rule, however, provides as follows: if a secured party files with respect to a PMSI during a ten-day period after the debtor receives possession of the collateral, the secured party has priority over the lien creditor's rights that arise between the time the security interest attaches and the time of filing [UCC 9–301(2)]. In many states, this so-called grace period has been extended to twenty days.

## WHEN MORE THAN ONE PARTY IS SECURED

When more than one party has a secured interest in the collateral of a defaulting debtor, the issues of perfection and timing become critical, as does the type of collateral involved. There are several general rules and, of course, exceptions to those rules.

**THE GENERAL RULE**   Among secured parties, the general rule of priority is as follows: The first security interest to be filed or perfected has priority over other filed or perfected security interests. If, however, none of the conflicting security interests has been perfected, the first security interest to attach has priority [UCC 9–312(5)].

For example, suppose that West Bank filed a financing statement covering Alger's inventory on March 1, and Friendly Savings and Loan filed a financing statement covering the same inventory on April 1. West Bank's interest would have priority over Friendly's interest. It would not matter which lender made its loan and attached its security interest first. If West Bank failed to perfect its security interest, however, and Friendly perfected its interest, then Friendly's interest would have pri-

---

7.   This definition also includes a receiver in equity, a trustee in bankruptcy, and an assignee for the benefit of creditors.

ority as the *only* perfected security interest. If both failed to perfect their interests, then the first to attach would have priority. Thus, if West Bank had a security agreement covering Alger's inventory on March 1 and advanced money to Alger on the same day, and Friendly's agreement and advance were made on April 1, West Bank would have priority over Friendly.

### AN EXCEPTION: PURCHASE-MONEY SECURITY INTEREST

The general rule, as previously stated, is that the first in time to file or perfect is first in priority rights to the collateral. This rule is always applicable when the first in time to perfect is a PMSI. The UCC provides, however, that under certain conditions a PMSI, properly perfected, will prevail over a non-PMSI in after-acquired collateral, even though the non-PMSI was the first in time to perfect.

If the collateral is *inventory,* a perfected PMSI will prevail over a previously perfected non-PMSI provided that the holder of the PMSI perfects *and* gives the holder of the non-PMSI security interest written notice of his or her interest *before* the debtor takes possession of the newly acquired inventory [UCC 9–312(3)].

If the collateral is other than inventory, a PMSI will have priority over a previously perfected non-PMSI provided that the PMSI is perfected either before or within ten days *after* the debtor takes possession. No notice is required [UCC 9–312(4)].

To illustrate: Retailer Elena needs a loan of money to be used as working capital. On May 1, she obtains a one-year installment loan from West Bank, signing a security agreement and putting up her present inventory plus any after-acquired inventory as collateral. That same date, West Bank perfects its non-PMSI by filing a financing statement centrally. On August 1, Elena learns that she can purchase directly from Martin, a manufacturer, $10,000 worth of new inventory, which is a bargain. Because she cannot pay this amount in cash, she signs a security agreement with Martin, giving Martin a security interest in the newly purchased inventory.

The new inventory is delivered on September 1, as ordered. On September 7, a fire destroys most of Elena's store and warehouse. There remains only a part of the new inventory, and its value is insufficient to cover both debts. Who has priority with regard to the remaining inventory, West Bank or Martin?

If Martin perfected by filing *and* gave West Bank written notice of its security interest prior to September 1, the date Elena received possession, Martin prevails. If Martin did not meet these conditions, West Bank prevails.

Suppose that the collateral is equipment, rather than inventory, and Martin perfected on September 8, after the fire. Because Martin properly perfected its PMSI within ten days after Elena received delivery, Martin prevails over West Bank for the remaining after-acquired equipment.

### SECURED PARTY VERSUS BUYER

In general, a security interest in collateral continues even after the collateral has been sold unless the secured party has authorized the sale [UCC 9–306(2)]. There are exceptions, however, and they allow the buyers of collateral sold without the secured party's authorization to take that collateral free of the security interest, even in situations when the security interest has been perfected. We examine those situations now.

### BUYERS IN THE ORDINARY COURSE OF BUSINESS

To require buyers to find out if there is an outstanding security interest on a merchant's inventory would impose a time-consuming restriction and would certainly inhibit commerce. Therefore, the UCC provides that a person who buys ''in the ordinary course of business'' will take the goods free from any security interest attached to those goods, even if the security interest is perfected and even if the buyer knows of its existence [UCC 9–307(1)]. A *buyer in the ordinary course of business* is defined as any person who, in good faith and without knowledge that the sale is *in violation* of the ownership rights or security interest of a third party in the goods, buys in ordinary course from a person in the business of selling goods of that kind [UCC 1–201(9)].[8]

Suppose retail seller Chad secures a loan from West Bank and puts up his existing appliance inventory and any appliance inventory thereafter acquired as collateral. Chad signs a security agreement and a financing statement, which West Bank

---

8. Note that a buyer may know of the *existence* of a security interest and still retain the status of a buyer in ordinary course. That status will be lost only if the buyer knows that his or her purchase of goods will *violate* a third party's security interest or other ownership rights.

properly perfects. Later Chad sells an appliance from inventory covered by the security agreement to Lee, and Lee pays cash. If Chad goes into default on the loan, West Bank's prior perfected security interest has no effect on Lee. Lee took the appliance completely free of West Bank's security interest, even though perfected, and West Bank loses this item of collateral for satisfaction of the debt. (Of course, West Bank has rights in any identifiable cash proceeds.)

In the following case, the court must determine at what point a buyer becomes a buyer in the ordinary course of the seller's business.

---

**BACKGROUND AND FACTS**   *The Big Knob Volunteer Fire Company agreed to buy a fire truck from Hamerly Custom Productions, Inc., which was in the business of assembling component parts into fire trucks. The Volunteer Fire Company paid Hamerly $48,000 toward the $51,836 purchase price. Under their contract, Hamerly agreed to deliver the truck within twenty to seventy days of receiving the chassis from a third party supplier. The contract also provided that title to the truck would not pass to the Volunteer Fire Company until the price had been paid in full. Hamerly ordered the chassis from Lowe & Moyer Garage, Inc., and on receiving the chassis began transforming it into a fire truck, painting "Big Knob Volunteer Fire Department" on the cab. The chassis was subject to a security interest. Hamerly, however, did not pay Lowe & Moyer for the chassis, nor did it complete the truck or deliver it to the Volunteer Fire Company. Consequently, both the Volunteer Fire Company and Lowe & Moyer sued Hamerly. Hamerly surrendered the truck to Lowe & Moyer, which dropped its suit. The Volunteer Fire Company obtained a default judgment against Hamerly for specific performance and then sued Hamerly and Lowe & Moyer to replevy (repossess) the truck. The trial court found in favor of Lowe & Moyer for the chassis or its value, reasoning that because title had not passed, the Volunteer Fire Company was not a buyer in the ordinary course of business. The Volunteer Fire Company appealed.*

| CASE 31.3 |

**BIG KNOB VOLUNTEER FIRE CO. v. LOWE & MOYER GARAGE, INC.**

Superior Court of Pennsylvania, 1985.
338 Pa.Super. 257,
487 A.2d 953.

---

*SPAETH,* President Judge:

\*   \*   \*   \*

\*   \*   \* The trial court held that the Volunteer Fire [Company] was not a buyer in ordinary course because there was no sale to it. Relying on the definition of "sale" as "the passing of title from the seller to the buyer for a price," [Section] 2106(a), the trial court held that "[n]either title to the truck passed, nor was delivery made to plaintiff."

The point at which a person becomes a buyer in ordinary course is subject to considerable controversy because the Code does not specify the moment at which the status is conferred. The controversy arises in the context of both [Section] 9307(a) and [Section] 2403(b) of the Code. \*   \*   \*

The cases are \*   \*   \* divided. Cases denying recovery to a party on the ground that the party was not a buyer in ordinary course reason that a sale is required, [Section] 1–201; a sale requires transfer of title, [Section] 2106(a); and a transfer of title occurs either when agreed upon by the parties or upon physical delivery, [Section] 2401(2). Absent satisfaction of these criteria, the buyer will not prevail even though some or all of the purchase price has been paid. \*   \*   \* This reasoning places the buyer who has paid in advance for goods not yet delivered in an extremely vulnerable position.

\*   \*   \*   \*

The modern trend in contests between a buyer without possession and a secured creditor, typically the inventory financer, is to ignore or deemphasize the concept of ''sale.'' Instead of focusing on passage of title (delivery), courts and commentators increasingly favor identification as the critical moment that determines when a buyer becomes a buyer in ordinary course. * * *

* * * *

* * * [C]ourts have with increasing frequency held that passing of title (when agreed to or occurring upon delivery, [Section] 2401(2)) is not essential to a person becoming a buyer in ordinary course of business. We agree with these courts, and hold that identification rather than delivery is the point at which a person becomes a buyer in ordinary course of business. Since here the fire truck was identified to the contract, the Volunteer Fire Company did become a buyer in ordinary course of business. Upon entrusting the goods to Hamerly, which dealt in goods of that kind, Lowe & Moyer gave Hamerly the power to transfer its rights to a buyer in ordinary course of business, and Hamerly exercised that power when it painted the Volunteer Fire Department's name on the cab of the fire truck, identifying the goods to the contract and making the Volunteer Fire [Company] a buyer in ordinary course of business.

**DECISION AND REMEDY** *The court held that the Volunteer Fire Company was entitled to possession of the truck free of the security interest.*

---

**BUYERS OF FARM PRODUCTS** Under the UCC, a buyer of farm products takes the products subject to a security interest, even if the buyer knows nothing about the existence of a security agreement [UCC 9–307(1)]. Under the Food Security Act of 1985,[9] however, buyers in the ordinary course of business include buyers of farm products from farmers. Under the Food Security Act, a secured party is not protected against a buyer of farm products from a farmer unless one of the following events occurs:

1. The buyer has received notice of the security interest within one year before the purchase.
2. The buyer fails to register with the secretary of state before the purchase, and the secured party has properly perfected his or her interest centrally.
3. The buyer has received notice from the secretary of state that the farm products being sold are subject to an *effective financing statement (EFS).*[10] An EFS is a form that a secured party must file in addition to an Article 9 financing

statement to protect his or her interest in a farmer's products in those states with EFS filing systems.

**BUYERS OF CONSUMER GOODS FROM CONSUMERS** Carla, a consumer, purchases a refrigerator from an appliance store on credit, because she cannot pay the full purchase price. A written security agreement exists in which the seller takes a PMSI in the consumer goods. Further, the seller need not file a financing statement, because, when a PMSI is taken in consumer goods, *perfection occurs automatically* [UCC 9–302(1)(d)]. Later, Carla sells the refrigerator to her next-door neighbor, Nan, who purchases it—as a purchaser not in the ordinary course of business—for home use without any knowledge of the credit arrangements between Carla and the original seller. Subsequently, Carla defaults on the credit payments to the seller. What are the seller's rights? The seller had a perfected PMSI in the refrigerator when it was held by Carla. Under UCC 9–307(2), however, the perfection is not good against the next-door neighbor.

UCC 9–307(2) requires that a person in the position of this next-door neighbor must purchase (give value for) the goods for personal, family, or household use, and without knowledge of the original seller's security interest, and that the purchase must take place *before* the secured party has filed a financing statement. In this case, recall that the

---

9. 7 U.S.C. Section 1631.
10. As of June 15, 1994, the following nineteen states have been certified by the U.S. Department of Agriculture for EFS filing: Alabama, Colorado, Idaho, Louisiana, Maine, Minnesota, Mississippi, Montana, Nebraska, New Hampshire, New Mexico, North Dakota, Oklahoma, Oregon, South Dakota, Utah, Vermont, West Virginia, and Wyoming.

# ■ CONCEPT SUMMARY 31.1 Priority of Claims to a Debtor's Collateral

| PARTIES | PRIORITY |
|---|---|
| **Unperfected Secured Party** | Prevails over unsecured creditors and creditors who have obtained judgments against the debtor but who have not begun the legal process to collect on those judgments [UCC 9–301]. |
| **Perfected Secured Parties to Same Collateral** | The first to file or perfect is first in right to the collateral [UCC 9–312(5)]. An exception is a purchase-money security interest (PMSI). Even if second in time of perfection, it has priority over a non-PMSI providing:<br>a. In the case of inventory, that the PMSI is perfected and written notice is given to the holder of the other perfected security interest *on* or *before* the time that the debtor takes possession [UCC 9–312(3)].<br>b. In the case of other collateral, that the PMSI has been perfected within ten days after the debtor receives possession [UCC 9–312(4)]. |
| **Purchaser of Debtor's Collateral** | 1. Goods purchased in the ordinary course of the seller's business—Purchaser prevails over a perfected secured party even if the purchaser knows of the security interest [UCC 9–307(1)].<br>2. Farm products purchased in the ordinary course of business—Purchaser prevails unless the purchaser:<br>  a. Received notice of the security interest within one year before the purchase.<br>  b. Fails to register with the secretary of state before the purchase, and the secured party has properly perfected his or her interest centrally.<br>  c. Received notice from the secretary of state that the farm products being sold are subject to an effective financing statement.<br>3. Consumer goods purchased out of the ordinary course of business—Purchaser prevails over a perfected secured party, providing the purchaser purchased:<br>  a. For value.<br>  b. Without actual knowledge of the security interest.<br>  c. For use as a consumer good.<br>  d. Prior to secured party's perfection by *filing* [UCC 9–307(2)].<br>4. The chattel paper purchaser prevails over a perfected secured party, providing the purchaser:<br>  a. Gave new value.<br>  b. Took possession.<br>  c. Took in the ordinary course of the purchaser's business.<br>  d. Took without *actual* knowledge of the secured party's perfection [UCC 9–308].<br>5. The purchaser of negotiable instruments, documents, and securities prevails over a perfected secured party, particularly if the purchaser is a holder in due course, a holder to whom the document has been duly negotiated, or a *bona fide* purchaser of a security [UCC 9–308; UCC 9–309]. |

seller took a PMSI, which is perfected automatically. No filing was required. Hence, the next-door neighbor purchased the refrigerator free and clear before the seller had filed a financing statement. The seller could have avoided this possibility simply by *filing* a financing statement, even though a PMSI had been perfected.

**BUYERS OF CHATTEL PAPER AND INSTRUMENTS** Another purchaser who may not be subject to a secured party's interest despite perfection is the purchaser of chattel paper and instruments. This protection is provided by UCC 9–308. As previously defined, *chattel paper* is a writing or writings that evidence both a monetary obligation and a security interest in specific goods. *Instrument* means a negotiable instrument as defined in UCC 3–104, or a certificated security as defined in UCC 8–102, or basically any other writing that evidences a right to the payment of money and is not itself a security agreement or lease transferred in the ordinary course of business by delivery with any necessary indorsement or assignment [UCC 9–105(1)(i)]. Security interests in instruments can be perfected only by possession.

Chattel paper is a very important class of collateral used in financing arrangements, especially in automobile financing. When chattel paper is sold by a creditor, the creditor can deliver it over to the assignee, who is then responsible for collecting the debt directly from the debtor. This arrangement is known as *notification* or *direct collection.* As an alternative, a creditor can sell chattel paper to an assignee with the understanding that the creditor will retain the chattel paper, make collections from the debtor, and then remit the money to the assignee. This kind of transaction is *nonnotification* or *indirect collection.* The widespread use of both methods of dealing with chattel paper is recognized by the UCC, and hence the UCC permits perfection of a chattel paper security interest either by filing or by taking possession of the chattel paper.

Problems arise when perfection of chattel paper is made by filing only. If the chattel paper is thereafter sold to another purchaser who gives *new value* and takes *possession* of the paper in the *ordinary course of the purchaser's business, without knowledge* that it is subject to a security interest, the new purchaser will have priority over the secured creditor. (Of course, the creditor has rights in the proceeds.)

SECTION 7

# RIGHTS AND DUTIES OF DEBTOR AND CREDITOR

The security agreement itself determines most of the rights and duties of the debtor and creditor. The UCC, however, imposes some rights and duties that are applicable in the absence of a security agreement to the contrary.

## INFORMATION REQUEST BY CREDITORS

Under UCC 9–407(1), a creditor has the option, when making the filing, of asking the filing officer to make a note of the file number, the date, and the hour of the original filing on a copy of the financing statement. The filing officer must send this copy to the person making the request. Under UCC 9–407(2), a filing officer must also give information to a person who is contemplating obtaining a security interest from a prospective debtor. The filing officer must give a certificate that provides information on possible perfected financing statements with respect to the named debtor. The filing officer will charge a fee for the certification and for any information copies provided.

## ASSIGNMENT, AMENDMENT, AND RELEASE

Whenever desired, a secured party of record can release part or all of the collateral described in a filed financing statement. This ends his or her security interest in the collateral [UCC 9–406]. A secured party can assign part or all of the security interest to another, called the assignee. That assignee becomes the secured party of record if, for example, he or she either makes a notation of the assignment somewhere on the financing statement or files a written statement of assignment [UCC 9–405(1), (2)].

It is also possible to amend a financing statement that has already been filed. *The amendment must be signed by both parties.* The debtor signs the security agreement, the original financing statement, and the amendments [UCC 9–402]. All other secured transaction documents, such as releases, assignments, continuations of perfection, perfections of collateral moved into another jurisdiction, and termination statements, need only be signed by the secured party.

## REASONABLE CARE OF COLLATERAL

If a secured party is in possession of the collateral, he or she must use reasonable care in preserving it. Otherwise, the secured party is liable to the debtor [UCC 9–207(1); UCC 9–207(3)]. If the collateral increases in value, the secured party can hold this increased value or profit as additional security unless it is in the form of money, which must be remitted to the debtor or applied toward reducing the secured debt [UCC 9–207(2)(c)]. Additionally, the collateral must be kept in identifiable condition unless it consists of fungible goods (goods that are naturally alike, such as wheat or oil) [UCC 9–207(2)(d)]. Finally, the debtor must pay for all reasonable charges incurred by the secured party in preserving, operating, and taking care of the collateral in possession [UCC 9–207(2)(a)].

## THE STATUS OF THE DEBT

During the time that the secured debt is outstanding, the debtor may wish to know the status of the debt. If so, the debtor need only sign a statement that indicates the aggregate amount of the unpaid debt at a specific date (and perhaps a list of the collateral covered by the security agreement). The secured party must then approve or correct this statement in writing. The creditor must comply with the request within two weeks of receipt; otherwise, the creditor is liable for any loss caused to the debtor by the failure to do so [UCC 9–208(2)]. One such request is allowed without charge every six months. For each additional request, the secured party can require a fee not exceeding $10 per request [UCC 9–208(3)].

## TERMINATION STATEMENT

When a secured debt is paid, the secured party generally must send a termination statement to the debtor or file such a statement with the filing officer to whom the original financing statement was given. If the financing statement covers consumer goods, the termination statement must be filed by the secured party within one month after the debt is paid, or—if the debtor requests the termination statement in writing—it must be filed within ten days of receipt of such request after the debt is paid, whichever is earlier [UCC 9–404(1)]. In all other cases, the termination statement must be filed or furnished to the debtor within ten days after a written request is made by the debtor.

If the affected secured party fails to file such a termination statement, as required by UCC 9–404(1), or fails to send the termination statement within ten days after proper demand, the secured party will be liable to the debtor for $100. Additionally, the secured party will be liable for any loss caused to the debtor.

# DEFAULT

Article 9 of the UCC defines the rights, duties, and remedies of a secured party and of the debtor upon the debtor's default. Should the secured party fail to comply with his or her duties, the debtor is afforded particular rights and remedies.

The topic of default is one of great concern to secured lenders and to the lawyers who draft security agreements. What constitutes default is not always clear. In fact, Article 9 does not define the term. Consequently, parties are encouraged in practice and by the UCC to include in their security agreements certain standards to be applied should default occur. In so doing, parties can stipulate the conditions that will constitute a default [UCC 9–501(3)].

Typically, because of the disparity in bargaining position between a debtor and a creditor, these critical terms are shaped by the creditor in an attempt to provide the maximum protection possible. The ultimate terms, however, are not allowed to go beyond the limitations imposed by the good faith requirement of UCC 1–203 and the unconscionability doctrine.

Although any breach of the terms of the security agreement can constitute default, default occurs most commonly when the debtor fails to meet the scheduled payments that the parties have agreed upon or when the debtor becomes bankrupt. If the security agreement covers equipment, however, the debtor may have warranted that he or she is the owner of the equipment or that no liens or other security interests are pending on that equipment. Breach of any of these representations can result in default.

## BASIC REMEDIES

A secured party's remedies can be divided into two basic categories:

1. A secured party can relinquish a security interest and proceed to judgment on the underlying debt, followed by **execution** and **levy.** Execution is an action to carry into effect the directions in a court decree or judgment. Levy is the obtaining of money by legal process through the seizure and sale of property,

usually done after an execution has been issued. Execution and levy are rarely done unless the value of the secured collateral has been reduced greatly below the amount of the debt and the debtor has other nonexempt assets available to satisfy the debt.

2. A secured party can take possession of the collateral covered by the security agreement [UCC 9–503]. Upon taking possession, the secured party can retain the collateral for satisfaction of the debt [UCC 9–505(2)] or can sell the collateral and apply the proceeds toward the debt [UCC 9–504].

The rights and remedies under UCC 9–501(1) are *cumulative*. Therefore, if a creditor is unsuccessful in enforcing rights by one method, another method can be pursued. The UCC does not require election of remedies—that is, the creditor need not choose between an action on the obligation and the repossession of the collateral.

When a security agreement covers both real and personal property, the secured party can proceed against the personal property in accordance with the remedies of Article 9. Alternatively, the secured party can proceed against the entire collateral under procedures set down by local real estate law, in which case the UCC does not apply [UCC 9–501(4)].

For example, this situation occurs when the security interest on a corporate loan applies to the manufacturing plant (real property) and also to the inventory (personal property). Determining whether particular collateral is personal or real property can prove difficult, especially in dealing with fixtures—things affixed to real property. Under certain circumstances, the UCC allows the removal of fixtures upon default; such removal, however, is subject to the provisions of Article 9 [UCC 9–313].

## SECURED PARTY'S RIGHT TO TAKE POSSESSION

UCC 9–503 states that "[u]nless otherwise agreed, a secured party has on default the right to take possession of the collateral. In taking possession, a secured party may proceed without judicial process if this can be done without a breach of the peace." The underlying rationale for this "self-help" provision of Article 9 is that it simplifies the process of repossession for creditors and reduces the burden on the courts. Because the UCC does

not define *breach of the peace,* however, it is not always easy to predict what will or will not constitute a breach of the peace.

Generally, the creditor or the creditor's agent cannot enter a debtor's home, garage, or place of business without permission. Consider a situation in which an automobile is collateral. If the repossessing party walks onto the debtor's premises, proceeds up the driveway, enters the vehicle without entering the garage, and drives off, it probably will not amount to a breach of the peace. In some states, however, an action for wrongful trespass could start a cause of action for breach of the peace or other tortious action.

## DISPOSITION OF COLLATERAL

Once default has occurred and the secured party has obtained possession of the collateral, the secured party may sell, lease, or otherwise dispose of the collateral in any commercially reasonable manner [UCC 9–504(1)]. Any sale is always subject to procedures established by state law.

**RETENTION OF COLLATERAL BY SECURED PARTY** The UCC recognizes that parties are sometimes better off if they do not sell the collateral. Therefore, a secured party can retain collateral, but this general right is subject to several conditions. The secured party must send written notice of the intention to retain the collateral to the debtor if the debtor has not signed a statement renouncing or modifying his or her rights after default. In the case of consumer goods, no other notice need be given. In all other cases, notice must be sent to any other secured party from whom the secured party in possession of the collateral has received written notice of a claim of interest in the collateral in question.

If within twenty-one days after the notice is sent, the secured party receives an objection in writing from a person entitled to receive notification, then the secured party must sell or otherwise dispose of the collateral in accordance with the provisions of UCC 9–504 (disposition procedures under UCC 9–504 will be discussed shortly). If no such written objection is forthcoming, the secured party can retain the collateral in full satisfaction of the debtor's obligation [UCC 9–505(2)].

**CONSUMER GOODS** When the collateral is consumer goods with a PMSI, and the debtor has paid 60 percent or more of the cash price or loan, then the secured party must sell or otherwise dispose of the collateral in accordance with the provisions of UCC 9–504 within ninety days. Failure to comply opens the secured party to an action for conversion (the wrongful taking of another's property—see Chapter 6) or other liability under UCC 9–507(1) unless the consumer-debtor signed a written statement *after default* renouncing or modifying the right to demand the sale of the goods [UCC 9–505(1)].

**DISPOSITION PROCEDURES** A secured party who does not choose to retain the collateral must resort to the disposition procedures prescribed under UCC 9–504. The UCC allows a great deal of flexibility with regard to disposition. The only real limitation is that it must be accomplished in a commercially reasonable manner. UCC 9–507(2) supplies some examples of what does or does not meet the standard of commercial reasonableness:

> The fact that a better price could have been obtained by a sale at a different time or in a different method from that selected by the secured party is not of itself sufficient to establish that the sale was not made in a commercially reasonable manner. If the secured party either sells the collateral in the usual manner in any recognized market therefor or if he sells at the price current in such a market at the time of sale or if he has otherwise sold in conformity with reasonable commercial practices among dealers in the type of property sold, he has sold in a commercially reasonable manner.

A secured party is not compelled to resort to public sale to dispose of the collateral. The party is given latitude under the UCC to seek out the best terms possible in a private, commercially reasonable sale. Generally, no specific time requirements must be met; however, the time must ultimately meet the standard of commercial reasonableness.

The secured party should diligently arrange to sell the collateral at the best price possible and avoid self-serving acts that raise suspicions of commercial unreasonableness. Assume that Boender, a secured party, advertises a private sale in a newspaper that is not likely to be read by potential purchasers, requires a minimum deposit of $50,000 with each purchaser's bid (while exempting himself from the deposit requirement), and then purchases the property at the sale for himself, only to resell it shortly thereafter at a substantial profit to a prearranged buyer. Boender's conduct unreasonably diminished the number of potential purchasers available at the sale. With fewer participants at the sale, the final purchase price was likely to be reduced. When the purchase price is low, the debtor may fail to satisfy its outstanding debt to Boender or to enjoy a surplus from the sale of the collateral (deficiency and surplus are discussed later in this chapter). In such a situation, the debtor may recover any loss caused by Boender's failure to comply with the requirement of commercial reasonableness under the UCC [UCC 9–507].[11]

Notice of any sale must be sent by the secured party to the debtor if the debtor has not signed a statement renouncing or modifying the right to notification of sale after default. For consumer goods, no other notification need be sent. In all other cases, notification must be sent to any other secured party from whom the secured party in possession of the collateral has received written notice of a claim of interest in the collateral [UCC 9–504(3)]. Such notice is not necessary, however, when the collateral is perishable or threatens to decline speedily in value or when it is of a type customarily sold on a recognized market. Generally, notice of the place, time, and manner of the sale is required if the sale is to be classified as a sale conducted in a commercially reasonable manner. At issue in the following case is whether a sale of collateral was conducted in a commercially reasonable manner.

---

11. *Boender v. Chicago North Clubhouse Association, Inc.,* 240 Ill.App.3d 622, 608 N.E.2d 207, 181 Ill.Dec. 134 (1992).

---

**BACKGROUND AND FACTS** *Guaranty Bank and Trust Company, a secured creditor in John Whatley's bankruptcy proceedings, was authorized to take possession of the collateral—Whatley's farm equipment—securing a debt that Whatley owed to Guaranty Bank. The proceeds from the sale of the collateral were to be put into an* escrow account *(a bank account held by a third party) pending an appellate court's decision as to whether Guaranty Bank's security interest took priority over that of the Small Business Administration (SBA), which also held a security interest*

**CASE 31.4**

**IN RE WHATLEY**

United States Bankruptcy Court,
Northern District of Mississippi,
1991.
126 Bankr. 231.

*in the farm equipment. Guaranty Bank posted public notices of its fore-closure sale and sent copies of the notice to local equipment dealers, Whatley's attorney, and the attorney representing the SBA. The notice was received by the SBA on September 2, 1987, and the foreclosure sale was to be conducted by the bank on September 10. Before the sale, Guaranty Bank had the equipment appraised by Yokley and Lundy Auction Company, which indicated that the total value was between $40,312.50 and $42,000.00. By subtracting expenses and other amounts from this value, Guaranty Bank calculated that it would bid $25,000 for the equipment at the foreclosure sale. At the sale, Guaranty Bank was the only bidder, and it purchased the equipment for $25,000. In accordance with the court or-der, this amount was deposited into the escrow account. The following day, Guaranty Bank sold the goods at auction for a net amount (after expenses of the sale) of $39,748.29. The SBA filed a motion to compel Guaranty Bank to pay SBA the difference between the $25,000 the bank had paid for the equipment at the foreclosure sale and the $39,748.29 that it had received on selling the equipment at the auction. Among other things, the SBA contended that the first sale—the foreclosure sale—had not been conducted in a commercially reasonable manner.*

*DAVID W. HOUSTON, III,* Bankruptcy Judge.
  * * * *

In this proceeding, Guaranty Bank based its foreclosure bid on the appraisal that it had received from Yokley and Lundy. The appraiser's worksheet, which reflected his evaluation for each item of equipment, indicated a total value for the equipment of between $40,312.50 and $42,000.00, although he did express that the equipment could have a value range of between $40,000.00 to $55,000.00. The commission and expenses estimated by Guaranty Bank were almost identical to the total amount of the actual commission and expenses incurred ($6,500.00 compared to $6,454.21).
* * * [T]he Yokley and Lundy appraiser considered the foreclosure bid price calculated by Guaranty Bank to be reasonable under the circumstances. The sale was noticed in keeping with customary standards of practice and in compliance with the requirements of the Mississippi Uniform Commercial Code. SBA was appropriately advised of the sale in a timely manner, but elected not to attend or bid on the property. From the evidence presented * * *, the Court is compelled to conclude that the foreclosure sale was conducted in a commercially reasonable manner. The fact that the auction sale enabled Guaranty Bank to receive an excess of $14,748.29, over and above the price it paid at the foreclosure sale, is not conclusive that the foreclosure sale was not conducted in a commercially reasonable manner. The argument of SBA as to this issue is not well taken.

**DECISION AND REMEDY** *Guaranty Bank was allowed to retain the profits it realized on the resale of the equipment.*

**INTERNATIONAL CONSIDERATIONS** **Waiver of Foreclosure-Sale Protections in England and the United States** *To prevent challenges to the reasonability of foreclosure sales, banks have sought to put waivers in loan contracts that prohibit such challenges even if some aspects of the sale are not commercially reason-able. Such waivers are enforceable in England. In the United States, how-ever, such waivers would generally not be enforceable because the UCC requires that foreclosure sales be conducted in a commercially reasonable manner.*

## ■ CONCEPT SUMMARY 31.2 Remedies of the Secured Party upon the Debtor's Default

| | |
|---|---|
| **Other Than Provided under the UCC** | The secured party may reduce the debt claim to judgment, foreclose, or enforce the security interest by any judicial procedure. For example, the secured party may proceed to a judgment on the underlying debt, followed by execution and levy on the debtor's nonexempt assets. |
| **Repossession of the Collateral** | The secured party may take possession (peacefully or by court order) of the collateral covered by the security agreement and then pursue one of two alternatives: <br> 1. Retain the collateral (unless the secured party has a purchase-money security interest in consumer goods and the debtor has paid 60 percent or more of the selling price or loan), in which case the creditor— <br>   a. Must give written notice to the debtor if the debtor has not signed a statement renouncing or modifying his or her rights after default. With consumer goods, no other notice is necessary. <br>   b. Must send notice to any other secured party with an interest in the same collateral. <br>   c. If an objection is received from the debtor or any other secured party within twenty-one days, in writing, the creditor must dispose of the collateral according to the requirements of UCC 9–504. Otherwise, the creditor may retain the collateral in full satisfaction of the debt. <br> 2. Sell the collateral, in which case the creditor— <br>   a. Must notify the debtor and (except in sales of consumer goods) other secured parties having claims to the collateral of the sale (unless the collateral is perishable or will decline rapidly in value). <br>   b. Must sell the goods in a commercially reasonable manner at a public or private sale. <br>   c. Must apply the proceeds in the following order: <br>     (1) Expenses incurred by the sale (which may include reasonable attorneys' fees and other legal expenses). <br>     (2) Balance of the debt owed to the secured party. <br>     (3) Subordinate security interests of creditors whose written demands have been received prior to the completion of the distribution of the proceeds. <br>     (4) Surplus to the debtor (except if the collateral is chattel paper or accounts). |

**PROCEEDS FROM DISPOSITION** Proceeds from the disposition of the collateral must be applied in the following order:

1. Reasonable expenses stemming from the retaking, holding, or preparing for sale are paid first. When authorized by law and if provided for in the agreement, these expenses can include reasonable attorneys' fees and legal expenses.

2. Satisfaction of the balance of the debt owed to the secured party must then be made.

3. Creditors with subordinate security interests whose written demands have been received prior to the completion of distribution of the proceeds are then entitled to receive the remaining proceeds from the sale [UCC 9–504(1)].

4. Any surplus generally goes to the debtor.

**DEFICIENCY JUDGMENT** Often, after proper disposition of the collateral, the secured party has not collected all that is still owed by the debtor. Unless otherwise agreed, the debtor is liable for any deficiency. Note, however, that if the underlying transaction was a sale of accounts or of chattel paper, the secured party can collect the deficiency by requesting a court to order a **deficiency judgment** only if the security agreement so provides [UCC 9–504(2)].

**REDEMPTION RIGHTS** Any time before the secured party disposes of the collateral or enters into a contract for its disposition, or before the debtor's obligation has been discharged through the secured party's retention of the collateral, the debtor or any other secured party can exercise the right of *redemption* of the collateral. The debtor or other secured party can do this by (1) tendering performance of all obligations secured by the collateral and (2) paying the expenses reasonably incurred by the secured party in retaking the collateral and maintaining its care and custody, including legal expenses and reasonable attorneys' fees if the security agreement so provides [UCC 9–506].

## TERMS AND CONCEPTS TO REVIEW

| | | |
|---|---|---|
| after-acquired property **600** | execution **607** | purchase-money security |
| attachment **590** | financing statement **595** | interest (PMSI) **592** |
| chattel paper **589** | floating lien **600** | secured party **589** |
| collateral **589** | levy **607** | secured transaction **588** |
| continuation statement **598** | lien creditor **601** | security agreement **589** |
| debtor **589** | perfection **593** | security interest **589** |
| default **593** | pledge **593** | |
| deficiency judgment **611** | proceeds **599** | |

## QUESTIONS AND CASE PROBLEMS

**31–1. Priority Disputes.** Ray is a seller of electric generators. He purchases a large quantity of generators from manufacturer Martin Corp. by making a down payment and signing a security agreement to make the balance of payments over a period of time. The agreement gives Martin Corp. a security interest in the generators and the proceeds. Martin Corp. files a financing statement on its security interest centrally. Ray receives the generators and immediately sells one of them to Green on an installment contract, with payment to be made in twelve equal installments. At the time of sale, Green knows of Martin's security interest. Two months later Ray goes into default on his payments to Martin. Discuss Martin's rights against purchaser Green in this situation.

**31–2. Perfection.** Marion has a prize horse named Thunderbolt. Marion is in need of working capital. To secure it, she borrows $5,000 from Rodriguez, and Rodriguez takes possession of Thunderbolt as security for the loan. No written agreement is signed. Discuss whether, in the absence of a written agreement, Rodriguez has a security interest in Thunderbolt *and* whether Rodriguez can be a perfected secured party without filing a financing statement.

**31–3. Perfection.** Discuss how each secured party would properly perfect his or her security interest in the following cases.

(a) Martin is a manufacturer of refrigerators. Ray, a retailer, buys a number of these refrigerators. Ray signs a security agreement giving Martin a security interest in the refrigerators.

(b) Mary sells a refrigerator to Carla, to be used in Carla's home. Carla signs a security agreement giving Mary a security interest in the refrigerator.

(c) Ray sells a refrigerator to Dr. Dodd, to be used in his office to store medicines. Dr. Dodd signs a security agreement giving Ray a security interest in the refrigerator.

(d) Mary sells a refrigerator to farmer Ames, who needs it to store eggs not sold at market. Ames signs a security agreement giving Mary a security interest in the refrigerator.

**31–4. Priority Disputes.** Martin is a manufacturer of washing machines. On September 1, in need of working capital, Martin's president contacts Smith, a loan officer for the First Bank. The president asks to borrow $200,000, and offers to put up all Martin's equipment as security. Smith agrees to make the loan. In the security agreement signed by Martin's president is a clause stating that this loan is secured not only by the existing equipment presently located at Martin's plant but by any equipment acquired in the future by Martin. The First Bank files a financing statement centrally on *September 5*. On *November 1*, Martin has an opportunity to purchase from Daniel Equipment Corp. some newly manufactured Daniel equipment at a bargain price of $50,000. On that same date, Martin contracts by a security agreement to purchase the equipment from Daniel, paying $20,000 down and the balance in monthly payments over a three-year period, with Daniel having a security interest in the purchased equipment. The new equipment is delivered on *December 1*. On *December 7*, Daniel perfects its security interest in the newly delivered equipment by filing a financing statement centrally. Later, Martin goes into default to both parties. Discuss whose interest in the new equipment has priority, First Bank's or Daniel's.

**31–5. Purchase-Money Security Interest.** Ray is a retail seller of television sets. Ray sells a color television set to Clara for her apartment for $600. Clara cannot pay cash and signs a security agreement, paying $100 down and agreeing to pay the balance in twelve equal installments of $50 each. The security agreement gives Ray a security interest in the television set. Clara makes six payments on time; then she goes into default because of unexpected financial problems. Ray repossesses the set and wants to keep it in full satisfaction of the debt. Discuss Ray's rights and duties in this matter.

**31–6. Sale of Collateral.** In 1969, Jones and Percell executed a promissory note and a security agreement covering a converted military aircraft built in the 1950s. Upon their default, the Bank of Nevada repossessed the aircraft. After providing the required notice to Jones and Percell, the bank placed advertisements in several trade journals, as well as in major newspapers in several large cities. In addition, the bank sent 2,000 brochures to 240 sales organizations. A sales representative was hired to market the aircraft. The plane was later sold for $71,000 to an aircraft broker, who in turn resold it for $123,000 after spending $33,000 on modifications. Because the price obtained on the sale of the plane was about $75,000 less than the amount Jones and Percell owed the bank, the bank initiated a lawsuit to obtain the amount of the deficiency. Can Jones and Percell object to the bank's manner of resale? Why or why not? [*Jones v. Bank of Nevada*, 91 Nev. 368, 535 P.2d 1279 (1975)]

**31–7. Sale of Collateral.** Calcote obtained an automobile loan from Citizens & Southern National Bank, with the bank maintaining a security interest in the car. On March 28, 1984, after Calcote had defaulted on the loan, the bank repossessed the vehicle. On the following day, the bank sent a certified letter, return receipt requested, to Calcote informing her of the repossession, of the bank's plans to sell the auto at a private sale in May 1984, and of her right to demand a public sale of the vehicle. Although the letter was sent to the address on the bank's records and at which the bank had repossessed the car, Calcote never received the letter. On April 19, 1984, it was returned to the bank stamped "unclaimed." On May 11, 1984, the car was sold at a private sale to which over 150 dealers had been invited. When Calcote learned that the car had been sold, she brought an action against the bank, claiming that she had not been properly notified of the repossession and sale and that the private sale was not a commercially

reasonable method of disposition. Was sufficient notice given to Calcote, and was the private sale commercially reasonable? [*Calcote v. Citizens & Southern National Bank*, 179 Ga.App. 132, 345 S.E.2d 616 (1986)]

**31–8. Priority Disputes.** For several years, Hugh Meyer had financial dealings with the First National Bank of Midland. On one occasion, Meyer delivered some stock certificates to the bank as security for a loan. The security agreement defined the collateral to include any "profits, interest and income from the listed property." Although the securities were in the bank's possession, the bank never registered the stock in its name, nor did it take other steps to ensure that any stock dividends would be sent to the bank instead of to Meyer. Meyer eventually received a stock dividend of $500,000 and turned over the dividend to his law firm as security for a debt he owed to the firm for legal services. Meyer went bankrupt, and the bank's successor, the Federal Deposit Insurance Corp., laid claim to the $500,000 as a perfected secured creditor. The law firm claimed that it, and not the bank, had a perfected security interest in the dividend because the dividend was in the law firm's possession. Which party had a perfected security interest in the $500,000 dividend? [*Federal Deposit Insurance Corp. v. W. Hugh Meyer & Associates, Inc.*, 864 F.2d 371 (5th Cir. 1989)]

**31–9. Oral Security Agreements.** John and Melody Fish bought various pieces of expensive jewelry, including a diamond ring, a diamond necklace, and a wedding band, from Odom's Jewelers. The Fishes agreed to make monthly installment payments to Odom's until the purchase price was paid in full. In 1988, the Fishes fell behind in their monthly payments on the account. The Fishes and Odom's orally agreed that the Fishes would return the jewelry to Odom's and that Odom's would hold the items for the Fishes until the account was paid. In 1991, the Fishes filed for bankruptcy protection. The jewelry was still in the possession of Odom's. One of the issues before the bankruptcy court was whether Odom's had a security interest in the jewelry. Did it? Explain. [*In re Fish*, 128 Bankr. 468 (N.D.Okla. 1991)]

**31–10. Purchase-Money Security Interest.** Barbara Wiegert and her daughter, Darcie Wiegert, went shopping at Sears, and Darcie bought a mattress and box spring for $396.11. Barbara later purchased from Sears a television set for $239.96. Both purchases of consumer goods were charged to the credit card of Barbara (and her husband, Harold). On both credit slips was printed the following statement: "I grant Sears a security interest or lien in this merchandise, unless prohibited by law, until paid in full." When the Wiegerts filed their bankruptcy petition, the balance due to Sears was $587.26, plus interest. The Wiegerts claimed that Sears was an unsecured creditor. Sears claimed that it was a secured creditor, arguing that the sales slip contained all of the information needed for a valid security agreement under UCC 9–203: (1) a description of the goods, (2) the signature of the debtor, and (3) language indicating that the debtor was granting Sears a security interest in the goods being purchased on credit. Sears further argued that it did not need to file a financing statement to perfect its security interest because UCC 9–302(1)(d) allows for automatic perfection for a purchase-money security interest in consumer goods. Was Sears correct in making these claims? Discuss fully. [*In the Matter of Wiegert,* 145 Bankr. 621 (D.Neb. 1991)]

**31–11. Perfection.** Richard E. Walker, Kelly E. Walker, and Kenneth W. Walker were partners in the Walker Brothers Dairy, a general partnership located in Florida. The Walkers purchased a "Model 2955 utility tractor, a round bale saw, and a feed mixer box" from the John Deere Company. John Deere took a security interest in the equipment. The security agreement stated that the debtor was a partnership known as "Walker Brothers Dairy." John Deere filed a financing statement, however, that listed the debtors as "Richard Walker, Kelly Walker, and Kenneth Wendell Walker." The statement was signed by each of the three partners. Their signatures were followed by a typewritten statement indicating that the partners were doing business as "Walker Brothers Dairy." When Walker Brothers Dairy voluntarily filed for bankruptcy, John Deere sought to repossess the equipment. The issue before the court was whether the financing statement, which listed the partners as debtors rather than the partnership, was sufficient to perfect John Deere's security interest in the partnership equipment. What should the court decide? Discuss. [*In re Walker,* 142 Bankr. 482 (M.D.Fla. 1992)]

### 31–12. A Question of Ethics

 *Raymond and Joan Massengill borrowed money from Indiana National Bank (INB) to purchase a van. Toward the end of the loan period, the Massengills were notified by mail that they were delinquent on their last two loan pay-*

*ments. Joan called INB on a Saturday and said that she did not agree with the amount that INB said was due. It was arranged that the Massengills would go to the bank the following Monday morning and take care of the matter. In the meantime, INB had made arrangements for the van to be repossessed. At 1:30 A.M. Sunday morning, two men appeared at the Massengills' driveway and began to hook up the van to a tow truck. Raymond, assuming that the van was being stolen, went outside to intervene and did so vociferously. During the course of events, Massengill became entangled in machinery at the rear of the tow truck and was dragged down the street and then run over by his towed van. The "repo men"—those hired by INB to repossess the van—knew of Raymond's plight but sped away. The trial court granted summary judgment for the bank, ruling that the bank was not liable for the injuries caused by the repossession company. On appeal, however, the court ruled that the bank could be liable for the acts of the repossession company and remanded the case for the determination of damages. [Massengill v. Indiana National Bank, 550 N.E.2d 97 (Ind.App.1st Dist. 1990)]*

1. Frequently, courts must decide, as in this case, whether the creditor should be held liable for the wrongful acts of persons hired by the creditor to undertake the actual repossession effort. Is it fair to hold the creditor liable for acts that the creditor did not commit? Why or why not?

2. Given the potential for violence during repossession efforts, why do you think Article 9 permits creditors to resort to "self-help" repossessions?

3. Should repossession companies be prohibited from taking collateral from debtors' property during the middle of the night, when debtors are more likely to conclude that the activity is wrongful?

# CHAPTER 32

# OTHER CREDITORS' REMEDIES AND SURETYSHIP

T he law governing debtor-creditor relations has undergone various changes over the years. Historically, debtors and their families have been subjected to punishment, including involuntary servitude and imprisonment, for their inability to pay debts. The modern legal system has moved away from a punishment philosophy in dealing with debtors. In fact, many observers say that it has moved too far in the other direction, to the detriment of creditors. Today, consumer protection is emphasized, and the legal system is designed to aid and protect the debtor and the debtor's family. Nonetheless, creditors continue to have numerous remedies available to them.

## SECTION 1

## LAWS ASSISTING CREDITORS

As pointed out in Chapter 31, if a debtor defaults, a secured creditor's priority can determine whether the creditor recoups complete, partial, or no payment of amounts he or she is owed. Creditors with no priority are paid last, of course—if at all.

A perfected security interest, in the case of personal property, or a mortgage, in the case of real estate, may be referred to as a *consensual lien*. A **lien** is a claim or charge on a debtor's property that must be satisfied before the property (or its proceeds) is available to satisfy the claims of other creditors. Referring to the lien as *consensual* indicates that its basis is the parties' agreement. Consensual liens on personal property are the subject of Article 9 of the UCC and were discussed in Chapter 31. Enforcing payment under a consensual lien on real estate is discussed later in this chapter.

A lien may also arise under a statute or the common law or through a judicial proceeding. Statutory liens include *mechanic's liens*. Liens created at common law include *artisan's liens* and *innkeeper's liens*. Judicial liens include those that represent a creditor's efforts to collect on a debt before a judgment (for example, through *prejudgment attachment*) or after it (for example, through a *writ of execution*). These terms are defined in the discussion of remedies that follows.

It is important to remember that a lien creditor has priority only to the extent of the value of his or her collateral. To illustrate, imagine that McInerney owns property worth $100,000, including a cache of furs worth $40,000. McInerney owes Bret $40,000, Easton $50,000, and Ellis $60,000. Bret has a lien on the furs. On McInerney's default, Bret has the first right to the furs or the proceeds from their sale. If the furs turned out to be worth only $20,000, Bret's claim for the other $20,000 would have no greater priority than the claims of Easton and Ellis.

Generally, a lien creditor has priority over an unperfected security interest but not over a perfected security interest. Thus, a person who becomes a lien creditor before another security interest in the same property is perfected has priority, but one who acquires the lien after perfection does not have priority. Mechanic's and artisan's liens, however, have priority over perfected security interests unless a statute provides otherwise. These types of liens are discussed below.

## MECHANIC'S LIEN

When a person contracts for labor, services, or material to be furnished for the purpose of making improvements on real property but does not immediately pay for the improvements, the creditor can place a **mechanic's lien** on the property. This creates a special type of debtor-creditor relationship in which the real estate itself becomes security for the debt.

For example, a painter agrees to paint a house for a homeowner for an agreed-upon price to cover labor and materials. If the homeowner cannot pay or pays only a portion of the charges, a mechanic's lien against the property can be created. The painter is the lienholder, and the real property is encumbered with a mechanic's lien for the amount owed. If the homeowner does not pay the lien, the property can be sold to satisfy the debt. Notice of the foreclosure and sale must be given to the debtor in advance, however.

The procedures by which a mechanic's lien is created are controlled by state law. Generally, the lienholder must file a written notice of lien against the particular property involved. The notice of lien must be filed within a specific time period, measured from the last date on which materials or labor were provided (usually within 60 to 120 days). Failure to pay the debt entitles the lienholder to foreclose on the real estate on which the improvements were made and to sell it to satisfy the amount of the debt. Of course, the lienholder is required by statute to give notice to the owner of the property prior to foreclosure and sale. The sale proceeds are used to pay the debt and the costs of the legal proceedings; the surplus, if any, is paid to the former owner.

At issue in the following case was whether a party who performed engineering work, but who was not licensed as an engineer, could enforce a mechanic's lien.

| CASE 32.1 |
| --- |
| **MIDWEST ENVIRONMENTAL CONSULTING & REMEDIATION SERVICES, INC. v. PEOPLES BANK OF BLOOMINGTON**<br>Appellate Court of Illinois, Fourth District, 1993.<br>251 Ill.App.3d 256,<br>620 N.E.2d 469,<br>189 Ill.Dec. 501. |

**COMPANY PROFILE** *During the Great Depression, many banks suffered huge losses on their investments and, with depositors lining up to withdraw all of their funds, were forced to close. To take over some of the assets of two closed Detroit banks, the National Bank of Detroit was organized with help from General Motors Corporation in 1933. Forty years later, the National Bank of Detroit merged with Detroit National Bank. The new company called itself National Bank of Detroit until 1990, when it changed to NBD Bank, N.A. NBD is the largest bank in Michigan and the leader in a five-state system of eighteen bank subsidiaries owned by NBD Bancorp, Inc., which has offices in London, Frankfurt, Tokyo, Australia, Canada, and Hong Kong, and an offshore banking facility in Nassau, Bahamas. NBD Bancorp became the sixteenth largest U.S. banking company in 1992, when it merged NBD Indiana, Inc., one of its subsidiaries, with INB Financial Corporation, Indiana's leading banking* *company. Headquartered in Indianapolis, INB operated 130 offices through six banks, the oldest of which was founded in 1834. Originally named Commerce America Banking Company, which was formed in a merger between Citizens Bank and Trust Company of Jeffersonville, Indiana, and Clark County State Bank in 1984, INB had expanded into Illinois in 1990 by acquiring Peoples Mid-Illinois Corporation. Organized in 1972, the principal asset of Peoples had been Peoples Bank of Bloomington.*

**BACKGROUND AND FACTS**   *Allan Green worked for an Illinois engineering firm, Lewis, Yockey, and Brown (LYB), as an environmental engineer and project manager. Green was not, however, licensed as an engineer in Illinois. In October 1991, Green performed engineering work on a subsurface investigation for Snyder Development, Inc., concerning property on which a gas station had been located in Bloomington, Illinois. Snyder wanted to sell the property. Green discovered that the soil was contaminated and told Snyder that according to the regulations of the Illinois Environmental Protection Agency (IEPA), the contamination would have to be removed. Green left LYB in November to form his own company—Midwest Environmental Consulting & Remediation Services, Inc. At the end of November, Snyder asked Green if he would provide engineering services with regard to the clean-up. Green agreed. Midwest removed the contaminated soil according to IEPA specifications, but Snyder failed to pay for the removal. Midwest (Green) brought an action against Snyder and its bank, the Peoples Bank of Bloomington, to foreclose on the property on the basis of its filed mechanic's lien. The trial court issued a judgment that included an award of more than $40,000 in Midwest's favor, and the defendants appealed. Among the issues on appeal was whether Midwest could assert a mechanic's lien given the fact that Green was not licensed as an engineer in Illinois.*

Justice *McCULLOUGH* delivered the opinion of the court:

\*   \*   \*   \*

\*   \*   \* The persons entitled to a mechanic's lien are defined in section 1 of the [Illinois Mechanics Lien] Act. That statute states in part: ''Any person who shall by any contract or contracts, express or implied, or partly expressed or implied, with the owner of a lot or tract of land, or with one whom the owner has authorized or knowingly permitted to contract, to improve the lot or tract of land or to manage a structure thereon \*   \*   \* or perform any services or incur any expense as an architect, structural engineer, professional engineer, land surveyor or property manager in, for or on a lot or tract of land for any such purpose; \*   \*   \* is known under this Act as a contractor, and has a lien upon the whole of such lot or tract of land and upon adjoining or adjacent lots or tracts of land of such owner constituting the same premises and occupied or used in connection with such lot or tract of land as a place of residence or business \*   \*   \* . This lien attaches as of the date of the contract.''

Contrary to defendant's position, plaintiff need not be an architect, structural engineer, professional engineer, land surveyor, or property manager to assert a mechanic's lien. Any person who does improvement work on the land under a contract with the owner can assert a mechanic's lien.

\*   \*   \*   \*

\*   \*   \* [T]he contract was not illegal. Nor has defendant proved that, in order to do the job, Green must have been a licensed professional engineer. When defendant began dealing with Green, he was an employee of another engineering firm, Lewis,

Yockey, and Brown (LYB). It was at this time that Green made the original estimates. Defendant does not complain that LYB was not licensed in Illinois. Nor has defendant presented any evidence suggesting that only an engineer can enter into a contract to remove contaminated soil from the site of a former gasoline service station.

**DECISION AND REMEDY**    *The appellate court affirmed the judgment of the trial court but reduced the award by 15 percent to reflect a markup to which Snyder had not agreed in the contract.*

## ARTISAN'S LIEN

An **artisan's lien** is a security device created at common law through which a creditor can recover payment from a debtor for labor and materials furnished in the repair of personal property. For example, Whitney leaves her diamond ring at the jewelry shop to be repaired and to have her initials engraved on the band. In the absence of an agreement, the jeweler can keep the ring until Whitney pays for the services that the jeweler provides. Should Whitney fail to pay, the jeweler has a lien on Whitney's ring for the amount of the bill and can sell the ring in satisfaction of the lien.

In contrast to a mechanic's lien, an artisan's lien is *possessory*. The lienholder ordinarily must have retained possession of the property and have expressly or impliedly agreed to provide the services on a cash, not a credit, basis. Usually, the lienholder retains possession of the property. When this occurs, the lien remains in existence as long as the lienholder maintains possession, and the lien is terminated once possession is voluntarily surrendered—unless the surrender is only temporary. If it is a temporary surrender, there must be an agreement that the property will be returned to the lienholder. Even with such an agreement, if a third party obtains rights in that property while it is out of the possession of the lienholder, the lien is lost. The only way that a lienholder can protect a lien and surrender possession at the same time is to record notice of the lien in accordance with state lien and recording statutes.

The artisan's lien has priority over a filed statutory lien, such as a title lien on an automobile or a lien filed under Article 9 of the UCC. This may not be true for a bailee's lien (such as a storage lien), however.

Modern statutes permit the holder of an artisan's lien to foreclose and sell the property subject to the lien to satisfy payment of the debt. As with the mechanic's lien, the lienholder is required to give notice to the owner of the property prior to foreclosure and sale. In some states, holders of artisan's liens must give notice to title lienholders of automobiles prior to foreclosure. The sale proceeds are used to pay the debt and the costs of the legal proceedings, and the surplus, if any, is paid to the former owner.

Can towing and storage services give rise to an artisan's lien? The court deals with this issue in the following case.

---

CASE 32.2

**CHRYSLER CREDIT CORP. v. KEELING**

Missouri Court of Appeals, 1990.
793 S.W.2d 222.

**BACKGROUND AND FACTS** *Chrysler Credit Corporation had a perfected security interest in a 1988 Dodge pickup that had been purchased by Robert Keeling. When Keeling defaulted on his payments, Chrysler attempted to repossess the vehicle but could not locate it for some time. Finally, the pickup was found in a lot operated by Joe Booth, doing business as Highway Tow Service. Booth had towed the pickup from an apartment complex parking lot to Booth's lot at the request of the apartment manager and had stored the pickup on his auto lot for over two months. Chrysler requested Booth to deliver possession of the car to Chrysler, but Booth refused to do so until he was paid for the towing ($50) and storage ($1,235) services. Chrysler then sued Booth to gain possession of the pickup. Booth contended that he had an artisan's lien on the truck and that under Missouri law, the common law artisan's lien took priority over*

*Chrysler's perfected security interest. The trial court held for Chrysler, and Booth appealed.*

*TURNAGE,* Presiding Judge.
    \*   \*   \*   \*

Booth is correct that the common law artisan's lien has not been abrogated by statute as held by this court in [a previous case]. The difficulty with Booth's contention is that the artisan's lien is only for one who furnishes labor or materials in the repair of a vehicle. Here, Booth makes no claim that he furnished labor or materials for the repair of the pickup. He makes some claim that towing the vehicle constituted a basis for an artisan's lien, but it is apparent that *towing a vehicle does not constitute the furnishing of labor or materials for the repair of a vehicle.* [Emphasis added.] Under the facts here Booth did not have a common law artisan's lien.

Booth's claim is for towing and storage. At common law there was no lien for storage. Thus, Booth did not have a common law lien for storage.

What Booth did have was a statutory lien for storage under [Section] 430.020 [a Missouri statute] which provides that every person who stores any vehicle shall have a lien for the amount due. Section 430.040.1 provides that no person shall have the right to take any vehicle out of the possession of any person who has a storage lien without paying the amount lawfully due.

Booth conveniently overlooks [Section] 430.040.2 which provides that a storage lien shall not take precedence over or be superior to any prior lien duly perfected in accordance with the laws of this state without the written consent of the holder of such prior lien.

*The appellate court affirmed the trial court's holding that Chrysler was entitled to possession of the pickup. Although under Missouri law, an artisan's lien would be superior to a duly perfected security interest, such as Chryler's, Booth did not have an artisan's lien, because he had furnished no labor or materials for the repair of the vehicle.*

**DECISION
AND REMEDY**

## INNKEEPER'S LIEN

An **innkeeper's lien** is another security device created at common law. An innkeeper's lien is placed on the baggage of guests for the agreed-upon hotel charges that remain unpaid. If no express agreement has been made on the amount of those charges, then the lien will be for the reasonable value of the accommodations furnished. The innkeeper's lien is terminated either by the guest's payment of the hotel charges or by the innkeeper's surrender of the baggage to the guest, unless the surrender is temporary. Most state statutes permit the innkeeper to satisfy the debt by means of a public sale of the guest's baggage. There is a trend toward requiring that the guest first be given an impartial judicial hearing.[1]

## JUDICIAL LIENS

A debt must be past due before a creditor can commence legal action against a debtor. Once legal action is brought, the debtor's property may be seized to satisfy the debt. If the property is seized prior to trial proceedings, the seizure is referred to as an *attachment* of the property. The seizure may also occur following a court judgment in the creditor's favor. In that case, the court's order to seize the property is referred to as a *writ of execution.*

**ATTACHMENT** *Attachment* under Article 9 of the UCC, as discussed in Chapter 31, refers to the process through which a security interest becomes enforceable against a debtor with respect to the debtor's collateral [UCC 9–203]. In the present context, **attachment** refers to a court-ordered seizure and taking into custody of property prior to the securing of a judgment for a past-due debt.

---

1. *Klim v. Jones,* 315 F.Supp. 109 (N.D.Cal. 1970).

Attachment rights are created by state statutes. Normally a *prejudgment* remedy, attachment occurs either at the time of or immediately after the commencement of a lawsuit and before the entry of a final judgment. By statute, the restrictions and requirements for a creditor to attach before judgment are specific and limited. The due process clause of the Fourteenth Amendment to the Constitution limits the courts' power to authorize seizure of a debtor's property without notice to the debtor or a hearing on the facts. In recent years, a number of state attachment laws have been held to be unconstitutional.

To use attachment as a remedy, the creditor must have an enforceable right to payment of the debt under law, and the creditor must follow certain procedures. Otherwise, the creditor can be liable for damages for wrongful attachment. He or she must file with the court an **affidavit** (a written or printed statement, made under oath or sworn to) stating that the debtor is in default and stating the

statutory grounds under which attachment is sought. A bond must be posted by the creditor to cover at least court costs, the value of the loss of use of the good suffered by the debtor, and the value of the property attached. When the court is satisfied that all the requirements have been met, it issues a **writ of attachment,** which is similar to a writ of execution (to be discussed shortly) in that it directs the sheriff or other officer to seize nonexempt property. If the creditor prevails at trial, the seized property can be sold to satisfy the judgment.

As the following case illustrates, strict compliance with every specific procedure established by the state's attachment statute is required for the property to be subject to an enforceable writ of attachment. Exact compliance with state law is required because a writ of attachment operates against a debtor's property simply on the strength of the creditor's sworn statement that a debt is owed.

## CASE 32.3

### TOPJIAN PLUMBING AND HEATING, INC. v. BRUCE TOPJIAN, INC.

Supreme Court of New Hampshire, 1987.
129 N.H. 481,
529 A.2d 391.

**BACKGROUND AND FACTS**  *Topjian Plumbing and Heating, Inc., the plaintiff, sought prejudgment writs of attachment to satisfy an anticipated judgment in a contract action against Bruce Topjian, Inc., the defendant. Topjian Plumbing did not petition the court for permission to effect the attachments but merely completed the forms, served them on the defendant and on the Fencers (the owners of a parcel of land that had previously belonged to the defendant), and recorded them at the registry of deeds. The Fencers objected to the attachment of their property, and in the course of the hearing on their objection, the superior court invalidated all of the attachments, holding that they were not in compliance with the New Hampshire prejudgment attachment statute as stated in Revised Statutes Annotated (RSA) Section 511-A:8. This statute requires application to the court for an order to attach property. Topjian Plumbing appealed.*

*THAYER,* Justice.
\* \* \* \*

The superior court invalidated the plaintiff's attachments because of the plaintiff's failure to petition the court for permission to attach the property prior to serving the attachments on the defendants and recording them at the registry of deeds. RSA 511-A:8 clearly requires that application must be made to the court for an order authorizing an *ex parte* [a hearing at which the defendant is not required to be present] prejudgment attachment, "[t]he purpose of [which] is to obtain security for the payment of a plaintiff's judgment should [plaintiff] prevail."
\* \* \* \*

In 1984, this court, interpreting RSA chapter 511-A, determined that the standard requirements of due process, such as notice and hearing, must be adhered to before property interests can be encumbered by a pre-judgment attachment. [T]he proper procedure for obtaining an *ex parte* attachment is for the plaintiff to petition the court for permission to obtain an *ex parte* attachment order before serving the attachment on the defendant and recording it at the registry of deeds.

Furthermore, the Superior Court Rules pertaining to *ex parte* pre-judgment attachments require plaintiffs to petition the court for permission to attach the property prior to service or entry of any writ of summons or other pleading.

*The Supreme Court of New Hampshire affirmed the decision of the lower court, holding that the attachments were invalid because the plaintiff had failed to comply with the attachment statute.*

**DECISION AND REMEDY**

**Fair Procedures and International Enforcement of Attachments** *In general, a U.S. court will give full effect to a foreign judgment and enforce the judgment in an action to attach assets in the United States. The judgment will not be enforced, however, if the procedures underlying the foreign judgment seem too unfair. For example, in one case, a U.S. court refused to enforce a pretrial judgment of a Spanish court. The U.S. court refused to "tie up all the assets of an enterprise in Illinois" because the Spanish defendant had no opportunity to appear before the Spanish court to contest the order.*[a]

**INTERNATIONAL CONSIDERATIONS**

a.  *Cerezo v. Babson Brothers Co.,* No. 91 C 7622, 1992 WL 18875 (N.D.Ill. 1992).

---

**WRIT OF EXECUTION**    If a creditor is successful in a legal action against a debtor, the court awards the creditor a judgment against the debtor (usually for the amount of the debt plus any interest and legal costs incurred in obtaining the judgment). Frequently, the creditor finds it easy to secure a judgment against the debtor but nevertheless fails to collect the awarded amount. If the debtor will not or cannot pay the judgment, the creditor is entitled to go back to the court and obtain a **writ of execution,** which is an order, usually issued by the clerk of the court, directing the sheriff to seize (levy) and sell any of the debtor's nonexempt real or personal property that is within the court's geographical jurisdiction (usually the county in which the courthouse is located). The proceeds of the sale are used to pay off the judgment and the costs of the sale. Any excess is paid to the debtor. The debtor can pay the judgment and redeem the nonexempt property any time before the sale takes place. Because of exemption laws (which cover the debtor's homestead and designated items of personal property) and bankruptcy laws, however, many judgments are virtually uncollectible.

## GARNISHMENT

An order for **garnishment** permits a creditor to collect a debt by seizing property of the debtor (such as wages or money in a bank account) that is being held by a third party (such as an employer or a bank). Typically, a garnishment judgment is served on a debtor's employer so that part of the debtor's usual paycheck will be paid to the creditor.

The legal proceeding for a garnishment action is governed by state law. As a result of a garnishment proceeding, a third party (such as the debtor's employer) is ordered by the court to turn over property owned by the debtor (such as wages) to pay the debt. Garnishment operates differently from state to state, however. According to the laws in some states, the judgment creditor needs to obtain only one order of garnishment, which will then continuously apply to the judgment debtor's weekly wages until the entire debt is paid. In other states, the judgment creditor must go back to court for a separate order of garnishment for each pay period.

Both federal laws and state laws limit the amount of money that can be garnisheed from a debtor's weekly take-home pay.[2] Federal law provides a minimal framework to protect debtors from losing all their income in order to pay judgment

---

2.  A few states (for example, Texas) do not permit garnishment of wages by private parties except under a child-support order.

debts.[3] State laws also provide dollar exemptions, and these amounts are often larger than those provided by federal law. State and federal statutes can be applied together to help create a pool of funds sufficient to enable a debtor to continue to provide for family needs while also reducing the amount of the judgment debt in a reasonable way.

Under federal law, garnishment of an employee's wages for any one indebtedness cannot be grounds for dismissal of an employee. But what if the employee is dismissed after the employer learns of the garnishment proceeding but before any wages are actually garnished? Does the law prohibiting dismissal for any one garnishment proceeding apply in such a situation? The court addresses this issue in the following case.

---

3. For example, the federal Consumer Credit Protection Act of 1968, 15 U.S.C. Sections 1601–1693, provides that a debtor can retain either 75 percent of the disposable earnings per week or the sum equivalent to thirty hours of work paid at federal minimum wage rates, whichever is greater.

---

| CASE 32.4 |
| :---: |

**JOHNSON v. TOWN OF TRAIL CREEK**

United States District Court, Northern District of Indiana, 1991.
771 F.Supp. 271.

**BACKGROUND AND FACTS**  *John Johnson worked for the street department of the Town of Trail Creek. In August 1989, Trail Creek received notice from a court that one of Johnson's creditors had received a court judgment against Johnson for an unpaid debt. The notice also stated that Johnson's wages would be subject to garnishment, pending a determination of whether Trail Creek owed any obligations or credits (for example, wages) to Johnson that could be garnished. Johnson was fired two days after this notice was received. Johnson brought an action against the town, the president of the town council, and the superintendent of the town's street department (the defendants), alleging, among other things, that the defendants had violated federal law because he was dismissed as a result of the notice of possible garnishment. The defendants moved to dismiss Johnson's complaint on the ground that they could not have violated the law, because Johnson's wages were not actually being withheld at the time of his discharge—in other words, no garnishment proceeding had yet occurred.*

*MILLER*, District Judge.

\* \* \* \*

15 U.S.C. [Section] 1674(a) provides, ''No employer may discharge any employee by reason of the fact that his earnings have been subjected to garnishment for any one indebtedness.'' 15 U.S.C. [Section] 1672(c) defines ''garnishment'' as meaning ''any legal or equitable procedure through which the earnings of any individual are required to be withheld for payment of any debt.''

Indiana's procedure for garnishment of wages consists of two steps. First, upon the filing of a verified motion by the judgment creditor, the employer is required to answer interrogatories or appear at a hearing to disclose whether it has an obligation owing to the judgment debtor \* \* \*. If the employer is found to have an obligation owing to the judgment debtor-employee, the court may order the payment of [the] obligation to the judgment-creditor. Thus, the judgment creditor's filing of the verified motion and the state court's order to Trail Creek were part of a garnishment: legal procedure through which Mr. Johnson's earnings were required to be withheld for a debt.

\* \* \* \*

If the defendants discharged Mr. Johnson by reason of the garnishment proceedings embodied by the [court's] order, they may be found to have deprived Mr. Johnson of his rights under 15 U.S.C. [Section] 1674(a).

**DECISION AND REMEDY**  *The court denied Trail Creek's motion to dismiss the complaint.*

*Clearly, the defense against Johnson's claim was a technical defense that violated the "spirit" (as well as the "letter") of 15 U.S.C. Section 1674(a). But before judging too harshly the defendants' attempts to evade the law, consider the effect of garnishment proceedings on employers. Compliance by employers with garnishment procedures (appearing at a court hearing, filing the appropriate documents, establishing and maintaining records relating to the garnishment, and so on) requires time. For employers, time is a costly resource, and garnishment proceedings are burdensome for employers because they are not compensated for these time costs. When considering these costs and the fact that an employer is an innocent third party caught in the middle of a creditor-debtor dispute, it should come as no surprise that the employer would want to avoid the hassle of garnishment if at all possible.*

**ETHICAL CONSIDERATIONS**

## CREDITORS' COMPOSITION AGREEMENTS

Creditors may contract with the debtor for discharge of the debtor's liquidated debts (debts that are definite, or fixed, in amount) upon payment of a sum less than that owed. These agreements are called *composition agreements* or **creditors' composition agreements** and, unless they are formed under duress, are usually held to be enforceable.

## MORTGAGE FORECLOSURE

Mortgage holders have the right to *foreclose* on mortgaged property in the event of a debtor's default. The usual method of foreclosure is by judicial sale of the property, although the statutory methods of foreclosure vary from state to state. If the proceeds of the foreclosure sale are sufficient to cover both the costs of the foreclosure and the mortgaged debt, any surplus is received by the debtor. If the sale proceeds are insufficient to cover the foreclosure costs and the mortgaged debt, however, the **mortgagee** (the creditor-lender) can seek to recover the difference from the **mortgagor** (the debtor) by obtaining a *deficiency judgment* representing the difference between the mortgaged debt plus foreclosure costs and the amount actually received from the proceeds of the foreclosure sale. A deficiency judgment is obtained in a separate legal action that is pursued subsequent to the foreclosure action. It entitles the creditor to recover from other property owned by the debtor. Some

states do not permit deficiency judgments for some types of real estate interests.

Before the foreclosure sale, a defaulting mortgagor can redeem the property by paying the full amount of the debt, plus any interest and costs that have accrued. This right is known as the **equity of redemption.** In some states, a mortgagor may even redeem the property within a certain period of time—called a **statutory period of redemption**—after the sale. In these states, the deed to the property is not usually delivered to the purchaser until the statutory period has expired.

## ASSIGNMENT FOR BENEFIT OF CREDITORS

Both common law and statutes may provide for a debtor's assignment of assets to a trustee or assignee for the benefit of the debtor's creditors. In these situations, that debtor voluntarily transfers title to assets owned to a trustee or assignee, who in turn sells or liquidates these assets, tendering payment to the debtor's creditors on a *pro rata* (proportionate) basis. Each creditor may accept the tender (and discharge the debt owed to him or her) or reject it (and attempt to collect the debt in another way).

The flexibility and informality of an assignment for the benefit of creditors may save creditors time and expense and result in better prices when a debtor's property is liquidated. Nevertheless, creditors may decide that this option does not adequately protect their rights. Under the bankruptcy laws, creditors of a certain number with a certain amount

## ■ CONCEPT SUMMARY 32.1 Remedies Available to Creditors

| REMEDY | DEFINITION |
|---|---|
| Mechanic's Lien | A nonpossessory, filed lien on an owner's real estate for labor, services, or materials furnished to or made on the realty. |
| Artisan's or Innkeeper's Lien | A possessory lien on an owner's personal property for labor performed, value added, or care of the personal property (in many states) for which no payment was received or credit extended. |
| Attachment | A court-ordered seizure of property (generally prior to full resolution of the creditor's rights resulting in judgment). Attachment is available only upon posting of bond and in strict compliance with the applicable state statutes. |
| Writ of Execution | In cases of unsatisfied judgments, a court order directing the sheriff or other officer to seize and sell sufficient nonexempt property of the judgment debtor to satisfy the judgment. |
| Garnishment | A collection remedy that allows the creditor to attach a debtor's money (such as wages owed or bank accounts) or other property that is held by a third party. |
| Creditors' Composition Agreement | A contract between the debtor and creditors whereby the debtor's debts are discharged by payment of a sum less than that owed in the original debt. |
| Mortgage Foreclosure | The creditor's selling or taking title to realty to satisfy the mortgage debt upon the debtor's default on the mortgage payments. |
| Assignment for Benefit of Creditors | The debtor's assignment of certain assets to a trustee or assignee, who sells or liquidates these assets and tenders payments to creditors on a *pro rata* basis. Acceptance of this payment by a creditor is discharge of the debt. |

of claims may have administration of the debtor's property transferred to the bankruptcy court—in other words, force the debtor into involuntary bankruptcy (see Chapter 33). Thus, a debtor's bankruptcy may supersede assignment for the benefit of creditors—even if the bankruptcy is initiated by creditors.

## ■ SECTION 2

# SURETYSHIP AND GUARANTY

When a third person promises to pay a debt owed by another in the event the debtor does not pay, either a *suretyship* or a *guaranty* relationship is created. Exhibit 32–1 illustrates these relationships. The third person's credit becomes the security for the debt owed.

## SURETYSHIP

A contract of strict **suretyship** is a promise made by a third person to be responsible for the debtor's obligation. It is an express contract between the **surety** and the creditor. The surety in the strictest sense is *primarily* liable for the debt of the principal. The creditor can demand payment from the surety from the moment that the debt is due. A suretyship contract is not a form of indemnity; that is, it is not merely a promise to make good any loss that a creditor may incur as a result of the debtor's failure to pay. The creditor need not exhaust all legal remedies against the principal debtor before holding the surety responsible for payment. Moreover, a surety agreement does not have to be in writing to be enforceable, although usually such agreements are in writing.

For example, Jason Ogger wants to borrow money from the bank to buy a used car. Because Jason is still in college, the bank will not lend him the money unless his father, Stacey Ogger, who

### ■ Exhibit 32–1 Suretyship and Guaranty Parties

In a suretyship or guaranty arrangement, a third party promises to be responsible for a debtor's obligations. A third party who agrees to be responsible for the debt even if the primary debtor does not default is known as a surety; a third party who agrees to be *secondarily* responsible for the debt only if the primary debtor defaults is known as a guarantor. As noted in Chapter 16, normally a promise of guaranty (a collateral, or secondary, promise) must be in writing to be enforceable.

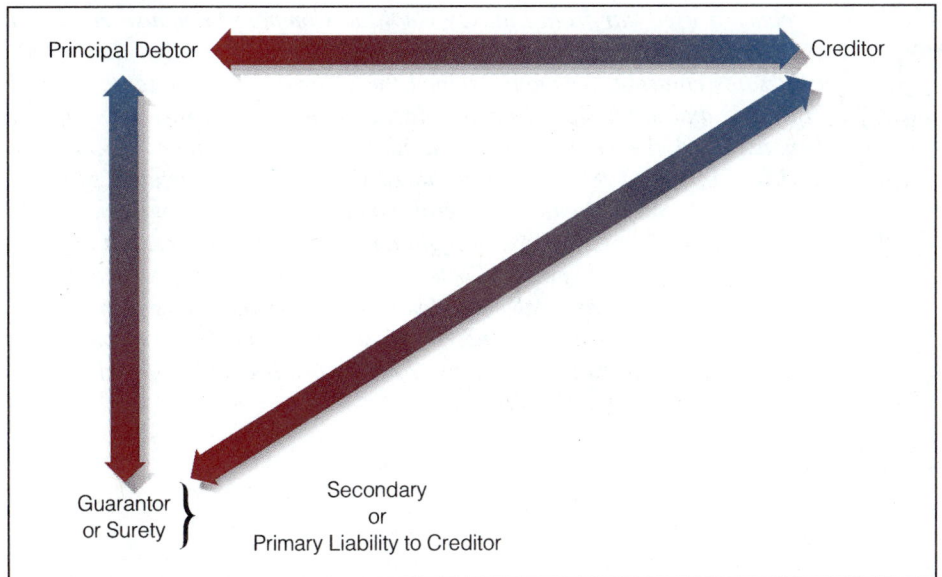

Principal Debtor — Creditor

Guarantor or Surety } Secondary or Primary Liability to Creditor

has dealt with the bank before, will **cosign** the note (add his signature to the note, thereby becoming jointly liable for payment of the debt). When Mr. Ogger cosigns the note, he becomes primarily liable to the bank. On the note's due date, the bank has the option of seeking payment from either Jason or Stacey Ogger, or both jointly.

## GUARANTY

A guaranty contract is similar to a suretyship contract in that it includes a promise to answer for the debt or default of another. With a suretyship arrangement, however, the surety is primarily liable for the debtor's obligation. With a guaranty arrangement, the **guarantor**—the third person making the guaranty—is *secondarily* liable. The guarantor can be required to pay the obligation only after the principal debtor defaults, and usually only after the creditor has made an attempt to collect from the debtor.

For example, a closely held corporation, BX Enterprises, needs to borrow money to meet its payroll. The bank is skeptical about the creditworthiness of BX and requires Dawson, its president, who is a wealthy businessperson and owner of 70 percent of BX Enterprises, to sign an agreement making himself personally liable for payment if BX does not pay off the loan. As a guarantor of the loan, Dawson cannot be held liable until BX Enterprises is in default.

The Statute of Frauds requires that a guaranty contract between the guarantor and the creditor must be in writing to be enforceable unless the *main-purpose* exception applies. Briefly, this exception provides that if the main purpose of the guaranty agreement is to benefit the guarantor, then the contract need not be in writing to be enforceable. (See Chapter 16 for a more detailed discussion of this exception.)

The guaranty contract terms determine the extent and time of the guarantor's liability. For example, the guaranty can be *continuing,* designed to cover a series of transactions by the debtor. Also, the guaranty can be *unlimited* or *limited* as to time and amount. In addition, the guaranty can be *absolute,* in which case the guarantor becomes liable immediately upon the debtor's default, or *conditional,* in which case the guarantor becomes liable only upon the happening of a certain event.

In the following case, the defendant claimed that he was a guarantor, not a surety, on a contract for the purchase of an automobile.

CASE 32.5

**GENERAL MOTORS ACCEPTANCE CORP. v. DANIELS**

Court of Appeals of Maryland, 1985.
303 Md. 254,
492 A.2d 1306.

**BACKGROUND AND FACTS** *In June 1981, John Daniels agreed to purchase a used car from Lindsay Cadillac Company. Because John had a poor credit rating, his brother, Seymoure, agreed to cosign the install- ment sales contract. Seymoure signed the contract on the line designated "Buyer," and John signed on the line designated "Co-Buyer." Lindsay then assigned the contract to General Motors Acceptance Corporation (GMAC). In May 1982, GMAC declared the contract in default. After at- tempting to locate the car for several months, GMAC finally found it in a condition of total loss. GMAC brought an action for damages, but because service of process was never effected on John, the action proceeded only against Seymoure. The trial court found that Seymoure was a guarantor of the contract between John and GMAC and held that GMAC would have to attempt to bring suit first against John before it could proceed against Seymoure. GMAC appealed the ruling.*

*COLE,* Judge.
\* \* \* \*

A suretyship and guaranty are contractual agreements. \* \* \* It is well settled that Maryland follows the objective law of contracts. A court construing an agreement under this test must first determine from the language of the agreement itself what a reasonable person in the position of the parties would have meant at the time it was effectuated. In addition, when the language of the contract is plain and unam- biguous there is no room for construction, and a court must presume that the parties meant what they expressed. In these circumstances, the true test of what is meant is not what the parties to the contract intended it to mean, but what a reasonable person in the position of the parties would have thought it meant. \* \* \*
\* \* \* \*

Our review of the evidence in this case convinces us that the District Court erred in finding that Seymoure was a guarantor rather than a surety with respect to the installment contract. \* \* \*

\* \* \* Seymoure agreed to purchase the subject automobile by affixing the signature to the installment sales contract on the line designated "Buyer." The contract clearly stated that all buyers agreed to be jointly and severally [individually] liable for the purchase of that vehicle. Therefore, under the objective law of contracts, a reasonable person knew or should have known that he was subjecting himself to primary liability for the purchase of the automobile. In short, although uncompensated sureties are favorites of the law, Seymoure's careless indifference does not insulate him from primary liability on that agreement.

Seymoure executed the same contract as his brother, thereby making himself a party to the original contract. There is no evidence that Seymoure executed an agreement collateral to and independent of this contract. This fact, standing alone, ordinarily negates the existence of a guaranty. \* \* \*

Both Seymoure and John signed the contract at the same time. \* \* \* [T]his fact tends to establish the existence of a contract of suretyship rather than a contract of guaranty. Furthermore, there are no competent facts indicating that Seymoure expressly agreed to pay for the automobile only upon the default of John.

*The appellate court reversed the lower court's ruling.*

**DECISION
AND REMEDY**

## DEFENSES OF THE SURETY AND THE GUARANTOR

The defenses of the surety and the guarantor are basically the same. Therefore, the following discussion applies to both, although it refers only to the surety.

Certain actions will release the surety from the obligation. For example, making any material modification in the terms of the original contract between the principal debtor and the creditor, including the awarding of a binding extension of time for making payment, without first obtaining the consent of the surety will discharge a gratuitous surety completely and a surety who is compensated to the extent that the surety suffers a loss.

Naturally, if the principal obligation is paid by the debtor or by another person on behalf of the debtor, the surety is discharged from the obligation. Similarly, if valid tender of payment is made, and the creditor for some reason rejects it with knowledge of the surety's existence, then the surety is released from any obligation on the debt.

Generally, any defenses available to a principal debtor can be used by the surety to avoid liability on the obligation to the creditor. Defenses available to the principal debtor that the surety *cannot* use include the principal debtor's incapacity, bankruptcy, and the statute of limitations. The ability of the surety to assert any defenses the debtor may have against the creditor is the most important concept in suretyship, because most of the defenses available to the surety are also those of the debtor.

Obviously, a surety may also have his or her own defenses—for example, incapacity or bankruptcy. If the creditor fraudulently induced the surety to guarantee the debt of the debtor, the surety can assert fraud as a defense. In most states, the creditor has a legal duty to inform the surety, prior to the formation of the suretyship contract, of material facts known by the creditor that would substantially increase the surety's risk. Failure to so inform is fraud and makes the suretyship obligation voidable.

In addition, if a creditor surrenders or impairs the debtor's collateral while knowing of the surety and without the surety's consent, the surety is released to the extent of any loss suffered from the creditor's actions. The primary reason for this is to protect the surety who agreed to become obligated only because the debtor's collateral was in the possession of the creditor.

## RIGHTS OF THE SURETY AND THE GUARANTOR

The rights of the surety and the guarantor are basically the same. Therefore, again, the following discussion applies to both.

When the surety pays the debt owed to the creditor, the surety is entitled to certain rights. First, the surety has the legal **right of subrogation.** Simply stated, this means that any right the creditor had against the debtor now becomes the right of the surety. Included are creditor rights in bankruptcy, rights to collateral possessed by the creditor, and rights to judgments secured by the creditor. In short, the surety now stands in the shoes of the creditor and may pursue any remedies that were available to the creditor against the debtor.

Second, the surety has a right to be reimbursed by the debtor. This **right of reimbursement** may stem either from the suretyship contract or from equity. Basically, the surety is entitled to receive from the debtor all outlays made on behalf of the suretyship arrangement. Such outlays can include expenses incurred, as well as the actual amount of the debt paid to the creditor.

Third, in the case of **co-sureties** (two or more sureties on the same obligation owed by the debtor), a surety who pays more than his or her proportionate share upon a debtor's default is entitled to recover from the co-sureties the amount paid above the surety's obligation. This is the **right of contribution.** Generally, a co-surety's liability either is determined by agreement or, in the absence of agreement, is set at the maximum liability under the suretyship contract.

For example, assume that two co-sureties are obligated under a suretyship contract to guarantee the debt of a debtor. Together, the sureties' maximum liability is $25,000. Surety A's maximum liability is $15,000, and surety B's is $10,000. The debtor owes $10,000 and is in default. Surety A pays the creditor the entire $10,000. In the absence of agreement, surety A can recover $4,000 from surety B ($10,000 ÷ $25,000 x $10,000 = $4,000, surety B's obligation).

## SECTION 3

# PROTECTION FOR DEBTORS

The law protects debtors, as well as creditors. Certain property of the debtor, for example, is exempt from creditors' actions. Consumer protection statutes also protect debtors' rights. Of course, bankruptcy laws, which will be discussed in the next chapter, are designed specifically to assist debtors in need of help.

## EXEMPTIONS

In most states, certain types of real and personal property are exempt from levy of execution or attachment. Probably the most familiar of these exemptions is the **homestead exemption.** Each state permits the debtor to retain the family home, either in its entirety or up to a specified dollar amount, free from the claims of unsecured creditors or trustees in bankruptcy. The purpose is to ensure that the debtor will retain some form of shelter.

Suppose that Beere owes Veltman $40,000. The debt is the subject of a lawsuit, and the court awards Veltman a judgment of $40,000 against Beere. Beere's homestead is valued at $50,000. There are no outstanding mortgages or other liens on his homestead. To satisfy the judgment debt, Beere's family home is sold at public auction for $45,000. Assuming that the homestead exemption is $25,000, the proceeds of the sale are distributed as follows:

1. Beere is given $25,000 as his homestead exemption.

2. Veltman is paid $20,000 toward the judgment debt, leaving a $20,000 deficiency judgment (that is, "leftover debt" ) that can be satisfied from any other nonexempt property (personal or real) that Beere may have, if allowed by state law.

In a few states, statutes permit the homestead exemption only if the judgment debtor has a family. The policy behind this type of statute is to protect the family. If a judgment debtor does not have a family, a creditor may be entitled to collect the full amount realized from the sale of the debtor's home.

State exemption statutes usually include both real and personal property. Personal property that is most often exempt from satisfaction of judgment debts includes the following:

1. Household furniture up to a specified dollar amount.
2. Clothing and certain personal possessions, such as family pictures or a Bible.
3. A vehicle (or vehicles) for transportation (at least up to a specified dollar amount).
4. Certain classified animals, usually livestock but including pets.
5. Equipment that the debtor uses in a business or trade, such as tools or professional instruments, up to a specified dollar amount.

## SPECIAL PROTECTION FOR CONSUMER DEBTORS

Numerous consumer protection statutes and rules apply to the debtor-creditor relationship. We have already discussed the Federal Trade Commission's rule limiting the rights of a holder in due course (HDC) who holds a negotiable promissory note executed by a debtor-buyer as part of a consumer transaction. This rule, discussed in Chapter 27, provides basically that any personal defenses that the buyer can assert against the seller can also be asserted against an HDC. The seller must disclose this information clearly on the sales agreement.

Other laws regulating debtor-creditor relationships include the Truth-in-Lending Act, which protects consumers by requiring creditors to disclose specific types of information when making loans to consumers. This act, along with other consumer protection statutes, will be discussed in Chapter 46.

# TERMS AND CONCEPTS TO REVIEW

affidavit 620
artisan's lien 618
attachment 619
cosign 625
co-surety 627
creditors' composition
   agreement 623
equity of redemption 623
garnishment 621

guarantor 625
homestead exemption 628
innkeeper's lien 619
lien 615
mechanic's lien 616
mortgagee 623
mortgagor 623
right of contribution 627
right of reimbursement 627

right of subrogation 627
statutory period of
   redemption 623
surety 624
suretyship 624
writ of attachment 620
writ of execution 621

# QUESTIONS AND CASE PROBLEMS

**32–1. Liens.** Sylvia takes her car to Crank's Auto Repair Shop. A sign in the window states that all repairs must be paid for in cash unless credit is approved in advance. Sylvia and Crank agree that Crank will repair Sylvia's car engine and put in a new transmission. No mention is made of credit. Because Crank is not sure how much engine repair will be necessary, he refuses to give Sylvia an estimate. He repairs the engine and puts in a new transmission. When Sylvia comes to pick up her car, she learns that the bill is $795. Sylvia is furious, refuses to pay Crank that amount, and demands possession of her car. Crank demands payment. Discuss the rights of the parties in this matter.

**32–2. Creditors' Remedies.** Kanahara is employed by the Cross-Bar Packing Corp. and earns take-home pay of $400 per week. He is $2,000 in debt to the Holiday Department Store for goods purchased on credit over the past eight months. Most of this property is nonexempt and is presently located in Kanahara's apartment. Kanahara is in default on his payments to Holiday. Holiday learns that Kanahara has a girlfriend in another state and that he plans on giving her most of this property for Christmas. Discuss what actions are available and should be taken by Holiday to resolve the debt owed by Kanahara.

**32–3. Guaranty.** Natali is a student at Slippery Stone University. In need of funds to pay for tuition and books, she attempts to secure a short-term loan from West Bank. The bank agrees to make a loan if Natali will have someone financially responsible guarantee the loan payments. Sheila, a well-known businesswoman and a friend of Natali's family, calls the bank and agrees to pay the loan if Natali cannot. Because of Sheila's reputation, the loan is made. Natali is making the payments, but because of illness she is not able to work for one month. She requests that West Bank extend the loan for three months. West Bank agrees, raising the interest rate for the extended period. Sheila is not notified of the extension (and therefore does not consent to it). One month later Natali drops out of school. All attempts to collect from Natali fail. West Bank wants to hold Sheila liable. Discuss West Bank's claim against Natali.

**32–4. Creditors' Remedies.** Iacco is the owner of a relatively old home valued at $45,000. He notices that the bathtubs and fixtures in both bathrooms are leaking and need to be replaced. He contracts with Plumber to replace the bathtubs and fixtures. Plumber replaces them, and on June 1 she submits her bill of $4,000 to Iacco. Because of financial difficulties, Iacco does not pay the bill. Iacco's only asset is his home, which, under state law, is exempt up to $40,000 as a homestead. Discuss fully Plumber's remedies in this situation.

**32–5. Mechanic's Lien.** Kloster-Madsen, Inc., a general contractor, entered into a contract with the owner of a building to do certain remodeling work. About a month later, pursuant to the contract, an electrical subcontractor removed several light fixtures from one of the ceilings, cutting four new holes in the ceiling and placing the removed light fixtures in these holes. Immediately after this work was begun, a new owner, Tafi's, Inc., purchased the building. Material and labor worth several thousand dollars were expended before Tafi's informed the general contractor that it did not wish to have the building remodeled. Discuss whether Kloster-Madsen can impose a mechanic's lien on the building even though it entered into the building contract with a different owner. [*Kloster-Madsen, Inc. v. Tafi's, Inc.*, 303 Minn. 59, 226 N.W.2d 603 (1975)]

**32–6. Garnishment.** Harmony Unlimited, Inc., obtained a judgment against John Chivetta and his company, JMC Enterprises. At the time of the judgment, John lacked sufficient funds to pay. Just before Harmony obtained the judgment, John had transferred $126,000 to his mother, Nettie, who had signed a promissory note. The note for $126,000 was payable on demand, carried no interest, and contained a provision that barred John from obtaining a money judgment against his mother. Nettie paid some of John's bills after the transfer of money from her son to her. Harmony served a garnishment summons on Nettie, claiming that she was a party to a fraudulent scheme by her son to conceal his assets and was holding funds that belonged to her son. Nettie argued that Harmony's rights against her could not be any greater than John's rights against her and that because John could not obtain a judgment against her for the money, Harmony could not do so either. Discuss Harmony's right of garnishment against Nettie. [*Harmony Unlimited, Inc. v. Chivetta,* 743 S.W.2d 884 (Mo.App. 1987)]

**32–7. Artisan's Lien.** In February 1973, Gladys Schmidt borrowed $4,120 from the National Bank of Joliet to finance the purchase of a Cadillac. The bank held a security interest in the automobile and perfected this interest by filing in the office of the secretary of state. In August 1973, Schmidt took the car to Bergeron Cadillac, Inc., for repairs, which cost approximately $2,000. When Schmidt failed to pay for the repairs, Bergeron Cadillac retained possession of the car and placed an artisan's lien on it. In September, Schmidt defaulted on her payments to the bank, and the bank later filed an action to gain possession of the Cadillac from Bergeron. Discuss which party had a right to possession of the vehicle—Bergeron Cadillac or the National Bank. [*National Bank of Joliet v. Bergeron Cadillac, Inc.,* 66 Ill.2d 140, 361 N.E.2d 1116, 5 Ill.Dec. 588 (1977)]

**32–8. Right of Subrogation.** Levinson and Johnson, who had both signed a promissory note, did not pay the note when it was due. Instead, American Thermex, Inc., a corporation in which Johnson had a controlling interest, voluntarily paid the note. American Thermex later brought suit against Levinson, seeking reimbursement for the payment. American Thermex argued, among other things, that because it had paid the note, it had the legal right of subrogation against the note's co-maker, Levinson. Will the court agree that American Thermex has a legal right of subrogation? Why or why not? [*Levinson v. American Thermex, Inc.,* 196 Ga.App. 291, 396 S.E.2d 252 (1990)]

**32–9. Rights of the Guarantor.** Hallmark Cards, Inc., sued Edward Peevy, who had guaranteed an obligation owed to Hallmark by Garry Peevy. At the time of Edward's guaranty, Hallmark had in its possession property pledged as security by Garry. Before suit was filed, Hallmark sold the pledged property without notice to Edward. Because the property sold did not cover the loan balance, Hallmark sued for the balance, seeking a deficiency judgment. Edward contended that because Hallmark had sold the property pledged by Garry as security for the obligation without notifying him (Edward), Hallmark was not entitled to a deficiency judgment against him. Hallmark contended that

Edward was not entitled to notice of the sale of the collateral and was not required to give consent. Which party will prevail in court? Discuss. [*Hallmark Cards, Inc. v. Peevy,* 293 Ark. 594, 739 S.W.2d 691 (1987)]

**32–10. Rights of the Guarantor** On October 1, 1985, Wallace and Helen Brunson contracted with Bear Park, Inc., to sell certain real estate in Taney County, Missouri, for $366,200. At the closing, Bear Park gave the Brunsons a promissory note for $285,000 in partial payment. Several of Bear Park's shareholders and directors, including Ronald Todd, signed a guaranty agreement on the back of the note. According to the terms of the note, Bear Park was to make quarterly payments of principal and interest, with the first payment of $68,800 due on January 7, 1986. The remaining quarterly payments, beginning April 7, 1986, would each be $7,226.80. When Bear Park failed to make the first payment, the Brunsons agreed to accept $7,000 in lieu of the full $68,800 and to increase the amount of the subsequent payments to cover the difference. Todd and the others knew nothing about the new terms. When Bear Park failed to make the next payment, the Brunsons declared the note in default and eventually demanded that the guarantors pay the amount due. No payments were made. The Brunsons assigned their interest in the note to Jake Kirkland, who foreclosed on the property. After the foreclosure sale, there was a deficiency of $36,454.84, plus interest, expenses, and attorneys' fees. Kirkland sued Todd and the others for this amount. Discuss the liability of Todd and the others in this situation. [*Kirkland v. Todd,* 856 S.W.2d 936 (Mo.App. 1993)]

**32–11. Case Briefing Assignment**

 *Examine Case A.5 [Allison-Bristow Community School District v. Iowa Civil Rights Commission, 461 N.W.2d 456 (Iowa 1990)] in Appendix A. The case has been excerpted there in great detail. Review and then brief the case, making sure that you include answers to the following questions in your brief.*

1. Why did Rowland claim that the back pay, plus interest, that the Civil Rights Commission ordered his employer to pay him were exempt earnings, not subject to garnishment under Iowa law?

2. How did the relevant Iowa statute define *earnings?*

3. On what grounds did the district court rule against Rowland?

4. What arguments were advanced by the judgment creditor, Willow Tree, to convince the court that Rowland's award of back pay, plus interest, should be subject to garnishment?

5. What was the reasoning behind the state supreme court's conclusion on the issue? In what way did the supreme court's ruling differ from that of the district court?

# CHAPTER 33

# BANKRUPTCY AND REORGANIZATION

Historically, debtors had few rights. As mentioned in the previous chapter, at one time debtors who could not pay their debts as they came due faced harsh consequences, including imprisonment and involuntary servitude. Today's debtors have numerous rights, including the right to petition for bankruptcy relief under federal law. Modern bankruptcy law is designed to accomplish two main goals. The first is to provide relief and protection to debtors who have ''gotten in over their heads.'' The second is to provide a fair means of distributing a debtor's assets among all creditors. Thus, the law attempts to protect the rights of both the debtor and the creditor.

Congressional authority to provide bankruptcy relief for debtors is based on Article I, Section 8, of the U.S. Constitution, which gives Congress the power to establish ''uniform Laws on the subject of Bankruptcies throughout the United States.'' Federal bankruptcy legislation was first enacted in 1898 and since then has undergone several modifications. Current bankruptcy law is based on the Bankruptcy Reform Act of 1978, as amended—hereinafter called the Bankruptcy Code, or more simply the Code (not to be confused with the Uniform Commercial Code, which is also sometimes called the Code). Significant changes to the Code were made by the Bankruptcy Reform Act of 1994. These changes are included in our discussion in this chapter.

Bankruptcy proceedings are held in federal bankruptcy courts, which are under the authority of U.S. district courts, and rulings from bankruptcy courts can be appealed to the district courts. Essentially, a bankruptcy court fulfills the role of an administrative court for the federal district court concerning matters in bankruptcy. The bankruptcy court holds proceedings dealing with the procedures required to administer the estate of the debtor in bankruptcy. Bankruptcy court judges are federally appointed. A bankruptcy court can conduct a jury trial if the appropriate district court has authorized it and the parties to the bankruptcy consent.

## SECTION 1

## TYPES OF BANKRUPTCY RELIEF

The Bankruptcy Code is contained in Title 11 of the United States Code (U.S.C.) and has eight chapters. Chapters 1, 3, and 5 of the Code include

631

general definitional provisions and provisions governing case administration, creditors, the debtor,[1] and the estate. These three chapters apply generally to all kinds of bankruptcies. The next five chapters of the Code set forth the different types of relief that debtors may seek. Chapter 7 provides for **liquidation** proceedings (the selling of all nonexempt assets and the distribution of the proceeds to the debtor's creditors). Chapter 9 governs the adjustment of debts of a municipality. Chapter 11 governs reorganizations. Chapters 12 and 13 provide for the adjustment of debts by parties with regular incomes (family farmers under Chapter 12 and individuals under Chapter 13).[2]

To fully inform a consumer-debtor of the various types of relief available, the Code requires that the clerk of the court give all **consumer-debtors** (defined as individuals whose debts are primarily consumer debts) written notice of each chapter under which they may proceed prior to the commencement of a bankruptcy filing.

In the following sections, we deal first with liquidation proceedings under Chapter 7 of the Code. We then examine the procedures required for Chapter 11 reorganizations, and Chapter 12 and 13 plans. The latter three chapters have been referred to as ''rehabilitation'' chapters.

## SECTION 2

# LIQUIDATION PROCEEDINGS

Liquidation under Chapter 7 of the Bankruptcy Code is generally the most familiar type of bankruptcy proceeding and is often referred to as an *ordinary,* or *straight, bankruptcy.* Put simply, a debtor in a liquidation bankruptcy turns all assets over to a **trustee.** The trustee sells the nonexempt assets and distributes the proceeds to creditors.

With certain exceptions, the remaining debts are then **discharged** (extinguished), and the debtors are relieved of their obligation to pay the debts.

Any ''person''—defined as including individuals, partnerships, and corporations[3]—may be a debtor in a liquidation proceeding. Railroads, insurance companies, banks, savings and loan associations, investment companies licensed by the Small Business Administration, and credit unions cannot be debtors in a liquidation bankruptcy, however. Rather, other chapters of the Bankruptcy Code or federal or state statutes apply to them.

## FILING THE PETITION

A straight bankruptcy may be commenced by the filing of either a voluntary or an involuntary **petition in bankruptcy**—the document that is filed with a bankruptcy court to initiate bankruptcy proceedings.

**VOLUNTARY BANKRUPTCY**  When a voluntary petition in bankruptcy is brought by the debtor, he or she files official forms designated for that purpose in the bankruptcy court. The Code requires a consumer-debtor who has opted for liquidation bankruptcy proceedings to state in the petition, at the time of filing, that he or she understands the relief available under other chapters of the Code and has chosen to proceed under Chapter 7. If the consumer-debtor is represented by an attorney, the attorney must file an affidavit stating that he or she has informed the debtor of the relief available under each chapter. A debtor does not have to be insolvent[4] to file for bankruptcy relief. Anyone liable to a creditor can declare bankruptcy.

The voluntary petition contains the following schedules:

1. A list of both secured and unsecured creditors, their addresses, and the amount of debt owed to each.

---

1. It is noteworthy that the term *bankrupt* no longer exists under the Code. Those who were *bankrupts* under bankruptcy law prior to the Bankruptcy Reform Act of 1978 are now merely *debtors* under the Code.
2. There are no Chapters 2, 4, 6, 8, or 10 in Title 11. Such ''gaps'' are not uncommon in the U.S.C. This is because chapter numbers (or other subdivisional unit numbers) are sometimes reserved for future use when a statute is enacted. (A gap may also appear if a law has been repealed.)

3. The definition of *corporation* includes unincorporated companies and associations. It also covers labor unions.
4. The inability to pay debts as they become due is known as *equitable* insolvency. A *balance sheet* insolvency, which exists when a debtor's liabilities exceed assets, is not the test. Thus, it is possible for debtors to voluntarily petition for bankruptcy or to be thrown into involuntary bankruptcy even though their assets far exceed their liabilities. This may occur when a debtor's cash flow problems become severe.

2. A statement of the financial affairs of the debtor.
3. A list of all property owned by the debtor, including property claimed by the debtor to be exempt.
4. A listing of current income and expenses. (This schedule provides creditors and the court with relevant information on the debtor's ability to pay creditors a reasonable amount from future income. This information *could* permit a court, on its own motion, to dismiss a debtor's Chapter 7 petition after a hearing, and to encourage the filing of a repayment plan under Chapter 13, when that would substantially improve the chances that creditors would be paid.)

The official forms must be completed accurately, sworn to under oath, and signed by the debtor. To conceal assets or knowingly supply false information on these schedules is a crime under the bankruptcy laws. If the voluntary petition for bankruptcy is found to be proper, the filing of the petition will itself constitute an **order for relief.** (An order for relief is a court's grant of assistance to a complainant. In the context of bankruptcy, relief consists of discharging a complainant's debts.) Once a consumer-debtor's voluntary petition has been filed, the clerk of the court or other appointee must give the trustee and creditors mailed notice of the order for relief not more than twenty days after entry of the order. A husband and wife may file jointly for bankruptcy under a single petition.

As mentioned above, debtors do not have to be insolvent to file for voluntary bankruptcy. Debtors do not have unfettered access to Chapter 7 bankruptcy proceedings, however. Section 707(b) of the Bankruptcy Code allows a bankruptcy court to dismiss a petition for relief under Chapter 7 if the granting of relief would constitute substantial abuse of Chapter 7. What constitutes "substantial abuse" under this section is at issue in the following case.

---

**BACKGROUND AND FACTS** *Tommy C. Richmond and his wife, Nancy, filed for bankruptcy relief under Chapter 7. At the time of their petition, Tommy had been employed for twenty-four years and Nancy, for eight years. The Richmonds' secured debts amounted to $72,233, and their unsecured debts totaled $19,525. Part of their secured debts was for a motor home, which they wanted to keep by reaffirming the debt.[a] The unsecured debts included $19,300 in credit-card charges, $140 in medical bills, and $85 in miscellaneous debts. The Richmonds had no legal dependents, but they voluntarily contributed to the support of seven grandchildren. On their bankruptcy schedule, they stated that their monthly expenses for food, cleaning and laundry, medical care, dental care, and recreation totaled $775. The bankruptcy trustee concluded that the Richmonds' monthly expenses, if they ceased supporting their grandchildren, could be reduced to $475 per month, leaving an additional $300 per month to repay creditors. Asserting that the Richmonds could repay 90 percent of their debts with their future earnings within three years under a Chapter 13 repayment plan (discussed later in this chapter), the trustee filed a motion to dismiss the case. To grant relief under Chapter 7 in these circumstances, argued the trustee, would constitute a substantial abuse of Chapter 7. The Richmonds contended that relief should be granted because Nancy had been ill, and even though she had not been ill for*

| CASE 33.1 |

**IN RE RICHMOND**

United States Bankruptcy Court,
Western District of Oklahoma,
1992.
144 Bankr. 539.

---

a. In a reaffirmation agreement, the debtor agrees to pay a creditor a debt that could be discharged in bankruptcy. See the discussion of reaffirmation agreements later in this chapter.

*an extended period of time, they had suffered a loss of income. Further, they wanted to continue to assist in the support of their grandchildren.*

*PAUL B. LINDSEY,* Bankruptcy Judge.

\* \* \* \*

\* \* \* The Bankruptcy Code does not define ''substantial abuse,'' but legislative history indicates that the purpose of [Section] 707(b) was to stop the use of Chapter 7 relief for unneedy debtors.

In deciding whether to apply [Section] 707(b), it has been held that a court should decide from the totality of the circumstances whether a debtor is seeking an advantage over his creditors or whether he is ''needy'' in the sense that his financial situation authorizes a discharge for his debts. In making this determination, in addition to debtor's ability to repay his debts, other factors to be considered include (1) whether the bankruptcy petition was filed because of a sudden illness, calamity, disability, or unemployment; (2) whether debtor incurred cash advances and made consumer purchases far in excess of his ability to repay; (3) whether debtor's proposed family budget is excessive or unreasonable; (4) whether debtor's schedules and statement of current income and expenses reasonably reflect the true financial condition; and (5) whether the petition was filed in good faith.

In this case, dismissal under [Section] 707(b) would be appropriate under virtually any rational analysis. \* \* \*

Debtors' schedules list only minimal medical bills, and although debtors asserted that Mrs. Richmond was ill, there is no evidence of any sudden or extended illness.

Mr. and Mrs. Richmond have been employed with the same substantial employer for 24 and 8 years, respectively.

The magnitude of the credit card debt scheduled by debtors is sufficient to warrant a determination that they knew, or should have known, of their inability to repay the debts when they were incurred. The debtors' schedule of current income and expenditures contains excessive prospective expenditures which, at least in part, apparently relate to their voluntary contributions to the support of their grandchildren and to the operation, maintenance and upkeep of the motor home which they propose to retain. This court does not believe that debtors' unsecured creditors should be required to contribute to the voluntary support of family members who are not dependents of debtors, or to in effect pay the expenses of debtors' recreational vehicle.

**DECISION AND REMEDY** *The bankruptcy court granted the trustee's motion to dismiss the case. To grant the Richmonds relief in these circumstances would constitute a substantial abuse of Chapter 7.*

**ETHICAL CONSIDERATIONS** *By its very nature, bankruptcy law favors debtors' interests over those of creditors. As this case shows, however, the rights of creditors are very much of concern to a bankruptcy court, and a debtor will rarely be offered refuge under bankruptcy law when the debtor can pay debts rightfully owed without undue hardship.*

**INVOLUNTARY BANKRUPTCY** An involuntary bankruptcy occurs when the debtor's creditors force the debtor into bankruptcy proceedings. An involuntary case cannot be commenced against a farmer[5] or a charitable institution. For an

5. The definition of *farmer* includes persons who receive more than 80 percent of their gross income from farming operations, such as tilling the soil, dairy farming, ranching, or the production or raising of crops, poultry, or livestock. Corporations and partnerships may qualify under certain conditions.

involuntary action to be filed against other debtors, the following requirements must be met: If the debtor has twelve or more creditors, three or more of these creditors having unsecured claims totaling at least $10,000 must join in the petition. If a debtor has fewer than twelve creditors, one or more creditors having a claim of $10,000 may file.

If the debtor challenges the involuntary petition, a hearing will be held, and the bankruptcy court will enter an order for relief if it finds either of the following:

1. The debtor is generally not paying debts as they become due.
2. A general receiver, assignee, or custodian took possession of, or was appointed to take charge of, substantially all of the debtor's property within 120 days before the filing of the petition.

If the court grants an order for relief, the debtor will be required to supply the same information in the bankruptcy schedules as in a voluntary bankruptcy.

An involuntary petition should not be used as an everyday debt-collection device, and the Code provides penalties for the filing of frivolous petitions against debtors. Judgment may be granted against the petitioning creditors for the costs and attorneys' fees incurred by the debtor in defending against an involuntary petition that is dismissed by the court. If the petition is filed in bad faith, damages can be awarded for injury to the debtor's reputation. Punitive damages may also be awarded.

## AUTOMATIC STAY

The moment a petition, either voluntary or involuntary, is filed, there exists an **automatic stay,** or suspension, of virtually all litigation and other action by creditors against the debtor or the debtor's property. In other words, once a petition has been filed, creditors cannot commence or continue most legal actions, such as foreclosure of liens, execution on judgments, trials, or any action to repossess property in the hands of the debtor. A secured creditor, however, may petition the bankruptcy court for relief from the automatic stay in certain circumstances. Also, the automatic stay does not apply to paternity, alimony, maintenance, and support debts. The Code provides that if a creditor

*knowingly* violates the automatic stay (a willful violation), any party injured, including the debtor, is entitled to recover actual damages, costs, and attorneys' fees and may be entitled to recover punitive damages as well.

Underlying the Code's automatic stay provision for a secured creditor is a concept known as *adequate protection.* The **adequate protection doctrine,** among other things, protects secured creditors from losing their security as a result of the automatic stay. The bankruptcy court can provide adequate protection by requiring the debtor or trustee to make periodic cash payments or a one-time cash payment (or to provide additional collateral or replacement liens) to the extent that the stay may actually cause the value of the property to decrease. Or the court may grant other relief that is the "indubitable equivalent" of (that is, equivalent to, without any doubt) the secured party's interest in the property, such as a guaranty by a solvent third party to cover losses suffered by the secured party as a result of the stay.

## PROPERTY OF THE ESTATE

Upon the commencement of a liquidation proceeding under Chapter 7, an *estate in property* is created. The estate consists of all the debtor's legal and equitable interests in property presently held, wherever located, together with community property, property transferred in a transaction voidable by the trustee, proceeds and profits from the property of the estate, and certain after-acquired property. Interests in certain property—such as gifts, inheritances, property settlements (divorce), and life insurance death proceeds—to which the debtor becomes entitled *within 180 days after filing* may also become part of the estate. Thus, the filing of a bankruptcy petition generally fixes a dividing line: property acquired prior to the filing of the petition becomes property of the estate, and property acquired after the filing of the petition, except as just noted, remains the debtor's.

## CREDITORS' MEETING AND CLAIMS

Within a reasonable time after the order for relief has been granted (not less than ten days or more than thirty days), the bankruptcy court must call a meeting of creditors listed in the schedules filed by the debtor. The bankruptcy judge does not attend this meeting.

The debtor is required to attend the meeting (unless excused by the court) and to submit to examination under oath by the creditors and the trustee. Failing to appear when required or making false statements under oath may result in the debtor's being denied a discharge of bankruptcy. At the meeting, the trustee ensures that the debtor is aware of the potential consequences of bankruptcy and of his or her ability to file for bankruptcy under a different chapter.

To be entitled to receive a portion of the debtor's estate, each creditor must normally file a *proof of claim* with the bankruptcy court clerk within ninety days of the creditors' meeting.[6] The proof of claim lists the creditor's name and address, as well as the amount that the creditor asserts is owed to the creditor by the debtor. If a creditor fails to file a proof of claim, the bankruptcy court or trustee may file the proof of claim on the creditor's behalf but is not obligated to do so.

Generally, any legal obligation of the debtor is a claim. In the case of a disputed, or unliquidated, claim, the bankruptcy court will set the value of the claim. Any creditor holding a debtor's obligation can file a claim against the debtor's estate. These claims are automatically allowed unless contested by the trustee, the debtor, or another creditor. A creditor who files a false claim commits a crime.

The Code, however, does not allow claims for breach of employment contracts or real estate leases for terms longer than one year. Such claims are limited to one year's wages or rent, despite the remaining length of either contract in breach.

## EXEMPTIONS

The trustee takes control over the debtor's property, but an individual debtor is entitled to exempt certain property from the bankruptcy. The Bankruptcy Code exempts the following property:[7]

1. Up to $15,000 in equity in the debtor's residence and burial plot (the homestead exemption).

2. Interest in a motor vehicle up to $2,400.
3. Interest, up to $400 for a particular item, in household goods and furnishings, wearing apparel, appliances, books, animals, crops, and musical instruments (the aggregate total of all items is limited, however, to $8,000).
4. Interest in jewelry up to $1,000.
5. Interest in any other property up to $800, plus any unused part of the $15,000 homestead exemption up to $7,500.
6. Interest in any tools of the debtor's trade up to $1,500.
7. Any unmatured life insurance contract owned by the debtor.
8. Certain interests in accrued dividends and interest under life insurance contracts owned by the debtor.
9. Professionally prescribed health aids.
10. The right to receive Social Security and certain welfare benefits, alimony and support, and certain pension benefits.
11. The right to receive certain personal injury and other awards, up to $15,000.

Individual states have the power to pass legislation precluding debtors from using the federal exemptions within that state; a majority of the states have done this (see Chapter 32). In those states, debtors may use only state, not federal, exemptions. In the rest of the states, an individual debtor (or a husband and wife filing jointly) may choose either the exemptions provided under state law or the federal exemptions.[8]

## THE TRUSTEE

Promptly after the order for relief in the liquidation proceeding has been entered, an interim or provisional trustee is appointed by the **U.S. Trustee** (a government official who performs appointing

---

6. This same ninety-day rule applies in Chapter 12 and Chapter 13 bankruptcies as well.
7. A debtor cannot avoid a judicial lien for paternity, alimony, maintenance, and support debts, however, even if the lien is imposed on exempt property.

8. State exemptions may or may not be limited with regard to value. Under state exemption laws, a debtor may enjoy an unlimited value exemption on a motor vehicle, for example, even though the federal bankruptcy scheme exempts a vehicle only up to a value of $2,400. A state's law may also define the property coming within an exemption differently than the federal law or may exclude, or except, specific things from an exemption, making it unavailable to a debtor who fits within the exception.

and other administrative tasks that a bankruptcy judge would otherwise have to perform). The interim or provisional trustee presides over the debtor's property until the first meeting of creditors. At this first meeting, either a permanent trustee is elected or the interim trustee becomes the permanent trustee. The trustee's principal duty is to collect and reduce to money the "property of the estate" and to close up the estate as expeditiously as is compatible with the best interests of the parties.

**TRUSTEE'S POWERS**  The basic duty of the trustee is to collect the debtor's available estate and reduce it to money for distribution, preserving the interests of both the debtor and unsecured creditors. This requires that the trustee be accountable for administering the debtor's estate. To enable the trustee to accomplish this duty, the Code gives the trustee certain powers, stated in both general and specific terms. These powers must be exercised within two years of the order for relief (even if a trustee has not been appointed).

General powers are described by the statement that the trustee occupies a position *equivalent* in rights to that of certain other parties. For example, the trustee has the same rights as a *lien creditor* who could have obtained a judicial lien on the debtor's property or who could have levied execution on the debtor's property. This means that a trustee has priority over an unperfected secured party to the debtor's property. A trustee also has power equivalent to that of a *bona fide purchaser* of real property from the debtor.

Nevertheless, a creditor with a purchase-money security interest may prevail against a trustee, if the creditor files within ten days of the debtor's receipt of the collateral, even if the bankruptcy petition is filed before the creditor perfects. For example, Baker loaned Newbury $20,000 on January 1, taking a security interest in the machinery Newbury purchased with the $20,000 on that same date. On January 27, before Baker perfected her security interest, Newbury filed for bankruptcy. The trustee can invalidate Baker's security interest, because it was unperfected when Newbury filed the bankruptcy petition. Baker can only assert a claim as an unsecured creditor. But if Newbury had filed for bankruptcy on January 7, and Baker had perfected her security interest on January 8,

she would have prevailed, because she perfected her purchase-money security interest within ten days of Newbury's receipt of the machinery.

The trustee has the power to require persons holding the debtor's property at the time the petition is filed to deliver the property to the trustee. The trustee also has specific *powers of avoidance*—that is, the trustee can set aside a sale or other transfer of the debtor's property, taking it back as a part of the debtor's estate. These powers include any voidable rights available to the debtor, preferences, certain statutory liens, and fraudulent transfers by the debtor. Each is discussed in more detail below.

The debtor shares most of the trustee's avoidance powers. Thus, if the trustee does not take action to enforce one of his or her rights (for example, to recover a preference), the debtor in a liquidation bankruptcy can nevertheless enforce that right.[9]

**VOIDABLE RIGHTS**  A trustee steps into the shoes of the debtor. Thus, any reason that a debtor can use to obtain the return of his or her property can be used by the trustee as well. These grounds include fraud, duress, incapacity, and mutual mistake.

For example, Ben sells his boat to Zabella. Zabella gives Ben a check, knowing that there are insufficient funds in his bank account to cover the check. Zabella has committed fraud. Ben has the right to avoid that transfer and recover the boat from Zabella. Once an order for relief under Chapter 7 of the Code has been entered for Ben, the trustee can exercise the same right to recover the boat from Zabella, and it becomes a part of the debtor's estate.

**PREFERENCES**  A debtor is not permitted to transfer property or to make a payment that favors—or gives a **preference** to—one creditor over others. The trustee is allowed to recover payments made both voluntarily and involuntarily to one creditor in preference over another.

---

9. Under Chapter 11 (to be discussed later), for which no trustee other than the debtor generally exists, the debtor has the same avoidance powers as a trustee under Chapter 7. Under Chapters 12 and 13 (also to be discussed later), a trustee must be appointed.

To have made a preferential payment that can be recovered, an _insolvent_ debtor generally must have transferred property, for a _preexisting_ debt, within _ninety days_ of the filing of the petition in bankruptcy. The transfer must give the creditor more than the creditor would have received as a result of the bankruptcy proceedings. The trustee does not have to prove insolvency, as the Code provides that the debtor is presumed to be insolvent during this ninety-day period.

Sometimes the creditor receiving the preference is an **insider**—an individual, a partner, a partnership, or an officer or a director of a corporation (or a relative of one of these) who has a close relationship with the debtor. If this is the case, the avoidance power of the trustee is extended to transfers made within _one year_ before filing; however, the _presumption_ of insolvency is confined to the ninety-day period. Therefore, the trustee must prove that the debtor was insolvent at the time of earlier transfer.

Not all transfers are preferences. To be a preference, the transfer must be made for something other than current consideration. Therefore, it is generally assumed by most courts that payment for services rendered within ten to fifteen days prior to the payment of the current consideration is not a preference. If a creditor receives payment in the ordinary course of business, such as payment of last month's telephone bill, the payment cannot be recovered by the trustee in bankruptcy. To be recoverable, a preference must be a transfer for an antecedent (preexisting) debt, such as a year-old printing bill. In addition, the Code permits a consumer-debtor to transfer any property to a creditor up to a total value of $600, without the transfer's constituting a preference. Also, payment of paternity, alimony, maintenance, and support debts is not a preference.

If a preferred creditor has sold the property to an innocent third party, the trustee cannot recover the property from the innocent party. The creditor, however, generally can be held accountable for the value of the property.

**LIENS ON DEBTOR'S PROPERTY**    The trustee has the power to avoid certain statutory liens against the debtor's property, such as a landlord's lien for unpaid rent. The trustee can avoid statutory liens that first became effective against the debtor when the bankruptcy petition was filed or when the debtor became insolvent. The trustee can also avoid any lien against a _bona fide_ purchaser that was not perfected or enforceable on the date of the bankruptcy petition.

**FRAUDULENT TRANSFERS**    The trustee may avoid fraudulent transfers or obligations if they are made within one year of the filing of the petition or if they are made with actual intent to hinder, delay, or defraud a creditor. Transfers made for less than a reasonably equivalent consideration are also vulnerable if by making them, the debtor became insolvent, was left engaged in business with an unreasonably small amount of capital, or intended to incur debts that he or she could not pay. When a fraudulent transfer is made outside the Code's one-year limit, creditors may seek alternative relief under state laws. State laws often allow creditors to recover for transfers made up to three years prior to the filing of a petition. The following case illustrates fraudulent transfers made by a debtor to his daughters.

| CASE 33.2 | **BACKGROUND AND FACTS**    _Ralph I. Lazar (the debtor) was sued for_ |
|---|---|

**IN RE LAZAR**

United States Bankruptcy Court, Southern District of Florida, 1988. 81 Bankr. 148.

**BACKGROUND AND FACTS**    _Ralph I. Lazar (the debtor) was sued for wrongful interference with a contractual relationship. Three weeks later, Lazar made the first of several transfers of his assets to his daughters, Arlene and Betty Lazar. One such transfer was his entire interest in a note and mortgage ($180,000), which was paid to his daughters. His daughters deposited the funds in certificates of deposit for approximately four months. The funds were then withdrawn. With these funds and with a transfer by Ralph Lazar of personal funds, plus $104,000 transferred from his solely owned pension trust fund, Arlene purchased a yacht. Title to the yacht was held by Arbet Enterprises, Inc., a closely held corporation in which the daughters were the sole shareholders. Arbet Enterprises was formed solely to take title to the yacht. The yacht was then sold, a sixty-foot Chris-Craft yacht was purchased (with title held by Arbet Enterprises) with half the proceeds, and the remaining funds were deposited to be used by the debtor_

*and his daughters for their support. The debtor used the Chris-Craft as his place of residence and for his personal benefit and enjoyment. Ralph Lazar lost the lawsuit for wrongful interference with a contractual relationship, resulting in a judgment against him for $2 million. When the judgment creditors attempted to execute the judgment, Lazar filed a Chapter 7 bankruptcy petition, having stripped himself of his assets by the transfers to his daughters. The trustee filed a claim against Lazar for fraudulent transfer and sought to have the money held by Arbet Enterprises (as Lazar's* alter ego, *or second self) and the Chris-Craft yacht turned over to the trustee as part of the debtor's estate. The creditors and Lazar's wife filed independent actions seeking to deny him a discharge in bankruptcy because of his fraudulent actions.*

*Sidney M.* WEAVER, Bankruptcy Judge.

\* \* \* \*

\* \* \* The transfers of the Note and Mortgage and the Pension Trust funds described above are marked by several of the ''badges of fraud'' which the Florida courts have identified as factors tending to indicate the presence of a fraudulent transfer. Specifically, the subject transfers were made to family members for no consideration, and after the transfers the debtor retained full control over, and derived the primary benefit from, the use of the funds and the assets subsequently purchased therewith.

The Court finds that the debtor's intent in making the aforesaid transfers, and the legal effect of said transfers, was to hinder, delay and defraud the creditors. Under these circumstances, the trustee has sufficiently proven his claim. \* \* \*

As a separate and independent basis for awarding the turnover of the yacht \* \* \* to the trustee, this Court finds that the corporation known as Arbet Enterprises, Inc. is the alter ego of the debtor. Arbet Enterprises, Inc. was at all times the mere instrumentality of the debtor [that is, completely under the debtor's control], created to aid the debtor in defrauding the creditors and concealing his ownership of [the yachts].

\* \* \* In connection with the claimed objections [of the creditors and the debtor's spouse] to the debtor's discharge, the Court finds that the debtor, with the intent to hinder, delay and defraud the creditors, did engage in the continuous concealment of his assets during the one year period prior to the filing of the bankruptcy petition, which satisfies the requirements of [Section] 727(a)(2) of the Bankruptcy Code.

**DECISION AND REMEDY**

*The court held that the transfers Ralph Lazar made to his daughters were fraudulent and that the trustee could set aside those transfers, which included the yacht and remaining funds. In addition, Lazar was denied the right to receive a discharge in bankruptcy.*

**INTERNATIONAL CONSIDERATIONS**

**Preventing International Fraudulent Transfers** *In anticipation of bankruptcy, persons may attempt a fraudulent transfer by conveying assets to parties located overseas. If a foreign debtor seeks to convey assets to a person or entity in the United States, a court of this nation may void the transfer in deference to the foreign bankruptcy court. Under principles of comity (discussed in Chapter 56), foreign courts grant similar deference to U.S. bankruptcy courts.*

## DISTRIBUTION OF PROPERTY

The rights of perfected secured creditors were discussed in Chapter 31. The Code provides that a consumer-debtor, within thirty days of filing a liquidation petition or before the date of the first meeting of the creditors (whichever is first), must file with the clerk a statement of intention with respect to the secured collateral. The statement must indicate whether the debtor will retain or surrender the collateral to the secured party.[10] The trustee is obligated to enforce the debtor's statement within forty-five days after it is filed.

If the collateral is surrendered to the perfected secured party, the secured creditor can enforce the security interest either by accepting the property in full satisfaction of the debt or by foreclosing on the collateral and using the proceeds to pay off the debt. Thus, the perfected secured party has priority over unsecured parties as to the proceeds from the disposition of the collateral. Indeed, the Code provides that if the value of the collateral exceeds the perfected secured party's claim, the secured party also has priority as to the proceeds in an amount that will cover reasonable fees and costs incurred because of the debtor's default. Any excess over this amount is used by the trustee to satisfy the claims of unsecured creditors. Should the collateral be insufficient to cover the secured debt owed, the secured creditor becomes an unsecured creditor for the difference.

Bankruptcy law establishes an order of priority for classes of debts owed to *unsecured* creditors, and they are paid in the order of their priority. Each class must be fully paid before the next class is entitled to any of the remaining proceeds. If there are insufficient proceeds to pay fully all the creditors in a class, the proceeds are distributed *proportionately* to the creditors in the class, and classes lower in priority receive nothing. The order of priority among classes of unsecured creditors is as follows:

1. Administrative expenses—including court costs, trustee fees, and attorneys' fees.
2. In an involuntary bankruptcy, expenses incurred by the debtor in the ordinary course of business from the date of the filing of the petition up to the appointment of the trustee or the issuance by the court of an order for relief.
3. Unpaid wages, salaries, and commissions earned within ninety days of the filing of the petition, limited to $4,000 per claimant. Any claim in excess of $4,000 or earned before the ninety-day period is treated as a claim of a general creditor (listed as number 9 below).
4. Unsecured claims for contributions to be made to employee benefit plans, limited to services performed during 180 days prior to the filing of the bankruptcy petition and $4,000 per employee.
5. Claims by farmers and fishers, up to $4,000, against debtor operators of grain storage or fish storage or processing facilities.
6. Consumer deposits of up to $1,800 given to the debtor before the petition was filed in connection with the purchase, lease, or rental of property or purchase of services that were not received or provided. Any claim in excess of $1,800 is treated as a claim of a general creditor (listed as number 9 below).
7. Paternity, alimony, maintenance, and support debts.
8. Certain taxes and penalties due to government units, such as income and property taxes.
9. Claims of general creditors.

If any amount remains after the priority classes of creditors have been satisfied, it is turned over to the debtor.

In a bankruptcy case in which the debtor has no assets,[11] creditors are notified of the debtor's petition for bankruptcy but are instructed not to file a claim. In such a case, the unsecured creditors will receive no payment and most, if not all, of these debts will be discharged.

## DISCHARGE

From the debtor's point of view, the primary purpose of liquidation is to obtain a fresh start through a discharge of debts.[12] Certain debts, however, are not dischargeable in bankruptcy. Also, certain debtors may not qualify to have all debts dis-

---

10. Also, if applicable, the debtor must specify whether the collateral will be claimed as exempt property and whether the debtor intends to redeem the property or reaffirm the debt secured by the collateral.

11. This type of bankruptcy is called a "no asset" case.
12. Discharges are granted under Chapter 7 only to *individuals*, not to corporations or partnerships. The latter may use Chapter 11, or they may terminate their existence under state law.

charged in bankruptcy. These situations are discussed below.

### EXCEPTIONS TO DISCHARGE

Discharge of a debt may be denied because of the nature of the claim or the conduct of the debtor. Claims that are not dischargeable in a liquidation bankruptcy include the following:

1. Claims for back taxes accruing within three years prior to bankruptcy.
2. Claims for amounts borrowed by the debtor to pay federal taxes.
3. Claims against property or money obtained by the debtor under false pretenses or by false representations. · *Fraud*
4. Claims by creditors who were not notified and did not know of the bankruptcy; these claims did not appear on the schedules the debtor was required to file.
5. Claims based on fraud or misuse of funds by the debtor while he or she was acting in a fiduciary capacity or claims involving the debtor's embezzlement or larceny.
6. Alimony, child support, and (with certain exceptions) property settlements.
7. Claims based on willful or malicious conduct by the debtor toward another or the property of another.
8. Certain government fines and penalties.
9. Certain student loans, unless payment of the loans imposes an undue hardship on the debtor and the debtor's dependents. *-w/i 5yrs.*
10. Consumer debts of more than $1,000 for luxury goods or services owed to a single creditor incurred within sixty days of the order for relief. This denial of discharge is *a rebuttable presumption* (that is, the denial may be challenged by the debtor), however, and any debts reasonably incurred to support the debtor or dependents are not classified as luxuries. *$500*
11. Cash advances totaling more than $1,000 that are extensions of open-end consumer credit obtained by the debtor within sixty days of the order for relief. A denial of discharge of these debts is also a rebuttable presumption. *40*
12. Judgments or consent decrees against a debtor as a result of the debtor's operation of a motor vehicle while intoxicated.
13. *Debts that survive previous bankruptcy*

In the following case, the question of the discharge of a student loan is at issue.

---

**BACKGROUND AND FACTS** *Mary Lou Baker attended three different institutions of higher learning, the University of Tennessee at Chattanooga, Cleveland State Community College, and the Baroness Erlanger School of Nursing. At these three schools, she received educational loans totaling $6,635. After graduation, she was employed, but her monthly take-home pay was less than $650. Monthly expenses for herself and her three children were approximately $925. Her husband had left town and provided no child or other financial support. She received no public aid and had no other income. In January 1981, just prior to this action, Mary Lou Baker's church paid her gas bill so that she and her children could have heat in their home. One child had difficulty reading, and another required expensive shoes. Baker had not been well and had been unable to pay her medical bills. She filed for bankruptcy. In her petition, she sought a discharge of her educational loans based on the hardship provision, which is the issue before the court.*

### CASE 33.3

**IN RE BAKER**

United States Bankruptcy Court,
Eastern District of Tennessee,
1981.
10 Bankr. 870.

*Ralph H. KELLEY, Bankruptcy Judge.*

This cause came on to be heard on May 5, 1981, on debtor's complaint to determine dischargeability of certain educational loans. The complaint alleges that debtor is entitled to relief under 11 U.S.C. [Section] 523 (a)(8) which reads as follows:

Exceptions to discharge.

(a) A discharge under section 727, 1141, or 1328(b) of this title does not discharge an individual debtor from any debt—. . . .

(8) to a governmental unit, or a nonprofit institution of higher education, for an educational loan, unless

(B) excepting such debt from discharge under this paragraph will impose an undue hardship on the debtor and the debtor's dependents;

\* \* \* \*

In 1976 the Congress passed the Educational Amendments which restricted a discharge in bankruptcy. The restriction was designed to remedy an abuse by students who, immediately upon graduation, would file bankruptcy to secure a discharge of educational loans. These students often had no other indebtedness and could easily pay their debts from future wages.

\* \* \* \*

The court concludes that under the circumstances of this case, requiring the debtor to repay the debts owed to the *three* defendants in the amount of $6,635.00 plus interest would impose upon her and her dependents an undue hardship. In passing the Educational Amendments of 1976 and including these amendments in the Bankruptcy Reform Act of 1978, Congress intended to correct an abuse. It did not intend to deprive those who have truly fallen on hard times of the ''fresh start'' policy of the new Bankruptcy Code.

**DECISION AND REMEDY**   *The debtor's student loans were discharged. Given the fact that she had ''truly fallen on hard times,'' Baker should be allowed to have her debts discharged in bankruptcy to avoid undue hardship.*

---

**OBJECTIONS TO DISCHARGE**   In addition to the exceptions to discharge previously listed, a bankruptcy court may also deny the discharge of the *debtor* (as opposed to the debt). In the latter situation, the assets of the debtor are still distributed to the creditors, but the debtor remains liable for the unpaid portion of all claims. Some grounds for the denial of discharge of the debtor follow.

1. The debtor's concealment or destruction of property with the intent to hinder, delay, or defraud a creditor.
2. The debtor's fraudulent concealment or destruction of financial records.
3. The granting of a discharge to the debtor within six years of the filing of the petition.

**EFFECT OF DISCHARGE**   The primary effect of a discharge is to void any judgment on a discharged debt and enjoin any action to collect a discharged debt. A discharge does not affect the liability of a co-debtor.

**REVOCATION OF DISCHARGE**   The Code provides that a debtor may lose his or her bankruptcy discharge by revocation upon petition by the trustee or a creditor. The bankruptcy court may, within one year, revoke the discharge decree if it is discovered that the debtor acted fraudulently or dishonestly during the bankruptcy proceedings. The revocation renders the discharge void, allowing creditors not satisfied by the distribution of the debtor's estate to proceed with their claims against the debtor.

## REAFFIRMATION OF DEBT

A debtor may voluntarily wish to pay a debt—such as, for example, a debt owed to a family member, family doctor, close friend, or some other party—notwithstanding the fact that the debt could be discharged in bankruptcy. An agreement to pay a debt dischargeable in bankrtupcy is called a **reaffirmation agreement.** To be enforceable, reaffirmation agreements must be made before the debtor is granted a discharge. The agreement must be filed with the court. Approval by the court is required unless the debtor's attorney files an affidavit stating that the reaffirmation agreement is voluntarily made, that the debtor understands the consequences of the agreement and of a default under the agreement, and that the agreement will not result in an undue hardship on the debtor or the debtor's family.

The agreement must contain a clear and conspicuous statement advising the debtor that reaffirmation is not required. The debtor can rescind, or cancel, the agreement at any time prior to discharge or within sixty days of the filing of the agreement, whichever is later. This rescission period must be stated *clearly* and *conspicuously* in the reaffirmation agreement.

## SECTION 3

# REORGANIZATIONS

The type of bankruptcy proceeding used most commonly by a corporate debtor is the Chapter 11 *reorganization*. In a reorganization, the creditors and the debtor formulate a plan under which the debtor pays a portion of his or her debts and is discharged of the remainder. The debtor is allowed to continue in business. Although this type of bankruptcy is commonly a corporate reorganization, any debtor (except a stockbroker or a commodities broker) who is eligible for Chapter 7 relief is eligible for relief under Chapter 11.[13] Prior to 1991, some courts had barred individuals from petitioning for reorganization, even though the language of the Code does not limit the use of reorganization to business debtors. The United States Supreme Court, however, has since ruled that a nonbusiness debtor may petition for relief under Chapter 11.[14]

The same principles that govern the filing of a liquidation petition apply to reorganization proceedings. The case may be brought either voluntarily or involuntarily. The same principles govern

the entry of the order for relief. The automatic stay and adequate protection provisions are applicable in reorganizations.

In some instances, creditors may prefer private, negotiated adjustments of creditor-debtor relations, also known as **workouts,** to bankruptcy proceedings. Often these out-of-court workouts are much more flexible and thus more conducive to a speedy settlement. Speed is critical, because delay is one of the most costly elements in any bankruptcy proceeding.

Another advantage of workouts is that they avoid the various administrative costs of bankruptcy proceedings. Thus, under Section 305(a) of the Bankruptcy Code, a court, after notice and a hearing, may dismiss or suspend all proceedings in a case at any time if dismissal or suspension would better serve the interests of the creditors. Section 1112 also allows a court, after notice and a hearing, to dismiss a case under reorganization "for cause." Cause includes the absence of a reasonable likelihood of rehabilitation, the inability to effect a plan, and an unreasonable delay by the debtor that is prejudicial to (may harm the interests of) creditors.[15]

In the following case, creditors of the Johns-Manville Corporation sought to dismiss, under Section 1112, a voluntary petition filed by Manville.

---

13. In addition, railroads are eligible for Chapter 11 relief.
14. *Toibb v. Radloff,* 501 U.S. 157, 111 S.Ct. 2197, 115 L.Ed.2d 145 (1991).

15. See 11 U.S.C. Section 1112(b). Debtors are not prohibited from filing successive petitions, however. A debtor whose petition is dismissed, for example, can file a new Chapter 11 petition (which may be granted unless it is filed in bad faith).

---

**COMPANY PROFILE** *In 1858, H. W. Johns founded a roofing materials business in Brooklyn. By 1901, Johns had patented a line of products containing asbestos and merged with the Manville Covering Company, which had begun in 1886 in Milwaukee to produce pipe coverings and insulation materials. Control of the renamed Johns-Manville Company was acquired by J. P. Morgan & Company in 1927. Under Morgan, the company concentrated on making building materials. Johns-Manville moved to Colorado in the early 1970s and in 1981 renamed itself Manville Corporation. In 1974, nearly 500 men who had worked with Manville products in the construction of ships during World War II filed the first major asbestos lawsuit against the company. By 1982, Manville had settled more than 4,000 asbestos-related lawsuits but faced a backlog of nearly 17,000. Manville phased out all activities related to asbestos and in 1988 began to focus on forest products, fiberglass, and mining.*

CASE 33.4

**IN RE JOHNS-MANVILLE CORP.**
United States Bankruptcy Court,
Southern District of New York,
1984.
36 Bankr. 727.

**BACKGROUND AND FACTS**   *On August 26, 1982, the Johns-Manville Corporation filed for protection under Chapter 11 of the Bankruptcy Code. This filing came as quite a surprise to some of Manville's creditors, as well as to some of the other corporations that were being sued, along with Manville, for injuries caused by asbestos exposure. Manville asserted that the nearly 17,000 lawsuits pending as of the filing date and the potential lawsuits of people who had been exposed to asbestos but who would not manifest asbestos-related diseases until some time in the future necessitated its filing. The creditors of Manville, including people harmed by asbestos exposure who had won lawsuits or settlements, contended that Johns-Manville had not filed in good faith and that the voluntary reorganization petition should thus be dismissed under Section 1112 of the Bankruptcy Code.*

Burton R. LIFLAND, Bankruptcy Judge.
\* \* \* \*

In determining whether to dismiss under Code Section 1112(b), a court is not necessarily required to consider whether the debtor has filed in ''good faith'' because that is not a specified [requirement] under the Code for filing. Rather, according to Code Section 1129(a)(3), good faith emerges as a requirement for the confirmation of a plan. \* \* \* It is thus logical that the good faith of the debtor be deemed a predicate primarily for emergence out of a Chapter 11 case. It is after confirmation of a concrete and immutable reorganization plan that creditors are foreclosed from advancing their distinct and parochial interests in the debtor's estate.
\* \* \* \*

In the instant case, not only would liquidation be wasteful and inefficient in destroying the utility of valuable assets of the companies as well as jobs, but, more importantly, liquidation would preclude just compensation of some present asbestos victims and all future asbestos claimants. This unassailable reality represents all the more reason for this Court to adhere to this basic potential liquidation avoidance aim of Chapter 11 and deny the motions to dismiss. Manville must not be required to wait until its economic picture has deteriorated beyond salvation to file for reorganization.

**DECISION AND REMEDY**   *The motions to dismiss the Manville petition were denied. The court concluded that a bankruptcy proceeding was appropriate in this situation.*

## DEBTOR IN POSSESSION

Upon entry of the order for relief, the debtor generally continues to operate his or her business as a **debtor in possession (DIP).** The court, however, may appoint a trustee (often referred to as a *receiver*) to operate the debtor's business if gross mismanagement of the business is shown or if appointing a trustee is in the best interests of the estate.

The DIP's role is similar to that of a trustee in a liquidation. The DIP is entitled to avoid pre-petition preferential payments made to creditors and pre-petition fraudulent transfers of assets. The DIP has the power to decide whether to cancel or assume pre-petition executory contracts (those that are not yet performed) or unexpired leases.

Under the ''strong-arm clause''[16] of the Bankruptcy Code, a DIP can avoid any obligation or any transfer of property of the debtor that could be avoided by certain parties. These parties include (1) a creditor who extended credit to the debtor at the time of bankruptcy (petition) and who conse-

---

16.   11 U.S.C. Section 544(a).

quently obtained a lien on the debtor's property; (2) a creditor who extended credit to the debtor at the time of bankruptcy and who consequently obtained a writ of execution against the debtor that was returned unsatisfied; and (3) a *bona fide* purchaser of real property from the debtor, if at the time of the bankruptcy the transfer was perfected.

The DIP has the powers that these parties would have, even if these parties do not actually exist. For example, Fogerty loans Wilson $10,000, secured by a mortgage on Wilson's real property. Fogerty fails to record the mortgage with the proper authorities. If Wilson were to sell the property to Bishop, a *bona fide* purchaser, Bishop would take the property free of the mortgage. Imagine, instead, that Wilson does not sell the property to anyone but files for bankruptcy. Under the strong-arm clause, Wilson's trustee can assert the rights of a hypothetical *bona fide* purchaser and take the property free of the mortgage.

## COLLECTIVE BARGAINING AGREEMENTS

Under the Bankruptcy Reform Act of 1978, questions arose as to whether a reorganization debtor could reject a recently negotiated collectively bargained labor contract. In *National Labor Relations Board v. Bildisco and Bildisco*, the United States Supreme Court held that a collective bargaining agreement subject to the National Labor Relations Act of 1935 (see Chapter 36) is an ''executory contract'' and thus subject to *rejection* by a debtor in possession.[17] The Court emphasized that such a rejection should not be permitted unless there is a finding that the policy of Chapter 11 (successful rehabilitation of debtors) would be served by the action. Hence, when the bankruptcy court determines that a rejection of a collective bargaining agreement should be permitted, it must make a reasoned finding *on the record* as to *why* it has determined that a rejection should be permitted.

The Code attempts to reconcile federal policies favoring collective bargaining with the need to allow a debtor company to reject executory labor contracts while trying to reorganize. The Code sets forth standards and procedures under which collective bargaining contracts can be assumed or rejected under a reorganization filing. In general, a collective bargaining contract can be rejected if the debtor has first proposed necessary contractual modifications to the union and the union has failed to adopt them without *good cause*. The company is required (1) to provide the union with the relevant information needed to evaluate this proposal and (2) to confer in *good faith* in attempting to reach a mutually satisfactory agreement on the modifications.

## CREDITORS' COMMITTEES

As soon as practicable after the entry of the order for relief, a creditors' committee of unsecured creditors is appointed. The committee may consult with the trustee or the DIP concerning the administration of the case or the formulation of the plan. Additional creditors' committees may be appointed to represent special-interest creditors. Orders affecting the estate generally will not be entered without either the consent of the committee or a hearing in which the judge hears the position of the committee.

Businesses with debts of less than $2 million that do not own or manage real estate can avoid creditors' committees. In these cases, orders can be entered without a committee's consent.

## THE REORGANIZATION PLAN

A reorganization plan to rehabilitate the debtor is a plan to conserve and administer the debtor's assets in the hope of an eventual return to successful operation and solvency. The plan must be fair and equitable and must do the following:

1. Designate classes of claims and interests.
2. Specify the treatment to be afforded the classes. (The plan must provide the same treatment for each claim in a particular class.)
3. Provide an adequate means for execution.

Only the debtor may file a plan within the first 120 days after the date of the order for relief. If the debtor does not meet the 120-day deadline, however, or if the debtor fails to obtain the required creditor consent (see below) within 180 days, any party may propose a plan. If a small-business debtor chooses to avoid creditors' committees, the time for the debtor's filing is shortened to 100 days, and any other party's plan must be filed within 160 days.

---

17. 465 U.S. 513, 104 S.Ct. 1188, 79 L.Ed.2d 482 (1984).

# EMERGING TRENDS IN BUSINESS LAW

## Revising the Bankruptcy Code: Chapter 11 under Attack

Once thought of as a refuge of the poor and less educated, personal bankruptcies now normally involve well-educated middle class baby boomers with big-time credit-card debt (about 60 percent of personal bankruptcies involve people born between 1946 and 1964). The majority of these bankruptcies fall under Chapter 7 of the U.S. Bankruptcy Code, which provides for liquidation. A relatively small number of the almost 900,000 bankruptcies filed each year are filed under Chapter 11 of the U.S. Bankruptcy Code. Indeed, there are approximately 20,000 such filings yearly. But they involve usually the largest amounts of money. You can get an idea of the size and assets of the companies involved by looking at the table presented below.

### Uses and Abuses of Chapter 11

Under current bankruptcy law, a corporation does not even need to be insolvent to go into Chapter 11. Johns-Mansville, A. H. Robbins (a pharmaceutical company), Texaco, and a number of other leading firms have had substantial assets when they entered Chapter 11 proceedings.

### The Largest Bankruptcies

| Company | Date of Filing | Assets (in Billions) |
|---|---|---|
| Texaco, Inc. | 1987 | $35.9 |
| Financial Corporation of America | 1988 | 33.9 |
| M Corporation | 1989 | 20.2 |
| First Executive | 1991 | 15.2 |
| Gibraltar Financial | 1990 | 15.0 |
| Imperial Corporation of America | 1990 | 12.3 |
| Allied Stores/Federated Department Stores | 1991 | 11.4 |
| First Capital Holdings | 1991 | 9.7 |
| Baldwin-United Company | 1983 | 9.4 |
| Southmark Corporation | 1989 | 9.2 |

Under Chapter 11, there is normally no trustee to watch out for creditors' interests. Chapter 11 is supposed to be a hospital for sick companies, but the chances that any one company that goes into Chapter 11 will survive are less than 7 percent. Only the very largest corporations seem to have a fighting chance of emerging from Chapter 11 proceedings as viable business entities.

Additionally, an apparently growing amount of fraud colors the ongoing use of Chapter 11 reorganizations. There have been an increasing number of suits filed by federal regulators against those who mishandle corporate assets during the reorganization process.

### A Call for Scrapping Chapter 11 Reorganizations

Because of the above-mentioned problems and others, some legal scholars and attorneys are arguing that Chapter 11 reorganization should be scrapped. In an article in the *Yale Law Review,* Michael Bradley and Michael Rosenzweig concluded that shareholders and bondholders are worse off because of Chapter 11.[a] The authors argue that attorneys and current management—rather than creditors and

---

a. "The Untenable Case for Chapter 11," 101 *Yale Law Journal* 1043 (March 1992).

stockholders—are the chief beneficiaries of Chapter 11. Basically, their research shows that Chapter 11 reorganizations do not preserve companies' assets because firms must pay millions of dollars for attorneys and accountants during the reorganization process. The bankruptcy courts allow such reorganizations to drag on for years. Eastern Airlines is a good example. When a bankruptcy judge allowed chief executive officer Frank Lorenzo to run the airline for one more year after it went into Chapter 11, the company lost $1 billion.

Some suggested changes in the law, other than scrapping Chapter 11 reorganizations completely, include the following:

- Place a time limit on a reorganization plan, such as six months or one year, and stick to it.
- Remove such issues as pension reform, environmental clean-ups, and product liability from the bankruptcy judge's dockets.
- Establish a minimum

credible level of business that can reasonably be obtained by the bankrupt company; otherwise, force it into liquidation immediately.

## ■ Implications for the Businessperson

1. Until Chapter 11 is reformed or scrapped altogether, lenders and others who extend credit to business firms must realize that the debts owed may be frozen in a reorganization plan. Consequently, to guard against potential losses, businesspersons are well advised to perfect a security interest in the debtor's collateral, as provided for under Article 9 of the UCC.
2. Every businessperson should be aware of the advantages of Chapter 11 and realize that there is an optimal time to initiate Chapter 11 proceedings. Rather than wait until creditors force troubled businesses into bankruptcy, the business firm might negotiate a reorganization plan in advance, by consulting with its creditors to find out what will or will not be acceptable to

them. Such advance planning speeds up the reorganization proceedings and saves on costs that are caused by delays. Because such a large percentage of Chapter 11 reorganizations end in failure, every alternative solution should be fully explored before petitioning for a reorganization.

## ■ For Critical Analysis

1. Contrast the protection afforded to creditors by Article 9 of the UCC and by such common law protections as liens with the protection afforded debtors under bankruptcy law. Is it possible to protect both debtors and creditors at the same time? Can a better balance than that achieved under existing laws be attained?
2. What distortions in the economy are caused by keeping companies alive in Chapter 11 reorganization? (One potential distortion would be excess capacity in an industry.)
3. Who besides bankruptcy attorneys might be against removing Chapter 11 from the U.S. Bankruptcy Code? Why?

Once the plan has been developed, it is submitted to each class of creditors for acceptance. Each class must accept the plan unless the class is not adversely affected by the plan. A class has accepted the plan when a majority of the creditors, representing two-thirds of the amount of the total claim, vote to approve it.[18]

Even when all classes of claims accept the plan, the court may refuse to confirm it if it is not "in

the best interests of the creditors." A spouse or child of the debtor can block the plan if it does not provide for payment of their claims in cash.

The plan is binding upon confirmation. The debtor is given a reorganization discharge from all claims not protected under the plan. This discharge does not apply to any claims that would be denied discharge under liquidation.

Even if only one class of claims has accepted the plan, the court may still confirm the plan under the Code's so-called **cram-down provision.** In other words, the court may confirm the plan over the objections of a class of creditors. Before the

---

18.   The plan need not provide for full repayment to unsecured creditors. Instead, creditors receive a percentage of each dollar owed to them by the debtor.

court can exercise this right of cram-down confirmation, it must be demonstrated that the plan "does not discriminate unfairly" against any creditors and that the plan is "fair and equitable."

# SECTION 4

# ADDITIONAL FORMS OF BANKRUPTCY RELIEF

In addition to bankruptcy relief through liquidation and reorganization, the Code also provides for individuals' repayment plans (Chapter 13) and family-farmer debt adjustments (Chapter 12).

## INDIVIDUALS' REPAYMENT PLANS

Chapter 13 of the Bankruptcy Code provides for "Adjustment of Debts of an Individual with Regular Income." Individuals (not partnerships or corporations) with *regular income* who owe fixed unsecured debts of less than $250,000 or fixed secured debts of less than $750,000 may take advantage of bankruptcy repayment plans.[19] This includes salaried employees; individual proprietors; and individuals who live on welfare, Social Security, fixed pensions, or investment income. Many small business debtors have a choice of filing a plan for reorganization or for repayment. There are several advantages, however, with repayment plans. One advantage is that they are less expensive and less complicated than reorganization proceedings or, for that matter, even liquidation proceedings.

## FILING THE PETITION

A repayment plan case can be initiated only by the filing of a voluntary petition by the debtor. Certain liquidation and reorganization cases may be converted to repayment plan cases with the consent of the debtor.[20] A trustee, who will make payments under the plan, must be appointed.

## AUTOMATIC STAY

Upon the filing of a repayment plan petition, the automatic stay previously discussed takes effect. It enjoins creditors from taking action against co-obligors of the debtor. Although the stay applies to all or part of a consumer debt, it does not apply to any business debt incurred by the debtor. A creditor has the right to seek relief from the automatic stay. To save the creditor time and money in seeking court approval to vacate (remove) the stay and recover from the co-debtor, the law provides that on the creditor's request to vacate the stay against the co-debtor, unless written objection is filed, twenty days later the stay against the co-debtor is automatically terminated without a hearing.

## THE REPAYMENT PLAN

A plan of rehabilitation by repayment must provide for the following:

1. The turnover to the trustee of such future earnings or income of the debtor as is necessary for execution of the plan.
2. Full payment in deferred cash payments of all claims entitled to priority.[21]
3. The same treatment of each claim within a particular class. (The Code permits the debtor to list co-debtors, such as guarantors or sureties, as a separate class.)

*Filing the Plan.* Only the debtor may file for a repayment plan. This plan may provide either for payment of all obligations in full or for payment of a lesser amount. The time for payment under the plan may not exceed three years unless the court approves an extension. The term, with extension, may not exceed five years.

The Code requires the debtor to make "timely" payments, and the trustee is required to ensure that the debtor commences these payments. The debtor must commence making payments under the proposed plan within thirty days after the plan has been *filed*. If the plan has not been confirmed, the trustee is instructed to retain the payments until the plan is confirmed and then distribute them accordingly. If the plan is denied, the trustee will return the payments to the debtor less any costs. Failure of the debtor to make timely payments or to commence payments within the thirty-day period will

---

19. Under the proposed amendments discussed in footnote 7, individuals with regular income who owe "debts of less than $1,000,000" may file an individual repayment plan under Chapter 13.

20. A Chapter 13 case may be converted to a Chapter 7 case at the request of either the debtor or, under certain circumstances, "for cause" by a creditor. A Chapter 13 case may be converted to a Chapter 11 case after a hearing.

---

21. As with a Chapter 11 reorganization plan, full repayment of all claims is not always required.

allow the court to convert the case to a liquidation bankruptcy or to dismiss the petition.

*Confirmation of the Plan.*   After the plan is filed, the court holds a confirmation hearing, at which interested parties may object to the plan. The court will confirm a plan with respect to each claim of a secured creditor under any of the following circumstances:

1.  If the secured creditors have accepted the plan.
2.  If the plan provides that creditors retain their liens and if the value of the property to be distributed to them under the plan is not less than the secured portion of their claims.
3.  If the debtor surrenders the property securing the claim to the creditors.

*Objection to the Plan.*   Unsecured creditors do not have a vote to confirm a repayment plan, but they can object to it. The court can approve a plan over the objection of the trustee or any unsecured creditor only in either of the following situations:

1.  When the value of the property to be distributed under the plan is at least equal to the amount of the claims.
2.  When all the debtor's projected disposable income to be received during the three-year plan period will be applied to making payments. Disposable income is all income received *less* amounts needed to support the debtor and dependents and/or amounts needed to meet ordinary expenses to continue the operation of a business.

*Modification of the Plan.*   Prior to completion of payments, the plan may be modified at the request of either the debtor, the trustee, or an unsecured creditor. If there is an objection to the modification by any interested party, the court must hold a hearing to determine approval or disapproval of the modified plan.

**DISCHARGE**   After completion of all payments, the court grants a discharge of all debts provided for by the repayment plan. Except for allowed claims not provided for by the plan, certain long-term debts provided for by the plan, and claims for alimony and child support, all other debts are dischargeable. A discharge of debts under a Chapter 13 repayment plan is sometimes referred to as a ''super-discharge.'' One of the reasons for this is

that the law allows a Chapter 13 discharge to include fraudulently incurred debt and claims resulting from malicious or willful injury. Therefore, a discharge under Chapter 13 may be much more beneficial to some debtors than a liquidation discharge under Chapter 7 might be.

Even if the debtor does not complete the plan, a hardship discharge may be granted if failure to complete the plan was due to circumstances beyond the debtor's control and if the value of the property distributed under the plan was greater than would have been paid in a liquidation. A discharge can be revoked within one year if it was obtained by fraud.

## FAMILY-FARMER PLANS

In 1986, to help relieve economic pressure on small farmers, Congress created Chapter 12 of the Bankruptcy Code by passing the Family Farmer Bankruptcy Act. The act, which was to remain in effect until October 1, 1993, was recently extended for another five years. The act defines a *family farmer* as one whose gross income is at least 50 percent farm dependent and whose debts are at least 80 percent farm related. The total debt must not exceed $1.5 million. A partnership or closely held corporation (at least 50 percent owned by the farm family) can also take advantage of this law.

The procedure for filing a family-farmer bankruptcy plan is very similar to the procedure for filing a repayment plan under Chapter 13. The farmer-debtor must file a plan not later than ninety days after the order for relief. The filing of the petition acts as an automatic stay against creditors' and co-obligors' actions against the estate.

The content of a family-farmer plan is basically the same as that of a Chapter 13 repayment plan. The plan can be modified by the farmer-debtor but, except for cause, must be confirmed or denied within forty-five days of the filing of the plan.

Court confirmation of the plan is the same as for a repayment plan. In summary, the plan must provide for payment of secured debts at the value of the collateral. If the secured debt exceeds the value of the collateral, the remaining debt is unsecured. For unsecured debtors, the plan must be confirmed if either the value of the property to be distributed under the plan equals the amount of the claim or the plan provides that all of the farmer-debtor's disposable income to be received in a three-year period (or longer, by court approval) will

■ CONCEPT SUMMARY 33.1 **Forms of Bankruptcy Relief Compared**

| ISSUE | CHAPTER 7 | CHAPTER 11 | CHAPTERS 12 AND 13 |
|---|---|---|---|
| **Purpose** | Liquidation. | Reorganization. | Adjustment. |
| **Who Can Petition** | Debtor (voluntary) or creditors (involuntary). | Debtor (voluntary) or creditors (involuntary). | Debtor (voluntary) only. |
| **Who Can Be a Debtor** | Any "person" (including partnerships and corporations) except railroads, insurance companies, banks, savings and loan institutions, and credit unions. Farmers and charitable institutions cannot be involuntarily petitioned. | Any debtor eligible for Chapter 7 relief; railroads are also eligible. | *Chapter 12*—Any family farmer whose gross income is at least 50 percent farm dependent and whose debts are at least 80 percent farm related or any partnership or closely held corporation at least 50 percent owned by a farm family, when total debt does not exceed $1.5 million. *Chapter 13*—Any individual (not partnerships or corporations) with regular income who owes fixed unsecured debts of less than $250,000 or secured debts of less than $750,000. |
| **Procedure Leading to Discharge** | Nonexempt property is sold with proceeds to be distributed (in order) to priority groups. Dischargeable debts are terminated. | Plan is submitted; if it is approved and followed, debts are discharged. | Plan is submitted (must be approved if debtor turns over disposable income for a three-year period); if it is approved and followed, debts are discharged. |
| **Advantages** | Upon liquidation and distribution, most debts are discharged, and the debtor has the opportunity for a fresh start. | Debtor continues in business. Creditors can accept the plan, or it can be "crammed down" on them. Plan allows for reorganization and liquidation of debts over the plan period. | Debtor continues in business or possession of assets. If plan is approved, most debts are discharged after a three-year period. |

be applied to making payments. Disposable income is all income received less amounts needed to support the farmer-debtor and family and to continue the farming operation. Completion of payments under the plan discharges all debts provided for by the plan.

A farmer who has already filed a reorganization or repayment plan may convert the plan to a family-farmer plan. The farmer-debtor may also convert a family-farmer plan to a liquidation plan.

## TERMS AND CONCEPTS TO REVIEW

adequate protection doctrine 635
automatic stay 635
consumer-debtor 632
cram-down provision 647
debtor in possession (DIP) 644

discharge 632
insider 638
liquidation 632
order for relief 633
petition in bankruptcy 632

preference 637
reaffirmation agreement 642
trustee 632
U.S. Trustee 637
workout 643

# QUESTIONS AND CASE PROBLEMS

**33–1. Voluntary versus Involuntary Bankruptcy.**
Burke has been a rancher all her life, raising cattle and crops. Her ranch is valued at $500,000, almost all of which is exempt under state law. Burke has eight creditors and a total indebtedness of $70,000. Two of her largest creditors are Oman ($30,000 owed) and Sneed ($25,000 owed). The other six creditors have claims of less than $5,000 each. A drought has ruined all of Burke's crops and forced her to sell many of her cattle at a loss. She cannot pay off her creditors.

    (a) Under the Bankruptcy Code, can Burke, with a $500,000 ranch, voluntarily petition herself into bankruptcy? Explain.

    (b) Could either Oman or Sneed force Burke into involuntary bankruptcy? Explain.

**33–2. Priority of Creditors.** Sam is a retail seller of television sets. He sells Gracen a $900 set on a retail installment security agreement in which she pays $100 down and agrees to pay the balance in equal installments. Sam retains a security interest in the set, and he perfects that interest by filing a financing statement locally. Two months later, Gracen is in default on her payments to Sam and is involuntarily petitioned into bankruptcy by her creditors. Sam wants to repossess the television set, as provided for in the security agreement, and he wants to have priority over the trustee in bankruptcy as to any proceeds from the disposal of the set. Discuss fully Sam's right to repossess and whether he has priority over the trustee in bankruptcy as to any proceeds from the disposal of the set.

**33–3. Preferences.** Peaslee is not known for his business sense. He started a greenhouse and nursery business two years ago, and because of his lack of experience, he soon was in debt to a number of creditors. On February 1, Peaslee borrowed $5,000 from his father to pay some of these creditors. On May 1, Peaslee paid back the $5,000, depleting his entire working capital. One creditor, the Cool Springs Nursery Supply Corp., extended credit to Peaslee on numerous purchases. Cool Springs pressured Peaslee for payment, and on July 1, Peaslee paid Cool Springs half the money owed. On September 1, Peaslee voluntarily petitioned

himself into bankruptcy. The trustee in bankruptcy claimed that both Peaslee's father and Cool Springs must turn over to the debtor's estate the amounts Peaslee paid to them. Discuss fully the trustee's claims.

**33–4. Distribution of Assets.** Montoro petitioned himself into voluntary bankruptcy. There were three major claims against his estate. One was made by Carlton, a friend who held Montoro's negotiable promissory note for $2,500; one was made by Elmer, an employee who was owed three months' back wages of $4,500; and one was made by the United Bank of the Rockies on an unsecured loan of $5,000. In addition, Dietrich, an accountant retained by the trustee, was owed $500, and property taxes of $1,000 were owed to Rock County. Montoro's nonexempt property was liquidated, with proceeds of $5,000. Discuss fully what amount each party will receive, and why.

**33–5. Discharge in Bankruptcy.** East Bank was a secured party on a $5,000 loan it made to Kirksey. Kirksey experienced financial difficulty, and creditors other than East Bank petitioned her into involuntary bankruptcy. The value of the secured collateral had substantially decreased in value. On its sale, the debt to East Bank was reduced to $2,500. Kirksey's estate consisted of $100,000 in exempt assets and $2,000 in nonexempt assets. After the bankruptcy costs and back wages to Kirksey's employees had been paid, nothing was left for unsecured creditors. Kirksey received a discharge in bankruptcy. Later she decided to go back into business. By selling a few exempt assets and getting a small loan, she would be able to buy a small, but profitable, restaurant. She went to East Bank for the loan. East Bank claimed that the balance of its secured debt had not been discharged in bankruptcy. Kirksey signed an agreement to pay East Bank the $2,500, as the bank had not been a party to petitioning her into bankruptcy. Because of this, East Bank made the new unsecured loan to Kirksey.

    (a) Discuss East Bank's claim that the balance of its secured debt had not been discharged in bankruptcy.

    (b) Discuss the legal effect of Kirksey's agreement to pay East Bank $2,500 after the discharge in bankruptcy.

    (c) If one year after buying the restaurant, Kirksey went into voluntary bankruptcy, what effect would the bankruptcy proceedings have on the new unsecured loan?

**33–6. Reorganization.** Tracey Service Co. filed a petition for a Chapter 11 reorganization. Acar Supply Co., one of Tracey's creditors, filed a motion to convert the case to a Chapter 7 liquidation. The court found that the debtor corporation had no place of business, no inventory, no equipment, no employees, and no business phone. Should Tracey Service be permitted to reorganize under Chapter 11? Explain. [*In re Tracey Service Co.,* 17 Bankr. 405 (Bankr.E.D.Pa. 1982)]

**33–7. Code Violations.** Prior to filing for bankruptcy, Bray was making loan payments to his company's credit union through payroll deductions. Bray's employer continued to deduct the loan payments from Bray's paychecks after being notified of the bankruptcy petition. Is this a violation of the Bankruptcy Code? Discuss. [*In re Bray,* 17 Bankr. 152 (Bankr.N.D.Ga. 1982)]

**33–8. Preferences.** In 1983, Beech Acceptance Corp. financed the sale of three airplanes to Gull Air, Inc. Approximately three years later, Gull Air defaulted on its obligations to Beech Acceptance, and Beech filed suit. Before the trial, Gull Air and Beech negotiated a workout agreement that provided for large monthly payments over a certain period. Despite the workout agreement, Gull Air filed a Chapter 11 petition in bankruptcy. Gull Air claimed that payments made under the workout agreement during the ninety days prior to the filing of the Chapter 11 petition amounted to a preference and must be returned to the debtor in possession (Gull Air). There was no question that Beech had received more than it would have under a Chapter 7 liquidation. Beech claimed that the payments had been made in the ordinary course of business. Discuss who is correct. [*In re Gull Air, Inc.,* 82 Bankr. 1 (Bankr.D.Mass. 1988)]

**33–9. Preferences.** Fred Currey purchased cattle from Itano Farms, Inc. As payment for the cattle, Currey gave Itano Farms worthless checks in the amount of $50,250. Currey was later convicted of passing bad checks, and the state criminal court ordered him to pay Itano Farms restitution in the amount of $50,250. About four months after this court order, Currey and his wife filed for Chapter 7 bankruptcy protection. During the ninety days prior to the filing of the petition, Currey had made three restitution payments to Itano, totaling $14,821. The Curreys sought to recover these payments as preferences. What should the court decide? Explain. [*In re Currey,* 144 Bankr. 490 (D.Ida. 1992)]

**33–10. Substantial Abuse of Chapter 7.** Ronald and Rhonda Harris filed a petition for liquidation under Chapter 7. They submitted a schedule that listed their debts at $9,735, their assets (other than real estate) at $7,295, their net monthly income at $2,249, and their monthly expenses at $1,973. The U.S. Trustee, concluding that the debtors could pay a significant portion of their unsecured debt under a three-year Chapter 13 plan, moved to dismiss the petition on the ground that to grant the Harrises relief would constitute a substan-

tial abuse of Chapter 7 under Section 707(b) of the Bankruptcy Code. The bankruptcy court denied the U.S. Trustee's motion, holding that two conditions must be met before a case can be dismissed for substantial abuse and that the trustee had failed to establish the existence of these conditions. The two conditions were (1) that the debtors exhibited "egregious behavior" (such as repeated bankruptcy filings evidencing bad faith, fraud, or misconduct) and (2) that a significant portion of the unsecured debt could be paid under a three-year Chapter 13 plan. Assuming that the debtors had not committed any egregious acts and that they did have the ability to pay all of their debts over a three-year period, how should the court rule on appeal? What is the primary factor to be considered when determining whether a debtor's actions constitute "substantial abuse" of Chapter 7? Discuss. [*U.S. Trustee v. Harris,* 960 F.2d 74 (8th Cir. 1992)]

**33–11. A Question of Ethics**

*In September 1986, Edward and Debora Davenport pleaded guilty in a Pennsylvania court to welfare fraud and were sentenced to probation for one year. As a condition of their probation, the Davenports were ordered to make monthly restitution payments to the county probation department, which would forward the payments to the Pennsylvania Department of Public Welfare, the victim of the Davenports' fraud. In May 1987, the Davenports filed a petition for Chapter 13 relief and listed the restitution payments among their debts. The bankruptcy court held that the restitution obligation was a dischargeable debt. On appeal, the district court reversed, holding that state-imposed criminal restitution obligations cannot be discharged in Chapter 13 bankruptcy. The Court of Appeals for the Third Circuit reversed the district court's decision, concluding that "the plain language of the chapter" demonstrated that restitution orders are debt within the meaning of the Code and hence dischargeable in proceedings under Chapter 13. Ultimately, the case was reviewed by the United States Supreme Court, which affirmed the Third Circuit's ruling. The Court noted that under the Bankruptcy Code, a debt is defined as a liability on a claim, and a claim is defined as a right to payment. Because the restitution obligations clearly constituted a right to payment, the Court held that the obligations were dischargeable in bankruptcy. [Pennsylvania Department of Public Welfare v. Davenport, 495 U.S. 552, 110 S.Ct. 2126, 109 L.Ed.2d 588 (1990)]*

1. Critics of this decision contend that the Court adhered to the letter, but not the spirit, of bankruptcy law in arriving at its conclusion. In what way, if any, did the Court not abide by the "spirit" of bankruptcy law?

2. Do you think that individuals' repayment plans, which allow nearly all types of debts to be discharged, tip the scales of justice too far in favor of debtors?

# FOCUS ON ETHICS

## Creditors' Rights and Bankruptcy

There is obviously no way in which the law can protect both debtors and creditors at all times under all circumstances. Trade-offs must be made in attempting to balance the rights of both groups, and the trade-offs made often lead to questions of fairness and justice. We look below at several aspects of debtor-creditor relationships that frequently pose ethical questions.

### Who Pays When the Debtor Defaults?

Although there is clearly a distinction in people's minds between the failure to pay a loan and the theft of personal property, the result is the same—the wealth of the creditor-seller is reduced. Whatever the ethical issue may be when a debtor fails to perform, the economic consequence is clear: the cost of a debtor's nonperformance is imposed on all other debtors who do perform. This cost takes the form of higher average interest rates.

That is, the greater the percentage of loan agreements that are not consummated according to the agreement, the larger will be the risk factor for creditors when extending credit. This larger risk factor is reflected in higher interest rates. Creditors

deal in a highly competitive market. They expect to earn a normal rate of return on their investments. If costs increase because of nonperformance by debtors, those costs will have to be recouped somewhere. In general, the only way to recoup them is to charge all debtors a higher interest rate.

This means that it is not only creditors who are harmed economically when debtors default but also ultimately all other debtors, actual and potential. Therefore, laws protecting debtors who default may, in fact, not be protecting the interests of debtors (as a group) in the long run.

### "Self-Help" Repossession

UCC 9–503 states that "[u]nless otherwise agreed, a secured party has on default the right to take possession of the collateral. In taking possession, a secured party may proceed without judicial process if this can be done without breach of the peace." The underlying rationale for this "self-help" provision of Article 9 is that it simplifies the process of repossession for creditors and reduces the burden on the courts. Because the UCC does not define "breach of the peace," it is not always easy to predict what will or will not constitute a breach of the peace.

From the debtor's point of view, it is not always clear what is happening when agents of the creditor appear to repossess collateral. Often, to avoid confrontation with the debtor and any potential violence or breach of the peace, a secured creditor will arrange to have collateral repossessed during the night or in the early-morning hours, when the repossession effort is least likely to be observed. For the debtor, repossession can therefore be very stressful. A debtor may awaken in the night and notice that his or her car is being towed away—without realizing that it is being repossessed.

At the same time, repossession can be risky for the creditor; if the repossession results in a breach of the peace, the creditor may be liable for substantial damages. For example, consider the case of *McCall v. Owens.*[1] The debtor, Boyce McCall, purchased a new Ford Pinto from a Ford dealer in May 1979, financing the purchase through a loan from the United American Bank. The installment sales contract stipulated that McCall would purchase and maintain insurance coverage on the Pinto, and if he did not, the

---

1. 820 S.W.2d 748 (Tenn.App. 1991).

bank would purchase the insurance and charge McCall for the premiums. McCall, however, opted to "self-insure" the car and refused to obtain the required coverage. The bank subsequently purchased insurance and charged McCall for the premiums, which McCall persistently refused to pay. Eventually, United American assigned the contract to First Tennessee Bank.

When McCall finished paying for the car, he still owed the bank $370 for insurance premiums and continued in his refusal to pay them. First Tennessee Bank decided to repossess the car and hired Ron Beverly of East Tennessee Auto Recovery to undertake the repossession. To tow the car, Beverly arranged to use a wrecker owned by Ted Owens and his son, Ted Douglas Owens, who jointly operated Ted's Chevron Service Station.

During the middle of a November night in 1983, McCall and his wife heard someone "stealing their car." Mrs. McCall phoned the police, while her husband got dressed and ran out to confront Ron Beverly and another man, who were about to tow the car from the property. The men were in such a hurry to tow the car that the wrecker ran over McCall's foot and knocked him to the ground. As a result of the affair, McCall required medical attention and six to eight weeks of bed rest.

Ultimately, McCall paid the disputed premiums, regained possession of his car, hired a lawyer, and sued all of the parties involved in the repossession—First

Tennessee Bank, East Tennessee Auto Recovery, Ron Beverly, Ted's Chevron, Ted Owens, and Ted Douglas Owens. McCall sought damages for a long list of wrongful acts: wrongful repossession, trespass to realty, chattel conversion (some personal property had been taken from the car), assault and battery, outrageous conduct, and defamation (based on the bank's report to a credit bureau about the repossession).

The court found that although the bank had a right to repossess the car to recover the $370, it had wrongfully breached the peace and could therefore be held liable for damages. The jury awarded a total of $115,000 in actual damages and $385,000 in punitive damages.

The point is that this incident—and others similar to it—would not have happened were it not for the UCC's self-help provision. And yet, there is no way to ensure that such confrontations will not occasionally result from repossession attempts. The trade-off here is clear: debtors are exposed, at times, to abuse and violence resulting from self-help repossessions so that creditors may collect on their debts quickly and without legal proceedings.

## Priority Disputes

Questions of fairness often arise when two or more creditors claim rights in the same collateral. Article 9 of the UCC, by establishing the order of priorities that apply in such situations, has attempted to

resolve priority disputes as equitably as possible. Still, however, situations arise in which there appears to be no way to avoid seemingly unjust results for one or more of the creditors involved.

Consider, for example, a recent case in which two creditors, a jeweler and a pawnbroker, each claimed superior rights to the same collateral—jewelry valued at nearly $40,000 that had been purchased from the jeweler with a bad check. The purchaser, Donald Pippin, wrote a check, on a bank account that had been closed, for $30,000 to purchase the jewelry, promising to pay the balance of the purchase price in installments. The jeweler, Osterman, Inc., took a security interest in the jewelry and subsequently perfected its interest by filing a financing statement. Before Osterman filed its financing statement, however, Pippin had pawned the jewelry for a $6,995 loan from National Pawn Brokers (NPB). Pippin was later caught and prosecuted for the fraud, and the jewelry was seized by the police. The question then arose as to which party had superior rights in the jewelry, Osterman or NPB.

Osterman claimed that it had superior rights in the jewelry because it had perfected its security interest by properly filing a financing statement, which the pawnbroker had not done. Osterman further argued that NPB could not take a security interest in the goods because before a security interest can attach to collateral, the debtor must have rights in the collateral—which Pippin did not have.

Enter the UCC. Recall from Chapter 21 that under UCC 2–403(1), a person with voidable title has the power to transfer good title to a good faith purchaser for value. The court deciding the issue looked to this provision of the UCC, as well as to case law, and concluded that Pippin, because he had voidable title (having procured the jewelry by fraud), had sufficient rights in the collateral to which a security interest could attach. Recall also from Chapter 31 that under UCC 9–305, a creditor who takes possession of the collateral automatically perfects a security interest in the goods. The court held, therefore, that both Osterman and NPB had perfected security interests in the jewelry and that because NPB had perfected its security interest first (its security interest was perfected the moment it took possession of the collateral), it had prior rights to the collateral.[2]

## The Problem of Proceeds

One of the ways the legal system protects creditors is by making it possible for a creditor to have not only a security interest in collateral but also an interest in the proceeds from the sale of the collateral. UCC 9–306(1) states that proceeds include "whatever is received upon the sale, exchange, collection or other disposition of collateral." If a debtor sells to a third party

equipment in which a creditor has a security interest, the payment received by the debtor in that sale will be proceeds of the collateral. Even if the goods in which there is a security interest are mixed with other goods and cannot be identified, the security interest still continues in the mass of mixed-up goods, such as wheat.

But what happens when flour is the collateral, and it is turned into bread? Obviously, the flour does not exist anymore, but the bread does, so the security interest persists in the bread. The same holds for flour, sugar, and eggs when they are made into a cake mix or a cake. Is there any point at which the proceeds of collateral are longer sufficiently related to the original collateral to allow the security interest to persist?

What about cattle or hog feed? If there is a security interest in the feed and it is fed to animals, does the security interest continue in the animals? If we based our logic on the flour example above, the answer would have to be yes. At least one court, however, has come to the opposite conclusion. In *Farmers Cooperative Elevator Co. v. Union State Bank,*[3] the issue was hog feed and hogs. The bank argued that the hogs were a form of proceeds; and because the UCC allows that a security interest continues in collateral "and also continues in any identifiable proceeds," the hogs were subject to a security interest as proceeds.

The court said no. Fattened hogs as proceeds are

unacceptable. The court reasoned that some distinct end product or mass from the biological transformation of the feed had to exist for the UCC to be operative. The hogs were the same before and after feeding, and therefore there were "no traceable proceeds." The feed was ingested, rather than manufactured, processed, or assembled. Through the process of biological transformation, the feed had been transformed into the animals. At that point, according to the court, the feed (and the bank's security interest) ceased to exist.

## Bankruptcy

The first goal of bankruptcy law is to provide relief and protection to debtors who have "gotten in over their heads." But consider the concept of bankruptcy from the point of view of the creditor. The creditor has extended a transfer of purchasing power from himself or herself to the debtor. That transfer of purchasing power represents a transfer of an asset for an asset. The debtor obtains the asset of money, goods, or services, and the creditor obtains the asset called a *secured* or *unsecured* legal obligation to pay. Once the debtor is in bankruptcy, voluntarily or involuntarily, the asset that the creditor owns most often has a diminished value. Indeed, in many circumstances, that asset has no value. Bankruptcy law attempts to provide a fair means of distributing to creditors the assets remaining in the debtor's possession.

---

2. *National Pawn Brokers Unlimited v. Osterman, Inc.,* 176 Wis.2d 418, 500 N.W.2d 407 (Wis. 1993).

---

3. 409 N.W.2d 178 (Iowa 1987).

Society has generally concluded that everyone should be given the chance to start over again. Thus, bankruptcy law is a balancing act between providing such a chance and ensuring that creditors are given "a fair shake." But the easier it becomes for debtors to hide behind bankruptcy laws, the greater will be the incentive for debtors to use such laws to avoid payment of legally owed sums of money. That also means that the more easily a debtor can hide behind bankruptcy laws, the more a creditor will charge, because of the increased degree of risk.

## Bankruptcy and Economics

The total number of bankruptcies per year has increased dramatically since the enactment of the Bankruptcy Reform Act of 1978. In 1976, for example, 193,000 debtors petitioned for bankruptcy relief. Today, that number has climbed to approximately 900,000 bankruptcies per year.

The increased number of bankruptcies means that creditors incur higher risks in making loans, because bankruptcy shifts the cost of the debt from the debtor to the creditor. To compensate for these higher risks, creditors will do one or more of the following: increase the interest rates charged to everyone, require more security (collateral), or be more selective in the granting of credit. Thus, a trade-off exists: the more lenient bankruptcy laws are, the better off will be those debtors who find themselves in bankruptcy; but those debtors who will never be in bankruptcy will be worse off. Ethical concerns here must be matched with the economic concerns of other groups of individuals affected by the law.

## ■ Discussion Questions

**1.** Is it unethical to avoid paying one's debts by going into bankruptcy? Does a person have a moral responsibility to pay his or her debts? After his haberdashery went bankrupt in the 1930s, President Harry Truman went on to pay all his creditors over the next decade, even though he had no legal obligation to do so. Should all bankrupt individuals acknowledge their responsibilities, as President Truman did?

**2.** Do you think that the law favors debtors at the expense of creditors, or vice versa? Is there any way a better balance between creditors' and debtors' interests could be achieved?

**3.** Although filing for bankruptcy is now much easier than it used to be and many more debtors are choosing bankruptcy as a solution to their financial difficulties, bankruptcy also has its negative side: those who go through bankruptcy have a difficult time reestablishing credit because of the "black mark" on their credit records. Is it ethical for a business to refuse to deal with a customer simply because that person once went into bankruptcy, even though that person is now a good credit risk in every other way? Is it consistent with bankruptcy law—the whole purpose of which is to rehabilitate debtors—for debtors to be burdened by this consequence? Can it be avoided?

**4.** So long as a breach of the peace does not result, a lender may repossess goods on the debtor's default under the self-help provision of the UCC. Do you think that this provision is fair to debtors? Should debtors have a right to be notified in advance of the creditors' intentions to repossess collateral?

# UNIT SIX

# AGENCY

## CONTENTS

**34** **Agency Formation and Duties**

**35** **Liability to Third Parties and Termination**

# CHAPTER 34

# AGENCY FORMATION AND DUTIES

**A**n **agency** relationship exists when one party, called the **agent,** agrees to represent or act for another party, called the **principal.** The principal has the right to control the agent's conduct in matters entrusted to the agent. An agency relationship may be created orally; by a writing; and in certain cases, merely by conduct. A court might even find that an agency relationship existed when the parties to it had no intention to create such a relationship. An agent may be engaged to accomplish a single task or to carry out many tasks.

Agency relationships permeate every aspect of modern economic life. By using agents, a principal can conduct multiple business operations simultaneously in various locations. Thus, for example, contracts that bind the principal can be made at different places with different persons at the same time. A familiar example of an agent is a corporate officer who serves in a representative capacity for the owners of the corporation. In this capacity, the officer has the authority to bind the principal (the corporation) to a contract. Indeed, agency law is essential to the existence and operation of a corporate entity, because only through its agents can a corporation function and enter into contracts.

## SECTION 1

## AGENCY RELATIONSHIPS

The Restatement (Second) of Agency defines *agency* as ''the fiduciary relation which results from the manifestation of consent by one person to another that the other shall act in his behalf and subject to his control, and consent by the other so to act.''[1] The term **fiduciary** is at the heart of agency law. The term can be used both as a noun and as an adjective. When used as a noun, it refers to a person having a duty created by his or her undertaking to act primarily for another's benefit in matters connected with the undertaking. When used as an adjective, as in ''fiduciary relationship,'' it means that the relationship is one involving trust and confidence.

In a principal-agent relationship, the parties have agreed that the agent will act *on behalf and instead of* the principal in negotiating and transacting business with third persons. An agent is empowered to perform legal acts that are binding on the principal and can bind a principal in a contract with a third person. For example, Porter is hired as a booking agent for a rock group, The Players. As the group's agent, Porter can negotiate and sign contracts for the rock group to appear at concerts. The contracts will be binding and thus legally enforceable against the group.

Agency relationships commonly exist between employers and employees and sometimes between employers and independent contractors who are hired to perform special tasks or services.

## EMPLOYER-EMPLOYEE RELATIONSHIPS

Prior to the industrial revolution, the terms *employer* and *employee* had no significance in the common law rules of agency. The term originally used to denote an employer-employee relationship was *master-servant relationship*. The terms *master* and *servant* are now archaic and outdated; but because they have been traditionally used in the law governing agency relationships, they are still encountered occasionally.

Today's law defines a *servant* as an employee and a *master* as an employer. An employee is defined as one whose physical conduct is *controlled, or subject to* control, by the employer. Normally, all employees who deal with third parties are deemed to be agents. For example, a sales clerk in a department store is deemed to be an agent of the store.

State and federal employment laws apply only to the employer-employee relationship. Statutes governing Social Security, withholding taxes, workers' compensation, unemployment compensation, workplace safety laws, and the like (see Chapter 36) are applicable only if there is an employer-employee status. *These laws do not apply to the independent contractor.*

## EMPLOYER–INDEPENDENT CONTRACTOR RELATIONSHIPS

Independent contractors are not employees, because those who hire them have no control over the details of their physical performance. The Restatement (Second) of Agency, Section 2, defines an **independent contractor** as follows:

> a person who contracts with another to do something for him but who is not controlled by the other nor subject to the other's right to control with respect to his physical conduct in the performance of the undertaking. He may or may not be an agent.

Building contractors and subcontractors are independent contractors, and a property owner does not control the acts of either of these professionals. Truck drivers who own their equipment and hire out on a per-job basis are independent contractors, but truck drivers who drive company trucks on a regular basis are usually employees. A collection agent and a real estate broker are other examples of independent contractors.

The relationship between a principal and an independent contractor may or may not involve an agency relationship. To illustrate: An owner of real estate who hires a real estate broker to negotiate a sale of his or her property has not only contracted with an independent contractor (the real estate broker) but has also established an agency relationship for the specific purpose of assisting in the sale of the property. Another example is an insurance agent, who is both an independent contractor and an agent of the insurance company for which he or she sells policies.

A question frequently faced by the courts in determining liability under agency law is whether a person hired by another to do a job is an employee or an independent contractor. Because employers are normally held liable as principals for the actions

---

1. Restatement (Second) of Agency, Section 1(1). The Restatement is an authoritative summary of the law of agency and is often referred to by jurists in decisions and opinions.

■ **Exhibit 34–1 IRS Factors for Determining Employee Status**

| | | |
|---|---|---|
| Generally, a worker will be classified by the Internal Revenue Service as an employee if the answers to the following questions are "yes": | | |
| ☐ Yes ☐ No | 1. | *Does the worker receive training from the employer?* |
| ☐ Yes ☐ No | 2. | *Is the worker given detailed instructions about performing particular tasks?* |
| ☐ Yes ☐ No | 3. | *Does the worker provide services that must be rendered personally?* |
| ☐ Yes ☐ No | 4. | *Does the worker maintain a continuous working relationship with the employer?* |
| ☐ Yes ☐ No | 5. | *Does the worker abide by the employer's work schedule?* |
| ☐ Yes ☐ No | 6. | *Does the worker work primarily at the employer's office or plant?* |
| ☐ Yes ☐ No | 7. | *Does the worker receive regular payments at periodic intervals?* |
| ☐ Yes ☐ No | 8. | *Does the worker use the employer's tools to perform work-related tasks?* |
| ☐ Yes ☐ No | 9. | *Does the worker work for only one employer at a time?* |
| ☐ Yes ☐ No | 10. | *Is the worker unable to offer work-related services to the general public?* |
| ☐ Yes ☐ No | 11. | *May the worker be fired by the employer?* |

made by their employee-agents within the scope of employment (as will be discussed later in this chapter), the court's decision as to employee versus independent-contractor status can be significant for the parties. In making this determination, courts often consider the following questions:

1.  How much control can the employer exercise over the details of the work?
2.  Is the employed person engaged in an occupation or business distinct from that of the employer?
3.  Is the work usually done under the employer's direction or is it done by a specialist without supervision?
4.  Does the employer supply the tools at the place of work?
5.  For how long is the person employed?
6.  What is the method of payment—by time period or at the completion of the job?
7.  What degree of skill is required of the person employed?

Generally, the greater the employer's control over the work, the more likely it is that the worker will be considered an employee. Another key factor is whether the employer withholds taxes from payments made to the worker and pays unemployment and Social Security taxes covering the worker.

Whether a worker is classified as an employee or an independent contractor also has significant tax ramifications. Independent contractors can avoid certain tax liabilities by taking advantage of business organizational forms available to small businesses (see Chapter 38). Therefore, the Internal Revenue Service (IRS) tends to scrutinize closely a firm's classification of a worker who provides services for the firm as an independent contractor rather than an employee. Regardless of the firm's classification of a worker's status as an independent contractor, if the IRS decides that the worker should be classified as an employee, then the employer will be responsible for paying any applicable Social Security, withholding, and unemployment taxes.

In making its determination, the IRS takes into account any number of the twenty factors contained in its Revenue Ruling 87–41. The IRS will compare the relative importance of these factors in making a final determination. Exhibit 34–1 lists eleven of the key factors that will be evaluated by the IRS in making its decision.

Although in some circumstances it is advantageous to have independent-contractor status, in others, employee status may confer desirable benefits on the worker. In the following case, for example, an insurance agent who lost his job wanted to take advantage of the protection offered to older employees by the Age Discrimination in Employment Act of 1967. Because that act governs only employer-employee relationships, the agent tried to convince the court that he was an employee rather than an independent contractor.

**BACKGROUND AND FACTS** *Elmer Oestman was an insurance agent for National Farmers Union Insurance Company. The company's contract, called a "local agent agreement," provided—among other things—that the "[l]ocal agent, acting solely as an independent contractor, is hereby authorized to solicit and submit written applications for insurance policies and other contracts of insurer strictly in accordance with the instructions and direction of insurer." The contract specifically stated that "[n]othing contained herein shall be construed as creating the relationship of employer and employee between the local agent and insurer." Oestman was paid on a commission basis, and no Social Security or income taxes were paid or withheld for him by the company. He filed taxes as a self-employed individual. He set his own and his staff's working hours, had complete discretion over hiring and firing his staff, bore all expenses incurred in selling insurance, and provided his own transportation and office equipment. When his "employment" was terminated, Oestman sued the company, alleging violation of the Age Discrimination in Employment Act of 1967. The trial court found that Oestman was an independent contractor and therefore, because the ADEA governs only employer-employee relationships, had no cause of action under the ADEA. Oestman appealed.*

| CASE 34.1 |
| --- |
| **OESTMAN v. NATIONAL FARMERS UNION INSURANCE CO.** United States Court of Appeals, Tenth Circuit, 1992. 958 F.2d 303. |

*SETH*, Circuit Judge.

\* \* \* \*

The question of whether an insurance agent is an employee or an independent contractor under ADEA is one of first impression in this circuit. \* \* \*

\* \* \* \*

\* \* \* The facts in the present case, taken as a whole, lead us to the conclusion that Mr. Oestman was an independent contractor and not an employee under ADEA.

The focus \* \* \* is the employer's right to control the "means and manner" of the worker's performance. In this case, Appellant's performance was subject to virtually no restrictions. Appellant's daily activities were not supervised and he was free to work as he chose. Appellant was not required to report to his office or to spend certain hours in pursuit of sales.

\* \* \* \*

We note that there are some elements of the working relationship between the parties that when looked at alone seem to indicate an employer/employee relationship. However, on balance, the relationship is more accurately characterized as employer/independent contractor.

**DECISION AND REMEDY**  *The appellate court affirmed the trial court's decision. Oestman was an independent contractor and thus had no cause of action under the ADEA.*

**ETHICAL CONSIDERATIONS**  *Clearly, independent contractors enjoy benefits that are not allowed to employees. For example, independent contractors are usually free to establish their own time schedules and work without any direct supervision by their "employers." Yet employees, in contrast, normally have benefits that are not accorded to independent contractors, including employee benefit plans, taxation benefits (the employer pays half of the employee's Social Security taxes, for example), and standing to sue under laws passed specifically to protect employees. In essence, those who opt for independent-*

*contractor status trade off the rights and benefits that they could obtain as employees. Therefore, when independent contractors allege employee status to benefit from laws governing employer-employee relationships, courts will normally hold that those benefiting from independent-contractor status cannot, as the old adage phrases it, "have their cake and eat it, too."*

# FORMATION OF THE AGENCY RELATIONSHIP

The following discussions will emphasize the usual form taken by agency relationships. Such relationships are *consensual;* that is, they come about by voluntary consent and agreement between the parties. Generally, the agreement need not be in writing,[2] and consideration is not required.

A principal must have legal capacity to enter into contracts. A person who cannot legally enter into contracts directly should not be allowed to do so indirectly through an agent. Because an agent derives the authority to enter into contracts from the principal, and a contract made by an agent is legally viewed as a contract of the principal, it is immaterial whether the agent personally has the legal capacity to make that contract. Thus, a minor can be an agent but in some states cannot be a principal appointing an agent.[3] When a minor is permitted to be a principal, however, any resulting contracts will be voidable by the minor principal but not by the adult third party. In sum, any person can be an agent, regardless of whether he or she has the capacity to contract. Even a person who is legally incompetent can be appointed an agent.

An agency relationship can be created for any legal purpose. One created for an illegal purpose or contrary to public policy is unenforceable. If LaSalle (as principal) contracts with Burke (as agent) to sell illegal narcotics, the agency relationship is unenforceable, because selling illegal narcotics is a felony and is contrary to public policy. It is also illegal for medical doctors and other licensed professionals to employ unlicensed agents to perform professional actions.

Generally, no formalities are required to create an agency. The agency relationship can arise by acts of the parties in one of the four ways discussed in the following sections.

## AGENCY BY AGREEMENT

Because agency is a consensual relationship, normally it must be based on an express or implied agreement that the agent will act for the principal and the principal agrees to have the agent so act. An agency agreement can take the form of an express written contract. For example, Arnstein enters into a written agreement with Vogel, a realtor, to sell Arnstein's house. An agency relationship exists between Arnstein and Vogel for the sale of the house and is detailed in a written document that both parties sign.

Many express agency agreements are oral. If Arnstein orally asks Gracen, a gardener, to contract with others for the care of his lawn on a regular basis, and Gracen orally agrees, an agency relationship exists between Arnstein and Gracen for the lawn care.

An agency agreement can also be implied by conduct. For example, a hotel expressly allows only Hans Cooper to park cars, but Hans has no employment contract there. The hotel's manager tells Hans when to work and where and how to park the cars. The hotel's conduct amounts to a manifestation of its willingness to have Hans park its customers' cars, and Hans can infer from the hotel's conduct that he has authority to act as a parking valet. It can be inferred that Hans is an

---

2. There are two main exceptions to the statement that agency agreements need not be in writing: (1) Whenever agency authority empowers the agent to enter into a contract that the Statute of Frauds requires to be in writing, then the agent's authority from the principal must likewise be in writing (this is called the *equal dignity rule*). (2) A power of attorney, which confers authority to an agent, must be in writing. Both of these exceptions will be discussed in Chapter 35.

3. Some courts have granted exceptions to allow a minor to appoint an agent for the limited purpose of contracting for the minor's necessities of life. See *Casey v. Kastel,* 237 N.Y. 305, 142 N.E. 671 (1924).

agent for the hotel, his purpose being to provide valet parking services for hotel guests.

## AGENCY BY RATIFICATION

On occasion, a person who is in fact not an agent may make a contract on behalf of another (a principal). If the principal approves or affirms that contract by word or by action, an agency relationship is created by **ratification.** Ratification is a question of intent, and intent can be expressed by either words or conduct. The basic requirements for ratification are discussed in Chapter 35.

## AGENCY BY ESTOPPEL

When a principal causes a third person to believe that another person is his or her agent, and the third person deals with the supposed agent, the principal is ''estopped to deny'' the agency relationship. In such a situation, the principal's actions create the *appearance* of an agency that does not in fact exist.

Suppose Jerry accompanies Grant, a seed sales representative, to call on a customer, Palko, the proprietor of the Neighborhood Seed Store. Jerry has done sales work but is not employed by Grant at this time. Grant boasts to Palko that he wishes he had three more assistants ''just like Jerry.'' Palko has reason to believe from Grant's statements that Jerry is an agent for Grant. Palko then places seed orders with Jerry. If Grant does not correct the impression that Jerry is an agent, Grant will be bound to fill the orders just as if Jerry were really Grant's agent. Grant's representation to Palko created the impression that Jerry was Grant's agent and had authority to solicit orders.

Agency by estoppel does not extend to all acts under all circumstances. For example, the acts or declarations of the purported agent in and of themselves do not create an agency by estoppel. It is the deeds or statements of the principal, not the agent, that create an agency. In addition, the third person must prove that he or she *reasonably* believed that an agency relationship existed and that the agent had authority. Facts and circumstances must show that an ordinary, prudent person familiar with business practice and custom would have been justified in concluding that the agent had authority. The following case illustrates these requirements.

---

**BACKGROUND AND FACTS** *During 1988 and 1989, Jerry Hall performed services as an independent contractor for the King & Wills Insurance Agency. Hall's contract with the agency authorized him to solicit insurance customers and to sell health, home, automobile, and commercial insurance policies. King & Wills provided Hall with an office and business cards identifying Hall as a King & Wills sales representative. King & Wills also took out a life insurance policy on Hall's life, listing King & Wills as Hall's employer and the beneficiary of the policy. King & Wills's advertisements in the yellow pages, on billboards, and on the outdoor office sign held Hall out to be a member of King & Wills. King & Wills did not monitor Hall's activities and did not require that he provide an itinerary of the businesses that he solicited. In the fall of 1988, Hall created a fictitious commercial insurance policy for the Wabash Independent Oil Company. Wabash gave Hall a check payable to King & Wills as a down payment for the policy and made regular premium payments to King & Wills for nearly a year thereafter. Hall never procured the insurance policy. Instead, he deposited the down payment and all further payments made by Wabash (which he intercepted at King & Wills's post office box) into his personal bank account. In all, Hall acquired more than $60,000 from Wabash and used it for his own benefit. Throughout this period, King & Wills was unaware of Hall's fraudulent activities. Wabash later filed suit against King & Wills, claiming, among other things, that King & Wills was liable for Hall's misappropriation of funds and failure to procure insurance. The trial court, finding that an agency existed between Hall and King & Wills, found in Wabash's favor, and King & Wills appealed.*

**CASE 34.2**

**WABASH INDEPENDENT OIL CO. v. KING & WILLS INSURANCE AGENCY**

Appellate Court of Illinois, Fifth District, 1993.
248 Ill.App.3d 719,
618 N.E.2d 1214,
188 Ill.Dec. 644.

*Justice MAAG* delivered the opinion of the court:

\* \* \* \*

A principal who has placed an agent in a situation where he may be presumed to have authority to act is estopped as against third persons from denying the agent's apparent authority. We believe that the trial court properly found Hall to be an agent of King & Wills. They placed Hall in a position equivalent to the agent in a principal-agent relationship, and King & Wills are estopped from denying that Hall was acting as their agent.

\* \* \* \*

The doctrine of estoppel [was] developed to prevent injustice or fraud, and where injury has resulted from the wrongful act of a third person, the damages flowing from the wrongful act must be borne by the party whose conduct made possible the wrongdoer's act, breach of trust, fraud, or negligence. When one of two innocent persons must suffer by the act of a third, he who by his conduct, act, or omission enabled the third person to occasion the loss must sustain the loss. And when one of two innocent persons \* \* \* must suffer a loss, it must be borne by that one of them who by his conduct has rendered the injury possible or who could have prevented it.

**DECISION AND REMEDY** *The appellate court affirmed the trial court's holding.*

**INTERNATIONAL CONSIDERATIONS** **Apparent Agency Authority and Ambassadors** *As will be discussed in the next chapter, issues may arise over whether a person who is clearly an agent for a known principal has exceeded his or her authority. For example, there is no question that ambassadors are agents for their governments. But sometimes questions arise as to whether an ambassador is authorized to bind his or her government in contract with a third party. In one case, the ambassador of Antigua took out a $250,000 loan on behalf of his government. The bank claimed that the ambassador had apparent authority to make such a contract. The government of Antigua argued that the ambassador had no such authority. The court disagreed with both sides and held that whether the ambassador was authorized to bind the government of Antigua to the contract was a disputed issue of fact that required a full trial. [First Fidelity Bank, N.A. v. Government of Antigua & Barbuda, 877 F.2d 189 (2d Cir. 1989)]*

## AGENCY BY OPERATION OF LAW

In some cases, the courts have found it desirable to find an agency relationship in the absence of a formal agreement. This may occur in family relationships. For example, suppose one spouse purchases certain basic necessaries and charges them to the other spouse's charge account. The courts will often rule that the latter is liable for payment of the necessaries, either because of a social policy of promoting the general welfare of the spouse or because of a legal duty to supply necessaries to family members.

Agency by operation of law may also occur in emergency situations, when an employee who has no agency authority to contract with others does so anyway due to an emergency. For example, a railroad engineer may contract on behalf of his or her employer for medical care for an injured motorist hit by the train.

## SECTION 3

# DUTIES OF AGENTS AND PRINCIPALS

Once the principal-agent relationship has been created, both parties have duties that govern their con-

# ■ CONCEPT SUMMARY 34.1  Formation of Principal-Agent Relationship

| METHOD OF FORMATION | DESCRIPTION |
|---|---|
| **By Agreement** | Agency relationship is formed through express consent (oral or written) or implied from conduct. |
| **By Ratification** | Principal either by act or agreement ratifies conduct by a person who is not in fact an agent. |
| **By Estoppel** | Principal causes a third person to believe that another person is his or her agent, and the third person acts to his or her detriment in reasonable reliance on that belief. |
| **By Operation of Law** | Agency relationship is based on a social duty (such as the need to support family members) or formed in emergency situations when the agent is unable to contact the principal. |

duct. As discussed previously, the principal-agent relationship is *fiduciary*—one of trust. In a fiduciary relationship, each party owes the other the duty to act with the utmost good faith. In this section, we examine the various duties of agents and principals.

## AGENT'S DUTIES

The duties that an agent owes to a principal are set forth in the agency agreement or arise by operation of law. They are implied from the agency relationship *whether or not the identity of the principal is disclosed to a third party.* When an agent employs or appoints a *subagent,* a fiduciary duty exists between the subagent and the principal, as well as between the subagent and the agent. Subagents owe the same duties to agents and to principals as agents owe to principals. Generally, the agent owes the principal five duties—performance, notification, loyalty, obedience, and accounting.

**DUTY OF PERFORMANCE**  An implied condition in every agency contract is the agent's agreement to use reasonable diligence and skill in performing the work. When an agent fails to perform his or her duties entirely, liability for breach of contract generally will result. The degree of skill or care required of an agent is usually that expected of a reasonable person under similar circumstances.

In most cases, this is interpreted to mean ordinary care (see Chapter 6). An agent may, however, have represented himself or herself as possessing special skills (such as those that an accountant or attorney possesses). In these situations, the agent is expected to exercise the skill or skills claimed. Failure to do so constitutes a breach of the agent's duty.

Not all agency relationships are based on contract. In some situations, an agent acts gratuitously—that is, not for money. A gratuitous agent cannot be liable for breach of contract, as there is no contract; he or she is subject only to tort liability. Once a gratuitous agent has begun to act in an agency capacity, he or she has the duty to continue to perform in that capacity in an acceptable manner and is subject to the same standards of care and duty to perform as contractual agents. Consider an example: Bower's friend, Alcott, is a real estate broker. Alcott gratuitously offers to sell Bower's farm. If Alcott never attempts to sell the farm, Bower has no legal cause of action to force Alcott to do so. If Alcott does find a buyer and keeps promising a sales contract, but fails to provide one within a reasonable period of time, causing the buyer to seek other property, then Bower has a cause of action in tort for negligence.

The following case raises an interesting question: Did an agent breach his duty to perform by failing to procure a life insurance policy notwithstanding the fact that no life insurance company would have insured the principal—because he used drugs?

CASE 34.3

**BIAS v. ADVANTAGE INTERNATIONAL, INC.**
United States Court of Appeals,
District of Columbia Circuit,
1990.
905 F.2d 1558.

**COMPANY PROFILE**    *Walter Brown founded the Boston Celtics basketball team in 1946. In the 1950s and 1960s, with Arnold "Red" Auerbach's coaching skills and Bill Russell's gifted playing ability and later coaching, the Celtics became the greatest dynasty in basketball history, winning eleven National Basketball Association (NBA) championships (eight in a row). The Celtics overcame a slump in the late 1970s with the help of players Larry Bird, Kevin McHale, and Robert Parish to win their fourteenth title in 1981. In 1986, the owners set the team up as a limited partnership. The Boston Celtics Limited Partnership operates what has been called the most successful sports franchise in history. As a franchise, the Celtics are valued at $91 million, the fourth highest value in the NBA. The team has won sixteen NBA titles, with seventeen players included in basketball's Hall of Fame and fifteen designated Most Valuable Player. The team's general partner is a corporation owned by Don Gaston, Alan Cohen, and Paul Dupee, Jr., but nearly 80,000 other investors own about half of the partnership units. The Celtics generate revenues through home-game ticket sales, television and radio rights, and Celtic merchandise. The Celtics play most of their home games in the old Boston Garden. A new Boston Garden was scheduled to open in 1995, although the waiting list for season tickets is fifteen years.*

**BACKGROUND AND FACTS**    *Leonard Bias, a basketball player, entered into an agency agreement with Advantage International, Inc., under which Advantage agreed to advise and represent Bias in his affairs. On June 17, 1986, Bias was picked by the Boston Celtics in the first round of the National Basketball Association draft. On the morning of June 19, 1986, Bias died of cocaine intoxication. Bias's estate sued Advantage, alleging, among other things, that Advantage had failed to procure a $1 million ("jumbo") life insurance policy on Bias, as it had been directed to do. Bias's parents maintained that Advantage had represented to Bias and to them that it had secured such a policy, and in reliance on these assurances, Bias's parents had not independently sought to buy an insurance policy on Bias's life. The trial court granted summary judgment for Advantage, holding that, in effect, the estate had not suffered any damage from Advantage's failure to obtain life insurance for Bias because even if Advantage had tried to obtain the life insurance policy, it would not have been able to do so because of Bias's cocaine use. The estate appealed, arguing that the questions of whether Bias was a drug user and was uninsurable were triable issues of fact and should have gone to the jury.*

*SENTELLE,* Circuit Judge.
\*    \*    \*    \*

\*    \*    \* The testimony of Long and Gregg [former teammates of Bias] clearly tends to show that Bias was a cocaine user. \*    \*    \* The testimony of Bias's parents to the effect that they knew Bias well and did not know him to be a drug user does not rebut the Long and Gregg testimony about Bias's drug use on particular occasions. \*    \*    \* Bias's parents and coach did not have personal knowledge of Bias's activities at the sorts of parties and gatherings about which Long and Gregg testified. The drug test results offered by the Estate may show that Bias had no cocaine in his system on the dates when the tests were administered, but, as the District Court correctly noted, these tests speak only to Bias's abstention during the periods preceding the tests. The tests do not rebut the Long and Gregg testimony that on a number of occasions Bias ingested cocaine in their presence.

The Estate could have deposed Long and Gregg, or otherwise attempted to impeach their testimony. The Estate also could have offered the testimony of other friends or teammates of Bias who were present at some of the gatherings described by Long and Gregg, who went out with Bias frequently, or who were otherwise familiar with his social habits. The Estate did none of these things. The Estate is not entitled to reach the jury merely on the supposition that the jury might not believe the defendants' witnesses. We thus agree with the District Court that there was no genuine issue of fact concerning Bias's status as a cocaine user.

\*   \*   \*   \*

\*   \*   \* The defendants offered evidence that every insurance company inquires about the prior drug use of an applicant for a jumbo policy at some point in the application process. \*   \*   \* The Estate failed to name a single particular company or provide other evidence that a single company existed which would have issued a jumbo policy in 1986 without inquiring about the applicant's drug use. Because the Estate has failed to do more than show that there is "some metaphysical doubt as to the material facts," the District Court properly concluded that there was no genuine issue of material fact as to the insurability of a drug user.

*The trial court's judgment was affirmed.*

**DECISION AND REMEDY**

**DUTY OF NOTIFICATION** It is a maxim in agency law that all that the agent knows, the principal knows. Thus, it is only logical that the agent be required to notify the principal of all matters that come to his or her attention concerning the subject matter of the agency. This is the duty of notification. What the agent actually tells the principal is not relevant; what the agent *should have told* the principal is crucial. Under the law of agency, notice to the agent is notice to the principal.

**DUTY OF LOYALTY** Loyalty is one of the most fundamental duties in a fiduciary relationship. Basically stated, the agent has the duty to act solely for the benefit of his or her principal and not in the interest of the agent or a third party. For example, an agent cannot represent two principals in the same transaction unless both know of the dual capacity and consent to it. Thus, a real estate agent cannot represent both the seller and the buyer in a transaction, unless the seller and the buyer so agree. The duty of loyalty also means that any information or knowledge acquired through the agency relationship is considered confidential. It would be a breach of loyalty to disclose such information either during the agency relationship or after its termination. Typical examples of confidential information are trade secrets and customer lists compiled by the principal.

Furthermore, an agent employed by a principal to buy cannot buy from himself or herself, and an agent employed to sell cannot become the purchaser, without the principal's consent. In short, the agent's loyalty must be undivided. The agent's actions must be strictly for the benefit of the principal and must not result in any secret profit for the agent.

**DUTY OF OBEDIENCE** When an agent is acting on behalf of the principal, a duty is imposed on that agent to follow all lawful and clearly stated instructions of the principal. Any deviation from such instructions is a violation of this duty. During emergency situations, however, when the principal cannot be consulted, the agent may deviate from such instructions without violating this duty if the circumstances so warrant. Whenever instructions are not clearly stated, the agent can fulfill the duty of obedience by acting in good faith and in a manner reasonable under the circumstances.

**DUTY OF ACCOUNTING** Unless an agent and a principal agree otherwise, the agent has the duty to keep and make available to the principal an account of all property and money received and paid out on behalf of the principal. This includes gifts from third persons in connection with the agency. For example, a gift from a customer to a salesperson for prompt deliveries made by the salesperson's firm belongs to the firm. The agent has a duty to maintain separate accounts for the principal's funds and for the agent's personal funds, and no intermingling of these accounts is allowed. Whenever a licensed professional (such as an attorney) violates this duty to account, he or she may be subject to disciplinary proceedings carried out by the appropriate regulatory institution (such as the state bar association) in addition to being liable to the principal for failure to account.

## PRINCIPAL'S DUTIES

The principal also has certain duties to the agent, either expressed or implied by law. The four duties of the principal—compensation, reimbursement and indemnification, cooperation, and safe working conditions—are discussed here.

**DUTY OF COMPENSATION**  In general, when a principal requests certain services from an agent, the agent reasonably expects payment. A duty is therefore implied for the principal to pay the agent for services rendered. For example, when an accountant or an attorney is asked to act as an agent, an agreement to compensate the agent for such service is implied. The principal also has the duty to pay that compensation in a timely manner.

Except in a gratuitous agency relationship, in which an agent does not act for money, the principal must pay the agreed-upon value for an agent's services. When the amount of compensation has been agreed upon by the parties, the principal owes the duty to pay it on completion of the agent's specified activities. If no amount has been expressly agreed upon, then the principal owes the agent the customary compensation for such services.

**DUTY OF REIMBURSEMENT AND INDEMNIFICATION**  Whenever an agent disburses sums of money at the request of the principal, and whenever the agent disburses sums of money to pay for necessary expenses in the course of a reasonable performance of his or her agency duties, the principal has the duty to reimburse the agent for these payments. Agents cannot recover for expenses incurred by their own misconduct or negligence, however.

Subject to the terms of the agency agreement, the principal has the duty to *indemnify* (compensate) an agent for liabilities incurred because of authorized and lawful acts and transactions. For example, if the agent, on the principal's behalf, forms a contract with a third party and the principal fails to perform the contract, the third party may sue the agent for damages. In this situation, the principal is obligated to compensate the agent for any costs incurred by the agent as a result of the principal's failure to perform the contract. The amount of indemnification may be specified in the agency contract. If it is not, the courts will look to the nature of the business and the type of loss to determine the amount.

**DUTY OF COOPERATION**  A principal has a duty both to cooperate with and to assist an agent in performing his or her duties. The principal must do nothing to prevent such performance. For example, when a principal grants an agent an exclusive territory, creating an *exclusive agency*, the principal cannot compete with the agent or appoint or allow another agent to so compete in violation of the exclusive agency. Such competition would expose the principal to liability for the agent's lost sales or profits.

**DUTY TO PROVIDE SAFE WORKING CONDITIONS**  The common law requires the principal to provide safe working premises, equipment, and conditions for all agents and employees. The principal has a duty to inspect working conditions and to warn agents and employees about any unsafe areas. When the agency is one of employment, the employer's liability is frequently covered by workers' compensation insurance, which is the primary remedy for an employee's injury on the job (see Chapter 36).

## SECTION 4

# REMEDIES AND RIGHTS OF AGENTS AND PRINCIPALS

It is said that every wrong has its remedy. In business situations, disputes between agents and principals may arise out of either contract or tort laws and carry corresponding remedies. These remedies include monetary damages, termination of the agency relationship, injunction, and required accountings.

## AGENT'S RIGHTS AND REMEDIES AGAINST PRINCIPAL

For every duty of the principal, the agent has a corresponding right. Therefore, the agent has the right to be compensated, reimbursed, and indemnified and to work in a safe environment. An agent also has the right to perform agency duties without interference by the principal.

Remedies of the agent for breach of duty by the principal follow normal contract and tort remedies. For example, under appropriate circumstances, an agent can lawfully withhold further performance and demand that the principal give an accounting.

When the principal-agent relationship is not contractual, an agent has no right to specific performance. An agent can recover for past services and future damages but cannot force the principal to allow him or her to continue acting as an agent.

## PRINCIPAL'S RIGHTS AND REMEDIES AGAINST AGENT

In general, a principal has contract remedies for an agent's breach of fiduciary duties. The principal also has tort remedies for fraud, misrepresentation, negligence, deceit, libel, slander, and trespass committed by the agent. In addition, any breach of a fiduciary duty by an agent may justify the principal's termination of the agency. The main actions available to the principal are constructive trust, avoidance, and indemnification.

**CONSTRUCTIVE TRUST**  Anything an agent obtains by virtue of the employment or agency relationship belongs to the principal. It is a breach of an agent's fiduciary duty to retain secretly benefits or profits that, by right, belong to the principal. Courts in this case will impose a **constructive trust.** The agent actually holds the money on behalf of the principal, and the principal can recover it in a lawsuit. For example, Andrews, a purchasing agent, gets cash rebates from a customer. If Andrews keeps the rebates, he violates his fiduciary duty to his principal, Metcalf. On finding out about the cash rebates, Metcalf can sue Andrews and recover them.

An agent is also prohibited from taking advantage of the agency relationship to obtain goods or property that the principal wants to purchase. For example, Peterson (the principal) wants to purchase property in the suburbs. Cox, Peterson's agent, learns that a valuable tract of land has just become available. Cox cannot buy the land for herself. Peterson gets the right of first refusal. If Cox purchases the land for her own benefit, the courts will impose a constructive trust on the land; that is, the land will be held for, and on behalf of, the principal despite the fact that the agent attempted to buy it in her own name.

**AVOIDANCE**  When an agent breaches the agency agreement or agency duties under a contract, the principal has a right to avoid any contract entered into with the agent. This right of avoidance is at the election of the principal.

In the following case, a real estate agent was supposedly acting on behalf of a landowner for the sale of real estate. The trial court had to decide whether the agent had breached his fiduciary duties.

---

**BACKGROUND AND FACTS**  *Ramsey, the plaintiff, was a licensed real estate broker and was also in the business of buying and holding land for resale. Gordon, the defendant, was the owner of approximately 181 acres of land and engaged Ramsey's services as a broker to find a buyer for the property. Ramsey, when he heard that the land was rapidly appreciating in value, told Gordon that he would buy the land himself. Gordon then agreed to sell Ramsey the tract of land for $800 per acre. A contract of sale to convey the property was drawn up; but before the contract was executed, Gordon conveyed the property to a third party for the same price ($800 per acre). Meanwhile, Ramsey, acting for himself, began negotiating for the resale of that property to another customer for a price of $1,250 per acre. Naturally, when Ramsey learned that Gordon had conveyed the*

CASE 34.4

**RAMSEY v. GORDON**

Court of Civil Appeals of Texas—Waco, 1978.
567 S.W.2d 868.

*property to another buyer, he blamed Gordon for his lost profits. Ramsey claimed that he had lost over $90,000 in profits on the resale of the property and brought an action against Gordon to recover this amount. Gordon maintained that Ramsey had breached his fiduciary duties as Gordon's agent by not finding a purchaser for the best price available. The trial court held for Gordon, and Ramsey appealed.*

*HALL,* Justice.
\* \* \* \*

Ramsey does not challenge the finding that the property was increasing in value when the contract was being negotiated and made with Gordon, nor the findings that he knew the value as increasing and failed to disclose that fact to Gordon. Indeed, he may not do so because [the findings] are amply supported by the evidence and its inferences. His response to the conclusion that he breached his duties as Gordon's agent is to argue that he was only a purchaser and to cite Gordon's testimony that Gordon believed $800.00 per acre was a fair price when he made the contract. The over-all import of the record is that when it served Ramsey's purposes he would claim that under the contract he was Gordon's agent, but that in fact he used the contract to speculate with the property to his personal advantage without disclosure to Gordon. As we have said, the [trial] court found that Ramsey was Gordon's agent. Ramsey's testimony supports that finding.

*Whenever an agent breaches his duty to his principal by becoming personally interested in an agency agreement, the contract is voidable at the election of the principal without full knowledge of all the facts surrounding the agent's interest.* [Emphasis added.] \* \* \* [It is a] "settled rule" that "an agent in dealing with a principal on his own account owes it to the principal not only to make no misstatements concerning the subject matter of the transaction, but also to disclose to him fully and completely all material facts known to the agent which might affect the principal; and that unless this duty on the part of the agent has been met, the principal cannot be held to have ratified the transaction."

**DECISION AND REMEDY**   *The judgment of the trial court was affirmed.*

---

**INDEMNIFICATION**   A principal can be sued by a third party for an agent's negligent conduct, and in certain situations the principal can sue the agent for an equal amount of damages. This is called *indemnification.* The same holds true if the agent violates the principal's instructions. For example, Lewis (the principal) tells his agent, Moore, who is a used-car salesman, to make no warranties for the used cars. Moore is eager to make a sale to Walters, a third party, and makes a warranty for the car's engine. Lewis is not absolved from liability to Walters for engine failure, but if Walters sues Lewis, Lewis normally can then sue Moore for indemnification for violating his instructions.

Sometimes it is difficult to distinguish between instructions of the principal that limit an agent's authority and those that are merely advice. For example, Willis (the principal) owns an office supply company; Jones (the agent) is the manager. Willis tells Jones, "Don't order any more inventory this month." Willis goes on vacation. A large order comes in from a local business, and the present inventory is insufficient to meet it. What is Jones to do? In this situation, Jones probably has the inherent authority to order more inventory despite Willis's command. It is unlikely that Jones would be required to indemnify Willis in the event that the local business subsequently canceled the order.

## TERMS AND CONCEPTS TO REVIEW

agency 658
agent 658
constructive trust 669

fiduciary 659
independent contractor 659
principal 658

ratification 663

# QUESTIONS AND CASE PROBLEMS

**34–1. Agency Formation.** Paul Gett is a well-known, wealthy financier living in the city of Torris. Adam Wade, Gett's friend, tells Timothy Brown that he is Gett's agent for the purchase of rare coins. Wade even shows Brown a local newspaper clipping mentioning Gett's interest in coin collecting. Brown, knowing of Wade's friendship with Gett, contracts with Wade to sell a rare coin valued at $25,000 to Gett. Wade takes the coin and disappears with it. On the date of contract payment, Brown seeks to collect from Gett, claiming that Wade's agency made Gett liable. Gett does not deny that Wade was a friend, but he claims that Wade was never his agent. Discuss fully whether an agency was in existence at the time the contract for the rare coin was made.

**34–2. Agent's Duties to Principal.** Alice is hired by Peter as an agent to sell a piece of property owned by Peter. The price to be obtained is to be at least $30,000. Alice discovers that because a shopping mall is planned for the area of Peter's property, the fair market value of the property will be at least $45,000 and could be higher. Alice forms a real estate partnership with her cousin Carl, and she prepares for Peter's signature a contract for $32,000 for sale of the property to Carl. Peter signs the contract. Just before closing and passage of title, Peter learns about the shopping mall and the increased fair market value of his property. Peter refuses to deed the property to Carl. Carl claims that Alice, as agent, solicited a price above that agreed on in the creation of the agency and that the contract is therefore binding and enforceable. Discuss fully whether Peter is bound to this contract.

**34–3. Agency Formation.** John Paul Corp. made the following contracts:

   (a) A contract with Able Construction to build an addition to the corporate office building.

   (b) A contract with a certified public accountant (CPA), a recent college graduate, to head the cost accounting section.

   (c) A contract with a salesperson to travel a designated area to solicit orders (contracts) for the corporation.

Able contracts with Apex for materials for the addition; the CPA hires an experienced accountant to advise her on certain accounting procedures; and the salesperson contracts to sell a large order to Green, agreeing to deliver the goods in person within twenty days. Later, Able refuses to pick up the materials, the CPA is in default in paying the hired consultant, and the salesperson does not deliver on time. Apex, the accountant, and Green claim John Paul Corp. is liable under agency law. Discuss fully whether an agency relationship was created by John Paul with Able, the CPA, or the salesperson.

**34–4. Agent's Duties to Principal.** Ankir is hired by Peters as a traveling salesperson. Ankir not only solicits orders but also delivers the goods and collects payments from his customers. Ankir places all payments in his private checking account and at the end of each month draws sufficient cash from his bank to cover the payments made. Peters is totally unaware of this procedure. Because of a slowdown in the economy, Peters tells all his salespeople to offer 20 percent discounts on orders. Ankir solicits orders, but he offers only 15 percent discounts, pocketing the extra 5 percent paid by customers. Ankir has not lost any orders by this practice, and he is rated one of Peters's top salespersons. Peters learns of Ankir's actions. Discuss fully Peters's rights in this matter.

**34–5. Employee versus Independent Contractor.** L.M.T. Steel Products, Inc., contracted with a school to install numerous room partitions. To accomplish this work, L.M.T. hired a man named Webster. Webster was not a regular employee of L.M.T., and it was stipulated that he was to be paid by the number of feet of partitions installed. Webster did not have a contractor's license. He hired other workers to do the installing, and these workers were paid by L.M.T. Webster was given blueprints by L.M.T., but he was not otherwise at any time actively supervised by L.M.T. on the job. Needing to place a telephone call to L.M.T., Webster drove his own personal vehicle to a public telephone. On the way, he negligently collided with another car, and an occupant of that car, Peirson, was injured. Peirson sued L.M.T., claiming that Webster was an employee. L.M.T. claimed that Webster was an independent contractor. Who was correct? Explain. [*L.M.T. Steel Products, Inc. v. Peirson,* 47 Md.App. 633, 425 A.2d 242 (1981)]

**34–6. Agent's Duties to Principal.** Broyles signed a sales representative's agreement with NCH Corp. that included covenants not to compete and not to solicit NCH customers after termination of the agreement. NCH maintained detailed and costly records of its routes and customers. It considered this information to be valuable and sensitive, although all the data were readily ascertainable from other sources. Broyles transcribed the names and information with intent to use this material after he left NCH's employ. He later voluntarily terminated his employment with NCH and went to work for a competing firm. Based on the information he had transcribed while an employee of NCH, he solicited business from some of his former customers. NCH sued Broyles, claiming that the use of his list was a breach of his employment contract and a breach of his fiduciary duty to NCH. Discuss whether NCH was successful in its claim that Broyles had breached his fiduciary duty. [*NCH Corp. v. Broyles,* 749 F.2d 247 (5th Cir. 1985)]

**34–7. Principal's Duties to Agent.** Aztec Petroleum Corp. arranged to have Douglas buy oil and gas leases for Aztec. In return for his services, Douglas was to receive an initial $5,000 plus a royalty interest in the leases he obtained. Douglas obtained a number of leases for Aztec but represented to Aztec that the prices paid for the leases were higher than they actually were. By sending Aztec photocopies of checks altered both as to payee and amount, along with forged receipts, Douglas was able to keep for himself a substantial amount of the money that Aztec had entrusted to him for payment of the leases. This money was used by Douglas for personal purchases, including two new cars, a boat, and other personal items. When Aztec refused to grant Douglas the promised royalty interest in the leases, Douglas brought suit to obtain it. The trial court held for Aztec, and Douglas appealed. In view of Douglas's deceptive activities, is Aztec required to grant the royalty interest? Discuss fully. [*Douglas v. Aztec Petroleum Corp.,* 695 S.W.2d 312 (Tex.App. 1985)]

**34–8. Employee versus Independent Contractor.** Clifford Aymes was hired by Jonathan Bonelli of Sun Island Sales, Inc., to create a computer program for Sun Island to use in maintaining records of its cash receipts, inventory, sales figures, and other data. No agreement was reached as to ownership rights in the program that Aymes developed, called CSALIB. Aymes did most of his programming at the Sun Island office. Although Bonelli gave Aymes frequent instructions as to what he wanted from the program, Aymes generally worked alone and enjoyed considerable autonomy in his work. He worked fairly regular hours, but he was not always paid by the hour—occasionally, he submitted bills (invoices) to Sun Island for his work. Aymes never received any employee benefits, such as health insurance, and Sun Island never withheld federal and state taxes from Aymes's paycheck. Furthermore, it did not pay any Social Security taxes on Aymes's earnings. When Bonelli unilaterally cut Aymes's hours in violation of an alleged oral agreement, Aymes left Sun Island

and demanded compensation for Sun Island's use of CSALIB. Bonelli refused to pay Aymes for the program's use and also stated that he would not pay Aymes $14,560 in back wages unless Aymes signed a form releasing all rights in CSALIB. Aymes then sued Bonelli and Sun Island for copyright infringement, and the court had to decide who owned the copyright in the program. Central to the determination of this issue was whether Aymes was an employee of Sun Island or an independent contractor. What should the court decide, and why? [*Aymes v. Bonelli,* 980 F.2d 857 (2d Cir. 1992)]

**34–9. A Question of Ethics**

*Erwin Ernst was the sole shareholder and chief executive officer of Matchmaker Real Estate Sales Center, Inc., located in Chicago. During 1987 and 1988, the Leadership Council for Metropolitan Open Communities, a nonprofit corporation, conducted a series of tests to see if Matchmaker sales agents engaged in "racial steering." In each test, one white couple and one black couple, evenly matched with regard to financial qualifications and housing needs, were sent to Matchmaker and told Matchmaker that they were looking for homes in southwest Chicago. Matchmaker agents consistently directed the white couples to higher-priced homes in white neighborhoods and the black couples to lower-priced homes in black or racially mixed neighborhoods. The city of Chicago, the Leadership Council, and the individual testers (the plaintiffs) all sued Matchmaker for violations of federal laws prohibiting racial discrimination and discrimination in housing. The court found the real estate agents to be employees, not independent contractors, and both Ernst and his corporation, Matchmaker, were held liable for compensatory damages under the doctrine of* respondeat superior. [*Under this doctrine, an employer is liable for the actions of his or her employees that are committed within the scope of employment—see Chapter 35.*] *The agents were held liable for both compensatory and punitive damages.* [Chicago v. Matchmaker Real Estate Sales Center, Inc., *982 F.2d 1086 (7th Cir. 1992)*]

1. In view of the fact that Ernst had specifically instructed his agents not to engage in discriminatory practices, is it fair to hold Ernst and Matchmaker liable for damages? Why or why not?

2. The court concluded that Ernst and Matchmaker should not be held liable for punitive damages in this case. Do you agree with this conclusion? Why or why not?

3. Ernst argued that the plaintiffs had no standing to sue because they had sustained no injury. The court, however, held that each of the plaintiffs had standing to bring suit. How might you justify the court's conclusion that the plaintiffs had met the injury requirement for standing to sue?

# CHAPTER 35

# LIABILITY TO THIRD PARTIES AND TERMINATION

A s discussed in the previous chapter, the law of agency focuses on the special relationship that exists between a principal and an agent—how the relationship is formed and the duties the principal and agent assume once the relationship is established. This chapter deals with another important aspect of agency law—the liability of principals and agents to third parties. We first look at the rights of third parties who enter into *contracts* with agents. Such contracts will make an agent's principal liable to the third party only if the agent had authority to make the contract or if the principal ratified, or was estopped from denying, the agent's acts.

The second part of the chapter will deal with an agent's liability to third parties in contract and tort and the principal's liability to third parties because of an agent's torts. The chapter concludes with a discussion of how agency relationships are terminated.

## SECTION 1

## SCOPE OF AGENT'S AUTHORITY

A principal's liability in a contract with a third party arises from the authority given the agent to enter legally binding contracts on the principal's behalf. An agent's authority can be either *actual* (express or implied) or *apparent.*

### EXPRESS AUTHORITY

**Express authority** is embodied in that which the principal has engaged the agent to do. Express authority can be given orally or in writing. The **equal dignity rule** in most states requires that if the contract being executed is or must be in writing, then the agent's authority must also be in writing. Failure to comply with the equal dignity rule can make a contract voidable *at the option of the principal.* The law regards the contract at that point as a mere offer. If the principal decides to accept the offer, acceptance must be ratified, or affirmed, in writing. Assume that Pattberg (the principal) orally asks Austin (the agent) to sell a ranch that Pattberg owns. Austin finds a buyer and signs a sales contract (a contract for an interest in realty must be in writing) on behalf of Pattberg to sell the ranch. The buyer cannot enforce the contract unless Pattberg subsequently ratifies Austin's agency status in writing. Once the contract is ratified, either party can enforce rights under the contract.

An exception to the equal dignity rule exists in modern business practice. An executive officer of a corporation, when acting for the corporation in an ordinary business situation, is not required to obtain written authority from the corporation. In addition, the equal dignity rule does not apply when an agent acts in the presence of a principal or when the agent's act of signing is merely perfunctory. Thus, if Healy (the principal) negotiates a contract but is called out of town the day it is to be signed and orally authorizes Scougall to sign, the oral authorization is sufficient.

Giving an agent a **power of attorney** confers express authority.[1] The power of attorney is a writ-

---

1.   An agent who holds the power of attorney is called an *attorney-in-fact* for the principal. The holder does not have to be an attorney-at-law (and often is not).

ten document and is usually notarized. (A document is notarized when a **notary public**—a public official authorized to attest to the authenticity of signatures—signs and dates the document and imprints it with his or her seal of authority.) A power of attorney can be special (permitting the agent to do specified acts only), or it can be general (permitting the agent to transact all business dealings for the principal). Because of the extensive authority granted to an agent by the latter (see Exhibit 35–1 on page 676), a general power of attorney is used with great caution and usually only in exceptional circumstances.

An ordinary power of attorney terminates on the incapacity or death of the person giving the power. A *durable* power of attorney, however, provides an agent with very broad powers to act and make decisions for the principal and specifies that it is not affected by the principal's incapacity. An elderly person, for example, might grant a durable power of attorney to provide for the handling of property and investments or specific health-care needs should he or she become incompetent.

The following case illustrates the formalities required for a power of attorney to give the holder the right to convey real estate.

---

| CASE 35.1 |
| --- |

**BLOOM v. WEISER**

District Court of Appeal of
Florida,
Third District, 1977.
348 So.2d 651.

**BACKGROUND AND FACTS**   *Joseph Weinberg and Rachela Weiser purchased a condominium unit as joint tenants.[a] Thereafter, Weinberg executed a general power of attorney making his son, Arthur Winters, his agent. Winters conveyed Weinberg's one-half interest in the condominium to Weinberg's daughter, Miriam Bloom. After Weinberg's death, Bloom wanted to sell the condominium, but Weiser claimed complete ownership by right of survivorship on the ground that the agent had no authority to transfer the real estate to Bloom. The trial court held for Weiser, and Bloom appealed.*

*HAVERFIELD, Judge.*
  *   *   *   *

The established rule is that a power of attorney must be strictly construed and the instrument will be held to grant only those powers which are specified. We are of the view that for a power of attorney to authorize a conveyance of real estate, the authority of the agent to do so must be plainly stated. Reviewing the power of attorney granted Winters, we find the instrument contains no specific grant of power autho-

---

a.   As will be discussed in Chapter 49, in a joint tenancy each tenant owns an undivided interest in the property; on the death of a tenant, his or her interest becomes the property of the surviving tenant. This is called the right of survivorship.

rizing him to convey real estate. Therefore, the July 18 deed executed by Winters and purporting to convey Weinberg's one-half interest in the subject condominium unit to Miriam Bloom is void.

*The appellate court affirmed the trial court's ruling. The deed executed by Winters was void, and title to the condominium belonged to Weiser.*

**DECISION AND REMEDY**

## IMPLIED AUTHORITY

**Implied authority** is conferred by custom, can be inferred from the position the agent occupies, or is implied by virtue of being reasonably necessary to carry out express authority. For example, Carlson is employed by Packard Grocery to manage one of its stores. Packard has not specified (expressly stated) Carlson's authority to contract with third persons. In this situation, authority to manage a business implies authority to do what is reasonably required (as is customary or can be inferred from a manager's position) to operate the business. This includes making contracts for obtaining employee help, for buying merchandise and equipment, and even for advertising the products sold in the store.

Because implied authority is conferred on the basis of custom, it is important for third persons to be familiar with the custom of the trade. The list of rules that have developed to determine what authority is implied based on custom or on the agent's position is extensive. In general, implied authority is authority customarily associated with the position occupied by the agent or authority that can be inferred from the express authority given to the agent to perform fully his or her duties. The test is whether it was reasonable for the agent to believe that he or she had the authority to enter the contract in question.

## APPARENT AUTHORITY AND ESTOPPEL

Actual authority (express or implied) arises from what the principal manifests *to the agent.* An agent has **apparent authority** when the principal, by either word or action, causes a *third party* reasonably to believe that an agent has authority to act, even though the agent has no express or implied authority. If the third party changes his or her position in reliance on the principal's representations, the principal may be *estopped* from denying that the agent had authority.

For example, a traveling salesperson has no express authority to collect for orders solicited from customers. Because the agent neither possesses the goods ordered nor delivers them, the agent also has no implied authority to collect. Assume that a customer, Ling, pays an agent, Adam, for a solicited order. Adam then takes the payment to the principal's accounting department. An accountant accepts payment and sends Ling a receipt. This procedure is thereafter followed for other orders solicited and paid for by Ling. Later Adam solicits an order, and Ling pays Adam as before. This time, however, Adam absconds with the money. Can Ling claim that the payment to Adam was authorized and thus, in effect, a payment to the principal? The answer is yes, because the principal's *repeated* acts of accepting Ling's payment led Ling reasonably to believe that Adam had authority to receive payments for goods solicited. Although Adam did not have express or implied authority, the principal's conduct gave Adam apparent authority to collect. The principal would be estopped from claiming that the agent had no authority to collect in this particular case.

There are other ways that a principal may go beyond mere statements that convince a third party that a certain person is the principal's agent. If, for example, the principal has "clothed the agent" with both possession and apparent ownership of the principal's property, the agent has very broad powers and can deal with the property as if he or she were the true owner.

For example, to deceive certain creditors, Sikora (the principal) and Hunter (the agent) agree verbally that Hunter will hold certain stock certificates for Sikora. Because the certificates are bearer paper (that is, they do not require indorsement to be transferred), Hunter's possession and apparent ownership of the stock certificates are such strong indications of ownership that a reasonable person would conclude that Hunter was the actual owner. If Hunter negotiates the stock certificates to a third

■ **Exhibit 35–1 Sample General Power of Attorney**

# POWER OF ATTORNEY
### GENERAL

**Know All Men by These Presents:** That I, _____
_____

the undersigned (jointly and severally, if more than one) hereby make, constitute and appoint _____
_____

as true and lawful Attorney for me and in my name, place and stead and for my use and benefit:

(a) To ask, demand, sue for, recover, collect and receive each and every sum of money, debt, account, legacy, bequest, interest, dividend, annuity and demand (which now is or hereafter shall become due, owing or payable) belonging to or claimed by me, and to use and take any lawful means for the recovery thereof by legal process or otherwise, and to execute and deliver a satisfaction or release therefor, together with the right and power to compromise or compound any claim or demand;

(b) To exercise any or all of the following powers as to real property, any interest therein and/or any building thereon: To contract for, purchase, receive and take possession thereof and of evidence of title thereto; to lease the same for any term or purpose, including leases for business, residence, and oil and/or mineral development; to sell, exchange, grant or convey the same with or without warranty; and to mortgage, transfer in trust, or otherwise encumber or hypothecate the same to secure payment of a negotiable or non-negotiable note or performance of any obligation or agreement;

(c) To exercise any or all of the following powers as to all kinds of personal property and goods, wares and merchandise, choses in action and other property in possession or in action: To contract for, buy, sell, exchange, transfer and in any legal manner deal in and with the same; and to mortgage, transfer in trust, or otherwise encumber or hypothecate the same to secure payment of a negotiable or non-negotiable note or performance of any obligation or agreement;

(d) To borrow money and to execute and deliver negotiable or non-negotiable notes therefor with or without security; and to loan money and receive negotiable or non-negotiable notes therefor with such security as he shall deem proper;

(e) To create, amend, supplement and terminate any trust and to instruct and advise the trustee of any trust wherein I am or may be trustor or beneficiary; to represent and vote stock, exercise stock rights, accept and deal with any dividend, distribution or bonus, join in any corporate financing, reorganization, merger, liquidation, consolidation or other action and the extension, compromise, conversion, adjustment, enforcement or foreclosure, singly or in conjunction with others of any corporate stock, bond, note, debenture or other security; to compound, compromise, adjust, settle and satisfy any obligation, secured or unsecured, owing by or to me and to give or accept any property and/or money whether or not equal to or less in value than the amount owing in payment, settlement or satisfaction thereof;

(f) To transact business of any kind or class and as my act and deed to sign, execute, acknowledge and deliver any deed, lease, assignment of lease, covenant, indenture, indemnity, agreement, mortgage, deed of trust, assignment of mortgage or of the beneficial interest under deed of trust, extension or renewal of any obligation, subordination or waiver of priority, hypothecation, bottomry, charter-party, bill of lading, bill of sale, bill, bond, note, whether negotiable or non-negotiable, receipt, evidence of debt, full or partial release or satisfaction of mortgage, judgment and other debt, request for partial or full reconveyance of deed of trust and such other instruments in writing of any kind or class as may be necessary or proper in the premises.

**Giving and Granting** unto my said Attorney full power and authority to do and perform all and every act and thing whatsoever requisite, necessary or appropriate to be done in and about the premises as fully to all intents and purposes as I might or could do if personally present, hereby ratifying all that my said Attorney shall lawfully do or cause to be done by virtue of these presents. The powers and authority hereby conferred upon my said Attorney shall be applicable to all real and personal property or interests therein now owned or hereafter acquired by me and wherever situate.

My said Attorney is empowered hereby to determine in his sole discretion the time when, purpose for and manner in which any power herein conferred upon him shall be exercised, and the conditions, provisions and covenants of any instrument or document which may be executed by him pursuant hereto; and in the acquisition or disposition of real or personal property, my said Attorney shall have exclusive power to fix the terms thereof for cash, credit and/or property, and if on credit with or without security.

The undersigned, if a married woman, hereby further authorizes and empowers my said Attorney, as my duly authorized agent, to join in my behalf, in the execution of any instrument by which any community real property or any interest therein, now owned or hereafter acquired by my spouse and myself, or either of us, is sold, leased, encumbered, or conveyed.

When the contest so requires, the masculine gender includes the feminine and/or neuter, and the singular number includes the plural.

WITNESS my hand this _____ day of _____ , 19_____

_____        _____

_____        _____

State of California,
County of _____ } SS.

On _____ , before me, the undersigned, a Notary Public in and for said State, personally appeared _____
_____
known to me to be the person _____ whose name _____ subscribed
to the within instrument and acknowledged that _____ executed the same.
Witness my hand and official seal.                                    (Seal) _____
                                                                              Notary Public in and for said State.

person, Sikora will be estopped from denying Hunter's authority to transfer the stock.

When land is involved, courts have held that possession alone is not a sufficient indication of ownership (see Chapter 51 for details). If, however, the agent also possesses the deed to the property and sells the property against the principal's wishes to an unsuspecting buyer, the principal normally cannot cancel the sale or assert a claim to title.

The following case illustrates a situation dealing with apparent authority.

---

**BACKGROUND AND FACTS** *Red River Commodities, Inc. (RRC), entered into a contract with Kelby Eidsness under which RRC agreed to purchase 250,000 pounds of sunflowers. Because of a drought, Eidsness was able to deliver only 75,084 pounds. The contract contained an excuse clause in which it was stated that if Eidsness could not deliver the promised 250,000 pounds because of an event unanticipated at the time that the contract was formed, Eidsness would be excused from performance only if he seasonably notified RRC of his inability to perform. Eidsness orally notified RRC's contracting representative, Richard Frith, whom Eidsness assumed was RRC's agent, about his poor crop in September before the harvest. RRC insisted that Frith was not a contracting agent and had no authority to bind RRC in any way. The RRC-Eidsness contract included the following statement: "The contracting representative identified below [Frith] does not have the authority to alter or vary the terms of this agreement. He is not an agent of RRC." Nevertheless, after contracts were made, Frith frequently contacted growers for RRC to help with their production problems. Frith talked to growers, inspected fields, and reported to RRC. RRC's manager testified that Frith was his "go-between" with growers such as Eidsness. Eidsness assumed that Frith was an agent of RRC and therefore that notice to Frith of the drought and of Eidsness's inability to perform the contract completely would suffice as notice to RRC. In RRC's suit against Eidsness for breach of contract, the trial court directed a verdict for RRC, holding, among other things, that Eidsness had failed to give notice of his inability to perform, because Frith was "an independent sales representative" and "not an agent ... insofar as production, acts of God, waivers, and the like are concerned." Eidsness appealed.*

**CASE 35.2**

**RED RIVER COMMODITIES, INC. v. EIDSNESS**

Supreme Court of North Dakota, 1990.
459 N.W.2d 805.

*MESCHKE*, Justice.
\* \* \* \*

RRC's characterization of Frith as "independent" of RRC is not controlling. *How a principal and agent describe their relationship between themselves does not regulate their relationship to others.* [Emphasis added.] \* \* \*

An agency "is ostensible [appears to exist] when the principal intentionally or by want of ordinary care causes a third person to believe another to be his agent, who really is not employed by him." An ostensible agency exists where the conduct of the supposed agent is consistent with an agency, and where, in a particular transaction, someone is justified in dealing with the supposed agent. An apparent or ostensible agency "must rest upon conduct or communications of the principal which, reasonably interpreted, causes a third person to believe that the agent has authority to act for and on behalf of the principal." \* \* \*

There was evidence that Frith knew about Kelby's [Eidsness's] poor production, other than through generalized knowledge of drought conditions. Kelby testified that

Frith contacted him during the fall before harvest, and that he told Frith that he expected his crop production to be * * * between 20% and 50% of the contracted quantity per acre. * * *

Notice to an agent is ordinarily notice to the principal. Evidence of Kelby's actual notice to Frith should be reconsidered by the trial court with a correct understanding of the law of agency.

**DECISION AND REMEDY** *The Supreme Court of North Dakota reversed the trial court's decision and remanded the case for further proceedings consistent with this opinion.*

**ETHICAL CONSIDERATIONS** *There was sufficient evidence to indicate that an ostensible, or apparent, agency existed between RRC and Frith. RRC admittedly relied on Frith to perform a variety of agent's duties. One could argue that it was unethical for RRC to deny the agency relationship when such denial favored RRC to the detriment of Eidsness.*

## EMERGENCY POWERS

When an unforeseen emergency demands action by the agent to protect or preserve the property and rights of the principal, but the agent is unable to communicate with the principal, the agent has emergency power.

For example, Falu (an employee) is an engineer for Pacific Railroad (the principal). While Falu is acting within the scope of his employment, he falls under the train many miles from home and is severely injured. Dusky, the conductor (an agent), directs Thompson, a doctor, to give medical aid to Falu and to charge Pacific for the medical services. Dusky has no express or implied authority to bind Pacific Railroad for the services of Thompson. Yet, because of the emergency situation, the law recognizes Dusky as having authority to act appropriately under the circumstances.

## RATIFICATION

**Ratification** is the affirmation of a previously unauthorized contract or act. Ratification can be either express or implied. Generally, only a principal can ratify. The principal must be aware of all material facts; otherwise, the ratification is not effective. Ratification binds the principal to the agent's acts and treats the acts or contracts as if they had been authorized by the principal *from the outset*. If the principal does not ratify, there is no contract binding the principal, and the third party's agreement with the agent is viewed merely as an unaccepted offer. Because the third party's agreement is treated as an unaccepted offer, the third

party can revoke the offer (rescind the agreement) at any time before the principal ratifies, without liability. The agent, however, may well be liable to the third party for misrepresenting his or her authority.

If a principal ratifies a contract *without knowledge* of all its terms, the principal can thereafter rescind the ratification unless, of course, the third party has proceeded to change position in reliance on the contract.

Suppose an agent, without authority, contracts with a third person on behalf of a principal for repair work to the principal's office building. The principal learns of the contract from the agent and agrees to ''some repair work,'' thinking that it will involve only patching and painting the exterior of the building. In fact, the contract includes resurfacing the parking lot, which the principal does not want done. On learning of the additional provision, the principal rescinds the contract. If the third party has made no preparations to do the work (such as purchasing materials, hiring additional workers, or renting equipment), then the principal can still rescind. But if the third party has, to his or her detriment, relied on the principal's ratification by making preparations, the principal must reimburse the third party for the cost of the preparations.

Two important points must be stressed. First, it is immaterial whether the principal's lack of knowledge results from the agent's fraud or is simply a mistake on the principal's part. If the third party has not changed position in reliance on the principal, the principal can repudiate the ratification. The unauthorized contract remains an offer,

## ■ CONCEPT SUMMARY 35.1 **Requirements for Ratification**

1. The purported agent must have acted on behalf of a principal who subsequently ratified the action.
2. The principal must know of all material facts involved in the transaction.
3. The agent's act must be affirmed in its entirety by the principal.
4. The principal must have the legal capacity to authorize the transaction at the time the agent engages in the act and at the time the principal ratifies.
5. The principal's affirmance must occur prior to the withdrawal of the third party from the transaction or prior to the third party's change of position in reliance on the contract.
6. The principal must observe the same formalities when he or she approves the act purportedly done by the agent on his or her behalf as would have been required to authorize it initially.

and the principal's acceptance is not valid, because contract law provides that one cannot accept terms about which one does not know. Second, the entire transaction must be ratified; a principal cannot affirm the desirable parts of a contract and reject the undesirable parts.

Death or incapacity of the third party *before* ratification will void an unauthorized contract. Most courts will also recognize an intervening and extraordinary change of circumstances as a basis for setting aside a principal's ratification to permit a third party to revoke.

Assume that Abend, without authority, enters into a contract with a third party who wants to purchase Paula's shopping center. The following night the shopping center is destroyed by fire. Paula's subsequent ratification will not be effective to bind the third party. The courts will reason that it is unjust to hold a third party liable in such a case and will permit the transaction to be avoided despite ratification.

The requirements for ratification are summarized in *Concept Summary 35.1*.

**EXPRESS RATIFICATION**   If a principal's statements or conduct express an intent to be bound,

the prior unauthorized act will be ratified, and the principal will become a party to the contract. For example, Berber (the agent) negotiates the sale of a shipment of oranges to World Markets without the authorization of Samuelson (the principal). Samuelson sees the completed paperwork and tells Berber to go ahead with it. Samuelson thus expressly ratifies the sale and is now bound to the terms of the sales contract.

**IMPLIED RATIFICATION**   Implied ratification occurs most commonly when a principal decides to accept the benefits of a previously unauthorized transaction. In the preceding example, if Samuelson had said nothing to Berber but had known of the unauthorized acts and failed to repudiate or object to them within a reasonable time, the contract would have been ratified. In addition, if World Markets had paid for the oranges and if Samuelson, on learning that World Markets had paid, did not object or repudiate, Samuelson would have impliedly ratified the contract.

The following case illustrates the need of the principal to promptly repudiate unauthorized acts of an agent, once he or she knows about them, to avoid ratification.

---

**BACKGROUND AND FACTS**   *Charles Theis, the plaintiff, maintained an investment account with the brokerage firm of duPont, Glore Forgan Inc., the defendant. Theis discovered that Benjamin, a duPont account executive, was making unauthorized transactions in his account and reprimanded him. Theis finally closed the account when Benjamin directly contravened Theis's order not to buy on May 24, 1968. Theis filed suit against duPont for all the unauthorized trading by Benjamin from the inception of the Theis account. The trial court allowed recovery on only the May 24 transaction. The defendant, duPont, appealed.*

CASE 35.3

**THEIS v. duPONT, GLORE FORGAN INC.**

Supreme Court of Kansas, 1973.
212 Kan. 301,
510 P.2d 1212.

*FROMME,* Justice.

\* \* \* \*

\* \* \* On acquiring knowledge of the unauthorized act of an agent, the principal should promptly repudiate the act, otherwise it will be presumed he has ratified and affirmed the act.

\* \* \* \*

The record is clear the trial court correctly applied [the principles governing ratification. T]here were 36 transactions in the Theis account. The court determined that by Theis's failure to promptly repudiate unauthorized transactions he had either authorized or ratified the first 35 transactions. However, the court found that Theis promptly repudiated the final transaction of May 24 when he learned it had been made contrary to his express orders. This was evidenced not only by registering a protest with Benjamin but also by closing his commodities account with the broker.

It is pointed out [that] the requirement of prompt repudiation is to prevent an investor from withholding his disapproval until the market has taken a turn for the worse, and then deciding to assert the alleged wrongdoing. In such case if prompt repudiation were not required he might sit back and quietly accept profits resulting from an unauthorized trade when it turned out to be to his advantage.

In the present case Theis had previously absorbed the losses, as well as the gains, resulting from Benjamin's unauthorized transactions. However, on May 24 Theis did not hesitate in closing his account as soon as he learned that Benjamin had bought \* \* \* contrary to express instructions. The record shows he did so without waiting to see whether the market price would ultimately rise or fall. His actions indicate he was unconcerned with the wisdom of the May 24 purchase. He was irate over the unauthorized purchase by Benjamin. The action of Theis in closing his account with duPont was found by the trial court to be an express repudiation of the May 24 transaction and this finding is supported by substantial evidence. Whether there has been a repudiation within a reasonable time is a question of fact and the ratification of a former unauthorized act is not the ratification of another entirely distinct act.

**DECISION AND REMEDY**   *Although the court found that Theis had ratified Benjamin's earlier actions, duPont, Glore Forgan Inc. was liable for the unauthorized act of its employee on May 24.*

## SECTION 2

# LIABILITY FOR CONTRACTS

Principals are classified as disclosed, partially disclosed, or undisclosed.[2] A **disclosed principal** is a principal whose identity is known by the third party at the time the contract is made by the agent. A **partially disclosed principal** is a principal whose identity is not known by the third party, but the third party knows that the agent is or may be acting for a principal at the time the contract is made. An **undisclosed principal** is a principal whose identity is totally unknown by the third party, and the third party has no knowledge that the agent is acting in an agency capacity at the time the contract is made.

## DISCLOSED AND PARTIALLY DISCLOSED PRINCIPALS

If an agent acts within the scope of his or her authority, a disclosed or partially disclosed principal is liable to a third party for a contract made by the agent. Ordinarily, if the principal is disclosed, an agent has no contractual liability for the nonperformance of the principal or of the third party.

---

2.  Restatement (Second) of Agency, Section 4.

If the agent has no authority but nevertheless contracts purportedly on behalf of a disclosed principal, the principal cannot be held liable in contract by a third party. The agent, however, is liable on a warranty theory (discussed below).

In most states, if the principal is partially disclosed, the principal and agent are both treated as parties to the contract, and the third party can hold either liable for contractual nonperformance.[3]

In the following case, the issue was whether an agent, through a written agreement, could assume liability for a contract with a third party when the identity of the principal was fully disclosed to the third party.

---

3. Restatement (Second) of Agency, Section 321.

---

CASE 35.4

**FAIRCHILD PUBLICATIONS DIVISION OF CAPITAL CITIES MEDIA, INC. v. ROSSTON, KREMER & SLAWTER, INC.**

Supreme Court, New York County, 1992.
584 N.Y.S.2d 389.

**COMPANY PROFILE** *In 1941, the Federal Communications Commission ordered Radio Corporation of America (RCA) to sell one of its two radio networks (NBC Red and NBC Blue). NBC Blue was sold to Edward Noble, heir to the Lifesavers candy fortune, and became the American Broadcasting Company (ABC). ABC, with only five television stations and no daytime programming, had nearly gone out of business by 1953, when it merged with United Paramount Theatres. In the 1950s, ABC pioneered the westerns* Cheyenne, Maverick, Colt .45, *and* Wyatt Earp, *but remained at the bottom of the audience ratings until the mid-1970s, when it suddenly topped the other networks with such shows as* Happy Days, The Love Boat, *and* Fantasy Island. *Capital Cities was founded in 1954 to buy and operate radio and television stations. Capital Cities began adding publishing properties in the 1960s, when it acquired Fairchild Publications. In 1986, Capital Cities bought ABC for $3.5 billion, at the time the largest purchase in media history. Today, Capital Cities/ABC, Inc., has 228 television affiliates and 3,175 radio affiliates, and owns 8 television stations, 17 radio stations, and parts of cable channels ESPN, Arts & Entertainment Network, and Lifetime. In publishing, Capital Cities/ABC owns the* Fort Worth Star-Telegram, Kansas City Star, Los Angeles *magazine, and a variety of trade publications, farm journals, and medical news publications.*

**BACKGROUND AND FACTS** *Fabrican, Inc., a home furnishings manufacturer, hired an advertising agency, Rosston, Kremer & Slawter, Inc. (RKS), to advertise Fabrican's products in national magazines. In early 1989, RKS arranged for Fabrican's ads to be placed in two magazines published by Fairchild Publications Division of Capital Cities Media, Inc. Daniel Kremer of RKS signed two contracts covering the advertising arrangement, both of which clearly designated Fabrican as the "advertiser." Both contracts, which consisted of preprinted forms containing filled-in blanks and typed and handwritten additions, provided that Fairchild agreed to publish the ads subject to the terms of advertising contracts adopted by the American Association of Advertising Agencies, Inc., "which terms are hereby incorporated herein and made part of this contract." The attached AAAA form stated that the advertising agency and the publisher agreed that the publisher would hold the advertising agency solely liable for payment. Fairchild published Fabrican's ads and sent invoices to RKS totaling $85,157. Neither Fabrican (which had since filed for bankruptcy) nor RKS paid the invoices, and Fairchild Publications sued RKS to recover the price of the ads. Kremer argued that RKS could not be liable because*

*(1) he was unaware of the AAAA term holding the advertising agency solely liable for payment and (2) RKS was acting as an agent for a disclosed principal.*

*HELEN E. FREEDMAN, Justice:*

\*    \*    \*    \*

Since it is undisputed that, in its dealings with Fairchild, RKS acted as the disclosed agent for Fabrican, in order to prevail, Fairchild must prove either that RKS agreed to be liable for Fabrican's debts or that custom and usage rendered RKS liable. After considering all the evidence, the Court finds that Fairchild has met its burden of proof on both grounds.

\*    \*    \*    \*

The fact that Mr. Kremer was unaware that the AAAA terms regarding agency liability were incorporated by reference in the Contracts does not affect their validity. Under these terms, RKS is liable for payment.

Other circumstances surrounding the transaction also contribute to the Court's finding of RKS' liability under the Contracts. At the time it entered into the Contracts, RKS had been placing advertising with Fairchild for more than forty years. \*   \*   \* Fairchild's policy was to hold agencies solely liable \*   \*   \* ; as Fairchild's regular customer, RKS knew or should have known of this policy. \*   \*   \* RKS acknowledged familiarity with the concept of sole agency liability, and did not dispute its liability, despite receiving regular bills, invoices, and dunning letters [letters demanding payment from a delinquent debtor], until a number of months after executing the Contracts. All these factors combine to estop RKS from denying liability.

**DECISION AND REMEDY**    *RKS was held liable for payment of the price of the ads.*

## UNDISCLOSED PRINCIPALS

When neither the fact of agency nor the identity of the principal is disclosed, a third party is deemed to be dealing with the agent personally, and the agent is liable as a party on the contract. For example, in a contract for the sale of a horse, a third party knows only that Scammon (the agent) wants to purchase the horse. The third party does not know that Scammon is actually an agent for Johnson (the principal). Scammon signs a written contract in her own name, not indicating any agency relationship, and the third party delivers the horse to Scammon. Scammon delivers the horse to Johnson, who is in fact the principal. Johnson refuses to pay Scammon for the horse, claiming that she had no authority to purchase it. Scammon tries to return the horse to the third party, who refuses to take it. The third party is entitled to hold Scammon liable for payment. The agent's subjective intent is not relevant. The third party contracted with the agent on the basis of the *agent's* credit and reputation, not the undisclosed principal's. Therefore, the agent is liable.

In contrast, if the agent has acted within the scope of authority, the undisclosed principal is fully bound to perform just as if the principal had been fully disclosed at the time the contract was made. Exceptions to this rule are made in the following circumstances:

1. The undisclosed principal was expressly excluded as a party in the contract. For example, an agent contracts for a lease of a building with a landlord. The landlord does not know of the agency, and the lease specially lists the agent as tenant, with no right of assignment without the landlord's consent. The undisclosed principal cannot enforce the lease.

2. The contract is a negotiable instrument. Here, the UCC provides that only the agent is liable

if the instrument neither names the principal nor shows that the agent signed in a representative capacity.[4]

3. The performance of the agent is personal to the contract, allowing the third party to refuse the principal's performance. Typical examples involve extensions of credit and highly personal service contracts.

4. The third party would not have entered into a contract with the principal had the third party known the principal's identity, the agent or the principal knew this, and the third party rescinds the contract.

If the agent is forced to pay the third party, and if the agent has contracted within the scope of authority granted, the agent is entitled to indemnification by the principal. It was the principal's duty to perform, even though his or her identity was undisclosed,[5] and failure to do so will make the principal ultimately liable. Once the undisclosed principal's identity is revealed, the third party has the right to *elect* to hold either the principal or the agent liable on the contract. (In some states no election is necessary.)

## WARRANTIES OF AGENT

When the agent lacks authority or exceeds the scope of authority, the agent's liability to a third party is based on the theory of breach of implied warranty of authority, not on breach of the contract itself.[6] The agent's implied warranty of authority can be breached intentionally or by a good faith mistake.[7] The agent's liability remains, as long as the third party has relied on the agency status. Conversely, when the third party knows at the time the contract is made that the agent is mistaken about the extent of his or her authority, or when the agent indicates to the third party *uncertainty* about the extent of authority, the agent is not personally liable for breach of warranty.

---

4.  UCC 3–401(1); UCC 3–403(2)(a); UCC R3–401(1); UCC R3–402(b)(2). Extrinsic evidence to show an agency relationship is not normally admissible.

5.  If the agent is a gratuitous agent, and the principal accepts the benefits of the agent's contract with a third party, then the principal will be liable to the agent on the theory of quasi contract (see Chapter 11).

6.  The agent is not liable on the contract because the agent was never intended personally to be a party to the contract.

7.  If the agent intentionally misrepresents his or her authority, then the agent can also be liable in tort for fraud.

# LIABILITY FOR AGENT'S TORTS

Obviously, an agent is liable for his or her own torts. A principal may also be liable for an agent's torts if they result from one of the following:

1. The principal's own tortious conduct.
2. The principal's authorization of a tortious act.
3. The agent's unauthorized but tortious misrepresentation.

If the agent is an employee, whose conduct the principal-employer controls, the employer may also be liable for torts committed by the employee in the course of employment under the doctrine of *respondeat superior,* as discussed below.

## PRINCIPAL'S TORTIOUS CONDUCT

A principal conducting an activity through an agent may be liable for harm resulting from the principal's own negligence or recklessness, which may include giving improper instructions; authorizing the use of improper materials, tools, or the like; establishing improper rules; or failing to prevent others' tortious conduct while they are on the principal's property or using the principal's equipment, materials, or tools. For instance, if Jack knows that Jill cannot drive but nevertheless authorizes her to take the company truck to pick up water pails for his business inventory, he will be liable for his own negligence to anyone injured by her negligent driving.

## PRINCIPAL'S AUTHORIZATION OF AGENT'S TORTIOUS CONDUCT

Similarly, a principal who authorizes an agent to commit a tortious act may be liable to persons or property injured thereby, because the act is considered to be the principal's. For example, Selkow directs Warren—an agent Selkow retained to oversee the harvest of crops he bought—to cut the corn on specific acreage, which neither of them has the right to do. The harvest is therefore a trespass, and Selkow is liable to whoever owns the corn.

In the same light, assume that Victoria instructs Guthrie, her real estate agent, to tell prospective

# ■ CONCEPT SUMMARY 35.2 Authority of Agent to Bind Principal and Third Party

| AUTHORITY OF AGENT | DEFINITION | EFFECT ON PRINCIPAL AND THIRD PARTY |
|---|---|---|
| **Express Authority** | Authority expressly given by the principal to the agent. | Principal and third party are bound in contract. |
| **Implied Authority** | Authority implied by custom, from the position in which the principal has placed the agent, or because it is necessary to carry out expressly authorized duties and responsibilities. | |
| **Apparent Authority** | Authority created when the conduct of the principal leads a third party to believe the principal's agent has authority. | |
| **Unauthorized Acts** | Acts committed by an agent that are outside the scope of his or her express, implied, or apparent authority. | Principal and third party are not bound in contract—*unless* the principal ratifies prior to the third party's withdrawal. |

purchasers that there is oil beneath her property, when she knows there is not. Victoria will be liable to anyone who buys the property in reliance on the statements.

## MISREPRESENTATION

A principal is exposed to tort liability whenever a third person sustains loss due to the agent's misrepresentation. The keys to a principal's liability are whether the agent was actually or apparently authorized to make representations and whether such representations were made within the scope of the agency.

**FRAUDULENT MISREPRESENTATION** Assume that Batsakis is a demonstrator for Moore's products. Moore sends Batsakis to a home show to demonstrate products and to answer questions from consumers. Moore has given Batsakis authority to make statements about the products. If Batsakis makes only true representations, all is fine; but if he makes false claims, Moore will be liable for any injuries or damages sustained by third parties in reliance on Batsakis's false representations.

An interesting series of cases has arisen on the theory that when a principal has placed an agent

in a position to defraud a third party, the principal is liable for the agent's fraudulent acts. For example, Frendak is a loan officer at First Security Bank. In the ordinary course of the job, Frendak approves and services loans and has access to the credit records of all customers. Frendak falsely represents to a borrower, McMillan, that the bank feels insecure about McMillan's loan and intends to call it in unless McMillan provides additional collateral, such as stocks and bonds. McMillan gives Frendak numerous stock certificates, which Frendak keeps in her own possession and later uses to make personal investments. The bank is liable to McMillan for losses sustained on the stocks even though the bank had no direct role in or knowledge of the fraudulent scheme.

The legal theory used here is that the agent's position conveys to third persons the impression that the agent has the authority to make statements and perform acts consistent with the ordinary duties that are within the scope of the position. When an agent appears to be acting within the scope of the authority that the position of agency confers but is actually taking advantage of a third party, the principal who placed the agent in that position is liable. In the example above, if a bank teller or a security guard had told McMillan that the bank required additional security for a loan, McMillan would not have been justified in relying on either person's authority to make that representation. McMillan, however, could reasonably expect that the loan officer was telling the truth.

**INNOCENT MISREPRESENTATION**   Tort liability based on fraud requires proof that a material misstatement was made knowingly and with the intent to deceive. An agent's innocent mistakes occurring in a contract transaction or involving a warranty contained in the contract can provide grounds for the third party's rescission of the contract and the award of damages. Moreover, justice dictates that when a principal knows that an agent is not accurately advised of facts but does not correct either the agent's or the third party's impressions, the principal is directly responsible to the third party for resulting damages. The point is that the principal is always directly responsible for an agent's misrepresentation made within the scope of authority.

## THE DOCTRINE OF RESPONDEAT SUPERIOR

Under the doctrine of *respondeat superior*,[8] the principal-employer is liable for any harm caused to a third party by an agent-employee in the scope of employment. This doctrine imposes **vicarious liability** on the employer—that is, liability without regard to the personal fault of the employer for torts committed by an employee in the course or scope of employment.[9] Third persons injured through the negligence of an employee can sue either the employee who was negligent or the employer, if the employee's negligent conduct occurred while the employee was acting within the scope of employment.

At early common law, a servant (employee) was viewed as the master's (employer's) property. The master was deemed to have absolute control over the servant's acts and was held strictly liable for them no matter how carefully the master supervised the servant. The rationale for the doctrine

of *respondeat superior* is based on the principle of social duty that requires every person to manage his or her affairs, whether accomplished by the person or through agents or servants, so as not to injure another. Liability is imposed on employers because they are deemed to be in a better financial position to bear the loss. The superior financial position carries with it the duty to be responsible for damages.

Today the doctrine continues, but employers carry liability insurance and spread the cost of risk over the entire business enterprise. Public policy requires that an injured person be afforded effective relief, and recovery from a business enterprise provides far more effective relief than recovery from an individual employee. Liability rights exist under law because of public policy protections of third parties. Thus, a master (employer) cannot contract with a servant (employee) to disclaim responsibilities for injuries resulting from the servant's acts, because such disclaimers are against public policy.

**SCOPE OF EMPLOYMENT**   The Restatement (Second) of Agency, Section 229, indicates the following general factors that courts will consider in determining whether or not a particular act occurred within the course and scope of employment:

1.  Whether the employee's act was authorized by the employer.
2.  The time, place, and purpose of the act.
3.  Whether the act was one commonly performed by employees on behalf of their employers.
4.  The extent to which the employer's interest was advanced by the act.
5.  The extent to which the private interests of the employee were involved.
6.  Whether the employer furnished the means or instrumentality (for example, a truck or a machine) by which an injury was inflicted.
7.  Whether the employer had reason to know that the employee would do the act in question and whether the employee had done it before.
8.  Whether the act involved the commission of a serious crime.

**LIABILITY FOR EMPLOYEE'S NEGLIGENCE** For the employer to be liable, the act causing injury must have occurred within the scope of the employee's employment. For example, Mandel (the employee) is a delivery driver for Schwartz (the employer). Schwartz provides Mandel with a

---

8.  Pronounced ree-*spahn*-dee-uht soo-*peer*-ee-your. The doctrine of *respondeat superior* applies not only to employer-employee relationships but also to principal-agent relationships as long as the principal has the right of control over the agent.
9.  The theory of *respondeat superior* is similar to the theory of strict liability covered in Chapters 6 and 25.

vehicle and instructs him to use it for making company deliveries. Nevertheless, one day Mandel drives his own car instead of the company vehicle and negligently injures Chou. Even though Mandel's act (driving his own car) was unauthorized, the negligence occurred as part of Mandel's regular duties of employment (making deliveries). Hence, Schwartz is still liable to Chou for the injuries caused by Mandel, even though Mandel used his own car contrary to Schwartz's instructions. Only if Mandel's acts had exceeded the scope of employment duties in a way that the employer could not reasonably have expected would Schwartz have been relieved of liability.

An employee going to and from work or to and from meals is usually considered outside the scope of employment. All travel time of a traveling salesperson or others whose jobs require them to travel, however, is normally considered within the scope of employment for the duration of the business trip, including the return trip home.

When an employee goes off on his or her own—that is, departs from the employer's business to take care of personal affairs—is the employer liable? It depends. If the employee's activity is a substantial departure akin to an utter abandonment of the employer's business, then the employer is not liable.

For example, a traveling salesperson is driving the employer's vehicle to call on a customer for a possible sales order. On the way to the customer's place of business, the employee deviates one block to mail a letter at the post office. As the employee approaches the post office, she negligently runs into a parked vehicle owned by Inga. The departure of the employee from the employer's business to take care of a personal affair is not substantial. The employee is still within the scope of employment, and the employer is liable to Inga. If the employee had decided to pick up a few friends for cocktails in another city, and in the process had negligently run her vehicle into Inga's, Inga could not have held the employer liable, only the employee.

The following case is a classic in master-servant law. Although it is over 150 years old, the legal principle for which it stands is still viable in employment law today.

---

| CASE 35.5 | **BACKGROUND AND FACTS** *The plaintiff was walking across* |
|---|---|

**JOEL v. MORISON**

Court of Exchequer,
England, 1834.
172 Eng. Rep. 1338.

**BACKGROUND AND FACTS** *The plaintiff was walking across Bishopsgatestreet when he was knocked down by a cart driven negligently by a servant of the defendant. The plaintiff suffered a fractured leg and multiple injuries. The plaintiff took the position that the defendant was liable for his injuries because the defendant's servant was driving the cart that caused the injuries. The defendant argued that his cart was never driven in the neighborhood in which the plaintiff was injured. Moreover, it was suggested that the defendant's servant had gone out of his way for his own purposes and might have taken the cart at a time when it was not wanted for business purposes to pay a visit to some friends.*

*PARKE,* Judge.
* * * *

His Lordship afterwards, in summing up, said—This is an action to recover damages for an injury sustained by the plaintiff, in consequence of the negligence of the defendant's servant. There is no doubt that the plaintiff has suffered the injury, and there is no doubt that the driver of the cart was guilty of negligence, and there is no doubt also that the master, if that person was driving the cart on his master's business, is responsible. If the servants, being on their master's business, took a detour to call upon a friend, the master will be responsible. If you think the servants lent the cart to a person who was driving without the defendant's knowledge, he will not be responsible. Or, if you think that the young man who was driving took the cart surreptitiously, and was not at the time employed on his master's business, the defendant will not be liable. The master is only liable where the servant is acting in the course of his employment. If he was going out of his way, against his master's implied commands, when driving on his master's business, he will make his master liable; *but if he was going on a frolic of his own, without being at all on his master's business, the master will not be liable.* As to the damages, the master * * * [although not himself] guilty of any offence, * * * is only responsible in law, therefore the amount should be reasonable. [Emphasis added.]

*The verdict was for the plaintiff, and he was awarded damages of £30. In this case, the master was held liable for the acts of his servant.*

**DECISION AND REMEDY**

*Respondeat Superior* **in Saudi Arabia** *The doctrine of* respondeat superior *is well established in the legal systems of the United States and most Western countries. Middle Eastern countries, however, do not employ the principle. Islamic law, codified in the* Shari'a, *holds to a strict principle that responsibility for human actions lies with the individual and cannot be vicariously extended to others. This principle and other concepts of Islamic law are based on a seventh-century conversation between the Angel Gabriel and the Prophet Mohammad.*

**INTERNATIONAL CONSIDERATIONS**

*Borrowed Servants.* Employers can lend the services of their employees to other employers. Suppose that an employer leases ground-moving equipment to another employer and sends along an employee to operate the machinery. Who is liable for injuries caused by the employee's negligent actions on the job site? Liability turns on *which employer had the primary right to control* the employee at the time the injuries occurred. Generally, the employer who rents out the equipment is presumed to retain control over his or her employee. If the rental is for a relatively long period of time, however, control may be deemed to pass to the employer who is renting the equipment and presumably controlling and directing the employee.

*Notice of Dangerous Conditions.* The employer is charged with knowledge of any dangerous conditions discovered by an employee and pertinent to the employment situation. To illustrate: A maintenance employee in Martin's apartment building notices a lead pipe protruding from the ground in the building's courtyard. The employee neglects either to fix it or to inform the employer of the danger. Jahnke falls on the pipe and is injured. The employer is charged with knowledge of the dangerous condition regardless of whether or not the employee actually informed the employer. That knowledge *is imputed to the employer* by virtue of the employment relationship.

**LIABILITY FOR EMPLOYEE'S INTENTIONAL TORTS** Most intentional torts that employees commit have no relation to their employment; thus, their employers will not be held liable. Under *respondeat superior,* however, the employer is liable for intentional torts of the employee that are committed within the scope of employment, just as the employer is liable for negligence. For example, an employer is liable when an employee commits assault and battery or false imprisonment while acting within the scope of employment.

An employee acting at the employer's direction can be liable as a **tortfeasor** (one who commits a wrong, or tort), along with the employer, for committing the tortious act even if the employee was unaware of the wrongfulness of the act. For example, an employer directs an employee to burn out a field of crops. The employee does so, assuming that the field belongs to the employer, which it does not. Both can be found liable to the owner of the field for damages.

An employer who knows or should know that an employee has a propensity for committing tortious acts is liable for the employee's acts even if they would not ordinarily be considered within the scope of employment. For example, the Blue Moon employs Arnold Muensch as a bouncer, knowing that he has a history of arrests for assault and battery. While he is working one night, and within the scope of his employment, he viciously attacks a patron who "looks at him funny." The Blue Moon will bear the responsibility for Muensch's acts, because it knew that he had a propensity for committing tortious acts.

Also, an employer is liable for permitting an employee to engage in reckless acts that can injure others. For example, an employer observes an employee smoking while filling containerized trucks with highly flammable liquids. Failure to stop the employee will cause the employer to be liable for any injuries that result.

To reduce the likelihood of liability losses, employers set up stringent work rules. For example, employees who drive company vehicles may be prohibited from giving rides to other passengers. Employees who violate these rules by being careless or committing unlawful or tortious acts may be subject to discipline, including discharge. Almost without exception, employers purchase liability insurance to cover the actions of certain employees.

SECTION 4

# LIABILITY FOR INDEPENDENT CONTRACTOR'S TORTS

The general rule concerning liability for the acts of independent contractors is that the employer is not liable for physical harm caused to a third person by the negligent act of an independent contractor in the performance of the contract. An employer who has no legal power to control the details of the physical performance of a contract cannot be held liable. Here again, the test is the *right to control*. Because an employer bargains with an independent contractor only for results and retains no control over the manner in which those results are achieved, the employer is generally not expected to bear the responsibility for torts committed by an independent contractor. A collection agency is a typical example of an independent contractor. The creditor is generally not liable for the acts of the collection agency, because collection is a distinct business occupation.

Generally, an exception to this doctrine prevails when exceptionally hazardous activities are involved. Typical examples of such activities include blasting operations, the transportation of highly volatile chemicals, and the use of poisonous gases. In these cases, an employer cannot be shielded from liability merely by using an independent contractor. Strict liability is imposed upon the employer-principal as a matter of law. Also, in some states, strict liability is imposed by statute.

In the following case, one of the issues before the court is whether the repossession of collateral is an inherently dangerous activity, in which case the secured creditor could be held liable for the damages caused by the independent contractor's tortious actions.

---

CASE 35.6

**MBANK OF EL PASO v. SANCHEZ**

Supreme Court of Texas,
1992.
836 S.W.2d 151.

**BACKGROUND AND FACTS** *MBank of El Paso contracted with El Paso Recovery Service (El Paso) to have El Paso repossess Yvonne Sanchez's 1978 Pontiac Trans-Am, which had been purchased through MBank financing. Two men hired by El Paso went to Sanchez's home with a tow truck and proceeded to hook the tow truck to the car, which was in the driveway. Sanchez, who was cutting the grass in the yard at the time, asked the men their purpose and demanded that they cease their attempt to take the automobile and that they leave the premises. When they ignored her, she locked herself in the car in an effort to stall them until the police or her husband could arrive. It was only after they got the automobile in the street that they identified their purpose and told her to get out of the car, which she refused to do. They then took the vehicle, with Sanchez locked in it, on a high-speed ride from her home to the repossession lot and parked the car in a fenced and locked yard with a loose guard dog. Sanchez was rescued some time later by her husband and the police.*

*Sanchez filed suit against MBank for damages, alleging that El Paso and its employees were MBank's agents and that they had willfully breached the peace in violation of UCC 9–503.[a] The trial court granted the bank's motion for summary judgment, holding that the bank could not be liable because El Paso was an independent contractor and not an employee or agent of MBank. Sanchez appealed, and the appellate court, holding that MBank had a nondelegable duty to repossess the vehicle without a breach of the peace, reversed the trial court's decision and remanded the case. MBank appealed to the state supreme court.*

MAUZY, Justice.
    *   *   *   *

Section 9–503 *   *   * provides in part: Unless otherwise agreed a secured party has on default the right to take possession of the collateral. *   *   * This provision, by its terms, gives a secured party two choices: it may repossess the collateral "if this can be done without breach of the peace," or it may take legal action. If the secured party chooses the first of those options, it runs the risk that the repossession may, in fact, breach the peace. When that happens, the secured party may be held liable in tort.
    *   *   *   *

As a general rule, when a duty is imposed by law on the basis of concerns for public safety, the party bearing the duty cannot escape it by delegating it to an independent contractor. Section 424 of the Restatement (Second) of Torts (1965) provides: One who by statute or by administrative regulation is under a duty to provide specified safeguards or precautions for the safety of others is subject to liability to the others for whose protection the duty is imposed for harm caused by the failure of a contractor employed by him to provide such safeguards or precautions. [Comment a to Section 424] further explains that a duty to take safety precautions cannot be delegated to an independent contractor: The rule stated in this Section applies whenever a statute or an administrative regulation imposes a duty upon one doing particular work to provide safeguards or precautions for the safety of others. In such a case the employer cannot delegate his duty to provide such safeguards or precautions to an independent contractor.

We believe that section 9–503 of the UCC imposes a duty on secured creditors pursuing nonjudicial repossession to take precautions for public safety. Applying section 424 of the Restatement, a secured creditor is prohibited from delegating this duty to an independent contractor.
    *   *   *   *

A secured creditor certainly has a strong interest in obtaining collateral from a defaulting debtor. That interest, however, must be balanced against society's interest in the public peace. If a creditor chooses to pursue self-help, it must be expected to take precautions in doing so. If this burden is too heavy, the creditor may seek relief by turning to the courts. By pursuing a legal remedy, a creditor shifts the responsibility for repossession to officers of the law.

*The state supreme court affirmed the lower appellate court's judgment.*

**DECISION
AND REMEDY**

a.   This is the "self-help" provision that allows secured creditors to repossess collateral on their own initiative, without resorting to judicial assistance—see Chapter 31.

# LIABILITY FOR AGENT'S CRIMES

Obviously, an agent is liable for his or her own crimes. A principal or employer is not liable for an agent's or employee's crime simply because the agent or employee committed the crime while otherwise acting within the scope of authority or employment, unless the principal or employer participated by conspiracy or other action. In some jurisdictions, under specific statutes, a principal may be liable for an agent's violating, in the course and scope of employment, such regulations as those governing sanitation, prices, weights, and the sale of liquor.

# LIABILITY FOR SUBAGENT'S ACTS

There are three instances in which an agent can hire a subagent:

1. To perform simple, definite duties.
2. When it is the business custom.
3. For unforeseen emergencies.

If an agent is authorized to hire subagents for the principal under any one of these circumstances, then the principal is liable for the acts of the subagents. There is a slight difference in result if the agent hires subagents for an *undisclosed principal.* In that case, the agent is responsible for the subagent in contract law for such things as wages. The undisclosed principal, however, is generally held to be liable for tort injuries. An agent's unauthorized hiring of a subagent generally does not create any legal relationship between the principal and the subagent.

# TERMINATION OF AN AGENCY

Agency law is similar to contract law in that both an agency and a contract terminate by an act of the parties or by operation of law. Once the relationship between the principal and the agent has ended, the agent no longer has actual authority to bind the principal—that is, he or she lacks the principal's consent to act in the principal's behalf. Under some circumstances, third persons may also need to be notified when the agency has been terminated.

## TERMINATION BY ACT OF THE PARTIES

The parties may terminate the authority by including in their agreement some express or implied condition or limitation, the occurrence of which will terminate the agency. This may consist of a certain date or some particular event. Furthermore, at any time, the parties may simply agree to end their relationship.

**LAPSE OF TIME** An agency agreement may specify the time period during which the agency relationship will exist. If so, the agency ends when that time expires. For example, Akers signs an agreement of agency with Palko ''beginning January 1, 1995, and ending December 31, 1997.'' The agency is automatically terminated on December 31, 1997. Of course, the parties can agree to continue the relationship, in which case the same terms will apply.

If no definite time is stated, then the agency continues for a reasonable time and can be terminated at will by either party. What constitutes a reasonable time depends on the circumstances and the nature of the agency relationship. For example, Palko asks Akers to sell her car. If after two years Akers has not sold Palko's car and there has been no communication between Palko and Akers, it is safe to assume that the agency relationship has terminated. Akers no longer has the authority to sell Palko's car.

**PURPOSE ACHIEVED** An agent can be employed to accomplish a particular objective, such as the purchase of stock for a cattle rancher. In that case, the agency automatically ends after the cattle have been purchased.

If more than one agent is employed to accomplish the same purpose, such as the sale of real estate, the first agent to complete the sale automatically terminates the agency relationship for all the others.

**OCCURRENCE OF A SPECIFIC EVENT** An agency can be created to terminate upon the happening of a certain event. For example, Palko appoints Akers to handle her business affairs while she is away. When Palko returns, the agency automatically terminates.

Sometimes one aspect of the agent's authority terminates on the occurrence of a particular event, but the agency relationship itself does not terminate. For example, Palko, a banker, permits Akers, the credit manager, to grant a credit line of $1,000 to certain depositors who maintain a balance of $1,000 in a savings account. If any customer's savings account balance falls below $1,000, Akers can no longer make the credit line available to that customer. But Akers's right to extend credit to the other customers maintaining the minimum balance will continue.

**MUTUAL AGREEMENT** Recall from basic contract law that parties can cancel (rescind) a contract by mutually agreeing to terminate the contractual relationship. The same holds true in agency law regardless of whether the agency contract is in writing or whether it is for a specific duration. For example, Palko no longer wishes Akers to be her agent, and Akers does not want to work for Palko any more. Either party can communicate to the other the intent to terminate the relationship. Agreement to terminate effectively relieves each of the rights, duties, and powers inherent in the relationship.

**TERMINATION BY ONE PARTY** As a *general* rule, either party can terminate the agency relationship. The agent's act is said to be a renunciation of authority. The principal's act is a revocation of authority. Although both parties may have the *power* to terminate—because agency is a consensual relationship, and thus neither party can be compelled to continue in the relationship—they may not possess the *right* to terminate and may therefore be liable for breach of contract. Wrongful termination can subject the canceling party to a suit for damages.

For example, Akers has a one-year employment contract with Palko to act as her agent for $18,000. Palko can discharge Akers before the contract period expires (Palko has the *power* to breach the contract); however, Palko will be liable to Akers for money damages, because Palko has no *right* to breach the contract.

Even in an agency at will (that is, an agency that either party may terminate at any time), the principal who wishes to terminate must give the agent a reasonable notice—that is, at least sufficient notice to allow the agent to recoup his or her expenses and, in some cases, to make a normal profit.

**AGENCY COUPLED WITH AN INTEREST** An *agency coupled with an interest* (also referred to as a *power coupled with an interest* or a *power given as a security*) is a relationship created for the benefit of the agent. The agent actually acquires a beneficial interest in the subject matter of the agency. Under these circumstances, it is not equitable to permit a principal to terminate at will. Hence, this type of agency is irrevocable.

In an agency coupled with an interest, the interest is not created for the benefit of the principal, so it is not really an agency in the usual sense. Therefore, any attempt by the principal to revoke an agency coupled with an interest normally has no legal force or effect. Also, an agency coupled with an interest is not terminated by the death of either the principal or the agent.

For example, Tamara Roberts needs $10,000. John Ocasek agrees to lend her the money, but not without security. Consequently, Roberts delivers some of her jewelry to Ocasek and signs a letter giving him the power, in case she fails to repay the loan, to sell the jewelry as her agent for the best price that can be obtained and to pay out of the proceeds the unpaid amount of the loan, giving any surplus to her. Having obtained the money, Roberts tells Ocasek that she revokes the power to sell. Under the law of agency, the power is not revoked because the agency, which was created for Roberts's benefit, gave Ocasek, the agent, a beneficial interest in the jewelry. Subsequently, Roberts dies. The power is still not affected.

An agency coupled with an interest should not be confused with a situation in which the agent merely derives proceeds or profits from the sale of the subject matter. For example, an agent who merely receives a commission from the sale of real property does not have a beneficial interest in the property itself. Likewise, an attorney whose fee is a percentage of the recovery (a *contingency fee*— see Chapter 4) merely has an interest in the proceeds. These agency relationships are revocable by the principal, subject to any express contractual arrangements between the principal and the agent.

## TERMINATION BY OPERATION OF LAW

Certain events will terminate agency authority automatically, because their occurrence makes it impossible for the agent to perform or improbable that the principal would continue to want performance. These events include death or insanity, loss of the agency's subject matter (impossibility), changed circumstances, bankruptcy, and war.

**DEATH OR INSANITY**    The general rule is that death or insanity of either the principal or the agent automatically and immediately terminates the ordinary agency relationship. Knowledge of the death is not required. For example, Palko sends Akers to the Far East to purchase a rare book. Before Akers makes the purchase, Palko dies. Akers's agent status is terminated at the moment of death, even though Akers does not know that Palko has died. (Some states, however, have changed the common law by statute to make knowledge of the principal's death a requirement for agency termination.)

An agent's transactions that occur after the death of the principal are not binding on the principal's estate. Assume Akers is hired by Palko to collect a debt from Tom (a third party). Palko dies, but Akers still collects the money from Tom, not knowing of Palko's death. Tom's payment to Akers is no longer legally sufficient to discharge Tom's debt to Palko, because Akers no longer has Palko's authority to collect the money. If Akers absconds with the money, Tom must pay the debt again, to Palko's estate.

**IMPOSSIBILITY**    When the specific subject matter of an agency is destroyed or lost, the agency terminates. For example, Palko employs Akers to sell Palko's house. Prior to any sale, the premises are destroyed by fire. Akers's agency and authority to sell Palko's house terminate. Similarly, when it is impossible for the agent to perform the agency lawfully because of war or because of a change in the law, the agency terminates.

**CHANGED CIRCUMSTANCES**    When an event occurs that has such an unusual effect on the subject matter of the agency that the agent can reasonably infer that the principal will not want the agency to continue, the agency terminates. Palko hires Akers to sell a tract of land for $10,000. Subsequently, Akers learns that there is oil under the land and that the land is therefore worth $1 million. The agency and Akers's authority to sell the land for $10,000 are terminated.

**BANKRUPTCY**    Bankruptcy of the principal or the agent *usually* terminates the agency relationship. In certain circumstances, as when the agent's financial status is irrelevant to the purpose of the agency, the agency relationship may continue. Insolvency (defined as the inability to pay debts when they become due or when liabilities exceed assets), as distinguished from bankruptcy, does not necessarily terminate the relationship.

**WAR**    When the principal's country and the agent's country are at war with each other, the agency is terminated. In this situation, the agency is automatically suspended or terminated because there is no way to enforce the legal rights and obligations of the parties.

## NOTICE REQUIRED FOR TERMINATION

When an agency terminates by operation of law because of death, insanity, or some other unforeseen circumstance, there is no duty to notify third persons, unless the agent's authority is coupled with an interest.[10] If, however, the parties themselves have terminated the agency, it is the principal's duty to inform any third parties who know of the existence of the agency that the agency has been terminated. The reason for the notice requirement is generally to prevent fraud. Fairness requires that third parties who have relied on the agent's continuing authority be given notice of the termination of the agent's authority.

An agent's *actual authority* continues until the agent receives some notice of termination. Notice to third parties, however, follows the general rule that an agent's *apparent authority* continues until

---

10.    There is an exception to this rule in banking. UCC R4–405 provides that the bank, as the agent, can continue to exercise specific types of authority even after the customer's death or insanity unless it has knowledge of the death or insanity. When the bank has knowledge of the customer's death, it has authority for ten days after the death to pay checks (but not notes or drafts) drawn by the customer unless it receives a stop-payment order from someone who has an interest in the account, such as an heir. (This ten-day rule does not apply to insanity.)

## ■ CONCEPT SUMMARY 35.3 Termination of an Agency

| METHOD OF AGENCY TERMINATION | RULES | TERMINATION OF AGENT'S AUTHORITY |
|---|---|---|
| **Act of the Parties** <br>1. Lapse of time <br>2. Purpose achieved <br>3. Mutual agreement <br><br>4. Occurrence of a specific event <br>5. Termination by one party <br>  a. Revocation by principal <br>  b. Renunciation by agent | Automatic at end of stated time. <br>Automatic upon completion of purpose. <br>Need mutual consent or acceptance of consideration. <br>Normally automatic upon the happening of the event. <br>At-will agencies—generally no breach. Cannot revoke an agency coupled with an interest. Specified time agencies— breach unless legal cause. | **Notice to Third Persons Required** <br>1. Direct to those who have dealt with agency. <br>2. Constructive to all others. |
| **Operation of Law** <br>1. Death or insanity <br><br><br>2. Impossibility—destruction of the specific subject matter <br>3. Changed circumstances <br><br><br>4. Bankruptcy <br><br>5. War between principal's and agent's countries | Automatic upon death or insanity of either principal or agent (except when agency is coupled with an interest). Applies any time agency cannot be performed because of event beyond parties' control. <br>Events so unusual, it would be inequitable to allow agency to continue to exist. <br>Bankruptcy decree—not mere insolvency—terminates agency. <br>Automatically suspends or terminates agency—no way to enforce legal rights. | **No Notice Required—** Automatic upon the happening of the event. |

the third person is notified (from any source of information) that such authority has been terminated.

The principal is expected to notify *directly* any third person who the principal knows has dealt with the agent. For third persons who have heard about the agency but have not dealt with the agent, *constructive notice* is sufficient.[11]

No particular form of notice is required. The principal can actually notify the agent, or the agent can learn of the termination through some other means. For example, Rice bids on a shipment of steel and hires Weinstein as an agent to arrange transportation of the shipment. When Weinstein learns that Rice has lost the bid, Weinstein's authority to make the transportation arrangement terminates.

If the agent's authority is written, it must be revoked in writing, and the writing must be shown to all people who saw the original writing that established the agency relationship. Otherwise, the principal may still be bound by the agent's apparent authority. Sometimes a written authorization (like that granting power of attorney) contains an expiration date. The passage of the expiration date is sufficient notice of termination for third parties.

---

11. *Constructive notice* is information or knowledge of a fact imputed by law to a person if he or she could have discovered the fact by proper diligence. Constructive notice is often accomplished pursuant to a statute by newspaper publication.

## TERMS AND CONCEPTS TO REVIEW

apparent authority 675

disclosed principal 680

equal dignity rule 673

express authority 673

implied authority 675

notary public 674

partially disclosed
  principal 680

power of attorney 674

ratification 678

*respondeat superior* 685

tortfeasor 687

undisclosed principal 680

vicarious liability 685

# QUESTIONS AND CASE PROBLEMS

**35–1. Liability for Agent's Contracts.** Adam is a traveling salesperson for Peter Petri Plumbing Supply Corp. Adam has express authority to solicit orders from customers and to offer a 5 percent discount if payment is made within thirty days of delivery. Petri has said nothing to Adam about extending credit. Adam calls on a new prospective customer, John's Plumbing Firm. John tells Adam that he will place a large order for Petri products if Adam will give him a 10 percent discount with payment due in equal installments thirty, sixty, and ninety days from delivery. Adam says he has authority to make such a contract. John calls Petri and asks if Adam is authorized to make contracts giving a discount. No mention is made of payment terms. Petri replies that Adam has authority to make discounts on purchase orders. On the basis of this information, John orders $10,000 worth of plumbing supplies and fixtures. The goods are delivered and are being sold. One week later John receives a bill for $9,500, due in thirty days. John insists he owes only $9,000 and can pay it in three equal installments, at thirty, sixty, and ninety days from delivery. Discuss the liability of Petri and John only.

**35–2. Liability for Agent's Contracts.** Alice Adams is a purchasing agent-employee for the A & B Coal Supply partnership. Adams has authority to purchase the coal needed by A & B to satisfy the needs of its customers. While Adams is leaving a coal mine from which she has just purchased a large quantity of coal, her car breaks down. She walks into a small roadside grocery store for help. While there, she runs into Will Wilson. Wilson owns 360 acres back in the mountains with all mineral rights. Wilson, in need of money, offers to sell Adams the property at $1,500 per acre. On inspection of the property, Adams forms the opinion that the subsurface contains valuable coal deposits. Adams contracts to purchase the property for A & B Coal Supply, signing the contract "A & B Coal Supply, Alice Adams, agent." The closing date is August 1. Adams takes the contract to the partnership. The managing partner is furious, as A & B is not in the property business. Later, just before closing, both Wilson and the partnership learn

that the value of the land is at least $15,000 per acre. Discuss the rights of A & B and Wilson concerning the land contract.

**35–3. Undisclosed Principal.** Paula Enterprises hires Able to act as its agent to purchase a one-thousand-acre tract of land from Thompson for $1,000 per acre. Paula Enterprises does not wish Thompson to know that it is the principal or that Able is its agent. Paula wants the land for a new country housing development, and Thompson may not sell the land for that purpose or may demand a premium price. Able makes the contract for the purchase, signing only his name as purchaser and not disclosing to Thompson the agency relationship. The closing and transfer of deed are to take place on September 1.

(a) If Thompson learns of Paula's identity on August 1, can Thompson legally refuse to deed the property on September 1? Explain.

(b) Paula gives Able the money for the closing, but Able absconds with the money, causing a breach of Able's contract at the date of closing. Thompson then learns of Paula's identity and wants to enforce the contract. Discuss fully Thompson's rights under these circumstances.

**35–4. Principal's Liability for Agent's Torts.** Able is hired as a traveling salesperson for the ABC Tire Corp. Able has a designated geographical area and time schedule within which to solicit orders and service customers. Able is given a company car to use in covering the territory. One day, Able decides to take his personal car to cover part of his territory. It is 11:00 A.M., and Able has just finished calling on all customers in the city of Tarrytown. Able's next appointment is in the city of Austex, twenty miles down the road, at 2:00 P.M. Able starts out for Austex, but halfway there he decides to visit a former college roommate who runs a farm ten miles off the main highway. Able is enjoying his visit with his former roommate when he realizes that it is 1:45 P.M. and that he will be late for the appointment in Austex. Driving at a high speed down the country road to reach the main highway, Able crashes his car into Thomas's tractor, severely injuring Thomas, a farmer. Thomas claims he can hold the ABC Tire Corp. liable for his injuries. Discuss fully ABC's liability in this situation.

**35–5. Termination of Agency.** Adam is an agent for Fish Galore, Inc. Adam has express authority to solicit orders and receive payments in advance of shipment. He is well known as an agent in the region. One of his customers, Seafood Quality, has been a regular customer for five years, has usually made large orders, and has always paid Adam in advance to get the discount offered by Fish Galore. Fish Galore learns that Adam has incurred large gambling debts and has recently used some of the customers' payments to pay off these debts. When Adam cannot reimburse Fish Galore, he is fired. Fish Galore hires a new agent and publishes in regional newspapers the fact that the new agent will be covering the territory. Desperately in need of cash, Adam solicits a large order from Seafood Quality and receives payment. Then he calls on a new customer, Catfish Heaven, which also gives Adam an order and payment. Adam absconds with the money. Fish Galore refuses to honor either order. Seafood Quality and Catfish Heaven claim that Fish Galore is in breach of contract. Discuss fully their claims.

**35–6. Agent's Apparent Authority.** The City of Delta Junction (Delta) in Alaska decided to purchase a fire tanker and sought bids from several truck dealers. The city eventually purchased a truck from Alaska Mack, Inc., a Mack truck dealer in Fairbanks. Alaska Mack modified a Mack chassis to carry a five-thousand-gallon tank, but the truck exceeded the manufacturer's specified weight limits and was dangerously unbalanced and difficult to drive. When subsequent modifications failed to remedy these problems, the city brought suit for breach of warranty against Alaska Mack and against Mack Trucks, Inc., of Allentown, Pennsylvania, as principal, under the theory of apparent agency, or apparent authority. Mack Trucks, Inc., the manufacturer of Mack trucks, claimed that Alaska Mack was not its agent and that it was not responsible for any actions undertaken by Alaska Mack. Delta argued that Alaska Mack was listed in trade journals and the Fairbanks telephone directory under the heading "Mack Trucks" and that its advertisements carried the familiar Mack bulldog trademark. On the basis of these representations, both Delta's mayor and the fire chief, at the time of the purchase, believed that Alaska Mack was an agent for the manufacture of Mack trucks. Alaska Mack's bid was accepted by the city council, even though it was the highest bid received for the truck, because of the manufacturer's reputation. The trial court granted a directed verdict for Mack Trucks, Inc. What will happen on appeal? Discuss fully. [*City of Delta Junction v. Mack Trucks, Inc.,* 670 P.2d 1128 (Alaska 1983)]

**35–7. Liability for Agent's Acts.** Richard Lanno worked for the Thermal Equipment Corp. as a project engineer. Lanno was allowed to keep a company van and tools at his home because he routinely drove to work sites directly from his home and because he was often needed for unanticipated trips during his off-hours. The arrangement had been made for the convenience of Thermal Equipment, even though Lanno's managers permitted him to make personal use of the van. Lanno was involved in a collision with Lazar while driving the van home from work. At the time of the accident, Lanno had taken a detour to stop at a store—he had intended to purchase a few items and then go home. Lazar sued Thermal Equipment, claiming that Lanno had acted while within the scope of his employment. Discuss whether Lazar was able to recover, and why. Can employees act on behalf of their employers and themselves at the same time? Explain. [*Lazar v. Thermal Equipment Corp.,* 148 Cal.App.3d 458, 195 Cal.Rptr. 890 (1983)]

**35–8. Ratification by Principal.** Fred Hash worked for Van Stavern Construction Co. as a field supervisor in charge of constructing a new plant facility. Hash entered into a contract with Sutton's Steel & Supply, Inc., to supply steel to the construction site in several installments. Hash gave the name of B. D. Van Stavern, the president and owner of the construction firm, instead of the firm name as the party for whom he was acting. The contract and the subsequent invoices all had B. D. Van Stavern's name on them. Several loads were delivered by Sutton. All of the invoices were signed by Van Stavern employees, and corporate checks were made out to Sutton. When Sutton Steel later sued Van Stavern personally for unpaid debts totaling $40,437, it claimed that Van Stavern had ratified the acts of his employee, Hash, by allowing payment on previous invoices. Although Van Stavern had had no knowledge of the unauthorized arrangement, had he legally ratified the agreement by his silence? Explain. [*Sutton's Steel & Supply, Inc. v. Van Stavern,* 496 So.2d 1360 (La.App. 3d Cir. 1986)]

**35–9. Respondeat Superior.** Garcia was an employee of Van Groningen & Sons, Inc., which operated an orchard, and one of Garcia's duties was to drive a tractor through the orchard while pulling machinery behind. On one occasion, Garcia invited his nephew Perez to accompany him on the job as he drove the tractor through the orchard. Perez had to sit on the toolbox, because there was only one seat on the tractor. Perez was knocked off by a tree branch and was severely injured when the tractor machinery ran over his leg. Perez sued Van Groningen & Sons under the theory of *respondeat superior.* Van Groningen testified that the company forbade anyone but the driver to ride on the tractor because of the danger and that Garcia had personally been advised of this rule. Discuss what chance Perez has of recovering under the doctrine of *respondeat superior.* [*Perez v. Van Groningen & Sons, Inc.,* 41 Cal.3d 962, 719 P.2d 676, 227 Cal.Rptr. 106 (1986)]

**35–10. Disclosure of Principal's Identity.** Port Ship Service, Inc., a water taxi service, ferried crew members, customs agents, supplies, and the like between ships and the shore at the Port of New Orleans. Norton, Lilly & Co. acted as an agent for various ships entering the harbor that required water taxi services. Ships needing water taxi services would call Norton, and Norton would communicate the names of the vessels needing such services to Port Ship. Although Norton never informed Port Ship of the names of the vessels' owners, such information was readily available to Port Ship in publications commonly used by port authorities. In addition, Norton maintained a twenty-four-hour telephone service through which Port Ship could ascertain the identities of any of the ship owners. Port Ship sought to hold Norton liable for unpaid taxi services, and the issue turned on whether the ship owners were fully disclosed principals (in which case Norton could not be held liable). The court stated that the Restatement (Second) of Agency, Section 4, "makes ... clear" that "it is the agent's duty to disclose the principal's identity, and not a third party's duty to ascertain that identity." Had Norton disclosed the principals' identities by giving Port Ship the names of the vessels? Discuss fully. [*Port Ship Service, Inc. v. Norton, Lilly & Co.*, 883 F.2d 23 (5th Cir. 1989)]

**35–11. *Respondeat Superior.*** W. Stephen Brooks was employed as a sales representative for the Bob King Mitsubishi car dealership. Reba Stanley, age eighteen, met with Brooks to test-drive a Mitsubishi pickup truck. During the test drive, Brooks assaulted Stanley "by touching and grabbing her about her arms, hands, groin area, and breasts. He also ... exposed his genitals and placed her hand on his private parts." When they returned from the test drive, Brooks took her to the Mitsubishi service department and "again exposed himself and tried to force her to touch him." Stanley was able to free herself and left the dealership. Brooks was later convicted on charges arising out of the incident. Stanley sued both Brooks and the car dealership, claiming that she had suffered severe emotional distress as a result of the assault. The trial court granted the dealership's motion for summary judgment and entered a default judgment against Brooks. Stanley appealed, arguing that the dealership should be held liable for Brooks's torts under the doctrine of *respondeat superior.* What should the appellate court decide? Discuss. [*Stanley v. Brooks*, 436 S.E.2d 272 (N.C.App. 1993)]

**35–12. Case Briefing Assignment**

 *Examine Case A.6 [*Green v. Shell Oil Co., 181 Mich.App. 439, 450 N.W.2d 50 (1989)*] in Appendix A. The case is excerpted there in great detail. Review and then brief the case, making sure that you include answers to the following questions in your brief.*

1. Green sued Shell and Lanford on two grounds. What are they?
2. Why did the court hold that summary judgment on the issue of Lanford's agency status was inappropriate?
3. Why did the court hold that the service station attendant was not acting within the scope of employment while he was participating in the assault and battery?

# FOCUS ON ETHICS

## Agency

When one person agrees to act on behalf of another, as an agent does in an agency relationship, that person assumes certain ethical responsibilities. An agent acting *on behalf of* a principal implicitly promises to place the principal's interests above his or her own interests. Similarly, a principal in an agency relationship assumes certain ethical duties. If an agent incurs expenses or liability while acting on the principal's behalf, for example, it is only fair that the principal should assume responsibility for those expenses or that liability. In essence, agency law gives legal force to the ethical duties arising in an agency relationship. Although agency law also focuses on the rights of agents and principals, those rights are framed by the concept of duty—that is, an agent's duty becomes a right for the principal and vice versa.

Significantly, most of the duties of the principal and agent described below are negotiable at law. In forming a contract, the principal and the agent can extend or abridge many of the ordinary duties owed in such a relationship. Legal rules generally come into play when the contract is silent or ambiguous on an issue. Allowing the parties to negotiate their relative duties seems ethically fair, as long as the parties are able to understand their rights and make informed decisions.

### The Duty of the Agent to the Principal

What is the nature of the duty that an agent owes to a principal in an employment situation? Does the agent have the duty to disclose *all* favorable information that could be used by the principal to increase the principal's profits? Or does the agent have the right to use some of the information gleaned during the course of normal employment for his or her own benefit? To understand the answers to these questions, we must understand the kind of relationship that exists between a principal and an agent.

The very nature of the principal-agent relationship is one of trust, which we call a fiduciary relationship. Because of this, it is expected that an agent owes certain duties to the principal. These duties include being loyal and obedient, informing the principal of important facts concerning the agency, accounting to the principal for property or money received, and performing with reasonable diligence and skill.

Thus, ethical conduct would prevent an agent from representing two principals in the same transaction, making a secret profit from the agency relationship, or failing to disclose the interest of the agent in property the principal was purchasing. The expected ethical conduct of the agent has evolved into rules that, if breached, cause the agent to be held legally liable.

What about looking beyond the duty to the principal and considering one's duty to society? Consider, for example, the situation faced by employees of Firestone in regard to faulty tires produced by that company. The employees who knew of the company's defective tires in the early 1980s presumably could have divulged that information to the public (at the risk of losing their jobs, of course). Some scholars have argued that many of the greatest "evils" in the past twenty-five years have been accomplished in the name of "duty" to the principal. Duty in this context means placing the well-being of the principal above that of the public.

### The Duty of the Principal to the Agent

Just as agents owe certain fiduciary duties to their principals, so do principals owe ethical duties to their agents. Under agency law, principals have certain defined duties, such as compensating or reimbursing their agents for expenses incurred in the course of performing their duties as agents.

Principals also owe their agents a duty of cooperation. One might expect most principals to cooperate with their agents out of self-interest, but this is not universally so. Suppose that a principal hires an agent on commission to sell a building, and the agent puts considerable time and expense into the process. If the principal changes his or her mind and decides to retain the building, he or she might want to prevent the agent from completing a sale. Is such action ethical? Does it violate a principal's duty of cooperation? What alternatives would such a principal have?

Another duty of principals is to provide safe working conditions. The principal therefore should not expose agents to unreasonable hazards as they go about their work. The definition of *safe* remains a difficult one, however, as every job probably entails some degree of unavoidable risk. Suppose, for example, that an employer hires a sales representative and supplies the representative with a car. Must the car contain air bags to ensure safe working conditions? Or would a car with seat belts be "safe enough"?

Although a principal is legally obligated to fulfill certain duties to the agent, these duties do not include any specific duty of loyalty. Some argue that the lack of employer loyalty to employees leads to a reduction of employee loyalty to employers. After all, they maintain, why should an employee be loyal to an employer's interests over the years when the employee knows that there is no corresponding legal duty on the part of the employer to be loyal to the employee's interests? Employers who do show a sense of loyalty to employees—for example, by not laying off longtime, faithful employees when business is slow or when those employees could be replaced by younger workers at lower cost—base that sense of loyalty primarily on ethical, not legal, considerations.

## Employee versus Independent Contractor

There is a distinction between an employer-employee relationship and the relationship that exists between an employer and an independent contractor. Is it fair, when two parties contract to create an employer–independent contractor relationship, that in spite of what the parties stated in their contract, a court holds that an employer-employee relationship exists instead?

Consider the case of Christopher Heard, who was hired by a pizza franchise, Numero Uno No. 12, to deliver pizza. Heard signed an independent contractor agreement with Numero Uno, which explicitly stated that Heard was being hired not as an employee but as an independent contractor. The agreement read, in part, as follows: "Independent Contractor [Heard] acknowledges that he is not being hired by the Client [Numero Uno], but the Client is strictly contracting services." The agreement also stated, "Independent Contractor agrees that the Client shall be held harmless against any lawsuits which may result from any act of the Independent Contractor's services." The term *independent contractor* is mentioned no less than ten times in the agreement.

When Heard's truck hit another vehicle while he was on the way to deliver pizza to a customer, the driver of the other car sustained $14,000 in medical and property damages. The driver-plaintiff sued Heard and the owners of Numero Uno.[1] In determining whether the owners of Numero Uno should be liable to the plaintiff, the court had to determine whether Heard, as a pizza deliverer, was an employee of Numero Uno or an independent contractor. The trial court concluded that Heard was an independent contractor.

On review, however, the appellate court held that the evidence indicated otherwise. The appellate court stated that

---

1. *Toyota Motor Sales U.S.A., Inc. v. Superior Court,* 220 Cal.App.3d 864, 269 Cal.Rptr. 647 (1990). (The plaintiff also sued Toyota, alleging that the seat belt in the Toyota she was driving was defective.)

employer control "is clearly the most important" of the numerous factors to be weighed in determining whether an individual is an employee or an independent contractor. The appellate court in this case used the same logic that the Internal Revenue Service uses when it examines independent contractor situations. That Heard had a certain amount of freedom of action and provided his own vehicle, expenses, and insurance did not outweigh the amount of control that Numero Uno had over Heard's actions. Numero Uno "determined what would be delivered, when and to whom and what price would be charged."

In regard to determinations of employee or independent contractor status, it is not what parties say about their relationship that counts but what they actually do. This rule seems to fly in the face of social and ethical principles underlying the doctrine of freedom of contract. But it does reflect other social and ethical values, particularly the principle that those who are harmed should be compensated. Given the fact that employers are liable for the wrongful acts of their employees under the doctrine of *respondeat superior,* would it be fair to let some employers "off the hook" simply because they contracted with individuals as independent contractors rather than as employees? Would it be fair to victims who are harmed by so-called independent contractors not to allow them to be compensated by the principal-employers?

## Apparent Authority and Agency by Estoppel

Agency law is designed to enforce the ethical or fiduciary duties that arise once an agency relationship is established. If the agent or the principal breaches his or her duties, the law will come to the aid of the innocent party. To perhaps an even greater extent, agency law is designed to protect third parties—people outside the agency relationship. The doctrines of apparent authority and agency by estoppel stem primarily from ethical considerations that arise when third parties suffer a loss from an apparent agency relationship.

Sometimes, for example, a third person may be led by the actions of the principal to believe that an individual is acting in the capacity of an agent, when in fact the individual is not an agent at all. If the principal, for example, allowed a person to use the principal's stationery when contracting with third parties, a court may conclude that it would only be fair in such a situation to estop (prevent) the principal from later denying the agency relationship. In other situations, a third party might assume that someone who is clearly an agent has authority to speak for the principal in regard to certain matters, but the principal denies that such authority for these matters exists. Again, the courts will evaluate the circumstances to decide whether the principal should be estopped from denying the agent's authority.

As in other areas of the law, whenever there is a choice as to which of two relatively innocent parties should bear responsibility for harms resulting from a transaction, the law generally holds that the person who was in the best position to prevent the harm should be liable. The concepts of apparent authority and agency by estoppel reflect this general legal principle. For example, in one case, a contractor, S&S Construction Company, entered into contracts with a small college in Mississippi to construct some buildings on the campus. Part of the funding for the construction was to come from the Christian Methodist Episcopal Church (CME).

When the college fell behind on its payments due under the contract, S&S refused to do further work. CME's general secretary of finance, O. T. Peeples, wrote to S&S that the funds "necessary to complete the construction" had been set aside in a special account and that S&S would be paid on a regular monthly basis up to the project's completion. S&S resumed construction and later, when the college fell behind in its payments and entered into bankruptcy proceedings, sought to recover the payments from CME.

CME argued that Peeples had exceeded his authority as an agent when he promised S&S that funds had been set aside for the construction work. The court did not agree. It concluded that CME, by naming Peeples as the church's finance secretary and authorizing Peeples to handle financial matters, had clothed Peeples with the authority to "make statements on such matters" and that S&S had acted reasonably in relying on Peeples's written assurances that S&S would be paid. The court held that even though CME claimed that it was an innocent party injured by Peeples's actions, it was, after all, the entity that had placed Peeples in the position of finance secretary, and it therefore "was in a better position than was S&S to protect itself from losses resulting from Peeples' conduct."[2]

### Respondeat Superior

Another legal concept that addresses the effect on third parties of agency relationships is the doctrine of *respondeat superior.* The doctrine raises a significant ethical question: Why should innocent employers be required to assume responsibility for the tortious actions of their agent-employees? Again, the answer has to do with the courts' perception that when one of two innocent parties must bear a loss, the party in the best position to prevent that loss should bear the burden of loss. In an employment relationship, for example, the employer has more control over the employee's behavior than a third party to the relationship does. Also, the courts assume that holding employers responsible for their employees' torts will act as a deterrent. In other words, employers will supervise their employees more carefully to avoid liability.

Another reason for retaining the doctrine of *respondeat superior* in our laws is based on the employer's assumed ability to pay. Our collection of shared beliefs suggests that an injured party should be afforded the most effective relief possible. Thus, even though an employer may be absolutely innocent, the employer has a "deeper pocket" and will be more likely to have the funds necessary to make the injured party whole.

### ■ Discussion Questions

**1.** How much obedience and loyalty does an employee owe an employer? What if the employer engages in an activity—or requests the employee to engage in an activity—that violates the employee's ethical standards but does not necessarily violate any public policy or law? In such a situation, does an employee's duty to abide by his or her own ethical standards override the employee's duty of loyalty to the employer?

**2.** If an agent injures a third party during the course of employment, under the doctrine of *respondeat superior,* the employer may be held liable for the agent's actions even though the employer did not authorize the action and was not even aware of it. Do you think that it is fair to hold employers liable in such situations? Do you think that it would be fairer to hold that the employee alone should bear responsibility for his or her tortious actions to third parties, even when the actions are committed within the scope of employment?

**3.** Agency by estoppel occurs when the presumed principal's actions create the appearance of authority in a presumed agent and a third party reasonably relies, to his or her detriment, on the agent's authority. In what ways are the ethical considerations underlying the doctrine of agency by estoppel or apparent authority similar to those underlying the doctrine of *respondeat superior?* In what ways are the ethical considerations different?

**4.** When an agency is terminated by an act of the parties, the law requires that third parties who have dealt with the agency be notified of the termination. What purpose does notification serve? Are the reasons for this requirement based on any ethical considerations?

---

2. *Christian Methodist Episcopal Church v. S&S Construction Co.,* 615 So.2d 568 (Miss. 1993).

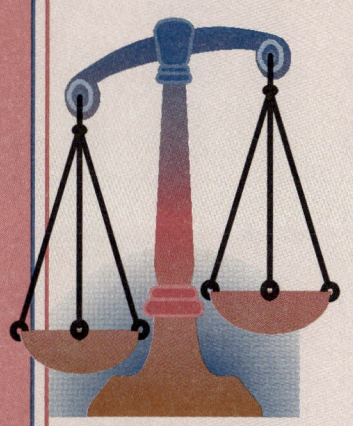

# Unit Seven

# Employment and Labor Relations

## Contents

**36** **Employment and Labor Law**

**37** **Employment Discrimination**

# CHAPTER 36

# EMPLOYMENT AND LABOR LAW

I n the United States, employment relationships have traditionally been governed by the law of contracts, agency, and torts. Before the industrial revolution, workers and employers enjoyed relatively equal bargaining power. At that time, employment relationships were generally governed by the common law doctrine of **employment at will.** Under this doctrine, either party may terminate the employment relationship at any time and for any reason—provided, of course, that the employment termination does not violate the provisions of an employment contract.

In the 1930s, during the Great Depression, both state and federal governments began to protect the rights of workers. In 1931, Congress enacted the Davis-Bacon Act,[1] which requires the payment of "prevailing wages" to employees of contractors and subcontractors working on government construction projects. In 1936, an act that extended the Davis-Bacon Act was put into effect—the Walsh-Healey Act.[2] This act requires a minimum wage, as well as overtime pay of time and a half, for employees of manufacturers or suppliers entering into contracts with agencies of the federal government.

Other legislation during the 1930s and subsequent decades established the right of employees to form labor unions, to bargain as a group with management, and to engage in peaceful strikes. A succession of laws regulating health and safety in the workplace, income security for workers, equal opportunity for employees, and other aspects of employment relationships further protected employee rights. Today's employers must comply with a myriad of laws and regulations to ensure that employee rights are protected.

---

1.  40 U.S.C. Sections 276a–276a-5.
2.  41 U.S.C. Sections 35–45.

In this chapter, we look at the most significant laws regulating employment relationships. Other significant laws regulating the workplace—those prohibiting employment discrimination—will be dealt with in the next chapter.

# EMPLOYMENT AT WILL

As previously discussed, under the traditional employment-at-will doctrine, either party may terminate an employment contract at any time and for any reason (unless the contract specifically provides to the contrary). As also mentioned, federal and state statutes have modified this doctrine. Today's employer is not permitted to fire an employee if to do so would violate a federal or state employment statute, such as one prohibiting employment termination for discriminatory reasons (see Chapter 37). Whenever an employer discharges an employee in violation of the law, the employee may bring an action for **wrongful discharge.**

The employment-at-will doctrine has also been eroded through a series of court rulings that restrict the right of employers to fire workers. Because this is a common law issue, the rules vary from state to state. The trend among the states has been to recognize exceptions to the employment-at-will doctrine. Exceptions to the employment-at-will doctrine include those based on contract theory, public policy, and tort law.

## EXCEPTIONS BASED ON CONTRACT THEORY

Some courts have held that an *implied* employment contract exists between the employer and the employee. If the employee is fired outside the terms of the implied contract, he or she may succeed in a breach-of-contract action even though no written employment contract exists.

For example, an employer's manual or personnel bulletin may state that, as a matter of policy, workers will be dismissed only for good cause. If the employee is aware of this policy and continues to work for the employer, a court may find that there is an implied contract based on the terms stated in the manual or bulletin. Promises that an employer makes to employees regarding discharge policy may also be considered part of an implied contract. If the employer fires the worker in a manner contrary to the manner promised, a court may hold that the employer has violated the implied contract and is liable for damages. Most state courts will consider this claim and judge it by traditional contract standards.

A few states have gone further and held that all employment contracts contain an implied covenant of good faith. This means that both sides promise to abide by the contract in good faith. If an employer fires an employee for an arbitrary or unjustified reason, the employee can claim that the covenant of good faith was breached and the contract violated.

## EXCEPTIONS BASED ON PUBLIC POLICY

The most widespread common law exception to the employment-at-will doctrine is the public-policy exception. Under this rule, an employer may not fire a worker for reasons that violate a fundamental public policy of the jurisdiction. For example, a court may prevent an employer from firing a worker who serves on a jury and therefore cannot work during his or her normally scheduled working hours. Sometimes, an employer will direct an employee to do something that violates the law. If the employee refuses to perform the illegal act, the employer might decide to fire the worker. Most states have held that firing the worker under these circumstances violates public policy.

**Whistleblowing** occurs when an employee tells a government official, upper-management authorities, or the press that his or her employer is engaged in some unsafe or illegal activity. Employees who expose the wrongdoing of employers often find themselves disciplined or even out of a job. In a few cases, whistleblowers have been protected from wrongful discharge for reasons of public policy. For example, a bank was held to have wrongfully discharged an employee who pressured the employer to comply with state and federal consumer credit laws.[3]

---

3. *Harless v. First National Bank in Fairmont,* 162 W.Va. 116, 246 S.E.2d 270 (1978).

In another case, an at-will employee—a probation officer with the police department of the city of Globe, Arizona—discovered that a man had been arrested for vagrancy under an obsolete statute, had been sentenced to ten days in prison, and had been in jail for twenty-one days. The officer pointed out to a magistrate that this was illegal. The magistrate informed the police chief, who then fired the officer, and the officer sued the city for wrongful discharge. Holding that the discharge violated public policy, the court said, "So long as employees' actions are not merely private or proprietary, but instead seek to further the public good, the decision to expose illegal or unsafe practices should be encouraged *   *   *. There is no public policy more important or fundamental than the one favoring the effective protection of the lives, liberty, and property of the people. The officer's successful attempt to free the arrestee from illegal confinement was a refreshing and laudable exercise that should be protected, not punished."[4]

## EXCEPTIONS BASED ON TORT THEORY

In a few cases, the discharge of an employee may give rise to an action for wrongful discharge under tort theories. Abusive discharge procedures may result in intentional infliction of emotional distress or defamation. In one case, a restaurant had suffered some thefts of supplies, and the manager announced that he would start firing waitresses alphabetically until the thief was identified. The first waitress fired said that she suffered great emotional distress as a result. The state's highest court upheld her claim as stating a valid cause of action.[5]

## SECTION 2

# STATUTORY PROTECTION FOR WHISTLEBLOWERS

As discussed in the preceding section, whistleblowers may be protected from retaliatory dis-

charge on the basis of public policy. But this public-policy exception to the employment-at-will doctrine is just that—an exception. To encourage workers to report employer wrongdoing, such as fraud, a number of states[6] and the federal government have enacted so-called whistleblower statutes. These statutes protect whistleblowers from subsequent retaliation on the part of employers. They may also provide an incentive to disclose information by providing the whistleblower with a monetary reward. For example, the False Claims Reform Act of 1986[7] requires that a whistleblower who has disclosed information relating to a fraud perpetrated against the U.S. government receive between 15 and 25 percent of the proceeds if the government brings suit against the wrongdoer. Another federal statute, the Whistleblower Protection Act of 1989,[8] protects federal employees who blow the whistle on their employers from their employers' retaliatory actions.

In one case, an employee of the General Electric Corporation (GE) was awarded $13,387,500 under the False Claims Reform Act. The employee, Chester Walsh, was assigned to manage an overseas aircraft operation in Israel. Walsh learned that a substantial amount of the project money that had been provided by the U.S. government was being diverted to other projects and embezzled by Israeli officials and some other GE employees. Walsh smuggled evidence of the embezzlement out of Israel, into Switzerland, and then into the United States, where he delivered the information to the U.S. Department of Justice (DOJ). The DOJ proceeded with a lawsuit against the perpetrators of the fraud, including GE, and recovered a total of $59,500,000.[9]

Most states also provide statutory incentives for the whistleblower to disclose information to the government about the suspicious acts of an employer. As illustrated by the following case, a state statute may provide a wide range of remedies for the whistleblower.

---

4. *Wagner v. City of Globe*, 150 Ariz. 82, 722 P.2d 250 (1986).
5. *Agis v. Howard Johnson Co.*, 371 Mass. 140, 355 N.E.2d 315 (1976).

6. At least thirty-seven states now have whistleblower statutes.
7. 31 U.S.C. Sections 3729–3733. This act amended the False Claims Act of 1863.
8. 5 U.S.C. Section 1201.
9. *United States v. General Electric*, 808 F.Supp. 580 (D. Ohio 1992).

**BACKGROUND AND FACTS**   *George Green worked as an architect for the Texas Department of Human Services (DHS). His job entailed reviewing construction contracts between the DHS and private contractors and advising his supervisors generally on the compliance with the contracts. Green believed that the DHS procurement officers displayed a pattern of corruption, including fraud, extortion, and kickbacks. He reported this observation to his supervisors but was dissatisfied with their lack of response to his concerns of wrongdoing. He then notified several DHS workers that he was going to report the corruption to authorities outside the department. Shortly thereafter, the DHS examined Green's office telephone records for the past two years and discovered one unauthorized long-distance telephone call that cost thirteen cents. Due to a job-related back injury, Green regularly took time off work to attend therapy sessions. The DHS, in an investigation of Green's use of sick leave, found one instance in which Green failed to attend his therapy session. Based on these investigations, the DHS fired Green on grounds of "abuse of sick leave, falsification of official DHS documents, and telephone misuse." Green sued the DHS under the Texas Whistleblower Act, claiming that the DHS fired him in retaliation for his concerns about the procurement officers' activities. The jury awarded Green actual damages of $3,459,832, punitive damages of $10,000,000, attorneys' fees amounting to $160,000, and interest. The DHS appealed in part on the ground that the evidence was insufficient to support Green's claim.*

CASE 36.1

**TEXAS DEPARTMENT OF HUMAN SERVICES v. GREEN**
Court of Appeals of Texas— Austin, 1993.
855 S.W.2d 136.

*BEA ANN SMITH,* Justice.
 *  *  *  *

The relevant portions of the [Texas Whistleblower] Act prohibiting retaliation and creating certain remedies for public employees [are as follows:] Sec. 2. A state or local governmental body may not suspend or terminate the employment of, or otherwise discriminate against, a public employee who reports a violation of law to an appropriate law enforcement authority if the employee report is made in good faith. Sec. 3. (a) A public employee who alleges a violation of this Act may sue for injunctive relief, damages, or both. . . . . Sec. 4. (a) A public employee who sues under this Act may recover: (1) actual damages; (2) exemplary damages; (3) costs of court; and (4) reasonable attorney's fees. (b) In addition to amounts recovered under Subsection (a) of this section, a public employee whose employment is suspended or terminated in violation of this Act is entitled to: (1) reinstatement in his former position; (2) compensation for wages lost during the period of suspension or termination; and (3) reinstatement of any fringe benefits or seniority rights lost because of the suspension or termination.
 *  *  *  *

The Whistleblower Act seeks to protect the individual employee against the collective acts of the agency, the bureaucracy, the institution, the system that retaliates, and does not seek to protect the employee solely against the acts of an individual supervisor. *  *  *
 *  *  *  *

 *  *  * [The] DHS ordered an investigation of Green's "telephone abuse." Even when certain suspect calls apparently giving rise to the investigation turned out to be authorized, DHS did not curtail the telephone investigation. Rather than handle any unauthorized calls as an administrative matter, DHS tried to prosecute Green for an unauthorized thirteen-cent call. Next, DHS began an unprecedented investigation of Green's sick leave; at one point in this investigation, five investigators followed Green because he supposedly missed a physical therapy session. *  *  * [The] DHS simultaneously terminated the telephone and sick-leave investigations,

referred both matters to the district attorney for criminal prosecution, and fired Green. We conclude that this is more than the scintilla [a minuscule amount] of evidence required to defeat the no-evidence challenge to the jury's finding that Green's whistleblowing activities resulted in DHS's retaliatory firing * * * .

**DECISION AND REMEDY**   *The appellate court affirmed the lower court's judgment. The DHS's discharge of Green constituted a retaliatory discharge in violation of the Texas Whistleblower Act.*

**INTERNATIONAL CONSIDERATIONS**   **Whistleblowing in England** *England has passed legislation protecting workers who report health and safety violations by their employers. In a recent case, a company dismissed a worker who reported unsafe levels of a chemical, lindane, and called in a health and safety inspector. After the company fired the worker, the worker sued the employer for violating the law protecting whistleblowers and recovered approximately $12,000 in damages.*

---

## SECTION 3

# PRIVACY RIGHTS OF EMPLOYEES

Recall from Chapter 5 that there is no provision in the U.S. Constitution that guarantees a right to privacy. Yet a personal right to privacy has been inferred from other constitutional guarantees provided by the First, Third, Fourth, Fifth, and Ninth Amendments to the Constitution. In the last two decades, concerns about the privacy rights of employees have arisen in response to the sometimes invasive tactics used by employers in their efforts to monitor and screen workers. Lie-detector tests, drug tests, and other practices have increasingly been subject to challenge as violations of employee privacy rights.

### LIE-DETECTOR TESTS

At one time, many employers required employees or job applicants to take polygraph examinations in connection with their employment. The results of these lie-detector tests are not admissible as evidence in criminal trials, and many persons consider the tests to be an invasion of privacy.

In 1988, Congress passed the Employee Polygraph Protection Act.[10] The act prohibits certain employers from (1) requiring or causing employees or job applicants to take lie-detector tests

or suggesting or requesting that they do so; (2) using, accepting, referring to, or asking about the results of lie-detector tests taken by employees or applicants; and (3) taking or threatening negative employment-related action against employees or applicants based on results of lie-detector tests or on their refusal to take the tests.

Employers excepted from these prohibitions include federal, state, and local government employers; certain security service firms; and companies manufacturing and distributing controlled substances. Other employers may use polygraph tests when investigating losses attributable to theft—including embezzlement and stealing of trade secrets.

### DRUG TESTING

Workers whose ability to perform is impaired as a result of drug use can pose a substantial threat to the safety of others. For example, railway or airline employees may seriously endanger the public safety if they perform their jobs under the influence of alcohol or other drugs. Drug and alcohol use also is very costly for employers, who lose billions of dollars each year as a result of absenteeism, impaired performance, and accidents caused by employee drug use. In the interest of public safety and to reduce unnecessary costs, many of today's employers, including the government, require their employees to submit to drug testing.

Laws relating to the privacy rights of private-sector employees vary from state to state. Some state constitutions may prohibit private employers

---

10.   29 U.S.C. Sections 2001–2009.

from testing for drugs, and state statutes may restrict drug testing by private employers in any number of ways. A collective bargaining agreement may also provide protection against drug testing. In some instances, employees have brought an action against the employer for the tort of invasion of privacy (discussed in Chapter 6).

Constitutional limitations apply to the testing of government employees. The Fourth Amendment provides that individuals have the right to be "secure in their persons" against "unreasonable searches and seizures" conducted by government agents. Drug tests have been held constitutional, however, when there was a reasonable basis for suspecting government employees of using drugs. Also, when drug use in a particular government job could threaten public safety, testing has been upheld. For example, a Department of Transpor-

tation rule that requires employees engaged in oil and gas pipeline operations to submit to random drug testing was upheld, even though the rule did not require that before being tested the individual must have been suspected of drug use.[11] The court held that the government's interest in promoting public safety in the pipeline industry outweighed the employees' privacy interests.

In the following case, employees of the Department of Labor claimed that drug testing based on the reasonable suspicion of off-duty drug use violated their constitutional rights under the Fourth Amendment.

---

11. *Electrical Workers Local 1245 v. Skinner*, 913 F.2d 1454 (9th Cir. 1990).

---

**HISTORICAL AND POLITICAL SETTING**  *In the 1980s, President Ronald Reagan deployed Cruise missiles in Europe and supported the development of the Stealth bomber and a range of laser-guided missiles known as the Strategic Defense Initiative (SDI, or "Star Wars"). In defense of American interests, President Reagan authorized the landing of U.S. troops in Grenada and an attack on military headquarters in Libya. Domestically, the president supported a restructuring of the federal income tax system and other economic stimulants, including "deregulation"—a reduction in the number of administrative regulations created by government agencies. By the mid-1980s, the greatest threat to domestic tranquility appeared to be an increasing use of illegal drugs. As part of a war on drugs, President Reagan issued Executive Order 12564.*

**BACKGROUND AND FACTS**  *In 1986, President Reagan issued an executive order requiring all agencies and departments in the executive branch of the government to "develop a plan for achieving the objective of a drug-free workplace with due consideration of the rights of the government, the employee, and the general public." In 1988, in response to the order, the Department of Labor (DOL) developed a "Drug-Free Workplace Plan." The plan designated certain DOL employment positions to be sensitive positions in regard to public health and safety or national security. The plan provided that employees holding these positions—called "testing-designated positions," or TDPs—could be subjected to drug testing, including drug testing based on a reasonable suspicion of on-duty or off-duty drug use. The American Federation of Government Employees and two individual DOL employees sought to enjoin the DOL from certain types of drug testing, including drug testing based on a reasonable suspicion of on-duty or off-duty drug use. The trial court approved the DOL's drug-testing plan except for testing based on the reasonable suspicion of off-duty use. The court granted an injunction against such testing, holding that the Fourth Amendment permits such testing only when it is based on a*

**CASE 36.2**

**AMERICAN FEDERATION OF GOVERNMENT EMPLOYEES, AFL-CIO, LOCAL 2391 v. MARTIN**

United States Court of Appeals, Ninth Circuit, 1992. 969 F.2d 788.

*reasonable suspicion of on-duty, and not off-duty, illegal drug use or impairment. The DOL appealed the court's decision.*

*PREGERSON*, Circuit Judge:

\* \* \* \*

We note at the outset that urinalysis drug tests necessarily invade reasonable expectations of privacy rendering them searches within the meaning of the Fourth Amendment. \* \* \* [W]hether the government may validly require its employees to submit to drug testing is determined "by balancing its intrusion on the [employees'] Fourth Amendment interests against its promotion of legitimate governmental interests." \* \* \*

\* \* \* \*

We recognize that significant privacy interests of DOL employees are infringed by urinalysis drug testing for off-duty drug use. Nevertheless, under the circumstances \* \* \* we find these interests outweighed by the DOL's interest in preventing on- or off-duty drug use from impairing TDP [testing-designated position] employees in the performance of their duties. \* \* \*

The safety- and security-sensitive nature of TDPs justifies the DOL's drug testing of TDP employees based on a reasonable suspicion arising from observed off-duty illegal drug use or impairment. We are convinced that under these limited circumstances the reasonable suspicion requirement of the DOL's Plan adequately protects its TDP employees from arbitrary and unreasonable drug testing.

**DECISION AND REMEDY**  *The appellate court reversed the trial court's ruling.*

## AIDS TESTING

An increasing number of employers are testing their workers for acquired immune deficiency syndrome (AIDS). Few public issues are more controversial than this practice.

Some state laws restrict AIDS testing, and federal statutes offer some protection to employees or job applicants who have AIDS or have tested positive for the AIDS virus. The federal Americans with Disabilities Act of 1990[12] (discussed in Chapter 37), for example, prohibits discrimination against individuals with disabilities, and the term *disability* has been broadly defined to include those individuals with diseases such as AIDS. The law also requires employers to reasonably accommodate the needs of persons with disabilities. Generally, although the law may not prohibit AIDS testing, it may prohibit the discharge of employees based on the results of those tests.

## PERFORMANCE MONITORING

In the last decade, many employers have begun to monitor the performance of their employees through electronic means. Some employers electronically monitor their employees' use of computer terminals or company telephones. In some situations, employers use video cameras to evaluate their employees' performance.

**TELEPHONE CONVERSATIONS** Listening to employees' telephone conversations may violate the Electronic Communications Privacy Act (ECPA) of 1986,[13] which amended existing federal wiretapping law to cover new forms of communications, such as those that take place via cellular telephones or electronic mail (E-mail). This act prohibits the intentional interception of any wire or electronic communication or the intentional disclosure or use of the information obtained by the interception. The ECPA excludes from coverage, however, any electronic communications through devices that are "furnished to the subscriber or user by a provider of wire or electronic communication service" and that are being used by the subscriber or user, or by the provider of the service, "in the ordinary course of its business." Does this exception—which is often referred to as the "business-

---

12. 42 U.S.C. Sections 12102–12118.

13. 18 U.S.C. Sections 2510–2521.

extension exception'' to the ECPA—permit employers to monitor employee telephone conversations in the ordinary course of their businesses? Some courts have held that it does, so long as the telephone communication does not qualify as a personal call.[14]

**ELECTRONICS COMMUNICATIONS**    A particularly troublesome issue for many employees is employer monitoring of their computer files, voice mail, E-mail, or other electronic communications. According to a recent survey, 22 percent of the employers sampled monitored such communications, and in firms with less than a thousand employees, the figure was 30 percent.[15] To date, there have been no reported court decisions on whether the business-extension exception applies to monitoring these forms of communications. The Supreme Court of California has suggested, however, that if the exception were applied, it would cover only monitoring that was undertaken for a specified purpose and conducted at a particular place and time. The exception would not apply to ''surreptitious electronic monitoring.''[16]

**EMPLOYER LIABILITY**    Generally, there is little specific government regulation of monitoring activities, and an employer may be able to avoid what laws do exist by simply informing employees that they are subject to monitoring. Then, if employees challenge the monitoring practice, the employer

can raise the defense of consent by claiming that the employees consented to the monitoring. Employers should be cautious, however, when monitoring employees, because an employee may bring an action for invasion of privacy, and a court may decide that the employee's reasonable expectation of privacy outweighs the employer's need for surveillance. Similarly, an employer should consider alternatives before searching an employee's desk, filing cabinet, or office. If a search is conducted and the employee sues, a court may balance the purposes of the search against its intrusiveness. The court may also consider the availability of less intrusive alternatives that would have accomplished the same purposes.

## SCREENING PROCEDURES

An area of concern to potential employees has to do with preemployment screening procedures. What kinds of questions on an employment application or a preemployment test are permissible? What kinds of questions go too far in terms of invading the potential employee's privacy? Is it an invasion of the potential employee's privacy, for example, to ask questions about his or her sexual inclinations or religious convictions? Although an employer may believe that such information is relevant to the job for which the individual has applied, the applicant may feel differently about the matter.

A key factor in determining whether preemployment screening tests violate the privacy rights of potential employees is whether there exists a nexus, or connection, between the questions and the job for which an applicant is applying. The following case is illustrative in this respect.

---

14.  See, for example, *Epps v. St. Mary's Hospital of Athens, Inc.*, 802 F.2d 412 (11th Cir. 1986).
15.  Michael Traynor, ''Computer E-Mail Privacy Issues Unresolved,'' *National Law Journal*, January 31, 1994, p. S2.
16.  *People v. Otto,* 2 Cal.4th 1088, 831 P.2d 1178, 9 Cal.Rptr.2d 596 (1992).

---

**COMPANY PROFILE**    *The Panic of 1873 bankrupted Joseph Hudson, but by 1881 he had saved enough money to open a clothing store in Detroit. Using marketing techniques that were new at the time, Hudson marked his goods with prices (instead of bargaining with the customers) and accepted merchandise returns. By 1891, Hudson's was the largest retailer of men's clothing in the United States. In 1902, in Minneapolis, Minnesota, George Dayton established Dayton's, a department store that, like Hudson's, accepted customers' returns of merchandise. In 1954, in Detroit, Hudson's built Northland, then the largest shopping center in the United States. Two years later, in Minneapolis, Dayton's built Southdale,*

| CASE 36.3 |
| --- |

**SOROKA v. DAYTON HUDSON CORP.**

California Court of Appeal, First District, Division 4, 1991.
7 Cal.App.4th 203,
1 Cal.Rptr.2d 77.

*the world's first fully enclosed shopping mall. Dayton's opened the first Target store in 1962. Seven years later, Dayton's bought Hudson's and formed Dayton Hudson Corporation. Today, Dayton Hudson Corporation also includes Marshall Field's of Chicago and Mervyn's. Dayton Hudson operates nearly a thousand stores across the United States. The Target stores account for nearly 60 percent of the corporation's sales.*

**BACKGROUND AND FACTS** *Target hires store security officers (SSOs) to observe, apprehend, and arrest suspected shoplifters. SSOs are not armed, but they carry handcuffs and may use force, in self-defense, against suspected shoplifters. Target views good judgment and emotional stability as important SSO job skills. To determine whether applicants for SSO positions possess these qualities, Target uses a psychological test that it calls the Psychscreen. All job applicants must take the test as a condition of employment. A number of the questions included in the Psychscreen test are highly personal and intimate. Some of the questions relate to the applicant's religious beliefs ("I believe in the second coming of Christ" and "I believe my sins are unpardonable"); other questions concern the job candidate's sexual orientation ("I have often wished that I were a girl" and "Many of my dreams are about sex matters"). Sibi Soroka and two other applicants (the plaintiffs) found the test objectionable and brought a class-action suit against Dayton Hudson, challenging the test as violating their privacy rights. The trial court found that Target's use of the test was reasonable, and the plaintiffs appealed.*

*REARDON,* Associate Justice.

\* \* \* \*

Target concedes that the Psychscreen intrudes on the privacy interests of its job applicants. \* \* \*

While Target unquestionably has an interest in employing emotionally stable persons to be SSO's, testing applicants about their religious beliefs and sexual orientation does not further this interest. To justify the invasion of privacy resulting from use of the Psychscreen, Target must demonstrate a compelling interest and must establish that the test serves a job-related purpose. \* \* \* Target made no showing that a person's religious beliefs or sexual orientation have any bearing on the emotional stability or on the ability to perform an SSO's job responsibilities. It did no more than to make generalized claims about the Psychscreen's relationship to emotional fitness and to assert that it has seen an overall improvement in SSO quality and performance since it implemented the Psychscreen. This is not sufficient to constitute a compelling interest, nor does it satisfy the \* \* \* requirement [that the questions be related to the job]. Therefore, Target's inquiry into the religious beliefs and sexual orientation of SSO applicants unjustifiably violates the state constitutional right to privacy.

**DECISION AND REMEDY** *The appellate court reversed the trial court's decision and remanded the case for further proceedings.*

# HEALTH AND SAFETY PROTECTION

Under the common law, employees injured on the job had to rely on tort law or contract law theories in suits brought against their employers. Today, numerous state and federal statutes protect employees and their families from the risk of accidental injury, death, or disease resulting from their employment. This section discusses the Occupational Safety and Health Act of 1970[17] and state workers' compensation acts, both of which are specifically designed to protect employees and their families.

## OSHA

At the federal level, the primary legislation for employee health and safety protection is the Occupational Safety and Health Act of 1970. This act was passed in an attempt to ensure safe and healthful working conditions for practically every employee in the country. The act provides for specific standards that must be met by employers, plus a general duty to keep workplaces safe.

### OSHA ENFORCEMENT
Three federal agencies were created to develop and enforce the standards set by this act. The Occupational Safety and Health Administration (OSHA) is part of the Department of Labor and has the authority to promulgate standards, make inspections, and enforce the act. OSHA has safety standards governing many workplace details, such as the structural stability of ladders and the requirements for railings. OSHA also establishes standards that protect employees against exposure to substances that may be harmful to their health and requires some employers to provide workers with information and training on the use of personal protective equipment. The National Institute for Occupational Safety and Health is part of the Department of Health and Human Services. Its main duty is to conduct research on safety and health problems and to recommend standards for OSHA to adopt. Finally, the Occupational Safety and Health Review Commission is an independent agency set up to handle appeals from actions taken by OSHA administrators.

Criminal penalties for willful violation of the federal Occupational Safety and Health Act are limited. Employers may be prosecuted under state laws, however. In 1988, the Justice Department stated its view that criminal penalties in the act did not preempt state and local criminal laws.[18] In other words, the act could no longer be used to shield employers from state criminal prosecution if they showed willful disregard for worker safety. In 1991, the Court of Appeals for the First Circuit held that the act also did not shield employers from liability under state tort laws.[19]

### OSHA PROCEDURES
Employees can file complaints of OSHA violations. Under the Occupational Safety and Health Act, an employer cannot discharge an employee who files a complaint or who, in good faith, refuses to work in a high-risk area if bodily harm or death might result. Employers with eleven or more employees are required to keep occupational injury and illness records for each employee. Each record must be made available for inspection when requested by an OSHA inspector. Whenever a work-related injury or disease occurs, employers must make reports directly to OSHA. Whenever an employee is killed in a work-related accident, or when three or more employees are hospitalized in one accident, the Department of Labor must be notified within eight hours. If it is not, the company is fined. Following the accident, a complete inspection of the premises is mandatory.

OSHA compliance officers may enter and inspect facilities of any establishment covered by the act.[20] In the past, warrantless inspections were conducted. As the following case illustrates, however, it is now recognized that such inspections violate the warrant clause of the Fourth Amendment.

---

17. 29 U.S.C. Sections 553, 651–678.

18. Letter to Chairman, House Committee on Government Operations, 100th Cong., 2d Sess. (1988).

19. *Pedraza v. Shell Oil Co.,* 942 F.2d 48 (1st Cir. 1991); *cert.* denied, *Shell Oil Co. v. Pedraza,* ___ U.S. ___, 112 S.Ct. 993, 117 L.Ed.2d 154 (1992). The phrase "*cert.* denied" is short for *certiorari* denied—in this case, by the United States Supreme Court. See Chapter 3.

20. Among other things, OSHA inspectors can videotape employees at their work stations as part of an investigation of workplace ergonomics. *Matter of Establishment Inspection of Kelly-Springfield Tire Co.,* 13 F.3d 1160 (7th Cir. 1994).

**CASE 36.4**

**MARSHALL v.
BARLOW'S, INC.**
Supreme Court of the
United States, 1978.
436 U.S. 307,
98 S.Ct. 1816,
56 L.Ed.2d 305.

**BACKGROUND AND FACTS**   *In 1975, an OSHA inspector entered the customer service area of Barlow's, Inc., an electrical and plumbing installation business. After showing his credentials, the inspector informed the president and general manager, Barlow, that he wished to conduct a search of the working areas of the business. Upon inquiry, Barlow learned that no complaint had been received about his company. The inspection was simply the result of a random selection process, and the inspector did not have a search warrant. Barlow refused to permit the inspector to enter the working area of his business, claiming rights guaranteed by the Fourth Amendment of the U.S. Constitution. OSHA filed suit in the district court and received an order compelling Barlow to admit the inspector for purposes of conducting an occupational safety and health inspection. When the OSHA inspector presented himself, however, Barlow again refused him admission. Barlow then sought an injunction against the warrantless search on the ground that it violated the Fourth Amendment. A panel of three judges issued a permanent injunction, and OSHA appealed.*

Mr. Justice *WHITE* delivered the opinion of the Court.

\*   \*   \*   \*

The Warrant Clause of the Fourth Amendment protects commercial buildings as well as private homes. To hold otherwise would belie the origin of that Amendment, and the American colonial experience. An important forerunner of the first 10 Amendments to the United States Constitution, the Virginia Bill of Rights, specifically opposed ''general warrants, whereby an officer or messenger may be commanded to search suspected places without evidence of a fact committed.'' The general warrant was a recurring point of contention in the colonies immediately preceding the Revolution. \*   \*   \*

\*   \*   \*   \*

The Secretary urges that an exception from the search warrant requirement has been recognized for ''pervasively regulated business[es],'' \*   \*   \*   .

\*   \*   \*   \*

\*   \*   \* Invoking the Walsh-Healey Act of 1936,[a] the Secretary attempts to support a conclusion that all businesses involved in interstate commerce have long been subjected to close supervision of employee safety and health conditions. But the degree of federal involvement in employee working circumstances has never been of the order of specificity and pervasiveness that OSHA mandates. It is quite unconvincing to argue that the imposition of minimum wages and maximum hours on employers who contracted with the Government under the Walsh-Healey Act prepared the entirety of American interstate commerce for regulation of working conditions to the minutest detail. Nor can any but the most fictional sense of voluntary consent to later searches be found in the single fact that one conducts a business affecting interstate commerce; under current practice and law, few businesses can be conducted without having some effect on interstate commerce.

\*   \*   \*   \*

\*   \*   \* We conclude that the concerns expressed by the Secretary do not suffice to justify warrantless inspections under OSHA or vitiate the general constitutional requirement that for a search to be reasonable a warrant must be obtained.

**DECISION
AND REMEDY**   *The permanent injunction was upheld. OSHA inspections conducted without warrants were held to be unconstitutional.*

a.   Recall from this chapter's introduction that this act requires a minimum wage, as well as overtime pay of time and a half, for employees of manufacturers or suppliers entering into contracts with agencies of the federal government.

## STATE WORKERS' COMPENSATION LAWS

State **workers' compensation laws** establish an administrative procedure for compensating workers injured on the job. Instead of suing, an injured worker files a claim with the administrative agency or board that administers the local workers' compensation claims.

Most workers' compensation statutes are similar. No state covers all employees. Typically excluded are domestic workers, agricultural workers, temporary employees, and employees of common carriers (companies that provide transportation services to the public). Typically, the statutes cover minors. Usually, the statutes allow employers to purchase insurance from a private insurer or a state fund to pay workers' compensation benefits in the event of a claim. Most states also allow employers to be *self-insured*—that is, employers who show an ability to pay claims do not need to buy insurance.

In general, the right to recover benefits is predicated wholly on the existence of an employment relationship and the fact that the injury was *accidental* and *occurred on the job* or *in the course of employment*, regardless of fault. Intentionally inflicted self-injury, for example, would not be considered accidental and hence would not be covered. If an injury occurred while an employee was commuting to or from work, it would not usually be considered to have occurred on the job or in the course of employment and hence would not be covered.

An employee must notify his or her employer promptly (usually within thirty days) of an injury. Generally, an employee also must file a workers' compensation claim with the appropriate state agency or board within a certain period (sixty days to two years) from the time the injury is first noticed, rather than from the time of the accident.

An employee's acceptance of workers' compensation benefits bars the employee from suing for injuries caused by the employer's negligence. By barring lawsuits for negligence, workers' compensation laws also bar employers from raising common law defenses to negligence. For example, an employer can no longer raise such defenses as contributory negligence or assumption of risk to avoid liability for negligence. A worker may sue an employer who *intentionally* injures the worker, however.

# RETIREMENT AND SECURITY INCOME

Federal and state governments participate in insurance programs designed to protect employees and their families by covering the financial impact of retirement, disability, death, hospitalization, and unemployment. The key federal law on this subject is the Social Security Act of 1935.[21]

## OLD AGE, SURVIVORS, AND DISABILITY INSURANCE

The Social Security Act provides for old age (retirement), survivors, and disability insurance. The act is therefore often referred to as OASDI. Both employers and employees must ''contribute'' under the Federal Insurance Contributions Act (FICA)[22] to help pay for the employees' loss of income on retirement. The basis for the employee's and the employer's contribution is the employee's annual wage base—the maximum amount of the employee's wages that are subject to the tax. Benefits are fixed by statute but increase automatically with increases in the cost of living.

## MEDICARE

A health insurance program, Medicare is administered by the Social Security Administration for people sixty-five years of age and older and for some under sixty-five who are disabled. It has two parts, one pertaining to hospital costs and the other to nonhospital medical costs, such as visits to doctors' offices. People who have Medicare hospital insurance can also obtain additional federal medical insurance if they pay small monthly premiums, which increase as the cost of medical care increases.

As with Social Security contributions, both the employer and the employee contribute to Medicare. Currently, 2.9 percent of the amount of all wages and salaries paid to employees goes toward financing Medicare.

---

21.  42 U.S.C. Sections 301–1397e.
22.  26 U.S.C. Sections 3101–3125.

## PRIVATE RETIREMENT PLANS

There has been significant legislation to regulate retirement plans set up by employers to supplement Social Security benefits. The major federal act covering these retirement plans is the Employee Retirement Income Security Act of 1974 (ERISA).[23] This act empowers the Labor Management Services Administration of the Department of Labor to enforce its provisions to regulate individuals who operate private pension funds. ERISA does not require an employer to establish a pension plan. When a plan exists, however, ERISA establishes standards for its management.

A key provision of ERISA concerns **vesting.** Vesting gives an employee a legal right to receive pension benefits at some future date when he or she stops working. Before ERISA, some employees who had worked for companies for as long as thirty years received no pension benefits when their employment terminated, because those benefits had not vested. ERISA establishes complex vesting rules. Generally, however, all employee contributions to pension plans vest immediately, and employee rights to employer pension-plan contributions vest after five years of employment.

In an attempt to prevent mismanagement of pension funds, ERISA has established rules on how they must be invested. Pension managers must be cautious in their investments and refrain from investing more than 10 percent of the fund in securities of the employer. ERISA also contains detailed record-keeping and reporting requirements.

## UNEMPLOYMENT COMPENSATION

The United States has a system of unemployment insurance in which employers pay into a fund, the proceeds of which are paid out to qualified unemployed workers. The Federal Unemployment Tax Act[24] of 1935 created a state system that provides unemployment compensation to eligible individuals. Employers that fall under the provisions of the act are taxed at regular intervals. Taxes are typically paid by the employers to the states, which then deposit them with the federal government. The federal government maintains an unemployment insurance fund, in which each state has an account.

---

23. 29 U.S.C. Sections 1001–1461.
24. 26 U.S.C. Sections 3301–3310.

---

### SECTION 6

# COBRA AND OTHER EMPLOYMENT LAWS

Legislation affecting employment relationships addresses a broad range of other issues. In this section, we examine several important statutes governing such issues as health insurance for former employees, family and medical leave, child labor, overtime pay, minimum wages, and immigrant workers.

## COBRA

The Consolidated Omnibus Budget Reconciliation Act (COBRA) of 1985[25] prohibits the elimination of a worker's medical, optical, or dental insurance coverage upon the voluntary or involuntary termination of the worker's employment. The act includes most workers who have either lost their jobs or had their hours decreased such that they are no longer eligible for coverage under the employer's health plan. Only those workers fired for gross misconduct are excluded from protection.

**APPLICATION OF COBRA** The worker has sixty days (beginning with the date that the group coverage would stop) to decide whether to continue with the employer's group insurance plan or not. If the worker chooses to discontinue the coverage, then the employer has no further obligation. If the worker chooses to continue coverage, however, the employer is obligated to keep the policy active for up to eighteen months. If the worker is disabled, the employer must extend coverage up to twenty-nine months. The coverage provided must be the same as that enjoyed by the worker prior to the termination or reduction of work. If family members were originally included, for example, COBRA would prohibit their exclusion. This is not a free ride for the worker, however. To receive continued benefits, he or she may be required to pay all of the premium, as well as a 2 percent administrative charge.

**EMPLOYERS' OBLIGATIONS** Employers, with some exceptions, must comply with COBRA if

---

25. 29 U.S.C. Sections 1161–1169.

they employ twenty or more workers and provide a benefit plan to those workers. They must inform an employee of COBRA's provisions when a group health plan is established and if that worker faces termination or a reduction of hours that would affect his or her eligibility for coverage under the plan.

The employer is relieved of the responsibility to provide benefit coverage if it completely eliminates its group benefit plan. An employer is also relieved of responsibility when the worker becomes eligible for Medicare, falls under a spouse's health plan, becomes insured under a different plan (with a new employer, for example), or fails to pay the premium. An employer that fails to comply with COBRA risks substantial penalties, such as a tax of up to 10 percent of the annual cost of the group plan or $500,000, whichever is less.[26]

## FAMILY AND MEDICAL LEAVE ACT

A majority of the states have legislation allowing for a leave from employment for family or medical reasons, and many employers maintain private family-leave plans for their workers. The federal Family and Medical Leave Act of 1993 (FMLA),[27] however, significantly improves job security for most workers whose employers have fifty or more employees.

The act requires qualifying employers to provide employees with up to twelve weeks of family or medical leave during any twelve-month period. During the employee's leave, the employer must continue the worker's health-care coverage and guarantee employment in the same position or a comparable position when the employee returns to work. An important exception to the FMLA, however, allows the employer to avoid reinstatement of a *key employee*—defined as an employee whose pay falls within the top 10 percent of the firm's work force.

Generally, family leave may be taken when an employee wishes to care for a newborn baby, an adopted child, or a foster child.[28] Medical leave may be taken when the employee or the employee's spouse, child, or parent has a "serious health con-

dition" requiring care. The FMLA also allows for intermittent leave when medically necessary.

The FMLA provides a wide array of statutory remedies to the injured employee. Remedies include damages for unpaid wages (or salary), lost benefits, denied compensation, actual monetary losses (such as the cost of providing for care) up to an amount equivalent to the employee's wages for twelve weeks, job reinstatement, and promotion. The successful plaintiff is entitled to court costs and attorneys' fees and, in cases involving bad faith on the part of the employer, double damages.

## FAIR LABOR STANDARDS ACT

The Fair Labor Standards Act of 1938 (FLSA),[29] also known as the Wage-Hour Law, covers many employers, including those who are engaged in interstate commerce or engaged in the production of goods for interstate commerce and certain specified businesses. The FLSA is concerned with child labor, maximum hours, and minimum wages.

**CHILD LABOR** The act prohibits oppressive child labor. Children under fourteen years of age are allowed to deliver newspapers, work for their parents, and work in the entertainment and (with some exceptions) agricultural areas. Children who are fourteen or fifteen years of age are allowed to work but not in hazardous occupations. There are also numerous restrictions on how many hours per day and per week they can work. For example, they cannot work during school hours, for more than three hours on a school day (or eight hours on a nonschool day), for more than eighteen hours during a school week (or forty hours during a nonschool week), or before 7 A.M. or after 7 P.M. (9 P.M. during the summer).

Most states require persons under sixteen years of age to obtain work permits. Persons between the ages of sixteen and eighteen do not face such restrictions on working times and hours, but they cannot be employed in hazardous jobs or in jobs detrimental to their health and well-being. Persons over the age of eighteen are not affected by any of the above-mentioned restrictions.

---

26. Health-care legislation proposed by the Clinton administration may supersede COBRA.
27. 29 U.S.C. Sections 2601, 2611–2619, 2651–2654.
28. The foster care must be state sanctioned before such an arrangement falls within the coverage of the FMLA.

---

29. 29 U.S.C. Sections 201–260.

**MAXIMUM HOURS** Under the FLSA, any employee who agrees to work more than forty hours per week must be paid no less than one and a half times his or her regular pay for all hours over forty. Certain employees are exempted from the overtime provisions of the act. Exempt employees fall into four categories: executives, administrative employees, professional employees, and outside salespersons. The FLSA has specific tests to determine whether an employee qualifies as an executive, an administrative employee, or a professional employee. Generally, to fall into one of these three categories, an employee must earn more than a specified amount of income per week and devote a certain percentage of work time to the performance of specific types of duties. To qualify as an outside salesperson, the employee must regularly engage in sales work away from the office and spend no more than 20 percent of work time per week performing other than sales duties.

**MINIMUM WAGE** The FLSA provides that a **minimum wage** of a specified amount ($4.25 per hour as of April 1, 1991) must be paid to employees in covered industries. Congress periodically revises such minimum wages. The term *wages* is meant to include the reasonable cost of the employer in furnishing employees with board, lodging, and other facilities if they are customarily furnished by that employer.

## THE IMMIGRATION ACT OF 1990

The Immigration Act of 1990[30] limits the number of legal immigrants entering the United States by capping the number of visas (entry permits) that are issued each year. Under the act, employers recruiting workers from other countries must complete a certification process and satisfy the Department of Labor that there is a shortage of qualified U.S. workers capable of performing the work. The employer must also establish that bringing aliens into this country will not adversely affect the existing labor market in that particular area. In this way, the act attempts to serve two purposes: encouraging skilled workers to enter this country and at the same time restricting competition for American jobs.

# UNIONS AND COLLECTIVE BARGAINING

Most of the early legislation to protect employees focused on the rights of workers to join unions and to engage in collective bargaining. **Collective bargaining** can be defined as the process by which labor and management negotiate the terms and conditions of employment, including wages, benefits, working conditions, and other matters. Collective bargaining allows union representatives to be elected by union members and speak on behalf of the members at the bargaining table.

## NORRIS-LAGUARDIA ACT

Congress protected peaceful strikes, picketing, and boycotts in 1932 in the Norris-LaGuardia Act.[31] The statute restricted federal courts in their power to issue injunctions against unions engaged in peaceful strikes. In effect, this act declared a national policy permitting employees to organize.

## NATIONAL LABOR RELATIONS ACT

The National Labor Relations Act (NLRA) of 1935, which is also known as the Wagner Act,[32] established the rights of employees to engage in collective bargaining and to strike. The act also created the National Labor Relations Board (NLRB) to oversee union elections and to prevent employers from engaging in unfair and illegal union-labor activities and unfair labor practices. The purpose of the NLRA was to secure for employees the rights to organize, to bargain collectively through representatives of their own choosing, and to engage in concerted activities for organizing, collective bargaining, and other purposes. The act specifically defined a number of employer practices as unfair to labor:

1. Interference with the efforts of employees to form, join, or assist labor organizations or to engage in concerted activities for their mutual aid or protection.

---

30. This act amended various provisions of the Immigration and Nationality Act of 1952, 8 U.S.C. Sections 1101–1524.

31. 29 U.S.C. Sections 101–110, 113–115.
32. 29 U.S.C. Sections 151–169.

2. An employer's domination of a labor organization or contribution of financial or other support to it.
3. Discrimination in the hiring or awarding of tenure to employees for reason of union affiliation.
4. Discrimination against employees for filing charges under the act or giving testimony under the act.
5. Refusal to bargain collectively with the duly designated representative of the employees.

Another purpose of the act was to promote fair and just settlements of disputes by peaceful processes and to avoid industrial warfare. The NLRB was granted investigatory powers and was authorized to issue and serve complaints against employers in response to employee charges of unfair labor practices. The NLRB was further empowered to issue **cease-and-desist orders**—orders compelling employers to cease engaging in the unfair practices—when violations were found. Cease-and-desist orders could be enforced by circuit courts of appeals if necessary.

Arguments over alleged unfair labor practices are first decided by the NLRB and may then be appealed to a federal court. The following case, which involved an allegedly unfair labor practice, illustrates this process.

---

**BACKGROUND AND FACTS** *Salvatore Monte was the president of Kenrich Petrochemicals, Inc., a family-owned business. Helen Chizmar had been Kenrich's office manager since 1963. Among the clerical staff that Chizmar supervised were her sister, her daughter, and her daughter-in-law. In May 1987, Chizmar's three relatives and four other clerical staff members designated the Oil, Chemical and Atomic Workers International Union as their bargaining representative. Chizmar was not involved, but when Monte received notice that his office was unionizing, he told Chizmar that someone else could do her job for "$20,000 less" and fired her. Later, he told another employee that one of his reasons for firing Chizmar was that he "was not going to put up with any union bullsh___." A few days later, he told the clerical workers that if they voted for the union they would have to "start from scratch. No benefits, no salary, no vacations." Monte shoved one of the women against a filing cabinet. Still later, during negotiations with the union, Monte said that he planned to "get rid of the whole family." Chizmar's family complained to the National Labor Relations Board that Chizmar's firing was an unfair labor practice. The NLRB agreed and ordered that Chizmar be reinstated with back pay. Kenrich appealed.*

CASE 36.5

**KENRICH PETROCHEMICALS, INC. v. NATIONAL LABOR RELATIONS BOARD**

United States Court of Appeals, Third Circuit, 1990.
907 F.2d 400.

---

*STAPLETON,* Circuit Judge:
 * * * *
Kenrich's * * * argument is that the Board may not reinstate a supervisor because the Act does not protect a supervisor who engages in union activity. * * * While it is uncontestably true that the Act does not protect a supervisor from being discharged for engaging in concerted activity, this does not deprive the Board of the authority to order the reinstatement of a supervisor whose firing resulted not from her own pro-union conduct, but from the employer's efforts to thwart the exercise of * * * rights by protected rank-and-file employees. * * *
 * * * *
 * * * [W]hen an employer fires a supervisor in order to discourage the exercise of * * * rights by protected employees closely related to the supervisor, the Board, based upon its experience, is entitled to infer in the absence of evidence to the contrary that the intended message was an effective one. Indeed, we do not believe one needs extensive experience with behavior in response to coercive tactics in the workplace

to conclude that such a discharge must communicate to rank-and-file employees that the employer is willing to go to any lengths to crush [unionizing] activity. *   *   * *   *   *   *

If that discharge is left unremedied, the fears engendered by that discharge and Monte's later threats will not be dispelled. Rather, a powerful message will be sent out to the supervisors and employees of Kenrich that the company may, without fear of redress, use family member supervisors as hostages. *   *   *

By reinstating Chizmar and compensating her for lost wages, the Board's order protects the *   *   * rights of Kenrich's employees by assuring them that they need not fear that the exercise of their rights will give the company a license to inflict harm on their family. It also protects the employees by reassuring their relatives who are supervisors that they need not feel that their jobs are dependent on their ability to dissuade their family members from engaging in protected activity.

**DECISION AND REMEDY**   *The court concluded that the NLRB's reinstatement and back pay order was reasonably calculated to dispel the intimidation caused by Chizmar's firing and ruled that the order be enforced.*

## LABOR-MANAGEMENT RELATIONS ACT

The Labor-Management Relations Act of 1947 (the Taft-Hartley Act)[33] was passed to proscribe certain unfair union practices, such as the *closed shop*. A **closed shop** is a firm that requires union membership by its workers as a condition of employment. The closed shop was made illegal under the Taft-Hartley Act. The act preserved the legality of the **union shop,** which does not require membership as a prerequisite for employment but can, and usually does, require that workers join the union after a specified amount of time on the job.

The act also prohibited unions from refusing to bargain with employers, engaging in certain types of picketing, and featherbedding (causing employers to hire more employees than necessary). The act also allowed individual states to pass their own **right-to-work laws**—laws making it illegal for union membership to be required for *continued* employment in any establishment. Thus, union shops are technically illegal in states with right-to-work laws.

## LABOR-MANAGEMENT REPORTING AND DISCLOSURE ACT

The Labor-Management Reporting and Disclosure Act of 1959 (the Landrum-Griffin Act)[34] estab-lished an employee bill of rights and reporting requirements for union activities. The Landrum-Griffin Act strictly regulates internal union business procedures. Union elections, for example, are regulated by the Landrum-Griffin Act, which requires that regularly scheduled elections of officers occur and that secret ballots be used. Ex-convicts and Communists are prohibited from holding union office. Moreover, union officials are accountable for union property and funds. Members have the right to attend and to participate in union meetings, to nominate officers, and to vote in most union proceedings.

The Landrum-Griffin Act also outlawed certain agreements—called **hot-cargo agreements**—in which employers voluntarily agreed with unions not to handle, use, or deal in non-union-produced goods of other employers. In principle, the Taft-Hartley Act had made all such boycotts (called **secondary boycotts**) illegal. This particular type of secondary boycott was not made illegal by the Taft-Hartley Act, however, because that act only prevented unions from inducing *employees* to strike or otherwise act to force the employer not to handle these goods. The Landrum-Griffin Act addressed this problem by declaring that secondary boycotts resulting from hot-cargo agreements were illegal.

33.  29 U.S.C. Sections 141–144.
34.  29 U.S.C. Sections 401–531.

# TERMS AND CONCEPTS TO REVIEW

| | | |
|---|---|---|
| cease-and-desist order **717** | minimum wage **716** | whistleblowing **703** |
| closed shop **718** | right-to-work law **718** | workers' compensation |
| collective bargaining **716** | secondary boycott **718** | laws **713** |
| employment at will **702** | union shop **718** | wrongful discharge **703** |
| hot-cargo agreement **718** | vesting **714** | |

# QUESTIONS AND CASE PROBLEMS

**36–1. Labor Laws.** Calzoni Boating Co. is an interstate business engaged in manufacturing and selling boats. The company has five hundred nonunion employees. Representatives of these employees are requesting a four-day, ten-hours-per-day workweek, and Calzoni is concerned that this would require paying time and a half after eight hours per day. Which federal act is Calzoni thinking of that might require this? Will the act in fact require paying time and a half for all hours worked over eight hours per day if the employees' proposal is accepted? Explain.

**36–2. Health and Safety Regulations.** Denton and Carlo were employed at an appliance plant. Their job required them to do occasional maintenance work while standing on a wire mesh twenty feet above the plant floor. Other employees had fallen through the mesh, one of whom had been killed by the fall. When Denton and Carlo were asked by their supervisor to do work that would likely require them to walk on the mesh, they refused due to their fear of bodily harm or death. Because of their refusal to do the requested work, the two employees were fired from their jobs. Was their discharge wrongful? If so, under what federal employment law? To what federal agency or department should they turn for assistance?

**36–3. Unfair Labor Practices.** Suppose that Consolidated Stores is undergoing a unionization campaign. Prior to the union election, management says that the union is unnecessary to protect workers. Management also provides bonuses and wage increases to the workers during this period. The employees reject the union. Union organizers protest that the wage increases during the election campaign unfairly prejudiced the vote. Should these wage increases be regarded as an unfair labor practice? Discuss.

**36–4. Workers' Compensation.** Gary Segler worked for Caterpillar Tractor Co. in one of its factories. Near his work station there was a conveyor belt that ran through a large industrial oven. Sometimes, the workers would use the oven to heat their meals. Thirty-inch-high flasks containing molds were fixed at regular intervals

on the conveyor and were transported into the oven. Segler had to walk between the flasks to get to his work station. One morning, the conveyor was not moving, and Segler used the oven to cook a frozen pot pie. As he was removing the pot pie from the oven, the conveyor came on, and a flask struck Segler, seriously injuring him. Segler sought recovery under the state workers' compensation law. Should he recover? Why or why not?

**36–5. Health and Safety Regulations.** At an REA Express, Inc., shipping terminal, a conveyor belt was inoperative because an electrical circuit had shorted out. The manager called a licensed electrical contractor. When the contractor arrived, REA's maintenance supervisor was in the circuit breaker room. The floor was wet, and the maintenance supervisor was using sawdust to try to soak up the water. While the licensed electrical contractor was standing on the wet floor, attempting to fix the short circuit, he was electrocuted. Simultaneously, REA's maintenance supervisor, who was standing on a wooden platform, was burned and knocked unconscious. The Occupational Safety and Health Administration (OSHA) sought to fine REA Express $1,000 for failure to furnish a place of employment free from recognized hazards. Will the court uphold OSHA's decision? Discuss fully. [*REA Express, Inc. v. Brennan*, 495 F.2d 822 (2d Cir. 1974)]

**36–6. Whistleblowing.** Richard Winters was an at-will employee for the Houston *Chronicle* from April 1977 to June 1986. Beginning in 1980, he became aware of alleged illegal activities carried out by other employees. He claimed that the *Chronicle* was falsely reporting an inflated number of paid subscribers, that several employees were engaged in inventory theft, and that his supervisor had offered him an opportunity to participate in a kickback scheme with the manufacturers of plastic bags. Winters reported all these activities to upper-level management in January 1986 but made no report to law enforcement agencies. He was fired six months later. He sued the *Chronicle* for wrongful termination. How should the court decide? Discuss fully. [*Winters v. Houston Chronicle Publishing*, 795 S.W.2d 723 (Tex. 1990)]

**36–7. Employment at Will.** Robert Adams worked as a delivery truck driver for George W. Cochran & Co.

Adams persistently refused to drive a truck that lacked a required inspection sticker and was subsequently fired as a result of his refusal. Adams was an at-will employee, and Cochran contended that because there was no written employment contract stating otherwise, Cochran was entitled to discharge Adams at will—that is, for cause or no cause. Adams sought to recover $7,094 in lost wages and $200,000 in damages for the "humiliation, mental anguish and emotional distress" that he had suffered as a result of being fired from his job. Under what legal doctrines discussed in this chapter—or exceptions to those doctrines—might Adams be able to recover damages from Cochran? Discuss fully. [*Adams v. George W. Cochran & Co.,* 597 A.2d 28 (D.C.App. 1991)]

**36–8. Whistleblowing.** Debra Roxberry supervised the dry-cleaning department for Robertson and Penn, Inc. (R&P), a private contractor to the U.S. government for laundry and dry-cleaning services at Fort Riley, Kansas. Willie Dawson was an employee of another private contractor to the U.S. government, which operated the Central Issue Facility at Fort Riley. On one occasion, when Dawson was picking up some shirts from R&P, Roxberry informed him that the shirts had been washed instead of dry-cleaned, the process for which they had been delivered and that R&P was contractually obligated to perform. Roxberry was fired a short time later, and she sued R&P for wrongful discharge, alleging that she had been fired for "blowing the whistle" on her employer's violation of its contract with the government. Under the relevant state law, at-will employees have a cause of action against an employer for discharge in retaliation for whistleblowing. R&P contended, among other things, that Roxberry was not a whistleblower because she did not report the incident to the proper authorities but only to an employee of a private company. Will the court agree with R&P's conclusion that Roxberry was not a whistleblower? Discuss. [*Roxberry v. Robertson and Penn, Inc.,* 963 F.2d 382 (10th Cir. 1992)]

**36–9. Workers' Compensation.** Earl Angus, as a condition of his employment, lived in a mobile home owned by his employer, Deffenbaugh Industries. The mobile home was located on the grounds of Deffenbaugh's plant and was purchased by Deffenbaugh to house the Angus family because it wanted Angus to "maintain a constant presence on the premises." Although Angus ordinarily worked out of an office located in a different building, the mobile home had a telephone, so Angus would be able to contact company drivers and customers as needed. One day, Angus returned to the mobile home and awaited the arrival of a truck on company business. About fifteen minutes after Angus had arrived at the mobile home, and while the family was eating dinner, a tornado struck. The tornado left Angus's wife dead and Angus and his daughter severely injured. Angus filed a workers' compensation claim against Deffenbaugh, alleging that his injuries "arose out of his employment." Among other things, Deffenbaugh argued that the injury did not occur within the course of employment, because Angus was not working but eating dinner with his family when the tornado struck. How should the court decide? [*Deffenbaugh Industries v. Angus,* 313 Ark. 100, 852 S.W.2d 804 (1993)]

**36–10. Case Briefing Assignment**

 *Examine Case A.7 [Johnston v. Del Mar Distributing Co., 776 S.W.2d 768 (Tex.App.— Corpus Christi 1989)] in Appendix A. The case has been excerpted there in great detail. Review and then brief the case, making sure that you include answers to the following questions in your brief.*

1. Why did Del Mar Distributing Co. terminate Nancy Johnston's employment?
2. What defense did Del Mar raise against Johnston's claim of wrongful discharge?
3. On what case precedent did the appellate court base its reasoning?
4. Why did the appellate court conclude that, given the circumstances of this case, it was irrelevant whether the act itself that Johnston was asked to perform was legal or illegal?

# CHAPTER 37

# EMPLOYMENT DISCRIMINATION

**D**uring the early 1960s we, as a nation, focused our attention on the civil rights of all Americans. Out of this movement to end racial and other forms of discrimination grew a body of law protecting workers against discrimination in the workplace. This protective legislation further eroded the employment-at-will doctrine, which was discussed in the previous chapter. In the past several decades, judicial decisions, administrative agency actions, and legislation have restricted the ability of employers, as well as unions, to discriminate against workers on the basis of race, color, religion, national origin, gender, age, or disability. A class of persons defined by one or more of these criteria is known as a **protected class.**

Several federal statutes prohibit **employment discrimination** against members of protected classes. The most important statute is Title VII of the Civil Rights Act of 1964[1] and its amendments. Title VII prohibits employment discrimination on the basis of race, color, religion, national origin, or gender. Discrimination on the basis of age and disability are prohibited by the Age Discrimination in Employment Act of 1967[2] and the Americans with Disabilities Act of 1990,[3] respectively.

The focus of this chapter is on the kinds of discrimination prohibited by these federal statutes. As will be discussed in the final section of this chapter, however, discrimination against employees on the basis of any of the above-mentioned criteria may also violate state human rights statutes or other state laws prohibiting discrimination.

---

1. 42 U.S.C. Sections 2000e–2000e-17.
2. 29 U.S.C. Sections 621–634.
3. 42 U.S.C. Sections 12102–12118.

# TITLE VII OF THE CIVIL RIGHTS ACT OF 1964

Title VII of the Civil Rights Act of 1964 and its amendments prohibit job discrimination against employees, applicants, and union members on the basis of race, color, national origin, religion, and gender at any stage of employment. Title VII applies to employers with fifteen or more employees, labor unions with fifteen or more members, labor unions that operate hiring halls (to which members go regularly to be rationed jobs as they become available), employment agencies, and state and local governing units or agencies. A special section of the act prohibits discrimination in most federal government employment.

A person who has suffered discrimination may not simply file a lawsuit under Title VII. Compliance with Title VII is monitored by the Equal Employment Opportunity Commission (EEOC). The EEOC has the power to issue guidelines for interpreting the law and to bring lawsuits against organizations that violate the law. Thus, first the victim must file a claim with the EEOC, which investigates the facts and seeks to achieve a voluntary agreement on the part of the employer and employee to settle the dispute. If voluntary agreement is not reached, the EEOC may sue the employer under Title VII. If the EEOC chooses not to sue—for example, if it does not believe that the complaining individual was discriminated against—the victim may bring his or her own lawsuit.

## DISCRIMINATION BASED ON RACE, COLOR, NATIONAL ORIGIN, AND RELIGION

If a company's standards or policies for selecting or promoting employees have the effect of discriminating against employees or job applicants on the basis of race, color, or national origin and do not have a substantial, demonstrable relationship to realistic qualifications for the job in question, they are illegal. Discrimination against these protected classes in regard to employment conditions and benefits is also illegal. An employer cannot maintain all-white or all–African-American crews for no demonstrable reason, for example, nor can an employer grant higher average Christmas bonuses to whites than to African Americans.

Title VII also prohibits employment discrimination based on religion. As discussed in Chapter 5, employers must reasonably accommodate the religious needs of their employees.

## DISCRIMINATION BASED ON GENDER

Under Title VII, as well as other federal acts, employers are forbidden to discriminate against employees on the basis of gender. Employers are prohibited from classifying jobs as male or female and from advertising in help-wanted columns that are designated male or female unless the employer can prove that the gender of the applicant is essential to the job. Furthermore, employers cannot have separate male and female seniority lists. As discussed below, employers also cannot discriminate against women who are pregnant, and increasingly employers face liability for the sexual harassment of women in the workplace.

**PREGNANCY DISCRIMINATION** The Pregnancy Discrimination Act of 1978,[4] which amended Title VII, expanded the definition of gender discrimination to include discrimination based on pregnancy. Women affected by pregnancy, childbirth, or related medical conditions must be treated—for all employment-related purposes, including the receipt of benefits under employee-benefit programs—the same as other persons not so affected but similar in ability to work. An employer is required to treat an employee temporarily unable to perform her job owing to a pregnancy-related condition in the same manner as the employer would treat other temporarily disabled employees. The employer must change work assignments, grant paid disability leaves, or grant leaves without pay if that is how other temporarily disabled employees would be treated. Policies concerning an employee's return to work, accrual of seniority, pay increases, and so on must also result in equal treatment.[5]

---

4.   42 U.S.C. Section 2000e(k).

5.   A cause of action under the Pregnancy Discrimination Act is not limited to women—a man may also have standing to sue for discrimination under the act. In *Nicol v. Imagematrix, Inc.*, 773 F.Supp. 802 (E.D.Va. 1991), the court held that the husband of a pregnant woman had standing to sue his former employer. The husband alleged that he had been fired because his wife (who worked for the same employer and was also fired) was pregnant.

**SEXUAL HARASSMENT** Employees also have some protection against **sexual harassment** in the workplace under Title VII provisions. Courts generally distinguish between *quid pro quo* harassment and hostile-environment harassment. *Quid pro quo* is a Latin phrase that is often translated to mean ''something in exchange for something else.'' *Quid pro quo* harassment occurs when job opportunities, promotions, and the like are doled out in exchange for sexual favors. *Hostile-environment* harassment occurs when an employee is subjected to sexual comments, jokes, or physical contact perceived to be offensive. Guidelines issued by the EEOC describe hostile-environment harassment as conduct that ''has the purpose or effect of unreasonably interfering with an individual's work performance or creating an intimidating, hostile, or offensive working environment.''[6]

In a sexual harassment case, the employer may be liable even though an employee did the harassing. If the employee is in a supervisory position, the employer will usually automatically be held liable for the behavior. The EEOC guidelines provide that an employer will be liable when a co-worker or even a nonemployee did the harassing, provided that the employer knew, or should have known, about the harassment and failed to take immediate corrective action.

If a restaurant owner or manager knows that a certain customer repeatedly harasses a waitress, for example, and permits the harassment to continue, the restaurant owner may be liable under Title VII even though the customer is not an employee of the restaurant. The issue turns on the control that the employer exerts over a nonemployee. In the situation just described, a court would likely conclude that the restaurant manager or owner could have taken action to prevent the customer from harassing the waitress.

*Proving Sexual Harassment.* Sexual harassment is often very difficult to prove, because there may be no third party witnesses and no written evidence. The question thus comes down to who is more believable, the alleged victim or the alleged offender.

Even if an employee can prove that sexually offensive conduct occurred, at what point does such conduct result in an ''intimidating, hostile, or offensive working environment''? In other words, how offensive must the conduct be and how many times must it occur before an employee has a cause of action under Title VII for hostile-environment harassment? In recent years, courts have had to struggle with such questions and usually render their decisions on a case-by-case basis. At least one court has concluded that even one incident of sexually offensive conduct can result in a hostile, offensive working environment.[7]

In the case presented below, the United States Supreme Court addresses another controversial issue relating to hostile-environment claims. Prior to this decision, many jurisdictions had held that a worker claiming to be a victim of hostile-environment harassment must establish that he or she suffered serious psychological effects as a result of the offensive conduct.

---

6.   29 C.F.R. Section 1604.11(a)(3).

7.   See *Radtke v. Everett*, 442 Mich. 368, 501 N.W.2d 155 (1993).

---

**BACKGROUND AND FACTS** *Teresa Harris was the manager of Forklift Systems, Inc. In the presence of other employees, the president of the company, Charles Hardy, said to Harris, ''You're a woman, what do you know?'' and ''We need a man as a rental manager.'' He called her a ''dumb ass woman'' and suggested that she join him at a motel to negotiate a raise. Hardy occasionally asked Harris to ''get coins from his front pants pocket'' and once threw coins on the floor, asking Harris to retrieve them. He also made ''sexual innuendos'' about Harris's and other women's clothing. At one point, Hardy asked Harris the following question about a Forklift customer: ''What did you do, promise the guy . . . some [sex] Saturday night?'' Shortly thereafter, Harris quit and eventually sued Forklift for sex discrimination in violation of Title VII, alleging that Hardy's*

**CASE 37.1**

**HARRIS v. FORKLIFT SYSTEMS, INC.**

Supreme Court of the United States, 1993.

____ U.S. ____,
114 S.Ct. 367,
126 L.Ed.2d 295.

*conduct had turned her workplace into a hostile environment. The district court dismissed the suit. Although the court acknowledged that a reasonable woman in Harris's position would have been offended, Harris failed to show that she had suffered serious psychological injury as a result of Hardy's conduct and failed to establish a work environment "so poisoned as to be intimidating or abusive." Harris appealed, and the court of appeals affirmed the trial court's judgment. Harris then appealed to the United States Supreme Court.*

Justice *O'CONNOR* delivered the opinion of the Court.
* * * *

Title VII of the Civil Rights Act of 1964 makes it "an unlawful employment practice for an employer . . . to discriminate against any individual with respect to his [or her] compensation, terms, conditions, or privileges of employment, because of such individual's race, color, religion, sex, or national origin." . . . [T]his language "is not limited to 'economic' or 'tangible' discrimination. The phrase 'terms, conditions, or privileges of employment' evinces a congressional intent 'to strike at the entire spectrum of disparate treatment of [intentional discrimination against] men and women' in employment," which includes requiring people to work in a discriminatorily hostile or abusive environment. When the workplace is permeated with "discriminatory intimidation, ridicule, and insult," that is "sufficiently severe or pervasive to alter the conditions of the victim's employment and create an abusive working environment," Title VII is violated.
* * * *

* * * Title VII comes into play before the harassing conduct leads to a nervous breakdown. A discriminatorily abusive work environment, even one that does not seriously affect employees' psychological well-being, can and often will detract from employees' job performance, discourage employees from remaining on the job, or keep them from advancing in their careers. * * *

* * * *Title VII bars conduct that would seriously affect a reasonable person's psychological well-being, but the statute is not limited to such conduct. So long as the environment would reasonably be perceived, and is perceived, as hostile or abusive, there is no need for it also to be psychologically injurious.* [Emphasis added.]

* * * [Whether an] environment is "hostile" or "abusive" can be determined only by looking at all the circumstances. These may include the frequency of the discriminatory conduct; its severity; whether it is physically threatening or humiliating, or a mere offensive utterance; and whether it unreasonably interferes with an employee's work performance. The effect on the employee's psychological well-being is, of course, relevant to determining whether the plaintiff actually found the environment abusive. But while psychological harm, like any other relevant factor, may be taken into account, no single factor is required.

**DECISION AND REMEDY**    *The United States Supreme Court reversed the holding of the court of appeals and remanded the case to the trial court for further proceedings.*

**INTERNATIONAL CONSIDERATIONS**    **Sexual Harassment in Japan** *Japan has no laws that expressly prohibit sexual harassment, but Article 14 of the Japanese Constitution prohibits sexual discrimination. In 1991, a magazine editor filed the first sexual harassment lawsuit in Japan under this article. Her employer had been spreading rumors about her sex life. She won the case and received damages of over $15,000.*

*The Applicability of the "Reasonable Person" Standard.* One of the difficulties in evaluating sexual harassment claims is the fact that men and women often have different opinions on what constitutes socially offensive conduct. The traditional legal standard for determining what is or is not appropriate behavior is the "reasonable person" standard. If a reasonable person in the same circumstances as the offended employee would have responded similarly to the alleged wrong, then the actual conduct of the employee is considered reasonable.

Some courts have held that sexual harassment should not be viewed from the gender-neutral "reasonable person" perspective but from a "reasonable woman" perspective. In *Ellison v. Brady,* for example, the U.S. Court of Appeals for the Ninth Circuit held that a woman's claim of sexual harassment should be viewed in light of a reasonable woman standard. Any other standard, said the court, "tends to systematically ignore the experiences of women."[8] Other courts have applied a reasonable man standard to claims of sexual harassment.[9] Still other courts have adopted a gender-sensitive standard, in which the gender of the reasonable person mirrors that of the employee-plaintiff.[10]

In 1993, the EEOC proposed new guidelines on harassment in the workplace.[11] The guidelines adopt a reasonable person standard for determining whether harassment in the workplace rises to the level of hostile or abusive environment sufficient for a Title VII violation. The guidelines provide, however, that in establishing whether the standard has been met, the employee-plaintiff's race, color, religion, gender, national origin, age, or disability must be considered. In the *Harris* case presented above, the Supreme Court also adopted a broad standard by holding that in cases of alleged sexual harassment, the conduct at issue must be abusive both objectively (as perceived by a reasonable person) and subjectively (as perceived by the victim).

---

8. 924 F.2d 872 (9th Cir. 1991).

9. See, for example, *Daniels v. Essex Group, Inc.,* 937 F.2d 1264 (7th Cir. 1991).

10. See, for example, *Lehmann v. Toys 'Я' Us,* 132 N.J. 587, 626 A.2d 445 (1993), in which the court announced a reasonableness standard that applies to "sexual harassment of women by men, men by women, men by men, and women by women."

11. Proposed 29 C.F.R. Part 1609.

## INTENTIONAL VERSUS UNINTENTIONAL DISCRIMINATION

Title VII prohibits both intentional and unintentional discrimination. Intentional discrimination by an employer against an employee is known as **disparate-treatment discrimination.** Because intent may sometimes be difficult to prove, courts have established certain procedures for resolving disparate-treatment cases. Suppose that a woman applies for employment with a construction firm and is rejected. If she sues on the basis of disparate-treatment discrimination in hiring, she must show that (1) she is a member of a protected class, (2) she applied and was qualified for the job in question, (3) she was rejected by the employer, and (4) the employer continued to seek applicants for the position or filled the position with a person not in a protected class.

If the woman can meet these relatively easy requirements, she makes out a *prima facie* **case** of illegal discrimination. Making out a *prima facie* case of discrimination means that the plaintiff has met her initial burden of proof and will win in the absence of a legally acceptable employer defense (defenses to claims of employment discrimination are discussed later in this chapter). The burden then shifts to the employer-defendant, who must articulate a legal reason for not hiring the plaintiff. For example, the employer might say that the plaintiff was not hired because she lacked sufficient experience or training. To prevail, the plaintiff must then show that the employer's reason is a pretext (not the true reason) and that discriminatory intent actually motivated the employer's decision.

Employers often find it necessary to use interviews and testing procedures to choose from among a large number of applicants for job openings. Minimum educational requirements are also common. Employer practices, such as those involving educational requirements, may have an unintended discriminatory impact on a protected class. **Disparate-impact discrimination** occurs when, as a result of educational or other job requirements or hiring procedures, an employer's work force does not reflect the percentage of nonwhites, women, or members of other protected classes that characterizes qualified individuals in the local labor market. If a person challenging an employment practice having a discriminatory effect can show a connection between the practice and the disparity, he or she makes out a *prima facie* case, and no evidence of discriminatory intent needs to be shown. Disparate-impact discrimination can also occur when an educational or other job requirement or hiring procedure excludes members of a protected class from an employer's work force at a substantially higher rate than nonmembers, regardless of the racial balance in the employer's work force. The following case illustrates how a job requirement can create this type of discriminatory impact.

---

### CASE 37.2

**BRADLEY v. PIZZACO OF NEBRASKA, INC.**
United States Court of Appeals,
Eighth Circuit, 1991.
939 F.2d 610.

**BACKGROUND AND FACTS** *Pizzaco of Nebraska, Inc., a Domino's Pizza franchisee, hired Langston Bradley to deliver pizzas but fired him within two weeks because he would not remove his beard, which violated Domino's no-beard policy. Bradley, an African American, suffered from pseudofolliculitis barbae (PFB), a skin disorder affecting almost half of all African-American males. The symptoms of PFB—skin irritation and scarring—are brought on by shaving, and in severe cases, men with PFB must abstain from shaving altogether. Domino's policy, however, provided for no exceptions. Bradley brought a disparate-impact case against Domino's, alleging that Domino's policy discriminated against African-American males in violation of Title VII. The EEOC intervened on behalf of Bradley and other African-American males adversely affected by the policy. The EEOC sought an injunction requiring Domino's to recognize an exception to the policy for African-American males who are medically unable to shave. The trial court held, among other things, that the EEOC had failed to establish that the policy had a disparate impact on African-American males. Bradley and the EEOC appealed.*

*FAGG,* Circuit Judge.
\* \* \* \*

This case \* \* \* is about a facially neutral employment policy that discriminates against black males when applied. Title VII forbids employment policies with a disparate impact unless the policy is justified by legitimate employment goals. To make a *prima facie* case of disparate impact, the EEOC must identify a specific employment practice that has a significantly disparate impact on black males. The EEOC contends the district court committed error in holding the EEOC failed to satisfy these requirements. We agree. \* \* \*
\* \* \* \*

The EEOC's evidence makes clear that Domino's strictly enforced no-beard policy has a discriminatory impact on black males. PFB prevents a sizable segment of the black male population from appearing clean-shaven, but does not similarly affect white males. Domino's policy—which makes no exceptions for black males who medically are unable to shave because of a skin disorder peculiar to their race—effectively operates to exclude these black males from employment with Domino's.

**DECISION AND REMEDY**   *The appellate court reversed the district court's holding that the EEOC failed to make a* prima facie *showing of disparate impact and remanded the case for further proceedings.*

---

## REMEDIES UNDER TITLE VII

Employer liability under Title VII may be extensive. If the plaintiff successfully proves that unlawful discrimination occurred, he or she may be awarded reinstatement, back pay, retroactive promotions, and damages. Prior to the Civil Rights Act of 1991, damages were not available under

Title VII. Plaintiffs alleging racial discrimination therefore often brought actions under 42 U.S.C. Section 1981. Section 1981, which was enacted as part of the Civil Rights Act of 1866, prohibits discrimination on the basis of race or ethnicity in the formation or enforcement of contracts. Until the 1991 Civil Rights Act, however, damages were not available for victims of intentional employment discrimination based on gender, religion, age, or disability. By allowing compensatory damages to be awarded in cases brought under other employment laws, such as Title VII, the 1991 act thus significantly broadened the rights of persons suffering from employment discrimination.

Under the 1991 act, compensatory damages are available only in cases of intentional discrimination. The statute also stipulates that compensatory damages shall not include back pay, interest on back pay, or other relief already available under Title VII. Punitive damages may be recovered against a private employer only if the employer acted with malice or reckless indifference to an individual's rights. The sum of the amount of compensatory and punitive damages is limited by the statute to specific amounts against specific employers—ranging from $50,000 against employers with one hundred or fewer employees to $300,000 against employers with more than five hundred employees.

SECTION 2

# DISCRIMINATION BASED ON AGE

Age discrimination is potentially the most widespread form of discrimination, because anyone—regardless of race, color, national origin, or gender—could be a victim at some point in life. The Age Discrimination in Employment Act (ADEA) of 1967, as amended, prohibits employment discrimination on the basis of age against individuals forty years of age or older. An amendment to the act prohibits mandatory retirement for nonmanagerial workers. For the act to apply, an employer must have twenty or more employees, and the employer's business activities must affect interstate commerce.

The ADEA is similar to Title VII in that it offers protection against both intentional (disparate-treatment) age discrimination and unintentional (disparate-impact) age discrimination. The burden-shifting procedure under the ADEA is also similar to that under Title VII. If a plaintiff can establish that he or she (1) was a member of the protected age group, (2) was qualified for the position from which he or she was discharged, and (3) was discharged under circumstances that give rise to an inference of discrimination, the plaintiff has established a *prima facie* case of unlawful age discrimination. The burden then shifts to the employer, who must articulate a legitimate reason for the discrimination. If the plaintiff can prove that the employer's reason is only a pretext and that the plaintiff's age was a determining factor in the employer's decision, the employer will be held liable under the ADEA.

Numerous cases of alleged age discrimination have been brought against employers who, to cut costs, replaced older, higher-salaried employees with younger, lower-salaried workers. In one case, for example, a fifty-four-year-old manager of a plant who earned approximately $15.75 an hour was temporarily laid off when the plant was closed for the winter. When spring came, the manager was replaced by a forty-three-year-old worker who earned approximately $8.05 an hour. The older manager, who had worked for the firm for twenty-seven years, was given no opportunity to accept a lower wage rate or otherwise accommodate the firm's need to reduce costs. The court, which referred to the firm's dismissal of the manager as an exercise in "industrial capital punishment," held that the manager's dismissal in these circumstances violated the ADEA.[12]

Whether a firing is discriminatory or simply part of a rational business decision to prune the company's ranks is not always clear. Companies will generally defend a decision to discharge a worker by asserting that the worker could no longer perform his or her duties or that the worker's skills were no longer needed. The employee must prove that the discharge was motivated, at least in part, by age bias. Proof that qualified older employees are generally discharged before younger employees or that co-workers continually made unflattering age-related comments about the discharged

---

12. *Metz v. Transit Mix, Inc.*, 828 F.2d 1202 (7th Cir. 1987).

worker may be enough. The following case is typical of many age-discrimination cases involving companies that try to trim the payrolls and become more cost effective by reorganizing the firm and consolidating various job positions.

---

| CASE 37.3 |
| --- |

**MARESCO v. EVANS CHEMETICS, DIVISION OF W. R. GRACE & CO.**
United States Court of Appeals, Second Circuit, 1992. 964 F.2d 106.

**COMPANY PROFILE** *In 1848, after two years at sea, William Russell Grace, who was then sixteen years old, was hired in Liverpool, England, by a ship chandlery (a firm that buys and sells ships). Two years later, Grace went to work in Callao, Peru, for a similar firm, which he and his brother eventually took over. In 1865, Grace founded W. R. Grace & Company in New York to engage in trade in South America. To help the government of Peru avoid bankruptcy in 1890, Grace assumed the debt of two Peruvian government bond issues in exchange for control of nearly all of the country's resources, including silver mines, oil and mineral rights, and railroads. A year later, Grace founded the New York & Pacific Steamship Company, later adding the Grace Steamship Company. In 1895, at the age of sixty-three, Grace combined his New York and Peruvian holdings into W. R. Grace and Company, which ultimately expanded into agricultural, banking, chemical, mercantile, and utility investments in North and South America. In December 1978, the company acquired Evans Chemetics, which became part of the firm's Organic Chemicals Division, with offices in Nashua, New Hampshire; Lexington, Massachusetts; and Darien, Connecticut.*

**BACKGROUND AND FACTS** *Eugene Maresco had worked for Evans Chemetics from 1967 to 1986. In 1986, the company closed its branch office in Darien, Connecticut, in which Maresco worked as an accountant and credit manager, for legitimate cost-saving reasons. All of Darien's accounting functions were transferred to the Lexington, Massachusetts, office. Four of the workers in the Darien office were allowed to relocate to the Lexington office. Of this group, three were nonaccounting employees over the age of forty, and one was an accountant. The accountant was under forty but had more education and experience than Maresco. Maresco, who was sixty years old, and several other employees were discharged, and Maresco's responsibilities were assumed by two accountants in the Lexington office. After the consolidation, the Lexington accounting department consisted of twenty employees, only one of whom was over the age of forty. Maresco sued Evans Chemetics, alleging that his termination constituted age discrimination in violation of the Age Discrimination in Employment Act. The trial court granted Evans's motion for summary judgment, holding that Maresco had not established that the circumstances of his discharge gave rise to an inference of age discrimination. Maresco appealed.*

MAHONEY, Circuit Judge:
\* \* \* \*

Whether an analysis of the evidence proffered by Maresco yields an inference of discrimination depends largely upon the vantage from which this case is viewed. Evans argues, and the district court agreed, that the case involves a simple decision to close the Darien office. Under this scenario, it is natural to assume that the resulting reduction-in-force would be borne entirely by the Darien work force. According to this view, Evans reviewed the twelve Darien employees and decided to transfer only those with special qualifications or abilities to the Lexington office. Because the age distribution of those transferred (three of four were in the protected class) was approximately the same as that of those terminated, no inference of discrimination arises.

Maresco posits a different theory of the case, contending that what occurred was a consolidation of the Darien and Lexington offices. Under this view, upon consolidation there were more employees than available positions, but because what transpired was a combination of existing functions and not an elimination of the Darien functions, there was no valid presumption that layoffs would come from the Darien office. \* \* \* Viewed in this light, there were twenty-three accounting personnel in the work force. Three of the accounting employees were from the Darien office, two of whom were in the protected class. The Lexington office had twenty preconsolidation accounting employees, only one of whom was in the protected class. \* \* \*

\* \* \* \*

The decision to terminate two of the three older accounting employees, and none of the twenty younger employees, presents circumstances which give rise to an inference sufficient to withstand a motion for summary judgment that age was impermissibly considered in allocating the post-consolidation employment positions.

*The trial court's decision was reversed and the case remanded for trial.* **DECISION AND REMEDY**

---

# DISCRIMINATION BASED ON DISABILITY

In 1990, Congress passed the Americans with Disabilities Act (ADA), which became effective in 1992. The ADA, like earlier civil rights legislation, was designed to eliminate discriminatory hiring and firing practices that prevent otherwise qualified disabled workers from fully participating in the national labor force.

The ADA is broadly drafted to define disabled persons as persons with a physical or mental impairment that ''substantially limits'' their everyday activities. More specifically, the ADA defines *disability* as ''(1) a physical or mental impairment that substantially limits one or more of the major life activities of such individuals; (2) a record of such impairment; or (3) being regarded as having such an impairment.'' Health conditions that have been considered disabilities under federal law include blindness, heart disease, cancer, muscular dystrophy, cerebral palsy, paraplegia, diabetes, acquired immune deficiency syndrome (AIDS), and morbid obesity (defined as existing when an individual's weight is two times that of the normal

person).[13] The ADA excludes from coverage certain conditions, including homosexuality and kleptomania.

## REASONABLE ACCOMMODATIONS

The ADA prohibits employers from refusing to hire disabled persons who are otherwise qualified for a particular position. It does not, however, require that *unqualified* disabled applicants be hired. That the employer may have to make some reasonable accommodations for a disabled applicant, such as installing ramps for a wheelchair, will not cause the applicant to be considered unqualified. Reasonable accommodations might also include establishing more flexible working hours, creating new job assignments, and creating or improving training materials and procedures. Employers who do not wish to make such accommodations must demonstrate that the accommodations will cause ''undue hardship.'' The law offers no uniform standards for identifying what is an undue hardship other than the imposition of a ''significant difficulty or expense'' on the employer.

---

13. *Cook v. Rhode Island Department of Mental Health,* 10 F.3d 17 (1st Cir. 1993).

There are limits to the employer's obligation to accommodate an employee under the ADA. If a disabled employee can perform the essentials of his or her job without accommodation, then no violation of the ADA has occurred, as the following case illustrates.

CASE 37.4

**HARMER v. VIRGINIA ELECTRIC AND POWER CO.**

United States District Court, Eastern District of Virginia, 1993.
831 F.Supp. 1300.

**BACKGROUND AND FACTS**   *Robert E. Harmer, a bronchial asthmatic, worked as a buyer for the Virginia Electric and Power Company. His unenclosed modular office in the purchasing department was located on the twelfth floor of Virginia Power's corporate headquarters. Harmer's physician stated that Harmer's pulmonary condition "substantially limit[ed] his ability to care for himself, his ability to breathe, his ability to walk and his life expectancy"; he also stated that the existence of tobacco smoke in Harmer's workplace seriously aggravated Harmer's condition. In 1986, Virginia Power was notified of Harmer's disabling condition and the effect of the smoke on Harmer's health. Harmer later requested a transfer to the Surry Nuclear Power Station, where smoking was prohibited. When Virginia Power offered the job to Harmer, however, he rejected it. Although Virginia Power declined to ban smoking entirely on the twelfth floor, as Harmer and a group of other employees had initially requested, it did significantly modify its smoking policy by 1990. Smokeless ashtrays and air purifiers were made available; fans were installed; smoking employees were moved farther away from nonsmoking employees; and smoking was prohibited in elevators, service lines, cafeterias, auditoriums, stairways, and hallways. In 1992, Harmer requested that the company declare the entire building smoke free, but Virginia Power did not do so at that time. Harmer sued Virginia Power, claiming, among other things, that the company's failure to accommodate his disability violated the ADA.*

*RICHARD L. WILLIAMS,* District Judge.

\* \* \* \*

\* \* \* [T]he ADA protects Harmer from discrimination due to his disability. But Harmer still must show that he is entitled to a complete smoking ban as a reasonable accommodation to his disability, and he is unable to do so. As the Court reads the ADA, the purpose of reasonable accommodation is to allow a disabled employee to perform the essential functions of his job or to enable him to enjoy equal privileges of nondisabled employees, such as access to bathrooms and cafeterias, etc. Harmer is not entitled to absolute accommodation under the ADA because he can perform the essential functions of his position with the reasonable accommodations made by Virginia Power as evidenced by his job performance appraisals, which indicate that he consistently met his job requirements. No evidence has been offered to suggest that Harmer's productivity was not comparable to that of other employees, and Harmer's average job performance appraisals constitute affirmative evidence that his productivity was satisfactory.

Therefore, because the evidence established that Harmer could at all times adequately perform his employment duties, Harmer is not entitled to further accommodation under the ADA.

**DECISION AND REMEDY**   *The district court granted Virginia Power's motion for summary judgment. The court held that Virginia Power did not need to provide a smoke-free office environment to satisfy the ADA's requirement of reasonable accommodation.*

## PREEMPLOYMENT PHYSICALS

Under the ADA, employers are not permitted to ask job applicants about the nature or extent of any known disabilities. Furthermore, they cannot require disabled persons to submit to preemployment physicals unless such exams are required of all other applicants. Employers can condition an offer of employment on the employee's successfully passing a medical examination, but disqualifications must result from the discovery of problems that render the applicant unable to perform the job for which he or she is to be hired.

## DANGEROUS WORKERS

An employer may defend a decision not to hire a disabled worker if the applicant would pose a "direct threat to the health or safety" of his or her co-workers. This danger must be substantial and immediate; it cannot be speculative. A worker who suffers from hallucinations that cause him to attack his co-workers would probably be considered such a threat, for example. Other federal regulations also permit employers to terminate the employment of qualified workers whose disabilities are such that they may pose a danger to their own personal well-being.

In the wake of the AIDS epidemic, many employers are concerned about hiring or continuing to employ a worker who has AIDS under the assumption that the worker might pose a direct threat to the health or safety of others in the workplace. Courts have generally held, however, that AIDS is not so contagious as to disqualify employees in most jobs. Therefore, employers must reasonably accommodate job applicants or employees who have AIDS or who test positive for the AIDS virus.

## PROCEDURES AND REMEDIES UNDER THE ADA

As in Title VII cases, claims alleging violations of the ADA may be commenced only after the plaintiff has pursued the claim through the EEOC. Plaintiffs may sue for many of the same remedies available under Title VII. They may seek reinstatement, back pay, a limited amount of compensatory and punitive damages (for intentional discrimination), and certain other forms of relief. Repeat violators may be ordered to pay fines of up to $100,000.

## OTHER LAWS PROTECTING WORKERS WITH DISABILITIES

Employers' violations of the ADA may also violate the Rehabilitation Act of 1973.[14] The Rehabilitation Act includes essentially the same provisions as the ADA but applies to federal employers; employers who receive federal aid (such as airports) or operate federal programs; and employers with federal service, supply, or construction contracts of $2,500 or more.

Under the Rehabilitation Act, private individuals claiming discrimination can sue federal employers and employers who receive federal aid or operate federal programs, but individuals cannot sue federal contractors. Contractors may be investigated by the Office of Federal Contract Compliance Programs of the Department of Labor.

Relief available against federal employers under the Rehabilitation Act includes all remedies available to federal employees under Title VII. Remedies available against the recipients of federal aid and those who operate federal programs include back pay, but not compensatory or punitive damages, and the recipients may also have their financial assistance withdrawn. Relief awarded against federal contractors may include reinstatement or hiring, as well as back pay, and sanctions imposed may include the loss of any government contracts.

Violations of the ADA may also be violations of state laws prohibiting discrimination based on disability. Many state laws provide for increased damages. The New Jersey law prohibiting discrimination,[15] for example, allows damages for pain, suffering, and emotional distress, as well as punitive damages, in addition to federal remedies.

## SECTION 4

# AFFIRMATIVE ACTION

Federal statutes and regulations providing for equal opportunity in the workplace were designed to reduce or eliminate discriminatory practices with respect to hiring, retaining, and promoting

14. 29 U.S.C. Sections 791–796i.
15. New Jersey Statutes Sections 10:5–1 to 10:5–42.

# EMERGING TRENDS IN BUSINESS LAW

## Accommodating Workers with Disabilities

When the Americans with Disabilities Act (ADA) was passed in 1990, Congress estimated that about 17 percent of the U.S. population was living with a disability. Prior to 1990, the major federal law providing protection to those with disabilities was the Rehabilitation Act of 1973. That act covered only federal government employees or those employed under federally funded programs. As of 1994, the ADA extended federal protection against disability-based discrimination to all workplaces with twenty-five or more workers.

### A Growing ADA Case Load

According to the Equal Employment Opportunity Commission (EEOC), over 17 percent of the almost 90,000 discrimination cases filed with that office during the first full year of the ADA's implementation were for disability-based discrimination. The EEOC predicts that this percentage will rise over time. Employees who believe that they have been discriminated against on the basis of a disability have two reasons to file a charge of such discrimination with the EEOC: (1) if successful, they may obtain back pay, damages, and other remedies; and (2) the Internal Revenue Service has ruled that such damages

and back pay are not subject to taxation.[a]

Clearly, employers also have an incentive to satisfy the ADA's requirement that they "reasonably" accommodate workers with disabilities.

### Reasonable Accommodation versus Undue Hardship

Under the ADA, an employer's accommodation is considered reasonable if such accommodation permits a worker with a disability to perform the essential functions of the job in question. Therefore, employers must modify their job-application process so that those with disabilities can compete for jobs with those who do not have disabilities. Consequently, a job announcement that has only a phone number would discriminate against hearing-impaired potential job applicants. Therefore, an address must also be provided.

In addition, employers must modify the physical work

environment if necessary so that a disabled worker can perform the essential job functions. Some modifications can be easily made, such as lowering a water fountain to accommodate those in wheelchairs. In general, the EEOC suggests that employers should give "primary consideration" to an employee's preference in deciding what accommodations should be made. Employees suffering from a disability can, though, reject a reasonable accommodation offered by the employer.

### Undue Hardship

If an accommodation would constitute an "undue hardship," the employer would not normally be required to undertake it. There is no exact definition of what constitutes an undue hardship, however. The employer must determine the point at which accommodating a worker with a disability results in an undue hardship to the employer. The standard for what constitutes a reasonable accommodation is not yet well established. Consider some examples:

---

a. The Court of Appeals for the Federal Circuit ruled in 1994 that punitive damages are taxable, however. See *Reese v. United States,* 24 F.3d 228 (Fed.Cir. 1994).

1. An employee qualifies as being disabled under the ADA because he has severe bouts of depression. His medication causes drowsiness such that he routinely falls asleep on the

job. Can the employer be required to accommodate this employee? The U.S. Court of Appeals for the Seventh Circuit held that "[t]he government may presumably require its employees to stay awake as a matter of decorum. But that is not necessarily to say that an occasional nap would make any federal employee unfit."[b]

**2.** A ski resort owner decides to upgrade the resort's image to obtain a higher rating. One of the resort's chambermaids refuses to wear her dentures because they hurt. Can the owner of the resort fire the worker without liability under the ADA? The answer is, probably not. The ADA protects not only those with disabilities but also those who are *perceived* to have disabilities. In this situation, if the owner of the resort perceives that the employee's refusal to wear her false teeth results in a cosmetic disfigurement (which is a disability under federal law), the employee is a protected individual. If she is fired, that "disability" will substantially limit a major life activity, i.e., her job.[c]

---

b. *Overton v. Reilly*, 977 F.2d 1190 (7th Cir. 1992).
c. See, for example, *Hodgdon v. Mt. Mansfield Co.*, 624 A.2d 1122 (Vt. 1992). Although this case was decided under a state law protecting workers with disabilities, the court looked to federal law—particularly, the Rehabilitation Act of 1973—for guidance. The provisions of the ADA closely parallel those of the Rehabilitation Act.

## The Disabled and Health Insurance Plans

Employers may wish to hire or refuse to hire workers with disabilities because of their impact on group health-insurance costs. Pursuant to the ADA, the EEOC has developed guidelines that clearly indicate that disabled workers must be given equal access to any health insurance provided to other employees. Employers can exclude from coverage preexisting health conditions and certain types of diagnostic or surgical procedures, however. And an employer can also put a limit, or cap, on health-care payments in its particular group-health policy—as long as such caps are "applied equally to all insured employees" and do not "discriminate on the basis of disability."

Whenever a group health-care plan makes a disability-based distinction in its benefits, the plan violates the ADA. The employer must then be able to justify the distinction by doing one of the following:

● Offering proof that limiting coverage of certain ailments is required to keep the plan financially sound.
● Proving that coverage of certain ailments would cause a significant increase in premium payments or their equivalent such that the plan would be unappealing to a significant number of workers.
● Proving that the disparate treatment is justified by the risks and costs associated with a particular disability.

## The ADA and Substance Abusers

Many employers and employees are unclear about the protection given by the ADA to substance abusers. Under the ADA, alcoholism is a disability. Consequently, employers cannot legally discriminate against employees simply because they are alcoholics. Thus employers must treat alcoholics in the same way as they treat other employees. An alcoholic employee cannot be disciplined any differently than anyone else simply because he or she was drinking the night before and came to work late. In other words, alcoholics must be held to the same standards of performance as others. Employers do have the right to prohibit the use of alcohol in the workplace. Employers can require that employees not be under the influence of alcohol while working. Finally, employers can either fire or refuse to hire an alcoholic if he or she poses a substantial risk of harm to either himself or herself or to others and the risk cannot be reduced by reasonable accommodation.

Drug addiction is a disability under the act because it is a substantially limiting impairment. Those who are currently using illegal drugs are not protected by the act, though. The ADA only protects *former* drug addicts—those who have completed a supervised drug-rehabilitation program or who are currently in a supervised rehabilitation program. Individuals who have used drugs casually in the past are not protected under the act. They are not considered addicts and therefore do not have a disability (addiction).

### ■ Implications for the Businessperson

1. Because of the growing importance of the ADA, employers need to become familiar with the specific provisions of that act as well as current and future interpretive guidelines issued by the EEOC. Most likely, many employers will need to modify their policies and practices in regard to hiring and firing employees. Employers may have to alter the way that they advertise, conduct job interviews, and even the way they word their job applications. Employers must focus on job functions and whether applicants feel they can perform those functions—not on applicants' disabilities, past histories of drug use, workers' compensation claims or benefits, and so on. Employers must scrutinize their existing health-care plans to make sure that if any disability-based distinction exists, it is justified under the ADA. Employers

must learn how to "reasonably accommodate" existing and potential employees with disabilities.

To avoid a lawsuit for disability-based discrimination, it is in the employer's interest to work closely with the disabled worker in deciding what accommodations must be made. If the accommodation is one recommended by the employee, the employee will likely be more satisfied with the arrangement.

### ■ For Critical Analysis

1. Until the ADA, laws prohibiting employment discrimination, such as Title VII of the Civil Rights Act of 1964 and the Age Discrimination in Employment Act of 1967, focused mainly on prohibiting discrimination against a protected class. The ADA, in contrast, requires the employer to take action—to reasonably accommodate employees with disabilities. One could say that the ADA requires employers to treat employees unequally. Does this mean that Americans are moving away from the traditional notion that fairness is synonymous with equal

treatment? Or does the ADA promote the goal of equal protection under the laws? Discuss.

2. It is one thing for employers to reasonably accommodate the needs of employees with obvious *physical* disabilities. But it may be quite another for employers to accommodate employees who claim to suffer from mental impairments. How can an employer be certain that an employee is being truthful about a mental impairment, such as depression or stress? When employees claiming to suffer from such mental impairments request time off to see a psychiatrist or counselor, how much time off is reasonable? Will there ever be any way for employers to be certain about the nonobvious disabilities of their employees?

3. A former rock star admits on a job application for the police department that he casually used drugs in the 1970s. He is refused employment. He sues under the ADA. Will he prevail? Why or why not? Is the result "fair"?

---

employees. **Affirmative action** programs go a step further and attempt to "make up" for past patterns of discrimination by giving members of protected classes preferential treatment in hiring or promotion. Affirmative action programs have caused much controversy, particularly when they result in what is frequently called "reverse discrimination"—discrimination against "majority" workers, such as white males. Although affirmative action programs have been under attack in recent

years, the United States Supreme Court has generally held that they are legitimate if they are designed to correct existing imbalances in the work force and as long as employers consider factors in addition to race or gender when making employment decisions. The Supreme Court usually looks at the special circumstances surrounding each case when determining whether challenged affirmative action plans are legitimate.

# DEFENSES TO CLAIMS OF EMPLOYMENT DISCRIMINATION

After an employee makes out a *prima facie* case of discrimination, the employer has an opportunity to respond. The employer may attempt to disprove the case, or the employer may use certain defenses to justify the discriminatory practice.

## BUSINESS NECESSITY

An employer may defend against a claim of disparate-impact discrimination by asserting that a practice that has a discriminatory effect is a business necessity. If requiring a high school diploma, for example, is shown to have a discriminatory effect, an employer might argue that a high school education is required for workers to perform the job at a required level of competence. If the employer can demonstrate to the court's satisfaction that there exists a definite connection between a high school education and job performance, then the employer will succeed in this **business necessity defense.**

## BONA FIDE OCCUPATIONAL QUALIFICATION

Another defense applies when discrimination against a protected class is essential to a job—that is, when a particular trait is a *bona fide* **occupational qualification** (BFOQ). For example, a men's fashion magazine might legitimately hire only male models. Similarly, the Federal Aviation Administration can legitimately impose age limits for airline pilots. Race, however, can never be a BFOQ. Much controversy has arisen over the BFOQ defense, particularly in gender-based discrimination cases. Some companies have argued that being male is a BFOQ for jobs requiring heavy lifting,[16] whereas others have contended that being female is a BFOQ for flight attendants.[17] Courts have rejected both these arguments and have generally restricted the BFOQ defense to instances in which the employee's gender is essential to the job. In 1991, the United States Supreme Court held that a so-called fetal-protection policy that prohibited fertile women of child-bearing age from working for a particular division within a company was an unacceptable BFOQ.[18]

## SENIORITY SYSTEMS

An employer with a history of discrimination may have no members of protected classes in upper-level positions. Even if the employer now seeks to be unbiased, it may face a lawsuit seeking an order that minorities be promoted ahead of schedule to compensate for past discrimination. If no present intent to discriminate is shown, and promotions or other job benefits are distributed according to a fair **seniority system** (in which workers with more years of service are promoted first, or laid off last), however, the employer has a good defense against the suit.

## EMPLOYEE MISCONDUCT

In some situations, an employer may avoid liability for employment discrimination under the so-called **after-acquired evidence** doctrine. Under this doctrine, which was first articulated by a U.S. Court of Appeals for the Tenth Circuit in 1988,[19] an employer who discovers that an employee had engaged in misconduct while on the job may be able to use that misconduct as a defense to claims of discriminatory firing or wrongful discharge. For example, if an employer fires a worker and subsequently learns that the worker had made material misrepresentations on his or her employment application, the employer might argue that had the employer known earlier of these misrepresentations, the employee would have been fired for such

---

16. *Rosenfeld v. Southern Pacific Co.,* 444 F.2d 1219 (9th Cir. 1971).

17. *Diaz v. Pan American World Airways, Inc.,* 442 F.2d 385 (5th Cir. 1971).

18. *United Automobile Workers v. Johnson Controls, Inc.,* 113 U.S. 158,111 S.Ct. 1196, 113 L.Ed.2d 158 (1991). (This case is presented in Chapter 2 as Case 2.3.)

19. *Summers v. State Farm Mutual Automobile Insurance Co.,* 864 F.2d 700 (10th Cir. 1988).

misconduct. The employer would have to establish that the worker's misrepresentation was material, or job related, and that the employer relied on the misrepresentation when it hired the applicant.[20]

As the following case illustrates, evidence of other types of employee misconduct may also serve, after the fact, as nondiscriminatory grounds for firing an employee.

---

20. See, for example, *Johnson v. Honeywell Information Systems, Inc.,* 955 F.2d 409 (6th Cir. 1992).

---

### CASE 37.5

**McKENNON v. NASHVILLE BANNER PUBLISHING CO.**

Supreme Court of the United States, 1995. ____ U.S. ____ , 115 S.Ct. 879, ____ L.Ed.2d ____.

**BACKGROUND AND FACTS**   *Christine McKennon, a sixty-two-year-old secretary, had been employed with the Nashville Banner Publishing Company for thirty-nine years when her employment was terminated in 1990. McKennon brought an action against Nashville Banner under the Age Discrimination in Employment Act, claiming that she was terminated from her job only because of her age. Prior to her employment termination, McKennon had removed confidential documents from her employer's premises and showed them to her husband. Later, during pretrial proceedings, McKennon admitted to this misconduct, stating that she had copied the documents "in an attempt to learn information regarding my job security concerns." She felt that the confidential documents were her "insurance" and "protection" against wrongful termination. In response to McKennon's admission, Nashville Banner claimed that it would have terminated her immediately had it known of her actions. The district court granted summary judgment in favor of Nashville Banner, and the appellate court affirmed. McKennon appealed.*

*JUSTICE KENNEDY,* delivered the opinion of the Court.
  \* \* \* \*
  \* \* \* [T]he legal conclusion reached by [the lower] courts that after-acquired evidence of wrongdoing which would have resulted in discharge bars employees from any relief under the ADEA \* \* \* is incorrect.
  \* \* \* \*
  The [Age Discrimination in Employment Act (ADEA) of 1967] and Title VII share common substantive features and also a common purpose: "the elimination of discrimination in the workplace." Congress designed the remedial measures in these statutes to serve as a "spur or catalyst" to cause employers "to self-examine and to self-evaluate their employment practices and to endeavor to eliminate, so far as possible, the last vestiges" of discrimination. Deterrence is one object of these statutes. Compensation for injuries caused by the prohibited discrimination is another. The ADEA, in keeping with these purposes, contains a vital element \* \* \*: it grants an injured employee a right of action to obtain the authorized relief. The private litigant who seeks redress for his or her injuries vindicates both the deterrence and the compensation objectives of the ADEA. It would not accord with this scheme if after-acquired evidence of wrongdoing that would have resulted in termination operates, in every instance, to bar all relief for an earlier violation of the Act.

**DECISION AND REMEDY**   *The Supreme Court reversed the judgment of the lower courts and remanded the case to allow McKennon's case to proceed.*

# STATE LAWS PROHIBITING EMPLOYMENT DISCRIMINATION

Although the focus of this chapter is on federal legislation, most states also have statutes that prohibit employment discrimination. Generally, the kinds of discrimination prohibited under federal legislation are also prohibited by state laws. In addition, state statutes often provide protection for certain individuals, such as homosexuals, who are not protected under Title VII.

Numerous plaintiffs who allege employment discrimination seek relief under state statutes instead of Title VII. In the following case, the plaintiff alleged that he was discriminated against in his employment because of his foreign accent (he was from Cambodia), in violation of a Washington state statute.

---

**HISTORICAL AND POLITICAL SETTING**   *During the 1950s, the 1960s, and the 1970s, the United States was militarily involved in actions against the Vietnamese Communists, who were attempting to control Southeast Asia. Cambodia (or Kampuchea), which lies between Vietnam and Thailand, attempted to remain neutral. Cambodia's ruler, Prince Norodom Sihanouk, refused to cooperate with either the Vietnamese or the Americans. Despite Sihanouk's policy, U.S. military commanders believed that the Vietnamese Communists had command centers in Cambodia. Sihanouk was overthrown in 1970 by Lon Nol, who began persecuting Cambodia's 400,000 ethnic Vietnamese and asked for U.S. aid to prevent a Vietnamese takeover. President Richard Nixon authorized U.S. military forces to move into eastern Cambodia. Meanwhile, Cambodian Communists, known as the Khmer Rouge, fought against Lon Nol. As U.S. involvement in Southeast Asia decreased in the early 1970s, the balance of military power shifted. In April 1975, Communists seized power by force all over Southeast Asia. Lon Nol's government fell to the Khmer Rouge, who began a systematic program of genocide that eventually resulted in the deaths of more than one million people—a fifth of Cambodia's population.*

**CASE 37.6**

**XIENG v. PEOPLES NATIONAL BANK OF WASHINGTON**

Supreme Court of Washington, 1993.
120 Wash.2d 512,
844 P.2d 389.

**BACKGROUND AND FACTS**   *Phanna Xieng first came to the United States in 1974, when he was sent here from Cambodia for "advanced military training." When the Cambodian government fell in 1975, Xieng remained in the United States, eventually finding employment with Peoples National Bank of Washington in 1979. In performance appraisals from 1980 through 1985, Xieng was rated by his supervisors as "capable of dealing effectively with customers" and qualified for promotion, although in each appraisal it was noted that Xieng might improve his communication skills to maximize his possibilities for future advancement. Xieng sought job promotions on numerous occasions but was never promoted. In 1986, he filed a complaint against the bank, alleging employment discrimination based on national origin. The trial court found that Xieng was qualified for many of the promotions for which he applied, that his accent would not have materially interfered with his job performance in the positions for which he applied, and that the bank's failure to promote him because of his accent constituted discrimination based on national origin. The bank appealed, and the appellate court affirmed the trial court's decision. The bank then appealed to the Supreme Court of Washington.*

*BRACHTENBACH, Justice.*

\* \* \* \*

\* \* \* [T]he following are established facts: (1) that defendant's reason for not promoting plaintiff was because of his "foreign" accent, (2) that plaintiff's accent did not interfere materially with his job performance, and (3) that plaintiff's accent would not have interfered materially with his job performance if he had been promoted to the position for which the court also found he was qualified.

\* \* \* \*

\* \* \* There is nothing improper about an employer making an honest assessment of the oral communications skills of a candidate for a job when such skills are reasonably related to job performance. \* \* \* Accent and national origin are obviously inextricably intertwined in many cases. It would therefore be an easy refuge in this context for an employer unlawfully discriminating against someone based on national origin to state falsely that it was not the person's national origin that caused the employment or promotion problem, but the candidate's inability to measure up to the communications skills demanded by the job.

**DECISION AND REMEDY**   *The Supreme Court of Washington affirmed the lower courts' decisions. Xieng prevailed.*

**ETHICAL CONSIDERATIONS**   *On one of the occasions on which Xieng sought a promotion, he was interviewed by a managerial-level supervisor who threw Xieng's résumé into the wastebasket as soon as Xieng left the office. On another occasion, Xieng was told that he would be promoted if he could guarantee that all of the ethnic Cambodians in the city would become customers of the bank. When he explained that it would be impossible to make that guaranty, the promotion went to someone else. On a third occasion, he was told that he would be promoted automatically as soon as a position became available, but when a position opened, the promotion went to someone less qualified. The bank claimed that it had acted in good faith in rejecting Xieng for promotion because of his "communications skills." The trial court found that "the reason for the rejection [for promotion] was not worthy of credence."*

# TERMS AND CONCEPTS TO REVIEW

affirmative action 734
after-acquired evidence 735
*bona fide* occupational
   qualification (BFOQ)
   735
business necessity defense 735

disparate-impact
   discrimination 725
disparate-treatment
   discrimination 725
employment
   discrimination 721

*prima facie* case 725
protected class 721
seniority system 735
sexual harassment 723

# QUESTIONS AND CASE PROBLEMS

**37–1. Title VII Violations.** Discuss fully whether any of the following actions would constitute a violation of the 1964 Civil Rights Act, Title VII, as amended:

(a) Tennington, Inc., is a consulting firm and has ten employees. These employees travel on consulting jobs in seven states. Tennington has an employment record of hiring only white males.

(b) Novo Films, Inc., is making a film about Africa and needs to employ approximately one hundred extras for this picture. Novo advertises in all major newspapers in southern California for the hiring of these extras. The ad states that only African Americans need apply.

**37–2. Discrimination Based on Age.** Tavo Jones had worked for Westshore Resort since 1974, maintaining golf carts. During the next decade, he received positive job evaluations and numerous merit pay raises. He was promoted to the position of supervisor of golf cart maintenance at three courses. Then a new employee, Ben Olery, was placed in charge of the golf courses. He demoted Jones, who was over the age of forty, to running one of the three cart facilities, and he froze Jones's salary indefinitely. Olery also demoted five other men over the age of forty. Another cart facility was placed under the supervision of Blake Blair. Later, the cart facilities for three courses were again consolidated, but Blair—not Jones—was put in charge. At the time, Blair was in his twenties. Jones overheard Blair say that "we are going to have to do away with these old and senile" men. Jones quit and sued Westshore for employment discrimination. Should he prevail? Explain.

**37–3. Disparate-Impact Discrimination.** Several African-American employees of the Connecticut Department of Income Maintenance who sought promotion to supervisory positions took the required written examination but failed to pass it. Of all who took the examination, 54 percent of the African-American employees passed it, whereas nearly 80 percent of the white employees who took the test passed. Following the examination, the state of Connecticut promoted eleven African-American employees (representing 23 percent of all African-American employees) and thirty-five white employees (representing 14 percent of all white employees). Teal and three other African-American employees who failed the test sued the state of Connecticut and the Department of Income Maintenance. The employees asserted that the written test excluded a disproportionate number of African-American employees from promotion to supervisory positions and therefore violated Title VII of the Civil Rights Act. The state argued that because a greater percentage of African-American employees had been promoted, relative to white employees, the test was not discriminatory. Which party was correct?

**37–4. Disparate-Impact Discrimination.** Chinawa, a major processor of cheese sold throughout the United States, employs one hundred workers at its principal processing plant. The plant is located in Heartland Corners, in which the population is 50 percent white and 25 percent African American, with the balance Hispanic American, Asian American, and others. Chinawa requires a high school diploma as a condition of employment for its cleaning crew. Three-fourths of the white population complete high school, compared with only one-fourth of those in the minority groups. Chinawa has an all-white cleaning crew. Has Chinawa violated Title VII of the Civil Rights Act of 1964? Explain.

**37–5. Discrimination Based on Disability.** Ananda is a hearing-impaired repairperson currently employed with the Southwestern Telephone Company. Her job requires her to drive the company truck to remote rural areas in all kinds of weather, to climb telephone poles, to make general repairs to telephone lines, and so on. She has held this position for five years, a full year longer than any other employee, and she is quite competent. Ananda applied for a promotion to the position of repair crew coordinator, a position that would require Ananda to be in constant communication with all repairpersons in the field. Southwestern rejected Ananda's application, stating that the company "needed someone in this critical position who can speak and hear clearly, someone who did not suffer from any hearing disability." Ananda says she could easily perform the essentials of the job if Southwestern would provide her with a sign interpreter. Although agreeing that Ananda was otherwise qualified for the coordinator position, Southwestern concluded that the cost of hiring an interpreter would be prohibitive, and therefore it should not be required to accommodate her disability under the Americans with Disabilities Act. Who is correct? Discuss.

**37–6. Discrimination Based on Gender.** Beginning in June 1966, Corning Glass Works started to open up jobs on the night shift to women. The previously separate male and female seniority lists were consolidated, and the women became eligible to exercise their seniority on the same basis as men and to bid for higher-paid night inspection jobs as vacancies occurred. But on January 20, 1969, a new collective bargaining agreement went into effect; it established a new job evaluation system for setting wage rates. This agreement abolished (for the future) separate base wages for night- and day-shift inspectors and imposed a uniform base wage for inspectors that exceeded the wage rate previously in effect for the night shift. The agreement, however, did allow for a higher "red circle" rate for employees hired prior to January 20, 1969, when they were working as inspectors on the night shift. This "red circle" wage served essentially to perpetuate the differential in base wages between day and night inspectors. Had Corning violated Title VII of the Civil Rights Act of 1964? Discuss. [*Corning Glass Works v. Brennan,* 417 U.S. 188, 94 S.Ct. 2223, 41 L.Ed.2d 1 (1974)]

**37–7. Discrimination Based on Race.** Patricia Jackson, an African-American female and an experienced waitress, applied for a job as a part-time waitress at a restaurant owned by Jackie McCleod in Foley, Alabama. An interview was arranged for the afternoon of June 2, 1989, which was a Friday. During the course of the interview, Jackson and McCleod entered into a verbal contract for Jackson to be hired as a part-time waitress, beginning Monday, June 5. Jackson was to work her first two days in the kitchen and following that orientation period would start working as a waitress. On Sunday, June 4, McCleod made up the work schedule for the period June 5 through June 11. Jackson was scheduled to work four days during the week and on each of those days would be doing kitchen work. Jackson appeared for work on Monday, June 5, as agreed. When she discovered that she had been scheduled to work in the kitchen for four days, as opposed to the two-day orientation period she expected, she confronted McCleod and asked to be put on the floor as a waitress. When her request was not granted, Jackson left the restaurant. On that same day, McCleod hired a white female for the position of waitress. Jackson sued McCleod for discrimination on the basis of race in McCleod's hiring procedures, and the issue turned on whether any discrimination occurred during the ''hiring'' of Jackson. Will Jackson prevail in court? Discuss fully. [*Jackson v. McCleod*, 748 F.Supp. 831 (S.C.Ala. 1990)]

**37–8. Discrimination Based on Race.** Duke Power Co. was sued by a number of its African-American employees for practicing racial discrimination in the hiring and assigning of employees at its Dan River plant. The plant was organized into five operating departments: (1) labor, (2) coal handling, (3) operations, (4) maintenance, and (5) laboratory testing. African Americans were employed only in the labor department, in which the highest-paying jobs paid less than the lowest-paying jobs in the other four departments (which employed only whites). Promotions were normally made within each department on the basis of seniority. Transferees into a department usually began in the lowest position. In 1955, the company began to require a high school education for an initial assignment into any department except the labor department. In addition, it required a high school education for any transfer from the coal-handling department to any inside department (operations, maintenance, or laboratory). For ten years, this company-wide policy was enforced. In 1965, when the company abandoned its policy of restricting African Americans to the labor department, a high school diploma or equivalency test was nevertheless made a prerequisite to transfer from the labor department into any other department. This requirement rendered a markedly disproportionate number of African Americans ineligible for employment advancement in the company. Did these employer practices violate Title VII of the Civil Rights Act? Discuss fully. [*Griggs v. Duke Power Co.*, 401 U.S. 424, 91 S.Ct. 849, 28 L.Ed.2d 158 (1971)]

**37–9. Disparate-Treatment Discrimination.** Melvin Hicks was an African-American shift supervisor at the St. Mary's Honor Center, a halfway house operated by the Missouri Department of Corrections and Human Resources. Prior to the replacement of his immediate supervisor (the shift commander) and the appointment of a new superintendent, Hicks had always had a satisfactory employment record. After the change in personnel, however, Hicks was disciplined repeatedly and with increasing severity until he was eventually fired. He then brought an action under Title VII, alleging racial discrimination. Hicks successfully presented a *prima facie* case: he was an African American, he was qualified for the job of shift commander, he was demoted and then discharged, and the position he vacated was filled by a white man. The burden then shifted to St. Mary's Honor Center to prove that it had acted for legitimate, nondiscriminatory reasons. The center asserted that Hicks had violated procedures and threatened his supervisor. The district court found the claims to be a mere pretext (a fabricated reason for dismissing Hicks). The court nonetheless held for the center because Hicks had failed to prove that the center's actions were motivated by any racial bias—in other words, Hicks had not been discriminated against on the basis of race, as he had contended. The appellate court reversed, holding that once the district court had found that the center's reasons were pretextual, Hicks was entitled to judgment as a matter of law. The case was appealed to the United States Supreme Court. Discuss how the Supreme Court should decide this case, and why. [*St. Mary's Honor Center v. Hicks*, ___ U.S. ___, 113 S.Ct. 2742, 125 L.Ed.2d 407 (1993)]

**37–10. Defenses to Employment Discrimination.** Dorothea O'Driscoll had worked as a quality-control inspector for Hercules, Inc., for six years when her employment was terminated in 1986. O'Driscoll sued Hercules for age discrimination in violation of the Age Discrimination in Employment Act of 1967. While preparing for trial, Hercules discovered evidence of misconduct on the part of O'Driscoll that it had been unaware of when it terminated her employment. Among other things, Hercules learned that O'Driscoll had misrepresented her age on both her employment application and her application for a government security clearance (necessary to handle confidential information). She also did not disclose a previous employer, falsely represented that she had never applied for work with Hercules before, and falsely stated that she had completed two quarters of study at a technical college. Additionally, on her application for group insurance coverage, she misrepresented the age of her son, who would otherwise have been ineligible for coverage as her dependent. Hercules defended against O'Driscoll's claim of age discrimination by stating that had it known of this misconduct, it would have terminated her employment anyway. What should the court decide? Discuss fully. [*O'Driscoll v. Hercules, Inc.*, 12 F.3d 176 (10th Cir. 1994)]

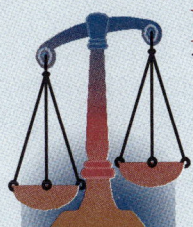

# FOCUS ON ETHICS

# Employment and Labor Relations

Traditionally, employers were free to hire and fire their employees "at will"—for any reason (or no reason) and at any time. Today, many employers face just the opposite situation. Statutes providing for employee safety, equal employment opportunity, and, to a more limited extent, privacy rights have significantly restricted the rights of employers to sculpt their workplaces as they will. In areas not covered by statutory law, the courts have also increasingly showed a willingness to carve out exceptions to the at-will doctrine to protect employees' rights. In effect, the legal pendulum has swung from employer protection to employee protection.

Statutes and court decisions affecting employment relationships rest ultimately on society's ethical convictions of what is right or wrong behavior in the employment context. We focus below on some of the ethical dimensions of the laws governing employment relationships.

## Implied Employment Contracts

As discussed in Chapter 36, courts sometimes make exceptions to the employment-at-will doctrine—including exceptions based on contract theory. Increasingly, courts have found that an employer's oral promises or written statements in an employment manual constitute an implied contract. But is it fair to the employer to hold that he or she is bound by an employment contract that the employer had no intention of creating?

Consider, for example, the situation recently faced by American Colloid Company. That company's president distributed to the firm's employees a letter stating that there was an "important change" in the way in which the company wanted to deal with its employees. The president wrote that the company was "dedicated to the objective of job stability," that management would do all it could to eliminate any need for layoffs, and so on. The letter went on to state, "This does not mean that firings for good reason, such as poor performance or unsafe work, will not occur."

Does this letter mean that the employees are no longer "at will" and can be fired only for good reason, or just cause? Does the letter constitute an employment contract? The company certainly did not intend the letter to be a contract. An employee of the firm, however, claimed that the letter was just that. When the employee, Michael Lesmeister, was later fired, he sued the employer for discharging him without "good reason" in violation of the employment contract. A federal district court agreed with Lesmeister that the letter had created an implied contract, and it awarded him $30,899 in damages. The decision was upheld on appeal.[1]

Now consider the issue of implied contracts from the employee's perspective. In this situation, the ethical question is just the opposite: Would it be fair for a court *not* to hold that an implied employment contract exists, especially if an employee reasonably relied on statements made by the employer, orally or in a written employment manual? In one case, for example, a company handbook promised that any employee returning from an employer-approved leave of absence would be reinstated in the same or similar position. An employee, relying on this provision, took a nine-month leave of absence (with the express permission of the

---

1. 4 F.3d 631 (8th Cir. 1993).

employer). At the end of the nine months, however, the employer refused to rehire the employee for any position.

Here, given the employee's reliance on the promise made in the company handbook, it would seem only fair that the court find an implied contract—which the court did, when the employee sued the employer for breach of an implied employment contract. In its defense, the employer pointed out that the employment manual also had stated that the employment relationship remained "at will" and that either party could terminate the relationship at any time. Nonetheless, the court sided with the employee and declared that the promise regarding reinstatement, upon which the employee had relied when deciding to take the leave, created an implied contract.[2]

Obviously, the courts do not have an easy task when grappling with such issues. Ultimately, the courts must weigh several factors in deciding such cases, including the nature of the promises made by the employer and the extent of reliance on these promises by employees.

## Rewarding Whistleblowers

Arguing that whistleblowers should be protected against retaliation for their efforts is one thing, but whether they should be allowed to "hit the jackpot" for disclosing fraud against the government is another. The False Claims

Reform Act of 1986[3] rewards those who report fraud perpetrated against the government by allowing the whistleblower to receive a percentage of the funds recovered. In Chapter 36, we discussed a fraud case that was brought by an employee under the False Claims Reform Act. That case led to a reward of over $13 million to the person who reported the fraud. Ever-increasing numbers of employees are making substantial sums by detecting evidence of fraud on the part of their employers and reporting the fraud to government officials.

Government rewards to persons who blow the whistle on others' activities are not new. The Internal Revenue Service, for example, has a lengthy history of rewarding persons who disclose other persons' tax fraud. The ethical argument supporting such rewards essentially is that the end (preventing the waste of government funds and protecting the public interest) justifies the means. But even though giving monetary awards encourages whistleblowing and helps to detect fraud against the government, is it ethical when the motive for reporting fraud is solely monetary?

## Employment Discrimination

Laws prohibiting discrimination in employment are founded on the public policy that all persons, regardless of race, color, national origin, religion,

age, or (for some persons) disabilities, should have a fair and equal opportunity to obtain employment. This policy, however, often conflicts with other public policies, such as those underlying the employment-at-will doctrine and freedom of contract. The policy also conflicts with laws encouraging advancements and promotions based solely on merit.

Essentially, antidiscrimination laws raise questions of fairness. On the one hand, society has deemed that it is fair to ensure that all persons have equal employment opportunities. On the other hand, many people question whether it is fair that to achieve equal-opportunity goals, those persons (such as white males) who do not fall within a protected class must step aside. While equal employment opportunity laws prohibit discrimination against some persons, they also permit discrimination against others—or reverse discrimination.

### Reverse Discrimination

A leading case on the issue of reverse discrimination is *Regents of the University of California v. Bakke.*[4] The case arose after Alan Bakke, a Vietnam veteran and engineer who had been turned down for medical school at the Davis campus of the University of California, discovered that his academic record was better than those of some of the minority applicants who had been admitted to the program.

---

2. *Niehaus v. Delaware Valley Medical Center,* 631 A.2d 1314 (Pa.Sup. 1993).

3. 31 U.S.C. Sections 3729–3733. This act amended the False Claims Act of 1863.

4. 438 U.S. 265, 98 S.Ct. 2733, 57 L.Ed.2d 750 (1978).

He sued the University of California regents, alleging reverse discrimination. The United States Supreme Court held that a public university may give favorable weight to minority applicants as part of a plan to increase minority enrollment. The Court, however, stated that the use of a quota system, in which a certain number of places is explicitly reserved for minority applicants, is unconstitutional. In other words, although public universities may consider race or ethnic background as a factor in attempting to obtain the benefits that flow from an ethnically diverse student body, they may not utilize a quota system for the benefit of minorities.

Although *Bakke* and subsequent court decisions have alleviated the harshness of the quota system, reverse discrimination against white males sometimes continues to occur in the employment context in the interests of achieving equal employment opportunity.

## Disability-based Discrimination

In providing protection for disabled persons in the employment context through the Americans with Disabilities Act (ADA),[5] Congress expressed society's concern that disabled persons should be given a fair opportunity to compete in the workplace. As mentioned in the *Emerging Trends in Business Law* presented in Chapter 37, this act differs from other federal antidiscrimination laws in that it requires employers to treat disabled employees *unequally* as opposed to equally—under the ADA, a disabled person is entitled to be reasonably accommodated by the employer.

The ADA thus forces employers to view their workplaces in a new light. They must now look beyond an employee's disability and determine whether that employee is able to fulfill the essential requirements of the job. This was clearly illustrated by the first case decided under the ADA, *EEOC v. AIC Security*.[6] In that case, an employee, Charles Wessel, was fired from his position as executive director of AIC Security's security guard division. Wessel, a heavy smoker for over two decades, had been first diagnosed with emphysema, then lung cancer, and finally cancer of the brain. His right lung had been removed, he suffered from short-term memory loss as well as seizures, and he was told by his physician not to drive an automobile.

Wessel claimed that with reasonable accommodations (such as leaving work early on the days that he had radiation treatments scheduled or having someone drive his car on those few occasions when he needed transportion to fulfill job requirements), he could still do his job. Nonetheless, AIC fired Wessel. Wessel sued his employer, claiming that AIC Security had violated the terms of the ADA. The court denied AIC's motion for summary judgment, holding that there was insufficient evidence to conclude that Wessel could not perform the essential functions of his job. The case should therefore go to trial.

AIC Security argued its case solely on the premise that Wessel was incapable of performing the essential functions of his job. The evidence presented to the court, however, was clearly conflicting. Wessel had been a prominent person in the security industry, was well known, and by all indications, continued to work efficiently—with some time off for medical and surgical treatments.

One could speculate that the real reason Wessel was fired may have been because of the discomfort he caused to his employer and other AIC employees, who had to work daily with someone suffering from terminal cancer. One of the interesting aspects of the ADA is that it not only protects persons who actually suffer from a disability but also those persons who are *perceived* by employers to have a disability. The ADA requires, among other things, an attitudinal change on the part of employers and employees alike in regard to workers with disabilities.

## Sexual Harassment

Sexual harassment in the workplace is not new, but only in the last few years have courts extended laws prohibiting sex discrimination to cover sexual harassment. In doing so, however, the courts have faced some perplexing

---

5. 42 U.S.C. Sections 12102–12118.

6. 820 F.Supp. 1060 (N.D.Ill. 1993).

questions. For example, at what point does a sexually offensive action or series of actions create an environment sufficiently hostile to women that a woman would have a cause of action for sexual harassment? And what standard should be used in determining what constitutes a sexually offensive action—the traditional "reasonable person" standard, a "reasonable woman" or a "reasonable man" standard, a "reasonable victim" standard, or a combination of these? In deciding such issues, the courts must deal with questions of fairness that society as a whole is facing in regard to women in the workplace.

Recently, another question has had to be addressed by the courts. Should men who are harassed by other men also be protected by laws that prohibit sex discrimination in the workplace? For example, what if the male president of a firm demands that a male employee sleep with him or be terminated from his employment? Does this action qualify as sexual harassment? Courts have varied in their treatment of such claims, but increasingly, this type of harassment is being brought under the protective umbrella of state and federal laws prohibiting sex discrimination.

The example of same-gender harassment just mentioned actually occurred. In deciding the issue, the California Court of Appeal stated as follows: "We find no basis of support in the statutory language for the contention that the Legislature intended to limit protection from sexual harassment to male-female harassment. Although the statute does not specify whether it prohibits 'same gender' harassment or 'other gender' harassment, no ambiguity is created by this omission. Common usage indicates that in the absence of a modifying adjective, the Legislature intended to prohibit sexual harassment in all cases."[7]

## Family and Medical Leave

Society does not stand still, and neither can the law that governs it. A clear example of a law necessitated by social changes in the United States is the Family and Medical Leave Act of 1993 (FMLA).[8] The act reflects the realities of today's world. Nearly two-thirds of women with children now work, by choice or necessity. Also, about a fourth of all adults now provide care for elderly relatives or anticipate the need to provide such care within the next five years. With so many women now working, there is often no caretaker available to attend to medical emergencies or other family needs in the home. By allowing employees to take a leave from work for family or medical reasons, the FMLA recognizes the changing face of America.

From an ethical perspective, the act may be viewed as a choice on the part of society to shift to the employer family burdens caused by changing economic and social needs. In effect, Congress, by passing the act, addressed the pressing needs of the so-called baby-boomer (or "sandwich") generation—caught between the pressures of providing child care on the one hand and care for aging parents on the other.

## Labor Law and Quality Control

One of the ways in which today's corporations have increased their productivity and product quality—and, hence their ability to compete effectively—is by using some type of employee-participation program. Such programs are established not only to promote labor-management cooperation but also to incorporate employee input into the decision-making process in order to improve the quality of the firm's products or services.

While employee-participation programs appear to be an effective approach to the problems of productivity and product quality, they have recently come under attack as violating labor laws. To illustrate: Electromation, Inc., an electrical-components manufacturer, set up a series of committees involving employee and management participation. The committees were initially established to counter employee dissatisfaction with new employment policies that related to absenteeism, nonsmoking rules, and so on.

The workers who participated in these committees involved themselves in developing

_____

7. *Mogilevsky v. Superior Court,* 20 Cal.App.4th 1409, 26 Cal.Rptr.2d 116 (1993).
8. 29 U.S.C. Sections 2601, 2611–2619, 2651–2654.

solutions to these and various other problems, including worker benefits. The Teamsters Union, which was attempting to unionize Electromation's work force, successfully argued to the National Labor Relations Board (NLRB) that the committees violated the National Labor Relations Act (NLRA) because, in essence, the committees were labor organizations that were unlawfully "dominated" by the employer.[9]

Because numerous companies throughout the United States use similar action committees, the corporate community felt that it had been dealt a severe blow by the NLRB's decision. Almost any type of employee-participation program, regardless of how beneficial for employer and employee alike, could possibly be characterized as a labor organization as defined under the NLRA. As a result, employers will be wary of employee-participation programs, regardless of how beneficial they are.

The U.S. Constitution is premised on the belief that we benefit as a society by the free exchange of ideas and political beliefs. Should labor laws function to restrict the expression of ideas? Can a balance be struck between the goals of free speech and assembly and the prevention of an employer-dominated workplace in which the employee is underrepresented?

---

9. *Electromation, Inc.,* 309 N.L.R.B. No. 163 (1992).

## Fatigued Employees

Companies are required by law to protect the safety of workers in the workplace. Employers may also be held liable when their employees are injured outside the workplace if the employees are performing work-related tasks, such as driving delivery trucks. But questions sometimes arise as to whether an employer's liability should extend even further. For example, say a fatigued worker falls asleep at the wheel on the way home from work and causes an accident. Should the employer be liable for any injuries sustained as a result of that accident?

Several cases have reached the courts in which this or a similar issue is involved. In one case, a court held that a fatigued employee-driver was analogous to an intoxicated driver, and therefore the court applied the principles underlying so-called "dram shop acts" (see Chapter 6) to the situation. The court held that the employer, because it allowed the employee to leave work in such a fatigued state, was liable for injuries resulting from an accident caused by the fatigued employee.[10]

Another aspect of the problems presented by fatigued employees was recently dealt with in *Yellow Freight Systems, Inc. v. Reich.*[11] In that case, a truck driver was disciplined by his employer for stopping to nap during a long run. The driver was fatigued

---

10. *Senn v. Scudieri,* 165 A.D.2d 346, 567 N.Y.S.2d 665 (1991).
11. 8 F.3d 980 (4th Cir. 1993).

from nineteen hours of driving and had been weaving on the road before he finally stopped for a rest. The driver filed a complaint with the Department of Labor, contending that the disciplinary action violated federal statutes and regulations prohibiting drivers from operating vehicles while fatigued.

The employer argued that had the driver taken advantage of the employer's protective procedures, such as taking a rest period of eight to twelve hours between runs, the driver would not have been so fatigued in the first place. The employer had instituted such procedures not only to protect the safety of other drivers on the road but also to ensure that its shipments arrived on time, without delays caused by naps, breaks, and so on. The secretary of labor agreed with the driver, as did a federal appellate court when the secretary's decision was appealed.

The dissent in the case, though, concluded that the majority's decision allowed the driver to "have it both ways," as it were. On the one hand, the driver had a history of repeatedly taking on runs while he was fatigued. On the other hand, the court allowed the driver to avoid the consequences of his action— the disciplinary sanctions for stopping, resting, and delivering the goods late.

## Worker Safety and Efficiency versus Privacy Rights

A significant issue in the employment arena has to do with how far an employer can go in invading employee privacy rights in the interests of worker safety and efficiency. As discussed in Chapter 36, such actions as drug testing, performance monitoring, and preemployment screening have all been challenged by employees as constituting an invasion of privacy.

An especially problematic practice undertaken by some employers is the use of "spies" to gather information about an employee's after-hours activities. Imagine going over to a co-worker's apartment after work to watch a televised basketball game. You get along well, and you think you are developing a close and trusting friendship with this person. But, as it turns out, you are socializing with a company spy who wants to know everything about you and what your activities are "after working hours"—so that he or she can relay that information to your employer.

Should the employer be allowed to hire spies to become "false friends" of employees after work? What if the employer was aware of an illegal drug ring that is operating out of the plant and is using spies to expose the ringleader? Clearly, the courts face a difficult challenge in defining the point at which an employer's actions cross the line between legitimate actions in the interest of protecting the safety and efficiency of its employees and illegal activities that violate employees' privacy rights.

## ■ Discussion Questions

1. Occupational safety laws strive to protect the public health from hazardous substances, inadequate emergency procedures, unsafe equipment, and so on. Certain jobs (such as that of a bridge builder) necessarily involve greater risks than others (such as that of a telephone operator). Should employees be allowed to bargain freely with their employers and accept some greater risk in exchange for higher wages? Should the employee be free to bargain away the safety measures provided under occupational laws?

2. An employer's affirmative action policy may conflict with the interests of its current employees and their union. How should such a company balance its duties under labor laws with its duties under antidiscrimination laws?

3. The traditional doctrine of employment at will allows employers to fire whomever they choose for any or no reason. Developments in both statutory and common law have eroded the effectiveness of this doctrine. Do you believe that society has gone too far in the direction of protecting the interests of employees as opposed to the interests of employers? How can the often-conflicting interests of these two groups most appropriately be balanced? Can they ever be balanced, considering the difference in economic power between employers and employees?

# UNIT EIGHT

# BUSINESS ORGANIZATIONS

## CONTENTS

**38** **Forms of Business Organizations and Private Franchises**

**39** **Partnerships—Nature, Formation, and Operation**

**40** **Partnerships—Termination and Limited Partnerships**

**41** **Corporations—Formation and Financing**

**42** **Corporations—Directors, Officers, and Shareholders**

**43** **Corporations—Merger, Consolidation, and Termination**

**44** **Corporations—Investor Protection**

# CHAPTER 38

# FORMS OF BUSINESS ORGANIZATIONS AND PRIVATE FRANCHISES

**A** basic question facing anyone who wishes to start up a business is which of the several forms of business organization will be most appropriate for the business endeavor. In deciding this question, the **entrepreneur** (one who initiates and assumes the financial risk of a new enterprise) needs to consider the advantages and disadvantages associated with each form.

In this chapter, we examine the basic features of the three major business forms: sole proprietorships, partnerships, and corporations. We also touch on joint ventures, syndicates, joint stock companies, business trusts, cooperatives, and a relatively new business form known as the limited liability company. A discussion of private franchises concludes the chapter.

## SECTION 1

## SOLE PROPRIETORSHIPS

A **sole proprietorship** is the simplest form of business. In this form, the owner is the business; thus, anyone who does business without creating a separate business entity, such as a partnership or corporation, has a sole proprietorship. Sole proprietorships are very common and constitute over two-thirds of all American businesses. They are also usually small enterprises—less than 1 percent of the sole proprietorships existing in the United States earn over $1 million per year. Sole proprietors can own and manage any type of business from an informal, home-office undertaking to a large restaurant or construction firm.

### ADVANTAGES OF SOLE PROPRIETORSHIPS

A major advantage of the sole proprietorship is that the proprietor receives all the profits (because he or she takes all the risk). In addition, it is often easier and less costly to start a sole proprietorship than to start any other kind of business, as few legal forms are involved. This business form also entails more flexibility than does a partnership or a corporation. The sole proprietor is free to make any decision he or she wishes concerning the business—whom to hire, when to take a vacation, what kind of business to pursue, and so on. Sole proprietors are also allowed to establish tax-exempt retirement accounts, such as a Keogh plan. (A **Keogh plan** is a retirement program designed for self-employed persons by which a certain percentage of their income can be contributed to the plan, and interest earnings will not be taxed until funds are withdrawn from the plan.)

## DISADVANTAGES OF SOLE PROPRIETORSHIPS

The major disadvantage of the sole proprietorship is that the proprietor alone, as the firm's sole owner, bears the burden of any losses or liabilities incurred by the business enterprise. In other words, the sole proprietor has unlimited liability, or legal responsibility, for all obligations incurred in doing business. The unlimited liability of the sole proprietor, in contrast to the limited liability of the limited partner or corporate shareholder (discussed below), is a major factor to be considered when choosing a business form.

Another disadvantage is that the proprietor's opportunity to raise capital is limited to personal funds and the funds of those who are willing to make loans. The sole proprietorship also has the disadvantage of lacking continuity of business upon the death of the proprietor. When the owner dies, so does the business—it is automatically dissolved. If the business is to be transferred to family members or other heirs, a new proprietorship is created.

In spite of the above disadvantages, sole proprietorships are predominant among types of business organizations in the United States.

## SECTION 2

# PARTNERSHIPS

Partnerships can take the form of general partnerships or limited partnerships. The two forms of partnership differ considerably in regard to legal requirements and the rights and liabilities of partners.

## GENERAL PARTNERSHIPS

General partnerships are usually referred to simply as partnerships. A **partnership** is a joint undertaking that arises from an agreement, express or implied, between two or more persons to carry on a business for profit. Partners are co-owners of a business, and they have joint control over its operation and the right to share in its profits. No particular form of partnership agreement is necessary for the creation of a partnership, although the partners should normally put their agreement in writing. Both partnerships and sole proprietorships are creatures of the common law rather than of statute. Basically, the partners may agree to almost any terms when establishing the partnership so long as they are not illegal or contrary to public policy.

A partnership is a legal entity only for limited purposes, such as the partnership name and title of ownership and property. The partners are subject to personal liability for partnership obligations, and the partnership itself is not subject to levy for federal income taxes, although an **information return** must be filed. That is, the partnership as an entity only *reports* (does not pay taxes on) the income received by the partnership. A partner's profit from the partnership (whether distributed or not) is taxed as individual income to the individual partner.

The nature, formation, operation, and termination of general partnerships are discussed in further detail in Chapters 39 and 40.

## LIMITED PARTNERSHIPS

A special and quite popular form of partnership is the **limited partnership,** which consists of at least one general partner and one or more limited partners. The general partner or partners run the business and are subject to personal liability for partnership debts and obligations. The limited partner or partners, however, have limited liability, both with respect to lawsuits brought against the partnership and money at risk. The maximum money at risk is defined by the limited partnership agreement, which specifically states how much each limited partner must contribute to the partnership.

Unlike a general partnership, a limited partnership is completely a creature of statute. If the statute is not followed almost to the letter, the courts will hold that a general partnership exists instead. Then those who thought their liability was limited by their investment in a limited partnership will be held generally liable to the full extent of their personal net worth. Limited partnerships are discussed in more detail in Chapter 40.

# CORPORATIONS

A third and widely used type of business organizational form is the **corporation.** Corporations consist of shareholders, who are the owners of the business. A board of directors, elected by the shareholders, manages the business. The board of directors normally employs officers to oversee day-to-day operations.

The corporation is a creature of statute, and it is therefore a legal entity. Its existence depends generally upon state law, although some corporations, especially public organizations, can be created under federal law. The law governing the formation, management and operation, liability, and termination of corporations will be discussed in detail in Chapters 41 through 44.

One of the key advantages of the corporate form of business is that the liability of its owners (shareholders) is limited to their investments. Their personal estates are usually not liable for the obligations of the corporation. A key disadvantage of the corporate form is that any distributed corporate income is taxed twice. The corporate entity pays taxes on the firm's income, and when income is distributed to shareholders, the shareholders again pay taxes on that income.

Some small corporations are able to avoid this double-taxation feature of the corporation by electing to be treated as an **S corporation** for tax purposes. Subchapter S of the Internal Revenue Code allows qualifying corporations to be taxed in a way similar to the way a partnership is taxed. In other words, a corporation electing S corporation status will not be taxed at the corporate level. As with partners in a partnership, the income is taxed only once—when it is distributed to the shareholder-owners, who pay personal income taxes on their respective shares of the profits.

# MAJOR BUSINESS FORMS COMPARED

Exhibit 38–1 lists the essential advantages and disadvantages of each of the three major forms of business organization. We select for further discussion here four important concerns for anyone starting a business—the ease of creation, the liability of the owners, tax features, and the need for capital—and then offer some suggestions on which business form is the most appropriate for different types of business situations.

## EASE OF CREATION

No formalities are required in starting a business as a sole proprietorship. A general partnership can be organized easily and inexpensively. A corporation must be organized according to specific statutory procedures, must have sufficient capitalization, and must pay other costs of formal incorporation. In fact, throughout its life, a corporation is subject to more governmental supervision and reporting requirements than is a partnership.

## LIABILITY OF OWNERS

Generally, sole proprietors and general partners have personal liability, whereas the liability of limited partners and shareholders of corporations is limited to their investment. The issue of liability is an important one for the firm's owners, who may not want to place their personal assets at risk in the event the business cannot meet its obligations.

The form of the organization does not always in and of itself determine the liability of the owners, however. For example, a court may ''pierce the corporate veil'' in certain circumstances (as will be discussed in Chapter 41) and hold corporate shareholders liable for corporate obligations.

Furthermore, creditors may not be willing to extend credit to a newly formed or small corporation precisely because of the limited liability of corporate owners. Typically, if a corporation has relatively few shareholders, a bank or other lender will require the shareholders to personally cosign or guarantee any loans made to the corporation. That is, the shareholders agree to become personally liable for the loan if the corporation goes under or cannot meet its debts. In essence, the share-

# ■ Exhibit 38–1 Major Business Forms Compared

| Characteristic | Sole Proprietorship | Partnership | Corporation |
|---|---|---|---|
| **Method of Creation** | Created at will by owner. | Created by agreement of the parties. | Charter issued by state—created by statutory authorization. |
| **Legal Position** | Not a separate entity; owner is the business. | Not a separate legal entity in many states. | Always a legal entity separate and distinct from its owners—a legal fiction for the purposes of owning property and being a party to litigation. |
| **Liability** | Unlimited liability. | Unlimited liability. | Limited liability of shareholders—shareholders are not liable for the debts of the corporation. |
| **Duration** | Determined by owner; automatically dissolved on owner's death. | Terminated by agreement of the partners, by the death of one or more of the partners, by withdrawal of a partner, by bankruptcy, etc. | Can have perpetual existence. |
| **Transferability of Interest** | Interest can be transferred, but individual's proprietorship then ends. | Although partnership interest can be assigned, assignee does not have full rights of a partner. | Share of stock can be transferred. |
| **Management** | Completely at owner's discretion. | Each general partner has a direct and equal voice in management unless expressly agreed otherwise in the partnership agreement. | Shareholders elect directors, who set policy and appoint officers. |
| **Taxation** | Owner pays personal taxes on business income. | Each partner pays *pro rata* share of income taxes on net profits, whether or not they are distributed. | Double taxation—corporation pays income tax on net profits, with no deduction for dividends, and shareholders pay income tax on disbursed dividends they receive. |
| **Organizational Fees, Annual License Fees, and Annual Reports** | None. | None. | All required. |
| **Transaction of Business in Other States** | Generally no limitation. | Generally no limitation.[a] | Normally must qualify to do business and obtain certificate of authority. |

a. A few states have enacted statutes requiring that foreign partnerships qualify to do business there—for example, 3 N.H.Rev.Stat.Ann. Chapter 305-A in New Hampshire.

■ **Exhibit 38–2  Tax Aspects of Partnerships and Corporations[a]**

| Tax Aspect | Partnership | Corporation |
|---|---|---|
| **Federal Income Tax** | Partners are taxed on proportionate shares of partnership income, even if not distributed; the partnership files information returns only. | Income of the corporation is taxed; stockholders are also taxed on distributed dividends. The corporation files corporate income tax forms. |
| **Accumulation** | Partners are taxed on accumulated as well as distributed earnings. | Corporate stockholders are not taxed on accumulated earnings. There is, however, a penalty tax, in some instances, that the corporation must pay for unreasonable accumulations of income. |
| **Capital Gains** | Partners are taxed on their proportionate shares of capital gains, which are taxed at ordinary income rate. | The corporation is taxed on capital gains and losses. |
| **Exempt Income** | Partners are not taxed on exempt income received from the firm. | Any exempt income distributed by a corporation is fully taxable income to the stockholders. |
| **Pension Plan** | Partners can adopt a Keogh plan, an IRA, or a 401-K plan. | Employees and officers who are also stockholders can be beneficiaries of a pension trust. The corporation can deduct its payments to the trust. |
| **Social Security** | Partners must pay a self-employment tax (in 1994, 12.4 percent on income up to $57,600, plus 2.9 percent Medicare tax on all income). | All compensation to officers and employee stockholders is subject to Social Security taxation up to the maximum. |
| **Death Benefits (excluding those provided by insurance)** | There is no exemption for payments to partners' beneficiaries. | Benefits up to $5,000 can be received tax-free by employees' beneficiaries. |
| **State Taxes** | The partnership is not subject to taxes. State income taxes are paid by each partner. | The corporation is subject to state income taxes (although these taxes can be deducted on federal returns). |

a.   As of 1994.

holders become guarantors for the corporation's debt. Hence, the corporate form of business does not prevent the shareholders from having personal liability in such a situation, because they have assumed the liability voluntarily.

## TAX CONSIDERATIONS

Various tax considerations must be taken into account when one decides how best to organize a business. Taxes on income earned by a sole proprietor are simply taxed as personal income. Tax aspects of partnerships and corporations are summarized in Exhibit 38–2.

## THE NEED FOR CAPITAL

One of the most common reasons for changing from a sole proprietorship to a partnership or a corporation is the need for additional capital to finance expansion. A sole proprietor can seek partners who will bring capital with them. The partnership might be able to secure more funds from potential lenders than could the sole proprietor.

When a firm wants to expand greatly, however, simply increasing the number of partners can result in too many partners and make it difficult for the firm to operate effectively. Therefore, incorporation might be the best choice for an expanding business organization. There are many possibilities for obtaining more capital by issuing shares of stock. The original owners will find that, although their proportionate ownership of the company is reduced, they are able to expand much more rapidly by selling shares in the company.

## THE APPROPRIATE ORGANIZATIONAL FORM

If a business is relatively small, is not diversified, employs relatively few people, has modest profits, and is not likely to expand significantly or require extensive financing in the immediate future, the most appropriate form for doing business may be a sole proprietorship. If it is advantageous to do so for tax purposes, though, even a small business might consider electing S corporation status.

If the business is larger and has greater capital needs but few owners, the most appropriate form may be a partnership. When the business is expanding, becoming more profitable and diversified, it may be most advantageous to do business in the corporate form.

---

### SECTION 5

# OTHER ORGANIZATIONAL FORMS

A business venture does not have to be organized as a sole proprietorship, a partnership, or a corporation. Several other organizational forms exist, although for the most part they are hybrid organizations—that is, they have characteristics similar to those of partnerships or corporations, or they combine features of both. We look at several of these forms here.

## JOINT VENTURES

A **joint venture,** which is sometimes referred to as a *joint adventure,* is a relationship in which two or more persons combine their efforts or their property for a single transaction or project, or a related series of transactions or projects. Unless otherwise agreed, joint venturers share profits and losses equally. For example, when several contractors combine their resources to build and sell houses in a single development, their relationship is a joint venture.

Joint ventures range in size from very small activities to huge, multimillion-dollar joint actions engaged in by some of the world's largest corporations. Large organizations often investigate new markets or new ideas by forming joint ventures with other enterprises. For instance, General Motors Corporation and Volvo Truck Corporation were involved in a joint venture—Volvo GM—to manufacture heavy-duty trucks and market them in the United States.

**CHARACTERISTICS OF JOINT VENTURES** A joint venture resembles a partnership and is taxed like a partnership. The essential difference is that a joint venture typically involves the pursuit of a single project or series of transactions, and a partnership usually concerns an ongoing business. Of course, a partnership may be created to conduct a single transaction. For this reason, most courts apply the same principles to joint ventures as they apply to partnerships. Exceptions to the application of partnership principles to joint ventures include the following:

1. The members of a joint venture have less implied and apparent authority than the partners in a partnership (under partnership law, each partner is an agent of the other partners), because the activities of a joint venture are more limited than the business of a partnership.
2. Although the death of a partner terminates a partnership, the death of a joint venturer ordinarily does not terminate a joint venture.

**DURATION** The members of a joint venture can specify its duration. If the members do not specify a duration, a joint venture normally terminates when the project or the transaction for which it was formed has been completed. Thus, the termination of the joint venture to build and sell houses in a single development would occur once the houses were built and sold. If the members (housing contractors) do not specify a particular duration and the joint venture does not clearly relate to the achievement of a certain goal, a joint venture is terminable at the will of any of its members.

**DUTIES, RIGHTS, AND LIABILITIES AMONG JOINT VENTURERS** The duties that joint venturers owe to each other are the same duties that partners owe to each other (discussed in Chapter 39). Thus, the contractors in the previous example owe each other fiduciary duties, including a duty of loyalty. If two of the contractors secretly buy the land that was to be acquired by the joint venture, the other joint venturers may be awarded damages for the breach of loyalty.

When the members of a joint venture are ordinarily engaged in business operations that are similar to the activity of the joint venture, there are two areas of the law in which conflicts may develop. First, when the members of a joint venture are competitors, each member may face a choice between disclosing trade secrets to a competitor and breaching the duty to disclose. Second, in those circumstances, there is also a potential for a violation of the antitrust laws (see Chapter 48). For both reasons, joint venturers should specify exactly the information that each will be required to disclose.

Each joint venturer has an equal right to manage the activities of the enterprise. Control of the operation may be given to no more than one of the members, however, without affecting the status of the relationship. For instance, if the contractors agree that one of them will serve as the general contractor to oversee the construction of the houses, it may appear that this contractor is the owner of the business, but this appearance does not affect the members' relationship as a joint venture.

Each joint venturer is liable to third parties for the actions of the other members of the joint venture in pursuit of the goal of the enterprise. This is illustrated by the following case.

CASE 38.1

**HILL v. ZIMMERER**
Supreme Court of Wyoming,
1992.
839 P.2d 977.

**BACKGROUND AND FACTS** *In March 1988, Ron Hill arranged to buy alfalfa hay from Bob Zimmerer. Ron, Johnny Hill, Bobby Hill, and Bobby Hill, Jr., went to Zimmerer's farm and loaded the hay into Johnny's trailer, which was pulled by Ron's tractor. The hay was delivered to various feedlots to satisfy contracts held by Johnny. Ron and Johnny Hill agreed to split the profits according to a 60/40 ratio. By mid-April, the Hills had hauled eleven loads of hay without paying for them. Zimmerer halted the operation and demanded payment, which was made by late May with checks that were drafted on Johnny Hill's account. When the operation resumed, Ron Hill no longer actively participated, but the others continued to use his tractor. The Hills had hauled another twenty-three-and-one-half loads of hay from Zimmerer's farm by early July, when they again fell behind in their payments. This time, when Zimmerer demanded payment, the Hills left and never returned. Zimmerer filed a suit against Johnny and Ron Hill for, among other things, the amount of the unmade payments on the hay that had been taken and the value of the hay that had not been taken and that was subsequently damaged by the weather. Johnny Hill declared bankruptcy. A trial was held on the suit against Ron Hill. Ron Hill argued, in part, that he was not a joint venturer with Johnny but that he only accommodated Johnny Hill by contacting Zimmerer and by "leasing" his tractor to Johnny for a share of the profits. The court concluded that Ron and Johnny Hill were joint venturers in the hay-hauling operation and ordered a judgment to be entered against Ron Hill in the amount of $17,507.50, plus costs of $111.34, at 7 percent interest. Ron Hill appealed.*

*GOLDEN*, Justice.
\* \* \* \*
\* \* \* A joint adventure is defined generically as an "association of persons to carry out a single business enterprise for profit, for which purpose they combine their property, money, effects, skill, and knowledge." As between the parties, a joint adventurer relationship may be formed only by contract. Consequently, such a relationship will be found when there exists (1) an agreement, express or implied,

(2) to carry out a common business purpose, (3) for pecuniary gain, (4) in which each party has an equal voice in control and direction of the undertaking. As to third persons, however, *the law will impose joint adventurer status upon individuals or entities conducting their affairs as though they are joint adventurers, regardless of their actual intent. *   *   * [Emphasis added.]*

The district court *   *   * determined that Ron Hill was an apparent joint adventurer with his cousin, Johnny Hill, and that Ron Hill should be held jointly and severally liable for the hay purchase debt incurred with Bob Zimmerer. *   *   * [W]e are satisfied that the district court's determinations are amply supported. The record reflects that both Ron Hill and Johnny Hill negotiated with Bob Zimmerer to purchase hay; that the purpose of the negotiations was to satisfy supply contracts which Johnny Hill held with various feed lots; that Ron Hill and Johnny Hill both contributed their time, talents and property to the undertaking; that they agreed to share the profits and losses on a 60/40 ratio; and that Bob Zimmerer thought that Johnny Hill and Ron Hill were jointly involved in the hay hauling operation. While Johnny Hill explained that he was merely leasing Ron Hill's tractor, the most favorable inference that may reasonably be drawn from the evidence is that Johnny Hill and Ron Hill were engaged in a joint adventure.

*The appellate court affirmed the judgment of the trial court.*

**DECISION AND REMEDY**

## SYNDICATE

A group of individuals getting together to finance a particular project, such as the building of a shopping center or the purchase of a professional basketball franchise, is called a **syndicate** or an *investment group*. The forms of such groups vary considerably. They may exist as corporations or as general or limited partnerships. In some cases, the members merely own property jointly and have no legally recognized business arrangement.

## JOINT STOCK COMPANY

A **joint stock company** is a true hybrid of a partnership and a corporation. It has many characteristics of a corporation in that (1) its ownership is represented by transferable shares of stock, (2) it is usually managed by directors and officers of the company or association, and (3) it can have a perpetual existence. Most of its other features, however, are more characteristic of a partnership, and it is usually treated like a partnership. Like a partnership, a joint stock company is formed by agreement (not statute), property is usually held in the names of the members, shareholders have personal liability, and generally the company is not treated as a legal entity for purposes of a lawsuit. In a joint stock company, however, shareholders are not considered to be agents of one another, as would be the case if the company were a true partnership.

## BUSINESS TRUST

A **business trust** is created by a written trust agreement that sets forth the interests of the beneficiaries and the obligations and powers of the trustees. With a business trust, legal ownership and management of the property of the business stay with one or more of the trustees, and the profits are distributed to the beneficiaries. The business trust resembles a corporation in many respects. Death or bankruptcy of a beneficiary, for example, does not terminate the trust, and beneficiaries are not personally responsible for the debts or obligations of the business trust. In fact, in a number of states, business trusts must pay corporate taxes.

The business trust was started in Massachusetts in an attempt to obtain the limited liability of corporate status while avoiding certain restrictions that at one time were imposed on a corporation's ownership and development of real property. In the 1800s, some business trusts acquired substantial assets and, in some industries, began to assert significant control over the marketplace. One of the most famous business trusts was John D. Rockefeller's Standard Oil Company. To curb the anticompetitive effects of these trusts, Congress passed the Sherman Antitrust Act of 1890 and the other antitrust laws discussed in Chapter 48.

## COOPERATIVE

A **cooperative** is an association that is organized to provide an economic service without profit to its members (or shareholders). An incorporated cooperative is subject to state laws governing nonprofit corporations. It makes distributions of dividends, or profits, to its owners on the basis of their transactions with the cooperative rather than on the basis of the amount of capital they contributed. Unincorporated cooperatives are often treated like partnerships. The members have joint liability for the cooperative's acts.

This form of business is generally adopted by groups of individuals who wish to pool their resources to gain some advantage in the marketplace. Consumer purchasing cooperatives are formed to obtain lower prices through quantity discounts. Seller marketing cooperatives are formed to control the market and thereby obtain higher sales prices from consumers. Credit cooperatives and farmers' cooperatives are other examples of this form of business enterprise. Cooperatives are often exempt from certain federal laws—for example, antitrust statutes—because of their special status.

## LIMITED LIABILITY COMPANY (LLC)

Since 1977, an increasing number of states have authorized a new form of business organization called the **limited liability company (LLC).** The LLC is a hybrid form of business enterprise that offers the limited liability of the corporation but the tax advantages of a partnership. The origins and characteristics of this increasingly significant form of business organization are discussed in this chapter's *Emerging Trends in Business Law.*

## SECTION 6

# PRIVATE FRANCHISES

Times have changed dramatically since Ray Kroc, the late founder of McDonald's, launched the franchising boom over forty years ago. Today, over a third of all retail sales and an increasing part of the gross domestic product of the United States are generated by private franchises. A **franchise** is any arrangement in which the owner of a trademark, a trade name, or a copyright has licensed others to use it in selling goods or services. A **franchisee** (a purchaser of a franchise) is generally legally independent, but economically dependent, on the integrated business system of the **franchisor** (the seller of the franchise). In other words, a franchisee can operate as an independent businessperson but still obtain the advantages of a regional or national organization. Well-known franchises include McDonald's, Hilton Hotels, Holiday Inns, and Burger King.

## THE LAW OF FRANCHISING

The growth in franchise operations has outdistanced the law of franchising. There has yet to be developed a solid body of appellate decisions under federal or state laws relating to franchises. In the absence of case law precisely addressed to franchising, the courts tend to apply general common law principles and appropriate federal or state statutory definitions and rules. Characteristics associated with a franchising relationship are similar in some respects to those of principal-agent, employer-employee, and employer–independent contractor relationships—yet a franchising relationship does not truly fit into any of these traditional classifications.

**FEDERAL REGULATION OF FRANCHISING** Some statutory requirements specifically relating to franchising have been enacted at the federal level. Automobile dealership franchisees are protected from automobile manufacturers' bad faith termination of their franchises by the Automobile Dealers' Franchise Act (enacted in 1956), also known as the Automobile Dealers' Day in Court Act.[1] If a manufacturer-franchisor terminates a franchise because of a dealer-franchisee's failure to comply with unreasonable demands (for example, failure to attain an unrealistically high sales quota), the manufacturer may be liable for damages.

Another federal statute is the Petroleum Marketing Practices Act (PMPA),[2] which was adopted in 1979 to protect gasoline station franchisees' reasonable expectations in the continuation of their franchises. Before the PMPA's passage, gas-

---

1.  15 U.S.C. Sections 1221–1225.
2.  15 U.S.C. Sections 2801–2841.

oline franchisors sometimes imposed high minimum rents and gallonage requirements, and the situation only worsened during the energy crisis in the early 1970s. The PMPA prescribes the grounds and conditions under which a franchisor may terminate or decline to renew a franchise. Federal antitrust laws (discussed in Chapter 48) may also apply if there is an illegal price-fixing agreement affecting the relationship between a franchisor and franchisee.

In 1979, the Federal Trade Commission (FTC) issued regulations that require franchisors to disclose material facts necessary to a prospective franchisee's making an informed decision concerning the purchase of a franchise.

**STATE REGULATION OF FRANCHISING**  Most states currently have statutes dealing with franchise law. State legislation tends to be similar to federal statutes and the FTC regulations. That is, state laws are generally designed to protect prospective franchisees from dishonest franchisors and to prohibit franchisors from terminating franchises without good cause. For example, a law might require the disclosure of information that is material to making an informed decision regarding the purchase of a franchise. This could include such information as the actual costs of operation, recurring expenses, and profits earned, along with facts substantiating these figures.

In response to the need for a uniform franchise law, the National Conference of Commissioners on Uniform State Laws drafted a model law that standardizes the various state franchise regulations. Because the uniform law represents a compromise of so many diverse interests, it has met with little success in being adopted as law by the various states.

When a franchise exists primarily for the sale of products manufactured by the franchisor, the law governing sales as expressed in Article 2 of the Uniform Commercial Code applies (see Chapters 20 through 25).

## TYPES OF FRANCHISES

Franchises can take the form of distributorships, chain-style business operations, or manufacturing or processing-plant arrangements. We briefly describe each of these forms below:

1.  A *distributorship* is established when a manufacturing concern (franchisor) licenses a dealer (franchisee) to sell its product. Often, a distributorship covers an exclusive territory. An example of this type of franchise is an automobile dealership.

2.  A *chain-style business franchise* results when a franchise operates under a franchisor's trade name and is identified as a member of a select group of dealers that engages in the franchisor's business. The franchisee is generally required to follow standardized or prescribed methods of operation. Often, the franchisor requires that the franchisee maintain certain standards of operation. In addition, sometimes the franchisee is obligated to deal exclusively with the franchisor to obtain materials and supplies. An example of this type of franchise is McDonald's and most other fast-food chains.

3.  A *manufacturing* or *processing-plant franchise* is created when the franchisor transmits to the franchisee the essential ingredients or formula to make a particular product. The franchisee then markets it either at wholesale or at retail in accordance with the franchisor's standards. Examples of this type of franchise are Coca-Cola and other soft-drink bottling companies.

## THE FRANCHISE AGREEMENT

The franchise relationship is created by a contract between the franchisor and the franchisee. To avoid future problems arising from the relationship, prospective franchisees should obtain all of the relevant details of the business and scrutinize carefully the franchise agreement and its economic and legal implications. As mentioned above, federal and state disclosure laws require that franchisors supply prospective franchisees with all material facts and information relating to the franchise.

Each franchise relationship and each industry has its own characteristics, so it is difficult to describe the broad range of details a franchising contract may include. The following sections, however, will define the essential characteristics of the franchise relationship.

**PAYING FOR THE FRANCHISE**  The franchisee ordinarily pays an initial fee or lump-sum price for the franchise license (the privilege of being granted a franchise). This fee is separate from the fee for the various products that the franchisee purchases from or through the franchisor. In some industries,

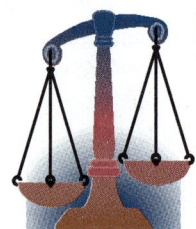

# EMERGING TRENDS IN BUSINESS LAW

## Limited Liability Companies (LLCs)

Corporations offer the advantage of limited liability for shareholders. A disadvantage of the corporate form, however, is that income received by corporations is taxed twice. Partnerships offer tax advantages to their members, because all income is "passed through" the partnership entity to the partners themselves, who are taxed only as individuals. But in contrast to the limited liability of corporate shareholders, the liability of partners in ordinary partnerships is unlimited. For many entrepreneurs and investors, the ideal business form would combine the tax advantages of the partnership form of business with the limited-liability feature of the corporate enterprise.

Two types of existing U.S. business forms partially address these needs. One of them is the limited partnership. Limited partners enjoy both the tax benefits of the partnership *and* limited liability. Yet the limited liability of limited partners is conditional: limited liability exists only so long as the limited partner does not participate in management. The other business form is the S corporation—although this is less a business form than a special corporate tax status. S corporation status allows small corporations to avoid the

double-taxation feature of corporations. Like partnerships, S corporations are "pass-through" entities with regard to taxes. S corporation shareholders pay taxes personally on their respective shares of the profits, and the corporation itself is not taxed. The problem with S corporations is that only small corporations (those with thirty-five or fewer shareholders) may acquire S corporation status. Furthermore, with few exceptions, only *individuals* may be shareholders in an S corporation; partnerships and corporations cannot be shareholders. Finally, no nonresident alien can be a shareholder in an S corporation. This means that if, say, a European investor wanted to purchase shares in an S corporation, it would not be permissible.

### LLC Statutes

In 1977, the state of Wyoming passed legislation authorizing the creation of a limited liability company (LLC), which is a hybrid form of business enterprise that combines the pass-through tax benefits of S corporations and partnerships with the limited liability of limited partners and corporate shareholders. Interest in LLCs mushroomed after a 1988 ruling by the Internal Revenue

Service (IRS) that Wyoming LLCs would be taxed as partnerships instead of as corporations. Before that ruling, the only other state to enact a statute authorizing LLCs was Florida, in 1982. After the IRS ruling, however, numerous states adopted LLC statutes. By the beginning of 1994, at least thirty-six states had enacted laws authorizing LLCs, and legislatures in many of the remaining states were considering the adoption of such statutes.

The state LLC statutes are far from uniform, but typically they are based on the Wyoming act's provisions, with variations according to each state's corporate and partnership laws.[a] Generally, to achieve the special pass-through tax treatment, the LLC must be properly formed in accordance with the requirements imposed by the state's LLC statute. Also, if an LLC possesses more than two of the following four characteristics, the LLC as an entity will be liable for income taxes, and the benefits of

---

a. In an attempt to create some uniformity among the states in regard to LLC statutes, the National Conference of Commissioners on Uniform State Laws has drafted a model LLC act.

pass-through taxation will be lost:

- Limited liability.
- Continuity of life.
- Free transferability of interest.
- Centralization of management.

## Advantages of the LLC

A major advantage of the LLC is, of course, that it is taxed as a partnership: profits are passed through the LLC entity, and taxes are paid personally by the members of the company. Another advantage is that the liability of members is limited to the amount of their investments. Furthermore, unlike limited partnerships, the LLC does not grant limited liability on the condition that the members refrain from active participation in the management of the company.

In an LLC, members are allowed to participate fully in management activities, and under at least one state's statute, the firm's managers need not even be members of the LLC. Yet another advantage is that corporations and partnerships, as well as foreign investors, can be LLC members, whereas these entities cannot be shareholders in S corporations. Also in contrast to S corporations, there is no limit on the number of shareholder-members of the LLC.

## Disadvantages of the LLC

The disadvantages of the LLC are relatively few. Perhaps the greatest disadvantage is that until uniform LLC statutes are

adopted by all the states, or most of the states, any firm engaged in multistate operations may face difficulties. For example, members of an LLC formed in one state may have limited liability in that state but face unlimited liability in another state. Another disadvantage is the fact that because the LLC is a relatively new form of enterprise, little case law exists in regard to LLCs. In some situations, the restrictions placed by statute on the transfer of ownership interests in LLCs may also be a disadvantage.

## LLCs in Other Countries

LLCs emerged in the United States only in 1977, with the passage of the Wyoming LLC statute, but they have been in existence for over a century in other countries. They were first allowed in Germany, which passed legislation in 1892 providing for a form of business called a *Gesellschaft mit beschranker Haftung* (GmbH), or "company with limited liability." Over the next few decades, the LLC form of enterprise spread to Portugal (1901), Panama (1917), Brazil (1919), Chile (1923), France (1925), Turkey (1926), Cuba (1929), Argentina (1932), Mexico (1934), Belgium (1935), Switzerland (1936), and Italy (1936).

## ■ Implications for the Businessperson

**1.** In those states that have LLC statutes, businesspersons now have the option of

organizing as an LLC to secure both the tax benefits of the partnership and the limited personal liability of the corporation. At the same time, those who opt to do business as an LLC may be faced with a degree of legal uncertainty. This is because LLC statutes vary from state to state, and thus far, there has been little case law to indicate how the courts will interpret these statutes.

**2.** The IRS has ruled on the tax status of LLCs in an increasing number of states. But as more states pass their own acts, the IRS is lagging behind. Consequently, an LLC formed in a state that has not yet received an IRS ruling may be at risk in terms of its tax status as a partnership.

**3.** Part of the impetus behind creating LLCs in this country is that foreign investors may become LLC members. Moreover, many potential foreign investors are familiar with the LLC form and feel comfortable with it. Generally, the LLC offers U.S. firms and potential investors from other countries opportunities and flexibility greater than those available through partnerships or corporations.

## ■ For Critical Analysis

**1.** Why do you think that, after some states passed legislation authorizing LLCs, numerous other states passed similar legislation?

**2.** The IRS can determine if an LLC will or will not be liable for income taxes on any profits earned. Why should the IRS care?

the franchisor relies heavily on the initial sale of the franchise for realizing a profit. In other industries, the continued dealing between the parties brings profit to both.

In most situations, the franchisor will receive a stated percentage of the annual sales or annual volume of business done by the franchisee. The franchise agreement may also require the franchisee to pay a percentage of advertising costs and certain administrative expenses incurred under the franchise agreement.

**LOCATION OF THE FRANCHISE**   Typically, the franchisor will determine the territory to be served. The franchise agreement may specify whether the premises for the business must be leased or purchased outright. In some cases, construction of a building is necessary to meet the terms of the franchise agreement.

Certainly, the agreement will specify whether the franchisor supplies equipment and furnishings for the premises or whether this is the responsibility of the franchisee. When the franchise is a service operation, such as a motel, the contract often provides that the franchisor will establish certain standards for the facility and will make inspections to ensure that the standards are being maintained in order to protect the franchise name and reputation.

One area of franchises that causes a great deal of conflict is the territorial exclusivity of the franchise. Many franchise agreements, while they do define the territory allotted to a particular franchise, specifically state that the franchise is nonexclusive. The ramifications of nonexclusivity can be severe, because it allows the franchisor to establish additional franchises in the same territory as the existing franchisee. The following case illustrates this problem.

---

CASE 38.2

**BURGER KING CORP. v. WEAVER**

United States District Court, Southern District of Florida, 1992. 798 F.Supp. 684.

**BACKGROUND AND FACTS**   *C. R. Weaver purchased franchises from the Burger King Corporation (BKC) between 1976 and 1988 to operate two Burger King restaurants (restaurants #1666 and #6158) in the Great Falls, Montana, area and one in a nearby town. In 1989, a Burger King restaurant opened on the Malmstrom Air Force Base, which is situated on the outskirts of Great Falls. BKC had granted to the Army and Air Force Exchange Service (AAFES) the right to operate a restaurant on the base in accordance with a worldwide contract entered into between the AAFES and BKC in 1984. That agreement allowed the AAFES to unilaterally choose the sites or bases on which to place Burger King restaurants. The new franchise at Malmstrom caused profits to decline at Weaver's two Great Falls restaurants. Concluding that BKC had breached its franchise agreements, Weaver refused to pay BKC the customary rents, fees, and related charges. When BKC sued Weaver for breach of the franchise agreements, Weaver counterclaimed that BKC had, among other things, breached the covenant of good faith and fair dealing.*

*ARONOVITZ*, District Judge.

\* \* \* \*

The franchise agreements for restaurants #1666 and #6158 differ in their respective treatment of the franchisee's ''territorial rights.'' In particular, the franchise agreement for restaurant #1666 contains no language specifically directed at the territorial or geographical parameters of the agreement. That is, the agreement makes no specific mention of either party's ''territorial rights.'' \* \* \*

The franchise agreement for restaurant #6158, on the other hand, has language which appears to be specifically directed at addressing the respective ''territorial rights'' of the parties. Under the heading ''Franchise Grant: Term and Location,'' the agreement provides that ''[t]his franchise is for the specified location only and does not in any way grant or imply any area, market or territorial rights proprietary to franchisee.''

\* \* \* \*

While this Court acknowledges that the existence of a "territorial rights" clause which affirmatively grants to BKC the right to place a Burger King restaurant at any location would foreclose a cause of action based on the implied covenant, we do not believe that the two agreements in question contain such a clause. First, the "site specific" clauses contained in franchise agreement #1666, even taken together, hardly constitute a definitive declaration of the parties' respective "territorial rights." More significant, these clauses cannot be said to expressly authorize BKC to place a Burger King restaurant at any location it wishes.

Second, the "territorial rights" clause of franchise agreement #6158 * * * similarly cannot be said to affirmatively authorize the placement of a BKC franchise on any site. * * *

* * * *

* * * Taken to its logical extreme, BKC's construction of the franchise agreements would entitle it to set up a competing franchise next door to an existing franchise the day after the existing franchise had opened for business. If that were the plain and intended meaning of the "territorial rights" language contained in the two franchise agreements, this Court entertains serious doubts about whether a rational franchisee would ever enter into a franchise agreement with BKC.

**DECISION AND REMEDY**  *The court denied BKC's motion for summary judgment, holding that Weaver had stated a cause of action based on the implied covenant of good faith and fair dealing and that the case should therefore go to trial.*

---

**PRICE CONTROLS**  Franchises provide the franchisor with an outlet for the firm's goods and services. Depending on the nature of the business, the franchisor may require the franchisee to purchase certain supplies from the franchisor at an established price.[3] Of course, a franchisor cannot set the prices at which the franchisee will resell the goods, as this is a violation of state antitrust laws, federal antitrust laws, or both. A franchisor can suggest retail prices but cannot insist on them.

**BUSINESS ORGANIZATION AND QUALITY CONTROLS**  The business organization of the franchisee is of great concern to the franchisor. Depending on the terms of the franchise agreement, the franchisor may specify particular requirements for the form and capital structure of the business. The franchise agreement can provide that the franchisee must meet standards of operation relating to such aspects of the business as sales quotas, quality standards, or record keeping. Furthermore, a franchisor may wish to retain stringent control over the training of personnel involved in the operation and over administrative aspects of the business. Although the day-to-day operation of the franchise business is normally left up to the franchisee, the franchise agreement may provide for whatever amount of supervision and control is agreed on by the parties.

As a general rule, the validity of a provision permitting the franchisor to enforce certain quality standards is unquestioned. Because the franchisor has a legitimate interest in maintaining the quality of the product or service in order to protect its name and reputation, it can exercise greater control in this area than would otherwise be tolerated.

**TERMINATION OF THE FRANCHISE**  The duration of the franchise is a matter to be determined between the parties. Often, a franchise will start out for a short period, such as a year, so that the franchisee and the franchisor can determine whether they want to stay in business with each other. Usually the franchise agreement will specify that termination must be "for cause," such as death or disability of the franchisee, insolvency of the franchisee, breach of the franchise agreement, or failure to meet specified sales quotas. Most franchise contracts provide that notice of termination must be given. If no set time for termination is given, then a reasonable time with notice will be implied. A franchisee must be given reasonable time to wind up the business—that is, to do the

---

3.  Requiring a franchisee to purchase *exclusively* from the franchisor may violate federal antitrust laws. See Chapter 48.

accounting and return the copyright, trademark, or any other property of the franchisor.

Much franchise litigation has arisen over termination provisions. The termination provisions of contracts are generally more favorable to the franchisor. This means that the franchisee, who normally invests a substantial amount of time and money in the franchise operation to make it successful, may receive little or nothing for the business upon termination. The franchisor owns the trademark and hence the business.

It is in this area that the lack of statutory law and case law is felt most keenly by the franchisee. Automobile dealerships and gasoline stations subject to franchise contracts now have some statutory protection, however, under the Automobile Dealers' Franchise Act and the Petroleum Marketing Practices Act, respectively. In determining whether a franchisor has acted in good faith when terminating a franchise agreement, the courts need to balance the rights of both parties. The following case illustrates this point.

---

### CASE 38.3

**BECK OIL CO. v. TEXACO REFINING & MARKETING, INC.**

United States District Court, Central District of Illinois, 1993.
822 F.Supp. 1326.

**COMPANY PROFILE**  *Anthony Luchich discovered more oil beneath Spindletop Hill near Beaumont, Texas, in 1901, than was contained in the rest of the United States combined. To exploit the discovery, nearly two hundred oil companies swarmed over east Texas. Joseph ''Buckskin Joe'' Cullinan, a former Standard Oil executive, founded the Texas Company in 1902, bought up oil fields near Spindletop Hill, and began selling oil under the Texaco brand. Texas Company executives bought out Cullinan in 1916 and moved the company's base to New York. From there, the company expanded across the globe. With Standard Oil of California (now Chevron), the Texas Company formed Caltex in 1936 to market Saudi Arabian oil. At the same time, the Texas Company became the only U.S. oil company with gas stations in all fifty states. Renamed Texaco, Inc., in 1959, the company's U.S. resources began to dry up in the 1960s and 1970s, and it lost overseas supplies to the expropriations of foreign governments. In the early 1980s, to secure new sources of oil, Texaco acquired the Getty Oil Company. Getty had already made a deal with Pennzoil, however, and for interfering with that contract, Texaco was ordered to pay damages to Pennzoil. Texaco filed for bankruptcy and reorganized. As part of the reorganization and to fend off a later takeover attempt, Texaco upgraded its refinery operations to increase efficiency and produce cleaner fuels.*

**BACKGROUND AND FACTS**  *Texaco Refining & Marketing, Inc. (TRMI), a wholly owned subsidiary of Texaco, Inc., refines and markets motor fuels and other petroleum products for wholesale and retail distribution. After acquiring the Getty Oil Company, Texaco formed TRMI as part of Texaco's reorganization. The Beck Oil Company and four other firms each held three-year distribution franchises with TRMI, the franchisor. TRMI withdrew from the geographical areas in which the franchisees had been distributing TRMI petroleum products, closed its outdated Lawrenceville, Illinois, refinery, and terminated the franchise agreements with Beck and the others. The franchisees sued TRMI for terminating the franchise agreements. The question before the court was whether TRMI had acted in good faith and in the normal course of business, as required by the Petroleum Marketing Practices Act, when it withdrew from the plaintiffs' marketing area. Both TRMI (the defendant) and the franchisees (the plaintiffs) moved for summary judgment.*

*RICHARD MILLS,* District Judge:

\* \* \* \*

\* \* \* Defendant states that the decision to terminate was based on three factors: 1) the closing of Defendant's Lawrenceville, Illinois, refinery; 2) the inability of Defendant to economically supply the withdrawal area; and 3) the unreasonable and uneconomical Getty supply system in the withdrawal area. The Lawrenceville refinery was technologically outdated and by late 1984, the cost of finished gasoline produced there resulted in a $2.00 per barrel loss for each barrel of oil refined. In addition, Defendant did not have another refinery in the location with an efficient means of transporting Defendant's products to the withdrawal area.

The Petroleum Marketing Practices Act (PMPA) governs the termination of motor fuel product franchises. Under the PMPA, the following are grounds for termination of any franchise: \* \* \* a determination made by the franchisor in good faith and in the normal course of business to withdraw from the marketing of motor fuel through retail outlets in the relevant geographic market area in which the marketing premises are located, if—(i) such determination—(I) was made after the date such franchise was entered into or renewed, and (II) was based upon the occurrence of changes in relevant facts and circumstances after such date; (ii) the termination or nonrenewal is not for the purpose of converting the premises, which are the subject of the franchise, to operation by employees or agents of the franchisor for such franchisor's own account; \* \* \*

\* \* \* \*

In this case, after the Getty acquisition, Texaco reorganized and reevaluated its operations to determine their efficiency and profitability. The affidavits submitted by TRMI demonstrate concerns about uneconomical distribution methods in the area served by the Lawrenceville refinery. Accordingly, the Court must conclude that TRMI's decision to withdraw was made in good faith and was part of the normal decision making process once TRMI began examining its operations after the Getty acquisition.

**DECISION AND REMEDY**

*Holding that TRMI had not discriminated against, or acted arbitrarily toward, its franchisees, the district court granted summary judgment in favor of TRMI.*

**INTERNATIONAL CONSIDERATIONS**

**Franchise Termination Abroad** *Many countries have no specific laws governing franchising arrangements, which are governed by general contract law. Most countries require that franchise terminations be made in good faith and with reasonable notice. Japanese law characterizes franchises as ''continuous contracts'' that require good cause for termination or nonrenewal at the end of the franchise term.*

# TERMS AND CONCEPTS TO REVIEW

business trust 755
cooperative 756
corporation 750
entrepreneur 748
franchise 756
franchisee 756
franchisor 756

information return 749
joint stock company 755
joint venture 753
Keogh plan 749
limited liability company
(LLC) 756
limited partnership 749

partnership 749
S corporation 750
sole proprietorship 748
syndicate 755

# QUESTIONS AND CASE PROBLEMS

**38–1. Choice of Business Form.** Suppose that Subir, Brad, and Lori are college graduates, and Subir has come up with an idea for a new product that he believes could make the three of them very rich. His idea is to manufacture soft-drink dispensers for home use, and his goal is to market them to consumers throughout the Midwest. Subir's personal experience qualifies him to be both first-line supervisor and general manager of the new firm. Brad is a born salesperson. Lori has little interest in sales or management but would like to invest a large sum of money that she has inherited from her aunt. Discuss fully what factors Subir, Brad, and Lori should consider in deciding which form of business organization to adopt.

**38–2. Choice of Business Form.** In the situation described in Question 38–1, assume that Lori is willing to put her inherited money in the business but does not want any further liability should the soft-drink dispenser manufacturing business fail. Alternatively, the bank is willing to lend some capital at a 12 percent interest rate, but it will do so only if certain restrictions are placed on management decisions. The bank's plan is not satisfactory to Subir or Brad, and the two decide to bring Lori into the business. Under these circumstances, discuss which types of business organizations are best suited to meet Lori's needs.

**38–3. Business Forms and Liability.** The limited liability of corporate shareholders is one of the most important reasons that firms choose to organize as corporations rather than as partnerships or sole proprietorships. Limited liability means that if a corporation is not able to meet its obligations with corporate assets, creditors will not be allowed to look to the owners (stockholders) of the corporation to satisfy their claims. Assume that Subir and Brad (in Question 38–1) do not have a wealthy friend like Lori who wishes to go into business with them, and they therefore must borrow money to start their business. Subir and Brad decide to incorporate. What do you think a lender will ask them when they seek a loan? What effect does this have on the "advantage" of limited liability under incorporation?

**38–4. Business Forms and Liability.** Assume that Bateson Corp. is considering entering into two contracts—one with a joint stock company that distributes home products east of the Mississippi River and the other with a business trust formed by a number of sole proprietors who are sellers of home products on the West Coast. Both contracts involve large capital outlays for Bateson to supply each business with restaurant equipment. In both business organizations, at least two shareholders or beneficiaries are personally wealthy, but each business organization has limited financial resources. The owner-managers of Bateson are not familiar with either form of business organization. Because each form resembles a corporation, they are concerned with the possibility of liability in the event that either business organization breaches the contract by failing to make the deferred payments. Discuss fully Bateson's concern.

**38–5. Franchise Agreements.** Otmar has been interested in securing a particular high-quality ice cream franchise. The franchisor is willing to give him a franchise. A franchise agreement is made that calls for Otmar to sell the ice cream only at a specific location; to buy all the ice cream from the franchisor; to order and sell all the flavors produced by the franchisor; and to refrain from selling any ice cream stored for more than two weeks after delivery by the franchisor, as this ice cream decreases in quality after that period. After two months of operation, Otmar believes that he can increase his profits by moving the store to another part of the city. He also refuses to order even a limited quantity of the "fruit delight" flavor because of its higher cost, and he has sold ice cream that has been stored longer than two weeks without customer complaint. Otmar claims that the franchisor has no right to restrict him in these practices. Discuss his claims.

**38–6. Franchise Termination.** H. C. Blackwell Co. was a truck dealership owned by the Blackwell family. In 1961 they purchased a franchise from Kenworth Truck Co. to sell Kenworth trucks. The franchise agreement had been renewed several times. In November 1975 the Blackwells began negotiations with Kenworth to renew the recently expired franchise, and disagreements arose concerning the franchise. On February 4, 1976, Kenworth wrote to Blackwell that the franchise would be terminated in ninety days unless Blackwell met twelve specific demands made by Kenworth. In trying to meet these demands—which included increased sales, a better method of keeping business records, and capital improvements at its dealership—Blackwell spent approximately $90,000. By the end of the ninety-day period, however, the demands had not been met, so Kenworth terminated the franchise. Blackwell sued Kenworth for damages on the grounds that Kenworth had wrongfully terminated the franchise agreement and, in so doing, had violated the Automobile Dealers' Franchise Act. During the trial, Kenworth's own regional sales manager stated that the demands imposed by Kenworth upon Blackwell would have taken at least a year to meet. Has Kenworth wrongfully terminated the franchise under the Automobile Dealers' Franchise Act? Discuss fully. [*H. C. Blackwell Co. v. Kenworth Truck Co.,* 620 F.2d 104 (5th Cir. 1980)]

**38–7. Franchise Termination.** In 1953, Atlantic Richfield Co. (Arco) and Razumic signed a printed form titled a "Dealer Lease." The agreement referred to the parties as lessor and lessee. It authorized Razumic to operate an Arco service station and provided, among other things, for Arco's signs and trade name to be prominently displayed at the service station and for gasoline and other related products to be sold. The agreement detailed other aspects of the parties' business relationship, including Razumic's obligation to operate the service station in such a manner as to reflect favorably on Arco's goodwill.

These basic terms were in all renewal agreements made by the parties over the years. In 1973, Arco notified Razumic that the agreement was being terminated and gave him thirty days to vacate the premises. Razumic refused, and Arco filed suit to force termination of the agreement. Did the "Dealer Lease" constitute a franchise agreement? If so—in view of the fact that the Petroleum Marketing Practices Act had not yet been passed when this case was decided—on what grounds might the court hold that Arco could not terminate the franchise at will? Discuss. [*Atlantic Richfield Co. v. Razumic,* 480 Pa. 366, 390 A.2d 736 (1978)]

**38–8. Joint Ventures.** Gustave Peterson contacted his family doctor, Leland Reichelt, complaining of abdominal pain. The doctor recommended gallbladder surgery. Dr. George Fortier performed the surgery, and Reichelt assisted. It was Reichelt's normal practice to refer patients to Fortier for surgery, and each doctor charged the patient separately for his services. During the operation, a metal clip was inadvertently left inside Peterson's abdominal cavity. It eventually formed a stone, which later caused Peterson chest and gastric pain. Peterson repeatedly complained to Reichelt, who diagnosed the problem as being related to either a hernia or stress. Peterson finally sought the advice of another physician, who, upon performing surgery, discovered the metal clip. Peterson filed suit against both Reichelt and Fortier for malpractice under the theory that Fortier and Reichelt were engaged in a joint enterprise (joint venture). Discuss fully whether the two doctors were joint venturers. [*Peterson v. Fortier,* 406 N.W.2d 563 (Minn.App. 1987)]

**38–9. Good Faith in Franchising Relationships.** Ernst and Barbara Larese entered into a ten-year franchise agreement with Creamland Dairies, Inc., in 1974. The agreement provided that the franchisee "shall not assign, transfer or sublet this franchise, or any of [the] rights under this agreement, without the prior written consent of Area Franchisor [Creamland] and Baskin Robbins." The Lareses attempted to sell their franchise rights in February and August 1979, but Creamland refused to consent to the sale. The Lareses brought suit, alleging that Creamland had interfered with their contractual relations with the prospective buyers by unreasonably withholding its consent; they held that Creamland had a duty to act in good faith and in a commercially reasonable manner when a franchisee sought to transfer its rights under the franchise agreement. Creamland contended that the contract gave it an unqualified right to refuse to consent to proposed sales of the franchise rights. Which party prevailed? Explain. [*Larese v. Creamland Dairies, Inc.,* 767 F.2d 716 (10th Cir. 1985)]

**38–10. Franchise Termination.** AB&B, Inc., sold wines produced by Banfi Products, Inc., under a distributorship agreement. In 1986, AB&B experienced a se-

vere decline in the demand for one of Banfi's wines, Riunite, mostly because of a recall of that wine resulting from contamination problems in the fall of 1985. Because of decreasing sales, Banfi sent a letter to AB&B, which stated as follows: "You are aware that Banfi's corporate policy requires our distributors to maintain no less than a 60-day inventory of products. Not only are you out of stock on most items in our line, but our records indicate that the last activity on your account was a credit in January of 1986, and your last purchase was in April of 1985. Your lack of interest in and support of the Banfi line leaves us no alternative but to terminate our distributorship relationship with you, effective sixty (60) days from your receipt of this notice." In fact, AB&B held, on average, a ninety-six-day inventory of Banfi wines. In support of its allegation that AB&B showed a "lack of interest in and support of the Banfi line," Banfi had indicated that AB&B routinely failed to send a representative to Banfi's sales meetings. Yet there was no evidence that those meetings were mandatory, and AB&B always received notebooks from Banfi containing the information from those meetings. Although AB&B requested a meeting with Banfi to discuss these issues, Banfi terminated the franchise relationship without responding to AB&B's request. In AB&B's lawsuit against Banfi for wrongful termination of the franchise relationship, what should the court decide? Discuss. [*AB&B, Inc. v. Banfi Products, Inc.,* 71 Ohio App.3d 650, 594 N.E.2d 1151 (1991)]

**38–11. Joint Ventures.** Windy City Balloon Port, Ltd., operated a balloon launching facility near Barrington Hills, Illinois, offering public commercial sightseeing flights in hot-air and helium balloons owned by third parties. Windy City sold tickets for the balloon rides for $100 to $150 per person per ride. The pilot of the balloon would receive $60 to $70 directly from Windy City for each ticket sold but otherwise received no consideration from Windy City. Although Windy City provided refueling and repair facilities for the balloons and canceled balloon flights when the weather conditions were unsafe, Windy City had no control over the balloons after they departed from the balloon launch. On August 15, 1981, a hot-air balloon piloted by James Bickett departed from a launching site at Windy City. It was carrying five passengers—Kenneth Coleman, Jr., Terry Ritter, Brian Baker, William Keating, and Harry Evans. Shortly after takeoff, the balloon struck power lines and crashed to the ground, killing Bickett, Coleman, Ritter, Baker, and Keating. Evans survived, but sustained severe burns and injuries. In a lawsuit filed by representatives of the deceased passengers and others, one of the issues was whether Windy City and Bickett were involved in a joint venture. How did the court rule? Discuss fully. [*Coleman v. Charlesworth,* 157 Ill.2d 257, 623 N.E.2d 1366, 191 Ill.Dec. 480 (1993)]

# CHAPTER 39

# PARTNERSHIPS— NATURE, FORMATION, AND OPERATION

**W**hen two or more persons agree to do business as partners, they enter into a special relationship with one another. To an extent, their relationship is similar to an agency relationship, because each partner is deemed the agent of the other partners and of the partnership. The agency concepts discussed in Chapters 34 and 35 thus apply—specifically, the imputation of knowledge of, and responsibility for, acts done within the scope of the partnership relationship. In their relationship to one another, partners are also bound by the fiduciary ties that bind an agent and principal under agency law.

Partnership law is distinct from agency law in one significant way, however. A partnership is based on a voluntary contract between two or more competent persons who agree to place some or all of their money or other assets, labor, and skills in a business with the understanding that profits and losses will be shared. In a nonpartnership agency relationship, the agent usually does not have an ownership interest in the business, nor is he or she obligated to bear a portion of the ordinary business losses.

The Uniform Partnership Act (UPA) governs the operation of partnerships *in the absence of express agreement* and has done much to reduce controversies in the law relating to partnerships. Except for Louisiana, the UPA has been adopted in all of the states, as well as in the District of Columbia. The entire text of the UPA is presented in Appendix E at the end of this text. A revised version of the UPA, known as the Revised Uniform Partnership Act (RUPA), was formally adopted by the National Conference of Commissioners on Uniform State Laws in 1992 and has already been adopted in at least two states.[1] The RUPA significantly changes some of the rules governing partnership, as we will note in the discussion of partnership law in this chapter and in Chapter 40.

---

1. Montana and Wyoming. Texas has adopted a new partnership act that is similar in some ways to an earlier draft of the RUPA. Other states are considering adoption of the RUPA. Appendix F contains excerpts from the RUPA.

# DEFINITION OF PARTNERSHIP

Parties commonly find themselves in conflict over whether their business enterprise is a legal partnership, especially in the absence of a formal, written partnership agreement. Under the UPA, a *partnership* is defined as ''an association of two or more persons to carry on as co-owners a business for profit'' [UPA 6(1)]. In resolving disputes over whether partnership status exists, courts will usually look for the following three essential elements of partnership implicit in this definition:

1. A sharing of profits or losses.
2. A joint ownership of the business.
3. An equal right in the management of the business.

In the event that the evidence is insufficient to establish all three factors, the UPA provides a set of guidelines to be used. For example, the existence of a partnership will be inferred if profits and losses from a business are shared. No such inference is made, however, if the profits were received as payment of the following:

1. A debt by installments or interest on a loan.
2. Wages of an employee.
3. Rent to a landlord.
4. An annuity to a widow or representative of a deceased partner.
5. A sale of goodwill of a business or property [UPA 7(4)].

To illustrate: Suppose that a debtor owes a creditor $5,000 on an unsecured debt. To repay the debt, the debtor agrees to pay (and the creditor, to accept) 10 percent of the debtor's monthly business profits until the loan with interest has been paid. Although the creditor is sharing profits from the business, the debtor and creditor are not presumed to be partners.

Joint ownership of property, obviously, does not in and of itself create a partnership. Therefore, the fact that, say, MacPherson and Bunker own real property as joint tenants or as tenants in common (a form of joint ownership) does not establish a partnership. In fact, the sharing of gross returns and even profits from such ownership is usually not enough to create a partnership [UPA 7(2), (3)]. Thus, if MacPherson and Bunker jointly owned a piece of rural property and leased the land to a farmer, the sharing of the profits from the farming operation by the farmer in lieu of set rental payments would ordinarily not make MacPherson, Bunker, and the farmer partners.

# THE NATURE OF PARTNERSHIPS

A partnership is sometimes called a *firm* or a *company,* terms that connote an entity separate and apart from its aggregate members. Sometimes the law of partnership recognizes the independent entity for some purposes but may treat the partnership as an aggregate of individual partners for other purposes. At common law, a partnership was never treated as a separate legal entity. Thus, a common law suit could never be brought by or against the firm in its own name; each individual partner had to sue or be sued.

## PARTNERSHIP AS AN ENTITY

Many states today provide specifically that the partnership can be treated as an entity for certain purposes. These usually include the capacity to sue or be sued, to collect judgments, and to have all accounting procedures in the name of the partnership. In addition, the UPA recognizes that partnership property may be held in the name of the partnership rather than in the names of the individual partners. Finally, federal procedural laws frequently permit the partnership to be treated as an entity in such matters as lawsuits in federal courts, bankruptcy proceedings, and the filing of informational federal tax returns. These matters will be discussed here in some detail.

**LEGAL CAPACITY**    States vary on how a partnership is viewed as a party in a legal suit. Some permit a partnership to sue and be sued in the firm name; others allow a partnership to be sued as an entity but do not allow the partnership, as a plaintiff, to sue others in its firm name (that is, the partnership must use the names of the individual partners). Federal courts recognize the partnership as an entity that can sue or be sued when a federal question is involved. Otherwise, federal courts follow the practice adopted by the state in which the federal court is located.

**JUDGMENTS**   Partnership liability is first paid out of partnership assets when a judgment is rendered *against the firm name.* In a general partnership, the personal assets of the individual members are subject to liability if the partnership's assets are inadequate. Even in limited partnerships, at least one of the partners—the general partner—subjects his or her personal assets to liability for the partnership's obligations. Good legal practice dictates that when state law permits a firm to be sued, the individual partners should also be sued. This ensures that a wide range of assets will be available for paying the judgment.

**MARSHALING ASSETS**   The general rule is that a judgment creditor of a partnership (a creditor in whose favor a money judgment has been entered by a court) can execute the judgment against the partners either jointly or severally (joint and several liability will be discussed later in this chapter). In some states, however, the judgment creditor must exhaust the remedies against partnership property before proceeding to execute against the individual property of the partners. This is referred to as the doctrine of **marshaling assets.** Marshaling assets is a common law equitable doctrine; it is not statutory.

In marshaling assets, assets are arranged, or ranked, in a certain order toward the payment of debts outstanding. In some situations, there are two classes of assets, and some creditors can enforce their claims against both whereas others can enforce their claims against only one. When this occurs, the creditors of the former class are compelled to exhaust the assets against which they alone have a claim before they can have recourse to the other assets. This provides for the settlement of as many claims as possible.

As applied to a partnership, the doctrine of marshaling assets requires that partnership creditors have first priority to the partnership's assets and that personal creditors of the individual partners have first priority to the individual assets of each partner. When the partnership's assets are insufficient to satisfy a partnership creditor, that creditor does not have access to the assets of any individual

partner until the personal creditors of that partner have been satisfied from those assets. This doctrine does not apply to partnerships that are in liquidation proceedings under Chapter 7 of the Bankruptcy Code (see Chapter 33).

**BANKRUPTCY**   In federal court, an adjudication of bankruptcy *in the firm name* applies only to the partnership entity. It does not constitute personal bankruptcy for the partners. Similarly, the personal bankruptcy of an individual partner does not bring the partnership entity or its assets into bankruptcy.

The doctrine of marshaling assets is modified when a partnership is granted an order of relief in bankruptcy. In such situations, if partnership assets are insufficient to cover debts owed to partnership creditors, each general partner becomes *personally* liable to the bankruptcy trustee for the amount of the deficiency.

**CONVEYANCE OF PROPERTY**   The title to real or personal property can be held in the partnership's firm name. In other words, the partnership as an entity can own property apart from that owned by its individual members [UPA 8(3)]. Thus, the property held in the firm name can be conveyed (transferred) without each individual partner's joining in the transaction.

At common law, title to real estate could not be held in a partnership's firm name. Each partner had to join in all conveyances (transfers of rights in the real estate), because each partner was regarded as a co-owner (known in legal terminology as a *tenant in partnership*).[2] Tenancy in partnership will be discussed later in this chapter. Although the modern rule of partnership property ownership disregards the need for aggregate action (action by all the partners jointly) to convey property, there are some practical difficulties to consider.

Most states do not require that public records keep lists of the members of a partnership. Hence,

---

2.   The UPA retained this concept in UPA 25(1). Although property may be held in the name of the partnership, as tenants in partnership, partners are still regarded as co-owners. The RUPA, however, discards the concept of tenancy in partnership, stating simply that "[a] partner is not a co-owner of partnership property" [RUPA 501]. Further, "[p]roperty transferred to or otherwise acquired by a partnership is property of the partnership and not of the partners individually" [RUPA 203].

in determining the validity of a conveyance in a partnership's name, it may be impossible to tell whether the person executing the deed is actually a partner and has authority to convey. Some states, however, have passed laws requiring firms to file a statement of partnership. This list names members of the firm authorized to execute conveyances on behalf of the firm.

## AGGREGATE THEORY OF PARTNERSHIP

When the partnership is not regarded as a separate legal entity, it is treated as an *aggregate* of the individual partners. For example, for federal income tax purposes, a partnership is not a tax-paying entity. Recall from Chapter 38 that the income or losses incurred by a partnership are "passed through" the partnership framework and attributed to the partners on their individual tax returns. The partnership as an entity has no tax liability. It is an entity only for the filing of an informational return with the Internal Revenue Service, indicating the profit and loss that each partner will report on his or her individual tax return.

## SECTION 3

# PARTNERSHIP FORMATION

A partnership is a voluntary association of individuals. A partnership is generally based on an agreement among the parties that reflects their intention to create a partnership, contribute capital, share profits and losses, and participate in management. The partnership relationship involves a high degree of trust and reliance. As mentioned previously, each partner is an agent for the other partners and stands in a fiduciary relationship to the other partners and the partnership.

## FORMALITIES

As a general rule, agreements to form a partnership can be *oral, written,* or *implied by conduct.* Some partnership agreements, however, must be in writing to be legally enforceable within the Statute of Frauds (see Chapter 16 for details). For example, a partnership agreement that, by its terms, is to continue for more than one year or a partnership agreement that authorizes the partners to deal in real-property transfers must be evidenced by a suf-

ficient writing. Generally, a partnership agreement can include virtually any terms that the partners wish, unless they are illegal or contrary to public policy. A sample partnership agreement is shown in Exhibit 39–1.[3]

Practically speaking, it is better if the provisions of any partnership agreement are in writing. The terms of an oral agreement are difficult to prove, because a court must evaluate oral testimony given by persons with an interest in the eventual decision. In addition, in the course of drafting a written agreement, the partners may see potential problems that they would not have otherwise seen.

For instance, assume that Tang and Fred plan to enter into a partnership agreement to sell tires. Among the provisions to be included is that Tang is to provide two-thirds of the capital to start up the business and is to receive two-thirds of the profits in return. The agreement is made orally. Tang now sues Fred because Fred claims that one-half of the profits should be his. Without a writing, Tang may have a hard time overcoming the presumption that he is entitled to only one-half of the profits of a two-person partnership.[4] A partnership agreement, called **articles of partnership,** usually specifies each partner's share of the profits and is binding regardless of how uneven the distribution appears to be.

## DURATION OF THE PARTNERSHIP

The partnership agreement can specify the duration of the partnership in terms of a date or the completion of a particular project. This is called a *partnership for a term.* A dissolution without the consent of all the partners prior to the expiration of the partnership term constitutes a breach of the agreement, and the partner responsible for the breach can be liable for any losses resulting from it.

If no fixed duration is specified, the partnership is a *partnership at will.* Any partner can dissolve

---

3. The RUPA provides for the voluntary filing of a partnership statement, containing such information as the agency authority of the partners, with the secretary of state. The statement must be executed by at least two partners, a copy must be sent to all partners, and a certified copy must be filed in the office for recording transfers of real property (in most states, in the county in which the property is located).

4. The law assumes that members of a partnership share profits equally and losses in the same ratio as profits unless a partnership agreement provides otherwise [UPA 18(a)].

■ **Exhibit 39–1 Sample Partnership Agreement**

# PARTNERSHIP AGREEMENT

This agreement, made and entered into as of the _____, by and among _____ _____ (hereinafter collectively sometimes referred to as "Partners").

## WITNESSETH:

Whereas, the Parties hereto desire to form a General Partnership (hereinafter referred to as the "Partnership"), for the term and upon the conditions hereinafter set forth;

Now, therefore, in consideration of the mutual covenants hereinafter contained, it is agreed by and among the Parties hereto as follows:

### Article I
### BASIC STRUCTURE

**Form.** The Parties hereby form a General Partnership pursuant to the Laws of _____ _____.

**Name.** The business of the Partnership shall be conducted under the name of _____ _____.

**Place of Business.** The principal office and place of business of the Partnership shall be located at _____, or such other place as the Partners may from time to time designate.

**Term.** The Partnership shall commence on _____, and shall continue for _____years, unless earlier terminated in the following manner: (a) By the completion of the purpose intended, or (b) Pursuant to this Agreement, or (c) By applicable _____law, or (d) By death, insanity, bankruptcy, retirement, withdrawal, resignation, expulsion, or disability of all of the then Partners.

**Purpose—General.** The purpose for which the Partnership is organized is _____

### Article II
### FINANCIAL ARRANGEMENTS

Each Partner has contributed to the initial capital of the Partnership property in the amount and form indicated on Schedule A attached hereto and made a part hereof. Capital contributions to the Partnership shall not earn interest. An individual capital account shall be maintained for each Partner. If at any time during the existence of the Partnership it shall become necessary to increase the capital with which the said Partnership is doing business, then (upon the vote of the Managing Partner(s)): each party to this Agreement shall contribute to the capital of this Partnership within _ days notice of such need in an amount according to his then Percentage Share of Capital as called for by the Managing Partner(s).

The Percentage Share of Profits and Capital of each Partner shall be (unless otherwise modified by the terms of this Agreement) as follows:

| Names | Initial Percentage Share of Profits and Capital |
|---|---|
| | |

No interest shall be paid on any contribution to the capital of the Partnership. No Partner shall have the right to demand the return of his capital contributions except as herein provided. Except as herein provided, the individual Partners shall have no right to any priority over each other as to the return of capital contributions except as herein provided.

Distributions to the Partners of net operating profits of the Partnership, as hereinafter defined, shall be made at _____. Such distributions shall be made to the Partners simultaneously.

For the purpose of this Agreement, net operating profit for any accounting period shall mean the gross receipts of the Partnership for such period, less the sum of all cash expenses of operation of the Partnership, and such sums as may be necessary to establish a reserve for operating expenses. In determining net operating profit, deductions for depreciation, amortization, or other similar charges not requiring actual current expenditures of cash shall *not* be taken into account in accordance with generally accepted accounting principles.

■ **Exhibit 39–1 Sample Partnership Agreement (Continued)**

No Partner shall be entitled to receive any compensation from the Partnership, nor shall any Partner receive any drawing account from the Partnership.

### Article III
### MANAGEMENT

The Managing Partner(s) shall be _____.

The Managing Partner(s) shall have the right to vote as to the management and conduct of the business of the Partnership as follows:

| Names | Vote |
|-------|------|

### Article IV
### DISSOLUTION

˙In the event that the Partnership shall hereafter be dissolved for any reason whatsoever, a full and general account of its assets, liabilities and transactions shall at once be taken. Such assets may be sold and turned into cash as soon as possible and all debts and other amounts due the Partnership collected. The proceeds thereof shall thereupon be applied as follows:

(a) To discharge the debts and liabilities of the Partnership and the expenses of liquidation.

(b) To pay each Partner or his legal representative any unpaid salary, drawing account, interest or profits to which he shall then be entitled and in addition, to repay to any Partner his capital contributions in excess of his original capital contribution.

(c) To divide the surplus, if any, among the Partners or their representatives as follows: (1) First (to the extent of each Partner's then capital account) in proportion to their then capital accounts. (2) Then according to each Partner's then Percentage Share of [*Capital/Income*].

No Partner shall have the right to demand and receive property in kind for his distribution.

### Article V
### MISCELLANEOUS

The Partnership's fiscal year shall commence on January 1st of each year and shall end on December 31st of each year. Full and accurate books of account shall be kept at such place as the Managing Partner(s) may from time to time designate, showing the condition of the business and finances of the Partnership; and each Partner shall have access to such books of account and shall be entitled to examine them at any time during ordinary business hours. At the end of each year, the Managing Partner(s) shall cause the Partnership's accountant to prepare a balance sheet setting forth the financial position of the Partnership as of the end of that year and a statement of operations (income and expenses) for that year. A copy of the balance sheet and statement of operations shall be delivered to each Partner as soon as it is available.

Each Partner shall be deemed to have waived all objections to any transaction or other facts about the operation of the Partnership disclosed in such balance sheet and/or statement of operations unless he shall have notified the Managing Partner(s) in writing of his objectives within thirty (30) days of the date on which such statement is mailed.

The Partnership shall maintain a bank account or bank accounts in the Partnership's name in a national or state bank in the State of _____. Checks and drafts shall be drawn on the Partnership's bank account for Partnership purposes only and shall be signed by the Managing Partner(s) or their designated agent.

Any controversy or claim arising out of or relating to this Agreement shall only be settled by arbitration in accordance with the rules of the American Arbitration Association, one Arbitrator, and shall be enforceable in any court having competent jurisdiction.

| Witnesses | Partners |
|-----------|----------|
| _____ | _____ |
| _____ | _____ |

Dated: _____

this type of partnership at any time without violating the agreement and without incurring liability for losses to other partners that result from the termination.

## CAPACITY

Any person having the capacity to enter a contract can become a partner. A partnership contract entered into with a minor as a partner is voidable and can be disaffirmed by the minor (see Chapter 14 for details). Lack of legal capacity due to insanity at the time of the agreement likewise allows the purported partner either to avoid the agreement or to enforce it. If a partner is adjudicated mentally incompetent during the course of the partnership, the partnership is not automatically dissolved, but dissolution can be decreed by a court upon petition.

## THE CORPORATION AS PARTNER

General partners are personally liable for the debts incurred by the partnership. But if one of the general partners is a corporation, then what does personal liability mean? Basically, the capacity of corporations to contract is a question of corporation law. The Revised Model Business Corporation Act (see Appendix F) allows corporations generally to make contracts and incur liabilities. The UPA specifically permits a corporation to be a partner. By definition, ''a partnership is an association of two or more persons,'' and the UPA defines a person as including corporations [UPA 2].

Many states restrict the ability of corporations to become partners, though such restrictions have become less common over the years. Many decisions in jurisdictions that do not permit corporate partners nevertheless validate the arrangements by characterizing them as joint ventures rather than as partnerships.

## PARTNERSHIP BY ESTOPPEL

Parties who are not partners can hold themselves out as partners and make representations that third persons rely on in dealing with the alleged partners. In such a situation, a court may conclude that a **partnership by estoppel** exists, in which case liability is imposed on the alleged partner or partners (although partnership *rights* are not conferred on these persons).

There are two aspects of such liability. The person representing himself or herself to be a partner in an actual or alleged partnership is liable to any third person who extends credit in good faith reliance on such representations. Similarly, a person who expressly or impliedly *consents* to such misrepresentation of an alleged partnership relationship is also liable to third persons who extend credit in good faith reliance [UPA 16].

For example, Moreno owns a small shop. Knowing that the Midland Bank will not make a loan on his credit alone, Moreno represents that Lukas, a financially secure businessperson, is a partner in Moreno's business. Lukas knows of Moreno's misrepresentation but fails to correct the bank's information. Midland Bank, relying on the strength of Lukas's reputation and credit, extends a loan to Moreno. Moreno will be liable to the bank for the loan repayment. In many states, Lukas would also be held liable to the bank in such a loan transaction. Lukas has impliedly consented to the misrepresentation and will normally be estopped from denying that she is a partner of Moreno. She will be regarded as if she were in fact a partner in Moreno's business to the extent that this loan is concerned.

When a real partnership exists and a partner represents that a nonpartner is a member of the firm, the nonpartner is regarded as an agent whose acts are binding on the partner (but normally not on the partnership). For example, Middle Earth Movers has three partners—Jansen, Mathews, and Harran. Mathews represents to the business community that Tully is also a partner. If Tully negotiates a contract in the name of Middle Earth Movers, the contract will be binding on Mathews but normally not on Jansen and Harran (unless, of course, Jansen and Harran knew about, and consented to, Mathews's representation about Tully). Again, partnership by estoppel requires that a third person reasonably and detrimentally rely on the representation that a person was part of the partnership.

## SECTION 4

# PARTNERSHIP OPERATION

The rights and duties of partners are governed largely by the specific terms of their partnership agreement. In the absence of provisions to the contrary in the partnership agreement, the law imposes the rights and duties discussed in this chapter. The character and nature of the partnership business generally influence the application of these rights and duties.

## RIGHTS AMONG PARTNERS

The rights held by partners in a partnership relate to the following areas: management, interest in the partnership, compensation, inspection of books, accounting, and property rights.

**MANAGEMENT**   "All partners have equal rights in the management and conduct of partnership business" [UPA 18(e)]. Management rights belong to all partners in a general partnership.[5] Unless the partners agree otherwise, each partner has one vote in management matters *regardless of the proportional size of his or her interest in the firm.* Often, in a large partnership, partners will agree to delegate daily management responsibilities to a management committee made up of one or more of the partners.

The majority rule controls decisions in ordinary matters connected with partnership business, unless otherwise specified in the agreement. Unanimous consent of the partners is required, however, to bind the firm in any of the following actions, which significantly affect the nature of the partnership:

1.  To alter the essential nature of the firm's business as expressed in the partnership agreement or to alter the capital structure of the partnership.
2.  To admit new partners or to enter a wholly new business [UPA 18(g), (h)].
3.  To assign partnership property into a trust for the benefit of creditors.
4.  To dispose of the partnership's goodwill.
5.  To confess judgment against the partnership or submit partnership claims to arbitration. (A **confession of judgment** is the act of a debtor in permitting a judgment to be entered against him or her by a creditor, for an agreed sum, without the institution of legal proceedings.)

6.  To undertake any act that would make further conduct of partnership business impossible [UPA 9(3), various subsections].
7.  To amend the articles of the partnership agreement.

**INTEREST IN THE PARTNERSHIP**   Each partner is entitled to the proportion of business profits and losses that is designated in the partnership agreement. If the agreement does not apportion profits or losses, the UPA provides that profits are to be shared equally and losses are to be shared in the same ratio as profits [UPA 18(a)].

**COMPENSATION**   Devoting time, skill, and energy to partnership business is a partner's duty and generally not a compensable service. Partners can, of course, agree otherwise. For example, the managing partner of a law firm often receives a salary in addition to his or her share of profits for performing special administrative duties in office and personnel management. UPA 18(f) provides that on the death of a partner, a surviving partner is entitled to compensation for services in winding up partnership affairs (and reimbursement for expenses incurred in the process) above and apart from his or her share in the partnership profits.

**INSPECTION OF BOOKS**   Partnership books and records must be kept accessible to all partners. Each partner has the right to receive (and the corresponding duty to produce) full and complete information concerning the conduct of all aspects of partnership business [UPA 20]. Each firm retains books in which to record and secure such information. Partners contribute the information, and a bookkeeper typically has the duty to preserve it. The books must be kept at the firm's principal business office unless the partners agree otherwise [UPA 19]. Every partner, whether active or inactive, is entitled to inspect all books and records upon demand and can make copies of the materials. The personal representative of a deceased partner's estate has the same right of access to partnership books and records that the decedent would have had.

**ACCOUNTING**   An accounting of partnership assets or profits is done to determine the value of each partner's proportionate share in the partnership. An accounting can be called for voluntarily, or it can be compelled by the order of a court in

---

5.   In limited partnerships, limited partners may not generally participate in management without affecting their limited liability status. See Chapter 40.

equity.[6] Formal accounting occurs by right in connection with dissolution proceedings, but under UPA 22, a partner also has the right to a formal accounting in the following situations:

1.   When the partnership agreement provides for a formal accounting.

---

6.   The principal remedy of a partner against co-partners is an equity suit for dissolution, an accounting, or both. With minor exceptions, a partner cannot maintain an action against other firm members for damages until partnership affairs are settled and an accounting is done. This rule is necessary because legal disputes among partners invariably involve conflicting claims to shares in the partnership. Logically, the value of each partner's share must first be determined by an accounting.

2.   When a partner is wrongfully excluded from the business, from access to the books, or from both.

3.   When any partner is withholding profits or benefits belonging to the partnership in breach of the fiduciary duty.

4.   When circumstances "render it just and reasonable."

In the following case, two partners petitioned the court for a formal accounting, alleging that the managing partners of the partnership had misappropriated partnership assets.

---

| CASE 39.1 |
| --- |

**LAWSON v. ROGERS**
Supreme Court of South
Carolina, 1993.
435 S.E.2d 853.

**BACKGROUND AND FACTS**   *In 1981, Mandeville Rogers, Walter Lawson, and Hugh Leatherman formed a partnership called Howard Johnson's Riverfront Enterprises for the purpose of purchasing and operating a hotel. Under the partnership agreement, each partner would share equally in the profits and losses of the business, and although each partner had an equal vote, Leatherman and Rogers were the managing partners. The following year, Lawson formally conveyed half of his partnership interest to C. Weston Houck. In 1989, Rogers and Leatherman instructed the hotel's general manager, Alan Harrison, to collect the hotel's cash revenues (which included cash collected from the hotel's vending and arcade machines, VCR rental fees, telephone commissions, parking fees, and so on) and divide the cash equally among Harrison, Rogers, and Leatherman. A "slush" fund was also set up with insurance proceeds from a damaged hotel vehicle, compensation for a damaged hotel room, and a hotel telephone system refund. With Rogers's permission, Harrison spent the slush fund on a family vacation. Like the cash fund, the slush fund was not reflected in the partnership records. In 1989, Rogers and Leatherman spent over $46,000 of partnership funds to pay for repairs to the hotel after Hurricane Hugo. Few of these expenses were documented. Lawson and Houck brought an action for an accounting, alleging that Rogers and Leatherman had misappropriated partnership assets. A formal accounting of the partnership assets was conducted. A court-appointed accountant estimated the cash and slush funds to total $39,278.87. The trial court rejected that estimate as too speculative and also concluded that Harrison's one-third of the cash revenues constituted authorized compensation. In all, the partners were ordered by the trial court to return only $19,500 to the partnership. Houck and Lawson appealed to the Supreme Court of South Carolina.*

*PER CURIAM* [by the whole court]:
\* \* \* \*

\* \*  \* It is one of the ordinary duties of partners to keep true and correct books showing the firm accounts. In the absence of an agreement on the subject, the duty of keeping such accounts rests equally on each partner; but if one of the partners is the managing partner, the duty to keep books is on him. A partner's right in the partnership property carries with it a right to an accounting.

\* \* \* \*

Although the managing partners, Rogers and Leatherman, may have expended some of their own money in the management of the partnership property and were entitled to reimbursement for this expense, we agree with the trial court that they showed no justification for the cash disbursements they received.\* \* \*

Furthermore, we disagree with the trial court that the monies retained by Harrison were a proper part of his compensation. To characterize this cash-splitting scheme as merely part of Harrison's compensation is to ignore the scheme as a whole. This ''cash'' fund did not consist merely of the vending machine commissions but virtually all of the cash proceeds collected at the hotel which could remain unrecorded without detection. Leatherman and Rogers agreed to give Harrison one-third of this sum even though they had no idea how much money was involved and gave him not just the profits from the machines but all the proceeds collected from these machines. Meanwhile, the partnership was paying for all the soft drinks and food items for the machines. Furthermore, they did not account for this compensation in the partnership books nor did they inform their co-partners of this arrangement. \* \* \*

Likewise, Leatherman and Rogers failed to account for the cash disbursements made after Hurricane Hugo. Although desperate times may call for desperate measures, managing partners must still account for what has been done. \* \* \* [W]e have accepted all expenses reflected by any legible documentation during this period. Therefore, we find an additional $7,079.82 as properly accounted for by Rogers and Leatherman. Nevertheless, there remains $31,950.18 of the $46,030.00 cash disbursed during the post-Hurricane period for which there has not been a proper accounting. \* \* \* Therefore, the total amount of the judgment against Rogers and Leatherman should be $71,229.05.

*The Supreme Court of South Carolina held that the managing partners were liable for the full amount appropriated by them and the hotel manager through cash disbursements, as well as for the amount of posthurricane cash disbursements for which they failed to account.*

**DECISION AND REMEDY**

---

**PROPERTY RIGHTS**  A partner has the following three basic property rights:

1. An interest in the partnership.
2. A right in specific partnership property.
3. A right to participate in the management of the partnership, as previously discussed [UPA 24].

There is an important legal distinction between a partner's rights in specific property belonging to the firm to be used for business purposes and a partner's right to share in the firm's earned profits to the extent of his or her interest in the firm. A partner is co-owner with his or her partners of specific partnership property, holding the property as a tenant in partnership. A specific asset may constitute partnership property even when title to it is in an individual partner's name.

The rights of creditors in regard to partnerships were discussed earlier in this chapter. A judgment creditor of an individual partner has no right to execute or attach specific partnership property, but he or she can obtain the partner's share of profits. A creditor of the firm can levy directly upon partnership property.

*Partner's Interest in the Firm.*  A partner's interest in the firm is a personal asset consisting of a proportionate share of the profits earned [UPA 26] and a return of capital on the partnership's termination. A partner's interest is susceptible to assignment or to a judgment creditor's lien. Judgment creditors can attach a partner's interest by petitioning the court that entered the judgment to grant the creditors a **charging order.** This order entitles the creditors to the profits of the partner and to any assets available to the partner upon dissolution [UPA 28]. Neither an assignment nor a court's charging order entitling a creditor to receive a share of the partner's money will cause dissolution of the firm [UPA 27].

*Partnership Property.* UPA 8(1) provides that "all property originally brought into the partnership's stock or subsequently acquired, by purchase or otherwise, *on account of the partnership,* is partnership property" (emphasis added). Indications that an asset was acquired with the intention that it be a partnership asset is the heart of the phrase *on account of the partnership.* Thus, the more closely an asset is associated with the business operations of the partnership, the more likely it is to be a partnership asset.[7] Moreover, when such an asset is purchased with partnership funds, it will belong to the partnership unless a contrary intention is shown. If, for example, a piece of property is purchased with partnership funds, it is presumed

---

7. Under the RUPA, property that is not acquired in the name of the partnership is nonetheless partnership property if the instrument transferring title refers to (1) the person taking title as a partner or (2) the existence of the partnership [RUPA 204(a)(2)]. If neither of these occurs, the property is still presumed to be partnership property if it is acquired with partnership funds [RUPA 204(c)]. If none of the above occurs, the property is presumed to be the property of individual partners, even if it is used in the partnership business [RUPA 204(d)].

to be partnership property even if title is taken in the name of one of the partners.

Partners are *tenants in partnership* of all firm property [UPA 25(1)]. Tenancy in partnership has several important effects. If a partner dies, the surviving partners, not the heirs of the deceased partner, have the right of survivorship to the specific property. Although surviving partners are entitled to possession, they have a duty to account to the decedent's estate for the *value* of the deceased partner's interest in that property [UPA 25(2)(d), (e)].

A partner has no right to sell, assign, or in any way deal with a particular item of partnership property other than for partnership purposes [UPA 25(2)(a), (b)]. Nor is a partner's personal credit related to partnership property; his or her creditors cannot use partnership property to satisfy the personal debts of the partner. Partnership property is available only to satisfy partnership debts, to enhance the firm's credit, or to achieve other business purposes.

Every partner is a co-owner with all other partners of specific partnership property, such as office equipment, office supplies, and vehicles. Each partner has equal rights to possess partnership property for business purposes or in satisfaction of firm debts, but not for any other purpose without the consent of all the other partners.

The following case deals with an attempt by a deceased partner's widow to claim, as her husband's heir, an interest in partnership property.

---

CASE 39.2

**CATES v. INTERNATIONAL TELEPHONE AND TELEGRAPH CORP.**

United States Court of Appeals, Fifth Circuit, 1985. 756 F.2d 1161.

**COMPANY PROFILE** *Sosthenes Behn founded the International Telephone and Telegraph Corporation (ITT) in 1920 to manage telephone companies in Cuba and Puerto Rico. By 1925, Behn had bought three small Spanish telephone companies to form Compañia Telefònica Nacional de España. From the 1920s through the 1970s, ITT bought and sold a variety of companies, including Societatea Anonima Romana de Telefoane (a Romanian telephone company), United River Plate Telephone of Buenos Aires, Avis, Inc., Levitt & Sons, Inc., the Canteen Corporation, and telephone companies in Uruguay, Chile, and Brazil. To improve its earnings, in the 1980s ITT sold part or all of more than one hundred companies, including its remaining telephone businesses, and slashed its work force by more than 60 percent. Today, ITT is a diversified conglomerate that operates in eight industries, including publishing (ITT World Directories, Inc.), forest products (ITT Rayonier, Inc.), finance (ITT Financial Corporation), hotel operations (ITT Sheraton Corporation), and insurance (ITT Hartford Insurance Company). ITT Hartford suffered huge losses in Hurricane Andrew (1992), the World Trade Center bombing (1993), and other disasters, but subsequently improved its financial position through* *its life insurance operations, and currently accounts for nearly 40 percent of ITT's profits. ITT Hartford is one of the oldest and largest insurance companies in the United States.*

**BACKGROUND AND FACTS**  *James Cates and three other persons formed two partnerships, SanJac International (SJI) and SanJac Association (SJA). The partnerships provided group life, health, and accident insurance to small-business employers who could not obtain the lower rates charged to bigger businesses. To facilitate their program, the partnerships contracted with insurance providers, including the defendant firms, ITT Life Insurance Company and Lloyds of London. The partnerships were later dissolved. In the process of winding up the affairs of the partnerships, Cates filed a lawsuit against ITT Life and Lloyds of London for—among other things—failure to pay claims promptly and entering into contracts with the fraudulent intent not to perform them. The trial court dismissed the suit and Cates appealed. Before the appellate court heard the parties' oral arguments, Cates died. Cates's wife intervened in the suit, claiming that as Cates's heir, she could pursue the action on behalf of the partnership.*

*GARWOOD,* Circuit Judge:
\* \* \* \*
\* \* \* [T]he widow, heirs, legatees, or personal representatives of a deceased partner have neither any interest in or right to possess specific partnership property nor any right to the management or administration of partnership affairs, all such interests and rights vesting in the remaining partner or partners. Accordingly, even if any or all of the \* \* \* contentions of Cates are well taken, a point we do not decide, nevertheless, his widow \* \* \*, Mrs. Cates, would not, merely by reason of any or all such matters, be able to maintain suit on the partnership causes of action.

Mrs. Cates, however, urges that the situation is otherwise because, although neither partnership had terminated, "the partnerships were not only in dissolution, but . . . Cates took charge of the winding-up process and thus had the right to institute suits or take other steps to complete the winding-up process." \* \* \* She contends that where a partnership is in dissolution and the partner conducting the winding-up process dies, that the right to complete the winding up passes to the deceased partner's personal representative. That is true, however, *only* with respect to the death of the *last* surviving partner. At his death, Cates was not the last surviving partner in either SJA or SJI. [Under the Texas Uniform Partnership Act] section 25(2)(d) the rights of a deceased partner to specific partnership property vest "in the surviving partner" and *not* in the deceased partner's personal representative, except only "where the deceased was the last surviving partner." And, section 37 provides that "the legal representative of the last surviving partner, not bankrupt, has the right to wind up the partnership affairs."

**DECISION AND REMEDY**

*The court ruled that Mrs. Cates could not bring an action on behalf of the partnership solely because she was the heir of one of the partners. Partnership property rights pass to the partnership's surviving partners and not to the heirs of a deceased partner. The court remanded the case, however, for a determination as to whether there were other grounds on which she could bring the suit.*

## DUTIES AND POWERS OF PARTNERS

The duties and powers of partners consist of a fiduciary duty of each partner to the others and general agency powers.

**FIDUCIARY DUTIES**    Partners stand in a fiduciary relationship to one another just as principals and agents do (see Chapter 34). It is a relationship of extraordinary trust and loyalty. The fiduciary duty imposes a responsibility upon each partner to act in utmost good faith for the benefit of the partnership. It requires that each partner subordinate his or her personal interests to the mutual welfare of the partners.[8] Thus, a partner cannot engage in any independent competitive activities without the other partners' consent.

This fiduciary duty underlies the entire body of law pertaining to partnership and to agency. From it, certain other duties are commonly implied. Thus, a partner must account to the partnership for any personal profits or benefits derived without the consent of all of the partners in any partnership transaction.[9] These include transactions among partners or with third parties connected with the formation, conduct, or liquidation of the partnership or with any use of partnership property [UPA 21]. The following case involves an alleged breach of a partner's fiduciary duty to the deceased partner's widow.

---

8.   The RUPA states that partners may pursue their own interests without automatically violating their fiduciary duties [RUPA 404(e)].

9.   In this sense, to account to the partnership means not only to divulge the information but also to determine the value of any benefits or profits derived and to hold that money or property in trust on behalf of the partnership.

---

| CASE 39.3 |
| :---: |

**ESTATE OF WITLIN v. RIO HONDO ASSOCIATES**

California Court of Appeal, Second District, Division 3, 1978. 83 Cal.App.3d 167, 147 Cal.Rptr. 723.

**BACKGROUND AND FACTS**    *About forty-five doctors, including Dr. Witlin, owned and operated a health center as a partnership (Rio Hondo Associates). When Witlin died, the other doctors, in accordance with their partnership agreement, purchased his share of the center, paying his widow $65,228. The partnership agreement provided that on Witlin's death, a management committee of the partnership was required to make a good faith determination of the fair market value of Witlin's share. The partnership had the option to offer this amount to Witlin's widow. The $65,228 offer, however, was based only on the book value of the partnership's assets. (Book value is the value at which assets are carried on the books—that is, cost less depreciation. It does not include the goodwill or the ongoing business value of a successful business, factors that are likely to be considered in determining fair market value.) In addition, although the partnership was in the process of bargaining to sell the health center at a price that would have doubled Mrs. Witlin's proportionate share, the partnership did not inform her of that fact. Later, Mrs. Witlin sought a greater amount for her husband's share, even though she had accepted the partnership's offer. The trial court held for Witlin's widow, and the doctors appealed.*

*COBEY*, Associate Justice.
\*    \*    \*    \*

Appellants [forty-five doctors] owed [a fiduciary] duty to plaintiff as the widow and executrix [personal representative] of their deceased partner in purchasing from her their deceased partner's interest in the partnership. Throughout the transaction they were bound to act toward her ''in the highest good faith'' and they were forbidden to obtain any advantage over her in the matter by, among other things, the slightest concealment. Yet the management committee never revealed to plaintiff or her representative, King, that the basic value in their formula for determining the fair market value of the partnership was book value alone. Likewise, as already noted, the management committee did not mention to King the possibility that the hospital might be shortly sold.

This possibility of sale was quite real. It appears from plaintiff's improperly rejected offers of proof that the management committee reached in 1969 a tentative agreement with General Health Services to sell the partnership's assets to it for approximately $60,000 a percentage point [1 percent of the total partnership assets], that between April and September 28, 1971, the management committee and the American Cyanamid Corporation were discussing a sale of the partnership to it for at least $93,000 a percentage point, and, as already noted from the evidence itself, that the partnership's assets were finally sold in June 1972 to Hospital Corporation of America for about $84,000 a percentage point.

The management committee knew all of this, but they apparently never breathed a word of it to either plaintiff or her attorney. It seems that in discussing the fair market value of the partnership they talked out of both sides of their mouths. They talked to plaintiff and her attorney in terms of $16,000 and $24,600 per percentage point while they were more or less simultaneously talking to conglomerates interested in purchasing the hospital and the other assets of the partnership in terms of selling prices ranging from $60,000 to $93,500 per percentage point. Given this situation, how could their offer of $24,600 per percentage point to plaintiff have been a good faith determination on their part of the fair market value of the partnership? Obviously the jury's verdict was correct and solidly supported in this respect.

*The trial court's judgment was affirmed on appeal. The partners were held to have breached their fiduciary duty to their deceased partner by failing to make a full and fair disclosure.*

**DECISION AND REMEDY**

**Partnership Law in Other Countries** *Most nations recognize the partnership form of business and impose fiduciary duties upon managing partners. The law in Japan makes no specific provision for business partnerships. Although resident Japanese nationals tend not to use the partnership form, some foreign firms have established partnership-like entities in Japan. Korean law provides for partnerships but prohibits foreign investments in such partnerships.*

**INTERNATIONAL CONSIDERATIONS**

GENERAL AGENCY POWERS   Each partner is an *agent* of every other partner and acts as both a principal and an agent in any business transaction within the scope of the partnership agreement. Each partner is a general agent of the partnership in carrying out the usual business of the firm.[10] Thus, every act of a partner concerning partnership business and every contract signed in the partnership name bind the firm [UPA 9(1)].

The UPA affirms general principles of agency law that pertain to the authority of a partner to bind a partnership in contract. Under the same principles, a partner may subject a partnership to liability in tort. When a partner is apparently carrying on partnership business with third persons in the usual way, both the partner and the firm share liability. It is only when third persons *know* that the partner has no such authority that the partnership is not liable. For example, Patricia, a partner in the partnership of Heise, Green, and Stevens, applies for a loan on behalf of the partnership without authorization from the other partners. The bank manager knows that Patricia has no authority. If the bank manager grants the loan, Patricia will be personally bound, but the firm will not be liable.

*Joint Liability.*   In most states, partners are subject to joint liability on partnership debts and

10. The RUPA adds ''or business of the kind carried on by the partnership'' [RUPA 301(1)]. Basically, this addition gives added protection to third persons who deal with a partnership that is not familiar to them.

# EMERGING TRENDS IN BUSINESS LAW

# Limited Liability Partnerships (LLPs)

**M**any professionals, such as attorneys and accountants, work together using the business form of the partnership. One of the major advantages of a partnership is that the partnership's income is "passed through" to the partners as personal income. Consequently, partners avoid the double-taxation feature of the corporate form of business. But there is a price to pay for this tax advantage: partners face unlimited personal liability.

Consider a group of lawyers operating as a partnership. One lawyer improperly defends a client. The client sues that attorney and wins a large judgment. When the firm's malpractice insurance is insufficient to cover the obligation and that attorney's personal assets are exhausted, the personal assets of the other, innocent partners can be used to satisfy the judgment.

Attorneys and accountants in many states can avoid such personal liability by forming a professional corporation. But the trade-off here is that they then have to pay corporate income taxes. Enter the registered limited liability partnership (LLP). This form of business organization allows professionals to enjoy the tax benefits of a partnership while avoiding personal liability

for the malpractice of other partners.

## Limited Liability Partnership Statutes

The first state to enact an LLP statute was Texas, in August 1991. Delaware, Louisiana, North Carolina, and Washington, D.C., quickly followed suit. As of the beginning of 1994, similar LLP bills were pending in Illinois, Massachusetts, Mississippi, New Mexico, Pennsylvania, and South Carolina. It is predicted that the majority of states will enact similar statutes in the near future.[a]

In essence, each individual state statute limits in some way the normal joint and several liability of partners. For example, Delaware law protects each innocent partner from the "debts and obligations of the partnership arising from negligence, wrongful acts, or misconduct." In North Carolina, Texas, and Washington, D.C., the statutes protect innocent partners from obligations arising from "errors, omissions, negligence, incompetence, or malfeasance." Louisiana also includes "willful or intentional

_____
a. A similar organizational entity in the corporate field, the limited liability company (LLC), now exists in at least thirty-six states. See Chapter 38.

misconduct." The LLP form of business organization is not limited to attorneys but can be used by virtually any professionals.

## Potential Problems with LLPs

LLPs do not come without certain potential problems. Apparently, the Internal Revenue Service (IRS) has committed itself only once, in a private-letter ruling,[b] as to how it will tax an LLP. The IRS stated that LLPs in Texas will be treated as partnerships for tax liability purposes.

What happens when an LLP formed under the law of one state is sued in another state that does not have an LLP statute? Here a potential problem arises. The Delaware and Washington, D.C., LLP statutes specifically state that an LLP registered in those jurisdictions can carry on its business in any jurisdiction. But does that mean that all other states will recognize such LLPs? Constitutional experts point out that each

_____
b. A private-letter ruling is a written statement by the IRS in response to a taxpayer's request for advice. The taxpayer specifies a set of facts that usually resembles a transaction in which he or she is about to participate, and the IRS applies the tax laws to those facts.

state is supposed to respect the laws of another state, but "the jury is still out." Currently, only Minnesota, New Jersey, and Washington, D.C., specifically recognize the LLPs of other states.

## Setting Up an LLP

In most states that have enacted LLP statutes, the process for setting up an LLP is quite simple. For example, to become an LLP in Texas, a partnership must do the following:

1. File the appropriate form with the secretary of state.
2. Pay an annual fee of $200 per partner.
3. Maintain at least $100,000 in professional liability insurance.
4. Add either "L.L.P." or "Registered Limited Liability Partnership" to its name.

Usually the reason why it is so easy to form an LLP is because LLP statutes are simply amendments to a state's already existing partnership law.

### ■ Implications for the Businessperson

1. Individual professionals who wish to join with other professionals in a partnership may wish to seek LLP status to avoid problems stemming from the joint and several liability of partners. This is particularly relevant in today's atmosphere of large judgments against professional partnerships, especially those involving attorneys, physicians, and accountants.
2. On the other side of the coin, a businessperson suing a professional for malpractice will want to know whether that professional is part of an LLP. If so, then even after a favorable judgment, the assets that the successful plaintiff can reach to satisfy the judgment will not be as great as they would be if the business were a partnership. In an LLP, once the partnership assets and any appropriate insurance are exhausted, the judgment creditor's only recourse will be the personal assets of the individual partner who committed the wrongdoing.

### ■ For Critical Analysis

1. Typically, when an individual partner is sued, the other partners rally to his or her defense. There are at least two reasons for this: (1) loyalty and (2) fear of the consequences of joint and several liability. Would innocent partners in an LLP experience a reduced pressure to help defend the partner being sued? Why or why not?
2. The LLP has been created to relieve partners of the burden of joint and several liability. Why do you think partnership law imposes such liability in the first place? Who might suffer if such liability is eliminated through LLPs? Explain.

---

contracts [UPA 15(b)]. **Joint liability** means that if a third party sues a partner on, for example, a partnership debt, the partner has the right to insist that the other partners be sued with him or her. In fact, if the third party does not sue all of the partners, those partners sued cannot be required to pay a judgment, and the assets of the partnership cannot be used to satisfy the judgment. (Similarly, the third party's release of one partner releases all partners.) In other words, to bring a successful claim against the partnership on a debt or contract, a plaintiff must name all the partners as defendants. To simplify this rule, some states have enacted statutes providing that a partnership may be sued in its own name, and a judgment will be binding on the partnership and the individual partners even though not all the partners are named in the complaint.[11]

If the third party is successful, he or she may collect on the judgment against the assets of one or more of the partners. In other words, each partner

---

11. California is an example of such a state.

is liable and may be required to pay the entire amount of the judgment. When one partner pays the entire amount, the partnership is required to indemnify (reimburse) that partner [UPA 18(b)]. If the partnership cannot do so, the obligation falls on the other partners.

### Joint and Several Liability.

In a few states, partners are jointly and severally liable for partnership debts and contracts. In all states, partners are jointly and severally liable for torts and breaches of trust [UPA 15(a)].[12]

**Joint and several liability** means a third party may sue any one or more of the partners without suing all of them or the partnership itself. In other words, a third party may sue one or more of the partners separately (severally) or all of them together (jointly), at his or her option. This is true even if the partner did not participate in, ratify, or know about whatever it was that gave rise to the cause of action.[13]

A judgment against one partner on his or her several liability does not extinguish the others' liability. (Similarly, a release of one partner discharges the partners' joint, but not several, liability.) Thus, those not sued in the first action may be sued subsequently. The first action, however, may have been conclusive on the question of liability. If, for example, in an action against one partner, the court held that the partnership was in no way liable, the third party cannot bring an action against another partner and succeed on the issue of the partnership's liability.

If the third party is successful, he or she may collect on the judgment only against the assets of those partners named as defendants. The partner who committed the tort, though, is required to indemnify the partnership for any damages it pays.

### Liability of Incoming Partner.

A newly admitted partner to an existing partnership has limited liability for whatever debts and obligations the partnership incurred *prior* to the new partner's admission. UPA 17 provides that the new partner's liability can be satisfied only from partnership assets. This means that the new partner has no personal liability for these debts and obligations, but the new partner's capital contribution may be used to satisfy the debts and obligations.

### Authority of Partners.

The agency concepts relating to apparent authority, actual authority, and ratification that were discussed in Chapter 35 are also applicable to partnerships. The extent of *implied authority* is generally broader for partners than for ordinary agents. The character and scope of the partnership business and the customary nature of the particular business operation determine the scope of implied powers. For example, each partner in a trading partnership—essentially, any partnership business that has goods in inventory and makes profits buying and selling those goods—has a wide range of implied powers to borrow money in the firm name and to extend the firm's credit in issuing or indorsing instruments.

In an ordinary partnership, firm members can exercise all implied powers reasonably necessary and customary to carry on that particular business. Some customarily implied powers include the authority to make warranties on goods in the sales business, the power to convey real property in the firm name when such conveyances are part of the ordinary course of partnership business, the power to enter contracts consistent with the firm's regular course of business, and the power to make admissions and representations concerning partnership affairs [UPA 11].

If a partner acts within the scope of authority, the partnership is bound to third parties. For example, a partner's authority to sell partnership products carries with it the implied authority to transfer title and to make usual warranties. Hence, in a partnership that operates a retail tire store, any partner negotiating a contract with a customer for the sale of a set of tires can warrant that "each tire will be warranted for normal wear for 40,000 miles."

This same partner, however, does not have the authority to sell office equipment, fixtures, or the partnership office building without the consent of all the other partners. In addition, because partnerships are formed for profit, a partner does not generally have the authority to make charitable contributions without the consent of the other partners. No such action is binding on the partnership unless it is ratified by all of the other partners.

---

12. Under the RUPA, partners' liability is joint and several for all debts [RUPA 306].

13. The RUPA prevents creditors from bringing an action to collect debts from the partners of a nonbankrupt partnership without first attempting unsuccessfully to collect from the partnership (or convincing a court that the attempt would be unsuccessful) [RUPA 307(d)].

## TERMS AND CONCEPTS TO REVIEW

articles of partnership **769**       joint and several liability **782**       partnership by estoppel **772**
charging order **775**                joint liability **781**
confession of judgment **773**        marshaling assets **768**

## QUESTIONS AND CASE PROBLEMS

**39–1. Indications of Partnership.** Daniel is the owner of a chain of shoe stores. He hires Rubya as the manager of a new store, which is to open in Grand Rapids, Michigan. Daniel, by written contract, agrees to pay Rubya a monthly salary. Also, Daniel agrees to pay Rubya 20 percent of the profits. Without Daniel's knowledge, Rubya represents himself to Classen as Daniel's partner, showing Classen the agreement to share profits. Classen extends credit to Rubya. Rubya defaults. Discuss whether Classen can hold Daniel liable as a partner.

**39–2. The Nature of Partnerships.** Aretha wishes to purchase some real property owned by Tropical Gardens. She learns that Tropical Gardens is a partnership owned by Waldheim, Berry, and Lamont. She also learns that the partnership needs capital and that the need for capital is one of the major reasons the partners are selling their real property. Because Tropical Gardens is a partnership, Aretha has the following concerns:

    (a) Can the partnership convey the land in the name of Tropical Gardens?

    (b) If there is a breach of contract, against whom must Aretha file a lawsuit?

    (c) If Aretha obtains a judgment against Tropical Gardens, against whom can she execute it?

Discuss fully each of Aretha's concerns.

**39–3. Rights of Partners.** Meyer, Knapp, and Cavanna formed a partnership to operate a window-washing service. Meyer contributes $10,000 to the partnership, and Knapp and Cavanna contribute $1,000 each. The partnership agreement is silent on how profits and losses will be shared. One month after the partnership has begun operation, Knapp and Cavanna vote, over Meyer's objection, to purchase another truck for the firm's operation. Meyer believes that because he contributed $10,000, no major commitment to purchase by the partnership can be made over his objection. In addition, Meyer claims that, in absence of agreement, profits must be divided in the same ratio as capital contributions. Discuss Meyer's contentions.

**39–4. Compensation.** Tandoori, Beth, and Nadia form a partnership to operate a hairstyling salon. After one year's operation, the salon has become very busy and profitable. Most customers have a preference as to which partner's services they use. Tandoori becomes ill, and Beth and Nadia start working sixty-hour weeks. It appears that Tandoori will not return to work for at least two months. Beth and Nadia want to bring in Dana as a new partner. Tandoori objects to Dana and refuses to consent to Dana's admission into the partnership. Beth and Nadia insist that they be paid extra compensation for having to work additional hours because of Tandoori's illness. Discuss whether Beth and Nadia are entitled to the compensation claimed and whether Dana can be admitted as a new partner by majority vote.

**39–5. Partnership Property.** Two brothers, Eugene and Marlowe Mehl, operated their family farm as a partnership. Property held by the partnership consisted primarily of farming equipment and machinery. The partnership did not own any real property but leased land from the family and other people. The brothers had agreed to split all profits on an equal basis, but there had never been a written partnership agreement. In 1973, Eugene withdrew $7,200 from the partnership bank account and bought the Dagmar Bar, located in Dagmar, Montana. The warranty deed and the liquor license to the bar were held in the names of Eugene Mehl and his wife, Bonnie. In 1980, Eugene and Bonnie were divorced, and Bonnie received the bar and liquor license as part of the property settlement. In 1983, Marlowe gave written notice to Eugene that he was dissolving the partnership. Eventually, a district court in Montana distributed the assets of the partnership. The court concluded that the Dagmar Bar was a partnership asset. On appeal, Eugene contended that the bar was not partnership property and entered into evidence a number of documents that tended to indicate that he was the owner of the bar. What should the appellate court decide? Discuss fully. [*Mehl v. Mehl*, 241 Mont. 310, 786 P.2d 1173 (1990)]

**39–6. Indications of Partnership.** Three brothers, James, John, and Claude, purchased several parcels of land, taking title to the land either in their names or in their partnership name, Strother Brothers. The brothers never executed a written partnership agreement. After James died, John and Claude, along with their mother, Minnie, brought suit to have Minnie declared owner of a one-fourth interest in the lands. This would leave James's heirs with only a one-fourth interest in the partnership instead of a one-third interest. Before the trial, Minnie died, leaving all her property to John and Claude. Discuss whether John and Claude succeeded in their attempt to increase their shares of the partnership's property at the expense of their deceased brother's estate. [*Strother v. Strother,* 436 So.2d 847 (Ala. 1983)]

**39–7. Partners as Fiduciaries.** In 1974, Dunay, Weisglass, and Koenig formed a partnership to engage in the brokerage business. They made no capital contributions to the partnership and agreed to share all revenue and expenses on an equal basis. The partnership entered into an agreement with Ladenburg, Thalmann & Co. to manage the latter's institutional investors services. The agreement did not provide any specific time limit. Each partner was appointed vice president of Ladenburg. Later, Dunay was appointed president of Ladenburg and was promised an additional share of profits for additional work on a year-to-year basis. Dunay contributed his salary as Ladenburg president and his additional share of profits to the partnership. On April 2, 1979, Weisglass and Koenig told Dunay that they wished to dissolve the partnership and did so immediately, forming their own partnership, W.K. Associates, the same day. Dunay received from the original partnership $15,044, the amount reflected on the partnership's records as his unpaid share of partnership income. Dunay remained with Ladenburg for a short period of time, leaving when the Ladenburg board of directors removed him as president and appointed in his place Weisglass on May 10. Dunay then filed a lawsuit, alleging, among other things, that Weisglass and Koenig had breached their fiduciary duty in dissolving the partnership and forming a new partnership. As part of the suit, Dunay sought some of the profits earned by Weisglass and Koenig after the dissolution. The defendants filed a motion to dismiss Dunay's complaint. In whose favor did the court rule, and why? Discuss fully. [*Dunay v. Ladenburg, Thalmann & Co.,* 170 A.D.2d 335, 565 N.Y.S.2d 819 (1991)]

**39–8. Indications of Partnership Status.** Carmen Allen and Sandy Newsome, in accordance with a written agreement dated March 11, 1987, conducted a carpet and wall-covering business under the name of Newsome Carpets and Wallcovering. The agreement provided that Allen would invest $5,000 cash in the business and that Newsome would invest carpet stock, fixtures, and equipment equal in value to $5,000. On November 4, 1987, Allen and Newsome executed a document entitled "Partnership Agreement" that established the name, place, nature, and duration of the business and outlined the operating procedures of the firm and the rights and responsibilities of the parties. The document referred to Newsome Carpets as a partnership and to Allen and Newsome as partners, each of whom received 50 percent ownership in the firm in return for their capital investment. The next day, on November 5, articles of incorporation designating Newsome and Allen as directors of Newsome Carpets, Inc., were filed in the office of the secretary of state. Evidence at trial indicated that Allen shared profits, rendered business advice, and signed doc-

uments as a general partner of Newsome Carpets. When the corporation was subsequently dissolved, one of the creditors, Orders Distributing Co., sued Allen and Newsome as partners to recover an outstanding debt. Allen (Newsome's whereabouts were unknown when the suit was brought) claimed that the business was a corporation, not a partnership, and that she therefore could not be held personally liable for the debt. Will the court hold that Newsome Carpets was a partnership and not a corporation? Discuss. [*Orders Distributing Co. v. Newsome Carpets & Wallcovering,* 418 S.E.2d 550 (S.C. 1992)]

**39–9. Liability of Partners.** Dr. J. Gregg Sikes was a general partner with Thomas Ledford in a partnership formed to build and sell condominiums in Nashville, Tennessee. Ledford also managed the partnership's business; Sikes took no part in day-to-day operations. BancBoston Mortgage Corp. loaned the partnership $1.6 million to buy the land on which the project was to be built and agreed to lend the partnership construction funds of $4,625,000. The construction loan was contingent on, among other requirements, the partnership's submission of contracts for the purchase of at least fourteen condominiums. Eventually, Ledford submitted fourteen contracts, but several of them were subject to undisclosed side agreements that violated the terms of the loan (for example, two of the contracts were signed as an accommodation to Ledford—one by a Ledford employee and the other by a friend of an employee, neither of whom had any intention of actually going through with a purchase). Without checking the contracts, the bank gave the construction money to the partnership. By the time the condominiums were built, all of the purchase contracts had expired. The partnership defaulted on the loans, and the two partners filed for bankruptcy, asking the court to discharge the loans. Ledford had clearly committed fraud, and the court refused to discharge him from personal liability for the loans. Sikes contended that his indebtedness on the construction loan was dischargeable because he had been ignorant of Ledford's fraud. In these circumstances, can Sikes be held responsible for the partnership debt? What should the court decide? [*In re Ledford,* 970 F.2d 1556 (8th Cir. 1992)]

**39–10. A Question of Ethics**

*David Murphy and James Canion formed a general partnership to conduct real estate business. A provision in their partnership agreement provided that both partners would devote their full-time efforts to conducting partnership business, that all personal earnings from personal services would be included as partnership income, and that any real estate or other partnership business conducted by either partner during the term of the partnership agreement should be for the joint account of the partnership. Through his business associates and contacts, Canion learned of several profitable real estate opportunities. Canion never informed Murphy of*

*these opportunities but, instead, secretly took advantage of them for his own gain. When Murphy found out about Canion's activities, he told Canion that he was canceling the partnership under a clause in the partnership agreement that allowed termination by a partner with ninety days' notice. In the lawsuit that followed, Murphy alleged that Canion had breached the partnership agreement and his fiduciary duty to the partnership. The trial court agreed with Murphy and awarded him damages, which the court held to be proximately caused by Canion's wrongful appropriation of partnership business opportunities. On appeal, Canion contended, among other things, that his breach of his fiduciary duty did not proximately cause any damages to Murphy, because the income generated by Canion's "secret" projects was received after the partnership had terminated. [Murphy v. Canion, 797 S.W.2d 944 (Tex.App.–Houston [14th Dist.] 1990)]*

1. Should Murphy be entitled, in the form of damages, to a share of the profits made by Canion by his secret dealings, in view of the fact that Canion received the income *after* the partnership terminated? If you were the judge, how would you decide this issue, and on what legal basis? From an ethical point of view, what solution would be the fairest?

2. What ethical considerations are involved in the rule that partners have a fiduciary duty to subordinate their personal interests to the mutual welfare of all of the partners? Do you think that a partnership would be a viable form of business organization if partners were not held to such a fiduciary duty?

# CHAPTER 40

# PARTNERSHIPS— TERMINATION AND LIMITED PARTNERSHIPS

**P**artnerships can be terminated for a variety of reasons. For example, the partnership agreement may specify a termination date, or the partners may simply agree among themselves to terminate the business. A partner's withdrawal will automatically dissolve the partnership. The partnership may end for other reasons, such as by court decree.

In this chapter, we examine the law governing the termination of partnerships. We then look at a special form of partnership, the limited partnership. This business form is sufficiently important in the business world, particularly as an investment vehicle, to warrant a special section in this chapter.

## PARTNERSHIP TERMINATION

Any change in the relations of the partners that demonstrates unwillingness or inability to carry on partnership business dissolves the partnership, resulting in termination [UPA 29]. If any of the partners wishes to continue the business, he or she is free to reorganize into a new partnership with the remaining partners.

The termination of a partnership has two stages—dissolution and winding up. Both stages must take place before termination is complete. **Dissolution** occurs when any partner ceases to be associated with the carrying on of partnership business. **Winding up** is the actual process of collecting and distributing the partnership's assets. Dissolution terminates the right of a partnership to exist as a going concern, but the partnership continues to exist long enough to wind up its affairs. When winding up is complete, the partnership's *legal* existence is terminated.

# DISSOLUTION

Dissolution, the first stage in the termination of a partnership, can be brought about by acts of the partners, by operation of law, or by judicial decree.

## DISSOLUTION BY ACTS OF THE PARTNERS

Dissolution of a partnership may come about through the following acts of the partners: by agreement, by the withdrawal of a partner,[1] by the addition of a partner, or by the transfer of a partner's interest.

*Dissolution by Agreement.* A partnership can be dissolved when certain events stipulated in the partnership agreement occur. For example, when a partnership agreement expresses a fixed time or a particular business objective to be accomplished, the passing of the date or the accomplishment of the project dissolves the partnership. Partners do not have to abide by the stipulations in the agreement, however. They can mutually agree to dissolve the partnership early or to extend it. If they agree to continue in the partnership, they become *partners at will*—meaning that any partner can dissolve the partnership at any time by withdrawing from the firm.

*Partner's Power to Withdraw.* A partnership is a personal legal relationship among co-owners. No person can be compelled either to become a partner or to remain one. Implicit in a partnership is each partner's *power* to dissociate from the partnership at any time and thus dissolve the partnership. Note that although a partner always has the *power* to withdraw from the partnership, he or she may not always have the *right* to do so. In a partnership for a specified term or for a specified purpose, a partner does not have the right to withdraw until the term has lapsed or the purpose has been fulfilled. If a partner withdraws in contravention of the partnership agreement, he or she will be liable to the other partners for damages resulting from wrongful dissolution of the partnership.

*Admission of a New Partner.* A change in the composition of the partnership by the *admission of a new partner* results in dissolution. The new partnership carries the debts of the dissolved partnership. Creditors of the prior partnership become creditors of the partnership that is continuing the business [UPA 41].

*Transfer of a Partner's Interest.* The UPA provides that neither a voluntary transfer of a partner's interest[2] nor an involuntary sale of a partner's interest for the benefit of creditors [UPA 28] by itself dissolves the partnership. (A transferee—the one to whom the interest is transferred—acquires the right to the transferring partner's profits but does not become a partner; thus, a transferee has no say in the management or administration of the partnership affairs and no right to inspect the partnership books.) Either occurrence, however, can ultimately lead to judicial dissolution of the partnership, as will be discussed.

## DISSOLUTION BY OPERATION OF LAW

A partnership is dissolved by operation of law in the event of death, bankruptcy, or illegality.

*Death.* A partnership is dissolved upon the death of any partner, even if the partnership agreement provides for carrying on the business with the executor of the decedent's estate.[3] Any change in the composition among partners results in a new partnership.

*Bankruptcy.* The bankruptcy of a partner will dissolve a partnership. Insolvency alone will not result in dissolution. Naturally, bankruptcy of the firm itself will result in dissolution of the partnership.

*Illegality.* Any event that makes it unlawful for the partnership to continue its business or for any partner to carry on in the partnership will result in dissolution. Even if the illegality of the partnership business is a cause for dissolution, however, the

---

1. The Revised Uniform Partnership Act (RUPA) distinguishes the withdrawal of a partner that causes a breakup of a partnership from a withdrawal that causes only the end of a partner's participation in the business (and results in a buy-out of that partner's interest) [RUPA 601, 701, 801]. Dissolution results only if the partnership must be liquidated [RUPA 801].

2. A single partner cannot make another person a partner in a partnership merely by transferring his or her interest to that person [UPA 27].
3. Under the RUPA, the death of a partner represents that partner's ''dissociation'' from the partnership, but it is not an automatic ground for the partnership's dissolution [RUPA 601].

partners can decide to change the nature of their business and continue in the partnership. When the illegality applies to an individual partner, the dissolution *must* occur. For example, suppose that the state legislature passes a law making it illegal for magistrates to engage in the practice of law. If an attorney in a law firm is appointed a magistrate, the partnership must be dissolved. The next case deals with dissolution of a partnership due to illegality.

---

CASE 40.1

**WILLIAMS v. BURRUS**
Court of Appeals of
Washington, Division 1, 1978.
20 Wash.App. 494,
581 P.2d 164.

**BACKGROUND AND FACTS**   *The plaintiff, Williams, sued the defendant, Burrus, for an accounting and dissolution of their partnership. To form the partnership, Williams had provided property to serve as collateral so that Burrus could obtain a bank loan to assist in the purchasing of a restaurant. The partnership agreement, in addition to providing that Williams would supply the collateral, stated that the business would be in Burrus's name and that Burrus alone would apply for a liquor license, without mentioning Williams. At the time, Williams was an unacceptable licensee, according to the Washington State Liquor Control Board. To receive a license issued to a partnership, all members of the partnership have to be qualified to obtain a license. The trial court found the partnership agreement illegal and unenforceable and dismissed Williams's complaint. Williams appealed.*

*ANDERSEN*, Judge.
          *   *   *   *

No state retail liquor license of any kind can be issued to a partnership unless all of the members thereof are qualified to obtain a license, and no licenseholder can allow any other person to use such a license.

Furthermore, a partnership is dissolved by any event which makes it unlawful for the business of the partnership to be carried on or for the members to carry it on in partnership.

The issue of illegality may be raised at any time.

Under the general rule that the courts will not aid either party to an illegal agreement where a partnership is formed to carry out an illegal business or to conduct a lawful business in an illegal manner, the courts will refuse to aid any of the parties thereto in an action against the other.

**DECISION AND REMEDY**   *The appellate court affirmed the trial court's dismissal of Williams's case. Because the partnership was illegal, neither party had any rights that a court would enforce.*

---

**DISSOLUTION BY JUDICIAL DECREE**   Dissolution of a partnership can result from judicial decree. For dissolution to occur, an application or petition must be made in an appropriate court. The court then either denies the petition or grants a decree of dissolution. Under UPA 32, a court can dissolve a partnership for the reasons discussed below or whenever circumstances render it equitable.

*Insanity.*   A partnership can obtain a judicial declaration of dissolution when a partner is adjudicated insane or is shown to be of unsound mind. This action often involves a series of complex tests and standards.

*Incapacity.*   When it appears that a partner has become incapable of performing his or her duties under the partnership agreement, a decree of dissolution may be required. It must appear that the incapacity is permanent and will substantially affect the partner's ability to discharge his or her duties to the firm.

***Business Impracticality.*** When it becomes obvious that the firm's business can be operated only at a loss, judicial dissolution may be ordered.

***Improper Conduct.*** A partner's impropriety involving partnership business (for example, fraud perpetrated upon the other partners) or improper behavior reflecting unfavorably upon the firm (for

example, habitual drunkenness resulting in gross neglect of the partnership's business) will provide grounds for a judicial decree of dissolution.

***Other Circumstances.*** Dissolution may also be granted in other circumstances when the court finds it equitable to do so. (In general, courts are reluctant to allow partners to sue each other except for dissolution.) For example, a court might order dissolution when personal dissension between partners becomes so persistent and harmful as to undermine the confidence and cooperation necessary to carry on the firm's business. The following case is illustrative.

---

**BACKGROUND AND FACTS** *Wayne Taurman was an employee of John Felton's Felton Construction Company (FCC). In 1969, Felton formed Felton Investment Group (FIG) as a general partnership consisting of deserving employees of FCC. Each member of FIG made weekly contributions—deducted from the employee's paycheck—to the investment fund. The money was then placed in investments agreed upon by all the partners. Taurman was a charter member of FIG. In 1974, Felton began to promote the idea that FIG should become a limited partnership with Felton in charge as general partner. Taurman opposed Felton's idea. His employment by the company was later terminated on the ground that he had refused to renounce his union membership to work on a nonunion job. Shortly after his termination, Taurman received a check for $21,448.98 from FIG. The check represented Taurman's contributions to FIG, plus 4 percent annual interest. In the FIG partnership agreement, this was the amount payable in situations in which employees were discharged for misconduct. Taurman did not feel he had been guilty of misconduct and wanted his full share of the partnership assets upon withdrawing from the partnership. Felton disagreed. Taurman, joined by Derrold Paige, another employee and FIG member who had received similar treatment, then brought an action to have the partnership dissolved, its assets sold, and the proceeds distributed to its partners. The trial court granted the dissolution, and Felton appealed to the Supreme Court of Montana.*

**CASE 40.2**

**FELTON INVESTMENT GROUP v. TAURMAN**

Supreme Court of Montana, 1986.
222 Mont. 238,
722 P.2d 1135.

---

*MORRISON*, Justice.

\* \* \* \*

\* \* \* The [National Labor Relations] Act provides that a wrongful discharge from employment occurs when one is discharged for supporting a union.

\* \* \* \*

\* \* \* [T]here is substantial credible evidence to support [the trial court's] determination. Both individuals worked for FCC [Felton Construction Company] for a substantial number of years. Numerous people associated with FCC testified that neither individual was a problem employee. Their employment, or lack thereof, hinged completely on their willingness to disassociate with their union.

\* \* \* [W]e find no error in the trial court's decision that pursuant to [Section] 35–10–401(1), MCA [Montana's adaptation of the Uniform Partnership Act], Taurman and Paige must be repaid their contributions into the partnership and receive their *pro rata* [proportionate] share of the assets of the partnership. Section 35–10–401, MCA, states at the outset that ''[t]he rights and duties of the partners in relation to the partnership shall be determined subject to any agreement between them \* \* \*.'' The agreement between the partners covers the voluntary termination of a partner's employment with FCC as well as his discharge for misconduct. It also covers involuntary termination caused by disability, death or retirement. However, there is nothing in the partnership agreement concerning the effect of a partner's involuntary termination from FCC absent misconduct. Numerous members of FIG, including its controller, testified that this contingency was not covered in FIG's partnership agreement. Since the rights of partners of FIG who were involuntarily terminated from FCC without cause were not expressed in the agreement, [Section] 35–10–401(1), MCA, controls:

(1) Each partner shall be repaid his contributions whether by way of capital or advances to the partnership property and share equally in the profits and surplus remaining after all liabilities, including those to partners, are satisfied \* \* \* .

**DECISION AND REMEDY**   *The Supreme Court of Montana affirmed the trial court's judgment. Taurman and Paige were entitled to have the partnership dissolved by judicial decree and to receive their contributions and their* pro rata *shares of partnership assets.*

**NOTICE OF DISSOLUTION**   The intent to dissolve or to withdraw from a firm must be communicated to each partner. This notice of intent can come from the words of a partner (actual notice) or from the actions of a partner (constructive notice). All partners will share liability for the acts of any partner who continues to conduct business for the firm without knowing that the partnership has been dissolved. For example, Alzor, Jennifer, and Carla have a partnership. Alzor tells Jennifer of her intent to withdraw. Before Carla learns of Alzor's intentions, she enters into a contract with a third party. The contract is equally binding on Alzor, Jennifer, and Carla. Unless the other partners have notice, the withdrawing partner will continue to be bound as a partner to all contracts created for the firm.

To avoid liability for obligations a partner incurs after dissolution of a partnership, notice must be given to all affected third persons. The manner of giving notice depends on the third person's relationship to the firm. Any third person who has extended credit to the partnership must receive *actual notice*. For all others, a newspaper announcement or similar public notice is sufficient.

## WINDING UP

Once dissolution has occurred and partners have been notified, they cannot create new obligations on behalf of the partnership. Their only authority is to complete transactions begun but not finished at the time of dissolution and to wind up the business of the partnership. Winding up includes collecting and preserving partnership assets, discharging liabilities (paying debts), and accounting to each partner for the value of his or her interest in the partnership.

When dissolution is caused by a partner's act that violates the partnership agreement, the innocent partners may have rights to damages resulting from the dissolution. Also, the innocent partners have the right to buy out the offending partner and to continue the business instead of winding up the partnership. A partner who has committed a wrongful act is barred from participating in the winding up of partnership business.

Dissolution resulting from the death of a partner vests all partnership assets in the surviving partners. The surviving partners act as fiduciaries in settling partnership affairs in a quick, practicable manner and in accounting to the estate of the deceased partner for the value of the decedent's interest in the partnership. The surviving partners are entitled to payment for their services in winding up the partnership, as well as to reimbursement for any costs incurred in the process [UPA 18(f)].

The court stresses in the following case that a partnership is not terminated until the winding up of partnership affairs is completed and all obligations of the partnership are discharged.

**CASE 40.3**

**LENKIN v. BECKMAN**
District of Columbia Court of Appeals, 1990.
575 A.2d 273.

**COMPANY PROFILE** *Beckman & Kirstein is a law firm located in Washington, D.C. The firm's practice includes general civil and trial work in the international, administrative, and legislative arenas. The areas of law in which the firm has practiced include aviation, antitrust, banking, commercial, corporate, and franchise law. The partners are Robert Beckman and David Kirstein. Beckman received his undergraduate and law degrees from the University of Pennsylvania. Among other positions, he has served as a trial attorney for the Antitrust Division of the Department of Justice and as a lecturer in administrative law and property law for the Washington College of Law at American University. Kirstein received his undergraduate degree from the University of Connecticut and his law degree from the University of Virginia. He has taught at the University of Tennessee Law School, Boston College Law School, and Harvard Law School. He has also served as counsel to the Civil Aeronautics Board and the Aviation Subcommittee of the Senate Committee on Commerce, Science, and Transportation.*

**BACKGROUND AND FACTS** *In May 1983, the partnership of Beckman, Farmer & Kirstein (B, F & K) entered into a ten-year lease agreement with Melvin Lenkin to lease office space from Lenkin in a building in Washington, D.C. The lease included a clause—clause 23(b)—that released the individual partners, as well as their successors in interest, from any personal liability under the lease. B, F & K was dissolved in May 1984, and a new partnership, Beckman & Kirstein (B & K), was formed. The parties disagreed as to whether Robert Beckman had personally assumed the lease obligation (as Beckman contended) or B & K had assumed the lease obligation (as Lenkin contended). In October 1985, almost eight years before the lease was to expire, Beckman informed Lenkin by letter that the lease was being terminated effective November 30, 1985. Lenkin later filed suit against Beckman and Kirstein, "on behalf of Beckman & Kirstein, a partnership," seeking damages under the lease. The trial court granted Beckman and Kirstein's motion to dismiss, holding that Beckman and Kirstein, as individuals, were released from all liability by the provision in the lease agreement. It further concluded that, as a matter of law, because a partnership entity cannot be sued in the District of Columbia, Lenkin could not obtain a judgment against the firm of B & K. Therefore, there could be neither personal nor partnership liability for the lease obligation. Lenkin appealed.*

*FERREN,* Associate Judge:
\* \* \* \*

The assumption that all partnership property automatically becomes personal property upon dissolution of the partnership (and thus would be insulated against

Lenkin's claim by clause 23(b) of the lease) is *   *   * incorrect. A partnership is not terminated for all purposes upon dissolution; it "continues until the winding up of partnership affairs is completed." "The dissolution of a partnership affects only future obligations of the business. As to past transactions the partnership continues until it shall have satisfied all of its pre-existing obligations." Once in dissolution, moreover, the partnership is deemed to have two categories of assets: "partnership property" and the "contributions of the partners necessary for the payment of all liabilities" of the partnership, beginning with those owing to "creditors other than partners." Partnership property must be exhausted before partners are required to contribute to the assets of the partnership for the purpose of satisfying any of the enumerated categories of partnership liabilities.

If, as in this case, a creditor permits a partner to contract out of personal liability—so that there is no obligation to make a "contribution" to satisfy the creditor—this does not necessarily eliminate creditor access to the other kind of partnership asset, "partnership property," whoever happens to have it. Accordingly, vis-a-vis creditor Lenkin, the partnership assets of B, F & K, upon dissolution, did not necessarily become the personal property—unreachable by virtue of clause 23(b) of the lease—of Beckman, Kirstein, or anyone else.

Finally, we address the assumption that partnership property cannot be reached because a partnership, as such, cannot be sued. We agree with [the trial court judge] that, under the law of this jurisdiction, a partnership entity lacks capacity to be sued. On the other hand, a partnership may be held accountable for partner wrongs, provided the action is "brought in the names of the partners, with service of process upon them individually." In sum, the rule precluding suit against a partnership entity does not prevent suit against the partnership through an action against the individual partners.

**DECISION AND REMEDY**  *The appellate court reversed the trial court's decision and remanded the case for further proceedings consistent with the legal premises set out by the appellate court in this opinion.*

## DISTRIBUTION OF ASSETS

Creditors of the partnership, as well as creditors of the individual partners, can make claims on the partnership's assets. Creditors of the partnership have priority over creditors of individual partners in the distribution of partnership assets; the converse priority is followed in the distribution of individual partner assets—except under bankruptcy law, which provides that a partner's individual assets may be utilized to pay claims against a partnership involved in certain bankruptcy proceedings.[4] (Bankruptcy law in general is discussed in Chapter 33.)

The priorities in the distribution of a partnership's assets are as follows [UPA 40(b)]:[5]

1. Payment of third party debts.
2. Refund of advances (loans) made to or for the firm by a partner.
3. Return of capital contribution to a partner.
4. Distribution of the balance, if any, to partners in accordance with the relative proportions of their respective shares in the profits.

If the partnership's liabilities are greater than its assets, the partners bear the losses—in the absence

---

4.   11 U.S.C. Section 723.

5.   Under the RUPA, partner creditors are included among creditors who take first priority [RUPA 808]. Capital contributions and profits or losses are then calculated together to determine the amounts that the partners receive or the amounts that they must pay.

of a contrary agreement—in the same proportion in which they shared the profits (rather than, for example, in proportion to their contributions to the partnership's capital). If the partnership is insolvent, the partners must still contribute their respective shares. If one of the partners does not contribute, the other or others must provide the additional amounts necessary to pay the liabilities; but he, she, or they have a **right of contribution** against (that is, a right to be reimbursed by) whoever has not paid his or her share.[6]

_____

6.  If an individual partner is insolvent and for that reason cannot pay his or her share of the loss, however, the solvent partner or partners will be unable to recover their additional contributions from the insolvent partner.

The distribution of partnership assets begins with the subtraction of the partnership's total liabilities from its total assets. Liabilities include amounts owed to creditors and to partners for other than capital and profit, and to partners for their capital contributions. Amounts that remain after payment of the liabilities are distributed to the partners according to the profit-sharing ratio. If, however, the partnership has suffered an aggregate loss, the total loss is shared as agreed or in the same ratio as the partners share profits.

The following case illustrates that nonpartner (third party) creditors have first priority to partnership assets.

---

**BACKGROUND AND FACTS**  *Robert Lowther, Fred Riggleman, and Granville Zopp were equal partners in the Four Square Partnership. The partnership was created to acquire and develop real estate for commercial retail use. In the course of the partnership, Riggleman loaned $30,000 to the partnership, and Zopp loaned the partnership $50,000. Donald H. Lowther, Robert's brother and not a partner of the firm, loaned Four Square $80,000 and took a promissory note signed by the three partners. Four Square encountered financial difficulties shortly after the commercial venture began and eventually defaulted on payments due on a construction loan it had received from a bank. The bank foreclosed on the property securing the debt. The proceeds of the subsequent foreclosure sale satisfied the bank's interest and left a surplus of $87,783 to be returned to the partnership. In the meantime, the partnership had been dissolved and was in the process of winding up its affairs. Robert Lowther filed suit, asking the court to prevent any distribution of the firm's assets to the partners until a determination was made as to who was legally entitled to those assets. Donald Lowther intervened in the suit to establish his priority as a nonpartner creditor. The trial court found that the claims of Riggleman and Zopp, as secured creditors, took priority over that of Donald Lowther. Donald Lowther appealed.*

| CASE 40.4 |
| --- |

**LOWTHER v. RIGGLEMAN**

Supreme Court of Appeals of West Virginia, 1993.

428 S.E.2d 49,

189 W.Va. 68.

*MILLER*, Justice:

\* \* \* \*

Under the Uniform Partnership Act, the order of priorities in settling accounts of a partnership upon its dissolution is found in W.Va.Code, 47–8A-40, which provides, in relevant part: "In settling accounts between the partners after dissolution, the following rules shall be observed \*   \*   \* "(b) The liabilities of the partnership shall rank in order of payment as follows: "(I) Those owing to creditors other than partners, "(II) Those owing to partners other than for capital and profits, "(III) Those owing to partners in respect of capital, "(IV) Those owing to partners in respect of profits."

Thus, under the foregoing statute, the liability of a partnership to creditors other than partners, such as the appellant, must be given greater priority in the order of payment than the liability owed by a partnership to its partners, such as the appellees [Riggleman and Zopp], when the partnership is dissolved. The common law partnership rules regarding distribution of the assets of a partnership upon dissolution are much the same * * *.

\* \* \* \*

* * * [T]he common law was that a partner in a partnership dissolution could not assert a lien on partnership assets that would create a preferential claim over its general creditors. This same result has been reached interpreting the Uniform Partnership Act. We agree with this rule, and, therefore, conclude that the appellees are not general creditors of the partnership on a par with the appellant.

**DECISION AND REMEDY**  *The appellate court reversed the trial court's holding and remanded the case for further proceedings consistent with its opinion.*

## PARTNERSHIP BUY-SELL AGREEMENTS

Usually, when people enter into partnerships, they are getting along with one another. To prepare for the possibility that the situation may change and they may become unable to work together amicably, the partners should make express arrangements during the formation of the partnership to provide for its smooth dissolution. An agreement may be made for one or more partners to buy out the other or others, should the situation warrant. Such an agreement is called a **buy-sell agreement,** or simply a buy-out agreement. To agree beforehand on who buys what, under what circumstances, and, if possible, at what price, may eliminate costly negotiations or litigation later. Alternatively, it may be agreed that one or more partners will determine the value of the interest being sold, and the other or others can decide whether to buy or sell.

A similar agreement can be formed for the transfer of a partner's interest on his or her death to the surviving partners. The partners can agree that the survivors will pay the value of the deceased partner's interest in the partnership to his or her representative. To fund the payment of the value of each partner's interest on his or her death, partnership funds can be used to purchase insurance.[7]

**SECTION 2**

# LIMITED PARTNERSHIPS

Limited partnerships consist of at least one **general partner** and one or more **limited partners.** The general partner (or partners) assumes management responsibility of the partnership and, as such, has full responsibility for the partnership and for all debts of the partnership. The limited partner (or partners) contributes cash (or other property) and owns an interest in the firm but does not undertake any management responsibilities and is not personally liable for partnership debts beyond the amount of his or her investment. A limited partner can forfeit limited liability by taking part in managing the business.

Limited partnerships are sometimes referred to as *special partnerships,* in contrast to *general partnerships.* A comparison of the basic characteristics of general partnerships and limited partnerships appears in Exhibit 40–1.[8]

Until 1976, the law governing limited partnerships in all states except Louisiana was the Uniform Limited Partnership Act (ULPA). Since 1976, most states and the District of Columbia have adopted

---

7.  Under the RUPA, if a partner's dissociation does not result in a dissolution of the partnership, a buy-out of the partner's interest is mandatory [RUPA 701(a)]. The RUPA contains an extensive set of buy-out rules. Basically, a departing partner gets the same amount through a buy-out that he or she would get if the business were winding up [RUPA 701(b)].

8.  Under the RUPA, a general partnership can be converted into a limited partnership and vice versa [RUPA 902, 903]. The RUPA also provides for the merger of a general partnership with one or more general or limited partnerships under rules that are similar to those governing corporate mergers [RUPA 905].

■ **Exhibit 40–1  A Basic Comparison of Types of Partnerships**

| Characteristic | General Partnership (UPA) | Limited Partnership (RULPA) |
|---|---|---|
| **Creation** | By agreement of two or more persons to carry on a business as co-owners for profit. | By agreement of two or more persons to carry on a business as co-owners for profit. Must include one or more general partners and one or more limited partners. Filing of certificate with secretary of state is required. |
| **Sharing of Profits and Losses** | By agreement, or in the absence thereof, profits are shared equally by partners, and losses are shared in the same ratio as profits. | Profits are shared as required in certificate agreement, and losses are shared likewise up to their capital contributions. In the absence of provision in certificate agreement, profits and losses are shared on the basis of percentages of capital contributions. |
| **Liability** | Unlimited personal liability of all partners. | Unlimited personal liability of all general partners; limited partners only to extent of capital contributions. |
| **Capital Contribution** | No minimal or mandatory amount; set by agreement. | Set by agreement; may be cash, property, services, or any obligation. |
| **Management** | By agreement, or in the absence thereof, all partners have an equal voice. | General partners by agreement, or else each has an equal voice. Limited partners have no voice, or else are subject to liability as a general partner, but *only* if a third party has knowledge of such involvement. Limited partner may act as agent or employee of the partnership and may vote on amending the certificate or on the sale or dissolution of the partnership. |
| **Duration** | By agreement, or can be dissolved by action of partner (withdrawal), operation of law (death or bankruptcy), or court decree. | By agreement in certification, or by withdrawal, death, or mental incompetence of general partner in absence of right of other general partners to continue the partnership. Death of a limited partner, unless he or she is the only remaining limited partner, does not terminate the partnership. |
| **Assignment** | Interest can be assigned, although assignee does not have rights of substituted partner without consent of other partners. | Same as general partnership; if partners consent to assignee's becoming a partner, certificate must be amended. Upon assignment of all interest, the partner ceases to be a partner. |
| **Priorities (order) upon Liquidation** | 1. Outside creditors.<br>2. Partner creditors.<br>3. Partners, according to capital contribution.<br>4. Partners, according to profits. | 1. Outside creditors and partner creditors.<br>2. Partners and former partners entitled to distributions before withdrawal under the agreement or RULPA.<br>3. Partners, according to capital contributions.<br>4. Partners, according to profits. |

the revision of the ULPA, the Revised Uniform Limited Partnership Act (RULPA). Because the RULPA is the dominant law governing limited partnerships in the United States, references within this section will be to the RULPA.

## FORMATION OF A LIMITED PARTNERSHIP

Compared with the informal, private, and voluntary agreement that usually suffices for a general partnership, the formation of a limited partnership is a public and formal proceeding that must follow statutory requirements. A limited partnership must have at least one general partner and one limited partner, and the partners must sign a **certificate of limited partnership,** which requires information similar to that found in a corporate charter (see Chapter 41). The certificate must be filed with the designated state official—under the RULPA, the secretary of state. The certificate is usually open to public inspection. In essence, the content of the certificate and the method of filing are similar to those for the corporate charter [RULPA 101(7); RULPA 201].

## RIGHTS AND LIABILITIES OF LIMITED PARTNERS

General partners, unlike limited partners, are personally liable to the partnership's creditors; thus, at least one general partner is necessary in a limited partnership so that someone has personal liability. This policy can be circumvented in states that allow a corporation to be the general partner in a partnership. Because the corporation has limited liability by virtue of corporate laws, no one in the limited partnership in this situation has personal liability.

**RIGHTS OF LIMITED PARTNERS** Subject to the limitations that will be discussed here, limited partners have essentially the same rights as general partners, including the right of access to partnership books and the right to other information regarding partnership business. Upon dissolution, limited partners are entitled to a return of their contributions in accordance with the partnership certificate [RULPA 804(c)]. They can also assign their interests subject to specific clauses in the certificate [RULPA 702; RULPA 704].

The RULPA provides a limited partner with the right to sue on behalf of the firm if the general partners with authority to do so have refused to file suit [RULPA 1001]. In addition, legislation protecting investors, such as securities laws (discussed in Chapter 44), may give some protection to limited partners.

**LIABILITIES OF LIMITED PARTNERS** A limited partner is liable to creditors to the extent of any contribution that had been promised to the firm or any part of a contribution that was withdrawn from the firm [RULPA 502]. If the firm is organized in an improper manner and the limited partner fails to renunciate (withdraw from the partnership) on discovery of the defect, the limited partner can be held personally liable by the firm's creditors. Note, though, that the RULPA allows people to remain limited partners regardless of whether they comply with statutory technicalities. Liability for false statements in a partnership certificate runs in favor of persons relying on the false statements and against members who sign the certificate knowing of the falsities [RULPA 207]. A limited partnership is formed by good faith compliance with the requirements for signing and filing the certificate, even if it is incomplete or defective. When a limited partner discovers a defect in the formation of the limited partnership, he or she can obtain shelter from future liability by causing an appropriate amendment or certificate to be filed or by renouncing an interest in the profits of the partnership, thereby avoiding any future reliance by third parties [RULPA 304].

The liability of a limited partner is limited to the capital that he or she contributes or agrees to contribute to the partnership. By contrast, the liability of a general partner for partnership indebtedness is virtually unlimited.

**LIMITED PARTNERS AND MANAGEMENT** The exemptions from personal liability of the limited partners rest on their not participating in management [RULPA 303]. The surname of a limited partner cannot be included in the partnership name [RULPA 102]. A violation of this provision renders the limited partner just as liable as a general partner to any creditor who does not know that he or she is a limited partner. Note that no law expressly bars the participation of limited partners in the management of the partnership. Rather, the threat of personal liability normally deters their participation.

Under the RULPA, a limited partner will be liable as a general partner only if the third party had knowledge of the limited partner's management activities [RULPA 303]. How much actual review and advisement a limited partner can engage in before being exposed to liability is an unsettled question.[9]

_____

9.  It is an unsettled question partly because there are differences among the laws in different states. Factors to be considered under the RULPA are listed in RULPA 303(b), (c).

In the following case, a limited partner was alleged to have participated in the control of the business by interceding on the partnership's behalf to secure credit.

---

**BACKGROUND AND FACTS**  *Robert Pitman was one of two limited partners in Ramsey Homebuilders, a limited partnership that engaged in the business of residential construction. Michael Ramsey was the sole general partner in the partnership. Because Ramsey had a poor credit history, he was unable to borrow the money or obtain the credit that was needed to sustain the partnership's business. Pitman, who had a personal account with Flanagan Lumber Company, contacted Flanagan's credit manager and secured an account in the partnership's name. After the partnership failed to pay the account, Flanagan sued Pitman, alleging that although Pitman was a limited partner in Ramsey Homebuilders, he was responsible for the partnership's debt under RULPA 303. Pitman argued that, if anything, he was operating within the waters of the "safe harbor" provided by RULPA 303(b)(3), which states that a limited partner does not participate in the control of the partnership solely by acting as a surety or guarantor for any liabilities incurred by the partnership. The trial court found that Pitman had participated in the control of the business by securing credit for the partnership, that Flanagan had reasonably relied on that participation in extending credit, and that Pitman was therefore liable to Flanagan for the debt subsequently incurred by the partnership. Pitman appealed.*

| CASE 40.5 |
| --- |
| **PITMAN v. FLANAGAN LUMBER CO.** |
| Supreme Court of Alabama, 1990. |
| 567 So.2d 1335. |

*HOUSTON,* Justice.

\*   \*   \*   \*

Pitman argues that the evidence does not support the trial court's finding that he participated in the control of the partnership's business. \*   \*   \* He also contends that he had no written agreement with Flanagan to pay the partnership's account and, therefore, that under [the Alabama Statute of Frauds], he cannot be held responsible for the debt.

\*   \*   \*   \*

Flanagan contends, however, that the evidence supports the trial court's finding that Pitman participated in the control of the partnership's business. Furthermore, Flanagan argues, [the Statute of Frauds] is not applicable because the judgment was not predicated upon an agreement between it [Flanagan] and Pitman to pay the partnership's account, but, instead, upon Pitman's loss of limited partner status under [RULPA 303(a)]. We agree.

\*   \*   \*   \*

"Control" is defined in Black's Law Dictionary as "the [p]ower or authority to manage, direct, superintend, restrict, regulate, govern, administer, or oversee." In the present case, the evidence showed that Pitman interceded on behalf of the partnership in order to secure an account with Flanagan. The trial court could have found from this evidence that Pitman participated in the "control" of the partnership's business by securing one of the things that the partnership needed to survive—a source of building materials that would be provided on credit. Furthermore, the evidence supports the trial court's finding that Flanagan reasonably relied on Pitman's participation in the partnership's business by extending credit to the partnership. The trial court's judgment was not plainly and palpably wrong.

With regard to Pitman's second contention (i.e., that [the Statute of Frauds] protects him from liability because he had no written agreement with Flanagan to pay the partnership's debt), the trial court did not adjudge Pitman liable on the ground that he had an agreement with Flanagan to pay the account, but on the ground that he had lost his limited partner status under [RULPA 303(a)], and, therefore[,] became liable as a general partner for the partnership's debt * * *.

**DECISION AND REMEDY**    *The appellate court affirmed the trial court's decision.*

**INTERNATIONAL CONSIDERATIONS**    **Liability of Limited Partners in Argentina** *Many nations permit businesspersons to establish limited partnerships. In Argentina, the limited partnership is called a* sociedad en comandita *and is closely regulated by the government. Limited partners, known as "sleeping partners," have limited liability so long as they do not participate in management. Argentinian law, however, does permit limited partners to inspect the books, express their views to managers, or offer advice at partnership meetings.*

## DISSOLUTION OF A LIMITED PARTNERSHIP

A limited partnership is dissolved in much the same way as an ordinary partnership. The retirement, death, or mental incompetence of a general partner can dissolve the partnership, but not if the business can be continued by one or more of the other general partners in accordance with their certificate or by consent of all members [RULPA 801]. The death or assignment of interest of a limited partner does not dissolve the limited partnership [RULPA 702, 704, 705]. A limited partnership can be dissolved by court decree [RULPA 802].

Illegality, expulsion, and bankruptcy of the general partners dissolve a limited partnership.

Bankruptcy of a limited partner, however, does not dissolve the partnership unless it causes the bankruptcy of the firm. The retirement of a general partner causes a dissolution unless the members consent to a continuation by the remaining general partners or unless this contingency is provided for in the certificate.

Upon dissolution, creditors' rights, including those of partners who are creditors, take first priority. Then partners and former partners receive unpaid distributions of partnership assets and, except as otherwise agreed upon, amounts representing a return on their contributions and amounts proportionate to their shares of the distributions [RULPA 804].

## TERMS AND CONCEPTS TO REVIEW

| | | |
|---|---|---|
| buy-sell agreement 794 | dissolution 786 | right of contribution 793 |
| certificate of limited partnership 796 | general partner 794 | winding up 786 |
| | limited partner 794 | |

# QUESTIONS AND CASE PROBLEMS

**40–1. Partnership Dissolution.** Alister, Beesum, and McCoy have formed a twenty-year partnership to purchase land, develop it, manage it, and then sell the property. The partnership agreement calls for the partners to devote their full time to the business. Discuss fully which of the following acts will constitute a dissolution of the partnership and whether there is any ensuing liability of Alister.

    (a) After two years, Beesum and McCoy agree that the working hours of the partnership will be from 8:00 A.M. to 6:00 P.M. rather than the previously established schedule of 9:00 A.M. to 5:00 P.M. Alister refuses to come to work before 9:00 A.M. and quits promptly at 5:00 P.M.

    (b) After two years, Alister quits the partnership and walks out.

    (c) After two years, Alister becomes insolvent.

    (d) After two years, Alister dies.

**40–2. Distribution of Partnership Assets.** Susan and Dominic formed a partnership. At the time of formation, Susan's capital contribution was $10,000, and Dominic's was $15,000. Later, Susan made a $10,000 loan to the partnership when it needed working capital. The partnership agreement provided that profits were to be shared, with 40 percent for Susan and 60 percent for Dominic. The partnership was dissolved by Dominic's death. At the end of the dissolution and the winding up of the partnership, the partnership's assets were $50,000, and the partnership's debts were $8,000. Discuss fully how the assets should be distributed.

**40–3. Fiduciary Duties of Partners.** Kaarin, Dak, and Charles were partners in a partnership at will. Kaarin and Dak excluded Charles from partnership management affairs and then sought a dissolution of the partnership. A trial court dissolved the partnership and ordered a sale of the partnership asset, a shopping center. Kaarin and Dak were the highest bidders at the court-ordered sale and were therefore able to retain the shopping center. Will the courts protect Charles in this situation? Discuss.

**40–4. Liability of Limited Partners.** Asner and Burton form a limited partnership with Asner as the general partner and Burton as the limited partner. Burton puts up $15,000, and Asner contributes some office equipment that he owns. A certificate of limited partnership is properly filed, and business is begun. One month later, Asner becomes ill. Instead of hiring someone to manage the business, Burton takes over complete management himself. While Burton is in control, he makes a contract with Thomas involving a large sum of money. Asner returns to work. Because of other commitments, the Thomas contract is breached. Thomas contends that Asner and Burton will be personally liable for damages caused by the breach if they cannot be satisfied out of the assets of the limited partnership. Discuss this contention.

**40–5. Limited Partnerships.** Dru, Lizbet, and Elena form a limited partnership. Dru is a general partner, and Lizbet and Elena are limited partners. Consider each of the separate events below, and discuss fully which event or events constitute a dissolution of the limited partnership.

    (a) Lizbet assigns her partnership interest to Arian.

    (b) Elena is petitioned into involuntary bankruptcy.

    (c) Dru dies.

**40–6. Partnership Dissolution.** Carola and Grogan were partners in a law firm. The partnership began business in 1974 and was created by an oral agreement. On September 6, 1976, Carola withdrew from the partnership some of its files, furniture, and books, along with various other items of office equipment. The next day, Carola informed Grogan he had withdrawn from the partnership. Discuss whether Carola's actions on September 6, 1976, constituted effective notice of dissolution to Grogan. [*Carola v. Grogan*, 102 A.D.2d 934, 477 N.Y.S.2d 525 (1984)]

**40–7. Partnership Dissolution.** Alex Gershunoff and Lawrence Silk formed a partnership in 1964 to syndicate and manage apartment houses. Jacob Oliker served the partnership as legal counsel. In 1969, Oliker joined the partnership, known as the Alex Co., as an equal partner. Oliker paid $5,000 to the partnership and gave up his legal practice as consideration for entering the partnership, but there was never a written partnership agreement. The partnership functioned smoothly from 1969 until 1974. In March 1974, Oliker withdrew from the partnership. After Oliker's withdrawal, the value of land owned by the partnership greatly appreciated. For two and a half years, the parties failed to agree on the amount of Oliker's interest. In November 1976, Gershunoff and Silk sent Oliker a "final accounting," which Oliker rejected. Oliker filed suit, requesting a formal accounting and a court-supervised winding up of affairs, with his interest to be determined as of its value at the time of the court-ordered accounting. Discuss whether Oliker was entitled to an equal share in the increased value of partnership assets. [*Oliker v. Gershunoff*, 195 Cal.App.3d 1288, 241 Cal.Rptr. 415 (2d Dist. 1987)]

**40–8. Partnership Dissolution.** In January 1987, Westbrook Pharmacy and Surgical Supply (doing business as Canter's Pharmacy, Inc.), Orrie Rockwell, Jr., and another business entity entered into a partnership agreement for the purpose of operating a personal care facility in Elizabeth, Pennsylvania. The partnership agreement provided that any disputes among the partners were to be submitted to arbitration. Two years later, the partnership sued Westbrook to recover capital contributions allegedly owed by Westbrook to the partnership. Westbrook filed a counterclaim against the partnership, seeking an accounting and a dissolution of the partnership. The partnership filed a motion to stay the proceedings pending arbitration pursuant to the arbitration provision in the partnership agreement. The trial court granted the partnership's motion. The question on appeal is whether the arbitration provision was enforceable, given the fact that Westbrook had sought an accounting and dissolution of the firm. Did Westbrook's action dissolve the partnership, thus rendering the provisions of the partnership—including the arbitration provision—ineffective? Discuss fully. [*Canter's Pharmacy, Inc. v. Elizabeth Associates,* 396 Pa.Super. 505, 578 A.2d 1326 (1990)]

**40–9. Liability of Limited Partners.** Combat Associates was formed as a limited partnership to promote an exhibition boxing match between Lyle Alzado (a professional football player) and Muhammad Ali. Alzado and others had formed Combat Promotions; this organization was to be the general partner and Blinder, Robinson & Co. (Blinder), the limited partner, in Combat Associates. The general partner's contribution consisted of assigning all contracts pertaining to the match, and the limited partner's contribution was a $250,000 letter of credit to ensure Ali's compensation. Alzado personally guaranteed to repay Blinder for any amount of loss if the proceeds of the match were less than $250,000. In preparation for the match, at Alzado's request, Blinder's president participated in interviews and a promotional rally, and the company sponsored parties and allowed its local office to be used as a ticket sales outlet. The proceeds of the match were insufficient, and Blinder sued Alzado on his guaranty. Alzado counterclaimed by asserting that Blinder took an active role in the control and management of Combat Associates and should be held liable as a general partner. How did the court rule on Alzado's counterclaim? Discuss. [*Blinder, Robinson & Co. v. Alzado,* 713 P.2d 1314 (Colo.App. 1985)]

**40–10. Partnership Dissolution.** Elfon Realty Co. was a limited partnership in which Harry Macklowe was the sole general partner and 42nd Street Development Corp. was the sole limited partner. The limited partner assigned its right to receive partnership distributions to a third party, in violation of the express conditions of the partnership agreement. In the litigation that followed, a central issue was whether 42nd Street Development Corp. should be entitled to an accounting in view of the fact that it had breached the partnership agreement. Discuss fully whether 42nd Street's assignment was sufficient misconduct to bar it from an accounting of partnership assets and profits. [*Macklowe v. 42nd Street Development Corp.,* 157 A.D.2d 566, 550 N.Y.S.2d 309 (1990)]

**40–11. Winding Up Partnership Affairs.** Rex Thorne of Diesel Repower Systems, Inc., contracted to sell five diesel engines to C&S Sales Group, a partnership owned by Don Crosby and Dennis Stringer. C&S planned to resell the engines to Oregon Parts Co. Thorne provided Crosby with the serial numbers of the engines and agreed to have them ready for shipment no later than November 4, 1987. On October 19 and 28, C&S sent payments to Thorne to cover the $25,000 contract price for the engines. When Diesel Repower did not deliver the engines as promised, Stringer discovered that Thorne did not have the engines with the serial numbers he had provided. Instead, Thorne gave C&S three incomplete engines, including one that had been burned and could not be used. Oregon Parts sued C&S and received a judgment for $32,121.76. C&S dissolved as a partnership, but subsequently sued Thorne and Diesel Repower for the amount that C&S had been ordered to pay to Oregon Parts. The jury returned a verdict against Thorne, individually, for $32,121.76 in compensatory damages. The court entered a judgment on that verdict, and Thorne appealed. Thorne argued in part that C&S had lacked the capacity to file a complaint against him, because the C&S partnership had been dissolved before the complaint was filed. What did the court decide? Discuss fully. [*Thorne v. C&S Sales Group,* 577 So.2d 1264 (Ala. 1991)]

**40–12. Partnership Agreements.** In 1980, Frederick Badger, Jr., Willard Linscott, and Orman Twitchell formed a partnership for the purpose of acquiring and managing certain commercial real estate in Bangor, Maine. The partners executed a written agreement that specified, among other things, the effect on the partnership and the procedures to be followed on a partner's death, expulsion, or withdrawal from the partnership. The agreement further provided that all disputes arising out of the agreement would be resolved through arbitration. In 1986, Twitchell was expelled from the partnership. He contested the expulsion. In 1988, Willard Linscott died. In accordance with the partnership agreement, Linscott's wife and personal representative undertook negotiations regarding the partnership's purchase of her late husband's interest in the partnership, but no agreement was reached as to the fair value of Linscott's shares. In 1991, Badger petitioned the court to dissolve the partnership, citing the disputes among the parties and alleging that the partnership could only be carried on at a loss. Should the court dissolve the partnership? Must the existing disputes be settled by the partners through arbitration? What will the court decide? [*Badger v. Linscott,* 622 A.2d 1161 (Me. 1993)]

# CHAPTER 41

# CORPORATIONS— FORMATION AND FINANCING

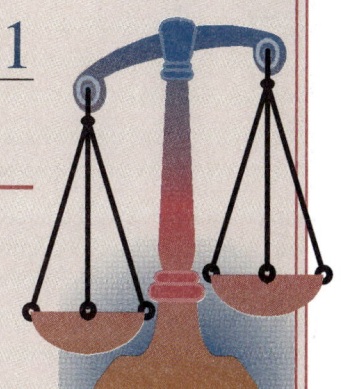

A corporation can be owned by a single person, or it can have hundreds, thousands, or even millions of shareholders. The shareholder form of business organization developed in Europe at the end of the seventeenth century. Called *joint stock companies,* these organizations frequently collapsed because their organizers absconded with the funds or proved to be incompetent. Because of this history of fraud and collapse, organizations resembling corporations were regarded with suspicion in the United States during its early years. Although several business corporations were formed after the Revolutionary War, it was not until the nineteenth century that the corporation came into common use for private business. Today, the corporation is one of the most important forms of business organization in the United States.

The corporation is a creature of statute. A corporation is an artificial being, existing in law only and neither tangible nor visible. Its existence depends generally upon state law, although some corporations, especially public organizations, can be created under federal law. Each state has its own body of corporate law, and these laws are not entirely uniform. The Model Business Corporation Act (MBCA) is a codification of modern corporation law that has been influential in the codification of state corporation statutes. Today, the majority of state statutes are guided by the revised MBCA, known as the Revised Model Business Corporation Act (RMBCA). The most recent edition of the latter is included in its entirety in Appendix H of this text. You should keep in mind, however, that there is considerable variation among the statutes of the states that have used the MBCA or the RMBCA as a basis for their statutes, and several states do not follow either act. Because of this, individual state corporation laws should be relied on to determine corporate law rather than the MBCA or RMBCA.

In this chapter, we examine the nature of the corporate form of business enterprise and the various classifications of corporations. We then discuss the formation and financing of today's corporation.

## SECTION 1

# THE NATURE OF THE CORPORATION

A *corporation* is a legal entity created and recognized by state law. It can consist of one or more persons identified under a common name.

## THE CORPORATION AS A LEGAL PERSON

A corporation is recognized under state and federal law as a "person," and it enjoys many of the same rights and privileges that U.S. citizens enjoy. The Bill of Rights guarantees a "person," as a citizen, certain protections; and corporations are considered persons in most instances. Accordingly, a corporation has the same constitutional rights as a natural person does (see Chapter 5). The corporation has a right to equal protection of the laws under the Fourteenth Amendment. It has the right of access to the courts as an entity that can sue or be sued. It also has the right of due process before denial of life, liberty, or property, as well as freedom from unreasonable searches and seizures and from double jeopardy.

Under the First Amendment, corporations are entitled to freedom of speech, but commercial speech (such as advertising) and political speech (such as contributions to political causes or candidates) receive significantly less protection than noncommercial speech (see Chapter 5 for a fuller discussion of commercial and political speech).

Only the corporation's individual officers and employees possess the Fifth Amendment right against self-incrimination.[1] And the privileges and immunities clause of the Constitution does not fully protect corporations, nor does it protect an unincorporated association.[2] Recall from Chapter 5 that the privileges and immunities clause requires each state to treat citizens of other states equally with respect to access to courts, travel rights, and so forth.

---

1.  *In re Grand Jury No. 86–3 (Will Roberts Corp.),* 816 F.2d 569 (11th Cir. 1987).
2.  *W. C. M. Window Co. v. Bernardi,* 730 F.2d 486 (7th Cir. 1984).

## CHARACTERISTICS OF THE CORPORATE ENTITY

A corporation is an artificial person, with its own corporate name, owned by individual shareholders. It is a legal entity with rights and responsibilities. The corporation substitutes itself for its shareholders in conducting corporate business and in incurring liability, yet its authority to act and the liability for its actions are separate and apart from the individuals who own it. (In certain limited situations, the "corporate veil" can be pierced—that is, liability for the corporation's obligations can be extended to shareholders, a topic to be discussed later in this chapter.) Responsibility for the overall management of the corporation is entrusted to a board of directors, which is elected by the shareholders [RMBCA 8.01; RMBCA 8.03]. Corporate officers and other employees are hired by the board of directors to run the daily business operations of the corporation.

When an individual purchases a share of stock in a corporation, that person becomes a shareholder and an owner of the corporation. Unlike the members in a partnership, the body of shareholders can change constantly without affecting the continued existence of the corporation. A shareholder can sue the corporation, and the corporation can sue a shareholder. Also, under certain circumstances, a shareholder can sue on behalf of a corporation. The rights and duties of all corporate personnel will be examined in Chapter 42.

Because a corporation is a separate legal entity, corporate profits are taxed by state and federal governments. Corporations can do one of two things with corporate profits—retain them or pass them on to shareholders in the form of dividends. The corporation receives no tax deduction for dividends distributed to shareholders. Dividends are again taxable (except when they represent distributions of capital) as ordinary income to the shareholder receiving them. As mentioned in Chapter 38, this double-taxation feature of the corporation organization is one of its major disadvantages. Profits not distributed are retained by the corporation. **Retained earnings,** if invested properly, will yield corporate profits in the future and thus may cause the price of the company's stock to rise. Individual shareholders can then reap the benefits of these retained earnings in the gains they receive when they sell their shares.

## TORTS

A corporation is liable for the torts committed by its agents or officers within the course and scope of their employment. This principle applies to a corporation exactly as it applies to the ordinary agency relationships discussed in Chapters 34 and 35. It follows the doctrine of *respondeat superior.*

## CRIMINAL ACTS

An unsettled area of corporation law has to do with the criminal acts of a corporation. Because a corporation cannot be sent to prison—even though, under law, it is a person—most courts hold a corporation that has violated a criminal statute liable for fines. When criminal conduct can be attributed to corporate officers or agents, those individuals, as *natural* persons, are held liable and can be imprisoned for their acts. The criminal liability of corporations and corporate officers and agents is discussed in detail in Chapter 9.

SECTION 2

# CORPORATE POWERS

Under modern law, except as limited by charters, statutes, or constitutions, *a corporation can engage in all acts and enter into any contract available to a natural person in order to accomplish the purposes for which it was created.* When a corporation is created, the express and implied powers necessary to achieve its purpose also come into existence.

## EXPRESS AND IMPLIED POWERS

The express powers of a corporation are found in its **articles of incorporation** (a document containing information about the corporation, including the corporation's organization and functions), in the law of the state of incorporation, and in the state and federal constitutions. Corporate **bylaws** (rules of management adopted by the corporation at its first organization meeting) and the resolutions of the corporation's board of directors also grant or restrict certain powers. The following order of priority is used when conflicts arise among documents involving corporations:

1. The U.S. Constitution.
2. State constitutions.
3. State statutes.
4. The articles of incorporation.
5. Bylaws.
6. Resolutions of the board of directors.

Certain implied powers arise when a corporation is created. Barring express constitutional, statutory, or charter prohibitions, the corporation has the implied power to perform all acts reasonably appropriate and necessary to accomplish its corporate purposes. For this reason, a corporation has the implied power to borrow money within certain limits, to lend money, to extend credit to those with whom it has a legal or contractual relationship, and to make charitable contributions.[3]

To borrow money, the corporation acts through its board of directors to authorize the loan. Most often, the president or chief executive officer of the corporation will execute the necessary papers on behalf of the corporation. In so doing, corporate officers have the implied power to bind the corporation in matters directly connected with the *ordinary* business affairs of the enterprise. A corporate officer does not have the authority to bind the corporation in matters of great significance to the corporate purpose or undertaking, such as the sale of substantial corporate assets, however.

## ULTRA VIRES DOCTRINE

The term ***ultra vires*** means "beyond the powers." In corporate law, acts of a corporation that are beyond the authority given to it under its charter or under the statutes by which it was incorporated are *ultra vires* acts. In other words, acts in furtherance of the corporation's expressed purposes are within the corporate power; acts beyond the scope of corporate business as described in the charter are *ultra vires* acts. Thus *ultra vires* acts can be understood only within the context of the particular stated purpose for which the corporation was organized.

The stated purposes in the articles of incorporation set the limits of the activities the

---

3. A corporation is prohibited from making political contributions in federal elections by the Federal Elections Campaign Act of 1974 (18 U.S.C. Section 321).

corporation can legally pursue. Any time the corporation takes on activities outside the stated purpose or purposes, the corporation can be charged with committing an *ultra vires* act. Because of this, corporations are increasingly aware of the benefits of adopting a very broad statement of purpose in their articles of incorporation to include virtually all conceivable activities. Corporate statutes in many states permit the expression ''any lawful purpose'' to be a legally sufficient stated purpose in the articles of incorporation.

A majority of cases dealing with *ultra vires* acts have involved contracts made for unauthorized purposes. For example, it is difficult to see how a contract made by a plumbing company for the purchase of six thousand cases of brandy is reasonably related to the conduct and furtherance of the corporation's stated purpose of providing plumbing installation and services. Hence, such a contract would probably be held *ultra vires.*

In some states, when a contract is entirely executory (a contract not yet performed by either party), a defense of *ultra vires* can be used by either party to prevent enforcement of the contract. In cases in which an *ultra vires* contract is partially or fully executed at the time of challenge, courts may enforce, or uphold, the contract if the circumstances are such that it would be inequitable to allow a party to assert the defense of *ultra vires.*

Section 3.04 of the RMBCA upholds the validity and enforceability of an *ultra vires* contract *as between the parties involved,* subject to the following rights:

1.  The right of shareholders on behalf of the corporation to bring an action to obtain an injunction and damages.
2.  The right of the corporation itself to recover damages from the officers and directors who caused the *ultra vires* transactions.
3.  The right of the attorney general of the state to institute a proceeding to obtain an injunction against the *ultra vires* transactions or to institute dissolution proceedings against the corporation for *ultra vires* acts.

Although still of some importance, the *ultra vires* doctrine is of declining significance in corporate law because courts have held that any legal action that a corporation undertakes to profit its shareholders is allowable and proper.

# CLASSIFICATION OF CORPORATIONS

The classification of a corporation normally depends upon its location, purpose, and ownership characteristics.

## DOMESTIC, FOREIGN, AND ALIEN CORPORATIONS

A corporation is referred to as a **domestic corporation** in its home state (the state in which it incorporates). A corporation formed in one state but doing business in another is referred to in that other state as a **foreign corporation.** A corporation formed in another country (say, Mexico) but doing business within the United States is referred to in the United States as an **alien corporation.**

A corporation does not have an automatic right to do business in a state other than its state of incorporation. It normally must obtain a *certificate of authority* in any state in which it plans to do business. Once the certificate has been issued, the powers conferred upon a corporation by its home state generally can be exercised in the other state. Should a foreign corporation do business without obtaining a certificate of authority, the state can fine the corporation; deny it the privilege of using state courts; and even hold its officers, directors, or agents personally liable for corporate obligations, including contractual obligations, incurred in that state.[4]

As discussed in Chapter 3, before a state court can hear a dispute in which a foreign corporation is the defendant, the state court must have *jurisdiction* over the defendant; this requires that the foreign corporation have sufficient *contacts* with the state. A foreign corporation that has its home office within the state or has manufacturing plants in the state generally meets this *minimum-contacts* requirement.[5] A foreign corporation whose only contact with the state is the fact that

---

4.  *Robertson v. Levy,* 197 A.2d 443 (D.C.App. 1964).
5.  The minimum-contacts standard was established in *International Shoe Co. v. State of Washington,* 326 U.S. 310, 66 S.Ct. 154, 90 L.Ed. 96 (1945).

one of its directors resides there usually does not have sufficient contacts with the state for the state court to exercise jurisdiction over it.

What about a Japanese corporation whose only contact with a state is through its wholly owned subsidiary? Can a state exercise jurisdiction over the Japanese corporation in these circumstances? This issue is raised in the following case, in which the court bases its decision on a "stream of commerce" theory of minimum contacts.

---

**BACKGROUND AND FACTS**  *In 1991, Loral Fairchild Corporation brought suit in a federal court against Victor Company of Japan, Ltd., and a number of other Japanese firms for patent infringement. One of the firms, Murata Machinery, Ltd. (Murata-Japan), manufactured facsimile (fax) machines that were distributed in the state of Virginia through its wholly owned subsidiary, Murata Business Systems, Inc. (Murata-America). Loral, which also sold fax machines in Virginia, alleged that Murata-Japan's fax machines used a device that had been patented by Loral. Murata-Japan moved to dismiss the complaint for lack of personal jurisdiction, and the issue in this case centered on whether Murata-Japan had sufficient contacts with Virginia to justify jurisdiction over Murata-Japan by a U.S. court. The evidence indicated that Murata-Japan itself did not sell products or services in Virginia, had no offices or bank accounts in Virginia, and shipped its goods to ports in states other than Virginia. All advertising, marketing, and distribution of Murata-Japan fax machines in Virginia were controlled solely by Murata-America. In short, Murata-Japan's sole "contacts" with Virginia existed by virtue of the fact that its subsidiary served the Virginia market and that its products allegedly caused tortious injury (to Loral) in Virginia.*

**CASE 41.1**

**LORAL FAIRCHILD CORP. v. VICTOR COMPANY OF JAPAN, LTD.**

United States District Court, Eastern District of New York, 1992.

803 F.Supp. 626.

*JOHNSON*, District Judge:

\* \* \* \*

\* \* \* [Under *World-Wide Volkswagen Corp. v. Woodson*, the] forum State does not exceed its powers \* \* \* if it asserts personal jurisdiction over a corporation that delivers its products into the stream of commerce with the expectation that they will be purchased by consumers in the forum State. \* \* \* ["The] foreseeability that is critical \* \* \* is that the defendant's conduct and connection with the forum state are such that [they] should reasonably anticipate being haled into court there."

\* \* \* \*

\* \* \* [T]he reasons for exercising jurisdiction over Murata-Japan in this case are \* \* \* compelling.

First, parent-Murata-Japan owns not 96% but 100% of its subsidiary/distributor's stock. Second, Murata-Japan has majority representation on the subsidiary's board \* \* \* .

\* \* \* \*

\* \* \* In addition, Murata-Japan derived substantial economic benefit from the Virginia sales and protection of Virginia laws. In total, Murata-Japan knew it had indirectly established contacts with the forum and intended such a result. Stated differently, Murata-Japan could have anticipated this lawsuit from its manufacture of infringing products sold by its distributor in Virginia.

---

*The court held that by placing its machines in the stream of commerce and purposefully directing them toward the Virginia marketplace,*  **DECISION AND REMEDY**

*Murata-Japan had satisfied the "minimum contacts" requirements for personal jurisdiction.*

**ETHICAL CONSIDERATIONS** *Murata-Japan argued, among other things, that being "haled into court" in the United States would impose an extreme burden on it, because its employees would be required to travel from Japan to the United States. In response to this argument, the court stated that "[a]ny inconvenience that Murata-Japan may suffer must be weighed against a public policy which favors providing a forum for an injured resident to bring an action against a non-resident manufacturer." The court concluded that this public policy outweighed "any inconvenience to Murata-Japan in defending this lawsuit."*

## PUBLIC AND PRIVATE CORPORATIONS

A public corporation is one formed by the government to meet some political or governmental purpose. Cities and towns that incorporate are common examples. In addition, many federal government organizations, such as the U.S. Postal Service, the Tennessee Valley Authority, and AMTRAK, are public corporations.

Private corporations, in contrast, are created either wholly or in part for private benefit. Most corporations are private. Although they may serve a public purpose, as a public utility does, they are owned by private persons rather than by the government.

## NONPROFIT CORPORATIONS

Corporations formed without a profit-making purpose are called *nonprofit, not-for-profit,* or *eleemosynary* (charitable) corporations. Nonprofit corporations are usually (although not necessarily) private corporations. Private hospitals, educational institutions, charities, religious organizations, and the like are frequently organized as nonprofit corporations. The nonprofit corporation is a convenient form of organization that allows various groups to own property and to form contracts without the individual members being personally exposed to liability.

## CLOSE CORPORATIONS

A **close corporation** is one whose shares are held by members of a family or by relatively few persons. Close corporations are also referred to as *closely held, family,* or *privately held* corpora-

tions. Usually, the members of the small group constituting a close corporation are personally known to one another. Because the number of shareholders is so small, there is no trading market for the shares. In practice, a close corporation is often operated like a partnership. A few states recognize this similarity in special statutory provisions that cover close corporations.

**STATUTES FOR CLOSE CORPORATIONS** To be eligible for close corporation status, a corporation has to have a limited number of shareholders, the transfer of corporation stock must be subject to certain restrictions, and the corporation must not make any public offering of its securities.[6] Close corporation statutes provide greater flexibility by expressly permitting electing corporations to vary significantly from those subject to traditional corporation law.[7]

A Statutory Close Corporation Supplement to the MBCA has been promulgated by the Committee on Corporate Laws of the Section of Corporation, Banking, and Business Law of the American Bar Association (ABA). In states that have adopted this supplement, it applies only to eligible corporations that elect close corporation status. To be eligible, a corporation must have fewer than fifty shareholders. As under some states' statutes, the supplement relaxes most of the nonessential formalities in the operation of a closely held corporation.

---

6. See, for example, 8 Del. Code Ann. Section 342, which provides that close corporations can have no more than thirty shareholders.

7. For example, in some states (such as Maryland), the close corporation need not have a board of directors.

Because close corporations come in many sizes and shapes, however, special close corporation statutes often fail to address issues relevant to many organizations. Also, given the informal style in which many close corporations are operated, the statutory requirement that a corporation must formally elect special status and continuously qualify often makes the process difficult for those whom the statutes are intended to benefit. For these and other reasons, in 1991 the ABA approved RMBCA 7.32.

Under RMBCA 7.32, if all of the shareholders of a corporation agree in writing, the corporation can operate without directors, bylaws, annual or special shareholders' or directors' meetings, stock certificates, or formal records of shareholders' or directors' decisions.[8] Such shareholder agreements are of primary benefit to close corporations, whose few shareholders are most likely to agree unanimously on such formalities.

## MANAGEMENT OF CLOSE CORPORATIONS

The close corporation has a single shareholder or a closely knit group of shareholders who usually hold the positions of directors and officers. Management of a close corporation resembles that of a sole proprietorship or a partnership, although as a corporation, the firm must meet the same legal requirements as other corporations—unless special statutes have been enacted, as mentioned previously. In states without such special statutes, close corporations have sometimes found it difficult to meet the requirements of state corporation law.

Consider a situation in which a state law requires that a corporation have two directors, but the close corporation has only one shareholder. One way of satisfying this law is to set two as the number of directors in the articles of incorporation but to operate the corporation with a permanent vacancy on the board of directors. Alternatively, a disinterested person, usually a friend, might be convinced to put his or her name down as director.

To prevent a majority shareholder from dominating a close corporation, the corporation may require that action can be taken by the board only on approval of more than a majority of the directors. Typically, this would not be required for ordinary business decisions but only for extraordinary actions—such as changing the amount of dividends or dismissing an employee-shareholder.

## TRANSFER OF SHARES IN CLOSE CORPORATIONS

Because, by definition, a close corporation has a small number of shareholders, the transfer of shares of one shareholder to someone else can cause serious management problems. In other words, the other shareholders can find themselves required to share control with someone they may not know or like. To avoid this problem, it is usually advisable for the close corporation with several shareholders to specify restrictions on the transferability of stock in its articles of incorporation. A few states have statutes prohibiting the transfer of close corporation shares unless certain persons—including shareholders, family members, and the corporation—have been given the opportunity to purchase the shares for the same price first.

Consider an example. Three sisters, Tisa, Dina, and Helene Jordan, form a corporation, Jordan's Car Wash, Inc. The three sisters are the only shareholders. Tisa and Dina do not want Helene to sell her shares to an unknown third person. When they write the articles of incorporation, they therefore restrict the transferability of shares to outside persons by stipulating that shareholders offer their shares to the corporation or other shareholders before selling them to an outside purchaser.

Another way that control of a close corporation can be stabilized is through the use of a shareholder agreement. Agreements among shareholders to vote their stock in a particular way are generally upheld.[9] Shareholder agreements can also provide that when one of the original shareholders dies, his or her shares of stock in the corporation will be divided in such a way that the proportionate holdings of the survivors, and thus their proportionate control, will be maintained.

Courts are generally reluctant to interfere with private agreements, including shareholder agreements, as illustrated by the following case.

---

8. Shareholders cannot agree, however, to eliminate shareholders' rights to inspect corporate books and records, to bring derivative actions (lawsuits on behalf of the corporation—see Chapter 42), to seek dissolution for corporate waste, or to dissent from extraordinary corporate actions.

---

9. An important case upholding the validity of shareholder agreements is *Ringling Bros.–Barnum and Bailey Combined Shows v. Ringling,* 29 Del.Ch. 610, 53 A.2d 441 (1947).

**CASE 41.2**

**ROSINY v. SCHMIDT**
New York Supreme Court,
Appellate Division, 1992.
185 A.D.2d 727,
587 N.Y.S.2d 929.

**BACKGROUND AND FACTS**   *In 1981, a shareholder agreement was formed among the four shareholders of Ched Realty, each of whom held 25 percent of the corporation's shares. Among other things, the agreement provided that in the event of a shareholder's death, the surviving shareholders could buy the decedent's shares at "book value" or $200 per share, whichever was greater. Two of the shareholders, Allen and Frank Rosiny, were young, well-educated attorneys. The other two shareholders, Charles McGuire and Jeanette Priddy, were elderly, and neither of them had completed high school. McGuire and Priddy had signed several shareholder agreements prior to 1981, including a 1971 agreement in which the "book value" had been used to measure the value of corporate shares. When the 1981 agreement was formed, the book value of the corporation was negative (given the depreciation of the premises, as recorded in the corporate books), but the market value was $4,225 per share and gaining in value. Both Priddy and McGuire died in 1988. Allen and Frank Rosiny sought to purchase the decedents' stock—which still had a negative book value but a market value of $41,500 per share—for $200 per share. When the decedents' representatives protested, the Rosinys sued to enforce the buy-out provision of the shareholder agreement. The heirs of McGuire and Priddy argued that there was no "meeting of the minds" [mutual assent] when the 1981 agreement was formed, and therefore the agreement was unenforceable. The heirs asserted that when the 1981 agreement was formed, Priddy was preoccupied with the death of her husband and McGuire's mental condition was "not good." They also claimed that the agreement was unconscionable because the younger shareholders, knowing that neither McGuire nor Priddy was aware of what they were signing, took advantage of this fact for their personal advantage. The court declared the 1981 agreement unenforceable, and the Rosinys appealed.*

**MEMORANDUM DECISION.**
\*   \*   \*   \*

\*   \*   \* [With regard to] the defendants' claim of unconscionability \*   \*   \* [t]he record \*   \*   \* reveals that this was the fourth Ched shareholders' agreement and the only one to which the plaintiffs [the Rosinys] were signatories. With the exception of one agreement in 1964 which contained a market value-based post-mortem buyout provision, which was later discarded, the others all provided for a book value formula to determine the value of a decedent's shares.
\*   \*   \*   \*

Nor does the record support the implication that because of the disparity in age and educational background, the decedents were deceived by the young attorneys. \*   \*   \* It may not nor should it be presumed that because one is of a certain advanced age that a contract is void or even voidable.
\*   \*   \*   \*

Also \*   \*   \* the 1981 agreement provided for its termination by the sale of the property or by the voluntary or involuntary dissolution of the corporation. Priddy and McGuire \*   \*   \* had the option of selling the property or dissolving the corporation. \*   \*   \* Despite representation by counsel, neither Priddy nor McGuire opted to sell the property or dissolve the corporation during the seven years following their execution of the 1981 agreement \*   \*   \*.
\*   \*   \*   \*

Nor is there support in the record for the conclusion that there was no meeting of the minds with respect to the term "book value." \*   \*   \* Priddy and McGuire had signed a 1971 agreement containing the identical buyout provision after rejecting a fair market value approach contained in an earlier agreement. The return to the use of "book value," an unambiguous term, from fair market value, as well as the use of this term in previous agreements, evinces a meeting of the minds as to this term of the agreement.

*The appellate court held in favor of the Rosinys. The 1981 shareholder agreement's postmortem buy-out provision was enforceable against the estates of Priddy and McGuire.*

**DECISION AND REMEDY**

## S CORPORATIONS

In 1982, Congress enacted the Subchapter S Revision Act. The act provided that small corporations, if they meet certain requirements (discussed below), can be treated for tax purposes as *S corporations* under Subchapter S of the Internal Revenue Code. As mentioned in Chapter 38, those electing for S corporation status can avoid the imposition of income taxes at the corporate level while retaining many of the advantages of a corporation, particularly limited liability. Although the S corporation has the advantages of the corporate form without the double taxation of income (corporate income is generally not taxed separately), it does have some disadvantages. One of the most important disadvantages relates to the fact that an S corporation's fringe-benefit payments to employee-shareholders who own more than 2 percent of the stock are generally nondeductible.

**QUALIFICATION REQUIREMENTS FOR S CORPORATION STATUS** Numerous requirements must be met for a corporation to qualify for S corporation status. The most important requirements are listed here.

1. The corporation must be a domestic corporation.
2. The corporation must not be a member of an affiliated group of corporations.
3. The shareholders of the corporation must be individuals, estates, or certain trusts. Corporations, partnerships, and nonqualifying trusts cannot be shareholders.
4. The corporation must have thirty-five or fewer shareholders.
5. The corporation can have only one class of stock. Not all shareholders need have the same voting rights.

6. No shareholder of the corporation can be a nonresident alien.

**BENEFITS OF S CORPORATIONS** At times it is beneficial for a regular corporation to elect S corporation status, as detailed in the following checklist.

1. When the corporation has losses, the S election allows the shareholders to use such losses to offset other income.
2. Whenever the shareholders are in lower tax brackets than the corporation, the S election causes the corporation's entire income to be taxed in the shareholders' brackets, whether or not it is distributed. This is particularly attractive when the corporation wants to accumulate earnings for some future business purpose.
3. Only a single tax on corporate income is imposed at individual income tax rates at the shareholder level (taxable to shareholders whether or not the income is actually distributed).

## PROFESSIONAL CORPORATIONS

Professional persons such as physicians, lawyers, dentists, and accountants can incorporate. Their corporations are typically identified by the letters S.C. (service corporation), P.C. (professional corporation), Inc. (incorporated), or P.A. (professional association). In general, the laws governing professional corporations are similar to those governing ordinary business corporations, although three basic areas of liability deserve brief attention.

First, a court might, for liability purposes, regard the professional corporation as a partnership in which each partner can be held liable for whatever malpractice liability is incurred by the others within the scope of the partnership. Second, a shareholder in a professional corporation is protected from the liability imposed because of torts (unrelated to malpractice) committed by other members. Third, although any shareholder of a professional corporation who engages in a negligent action and who is guilty of malpractice is *personally* liable for the damage caused, many professional corporation statutes impose personal liability on professional persons not only for their acts but also for the professional acts performed under their supervision.

Recently enacted statutes providing for limited liability companies (and, in a few states, limited liability partnerships) öffer some options for pro-

fessionals—see the *Emerging Trends in Business Law* in Chapters 38 and 39.

What if a business enterprise is by law defined as a corporation but is in fact conducted as if it were a partnership? This question has often come before the courts. In some cases, courts have imposed partnership law on the shareholders and held them personally liable for business obligations. In the following case, for example, a law partnership incorporated as a professional corporation in 1977 primarily for the purpose of obtaining certain tax benefits. The firm continued to operate, in fact, as a partnership. A central issue before the court was whether the firm should be governed by partnership law or corporation law.

---

### CASE 41.3

**BOYD, PAYNE, GATES & FARTHING, P.C. v. PAYNE, GATES, FARTHING & RADD, P.C.**

Supreme Court of Virginia, 1992.
422 S.E.2d 784.

**BACKGROUND AND FACTS**  *In 1977, Robert Boyd, Charles Payne, Ronald Gates, and Philip Farthing, who practiced law together as a partnership, formed a professional corporation known as Boyd, Payne, Gates & Farthing, P.C. (Boyd P.C.). In a letter sent to its clients and the legal community, Boyd P.C. stated that the "partnership" would continue to practice under the new firm name. Corporate stock was issued to the four partners in the same percentages as their profit percentages. Changes in the profit percentages occurred over time, but the stock ratio remained the same. In 1983, when Anthony Radd joined the practice, he received no stock but began receiving 5 percent of the profits. No partnership assets were ever transferred to the corporation. The members of the firm continued to refer to one another as "partners" and to Boyd as the "managing partner." "Partners' meetings" were held to discuss the firm's business matters. In 1987, Payne, Gates, Farthing, and Radd left Boyd P.C. and formed their own professional corporation under the name of Payne, Gates, Farthing & Radd, P.C. (Payne P.C.). A dispute arose over the ownership of Boyd P.C.'s assets, including accounts receivable, and the trial court found that Boyd P.C. was in fact a partnership and that the former partners were entitled to an accounting and a distribution of the partnership's assets. The court ordered Boyd P.C. to pay Payne and the others their respective percentages of the value of the partnership (in all, over $550,000). Boyd P.C. appealed this decision, contending that the trial court erred in applying partnership law to a corporation.*

---

*CARRICO,* Chief Justice.
\* \* \* \*

No formal partnership agreement existed during any of the periods in question and no partnership certificate was ever filed. However, tax returns described the law firm as a partnership and indicated that the members shared in losses as well as profits. \*  \*  \*
\* \* \* \*

\*  \*  \* Significantly, after the corporation was formed, the partners executed an agreement dealing with the possibility of a tax audit. The agreement provided that in the event of such an audit, "any tax liability . . . shall become the responsibility

. . . of each partner . . . according to [the] percentage of profits which he received in that particular year.'' Hence, the tax liability was apportioned on the basis of partnership percentages, not stock ownership.

\* \* \* \*

Because Boyd P.C. was a close corporation and its shareholders validly conducted the internal affairs of their law practice as a partnership, we hold that the trial court properly settled their rights and liabilities according to partnership law.

*The trial court's judgment was affirmed.*

**DECISION AND REMEDY**

---

## SECTION 4

# CORPORATE FORMATION

The formation of a corporation involves two steps: (1) preliminary organizational and promotional undertakings—particularly, obtaining capital for the future corporation—and (2) the legal process of incorporation.

### PROMOTIONAL ACTIVITIES

Before a corporation becomes a reality, people invest in the proposed corporation as subscribers, and contracts are frequently made by **promoters** on behalf of the future corporation. Promoters are those who, for themselves or others, take the preliminary steps in organizing a corporation. One of the tasks of the promoter is to issue a **prospectus,** which is a document required by federal or state securities laws (see Chapter 44) that describes the financial operations of the corporation, thus allowing an investor to make an informed decision. The promoter also secures the *corporate charter,* which, as will be discussed in the section on incorporation procedures, is a document issued by a state agency or authority—usually the secretary of state—that grants a corporation legal existence and the right to function.

**PROMOTER'S LIABILITY**  It is not unusual for a promoter to purchase or lease property with a view to selling it to the corporation when the corporation is formed. In addition, a promoter may enter into contracts with attorneys, accountants, architects, or other professionals whose services will be needed in planning for the proposed corporation. Finally, a promoter induces people to purchase stock in the corporation.

Some interesting legal questions arise in regard to promoters' activities, the most important centering on whether the promoter is personally liable for contracts made on behalf of a corporation that does not yet have any legal existence. In addition, once the corporation is formed, does the corporation assume liability on these contracts, or is the promoter still personally liable?

As a general rule, a promoter is held personally liable on preincorporation contracts. Courts simply hold that promoters are not agents when a corporation has yet to come into existence. If, however, the promoter secures the contracting party's agreement to hold only the corporation (not the promoter) liable on the contract, the promoter will not be liable in the event of any breach of contract.

Basically, the personal liability of the promoter continues even after incorporation unless the third party *releases* the promoter. In most states, this rule is applied whether or not the promoter made the agreement in the name of, or with reference to, the proposed corporation.

Incorporation does not make the corporation automatically liable for preincorporation contracts. Until the newly formed corporation consents, the third party cannot enforce the promoter's contract against the corporation.

Once the corporation is formed (the charter issued), the promoter remains personally liable until the corporation assumes the preincorporation contract by *novation* (see Chapter 18). Novation releases the promoter and makes the corporation liable for performing the contractual obligations. In some cases the corporation *adopts* the promoter's contract by undertaking to perform it. Most courts hold that adoption in and of itself does not discharge the promoter from contractual liability. Obviously, a corporation cannot normally *ratify* a preincorporation contract, as no principal was in existence at the time the contract was made.

# ■ CONCEPT SUMMARY 41.1 Classification of Corporations

| CLASSIFICATION | DESCRIPTION |
|---|---|
| **Domestic, Foreign, and Alien Corporations** | A corporation is referred to as a *domestic corporation* within its home state (the state in which it incorporates). A corporation is referred to as a *foreign corporation* by any state that is not its home state. A corporation is referred to as an *alien corporation* if it originates in another country but does business in the United States. |
| **Public and Private Corporations** | A *public corporation* is one formed by government (e.g., cities, towns, and public projects). A *private corporation* is one formed wholly or in part for private benefit. Most corporations are private. |
| **Nonprofit Corporation** | A corporation formed without a profit-making purpose (e.g., charitable, educational, and religious organizations and hospitals). |
| **Close Corporation** | A corporation owned by a family or a relatively small number of individuals. Transfer of shares is usually restricted, and the corporation cannot make a public offering of its securities. |
| **S Corporation** | A small domestic corporation (must have thirty-five or fewer shareholders as members) that, under Subchapter S of the Internal Revenue Code, is given special tax treatment. These corporations allow shareholders to enjoy the limited legal liability of the corporate form but to avoid its double-taxation feature (taxes are paid by shareholders as personal income, and the S corporation is not taxed separately). |
| **Professional Corporation** | A corporation formed by professionals (e.g., physicians or lawyers) to obtain the benefits of incorporation (pension plans, tax benefits, and limited liability). In most cases, the professional corporation is treated like other corporations, but sometimes the courts will disregard the corporate form and treat the shareholders as partners. |

**SUBSCRIBERS AND SUBSCRIPTIONS**   Prior to the actual formation of the corporation, the promoter can contact potential individual investors, and they can agree to purchase capital stock in the future corporation. This agreement is often called a *subscription agreement,* and the potential investor is called a *subscriber.* Depending on state law, subscribers become shareholders as soon as the corporation is formed or as soon as the corporation accepts the agreement. This way, if Corporation X becomes insolvent, the trustee in bankruptcy (see Chapter 33) can collect the consideration for any unpaid stock from a preincorporation subscriber.

Most courts view preincorporation subscriptions as continuing offers to purchase corporate stock. On or after its formation, the corporation can choose to accept the offer to purchase stock. Many courts also treat a subscription as a contract be-

tween the subscribers, making it irrevocable except with the consent of all of the subscribers. A subscription is irrevocable for a period of six months unless otherwise provided in the subscription agreement or unless all the subscribers agree to the revocation of the subscription [RMBCA 6.20]. In some courts and jurisdictions, the preincorporation subscriber can revoke the offer to purchase before acceptance without liability, however.

## INCORPORATION PROCEDURES

Exact procedures for incorporation differ among states, but the basic requirements are similar.

**STATE CHARTERING**   The first step in the incorporation procedure is to select a state in which to incorporate. Because state incorporation laws differ, individuals have found some advantage in looking for the states that offer the most advantageous tax or incorporation provisions. Delaware has historically had the least restrictive laws. Consequently, many corporations, including a number of the largest, have incorporated there. Delaware's statutes permit firms to incorporate in Delaware and carry out business and locate operating headquarters elsewhere. (Most other states now permit this as well.) Closely held corporations, however, particularly those of a professional nature, generally incorporate in the state in which their principal stockholders live and work.

**ARTICLES OF INCORPORATION** The primary document needed to begin the incorporation process is called the *articles of incorporation* (see Exhibit 41–1 for sample articles of incorporation for a close corporation). The articles include basic information about the corporation and serve as a primary source of authority for its future organization and business functions. The person or persons who execute the articles are called *incorporators* and will be discussed shortly. Generally, the information indicated below should be included in the articles of incorporation.

*Corporate Name.* The choice of a corporate name is subject to state approval to ensure against duplication or deception. State statutes usually require that the secretary of state run a check on the proposed name in the state of incorporation. Some states require that the incorporators, at their own expense, run a check on the proposed name for the newly formed corporation. Once cleared, a name can be reserved for a short time, for a fee, pending the completion of the articles of incorporation. All corporate statutes require the corporation name to include the word *Corporation, Incorporated, Company,* or *Limited,* or abbreviations of these terms [RMBCA 4.01; RMBCA 4.02].

A corporate name is prohibited from being the same as, or deceptively similar to, the name of an existing corporation doing business within the state. For example, if an existing corporation is named General Dynamics, Inc., the state will not allow another corporation to be called General Dynamic, Inc., because that name is deceptively similar to the first, and it impliedly transfers a part of the goodwill established by the first corporate user to the second corporation.

*Nature and Purpose.* The intended business activities of the corporation must be specified in the articles, and naturally, they must be lawful. Stating a general corporate purpose is usually sufficient to give rise to all of the powers necessary or convenient to the purpose of the organization. The corporate charter can state, for example, that the corporation is organized ''to engage in the production and sale of agricultural products.'' As stated before, there is a trend toward allowing corporate charters to state that the corporation is organized for ''any legal business.'' A broadly stated purpose creates greater flexibility and avoids unnecessary future amendments to the corporate charter should the corporation change or modify its line of business [RMBCA 2.02(b)(2)(i); RMBCA 3.01].

Some states prohibit the incorporation of certain professionals, such as doctors or lawyers, except pursuant to a professional incorporation statute. Also, in some states, certain industries—such as banks, insurance companies, or public utilities—cannot be operated in the general corporate form and are governed by special incorporation statutes.

*Duration.* A corporation can have perpetual existence under the corporate statutes of most states. A few states, however, prescribe a maximum duration, after which the corporation must formally renew its existence.

*Capital Structure.* The capital structure of the corporation is generally set forth in the articles. A few state statutes require a relatively small capital investment (for example, $1,000) for ordinary business corporations but a greater capital investment for those engaged in insurance or banking. The number of shares of stock authorized for issuance; their valuation; the various types or classes of stock authorized for issuance; and other relevant information concerning equity, capital, and credit must be outlined in the articles.

*Internal Organization.* Whatever the internal management structure of the corporation, it should be described in the articles, although it can be included in bylaws adopted after the corporation is formed [RMBCA 2.02]. The articles of incorporation commence the corporation; the bylaws are formed after commencement by the board of directors. Bylaws are subject to, and cannot conflict

■ **Exhibit 41–1 Sample Articles of Incorporation—Short Form**

Filed with Secretary of State

_____ , 19 _____

ARTICLES OF INCORPORATION
OF

_____

ARTICLE I

The name of this corporation is _____

ARTICLE II

The purpose of this corporation is to engage in any lawful act or activity for which a corporation may be organized under the General Corporation Law of New Pacum other than the banking business, the trust company business or the practice of a profession permitted to be incorporated by the New Pacum Corporation Code.

ARTICLE III

The name and address in the State of New Pacum of this corporation's initial agent for service of process is: _____

_____

ARTICLE IV

The corporation is authorized to issue only one class of shares of stock; and the total number of shares which this corporation is authorized to issue is _____

ARTICLE V

This corporation is a close corporation. All the corporation's issued shares of stock shall be held of record by not more than ten (10) persons.

DATED: _____

_____          _____

_____          _____

[Signature(s) of Incorporator/Director(s)]

I (we) hereby declare that I (we) am (are) the person(s) who executed the foregoing Articles of Incorporation, which execution is my (our) act and deed.

_____          _____

_____          _____

with, the incorporation statute or the corporation's charter [RMBCA 2.06]. Under the RMBCA, shareholders may amend or repeal bylaws. The board of directors may also amend or repeal bylaws unless the articles of incorporation or provisions of the incorporation statute reserve that power to shareholders exclusively [RMBCA 10.20]. Typical bylaw provisions describe voting procedures and requirements for shareholders, the election of the board of directors, the methods of replacing directors, and the manner and time of scheduling shareholders' meetings and board meetings.

*Registered Office and Agent.* The corporation must indicate the location and address of its registered office within the state [RMBCA 2.02(a)(3)]. Usually, the registered office is also the principal office of the corporation. The corporation must give the name and address of a specific person who has been designated as an *agent* and who can receive legal documents on behalf of the corporation. These legal documents include service of process (the delivery of a court order requiring an appearance in court).

*Incorporators.* Each incorporator must be listed by name and must indicate an address [RMBCA 2.202(a)(4)]. An incorporator is a person—often, the corporate promoter—who applies to the state on behalf of the corporation to obtain its corporate charter. The incorporator need not be a subscriber and need not have any interest at all in the corporation. Many states do not impose residency or age requirements for incorporators. States vary on the required number of incorporators; it can be as few as one or as many as three. Incorporators are required to sign the articles of incorporation when they are submitted to the state; often, this is their only duty. In some states, they participate at the first organizational meeting of the corporation.

**CERTIFICATE OF INCORPORATION** Once the articles of incorporation have been prepared, signed, and authenticated by the incorporators, they are sent to the appropriate state official, usually the secretary of state, along with the appropriate filing fee. In many states, the secretary of state then issues a **certificate of incorporation** representing the state's authorization for the corporation to conduct business. (This may be called the **corporate charter.**) The certificate and a copy of the articles are returned to the incorporators, who then hold the initial organizational meeting that completes the details of incorporation [RMBCA 2.03].

**FIRST ORGANIZATIONAL MEETING** The first organizational meeting is often provided for in the articles of incorporation but is held after the charter is actually granted. At this meeting, the incorporators elect the first board of directors and complete the routine business of incorporation (pass bylaws, issue stock, and so forth). Sometimes, the meeting is held after the election of the board of directors, and the business to be transacted depends upon the requirements of the state's incorporation statute, the nature of the business, the provisions made in the articles, and the desires of the promoters [RMBCA 2.05].

Adoption of bylaws—the internal rules of management for the corporation—is probably the most important function of the first organizational meeting. The shareholders, directors, and officers must abide by the bylaws in conducting corporate business. Corporate employees and third persons dealing with the corporation are not bound by them, however, unless they have reason to be familiar with them.

# IMPROPER INCORPORATION

The procedures for incorporation are very specific. If they are not followed precisely, others may be able to challenge the existence of the corporation.

Errors in the incorporation procedures can become important when, for example, a third person who is attempting to enforce a contract or bring suit for a tort injury fortuitously learns of them. On the basis of improper incorporation, the plaintiff could seek to make the would-be shareholders personally liable. Also, when the corporation seeks to enforce a contract against a defaulting party, if the defaulting party learns of a defect in the incorporation procedure, he or she may be able to avoid liability on that ground.

To prevent injustice, courts will sometimes attribute corporate existence to an improperly formed corporation by holding it to be a *de jure* corporation or a *de facto* corporation, as discussed below. In some cases, corporation by estoppel may also occur.

## DE JURE AND DE FACTO CORPORATIONS

In the event of substantial compliance with all conditions precedent to incorporation, a corporation is said to have *de jure* existence in law. In most states and under RMBCA 2.03(b), the certificate of incorporation is viewed as evidence that all mandatory statutory provisions have been met. This means that the corporation is properly formed, and neither the state nor a third party can attack its existence. If, for example, an incorporator's address was incorrectly listed, this would mean that the corporation was improperly formed. The law, however, does not regard such inconsequential procedural defects as detracting from substantial compliance, and courts will uphold the *de jure* status of the corporate entity.

Sometimes there is a defect in complying with statutory mandates—for example, the corporation charter may have expired. Under these circumstances, the corporation may have a *de facto* status, meaning that its existence cannot be challenged by third persons (except the state). The following elements are required for *de facto* status:

1. There must be a state statute under which the corporation can be validly incorporated.
2. The parties must have made a good faith attempt to comply with the statute.
3. The enterprise must have already undertaken to do business as a corporation.

## CORPORATION BY ESTOPPEL

If an association that is neither an actual corporation nor a *de facto* or *de jure* corporation holds itself out as being a corporation, it will be estopped from denying corporate status in a lawsuit by a third party. This usually occurs when a third party contracts with an association that claims to be a corporation but does not hold a certificate of incorporation. When the third party brings suit naming the so-called corporation as the defendant, the association may not escape from liability on the ground that no corporation exists. When justice requires, the courts treat an alleged corporation as if it were an actual corporation for the purpose of determining the rights and liabilities involved in a particular situation. Corporation by estoppel is thus determined by the situation. It does not extend recognition of corporate status beyond the resolution of the problem at hand.

## SECTION 6

# DISREGARDING THE CORPORATE ENTITY

In some unusual situations, a corporate entity is used by its owners to perpetrate a fraud, circumvent the law, or in some other way accomplish an illegitimate objective. In these cases, the court will ignore the corporate structure by "piercing the corporate veil," exposing the shareholders to personal liability [RMBCA 2.04].

The following are some of the factors that may cause the courts to pierce the corporate veil:

1. A party is tricked or misled into dealing with the corporation rather than the individual.
2. The corporation is set up never to make a profit or always to be insolvent, or it is too "thinly" capitalized—that is, a corporation may have insufficient capital at the time the corporation is formed to meet its prospective debts or potential liabilities.
3. Statutory corporate formalities, such as holding required corporation meetings, are not followed.
4. Personal and corporate interests are mixed together, or **commingled,** to the extent that the corporation has no separate identity.

To elaborate on the fourth factor in the preceding list, consider a close corporation that is formed according to law by a single person or by a few family members. In such a case, the corporate entity and the sole stockholder (or family-member stockholders) must carefully preserve the separate status of the corporation and its owners. Certain practices invite trouble for the one-person or family-owned corporation: the commingling of corporate and personal funds; the failure to hold and record minutes of board of directors' meetings; or the shareholders' continuous, personal use of corporate property (for example, vehicles). When the corporate privilege is abused for personal benefit and the corporate business is treated in such a careless manner that the corporation and the shareholder in control are no longer separate entities, the court usually will require an owner to assume personal liability to creditors for the corporation's debts. In short, when the facts show that great injustice would result from the use of a corporation to avoid individual responsibility, a court of equity will look behind the corporate structure to the individual stockholder.

General corporation law has no specific prohibition against a stockholder's lawfully lending money to his or her corporation. When an officer, director, or majority shareholder lends the corporation money and takes back security in the form of corporate assets, however, the courts will scrutinize the transaction closely. Any such transaction must be made in good faith and for fair value.

The following case involves two shareholders who loaned money to the corporation in return for a security interest in corporate property.

---

**CASE 41.4**

**INTERTHERM, INC. v. OLYMPIC HOMES SYSTEMS, INC.**
Court of Appeals of Tennessee, 1978.
569 S.W.2d 467.

**BACKGROUND AND FACTS** *The plaintiffs (InterTherm, Inc.) were creditors of Olympic Homes Systems, Inc. Two of Olympic's shareholders, Langley and Clayton, the defendants, had made a sizable loan to the corporation. In return, they took a security interest in certain corporate property. When the corporation became insolvent, the general creditors attempted to set aside the priority of the defendants' security interest. The defendants argued that the general creditors had failed to show either that there was any fraud involved in the making of the loan or that the loan was not a legitimate transaction. Moreover, according to the defendants, the general creditors had not established that the defendants' relationship to the corporation was fiduciary or that they showed a lack of good faith in the loan transaction. The trial court entered judgment for the general creditors, and the shareholders appealed.*

*DROWOTA,* Judge.
\* \* \* \*

It is \* \* \* generally held that courts will closely scrutinize the transactions of a majority, dominant, or controlling shareholder with his corporation, and will place the burden of proof upon the shareholder when the good faith and fairness of such a transaction is challenged. \* \* \* It is obvious, however, that the reason for applying the rule to a shareholder is the same as the reason for applying it to an officer or director, that is, that he occupies a fiduciary position with regard to the corporation and those interested in it. Unless it is shown that a shareholder owns a majority of the stock or that he otherwise controls or dominates a corporation, however, a shareholder cannot be said to be a fiduciary and the reason for closely scrutinizing his transactions with the corporation disappears. \* \* \*

\* \* \* We hold that the instant transaction should not be subjected to close scrutiny, and that the burden of proof should not be on defendant shareholders, because plaintiffs have offered no evidence from which we could conclude that defendants owned a majority of Olympic's stock or otherwise dominated it in such a way as to justify imposing fiduciary responsibilities on them.

There is no evidence in this record that either defendant Langley or defendant Clayton was ever an officer or director of Olympic. The evidence is that each owned 15% of the capital stock of Olympic. It is clear that both were involved in setting up the corporation, but there is nothing to show that they participated in the business afterward. There is evidence that they did not intend to participate in the corporation's everyday affairs. \* \* \* In short, there is no evidence of any degree of power or control by defendants over the corporation at any time. \* \* \*

Plaintiffs, then, by failing to show that defendants Langley and Clayton had any fiduciary capacity with Olympic, have failed to shift from themselves the burden of proving fraud or absence of good faith in the loan transaction.

**DECISION AND REMEDY**

*The Supreme Court of Tennessee reversed the lower court's decision and held that the defendants, Langley and Clayton, held a valid security interest in the property of Olympic and were entitled to priority over the general creditors.*

**INTERNATIONAL CONSIDERATIONS** **Piercing the Corporate Veil in Europe** *Nations that recognize limited-liability entities also provide for "piercing the corporate veil" to avoid abuse. Some nations, such as Germany, have been most hesitant to do so, however. The developing European law has made it easier to pierce the corporate veil. When there is a single controlling shareholder, some European cases have established a presumption that the shareholder is personally liable. The shareholder bears the burden of proving that the company was truly a separate entity.*

## SECTION 7

# CORPORATE FINANCING

Corporations are financed by the issuance and sale of corporate securities—bonds and stock. To obtain financing, corporations issue **securities**—evidence of the obligation to pay money or of the right to participate in earnings and the distribution of corporate trusts and other property. The principal method of long-term and initial corporate financing is the issuance of stocks (equity) and bonds (debt), both of which are sold to investors. **Stocks,** or *equity securities,* represent the purchase of ownership in the business firm. **Bonds,** or *debt securities,* represent the borrowing of money by firms (and governments). Of course, not all debt is in the form of debt securities. Some is in the form of accounts payable, some is in the form of notes payable, and some is in the form of leaseholds. Accounts and notes payable are typically short-term debts. Bonds are simply a way for the corporation to split up its long-term debt so that it can market it more easily.

## BONDS

*Bonds* are issued by business firms and by governments at all levels as evidence of the funds they are borrowing from investors. Bonds almost always have a designated *maturity date*—the date when the principal or face amount of the bond (or loan) is returned to the investor—and are sometimes referred to as *fixed-income securities,* because their owners receive a fixed-dollar interest payment during the period of time prior to maturity.

The characteristics of corporate bonds vary widely, in part because corporations differ in their abilities to generate the earnings and cash flow necessary to make interest payments and to repay the principal amount of the bonds at maturity. Furthermore, corporate bonds are only a part of the total debt and the overall financial structure of corporate business. The different types of corporate bonds are described in Exhibit 41–2.

## STOCKS

Issuing *stocks* is another way that corporations can obtain financing [RMBCA 6.01]. The ways in

### ■ Exhibit 41–2 Types of Corporate Bonds

| Type | Definition |
|------|-----------|
| **Debenture Bonds** | Bonds for which no specific assets of the corporation are pledged as backing. Rather, they are backed by the general credit rating of the corporation, plus any assets that can be seized if the corporation allows the debentures to go into default. |
| **Mortgage Bonds** | Bonds that pledge specific property. If the corporation defaults on the bonds, the bondholders can take the property. |
| **Convertible Bonds** | Bonds that can be exchanged for a specified number of shares of common stock under certain conditions. |
| **Callable Bonds** | Bonds that may be called in and the principal repaid at specified times or under conditions specified in the bond when it is issued. |

■ **Exhibit 41–3  How Do Stocks and Bonds Differ?**

| Stocks | Bonds |
|---|---|
| 1. Stocks represent ownership. | 1. Bonds represent debt. |
| 2. Stocks (common) do not have a fixed dividend rate. | 2. Interest on bonds must always be paid, whether or not any profit is earned. |
| 3. Stockholders can elect a board of directors, which controls the corporation. | 3. Bondholders usually have no voice in, or control over, management of the corporation. |
| 4. Stocks do not have a maturity date; the corporation does not usually repay the stockholder. | 4. Bonds have a maturity date when the bondholder is to be repaid the face value of the bond. |
| 5. All corporations issue or offer to sell stocks. This is the usual definition of a corporation. | 5. Corporations do not necessarily issue bonds. |
| 6. Stockholders have a claim against the property and income of a corporation after all creditors' claims have been met. | 6. Bondholders have a claim against the property and income of a corporation that must be met before the claims of stockholders. |

which stocks differ from bonds are summarized in Exhibit 41–3. Basically, stocks represent ownership in a business firm, whereas bonds represent borrowing by the firm.

Exhibit 41–4 offers a summary of the types of stocks issued by corporations. The two major types are *common stock* and *preferred stock.*

COMMON STOCK  **Common stock** represents the true ownership of a corporation. It provides a proportionate interest in the corporation with regard to (1) control, (2) earnings, and (3) net assets. A shareholder's interest is generally in proportion to the number of shares owned out of the total number of shares issued.

Any person who purchases shares acquires voting rights—one vote per share held. Voting rights in a corporation apply to the election of the firm's board of directors and to any proposed changes in the ownership structure of the firm.[10] For example, a holder of common stock generally has the right to vote in a decision on a proposed merger, as mergers can change the proportion of ownership.

Firms are not obligated to return a principal amount per share to each holder of common stock, because no firm can ensure that the market price

---

10.  State corporation law specifies the types of actions for which shareholder approval must be obtained.

■ **Exhibit 41–4  Types of Stocks**

| Type | Definition |
|---|---|
| **Common Stock** | Voting shares that represent ownership interest in a corporation. Common stock has the lowest priority with respect to payment of dividends and distribution of assets upon the corporation's dissolution. |
| **Preferred Stock** | Shares of stock that have priority over common-stock shares as to payment of dividends and distribution of assets upon dissolution. Dividend payments are usually a fixed percentage of the face value of the share. |
| **Cumulative Preferred Stock** | Stock in which required dividends not paid in a given year must be paid in a subsequent year before any common-stock dividends are paid. |
| **Participating Preferred Stock** | Stock in which the owner is entitled to receive the preferred-stock dividend and additional dividends after payment of dividends on common stock. |
| **Convertible Preferred Stock** | Preferred shares giving shareholders the option to convert their shares into a specified number of common shares either in the issuing corporation or, sometimes, in another corporation. |
| **Redeemable, or Callable, Preferred Stock** | Preferred shares issued with the express condition that the issuing corporation has the right to repurchase the shares as specified. |

■ **Exhibit 41–5  Cumulative Convertible Preferred-Stock Certificate**

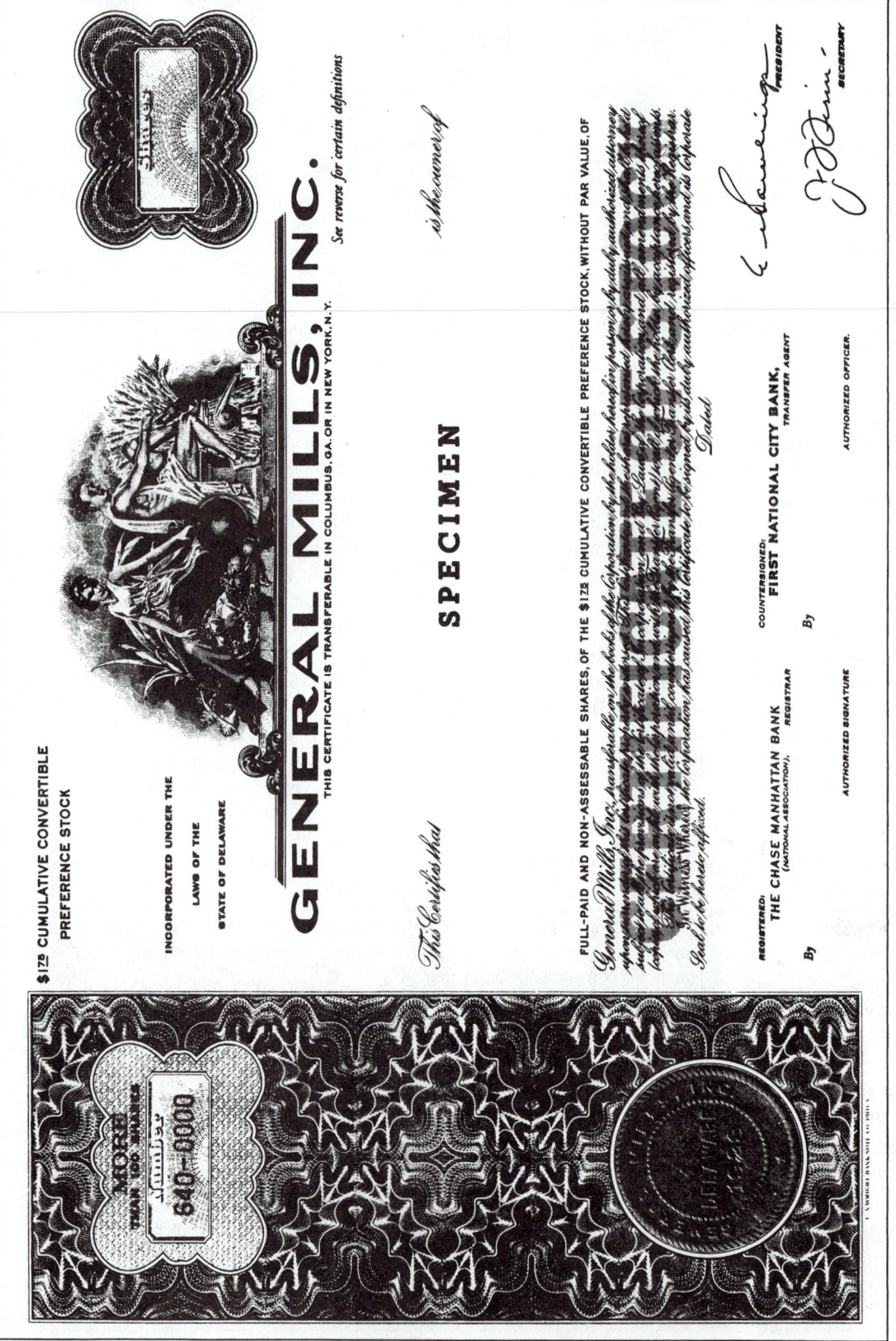

per share of its common stock will not decline over time. Nor does the issuing firm have to guarantee a dividend; indeed, some corporations never pay dividends.

Holders of common stock are a group of investors who assume a *residual* position in the overall financial structure of a business. In terms of receiving payment for their investments, they are last in line. The earnings to which they are entitled also depend on all the other groups—suppliers, employees, managers, bankers, governments, bondholders, and holders of preferred stock—being paid what is due them first. Once those groups are paid, however, the owners of common stock may be entitled to *all* the remaining earnings. (But the board of directors is not normally under any duty to declare the remaining earnings as dividends.)

**PREFERRED STOCK**    **Preferred stock** is stock with *preferences*. Usually, this means that holders of preferred stock have priority over holders of common stock as to dividends and to payment upon

dissolution of the corporation. Preferred stockholders may or may not have the right to vote (the trend is toward giving preferred stockholders the right to vote).

From an investment standpoint, preferred stock is more similar to bonds than to common stock. Preferred shareholders receive periodic dividend payments, usually established as a fixed percentage of the face amount of each preferred share. A 6 percent preferred stock with a face amount of $100 per share would pay its owner a $6 dividend each year. This is not a legal obligation on the part of the firm. Preferred stock is not included among the liabilities of a business, because it is technically equity. Like other equity securities, preferred shares have no fixed maturity date on which they must be retired by the firm. Although occasionally firms retire preferred stock, they are not legally obligated to do so. A sample cumulative convertible preferred-stock certificate is shown in Exhibit 41–5.

---

# TERMS AND CONCEPTS TO REVIEW

| | | |
|---|---|---|
| alien corporation 804 | commingle 816 | prospectus 811 |
| articles of incorporation 803 | common stock 819 | retained earnings 802 |
| bond 818 | corporate charter 815 | securities 818 |
| bylaw 803 | domestic corporation 804 | stock 818 |
| certificate of | foreign corporation 804 | *ultra vires* 803 |
|    incorporation 815 | preferred stock 821 | |
| close corporation 806 | promoter 811 | |

---

# QUESTIONS AND CASE PROBLEMS

**41–1. Nature of Corporations.** Jonathan, Gary, and Rob are active members of a partnership called Swim City. The partnership manufactures, sells, and installs outdoor swimming pools in the states of Texas and Arkansas. The partners want to continue to be active in management and to expand the business into other states as well. They are concerned about rather large recent judgments entered against swimming pool companies throughout the United States. Based on these facts only, discuss whether the partnership should incorporate.

**41–2. Liability for Preincorporation Contracts.** Cummings, Marvin, and Taft are recent college grad-

uates who want to form a corporation to manufacture and sell personal computers. Peterson tells them he will set in motion the formation of their corporation. First, Peterson makes a contract for the purchase of a piece of land for $20,000 with Owens. Owens does not know of the prospective corporate formation at the time of the signing of the contract. Second, Peterson makes a contract with Babcock to build a small plant on the property being purchased. Babcock's contract is conditional on the corporation's formation. Peterson secures all necessary subscription agreements and capitalization, and he files the articles of incorporation. A charter is issued.
  (a) Discuss whether the newly formed corporation, Peterson, or both are liable on the contracts with Owens and Babcock.
  (b) Discuss whether the corporation is automatically liable to Babcock upon being formed.

**41–3. Subscription Agreements.** As a promoter forming a new corporation, Peterson enters into three preincorporation subscription agreements with Mary, Anne, and Harry. The three subscribers each agree to purchase one thousand shares of stock of the future corporation for $2,000. Two months later, just prior to the issuance of the corporate charter, Mary tells Peterson she is withdrawing from the agreement. The charter is issued the next week. Just before the first organizational meeting of the corporation, Harry also withdraws from the agreement. Discuss fully whether Mary, Harry, or both can withdraw from their subscription agreements without liability.

**41–4. Corporate Status.** Three brothers inherited a small paper-supply business from their father, who had operated the business as a sole proprietorship. The brothers decided to incorporate under the name of Miwa Corp. and retained an attorney to draw up the necessary documents. The attorney drew up the papers and had the brothers sign them but neglected to send the application for a corporate charter to the secretary of state's office. The brothers assumed that all necessary legal work had been taken care of, and they proceeded to do business as Miwa Corp. One day, a Miwa Corp. employee was delivering a carton of paper supplies to one of Miwa's customers. On the way to the customer's office, the employee negligently ran a red light and caused a car accident. Harman, the driver of the other vehicle, was injured as a result and sued Miwa Corp. for damages. Harman then learned that no state charter had ever been issued to Miwa Corp., so he sued each of the brothers personally for damages. Can the brothers avoid personal liability for the tort of their employee? Explain.

**41–5. Corporate Powers.** Oya Paka and two business associates formed a corporation called Paka Corp. for the purpose of selling computer services. Oya, who owned 50 percent of the corporate shares, served as the corporation's president. Oya wished to obtain a personal loan from her bank for $250,000, but the bank required the note to be cosigned by a third party. Oya cosigned the note in the name of the corporation. Later, Oya defaulted on the note, and the bank sued the corporation for payment. The corporation asserted, as a defense, that Oya had exceeded her authority when she cosigned the note on behalf of the corporation. Had she? Explain.

**41–6. Liability for Preincorporation Contracts.** Skandinavia, Inc., manufactured and sold polypropylene underwear. Following two years of poor sales, Skandinavia entered into negotiations to sell the business to Odilon Cormier, an experienced textile manufacturer. Skandinavia and Cormier agreed that Cormier would take Skandinavia's underwear inventory and use it in a new corporation, which would be called Polypro, Inc. In return, Skandinavia would receive a commission on future sales from Polypro. Polypro was subsequently established and began selling the underwear. Skandinavia, however, never received any commissions from the sales. It therefore brought suit against

Polypro and Cormier to recover its promised commissions. The claim against Polypro was dismissed by the trial court, but the trial court found Cormier to be personally liable for the commissions owed. Cormier appealed to the Supreme Court of New Hampshire. Is Cormier personally liable for the contract he signed in the course of setting up a new corporation? Discuss. [*Skandinavia, Inc. v. Cormier,* 128 N.H. 215, 214 A.2d 1250 (1986)]

**41–7. Professional Corporations.** The defendant, Cohen, Stracher & Bloom, P.C., a law firm organized as a professional corporation under New York law, entered into an agreement with the plaintiff, We're Associates Co., for the lease of office space located in Lake Success, New York. The lease was signed for We're Associates by one of the partners of the plaintiff's company and for the defendant professional corporation by Paul J. Bloom, as vice president. Bloom and the other two defendants, Cohen and Stracher, were the sole officers, directors, and shareholders of the professional corporation. The corporation became delinquent in paying its rent, and the plaintiff brought an action to recover rents and other charges of approximately $9,000 alleged to be due and owing under the lease. The complaint was filed against the professional corporation and each individual shareholder of the corporation. The individual shareholders moved to dismiss the action against them individually. Will the court grant their motion? Discuss. [*We're Associates Co. v. Cohen, Stracher & Bloom, P.C.,* 103 A.D.2d 130, 478 N.Y.S.2d 670 (1984)]

**41–8.** *Ultra Vires* **Acts.** The Midtown Club, Inc., was a nonprofit corporation whose certificate of incorporation stated that the sole purpose of the club was "to provide facilities for the serving of luncheon or other meals to members." Samuel Cross, a member of the club, brought a female guest to lunch at the club, but he and his friend were both refused seating. On several occasions, Cross made applications on behalf of females for their admission to the club, but the club either ignored or rejected them. Cross brought an action against the club, alleging that the club's actions were *ultra vires.* Did he succeed? Explain. [*Cross v. Midtown Club, Inc.,* 33 Conn.Supp. 150, 365 A.2d 127 (1976)]

**41–9. Corporate Status.** Pat Daniels, John Daniels, and Bill Mandell (the defendants) planned to purchase a tavern and restaurant business in St. Charles, Illinois, and to organize their business in the form of a corporation under the name of D&M, Inc. The defendants negotiated with Howard Realty Group to lease the premises on which the tavern and restaurant were located. While the sale of the business and the negotiation of the lease were proceeding, neither the seller of the business nor Howard contemplated personal guarantees from the defendants. On January 18, 1987, although D&M had not yet been incorporated, the lease was signed in the name of D&M, Inc., by Pat Daniels and Bill Mandell, in their capacities as president and secretary, respectively, of the future corporation. On February 11, 1987, the defendants filed the articles of incorporation for D&M with the secretary of state. The articles were returned by the secretary of state's office because the name "D&M, Inc." was already in use by another Illinois corporation. The defendants then decided to file the articles of incorporation under the name of The Lodge at Tin Cup Pass, Inc. (the Lodge). They first checked with the landlord to see if they could use that name, because it was similar to the name of the property, Tin Cup Pass. The Lodge was duly incorporated on March 5, 1987. In late 1988, when the Lodge defaulted on its lease payments, Tin Cup Pass Limited Partnership, to whom Howard had assigned the lease, sued the defendants personally to recover the lease payments due, alleging that the defendants should be held liable as corporate promoters for D&M, Inc., a corporation that was never formed. What will result in court? Discuss fully. [*Tin Cup Pass Limited Partnership v. Daniels,* 195 Ill.App.3d 847, 553 N.E.2d 82, 142 Ill.Dec. 732 (1990)]

**41–10. Liability of Shareholders.** In the early 1950s, Mary Emmons opened an account at M&M Wholesale Florist, Inc., to purchase flowers and florist supplies for her flower shop, called Bay Minette Flower Shop, which she operated as a sole proprietorship. In 1973, the flower shop was incorporated as Bay Minette Flower Shop, Inc. Emmons continued to order supplies from M&M, as did her son when he began to manage the day-to-day operations of the shop during the 1980s. M&M, which had no knowledge that Bay Minette was now a corporation, sued Emmons and her son personally to recover a balance owing on the Bay Minette account (for purchases made after Bay Minette had incorporated). Is the fact that M&M was never informed of the subsequent incorporation of the Bay Minette Flower Shop a sufficient ground for piercing the corporate veil and holding Emmons and her son personally liable for the debt? Explain. [*M&M Wholesale Florist, Inc. v. Emmons,* 600 So.2d 998 (Ala. 1992)]

**41–11. Liability for Preincorporation Contracts.** Joe Alexander contracted with Robert Harris for the sale of Harris's business on February 1, 1988. Alexander purported to act on behalf of J&R Construction (J&R), a newly formed corporation. As the incorporators, Joe and Rita Alexander and Avanell Looney signed the articles of incorporation for J&R on the same day that Joe contracted with Harris. The articles were not filed with the secretary of state, however, until February 3. When J&R defaulted on its payments due under the contract with Harris in 1991, Harris sued the Alexanders and Looney personally for the $49,696.21 still owed. The trial court held Joe Alexander personally liable for the debt (because he had signed the contract with Harris) but not Rita Alexander or Avanell Looney. The relevant state statute imposes joint and several liability on those

purporting to act as, or on behalf of, a corporation while knowing that the corporation has not yet come into existence. On appeal, Harris argued that because the Alexanders and Looney acted on behalf of J&R while knowing that no corporation existed, all three incorporators should be held jointly and severally liable as partners. Did Rita Alexander and Avanell Looney also "act as, or on behalf of," the corporation? On appeal, how should the court decide? [*Harris v. Looney,* 43 Ark.App. 127, 862 S.W.2d 282 (1993)]

### 41–12. A Question of Ethics

 *On November 3, 1981, Garry Fox met with a representative of Coopers & Lybrand (Coopers), a national accounting firm, to obtain tax advice from Coopers and other accounting services on behalf of a corporation Fox was in the process of forming. Coopers agreed to perform the services. The new corporation, G. Fox and Partners, Inc., was incorporated on December 4, 1981. Coopers completed its work by mid-December and billed G. Fox and Partners for $10,827 for its accounting services. When neither the new corporation nor Fox paid the bill, Coopers sued Garry Fox personally for the amount. Coopers claimed that Fox had breached express and implied contracts and that, as a corporate promoter, Fox was liable for the unpaid debt. Fox argued that Coopers had agreed to look solely to the corporation for payment. The trial court found that there was no agreement, either express or implied, that would obligate Fox individually to pay Coopers's fee, because Coopers failed to prove the existence of any such agreement. On appeal, however, the trial court's judgment was reversed. Fox was held liable as a corporate promoter for the unpaid debt.* [Coopers & Lybrand v. Fox, 758 P.2d 683 (Colo. 1988)]

1. In view of the fact that Coopers & Lybrand knew that Fox was acting on behalf of a future corporation, do you think that it is fair that Fox should be held personally liable for the contract?

2. Undertaking preliminary corporate organization and promotion is an essential step in the process of corporate formation. Do you think that the risks imposed on promoters by holding them personally liable for preincorporation contracts counter the public policy of promoting business enterprises?

3. What might result if corporate promoters could never be held personally liable for preincorporation contracts? Would such a law also pose a barrier to commerce by increasing the difficulty in obtaining necessary preincorporation contracts, such as for office space, equipment, credit, and so on?

# CHAPTER 42

# CORPORATIONS— DIRECTORS, OFFICERS, AND SHAREHOLDERS

orporate directors, officers, and shareholders all play different roles within the corporate entity. The directors play a key role, because they control the firm. They decide on corporate policy and appoint corporate officers to manage the day-to-day affairs of the firm. The shareholders, because they elect the directors, also play a vital role, albeit a less direct one. Each of these roles carries with it certain rights and responsibilities.

Sometimes, actions that may benefit the corporation as a whole do not coincide with the separate interests of the individuals making up the corporation. In such situations, it is important to know the rights and duties of all participants in the corporate enterprise. This chapter focuses on these rights and the ways in which conflicts among corporate participants are resolved.

## SECTION 1

## ROLE OF DIRECTORS AND OFFICERS

Every corporation is governed by a board of directors. A director occupies a position of responsibility unlike that of other corporate personnel. Directors are sometimes inappropriately characterized as *agents* because they act for and on behalf of the corporation. No *individual* director, however, can act as an agent to bind the corporation, and as a group, directors collectively control the corporation in a way that no agent is able to control a principal. Directors are often incorrectly characterized as *trustees* because they occupy positions of trust and control over the corporation. Unlike trustees, however, they do not own or hold title to property for the use and benefit of others.

## ELECTION OF DIRECTORS

Subject to statutory limitations, the number of directors is set forth in the corporation's articles of incorporation (corporate articles) or bylaws. Historically, the minimum number of directors has been three, but today many states permit fewer. Indeed, the Revised Model Business Corporation Act (RMBCA), in Section 8.01, permits corporations with fewer than fifty shareholders to eliminate the board of directors.

The first board of directors is normally appointed by the incorporators upon the creation of the corporation, or directors are named by the corporation itself in the articles. The first board serves until the first annual shareholders' meeting. Subsequent directors are elected by a majority vote of the shareholders [RMBCA 2.05].

The term of office for a director is usually one year—from annual meeting to annual meeting. Longer and staggered terms are permissible under most state statutes. A common practice is to elect one-third of the board members each year for a three-year term. In this way, there is greater management continuity [RMBCA 8.05; RMBCA 8.06].

A director can be removed *for cause* (such as the breach of a duty or other misconduct), either as specified in the articles or bylaws or by shareholder action. Even the board of directors itself may be given power to remove a director for cause, subject to shareholder review. In most states, unless the shareholders have reserved the right at the time of election, a director cannot be removed without cause [RMBCA 8.08].

When vacancies occur on the board of directors due to death or resignation, or when a new position is created through amendment of the articles or bylaws, either the shareholders or the board itself can fill the position, depending on state law or on the provisions of the bylaws [RMBCA 8.10].

## DIRECTORS' QUALIFICATIONS AND COMPENSATION

Few legal qualifications exist for directors. Only a handful of states retain minimum age and residency requirements. A director is sometimes a shareholder, but this is not a necessary qualification unless, of course, statutory provisions or corporate articles or bylaws require ownership [RMBCA 8.02].

Compensation for directors is ordinarily specified in the corporate articles or bylaws. Because directors have a fiduciary relationship to the shareholders and to the corporation, an express agreement or provision for compensation is necessary for them to receive money from the funds that they control and for which they have responsibilities.

## BOARD OF DIRECTORS' MEETINGS

The board of directors conducts business by holding formal meetings with recorded minutes. The date upon which regular meetings are held is usually established in the articles and bylaws or by board resolution, and no further notice is customarily required. Special meetings can be called with notice sent to all directors [RMBCA 8.20].

Quorum requirements can vary among jurisdictions. Many states leave the decision to the corporate articles or bylaws. (A **quorum** is the minimum number of members of a body of officials or other group that must be present before business can validly be transacted.) In the absence thereof, most states provide that a quorum is a majority of the number of directors authorized in the articles or bylaws. Voting is done in person (unlike voting at shareholders' meetings, which can be done by proxy—proxies will be discussed later in this chapter).[1] The rule is one vote per director. Ordinary matters generally require a majority vote; certain extraordinary issues may require a greater-than-majority vote [RMBCA 8.24].

## RIGHTS OF DIRECTORS

A director of a corporation has a number of rights, including the rights of participation, inspection, compensation, and indemnification.

**PARTICIPATION AND INSPECTION**    Among the rights that a corporate director must have to function properly in that position, the main right is one of participation—meaning that the director must be notified of board of directors' meetings so as to participate in them. As pointed out earlier in this chapter, regular board meetings are usually established by the bylaws or by board resolution, and no notice of these meetings is required. If special meetings are called, however, notice is required

---

1.  Except in Louisiana, which allows a director to vote by proxy under certain circumstances. Some states, such as Michigan and Texas, and Section 8.20 of the RMBCA permit telephone conferences for board of directors' meetings.

unless waived by the director [RMBCA 8.22; RMBCA 8.23].

A director must have access to all corporate books and records to make decisions and to exercise the necessary supervision over corporate officers and employees. This right is virtually absolute and cannot be restricted.

### COMPENSATION AND INDEMNIFICATION

Historically, directors have had no inherent right to compensation for their services as directors. Officers receive compensation, and nominal sums are often paid as honoraria to directors. In many cases, directors are also chief corporate officers and receive compensation in their managerial positions. Most directors, however, gain through indirect benefits, such as business contacts, prestige, and other rewards. There is a trend toward providing more than nominal compensation for directors, especially in large corporations in which directorships can be enormous burdens in terms of time, work, effort, and risk. Many states permit the corporate articles or bylaws to authorize compensation for directors, and in some cases the board can set its own compensation unless the articles or bylaws provide otherwise [RMBCA 8.11].

It is not unusual for corporate directors to become involved in lawsuits by virtue of their position and their actions as directors. Most states (and RMBCA 8.51) permit a corporation to indemnify (guarantee reimbursement to) a director for legal costs, fees, and judgments involved in defending against corporation-related lawsuits. Criminal convictions usually require bad faith, but bad faith is not presumed merely because the director settles the litigation, pleads *nolo contendere* (no contest), or even is found liable in a civil suit. Many states specifically permit a corporation to purchase liability insurance for the directors and officers to cover indemnification. When the statutes are silent on this matter, the power to purchase such insurance is usually considered to be part of the corporation's implied power.

### DIRECTORS' MANAGEMENT RESPONSIBILITIES

Directors have responsibility for all policymaking decisions necessary to the management of all corporate affairs. Just as shareholders cannot act individually to bind the corporation, the directors must act as a body in carrying out routine corporate business. One director has one vote, and generally the majority rules.

The general areas of responsibility of the board of directors include the following:

1. Authorization for major corporate policy decisions—for example, the initiation of proceedings for the sale or lease of corporate assets outside the regular course of business, the determination of new product lines, and the overseeing of major contract negotiations and major management-labor negotiations.
2. Appointment, supervision, and removal of corporate officers and other managerial employees and the determination of their compensation.
3. Financial decisions, such as the declaration and payment of dividends to shareholders or the issuance of authorized shares or bonds.

The board of directors can delegate some of its functions to an executive committee or to corporate officers. In doing so, the board is not relieved of its overall responsibility for directing the affairs of the corporation, but corporate officers and managerial personnel are empowered to make decisions relating to ordinary, daily corporate affairs within well-defined guidelines [RMBCA 8.25].

**EXECUTIVE COMMITTEE** Most states permit the board of directors to elect an executive committee from among the directors to handle the interim management decisions between board of directors' meetings, as provided in the bylaws. The executive committee is limited to making management decisions about ordinary business matters.

**CORPORATE OFFICERS AND EXECUTIVES** The officers and other executive employees are hired by the board of directors or, in rare instances, by the shareholders. In addition to carrying out the duties articulated in the bylaws, corporate and managerial officers act as agents of the corporation, and the ordinary rules of agency (see Chapters 34 and 35) apply or have been applied to their employment (unlike the board of directors, whose powers are conferred by the state).

Qualifications for officers and other executive employees are determined at the discretion of the corporation and may be included in the articles or bylaws. In most states, a person can hold more than one office and can be both an officer and a director of the corporation.

The rights of corporate officers and other high-level managers are defined by employment contracts, because they are employees of the company. Corporate officers normally can be removed by the board of directors at any time with or without cause and regardless of the terms of the employment contract, however, although it is possible for the corporation to be liable for breach of contract. The duties of corporate officers are the same as those of directors, because their respective corporate positions involve both of them in decision making and place them in similar positions of control. Hence, officers are viewed as having the same fiduciary duties of care and loyalty in their conduct of corporate affairs as directors have, a subject to which we now turn [RMBCA 8.42].

## DUTIES OF DIRECTORS AND OFFICERS

Directors and officers are deemed *fiduciaries* of the corporation, because their relationship with the corporation and its shareholders is one of trust and confidence. The fiduciary duties of the directors and officers include the duty of care and the duty of loyalty.

**DUTY OF CARE**   Directors are obligated to be honest and to use prudent business judgment in the conduct of corporate affairs. Directors must exercise the same degree of care that reasonably prudent people use in the conduct of their own personal affairs (see Chapter 6).

Directors can be held answerable to the corporation and to the shareholders for breach of their duty of care. When directors delegate work to corporate officers and employees, they are expected to use a reasonable amount of supervision. Otherwise, they will be held liable for *negligence* or *mismanagement* of corporate personnel. For example, assume that a corporate bank director failed to attend any board of directors' meetings in five-and-one-half years, never inspected any of the corporate books or records, and generally failed to supervise the efforts of the bank president and the loan committee. Meanwhile, the bank president made various improper loans and permitted large overdrafts. In this situation, the corporate director may be held liable to the corporation for losses resulting from the unsupervised actions of the bank president and the loan committee.

The standard of *due care* has been variously described and codified in many corporation codes and by judicial decisions.[2] The impact of the standard is to require that directors carry out their responsibilities in an informed, businesslike manner.

Depending on the nature of the business, directors and officers are often expected to act in accordance with their own knowledge and training. Most states and the RMBCA [see RMBCA 8.30], however, allow a director to make decisions in reliance on information furnished by competent officers or employees, professionals such as attorneys and accountants, or even an executive committee of the board, without being accused of acting in bad faith or failing to exercise due care if such information turns out to be faulty.

Directors are expected to attend board of directors' meetings, and their votes should be entered into the minutes of corporate meetings. Unless a dissent is entered, the director is presumed to have assented. Directors who dissent rarely are held individually liable for mismanagement of the corporation. For this reason, a director who is absent from a given meeting sometimes registers with the secretary of the board a dissent to actions taken at the meeting [RMBCA 8.24].

Directors are expected to be informed on corporate matters and to understand legal and other professional advice rendered to the board. In *Smith v. Van Gorkom,* for example, directors were held liable for accepting an offer for the purchase of a corporation because they purportedly failed to investigate the value of the business and whether a higher price could be obtained.[3] A director who is unable to carry out such responsibilities must resign. When the required duty of care has not been exercised, directors and officers are liable for the damages caused to the corporation by their negligence.

**DUTY OF LOYALTY**   One can define *loyalty* as faithfulness to one's obligations and duties. The essence of the fiduciary duty requires the subordination of self-interest to the interest of the entity to which the duty is owed. It presumes constant loyalty to the corporation on the part of the directors and officers. In general, the duty of loyalty prohibits directors from using corporate funds or confidential

---

2.   See, for example, RMBCA 8.30(a).
3.   488 A.2d 858 (Del. 1985).

corporate information for their personal advantage. It requires officers and directors to disclose fully any corporate opportunity or any possible conflicts of interest that might occur in a transaction involving the directors of the corporation.

Cases dealing with fiduciary duty typically involve one or more of the following:

1. Competing with the corporation.
2. Usurping (taking advantage of) a corporate opportunity.
3. Having an interest that conflicts with the interest of the corporation.

4. Engaging in insider trading (using information that is not public to make a profit trading securities—see Chapter 44).
5. Authorizing a corporate transaction that is detrimental to minority shareholders.
6. Selling control over the corporation.

In the following case, a corporation sued two of its former officers, alleging that they had breached their duty of loyalty by planning and creating a competing enterprise while still employed by the corporation.

---

| CASE 42.1 |
| --- |
| **VECO CORP. v. BABCOCK** |
| Appellate Court of Illinois, First District, Second Division, 1993. 243 Ill.App.3d 153, 611 N.E.2d 1054, 183 Ill.Dec. 406. |

**BACKGROUND AND FACTS** *Two high-ranking officers of Veco Corporation, an Illinois financial services company, started talking about forming their own financial services company, to be called CorMac, Inc. The officers, Robert Babcock and Margaret Michails, expanded their discussions to include other employees of Veco, including Jeanne Tucker and Patricia Walker. While they were still working for Veco, Babcock prepared the business plan for CorMac, and Michails typed it up. The plan listed the then-current Veco employees who would join CorMac and also detailed the ''taking over'' of an important Veco client. When Veco's founder and sole shareholder, David Vear, discovered what Babcock had done, he summarily fired him. Immediately thereafter, Michails, Tucker, and Walker resigned and began working with CorMac. In the wake of those resignations, Veco was left with no personnel who were experienced in handling one of its major accounts (National Exchange Benefit Trust, or N.E.B.T.). As a result, Veco claimed that it had suffered losses totaling at least $100,000. Veco sued Babcock and Michails, alleging that they had breached their fiduciary duty of loyalty by forming their business plan and recruiting other key Veco employees to join their new competing entity while they were still employed by Veco. The trial court held for Babcock and the others. Although what Babcock and the others had done may have been unethical, the court did not see their actions as illegal. Veco appealed.*

Justice *HARTMAN* delivered the opinion of the court:
  \*    \*    \*    \*

  \*    \*    \* Corporate officers are liable for breaching their fiduciary duties where, while still affiliated with the company, they solicit fellow employees to join a rival business or orchestrate a mass exodus of employees to follow shortly the officer's resignation from the company. In the present case, it is undisputed that Babcock recruited Michails, Tucker, and Walker to join him prior to his termination; he also cautioned them not to tell Vear of their plans. At Babcock's direction and while still employed at Veco, Michails retrieved, copied, and typed various documents belonging to Veco for CorMac. While still employed at Veco, Tucker joined Babcock in a meeting where Babcock solicited N.E.B.T. members for CorMac. After Vear fired Babcock, Michails, Tucker, and Walker immediately resigned. This evidence is uncontradicted. Clearly, defendants secretly solicited Veco employees for CorMac and orchestrated a mass exodus of Veco's N.E.B.T. servicing employees to follow Babcock's resignation. Such conduct is a breach of fiduciary duties.

*The appellate court, holding that the trial court's ruling was against the "manifest weight of the evidence," reversed the trial court's decision and remanded the case for further proceedings consistent with its opinion.*

**DECISION AND REMEDY**

---

**CONFLICTS OF INTEREST** Corporate directors often have many business affiliations, and they can even sit on the board of more than one corporation. Of course, they are precluded from entering into or supporting any business that operates in direct competition with the corporation. The fiduciary duty requires them to make a full disclosure of any potential conflicts of interest that might arise in any corporate transaction [RMBCA 8.60].

Sometimes a corporation enters into a contract or engages in a transaction in which an officer or director has a personal interest. The director or officer must make a *full disclosure* of that interest and must abstain from voting on the proposed transaction. For example, Ballo Corporation needs office space. Stephan Colson, one of its five directors, owns the building adjoining the corporation. He negotiates a lease with Ballo for the space, making a full disclosure to Ballo and the other four board directors. The lease arrangement is fair and reasonable, and it is unanimously approved by the corporation's board of directors. In such a case, the contract is valid. The rule is one of reason; otherwise, directors would be prevented from ever giving financial assistance to the corporations they serve.

The various state statutes contain different standards, but a contract will generally not be voidable if it was fair and reasonable to the corporation at the time the contract was made, there was a full disclosure of the interest of the officers or directors involved in the transaction, and the contract was approved by a majority of the disinterested directors or shareholders [RMBCA 8.62].

Often contracts are negotiated between corporations having one or more directors who are members of both boards. Such transactions require great care, as they are closely scrutinized by the courts. (As will be discussed in Chapter 48, in certain circumstances—if two large corporations are competing with each other, for example—it may constitute a violation of antitrust laws if the same director sits on the boards of both companies.)

## LIABILITY OF DIRECTORS AND OFFICERS

Directors and officers are exposed to liability on many fronts. Not only are they personally liable for the torts and crimes that they commit within the scope of their employment, but they also may be held personally liable for the wrongful acts committed by corporate personnel under their direct supervision (see Chapter 9). Shareholders may perceive that the corporate directors are not acting in the best interests of the corporation and sue the directors, in what is called a *shareholder's derivative suit,* on behalf of the corporation. This type of action is discussed later in this chapter, in the context of the rights of shareholders. In this section, we examine the so-called **business judgment rule,** under which a corporate director or officer may be able to avoid liability for poor business judgments.

Directors are expected to use their best judgment in guiding corporate management, but they are not insurers of business success. Honest mistakes of judgment and poor business decisions on their part do not make them liable to the corporation for resulting damages. The business judgment rule immunizes directors—and officers—from liability when a decision is within managerial authority, as long as the decision complies with management's fiduciary duties and as long as acting on the decision is within the powers of the corporation. Consequently, if there is a reasonable basis for a business decision, it is unlikely that the court will interfere with that decision, even if the corporation suffers thereby.

To benefit from the rule, directors and officers must act in good faith, in what they consider to be the best interests of the corporation, and with the care that an ordinarily prudent person in a similar position would exercise in similar circumstances. This requires an informed decision, with a rational basis, and with no conflict between the decision maker's personal interest and the interest of the corporation [RMBCA 8.30].

To be informed, the director or officer must do what is necessary to become informed: attend presentations, ask for information from those who have it, read reports, and review other written materials such as contracts—in other words, carefully study a situation and its alternatives. To be free of conflicting interests, the director must not engage in self-dealing. For instance, a director should not oppose a *tender offer* (another company's offer made directly to the shareholders to purchase their shares) that is in the corporation's best interest simply because its acceptance may cost the director his or her position. For a decision to have an apparently rational basis, the decision itself must appear to have been made reasonably. For example, a director should not accept a tender offer with only a moment's consideration based solely on the market price of the corporation's shares.

SECTION 2

# THE ROLE OF SHAREHOLDERS

The acquisition of a share of stock makes a person an owner and shareholder in a corporation. Shareholders thus own the corporation. Although they have no legal title to corporate property vested in the corporation, such as buildings and equipment, they do have an *equitable* (ownership) interest in the firm.

As a general rule, shareholders have no responsibility for the daily management of the corporation, although they are ultimately responsible for choosing the board of directors, which does have such control. Ordinarily, corporate officers and other employees owe no direct duty to individual stockholders. Their duty is to the corporation as a whole. A director, however, is in a fiduciary relationship to the corporation and therefore serves the interests of the shareholders as a whole. Generally, there is no legal relationship between shareholders and creditors of the corporation. Shareholders can, in fact, be creditors of the cor-

poration and have the same rights of recovery against the corporation as any other creditor.

In this section, we look at the powers, rights, and liabilities of shareholders, which may be generally established in the articles of incorporation and under the state's general incorporation law.

## SHAREHOLDERS' POWERS

Shareholders must approve fundamental changes affecting the corporation before the changes can be effected. Hence, shareholders are empowered to amend the articles of incorporation (charter) and bylaws, approve a merger or the dissolution of the corporation, and approve the sale of all or substantially all of the corporation's assets. Some of these powers are subject to prior board approval.

Election and removal of the board of directors are accomplished by a vote of the shareholders. The first board of directors is either named in the articles of incorporation or chosen by the incorporators to serve until the first shareholders' meeting. From that time on, selection and retention of directors are exclusively shareholder functions.

Directors usually serve their full terms; if they are unsatisfactory, they are simply not reelected. Shareholders have the inherent power, however, to remove a director from office *for cause* (breach of duty or misconduct) by a majority vote.[4] Some state statutes even permit removal of directors *without cause* by the vote of a majority of the holders of outstanding shares entitled to vote.[5] Some corporate charters also expressly provide that shareholders, by majority vote, can remove a director at any time *without cause*.

## SHAREHOLDERS' MEETINGS

Shareholders' meetings must occur at least annually, and in addition, special meetings can be called to take care of urgent matters. The notice and time of meetings, including the day and the hour, are announced in writing to each shareholder

---

4. A director can often demand court review of removal for cause.

5. Most states allow *cumulative voting* (which will be discussed shortly) for directors. If cumulative voting is authorized, a director may not be removed if the number of votes sufficient to elect him or her under cumulative voting is voted against his or her removal. See, for example, California Corporate Code Section 303A. Also see Section 8.08(c) of the RMBCA.

■ CONCEPT SUMMARY 42.1 **Role of Directors and Officers**

| | |
|---|---|
| **Election of Directors** | The first board of directors is usually appointed by the incorporators; thereafter, directors are elected by the shareholders. Directors usually serve a one-year term, although it can be longer. |
| **Directors' Qualifications and Compensation** | Few qualifications are required; a director can be a shareholder but is not required to be by statute. Compensation is usually specified in the corporate articles or bylaws. |
| **Board of Directors' Meetings** | The board of directors conducts business by holding formal meetings with recorded minutes. The date of regular meetings is usually established in the corporate articles or bylaws; special meetings can be called with notice sent to all directors. Quorum requirements vary from state to state; usually, a quorum is the majority of corporate directors. Voting is usually required in person, and in ordinary matters only a majority vote is required. |
| **Rights of Directors** | Directors' rights include the rights of participation, inspection, indemnification, and compensation. |
| **Directors' Management Responsibilities** | 1. Directors' management responsibilities include the following:<br>  a. All policymaking decisions necessary to the management of corporate affairs.<br>  b. Appointment, supervision, and removal of corporate officers and other managerial employees; determination of employees' compensation.<br>  c. Authorization for major corporate decisions.<br>  d. Declaration and payment of corporate dividends to shareholders; issuance of authorized shares or bonds.<br>2. Directors may delegate some of their responsibilities to executive committees or corporate officers and executives. |
| **Duties of Directors and Officers** | 1. *Duty of care*—Directors and officers are obligated to be honest and to use prudent business judgment in the conduct of corporate affairs. If a director fails to exercise this duty of care, he or she can be answerable to the corporation and to the shareholders for breaching the duty of care.<br>2. *Duty of loyalty*—Directors and officers have a fiduciary duty to subordinate their own interests to those of the corporation in matters relating to the corporation. Loyalty to the corporation and its interests is required of all directors. They must make full disclosure of any potential conflicts of interest between their personal interests and those of the corporation. |
| **Liability of Directors and Officers** | 1. Corporate directors and officers are liable for their own torts and crimes committed within the scope of employment and may be held personally liable for the torts and crimes committed by corporate personnel under their direct supervision.<br>2. The *business judgment rule* immunizes a director from liability in a corporate transaction as long as the transaction was within the powers of the corporation and the authority of the director and as long as due care was exercised by the director. |

at a reasonable length of time prior to the date of the shareholders' meeting.[6] Notices of special meetings must include a statement of the purpose of the meeting; business transacted at a special meeting is limited to that purpose.

## PROXIES AND SHAREHOLDER PROPOSALS

Because it is usually not practical for owners of only a few shares of stock of publicly traded corporations to attend shareholders' meetings, such stockholders normally give third parties a written authorization to vote their shares at the meeting. This authorization is called a **proxy.** Proxies are often solicited by management, but any person can solicit proxies to concentrate voting power. Proxies have been used by a group of shareholders as a device for taking over a corporation (corporate takeovers are discussed in Chapter 43). Proxies are normally revocable (that is, they can be withdrawn), unless they are specifically designated as irrevocable. Under RMBCA 7.22(c), proxies last for eleven months.

To vote by proxy on proposals for corporate action, shareholders must be informed. The Securities and Exchange Commission (SEC), which regulates the purchase and sale of securities (see Chapter 44), has special provisions relating to proxies. SEC Rule 14a-8 requires that when a company sends proxy materials to its shareholders, the company must also include whatever proposals will be considered at the meeting and provide shareholders with the opportunity to vote on the proposals by marking and returning their proxy cards. Under SEC Rule 14a-8, shareholders who own at least $1,000 worth of stock are eligible to submit proposals for inclusion in corporate proxy material.

A corporation is not required to include proposals that relate to "ordinary business operations" in proxy materials. Normally, only those proposals that relate to significant policy considerations must be included. Often, however, it is difficult to draw the line between proposals that relate to "ordinary business operations" and proposals that concern significant policy issues. In a 1976 interpretive ruling, the SEC recognized that equal employment opportunity and affirmative action issues raise significant policy considerations.[7] Yet in 1992, the SEC ruled that proposals relating to these issues could be excluded from proxy materials because the line "between policies implicating broad social issues and the conduct of day-to-day business [is] simply too hard to draw" in the area of employment.[8] In 1993, the SEC again sided with management when it allowed the Walt Disney Company to exclude from proxy materials a shareholders' proposal asking management to prohibit visitors to Disneyland from smoking.

The court in the following case was less reluctant than the SEC to draw a line between includable and excludable proposals.

---

6. The shareholder can waive the requirement of written notice by signing a waiver form [RMBCA 7.06]. A shareholder who does not receive written notice, but who learns of the meeting and attends without protesting the lack of notice, is said to have waived notice by such conduct. State statutes and corporate bylaws typically set forth the time within which notice must be sent, what methods can be used, and what the notice must contain.

7. *Adoption of Amendments Relating to Proposals by Security Holders,* Exchange Act Release No. 12999, 41 Fed.Reg. 52,994 (December 3, 1976).

8. *Cracker Barrel Old Country Stores, Inc.,* SEC No-Action Letter, 1992 W.L. 289095 (October 13, 1992). [W.L. refers to WESTLAW.]

---

| CASE 42.2 | **COMPANY PROFILE** *Wal-Mart Stores, Inc., began as a single store—* |
| --- | --- |
| **AMALGAMATED CLOTHING AND TEXTILE WORKERS UNION v. WAL-MART STORES, INC.** United States District Court, Southern District of New York, 1993. 821 F.Supp. 877. | *Wal-Mart Discount City—in Rogers, Arkansas, in 1962. Wal-Mart was the idea of Sam Walton, who had worked for J. C. Penney in Des Moines, Iowa, in the 1940s and had operated nine Ben Franklin Store franchises in the 1950s. Walton's strategy was to sell brand-name merchandise at low prices, keep the merchandise in stock, and accept all returns of any items from any customers. In 1970, company shares were first sold to the public. Opening stores in small towns and the suburban areas of large cities, Wal-Mart sold household goods, clothes, lawn and garden supplies, and other merchandise. By 1980, Wal-Mart was America's thirty-ninth largest store operator in terms of sales. By the 1990s, Wal-Mart was num-* |

*ber one, with nearly $60 billion in sales. Wal-Mart offers employees a profit-sharing plan (which invests mostly in Wal-Mart stock), bonuses related to profits and reductions in shoplifting and employee theft, and a stock purchase plan. Wal-Mart stock bought in 1980 for $1,000 sold a decade later for more than $43,000.*

**BACKGROUND AND FACTS** *Amalgamated Clothing and Textile Workers Union (ACTWU) is a labor union and a shareholder of Wal-Mart Stores, Inc. The ACTWU and other Wal-Mart shareholders submitted a proposal for inclusion in Wal-Mart's 1993 proxy materials. The proposal sought to submit certain requests for a shareholder vote. Essentially, the requests called for Wal-Mart's directors to prepare and distribute reports about Wal-Mart's equal employment opportunity (EEO) and affirmative action policies, programs, and data, along with a description of Wal-Mart's efforts to publicize its EEO policies to suppliers and to buy goods and services from firms owned by minorities and females. Wal-Mart refused to include the proposal. The shareholders filed a lawsuit, alleging that Wal-Mart's omission of their proposal violated SEC Rule 14a-8. Wal-Mart filed a motion to dismiss, asserting that it could exclude the proposal because it dealt with a matter relating to the conduct of its "ordinary business operations." The shareholders filed a motion for summary judgment.*

*WOOD*, D.J. [District Judge]
 \* \* \* \*
 \* \* \* [C]ongress delegated to the SEC the task of ensuring that shareholders are informed on all the major questions of policy to be raised at an annual meeting. The SEC continues to implement Congress's goals by providing shareholders with the right to communicate with other shareholders and with management through the dissemination of proxy material on matters of broad social import such as plant closings, tobacco production, cigarette advertising and executive compensation. The SEC cannot, in effect, eliminate this avenue of shareholder communication with management and other shareholders on a topic of broad social import simply because it finds the line between proper and improper issues for communication hard to draw, and still act consistently with the principles enunciated in the 1976 Interpretive [Ruling]. If the SEC wishes to amend its rules \* \* \*, it may do so. Or if the SEC no longer considers EEO [equal employment opportunity] and affirmative action policies to have broad social import—if a shift in public concerns has diminished interest in these social issues—the SEC simply can so state, consistent with the 1976 Interpretive [Ruling]. The SEC's difficulties in drawing these lines do not excuse it or the courts from making these decisions, which Congress has entrusted to the SEC and, ultimately, to the courts. The court draws a line here between includable and excludable proposals that is consistent with the line previously drawn by the SEC and the courts between "matters involving substantial policy considerations" and matters involving only "ordinary business operations."

*The district court granted the ACTWU's motion for summary judgment. The court held that the proposal was not excludable, and Wal-Mart was enjoined from omitting the proposal from Wal-Mart's proxy material.*

**DECISION AND REMEDY**

## SHAREHOLDER VOTING

Shareholders exercise ownership control through the power of their votes. Each common shareholder is entitled to one vote per share, although the voting techniques discussed below all enhance the power of the shareholder's vote. The articles of incorporation can exclude or limit voting rights, particularly to certain classes of shares. For example, owners of preferred shares are usually denied the right to vote [RMBCA 7.21].

For shareholders to act, a *quorum* (a minimum number of shareholders, in terms of the number of shares held) must be present at a meeting. Generally, a quorum is more than 50 percent. Corporate business matters are presented in the form of *resolutions,* which shareholders vote to approve or disapprove. If a state statute sets forth specific voting requirements, the corporation's articles or bylaws must be consistent with these statutory limitations. Some states provide that the unanimous written consent of shareholders is a permissible alternative to holding a shareholders' meeting [RMBCA 7.25].

Once a quorum is present, a majority vote of the shares represented at the meeting is usually required to pass resolutions. Assume that Novo Pictures, Inc., has 10,000 outstanding shares of voting stock. Its articles of incorporation set the quorum at 50 percent of outstanding shares and provide that a majority vote of the shares present is necessary to pass on ordinary matters. Therefore, for this firm, at the shareholders' meeting, a quorum of stockholders representing 5,000 outstanding shares must be present to conduct business, and a vote of at least 2,501 of those shares represented at the meeting is needed to pass ordinary resolutions. If more than 5,000 are present, a larger vote will be required.

At times, a larger-than-majority vote will be required either by statute or by corporate charter. Extraordinary corporate matters, such as a merger, consolidation, or dissolution of the corporation (see Chapter 43), require a higher percentage of the representatives of all corporate shares entitled to vote, not just a majority of those present at that particular meeting [RMBCA 7.27].

**VOTING LISTS** Voting lists are prepared by the corporation prior to each shareholders' meeting. Persons whose names appear on the corporation's stockholder records as owners are the ones ordinarily entitled to vote.[9] The voting list contains the name and address of each shareholder as shown on the corporate records on a given cutoff date, or record date. (Under RMBCA 7.07, the record date may be as much as seventy days before the meeting.) The voting list also includes the number of voting shares held by each owner. The list is usually kept at the corporate headquarters and is available for shareholder inspection [RMBCA 7.20].

**CUMULATIVE VOTING** Most states permit or require shareholders to elect directors by *cumulative voting,* a method of voting designed to allow minority shareholders representation on the board of directors.[10] When cumulative voting is allowed or required, the number of members of the board to be elected is multiplied by the total number of voting shares. The result equals the number of votes a shareholder has, and this total can be cast for one or more nominees for director. All nominees stand for election at the same time. When cumulative voting is not required either by statute or under the articles, the entire board can be elected by a majority of shares at a shareholders' meeting.

Suppose, for example, that a corporation has 10,000 shares issued and outstanding. The minority shareholders hold only 3,000 shares, and the majority shareholders hold the other 7,000 shares. Three members of the board are to be elected. The majority shareholders' nominees are Alomon, Beasley, and Caravel. The minority shareholders' nominee is Dovrik. Can Dovrik be elected by the minority shareholders?

If cumulative voting is allowed, the answer is yes. The minority shareholders have 9,000 votes among them (the number of directors to be elected times the number of shares equals 3 times 3,000, which equals 9,000 votes). All of these votes can be cast to elect Dovrik. The majority shareholders have 21,000 votes (3 times 7,000 equals 21,000 votes), but these votes have to be distributed among their three nominees. The principle of cumulative voting is that no matter how the majority shareholders cast their 21,000 votes, they will not be

---

9. When the legal owner is deceased, bankrupt, incompetent, or in some other way under a legal disability, his or her vote can be cast by a person designated by law to control and manage the owner's property.

10. See, for example, California Corporate Code Section 708. Under RMBCA 7.28, however, no cumulative voting rights exist unless the articles of incorporation so provide.

■ **Exhibit 42–1 Results of Cumulative Voting**

| Ballot | Majority Shareholder Votes | | | Minority Shareholder Votes | Directors Elected |
|---|---|---|---|---|---|
| | *Alomon* | *Beasley* | *Caravel* | *Dovrik* | |
| 1 | 10,000 | 10,000 | 1,000 | 9,000 | Alomon, Beasley, Dovrik |
| 2 | 9,001 | 9,000 | 2,999 | 9,000 | Alomon, Beasley, Dovrik |
| 3 | 6,000 | 7,000 | 8,000 | 9,000 | Beasley, Caravel, Dovrik |

able to elect all three directors if the minority shareholders cast all of their 9,000 votes for Dovrik, as illustrated in Exhibit 42–1.

**OTHER VOTING TECHNIQUES** A group of shareholders can agree in writing prior to a shareholders' meeting to vote their shares together in a specified manner. Such *shareholder voting agreements* are usually held to be valid and enforceable. A shareholder can also appoint a voting agent and vote by proxy. As mentioned previously, a proxy is a written authorization to cast the shareholder's vote, and a person can solicit proxies from a number of shareholders in an attempt to concentrate voting power [RMBCA 7.31].

Another technique is for shareholders to enter into a **voting trust,** which is an agreement (a trust contract) under which legal title (recorded ownership on the corporate books) is transferred to a trustee who is responsible for voting the shares. The agreement can specify how the trustee is to vote, or it can allow the trustee to use his or her discretion. The trustee takes physical possession of the actual stock certificate and in return gives the shareholder a *voting trust certificate.* The shareholder retains all of the rights of ownership (for example, the right to receive dividend payments) except for the power to vote the shares [RMBCA 7.30].

## RIGHTS OF SHAREHOLDERS

Shareholders possess numerous rights. A significant right—the right to vote their shares—has already been discussed. In addition to voting rights, a shareholder has the rights, based on ownership of stock, to stock certificates (depending on the jurisdiction), to purchase newly issued stock, to dividends, to inspect corporate records, to transfer shares (with some exceptions), to a proportionate share of corporate assets on corporate dissolution,

and to file suit on behalf of the corporation. These rights are discussed in the following subsections.

**STOCK CERTIFICATES** A **stock certificate** is a certificate issued by a corporation that evidences ownership of a specified number of shares in the corporation. In jurisdictions that require the issuance of stock certificates, shareholders have the right to demand that the corporation issue a certificate and record their names and addresses in the corporate stock record books. In most states (and under RMBCA 6.26), boards of directors may provide that shares of stock be uncertificated (that is, that actual, physical stock certificates need not be issued). In that circumstance, it may be required that the corporation send the holders of uncertificated shares letters or some other form of notice containing the same information required to be included on the face of stock certificates.

Stock is intangible personal property, and the ownership right exists independently of the certificate itself. A stock certificate may be lost or destroyed, but ownership is not destroyed with it. A new certificate can be issued to replace one that has been lost or destroyed.[11] Notice of shareholder meetings, dividends, and operational and financial reports are all distributed according to the recorded ownership listed in the corporation's books, not on the basis of possession of the certificate.

**PREEMPTIVE RIGHTS** A **preemptive right** is a common law concept under which a preference is given to a shareholder over all other purchasers

---

11. For a lost or destroyed certificate to be reissued, a shareholder normally must furnish an indemnity bond (a guaranty of payment) to protect the corporation against potential loss should the original certificate reappear at some future time in the hands of a *bona fide* purchaser [UCC 8–302; UCC 8–405(2)].

to subscribe to or purchase a prorated share of a new issue of stock. This allows the shareholder to maintain his or her portion of control, voting power, or financial interest in the corporation. Most statutes either (1) grant preemptive rights but allow them to be negated in the corporation's articles or (2) deny preemptive rights except to the extent that they are granted in the articles [RMBCA 6.30]. The result is that the articles of incorporation determine the existence and scope of preemptive rights. Generally, preemptive rights apply only to additional, newly issued stock sold for cash and must be exercised within a specified time period (usually thirty days).

For example, Tron Corporation authorizes and issues 1,000 shares of stock, and Omar Loren purchases 100 shares, making him the owner of 10 percent of the company's stock. Subsequently, Tron, by vote of its shareholders, authorizes the issuance of another 1,000 shares (amending the articles of incorporation). This increases its capital stock to a total of 2,000 shares. If preemptive rights have been provided, Loren can purchase one additional share of the new stock being issued for each share currently owned—or 100 additional shares. Thus, he can own 200 of the 2,000 shares outstanding, and his relative position as a shareholder will be maintained. If preemptive rights are not reserved, his proportionate control and voting power will be diluted from that of a 10 percent shareholder to that of a 5 percent shareholder because of the issuance of the additional 1,000 shares.

Preemptive rights are far more significant in a close corporation because of the relatively few number of shares and the substantial interest that each shareholder controls.

**STOCK WARRANTS** When preemptive rights exist and a corporation is issuing additional shares, each shareholder is usually given **stock warrants,** which are transferable options to acquire a given number of shares from the corporation at a stated price. Warrants are often publicly traded on securities exchanges. When the warrant option is for a short period of time, the stock warrants are usually referred to as *rights*.

**DIVIDENDS** A **dividend** is a distribution of corporate profits or income *ordered by the directors* and paid to the shareholders in proportion to their respective shares in the corporation. Dividends can be paid in cash, property, stock of the corporation

that is paying the dividends, or stock of other corporations.[12]

State laws vary, but every state determines the general circumstances and legal requirements under which dividends are paid. State laws also control the sources of revenue to be used; only certain funds are legally available for paying dividends. Once declared, a cash dividend becomes a corporate debt enforceable at law like any other debt.

Under statutes that limit the sources of funds from which dividends may be paid, prescribed sources include the following:

1. *Retained earnings.* All state statutes allow dividends to be paid from the undistributed net profits earned by the corporation, including capital gains from the sale of fixed assets. The undistributed net profits are called *earned surplus,* or *retained earnings.*
2. *Net profits.* A few state statutes allow dividends to be issued from current net profits without regard to deficits in prior years.
3. *Surplus.* A number of state statutes allow dividends to be paid out of any kind of surplus.

**Illegal Dividends.** Sometimes dividends are improperly paid from an unauthorized account, or their payment causes the corporation to become insolvent. Generally, in such cases, shareholders must return illegal dividends only if they knew that the dividends were illegal when they received them. If a dividend is paid while the corporation is *insolvent,* it is automatically an illegal dividend, and shareholders may be liable for returning the payment to the corporation or its creditors. In all cases of illegal and improper dividends, the board of directors can be held personally liable for the amount of the payment. When directors can show that a shareholder knew a dividend was illegal when it was received, however, the directors are entitled to reimbursement from the shareholder.

**Directors' Failure to Declare a Dividend.** When directors fail to declare a dividend, shareholders can ask a court of equity for an injunction to compel the directors to meet and to declare a

---

12. Technically, dividends paid in stock are not dividends. They maintain each shareholder's proportional interest in the corporation. On one occasion a distillery declared and paid a "dividend" in bonded whiskey.

dividend. For the injunction to be granted, it must be shown that the directors have acted so unreasonably in withholding the dividend that their conduct is an abuse of their discretion.

Often large money reserves are accumulated for a *bona fide* purpose, such as expansion, research, or other legitimate corporate goals. The mere fact that sufficient corporate earnings or surplus is available to pay a dividend is not enough to compel directors to distribute funds that, in the board's opinion, should not be paid. The courts are hesitant to interfere with corporate operations and will not compel directors to declare dividends unless abuse of discretion is clearly shown.[13]

**INSPECTION RIGHTS**   Shareholders in a corporation enjoy both common law and statutory inspection rights.[14] The shareholder's right of inspection is limited, however, to the inspection and copying of corporate books and records for a *proper purpose*, provided the request is made in

advance. Either the shareholder can inspect in person, or an attorney, agent, accountant, or other type of assistant can do so. The RMBCA requires the corporation to maintain an alphabetical voting list of shareholders with addresses and number of shares owned; this list must be kept open at the annual meeting for inspection by any shareholder of record [RMBCA 7.20].

The power of inspection is fraught with potential abuses, and the corporation is allowed to protect itself from them. For example, a shareholder can properly be denied access to corporate records to prevent harassment or to protect trade secrets or other confidential corporate information. Some states require that a shareholder must have held his or her shares for a minimum period of time immediately preceding the demand to inspect or must hold a minimum number of outstanding shares. The RMBCA provides that every shareholder is entitled to examine specified corporate records [RMBCA 16.02].

In the following case, a shareholder sought to inspect and copy corporate records to locate other shareholders who might want to join in an action against the corporation for alleged wrongdoing. The question before the court was whether the shareholder's reason for inspecting the corporate records, given these circumstances, qualified as a ''proper purpose.''

---

13.   A striking exception to this rule was made in *Dodge v. Ford Motor Co.*, 204 Mich. 459, 170 N.W. 668 (1919), when Henry Ford, the president and major stockholder of Ford Motor Company, refused to declare a dividend notwithstanding the firm's large capital surplus. The court, holding that Ford had abused his discretion, ordered the company to declare a dividend.

14.   See, for example, *Schwartzman v. Schwartzman Packing Co.*, 99 N.M. 436, 659 P.2d 888 (1983).

---

**BACKGROUND AND FACTS**   *In July 1991, Charles Horton and seventy-eight other shareholders of Compaq Computer Corporation sued Compaq, some of its advisors, and certain management personnel (the defendants), alleging that Compaq and its co-defendants had engaged in fraud and other misconduct in violation of Texas statutory law and common law. The plaintiffs' claims arose from the contention that Compaq misled the public as to the true value of its stock at a time when members of management were selling their own shares. In September 1992, Horton sought to inspect Compaq's stock ledger and related information. Horton's demand letter stated that the purpose of the request was to inform other Compaq shareholders of the lawsuit and learn whether any of them wanted to join in the action against the defendants. Compaq refused Horton's demand, stating that the purpose described in the letter was not a ''proper purpose'' under Delaware law. A Delaware chancery court entered a judgment in the plaintiffs' favor, and Compaq appealed.*

CASE 42.3

**COMPAQ COMPUTER CORP. v. HORTON**
Supreme Court of Delaware, 1993.
631 A.2d 1.

---

*MOORE*, Justice.
\* \* \* \*

Horton's ultimate objective, to solicit additional parties to the Texas litigation, may impose substantial expenses upon the company. Compaq argues, therefore, that

such a purpose is *per se* improper as adverse to the interests of the corporation.
* * *

Horton, as a current stockholder of Compaq, has nothing to gain by harming the legitimate interests of the company. Moreover, as he argues, the prospect of the Texas litigation poses no legitimate threat to Compaq's interests. The Texas litigation is already pending with seventy-nine plaintiffs. The inclusion of more plaintiffs will not substantially increase Compaq's costs of defending the action. The real risk to Compaq is that any additional plaintiffs, who may join the suit, potentially increase the damage award against the company. Yet, insofar as law and policy require corporations and their agents to answer for the breaches of their duties to shareholders, Compaq has no legitimate interest in avoiding the payment of compensatory damages which it, its management or advisors may owe to those who own the enterprise. Thus, common sense and public policy dictate that a proper purpose may be stated in these circumstances, notwithstanding the lack of a direct benefit flowing to the corporation.

Equally important is the fact that if damages are assessed against Compaq in the Texas litigation, the company is entitled to seek indemnification from its co-defendant managers and advisors or to pursue its own claims against them. The availability of this diminishes the possibility that Compaq will suffer any harm at all.

**DECISION AND REMEDY** *The Supreme Court of Delaware affirmed the chancery court's decision. Horton had stated a proper purpose for wanting to inspect the corporate stockholder records.*

**TRANSFER OF SHARES** Corporate stock represents an ownership right in intangible personal property. The law generally recognizes the right of an owner to transfer property to another person unless there are valid restrictions on its transferability. Although stock certificates are negotiable and freely transferable by indorsement and delivery, transfer of stock in closely held corporations is generally restricted by the bylaws, by a restriction stamped on the stock certificate, or by a shareholder agreement (see Chapter 41). The existence of any restrictions on transferability must always be noted on the face of the stock certificate, and these restrictions must be reasonable.

Sometimes corporations or their shareholders restrict transferability by reserving the option to purchase any shares offered for resale by a shareholder. This **right of first refusal** remains with the corporation or the shareholders for only a specified time or a reasonable time. Variations on the purchase option are possible. For example, a shareholder might be required to offer the shares to other shareholders or to the corporation first.

When shares are transferred, a new entry is made in the corporate stock book to indicate the new owner. Until the corporation is notified and the entry is complete, voting rights, notice of share-holders' meetings, dividend distribution, and so forth are all held by the current record owner.

**RIGHTS ON DISSOLUTION** When a corporation is dissolved and its outstanding debts and the claims of its creditors have been satisfied, the remaining assets are distributed on a *pro rata* basis among the shareholders. If no preferences to distribution of assets upon liquidation are given to any class of stock, then the stockholders share the remaining assets.

Shareholders also have the right to petition the court to dissolve the corporation. Suppose that a minority shareholder knows that the board of directors is mishandling corporate assets or is permitting a deadlock to threaten or irreparably injure the corporation's finances. The minority shareholder is not powerless to intervene. He or she can petition a court to appoint a receiver and to liquidate the business assets of the corporation.

The RMBCA permits any shareholder to initiate such an action in any of the following circumstances [RMBCA 14.30]:

1. The directors are deadlocked in the management of corporate affairs; shareholders are unable to break that deadlock; and irreparable

injury to the corporation is being suffered or threatened.

2. The acts of the directors or those in control of the corporation are illegal, oppressive, or fraudulent.

3. Corporate assets are being misapplied or wasted.

4. The shareholders are deadlocked in voting power and have failed, for a specified period (usually two annual meetings), to elect successors to directors whose terms have expired or would have expired with the election of successors.

**SHAREHOLDER'S DERIVATIVE SUIT** When those in control of a corporation—the corporate directors—fail to sue in the corporate name to redress a wrong suffered by the corporation, shareholders are permitted to do so ''derivatively'' in what is known as a **shareholder's derivative suit.** Some wrong must have been done to the corporation, and before a derivative suit can be brought, the shareholders must first state their complaint to the board of directors. Only if the directors fail to solve the problem or to take appropriate action can the derivative suit go forward. The right of shareholders to bring a derivative action is especially important when the wrong suffered by the corporation results from the actions of corporate directors, because in such cases, the directors and officers would probably want to prevent any action against themselves.[15]

The shareholder's derivative suit is singular in that those suing are not pursuing rights or benefits for themselves personally but are acting as guardians of the corporate entity. Therefore, any damages recovered by the suit normally go into the corporation's treasury, not to the shareholders personally. The derivative nature of this type of lawsuit is stressed in the following case.

---

15. See RMBCA 7.40–7.47.

---

**BACKGROUND AND FACTS** *Jacob Schachter and Herbert Kulik, the founders of Ketek Electric Corporation, each owned 50 percent of the corporation's shares and served as the corporation's only officers. Arnold Glenn, as trustee, and Kulik brought a shareholder's derivative suit against Schachter, alleging that Schachter had diverted Ketek assets and opportunities to Hoteltron Systems, Inc., a corporation wholly owned by Schachter. The trial court initially held that neither Schachter nor Kulik had proved a breach of duty by the other. The appellate court reversed this decision. The trial court later determined damages and also decided that the damages should be paid to Kulik, not to Ketek. Schachter appealed, and the appellate court ruled that the damages should be awarded to the injured corporation, Ketek, rather than to the injured shareholder, Kulik. Kulik argued that awarding damages to the corporation was inequitable, because Schachter, as a shareholder of Ketek, would ultimately share in the proceeds of the award. Eventually, the case was heard by the New York Court of Appeals.*

| CASE 42.4 |
| --- |
| **GLENN v. HOTELTRON SYSTEMS, INC.** |
| Court of Appeals of New York, 1989. |
| 74 N.Y.2d 386, |
| 547 N.E.2d 71, |
| 547 N.Y.S.2d 816. |

*WACHTLER*, Chief Judge.

\* \* \* \*

It is the general rule that, because a shareholders' derivative suit seeks to vindicate a wrong done to the corporation through enforcement of a corporate cause of action, any recovery obtained is for the benefit of the injured corporation. Where, however, the plaintiff sues in an individual capacity to recover damages resulting in harm, not to the corporation, but to individual shareholders, the suit is personal, not derivative, and it is appropriate for damages to be awarded directly to those shareholders.

In this case, the diversion of Ketek's corporate assets by Schachter for his own profit resulted in a corporate injury because it deprived Ketek of those profits. Kulik, the innocent shareholder, was injured only to the extent that he was entitled to share in those profits. His injury was real, but it was derivative, not direct. Thus, the [lower court] properly ruled that those profits should be returned to Ketek Corp.

**DECISION AND REMEDY**      *The New York Court of Appeals affirmed the lower court's ruling. Damages should be paid to Ketek Electric Corporation and not to Kulik, because the injury Kulik suffered was derivative, or secondary to the corporate injury, and not direct.*

**INTERNATIONAL CONSIDERATIONS**      **Limits on Shareholder's Derivative Actions in Foreign Nations** *Foreign nations are more restrictive than the United States in regard to the use of the shareholder's derivative suit. In Germany, for example, there is no provision for derivative litigation, and a corporation's duty to its employees is just as significant as its duty to the shareholder-owners of the company. The United Kingdom has no statute authorizing derivative actions, which are permitted only to challenge directors' actions that the shareholders could not legally ratify. Japan authorizes derivative actions but also permits a company to sue the shareholder-plaintiff for damages if the action is unsuccessful.*

## LIABILITY OF SHAREHOLDERS

One of the hallmarks of the corporate organization is that shareholders are not personally liable for the debts of the corporation. If the corporation fails, shareholders can lose their investments, but that is generally the limit of their liability. As discussed in Chapter 41, in certain instances of fraud, undercapitalization, or careless observance of corporate formalities, a court will pierce the corporate veil (disregard the corporate entity) and hold the shareholders individually liable. But these situations are the exception, not the rule. Although rare, there are certain other instances where a shareholder can be personally liable. One relates to illegal dividends, which were discussed previously. Two others relate to *stock subscriptions* and *watered stock,* which will be discussed here.

**STOCK-SUBSCRIPTION AGREEMENTS**      Sometimes stock-subscription agreements—written contracts by which one agrees to buy capital stock of a corporation—exist prior to incorporation. Normally, these agreements are treated as continuing offers and are usually irrevocable (for up to six months under RMBCA 6.20). Once the corporation has been formed, it can sell shares to shareholder investors. In either case, once the subscription agreement or stock offer is accepted, a binding contract is formed. Any refusal to pay constitutes a breach resulting in the personal liability of the shareholder.

**WATERED STOCK**      Shares of stock can be paid for by property or by services rendered instead of cash. Shares cannot be purchased with promissory notes, however. The general rule is that for **par-value shares** sold (that is, shares that have a specific face value, or formal cash-in value, written on them, such as one penny or one dollar), the corporation must receive a value at least equal to the par-value amount. For any **no-par shares** sold (that is, shares that have no face value—no specific amount printed on their faces), the corporation must receive the value of the shares as determined by the board or the shareholders. When shares are issued by the corporation for less than these stated values, the shares are referred to as **watered stock.** In most cases, the shareholder who receives watered stock must pay the difference to the corporation (the shareholder is personally liable). In some states, the shareholder who receives watered stock may be liable to creditors of the corporation for unpaid corporate debts.

To illustrate the concept of watered stock, suppose that during the formation of a corporation, Gomez, as one of the incorporators, transfers his property, Sunset Beach, to the corporation for 10,000 shares of stock at a par value of $100 per

## ■ CONCEPT SUMMARY 42.2 Role of Shareholders

| | |
|---|---|
| **Shareholders' Powers** | Shareholders' powers include approval of all fundamental changes affecting the corporation and election of the board of directors. |
| **Shareholders' Meetings** | Shareholders' meetings must occur at least annually; special meetings can be called when necessary. Notice of the time and place of the meeting (and its purpose, if the meeting is specially called) must be sent to shareholders. Voting requirements and procedures are as follows:<br><br>1. A minimum number of shareholders (a quorum—generally, more than 50 percent of shares held) must be present at a meeting; resolutions are normally passed by majority vote.<br>2. Voting lists of shareholders on record must be prepared by the corporation prior to each shareholders' meeting.<br>3. Cumulative voting may or may not be required or permitted so as to give minority shareholders a better chance to be represented on the board of directors.<br>4. Shareholders' voting agreements to vote their shares together are usually held to be valid and enforceable.<br>5. A shareholder may appoint a proxy (substitute) to vote his or her shares.<br>6. A shareholder may enter into a voting trust agreement by which title (record ownership) of his or her shares is given to a trustee, and the trustee votes the shares in accordance with the trust agreement. |
| **Shareholders' Rights** | Shareholders have numerous rights, including voting rights, the right to a stock certificate, preemptive rights and the right to stock warrants (depending on the corporate charter), the right to obtain a dividend (at the discretion of the directors), the right to inspect the corporate records, the right to transfer their shares (this right may be restricted in close corporations), the right to their shares of corporate assets when the corporation is dissolved, and the right to sue on behalf of the corporation (bring a shareholder's derivative suit) when the directors fail to do so. |
| **Shareholders' Liability** | Shareholders may be liable for the retention of illegal dividends, for breach of a stock-subscription agreement, and for watered stock. In certain situations, majority shareholders may be regarded as having a fiduciary duty to minority shareholders and will be liable if that duty is breached. |

share for a total price of $1 million. After the property is transferred and the shares are issued, Sunset Beach is carried on the corporate books at a value of $1 million. Upon appraisal, it is discovered that the market value of the property at the time of transfer was only $500,000. The shares issued to Gomez are therefore watered stock, and he is liable to the corporation for the difference.

## DUTIES OF MAJORITY SHAREHOLDERS

In some cases, a majority shareholder is regarded as having a fiduciary duty to the corporation and to the minority shareholders. This occurs when a single shareholder (or a few shareholders acting in concert) owns a sufficient number of shares to exercise *de facto* (actual) control over the corporation. In these situations, majority shareholders owe a fiduciary duty to the minority shareholders and creditors when they sell their shares, because such a sale would be, in fact, a transfer of control of the corporation.

Whether the controlling majority of shareholders owed a fiduciary duty to a minority shareholder is at issue in the following case.

---

CASE 42.5

**PEDRO v. PEDRO**
Court of Appeals of Minnesota,
1992.
489 N.W.2d 798.

**BACKGROUND AND FACTS** *Alfred, Carl, and Eugene Pedro each owned a one-third interest in The Pedro Companies (TPC), a close corporation that manufactured and sold luggage and leather products. All of the brothers had worked for the corporation for most of their adult lives. The relationship between Alfred and the other two brothers began to deteriorate in 1987 after Alfred discovered a discrepancy between the internal accounting records and the TPC checking account. Alfred was concerned and insisted that an independent accountant be retained to locate the source of the discrepancy. Subsequently, two different accountants examined the records, but neither could identify the source of a $140,000 discrepancy, and one accountant said that he was denied access to numerous documents during the investigation. Alfred testified that during this time, Eugene would interfere with his area of responsibility in the TPC plant and undermine his management authority. Alfred also stated that his brothers told him that if he did not forget about the discrepancy, they would fire him—which they did in December 1987. Employees were told that Alfred had had a nervous breakdown, which was not true. At the time he was fired, Alfred was sixty-two years old and had worked for TPC for forty-five years. Alfred sued the brothers for breach of fiduciary duty and wrongful discharge. The trial court held for Alfred and awarded him over $1.8 million in damages, plus interest, for the value of his shares, lost wages, and attorneys' fees. The brothers appealed.*

NORTON, Judge.
\* \* \* \*

The relationship among shareholders in closely held corporations is analogous to that of partners. Shareholders in closely held corporations owe one another a fiduciary duty. In a fiduciary relationship "the law imposes upon them highest standards of integrity and good faith in their dealings with each other." Owing a fiduciary duty includes dealing "openly, honestly and fairly with other shareholders."

The court's findings of fact contain many examples where appellants did not act openly, honestly, and fairly with respondent Alfred Pedro. \* \* \*
\* \* \* \*

\* \* \* In a closely held corporation the nature of the employment of a shareholder may create a reasonable expectation by the employee-owner that his employment is not terminable at will.

The unique facts in the record support the trial court's finding of an agreement to provide lifetime employment to respondent. Carl Pedro, Sr. worked at the corporation until his death. Eugene Pedro, who worked for over 50 years at TPC, testified that he intended to always work for the company. Carl Pedro, Jr. worked at TPC for over 34 years. Alfred Pedro testified of his expectation of a lifetime job like his father. He had already been employed by TPC for 45 years. Even the corporate accountant testified regarding Carl's and Eugene's expectations that they would work for the corporation as long as they wanted. Based upon this evidence it was reasonable for the trial court to determine that the parties did in fact have a contract that was not terminable at will.

*The trial court's judgment was affirmed.*

*Carl and Eugene argued that because there was no diminution in the value of the corporation or the value of Alfred's shares in the company, they had not breached their fiduciary duties. The court pointed out, however, that depleting corporate value is not the only method of breaching fiduciary duties. Carl and Eugene had made no payments to Alfred for the value of his shares (as determined by the trial court), had interfered with his responsibilities at TPC, had hired a private investigator to follow him when he was not in the office, had fabricated accusations of neglect and malfeasance, had told employees that he had had a nervous breakdown, and had threatened to fire him. Finally, Carl and Eugene admitted that they acted "in a manner unfairly prejudicial" toward Alfred. "This admission," the court concluded, "supports a finding of breach of fiduciary duty."*

# Terms and Concepts to Review

| | | |
|---|---|---|
| business judgment rule 829 | proxy 832 | stock certificate 835 |
| dividend 836 | quorum 825 | stock warrant 836 |
| no-par share 840 | right of first refusal 838 | voting trust 835 |
| par-value share 840 | shareholder's derivative | watered stock 840 |
| preemptive right 835 | suit 839 | |

# QUESTIONS AND CASE PROBLEMS

**42–1. Duties of Directors.** Otts Corp. is negotiating with the Wick Construction Co. for the renovation of the Otts corporate headquarters. Wick, owner of the Wick Construction Co., is also one of the five members of the board of directors of Otts. The contract terms are standard for this type of contract. Wick has previously informed two of the other directors of his interest in the construction company. The contract is approved by Otts's board on a three-to-two vote, with Wick voting with the majority. Discuss whether this contract is binding on the corporation.

**42–2. Duties of Directors.** AstroStar, Inc., has a board of directors consisting of three members (Eckhart, Golum, and Macero) and approximately five hundred shareholders. At a regular meeting of the board, the board selects Galiard as president of the corporation by a two-to-one vote, with Eckhart dissenting. The minutes of the meeting do not register Eckhart's dissenting vote. Later, upon an audit, it is discovered that Galiard is a former convict and has openly embezzled $500,000 from AstroStar, Inc. This loss is not covered by insurance. The corporation wants to hold directors Eckhart, Golum, and Macero liable. Eckhart claims no liability. Discuss the personal liability of the directors to the corporation.

**42–3. Rights of Shareholders.** Avril owns 10,000 shares (10 percent) of Superal Corp. Superal authorized 100,000 shares and issued all of them during its first six months in operation. Later, Superal reacquired 10,000 of these shares. With shareholder approval, Superal amended its articles so as to authorize and issue another 100,000 shares and also, by a resolution of the board of directors, to reissue the 10,000 shares of treasury stock (the shares reaquired by the corporation). There is no provision in the corporate articles dealing with shareholders' preemptive rights. Because of her previous ownership of 10 percent of Superal, Avril claims that she has the preemptive right to purchase 10,000 shares of the new issue and 1,000 shares of the stock being reissued. Discuss her claims.

**42–4. Rights of Shareholders.** Lucia has acquired one share of common stock of a multimillion-dollar corporation with over 500,000 shareholders. Lucia's ownership is so small that she is questioning what her rights are as a shareholder. For example, she wants to know whether this one share entitles her to (1) attend and vote at shareholders' meetings, (2) inspect the corporate books, and (3) receive yearly dividends. Discuss Lucia's rights in these three matters.

**42–5. Liability of Shareholders.** Riddle has made a preincorporation subscription agreement to purchase 500 shares of a newly formed corporation. The shares have a par value of $100 per share. The corporation is formed, and Riddle's subscription is accepted by the corporation. Riddle transfers a piece of land he owns to the corporation, and the corporation issues 250 shares for it. One year later, with the corporation in serious financial difficulty, the board declares and pays a dividend of $5 per share. It is now learned that the land transferred by Riddle had a market value of $18,000. Discuss any liability that shareholder Riddle has to the corporation or to creditors of the corporation.

**42–6. Duties of Directors.** Midwest Management Corp. was looking for investment opportunities. Morris Stephens, one of Midwest's directors and the chairman of the investment committee, proposed that Midwest provide financing for Stephens's son and his business colleagues, who were in need of financing to open a broker-dealer business. Midwest agreed to propose to the shareholders for their approval an investment of $250,000 in the new business on the condition that Stephens would manage the business and would purchase 100,000 shares of stock in the new firm. At each of two shareholders' meetings, the directors informed the shareholders that Stephens agreed to the condition. Stephens was present at both meetings and did not deny that he had agreed to purchase the 100,000 shares of stock and manage the new corporation. Upon the shareholders' approval, the $250,000 investment was made, and later another $150,000 was invested when the new business suffered losses. About a year after it had opened, the business closed, and Midwest ended up losing over $325,000. Midwest then learned that Stephens had not kept his agreement to purchase stock in, or to manage, the corporation. Midwest sued Stephens for breaching his fiduciary duties and asked for compensatory and punitive damages. Did Midwest succeed? Explain. [*Midwest Management Corp. v. Stephens,* 353 N.W.2d 76 (Iowa 1984)]

**42–7. Rights of Shareholders.** Frederick Valerino and his family owned 50 percent of the stock in EMA (Electrical-Mechanical of America, Inc.), and the remaining 50 percent was owned by Charles Little. Both Valerino and Little participated actively in operating the corporation until 1979, when a dispute arose, resulting in a stalemate. For two years no shareholders' meeting was held and no board of directors could be elected. Little held a shareholders' meeting in 1981 and sent a telegram to Valerino stating that the purpose of the meeting was "[f]or the sale and purchase of the Capital Stock of EMA." Valerino did not attend and sent a reply letter indicating that he did not wish to sell any of his stock. Actually, Little held the meeting with the intention of issuing more stock to himself and his family, thus reducing Valerino's ownership to 25 percent. Valerino sued to enforce his preemptive rights in the corporation and to set aside the new stock issuance because of fraud. Discuss whether Valerino should succeed in his claim. [*Valerino v. Little,* 62 Md.App. 588, 490 A.2d 756 (1985)]

**42–8. Liability of Directors and Officers.** Abe Schultz, Sol Schultz, and Lawrence Newfeld were the managing directors and officers of Chemical Dynamics, Inc., a close corporation. In 1967, the corporation leased a building in which to house its offices and operations. Included in the lease agreement was a provision giving Chemical Dynamics an option to purchase the property for $300,000. In 1970, because the corporation was experiencing financial problems and could not pay its rent, it assigned the lease and the purchase option to Newfeld in return for Newfeld's loan to the corporation of approximately $21,500. In 1973, Newfeld purchased the property. Eventually, when the corporation's financial situation had improved and its debts were paid, Abe Schultz sued Newfeld on behalf of the corporation, claiming that Newfeld had breached his fiduciary duty by usurping a corporate opportunity to purchase the property. Evaluate Schultz's claim. [*Chemical Dynamics, Inc. v. Newfeld,* 728 S.W.2d 590 (Mo.App. 1987)]

**42–9. Rights of Shareholders.** A group of stockholders of Ono Development Co. and Ono East, Inc., brought suit, on behalf of themselves and the other stockholders of the corporations, and derivatively, on behalf of the corporations, against Pannell Kerr Forster, an accounting firm, and two of its employees (the defendants) to recover damages for breach of contract and fraud. The stockholders alleged that the defendants had failed to disclose in annual audits of the corporations' books that certain commissions were being improperly paid to and by three of the corporation's principal officers and directors. As a result, the corporations had been deprived of the use of large sums of money over an approximate ten-year period. While the action was pending, the plaintiff stockholders all sold their stock back to the corporations. The defendants argued that the stockholders lacked standing to sue the corporations either on their own behalf or on behalf of the corporations. What should the court decide, and why? [*McLaughlin v. Pannell Kerr Forster,* 589 So.2d 143 (Ala. 1991)]

**42–10. Shareholder Proposals.** Ohio Edison Co. is a public utility. Ohio Edison's articles of incorporation vest the authority to make capital expenditures solely in the board of directors. Since 1982, the company's capital expenditures have averaged $595 million per year. C. L. Grimes, a shareholder in Ohio Edison, proposed that the company amend its articles of incorporation to require shareholder approval of certain capital expenditures in excess of $300 million. In other words, under Grimes's proposal, once the spending threshold of $300 million was reached, each expenditure, including such routine expenditures as the purchase of a typewriter or a new desk, would require shareholder approval. On October 23, 1990, Grimes asked Ohio Edison to enclose his proposal in the proxy materials for the next shareholders' meeting. Ohio Edison submitted the proposal to the Securities and Exchange Commission (SEC) for an opinion as to whether it needed to be included with the proxy materials. The SEC ruled that the proposal could be omitted, because it concerned ordinary business operations. When Ohio Edison distributed proxy materials for the meeting without mentioning Grimes's proposal, Grimes filed suit. Grimes contended that Ohio Edison violated SEC rules by failing to include his proposal in its proxy materials and by failing to inform its shareholders that he would offer his proposal at the meeting (which, Grimes argued, made the proxy materials "false and misleading"). Ohio Edison responded with a motion to dismiss the complaint. The court granted the motion. Grimes appealed. How will the appellate court rule? Discuss fully. [*Grimes v. Ohio Edison Co.,* 992 F.2d 455 (2d Cir. 1993)]

**42–11. Duty of Care.** J. R. Mullins, the sole director and shareholder of the Food Stores of South Carolina, Inc. (FSSC), opened two Sav-A-Lot grocery stores in Myrtle Beach. He then established another corporation, Food Stores of Greenville (FSG), and opened a Sav-A-Lot store in the Greenville community. Mullins was also FSG's sole shareholder and director. He instructed FSG's vice president to place Sav-A-Lot advertisements with the *Greenville News-Piedmont*, which was owned by Multimedia Publishing of South Carolina, Inc. The two Myrtle Beach stores were later closed and their inventory transferred to the Greenville store. FSG then transferred $144,000 to Mullins and his other cor-

porations—purportedly to repay debts owed by FSG. When the Greenville Sav-A-Lot closed following this transfer, Multimedia was left unpaid for the advertising services that it had provided to FSG. Mullins claimed that he had relinquished management of FSG to others and did not know that Multimedia had not been paid. Can Mullins, as corporate director and sole shareholder of FSG, avoid liability for the debts of the FSG corporation when he was on notice that the advertising had been ordered from Multimedia? Is Mullins's statement that he did not know of the debt tantamount to negligence and a breach of his duties as a director? Should Mullins have inquired into whether the Multimedia account had been paid? Discuss these issues and whether Mullins should escape liability for the Multimedia debt. [*Multimedia Publishing of South Carolina, Inc. v. Mullins,* 431 S.E.2d 569 (S.C. 1993)]

**42–12. Case Briefing Assignment**

 *Examine Case A.8 [Maschmeier v. Southside Press, Ltd., 435 N.W.2d 377 (Iowa App. 1989)] in Appendix A. The case has been excerpted there in great detail. Review and then brief the case, making sure that you include answers to the following questions in your brief.*

1. What was the primary reason for this lawsuit?
2. What restriction did the corporate bylaws place on the transfer of corporate shares? Upon transfer, how was the price of shares to be determined?
3. How did the majority shareholders (the parents) effectively "freeze out" or "squeeze out" the minority shareholders (the sons)?
4. Why was it necessary for the court to determine the fair value of shares, as the shareholders had agreed in the bylaws on a method for accomplishing this?
5. Why was it necessary to establish that the majority shareholders had acted oppressively toward the minority shareholders or wasted corporate assets before the court could fashion its particular remedy in this case?

# CHAPTER 43

# CORPORATIONS—
## MERGER,
### CONSOLIDATION,
### AND TERMINATION

**T**he French author and historian André Maurois (1885–1967) once commented that business is "a combination of war and sport." Certainly, the terminology associated with a number of corporate acquisitions and takeovers buttresses that conclusion. Consider the warlike sound of such terms as *aggressor, target, white knight, poison pill,* and *Pac-Man defense*—terms that are heard in corporate boardrooms around the country. For all their colorfulness, such terms reflect the fact that any corporate expansion and reorganization can generate conflict both among the corporate entities involved and among the directors, officers, and shareholders of each corporation. Corporate participants may have conflicting views, for example, on the merits of acquiring or combining with another corporation.

A corporation typically extends or reorganizes its operations through a merger or consolidation, a purchase of another corporation's assets, or a purchase of a controlling interest in another corporation. This chapter will examine these four types of corporate events. The last part of this chapter will discuss the typical reasons for, and methods used in, terminating a corporation.

## MERGER AND CONSOLIDATION

The terms *merger* and *consolidation* are often used interchangeably, but they refer to two legally distinct proceedings. Whether a combination is in fact a merger or a consolidation, however, the rights and liabilities of shareholders, the corporation, and its creditors are the same.

### ■ Exhibit 43–1 Merger

In this illustration, Corporations A and B decide to merge. They agree that A will absorb B, so on merging, B ceases to exist as a separate entity, and A continues as the surviving corporation.

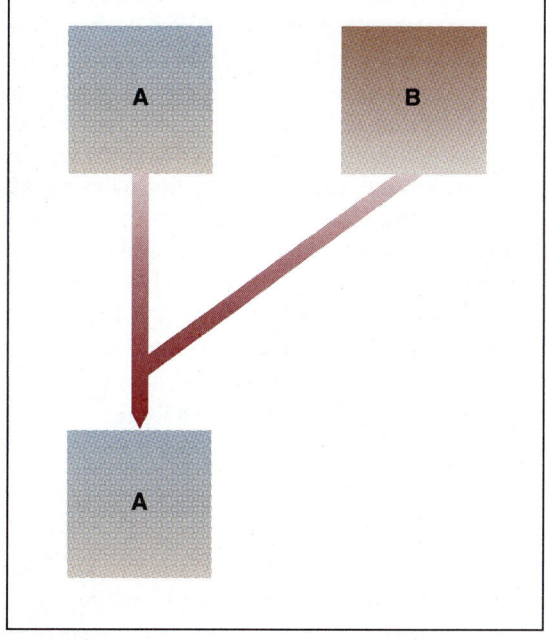

### ■ Exhibit 43–2 Consolidation

In this illustration, Corporations A and B consolidate to form an entirely new organization, Corporation C. In the process, A and B terminate, and C comes into existence as an entirely new entity.

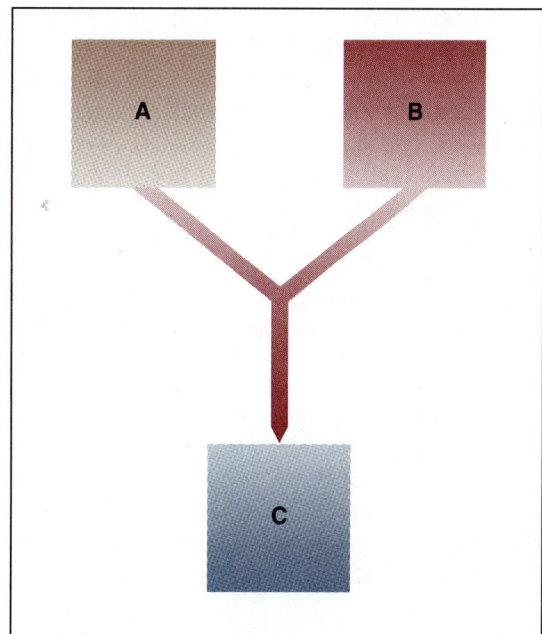

## MERGER

A **merger** involves the legal combination of two or more corporations. After a merger, only one of the corporations continues to exist. For example, Corporation A and Corporation B decide to merge. It is agreed that A will absorb B; so upon merger, B ceases to exist as a separate entity, and A continues as the **surviving corporation.** This process is illustrated in Exhibit 43–1.

After the merger, A is recognized as a single corporation possessing all the rights, privileges, and powers of itself and B. A automatically acquires all of B's property and assets without the necessity of formal transfer. A becomes liable for all of B's debts and obligations.[1] Finally, A's articles of incorporation are deemed *amended* to include any changes that are stated in the *articles of merger.*

In a merger, the surviving corporation is vested with the disappearing corporation's preexisting legal rights and obligations. For example, if the disappearing corporation had a right of action against a third party, the surviving corporation could bring suit after the merger to recover the disappearing corporation's damages.

## CONSOLIDATION

In the case of a **consolidation,** two or more corporations combine so that each corporation ceases to exist and a new one emerges. Corporation A and Corporation B consolidate to form an entirely new organization, Corporation C. In the process, A and B both terminate. C comes into existence as an entirely new entity. This process is illustrated in Exhibit 43–2.

The results of consolidation are essentially the same as the results of merger. C is recognized as a new corporation and a single entity; A and B

---

1. A corporation that is subject to suit in some jurisdictions cannot avoid liability by merging with a corporation that could not otherwise have been sued in those jurisdictions. See, for example, *In re Silicone Gel Breast Implants Product Liability Litigation,* 837 F.Supp. 1123 (N.D.Ala. 1993).

cease to exist. C accedes to all the rights, privileges, and powers previously held by A and B. Title to any property and assets owned by A and B passes to C without formal transfer. C assumes liability for all debts and obligations owed by A and B. The articles of consolidation *take the place of* A's and B's original corporate articles and are thereafter regarded as C's corporate articles.

When a merger or consolidation takes place, the surviving corporation or newly formed corporation will issue shares or pay some fair consideration to the shareholders of the corporation that ceases to exist.

## THE MERGER AND CONSOLIDATION PROCEDURE

All states have statutes authorizing mergers and consolidations for domestic (in-state) corporations, and most states allow the combination of domestic and foreign (out-of-state) corporations. Although the procedures vary somewhat among jurisdictions, in each case the basic requirements are as outlined below [RMBCA 11.01–11.07].

1.  The board of directors of *each* corporation involved must approve a merger or consolidation plan.[2]
2.  The shareholders of *each* corporation must vote approval of the plan at a shareholders' meeting. Most state statutes require the approval of two-thirds of the outstanding shares of voting stock, although some states require only a simple majority, and others require a four-fifths vote. Frequently, statutes require that each class of stock approve the merger; thus, the holders of nonvoting stock must also approve. A corporation's bylaws can dictate a stricter requirement.
3.  Once approved by *all* the directors and the shareholders, the plan (articles of merger or consolidation) is filed, usually with the secretary of state.

---

2.  When a corporation undertakes a transaction that will cause a change in corporate control or that will break up the corporate entity, the directors have an obligation ''to seek the best value reasonably available to the stockholders.'' See, for example, *Paramount Communications, Inc., v. QVC Network, Inc.,* 637 A.2d 34 (Del. 1994).

4.  When state formalities are satisfied, the state issues a certificate of merger to the surviving corporation or a certificate of consolidation to the newly consolidated corporation.

RMBCA 11.04 provides a simplified procedure for the merger of a substantially owned subsidiary corporation into its parent corporation. Under these provisions, a **short-form merger**—also referred to as a *parent-subsidiary merger*—can be accomplished *without approval of the shareholders* of either corporation. The short-form merger can be used only when the parent corporation owns at least 90 percent of the outstanding shares of each class of stock of the subsidiary corporation. The simplified procedure requires that a plan for the merger be approved by the board of directors of the parent corporation before it is filed with the state. A copy of the merger plan must be sent to each shareholder of record of the subsidiary corporation.

## APPRAISAL RIGHTS

The law recognizes that a dissenting shareholder should not be forced to become an unwilling shareholder in a corporation that is new or different from the one in which the shareholder originally invested. The shareholder has the right to dissent and may be entitled to be paid *fair value* for the number of shares held on the date of the merger or consolidation [RMBCA 13.02]. This right, which is referred to as the shareholder's **appraisal right,** is given by state statute and is available only when the statute specifically provides for it. The right is normally extended to regular mergers, consolidations, short-form mergers, sales of substantially all the corporate assets not in the ordinary course of business, and in certain states, adverse amendments to the articles of incorporation. The appraisal right may be lost if the elaborate statutory procedures are not precisely followed. Whenever the right is lost, the dissenting shareholder must go along with the transaction to which he or she objects.

One of the basic procedures usually followed requires that a written notice of dissent be filed by the dissenting shareholder or shareholders prior to the vote of the shareholders on the proposed transaction. This notice of dissent is also basically a notice to all shareholders of costs that may be imposed by dissenting shareholders should the merger or consolidation be approved. In addition, after the merger or consolidation has been approved, the dissenting shareholders must make a written demand for payment and for fair value [RMBCA 13.20–13.28].

*Valuation* of shares is often a point of contention between the dissenting shareholder and the corporation. RMBCA 13.01 provides that the "fair value of shares" is the value on the day prior to the date on which the vote was taken.[3] The corporation must make a *written* offer to purchase a dissenting shareholder's stock, accompanying the offer with a current balance sheet and income statement for the corporation. If the shareholder and the corporation do not agree on the fair value, a court will determine it [RMBCA 13.30].

---

3. Any appreciation or depreciation of the stock in anticipation of the approval is excluded.

In some jurisdictions, once a dissenting shareholder elects appraisal rights under statute, the shareholder loses his or her shareholder status. Without that status, a shareholder cannot vote, receive dividends, or sue to enjoin whatever action prompted his or her dissent. In some of those jurisdictions, statutes provide, or courts have held, that shareholder status may be reinstated during the appraisal process (for example, if the shareholder decides to withdraw from the process and the corporation approves). In other jurisdictions, shareholder status may not be reinstated until the appraisal has concluded. Even if the status is lost, courts may allow an individual to sue on grounds of fraud or other illegal conduct associated with the merger.

The following case illustrates the frequently encountered problem of determining the fair value of shares under appraisal rights.

**BACKGROUND AND FACTS** *Springboard Software, Inc., creates and markets software programs for personal computers. Anthony Nicholson, a Springboard shareholder, held 103,853 shares of common stock and 28,814 shares of preferred stock, as well as 3,250 shares of common stock for each of his two sons. On May 1, 1989, the Springboard board of directors met to consider a proposed merger between Springboard and Spinnaker Software Corporation. The merger would involve an exchange of shares for a percentage of ownership in the resulting entity. The board voted to approve the merger and submitted the matter to the shareholders. At the end of June, Springboard and Spinnaker issued a prospectus that described the merger to their respective shareholders. A footnote to Spinnaker's financial report, attached to the prospectus, indicated that Spinnaker would show the merger, for accounting purposes, as a purchase of Springboard for approximately $5.4 million. The shareholders approved the merger on July 19. On that date, Nicholson exercised his rights as a dissenting shareholder, entitling him to the fair value of his shares. In December, Spinnaker offered Nicholson $.90 per common share and $1.575 per preferred share, basing these figures on a* pro rata *share of the $5.4 million noted in Spinnaker's report. The market price for Springboard shares had never fallen below $1.625 per share, however, and Nicholson rejected Spinnaker's evaluation. Nicholson argued that the fair value of his shares should be based on the midpoint of the market price per share of Springboard common stock on May 1. Spinnaker asked a court to evaluate Nicholson's interest. Based on the testimony of Nicholson's expert witness, the court concluded that the fair value of Nicholson's common shares was $2.16, and the fair value of his preferred shares was $3.00. Spinnaker appealed.*

CASE 43.1

**SPINNAKER SOFTWARE CORP. v. NICHOLSON**

Court of Appeals of Minnesota, 1993.
495 N.W.2d 441.

*DAVIES,* Presiding Judge.

\* \* \* \*

In determining ''fair value'' of the shares, Minn.Stat. [Section] 302A.473, [Subdivision] 7, provides: The court \* \* \* shall determine the fair value of the shares, taking into account any and all factors the court finds relevant, computed by any method or combination of methods that the court, in its discretion, sees fit to use, whether or not used by the corporation or by a dissenter.

\* \* \* \*

\* \* \* Spinnaker argues that the purchase price for Springboard was $5.4 million, based on the footnote to Spinnaker's financial records attached to the prospectus. The evidence shows that the merger transaction involved an exchange of shares for a percentage of ownership in the merged entity and that the $5.4 million was merely the amount that Spinnaker's accountants used to represent the transaction for accounting purposes. We are not persuaded that a preponderance of the evidence shows the $5.4 million was the purchase price or fair value of Springboard as negotiated in an arms-length transaction.

Valuation of property is a finding of fact which an appellate court will reverse only if clearly erroneous. We conclude that the trial court's findings in support of its valuation are supported by the evidence and the testimony of Nicholson's expert witness. The method of valuation used by Nicholson's expert and adopted by the trial court in determining the value of Nicholson's common shares falls within the broad discretion accorded the trial court under Minn.Stat. [Section] 302A.473. The evidence also supports the trial court's finding regarding the value of Nicholson's preferred shares.

**DECISION AND REMEDY**    *The appellate court affirmed the lower court's decision.*

## SHAREHOLDER APPROVAL

Shareholders invest in a corporate enterprise with the expectation that the board of directors will manage the enterprise and will approve ordinary business matters. Actions taken on extraordinary matters must be authorized by the board of directors and the shareholders. Often, modern statutes require that certain types of extraordinary matters be approved by a vote of the shareholders. Typically, matters requiring shareholder approval include the sale, lease, or exchange of all or substantially all corporate assets outside of the corporation's regular course of business [RMBCA 12.01–12.02]. Other examples include amendments to the articles of incorporation, transactions concerning merger or consolidation, and dissolution.

The following case involves a sale of corporate assets that was negotiated without the shareholders' approval. The shareholders opposing the sale sought injunctive relief from the court.

| CASE 43.2 | |
|---|---|
| **SCHWADEL v. UCHITEL** District Court of Appeal of Florida, Third District, 1984. 455 So.2d 401. | **BACKGROUND AND FACTS**  *Mike and Peter Schwadel, the plaintiffs, were two of the three major shareholders in HJU Sales & Investments, Inc. Over several years the assets of the corporation had been sold off until only one asset remained—a restaurant called ''The Place for Steak.'' The plaintiffs sued the president and third major shareholder of the corporation, Hy Uchitel, when he entered into a contract to sell this remaining asset. Florida state law prohibits the sale of all or substantially all of a corporation's assets without shareholder approval. The Schwadels sought an injunction to prevent the sale of the restaurant, but the lower court denied the request. The plaintiffs appealed.* |

*BASKIN,* Judge.

\* \* \* \*

The prerequisites of section 607.241 [of Florida statutes] must be satisfied when a contemplated sale of major assets of a corporation will substantially limit the corporate business. The Place for Steak was the sole asset of Southern Caterers of North Bay Village, Inc., the wholly owned subsidiary of HJU, and the last of several restaurants owned by parent corporation HJU. It is undisputed that the fundamental purpose in forming the parent corporation and in operating the corporate enterprise through various subsidiaries was, and continues to be, to engage in the restaurant business. Thus, the sale of The Place for Steak constitutes a sale of "substantially all" the corporate assets and is subject to the statutory rights and protections extended to stockholders under Florida's shareholder "consent" provisions governing such transactions.

The purpose of a shareholder "consent" provision is "to protect the shareholders from fundamental change, or more specifically to protect the shareholders from the destruction of the means to accomplish the purposes or objects for which the corporation was incorporated and actually performs." When Hy Uchitel entered into a contract for the sale of the last major corporate asset, he violated shareholders' statutory rights to receive prior notice to consider the transaction and effectively barred their participation in a decision which fundamentally changes the nature of the corporation. This court must therefore decide whether injunctive relief is appropriate under these circumstances.

The general rule is that a court of equity is empowered to issue injunctive relief to prevent officers or directors of a corporation from wrongfully dealing with corporate assets and to prevent such wrongful actions from infringing upon shareholders' voting rights. The proposed sale of the remaining corporate asset constituted a breach of Uchitel's fiduciary duties to the corporation and to its stockholders, and deprived shareholders of their statutory rights to notice and to vote prior to the transfer of the last corporate asset. Injunctive relief is appropriate because appellants have a clear legal right to prior notice and a vote, and legal remedies are inadequate to prevent the irreparable harm that would result from Uchitel's unilateral decision to change the fundamental nature of the corporate enterprise. An award of damages would not compensate the shareholders for the destruction of the corporation caused by the transfer of the last major corporate asset. The pending sale is therefore enjoined.

*The appellate court reversed the lower court's decision and granted an injunction to the plaintiffs.*

**DECISION AND REMEDY**

---

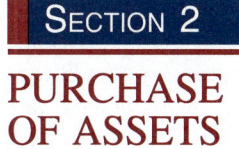

# PURCHASE OF ASSETS

When a corporation acquires all or substantially all of the assets of another corporation by direct purchase, the purchasing corporation, or *acquiring corporation,* simply extends its ownership and control over more physical assets. Because no change in the legal entity occurs, the acquiring cor-

poration is not required to obtain shareholder approval for the purchase.[4]

---

4.   If the acquiring corporation plans to pay for the assets with its own corporate stock and not enough authorized unissued shares are available, the shareholders must vote to approve issuance of additional shares by amendment of the corporate articles. Also, acquiring corporations whose stock is traded on a national stock exchange can be required to obtain their own shareholders' approval if they plan to issue a significant number of shares, such as a number equal to 20 percent or more of the outstanding shares.

Although the acquiring corporation may not be required to obtain shareholder approval for such an acquisition, the U.S. Department of Justice has issued guidelines that significantly constrain and often prohibit mergers that could result from a purchase of assets. These guidelines are part of the federal antitrust laws to enforce Section 7 of the Clayton Act (discussed in Chapter 48).

Note that the corporation that is *selling* all its assets is substantially changing its business position and perhaps its ability to carry out its corporate purposes. For that reason, the corporation whose assets are *acquired* must obtain both board of director and shareholder approval. In most states and under the RMBCA, a dissenting shareholder of the selling corporation can demand appraisal rights.

Generally, a corporation that purchases the assets of another corporation is not responsible for the liabilities of the selling corporation. Exceptions to this rule are made in the following circumstances:

1. When the purchasing corporation impliedly or expressly assumes the seller's liabilities.
2. When the sale amounts to what in fact is a merger or a consolidation.
3. When the purchaser continues the seller's business and retains the same personnel (same shareholders, directors, and officers).
4. When the sale is fraudulently executed to escape liability.

In any of these situations, the acquiring corporation will be held to have assumed both the assets and the liabilities of the selling corporation.

The following case addresses the issue of whether a corporation that purchased the assets of another firm and assumed its liabilities is subject to liability for punitive damages based on the conduct of the predecessor.

---

### CASE 43.3

**DAVIS v. CELOTEX CORP.**

Supreme Court of Appeals of
West Virginia, 1992.
187 W.Va. 566,
420 S.E.2d 557.

**COMPANY PROFILE**   *Philip Carey Manufacturing Company was incorporated in Ohio in 1888. Philip Carey manufactured building products that contained asbestos. The dangers of asbestos were documented as early as 1918 in American medical literature. During the 1930s, there was considerable publicity on the risk of breathing asbestos dust. For example, in 1930, an article published in the asbestos-industry magazine* Asbestos *concluded that fifteen cases of pulmonary fibrosis among factory workers were caused by asbestos dust. By 1942, there were enough cases of lung cancer associated with asbestos for this topic to be included in a medical textbook on occupational cancer. After several employees filed workers' compensation claims alleging that they suffered from work-related asbestosis, in 1962 Philip Carey hired a consultant to advise it on protecting its workers from asbestosis. The consultant discussed the risks associated with exposure to asbestos, recommended steps to protect workers, and outlined what the company should do to limit its future legal liability. The company did not act on the recommendations. In 1967, Philip Carey merged with the Glen Alden Corporation. Philip Carey transferred all of its assets, subject to liabilities, to Glen Alden and became its subsidiary. In 1969, this new corporation merged with another Glen Alden subsidiary, the Briggs Manufacturing Company. The surviving company was named the Panacon Corporation.*

**BACKGROUND AND FACTS**   *From 1965 to 1974, Jennings Davis was employed as a plumber and pipe fitter by several electric power generating plants. During his employment, Davis was exposed to asbestos-containing products that were manufactured by numerous companies. As a purported result, Davis developed asbestosis and lung cancer and died from lung* *cancer in 1987. One of the companies supplying asbestos to the power plants for which Davis had worked was Panacon Corporation. In 1972, Celotex Corporation had purchased the assets of Panacon and expressly assumed all of the liabilities and duties of Panacon. On Davis's death, his son, Ronald Davis, sued Celotex Corporation for damages, alleging that Celotex had assumed Panacon's liability for health hazards associated with its products. The trial court found for Davis and awarded both compensatory and punitive damages. On appeal, Celotex claimed that although it continued to manufacture and market asbestos products, it placed warning labels on its product and therefore was not "engaged in the sort of egregious conduct that warrants punitive damages." According to Celotex, it was guilty only of acquiring a company that knowingly concealed the dangers of asbestos.*

**MILLER,** Justice:

\* \* \* \*

At common law, it was generally held that the purchaser of all the assets of a corporation was not liable for the debts or liabilities of the corporation purchased. This rule has since been tempered by a number of exceptions and statutory provisions.

\* \* \*

\* \* \* These exceptions are outlined [as follows]: "—there is an express or implied assumption of liability; "—the transaction amounts to a consolidation or merger; "—the transaction was fraudulent; "—some of the elements of a purchase in good faith were lacking, as where the transfer was without consideration and the creditors of the transferor were not provided for; "—the transferee corporation was a mere continuation or reincarnation of the old corporation."

\* \* \* \*

While we find Celotex's argument without merit, this is not to say that every acquisition or merger will automatically result in punitive damage liability. Here, at the time of the merger, the extreme health hazards associated with asbestos products were well known. The continuation of the business was a direct and deliberate product of the merger. Thus, we conclude that when a corporation acquires or merges with a company manufacturing a product that is known to create serious health hazards, and the successor corporation continues to produce the same product in the same manner, it may be found liable for punitive damages for liabilities incurred by the predecessor company in its manufacture of such product.

*The trial court's judgment was affirmed. Celotex could be held liable, as a successor corporation, for both compensatory and punitive damages.*

**DECISION AND REMEDY**

## SECTION 3

# PURCHASE OF STOCK

An alternative to the purchase of another corporation's assets is the purchase of a substantial number of the voting shares of its stock. This enables the acquiring corporation, sometimes referred to as the **aggressor,** to control the acquired corporation, or **target corporation.** The acquiring corporation deals directly with the shareholders in seeking to purchase the shares they hold.

## TENDER OFFERS

When the acquiring corporation makes a public offer to all shareholders of the target corporation, it is called a **tender offer** (an offer that is publicly advertised and addressed to all shareholders of the target company). The price of the stock in the tender offer is generally higher than the market price of the target stock prior to the announcement of the tender offer. The higher price induces shareholders to tender (offer to sell) their shares to the acquiring firm. The tender offer can be conditional upon the receipt of a specified number of outstanding shares by a specified date. The offering corporation can make an *exchange* tender offer in which it offers target stockholders its own securities in exchange for their target stock. In a cash tender offer, the offering corporation offers the target stockholders cash in exchange for their target stock.

Federal securities laws strictly control the terms, duration, and circumstances under which most tender offers are made. In addition, a majority of states have passed takeover statutes that impose additional regulations on tender offers when instate companies are involved.

## LEVERAGED BUY-OUTS (LBOs)

In the last decade, a number of corporations have arranged to ''go private'' through so-called **leveraged buy-outs (LBOs).** In an LBO, the management of a corporation—or any other group, but management is usually included—purchases all outstanding corporate stock held by the public and in this way gains control over the corporate enterprise. The LBO is financed by borrowing money against the assets of the corporation, which may include real estate or plant and equipment. The borrowing may take the form of the issuance of bonds, a straight bank loan, or a loan from an investment bank. Because an LBO often results in a high debt load for the corporation, the interest payments on the debt may become so burdensome that the corporation cannot later survive. Some corporations have failed to survive following LBOs for this reason.

## TARGET RESPONSES

As discussed in Chapter 42, the directors of a corporation owe a fiduciary duty to the shareholders. In the context of a tender offer, this requires that, after full consideration, the directors of the target firm make a good faith decision as to whether the shareholders' acceptance or rejection of the offer would be most beneficial. In making any recommendation, the directors must fully disclose all *material facts.* A fact is material if there is a substantial likelihood that a reasonable shareholder would consider it important in deciding how to vote. For example, information indicating a good price for the stock would be considered material.

Sometimes, a target firm's board of directors will see a tender offer as favorable and recommend to the shareholders that they accept it. To resist a takeover, a target company may make a *self-tender,* which is an offer to acquire stock from its own shareholders and thereby retain corporate control. Alternatively, a target corporation might resort to one of several other tactics to resist a takeover (see Exhibit 43–3).

A target may also seek an injunction against an acquiring corporation on grounds that the attempted takeover violates antitrust laws (the subject of Chapter 48), which are intended to prevent the illegal restraint of competition. This defense may succeed if the takeover would, in the eyes of a court, result in a substantial increase in the acquiring corporation's market power.

## SECTION 4

# TERMINATION

Termination of a corporate life, like termination of a partnership, has two phases—dissolution and liquidation. **Dissolution** is the legal death of the artificial ''person'' of the corporation. **Liquidation** is the process by which corporate assets are converted into cash and distributed among creditors and shareholders according to specific rules of preference.[5]

## DISSOLUTION

Dissolution can be brought about voluntarily by the directors and shareholders or involuntarily by the state or through a court's order.

**VOLUNTARY DISSOLUTION** There are basically two ways in which a corporation can be voluntarily dissolved once a corporation has issued

---

5.  Upon dissolution, the liquidated assets are first used to pay creditors. Any remaining assets are distributed to shareholders according to their respective stock rights; preferred stock has priority over common stock, generally by charter.

■ **Exhibit 43–3  The Terminology of Takeover Defenses**

| Term | Definition |
|---|---|
| **Crown Jewel** | When threatened with a takeover, management makes the company less attractive to the raider by selling to a third party the company's most valuable asset (hence the term *crown jewel*). |
| **Golden Parachute** | When a takeover is successful, top management is usually changed. With this in mind, a company may establish special termination or retirement benefits that must be paid to top management if they are ''retired.'' In other words, a departing high-level manager's parachute will be ''golden'' when he or she is forced to ''bail out'' of the company. |
| **Greenmail** | To regain control, a target company may pay a higher-than-market price to repurchase the stock that the acquiring corporation bought. When a takeover is attempted through a gradual accumulation of target stock rather than a tender offer, the intent may be to get the target company to buy back the accumulated shares at a premium price—a concept similar to blackmail. |
| **Lobster Trap** | Lobster traps are designed to catch large lobsters but to allow small lobsters to escape. In the ''lobster trap'' defense, holders of convertible securities (corporate bonds or stock that is convertible into common shares) are prohibited from converting the securities into common shares if the holders already own, or would own after conversion, 10 percent or more of the voting shares of stock. |
| **Pac-Man** | Named after the Atari video game, this is an aggressive defense by which the target corporation attempts its own takeover of the acquiring corporation. |
| **Poison Pill** | The target corporation issues to its stockholders shares that can be turned in for cash if a takeover is successful. This makes the takeover undesirably or even prohibitively expensive for the acquiring corporation. |
| **Scorched Earth** | The target corporation sells off assets or divisions or takes out loans that it agrees to repay in the event of a takeover, thus making itself less financially attractive to the acquiring corporation. |
| **Shark Repellant** | To make a takeover more difficult, a target company may change its articles of incorporation or bylaws. For example, the bylaws may be amended to require that a large number of shareholders approve the firm's combination. This tactic casts the acquiring corporation in the role of a shark that must be repelled. |
| **White Knight** | The target corporation solicits a merger with a third party, which then makes a better (often simply a higher) tender offer to the target's shareholders. The third party that ''rescues'' the target is the ''white knight.'' |

shares and commenced business operations.[6] First, the shareholders can initiate corporate dissolution proceedings by a unanimous vote to dissolve the corporation. Second, the directors may propose that the corporation be dissolved and submit the proposal to the shareholders for a vote at a share-holders' annual meeting or a specially called shareholders' meeting.

Under RMBCA 14.03, once a decision is reached to dissolve the corporation, the corporation must file *articles of dissolution* with the secretary of state. These articles must include the name of the corporation, the date that the dissolution was authorized, and how it was authorized. The effective date of dissolution will be the date of its articles of dissolution. The corporation must also notify its creditors of the dissolution and establish a date (at least 120 days following the date of dissolution)

---

6.  If the corporation was formed but has not yet undertaken any business or issued any shares, a majority of the incorporators can dissolve the corporation relatively simply—by filing *articles of dissolution* with the secretary of state's office, which will then issue a *certificate of dissolution.*

by which all claims against the corporation must be received [RMBCA 14.06].

**INVOLUNTARY DISSOLUTION** Corporations are creatures of statute, as stated earlier. Just as the state can allow a corporation to come into existence, so can it end that existence. The state, in an action brought by the secretary of state or the state attorney general, may dissolve a corporation for any of the following reasons [RMBCA 14.20]:

1. The failure of the corporation to comply with administrative requirements (such as the failure to pay annual taxes, submit an annual report, or have a designated registered agent).
2. The procurement of a corporate charter through fraud or misrepresentation upon the state.
3. The abuse of corporate powers (*ultra vires* acts).
4. The violation of the state criminal code after the demand to discontinue the violation has been made by the secretary of state.
5. The failure to commence business operations.
6. The abandonment of operations before starting up.

The Statutory Close Corporation Supplement provides that the articles of incorporation of a close corporation may empower any shareholder to dissolve the corporation at will or on the occurrence of a specified event—such as the death of another shareholder. This provides a shareholder in a close corporation with the same power to dissolve his or her business organization as a partner in a partnership.

Sometimes an involuntary dissolution of a corporation is necessary—for example, when a board of directors is deadlocked. Courts hesitate to order involuntary dissolution in such circumstances unless there is specific statutory authorization to do so, but if the deadlock cannot be resolved by the shareholders and if it will irreparably injure the corporation, the court will proceed with an involuntary dissolution. Courts can also dissolve a corporation for mismanagement [RMBCA 14.30].

In the following case, a minority shareholder—one of the two shareholders in a close corporation—sued to have the corporation dissolved because he had been "frozen out" of the business by the allegedly oppressive tactics of the majority shareholder.

---

| CASE 43.4 |
|---|

**BALVIK v. SYLVESTER**

Supreme Court of North Dakota, 1987.
411 N.W.2d 383.

**BACKGROUND AND FACTS** *In 1984, Elmer Balvik and Thomas Sylvester decided to turn their partnership into a corporation because of the tax benefits that would result. The new Weldon Corporation carried on the partnership's old business of electrical contracting. Sylvester received 70 percent of the stock of the new corporation and Balvik, the remaining 30 percent, in proportion to the capital that each contributed. Both took positions as directors and officers of the corporation, and each was entitled to one vote per share of stock. Balvik was at all times a minority voice in the company. Although Sylvester and Balvik had had no problems during their years as partners, difficulties emerged soon after incorporation. Sylvester believed that excess profits should be reinvested in the corporation, whereas Balvik wanted them withdrawn and paid out as bonuses or dividends. Balvik was fired from his job, allegedly because of poor performance, and he began working for another company. He was unable to take any of his capital contribution in the corporation with him, and he no longer received a salary from the corporation. Balvik sued to have the corporation dissolved under North Dakota law, which allows dissolution for illegal, oppressive, or fraudulent acts by corporate directors or those in control of the corporation toward minority shareholders. The district court ordered dissolution and appointed a receiver, and Sylvester appealed.*

*VANDE WALLE*, Justice.
* * * *

The limited market for stock in a close corporation and the natural reluctance of potential investors to purchase a noncontrolling interest in a close corporation that has been marked by dissension can result in a minority shareholder's interest being held "hostage" by the controlling interest, and can lead to situations where the majority "freeze out" minority shareholders by the use of oppressive tactics.
* * * *

Because of the predicament in which minority shareholders in a close corporation are placed by a "freeze out" situation, courts have analyzed alleged "oppressive" conduct by those in control in terms of "fiduciary duties" owed by the majority shareholders to the minority and the "reasonable expectations" held by the minority shareholders in committing their capital and labor to the particular enterprise.
* * * *

* * * [C]onsidering Sylvester's inclination to reinvest profits in the corporation, the possibility of a declaration of dividends in the near future appears remote. We find little relevance in whether Sylvester discharged Balvik from employment for cause, or in the fact that Balvik's removal as a director and officer of the corporation occurred only after Balvik brought the instant suit. The ultimate effect of these actions is that Balvik clearly has been "frozen out" of a business in which he reasonably expected to participate. As a result, Balvik is entitled to relief.
* * * *

We have recognized that forced dissolution of a corporation is a drastic remedy which should be invoked with extreme caution and only when justice requires it. In a sense, a forced dissolution allows minority shareholders to exercise retaliatory "oppression" against the majority. * * *

Under the circumstances, we believe the trial court abused its discretion in ordering the extreme remedy of dissolution. Weldon is apparently an on-going business and, under the facts presented, ordering its dissolution and liquidation is unduly harsh. Balvik, in his complaint, sought as an alternative remedy that "the Defendant pay to the Plaintiff the true value of his stock in the Corporation. . . ." * * * [W]e believe [this] is the appropriate remedy here. Consequently, we remand this case for the entry of an order requiring either Weldon or Sylvester to purchase Balvik's stock at a price determined by the court to be the fair value thereof. The court may conduct any further proceedings it deems necessary for resolution of the issue. The parties are, of course, free to agree to other alternative methods of resolving this dispute.

**DECISION AND REMEDY**

*The Supreme Court of North Dakota affirmed the decision of the lower court that Balvik had been "frozen out" of the corporation.*

**INTERNATIONAL CONSIDERATIONS**

**Rights of Minority Shareholders in Canada** *In Canada, ownership of corporations is frequently concentrated in the hands of a few controlling shareholders. Unlike the United States, Canada does not recognize a fiduciary duty of controlling shareholders toward minority shareholders. Canada does have a doctrine of "fraud on the minority," however. This doctrine applies to extreme misbehavior. Canada also has "oppression statutes" that place some restrictions on the actions of majority shareholders.*

## LIQUIDATION

When dissolution takes place by voluntary action, the members of the board of directors act as trustees of the corporate assets. As trustees, they are responsible for winding up the affairs of the corporation for the benefit of corporate creditors and shareholders. This makes the board members personally liable for any breach of their fiduciary trustee duties.

Liquidation can be accomplished without court supervision unless the members of the board do not wish to act in this capacity or unless shareholders or creditors can show cause to the court why the board should not be permitted to assume the trustee function. In either case, the court will appoint a **receiver** to wind up the corporate affairs and liquidate corporate assets. A receiver is always appointed by the court if the dissolution is involuntary.

# TERMS AND CONCEPTS TO REVIEW

| | | |
|---|---|---|
| aggressor  853 | leveraged buy-out (LBO)  854 | short-form merger  848 |
| appraisal right  848 | liquidation  854 | surviving corporation  847 |
| consolidation  847 | merger  847 | target corporation  853 |
| dissolution  854 | receiver  858 | tender offer  853 |

# QUESTIONS AND CASE PROBLEMS

**43–1. Corporate Combinations.** Gretz is chairperson of the board of directors of Faraday, Inc., and Williams is chairperson of the board of directors of Firebrand, Inc. Faraday is a manufacturing corporation, and Firebrand is a transportation corporation. Gretz and Williams meet to consider the possibility of combining their corporations and activities into a single corporate entity. They consider two alternative courses of action: acquisition by Faraday of all the stock and assets of Firebrand or combination of the two corporations to form a new corporation, Farabrand, Inc. Both chairpersons are concerned about the necessity of formal transfer of property, liability for existing debts, and the problem of amending articles of incorporation. Discuss what the two proposed combinations are called and what legal effect each has on the transfer of property, the liabilities of the combined corporations, and the need to amend the articles of incorporation.

**43–2. Shareholders' Rights.** Alir owns 10,000 shares of Ajax Corp. Her shares represent a 10 percent ownership in Ajax. Zeta Corp. is interested in acquiring Ajax in a merger, and the board of directors of each corporation has approved the merger. The shareholders of Zeta have already approved the acquisition, and Ajax has called for a shareholders' meeting to approve the merger. Alir disapproves of the merger and does not want to accept Zeta shares for the Ajax shares she holds. The market price of Ajax shares is $20 per share the day before the shareholder vote and drops to $16 on the day the shareholders of Ajax approve the merger. Discuss Alir's rights in this matter, beginning with the notice of the proposed merger.

**43–3. Purchase of Assets.** Green Corp. wants to acquire all the assets of Red Dot Corp. Green plans to pay for the assets by issuing its own corporate stock. Green's board of directors has already approved the merger. Discuss whether shareholder approval is required for this merger.

**43–4. Corporate Expansion.** Alitech Corp. is a small midwestern business that owns a valuable patent. Alitech has approximately 1,000 shareholders with 100,000 authorized and outstanding shares. Block Corp. would like to have use of the patent, but Alitech refuses to give Block a license. Block has tried to acquire Alitech by purchasing Alitech's assets, but Alitech's board of directors has refused to approve the acquisition. Alitech's shares are presently selling for $5 per share. Discuss how Block Corp. might proceed to gain the control and use of Alitech's patent.

**43–5. Termination.** Saunders Corp. has been losing money for several years but still has valuable fixed assets. The shareholders see little hope that the corporation will ever make a profit. Another corporation, Topway Corp., has failed to pay state taxes for several years or to file annual reports required by statute. In addition, Topway is accused of being guilty of gross and persistent *ultra vires* acts. Discuss whether these corporations will be terminated and how the assets of each would be handled upon dissolution.

**43–6. Corporate Dissolution.** I. Burack, Inc., was a family-operated close corporation that sold plumbing supplies in New York. The founder and president, Israel Burack, transferred his shares in the corporation to other family members; and when Israel died in 1974, the position of president passed to his son, Robert Burack. Robert held a one-third interest in the company, and the remainder was divided among Israel's other children and grandchildren. All shareholders participated in the corporation as employees or officers and thus relied on salaries and bonuses, rather than dividends, for distribution of the corporation's earnings. In 1976, several of the family-member employees requested a salary increase from Robert, who claimed that company earnings were not sufficient to warrant any employee salary increases. Shortly thereafter, a shareholders' meeting was held (the first in the company's fifty-year history), and Robert was removed from his position as president and denied the right to participate in any way in the corporation. Robert sued to have the company dissolved because he had been frozen out. Discuss whether Robert should succeed in his suit or whether the court would choose another alternative. [*Burack v. I. Burack, Inc.,* 137 A.D.2d 523, 524 N.Y.S.2d 457 (1988)]

**43–7. Purchase of Assets.** On March 6, 1981, Carolyn Hamaker lost three fingers from her left hand while operating a notcher machine (lathe) at Pallets and Wood Products, her place of employment in South Dakota. The notching machine had been manufactured by Kenwel Machine Co. On December 31, 1975, Kenwel sold its assets to John and Rosemary Jackson, who created a new company called Kenwel-Jackson Machine Co. Kenwel Machine Co. terminated its existence in August 1977. Kenwel-Jackson Machine Co. continued to manufacture notchers, but it made several design changes and was in fact producing a different machine from the one that injured Carolyn Hamaker. As a result of her injuries, Hamaker brought a suit for damages against Kenwel-Jackson, because Kenwel Machine Co. no longer existed. Discuss whether Kenwel-Jackson is liable for injuries caused by a machine manufactured by a company it purchased. [*Hamaker v. Kenwel-Jackson Machine Co.,* 387 N.W.2d 515 (S.D. 1986)]

**43–8. Involuntary Dissolution.** Two brothers, Albert and Raymond Martin, each owned 50 percent of the stock in Martin's News Service, Inc. Albert and Raymond had difficulty working together and communicated only through their accountant. For ten years, there were no corporate meetings, elections to the board of directors, or other corporate formalities. During that time, Raymond operated the business much as a sole proprietorship, failing to consult Albert on any matter and making all of the decisions himself. The corporation, however, was a viable concern that had grown successfully through the years. Albert sued to have the corporation dissolved. Should he succeed? Discuss. [*Martin v. Martin's News Service, Inc.,* 9 Conn.App. 304, 518 A.2d 951 (1986)]

**43–9. Purchase of Assets.** In 1987, William Myers sustained injuries to his hand while operating a cement pump that had been manufactured by Thomsen Equipment Co. Myers alleged that the pump was unreasonably dangerous because it had an ''unguarded nip point in a flapper valve.'' Putzmeister, Inc., purchased Thomsen's assets in 1982. If Myers has a valid product liability claim, what factors will the court consider in determining whether Putzmeister can be held liable for injuries caused by Thomsen's product? [*Myers v. Putzmeister, Inc.,* 232 Ill.App.3d 419, 596 N.E.2d 754, 173 Ill.Dec. 130 (1992)]

**43–10. Sale of Assets.** Lori Ann Nilsson, in the course of her employment as a machine operator, was injured by a pipe and tube cutoff machine that had been manufactured and sold by Continental Machine Co. prior to 1978. In 1986, Fredor Corp. purchased all of the production assets of Continental, including the pipe and tube machine product line, and formed Continental Machine Manufacturing Co. (CMM). The assets purchased from Continental were transferred to CMM. CMM continued to manufacture the same product lines as Continental had. The shareholders of Continental did not become shareholders, officers, or employees of Fredor or CMM. Most of the employees of Continental became employees of CMM, however. There was no evidence that the transaction was undertaken for a fraudulent purpose, nor did Fredor or CMM agree to assume Continental's liabilities. After the sale of assets, Continental continued to exist, but it had no productive assets. Continental continued to own the building in which the assets had been located, however, and leased the building to CMM. Nilsson brought a product liability suit against CMM. Will the court hold CMM liable for injuries caused by a machine manufactured by Continental? What factors will the court consider in reaching its decision? Discuss fully. [*Nilsson v. Continental Machine Manufacturing Co.,* 251 Ill.App.3d 415, 621 N.E.2d 1032, 190 Ill.Dec. 579 (1993)]

### 43–11. A Question of Ethics

*In a corporate merger, Diamond Shamrock Corp. retained its corporate identity, and the Natomas Co. was absorbed into the former's corporate hierarchy. As part of the merger agreement, five inside directors (directors who are also officers of the corporation) of Natomas were offered golden parachutes, which provided that the five individuals would be paid three years of compensation if they left their positions at Natomas for any reason other than termination for just cause. Three of the five voluntarily left their positions after three years. Under the terms of their parachute agreements, they collected over $10 million. A suit challenging the golden parachutes was brought by Gaillard, a shareholder of Natomas. A trial court sustained the golden parachutes on the ground that the directors were protected by the business judgment rule in effecting the agreement. The appellate court held that the business judgment rule does not apply in a review of the conduct of inside directors and remanded the case for trial. [Gaillard v. Natomas Co., 208 Cal.App.3d 1250, 256 Cal.Rptr. 702 (1989)]*

1. Regardless of the legal issues, are golden parachutes ethical in a general sense?

2. Why would a corporation *want* to grant its top management such seemingly one-sided agreements?

3. In *Gaillard,* how would your views be affected by evidence showing that the golden parachutes were developed and presented to the board by the very individuals who were the beneficiaries of the agreements—that is, by the five inside directors?

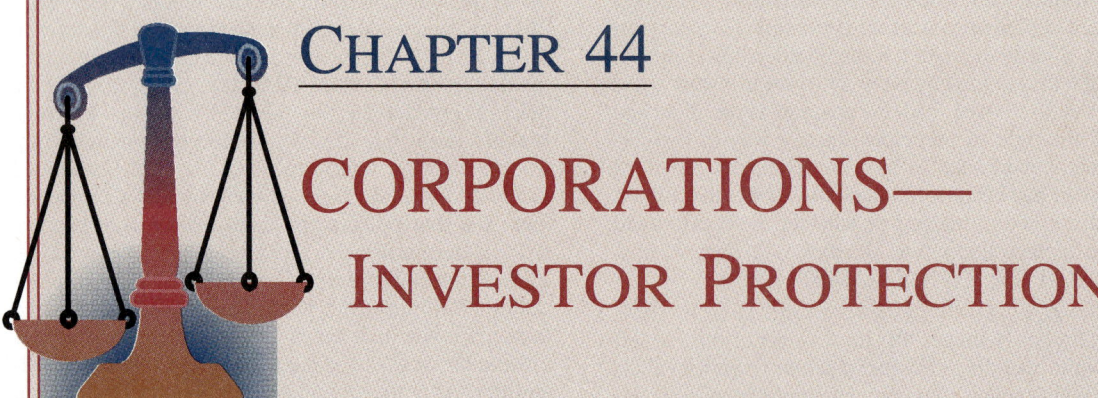

# CHAPTER 44

# CORPORATIONS—
# INVESTOR PROTECTION

After the great stock market crash of 1929, various studies showed a need for regulating securities markets. Basically, legislation for such regulation was enacted to provide investors with more information to help them make buying and selling decisions about *securities*—generally defined as any documents evidencing corporate ownership (stock) or debts (bonds)—and to prohibit deceptive, unfair, and manipulative practices in the purchase and sale of securities. Today, the sale and transfer of securities are heavily regulated by federal and state statutes and by government agencies. This chapter will discuss the nature of federal securities regulations and their effect on the business world.

## THE SECURITIES AND EXCHANGE COMMISSION

The stock market crash of October 29, 1929, and the ensuing economic depression caused the public to focus on the importance of securities markets for the economic well-being of the nation. The feverish trading in securities during the preceding decade became the subject of widespread attention, and numerous reports were circulated concerning the speculative, manipulative, and at times unscrupulous trading that occurred in the stock markets.

The public, outraged by such practices, pressured Congress into action. As a result, in 1931 the Senate passed a resolution calling for an extensive investigation of securities trading. The investigation led, ultimately, to the passage by Congress of the Securities Act of 1933, which is also known as the *truth-in-securities* bill. In the following year, the Securities Exchange Act was passed by Congress. This 1934 act created the Securities and Exchange Commission (SEC) as an independent regulatory agency whose function was to administer the 1933 and 1934 acts. Its major responsibilities in this respect are as follows:

1. Requiring disclosure of facts concerning offerings of securities listed on national securities exchanges and offerings of certain securities traded over the counter (OTC).
2. Regulating the trade in securities on the thirteen national and regional securities exchanges and in the OTC markets.
3. Investigating securities frauds.
4. Regulating the activities of securities brokers, dealers, and investment advisers and requiring their registration.
5. Supervising the activities of mutual funds.
6. Recommending administrative sanctions, injunctive remedies, and criminal prosecution against those who violate securities laws. (The Fraud Section of the Criminal Division of the Department of Justice prosecutes violations of federal securities laws.)

From the time of its creation until the present, the SEC's regulatory functions have gradually been increased by legislation granting it authority in different areas. In recent years the SEC has been active in promoting stiffer penalties for *insider trading* and in effecting regulatory changes addressing the problem of the proliferation of hostile takeovers and corporate-control contests, in which outsiders attempt to wrest control of the corporation from its current board of directors. Another current major concern of the SEC is to effect fundamental changes in the basic regulatory framework applying to the financial services industry. Under the Securities Enforcement Remedies Act of 1990, the SEC was granted substantial new powers, increasing the range of SEC enforcement options.

<br>

| | SECTION 2 |
|---|---|

# SECURITIES ACT OF 1933

The Securities Act of 1933[1] was designed to prohibit various forms of fraud and to stabilize the

securities industry by requiring that all essential information concerning the issuance of stocks be made available to the investing public. Essentially, the purpose of this act is to require disclosure. Under Section 2(1) of the Securities Act, securities include

> any note, stock, treasury stock, bond, debenture, evidence of indebtedness, certificate of interest or participation in any profit-sharing agreement, collateral-trust certificate, preorganization certificate or subscription, transferable share, investment contract, voting-trust certificate, certificate of deposit for a security, fractional undivided interest in oil, gas, or other mineral rights, or, in general, any interest or instrument commonly known as a "security," or any certificate of interest or participation in, temporary or interim certificate for, receipt for, guarantee of, or warrant or right to subscribe to or purchase, any of the foregoing.[2]

Basically, the courts have interpreted this definition to mean that a security exists in any transaction in which a person (1) invests (2) in a common enterprise (3) reasonably expecting profits (4) derived *primarily* or *substantially* from others' managerial or entrepreneurial efforts.[3]

For our purposes, it is probably most convenient to think of securities in their most common form—stocks and bonds issued by corporations. Bear in mind that securities can take many forms and have been held to include whiskey, cosmetics, worms, beavers, boats, vacuum cleaners, muskrats, and cemetery lots, as well as investment contracts in condominiums, franchises, limited partnerships, oil or gas or other mineral rights, and farm animals accompanied by care agreements.

## REGISTRATION STATEMENT

Section 5 of the Securities Act of 1933 broadly provides that if a security does not qualify for an exemption, that security must be *registered* before it is offered to the public either through the mails or through any facility of interstate commerce, including securities exchanges. Issuing corporations must file a *registration statement* with the SEC.

---

1. 15 U.S.C. Sections 77–77aa.

2. 15 U.S.C. Section 77b(1). Amendments in 1982 added stock options.
3. *SEC v. W. J. Howey Co.,* 328 U.S. 293, 66 S.Ct. 1100, 90 L.Ed. 1244 (1946).

Investors must be provided with a *prospectus* that describes the security being sold, the issuing corporation, and the investment or risk attaching to the security. In principle, the registration statement and the prospectus supply sufficient information to enable unsophisticated investors to evaluate the financial risk involved.

**CONTENTS OF THE STATEMENT**   The registration statement must include the following:

1. A description of the significant provisions of the security offered for sale, including the relationship between that security and the other capital securities of the registrant. Also, the corporation must disclose how it intends to use the proceeds of the sale.
2. A description of the registrant's properties and business.
3. A description of the management of the registrant; its security holdings; and its remuneration and other benefits, including pensions and stock options. Any interests of directors or officers in any material transactions with the corporation must be disclosed.
4. A financial statement certified by an independent public accounting firm.
5. A description of pending lawsuits.

**OTHER REQUIREMENTS**   Before filing the registration statement and the prospectus with the SEC, the corporation is allowed to obtain an underwriter who will monitor the distribution of the new issue. There is a twenty-day waiting period (which can be accelerated by the SEC) after registration before the sale can take place. During this period, oral offers between interested investors and the issuing corporation concerning the purchase and sale of the proposed securities may take place, and very limited written advertising is allowed. At this time the so-called **red herring** prospectus may be distributed. It gets its name from the red legend printed across it stating that the registration has been filed but has not become effective.

After the waiting period, the registered securities can be legally bought and sold. Written advertising is allowed in the form of a so-called **tombstone ad,** so named because the format resembles a tombstone. Such ads simply tell the investor where and how to obtain a prospectus. Normally, any other type of advertising is prohibited.

**VIOLATIONS**   Registration violations of the 1933 act are not treated lightly. In the following case, the BarChris Construction Corporation was sued by the purchasers of the corporation's debentures (see Chapter 41) under Section 11 of the Securities Act of 1933. Section 11 imposes liability when a registration statement or a prospectus contains material false statements or material omissions.

---

| CASE 44.1 |
| :---: |
| **ESCOTT v. BARCHRIS CONSTRUCTION CORP.** |
| United States District Court, Southern District of New York, 1968. |
| 283 F.Supp. 643. |

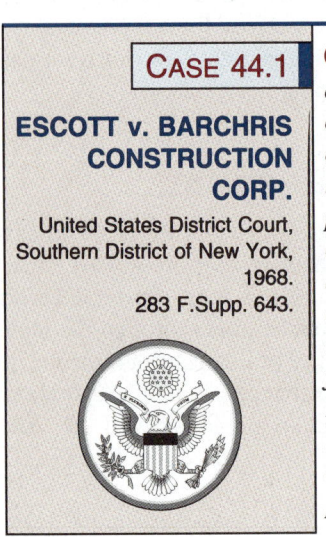

**COMPANY PROFILE**   *BarChris Construction Corporation grew out of a business that was started in 1946 to build bowling alleys. The availability of automatic pin-setting machines to the owners of bowling alleys in the early 1950s sparked rapid growth in the bowling industry. Due in part to the speed and accuracy with which an automatic pinsetter could reset the pins, bowling increased in popularity in bowling alleys that used the new equipment, and bowling became the leading U.S. indoor sport. BarChris benefited from this increased interest in bowling, and its construction operations expanded rapidly. BarChris's sales increased dramatically between 1956 and 1960, and the company was recognized as a significant factor in the bowling construction industry. It was estimated that in 1960, BarChris installed approximately 3 percent of all bowling lanes built in the United States. BarChris was in constant need of cash to finance its operations, a need that grew more and more pressing as operations expanded. In 1959, BarChris sold over a half-million shares of its common stock to the public. By early 1961, it needed additional working capital, and this time it decided to sell debentures (see Chapter 41). BarChris filed a registration statement for the debentures with the SEC and received the*

*proceeds of the financing. Nevertheless, BarChris experienced increasing financial difficulties, which in time became insurmountable. By early 1962, it was painfully apparent that BarChris was beginning to fail. In October of that year, BarChris filed a petition for bankruptcy, and the next month it defaulted on the interest due on the debentures.*

**BACKGROUND AND FACTS**  *This lawsuit was brought by purchasers of the BarChris Construction Corporation bonds under Section 11 of the Securities Act of 1933. Before issuing the bonds, BarChris had filed a registration statement with the Securities and Exchange Commission and had issued a prospectus relating the state of BarChris's affairs in the first months of 1961. The plaintiffs challenged the accuracy of the registration statement and charged that the text of the prospectus contained material false statements and material omissions. The plaintiffs alleged that BarChris had overstated its sales, profits, liabilities, and customer orders, and had failed to disclose its loans to company officers, the failure of some of its customers to pay amounts due, its use of the money that it received in payment from other customers, and the projected success or failure of several bowling alleys.*

*McLEAN,* District Judge.
\*   \*   \*   \*

It is a prerequisite to liability under Section 11 of the [Securities] Act [of 1933] that the fact which is falsely stated in a registration statement, or the fact that is omitted when it should have been stated to avoid misleading, be ''material.'' The regulations of the Securities and Exchange Commission pertaining to the registration of securities define the word as follows:

> ''The term 'material,' when used to qualify a requirement for the furnishing of information as to any subject, limits the information required to those matters as to which an average prudent investor ought reasonably to be informed before purchasing the security registered.''

\*   \*   \*   \*

The average prudent investor is not concerned with minor inaccuracies or with errors as to matters which are of no interest to him. The facts which tend to deter him from purchasing a security are facts which have an important bearing upon the nature or condition of the issuing corporation or its business.

Judged by this test, there is no doubt that many of the misstatements and omissions in this prospectus were material. This is true of all of them which relate to the state of affairs in 1961, i.e., the overstatement of sales and gross profit  \*   \*   \* , the understatement of contingent liabilities  \*   \*   \* , the overstatement of orders on hand and the failure to disclose the true facts with respect to officers' loans, customers' delinquencies, application of proceeds and the prospective operation of several alleys.

**DECISION AND REMEDY**

*BarChris Construction Corporation was held liable. Also held liable were the underwriters of the issuance (including eight investment banking firms), BarChris's auditors (Peat, Marwick, Mitchell & Company), and all of the signers of the registration statement (including BarChris's directors, controller, attorney, and others).*

## EXEMPT SECURITIES

A number of specific securities are exempt from the registration requirements of the Securities Act of 1933. These securities—which can also generally be resold without being registered—include the following:[4]

1. All bank securities sold prior to July 27, 1933.
2. Commercial paper if the maturity date does not exceed nine months.
3. Securities of charitable organizations.
4. Securities resulting from a corporate reorganization issued for exchange with the issuer's existing security holders and certificates issued by trustees, receivers, or debtors in possession under the bankruptcy laws (bankruptcy is discussed in Chapter 33).
5. Securities issued exclusively for exchange with the issuer's existing security holders, provided no commission is paid (for example, stock dividends and stock splits).
6. Securities issued to finance the acquisition of railroad equipment.
7. Any insurance, endowment, or annuity contract issued by a state-regulated insurance company.
8. Government-issued securities.
9. Securities issued by banks, savings and loan associations, farmers' cooperatives, and similar institutions subject to supervision by governmental authorities.
10. In consideration of the "small amount involved,"[5] an issuer's offer of up to $5 million in securities in any twelve-month period (including up to $1.5 million in nonissuer resales).

For the last exemption, under Regulation A,[6] the issuer must file with the SEC a notice of the issue and an offering circular, which must also be provided to investors before the sale. This is a much simpler and less expensive process than the procedures associated with full registration. Companies are allowed to "test the waters" for potential interest before preparing the offering circular. To *test the waters* means to determine potential in-

terest without actually selling any securities or requiring any commitment on the part of those who are interested. Small business issuers (companies with less than $25 million in annual revenues and less than $25 million in outstanding voting stock) can also use an integrated registration and reporting system that uses simpler forms than the full registration system.

## EXEMPT TRANSACTIONS

An issuer of securities that are not exempt under one of the categories listed above can avoid the high cost and complicated procedures associated with registration by taking advantage of certain transaction exemptions. An offering may qualify for more than one exemption.

These exemptions are very broad, and thus many sales occur without registration. The exemptions are available only in the transaction in which the securities are issued, however (except for securities issued under Rule 504, which will be discussed shortly). A resale of the securities may be made only after registration (unless the resale qualifies as an exempt transaction).

**REGULATION D**  The SEC's Regulation D contains four separate exemptions from registration requirements for limited offers (offers that involve either a small amount of money or are made in a limited manner). Regulation D provides that any of these offerings made during any twelve-month period are exempt from the registration requirements.

*Rule 504.*  Noninvestment company offerings up to $1 million in any one year are exempt.[7] A noninvestment company is a firm that is not engaged primarily in the business of investing or trading in securities.

*Rule 504a.*  Offerings up to $500,000 in any one year by so-called blank check companies—companies with no specific business plans except to locate and acquire presently unknown businesses or opportunities—are exempt if no general solicitation or advertising is used; the SEC is notified of the sales; and precaution is taken against non-

4. 15 U.S.C. Section 77c.
5. 15 U.S.C. Section 77c(b).
6. 17 C.F.R. Sections 230.251–230.263.
7. 17 C.F.R. Section 230.504.

exempt, unregistered resales.[8] The limits on advertising and unregistered resales do not apply if the offering is made solely in states that provide for registration and disclosure and the securities are sold in compliance with those provisions.[9]

*Rule 505.* Private, noninvestment company offerings up to $5 million in any twelve-month period are exempt, regardless of the number of **accredited investors** (banks, insurance companies, investment companies, the issuer's executive officers and directors, and persons whose income or net worth exceeds certain limits), so long as there are no more than thirty-five unaccredited investors; no general solicitation or advertising is used; the SEC is notified of the sales; and precaution is taken against nonexempt, unregistered resales. If the sale involves *any* unaccredited investors, *all* investors must be given material information about the offering company, its business, and the securities before the sale. The issuer is not required to believe that each unaccredited investor "has such knowledge and experience in financial and business matters that he is capable of evaluating the merits and the risks of the prospective investment."[10]

*Rule 506.* Private offerings in unlimited amounts that are not generally solicited or advertised are exempt if the SEC is notified of the sales, precaution is taken against nonexempt, unregistered resales, and the issuer believes that each unaccredited investor has sufficient knowledge or experience in financial matters to be capable of evaluating the investment's merits and risks. There may be no more than thirty-five unaccredited investors, although there may be an unlimited number of accredited investors. If there are *any* unaccredited investors, the issuer must provide to *all* purchasers material information about itself, its business, and the securities before the sale.[11]

This exemption is perhaps most important to those firms that want to raise funds through the sale of securities without registering them. It is often referred to as the *private placement* exemption, because it exempts "transactions not involving any public offering."[12] This provision applies to private offerings to a limited number of persons who are sufficiently sophisticated and in a sufficiently strong bargaining position so as to be able to assume the risk of the investment (and who thus have no need for federal registration protection) and to private offerings to similarly situated institutional investors.

**RULE 147—INTRASTATE ISSUES**  Also exempt are intrastate transactions involving purely local offerings.[13] This exemption applies to offerings restricted to residents of the state in which the issuing company is organized and doing business. The exemption requires that 80 percent of the issuer's assets be located in the state of issue, 80 percent of the issuer's gross revenue be from business conducted within the state, and 80 percent of the net income from the sale of the issue be used in the state. Also, for nine months after the last sale, no resale may be made to a nonresident, and precautions must be taken against this possibility. (Precautions include obtaining a statement of residence in writing from each investor, as well as indicating on the securities certificates that they are unregistered and subject to resale only to state residents.) These offerings remain subject to applicable laws in the state of issue.

**SECTION 4(6)**  Under Section 4(6) of the Securities Act of 1933, an offer made *solely* to accredited investors is exempt if its amount is not more than $5 million. Any number of accredited investors may participate, but no unaccredited investors may do so. No general solicitation or advertising may be used; the SEC must be notified of all sales; and precaution must be taken against nonexempt, unregistered resales (because these are restricted securities and may be resold only by registration or in an exempt transaction).[14]

---

8. Precautions to be taken against nonexempt, unregistered resales include asking the investor whether he or she is buying the securities for others; before the sale, disclosing to each purchaser in writing that the securities are unregistered and thus cannot be resold, except in an exempt transaction, without first being registered; and indicating on the certificates that the securities are unregistered and restricted.

9. 17 C.F.R. Section 230.504a.

10. 17 C.F.R. Section 230.505.

11. 17 C.F.R. Section 230.506.

---

12. 15 U.S.C. Section 77d(2).

13. 15 U.S.C. Section 77c(a)(11); 17 C.F.R. Section 230.147.

14. 15 U.S.C. Section 77d(6).

### ■ Exhibit 44–1 Exemptions under the 1933 Securities Act

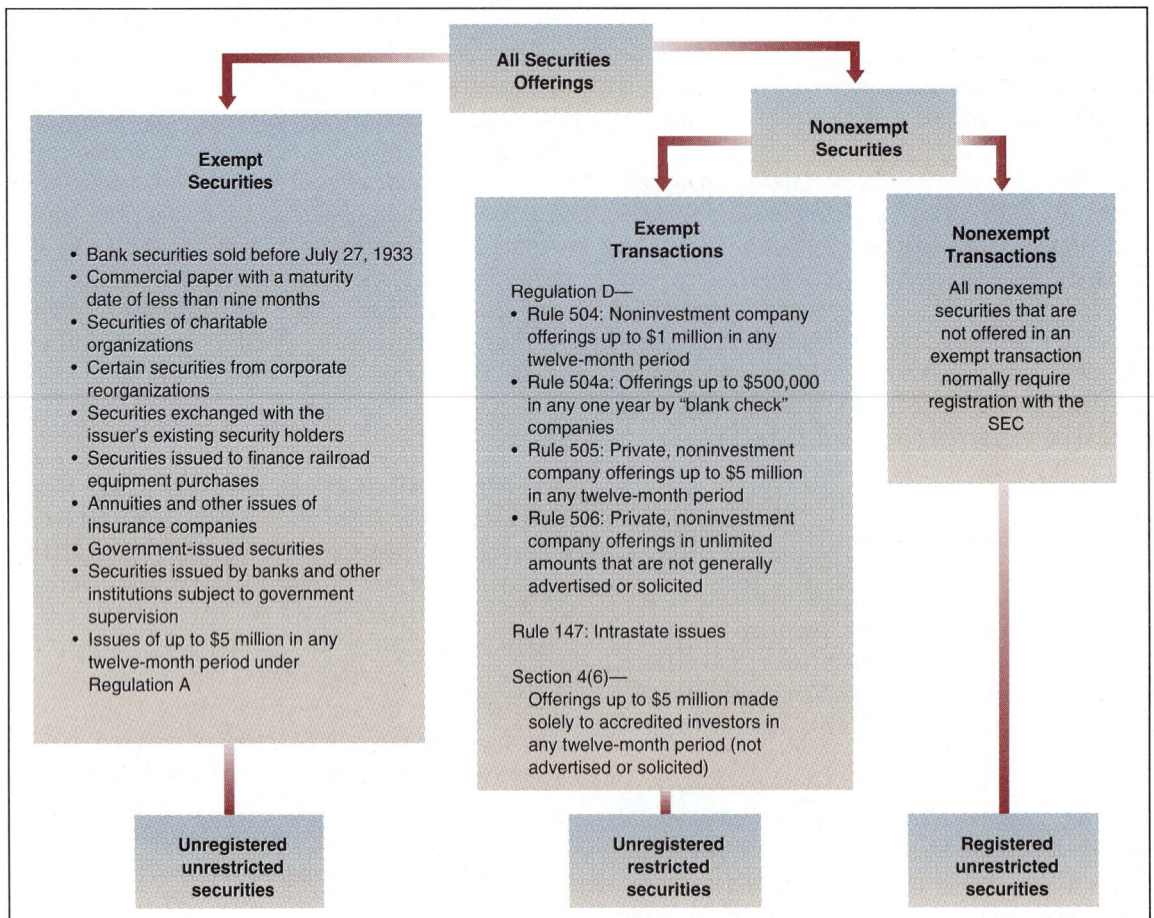

Transactions that are exempt from the registration requirements under the Securities Act of 1933 and SEC regulations are summarized in Exhibit 44–1.

**RESALES**  Most securities can be resold without registration (although some resales may be subject to some restrictions, which are discussed above in connection with specific exemptions). The Securities Act of 1933 provides exemptions for resales by most persons other than issuers or underwriters. Resales of restricted securities acquired under Rule 504a, Rule 505, Rule 506, or Section 4(6), however, trigger the registration requirements unless the party selling them complies with Rule 144 or Rule 144A. These rules, which are discussed below, are sometimes referred to as ''safe harbors.''

*Rule 144.*  Rule 144 exempts restricted securities from registration on resale if there is adequate current public information about the issuer, the person selling the securities has owned them for at least two years, they are sold in certain limited amounts in unsolicited brokers' transactions, and the SEC is given notice of the resale.[15] ''Adequate current public information'' consists of the reports that certain companies are required to file under the Securities Exchange Act of 1934. Any person (except an affiliate) who has owned the securities for at least three years is subject to none of these requirements. An *affiliate* is a person who controls,

---

15.   17 C.F.R. Section 230.144.

is controlled by, or is in common control with the issuer. Sales of *nonrestricted* securities by an affiliate are also subject to the requirements for an exemption under Rule 144 (except that the affiliate need not have owned the securities for at least two years).

*Rule 144A.*    Securities that at the time of issue are not of the same class as securities listed on a national securities exchange or quoted in a U.S. automated interdealer quotation system may be resold under Rule 144A.[16] They may be sold only to a qualified institutional buyer (an institution, such as an insurance company, an investment company, or a bank, that owns and invests at least $100 million in securities). The seller must take reasonable steps to ensure that the buyer knows that the seller is relying on the exemption under Rule 144A. A sample restricted stock certificate is shown in Exhibit 44–2.

## SECTION 3

# SECURITIES EXCHANGE ACT OF 1934

The Securities Exchange Act of 1934 provides for the regulation and registration of securities exchanges; brokers; dealers; and national securities associations, such as the National Association of Securities Dealers (NASD). The SEC regulates the markets in which securities are traded by maintaining a continuous disclosure system for all corporations with securities on the securities exchanges and for those companies that have assets in excess of $5 million and five hundred or more shareholders. These corporations are referred to as Section 12 companies, as they are required to register their securities under Section 12 of the 1934 act. The act regulates proxy solicitation for voting (see Chapter 42), and it allows the SEC to engage in market surveillance to regulate undesirable market practices such as fraud, market manipulation, misrepresentation, and stabilization. (*Stabilization*

is a market-manipulating technique by which securities underwriters bid for securities to stabilize their prices during their issuance.)

## SECTION 10(b) AND RULE 10b-5

Section 10(b) is one of the most important sections of the Securities Exchange Act of 1934. This section prohibits the use of ''any manipulative or deceptive device or contrivance in contravention of such rules and regulations as the [SEC] may prescribe.'' Among the rules that the SEC has prescribed is **Rule 10b-5,** which prohibits the commission of fraud in connection with the purchase or sale of any security.

## INSIDER TRADING

One of the most important purposes of Section 10(b) and Rule 10b-5 relates to so-called **insider trading.** Because of their positions, corporate directors and officers often obtain advance inside information that can affect the future market value of the corporate stock. Obviously, their positions can give them a trading advantage over the general public and shareholders. The 1934 Securities Exchange Act defines inside information and extends liability to officers and directors in their personal transactions for taking advantage of such information when they know that it is unavailable to the person with whom they are dealing.

Section 10(b) of the 1934 act and SEC Rule 10b-5 cover not only corporate officers, directors, and majority shareholders but also any persons having access to or receiving information of a nonpublic nature on which trading is based. Those found liable under Rule 10b-5 have a right to seek contribution from those who may have shared responsibility for the violations, including accountants, attorneys, and corporations.[17]

In the following case, a shareholder alleged that a corporate officer and a corporate director breached their fiduciary duties by trading corporate shares on the basis of nonpublic information.

---

16.   17 C.F.R. Section 230.144A.

17.   *Musick, Peeler & Garrett v. Employers Insurance of Wausau,* \_\_\_\_U.S. \_\_\_\_, 113 S.Ct. 2085, 124 L.Ed.2d 194 (1993).

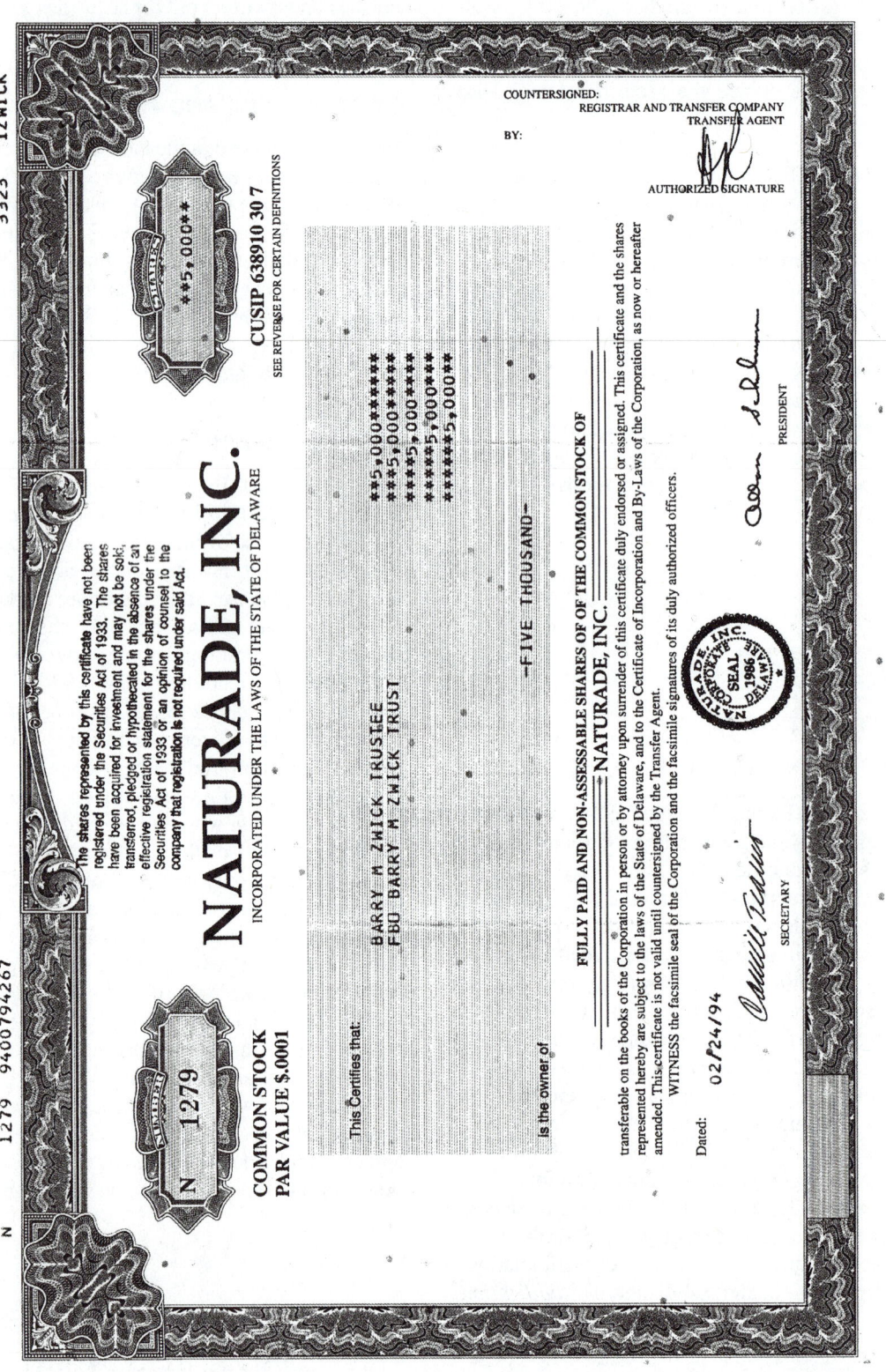

■ **Exhibit 44–2  A Sample Restricted Stock Certificate**

**HISTORICAL AND ETHICAL SETTING**    *Officers and directors owe fiduciary duties to their corporation and its shareholders with respect to corporate business and property. Shares in the corporation are private property, however, and trading in those shares is not usually a corporate transaction. Thus, at common law a century ago, directors and officers were considered to owe no fiduciary duties when they traded in the shares of their corporations. Directors or officers with inside information could trade with impunity without disclosing the information (as long as they avoided outright fraud). Although this rule is sometimes stated to be the majority rule, it has been applied in few cases over the last ninety-five years. Instead, the courts have developed a number of "exceptions." Some state courts have developed an agency law theory. According to agency law, an agent may not profit from using the property of his or her principal. It is reasoned by analogy that a director or officer may not profit from using inside information belonging to the corporation. In other words, under this reasoning, officers or directors owe a fiduciary duty to their corporation not to engage in the trading of shares in the corporation on the basis of inside information.*

**CASE 44.2**

**DIAMOND v. OREAMUNO**

Court of Appeals of New York, 1969.
24 N.Y.2d 494,
248 N.E.2d 910,
301 N.Y.S.2d 78.

**BACKGROUND AND FACTS**    *The defendants in this case were the chairman of the board (Oreamuno) and president (Gonzalez) of Management Assistance, Inc. (MAI), a corporation that bought and leased computers, with maintenance services being provided by IBM. The defendants learned that IBM was going to increase its maintenance prices dramatically, to such an extent that it would cut MAI's profits by 75 percent per month. Just before the IBM maintenance price increase was announced, the defendants sold their MAI stock for $28 per share. After IBM publicly announced its price increase, MAI stock fell to $11 per share. The plaintiff (Diamond) brought a shareholder's derivative lawsuit on behalf of MAI to recover the difference in profits. The trial court granted the defendants' motion to dismiss, and the plaintiff appealed.*

*FULD*, Chief Judge.
    *    *    *    *

Accepting the truth of the complaint's allegations, there is no question but that the defendants were guilty of withholding material information from the purchasers of the shares and, indeed, the defendants acknowledge that the facts asserted constitute a violation of rule 10b-5. *    *    * Of course, any individual purchaser, who could prove an injury as a result of a rule 10b-5 violation can bring his own action for rescission but we have not been referred to a single case in which such an action has been successfully prosecuted where the public sale of securities is involved. The reason for this is that sales of securities, whether through a stock exchange or over-the-counter, are characteristically anonymous transactions, usually handled through brokers, and the matching of the ultimate buyer with the ultimate seller presents virtually insurmountable obstacles. *    *    *

In view of the practical difficulties inherent in an action under the Federal law, the desirability of creating an effective common-law remedy is manifest. *    *    * There is ample room in a situation such as is here presented for a "private Attorney General" to come forward and enforce proper behavior on the part of corporate officials through the medium of the derivative action brought in the name of the corporation. Only by sanctioning such a cause of action will there be any effective method to prevent the type of abuse of corporate office complained of in this case.

**DECISION AND REMEDY**  *The court of appeals held that when corporate fiduciaries have breached their duty to the corporation by the use of nonpublic information, a shareholder may bring a derivative action for any profit resulting from the breach of duty.*

---

**DISCLOSURE UNDER RULE 10b-5**  Any material omission or misrepresentation of material facts in connection with the purchase or sale of a security may violate Section 10(b) and Rule 10b-5. The key to liability (which can be civil or criminal) under this rule is whether the insider's information is *material.* The following are some examples of material facts calling for a disclosure under the rule:

1. A new ore discovery.
2. Fraudulent trading in the company stock by a broker-dealer.
3. A dividend change (whether up or down).
4. A contract for the sale of corporate assets.
5. A new discovery (process or product).
6. A significant change in the firm's financial condition.

Courts have struggled with the problem of when information becomes public knowledge. Clearly, when inside information becomes public knowledge, all insiders should be allowed to trade without disclosure. The courts have suggested that insiders should refrain from trading for a "reasonable waiting period" when the news is not readily translatable into investment action. Presumably, this gives the news time to filter down to, and to be evaluated by, the investing public.

The following is one of the landmark cases interpreting Rule 10b-5. The SEC sued several of Texas Gulf Sulphur's directors, officers, and employees under Rule 10b-5 after these persons had purchased large amounts of the corporate stock prior to the announcement of the corporation's rich ore discovery.

---

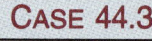

**CASE 44.3**

**SEC v. TEXAS GULF SULPHUR CO.**
United States Court of Appeals,
Second Circuit, 1968.
401 F.2d 833.

**BACKGROUND AND FACTS**  *In 1957, the Texas Gulf Sulphur Company (TGS) began exploring for minerals in eastern Canada. In March 1959, aerial geophysical surveys were conducted over more than 15,000 square miles of the area. The operations revealed numerous and extraordinary variations in the conductivity of the rock, which indicated a remarkable concentration of commercially exploitable minerals. One site of such variations was near Timmins, Ontario. On October 29 and 30, 1963, a ground survey of the site near Timmins indicated a need to drill for further evaluation. TGS drilled a hole on November 12 that appeared to yield a core with an exceedingly high mineral content. TGS kept secret the results of the core sample. Officers and employees of the company made substantial purchases of TGS's stock or accepted stock options after learning of the ore discovery, even though further drilling was necessary to establish whether there was enough ore to be mined commercially. Several months later, TGS's announcement of the strike of at least 25 million tons of ore substantially drove up the price of TGS stock. The SEC brought suit against the officers and employees of TGS for violating the insider-trading prohibition of Rule 10b-5. The officers and employees argued that the information on which they had traded had not been material at the time of their trades because the mine had not then been commercially proved. The trial court held that most of the defendants had not violated Rule 10b-5, and the SEC appealed.*

*WATERMAN, Circuit Judge.*
\* \* \* \*
\* \* \* [W]hether facts are material within Rule 10b-5 when the facts relate to

a particular event and are undisclosed by those persons who are knowledgeable thereof will depend at any given time upon a balancing of both the indicated probability that the event will occur and the anticipated magnitude of the event in light of the totality of the company activity. Here, * * * knowledge of the possibility, which surely was more than marginal, of the existence of a mine of the vast magnitude indicated by the remarkably rich drill core located rather close to the surface (suggesting mineability by the less expensive openpit method) within the confines of a large anomaly (suggesting an extensive region of mineralization) might well have affected the price of TGS stock and would certainly have been an important fact to a reasonable, if speculative, investor in deciding whether he should buy, sell, or hold. After all, this first drill core was ''unusually good and * * * excited the interest and speculation of those who knew about it.''

&ast; &ast; &ast; &ast;

Finally, a major factor in determining whether the * * * discovery was a material fact is the importance attached to the drilling results by those who knew about it. In view of other unrelated recent developments favorably affecting TGS, participation by an informed person in a regular stock-purchase program, or even sporadic trading by an informed person, might lend only nominal support to the inference of the materiality of the * * * discovery; nevertheless, the timing by those who knew of it of their stock purchases and their purchases of *short-term* calls—purchases in some cases by individuals who had never before purchased calls or even TGS stock—virtually compels the inference that the insiders were influenced by the drilling results.

**DECISION AND REMEDY** *The appellate court ruled in favor of the SEC. All of the trading by insiders who knew of the mineral find before its true extent was publicly announced violated Rule 10b-5.*

**APPLICABILITY OF RULE 10b-5** Rule 10b-5 applies in virtually all cases concerning the trading of securities, whether on organized exchanges, in over-the-counter markets, or in private transactions. The rule covers notes, bonds, certificates of interest and participation in any profit-sharing agreement, agreements to form a corporation, and joint-venture agreements; in short, the rule covers just about any form of security. It is immaterial whether a firm has securities registered under the 1933 act for the 1934 act to apply.

Rule 10b-5 is applicable only when the requisites of federal jurisdiction (such as the use of the mails, of stock exchange facilities, or of any instrumentality of interstate commerce) are present. Virtually no commercial transaction, however, can be completed without such contact. In addition, the states have corporate securities laws, many of which include provisions similar to Rule 10b-5.

In the case below, the United States Supreme Court examines the liability of a person who had received material nonpublic information from insiders of a corporation with which he had no connection.

---

**CASE 44.4**

**DIRKS v. SEC**
Supreme Court of the United States, 1983.
463 U.S. 646,
103 S.Ct. 3255,
77 L.Ed.2d 911.

**BACKGROUND AND FACTS** *Raymond Dirks was an officer of a New York broker-dealer firm. Dirks specialized in providing investment analysis of insurance company securities to institutional investors. In March 1973, Dirks received information from Ronald Secrist, a former officer of Equity Funding of America, who alleged that the assets of Equity Funding were vastly overstated as a result of fraudulent corporate practices. Secrist urged Dirks to verify the fraud and to disclose it publicly. Dirks decided to investigate the allegations, and throughout his investigation he openly* *discussed the information he had obtained with a number of clients and investors. The Securities and Exchange Commission (SEC) subsequently filed a complaint against Equity Funding and also found that Dirks had aided and abetted violations of Section 17(a) of the Securities Act of 1933, Section 10(b) of the Securities Exchange Act of 1934, and SEC Rule 10b-5 by repeating the allegations of fraud to members of the investment community who later sold their Equity stock. Dirks sought review in the court of appeals, which entered a judgment against him. The United States Supreme Court granted certiorari.*

Justice *POWELL* delivered the opinion of the Court.
\*   \*   \*   \*

\*   \*   \* [T]he SEC recognized that the common law in some jurisdictions imposes on ''corporate 'insiders,' particularly officers, directors, or controlling stockholders'' an ''affirmative duty of disclosure when dealing in securities.'' The SEC found that not only did breach of this common-law duty also establish the elements of a Rule 10b-5 violation, but that individuals other than corporate insiders could be obligated either to disclose material nonpublic information before trading or to abstain from trading altogether. \*   \*   \*
\*   \*   \*   \*

\*   \*   \* [T]here can be no duty to disclose where the person who has traded on inside information ''was not [the corporation's] agent, was not a fiduciary, [or] was not a person in whom the sellers [of the securities] had placed their trust and confidence.'' \*   \*   \*
\*   \*   \*   \*

The conclusion that recipients of inside information do not invariably acquire a duty to disclose or abstain does not mean that such tippees [those who receive ''tips'' from insiders] always are free to trade on the information. The need for a ban on some tippee trading is clear. Not only are insiders forbidden by their fiduciary relationship from personally using undisclosed corporate information to their advantage, but they may not give such information to an outsider for the same improper purpose of exploiting the information for their personal gain. \*   \*   \*
\*   \*   \*   \*

In determining whether a tippee is under an obligation to disclose or abstain, it thus is necessary to determine whether the insider's ''tip'' constituted a breach of the insider's fiduciary duty. \*   \*   \* Thus, the test is whether the insider personally will benefit, directly or indirectly, from his disclosure. Absent some personal gain, there has been no breach of duty to stockholders. And absent a breach by the insider, there is no derivative breach. \*   \*   \*
\*   \*   \*   \*

Under the inside-trading and tipping rules set forth above, we find that there was no actionable violation by Dirks. It is undisputed that Dirks himself was a stranger to Equity Funding, with no pre-existing fiduciary duty to its shareholders. He took no action, directly or indirectly, that induced the shareholders or officers of Equity Funding to repose trust or confidence in him. There was no expectation by Dirks' sources that he would keep their information in confidence. Nor did Dirks misappropriate or illegally obtain the information about Equity Funding. Unless the insiders breached their \*   \*   \* duty to shareholders in disclosing the nonpublic information to Dirks, he breached no duty when he passed it on.

*The decision of the court of appeals was reversed. The Supreme Court held that Dirks, under the circumstances, had no duty to refrain from using the inside information that he had acquired.*

**DECISION AND REMEDY**

**OUTSIDERS AND RULE 10b-5**    The traditional insider-trading case involves true insiders—corporate officers, directors, and majority shareholders who have access to, and trade on, inside information. Increasingly, liability under Section 10(b) of the 1934 act and SEC Rule 10b-5 has been extended to include certain ''outsiders''—those who trade on inside information acquired *indirectly.* Two theories have been developed in recent years under which outsiders may be held liable for insider trading: the *tipper/tippee theory* and the *misappropriation theory.*

*Tipper/Tippee Theory.*    Anyone who acquires inside information as a result of a corporate insider's breach of his or her fiduciary duty can be liable under Rule 10b-5. This liability extends to **tippees** (those who receive ''tips'' from insiders) and even remote tippees (tippees of tippees). The key to liability under this theory is that inside information was obtained as a result of someone's breach of a fiduciary duty to the corporation whose shares are traded. Unless there has been a breach of a duty not to disclose inside information, and the tippee knows of this breach (or should know of it), liability under this theory cannot result.

For example, in *Chiarella v. United States,*[18] the United States Supreme Court considered the role Rule 10b-5 plays when there was no breach of duty and no use of interstate commerce, the mails, or any of the facilities of any national securities exchange. Chiarella was a printer who worked at a New York composing room and handled announcements of corporate takeover bids. Even though the documents that were delivered to the printer concealed the identity of the target corporations by blank spaces and false names, Chiarella was able to deduce the names of the target companies. Without disclosing his knowledge, he purchased stock in the target companies and sold the shares immediately after the takeover attempts were made public. He realized a gain of

slightly more than $30,000 in the course of fourteen months.

In 1978, Chiarella was indicted on seventeen counts of violating Section 10(b) of the Securities Exchange Act of 1934 and SEC Rule 10b-5. The trial court convicted him on all counts, and the court of appeals affirmed that conviction. The United States Supreme Court, however, reversed the trial court's decision. The Supreme Court held that Chiarella could not be convicted for his failure to disclose his knowledge to stockholders or to target companies, because he was under no duty to disclose his knowledge. Chiarella was under no duty to disclose because he had no prior dealing with the stockholders and was not their agent, nor was he a person in whom sellers had placed their trust and confidence. Thus, the Court held that Chiarella was not liable as a tippee.[19]

*Misappropriation Theory.*    Liability for insider trading may also be established under the misappropriation theory. This theory of liability holds that if an individual wrongfully obtains—misappropriates—inside information and trades on it to his or her personal gain, then the individual should be held liable, because in essence, he or she stole information rightfully belonging to another. This theory has significantly extended the reach of Rule 10b-5 to outsiders who would not ordinarily be deemed fiduciaries of the corporations in whose stock they trade. Courts will normally hold, however, that some fiduciary duty to some lawful possessor of material nonpublic information must have

---

18.   445 U.S. 222, 100 S.Ct. 1108, 63 L.Ed. 348 (1980).

19.   Note, though, that Chiarella might not have escaped liability if the jury had been instructed to find liability under the misappropriation theory discussed next. Under that theory, it could be argued that Chiarella violated his duty of loyalty to his employer, the printing firm, by engaging in actions that could foreseeably be harmful to the printing firm's reputation. Note also that after *Chiarella,* the SEC adopted Rule 14e-3 (17 C.F.R. Section 240.14e-3), which makes it unlawful for a person who acquires advance knowledge of a tender offer to use that information in securities transactions.

been violated and some harm to the defrauded party must have occurred for liability to exist.

The following case raises the question of whether the tipper, to be liable under Rule 10b-5, must have known that his or her breach of a fiduciary obligation would lead to the tippee's trading on the misappropriated information.

---

<table>
<tr><td>

**CASE 44.5**

**UNITED STATES v. LIBERA**

United States Court of Appeals, Seventh Circuit, 1993 989 F.2d 596

</td><td>

**BACKGROUND AND FACTS** *R. R. Donnelley & Sons Company operates a printing plant in Old Saybrook, Connecticut, which prints* Business Week, *a weekly publication owned by McGraw-Hill, Inc. McGraw-Hill and Donnelley follow a policy of keeping the contents of each weekly issue confidential until 5:00 P.M. on Thursday. This policy is based on the fact that the contents of the magazine may affect the price of particular stocks and, prior to release, are regarded as inside information by the Securities and Exchange Commission. Donnelley employees knew that company rules forbade the removal of magazines from the plant. William Dillon tracked the stocks of companies analyzed in* Business Week *and observed that the trading in favorably mentioned securities often began increasing in volume and price on the Wednesday before publication and continued through the next Monday. Dillon, recognizing the value of receiving advance copies of* Business Week, *sought out Donnelley employees who would give him copies of the magazine on Thursday mornings. Dillon, Benjamin Libera, and Francis Sablone used the information to trade regularly on Thursday mornings in the securities reported in* Business Week. *When their scheme was discovered, Dillon agreed to plead guilty to certain criminal charges and to testify against Libera and Sablone, who were convicted of violations of Section 10(b) under the misappropriation theory. Libera and Sablone appealed, arguing that they could not be liable for insider trading unless the tipper (in this case, the Donnelley employees who gave them advance copies of* Business Week*) knew that the breach of a fiduciary obligation would lead to the tippee's trading on the misappropriated information.*

</td></tr>
</table>

*WINTER,* Circuit Judge:

 \*   \*   \*   \*

\*   \*   \* [T]he misappropriation theory requires the establishment of two elements: (i) a breach by the tipper of a duty owed to the owner of the nonpublic information; and (ii) the tippee's knowledge that the tipper had breached the duty. We believe these two elements, without more, are sufficient for tippee liability. The tipper's knowledge that he or she was breaching a duty to the owner of confidential information suffices to establish the tipper's expectation that the breach will lead to some kind of a misuse of the information. This is so because it may be presumed that the tippee's interest in the information is, in contemporary jargon, not for nothing. To allow a tippee to escape liability solely because the government cannot prove to a jury's satisfaction that the tipper knew exactly what misuse would result from the tipper's wrongdoing would not fulfill the purpose of the misappropriation theory, which is to protect property rights in information. Indeed, such a requirement would serve no purpose other than to create a loophole for such misuse.

**DECISION AND REMEDY**    *The appellate court affirmed the convictions of Libera and Sablone.*

**INTERNATIONAL CONSIDERATIONS**

**Insider Trading in Germany** *Germany does not have laws prohibiting insider trading. Instead, insider trading is regulated by voluntary guidelines that are included in employment contracts with banks and stock corporations. The guidelines prohibit trading by corporate insiders but have not been extended to cover the misappropriation of inside information by outsiders, who normally are not subject to the guidelines. In addition, the guidelines are not consistently enforced.*

## INSIDER REPORTING AND TRADING—SECTION 16(b)

Officers, directors, and certain large stockholders[20] of Section 12 corporations are required to file reports with the SEC concerning their ownership and trading of the corporation's securities.[21] To discourage such insiders from using nonpublic information about their company to their personal benefit in the stock market, Section 16(b) of the 1934 act provides for the recapture by the corporation of all profits realized by the insider on any purchase and sale or sale and purchase of the corporation's stock within any six-month period.[22] It is irrelevant whether the insider actually uses inside information; all such *short-swing* profits must be returned to the corporation.

Section 16(b) applies not only to stock but to warrants, options, and securities convertible into stock. In addition, the courts have fashioned complex rules for determining profits. Corporate insiders are wise to seek competent counsel prior to trading in the corporation's stock. Exhibit 44–3 compares the effects of Rule 10b-5 and Section 16(b).

## INSIDER-TRADING SANCTIONS

The Insider Trading Sanctions Act of 1984[23] permits the SEC to bring suit in a federal district court against anyone violating or aiding in a violation of the 1934 act or SEC rules by purchasing or selling a security while in the possession of material non-

public information. The violation must occur on or through the facilities of a national securities exchange or from or through a broker or dealer. Transactions pursuant to a public offering by an issuer of securities are excepted.

The court may assess as a penalty as much as triple the profits gained or the loss avoided by the guilty party. For purposes of the act, profit or loss is defined as "the difference between the purchase or sale price of the security and the value of that security as measured by the trading price of the security at a reasonable period of time after public dissemination of the nonpublic information."[24]

The Insider Trading and Securities Fraud Enforcement Act of 1988 enlarged the class of persons who may be subject to civil liability for insider-trading violations, gave the SEC authority to award **bounty payments** (rewards given by government officials for acts beneficial to the state) to persons providing information leading to the prosecution of insider-trading violations, gave the SEC rule-making authority to require specific policies and procedures to prevent insider trading, and increased the criminal penalties for violations. Maximum jail terms were increased from five to ten years; fines were increased to $1 million for individuals and to $2.5 million for partnerships and corporations.[25] Neither the 1984 act nor the 1988 act has any effect on other actions the SEC or private investors may take.

## PROXY STATEMENTS

Section 14(a) of the Securities Exchange Act of 1934 regulates the solicitation of proxies (see Chapter 42) from shareholders of Section 12 companies. The SEC regulates the content of proxy statements, which are statements sent to

---

20. Those stockholders owning 10 percent of the class of equity securities registered under Section 12 of the 1934 act.
21. 15 U.S.C. Section 78*l*.
22. In a predicted declining market for a particular stock, one can realize profits by "selling short"—selling at a high price and repurchasing at a later time at a lower price to cover the "short sale." The short seller typically has to borrow the stock in the meantime (and pay interest on the borrowed stock).
23. 15 U.S.C. Section 78u(d)(2)(A).

24. 15 U.S.C. Section 78u(d)(2)(C).
25. 15 U.S.C. Section 78ff(a).

■ **Exhibit 44–3 Comparison of Coverage, Application, and Liabilities under Rule 10b-5 and Section 16(b)**

|  | **Rule 10b-5** | **Section 16(b)** |
|---|---|---|
| Subject matter of transaction | Any security (does not have to be registered) | Any security (does not have to be registered) |
| Transactions covered | Purchase or sale | Short-swing purchase and sale or short-swing sale and purchase |
| Who is subject to liability? | Virtually anyone with inside information under a duty to disclose—including officers, directors, controlling stockholders, and tippees | Officers, directors, and certain 10 percent stockholders |
| Is omission or misrepresentation necessary for liability? | Yes | No |
| Any exempt transactions? | No | Yes, a variety of exemptions |
| Is direct dealing with the party necessary? | No | No |
| Who may bring an action? | A person transacting with an insider, the SEC, or a purchaser or seller damaged by a wrongful act | Corporation and shareholder by derivative action |

shareholders by corporate managers who are requesting authority to vote on behalf of the shareholders in a particular election on specified issues. Whoever solicits a proxy must fully and accurately disclose in the proxy statement all of the facts that are pertinent to the matter on which the shareholders are to vote. SEC Rule 14a-9 is similar to the antifraud provisions of Rule 10b-5. Remedies for violation are extensive, ranging from injunctions to prevent a vote from being taken to monetary damages.

## SECTION 4

# REGULATION OF INVESTMENT COMPANIES

Investment companies, and mutual funds in particular, grew rapidly after World War II. **Investment companies** act on behalf of many smaller shareholders/owners by buying a large portfolio of securities and managing that portfolio professionally. A **mutual fund** is a specific type of investment company that continually buys or sells to investors shares of ownership in a portfolio. Such companies are regulated by the Investment Company Act of 1940,[26] which provides for SEC regulation of their activities. The 1940 act was expanded by the Investment Company Act Amendments of 1970. Further minor changes were made in the Securities Act Amendments of 1975.

The 1940 act requires that every investment company register with the SEC and imposes restrictions on the activities of such companies and persons connected with them. For the purposes of the act, an investment company is defined as any entity that (1) "is * * * engaged primarily * * * in the business of investing, reinvesting, or trading in securities" or (2) is engaged in such business and more than 40 percent of the company's assets consist of investment securities. Excluded from coverage by the act are banks, insurance companies, savings and loan associations, finance companies, oil and gas drilling firms, charitable foundations, tax-exempt pension funds, and other special types of institutions, such as closely held corporations.

All investment companies must register with the SEC by filing a notification of registration. Each

---

26.   15 U.S.C. Sections 80a–1 to 80a–64.

year registered investment companies must file reports with the SEC. To safeguard company assets, all securities must be held in the custody of a bank or stock-exchange member, and that bank or stock-exchange member must follow strict procedures established by the SEC.

No dividends may be paid from any source other than accumulated, undistributed net income. Furthermore, there are some restrictions on investment activities. For example, investment companies are not allowed to purchase securities on the margin (pay only part of the total price, borrowing the rest), sell short (sell shares not yet owned), or participate in joint trading accounts.

## SECTION 5

# STATE SECURITIES LAWS

Today, all states have their own corporate securities laws that regulate the offer and sale of securities within individual state borders.[27] Often referred to

---

27. These laws are catalogued and annotated in the Commerce Clearing House's *Blue Sky Law Reporter,* a loose-leaf service.

as **blue sky laws,** they are designed to prevent "speculative schemes which have no more basis than so many feet of blue sky."

Since the adoption of the 1933 and 1934 federal securities acts, the state and federal governments have regulated securities concurrently. Issuers must comply with both federal and state securities laws, and exemptions from federal law are not exemptions from state laws. Certain features are common to all state blue sky laws. They have antifraud provisions, many of which are patterned after Rule 10b-5. Also, most state corporate securities laws regulate securities brokers and dealers.

Typically, these laws also provide for the registration or qualification of securities offered or issued for sale within the state. Unless an applicable exemption from registration is found, issuers must register or qualify their stock with the appropriate state official, often called a *corporations commissioner.* There are differences in philosophy among state statutes. Many are like the Securities Act of 1933 and mandate certain disclosures before registration is effective and a permit to sell the securities is issued. Others have fairness standards that a corporation must meet to offer or sell stock in the state. The Uniform Securities Act, which has been adopted in part by several states, was drafted to be acceptable to states with differing regulatory philosophies.

---

## TERMS AND CONCEPTS TO REVIEW

| | | |
|---|---|---|
| accredited investor  865 | investment company  876 | Rule 10b–5  867 |
| blue sky law  877 | mutual fund  876 | tippee  873 |
| bounty payment  875 | red herring  862 | tombstone ad  862 |
| insider trading  867 | | |

---

# QUESTIONS AND CASE PROBLEMS

**44–1. Registration Requirements.** Estrada Hermanos, Inc., a corporation incorporated and doing business in Florida, decides to sell $1 million worth of its no-par-value common stock to the public. The stock will be sold only within the state of Iowa. Jose Estrada, the chairman of the board, says the offering need not be registered with the Securities and Exchange Commission. His brother,

Gustavo, disagrees. Who is right? Explain.

**44–2. Registration Requirements.** Huron Corp. had 300,000 common shares outstanding. The owners of these outstanding shares lived in several different states. Huron decided to split the 300,000 shares two for one. Will Huron Corp. have to file a registration statement and prospectus on the 300,000 new shares to be issued as a result of the split? Explain.

**44–3. Securities Fraud.** Leston Nay owned 90 percent of the stock of First Securities Co. Between the years

1942 and 1966, Hochfelder sent large sums of money to Nay to be invested in *escrow accounts*—accounts belonging to one entity but held by another entity—of First Securities. The whole investment scheme was a fraud, and Nay converted the money sent by Hochfelder to his own use. When Hochfelder discovered the fraud, he sued Ernst & Ernst, the auditor of First Securities, for failing to use proper auditing procedures and thus negligently failing to discover the fraudulent scheme. Should the firm of Ernst & Ernst be found guilty of violating Section 10(b) of the 1934 Securities Exchange Act and the Securities and Exchange Commission Rule 10b-5? Explain. [*Ernst & Ernst v. Hochfelder*, 425 U.S. 185, 96 S.Ct. 1375, 47 L.Ed.2d 668 (1976)]

**44–4. Rule 10b-5.** Danny Cherif was employed by the First National Bank of Chicago in its International Financial Institutions Department from 1979 until 1987, when Cherif's position was eliminated due to an internal reorganization. Cherif, by a forged memo to the bank's security department, caused his magnetic identification (ID) card—which he had received as an employee to allow him to enter the bank building—to remain activated after his employment was terminated. Cherif used his ID card to enter the building at night to obtain confidential financial information from the bank's Specialized Finance Department regarding extraordinary business transactions, such as tender offers. During 1988 and 1989, Cherif made substantial profits by securities trading based on this information. Eventually, Cherif's activities were investigated by the Securities and Exchange Commission (SEC), and Cherif was charged with violating Section 10(b) and Rule 10b-5 by misappropriating and trading on inside information in violation of his fiduciary duties to his former employer. Cherif argued that the SEC wrongfully applied the misappropriation theory to his activities, because as a former employee, he no longer had a fiduciary duty to the bank. Explain whether Cherif is liable under Rule 10b-5. [*SEC v. Cherif*, 933 F.2d 403 (7th Cir. 1991)]

**44–5. Definition of a Security.** The W. J. Howey Co. (Howey) owned large tracts of citrus acreage in Lake County, Florida. For several years it planted about five hundred acres annually, keeping half of the groves itself and offering the other half to the public to help finance additional development. Howey-in-the-Hills Service, Inc., was a service company engaged in cultivating and developing these groves, including the harvesting and marketing of the crops. Each prospective customer was offered both a land sales contract and a service contract, after being told that it was not feasible to invest in a grove unless service arrangements were made. Of the acreage sold by Howey, 85 percent was sold with a service contract with Howey-in-the-Hills Service, Inc. Howey did not register with the Securities and Exchange Commission (SEC) or meet the other administrative requirements that issuers of securities must fulfill. The SEC sued to enjoin Howey from continuing to offer the land sales and service contracts. Howey responded that no SEC violation existed because no securities were issued. Which party will prevail in court, Howey or the SEC? For what reasons? [*SEC v. W. J. Howey Co.*, 328 U.S. 293, 66 S.Ct. 1100, 90 L.Ed. 1244 (1946)]

**44–6. Rule 10b-5.** Susan Waldbaum was a niece of the president and controlling shareholder of Waldbaum, Inc. Susan's mother (the president's sister) told Susan that the company was going to be sold at a favorable price and that a tender offer was soon to be made. She told Susan not to tell anyone except her husband, Keith Loeb, about the sale. The next day, Susan told her husband of the sale and cautioned him not to tell anyone, because "it could possibly ruin the sale." The day after he learned of the sale, Loeb called Robert Chestman, his broker, and told him that he "had some accurate information" that the company was about to be sold at a "substantially higher" price than the market value of its stock. That day, Chestman purchased shares of the company for himself, as well as for Loeb. Chestman was later convicted by a jury of, among other things, trading on misappropriated inside information in violation of Rule 10b-5. On appeal, the central question in regard to liability under the misappropriation theory was whether Chestman had acquired the inside information about the Waldbaum company as a result of an insider's breach of a fiduciary duty. Essentially, the inquiry focused on whether Loeb owed a fiduciary duty to his wife's family or to his wife to keep the information confidential. How should the court rule? [*United States v. Chestman*, 947 F.2d 551 (2d Cir. 1991)]

**44–7. Investor Protection.** U.S. News & World Report, Inc., set up a profit-sharing plan in 1962 that allotted to certain employees specially issued stock known as bonus or anniversary stock. The stock was given to the employees for past services and could not be traded or sold to anyone other than the corporate issuer, U.S. News. This special stock was issued only to employees and for no other purpose than as bonuses. Because there was no market for the stock, U.S. News hired an independent appraiser to estimate the fair value of the stock so that the employees could redeem the shares. Charles Foltz and several other employees held stock through this plan and sought to redeem the shares with U.S. News, but Foltz disputed the value set by the appraisers. Foltz sued U.S. News for violation of securities regulations. What defense would allow U.S. News to resist successfully Foltz's claim? [*Foltz v. U.S. News & World Report, Inc.*, 627 F.Supp. 1143 (D.D.C. 1986)]

**44–8. Section 10(b).** In early 1986, FMC Corp. finalized plans to buy some of its own stock as part of a restructuring of its balance statement. Unknown to FMC management, the brokerage firm FMC employed—Goldman, Sachs & Co.—disclosed information on the stock purchase that found its way to Ivan Boesky. FMC was one of the seven major corporations in whose stock Ivan Boesky allegedly traded using inside information. Boesky made purchases of FMC's stock between

February 18 and February 21 and between March 12 and April 4. Boesky's purchases amounted to a substantial portion of the total volume of FMC stock traded during these periods. The price of FMC stock increased from $71.25 on February 18, 1986, to $97.00 on April 25, 1986. As a result, FMC paid substantially more for the repurchase of its own stock than anticipated. Upon the discovery of Boesky's knowledge of FMC's recapitalization plan, FMC sued Boesky for the excess price it had paid—approximately $220 million. Discuss whether FMC should recover under Section 10(b) of the Securities Exchange Act and the Securities and Exchange Commission Rule 10b-5. [*FMC Corp. v. Boesky,* 673 F.Supp. 242 (N.D.Ill. 1987)]

**44–9. Short-swing Profits.** Emerson Electric Co. purchased 13.2 percent of Dodge Manufacturing Co.'s stock in an unsuccessful takeover attempt in June 1967. Later, when Dodge merged with Reliance Electric Co., Emerson decided to sell its shares. To avoid being subject to the restrictions of Section 16 of the Securities Exchange Act of 1934, which pertain to any purchase and sale by any owner of 10 percent or more of a corporation's stock, Emerson decided on a two-step selling plan. First, it sold off sufficient shares to reduce its holdings to 9.96 percent, and then it sold the remaining stock—all within a six-month period. Because under Section 16(b) of the act, the owner must be a 10 percent owner "both at the time of the purchase and sale . . . of the security involved," Emerson in this way succeeded in avoiding Section 16(b) requirements. Reliance demanded that Emerson return the profits made on both sales. Emerson sought a declaratory judgment from the court that it was not liable, arguing that because at the time of the second sale it had not owned 10 percent of Dodge stock, Section 16 did not apply. Does Section 16 of the Securities Exchange Act of 1934 apply to Emerson's transactions, and is Emerson liable to Reliance for its profits? [*Reliance Electric Co. v. Emerson Electric Co.,* 404 U.S. 418, 92 S.Ct. 596, 30 L.Ed.2d 575 (1972)]

**44–10. Rule 10b-5.** Energy Resource Group, Inc. (ERG), entered into a written agreement with Ivan West for West to find an investor willing to purchase ERG stock. West later formed a partnership, called Investment Management Group (IMG), with Don Peters and another

person. According to the terms of the partnership agreement, West's consulting work for ERG was excluded from the work of the IMG partnership. West learned through his consulting position with ERG that ERG was to be acquired by another corporation for $6.00 per share. At the time West learned of the acquisition, ERG stock was trading at $3.50 per share. Apparently, Peters learned of the acquisition from papers on West's desk in the IMG office and then shared the information with Ken Mick, his stockbroker. Mick then encouraged several clients to buy ERG stock prior to the public announcement of the acquisition. Mick, in return for leaking this inside information to clients, received a special premium from the enriched investors. Mick then paid a portion of the premium to Peters. The Securities and Exchange Commission brought an action against Peters for violating Rule 10b-5. Under what theory might Peters be held liable for insider trading in violation of Rule 10b-5? Discuss fully. [*SEC v. Peters,* 735 F.Supp. 1505 (D.Kans. 1990)]

**44–11. Securities Fraud.** William Gotchey owned 50 percent of the shares of First American Financial Consultants, Inc. (FAFC), an investment company registered with the Securities and Exchange Commission. In the fall of 1987, Paul Hatfield, a client of FAFC, spoke with Gotchey about investing. In December, Hatfield told Gotchey that he wished to invest $15,000 in a secure investment. Gotchey told Hatfield that he would be placing the $15,000 in mortgage-backed securities to be invested through a mortgage company. Hatfield received interest payments from FAFC purportedly from the alleged investment. He also received statements confirming that the investment had been made. In fact, Gotchey had deposited the entire amount into an FAFC bank account. When Hatfield did not receive his interest payment due at the beginning of July 1988, he confronted Gotchey. Gotchey responded by asking Hatfield to sign an agreement whereby FAFC would repay the $15,000 in monthly installments over ten years. Hatfield refused. To date, Gotchey has not accounted for the $15,000, nor has Hatfield received any interest payments since June 1988. Has Gotchey violated Section 10b-5 of the Securities Exchange Act? Why or why not? [*SEC v. Gotchey,* 981 F.2d 1251 (4th Cir. 1992)]

## FOCUS ON ETHICS

# Business Organizations

**B**ecause all business activities take place in one of the types of business organizations discussed within this unit, all ethical issues in the business context relate to the relationships that exist within these forms of business organization. In the previous unit, we discussed some of the significant ethical issues that arise in employment relations. In this *Focus on Ethics,* we examine selected areas in which ethical problems relate to the specific form in which business takes place.

## Fiduciary Duties—Revisited
The law of agency, as outlined in Chapters 34 and 35, permeates virtually all relationships within any partnership or corporation. An important duty that arises in the law of agency, and that applies to all partners and corporate directors, officers, and management personnel, is the duty of loyalty. As caretakers of the shareholders' wealth, corporate directors and officers also have a fiduciary duty to exercise care when making decisions affecting the corporate enterprise.

### Duty of Loyalty
Every individual has his or her own personal interests, which may at times conflict with the interests of the partnership or corporation with which he or she is affiliated. In particular, a partner or a corporate director may face a conflict between personal interests and the interests of the business entity. Corporate officers may find themselves in a position to acquire assets that would also benefit the corporation if acquired in the corporation's name.

In one landmark case, *Guth v. Loft, Inc.,*[1] Charles G. Guth, the president and a director of Loft, Inc., a soft-drink bottling company, negotiated with the Coca-Cola Company for a discount on its syrups. When negotiations with Coca-Cola failed to result in a discount for Loft, Guth decided to see what Pepsi Cola could offer. During his investigation of this possibility, Guth set up a new corporation to acquire the secret formula and trademark for the manufacture of Pepsi Cola. He did so without offering the opportunity to Loft. A shareholder brought a suit against Guth, arguing that the shares of the new corporation should belong to Loft, and not to Guth personally. The shareholder prevailed. The court ruled that Guth had

*usurped* a corporate opportunity in violation of his duty of loyalty to the corporation.

### Duty of Care
In addition to the duty of loyalty, every corporate director or officer has a duty of care, which clearly involves a duty to make informed decisions. That means that the partner, director, or officer must take sufficient care to make sure that decisions reached are based on an appropriate amount of information. For example, before corporate directors submit a merger offer to the shareholders, they need to carefully evaluate the offer. Is the offered price for the company shares fair to the shareholders?

A leading case in this area, *Smith v. Van Gorkom,*[2] occurred in Delaware when the chairman of the board of Trans Union Corporation, Jerome W. Van Gorkom (who was about to retire), asked his chief financial officer (CFO) to work out a per-share value at which a leveraged buy-out by the current management could take place. The CFO hastily came up with a $55-per-share figure, compared with the

---

1.  5 A.2d 503 (Del. 1939).

2.  488 A.2d 858 (Del. 1985).

current stock market value of $37 per share. Van Gorkom then called a board meeting on one day's notice to obtain approval for a merger that he had worked out at $55 per share. A merger agreement was delivered to the board members only a few hours before the next day's board meeting. At that meeting, Van Gorkom gave a twenty-minute oral presentation. The board approved the deal.

At trial, the shareholders who were suing lost, but on appeal the court ruled that the directors were grossly negligent in reaching an "informed" decision. In spite of the fact that there had been no bad faith, no conflict of interest, and no fraud, the directors were not protected by the business judgment rule. They could *not* have reasonably based their decision on the CFO's reports; they should have had an independent valuation of the company prior to accepting the leveraged buy-out offer. Note here that the court's ruling was in spite of the fact that the merger offer was at a price per share of stock that was at a substantial premium over the market price of the stock.

In *Van Gorkom,* the Delaware Supreme Court held that the directors were personally liable "to the extent that the fair market value of Trans Union exceeded $55 per share." The action was ultimately settled for $23.5 million. Part of this liability was covered by the insurance company that Trans Union used for directors' and officers' insurance—otherwise known as D&O insurance. The D&O

insurance carried by the company only provided $10 million of coverage, however.

In more recent decisions, the Delaware Supreme Court has continued to emphasize that corporate directors have an obligation to strike deals that are fair to shareholders. For example, in one case, the directors of Paramount Communications, Inc., formed an agreement with Viacom, Inc., to undertake a merger. While the Paramount-Viacom negotiations were under way, another corporation, QVC Network, Inc., attempted a hostile takeover of Paramount. QVC announced its offer to purchase Paramount stock at $90 per share, compared with the $85 per share offered by Viacom. In all, the QVC tender offer exceeded the Viacom tender offer by approximately $1.3 billion. Nonetheless, the directors of Paramount refused to consider the QVC offer. QVC and some of Paramount's stockholders sought to enjoin the Paramount-Viacom merger.

The trial court granted the requested injunction. The court found that the Paramount-Viacom "merger" agreement in fact provided for a change in the control of Paramount. Once the merger was effected, Viacom's chairman and chief executive officer, Sumner Redstone, would own approximately 70 percent of Paramount's voting stock. As the majority shareholder, Redstone would have the power, under certain circumstances, to make decisions that could materially alter the interests of the minority shareholders.

Paramount appealed to the Delaware Supreme Court. On appeal, the Paramount directors argued that in their business judgment, the Paramount-Viacom transaction constituted a sound business decision. The court, however, held that in the context of a sale of control, the directors had a duty to obtain the best value available to the Paramount shareholders. In the eyes of the court, the Paramount directors' decision to proceed with the Paramount-Viacom transaction, in view of the circumstances, constituted a breach of the directors' fiduciary duties.[3]

## The Plight of Minority Shareholders

Minority shareholders, particularly those in close corporations, often have little recourse when they suffer what they perceive to be unfair treatment by the majority shareholders. For example, assume that a corporation has four shareholders. Each shareholder owns 25 percent of the corporate shares, serves on the board of directors, and is employed by the corporation as an officer. Further assume that one of the shareholders has a falling-out, for whatever reason, with the other three shareholders.

In these circumstances, the minority shareholder will have little recourse against certain coercive policies of the

---

3. *Paramount Communications, Inc. v. QVC Network, Inc.,* 637 A.2d 34 (Del. 1994).

majority shareholders. For example, the majority shareholders may vote to fire the minority shareholder from his job with the firm. Further, they may decide to reinvest company profits in the business rather than issue dividends. In effect, the minority shareholder is now without a job and without income in any form from the corporate enterprise. As another alternative, the majority shareholders may increase their own salaries to reduce the size of dividends distributed to shareholders. By receiving more corporate income in the form of salaries, the majority shareholders are able to lower their tax liability—because dividends are taxed twice and salaries are taxed only once, as personal income.

The minority shareholder is, in effect, locked out of the corporation. Of course, the minority shareholder could bring a derivative suit against the corporation if he feels that the majority shareholders are abusing their discretion or mismanaging corporate assets. But litigation is costly, and even if the minority shareholder wins such a suit, he will have no personal right to damages. Rather, any damages obtained will go into the corporate coffers.

To protect the interests of minority shareholders, courts have shown an increasing willingness to allow minority shareholders to sue majority shareholders directly for breach of fiduciary duties. Some courts have also ordered close corporations to purchase minority

shareholders' shares at fair value to resolve shareholder disputes. At least two states have enacted statutes that provide for such buy-outs.[4]

## Insider Trading

Only in the last ten years have Americans seen rich, successful financiers end up in jail because of some violation of securities laws. One law prohibits the use of inside information to profit in the trading of shares of stock in the corporation from which the information is gleaned. Even a *tippee* (an outsider) can be liable for insider trading under securities law if the tippee's acquisition of inside information followed from an officer's or director's breach of his or her fiduciary duties. Tippees of tippees (remote tippees) can also be held liable if they knew, or should have known, that they were trading on improperly obtained inside information.

For example, in *SEC v. Musella*,[5] a manager of a law firm passed inside information about corporate mergers and acquisitions planned by the firm's clients to a friend and the friend's stockbroker. The stockbroker passed the information on to a third party. That third party then shared the information with his brother, a police officer. The police officer then recommended to two other

police officers that they purchase certain securities. All parties involved, including the latter two police officers, profited substantially from their investments, and other tips and investments followed.

Could the two police officers, who never were told (and never inquired about) the source of the information, be held liable for insider trading as remote tippees? Yes, according to the court. Their liability was not founded on the fact that they *knew* that they were trading on improperly acquired inside information but on the fact that they *should have known* that such was the case. The court held that the two police officers "did not ask because they did not want to know," and just because they consciously avoided knowledge about the source of the information did not mean that they were not guilty under laws prohibiting insider trading.

Outsiders trading on inside information are normally held liable for violating securities laws only if the trading is related to a breach of some duty. Recall from Chapter 44 that in *Chiarella v. United States*,[6] Chiarella was not held liable for trading on information obtained in the course of his work as a printer because the court held that no fiduciary duty had been breached. Yet, had the jury been instructed to find liability under the misappropriation theory, Chiarella may have been held liable for violating insider-trading laws on the basis that

---

4. See Minnesota Statutes Section 302A.751(2); New Jersey Statutes Section 14A: 12–7(c)(8).

5. 678 F.Supp. 1060 (S.D.N.Y. 1988).

---

6. 445 U.S. 222, 100 S.Ct. 1108, 63 L.Ed.2d 348 (1980).

he had violated a duty of loyalty to his employer. In a sense, the development of the misappropriation theory of liability has allowed courts to address more directly the simple ethical question, "Is such behavior right?"

## Franchise Relationships and Agency Law

A significant issue in franchise relationships has to do with agency law. For example, consider the following situation. A customer is ejected by two "bouncers" from a lounge in a Radisson Inn and suffers injuries as a result. The customer sues the owners of the franchise (Radisson Inn), as well as the franchisor (Radisson Hotels International, Inc.), to recover damages. Can the franchisor be held liable for the injuries caused by its franchisee's employees as an employer or principal under agency theory?

According to the Georgia appellate court that reviewed this case, the answer to this question is no.[7] Although Radisson Hotels required its franchisees to adhere to operating standards set forth in an operating manual, Radisson Hotels did not exercise sufficient control over its franchisees' operations to create an employer-employee relationship. Neither the manual nor the franchise agreement gave Radisson Hotels the authority to exercise direct supervisory control over

its franchisees' employees. Furthermore, the franchise agreement between Radisson Hotels and the Radisson Inn specifically stated that the Radisson Inn was an independent contractor and that "[n]either party shall be considered an agent, legal representative, partner, subsidiary, joint venturer or employee of the other."

Traditionally, courts have held, as the Georgia court did in the above case, that a franchising agreement does not give rise to an agency relationship—although occasionally a court might find that an apparent agency exists.[8] Increasingly, however, franchisors are finding that if they exercise too much control over the operations of their franchisees, they may incur liability, as principals, for the torts of their franchisees' employees.

The lawsuits brought against Domino's Pizza, Inc., in recent years illustrate this problem for franchisors. In one case, for example, Ralph and Ricky Parker were injured as a result of an accident caused by a Domino's Pizza delivery driver. The Parkers sued both the franchisor (Domino's Pizza) and the franchisee (J & B Enterprises) for damages. In the lawsuit, the Parkers alleged that Domino's Pizza, because it exercised so much control over its franchisees' business practices, was liable as an

employer under the doctrine of *respondeat superior* (discussed in Chapter 35).

The trial court found that, as a matter of law, J & B Enterprises was an independent contractor, as provided in the franchise agreement between the parties. Consequently, Domino's Pizza could not be held liable for the negligence of J & B's agents and employees. The appellate court, though, reversed the trial court's ruling and remanded the case for trial, holding that Domino's Pizza exercised such extensive control over its franchisees that it was erroneous to conclude that, as a matter of law, Domino's Pizza could not be held liable as an employer.

The appellate court reached this conclusion after closely scrutinizing the franchise agreement and the operating manual (the latter specifies the standards that all Domino's Pizza franchisees must follow). According to the court, the franchise agreement contained very specific instructions to Domino's Pizza franchisees. As to the manual, the court stated that it was a "veritable bible for overseeing a Domino's operation. It contains prescriptions for every conceivable facet of the business: from the elements of preparing the perfect pizza to maintaining accurate books; from advertising and promotional ideas to routing and delivery guidelines; from order-taking instructions to oven-tending rules; from organization to sanitation." The manual described "a wide array of techniques for 'boxing

---

7. *McGuire v. Radisson Hotels International, Inc.,* 209 Ga.App. 740, 435 S.E.2d 51 (1993).

8. See, for example, *City of Delta Junction v. Mack Trucks, Inc.,* 670 P.2d 1128 (Alaska 1983).

and cutting' the pizza, as well as tips on running the franchise to achieve an optimum profit. The manual literally leaves nothing to chance."[9]

The cases against Domino's Pizza and similar cases have alerted franchisors to the fact that they should make sure that they do not go too far in controlling their franchisees' operations in the interests of quality control. Even though an independent business entity may purchase a franchise and even though the franchise agreement specifies that no agency relationship exists, the courts may find otherwise.

## ■ Discussion Questions

**1.** There are laws against "interlocking directorates," in which one individual serves on

---

9. *Parker v. Domino's Pizza, Inc.*, 629 So.2d 1026 (Fla.App. 1993). As a result of several lawsuits brought by plaintiffs who had been injured by Domino's Pizza delivery drivers, Domino's changed some of its policies in regard to its franchisees. Particularly, it stopped insisting that its franchisees abide by the "thirty-minute delivery" requirement.

the boards of directors of competing companies. Normally, however, there is no law prohibiting a major shareholder in one corporation from purchasing the securities of a competing corporation. If a law were passed making such a purchase illegal, who would benefit? Who would lose? Would society be better or worse off, on net, if such a law were passed?

**2.** Many ethical issues involved in a franchising relationship are unique to that relationship—compared with, say, the relationship between an employee and an employer or between a corporate officer and the shareholders. What are the unique ethical concerns in franchising relationships? To what extent does current law address these concerns? Why do you think it has been so difficult to create an acceptable uniform law of franchising?

**3.** The shareholder's derivative suit is founded in equity. It is a mechanism for providing shareholders with a remedy against corporate directors, officers, key management personnel, and majority shareholders whose actions might be detrimental to the interests of the corporation as a whole. By its very nature,

such a suit is derivative—that is, it derives from an injury sustained by the corporate enterprise. Hence, any court-awarded damages go directly to the corporation rather than to the injured shareholder or shareholders. What are the advantages and disadvantages of the derivative suit for minority shareholders, particularly those who own shares in close corporations? Can you think of a fairer way for minority shareholders to obtain redress for corporate mismanagement or other wrongdoing?

**4.** Shareholders in close corporations often rely on their corporate salaries, rather than on dividends, for income. In such situations, is it fair that majority shareholders should be able to "freeze out" or "squeeze out" a minority shareholder from corporate operations by firing the shareholder? Assuming that the fired employee-shareholder has no cause of action against the firm for discriminatory treatment, what recourse does the fired employee have against the firm and the other shareholders? Should the law intervene to protect a minority shareholder's job in these circumstances?

# UNIT NINE

# GOVERNMENT REGULATION

## CONTENTS

**45** **Administrative Law**

**46** **Consumer Law**

**47** **Environmental Law**

**48** **Antitrust Law**

# CHAPTER 45

# ADMINISTRATIVE LAW

**A**dministrative agencies were largely unknown in the early years of our nation. At the time, the United States had a relatively simple, non-industrial economy that required little regulation. Today, administrative agencies regulate virtually every aspect of a business's operation. At the federal level, the Securities and Exchange Commission regulates the firm's capital structure and financing, as well as its financial reporting. The National Labor Relations Board oversees relations between the firm and any unions with which it may deal. The Equal Employment Opportunity Commission also regulates employment relationships. The Environmental Protection Agency and the Occupational Safety and Health Administration may affect the way the firm manufactures its products. The Federal Trade Commission may affect the way it markets these products.

Added to this layer of federal regulation is a second layer of state regulation that, when not preempted by federal legislation, may cover many of the same activities or regulate independently those activities not covered by federal regulation. Finally, agency regulations at the county or municipal level also affect certain types of business activities.

Administrative agencies issue rules, orders, and decisions. These regulations make up the body of *administrative law*. You were introduced briefly to some of the main principles of administrative law in Chapter 1. In the following pages, these principles are presented in much greater detail.

## SECTION 1

## AGENCY CREATION

There is virtually no way that Congress can oversee the actual implementation of all the laws that it enacts. It therefore must delegate such tasks to others, particularly when the issues relate to highly technical areas. By creating and delegating some of its authority to an administrative agency, Congress may indirectly monitor a particular area in which it has passed legislation without becoming bogged down in the details relating to enforcement—details that are best left to specialists. The delegation of such authority is also mandated by the limited resources available to Congress.

To create an administrative agency, Congress passes **enabling legislation,** which specifies the name, composition, and powers of the agency being created. The Federal Trade Commission (FTC), for example, was created in 1914 by the Federal Trade Commission Act.[1] The act prohibits unfair and deceptive trade practices. It also describes the procedures that the agency must follow to charge persons or organizations with violations of the act, and it provides for judicial review of agency orders. Other portions of the act grant the agency powers to "make rules and regulations for the purpose of carrying out the Act," to conduct investigations of business practices, to obtain reports from interstate corporations concerning their business practices, to investigate possible violations of federal antitrust statutes,[2] to publish findings of its investigations, and to recommend new legislation. The act also empowers the FTC to hold trial-like hearings and to adjudicate certain kinds of trade disputes that involve FTC regulations or federal antitrust laws.

Note that Congress, although it delegated substantial authority to the FTC, did not delegate—and cannot delegate to an administrative agency—the authority to decide which agency regulations will be treated as criminal offenses. Only Congress can make that determination.

1.   15 U.S.C. Sections 41–58.
2.   The FTC shares enforcement of the Clayton Act with the Antitrust Division of the U.S. Department of Justice. See Chapter 48.

## SECTION 2

# TYPES OF AGENCIES

Whenever a new federal administrative agency is created, a decision is made by the president and Congress as to where it will be located within the federal bureaucracy. Most agencies are **executive agencies**—that is, they are agencies that constitute the cabinet departments of the executive branch or subagencies within those departments. The Occupational Safety and Health Administration, for example, is a subagency within the Department of Labor. Exhibit 45–1 lists the fourteen cabinet departments and their most important subagencies.

**Independent regulatory agencies** are agencies that are outside the major executive departments. The earliest such agency was the Interstate Commerce Commission (ICC), which was established in 1887. The agency was supposed to make technical, nonpolitical decisions about rates, profits, and rules governing transportation that would benefit the public interest. In the years that followed the creation of the ICC, other agencies were formed to regulate banking (the Federal Reserve System), unfair trade practices (the Federal Trade Commission), the purchase and sale of securities (the Securities and Exchange Commission), and so on. These and other selected independent regulatory agencies, as well as their principal functions, are listed in Exhibit 45–2.

The significant difference between the two types of agencies lies in the accountability of the regulators. Agencies that are considered part of the executive branch are subject to the authority of the president, who has the power to appoint and remove federal officers. In theory, this power is less pronounced in regard to independent agencies, whose officers serve for fixed terms and cannot be removed without just cause. In practice, however, the president's power to exert influence over independent agencies is often considerable.

## SECTION 3

# AGENCY POWERS AND FUNCTIONS

Administrative agencies occupy an unusual niche in the American legal scheme, because they exercise powers that are normally divided among the three branches of government. Notice that in the FTC's enabling legislation discussed above, the FTC's grant of power incorporates functions associated with the legislature *(rulemaking),* the executive branch *(enforcement),* and the courts *(adjudication).* Combining these functions in one governmental entity concentrates considerable power in a single organization.

As another example, consider the powers exercised by the Securities and Exchange Commission

### ■ Exhibit 45–1 Executive Departments and Important Subagencies

| Department | Date Formed | Important Subagencies |
|---|---|---|
| State | 1789 | Passport Office; Bureau of Diplomatic Security; Foreign Service; Bureau of Human Rights and Humanitarian Affairs; Bureau of Consular Affairs; Bureau of Intelligence and Research |
| Treasury | 1789 | Internal Revenue Service; Bureau of Alcohol, Tobacco, and Firearms; U.S. Secret Service; U.S. Mint; Customs Service |
| Interior | 1849 | U.S. Fish and Wildlife Service; National Park Service; Bureau of Indian Affairs; Bureau of Land Management |
| Justice | 1870[a] | Federal Bureau of Investigation; Drug Enforcement Administration; Bureau of Prisons; U.S. Marshals Service; Immigration and Naturalization Service |
| Agriculture | 1889 | Soil Conservation Service; Agricultural Research Service; Food Safety and Inspection Service; Federal Crop Insurance Corporation; Farmers Home Administration |
| Commerce | 1913[b] | Bureau of the Census; Bureau of Economic Analysis; Minority Business Development Agency; Patent and Trademark Office; National Oceanic and Atmospheric Administration; U.S. Travel and Tourism Administration |
| Labor | 1913[b] | Occupational Safety and Health Administration; Bureau of Labor Statistics; Employment Standards Administration; Office of Labor–Management Standards; Employment and Training Administration |
| Defense | 1949[c] | National Guard; Defense Investigative Service; National Security Agency; Joint Chiefs of Staff; Departments of the Air Force, Navy, Army |
| Housing and Urban Development | 1965 | Assistant Secretary for Community Planning and Development; Government National Mortgage Association; Assistant Secretary for Housing—Federal Housing Commissioner; Assistant Secretary for Fair Housing and Equal Opportunity |
| Transportation | 1967 | Federal Aviation Administration; Federal Highway Administration; National Highway Traffic Safety Administration; U.S. Coast Guard; Federal Transit Administration |
| Energy | 1977 | Office of Civilian Radioactive Waste Management; Bonneville Power Administration; Office of Nuclear Energy; Energy Information Administration; Office of Conservation and Renewable Energy |
| Health and Human Services | 1980[d] | Food and Drug Administration; Health Care Financing Administration; Public Health Service |
| Education | 1980[e] | Office of Special Education and Rehabilitation Services; Office of Elementary and Secondary Education; Office of Postsecondary Education; Office of Vocational and Adult Education |
| Veterans' Affairs | 1989 | Veterans Health Administration; Veterans Benefits Administration; National Cemetery System |

a.　Formed from the Office of the Attorney General (created in 1789).
b.　Formed from the Department of Commerce and Labor (created in 1903).
c.　Formed from the Department of War (created in 1789) and the Department of the Navy (created in 1798).
d.　Formed from the Department of Health, Education, and Welfare (created in 1953).
e.　Formed from the Department of Health, Education, and Welfare (created in 1953).

(SEC). Under its rulemaking authority, the SEC drafts and issues rules regarding what disclosures must be made in a stock-offering prospectus. Under its enforcement authority, the SEC also prosecutes alleged violations of these regulations. Fi-nally, it sits as judge and jury in deciding whether its rules have been violated and, if so, what punishment to impose on the offender (although the judgment may be appealed to a court).

■ **Exhibit 45–2 Selected Independent Regulatory Agencies**

| Name | Date Formed | Principal Duties |
|---|---|---|
| Interstate Commerce Commission (ICC) | 1887 | Regulates interstate surface transportation via trucks, buses, trains, and inland waterways. |
| Federal Reserve System Board of Governors (Fed) | 1913 | Determines policy with respect to interest rates, credit availability, and the money supply. |
| Federal Trade Commission (FTC) | 1914 | Prevents businesses from engaging in unfair trade practices; stops the formation of monopolies in the business sector; protects consumer rights. |
| Securities and Exchange Commission (SEC) | 1934 | Regulates the nation's stock exchanges, in which shares of stock are bought and sold; enforces the securities laws, which require full disclosure of the financial profiles of companies that wish to sell stocks and bonds to the public. |
| Federal Communications Commission (FCC) | 1934 | Regulates all communications by telegraph, cable, telephone, radio, satellite, and television. |
| National Labor Relations Board (NLRB) | 1935 | Protects employees' rights to join unions and bargain collectively with employers; attempts to prevent unfair labor practices by both employers and unions. |
| Equal Employment Opportunity Commission (EEOC) | 1964 | Works to eliminate discrimination in employment based on religion, sex, race, color, disability, national origin, or age; investigates claims of discrimination. |
| Environmental Protection Agency (EPA) | 1970 | Undertakes programs aimed at reducing air and water pollution; works with state and local agencies to help fight environmental hazards. (It has been suggested recently that its status be elevated to that of a department.) |
| Nuclear Regulatory Commission (NRC) | 1975 | Ensures that electricity-generating nuclear reactors in the United States are built and operated safely; regularly inspects operations of such reactors. |

## AGENCY POWERS AND THE CONSTITUTION

Recall from Chapter 5 that the constitutional principle of *checks and balances* allows each branch of government to act as a check on the actions of the other two branches. Furthermore, under the Constitution, only the legislative branch is authorized to create laws. Yet administrative agencies, which are not specifically referred to in the Constitution, can and do make **legislative rules,** or *substantive rules,* that are as legally binding as a law passed by Congress.

The constitutional authority for delegating congressional powers to administrative agencies—and the basis of all administrative law—is generally held to be implied by Article I of the U.S. Constitution. Section 1 of that article grants all legislative powers to Congress and requires Congress to oversee the implementation of all laws. Article I, Section 8, gives Congress the power to make all laws necessary for executing its specified powers. These passages have been construed by the courts, under what is known as the **delegation doctrine,** as granting to Congress the power to establish administrative agencies that can create rules for implementing those laws. The expansive interpretation given to this grant of authority has been dictated by the practical considerations mentioned previously.

## AGENCY FUNCTIONS AND PROCEDURES

Three types of operations—rulemaking, enforcement, and adjudication—make up the functions of most administrative agencies. Taken together, these three functions constitute what may be termed the **administrative process.** The enforcement function, although discussed separately below, is carried out within the context of rulemaking and adjudication.

The Administrative Procedure Act (APA) of 1946[3] is an integral part of the adminstrative process. This act imposes procedural requirements on agencies that they must follow in their rulemaking, adjudication, and other functions. The application of the act will be examined as we go through the basic functions carried out by administrative agencies.

## SECTION 4

# RULEMAKING

A major function of an administrative agency is the formulation of new regulations—the so-called **rulemaking** function. The power an agency has to make rules is conferred on it by Congress in the agency's enabling legislation. Enabling legislation is almost always written in very broad terms, and generally, administrative agencies have substantial control over their rulemaking agendas.

This control is somewhat limited, however, by Section 553(e) of the APA, which provides that "each agency shall give an interested person the right to petition for the issuance, amendment, or repeal of a rule." Agencies must consider any such petitions promptly and decide whether to take any action in response to them. If an agency decides to deny the petitioner's request, it must notify the petitioner of the denial and give a reasonable explanation as to why the petition was denied. Another limitation on an agency's control over its rulemaking agenda exists when Congress, in its enabling legislation, requires that the agency create rules governing a certain area within a specified period of time.

Once an agency decides to promulgate a legislative rule, the rulemaking process begins. The APA establishes procedures for both *informal rulemaking* and *formal rulemaking*. Agencies most commonly use informal rulemaking procedures when creating rules, because formal rulemaking involves extensive and cumbersome proceedings. Under the APA, an agency is only required to engage in formal rulemaking when the agency's enabling legislation requires the agency to do so. The APA also provides for *exempted rulemaking,* but because it applies only in special circumstances (such as military matters or foreign

affairs), we will not examine it here. Other types of rulemaking that will be discussed below include *hybrid rulemaking* and *negotiated rulemaking.*

## INFORMAL RULEMAKING

Three requirements are imposed by the APA for **informal rulemaking,** or *notice-and-comment rulemaking:* (1) the publication of a notice of proposed rulemaking, (2) opportunity for comment, and (3) the publication of the final rule accompanied by a general statement of the rule's basis and purpose. These requirements establish the sequence of events that must occur before a rule becomes law.

**NOTICE OF PROPOSED RULEMAKING** Section 553(b) of the APA requires agencies to begin any rulemaking proceedings by publishing a **notice of proposed rulemaking** in the *Federal Register.* The *Federal Register* is a daily publication of the executive branch that prints government orders, rules, and regulations. It is assumed by the federal government that notice in the *Federal Register* constitutes notice to the public. The notice of proposed rulemaking must state the time and place in which agency proceedings on the proposed rule will be held, the proposed rule or a description of the substance of the proposed rule, and the nature of the proceedings. The notice also must state the legal authority for the proceedings, which is usually the agency's enabling legislation.

Courts now generally require that the agency also disclose the research data and methods on which it relied in establishing the rule. The purpose of requiring these disclosures is to ensure that meaningful comments on the rule can be elicited from the private sector. Often, to avoid being challenged for inadequate notice, an agency will publish the full text of the proposed rule along with an appendix that describes its research results and methodology in more technical language.

**COMMENT PERIOD** Publication of the notice of the proposed rulemaking is followed by a **comment period.** The purpose of requiring a comment period is to give interested parties the opportunity to express their views on the proposed rule in an effort to influence agency policy. The comments may be in writing or, if a hearing is held, given orally. The agency need not respond to all comments, but it must respond to any significant

---

3.  5 U.S.C. Sections 551–706.

comments that bear directly on the proposed rule by either modifying its final rule or explaining, in the statement of basis and purpose accompanying the final rule, why it did not modify the final rule.

THE FINAL RULE    After the public has been given an opportunity to comment on the proposed rule, the agency reviews this information and publishes a final rule in the *Federal Register.* The date of publication must precede the rule's effective date by at least thirty days. Exhibit 45–3 shows a sample page from a rule published in the *Federal Register.*

The final rule will have binding legal effect unless overturned by subsequent judicial review. In many instances, an agency may adopt only those rules that find support in the rulemaking record, which also forms the basis of any court review of the agency decision. The agency's **rulemaking record** will differ with the type of rulemaking procedure but generally consists of at least the notice of the proposed rulemaking, the comments filed by the public, the final rule, and most of the relevant documents prepared by the agency itself.

Although the final rule may differ from the proposed rule, based on modifications made in response to comments received during the comment period, it cannot vary too substantially from the proposed rule. If it does, a court may order the agency to undertake another notice-and-comment proceeding so that adequate notice of the rule is given. Generally, the final rule must be a "logical outgrowth" of the proposed rule.[4]

EX PARTE CONTACTS    A problem may be presented by *ex parte* **contacts**—informal communications to the agency that are not contained within the rulemaking record. Sometimes, other agencies or private parties communicate their rulemaking advice to agencies privately and off the record. Although such comments are not necessarily illegal in informal rulemaking, they have become controversial and have been the subject of some criticism. The APA does not prohibit the agency from listening to such comments, but a rule adopted by the agency must find adequate support in the public record and cannot rely exclusively on *ex parte* contacts.

## FORMAL RULEMAKING

As with informal rulemaking, **formal rulemaking,** or *rulemaking on a record,* begins with publication of a notice of proposed rulemaking in the *Federal Register.* In formal rulemaking, though, the announced proceedings are much more extensive, amounting to a public hearing conducted in the manner of a trial. At the hearing, the agency presents evidence intended to justify the proposed rule. Anyone opposing the proposed rule may present evidence to counter the agency's claims. Both sides are permitted to examine the evidence presented and to cross-examine each other's witnesses. After the formal hearing is concluded, the agency is required to prepare a formal written statement—which becomes the rulemaking record—describing its findings based on the evidence presented by both sides.

## HYBRID RULEMAKING

As rulemaking became an increasingly important part of agency decision making, and as frustration over the shortcomings of APA procedures increased, the courts and, later, Congress began a search for alternatives. The result has been a set of ill-defined procedures referred to as **hybrid rulemaking.** These procedures incorporate advantages of both the formal and informal procedures. As with formal rulemaking, there is an opportunity for direct participation through a public hearing, but the right of interested parties to cross-examine witnesses is much more restricted.

## NEGOTIATED RULEMAKING

If an agency promulgates a rule that will have a significantly adverse effect on an industry, the agency will likely face compliance problems. One way to conserve limited government resources and avoid protracted litigation is to negotiate the substance of a new rule with representatives of the industry or group to be regulated. Congress gave formal approval to such a process, which is called **negotiated rulemaking,** in the Negotiated Rulemaking Act of 1990.[5] The act authorizes agencies to allow those who will be affected by a new rule to participate in the rule-drafting process, but it does not require them to do so.

---

4.   See, for example, *Chocolate Manufacturers Association v. Block,* 755 F.2d 1098 (4th Cir. 1985).

5.   5 U.S.C. Section 581.

■ **Exhibit 45–3  A Page from the *Federal Register***

**64004**    Federal Register / Vol. 56, No. 235 / Friday, December 6, 1991 / Rules and Regulations

**DEPARTMENT OF LABOR**

**Occupational Safety and Health Administration**

**29 CFR Part 1910.1030**

**[Docket No. H–370]**

**Occupational Exposure to Bloodborne Pathogens**

**AGENCY:** Occupational Safety and Health Administration (OSHA), Labor.
**ACTION:** Final rule.

**SUMMARY:** The Occupational Safety and Health Administration hereby promulgates a standard under section 6(b) of the Occupational Safety and Health Act of 1970 (the Act), 29 U.S.C. 655 to eliminate or minimize occupational exposure to Hepatitis B Virus (HBV), Human Immunodeficiency Virus (HIV) and other bloodborne pathogens. Based on a review of the information in the rulemaking record, OSHA has made a determination that employees face a significant health risk as the result of occupational exposure to blood and other potentially infectious materials because they may contain bloodborne pathogens, including hepatitis B virus which causes Hepatitis B, a serious liver disease, and human immunodeficiency virus, which causes Acquired Immunodeficiency Syndrome (AIDS). The Agency further concludes that this exposure can be minimized or eliminated using a combination of engineering and work practice controls, personal protective clothing and equipment, training, medical surveillance, Hepatitis B vaccination, signs and labels, and other provisions.
**DATES:** This standard shall become effective on March 6, 1992.

Any petitions for review must be filed not later than the 59th day following the promulgation of the standard. See Section 6(f) of the OSH Act; 29 CFR 1911.18(d) and *United Mine Workers of America* v. *Mine Safety and Health Administration,* 900 F.2d 384 (D.C. Cir. 1990).
**ADDRESSES:** For additional copies of this standard, contact: OSHA Office of Publications; U.S. Department of Labor, room N3101, 200 Constitution Ave., NW., Washington, DC 20210, Telephone (202) 523–9667.

For copies of materials in the docket, contact: OSHA Docket Office, Docket No. H–370, room N2625, U.S. Department of Labor, 200 Constitution Ave, NW., Washington, DC 20210, Telephone (202) 523–7894. The hours of operation of the Docket Office are 10 a.m. until 4 p.m.

In compliance with 28 U.S.C. 2112(a), the Agency designates for receipt of

petitions for review of the standard, the Associate Solicitor for Occupational Safety and Health, Office of the Solicitor, room S–4004, U.S. Department of Labor, 200 Constitution Avenue, NW., Washington, DC 20210.
**FOR FURTHER INFORMATION CONTACT:** Mr. James F. Foster, OSHA, U.S. Department of Labor, Office of Public Affairs, Room N3647, 200 Constitution Avenue, NW., Washington, DC 20210, telephone (202) 523–8151.
**SUPPLEMENTARY INFORMATION:**

Table of Contents
I. Introduction
II. Pertinent Legal Authority
III. Events Leading to the Standard
IV. Health Effects
V. Quantitative Risk Assessment
VI. Significance of Risk
VII. Regulatory Impact Analysis and
 Regulatory Flexibility Analysis
VIII. Environmental Impact
IX. Summary and Explanation of the
 Standard
X. Authority and Signature
XI. The Standard

References to the rulemaking record are in the text of the preamble. References are given as "Ex," followed by a number to designate the reference in the docket. For example, "Ex. 1" means exhibit 1 in the Docket H–370. This document is a copy of the Advance Notice of Proposed Rulemaking for Bloodborne Pathogens that was published in the Federal Register on November 27, 1987 (52 FR 45438). References to the transcripts of the public hearings are given as "Tr." followed by the date and page. For example, "Mr. Clyde R. Bragdon, Jr. Tr. 9/14/89, p. 100" refers to the first page of the testimony of Mr. Clyde A. Bragdon, Jr., Administrator of the U.S. Fire Administration, given at the public hearing on September 14, 1989. A list of the exhibits, copies of the exhibits, and copies of the transcripts are available in the OSHA Docket Office.

**I. Introduction**

The preamble to the Final Standard for Occupational Exposure to Bloodborne Pathogens discusses the events leading to the promulgation of final standard, health effects of exposure, degree and significance of the risk, an analysis of the technological and economic feasibility of the standard's implementation, regulatory impact and regulatory flexibility analysis, and the rationale behind the specific provisions of the standard.

The public was invited to comment on these matters following publication of the Advance Notice of Proposed Rulemaking on November 27, 1987 (52 FR 45436) and following publication of

the Proposed Standard on May 30, 1989 (54 FR 23042).

The Agency recognizes the unique nature of both the healthcare industry and other operations covered by this standard. The Agency concludes the employee protection can be provided in a manner consistent with a high standard of patient care.

*Hazardous Waste Operations and Emergency Response Standard*

The Hazardous Waste Operations and Emergency Response (HAZWOPER) Standard (29 CFR 1910.120) covers three groups of employees: workers at uncontrolled hazardous waste remediation sites; workers at Resource Conservation Recovery Act (RCRA) permitted hazardous waste treatment, storage, and disposal facilities; and those workers expected to respond to emergencies caused by the uncontrolled release of hazardous substances.

The definition of hazardous substance includes any biological agent or infectious material which may cause disease or death. There are three potential scenarios where the bloodborne and hazardous waste operations and emergency response standard may interface. These scenarios include: workers involved in cleanup operations at hazardous waste sites involving regulated waste; workers at RCRA permitted incinerators that burn infectious waste; and workers responding to an emergency caused by the uncontrolled release of regulated waste (e.g., a transportation accident).

Employers of employees engaged in these three activities must comply with the requirements in 29 CFR 1910.120 as well as the Bloodborne Pathogens Standard. If there is a conflict or overlap, the provision that is more protective of employee health and safety applies.

*Information Collection Requirements*

5 CFR part 1320 sets forth procedures for agencies to follow in obtaining OMB clearance for information collection requirements under the Paperwork Reduction Act of 1980, 44 U.S.C. 3501 et seq. The final bloodborne pathogen standard requires the employer to allow OSHA access to the exposure control plan, medical and training records. In accordance with the provisions of the Paperwork Reduction Act and the regulations issued pursuant thereto, OSHA certifies that it has submitted the information collection to OMB for review under section 3504(h) of that Act.

Public reporting burden for this collection of information is estimated to average five minutes per response to

If an agency chooses to engage in negotiated rulemaking, it must publish in the *Federal Register* the subject and scope of the rule to be developed, the parties who will be significantly affected by the rule, and other information. Representatives of the affected groups and other interested parties may then apply to be members of the negotiating committee. The agency is also represented on the committee, but a neutral third party—not the agency—presides over the proceedings. Once the committee members have reached agreement on the terms of the proposed rule, notice of the proposed rule is then published in the *Federal Register,* followed by a comment period.

## INTERPRETATIVE AND PROCEDURAL RULES

An administrative agency may create three types of rules. The APA's rulemaking requirements discussed in this section apply only to *legislative* rules, which, as already mentioned, carry the same weight as congressionally enacted statutes. In addition to legislative rules, however, agencies also make interpretative rules and procedural rules.

**Interpretative rules** are simply statements and opinions issued by an agency explaining how the agency interprets and intends to apply the statutes it enforces. Because interpretative rules do not have the force of rules of law, they are not automatically binding on private individuals or organizations. They also are not binding on the courts in the way that rules of law are. In practice, however, the courts tend to give considerable weight to interpretative rules when deciding cases involving agency regulations.

**Procedural rules** describe an agency's methods of operation and establish procedures for dealings with the agency in and through hearings, negotiations, settlements, presentation of evidence, and other activities.

## SECTION 5

# ENFORCEMENT

To make and enforce its rules, and to enforce the provisions of its enabling legislation, agencies must have access to relevant information. The enforcement function of an administrative agency

thus occurs largely within the framework of its rulemaking and adjudication functions. Agency enforcement involves the exercise of investigative powers and prosecutorial powers.

## INVESTIGATIONS

Virtually every aspect of the administrative process requires that agencies obtain a wide array of information concerning the activities and organizations that they are charged with overseeing. Agencies, for example, frequently hold hearings during the rulemaking process and thus must have knowledge of facts and circumstances pertinent to the proposed rules. Agencies must also obtain information and investigate conduct to ascertain whether the enabling statute or the agency's rules are being violated.

**INVESTIGATIVE TOOLS**   The two most important investigative tools available to an administrative agency are subpoenas and searches and seizures.

*Subpoenas.*   A **subpoena** is a writ, or order, compelling an individual to appear before a tribunal, such as a court or an administrative hearing. The subpoena *ad testificandum* (''to testify''), the technical name for an ordinary subpoena, may be issued as part of an agency's adjudicative function. The subpoena *duces tecum* (''bring it with you'') compels an individual or organization to hand over books, papers, records, or documents that are specified on the subpoena. The subpoena *duces tecum* may thus be used in any investigation to obtain documents or other evidence.

*Searches and Seizures.*   Many agencies gather information through on-site inspections. Sometimes a search of a home, office, or factory is the only means of obtaining evidence needed to prove a regulatory violation. At other times, a physical inspection or testing is used in place of a formal hearing to correct or prevent an undesirable condition. Inspection and testing cover a wide range of activities, including safety inspections of underground coal mines, safety tests of commercial equipment and automobiles, and environmental monitoring of factory emissions.

The Fourth Amendment protects against unreasonable searches and seizures by requiring that in most instances a physical search for evidence must be conducted under the authority of a search warrant. Although it was once thought that administrative inspections were exempt from the warrant requirement, the United States Supreme Court, noting the peculiarity of affording protection only in cases of suspected criminal activity, held in *Marshall v. Barlow's, Inc.,*[6] that the requirement does apply to the administrative process.

## LIMITATIONS ON INVESTIGATIVE POWERS

The intrusive nature of an agency's investigatory actions brings into play several legal safeguards against an agency's abuse in exercising its investigatory powers. The Fourth Amendment protection against unreasonable searches and seizures, as just discussed, is one of these safeguards. The APA, in Section 555(c), provides another safeguard by incorporating the general principle that an agency can exercise only such powers as have been delegated to it by Congress. Thus, an agency's power to conduct a particular investigation must be based in some way on the powers conferred on the agency by the enabling legislation creating the agency. Generally, this limitation is easy to satisfy in practice, because the grant of regulatory power and investigative authority is usually drafted in broad terms by the legislature.

Even if the investigation is carried out with legal authorization and for a legitimate purpose, any information sought must be relevant to that purpose. Additionally, investigative demands must be specific and not unreasonably burdensome. The United States Supreme Court has held that al-

though, under the Fourth Amendment, an administrative subpoena must adequately describe the material sought, "the sufficiency of the specifications is variable in relation to the nature, purposes, and scope of [the agency's] inquiry."[7] Although firms often claim that agency demands are unreasonably burdensome, such claims are seldom successful.

The Fifth Amendment privilege against self-incrimination may come into play, but this constitutional protection is limited in the administrative context. An agency has fairly broad power to require that certain records be kept by an individual or organization and that the records be made available to the agency on demand as part of a regulatory program. Also, the privilege against self-incrimination is available only to the person asserting it; it cannot be asserted on behalf of another individual or on behalf of an organization.[8]

Finally, privileged information, including attorney-client or accountant-client communications (see Chapter 6), may be protected. The protection given to privileged information under the common law has seldom been tested in connection with administrative agency investigations, and it is unclear how and to what extent this protection applies in the administrative law context.

In the following case, the plaintiff challenged the right of an administrative agency to subpoena its financial records. The court considers the extent of an agency's investigative powers.

---

6. 436 U.S. 307, 98 S.Ct. 1816, 56 L.Ed.2d 305 (1978). This case was presented in Chapter 36 as Case 36.4.

7. *Oklahoma Press Publishing Co. v. Walling,* 327 U.S. 186, 66 S.Ct. 494, 90 L.Ed. 614 (1946).

8. A corporation is not a "person" for the purpose of the self-incrimination provision of the Fifth Amendment.

---

| CASE 45.1 |
| --- |
| **SANDSEND FINANCIAL CONSULTANTS, LTD. v. FEDERAL HOME LOAN BANK BOARD** |
| United States Court of Appeals, Fifth Circuit, 1989. 878 F.2d 875. |

**BACKGROUND AND FACTS** *The Federal Home Loan Bank Board (FHLBB) operated the Federal Savings and Loan Insurance Corporation (FSLIC). The FHLBB's duties included examining all FSLIC-insured institutions to determine whether they were being operated properly under applicable laws and regulations. As part of an investigation of Texas-based Vision Banc Savings and Loan, the FHLBB became suspicious of a large loan made to Sandsend Financial Consultants, Ltd. Hoping to trace the proceeds of the loan, the FHLBB subpoenaed Sandsend's financial records from a second bank, West Belt. Sandsend requested a federal district court to void the subpoena, which the court did. The FHLBB appealed.*

*GEE,* Circuit Judge:

\* \* \* \*

The FHLBB's subpoena power extends to Sandsend's financial records; it is not limited to parties directly associated with the target of an investigation. \* \* \* [W]e note two important principles that inform our inquiry: First, an administrative agency's power to issue subpoenas is a broad-ranging one which courts are reluctant to trammel [restrict]. \* \* \* Second, when reviewing an administrative subpoena, the court plays a ''strictly limited'' role. The court's inquiry is limited to two questions: (1) whether the investigation is for a proper statutory purpose and (2) whether the documents the agency seeks are relevant to the investigation. \* \* \*

\* \* \* \*

We find no basis in the record for quashing [voiding] the subpoena. First, it is undisputed that the FHLBB's examination of Vision Banc is a legitimate law enforcement inquiry. Second, Sandsend's records are relevant to the FHLBB's inquiry. \* \* \* So long as the material requested '' 'touches a matter under investigation,' '' an administrative subpoena will survive a challenge that the material is not relevant. Certainly, Sandsend has only a tangential relationship to Vision Banc, the target of the investigation. But the FHLBB suspects that Sandsend is part of a scheme to defraud Vision Banc or to misuse Vision Banc's funds. \* \* \* Sandsend may have only a loose connection with Vision Banc. Its financial records, however, touch on a matter under investigation and, thus, are relevant to the FHLBB's examination.

*The United States Court of Appeals reversed the district court's decision and directed the court to enforce the subpoena.*

**DECISION AND REMEDY**

## PROSECUTION

After conducting its own investigation of a suspected rule violation, an agency may decide to take administrative action against specific parties. In some cases (for example, in an action brought by the FTC for alleged false advertising), an agency's actions may be prompted by private individuals or interest groups. During this phase of the process, the agency may make an offer to negotiate and reach some settlement or agreement concerning the action with which the agency is concerned.

If a settlement cannot be reached, the agency may issue a formal *complaint*. If the Environmental Protection Agency (EPA), for example, finds that a manufacturing plant is responsible for excessively polluting the groundwater in violation of federal pollution laws, the EPA will issue a complaint against the violator in an effort to bring the plant into compliance with the federal regulations. This complaint is a public document and may even be accompanied by a press release. The manufacturing plant charged in the complaint will respond by filing an answer to the EPA's allegations.

In an effort to deal with the violation informally, without the need for a formal hearing, set-

tlement negotiations between the agency and the plant may be scheduled. The savings in time and cost may make the informal settlement process an economical vehicle for both the agency and the charged party. During the settlement negotiations, each party has an opportunity to discuss its position on the relevant issues. The EPA will attempt to win voluntary compliance from the plant with the federal pollution laws. The manufacturing plant may argue that it is operating within the federal guidelines already or that a neighboring chemical plant is the primary polluter. The plant and the EPA may reach a temporary settlement and agree to the drilling of several test wells to determine if indeed the manufacturing plant is (or is not) the primary polluter as charged.

## SECTION 6

# ADJUDICATION

The majority of agency actions against individuals or businesses are resolved through settlements at the initial stage, without the need for formal adjudication. If a settlement is not reached, then the dispute will have to be resolved through adjudication.

## Hearing Procedures

**Adjudication** involves the resolution of disputes through a hearing conducted by the agency. A formal adjudicatory hearing resembles a trial in many respects. Prior to the hearing, the parties are permitted to undertake extensive discovery proceedings (involving depositions, interrogatories, and requests for documents or other information—see Chapter 4). During the hearing, the parties may give testimony, present other evidence, and cross-examine adverse witnesses. A significant difference between a trial and an administrative agency hearing, though, is the relaxation of evidentiary rules in the latter. Much more information, including hearsay (secondhand information offered for its truth), can be introduced as evidence during an administrative hearing than at a trial.

An **administrative law judge (ALJ)** presides over the hearing itself and has the power to administer oaths, take testimony, rule on questions of evidence, and make determinations of fact. Although an ALJ is a member of the very agency prosecuting the case, certain safeguards exist to promote fairness in the proceedings. The ALJ is separated in the agency's organization from the investigative and prosecutorial staff according to provisions of the APA. The APA also prohibits private (*ex parte*) communications between the ALJ and anyone who is party to an agency proceeding. Finally, provisions of the APA protect the ALJ from agency discipline except on a clear showing of good cause for such action.

Hearing procedures vary widely from agency to agency. Frequently, disputes are resolved through less formal adjudication proceedings. For example, the parties, their counsel, and the ALJ may simply meet at a table in a conference room for the dispute-settlement proceedings. Administrative agencies generally can exercise substantial discretion over the type of hearing procedures that will be used.

## Agency Orders

After a hearing is concluded, the ALJ renders an **initial order.** The order may compel the charged party to pay damages, or it may forbid the party from carrying on some specified activity. The latter is referred to as a *cease-and-desist order* and in effect is identical to an ordinary court's injunction. Either side may appeal the ALJ's initial order. An appeal is usually taken to a federal appeals court, though some intermediate decisions may be appealed to a federal district court. The commission that governs the agency may occasionally decide on its own to review the case. If the commission does so, it may consider all aspects of the case freshly, as though no prior decisions had been rendered.

If no appeal is taken, or if the case is not reviewed or considered anew by the agency commission, the ALJ's initial order becomes the **final order** of the agency. Otherwise, the final order must come from the commission's decision or that of the reviewing court.

## Section 7

# JUDICIAL REVIEW

As will be discussed in the next section, the legislative and executive branches exercise considerable influence over the regulatory policies of administrative agencies. The courts also exercise considerable control over the regulatory process through the process of judicial review of agency actions.

Recall from Chapter 3 that appellate, or reviewing, courts normally defer to the decisions of trial courts regarding questions of fact. In reviewing administrative actions, the courts are similarly reluctant to review questions of fact, and in most cases, the appellate court defers to the facts as found in the initial agency proceeding. The courts, however, will conduct a *de novo* review (review the case anew, as if it had not been decided before) to make an independent finding of facts in the following circumstances: (1) when such a review is required by statute, (2) if inadequate fact-finding proceedings were employed by the agency initially adjudicating the case, or (3) if new facts are raised in a proceeding to enforce a nonadjudicatory action (an action taken without a trial or a similar hearing).

Although the APA provides for judicial review of most agency actions, certain requirements must be met before a court will review an agency's decision.

## REQUIREMENTS FOR JUDICIAL REVIEW

Parties seeking judicial review of administrative agency decisions must satisfy several preliminary requirements. First, the party challenging the agency action (the challenger, or plaintiff) must show that the nature of the action is *reviewable* before the court. The APA creates a presumption that agency actions are reviewable, thus making this requirement easy to satisfy.

Second, the challenger must have *standing to sue* the agency. As discussed in Chapter 3, standing to sue is a requirement every plaintiff must meet by showing that he or she has a direct stake in the outcome of a controversy. To establish standing in the administrative context, the challenger must show that the challenger's interests have been substantially affected by the agency's action.

Third, because the courts are reluctant to interfere with the regulatory process, they will not review an agency's action unless the challenger has *exhausted all possible administrative remedies*. This requirement forces the challenger to cooperate with the agency to resolve the dispute. If the dispute still cannot be resolved and alternative means have been exhausted, the court will review the action.

Finally, Article III, Section 2, of the U.S. Constitution, as interpreted by the United States Supreme Court, requires that an *actual controversy* be at issue. In other words, a court is prohibited from giving an opinion on an issue unless an actual dispute exists. This requirement is referred to as *ripeness*—the court will not review cases before it is necessary to decide them. When considering whether a dispute meets this requirement, courts have been willing to weigh the benefits of allowing time to refine the controversy against the harm of delaying review.

The above requirements relate to the review of agency decisions by the federal courts *after* a dispute has been adjudicated by the agency. In some circumstances, however, parties who will be affected by an agency rule may petition the court to review the rule *before* they have violated the rule in question. In the case presented below, for example, the American Dental Association and other health-care providers challenged a rule promulgated in 1991 by the Occupational Safety and Health Administration to contain the spread of blood-borne diseases in the health-care industry.[9]

---

9. 29 C.F.R. Section 1910.1030.

---

**BACKGROUND AND FACTS** *In 1991, the Occupational Safety and Health Administration (OSHA) promulgated a rule on occupational exposure to blood-borne pathogens (disease-causing agents). OSHA's aim in promulgating the rule was to protect health-care workers from viruses, particularly those causing hepatitis B (a serious liver disease) and acquired immune deficiency syndrome (AIDS), which can be transmitted in the blood of patients. The rule requires employers in the health-care industry to take certain precautions relating to the handling of contaminated instruments, the disposal of waste materials, and the use of protective clothing. The rule also requires employers to provide vaccinations for hepatitis B for their employees and confidential blood testing of workers following accidental exposures. The rule applies universally to all health-care workers, regardless of the type of patients treated. OSHA estimated that compliance with the new rule would cost the health-care industry $813 million annually, or, phrased in different terms, about $4 million for every life saved. Most employers in the health-care industry accepted the rule. The American Dental Association (ADA) and two other groups, however, challenged it. Among other things, the ADA argued that OSHA had failed to establish that dental workers were sufficiently at risk to benefit from the rule. Furthermore, the rule would unnecessarily burden consumers with increased medical costs and, hence, diminished care.*

| CASE 45.2 |
| --- |

**AMERICAN DENTAL ASSOCIATION v. MARTIN**
United States Court of Appeals,
Seventh Circuit, 1993.
984 F.2d 823.

*POSNER,* Circuit Judge.

\* \* \* \*

In deciding to impose this extensive array of restrictions on the practice of medicine, nursing, and dentistry, OSHA \* \* \* asked whether the restrictions would materially reduce a significant workplace risk to human health without imperiling the existence of, or threatening massive dislocation to, the health care industry. For this is the applicable legal standard. \* \* \*

\* \* \* \*

OSHA cannot impose onerous requirements on an industry that does not pose substantial hazards to the safety or health of its workers merely because the industry is a part of some larger sector or grouping [that] the agency has decided to regulate \* \* \* wholesale. That would be an irrational way to proceed. But neither is the agency required to proceed workplace by workplace, which in the case of bloodborne pathogens would require it to promulgate hundreds of thousands of separate rules. It is not our business to pick the happy medium between these extremes. It is OSHA's business. If it provides a rational explanation for its choice, we are bound. \* \* \* The risk of blood splatters and needlesticks is greater in some medical procedures than in others, but a dental hygienist is as likely to be splattered by blood contained in saliva as is many a worker in a hospital or a doctor's office. \* \* \*

\* \* \* \*

\* \* \* [T]he dental association's argument that OSHA's rule is likely to cause a deterioration in dental care as dental patients flee the higher prices resulting from the industry's efforts to shift some of the costs of compliance with the rule to its customers [is untenable]. There are some omitted costs [costs omitted in OSHA's analysis] \* \* \* but not enough to make a decisive difference[.]

**DECISION AND REMEDY**  *The court denied the American Dental Association's petition to review the blood-borne pathogen rule.*

## THE SCOPE OF REVIEW

The court will review whether the agency has exceeded its authority under the enabling legislation; whether the agency has properly interpreted laws applicable to the agency action under review; and whether the agency has violated any constitutional provisions. It also will review whether the agency has acted in accordance with procedural requirements of the law; whether the agency's actions were arbitrary, capricious, or an abuse of discretion; and whether any conclusions drawn by the agency are not supported by substantial evidence.

## STANDARDS OF REVIEW

The **standard of review** is the test that the court applies when it reviews an agency action. The APA provides for two standards of review: the substantial evidence test and the arbitrary and capricious test. Courts apply the **substantial evidence test** when they review formal agency actions, such as an administrative hearing. Under this test, only those agency findings that were not supported by substantial evidence may be overturned by the reviewing court. The court, in applying this test, determines whether the agency acted reasonably based on the facts it had before it.

The **arbitrary and capricious test** is generally applied to informal agency actions, such as an Environmental Protection Agency decision to include a certain organic chemical, such as ethanol, in its list of pollutants. In applying this test, the court avoids substituting its own judgment for that of the agency and gives deference to the agency's decisions. Out of necessity, an agency develops a certain technical expertise in its subject matter—an expertise that the court does not ordinarily have. The court merely ascertains whether the agency had an adequate factual basis for its decision. Unless the court can point to a clear error in the agency's judgment, it will not strike down the agency's decision as arbitrary and capricious. This standard of review is the easiest to satisfy and allows the majority of agency actions to pass judicial muster. The following case involved an application of the arbitrary and capricious test.

---

**HISTORICAL AND ENVIRONMENTAL SETTING** *Oregon's Rogue River basin includes some of the finest fishing grounds in the United States. In the 1930s, federal and state agencies began planning a project to prevent recurring floods in the basin. In 1961, a study recommended the construction of three dams: the Lost Creek Dam on the Rogue River, the Applegate Dam on the Applegate River, and the Elk Creek Dam on the Elk Creek near its confluence with the Rogue River. Congress authorized the Army Corps of Engineers to build the dams. The Lost Creek Dam was completed in 1977, and the Applegate Dam was completed in 1981. Construction of the Elk Creek Dam was halted in 1975, however, to analyze the environmental consequences. Studies undertaken by the corps in 1974 and 1979 indicated that the Elk Creek Dam might increase the Rogue River's temperature and turbidity (muddiness), which, according to the studies, would have no major effect on fish production but might occasionally impair fishing. Studies by other government agencies suggested that the dam's effect on fishing and turbidity could be greater, but in 1982, a decision was made to proceed with construction, and in August 1985, Congress appropriated the funds.*

| CASE 45.3 |
| --- |

**MARSH v. OREGON NATURAL RESOURCES COUNCIL**
Supreme Court of the United States, 1989.
490 U.S. 360,
109 S.Ct. 1851,
104 L.Ed.2d 377.

**BACKGROUND AND FACTS** *In October 1985, four nonprofit organizations sued the Army Corps of Engineers, claiming that the corps had violated the National Environmental Policy Act of 1969.[a] The organizations asserted that the corps had failed to prepare a supplemental environmental impact statement (EIS)[b] based on information contained in two studies—an Oregon Department of Fish and Wildlife memorandum and a U.S. Soil Conservation Service survey—suggesting that construction of the third dam would increase the temperature and turbidity of the Rogue River. The corps contended that the EIS was unnecessary, because on the basis of its own analysis, as well as that of independent research commissioned by the corps, the two studies were not indisputable and in any event were of exaggerated importance in assessing the project. A federal district court denied the request that the corps be enjoined from completing the project. On appeal, the appellate court reversed the decision to deny the injunction and remanded the case to the district court. The corps appealed to the United States Supreme Court.*

Justice *STEVENS* delivered the opinion of the Court.
&ast; &ast; &ast; &ast;
&ast; &ast; &ast; [R]eview of the narrow question before us &ast; &ast; &ast; is controlled by the "arbitrary and capricious" standard &ast; &ast; &ast; .
&ast; &ast; &ast; &ast;

---

a.  42 U.S.C. Sections 4321–4370d.
b.  Environmental impact statements and the types of actions that require them are discussed in Chapter 47.

The question presented for review in this case is a classic example of a factual dispute the resolution of which implicates substantial agency expertise. * * * Because analysis of the relevant documents "requires a high level of technical expertise," we must defer to "the informed discretion of the responsible federal agencies." * * *

* * * [I]n making the factual inquiry concerning whether an agency decision was "arbitrary or capricious," the reviewing court "must consider whether the decision was based on a consideration of the relevant factors and whether there has been a clear error of judgment." * * *

* * * *

* * * Even if another decisionmaker might have reached a contrary result, it was surely not "a clear error of judgment" for the Corps to have found that the new and accurate information in the documents was not significant and that the significant information was not new and accurate. * * * [T]he Corps conducted a reasoned evaluation of the relevant information and reached a decision that, although perhaps disputable, was not "arbitrary or capricious."

**DECISION AND REMEDY**  *The Supreme Court of the United States reversed the appellate court's decision and remanded the case for further proceedings.*

# OTHER CONTROLS OVER ADMINISTRATIVE AGENCIES

The courts, through the process of judicial review, provide a substantial check on the authority of administrative agencies. Other sources of control over agency authority have also already been mentioned in this chapter, including the APA, which significantly controls the administrative process. Additionally, the enabling legislation of the agency is a source of limitation, because it defines an agency's authority. We look here at how the executive and legislative branches of government exercise further controls over agency authority.

## EXECUTIVE CONTROLS

Executive control over agency power is exercised through several means. First, the president may exercise veto power over any enabling legislation or subsequent modifications to agency authority that Congress seeks to enact. Another important power over agency affairs is the president's authority to appoint and remove federal officers. In theory, this power is less pronounced in the case of independent agencies, whose officers serve for fixed terms and cannot be removed without just cause. In practice, however, the president's power to exert influence over independent agencies is often considerable.

## LEGISLATIVE CONTROLS

Congress gives power to an agency, and it can, through subsequent legislation, take away that power or even abolish an agency altogether. Congress can amend an enabling act, for example, to prohibit an agency from issuing certain types of rules. Congress's power of the purse (the constitutional taxing and spending powers) allows it to exercise considerable influence over agency policy. There must be legislative authorization for any allocation of government funds for a specific agency. This authorization is usually contained in the enabling legislation and may set certain time and monetary limits for funding particular programs. Congress, of course, can always revise these limits.

In addition to the formal legislating and funding powers that Congress exercises, it has the authority to investigate the implementation of its statutory laws and the agencies that it has created. It may also affect agency policy through its "casework" activities, which involve individual legislators' attempts to help their constituents deal with agencies.

# PUBLIC ACCOUNTABILITY

As a result of growing public concern over the powers exercised by administrative agencies in the 1960s and subsequent decades, Congress passed several laws to make agencies more accountable through public scrutiny. We discuss here the most significant of these laws.

## THE FREEDOM OF INFORMATION ACT

The Freedom of Information Act (FOIA)[10] of 1966 requires the federal government to disclose certain "records" to "any person" on request, even without any reason being given for the request. The FOIA exempts certain types of records. For other records, though, a request that complies with the FOIA procedures need only contain a reasonable description of the information sought (see Exhibit 45–4). An agency's failure to comply with a request may be challenged in a federal district court. The media, industry trade associations, public interest groups, and even companies seeking information about competitors rely on these FOIA provisions to obtain information from government agencies.

## THE GOVERNMENT- IN-THE-SUNSHINE ACT

The Government-in-the-Sunshine Act,[11] or open meeting law, was passed in 1976. It requires that "every portion of every meeting of an agency" that is headed by a "collegial body" must be open to "public observation." The act also requires procedures to ensure that the public is provided with adequate advance notice of the agency's scheduled meeting and agenda. As with the FOIA, the Sunshine Act contains certain exceptions. Closed meetings are permitted when (1) the subject of the meeting concerns accusing any person of a crime, (2) open meetings would frustrate implementation of future agency actions, or (3) the subject of the meeting involves matters relating to future litigation or rulemaking. Courts interpret these exceptions strictly so as to allow open access whenever possible.

## THE REGULATORY FLEXIBILITY ACT

Concern over the effects of regulation on the efficiency of businesses, particularly smaller ones, led Congress to pass the Regulatory Flexibility Act in 1980.[12] Under this act, whenever a new regulation will have a "significant impact upon a substantial number of small entities," the agency must conduct a regulatory flexibility analysis. The analysis must measure the cost imposed by the rule on small businesses and must consider less burdensome alternatives. The act also contains provisions to alert small businesses about forthcoming regulations. The act has relieved some record-keeping burdens for small businesses, especially with regard to hazardous waste management.

# STATE AGENCIES

Although much of this chapter has dealt with federal administrative agencies, state administrative agencies play an important role in the regulatory process. The growing presence of such agencies has been fostered by many of the same factors that have encouraged the proliferation of federal agencies, particularly the inability of state legislatures to oversee the actual implementation of their laws and the greater technical competence of such agencies.

## PARALLEL AGENCIES AND THE SUPREMACY CLAUSE

Commonly, a state agency is created as a parallel to a federal agency to provide similar services on a more localized basis. Such parallel agencies include the federal Social Security Administration and the state welfare agency, the Internal Revenue Service and the state revenue department, and the Environmental Protection Agency (EPA) and the state pollution-control agency. Not all federal

---

10. 5 U.S.C. Section 552.
11. 5 U.S.C. Section 552b.

12. 5 U.S.C. Sections 601–612.

■ **Exhibit 45–4 Sample Letter Requesting Information from an Executive Department or Agency**

Agency Head or FOIA Officer            Date
Title
Name of Agency
Address of Agency
City, State, Zip

Re: Freedom of Information Act Request.

Dear _____:

    Under the provisions of the Freedom of Information Act, 5 U.S.C. 552, I am requesting access to _____
[identify the records as clearly and specifically as possible].

    If there are any fees for searching for, or copying, the records I have requested, please inform me before you fulfill the request [Or:] please supply the records without informing me [if the fees do not exceed $_____.]

    [Optional] I am requesting this information because _____
_____
[state the reason for your request if you think it will assist you in obtaining the information].

    [Optional] As you know, the act permits you to reduce or waive fees when the release of the information is considered as "primarily benefiting the public." I believe that this request fits that category and I therefore ask that you waive any fees.

    If all or any part of this request is denied, please cite the specific exemption(s) that you think justifies your refusal to release the information, and inform me of the appeal procedures available to me under the law.

    I would appreciate your handling this request as quickly as possible, and I look forward to hearing from you within ten days, as the law stipulates.

                               Sincerely,
                               [Signature]
                               Name
                               Address
                               City, State, Zip

SOURCE: U.S. Congress, House Committee on Government Operations, *A Citizen's Guide on How to Use the Freedom of Information Act and the Privacy Act Requesting Government Documents,* 95th Congress, 1st Session (1977).

agencies have parallel state agencies, however. For example, the Federal Bureau of Investigation and the Nuclear Regulatory Commission have no parallel agency at the state level.

As discussed in Chapter 5, when Congress creates a law, the supremacy clause of the U.S. Constitution requires that the federal law be held supreme. Any inconsistent state law must give way to the federal law. When Congress enables a federal agency and a state legislature enables a similar agency to regulate the same subject matter (such as pollution), the supremacy clause requires that the federal agency's operation prevail over an inconsistent state agency's action. For example, if the EPA determines that a manufacturing plant is polluting the groundwater, the state pollution-control agency is prohibited from determining that the same plant is not polluting the groundwater.

## FEDERAL AND STATE AGENCIES COMPARED

Federal agencies generally enjoy greater autonomy and organizational resources than do state agencies, and federal administrative law has expanded much more rapidly, embracing a wider variety of complex subjects. Moreover, many state courts—unlike their federal counterparts—have continued to require that statutes authorizing agency actions contain specific restrictions and limitations on the scope of agency powers.

State regulatory agencies—particularly occupational licensing boards—are more likely to be challenged for unfairly depriving a party of some right or privilege than are federal agencies. Because of the lesser degree of political autonomy of state agencies, state legislatures have been more reluctant than Congress to grant administrative agencies the power to punish criminal behavior. A number of states have adopted versions of the Model State Administrative Procedure Act—which is based on the APA—to regulate state administrative procedures.

---

# TERMS AND CONCEPTS TO REVIEW

adjudication 896
administrative law judge
  (ALJ) 896
administrative process 889
arbitrary and capricious
  test 898
comment period 890
delegation doctrine 889
enabling legislation 887
*ex parte* contact 891

executive agency 887
final order 896
formal rulemaking 891
hybrid rulemaking 891
independent regulatory
  agency 887
informal rulemaking 890
initial order 896
interpretative rule 893
legislative rule 889

negotiated rulemaking 891
notice of proposed
  rulemaking 890
procedural rule 893
rulemaking 890
rulemaking record 891
standard of review 898
subpoena 893
substantial evidence test 898

---

# QUESTIONS AND CASE PROBLEMS

**45–1. Rulemaking Procedures.** Assume that the Securities and Exchange Commission (SEC) has a policy not to enforce rules prohibiting insider trading except when the insiders make monetary profits for themselves. Then the SEC modifies this policy by a determination that the agency has the statutory authority to bring an enforcement action against an individual even if he or she does not personally profit from the insider trading. In modifying the policy, the SEC does not conduct a rulemaking but simply announces its new decision. A securities organization objects and says that the policy was unlawfully developed without opportunity for public comment. In a lawsuit challenging the new policy, should the policy be overruled under the Administrative Procedure Act? Discuss.

**45–2. Rulemaking Procedures.** Assume that the Food and Drug Administration (FDA), using proper procedures, adopts a rule describing its future investigations. This new rule covers all future cases in which the FDA wants to regulate food additives. Under the new rule, the FDA says that it will not regulate food additives without giving food companies an opportunity to cross-examine witnesses. Some time later, the FDA wants to regulate methylisocyanate, a food additive. In doing so, the FDA undertakes an informal rulemaking procedure, without cross-examination, and regulates methylisocyanate. Producers protest, saying that the FDA promised cross-examination. The FDA responds that the Administrative Procedure Act does not require such cross-examination and that it could freely withdraw the promise made in its new rule. Discuss fully how the court should decide this issue.

**45–3. Rulemaking and Adjudication Powers.** For decades, the Federal Trade Commission (FTC) resolved fair trade and advertising disputes through individual adjudications. In the 1960s, the FTC began promulgating rules that defined fair and unfair trade practices. In cases involving violations of these rules, the due process rights of participants were more limited and did not include cross-examination. This was because, although anyone found violating a rule would receive a full adjudication, the legitimacy of the rule itself could not be challenged in the adjudication. Any party violating a rule was almost certain to lose the adjudication. Affected parties complained, arguing that their rights before the FTC were unduly limited by the new rules. Were the rules illegal? Explain.

**45–4. Rulemaking Procedures.** The Department of Commerce issued a flammability standard that required all mattresses, including crib mattresses, to pass a test that involved contact with a burning cigarette. The manufacturers of crib mattresses petitioned the department to exempt their product from the test procedure, but the department refused to do so. The crib mattress manufacturers sued the department and argued that applying such a rule to crib mattresses was arbitrary and capricious because infants do not smoke. Discuss fully whether this rule should be overturned. [*Bunny Bear, Inc. v. Peterson,* 473 F.2d 1002 (1st Cir. 1973)]

**45–5. Rulemaking Procedures.** The Atomic Energy Commission (AEC) was engaged in rulemaking proceedings for nuclear reactor safety. An environmental group sued the commission, arguing that its proceedings were inadequate. The commission had carefully complied with all requirements of the Administrative Procedure Act. The environmentalists argued, however, that the very hazardous and technical nature of the reactor safety issue required elaborate procedures above and beyond those of the act. A federal court of appeals agreed and overturned the AEC rules. The commission appealed the case to the United States Supreme Court. How should the Court rule? Discuss. [*Vermont Yankee Nuclear Power Corp. v. Natural Resources Defense Council, Inc.,* 435 U.S. 519, 98 S.Ct. 1197, 55 L.Ed.2d 460 (1978)]

**45–6. Executive Controls.** In 1982, the president of the United States appointed Matthew Chabal, Jr., to the position of U.S. marshal. U.S. marshals are assigned to the federal courts. In the fall of 1985, Chabal received an unsatisfactory annual performance rating, and he was fired shortly thereafter by the president. Given that U.S. marshals are assigned to the federal courts, are these appointees members of the executive branch? Did the president have the right to fire Chabal without consulting Congress about the decision? [*Chabal v. Reagan,* 841 F.2d 1216 (3d Cir. 1988)]

**45–7. Agency Investigations.** A state statute required vehicle dismantlers—persons whose business includes dismantling automobiles and selling the parts—to be licensed and to keep records regarding the vehicles and parts in their possession. The statute also authorized warrantless administrative inspections; that is, without first obtaining a warrant, agents of the state department of motor vehicles or police officers could inspect a vehicle dismantler's license and records, as well as vehicles on the premises. Pursuant to this statute, police officers entered an automobile junkyard and asked to see the owner's license and records. The owner replied that he did not have the documents. The officers inspected the premises and discovered stolen vehicles and parts. Charged with possession of stolen property and unregistered operation as a vehicle dismantler, the junkyard owner argued that the warrantless inspection statute was unconstitutional under the Fourth Amendment. The trial court disagreed, reasoning that the junkyard business was a highly regulated industry. On appeal, the highest state court concluded that the statute had no truly administrative purpose and impermissibly authorized searches only to discover stolen property. The state appealed to the United States Supreme Court. Should the Court uphold the statute? Discuss. [*New York v. Burger,* 482 U.S. 691, 107 S.Ct. 2636, 96 L.Ed.2d 601 (1987)]

**45–8. *Ex Parte* Comments.** In 1976, the Environmental Protection Agency (EPA) proposed a rule establishing new pollution-control standards for coal-fired steam generators. The agency gave notice and received comments in the manner prescribed by the Administrative Procedure Act. After the public comments had been received, the EPA received informal suggestions from members of Congress and other federal officials. In 1979, the EPA published its final standards. Several environmental groups protested these standards, arguing that they were too lax. As part of this protest, the groups complained that political influence from Congress and other federal officials had encouraged the EPA to relax the proposed standards. The groups went on to argue that these *ex parte* comments were themselves illegal or that such comments at least should have been summarized in the record. What will the court decide? Discuss fully. [*Sierra Club v. Costle,* 657 F.2d 298 (D.C. Cir. 1981)]

**45–9. Arbitrary and Capricious Test.** In 1977, the Department of Transportation (DOT) adopted a passive-restraint standard (known as Standard 208) that required new cars to have either air bags or automatic seat belts. By 1981, it had become clear that all the major auto manufacturers would install automatic seat belts to comply with this rule. The DOT determined that most purchasers of cars would detach their automatic seat belts, thus making them ineffective. Consequently, the department repealed the regulation. State Farm Mutual Automobile Insurance Co. and other insurance companies sued in the District of Columbia Circuit Court of Appeals for a review of the DOT's repeal of the regulation. That court held that the repeal was arbitrary and capricious because the DOT had reversed its rule without sufficient support. The motor vehicle manufacturers then appealed this decision to the United States Supreme Court. What will result? Discuss. [*Motor Vehicle Manufacturers Association v. State Farm Mutual Automobile Insurance Co.,* 463 U.S. 29, 103 S.Ct. 2856, 77 L.Ed.2d 443 (1983)]

## 45–10. A Question of Ethics

*The Marine Mammal Protection Act was enacted in 1972 to reduce incidental killing and injury of marine mammals during commercial fishing operations. Under the act, commercial fishing vessels are required to allow an employee of the National Oceanic and Atmospheric Administration (NOAA) to accompany the vessels to conduct research and observe operations. In December 1986, after NOAA had adopted a new policy of recruiting female as well as male observers, NOAA notified Caribbean Marine Services Co. that female observers would be assigned to accompany two of the company's fishing vessels on their next voyages. The owners and crew members of the ships (the plaintiffs) moved for an injunction against the implementation of the NOAA directive. The plaintiffs contended that the presence of a female on board a fishing vessel would be very awkward, because the female would have to share the crew's quarters, and crew members enjoyed little or no privacy with respect to bodily functions. Further, they alleged that the presence of a female would be disruptive to fishing operations, because some of the crew members were "crude" men with little formal education who might harass or sexually assault a female observer, and the officers would therefore have to devote time to protecting the female from the crew. Finally, the plaintiffs argued that the presence of a female observer could destroy morale and distract the crew, thus affecting the crew's efficiency and decreasing the vessel's profits. [Caribbean Marine Services Co. v. Baldrige, 844 F.2d 668 (9th Cir. 1988)]*

1. In general, do you think that the public policy of promoting equal employment opportunity should override the concerns of the vessel owners and crew members? If you were the judge, would you grant the injunction? Why or why not?

2. The plaintiffs pointed out that fishing voyages could last three months or longer. Would the length of a particular voyage affect your answer to the preceding question?

3. The plaintiffs contended that even if the indignity of sharing bunk rooms and toilet facilities with a female observer could be overcome, the observer's very presence in the common areas of the vessel, such as the dining area, would unconstitutionally infringe on the crew members' right to privacy in these areas. Evaluate this claim.

# CHAPTER 46

# CONSUMER LAW

All statutes, agency rules, and common law judicial decisions that serve to protect the interest of consumers are classified as **consumer law.** Consumer transactions take a variety of forms but broadly include those that involve an exchange of value for the purpose of acquiring goods, services, land, or credit for personal or family use.

Traditionally in disputes involving consumers, it was assumed that the freedom to contract carried with it the obligation to live by the deal made. Therefore, the watchword in most such transactions was *caveat emptor*—''let the buyer beware.'' Over time, this attitude has changed considerably. Today myriad federal and state laws protect consumers from unfair trade practices, unsafe products, discriminatory or unreasonable credit requirements, and other problems related to consumer transactions. Nearly every agency and department of the federal government has an office of consumer affairs, and most states have one or more such offices to assist consumers. Typically, the attorney general's office assists consumers at the state level.

In this chapter, we focus primarily on federal legislation, partly because of its wider applicability and partly because much state legislation closely parallels the federal laws. As a general rule, state consumer protection is more stringent, as will be discussed in the final section of this chapter.

## ADVERTISING

One of the earliest—and still one of the most important—federal consumer protection laws was the Federal Trade Commission Act of 1914.[1] As discussed in the preceding chapter, the act created the Federal Trade Commission

---

1.  15 U.S.C. Sections 41–58.

(FTC) to carry out the broadly stated goal of preventing unfair and deceptive trade practices, including deceptive advertising.[2]

## UNFAIR AND DECEPTIVE ADVERTISING

Advertising will be deemed deceptive if a consumer would be misled by the advertising claim. Vague generalities and obvious exaggerations are permissible. These claims are known as *puffing*. When a claim takes on the appearance of literal authenticity, however, it may create problems. Advertising that would *appear* to be based on factual evidence but that in fact is scientifically untrue will be deemed deceptive. A classic example is provided by a 1944 case in which the claim that a skin cream would restore youthful qualities to aged skin was deemed deceptive.[3]

Another advertising practice that has been attacked by the FTC as deceptive involves misleading price claims. For example, advertising to sell two cans of paint for the price of one and then setting a very high unit price has been held to be deceptive. The FTC also regulates advertising that contains the endorsements of celebrities. An advertisement may be deemed deceptive if the celebrity actually makes no use of the product. In the following case, advertisements of a sunburn treatment were alleged to be deceptive.

---

2.  15 U.S.C. Section 45.

---

3.  *Charles of the Ritz Distributing Corp. v. Federal Trade Commission,* 143 F.2d 676 (2d Cir. 1944).

---

**BACKGROUND AND FACTS**   *The Federal Trade Commission staff's advertising substantiation rule held that advertisements must be substantiated by well-controlled scientific studies, or the claims would be considered deceptive. The staff brought an action against Pfizer, Inc., because the claims made by Pfizer in its advertisements for a sunburn treatment were allegedly unsupported by direct studies on humans. Pfizer argued that it had other forms of evidence sufficient to support its advertising claims. The administrative law judge who heard this adjudication dismissed the complaint against Pfizer, holding that no controlled scientific studies should be required. The staff appealed this dismissal to the commission itself.*

CASE 46.1

**IN RE PFIZER, INC.**
Federal Trade Commission, 1972.
81 F.T.C. 23.

*KIRKPATRICK,* Commissioner.

The Commission's staff counsel, who have the burden of proving the allegations of the complaint, challenge certain advertising by Pfizer for the product "UN-BURN," a nonprescription product recommended for use on minor burns and sunburn. The complaint cited the following radio and television advertising for Un-Burn as typical and representative:

New Un-Burn actually anesthetizes *nerves* in sensitive sunburned skin.

Un-Burn relieves pain *fast.* Actually *anesthetizes nerves* in sensitive sunburned skin.

\* \* \* Sunburned skin is sensitive skin \* \* \* Sensitive sunburned skin needs \* \* \* UN-BURN. New UN-BURN contains the same local anesthetic doctors often use. \* \* \* Actually anesthetizes nerves in sensitive sunburned skin. I'll tell you what I like about UN-BURN. It's the best friend a blonde ever had! \* \* \* I'm a blonde \* \* \* and I know what it means to have sensitive skin. Why I'm half afraid of moon burn! That's why I'm mad about UN-BURN. It stops sunburn pain in \* \* \* less time than it takes me to slip out of my bikini. \* \* \*
\* \* \* \*

Pfizer's director of Marketing testified that he took three measures to satisfy himself as to the efficacy of the product Un-Burn. First, he received "complete assurance" from Pfizer's medical people that the claims he planned to use for

Un-Burn could be supported by the two active ingredients in the quantities in which they were to be used in the product. He was assured that the way a topical anesthetic works is to anesthetize nerves and thereby stop pain. He was also assured by the "medical people" that the product was patterned very closely after the market leader, Solarcaine. Secondly, he was assured that all available literature or information on these two active ingredients had been thoroughly reviewed and favorable conclusions derived from this review as to the efficacy of the ingredients as topical anesthetics. Finally, he personally reviewed all competitive advertising to satisfy himself that Pfizer would not be claiming anything more than other products with the same active ingredients. The director of marketing testified that Pfizer did not conduct tests on humans to determine whether the efficacy claims could be supported, but consciously "accepted another method of satisfying" themselves by going over the history of the ingredients. No specific tests were conducted on human beings to prove that Un-Burn anesthetizes nerve ends.

\* \* \* \*

While the Commission finds that respondent failed in its attempt to demonstrate affirmatively the existence of a reasonable basis for its Un-Burn advertising, the evidence is not sufficient to prove that respondent in fact *lacked* a reasonable basis for its advertising claims. The record evidence is simply inconclusive with regard to the adequacy of the medical literature and clinical experience relied upon by respondent, and with regard to the reasonableness of such reliance.

**DECISION AND REMEDY**  *The FTC affirmed the administrative law judge's decision and dismissed the complaint against Pfizer. In so doing, the FTC upheld the concept that advertising must be substantiated, but it went on to hold that the staff had not met its burden of proof in demonstrating that Pfizer's advertising was insufficiently substantiated.*

**INTERNATIONAL CONSIDERATIONS**  **Advertising Regulation in the European Union** *In 1984, the European Community (now known as the European Union) adopted the "Misleading Advertising Directive" in an attempt to establish some uniformity among the member nations in regard to the regulation of advertising. This directive calls on member nations to prohibit misleading ads and requires them to create means to enforce these prohibitions. The directive specifically requires that the relevant courts and administrative agencies be empowered to require substantiation of factual claims in advertising. If advertisers fail to offer sufficient evidence to substantiate their claims, it will be presumed that the claims are inaccurate.*

## BAIT-AND-SWITCH ADVERTISING

The FTC has promulgated specific rules to govern advertising techniques. One of the most important rules is contained in the FTC's "Guides on Bait Advertising,"[4] issued in 1968. The rule seeks to prevent **bait-and-switch advertising**—that is, advertising a very low price for a particular item that will likely be unavailable to the consumer, who will then be encouraged to purchase a more expensive item. The low price is the "bait" to lure the consumer into the store. The salesperson is instructed to "switch" the consumer to a different, more expensive item. Under the FTC guidelines, bait-and-switch advertising occurs if the seller refuses to show the advertised item, fails to have in stock a reasonable quantity of the item, fails to promise to deliver the advertised item within a reasonable time, or discourages employees from selling the item.

4. 16 C.F.R. Part 238.

## FTC ACTIONS AGAINST DECEPTIVE ADVERTISING

The FTC receives complaints from many sources, including competitors of alleged violators, consumers, consumer organizations, trade associations, Better Business Bureaus, government organizations, and state and local officials. If enough consumers complain and the complaints are widespread, the FTC will investigate the problem and perhaps take action. If, after its investigations, the FTC believes that a given advertisement is unfair or deceptive, it drafts a formal complaint, which is sent to the alleged offender. The company may agree to settle the complaint without further proceedings.

If the company does not agree to settle a complaint, the FTC can conduct a hearing in which the company can present its defense. As discussed in Chapter 45, a hearing conducted by an administrative agency is held before an administrative law judge (ALJ) instead of a federal district court judge. If the FTC succeeds in proving that an advertisement is unfair or deceptive, it usually issues a **cease-and-desist order** requiring that the challenged advertising be stopped. It might also impose a sanction known as **counteradvertising** by requiring the company to advertise anew—in print, on radio, and on television—to inform the public about the earlier misinformation. The FTC may institute **multiple product orders,** which require a firm to cease and desist from false advertising not only in regard to the product that was the subject of the action but also in regard to all of the firm's other products.

In the following case, the FTC ruled that Kraft, Inc., had engaged in deceptive advertising in marketing its cheese slices and ordered Kraft to cease and desist from such advertising.

---

**BACKGROUND AND FACTS** *Kraft's individually wrapped cheese slices, or ''Singles Slices,'' which are made from real cheese, cost more than the imitation cheese slices on the market. In the early 1980s, Kraft began losing its market share to an increasing number of producers of imitation cheese slices. Kraft responded with a series of advertisements, collectively known as the ''Five Ounces of Milk'' campaign. The ads claimed that Kraft Singles cost more than imitation slices because they were made from five ounces of milk rather than less expensive ingredients. The ads also implied that because each slice contained five ounces of milk, Kraft Singles contained a higher calcium content than imitation cheese slices. The FTC filed a complaint against Kraft, charging that Kraft had materially misrepresented the calcium content and relative calcium benefit of Kraft Singles. The administrative law judge (ALJ) ruled that Kraft was misleading consumers, because, although Kraft did use five ounces of milk in making each Kraft Single, roughly 30 percent of the calcium contained in the milk was lost during processing—and Kraft had neglected to inform consumers of this fact. Furthermore, the ALJ found that the vast majority of imitation cheese slices sold in the United States contained approximately the same amount of calcium as Kraft Singles. The ALJ therefore ordered Kraft to cease and desist from making these claims. The FTC commissioners affirmed the order, with some modifications, and Kraft appealed.*

CASE 46.2

**KRAFT, INC. v. FEDERAL TRADE COMMISSION**
United States Court of Appeals,
Seventh Circuit, 1992.
970 F.2d 311.

*FLAUM,* Circuit Judge.
\* \* \* \*

Kraft makes numerous arguments on appeal, but its principal claim is that the FTC erred as a matter of law in not requiring extrinsic evidence of consumer deception. \* \* \*.
\* \* \* \*

\* \* \* Courts, including the Supreme Court, have uniformly rejected imposing such a requirement on the FTC, and we decline to do so as well. We hold that the Commission may rely on its own reasoned analysis to determine what claims, including implied ones, are conveyed in a challenged advertisement, so long as those claims are reasonably clear from the face of the advertisement.

Kraft's [claim] has two flaws. First, it rests on the faulty premise that implied claims are inescapably subjective and unpredictable. \* \* \* The implied claims Kraft made are reasonably clear from the face of the advertisements, and hence the Commission was not required to utilize consumer surveys in reaching its decision.

\* \* \* The Commissioners' personal experiences quite obviously affect their perceptions, but it does not follow that they are incapable of predicting whether a particular claim is likely to be perceived by a reasonable number of consumers.

**DECISION AND REMEDY** *The court, holding that Kraft's advertising campaign was deceptive and likely to mislead consumers, affirmed the FTC's ruling.*

## TELEMARKETING AND FAX ADVERTISING

The pervasive use of the telephone to market goods and services to the home and other businesses led to the passage in 1991 of the Telephone Consumer Protection Act (TCPA).[5] The act generally prohibits telephone solicitation using an automatic telephone dialing system or a prerecorded voice.[6] Over half of the states also have laws regulating telephone solicitation.

Not surprisingly, the widespread use of facsimile (fax) machines has led to the use of faxes as a tool for direct marketing. Advertising by fax is usually less expensive than mailing a letter, and faxes normally receive greater attention than ''junk mail.'' At the same time, unsolicited fax messages tie up the recipient's fax machine and impose a cost on the recipient, who must pay for fax paper, toner, and other supplies. The TCPA also makes it illegal to transmit ads via fax without first obtaining the recipient's permission.

The act is enforced by the Federal Communications Commission and also provides for a private right of action. Consumers can recover any actual monetary loss resulting from a violation of the act or receive $500 in damages for each violation,

whichever is greater. If a court finds that a defendant willfully or knowingly violated the act, the court has the discretion to treble the damages awarded.

## SECTION 2

# LABELING AND PACKAGING LAWS

In addition to the broad restrictions on advertising, a number of federal and state laws deal specifically with the information given on labels and packages. The restrictions are designed to provide accurate information about the product and to warn about possible dangers from its use or misuse. In general, labels must be accurate. That is, they must use words as those words are understood by the ordinary consumer. For example, a box of cereal cannot be labeled ''giant'' if it would exaggerate the amount of cereal contained in the box. In some instances, labels must specify the raw materials used in the product, such as the percentage of cotton, nylon, or other fibers used in a garment. In other instances, the products must carry a warning. Cigarette packages and advertising, for example, must include one of several warnings about the health hazards associated with smoking.[7]

The numerous federal laws include the Fur Products Labeling Act of 1951,[8] the Wool Products

---

5.  47 U.S.C. Section 227.
6.  Courts are divided on whether the restraints on commercial speech provided for under the TCPA and similar state statutes violate the First Amendment. See, for example, *Moser v. Federal Communications Commission,* 826 F.Supp. 360 (D.Or. 1993); *State v. Casino Marketing Group, Inc.,* 491 N.W.2d 882 (Minn. 1992); and *Lysaght v. State of New Jersey,* 837 F.Supp. 646 (D.N.J. 1993).

---

7.  15 U.S.C. Sections 1331–1341.
8.  15 U.S.C. Section 69.

Labeling Act of 1939,[9] the Flammable Fabrics Act of 1953,[10] the Smokeless Tobacco Health Education Act of 1986,[11] and the Fair Packaging and Labeling Act of 1966.[12] The Smokeless Tobacco Health Education Act, for example, requires that producers, packagers, and importers of smokeless tobacco label their product with one of several warnings about the health hazards associated with the use of smokeless tobacco; the warnings are similar to those contained on ordinary tobacco product packages.

The Fair Packaging and Labeling Act requires that products possess labels that identify the product; the net quantity of the contents, as well as the quantity of servings, if the number of servings is stated; the manufacturer; and the packager or distributor. The act also provides authority to add requirements concerning words used to describe packages, terms that are associated with savings claims, information disclosures for ingredients in nonfood products, and standards for the partial filling of packages. The most recent standard requires that food products bear labels detailing nutrition information, including how much fat a product contains and what kind of fat it is. These restrictions are enforced by the Department of Health and Human Services, as well as the Federal Trade Commission.

## SECTION 3

# SALES

Many of the laws that protect consumers concern the disclosure of certain terms in sales transactions and provide rules governing the various forms of sales, such as door-to-door sales, mail-order sales, referral sales, and the unsolicited receipt of merchandise. Much of the federal regulation of sales is conducted by the FTC under its regulatory authority to curb unfair trade practices. Other federal agencies, however, are involved to various degrees. For example, the Federal Reserve Board of Governors has issued **Regulation Z,**[13] which governs credit provisions associated with sales

contracts. Numerous state laws are also relevant. Many states, for example, have enacted laws governing home sale transactions. Moreover, states have provided a number of consumer protection provisions through the adoption of the Uniform Commercial Code and, in those states that have adopted it, by the Uniform Consumer Credit Code.

## DOOR-TO-DOOR SALES

A door-to-door sale is any transaction that is initiated by a visit to, and is concluded at, the buyer's home—as distinct from some other place, such as the seller's showroom or office. Certain features of this type of sales activity have prompted concern. For one thing, because repeat purchases are less likely than with store sales, sellers are less constrained by the need to build up goodwill with regular customers. Additionally, individuals may feel more pressure when cornered in their own home by a persistent salesperson; they may simply buy to get rid of an obnoxious salesperson standing at the front door.

For these reasons, door-to-door sales are regulated both at the state level and by the federal government. States have enacted ''cooling-off'' legislation, which permits a buyer to rescind a door-to-door purchase if the election is made within a certain period of time. The FTC has mandated a three-day cooling-off period, but when state legislation is more favorable to the buyer, the latter will govern the sale. In addition, the FTC requires the seller to notify the buyer of the right to cancel the sale within the specified time, and if the sale is originally conducted in Spanish, notice must also be given in Spanish.[14]

## TELEPHONE AND MAIL-ORDER SALES

Sales made by either telephone or mail order are the greatest source of complaints to the nation's Better Business Bureaus. Many mail-order houses are far removed from the buyers to whom the houses sell, thus making the burden greater in bringing a complaint against the seller. To a certain extent, consumers are protected under federal laws prohibiting mail fraud, which were discussed in Chapter 9, and under state consumer protection laws that parallel and supplement the federal laws.

---

9.  15 U.S.C. Section 68.
10.  15 U.S.C. Section 1191.
11.  15 U.S.C. Sections 4401–4408.
12.  15 U.S.C. Sections 1451–1461.
13.  12 C.F.R. Sections 226.1–226.30.

---

14.  16 C.F.R. Section 429.1.

The FTC "Mail or Telephone Order Merchandise Rule" of 1993, which amended the FTC "Mail Order Rule" of 1975,[15] provides specific protections for consumers who purchase goods via phone lines or through the mails. The 1993 rule extended the 1975 rule to include sales in which orders are transmitted using computers, facsimile (fax) machines, or some similar means involving telephone lines. Among other things, the rule requires mail-order merchants to ship orders within the time promised in their catalogs or advertisements, to notify consumers when orders cannot be shipped on time, and to issue a refund within a specified period of time when a consumer cancels an order.

In addition, the Postal Reorganization Act of 1970[16] provides that *unsolicited* mechandise sent by U.S. mail may be retained, used, discarded, or disposed of in any manner deemed appropriate, without the recipient's incurring any obligation to the sender.

## FTC REGULATION OF SPECIFIC INDUSTRIES

Over the last decade, the FTC has begun to target certain sales practices on an industrywide basis. Two examples are the used-car business and the funeral-home trade. In 1984, the FTC enacted the "Used Motor Vehicle Regulation Rule,"[17] which is more commonly known as the "used-car rule." This rule requires used-car dealers to affix a "Buyers Guide" label to all cars sold on their lots. The label must disclose the following information: (1) the car's warranty or a statement that the car is being sold "as is," (2) information regarding any service contract or promises being made by the dealer, and (3) a suggestion that the purchaser obtain both an inspection of the car and a written statement of any promises made by the dealer.

In 1984, the FTC also enacted rules requiring that funeral homes provide customers with itemized prices of all charges incurred for a funeral.[18] In addition, the regulations prohibit funeral homes from requiring specific embalming procedures or specific types of caskets for bodies that are to be cremated.

---

15. 16 C.F.R. Sections 435.1–435.2.
16. 39 U.S.C. Section 3009.
17. 16 C.F.R. Sections 455.1–455.5.
18. 16 C.F.R. Section 453.2.

## REAL ESTATE SALES

Various federal and state laws apply to consumer transactions involving real estate. These laws are designed to prevent fraud and to provide buyers with certain types of information. In some cases, these protections mirror those provided in non–real estate sales. The disclosure requirements of the Truth-in-Lending Act apply to a number of real estate transactions, as will be discussed shortly.

### INTERSTATE LAND SALES FULL DISCLOSURE ACT

The Interstate Land Sales Full Disclosure Act[19] was passed by Congress in 1968, and it is administered by the Department of Housing and Urban Development (HUD). The purpose of the act is to ensure disclosure of certain information to consumers so that they can make reasoned decisions about land purchases. The act is similar to the Securities Act of 1933 in both purpose and design. The act requires any seller or lessor of one hundred or more lots of unimproved land, if the sale or lease is part of a common promotional plan, to file an initial "statement of record" with HUD's Office of Interstate Land Sales Registration.

The act only applies if the promotional plan can be deemed part of interstate commerce. But, as in cases involving securities, this is generally an easy requirement to meet. For example, even strictly local sales might be considered interstate commerce if transacted in part over the phone; although the calls might be local, the phone lines traverse state boundaries. For the same reason, use of the mail system is likely to ensure that a promotional plan is in the stream of interstate commerce.

Once the initial statement is filed, it must be approved by HUD before the developer can begin to offer the land for sale or lease. The act also provides purchasers with a private right of action for the land promoter's fraud, misrepresentation, or noncompliance with pertinent provisions of the act. Criminal penalties are provided under the act, and HUD is given certain rights with regard to inspections, injunctions, and prosecution of offenses. Three provisions of the act provide purchasers with rights of rescission (cancellation).

### REAL ESTATE SETTLEMENT PROCEDURES ACT

For many individuals, purchasing a home involves a bewildering array of procedures and re-

---

19. 15 U.S.C. Sections 1701–1720.

quirements. Settlement (finalizing a real estate transaction) may require title insurance, attorneys' fees, appraisal fees, taxes, insurance, and brokers' fees. To aid home buyers, federal legislation requires specific disclosures regarding settlement procedures. The 1976 revisions of the Real Estate Settlement Procedures Act[20] make the following stipulations:

1. Within three business days after a person applies for a mortgage loan, the lender must send a booklet prepared by HUD that explains the settlement procedures, describes the costs to the potential buyer, and outlines the applicant's legal rights.
2. Within the three-day period, the lender must give an estimate of most of the settlement costs.
3. The lender must clearly identify individuals or firms that the applicant is required to use for legal or other services, including title search and insurance.
4. If the loan is approved, the lender must provide a truth-in-lending statement that shows the annual percentage rate on the mortgage loan.
5. Lenders, title insurers, and others involved in the transaction cannot pay kickbacks for business referred to them.

■ Section 4

# CREDIT PROTECTION

Because credit has assumed such an important role in consumer transactions, it is not surprising that some of the most important consumer protection laws have to do with credit. We look now at some of the most significant laws regulating consumer credit transactions.

## THE TRUTH-IN-LENDING ACT

The Truth-in-Lending Act (TILA), Title I of the Consumer Credit Protection Act (CCPA),[21] was enacted by Congress in 1968. The TILA is basically

a disclosure law. Administered by the Federal Reserve Board, it requires sellers and lenders to disclose credit or loan terms to debtors so that the latter can shop around for the best available financing terms.

The TILA applies to creditors who, in the ordinary course of business, lend money to consumers, sell goods on credit to consumers, or arrange for the extension of credit to consumers. Thus, sales between two consumers are not subject to the act. Only debtors who are *natural* persons are protected by the TILA; corporations and other entities created by law are not.

**DISCLOSURE REQUIREMENTS** The disclosure requirements are found in Regulation Z, which, as mentioned earlier, was promulgated by the Federal Reserve Board. If the contracting parties are subject to the TILA, the requirements of Regulation Z apply to any transaction involving an installment sales contract in which payment is to be made in more than four installments. These transactions typically include installment loans, retail and installment sales, car loans, home improvement loans, and certain real estate loans if the amount of financing is less than $25,000.

Whenever credit is extended to consumers in these kinds of transactions, the lender must disclose to the consumer, in the installment contract, all material facts relating to the credit transaction, including the specific dollar amount being financed; the annual percentage rate of interest; any financing charges, premiums, or points; the number, amounts, and due dates of payments; any penalties imposed on delinquent payments or prepayment; and a description of any security interest in the property being financed or in other property of the consumer. The regulations require these disclosures to be clear, conspicuous, and segregated from irrelevant information. Compliance with these regulations is satisfied when the creditor places all of the disclosures on one side of one document (unless there is not enough room) or groups the disclosures together within a box outlined by boldfaced lines. Commonly, creditors set off the disclosures in a box (often referred as the ''Federal Box'' ) within the credit contract or other document. The creditor must also give a copy of these disclosures to the consumer.

The TILA also provides that if a lender takes a security interest in the consumer's principal dwelling, the consumer may rescind the transaction

---

20. 12 U.S.C. Sections 2601–2617.
21. 15 U.S.C. Sections 1601–1693r. The act was amended in 1980 by the Truth-in-Lending Simplification and Reform Act.

within three days. The creditor must notify the consumer of this right of rescission in writing and provide the consumer with two copies of the notice. The creditor must also indicate on the notice the date on which the three-day period will end. If the creditor fails to comply with these requirements, the three-day rescission period will be extended to three years.

**VIOLATIONS OF THE TILA**   Various penalties apply to creditors who violate the TILA by either failing to provide the required disclosures or failing to discover an error in the statement provided. The act confers a *private right of action* on consumers who have been injured by a creditor's violation. If the suit is brought within one year of the date of the violation, the creditor will be liable for twice the amount of the finance charge, plus attorneys' fees. No more than $1,000 in damages may be recovered, but in no event will the penalty be less than $100. Federal agencies, including the Department of Justice and the FTC, may sue violators for criminal, as well as civil, violations. The criminal penalties include as much as a $5,000 fine and up to one year in jail. The following case illustrates how strictly TILA requirements will be enforced.

---

CASE 46.3

**ELSNER v. ALBRECHT**

Court of Appeals of Michigan, 1990.
185 Mich.App. 72,
460 N.W.2d 232.

**BACKGROUND AND FACTS**   *In February 1986, Max and Jacquelyn Elsner met with a representative of Diamond Mortgage to discuss the possibility of obtaining a loan to pay the balance on their land contract and to pay for home improvements. The representative asked the Elsners to sign some preliminary documents, including a loan application, and allegedly advised the Elsners that they would not sign the final binding papers until they received the money. The representative also gave each of the Elsners one copy of a "Notice of Right to Cancel." In fact, the documents signed by the Elsners included a mortgage contract and a promissory note, which Diamond shortly thereafter assigned to Harley and Donna Albrecht in exchange for $26,500. The Elsners never received the money. When the Albrechts sought payment on the note, the Elsners brought an action to rescind the contract, claiming that Diamond had violated the TILA because the representative gave them each only one copy of the "Notice of Right to Cancel"—instead of two copies, as required under the act. The trial court granted rescission, and the Albrechts appealed. The Albrechts argued that, as holders in due course (see Chapter 27), they were entitled to payment of the note, and therefore the contract could not be rescinded.*

*PER CURIAM.*
    *  *  *  *
   First, we find that plaintiffs were entitled to rescind the mortgage contract under the TILA, and Regulation Z. The TILA and Reg. Z provide for rescission until three days after the latest of the following events: (1) consummation of the transactions, (2) delivery of two copies to each borrower of the notice of right to cancel, or (3) delivery of all "material disclosures." We find that plaintiffs were entitled to rescind the transaction because Diamond Mortgage failed to deliver two copies to each borrower of the notice of right to cancel.

   This case is virtually identical to a federal district court case involving two other parties victimized by the Diamond-Obie mortgage scheme. In *Stone v. Mehlberg,* the federal district court granted summary disposition to plaintiffs who had rescinded their mortgage transaction. In *Stone,* as in the present case, the trial court found that each plaintiff had not received two copies of their right to cancel as required under [the TILA and Regulation Z]. As the *Stone* court held, this requirement is not a mere technicality and requires that two copies be provided to each spouse since both had an ownership interest in the residence. ''The fact that joint obligors may be husband and wife is irrelevant. Spouses are no more interchangeable under the TILA's rescission provisions than any other group of persons. Where the notice of right to cancel is not delivered, plaintiffs' right to rescind continues, subject to the statute of limitations.'' The *Stone* court went on to note that plaintiffs were not prevented from rescinding their mortgage agreement because of defendants' status as holders in due course, holding the TILA's rescission remedy preempts the holder in due course doctrine.

| | |
|---|---|
| *The trial court's decision was affirmed. The Elsners were entitled to rescission, notwithstanding the fact that the mortgage contract and note had been transferred to a good faith purchaser for value.* | **DECISION AND REMEDY** |
| *It is important to realize that the courts generally assume that the best way to protect the greatest number of consumers is by strict enforcement of consumer protection legislation, such as the TILA, even though occasional injustices are bound to result and even, in this case, at the expense of the holder-in-due-course doctrine—which itself rests on the ethical conviction that innocent third parties should be protected.* | **ETHICAL CONSIDERATIONS** |

## THE CONSUMER LEASING ACT

The Consumer Leasing Act (CLA) of 1988[22] amended the TILA to provide protection for consumers who lease automobiles and other goods. The CLA applies to those who lease or arrange to lease consumer goods in the ordinary course of their business. The act only applies if the goods are priced at $25,000 or less and if the lease term exceeds four months. The CLA and its implementing regulation, Regulation M,[23] requires lessors to disclose in writing all of the material terms of the lease, including the following: a description of the goods subject to the lease, finance charges, the dates on which payments are due and the amount of the payments, applicable warranties, insurance costs that the consumer must pay, costs and conditions relating to terminating the lease prior to the end of the lease period, and other charges for which the consumer may be responsible.

As under the TILA, disclosures must be made accurately, in a clear and conspicuous manner, and in a meaningful sequence. The FTC enforces the CLA, and those who violate the requirements of the act face the same civil and criminal liability as those who violate the TILA.

## THE EQUAL CREDIT OPPORTUNITY ACT

In 1974, Congress enacted the Equal Credit Opportunity Act (ECOA)[24] as an amendment to the Consumer Credit Protection Act. The ECOA prohibits the denial of credit solely on the basis of race, religion, national origin, color, sex, marital status, or age. The act also prohibits credit discrimination on the basis of whether an individual receives certain forms of income, such as public assistance benefits. Under the ECOA, a creditor may not require the signature of an applicant's spouse, other than a joint applicant, on a credit instrument if the applicant qualifies under the creditor's standards of creditworthiness for the amount and terms of the credit request. Creditors are permitted to request any information from a credit applicant except that which would be used for the type of discrimination covered in the act or its amendments.

## THE FAIR CREDIT BILLING ACT

In 1974, Congress also enacted the Fair Credit Billing Act[25] as an amendment to the TILA. Under the terms of the act, a purchaser can withhold

---

22. 15 U.S.C. Sections 1667–1667e.
23. 12 C.F.R. Sections 213.1–213.8.

24. 15 U.S.C. Sections 1691–1691f.
25. 15 U.S.C. Sections 1666–1666j.

payment for an allegedly defective product that was purchased with a credit card. It is up to the credit-card issuer to intervene and attempt to settle the dispute. A purchaser does not have an unlimited right to stop payment, however. The purchaser must first exercise a good faith effort to get satisfaction from the seller.

Other provisions of the act relate to disputes over billing. If the debtor believes there is an error in a bill, the debtor may suspend payment until the credit-card company investigates the complaint. The consumer, within sixty days of receipt of the disputed bill, must write to the company that issued the card and explain the basis of the alleged error. The company must resolve the dispute within ninety days, during which time it can neither close the account nor issue additional financing charges. If, however, the error is unfounded and is resolved against the debtor, the creditor may seek to collect finance charges for the entire period for which payments were not made.

## LOST AND UNAUTHORIZED CREDIT CARDS

The TILA contains other provisions regarding credit cards. One of these provisions limits the liability of the cardholder to $50 per card for unauthorized charges made before the credit-card issuer is notified that the card has been lost. Another provision prohibits a credit-card company from billing a consumer for any unauthorized charges if the credit card was improperly issued by the company.

## THE FAIR CREDIT REPORTING ACT

In 1970, to protect consumers against inaccurate credit reporting, Congress enacted the Fair Credit Reporting Act (FCRA).[26] The act provides that consumer credit reporting agencies may issue credit reports to users only for specified purposes, including the extension of credit, the issuance of insurance policies, compliance with a court order, and compliance with a consumer's request for a copy of his or her own credit report. The act further provides that any time a consumer is denied credit or insurance on the basis of the consumer's credit report, or is charged more than others ordinarily would be for credit or insurance, the consumer must be notified of that fact and of the name and address of the credit-reporting agency that issued the credit report.

Under the act, consumers may request the source of any information being given out by a credit agency, as well as the identity of anyone who has received an agency's report. Consumers are also permitted to have access to the information contained about them in a credit reporting agency's files. If a consumer discovers that a credit reporting agency's files contain inaccurate information about the consumer's credit standing, the agency, upon the consumer's written request, must investigate the matter and delete any unverifiable or erroneous information within a reasonable period of time. The following case illustrates the liability exposure of companies that maintain credit reports and ratings.

---

26.   15 U.S.C. Sections 1681–1681t.

---

| CASE 46.4 | **COMPANY PROFILE** *In 1904, Charles Thompson, a welder for the Cleveland Cap Screw Company, devised an improved method for assembling automobile valves. By 1908, Cleveland Cap Screw was making most of the engine valves for the automobile industry. Charles Thompson became president in 1915; the company became Thompson Products in 1926. Thompson Products began to diversify in the 1930s, and by 1945, sales had increased sevenfold. In 1953, the company provided financial support for the Ramo-Wooldridge Corporation, founded by engineers Simon Ramo and Dean Wooldridge to build an intercontinental ballistic missile. In 1958, the companies merged to form Thompson Ramo Wooldridge (renamed TRW, Inc., in 1965). In the 1960s, TRW built rocket engines for the Apollo program, satellites, and missiles, and worked on many other space and defense projects. Today, TRW supplies the automotive, aerospace, defense, and information systems industries. TRW is the world's leading airbag maker and a leading producer of power steering systems. TRW has* |

**STEVENSON v. TRW, INC.**

United States Court of Appeals, Fifth Circuit, 1993. 987 F.2d 288.

*built over 170 spacecraft and produces surveillance and communica-
tions equipment and satellites for the U.S. government. TRW's information systems and services arm includes one of the world's largest credit-
reporting services.*

**BACKGROUND AND FACTS**   *John Stevenson obtained a copy of his
credit report from TRW, Inc., a credit-reporting agency, after he began
receiving phone calls from bill collectors concerning debts that he did not
owe. He discovered that the credit report listed sixteen accounts that he
had not opened. Some of the accounts belonged to another John Stevenson,
and others appeared to belong to his estranged son, John Stevenson, Jr.
On October 9, 1989, Stevenson wrote a letter requesting TRW to correct
his credit report. TRW began its investigation by sending ''Consumer
Dispute Verification'' forms (CDVs) to the subscribers that had reported
the disputed accounts. CDVs ask subscribers to check whether the information they have about a consumer matches the information in TRW's credit
report. If a subscriber fails to respond within twenty days or indicates
that TRW's account information is incorrect, TRW deletes the disputed
information. By February 9, 1990, TRW had completed its investigation
and claimed that all disputed accounts containing ''negative'' credit information had been removed. Nonetheless, inaccurate information continued to
appear on Stevenson's reports. Stevenson filed suit against TRW, alleging,
among other things, that TRW had violated the Fair Credit Reporting Act
(FCRA) by its failure to delete erroneous information promptly from
Stevenson's credit report. The court, holding that TRW had negligently
and willfully violated the FCRA, entered a judgment in Stevenson's
favor. Stevenson was awarded actual damages of $30,000 for mental
anguish, punitive damages of $100,000, and attorneys' fees of $20,700.
TRW appealed.*

*JERRE S. WILLIAMS,* Circuit Judge:
   \*   \*   \*   \*
   \*   \*   \* [The trial] court found that TRW had negligently and willfully violated
[the FCRA] by not deleting inaccurate and unverifiable information promptly and
by allowing deleted information to reappear.
   \*   \*   \*   \*
   Allowing inaccurate information back onto a credit report after deleting it because
it is inaccurate is [negligence]. Additionally, in spite of the complexity of Stevenson's
dispute, TRW contacted the subscribers only through the CDVs. Although testimony
at trial revealed that TRW sometimes calls subscribers to verify information, it made
no calls in Stevenson's case. TRW relied solely on the CDVs despite the number of
disputed accounts and the allegations of fraud. TRW also relied on the subscribers
to tell TRW whether to delete information from Stevenson's report. In a reinvestigation of the accuracy of credit reports, a credit bureau must bear some responsibility
for evaluating the accuracy of information obtained from subscribers.
   TRW argues in its defense that the reinvestigation was complicated by the accounts fraudulently obtained in Stevenson's name and based upon accurate information. TRW urged at trial, however, that where fraud has occurred, the consumer
must resolve the problem with the creditor. TRW's only obligation, it urges, is to
publish a ''victim of fraud'' statement at the end of a credit report if fraud has been
established by the parties. This response by TRW to Stevenson's complaint falls
short of [the FCRA's] mandate that the ''consumer reporting agency shall within a
reasonable period of time reinvestigate'' and ''promptly delete'' inaccurate or

unverifiable information. The statute places the burden of investigation squarely on TRW. We conclude that there was no clear error in the district court's finding of negligence in failure to meet the prompt deletion requirement.

**DECISION AND REMEDY**    *The appellate court affirmed the trial court's judgment, as well as the award of $30,000 in actual damages and $20,700 in attorneys' fees. The court did not agree with the trial court that TRW's noncompliance with the FCRA was willful, however, and therefore reversed the award of punitive damages.*

## THE FAIR DEBT COLLECTION PRACTICES ACT

In 1977, Congress enacted the Fair Debt Collection Practices Act (FDCPA)[27] in an attempt to curb what were perceived to be abuses by collection agencies. The act applies only to specialized debt-collection agencies that, usually for a percentage of the amount owed, regularly attempt to collect debts on behalf of someone else. Creditors who attempt to collect a debt are not covered by the act unless, by misrepresenting themselves to the debtor, they cause the debtor to believe they are a collection agency. The act explicitly prohibits a collection agency from using any of the following tactics:

1. Contacting the debtor at the debtor's place of employment if the debtor's employer objects.
2. Contacting the debtor during inconvenient or unusual times (for example, calling the debtor at three o'clock in the morning) or at any time if the debtor is being represented by an attorney.
3. Contacting third parties other than the debtor's parents, spouse, or financial advisor about payment of a debt unless a court authorizes such action.

4. Using harassment or intimidation (for example, using abusive language or threatening violence), or employing false and misleading information (for example, posing as a police officer).
5. Communicating with the debtor at any time after receiving notice that the debtor is refusing to pay the debt, except to advise the debtor of further action to be taken by the collection agency.

The FDCPA also requires collection agencies to include a **validation notice** whenever they initially contact a debtor for payment of a debt or within five days of that initial contact. The notice must state that the debtor has thirty days within which to dispute the debt and to request a written verification of the debt from the collection agency. The debtor's request for debt validation must be in writing.

The enforcement of the FDCPA is primarily the responsibility of the Federal Trade Commission. The act provides that a debt collector who fails to comply with the act is liable for actual damages, plus additional damages not to exceed $1,000 and attorneys' fees. In the following case, a debtor sued a collection agency for failure to comply with the act's requirements.

---

27.  15 U.S.C. Sections 1692–1692o.

---

**CASE 46.5**

**MILLER v. PAYCO–GENERAL AMERICAN CREDITS, INC.**

United States Court of Appeals, Fourth Circuit, 1991. 943 F.2d 482.

**BACKGROUND AND FACTS**    *Lenvil Miller owed $2,501.61 to the Star Bank of Cincinnati. Star Bank referred the account to a collection agency, Payco–General American Credits, Inc., for collection. Payco sent Miller a one-page collection form. In the middle of the front side of the form, in large, red, boldface type, was the statement, "THIS IS A DEMAND FOR IMMEDIATE FULL PAYMENT OF YOUR DEBT," followed by the words, "YOUR SERIOUSLY PAST DUE ACCOUNT HAS BEEN GIVEN TO US FOR IMMEDIATE ACTION. YOU HAVE HAD AMPLE TIME TO PAY YOUR DEBT, BUT YOU HAVE NOT. IF THERE IS A VALID REASON, PHONE US AT [telephone number] TODAY. IF NOT, PAY US—NOW."*

*At the very bottom of the page, in the smallest type on the page, was the statement, "NOTICE: SEE REVERSE SIDE FOR IMPORTANT INFORMATION." On the reverse side of the form, printed in gray ink, was the validation notice required by the Fair Debt Collection Practices Act (FDCPA). Miller sued Payco, alleging that the validation notice violated the FDCPA because the notice was contradicted by other parts of the collection letter, was overshadowed by the demands for immediate payment, and was not effectively conveyed to the consumer. The trial court granted summary judgment for Payco, and Miller appealed.*

*WILKINSON,* Circuit Judge:

   \*   \*   \*   \*

We agree with Miller that the form he received from Payco both contradicted and overshadowed the required validation notice, preventing the notice's effective communication. \*   \*   \*

A consumer who wished to obtain validation of his debt could lose his rights under the statute if he followed the commands to telephone. [The FDCPA] guarantees that validation will be sent and collection activities will cease only when the consumer disputes the debt in writing. \*   \*   \* The language on the front of the form emphatically instructs consumers to dispute their debt by telephone, in opposition to the statutory requirements.

The emphasis on immediate action also stands in contradiction to the FDCPA, which provides consumers a thirty day period to decide to request validation. A consumer who received Payco's form could easily be confused between the commands to respond "immediately," "now," and "today," and the thirty day response time contemplated by the statute.

*The appellate court reversed the trial court's judgment and remanded the case for further proceedings.*

**DECISION AND REMEDY**

*This case clearly illustrates a collection agency's attempt to comply with the letter but not the spirit of the FDCPA. The court recognized this in the concluding lines of its opinion: "There are numerous and ingenious ways of circumventing [the requirements of the FDCPA] under a cover of a technical compliance. Payco has devised one such way, and we think that to uphold it would strip the statute of its meaning."*

**ETHICAL CONSIDERATIONS**

## GARNISHMENT OF WAGES

Despite the increasing number of protections afforded debtors, creditors are not without their own means of securing payment on a debt. One of these is the right to garnish a debtor's wages after the debt has gone uncollected for a prolonged period. Recall from Chapter 32 that *garnishment* is the legal procedure by which a creditor may collect on a debt by directly attaching, or seizing, a portion of the debtor's assets (such as wages) that are in the possession of a third party (such as an employer).

State law provides the basis for a process of garnishment, but the law varies among the states as to how easily garnishment may be obtained. Indeed, a few states prohibit garnishment of wages altogether. In addition, the Constitution and, more recently, federal legislation under the TILA provide further protections against abuse.[28] In general, the debtor is entitled to notice and an opportunity to be heard in a process of garnishment. Moreover, wages cannot be garnished beyond 25 percent of the debtor's after-tax earnings, and the garnishment must leave the debtor with at least a specified minimum income.

---

28.   15 U.S.C. Sections 1671–1677.

# CONSUMER HEALTH AND SAFETY

Laws discussed earlier regarding the labeling and packaging of products go a long way toward promoting consumer health and safety. But there is a significant distinction between regulating the information dispensed about a product and regulating the content of the actual product. The classic example is tobacco products. Tobacco products have not been altered by regulation or banned outright despite their obvious hazards. What has been regulated are the warnings that producers are required to give consumers about the hazards of tobacco.[29] This section focuses on laws that regulate the actual products made available to consumers.

## THE FEDERAL FOOD, DRUG, AND COSMETIC ACT

The first federal legislation regulating food and drugs was enacted in 1906 as the Pure Food and Drugs Act. That law, as amended in 1938, exists presently as the Federal Food, Drug, and Cosmetic Act (FFDCA).[30] The act protects consumers against adulterated and misbranded foods and drugs. More recent amendments have added additional substantive and procedural requirements to the act. In its present form, the act establishes food standards, specifies safe levels of potentially hazardous food additives, and sets classifications of food and food advertising.

Most of these statutory requirements are monitored and enforced by the Food and Drug Administration (FDA). Under an extensive set of procedures established by the FDA, drugs must be shown to be effective as well as safe before they may be marketed to the public, and the use of some food additives suspected of being carcinogenic is prohibited. A 1976 amendment to the FFDCA[31]

authorizes the FDA to regulate medical devices, such as pacemakers and other health devices or equipment, and to withdraw from the market any such device that is mislabeled.

## THE CONSUMER PRODUCT SAFETY ACT

Consumer product safety legislation began in 1953 with enactment of the Flammable Fabrics Act, which prohibits the sale of highly flammable clothing or materials. Over the next two decades, Congress enacted legislation for specific classes of products regarding the design or composition of the products. Then in 1972, Congress, by enacting the Consumer Product Safety Act,[32] created a comprehensive scheme of regulation over matters concerning consumer safety. The act also established far-reaching authority over consumer safety under the Consumer Product Safety Commission (CPSC).

The CPSC conducts research on the safety of individual products, and it maintains a clearinghouse on the risks associated with different consumer products. The Consumer Product Safety Act authorizes the CPSC to set standards for consumer products and to ban the manufacture and sale of any product that it deems to be potentially hazardous to consumers. The CPSC also has authority to remove from the market any products it believes to be imminently hazardous and to require manufacturers to report on any products already sold or intended for sale if the products have proved to be hazardous. The CPSC also has authority to administer other product safety legislation, such as the Child Protection and Toy Safety Act of 1969,[33] the Federal Hazardous Substances Act of 1960,[34] and the Flammable Fabrics Act.

The CPSC's authority is sufficiently broad to allow it to ban any product that the CPSC believes poses merely an "unreasonable risk" to the consumer. Some of the products that the CPSC has banned include various types of fireworks, cribs, and toys, as well as many products containing asbestos or vinyl chloride.

---

29. We are ignoring recent civil litigation concerning the liability of tobacco product manufacturers for injuries that arise from the use of tobacco.

30. 21 U.S.C. Sections 301–393.

31. 21 U.S.C. Sections 352(o), 360(j), 360(k), and 360c–360k.

32. 15 U.S.C. Sections 2051–2083.

33. This act consisted of amendments to 15 U.S.C. Sections 1261, 1262, and 1274.

34. 15 U.S.C. Sections 1261–1277.

<br>

<br>

## SECTION 6

# STATE CONSUMER PROTECTION LAWS

Thus far, our primary focus has been on federal legislation. Although variation among the state laws prevents making any broad generalizations, state laws often provide more sweeping and significant protections for the consumer than do federal laws. Precisely because of the variation among the states, a businessperson is well advised to consider all aspects of the laws of the states in which he or she does business. Even remote connections with a state may bring a transaction within the authority of a particular state's laws. Furthermore, basic principles of contract law include the considerable discretion of the contracting parties to

choose to have the laws of a particular state govern the terms of their agreement.[35]

Although state laws vary widely, there is a common thread running through most of them. Typically, state consumer protection laws are directed at deceptive trade practices, such as a seller's providing false or misleading information to the consumer. As just mentioned, some of the legislation provides broad protection for consumers. A prime example is the Texas Deceptive Trade Practices Act of 1973, which forbids a seller from selling to a buyer anything that the buyer does not need or cannot afford. The following case illustrates an application of the Tennessee Consumer Protection Act of 1977.

---

35. So-called conflicts of law may arise in any transaction that crosses state boundaries.

---

**BACKGROUND AND FACTS** *In September 1985, Darrell Morris bought a 1979 Ford truck from Mack's Used Cars & Parts, Inc. He traded in an older truck as a down payment and financed the remainder of the purchase price over a three-year period. The bill of sale contained the following disclaimer: "This unit is sold as is. No warranties have been expressed or implied." After paying the last installment, Morris received the certificate of title and learned that the truck had been previously wrecked and reconstructed. Mack's was aware of this fact but had not disclosed it to Morris at the time of the purchase. Morris sued Mack's, alleging that Mack's had breached express and implied warranties and had violated the Tennessee Consumer Protection Act of 1977, which prohibits unfair or deceptive acts. Mack's contended that the warranty disclaimer in the bill of sale relieved it from any liability for failing to disclose to Morris the fact that the pickup had been wrecked and reconstructed. The trial court agreed with Mack's and dismissed the suit. Morris appealed, contending that the disclaimer (valid under the Uniform Commercial Code—see Chapter 24) did not bar an action for violation of the Tennessee Consumer Protection Act. The appellate court affirmed the dismissal, saying that to hold Mack's liable under the Tennessee Consumer Protection Act "would, in effect, be creating liability under an 'as is' sale which is waived under [UCC] 2–316(3)(a)." Morris appealed the case to the Supreme Court of Tennessee.*

CASE 46.6

**MORRIS v. MACK'S USED CARS**

Supreme Court of Tennessee, 1992.
824 S.W.2d 538.

*REID*, Chief Justice.

\* \* \* \*

\* \* \* Disclaimers permitted by [Section] 47–2–316 of [Tennessee's version of] the Uniform Commercial Code (UCC) may limit or modify liability otherwise imposed by the code, but such disclaimers do not defeat separate causes of action for unfair or deceptive acts or practices under the [Tennessee] Consumer Protection Act.

\* \* \* \*

Automobile sales cases from other jurisdictions have held that an "as is" disclaimer of warranties does not bar an action for deceptive trade practices. * * *

The Tennessee Consumer Protection Act is to be liberally construed to protect consumers and others from those who engage in deceptive acts or practices. * * * To allow the seller here to avoid liability for unfair or deceptive acts or practices by disclaiming contractual warranties under the UCC would contravene the broad remedial intent of the Consumer Protection Act.

**DECISION AND REMEDY**    *The Supreme Court of Tennessee reversed the appellate court's decision.*

**ETHICAL CONSIDERATIONS**    *Traditionally, in transacting business, superior information and business acumen are legitimate advantages, which lead to no liability. But the continuing development of modern business ethics has limited sellers' attempts to take advantage of ignorance. Thus, if (1) one party knows a fact basic to a transaction, (2) the other party is ignorant of the fact, and (3) under the customs of the trade or other circumstances a disclosure of the fact is reasonably to be expected, the party who does not disclose it may be liable. In such a situation, good faith and fair dealing require disclosure.*

## THE UNIFORM COMMERCIAL CODE

Consumers are afforded the protections offered by the sections in the Uniform Commercial Code (UCC) on express and implied warranties. These were covered in detail in Chapters 20 through 25, and the reader should consider the importance of these protections in the context of our present discussion. UCC 2–719(3) also restricts the ability of sellers to limit their liability for personal injuries caused by defective consumer products. Perhaps the most significant UCC consumer protection, however, is the principle of unconscionability based on UCC 2–302. This section allows the courts to refuse to enforce contracts that are so one sided and unfair that they "shock the conscience" of the court. In discussing consumer protections under the UCC, it is important to recall the Magnuson-Moss Warranty Act, which was discussed in Chapter 24. This federal law supplements the UCC provisions in cases involving both a consumer transaction of at least $10 and an express written warranty.

## THE UNIFORM CONSUMER CREDIT CODE

Far less widely adopted than the UCC is the Uniform Consumer Credit Code (UCCC). Pro-

mulgated in 1968 by the National Conference of Commissioners on the Uniform State Laws, the UCCC is an attempt to draft a comprehensive body of rules governing the most important aspects of consumer credit. The UCCC includes sections on truth in lending, maximum credit ceilings, door-to-door sales, and referral sales. The UCCC also contains provisions concerning fine-print clauses and creditor remedies, including provisions regarding deficiency judgments[36] and garnishments. In states that have adopted it, the UCCC applies to most sales, including those involving real estate. Its adoption also displaces the adopting state's consumer credit laws, as well as laws governing installment loans, usury, and retail installment sales.

The UCCC is controversial, and it has been adopted in only a handful of states. Even those states that have adopted the UCCC have adopted only portions. Moreover, substantial differences in the various state versions remove much of the uniformity from the act among the various adopting states.

---

36.  A deficiency judgment is a judgment for the portion of a debt not recovered from the forced sale of property securing that debt.

# TERMS AND CONCEPTS TO REVIEW

| | | |
|---|---|---|
| bait-and-switch advertising **908** | consumer law **906** | Regulation Z **911** |
| cease-and-desist order **909** | counteradvertising **909** | validation notice **918** |
| | multiple product orders **909** | |

# QUESTIONS AND CASE PROBLEMS

**46–1. Unsolicited Merchandise.** Andrew, a California resident, received a flyer in the U.S. mail announcing a new line of regional cookbooks distributed by the Every-Kind Cookbook Co. Andrew was not interested and threw the flyer away. Two days later, Andrew received in the mail an introductory cookbook entitled *Lower Mongolian Regional Cookbook,* as announced in the flyer, on a "trial basis" from Every-Kind. Andrew was not interested but did not go to the trouble to return the cookbook. Every-Kind demanded payment of $20.95 for the *Lower Mongolian Regional Cookbook.* Discuss whether Andrew can be required to pay for the cookbook.

**46–2. Consumer Protection.** Fireside Rocking Chair Co. advertised in the newspaper a special sale price of $159 on machine-caned rocking chairs. In the advertisement was a drawing of a natural-wood rocking chair with a caned back and seat. The average person would not be able to tell from the drawing whether the rocking chair was machine caned or hand caned. The hand-caned rocking chairs sold for $259. Lowell and Celia Gudmundson went to Fireside because they had seen the ad for the machine-caned rocking chair and were very interested in purchasing one. The Gudmundsons arrived on the morning the sale began. Fireside's agent said the only machine-caned rocking chairs he had were painted lime green and were priced at $159. He immediately turned the Gudmundsons' attention to the hand-caned rocking chairs, praising their quality and pointing out that for the extra $100, the hand-caned chairs were surely a good value. The Gudmundsons, preferring the natural-wood, machine-caned rocking chair for $159 as pictured in the advertisement, said they would like to order the one in the ad. The Fireside agent said he could not order a natural-wood, machine-caned rocking chair. Discuss fully whether Fireside has violated any consumer protection laws.

**46–3. Door-to-Door Sales.** On June 28, a sales representative for Renowned Books called on the Gonchars at their home. After a very persuasive sales pitch on the part of the sales agent, the Gonchars agreed in writing to purchase a twenty-volume set of historical encyclopedias from Renowned Books for a total of $299. An initial down payment of $35 was required, with the re-

mainder of the price to be paid in monthly payments over a one-year period. Two days later the Gonchars, having second thoughts, contacted the book company and stated they had decided to rescind the contract. Renowned Books said this would be impossible. Has Renowned Books violated any consumer law by not allowing the Gonchars to rescind their contract? Explain.

**46–4. Truth in Lending.** Michael and Patricia Jensen purchased a new 1989 Ford Tempo from Ray Kim Ford, Inc. The Jensens signed a retail installment contract that provided for an estimated trade-in value of $800 for their old car. When the traded-in car turned out to be worth $1,388.08, Ray Kim prepared a second retail installment contract, without the Jensens' knowledge. The second contract, although it credited the increased trade-in value of the car, compensated for this credit by increasing the interest rate, increasing the sales price of the car, and making other adjustments so that the second contract basically called for future cash payments by the Jensens of about the same amount as the first contract. In effect, the second contract gave the Jensens almost no benefit for the increased value of their traded-in car. The Jensens made payments under the contract until they noticed the five-cent difference in monthly payments, asked for a copy of the contract, and realized that it was not the contract that they had signed. The Jensens sued Ray Kim, alleging that the second contract was a forgery and that Ray Kim had violated the Truth-in-Lending Act (TILA) by not disclosing to them the credit terms of the second contract. Has Ray Kim violated the TILA? If the Jensens choose to adopt the terms of the second contract, despite the forgery, has the act been violated? Discuss fully. [*Jensen v. Ray Kim Ford, Inc.,* 920 F.2d 3 (7th Cir. 1990)]

**46–5. Deceptive Advertising.** Thompson Medical Co. marketed a new cream called Aspercreme that was supposed to help arthritis victims and others suffering from minor aches. Aspercreme contained no aspirin. Thompson's television advertisements stated that the product provided "the strong relief of aspirin right where you hurt" and showed the announcer holding up aspirin tablets as well as a tube of Aspercreme. The Federal Trade Commission held that the advertisements were misleading, because they led consumers to believe that Aspercreme contained aspirin. Thompson Medical Co. appealed this decision and argued that the advertisements never actually stated that its product contained aspirin. How should the court rule? Discuss. [*Thompson Medical Co. v. Federal Trade Commission,* 791 F.2d 189 (D.C. Cir. 1986)]

**46–6. Deceptive Advertising.** Dennis and Janice Geiger saw an advertisement in a newspaper for a Kimball Whitney spinet piano on sale for $699 by McCormick Piano & Organ Co. Because the style of the piano drawn in the advertisement matched their furniture, the Geigers were particularly interested in the Kimball. When they went to McCormick Piano & Organ, however, they learned that the drawing closely resembled another, more expensive Crest piano, and that the Kimball spinet looked quite different than the piano sketched in the drawing. The salesperson told the Geigers that she was unable to order a spinet piano of the style requested by the Geigers. When the Geigers asked for the names of other customers who had purchased the advertised pianos, the salesperson became extremely upset and said she would not, under any circumstances, sell the Geigers a piano. The Geigers then brought suit against the piano store, alleging that the store had engaged in deceptive advertising in violation of Indiana law. Was the McCormick Piano & Organ Co. guilty of deceptive advertising? Explain. [*McCormick Piano & Organ Co. v. Geiger,* 412 N.E.2d 842 (Ind.App. 1980)]

**46–7. Land Sales.** Branigar Organization, Inc., began a residential development in the 1970s. The development included a large country club with golf courses and tennis courts. The purchase price of a house or lot, however, did not include the initiation fees and dues required for club membership—although all residents could join the club if they paid these fees. Branigar later transferred the ownership and management of the club, and according to the plan of the new ownership, all members of the club were told that they would lose their usage rights as of December 31, 1990. After that date, only members owning an equity interest in—that is, members who had purchased shares in—the club would be allowed to use the facilities. All nonequity members were offered the right to become equity members. Shirley Rice and others who had purchased lots or houses in the development claimed that Branigar's failure to disclose that the nonequity club members would eventually be required to buy equity membership to use the club violated the Interstate Land Sales Full Disclosure Act. The act requires developers to furnish prospective subdivision-lot purchasers with a property report that includes, among other things, information regarding recreational facilities associated with the subdivision. Will Rice and the others succeed in their claim? Discuss fully. [*Rice v. Branigar Organization, Inc.,* 922 F.2d 788 (11th Cir. 1991)]

**46–8. Fair Debt Collection.** Josephine Rutyna was a sixty-year-old widow who, in late 1976 and early 1977, had incurred a debt for medical treatment of her high blood pressure and epilepsy. She assumed that the cost of the services had been paid by either Medicare or her private insurance company. In July 1978, however, she was contacted by an agent of Collection Accounts Terminal, Inc., who stated that Rutyna still owed a debt of $56 for those services. She denied that she owed the debt, and the following month she received a letter from the collection agency threatening to contact her neighbors and employer concerning the debt if the $56 was not paid immediately. Discuss fully whether the collection agency's letter violates any consumer protection law. [*Rutyna v. Collection Accounts Terminal, Inc.,* 478 F.Supp. 980 (N.D.Ill. 1979)]

**46–9. Truth in Lending.** On December 5, 1988, John and Carol Rowland met with a sales representative from Nu View Window of Illinois, Inc., and agreed to buy six windows for $4,364. On the same day, the Rowlands and the sales representative also partially completed a "Retail Installment Contract" and a "Notice of Right of Rescission," a copy of which was given to the Rowlands. The copy, however, was nearly illegible, and it was impossible to read the finance charges, the total price, the total number of payments, and other information. A few days later, the Rowlands gave Magna Millikin Bank of Decatur, N.A., a mortgage on their home in return for a loan of $4,364 to finance the purchase of the windows. (The bank worked closely with Nu View and financed hundreds of contracts annually for Nu View customers.) On January 18, 1989, Magna Millikin dated its copy of the Retail Installment Contract. On February 5, 1991, the Rowlands, having had second thoughts about the purchase, rescinded the transaction by letter to Magna Millikin and demanded release from their mortgage on their residence. Magna Millikin refused to terminate the transaction or release the mortgage. Should the Rowlands be allowed to rescind the transaction? Why or why not? Discuss fully. [*Rowland v. Magna Millikin Bank of Decatur, N.A.,* 812 F.Supp. 875 (C.D.Ill. 1992)]

### 46–10. Case Briefing Assignment

 *Examine Case A.9 [Roberts v. Walmart Stores, Inc., 736 F.Supp. 1527 (E.D.Mo. 1990)] in Appendix A. The case has been excerpted there in great detail. Review and then brief the case, making sure that you include answers to the following questions in your brief.*

**1.** What was the basis of the Roberts' claim?
**2.** What defense did Walmart raise?
**3.** What was the court's decision?

# CHAPTER 47

# ENVIRONMENTAL LAW

W hen the human population was small and dispersed and industry was limited, the earth was relatively unspoiled. Environmental degradation was not a significant problem. Today, however, industrial society's generation of waste threatens the quality of human life.

**Environmental law**—all law pertaining to environmental protection—is not new. Indeed, the federal government began to regulate some activities, such as those involving the pollution of navigable waterways, in the late 1800s. In the last few decades, however, the body of environmental law has expanded substantially in an attempt to control industrial waste and to protect dwindling natural resources and endangered species. In this chapter, we first discuss the common law actions that can be brought against business firms and individuals for damages caused by polluting activities. The remainder of the chapter examines the numerous federal statutes and regulations that have been created to protect the environment.

## SECTION 1

## COMMON LAW ACTIONS

Common law remedies against environmental pollution originated centuries ago in England. Those responsible for operations that created dirt, smoke, noxious odors, noise, or toxic substances were sometimes held liable under common law theories of nuisance or negligence. Today, injured individuals continue to rely on the common law to obtain damages and injunctions against business polluters. (Statutory remedies are also available, a topic that we treat later.)

### NUISANCE

Under the common law doctrine of **nuisance,** persons may be held liable if they use their property in a manner that unreasonably interferes with others' rights to use or enjoy their own property. In these situations, it is common for courts to balance the equities between the harm caused by the pollution and the costs of stopping it.

Courts have often denied *injunctive relief* on the ground that the hardships to be imposed on the polluter and on the community are relatively greater than the hardships to be suffered by the plaintiff. For example, a factory that causes neighboring landowners to suffer from smoke, dirt, and vibrations may be left in operation if it is the core of a local economy. The injured parties may be awarded only their money damages. These damages may include compensation for the decreased value of the neighbors' property that results from the factory's operation.

A property owner may be given relief from pollution in situations in which he or she can identify a distinct harm separate from that affecting the general public. This is referred to as a "private" nuisance. Under the common law, citizens were denied standing (access to the courts—see Chapter 3) unless they suffered a harm distinct from the harm suffered by the public at large. Some states still require this. Therefore, a group of citizens who wished to stop a new development that would cause significant water pollution was denied access to the courts on the ground that the harm to them did not differ from the harm to the general public.[1] A public authority (such as a state's attorney general) can sue to abate a "public" nuisance.

## NEGLIGENCE AND STRICT LIABILITY

An injured party may sue a business polluter in tort under the negligence and strict liability theories discussed in Chapter 6. The basis for a negligence action is the business's alleged failure to use reasonable care toward the party whose injury was foreseeable and, of course, caused by the lack of reasonable care. For example, employees might sue an employer whose failure to use proper pollution controls contaminated the air, causing the employees to suffer respiratory illnesses.

Businesses that engage in ultrahazardous activities—such as the transportation of radioactive materials—are strictly liable for whatever injuries the activities cause. In a strict liability action, the injured party does not need to prove that the business failed to exercise reasonable care.

A developing area of tort law involves **toxic torts**—actions against toxic polluters based on common law theories. In the following toxic tort case, the court outlines reasons for holding a particular polluter liable under theories of common law negligence and strict liability.

---

1. *Save the Bay Committee, Inc. v. Mayor of City of Savannah,* 227 Ga. 436, 181 S.E.2d 351 (1971).

---

**CASE 47.1**

**STERLING v. VELSICOL CHEMICAL CORP.**

United States District Court, Western District of Tennessee, 1986.
647 F.Supp. 303.

**BACKGROUND AND FACTS** *In 1964, Velsicol Chemical Corporation began operating a chemical waste burial site on a farm in Tennessee. At the 242-acre site, over the better part of the next decade, Velsicol buried more than 300,000 fifty-five-gallon drums and hundreds of boxes filled with chemical waste. In 1973, the state of Tennessee determined the site to be hazardous and closed it. Local residents sued Velsicol on a number of legal theories, including negligence and strict liability, claiming that the aquifer from which they drew their drinking water was contaminated with hazardous chemicals that leaked from the farm. The residents sought damages for a variety of alleged physical and emotional injuries, as well as property damage.*

*HORTON,* Judge.
\* \* \* \*
*Strict Liability* \* \* \*
\* \* \* \*

\* \* \* [T]he Court concludes that Velsicol's activity on the farm was not only [an] ultrahazardous activity, but also [an] abnormally dangerous activity and therefore the defendant is strictly liable for any damages that have occurred. This conclusion is made for \* \* \* the following reasons:

1.    There was a high degree of risk of harm to the person, land or chattels [personal property] of others \* \* \* ;

2.    There was a likelihood that the harm that results would be great, such as the increased risk of many diseases including cancer, and the destruction of the plaintiffs' quality of life;

3.    The inability to eliminate the risk by the exercise of reasonable care;

4.    The extent to which the activity at the dump was not a matter of common usage and as a means of disposal and violated the state of the art;

5.    The inappropriateness of the location of the dump where it was carried out; and

6.    The extent to which its value to the community (none) was outweighed by its dangerous attributes (great).

*Common Law Negligence*

The Court concludes that the doctrine of common law negligence applies to this case and Velsicol is clearly guilty of negligence in this case for the following reasons:

1.    The Court concludes that there was a duty, a standard of conduct, imposed by law on Velsicol to protect others from unreasonable harm arising from the dumping of chemicals on its farm; and

2.    The Court further concludes that defendant breached that duty by its failure to do the following:

   a.   Defendant failed to investigate the geological makeup or strata under the dumpsite prior to its purchase or operation;

   b.   Defendant failed to investigate the hydrological, or water bearing zones under the dumpsite prior to its purchase or operation;

   c.   Defendant failed to hire knowledgeable persons to investigate the geological and hydrogeological area under the dumpsite prior to its purchase or operation;

   d.   Defendant failed to install proper monitoring procedures in and around the dumpsite prior to commencing dumping operations at the dumpsite;

   e.   Defendant failed to investigate the geological and hydrogeological situation at the dumpsite after being warned by the [U.S. Geological Survey] in 1967 that their chemicals were escaping from their burial trenches and were in fact contaminating the local water table aquifer.

*The district court awarded the residents more than $5.2 million in compensatory damages, $7.5 million in punitive damages, and prejudgment interest (interest that accrues on the amount of the judgment from the time of the filing of the suit to the issuing of the judgment) at the rate of 8 percent per year on the compensatory damages. On appeal, the U.S. Court of Appeals for the Sixth Circuit found that the district court properly held Velsicol liable but that it erred in the damage awards. The case was remanded for recalculation of some of the damages.*[a]

**DECISION AND REMEDY**

a.   *Sterling v. Velsicol Chemical Corp.*, 855 F.2d 1188 (6th Cir. 1988).

## SECTION 2

# FEDERAL REGULATION

Congress has passed a number of statutes to control the impact of human activities on the environment.

The major federal environmental statutes discussed in this chapter are listed and summarized in Exhibit 47–1. Some of these statutes have been passed in an attempt to improve the quality of air and water. Some of them specifically regulate toxic chemicals—including pesticides, herbicides, and hazardous wastes. Some are concerned with radiation.

■ **Exhibit 47–1 Federal Environmental Statutes**

| Popular Name | Purpose | Statute Reference |
|---|---|---|
| Rivers and Harbors Appropriations Act (1899) | To prohibit ships and manufacturers from discharging and depositing refuse in navigable waterways. | 33 U.S.C. Sections 401–418. |
| Federal Insecticide, Fungicide, and Rodenticide Act (FIFRA) (1947) | To control the use of pesticides and herbicides. | 7 U.S.C. Sections 135–136y. |
| Federal Water Pollution Control Act (FWPCA) (1948) | To eliminate the discharge of pollutants from major sources into navigable waters. | 33 U.S.C. Sections 1251–1387. |
| Atomic Energy Act (1954) | To limit environmental harm from the private nuclear industry. | 42 U.S.C. Sections 2011 to 2297g–4. |
| Clean Air Act (1963) | To control air pollution from mobile and stationary sources. | 42 U.S.C. Sections 7401–7671q. |
| National Environmental Policy Act (NEPA) (1969) | To limit environmental harm from federal government activities. | 42 U.S.C. Sections 4321–4370d. |
| Marine Protection, Research, and Sanctuaries Act of 1972 (Ocean Dumping Act) | To regulate the transporting and dumping of material into ocean waters. | 16 U.S.C. Sections 1401–1445. |
| Noise Control Act (1972) | To regulate noise pollution from transportation and nontransportation sources. | 42 U.S.C. Sections 4901–4918. |
| Endangered Species Act (1973) | To protect species that are threatened with extinction. | 16 U.S.C. Sections 1531–1544. |
| Safe Drinking Water Act (1974) | To regulate pollutants in public drinking water systems. | 42 U.S.C. Sections 300f to 300j–25. |
| Resource Conservation and Recovery Act (RCRA) (1976) | To establish standards for hazardous waste disposal. | 42 U.S.C. Sections 6901–6986. |
| Toxic Substances Control Act (1976) | To regulate toxic chemicals and chemical compounds. | 15 U.S.C. Sections 2601–2692. |
| Comprehensive Environmental Response, Compensation, and Liability Act (CERCLA) (Superfund) (1980) | To regulate the clean-up of hazardous waste disposal sites. | 42 U.S.C. Sections 9601–9675. |
| Low Level Radioactive Waste Policy Act (1980) | To assign to the states responsibility for nuclear power plants' low-level radioactive waste. | 42 U.S.C. Sections 2021b–2021j. |
| Nuclear Waste Policy Act (1982) | To provide for the designation of a permanent radioactive waste disposal site. | 42 U.S.C. Sections 10101–10270. |
| Oil Pollution Act (1990) | To establish liability for the clean-up of navigable waters after oil-spill disasters. | 33 U.S.C. Sections 2701–2761. |

## NATIONAL ENVIRONMENTAL POLICY ACT

The National Environmental Policy Act (NEPA) of 1969[2] requires that all agencies of the federal government consider environmental factors when making significant decisions. For every major federal action that significantly affects the quality of the environment, an **environmental impact statement (EIS)** must be prepared. An action qualifies as "major" if it involves a substantial commitment of resources (monetary or otherwise). An

---

2. 42 U.S.C. Sections 4321–4370d.

action is "federal" if a federal agency has the power to control it. Construction by a private developer of a ski resort on federal land, for example, may require an EIS.[3] So would building or operating a nuclear plant, which requires a federal permit,[4] or constructing a dam as part of a federal project.[5]

An EIS must analyze (1) the impact on the environment that the action will have, (2) any adverse effects to the environment and alternative actions that might be taken, and (3) irreversible effects the action might generate. If an agency decides that an EIS is unnecessary, it must issue a statement supporting this conclusion. EISs have become instruments for private citizens, consumer interest groups, businesses, and others to challenge federal agency actions on the basis that the actions improperly threaten the environment.

## COMPLEMENTARY FEDERAL LAWS

Other federal laws also require that environmental values be considered in agency decision making. Among the most important of these laws are those that have been enacted to protect fish and wildlife. Under the Fish and Wildlife Coordination Act of 1958,[6] federal agencies proposing to approve the impounding or diversion of the waters of a stream must consult with the Fish and Wildlife Service with a view to preventing the loss of fish and wildlife resources. Also important is the Endangered Species Act of 1973.[7] Under this act, all federal agencies are required to take steps to ensure that their actions "do not jeopardize the continued existence of endangered species" or the habitat of an endangered species. An action may jeopardize the continued existence of a species if it sets in motion a chain of events that reduces the chances that the species will survive.

## ENVIRONMENTAL PROTECTION AGENCY

In 1970 the Environmental Protection Agency (EPA) was created to coordinate federal environmental responsibilities. The EPA administers most federal environmental policies and statutes. Other federal agencies with authority for regulating specific environmental matters include the Department of the Interior, the Department of Defense, the Department of Labor, the Food and Drug Administration, and the Nuclear Regulatory Commission.

## SECTION 3

# AIR POLLUTION

Federal involvement with air pollution goes back to the 1950s, when Congress authorized funds for air-pollution research. In 1963, the federal government passed the Clean Air Act,[8] which focused on multistate air pollution and provided assistance to states. Various amendments, particularly in 1970, 1977, and 1990, strengthened the government's authority to regulate the quality of air. These laws provide the basis for issuing regulations to control pollution coming primarily from mobile sources (such as automobiles) and stationary sources (such as electric utilities and industrial plants).

## MOBILE SOURCES

Regulations governing air pollution from automobiles and other mobile sources specify pollution standards and time schedules. For example, the 1970 Clean Air Act required a reduction of 90 percent in the amount of carbon monoxide and other pollutants emitted by automobiles by 1975. (This did not happen, however, and the 1977 amendments extended the deadline to 1983. Generally, automobile manufacturers met the 90 percent reduction goal by installing catalytic converters on automobiles.)

An automobile purchased today emits only about 4 percent of the pollutants that a new 1970 model did. Nevertheless, there are so many more automobiles being driven today that the urban ground-level ozone, which decreased between the late 1970s and the late 1980s, has risen to former levels. Under the 1990 amendments, automobile manufacturers must cut new automobiles' exhaust emission of nitrogen oxide by 60 percent and

---

3.  *Robertson v. Methow Valley Citizens' Council*, 490 U.S. 332, 109 S.Ct. 1835, 104 L.Ed.2d 351 (1989).

4.  *Calvert Cliffs Coordinating Committee v. Atomic Energy Commission*, 449 F.2d 1109 (D.C. Cir. 1971).

5.  *Marsh v. Oregon Natural Resources Council*, 490 U.S. 360, 109 S.Ct. 1851, 104 L.Ed.2d 377 (1989). This case is presented in Chapter 45 as Case 45.3.

6.  16 U.S.C. Sections 661–666c.

7.  16 U.S.C. Sections 1531–1544.

8.  42 U.S.C. Sections 7401–7671q.

emission of other pollutants by 35 percent. Beginning in 1994, increasing numbers of new automobiles had to meet these standards. By 1998, all new automobiles must do so. Another set of emission controls may be ordered after 2000. To ensure compliance, the EPA certifies the prototype of a new automobile whose emission controls are effective up to 50,000 miles. The EPA may also inspect production models. If a vehicle does not meet the standards in actual driving, the EPA can order a recall and the repair or replacement of pollution-control equipment at the manufacturer's expense.

To further reduce pollutants in automobile emissions, the 1990 amendments require that "employer trip-reduction" programs be implemented beginning in 1994. Businesses have been targeted for these programs because they necessarily contribute to air pollution when their employees drive to work. These employer-created programs must increase the number of employee passengers per vehicle traveling to and from the job site by 25 percent in four years. Affected employers include those with over one hundred employees and located in major metropolitan areas, such as Los Angeles and New York. Employer trip-reduction programs will require many commuters to use alternative forms of transportation, such as mass transit or carpooling.

Service stations are also subject to environmental regulations. The 1990 amendments required that in 1992, service stations had to sell gasoline with a higher oxygen content in forty-one cities that experienced carbon monoxide pollution in the winter. This could be accomplished by selling fuel containing corn ethanol. Beginning in 1995, service stations must sell even cleaner burning gasoline in Los Angeles and another eight of the most polluted urban areas.

## STATIONARY SOURCES

The Clean Air Act authorizes the EPA to establish air quality standards for stationary sources (such as manufacturing plants) also but recognizes that the primary responsibility for preventing and controlling air pollution rests with state and local governments. The EPA sets two levels (primary and secondary) of ambient standards—that is, the maximum level of certain pollutants—and the states formulate plans to achieve those standards. The plans are to provide for the attainment of primary standards within three years and secondary standards within a reasonable time. For economic, political, or technological reasons, however, the deadlines are often subject to change.

Different standards apply to existing sources of pollution and major new sources. Different standards also apply to sources in clean areas and sources in polluted areas. Major new sources include existing sources modified by a change in a method of operation that increases emissions. Performance standards for these sources require use of the maximum achievable control technology, or MACT, to reduce emissions from the combustion of fossil fuels (coal and oil).

Under the 1990 amendments to the Clean Air Act, 110 of the oldest coal-burning power plants in the United States must cut their emissions by 40 percent by the year 2001 to reduce acid rain. Utilities were granted "credits" to emit certain amounts of sulfur dioxide, and those that emit less than the allowed amounts can sell their credits to other polluters. Controls on other factories and businesses are intended to reduce ground-level ozone pollution in ninety-six cities to healthful levels by 2005 (except Los Angeles, which has until 2010). Industrial emissions of 189 hazardous air pollutants must be reduced by 90 percent by 2000. By 2002, the production of chlorofluorocarbons, carbon tetrachloride, and methyl chloroform—used in air conditioning, refrigeration, and insulation and linked to depletion of the ozone layer—must stop.

Hazardous air pollutants are those likely to cause an increase in mortality or in serious irreversible or incapacitating illness. As noted, there are 189 of these pollutants, including asbestos, benzene, beryllium, cadmium, mercury, vinyl chloride, and other cancer-causing materials. These pollutants may also cause neurological and reproductive damage. They are emitted by a variety of business activities, including smelting, dry cleaning, house painting, and commercial baking. Instead of establishing specific emissions standards for each hazardous air pollutant, the new law requires industry to use the best available technology to limit those emissions. The EPA may strengthen this requirement if necessary to protect the public health.

## PENALTIES

For violations of emission limits under the Clean Air Act, the EPA can assess civil penalties of up to $25,000 per day. To penalize those for whom this amount makes a violation more cost effective than compliance, the EPA can obtain a penalty equal to the violator's economic benefits from noncompliance. Private citizens can also sue violators. Those who knowingly violate the act may be subject to criminal fines.

# WATER POLLUTION

Federal regulations governing the pollution of water can be traced back to the Rivers and Harbors Appropriations Act of 1899.[9] These regulations prohibited ships and manufacturers from discharging or depositing refuse in navigable waterways.

## NAVIGABLE WATERS

Once limited to waters actually used for navigation, the term *navigable waters* is today interpreted to include coastal and freshwater wetlands (how the EPA defines wetlands will be discussed shortly), as well as intrastate lakes and streams used by interstate travelers and industries. In 1948, Congress passed the Federal Water Pollution Control Act (FWPCA),[10] but its regulatory system and enforcement proved inadequate. In 1972, amendments to the FWPCA—known as the Clean Water Act—established the following goals: (1) make waters safe for swimming, (2) protect fish and wildlife, and (3) eliminate the discharge of pollutants into the water. They set forth specific time sched-

ules, which were extended by amendment in 1977 and by the Water Quality Act of 1987.[11] Under these schedules, the EPA establishes limitations for discharges of types of pollutants based on the technology available for controlling them. Regulations, for the most part, specify that the best available technology be installed. The 1972 amendments also required that municipal and industrial polluters apply for permits before discharging wastes into navigable waters.

Under the act, violators are subject to a variety of civil and criminal penalties. Civil penalties for each violation range from as low as a maximum of $10,000 per day, and not more than $25,000 per violation, to as much as $25,000 per day. Criminal penalties range from a fine of $2,500 per day and imprisonment of up to one year to a fine of $1 million and fifteen years' imprisonment. Injunctive relief and damages can also be imposed. The polluting party can be required to clean up the pollution or pay for the cost of doing so.

The Clean Water Act prohibits the filling or dredging of **wetlands** unless a permit is obtained from the Army Corps of Engineers. The EPA defines wetlands as ''those areas that are inundated or saturated by surface or ground water at a frequency and duration sufficient to support, and that under normal circumstances do support, a prevalence of vegetation typically adapted for life in [water] saturated soil conditions.'' In recent years, federal regulatory policy in regard to wetlands has elicited substantial controversy because of the broad interpretation of what constitutes a wetland subject to the regulatory authority of the federal government. The following case is illustrative.

---

9. 33 U.S.C. Sections 401–418.
10. 33 U.S.C. Sections 1251–1387.

---

11. This act amended 33 U.S.C. Section 1251.

---

**COMPANY PROFILE** *Sam and Jack Hoffman started F&S Construction in Phoenix in 1947. Over the next few years, the company—renamed the Hoffman Group—built thousands of low-priced houses throughout the United States, becoming the nation's third largest builder by 1955. The firm relocated to Chicago, where the Hoffmans began to build Hoffman Estates and a number of other subdivisions. Norman Hassinger, a residential marketing expert, became president of the Hoffman Group in 1982 and gradually took over the firm. In 1987, the Hoffman Group became the Hassinger Companies. Hassinger created Hoffman Homes as a home-building subsidiary. At the time, the firm had seventeen residential subdivisions under development in Chicago and its suburbs, with home prices ranging from $95,000 to $800,000. Hassinger planned to expand through*

**CASE 47.2**

**HOFFMAN HOMES, INC. v. ADMINISTRATOR, UNITED STATES ENVIRONMENTAL PROTECTION AGENCY**

United States Court of Appeals, Seventh Circuit, 1993. 999 F.2d 256.

*other subsidiaries to acquire, develop, and market land and residential and commercial properties in other cities, including Minneapolis, Cincinnati, and St. Louis.*

**BACKGROUND AND FACTS**   *Hoffman Homes, Inc., in preparation for the construction of a housing subdivision, filled and graded a 0.8-acre, bowl-shaped depression ("Area A"), which was located on property owned by Hoffman in Hoffman Estates, Illinois. Before Hoffman filled Area A, rainwater periodically collected there. The EPA issued an order stating that Hoffman had filled wetlands without a permit in violation of the Clean Water Act and ordered Hoffman, among other things, to cease its filling activities and pay a fine of $50,000 for violating the act. In response to Hoffman's protests that the EPA had no regulatory authority over Area A because the area in no way affected interstate commerce, the EPA stated that it had authority to regulate discharges of fill materials into intrastate wetlands that have a "minimal, potential effect" on interstate commerce. The EPA found that Area A had such a minimal, potential effect on interstate commerce because migratory birds could potentially use the area. Hoffman appealed the decision to the Seventh Circuit Court of Appeals.*

*HARLINGTON WOOD, Senior Circuit Judge.*
*    *    *    *

Based on our examination of the record, we find the [EPA's] conclusion that Area A was suitable for migratory bird habitat to be unsupported by substantial evidence on the record as a whole. *    *    *

It is true, of course, that migratory birds can alight most anywhere. As [a witness] testified, he has seen mallards in parking lot puddles. The ALJ [administrative law judge of the EPA], however, was in the unique position to view the evidence, to hear the testimony, and to judge the credibility of the witnesses. He concluded that the evidence did not support the conclusion that Area A had characteristics whose use by and value to migratory birds is well established. We agree. The migratory birds are better judges of what is suitable for their welfare than are we [or anyone at the EPA]. Having avoided Area A the migratory birds have thus spoken and submitted their own evidence. We see no need to argue with them. No justification whatsoever is seen from the evidence to interfere with private ownership based on what appears to be no more than a well intentioned effort in these particular factual circumstances to expand government control beyond reasonable or practical limits. After April showers not every temporary wet spot necessarily becomes subject to government control.

**DECISION AND REMEDY**   *The court, holding that Area A was not subject to regulation under the Clean Water Act, vacated the EPA's order requiring Hoffman Homes to pay a $50,000 administrative penalty for the filling of Area A.*

# DRINKING WATER

Another statute governing water pollution is the Safe Drinking Water Act.[12] Passed in 1974, this act requires the EPA to set maximum levels for pollutants in public water systems. Public water supply system operators must come as close as possible to meeting the EPA's standards by using the best available technology that is economically and technologically feasible. The EPA is particu-

---

12.   42 U.S.C. Sections 300f to 300j–25.

larly concerned with contamination from underground sources. Pesticides and wastes leaked from landfills or disposed of in underground injection wells are among the more than two hundred pollutants known to exist in groundwater used for drinking in at least thirty-four states. Many of these substances are associated with cancer and damage to the central nervous system, liver, and kidneys.

## OCEAN DUMPING

The Marine Protection, Research, and Sanctuaries Act of 1972[13] (known popularly as the Ocean Dumping Act), as amended in 1983, regulates the transportation and dumping of material into ocean waters. (The term *material* is synonymous with the term *pollutant* as used in the Federal Water Pollution Control Act.) The Ocean Dumping Act prohibits entirely the ocean dumping of radiological, chemical, and biological warfare agents and high-level radioactive waste. The act establishes a permit program for transporting and dumping other materials. There are specific exemptions—materials subject to the permit provisions of other pollution legislation, wastes from structures regulated by other laws (for example, offshore oil exploration and drilling platforms), sewage, and other wastes. The Ocean Dumping Act also authorizes the designation of marine sanctuaries for "preserving or restoring such areas for their conservation, recreational, ecological, or esthetic values."

Each violation of any provision or permit may result in a civil penalty of not more than $50,000 or revocation or suspension of the permit. A knowing violation is a criminal offense that may result in a $50,000 fine, imprisonment for not more than a year, or both. Acts amounting to violations can also be enjoined.

## OIL POLLUTION

In 1989, the supertanker *Exxon Valdez* caused the worst oil spill in North American history in the waters of Alaska's Prince William Sound. A quarter of a million barrels of crude oil—more than ten million gallons—leaked out of the ship's broken hull. In response to the *Exxon Valdez* oil spill dis-

aster, Congress passed the Oil Pollution Act of 1990.[14] Any onshore or offshore oil facility, oil shipper, vessel owner, or vessel operator that discharges oil into navigable waters or onto an adjoining shore may be liable for clean-up costs, as well as damages. The act created a $1 billion oil clean-up and economic compensation fund and decreed that by the year 2011, oil tankers using U.S. ports must be double hulled to limit the severity of accidental spills.

Under the act, damage to natural resources, private property, and the local economy, including the increased cost of providing public services, is compensable. The act provides for civil penalties of $1,000 per barrel spilled or $25,000 for each day of the violation. The party held responsible for the clean-up costs can bring a civil suit for contribution from other potentially liable parties.

## SECTION 5

# NOISE POLLUTION

Regulations concerning noise pollution include the Noise Control Act of 1972.[15] This act requires the EPA to establish noise emission standards (maximum noise levels below which no harmful effects occur due to interference with speech or other activity). The act directs the EPA to establish standards—for example, for railroad noise emissions. The standards must be achievable by the best available technology, and they must be economically within reason.

The act prohibits, among other things, distributing products manufactured in violation of the noise emission standards and tampering with noise control devices. Either of these activities can result in an injunction or whatever other remedy "is necessary to protect the public health and welfare." Illegal product distribution can also result in a fine and imprisonment. Violations of provisions of the Noise Control Act can result in penalties of not more than $50,000 per day and imprisonment for not more than two years.

---

13.  16 U.S.C. Sections 1401–1445.

14.  33 U.S.C. Sections 2701–2761.

15.  42 U.S.C. Sections 4901–4918.

# EMERGING TRENDS IN BUSINESS LAW

## Expanding CERCLA Liability

We have stated previously in this text that were it not for credit, the business world, as we know it, would cease to exist. The Comprehensive Environmental Response, Compensation, and Liability Act (CERCLA, or Superfund) acknowledged the importance of credit to the business community by exempting banks or other lenders that have made loans to polluters so long as the banks or lenders do not participate in the firms' management.[a]

But how far can a lender go in protecting its interests before it will be considered to be participating in management? And what if a lender forecloses on business property that was used to secure a loan? The lender thereby becomes an "owner" of polluted premises. Does its ownership of those premises subject it to liability under CERCLA as an "owner"—one of the potentially responsible parties (PRPs) under the act? How the courts answer these questions has significant policy implications for lenders and borrowers alike.

### Landmark Cases in Lender Liability under CERCLA

In a 1986 landmark case, the Maryland Bank and Trust Company had foreclosed on real estate in which it held a security interest and then purchased the property at the foreclosure sale.
Approximately a year later, the EPA discovered hazardous waste on the site. The EPA sued the bank for the clean-up costs, which exceeded the value of the loan. The court held that the bank was responsible. The court reasoned that whenever a lender qualifies as an owner or operator of a polluted site, the lender can also be deemed responsible.[b]

The scope of lender liability was greatly expanded in *United States v. Fleet Factors Corp.*[c] In *Fleet Factors,* the court held that the lender's mere "capacity to influence the waste disposal decisions" of the polluting firm and

participation in the firm's management might establish lender liability for clean-up costs. Actual decision making or action on the part of the lender was not necessary to establish liability.

### The EPA's Response

In 1992, the EPA responded to the uncertainty in the lending community following the *Fleet Factors* case and other decisions by promulgating a rule that reinforced the lender exemption.[d] Under the 1992 EPA rule, which applied only to owners or operators of hazardous waste sites, a lender was exempted from liability under CERCLA unless the lender participated in the day-to-day operations or environmental activities of the firm or directed the firm's hazardous waste handling or disposal practices. A lender would not be liable if it simply monitored a borrower's business, provided financial advice, or restructured the terms of the loan. Even the temporary acquisition (for a year or less) of a hazardous waste site through foreclosure would not generally result in lender liability.

---

a. 42 U.S.C. Section 9601(20)(A).

b. *United States v. Maryland Bank and Trust Co.*, 632 F.Supp. 573 (D.Md. 1986).
c. 901 F.2d 1550 (11th Cir. 1990); *cert.* denied, 498 U.S. 1046, 111 S.Ct. 752, 112 L.Ed.2d 772 (1990).

d. 40 C.F.R. Section 1100.

## Subsequent Court Decisions

In 1993, two federal circuit courts of appeals, without relying on the EPA rule, also concluded that lenders who acquired ownership of property by foreclosure were exempt from liability under CERCLA. In both cases, the lenders did not attempt to manage the property, acted solely to protect their security interests, and acted reasonably and seasonably to divest their ownership interests.[e]

In 1994, the EPA rule was vacated by the U.S. Court of Appeals for the District of Columbia Circuit in *Kelley v. EPA.*[f] The court held that the EPA had exceeded its authority by determining the scope of lender liability under CERCLA. The court stated that Congress did not intend the EPA, itself "one of many potential plaintiffs," to "have authority to, by regulation, define liability for a class of potential defendants." According to the court, "Congress, by providing for private rights of action, . . . has designated the courts and not [the] EPA as the adjudicator of the scope of CERCLA liability."

## Looking Ahead

In 1994, the Clinton administration was revisiting the issue of Superfund requirements. By the time you

---

e. See *United States v. McLamb,* 5 F.3d 69 (4th Cir. 1993), and *Waterville Industries, Inc. v. Finance Authority of Maine,* 984 F.2d 549 (1st Cir. 1993).

f. 15 F.3d 1100 (D.C. Cir. 1994).

read this book, Congress may have enacted amendments to CERCLA that, among other things, explicitly address the issue of lender and trustee liability. The proposed bill specifically states that the term "owner or operator" does not include persons who hold title to a site solely as a trustee, custodian, or fiduciary as required by law. Such persons may be held liable only if they are affiliated with liable parties, contribute to the release (or threatened release), or fail to comply with EPA requirements.

## ■ Implications for the Businessperson

1.  The implications for businesspersons of the 1994 interpretation and application of lender liability under CERCLA are clear. Lenders will be more reluctant to make secured loans to business firms if there is even a remote possibility that the real property securing the loans may be contaminated—or will be contaminated by the businesses to whom the loans are made.

2.  The implications for businesspersons who want to obtain financing are equally clear. They may face higher interest rates to justify the greater risks assumed by lenders or greater expenses in investigating the previous use of the property.

3.  Lenders will also be more reluctant to foreclose on property—out of fear of CERCLA liability if they become owners and because they might not be able to sell the property as readily.

## ■ For Critical Analysis

1.  Many persons have claimed that the expansive interpretation of lender liability under CERCLA effectively discriminates against inner-city improvements. This discrimination occurs because many factories and businesses in those areas existed prior to the regulation of toxic waste disposal, and therefore those properties are more likely than others to be contaminated. Do you think that such discrimination is fair, especially in view of the policy of encouraging inner-city improvements? Do you see any way to resolve this problem?

2.  In your opinion, should lenders and borrowers be permitted to include provisions in their loan contracts designating which of the parties will be liable for any toxic-waste clean-up operations that may be necessary?

3.  It has been estimated that for every dollar spent cleaning up toxic sites, administrative agencies spend seven dollars in overhead. Can you think of any way to trim the administrative costs associated with the clean-up of contaminated sites?

# TOXIC CHEMICALS

Originally, most environmental clean-up efforts were directed toward reducing smog and making water safe for fishing and swimming. Over time, however, control of toxic chemicals has become an important part of environmental law.

## PESTICIDES AND HERBICIDES

The first toxic chemical problem to receive widespread public attention was that posed by pesticides and herbicides. Using these chemicals to kill insects and weeds has increased agricultural productivity, but their residue remains in the environment. In some instances, accumulations of this residue have killed animals, and scientists have identified potential long-term effects that are detrimental to people.

The federal statute regulating pesticides and herbicides is the Federal Insecticide, Fungicide, and Rodenticide Act (FIFRA) of 1947.[16] Under FIFRA, pesticides and herbicides must be (1) registered before they can be sold, (2) certified and used only for approved applications, and (3) used in limited quantities when applied to food crops. If a substance is identified as harmful, the EPA can cancel its registration after a hearing. If the harm is imminent, the EPA can suspend registration pending the hearing. The EPA, or state officers or employees, may also inspect factories in which these chemicals are manufactured.

It is a violation of FIFRA to sell a pesticide or herbicide that is unregistered, a pesticide or herbicide with a registration that has been canceled or suspended, or a pesticide or herbicide with a false or misleading label. For example, it is an offense to sell a substance that is adulterated (that has a chemical strength different than the concentration declared on the label). It is also an offense to destroy or deface any labeling required under the act. The act's labeling requirements include directions for the use of the pesticide or herbicide, warnings to protect human health and the environment, a statement of treatment in the case of poisoning, and a list of the ingredients.

A private party can petition the EPA to suspend or cancel the registration of a pesticide or herbicide.

If the EPA fails to act, the private party can petition a federal court to review the EPA's failure. Penalties for registrants and producers for violating FIFRA include imprisonment for up to one year and a fine of no more than $50,000. Penalties for commercial dealers include imprisonment for up to one year and a fine of no more than $25,000. Farmers and other private users of pesticides or herbicides who violate the act are subject to a $1,000 fine and imprisonment for up to thirty days.

## TOXIC SUBSTANCES

The first comprehensive law covering toxic substances was the Toxic Substances Control Act of 1976.[17] The act was passed to regulate chemicals and chemical compounds that are known to be toxic—such as asbestos and polychlorinated biphenyls, popularly known as PCBs—and to institute investigation of any possible harmful effects from new chemical compounds. The regulations authorize the EPA to require that manufacturers, processors, and other organizations planning to use chemicals first determine their effects on human health and the environment. The EPA can regulate substances that potentially pose an imminent hazard or an unreasonable risk of injury to health or the environment. The EPA may require special labeling, limit the use of a substance, set production quotas, or prohibit the use of a substance altogether.

## HAZARDOUS WASTES

Some industrial, agricultural, and household wastes pose more serious threats than others. If not properly disposed of, these toxic chemicals may present a substantial danger to human health and the environment. If released into the environment, they may contaminate public drinking water resources.

**RESOURCE CONSERVATION AND RECOVERY ACT** In 1976, Congress passed the Resource Conservation and Recovery Act (RCRA)[18] in reaction to an ever-increasing concern with the effects of hazardous waste materials on the environment. The RCRA required the EPA to establish regulations to monitor and control hazardous waste disposal and to determine which

---

16. 7 U.S.C. Sections 135–136y.

17. 15 U.S.C. Sections 2601–2692.
18. 42 U.S.C. Sections 6901–6986.

forms of solid waste should be considered hazardous and thus subject to regulation. The act authorized the EPA to promulgate various technical requirements for limited types of facilities for storage and treatment of hazardous waste. The act also requires all producers of hazardous waste materials to label and package properly any hazardous waste to be transported.

The RCRA was amended in 1984 and 1986 to decrease the use of land containment in the disposal of hazardous waste and to require compliance with the act by some generators of hazardous waste—such as those generating less than 1,000 kilograms (2,200 pounds) a month—that had previously been excluded from regulation under the RCRA.

Under the RCRA, a company may be assessed a civil penalty based on the seriousness of the violation, the probability of harm, and the extent to which the violation deviates from RCRA requirements. The assessment may be up to $25,000 for each violation.[19] Criminal penalties include fines up to $50,000 for each day of violation, imprisonment for up to two years (in most instances), or both.[20] Criminal fines and the time of imprisonment can be doubled for certain repeat offenders.

**SUPERFUND** In 1980, Congress passed the Comprehensive Environmental Response, Compensation, and Liability Act (CERCLA),[21] commonly known as Superfund. The basic purpose of Superfund, which was amended in 1986 by the Superfund Amendments and Reauthorization Act, is to regulate the clean-up of leaking hazardous waste disposal sites. A special federal fund was created for that purpose.

Superfund provides that when a release or a threatened release of hazardous chemicals from a site occurs, the EPA can clean up the site and recover the cost of the clean-up from the following persons: (1) the person who generated the wastes disposed of at the site, (2) the person who transported the wastes to the site, (3) the person who owned or operated the site at the time of the disposal, or (4) the current owner or operator. A person falling within one of these categories is referred to as a **potentially responsible party (PRP).** We discuss below the liability that PRPs face under Superfund.

*Liability under Superfund.* Liability under Superfund is usually joint and several—that is, a person who generated only a fraction of the hazardous waste disposed of at the site may nevertheless be liable for all of the clean-up costs. CERCLA authorizes a party who has incurred clean-up costs to bring a "contribution action" against any other person who is liable or potentially liable for a percentage of the costs.

Courts often focus on the meaning of the words "owner or operator" to determine who is a PRP. A parent company has been held liable as an "operator" for clean-up costs for a chemical spill at a plant owned by its subsidiary. The court pointed out that the parent company controlled the subsidiary's finances, real estate transactions, and contact with the government and that the parent company's personnel held most of the subsidiary's officer and director positions.[22] In other cases, courts have held officers and shareholders liable based on their authority to exercise control over their corporations.[23] In the following case, the court considers whether a successor corporation (see Chapter 43) can be held liable under CERCLA.

---

19. 42 U.S.C. Section 6929(g).
20. 42 U.S.C. Section 6929(d).
21. 42 U.S.C. Sections 9601–9675.

22. *United States v. Kayser-Roth Corp.,* 910 F.2d 24 (1st Cir. 1990).
23. See, for example, *State of New York v. Shore Realty Corp.,* 759 F.2d 1032 (2d Cir. 1985).

---

**BACKGROUND AND FACTS** *The Anspec Company purchased a parcel of land from Ultraspherics, Inc., in 1978. After the sale, Ultraspherics merged into the Hoover Group, which was designated as the surviving corporation. Johnson Controls, Inc., was the sole shareholder of the Hoover Group and of Hoover Universal, which was the sole shareholder of Ultraspherics. Prior to the sale of the property to Anspec, Ultraspherics had placed three tanks on the property—one underground and two above the ground—which were used to store hazardous waste materials. Leaks*

CASE 47.3

ANSPEC CO. v. JOHNSON CONTROLS, INC.

United States Court of Appeals, Sixth Circuit, 1991. 922 F.2d 1240.

*and spills of the hazardous waste contaminated the soil at the site and the groundwater beneath the site. Anspec requested the Hoover Group, as the corporate successor of Ultraspherics, to pay the costs associated with cleaning up the site. When the Hoover Group refused to comply, Anspec brought this action against Ultraspherics and its corporate successors. The trial court held that Ultraspherics could not be liable, because it no longer existed. The other defendants—the Hoover Group, Hoover Universal, and Johnson Controls—moved for dismissal. On the grounds that none of them had ever owned, occupied, or stored chemicals on the property and that the Comprehensive Environmental Response, Compensation, and Liability Act (CERCLA) did not provide that successor corporations were liable for clean-up costs, the trial court granted the motion for dismissal, and Anspec appealed.*

LIVELY, Senior Circuit Judge.

\* \* \* \*

\* \* \* In this dispute between private parties, CERCLA is concerned only that the persons listed in [Section] 9607(a) be responsible for cleanup costs. Since successor corporations are not so listed, the defendants argue, the district court correctly dismissed Hoover Group, Hoover Universal and Johnson Controls.

With respect to Ultraspherics, the plaintiffs contend that this defendant comes within the clear statutory designation of a person potentially liable; that [Section] 9607(a)(2) makes liable for cleanup costs ''any person who at the time of disposal of any hazardous substance owned or operated any facility at which such hazardous substances were disposed of[.]'' \* \* \* Moreover, Michigan [corporate law] provides that although the separate existence of every corporation except the surviving corporation in a merger ceases, the surviving corporation has all liabilities of every corporation that was a party to the merger. For purposes of liability, the surviving corporation and the merged corporation are one and the same. If Ultraspherics is not liable for cleanup costs, it is only because Hoover Group stands in its shoes as the surviving party that became liable for its obligations. \* \* \*

\* \* \* \*

\* \* \* [C]onstruing the statute [CERCLA] in light of a universally accepted principle of private corporation law, we conclude that Congress included successor corporations within the description of entities that are potentially liable under CERCLA for cleanup costs. That is to say, when Congress wrote ''corporation'' in CERCLA it intended to include a successor corporation.

**DECISION AND REMEDY** *The appellate court reversed the trial court's judgment and remanded the case for further proceedings consistent with this opinion. The district court was instructed to follow Michigan law in its application of successor liability.*

---

*Trustee Liability.* There is no exemption from CERCLA liability for trustees who manage property held in trust. As will be discussed in Chapter 51, a trust is a legal arrangement in which property is held by one party (the trustee) for the benefit of another party (the beneficiary). Title to property held in trust is ordinarily placed in the name of the trustee. If a trustee becomes the recorded owner of a contaminated site, the trustee is an ''owner'' for purposes of Superfund liability, but liability ensues only upon the trustee's administration of the trust property. As a result, a trustee may be liable for the clean-up costs on the trust property—as illustrated by the following case.

**BACKGROUND AND FACTS** *Wilbur Estes owned a landfill on the south bank of the Salt River in Phoenix, Arizona. He was also the sole shareholder and president of the Garbage Services Company (GSC), which managed the landfill. Estes sold the property but retained an option to repurchase it. The new owners of the site leased the property to GSC. When Estes died in 1965, the Valley National Bank (VNB) became trustee under Estes's will. Ownership of the stock in GSC and the option to purchase the landfill was transferred to VNB. VNB exercised the repurchase option and purchased the landfill, and it continued to lease the landfill to GSC. VNB's involvement in the operation of the landfill was limited. VNB procured liability insurance and paid the property taxes but left the day-to-day operations of the landfill entirely to GSC. The landfill closed in 1972, and in 1980 the city of Phoenix condemned the property as contaminated. By 1989, the city had incurred substantial hazardous waste clean-up costs at the site. The city filed an action to recover its costs from the Estes estate and from VNB as trustee. VNB filed a motion for summary judgment, arguing that, as a matter of law, it could not be held liable for clean-up costs that exceeded the assets in the Estes trust.*

| CASE 47.4 |
| --- |
| **PHOENIX v. GARBAGE SERVICES CO.** |
| United States District Court, District of Arizona, 1993. |
| 816 F.Supp. 564. |

*CONTI*, District Judge.

\* \* \* \*

\* \* \* [CERCLA] imposes liability on current or past owners, provided that they owned the site at the time of disposal of the hazardous substances. In enacting CERCLA, the legislature in effect codified the common law rule of strict liability for ultrahazardous activities, and classified the disposal of hazardous substances as an ultrahazardous activity. Thus, when a property owner allows his property to be used for the disposal of hazardous substances, [CERCLA] imposes strict liability for any damages due to a release or threatened release of the hazardous substances into the environment. Liability under this subsection is not based on mere ownership of property, but on the property owner's decision to allow his property to be used for an ultrahazardous activity. The rationale \* \* \* is that the owner has both the power and the responsibility to control the use of his property.

\* \* \* \*

\* \* \* [I]f a trustee has control over trust property, and knowingly allows it to be used for the disposal of hazardous substances, then it is the trustee who is responsible for the decision to use the property for an ultrahazardous activity. The trustee is not liable merely because he held title to the property, but because it was in his power to control the use of the property, and he opted to use it for the disposal of hazardous substances. Although the trustee's status as the holder of legal title is the vehicle by which [CERCLA] imposes liability, there would not be any liability but for the trustee's decision. This liability, therefore, is incurred in the course of administration of the trust, and the trustee is personally liable regardless of the trust's ability to indemnify [compensate] him.

**DECISION AND REMEDY** *The court held in favor of the city of Phoenix and denied VNB's motion for partial summary judgment. VNB could be held personally liable for the costs incurred in cleaning up the site.*

**INTERNATIONAL CONSIDERATIONS** **Liability for Hazardous Waste Disposal in the European Union** *The "European Directive on Civil Liability for Damage Caused by Waste"* *follows CERCLA in several respects, including its imposition of strict liability for environmental harms. The directive differs from CERCLA, however, in limiting liability to the person or persons in possession of the waste at the time that any harm results. Companies in Europe can generally avoid liability by arranging for waste disposal at a licensed facility.*

## SECTION 7

# RADIATION

At the beginning of its development, nuclear energy was regarded as a cleaner and less expensive alternative to fossil fuels (coal and oil). During the production of nuclear energy, however, plutonium, uranium, and other radioactive materials emit dangerous levels of radiation. Radiation at these levels is believed to cause cancer and other diseases. The waste produced by a nuclear power plant remains radioactive for thousands of years. Despite continuing research, a method for permanent disposal of nuclear waste has not been developed.

Nuclear power plants are built and operated by private industry. The private nuclear industry is regulated almost exclusively by the federal government under the Atomic Energy Act of 1954.[24] The Nuclear Regulatory Commission (NRC) is the federal agency responsible for regulating the private nuclear industry. The NRC reviews the plans for each proposed nuclear plant and issues a construction permit only after preparing an environmental impact statement that considers the impact of an accidental release of radiation. After construction, the NRC licenses the plant's operation.

The Environmental Protection Agency sets standards for radioactivity in the overall environment and for the disposal of some radioactive waste. Low-level radioactive waste generated by private facilities is the responsibility of each state under the Low Level Radioactive Waste Policy Act of 1980.[25] The NRC regulates the use and disposal of other nuclear materials and radioactive waste. Some radioactive waste is buried, burned, or dumped in the ocean. Currently, however, most of it is stored at the plants in which it is produced. Under the Nuclear Waste Policy Act of 1982,[26] the

government is looking for a permanent disposal site scheduled to be opened in the year 2000.

Liability may be predicated on some of the same grounds discussed in other sections of this chapter. A common law theory may serve as the basis for liability for harms caused by radiation. For example, Safety Light Corporation was held liable under a strict liability theory for the acts of its predecessor company, the United States Radium Company (USRC). USRC had extracted radium from uranium ore and deposited radioactive residue from the process on vacant portions of its property in New Jersey between 1917 and 1926. T&E Industries, Inc., bought the property in 1974. In 1979, the state advised T&E that radiation levels on the property were excessive. In T&E's suit against Safety Light, the court held that the party creating a radiation hazard is strictly responsible for its clean-up and any damages.[27]

Liability for injury resulting from radiation may also arise under one of the statutes discussed elsewhere in this chapter. In 1986, the state of Ohio sued the Department of Energy and private contractors who had operated a nuclear weapons facility at Fernald, Ohio, alleging, among other things, that they improperly released radioactive materials into the environment in violation of the Clean Water Act, the RCRA, and CERCLA. In 1988, energy officials admitted that an operator of the facility had been ordered to continue dumping radioactive material at the site over a period of years. Federal officials agreed to pay Ohio more than $1 million to settle two suits and agreed to allow the state to oversee the clean-up of the site. In 1990, a federal appeals court ordered the Department of Energy to pay $250,000 in civil penalties to Ohio.[28]

---

24.   42 U.S.C. Sections 2011 to 2297g–4.
25.   42 U.S.C. Sections 2021b–2021j.
26.   42 U.S.C. Sections 10101–10270.

27.   *T&E Industries, Inc. v. Safety Light Corp.,* 123 N.J. 371, 587 A.2d 1249 (1991).
28.   *Ohio v. Department of Energy,* 904 F.2d 1058 (6th Cir. 1990).

# STATE AND LOCAL REGULATION

Many states regulate the degree to which the environment may be polluted. Thus, for example, even when state zoning laws permit a business's proposed development, the proposal may have to be altered to change the development's impact on the environment. State laws may restrict a business's discharge of chemicals into the air or water, or regulate its disposal of toxic wastes. States may also regulate the disposal or recycling of other wastes, including glass, metal, and plastic containers and paper. Additionally, states may restrict the emissions from motor vehicles.

City, county, and other local governments control some aspects of the environment. For instance, local zoning laws control some land use. These laws may be designed to inhibit or direct the growth of cities and suburbs or to protect the natural environment. Other aspects of the environment may be subject to local regulation for other reasons. Methods of waste and garbage removal and disposal, for example, can have a substantial impact on a community. The appearance of buildings and other structures, including advertising signs and billboards, may affect traffic safety, property values, or local aesthetics. Noise generated by a business or its customers may be annoying, disruptive, or damaging to its neighbors. The location and condition of parks, streets, and other public uses of land subject to local control affect the environment and can also affect business.

---

## TERMS AND CONCEPTS TO REVIEW

environmental impact
   statement (EIS)  **928**
environmental law  **925**

nuisance  **925**
potentially responsible party
   (PRP)  **937**

toxic tort  **926**
wetland  **931**

---

# QUESTIONS AND CASE PROBLEMS

**47–1. Clean Air Act.** The Environmental Protection Agency (EPA) has set ambient standards for several pollutants, including sulfur dioxide, specifying the maximum concentration allowable in the outdoor air. One way to meet these standards is to reduce emissions. Companies discovered, however, that they could also meet the standards at less cost by building very high smokestacks. When emitted from such high stacks, pollutants were more widely dispersed and remained below the concentration level specified by the ambient standards. Environmental groups claimed that the Clean Air Act was designed to reduce pollution, not to disperse it, and argued that industry should not be allowed to rely on tall stacks. Are the environmental groups correct, or should industry be allowed to use the less expensive dispersal method? Discuss.

**47–2. Clean Air Act.** Some scientific knowledge indicates that there is no safe level of exposure to a cancer-causing agent. In theory, even one molecule of such a substance has the potential for causing cancer. Section 112 of the Clean Air Act requires that all cancer-causing substances be regulated to ensure a margin of safety.

Some environmental groups have argued that all emissions of such substances must be eliminated in order for such a margin of safety to be reached. Such a total elimination would likely shut down many major U.S. industries. Should the Environmental Protection Agency totally eliminate all emissions of cancer-causing chemicals? Discuss.

**47–3. Environmental Laws.** Moonbay is a real estate development corporation that primarily develops retirement communities. Farmtex owns a number of feedlots in Sunny Valley. Moonbay purchased twenty thousand acres of farmland in the same area and began building and selling retirement homes on this acreage. In the meantime, Farmtex continued to expand its feedlot business, and eventually only five hundred feet separated the two operations. Because of the odor and flies from the feedlots, Moonbay found it difficult to sell the homes in its development. Moonbay wants to enjoin Farmtex from operating its feedlots in the vicinity of the retirement home development. Discuss under what theory Moonbay would file this action. Discuss fully whether Farmtex has violated any federal environmental laws.

**47–4. Environmental Laws.** Fruitade, Inc., is a processor of a soft drink called Freshen Up. Fruitade uses returnable bottles, as well as a special acid to clean its bottles for further beverage processing. The acid is diluted by water and then allowed to pass into a navigable stream. Fruitade crushes its broken bottles and throws the crushed glass into the stream. Discuss fully any environmental laws that Fruitade has violated.

**47–5. Superfund.** Asarco, Inc., had a copper smelter at Ruston, Washington. As part of its operations, Asarco produced a by-product called "slag," a hard, rocklike substance. Industrial Mineral Products (IMP) sold the slag for Asarco to Louisiana-Pacific Corp. and other businesses, which used the slag as a ballast to stabilize the ground at log-sorting yards in the Tacoma, Washington, area. About nine months after IMP stopped selling the slag, it sold substantially all of its assets to L-Bar Products, Inc. Government agencies later discovered that the slag reacted with the acidic wood waste in the log-sorting yards, causing heavy metals from the slag to leach into the groundwater and soil. Louisiana-Pacific and the Port of Tacoma sued Asarco under the Comprehensive Environmental Response, Compensation, and Liability Act (CERCLA), claiming that Asarco was liable for clean-up costs. Asarco brought a third party claim against L-Bar as corporate successor to IMP. L-Bar moved for summary judgment, claiming that it was not the successor to IMP and could not be liable under CERCLA for IMP's actions. Will the court agree with L-Bar? Discuss fully. [*Louisiana-Pacific Corp. v. Asarco, Inc.,* 909 F.2d 1260 (9th Cir. 1990)]

**47–6. Pesticide Regulation.** The Environmental Protection Agency (EPA) canceled the registration of the pesticide Diazinon for use on golf courses and sod farms because of concern about the effects of Diazinon on birds. The Federal Insecticide, Fungicide, and Rodenticide Act authorizes cancellation of the registration of products that "generally cause unreasonable adverse effects on the environment." The statute further defines "unreasonable adverse effects on the environment" to mean "any unreasonable risk to man or the environment, taking into account the . . . costs and benefits." Thus, in determining whether a pesticide should continue to be used, one must balance the risks and benefits of the use of the pesticide. Does this mean that one must find that the pesticide killed birds more often than not before its use can be prohibited? Or to prohibit the pesticide's use, is it sufficient to find only that the use of the pesticide results in recurrent bird kills? [*CIBA-Geigy Corp. v. Environmental Protection Agency,* 874 F.2d 277 (5th Cir. 1989)]

**47–7. Common Law Nuisance.** Taylor Bay Protective Association is a nonprofit corporation established for the purpose of restoring and improving the water quality of Taylor Bay. Local water districts began operating a flood control project in the area. As part of the project, a pumping station was developed. Testimony at trial revealed that the pumps were operated contrary to the instructions provided in the operation and maintenance manual. The pumps acted as vacuums, sucking up increased amounts of silt and depositing the silt in Taylor Bay. Thus, the project resulted in sedimentation and turbidity problems in the downstream watercourse of Taylor Bay. The association sued the local water districts, alleging that the pumping operations created a nuisance. Do the pumping operations qualify as a common law nuisance? Who should be responsible for the clean-up costs? Discuss both questions fully. [*Taylor Bay Protective Association v. Environmental Protection Agency,* 884 F.2d 1073 (8th Cir. 1989)]

**47–8. Water Pollution.** The Environmental Protection Agency (EPA) promulgated water-pollution discharge limits for several mining industries. These standards authorized variances exempting mining operations from coverage by the standards if the operations could show that they used special processes or facilities that made the standards inapplicable. Cost was not a consideration in granting the variances. An industry trade association sued, claiming that the EPA should consider costs in granting variances, and the Fourth Circuit Court of Appeals agreed. Discuss whether the United States Supreme Court should overturn this decision or affirm it and let costs be considered in the granting of variances under the Clean Water Act. [*Environmental Protection Agency v. National Crushed Stone Association,* 449 U.S. 64, 101 S.Ct. 295, 66 L.Ed.2d 268 (1980)]

**47–9. Superfund.** In the 1970s, South Carolina Recycling and Disposal, Inc. (SCRDI), ran a hazardous waste disposal and recycling operation. A number of chemical companies (so-called generators) brought their wastes to the SCRDI facility. Handling of wastes at the site was itself hazardous; 7,200 fifty-five-gallon drums of hazardous substances—including materials that were toxic, carcinogenic, mutagenic, explosive, and highly flammable—accumulated. Stacked without regard to the source or the compatibility of the substances within, many drums deteriorated to the point that their contents spilled onto other drums, mixed with other leaking substances, and oozed into the ground. This caused noxious and toxic fumes and a number of fires and explosions. The Environmental Protection Agency (EPA) began clean-up operations and sued some of the generators (plus others) for the costs. Should the EPA be required to show that a certain generator's waste was a cause of the environmental harm? Should a generator be responsible for the costs of cleaning up only its contribution? Discuss fully. [*United States v. South Carolina Recycling and Disposal, Inc.,* 653 F.Supp. 984 (D.S.C. 1986)]

**47–10. Hazardous Waste.** The Resource Conservation and Recovery Act gives the Environmental Protection Agency (EPA) authority to require a company to clean up a hazardous waste site that presents an "imminent and substantial endangerment" to public health or to the environment. A company disposed of dioxin by discharging it into a pond located on its property. The EPA ordered that the company stop the disposal and clean up the site. The company argued that the EPA had no evidence of any actual harm to the health of nearby residents. Should the company be compelled to clean up the dioxin even in the absence of evidence of actual harm? Discuss. [*United States v. Vertac Chemical Corp.,* 489 F.Supp. 870 (E.D.Ark. 1980)]

**47–11. Common Law Nuisance.** In 1987, John and Jean Zarlenga purchased a new home in Bloomingdale, Illinois. Bloomingdale Partners (BP) then built an eight-story apartment complex across the street from the Zarlenga home. Each of the 168 apartments had an air conditioner weighing about nine hundred pounds. Over sixty air conditioners were on the side of the complex that faced the Zarlenga home. The Zarlengas testified that the noise from these air conditioners during the summer was a ''loud rumbling sound'' that was ''continuous and monotonous.'' The machines disrupted their sleep. Jean Zarlenga suffered from headaches and irritability. In her testimony, she stated, ''It's made my life miserable. I cannot use my deck. I cannot have company over . . . I can't open my windows in my bedroom. I toss and turn all night.'' The Zarlengas sued BP for creating a nuisance, claiming that the apartment complex substantially interfered with the use and enjoyment of their home. The Zarlengas sought damages from BP for the devaluation of their home due to the noise and for their suffering. How should the court decide this case? Discuss fully. [*In re Bloomingdale Partners,* 160 Bankr. 101 (N.D.Ill. 1993)]

# CHAPTER 48

# ANTITRUST LAW

**T**oday's antitrust laws are the direct descendants of common law actions intended to limit **restraints on trade** (agreements between firms that have the effect of reducing competition in the marketplace). Concern over monopolistic practices arose following the Civil War with the growth of large corporate enterprises and their attempts to reduce or eliminate competition. They did this by legally tying themselves together in a **trust,** which is a legal entity in which a trustee holds title to property for the benefit of another. The participants in the most famous trust—the Standard Oil trust in the late 1800s—transferred their stock to a trustee and received trust certificates in exchange. The trustee then made decisions fixing prices, controlling production, and determining the control of exclusive geographical markets for all of the oil companies that were in the Standard Oil trust. It became apparent that the trust wielded such economic power that corporations outside the trust could not compete effectively.

Many states attempted to control such monopolistic behavior by enacting statutes outlawing the use of trusts. That is why all of the laws that regulate economic competition today are referred to as **antitrust laws.** At the national level, the government recognized the problem in 1887 and passed the Interstate Commerce Act, followed by the Sherman Antitrust Act in 1890. In 1914, Congress passed the Clayton Act and the Federal Trade Commission Act to further curb anticompetitive or unfair business practices. Since their passage, the 1914 acts have been amended by Congress to broaden and strengthen their coverage.

This chapter examines these major antitrust statutes, focusing particularly on the Sherman Act and the Clayton Act, as amended, and the types of activities prohibited by those acts. Remember in reading this chapter that the basis of antitrust legislation is the desire to foster competition. Antitrust legislation was initially created—and continues to be enforced—because of our belief that competition leads to lower prices, more product information, and a better distribution of wealth between consumers and producers.

# THE SHERMAN ANTITRUST ACT

The author of the Sherman Antitrust Act of 1890, Senator John Sherman, brother of the famed Civil War general and a recognized financial authority, had been concerned for years with the diminishing competition within American industry. He told Congress that the Sherman Act "does not announce a new principle of law, but applies old and well-recognized principles of the common law."[1]

The common law regarding trade regulation was not always consistent. Certainly it was not very familiar to the legislators of the Fifty-first Congress of the United States in 1890. The public concern over large business integrations and trusts was familiar, however, and in 1890 Congress passed "An Act to Protect Trade and Commerce against Unlawful Restraints and Monopolies"—commonly known as the Sherman Antitrust Act, or more simply, the Sherman Act.

## MAJOR PROVISIONS OF THE SHERMAN ACT

Sections 1 and 2 contain the main provisions of the Sherman Act.

1: Every contract, combination in the form of trust or otherwise, or conspiracy, in restraint of trade or commerce among the several States, or with foreign nations, is hereby declared to be illegal [and is a felony punishable by fine and/or imprisonment].

2: Every person who shall monopolize, or attempt to monopolize, or combine or conspire with any other person or persons, to monopolize any part of the trade or commerce among the several States, or with foreign nations, shall be deemed guilty of a felony [and is similarly punishable].

These two sections of the Sherman Act are quite different. Section 1 requires two or more persons, as a person cannot contract, combine, or conspire alone. Thus, the essence of the illegal activity is *the act of joining together*. Section 2 applies both to an individual person and to several people, because it refers to "[e]very person." Thus, unilateral conduct can result in a violation of Section 2.

The cases brought to the courts under Section 1 of the Sherman Act differ from those brought under Section 2. Section 1 cases are often concerned with finding an agreement (written or oral) that leads to a restraint of trade. Section 2 cases deal with the structure of a **monopoly** that exists in the marketplace. The term *monopoly* is generally used to describe a market in which there is a single seller. Whereas Section 1 focuses on agreements that are restrictive—that is, agreements that have a wrongful purpose—Section 2 looks at the so-called misuse of **monopoly power** in the marketplace. Monopoly power exists when a firm has an extreme amount of **market power**—the power to affect the market price of its product. Both Section 1 and Section 2 seek to curtail market industrial practices that result in undesired monopoly pricing and output behavior. Any case brought under Section 2, however, must be one in which the "threshold" or "necessary" amount of monopoly power already exists. We will return to a discussion of these two sections of the Sherman Act after we look at the act's jurisdictional requirements.

## JURISDICTIONAL REQUIREMENTS

The Sherman Act applies only to restraints that have a significant impact on commerce. Because Congress can regulate only interstate commerce, in principle only interstate commerce is affected by this act.[2] The Sherman Act also extends to U.S. nationals abroad who are engaged in activities that have an effect on U.S. foreign commerce. The extraterritorial application of U.S. antitrust laws is discussed in Chapter 56. State regulation of anticompetitive practices addresses purely local restraints on competition. Courts have generally held that any activity that substantially affects interstate commerce falls within the ambit of the Sherman Act. As discussed in Chapter 5, courts have construed the meaning of *interstate commerce* more and more broadly, bringing even local activities within the regulatory power of the national government. Whether a seemingly local activity touched sufficiently on interstate commerce to come under the purview of the Sherman Act is at issue in the following case.

---

1.   21 Congressional Record 2456 (1890).

2.   See the discussion of the commerce clause in Chapter 5.

## CASE 48.1

### SUMMIT HEALTH, LTD. v. PINHAS

Supreme Court of the
United States, 1991.
500 U.S. 322,
111 S.Ct. 1842,
114 L.Ed.2d 366.

**HISTORICAL AND POLITICAL SETTING** *The record of the congressional debates on the Sherman Act reveals, in Senator John Sherman's words, an intent to ''g[o] as far as the Constitution permits Congress to go.''[a] Congress intended to deal comprehensively and effectively with ''the evils resulting from contracts, combinations and conspiracies in restraint of trade, and to that end to exercise all the power it possessed.''[b] Since the passage of the Sherman Act more than a century ago, the U.S. economy has grown, and the federal power over commerce has experienced similar expansion. The United States Supreme Court has long allowed the reach of the Sherman Act to expand with the expanding notions of congressional power. In the words of the Court, ''[t]he Act is comprehensive in its terms and coverage, protecting all who are made victims of the forbidden practices by whomever they may be perpetrated.''[c]*

**BACKGROUND AND FACTS** *Dr. Simon Pinhas was an ophthalmologist on the staff of Midway Hospital Medical Center (a subsidiary of Summit Health, Ltd.) in Los Angeles. Prior to 1986, most eye surgeries in Los Angeles were performed by a primary surgeon with the assistance of a second surgeon. In February 1986, the administrators of the Medicare program announced that they would no longer reimburse physicians for the services of assistants, and most hospitals in the Los Angeles area abolished the assistant-surgeon requirement. Midway refused to do so. For Pinhas, who performed numerous surgeries at Midway, this meant that it would cost him $60,000 a year to pay for assistant surgeons that he did not need. He told Midway that if the assistant-surgeon requirement was not eliminated, he would leave. In response, the medical staff initiated peer-review proceedings against Pinhas, terminated his staff privileges, and began preparing an adverse report about Pinhas to distribute to all hospitals in the area. Pinhas filed a complaint alleging that the Midway medical staff had violated the Sherman Act by entering into a conspiracy to drive him out of business so that other ophthalmologists would obtain a greater share of the market for ophthalmologic services in Los Angeles. The trial court dismissed his complaint on the ground that interstate commerce was not affected by Pinhas's removal from the Midway medical staff, and therefore the Sherman Act did not apply. Pinhas appealed, and ultimately the case was reviewed by the United States Supreme Court.*

Justice *STEVENS* delivered the opinion of the Court.

\* \* \* \*

\* \* \* [T]his case involves the provision of ophthalmological services. It seems clear \* \* \* that these services are regularly performed for out-of-state patients and generate revenues from out-of-state sources; their importance as part of the entire operation of the hospital is evident from the allegations of the complaint. A conspiracy to eliminate the entire ophthalmological department of the hospital, like a conspiracy to destroy the hospital itself, would unquestionably affect interstate commerce.

a. 20 Congressional Record 1167 (1889).

b. *Atlantic Cleaners & Dyers, Inc. v. United States*, 286 U.S. 427, 52 S.Ct. 607, 76 L.Ed. 1204 (1932).

c. *Mandeville Island Farms, Inc. v. American Crystal Sugar Co.*, 334 U.S. 219, 68 S.Ct. 996, 92 L.Ed. 1328 (1948).

\* \* \* Petitioners argue that respondent's complaint is insufficient because there is no factual nexus between the restraint on this one surgeon's practice and interstate commerce.

There are two flaws in petitioners' argument. First, \* \* \* proper analysis focuses, not upon actual consequences, but rather upon the potential harm that would ensue if the conspiracy were successful. \* \* \*

Second, if the conspiracy alleged in the complaint is successful, ''as a matter of practical economics'' there will be a reduction in the provision of ophthalmological services in the Los Angeles market. \* \* \*

*The United States Supreme Court held that the medical staff's peer-review proceedings affected interstate commerce, and thus the staff's actions against Pinhas fell within the jurisdiction of the Sherman Act.*

**DECISION
AND REMEDY**

<br>

## SECTION 2

# SECTION 1 OF THE SHERMAN ACT

The underlying assumption of Section 1 of the Sherman Act is that society's welfare is harmed if rival firms are permitted to join in an agreement that consolidates their market power or otherwise restrains competition. Not all agreements between rivals, however, result in enhanced market power or *unreasonably* restrain trade. Under what is called the **rule of reason,** anticompetitive agreements that allegedly violate Section 1 of the Sherman Act are analyzed with the view that they may, in fact, constitute reasonable restraints on trade. When applying this rule, the court considers the purpose of the arrangement, the powers of the parties, and the effect of their actions in restraining trade. If the court deems that legitimate competitive benefits outweigh the anticompetitive effects of the agreement, it will be held lawful.

The need for a rule-of-reason analysis of some agreements in restraint of trade is obvious—if the rule of reason had not been developed, virtually any business agreement could conceivably violate the Sherman Act. Justice Louis D. Brandeis effectively phrased this sentiment in *Chicago Board of Trade v. United States,* a case decided in 1918:

Every agreement concerning trade, every regulation of trade, restrains. To bind, to restrain, is of their very essence. The true test of legality is whether the restraint imposed is such as merely regulates and perhaps thereby promotes competition or whether it is such as may suppress or even destroy competition.[3]

When analyzing an alleged Section 1 violation under the rule of reason, a court will consider several factors, including the purpose of the agreement, the parties' power to implement the agreement to achieve that purpose, and the effect or potential effect of the agreement on competition. Another possible factor that might be considered is whether the parties could have relied on less restrictive means to achieve their purpose.

Some agreements, however, are so blatantly and substantially anticompetitive that they are deemed illegal *per se* (on their face, or inherently) under Section 1. If an agreement is found to be of a type that is deemed a *per se* **violation,** a court is precluded from determining whether the agreement's benefits outweigh its anticompetitive effects.

The dividing line between agreements that constitute *per se* violations and agreements that should be judged under a rule of reason is seldom clear. Moreover, in some cases, the United States Supreme Court has stated that it is applying a *per se* rule, and yet a careful reading of the Court's analysis suggests that the Court is weighing benefits against harms under a rule of reason. Some have termed this a ''soft,'' or ''limited,'' *per se* rule. Others have called it a ''narrow'' rule of reason. Perhaps the most that can be said with certainty is that although the distinction between the two rules seems clear in theory, in the actual

---

3.   246 U.S. 231, 38 S.Ct. 242, 62 L.Ed. 683 (1918).

application of antitrust laws, the distinction has not always been so clear.

We turn now to the types of trade restraints prohibited by Section 1 of the Sherman Act. Generally, these restraints fall into two broad categories: *horizontal restraints* and *vertical restraints*. Some restraints are *per se* violations of Section 1, but others may be permissible; those that are not *per se* violations are tested under the rule of reason.

## HORIZONTAL RESTRAINTS

The term **horizontal restraint** is encountered frequently in antitrust law. A horizontal restraint is any agreement that in some way restrains competition between rival firms competing in the same market.

**PRICE FIXING**   Any agreement among competitors to fix prices, or **price-fixing agreement,** constitutes a *per se* violation of Section 1 of the Sherman Act. Perhaps the definitive case regarding price-fixing agreements remains the 1940 case of *United States v. Socony-Vacuum Oil Co.*[4] In that case, a group of independent oil producers in Texas and Louisiana were caught between falling demand due to the Great Depression of the 1930s and increasing supply from newly discovered oil fields in the region. In response to these conditions, a group of the major refining companies agreed to buy ''distress'' gasoline (excess supplies) from the independents so as to dispose of it in an ''orderly manner.'' Although there was no explicit agreement as to price, it was clear that the purpose of the agreement was to limit the supply of gasoline on the market and thereby raise prices.

There may have been good reasons for the agreement. Nonetheless, the United States Supreme Court recognized the dangerous effects that such an agreement could have on open and free competition. The Court held that the reasonableness of a price-fixing agreement is never a defense; any agreement that restricts output or artificially fixes price is a *per se* violation of Section 1. The rationale of the *per se* rule was best stated in what is now the most famous portion of the Court's opinion. In footnote 59, Justice William O. Douglas compared a freely functioning price system to a body's central nervous system, condemning price-fixing agreements as threats to ''the central nervous system of the economy.''

**GROUP BOYCOTTS**   A **group boycott** is an agreement by two or more sellers to refuse to deal with, or to boycott, a particular person or firm. Such group boycotts have been held to constitute *per se* violations of Section 1 of the Sherman Act. Section 1 will be violated if it can be demonstrated that the boycott or joint refusal to deal was undertaken with the intention of eliminating competition or preventing entry into a given market. Some boycotts, such as group boycotts against a supplier for political reasons, may be protected under the First Amendment right to freedom of expression.

**HORIZONTAL MARKET DIVISION**   It is a *per se* violation of Section 1 of the Sherman Act for competitors to divide up territories or customers. For example, manufacturers A, B, and C compete against one another in the states of Kansas, Nebraska, and Iowa. By agreement, A sells products only in Kansas; B sells only in Nebraska; and C sells only in Iowa. This concerted action reduces costs and allows each of the three (assuming there is no other competition) to raise the price of the goods sold in its own state. The same violation would take place if A, B, and C had simply agreed that A would sell only to institutional purchasers (school districts, universities, state agencies and departments, cities, and so on) in the three states, B only to wholesalers, and C only to retailers.

**TRADE ASSOCIATIONS**   Businesses within the same general industry or profession frequently organize trade associations to pursue common interests. Their joint activities may provide for exchanges of information, representation of the members' business interests before governmental bodies, advertising campaigns, and the setting of regulatory standards to govern their industry or profession. Generally, the rule of reason is applied to many of these horizontal actions. For example, if a court finds that a trade association practice or agreement that restrains trade is nonetheless sufficiently beneficial both to the association and to the public, it may deem the restraint reasonable.

Other trade association agreements may have such substantially anticompetitive effects that the court will consider them to be in violation of Section 1 of the Sherman Act. In *National Society of*

---

4.   310 U.S. 150, 60 S.Ct. 811, 84 L.Ed.2d 1129 (1940).

*Professional Engineers v. United States,*[5] for example, it was held that the society's Code of Ethics—which prohibited discussion of prices with a potential customer until after the customer had chosen an engineer—was a Section 1 viola-

tion. The United States Supreme Court found that this ban on competitive bidding was "nothing less than a frontal assault on the basic policy of the Sherman Act." In the following case, the court closely scrutinizes an action undertaken by a health-care professional group allegedly for the sole purpose of protecting the public.

5.   453 U.S. 679, 98 S.Ct. 1355, 55 L.Ed.2d 637 (1978).

---

**BACKGROUND AND FACTS**   *In 1966, the American Medical Association (AMA) passed a resolution labeling chiropractic an unscientific cult. (Chiropractors attempt to cure or relieve bodily ailments by making skeletal adjustments.) In effect, this label prevented physicians from associating with chiropractors, because Principle 3 of the Principles of Medical Ethics—the AMA's code of ethical conduct—provided that a "physician should practice a method of healing founded on a scientific basis; and he should not voluntarily associate with anyone who violates this principle." Medical doctors used Principle 3 to justify their refusal to have anything to do with chiropractors or to allow chiropractors to use hospital diagnostic services or become members of hospital medical staffs. Despite the AMA's efforts, chiropractic became licensed in all fifty states, and in a 1980 revision of the AMA's ethical code, Principle 3 was eliminated. In 1976, Chester Wilk and four other chiropractors brought an action against the AMA, claiming that the boycott had violated Section 1 of the Sherman Act and seeking injunctive relief from the boycott's "lingering effects" on chiropractors. The trial court, holding that the AMA had violated Section 1 of the Sherman Act by conducting an illegal boycott in restraint of trade, granted an injunction that, among other things, required the AMA to publish widely the trial court's order. The AMA appealed.*

**CASE 48.2**

**WILK v. AMERICAN MEDICAL ASSOCIATION**

United States Court of Appeals, Seventh Circuit, 1990.
895 F.2d 352.

*MANION,* Circuit Judge.
\*   \*   \*   \*

Despite the fact that \*   \*   \* the conspiracy ended in 1980, \*   \*   \* the illegal boycott's "lingering effects" still threatened plaintiffs with current injury \*   \*   \*. \*   \*   \* [T]he boycott caused injury to chiropractors' reputations which had not been repaired, and current economic injury to chiropractors. Further, the AMA never affirmatively acknowledged that there are no impediments to professional association and cooperation between chiropractors and medical physicians \*   \*   \*.
\*   \*   \*   \*

\*   \*   \* Essentially, the AMA argues that \*   \*   \* health care consumers almost invariably lack sufficient information needed to evaluate the quality of medical services. This increases the risk of fraud and deception on consumers by unscrupulous health care providers \*   \*   \*. The AMA's conduct, the theory goes on, \*   \*   \* allowed consumers to be assured that physicians would use only scientifically valid treatments. This in effect \*   \*   \* provided consumers with essential information \*   \*   \*.

Getting information to the market is a fine goal, but \*   \*   \* the AMA was not motivated solely by such altruistic concerns. Indeed, \*   \*   \* the AMA intended to "destroy a competitor," namely, chiropractors. It is not enough to carry the day to argue that competition should be eliminated in the name of public safety.

<table>
<tr>
<td>**DECISION AND REMEDY**</td>
<td>*The appellate court affirmed both the trial court's ruling that the AMA had violated Section 1 of the Sherman Act by conducting an illegal boycott of chiropractors and the trial court's decision to grant an injunction against the AMA.*</td>
</tr>
</table>

**JOINT VENTURES** Joint ventures undertaken by competitors are also subject to antitrust laws. As discussed in Chapter 38, a *joint venture* is an undertaking by two or more individuals or firms for a specific purpose. If a joint venture does not involve price fixing or market divisions, the agreement will be analyzed under the rule of reason. Whether the venture will then be upheld under Section 1 depends on an overall assessment of the purposes of the venture, a strict analysis of the potential benefits relative to the likely harms, and in some cases, an assessment of whether there are less restrictive alternatives for achieving the same goals.[6]

## VERTICAL RESTRAINTS

A **vertical restraint** of trade is one that results from an agreement between firms at different levels in the manufacturing and distribution process. In contrast to horizontal relationships, which occur at the same level of operation, vertical relationships encompass the entire chain of production: the purchase of inputs, basic manufacturing, distribution to wholesalers, and eventual sale of a product at the retail level. For some products, it is possible that these distinct phases are carried on by different firms. In other instances, a single firm may carry out two or more of the different functional phases. Such firms are considered to be **vertically integrated firms.**

Even though firms operating at different functional levels are not in direct competition with one another, they are in competition with other firms operating at their own respective levels of operation. Thus, agreements between firms standing in a vertical relationship do significantly affect competition. Some vertical restraints are *per se* violations of Section 1; others are judged under the rule of reason.

**TERRITORIAL OR CUSTOMER RESTRICTIONS** In arranging for the distribution of a firm's products, manufacturers often wish to insulate dealers from direct competition with other dealers selling the firm's product. In this endeavor, they may institute territorial restrictions, or they may attempt to prohibit wholesalers or retailers from reselling the products to certain classes of buyers, such as competing retailers. There may be legitimate, procompetitive reasons for imposing such territorial or customer restrictions. For example, a manufacturer may wish to prevent a dealer from cutting costs and undercutting rivals by providing the product without promotion or customer service, while relying on a nearby dealer to provide these services. In this situation, the cost-cutting dealer would reap the benefits (sales of the product) paid for by other dealers who undertake promotion and arrange for customer service. This is an example of the "free rider" problem.[7] The cost-cutting dealer, by not providing customer service, could also harm the manufacturer's reputation.

Territorial and customer restrictions are judged under a rule of reason. In the following case, *Continental T.V., Inc. v. GTE Sylvania, Inc.,* the United States Supreme Court overturned its earlier stance, which had been set out in *United States v. Arnold, Schwinn & Co.*[8] In *Schwinn,* the Court had held territorial and customer restrictions to be *per se* violations of Section 1 of the Sherman Act. The *Continental* case has been heralded as one of the most important antitrust cases since the 1940s. It marked a definite shift from rigid characterization of these kinds of vertical restraints to a more flexible, economic analysis of the restraints under the rule of reason.

---

6. See, for example, *United States v. Morgan,* 118 F.Supp. 621 (S.D.N.Y. 1953). This case is often cited as a classic example of how to judge joint ventures under the rule of reason.

7. For a discussion of the free rider problem in the context of sports telecasting, see *Chicago Professional Sports Limited Partnership v. National Basketball Association,* 961 F.2d 667 (7th Cir. 1993).

8. 388 U.S. 365, 87 S.Ct. 1856, 18 L.Ed.2d 1249 (1967).

**BACKGROUND AND FACTS**  *GTE Sylvania, Inc., a manufacturer of television sets, adopted a franchise plan limiting the number of franchises granted in any given geographical area and requiring each franchise to sell Sylvania products only from the location or locations at which they were franchised. A franchise did not constitute an exclusive territory, and Sylvania retained sole discretion to increase the number of retailers in an area, depending on the success or failure of existing retailers in developing their markets. (This is called* intrabrand *competition.) Continental T.V., Inc., was a retailer under Sylvania's franchise plan. When Sylvania proposed a new franchise that would compete with Continental, Continental announced that it was opening its own new store in another location. Sylvania cut Continental's credit with the company, and Continental in turn withheld payments for previously received merchandise. Sylvania terminated Continental's franchise, and a suit was brought for the money owed. Continental claimed that Sylvania's vertically restrictive franchise system violated Section 1 of the Sherman Act. The district court ruled in Continental's favor, and Sylvania appealed. The appellate court reversed the trial court's decision. Continental appealed to the United States Supreme Court.*

CASE 48.3

**CONTINENTAL T.V., INC. v. GTE SYLVANIA, INC.**

Supreme Court of the United States, 1977.
433 U.S. 36,
97 S.Ct. 2549,
53 L.Ed.2d 568.

Mr. Justice *POWELL* delivered the opinion of the Court.

\* \* \* \*

Vertical restrictions reduce intrabrand competition by limiting the number of sellers of a particular product competing for the business of a given group of buyers. Location restrictions have this effect because of practical constraints on the effective marketing area of retail outlets. Although intrabrand competition may be reduced, the ability of retailers to exploit the resulting market may be limited both by the ability of consumers to travel to other franchised locations and, perhaps more importantly, to purchase the competing products of other manufacturers. \* \* \*

Vertical restrictions promote interbrand competition by allowing the manufacturer to achieve certain efficiencies in the distribution of his products. \* \* \* Economists have identified a number of ways in which manufacturers can use such restrictions to compete more effectively against other manufacturers. For example, new manufacturers and manufacturers entering new markets can use the restrictions in order to induce competent and aggressive retailers to make the kind of investment of capital and labor that is often required in the distribution of products unknown to the consumer. Established manufacturers can use them to induce retailers to engage in promotional activities or to provide service and repair facilities necessary to the efficient marketing of their products. Service and repair are vital for many products, such as automobiles and major household appliances. The availability and quality of such services affect a manufacturer's goodwill and the competitiveness of his product. Because of market imperfections \* \* \*, these services might not be provided by retailers in a purely competitive situation, despite the fact that each retailer's benefit would be greater if all provided the services than if none did.

\* \* \* \*

\* \* \* Such restrictions, in varying forms, are widely used in our free market economy. \* \* \* [T]here is substantial scholarly and judicial authority supporting their economic utility. There is relatively little authority to the contrary. Certainly, there has been no showing in this case, either generally or with respect to Sylvania's agreements, that vertical restrictions have or are likely to have a "pernicious effect on competition" or that they "lack . . . any redeeming virtue" [which is required for the application of *per se* rules of illegality]. Accordingly, we conclude that the *per se* rule stated in *Schwinn* must be overruled. \*  \*  \*

\*  \*  \*  \*

\*  \*  \* When anticompetitive effects are shown to result from particular vertical restrictions they can be adequately policed under the rule of reason, the standard traditionally applied for the majority of anticompetitive practices challenged under [Section] 1 of the [Sherman] Act.

**DECISION AND REMEDY**   *The United States Supreme Court affirmed the appellate court's holding that Sylvania had not violated Section 1 of the Sherman Act. The decision that all such restraints would be treated as* per se *violations does not mean that all such restraints are necessarily legal, but that in the future the legality of all such restraints will be tested under a rule of reason.*

**RESALE PRICE MAINTENANCE AGREEMENTS**
An agreement between a manufacturer and a distributor or retailer in which the manufacturer specifies what the retail prices of its products must be is referred to as a **resale price maintenance agreement.** Resale price maintenance agreements, also known as *fair trade agreements,* were authorized for many years under *fair trade laws.* Today, these vertical price-fixing agreements are normally considered to be *per se* violations of Section 1 of the Sherman Act. Although manufacturers can determine the retail prices of their products when they are sold through their own stores or outlets, they may only *suggest* retail prices for their products when they are sold by independent retailers.

**REFUSALS TO DEAL**   As discussed previously, joint refusals to deal (group boycotts) are subject to sharp scrutiny under Section 1 of the Sherman Act. A single manufacturer acting unilaterally (by itself), however, is free to deal, or not to deal, with whomever it wishes. In vertical arrangements, even though a manufacturer cannot set retail prices for its products, it can refuse to deal with retailers or dealers that cut prices to levels substantially below the manufacturer's suggested retail prices. In *United States v. Colgate & Co.,*[9] for example, the United States Supreme Court held that a manufacturer's advance announcement that it would not sell to price cutters was not a violation of the Sherman Act.

SECTION 3

# SECTION 2 OF THE SHERMAN ACT

Section 1 of the Sherman Act proscribes certain *concerted* (joint) activities that restrain trade. In contrast, Section 2 condemns "every person who shall monopolize or attempt to monopolize." As the phrasing of Section 2 suggests, there are two distinct types of behavior that are subject to sanction under Section 2: *monopolization* and *attempts to monopolize.* In this section, we examine both of these Section 2 offenses.

A tactic that may be involved in either offense is **predatory pricing.** Predatory pricing, by definition, involves an attempt by one firm to drive its competitors from the market by selling its product substantially *below* the normal costs of production; once the competitors are eliminated, the firm will attempt to recapture its losses and go on to earn very high profits by driving prices up far above their competitive levels.

## MONOPOLIZATION

In *United States v. Grinnell Corp.,*[10] the United States Supreme Court defined the offense of **monopolization** as involving the following two elements: "(1) the possession of monopoly power in the relevant market and (2) the willful acquisition or maintenance of the power as distinguished from

---

9.   250 U.S. 300, 39 S.Ct. 465, 63 L.Ed 992 (1919).

10.   384 U.S. 563, 86 S.Ct. 1698, 16 L.Ed.2d 778 (1966).

growth or development as a consequence of a superior product, business acumen, or historic accident.'' A violation of Section 2 requires that both these elements—monopoly power and intent to monopolize—be established.

**MONOPOLY POWER**   The Sherman Act does not define *monopoly.* In economic parlance, monopoly refers to control by a single entity. It is well established in antitrust law, however, that a firm may be a monopoly even though it is not the sole seller in a market. Nor is a monopoly a function of size alone (for example, a ''mom and pop'' grocery located in an isolated desert town is a monopolist if it is the only grocery serving that particular market). Size in relation to the market is what matters, because monopoly involves power to affect prices and output. *Monopoly power,* as mentioned earlier in this chapter, exists when a firm has an extreme amount of market power. If a firm has sufficient market power to control prices and exclude competition, that firm has monopoly power.

As difficult as it is to define market power precisely, it is even more difficult to measure it. As a workable proxy, courts often look to the firm's percentage share of the ''relevant market.'' This is the so-called **market-share test.**[11] A firm generally is considered to have monopoly power if its share of the relevant market is 70 percent or more. This is not an absolute dictum, however. It is only a loose rule of thumb; in some cases, a smaller share may be held to constitute monopoly power.[12]

The relevant market consists of two elements: (1) a relevant *product* market and (2) a relevant *geographical* market. No doubt, the relevant product market should include all products that, although produced by different firms, nonetheless have identical attributes. Yet products that are not identical may be substituted for one another. Coffee may be substituted for tea, for example, or cellophane plastic wrap for wax paper. In defining the relevant product market, the key issue is the degree of interchangeability between products. If one product is a sufficient substitute for another, the two products are considered to be part of the same product market.

The second component of the relevant market is the geographical boundaries of the market. For products that are sold nationwide, the geographical boundaries of the market encompass the entire United States. If a producer and its competitors sell in only a limited area (one in which customers have no access to other sources for the product), then the geographical market is limited to that area. A national firm may thus compete in several distinct areas, having monopoly power in one area but not in another.

**THE INTENT REQUIREMENT**   The fact that a firm has monopoly power, in and of itself, does not constitute the offense of monopolization under Section 2 of the Sherman Act. The offense also requires intent to monopolize, or, in the words of Section 2, the ''willful acquisition or maintenance of the power.'' A dominant market share may be the result of business acumen or the development of a superior product. It may be simply the result of historical accident. In these situations, the acquisition of monopoly power is not an antitrust violation. Indeed, it would be counter to society's interest to condemn every firm that acquired a position of power because it was well managed, was efficient, and marketed a product desired by consumers. If, however, a firm possesses market power as a result of some purposeful act to acquire or maintain that power through anticompetitive means, then this is a violation of Section 2.

In most monopolization cases, intent may be inferred from evidence that the firm had monopoly power and engaged in anticompetitive behavior.

## ATTEMPTS TO MONOPOLIZE

Section 2 of the Sherman Act also prohibits **attempted monopolization** of a market. Any action challenged as an attempt to monopolize must be specifically intended to exclude competitors and garner monopoly power. In addition, the attempt must have had a ''dangerous'' probability of success; that is, actual monopolization is not required —*serious* threats of monopolization constitute violations. A probability cannot be dangerous unless

---

11.   Other measures of market power have been devised, but the market-share test is the most widely used.

12.   This standard was first articulated by Justice Learned Hand in *United States v. Aluminum Co. of America,* 148 F.2d 416 (2d Cir. 1945). A 90 percent share was held to be clear evidence of monopoly power. Anything less than 64 percent, said Justice Hand, made monopoly power doubtful, and anything less than 30 percent was clearly not monopoly power.

the alleged offender possesses at least some degree of market power. In the following case, the United States Supreme Court considered whether a dan-gerous probability may be inferred from evidence of anticompetitive behavior.

---

CASE 48.4

**SPECTRUM SPORTS, INC. v. McQUILLAN**

Supreme Court of the United States, 1993. ___ U.S. ___, 113 S.Ct. 884, 122 L.Ed.2d 247.

**BACKGROUND AND FACTS** *Sorbothane is an elastic polymer with shock-absorbing characteristics that make it useful in a variety of medical, athletic, and equestrian products. BTR, Inc., owns the patent rights to sorbothane. In 1980, BTR granted Shirley and Larry McQuillan, doing business as Sorboturf Enterprises, all manufacturing and distribution rights to sorbothane and exclusive rights to purchase sorbothane for use in equestrian products. In 1981, BTR changed the distribution arrangements—the McQuillans were to distribute sorbothane products in the southwestern states, and Spectrum Sports, Inc., was selected as a distributor for another region. In April 1982, BTR told the McQuillans that it wanted them to relinquish their athletic shoe distributorship as a condition for retaining the right to develop and distribute equestrian products. The McQuillans refused. In the fall of 1982, BTR told the McQuillans that another company had been appointed as the national distributor for sorbothane equestrian products. In August 1983, BTR told the McQuillans that it would no longer accept their orders, and Spectrum became the national distributor of sorbothane athletic shoe inserts. The McQuillans' business failed. The McQuillans sued BTR and Spectrum for, among other things, attempted monopolization in violation of Section 2 of the Sherman Act. The jury found attempted monopolization by inferring from the defendants' conduct an intent to monopolize and a dangerous probability of success. The trial court ruled in favor of the McQuillans, and the defendants appealed. When the appellate court affirmed the judgment, the defendants asked the United States Supreme Court to review the decision.*

Justice *WHITE* delivered the opinion of the Court.

\* \* \* \*

\* \* \* [T]o demonstrate attempted monopolization a plaintiff must prove (1) that the defendant has engaged in predatory or anticompetitive conduct with (2) a specific intent to monopolize and (3) a dangerous probability of achieving monopoly power. In order to determine whether there is a dangerous probability of monopolization, \* \* \* it [is] necessary to consider the relevant market and the defendant's ability to lessen or destroy competition in that market.

\* \* \* \*

\* \* \* The purpose of the [Sherman] Act is not to protect businesses from the working of the market; it is to protect the public from the failure of the market. The law directs itself not against conduct which is competitive, even severely so, but against conduct which unfairly tends to destroy competition itself. It does so not out of solicitude for private concerns but out of concern for the public interest. Thus, this Court and other courts have been careful to avoid constructions of [Section] 2 which might chill competition, rather than foster it. \* \* \* The concern that [Section] 2 might be applied so as to further anticompetitive ends is plainly not met by inquiring only whether the defendant has engaged in "unfair" or "predatory" tactics. \* \* \*

\* \* \* \*

\* \* \* In this case, [the jury inferred] specific intent and dangerous probability of success from the defendants' predatory conduct, without any proof of the relevant market or of a realistic probability that the defendants could achieve monopoly power in that market. \* \* \* [T]he affirmance of the [Section] 2 judgment against [the defendants] rested solely on the legally erroneous conclusion that [the defendants] had attempted to monopolize in violation of [Section] 2 \* \* \* .

*The Supreme Court reversed the decision of the appellate court and re-manded the case.*

**DECISION
AND REMEDY**

## SECTION 4

# THE CLAYTON ACT

In 1914, Congress attempted to strengthen federal antitrust laws by enacting the Clayton Act. The Clayton Act was aimed at specific anticompetitive or monopolistic practices that were not covered by the Sherman Act. The substantive provisions of the act deal with four distinct forms of business behavior, which are declared illegal but not criminal. With regard to each of the four provisions, the act's prohibitions are qualified by the general condition that the behavior is illegal only if it substantially tends to lessen competition or tends to create monopoly power. The major offenses under the Clayton Act are set out in Sections 2, 3, 7, and 8 of the act.

## PRICE DISCRIMINATION

Section 2 of the Clayton Act prohibits **price discrimination,** which occurs when a seller charges different prices to competitive buyers for identical goods. Because businesses frequently circumvented Section 2, Congress strengthened this section by amending it with the passage of the Robinson-Patman Act in 1936.

As amended, Section 2 prohibits certain forms of price discrimination that cannot be justified by differences in production, transportation, sale, or other costs. To violate Section 2, the seller must be engaged in interstate commerce, and the effect of the price discrimination must be to substantially lessen competition or create a competitive injury. Under the Robinson-Patman Act, a seller is prohibited from reducing a price to one buyer below the price charged to that buyer's competitor.

An exception is made if it can be shown that the seller charged a lower price temporarily to one of the buyers to meet in good faith another seller's

low price to a competitor of the buyer. To be predatory, a seller's pricing policies must also include a reasonable prospect of the seller's recouping its losses.[13]

## EXCLUSIONARY PRACTICES

Under Section 3 of the Clayton Act, sellers or lessors cannot sell or lease "on the condition, agreement or understanding that the \* \* \* purchaser or lessee thereof shall not use or deal in the goods \* \* \* of a competitor or competitors of the seller." In effect, this section prohibits two types of vertical agreements involving exclusionary practices—exclusive-dealing contracts and tying arrangements.

**EXCLUSIVE-DEALING CONTRACTS** A contract under which a seller forbids the buyer to purchase products from the seller's competitors is called an **exclusive-dealing contract.** An exclusive-dealing contract is prohibited under Section 3 if the effect of the contract is "to substantially lessen competition or tend to create a monopoly."

The leading exclusive-dealing decision is that of *Standard Oil Co. of California v. United States.*[14] In this case, the then-largest gasoline seller in the nation made exclusive-dealing contracts with independent stations in seven western states. The contracts involved 16 percent of all retail outlets, whose sales were approximately 7 percent of all retail sales in that market. The United States Supreme Court noted that the market was

---

13. See, for example, *Brooke Group, Ltd. v. Brown & Williamson Tobacco Corp.,* ___ U.S. ___, 113 S.Ct. 2578, 125 L.Ed.2d 168 (1993), in which the Supreme Court held that a seller's price-cutting policies could not be predatory "[g]iven the market's realities"—the size of the seller's market share, the expanding output by other sellers, plus other factors.
14. 37 U.S. 293, 69 S.Ct. 1051, 93 L.Ed. 1371 (1949).

substantially concentrated, because the seven largest gasoline suppliers all used exclusive-dealing contracts with their independent retailers and together controlled 65 percent of the market. Looking at market conditions after the arrangements were instituted, the Court found that market shares were extremely stable, and entry into the market was apparently restricted. Thus, the Court held that Section 3 had been violated, because competition was "foreclosed in a substantial share" of the relevant market.

**TYING ARRANGEMENTS**   When the seller conditions the sale of a product (the tying product) on the buyer's agreement to purchase another product (the tied product) produced or distributed by the same seller, a **tying arrangement**, or *tie-in sales agreement,* results. The legality of such an agreement depends on many factors, particularly the purpose of the agreement and the agreement's likely effect on competition in the relevant markets (consider that there are two markets, because the agreement involves both the tying and the tied product). In 1936, for example, the United States Supreme Court held that International Business Machines' and Remington Rand's practice of requiring the purchase of their own machine cards (the tied product) as a condition to leasing their tabulation machines (the tying product) violated Section 3 of the Clayton Act. The two firms were the only ones in the market with completely automated tabulation machines, so the Court concluded that they each possessed market power sufficient to "substantially lessen competition" through their respective tying arrangements.[15]

Section 3 of the Clayton Act has been held to apply only to commodities, not to services. But tying arrangements may also violate Section 1 of the Sherman Act. Thus, those cases involving tying arrangements of services have been brought under Section 1 of the Sherman Act. Traditionally, the courts have held tying arrangements brought under the Sherman Act to be illegal *per se.* In recent years, however, courts have shown a willingness to look at factors that are important in a rule-of-reason analysis. This is another example of the "soft" *per se* rule referred to earlier in this chapter.

## MERGERS

Under Section 7 of the Clayton Act, a person or business organization cannot hold stock and/or assets in another business "where the effect . . . may be to substantially lessen competition." This section is the statutory authority for preventing mergers that could result in monopoly power or a substantial lessening of competition in the marketplace.

A crucial consideration in most merger cases is **market concentration.** Market concentration roughly translates into the allocation of percentage market shares among the various firms in the relevant market. For example, if the four largest grocery stores in Chicago accounted for 80 percent of all retail food sales, the market clearly would be concentrated in those four firms. Competition, however, is not necessarily diminished solely as a result of market concentration, and other factors will be considered in determining whether a merger will violate Section 7. Another concept of particular importance in evaluating the effects of a merger is whether the merger will make it more difficult for potential competitors to enter the relevant market.

We look here at how Section 7 applies to three types of mergers: horizontal mergers, vertical mergers, and conglomerate mergers.

**HORIZONTAL MERGERS**   Mergers between firms that compete with each other in the same market are called **horizontal mergers.** If a horizontal merger creates an entity whose increased market share unduly restricts competition, the merger will be presumed illegal. This is because of the United States Supreme Court's interpretation that Congress, in amending Section 7 of the Clayton Act in 1950, intended to prevent mergers that increase market concentration.[16] Three other factors that are also considered in analyzing the legality of a horizontal merger are overall concentration of the relevant market, the relevant market's history of tending toward concentration, and whether the apparent design of the merger is to establish market power or restrict competition.

The Federal Trade Commission (FTC) and the Department of Justice (DOJ) have established

---

15.   *International Business Machines Corp. v. United States,* 298 U.S. 131, 56 S.Ct. 701, 80 L.Ed. 1085 (1936).

16.   *Brown Shoe v. United States,* 370 U.S. 294, 82 S.Ct. 1502, 8 L.Ed.2d 510 (1962).

guidelines indicating which mergers will be challenged.

Under the guidelines, the first factor to be considered in determining whether a merger will be challenged is the degree of concentration in the relevant market. In determining market concentration, the FTC and the DOJ employ what is known as the **Herfindahl-Hirschman Index (HHI).**

The HHI is computed by summing the squares of each of the percentage market shares of firms in the relevant market. For example, if there are four firms with shares of 30 percent, 30 percent, 20 percent, and 20 percent, respectively, then the pre-merger HHI equals 2,600 ($30^2 + 30^2 + 20^2 + 20^2 = 2,600$).

If the pre-merger HHI is less than 1,000, then the market is unconcentrated, and the merger will not likely be challenged. If the pre-merger HHI is between 1,000 and 1,800, the industry is moderately concentrated, and the merger will be challenged only if it increases the HHI by 100 points or more.[17] If the pre-merger HHI is greater than 1,800, the market is highly concentrated. In a highly concentrated market, a merger that produces an increase in the HHI between 50 and 100 points raises significant competitive concerns. Mergers that produce an increase in the HHI of more than 100 points in a highly concentrated market are deemed likely to enhance market power.[18]

The guidelines stress that the determination of market share and market concentration is only the starting point in analyzing the potential anticompetitive effects of a merger. Before deciding to challenge a merger, the FTC and the DOJ will look at a number of other factors, including the ease of entry into the relevant market, economic efficiency, the financial condition of the merging firms, the nature and price of the product or products involved, and so on. If a firm is a leading one—having at least a 35 percent share and twice that of the next leading firm—any merger with a firm having as little as a 1 percent share will be challenged.

**VERTICAL MERGERS**  A **vertical merger** occurs when a company at one stage of production acquires a company at a higher or lower stage of production. Courts in the past have almost exclusively focused on "foreclosure" in assessing vertical mergers. Foreclosure occurs because competitors of the merging firms lose opportunities to either sell or buy products from the merging firms. For example, in *United States v. E. I. du Pont de Nemours & Co.,*[19] du Pont was challenged for acquiring a considerable amount of General Motors (GM) stock. In holding that the transaction was illegal, the United States Supreme Court noted that the stock acquisition would enable du Pont to foreclose other sellers of fabrics and finishes from selling to GM, which then accounted for 50 percent of all auto fabric and finishes purchases.

More recently, whether a vertical merger will be deemed illegal has depended on several factors, including market concentration, barriers to entry into the market, and the apparent intent of the merging parties. Mergers that do not prevent competitors of either of the merging firms from competing in a segment of the market will not be condemned as "foreclosing" competition and are legal.

**CONGLOMERATE MERGERS**  There are three general types of **conglomerate mergers:** market-extension, product-extension, and diversification mergers. A market-extension merger occurs when a firm seeks to sell its product in a new market by merging with a firm already established in that market. A product-extension merger occurs when a firm seeks to add a closely related product to its existing line by merging with a firm already producing that product. For example, a manufacturer might seek to extend its product line of household products to include floor wax detergent by acquiring a leading manufacturer of floor wax. A diversification merger occurs when a firm merges with another firm that offers a product or service wholly unrelated to the first firm's existing activities. An example of a diversification merger would be Chrysler Corporation's acquisition of Holiday Inns. The following case involves a product-extension conglomerate merger.

---

17.   Compute the change in the index by doubling the product of the merging firms' pre-merger market shares. For example, a merger between a firm with a 5 percent share and one with a 6 percent share will increase the HHI by $2 \times (5 \times 6) = 60$. For an analysis of the HHI concentration of companies in the credit-card market, see *SCFC ILC, Inc. v. Visa U.S.A. Inc.,* 819 F.Supp. 956 (D.Utah 1993).

18.   See, for example, *United States v. United Tote, Inc.,* 768 F.Supp. 1064 (D.Del. 1991), in which the court ordered the divestiture of a firm whose HHI was 3,940 before a merger and 4,640 after the merger.

---

19.   353 U.S. 586, 77 S.Ct. 872, 1 L.Ed.2d 1057 (1957).

## CASE 48.5

### FEDERAL TRADE COMMISSION v. PROCTER & GAMBLE CO.

Supreme Court of the
United States, 1967.
386 U.S. 568,
87 S.Ct. 1224,
18 L.Ed.2d 303.

**COMPANY PROFILE**   *The Procter & Gamble Company (P&G) started in 1837 in Cincinnati, Ohio, when William Procter and James Gamble merged their candlemaking and soapmaking businesses. In 1878, P&G, which had by then become one of the largest companies in Cincinnati, introduced The White Soap. The White Soap's appeal was that it floated. Renamed Ivory in 1882, the soap was advertised as "99 and 44/100ths percent pure." The advertising campaign for Ivory was one of the first to advertise directly to the consumer. Between 1930 and 1959, P&G became the largest seller of packaged consumer goods in the United States. The company has introduced or acquired more than 160 products under such familiar brand names as Bounce, Charmin, Cheer, Crest, Crisco, Duncan Hines, Folgers Coffee, Hawaiian Punch, Head & Shoulders, Icy Hot, Old Spice, Safeguard, Spic and Span, Tide, and Vicks.*

**BACKGROUND AND FACTS**   *The Procter & Gamble Company acquired Clorox Chemical Company in 1957. At the time, P&G was the dominant manufacturer of household soaps, detergents, and cleansers. Clorox and Purex were the leading manufacturers of household bleach in a highly concentrated market. P&G's large advertising budget, along with other factors, seemingly allowed it to enjoy cost advantages in advertising its products. The Federal Trade Commission (FTC) brought an action against P&G claiming that P&G's acquisition of Clorox substantially lessened competition in the market for liquid bleach and thus violated Section 7 of the Clayton Act. Arguing that the merger prevented other bleach products from entering the market, thereby eliminating potential competitors, the FTC ordered P&G to divest itself of the Clorox Company. P&G appealed.*

Mr. Justice *DOUGLAS* delivered the opinion of the Court.

\* \* \* \*

At the time of the acquisition, Clorox was the leading manufacturer of household liquid bleach, with 48.8% of the national sales \* \* \* . The industry is highly concentrated; in 1957, Clorox and Purex accounted for almost 65% of the Nation's household liquid bleach sales, and, together with four other firms, for almost 80%. \* \* \*

\* \* \* \*

Since all liquid bleach is chemically identical, advertising and sales promotion are vital. In 1957 Clorox spent almost $3,700,000 on advertising, imprinting the value of its bleach in the mind of the consumer. \* \* \* The Commission found that these heavy expenditures went far to explain why Clorox maintained so high a market share despite the fact that its brand, though chemically indistinguishable from rival brands, retailed for a price equal to or, in many instances, higher than its competitors.

\* \* \* \*

The anticompetitive effects with which this product-extension merger is fraught can easily be seen: (1) the substitution of the powerful acquiring firm for the smaller, but already dominant, firm may substantially reduce the competitive structure of the industry by raising entry barriers and by dissuading the smaller firms from aggressively competing; (2) the acquisition eliminates the potential competition of the acquiring firm.

*The court upheld the FTC order that Proctor & Gamble divest itself of the Clorox Company.*

**Regulation of Mergers in the European Union** *In 1989, the European Community (now known as the European Union) adopted a regulation to control mergers. The regulation gave the European Commission the authority to approve or reject mergers of a "Community dimension," which are defined as mergers of two very large companies with annual sales exceeding a specified threshold amount. Such mergers are most likely to be conglomerate mergers, and companies must provide advance notification of any such combination.*

## INTERLOCKING DIRECTORATES

Section 8 of the Clayton Act deals with *interlocking directorates*—that is, the practice of having individuals serve as directors on the boards of two or more competing companies simultaneously. Specifically, no person may be a director in two or more corporations at the same time if either of the corporations has capital, surplus, or undivided profits aggregating more than $12.092 million or if the competitive sales of the company are $1.209 million or more. The threshold amounts are adjusted each year by the Federal Trade Commission (FTC). (The amounts given here are those announced by the FTC in 1994.)

## SECTION 5

# THE FEDERAL TRADE COMMISSION ACT

The Federal Trade Commission Act was enacted in 1914, the same year that the Clayton Act was written into law. Section 5 is the sole substantive provision of the act. It provides, in part, as follows: "Unfair methods of competition in or affecting commerce, and unfair or deceptive acts or practices in or affecting commerce are hereby declared illegal." Section 5 condemns all forms of anticompetitive behavior that are not covered under other federal antitrust laws. The act also created the Federal Trade Commission, an administrative agency with functions that include antitrust enforcement, as well as other duties relating to consumer protection (see Chapter 46).

## SECTION 6

# ENFORCEMENT OF ANTITRUST LAWS

The federal agencies that enforce the federal antitrust laws are the Department of Justice (DOJ) and the Federal Trade Commission (FTC). The DOJ can prosecute violations of the Sherman Act as either criminal or civil violations. Violations of the Clayton Act are not crimes, and the DOJ can enforce that statute only through civil proceedings. The various remedies that the DOJ has asked the courts to impose include **divestiture** (making a company give up one or more of its operating functions) and dissolution. The DOJ might force a group of meat packers, for example, to divorce itself from controlling or owning butcher shops.

The FTC enforces the Clayton Act and has sole authority to enforce violations of Section 5 of the Federal Trade Commission Act. FTC actions are effected through administrative orders, but if a firm violates an FTC order, the FTC can seek court sanctions for the violation.

A private party can sue for treble damages and attorneys' fees under Section 4 of the Clayton Act if the party is injured as a result of a violation of any of the federal antitrust laws, except Section 5 of the Federal Trade Commission Act. In some instances, private parties may also seek injunctive relief to prevent antitrust violations. The courts have determined that the ability to sue depends on the directness of the injury suffered by the would-be plaintiff. Thus, a person wishing to sue under the Sherman Act must prove (1) that the antitrust violation either caused or was a substantial factor in causing the injury that was suffered and (2) that the unlawful actions of the accused party affected business activities of the plaintiff that were protected by the antitrust laws.

In recent years, more than 90 percent of all antitrust actions have been brought by private plaintiffs. One reason for this is, of course, that successful plaintiffs recover three times the damages that they have suffered as a result of the violation. Such recoveries by private plaintiffs for antitrust violations have been rationalized as encouraging "private attorneys general" who will vigorously pursue antitrust violators on their own initiative.

SECTION 7

# EXEMPTIONS FROM ANTITRUST LAWS

There are many legislative and constitutional limitations on antitrust enforcement. Most are statutory and judicially created exemptions applying to the following areas:

1. *Labor.* Section 6 of the Clayton Act generally permits labor unions to organize and bargain without violating antitrust laws. Section 20 of the Clayton Act specifies that strikes and other labor activities are not violations of any law of the United States. But a union can lose its exemption if it combines with a nonlabor group rather than acting simply in its own self-interest.

2. *Agricultural associations and fisheries.* Section 6 of the Clayton Act (along with the Capper-Volstead Act of 1922) exempts agricultural cooperatives from the antitrust laws. The Fisheries Cooperative Marketing Act of 1976 exempts from antitrust legislation individuals in the fishing industry who collectively catch, produce, and prepare for market their products. Both exemptions allow members of such co-ops to combine and set prices for a particular product, but the exemptions do not allow them to engage in exclusionary practices or restraints of trade directed at competitors.

3. *Insurance.* The McCarran-Ferguson Act of 1945 exempts the insurance business from the antitrust laws whenever state regulation exists. This exemption does not cover boycotts, coercion, or intimidation on the part of insurance companies.

4. *Foreign trade.* Under the provisions of the 1918 Webb-Pomerane Act, American exporters may engage in cooperative activity to compete with similar foreign associations. Such cooperative activity may not, however, restrain trade within the United States or injure other American exporters. In 1982 the Export Trading Company Act was passed, broadening the Webb-Pomerane Act by permitting the Department of Justice to certify properly qualified export trading companies. Any activity within the scope described by the certificate is exempt from public prosecution under the antitrust laws.

5. *Baseball.* In 1922, the United States Supreme Court held that professional baseball was not within the reach of federal antitrust laws, because it was not "interstate commerce."[20] Under the Court's modern interpretations of the Constitution's commerce clause, this decision is clearly wrong.[21] Nonetheless, professional baseball retains its antitrust exemption; but this exemption applies only to baseball, not to other sports.

6. *Oil marketing.* The Interstate Oil Compact of 1935 allows states to determine quotas on oil that will be marketed in interstate commerce.

7. *Other exemptions.* Other activities exempt from antitrust laws include the following:
   a. Activities approved by the president in furtherance of the defense of our nation (under the Defense Production Act of 1950, as amended).
   b. Cooperative research among small business firms (under the Small Business Administration Act of 1958, as amended).

---

20. *Federal Baseball Club of Baltimore, Inc. v. National League of Professional Baseball Clubs,* 259 U.S. 200, 42 S.Ct. 465, 66 L.Ed. 898 (1922).

21. Recently, a federal court held that baseball's exemption applies only to the game's reserve system. (Under the reserve system, teams hold players' contracts for the players' entire careers. The reserve system is generally being replaced by the free agency system.) See *Piazza v. Major League Baseball,* 831 F.Supp. 420 (E.D.Pa. 1993).

c. Research or production of a product, process, or service by joint ventures consisting of competitors (under special federal legislation, including the National Cooperative Research Act of 1984 and the National Cooperative Production Amendments of 1993).

d. State actions, when the state policy is clearly articulated and the policy is actively supervised by the state.[22]

e. Activities of regulated industries (such as the transportation, communication, and banking industries) when federal commissions, boards, or agencies (such as the Federal Communications Commission, the Federal Maritime Commission, or the Interstate Commerce Commission) have primary regulatory authority.

f. Joint efforts by businesspersons to obtain legislative, judicial, or executive action

under what is often referred to as the *Noerr-Pennington* doctrine.[23] For example, video producers might jointly lobby Congress to change the copyright laws, or a video-rental company might sue another video-rental firm, without being held liable for attempting to restrain trade. Although selfish rather than purely public-minded conduct is permitted, there is an exception: an action will not be protected if it is clear that the action is "objectively baseless in the sense that no reasonable [person] could reasonably expect success on the merits" and it is an attempt to make anticompetitive use of government processes.[24]

22. See *Parker v. Brown*, 347 U.S. 341, 63 S.Ct. 307, 87 L.Ed. 315 (1943).

23. *United Mine Workers of America v. Pennington*, 381 U.S. 657, 89 S.Ct. 1585, 14 L.Ed.2d 626 (1965); and *Eastern Railroad Presidents Conference v. Noerr Motor Freight, Inc.*, 365 U.S. 127, 81 S.Ct. 523, 5 L.Ed.2d 464 (1961).

24. *Professional Real Estate Investors Inc. v. Columbia Pictures Industries Inc.*, ____ U.S. ____, 113 S.Ct. 1920, 123 L.Ed.2d 611 (1993).

## TERMS AND CONCEPTS TO REVIEW

antitrust law  944
attempted
    monopolization  953
conglomerate merger  957
divestiture  959
exclusive-dealing contract  955
group boycott  948
Herfindahl-Hirschman Index
    (HHI)  957
horizontal merger  956

horizontal restraint  948
market concentration  956
market power  945
market-share test  953
monopolization  952
monopoly  945
monopoly power  945
*per se* violation  947
predatory pricing  952
price discrimination  955

price-fixing agreement  948
resale price maintenance
    agreement  952
restraint on trade  944
rule of reason  947
trust  944
tying arrangement  956
vertical merger  957
vertical restraint  950
vertically integrated firm  950

# QUESTIONS AND CASE PROBLEMS

**48–1. Sherman Act.** An agreement that is blatantly and substantially anticompetitive is deemed a *per se* violation of Section 1 of the Sherman Act. Under what rule is an agreement analyzed if it appears to be anticompetitive but is not a *per se* violation? In making this analysis, what factors will a court consider?

**48–2. Clayton Act.** The Clayton Act deals with specific practices that are considered to reduce competition or lead to monopoly power but that are not expressly covered by the Sherman Act. What are these practices?

**48–3. Antitrust Laws.** Assume that the following events take place. Which antitrust law has been *primarily* violated in each event, and why?

(a) Allitron, Inc., and Donovan, Ltd., are interstate competitors selling similar appliances principally in the states of Indiana, Kentucky, Illinois, and Ohio. Allitron and Donovan agree that Allitron will no longer sell in Ohio and Indiana, and Donovan will no longer sell in Kentucky and Illinois.

(b) The partnership of Alvaredo and Parish is engaged in the oil-wellhead service industry in the states of New Mexico and Colorado. It presently has about 40 percent of the market for this service. Webb Corp. is engaged in competition with the Alvaredo-Parish partnership in the same state area. Webb has approximately 35 percent of the market. Alvaredo and Parish acquire the stock and assets of the Webb Corp.

**48–4. Restraints of Trade.** Jorge's Appliance Corp. is a new retail seller of appliances in Sunrise City. Jorge's innovative sales techniques and financing have caused a substantial loss of sales from the appliance department of No-Glow Department Store, a large chain store with substantial buying power. No-Glow told a number of appliance manufacturers that if they continued to sell to Jorge's, No-Glow would discontinue its large volume of purchases from these manufacturers. The manufacturers immediately stopped selling appliances to Jorge's. Jorge's filed suit against No-Glow and the manufacturers, claiming that their actions constituted an antitrust violation. No-Glow and the manufacturers were able to prove that Jorge's was a small retailer with a small portion of the market, and because the relevant market was not substantially affected, they claimed that they were not guilty of restraint of trade. Discuss fully whether there was an antitrust violation.

**48–5. Restraints of Trade.** Instant Foto Corp. is a manufacturer of photography film. At the present time, Instant Foto has approximately 50 percent of the market. Instant Foto advertises that the purchase price for Instant Foto film includes photo processing by Instant Foto Corp. Instant Foto claims that its film processing is specially designed to improve the quality of the finished photos when using Instant Foto's film. Is Instant Foto's combination of film purchase and film processing an antitrust violation? Explain.

**48–6. Sherman Act, Sections 1 and 2.** In contracts with television networks for the 1982–1985 football seasons, the National Collegiate Athletic Association (NCAA), a nonprofit organization, gave the ABC, CBS, and Turner broadcasting networks exclusive rights to negotiate with NCAA colleges to televise games. The contracts limited the number of games that could be televised by the networks, the number of appearances that any one team could make on television, and the amount of money a school could have for televising its games. The NCAA plan also required that a certain number of games between small colleges be televised, and it prohibited any individual institution from contracting separately for television coverage of its games. Not surprisingly, the NCAA plan drew criticism from major college teams, which felt that they deserved more network appearances and more money than teams

from smaller schools. Their efforts to gain a greater voice in the NCAA television policy, though supported by the College Football Association, proved unsuccessful. As a result, the University of Oklahoma and the University of Georgia brought an action against the NCAA, alleging that its contracts with the television networks violated Sections 1 and 2 of the Sherman Act. Specifically, the NCAA was charged with price fixing, horizontal limitations on production, group boycott, and monopolization. The NCAA argued, among other things, that as a nonprofit organization with ''noneconomic'' motives, it should not be subject to antitrust laws. How should the United States Supreme Court rule? [*NCAA v. Board of Regents of the University of Oklahoma,* 468 U.S. 85, 104 S.Ct. 2948, 82 L.Ed.2d 70 (1984)]

**48–7. Sherman Act, Section 2.** American Academic Suppliers, Inc., and Beckley-Cardy, Inc., were wholesalers engaged in the sale of school supplies. American's major markets were largely concentrated in the Midwest; Beckley's markets were on a more national scale. American had been started by Beckley's former president on a small initial investment of less than $500,000. American had also hired a number of salespersons away from Beckley. Initially, American had experienced fairly rapid expansion in the markets in which it competed with Beckley. Beckley responded by giving steep discounts in the prices of some of its products and, according to American, by making disparaging remarks and starting rumors about American's business operations. American sued Beckley, alleging, among other things, that Beckley had violated Section 2 of the Sherman Act by attempting to monopolize the school-supply market. Did Beckley's actions constitute an attempt to monopolize the school-supply market in violation of Section 2 of the Sherman Act? Discuss fully. [*American Academic Suppliers, Inc. v. Beckley-Cardy, Inc.,* 922 F.2d 1317 (7th Cir. 1991)]

**48–8. Sherman Act, Section 1.** To offer a competitive alternative to health-maintenance organizations and to promote fee-for-service medicine, members of the Maricopa County Medical Society and another medical society established a fee schedule that prescribed the maximum fees that the physicians could charge patients who were insured under specified health-insurance plans. The state of Arizona filed a complaint against the medical societies, alleging that the fee schedule constituted a horizontal price-fixing conspiracy and a *per se* violation of Section 1 of the Sherman Act. The medical societies claimed that the *per se* rule should not apply because (1) the medical societies were professional organizations; (2) the agreement fixed maximum prices, not minimum or uniform prices; (3) the judiciary had insufficient experience in the medical industry to justify applying the *per se* rule; and (4) the fee schedule was justified by its procompetitive effects. The district and appellate courts both agreed with the medical societies that the case should not be judged under the *per se* rule. What will the United States Supreme Court decide? [*Arizona v. Maricopa County Medical Society,* 457 U.S. 332, 102 S.Ct. 2466, 73 L.Ed.2d 48 (1982)]

**48–9. Sherman Act, Section 2.** For some time, the four major and independently owned downhill skiing facilities in Aspen, Colorado—Ajax, Aspen Highlands, Buttermilk, and Snowmass—had offered an "all-Aspen" skiing ticket that could be used at any of the four facilities. The proceeds of the all-Aspen ticket sales were distributed to the four facilities proportionately to the number of skiers using each one. By 1977, Aspen Skiing Co. had acquired ownership of Ajax, Buttermilk, and Snowmass and discontinued the all-Aspen ticket, offering instead a ticket that could be used by skiers only at its three facilities. As a result of Aspen Skiing Co.'s activities, the Aspen Highlands share of the skiing market declined from 20 percent in 1977 to only 11 percent by 1981. Aspen Highlands Skiing Corp. brought an action against Aspen Skiing Co., alleging that the latter had monopolized the Aspen skiing market and that its discontinuation of the all-Aspen ticket sales constituted an intentional attempt to misuse its monopoly power in violation of Section 2 of the Sherman Act. Aspen Skiing Co. claimed that its actions represented nothing more than a refusal to participate in a cooperative venture with a competitor and therefore could not possibly be illegal under antitrust laws. Which party will prevail in court, and why? [*Aspen Skiing Co. v. Aspen Highlands Skiing Corp.,* 472 U.S. 585, 105 S.Ct. 2847, 86 L.Ed.2d 467 (1985)]

**48–10. Sherman Act, Section 1.** In an attempt to control costs, dental health insurers adopted a policy that required dentists to submit diagnostic dental X-rays to the insurance company for review before the company would approve payment for treatment. The Indiana Federation of Dentists objected to this policy and adopted a resolution not to submit X-rays as requested by the insurers. Most dentists complied with this resolution and refused to submit X-rays. In 1978, the Federal Trade Commission (FTC) issued a complaint against the federation and found that the joint refusal to submit X-rays was a violation of antitrust laws. According to the FTC, the policy of not submitting X-rays had the effect of encouraging unnecessary dental procedures and raising costs. The federation appealed this finding, and the court of appeals overturned the FTC's ruling. The appellate court contended that the FTC had not shown that the federation's policy had an anticompetitive effect. The FTC then appealed to the United States Supreme Court. How should the Supreme Court rule? Discuss fully. [*Federal Trade Commission v. Indiana Federation of Dentists,* 476 U.S. 447, 106 S.Ct. 2009, 90 L.Ed.2d 445 (1986)]

**48–11. Sherman Act, Section 1.** Harcourt Brace Jovanovich Legal and Professional Publications (HBJ), the nation's largest provider of bar review materials and lecture services, began offering a Georgia bar review course in 1976 and was in direct, and often intense, competition with BRG of Georgia, Inc., the other main provider of bar review courses in Georgia, from 1977 to 1979. In early 1980, HBJ and BRG entered into an agreement that gave BRG the exclusive right to market HBJ's materials in Georgia and to use its trade name, Bar/Bri. The parties agreed that HBJ would not compete with BRG in Georgia and that BRG would not compete with HBJ outside of Georgia. Immediately after the 1980 agreement, the price of BRG's course was increased from $150 to over $400. Jay Palmer, a former law student, brought an action against the two firms, alleging that the 1980 agreement violated Section 1 of the Sherman Act. What will the court decide? Discuss fully. [*Palmer v. BRG of Georgia, Inc.,* 498 U.S. 46, 111 S.Ct. 401, 112 L.Ed.2d 349 (1990)]

**48–12. Tying Arrangements.** Eastman Kodak Co. has about a 20 percent share of the highly competitive market for high-volume photocopiers and microfilm equipment, and it controls nearly the entire market for replacement parts for the equipment (parts that are not interchangeable with parts for other manufacturers' equipment). Prior to 1985, Kodak sold replacement parts for its equipment without significant restrictions. As a result, a number of independent service organizations (ISOs) purchased Kodak parts to use when repairing and servicing Kodak copiers. In 1985, Kodak changed its policy to prevent the ISOs from competing with Kodak's own service organizations. It ceased selling parts to ISOs and refused to sell its replacement parts to its customers unless they agreed *not* to have their equipment serviced by ISOs. In 1987, Image Technical Services, Inc., and seventeen other ISOs sued Kodak, alleging that Kodak's policy was a tying arrangement in violation of Section 1 of the Sherman Act. Kodak claimed that its policy was not an illegal tying arrangement because it had no market power with respect to its equipment. Therefore, it did not have market power with respect to replacement parts—it could not raise the price of replacement parts and service beyond competitive rates because if it did, it would lose customers, who would purchase other manufacturers' equipment. Assuming that Kodak does not have market power in the market for the photocopying and microfilm equipment, does Kodak's restrictive policy constitute an illegal tying arrangement? Does it violate antitrust laws in any way? Discuss fully. [*Eastman Kodak Co. v. Image Technical Services, Inc.,* ___ U.S. ___, 112 S.Ct. 2072, 119 L.Ed.2d 265 (1992)]

# Government Regulation

I f this text had been written 150 years ago, it would have had little to say about federal government regulation. In the 1890s, the beginnings of federal regulation and antitrust law were manifested in the form of the Interstate Commerce Act and the Sherman Act, but there was little or no legislation designed to protect consumers or the environment. Today, in contrast, virtually every area of economic activity is regulated by the government.

From a very broad perspective, ethical issues in government regulation arise because regulation, by its very nature, means that some traditional rights and freedoms have to be given up to ensure that other rights and freedoms are protected. Essentially, government regulation brings two ethical principles into conflict. On the one hand, deeply embedded in American culture is the idea that the government should play a limited role in directing our lives. Indeed, this nation was founded so that Americans could be free from the "heavy hand of government" experienced by the colonists under English rule. On the other hand, one of the basic functions of government is to protect the constitutional rights of individuals and, in the

business community, to protect competition in the marketplace.

In this *Focus on Ethics,* we look at selected examples of some of the ways in which government regulation reflects the trade-offs that society has been willing to make in the interests of protecting consumers, the environment, and free competition in our society.

## Environmental Law

Questions of fairness inevitably arise in regard to environmental law. Has the government gone too far in regulating businesses in the interest of protecting the environment? Has the government gone far enough? At what point do the costs of environmental regulations become too burdensome for society to bear? These are broad questions, but they are ethical in nature, because they ultimately relate to society's notions of what is right, just, or good.

If manufacturers ceased all production and Americans returned to the rural life of earlier times, the environment would certainly benefit. Obviously, Americans do not want to pay that high a cost. Certainly, we want to enjoy the fruits of our advanced economy. But environmental

protection means that some sacrifices will have to be made. How much are we willing to sacrifice today to ensure that future generations have a more healthful world in which to live?

### Superfund and Toxic Waste

Although everybody is in favor of cleaning up America's toxic waste dumps, nobody has the slightest idea what this task will ultimately cost. Much of the problem in determining the ultimate costs of the Superfund (CERCLA—see Chapter 47) program stems from the difficulty of estimating the costs of cleaning up a site. Until the clean-up is actually undertaken, it is often difficult to assess the extent of contamination. Moreover, there is no agreed-on standard as to how clean these sites need to be before they no longer pose any threat of harm to life. Do you have to remove *all* of the contamination, or would removal of some lesser amount satisfy a reasonable degree of environmental quality? On the cost side of the picture, another question exists: If, say, 90 percent of the waste at a given site could be removed for $50,000, but the removal of the other 10 percent would cost $2 million, is it reasonable to remove that remaining 10 percent?

Perhaps the real question that Congress now needs to ask is how effective the Superfund has been. As of 1994, of the $12.5 billion paid out by insurance companies for CERCLA liability, about 85 percent went to legal and administrative fees. That means that only 15 percent was used for actual clean-up. The reality today is that there is a multibillion-dollar Superfund industry. This industry comprises thousands of scientists, engineers, government officials, lawyers, lobbyists, and policy specialists. Given the complex nature of CERCLA, as well as the absence of guidance as to what is meant by "clean up" in the context of hazardous wastes, the industry will only get larger in the future.

### Interstate Water Pollution

Another issue has to do with the extent to which states should be able to regulate the pollution of interstate waterways. Disputes over interstate waterways often involve pollution by firms in one state of a waterway that flows into another state. Because states have different water-quality standards, a question of fairness arises as to which state's laws should govern in this situation. Furthermore, the federal Environmental Protection Agency (EPA) also regulates water pollution under the authority of the Clean Water Act of 1972 and its amendments. Should the states' water-quality standards take priority over federal regulation by the EPA, or do

the standards issued by the EPA preempt state laws?

In 1992, the United States Supreme Court tackled such questions in *Arkansas v. Oklahoma*.[1] In that case, a Fayetteville, Arkansas, sewage treatment plant had obtained a permit from the EPA to discharge effluent (waste) into a stream that ultimately reached the Illinois River before it flowed into Oklahoma. The state of Oklahoma and other Oklahoma parties challenged the EPA-issued permit, contending that the Fayetteville discharge violated Oklahoma water-quality standards—which required that there be "no degradation" of the upper Illinois River—and that the EPA should have taken these standards into consideration. The EPA had, in fact, taken Oklahoma's standards into consideration, but it decided that Oklahoma's standards would only be violated if the Fayetteville discharge effected an "actually detectable or measurable" change in the water quality of the upper Illinois River in Oklahoma.

After making detailed findings of fact, an EPA administrative law judge (ALJ) found that the Fayetteville discharge would not lead to a detectable change in water quality under any of Oklahoma's four primary measures of water pollution. Therefore, the Fayetteville plant could keep on pouring its effluent into the Arkansas

_____

1. ____ U.S.____, 112 S.Ct. 1046, 117 L.Ed.2d 239 (1992).

stream. Oklahoma appealed the ALJ's decision to a federal court of appeals, which reversed the ALJ's decision; ultimately, the case reached the United States Supreme Court.

The Supreme Court first assessed the relative authority of state regulations affecting interstate waterways, concluding that when an interstate waterway is involved and the downstream state objects to an upstream state's discharge, the only state law applicable is the law of the upstream state. Therefore, when a permit to discharge waste into a waterway is being issued by the upstream state's regulatory agency, the downstream state "does not have the authority to block the issuance of the permit if it is dissatisfied with the proposed standards. An affected State's only recourse is to apply to the EPA Administrator, who then has the discretion to disapprove the permit if he concludes that the discharges will have an undue impact on interstate waters. * * * Thus the Act makes it clear that affected States occupy a subordinate position to source States in the federal regulatory program."

The Court then addressed the issue of whether the EPA had the authority to interpret Oklahoma's standard of "no degradation" of its waterways to mean no "detectable or measurable" change in the water quality of its waterways. The Court held that the EPA did have such authority. The Clean Water Act "vests in the EPA and the States broad authority to develop long-range area-wide programs to alleviate and eliminate existing pollution."

The EPA had validly exercised its discretionary powers when it determined that the Fayetteville discharge had to comply with Oklahoma's water-quality standards and also when it determined that Oklahoma's standards would not be violated unless there was a detectable deterioration in the water quality of the upper Illinois River in Oklahoma. The EPA had stressed that "unless there is some method for measuring compliance, there is no way to ensure compliance." The Court agreed with this approach and stated that the EPA's "interpretation of the Oklahoma standards makes eminent sense in the interstate context: if every discharge that had some theoretical impact on a downstream State were interpreted as 'degrading' the downstream waters, downstream States might wield an effective veto over upstream discharges."

## Equal Credit Opportunity

The Equal Credit Opportunity Act (ECOA), by prohibiting creditors from discriminating against credit applicants on the basis of race, religion, national origin, color, sex, marital status, or age, reflects society's ethical goal of ending discrimination on these bases in all areas of life. Before the passage of the act, women were particularly disadvantaged, because potential creditors normally

requested their spouses to cosign credit agreements.

The ECOA, among other things, prohibits this practice. A creditor may request a spouse's signature, but only if the credit applicant does not have sufficient income to meet the creditor's standards of creditworthiness. If a creditor unlawfully demands that a spouse cosign a credit agreement, the cosigning spouse is allowed to sue the creditor for damages for violating the ECOA. But does the creditor's breach of the ECOA render the credit agreement invalid? No. Under the ECOA, the agreement is enforceable against the cosigning spouse. State laws, though, may go further in protecting consumers against such practices.

Consider, for example, a case that was reviewed by the Wyoming Supreme Court in 1992. It involved Richard Naef and his wife, Linda Naef. Richard, when he obtained a franchise to sell Polaris snowmobiles, financed the purchase through credit arrangements made with Transamerica Commercial Finance Corporation. Later, when Richard's dealership failed to pay Transamerica as promised, Transamerica promised him that if he would sign a promissory note for the amount owed ($41,000), Transamerica would not foreclose on the debt, and he could continue his business operations. Transamerica insisted that Linda also had to sign the note. Linda expressed her concern about signing the note, because she would be unable to pay such an

amount. The Transamerica representative assured her that it was just a formality and that she would never be obligated to pay the note. Linda signed the papers, and the next day Transamerica repossessed the snowmobiles. Transamerica then sued the Naefs for payment of the note. Richard petitioned for bankruptcy relief, but Transamerica continued the suit against Linda.

The court noted that Transamerica, when requesting Linda's signature, had induced her to sign the note by misrepresenting to her that she would never be obligated to pay it. According to the court, this misrepresentation alone was not enough to release Linda from liability for payment of the note. The court concluded, however, that Transamerica's reprehensible conduct, when combined with its "blanket, illegal and unreasonable policy of requiring spousal signatures," was sufficient to nullify, or invalidate, the note.[2]

## Fair Debt Collection

By the passage of the Fair Debt Collection Practices Act (FDCPA), Congress expressed society's concern with unfair debt-collection practices. The act prohibits those who collect debts for other parties, such as collection agencies, from engaging in certain abusive tactics, as discussed in Chapter 46. Some have

---

2.  *Transamerica Commercial Finance Corp. v. Naef*, 842 P.2d 539 (Wyo. 1992).

argued that the act did not go far enough in the direction of protecting consumer debtors, because the act does not cover creditors who collect their own debts rather than have a third party, such as a collection agency, do so.

Consider, for example, the situation in *Sterling Mirror of Maryland, Inc. v. Gordon*.[3] Sterling Mirror of Maryland, Inc., had installed mirrors in the home of John and Daisy Gordon. Only John signed the contract. Because one of the mirrors was chipped while it was being installed, John Gordon refused to pay the balance due to Sterling Mirror. Sterling Mirror tried to pressure the Gordons into paying for the mirrors by making numerous calls to Daisy at her place of employment. When Sterling Mirror sued the Gordons for the balance due, Daisy counterclaimed for damages under the FDCPA, asserting, among other things, that Sterling Mirror had violated the provisions of that act by contacting her at work. Had Sterling Mirror violated the FDCPA? No, it had not, because Sterling Mirror was not a collection agency, and thus the FDCPA did not apply. Had it been a collection agency, however, it would have violated the FDCPA, because under the act, collection agencies are allowed to contact only the debtor (not the debtor's spouse) at the debtor's place of employment, and then

_____
3.  619 A.2d 64 (D.C.App. 1993).

only if the employer does not object.

## Antitrust Law and the Ivy League

Antitrust policy expresses American attitudes toward big business and government. Current antitrust law stems from public concern in the 1880s over the large corporate mergers resulting from new technology and improved transportation links. Some people question, however, whether these attitudes and concerns are fully transferable to every sector of the economy, particularly nonprofit colleges and universities. Should centers for higher education be excluded from antitrust laws?

Consider the case of *United States v. Brown University*.[4] Since 1958, the Massachusetts Institute of Technology (MIT) and eight of the nation's most prestigious colleges and universities—the Ivy League schools[5]—have met two times a year to exchange information on the financial-aid packages that would be offered to incoming students and their families. In 1989, the Department of Justice (DOJ) undertook an investigation of the alleged price-fixing behavior. The DOJ discovered that the "Ivy Overlap Group" developed methods for analyzing students' financial needs,

_____
4.  805 F.Supp. 288 (E.D.Pa. 1992).
5.  Brown, Columbia, Cornell, Dartmouth, Harvard, Princeton, the University of Pennsylvania, and Yale.

agreed not to award any merit scholarships, and compared and adjusted proposed family contributions. The goal of each review meeting was to make sure that each of the ten thousand or so students who applied to more than one of the schools in the group would be offered essentially the same basic financial-aid package.

The Ivy Group also shared information about proposed tuition increases. Throughout the year, the universities exchanged information on proposed tuition increases for the following year and adjusted their tuition rates accordingly. Rates for room and board were also discussed and resulted in similar rates being charged across a wide variety of universities. Room and board at Harvard, for example, located in very expensive Cambridge, Massachusetts, was the same as it was at Brown, in much less expensive Providence, Rhode Island.

The Ivy Group schools argued that such meetings were necessary to prevent the schools from engaging in a bidding war for talented students. According to the Ivy Group, if each school offered similar financial aid, students would be free to choose a college based on academic, rather than financial, considerations. The DOJ disagreed. After a two-year investigation, the DOJ charged the colleges with price fixing in violation of Section 1 of the Sherman Act. All of the colleges except MIT eventually entered into "consent decrees," agreeing that they would no longer discuss current financial-aid information among themselves. MIT, however, confident in the integrity of its financial-aid process, refused to give in and went to trial.

At trial, one of MIT's arguments focused on the fact that educational institutions are not commercial and should not be subject to laws governing the commercial world, including antitrust laws. In response to MIT's contention, the judge stated that he could "conceive of few aspects of higher education that are more commercial than the price charged to students."

The court also disagreed with MIT's argument that the Ivy Group's agreements on financial aid were beneficial to students because the nearly uniform costs left students free to select colleges based on factors other than price. The court found that the agreements "created a horizontal restraint which interfered with the natural functioning of the marketplace by eliminating students' ability to consider price differences when choosing a school and by depriving students of the ability to receive financial incentives which competition between those schools may have generated." "Indeed," said the judge, "the member institutions formed the Ivy Overlap Group for the very purpose of eliminating economic competition for students." Declaring that the court "[had] no choice but to respect 102 years of our nation's antitrust policy," the judge ruled that the participation of MIT in the Ivy

Group's agreements in respect to financial aid violated the antitrust laws.

On appeal, however, the trial court's ruling was reversed and the case remanded. According to the appellate court, the Ivy Group had not necessarily engaged in unlawful price fixing. The lower court's analysis had failed to examine social-welfare factors unique to higher education. After the appellate court's decision, the DOJ and MIT reached a settlement, which essentially allows MIT and the other Ivy League schools to continue their previous practice of comparing financial-aid packages. The trade-off reflected in the DOJ-MIT settlement is clear: one social goal (the ability of students to negotiate better financial-aid packages) was sacrificed to attain another (the protection of institutions of higher learning against the financial effects of bidding wars for students).[6]

## ■ Discussion Questions

**1.** In the discussion of the Superfund in this *Focus on Ethics,* the following question was raised: "If, say, 90 percent of the waste at a given site could be removed for $50,000, but the removal of the other 10 percent would cost $2 million, is it reasonable to remove that remaining 10 percent?" How would you answer this question?

6. *United States v. Brown University,* 5 F.3d 658 (3rd Cir. 1993).

**2.** Both environmental and occupational safety laws strive to protect the public health from hazardous substances. Should standards in these two contexts be the same? Or should employees be allowed to voluntarily accept some greater risk in return for a higher wage scale?

**3.** Assume that if all asbestos were removed from all public buildings in the nation, it would save perhaps ten lives per year. If the cost of the asbestos removal were $250 billion, in effect, Americans would be paying $250 million per life saved. Is this too high a price to pay? Should cost ever be a consideration when considering human lives?

**4.** Creditors must comply strictly with the requirements of such consumer protection laws as the Truth-in-Lending Act, the Equal Credit Opportunity Act, and the Fair Debt Collection Practices Act. Even a minor violation may permit a consumer to sue a creditor for damages. In some cases, consumers have sought damages for violations even though the creditor had abided by the "spirit" of the law but not the "letter." Should courts make exceptions when consumers are clearly abusing these protective laws for their own gain? Or should the courts hold creditors liable even when, by doing so, the result is unfair to the creditor?

# UNIT TEN

# PROPERTY

**CONTENTS**

**49** The Nature of Property and Personalty

**50** Bailments

**51** Real Property

**52** Landlord-Tenant Relationships

# CHAPTER 49

# THE NATURE
# OF PROPERTY
# AND PERSONALTY

The word *property* is familiar to everybody. And so far in this text, the term has been used again and again. In Chapter 8, for example, you read about one form of property—intellectual property. Chapters 20 through 25 examined the law governing the sale of goods, which is another form of property. Here we look more closely at this term in the context of what has become known as property law.

**Property** consists of the legally protected rights and interests a person has in anything with an ascertainable value that is subject to ownership. Property would have little value if the law did not define the right to use it, to sell or dispose of it, and to prevent trespassing upon it. In the United States, the ownership of property receives unique protection under the law. The Fifth Amendment to the U.S. Constitution states that no person shall ''be deprived of life, liberty, or property, without due process of law; nor shall private property be taken for public use, without just compensation.'' The Fourteenth Amendment provides that no state shall ''deprive any person of life, liberty, or property, without due process of law.''

Property may be divided into real property and personal property. **Real property** (sometimes called *realty* or *real estate*) means the land and everything permanently attached to it. When structures are permanently attached to the land, then everything attached permanently to the structures is also realty. Everything else is **personal property,** or *personalty*. Attorneys sometimes refer to personal property as **chattel,** a term used under the common law to denote all forms of personal property.

In this chapter, we first examine the basic attributes of personal and real property and then look at the ways in which ownership rights in both of these forms of property can be held. The remainder of the chapter focuses on ownership rights in personal property, as well as on the laws governing rights in mislaid, lost, or abandoned property.

# THE NATURE OF PERSONAL PROPERTY

Personal property can be tangible or intangible. *Tangible personal property,* such as a television set, heavy construction equipment, or a car, has physical substance. *Intangible personal property* represents some set of rights and interests, but it has no real physical existence. Stocks and bonds are intangible personal property. So, too, are patents, trademarks, and copyrights, as discussed in Chapter 8.

Because we live in a dynamic society, new types of personal property—and therefore new types of ownership rights in personal property—emerge over time. For example, gas, water, and telephone services are now considered personal property for the purpose of criminal prosecution when they are stolen or used without payment. Federal and state statutes protect against the copying of musical compositions. It is a crime now to engage in the "bootlegging"—illegal copying for resale—of records and tapes. The theft of computer programs and services is considered in many states to be a theft of personal property.

# THE NATURE OF REAL PROPERTY

*Real property* consists of land and the buildings, plants, and trees that it contains. Whereas personal property is movable, real property is immovable. Real property usually means land, but it also includes subsurface and air rights, plant life and vegetation, and fixtures.

## LAND

Land includes the soil on the surface of the earth and the natural products or artificial structures that are attached to it. Land further includes all the waters contained on or under its surface and the air space above it (subject, of course, to the legal use of aviators). In other words, unless a statute or case law holds otherwise, a landowner has the right to everything existing permanently below the surface of his or her property to the center of the earth and above it to the heavens.

## AIR SPACE AND SUBSURFACE RIGHTS

The owner of real property has relatively exclusive rights to the air space above the land as well as the soil and minerals underneath it. Significant limitations on either air rights or subsurface rights normally have to be indicated on the document transferring title at the time of purchase. When no such limitations, or encumbrances, are noted, a purchaser can expect to have an unfettered right to possession of the property. The ways in which ownership rights in real property can be limited will be examined in detail in Chapter 51.

**AIR RIGHTS** Until seventy-five years ago, the right to use the air space over an owner's property was not too significant. Early cases involving air rights dealt with matters such as whether a telephone wire could be run across a person's property when the wire did not touch any of the property[1] and whether a bullet shot over a person's land constituted trespass.[2]

Today, cases involving air rights present questions such as the right of commercial and private planes to fly over property and the right of individuals and governments to seed clouds and produce artificial rain. Flights over private land do not normally violate the property owners' rights unless the flights are low and frequent, causing a direct interference with the enjoyment and use of the land.[3]

**SUBSURFACE RIGHTS** Ownership of the surface of land can be separated from ownership of

---

1. *Butler v. Frontier Telephone Co.,* 186 N.Y. 486, 79 N.E. 716 (1906). Stringing a wire across someone's property violates the air rights of that person. Leaning walls and projecting eave spouts and roofs also violate the air rights of the property owner.
2. *Herrin v. Sutherland,* 74 Mont. 587, 241 P. 328 (1925). Shooting over a person's land normally constitutes trespass.
3. *United States v. Causby,* 328 U.S. 256, 66 S.Ct. 1062, 90 L.Ed. 1206 (1946).

its subsurface. Subsurface rights can be extremely valuable when minerals, oil, or natural gas is located beneath the surface. But a subsurface owner's rights would be of little value if he or she could not use the surface to exercise those rights. Hence, a subsurface owner will have a right (called a *profit*—see Chapter 51) to go onto the surface of the land to, for example, find and remove minerals.

Of course, conflicts may arise between surface and subsurface owners when attempts are made to excavate below the surface. At common law, a landowner has the right to have the land supported in its natural condition by the owners of the interests under the surface. If the owners of the subsurface rights excavate, they are absolutely liable if their excavation causes the surface to collapse. Depending on the circumstances, the excavators may also be liable for any damage to structures on the land. Many states have statutes that extend excavators' liability to include damage to structures on the property. Typically, these statutes provide exact guidelines as to the requirements for excavations of various depths.

## PLANT LIFE AND VEGETATION

Plant life, both natural and cultivated, is also considered to be real property. In many instances, the natural vegetation, such as trees, adds greatly to the value of the realty. When a parcel of land is sold and the land has growing crops on it, the sale includes the crops, unless otherwise specified in the sales contract. When crops are sold by themselves, however, they are considered to be personal property or goods. Consequently, the sale of crops is a sale of goods, and it is governed by the Uniform Commercial Code rather than by real property law.[4]

## FIXTURES

Certain personal property can become so closely associated with the real property to which it is attached that the law views it as real property. Such property is known as a **fixture**—a thing affixed to

---

4. See UCC 2–107(2).

realty. A thing is *affixed* to realty when it is attached to it by roots; embedded in it; or permanently attached by means of cement, plaster, bolts, nails, or screws. The fixture can be physically attached to real property, be attached to another fixture, or even be without any actual physical attachment to the land, as long as the owner *intends* the property to be a fixture.

Fixtures are included in the sale of land if the sales contract does not provide otherwise. The sale of a house includes the land and the house and garage on it, as well as the cabinets, plumbing, and windows. Because these are permanently affixed to the property, they are considered to be a part of it. Unless otherwise agreed, however, the curtains and throw rugs are not included. Items such as drapes and window-unit air conditioners are difficult to classify. Thus, a contract for the sale of a house or commercial realty should indicate which items of this sort are included in the sale.

**THE ROLE OF INTENT** To determine whether or not a certain item is a fixture, the *intention* of the party who placed the property must be examined. If the facts indicate that the person intended the item to be a fixture, then it will be a fixture. When the intent of the party who placed the fixture on the realty is in dispute, the courts usually determine the intent based on either or both of the following factors:

1. If the property attached cannot be removed without causing substantial damage to the remaining realty, it is usually deemed a fixture.
2. If the property attached is so adapted to the rest of the realty as to become a part of it, the property is usually deemed a fixture.

Certain items can only be attached to property permanently; such items are fixtures. It is assumed that the owner intended them to be fixtures, because they had to be permanently attached to the property. A tile floor, cabinets, and carpeting are examples. Also, when an item of property is custom made for installation on real property, such as storm windows, the property is usually classified as a fixture. Again, it is assumed that the owner intended the item of property to become part of the real property.

What qualifies as a fixture is not always easy to predict, as the following case illustrates.

**BACKGROUND AND FACTS** *The city of North Charleston, South Carolina, needed land on which to construct a new coliseum. The city had title to twenty-nine acres but needed a few more. Exercising its power of eminent domain, North Charleston condemned three acres of private property. (The power of eminent domain allows the government to take private land—through what are known as condemnation proceedings—for public use, for just compensation; see Chapter 51.) By law, North Charleston was required to pay the fair market value of the real property taken from the private landowners. The law does not require that North Charleston compensate the landowners for any personal property or costs stemming from moving personal property off the condemned site. Janie and William Claxton owned part of the condemned land. The city initiated a condemnation proceeding against the Claxtons, who then requested a jury trial. The Claxtons were awarded $79,500 in compensation for the real property, plus $17,654.15 in attorneys' fees. On appeal, the Claxtons argued that the trial judge failed to include the cost of removing the Claxtons' mobile homes from the site, which they claimed were fixtures and part of the real property. Because the homes were real property, they argued, the cost of moving the homes was compensable under condemnation law.*

**CASE 49.1**

**CITY OF NORTH CHARLESTON v. CLAXTON**
Court of Appeals of South Carolina, 1993.
431 S.E.2d 610.

*GARDNER,* Judge.

\* \* \* \*

\* \* \* *A chattel does not become a fixture by mere affixation to realty.* Criteria for determining whether an item remains personalty or becomes a fixture when affixed to realty includes: (1) the mode of attachment; (2) the character of the structure of the article; (3) the intent of parties making the annexation; and (4) the relationship of the parties. [Emphasis added.]

Mobile homes have been held to be both fixtures and personal property. In this case, the record reflects that the Claxtons' trailers were connected to utility services. There is no evidence, however, that the trailers had other significant attachments to the property such as permanent foundations or additions. Based on these facts, we hold that the Claxtons' mobile homes are not fixtures \* \* \* .

*The appellate court affirmed the trial court's refusal to consider the costs involved in removing the mobile homes from the condemned site.*

**DECISION AND REMEDY**

---

**TRADE FIXTURES** An exception to the rule that fixtures are a part of the real property involves **trade fixtures.** A trade fixture is installed for a commercial purpose by the tenant and remains the property of the tenant, unless removal would irreparably damage the building or property. A walk-in cooler, for example, purchased and installed by a tenant who used the premises for a restaurant, is a trade fixture. The tenant can remove the cooler from the premises when the lease terminates but ordinarily must repair any damage that the removal causes or compensate the landlord for the damage.

**SECTION 3**

# PROPERTY OWNERSHIP

Property ownership can be viewed as a bundle of rights. These rights include the right to possession of the property and the right to dispose of the property—by sale, gift, rental, lease, and so on.

## FEE SIMPLE

A person who holds the entire bundle of rights is said to be the owner in **fee simple.** The owner in fee simple is entitled to use, possess, and dispose of the property as he or she chooses during his or her lifetime; and upon death, the owner's interest in the property descends to his or her heirs. We will look further at ownership in fee simple in Chapter 51, in the context of real property ownership.

## CONCURRENT OWNERSHIP

Persons who share ownership rights simultaneously in particular property are said to be *concurrent* owners. There are two principal types of **concurrent ownership:** *tenancy in common* and *joint tenancy.* Concurrent ownership rights can also be held in a *tenancy by the entirety* or as *community property,* although these latter two types of concurrent ownership are less common.

**TENANCY IN COMMON**    The term **tenancy in common** refers to a form of co-ownership in which each of two or more persons owns an *undivided* portion of the property. Such portions need not be equal. When a tenant in common dies, the property interest passes to the heirs. For example, suppose Reband and Charnock each owned an equal interest in a rare stamp collection as tenants in common. If Reband died before Charnock, one-half of the stamp collection would become the property of Reband's heirs. If Reband had sold her interest to French before she died, French and Charnock would have become co-owners as tenants in common. If French died, his interest in the personal property would pass to his heirs, and they in turn would own the property with Charnock as tenants in common.

**JOINT TENANCY**    In a **joint tenancy,** each of two or more persons owns an undivided interest in the whole (personal property), and a deceased joint tenant's interest *passes to the surviving joint tenant or tenants.* Joint tenancy can be terminated at any time before the joint tenant's death by gift or by sale. If no termination occurs, then upon the death of a joint tenant, his or her interest transfers to the remaining joint tenants, not to the heirs of the deceased joint tenant.

The fact that the surviving joint tenant or tenants acquires the deceased tenant's interests—instead of the interest passing to the deceased tenant's heirs—is the main feature distinguishing a joint tenancy from a tenancy in common. To illustrate: If Reband and Charnock from the preceding example were joint tenants, and if Reband died before Charnock, the entire stamp collection would become the property of Charnock. Reband's heirs would receive no interest in the collection. If, prior to Reband's death, she had sold her interest to French, French and Charnock would have become co-owners. Reband's sale, however, would have terminated the joint tenancy, and French and Charnock would have become owners as tenants in common—unless, of course, they established another joint tenancy or other form of ownership.

A joint tenancy can also be transferred by *partition;* that is, the tenants can physically divide the property into equal parts. Because a joint tenant's interest is capable of being conveyed without the consent of the other joint tenants, it can be levied against (seized by court order) to satisfy the tenant's judgment creditors. This characteristic is also true of the tenancy in common.

At common law, unless a clear intention to create a tenancy in common was shown, there was a presumption that any co-tenancy was a joint tenancy. Modern statutes, however, reverse this presumption. Most statutes now presume that a co-tenancy is a tenancy in common unless there is a clear intention to establish a joint tenancy. Thus, language such as ''to Jerrold and Eva as joint tenants with right of survivorship, and not as tenants in common'' would be necessary to create a joint tenancy.

The following case involves a situation in which two parties owned, as joint tenants, an investment account. The case illustrates the survivorship rights of a joint tenant.

| CASE 49.2 | **BACKGROUND AND FACTS**    *In August 1986, Marie McGinness used her own funds to open an account with Shearson Lehman Brothers, Inc. (Shearson), an investment company. She stated that the account would be owned by herself and her son, Chester Graves, as joint tenants. Later, Graves and his mother signed the joint tenancy agreement. On March 17, 1992, McGinness telephoned Shearson and ordered the account to be liq-* |
| --- | --- |
| **GRAVES v. KELLEY**<br>Court of Appeals of Indiana,<br>First District, 1993.<br>625 N.E.2d 493. | |

uidated *(converted into cash), which Shearson accomplished later that day. McGinness died the following day. A check for $17,453.60, issued by Shearson to "Marie McGinness and Chester Graves JTWROS [joint tenants with right of survivorship]," arrived at the McGinness address on March 19. The joint account with Shearson was closed. The personal representative of the McGinness estate, Marilyn Kelley, brought an action to determine ownership of the account proceeds. The trial court held that the telephone call from McGinness was sufficient to terminate the joint tenancy before she died, and therefore the estate was entitled to the proceeds. Graves appealed.*

*ROBERTSON,* Judge.

\* \* \* \*

The deposit agreement of a joint account establishes a party's right to withdraw funds and governs the relationship between the bank and the joint tenants. In the present case, the deposit agreement reads as follows: Each of the joint tenants shall have the authority . . . (c) to receive or withdraw money, securities, commodities, and other property, (d) to execute agreements relating to the foregoing matters and to terminate, modify or waive any of the provisions thereof, and (e) generally to deal with you [Shearson] as fully as if he alone were interested in said account, all without notice to the other tenant or joint tenants. Notwithstanding the foregoing, you [Shearson] are authorized, in your discretion, to require joint action by the joint tenants with respect to any matter concerning the joint account, including . . . the withdrawal of moneys, securities, or commodities.

\* \* \* Obviously, Shearson, in the exercise of its discretion as provided under the deposit agreement, did not permit McGinness to withdraw all the funds in the account in favor of herself over the telephone. Instead, Shearson, in the exercise of its discretion as provided under the deposit agreement, issued the funds jointly to McGinness and Graves, and maintained the right of survivorship between the parties.

\* \* \* \*

In the present case, the joint account or its proceeds, the check, remained jointly owned by McGinness and Graves with the right of survivorship as provided by express written instruments (the deposit agreement and the check). Therefore, the proceeds of the account became Graves' property at the time of McGinness' death.

**DECISION AND REMEDY** *The appellate court reversed the trial court's decision and remanded the case for proceedings consistent with its opinion.*

**INTERNATIONAL CONSIDERATIONS** **Joint Tenancy and Rights of Survivorship under Islamic Law** *Islamic law (*shari'a) *makes no provision for joint tenancy with rights of survivorship. Instead, concurrent tenancies are normally regarded as tenancies in common. In regard to survivorship rights, Islamic law provides that no more than one-third of an estate can be devised by will. The remainder must be inherited by heirs as specified in Islamic law.*

**TENANCY BY THE ENTIRETY** A **tenancy by the entirety** is less common today than it once was. Typically, it is created by a conveyance (transfer) of real property to a husband and wife. It is distinguished from a joint tenancy by the inability of either spouse to transfer separately his or her interest during his or her lifetime. In some states where statutes give the wife the right to convey her property, this form of concurrent ownership has been effectively abolished. A divorce, either spouse's death, or mutual agreement will terminate a tenancy by the entirety.

**COMMUNITY PROPERTY**   Only a limited number of states[5] allow property to be owned as **community property.** If property is held as community property, each spouse technically owns an *undivided* one-half interest in property. This type of ownership applies to most property acquired by the husband and/or the wife during the course of the marriage. It generally does not apply to property acquired prior to the marriage or to property acquired by gift or inheritance during the marriage. After a divorce, community property is divided equally in some states and according to the discretion of the court in other states.

## SECTION 4

# ACQUIRING OWNERSHIP OF PERSONAL PROPERTY

The ownership of personal property can be acquired by purchase, possession, production, gift, will or inheritance, accession, and confusion. The purchase of personal property, which was discussed in Chapters 20 through 25, is one of the most common forms of acquiring or transferring personalty. The other forms of acquisition are discussed below.

## POSSESSION

One example of acquiring ownership by possession is the capture of wild animals. Wild animals belong to no one in their natural states, and the first person to take possession of a wild animal normally owns it. The killing of a wild animal amounts to assuming ownership of it. Merely being in hot pursuit does not give title, however. There are two exceptions to this basic rule. First, any wild animals captured by a trespasser are the property of the landowner, not the trespasser. The fish in a pond on a farmer's land, for example, are the farmer's property, not the property of a trespasser who fishes for and catches them. Second, if wild animals are captured or killed in violation of wild game statutes, the capturer does not obtain title to the animals; rather,

the state does. Those who find lost or abandoned property also can acquire ownership rights through mere possession of the property, as will be discussed later in this chapter.

## PRODUCTION

Production—the fruits of one's labor—is another means of acquiring ownership of personal property. As discussed in Chapter 8, writers, inventors, manufacturers, and others who produce personal property may thereby acquire title to it. (In some situations—for example, when a researcher is hired as an employee to invent a new product or technique—the producer does not own what is produced, however.)

## GIFT

A **gift** is another fairly common means of acquiring or transferring ownership of property. A gift is essentially a *voluntary* transfer of property ownership. It is not supported by legally sufficient consideration (see Chapter 13), because the very essence of a gift is giving without consideration. Gifts can be made during a person's lifetime, or they can be made in a last will and testament. A gift made by will is called a *testamentary gift.*

   There are three requirements for an effective gift—delivery, donative intent on the part of the *donor* (the one giving the gift), and acceptance by the *donee* (the one receiving the gift). Each of these requirements is discussed below. Until these three requirements are met, no effective gift has been made. For example, suppose that your aunt tells you that she is going to give you a new Mercedes-Benz for your next birthday. This is simply a *promise* to make a gift. It is not considered a gift until the Mercedes-Benz is delivered.

**DELIVERY**   Delivery is obvious in most cases, but some objects cannot be relinquished physically. Then the question of delivery depends upon the surrounding circumstances. When the physical object cannot be delivered, a symbolic delivery, or **constructive delivery,** will be sufficient. Constructive delivery does not confer actual possession of the object in question. It is a general term for all those acts that the law holds to be equivalent to acts of real delivery. Suppose that you want to make a gift of various old rare coins that you have stored in a safe-deposit box at your bank. You cer-

---

5.   These states include Arizona, California, Idaho, Louisiana, Nevada, New Mexico, Texas, Washington, and Wisconsin. Puerto Rico allows property to be owned as community property as well.

tainly cannot deliver the box itself to the donee, and you do not want to take the coins out of the bank. Instead, you can simply deliver the key to the box to your donee and authorize the donee's access to the box and its contents. This constitutes symbolic, or constructive, delivery of the contents of the box. Delivery of intangible personal property, such as stock-ownership rights, *must* be accomplished by symbolic or constructive delivery, such as by the delivery of a stock certificate.

An effective delivery also requires giving up *complete dominion*[6] *and control* over the subject matter of the gift. The outcome of disputes often turns on the retaining or relinquishing of control over the subject matter of the gift. The Internal Revenue Service scrutinizes transactions between relatives when one relative has given away to another relative income-producing property. A relative who does not relinquish complete control over a piece of property will have to pay taxes on the income from that property. Under the tax laws, it may be illegal to assign or give away income while retaining control over the property that produces the income (unless a special trust is set up—see Chapter 54).

Delivery can be accomplished by means of a third person. The third person may be the agent of

the donor or of the donee. If the person is the agent of the donor, the gift is effective when the agent delivers the property to the donee. If, in contrast, the third person is the agent of the donee, the gift is effective when the donor delivers the property to the donee's agent.[7] When there is doubt as to whose agent the third party is, he or she is generally presumed to be the agent of the donor. Naturally, no delivery is necessary if the gift is already in the hands of the donee. All that is necessary to complete the gift in such a case is the required intent and acceptance by the donee.

**DONATIVE INTENT**  Donative intent (the intent to make a gift) is determined from the language of the donor and the surrounding circumstances. When a gift is challenged in court, for example, the court may look at the relationship between the parties and the size of the gift in relation to the donor's other assets. Donative intent might be questioned by a court if the gift was made to an archenemy. Likewise, when a person has given away a large portion of his or her assets, the court will scrutinize the transactions to determine whether the donor was mentally competent or whether fraud or duress was involved. In the following case, the court looks at the intent of the donor and the question of delivery.

---

6. The term *dominion* in this sense refers to absolute ownership rights in, and control over, property. One who has dominion over property both possesses and has title to the property.

---

7. *Bickford v. Mattocks,* 95 Me. 547, 50 A.894 (1901).

---

**BACKGROUND AND FACTS**  *Gladys Piper died intestate (without a will) in 1982. At the time of her death, she owned personal property consisting of household goods, two old automobiles, farm machinery, and "miscellaneous" items totaling $5,150. This did not include jewelry or cash. When Piper died, she had $206.75 in cash and her two diamond rings, known as the "Andy Piper" rings, in her purse. The contents of Piper's purse were taken by her niece Wanda Brown upon Piper's death, allegedly to preserve them for the estate. Clara Kauffman, a friend of Gladys Piper, filed a claim against the estate for $4,800. From October 1974 until Piper's death in 1982, Kauffman had taken Piper to the doctor, beauty shop, and grocery store; written her checks to pay her bills; and helped her care for her home. Kauffman maintained that Piper had*

**CASE 49.3**

**IN RE ESTATE OF PIPER**[a]

Missouri Court of Appeals, 1984.
676 S.W.2d 897.

---

a.  Recall that *In re* means "In the matter of," "concerning," or "regarding." Case titles that begin with *In re* indicate that the matter before the court was not one involving adversarial parties but rather a matter that called for some judicial action to be taken—in this case, a determination of who had ownership rights in Gladys Piper's rings.

*promised to pay her for these services and that the diamond rings were a gift to her. The trial court denied Kauffman's request for payment of $4,800 on the basis that the services had been voluntary. Kauffman then filed a petition for delivery of personal property (the rings), which was granted by the trial court. The defendants—Piper's heirs and her estate by the administrator—appealed.*

*GREENE*, Judge.

* * * *

* * * Clara's petition claimed the rings belonged to her by reason of "a consummated gift long prior to the death of Gladys Piper." The only evidence of the gift issue came from two witnesses. James Naylor, who had known Gladys for over 20 years, testified that when he saw Gladys "[b]etween the time of her last admission to the hospital and the date of her death," Gladys told him, after Naylor had complimented her on her rings, that "these are Clara's, but I am wearing them until I am finished with them, or until I am dead or whatever she may have said * * * ." Beverly Marcus testified that Gladys told her "when she was through with those rings, they were to be Clara's."

There was no evidence of any actual delivery to Clara, at any time, of the rings.

* * * *

While no particular form is necessary to effect a delivery, and while the delivery may be actual, constructive, or symbolical, there must be some evidence to support a delivery theory. What we have here, at best, through the testimony of James Naylor and Beverly Marcus, was an intention on the part of Gladys, at some future time, to make a gift of the rings to Clara. Such an intention, no matter how clearly expressed, which has not been carried into effect, confers no ownership rights in the property in the intended donee. *Language written or spoken, expressing an intention to give, does not constitute a gift, unless the intention is executed by a complete and unconditional delivery of the subject matter, or delivery of a proper written instrument evidencing the gift.* There is no evidence in this case to prove delivery, and, for such reason, the trial court's judgment is erroneous. [Emphasis added.]

**DECISION AND REMEDY** *The judgment of the trial court was reversed. No effective gift of the rings had been made, because Piper had never delivered the rings to Kauffman.*

---

**ACCEPTANCE** The final requirement of a valid gift is acceptance by the donee. This rarely presents any problems, because most donees readily accept their gifts. The courts generally assume acceptance unless shown otherwise.

**GIFTS *INTER VIVOS* AND GIFTS *CAUSA MORTIS***
A gift made during the donor's lifetime is called a **gift *inter vivos***. A **gift *causa mortis*** is made in contemplation of imminent death. Gifts *causa mortis* do not become absolute until the donor dies from the contemplated illness or disease. A gift *causa mortis* is revocable at any time up to the death of the donor and is automatically revoked if the donor recovers.

Suppose that Stiggur is to be operated on for a cancerous tumor. Before the operation, he delivers an envelope to a close business associate. The envelope contains a letter saying, "I realize my days are numbered, and I want to give you this check for $1 million in the event of my death from this operation." The business associate cashes the check. The surgeon performs the operation and removes the tumor. Stiggur recovers fully. Several months later, Stiggur dies from a heart attack that is totally unrelated to the operation. If Stiggur's personal representative (the party charged with administering Stiggur's estate) tries to recover the $1 million, normally she will succeed. The gift *causa mortis* is automatically revoked if the donor recovers. The *specific event* that was contemplated in making the gift was death from a particular operation. Because Stiggur's death was not the result of this event, the gift is revoked, and the $1 million passes to Stiggur's estate.[8]

Although a gift *causa mortis* is revocable at any time prior to the donor's death, to be effective, the gift must meet the three requirements of delivery, intent, and acceptance. The question of whether a gift *causa mortis* had been effectively delivered is at issue in the following case.

---

8. *Brind v. International Trust Co.*, 66 Colo. 60, 179 P. 148 (1919).

---

**BACKGROUND AND FACTS** *William Yee and S. Hing Woo had been lovers for nearly twenty years. They often lived together; they held themselves out as husband and wife; and Yee had even given Woo a wedding band, which she wore. Two days before his death, Yee told Woo that he felt "terribly bad," that he had a "heaviness" in his chest, and that he believed he would die. That night, he gave Woo two checks, one for $42,700 and one for $80,000, and told her that if he died, he wanted her "to be taken care of." The next day, he gave Woo a third check for $1,900. After Yee's death, Woo cashed the $42,700 check and the $1,900 check. The $80,000 check was never cashed. The administrator of Yee's estate petitioned the court to declare that Woo was not entitled to the money represented by the checks or to any of Yee's other assets. The central issue before the court was whether an effective gift* causa mortis *had been made.*

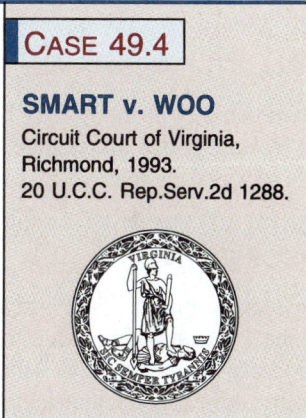

CASE 49.4

**SMART v. WOO**
Circuit Court of Virginia,
Richmond, 1993.
20 U.C.C. Rep.Serv.2d 1288.

JOHNSON, J.

\* \* \* \*

\* \* \* [T]he court has no problem finding that Yee fully intended to make a gift of money to Woo. The testimony of Woo and her sister, which the court finds perfectly credible, easily establishes that Yee intended to give Woo the funds represented by the three checks in question. When he gave her the checks, he told her that he wanted her to be taken care of; he wanted her to be provided for. The checks were given to her for that purpose.

The court also finds that the checks were given to Woo by Yee under the apprehension that death was imminent. \* \* \*

The court also makes the obvious finding that the subject of the alleged gift—money—is personal property. Accordingly, two of the three elements of a gift *causa mortis* \* \* \* are met. Also met is the required element of intent. The gifts fail, however, because delivery of the checks did not constitute delivery of the object of the gifts themselves; that is, the money in the bank.

\* \* \* \*

\* \* \* Section 3–409(1) of the Uniform Commercial Code provides: "A check or other draft does not of itself operate as an assignment of any funds in the hands of the drawee available for its payment, and the drawee is not liable on the instrument until he accepts it." Thus, while three checks were delivered by Yee to Woo, no money was delivered. And since no money was delivered, no money can be claimed by Woo as a gift *causa mortis.*

\* \* \* ("[T]he general rule appears to be that the donor's own check is not the subject of a valid gift, either *inter vivos* or *causa mortis,* prior to acceptance or payment by the bank.")

| | |
|---|---|
| **DECISION AND REMEDY** | *The court held that because the necessary element of delivery was not present, no gift occurred. Woo was not entitled to any part of the estate to satisfy the $80,000 check, and she was ordered to repay to the estate the $44,600 received when she cashed the other two checks.* |
| **ETHICAL CONSIDERATIONS** | *The court realized that enforcing the delivery requirement in this case led to harsh results and sympathized with Woo's plight. Nonetheless, in the eyes of the court, to grant an exception to the delivery requirement, as Woo had asked the court to do, would essentially abolish the legal principle that delivery was required for a gift to be effective.* |

## WILL OR INHERITANCE

Ownership of property may be transferred by will or by inheritance under state statutes. These types of transfers are dealt with at length in Chapter 54.

## ACCESSION

**Accession** means "something added." It occurs when someone adds value to a piece of personal property by use of either labor or materials. Generally, there is no dispute about who owns the property after accession has occurred, especially when the accession is accomplished with the owner's consent. For example, a Corvette-customizing specialist comes to Hoshi's house. Hoshi has all the materials necessary. The customizing specialist uses them to add a unique bumper to Hoshi's Corvette. Hoshi simply pays the customizer for the value of the labor, obviously retaining title to the property.

Ownership can be at issue after the occurrence of an accession if (1) a party has wrongfully caused the accession or (2) the materials added or labor expended greatly increase the value of the property or change the identity of the property. Some general rules can be applied when these situations occur.

When accession occurs without the owner's consent, the courts will tend to favor the owner over the improver—the one who improves the property—provided the accession is done in bad faith. This is true even if the value of the property was increased substantially. In addition, many courts will deny the improver (wrongdoer) any compensation for the value added; for example, a car thief who put new tires on the stolen car would obviously not be compensated for the value of the new tires.

If the accession is performed in good faith, however, even without the owner's consent, ownership of the improved item most often depends on whether the accession has increased the value of the property or changed its identity. The greater the increase, the more likely that ownership will pass to the improver. Obviously, when this occurs, the improver must compensate the original owner for the value the property had prior to the accession. If the increase in value is not sufficient for ownership to be passed to the improver, most courts require the owner to compensate the improver for the value added.

## CONFUSION

**Confusion** is defined as the commingling of goods so that one person's personal property cannot be distinguished from another's. It frequently involves goods that are fungible.[9] *Fungible goods* are goods consisting of identical particles, such as grain or oil. For example, if two farmers put their number 2 grade winter wheat into the same silo, confusion will occur. When goods are confused due to a wrongful and willful act and the wrongdoer is unable to prove what percentage of the confused goods belongs to him or her, then the innocent party ordinarily acquires title to the whole.

This rule does not apply when confusion occurs by agreement, honest mistake, or the act of some third party. When any of these three events occurs, the owners all share ownership as tenants in common. Suppose that you enter into a cooperative arrangement with five other farmers in your local community of Midway, Iowa. Each fall everyone

---

9. See UCC 1–201(17).

harvests the same amount of number 2 yellow corn. The corn is stored in silos that are held by the cooperative. Each of you owns one-sixth of the total corn in the silos. If anything happens to the corn, each of you will bear the loss in equal proportions of one-sixth.

Now suppose you share ownership in some other proportion. Often, owners do not have equal interests. In such a case, the owners must keep careful records of their respective proportions. If a dispute over ownership or loss arises, the courts will presume that everyone has an equal interest in the goods. Therefore, you must be prepared to prove that you own more or less than an equal part.

Suppose you own two-thirds of the corn in the Midway co-op silos. Further assume that the silos are damaged by a tornado and thunderstorm. How much have you lost if one-half of the corn is blown away by the storm? You have lost one-half of your two-thirds, or one-third of the total. When corn is stored by several owners, each owning a different proportion of the total, loss is shared proportionally.

# MISLAID, LOST, OR ABANDONED PROPERTY

As already noted, one of the methods of acquiring ownership of property is to possess it. Simply finding something and holding onto it, however, does not *necessarily* entitle the finder to it. Different rules apply, depending on whether the property was mislaid, lost, or abandoned.

## MISLAID PROPERTY

Property that has been voluntarily placed somewhere by the owner and then inadvertently forgotten is **mislaid property.** Suppose you go to the theater and leave your opera glasses at the concession stand. The glasses are mislaid property, and the theater owner is entrusted with the duty of reasonable care for the goods. When mislaid property is found, the finder does not obtain title to the goods.[10] Instead, the owner of the place where the

property was mislaid becomes the caretaker of the property, because it is highly likely that the true owner will return.[11]

## LOST PROPERTY

Property that is *involuntarily* left is **lost property.** A finder of lost property can claim title to the property against the whole world, *except the true owner*. If the true owner demands that the lost property be returned, the finder must return it. If a third party attempts to take possession of lost property from a finder, the third party cannot assert a better title than the finder.

When a finder knows who the true owners of property are and fails to return the property to them, that finder is guilty of a tort known as *conversion* (see Chapter 6). Finally, many states require the finder to make a reasonably diligent search to locate the true owner of lost property.

Suppose Kamal works in a large library at night. After work, as he is walking through the courtyard of the library, he finds a piece of gold jewelry that contains several apparently precious stones. Kamal decides to take it to a jewelry store to have it appraised. While pretending to weigh the jewelry, an employee of the jeweler removes several of the stones. If Kamal brings an action to recover the stones from the jeweler, he will win, because he found lost property and holds valid title against everyone except the true owner. Because the property was lost and not mislaid, the owner of the library is not the caretaker of the jewelry. Instead, Kamal acquires title good against the whole world (except the true owner).[12]

Many states have **estray statutes** to encourage and facilitate the return of property to its true owner and then to reward the finder for honesty if the property remains unclaimed. Such statutes provide an incentive for finders to report their discoveries by making it possible for them, after passage of a

---

10.  The finder is an involuntary bailee. See Chapter 50.

11.  The owner of the place where property is mislaid is a bailee with right of possession against all except the true owner.
12.  See *Armory v. Delamirie,* 93 Eng. Rep. 664 (K.B. 1722). If Kamal had found the jewelry during the course of his employment, however, his employer would be the involuntary bailee. Further, many courts now say that lost property recovered in a private place allows the owner of the place, *not* the finder, to become the bailee (even if the finder is not a trespasser).

specified period of time, to acquire legal title to the property they have found if the property remains unclaimed. Such statutes usually require the county clerk to advertise the property in an attempt to help the owner recover what has been lost. Some preliminary questions must always be resolved before the estray statute can be employed. The item must be lost property, not mislaid or abandoned property. When the situation indicates that the property was probably lost and not mislaid or abandoned, as a matter of public policy, loss is presumed, and the estray statute applies.

## ABANDONED PROPERTY

Property that has been *discarded* by the true owner, who has *no intention* of claiming title to it, is **abandoned property.** Someone who finds abandoned property acquires title to it, and such title is good against the whole world, *including the original owner.* The owner of lost property who eventually gives up any further attempt to find the lost property is frequently held to have abandoned the property.

For example, assume that Aleka is driving with the windows down in her car. Somewhere along her route, a valuable scarf blows out the window. She retraces her route and searches for the scarf but cannot find it. She finally decides that further search is futile and proceeds to her destination five hundred miles away. Six months later, Frye, a hitchhiker, finds the scarf. Frye has acquired title, which is good even against Aleka. By completely giving up her search, Aleka had abandoned the scarf just as effectively as if she had intentionally discarded it.

A trespasser who finds an item of abandoned personal property does not acquire title to it, however. The owner of the real property on which it was found does. The same rule applies if the property was lost. Similarly, if a landowner employs a crew to install an underground septic tank, for example, and the crew digs up a cache of pioneer relics, the landowner has first claim to the relics, because they were buried in his or her ground.

In contrast, if the crew had unearthed money, gold, silver, or bullion (instead of pewter dishes, tin cups, brass buttons, and old muskets), the find could be classified as **treasure trove** (treasure that is found), and the crew might be able to keep it. In the United States, in the absence of a statute, a finder has title to treasure trove against all but the true owner. (In Great Britain, the Crown gets it.) Generally, to constitute treasure trove, property need not have been buried—it could have been hidden in some other private place, such as behind loose bricks in an old chimney—but its owner must be unknown, and its finders must not have been trespassing.

In a widely publicized case, the Columbus-America Discovery Group, Inc. (CADG), located the sunken *S.S. Central America* 160 miles east of Charleston, South Carolina. The luxury passenger ship sank in 1857, on a voyage from Panama to New York. The vessel carried gold miners returning from California to the East to invest their gold, which was also on board. The CADG began its lengthy search of the ocean floor in 1986. When the CADG found the *Central America,* it sought to establish finder's rights in the gold (valued at between $450 million and $1 billion).[13] Several insurance companies, claiming to be the true owners, challenged the CADG's rights as finders. The insurance companies had issued policies covering the gold cargo. They argued that the rights of the original owners were subrogated to them (see Chapter 32) because they had paid on the original owners' insurance claims when the ship sank; this would give the insurers the same rights to the gold that the original owners had.

The district court applied the law of abandoned property and held in favor of the CADG. That decision was reversed on appeal, however. The appellate court held that the insurance companies had ownership rights in the gold and that the companies had not abandoned those rights.[14] As a result, the law of salvage, not the law of abandoned property, was appropriate. As salvagers, the CADG was entitled only to an award for its services in locating the *Central America.*

In the following case, the issue was whether some valuable property found by the plaintiff was lost or abandoned.

---

13. *Columbus-America Discovery Group, Inc. v. Unidentified, Wrecked and Abandoned Sailing Vessel,* 742 F.Supp. 1327 (E.D.Va. 1990).

14. *Columbus-America Discovery Group, Inc. v. Atlantic Mutual Insurance Co.,* 974 F.2d 450 (4th Cir. 1992).

**COMPANY PROFILE** *The federal government chartered the First National Bank of Chicago in 1863. First National doubled its size when it purchased the Union National Bank and the Metropolitan National Bank in the first two years of the twentieth century. Continuing to grow despite the Great Depression and World War II, First National opened a London office and entered the international marketplace in 1959. The bank reorganized as the First Chicago Corporation in 1969 and expanded in the early 1970s. By the middle of the decade, however, First Chicago found itself with $2 billion in problem loans and faced a possible shutdown by federal regulators. While recovering in the 1980s, the bank lost $571 million in loans to several Latin American countries. By the early 1990s, First Chicago held over $1 billion in nonperforming loans and real estate holdings. Despite these problems, First Chicago has continued to grow. Today, it is the largest bank in the Chicago area and the thirteenth largest bank (and the fifth largest credit-card issuer) in the United States. First Chicago owns the American National Corporation, which itself owns Chicago's fifth largest bank (American National Bank and Trust) and several smaller banks in the Chicago area.*

CASE 49.5

**MICHAEL v. FIRST CHICAGO CORP.**

Appellate Court of Illinois, Second District, 1985.
139 Ill.App.3d 374,
487 N.E.2d 403,
93 Ill.Dec. 736.

**BACKGROUND AND FACTS** *In June 1983, First Chicago sold some of its used office furniture to Walter Zibton, a new and secondhand office supply and furniture dealer. Included among the items of furniture were some file cabinets that were locked and presumed to be empty. Keys for the file cabinets were unavailable. Zibton sold one of the file cabinets to Charles Strayve, throwing three other file cabinets into the deal free of charge. Strayve later gave one of the cabinets to his friend Richard Michael, the plaintiff in this case. About six weeks after Michael received the cabinet, it fell over in Michael's garage, burst open, and exposed the contents: $6,687,948.85 worth of certificates of deposit (CDs). Michael took the CDs to the Federal Bureau of Investigation (FBI) for safekeeping and brought an action to determine their ownership. Michael claimed they were abandoned property and that he, as the finder, was thus the rightful owner. The trial court disagreed with Michael and gave First Chicago possession, holding that the CDs had not been abandoned but were instead lost property. As such, First Chicago was the rightful owner. Michael appealed.*

*REINHARD, Justice:*
* * * *
* * * A finder of property acquires no rights in mislaid property, is entitled to possession of lost property against everyone except the true owner, and is entitled to keep abandoned property.
* * * As a general rule, abandonment is not presumed and the party seeking to declare an abandonment must prove the abandoning party intended to do so.
* * * *
Plaintiffs failed to show First Chicago intended to abandon the certificates of deposit. It is readily apparent from the evidence that the certificates of deposit were to be transferred to other storage and some simply were overlooked and left in the file cabinets. The relinquishment of possession, under the circumstances here, without a showing of an intention to permanently give up all right to the certificates of deposit is not enough to show an abandonment.

**DECISION AND REMEDY**   *The appellate court upheld the trial court's judgment. First Chicago was the rightful owner of the CDs.*

## ■ CONCEPT SUMMARY 49.1 Personal Property

| CONCEPT | DESCRIPTION |
|---|---|
| **Personal Property** | Personal property (personalty) includes all property not classified as real property (realty). It can be tangible (such as a TV set or a car) or intangible (such as stocks or bonds). Referred to legally as *chattel*—a term that includes both living and inanimate property. |
| **Common Types of Property Ownership** | 1. *Fee simple*—Exists when individuals have the right to possess, use, or dispose of the property as they choose during their lifetimes and to pass on the property to their heirs at death.<br>2. *Concurrent ownership:*<br>  a. Tenancy in common—Co-ownership in which two or more persons own an undivided fractional interest in the property; upon one tenant's death, the property interest passes to his or her heirs.<br>  b. Joint tenancy—Exists when two or more persons own an undivided interest in property; upon the death of a joint tenant, the property interest transfers to the remaining tenant(s), not to the heirs of the deceased.<br>  c. Tenancy by the entirety—A form of co-ownership between a husband and wife that is similar to a joint tenancy, except that a spouse cannot transfer separately his or her interest during his or her lifetime.<br>  d. Community property—A form of co-ownership in which each spouse technically owns an undivided one-half interest in property acquired during the marriage. This type of ownership occurs in only a few states. |
| **Acquisition of Personal Property** | 1. *Purchase*—The most common means of acquiring and transferring ownership of personal property.<br>2. *Possession*—Ownership may be acquired by possession if no other person has ownership title (e.g., wild animals or abandoned property may be acquired by possession).<br>3. *Production*—Any product or item produced by an individual becomes the property of that individual (with minor exceptions).<br>4. *Gift*—An effective gift exists when:<br>  a. The gift is delivered (physically or constructively) to the donee or the donee's agent.<br>  b. There is evidence of *intent* to make a gift of the property in question.<br>  c. The gift is accepted by the donee or the donee's agent.<br>5. *Will or inheritance*—Upon death, the property of the deceased passes to family members or others by will or inheritance laws.<br>6. *Accession*—When someone adds value to a piece of property by labor or materials, the added value generally becomes the property of the owner of the original property (includes accessions made in bad faith). Good faith accessions that substantially increase the property's value or change the identity of the property may cause title to pass to the improver.<br>7. *Confusion*—In the case of fungible goods, if a person wrongfully and willfully commingles goods with those of another in order to render them indistinguishable, the innocent party acquires title to the whole. Otherwise, the owners become tenants in common of the intermingled goods. |

## ◼ CONCEPT SUMMARY 49.1 Personal Property *(continued)*

| CONCEPT | DESCRIPTION |
|---|---|
| **Mislaid, Lost, and Abandoned Property** | 1. *Mislaid property*—Property that is placed somewhere *voluntarily* by the owner and then inadvertently forgotten. A finder of mislaid property will not acquire title to the goods, and the owner of the place where the property was mislaid becomes a caretaker of the mislaid property. |
| | 2. *Lost property*—Property that is *involuntarily* left and forgotten. A finder of lost property can claim title to the property against the whole world *except the true owner.* |
| | 3. *Abandoned property*—Property that has been discarded by the true owner, who has no intention of claiming title to the property in the future. A finder of abandoned property can claim title to it against the whole world, *including the original owner.* |

## TERMS AND CONCEPTS TO REVIEW

| | | |
|---|---|---|
| abandoned property 982 | fee simple 973 | personal property 970 |
| accession 980 | fixture 972 | property 970 |
| chattel 970 | gift 976 | real property 970 |
| community property 976 | gift *causa mortis* 978 | tenancy by the entirety 975 |
| concurrent ownership 974 | gift *inter vivos* 978 | tenancy in common 974 |
| confusion 980 | joint tenancy 974 | trade fixture 973 |
| constructive delivery 976 | lost property 981 | treasure trove 982 |
| estray statute 981 | mislaid property 981 | |

## QUESTIONS AND CASE PROBLEMS

**49–1. Gifts.** Jaspal has a severe heart attack and is taken to the hospital. He is not expected to live, and he knows it. Because he is a bachelor without close relatives nearby, Jaspal gives his car keys to his close friend, Friedrich, telling Friedrich that he is expected to die and that the car is Friedrich's. Jaspal survives the heart attack, but two months later he dies from pneumonia. Jaspal's uncle, Sam, the executor of Jaspal's estate, wants Friedrich to return the car. Friedrich refuses, claiming that the car was given to him by Jaspal as a gift. Discuss whether Friedrich will be required to return the car to Jaspal's estate.

**49–2. Found Property.** Senga goes into Meyer's Department Store to do some Christmas shopping. She becomes engrossed in looking over a number of silk blouses but suddenly realizes she has a dinner engagement. She hastily departs from the store, inadvertently leaving her purse on a sales counter. Elena, a sales clerk at the store, notices the purse on the counter but leaves it there, expecting Senga to return for it. Later, when Senga returns, the purse is gone. Senga files an action against Meyer's Department Store for the loss of her purse. Discuss the probable success of her suit.

**49–3. Found Property.** Bill Heise is a janitor for the First Mercantile Department Store. While walking to work, Bill discovers an expensive watch lying on the curb. Bill gives the watch to his son, Otto. Two weeks later, Martin Avery, the true owner of the watch, discovers that Bill found the watch and demands it back from Otto. Discuss who is entitled to the watch and why.

**49–4. Gifts.** Fischel Levin has a son named Don. Fischel wants to give his son a new car that he has recently purchased. Fischel and his son have been on bad terms during the past few years, and Fischel feels part of this is his fault. He goes to his son's house, wanting to make amends by giving the car to Don. When Fischel arrives at Don's house, his daughter-in-law (Don's wife) tells

Fischel that Don is out of town and will return the next day. Fischel gives the keys to the new car to his daughter-in-law, tells her to hold the keys for his son, and says that he will return the next day. Two hours later, Fischel has second thoughts about giving Don the car. He retrieves the keys from his daughter-in-law before she can turn them over to Don. Don returns from his trip, learns of the events, and demands possession of the car, claiming a gift was made. Is Don entitled to the car? Explain.

**49–5. Rights of Possession.** Ilana DeCante owns a 1967 Chevy. The car has had continual mechanical problems, and Ilana's repair expenses have been considerable. One day, in disgust, Ilana parks the car on a city-owned vacant lot two blocks from her house. The car sits there for four months. During this period, Rhett Garnett observes the car, which has been unattended by Ilana. Rhett takes the car and makes improvements and repairs valued at $500. Later, Ilana learns that Rhett has the car, has it running smoothly, and is treating it as if it were his. Ilana demands the car, claiming title. Rhett refuses to surrender the car, claiming that he has title. Discuss who is correct and what rights, if any, each person has against the other.

**49–6. Fixtures.** Lawrence Reeves was a land-owning farmer whose land was being foreclosed upon by his mortgage holder, Metropolitan Life Insurance Co. Prior to the foreclosure, Reeves had contracted with Production Sale Co. to erect a grain-storage facility on the farm. Its total cost was $171,185.30. Prior to the foreclosure, Reeves had paid only $16,137.77. When Metropolitan brought the foreclosure proceedings, the question arose as to whether the grain-storage facility was a fixture to the realty or personal property. If it was considered to be a fixture, Metropolitan would receive the proceeds from the sale; if it was considered to be personal property, the proceeds would go to Production Sale Co. Discuss whether the facility was a fixture to the real property or personal property. [*Metropolitan Life Insurance Co. v. Reeves,* 223 Neb. 299, 389 N.W.2d 295 (1986)]

**49–7. Gifts.** For some time before she died, Merle Zimmerman allowed her good friend, Joan Robertson, to assist her with her financial affairs. Robertson was given access to Zimmerman's funds, through joint bank accounts, and to Zimmerman's safe-deposit box. At one point, Zimmerman gave Robertson a number of municipal bonds to "put . . . in safekeeping." Robertson noticed that the bonds had been placed in a series of manila envelopes, and each envelope contained a piece of paper on which was written the name of one of Zimmerman's relatives. One envelope, which contained bonds with a face value of $22,000, had Robertson's name on it. When Zimmerman died, Robertson distributed the bonds to the people whose names were on the envelopes and retained the bonds in the envelope with her own name on it. Zimmerman's estate claimed ownership of the bonds. Robertson asserted that Zimmerman had made a gift to her of the bonds. Discuss whether an effective gift had

been made. [*Robertson v. Estate of Zimmerman,* 778 S.W.2d 805 (Mo.App. 1989)]

**49–8. Abandoned Property.** Leonard Charrier, an amateur archaeologist in Louisiana, uncovered artifacts from an Indian burial ground that was several hundred years old. The artifacts had been made by the ancestors of the present-day Tunica Indian tribe of Louisiana. The Tunica tribe asked the court to award it custody of the property, which included burial pots, ornaments, and pottery. Charrier claimed that the property had been abandoned and that he had the right to title because he had taken possession of the property. Discuss whether the Tunica tribe, as heirs to the former owners of the property, should succeed in their claim to the artifacts, or whether the property was indeed abandoned. [*Charrier v. Bell,* 496 So.2d 601 (La.App.1st Cir. 1986)]

**49–9. Gifts.** Before her death, Melanie McCarthy had written and sent or otherwise delivered nine $3,000 checks intended as gifts to various relatives. None of the checks had been cashed prior to Melanie's death. Melanie's son, Daniel, who was one of the administrators of her estate, claimed that the Internal Revenue Service (IRS) should not levy estate taxes on the $27,000 still in Melanie's bank account to cover these checks, because the checks were completed gifts. The IRS contended that the gifts had not been effectively delivered prior to Melanie's death, because Melanie could have ordered the bank to stop payment on the uncashed checks and therefore had not relinquished complete dominion and control over the checks sufficient to establish a completed gift. What should the court decide? Discuss. [*McCarthy v. United States,* 806 F.2d 129 (7th Cir. 1986)]

**49–10. Concurrent Ownership.** Paul was the owner of real estate located in Putnam County, Florida. In 1982, while Paul was living with Lucille, he executed a deed conveying the property to himself and Lucille as joint tenants with right of survivorship. In 1985, Paul and Lucille stopped living together, and three months later Lucille conveyed her interest in the property to her daughter, Sandra. What type of interest does Sandra possess in the property, and why? [*Foucart v. Paul,* 516 So.2d 1035 (Fla.App. 1987)]

**49–11. Gifts.** Before her marriage to Herman Blettell in 1951, Mary Blettell owned a residence. Darlene Snider was Mary's daughter by a previous marriage. In 1965, Herman and Mary moved into the residence. Herman's name was never added to the title. In 1974, Mary executed a deed to the property to Darlene but did not deliver or record it. In 1978, Mary informed Darlene about the deed and told her that it was located in Mary and Darlene's joint safe-deposit box. In August 1987, Mary's health was declining, and she told Darlene to get the deed from their safe-deposit box, rent a safe-deposit box in Darlene's name only, and put the deed in it so "nobody can get [it] but you." Darlene removed the deed from the joint safe-deposit box and placed it in her own box. Herman was not aware of these events until shortly before Mary's death in 1989. On the day after Mary died, Darlene recorded the deed. Herman, as Mary's personal representative (the person appointed in Mary's will to look after her affairs after her death), contended that Mary's transfer of the deed to Darlene was not a valid gift *inter vivos* because the deed was never effectively delivered to Darlene. Darlene argued that there was a valid delivery in 1987, when Mary instructed Darlene to place the deed in her own safe-deposit box. What should the court decide? Explain. [*Estate of Blettell v. Snider,* 114 Or.App. 162, 834 P.2d 505 (1992)]

**49–12. Gifts.** James Wilson learned that he had terminal cancer in 1983 or 1984. At about that time, he arranged for a friend, Harold Buell, to have joint access to Wilson's safe-deposit box. Wilson gave Buell a key. The box contained, among other things, a copy of a promissory note for $65,000 from Michael Cronan. Wilson told Buell that the debt represented by the note was to be forgiven when he died and that on Wilson's death, Buell was to deliver the copy of the note to Cronan. In 1984, Cronan learned of Wilson's illness, and Wilson told Cronan on at least two occasions that Cronan's debt was to be forgiven on Wilson's death. In the meantime, Cronan continued to make payments on the note. Wilson died in July 1987. On the day after Wilson died, Buell delivered the copy of the note to Cronan, as directed. Wilson's personal representative (a person appointed to look after the deceased's affairs), Carol Kesterson, sought to recover from Cronan the balance owing on the $65,000 note, the original of which was found among Wilson's personal effects after his death. Cronan claimed that the debt had been forgiven, as a gift to Cronan. Were the requirements of a gift satisfied? How should this case be resolved? Discuss fully. [*Kesterson v. Cronan,* 105 Or.App. 551, 806 P.2d 134 (1991)]

# CHAPTER 50

# BAILMENTS

The law of bailments applies to many routine business transactions, such as the shipment of goods by a common carrier. The law of bailments also applies to personal transactions, such as an agreement to let a friend use your business law book. When individuals deal with bailments, whether they realize it or not, they are subject to the obligations and duties that arise from the bailment relationship.

A **bailment** is formed by the delivery of personal property, without transfer of title, by one person (called a **bailor**) to another (called a **bailee**), usually under an agreement for a particular purpose—for example, to loan, store, repair, or transport the property. Upon completion of the purpose, the bailee is obligated to return the bailed property in the same or better condition to the bailor or a third person, or to dispose of it as directed.

Most bailments are created by agreement, but not necessarily by contract, because in many bailments not all of the elements of a contract (such as mutual assent or consideration) are present. For example, if you loan your business law text to a friend, a bailment is created, but not by contract, because there is no consideration. Most commercial bailments, such as the delivery of your suit to the cleaners for dry cleaning, are based on contract, however.

A bailment is distinguished from a sale or a gift in that possession is transferred without passage of title or intent to transfer title. In a sale or a gift, title is transferred from the seller or donor to the buyer or donee.

The number, scope, and importance of bailments created daily in the business community and in everyday life make it desirable to understand the elements necessary for the creation of a bailment and to know what rights, duties, and liabilities flow from bailments.

# ELEMENTS OF A BAILMENT

Not all transactions involving the delivery of property from one person to another create a bailment. The required elements for the creation of a bailment are as follows:

1. Personal property.
2. Delivery of possession (without title).
3. Agreement that the property be returned to the bailor or otherwise disposed of according to its owner's directions.

## PERSONAL PROPERTY REQUIREMENT

Only personal property is bailable; there can be no bailment of persons. Although a bailment of your luggage is created when it is transported by an airline, as a passenger you are not the subject of a bailment. Also, you cannot bail realty; thus, leasing your house to a tenant is not a bailment. Bailments commonly involve *tangible* items—jewelry, cattle, automobiles, and the like. *Intangible* personal property may also be bailed, such as promissory notes and shares of corporate stock. One of the problems with bailments is the difficulty of defining what does or does not constitute personal property. In the following case, for example, the court had to determine whether the information contained in a letter was bailable personal property.

---

**BACKGROUND AND FACTS**  *Jole Liddle, a high school student in Salem School District 600, played basketball on the boy's varsity team. He planned to attend college after his graduation. The high school had a policy of delivering any mail sent to its students in care of the school. A letter from Monmouth College of West Long Branch, New Jersey, arrived at Liddle's high school a few days after it was mailed on July 18, 1990. The school did not deliver the letter to Liddle, however, until seven months later. The letter, which was addressed to Liddle in care of the boy's basketball coach, notified Liddle that he was being recruited by Monmouth for a basketball scholarship. Liddle did not receive the letter in time to compete for the scholarship. Liddle sued the school district, seeking damages equivalent to the value of a four-year Monmouth scholarship. Liddle alleged that the coach was negligent in his duties as a bailee of the letter. The school district filed a motion to dismiss the case, arguing that the letter was not bailable property. Liddle claimed that the information in the letter—the notice of a scholarship recruitment—was bailable. The trial court dismissed the action, and Liddle appealed. The only issue on appeal was whether the information in the letter from Monmouth was bailable property.*

**CASE 50.1**

**LIDDLE v. SALEM SCHOOL DISTRICT NO. 600**

Appellate Court of Illinois, Fifth District, 1993.
249 Ill.App.3d 768,
619 N.E.2d 530,
188 Ill.Dec. 905.

Justice *MAAG* delivered the opinion of the court:

\*   \*   \*   \*

Information may, under certain circumstances, be a valuable commodity. If a person learns that the price of a stock is going to increase the following day and purchases shares prior to the rise, that information absolutely has value. Each of the parties to this case is undoubtedly paying the attorneys representing them for legal advice. We doubt that these attorneys would claim their advice was valueless.

There are numerous older decisions in this State which recognize that the non-delivery or late delivery of a telegram may result in liability. \*   \*   \*

In some of the [decisions] referenced above, the information had value to only one person or entity. \*   \*   \*

Similarly, in this case, the letter and information it contained was only valuable to Mr. Liddle. He could not assign or sell that information, but the information still had value to him.

**DECISION AND REMEDY**  *The appellate court held that the information in the letter was intangible personal property and, as such, was bailable. The lower court's decision was thus reversed, and the case was remanded for further proceedings.*

## DELIVERY OF POSSESSION

*Delivery of possession* means transfer of possession of property to the bailee. Two requirements must be met for delivery of possession to occur:

1. The bailee must be given exclusive possession and control over the property.
2. The bailee must *knowingly* accept the personal property.[1] In other words, the bailee *intends* to exercise control over it.

If either delivery of possession or knowing acceptance is lacking, there is no bailment relationship. For example, suppose that Sudi is in a hurry to catch his plane. He has a package he wants to check at the airport. He arrives at the airport check-in station, but the person in charge has gone on a coffee break. Sudi decides to leave the package on the counter. Even though there has clearly been physical transfer of the package, the person in charge of the check-in station has not knowingly accepted the personal property. Therefore, there has been no effective delivery. The same result would occur in the following example: Delacroix checks her coat at a restaurant. In the coat pocket is a $20,000 diamond necklace. By accepting the coat, the bailee does not *knowingly* also accept the necklace.

**ACTUAL DELIVERY**  A distinction is made between a restaurant patron who checks a coat with an attendant and a patron who hangs a coat on a coatrack. Giving the coat to the attendant constitutes an actual, physical delivery and thereby creates a bailment. The attendant (hence the restaurant) has exclusive possession and control over the retention and removal of the coat. In contrast, the self-hung coat can be removed at any time by the patron or anyone else so inclined. The restaurant does not have substantial control over the property and normally is not considered a bailee.

**CONSTRUCTIVE DELIVERY**  Constructive delivery is an implied or symbolic delivery. What is physically delivered to the bailee is not the actual property bailed but something so related to the property that the requirement of delivery is satisfied. For example, Lyssenko owns a boat that she wishes to loan to Brady for the weekend. It is moored at a municipal marina. Lyssenko gives Brady the boat registration papers so that the harbormaster will allow Brady to board the boat. Lyssenko has made constructive delivery of the boat to Brady.

In certain unique situations, a bailment is found despite the apparent lack of the requisite elements of control and knowledge. In particular, safe-deposit box rental is usually held to constitute a bailor-bailee relationship between the bank and its customer, despite the bank's lack of knowledge of the contents and its inability to have exclusive control of the property.[2]

## THE BAILMENT AGREEMENT

A bailment agreement can be *express* or *implied*. Although no written agreement is required for bail-

---

1. We are dealing here with *voluntary* bailments. Under some circumstances, regardless of whether a person *intentionally* accepts possession of someone else's personal property, the law imposes on him or her the obligation to redeliver it. For example, if property is *accidentally* left in another's possession without negligence on the part of its owner, the person in whose possession it has been left may be responsible for its return. This is referred to as *involuntary* bailment.

2. By statute or by express contract, however, a safe-deposit box may be a lease of space or a license, depending on the jurisdiction, the facts, or both.

ments of less than one year (that is, the Statute of Frauds does not apply—see Chapter 16), it is a good idea to have a written agreement, especially when valuable property is involved.

The bailment agreement expressly or impliedly provides for the return of the bailed property to the bailor or to a third person or provides for disposal by the bailee. The agreement presupposes that the bailee will return the identical goods originally given by the bailor. In a bailment of *fungible goods*[3]—uniform, identical goods—or a bailment with the *option to purchase,* however, only equivalent property must be returned.

For example, if Hobson stores his grain (fungible goods) in Kwam's warehouse, a bailment is created. But at the end of the storage period, the warehouse is not obligated to return to Hobson exactly the same grain that was stored. As long as the warehouse returns goods of the same *type, grade,* and *quantity,* the warehouse—the bailee—has performed its obligation.

A bailment with an option or offer to purchase allows the prospective buyer the right to hold or use the property while deciding whether to purchase it. At the end of an agreed-upon period, the bailee must either return the property to the bailor-seller or agree to purchase the property (such as by paying cash to the seller). If he or she agrees to purchase the property, the bailee-buyer returns to the bailor-seller "equivalent" property (a promise or payment of money), terminating the bailment and creating a sale.

A typical example is a *sale on approval.* Suppose Tetsu is interested in buying a lawn mower. The seller gives her possession of a new model, telling her to take it home and try it out. The sales price is $280. If Tetsu does not like the lawn mower, she can bring it back within two weeks. If she does not bring it back within this period or if she approves the offer, the seller will bill her. Thus, a bailment is created, and Tetsu has the duty either to return the lawn mower or to approve the offer and return the equivalent in the form of the purchase price.

---

3. Fungible goods are defined in UCC 1–201(17) and discussed in Chapter 21. UCC 7–207(1) states clearly, "Fungible goods may be commingled."

## SECTION 2

# ORDINARY BAILMENTS

There are three types of ordinary bailments. The distinguishing feature among them is *which party receives a benefit from the bailment.* Ultimately, the courts may use this factor to determine the standard of care required of the bailee while in possession of the personal property, and this factor will dictate the rights and liabilities of the parties. The three types of ordinary bailments are as follows:

1. *Bailment for the sole benefit of the bailor.* This is a type of gratuitous bailment (one that involves no consideration) for the convenience and benefit of the bailor. The bailee is liable only for gross negligence. (Negligence is discussed in Chapter 6.)

2. *Bailment for the sole benefit of the bailee.* This is typically a loan of an article to a person (the bailee) solely for that person's convenience and benefit. The bailee is liable for even slight negligence.

3. *Bailment for the mutual benefit of the bailee and the bailor.* This is the most common kind of bailment and involves some form of compensation for storing items or holding property. It is a contractual bailment and is often referred to as a bailment for hire. The bailee is liable for ordinary negligence, or the failure to observe ordinary care, which is the care that a reasonably prudent person would use under the circumstances.

The degree of care that was traditionally required of the bailee in each of these three types of bailments is indicated in Exhibit 50–1. Recently, however, most courts have tended to impute a *standard of reasonable care* regardless of the type of bailment arrangement in effect.

## SECTION 3

# RIGHTS AND DUTIES OF THE BAILEE

In a bailment situation, both the bailee and the bailor have rights and duties. The rights and duties

■ **Exhibit 50–1 Degree of Care Required of a Bailee**

| Bailment for the Sole Benefit of the Bailor | Mutual-benefit Bailment | Bailment for the Sole Benefit of the Bailee |
|---|---|---|
| DEGREE OF CARE | | |
| SLIGHT | REASONABLE | GREAT |

of the bailee are discussed below. A bailor's rights and duties will be discussed in the following section.

## RIGHTS OF THE BAILEE

The bailee takes possession of personal property for a specified purpose, after which that property is returned (in the same or a *pre*specified altered form). Thus, implicit in the bailment agreement is the right of the bailee to take possession, to utilize the property in accomplishing the purpose of the bailment, and to receive some form of compensation (unless the bailment is intended to be gratuitous). Depending upon the nature of the bailment and the terms of the bailment agreement, these bailee rights are present (with some limitations) in varying degrees in all bailment transactions.

**RIGHT OF POSSESSION** Temporary control and possession of property that ultimately is to be returned to the owner is the hallmark of a bailment. The meaning of *temporary* depends upon the terms of the bailment agreement. If a specified period is expressed in the bailment agreement, then the bailment is continuous for that time period. Earlier termination by the bailor is a breach of contract (if the bailment involves consideration), and the bailee can recover damages from the bailor. If no duration is specified, the bailment ends when either the bailor or the bailee so demands and possession of the bailed property is returned to the bailor.

A bailee's right of possession, even though temporary, permits the bailee to recover damages from any third persons for damage or loss to the property. For example, No-Spot Dry Cleaners sends all suede leather garments to Cleanall Company for special processing. If Cleanall loses or damages any leather goods, No-Spot has the right to recover against Cleanall.

If the personal property is stolen from the bailee during the bailment, the bailee has a legal right to regain possession of (to recapture) the goods or to obtain damages from any third person who has wrongfully interfered with the bailee's possessory rights.

**RIGHT TO USE BAILED PROPERTY** Naturally, the extent to which bailees can use the personal property entrusted to them depends upon the terms of the bailment contract. When no provision is made, the extent of use depends upon how necessary it is for the goods to be at the bailee's disposal for the ordinary purpose of the bailment to be carried out. When leasing drilling machinery, for example, the bailee is expected to use the equipment to drill. In contrast, when providing long-term storage for a car, the bailee is not expected to use the car, because the ordinary purpose of a storage bailment does not include use of the property (unless an emergency dictates such use to protect the car).

**RIGHT OF COMPENSATION** A bailee has a right to be compensated as provided for in the bailment agreement, to be reimbursed for costs and services rendered in the keeping of the bailed property, or both. In mutual-benefit bailments, the amount of compensation is often expressed in the bailment contract. For example, in a rental (bailment) of a car, the contract provides for charges on the basis of time, mileage, or a combination of the two, plus other possible charges. In nonrental bailments, such as when a car is left at a service station for an oil change, the bailee makes a service charge for the work performed.

Even in a gratuitous bailment, a bailee has a right to be reimbursed or compensated for costs incurred in the keeping of the bailed property. For example, Hetta loses her pet dog, which is found by Jesse. Jesse takes Hetta's dog to his home and feeds it. Even though he takes good care of the dog, it becomes ill, and a veterinarian is called.

Jesse pays the bill for the veterinarian's services and the medicine. He is normally entitled to be reimbursed by Hetta for these reasonable costs incurred in the keeping of her dog.

To enforce the right of compensation, the bailee has a right to place a *possessory* lien (claim) on the specific bailed property until he or she has been fully compensated. This lien on specific bailed property is sometimes referred to as a **bailee's lien** or an **artisan's lien**, as discussed in Chapter 32. The lien is effective only so long as the bailee has not agreed to extend credit to the bailor and the bailee retains possession over the bailed property.

If the bailor refuses to pay or cannot pay the charges (compensation), the bailee is entitled in most states to foreclose on the lien. This means that the bailee can sell the property and be paid out of the proceeds for the amount owed from the bailment, returning any excess to the bailee.

For example, Sarito takes his car to the garage and enters into an agreement for repairs. The repairs are to be paid for in cash. Upon completion of the repairs, the garage tenders Sarito his car, but because of unexpected bills, he cannot pay the garage. The garage has a right to retain possession of Sarito's car, exercising a bailee's lien. Unless Sarito can make arrangements for payment, the garage will normally be entitled to sell the car to be compensated for the repairs.

### RIGHT TO LIMIT LIABILITY

In ordinary bailments, bailees have the right to limit their liability by type of risk, by monetary amount, or both, as long as (1) the limitations are called to the attention of the bailor and (2) the limitations are not against public policy.

Any enforceable limitation on liability imposed by the ordinary bailee must be brought to the bailor's attention. Although the bailee is not required to read orally or interpret the limitation for the bailor, the bailor must in some way know of the limitation. Thus, a sign in Nikolai's garage stating that Nikolai will not be responsible "for loss due to theft, fire, or vandalism" may or may not be held to be notice to the bailor. Whether the notice will be effective will depend on the size of the sign, its location, and any other circumstances affecting the likelihood of its being noticed by Nikolai's patrons. The same holds true with limitations placed on the back of identification receipts (stubs) for parked cars, checked coats, or stored bailed goods. Most courts require additional notice, because the bailor rarely reads the receipt and usually treats it merely as an identification number to be used when reclaiming the bailed goods.

Even if the bailor has received notice, certain types of disclaimers of liability are considered to be against public policy and therefore illegal. Clauses that limit a person's liability for his or her own wrongful acts, called *exculpatory clauses,* are carefully scrutinized by the courts, and in bailments they are often held to be illegal. The classic illustration of an exculpatory clause is found on parking receipts: "We assume no risk for damage to or loss of automobile or its contents regardless of cause. It is agreed that the vehicle owner assumes all such risks." Even though the language may vary, if the bailee attempts to exclude liability for the bailee's own negligence, the result is the same—the clause is unenforceable as being against public policy. This is especially true in the case of bailees providing quasi-public services, such as warehousers (discussed later in this chapter). The following case involves the attempted use of an exculpatory clause to limit a bailee's liability for its own negligence.

---

**BACKGROUND AND FACTS**    *R. W. Brockwell took his boat and its motor to Lake Gaston Sales and Service (Gaston) to be repaired. At the time Brockwell delivered the boat to Gaston, the boat contained many items of personal property, including fishing gear, navigation equipment, and electronic equipment. Before the boat could be repaired, Brockwell had to sign a repair order that contained the following disclaimer: "It is understood and agreed that [Gaston] assumes no responsibility whatsoever for loss or damage by theft, fire, vandalism, water or weather related damages, nor for any items of personal property left with the unit placed with [Gaston] for repair, storage or sale." About ten days later, after the boat*

**CASE 50.2**

**BROCKWELL v. LAKE GASTON SALES AND SERVICE**

Court of Appeals of North Carolina, 1992.
105 N.C.App. 226,
412 S.E.2d 104.

*had been repaired, Brockwell learned that equipment and other personal property worth over $2,000 was missing from the boat. Gaston contended that the disclaimer in the repair order absolved it from any liability for the missing property. Brockwell sued Gaston for negligence. The trial court held for Brockwell and awarded him damages. Gaston appealed.*

*HEDRICK,* Chief Judge.

\* \* \* \*

As a general rule, in an ordinary mutual benefit bailment, where there is no great disparity of bargaining power, the bailee may relieve himself from the liability imposed on him by the common law so long as the provisions of the contract do not run counter to the public interest. \* \* \*

\* \* \* Many courts hold that where the bailee makes it his business to act as bailee for hire, on a uniform and not an individual basis, it is against the public interest to permit him to exculpate himself from [avoid liability for] his own negligence. And the decided trend of modern decisions is against the validity of such exculpatory clauses or provisions in behalf of proprietors of parking lots, garages, parcel check rooms, and warehouses, who undertake to protect themselves against their own negligence by posting signs or printing limitations on the receipts or identification tokens delivered to the bailor-owner at the time of bailment.

In the present case, defendant, bailee, attempted to exculpate itself from liability for its own negligence where it ''was [its] business to act as a bailee for hire on a uniform . . . basis.'' Defendant, bailee, took plaintiff's boat, its contents, equipment and attachments into its sole possession in order to perform repairs on the boat in the regular course of its business, and we hold it was against public policy for defendant, bailee, to attempt to exculpate itself from the duty of ordinary care it owed to plaintiff, bailor. We therefore hold the liability disclaimer in the present case is void and unenforceable as a matter of law.

**DECISION AND REMEDY** *The trial court's decision was affirmed. Gaston could not, by contract, disclaim liability for its own negligence.*

## DUTIES OF THE BAILEE

The bailee has two basic responsibilities: (1) to take proper care of the property and (2) to surrender or dispose of the property at the end of the bailment. The bailee's duties are based on a mixture of tort law and contract law. The duty of care involves the standards and principles of tort law discussed previously and in Chapter 6. A bailee's failure to exercise appropriate care in handling the bailor's property results in tort liability. The duty to relinquish the property in a mutual-benefit bailment at the end of the bailment is grounded both in contract law principles and tort law. Failure to return the property is a breach of contract, and with one exception, the bailee is liable for damages. The exception exists when the obligation is excused because the goods or chattel has been destroyed,

lost, or stolen through no fault of the bailee (or claimed by a third party with a superior claim). Failure to return bailed property may also result in the tort of conversion (the wrongful taking of another's personal property).

**DUTY OF CARE** As previously discussed, bailees must exercise proper care over the property in their possession to prevent its loss or damage. As Exhibit 50–1 illustrated, the three types of bailments demand different degrees of care (although the trend is toward enforcement of standards of reasonable care). When a bailment exists for the sole benefit of the bailee, great care, or the highest level of care, is required. When the bailment exists for the mutual benefit of the bailor and the bailee, reasonable care is the standard. When the bailment exists for the sole benefit of the bailor, slight care, or something less than ordinary or reasonable care, is expected.

**DUTY TO RETURN BAILED PROPERTY**    At the end of the bailment, the bailee normally must relinquish the identical undamaged property (unless it is fungible) to either the bailor or someone the bailor designates, or must otherwise dispose of it as directed. This is usually a *contractual* duty arising from the bailment agreement (contract). Failure to give up possession at the time the bailment ends is a breach of contract and could result in the tort of conversion.

**DELIVERY OF GOODS TO THE WRONG PERSON**    Generally, the bailee has a duty to return the bailed goods to the bailor. A bailee may be liable if the goods being held or delivered are given to the wrong person. Hence, a bailee must be satisfied that the person to whom the goods are being delivered is the actual owner or has authority from the owner to take possession of the goods. Should the bailee deliver in error, then the bailee may be liable for conversion or misdelivery.

**PRESUMPTION OF NEGLIGENCE**    Sometimes the duty to return and the duty of care are combined to determine bailee liability. At the end of the bailment, a bailee has the duty to return the bailor's property in the condition in which it was received (allowing for ordinary wear and aging). In some cases, the bailor can sue the bailee in tort for damage to, or loss of, goods on the theory of *negligence* or *conversion*. But often it is not possible for the bailor to discover and prove what specific acts of negligence or conversion committed by the bailee caused damage or loss to the property.[4] Thus, the law of bailments recognizes a rule whereby a *presumption* that the bailee is guilty of negligence or conversion will be made if the bailee fails to return the property or dispose of it in accordance with the bailor's instructions, or if the bailee returns the property in a damaged condition. Once this is shown, the bailee must prove that he or she was not at fault. A bailee who is able to *rebut* (contradict) the presumption is not liable to the bailor.

When damage to goods is of the type that normally results only from someone's negligence, and when the bailee had full control of the goods, it is more likely than not that the damage was caused by the bailee's negligence. Therefore, the bailee's negligence is presumed.

Determining whether a bailee exercised an appropriate degree of care is usually a question of fact. This means that the trier of fact (a judge or a jury) weighs the facts of a particular situation and concludes that the bailee did or did not exercise the requisite degree of care at the time the loss or damage occurred. The failure to exercise appropriate care is negligence, and the bailee is liable for the loss or damage in tort.

The following case illustrates that once a bailment is created, failure of the bailee to return the bailed property to the bailor upon demand results in a presumption of negligence.

---

4. The basic formula for finding negligence requires proof that (1) a duty exists, (2) a breach of that duty occurred, (3) the breach is the proximate cause of damage or loss, and (4) an actual loss or damage resulted.

---

**BACKGROUND AND FACTS**    *Marvin Mueller, the president of Vin-Mar Supply, Inc., purchased approximately 1,150 railroad luggage carts from the Missouri Pacific Railroad. Mueller made an oral contract with Larry Soffer to store the luggage carts in Soffer's warehouse. Subsequently, a fire destroyed the warehouse, and the carts were either destroyed or severely damaged. Without Mueller's consent, the damaged carts were removed in the clean-up operation as scrap metal. Mueller demanded that Soffer return to him all of the carts in their postfire condition. When no carts were returned, Mueller filed suit, alleging that Soffer and the warehouse (the defendants) were negligent in the care they exercised over the bailed property. The trial court held that Mueller and Vin-Mar Supply (the plaintiffs) had established a* prima facie *case of bailment and that failure*

**CASE 50.3**

**MUELLER v. SOFFER**

Appellate Court of Illinois,
Fifth District, 1987.
160 Ill.App.3d 699,
513 N.E.2d 1198,
112 Ill.Dec. 589.

*to return the bailed property upon demand raised a presumption of negligence. The court also concluded that the defendants had failed to rebut [successfully argue against] the presumption of negligence and held for the plaintiffs. The defendants appealed.*

*KASSERMAN, Justice.*
\* \* \* \*

We conclude that [the] evidence does not rebut the presumption of negligence. Defendants, as bailees, were under a duty to exercise reasonable care under the circumstances. In the case at bar, \* \* \* Soffer testified that no effort was made to determine whether plaintiffs' property was salvageable, yet he authorized [the removal of] all the debris without seeking plaintiffs' authority or permission and without accounting to plaintiffs for the scrap value of the carts. We note that Powell received cash for some of the scrap from the site on September 20, and 21, 1984, *i.e.*, after Soffer received Mueller's demand letter. A bailee is not excused from failing to exercise ordinary care because the bailee would have been equally careless with his own property. Furthermore, in the face of the evidence presented by plaintiffs, defendants failed to present any evidence to rebut the presumption that the fire which resulted in a destruction of plaintiffs' property was a result of defendants' negligence.

**DECISION AND REMEDY**   *The appellate court affirmed the trial court's conclusions.*

---

# RIGHTS AND DUTIES OF THE BAILOR

As explained below, a bailee's duties and a bailor's rights are complementary. A bailor's basic duty is to provide a bailee with property free from latent defects that could injure the bailee.

## RIGHTS OF THE BAILOR

The bailor's rights are essentially a complement to the bailee's duties. A bailor has the right to expect the following:

1. The property will be protected with reasonable care while in the possession of the bailee.
2. The bailee will utilize the property as agreed in the bailment agreement (or not at all).
3. The property will be relinquished at the conclusion of the bailment according to directions given by the bailor.
4. The bailee will not convert (alter) the goods except as agreed.
5. The bailor will not be bound by any limitations on the bailee's liability unless these limitations

are known and are enforceable by law.
6. Repairs or service on the property will be completed without defective workmanship.

## DUTIES OF THE BAILOR

A bailor has a single, all-encompassing duty to provide the bailee with goods or chattel that are free from hidden defects that could injure the bailee. This duty translates into two rules:

1. In a *mutual-benefit bailment,* the bailor must notify the bailee of all known defects and any hidden defects that the bailor knew of or could have discovered with reasonable diligence and proper inspection.
2. In a *bailment for the sole benefit of the bailee,* the bailor must notify the bailee of any known defects.

The bailor's duty to reveal defects is based on a negligence theory of tort law. A bailor who fails to give the appropriate notice is liable to the bailee and to any other person who might reasonably be expected to come into contact with the defective article.

For example, assume that Rentco (the bailor) leases four tractors to Iniko. Unknown to Rentco (but discoverable by reasonable inspection), the brake mechanism on one of the tractors is defective at the time the bailment is made. Iniko uses the defective tractor without knowledge of the brake problem and is injured along with two other field workers when the tractor rolls out of control. Rentco is liable on a negligence theory for injuries sustained by Iniko and the two others.

This is the analysis: Rentco has a mutual-benefit bailment and a *duty* to notify Iniko of the discoverable brake defect. Rentco's failure to notify is the *proximate cause* of injuries to farm workers who might be expected to use, or have contact with, the tractor. Therefore, Rentco is liable for the resulting injuries.

A bailor can also incur *warranty liability* based on contract law (see Chapter 24) for injuries resulting from bailment of defective articles. Property leased by a bailor must be *fit for the intended*

*purpose of the bailment.* The bailor's knowledge of, or ability to discover, any defects is immaterial. Warranties of fitness arise by law in sales contracts and have been applied by judicial interpretation in the case of bailments "for hire." Article 2A of the UCC extends implied warranties of merchantability and fitness for a particular purpose to bailments whenever those bailments include rights to use the bailed goods.[5]

The resolution of the following case depended upon the degree of care owed by a bailor—the Atlanta Coca-Cola Bottling Company—to an injured third party. In determining the required degree of care, the court evaluates whether the bailment was a bailment for hire or a gratuitous bailment (bailment without consideration).

---

5. UCC 2A–212; UCC 2A–213.

---

**COMPANY PROFILE** *In 1886, John Pemberton, a druggist in Atlanta, invented Coca-Cola. Within a few years, Asa Candler, another Atlanta druggist, bought the Coca-Cola Company for $2,300. In less than a decade, Candler made Coca-Cola available throughout the United States, and in Canada and Mexico. In 1899, Candler sold most of the U.S. bottling rights to Benjamin Thomas and John Whitehead, who, with John Lupton, developed the regional franchise bottling system that is still in use. In 1919, Candler sold the Coca-Cola Company for $25 million to the Woodruff family. Robert Woodruff introduced the advertising slogans "The Pause That Refreshes" and "It's the Real Thing." Coca-Cola introduced Sprite in 1961, TAB in 1963, Diet Coke in 1982, and New Coke in 1985. In the early 1990s, Coca-Cola formed Coca-Cola Refreshments–Moscow, established an operation in Africa, and began planning additional expansion in Central America and China. Today, Coca-Cola dominates the global soft-drink market. With Coca-Cola products available in nearly two hundred countries, the company produces four of the world's five most popular carbonated beverages. In the U.S. market, however, Coca-Cola Classic barely has the lead over PepsiCo's Pepsi.*

CASE 50.4

**PRINCE v. ATLANTA COCA-COLA BOTTLING CO.**

Court of Appeals of Georgia, 1993.
210 Ga.App. 108,
435 S.E.2d 482.

**BACKGROUND AND FACTS** *Phar-Mor organized a promotional event to take place in the parking area of one of its stores. Phar-Mor arranged with the Atlanta Coca-Cola Bottling Company (ACCBC) to use one of its "special events wagons" during the event. An ACCBC employee delivered the wagon to Phar-Mor's premises and parked it in accordance with a Phar-Mor employee's instructions. ACCBC did not charge Phar-Mor for the use of the wagon, although Phar-Mor paid ACCBC for the beverages and food items (provided by ACCBC) that were sold from the wagon during the event. Phar-Mor employees operated the concession stand during*

*the event. ACCBC had no control over the premises on which the wagon was located. During the event, water leaked from the concession stand, causing a puddle to form. Lisa Prince was walking toward Phar-Mor to make a purchase when she stepped in the puddle, slipped, and fell. She sustained injuries as a result of the fall. ACCBC was unaware of the accident for several months. Prince sued ACCBC for negligence, claiming, among other things, that ACCBC had failed in its duty, as a bailor, to maintain the premises around its refreshment wagon. The trial court granted summary judgment in ACCBC's favor, and Prince appealed.*

BIRDSONG, Presiding Judge.
\*   \*   \*   \*

\*   \*   \* Normally \*   \*   \* "the character of a particular bailment, whether gratuitous or not, is to be determined by the contract between the parties to it." In determining whether a bailment is gratuitous or one for hire, "the possibility of some undisclosed benefit is not enough to render the bailment one for hire; there must be an understanding or arrangement, express or implied, between the parties, whereby the bailee has received or has a right to expect and demand something for his benefit. Casual or incidental benefits which he would have to surrender at the will of the bailor, do not amount to a consideration. There must be a compensation of some sort actually contemplated in the contract and bargained away by the bailor."
\*   \*   \*   \*

In this case, [ACCBC met its burden of showing that there was no evidence of Prince's] claim that appellee contracted with Phar-Mor to provide refreshments in the Coca-Cola special events wagon under a bailment for hire. \*   \*   \* As a gratuitous bailor, defendant ACCBC had no legal duty to maintain properly the area surrounding the refreshment wagon as averred in the complaint, particularly after the wagon was delivered and placed under the bailee's control for its use. Likewise, ACCBC had no legal duty to prevent drain water from the wagon from accumulating around the surrounding area, as such accumulation (whether or not giving rise to a dangerous condition) occurred only after the delivery of the chattel [personal property] to the bailee. Likewise, ACCBC had no legal duty to warn appellant of any slippery, dangerous, or unsafe conditions existing in the vicinity of its refreshment stand when such condition arose from water being allowed to drain on the ground after the wagon had been delivered and placed under the bailee's control. \*   \*   \*

**DECISION AND REMEDY**   *The appellate court affirmed the lower court's decision. A gratuitous bailment existed between Phar-Mor and ACCBC. ACCBC, as a gratuitous bailor, had no duty to maintain the property around the wagon once it had been delivered to the premises of the gratuitous bailee, Phar-Mor, and placed under Phar-Mor's control.*

**INTERNATIONAL CONSIDERATIONS**   **Bailments under European Civil Law**  *In Europe, bailment contracts are known as deposit contracts. Under the civil law tradition, which is derived from Roman law, deposit contracts are known as "consensual contracts." No formalities are required to create consensual contracts.*

# TERMINATION OF BAILMENTS

Bailments for a specific term end when the stated period lapses. When no duration is specified, the bailment can be terminated at any time by the following events:

1. The mutual agreement of both parties.
2. A demand by either party.
3. The completion of the purpose of the bailment.
4. An act by the bailee that is inconsistent with the terms of the bailment.
5. The operation of law.

# SPECIAL FEATURES OF SPECIFIC BAILMENTS

Most of this chapter has concerned itself with ordinary bailments—bailments in which bailees are expected to exercise ordinary care in the handling of bailed property. Some bailment transactions warrant special consideration. These include bailments in which the bailee's duty of care is extraordinary—that is, his or her liability for loss or damage to the property is absolute—as is generally true in cases involving common carriers and innkeepers. Warehouse companies have the same duty of care as ordinary bailees; but like carriers, they are subject to extensive coverage of federal and state laws, including the UCC's Article 7.

## DOCUMENTS OF TITLE AND ARTICLE 7

A shipment or storage of goods may be covered by a *bill of lading,* a *warehouse receipt,* or a *delivery order.* These documents of title are subject to Article 7 of the UCC.[6] To be a **document of title,** a document "must purport to be issued by or addressed to a bailee and purport to cover goods in the bailee's possession which are either identified or are fungible portions of an identified mass."[7]

A **bill of lading** is a document verifying the receipt of goods for shipment issued by a person engaged in the business of transporting or forwarding goods.[8] A **warehouse receipt** is a receipt issued by a person engaged in the business of storing goods for hire.[9] A **delivery order** is a written order to deliver goods directed to a warehouser, carrier, or other person who, in the ordinary course of business, issues warehouse receipts or bills of lading.[10]

Simply put, a document of title is a receipt for goods in the charge of a bailee-carrier or a bailee-warehouser and a contract for the shipment or storage of identified goods.

## NEGOTIABILITY OF DOCUMENTS OF TITLE

Negotiability is a concept that applies to documents of title when—as in situations involving commercial paper[11]—they contain the words "bearer" or "to the order of."[12] If a document of title is negotiable—that is, if it specifies that the goods are to be delivered to bearer or to the order of a named person—the following are also possible:

1. The possessor of the document of title is entitled to receive, hold, and dispose of the document and the goods it covers.
2. A good faith purchaser of the document may acquire greater rights to the document and the goods it covers than the transferor had or had the authority to convey (that is, a good faith purchaser may take free of the claims and defenses of prior parties).

If a document of title is nonnegotiable—that is, if it is not made payable to the order of any

---

6. Of course, where applicable, federal law takes priority [see UCC 7–103]. For example, the Federal Bills of Lading Act [49 U.S.C. Sections 81–124], enacted in 1916, applies to bills of lading issued by a common carrier for goods shipped in interstate or foreign commerce, and the United States Warehouse Act [7 U.S.C. Sections 241–243], also enacted in 1916, applies to receipts covering agricultural products stored for interstate or foreign commerce.

7. UCC 1–201(15); UCC 7–102(1)(e); see also UCC 7–401.
8. UCC 1–201(6).
9. UCC 1–201(45); see also UCC 7–201 and UCC 7–202. UCC 7–102(h) defines the person engaged in the storing of goods for hire as a *warehouseman.*
10. UCC 7–102(1)(d).
11. Commercial paper (negotiable instruments) is the subject of the UCC's Article 3, which is discussed in detail in Chapters 26 through 30.
12. UCC 7–104(1).

named person or to bearer—it may be transferred by assignment but not negotiation.[13]

In other words, documents of title constitute a class of commercial paper representing commodities in storage or transportation. Thus, for example, just as the holder in due course of a negotiable promissory note prevails over prior ownership claims, so too does the holder of a negotiable warehouse receipt who takes by *due negotiation*.[14]

The concepts of Articles 3 and 7 are similar.[15] There are important distinctions between them, however. For example, Article 7 refers to the negotiability process as due negotiation. **Due negotiation** requires not only that the purchaser of a document of title take it in good faith, for value, and without notice of a defense against or a claim to it, but also that he or she do so in the regular course of business or financing and not in the settlement or payment of a money obligation.[16] In other words, even if all other requirements are met, transfer of a negotiable document of title to a nonbusinessperson is *not* due negotiation. In such situations, the transferee acquires only those rights the transferor had or had the authority to convey.[17]

Upon due negotiation, however, a transferee can acquire greater rights in a document of title than the transferor had. The transferee obtains title to the document and to the goods, including rights to goods delivered to the bailee after the document was issued, and takes free of all prior claims and defenses of which he or she had no notice. The document's issuer remains obligated to store or deliver the goods according to the document's terms.[18] Under this provision, businesspersons can extend credit on documents of title without concern for adverse claims of third parties.

To prevent a thief or a finder of goods from defeating the rights of the true owner (by, for example, taking them to a warehouse and subsequently negotiating the warehouse receipt to a third party who would otherwise take the goods free of the claims of others), the goods must be delivered to the issuer of the document of title by their owner or the owner's agent.[19] Otherwise, the document does not represent title to the goods. Even if the document does not represent title, however, the bailee will not be liable if he or she acts in good faith and observes reasonable commercial standards in receiving and delivering the goods.[20]

In other words, a carrier or warehouser who receives goods from a thief or finder and delivers them according to that individual's instructions is not liable to the goods' true owner. The reason for this rule is that carriers and warehousers are not links in the chain of title and do not represent the owner in transactions affecting title but simply furnish a service necessary to trade and commerce.

## COMMON CARRIERS

Common carriers are publicly licensed to provide transportation services to the general public. They are distinguished from private carriers, which operate transportation facilities for a select clientele. A private carrier is not bound to provide service to every person or company making a request. The common carrier, however, must arrange carriage for all who apply, within certain limitations.[21]

The common-carrier contract of transportation creates a *mutual-benefit bailment*. Unlike the bailee in ordinary mutual-benefit bailments, however, the common carrier is held to a standard of care based on *strict liability,* rather than a standard of reasonable care, in protecting the bailed personal property. This means that the common carrier is absolutely liable, regardless of negligence, for all loss or damage to goods except for loss or damage caused by one of the five common law exceptions:

**1.** An act of God.
**2.** An act of a public enemy.

---

13. UCC 7–104(2).
14. Compare UCC 3–305 and UCC R3–302 with UCC 7–502.
15. For example, a delivery order under Article 7 is analogous to a draft under Article 3. A draft is an order by a drawer to a drawee to pay money to a payee. A delivery order is an order by a bailor to a bailee to deliver goods to a deliveree.
16. UCC 7–501(4).
17. UCC 7–504. And until the bailee is notified of the transfer, the transferee's rights may be defeated by certain creditors of the transferor; by a buyer from the transferor in the ordinary course of business, if the bailee has delivered the goods to the buyer; or by the bailee who has dealt with the transferor in good faith.
18. UCC 7–502.

19. UCC 7–503(1).
20. UCC 7–404.
21. A common carrier is not required to take any and all property anywhere in all instances. Public regulatory agencies govern common carriers, and carriers may be restricted to geographical areas. They may also be limited to carrying certain kinds of goods or to providing only special types of transportation equipment.

3. An order of a public authority.
4. An act of the shipper.
5. The inherent nature of the goods.

The UCC retained the common law liability of common carriers in UCC 7–309. Common carriers are treated as if they were absolute insurers for the safe delivery of goods to the destination, even though they are not. They cannot contract away this liability for damaged goods; subject to government regulations, they are permitted, however, to limit their dollar liability to an amount stated on the shipment contract.[22]

Except for the five exceptions given, the common carrier is liable for any damage to goods in shipment, even that caused by the willful acts of

_____

22. Federal laws and Interstate Commerce Commission regulations require common carriers to offer shippers the opportunity to obtain higher dollar limits for loss by paying a higher fee for the transport.

third persons or by sheer accident. Thus, a common-carrier trucking company moving cargo is liable for acts of vandalism, mechanical defects in refrigeration units, or a dam bursting, if any of these acts results in damage to the cargo. But damage caused by acts of God—an earthquake or lightning, for example—is the shipper's loss.

**SHIPPER'S LOSS** The shipper bears any loss occurring through its own faulty or improper crating or packaging procedures. For example, if a bird dies because its crate was poorly ventilated, the shipper, not the carrier, bears the loss.

In the following case, the United States Supreme Court deals with the question of whether a common carrier that has exercised reasonable care and has complied with the instructions of the shipper is nonetheless liable to the shipper for spoilage in transit of an interstate shipment of perishable commodities.

---

**BACKGROUND AND FACTS** *Elmore & Stahl, a fruit shipper, contracted with the Missouri Pacific Railway Company to ship 640 crates of honeydew melons from Rio Grande City, Texas, to Chicago. At trial, the jury was convinced that Missouri Pacific and its connecting carriers performed all the required transportation services without negligence. The jury also found that the evidence showed that the condition of the melons on arrival in Chicago was defective and that the condition was not due solely to an inherent defect in the melons. The trial judge ruled against the carrier, and the court of appeals affirmed the decision, as did the Texas Supreme Court. The ground for affirmation was, basically, that Missouri Pacific did not show that the spoilage or decay was due entirely to the inherent nature of the goods—in other words, that the damage was caused solely by natural deterioration. The carrier appealed to the United States Supreme Court.*

**CASE 50.5**

**MISSOURI PACIFIC RAILWAY CO. v. ELMORE & STAHL**

Supreme Court of the United States, 1964.
377 U.S. 134,
84 S.Ct. 1142,
12 L.Ed.2d 194.

Mr. Justice *STEWART* delivered the opinion of the Court.

\* \* \* \*

\* \* \* [I]n an action to recover from a carrier for damage to a shipment, the shipper establishes his prima facie case when he shows delivery [to the carrier] in good condition, arrival in damaged condition, and the amount of damages. Thereupon, the burden of proof is upon the carrier to show both that it was free from negligence and that the damage to the cargo was due to one of the expected causes relieving the carrier of liability.

\* \* \* [The carrier's] position is simply that if goods are perishable, and the nature of the damage is spoilage, and the jury affirmatively find[s] that the carrier was free from negligence and performed the transportation services as required by the shipper, then the law presumes that the cause of the spoilage was the natural tendency of perishables to deteriorate even though the damage might, in fact, have resulted from other causes, such as the acts of third parties, for which no exception from carrier liability is provided. \* \* \*

\* \* \* \*

Finally, all else failing, it is argued that as a matter of public policy, the burden ought not to be placed upon the carrier to explain the cause of spoilage, because when perishables are involved, the shipper is peculiarly knowledgeable about the commodity's condition at and prior to the time of shipment, and is therefore in the best position to explain the cause of the damage. Since this argument amounts to a suggestion that we now carve out an exception to an unquestioned rule of long standing upon which both shippers and carriers rely, and which is reflected in the freight rates set by the carrier, the petitioner must sustain a heavy burden of persuasion. The general rule of carrier liability is based upon the sound premise that the carrier has peculiarly within its knowledge "[a]ll the facts and circumstances upon which [it] may rely to relieve [it] of [its] duty. \*  \*  \* In consequence, the law casts upon [it] the burden of the loss which [it] cannot explain or, explaining, bring within the exceptional case in which [it] is relieved from liability." We are not persuaded that the carrier lacks adequate means to inform itself of the condition of goods at the time it receives them from the shipper, and it cannot be doubted that while the carrier has possession, it is the only one in a position to acquire the knowledge of what actually damaged a shipment entrusted to its care.

**DECISION AND REMEDY**   *The United States Supreme Court upheld the judgment of the Texas Supreme Court.*

---

## CONNECTING CARRIERS

A bill of lading that specifies one or more connecting carriers is called a *through bill of lading*. When connecting carriers are involved in transporting goods under a through bill of lading, the shipper can recover from the original carrier or any connecting carrier.[23] Normally, the *last* carrier is presumed to have received the goods in good condition.

## WAREHOUSE COMPANIES

Warehousing is the business of providing storage of property for compensation. Like ordinary bailees, warehouse companies are liable for loss or damage to property resulting from *negligence.* UCC 7–204(1) provides that a warehouser must "exercise such care ... as a reasonably careful [person] would exercise under like circumstances but unless otherwise agreed he is not liable for damages which could not have been avoided by the exercise of such care." Under UCC 7–204(2), a warehouse company can limit the dollar amount of liability, but the bailor must be given the option of paying an increased storage rate for an increase in the liability limit.

## INNKEEPERS

At common law, innkeepers, hotel owners, and similar operators were held to the same strict liability as common carriers with respect to property brought into the rooms by guests. Today, only those who provide lodging to the public for compensation as a *regular* business are covered under this rule of strict liability. Moreover, the rule applies only to those who are *guests,* as opposed to *lodgers.* A lodger is a permanent resident of the hotel or inn, whereas a guest is a traveler.

In many states, innkeepers can avoid strict liability for loss of guests' valuables and money by providing a safe in which to keep them. Each guest must be clearly notified of the availability of such a safe. Statutes often limit the liability of innkeepers with regard to articles that are not kept in the safe or that are of such a nature that they are not ordinarily kept in a safe. These statutes may limit the amount of monetary damages or even provide for no liability in the absence of innkeeper negligence.

Normally, the innkeeper assumes no responsibility for the safety of a guest's automobile, because the guest usually retains possession and control. If, however, the innkeeper provides parking facilities, and the guest's car is entrusted to the innkeeper or to an employee, the rules governing ordinary bailments will apply.

---

23.   UCC 7–302.

# ■ CONCEPT SUMMARY 50.1 Rights and Duties of the Bailee and Bailor

| Rights of a Bailee (Duties of a Bailor) | 1. A bailee has the right to be compensated or reimbursed for keeping bailed property. This right is based in contract or quasi contract.<br>2. Unpaid compensation or reimbursement entitles the bailee to a possessory lien on the bailed property and the right of foreclosure.<br>3. A bailee has the right to limit his or her liability. An ordinary bailee can limit types of risk, monetary amount, or both, provided proper notice is given and the limitation is not against public policy. In special bailments, limitations on types of risk are usually not allowed, but limitations on the monetary amount of loss are permitted by regulation.<br>4. The right of possession allows actions against third persons who damage or convert the bailed property and allows actions against the bailor for wrongful breach of the bailment.<br>5. The right to an insurable interest in the bailed property allows the bailee to insure and recover under the insurance policy for loss or damage to the property. |
|---|---|
| Duties of a Bailee (Rights of a Bailor) | 1. A bailee must exercise reasonable care over property entrusted to him or her. A common carrier (special bailee) is held to a standard of care based on *strict liability* unless the bailed property is lost or destroyed due to (a) an act of God, (b) an act of a public enemy, (c) an act of a governmental authority, (d) an act of a shipper, or (e) the inherent nature of the goods.<br>2. Bailed goods in a bailee's possession must be returned to the bailor or disposed of according to the bailor's directions. Failure of return gives rise to a presumption of negligence.<br>3. A bailee cannot use or profit from bailed goods except by agreement or in situations in which the use is implied to further the bailment purpose. |

## TERMS AND CONCEPTS TO REVIEW

bailee **988**
bailee's lien **993**
bailment **988**

bailor **988**
bill of lading **999**
delivery order **999**

document of title **999**
due negotiation **1000**
warehouse receipt **999**

# QUESTIONS AND CASE PROBLEMS

**50–1. Requirements of a Bailment.** Curtis is an executive on a business trip to the West Coast. He has driven his car on this trip and checks into the Hotel Ritz. The hotel has a guarded underground parking lot. Curtis gives his car keys to the parking lot attendant but fails to notify the attendant that his wife's $10,000 fur coat is in a box in the trunk. The next day, upon checking out, he discovers that his car has been stolen. Curtis wants to hold the hotel liable for both the car and the coat. Discuss the probable success of his claim.

**50–2. Duties of the Bailee.** Discuss the standard of care required from the bailee for the bailed property in the following situations, and determine whether the bailee breached that duty.

(a) Benedetto borrows Tom's lawn mower because his own lawn mower needs repair. Benedetto mows his front yard. In order to mow the backyard, he needs to move some hoses and lawn furniture. He leaves the mower in front of his house while doing so. When he returns, he discovers that the mower has been stolen.

(b) Atka owns a valuable speedboat. She is going on vacation and asks her neighbor, Regina, to store the boat in one stall of Regina's double garage. Regina consents, and the boat is moved into the garage. Regina, in need of some grocery items for dinner, drives to the store. In doing so, she leaves the garage door open, as is her custom. While she is at the store, the speedboat is stolen.

**50–3. Use of Bailed Property.** Lee owns and operates a service station. Yutu's car needs some minor repairs. Yutu takes her car to Lee's station. Lee tells Yutu that he will be unable to do the work until the next day and that Yutu can either bring the car back at that time or leave it overnight. Yutu leaves the car with Lee. The next afternoon Yutu comes to pick up her car. Lee presents Yutu with a bill for $220 and refuses to return the car until he is paid. Upon inspecting the car, Yutu discovers that the mileage indicator shows 150 more miles on the car than when she brought it in. Lee claims that he was legally allowed to let one of his employees road test the car by taking it to his home on the preceding evening and driving it around. Discuss Yutu's and Lee's legal rights under these circumstances.

**50–4. Liability of the Bailor.** Orlando borrows from his neighbor, Max, a gasoline-driven lawn edger. Max has not used the lawn edger for two years. Orlando is not familiar with using a lawn edger, because he has never owned one. Max previously used this edger often, and if he had made a reasonable inspection, he would have discovered that the blade was loose. Orlando is injured when the blade becomes detached while he is edging his yard.

    (a) Can Orlando hold Max liable for his injuries?
    (b) Would your answer be any different if Orlando had rented the edger from Max and paid a fee? Explain.

**50–5. Liability of Common Carriers.** Franklin Washer, Inc., delivered to the Western Central Railroad one hundred crated washing machines to be shipped to Rocky High Appliance Store in Denver, Colorado. Western Central received the goods on Thursday and stored them in its warehouse pending loading into boxcars the next day. On the Western Central shipping invoice was a clause printed in big, bold type that excluded the carrier from liability resulting from loss of goods under control of the carrier because of acts of vandalism, fire, or theft. The clause also limited liability to $500 per shipment unless a higher evaluation was declared and a fee paid. That evening a riot broke out. Some of the one hundred crated washing machines were stolen, some were damaged by the rioters, and some were destroyed by fire. Franklin wants to hold the carrier liable for the entire value of the one hundred machines. Western Central claims, first, that it has no liability by virtue of the contractual limitation against liability for loss by fire, theft, or vandalism, and second, that if it were liable, its damage cost responsibility would be only $500. Discuss the validity of Western Central's claims.

**50–6. Liability of the Bailee.** Robert Freeman owned a broken Bulova watch. Its band was encrusted with gold nuggets and contained two jade stones. He took the watch to John Garcia's jewelry store for repairs. Garcia did not have the necessary equipment to make all the repairs, so he sent the watch to Douglas Viers Base Watch Repair Lab. While it was at Viers's shop, the watch, along with several others, was stolen. Viers did not have insurance, nor did he have any burglar alarm or other safeguards on the premises. Freeman, claiming the watch had been worth $25,000, sued both Garcia and Viers for the value of the watch. Discuss whether Garcia, Viers, or both are liable for the loss of the watch. [*Freeman v. Garcia*, 495 So.2d 351 (La.App. 2d Cir. 1986)]

**50–7. Liability of the Bailee.** The plaintiffs, Rose and Obadiah Simmons, purchased a bedroom suite on layaway from Max's Discount Furniture, a store owned by Max Yelverton, the defendant. As part of the bargain, Yelverton's salesperson agreed that after the purchase price had been paid, Yelverton would continue to hold the furniture in storage until the Simmonses wanted to claim it or until Yelverton needed the warehouse space. Two years after the final payment had been made, the Simmonses attempted to pick up the furniture, only to discover that Yelverton had gone out of business and that the furniture was nowhere to be found. Discuss Yelverton's liability, assuming that there is no evidence that the loss of the furniture was due to lack of care on the part of Max's Discount Furniture. [*Simmons v. Yelverton*, 513 So.2d 504 (La.App. 2d Cir. 1987)]

**50–8. Duties of the Bailee.** K-2 Petroleum, Inc., and El Dorado Oil and Gas, Inc., were engaged in a joint-venture drilling project. They operated under an agreement whereby El Dorado provided a working electric generator for K-2's working interest in the well. The generator became nonfunctional, and K-2 sought to have El Dorado replace or repair it. El Dorado refused. K-2 subsequently contracted with Stewart & Stevenson Services, Inc. (S & S), for the repair of the generator. Shortly after receiving the generator for repair, S & S was notified by El Dorado that it was the true owner of the generator. El Dorado identified it by model and serial number and demanded its return upon completion of repairs. Because S & S knew of the common practice among oil field companies of switching, loaning, and borrowing equipment among themselves, it allowed El Dorado to take possession of the generator after El Dorado had paid for the repair. Before K-2 received any notice of S & S's delivery to El Dorado, K-2 and El Dorado terminated their joint venture and agreed that all salvageable equipment and supplies from the project were the property of K-2. K-2 later filed suit against S & S, claiming that S & S's failure to return the generator to K-2 and its delivery of the generator to El Dorado constituted the tort of conversion. Discuss K-2's claim. [*Stewart & Stevenson Services, Inc. v. Kratochvil*, 737 S.W.2d 65 (Tex.App.– San Antonio 1987)]

**50–9. Liability of the Bailee.** Several individuals placed personal property in a storage facility offered by the Winnebago County Fair Association, Inc. All who stored property in the building were required by the Winnebago County Fair Association to sign a storage agreement that included the following provision: "No liability exists for damage or loss to the stored equipment from the perils of fire." The storage building burned down, and all the property within was destroyed. A number of the people who had stored their property in the building brought suit against the fair association, claiming that the fire resulted from its negligence. Allstate Insurance Co., which had paid a number of claims for losses incurred due to the fire, joined the plaintiffs in the lawsuit. The Winnebago County Fair Association claimed that the exculpatory clause in its contract relieved it from any and all liability. The issue before the court was whether the bailee (the fair association) could validly contract away *all* liability for fire damage. What was the result? [*Allstate Insurance Co. v. Winnebago County Fair Association, Inc.,* 131 Ill.App.3d 225, 475 N.E.2d 230, 86 Ill.Dec. 233 (1985)]

**50–10. Duties of the Bailee.** Wanda Perry, who had an account with Farmers Bank of Greenwood, wanted to rent a safe-deposit box from the bank. The boxes were available only to bank customers, and no rent was charged. When renting the box, Wanda was asked to sign a signature card that stated the following: "The undersigned customer holds the Farmers Bank harmless for loss of currency or coin left in the box." A little over four years later, the bank was burglarized, and most of the safe-deposit boxes were broken into. Wanda's box was among those burglarized, and she lost all the currency and coins contained in it. At trial, evidence showed that the bank had been negligent in failing to restore a burglar alarm system that had been inoperative for more than a week prior to (and including) the day the bank was burglarized. Wanda sued the bank to recover the currency and coins, alleging negligence on the part of the bank. Discuss fully whether the bank should be held liable for the loss. [*Farmers Bank of Greenwood v. Perry,* 301 Ark. 547, 787 S.W.2d 645 (1990)]

**50–11. Liability of Innkeepers.** Marvin Gooden checked into a Day's Inn Motel in Atlanta, Georgia, on March 3, 1988, paying in advance for two days' lodging. The next day, Gooden temporarily left his room, in which he had a paper bag allegedly containing $9,000 in U.S. currency. Shortly after Gooden left the room, Mary Carter, a housekeeper, went into the room to clean it. She found the bag of money and, seeing no other personal effects, concluded that Gooden had checked out. Accordingly, she turned the bag and its contents over to her supervisor, Vivian Clark, who in turn gave the bag to another employee, Dempsey Wilson, to take to the motel office. Wilson had worked for the motel for about three years and had always before taken items of

value to the office when asked to do so. This time, however, he decided to abscond with the bag of money. A safe was located on the premises of the motel, and the motel posted a notice concerning the availability of the safe on the inside of the door of the room occupied by Gooden. In the notice, the motel disclaimed liability for guests' valuables unless they were placed in the safe. Gooden had not asked to use the safe. Gooden sued the motel and its employees (Carter and Clark) to recover the $9,000. Can Gooden recover the $9,000 from the hotel? Discuss fully. [*Gooden v. Day's Inn,* 196 Ga.App. 324, 395 S.E.2d 876 (1990)]

**50–12. Liability of the Bailee.** John Eifler, a sailor, spent months at a time away at sea. Eifler rented an enclosed storage unit (for his personal belongings) and an outdoor parking space (for his car) from a self-storage facility owned by Shurgard Capital Management Corp. Eifler signed a lease with Shurgard. The lease stated that a landlord-tenant relationship, not a bailment, existed. The agreement further stated that "ALL PERSONAL PROPERTY ON OR IN THE STORAGE UNIT IS AT THE RISK OF THE TENANT. * * * IF TENANT WISHES TO HAVE HIS PROPERTY COVERED BY INSURANCE, TENANT MUST OBTAIN SEPARATE COVERAGE." At the managers' request, Eifler left his car keys with them during his trips at sea so that they could move his car while he was gone. Eifler visited the storage unit periodically when he was home on shore leave and drove his car as he needed. When Eifler returned from one of his trips, his car was missing from Shurgard. There was a new manager of the facility, and the new manager knew nothing about the car or the car keys. Eifler sued Shurgard for failing to care for his car. He claimed that a bailment had been created and that Shurgard's attempt to limit its liability was ineffective because "a bailee cannot limit its liability for negligence." Did a bailment exist? If so, could Shurgard limit its liability for negligence? Explain. [*Eifler v. Shurgard Capital Management Corp.,* 71 Wash.App.684, 861 P.2d 1071 (1993)]

**50–13. Case Briefing Assignment**

*Examine Case A.10 [Strang v. Hollowell, 387 S.E.2d 664 (N.C.App. 1990)] in Appendix A. The case has been excerpted there in great detail. Review and then brief the case, making sure that you include answers to the following questions in your brief.*

1. Are there any facts in dispute in this case?
2. What was the only issue presented on appeal?
3. How was the bailment contract breached?
4. Why did the defendant, Hollowell, contend that he should not be held personally liable for the damages to the plaintiff's automobile?

# CHAPTER 51

# REAL PROPERTY

F rom earliest times, property has provided a means for survival. Primitive peoples lived off the fruits of the land, eating the vegetation and wildlife. Later, as the wildlife was domesticated and the vegetation cultivated, property provided pasturage and farmland. In the twelfth and thirteenth centuries, the power of feudal lords was exemplified by the amount of land that they held. After the age of feudalism passed, property continued to be an indicator of family wealth and social position. In the Western world, the protection of an individual's right to his or her property has become one of the most important rights of citizenship.

In this chapter, we first look at the nature of ownership rights in real property. We then examine the legal requirements involved in the transfer of real property, including the kinds of rights that are transferred by various kinds of deeds; the procedures used in the sale of real estate; and a way in which real property can, under certain conditions, be transferred merely by possession.

It is important to realize that real property rights are never absolute. There is a higher right—that of the government to take, for compensation, private land for public use. The concluding section in this chapter will discuss this right, called *eminent domain,* as well as zoning laws and other restrictions on the ownership of property.

## SECTION 1

## OWNERSHIP INTERESTS IN REAL PROPERTY

Ownership of property is an abstract concept that cannot exist independently of the legal system. No one can actually possess or *hold* a piece of land, the air above, the earth below, and all the water contained on it. One can only possess *rights* in real property. Numerous rights are involved in real property ownership. As discussed in Chapter 49, one who holds the entire bundle of rights owns the property in *fee simple.* We look below first at the fee simple absolute and then at the various types of limited property interests that can come into existence when an owner in fee simple absolute parts with some, but not all, of his or her rights in real property.

## FEE SIMPLE

In a **fee simple absolute,** the owner has the greatest aggregation of rights, privileges, and power possible. The owner can give the property away, sell the property for a price, or transfer the property by will to another. The fee simple absolute is limited to a person and his or her heirs and is assigned forever without limitation or condition. The rights that accompany a fee simple absolute include the right to use the land for whatever purpose the owner sees fit, subject to laws that prevent the owner from unreasonably interfering with another person's land and subject to applicable zoning laws. Furthermore, the owner has the rights of *exclusive* possession of the property. A fee simple is potentially infinite in duration and can be disposed of by deed

or by will (by selling or giving away). When there is no will, the fee simple passes to the owner's legal heirs.

Ownership in fee simple may become limited whenever the property is transferred to another *conditionally.* When this occurs, the fee simple is known as a **fee simple defeasible** (the word *defeasible* means capable of being terminated or annulled), or a *determinable fee.* For example, a **conveyance,** or transfer of real property, ''to A and his heirs as long as the land is used for charitable purposes'' creates a fee simple defeasible, because ownership of the property is conditioned on the land's being used for charitable purposes. The original owner retains a *partial* ownership interest, because if the specified condition does not occur (if the land ceases to be used for charitable purposes), then the land reverts, or returns, to the original owner. If the original owner is not living at the time, the land passes to his or her heirs.

The conveyance of a fee simple defeasible usually includes the words *as long as, until, while,* or *during.* The following case illustrates the importance of these words in determining exactly what sort of interest the original owner created—or failed to create.

---

**BACKGROUND AND FACTS**  *In 1948, Cecil and Edna Wood conveyed land in Riverton, Wyoming, to Fremont County. The deed stated that the land was conveyed ''for the purpose of constructing and maintaining thereon a County Hospital in memorial to the gallant men of the Armed Forces of the United States of America from Fremont County, Wyoming.'' The county built a hospital on the land and operated it until November 1983, when the property was sold to a private company. The buyer operated the hospital until September 1984, when it moved the hospital to new facilities and put the Wood property up for sale. The Woods filed a lawsuit against the county to recover the value of the land that they had conveyed to the county in 1948. The county filed a motion for summary judgment, which the court granted. The Woods appealed, contending in part that the language in the deed created a fee simple defeasible.*

| CASE 51.1 |
| --- |
| **WOOD v. BOARD OF COUNTY COMMISSIONERS OF FREMONT COUNTY** |
| Supreme Court of Wyoming, 1988. |
| 759 P.2d 1250. |

*BROWN,* Chief Justice.
\* \* \* \*

\* \* \* An estate in fee simple [defeasible] may be created so as to [revert] upon the occurrence of an event which is not certain ever to occur. Words such as ''so long as,'' ''until,'' or ''during'' are commonly used in a conveyance to denote the presence of this type of special limitation. The critical requirement is that the language \* \* \* must clearly state the particular circumstances under which the fee simple estate conveyed might expire. \* \* \*

The plain language in the 1948 deed, stating that appellants conveyed the land to Fremont County for the purpose of constructing a county hospital, does not clearly state that the estate conveyed will expire automatically if the land is not used for the stated purpose. As such, it does not evidence an intent of the grantors to convey a fee simple [defeasible] * * * .

Use of the language conveying the land in "memorial" similarly fails to create a fee simple [defeasible]. "Memorial" is defined in *Webster's Third New International Dictionary* as "[s]omething that serves to preserve memory or knowledge of an individual or event." The time for which the hospital should serve to "preserve" the memory or knowledge is not stated in the deed, just as the time for maintaining the hospital is not there stated. The language of conveyance fails to designate the time at which the hospital must be constructed as well as the time during which it must be maintained or during which the indicated memory must be preserved. The omission of such limiting language evidences an intent not to convey a fee simple [defeasible].

| | |
|---|---|
| **DECISION AND REMEDY** | *The Supreme Court of Wyoming held that the language in the deed did not create a fee simple defeasible. The Woods were denied recovery of the value of the land from the county.* |

## LIFE ESTATES

A **life estate** is an estate that lasts for the life of some specified individual. A conveyance "to A for his life" creates a life estate.[1] In a life estate, the life tenant has fewer rights of ownership than the holder of a fee simple defeasible, because the rights necessarily cease to exist on the life tenant's death. The life tenant has the right to use the land provided no waste (injury to the land) is committed. In other words, the life tenant cannot injure the land in a manner that would adversely affect its value to the owner of the future interest in it. The life tenant can use the land to harvest crops or, if mines and oil wells are already on the land, can extract minerals and oil from it, but the life tenant cannot exploit the land by creating new wells or mines.

The life tenant has the right to mortgage the life estate and create liens, easements, and leases; but none can extend beyond the life of the tenant. In addition, with few exceptions, the owner of a life estate has an exclusive right to possession during his or her lifetime.

Along with these rights, the life tenant also has some duties—to keep the property in repair and to pay property taxes. In short, the owner of the life estate has the same rights as a fee simple owner except that he or she must maintain the value of the property during his or her tenancy, less the decrease in value resulting from the normal use of the property allowed by the life tenancy.

## FUTURE INTERESTS

When an owner in fee simple absolute conveys the estate conditionally to another (such as with a fee simple defeasible) or for a limited period of time (such as with a life estate), the original owner still retains an interest in the land. The owner retains the right to repossess ownership of the land if the conditions of the fee simple defeasible are not met or when the life of the life-estate holder ends. The residuary (or leftover) interest in the property that the owner retains is called a **future interest** because if it arises, it will only arise in the future.

If the owner retains ownership of the future interest, then the future interest is described as a **reversionary interest,** because the property will *revert* to the original owner if the condition specified in a fee simple defeasible fails or when a life tenant dies. If, however, the owner of the future interest transfers ownership rights in that future interest to another, the future interest is described as a **remainder.** For example, a conveyance "to A for life, then to B" creates a life estate for A and a remainder (future interest) for B. An

---

1. A less common type of life estate is created by the conveyance "to A for the life of B." This is known as an estate *pur autre vie,* or an estate for the duration of the life of another.

**executory interest** is a type of future interest very similar to a remainder, the difference being that an executory interest does not take effect immediately on the expiration of another interest, such as a life estate. For example, a conveyance ''to A for life and one year after A's death to B'' creates an executory interest in the property for B.

## NONPOSSESSORY INTERESTS

Some interests in land do not include any rights of possession. These interests, known as nonpossessory interests, include *easements, profits,* and *licenses.* Because easements and profits are similar, and the same rules apply to both, they will be discussed together.

**EASEMENTS AND PROFITS**  An **easement** is the right of a person to make limited use of another person's real property without taking anything from the property. An easement, for example, can be the right to walk across another's property. In contrast, a **profit** is the right to go onto land in possession of another and take away some part of the land itself or some product of the land. For example, Mack, the owner of Sandy View, gives Ann the right to go there and remove all the sand and gravel that she needs for her cement business. Ann has a profit. Easements and profits can be classified as either *appurtenant* or *in gross.*

*Easement or Profit Appurtenant.*  An easement or profit appurtenant arises when the owner of one piece of land has a right to go onto (or remove things from) an *adjacent* piece of land owned by another. Suppose Owen, the owner of Whiteacres, has a right to drive his car across Green's land, Greenacres, which is adjacent to Whiteacres. This right-of-way over Greenacres is an easement appurtenant to Whiteacres and can be used only by the owner of Whiteacres. Owen can convey the easement when he conveys Whiteacres.

*Easement or Profit in Gross.*  An easement or profit in gross exists when the right to use or take things from another's land is not dependent upon the owner of the easement or profit owning an adjacent tract of land. When a utility company is granted an easement to run its power lines across another's property, it obtains an easement in gross. An easement or profit in gross requires the existence of only one parcel of land, which must be

owned by someone other than the owner of the easement or profit in gross.

*Effect of a Sale of Property.*  When a parcel of land that is *benefited* by an easement or profit appurtenant is sold, the property carries the easement or profit along with it. Thus, if Owen sells Whiteacres to Thomas and includes the appurtenant right-of-way across Greenacres in the deed to Thomas, Thomas will own both the property and the easement that benefits it.

When a parcel of land that has the *burden* of an easement or profit appurtenant is sold, the new owner must recognize its existence only if he or she knew or should have known of it or if it was recorded in the appropriate office of the county. Thus, if Owen records his easement across Greenacres in the appropriate county office before Green conveys the land, the new owner of Greenacres will have to allow Owen, or any subsequent owner of Whiteacres, to continue to use the path across Greenacres.

*Creation of an Easement or Profit.*  Profits and easements can be created by *deed* or *will* or by *contract, implication, necessity,* or *prescription.* Creation by *deed* or *will* simply involves the delivery of a deed or a transfer by a will by the owner of an easement stating that the grantee (the person receiving the profit or easement) is granted the rights in the easement or profit that the grantor had. Easements or profits can also be created by contract, with the contract terms defining the extent and length of time of use. An easement or profit may be created by *implication* when the circumstances surrounding the division of a parcel of property imply its creation. If Barrow divides a parcel of land that has only one well for drinking water and conveys the half without a well to Dan, a profit by implication arises, because Dan needs drinking water.

An easement may also be created by necessity. An easement by *necessity* does not require division of property for its existence. A person who rents an apartment, for example, has an easement by necessity in the private road leading up to the dwelling.

Easements and profits by *prescription* are created in much the same way as title to property is obtained by *adverse possession* (discussed later in this chapter). An easement arises by prescription when one person exercises an easement, such as a right-of-way, on another person's land without the landowner's consent, and the use is apparent and continues for a period of time equal to the applicable statute of limitations.

*Termination of an Easement or Profit.* An easement or profit can be terminated or extinguished in several ways. The simplest way is to deed it back to the owner of the land that is burdened by it. Also, if the owner of an easement or profit becomes the owner of the property burdened by it, then it is merged into the property. Another way is to abandon it with the intent to relinquish the right to use it.

LICENSES  A **license** is the revocable right of a person to come onto another person's land. It is a personal privilege that arises from the consent of the owner of the land and that can be revoked by the owner. A ticket to attend a movie at a theater is an example of a license. Assume that a Broadway theater owner issues to Clotilde a ticket to see a play. If Clotilde is refused entry into the theater because she is improperly dressed, she has no right to force her way into the theater. The ticket is only a revocable license, not a conveyance of an interest in property.

## LEASEHOLD ESTATES

A **leasehold estate** is created when a real property owner or lessor (landlord) agrees to convey the right to possess and use the property to a lessee (tenant) for a certain period of time. In every leasehold estate, the tenant has a *qualified* right to exclusive possession (qualified by the right of the landlord to enter upon the premises to assure that *waste*—destructive use—is not being committed). The tenant can use the land—for example, by harvesting crops—but cannot injure the land by such activities as cutting down timber for sale or extracting oil. The respective rights and duties of the landlord and tenant that arise under a lease agreement will be discussed in greater detail in Chapter 52. Here we look at the types of leasehold estates, or tenancies, that can be created when real property is leased.

TENANCY FOR YEARS  A **tenancy for years** is created by an express contract (which can sometimes be oral) by which property is leased for a specified period of time, such as a month, a year, or a period of years. For example, signing a one-year lease to occupy an apartment creates a tenancy for years. At the end of the period specified in the lease, the lease ends (without notice), and possession of the apartment returns to the lessor. If the tenant dies during the period of the lease, the lease interest passes to the tenant's heirs as personal property. Often, leases include renewal or extension provisions.

PERIODIC TENANCY  A **periodic tenancy** is created by a lease that does not specify how long it is to last but does specify that rent is to be paid at certain intervals. This type of tenancy is automatically renewed for another rental period unless properly terminated. For example, a periodic tenancy is created by a lease that states, "Rent is due on the tenth day of every month." This provision creates a tenancy from month to month. This type of tenancy can also be from week to week or from year to year. A periodic tenancy sometimes arises when a landlord allows a tenant under a tenancy for years to hold over (retain possession after the lease term ends) and continue paying monthly or weekly rent.

At common law, to terminate a periodic tenancy, the landlord or tenant must give one period's notice to the other party. If the tenancy is month to month, one month's notice must be given. If the tenancy is week to week, one week's notice must be given. State statutes often require a different period for notice of termination in a periodic tenancy, however.

TENANCY AT WILL  Suppose a landlord rents an apartment to a tenant "for as long as both agree." In such a case, the tenant receives a leasehold estate known as a **tenancy at will.** At common law, either party can terminate the tenancy without notice (that is, "at will" ). This type of estate usually arises when a tenant who has been under a tenancy for years retains possession after the termination date of that tenancy with the landlord's consent. Before the tenancy has been converted into a periodic tenancy (by the periodic payment of rent), it is a tenancy at will, terminable by either party without notice. Once the tenancy is treated as a periodic tenancy, a termination notice must conform to the one already discussed. The death of either party or the voluntary commission of waste by the tenant will terminate a tenancy at will.

**TENANCY AT SUFFERANCE**   The mere possession of land without right is called a **tenancy at sufferance.** A tenancy at sufferance is created when a tenant *wrongfully* retains possession of property. It is not a true tenancy for that reason. Whenever a life estate, tenancy for years, periodic tenancy, or tenancy at will ends and the tenant continues to retain possession of the premises without the owner's permission, a tenancy at sufferance is created.

## SECTION 2

# TRANSFER OF OWNERSHIP

Ownership of real property can pass from one person to another in a number of ways. Ownership rights in real property are commonly transferred through a sale of the property or by will or inheritance. Real property ownership can also be transferred by gift, by possession, or (as will be discussed later in the chapter) by eminent domain. When ownership rights in real property are transferred, the type of interest being transferred and the conditions of the transfer normally are set forth in a *deed* executed by the one who is conveying the property.

## DEEDS

Possession and title to land are passed from person to person by means of a **deed**—the instrument of conveyance of real property. A deed is a writing signed by an owner of real property by which title to it is transferred to another. Deeds must meet certain requirements.

Unlike a contract, a deed does not have to be supported by legally sufficient consideration. Gifts of real property are common, and they require deeds even though there is no consideration for the gift. The necessary components of a valid deed are the following:

1. The names of the *grantor* (the giver or seller) and the *grantee* (the donee or buyer).
2. Words evidencing an intent to convey (for example, "I hereby bargain," "I hereby sell," "I hereby grant," or "I hereby give").
3. A legally sufficient description of the land.
4. The grantor's (and usually his or her spouse's) signature.
5. Delivery of the deed.

**WARRANTY DEED**   The **warranty deed** makes the greatest number of warranties and thus provides the most extensive protection against defects of title. A sample warranty deed is illustrated in Exhibit 51–1. In most states, special language is required to make a warranty deed. Thus, if a contract calls for "a warranty deed" without specifying the covenants to be included in the deed, or if a deed states that the seller is providing the "usual covenants," most courts will infer from this language that the following covenants are being made: a covenant that the grantor has the title to, and the power to convey, the property; a convenant that the buyer will not be disturbed in his or her possession of the land; and a covenant that transfer of the property is made without unknown adverse claims of third parties.

**SPECIAL WARRANTY DEED**   In contrast to the warranty deed, the **special warranty deed** warrants only that the grantor or seller has not previously done anything to lessen the value of the real estate. If the special warranty deed discloses all liens or other encumbrances, the seller will not be liable to the buyer if a third person subsequently interferes with the buyer's ownership. If the third person's claim arises out of, or is related to, some act of the seller, however, the seller will be liable to the buyer for damages.

Both the special warranty deed and the warranty deed warrant that the seller has "marketable" title. Common defects that may render a title unmarketable include variations in the names of grantors and grantees, breaks in the chain of title, outstanding liens, and defectively executed deeds in the chain of title.

**QUITCLAIM DEED**   A **quitclaim deed** warrants less than any other deed. Essentially, it simply conveys to the grantee whatever interest the grantor had. In other words, if the grantor had nothing, then the grantee receives nothing. Naturally, if the grantor had a defective title or no title at all, a conveyance by warranty deed or special warranty deed would not cure the defects. Such deeds, however, will give the buyer a cause of action to sue the seller.

A quitclaim deed can and often does serve as a release of the grantor's interest in a particular parcel of property. For instance, suppose Sandor owns a strip of waterfront property on which he

■ **Exhibit 51–1  A Sample Warranty Deed**

Date:  May 31, 1996

Grantor:  GAYLORD A. JENTZ AND WIFE, JOANN H. JENTZ

Grantor's Mailing Address (including county):
     4106 North Loop Drive
     Austin, Travis County, Texas

Grantee:  DAVID F. FRIEND AND WIFE, JOAN E. FRIEND AS JOINT TENANTS
     WITH RIGHT OF SURVIVORSHIP

Grantee's Mailing Address (including county):
     5929 Fuller Drive
     Austin, Travis County, Texas

Consideration:
For and in consideration of the sum of Ten and No/100 Dollars ($10.00) and other
valuable consideration to the undersigned paid by the grantees herein named, the
receipt of which is hereby acknowledged, and for which no lien is retained, either
express or implied.

Property (including any improvements):
Lot 23, Block "A", Northwest Hills, Green Acres Addition, Phase 4, Travis County,
Texas, according to the map or plat of record in volume 22, pages 331-336 of the
Plat Records of Travis County, Texas.

Reservations from and Exceptions to Conveyance and Warranty:

This conveyance with its warranty is expressly made subject to the following:

Easements and restrictions of record in Volume 7863, Page 53, Volume 8430,
Page 35, Volume 8133, Page 152 of the Real Property Records of Travis County,
Texas, Volume 22, Pages 335-339, of the Plat Records of Travis County, Texas;
and to any other restrictions and easements affecting said property which are
of record in Travis County, Texas.

    Grantor, for the consideration and subject to the reservations from and exceptions to conveyance and warranty, grants, sells,
and conveys to Grantee the property, together with all and singular the rights and appurtenances thereto in any wise belonging, to
have and hold it to Grantee, Grantee's heirs, executors, administrators, successors, or assigns forever. Grantor binds Grantor
and Grantor's heirs, executors, administrators, and successors to warrant and forever defend all and singular the property to
Grantee and Grantee's heirs, executors, administrators, successors, and assigns against every person whomsoever lawfully
claiming or to claim the same or any part thereof, except as to the reservations from and exceptions to conveyance and warranty.

    When the context requires, singular nouns and pronouns include the plural.

BY: _Gaylord A. Jentz_
       Gaylord A. Jentz

BY: _JoAnn H. Jentz_
       JoAnn H. Jentz

**(Acknowledgment)**

STATE OF TEXAS
COUNTY OF

    This instrument was acknowledged before me on the    31st   day of   May      , 1996
by   Gaylord A. and JoAnn H. Jentz

_Rosemary Potter_
Notary Public, State of Texas
Notary's name (printed): Rosemary Potter

Notary Seal

Notary's commission expires: 1/31/2001

wants to build condominiums. Lanz has an interest in a section of the property, which he might assert either to prevent the development or to insist on a share of its earnings. Sandor can negotiate with Lanz for a release of the claim. Lanz's signing of a quitclaim deed would constitute such a release.

**GRANT DEED** With a **grant deed,** the grantor simply states, ''I grant the property to you'' or ''I convey, or bargain and sell, the property to you.'' By state statute, grant deeds may carry with them an implied warranty that the grantor owns the property being transferred and has not previously encumbered it or conveyed it to someone else.

**SHERIFF'S DEED** A **sheriff's deed** is a document giving ownership rights to a buyer at a sheriff's sale, which is a sale held by a sheriff to pay a court judgment against the owner of the property. Typically, the property was subject to a mortgage or tax payments and the owner defaulted on the payments. A deed is given to the buyer at the sale as part of the foreclosure process on the mortgage or tax lien. The giving of the deed begins the running of the period of time during which the defaulting owner can redeem the property (see Chapter 32).

**RECORDING STATUTES** In every jurisdiction, **recording statutes** are in force. The purpose of these statutes, which require land transfers to be recorded in public records, is to provide prospective buyers with a way to check whether there have been earlier transactions creating interests or rights in specific parcels of real property. Hence, recording a deed gives constructive notice to the world that a certain person is now the owner of a particular parcel of real estate.[2] Placing everyone on notice as to the true owner is intended to prevent the previous owners from fraudulently conveying the land to a subsequent purchaser.

Properly notarized deeds are generally recorded in the county where the property is located. Many state statutes require that the grantor sign the deed in the presence of two attesting witnesses

before it can be recorded. There are three basic types of recording statutes:

1. A *race statute* provides that the first purchaser to record a deed has superior rights to the property, regardless of whether he or she knew that someone else had already bought it but had failed to record the deed.[3] Under these statutes, recording is a ''race,'' and whoever files first ''wins.''

2. A *pure notice statute* provides that, regardless of who files first, a person who knows that someone else has already bought the property cannot claim priority. In contrast, a subsequent good faith purchaser who, at the time he or she acquires a deed, has no notice of a previous deed—because, for example, it has not been recorded—may successfully assert a superior claim to the property. (A *good faith purchaser* is one who purchases for value, in good faith, and without notice.)

3. A *notice-race statute* protects a purchaser who does not know that someone else has already bought the property and who records his or her deed first.

Irrespective of the particular type of recording statute adopted by a state, recording a deed involves a fee. The grantee typically pays this fee, because he or she is the one who will be protected by recording the deed.

## CONTRACTS FOR THE SALE OF REAL ESTATE

Transfers of ownership interests in real property are frequently accomplished by means of a sale. The sale of real estate is similar to the sale of goods, because it involves a transfer of ownership, often with specific warranties. In the sale of real estate, however, certain formalities are observed that are not required in the sale of goods. For example, to meet the requirements of law, a deed must be signed and delivered.[4]

---

2. In this situation, constructive notice operates to impute to a person knowledge of the ownership, regardless of whether the individual actually knows about it. This is because he or she is in a position that involves a duty to inquire; and proper diligence—for example, searching the public records—would reveal the fact of the ownership.

3. Only two states (Delaware and North Carolina) use race statutes. Usage in the rest of the states is split about evenly between the pure notice statute and the notice-race statute.

4. The phrase *signed, sealed, and delivered* once referred to the requirements for transferring title to real property by deed. The seal has fallen from use, but signature and delivery are still required.

Several steps are involved in any sale of real property. The first step is the formation of the land sales contract. Then a title search (to verify that the seller has good title to the property and that no other claims to the property exist) follows, along with, usually, negotiations to obtain financing for the purchase. The final step is the closing. We examine some of the legal considerations involved in these steps below, as well as other requirements relating to the sale of real property. First, however, we look at the important role played by real estate agents, or brokers, in the sale of real property.

**BROKERS**   Buyers and sellers of real property frequently enlist the services of a *real estate agent,* or broker. Real estate agents are information brokers. They provide buyers and sellers of real estate with information and specialize in matching the wants of buyers with the property being offered for sale by sellers.

Normally, the broker is retained by the seller and acts as the seller's agent in the sale of the property. In compensation for their services, brokers usually receive a commission (which can range from 1 to 10 percent of the purchase price) from the seller when the sale is concluded. A broker can also act as an agent of the buyer, in which case a dual agency exists. Generally, a broker may not act as an agent for more than one party without the consent of all parties involved, and state laws may place further restrictions on dual agencies. Most states require real estate brokers to be licensed, and in some states, brokers may be required to meet continuing-education or other requirements.

A seller engages the services of a broker through a written *listing agreement.* In an *open* listing, the seller contracts for the services of more than one broker, and the first broker to produce a buyer receives the commission. In an *exclusive* listing, the seller contracts with just one broker, who receives the exclusive right to find a buyer and receive the commission from the seller. Under an exclusive listing agreement, the broker is entitled to a commission even if another broker sells the property.

**FORMATION OF THE SALES CONTRACT**   Generally, when someone decides to purchase real estate, he or she makes a written offer to purchase the property and puts up *earnest money* to show that an earnest, or serious, offer is being made. (If the buyer decides to withdraw the offer, the earnest

money, or deposit binder money, will often be forfeited, as liquidated damages, to the seller.) The offer states in some detail the exact offering price for the property and lists any other conditions that may be appropriate. The offer may be conditioned on the offeror's ability to obtain financing, for example. Within a specified time period, the seller of the property either accepts or rejects the offer.

If the offer is accepted, then a contract of sale is drawn up. Because an oral agreement for a sale of land is not enforceable under the Statute of Frauds, the agreement should be put in writing. The written agreement should include at least the names and addresses of the parties, a description of the property, the time for the closing, the type of deed that will be delivered, and the price. The contract might also state which party bears the risk of loss if, after the contract is formed, the property is destroyed (for example, if the house burns down).[5] Usually, the signing of the sales contract is accompanied by a deposit, which, with the earnest money, may be 10 percent of the purchase price paid to the seller.

Deposits toward the purchase price normally are held in a special account, called an **escrow account,** until all of the conditions of sale have been met and the closing takes place, at which time the money is transferred to the seller. The *escrow agent,* which may be a title company, bank, or special escrow company, acts as a neutral party in the sales transaction and facilitates the sale by allowing the buyer and seller to close the transaction without having to exchange documents and funds.

**TITLE EXAMINATION**   After the sales contract has been negotiated, the buyer or the buyer's attorney (or the escrow agent, title insurance company, or lending institution from which the purchase price is borrowed) performs a *title examination.* This entails examining at the county recording office the history of all past transfers of, liens on, and sales of the property in question.

A contract for a sale of land includes the seller's implied obligation to transfer marketable title. **Marketable title** is title that is free from encumbrances (such as mortgages and restrictive cove-

---

5.   Unless the contract states otherwise, the buyer will suffer any loss (assuming the loss is not the seller's fault). Either party can take out an insurance policy against the risk, however.

nants, both of which are discussed below), defects in the chain of title (such as a previous sale of the property by the seller), and other events that affect title (such as adverse possession and eminent domain, both of which are discussed below). Title is considered marketable even if the property is subject to zoning restrictions or public easements, such as sidewalks and sewers. If a title examination uncovers a material defect that has not been disclosed in the contract, the seller is considered to have breached the contract, and the buyer may seek any appropriate remedies (damages, rescission, or specific performance with a price adjustment).

Title examinations are not foolproof, and buyers of real property generally purchase **title insurance** to protect their interests in the event that some defect in the title was not discovered during the examination. A title insurance policy insures against loss resulting from any defects in the title and guarantees that if any defects do arise, the title company issuing the policy will defend the owner's interests and pay all legal expenses involved.

### FINANCING

Unless a buyer pays cash for the property, the buyer must obtain financing for the purchase with a mortgage loan. A **mortgage** is a loan made by a financial institution or trust company for which the property is given as security. In some states, the *mortgagor* (the borrower) holds title to the property; in others, the *mortgagee* (the lender) holds title until the loan is completely repaid. In several states, a trustee—a third party—holds title on behalf of the lender. The trustee then deeds the property back to the borrower when the loan is repaid. If the payments are not made, the trustee can deed the property to the lender or dispose of it by auction, depending on state law.

### CLOSING

The final step in the sale of real estate is the **closing**—also called settlement or closing escrow. The escrow agent coordinates the closing with the recording of deeds, the obtaining of title insurance, and other concurrent closing activities. Several costs must be paid, in cash, at the time of closing. These costs comprise fees for services, including those performed by the lender, escrow agent, and title company, and they can range from several hundred to several thousand dollars, depending on the amount of the mortgage loan and other conditions of sale. As discussed in Chapter 46 in the context of consumer protection, the Real Estate Settlement Procedures Act of 1976 requires lending institutions to notify—within a specified time period—each applicant for a mortgage loan of the specific costs that must be paid at the closing.

### WARRANTY OF HABITABILITY

The common law rule of *caveat emptor* (''let the buyer beware'') held that the seller of a home made no warranties with respect to its soundness or fitness unless such a warranty was specifically included in the deed or contract of sale. Although *caveat emptor* is still the rule of law in a minority of states, there is currently a strong trend against it and in favor of an **implied warranty of habitability.** Under this modern approach, the courts hold that the seller of a new house warrants that it will be fit for human habitation regardless of whether any such warranty is included in the deed or contract of sale. This warranty is similar to the UCC's implied warranty of merchantability for sales of personal property. In recent years, some states, such as Virginia, have passed legislation creating such warranties for newly constructed residences.

Essentially, under an implied warranty of habitability, the seller warrants that the house is in reasonable working order and is of reasonably sound construction. To recover damages for breach of the implied warranty of habitability, the purchaser is required only to prove that the home he or she purchased was somehow defective and to prove that the damages were caused by the defect. Thus, under the warranty of habitability theory, the seller of a new home is in effect a guarantor of the home's fitness.

### SELLER'S DUTY TO DISCLOSE

Traditionally, under the rule of *caveat emptor,* a seller had no duty to disclose to the buyer defects in the property, even if the seller knew about the defects and the buyer had no reasonable way to discover them. Currently, in many jurisdictions, courts have placed on sellers a duty to disclose any known defect that materially affects the value of the property and that the buyer could not reasonably discover. Under these circumstances, nondisclosure is similar to representing that the defect does not exist, and the buyer may have grounds for a successful lawsuit based on fraud or misrepresentation.

For example, Nick sells Nora a five-year-old house that he knows has roof problems. Nick does not tell Nora about these problems. During the first rain after the sale, water gushes from the house's ceilings and light fixtures. Nora contacts a roofing contractor, who tells her that repair would be a temporary solution and that only a new roof would be watertight. Nora might sue Nick for breach of contract, fraud, and misrepresentation, seeking rescission of their contract and a return of whatever amount she paid Nick toward the purchase price of the house.

## TRANSFER BY INHERITANCE

Property that is transferred on an owner's death is passed either by will or by inheritance laws. If the owner of land dies with a will, that land passes according to the terms of the will. If the owner dies without a will, state statutes prescribe how and to whom the property will pass. The transfer of property by inheritance is the subject of Chapter 54.

## ADVERSE POSSESSION

**Adverse possession** is a means of obtaining title to land without delivery of a deed. Essentially, when one person possesses the property of another for a certain statutory period of time (three to thirty years, with ten years being most common), that person, called the adverse possessor, acquires title to the land and cannot be removed from it by the original owner. The adverse possessor may ultimately be vested with good title just as if there had been a conveyance by deed.

For property to be held adversely, four elements must be satisfied:

1. Possession must be actual and exclusive; that is, the possessor must take sole physical occupancy of the property.

2. The possession must be open, visible, and notorious, not secret or clandestine. The possessor must occupy the land for all the world to see.

3. Possession must be continuous and peaceable for the required period of time. This requirement means that the possessor must not be interrupted in the occupancy by the true owner or by the courts.

4. Possession must be hostile and adverse. In other words, the possessor must claim the property as against the whole world. He or she cannot be living on the property with the permission of the owner.

There are a number of public-policy reasons for the adverse possession doctrine. These reasons include society's interest in resolving boundary disputes, in quieting (determining) title when title to property is in question, and in assuring that real property remains in the stream of commerce. More fundamentally, policies behind the doctrine include punishing owners who sit on their rights too long and rewarding possessors for putting land to productive use.

In the following case, the question before the court is whether a couple had obtained title to a certain portion of land by adverse possession.

---

| CASE 51.2 |
| --- |

**KLOS v. MOLENDA**
Superior Court of
Pennsylvania, 1986.
355 Pa.Super. 399,
513 A.2d 490.

**BACKGROUND AND FACTS**  *In September 1950, Michael and Albina Klos purchased part of some property owned by John and Anne Molenda. The Kloses' lot was 50 feet wide and 135 feet deep. Rather than surveying the property, the seller and buyer paced off the lot and placed stakes in the ground as boundary markers. The Kloses built a house on the lot in 1952 and put in a sidewalk along the full front. They also put in a driveway 30 inches from the stake line. They planted grass and a hedge in that 30 inches and maintained it until 1984. In 1983, Mr. Molenda died, and his widow hired a surveyor to inventory the landholdings. The survey located the rightful property line between the Molendas' and Kloses' land as being 30 inches closer to the Kloses' house than it currently was. This placed the property line right along the Kloses' driveway, instead of 30 inches to the side of the driveway. Upon learning this, Mrs. Molenda dug up the grass strip and the hedgerow and erected a fence right along the Kloses'*

*driveway, marking the property line. The Kloses brought this action challenging Mrs. Molenda's conduct, claiming that they held title to the land by adverse possession. The trial court held that the Kloses had title to the land. Mrs. Molenda appealed.*

*WIEAND,* Judge:
\* \* \* \*

On appeal, Mrs. Molenda's principal contentions are that the Klos possession was (1) sporadic rather than continuous, and (2) permissive and neither hostile nor adverse. We reject these arguments. The evidence disclosed that appellees had continuously maintained the strip of land in lawn between 1952 and 1984, when their maintenance of the lawn was prevented by the fence which Anne Molenda had erected. The use of land for lawn purposes and the continuous maintenance thereof in connection with a residence, it has been held, are sufficient to establish adverse possession.

The hostile nature of the Klos possession was not destroyed because the stake line may have been placed along a property line mistakenly located by the adjoining landowners. This fact did not render Klos' possession permissive. The parties intended that the Kloses should have title to that line, and thereafter the Kloses kept their flag flying continuously on the thirty (30) inch strip of land. Their possession, open, notorious and exclusive for more than twenty-one years, presented a hostile front to any person or persons intending to make a conflicting pretension of ownership.

*The appellate court affirmed the trial court's decision. The Kloses held rightful title to the land by adverse possession.*

**DECISION
AND REMEDY**

---

## SECTION 3

# LIMITATIONS ON THE RIGHTS OF PROPERTY OWNERS

As mentioned earlier in this chapter, no ownership rights in real property can ever be absolute. That is, an owner of real property cannot always do whatever he or she wishes on or with the property. Nuisance and environmental laws, for example, restrict certain types of activities. Holding the property is also conditional on the payment of property taxes. If these taxes are not paid, ownership of the property will be forfeited to the state. In addition, if a property owner fails to pay debts, the property may be seized to satisfy judgment creditors. In a word, the rights of every property owner are subject to certain conditions and limitations. In this final section of the chapter, we look at some of the important ways in which owners' rights in real property may be limited.

## EMINENT DOMAIN

Even if ownership in real property is in fee simple absolute, there is still a superior ownership that limits the fee simple absolute. Just as in medieval England, the king was the ultimate landowner, so in the United States, the government has an ultimate ownership right in all land. This right is known as **eminent domain,** and it is sometimes referred to as the condemnation power of the government to take land for public use. It gives a right to the government to acquire possession of real property in the manner directed by the Constitution and the laws of the state whenever the public interest requires it. Property may not be taken for private benefit, but only for public use.

For example, when a new public highway is to be built, the government must decide where to build it and how much land to condemn. The power of eminent domain is generally invoked through condemnation proceedings. After the government determines that a particular parcel of land is necessary for public use, it brings a judicial proceeding to obtain title to the land. Then, in another proceeding, the court determines the *fair value* of the land, which is usually approximately equal to its market value. Under the Fifth Amendment, private property may not be taken for public use without ''just compensation.''

## ZONING

The state's power to control the use of land through legislation is derived from two sources: eminent domain and police power. Through eminent domain, the government can take land for public use, but it must pay just compensation. Consequently, eminent domain is an expensive method of land-use control. Under its police power, however, the state can pass laws aimed at protecting public health, safety, morals, and general welfare. These laws include *zoning laws*, which can regulate uses of land without the state's having to compensate the landowner. If, however, a state law restricts a landowner's property rights too much, the state's regulation will be deemed a *confiscation,* or a *taking,* and may be subject to the eminent domain requirement that just compensation be paid.

Suppose that Perez owns a large tract of land, which she purchased with the intent to subdivide it and develop it into residential properties. At the time of the purchase, there were no zoning regulations restricting use of the land. If the government attempts to zone Perez's entire tract of land as

''public parkland only'' and thus to prohibit her from developing any part of it, the action will be deemed confiscatory; this is because the government will be denying her the ability to use her property for any reasonable income-producing or private purpose for which it is suited and because she had reasonable, investment-backed expectations in her development plans. The zoning regulation normally will be held unconstitutional and void, or the government will have to compensate Perez, because it has effectively confiscated her land.

The state's power to regulate the use of land is limited in two other ways, both of which arise from the Fourteenth Amendment. First, the state cannot regulate the use of land arbitrarily or unreasonably, because this would be taking property without due process. There must be a *rational basis* for the classifications that the state imposes on property. Any act that is reasonably related to the health or general welfare of the public is deemed to have a rational basis. Second, a state's regulation of land-use control cannot be discriminatory. A zoning ordinance is considered discriminatory if it affects one parcel of land in a way in which it does not affect surrounding parcels and if there is no rational basis for the difference.

The following case involved a challenge to a classification in a zoning ordinance on the ground that there was no rational basis for it.

---

**CASE 51.3**

**KIRSCH v. PRINCE GEORGE'S COUNTY**

Court of Appeals of Maryland, 1993.
331 Md. 89,
626 A.2d 372.

**COMPANY PROFILE** *The University of Maryland is an internationally recognized university community that is expanding in the number of students and scope of degree offerings every year. Established in 1807, the university's largest campus is in College Park, Prince George's County, Maryland, which is located nine miles from Washington, D.C. The University of Maryland is a public, four-year, coeducational university, offering undergraduate and graduate programs. Among its unique facilities are a center for architectural design and research, a model nuclear reactor, and a wind tunnel. More than two-thirds of the students live off-campus.*

**BACKGROUND AND FACTS** *Donald Kirsch and Martha Kaye Dunn owned residential property in Prince George's County, Maryland. Kirsch and Dunn wished to rent their property to students. Stephanie Stockman and Daniel Cones were students at the University of Maryland living off-campus in Prince George's County. In 1989, the county council enacted a ''mini-dorm'' zoning ordinance. The ordinance regulated the rental of residential property to persons ''who are registered full-time or part-time students at an institution of higher learning.'' The ordinance imposed restrictions that were intended to address complaints about the noise, litter,* *and parking of mini-dorm residents from other residents of College Park, the site of the principal campus of the University of Maryland. The ordinance took effect on July 1, 1990. On July 3, Kirsch, Dunn, Stockman, and Cones filed a lawsuit against the county, seeking a declaration that the ordinance was invalid. The plaintiffs argued in part that the ordinance discriminated against students as a classification in violation of the Fourteenth Amendment. The county filed a motion for summary judgment, and the court granted the motion. The plaintiffs appealed.*

*KARWACKI,* Judge.
\* \* \* \*

The crucial question for this Court is whether the County by adopting the ordinance's classification advances its objective of clearing residential neighborhoods of noise, litter, and parking congestion within the command of the Equal Protection Clause of the Fourteenth Amendment \* \* \* . We hold that it does not. To differentiate between permissible residential tenant classes by creating more strenuous zoning requirements for some and less for others based solely on the occupation which the tenant pursues away from that residence is that sort of arbitrary classification forbidden under our [Constitution].
\* \* \* \*

\* \* \* [T]he Prince George's County ''mini-dorm'' ordinance does not differentiate based on the nature of the use of the property, such as a fraternity house or a lodging house, but rather on the occupation of the persons who would dwell therein. Therefore, under the ordinance a landlord of a building \* \* \* is permitted to rent the same for occupancy \* \* \* so long as [the tenants] are not pursuing a higher education without incurring the burdens of complying with the arduous requirements of the ordinance. Such occupancy would equally add motor vehicles to a congested parking situation and pose the threat of increased noise and litter. Such a zoning classification of residential property is wholly unrelated to the stated purpose of the ordinance, and its impact upon persons who are registered as full-time or part-time students at an institution of higher learning denies those students equal protection of the laws under the Fourteenth Amendment to the United States Constitution \* \* \* .

*The Maryland Court of Appeals reversed the judgment of the lower court and remanded the case for a declaration that the mini-dorm ordinance was invalid.*

**DECISION AND REMEDY**

---

**VARIANCES** A landowner whose land has been limited by a zoning ordinance to a particular use cannot make an alternative use of the land unless he or she first obtains a *zoning variance*. A landowner must meet three criteria to be entitled to a variance:

1. The landowner must find it impossible to realize a reasonable return on the land as zoned.
2. The adverse effect of the zoning ordinance must be particular to the person seeking the variance and not one that has a similar effect on the other landowners within the same zone.
3. A granting of the variance must not substantially alter the essential character of the zoned area.

Courts tend to be rather lenient about the first two requirements. By far the most important criterion used in granting a variance is whether it will substantially alter the character of the neighborhood.

**BUILDING PERMITS** As part of its power to control the use of land through legislation, the state can regulate such things as the overall appearance of a community. For example, local ordinances may prohibit a property owner's tearing down or remodeling a historic landmark. The state may also require property owners to make concessions for such public needs as transportation. Typically, these goals are accomplished in part by requiring that an owner obtain a building permit from a local review board before undertaking a building project. In issuing a permit, the board may impose certain restrictions. Builder-developers are routinely required, for example, to include sidewalks and access roads in their developments.

The United States Supreme Court has held that such restrictions do not constitute a taking of an owner's property if they "substantially advance legitimate state interests" and do not "den[y] an owner economically viable use of his land."[6] It is not clear, however, exactly what constitutes a "legitimate state interest" or what connection between that interest and a restriction satisfies the requirement that the restriction "substantially advance" the interest. The following case concerns the distinction between a restriction on the use of property and a taking of the property.

_____

6.  *Agins v. Tiburon,* 447 U.S. 255, 100 S.Ct. 2138, 65 L.Ed. 2d 106 (1980).

---

CASE 51.4

**NOLLAN v. CALIFORNIA COASTAL COMMISSION**

Supreme Court of the United States, 1987. 483 U.S. 825, 107 S.Ct. 3141, 97 L.Ed.2d 677.

**BACKGROUND AND FACTS**  *James and Marilyn Nollan sought a building permit from the California Coastal Commission (CCC) to replace a single-story house on the Nollans' beachfront property with a two-story structure approximately three times larger. The CCC concluded that the new house would obstruct the public's view of the ocean, increase private use of the beach, and create a "psychological barrier" to access to the public beaches that were on both sides of the Nollans' property. The CCC agreed to issue the permit if the Nollans would dedicate a strip of their land for public use. The strip, which ran next to the water's edge along the beach, would connect the public beaches. The Nollans appealed to a state court, contending that the CCC's condition was a taking of private property for public use without compensation. The court agreed with the Nollans, and the CCC appealed. The appellate court ruled in the CCC's favor, and the Nollans appealed to the United States Supreme Court.*

Justice *SCALIA* delivered the opinion of the Court.
*    *    *    *

Had California simply required the Nollans to make an easement across their beachfront available to the public on a permanent basis in order to increase public access to the beach, rather than conditioning their permit to rebuild their house on their agreeing to do so, we have no doubt there would have been a taking. *    *    *

*    *    * [T]he question becomes whether requiring it to be conveyed as a condition for issuing a land use permit alters the outcome. *    *    *

*    *    * [H]ere, the lack of nexus [connection] between the condition and the *    *    * purpose of the building restriction converts that purpose to something other than what it was. The purpose then becomes, quite simply, the obtaining of an easement to serve some valid governmental purpose, but without payment of compensation. Whatever may be the outer limits of "legitimate state interests" in the takings and land use context, this is not one of them. *    *    *

*    *    *    *

*    *    * It is quite impossible to understand how a requirement that people already on the public beaches be able to walk across the Nollans' property reduces any obstacles to viewing the beach created by the new house. It is also impossible to understand how it lowers any "psychological barrier" to using the public beaches, or how it helps to remedy any additional congestion on them caused by construction of the Nollans' new house. We therefore find that the Commission's imposition of

the permit condition cannot be treated as an exercise of its land use power for any of these purposes.

*The Supreme Court concluded that there was not a sufficient connection between the Nollans' proposed construction and the CCC's desired easement for the state to obtain the easement without paying the Nollans for it.*

**DECISION AND REMEDY**

**Takings Law in Germany** *Like the U.S. Constitution, the German constitution places restraints on government's ability to take private property for public use. The German constitution first affirmatively establishes the right of the government to take private property for public use and then requires some payment to the landowner for the property that is taken. The German constitution also states that private property owners have a duty to use their property for the public good.*

**INTERNATIONAL CONSIDERATIONS**

## COVENANTS RUNNING WITH THE LAND

A **covenant running with the land** goes with the land and cannot be separated from it. A covenant runs with the land when the original parties *and* their successors, as opposed to the original parties alone, will be entitled to its benefit or burdened with its obligation. In other words, its benefit or obligation passes with the land's ownership.

Consider an example. Owen is the owner of Grasslands, a twenty-acre estate whose northern half contains a small reservoir. Owen wishes to convey the northern half to Arid City, but before he does, he digs an irrigation ditch connecting the reservoir with the lower ten acres, which he uses as farmland. When Owen conveys the northern ten acres to Arid City, he enters into an agreement with the city. The agreement, which is contained in the deed, states, "Arid City, its heirs and assigns, promises not to remove more than five thousand gallons of water per day from the Grasslands reservoir." Owen has created a *covenant running with the land* under which Arid City and all future owners of the northern ten acres of Grasslands are limited as to the amount of water they can draw from its reservoir.

Four requirements must be met for a covenant running with the land to be enforceable. If they are not met, the covenant will apply to the two original parties to a contract only and will not run with the land to future owners. The requirements are as follows:

1. The covenant running with the land must be created in a written agreement (covenant). It is usually contained in the document that conveys the land.
2. The parties must intend that the covenant *run with the land.* In other words, the instrument that contains the covenant must state not only that the promisor is bound by the terms of the covenant but that all the promisor's "successors, heirs, or assigns" will be bound.
3. The covenant must *touch and concern* the land. The limitations on the activities of the owner of the burdened land must have some connection with the land. For example, a purchaser of land cannot be bound by a covenant requiring him or her to drive only Ford pickups, because such a restriction has no relation to the land purchased.
4. The original parties to the covenant must be in *privity of estate* at the time the covenant is created. This requirement means that the relationship between them must be that of landlord and tenant, vendor and purchaser, or the like.

## EQUITABLE SERVITUDES

Because of the confusion over the meaning and application of the privity of estate requirement, covenants running with the land are not always an effective device for guiding the development of residential and commercial land. Therefore, courts of equity have utilized an alternative means of private land-use control known as **equitable servitudes.** The most significant difference between covenants running with the land and equitable servitudes is that privity of estate is not required for enforcement of an equitable servitude.

An equitable servitude is created by an instrument that complies with the Statute of Frauds, an intention that the use of land be restricted, and *notice* of the restriction to the person acquiring the burdened land. The notice may be constructive.

For example, in the course of developing a fifty-lot suburban subdivision, Levitt records a declaration of restrictions that effectively limits construction on each lot to one single-family house. In each lot's deed is a reference to the declaration with a provision that the purchaser and his or her successors are bound to those restrictions. Thus, each purchaser assumes ownership with notice of the restrictions. If an owner attempts to build a duplex (or any structure that does not comply with the restrictions) on a lot, the other owners may obtain a court order enjoining the construction.

In fact, Levitt might simply have included the restrictions on the subdivision's map, filed the map in the appropriate public office, and included a reference to the map in each deed. In this way, each owner would also have been held to have constructive notice of the restrictions.

Equitable servitudes are usually upheld; however, equitable servitudes and covenants running with the land have sometimes been used to perpetuate neighborhood segregation, and in these cases they have been invalidated by the courts. In the United States Supreme Court case of *Shelley v. Kraemer,*[7] restrictive covenants proscribing resale to minority groups were declared unconstitutional and could no longer be enforced in courts of law. In addition, the Civil Rights Act of 1968 (also known as the Fair Housing Act) prohibits all discrimination based on race, color, religion, or national origin in the sale and leasing of housing.

In the following case, the court has to decide whether a restrictive covenant prohibiting any "outside radio, television, Ham broadcasting, or other electronic antenna or aerial" intended to prohibit satellite dishes, even though such dishes were not in use at the time the covenant was drafted.

---

7.   334 U.S. 1, 68 S.Ct. 836, 92 L.Ed. 1161 (1948).

---

| CASE 51.5 | **BACKGROUND AND FACTS**  *Claudia Churchill installed a satellite dish in the backyard of her residence, which was located in a residential subdivision called the Piedmont Subdivision. The Piedmont Subdivision was subject to a restrictive covenant that provided in part as follows: "No outside radio, television, Ham broadcasting, or other electronic antenna or aerial shall be erected or placed on any structure or on any lot. If used, any such antenna or aerial shall be placed in the attic of the house or in any other place in the house where it will be concealed from public view from any side of the house." Roy Breeling and a number of other homeowners in the subdivision filed an action, asking that Churchill be required to remove the satellite dish. The trial court held that the covenant applied to the satellite dish, even though such dishes were not in use in the early 1970s, when the covenant was drafted. The court therefore granted the homeowners' request and ordered Churchill to remove the dish from her property. Churchill appealed.* |

**BREELING v. CHURCHILL**

Supreme Court of Nebraska,
1988.
228 Neb. 596,
423 N.W.2d 469.

*CHEUVRONT,* District Judge.
\* \* \* \*

A restrictive covenant is to be construed in connection with the surrounding circumstances, which the parties are supposed to have had in mind at the time they made it; the location and character of the entire tract of land; the purpose of the restriction; whether it was for the sole benefit of the grantor or for the benefit of the grantee and subsequent purchasers; and whether it was in pursuance of a general building plan for the development of the property.

The restrictive covenants of Piedmont, read as a whole, not only specifically prohibit all outdoor antennas, they evidence a broad concern for aesthetics and prohibit many uses of the property within the subdivision which would detract from the appearance of the area as a whole. It is clear that in light of the surrounding circumstances, the character of the entire area, and the purposes of the restrictions, it was intended that structures such as a satellite dish were not to be permitted. We find that the restriction prohibiting all "outside radio, television, Ham broadcasting, or other electronic antenna or aerial" includes a satellite dish.

**DECISION AND REMEDY**

*The Supreme Court of Nebraska concluded that the trial court was correct in finding that the restrictive covenant prohibited the erection of a satellite dish. The trial court's judgment was thus affirmed.*

## TERMS AND CONCEPTS TO REVIEW

adverse possession 1016
closing 1015
conveyance 1007
covenant running with the
    land 1021
deed 1011
easement 1009
eminent domain 1017
equitable servitude 1022
escrow account 1014
executory interest 1008
fee simple absolute 1007

fee simple defeasible 1007
future interest 1008
grant deed 1013
implied warranty of
    habitability 1015
leasehold estate 1010
license 1010
life estate 1008
marketable title 1014
mortgage 1015
periodic tenancy 1010
profit 1009

quitclaim deed 1011
recording statute 1013
remainder 1008
reversionary interest 1008
sheriff's deed 1013
special warranty deed 1011
tenancy at sufferance 1011
tenancy at will 1010
tenancy for years 1010
title insurance 1015
warranty deed 1011

## QUESTIONS AND CASE PROBLEMS

**51–1. Deeds.** Madison owned a tract of land, but he was not sure that he had full title to the property. When Rafael expressed an interest in buying the property, Madison sold Rafael the land and executed a quitclaim deed. Rafael properly recorded the deed immediately. Several months later, Madison learned that he had had full title to the tract of land. He then sold the land to Linda by warranty deed. Linda knew of the earlier purchase by Rafael but took the deed anyway and later sued to have Rafael evicted from the land. Linda claimed that because she had a warranty deed, her title to the land was better than that of Rafael's quitclaim deed. Will Linda succeed in claiming title to the land? Explain.

**51–2. Deeds.** Wilfredo and Patricia are neighbors. Wilfredo's lot is extremely large, and his present and future use of it will not involve the entire area. Patricia wants to build a single-car garage and driveway along the present lot boundary. Because of ordinances requiring buildings to be set back fifteen feet from an adjoining property line, and because of the placement of her existing structures, Patricia cannot build the garage. Patricia contracts to purchase ten feet of Wilfredo's property along their boundary line for $3,000. Wilfredo is willing to sell but will give Patricia only a quitclaim deed, whereas Patricia wants a warranty deed. Discuss the differences between these deeds as they would affect the rights of the parties if the title to this ten feet of land later proved to be defective.

**51–3. Ownership of Real Property.** Glenn is the owner of a lakeside house and lot. He deeds the house and lot to "my wife, Livia, for life, then to my daughter, Sarina." Given these facts, answer the following questions.

    (a) Does Glenn have any ownership interest in the lakeside house after making these transfers? Explain.

    (b) What is Livia's interest called? Is there any limitation on her rights to use the property as she wishes? Discuss.

    (c) What is Sarina's interest called? Explain.

**51–4. Eminent Domain.** The Minneapolis Police Department, in trying to apprehend a suspect who had entered and hidden himself in Harriet Wegner's house, severely damaged the house. The police and a SWAT team called in to assist the police were unable to persuade the suspect to come out, so they fired twenty-five rounds of tear gas into the house, as well as three concussion ("flash-bang") grenades. The police finally apprehended the suspect as he crawled out of a basement window. Wegner alleged that these events caused damages of $71,000 to her home. Her insurance carrier, Milwaukee Mutual Insurance Company, paid her about $28,000 but refused to pay for the rest of the damage. Wegner and Milwaukee Mutual both sued the city of Minneapolis, alleging that the police department's actions constituted a compensable taking under the Minnesota constitution. (The insurance company sought reimbursement for the money it had paid to Wegner and for possible future liability on her claim.) The trial court granted summary judgment for the city on the taking issue, holding that "[e]minent domain is not intended as a limitation on [the] police power" of the state. The appellate court affirmed. Wegner and the insurance company appealed to the Minnesota Supreme Court. How should the court rule? Explain. [*Wegner v. Milwaukee Mutual Insurance Co.,* 479 N.W.2d 38 (Mn. 1991)]

**51–5. Covenant Running with the Land.** In 1961, Mary Schaefers divided her real property and conveyed it to her children, William, Elfreda, Julienne, and Rosemary. The deed from Mary Schaefers to her daughter Rosemary contained the following language: "It is further mutually agreed by and between the grantor and the grantee that as part of the consideration set out above, the grantee agrees to provide a permanent home for my daughter, Elfreda, should she desire or request one, and for my son, William Schaefers, should he desire or request one. Failure to perform the above will be considered a material breach of the consideration set out herein." In 1974, Rosemary conveyed her portion of her mother's property to Edward and Arthur Apel. Subsequently, William Schaefers attempted to prevent the sale to the Apels from taking place by telling them that the house was encumbered by a covenant running with the land and that if they purchased the house, they would be bound to provide a home for William and Elfreda Schaefers. Is Rosemary's promise to provide a home for William and Elfreda (should they demand one) a covenant running with the land? Explain. [*Schaefers v. Apel,* 295 Ala. 277, 328 So.2d 274 (1976)]

**51–6. Easements.** In 1882, Moses Webster owned a parcel of land that extended down to the Atlantic Ocean. He conveyed the strip of the property fronting the ocean to another party. The deed included the following statement: "Reserve being had for said Moses Webster the right of way by land or water." The strip of property is now owned by Margaret Williams, and the portion retained by Webster now belongs to Thomas O'Neill. Williams is denying O'Neill access to the ocean. O'Neill has brought an action to establish his title to an easement over Williams's property. What should the court decide? Discuss fully. [*O'Neill v. Williams,* 527 A.2d 322 (Me. 1987)]

**51–7. Zoning and Land-Use Restrictions.** Florence Dolan owns the A-Boy West Hardware store in downtown Tigard, Oregon. Wanting to expand the store and its parking lot, Dolan applied to the city for a permit. Under the Tigard Community Development Code (the local zoning regulations), the city could attach conditions to downtown development to provide for projected transportation and public facility needs. The city told Dolan that she could expand if she would dedicate a portion of her property for the improvement of a storm drainage system, including a public greenway along a creek, and dedicate an additional strip of land as a pedestrian/bicycle pathway. The dedication would represent about 10 percent of Dolan's property. Dolan sought a variance, which the city denied, and Dolan appealed. The city claimed that there was a sufficient connection between the expansion of the store and the dedication requirements, because the expansion would increase traffic to the area and would also increase storm runoff. Dolan conceded that there would be increases but contended that the increases would not be enough to justify taking 10 percent of her property. Dolan claimed that the city's restriction was an uncompensated taking of her property in violation of the Fifth Amendment. How should the court rule? Discuss fully. [*Dolan v. City of Tigard,* ____ U.S. ____, 114 S.Ct. 2309, 129 L.Ed.2d 304 (1994)]

**51–8. Adverse Possession.** Paul and Barbara Sue Flanagan owned property in Alma, Arkansas, which was being purchased by the Smiths under an installment land contract. It was assumed by all owners of the property since 1946 that a fence located at the southern end of the property was the southern boundary of the property. Over the years, all owners had maintained and generally exercised dominion over the property up to the fence. In 1985, when Jerry and Mildred Hicks purchased a lot bordering the southern side of the Flanagan property, a survey showed that the true boundary was approximately eleven feet north of the existing fence. The Hickses asked the Smiths to remove the fence, but they refused to do so. The Hickses then brought an action to compel their neighbors to remove the fence. What will the court decide? Discuss fully. [*Hicks v. Flanagan,* 30 Ark.App. 53, 782 S.W.2d 587 (1990)]

### 51–9. A Question of Ethics

 *The Stanards have owned lakeshore property since 1963. In 1969, the Urbans purchased lakeshore property adjoining the Stanards' lot and used the property for a summer cabin from 1969 through 1974. In 1975, the Urbans converted the summer cabin into a year-round home and moved there permanently. Since 1969, the Urbans have used a grassy area of land—part of which belonged to the Stanards—up to a wooded area between the two houses. Between 1969 and 1988, the Urbans mowed the grassy area up to the woods line and kept the weeds down, let their children and grandchildren play in the grassy area, and stored their boat dock on the grassy area each winter. In 1981, the Urbans constructed a white tin storage shed—mounted on a concrete slab—on the grassy area. Most of the shed was located on the Stanards' property. In 1988, the Stanards brought a lawsuit against the Urbans for trespass and sought removal of the white shed. The Urbans claimed that they acquired ownership of the property by adverse possession because they had used the property since 1969 (the state's statutory requirement for adverse possession was fifteen years). The Stanards claimed that the measurement of the statutory period should begin in 1981, when the permanent storage shed was constructed. Given these circumstances, con-sider the following questions. [Stanard v. Urban, 453 N.W.2d 733 (Minn.App. 1990)]*

1. Do you think that the Urbans' use of the Stanards' property *prior* to 1981 (when the shed was built) met the requirements for adverse possession? That is, was the use actual, open, hostile, continuous, and exclusive during those years? Or is this situation similar to many others in which there are no fences between neighboring lots and the respective owners and their families occasionally trespass on the others' property?

2. Would it affect your answer to the above question if you knew that the Urbans, sometime between 1980 and 1982, offered to purchase the parcel of property in question from the Stanards?

3. At what point should trespass on another's property constitute adverse possession? For example, if your neighbors customarily store their boat partially on your property, and you do not object, should this circumstance trigger a statutory period for adverse possession? What if your neighbors' children also customarily play on your side of the boundary line between your property and your neighbors' property?

4. Why do you think that state statutes permit people to acquire title to property by adverse possession? What public policy is reflected in these statutes?

# CHAPTER 52

# LANDLORD-TENANT RELATIONSHIPS

**A**nyone who rents housing or rents space for commercial purposes becomes subject to the laws governing landlord-tenant relationships. The owner of the property is the landlord, or **lessor;** the party assuming temporary possession is the tenant, or **lessee;** and their rental agreement is the **lease.** The property interest involved in a landlord-tenant relationship is known as a *leasehold estate,* as discussed in the previous chapter. The *temporary* nature of possession, under a lease, is what distinguishes a tenant from a purchaser, who acquires title to the property. The *exclusivity* of possession distinguishes a tenant from a licensee, who acquires the temporary right to a *nonexclusive* use, such as sitting in a theater seat.

In the past century—and particularly in the past three decades—landlord-tenant relationships have become much more complex than they once were, as have the laws governing them. Generally, the law has come to apply contract doctrines, such as those providing for implied warranties and unconscionability, to the landlord-tenant relationship. Increasingly, landlord-tenant relationships have become subject to specific state and local statutes and ordinances as well. In 1972, in an effort to create more uniformity in the law governing landlord-tenant relationships, the National Conference of Commissioners on Uniform State Laws approved the Uniform Residential Landlord and Tenant Act (URLTA) for adoption by the states. Over one-fourth of the states have adopted variations of the URLTA.

<table>
<tr><td>■ SECTION 1</td></tr>
</table>

## CREATION OF THE LANDLORD-TENANT RELATIONSHIP: THE LEASE

Leases may be oral or written. As is the case with most oral agreements, however, a party who seeks to enforce an oral lease may have difficulty proving its existence. In all states, statutes mandate that leases be in writing for some tenancies (such as those exceeding one year).

## THE LEASE FORM

To create a landlord-tenant relationship, a document must do the following:

1. Express an intent to establish the relationship.
2. Provide for transfer of the property's possession to the tenant at the beginning of the term.
3. Provide for the landlord's *reversionary* (future) interest, which entitles the property owner to retake possession at the end of the term.
4. Describe the property—for example, give its street address.
5. Indicate the length of the term, the amount of the rent, and how and when it is to be paid.

In the drafting of commercial leases, sound business practice dictates that the leases be written carefully and that the parties' rights and obligations be clearly defined in the lease agreements.

## ILLEGALITY

A property owner cannot legally discriminate against prospective tenants on the basis of race,
color, religion, national origin, or sex. Similarly, a tenant cannot legally promise to do something counter to laws prohibiting discrimination. A tenant, for example, cannot legally promise to do business only with members of a particular race. The public policy underlying these prohibitions is to treat all people equally.

State or local law often dictates permissible lease terms. The URLTA, for example, prohibits the inclusion in a lease agreement of a clause under which the tenant agrees to pay the landlord's attorneys' fees in a suit to enforce the lease. A statute or ordinance might prohibit leasing a structure that is in disrepair or is not in compliance with local building codes. Similarly, a statute may prohibit the leasing of property for a particular purpose, such as gambling. If a landlord and tenant intend that the leased premises be used only to house an illegal betting operation, their lease is unenforceable.

Often, rental properties are managed by agents of the landowner. Recall from Chapter 35 that under the theory of *respondeat superior,* a principal (in this situation, the landlord) is liable for the wrongful actions of his or her agent if the actions occurred within the scope of employment. At issue in the following case is whether a landlord can be held liable for his agent's discrimination on the basis of sex against a woman who sought to rent a particular apartment.

---

**BACKGROUND AND FACTS**  *Darlene Walker, a single parent with one son, was looking for an apartment in Falls Church, Virginia. A real estate agent, John Moore, was assisting her in her search and took Walker to view an apartment owned by Frank Whitesell III and managed by Constance Crigler. Walker liked the apartment because it was near a school for her son and near transportation, and Moore called Crigler and told her that he had an applicant for the apartment. Crigler told Moore, and later Walker, that she would never rent to a woman in any circumstances. Walker asked Crigler if she was speaking for the owner, and Crigler said that she was. Walker sued Crigler and Whitesell for violating federal laws prohibiting discrimination in housing. The trial court found Crigler liable for damages in the amount of $5,000 but held that Whitesell was not liable for Crigler's actions because he had previously instructed her, in writing, not to discriminate illegally against any potential renters. Walker appealed. (Shortly after the appeal was filed, Crigler filed for Chapter 7 bankruptcy, and a few months later the $5,000 judgment against her was discharged.)*

**CASE 52.1**

**WALKER v. CRIGLER**
United States Court of Appeals,
Fourth Circuit, 1992.
976 F.2d 900.

*MURNAGHAN,* Circuit Judge:

\* \* \* \*

\* \* \* The evidence is sufficient to support the conclusion that Whitesell specifically intended that Crigler not discriminate. In many cases, involving issues other than housing discrimination, such a finding would refute the assertion that Crigler had acted within the scope of employment, and would concurrently, shield Whitesell from any liability as principal. However, the arguable conclusion that Crigler acted outside the scope of her employment is irrelevant in the present case, for Whitesell could not insulate himself from liability for sex discrimination in regard to living premises owned by him and managed for his benefit merely by relinquishing the responsibility for preventing such discrimination to another party. \* \* \*

\* \* \* \*

\* \* \* Just as we feel no qualms in holding a property owner responsible for paying property taxes, meeting health code safety requirements, or ensuring that other responsibilities to protect the public are met, and we refuse to allow the owner to avoid these responsibilities with an assertion that he had conferred the duty to another, we must hold those who benefit from the sale and rental of property to the public to the specific mandates of anti-discrimination law if the goal of equal housing opportunity is to be reached.

**DECISION AND REMEDY** *The appellate court reversed the trial court's decision on this issue. Whitesell was ordered to pay $5,000 in damages to Walker.*

**ETHICAL CONSIDERATIONS** *The court was aware of the seeming unfairness of holding landlords liable in situations such as the one described in this case. "The central question to be decided in a case such as this," said the court, "is which innocent party, the owner whose agent acted contrary to instruction, or the potential renter who felt the direct harm of the agent's discriminatory failure to offer the residence for rent, will ultimately bear the burden of the harm caused." The court found that because the landlord had the power to control the acts of his or her agent, it was fairer that the landlord should bear the burden.*

## UNCONSCIONABILITY

The *unconscionability* concept is one of the most important of the contract doctrines applied to leases. Basically, in some jurisdictions (and under URLTA 1.303), the concept follows the provision of UCC 2–302. Under this provision, a court may declare an entire contract or any of its clauses unconscionable and thus illegal, depending on the circumstances surrounding the transaction and the parties' relative bargaining positions. In a residential lease, for example, a clause claiming to absolve a landlord from responsibility for interruptions in such essential services as central heating or air conditioning will not shield a landlord from liability if the systems break down when they are needed the most.

## SECTION 2

# PARTIES' RIGHTS AND DUTIES

At common law, the parties to a lease had relative freedom to include whatever terms they chose in the lease. Currently, the trend is to base the rights and duties of the parties on the principles of real estate law and contract law. These rights and duties generally pertain to the four broad areas of concern for landlords and tenants—the possession, use, maintenance, and, of course, rent of the leased property.

## POSSESSION

Possession involves the obligation of the landlord to deliver possession to the tenant at the beginning of the lease term and the right of the tenant to obtain possession and retain it until the lease expires.

### LANDLORD'S DUTY TO DELIVER POSSESSION

A landlord is obligated to give a tenant possession of the property that the tenant has agreed to lease. The ''English'' rule, followed in many states, requires the landlord to provide actual *physical possession* to the tenant. If, for example, a previous tenant is still living on the premises on the date the new tenant is entitled to possession, the landlord must remove the previous tenant or breach the obligation to the new tenant.

The ''American'' rule, followed in other states, requires the landlord to transfer only the *legal right to possession*. Under this rule, the new tenant in the preceding example would have been responsible for removing the previous tenant, who no longer had the legal right to possession.

The URLTA follows the English rule and requires the landlord to provide the tenant with actual physical possession of the leased property, unless the parties agree otherwise.

### TENANT'S RIGHT TO RETAIN POSSESSION

After obtaining possession, the tenant retains it exclusively until the lease expires, unless the lease provides otherwise or the tenant defaults under the terms of the lease. Most leases expressly give the landlord the right to come onto the property for the purpose of inspecting it, making necessary repairs, or showing the property to prospective purchasers or (toward the end of an expiring term) to possible future tenants.

### COVENANT OF QUIET ENJOYMENT

Under the *covenant of quiet enjoyment,* the landlord promises that during the lease term neither the landlord nor anyone having a superior title to the property will disturb the tenant's use and enjoyment of the property. This covenant forms the essence of the landlord-tenant relationship. If the covenant is breached, the tenant can terminate the lease and sue for damages.

### EVICTION

If the landlord deprives the tenant of the tenant's possession of the leased property or interferes with his or her use or enjoyment of it, an **eviction** occurs. This is the case, for example, when the landlord changes the lock and refuses to give the tenant a new key. A *partial eviction* occurs if the landlord deprives the tenant of the use of a part—one room, for example—of the leased premises. Assuming that the tenant has a legal right to possession of the property, he or she may either (1) sue for damages or possession or (2) consider the eviction a breach of condition and cease paying rent or terminate the lease.

*Constructive Eviction.* Whenever the landlord wrongfully performs, or fails to perform, any of the undertakings the lease requires, thereby making the tenant's further use and enjoyment of the property exceedingly difficult or virtually impossible, **constructive eviction** occurs. Examples of constructive eviction include a landlord's failure to provide heat in the winter, light, or other essential utilities. To claim that a constructive eviction has occurred, the tenant must first notify the landlord of the interference. If the landlord fails to remedy the situation within a reasonable period of time, the tenant must then abandon the premises. On vacating the premises, the tenant's obligation to pay further rent ceases. As in cases of wrongful eviction, the tenant may sue to move back onto the property or terminate the lease and seek damages.

*Retaliatory Eviction.* When a landlord evicts a tenant for complaining to a government agency about the improper condition of the leased premises, a **retaliatory eviction** occurs. Under some statutes, a retaliatory motive is presumed when eviction proceedings are begun within a certain time after a tenant has complained. If a tenant can prove that a landlord's primary purpose in evicting or attempting to evict the tenant is retaliation for reporting violations—of a housing or sanitation code, for example—regardless of the time elapsed, the tenant may be entitled to stop the eviction proceedings or collect damages.

## USING THE PREMISES

If the parties do not limit by agreement the uses to which the property may be put, the tenant may make any use of it, so long as the use is legal and reasonably relates to the purpose for which the property is adapted or ordinarily used and does not injure the landlord's interest.

Also, the tenant is not entitled to create a *nuisance* by substantially interfering with others' quiet enjoyment of their property rights. To constitute a nuisance, conduct must be more than simply aggravating. Arguing with the neighbors may be annoying behavior, for example, but it would probably not qualify as a nuisance, unless it constituted harassment. Consistently playing drums in the middle of the night in an apartment complex, however, probably would constitute a nuisance.

### TENANT'S DUTY NOT TO COMMIT WASTE

The tenant has no right to remove or otherwise damage leased property without the landlord's consent. The duty of a tenant not to damage the premises is a duty not to commit **waste**, which is the abuse or destructive use of property by one in rightful possession. A tenant cannot knock out an inside wall in a leased house to enlarge a living room, for example, or remove a fence or a grove of trees to accommodate grazing livestock unless he or she first obtains the landlord's permission to do so.

The tenant is responsible for all damage he or she causes, intentionally or negligently, and the tenant may be held liable for the cost of returning the property to the physical condition it was in at the lease's inception. Unless the parties have agreed otherwise, however, the tenant is not responsible for ordinary wear and tear and the property's consequent depreciation in value.

If, at some time during the lease term, the tenant decides to stop using the property but to continue paying the rent, the lease may require the tenant to give the landlord notice of the nonuse. There is always a greater chance of vandalism, fire, or some other cause of damage to property when it is not being used, and the nonuse may affect insurance coverage.

### ALTERING THE PREMISES

In most states, the tenant may make no alterations to the leased premises without the landlord's consent. In other jurisdictions, the tenant may make alterations, without being liable for the expense of their removal, if they were necessary for the tenant's use of the property and did not reduce its value. **Alterations** include improvements or changes that materially affect the condition of the property. Thus, for example, erecting additional structures probably would be considered making alterations, whereas painting interior walls would not. Unless the parties have agreed otherwise, neither the landlord nor the tenant is required to make specific alterations or otherwise improve the property.

Once a residential tenant affixes an item of personal property—such as a storage cabinet—to real property, it becomes a *fixture* (see Chapter 49). In some jurisdictions, fixtures become the landlord's property and may not be removed at the end of the lease term. In other jurisdictions, fixtures can be removed at the end of the lease period if they can be taken without damage to the landlord's property.

## MAINTAINING THE PREMISES

At common law the landlord was under no duty to repair the leased premises or to warrant that they were habitable or suitable for the tenant's purposes. The tenant took the property ''as is.'' Today, this common law rule has generally been replaced with statutes mandating a landowner's compliance with certain safety, health, and fire-protection standards. Also, in most states, statutes or judicial decisions impose a duty on a landlord who leases residential property to furnish premises that are *habitable*— that is, in a condition fit for human occupancy— and to make repairs for damages not caused by the tenant's actions. Nevertheless, under a long-term commercial lease, a tenant may still assume the responsibility of making all necessary repairs, including, for example, rebuilding a structure after its destruction in a fire.

### STATUTORY REQUIREMENTS

Usually, the landlord must comply with state statutes and city ordinances that delineate specific standards for the construction and maintenance of buildings. Typically, these codes contain structural requirements common to the construction, wiring, and plumbing of residential and commercial buildings. In some jurisdictions, landlords of residential property are required by statute to maintain the premises in good repair.

The landlord is also responsible for maintaining **common areas**—areas such as halls, stairways, elevators, and so on that are used by all tenants. This duty relates not only to defects of which the landlord has actual knowledge but also to those about which the landlord should reasonably know. A landlord, for example, cannot avoid responsibility for repairing a dilapidated but little-used back stairway by asserting that he or she never used it and did not know it needed to be fixed.

**OBLIGATIONS UNDER THE LEASE**  In a long-term lease for the use of commercial property, the parties may choose to designate in the lease which of them has the responsibility to maintain the leased premises and to what extent. Generally, an express promise to repair is legally binding.

Under most circumstances, a residential tenant is not required to make major repairs, such as replacing an old roof or laying a new foundation. And without a lease provision under which the tenant assumes a duty to maintain the leased property, the tenant is under no obligation to do so. The tenant is liable for repairs required as a result of his or her intentional or negligent actions.

The following case involves a dispute between a landlord and a tenant over the proper measure of damages for a tenant's failure to maintain the premises as promised in the lease agreement.

---

**BACKGROUND AND FACTS**  *ARG Enterprises, Inc., operated a Black Angus restaurant on premises leased from SDR Associates. The lease included a provision that required ARG to return the premises in the condition in which it had received them. In return for ARG's agreeing to maintain the premises, SDR charged lower rent payments than it otherwise would have. About six months before the lease was due to expire, SDR notified ARG of the need to return the premises in good condition if the lease was not renewed. When the lease expired, however, the premises were in disrepair. Extensive repairs were required for the roof as well as for the air-conditioning unit, the exhaust fans, and the parking lot. These problems prevented SDR from renting the premises to anyone else. Before the lease expired, SDR had been negotiating with Toys "Я" Us, Inc., about the possibility of demolishing the building and selling just the land, but SDR's preference was to relet the building as a restaurant. At the time of the trial, the structure had not been destroyed, but it subsequently was. SDR sued ARG, alleging that ARG had breached the lease agreement by failing to return the premises to SDR in good condition. Among other things, SDR sought damages in the amount of $200,000 as the cost for restoring the premises to good condition. The trial court held for SDR, and ARG appealed.*

**CASE 52.2**

**SDR ASSOCIATES v. ARG ENTERPRISES, INC.**

Court of Appeals of Arizona, Division 2, Department B, 1991. 170 Ariz. 1, 821 P.2d 268.

*ROLL,* Presiding Judge.
\* \* \* \*

ARG argues that the trial court used an incorrect method of calculating damages arising from ARG's breach of the lease. \* \* \* The correct measure, ARG maintains, is one based on diminution of market value, not cost of repair. Thus, because SDR ultimately elected to level the building following surrender of the premises, resulting in an increase in the value of the property, ARG caused no diminution in value.
\* \* \* \*

\* \* \* Here, the damage was not irremediable [impossible to repair or remedy]. Even if it was, however, the test for diminution in value is the difference immediately before and after the lease was terminated, and subsequent events affecting value are irrelevant to that determination. \* \* \*
\* \* \* \*

ARG failed to prove that the damages awarded SDR, arrived at immediately upon return of the property, were excessive. SDR gave ARG rent concessions.

Furthermore, SDR presented sufficient evidence to sustain the trial court's determination that the cost of restoring the premises to good condition was $200,000. Therefore, the trial court did not err in calculating damages sustained by SDR.

**DECISION AND REMEDY**    *The appellate court affirmed the trial court's decision. ARG was ordered to pay $200,000 in damages to SDR.*

---

**IMPLIED WARRANTY OF HABITABILITY**    The *implied warranty of habitability* requires that a landlord who leases residential property furnish the premises in a habitable condition—that is, in a condition that is safe and suitable for people to live in—at the beginning of a lease term and to maintain them in that condition for the lease's duration. Some state legislatures have enacted this warranty into law. In other jurisdictions, courts have based this warranty on the existence of a landlord's statutory duty to repair or simply have applied it as a matter of public policy.

Generally, this warranty applies to major—or *substantial*—physical defects that the landlord knows or should know about and has had a reasonable time to repair (for example, a big hole in the roof). In deciding whether a defect is sufficiently substantial to be in violation of the warranty, courts may consider the following factors:

1. Whether the tenant caused the defect or is otherwise responsible for it.
2. How long the defect has existed.
3. The age of the building, because a newer dwelling would be expected to have fewer problems.
4. The defect's impact—potential and real—on the tenant's health, safety, and activities such as sleeping and eating.
5. Whether the defect contravenes applicable housing, building, or sanitation statutes.

An unattractive or annoying feature, such as a crack in the wall, may be unpleasant, but unless the crack is evidence of a structural defect or affects the residence's heating capabilities, it is probably not sufficiently substantial to make the structure uninhabitable.

**REMEDIES FOR LANDLORD'S FAILURE TO MAINTAIN LEASED PROPERTY**    The tenant's remedies for the landlord's failure to maintain the leased premises vary with the circumstances and with state laws.

*Withholding Rent.*    Rent withholding is a remedy that is generally associated with the landlord's breach of the warranty of habitability. When rent withholding is authorized under a statute (sometimes referred to as a ''rent strike'' statute), the tenant must usually put the amount withheld into an *escrow account.* This account is held in the name of the depositor (in this case, the tenant) and an *escrow agent* (in this case, usually the court or a government agency), and the funds are returnable to the depositor if the third person (in this case, the landlord) fails to fulfill the escrow condition.

Generally, the tenant may withhold an amount equal to the amount by which the defect rendering the premises unlivable reduces the property's rental value. How much that is may be determined in different ways, and the tenant who withholds more than is legally permissible is liable to the landlord for the excessive amount withheld. In the following case, the tenant withheld rent because the landlord failed to maintain the premises in a habitable condition.

---

| CASE 52.3 | **BACKGROUND AND FACTS**    *Paula Sheets rented residential premises from Betty Light from October 1988 through January 1990. In September 1989, Sheets notified Light that the plumbing was deficient and that mold was gradually destroying her belongings. Because Light failed to remedy the problem over the next several months, Sheets withheld the rent for January 1990, although she occupied the premises during that month. Light served Sheets with a notice of eviction and brought this action to* |
|---|---|
| **LIGHT v. SHEETS**<br>Court of Appeals of Oregon,<br>1991.<br>105 Or.App. 298,<br>804 P.2d 1197. | |

*recover the unpaid January rent. Sheets counterclaimed, alleging that Light had failed to maintain the dwelling in a habitable condition, in violation of Oregon law. Sheets sought damages and an injunction ordering Light to comply with the statutory habitability requirements. The trial court, concluding that the plumbing problems reduced the monthly rental value of the premises by $60, awarded Sheets $240 in damages ($60 for each month from September 1989, when Sheets notified Light of the plumbing problems, through December 1989). Possession of the premises, however, was given to the landlord. Sheets appealed, seeking possession of the premises and contending that the trial court should have awarded $60 for the month of January 1990 also.*

BUTTLER, Presiding Judge.

\* \* \* \*

\* \* \* There is no explanation in the record why the trial court, having found habitability violations reducing the rental value by $60 per month, allowed that reduction for each of the months September through December, but not for January. There is no evidence that the conditions had been remedied during January, although tenant remained in possession during that month.

A tenant is entitled to damages for the entire period during which the landlord fails to maintain the premises in a habitable condition, after notice. In [a previous case], we upheld an award for diminution in rental value through the time when the required repairs were made. A similar award in this case would include $60 for January. The trial court erred in failing to do that.

The effect of increasing tenant's damages to $300 is to offset completely the rent that she owed [for the month of January 1990], so that she owed nothing at the time of trial. Because no rent remained due after application of tenant's recovery on her counterclaim, ''judgment shall be entered for the tenant in the action for possession.'' That will also make tenant the prevailing party, authorizing an award of attorney fees.

**DECISION AND REMEDY**

*The appellate court reversed and remanded the case for a decision consistent with its holding.*

**INTERNATIONAL CONSIDERATIONS**

**The Warranty of Habitability in England** *English law traditionally adhered to the principle of* caveat tenant *(''let the tenant beware''). The Landlord and Tenant Act of 1985, however, requires that leased premises be fit for human habitation, although the act applies mainly to dwellings rented for very low rates. The act also sets forth details relating to the landlord's obligations to maintain and repair leased premises. Unlike U.S. law governing landlord-tenant relationships, much of which evolved under the common law, English landlord-tenant law has been created, to a great extent, by statute.*

*Repairing and Deducting.* Under **repair-and-deduct statutes** or judicial recognition of a right to repair and deduct, the tenant pays for the repairs and deducts their cost from the rent. As in the case of rent withholding, this remedy is usually associated with the landlord's breach of the warranty of habitability.

Before a tenant can use this remedy, the problem—which in some states must concern a basic service, such as heat or water—must be the landlord's responsibility, and the landlord must be notified and fail to do anything about the problem within a reasonable time. Under some statutes, the deductible amount is restricted to a month's rent or some other fixed amount.

*Canceling the Lease.* Terminating the lease is a remedy available to the tenant normally only when the landlord's failure to repair amounts to either constructive eviction or a breach of the warranty of habitability.

*Suing for Damages.* Although a lawsuit for damages is always a possible course of action, it is not always economical. The amount a tenant can negotiate or be awarded may be based on the cost of a defect's repair or on the difference between the defective property's and the repaired property's rental values.

## RENT

*Rent* is the tenant's payment to the landlord for the tenant's occupancy or use of the landlord's real property. Generally, the tenant must pay the rent even if he or she refuses to occupy the property or moves out, as long as the refusal or the move is unjustifiable and the lease is in force. Rent is payable according to an applicable statute, to custom, or to what the parties decide. The amount may be subject to a legislated ceiling—as in Santa Monica, California, and New York City—or it may be as much or as little as the market will bear. Usually, rent is payable in advance or periodically throughout the lease term, but rent payable in crops may not be due until the end of a term.

Some states provide that the landlord must wait for as many as ten days after the rent's due date before initiating proceedings to terminate the lease for failure on the part of the tenant to pay rent. Notice may be required before a suit can be filed. Also, the landlord may impliedly waive the right to prompt payment if in the past he or she has accepted late payments.

**SECURITY DEPOSITS** At the lease's inception, the landlord may require a deposit to secure the tenant's obligation to fulfill the lease. If the tenant fails to pay the rent or damages the property, the landlord may retain the deposit.

Under the URLTA (for residential leases only), the amount of the deposit is limited to one month's rent and must be returned—less any amounts owed for damages or unpaid rent—within fourteen days of the tenant's request for the return of the deposit after the end of the lease term. Some states permit larger deposits and longer periods before their return. Under the URLTA and some state laws, if the landlord withholds any amount from the deposit to cover damages, the tenant must be given an itemized list of the damages. In some states, the landlord must also pay interest on the deposit, less an appropriate sum as compensation for the effort involved in meeting this obligation. If the landlord fails to meet these requirements, the tenant may recover at least the amount due. In some states, the tenant may recover triple the amount due and attorneys' fees.

*Late Charges* Legally, late charges can be imposed if a tenant does not pay rent when it is due. In general, the amount of a late charge may not be excessive, and it must bear some logical relation to the amount of the rent or to how long the payment has been overdue.

**RENT ESCALATION** Unless there is a clause in the lease providing otherwise, the amount of the rent cannot be increased during the lease term. If there is a clause allowing for the rent to be increased in the future—a **rent escalation clause**—the amount may be linked to the landlord's operating costs, indexed to increases in the cost of living, or subject to a real or anticipated increase in a commercial tenant's business activity.

**PROPERTY TAXES** In most jurisdictions, the tenant is not obligated to pay assessments and taxes on leased property. The responsibility of paying those charges may be transferred from the landlord to the tenant in the lease, however, or the lease may provide that the rent will be raised if the taxes increase. The tenant may be liable for the amount of the increase if the increase is due to improvements (such as the installation of trade fixtures in commercial premises) made by the tenant.

**LANDLORD'S REMEDIES FOR TENANT'S FAILURE TO PAY RENT** Under the common law and in many states, when a tenant vacates leased property unjustifiably (not as a result of constructive eviction or the landlord's breach of the warranty of habitability), the tenant remains obligated to pay the rent for the remainder of the lease term—however long that might be. The landlord may refuse to lease the premises to an acceptable new tenant and let the property stand vacant.

In a growing number of jurisdictions, however, the landlord is required to *mitigate* his or her damages—that is, the landlord is required to make a reasonable attempt to lease the property to another party. In those jurisdictions, the tenant's liability for unpaid rent is restricted to the period of time that it would reasonably take for the landlord to lease the property to another tenant. Damages may also be allowed for the landlord's costs in re-letting the property.

What is considered a reasonable period of time with respect to re-letting the property varies with the type of lease and the location of the leased premises. Under a long-term residential lease, for example, this period might be three months. In some jurisdictions, if reasonable—but unsuccessful—attempts are made to re-let, the tenant remains liable for the rent for the remainder of the lease.

Depending on the jurisdiction, if a tenant fails to pay rent or refuses to give up wrongful possession of leased property, the landlord can resort to one of three actions: a landlord's lien, a lawsuit, or recovery of possession.

***Landlord's Lien.***    Under the common law, when a tenant did not pay the rent, the landlord could simply take and keep or sell whatever of the defaulting tenant's personal property was on the leased premises. Today, the landlord does not have this alternative unless the parties have contracted for it or it is permitted under a statute.

Among states that by statute preserve this remedy, known as a **landlord's lien,** some states grant the landlord a lien on all of the tenant's personal property but require the landlord to initiate court proceedings to exercise the lien. Typically, the court will authorize a sheriff to seize the tenant's property. Other states allow the landlord to seize specific items of the tenant's property and hold them as *security* for unpaid rent (that is, as protection or assurance that the landlord will recoup something on the tenant's obligation), but the landlord must obtain a court order to sell the tenant's property.

***Lawsuit.***    Just as the landlord may sue the responsible tenant for damaging leased property, the landlord may also sue the defaulting tenant to collect unpaid rent.

***Recovery of Possession.***    Under the common law, on the tenant's breach of the lease, the landlord could—with force, if necessary—evict the tenant and recover possession of the leased property without legal proceedings. Today, the landlord must use legal process, even if the parties have stipulated in the lease that the landlord has, and may exercise without legal proceedings, a **right of entry** (a right to retake possession peaceably).

There are two procedures to which the landlord may resort to evict the tenant. One is the common law remedy of **ejectment,** which requires the landlord to appear in court and show that the defaulting tenant is in wrongful possession. An action in ejectment does not take priority over other proceedings and, consequently, may be delayed for a long time. During the delay, the tenant can remain in possession. Thus, this action is used infrequently.

The remedy of ejectment has been modified under statutes that provide for a summary judicial procedure, generally referred to as an **unlawful detainer.** During the unlawful detainer proceeding, the landlord attempts to prove that the tenant breached the lease or that the lease expired and the tenant refused to leave. The court makes its decision quickly, or summarily. If the landlord prevails, the court orders the sheriff to remove the tenant.

## SECTION 3

# LIABILITY FOR INJURIES ON THE PREMISES

Under the common law, whether a party in possession of property was liable to an individual who was injured on the property depended in part on that individual's classification as an invitee, a licensee, or a trespasser. Recall from Chapter 6 that an **invitee** is one whom the party in possession invites onto the premises for the possessing party's benefit, such as a business customer or a dinner-party guest. A **licensee** is one whom the party in possession invites or allows onto the premises for the licensee's benefit, such as a salesperson. A **trespasser** is one whom the party in possession does not invite and who has no other right to be on the premises. Each classification might require a different standard of care on the part of the person in possession of the property. Under certain circumstances, if the injured trespasser is a very young child who might be expected to be attracted to a dangerous condition on the property, such as an unfenced swimming pool, the **attractive nuisance doctrine** could apply to require yet a different standard of care.

These distinctions have not been entirely done away with, but today liability is more likely to depend on who controls the area where the injury occurred, and the governing standard is one of *reasonable care* under all circumstances. Applying the standard of reasonable care requires taking into consideration the predictability of a particular event (that is, applying the principle of *foreseeable risk*). The person who has responsibility for a particular part of the premises must take the same precautions regarding the area's safety as would a person of ordinary prudence in the same circumstances. Essentially, this is the same standard of care that is applied in cases of negligence (discussed in Chapter 6).

## LANDLORD'S LIABILITY

Traditionally, when the landlord surrendered possession of his or her property to the tenant, the landlord also relinquished responsibility for injuries occurring on the property. This was true regardless of whether the injury was caused by a condition that existed at the time the property was leased or a condition that developed later. Today, however, in recognition of the policies underlying the warranty of habitability, the landlord bears greater responsibility for the conditions of the premises and for injuries resulting from those conditions.

Currently, the landlord is generally liable for injuries occurring on the part of the property within the landlord's control—that is, common areas such as basements, hallways, and elevators. Also, when the landlord assumes an obligation to repair, the landlord's liability may extend to injuries attributable either to failure to make repairs or to negligently made repairs. Thus, the landlord may be responsible for injuries that occur on the part of the premises subject to the tenant's control—that is, the apartment, the house, or the store that the tenant leased from the landlord—when that responsibility is based on the landlord's duty to repair.

**INJURIES CAUSED BY DEFECTS ON THE PREMISES** The landlord's liability extends to injuries resulting from a dangerous condition about which the landlord knew or should have known, when the landlord fails to tell the tenant about it or actually conceals it. The landlord need not believe that the condition is unsafe; the situation need only be one that would lead a reasonable person to conclude that there is an unreasonable risk of harm. The landlord may be liable if he or she knows that the mortar is very loose in a brick wall, for example, and a brick subsequently falls and injures a tenant.

In most states, the landlord is not under a duty to inspect residential premises before leasing them, unless there is reason to suspect that a potentially harmful defect exists. Also, the landlord is under no obligation to tell the tenant about conditions about which the tenant knows when he or she signs the lease or that are obvious, such as a lumpy carpet in the hall.

**COMMERCIAL PROPERTY** When property is leased for public purposes, including commercial activities, the landlord does have an obligation to inspect the property and make repairs before the tenant takes possession to prevent unreasonable risks to members of the public. This does not include obvious conditions, which people can be expected to avoid. The landlord's liability covers only that part of the leased premises that is open to the public. If, for example, a customer disregards a sign reading "Employees Only," goes through the door, and is somehow injured on the other side, the landlord normally may not be held liable. Similarly, the landlord is normally not liable for the tenant's negligence in maintaining the premises, assuming they were in good condition when the tenant moved in.

The liability of a landlord of leased commercial property is at issue in the following case. Note the importance of the distinction between obvious and latent conditions in the court's determination of whether the landlord should be held liable.

**COMPANY PROFILE** *W. P. Lay, a steamboat captain, founded the Alabama Power Company in 1906 to develop electric power on Alabama's Coosa River. James Mitchell took over the company in 1912. Mitchell bought a number of Alabama's utilities and joined them with Alabama Power under the ownership of Alabama Traction Light & Power (ATL&P). When Mitchell died in 1920, Alabama Power's lawyer Tom Martin became president and reorganized ATL&P into Southeastern Power & Light. Southeastern acquired utility companies across the southern states until it was itself combined with Penn-Ohio Edison to form Commonwealth & Southern in 1929. The latter was dissolved in 1942 by the Securities and Exchange Commission, which put Alabama Power and three other southern utilities under the authority of the Southern Company. Today, the Southern Company is the second largest publicly owned electric utility in the United States, providing service to more than three million customers in four states. Southern provides electricity through five utilities, including Alabama Power. Alabama Power is entitled to half of the power generated by a Southern subsidiary, the Southern Electric Generating Company (SEGCO). SEGCO operates generating plants on Alabama's Coosa River.*

> CASE 52.4
>
> **ALABAMA POWER CO. v. DUNAWAY**
> Supreme Court of Alabama, 1987.
> 502 So.2d 726.

**BACKGROUND AND FACTS** *Alabama Power Company (APCO) leased property to David Garner, who operated Real Island Marina. The land was located on the waterfront of Lake Martin in Alabama, and under the lease, APCO had no duty to repair or maintain the land. Garner operated the marina and charged the public for recreational use of the facilities. An employee picnic held at the marina was attended by David Dunaway and his family. Dunaway's son, Daniel, drowned in the lake after the family had camped for the night on the marina premises. No direct evidence existed as to how the accident occurred. Mrs. Dunaway sued APCO, Real Island Marina, and the company that sponsored the picnic for the wrongful death of her son, claiming that the property was unsafe and that lifeguards and guardrails on the seawall by the lake should have been provided. The circuit court found in favor of Dunaway, and APCO appealed.*

*HOUSTON,* Justice.
\* \* \* \*

[A]s to the tenant, his servant, guest or others entering under his title, in the absence of a covenant to repair, the landlord is only liable for injuries resulting from *latent defects, known to him at the time of the leasing, and which he concealed from the tenant.*

\* \* \* \*

Under these principles there is simply no factual basis for liability for APCO as landlord under either of the plaintiff's theories of negligence. The picnic pavilion and seawall were built by the lessee (Garner) and if there were a "defect" arising from the pavilion's proximity to the water, it was obvious to any observer. This was no "latent" defect. The testimony showed that the plaintiff, as well as Daniel's father, had been to Real Island Marina with Daniel and both knew of the location of the pavilion with respect to the water and of the absence of guardrails on the seawall. There were no lifeguards at the marina, and Garner had erected a sign reading "Danger, swim at your own risk." The lack of lifeguards is a condition which could have been discovered by Garner's invitees by their reasonable and customary inspection. Therefore, this was not a "latent defect."

**DECISION AND REMEDY**     *The Supreme Court of Alabama reversed the lower court's decision. APCO was under no duty to warn the public of obvious hazards and was not liable for the death of Daniel Dunaway.*

---

**COMMON AREAS**   The landlord is responsible for—and liable for any injuries resulting from—the condition of common areas, as long as the areas are under his or her control. This responsibility includes a duty to inspect and repair such conditions as peeling lead-based paint, rotting stair railings, burned-out or dim lighting, and defective water heaters. It also includes a duty to otherwise correct such conditions as wet steps or a loose mat placed over the slippery surface of a polished floor.

When the landlord retains control over part of the premises leased to the tenant—for example, an apartment's walls—the landlord may be liable for injuries caused by that part's disrepair. The landlord is not, however, liable for injuries occurring on parts of his or her residential property where people could not be reasonably expected to go—for example, a roof or a closed basement.

**REPAIRS**   In many jurisdictions, under building, housing, or sanitation codes or the warranty of habitability, the landlord is required to put or keep premises for lease in good repair. The breach of this duty may constitute negligence and establish the landlord's liability for any injuries caused by this negligence.

The landlord's express agreement to repair may be a basis for the landlord's liability if an injury is caused by the landlord's failure to fulfill the agreement. Ordinarily, the landlord has a reasonable time, after discovering or being told that a condition requires repair, within which to do the repair work or see that it is done. Regardless of whether the landlord has agreed to make repairs, once the landlord undertakes them, he or she is liable for injuries attributable to negligence in the repair work.

**INJURIES CAUSED BY CRIMES OF THIRD PERSONS**   The landlord is not normally required to set up an elaborate security system to protect tenants from criminals. But when crimes are reasonably foreseeable and the landlord takes no steps to prevent them, he or she may be liable for negligence—failure to provide adequate security—if an injury results.

Courts consider several factors in determining whether a crime is foreseeable and preventable. It is logical to assume that some prior criminal activity in the geographical area in which the property is located is required to make future crimes reasonably predictable. Similarly, it is reasonable to base an expectation of future crime on how recently the previous crime occurred.

Also, courts may consider the *type* of crime that occurred previously. In this area, the courts are divided. Some follow the *prior similar incidents* rule, under which the existence of earlier similar crimes must be shown before foreseeability is established. Others follow what is known as the *totality of the circumstances* rule. These two rules and their implications for plaintiffs and defendants are explored in this chapter's *Emerging Trends in Business Law.*

**EXCULPATORY CLAUSES**   A lease may contain a clause that claims to relieve the landlord from any liability for injuries or other damages, including those caused by the landlord's own negligence. Known as **exculpatory clauses,** these provisions are unenforceable if injury or damage results from the landlord's failure to fulfill a statutory duty, such as compliance with a state's building code. When included in a lease for residential property, an exculpatory clause releasing a landlord from liability for his or her negligence is unenforceable.

## TENANT'S LIABILITY

A tenant has a duty to maintain in a reasonably safe condition those areas under his or her control. When commercial property is involved, this duty extends to all parts of the premises onto which a customer or other member of the public might be expected to go—such as the aisles in a grocery store. The grocer's duty includes using care in displaying his or her wares so that they present no threat to customers' safety. The goods should not be stacked, for example, so as to block an aisle or to fall onto a customer taking an item for purchase. Similarly, the grocer may be liable if a customer slips on the spilled contents of a broken jar and is injured.

In some situations—particularly when property is leased for commercial purposes—the tenant's duty may coincide with the landlord's duty. When this happens, both the landlord and the tenant may be liable for a third party's injuries.

## SECTION 4

# TRANSFERRING RIGHTS TO LEASED PROPERTY

Either the landlord or the tenant may wish to transfer his or her rights to the leased property during the term of the lease.

### TRANSFERRING THE LANDLORD'S INTEREST

Just as any other real property owner can sell, give away, or otherwise transfer his or her real property (see Chapter 51), so can a landlord—who is, of course, the leased property's owner. Furthermore, the landlord may make a deal involving only the lease, only the landlord's reversionary interest in the property after the lease has been terminated, only the rent accruable under the lease, or any of these property rights in combination.

If complete title—that is, the landlord's reversionary interest—to the leased property is transferred, the tenant becomes the tenant of the new owner. The new owner may collect subsequent rent but must then abide by the terms of the existing lease agreement.

### TRANSFERRING THE TENANT'S INTEREST

The tenant's transfer of his or her entire interest in the leased property to a third person is an **assignment** of the lease. The tenant's transfer of all or part of the premises for a period shorter than the lease term is a **sublease.** Under neither an assignment nor a sublease can the assignee's or sublessee's rights against the landlord be *greater* than those of the original tenant.

ASSIGNMENTS   A controlling statute or a clause in the lease may require the landlord's consent to the tenant's assignment of his or her interest in the lease. It may also require that the landlord not unreasonably withhold such consent, however. If the statute does not contain the latter condition, some courts will impose it nonetheless. Typically, clauses that require the landlord's consent to assignment are written as forfeiture restraints—that is, they provide that the landlord may terminate the tenancy if the tenant attempts to assign the lease without consent. This restriction is meant to protect the landlord from an assignee-tenant who might damage the property, fail to pay the rent, or otherwise be irresponsible. The landlord's knowing acceptance of rent from an assignee, however, may constitute a waiver of the consent requirement.

When an assignment is valid, the assignee acquires all of the tenant's rights under the lease. But an assignment does not release the assigning tenant from the obligation to pay rent should the assignee default. Also, if the assignee exercises an option under the original lease to extend the term, the assigning tenant remains liable for the rent during the extension, unless the landlord agrees otherwise.

SUBLEASES   The restrictions that apply to an assignment of the tenant's interest in the leased premises also apply to a sublease. For example, if the landlord's consent is required, a sublease without such permission is ineffective. Also, a sublease does not release the tenant from his or her obligations under the lease any more than an assignment does.

To illustrate: A student, Adya, leases an apartment for a two-year period. Adya has been planning to attend summer school, but she is offered a job in Europe for the summer months, and she accepts. To avoid paying three months' rent for an unoccupied apartment, she can sublease the apartment to another student. (Adya may have to obtain her landlord's consent for this sublease if the lease requires it.) The sublessee will take the apartment under the same lease terms as Adya. The landlord can hold Adya liable should the sublessee violate those terms.

# EMERGING TRENDS IN BUSINESS LAW

## The Limitation of Landlords' Liability for Crimes on Leased Premises

At common law, landlords are responsible for the safety of invitees on their business premises. Under landlord-tenant law, landlords are similarly responsible for the safety of their tenants and their tenants' invitees while they are in areas that are under the landlords' control, such as hallways and other common areas. Normally, however, courts will impose liability on landlords for crimes committed by third parties in common areas only if those crimes were *reasonably foreseeable*.

The important question has always been, at what point does a crime become reasonably foreseeable? Does a crime become reasonably foreseeable only if other *similar* crimes have been committed on the premises? What if previous but *dissimilar* crimes were committed on the premises? What if the neighborhood in which an apartment building is located is a high-crime area? Will this make crime in the apartment building's parking lot or hallways "reasonably foreseeable"?

How the courts have answered these questions has significant implications for landlords and victims alike.

### The "Prior Similar Incidents" Rule

Until 1985, the prevailing judicial rule was that prior similar incidents had to have occurred before a landlord would be put on notice that more adequate security measures were necessary to prevent future crimes. For example, under this rule a series of thefts from automobiles in an apartment complex parking garage may make subsequent apartment break-ins foreseeable. But such automobile break-ins would not necessarily make a murder foreseeable.

### The *Isaacs* Decision

The California Supreme Court made a significant departure from this rule in a landmark case, *Isaacs v. Huntington Memorial Hospital*.[a] In this case, the court ruled that the "prior similar incidents" rule was "fatally flawed" in many respects. The court stated that such a rule discouraged landowners from taking adequate measures to protect the premises. The court also pointed out that under the rule, the first victim loses while subsequent victims are

_____

a. 38 Cal.3d 112, 695 P.2d 653 (1985).

permitted recovery. The court also reasoned that such a rule leads to arbitrary results and distinctions because it is impossible to define exactly the word "similar."

There were also problems, according to the court, with the word "foreseeability." The court concluded that foreseeability should be determined in light of "all circumstances and not by a rigid application of a mechanical 'prior similar' rule." Thus, what must be foreseeable is the general character of the event or harm, not its precise nature or manner of occurrence.

After the *Isaacs* decision, about half of the states followed California's lead and adopted what has become known as the *totality of the circumstances* rule of foreseeability. More recently, though, the tide has turned again. A more conservative California Supreme Court revisited the *Isaccs* ruling in 1993 and, according to some observers, at least partially nullified its earlier "pro-victim" approach.

### "Random, Violent Crime Is Endemic"

The 1993 case concerned the Pacific Plaza Shopping Center,

a strip mall with twenty-five commercial tenants. A series of crimes had occurred at the mall, including bank robberies and purse snatchings. An employee of one of the mall's shops opened the shop for business at 8:00 A.M. as scheduled and shortly thereafter was raped by a man who was armed with a knife. The victim, Ann M., sued Pacific Plaza for negligence. She argued that the shopping mall had exposed her to an unreasonable risk of harm by failing to provide adequate security in the common areas. Pacific Plaza, arguing that it had no notice of any prior criminal incidents, moved for summary judgment in its favor. The motion was granted and affirmed on appeal. Ann M. appealed the case to the California Supreme Court.

The court stated that "[u]nfortunately, random, violent crime is endemic to today's society. It is difficult, if not impossible, to envision any locale open to the public where the occurrence of violent crime seems improbable. Upon further reflection and in light of the increase in violent crime, refinement of the rule enunciated in *Isaacs* is required."

The court then went on to "refine" the rule enunciated in the *Isaacs* case. The court pointed out that the hiring of guards is not an insignificant expense and anyway, "no one really knows what people commit crime, hence no one really knows what is 'adequate' deterrence in any given situation." The court therefore concluded that a "high degree of foreseeability" is required to hold landlords liable. According to the court, "the requisite degree of foreseeability rarely, if ever, can be proven in the absence of prior similar incidents of violent crime on the landowner's premises. To hold otherwise would be to impose an unfair burden upon landlords and, in effect, would force landlords to become the insurers of public safety."[b]

## ■ Implications for the Businessperson

1.   It would appear that the ruling in *Pacific Plaza Shopping Center* may steer the courts to the *prior similar incidents* rule. This may result in some relief to landlords from liability for crimes committed by third parties on leased premises. Consequently, there may be fewer security guards hired and subsequently lower commercial rents.
2.   Businesspersons who lease premises, such as space in a shopping mall, in high-crime districts face the

___

b. *Ann M. v. Pacific Plaza Shopping Center*, 6 Cal.4th 666, 863 P.2d 207, 25 Cal.Rptr. 2d 137 (1993).

opposite problem: How can they ensure the safety of themselves, their employees, and their invitees on the leased premises? If the expense of adequate security is not borne by the lessor, the message is clear: the lessee will bear the cost.
3.   If the *Pacific Plaza Shopping Center* decision is adopted in other jurisdictions, there may be more investment in leasable commercial buildings such as malls and hotels. In theory, the reversion to the prior similar incidents rule will reduce the costs of leasing commercial buildings.

## ■ For Critical Analysis

1.   Do you agree with the California Supreme Court's reasoning in the *Ann M.* case? Why or why not?
2.   Some commentators on the *Ann M.* case, including (not surprisingly) the attorney for the Pacific Plaza Shopping Center, regard the California Supreme Court's recent ruling as a common-sense approach to the problem of "endemic" crime. Do you agree? Explain your answer.
3.   One of the issues raised by the *Isaacs* and *Ann M.* decisions is whether the foreseeability of a crime is a question of law (for judges to decide) or a question of fact that should be put to a jury. If it were up to you, how would you decide this issue? Why?

# TERMINATION OR RENEWAL OF THE LEASE

Usually a lease terminates when its term ends. The tenant surrenders the property to the landlord, who retakes possession. If the lease does not contain an option for renewal and the parties have not agreed that the tenant may stay on, the tenant has no right to remain. If the lease is renewable and the tenant decides to exercise the option, the tenant must comply with any conditions requiring notice to the landlord of the tenant's decision.

## TERMINATION

In addition to the expiration of the lease term, a lease can be terminated in several other ways.

**TERMINATION BY NOTICE** If the lease states the time it will end, the landlord is not required to give the tenant notice—that is, to remind the tenant that the lease is going to expire—even as the time approaches. The lease terminates automatically. The lease may require that notice be given, however, or notice may be required under a statute. The procedures and time periods vary, but usually one or two months' notice is enough to end a tenancy for a year, and a week will suffice to end a tenancy for a shorter period.

In contrast, a *periodic tenancy* will renew automatically unless one of the parties gives timely notice (usually, one rental period) of termination. A periodic tenancy is a tenancy from week to week, month to month, or year to year. (Periodic tenancies are discussed in Chapter 51.)

**RELEASE AND MERGER** A lease may also give the tenant the opportunity to purchase the leased property during the term or at its end. Regardless of whether the lease provides this option, the landlord can convey his or her interest in the property to the tenant. This transfer is a **release,** and the tenant's interest in the property merges into the title to the property, which he or she now holds. Of course, a release effectively relieves the tenant of his or her obligations under the lease while bestowing on him or her title to the property, as well as all of the former landlord's responsibilities regarding the property. Because a release is a transfer of real property, it is subject to the Statute of Frauds (discussed in Chapter 16) and thus must be in writing.

**SURRENDER BY AGREEMENT** The parties may agree to end a tenancy before it would otherwise terminate. If the lease was subject to the Statute of Frauds, surrender of the property by agreement must be in writing, because technically, the tenant is conveying his or her possessory interest in the property to the landlord. Surrender of the property by operation of law, however, does not require a writing. A surrender by operation of law is sometimes held to occur when the tenant abandons the property (as discussed below).

**ABANDONMENT** A landlord may treat a tenant's **abandonment** of the property—that is, the tenant's moving off the premises completely with no intention of returning—before the end of the term as an offer of surrender. The landlord's retaking of possession of the property will relieve the tenant of the obligation to pay rent. Sometimes, actions that the landlord takes to mitigate his or her damages—for example, refinishing an abandoned apartment's floors when preparing to lease it to another party—may be interpreted as accepting the tenant's offer of surrender, thereby absolving the tenant of responsibility for future rent payment.

**FORFEITURE** The termination of a lease, according to its terms or the terms of a statute, when one of the parties fails to fulfill a condition under the lease and thereby breaches it, is referred to as a **forfeiture.** If, for instance, the lease provides that the tenant will forfeit his or her interest in the leased property on failing to pay rent when it is due, the tenant's late payment of rent could prompt the lease's forfeiture. Generally, the courts do not favor forfeiture, and when neither the lease nor a statute provides for it, the landlord may only claim damages.

**DESTRUCTION OF THE PROPERTY** Under statutes in most states, destruction of the leased property brought about by a fire, flood, or other cause beyond the landlord's control can terminate a residential lease. Usually, the landlord is under no obligation to restore the premises.

Similarly, the destruction of an entire building leased for business purposes may release the commercial tenant from any responsibility for continued payment of rent. (Terms vary among leases. If there is, for example, a fire, a commercial tenant's rent may only be reduced proportionally, according to how much property has been destroyed. The responsibility for restoring the property may rest on the tenant.)

## RENEWAL

The lease may provide for renewal, or the landlord and the tenant may simply agree to renew it. When the lease provides for an option to renew, there is typically a requirement that the tenant notify the landlord within a specific period of time—usually days or months—before the lease expires as to whether the tenant will exercise the option. The tenant must comply with any particulars regarding the notice's form (for example, that it be in writing) or the renewal will be invalid, even if the tenant stays on the property. The tenant's attempt to alter other terms to which the renewal is subject can be interpreted as a choice not to exercise the option to renew.

If a tenant neither renews a lease in accordance with its terms nor moves off the leased premises, but stays on without the landlord's consent, he or she can be treated as a trespasser. The tenant may be held liable to the landlord for damages.

## TERMS AND CONCEPTS TO REVIEW

| | | |
|---|---|---|
| abandonment 1042 | exculpatory clause 1038 | rent escalation clause 1034 |
| alteration 1030 | forfeiture 1042 | repair-and-deduct |
| assignment 1039 | invitee 1035 | statute 1033 |
| attractive nuisance | landlord's lien 1035 | retaliatory eviction 1029 |
| doctrine 1036 | lease 1026 | right of entry 1035 |
| common area 1030 | lessee 1026 | sublease 1039 |
| constructive eviction 1029 | lessor 1026 | trespasser 1036 |
| ejectment 1035 | licensee 1035 | unlawful detainer 1035 |
| eviction 1029 | release 1042 | waste 1030 |

## QUESTIONS AND CASE PROBLEMS

**52–1. Lease versus License.** Turner owns an apartment building. She contracts with Alvarez for one year to place coin-operated washing machines and dryers in laundry rooms in the building complex. The contract requires Alvarez to service the washers and dryers within twenty-four hours after notice is given that service is necessary. Some of the apartment leaseholders complain to Turner that Alvarez's service is poor and that Alvarez does not promptly refund money lost in the machines. After an argument, Turner orders Alvarez to remove all the machines within one week and not to come on the property again. Alvarez claims that he has a lease of the laundry rooms for one year. Turner claims that Alvarez has a revocable license (see Chapter 51). Discuss fully the property rights of the parties in this matter.

**52–2. Constructive Eviction.** James owns a three-story building. He leases the ground floor to Juan's Mexican restaurant. The lease is to run for a five-year period and contains an express covenant of quiet enjoyment. One year later, James leases the top two stories to the Upbeat Club, a discotheque. The club's hours run from 5:00 P.M. to 11:00 P.M. The noise from the Upbeat Club is so loud that it is driving away customers from Juan's restaurant. Juan has notified the landlord of the interference and has called the police on a number of occasions. The landlord refuses to talk to the owners of the Upbeat Club or to do anything to remedy the situation. Juan abandons the premises. James files suit for breach of the lease agreement and for the rental payments still due under the lease. Juan claims that he was constructively evicted and has filed a countersuit for damages. Discuss who will be held liable.

**52–3. Tenant's Rights.** Thomas has been a tenant of the Crestview Apartments for more than ten years. His tenancy is a month-to-month tenancy. During the ten years of his tenancy, the building's condition has steadily deteriorated. Indeed, the deterioration has reached the point at which the premises are in violation of city health and housing ordinances. Thomas has repeatedly complained to the landlord, but no repairs have been made. Thomas helps to organize a tenants' council, and the council reports numerous housing, building, and health violations to the authorities. The authorities bring actions against the landlord.

    (a) Assume that immediately after the authorities bring their actions, Thomas is given notice of termination of his lease. Thomas wants to prevent his eviction. Discuss how successful he will be.

    (b) Assume Thomas and the other tenants want to withhold rent payments until the premises are repaired. Discuss whether the tenants may withhold the rent payments and, if so, to what extent and on what grounds.

**52–4. Landlord's Responsibilities.** Sarah has rented a house from Franks. The house is only two years old. Sarah's roof leaks every time it rains. The water that has accumulated in the attic has caused plaster to fall off ceilings in the upstairs bedrooms, and one ceiling has started to sag. Sarah has complained to Franks and asked him to have the roof repaired. Franks says he caulked the roof, but the roof still leaks. Franks claims that because Sarah has sole control of the leased premises, she has the duty to repair the roof. Sarah insists that the repair of the roof is Franks's responsibility. Discuss fully who is responsible for repairing the roof and, if the responsibility belongs to Franks, what remedies are available to Sarah.

**52–5. Tenant's Rights and Responsibilities.** You are a student in college and plan to attend classes for nine months. You sign a twelve-month lease for an apartment and pay a security deposit of $150. Discuss fully each of the following situations.

    (a) You have a summer job in your hometown and wish to assign the balance of your lease (three months) to a fellow student who will be attending summer school. Can you do so?

    (b) You are graduating in May. The lease will have three months remaining. Can you terminate the lease without liability by giving a thirty-day notice to the landlord?

    (c) The lease period has expired. Are you entitled to the return of your $150 security deposit?

**52–6. Liability for Injuries on Leased Premises.** Spirn, a shopping-mall tenant, sustained injuries when he fell while on the property of Joseph, the mall's owner. At the time of the injury, Spirn was on his way to a furnace room in the mall to check the furnace, which seemed to be malfunctioning. The furnace room was only accessible by an outside door, approximately twelve feet from the street. There was no paved walkway leading to the door, but a "trodden path" had been created in the snow by persons who had been called earlier by Joseph to repair the furnace. The repairpersons' footprints had made depressions in the snow, which had subsequently been iced over. Spirn slipped

and injured himself. He filed suit against Joseph, alleging that the path was an unnatural (or aggravated natural) condition of the premises created by agents of Joseph and that Joseph had a duty to maintain safe premises. Joseph had therefore been negligent in failing to warn Spirn of the condition of the path. Discuss whether Spirn was successful. [*Spirn v. Joseph,* 144 Ill.App.3d 127, 493 N.E.2d 1197, 98 Ill.Dec. 176 (1986)]

**52–7. Breach of the Lease Contract.** Tachtronic Instruments, Inc., leased office and warehouse space in a building owned by Provident Mutual Life Insurance Co. The three-year lease ran until October 31, 1985, and specified monthly payments to Provident in the amount of $2,463. Within the first year of the lease term, Tachtronic defaulted on its payments. When Provident brought an action to evict Tachtronic, the small firm paid a portion of the rent due, and the action was dismissed. By February 1984, Tachtronic had largely vacated the premises. On March 1, 1984, Tachtronic met with representatives of Provident at the "leased" premises. The premises were inspected by Provident, and Tachtronic removed its remaining possessions, swept the floor with a broom, and turned over the keys to Provident. Immediately thereafter, Provident sought a new tenant for the premises. A new tenant was found, and a more lucrative lease beginning November 1, 1984, was created between Provident and the new tenant. In June 1984, Provident commenced an action to recover the rent due from Tachtronic prior to its departure from the leased premises and also the rent due and payable for the remainder of the lease. Discuss whether Provident could collect. [*Provident Mutual Life Insurance Co. v. Tachtronic Instruments, Inc.,* 394 N.W.2d 161 (Minn.App. 1986)]

**52–8. Landlord's Responsibilities.** Inwood North Professional Group—Phase I leased medical office space to Joseph Davidow, a physician. The terms of the five-year lease specified that Inwood would provide electricity, hot water, air conditioning, janitorial and maintenance services, light fixtures, and security services. During his tenancy, Davidow encountered a number of problems. The roof leaked, and the air conditioning did not function properly. The premises were not cleaned and maintained by Inwood as promised in the lease agreement, and as a consequence, rodents and pests infested the premises, and trash littered the parking area. There was frequently no hot water, and at one point Davidow was without electricity for several days because Inwood had not paid the bill. About a year prior to the lease's expiration, Davidow moved to another office building and refused to pay the remaining rent due under the lease. Inwood sued for the unpaid rent. Must Davidow pay the remaining rent due under the lease? Discuss. [*Davidow v. Inwood North Professional Group—Phase I,* 747 S.W.2d 373 (Tex. 1988)]

**52–9. Lease Renewal.** MCM Ventures, II, Inc., leased premises from Rushing Construction Co. on which to operate a restaurant. The lease term was for two years:

January 1, 1987, to December 31, 1988. The lease agreement stated in part that MCM "shall have a continuing option for a period of eight (8) consecutive years to renew this lease." Before the lease term expired on December 31, 1988, MCM did nothing to renew the lease and, after the lease expired, continued to make monthly rent payments in the same amount as before in January and February 1989. Then, on February 28, 1989, MCM notified Rushing by mail that it wanted to exercise its option to renew the lease. Rushing refused to renew the lease, contending that MCM had forfeited the option by not exercising it prior to the expiration of the lease agreement in which the option had been given. Discuss fully whether MCM still had a right to exercise the lease renewal option as late as February 28, 1989. [*Rushing Construction Co. v. MCM Ventures, II, Inc.*, 100 N.C.App. 259, 395 S.E.2d 130 (1990)]

**52–10. The Lease Contract.** Christine Callis formed a lease agreement with Colonial Properties, Inc., to lease property in a shopping center in Montgomery, Alabama. Callis later alleged that before signing the lease agreement, she had told a representative of Colonial that she wanted to locate in a shopping center that would attract a wealthy clientele, and the representative had assured her that no discount stores would be allowed to lease space in the shopping center. The written lease agreement, which Callis signed, contained a clause stating that "[n]o representation, inducement, understanding or anything of any nature whatsoever made, stated or represented on Landlord's behalf, either orally or in writing (except this Lease), has induced Tenant to enter into this lease." The lease also stipulated that Callis would not conduct any type of business commonly called a discount store, surplus store, or other similar business. Later, Colonial did, in fact, lease space to discount stores, and Callis sued Colonial for breach of the lease contract. Will Callis succeed in her claim? Discuss fully. [*Callis v. Colonial Properties, Inc.*, 597 So.2d 660 (Ala.1991)]

**52–11. Liability for Injuries on Leased Premises.** Commerce Properties, Inc. (CPI), owned the apartment complex in which Jonathan Linthicum, aged four, and his parents lived as tenants. There were no warning signs in the parking area adjacent to the rental units to notify automobile drivers that children might be playing there and to reduce driving speed. There were no speed bumps to slow the automobile traffic. Nor was any other traffic warning or safety device in place. Jonathan was playing in the parking lot when he was struck by a car driven by a neighbor and was seriously injured. Jonathan sued CPI for negligent maintenance of the parking lot. How should the court decide this case? If Jonathan's parents knew or should have known of the risk, will CPI escape liability? Discuss fully. [*Commerce Properties, Inc. v. Linthicum*, 209 Ga.App. 853, 434 S.E.2d 769 (1993)]

# FOCUS ON ETHICS

# Property

The legal structures that support our ideas about property are crucial to the continuation of the basically capitalist economic system in which we live and, at times, thrive. Private property is at the heart of capitalist ideology. That does not prevent ethical issues from arising, however, over the control, sale, and use of private property.

## Problems with New Forms of Personal Property

Most of our laws were written to deal with traditional, tangible forms of property, such as a car or a book. In the modern economy, however, intangible personal property is increasingly important. The protection of rights in intangible property raises new difficulties.

For example, a company may expend tremendous amounts of time and money in developing a new and improved software program. But a consumer, after buying one copy of the program, can often duplicate the software innumerable times on new diskettes at very little expense. The company thus receives relatively less economic benefit from developing the software. As a consequence, the incentives for innovation

in software development are diminished.

The consumer who copies software without permission is in a sense stealing the intangible personal property of the company. Yet many individuals do not even consider the ethics of copying intangible personal property. Even if this copying is deemed a civil or criminal wrong, the legal system can do little about it. Such small-scale and frequent theft could not be practicably prevented. We must depend largely upon the ethics of individuals in protecting property rights in many new forms of intangible property.

## Defining Rights in Personal Property

Who owns what becomes a serious question many times. One of these times, for many people, is during divorce proceedings. Other such situations include treatments for medical conditions and *in vitro* fertilization.

### Who Owns That Degree?

Family law judges constantly have to decide which spouse is entitled to what assets after the dissolution of a marriage. In community property states, most property acquired after marriage is owned equally by each spouse. In many other

states, upon dissolution of the marriage, there is an "equitable" distribution of the household's property. The term *equitable,* of course, has no objective definition. And even if it did, numerous questions would still remain about what actually is an asset that is subject to division during a divorce proceeding.

Is the value of a professional license, say, to practice medicine, part of marital property to be divided? In a majority of states, no.[1] But a few states, including California and New York, have held that professional licenses are marital property.[2] What about simply an academic degree earned during marriage by one party with the financial assistance of the other? Is such a degree to be considered distributable marital property? Yes again, said the Appellate Division of the New York Supreme Court in *McGowan v. McGowan.*[3] If, in contrast, the property is a

---

1. See, for example, *Johnson v. Johnson,* 855 P.2d 250 (Utah.App. 1993).
2. See, for example, *O'Brien v. O'Brien,* 66 N.Y.2d 576, 489 N.E.2d 712, 498 N.Y.S.2d 743 (1985).
3. 142 A.D.2d 355, 535 N.Y.S.2d 990 (1988).

teaching certificate that a spouse earned shortly after marriage, this would not be treated as marital property. Why not? Because the certificate was the result of the person's educational achievements completed prior to marriage.

## Who Owns Your Body Tissue?

Let us say that you are a patient in a research hospital because you have a rare disease. Do you own the rights to your body tissues that might be used by researchers to develop a cure for that rare disease? Such was the issue in *Moore v. Regents of the University of California.*[4] John Moore was a patient at the medical center of the University of California at Los Angeles. He was being treated for leukemia. His physician, Dr. David Golde, discovered that some of Moore's cells greatly overproduced a chemical that boosted his body's immune system.

Golde recommended surgery to reduce an enlarged spleen. He then used the spleen in his research. Golde and another researcher were able to grow a viable cell line that produced an anticancer compound. They patented the line in 1984 and contracted with two drug companies to develop an experimental drug. Upon learning this, Moore sued Golde, the other researcher, the university, and the two drug companies. The

4. 51 Cal.3d 120, 793 P.2d 479, 271 Cal.Rptr. 146 (1990).

California Supreme Court threw out Moore's complaint, holding that Moore could not sue for conversion because he did not have a property right in his body cells after they had been taken from his body.

The ethical question here, of course, is, at a minimum, whether Moore's doctor, Golde, had a duty to inform Moore about what he was doing. According to testimony, from 1976 through 1984, Moore continued to receive treatment from Golde, but Golde denied to Moore that he had discovered anything of value during his research on Moore's spleen cells.

## Are Frozen Embryos Persons or Property?

Should cryogenically preserved preembryos (commonly referred to as "frozen embryos") be categorized as persons, property, or something in between? These preembryos result from a process known as *in vitro* fertilization (IVF), in which a woman's ovum is fertilized by a man's sperm outside the human organism for later implantation into the woman's uterus. The IVF process has enabled many couples to have children when they otherwise could not have. Normally, the "frozen life" of an embryo is two years or so; after that time, embryos lose their potential to develop into human beings, and therefore the question of whether they should be treated as persons or property becomes tangled with major ethical implications.

In spite of the fact that over five thousand IVF babies have

been born in the United States and that some twenty thousand or more frozen embryos remain in storage, very few courts have had to wrestle with the problem. One case involved a divorce action brought by Junior Lewis Davis against his wife, Mary Sue Davis. The couple agreed on all terms of the divorce settlement except one: Who should have "custody" of the seven frozen embryos that they had created through IVF with the assistance of a Knoxville, Tennessee, fertility clinic? Mary Davis wanted to donate them to a childless couple. Junior Davis, however, wanted the embryos discarded; he did not want to become the parent of a child whom he would never know and who might end up being raised without a father, as Junior Davis had. The Tennessee Supreme Court held that frozen embryos were neither property nor persons but occupied an intermediate category that entitled them to "special respect." Control over the disposition of the embryos should be with the couple donating the sperm and ova. But this decision did not help the court decide which of the Davises should have that control.

Ultimately, the court concluded that Junior Davis should have custody of the embryos on the ground that his constitutional right to privacy mandated that he should not have to procreate if he chose not to do so. Weighing Junior's interest in avoiding being forced to beget a child against Mary's interest in donating the embryos to a childless couple, the court held that Junior's interest was the more compelling.[5]

## The Question of Land-Use Control

Laws and regulations governing land use are prevalent throughout the United States and provide a system for controlling the use of both public and private real property. These regulations are often created for the benefit of the public. For example, a regulatory board might prohibit the placement of a landfill next to a neighborhood school, a prohibition that would be in the public interest. Individual property owners, however, do not always benefit personally from land-use regulations.

For example, consider the consequences of legislation that alters the rights of private property owners in coastal regions of the United States. Suppose that prior to passage of land-use legislation, owners of land in coastal areas could develop golf courses, condominiums, private homes, and so on, with little interference. After the legislation is implemented, a regulatory board is created that has the authority to pass judgment on each requested change in the current use of the land by issuing (or not issuing) a building permit, for example. Suppose that a large area of unaltered coastal land is privately held property. If the board routinely prohibits development on the private coastal property, the property's market value diminishes.

Now we are entering into a taking issue, which is covered by the Fifth Amendment to the U.S. Constitution. Under this amendment, private property cannot be taken for a proper public purpose without "just compensation." Government agencies maintain that land-use controls do not involve a taking because the physical possession of the land remains in the hands of the private owner. From an economic point of view, however, a taking of potential income has certainly occurred, because the net worth of the property owner subsequently falls when the new land-use controls markedly restrict the way in which the land can be used. The issue of whether a regulatory taking has so restricted the use of private land as to be the equivalent of a taking of private property, thus requiring just compensation to the owner, is an issue that continues to be debated by the courts.[6]

In recent years, cases have arisen concerning the passage of state laws that allow the public to come onto private beaches. For example, in Maine, firmly established rules of property law had long dictated that the owners of beachfront property held title to intertidal lands—the part of the beach that is submerged at high tide but not at low tide. That intertidal land was subject to an easement permitting public use only for fishing, fowling, navigation, and any other uses reasonably incidental or related to those

activities. In 1986, however, the Public Trust and Intertidal Land Act was passed. This act gave the public the right to use, essentially without limitation, the intertidal land for recreation. Members of the public in unrestricted numbers were given the right to come onto this "private property" for boating, sunbathing, walking, ball games or other athletic events, camping, nighttime beach parties, and horseback riding.

One of the beachfront property owners decided to sue, claiming that the new law constituted an unconstitutional taking of private property without compensation and was therefore in violation of the Fifth Amendment. The court, when faced with this question, agreed with the property owner.[7] The court cited a similar case that arose in California and was decided in favor of the landowner.[8] In that case, the United States Supreme Court found that a permanent physical occupation occurs whenever the public is given a permanent and continuous right to pass to and fro on real property. Granting the public such a right over privately owned land constitutes a taking.

The ethical considerations at issue here are whether the public's right to use the intertidal lands is superior to that of the property owner. Some contend that the public should have access to virtually

---

5. *Davis v. Davis,* 842 S.W.2d 588 (Tenn. 1992).

6. *Dolan v. City of Tigard,* ____ U.S. ____ , 114 S.Ct. 2309, 129 L.Ed.2d 304 (1994).

7. *Bell v. Town of Wells,* 557 A.2d 168 (Me. 1989).
8. *Nollan v. California Coastal Commission,* 483 U.S. 825, 107 S.Ct. 3141, 97 L.Ed.2d 677 (1987). This case was presented in Chapter 51 as Case 51.4.

all beaches because such beaches are a gift from nature. Here we are again faced with a trade-off. To what extent should private property rights be given up for the benefit of the rest of society? Which weighs more heavily on the scales: maintaining the integrity of private property rights or ensuring public enjoyment of a natural resource—the beaches? Moreover, if private property owners are indeed required to allow their private property to benefit others, to what extent should the state compensate those private property owners?

## The Question of Bailments

Ethical issues regarding bailments often arise with respect to the duty of care of the bailee. Both legal and ethical questions sometimes arise when one party claims that a bailment existed and the other party disagrees. Take, for example, the common practice of hanging one's coat on a coatrack inside or outside a dining room, classroom, or hotel seminar room. In what circumstances does this action give rise to a bailment? This question arose when Timothy Augustine attended a seminar at a Marriott Hotel. Augustine was wearing a cashmere coat, which he placed on a rack outside the seminar room. At the noon recess, he discovered that the rack had been moved some distance down the lobby, to a position near an exit, and that his coat was missing. He sued the hotel to recover the value of his coat.

The court ruled against him, holding that a bailment never

existed because there had been no delivery to the hotel, nor was the hotel ever in actual or constructive custody of the coat. Additionally, Augustine was not even a guest of the hotel. The court concluded that "a reasonable man would have wondered about the safety of his coat which he hung on a rack in a public lobby of a hotel, without ascertaining if there were a guard."[9] What if a sign had been placed above the coatrack that read, "Hotel not responsible for coats left here"? Would Augustine still have felt that the hotel had an ethical obligation to protect his personal property?

Bailments are such commonplace occurrences that, in many instances, the parties to the bailment may not even be aware that they have entered into such a relationship. Consider the airline passenger who places her handbag on the conveyor belt that passes under the X-ray equipment at the airport's security checkpoint. Inside the handbag is jewelry worth $431,000. The passenger walks through the magnetized "archway," hears the beeping signal, and is detained by security personnel while they verify what caused the signal. By the time she reaches the other end of the checkpoint to retrieve her handbag, it has disappeared. Has a bailment been created in this situation? If so, what is the extent of the bailee's liability for the stolen handbag?

These questions were raised in a case that ultimately reached the Supreme Court of Florida. The court held that a bailment for the mutual benefit of the bailor and the bailee had been created between the passenger and the airline company whose agent controlled the security checkpoint. The court also held that the bailee's liability was limited to $1,250—a liability cap that had been set forth on the passenger's ticket. What if the handbag had belonged to a person who was not a ticketed passenger? In that situation, said the court, the liability cap would not apply, and the airline, if found to be negligent as a bailee, would be liable for the full value of the lost goods.[10]

## Landlord-Tenant Relationships

How much freedom should renters have? This question raises both legal and ethical issues. Numerous restraints are imposed on landlords by federal and state antidiscrimination laws, but sometimes these laws conflict with other constitutional rights, such as the freedom of religion. This conflict arose in a Minnesota case, *Cooper v. French*.[11] Layle French owned a two-bedroom house in Marshall, Minnesota, which he put up for rent when he decided to move to the country. French advertised the house and agreed to rent it to Susan Parsons. He accepted a $250 check from her as a security deposit. French then

---

9. *Augustine v. Marriott Hotel,* 132 Misc.2d 180, 503 N.Y.S.2d 498 (1986).

10. *Wackenhut Corp. v. Lippert,* 609 So.2d 1304 (Fla. 1993).
11. 460 N.W.2d 2 (Minn. 1990).

realized that Parsons planned to share the house with her fiancé, Wesley Jenson, and that the two would likely engage in sexual relations before they were married while inhabiting French's house. French, a member of the Evangelical Free Church, told Parsons that he had changed his mind because the living together of unmarried adults of the opposite sex violated his religious beliefs.

Parsons sued French, alleging that French was in violation of the Minnesota Human Rights Act, which prohibited discrimination on the basis of marital status. Minnesota's Department of Human Rights agreed with Parsons; so, too, did an administrative law judge, as well as an appellate court's panel of justices. The Supreme Court of Minnesota, however, did not agree. That court argued, among other things, that the landlord's right to exercise his religion under the Freedom of Conscience provision of the Minnesota constitution outweighed any interest of the tenant to cohabit with her fiancé in rented property prior to her marriage.

Two fundamental ethical principles—one promoting freedom from discrimination and the other promoting freedom of religion—had to be weighed against each other in this case. It is simply not possible to develop an objective rule to determine which principle should prevail in all cases.

## Discrimination in Housing

In the context of a home purchase, the Fair Housing Act prohibits mortgage lenders from refusing to lend money toward the purchase of homes in certain areas. Prohibiting this practice, known as *redlining*, severely restricts the lenders' ability to choose freely where (or where not) to invest their money. Should lenders be coerced by law into lending money toward the purchase of homes that are located in neighborhoods in which criminal activity is on the increase and property values are rapidly declining? The lender is in business to make money on its loan; it is not a charitable organization. Public policy protects disadvantaged borrowers in this context, by making more housing available to them. Lenders, however, are forced to extend credit in areas that may increase their risk of loss.

## ■ Discussion Questions

**1.** Why are we willing to grant property rights in such intangibles as computer software programs but unwilling to grant property rights in ideas?
**2.** Should individuals have a property right in their particular jobs? In other words, once a person obtains a job, should that person be given the right to continue working in that job, no matter what? How would such a right affect the doctrine of at-will employment?
**3.** Land-use control involves winners and losers. The losers are obviously those whose land is decreased in value because of a new rule, regulation, or law that eliminates some of the possible uses of that land. Who are the winners? Should the winners compensate the losers? What does it mean when it is said that land-use control is in the "best interests of society"?
**4.** What limits can be placed on a person's use of private property? Consider an owner of oceanfront property who wants to develop a resort. What if such development would threaten the habitat of an endangered species? Should the individual defer to species protection? Should the government intervene to compel species protection?
**5.** Some argue that tenants' rights have increased so dramatically in the United States that fewer individuals want to invest in rental property, particularly in major cities. Do you believe that the government has gone too far in protecting tenants' rights? Do you believe that tenants should have even greater protection?

# UNIT ELEVEN

# SPECIAL TOPICS

CONTENTS

**53** **Insurance**

**54** **Wills, Trusts, and Estates**

**55** **Liability of Accountants and Other Professionals**

**56** **The International Legal Environment**

# CHAPTER 53

# INSURANCE

**A** foremost concern of virtually every individual is protecting his or her life and property against the risk of loss. **Risk** is the probability of a potential loss based on known and unknown factors. For example, an individual may wear a seat belt to guard against the risk of injury in automobile accidents or install smoke detectors to guard against the risk of fire. Of course, no one can predict whether an accident or a fire will ever occur, but individuals and businesses must establish plans to protect their personal and financial interests should some event threaten to undermine their security.

The insurance industry has grown out of the need to insure personal and real property, as well as health and life, against various risks. **Insurance** is a contract in which, for a stipulated consideration, one party agrees to compensate the other for any future loss on a specified subject by a specified peril. Essentially, insurance is an arrangement for *transferring and allocating risk.* This concept is known as **risk management.** The most common method of risk management is the transfer of certain risks from the individual to the insurance company.

## SECTION 1.

## INSURANCE CONCEPTS AND TERMINOLOGY

As with other areas of law, the area of insurance has its own special concepts and terminology, a knowledge of which is essential to an understanding of insurance law.

### THE CONCEPT OF RISK POOLING

All types of insurance companies use the principle of risk pooling; that is, they spread the risk among a large number of people—the pool—to make the premiums small compared with the coverage offered. Life insurance companies, for example, know that only a small proportion of the individuals in any particular age group will die in any one year. If a large percentage of this age group pays premiums to the company in exchange for a benefit payment in case of death, there will be a sufficient amount of money to pay the beneficiaries of the policyholders who die. Through the extensive correlation of data over a period of time, insurers can estimate fairly accurately the total amount they will have to pay if they insure a particular group, as well as the rates they will have to charge each member of the group so they can make the necessary payments and still show a profit.

## CLASSIFICATIONS OF INSURANCE

Insurance is classified according to the nature of the risk involved. For example, fire insurance, casualty insurance, life insurance, and title insurance apply to different types of risk. Furthermore, policies of these types differ in the persons and interests that they protect. This is reasonable because the types of losses that are expected and the types that are foreseeable or unforeseeable vary with the nature of the activity. See Exhibit 53–1 for a list of various insurance classifications.

## INSURANCE TERMINOLOGY

An insurance contract is called a **policy;** the consideration paid to the insurer is called a **premium;** and the insurance company is sometimes called an **underwriter.** The *parties* to an insurance policy are the *insurer* (the insurance company) and the *insured* (the person covered by its provisions). Insurance contracts are usually obtained through an *agent,* who ordinarily works for the insurance company, or through a *broker,* who is ordinarily an independent contractor. When a broker deals with an applicant for insurance, the broker is, in effect, the *applicant's* agent. In contrast, an insurance agent is an agent of the insurance company, not an agent of the applicant. As a general rule, the insurance company is bound by the acts of its agents when they act within the scope of the agency relationship (see Chapters 34 and 35). In most situations, state law determines the status of all parties writing or obtaining insurance.

## INSURABLE INTEREST

A person can insure anything in which he or she has an **insurable interest**—an interest either in a person's life or well-being or in property that is sufficiently substantial that insuring against injury to the person or damage to the property does not amount to a mere wagering (betting) contract.

**LIFE INSURANCE**   In the case of life insurance, one must have a reasonable expectation of benefit from the continued life of another to have an insurable interest in that person's life. The benefit may be pecuniary (related to money), or it may be founded upon the relationship between the parties (by blood or affinity).

Close family relationships give a person an insurable interest in the life of another. Generally, blood or marital relationships fit this category. A husband can take out an insurance policy on his wife and vice versa; parents can take out life insurance policies on their children; brothers and sisters, on each other; and grandparents, on grandchildren—as all these are close family relationships.

*Key-person insurance* (sometimes referred to as business insurance) involves an organization's insuring the life of a person who is important to that organization. Because the organization expects to receive some pecuniary gain from the continuation of the key person's life or some financial loss from the key person's death, the organization has an insurable interest. Typically, a partnership will insure the life of each partner, because the death of any one partner will legally dissolve the firm and cause some degree of loss to the partnership. Similarly, a corporation has an insurable interest in the life expectancy of a key executive whose death would result in financial loss to the company.

The insurable interest in life insurance must exist *at the time the policy is obtained*. Because of this rule, in most states a divorce will not affect a policy. Similarly, under a key-person life insurance policy, it will not matter if the key person is no longer in the business's employ at the time of the loss—that is, the key person's death.

**PROPERTY INSURANCE**   In the case of real and personal property, an insurable interest exists when the insured derives a pecuniary benefit from the preservation and continued existence of the property. That is, one has an insurable interest in

■ **Exhibit 53–1 Insurance Classifications**

| Type of Insurance | Coverage |
|---|---|
| Accident | Covers expenses, losses, and suffering incurred by the insured because of accidents causing physical injury and consequent disability; sometimes includes a specified payment to heirs of the insured if death results from an accident. |
| All-risk | Covers all losses that the insured may incur except those resulting from fraud on the part of the insured. |
| Automobile | May cover damage to automobiles resulting from specified hazards or occurrences (such as fire, vandalism, theft, or collision); normally provides protection against liability for personal injuries and property damage resulting from the operation of the vehicle. |
| Casualty | Protects against losses that may be incurred by the insured as a result of being held liable for personal injuries or property damage sustained by others. |
| Credit | Pays to a creditor the balance of a debt upon the disability, death, insolvency, or bankruptcy of the debtor; often offered by lending institutions. |
| Decreasing-term | Provides life insurance; requires uniform payments over the life (term) of the policy, but with a decreasing face value. |
| Employer's Liability | Insures employers against liability for injuries or losses sustained by employees during the course of their employment; covers claims not covered under workers' compensation insurance. |
| Fidelity or Guaranty | Provides indemnity against losses in trade or losses caused by the dishonesty of employees, the insolvency of debtors, or breaches of contract. |
| Fire | Covers losses caused to the insured as a result of a hostile fire. |
| Floater | Covers movable property, as long as the property is within the territorial boundaries specified in the contract. |
| Group | Provides individual life, medical, or disability insurance coverage but is obtainable through a group of persons, usually employees; the policy premium is paid either entirely by the employer or partially by the employer and partially by the employee. |
| Health | Covers expenses incurred by the insured resulting from physical injury or illness, as well as other expenses relating to health and life maintenance. |
| Homeowners' | Protects homeowners against some or all of the risks of loss to their residences and the residences' contents or against liability related to such property. |
| Key-person | Protects a business in the event of the death or disability of a key employee. |
| Liability | Protects against liability imposed on the insured resulting from injuries to the person or property of another. |
| Life | Covers the death of the policyholder. Upon the death of the insured, an amount specified in the policy is paid by the insurer to the insured's beneficiary. |
| Major Medical | Protects the insured against major hospital, medical, or surgical expenses. |
| Malpractice | Protects professionals (doctors, lawyers, and others) against malpractice claims brought against them by their patients or clients; a form of liability insurance. |
| Marine | Covers movable property (ships, freight, or cargo) against certain perils or navigation risks during a specific voyage or time period. |
| Mortgage | Covers a mortgage loan; the insurer pays the balance of the mortgage to the creditor upon the death or disability of the debtor. |

■ **Exhibit 53–1 Insurance Classifications (Continued)**

| Type of Insurance | Coverage |
|---|---|
| No-fault Auto | Covers personal injury and (sometimes) property damage resulting from automobile accidents. The insured submits his or her claims to his or her own insurance company, regardless of who was at fault. A person may sue the party at fault or that party's insurer only in cases involving serious medical injury and consequent high medical costs. Governed by state "no-fault" statutes. |
| Term | Provides life insurance for a specified period of time (term) with no cash surrender value; usually renewable. |
| Title | Protects against any defects in title to real property and any losses incurred as a result of existing claims against or liens on the property at the time of purchase. |

property when one would sustain a pecuniary loss from its destruction. Both a mortgagor and a mortgagee, for example, have an insurable interest in the mortgaged property. So do a landlord and a tenant in leased property, a secured party in the property in which he or she has an interest, a partner in partnership property, and a stockholder in corporate property. But John or Jane Doe cannot obtain fire insurance on the White House or auto insurance on the Andrettis' racing cars.

The existence of an insurable interest is a primary concern in determining liability under an insurance policy. The insurable interest in property must exist *when the loss occurs*. In the following case, the insurance company claimed that the insured possessed no insurable interest in her former husband's house because she had deeded her interest to him one year before his death.

**BACKGROUND AND FACTS**  *Linda Richmond and Eddie Durham were married, the parents of two children, and homeowners in Kentucky. When Richmond and Durham divorced, Richmond, the plaintiff, deeded her legal interest in the title to their home to Durham and moved out with their children. Shortly thereafter, Durham died, leaving the two children as his only legal heirs. Richmond returned to the home with the children. She had been living there and making the mortgage payments for more than one year when the home was totally destroyed by fire. Ten months prior to the fire, Richmond had secured fire insurance with the defendant, Motorists Mutual Insurance Company. She sought payment from Motorists for the destruction of the house, but Motorists refused to pay, claiming that she had no insurable interest in the house. The trial court awarded Richmond, her children, and the mortgage company $29,000. Motorists appealed.*

**CASE 53.1**

**MOTORISTS MUTUAL INSURANCE CO. v. RICHMOND**

Court of Appeals of Kentucky, 1984.
676 S.W.2d 478.

*CLAYTON*, Judge.
* * * *

Seeking to avoid payment under the contract, Motorists would now cast Richmond as nothing more than a trespassing squatter who "surreptitiously" [secretly] returned to the residence and thereafter fraudulently represented her true lack of ownership interest. * * * We cannot accept [this] base characterization. [It is] not supposed by the record or the law.

Linda Richmond, both before and after the death of her late former husband, made substantial monetary contribution to the maintenance and improvement of the destroyed residence. As natural guardian for her minor children, * * * she was obligated to provide for the care and custody of their offspring, including the duty to protect their home, of which the children became sole owners * * * upon the death of their father. Thus, when Richmond returned to the property following Durham's death she was not a surreptitious trespasser. Her offspring and she as their guardian were fully entitled to use and dominion over the premises. While not possessed of title, Richmond certainly possessed an insurable interest in the residence; first, by her status as natural guardian for the protection of her minor children's interest; and second, by her extensive pecuniary investment in the residence.

**DECISION AND REMEDY** *The court held that Linda Richmond had an insurable interest in the home, for which Motorists was required to pay.*

---

## SECTION 2

# THE INSURANCE CONTRACT

An insurance contract is governed by the general principles of contract law, although the insurance industry is heavily regulated by each state. Policies generally are in standard form; and in some states, standardization of forms is required.

## APPLICATION FOR INSURANCE

The filled-in application form for insurance is usually attached to the policy and made a part of the insurance contract. Thus, an insurance applicant is bound by any false statements that appear in the application (subject to certain exceptions). Because the insurance company evaluates the risk factors based on the information included in the insurance application, misstatements or misrepresentations can void a policy, especially if the insurance company can show that it would not have extended insurance if it had known the facts.

## EFFECTIVE DATE

The effective date of an insurance contract is important. In some instances, the insurance applicant is not protected until a formal written policy is issued. In other situations, the applicant is protected between the time an application is received and the time the insurance company either accepts or rejects it. Four facts should be kept in mind:

1. A broker is merely the agent of an applicant. Therefore, if the broker fails to procure a policy, the applicant is normally not insured. According to general principles of agency law, if the broker fails to obtain policy coverage and the applicant is damaged as a result, then the broker is liable to the damaged applicant-principal for the loss.

2. A person who seeks insurance from an insurance company's agent will usually be protected from the moment the application is made, provided—in the case of life insurance—that some form of premium has been paid. Between the time the application is received and the time it is either rejected or accepted, the applicant is covered (possibly subject to certain conditions, such as passing a physical examination). Usually, the agent will write a memorandum, or **binder,** indicating that a policy is pending and stating its essential terms.

3. If the parties agree that the policy will be issued and delivered at a later time, the contract is not effective until the policy is issued and delivered or sent to the applicant, depending upon the agreement. Thus, any loss sustained between the time of application and the delivery of the policy is not covered.

4. Parties may agree that a life insurance policy will be binding at the time the insured pays the first premium, or the policy may be expressly contingent upon the applicant's passing a physical examination. (If the applicant pays the premium and passes the examination, then the policy coverage is continuously in effect.) If the applicant pays the premium but

dies before having the physical examination, then, in order to collect, the applicant's estate normally must show that the applicant would have passed the examination had he or she not died.

Coverage on an insurance policy can begin when a binder is written; when the policy is issued; or, depending on the terms of the contract, after a certain period of time has elapsed. In the following case, because of a clerical error, the insured's coverage was not reflected in a company's computer files. The question was whether insurance coverage ever became effective or even existed.

---

**HISTORICAL AND ECONOMIC SETTING** *In marketing any product or service, economy can be achieved through a high volume of transactions. Insurance is no different. The primary method of attaining economy in the insurance field is through selling group insurance (a single contract that provides coverage for many individuals). In the United States, the first modern group insurance policies were issued by the Equitable Life Assurance Society in 1911. These policies provided life or health insurance coverage for the employees of a single employer. Group insurance is now available for the members of many other groups, including unions, industry organizations that include the employees of more than one employer, and trade and professional associations.*

**BACKGROUND AND FACTS** *Charis Snyder-Gilbert, a school psychologist, enrolled herself and her husband in a group health plan offered through the school system. The insurance was to take effect on October 1, 1989, and thereafter monthly premiums ($1 a month for herself and $150.22 for her husband) were deducted from her paycheck. The insurer, Humana Health Care Plans, entered both names separately into its computer system, but due to a clerical mistake, the computer entry for Mr. Gilbert reflected that his coverage both began and ended on October 1, 1989. During the following year, Mr. Gilbert submitted two claims totaling $69, but Humana denied both claims. Because of the small amount, the couple chose not to dispute the denials and paid the amount themselves. In October 1990, the clerical error came to light. Humana told the couple that Mr. Gilbert was, in fact, covered under the group plan and had been since October 1, 1989. Ms. Snyder-Gilbert, apparently realizing that paying $69 for the two claims was cheaper than paying the $1,807.84 that had been deducted from her paycheck for Mr. Gilbert's coverage, filed suit to recover the premiums.[a] The trial court held that Humana, by denying the two claims, had materially breached the insurance contract, entitling Ms. Snyder-Gilbert to a refund of the premiums. Humana appealed.*

**CASE 53.2**

**HUMANA HEALTH CARE PLANS v. SNYDER-GILBERT**

Court of Appeals of Indiana, 1992.

596 N.E.2d 299.

---

*MILLER*, Judge.

\* \* \* \*

It is axiomatic that a court cannot award a refund of premiums paid to secure insurance once the insurance company has been put at risk on behalf of the insured.

\* \* \*

It is not disputed that a valid insurance contract existed between Mr. Gilbert and Humana. Once Charis mailed her enrollment form to Humana and Humana entered

---

a. Ms. Snyder-Gilbert filed and argued her case *pro se*—that is, she did not retain an attorney but represented herself in court.

both of them with coverage in its computer files, this constituted a valid offer and acceptance for insurance. Under its agreement, Humana agreed to provide coverage to Mr. Gilbert beginning October 1, 1989; therefore, Humana was at risk for any legitimate claims of Mr. Gilbert which accrued after that point.

Furthermore, we fail to see how Humana's computer error could legally shield it from risk. While our courts in Indiana have not directly addressed this issue, there is helpful authority from Mississippi. \* \* \* [T]he [Mississippi Supreme] Court [has] consistently held that "error or mistake does not constitute an arguable reason for failure to honor a just claim." \* \* \*

Based on this, we conclude that, regardless of its computer error, Humana was still legally at risk for any and all legitimate claims of Mr. Gilbert that occurred after his coverage was erroneously terminated. Because Humana remained at risk, the small claims court erred as a matter of law in awarding a refund of premiums.

**DECISION AND REMEDY**   *The appellate court reversed the trial court's judgment.*

## PROVISIONS AND CLAUSES

Some of the important provisions and clauses contained in insurance contracts are defined and discussed in the following subsections.

**PROVISIONS MANDATED BY STATUTE**   If a statute mandates that a certain provision be included in insurance contracts, a court will deem that an insurance policy contains the provision regardless of whether the parties actually included it in the language of their contract. If a statute requires that any limitations regarding coverage be stated in the contract, a court will not allow an insurer to avoid liability for a claim through reliance on an unexpressed restriction.

**INCONTESTABILITY CLAUSES**   Statutes commonly require that a life or health-insurance policy provide that after the policy has been in force for a specified length of time—often two or three years—the insurer cannot contest statements made in the application. This is known as an *incontestability clause.* Once a policy becomes incontestable, the insurer cannot later avoid a claim on the basis of, for example, the insured's fraud, unless the clause provides an exception for that circumstance. The clause does not prohibit an insurer's refusal or reduction of payment for a claim due to nonpayment of premiums, failure to file proof of death within a certain period, or lack of an insurable interest.

**COINSURANCE CLAUSES**   Often, when taking out fire insurance policies, property owners insure their property for less than full value. Part of the reason for this is that most fires do not result in a total loss. To encourage owners to insure their property for an amount as close to full value as possible, a standard provision of fire insurance policies is a *coinsurance clause.* Typically, a coinsurance clause provides that if the owner insures the property up to a specified percentage—usually 80 percent—of its value, he or she will recover any loss up to the face amount of the policy. If the insurance is for less than the fixed percentage, the owner is responsible for a proportionate share of the loss. Coinsurance applies only in instances of partial loss. For example, if the owner of property valued at $100,000 took out a policy in the amount of $40,000 and suffered a loss of $30,000, the recovery would be $15,000. The formula for calculating the recovery amount is as follows:

$$\frac{\text{amount of insurance } (\$40,000)}{\text{coinsurance percentage } (80\%) \times \text{property value } (\$100,000)} = \begin{array}{c}\text{recovery} \\ \text{percentage} \\ (50\%)\end{array}$$

recovery percentage (50%) × amount of loss ($30,000) = recovery amount ($15,000)

If the owner had taken out a policy in the amount of $80,000, then, according to the same formula, the full loss would have been recovered.

## APPRAISAL AND ARBITRATION CLAUSES

Most fire insurance policies provide that if the parties cannot agree on the amount of a loss covered under the policy or on the value of the property lost, an *appraisal* can be demanded. An appraisal is an estimate of the property's value determined by suitably qualified individuals who have no interest in the property. Typically, two appraisers are used—one being appointed by each party. A third party, or *umpire,* may be called on to resolve differences. Other types of insurance policies also contain provisions for appraisal and arbitration when the insured and insurer disagree as to the value of a loss.

## MULTIPLE INSURANCE COVERAGE

If an insured has *multiple insurance coverage*—that is, policies with several companies covering the same insurance interest—and the amount of coverage exceeds the loss, the insured can collect from each insurer only the company's proportionate share of the liability to the total amount of insurance. Many fire insurance policies include a *pro rata* clause, which requires any loss to be shared proportionately by all carriers. For example, if Grumbling insured $50,000 worth of property with two companies, each of whose policies had a liability limit of $40,000, on the property's total destruction Grumbling could collect only $25,000 from each insurer.

## ANTILAPSE CLAUSES

A life insurance policy may provide, or a statute may require a policy to provide, that it will not automatically lapse if no payment is made on the date due. Ordinarily, under an *antilapse provision*, the insured has a *grace period* of thirty or thirty-one days within which to pay an overdue premium. If the insured fails to pay a premium altogether, there are alternatives to cancellation. The insurance company may

1. Be required to extend the insurance for a period of time.
2. Issue a policy with less coverage to reflect the amount of the payments made.
3. Pay to the insured the policy's **cash surrender value**—the amount the insurer has agreed to pay on the policy's cancellation before the insured's death. (In determining this value, the following factors are considered: the period that the policy has already run, the amount of

the premium, the insured's age and life expectancy, and amounts to be repaid on any outstanding loans taken out against the policy.)

When the insurance contract states that the insurer cannot cancel the policy, these alternatives are important.

## INTERPRETING PROVISIONS OF AN INSURANCE CONTRACT

The courts are increasingly cognizant of the fact that most people do not have the special training necessary to understand the intricate terminology used in insurance policies. The words used in an insurance contract have their ordinary meanings and are interpreted by courts in light of the nature of the coverage involved. When there is an ambiguity in the policy, the provision is interpreted against the insurance company. When it is unclear whether an insurance contract actually exists because the written policy has not been delivered, the uncertainty will be determined against the insurance company. The court will presume that the policy is in effect unless the company can show otherwise.

## CANCELLATION

When an insurance company can cancel its insurance contract, the policy or a state statute usually requires that the insurer give advance written notice of the cancellation. Any premium paid in advance and not yet earned may be refundable. The insured may also be entitled to a life insurance policy's *cash surrender value.*

Cancellation of an insurance policy can occur for various reasons, depending on the type of insurance. For example, automobile insurance can be canceled for nonpayment of premiums or suspension of the insured's driver's license. Property insurance can be canceled for nonpayment of premiums or for other reasons, including the insured's fraud or misrepresentation, conviction for a crime that increases the hazard insured against, or gross negligence that increases the hazard insured against. Life and health policies can be canceled due to false statements made by the insured in the application, but cancellation can only take place before the effective date of an incontestability clause. An insurer cannot cancel—or refuse to renew—a policy because of the national origin or race of an applicant or because the insured has appeared as a witness in a case brought against the company.

State laws normally impose specific requirements relating to insurance policy cancellations. In the following case, the plaintiff claimed that the insurer had not complied with the state's statutory requirements governing policy cancellation.

---

CASE 53.3

**CLYBURN v. ALLSTATE INSURANCE CO.**
United States District Court, District of South Carolina, 1993.
826 F.Supp. 955.

**BACKGROUND AND FACTS** *When William Clyburn's house burned to the ground, two years had passed since he had paid a premium on his policy with the Allstate Insurance Company. Allstate refused to cover the loss of the house, and Clyburn brought suit against the insurer, claiming that the policy had not been legally canceled and that the insurer had therefore improperly denied coverage. Specifically, Clyburn argued that Allstate had not followed the state's statutory requirements governing a policy cancellation. The relevant state statute required an insurer to send written notice to both the insured and to the insurer's "agent of record"— the insurance agent who had issued the policy to the insured. Allstate argued that it had properly notified Clyburn in writing of the cancellation and that it had also sent its agent of record, Thomas Young, a computer diskette containing the cancellation notice. The jury found in Clyburn's favor, concluding that Allstate had sent written notice to Clyburn but not to Allstate's agent of record. Allstate made a motion for either a new trial or a judgment notwithstanding the verdict (j.n.o.v.). The key issue before the court was whether notice sent via a computer diskette constituted "written" notice.*

BLATT, Senior District Judge.
    \*   \*   \*   \*
    \*   \*   \* As noted by the parties in the briefs submitted to the court, there is no case that could be located on this exact issue \*   \*   \*. There have been some cases dealing with videotapes as a "writing" with regard to some states' rules of procedure. In addition, in other contexts, tape recordings have been deemed to be "writings."
    Although \*   \*   \* these cases arise in entirely different contexts and stem from different statutes or rules, the cases do suggest that other media forms are recognized as "writings." The storage of information on tape recordings and videotapes is not that much different from that on floppy diskettes for computers, but rather is more a difference in the devices used to read the information. The information can be retrieved and printed as "hardcopy" on paper. In today's "paperless" society of computer generated information, the court is not prepared, in the absence of some legislative provision or otherwise, to find that a computer floppy diskette would not constitute a "writing" \*   \*   \*.

**DECISION AND REMEDY** *The court held that a notice on diskette could constitute written notice. The court granted Allstate's motion.*

## BASIC DUTIES AND RIGHTS

Essentially, the parties to an insurance contract are responsible for the obligations the contract imposes. These include the basic contractual duties discussed in Chapters 11 through 19 of this text, which covered contract law.

When applying for insurance, for example, the obligation to act in good faith means that a party must reveal everything necessary for the insurer to evaluate the risk. In other words, the applicant must disclose all material facts. These include all facts that would influence an insurer in determining whether to charge a higher premium or to refuse to issue a policy altogether.

Once the insurer has accepted the risk, and on the occurrence of an event giving rise to a claim, the insurer has a duty to investigate to determine the facts. When a policy provides insurance against third party claims, the insurer is obligated to make reasonable efforts to settle such a claim. If a settlement cannot be reached, then, regardless of the claim's merit, the insurer must defend any suit against the insured. Usually, a policy provides that in this situation the insured must cooperate. A policy provision may expressly require the insured to attend hearings and trials, to assist in obtaining evidence and witnesses, and to assist in reaching a settlement.

## DEFENSES AGAINST PAYMENT

An insurance company can raise any of the defenses that would be valid in any ordinary action on a contract, as well as some defenses that do not apply in ordinary contract actions. If the insurance company can show that the policy was procured by fraud, misrepresentation, or violation of warranties, it may have a valid defense for not paying on a claim. (The insurance company may also have the right to disaffirm or rescind an insurance contract.) Improper actions, such as those that are against public policy or that are otherwise illegal, can also give the insurance company a defense against the payment of a claim or allow it to rescind the contract. In the following case, the issue was whether an inaccurate answer to a pertinent question on a life insurance application was sufficient to justify the denial of a claim following the policy-owner's death.

---

**COMPANY PROFILE** *Fifty-seven New York businessmen founded the Nautilus Insurance Company in 1841. Starting operations in 1845, within a year Nautilus had the first life insurance agent west of the Mississippi River. Nautilus became the New York Life Insurance Company in 1849. Before the end of the nineteenth century, New York Life developed the branch office system that is now used throughout the insurance industry. At the turn of the century, the company established a plan, which is still used today, for compensating agents with lifetime income after twenty years of active service. In the early 1950s, New York Life pioneered simplified insurance policy forms, reduced premium rates, and updated rate tables. In 1956, the company was the first life insurance firm to use data processing equipment on a large scale. Through the 1980s, the company continued to diversify, offering a variety of insurance and investment products. In the 1990s, the company expanded beyond the United States, Canada, and Ireland into Great Britain, Indonesia, Korea, and Taiwan. Today, New York Life is the fifth largest U.S. life insurance company. New York Life is committed to AIDS research and is a founding contributor to the National Community AIDS Partnership.*

| CASE 53.4 |
| --- |
| **NEW YORK LIFE INSURANCE CO. v. JOHNSON** |
| United States Court of Appeals, Third Circuit, 1991. 923 F.2d 279. |

**BACKGROUND AND FACTS** *Kirk Johnson applied for life insurance with the New York Life Insurance Company on October 7, 1986. One of the questions on the application form required Johnson to provide information as to his past and present smoking habits. In answer to the question, Johnson represented that he had not smoked in the past twelve months and*

*that he had never smoked cigarettes. In fact, Johnson had smoked for thirteen years, and during the month prior to the insurance application he was smoking approximately ten cigarettes per day. Johnson died on July 17, 1988, for reasons unrelated to smoking. Johnson's father, Lawrence Johnson, who was the beneficiary of the policy, filed a claim for the insurance proceeds. While investigating the claim, New York Life discovered Kirk Johnson's misrepresentation on the application about his smoking habits. The company denied the claim and sought to cancel the policy by returning to Lawrence Johnson a check for the premiums paid under the policy. Lawrence Johnson refused to accept the check, and New York Life undertook an action for declaratory judgment (a court's determination of the parties' respective rights and obligations in regard to this controversy). The trial court dismissed the action, and New York Life appealed.*

DEBEVOISE, District Judge.

\*    \*    \*    \*

Under Pennsylvania law an insurance policy is void for misrepresentation when the insurer establishes three elements: (1) that the representation was false; (2) that the insured knew that the representation was false when made or made it in bad faith; and (3) that the representation was material to the risk being insured.

The district court recognized this well-established statement of Pennsylvania law. Further, the court concluded that "[t]here is no question on this record that the smoking habits of the decedent are material to the risk assumed by the insurer." A misrepresented fact is material if being disclosed to the insurer it would have caused it to refuse the risk altogether or to demand a higher premium. In the present case disclosure of the true facts about Kirk Johnson's smoking practices would have caused New York Life to have demanded higher premiums and thus the misrepresentations were material.

One would have expected that application of this well recognized Pennsylvania law to the undisputed facts would have required a declaration that the policy was void *ab initio* [from the beginning]. However, the district court noted that in Pennsylvania this law typically had been applied in the context of misrepresentations about the state of one's medical condition or health background and had never been applied in the context of a misrepresentation about smoking habits. \*    \*    \*

\*    \*    \*    \*

Although Pennsylvania courts have not had occasion to apply the void *ab initio* rule in the smoking misrepresentation context, other courts have addressed the very issue presented in this case. Applying rescission standards similar to Pennsylvania's, these courts have uniformly voided policies for misrepresentations of smoking habits.

**DECISION AND REMEDY**

*The appellate court reversed the trial court's judgment and remanded the case for the entry of a judgment declaring that the policy in question was void* ab initio.

**INTERNATIONAL CONSIDERATIONS**

**False Statements on Insurance Applications in the United Kingdom**
*The United Kingdom has stricter rules than most states in the United States in regard to false statements made on insurance applications. In the United Kingdom, insurance applicants are held to a standard of* uberrima fides *(Latin for "the most abundant good faith"). Even an innocent (unintentional) misrepresentation on an insurance application makes the contract voidable at the option of the insurer.*

## REBUTTAL OF THE
## DEFENSES AGAINST PAYMENT

The insurance company can be prevented, or estopped, from asserting some defenses that are normally available. For example, if a company tells an insured that information requested on a form is optional and the insured provides it anyway, the company cannot use the information to avoid its contractual obligation under the insurance contract. Similarly, incorrect statements as to the age of the insured normally do not provide the insurance company with a way to escape payment upon the death of the insured. Some states follow the *concurrent causation doctrine*, which requires that the insurer pay on a claim when the accident was due to more than one cause, at least one of which was covered under the policy.[1]

In the following case, the court evaluates whether a false statement made on an application for a life insurance policy and the backdating of the application and policy should allow the insurer to avoid payment on the policy.

---

1. This doctrine was enunciated by the California Supreme Court in *State Farm Mutual Automobile Insurance Company v. Partridge,* 10 Cal.3d 94, 514 P.2d 123, 109 Cal.Rptr. 811 (1973). Subsequently, a number of other states, particularly in the Midwest, have adopted the doctrine. But see *Vanguard Insurance Co. v. Clarke,* 438 Mich. 463, 475 N.W.2d 48 (1991), in which the Michigan Supreme Court rejected the doctrine.

---

**BACKGROUND AND FACTS**   *In the spring of 1982, Paul Roberts, then fifty-nine years of age, applied to the National Liberty Group of Companies for a $30,000 life insurance policy available only to individuals under sixty years of age. This first application was lost or misplaced by the insurance company, and Roberts submitted a second application in November 1982. Because Roberts had by then had his sixtieth birthday, the second application was backdated to April 11, 1982 (a date prior to his birthday), as was the ensuing policy. Although Roberts had suffered slight hypertension in 1979 and had been seen and treated by a physician for this condition for a short time thereafter, he marked "no" to the question on the application concerning treatment for high blood pressure. In October 1982, Roberts was diagnosed as having cancer, and he died from this disease in June 1983. Roberts, although he knew of the cancer diagnosis when he submitted the second application, did not indicate this on the application form because the diagnosis had not been made at the time of his original application. Upon Roberts's death, his wife submitted a claim to the insurance company for $30,000. The insurance company denied the claim on the ground that the false statement concerning hypertension and the failure to mention the cancer diagnosis constituted misrepresentation. Mrs. Roberts sued the insurance company for the proceeds plus interest. The trial court found for the plaintiff, and the insurance company (the defendant) appealed.*

**CASE 53.5**

**ROBERTS v. NATIONAL LIBERTY GROUP OF COMPANIES**

Appellate Court of Illinois, Fourth District, 1987.
159 Ill.App.3d 706,
512 N.E.2d 792,
111 Ill.Dec. 403.

Justice *WOMBACHER* delivered the opinion of the court:
*    *    *    *

Under Illinois law, a false statement in an application for insurance is not in itself a ground for avoiding the insurance policy. The insurer must prove that the statements were made with intent to deceive or involved matters materially affecting the acceptance of the risk. *   *   *
*    *    *    *

Incomplete answers, or failure to disclose material information in response to a question in an application may constitute a material misrepresentation. Whether an applicant's statements are material is determined by the question of whether reasonably careful men would have regarded the facts stated as substantially increasing the chances of the events insured against, so as to cause a rejection of the application or different conditions. In the instant case, there was testimony at trial that high blood pressure such as indicated here did not usually result in the defendant refusing insurance. The defendant's representative testified that the rate of the premium would most likely be involved. The large volume of applications made to the company indicates that an affirmative response to the blood pressure question would result in only a telephone check to the applicant * * * .

Lastly, the defendant contends that the failure to disclose the cancer prior to the issuance of the policy in November of 1982 voided the policy. The cancer was diagnosed one month prior to the receipt of the application by the defendant. However, the policy which was issued predates by six months the date that the cancer was diagnosed. The trial court held that the backdating of the policy estopped [prevented] the defendant from asserting the defense of nondisclosure.

* * * The test of estoppel is whether, considering all the circumstances of the case, conscience and honest dealing require that the defendant be estopped. Estoppel generally is based upon an insurance carrier's conduct and/or representations which mislead an insured to his detriment. We agree with the trial court. The defendant may not now adopt an inconsistent position or course of conduct to the loss of the plaintiff. Indeed, had the policy not been backdated then no policy would exist because Mr. Roberts' sixtieth birthday occurred in April 1982. The insurance coverage in question was only available to individuals under 60 years of age. Equity requires that due to the defendants' action of backdating the application and policy, they now be barred from asserting the nondisclosure defense.

**DECISION AND REMEDY**    *The judgment of the trial court was affirmed; the insurance company could not avoid payment on the policy.*

# TYPES OF INSURANCE

There are five general types of insurance coverage: life insurance, fire and homeowners' insurance, automobile insurance, marine insurance, and business liability insurance. We will examine briefly the coverage available under each of these types of insurance. Then certain features and provisions will be pointed out, with special emphasis on life and fire insurance policies as they relate to the law.

## LIFE INSURANCE

There are five basic types of life insurance:

1. **Whole life** is sometimes referred to as straight life, ordinary life, or cash-value insurance. This type of insurance provides protection with a cumulated cash surrender value that can be used as collateral for a loan. Premiums are paid by the insured during the insured's entire lifetime, with a fixed payment to the beneficiary upon death.

2. **Limited-payment life** might be a twenty-payment life policy. Premiums are paid for a stated number of years, after which the policy is paid up and fully effective during the insured's life. Naturally, premiums are higher than for whole life. This insurance has a cash surrender value.

3. **Term insurance** is a type of policy for which premiums are paid for a specified term. Payment on the policy is due only if death occurs within the term period. Premiums are less expensive than for whole life or limited-payment life, and there is usually no cash surrender value. Frequently, this type of insurance can be converted to another type of life insurance.

4. **Endowment insurance** involves fixed premium payments that are made for a definite term. At the end of the term, a fixed amount is to be paid to the insured or, upon the death of the insured during the specified period, to

a beneficiary. Thus, this type of insurance represents both term insurance and a form of **annuity** (the right to receive fixed, periodic payments for life or—as in this case—for a term of years). Endowment insurance has a rapidly increasing cash surrender value, but premiums are high, as payment is required at the end of the term even if the insured is still living.

5. **Universal life** is a type of insurance that combines some aspects of term insurance and some aspects of whole life insurance. Every payment, usually called a "contribution," involves two deductions made by the issuing life insurance company. The first one is a charge for term insurance protection; the second is for company expenses and profit. The money that remains after these deductions earns interest for the policyholder at a rate determined by the company. The interest-earning money in the policy is called the policy's cash value, but that term does not mean the same thing as it does for a traditional whole life insurance policy. With a universal life policy, the cash value grows at a variable interest rate rather than at a predetermined rate.

The rights and liabilities of the parties in life insurance are basically dependent upon the insurance contract. A few features deserve special attention.

**LIABILITY** The life insurance contract determines not only the extent of the insurer's liability but, generally, whether the insurer is liable upon the death of the insured. Most life insurance contracts exclude liability for death caused by suicide, military action during war, execution by a state or federal government, or even something that occurs while the insured is a passenger in a commercial vehicle. In the absence of exclusion, most courts today construe any cause of death to be one of the insurer's risks.

**ADJUSTMENT DUE TO MISSTATEMENT OF AGE** The insurance policy constitutes the agreement between the parties. The application for insurance is part of the policy and is usually attached to the policy. When the insured misstates his or her age in the application, an error takes place, particularly as to the amount of premiums paid. Mis-

statement of age is not a material error sufficient to allow the insurer to void the policy. Instead, upon discovery of the error, the insurer will adjust the premium payments and/or benefits accordingly.

**ASSIGNMENT** Most life insurance policies permit the insured to change beneficiaries. When this is the case, in the absence of any prohibition or notice requirement, the insured has a right to assign the rights to the policy (for example, as security for a loan) without the consent of the insurer or the beneficiary. If the beneficiary right is *vested*—that is, has become absolute, entitling the beneficiary to payment of the proceeds—the policy cannot be assigned without the consent of the beneficiary. The vast majority of life insurance contracts permit assignment and only require notice to the insurer to be effective.

**CREDITORS' RIGHTS** Unless insurance proceeds are exempt under state law, the insured's interest in life insurance is an asset that is subject to the rights of judgment creditors. These creditors generally can reach insurance proceeds payable to the insured's estate, proceeds payable to anyone if the payment of premiums constituted a fraud on creditors, and proceeds payable to a named beneficiary if the insured has reserved the right to change beneficiaries. Creditors, however, cannot compel the insured to make available the cash surrender value of the policy or to change the named beneficiary to that of the creditor. Almost all states exempt at least a part of the proceeds of life insurance from creditors' claims.

**TERMINATION** Although the insured can cancel and terminate the policy, the insurer generally cannot do so. Therefore, termination usually takes place only upon the occurrence of the following:

1. Default in premium payments that causes the policy to lapse.
2. Death and payment of benefits.
3. Expiration of the term of the policy.
4. Cancellation by the insured.

## FIRE AND HOMEOWNERS' INSURANCE

There are basically two types of insurance policies for a home—standard fire insurance policies and homeowners' policies.

### ■ Exhibit 53–2 Typical Fire Insurance Policies

| Type of Policy | Coverage |
|---|---|
| Blanket | Covers a class of property rather than specific property, because the property is expected to shift or vary in nature. A policy covering the inventory of a business is an example. |
| Floater | Usually supplements a specific policy. It is intended to cover property that may change in either location or quantity. To illustrate, if the painting mentioned under ''specific policy'' were to be exhibited during the year at numerous locations throughout the state, a floater policy would be desirable. |
| Open | A policy in which the value of the property insured is not agreed upon. The policy usually provides for a maximum liability of the insurer, but payment for loss is restricted to the fair market value of the property at the time of loss or to the insurer's limit, whichever is less. |
| Specific | Covers a specific item of property at a specific location. An example is a particular painting located in a residence or a piece of machinery located in a factory or business. |
| Valued | A policy in which, by agreement, a specific value is placed on the subject to be insured to cover the eventuality of its total loss. |

**STANDARD FIRE INSURANCE POLICIES**    The standard fire insurance policy protects the homeowner against fire and lightning, as well as damage from smoke and water caused by the fire or the fire department. Most fire insurance policies are classified according to the type of property covered and the extent (amount) of the issuer's liability. Exhibit 53–2 lists typical fire insurance policies.

As with life insurance, certain features and provisions of fire insurance deserve special mention. In reading the following, it is important to note some basic differences in the treatment of life and fire policies.

*Liability.*    The insurer's liability is determined from the terms of the policy. Most policies, however, limit recovery to losses resulting from *hostile* fires—basically, those that break out or begin in places where no fire was intended to burn. A *friendly* fire—one burning in a place where it was intended to burn—is not covered. Therefore, smoke from a fireplace is not covered, but smoke from a fire caused by a defective electrical outlet is covered. Sometimes, owners add ''extended coverage'' to the fire policy to cover losses from ''friendly'' fires.

If the policy is a *valued* policy (see Exhibit 53–2) and the subject matter is completely destroyed, the insurer is liable for the amount spec-ified in the policy. If it is an *open* policy, then the extent of actual loss must be determined, and the insurer is liable only for the amount of the loss or for the maximum amount specified in the policy, whichever is less. For partial losses, actual loss must always be determined, and the insurer's liability is limited to that amount. Most insurance policies permit the insurer either to restore or replace the property destroyed or to pay for the loss.

*Proof of Loss.*    Fire insurance policies require the insured to file with the insurer, within a specified period or immediately (within a reasonable time), a proof of loss as a condition for recovery. Failure to comply *could* allow the insurance carrier to avoid liability. Courts vary somewhat on the enforcement of such clauses.

*Occupancy Clause.*    Most standard policies require that the premises be occupied at the time of loss. The relevant clause states that if the premises become vacant or unoccupied for a given period, unless consent by the insurer is given, the coverage is suspended until the premises are reoccupied. Persons going on extended vacations should check their policies on this matter.

*Assignment.*    Before a loss has occurred, a fire insurance policy is not assignable without the consent of the insurer. The theory is that the fire insurance policy is a personal contract between the insured and the insurer. The nonassignability of the policy is extremely important in the purchase of a house. The purchaser must procure his or her own insurance. If the purchaser wishes to assume the remaining insurance coverage period of the seller, consent of the insurer is essential.

To illustrate, Ann is selling her home and lot to Jeff. Ann has a one-year fire policy with Ajax Insurance Company, with six months of coverage remaining at the date on which the sale is to close. Ann agrees to assign the balance of her policy, but Ajax has not given its consent. One day after passage of the deed, a fire totally destroys the house. Can Jeff recover from Ajax?

The answer is no, as the policy is actually voided upon the closing of the transaction and the deeding of the property. The reason the policy is voided is that Ann no longer has an insurable interest at the time of loss, and Jeff has no rights in a nonassignable policy.

**HOMEOWNERS' POLICIES** A homeowners' policy provides protection against a number of risks under a single policy, allowing the policyholder to avoid the cost of buying each protection separately. There are two basic types of homeowners' policy coverage:

1. *Property coverage* includes the garage, house, and other private buildings on the policyholder's lot. It also includes the personal possessions and property of the policyholder at home, in travel, or at work. It pays additional living expenses for living away from home because of a fire or some other covered peril.
2. *Liability coverage* is for personal liability in case someone is injured on the insured's property, the insured damages someone else's property, or the insured injures someone else who is not in an automobile.

Similar to liability coverage is coverage for the medical payments of others who are injured on the policyholder's property and coverage for property of others that is damaged by a member of the policyholder's family.

*Forms of Homeowners' Policies.* There are five forms of homeowners' and condominium owners' policies. The essential difference among the five

forms is the number of perils insured against. For example, one form (called the basic form) covers eleven perils, or risks; another (the broad form) covers eighteen; and another (the comprehensive form) covers those eighteen and all others.

Renters, too, take out insurance policies to cover losses to personal property. Renters' insurance, called ''residence contents broad form,'' covers personal possessions against the eighteen perils and includes additional living expenses and liability coverage.

## AUTOMOBILE INSURANCE

There are two basic kinds of automobile insurance: liability insurance and collision and comprehensive insurance.

**LIABILITY INSURANCE** Automobile liability insurance covers bodily injury and property damage liability. Liability limits are usually described by a series of three numbers, such as 100/300/50. This means that the policy, for one accident, will pay a maximum of $100,000 for bodily injury to one person, a maximum of $300,000 for bodily injury to more than one person, and a maximum of $50,000 for property damage. Many insurance companies offer liability up to $500,000 and sometimes higher.

Individuals who are dissatisfied with the maximum liability limits offered by regular automobile insurance coverage can purchase separate coverage under an *umbrella* policy. Umbrella limits sometimes go as high as $5 million. They also cover personal liability in excess of the liability limits of a homeowners' policy.

**COLLISION AND COMPREHENSIVE INSURANCE** Collision insurance covers damage to the insured's car in any type of collision. Usually, it is not advisable to purchase full collision coverage (otherwise known as zero deductible). The price per year is relatively high, because it is likely that small but costly repair jobs will be required each year. Most people prefer to take out $100, $250, or $500 deductible coverage, which costs substantially less than zero-deductible coverage.

Comprehensive insurance covers loss, damage, and destruction by fire, hurricane, hail, vandalism, and theft. It can be obtained separately from collision insurance.

**OTHER AUTOMOBILE INSURANCE** Other types of automobile insurance coverage include the following:

1. *Uninsured motorist coverage.* Uninsured motorist coverage insures the driver and passengers against injury caused by any driver without insurance or by a hit-and-run driver. Certain states require that it be included in all insurance policies sold to drivers.
2. *Accidental death benefits.* Sometimes called *double indemnity,* accidental death benefits provide a lump sum to named beneficiaries if the policyholder dies in an automobile accident. This coverage generally costs very little, but it may not be necessary if the insured has a sufficient amount of life insurance.
3. *Medical payment coverage.* Medical payment coverage provided by an auto insurance policy pays hospital and other medical bills and sometimes funeral expenses. This type of insurance protects all the passengers in the insured's car when the insured is driving.
4. *Other-driver coverage.* An **omnibus clause,** or *other-driver clause,* protects the vehicle owner who has taken out the insurance and anyone who drives the vehicle with the owner's permission. This coverage may be held to extend to a third party who drives the vehicle with the permission of the person to whom the owner gave permission.
5. *No-fault insurance.* Under no-fault statutes, claims arising from an accident are made against the claimant's own insurer, regardless of whose fault the accident was. In some cases—for example, when injuries involve expensive medical treatment—an injured party may seek recovery from another party or insurer. In those instances, the injured party may collect the maximum amount of no-fault insurance and still sue for total damages from the party at fault, although usually, on winning an award, the injured party must reimburse the insurer for its no-fault payments.

## MARINE INSURANCE

**Marine insurance** developed as a means of protecting shippers and vessel owners from the inherent risks involved in transporting goods via water. The insured is protected from the damage to or loss of a vessel or its cargo due to perils at sea (such perils include shipwrecks, as well as pirates). Marine insurance is of particular importance in the shipment of oil.

Marine insurance policies are often *valued*—that is, they are entered into for coverage up to a set amount (the established value of the freight or vessel insured). They may be voyage policies or time policies. A *voyage policy* covers the insured for the duration of the trip, regardless of how long it takes. The *time policy* lapses, or expires, at a specified time, regardless of whether the voyage has been completed. Policies may cover inland marine travel or ocean marine travel. *Inland marine* policies insure vessels navigating the inland waterways, such as the Great Lakes. *Ocean marine* policies, of course, insure vessels traveling on the oceans.

To acquire marine insurance for a ship or cargo, a vessel owner or a shipper warrants that the vessel is seaworthy. A seaworthy vessel can withstand ordinary weather conditions and has a competent captain of good moral character, a satisfactory crew, and suitable equipment on board. A breach of the warranty of seaworthiness would normally void the marine insurance policy.

## BUSINESS LIABILITY INSURANCE

A business may be vulnerable to all sorts of risks. A key employee may die or become disabled; a customer may be injured when using a manufacturer's product; the patron of an establishment selling liquor may leave the premises and injure a third party in an automobile accident; or a professional may overlook some important detail, causing liability for malpractice. Should the first situation arise (for instance, if the company president dies), the business may have some protection under a key-person insurance policy, discussed previously. In the other circumstances, other types of insurance may apply.

**GENERAL LIABILITY** Comprehensive general liability insurance can cover virtually as many risks as the insurer agrees to cover. For example, among the types of coverage that a business might wish to acquire is protection from liability for injuries arising from on-premises events not otherwise insured against, such as company social functions.

Some specialized establishments may be subject to liability in individualized circumstances, and policies can be drafted to meet their needs. In many jurisdictions, for example, statutes impose liability on a seller of intoxicating liquor when a buyer of the liquor, intoxicated as a result of the sale, injures a third party. Legal protection may extend not only to immediately consequent injuries, such as quadriplegia in an automobile accident, but also to the loss of financial support suffered by a family because of the injuries. Insurance can provide coverage for these injuries and financial losses.

**PRODUCT LIABILITY** Manufacturers may be subject to liability for injuries that their products cause, and product liability insurance can be written to match specific products' risks. Coverage can be procured under a comprehensive general liability policy or under a separate policy. The coverage may include expenses involved in recalling and replacing a product that has proved to be defective. (For a comprehensive discussion of product liability, see Chapter 25.)

**PROFESSIONAL MALPRACTICE** In recent years, professionals—attorneys, physicians, architects, and engineers, for example—have increasingly become the targets of negligence suits. Professionals may purchase malpractice insurance to protect themselves against such claims. The large judgments in some malpractice suits have received considerable publicity and are sometimes cited in what has been termed ''the insurance crisis,'' because they have contributed to a considerable increase in malpractice insurance premiums.

**WORKERS' COMPENSATION** Workers' compensation insurance covers payments to employees who are injured in accidents arising out of and in the course of employment (that is, on the job). Workers' compensation, which was discussed in detail in Chapter 36, is governed by state statutes.

---

## TERMS AND CONCEPTS TO REVIEW

| | | |
|---|---|---|
| annuity 1065 | limited-payment life 1064 | risk management 1052 |
| binder 1056 | marine insurance 1068 | term insurance 1064 |
| cash surrender value 1059 | omnibus clause 1068 | underwriter 1053 |
| endowment insurance 1064 | policy 1053 | universal life 1065 |
| insurable interest 1053 | premium 1053 | whole life 1064 |
| insurance 1052 | risk 1052 | |

---

## QUESTIONS AND CASE PROBLEMS

**53–1. Insurable Interest.** Adia owns a house and has an elderly third cousin living with her. Adia decides she needs fire insurance on the house and a life insurance policy on her third cousin to cover funeral and other expenses that will result from her cousin's death. Adia takes out a fire insurance policy from Ajax Insurance Co. and a $10,000 life insurance policy from Beta Insurance Co. on her third cousin. Six months later, Adia sells the house to John and transfers title to him. Adia and her cousin move into an apartment. With two months remaining on the Ajax policy, a fire totally destroys the house; at the same time, Adia's third cousin dies. Both insurance companies tender back premiums

but claim they have no liability under the insurance contracts, as Adia did not have an insurable interest. Discuss their claims.

**53–2. Insurer's Defenses.** Patrick contracts with an Ajax Insurance Co. agent for a $50,000 ordinary life insurance policy. The application form is filled in to show Patrick's age as thirty-two. In addition, the application form asks whether Patrick has ever had any heart ailments or problems. Patrick answers no, forgetting that as a young child he was diagnosed as having a slight heart murmur. A policy is issued. Three years later Patrick becomes seriously ill. A review of the policy discloses that Patrick was actually thirty-three at the time of application and issuance of the policy and that he erred in answering the question about a history of heart ailments. Discuss whether Ajax can void the policy and escape liability upon Patrick's death.

**53–3. Assignment of Insurance.** Sapata has an ordinary life insurance policy on her life and a fire insurance policy on her house. Both policies have been in force for a number of years. Sapata's life insurance names her son, Rory, as beneficiary. Sapata has specifically removed her right to change beneficiaries, and the life policy is silent on right of assignment. Sapata is going on a one-year European vacation and borrows money from Leonard to finance the trip. Leonard takes an assignment of the life insurance policy as security for the loan, as the policy has accumulated a substantial cash surrender value. Sapata also rents out her house to Leonard and assigns to him her fire insurance policy. Discuss fully whether Sapata's assignment of these policies is valid.

**53–4. Coinsurance Clauses.** Fritz has an open fire insurance policy on his home for a maximum liability of $60,000. The policy has a number of standard clauses, including the right of the insurer to restore or rebuild the property in lieu of a monetary payment, and it has a standard coinsurance clause. A fire in Fritz's house virtually destroys a utility room and part of the kitchen. The fire was caused by an electric water heater's overheating. The total damage to the property is $10,000. The property at the time of loss is valued at $100,000. Fritz files a proof of loss claim for $10,000. Discuss the insurer's liability in this situation.

**53–5. Multiple Insurance Coverage.** Lori has a large house. She secures two open fire insurance policies on the house. Her policy with the Ajax Insurance Co. is for a maximum of $100,000, and her policy with Beta Insurance Co. is for a maximum of $50,000. Lori's house burns to the ground. The value of the house at the time of the loss is $120,000. Discuss the liability of Ajax and Beta to Lori.

**53–6. Brokers versus Agents.** James and Hazel Gray signed a joint application for health-insurance coverage with Great American Reserve Insurance Co. The application was taken by John L. Sides, who at the time was not an agent for Great American but an independent insurance broker. Upon signing the application, the Grays gave Sides $188.50, the first month's premium, and later alleged that Sides had told them the policy would become effective when the first payment was made. Sides then sent the application to Great American, along with his own application to become a salesperson for Great American. Sides subsequently was allowed to sell Great American insurance policies. After several initial problems, Great American received the Grays' policy application two and a half months after they had signed it, and only then did the company begin to process the application. Two days before Great American received the policy application, James Gray was thrown from a horse and was injured. Hazel Gray notified Sides of the injury, but Sides learned from Great American that the Grays were not covered as of the date of the injury. James Gray then brought suit against Great American and Sides for breach of an insurance contract. Did the Grays have a valid insurance policy with Great American on the date of James Gray's injury? Explain. [*Gray v. Great American Reserve Insurance Co.*, 495 So.2d 602 (Ala. 1986)]

**53–7. Insurer's Defenses.** On April 16, 1982, Frances and Michael Berthiaume made a written application for life insurance with the Minnesota Mutual Life Insurance Co. The policy sought was to provide $44,308.37 in insurance coverage to cover the amount of the Berthiaumes' loan balance on the mortgage for their house, for a monthly premium of $12.42. Mr. Berthiaume did not take a physical examination for the policy, but in filling out the application he answered no to a question asking whether he had ever been treated for, or had ever been advised that he had, high blood pressure. The answer Mr. Berthiaume gave was incorrect; in fact, he had been diagnosed as having hypertension four months before the application was made. In October 1982, Mr. Berthiaume became ill, and he died two months later. When his widow submitted a claim for the mortgage insurance, the insurance company denied payment, citing Mr. Berthiaume's inaccurate answer on the application. Minnesota Mutual sought summary judgment, which was granted by the trial court. Mrs. Berthiaume appealed. Discuss whether Mr. Berthiaume's inaccurate answer on the insurance policy application voided Minnesota Mutual's obligation to pay on the policy. [*Berthiaume v. Minnesota Mutual Life Insurance Co.*, 388 N.W.2d 15 (Minn.App. 1986)]

**53–8. Effective Date of Coverage.** Robert Gladney applied for disability insurance from Paul Revere Life Insurance Co., enclosing with the application a check for $3,100, which represented the first semiannual premium. The issuance of the policy was conditional upon the insurance company's receipt of a medical form that was to be completed by Gladney's doctor following a physical examination. Gladney was a busy man and kept putting off the physical examination. Over a month later, Gladney submitted a second application, because the first one was too old. The insurance agent advised Gladney to leave the application undated so that if Gladney failed to have the physical examination within a month, he would not have to submit yet a third application. Gladney told the agent that he would notify him when the examination was completed. Soon thereafter, Gladney fell ill. His doctor examined him but did not conduct all the tests normally required by Paul Revere for disability insurance. A month later, Gladney was hospitalized and underwent heart surgery. Gladney never told the insurance agent about his visit to the doctor and the fact that the doctor had examined him. Gladney now claims that he is entitled to disability benefits under the policy because he paid the premium and would have been approved for insurance had he notified the insurance company of his examination. Will the court agree? Discuss fully. [*Gladney v. Paul Revere Life Insurance Co.*, 895 F.2d 238 (5th Cir. 1990)]

**53–9. Insurer's Defenses.** Jeffrey Duke purchased a life insurance policy on his own life from New England Mutual Life Insurance Co. Duke listed as his beneficiary his lover and business advisor, William Remmelink. On his insurance application, however, Duke had described his beneficiary as merely his business partner. After Duke died of acquired immune deficiency syndrome (AIDS), New England Mutual brought an action against William Johnson, the executor of Duke's estate, to rescind (cancel) the insurance contract on the ground that Duke had "materially misrepresented his relationship with his beneficiary." Johnson claimed that New England Mutual's attempt to rescind the contract was in bad faith and asked for both punitive damages and attorneys' fees. During the trial, an underwriter with twenty-four years of experience testified that New England Mutual had never before rescinded a policy because of a misrepresentation regarding the relationship between the beneficiary and the insured. Did Duke mischaracterize his relationship with his beneficiary? If so, was such a misrepresentation material? How should the court decide? [*New England Mutual Life Insurance Co. v. Johnson,* 155 Misc.2d 680, 589 N.Y.S.2d 736 (1992)]

**53–10. Interpretation of an Insurance Contract's Terms.** Martha Frances purchased insurance coverage from Nationwide Mutual Insurance Co. prior to going on a cruise. The policy covered "accidental bodily injury occurring anywhere in the world which arises solely from accident" and "is not contributed to by sickness, disease or bodily or mental infirmity." The policy also stated that if the injury resulted in the loss of life "within 180 days after the date of the accident," the company would pay the beneficiary $75,000. While on the cruise, Frances fell and broke her hip. She was immediately taken to a Florida hospital for surgery, during which she had a fatal heart attack. The death certificate described the cause of death as "terminal cardiac arrest due to or as a consequence of arteriosclerotic cardiovascular disease due to or as a consequence of previous [heart problems]." Audrey Allison, Frances's beneficiary, sought payment under the policy, but Nationwide refused to pay because Frances's death was caused in part by her preexisting heart condition. Allison then sued Nationwide to collect the death benefit. Assuming that Frances would not have died (at least, at that time) from her heart problems had it not been for the surgery, how should the court decide? Discuss fully. [*Allison v. Nationwide Mutual Insurance Co.,* 964 F.2d 291 (3d Cir. 1992)]

# CHAPTER 54

# WILLS, TRUSTS, AND ESTATES

A s the old adage states, "You can't take it with you." All of the real and personal property that you own will be transferred on your death to others. For that reason, the laws governing the succession of property are a necessary corollary to the concept of private ownership of property. The law requires that upon death, title to the decedent's property must *vest* in someone. In other words, someone must acquire the right to possess, use, or transfer the property. The decedent can direct the passage of property after death by *will*, subject to certain limitations imposed by the state. If no valid will has been executed, the decedent is said to have died **intestate,** and state **intestacy laws** prescribe the distribution of the property among heirs or next of kin. If no heirs or kin can be found, the property **escheats** (title is transferred to the state).

In addition, a person can transfer property through a *trust.*[1] The owner (settlor) of the property transfers legal title to a *trustee*, who has a duty imposed by law to hold the property for the use or benefit of another (the beneficiary).

**SECTION 1**

## WILLS

A **will** is the final declaration of how a person desires to have his or her property disposed of after death. A will is referred to as a *testamentary disposition* of property, and one who dies after having made a valid will is said to have died **testate**. A will is a formal instrument that must follow exactly the requirements of the appropriate state's statutes to be effective.

---

1. A trust can be set up by the property owner *during his or her life* (by a deed accompanied by a trust document) or *at his or her death* (by a will containing or accompanied by a trust document). This chapter discusses both types of trusts.

The reasoning behind such a strict requirement is obvious. A will becomes effective only after death. No attempts to modify it after the death of the maker are allowed, because the court cannot ask the maker to confirm the attempted modifications. (But sometimes the wording in the will must be "interpreted" by the courts.)

A will can serve other purposes besides the distribution of property. It can appoint a guardian for minor children or incapacitated adults. It can also appoint a personal representative to settle the affairs of the deceased.

## PARTIES

A person who makes out a will is known as a **testator.** The court responsible for administering any legal problems surrounding a will is called a **probate court**. When a person dies, a *personal representative* settles the affairs of the deceased. An **executor** is the personal representative named in the will. An **administrator** is the personal representative appointed by the court for a decedent who dies without a will, who fails to name an executor in the will, who names an executor lacking the capacity to serve, or who writes a will that the court refuses to admit to probate.

## GIFTS

A gift of real estate by will is generally called a **devise,** and a gift of personal property under a will is called a **bequest,** or **legacy.** Gifts by will can be specific, general, or residuary.

**SPECIFIC** A *specific* devise or bequest (legacy) describes particular property that can be distinguished from all the rest of the testator's property. For example, Chao's will provides, "I give my nephew, Tuan, my gold pocket watch." Should the gold watch not be part of Chao's property at the time of his death (if, for example, it has been sold, destroyed, or given away), the legacy is extinguished, or canceled.

**GENERAL** A *general* devise or bequest (legacy) does not single out any particular item of property to be transferred by will. For example, "I give to my daughter, Dana, $10,000" is a general bequest. Usually, general legacies specify a sum of money.

**RESIDUARY (RESIDUUM)** Sometimes a will provides that any assets remaining after specific gifts are made and debts are paid—called the *residuum*—are to be distributed through a *residuary* clause. A residuary provision is used because the exact amount to be distributed cannot be determined until all other gifts and payouts are made. A residuary clause can pose problems, however, when the will does not specifically name the beneficiaries to receive the residuum. In such a situation, if the court cannot determine the testator's intent, the residuum passes according to state laws of intestacy. In the following case, the court had to decide whether the residual assets of an estate should go to the only named beneficiary in the testator's will or should be distributed under intestacy laws to all of the legal heirs of the deceased.

---

**BACKGROUND AND FACTS** *Edward Cancik, the testator, died with a net estate valued at more than $200,000. Edward had intentionally omitted all his relatives from his will except his cousin Charles Cancik. Edward specifically willed to Charles all his personal and household goods and placed the residuum in a testamentary trust for the maintenance of the Cancik family mausoleum (trusts are discussed later in the chapter). After Edward's death, Charles filed a complaint alleging that the value of the trust corpus (that is, the capital or principal, as distinguished from the interest) vastly exceeded the amount necessary to accomplish its purpose (to maintain the mausoleum), and he asked that the residuum be distributed to him as the only heir under the testator's will. Thomas, another relative of Edward, acting for any unknown heirs as guardian ad litem (a person appointed to protect the interests of parties unable to represent themselves), filed a petition to have the residuum distributed to all the testator's heirs by intestacy. (Twelve heirs were later found to be living in Czechoslovakia.)*

| CASE 54.1 |
| --- |
| **ESTATE OF CANCIK** |
| Appellate Court of Illinois, First District, Fifth Division, 1984. |
| 121 Ill.App.3d 113, 459 N.E.2d 296, 76 Ill.Dec. 659. |

*The trial court held that the residuum passed to all the heirs by the laws of intestacy. Charles appealed.*

*SULLIVAN,* Justice:

\* \* \* \*

[Edward Cancik (testator)] executed a will in which he bequeathed, in clause IV, all of his personal and household effects to Charles; and then, in clause V, placed the residue of his estate into a testamentary trust, the income of which was to be used for the perpetual maintenance of the mausoleum. \* \* \* In the final clause of the will (clause VII), testator stated:

> I have intentionally omitted the names of my relatives from this my Last Will and Testament for reasons I deem good and sufficient with the exception of my aforesaid cousin, CHARLES E. CANCIK.

\* \* \* \*

The object of testamentary construction is to ascertain the intention of the testator and, in so doing, the intention which must be given effect is that expressed in the language of the will, not one which the testator may have had in his mind but failed to express. \* \* \*

In our view, a reading of the will in its entirety, and of the language of clause VII in particular, does not give rise to an implication \* \* \* that the testator intended Charles to inherit the entire excess residuum of his estate. It appears that his major concern was for the care and maintenance of the family mausoleum, and it was to this purpose that he directed, through clause V, the overwhelming bulk of his assets; and although he referred to Charles with a certain degree of affection, as his "beloved cousin," the bequest to Charles in clause IV of the will consisted of only personal property of minimal value when compared to the total estate. In the light of this vastly disproportionate division of property between the trust and Charles, we cannot conclude, as Charles suggests, that he (Charles) was so favored by the overall scheme of the will as to raise an inference that clause VII evidenced testator's intention to disinherit all other heirs; or, more importantly, that it created an alternate residuary bequest to him upon the termination or failure of the trust.

**DECISION AND REMEDY**    *The court held that the residue of Edward's estate must go to his heirs rather than to Charles, who was merely the beneficiary of Edward's personal belongings.*

---

**ABATEMENT AND LAPSED LEGACIES** On occasion, assets are insufficient to pay in full all of the bequests provided for in a will, as well as the taxes, debts, and expenses of administering the estate. When this happens, an *abatement*—by which the **legatees** (the recipients of bequests) receive reduced benefits—takes place. For example, Chao's will leaves "$15,000 each to my children, Tomika and Lin." Upon Chao's death, only $10,000 is available to honor these bequests. By abatement, each child will receive $5,000. If bequests are more complicated, abatement may be more complicated. The testator's intent, as expressed in the will, controls.

If the legatee dies prior to the death of the testator or before the legacy is payable, a *lapsed*

*legacy* occurs. At common law, the legacy failed. Today, under a state antilapse statute, a legacy may not lapse if the legatee is in a certain blood relationship to the testator—such as a child, grandchild, brother, or sister—and if the legatee also left a child or other surviving heir.

## PROBATE VERSUS NONPROBATE

To **probate** (prove) a will means to establish its validity and to carry the administration of the estate through a special court, which, as mentioned above, is called a probate court. Probate laws vary from state to state. In 1969, the American Bar Association and the National Conference of Commissioners on Uniform State Laws approved the Uniform Probate Code (UPC) for adoption by the states. The UPC codifies general principles and procedures for the resolution of conflicts in settling estates and relaxes some of the requirements for a valid will contained in earlier state laws.

In 1990, the National Conference of Commissioners on Uniform State Laws issued significant revisions to the UPC. These revisions were intended to accomplish three objectives. The first goal was to further relax the formal will requirements in favor of policies that more effectively recognize the intent of a testator. The UPC was also revised to provide for the interpretation of will substitutes and other *inter vivos* transfers that constitute the major form of transferring wealth between generations today. Finally, the UPC was changed in recognition of the fact that a significant number of people are married more than once, with children and stepchildren from previous marriages, and that many people who are not married wish to share their property as if they were.

Fifteen states have adopted the original UPC in full, at least three of those states have adopted parts of the revised UPC, and nearly all of the other states have enacted some part of the UPC and incorporated it into their own probate codes. For this reason, references to its provisions will be included in the remainder of this chapter. Nonetheless, succession and inheritance laws do vary from state to state, and one should therefore always check the particular laws of the state involved.[2]

The process of probate is time consuming and costly, and the court is involved in every step of the proceedings. Attorneys and personal representatives of decedents' estates often become involved in probate.

Many states have statutes that allow for the distribution of assets without probate proceedings. Faster and less expensive methods are then used. For example, property can be transferred by affidavit (a written statement taken before a person who has authority to affirm it), and problems or questions can be handled during an administrative hearing. In addition, some state statutes provide that title to cars, savings and checking accounts, and certain other property can be passed merely by filling out forms. This is particularly true when

most of the property is held in joint tenancy with the right of survivorship (see Chapter 49) or when there is only one heir.

**FAMILY SETTLEMENT AGREEMENTS** A majority of states provide for *family settlement agreements*, which are private agreements among the beneficiaries. Once a will is admitted to probate, the family members can agree to settle among themselves the distribution of the decedent's assets. Although a family settlement agreement speeds the settlement process, a court order is still needed to protect the estate from future creditors and to clear title to the assets involved.

**SUMMARY PROCEDURES** The use of summary procedures in estate administration can save time and money when the estate is small. Summary procedures are simpler and less formal than normal probate procedures. The expenses of a personal representative's commission, attorneys' fees, appraisers' fees, and so forth can be eliminated or at least minimized if the parties utilize summary administration procedures. But in some situations— for example, when a guardian for minor children or for an incompetent person must be appointed, and a trust has been created to protect the minor or the incompetent person—probate procedures cannot be avoided. In the ordinary situation, a person can employ various will substitutes to avoid the cost of probate—for example, *inter vivos* trusts (discussed later in this chapter), life insurance policies with named beneficiaries, or joint-tenancy arrangements. Not all methods are suitable for every estate, but there are alternatives to a complete probate administration.

## TESTAMENTARY CAPACITY

Not everyone who owns property necessarily qualifies to make a valid disposition of that property by will. *Testamentary capacity* requires the testator to be of legal age and sound mind *at the time the will is made*. The legal age for executing a will varies, but in most states and under the UPC, the minimum age is eighteen years [UPC 2–501]. Thus, a will of a twenty-one-year-old decedent written when the person was sixteen would be invalid if, under state law, the legal age for executing a will is eighteen.

The concept of *sound mind* refers to the testator's ability to formulate and comprehend a

---

2. For example, California law differs substantially from the UPC.

personal plan for the disposition of property. Further, a testator must intend the document to be his or her will. Courts have grappled with the requirement of sound mind for a long time, and their decisions have been inconsistent. Mental incapacity is a highly subjective matter and thus is not easily measured. The general test for testamentary capacity requires that the following conditions be met:

1.  The testator must comprehend and remember the "natural objects of his or her bounty" (usually family members and persons for whom the testator has affection).

2.  The testator must comprehend the kind and character of the property being distributed.

3.  The testator must understand and formulate a plan for disposing of the property.

Less mental ability is required to make a will than to manage one's own business affairs or to enter into a contract. Thus, a testator may be feeble, aged, eccentric, or offensive in behavior and still possess testamentary capacity. Moreover, a person can be adjudged mentally incompetent or have delusions about certain subjects and yet, during lucid moments, still be of sound mind and make a valid will. In the following case, the question before the court was whether the testator had the required testamentary capacity to make a will.

---

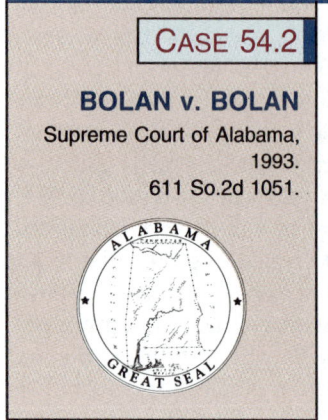

CASE 54.2

**BOLAN v. BOLAN**
Supreme Court of Alabama,
1993.
611 So.2d 1051.

**HISTORICAL AND CULTURAL SETTING** *In cases involving contested wills, English courts did not allow trial by jury. In actions of* ejectment *(actions in which a plaintiff seeks the removal of the defendant from land), English courts did allow trial by jury, even when one of the issues in the case was title to land that had been part of a testamentary disposition. When wills involving title to land came to be probated in the United States, it was believed that if those wills were contested, trial by jury should be allowed. Thus, trial by jury in will-contest cases came to be allowed in many states, including Alabama. Juries answer questions of fact. Incapacity is a question of fact. Because appellate courts do not generally consider questions of fact, an appellate court will normally not overturn the finding of a jury on the issue of incapacity as long as there is evidence to support the finding.*

**BACKGROUND AND FACTS** *Charley Bolan died on October 8, 1990, survived by six children. His will left one dollar to each of three of his children and to each child of his deceased son ("the contestants") and the remainder of his estate to the other three children ("the proponents"). The contestants claimed that the will was invalid, alleging, among other things, that Bolan lacked testamentary capacity at the time the will was made. The evidence before the court was conflicting. Witnesses present at the time the will was executed testified that Bolan was in sound mental condition on that occasion, and other family members testified to the same effect. But other testimony, including statements made by the contestants, indicated that Bolan was not in sound mental condition. The case was transferred from a probate court to a state trial court, and the trial jury held for the contestants. The proponents appealed.*

ALMON, *Justice.*
\* \* \* \*

\* \* \* Every testator is presumed to have the capacity to make a will, \* \* \* and the burden is on the contestant to prove the lack of testamentary capacity. The contestant need not show that the testator suffered from permanent insanity; the contestant's burden may be carried by demonstrating that the testator lacked testamentary capacity at the time the will was executed.

\* \* \* \*

Here, the witnesses to the September 9 will all testified that Charley was in sound mental condition on the date of the execution. There was testimony to the same effect from other family members. However, there was also testimony from Betty that Charley was in poor health before the date of execution; that he repeatedly held conversations with his dead wife; that he refused to bathe, change his clothes, or otherwise take care of himself; and that he had rigged up a dangerous spring-gun to protect himself from intruders when no real threat existed. \* \* \*

Although the evidence was conflicting, the contestants presented sufficient evidence of a lack of testamentary capacity to support the submission of the contest to the jury on this ground.

*The trial court's judgment was affirmed.*

**DECISION
AND REMEDY**

## FORMAL REQUIREMENTS OF A WILL

A will must comply with statutory formalities designed to ensure that the testator understood his or her actions at the time the will was made. These formalities are intended to help prevent fraud. Unless they are followed, the will is declared void, and the decedent's property is distributed according to the laws of intestacy of the state. The requirements are not uniform among jurisdictions. Most states, however, uphold the following basic requirements for executing a will:

1. *A will must be in writing.* A written document is generally required, although in some cases oral wills, called *nuncupative wills* (to be discussed later), are found valid [UPC 2–502]. The writing itself can be informal as long as it substantially complies with the statutory requirements. In some states, a will can be handwritten in crayon or ink. It can be written on a sheet or scrap of paper, on a paper bag, or on a piece of cloth. A will that is completely in the handwriting of the testator is called a **holographic** (or olographic) **will.**

   A will also can refer to a written memorandum that itself is not a will but that contains information necessary to carry out the will. For example, Thelma's will provides that a certain sum of money be divided among a group of charities named in a written memorandum that Thelma gave to the trustee *the same day the will was signed.* The written list of charities will be "incorporated by reference" into the

will only if it was in existence when the will was executed (signed) and if it is sufficiently described so that it can be identified.

2. *A formal (nonholographic) will must be signed by the testator.* It is a fundamental requirement in all jurisdictions that the testator's signature be made with the requisite intent to validate the will; but so long as the signature is in the body of the will, it need not be at the end of the will. Each jurisdiction dictates by statute and court decision what constitutes a signature. Initials, an "X" or other mark, and words like "Mom" have all been upheld as valid when it was shown that the testators intended them to be signatures.

3. *A formal (nonholographic) will must be witnessed.* A will must be attested by two, and sometimes three, witnesses. The number of witnesses, their qualifications, and the manner in which the witnessing must be done are generally set out in a state's statute. A witness can be required to be disinterested—that is, not a beneficiary under the will. The UPC, however, provides that a will is valid even if it is attested by an interested witness [UPC 2–505]. There are no age requirements for witnesses, but they must be mentally competent.

   The purpose of requiring wills to be witnessed is to verify that the testator actually executed (signed) the will and had the requisite intent and capacity at the time. A witness does not have to read the contents of the will. Usually, the testator and witnesses must all sign in the sight or the presence of one another, but the UPC deems it sufficient if the testator acknowledges his or her signature to the witnesses [UPC 2–502]. The UPC does not require all parties to sign in the presence of one another.

4. *A will may be required to be "published."* Publication is an oral declaration by the maker to the witnesses that the document they are about to sign is his or her "last will and testament." Publication is becoming an unnecessary formality in most states, and it is not required under the UPC.

In general, strict compliance with the preceding formalities (except the one relating to witnesses and the one relating to publication) is required before a formal document is accepted as the decedent's will. Holographic wills constitute another exception in some jurisdictions. A holographic will must be signed by the decedent, however, and its material provisions must be in the testator's handwriting for the will to be probated (validated) [UPC 2–502]. Also, under the revised UPC a document that does not comply with all of the formalities may be probated as a will if it is shown that the decedent intended it to constitute his or her will [UPC 2–503]. Exhibit 54–1 presents a copy of a sample will—one of the many wills purportedly written by Howard Hughes.

## NUNCUPATIVE WILLS

A **nuncupative will** is an oral will made before witnesses. It is not permitted in most states. When authorized by statute, however, a nuncupative will is valid only if made during the last illness or in expectation of the imminent death of the testator, and usually before at least three witnesses. Nuncupative wills are sometimes referred to as deathbed wills. Statutes frequently permit soldiers and sailors to make nuncupative wills when on active duty.

In most of those states that permit nuncupative wills, only personal property may pass by the will, and some of these states set value limits on the personal property that can be transferred.

## UNDUE INFLUENCE

A valid will is one that represents the maker's intention to transfer and distribute his or her property.

When it can be shown that the decedent's plan of distribution was the result of improper pressure by another person overriding the maker's intent, the will is declared invalid.

Undue influence may be inferred by the court if the testator ignores blood relatives and names as beneficiary a nonrelative who is in constant close contact and in a position to influence the making of the will. For example, if a nurse or friend caring for the deceased at the time of death was named as beneficiary to the exclusion of all family members, the validity of the will might well be challenged on the basis of undue influence.

## REVOCATION OF WILLS

An executed will is revocable by the maker at any time during the maker's lifetime. Wills can also be revoked by operation of law. Revocation can be partial or complete, and it must follow certain strict formalities.

**REVOCATION BY ACT OF THE MAKER** The maker can revoke an executed will in either of two ways—by physical act or in writing.

*Revocation by Physical Act.* The testator may revoke a will by intentionally burning, tearing, canceling, obliterating, or destroying it or by having someone else do so in the presence of the maker and at the maker's direction.[3] In some states, partial revocation by physical act of the maker is recognized. Thus, those portions of a will lined out or torn away are dropped, and the remaining parts of the will are valid. In no case, however, can a provision be crossed out and an additional or substitute provision written in. Such altered portions require reexecution (re-signing) and reattestation (rewitnessing).

To revoke a will by physical act, it is necessary to follow the mandates of a state statute exactly. When a state statute prescribes the exact methods for revoking a will by physical act, those are the only methods that will revoke the will.

---

3. The destruction cannot be inadvertent. The maker's intent to revoke must be shown. When a will has been burned or torn accidentally, it is normally recommended that the maker have a new document created so that it will not falsely appear that the maker intended to revoke the will.

■ **Exhibit 54–1  A Sample Will**

Jan. 11/72

This is my Last Will and Testament

(1)  I hereby revoke all Wills and testamentary dispositions of every nature or kind whatsoever made by me before this date.

(2)  I nominate, constitute, and appoint my counsel Chester C. Davis, sole executor and trustee of this my Last Will and Testament . . .

(3)  I give, devise, and bequeath all my monies, holdings, property of every nature and kind, all of my possessions and any profits of the before mentioned to the Howard Hughes Medical Institute for the use of medical research and the betterment of medical and health standards around the world.

(4)  I hereby direct my trustee Chester Davis and my assistants Nadine Henley and Frank Gay to continue in their positions and duties, and to also assume a controlling interest in management in the Medical Institute, to decide, direct, and implement policies and funds for the proper uses of the Medical Institute in the areas of medical research and the betterment of world health and medical standards.

(5)  I hereby request that my trustee make known to any business associates, aides, or confidants who wish to, or have undertaken a written documentation of any or all parts of my life, the terms of the Rosemont Enterprises agreement and possible infringements thereof—because of the conditions of that document.

(6)  I hereby direct my trustee to instruct Rosemont Enterprises to complete all written, visual, and audio documentation in the presentation of the factual representation of my life for public release two years to the day, after my death.

(7)  I authorize my trustee to make funds available limited to one quarter of the total estate to a private agency of my trustee's choice, in the event of my death by unnatural or man-made causes; to apprehend such person or group of persons and to bring them within full prosecution of the law; the funds being made available for legal expenses and costs incurred on behalf of the trustee's appointed agency.

(8)  I wish to make known to my trustee that I did not at any time enter into any contracts, agreements, or promises either oral or written, that transferred gave or bequeathed the bulk or any part of my estate to any person, persons, organizations, or whatever other than the Howard Hughes Medical Institute. I sign this as my Last Will and Testament.

/S/ Howard R. Hughes
Jan. 11, 1972

*Revocation by Another Writing.* A **codicil** is a written instrument separate from the will that amends or revokes provisions in the will. It eliminates the necessity of redrafting an entire will merely to add to it or amend it. A codicil can also be used to revoke an entire will. The codicil must be executed with the same formalities required for a will. It must refer expressly to the will. In effect, it updates a will, because the will is "incorporated by reference" into the codicil.

A *second will* can be executed that may or may not revoke the first or a prior will, depending upon the language used. The second will must use specific language such as "This will hereby revokes all prior wills." If the second will is otherwise valid and properly executed, it will revoke all prior wills. If the express *declaration of revocation* is missing, then both wills are read together. If any of the dispositions made in the second will are inconsistent with the prior will, the second will controls.

When a state statute details the requirements for revoking a will with another writing, those requirements must be strictly complied with, as illustrated by the following case.

---

CASE 54.3

**IN RE ESTATE OF THOMPSON**

Supreme Court of Nebraska, 1983.
214 Neb. 899,
336 N.W.2d 590.

**BACKGROUND AND FACTS**   *Frances Maude Thompson, the decedent, executed a will on September 2, 1964, in Nebraska. Upon her death, Victor Thompson, her husband, filed a petition for the probate of her will. John Finley, son of the decedent through a prior marriage, filed a petition seeking a formal adjudication of his deceased mother's estate by intestacy. Finley's petition claimed that his mother executed a subsequent will that revoked the 1964 document offered for probate by the husband. Finley could not find the subsequent will, however. Finley's petition was dismissed, and the will was admitted to probate. Finley appealed.*

*CAPORALE,* Justice.
*   *   *   *

*   *   * The only evidence concerning the issue is the testimony of the contestant son and his wife. It is to the effect that in July of 1965 they examined and read a one- or two-page typewritten document which the decedent, a Nebraska resident, showed them while she was visiting at their home in Colorado, and which she said was her will. The document began with the words, "Last Will and Testament of Frances Maude Thompson." It contained two signatures in addition to that of his mother, but they could not recall whose they were. According to the son, there was also "some kind of a mark on it for a notary." It bore a 1965 date, but he could not recall the month. The son believed, but could not "swear," that the document contained a clause revoking former wills. His wife recalled such a clause. *   *   *

It is the son's contention that although the above-cited testimony is insufficient to establish the distributive provisions of the 1965 will so as to entitle it to probate, the evidence is sufficient to establish that a will was duly made and executed after the 1964 will such as to destroy the earlier will. The effect of that circumstance would be that his mother would have died intestate and her property would therefore be subject to distribution under the laws of descent rather than under the 1964 document. *   *   *

In the posture of this case the threshold question becomes whether the contestant's evidence meets the "clear, unequivocal, and convincing" standard required to establish that a subsequent will was duly executed. We find that it does not.

One need look no further than the first two sentences of the Comment to [Section] 30–2332 [of the Nebraska statute] to reach that conclusion. Those sentences read: "Revocation of a will may be by either a subsequent will or an act done to the document. If revocation is by a subsequent will, it must be *properly executed.*" (Emphasis supplied.) The evidence does not tell us where the will was executed, what formalities, if any, the witnesses observed in affixing their signatures to the document, or what role a notary, if any, played in the execution process.

*The trial court's judgment was affirmed.*

**DECISION AND REMEDY**

### REVOCATION BY OPERATION OF LAW

Revocation by operation of law occurs when marriage, divorce or annulment, or the birth of children takes place after a will has been executed.

*Marriage.*　In most states, when a testator marries after executing a will that does not include the new spouse, the spouse upon the testator's death can receive the amount he or she would have taken had the testator died intestate. In effect, this revokes the will to the extent of providing the spouse with an intestate share. The rest of the estate is passed under the will [UPC 2–301; UPC 2–302]. If, however, the omission of a new spouse is intentional in the existing will or the spouse is otherwise provided for in the will (or by transfer of property outside of the will), the omitted spouse will not be given an intestate share.

*Divorce or Annulment.*　At common law and under the UPC, divorce does not necessarily revoke the entire will. A divorce or annulment occurring after a will has been executed will revoke those dispositions of property made under the will to the former spouse [UPC 2–508].

*Children Born after a Will Has Been Executed.*
If a child is born after a will has been executed and if it appears that the testator would have made a provision for the child, then the child is entitled to receive whatever portion of the estate he or she is allowed under state intestacy laws (to be discussed shortly). Most state laws allow a child to receive some portion of the estate if no provision is made in a will, unless it appears from the terms of the will that the testator intended to disinherit the child. Under the UPC, the rule is the same. The effect is to partially revoke the parent's will [UPC 2–302].

Under the revised UPC, a child born after a will has been executed shares on a *pro rata* basis in the property devised to the other surviving children (rather than receiving a full intestate share, which could be substantially more or less than whatever is given to the other children).

### RIGHTS UNDER A WILL

The law imposes certain limitations on the way a person can dispose of property in a will. For example, a married person who makes a will generally cannot avoid leaving a certain portion of the estate to the surviving spouse. In most states this is called an "elective share," a "forced share," or a "widow's (or widower's) share," and it is often one-third of the estate or an amount equal to a spouse's share under intestacy laws.

Beneficiaries under a will have rights as well. A beneficiary can renounce (disclaim) his or her share of the property given under a will. Further, a surviving spouse can renounce the amount given under a will and elect to take the "forced share" when the forced share is larger than the amount of the gift—this is the "widow's (or widower's) election," or "right of election." State statutes provide the methods by which a surviving spouse accomplishes renunciation. The purpose of these statutes is to allow the spouse to obtain whichever distribution would be most advantageous. The revised UPC gives the surviving spouse an elective right to take a percentage of the total estate determined by the length of time that the spouse and the decedent were married to each other [UPC 2–201].

### SECTION 2

# INTESTACY LAWS

Each state regulates by statute how property will be distributed when a person dies intestate (that is, without a valid will). These statutes are called statutes of descent and distribution, or more simply, intestacy laws, as mentioned in this chapter's introduction. Intestacy laws attempt to carry out the likely intent and wishes of the decedent. Intestacy laws assume that deceased persons would have intended that their natural heirs (spouses, children, grandchildren, or other family members) inherit

# ■ CONCEPT SUMMARY 54.1 **Wills**

| TYPE OF GIFT | DEFINITION |
|---|---|
| **Specific** | A devise or bequest of a particular piece of property in the testator's estate. |
| **General** | A devise or bequest that does not single out a particular item in the testator's estate; usually a sum of money. |
| **Residuary** | A devise or bequest of any properties left in the estate after all specific and general gifts have been made. |

| TYPE OF WILL | DEFINITION |
|---|---|
| **Attested** | A written will, signed by the testator, properly witnessed, and, where required, published; one that meets formal statutory requirements for a valid will. |
| **Holographic** | A will completely in the handwriting of the testator; valid where permitted by state statute. |
| **Nuncupative** | An oral will made before witnesses during the deathbed illness of the testator; it is only valid to transfer personal property, not real property. |

| METHOD OF REVOCATION OR MODIFICATION | DEFINITION |
|---|---|
| **_By Act of the Maker:_** | |
| **Physical Act** | Tearing up, canceling, obliterating, or deliberately destroying part or all of a will. |
| **Codicil** | A formal separate document to amend or revoke an existing will. |
| **New Will** | A new, properly executed will that expressly revokes the existing will. |
| **_By Operation of Law:_** | |
| **Marriage** | Generally revokes part of a will written before the marriage. (Under the UPC, marriage does not revoke a previously executed will. The spouse takes as he or she does under intestacy laws.) |
| **Divorce or Annulment** | Revokes dispositions made under a will to a former spouse. |
| **Subsequently Born Children** | It is _implied_ that the child is entitled to receive a portion of the estate. |

their property. Therefore, intestacy statutes set out rules and priorities under which these heirs inherit the property. If no heirs exist, then the property will escheat, or revert, to the state; that is, the state will assume ownership of the property.

## SURVIVING SPOUSE AND CHILDREN

The rules of descent vary widely from state to state. There is, however, usually a special statutory provision for the rights of the surviving spouse and children. In addition, the law provides that first the debts of the decedent must be satisfied out of his

or her estate, and then the remaining assets can pass to the surviving spouse and to the children.

A surviving spouse usually receives a share of the estate—one-half if there is also a surviving child and one-third if there are two or more children. Only when no children or grandchildren survive the decedent will a surviving spouse succeed to the _entire estate._

Assume that Foley dies intestate and is survived by his wife, Berek, and his children, Cirillo and Diane. Foley's property passes according to intestacy laws. After Foley's outstanding debts have been paid, Berek will receive the homestead (either in fee simple or as a life estate—see Chapter 51) and ordinarily a one-third to one-half interest in all other property, depending on state law. The remaining real and personal property will pass to Cirillo and Diane in equal portions.

Under the revised UPC, a surviving spouse receives the entire estate if no children survive the decedent [UPC 2–102]. A surviving spouse also receives the entire estate if there are children, but the children are descendants of both the decedent and the surviving spouse (and the surviving spouse has no other children). The surviving spouse receives different percentages of the estate, depending on whether the decedent leaves behind a parent, children who are not descendants of the surviving spouse, or children who are descendants of the surviving spouse but not descendants of the decedent.

## ORDER OF DISTRIBUTION

State statutes of descent and distribution specify the order in which heirs share in the estate of a person who dies intestate. When there is no surviving spouse or child, then grandchildren, brothers and sisters, and (in some states) parents of the decedents are the next in line to share. These relatives are usually called *lineal descendants*. Generally, on the testator's death, title will descend before it will ascend. For example, property will pass to the deceased's children before it will pass to his or her parents. (In either case, title by inheritance is called title by descent.) But because state statutes differ so widely, few other generalizations can be made about the laws of descent and distribution. It is extremely important to refer to the exact terms of

the applicable state statutes when addressing any problem of intestacy distribution.

If there are no lineal descendants, then *collateral heirs* are the next group to share. Collateral heirs include nieces, nephews, aunts, and uncles of the decedent. If there are no survivors in any of those groups of people related to the decedent, most statutes provide that the property is to be distributed among the next of kin of any of the collateral heirs. Stepchildren and other relatives by marriage are not considered kin. Legally adopted children, however, are recognized as lawful heirs of their adoptive parents.

Whether an illegitimate child inherits depends on state statutes. In some states, intestate succession between the father and the child can occur only when the child is "legitimized" by ceremony or the child has been "acknowledged" by the father. Under the revised UPC, the same rule applies to intestate succession between the child and the mother [UPC 2–114]. The United States Supreme Court has allowed state illegitimacy statutes to stand upon concluding that legitimate state purposes were served by the statutes.[4] In the following case, the constitutionality of an illegitimacy statute was affirmed by the Supreme Court of Ohio.

---

4.  *Labine v. Vincent,* 401 U.S. 532, 91 S.Ct. 1017, 28 L.Ed.2d 288 (1971). In *Trimble v. Gordon,* 430 U.S. 762, 97 S.Ct. 1459, 52 L.Ed.2d 31 (1977), the United States Supreme Court ruled that an Illinois illegitimacy statute was unconstitutional because it did not bear a rational relationship to a legitimate state purpose.

---

**BACKGROUND AND FACTS**  *Clarence Jackson died on January 17, 1975. His will left everything to his wife in the event she survived him. Because she had died earlier, the court appointed an administrator for his estate. The administrator, White, brought an action in probate court for a determination of the decedent's heirs-at-law. Alice Marie Jackson, who claimed to be the decedent's illegitimate daughter, was one of the defendants in this action. The probate court denied Alice Marie Jackson status to inherit as an heir-at-law, and she appealed.*

**CASE 54.4**

**WHITE v. RANDOLPH**
Supreme Court of Ohio, 1979.
59 Ohio St.2d 6,
391 N.E.2d 333.

*PER CURIAM* [by the whole court].
\* \* \* \*

"[Under Ohio statutes,] a child born out of wedlock is capable of inheriting from and through his mother, but may inherit from his father only under certain circumstances. [T]he father may legitimatize an illegitimate child by afterwards marrying the mother of the illegitimate child and acknowledging the child as his. Further, the natural father of an illegitimate child may confer upon such child a right of inheritance from such father by several means: (1) by formal acknowledgement in Probate Court that the child is his with consent of the mother; (2) by designating the illegitimate child as his heir-at-law; (3) by adopting the illegitimate child; and (4) by making a provision for the child in his will.

"Appellant concededly cannot meet any of the above criteria. However, appellant contends that the [Fourteenth Amendment of the U.S. Constitution] requires that she be permitted to inherit from decedent if she can establish with sufficient competent evidence that decedent is, in fact, her father. In the cases considering this general issue before us, it has been rather uniformly pointed out that the rationality of the classification must be examined in light of the legitimate state purposes to which it is related.

"It has long been recognized in Ohio that proof of paternity, especially after the death of the alleged father, is difficult, and peculiarly subject to abuse. One of the resultants of such abuse would be the instability of land titles of real estate left by intestate fathers of illegitimate children.

\* \* \* \*

"Clearly, the Ohio classification scheme is rationally related to the legitimate state purpose of assuring efficient disposition of property at death while avoiding spurious claims. Moreover, the Ohio provisions do not discriminate between legitimate and illegitimate children *per se*. All children may inherit from their mothers. Some illegitimate children and all legitimate children may inherit from their fathers. The group 'discriminated against' is that class of illegitimate children whose fathers did not formally acknowledge them or designate them as heirs-at-law."

**DECISION AND REMEDY**    *The judgment of the probate court was affirmed.*

**INTERNATIONAL CONSIDERATIONS**    **The Rights of Illegitimate Children in Europe**  *In 1979, the European Court of Human Rights considered the rights of illegitimate children. The court held that any difference between the rights of legitimate and illegitimate children was discriminatory and unlawful. Since that time, a number of European nations have passed laws prohibiting any such distinction.*

## DISTRIBUTION TO GRANDCHILDREN

When a person who dies is survived by descendants of deceased children, a question arises as to what share the grandchildren of the decedent will receive. *Per stirpes* is a method of dividing an intestate share by which a class or group of distributees (for example, grandchildren) take the share that their deceased parent would have been entitled to inherit had that parent lived.

Assume that Moss, a widower, has two children, Scott and Jules. Scott has two children (Bonita and Holly), and Jules has one child (Paul). At the time of Moss's death, Scott and Jules have predeceased their father. If Moss's estate is distributed *per stirpes,* the following distribution would take place:

1. Bonita and Holly: one-fourth each, taking Scott's share.
2. Paul: one-half, taking Jules's share.

Exhibit 54–2 illustrates the *per stirpes* method of distribution.

An estate may also be distributed on a *per capita* basis. This means that each person takes an equal share of the estate. If Moss's estate is distributed *per capita,* Bonita, Holly, and Paul will each receive a one-third share. Exhibit 54–3 illustrates the *per capita* method of distribution.

## ■ Exhibit 54–2 *Per Stirpes* Distribution

Under this method of distribution, an heir takes the share that his or her deceased parent would have been entitled to inherit, had the parent lived. This may mean that a class of distributees—the grandchildren, in this example—will not inherit in equal portions. (Note that Bonita and Holly only receive one-fourth of Moss's estate, whereas Paul inherits one-half.)

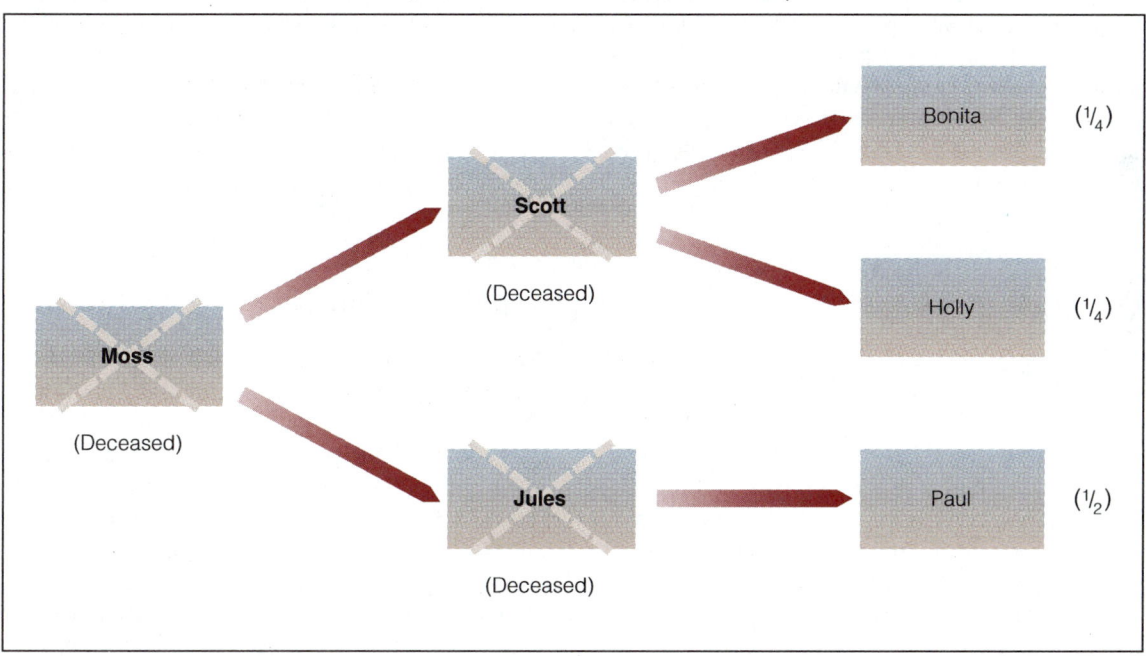

## ■ Exhibit 54–3 *Per Capita* Distribution

Under this method of distribution, all heirs in a certain class—in this case, the grandchildren—inherit equally. Note that Bonita and Holly in this situation each inherit one-third of Moss's estate (not one-fourth, as they do under the *per stirpes* method of distribution).

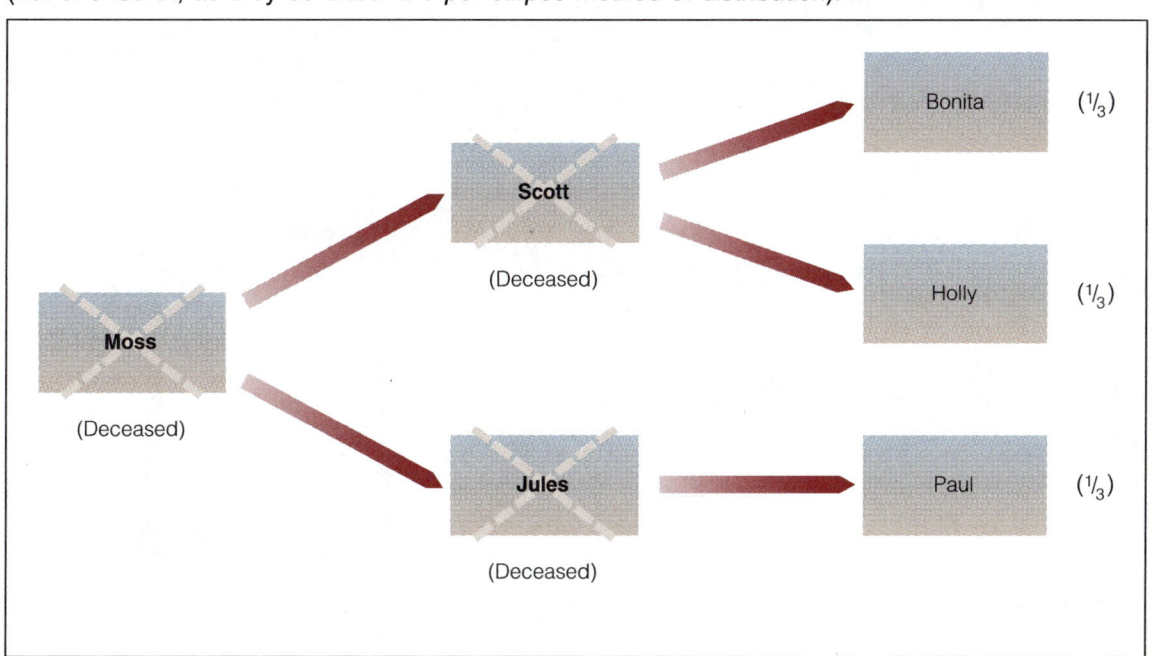

In most states and under the UPC, in-laws do not share in an estate. If a child dies before his or her parents, the child's spouse will not receive an inheritance. Assume that Moss's two children, Scott and Jules, are married and that Moss has no grandchildren. If Scott predeceases his father, under most state laws and under the UPC, Moss's entire estate would go to Jules. Scott's surviving wife would not inherit what would have been Scott's portion of the estate if Scott had not predeceased his father.

## SECTION 3

# TRUSTS

A trust involves any arrangement by which legal title to property is transferred from one person to be administered by a trustee for another's benefit. It can also be defined as a right of property (real or personal) held by one party for the benefit of another. A trust can be created for any purpose that is not illegal or against public policy. The essential elements of a trust follow.

1. A designated beneficiary.
2. A designated trustee.
3. A fund sufficiently identified to enable title to pass to the trustee.
4. Actual delivery to the trustee with the intention of passing title.

If Shanahan conveys his farm to First Bank of Minnesota to be held for the benefit of his daughters, Shanahan has created a trust. Shanahan is the settlor (the one creating the trust, or grantor), First Bank of Minnesota is the trustee, and Shanahan's daughters are the beneficiaries. This arrangement is illustrated in Exhibit 54–4.

## EXPRESS TRUSTS

An express trust is one created or declared in expressed terms, usually in writing. It differs from a trust that is inferred by the law from the conduct or dealings of the parties (an implied trust, to be discussed later). The two types of express trusts that will be discussed here are *inter vivos* trusts and testamentary trusts.

***INTER VIVOS* TRUSTS**   An *inter vivos* **trust** is a trust executed by a grantor during his or her lifetime. The grantor executes a "trust deed," and legal title to the trust property passes to the named trustee. The trustee has a duty to administer the

### ■ Exhibit 54–4 Trust Arrangement

In a trust, there is a separation of interests in the trust property. The trustee takes *legal* title, which appears to be complete ownership and possession but which does not include the right to receive any benefits from the property. The beneficiary takes *equitable* title, which is the right to receive all benefits from the property.

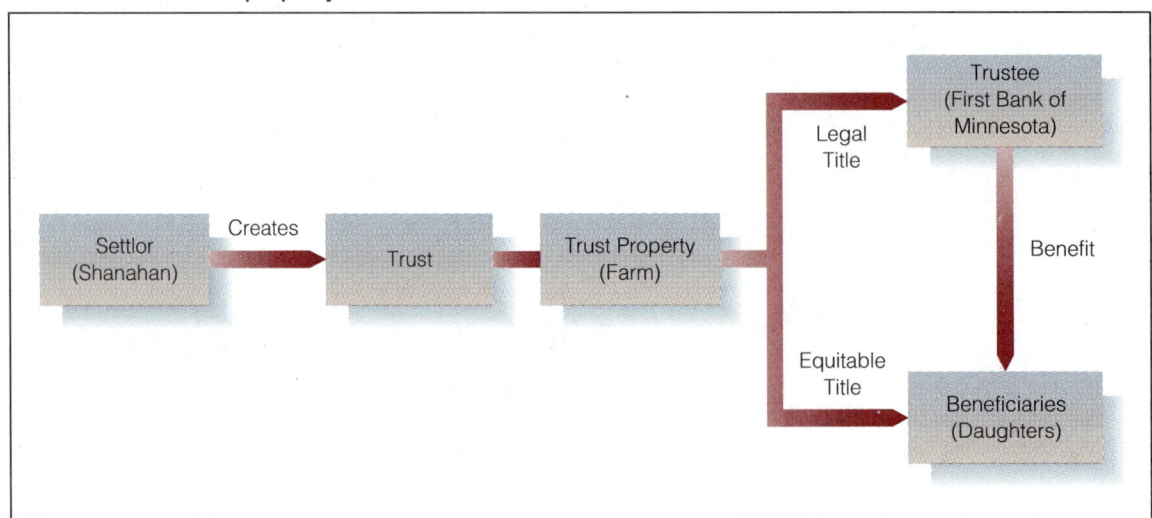

property as directed by the grantor for the benefit and in the interest of the beneficiaries. The trustee must preserve the trust property; make it productive; and if required by the terms of the trust agreement, pay income to the beneficiaries, all in accordance with the terms of the trust. Once the *inter vivos* trust is created, the grantor has, in effect, given over the property for the benefit of beneficiaries.

### TESTAMENTARY TRUSTS

A trust created by will to come into existence upon the settlor's death is referred to as a **testamentary trust.** Although a testamentary trust has a trustee who maintains legal title to the trust property, actions of the trustee are subject to judicial approval. The trustee of a testamentary trust can be named in the will or be appointed by the court. Thus, a testamentary trust will not fail because no trustee has been named in the will. The legal responsibilities of the trustees are the same in both an *inter vivos* and a testamentary trust. If the will setting up a testamentary trust is invalid, then the trust will also be invalid. The property that was supposed to be in the trust will then pass according to intestacy laws, not according to the terms of the trust.

### IMPLIED TRUSTS

Sometimes a trust is imposed by law, even in the absence of an express trust. Customarily, these implied trusts are characterized as either constructive trusts or resulting trusts.

### CONSTRUCTIVE TRUST

A **constructive trust** differs from an express trust in that it arises by operation of law as an equitable remedy that enables plaintiffs to recover property (and sometimes damages) from defendants who would otherwise be unjustly enriched. In a constructive trust, the legal owner is declared to be a trustee for the parties who, in equity, are actually entitled to the beneficial enjoyment that flows from the trust.

One source of a constructive trust is a wrongful action, such as violation of a fiduciary relationship. To illustrate: Arturo and Spring are partners in buying, developing, and selling real estate. Arturo learns through the staff of the partnership that two hundred acres of land will soon come on the market and that the staff will recommend that the partnership purchase the land. Arturo purchases the property secretly in his own name, violating his fiduciary relationship. When these facts are discovered, a court will determine that Arturo must hold the property in trust for the partnership.

Constructive trusts may be imposed for other reasons as well. In the following case, the issue concerns whether a constructive trust should be imposed to counter the effects of an insurance company's failure to change the beneficiary on a life insurance policy after the insured had requested the change.

---

**COMPANY PROFILE** *In 1927, in Birmingham, Alabama, Frank Samford founded an insurance company called the Heralds of Liberty. Two years later, the Heralds of Liberty became the Liberty National Life Insurance Company. Then and now, Liberty National markets its life, accident, and health-insurance policies in rural regions to lower-income customers. Liberty National concentrates its marketing in seven southern states and does half its business in Alabama. Liberty National life insurance costs three times more than other insurers' life insurance and ten times more than others' group coverage. But Liberty National sells policies without a physical examination and offers personal, monthly, premium-collection service. Liberty National is the ninth largest life insurer in the United States; in the early 1990s, its profit margin was twice as high as the average life insurance company. Liberty National is owned by Torchmark, a diversified insurance and financial services company headquartered in Birmingham.*

**BACKGROUND AND FACTS** *In March 1990, Antonio Suarez, Sr., purchased a $50,000 insurance policy on his life from Liberty National. The*

| CASE 54.5 |
| :--- |
| **ZEIGLER v. CARDONA** |
| United States District Court, Middle District of Alabama, 1993. |
| 830 F.Supp. 1395. |

*only designated beneficiary was Suarez's mother, Guarina Cardona. At the time the policy was issued, Suarez was living with his aunt, Ruby Zeigler. Suarez, Winifred Hamilton (the insurance agent), and Zeigler met in May or June to change the beneficiary on the policy from Cardona to Zeigler. At the meeting, Suarez made clear that he wanted the proceeds of the policy used for the benefit of his two children, Antonio (aged nine) and Ebony (aged eight). Zeigler agreed to this, and Suarez signed the change-of-beneficiary form. Hamilton then submitted the form to Liberty National. Apparently due to a clerical error, Liberty National never changed the name of the beneficiary on the policy. During the months that Suarez lived with Zeigler, Zeigler paid the insurance premiums that kept the policy in effect. Following Suarez's death in January 1991, a suit was brought to establish who had rights in the insurance proceeds. Because of Liberty National's error, Cardona was the only beneficiary of record. Antonio and Ebony sought to have the proceeds placed in a constructive trust on their behalf, as Suarez had intended.*

De MENT, District Judge.
    \*   \*   \*   \*

    \*   \*   \* As it relates to changing of beneficiaries, the law of equity regards as having been done that which ought to be done and the courts will give effect to the intention of the insured by holding that a change of beneficiary has been accomplished where he or she has done all that he or she could do in order to comply with the provisions of the policy. \*   \*   \*

    \*   \*   \* [It] is the court's opinion that Mr. Suarez did all that he could do in order to effectuate the change to name Ruby Zeigler as his primary beneficiary. Having found that Mrs. Zeigler is the proper beneficiary on the policy, the court now directs its attention to the issue of constructive trust.
    \*   \*   \*   \*

    \*   \*   \* The evidence is undisputed that Mr. Suarez wanted the proceeds of his life insurance policy to go to the benefit of the children. \*   \*   \* There was no discussion with Mr. Suarez as to the exact manner [in] which the money should be divided between Mrs. Zeigler and the children. The children clearly have an equitable interest in the proceeds of the policy since it was their father's intent that the policy proceeds be used for them. A constructive trust may be imposed on life insurance proceeds even though the designated beneficiary is not guilty of fraud or wrongdoing.

**DECISION AND REMEDY**     *The court held that Zeigler was entitled to $10,000. A constructive trust on the remainder of the proceeds was imposed for the benefit of Antonio and Ebony. Cardona received nothing.*

---

**RESULTING TRUST** A **resulting trust** arises from the conduct of the parties. Here the trust results, or is created, when circumstances raise an inference that the party holding legal title to the property does so for the benefit of another, unless the inference is refuted or the beneficial interest is otherwise disposed of.

To illustrate: Glenda wants to put one acre of land she owns on the market for sale. Because she is going out of the country for two years and would not be available to deed the property to a buyer during that period, she conveys the property to her good friend Oscar. Oscar can then sell and deed the property, with the proceeds to be turned over to Glenda. Because Glenda's intent in deeding the property to Oscar is neither a sale nor a gift, the property will be held in a resulting trust by Oscar (as trustee) for the benefit of Glenda. Therefore, on Glenda's return, Oscar will be required either to deed back the property to Glenda or, if the prop-

# ■ CONCEPT SUMMARY 54.2 **Trusts**

| TRUSTS | |
|---|---|
| **Definition** | Any arrangement through which property is transferred from one person to be administered by a trustee for another party's benefit. The essential elements of a trust are (1) a designated beneficiary, (2) a designated trustee, (3) a fund sufficiently identified to enable title to pass to the trustee, and (4) actual delivery to the trustee with the intention of passing title. |
| **Types of Trusts** | 1. *Express trusts*—Created by expressed terms, usually in writing.<br>  a. *Inter vivos* trust—A trust executed by a grantor during his or her lifetime.<br>  b. Testamentary trust—A trust created by will and coming into existence upon the death of the grantor.<br>2. *Implied trusts*—Trusts imposed by law.<br>  a. Constructive trust—Arises by operation of law whenever a transaction takes place in which the person who takes title to or possession of the property is in equity not entitled to enjoy the beneficial interest therein.<br>  b. Resulting trust—Arises from the conduct of the parties when an *apparent intention* to create a trust is present.<br>3. *Other kinds of trusts:*<br>  a. Charitable trust—A trust designed for the benefit of a public group or the public in general.<br>  b. Spendthrift trust—A trust created to provide for the maintenance of a beneficiary by allowing only a certain portion of the total amount to be received by the beneficiary at any one time.<br>  c. Totten trust—A trust created when one person deposits money in his or her own name as a trustee for another. |

erty has been sold, to turn over the proceeds (held in trust) to her.

## OTHER KINDS OF TRUSTS

Certain trusts are created for special purposes. Three such trusts are charitable, spendthrift, and Totten trusts.

**CHARITABLE TRUST** A trust designed for the benefit of a segment of the public or for the benefit of the public in general is a **charitable trust.** It differs from a private trust in that the identities of the beneficiaries are uncertain. Usually, to be deemed a charitable trust, a trust must be created for charitable, educational, religious, or scientific purposes.

**SPENDTHRIFT TRUST** A trust that contains a provision for the maintenance of a beneficiary by preventing the beneficiary's improvident use of the bestowed funds is a **spendthrift trust.** Essentially,

the beneficiary is not permitted to transfer his or her right to future payments of income or capital. To qualify as a spendthrift trust, the trust provisions must explicitly place restraints on the alienation (transfer to others) of the trust funds. The majority of states allow spendthrift trust provisions that prohibit creditors from subjecting to the payment of debts the beneficiary's interest in future distributions from the trust.

**TOTTEN TRUST** A special type of trust created when one person deposits money in his or her own name as a trustee for another is a **Totten trust,**[5] or *tentative trust.* This trust is tentative in that it is revocable at will until the depositor dies or completes the gift in his or her lifetime by some unequivocal act or declaration (for example, delivery of the funds to the intended beneficiary). If the

_____

5. This type of trust derives its unusual name from *In the Matter of Totten,* 179 N.Y. 112, 71 N.E. 748 (1904).

depositor dies before the beneficiary dies and if the depositor has not revoked the trust expressly or impliedly, a presumption arises that an absolute (a binding, irrevocable) trust has been created for the benefit of the beneficiary. At the death of the depositor, the beneficiary obtains property rights to the balance on hand.

## THE TRUSTEE

The trustee is the person holding the trust property. Anyone legally capable of holding title to, and dealing in, property can be a trustee. If the settlor of a trust fails to name a trustee, or if a named trustee cannot or will not serve, the trust does not fail—an appropriate court can appoint a trustee.

**TRUSTEE'S DUTIES**  A trustee must act with honesty, good faith, and prudence in administering the trust and exercise a high degree of loyalty toward the trust beneficiary. The general standard of care is the degree of care a prudent person would exercise in his or her personal affairs.[6] The duty of loyalty requires that the trustee act in the *exclusive* interest of the beneficiary.

Among specific duties, a trustee must keep clear and accurate accounts of the trust's administration and furnish complete and accurate information to the beneficiary. A trustee must keep trust assets separate from his or her own assets. A trustee has a duty to pay to an income beneficiary the net income of the trust assets at reasonable intervals. A trustee has a duty to distribute the risk of loss from investments by reasonable diversification and a duty to dispose of assets that do not represent prudent investments. Investments in federal, state, or municipal bonds; corporate bonds; and shares of preferred or common stock may be prudent investments under particular circumstances.

**TRUSTEE'S POWERS**  When a settlor creates a trust, he or she may prescribe the trustee's powers

and performance. Generally, state law[7] applies in the absence of specific terms in the trust.[8] When state law does apply, it is most likely to restrict the trustee's investment of trust funds. Typically, statutes confine trustees to investments in conservative debt securities such as government, utility, and railroad bonds and first-mortgage loans on realty. It is common, however, for a settlor to grant a trustee discretionary investment power. In that circumstance, any statute may be considered only advisory, with the trustee's decisions subject in most states to the prudent person rule.

A difficult question concerns the extent of a trustee's discretion to "invade" the principal and distribute it to an income beneficiary, if the income is found to be insufficient to provide for the beneficiary in an appropriate manner. A similar question concerns the extent of a trustee's discretion to retain trust income and add it to the principal, if the income is found to be more than sufficient to provide for the beneficiary in an appropriate manner. Generally, the answer to both questions is that the income beneficiary should be provided with a somewhat predictable annual income, but with a view to the safety of the principal. Thus, a trustee may make individualized adjustments in annual distributions.

Of course, a trustee is responsible for carrying out the purposes of the trust. If the trustee fails to comply with the terms of the trust or the controlling statute, he or she is personally liable for any loss.

**ALLOCATIONS BETWEEN PRINCIPAL AND INCOME**  Frequently, a settlor will provide one beneficiary with a life estate and another beneficiary with the remainder interest in a trust. A farmer, for example, may create a testamentary trust providing that the farm's income be paid to his or her surviving spouse and that on the surviving spouse's

---

6. Revised Uniform Principal and Income Act Section 2(a)(3); Restatement (Third) of Trusts, Section 227. This rule is in force in the majority of states by statute and in a small number of states under the common law. See also *O'Neill v. Commissioner of Internal Revenue,* 994 F.2d 302 (6th Cir. 1993).

7. In eight states, the law consists, in part, of the Uniform Principal and Income Act, published in 1931. The Revised Uniform Principal and Income Act, issued in 1962, has been adopted in thirty-four states. There are other uniform acts that may apply—for instance, about a third of the states have enacted the Uniform Trustees' Powers Act, promulgated in 1964. In addition, most states have their own statutes covering particular procedures and practices. Common law principles have been collected in the Restatement (Second) of Trusts.
8. Revised Uniform Principal and Income Act Section 2(a)(1); Restatement (Second) of Trusts, Section 164.

death, the farm be given to their children. Among the income and principal beneficiaries, questions may arise concerning the apportionment of receipts and expenses for the farm's management, as well as the trust's administration between income and principal. Even when income and principal beneficiaries are the same, these questions may occur.

To the extent that a trust instrument does not provide instructions, a trustee must refer to applicable state law. The general rule is that ordinary receipts and expenses are chargeable to the income beneficiary, whereas *extraordinary* receipts and expenses are allocated to the principal beneficiaries.[9] To illustrate: The receipt of rent from trust realty would be ordinary, as would the expense of paying the property's taxes. The cost of long-term improvements and proceeds from the property's sale, however, would be extraordinary.

## TRUST TERMINATION

The terms of a trust should expressly state the event on which the settlor wishes it to terminate—for example, the beneficiary's or the trustee's death. If the trust instrument does not provide for termination on the beneficiary's death, the beneficiary's death will not end it. Similarly, without an express provision, a trust will not terminate on the trustee's death.

Typically, a trust instrument specifies a termination date. For example, a trust created to educate the settlor's child may provide that the trust ends when the beneficiary reaches the age of twenty-five. If the trust's purpose is fulfilled before that date, a court may order the trust's termination. If no date is specified, a trust will terminate when its purpose has been fulfilled. Of course, if a trust's purposes become impossible or illegal, the trust will terminate.

---

## SECTION 4

# ESTATE ADMINISTRATION

The orderly procedure used to collect assets, settle debts, and distribute the remaining assets when a

person dies is the subject matter of estate administration. The rules and procedures for managing the estate of a deceased are controlled by statute. Thus, they vary from state to state. In every state, there is a special court, often called a probate court, that oversees the management of estates of decedents.

The first step after a person dies is usually to determine whether or not the decedent left a will. In most cases, the decedent's attorney will have that information. If there is uncertainty as to whether a valid will exists, the personal papers of the deceased must be reviewed. If a will exists, it probably names a personal representative (executor) to administer the estate. If there is no will, or if the will fails to name a personal representative, then the court must appoint an administrator. Under the UPC, the term *personal representative* refers to either an executor (person named in the will) or an administrator (person appointed by the court) [UPC 1–201(30)].

The personal representative has a number of duties. The first duty is to inventory and collect the assets of the decedent. If necessary, the assets are appraised to determine their value. Both the rights of creditors and the rights of beneficiaries must be protected during the estate administration proceedings. In addition, the personal representative is responsible for managing the assets of the estate during the administration period and for not allowing them to be wasted or unnecessarily depleted.

The personal representative receives and pays valid claims of creditors and arranges for the estate to pay federal and state income taxes and estate taxes (or inheritance taxes, depending on the state). A personal representative is required to post a bond to ensure honest and faithful performance. Usually, the bond exceeds the estimated value of the personal estate of the decedent. Under most state statutes, the will can specify that the personal representative need not post a bond.

When the ultimate distribution of assets to the beneficiaries is determined, the personal representative is responsible for distributing the estate pursuant to the court order. Once the assets have been distributed, an accounting is rendered to the court, the estate is closed, and the personal representative is relieved of any further responsibility or liability for the estate.

---

9. Revised Uniform Principal and Income Act, Sections 3, 6, 8, 13; Restatement (Second) of Trusts, Section 233.

# ESTATE TAXES

The death of an individual may result in tax liabilities at both the federal and state levels.

## FEDERAL ESTATE TAX

At the federal level, a tax is levied upon the total value of the estate after debts and expenses for administration have been deducted and after various exemptions have been allowed. The tax is on the estate itself rather than on the beneficiaries. Therefore, it does not depend on the character of any bequests or on the relationship of the beneficiary to the decedent, unless a gift to charity that is recognized by the Internal Revenue Service as deductible from the total estate for tax purposes is involved. Estate planning for larger estates also considers other deductions available under federal law. And an entire estate can pass free of estate tax if the estate is left to the surviving spouse.

## STATE INHERITANCE TAXES

The majority of states assess a death tax in the form of an inheritance tax imposed on the recipient of a bequest rather than on the estate. Some states also have a state estate tax similar to the federal estate tax. In general, inheritance tax rates are graduated according to the type of relationship between the beneficiary and decedent. The lowest rates and largest exemptions are applied to a surviving spouse and the children of the decedent.

## TERMS AND CONCEPTS TO REVIEW

| | | |
|---|---|---|
| administrator 1073 | *inter vivos* trust 1086 | probate court 1073 |
| bequest 1073 | intestacy laws 1072 | resulting trust 1088 |
| charitable trust 1089 | intestate 1072 | spendthrift trust 1089 |
| codicil 1080 | legacy 1073 | testamentary trust 1087 |
| constructive trust 1087 | legatee 1074 | testate 1072 |
| devise 1073 | nuncupative will 1078 | testator 1073 |
| escheat 1072 | *per capita* 1084 | Totten trust 1089 |
| executor 1073 | *per stirpes* 1084 | will 1072 |
| holographic will 1077 | probate 1074 | |

# QUESTIONS AND CASE PROBLEMS

**54–1. Estate Distribution.** Flint is a widower who has two married children, Janek and Abrial. Abrial has two children, Phil and Paula. Janek has no children. Flint dies, leaving a typewritten will that gives all his property equally to his children, Janek and Abrial. The will also provides that should a child predecease him, leaving grandchildren, the grandchildren are to take *per stirpes.* The will was witnessed by Abrial and Flint's lawyer and signed by Flint in their presence. Abrial has predeceased Flint. Janek claims the will is invalid.

    (a) Discuss whether the will is valid.

    (b) Discuss the distribution of Flint's estate if the will is invalid.

    (c) Discuss the distribution of Flint's estate if the will is valid.

**54–2. Wills and Subsequent Marriages or Children.** James was a bachelor. While single, he made out a will naming his mother, Carol, as sole beneficiary. Later, James married Lisa.

    (a) If James died while married to Lisa without changing his will, would the estate go to his mother, Carol? Explain.

    (b) Assume that James made out a new will upon his marriage to Lisa, leaving his entire estate to Lisa. Later he divorced Lisa and married Mandis, but he did not change his will. Discuss the rights of Lisa and Mandis to his estate after his death.

    (c) Assume that James divorced Lisa, married Mandis, and changed his will, leaving his estate to Mandis. Later, a daughter, Claire, was born. James died without having included Claire in his will. Discuss fully whether Claire had any rights in the estate.

**54–3. Types of Gifts by Will.** Ingrid has drafted and properly executed a will. Assume that the following clauses are included in her will and that the following events take place:

    (a) Ingrid's will provides, ''I leave my two-carat diamond ring to my sister, Sylvia.'' At the time of Ingrid's death, Sylvia has already died, leaving one child, Lindsay.

    (b) Ingrid's will provides, ''I leave $5,000 to each of my nieces, Fern and Dorothy.'' At the time of Ingrid's death, only $4,000 remains in her estate.

    (c) Ingrid's will provides, ''I leave to my nephew, Donald, my $30,000 Cadillac or its equivalent value.'' Just prior to Ingrid's death, she sold the Cadillac.

Discuss fully each situation, giving its name and describing its effect on the legatees.

**54–4. Undue Influence over Testator.** Rohan, an eighty-three-year-old invalid, employs a nurse, Sarah, to care for him. Prior to Sarah's employment, Rohan executed a will leaving his entire estate to his only living relative—his great-grandson, Leon. Sarah convinces Rohan that Leon is dead and gets Rohan to change his will, naming Sarah as his sole beneficiary. After Rohan's death, Leon appears and contests the will. Discuss the probable success of Leon's action.

**54–5. Trust Creation and Classification.** Assume that the transfers and events described below take place. Discuss fully whether a valid trust has been created in each situation, what each trust is called, and (when applicable) what its effect is.

    (a) John lives in Europe. He transfers $20,000 to his good friend Kate, and orally instructs her to invest and distribute the $20,000 and whatever it accrues so as to finance the MBA education of his daughter, JoAnn.

    (b) Fred is on the board of directors of the ABC Corp. and is the chairman of its research policy committee. Through his chairmanship he learns that ABC has come up with a cure for cancer. Fred purchases on the open market twenty thousand shares of ABC stock at $10 per share. When the announcement of the cure is made, the market value of ABC's stock increases to $200 per share.

    (c) Shana is a successful businessperson. She is engaged to marry Ty, a man of modest means who has ambitions to be an inventor. Shana creates a $20,000 joint savings account in the name of ''Shana, in trust for Ty.'' Shana tells Ty that the purpose of the account is to encourage him to move forward in his business ventures.

**54–6. Resulting Trusts.** Robert and Everett Kling, two brothers, purchased rental property in Fenton, Missouri. Robert contributed $5,544 and Everett, $5,624 toward the purchase price of $19,005. Title to the property was taken in the name of Everett's wife, Nancy. The brothers maintained an account in which they made deposits and from which they paid expenses related to the rental property. Although each brother had agreed to contribute $20 per month toward the remaining purchase price, Robert never did do so, and Everett consequently increased his contribution to $40 per month. When Robert died, Everett and Nancy claimed 100 percent ownership of the Fenton property. Robert's children, John and Janet, filed suit, claiming that Everett and Nancy held the property as a resulting trust and that they (John and Janet) were entitled to half of the property. Discuss whether a resulting trust had been created and, if so, what the distribution should be. [*Estate of Kling,* 736 S.W.2d 65 (Mo.App. 1987)]

**54–7. Revocation of a Will.** Myrtle Courziel executed a valid will that provided for the establishment of a scholarship fund designed to encourage the study of corrosion as it affects metallurgical engineering. The recipients were to be students in the upper half of their classes at the University of Alabama. Subsequently, Courziel died. John Calhoun, the eventual administrator of her estate, obtained access to Courziel's safe-deposit box to search for her will. He found the will intact, except that the last page of the will, which had contained Courziel's signature and the signatures of the witnesses, had been removed from the document and was not in the safe-deposit box or anywhere else to be found. Because Courziel had had sole control over the will, should it be presumed that by removing the last page of the will (or allowing it to be removed), she effectively revoked the will? [*Board of Trustees of University of Alabama v. Calhoun,* 514 So.2d 895 (Ala. 1987)]

**54–8. Publication of a Will.** Tennie Joyner was eighty years old and about to be hospitalized for an illness. To provide for her son, Calvin, Joyner wrote a will and took it to her neighbors for them to type and witness. In the document, she stated that she was giving all her possessions to Calvin because he had taken care of her for years. The will was contested on the basis that Joyner had not met the formal requirement of publication, because she did not tell her neighbors explicitly that the document was her ''last will and testament.'' Joyner had merely told her neighbors that she wanted ''a piece of paper fixed up so I can sign it and Calvin will have a place to live.'' Joyner intended the document to dispose of her property, and the neighbors were fully aware of her intention. Does Joyner's failure to state ''this is my last will and testament'' invalidate the will? Explain. [*Faith v. Singleton,* 286 Ark. 403, 692 S.W.2d 239 (1985)]

**54–9. Testamentary Trusts.** In 1956, Jack Adams executed a will, the terms of which established a charitable trust. The trust income was to go to the Prince Edward School Foundation as long as the foundation continued to operate and admitted to its schools "only members of the White Race." If the foundation admitted non-whites to its schools, the trust income was to go to the Miller School, under the same limitation, and so on to two other educational institutions. If all of the successively named educational beneficiaries violated the limitation, the income would go to Hermitage Methodist Homes of Virginia, Inc., without any limitation attending the bequest. In 1968, Adams died. Subsequent to the execution of the will, all of the educational beneficiaries enrolled African-American students. The trustee, uncertain as to how to distribute the trust income under these circumstances, sought counsel from the court. Assuming that the racially discriminatory provisions are unconstitutional and void, which, if any, of the named beneficiaries should receive the trust income? Discuss. [*Hermitage Methodist Homes of Virginia, Inc. v. Dominion Trust Co.,* 387 S.E.2d 740 (Va. 1990)]

**54–10. Testamentary Trusts.** Edwin Fickes died in 1943. His will provided for the creation of a trust, half of which was to be divided, upon the death of Fickes's last surviving child, "in equal portions between [the testator's] grandchildren then living." At the time of the death of Fickes's last surviving child, there were four biological grandchildren and four adopted grandchildren living. Two of the adopted grandchildren, both boys, had been adopted prior to Fickes's death. The other two, both girls, had been adopted after Fickes died. The trustee, Connecticut National Bank and Trust Co., sought a court determination of whether the adopted grandchildren were entitled to share in the trust distribution. The trial court found that the testator, Fickes, had intended to include his adopted grandsons as "grandchildren" within the meaning of his will but could not have intended to include his adopted granddaughters as "grandchildren," so they were not entitled to a share of the trust. What will happen on appeal? Discuss fully. [*Connecticut National Bank and Trust Co. v. Chadwick,* 217 Conn. 260, 585 A.2d 1189 (1991)]

**54–11. Spendthrift Trusts.** Billy Putman rented and occupied a house trailer owned by Douglas Sanders. Because Putman damaged the trailer while it was in his possession, Sanders sought and acquired a judgment against Putman for $2,429.36 in damages, plus court costs and interest. Sanders garnished Putman's bank account and learned of a certificate of deposit (CD) worth $20,000, which was held by a trustee (Georgia Putman) on behalf of Billy as the beneficiary. The CD was purchased with the proceeds from Billy's deceased father's life insurance policy. Sanders claimed that the insurance proceeds, or the CD, could be garnished. Putman argued that the CD funds were part of a spendthrift trust and therefore could not be reached by creditors, including Sanders. The only evidence in support of a spendthrift

trust was the insurance company's check made payable to Billy Putman's trustee. How should the court decide? Explain. [*Sanders v. Putman,* 315 Ark. 251, 866 S.W.2d 827 (1993)]

**54–12. A Question of Ethics**

 *Heber Burke (Heber) and his wife Evelyn spent most of their lives in Ohio and had jointly accumulated a substantial amount of property there. The Burkes, who had been married for fifty-three years, had two children, four grandchildren, and four great-grandchildren. Evelyn died in February 1985. Heber had originally hailed from Pike County, Kentucky, and in June 1985, he returned to Pike County and bought a house there. In the same month, he told his children that he was going to marry Lexie Damron, a widow who attended his church. Lexie and Heber were married on July 20. On July 27, Heber executed a will, which was drawn up by Lexie's attorney, in which he left all of his property to Lexie. Heber died three weeks later. Heber's children, Donald Burke and Beatrice Bates, contested the will, alleging that Heber lacked testamentary capacity and that Heber's will resulted from Lexie's undue influence over him. Friends and relatives of Heber in Pike County testified that they had never known Heber to drink and that, although he seemed saddened by his first wife's death, he was not incapacitated by it. According to the children's witnesses, however, after Evelyn's death, Heber allegedly drank heavily and constantly; had frequent crying spells; repeatedly visited his wife's grave; tried to dig her up so that he could talk to her; and had hallucinations, talking to people who were not present and claiming that Evelyn visited him regularly at night, which frightened him into sleeping in the attic. The jury found the will to be invalid on the grounds of undue influence, and Lexie appealed. [Burke v. Burke, 801 S.W.2d 691 (Ken.App. 1990)]*

1. The appellate court had to weigh two conflicting policies in deciding this issue. What two policies are in conflict here, and what criteria should be used in resolving the issue?

2. Given the circumstances described above, would you infer undue influence on the part of Lexie if you were the judge? Would you conclude that Heber lacked testamentary capacity? What would be the fairest solution, in your opinion?

3. In the above case, Heber's first wife, Evelyn, contributed substantially to the acquisition of the property subject to Heber's will. A natural assumption would be that Evelyn would want their children to inherit the jointly acquired property. Yet if Heber were found to be of sound mind and not the victim of any undue influence, the court would allow him to totally disregard the children, if he wished, in his will. Is this fair to Evelyn's presumed intentions? To the children? Is there any solution to the possible unfairness that can result from giving people the right to disregard natural heirs in their wills?

# Chapter 55

# Liability of Accountants and Other Professionals

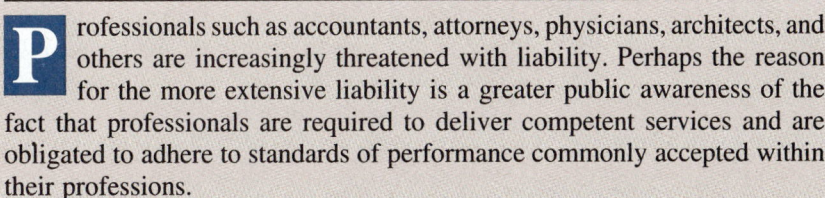

**P**rofessionals such as accountants, attorneys, physicians, architects, and others are increasingly threatened with liability. Perhaps the reason for the more extensive liability is a greater public awareness of the fact that professionals are required to deliver competent services and are obligated to adhere to standards of performance commonly accepted within their professions.

Considering the many potential sources of legal liability that may be imposed upon them, accountants, attorneys, and other professionals should be well aware of their legal obligations. In the first part of this chapter, we look at the potential common law liability of professionals and then examine the potential liability of accountants under securities laws and the Internal Revenue Code. The chapter concludes with a brief examination of the relationship of professionals, particularly accountants and attorneys, with their clients.

## SECTION 1

## POTENTIAL COMMON LAW LIABILITY TO CLIENTS

Under the common law, professionals may be liable to clients for breach of contract, negligence, or fraud.

### LIABILITY FOR BREACH OF CONTRACT

Accountants and other professionals face liability for any breach of contract under the common law. A professional owes a duty to his or her client to honor the terms of the contract and to perform the contract within the stated time period. If the professional fails to perform as agreed in the contract, then he or she has breached the contract, and the client has the right to recover damages from the professional. A professional may be held liable for expenses incurred by his or her client in securing another professional to provide the contracted-for services, for penalties imposed on the client for failure to meet time deadlines, and for any other reasonable and foreseeable monetary losses that arise from the professional's breach.

## LIABILITY FOR NEGLIGENCE

Accountants and other professionals may also be held liable under the common law for negligence in the performance of their services. As with any negligence claim, the elements that must be proved to establish negligence on the part of a professional are as follows:

1. A duty of care existed.
2. That duty of care was breached.
3. The plaintiff suffered an injury.
4. The injury was proximately caused by the defendant's breach of the duty of care.

All professionals are subject to standards of conduct established by codes of professional standards and ethics, by state statutes, and by judicial decisions. They are also governed by the contracts into which they enter with their clients. In their performance of contracts, professionals must exercise the established standard of care, knowledge, and judgment generally accepted by members of their professional group. We look below at the duty of care owed by two groups of professionals that frequently perform services for business firms: accountants and attorneys.

**ACCOUNTANT'S DUTY OF CARE** Accountants play a major role in a business's financial system. Accountants have the necessary expertise and experience in establishing and maintaining accurate financial records to design, control, and audit record-keeping systems; to prepare reliable statements that reflect an individual's or a business's financial status; and to give tax advice and prepare tax returns.

*GAAP and GAAS.* In the performance of their services, accountants must comply with **generally accepted accounting principles (GAAP)** and **generally accepted auditing standards (GAAS).** The Financial Accounting Standards Board (FASB, usually pronounced ''faz-bee'') determines what accounting conventions, rules, and

procedures constitute GAAP at a given point in time. GAAS are standards concerning an auditor's professional qualities and the judgment that he or she exercises in performing an examination and report. GAAS are established by the American Institute of Certified Public Accountants.

As long as an accountant conforms to generally accepted accounting principles and acts in good faith, he or she normally will not be held liable to the client for incorrect judgment. As a general rule, an accountant is not required to discover every impropriety, **defalcation** (embezzlement), or fraud in his or her client's books. If, however, the impropriety, defalcation, or fraud has gone undiscovered because of an accountant's negligence or failure to perform an express or implied duty, the accountant will be liable for any resulting losses suffered by his or her client. Therefore, an accountant who uncovers suspicious financial transactions and fails to investigate the matter fully or to inform his or her client of the discovery can be held liable to the client for the resulting loss.

A violation of GAAP and GAAS will be considered *prima facie* evidence of negligence on the part of the accountant. Compliance with GAAP and GAAS, however, does not *necessarily* relieve an accountant from potential legal liability. An accountant may be held to a higher standard of conduct established by state statute and by judicial decisions.

*Defenses to Negligence.* If an accountant is deemed guilty of negligence, the client may collect damages for losses that arose from the accountant's negligence. An accountant, however, is not without possible defenses to a cause of action for damages based on negligence. Possible defenses include the following allegations:

1. The accountant was not negligent.
2. If the accountant was negligent, this negligence was not the proximate cause of the client's losses.
3. The client was negligent (depending on whether state law allows contributory negligence as a defense).

*Unaudited Financial Statements.* Sometimes accountants are hired to prepare unaudited financial statements. (A financial statement is considered unaudited if no auditing procedures have been used in its preparation or if insufficient procedures have been used to justify an opinion.) In an unaudited financial statement, a lesser standard of care is typically required for a ''write-up'' (an increase in the valuation of an asset to reflect current value), but accountants may still be held liable in this situation. Accountants may be subject to liability for failing, in accordance with standard accounting procedures, to delineate a balance sheet as ''unaudited.'' An accountant will also be held liable for failure to disclose to a client facts or circumstances that give reason to believe that misstatements have been made or that a fraud has been committed.

**ATTORNEY'S DUTY OF CARE** The conduct of attorneys is governed by rules established by each state and by the American Bar Association's Model Rules of Professional Conduct. All attorneys owe a duty to provide competent and diligent representation. In judging an attorney's performance, the standard used will normally be that of a reasonably competent general practitioner of ordinary skill, experience, and capacity. If an attorney holds himself or herself out as having expertise in a special area of law (for example, domestic relations), then the attorney's standard of care in that area is higher than for attorneys without such expertise.

Attorneys are required to be familiar with well-settled principles of law applicable to a case and to discover law that can be found through a reasonable amount of research. The lawyer also must investigate and discover facts that could materially affect the client's legal rights.

When an attorney fails to exercise reasonable care and professional judgment, he or she breaches the duty of care. The plaintiff must then prove that the breach actually caused him or her some injury. For example, if the attorney allows the statute of limitations to lapse on a client's claim, he or she can be held liable for **malpractice** (professional negligence)—because the client can no longer file a cause of action in this case and has lost a potential award of damages. All attorneys are encouraged to keep calendars for their cases so that they will not carelessly miss crucial deadlines, such as the dates of court hearings. In the following case, an attorney was sued for legal malpractice because he failed to inform his client of a settlement offer.

---

**BACKGROUND AND FACTS** *Ralph W. Moores, Jr., was injured on the job while working as a dockworker in Maine. After collecting workers' compensation benefits in the amount of $43,000, Moores brought a third party liability suit against the shipowners. Nathan Greenberg was Moores's attorney. The shipowners informed Greenberg that they would settle the suit, making several offers, including, at one point, $90,000. Greenberg did not inform Moores of the offer because he did not deem it to be sufficiently significant. When Moores lost the case in court, he sued Greenberg, alleging that Greenberg had had a duty to inform him of these offers and had breached that duty by not doing so. The trial court jury held for Moores and awarded him $12,000 in damages ($90,000 less $35,000 in fees and expenses owed to Greenberg and less $43,000 recovered from the workers' compensation insurer). Neither party was satisfied with the verdict, and the case was appealed.*

CASE 55.1

**MOORES v. GREENBERG**

United States Court of Appeals, First Circuit, 1987. 834 F.2d 1105.

*SELYA,* Circuit Judge.
\* \* \* \*
\* \* \* In representing his client, *an attorney has a duty to use that degree of skill, diligence, and judgment ordinarily to be expected of a member of the bar practicing in the same (or a similar) locale.* As part and parcel of this duty, a lawyer must keep his client seasonably apprised of relevant developments, including opportunities for settlement. [Emphasis added.]

Greenberg says that, even if this be true, the sums mentioned to him were too [stingy] to be relayed. We need not decide today whether a lawyer has an obligation to transmit a patently unreasonable offer to his client. \* \* \* [T]he shipowners' $90,000 offer could not be said, as a matter of law, to be a patently ridiculous one. [On a record that was far from clear and less than obvious,] the district court did not err in permitting the jury to determine whether reasonably competent counsel would have informed Moores of the $90,000 offer and whether the client, had he been told, would have clasped it to his bosom.

\* \* \* \*

\* \* \* Short of punitive damages—and none were granted in this case—''[a]n attorney who [commits malpractice] is liable to his client for any reasonably foreseeable loss caused by his negligence.'' On this record, it was ''reasonably foreseeable'' that, by failing to communicate the offer, Greenberg would effectively deprive his client of the net benefit of the tendered bargain—nothing more.

**DECISION AND REMEDY** *The trial court's judgment was affirmed. The court found Greenberg to be liable to Moores for $12,000 ($90,000 less the $35,000 owed to Greenberg and the $43,000 received as workers' compensation).*

## PROFESSIONALS' LIABILITY FOR FRAUD

Actual fraud and constructive fraud present two different circumstances under which an accountant may be found liable. Recall from Chapter 15 that fraud, or misrepresentation, consists of the following elements:

1.  A misrepresentation of a material fact has occurred.
2.  There exists an intent to deceive.
3.  The innocent party has justifiably relied on the misrepresentation.
4.  For damages, the innocent party must have been injured.

A professional may be held liable for *actual fraud* when he or she intentionally misstates a material fact to mislead his or her client and the client justifiably relies on the misstated fact to his or her injury. A material fact is one that a reasonable person would consider important in deciding whether to act. In contrast, a professional may be held liable for *constructive fraud* whether or not he or she acted with fraudulent intent. For example, constructive fraud may be found when an accountant is grossly negligent in the performance of his or her duties. The intentional failure to perform a duty in reckless disregard of the consequences of such a failure would constitute gross negligence on the part of a professional. Both actual and constructive fraud are potential sources of legal liability under which a client may bring an action against an accountant or other professional.

When a client is dissatisfied with the performance of an accounting or legal firm, he or she will often sue on several theories. In the following case, which deals with accountants, the court had to sift through claims for negligence, constructive fraud, and breach of contract. Notice how the court disposes of the latter two counts by its treatment of the negligence claim.

---

**CASE 55.2**

**IN RE THE HAWAII CORP.**

United States District Court, District of Hawaii, 1983. 567 F.Supp. 609.

**COMPANY PROFILE** *The Von Hamm–Young Company was incorporated in 1899. It developed from a family-owned business into one of Hawaii's largest corporations. By 1964, when the company changed its name to The Hawaii Corporation (THC), it was engaged in construction, merchandising, real estate, laundry, and consumer finance services. American Pacific Group (APG) was formed in 1959 as Hawaii National Insurance Company. APG was primarily a holding company whose subsidiaries were mostly unprofitable. In the late 1960s, THC's officers, directors, and financial associates began planning for THC's expansion through acquisitions and mergers. When APG acquired more than 50 percent of THC's stock, representatives of the two companies discussed a merger. Peat, Marwick, Mitchell & Company (PMM) was a partnership in the practice of public accounting.*

**BACKGROUND AND FACTS**  *In planning a merger with The Hawaii Corporation (THC), the American Pacific Group (APG) engaged the accounting firm of Peat, Marwick, Mitchell & Company (PMM) to prepare financial statements for both companies and also to express opinions as to the most advantageous means of combining them. When the merger resulted in THC's arguably unnecessary loss of $22 million, the trustee who had overseen the merger of the two corporations sued PMM on grounds of, among other things, accountant malpractice, based on the unusual method PMM had used in restructuring the companies. The plaintiff contended that, had PMM used the accounting method generally applied in such transactions, its financial statements would have reflected a more negative picture, and the merger would never have occurred.*

*PANNER,* District Judge, Sitting by Designation.

\*    \*    \*    \*

I conclude that the plaintiff has failed to prove by a preponderance of the evidence that the defendant was negligent in the method of accounting for the transaction. It is not necessary to endorse such a procedure for application to all situations. Here it was appropriate. Even if \*  \*  \* purchase accounting[a] should have been used throughout the transaction, the results would have not been significantly different \*  \*  \*. The income statement on the *pro forma* statements [financial statements that are based on certain assumptions] would not have changed and the figure reported as retained earnings [undistributed corporate profits] on the balance sheet would have been somewhat higher. Under these circumstances, plaintiff has failed to prove that the merger would not have occurred, either by reason of director action or minority stockholder action.

Analysis of the testimony and the exhibits reflects thoughtful accounting decisions based on judgment in difficult matters \*  \*  \*.

\*    \*    \*    \*

Plaintiff alleges that PMM is liable for fraud because the comfort letter,[b] the financial statements and the *pro forma* balance sheets that PMM prepared contained material misrepresentations upon which THC relied in embarking on the THC-APG reorganization and related transactions. There is no contention of intentional fraud. Plaintiff asserts the misrepresentations were made with reckless disregard for their truth or falsity.

\*    \*    \*    \*

My findings with respect to the negligence claim are dispositive of [negate] plaintiff's fraud claim. Plaintiff has failed to prove that the comfort letter, financial statements, or *pro forma* balance sheets prepared by the defendant contained material misrepresentations.

\*    \*    \*    \*

Plaintiff contends that PMM breached its express and implied duties and obligations under the contracts by negligently and recklessly acting as previously set forth, and seeks contract damages including all compensation paid by plaintiff to PMM for the services it rendered.

\*    \*    \*    \*

a.  A method of accounting for mergers in which the total value paid for the acquired firm's assets is recorded in the acquiring firm's books. Any difference between the fair market value of the assets acquired and the purchase price is recorded as goodwill.

b.  A letter from PMM stating that the informal procedures used did not reveal any material changes in the financial statements and that only an audit with certain established procedures could reliably supply that information.

In concluding that plaintiff failed to prove by a preponderance of the evidence that defendant was negligent in performing auditing and accounting services for plaintiff, I have also necessarily concluded that plaintiff cannot recover for breach of contract.

**DECISION AND REMEDY**  *The court found that the accounting method employed by PMM, although admittedly "creative," did not violate the negligence standard, because it produced a result essentially similar to that of the standard method. Furthermore, the court concluded that even though the accounting was not done according to the usual method, it was arrived at by careful reasoning. Because that standard had been upheld, the court reasoned, there had been no breach of contract, fraud, or negligence. Judgment was for the defendant, PMM.*

---

## SECTION 2

# AUDITORS' LIABILITY TO THIRD PARTIES

Traditionally, an accountant or other professional did not owe any duty to a third person with whom he or she had no direct contractual relationship—that is, to any person not in *privity of contract* with the professional. A professional's duty was only to his or her client. Violations of statutory laws, fraud, and other intentional or reckless acts of wrongdoing were the only exceptions to this general rule.

Today, numerous third parties—including investors, shareholders, creditors, corporate managers and directors, regulatory agencies, and others—rely on professional opinions, such as those of auditors, when making decisions. In view of this extensive reliance, many courts have all but abandoned the privity requirement in regard to accountants' liability to third parties.

In this section, we focus on the potential liability of auditors to third parties. Understanding an auditor's common law liability to third parties is critical, because when a business fails, often its independent auditor (accountant) may be one of the few potentially solvent defendants. The majority of courts now hold that auditors can be held liable to third parties for negligence, but the standard for the imposition of this liability varies. There are generally three different views of accountants' liability to third parties, each of which we discuss below.

## THE *ULTRAMARES* RULE

The traditional rule regarding an accountant's liability to third parties was enunciated by Chief Judge Benjamin Cardozo in *Ultramares Corp. v. Touche,* a case decided in 1931.[1] In *Ultramares,* Fred Stern & Company (Stern) hired the public accounting firm of Touche, Niven & Company (Touche) to review Stern's financial records and prepare a balance sheet for the year ending December 31, 1923.[2] Touche prepared the balance sheet and supplied Stern with thirty-two certified copies. According to the certified balance sheet, Stern had a net worth (assets less liabilities) of $1,070,715.26. In reality, however, Stern was insolvent—the company's records had been falsified by Stern's insiders to reflect a positive net worth. In reliance on the certified balance sheets, a lender, Ultramares Corporation, loaned substantial amounts to Stern. After Stern was declared bankrupt, Ultramares brought an action against Touche for negligence in an attempt to recover damages.

The New York Court of Appeals (that state's highest court) refused to impose liability on the accountants and concluded that they owed a duty of care only to those persons for whose "primary benefit" the statements were intended. In this case, Stern was the only person for whose primary ben-

---

1.  255 N.Y. 170, 174 N.E. 441 (1931).
2.  A balance sheet is often relied on by banks, creditors, stockholders, purchasers, or sellers as a basis for making decisions relating to a company's business.

efit the statements were intended. The court held that in the absence of privity or a relationship "so close as to approach that of privity," a party could not recover from an accountant.

The court's requirement of privity or near privity has since been referred to as the *Ultramares* rule, or the New York rule. The rule was restated and somewhat modified in a 1985 New York case, *Credit Alliance Corp. v. Arthur Andersen & Co.*[3] In that case, the court held that if a third party has a sufficiently close relationship or nexus (link or connection) with an accountant, then the *Ultramares* privity requirement may be satisfied without establishing an accountant-client relationship. The rule enunciated in *Credit Alliance* is often referred to as the "near privity" rule. Only a minority of states have adopted this rule of accountants' liability to third parties.

## THE RESTATEMENT RULE

In the past several years, the *Ultramares* rule has been severely criticized. Auditors perform much of their work for use by persons who are not parties to the contract; and thus, it is asserted that they

3. 65 N.Y.2d 536, 483 N.E.2d 110 (1985): A "relationship sufficiently intimate to be equated with privity" is sufficient for a third party to sue another's accountant for negligence.

owe a duty to these third parties. Consequently, there has been an erosion of the *Ultramares* rule, and accountants have been exposed to potential liability to third parties.

The majority of courts have adopted the position taken by the Restatement (Second) of Torts, which states that accountants are subject to liability for negligence not only to their clients but also to *foreseen,* or *known,* users—or classes of users—of their reports or financial statements. Under Section 552(2) of the Restatement (Second) of Torts, an accountant's liability extends to those persons for whose benefit and guidance the accountant "intends to supply the information or knows that the recipient intends to supply it" and to those persons whom the accountant "intends the information to influence or knows that the recipient so intends." In other words, if an accountant prepares a financial statement for a client and knows that the client will submit that statement to a bank to secure a loan, the accountant may be held liable to the bank for negligent misstatements or omissions—because the accountant knew that the bank would rely on the accountant's work product when deciding whether to make the loan.

In the following case, the court considers the question of the extent of an accountant's liability to a third party. Note the court's reliance on the Restatement's position in determining the issue.

**BACKGROUND AND FACTS** *In April 1985, Max Mitchell, a certified public accountant (CPA) and president of Max Mitchell & Company, P.A., went to First Florida Bank for the purpose of negotiating a $500,000 unsecured line of credit for his client, C. M. Systems, Inc. Mitchell introduced himself to Stephen Hickman, the bank's vice president, as a CPA and gave to Hickman audited financial statements of C. M. Systems for the fiscal years ending October 31, 1983, and October 31, 1984, which had been prepared by Mitchell's firm. The 1984 statement did not indicate that C. M. Systems owed money to any bank, and in a later discussion with Hickman, Mitchell stated that as of April 16, 1985, C. M. Systems was not indebted to any bank and that he was not aware of any material change in the company's financial condition since October 31, 1984. After the bank approved the line of credit, C. M. Systems borrowed the entire $500,000 but never repaid the bank. The bank later discovered that the audit for the fiscal year ending October 31, 1984, had substantially overstated the assets, understated the liabilities, and overstated the net income of C. M. Systems. The audit also failed to reflect that the company owed at least $750,000 to several banks. In addition, several material changes*

**CASE 55.3**

**FIRST FLORIDA BANK, N.A.[a] v. MAX MITCHELL & CO.**

Supreme Court of Florida, 1990.
558 So.2d 9.

a. N.A. stands for National Association.

*had occurred in the company's balance sheet after the audit but prior to the approval of the line of credit. The bank filed a complaint against Mitchell and his firm, alleging negligence and gross negligence. Because of the absence of privity between either Mitchell or his firm and the bank, the trial court granted Mitchell summary judgment. The bank appealed.*

*GRIMES,* Judge.
\* \* \* \*

Upon consideration, we have decided to adopt the rationale of section 552, Restatement (Second) of Torts, as setting forth the circumstances under which accountants may be held liable in negligence to persons who are not in contractual privity. \* \* \*
\* \* \* \*

Because of the heavy reliance upon audited financial statements in the contemporary financial world, we believe permitting recovery only from those in privity or near privity is unduly restrictive. On the other hand, we are persuaded by the wisdom of the rule which limits liability to those persons or classes of persons whom an accountant "knows" will rely on his opinion rather than those he "should have known" would do so because it takes into account the fact that an accountant controls neither his client's accounting records nor the distribution of his reports. \* \* \*

There remains the need to apply this rule to the facts at hand. At the time Mitchell prepared the audits for C. M. Systems, it was unknown that they would be used to induce the reliance of First Florida Bank to approve a line of credit for C. M. Systems. Therefore, except for the unusual facts of this case, Mitchell could not be held liable to the bank for any negligence in preparing the audit. However, Mitchell actually negotiated the loan on behalf of his client. He personally delivered the financial statements to the bank with the knowledge that it would rely upon them in considering whether or not to make the loan. Under this unique set of facts, we believe that Mitchell vouched for the integrity of the audits and that his conduct in dealing with the bank sufficed to meet the requirements of the rule which we have adopted in this opinion.

**DECISION AND REMEDY** *The Supreme Court of Florida ruled that Mitchell could be held liable under the rule of liability adopted by the court. The case was remanded for further proceedings consistent with the court's opinion.*

**INTERNATIONAL CONSIDERATIONS** **Liability of Accountants to Third Parties in England** *After a long history of requiring privity, English courts began permitting foreseeable third parties to sue accountants for negligence. This produced a backlash, and a 1990 decision restricted such third party liability. The court described the "frightening" extent of accountants' liability in the United States and stressed that English courts should "demonstrate a greater concern for equity."*

## LIABILITY TO REASONABLY FORESEEABLE USERS

A small minority of courts hold accountants liable to any users whose reliance on an accountant's statements or reports was *reasonably foreseeable.*

This standard has been criticized as extending liability too far. In *Raritan River Steel Co. v.*

*Cherry, Bekaert & Holland,* for example, the North Carolina Supreme Court stated that "in fairness accountants should not be liable in circumstances where they are unaware of the use to which their opinions will be put. Instead, their liability should be commensurate with those persons or classes of persons whom they know will rely on their work. With such knowledge the auditor can, through purchase of liability insurance, setting fees, and adopting other protective measures appropriate to the risk, prepare accordingly.''[4]

The North Carolina court's statement echoes the view of the majority of the courts that the Restatement's approach is the more reasonable because it allows accountants to control their exposure to liability. Liability is ''fixed by the accountants' particular knowledge at the moment the audit is published,'' not by the foreseeability of the harm that might occur to a third party after the report is released.[5]

Even the California courts, which for several years had relied on reasonable foreseeability as the standard for determining an auditor's liability to third parties, have recently changed their position. In a 1992 case, the California Supreme Court held that an accountant ''owes no general duty of care regarding the conduct of an audit to persons other than the client.'' The court went on to say that if third parties rely on an auditor's opinion, ''there

is no liability even though the [auditor] should reasonably have foreseen such a possibility.''[6]

---

4. 322 N.C. 200, 367 S.E.2d 609 (1988).

5. *Bethlehem Steel Corp. v. Ernst & Whinney,* 822 S.W.2d 592 (Tenn. 1991).

---

6. *Bily v. Arthur Young & Co.,* 3 Cal.4th 370, 834 P.2d 745, 11 Cal.Rptr.2d 51 (1992).

## SECTION 3

# LIABILITY OF ATTORNEYS TO THIRD PARTIES

Like accountants, attorneys may also be held liable under the common law to third parties who rely on legal opinions to their detriment. The liability principles stated in Section 552 of the Restatement (Second) of Torts may apply to attorneys just as it may apply to accountants. Although the Restatement is not limited by its terms to accountants, the application to attorneys is still in dispute, as illustrated in the following case.

**BACKGROUND AND FACTS** *To raise money for a new municipal parking garage, which would be the first project to be implemented under an urban renewal plan, the town of Winter Park, Colorado, issued over $5 million in notes (a type of short-term bond). Central Bank Denver was considering the purchase of the notes when a lawsuit challenging the urban renewal plan was initiated by the county school district. The firm of Mehaffy, Rider, Windholz & Wilson represented Winter Park in the suit. Because of the lawsuit, Central Bank was unsure of whether it should purchase the notes. The bank, with authorization from Winter Park, therefore sought legal opinions from some law firms—including the firm of Mehaffy, Rider—as to whether the school district's lawsuit had any merit. In their opinion letters, the law firms stated that the lawsuit challenging the urban renewal plan had no merit. Relying on these opinions, the bank purchased the notes from Winter Park. When the school district's case came to trial, however, the judge found for the school district. The court voided the town's urban renewal plan and enjoined any further attempts by the town to implement it. The decision was affirmed on appeal. Following the disposition of that case, Central Bank filed suit against the law firms alleging negligent misrepresentation, among other things. The trial court dismissed the suit, finding that because Central Bank and the law firms did not have an attorney-client relationship, there was no basis for liability. Central Bank appealed the court's dismissal.*

**CASE 55.4**

**CENTRAL BANK DENVER, N.A. v. MEHAFFY, RIDER, WINDHOLZ & WILSON**

Colorado Court of Appeals, 1993.
865 P.2d 862.

Opinion by Judge *RULAND.*

\* \* \* \*

\* \* \* [A]n attorney's liability to a non-client has previously been limited to cases involving fraud or malice because of the attorney's duty of loyalty and effective advocacy to a client and because the potential liability might accrue to an unlimited number of third parties. Here, however, it is undisputed that the Bank has requested issuance of the opinion letters and that the client authorized such. Conversely, the potential liability is limited to those for whose benefit the letters were prepared.

Given these considerations, and given the fact that other professionals in this jurisdiction may be subjected to liability to third persons for negligent misrepresentation, we are unable to conclude that attorneys should enjoy an immunity from such claims. Instead, we consider this theory of recovery proper in such circumstances because counsel knows the purpose of the legal opinion and also knows or should know that it will be relied upon by the non-client as a basis for closing the transaction.

**DECISION AND REMEDY**
*The appellate court held that Central Bank may have a claim against the law firms for negligent misrepresentation. The lower court's decision was reversed on this issue and the case remanded for further proceedings consistent with the appellate court's decision.*

# POTENTIAL STATUTORY LIABILITY OF ACCOUNTANTS

Both civil and criminal liability may be imposed on accountants under the Securities Act of 1933 and the Securities Exchange Act of 1934.

## LIABILITY UNDER THE SECURITIES ACT OF 1933

The Securities Act of 1933 requires registration statements to be filed with the Securities and Exchange Commission (SEC) prior to an offering of securities (see Chapter 44).[7] Accountants frequently prepare and certify the issuer's financial statements that are included in the registration statement.

**LIABILITY UNDER SECTION 11** Section 11 of the Securities Act of 1933 imposes civil liability on accountants for misstatements and omissions of material facts in registration statements. Therefore, an accountant may be found liable if he or she prepared any financial statements included in the registration statement that "contained an untrue statement of a material fact or omitted to state a material fact required to be stated therein or necessary to make the statements therein not misleading."[8]

***Liability to Purchasers of Securities.*** Under Section 11, an accountant's liability for a misstatement or omission of a material fact in a registration statement extends to anyone who acquires a security covered by the registration statement. A purchaser of a security need only demonstrate that he or she has suffered a loss on the security. Proof of reliance on the materially false statement or misleading omission is not ordinarily required. Nor is there a requirement of privity between the accountant and the security purchasers.

***The Due Diligence Standard.*** Section 11 imposes a duty on accountants to use **due diligence** in the preparation of financial statements included in the filed registration statements. After the purchaser has proved the loss on the security, the accountant bears the burden of showing that he or she exercised due diligence in the preparation of the financial statements. To avoid liability, the accountant must show that he or she had, "after

---

7. Many securities and transactions are expressly exempted from the 1933 act.

8. 15 U.S.C. Section 77k(a).

reasonable investigation, reasonable grounds to believe and did believe, at the time such part of the registration statement became effective, that the statements therein were true and that there was no omission of a material fact required to be stated therein or necessary to make the statements therein not misleading.''[9] Further, the failure to follow GAAP and GAAS is also proof of a lack of due diligence.

In particular, the due diligence standard places a burden on accountants to verify information furnished by a corporation's officers and directors. The burden of proving due diligence requires an accountant to demonstrate that he or she is free from negligence or fraud. The accountants in *Escott v. BarChris Construction Corp.,*[10] for example, were held liable for a failure to detect danger signals in materials that, under GAAS, required further investigation under the circumstances. Merely asking questions is not always sufficient to satisfy the requirement of due diligence.

*Defenses to Liability.* Besides proving that he or she has acted with due diligence, an accountant may raise the following defenses to Section 11 liability:

1. There were no misstatements or omissions.
2. The misstatements or omissions were not of material facts.
3. The misstatements or omissions had no causal connection to the plaintiff's loss.
4. The plaintiff purchaser invested in the securities knowing of the misstatements or omissions.

**LIABILITY UNDER SECTION 12(2)** Section 12(2) of the Securities Act of 1933 imposes civil liability for fraud on anyone offering or selling a security.[11] Liability is based on the communication to an investor, whether orally or in the written prospectus,[12] of an untrue statement or omission of a material fact. Some courts have applied Section 12(2) to accountants who *aided and abetted* the seller or the offeror of the securities in violating

Section 12(2). In those jurisdictions that apply Section 12(2) to accountants for aiding and abetting, the accountant may be liable if he or she knew or should have known that an untrue statement or omission of material fact existed in the offer or sale.

In *Sandusky Land, Ltd. v. Uniplan Groups, Inc.,*[13] for example, an accounting firm had allegedly issued a misleading written opinion to investors concerning the tax benefits of investing in certain securities. Even though the firm was not the actual seller of the securities, the court found no reason to distinguish between persons exposed to liability under Section 12(2) and persons ''charged with aiding and abetting and conspiring in the violation of [that section].''

## LIABILITY UNDER THE SECURITIES EXCHANGE ACT OF 1934

Under Sections 18 and 10(b) of the Securities Exchange Act of 1934 and Rule 10b-5 of the Securities and Exchange Commission, an accountant may be found liable for fraud. A plaintiff has a substantially heavier burden of proof under the 1934 act than under the 1933 act. Unlike the 1933 act, the 1934 act provides that an accountant need not prove due diligence to escape liability.

**LIABILITY UNDER SECTION 18** Section 18 of the 1934 act imposes civil liability on an accountant who makes or causes to be made in any application, report, or document a statement that at the time and in light of the circumstances was false or misleading with respect to any material fact.[14]

Section 18 liability is narrow in that it applies only to applications, reports, documents, and registration statements filed with the SEC. This remedy is further limited in that it applies only to sellers and purchasers. Under Section 18, a seller or purchaser must prove one of the following:

1. That the false or misleading statement affected the price of the security.
2. That the purchaser or seller relied on the false or misleading statement in making the

---

9. 15 U.S.C. Section 77k(b)(3).

10. 283 F.Supp. 643 (S.D.N.Y. 1968). This case is presented in Chapter 44 as Case 44.1.

11. 15 U.S.C. Section 77*l*.

12. As discussed in Chapter 41, a *prospectus* contains financial disclosures about the corporation for the benefit of potential investors.

13. 400 F.Supp. 440 (N.D.Ohio 1975). See also *Gilbert Family Partnership v. Nido Corp.,* 697 F.Supp. 679 (E.D.Mich. 1988).

14. 15 U.S.C. Section 78r(a).

purchase or sale and was not aware of the inaccuracy of the statement.

Even if a purchaser or seller proves these two elements, an accountant can be exonerated of liability upon proof of "good faith" in the preparation of the financial statement. To demonstrate good faith, an accountant must show that he or she had no knowledge that the financial statement was false and misleading. Acting in good faith requires the total absence of an intention on the part of the accountant to seek an unfair advantage over, or to defraud, another party. Proving a lack of intent to deceive, manipulate, or defraud is frequently referred to as proving a lack of *scienter* (knowledge on the part of a misrepresenting party that material facts have been misrepresented or omitted with an intent to deceive). Absence of good faith can be demonstrated not only by proof of *scienter* but also by the accountant's reckless conduct and gross negligence. (Note that "mere" negligence in the preparation of a financial statement does not constitute liability under the 1934 act. This differs from provisions of the 1933 act, under which an accountant is liable for all negligent acts.) In addition to the good faith defense, accountants have available as a defense the buyer's or seller's knowledge that the financial statement was false and misleading.

A court, under Section 18 of the 1934 act, also has the discretion to assess reasonable costs, including attorneys' fees, against accountants.[15] Sellers and purchasers may maintain a cause of action "within one year after the discovery of the facts constituting the cause of action and within three years after such cause of action accrued."[16]

### LIABILITY UNDER SECTION 10(b) AND RULE 10b-5

The Securities Exchange Act of 1934 further subjects accountants to potential legal liability in its antifraud provisions. Section 10(b) of the 1934 act and SEC Rule 10b-5 contain the antifraud provisions. As stated in *Herman & MacLean v. Huddleston,* "a private right of action under Section 10(b) of the 1934 act and Rule 10b-5 has been consistently recognized for more than 35 years."[17]

Section 10(b) makes it unlawful for any person, including accountants, to use, in connection with the purchase or sale of any security, any manipulative or deceptive device or contrivance in contravention of SEC rules and regulations.[18] Rule 10b-5 further makes it unlawful for any person, by use of any means or instrumentality of interstate commerce, to do the following:

1. To employ any device, scheme, or artifice to defraud.
2. To make any untrue statement of a material fact or to omit to state a material fact necessary to make the statements made, in light of the circumstances, not misleading.
3. To engage in any act, practice, or course of business that operates or would operate as a fraud or deceit upon any person, in connection with the purchase or sale of any security.[19]

Accountants may be held liable only to sellers or purchasers under Section 10(b) and Rule 10b-5.[20] The scope of these antifraud provisions is extremely wide. Privity is not necessary for a recovery. Under these provisions, an accountant may be found liable not only for fraudulent misstatements of material facts in written material filed with the SEC but also for any fraudulent oral statements or omissions made in connection with the purchase or sale of any security.

For a plaintiff to recover from an accountant under the antifraud provisions of the 1934 act, he or she must, in addition to establishing status as a purchaser or seller, prove *scienter,*[21] a fraudulent action or deception, reliance, materiality, and causation. A plaintiff who fails to establish these elements cannot recover damages from an accountant under Section 10(b) or Rule 10b-5.

Federal courts in eleven circuits have held that accountants (and others) may be held liable in private actions for "aiding and abetting" violations of various provisions of the securities laws, including Section 10(b) and Rule 10b-5. In the following case, the United States Supreme Court addresses this issue.

---

15. 15 U.S.C. Section 78r(a).
16. 15 U.S.C. Section 78r(c).
17. 459 U.S. 375, 103 S.Ct. 683, 74 L.Ed.2d 548 (1983).
18. 15 U.S.C. Section 78j(b).
19. 17 C.F.R. Section 240.10b-5.
20. See *Blue Chip Stamps v. Manor Drug Stores,* 421 U.S. 723, 95 S.Ct. 1917, 44 L.Ed.2d 539 (1975).
21. See *Ernst & Ernst v. Hochfelder,* 425 U.S. 185, 96 S.Ct. 1375, 47 L.Ed.2d 668 (1976).

**CASE 55.5**

**CENTRAL BANK OF DENVER, N.A. v. FIRST INTERSTATE BANK OF DENVER, N.A.**

Supreme Court of the United States, 1994.
_____ U.S. _____,
114 S.Ct. 1439,
128 L.Ed.2d 119.

**BACKGROUND AND FACTS** *The Colorado Springs-Stetson Hills Public Building Authority wanted to issue bonds to finance public improvements at AmWest Development's Stetson Hills in Colorado Springs. The Central Bank of Denver, N.A., agreed to be the indenture trustee.[a] The bonds were to be secured by liens on more than five hundred acres of land in Stetson Hills. The bond agreements required that the land be worth at least 160 percent of the bonds' outstanding principal and interest. AmWest supplied appraisals showing that this test was met. In early 1988, before the bonds were issued, however, Central Bank learned that property values in Colorado Springs were declining, which indicated that the 160 percent test would not be met. AmWest asked Central Bank to delay an independent appraisal of the land until after the bonds were issued, and Central Bank agreed. First Interstate Bank of Denver, N.A., and others, purchased the bonds. Before Central Bank could complete the appraisal, the Authority defaulted on the bonds. First Interstate and others sued Central Bank and others, alleging in part that Central Bank was "secondarily liable under [Section] 10(b) for its conduct in aiding and abetting the fraud." The court granted summary judgment in favor of Central Bank. First Interstate appealed, and the appellate court ruled in First Interstate's favor. Central Bank appealed to the United States Supreme Court.*

Justice *KENNEDY* delivered the opinion of the Court.

\* \* \* \*

[A] survey of the express causes of action in the securities Acts reveals that each (like [Section] 10(b)) specifies the conduct for which defendants may be held liable. Some of the express causes of action specify categories of defendants who may be liable; others (like [Section] 10(b)) state only that "any person" who commits one of the prohibited acts may be held liable. The important point for present purposes, however, is that none of the express causes of action in the 1934 Act further imposes liability on one who aids or abets a violation.

\* \* \* [I]t would be \* \* \* anomalous to impute to Congress an intention in effect to expand the defendant class for 10b-5 actions beyond the bounds delineated for comparable express causes of action.

\* \* \* \*

\* \* \* [Further], when Congress enacts a statute under which a person may sue and recover damages from a private defendant for the defendant's violation of some statutory norm, there is no general presumption that the plaintiff may also sue aiders and abettors.

Congress instead has taken a statute-by-statute approach to civil aiding and abetting liability. \* \* \* Indeed, various provisions of the securities laws prohibit aiding and abetting, although violations are enforceable only in actions brought by the SEC.

\* \* \* \*

Because the text of [Section] 10(b) does not prohibit aiding and abetting, we hold that a private plaintiff may not maintain an aiding and abetting suit under [Section] 10(b).

**DECISION AND REMEDY** *The Supreme Court ruled that the trial court's grant of summary judgment to Central Bank was proper and reversed the judgment of the appellate court.*

a.   An *indenture* is an agreement under which bonds are issued. An *indenture trustee* is responsible for protecting the interests of the bondholders in the issue.

**COMMENT** *This ruling may have stemmed in part from the fear that if a private cause of action for "aiding and abetting" were recognized, there would be "excessive litigation," which could have "ripple effects." The Court explained that "newer and smaller companies may find it difficult to obtain advice from professionals. A professional may fear that a newer or smaller company may not survive and that business failure would generate securities litigation against the professional, among others. In addition, the increased costs incurred by professionals because of the litigation and settlement costs under 10b-5 may be passed on to their client companies, and in turn incurred by the company's investors, the intended beneficiaries of the statute."*

# POTENTIAL CRIMINAL LIABILITY

An accountant may be found criminally liable for violations of the Securities Act of 1933, the Securities Exchange Act of 1934, the Internal Revenue Code, and both state and federal criminal codes. Under both the 1933 act and the 1934 act, accountants may be subject to criminal penalties for *willful* violations—imprisonment of up to five years and/or a fine of up to $10,000 under the 1933 act and up to $100,000 under the 1934 act.

The Internal Revenue Code, Section 7206(2),[22] makes aiding or assisting in the preparation of a false tax return a felony punishable by a fine of $100,000 ($500,000 in the case of a corporation) and imprisonment for up to three years. Those who prepare tax returns for others also may face liability under the Internal Revenue Code. Note that one does not have to be an accountant to be subject to liability for tax-preparer penalties. The Internal Revenue Code defines a tax preparer as any person who prepares for compensation, or who employs one or more persons to prepare for compensation, all or a substantial portion of a tax return or a claim for a tax refund.[23]

Section 6694[24] of the Internal Revenue Code imposes on the tax preparer a penalty of $250 per return for negligent understatement of his or her client's tax liability and a penalty of $1,000 for willful understatement of tax liability or reckless or intentional disregard of rules or regulations. A tax preparer may also be subject to penalties under Section 6695[25] for failing to furnish the taxpayer with a copy of the return, failing to sign the return, or failing to furnish the appropriate tax identification numbers.

Section 6701[26] of the Internal Revenue Code imposes a penalty of $1,000 per document for aiding and abetting an individual's understatement of tax liability (the penalty is increased to $10,000 in corporate cases). The tax preparer's liability is limited to one penalty per taxpayer per tax year. If this penalty is imposed, no penalty can be imposed under Section 6694 with respect to the same document.

In most states, criminal penalties may be imposed for such actions as knowingly certifying false or fraudulent reports; falsifying, altering, or destroying books of account; and obtaining property or credit through the use of false financial statements.

# WORKING PAPERS

Performing an audit for a client involves an accumulation of **working papers**—the various documents used and developed during the audit. These include notes, computations, memoranda, copies, and other papers that make up the work product of an accountant's services to a client. Under the

---

22. 26 U.S.C. Section 7206(2).
23. 26 U.S.C. Section 7701(a)(36).
24. 26 U.S.C. Section 6694.

25. 26 U.S.C. Section 6695.
26. 26 U.S.C. Section 6701.

# ■ CONCEPT SUMMARY 55.1 Liability of Accountants and Other Professionals

| COMMON LAW LIABILITY | |
|---|---|
| **Liability to Client** | 1. *Breach of contract*—An accountant or other professional who fails to perform according to his or her contractual obligations can be held liable for breach of contract and resulting damages.<br>2. *Negligence*—An accountant or other professional, in performance of his or her duties, must use the care, knowledge, and judgment generally used by professionals in the same or similar circumstances. Failure to do so is negligence. An accountant's violation of generally accepted accounting principles and generally accepted auditing standards is *prima facie* evidence of negligence.<br>3. *Fraud*—Actual intent to misrepresent a material fact to a client, when the client relies on the misrepresentation, is fraud. Gross negligence in performance of duties is constructive fraud. |
| **Liability to Third Parties** | An accountant may be liable for negligence to any third person the accountant knows or should have known will benefit from the accountant's work. The standard for imposing this liability varies, but generally courts follow one of the following three rules:<br>1. *The* Ultramares *rule*—Liability will be imposed only if the accountant is in privity, or near privity, with the third party.<br>2. *The Restatement rule*—Liability will be imposed only if the third party's reliance is foreseen, or known, or if the third party is among a class of foreseeable, or known, users. The majority of courts adopt this rule.<br>3. *The "Reasonably foreseeable user" rule*—Liability will be imposed if the third party's use was reasonably foreseeable. |
| STATUTORY LIABILITY | |
| **Securities Act of 1933, Section 11** | An accountant who makes a false statement or omits a material fact in audited financial statements required for registration of securities under the law may be liable to anyone who acquires securities covered by the registration statement. The accountant's defense is basically the use of due diligence and the reasonable belief that the work was complete and correct. The burden of proof is on the accountant. Willful violations of this act may be subject to criminal penalties. |
| **Securities Act of 1933, Section 12(2)** | In some jurisdictions, an accountant may be liable for aiding and abetting the seller or offeror of securities when a prospectus or communication presented to an investor contained an untrue statement or omission of material fact. To be liable, the accountant must have known, or at least should have known, that an untrue statement or omission of material fact existed in the offer to sell the security. |
| **Securities Exchange Act of 1934, Sections 10(b) and 18** | Accountants are held liable for false and misleading applications, reports, and documents required under the act. The burden is on the plaintiff, and the accountant has numerous defenses, including good faith and lack of knowledge that what was submitted was false. Willful violations of this act may be subject to criminal penalties. |

■ CONCEPT SUMMARY 55.1 **Liability of Accountants and Other Professionals** *(continued)*

| STATUTORY LIABILITY | |
|---|---|
| **Internal Revenue Code** | 1. Aiding or assisting in the preparation of a false tax return is a felony. Aiding and abetting an individual's understatement of tax liability is a separate crime. |
| | 2. Tax preparers who negligently or willfully understate a client's tax liability or who recklessly or intentionally disregard Internal Revenue rules or regulations are subject to criminal penalties. |
| | 3. Tax preparers who fail to provide a taxpayer with a copy of the return, fail to sign the return, or fail to furnish the appropriate tax identification numbers may also be subject to criminal penalties. |

common law, which in this instance has been codified in a number of states, working papers remain the accountant's property. It is important for accountants to retain such records in the event that they need to defend against lawsuits for negligence or other actions in which their competence is challenged. But because an accountant's working papers reflect his or her client's financial situation, the client has a right of access to them. (An accountant must return to his or her client any of the client's records or journals upon the client's request, and failure to do so may result in liability.)

The client must give permission before working papers can be transferred to another accountant. Without the client's permission or a valid court order, the contents of working papers are not to be disclosed. Disclosure would constitute a breach of the accountant's fiduciary duty to the client. On grounds of unauthorized disclosure, the client could initiate a malpractice suit. The accountant's best defense would be that the client gave permission for the papers' release.

## SECTION 7

# CONFIDENTIALITY AND PRIVILEGE

Professionals are restrained by the ethical tenets of their professions to keep all communications with their clients confidential. The confidentiality of

attorney-client communications is also protected by law, which confers a *privilege* on such communications. This privilege is granted because of the need for full disclosure to the attorney of the facts of a client's case. To encourage frankness, confidential attorney-client communications relating to representation are normally held in strictest confidence and protected by law. The attorney and his or her employees may not discuss the client's case with anyone—even under court order—without the client's permission. The client holds the privilege, and only the client may waive it—by disclosing privileged information to someone outside the privilege, for example.

In a few states, accountant-client communications are privileged by state statute. In these states, accountant-client communications may not be revealed even in court or in court-sanctioned proceedings without the client's permission. The majority of states, however, abide by the common law, which provides that, if a court so orders, an accountant must disclose information about his or her client to the court. Physicians and other professionals may similarly be compelled to disclose in court information given to them in confidence by patients or clients.

Professional-client communications—other than those between an attorney and his or her client—are not privileged under federal law. In cases involving federal law, state-provided rights to confidentiality of accountant-client communications are not recognized. Thus, in those cases, in response to a court order, an accountant must provide the information sought.

## TERMS AND CONCEPTS TO REVIEW

defalcation 1096
due diligence 1104
generally accepted accounting
   principles (GAAP) 1096

generally accepted auditing
   standards (GAAS) 1096

malpractice 1097
working papers 1108

# QUESTIONS AND CASE PROBLEMS

**55–1.** *Ultramares* **Rule.** Larkin, Inc., retains Howard Perkins to manage its books and prepare its financial statements. Perkins, a certified public accountant, lives in Indiana and practices there. After twenty years, Perkins has become a bit bored with the format of generally accepted accounting principles and has become creative in his accounting methods. Now, though, Perkins has a problem, as he is being sued by Molly Tucker, one of Larkin's creditors. Tucker alleges that Perkins either knew or should have known that Larkin's financial statements would be distributed to various individuals. Furthermore, she asserts that these financial statements were negligently prepared and seriously inaccurate. What are the consequences of Perkins's failure to adopt generally accepted accounting principles? Under the traditional *Ultramares* rule, can Tucker recover damages from Perkins? Explain.

**55–2. Accountant's Liability to Third Parties and Public Policy.** The accounting firm of Goldman, Walters, Johnson & Co. prepared financial statements for Lucy's Fashions, Inc. After reviewing the various financial statements, Happydays State Bank agreed to loan Lucy's Fashions $35,000 for expansion. When Lucy's Fashions declared bankruptcy under Chapter 11 six months later, Happydays State Bank promptly filed an action against Goldman, Walters, Johnson & Co., alleging negligent preparation of financial statements. Assuming that the court has abandoned the *Ultramares* approach, what is the result? What are the policy reasons for holding accountants liable to third parties with whom they are not in privity?

**55–3. Accountant's Liability under Rule 10b-5.** In early 1995, Bennett, Inc., offered a substantial number of new common shares to the public. Harvey Helms had a long-standing interest in Bennett because his grandfather had once been president of the company. Upon receiving a prospectus prepared and distributed by Bennett, Helms was dismayed by the pessimism it embodied. Helms decided to delay purchasing stock in the company. Later, Helms asserted that the prospectus prepared by the accountants was overly pessimistic and contained materially misleading statements. Discuss fully how successful Helms would be in bringing a cause

of action under Rule 10b-5 against the accountants of Bennett, Inc.

**55–4. Auditor's Liability to Third Parties.** The plaintiffs, Harry and Barry Rosenblum, brought an action against Touche Ross & Co., a prominent accounting firm. The plaintiffs alleged that they had relied upon the correctness of audits in acquiring Giant common stock in conjunction with the sale of their business to Giant. The financial statements of Giant were found to be fraudulent, and the stock that the Rosenblums had acquired proved to be worthless. The plaintiffs alleged that Touche's negligence in conducting the audits was the proximate cause of their loss. Does an auditor owe a duty to third persons known and intended by the auditor to be recipients of the audit? Furthermore, does an independent auditor owe a duty to anyone when the opinion he or she furnishes does not include a statement limiting the dissemination of the information contained in the financial statements? Explain. [*H. Rosenblum, Inc. v. Adler,* 93 N.J. 324, 461 A.2d 138 (1983)]

**55–5. Auditor's Liability to Third Parties.** An accounting firm was engaged by two car rental companies to determine the net worth of those businesses by preparing an audited statement. At the request of their clients, the accountants did not audit the accounts receivable, made appropriate exceptions to the accounts receivable in the balance sheet, and qualified their opinion with a caveat stating that this had been done. After the audit had been performed and on the basis of the figures reflected in the balance sheet, Stephens Industries, Inc., purchased two-thirds of the car rental companies' stock. The car rental businesses thereafter failed, and Stephens Industries brought an action against the accounting firm for allegedly having misrepresented the status of the accounts receivable in the audit. What was the result? [*Stephens Industries, Inc. v. Haskins & Sells,* 438 F.2d 357 (10th Cir. 1971)]

**55–6. Accountant's Liability under Rule 10b-5.** The plaintiffs were the purchasers of all the stock in companies owned by the defendant sellers. Alleging fraud under the federal securities law and under the New York common law of fraud, the plaintiffs sued the defendant sellers and their accounting firm. What should be the result with respect to the accounting firm, assuming that the treatment of shipping costs, expenses, and other charges was not in accordance with generally accepted accounting principles and hence created an inaccurate financial picture in the financial statement? [*Berkowitz v. Baron,* 428 F.Supp. 1190 (S.D.N.Y. 1977)]

**55–7. Accountant's Liability to Third Parties.** Credit Alliance Corp. is a major financial service company engaged primarily in financing the purchase of capital equipment through installment sales and leasing agreements. As a condition of extending additional major financing to L. B. Smith, Credit Alliance required an audited financial statement. Smith provided Credit Alliance with an audited financial statement prepared by the accounting firm of Arthur Andersen & Co. Later, upon Smith's petitioning for bankruptcy, it was discovered that Smith, at the time of the audit, had been in a precarious financial position. Credit Alliance filed suit against Arthur Andersen, claiming that Andersen had failed to conduct investigations in accordance with proper auditing standards and that Andersen's recklessness had resulted in misleading statements that caused Credit Alliance to incur damages. In addition, it was claimed that Andersen knew, or should have known, that Credit Alliance would rely on these statements in issuing credit to Smith. Discuss whether Credit Alliance, as a third party, could hold Arthur Andersen liable in a negligence action. [*Credit Alliance Corp. v. Arthur Andersen & Co.,* 65 N.Y.2d 536, 483 N.E.2d 110, 493 N.Y.S.2d 435 (1985)]

**55–8. Accountant's Liability to Third Parties.** Toro Co. was a major supplier of equipment and credit to Summit Power Equipment Distributors. Toro required audited reports from Summit to evaluate the distributor's financial condition. Summit supplied Toro with reports prepared by Krouse, Kern & Co., an accounting firm. The reports allegedly contained mistakes and omissions regarding Summit's financial condition. According to Toro, it extended and renewed large amounts of credit to Summit in reliance on the audited reports. Summit was unable to repay these amounts, and Toro brought a negligence action against the accounting firm and the individual accountants. Evidence produced at the trial showed that Krouse knew that the reports it furnished to Summit were to be used by Summit to induce Toro to extend credit, but no evidence was produced to show either a contractual relationship between Krouse and Toro or a link between these companies evidencing Krouse's understanding of Toro's actual reliance on the reports. The relevant state law follows the *Ultramares* rule. What was the result? [*Toro Co. v. Krouse, Kern & Co.,* 827 F.2d 155 (7th Cir. 1987)]

**55–9. Accountant's Liability under Rule 10b-5.** The accounting firm of Arthur Young & Co. was employed by DMI Furniture, Inc., to conduct a review of an audit prepared by Brown, Kraft & Co., certified public accountants, for Gillespie Furniture Co. DMI planned to purchase Gillespie and wished to determine its net worth. Arthur Young, by letter, advised DMI that Brown, Kraft had performed a high-quality audit and that Gillespie's inventory on the audit dates was fairly stated on the general ledger. Allegedly as a result of these representations, DMI went forward with its purchase of Gillespie.

Subsequently, DMI charged Brown, Kraft & Co., Arthur Young, and Gillespie's former owners with violations of Section 10(b) of the Securities Exchange Act and SEC Rule 10b-5. DMI complained that Arthur Young's review had proved to be materially inaccurate and misleading, primarily because the inventory reflected in the balance sheet was grossly overstated. Arthur Young was charged "with acting recklessly in failing to detect, and thus failing to disclose, material omissions and reckless conduct on the part of Brown, Kraft, and in making affirmative misstatements in its letter" to DMI. Did DMI have a valid cause of action under either Section 10(b) or Rule 10b-5? Discuss. [*DMI Furniture, Inc. v. Brown, Kraft & Co.,* 644 F.Supp. 1517 (C.D.Cal. 1986)]

**55–10. Attorney's Duty of Care.** Sheila Simpson and the other two shareholders in H. P. Enterprises Corp. decided to sell the corporation and turned to Ed Oliver, an attorney, for assistance. Oliver formed a corporation, Tide Creek, for a group of investors, and Tide Creek then purchased the assets of Enterprises for $500,000, of which $100,000 was paid at the time of the sale in November 1983. As security for the sellers, Oliver provided a lien on the stock of Tide Creek and personal guaranties of the buyers on the corporation's $400,000 note to the sellers. Oliver was the sole source of legal advice for both parties. About six months after the sale, a fire destroyed Tide Creek's inventory. In October 1984, Oliver left the law firm in which he had been a partner, and one of the other partners, David James, took over the Simpson and Tide Creek accounts. In January 1985, James advised Simpson that Tide Creek was having financial difficulties and suggested that the note be restructured; this was done. When Simpson asked James what he would do if her interests and those of Tide Creek diverged, James replied, "We would have to support you." Tide Creek later filed for bankruptcy, as did the individuals who had personally guaranteed the note, and Simpson and the others received nothing. Will the sellers succeed in a lawsuit against James for negligence? Discuss fully. [*Simpson v. James,* 903 F.2d 372 (5th Cir. 1990)]

**55–11. Attorney-Client Privilege.** John and Christine Powell invested in a hotel-condominium development project. When legal problems with the project arose, the attorney representing the Powells was given access to certain documents and correspondence between the project developer, H. E. F. Partnership (HEF), and HEF's own legal counsel. When the project failed, the Powells sued HEF and others involved with the development scheme. In preparation for trial, the Powells sought discovery (see Chapter 4) of the documents and correspondence that HEF had released to them earlier. HEF refused to release the documents, alleging that they were confidential communications and protected under the attorney-client privilege. The Powells filed a motion with the court to compel discovery. How should the court rule on the motion to compel? Explain. [*Powell v. H.E.F. Partnership,* 835 F.Supp. 762 (D.Vt. 1993)]

# CHAPTER 56

# THE INTERNATIONAL LEGAL ENVIRONMENT

S ince ancient times, independent peoples and nations have traded their goods and wares with one another. In other words, international business transactions are not unique to the modern world, because people have always found that they can benefit from exchanging goods with others. What is new in our time is the emergence of an increasingly global business community. It is not uncommon, for example, for a U.S. corporation to have investments or manufacturing plants in a foreign country, or for a foreign corporation to have operations within the United States. Today, nearly every major business considers the potential of international markets for its products or services.

Because the exchange of goods, services, and ideas on a global level is now a common phenomenon, students of business law should be familiar with the laws pertaining to international business transactions. In this chapter, we examine the nature and sources of international law, some of the ways in which U.S. businesspersons commonly do business in or with foreign countries, and how those activities are regulated. The chapter goes on to discuss the application of U.S. antitrust, patent, and discrimination laws in a transnational setting, the settlement of disputes in the international context, and the bribing of foreign officials.

SECTION 1

## THE NATURE AND SOURCES OF INTERNATIONAL LAW

**International law,** which we discussed briefly in Chapter 1, was defined there as a body of written and unwritten laws observed by otherwise independent nations and governing the acts of individuals as well as states. The key difference between *national law* (the laws of specific nations—see Chapter 10) and international law is the fact that national law can be enforced by government authorities. But what government can enforce international law? By definition, a *nation* is a sovereign entity—which means that there is no higher authority to which that nation must submit. If a nation violates an international law, the most that other countries or international organizations can do (if persuasive tactics fail) is resort to coercive actions—from severance of diplomatic relations and boycotts to, at the last resort, war—against the violating nation.

In essence, international law is the result of centuries-old attempts to reconcile the traditional need of each nation to be the final authority over its own affairs with the desire of nations to benefit economically from trade and harmonious relations with one another. Sovereign nations can, and do, voluntarily agree to be governed in certain respects by international law for the purpose of facilitating international trade and commerce, as well as civilized discourse. As a result, a body of international law has evolved. In this section, we examine the primary sources and characteristics of that body of law.

## INTERNATIONAL CUSTOMS

One important source of international law consists of international customs that have evolved among nations in their relations with one another. Under Article 38(1) of the Statute of the International Court of Justice, an international custom is referred to as "evidence of a general practice accepted as law." The legal principles and doctrines discussed in Section 2 of this chapter are rooted in international customs and traditions that evolved over time in the international arena.

## TREATIES AND INTERNATIONAL AGREEMENTS

Treaties and other explicit agreements between or among foreign nations provide another important source of international law. A **treaty** is an agreement or contract between two or more nations that must be authorized and ratified by the supreme power of each nation. Under Article II, Section 2, of the U.S. Constitution, the president has the power "by and with the Advice and Consent of the Senate, to make Treaties, provided two-thirds of the Senators present concur."

A *bilateral* agreement, as the term implies, occurs when only two nations form an agreement that will govern their commercial exchanges or other relations with one another. *Multilateral* agreements are those formed by several nations. For example, regional trade associations such as the European Union (EU)—formerly called the European Community (EC)—or the North American Free Trade Agreement (NAFTA), both of which will be discussed later in this chapter, are the result of multilateral trade agreements. Other regional trade associations that have been created through multilateral agreements include the Association of Southeast Asian Nations (ASEAN) and the Andean Common Market (ANCOM).

## INTERNATIONAL ORGANIZATIONS AND CONFERENCES

International organizations and conferences further contribute to what is known as international law. In international law, the term **international organization** generally refers to an organization composed mainly of nations and usually established by treaty.

The United States is a member of more than one hundred multilateral and bilateral organizations, including at least twenty through the United Nations (see Exhibit 56–1). These organizations adopt resolutions, declarations, and other types of standards that often require a particular behavior of nations. The General Assembly of the United Nations, for example, has adopted numerous nonbinding resolutions and declarations that embody principles of international law. Disputes with respect to these resolutions and declarations may be brought before the International Court of Justice. That court, however, normally has jurisdiction to settle legal disputes only when nations voluntarily submit to its jurisdiction.

The United Nations Commission on International Trade Law has made considerable progress in establishing more uniformity in international law as it relates to trade and commerce. One of the commission's most significant creations to date is the 1980 Convention on Contracts for the International Sale of Goods (CISG). Recall from Chapters 20 through 25, which cover contracts for the sale of goods, that the CISG is similar to Article 2

■ **Exhibit 56–1 Multilateral International Organizations in Which the United States Participates**

| Name | Purpose |
|------|---------|
| Customs Cooperation Council | Established in 1950. Supervises the application and interpretation of an international code classifying goods and customs tariffs. |
| General Agreement on Tariffs and Trade (GATT); World Trade Organization (WTO) | Created in 1947, this was the first global commercial agreement in history and currently is the principal instrument for regulating international trade. Limits tariffs and other barriers to world trade on particular commodities and other items. |
| International Bank for Reconstruction and Development | Popularly known as the World Bank, a specialized agency of the United Nations since 1947. Promotes growth, trade, and balance of trade by facilitating investment and providing technical assistance, particularly in agriculture, energy, transportation, and telecommunications. |
| International Center for the Settlement of Investment Disputes | Established in 1966. Conciliates and arbitrates disputes between private investors and governments of other countries. |
| International Civil Aviation Organization | Established in 1947 and became a specialized agency of the United Nations seven months later. Develops international civil aviation by issuing rules and policies for safe and efficient airports and air navigation. |
| International Court of Justice (World Court) | Established in 1922 and became one of the principal organs of the United Nations in 1945. Jurisdiction comprises all cases that are referred to it. Decides disputes in accord with the rules of international law. |
| International Maritime Organization | Established in 1948. Promotes cooperation in the areas of government regulation, practices and technical matters of all kinds affecting shipping in international trade, the adoption of standards of maritime safety and efficiency, and the abolition of discrimination and unnecessary restrictions. |
| International Monetary Fund (IMF) | Created in 1944 at the United Nations Monetary and Financial Conference. Promotes economic stability by aiding the growth of international trade and the stability of currency exchange rates, as well as by providing for a system of international monetary assistance. |
| International Telecommunications Satellite Organization | Established in 1964. Operates an international public communications satellite system on a commercial, nondiscriminatory basis. |
| Permanent Court of Arbitration | Established in 1899 to facilitate the settlement of international disputes. The court has jurisdiction over all cases that it is requested to arbitrate. |
| United Nations (UN) | Established in 1945 to maintain international peace and security. Promotes international cooperation. |
| World Intellectual Property Organization | Established in 1967 and became a specialized agency of the United Nations in 1974. Promotes protection of intellectual property throughout the world. |

of the Uniform Commercial Code in that it is designed to settle disputes between parties to sales contracts. It spells out the duties of international buyers and sellers that will apply if the parties have not agreed otherwise in their contract. The CISG only governs sales contracts between trading partners in nations that have ratified the CISG, however, as discussed in Chapter 20.

# SECTION 2

# LEGAL PRINCIPLES AND DOCTRINES

Over time a number of legal principles and doctrines have evolved and have been employed—to a greater or lesser extent—by the courts of various nations to resolve or reduce conflicts that involve a foreign element. The three important legal principles discussed below are based primarily on courtesy and respect and are applied in the interests of maintaining harmonious relations among nations.

## THE PRINCIPLE OF COMITY

Under what is known as the principle of **comity,** one nation will defer and give effect to the laws and judicial decrees of another country, so long as those laws and judicial decrees are consistent with the law and public policy of the accommodating nation. This recognition is based primarily on courtesy and respect. For example, assume that a Swedish seller and an American buyer have formed a contract, which the buyer breaches. The seller sues the buyer in a Swedish court, which awards damages. But the buyer's assets are in the United States and cannot be reached unless the judgment is enforced by a U.S. court of law. In such a case, if a U.S. court determined that the procedures and laws applied in the Swedish court were consistent with U.S. national law and policy, the U.S. court would likely defer to, and enforce, the foreign court's judgment.

## THE ACT OF STATE DOCTRINE

The **act of state doctrine** is a judicially created doctrine that provides that the judicial branch of one country will not examine the validity of public acts committed by a recognized foreign government within its own territory. This doctrine is premised on the theory that the judicial branch should not "pass upon the validity of foreign acts when to do so would vex the harmony of our international relations with that foreign nation."[1]

The act of state doctrine can have important consequences for individuals and firms doing business with, and investing in, other countries. For example, this doctrine is frequently employed in cases involving **expropriation,** which occurs when a government seizes a privately owned business or privately owned goods for a proper public purpose and awards just compensation. When a government seizes private property for an illegal purpose and without just compensation, the taking is referred to as a **confiscation.** The line between these two forms of taking is sometimes blurred because of differing interpretations of what is illegal and what constitutes just compensation. To illustrate: Tim Flaherty, an American businessperson, owns a mine in Brazil. The government of Brazil seizes the mine for public use and claims that the profits Tim has realized from the mine in preceding years constitute just compensation. Tim disagrees, but the act of state doctrine may prevent Tim's recovery in a U.S. court of law.

When applicable, both the act of state doctrine and the doctrine of *sovereign immunity,* which we will discuss shortly, tend to immunize foreign nations from the jurisdiction of U.S. courts. What this means is that, generally, firms or individuals who own property overseas have little legal protection against government actions in the countries in which they operate.

The applicability of the act of state doctrine is at issue in the following case.

---

1. *Libra Bank Ltd. v. Banco Nacional de Costa Rica, S.A.,* 570 F.Supp. 870 (S.D.N.Y. 1983).

---

| CASE 56.1 |
| :---: |
| **W. S. KIRKPATRICK & CO. v. ENVIRONMENTAL TECTONICS CORP., INTERNATIONAL** |
| Supreme Court of the United States, 1990. |
| 493 U.S. 400, |
| 110 S.Ct. 701, |
| 107 L.Ed.2d 816. |

**BACKGROUND AND FACTS**  *W. S. Kirkpatrick & Company learned that the Republic of Nigeria was interested in contracting for the construction and equipment of a medical center in Nigeria. Kirkpatrick, with the aid of a Nigerian citizen, secured the contract as a result of bribing Nigerian officials. Nigerian law prohibits both the payment and receipt of bribes in connection with the awarding of government contracts, and the U.S. Foreign Corrupt Practices Act (FCPA) of 1977 expressly prohibits U.S. firms and their agents from bribing foreign officials to secure favorable contracts. Environmental Tectonics Corporation, International (ETC), an unsuccessful bidder for the contract, learned of the bribery and sued Kirkpatrick in a U.S. federal district court for damages. The district court granted summary judgment for Kirkpatrick because resolution of the case* *in favor of ETC would require imputing to foreign officials an unlawful motivation (the obtaining of bribes) and accordingly might embarrass the sovereign or interfere with the conduct of U.S. foreign policy. ETC appealed. The court of appeals reversed the judgment of the district court and remanded the case for trial. Kirkpatrick appealed to the United States Supreme Court.*

Justice *SCALIA* delivered the opinion of the Court.

\* \* \* \*

In every case in which we have held the act of state doctrine applicable, the relief sought or the defense interposed would have required a court in the United States to declare invalid the official act of a foreign sovereign performed within its own territory. \* \* \* In the present case, by contrast, neither the claim nor any asserted defense requires a determination that Nigeria's contract with Kirkpatrick International was, or was not, effective.

\* \* \* \*

The short of the matter is this: Courts in the United States have the power, and ordinarily the obligation, to decide cases and controversies properly presented to them. The act of state doctrine does not establish an exception for cases and controversies that may embarrass foreign governments, but merely requires that, in the process of deciding, the acts of foreign sovereigns taken within their own jurisdictions shall be deemed valid. That doctrine has no application to the present case because the validity of no foreign sovereign act is at issue.

*The Supreme Court affirmed the judgment of the court of appeals.*  **DECISION AND REMEDY**

## THE DOCTRINE OF SOVEREIGN IMMUNITY

When certain conditions are satisfied, the doctrine of **sovereign immunity** exempts foreign nations from the jurisdiction of the U.S. courts. In 1976, Congress codified this rule in the Foreign Sovereign Immunities Act (FSIA).[2] The FSIA also modified previous applications of the doctrine in certain respects by expanding the rights that plaintiff creditors have against foreign nations.

The FSIA exclusively governs the circumstances in which an action may be brought in the United States against a foreign nation. Section 1605 of the FSIA sets forth the major exceptions to the jurisdictional immunity of a foreign state. A foreign state is not immune from the jurisdiction of the courts of the United States when the state has "waived its immunity either explicitly or by implication" or when the state has engaged in actions that are taken "in connection with a commercial

activity carried on in the United States by the foreign state" that have "a direct effect in the United States."

Issues frequently arise as to what entities fall within the category of *foreign state*. The question of what is a *commercial activity* has also been the subject of dispute. Under Section 1603 of the FSIA, a *foreign state* is defined to include both a political subdivision of a foreign state and an instrumentality (an agency or entity acting for the state) of a foreign state. A *commercial activity* is broadly defined under Section 1603 to mean a commercial activity that is carried on by the foreign state having substantial contact with the United States. But the particulars of what constitutes a commercial activity are not defined in the act. Rather, it is left up to the courts to decide whether a particular activity is governmental or commercial in nature.

In the following case, a foreign government claimed immunity from the jurisdiction of U.S. courts on the basis of sovereign immunity. The issue turned on whether the actions of the foreign government were commercial activities.

---

2.   28 U.S.C. Sections 1602–1611.

CASE 56.2

**ECKERT INTERNATIONAL, INC. v. GOVERNMENT OF THE SOVEREIGN DEMOCRATIC REPUBLIC OF FIJI**

United States District Court, Eastern District of Virginia, 1993.
834 F.Supp. 167.

**BACKGROUND AND FACTS**  *In 1988, Eckert International, Inc., an American corporation, entered into a three-year contract with the government of the Sovereign Democratic Republic of Fiji (Fiji). The contract provided that Eckert would provide Fiji with government and public-relations consulting services in the Washington, D.C., area in return for an annual payment of $250,000. Both parties apparently performed their obligations satisfactorily for the three-year period. In 1991, the contract was renewed, without change, for an additional three years. The parties apparently performed their obligations satisfactorily for the first year of the 1991 contract. In 1992, however, Fiji's new prime minister terminated the contract and refused to pay Eckert for the two years remaining under the 1991 contract. Eckert sued Fiji for breach of contract, claiming that Fiji terminated the contract without cause or legal justification and therefore owed Eckert $500,000, the total remaining payments due under the 1991 agreement. Fiji moved to dismiss the claim, asserting, among other things, that it was immunized from the jurisdiction of U.S. courts by the Foreign Sovereign Immunities Act (FSIA).*

*ELLIS,* District Judge.
    \*   \*   \*   \*

    \*   \*   \* [The FSIA's] ''commercial activity'' exception operates here to preclude Fiji's [sovereign] immunity defense. This exception differentiates between a foreign state's public acts performed in its sovereign capacity and a foreign state's private acts performed as a market participant. Yet, the FSIA itself does not draw a sharply defined, bright line between a foreign state's public and private acts. Instead, the statute provides only a somewhat question begging definition of ''commercial activity'' as ''either a regular course of commercial conduct or a particular commercial transaction or act.'' Significantly, however, the Act goes on to mandate that the focus in drawing the distinction between public and private acts must be on the nature of the act performed rather than on its purpose. \*   \*   \*

    Measured by this standard, Fiji's act in entering into the 1991 contract was plainly a private act for the consulting contract is ''inherently commercial in nature'' and is governed by the rules of the marketplace. Fiji's argument that its contract was governmental, rather than commercial, in nature because Eckert represented Fiji in its ''political and diplomatic relationship'' with the United States is unpersuasive. This reasoning mistakenly focuses on the contract's purpose, while ignoring its essentially commercial nature. Indeed, the 1991 contract and its predecessor are simply garden variety consulting contracts, no different from myriad other consulting contracts between organizations and lobbyists. Foreign states entering into such contracts cannot be permitted to claim immunity from suit on such contracts merely by arguing that the contract had some governmental purpose. Were this Court to hold otherwise, foreign states would be free to enter into essentially commercial contracts with domestic entities and then, relying on sovereign immunity, abandon their obligation whenever it suited them to do so. \*   \*   \* The FSIA neither permits nor contemplates such a misuse of sovereign immunity. To the contrary, where, as here, a foreign state has entered into an essentially commercial contract for the performance of consulting services, it may not claim sovereign immunity under the FSIA.

**DECISION AND REMEDY**  *The court denied Fiji's motion to dismiss Eckert's claim.*

# DOING BUSINESS INTERNATIONALLY

A U.S. domestic firm can engage in international business transactions in a number of ways. Contracts for the international purchase and sale of goods were discussed earlier in this text, in Chapters 20 through 25. Here we look at other aspects of international business transactions, particularly at some of the ways in which business-persons extend their business operations into the international arena.

The simplest way of entering into international business operations is to seek out foreign markets for domestically produced products (or services). In other words, U.S. firms can **export** their goods and services to foreign markets. Alternatively, a U.S. firm can establish foreign production facilities so as to be closer to the foreign market or markets in which the firm's products are sold. The advantages may include lower labor costs, fewer government regulations, and lower taxes and trade barriers. It is also possible to obtain business from abroad by licensing technology that has been developed and is owned by the domestic firm to an existing foreign company. Finally, it is possible to expand abroad by selling franchises to overseas entities. The presence of McDonald's, Burger King, and KFC franchises throughout the world attests to the popularity of franchising.

## EXPORTING

The initial foray into international business by most U.S. companies is through exporting. Exporting can take two forms: direct exporting and indirect exporting. In *direct exporting,* a U.S. company signs a sales contract with a foreign purchaser that provides for the conditions of shipment and payment for the goods. (How payments are made in international transactions through the use of letters of credit was discussed in Chapter 22.) If business develops sufficiently in foreign countries, a U.S. corporation may develop a specialized marketing organization in the foreign market itself. Such *indirect exporting* can be undertaken by the appointment of a foreign agent or a foreign distributor.

**FOREIGN AGENT** When a U.S. firm desires a limited involvement in an international market, it will typically establish an *agency relationship* with a foreign firm. In an agency relationship, one person (the agent) agrees to act on behalf of, or instead of, another (the principal)—see Chapter 34. The foreign agent is thereby empowered to enter into contracts in the agent's country on behalf of the U.S. principal.

**FOREIGN DISTRIBUTOR** When a substantial market exists in a foreign country, a U.S. firm may wish to appoint a distributor located in that country. The U.S. firm and the distributor enter into a **distribution agreement,** which is a contract between the seller and the distributor setting out the terms and conditions of the distributorship—for example, price, currency of payment, guarantee of supply availability, and method of payment. The terms and conditions primarily involve contract law. Disputes concerning distribution agreements may involve jurisdictional or other issues. In addition, some **exclusive distributorships** have raised antitrust problems (see Chapter 48).

## MANUFACTURING ABROAD

An alternative to direct or indirect exporting is the establishment of foreign manufacturing facilities. Typically, U.S. firms want to establish manufacturing plants abroad if they believe that by doing so they will reduce costs—particularly for labor, shipping, and raw materials—and thereby be able to compete more effectively in foreign markets. Apple Computer, IBM, General Motors, and Ford are some of the many U.S. companies that have established manufacturing facilities abroad. Foreign firms have done the same in the United States. Sony, Nissan, and other Japanese manufacturers have established U.S. plants to avoid possible import duties that the U.S. Congress may impose on Japanese products entering this country.

There are several ways in which an American firm can manufacture in other countries. They include licensing and franchising, as well as investing in a wholly owned subsidiary or a joint venture.

**LICENSING** It is possible for U.S. firms to license their technologies to foreign manufacturers. **Technology licensing** may involve a process innovation that lowers the cost of production, or it may involve a product innovation that generates a superior product. Technology licensing may be an attractive alternative to establishing foreign production facilities, particularly if the process or product innovation has been patented, because the patent protects—at least to some extent—against the possibility that the innovation might be pirated. As with any licensing agreement, a licensing agreement with a foreign-based firm calls for a payment of royalties on some basis—such as so many cents per unit produced or a certain percentage of profits from units sold in a particular geographical territory.

In certain circumstances, even in the absence of a patent, a firm may be able to license the "know-how" associated with a particular manufacturing process—for example, a plant design or a secret formula. The foreign firm that agrees to sign the licensing agreement further agrees to keep the know-how confidential and to pay royalties. For example, the Coca-Cola Bottling Company licenses firms worldwide to use (and keep confidential) its secret formula for the syrup used in that soft drink, in return for a percentage of the income gained from the sale of Coca-Cola by those firms.

The licensing of technology benefits all parties to the transaction: those who receive the license can take advantage of an established reputation for quality, and the firms that grant the license receive income from the foreign sales of the firms' products, as well as establishing a worldwide reputation. Also, once a firm's trademark is known worldwide, the demand for other products manufactured or sold by that firm may increase—obviously an important consideration.

**FRANCHISING** Franchising is a well-known form of licensing. Recall from Chapter 38 that a franchise can be defined as an arrangement in which the owner of a trademark, trade name, or copyright (the franchisor) licenses another (the franchisee) to use the trademark, trade name, or copyright, under certain conditions or limitations, in the selling of goods or services in exchange. In return, the franchisee pays a fee, which is usually based on a percentage of gross or net sales. Examples of international franchises include McDonald's, the Coca-Cola Bottling Company, Holiday Inn, Avis, and Hertz.

**INVESTING IN A WHOLLY OWNED SUBSIDIARY OR A JOINT VENTURE** One way to expand into a foreign market is to establish a wholly owned subsidiary firm in a foreign country. The European subsidiary would likely take the form of the *société anonyme (S.A.),* which is similar to a U.S. corporation. In German-speaking nations, it would be called an *Aktiengesellschaft (A.G.).* When a wholly owned subsidiary is established, the parent company, which remains in the United States, retains complete ownership of all the facilities in the foreign country, as well as complete authority and control over all phases of the operation.

The expansion of a U.S. firm into international markets can also take the form of a joint venture. In a joint venture, the U.S. company owns only part of the operation; the rest is owned either by local owners in the foreign country or by another foreign entity. In a joint venture, responsibilities, as well as profits and liabilities, are shared by all of the firms involved in the venture. (See Chapter 38 for a more detailed discussion of joint ventures.)

---

**SECTION 4**

# REGULATION OF SPECIFIC BUSINESS ACTIVITIES

Doing business abroad can affect the economies, foreign policy, domestic politics, and other national interests of the countries involved. For this reason, nations impose laws to restrict or facilitate international business. Controls may also be imposed by international agreements.

## INVESTING

Investing in foreign nations involves a risk that the foreign government may expropriate the investment property. As mentioned earlier in this chapter, expropriation occurs when property is taken and the owner is paid just compensation for what is taken. This does not violate generally observed principles of international law. International law principles are normally violated, however, when property is confiscated by a government without compensation (or adequate compensation).

Few remedies are available for confiscation of property by a foreign government. Claims are often resolved by lump-sum settlements after negotiations between the United States and the taking nation. For example, investors whose claims arose out of confiscations following the Russian Revolution in 1917 were offered a lump-sum settlement by the Union of Soviet Socialist Republics in 1974. Still outstanding are $2 billion in claims against Cuba for confiscations that occurred in 1959 and 1960.

To counter the deterrent effect that the possibility of confiscation may have on potential investors, many countries guarantee compensation to foreign investors if property is taken. A guarantee can be in the form of national constitutional or statutory laws or provisions in international treaties. As further protection for foreign investments, some countries provide insurance for their citizens' investments abroad.

## EXPORT CONTROL

The U.S. Constitution provides in Article I, Section 9, that "No Tax or Duty shall be laid on Articles exported from any State." Thus, Congress cannot impose any export taxes. Congress can, however, use a variety of other devices to control exports. Congress may set export quotas on various items, such as grain being sold abroad. Under the Export Administration Act of 1979,[3] restrictions can be imposed on the flow of technologically advanced products and technical data.

Devices to stimulate exports and thereby aid domestic businesses include export incentives and subsidies. The Revenue Act of 1971, for example, gave tax benefits to firms marketing their products overseas through certain foreign sales corporations, exempting income produced by the exports.[4] Under the Export Trading Company Act of 1982,[5] U.S. banks are encouraged to invest in export trad-

ing companies. An export trading company consists of exporting firms joined to export a line of goods. The Export-Import Bank provides financial assistance, consisting primarily of credit guaranties given to commercial banks that in turn loan funds to U.S. exporting companies.

## IMPORT CONTROL

All nations have restrictions on imports, and the United States is no exception. Restrictions include strict prohibitions, quotas, and tariffs. Under the Trading with the Enemy Act of 1917,[6] for example, no goods may be imported from nations that have been designated enemies of the United States. Other laws prohibit the importation of illegal drugs, books that urge insurrection against the United States, and agricultural products that pose dangers to domestic crops or animals.

**Quotas** are limits on the amounts of goods that can be imported. At one time, the United States had legal quotas on the numbers of automobiles that could be imported from Japan. Currently, Japan "voluntarily" restricts the numbers of automobiles exported to the United States. **Tariffs** are taxes on imports. A tariff is usually a percentage of the value of the import, but it can be a flat rate per unit (such as on a barrel of oil). Tariffs raise the prices of goods, causing some consumers to purchase less expensive, domestically manufactured goods.

The United States has specific laws directed at what it sees as unfair international trade practices. **Dumping,** for example, is the sale of imported goods at "less than fair value." *Fair value* is usually determined by the price of those goods in the exporting country. Dumping is designed to undersell U.S. businesses to obtain a larger share of the U.S. market. To prevent this, an extra tariff—known as an *antidumping duty*—may be assessed on the imports.

The procedure for imposing antidumping duties involves two U.S. government agencies: the International Trade Commission (ITC) and the International Trade Administration (ITA). The ITC is an independent agency that makes recommen-

---

3. 50 U.S.C. App. Sections 2401–2420.
4. 26 U.S.C. Sections 991–994.
5. 15 U.S.C. Sections 4001, 4003.

6. 12 U.S.C. Section 95a.

dations to the president concerning temporary import restrictions. The ITC assesses the effects of dumping on domestic businesses. The ITA is part of the Department of Commerce and decides whether import sales were at less than fair value. The ITA determination establishes the amount of antidumping duties, which are set to equal the difference between the price charged in the United States and the price charged in the exporting country. A duty may be retroactive to cover past dumping.

## THE GENERAL AGREEMENT ON TARIFFS AND TRADE (GATT) AND WORLD TRADE ORGANIZATION

To minimize trade barriers among nations, most of the world's leading trade nations are signatories to the General Agreement on Tariffs and Trade (GATT). The GATT has become the principal instrument for regulating international trade. Originally negotiated in 1947, the GATT has gone through seven major tariff and trade renegotiations. Between 1964 and 1967, for example, forty-eight countries negotiated tariff reductions of 50 percent on a broad range of products. Between 1973 and 1979, one hundred countries negotiated nearly a dozen agreements relating to other trade barriers. An eighth round of negotiations (called the Uruguay Round) between 1986 and 1993 resulted in agreements relating to intellectual property rights, investment policies, dispute resolution, and other topics. The GATT became the World Trade Organization (WTO) in 1995.

Under Article I of the GATT, each member country agrees to grant **most-favored-nation status** to other member countries. This article obligates each GATT member to treat other GATT members at least as well as it treats that country that receives its most favorable treatment with regard to imports or exports. Excerpts from the GATT are presented in Appendix O at the end of this text.

## THE EUROPEAN UNION (EU)

Another way of minimizing trade barriers between nations is to form multilateral free trade agreements, or regional trade associations. Since the 1950s, European nations have been working toward a real common market by eliminating the financial, technical, and physical barriers that traditionally restrained trade between those nations. A united Europe began in 1951 with the establishment of the European Coal and Steel Community (ECSC), consisting of Belgium, West Germany, France, Italy, Luxembourg, and the Netherlands. In 1957, the European Atomic Energy Community (Euratom) was established, and in the same year, the Treaty of Rome created the European Economic Community (EEC). The Treaty of Rome outlined three goals: (1) to preserve European peace; (2) to establish a European common market—that is, a market in which goods, capital, and labor could move freely from one country to another; and (3) to form a politically unified Europe.

Originally, the ECSC, Euratom, and the EEC functioned separately. Under the Merger Treaty signed in 1965, however, the three entities agreed to have common institutions, and reference was typically made thereafter to the European Community, or EC. By 1968, most tariffs within the EC were eliminated, and in 1986, the EC countries ratified the Single European Act, which furthered the objective of attaining a unified European market. By 1995, the EC, which is now known as the European Union (EU), had become a single integrated European trading unit made up of fifteen European nations.

## THE NORTH AMERICAN FREE TRADE AGREEMENT (NAFTA)

The North American Free Trade Agreement (NAFTA), which was signed in 1993 and became effective on January 1, 1994, created a regional trading unit consisting of Mexico, the United States, and Canada. The primary goal of NAFTA is to eliminate tariffs among the United States, Mexico, and Canada on substantially all goods over a period of fifteen to twenty years. NAFTA gives the three countries a competitive advantage by retaining tariffs on goods imported from countries outside the NAFTA trading unit. Additionally, NAFTA provides for the elimination of barriers that traditionally have prevented the cross-border movement of services, such as financial or transportation services. For example, NAFTA provides that, with some exceptions, U.S. firms do not have to relocate in Mexico or Canada to provide services in those countries. NAFTA also attempts to eliminate citizenship requirements for the licensing of accountants, attorneys, physicians, and other professionals.

Over the last decade, countries competing for international trade have become more evenly matched competitors than in earlier years. In part, this is due to the increased use and success of regional international organizations such as the EU. In the eyes of many, NAFTA presents an opportunity for the United States to increase its global competitiveness and economic growth. Appendix P at the end of this text presents excerpts from the NAFTA.

SECTION 5

# U.S. LAWS IN A GLOBAL CONTEXT

The internationalization of business raises questions of the extraterritorial effect of a nation's laws—that is, the effect of a country's laws outside the country. To what extent do U.S. domestic laws affect the business activities of other nations? To what extent are U.S. businesses affected by the national laws of other countries when doing business abroad? The following sections discuss these questions in the context of U.S. antitrust, patent, and discrimination laws.

## U.S. ANTITRUST LAWS

U.S. antitrust laws, which were discussed in detail in Chapter 48, have a wide application. They may *subject* persons in foreign nations to their provisions as well as *protect* foreign consumers and competitors from violations committed by U.S. business firms. Consequently, *foreign persons,* a term that by definition includes foreign governments, may sue under U.S. antitrust laws in U.S. courts.

Section 1 of the Sherman Act of 1890[7] provides for the extraterritorial effect of the U.S. antitrust

laws. The United States is a major proponent of free competition in the global economy, and thus any conspiracy that has a substantial effect on U.S. commerce is within the reach of the Sherman Act. The violation may even occur outside the United States, and foreign governments as well as persons can be sued for violation of U.S. antitrust laws. Yet before U.S. courts will exercise jurisdiction and apply antitrust laws, it must be shown that the alleged violation had a *substantial effect* on U.S. commerce. U.S. jurisdiction is automatically invoked, however, when a *per se* violation occurs. As discussed in Chapter 48, certain types of restrictive contracts are deemed inherently anticompetitive and thus in restraint of trade as a matter of law. When such a restrictive contract is entered into, there is said to be a *per se* violation of the antitrust laws.

A *per se* violation may consist of price-fixing or tying (tie-in) contracts. If a domestic firm, for example, joins a foreign cartel to control the production, price, or distribution of goods, and this cartel has a *substantial restraining effect* on U.S. commerce, a *per se* violation may exist. Hence, both the domestic firm and the foreign cartel have the potential to be sued in violation of the U.S. antitrust laws. Likewise, if foreign firms doing business in the United States enter into a price-fixing or other anticompetitive agreement to control a portion of U.S. markets, a *per se* violation may exist.

In 1982, Congress amended the Sherman Act and the Federal Trade Commission Act of 1914[8] to limit their application when unfair methods of competition are involved in U.S. export trade or commerce with foreign nations. The acts are not limited, however, when there is a "direct, substantial, and reasonably foreseeable effect" on U.S. domestic commerce that results in a claim for damages.

An alleged conspiracy on the part of Japanese television manufacturers to gain control of the electronic products market in the United States—in violation of the Sherman Act and other antitrust and tariff legislation—was considered by the United States Supreme Court in the following case.

---

7.  15 U.S.C. Sections 1–7.

8.  15 U.S.C. Sections 41–51.

CASE 56.3

**MATSUSHITA ELECTRIC INDUSTRIAL CO. v. ZENITH RADIO CORP.**

Supreme Court of the
United States, 1986.
475 U.S. 574,
106 S.Ct. 1348,
89 L.Ed.2d 538.

**BACKGROUND AND FACTS**   *Zenith Radio Corporation and several other U.S. manufacturers of television sets alleged that Matsushita Electric Industrial Company and other Japanese firms "illegally conspired to drive American firms from the consumer electronic products market" by means of a "scheme to raise, fix and maintain artificially high prices for television receivers sold by [Matsushita and others] in Japan and, at the same time, to fix and maintain low prices for television receivers exported to and sold in the United States." The alleged conspiracy began, according to Zenith, in 1953. The American firms claimed that the Japanese were engaged in a "predatory pricing" arrangement whereby the losses sustained by selling at such low prices in the United States were offset by monopoly profits obtained in Japan. Once the Japanese gained control over an overwhelming portion of the American market for electronic products, their monopoly power would enable them to recover their losses by charging artificially high prices in the United States as well. The district court granted summary judgment in favor of the Japanese firms, and the case was appealed. The court of appeals reversed the judgment of the district court, and the case was appealed to the United States Supreme Court.*

Justice *POWELL* delivered the opinion of the Court.
*   *   *   *

*   *   * [R]espondents allege that a large number of firms have conspired over a period of many years to charge below-market prices in order to stifle competition. Such a conspiracy is incalculably more difficult to execute than an analogous plan undertaken by a single predator. The conspirators must allocate the losses to be sustained during the conspiracy's operation, and must also allocate any gains to be realized from its success. Precisely because success is speculative and depends on a willingness to endure losses for an indefinite period, each conspirator has a strong incentive to cheat, letting its partners suffer the losses necessary to destroy the competition while sharing in any gains if the conspiracy succeeds. *   *   * Yet if conspirators cheat to any substantial extent, the conspiracy must fail, because its success depends on depressing the market price for all buyers *   *   *.

[I]f predatory pricing conspiracies are generally unlikely to occur, they are especially so where, as here, the prospects of attaining monopoly power seem slight. *   *   * Two decades after their conspiracy is alleged to have commenced, petitioners appear to be far from achieving this goal: the two largest shares of the retail market in television sets are held by RCA and respondent Zenith, not by any of the petitioners. Moreover, those shares, which together approximate 40% of sales, did not decline appreciably during the 1970's. Petitioners' collective share rose rapidly during this period, from one-fifth or less of the relevant markets to close to 50%. Neither the District Court nor the Court of Appeals found, however, that petitioners' share presently allows them to charge monopoly prices; to the contrary, respondents contend that the conspiracy is ongoing—that petitioners are still artificially depressing the market price in order to drive Zenith out of the market. *   *   *

The alleged conspiracy's failure to achieve its ends in the two decades of its asserted operation is strong evidence that the conspiracy does not in fact exist.

**DECISION AND REMEDY**   *The United States Supreme Court reversed the decision of the court of appeals and remanded the case.*

## PATENT LAWS

In the United States, inventions are protected by patent law, which is intended to prevent others from copying an invention. U.S. patent laws provide no direct protection overseas, however. To be protected in another country, an invention must be patented under the laws of that country. Internationally, an agreement known as the Paris Convention[9] guarantees nondiscriminatory treatment under the laws of other nations, but it does not provide independent international patent protection.

## DISCRIMINATION LAWS

There are laws in the United States prohibiting discrimination on the basis of race, color, national origin, religion, sex, age, and disability. These laws, as they affect employment relationships (see Chapter 37), generally apply extraterritorially. Since 1984, for example, the Age Discrimination in Employment Act of 1967[10] has covered U.S. employees working abroad for U.S. employers. The Americans with Disabilities Act of 1990,[11] which requires employers to accommodate the needs of workers with disabilities, also applies to U.S. nationals working abroad for U.S. firms.

For some time, it was uncertain whether the major U.S. law regulating discriminatory practices in the workplace, Title VII of the Civil Rights Act of 1964, applied extraterritorially. Because the act did not specifically claim that it protected employees outside the boundaries of the United States, courts reached different conclusions. In 1991, the United States Supreme Court concluded that Title VII did not apply extraterritorially.[12] Later that same year, Congress passed the Civil Rights Act of 1991, which, among other things, provided that Title VII applied extraterritorially to all U.S. employees working for U.S. employers abroad.

U.S. discrimination laws, in regard to their extraterritorial application, generally stipulate that U.S. employers must abide by U.S. discrimination laws *unless* to do so would violate the laws of the countries in which their workplaces are located. This ''foreign laws exception'' allows employers to avoid being subjected to conflicting laws.

What happens if a Japanese firm doing business in the United States allegedly discriminates against U.S. employees in favor of Japanese citizens, which is permitted under a treaty between the United States and Japan? Is discrimination on the basis of citizenship the same thing as discrimination on the basis of national origin? These questions were addressed in the following case.

---

9. The agreement is known as the Paris Convention because on March 20, 1883, it was signed in Paris. See International Convention for the Protection of Industrial Property, 25 Stat. 1372, T.S. No. 379. A revision of the Paris Convention was signed in Stockholm on July 14, 1967. See International Convention for the Protection of Industrial Property, 21 U.S.T. 1629, T.I.A.S. No. 6923.

10. 29 U.S.C. Sections 621–634.

11. 42 U.S.C. Sections 12102–12118.

---

12. *. Equal Employment Opportunity Commission v. Arabian American Oil Co.,* 499 U.S. 244, 111 S.Ct. 1227, 113 L.Ed.2d 274 (1991).

---

**COMPANY PROFILE** *Motorola, Inc., manufactured automobile radios, police radios, and walkie-talkies before and during World War II. In the early years of television, Motorola marketed the first television sets priced under $200. By the 1970s, however, Motorola began losing its television-set market share to Japanese manufacturers, and in 1974, the company sold its Quasar television manufacturing facilities in Franklin Park, Illinois, to Matsushita Electric Industrial Company, which is based in Osaka, Japan. Matsushita made more than one million television sets in the Quasar plant in 1988, when it exported from Franklin Park to Japan a shipment of sets under the Panasonic label. The next year, Matsushita appointed an American, who had worked for Quasar before its sale by Motorola, to Matsushita's second highest executive position in North America.*

| CASE 56.4 |
| --- |
| **FORTINO v. QUASAR CO., A DIVISION OF MATSUSHITA ELECTRIC CORP. OF AMERICA** |
| United States Court of Appeals, Seventh Circuit, 1991. 950 F.2d 389. |

**BACKGROUND AND FACTS** *In 1953, the United States and Japan entered into a Treaty of Friendship, Commerce, and Navigation. The treaty provides, among other things, that Japanese companies doing business in the United States and U.S. companies doing business in Japan had, in either case, the right to choose citizens of their own nations as executives for their firms. Quasar Company, doing business in the United States as a subsidiary of the Japanese company Matsushita Electric Industrial Company, employed U.S. workers and management personnel but was largely controlled by executives of Matsushita. After suffering a $20 million loss in 1985, Matsushita executives restructured Quasar and cut its work force dramatically. Of eighty-nine managers working for the company, sixty-six were fired. None of the company's ten Japanese executives was laid off, and some of them received raises. John Fortino and two other American executives who had been fired (the plaintiffs) sued Quasar for, among other things, discriminating against them on the basis of national origin in violation of Title VII. Quasar defended by asserting that discrimination on the basis of citizenship, as allowed under the treaty, did not violate Title VII. The trial court held for the American executives, and Quasar appealed.*

POSNER, Circuit Judge.

&ast;  &ast;  &ast;  &ast;

&ast;  &ast;  &ast; [Title VII] protects Americans of non-Japanese origin from discrimination in favor of persons of Japanese origin. Title VII does not, however, forbid discrimination on grounds of citizenship. Of course, especially in the case of a homogeneous country like Japan, citizenship and national origin are highly correlated; almost all citizens of Japan were born there. &ast;  &ast;  &ast; By virtue of the treaty, "foreign businesses clearly have the right to choose citizens of their own nation as executives because they are such citizens." That right would be empty if the subsidiary could be punished for treating its citizen executives differently from American executives on the ground that, since the former were of Japanese national origin and the latter were not, it was discriminating on the basis of national origin. Title VII would be taking back from the Japanese with one hand what the treaty had given them with the other. This collision is avoided by holding national origin and citizenship separate.

**DECISION AND REMEDY** *The appellate court reversed the trial court's decision. The plaintiffs had no cause of action under Title VII.*

---

# RESOLVING INTERNATIONAL CONTRACT DISPUTES

Recall from Chapter 3 that the arbitration of civil disputes is becoming an increasingly attractive alternative to costly litigation through the court system. This is true on the international level as well. As already mentioned, arbitration clauses are frequently found in contracts governing the international sale of goods. By means of such clauses, the parties agree in advance to be bound by the decision of a specified third party in the event of a dispute.

The third party may be a neutral entity (such as the International Chamber of Commerce), a panel of individuals representing both parties' interests, or some other group or organization. The United Nations Convention on the Recognition and Enforcement of Foreign Arbitral Awards[13]—

---

13. June 10, 1958, 21 U.S.T. 2517, T.I.A.S. No. 6997 (the "New York Convention").

which has been implemented in more than fifty countries, including the United States—assists in the enforcement of arbitration clauses, as do provisions in specific treaties between nations. The American Arbitration Association, or AAA (discussed in Chapter 3) provides arbitration services for international as well as domestic disputes. In 1993, the AAA signed an agreement with the Miami International Arbitration and Mediation Institute, which provides for the arbitration of commercial cases in South Florida.

If no arbitration clause is contained in a sales contract, litigation may occur. If forum-selection and choice-of-law clauses (discussed in Chapter 20) are included in the contract, the lawsuit will be heard by a court in the forum country specified and decided according to that country's law. If no forum and choice of law have been specified, however, legal proceedings will be more complex and attended by much more uncertainty. For example, litigation may take place in two or more countries, with each country applying its own choice-of-law rules to determine which substantive law will be applied to the particular transactions. Furthermore, even if a plaintiff wins a favorable judgment in a lawsuit litigated in the plaintiff's country, there is no guaranty that the court's judgment will be enforced by judicial bodies in the defendant's country. As discussed earlier in this chapter, under the principle of comity, the judgment may be enforced in the defendant's country, particularly if the defendant's country is the United States and the foreign court's decision is consistent with U.S. national law and policy. Other nations, however, may not be as accommodating as the United States, and the plaintiff may be left empty handed.

## SECTION 7

# BRIBING FOREIGN OFFICIALS

In the 1970s, the U.S. press, and government officials as well, uncovered a number of business scandals involving large side payments by American corporations, such as Lockheed Aircraft, to foreign representatives for the purpose of securing advantageous international trade contracts. To pro-

hibit American firms from this unethical conduct, Congress passed the Foreign Corrupt Practices Act (FCPA)[14] in 1977.

The FCPA is divided into two major parts. The first part applies to all U.S. companies and their directors, officers, shareholders, employees, and agents. This part of the FCPA prohibits the bribery of most officials of foreign governments if the purpose of the payment is to get the official to act in his or her official capacity to provide business opportunities. The FCPA does not prohibit payment of substantial sums to minor officials whose duties are ministerial. These payments are often referred to as "grease," or facilitating payments. They are meant to ensure that administrative services that might otherwise be performed at a slow pace are sped up. Thus, for example, if a firm makes a payment to a minor official to speed up an import licensing process, the FCPA has not been violated. Generally, the act, as amended, permits payments to foreign officials if such payments are lawful within the foreign country. The act also does not prohibit payments to private foreign companies or other third parties unless the American firm knows that the payments will be passed on to a foreign government in violation of the FCPA.

The second part of the FCPA is directed toward accountants, because in the past, bribes were often concealed in corporate financial records. All companies must keep detailed records that "accurately and fairly" reflect the company's financial activities. In addition, all companies must have an accounting system that provides "reasonable assurance" that all transactions entered into by the company are accounted for and legal. These requirements assist in detecting illegal bribes. The FCPA further prohibits any person from making false statements to accountants or false entries in any record or account.

Business firms that violate the act may be fined up to $2 million. Individual officers or directors who violate the FCPA may be fined up to $100,000 (the fine cannot be paid by the company) and be imprisoned for up to five years.

---

14. 15 U.S.C. Sections 78m–78ff. The FCPA was amended by the Omnibus Trade and Competitiveness Act of 1988. These amendments modified some of the harsher provisions of the act so that U.S. firms could compete more effectively with foreign firms. 15 U.S.C. Sections 78m(b), 78dd-1, 78dd-2, 78ff.

## TERMS AND CONCEPTS TO REVIEW

act of state doctrine 1116
comity 1116
confiscation 1116
distribution agreement 1119
dumping 1121
exclusive distributorship 1119

export 1119
expropriation 1116
international law 1113
international
  organization 1114
most-favored-nation
  status 1122

quota 1121
sovereign immunity 1117
tariff 1121
technology licensing 1119
treaty 1114

## QUESTIONS AND CASE PROBLEMS

**56–1. Bribery of Foreign Officials.** Air Flight is a U.S. manufacturer of helicopters. Heise, vice president in charge of sales, wants to sell one hundred helicopters to North Zin, a foreign country. Secretary of Defense Zoro in North Zin has complete authority to purchase helicopters for his country. Zoro usually relies on evaluations made by his subordinates. Air Flight's main competition in the sale of these helicopters is from Top Flight, a European firm. The president of Top Flight has given Zoro his own personal helicopter and deposited $100,000 into Zoro's account. Heise immediately offers Zoro $200,000 in cash and, in addition, gives $10,000 to each of Zoro's subordinates to induce them to process Air Flight's evaluation before they process Top Flight's. ABC accountants, when auditing Air Flight's accounts, discover these payments that have been made to Zoro and his subordinates. Heise and Air Flight claim that without these payments, Air Flight cannot compete in foreign markets. Discuss whether these payments made by Air Flight are illegal.

**56–2. Sovereign Immunity.** Section 1610(d)(1) of the Foreign Sovereign Immunities Act (FSIA) provides that the property of a foreign state that is used for commercial activity in the United States is not immune from attachment prior to the entry of a judgment if the foreign state has "explicitly waived its immunity from attachment prior to judgment." Banco Nacional, an instrumentality of the government of Costa Rica, entered into a written agreement with Libra Bank, Ltd., the plaintiffs. In the agreement, Banco Nacional stated that it did not have "any right of immunity from suit with respect to the Borrower's obligations" under this particular agreement. Did Banco Nacional, the defendant, "explicitly" waive its immunity from prejudgment attachment, as required by the FSIA? [*Libra Bank, Ltd. v. Banco Nacional de Costa Rica, S.A.,* 676 F.2d 47 (2d Cir. 1982)]

**56–3. Antitrust Claims.** Both Mannington Mills, Inc., and Congoleum Corp. are American producers of carpets and other floor coverings. Mannington alleged that Congoleum had fraudulently obtained foreign patents

through false statements and misrepresentation of data. Mannington sued Congoleum, arguing that these actions violated U.S. antitrust laws. Congoleum argued that the U.S. courts had no jurisdiction. Congoleum contended that issuance of foreign patents came under the act of state doctrine or, at least, required deference to foreign nations. Should the United States exercise jurisdiction over this dispute? [*Mannington Mills, Inc. v. Congoleum Corp.,* 595 F.2d 1287 (3d Cir. 1979)]

**56–4. Dumping.** ICC Industries, Inc., was an importer of potassium permanganate from the People's Republic of China. The International Trade Administration (ITA) of the Department of Commerce conducted an anti-dumping investigation and concluded that this potassium permanganate was being imported at less than fair value, in violation of U.S. law. Fair value is an estimate of the value of the product in the home market—in this case, the People's Republic of China. As a consequence of its investigation of ICC, the ITA imposed retroactive antidumping duties on ICC's imports of potassium permanganate for the period 1981 to 1983. Imposition of these duties required a finding that ICC had known or should have known that the product was being imported at less than fair value. ICC argued that it was unaware of this fact. ICC emphasized that because the People's Republic of China had a nonmarket economy, the company was unable to ascertain a home market value for potassium permanganate. ICC therefore appealed the ITA's order to the Court of Appeals for the Federal Circuit. What will result? Discuss fully. [*ICC Industries, Inc. v. United States,* 812 F.2d 694 (Fed.Cir. 1987)]

**56–5. Jurisdictional Requirements.** Harris Corp., the plaintiff, entered into a contract with the defendant, National Iranian Radio and Television (NIRT), to manufacture and deliver 144 FM broadcast transmitters to Teheran, Iran. Due to the revolution in Iran, the plaintiff was unable to complete delivery of the transmitters. NIRT attempted to collect on a letter of credit that had been set up to guarantee performance. The plaintiff subsequently brought an action against the defendant, seeking to enjoin receipt of payment on the letter of credit. Bank Melli Iran, the issuer, was also made a defendant. Both defendants alleged that the district court lacked jurisdiction over them. From 1969 to 1982, Melli maintained an office in New York City, where it carried out significant business transactions. Moreover, this contract into which NIRT had entered required performance by Harris in the United States and also the training of NIRT personnel in the United States. Was this action consistent with due process? Was the "minimum contacts" standard established for foreign jurisdiction (discussed in Chapter 41) satisfied? [*Harris Corp. v. National Iranian Radio and Television,* 691 F.2d 1344 (11th Cir. 1982)]

**56–6. Sovereign Immunity.** Texas Trading & Milling Corp. and other companies brought an action for breach of contract against the Federal Republic of Nigeria and its central bank. Nigeria, a rapidly developing and oil-rich nation, had overbought huge quantities of cement from Texas Trading and others. Unable to accept delivery of the cement, Nigeria repudiated the contract, alleging immunity under the Foreign Sovereign Immunities Act of 1976. Because the buyer of the cement was the Nigerian government, does the doctrine of sovereign immunity remove the dispute from the jurisdiction of U.S. courts? [*Texas Trading & Milling Corp. v. Federal Republic of Nigeria,* 647 F.2d 300 (2d Cir. 1981)]

**56–7. Antitrust Claims.** Billy Lamb and Carmon Willis (the plaintiffs) are tobacco growers in Kentucky. Phillip Morris, Inc., and B.A.T. Industries, PLC, routinely purchase tobacco not only from Kentucky but also from producers in several foreign countries. In 1982, subsidiaries of Phillip Morris and B.A.T. (the defendants) entered into an agreement with *La Fundacion Del Nino* (the Children's Foundation) of Caracas, Venezuela. The president of the Children's Foundation was the wife of the president of Venezuela. The agreement provided that the two subsidiaries would donate a total of approximately $12.5 million to the Children's Foundation, and in exchange, the subsidiaries were to obtain price controls on Venezuelan tobacco, elimination of controls on retail cigarette prices in Venezuela, tax deductions for the donations, and assurances that existing tax rates applicable to tobacco companies would not be increased. The plaintiffs brought this action, alleging that the Venezuelan arrangement was an inducement designed to restrain trade in violation of U.S. antitrust laws. Such an arrangement, the plaintiffs contended, would result in the artificial depression of tobacco prices to the detriment of domestic tobacco growers, while ensuring lucrative retail prices for tobacco products sold abroad. The trial court held that the plaintiffs' claim was barred by the act of state doctrine. What will result on appeal? Discuss. [*Lamb v. Phillip Morris, Inc.,* 915 F.2d 1024 (6th Cir. 1990)]

**56–8. Sovereign Immunity.** As part of a plan to stabilize the Republic of Argentina's currency, that country and its central bank (collectively, Argentina) issued bonds that provided for repayment in U.S. dollars. Repayment would be made in several locations, including New York City. When the bonds began to mature, Argentina lacked sufficient funds to cover them, so it unilaterally extended the time for payment and offered bondholders substitute instruments as a means of rescheduling the debts. Weltover, Inc., of Panama, plus another Panamanian corporation and a Swiss bank (collectively, Weltover), declined to accept the rescheduling and insisted on repayment in New York. When Argentina refused, Weltover brought a breach-of-contract action in a U.S. district court. Argentina moved to dismiss the action, claiming immunity from the jurisdiction of the U.S. courts under the Foreign Sovereign Immunities Act. Weltover contended that Argentina's sale of the bonds fell under the "commercial activities" exception to sovereign immunity. What should the court decide? Discuss fully. [*Republic of Argentina v. Weltover, Inc.,* \_\_\_\_U.S.\_\_\_\_, 112 S.Ct. 2160, 119 L.Ed.2d 394 (1992)]

**56–9. Case Briefing Assignment**

 *Examine Case A.11* [Trans-Orient Marine Corp. v. Star Trading & Marine, Inc., *731 F.Supp. 619 (S.D.N.Y. 1990)]* in Appendix A. *The case has been excerpted there in great detail. Review and then brief the case, making sure that you include answers to the following questions in your brief.*

1. What specific circumstances led to this lawsuit?
2. What was the central international legal issue addressed by the court?
3. How did the court distinguish a "succession of state" from a "succession of government," and what was the effect of the distinction on executory contracts of the state?
4. To what "seminal decision" on this issue did the court refer? On what other cases did the court rely in its reasoning?

# FOCUS ON ETHICS

## Special Topics

**U** nique situations present special ethical problems. In this final *Focus on Ethics,* we consider some of the ethical dimensions of the special legal topics discussed within the chapters of this unit.

### Insurance and Moral Hazard

A number of ethical issues arise in the area of insurance. One of the major ethical concerns involves *moral hazard.* In the insurance industry, moral hazard occurs when individuals or companies have an incentive to act negligently or to engage in activities that will result in payment by an insurance company. For example, the businessperson who takes out a large insurance policy on a building has less incentive to make sure that the building is protected from fire than an individual without an insurance policy. What is the ethical responsibility of the owner of the building when insurance is in effect? Is he or she exempt from taking precautions against a fire?

The same issue arises for insurance policies that cover losses due to theft. The smaller the deductible in such policies, the less incentive the property owner has to prevent loss due to theft. With insurance in effect, for example, the property owner may have less incentive to install alarm systems, to pay for private patrol service, and so on. Of course, the more claims made on such insurance policies, the higher the average insurance rate per dollar amount insured. Thus, those individuals who are careless about protecting their own property impose costs on *all* individuals who buy property insurance.

### Ethics and Insurance Claims

Issues of fairness often arise when insurance companies attempt to avoid payment on policies. In one case, for example, the plaintiff, Cleopatra Haslip, had a medical policy with the Pacific Mutual Life Insurance Company. The company refused to pay a medical bill of $3,800, arguing that the company had no record of the policy because a dishonest insurance agent had pocketed the premiums. Certainly, from an ethical point of view, there is little question that Pacific Mutual had a duty to pay the medical bill. In this case, the attempt to avoid payment on the policy turned out to be a bad decision on Pacific Mutual's part.

Ultimately, the case reached the courts, and an Alabama jury awarded Haslip $1.04 million, including $840,000 in punitive damages—more than 200 times the plaintiff's out-of-pocket expenses. The United States Supreme Court upheld the trial court's decision.[1] Many plaintiffs who sue their insurers for payment meet with less success, however. Mistakes on applications for insurance have often allowed insurers to avoid payment on the policies even though the mistakes were unintentionally made.

Ethical issues also surface when insurance companies are forced to pay on policies because of technical errors on the part of the insurer. If an insurance company fails to comply with the letter of the law as spelled out in applicable insurance statutes, the insurer may have to pay on a policy even though it may seem unfair to do so. For example, if a policyholder ceases to make the premium payments, the insurer must follow specific notice requirements when canceling the coverage. If it does not, the insured may argue successfully that the insurance coverage is still in force,

---

1. *Pacific Mutual Life Insurance Co. v. Haslip,* 499 U.S. 1, 111 S.Ct. 1032, 113 L.Ed.2d 1 (1991).

despite the fact that the insured has not made the required payments on the policy.[2]

## Gender-based Insurance Rates

Insurance companies traditionally have charged men and women different rates for the same insurance coverage. Women have normally paid lower rates for life insurance than men have because statistically, women have longer life spans than men. Similarly, women have traditionally paid lower automobile insurance rates because they have fewer accidents than men. Gender-based insurance rates have long been endorsed by the insurance industry, as well as by the state laws that regulate the industry.

Over the last decade, however, gender-based insurance rates have been attacked as being discriminatory. Many believe—and many courts have held—that discriminatory insurance rates violate state and federal civil rights laws or constitutional clauses providing for equal protection. One state, Montana, mandated similar rates for men and women in 1985. Maryland nearly became the second state to bar insurers from basing rates on gender when the state insurance commissioner ordered that gender-based insurance rates violated the state's Equal Rights Amendment (ERA). In 1993,

however, a Maryland state court struck down the commissioner's order, finding that the insurance rates fell under an exception to the state's ERA.[3]

Insurance companies contend that gender-based rates are based on sound actuarial data. In other words, gender-based rates make economic sense. Women's rights groups and others, however, argue that insurers are already prohibited from charging differential rates based on racial criteria even though actuarial tables show that whites tend to outlive blacks. Why, then, should differential rates be applied to women and men? Which is the more equitable view continues to be debated.

## Inheritance Laws and Illegitimacy

In the ancient world, illegitimacy was often dealt with expeditiously by destroying the mother of the future illegitimate child. In biblical days, a woman who had committed adultery was stoned to death—unless, as in the case of David and Bathsheba, a marriage could be arranged. In Bathsheba's case, David saved her life at

the expense of her husband, Uriah, whom David arranged to have killed in battle so he could then marry Bathsheba. Under Islamic law, stoning was also the proper punishment for adultery. In the Christian world, illegitimate children and their mothers were always allowed to live, even though they were usually regarded as outcasts and pariahs until fairly recently.

At common law, the illegitimate child was regarded as a *filius nullius* (Latin for "child of no one" ) and had no right to inherit. Today, statutes vary from state to state in regard to the inheritance laws governing illegitimate offspring. Generally, an illegitimate child is treated as the child of the mother and can inherit from her and her relatives. The child is usually not regarded as the legal child of the father unless paternity is established through some legal proceeding. Many state statutes permit the illegitimate child to inherit from the father if paternity has been established prior to the father's death.

A landmark case in establishing the rights of illegitimate children was decided by the United States Supreme Court in 1977. In *Trimble v. Gordon,*[4] an illegitimate child sought to inherit property from her deceased natural father on the grounds that an Illinois statute prohibiting inheritance by illegitimate children in the absence of a will was unconstitutional. The child was Deta Mona Trimble, daughter

---

2. See, for example, *Clyburn v. Allstate Insurance Co.,* 826 F.Supp. 955 (D.S.C. 1993). This case was presented in Chapter 53 as Case 53.3.

---

3. The insurance commissioner's ruling and the appeal of that ruling were in conjunction with a case that began in 1978, when the Maryland Commission on Human Relations sued the Equitable Life Assurance Society. As of 1994, the case is pending in Maryland's Court of Special Appeals. See *Insurance Commissioner v. Equitable Life Assurance Society,* 330 Md. 458, 624 A.2d 954 (1993).

---

4. 430 U.S. 762, 97 S.Ct. 1459, 52 L.Ed.2d 31 (1977).

of Jessie Trimble and Sherman Gordon. The paternity of the father had been established before a Cook County, Illinois, circuit court in 1973. Gordon died intestate in 1974. The mother filed a petition on behalf of the child in the probate division of the county circuit court, which was denied by the court on the basis of an Illinois law disallowing the child's inheritance because she was illegitimate. Had she been legitimate, she would have been her father's sole heir. The Illinois Supreme Court in 1975 affirmed the petition's dismissal.

When the case came before the United States Supreme Court in 1977, the Court acknowledged that the "judicial task here is the difficult one of vindicating constitutional rights without interfering unduly with the State's primary responsibility in this area. . . . and the need for the States to draw 'arbitrary lines . . . to facilitate potentially difficult problems of proof.' " The Court found it hard to perceive any justification for the Illinois statute, nor for the lower court's insistence that the father could have avoided the problem had he just made a will.

In reversing the Illinois Supreme Court decision, the high court stated that the section of the Illinois Probate Act that forbade Deta Mona to inherit her father's property "cannot be squared with the command of the equal protection clause of the Fourteenth Amendment." Even though the Illinois statute rested to some extent on public policy supporting the family unit, the United States Supreme Court "expressly considered and rejected the argument that a State may attempt to influence the actions of men and women by imposing sanctions on the children born of their illegitimate relationships."

## Ethics and International Law

Differences in the laws and customs of the various nations of the globe present unique types of ethical issues for firms engaged in international business transactions. Some of these issues were discussed in Chapter 10. Here we look at a few other problems, focusing particularly on some ethical issues relating to international doctrines and to U.S. laws as they apply to international transactions.

### Sovereign Immunity

Sometimes, the application of the doctrine of sovereign immunity may lead to seemingly inequitable results. The economy of the United States is primarily controlled by private interests, whereas the economy of many foreign countries, particularly developing nations, is often extensively controlled by government. When a U.S. firm does business with a foreign firm in a developing country, therefore, the chances are that the U.S. firm will work closely with foreign government officials. Should a dispute arise between the parties, the question then becomes whether the U.S. firm may bring a lawsuit against the foreign firm. If the foreign defendant raises the defense of sovereign immunity, alleging that it is a government-controlled operation, then it may be immune from liability. The ethical issue in these situations is whether it is fair that U.S. firms be left without any legal recourse when they suffer damages as a result of actions controlled by foreign governments.

Consider, for example, the situation that arose in *Antares Aircraft, L.P. v. Federal Republic of Nigeria.*[5] In that case, Antares Aircraft, a New York limited partnership, had one asset—a DC-8–55 aircraft registered in Nigeria. Antares was required by the Nigerian government to leave the plane at the airport in Lagos, Nigeria, until certain fees (which had been incurred by a previous owner of the plane) were paid. Antares paid the $100,000 in fees, but the Nigerian government did not release the plane until five months later. In the meantime, the plane had been damaged by exposure to the elements. Antares filed suit against the Nigerian government for the tort of conversion, alleging that the Nigerian government had wrongfully detained the plane.

Antares argued that the Nigerian government's actions fell within the commercial-activity exception to the Foreign Sovereign Immunities Act (FSIA), and therefore the Nigerian government was not immune from the jurisdiction of U.S. courts. Although the court agreed with Antares that the fees collected by the Nigerian government were in connection with a commercial activity, it found that the

_____

5. 999 F.2d 33 (2d Cir. 1993).

activity did not have a "direct effect" in the United States—which must occur before the commercial-activity exception to the FSIA can apply. The court therefore held that the Nigerian government was immune from liability. The court stated that "the detention of Antares' sole asset affected the financial well-being of the American partnership. However, the fact that an American individual or firm suffers some financial loss from a foreign tort cannot, standing alone, suffice to trigger the [commercial-activity] exception."

Because the FSIA does not define exactly what types of activities on the part of a foreign government will fall under the commercial-activity exception, the courts exercise considerable discretion in deciding such issues. Although the majority on the court hearing the *Antares* case concluded that the loss suffered by Antares was not sufficiently significant to constitute a "direct effect in the United States," other courts might conclude differently. Certainly, the dissenting judge in *Antares* believed that the detention of the plane did constitute a direct effect in the United States. The partners lived in the United States and lost money because of a foreign government's interference with their property. The dissent concluded that the partnership's loss should be sufficient to establish an exception to immunity under the FSIA.

### The Foreign Corrupt Practices Act

Since its passage by Congress in 1977, the Foreign Corrupt Practices Act (FCPA) has been the target of substantial criticism. Many U.S. firms have criticized this act because it places them at a competitive disadvantage relative to foreign firms.

For example, assume that your company wants to do business with a foreign firm. A foreign official promises your company the contract, but only if you agree to "contribute," say, $500,000 to the official's bank account in another country. You say no to the deal because you know that the FCPA prohibits you from making such a "bribe." If you agreed to the deal, you could face criminal penalities, including up to five years in prison. A company from another nation, which has been competing for the contract, faces no such prohibition, however. That company agrees to pay the $500,000 and gets the contract.

For several years, the United States has been encouraging other nations to pass similar antibribery laws but as yet has met with little success. Many countries' governments echo the same criticisms as those voiced by U.S. businesspersons: laws prohibiting the bribery of foreign officials would put their countries at a competitive disadvantage relative to nations that do not adopt such laws.

Even assuming that all nations had laws similar to the FCPA, a further issue remains: How do you prove that a bribe has been tendered (or a side payment requested)? Recall from Chapter 9 that the crime of bribery occurs when a bribe is offered—the bribe does not have to be accepted for the crime to have occurred. When someone refuses a bribe, sometimes the only proof that the bribe was offered is the word of the person who refused the bribe. What would prevent a foreign government from retaliating when a U.S. firm's representative accuses a foreign official of requesting a bribe but cannot otherwise prove that the bribery occurred?

### U.S. Laws in an International Context

When doing business in a foreign country, a U.S. firm must abide by both U.S. laws and the foreign government's laws. The "foreign laws exception" to many U.S. discrimination laws, however, excuses domestic employers from liability if adherence to the U.S. laws would violate the law of the host country. Sometimes, though, U.S. employers abroad may encounter difficulty when their understanding of a foreign nation's law differs from a U.S. court's interpretation.

This kind of situation faced RFE/RL, Inc. (better known as Radio Free Europe and Radio Liberty)—a U.S. employer that had over three hundred U.S. citizens working at its principal place of business in Munich, Germany—when RFE/RL was charged with violating U.S. laws prohibiting age discrimination in employment. The concept of a mandatory retirement age is deeply embedded in German labor policy. Unlike U.S. laws, German laws do not prohibit this form of age discrimination.

German labor union contracts frequently require workers to retire at the age of sixty-five under mandatory retirement clauses.

RFE/RL and a German labor union bargained for, and agreed to, a mandatory retirement clause in 1982. In 1984, the U.S. Age Discrimination in Employment Act (ADEA) of 1967 was amended to apply extraterritorially. RFE/RL tried to accommodate the new U.S. law by signing individual employment contracts that allowed certain employees to continue working past the age of sixty-five. The company's "works council"—which is bound by German law to give effect to a union contract—rejected the individual contracts because they violated the mandatory retirement provision in the union contract. RFE/RL appealed to the German labor courts with no success; those courts held that the union contract did not permit a retirement age higher than sixty-five. When William Mahoney (and other American employees) reached the age of sixty-five, RFE/RL assumed that it had a legal obligation to terminate their employment, and it did so. As a result, Mahoney sued RFE/RL for age discrimination in violation of the ADEA, which prohibits mandatory retirement at the age of sixty-five.

In 1992, a U.S. federal court held that in spite of the German union contract's provisions and the German labor courts' decision, German law did not compel RFE/RL to fire Mahoney. According to the U.S. court, the decisions made by the German labor courts "involved a narrower issue than that addressed here. Those decisions simply held that the union contract did not permit a retirement age higher than 65; they merely enforced the contract upon the parties to it. . . . They did not hold that anything in German law compelled the decisions reached." The foreign laws exception only applied to laws enacted by the foreign government; it did not apply to RFE/RL's mandatory retirement of Mahoney, which was held to have been illegal.

Was it fair to ask RFE/RL to choose between breaching the foreign labor contract under the foreign country's practices and violating U.S. discrimination law? Assuming that RFE/RL acted in good faith in discharging Mahoney, one cannot but sympathize with RFE/RL and any other employer facing the challenge of trying to obey two masters, or sets of laws, at the same time.[6]

## ■ Discussion Questions

**1.** Suppose an applicant for insurance unknowingly makes a false statement concerning a material fact on the application form. Should an insurer have any responsibility to pay out on the subsequently issued insurance?

**2.** The Foreign Corrupt Practices Act was passed in an attempt to ensure more ethical conduct on the part of U.S. businesspersons doing business abroad. Do you think that the act is fair to U.S. firms in view of the fact that other countries do not have similar laws? The act permits so-called grease payments to minor government officials to expedite such things as paperwork. Do such payments amount to bribes? Should the act prohibit these kinds of payments as well?

**3.** The United States banned the pesticide DDT, primarily because of its adverse effects on wildlife. In Asia, however, DDT has been a critical component of the mosquito control necessary to combat malaria. Should the ban in the United States prevent U.S. firms from manufacturing DDT and shipping it to an Asian country, where it could be used to save lives? Should the U.S. chemical manufacturer be required to produce the DDT in the same country that uses the chemical?

---

6. In 1993, the Equal Employment Opportunity Commission issued guidelines on the extraterritorial application of Title VII of the Civil Rights Act of 1964 and the Americans with Disabilities Act of 1990. The guidelines adopt the *Mahoney* court's restrictive interpretation of what is a "law" for purposes of the foreign laws exception.

# PERSONAL LAW HANDBOOK

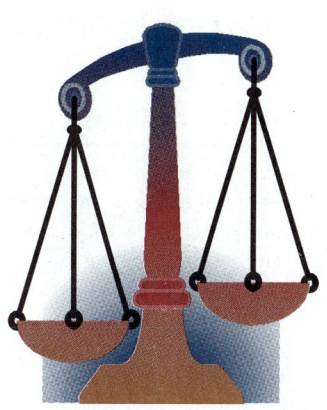

## Contents

Note to Student

**TOPIC 1  RENTING A HOME**
Leases
Eviction
Substandard Housing
Rent
Security Deposits
Liability for Injuries
Lockouts

**TOPIC 2  FAMILY LAW**
Getting Married
Financial Aspects of Marriage
Children
Wills and Estates
Homosexual Families

**TOPIC 3  CONSUMER LAW**
The Consumer Contract
Warranties
Product Liability
Deceptive Sales Practices
Consumer Credit
Small Claims Court

**TOPIC 4  EMPLOYMENT LAW**
The Civil Rights Act

Other Discrimination Laws
Sexual Harassment
Wrongful Discharge
Employee Privacy
Other Employee Protection Laws

**TOPIC 5  OWNING AND OPERATING
MOTOR VEHICLES**
Buying a New Car
Buying or Selling a Used Car
Renting or Leasing a Car
Insuring a Car
Repairing a Car
Driving Violations
Driving Accidents

**TOPIC 6  CRIMINAL LAW**
The Nature of Crimes
Arrest and Prosecution
Pretrial Procedures
Trial and Defenses
Sentencing
Juvenile Justice

**TOPIC 7  JURY DUTY**
Jury Venire and Selection
Trial
Jurors' Rights

# Note to Student

Business law and the legal environment do not just consist of theoretical concepts and vague statutes. Rather, you will find that you can use what you have learned from your course in many practical ways throughout your life. In this *Personal Law Handbook* you will discover suggestions for preventing costly legal problems, as well as ideas about how to handle those legal problems that you have not been able to avoid. To a large extent, personal law is preventive—the more you know about the legal consequences of your actions and the actions of those with whom you have dealings, the better you will be able to prevent legal problems.

In no way should you take this *Handbook* to be a substitute for licensed, professional legal assistance. Whenever you think that you have a legal problem, you should consult an attorney.

## TOPIC 1

# RENTING A HOME

Like millions of Americans, you may decide not to own your own home. Instead, you may choose to rent a house, an apartment, a mobile home, or some other form of housing. As a tenant, your relationship with your landlord is *generally governed by the law of the state in which you live.*

## Leases

The **lease** is the agreement between you and your landlord that sets out rights and duties regarding the rental property. A written lease is a legal document enforceable in court—a signature on a lease is generally proof that the person who signed it read it and agreed to it. Thus, if you sign a lease, you are bound to do what it says. For this reason, you should read an entire lease carefully before you sign it.

Most leases are written to favor the landlord's interests. If you are unsure of the meaning or effect of any of the terms, before signing the lease you should seek the advice of a lawyer, a tenants' rights organization, a legal aid office, or others experienced with leases.

### ORAL LEASES

In almost all states, an oral lease for a period of less than a year is valid and enforceable. The basic problem with an oral lease is the same as the basic problem with other oral contracts: it is difficult to prove the terms of the oral agreement. Generally, it is assumed an oral lease that requires rent to be paid monthly creates a **month-to-month tenancy.** This means that, with a month's written notice, a landlord can raise the rent or end the tenancy. Of course, you can also end the tenancy with a month's written notice. (The notice must be given a month before the rent is due. Sometimes, a local statute provides that the notice period is thirty days. In that case, the notice must be given thirty days before the rent is due.)

## LEASE TERMS

Leases include such terms as the following items:

1. The names of the parties to the agreement.
2. The address of the rental property.
3. The amount and the due date of the rent.
4. Other fees and charges.
5. The period of time for which the property is rented.
6. The rights and duties of the parties, which relate to use of the premises, alterations, maintenance, repairs, and other areas of responsibility.
7. The amount of a security deposit.
8. The conditions under which the rent can be raised.
9. Provisions for subleasing the property and terminating the lease.

**ALTERATIONS**   Can you make changes to rental property after you move in? In most circumstances, the answer depends on the terms of the lease. Most leases include a provision that prohibits alterations without the landlord's written approval. If you do not get the landlord's approval before making alterations, you will violate the lease and may be liable for any presumed destruction of the property. If there is no lease provision concerning alterations, you can make changes to the property that do not reduce the value of the property to the landlord.

If no lease provision applies and you have made a change—for example—if you have added bookshelves or installed new cabinets, who owns the new addition? If you cannot come to an agreement with your landlord, and you ask a court to decide the question, the court will look at the laws of your state to determine who owns what. In some states, the addition may be the property of the landlord; in other states, it may be yours, and you can sell it to the landlord or remove it. If it is your property and you choose to remove it, you should do so carefully to avoid any damage to the rental property. If the property is damaged, you are responsible.

**SUBLEASES**   Normally, a lease contains a provision that prohibits a tenant from **subleasing** the rental property without the landlord's written approval. If the lease does not require the landlord's approval, in most cases you can sublease for whatever period of time you could remain on the property under the lease. A sublease cannot be for a longer period than you could stay on the property. For instance, if you signed a one-year lease that contains no provision regarding subleasing and there are six months left before the lease expires, you could sublease the property for six months or less. *As the original tenant, however, you are still liable for the rent and any damage to the property.*

Whether or not your lease prohibits subleasing, can you move out before the lease expires? Generally, the answer is yes. You will be liable for the rent for the rest of the lease, however. There may be a limit on how much you pay: in some states, a landlord must make a reasonable effort to find a new tenant for the same amount of rent and the same period of time. If the property can be rented only for a smaller amount of money or a shorter time, you will be liable for the difference.

To minimize your losses, as soon as you know you will be moving out, send the landlord written notice (via certified or registered mail) of your plan to allow as much time as possible to find a new tenant. Keep a copy of the notice. You might also help find a new tenant by advertising that the property will be available.

**RENEWAL**  Typically, a lease requires that you move out when it expires. A lease can provide, however, that it renews automatically unless you tell the landlord in advance that you plan to move out. If you do not give the landlord this notice, you will be renewing the lease on the same terms for the same period of time. A different lease might provide that if you stay on the property after the lease expires and the landlord accepts a payment of rent, the lease renews according to the original terms.

If the lease does not mention renewal, in some states the landlord does not need to give you notice that the lease is ending. In these states, the reasoning is that you know when the lease expires because you signed it, and thus you must leave the property when the lease ends without additional notice. In other states, if you remain on the property after the lease ends and the landlord accepts a payment of rent, a new month-to-month tenancy is created or, in some states, the lease renews according to its original terms.

**OTHER RIGHTS**  You may have other rights and responsibilities as a tenant. Leases often cover such subjects as pets, parking, cleaning, noise, and so on. If you violate any of these rules, the landlord can give you notice to move or take you to court to have you evicted. The other tenants are probably subject to the same rules. If you have any complaints regarding other tenants' behavior under the lease, contact your landlord. If you are unhappy with the landlord's response, or if the complaint concerns a neighbor who is not a tenant, contact your attorney, a legal aid office, or a local tenants' rights organization.

## ILLEGAL TERMS

A landlord cannot legally discriminate against you on the basis of your race, color, religion, national origin, or gender. Also, a landlord cannot discriminate against you if you have a handicap or, in most cases, if you have children. Similarly, as a tenant, you cannot legally promise to do something counter to the laws prohibiting discrimination. The public policy underlying these prohibitions is to treat all people equally.

One of the reasons to read a lease carefully is to look for, and avoid, illegal terms. Generally, any clause that purports to waive your legal rights is unenforceable. For this reason, clauses that attempt to do any or all of the following may be unenforceable in your state:

1. Waiving your right to a jury trial in eviction proceedings.
2. Permitting your landlord to evict you in a court proceeding without your presence.
3. Providing for a nonrefundable security deposit.
4. Limiting your landlord's liability for hazardous conditions that injure you or your guests.
5. Requiring that you pay an unreasonably high fee or penalty for a late rent payment.
6. Requiring that you assume your landlord's responsibility for maintenance and repair of a private residence.
7. Requiring that you pay your landlord's attorneys' fees if the landlord sues to enforce the lease.

A lease is enforceable in most cases even if it contains an illegal clause. A court will strike the illegal clause from the lease and enforce the other terms. For example, some states prohibit a clause under which you agree to pay the landlord's attorneys' fees if the landlord sues to enforce the lease. If you fail to pay the rent and the landlord sues, the court could enforce the lease but order the landlord to pay his or her own attorneys' fees.

# Eviction

**Eviction** is a legal process by which your landlord can get you off the rental property. In most states, the procedure involves a written notice to you and a hearing in court.

## REASONS FOR EVICTION

Your landlord can have you evicted for violating the lease, the law, or other rules that apply to the rental property. Reasons that your landlord might want to evict you include:

1. Failing to pay the rent.
2. Remaining on the property after the lease expires.
3. Damaging the property.
4. Disturbing your neighbors' quiet enjoyment.

The most common reason for eviction is nonpayment of rent. Paying rent late, paying less than is due, and paying it to the wrong person or at the wrong place are related reasons that a landlord might want to evict you. Failing to pay a valid rent increase may justify eviction. If you believe that an increase is not valid, you may defend against an eviction on that ground. Another course of action is to pay the increase under protest and challenge it in court.

Can your landlord refuse to accept rent that is offered on time and evict you for nonpayment of rent? If your landlord refuses to accept your payment, send the landlord a certified, return-receipt-requested letter offering again to pay the rent. Keep a copy of the letter. If your landlord tries to evict you,

you can show the copy of the letter and receipt to the court to prove that you offered the rent and it was refused.

Your landlord can evict you for staying on the property after your lease expires. You might avoid an eviction after the last month of the term by offering the landlord the next month's rent. If the landlord accepts the payment, a new month-to-month tenancy begins or, in some states, the lease is renewed.

## EVICTION NOTICE

Ordinarily, your landlord has to give you written notice before beginning an eviction, to give you a chance to correct the violation. For example, if you have not paid the rent, you must be given an opportunity to pay it. The notice period is usually short—three days, in most states. Of course, if the lease has expired, in most states the landlord is not required to give notice. Many states have strict requirements about how the notice must be given. Sometimes it must be given to you personally or sent to you by registered or certified mail.

## EVICTION PROCEEDINGS

In most states, eviction requires going to court. An eviction proceeding is generally a brief proceeding in which the court acts quickly to determine who has the right to the rental property. In some states and in some cases, you have the right to a jury trial (ask the clerk of the court). You are not entitled to a court-appointed lawyer in an eviction proceeding, and you are not required to have one, but it is a good idea to be represented because the landlord will probably have an attorney. If you choose to represent yourself, you can do anything an attorney could do, but you will be expected to do it competently. If you do not show up to defend yourself, you normally automatically lose.

In the proceeding, your landlord must prove the truth of what he or she claims and show that what is proved is a cause for eviction. You have a right to prove that the landlord is wrong. For example, if the landlord is attempting to evict you for not paying all of the rent or not paying a rent increase, you might defend yourself on any of the following grounds:

1. You paid the rent.
2. No rent was owed.
3. You rightfully deducted the cost of a repair to the property from the amount of the rent.
4. The landlord's motive for the eviction or the rent increase violated the lease or was otherwise illegal.
5. The eviction notice did not give you necessary information within the required time.

The court decides whom to believe and if what is proved is a sufficient cause for eviction or a sufficient defense against it. The court can issue an order to the landlord to leave you alone, or the court can issue a judgment in favor of the landlord for the amount of the rent. The court can also issue an order to an officer (usually a sheriff) to put you out on the street. The officer may give you notice a few days before

acting, depending on local law. In many states, the court can order a **stay of eviction,** which temporarily postpones execution of the judgment, usually on the basis of a hardship such as cold winter weather or the lack of another place to live. The entire process, from the day you receive the notice of eviction to the day the sheriff appears at your door, may take as little as three weeks or as much as three months. Either party may appeal the judgment.

# Substandard Housing

Landlords must maintain rental property to meet certain minimum health and safety standards. These standards are generally established in state or local laws known as housing codes. In most states, the **implied warranty of habitability** also guarantees that landlords will provide decent, safe, sanitary, and livable housing, as defined by local housing codes.

## LOCAL HOUSING CODES

Housing codes normally include regulations that cover such details as the following:

1. Room temperature.
2. Water temperature, water pressure, and plumbing.
3. Electrical wiring and fire safety, including smoke alarms.
4. Rodent and insect infestation.
5. The number of garbage cans.
6. Building structure and related features, such as the kind of locks required on apartment doors.

To learn the exact requirements of your local housing code, contact your attorney, a legal aid office, a local tenants' rights organization, or the city or county building inspection department. Your local library may also have a reference copy of the housing code and other state and local laws.

## THE IMPLIED WARRANTY OF HABITABILITY

The implied warranty of habitability applies whether or not it is mentioned in your lease, and a clause in the lease that attempts to reject the warranty is unenforceable. Generally, this warranty covers only the most serious problems—a lack of heat in the winter, for example, rather than a few ants on the kitchen floor. If your landlord fails to fix a serious problem, you can go to court and charge the landlord with violation of the warranty. Your best evidence to prove the substandard condition of your home is your copy of the building inspection department's report (discussed below).

## STEPS TO TAKE TO FIX THE SITUATION

What can you do if your landlord fails to provide decent, safe, sanitary, and livable housing? You can contact the city or county to enforce your local housing code. There are steps you can take on your own, or with other tenants, to remedy the situation. Possible steps that you can take include moving out; repairing the condition that makes the housing unsafe, unsanitary, or unlivable and deducting the cost of the repair from the rent; reducing the amount of the rent that you pay; getting a court order to have the property repaired; and suing your landlord. Your landlord may challenge what you do, and this challenge may involve court action, but if you choose your remedy carefully and follow the appropriate steps, you should have a good defense.

## CONTACT YOUR LOCAL BUILDING INSPECTION DEPARTMENT

If you believe that your landlord is in violation of your local housing code, contact your local building inspection department. Explain what you think is wrong and ask for an inspection. When the inspector arrives, point out the conditions that need repair and ask the inspector to check the rest of the building for other violations. When the inspector files a report, get a copy from the building inspection department. If there are mistakes or something is missing, ask for a new inspection.

Your landlord will be given a copy of the report and an order to repair violations within a certain period of time (usually thirty days). The building inspection department and the courts are responsible for seeing that your landlord makes the repairs, but if there will be a hearing, you may want to go to explain what you think is wrong. A landlord who does not make the repairs is subject to a fine. If the violations are very serious, the property may be condemned and the building demolished.

## MOVE OUT

If the property is essentially uninhabitable, you can move out. Generally, it does not matter what caused the property to become uninhabitable—a fire, a storm, a flood, or your landlord's failure to maintain the property—so long as the cause was not something that you did. Frequently, you can move out without giving the landlord notice and without being liable for future rent. You should be aware, however, that the option to move out was created by the courts as the **doctrine of constructive eviction.** Its availability varies from state to state and from case to case. If you move out and your landlord sues you, the court may decide that the property was habitable, and you can be held liable for unpaid and future rent.

## MAKE REPAIRS AND DEDUCT THE COST FROM THE RENT

In some states, if the rental property includes a defective condition that will affect your health or safety (that is, if the condition violates the warranty of habitability), you can pay for the repairs and deduct the cost from the rent. To use this remedy, take the following steps:

1. Determine that the problem is the landlord's responsibility. This will depend on your local law or lease terms to the contrary. In some states, the condition must concern a basic service, such as heat or water.
2. Notify the landlord about the problem in writing (certified or registered mail), explaining that you intend to use this remedy if repairs are not made within a reasonable time. Normally, thirty days is sufficient. An emergency might warrant less time.
3. Make repairs (or hire someone to make repairs) if the landlord does not take steps to fix the problem. Some states require that you get written estimates first. Save all receipts and other paperwork.
4. Deduct the cost of the repairs from your next rent payment. Give the receipts to the landlord but keep copies. In some states, the deductible amount is restricted to a month's rent or some other fixed amount. To avoid this restriction in making a major repair, you and other tenants might act together and deduct a portion of the cost from each tenant's rent. Before doing so, however, ask your attorney, or someone else familiar with your local law, about this possibility.

If your landlord tries to evict you for nonpayment of rent, you can explain your side of the story in court. Generally, if you have followed the law and used common sense, you should have few problems. If the court decides that you were wrong, you will have to pay the entire rent, regardless of how much you spent on repairs.

## WITHHOLD RENT

In some states, if the rental property includes a defective condition that violates the warranty of habitability, you can withhold some of the rent. To use this remedy, take the following steps:

1. Determine that the condition violates the warranty of habitability.
2. Notify the landlord of the problem in writing (certified or registered mail).
3. Allow the landlord a reasonable time to make repairs.
4. Withhold all or part of your next rental payment. In some states, you may be able to withhold amounts for past months when the property was uninhabitable and you paid the rent. In a few states, you must deposit any withheld amounts in a special **escrow account.** The money in the account will be returned to you if the landlord does not make the repairs.

The basic difficulty with using this remedy is determining how much rent to withhold. Often, the decision is made by a court because usually, when rent is withheld, a landlord tries to evict the tenant for nonpayment of rent or asks a court to order the tenant to pay back rent. The court reviews the condition of the property and decides whether the amount withheld was correct. Generally, the court considers how much the defective condition affects the habitability of the property. There is no penalty for withholding too much rent if you act in good faith. If the court determines that you withheld too much, you pay the difference to the landlord.

## SUE THE LANDLORD

You can sue your landlord anytime you believe that the implied warranty of habitability has been breached. In your suit, you can ask the court for any of the following remedies.

1. A declaration of your rights and remedies in the relationship with your landlord.
2. An order to the landlord to pay you money for any injury to you or any damage to your property.
3. An order to the landlord to fix the condition of the property or to stop doing whatever it is that makes the property uninhabitable.

Before asking a court for relief, you should be aware that a court will usually declare parties' rights and remedies, but courts are reluctant to order landlords to do something or to stop doing something when constant supervision is required to ensure that the orders are followed. Also, although a lawsuit is always a possible course of action, it is not always economical.

If a serious dispute develops between you and your landlord, and the dispute cannot be resolved, you may take the matter to court. In some circumstances, this may be required. In most cases and in most states, the appropriate court is a small claims court. When taking a matter to small claims court, you should keep the following points in mind:

1. In many states, no attorney is necessary. In some states, an attorney cannot appear on behalf of a client in small claims court. Assistance can be obtained from the clerk of the court or some other designated official.
2. The proper party must be notified about the suit. You may know only the resident manager of the property, not the actual owner, or you may know the owner only as the name of a corporation. An owner's name may be available through the local tax assessor's office or the county clerk.
3. All relevant documents should be kept available for the court. These may include a copy of the lease, rent receipts, an inventory of the condition of the premises taken before you moved in, canceled checks, receipts and estimates for repairs, and notes taken during any negotiations between you and your landlord.
4. You might be able to recover attorneys' fees, if an attorney was consulted and paid. In some cases, you may recover double or triple the amount of a security deposit wrongfully retained by your landlord. For more information about small claims courts, see the discussion of consumer law later in this *Handbook*.

## RETALIATORY EVICTION

**Retaliatory eviction** occurs if your landlord evicts you for complaining to a government agency about the condition of the property. If you can prove that your landlord's primary purpose in evicting or attempting to evict you is retaliation for reporting violations—of a housing or sanitation code, for example—you may be entitled to stop the eviction proceedings or collect damages. This can be difficult to prove, unless your landlord admits his or her purpose in a note, in a statement to another person, or in testimony to a court.

In many states, a landlord is presumed to be acting in retaliation if the eviction proceedings are begun within a certain period of time (six to twelve months, in some states) after a tenant has contacted a government agency. In this case, the landlord must prove that he or she did not have a retaliatory purpose. If your landlord shows that you did not pay the rent or that you violated the lease, you could be evicted. If you win, however, you can stay on the premises.

When your lease comes up for renewal, the landlord may raise the rent to help cover the cost of the repairs. Your landlord cannot raise the rent simply to punish you for reporting the violations, however. In most of the states that protect tenants from retaliatory eviction, courts would consider this retaliatory and subject to the same limitations as a retaliatory eviction.

# Rent

The primary obligation of the tenant is to pay the agreed-upon rent at the time specified. You retain this obligation even after you have subleased the apartment. If the sublessee fails to pay, your lease obliges you to make payment. Rent is typically due on a certain date of the month. If payments are late, the landlord may charge interest for being late. Most leases provide that if rent is late by more than a certain amount, you will be charged a penalty fee. The amount and nature of this fee must be specified in the lease. The amount must also be reasonable. One Vermont case held that a dollar-a-day charge for late rent payments was excessive.

## RAISING THE RENT

As a general rule, your landlord cannot raise your rent during the term of your lease. An exception would exist if the lease itself provides some procedure for rent increases during its term. Such a provision is typically called an **escalation clause,** which permits periodic increases that usually are based upon rising costs for fuel or building upkeep.

After a lease expires, you may continue, with the landlord's consent, renting on a month-to-month basis. This means that the terms of the old lease continue in operation but can be terminated at any time either by you or the landlord (usually with one month's or thirty days' notice). Alternatively, you may execute a new lease with your landlord, who may require a higher rental payment. This is a matter to be negotiated.

## RENT CONTROL

While landlords may generally charge whatever the market will bear, many large cities have rent control laws that restrain rent increases. These ordinances place limits on how much rent can be raised by landlords, even after a lease expires. Rent can be increased only by a set percentage, which may be tied to the cost of living. Because the existence and substance of these ordinances vary from place to place and can change over time, those renting property should become familiar with their local laws.

# Security Deposits

Before renting an apartment, you probably will be required to make a **security deposit** in an amount such as one month's rent. The landlord holds this money during your lease to protect against damage that you may do to the property. Theoretically, you recover this deposit when you move out of the apartment. All security deposits must be potentially refundable. If you caused more damage than covered by your security deposit, the landlord may sue you for the remainder.

## USE OF THE SECURITY DEPOSIT

You may lose your security deposit if the landlord requires the money to repair damages that you have done to the premises. The security deposit is not applied to **ordinary wear and tear.** This term applies to ordinary deterioration of an apartment over time, such as fading paint, carpet wear, etc. The landlord may take your security deposit for larger damages, such as permanent stains or cigarette burns in carpeting, broken appliances or window frames, or holes punched in walls. Even a small hole to hang a picture might permit withholding (though repair costs would be quite small). Some landlords might attempt to use your security deposit to recover fees for late payment of rent, but this is illegal in most states.

## PROTECTING YOUR SECURITY DEPOSIT

When you attempt to recover your security deposit, a dispute may arise over the nature of damages and the condition of the apartment when you moved in. The following steps will help you protect your deposit:

1. Get a receipt for the amount of the deposit.
2. Before moving in, make a list of existing defects or problems and provide a copy of the list to your landlord.
3. Before moving out, clean the apartment and repair damages insofar as possible.
4. Before moving out, inspect the apartment yourself along with the landlord or other witness.
5. After moving out, leave a forwarding address and your keys to the apartment with the landlord.

You might also ask your landlord for interest on your deposit during your lease. This is required only in a few states.

## WITHHOLDING YOUR DEPOSIT

The landlord may decide to withhold some of your security deposit for repairs. Most jurisdictions require the landlord to provide you with an itemized list of repairs and their costs. In many states, to avoid a penalty, the landlord must provide this list or refund the deposit within thirty days of the date that you moved out and gave the landlord a forwarding address. If the landlord does not do this, he or she may forfeit the right to withhold any of your security deposit.

You may dispute your landlord's assessment. You may file suit against your landlord for withholding your deposit, probably in small claims court. You can question either the need for the repairs or whether the cost of the repairs was reasonable.

# Liability for Injuries

What if a guest of yours is injured while in your apartment? The guest might sue the landlord, or you, or both. Either one of you could be liable.

## COMMON AREAS

Liability for injuries in apartments depends on who has legal control over the area in question. **Common areas** are under the control of the landlord, who will be liable for injuries in this area. If your guest trips over a defective stair step on the way to your apartment, the landlord is liable and you probably are not. The landlord may also be responsible for slippery surfaces, inadequate lighting, or rotting wood.

## STRUCTURAL DEFECTS

Even if the injury occurs inside your apartment, the landlord may be liable. A defective water heater or outside railing, for example, is within the landlord's control. Similarly, if the landlord undertakes certain repairs in your apartment and performs the repairs negligently, the landlord is responsible for resultant damages.

## TENANT LIABILITY

You are potentially liable for certain injuries occurring within your apartment. You have some control over this area and are responsible for maintaining its safe condition. You are responsible for any injuries resulting from your furnishings or from your misuse of apartment fixtures, such as lights or plumbing. You may purchase renters' insurance to cover this liability, as well as to insure against the damage, loss, or destruction of your belongings.

# Lockouts

If a dispute with your landlord has reached an extreme level, your landlord may lock you out of your apartment and seize your possessions. In the vast majority of states, such lockouts are unlawful. The laws provide that a tenant has a right to notice and a hearing, but some landlords continue to conduct illegal lockouts. If you suffer an illegal lockout, you should call the police and complain of a criminal trespass and conversion of your personal property. If the police are unhelpful, you can get an attorney to obtain an order recovering possession. You may recover all your costs from the landlord and may continue to pursue a tort action.

In lieu of a lockout, the landlord may conduct a **utility shutoff,** in an effort to force you off the premises. This action is also illegal, and states provide both civil and criminal penalties against the offending landlord. As with a lockout, you may need to go to court to enforce your rights and get your utilities turned back on.

## TOPIC 2

# FAMILY LAW

Families ideally work out their relationships internally and settle their own problems without resorting to legal process. In reality, however, courts often become involved in family disputes. Moreover, the law establishes a basic framework through which parties may voluntarily resolve their disputes without going before a judge.

# Getting Married

The decision to get married has changed in recent decades. Couples are more frequently living together, or cohabiting, without first marrying. This is generally legal, though some states have normally unenforced laws prohibiting extramarital cohabitation. Many couples still get married and there are some practical advantages to marriage. Married couples may have an easier time obtaining insurance, credit, etc. Married partners, upon divorce, are more likely to receive child custody. Married couples also have more adoption opportunities. Many companies offer health insurance to spouses but not to unmarried partners.

## ENGAGEMENT

There are few legal requirements governing engagement. Traditionally, one left at the altar could sue a fiancé for breach of promise to marry. Today, most states have done away with this cause of action. If an engagement is broken, the law probably would force the party to return certain gifts, such as engagement rings, shower gifts, etc.

## MARRIAGE REQUIREMENTS

States place some limitations upon who may marry. The betrothed must be man and woman, currently unmarried, not closely related by blood, and over a certain age (often eighteen). State laws differ, and some actually prohibit marriages among those closely related even if the relation is only by marriage. Those who are underage may marry with parental consent or if judicially emancipated from their parents. Below a certain age, such as fourteen or sixteen, marriage may be absolutely prohibited by state law except with court approval.

## MARRIAGE CEREMONY

Certain procedures are generally required for a legally recognized marriage. The parties must first obtain a marriage license from the state government. Some states also require a blood test, in which the government checks for diseases, such as venereal diseases. Some states require a waiting period before getting the license or between the time of acquiring the license and officially getting married. In thirteen states and the District of Columbia, a license is the only requirement for a marriage.

In the other thirty-seven states, some form of marriage ceremony is also required. The parties must present the license to someone authorized to perform marriages (a state official or member of the clergy). The ceremony must involve a public statement of agreement to marriage. The remainder of the ceremony is generally within the couple's discretion. After the ceremony, the marriage license must be recorded.

## COMMON LAW MARRIAGE

About fifteen states recognize **common law marriage,** a procedure by which parties become married without a license or ceremony. There are four general requirements for a common law marriage:

1. The parties must be eligible to marry.
2. The parties must have a present and continuing intention and agreement to be husband and wife.
3. The parties must live together as husband and wife.
4. The parties must hold themselves out to the public as husband and wife.

There are a number of misapprehensions about common law marriage. Cohabitation alone cannot produce a common law marriage; the parties must additionally hold themselves out to others as husband and wife. There is no minimum time period required for a common law marriage. The parties may become married as soon as they both live as husband and wife and hold themselves out to the public as married.

There is no common law divorce. Once a couple is regarded as married—and particularly once a court has recognized them as married by common law—they must obtain a court decree to dissolve the marriage.

## DUTIES OF MARRIAGE

The law considers marriage to be a form of contract, and historically the marriage contract came complete with a full set of duties for the husband and wife. Formerly, the husband had the duty to be the provider, and could not purchase luxuries for himself until the family was provided with necessities. The wife had certain duties in the home. Times have changed, and courts today enforce few duties arising from the marriage contract. Spouses are generally allowed to arrange their own affairs however they see fit.

The law still holds that a spouse has a duty of financial support, providing such basics as food, shelter, and medical care, insofar as he or she is able. In many states, this duty lasts throughout the marriage, even if the spouses are living apart. Failure to provide support for a child may be a criminal violation. (In non-community property states, except for these basics, one spouse is not responsible for the debts of the other spouse unless he or she is ordered to pay them as part of a divorce decree.)

Additional duties may be created by a separate agreement between the spouses. Some decisions have held that a spouse may not deny sexual relations without good cause, though courts are becoming more hesitant to enforce such a requirement.

Traditional common law provided for **interspousal immunity.** This means that one spouse could not sue the other for torts, such as assault and battery. Most states now have modified this law and permit one spouse to sue the other for at least intentional torts. Interspousal immunity still means that one partner may not be required to testify against a spouse in court, though a spouse may voluntarily so testify. An increasing number of states recognizes the crime of marital rape.

It is, of course, illegal to batter a spouse. Unlawful abuse has been extended to include extreme cases of harassment and threats of physical beating or confinement. A victim of spousal battering should call the police and may seek other legal protection against the abuser, including an emergency restraining order, which requires the abusing spouse to stay away from the victim. Many shelters are available to assist an abused spouse.

# Financial Aspects of Marriage

## PRENUPTIAL AGREEMENTS

Brides and grooms are increasingly bringing substantial assets into a marriage, which has led to greater use of the **prenuptial,** or premarital, **agreement.** A prenuptial agreement is a contract between the parties entered into before the wedding occurs. Such an agreement generally provides for disposition of property in the event of the divorce or death of one spouse. One typical use of a prenuptial agreement would be to guarantee that children from a previous marriage receive a certain share of their parent's estate. Prenuptial agreements must be in writing to be enforceable.

There are certain advantages to prenuptial agreements. Such contracts enable the parties to settle possible disagreements in advance and provide some long-term financial certainty to the parties. Note, though, that prenuptial agreements are criticized for evincing a lack of mutual trust and for being unromantic. Such agreements may even prove unfair to a spouse in the event of divorce.

As with any contract, prenuptial agreements are presumptively valid but are not always so. While traditional courts refused to recognize prenuptial agreements, most states now uphold such contracts, even if they eliminate financial support in the event of divorce. Courts do look closely at the agreement for evidence of unfairness. There are several circumstances when courts have refused to enforce prenuptial agreements, such as:

- When the agreement would so impoverish the spouse as to make him or her eligible for welfare.

- When there was unfair bargaining at the time of the agreement, such as a failure to disclose all money and property assets.
- When one party was not represented by counsel.
- When the agreement was entered into immediately before the marriage (such agreements should be made weeks or months in advance).

In general, a party must show that the prenuptial agreement was made voluntarily and without threats or unfair pressure.

## PROPERTY OWNERSHIP

Separate property is property that a spouse owned before the marriage, plus inheritances and gifts acquired during the marriage. This property belongs to the spouse personally and not to the marital unit. Upon dissolution of the marriage, separate property is not divided but retained by the owner.

The separate property right may be lost during marriage, however. If the couple combines separate property with that acquired during the marriage, the two properties may be merged into jointly held property. Suppose that a wife owns a lot on which the couple builds a house after their marriage. The wife has lost her separate property rights in the land. Merely renovating a separately held property (e.g., sprucing up a vacation home) may transform the separate property into joint property. Placing separate property into a jointly held bank account may also transform the money into joint property. The separate property issue is important even if the couple is happy and trusting. For example, a wife's creditors may not attach her husband's separate property but may reach at least a portion of jointly held property.

The converse of separate property occurs when one spouse brings debts into the marriage. In most states, you are not liable for your spouse's premarital debts. In community property states (described below), under certain circumstances, a spouse may become liable for premarital debts.

Nine jurisdictions (Arizona, California, Idaho, Louisiana, Nebraska, New Mexico, Texas, Washington, and Wisconsin) have the system known as **community property.** These states provide that each spouse share equally in all income earned and most property acquired during the marriage. This is true even if one party supplied all the income and assets. The community property system is significant both for creditors and for the parties upon divorce. In community property states, one spouse may encumber the other with debts. In other states, one party generally may not incur debts for the other.

## SEPARATION AND DIVORCE

**Divorce** is generally preceded by a separation period. Such separation may be due to abandonment or may be through mutual consent. States may require a separation period prior to granting a divorce.

A divorce is a formal court proceeding used to legally dissolve a marriage. Divorce laws vary considerably among the states, with some having much easier procedures. All states provide for some form of **no-fault divorce.** This eliminates the requirement that divorce be justified by some demonstrable reason, such as abuse or abandonment. The most common basis for a no-fault divorce is irreconcilable differences. No-fault divorce laws make it practically impossible for one spouse to prevent a divorce desired by the other. Even in these states, courts may look to fault in deciding financial settlements between the parties.

Lawyers are not strictly required for a divorce proceeding. Most states permit ''do-it-yourself divorces,'' sometimes called *pro se* **divorces.** In this process, the individuals handle everything themselves before the court. Couples can obtain the necessary forms at the local courthouse (or in form books). If a significant amount of money is at stake, however, the divorcing spouses should obtain professional legal and accounting advice.

Most divorces are not actually tried in court. Only about ten percent of divorces go to trial. The parties typically settle their outstanding claims, though often only after lengthy negotiations. Divorcing spouses increasingly use **mediation** to settle disagreements. A mediator is typically trained and meets with the parties in the absence of lawyers. The mediator does not make decisions but tries to prod the parties into a mutually acceptable agreement.

In a divorce settlement, some written agreement is reached on contested issues, such as property settlement, child custody, continued support, etc. This agreement must be presented to the court for its approval. The court may disapprove the agreement as unconscionable (extremely unfair), though this is very rare. If only one side of the divorce had legal representation, courts will scrutinize settlement agreements more closely.

An **annulment** is more than a divorce and means that the marriage was never effective in the first place. Annulment may be available if the marriage is based upon fraud, if the marriage was unconsummated, if there was **bigamy,** and for a limited set of other reasons. Obtaining an annulment is especially significant for those belonging to certain religions (such as Catholicism) in order for a person to remarry.

## PROPERTY DIVISION AND ALIMONY

Although most divorcing parties settle their financial disputes, this settlement is colored by the requirements of the law. Whether the state has community property laws or not, the court may divide marital property without respect to formal papers of ownership. Judges have almost unlimited discretion in deciding which person receives what property, as long as the division is reasonably equitable.

Courts divide marital property and, in most circumstances, separate property remains with the owner. When deciding how to divide the common property, however, judges consider the existence of the separate property and its effect on the wealth and needs of the divorcing spouses. Retirement benefits are generally considered to be marital property, divided between the spouses. In community property states, the property is presumptively split equally. Judges

may change this division to suit the circumstances, however. Courts use a variety of standards in considering how to divide property, including the following:

- The duration of the marriage.
- The health of the parties.
- The individuals' occupations and vocational skills.
- The individuals' relative wealth and income.
- The standard of living during the marriage.
- The relative contributions to the marriage, both financially and in homemaker contributions.
- Needs and concerns of any children.
- Tax and inheritance considerations.

Marital debts must also be divided according to similar criteria.

A typical property controversy in divorce cases concerns rights to the marital residence. If there are minor children, the house is usually given to the parent with custody of the children. It may be difficult to balance the grant of the house with other property (many families have few substantial assets other than their homes). Once the children are grown, the court may order the house to be sold and the proceeds divided.

**Alimony** is money paid for support of the former spouse. Historically, the husband was the wage earner and was expected to pay alimony to his former wife, to permit her to maintain her standard of living. There are well-known cases involving wealthy entertainers, such as former NBC late-night T.V. host Johnny Carson, who have been directed to pay their ex-wives (or, in a few cases, ex-husbands) hundreds of thousands of dollars in annual alimony. Alimony ends when the recipient remarries.

The law of alimony is changing. One common form of alimony today is called **rehabilitative support.** Rather than providing indefinite support payments, rehabilitative support is designed to provide the ex-spouse with the education, training, or job experience necessary to support himself or herself. This form of alimony assists spouses who devoted their lives to homemaking or who left lucrative opportunities because of the marriage. Such rehabilitative support may only last for a limited period, particularly if the spouse finds a good job. Such temporary rehabilitative support has been criticized, because many divorcees are of an age that hampers their prospects of developing a new career. Many courts still award permanent support, if the recipient's earning prospects are far less than those of the wealthier spouse or if the recipient is of relatively advanced age. About half the states also consider fault in the divorce as a factor in awarding spousal support such as alimony. Alimony may be modified as the parties' situations change.

A common controversy involves one spouse supporting another through graduate school (such as law or medical school), followed by a divorce. The supporting spouse may claim a share of the income subsequently earned by the supported spouse as a lawyer or a doctor. Courts have been hesitant to grant the supporting spouse some property right in the advanced or professional degree obtained by the other spouse but have awarded payments to compensate for the supporting spouse's contributions to the education. One New York decision did hold that an academic degree earned by the husband was marital property.

## PALIMONY

**Palimony** is a common but nonlegal name for claims made by a member of an unmarried couple after they have split up. After cohabiting for years, a partner may claim some interest in the other's property. There is no statutory provision for such a claim, and courts have been reluctant to recognize an automatic right to palimony. Unmarried couples may enter a contract that specifies legal rights should they break up. Such contracts may be valid, but courts have tended to scrutinize them closely for legality. These contracts should be in writing, although this is not strictly required at law. The California Supreme Court has held that a contract between a cohabiting couple may even be implied from conduct or unspoken understandings. Other states, such as Illinois, are unwilling to recognize palimony actions. Palimony may be especially important for homosexual couples, who are barred from marrying legally.

## CHILD CUSTODY

The most contentious issue in many divorces is child custody—the right to live with and to care for the children on an everyday basis. Traditionally, the mother almost always received custody. Forty-four states have now adopted the Uniform Marriage and Divorce Act, which governs custody determinations. Mothers still usually receive custody, but courts now explicitly consider a list of factors, including:

- The wishes of the child.
- The nature of the relationship and emotional ties with each parent.
- The ability and interest of the parents in providing for the child's needs and education.
- Any required adjustments to a new house or community.
- The stability of the family relationship.

Family stability is probably the most important factor. Some recent decisions have put increased emphasis on whether one parent was a smoker, because secondary smoke may damage the child's lungs. Courts may appoint a **guardian *ad litem,*** usually an attorney, who directly represents the child's interests in court. Custody decisions are not permanent and may be changed by a court.

The noncustodial parent generally receives visitation rights. The parent may get to spend weekends or other time periods with the child. Visitation is denied in extreme cases, such as child abuse or when there is a reasonable fear of child snatching by the noncustodial parent.

The court may provide a system of **joint custody,** which many states now prefer. Joint legal custody means that both parents together make major decisions about the child. Some procedure, such as mediation, is available in the event of disagreement. In some states, including California, mediation is mandatory in child custody disputes. This may also involve joint physical custody, in which both parents maintain a home for the child and have roughly comparable time with the child.

Regardless of the custody arrangements, a court must make some provision for financial **child support.** Child support obligations arise even if the parents were never married. States have official guidelines to determine child support duties. These guidelines are often percentage formulas based on parental income. Judges must follow the guidelines, unless special facts justify a departure. Children with particularly large needs (for example, the disabled) may require a greater support award.

It is a common misconception that if one ex-spouse fails to meet his or her obligations under a divorce decree or other court order (such as withholding visitation rights), the other party can withhold payment of child support. Child support is a separate court order—it cannot be withheld because an ex-spouse does something that the other ex-spouse does not like. (What a parent can do is ask the court to modify a decree in some way.) A large number of noncustodial parents are failing to make their child support payments, and states are providing for automatic withholding of support payments from the wages of the parent. Child support orders may also be revised and adjusted according to need and ability to pay. The Uniform Reciprocal Enforcement of Support Act assists states in recovering support payments from parents living in other states. The failure to make child support payments is a crime.

# Children

The decision whether to have children is a central part of the family relationship. The law of childbearing has become increasingly complex with the advent of new arrangements, such as surrogate parenthood and artificial insemination. The law here is still unsettled. Within a marriage, the decision to have children obviously should be mutually reached. The woman ultimately has the right to use contraceptive devices or to go ahead and bear a child, and she does not need to obtain the husband's permission.

## PATERNITY

If a couple is married, the law presumes that any newborn child is the husband's, and he must support the child unless he can prove that he is not the biological father. Some states do not even allow the husband an opportunity to prove his lack of paternity. An unmarried mother may file a suit to establish the **paternity** of her child. If the unwed mother is on public welfare aid, the government may file a paternity suit to be reimbursed.

The paternity of a child may be proved scientifically. Science has advanced beyond historically used blood tests and now uses DNA testing or comparable procedures that check for genetic factors. Such tests reportedly are 98 to 99 percent accurate in determining parenthood. The biological father of the child has a legal obligation to provide support, regardless of marital status. These obligations are just as great as for married fathers and are determined by the child support guidelines of the state. The obligations usually last until the child is no longer a minor. The mother's subsequent marriage to another man does not necessarily extinguish the child support obligations of the biological father.

While all biological fathers have an obligation to provide child support regardless of marital status, children born out of wedlock still suffer disadvantages. Legally, an illegitimate child has no presumptive right to inherit as an heir of the father. An increasing number of children are born to unmarried parents (about one-third of all first births). In response, the law is evolving to provide added rights and protections to children born out of wedlock. Courts have held that the government cannot discriminate against illegitimate children and that such children have a right to recover damages for the deaths of their parents. In most states, the eventual marriage of the parents "legitimizes" a previous child of theirs.

## ADOPTION

**Adoption** is a procedure in which persons become the official legal parents of a child that is not their biological child. Adoption may be contrasted with **foster care,** which is a temporary arrangement in which a family is paid by the state to care for a child over a limited time period, often pending adoption. There are three minimum requirements for an adoption to be legal:

1. The legal rights of the biological parents must have been terminated by death or judicial decree.
2. The adopting parents must follow all procedures required by the state of adoption.
3. The adoption must be formally approved by a judge.

There may be additional requirements in specific circumstances. For example, adopting a teenage child generally requires the child's official consent.

Adoption is often done through a public or private agency that has received authority to agree to the adoption of children in its custody. The biological parents may convey the authority to the agency to find legal parents for their child. The agency investigates potential adopters and chooses a set of parents. In other circumstances, potential parents may pursue independent adoption, when a doctor or lawyer or other individual puts adopting parents together with a pregnant woman who must give up her child. These parties make their own private arrangements, which usually involve the adopting parents paying for the legal and medical expenses associated with childbirth and adoption. The intermediary also generally receives a fee. This approach has the potential for abuse and is prohibited by some states. There is a growing number of black market adoptions from developing nations (such as China and Romania).

Even entirely independent adoptions must be approved in court. The primary standard for approving an adoption is the best interests of the child. The court (and applicable private agency) considers the financial resources of the adopting parents, their family stability and home environment, their ages, religious and racial compatibility, and other factors relevant to the child's future health and welfare. Most states permit single persons to adopt, though married couples are generally preferred.

After the adoption, many states place the new parents on probation for a time. This period is usually from six months to one year. The agency or court appoints an individual to ensure that the adoptive parents are caring appropriately for the child's well-being. If not, the child may be removed and returned to an agency for placement in another home.

Once an adoption is formally completed, the adoptive parents have all the responsibilities of biological parents. Should they divorce, each adoptive parent still has all the child support obligations associated with biological parents. Depending on the state, the child may retain some legal connection with the biological parents, such as inheritance rights upon their deaths. The adopted child also has rights of inheritance from the adoptive parents.

## CHILDREN'S RIGHTS

The law has special concern for children. Legally, a child is an unmarried minor (under the age of eighteen), who is not emancipated. **Emancipation** occurs when children leave home to support themselves. Parents have duties toward their children to provide food, shelter, clothing, medical care, and other necessities. Parents must also ensure that their children attend school (normally until the age of sixteen). Parents are prohibited from abusing or neglecting their children. Parental duties to children generally end at age eighteen, but these duties may continue longer if the child is seriously disabled.

Along with these duties, parents have certain rights of control over children. Parents can direct the upbringing of their children and control where they live, what school they attend, and even what religion they practice. Parents also generally control the medical care to be given, though parents' refusal to provide for such care in life-threatening situations (usually for religious reasons) can be a crime. Parents have broad legal authority to control the behavior of their children, though this lessens as the children age and become more mature. Parents may punish children but not excessively.

Historically, children could not sue their parents for negligence, due to a governmental interest in family harmony. Today, most states permit such lawsuits, which are generally covered by insurance. The traditional common law rule was that parents were not liable for the tortious actions of their children. About half the states now provide partial parental liability for their children's intentional torts, up to a limit of about $10,000 (depending upon the state).

## CHILD ABUSE AND NEGLECT

All states have laws that prohibit the abuse and neglect of children by their parents or others. Child abuse primarily covers severe physical beatings and sexual molestation of minors by anyone. Child abuse may even extend to emotional abuse, when a person publicly humiliates a child in an extreme way. Child neglect occurs when parents or legal guardians fail to provide for basic needs, such as food, shelter, clothing, and medical treatment. Laws now require doctors and social workers to report suspected cases of child abuse.

In serious cases of child abuse or neglect, the government may remove the child from his or her parents. Ideally, this is temporary and the objective is to reunite the family after the parents' problems have been corrected through counseling or otherwise. If the parents are unrepentant, the state may ask the court to terminate all parental rights and make the children available for adoption.

## Wills and Estates

In a marriage, each spouse should have a will. State law automatically provides spouses with financial benefits after death, but that adds complications. If a spouse dies **intestate** (without a will), the family may still recover but may assume added administrative costs and tax burdens. The adjudication of inheritance rights is known as **probate,** and legal probate battles may be protracted and costly. If there is no will, a court will appoint someone to manage the estate. Couples also should revise the terms of their wills to take advantage of changes in the tax laws and the changing needs of their heirs. A will is even more important for unmarried couples. An unmarried partner has no automatic right to assets on death and will inherit only if provided for in a will.

In the absence of a will, the deceased's property is distributed according to a state's intestate succession law. The surviving spouse has a legal right to a certain share of the estate (usually one-third or one-half, depending upon the state). In the absence of a will, children also have a right to a share of the property.

When there is a will, the law restricts its terms in order to protect the surviving family. A married person cannot will an entire estate to charity, for example. The surviving spouse has a right to what is known as the **elective share.** The elective share is a certain guaranteed minimum of the deceased's estate. It is called elective, because the spouse may choose to take what is provided in the will or may elect the minimum share specified by state law. A spouse may lose this elective share option if he or she signed the deceased's will. A child may be disinherited, even when he or she is a minor, and thereby be denied a share of the deceased parent's estate. Such disinheritance must be clearly intended, however. Mere failure to mention a child in the will does not constitute disinheritance. In limited circumstances, the contents of a will may be challenged by potential heirs.

Some families partially avoid probate and wills by using a **living trust.** The living trust is a device in which a person known as the **trustee** holds legal title to property and manages it in the interest of named beneficiaries of the trust. A wife might establish such a trust with herself and her husband as beneficiaries for life. After her death, her husband may receive the property directly or continue the trust, with himself as beneficiary. The latter option requires appointment of a new trustee, which could be the husband himself. The trust option may allow greater flexibility than a will and also avoid certain taxes.

## Homosexual Families

Some of the most controversial family law topics involve gay or lesbian families. Many homosexual couples live in stable, long-term relationships. They may wish to formally recognize their relationships through a wedding ceremony. No state legally recognizes such same-sex marriages. Gays and lesbians may hold what have become known as ''commitment ceremonies,'' which are similar to marriage ceremonies. Such commitment ceremonies do not invoke the legal protections surrounding marriage, however. There is no legal provision for community property or alimony in such cases. Homosexual couples may provide for similar protections through a contract.

Some homosexual couples wish to adopt children, though this can be difficult. Two states, Florida and New Hampshire, have explicitly prohibited homosexual adoptions, but some local Florida courts have struck down that state's law as being unconstitutional. Even in the absence of such a law, an Ohio judge held in 1988 that gays and lesbians were ineligible to adopt. Despite the roadblocks, over two hundred homosexual couples have successfully adopted children. Gays and lesbians are also at a disadvantage in child custody battles that follow a divorce.

**TOPIC 3**

# CONSUMER LAW

The typical American undertakes hundreds of consumer transactions every year. Most such purchases prove ordinary and uncontroversial, but an occasional purchase goes awry. The product may be worthless or even dangerous. In these instances, the consumer may need the protection of the law. The traditional common law embraced the doctrine of *caveat emptor,* meaning ''let the buyer beware.'' Consumers had little recourse when purchases went sour. Today, there is an increasing number of consumer protection laws.

## The Consumer Contract

Whenever you purchase groceries or any other product, you enter a contract. Although grocery shopping does not involve a formal written contract, such purchases are contracts and are governed by the principles of contract law. Consumer purchases must meet all of the requirements of a contract in order to be binding on you and the seller. Most purchases easily satisfy the main requirements of contract law and present no loopholes for escaping a deal. An exception exists when a purchaser is a minor. The general rule is that a minor (someone under eighteen years of age) may disavow and escape a contract even after it has been completed.

## FRAUD

You can escape a contract if you were fraudulently induced into making the contract. Fraud requires proof of the following elements:

1. A misrepresentation of material fact.
2. An intent to deceive.
3. Justifiable reliance.

A seller who lies about the attributes of a product to make a sale may commit fraud. You must distinguish fraudulent lying from **puffing,** which refers to the seller's qualitative statements about the product. A seller who promises that its product is ''of great quality'' or ''fantastic'' is merely puffing about the product. To show fraud you would have to demonstrate a more specific statement of fact, such as a false statement about the number of miles on a used car. If you can prove fraud, you may either rescind (escape) the contract or collect the damages that you suffered as a consequence of the fraud.

## UNCONSCIONABILITY

The law ordinarily does not look into the fairness of contracts. It is the responsibility of the parties to obtain the best deal for themselves. Courts usually will not strike down contracts simply for unfairness. A limited exception exists for **unconscionability,** which means such extreme unfairness as to ''shock the conscience'' of a court. Courts can refuse to enforce unconscionable contracts.

Unconscionability may be found when there is a great disparity of bargaining power. Such disparity may arise with **contracts of adhesion.** These exist when a seller presents you with a ''take-it-or-leave-it'' form contract and refuses to negotiate over the terms on the form. You have little bargaining power in this circumstance. Note that not all contracts of adhesion are unconscionable—you could simply walk away from the deal. If circumstances force you to make a contract and you cannot bargain over the terms, and if those terms seem manifestly unfair to you, the contract may be deemed unconscionable.

# Warranties

Most products that you purchase will come with some form of warranty or promise regarding the quality of the product. If the product does not meet the warranted standard, you have a right to a remedy. Generally this remedy is readily provided by the manufacturer or retailer, but in some cases you may need to go to court. Warranties may come in several forms.

## EXPRESS WARRANTIES

An **express warranty** is any explicit factual assurance about a product. The express warranty may be a written promise of quality and performance or may be an oral assurance from a salesperson. An express warranty may even be visual. If the retailer shows you a model of the product, it is creating an express warranty that the item purchased will conform to that model. Of course, a written warranty is easier to enforce in court. You should also be aware that puffing does not create a warranty but is merely sales talk.

Many warranties contain a specific remedy should something go wrong with the product. A **full warranty** means that the product will be repaired or replaced free of charge within a reasonable time, or else you will receive a refund. Even a full warranty does not provide absolute protection, because the warranty will also set forth terms and conditions. For example, a microwave oven may be under full warranty for 180 days. After that time you are unprotected. A limited warranty provides even less protection. A limited warranty might provide for repair but not a refund. Moreover, to take advantage of such a warranty you may have to deliver or mail the product to a designated site.

Beware of disclaimers. Even after a salesperson makes detailed promises about a product, you may be expected to sign a written contract that disclaims all express warranties. Although this may seem unfair, it is a legal practice and can nullify anything that the salesperson said, as well as eliminate any other warranty protection. Disclaimers are discussed below. Be sure to read any warranty and understand your rights before you make a purchase.

## IMPLIED WARRANTIES

Many consumer contracts come with implied warranties that automatically come with the product. These warranties protect you even if the salesperson made no promises about the product. The law implies these warranties in sales of goods. Implied warranties of merchantability are created only by sellers who are merchants. Thus, a garage sale in your neighborhood would not include such a warranty.

The **implied warranty of merchantability** means that your purchase will be of at least average quality for that type of product and will perform its intended function. This means that if you buy a camera, it will successfully take pictures. The **implied warranty of fitness** applies when the salesperson helps you select a product for a particular purpose. If you inform the retailer of your purpose and rely on him or her to choose a suitable product, the company warrants that the product is suited for that purpose. If you ask for an underwater camera, the product a salesperson picks out must function under water. The **implied warranty of title** simply means that the seller warrants that he or she is the owner (or authorized agent) of the item for sale.

## DISCLAIMERS

Companies may choose to disclaim warranties or to limit their potential liability. The disclaimer may bluntly declare that there are no warranties on the product or may state that your only remedy is repair or replacement of the product. Merchants may even disclaim the implied warranties discussed above, but they must use specific and conspicuous language to do so. The implied warranties of merchantability and fitness may be disclaimed by declaring that the product is sold "as is." This language is understood to state that the product is being sold with possible flaws and that the buyer assumes the risk of the flaws.

Most disclaimers are legally effective and prevent you from claiming breach of warranty. Some courts will at least require that the disclaimer be conspicuous (for example, in capital letters on the front page of the contract) or in clear and understandable language. In any event, you are expected to read the contract and be aware of any disclaimers.

# Product Liability

If you are physically injured by a product, you may bring a product liability action. Under modern law, you may sue even if you did not personally purchase the product that injured you. This is the doctrine of **strict product liability.**

Under strict product liability, you need not prove that the manufacturer was negligent or careless, but you must show that the product contained a defect causing an unreasonable danger. Suppose that you received from your toaster a nasty shock that required medical attention. You might recover these damages in strict product liability. You could not get a new toaster, however. You cannot recover if you or anyone else altered the product after it was purchased.

You may recover product liability damages in negligence, though negligence tends to be difficult to prove. A breach of warranty action may also be available for unsafe products. Warranty tends to be limited to the actual purchasers of the product, however. Warranty actions are limited by the scope of the warranty and any disclaimers.

# Deceptive Sales Practices

Most of the protections discussed above are limited by the sales contract. In recent years, many legislatures have passed statutes that provide further protection to consumers against a variety of deceptive sales practices used by merchants.

## BAIT AND SWITCH

**Bait and switch** is a sales tactic that has been outlawed. The typical bait-and-switch scheme begins with a store advertising a popular product at an extremely low price. This is the "bait." Consumers see the advertisement and go to the store to purchase the advertised product. The store informs the consumers that it is sold out of the advertised product or otherwise discourages the sale of this product. Salespersons attempt to convince the consumer to purchase an alternative product that has a higher profit margin (the "switch"). The bait-and-switch scheme lures customers into the store, where they can be persuaded to "buy up" by the salesperson.

The federal government has prohibited bait-and-switch tactics. If you believe that a store is using this method, you should complain to the Federal Trade Commission, which enforces the law. Most states and many local government consumer protection agencies also act against unlawful bait-and-switch tactics.

Note the differences between illegal bait-and-switch scams and legal *loss-leader tactics.* Grocery stores may offer a very low price on milk or some other staple to get you into the store. Their theory is that once you buy the milk, you are also likely to purchase other groceries that have higher mark-ups. You should be aware of this tactic, but as long as the milk is available for your purchase, the tactic is a sound business practice and perfectly legal.

## MAIL ORDER SALES

Mail order sales are growing rapidly, as tens of millions of Americans rely on the convenience of ordering at home. Mail order purchases obviously represent some risk to consumers, however, because you don't obtain immediate possession of the product. Some laws have been passed to protect against mail order fraud.

A Federal Trade Commission rule states that the seller must inform you when the purchase will be shipped and must conform to promises about shipping. If no shipping date is given, the merchandise must be sent within thirty days. If the product is not shipped within thirty days, you have a right to cancel the order.

Sometimes, unsolicited products are sent to you by mail. You may treat these as gifts, and you have no obligation to pay for the unrequested merchandise. Sending you a bill for free samples may be mail fraud, which is a federal crime. This rule does not apply if you belong to a club, such as a book-of-the-month club or a record club. When you joined this club, it is likely that you contractually agreed to purchase the month's selection unless you took affirmative action and sent in a card rejecting the selection. If you failed to send in the card, you are legally obligated to pay for the selection shipped.

## "FREE" OFFERS

From time to time, you may receive what appear to be remarkable offers for free merchandise. One common form of such offers is a promise that if you visit a condominium complex you will receive one of a selection of valuable-sounding gifts. These offers are seldom as they appear. In one reported case, a person was promised an "all-terrain vehicle," but this proved to be a lawn chair on wheels. You might have a fraud action in response to such an offer, but it is wisest simply to have a healthy skepticism and protect yourself in the first place. Be particularly suspicious if you must pay any money to take advantage of some later offer.

## DOOR-TO-DOOR SALES

Door-to-door sales occur when a salesperson goes from house to house in a neighborhood offering a product. The law offers special protections for consumers in these transactions.

The law establishes a three-day **cooling-off period** for sales made in your home or anywhere that is not a fixed place of business for the seller. Under this rule, you may cancel the contract for any or no reason within three days of entering into the deal. The three-day period does not begin to run until you have been informed of your cooling-off-period rights. There can be no charge for your canceling the deal. If you have already made payment, the salesperson must refund your money in full within ten business days. If you have received the merchandise, you must make it available to be picked up during this time.

In addition to the cooling-off period, federal and state laws dictate that the door-to-door salesperson provide you with certain information on a receipt or otherwise. This information includes:

- A description of the goods or services sold.
- The seller's identity and place of business.
- The amount of money you paid or the value of the goods delivered to you.
- Your cooling-off-period rights.

# Consumer Credit

A large proportion of purchases in today's market is made with credit. While use of credit is convenient, the process creates its own legal issues. Several laws have been passed to settle credit issues.

## CREDIT CARDS

Most consumers use credit cards for purchases. These cards may be issued by a specific store or may be all-purpose cards, such as Visa or American Express. While such cards make shopping convenient, be sure that you understand how the cards operate.

Many credit cards, such as Visa and Mastercard and most department store credit cards, use a **revolving credit** system. Each month's purchases are added and a bill is sent to you. Many cards grant you a ''free ride period,'' meaning you need not pay interest during the weeks before you receive the bill. You may pay all or a minimum portion of the bill. The remaining unpaid balance represents a loan to you. Be careful about maintaining an unpaid balance on your charge cards. Interest rates charged on credit cards continue to be high, compared with market rates for bank loans. You may end up paying a considerable premium for use of your credit card. Some companies reserve the right to change their interest rates over time.

Some companies, such as American Express, issue cards that do not permit a revolving credit balance and require you to pay off your debts in full every month. If you fail to pay in full on these cards, you will be charged a contractual penalty that may well exceed the high interest rates of charge cards. Many cards also charge an annual fee for possession of the card. You should compare interest rates and other features before choosing a charge card for regular use.

One concern with credit-card ownership is theft. If your card is stolen, the thief could make many purchases and bill them to you. Indeed, a thief does not need your actual card—learning your card number enables such a person to make mail order purchases on your card. Credit-card theft is in-creasingly common. The law provides some strong protections for the consumer who suffers from credit-card theft.

Under the Truth-in-Lending Act, you have no liability on your credit card unless the granting company has followed required procedures. The credit grantor must prove that you used the card at least once yourself, that the company notified you of your potential liability, and that the company notified you of how to inform the company in the event the card was stolen or lost. Even if the company follows all these requirements, your potential liability is still quite limited.

The law normally restricts your total liability for improper use of your charge cards to $50 per card. Moreover, you have no liability for any charges that occur after you have reported the card as stolen. Consequently, you should report lost or stolen charge cards as soon as you discover them to be missing.

Another potential credit-card problem involves **billing errors.** Billing errors could include being charged for products you did not purchase, mistakes in computations, or failure to give credit for your payments or returned purchases. If you believe that you have discovered a billing error, the Fair Credit Billing Act provides procedures for you to use.

First, notify the credit-card company in writing within sixty days after the bill was mailed to you. Notification must be in writing—telephone calls do not protect your rights under the statute. Be sure to include your account number, the date of the error, and a specification of the nature of the error. The credit-card company must acknowledge your letter or correct the error within thirty days. If the error is not corrected, the company must explain to you within ninety days why it believes the bill to be correct. You may continue to correspond with the company. If you protest the company's explanation within ten days, your credit record will reflect the presence of the dispute. The following table summarizes the time limits of the law.

| |
|---|
| * Notify company of error—in writing, sixty days from error |
| * Company acknowledgment to you—thirty days from notification |
| * Company correction or final response—ninety days from notification |
| * Your notice of protest—ten days from final response |

If the company fails to follow the required legal procedures, it cannot collect the first $50 of the disputed amount or finance charges but can bill you for any remainder. If you fail to pay the remainder, the company may institute collection proceedings against you. At this point, your choice may be to pay or to go to court.

If you use a credit card to buy goods that are defective or damaged or services that are poor quality, you may withhold payment for the disputed item. You cannot withhold payment, however, unless you notify the merchant of your complaint at the same time and make a real attempt to resolve the problem with the merchant. If you bought the goods or services with a credit card other than the store's credit card, the right to withhold payment is limited to purchases over $50 that occurred in your state, or outside your state within one hundred miles of your home address.

## CREDIT REPORTS

After using credit cards or paying off other loans, you will establish a **credit record.** It is important to make payments on time, as this will create a good credit record and make it much easier to obtain a loan in the future. If you have a bad credit record, you may face difficulty getting a loan, even if you are gainfully employed.

Your credit record is summarized on **credit reports** that are maintained by credit bureaus and other companies. Despite your best efforts to pay responsibly, there is a risk that an error in your credit report could make you appear to have an unreliable credit record. To help correct this problem, Congress passed the Fair Credit Reporting Act in 1970.

The Fair Credit Reporting Act requires that those who deny you credit based on credit-bureau information must inform you of the name and address of the credit bureau. If you inquire of the bureau, it must disclose the substance of the information in your file, though you do not have a right to actual copies of the file. If the information in your credit record is inaccurate or incomplete, you can demand that the credit bureau investigate and correct these errors. If the disagreement continues, you can have your position included in your file. If the credit bureau refuses to cooperate at all, you may complain to the Federal Trade Commission, which enforces the act.

## BILL COLLECTION PRACTICES

If you have an overdue debt, a company may assign it to a debt collector. This is a person or company that effectively receives a percentage of the debt in exchange for efforts to collect overdue debts. In the past, collection agencies have been quite abusive in their efforts to collect past-due accounts.

In response to past abuses, Congress passed the Fair Debt Collection Practices Act in 1978. This act requires the debt collector to notify you of the following facts within five days of the initial contact:

1. The amount that you owe.
2. To whom you owe the money.
3. That the collector accepts the debt as authentic unless you challenge it within thirty days.
4. What to do if you dispute the debt.

Perhaps you accept that you owe the debt but are simply unable to pay at this time. You may be able to negotiate a payment schedule with the debt collector. The act prohibits a specific series of debt-collection practices, such as:

- Informing employers or others of the debt.
- Using obscene or harassing language.

- Using threats to harm you or your reputation.
- Making harassing telephone calls at inconvenient times.
- Misrepresenting the amount of the debt or the collector's identity.
- Threatening you with imprisonment or garnishment other than that provided at law.

If the debt-collection agency violates these provisions you may sue the collector and recover up to $1,000. You should also inform the Federal Trade Commission, any state or local consumer protection departments, and if appropriate, the telephone company.

You may choose to send a letter to the debt collector telling the agency not to contact you any further. The collector must also stop contacting you if you write within thirty days that you dispute the existence or amount of the debt. The collector may respond by sending you proof of the debt. In any event, the collector still may commence legal collection action against you for the unpaid debt.

If you are sued for an unpaid debt, you should contact a lawyer or go to a legal aid office if you cannot afford an attorney. You may have defenses to the alleged debt, such as your belief that you purchased a defective product. If the court enters a judgment against you for the debt, it may allow the creditor to seize your nonexempt property in the amount owed and sell it to satisfy the debt. In many states, the court might **garnish** your bank accounts or wages. This permits the creditor automatically to receive a portion of your take-home pay from your employer (up to a maximum of 25 percent).

# Small Claims Court

Some defective products may cause great harm, such as bodily injury, and these damages should be pursued with a lawyer in a general state court. Many consumer transactions, such as the purchase of a nonfunctioning product, result in only small damages, which make it impractical to hire a lawyer and pursue an ordinary claim. For these smaller harms, every state provides some form of **small claims court** (sometimes called pro se courts or magistrates' courts).

There are many advantages to the use of small claims court. The cost of bringing an action is much less than in regular court, and you probably will receive a decision much sooner. A typical small claims case is resolved in a couple of months, while ordinary litigation may take years. In small claims court, you will not need to retain a lawyer to represent you; many states prohibit the use of attorneys in small claims court. You will not need complicated forms or special language. You do make some sacrifices, however, such as the absence of a jury trial and pretrial discovery.

## JURISDICTIONAL LIMITS

Not every case can be filed in small claims court. The court's jurisdiction is limited to truly small claims and varies by state. The typical dollar limit for small claims court is about $2,500, which means you may not bring an action seeking more than that amount in damages. Some states have higher limits—for example, Tennessee, which permits small claims court to hear cases for up to $10,000, and Illinois, which places the limit at $15,000. Other states have lower limits, such as Arizona and Ohio, which limit jurisdiction to claims of under $1,000.

You may voluntarily choose to reduce your claim to slip under the jurisdiction of the small claims court. If you believe that you are owed $3,000, you might file a claim for only $2,500 in small claims court. While you lose the opportunity to recover the $500 difference, you gain the reduced costs of proceeding in small claims court. You cannot split a single claim into two separate cases and then try to bring them both in small claims court. In about half the states, small claims cases are limited to damages and the court cannot issue injunctions or other equitable remedies.

## FILING A CLAIM

As in a general court, a small claims court action begins with the filing of a claim at a specific government office. Before filing this claim, you should notify the prospective defendant through a **demand letter** that states the amount that you believe you are owed. The claim need follow few formalities but must contain certain essential information, such as:

- Your name and address.
- The correct name and address of the person that you are suing.
- The reason that you are owed money, such as when and where your damages arose or a debt was incurred.
- The amount of damages that you are claiming.

Some states give you a form on which you supply this information. Keep copies of all letters, forms, and other papers for your files.

**Statutes of limitations** apply to small claims actions. This means that you must bring your case within a reasonably prompt time after you suffered damages or learned of your claim. The statutes of limitations vary by state. In most states, the limitations period for actions under a written contract is four years; under an oral contract it is two years; and for a tort action it is two or three years, depending upon the tort.

There is a fee associated with filing a claim in small claims court. The amount of this fee is typically small (about $25 to $50), and the fee may vary based on the amount of your claim. You must pay this fee at the time that you file the claim. If you win, the fee may be refunded or added to the judgment.

After the claim is filed, the court will notify the person you are suing. That party will receive a summons to appear before the court. You must provide the court with the correct address, however, which is not always easy to obtain for out-of-state corporations. You may obtain this information from your state's secretary of state office, which maintains a roster of companies doing business in the state. In some states, the defendant must respond to your claim (if only by filing a

general denial), but in most jurisdictions, the defendant need file no papers in response to your claim.

## PRETRIAL PROCEDURES

In the traditional legal action, trial is preceded by extensive discovery, in which the parties exchange documents, question witnesses, etc. The small claims court dispenses with most of this expensive and time-consuming process. As a litigant, you can **subpoena** documents if necessary. While this procedure is seldom used in small claims court, it could be that the defendant or other party has documents that you need for your case. You can require the party to turn over these documents, but don't abuse this authority. If extensive discovery is necessary, you should go to a more traditional court.

You should also identify and arrange for the appearance of relevant witnesses. Go over their testimony with witnesses in advance of trial so that you are prepared for what they will say. You can have a subpoena issued to uncooperative witnesses. If a question of value is at issue, you may need an expert witness. If you are disputing the efficacy of an automobile repair, you should have your own mechanic render an opinion.

You will probably receive a hearing on your claim within thirty days. In most jurisdictions, this is an informal pretrial hearing without witnesses. The court may try to arrange a settlement between you and the defendant. If the defendant fails to appear, you can win a **default judgment,** which is a victory without a trial. If you fail to appear, your case may be dismissed. In the absence of a settlement, your case will promptly advance to trial.

Some states do not provide for these pretrial procedures. In those states, if the defendant fails to respond to your claim, a default judgment is entered against him or her. If the defendant does respond, the matter is scheduled for trial.

## TRIAL PROCEDURES

Because you will be presenting the case in small claims court, you should do some preparation. Arrange all your documentary evidence of support (receipts, canceled checks, contracts, etc.) and other physical evidence, such as the damaged product. Outline your case and go over your presentation. You should also consider sitting in on a few cases before your own trial, in order to familiarize yourself with the court's methods. Sitting in can also alert you to potential pitfalls.

When the trial time comes, you will stand up and present your case, along with your documents, witnesses, and other evidence. You and your witnesses can speak freely, without the constraints of the formal rules of evidence. Indeed, your witness need not appear in person but might provide a written statement. You may prepare maps or charts or write on a court blackboard. The defendant will have an opportunity to present its case to the court as well. The judge will ask questions of both sides.

When presenting your case, stand up. Be clear, organized, and concise. Limit yourself to the facts and treat the defendant with courtesy. Provide only that evidence which is relevant to your particular claim. Present your facts in a conversational manner; do not attempt to read or memorize every word of a prepared statement. Don't act like Perry Mason but simply present your facts in a straightforward fashion.

## JUDGMENT AND APPEAL

After deliberating, the small claims judge will render a decision. If you prevail, you will receive a **final judgment,** which is a document that states that you are authorized to recover a certain amount from the party that you sued. This amount will be whatever the court found you were owed, plus court fees and **prejudgment interest.** The court may provide that the judgment is to be paid out in installments over a period of time.

Even if you win and receive the final judgment, you still must collect the claim. The court does not serve as a collection agency. The court will inform you of how to go about collecting your judgment. If the defendant refuses to pay, you must go back to court to obtain a **writ of execution**—a legal document that you can present to the sheriff, who will seize the defendant's nonexempt property for you. When payment is complete, you file a **satisfaction of judgment** form with the court.

In most states, if you lose your case in small claims court, you may appeal. Some states, including Michigan and California, do not permit plaintiffs to appeal a small claims judgment. If appeal is allowed, you must file a notice of appeal within a brief time following the judgment, such as thirty days. There will be an additional fee to file an appeal, and attorneys may be used on appeal.

## TOPIC 4

# EMPLOYMENT LAW

Getting and holding a job is clearly important to your future well-being. In the past, an employer could hire and fire workers with virtually no legal restrictions. Today, many laws have been passed to restrict the employer's discretion and ensure that employees are treated more fairly. These laws do not guarantee fairness in the workplace, but they do prevent certain specific forms of unfairness.

## The Civil Rights Act of 1964

Until the early 1960s, private employers were free to discriminate openly against minorities, women, or any other group. The Civil Rights Act of 1964 prohibited much of this discrimination against certain groups of protected classes. The Equal Employment Opportunity Commission (EEOC) was created to help resolve or prosecute discrimination cases for employees. Only the protected classes are sheltered from discrimination, however, and employers may lawfully dis-

criminate against other unlisted groups (such as homosexuals). The Civil Rights Act applies to all those businesses that have fifteen or more employees.

## PROTECTED CLASSES

The Civil Rights Act prohibits discrimination against five specific protected classes, based on the following factors:

- Race
- Sex
- Color
- Religion
- National origin

With a few minor exceptions, employers may not discriminate based upon any of these factors. Other unlisted groups are not covered by the Civil Rights Act and must seek protection elsewhere in the law. The law has been interpreted broadly to protect ethnic groups that might not fit exactly in a protected class, such as Arabs, Latinos, and those of mixed race. Religion also is defined broadly. The Civil Rights Act does not prohibit discrimination based upon sexual orientation, but a number of states and localities do ban this form of discrimination.

## PROHIBITED ACTS

The law shelters the protected classes from all significant forms of employment discrimination at any stage of employment. A business may not discriminate in hiring. Contrary to popular belief, the law does not strictly prohibit an employer's questioning of potential workers about their race, religion, marital status, etc. Many employers avoid asking such questions, though, because the interrogation may be viewed as evidence of a discriminatory intent. Questioning should be limited to objectively necessary topics.

An employer may not consider the prohibited factors when firing workers, setting pay scales, or granting promotions. The law also prohibits discrimination regarding the ''terms and conditions of employment.'' This means that an employer cannot expect a given protected class of workers to work longer or suffer less desirable working conditions than other employees. Indeed, employers must be very careful about giving preferential treatment to the members of any protected class. Sexual or racial harassment, which is discussed below, is another prohibited act.

The law does permit employers to have different standards for men and women. For example, a company may have different dress codes, based upon the employee's gender. Such dress codes may become illegal, however, if they require women to wear demeaning clothing.

Employers may not discriminate based upon pregnancy. An employer cannot refuse to hire a pregnant woman, fire her because of her pregnancy, or force her to take maternity leave. Pregnancy must be treated the same as other temporary disabilities—covered under health insurance if other temporary disabilities are covered, for example.

## PROCEDURES

If you believe that you have suffered unlawful discrimination, you should first file a claim with a state government human-rights agency, which will investigate and pursue your case if it is deemed meritorious. If you receive no relief on the state level, you can file a claim with the EEOC. You must file a claim with the EEOC within 180 days of suffering the discrimination. The EEOC will try to reach a voluntary settlement with your employer that protects your interests. If no settlement can be reached, the EEOC will determine whether there is reasonable cause to suspect unlawful discrimination. If so, the Commission will take the case to court for you. If not, the Commission will give you a "right-to-sue" letter, and you can attempt to prove that you suffered illegal discrimination. If the EEOC does not act promptly (within six months), you are entitled to a right-to-sue letter. You must file your lawsuit within ninety days of obtaining a right-to-sue letter.

Even if you have suffered unlawful discrimination in hiring, you should seek out another job, as this can demonstrate your desire to work and will strengthen your claim. If your claim is successful, you may be awarded back pay (up to two years), compensatory damages, attorneys' fees, and job reinstatement.

## DISPARATE IMPACT

The initial focus of the Civil Rights Act of 1964 was upon intentional discrimination (called disparate-treatment discrimination) against protected classes. As the law evolved, courts began to recognize the presence of apparently unintentional discriminatory practices. The doctrine of **disparate impact** discrimination followed.

Illegal disparate-impact discrimination arises when an employer has a rule that is superficially neutral and nondiscriminatory, but that rule happens to have a significantly adverse impact upon members of a protected group. For example, suppose that a fire department had a rule requiring all job applicants to be at least six feet tall and weigh at least 175 pounds. Although this rule is applied equally to everyone, the requirements exclude a disproportionate number of women who might want to become firefighters. This rule has a disparate impact.

An employer may justify a rule with a disparate impact if it is a business necessity. The fire department could respond that firefighters need strength and so the rule is necessary for the job. The plaintiff could rebut this by showing that an alternative strength test or other measure could serve the fire department's interests without having a discriminatory impact upon women.

An employer may also justify a rule if it is a bona fide occupational qualification (BFOQ). The BFOQ exception is very limited, however, and generally applies only in obvious situations, such as those involving fashion models or actors.

## AFFIRMATIVE ACTION

The Civil Rights Act of 1964 protects everyone against discrimination, including white males. There is an exception for **affirmative action,** which may in effect create discrimination to a degree against white males or other groups that historically have been successful in employment and promotions. In some circumstances, an employer might favor a minority or woman in hiring.

While theoretically lawful, affirmative action is limited. First, the employer must show a reason or need for an affirmative action program. Such a reason might well be that the company has extremely few minority employees, relative to the community population of qualified workers. Any resultant program must be temporary, limited to correcting the need for affirmative action, restricted to qualified persons, and cannot unduly restrict the opportunities of a majority class. Courts have upheld affirmative action programs in hiring but have been very reluctant to accept affirmative action programs which might mean majority workers could be fired from their positions.

# Other Discrimination Laws

The Civil Rights Act of 1964 was followed by laws prohibiting discrimination against other groups of people. These laws generally track the operation of the Civil Rights Act, with some exceptions.

## AGE DISCRIMINATION

The Age Discrimination in Employment Act of 1967 ("ADEA") prohibits age discrimination against anyone forty or older. The protected class is limited to those forty years of age and older; the law implicitly permits age discrimination against those less than forty years old. As in the Civil Rights Act of 1964, the law prohibits many forms of discrimination, including promotions, and extends to disparate-impact discrimination as well. The law extends to businesses with twenty or more employees.

As amended, the law also prohibits mandatory retirement ages. A limited exception exists for corporate management. The ADEA does not mean that an employer cannot fire or force the retirement of an older worker. The law simply requires that the retirement be based on the employee's ability to do the job and not simply his or her age. The ADEA does permit an employer to offer voluntary retirement programs based on the age of the worker. Such a program must be truly voluntary, and the worker cannot be pressured to accept the program.

## DISABILITY DISCRIMINATION

In 1990, Congress passed the Americans with Disabilities Act (ADA), which expanded protection for persons with disabilities. Protected individuals include those with traditional disabilities (blindness, inability to walk) and other disabilities (AIDS, certain emotional illnesses). The law prohibits most forms of employment discrimination and extends to businesses with fifteen or more employees. The ADA explicitly outlaws an employer's questioning of an employee or potential employee about the presence or extent of a disability. It is also illegal not to hire potential employees out of a fear that they might generate large health-insurance claims.

The ADA requires businesses to make **reasonable accommodations** for disabled workers or job applicants. Such an accommodation is one that enables the disabled person to do a job without the employer's having to incur undue expense or difficulty. Larger companies with greater assets will be expected to do more to accommodate qualified disabled workers.

Another provision of the ADA forces employers to grant leaves of absence for disabilities, unless the company can show that the extended leave would cause "undue hardship" to the company. If you must take such an extended leave due to disability, the employer must hold your job open, unless the employer can demonstrate such hardship.

Discrimination against the disabled is allowed under certain circumstances. If the disabled worker would present a risk to self or others on the job, the employer normally need not hire the worker. For example, while it is illegal to discriminate against individuals with AIDS in general, an employer may refuse to hire someone with AIDS for a job that presents a realistic risk that the disease will be transmitted to others.

# Sexual Harassment

Harassment of employees based upon their membership in a protected class can be illegal under the antidiscrimination laws. The most common and frequent form of such harassment is sexual harassment, which is considered to be discrimination based upon sex.

## QUID PRO QUO HARASSMENT

The historically infamous form of sexual harassment is known as *quid pro quo*. This is the "casting couch" scenario where a boss demands sexual favors as a condition of promotion or continued employment. If the employee refuses and suffers adverse employment consequences, he or she may rightfully claim illegal discrimination.

## HOSTILE ENVIRONMENT HARASSMENT

The law also prohibits **hostile environment** harassment, which means the creation of a working environment so tainted by harassment that the worker's terms and conditions of employment are affected. Extreme cases of blatant harassment, such as grabbing parts of the worker's body and making blatantly obscene suggestive remarks, clearly qualify as hostile environment harassment. Other circumstances, such as flirting, are less clear-cut. Romance may arise on the job, and

sexual relations or advances among workers are only illegal if they are unwelcome.

It can be difficult to draw the line between a hostile environment and either flirtation or episodes of harassment so minor that they do not affect the terms and conditions of employment. A rare off-color joke is not normally illegal harassment. In general, you may ask a co-worker out on a date, but you should not persist if he or she refuses. Posting pornographic pictures at work is certainly questionable. The seriousness of harassment is judged in part by the perceptions of its victim. Because most victims are female, many courts apply the **reasonable woman** standard to test whether a reasonable woman would be seriously offended by the behavior in question.

Under the Civil Rights Act of 1964, only the employer is liable for sexual harassment, not the offending worker. The company is liable for harassment by a co-worker if it knew or had reason to know of the harassment and failed to prevent it. For this reason, the victim of harassment should first inform a supervisor or other corporate official and try to resolve the problem internally. If the harasser is a supervisor or a high corporate officer, the court may presume the employer's awareness. In a 1992 case, the chief executive of a company committed the harassment, and the victim was awarded over $1.3 million in damages, which included **punitive damages** (damages assessed to punish the wrongdoer).

# Wrongful Discharge

Suppose that you are fired from your job for no reason or because your boss is arbitrary and believed a lie told about you. You were not even given an opportunity to explain your side of the story. You had no right to any prior notice before your discharge. Historically, it would have been virtually impossible for you to file a successful lawsuit over your discharge. Antidiscrimination statutes imposed one important restriction on employer discharges. In recent years, courts have been placing even greater constraints on the employer's discretion to fire a worker, developing the doctrine of **wrongful discharge.**

## AT-WILL EMPLOYMENT

The customary common law recognizes a doctrine called **at-will employment.** This doctrine means that in most employment contracts (not for an explicit term of years), the worker may quit at any time or the employer may discharge the worker at any time. Neither action requires justification. Thus, an employer can fire a worker for no reason or even a bad reason, and courts will not interfere with this choice. This might seem unfair to you, but the law does not second-guess the employer's reasoning.

## IMPLIED CONTRACT

The employer may yield its at-will employment rights through an explicit or implied contract with the employee.

An implied contract may be created through an **employment manual.** Perhaps the employment manual promises that you will not be fired without good cause and a chance to explain yourself. If these promises are expressed in terms of your rights as an employee and then are violated, you might claim that the discharge was an illegal violation of your implied contract. Some employment manuals have disclaimers, however, which state that the employee rights as stated in the manuals are not enforceable. Such a disclaimer might undermine your wrongful discharge claim. Oral assurances by responsible corporate officers may also create an implied contract, though these can be more difficult for you to prove.

## PUBLIC-POLICY EXCEPTION

Courts also recognize a worker's wrongful discharge action if a firing violates public policy. The public-policy standard is limited, however, and simple unfairness does not constitute a wrongful discharge. Rather, you must demonstrate that the firing contravenes a fundamental principle of public policy.

An employee who has a generalized and even admirable concern for public safety is not protected from discharge by public policy. The public-policy exception applies in circumstances such as the following:

- You are fired for exercising a civic right or duty, such as jury duty or voting.
- You are fired for refusing to violate the law, such as refusal to participate in an environmental crime.
- You are fired in retaliation for exercising legal rights, such as filing a proper workers' compensation claim.

An employer normally may always fire an employee for good cause, such as absenteeism, incompetence, or disruptiveness.

## WHISTLEBLOWING

**Whistleblowing** is a term describing the situation in which an employee notifies management or the media of wrongdoing in the corporation. Perhaps you have discovered that an officer is engaged in an unlawful price-fixing scheme. After you ''blow the whistle'' on this individual, you are fired by the company.

Whistleblowing is partially protected by state law. Some states have statutes that protect whistleblowers, and other states use the public-policy exception. In either case, you should be sure of your facts before blowing the whistle. In addition, you should first blow the whistle internally and enable the corporation to correct the problem before airing the issue in the media. Even so, there is no guarantee of protection. In a California case, an employee was fired after informing management that his supervisor was under investigation by the FBI. The court held that the discharge was legal on the ground that an employee has no right to spread even accurate rumors about fellow employees. In some industries, such as defense contracting, whistleblowers are strongly protected by federal law.

## INDEPENDENT TORTS

In some cases, even if your firing is legal, the employer may conduct the discharge in a way that provides you with an independent tort action. Imagine that your employer wrongfully accuses you of stealing company property and fires you. If the employer called you a thief in front of other employees, you may have a strong **defamation** action against the employer. Other possible tort actions are **fraud** or **intentional infliction of emotional distress,** if the firing was conducted in a particularly abusive manner.

# Employee Privacy

Employee privacy rights are a major new concern of the law. In general, employees have little on-the-job privacy protection under common law. Some statutes have been passed to provide a measure of privacy protection to workers, but this protection is still quite limited.

## LIE-DETECTOR TESTS

Some companies used to conduct polygraph or other lie-detector examinations regularly and at random in order to detect employee theft or other problems. Congress was concerned about the widespread utilization of such tests and passed legislation in 1988 to limit their use.

In most occupations you cannot be forced to take a lie-detector test and therefore cannot be fired for refusing to take the test. There are some exceptions when polygraph testing is allowed. Workers holding certain sensitive jobs, such as security personnel and production of controlled substances, are subject to lie-detector testing. The employer may also force you to take such a test if the company is conducting an ongoing investigation of losses and has reasonable suspicion that you were involved in the losses because you had control over the property.

Even when you are lawfully subject to testing, federal law contains further protections. You cannot be asked needlessly intrusive or degrading questions. You must be informed of the purpose for the testing, and disclosure of the test results is limited. The testing must follow accepted standards for accuracy.

## DRUG TESTING

Recent years have seen a significant increase in the use of employer drug testing, as the costs of drug abuse are increasingly recognized. With the exception of a few states, such drug tests are legal. Although drug tests plainly intrude upon your privacy, the tests are generally held to be a reasonable exercise of the employer's rights. Courts may require that steps be taken to ensure the test's accuracy and that the privacy invasion of a drug test be no greater than needed. Other forms of medical tests have been acceptable, but the Americans with Disabilities Act now restricts such testing to cases of necessity.

## EMPLOYEE MONITORING

With the advance of new technologies, employers are increasingly able to monitor the work of their employees. Companies may keep track of the contents of your telephone calls or your computer work. Closed-circuit monitors may be installed in the workplace to observe your work habits. Like drug testing, such monitoring is considered a matter between employer and employee and is generally legal. A few states have limited laws restricting such monitoring, such as prohibiting monitoring of nonwork areas.

## PERSONNEL RECORDS

Federal law provides no right for workers to see their personnel records, though a number of states grant such a right, as do many employers' voluntary policies. Moreover, an employer may lawfully disclose the contents of your personnel file to individuals either inside or outside the company. If the revealed information is false, you may sue for defamation.

# Other Employee Protection Laws

In addition to the discrimination and privacy laws discussed above, there are a large number of statutes that provide a variety of protections to workers. Many of these protect the economic and safety interests of workers and are summarized below.

## LABOR UNIONS

The first significant law for worker protection was enacted in 1932 and gave legal protection to labor unions. Before federal legislation such as minimum wage or occupational safety laws, workers depended on unions to protect their interests. Today, unions are less significant than in the past but many work forces are still unionized and you always have the right to attempt to form a union and protect your interests.

If you wish to form a union you may enlist the assistance of a well-established, powerful organization such as the AFL-CIO. You then must demonstrate the interest of other workers in unionizing by getting them to sign authorization cards. If this is successful, you can obtain a vote among the workers over whether to form a union. If you are already represented but dissatisfied with your current union, you may obtain a vote to decertify that union. If you don't want to join an existing union, your rights will depend upon state law. Some "right to work" states prohibit a requirement of union membership, while other states allow it.

Once a union is formed, its primary responsibility is **collective bargaining** with the employer. Representatives from the union and the employer confer and seek to hammer out a contract that will govern all the covered workers. If an agreement cannot be reached, the union may call a strike against the employer. Only the union can call a strike, and a walkout by a small group of disgruntled workers will be an illegal wildcat strike. In most strikes, the employer may hire permanent replacement workers, and the unionized employees could lose their jobs.

## FAIR LABOR STANDARDS ACT

The Fair Labor Standards Act (FLSA), which dates back to 1938, governs the hours and wages of work. The coverage of the FLSA is very broad and reaches virtually every employer in the country. This law establishes a minimum wage, which is now set at $4.25 per hour. Some states have a higher minimum wage. Employers must pay the applicable minimum wage rate for up to the first forty hours worked in a week. If you work more than forty hours, you are entitled to one and a half times your regular wage rate (usually called "overtime"). Under the FLSA, the operative period is a week, and you are not automatically entitled to overtime simply because you worked more than eight hours in any single day. Some states provide for overtime pay for more than eight hours worked in a day.

The FLSA has detailed rules for calculating the number of hours worked. For example, brief coffee breaks of twenty minutes or less are counted as working time. In general, meal time is not counted as hours worked, even if the worker must eat on the premises. Of course, meals are working time if the employee has duties during this period, such as answering the phone. Travel time or "on-call" time may count as hours worked if the employer places material restrictions on the worker's use of this time.

The minimum wage standard is not limited to those employees who are paid by the hour. A salaried worker must be paid a salary equal to at least the number of hours worked multiplied by the minimum wage rate ($170 per forty-hour week as of 1994). The FLSA gives employers some flexibility, because the measured forty-hour workweek under the law need not begin on a Monday. Moreover, an employer may pay less than minimum wage when the difference is made up in cash tips. In some circumstances, a company may pay less than minimum wage if it provides free meals or lodging to employees.

Not every worker is protected by the FLSA. For example, agricultural workers, many salespeople, and professional, managerial, and supervisory employees are exempted from the law. The FLSA also has child-labor provisions that generally prevent employment of those younger than fourteen and that restrict the terms of employment of those aged fourteen to seventeen.

## ERISA

The Employee Retirement Income Security Act (ERISA) of 1974 was adopted to protect worker interests in pension plans and certain other benefit plans. ERISA is an enormously complicated statute that addresses the administration of such plans. ERISA does not require that an employer establish any form of benefit plan for its workers.

If an employer chooses to establish a pension plan or agrees to a plan in negotiations, ERISA regulates the operation of the plan to protect employee interests. ERISA imposes vesting requirements, which mean that the worker obtains an irrevocable interest in his or her plan benefits after a certain time, such as five years. ERISA also regulates the investments of pension plans and takes other measures to ensure the safety of these investments.

## WORKER SAFETY

The Occupational Safety and Health Act (OSHA) of 1970 was enacted to help ensure safe and healthful working conditions on the job. Numerous standards have been set under this law, including limits on exposures to harmful chemicals and numerous workplace standards to avert accidents. In addition, the law contains a **general duty clause,** which obligates employers to keep the workplace free of recognized hazards to health, even in the absence of a standard. Employees can file complaints about unsafe conditions and cannot be required to work when they have a good faith reason to fear that their safety is in jeopardy. Workers also have an OSHA duty to comply with federal safety and health rules.

When an on-the-job accident does occur, the employee may recover **workers' compensation.** Each state has a workers' compensation system that pays benefits for accidents or diseases that arise out of or occur in the course of normal employment. Most states also require employers to carry insurance to guarantee funds for payment. The worker need not prove any fault on the part of the employer, so recovery is relatively easy. A worker may recover even if his or her own negligence contributed to the injury, but there is no recovery for intentionally self-inflicted harms. The amount of recovery, though, is typically less than what is available in **litigation.** The injured worker may not file suit against the employer but may be able to bring a case against a manufacturer of the product that caused the injury.

Some workers have been afraid to file for compensation, lest they be fired. In most states, a person cannot be discharged in retaliation for filing a legitimate workers' compensation claim. Employers may still fire high-risk employees who have filed many such claims. The scope of workers' compensation has been expanding to cover stress-related circumstances such as a heart attack suffered by a white-collar employee.

## FAMILY LEAVE

In 1993, Congress passed the Family and Medical Leave Act, which covers entities that have fifty or more employees. This law requires covered employers to provide up to twelve weeks of unpaid, job-protected leave to ''eligible'' employees for certain family and medical reasons. You are ''eligible'' if you worked for the covered employer for at least one year and for 1,250 hours in the previous twelve months.

The law requires that this unpaid leave be granted ''for the care of the employee's child (birth or placement for adoption or foster care); for the care of the employee's spouse, son or daughter, or parent, who has a serious health condition; or for a serious health condition that makes the employee unable to perform their job.'' The Department of Labor has prepared a medical certification form to meet the act's requirement that workers certify that the leave requests are related to serious health conditions. Workers must provide thirty days' advance notice of their need for leave, if possible.

The Family and Medical Leave Act guarantees certain protections to workers who avail themselves of the guaranteed leave time. These workers must be restored to their original jobs or equivalent jobs upon their return from leave. The law also guarantees the protection of employment benefits that were accrued prior to the start of leave and the maintenance of health coverage during the time on leave.

## PLANT CLOSING LEGISLATION

In 1988, Congress passed the Worker Adjustment and Retraining Notification Act (WARNA) in order to provide workers with advance notice of certain job losses. WARNA applies to larger companies, such as those with one hundred or more employees. This law covers plant closings and mass layoffs (more than fifty workers and at least 33 percent of the workforce fired). In such circumstances, an employer must provide at least sixty days' advance written notice to workers. Failure to provide such notice entitles workers to pay and benefits for the period when the required warning was lacking.

## UNEMPLOYMENT COMPENSATION

The United States has an unemployment compensation system, in which employers pay taxes into a fund, and the proceeds are paid out to workers who qualify for such compensation. Each state has authority to set rules determining which workers are entitled to unemployment benefits. Some typical state requirements are as follows:

- The employee must have been fired without good cause or have quit the job with good cause.
- The employee must be unemployed for some minimum amount of time, such as a week.
- The employee must have worked on a reasonably regular basis prior to unemployment.
- The employee must register with a state-run employment agency, seek a new job, and accept any reasonably suitable new job offer.
- The employee must be able to work and not be a striker.

If the worker qualifies for unemployment compensation, he or she will receive regular but temporary benefits based on a formula. The formula is generally based on a fraction of the worker's average wages during a recent period up to a certain maximum. Benefits are available for up to twenty-six weeks, and this has been extended during times of serious unemployment. This income may be taxable.

## TOPIC 5

# OWNING AND OPERATING MOTOR VEHICLES

Motor vehicles are a significant part of the average American's life. In many areas of the country, a car or motorcycle is a necessity for commuting, shopping, etc. A car is also one of the most significant expenses that you may have. The laws of owning and operating motor vehicles vary by state jurisdiction, but the state requirements have many common features.

# Buying a New Car

When shopping for a new motor vehicle, you will inevitably be drawn to dealer advertising in newspapers or on television. Some states regulate automobile ads, requiring that they state the duration of a sale or the number of vehicles that the dealer has available. Automobile ads may nevertheless mislead you. Published prices may omit necessary or factory-installed option packages, dealer preparation costs, taxes, and other fees.

Once you have settled on a new motor vehicle, its purchase is a fairly standard contractual arrangement in which you obtain title to the vehicle in exchange for cash or loan financing. The contract must be in writing and should clearly set forth all important terms (such as total cost, value for trade-in, terms of financing, etc.). The contract also should set forth the vehicle identification number (''VIN'') and any other fundamental understandings between the buyer and seller. For example, the contract should state that the car is in fact new and has not been used as a demonstrator or rental car. Also, be sure to get promised warranties in writing in the contract.

## FINANCING

Most individuals cannot pay cash for a new car and must therefore arrange for financing. You may obtain such financing through a bank, savings and loan, or credit union, but many dealers now offer their own financing, often at a discount rate, in order to attract customers. Compare rates and be aware that dealers may increase the purchase price of the car to compensate for discount financing.

Federal law regulates contracts for financing products such as automobiles. The lender must inform you of the following facts:

1. The annual percentage rate charged.
2. How the lender sets the finance charge.
3. The balance on which the finance charge is computed.
4. The finance charge amount.
5. The amount to be financed.
6. The total dollar amount to be paid.
7. The number, amounts, and due dates of payments.

Lenders who violate the law owe you any damages you have suffered, plus a fine and court costs.

## TITLE

Once financing has been arranged, you obtain the vehicle plus a certificate of title to the vehicle. This title serves as proof of ownership and should be safely kept by the buyer. The title alone does not give you the right to drive the vehicle, however. States require that the car be registered with the state and be issued license plates. The driver also must have a driver's license.

If you fail to make required loan payments, the seller may take back the title and repossess the car. After a car is repossessed, you have a chance to redeem it by paying all overdue payments (and possibly the entire balance due), plus repossession costs.

## WARRANTIES

Most new cars come with some form of **express warranty.** This is a promise of quality or service that should be stated in the contract. A typical express warranty would provide that the seller will replace any defective parts without charge, for a certain time period or until the car has been driven a certain number of miles.

Automobile purchasers also automatically receive certain **implied warranties.** These warranties are presumed to be included in all contracts and need not be stated explicitly. The **implied warranty of title** declares that the seller is the true owner of the car and has legal right to transfer that ownership to you. The **implied warranty of merchantability** states that the vehicle at least meets ordinary standards of mechanical efficiency. This assures you that the car won't break down as soon as you drive it off the seller's lot.

While these implied warranties generally accompany any sale of a new car, the seller may avoid such warranties by using a **disclaimer.** A provision in the contract of sale, if properly worded, could clearly declare that the seller is making no warranties. The sale of a used car ''as is'' disclaims implied warranties. If you sign such a contract, you lose the legal protections associated with implied warranties of merchantability.

If a warranty or other contract provision is violated, you may cancel the sale of the car within a reasonable time after you have obtained it. A reasonable time is usually no more than a week or two. Alternatively, you may provide the dealer an opportunity to ''cure'' the defect. Once you cancel the sale of the car, it is no longer yours and you must stop using it.

If the warranty violation is discovered too late for cancellation, you can seek damages. As a general rule, you must continue to make your car payments while seeking legal recourse. If the violation is significant or costly to correct, you may need a lawyer to help you enforce your contractual rights.

## LEMON LAWS

Forty-five states have passed **lemon laws** to protect those who purchase defective vehicles. These laws provide you protection over and above any warranties. The precise terms of lemon laws vary from state to state. In general, a ''lemon'' is a vehicle that has a defect substantially affecting its use, value, or safety, even after reasonable efforts of repair. This may mean as many as four repair attempts on the same problem before repair is deemed futile. Alternatively, some states consider a car a lemon if it is out of commission for more than thirty days during the first year of ownership.

In order to take advantage of a lemon law, you must notify the dealer of the defect and keep a copy of all repair records and receipts. In most states, you will be required to take the dispute to **arbitration** before suing. If you win, you may obtain a satisfactory replacement vehicle or a refund of the purchase price plus associated taxes and fees (minus some allowance for the value of your use of the car). The states also provide other consumer protection laws that offer larger damages than those under lemon laws (such as triple the cost of the car), though these laws may require you to prove that the dealer knowingly or willfully sold you a defective vehicle.

## Buying or Selling a Used Car

Used vehicles represent a significant percentage of sales, and ordinary individuals may be on both sides of a used-car sale. The law provides some basic requirements for such a contract. First, if the price is $500 or more, the contract must be in writing to be enforceable in court. Second, the transaction must include a written **bill of sale.** The bill of sale should state the amount paid, the method of payment, and identifying details about the car, including its VIN. The bill of sale or transfer of title should be signed and dated and generally must be submitted to a specific government agency for registration. Note that applicable sales tax must be paid on used-car sales.

Used-car sales are subject to many of the same buyer-protection laws as are new-car sales. Lemon laws are increasingly being extended to apply to used-car sales. Warranties also apply to many used car sales. If you are selling a car with a material latent defect (one that is not readily discoverable by the buyer), you have a duty to disclose that defect. Otherwise you may be liable for fraud. The implied warranty of merchantability, however, only applies to merchants and does not exist if the sale is by an individual who is not in the business of selling used cars. Although an individual seller makes no implied warranty of quality, the seller may make an express warranty of quality. Any implied warranties may be disclaimed by selling the car ''as is.''

Additional regulatory requirements apply to dealers in used cars and provide further buyer protection. A dealer is anyone who sells six or more used cars in a twelve-month period. The Federal Trade Commission requires that dealers post a **Buyer's Guide** on the side window of each used car they sell. This includes a warning that oral promises are difficult to enforce as a practical matter and a recommendation that you get all promises in unambiguous writing. The Guide also lists the terms of any warranties provided and supplies details about any service contracts and significant recurrent problems with the car's mechanical or safety systems.

## Renting or Leasing a Car

A short-term automobile rental is another form of contractual arrangement subject to the agreement of the parties. Most automobile rental companies require that you have a driver's license and a major credit card, and some require that you be at least twenty-five years old before they will rent you a vehicle. These companies often waive the age requirement if the rental is business related or if you are a member of an established auto club.

The rental agreement contract will contain a variety of detailed terms and provide you some options. The most significant of these options is the **collision damage waiver.** If you pay for this collision protection, you are not liable for accidental damages to the rental car. The coverage does not extend to personal injuries or damage to others' property, however. Accepting the company's collision damage insurance may be unnecessary. Your existing automobile insurance policy may already provide for this coverage, as may your employer's policy (if this is a business rental) or your credit card itself.

Automobile leasing is a growing business and typically substitutes for the purchase of a car. Under a typical lease, you make monthly payments to the dealer for two to four years. These payments are in place of and typically much less than the monthly payments you would make on a new-car loan. Unlike such loan payments, however, lease payments do not provide you with an **equity (ownership) interest** in the vehicle. Leasing a car may in some states avoid the need to pay sales tax and avoid a down payment (although one- or two-months' advance lease payments are typically required).

When the lease expires, you return the vehicle to the dealer. You no longer have any obligation or interest in this car. If you want to keep the car, you may buy it from the dealer at the end of the lease. Some leases specify an end-of-lease purchase price. For other leases, you simply must negotiate a price with the dealer.

The terms of a lease are like any other contract. Many leases provide that you must make additional payments if you drive more than 15,000 miles per year or cause some irreparable damage to the vehicle. Other terms may include insurance, maintenance agreements, loaner-car arrangements, etc. These may be negotiated, but some dealers may be unwilling to modify their standard form leases.

In some respects, a lease of a motor vehicle may be as much of a commitment as a purchase. The contract binds you to keep the car for the duration of the lease, unless you can sublease the vehicle. Some lease contracts contain an early termination clause through which you may escape the lease early if you don't like the car. These clauses typically require you to pay a penalty, however. If your leased car is stolen or destroyed, it is considered to be an early termination, and your insurance probably will not cover the early termination penalty. **Gap insurance** is available to cover this possibility.

## Insuring a Car

### CATEGORIES OF INSURANCE

Many states require you to have automobile **liability insurance** and others require you to demonstrate ''financial responsibility'' (such as obtaining insurance or posting a bond). The laws specify a minimum basic level of coverage that is required. These requirements vary by state. Insurance laws are designed to ensure that you can pay damages if injury occurs to another person as a result of your careless driving. Failure to maintain such insurance is a driving violation that subjects you to a fine and potential loss of your license.

When you acquire liability insurance, your insurance company must pay for the damages that you caused. If you are sued for negligent driving, your insurance company generally will take charge of the suit and supply its own lawyer. You remain personally liable, however, for damages over and above the policy limits (which may be as low as $50,000). The compulsory liability insurance laws also help protect your ability to recover damages if you are injured by others.

When you obtain insurance, your periodic payment rate will be based upon a number of factors. These include type of car, your age, gender, driving record, and primary use of car, plus local accident rates. Although it may seem unfair, all young males pay an extra premium, because so many young males get into accidents. You may pay a higher rate if your type of car is particularly expensive to repair or especially likely to be stolen. As with any business deal, you can shop around to find the best rates.

When acquiring insurance, you may obtain **uninsured motorist coverage.** Indeed, seventeen states require you to have such a policy. This uninsured motorist coverage enables you to collect for your damages if you are injured by a negligent driver who lacks his or her own insurance. Even in states in which liability insurance is required, a significant number of drivers lack coverage. Under uninsured motorist coverage, your own insurance company pays for your damages and then attempts to recover this payment in an action against the uninsured driver. You are thus covered even if the negligent driver lacks the ability to pay.

To collect under uninsured motorist coverage, you generally must show that the other driver was at fault and lacked liability insurance. Many uninsured motorist policies provide protection even when the other party has insurance, but the party's policy limits are insufficient to cover all your damages. You can recover your damages only once, however, and cannot duplicate payments from both your own and the other party's insurers.

In addition to liability and uninsured motorist coverage, you have other insurance options. Many individuals purchase **collision insurance,** through which the insurer pays for any damages to your car from a collision, regardless of who was at fault. **Comprehensive insurance** protects against noncollision damage to your vehicle (including theft, vandalization, and hail damage). These policies generally do *not* cover personal items left in your vehicle. These policies also generally contain a **deductible,** which means that you must pay a certain amount of your loss, such as the first $200 of damages. You may also obtain insurance to cover medical payments for you and your passengers after an accident.

About half of the states have a system of **no-fault insurance.** This system largely eliminates lawsuits for negligence and requires every driver to carry insurance to pay for his or her own damages, regardless of who was at fault in the accident. Under this system, parties need not go to court to recover and need not worry that the other driver lacks insurance. Damage compensation in no-fault systems tends to be lower than in traditional jurisdictions.

## INSURANCE COVERAGE

If you obtain automobile insurance and inform your insurance company that others may drive your car, they too are protected by the policy. An automobile insurance policy typically extends coverage to the following parties:

- You and your spouse.
- Other residents of your household that you have declared to the insurance company.
- Other undeclared persons who drive the car with your permission (though this may be limited to infrequent borrowings).
- Nondrivers who may be liable due to your negligence, such as your employer.

If you fail to inform the insurance company that another party will be a regular driver of your car, that person may not be covered by the insurance.

If you purchase a new car, your old automobile insurance policy continues in effect for at least thirty days, while a new policy may be written and acquired. You should notify your insurance company of your purchase and obtain a new policy promptly in order to ensure continued protection. Your policy will also cover you when you drive an automobile owned by another person. If you go on vacation and have an accident while driving your sister's car, you will probably be covered by both your policy and her policy. In many cases, your policy will not provide coverage for driving in foreign countries (except Canada).

# Repairing a Car

When your car is damaged and requires repair, you will need to choose a mechanic. In some areas, auto mechanics are notorious for questionable or fraudulent practices. To defend yourself against such practices, investigate the reputation and past practices of mechanics and negotiate a repair contract that legally protects your interests.

The repair contract is often called a **repair order.** This order is customarily a form standard in the industry that describes the work to be done on your vehicle. Signing the order creates a contract authorizing the mechanic to make the described repairs. The repair order contains necessary identifying information about you and your car but does not generally state a price for the repairs.

It is a good practice to receive a cost estimate for repairs before authorizing the work, though some repair shops will charge for such estimates. At common law, this estimate is not binding, and if the cost proves greater than the estimate, you are still bound to pay the difference. Some states have legislation that provides that actual costs cannot exceed the estimate by more than a certain percentage.

After repair work, complaints may arise over the quality of the work, the cost, or warranties made by the mechanic. Most states have laws requiring that you be provided with a detailed invoice of parts and labor as well as the right to receive parts that have been replaced. If you believe that you have been cheated, you may be able to sue in contract or under a deceptive trade practices statute. If you inform your state attorney general, he or she may take action on your behalf.

If you refuse to pay for the repairs, the mechanic may keep your car. This is done through an **artisan's lien** (or mechanic's lien), which gives the repair shop the right to possession of your car to satisfy your debt. This lien is available only if the shop has complied with legal requirements for repair authorization. If you make payments, the mechanic must return your car.

# Driving Violations

A long list of criminal laws governs driving. These laws vary greatly in seriousness and in penalties. For the most significant violations, penalties may include prison time.

## STOP AND SEARCH

The police have a broad right to stop you while you are driving. When you see the police flashing lights in your rearview mirror, you should pull over to the side of the road as promptly and safely as possible. The police have a right to see your driver's license and to have you step out of the car.

After a stop, the officer may want to search your car. The officer need not have a warrant. Your car can only be searched, however, if either (a) you consent or (b) the officer has probable cause to believe that your vehicle contains incriminating evidence. If an illegal item (such as drugs or guns) is in plain view in your car, the officer may seize it without the need for a search warrant. The law defining the scope of police searches is ever changing as new cases are brought. At a minimum, the police may search the area within the driver's reach, including the glove compartment. Under some circumstances, the police can impound your car. If so, they may do a thorough search without a warrant or even probable cause.

## SPEEDING

A common driving violation is excessive speed. If you are caught speeding, you may be subject to a substantial fine. The officer may choose not to cite you for speeding if you have a particularly good reason (such as a health emergency). Most speeding violations are demonstrated by radar readings of your speed. You may have heard of cases in which radar results were thrown out of court for improper maintenance or other reasons. In the vast majority of cases, however, courts accept the results of radar guns as virtually conclusive evidence that you were speeding. In many jurisdictions, you may take a defensive driving course in lieu of a fine for speeding. Completion of the course may also keep the ticket off your driving record and avoid an increase in insurance rates.

Some people use radar detectors to avoid getting caught speeding. Connecticut and Virginia have outlawed the use of such radar detectors. In a recent New Jersey case, a person was arrested for flashing his headlights to warn oncoming traffic of the presence of a radar trap. The court, however, held that his actions were perfectly legal.

## DRIVING WHILE INTOXICATED

Perhaps the most serious driving violation is driving while intoxicated with alcohol or other drugs. Some states call this crime "driving under the influence." Intoxication is typically defined by blood-alcohol level, and different states have different standards for defining intoxication. Drunk driving is responsible for about 20,000 deaths annually.

The blood-alcohol level defining intoxication varies somewhat by state, with most using a .10 standard (meaning one-tenth of one percent blood-alcohol concentration). California and some other states have lowered this threshold to .08. Your blood-alcohol level is a function of your weight and alcohol consumption, plus some other factors. Having two regular-sized drinks (one ounce of alcohol each) within one hour may put you in the danger zone of violation.

The police may pull you over if your driving appears erratic, such as weaving from lane to lane. Indeed, the police may establish roadblocks in areas frequented by drinkers and stop cars randomly to check for drunk driving. Once you are stopped they will observe your coordination, your speech, whether you smell of alcohol, and the appearance of your eyes. They may administer a simple test of your ability to walk a straight line or your ability to focus your eyes on a point. If they continue to suspect that you were driving while intoxicated, they will ask you to take a breathalyzer examination.

You are not required to take the breathalyzer test, due to the constitutional protection against self-incrimination. If you refuse, however, states are authorized to suspend your driver's license, usually for several months. Many attorneys advise that you should refuse the breathalyzer if you suspect that you are indeed intoxicated beyond the legal limit. If you fail a breathalyzer test, your attorney may subsequently challenge the results, but the test is often powerful evidence. In many states, you have a right to a second, confirmatory test if you fail the first breathalyzer exam. If you refuse the breathalyzer, the case against you will be built upon the testimony of the police officer and others who observed your condition at the time.

## PENALTIES

The penalty for most driving violations is a fine, ranging from tens to hundreds of dollars. If you have accumulated a number of driving violations, the state may also suspend your license temporarily or revoke your license indefinitely. Revocation is generally limited to serious violations, such as driving while intoxicated, fleeing the police, or using a vehicle to commit a felony crime. You are entitled to notice and a hearing before revocation takes effect.

If you drive without a license (because it has been suspended or revoked), you may be arrested and held in jail until you can post bond. The amount of this bond will depend on your driving record and the nature of any other violation you may have committed to provoke the arrest. In this event, you should find an attorney as promptly as possible.

Serious violations, such as driving while intoxicated, may result in imprisonment. Fourteen states require mandatory imprisonment after the first offense of drunk driving. (The requirement may be only a few days.) Numerous other states require imprisonment after repeat violations and potential penalties include months or years in prison. A drunk-driving conviction also results in a substantial increase in insurance premiums or even insurance cancellation.

# Driving Accidents

## LIABILITY

Under the law, you have a duty to drive with reasonable care. If your negligent driving injures someone, you and/or your insurance company may be liable for the resultant damages. Negligence is a general term covering any sort of carelessness including driving violations. It is also negligence if you fail to keep your vehicle in good repair. If the accident was unavoidable, you are not liable.

You may be liable even if you were not the driver. The doctrine of **negligent entrustment** applies if you permit an underage, intoxicated, or other incapable person to use your car. In about half the states, parents or guardians are automatically liable if they have signed the driver's license application for their children who subsequently cause an accident. An employer is also typically liable for accidents caused by an employee acting within the scope of employment.

In many accidents, both involved parties were negligent in some manner. In this circumstance, the law provides for **comparative negligence.** Under this doctrine, each party must pay damages in proportion to his or her negligence. In most states, you cannot recover any damages if you were more than 50 percent to blame. Even in these states, the damages you owe will be reduced by the proportion of negligence assigned to the other driver. You also may be liable to passengers in your own car who are injured in an accident that was your fault.

## REPORTING REQUIREMENTS

The law requires that you report some driving accidents. A written report is required if the accident causes personal injury or if property damage exceeds a minimum threshold (usually about $250). This report generally must be filed with a specific government agency within five or ten days of the accident, depending on the state. To help ensure the report's accuracy, take careful note of weather and road conditions, speed estimates, time, and other relevant factors.

Failure to file the report is a misdemeanor and may be punishable by suspension of your driver's license. When you submit the report, you are automatically verifying that all the reported facts are true and that you are not omitting any material facts about the accident. Knowingly providing false information may be a felony.

## WHAT TO DO AFTER YOUR ACCIDENT

If you are in a significant accident, you should first park your car out of traffic, if possible. Driving away from the scene of the accident is illegal. Post warning flares by the side of the road or have a person warn oncoming vehicles. Exchange information with the other driver involved in the accident. This information should include the names and addresses of all passengers, vehicle license number, vehicle registration, and proof of insurance. Today's laws require a person to provide such identification. If police officers arrive on the scene, ask for their names and badge numbers. If you have a camera in your car, take pictures of the scene.

*Do not make statements about fault to the other driver, bystanders, or the police.* If you have injured someone, you may feel bad. There is nothing to be gained, however, by confessing fault immediately after the accident. At this time, you may be unaware of the true cause of the accident, and an admission of fault may be used against you even if you later realize that you were not at fault. After you are familiar with all the relevant facts and you have consulted with your insurance company and an attorney, you may choose to admit fault.

If someone is hurt or killed in the accident, you should alert the police and emergency medical services immediately. Be cautious about attempting to provide medical assistance unless you are qualified—you could aggravate an injury. After emergency concerns have been addressed, you should file required reports, contact your insurance company, and possibly contact an attorney.

Even if you do not seem to be injured, you should see a doctor for possible hidden or delayed conditions. If the insurance claims adjustor for the other party contacts you, refer the adjustor to your attorney. If you don't have an attorney, be careful what you say. Make no settlement until you have sufficiently explored your medical condition and legal opportunities. If you suspect that the accident was caused by a defect in your own vehicle, do not have the car repaired until after consulting with an attorney. In any event, keep careful records of any repairs done following the accident and retain replaced parts.

## RENDERING ASSISTANCE TO OTHERS

If you come across an accident while driving, you may consider stopping and rendering assistance. As a general rule, you have no duty to provide assistance if you were uninvolved in the accident. If you were involved in the accident, all states require you to stop and render assistance, even if you do not believe that you were at fault. Rendering assistance may simply involve telephoning the police and emergency medical services.

If you witness an accident, you may render assistance even when it is not legally required. If you stop and provide assistance to an accident victim, theoretically you could subsequently be sued by the victim for negligence in the manner of providing such assistance. The vast majority of states have adopted **Good Samaritan laws,** which shield you from any liability for simple negligence in assisting an accident victim. You could still be sued, though, for extreme or gross negligence in providing assistance.

## TOPIC 6

# CRIMINAL LAW

It is wise to obey the law and avoid the criminal justice system. Should you be charged with a crime, it is crucial for you to understand the charges and your constitutional rights. Except for the most minor crimes, you must consult an attorney.

## The Nature of Crimes

A criminal act is one that is prohibited by the legislature in a statute. An act does not become criminal simply because it is unethical or reprehensible—it must be specifically outlawed to be a crime.

There is considerable overlap between criminal law and civil law. If a person steals your car, that action is the crime of auto theft and also the civil tort of conversion. The responsible party may be prosecuted for the crime and also sued for the tort in separate judicial actions. The criminal action will be brought by the state government and tried by a **prosecutor** employed by the government. If convicted, the defendant will be required to pay a fine and/or do time in jail. The civil action must be brought by you and litigated by your lawyer. If you win, the defendant must pay you damages. The defendant cannot be sentenced to jail in a civil case. Although the two cases deal with the same action, they are pursued independently and employ different procedures, such as different burdens of proof.

Either the state or the federal legislature may make a certain action criminal. Most crimes are state crimes, prosecuted by the state and heard in state court. Other crimes, such as mail fraud or failure to pay federal income tax, are uniquely federal and enforced by federal authorities. A few crimes, such as possession of illegal drugs and bank robbery, are both federal and state crimes.

### TYPES OF CRIMES

A wide range of activities have been outlawed as criminal acts. The best known are the most serious and violent crimes, such as murder, rape, and kidnapping. These crimes are punishable by death or by an imprisonment sentence for a period such as twenty years to life. The **felony murder rule** makes a person guilty of murder, even if he or she does not personally murder anyone. Suppose an armed robbery of a con-

venience store involves three persons—two go into the store and one stays in the "getaway car." No violence is planned, but one of the robbers shoots and kills the clerk. All three persons are guilty of murder, even the one who did not go into the store.

The criminal justice system considers lesser but still severe crimes to include those such as armed robbery and manslaughter (for example, murder in a moment of passion or through negligence). Careless driving that results in a fatal accident may give rise to a negligent manslaughter prosecution. The sentence for these crimes may be three to five years or longer in prison.

Some crimes against property are also punished severely. For example, arson and extortion may be punished by years of imprisonment. Robbery, the taking of money or property directly from a person, is a more serious crime than burglary, the taking of property from a home in that person's absence. A burglary conviction may have greater penalties if it was conducted with a weapon, at night, or when the home was occupied. Receiving or buying property that you know or should know has been stolen is itself a crime sometimes referred to as obtaining stolen goods.

Crimes against public health, safety, and welfare form another category of criminal action. This category includes the possession, manufacture, or sale of certain prohibited drugs, such as cocaine or heroin. Selling alcohol to a minor is another example of this type of crime. Many of the laws against such crimes are aimed at businesses that may violate environmental laws or food safety laws.

Among the most controversial crimes are those "against public decency and morals." Such crimes include bigamy, prostitution, and illegal gambling. A controversial Supreme Court decision held that it was constitutional to prohibit homosexual sodomy, even in private. A number of states still have statutes that outlaw both homosexual and heterosexual sodomy, but these laws are seldom enforced. By contrast, molestation or other lewd and lascivious behavior toward a child is illegal and strictly enforced.

### MISDEMEANORS VERSUS FELONIES

Crimes are deemed to be either **misdemeanors** or **felonies.** A felony is a particularly serious crime. Examples of felonies are homicide, rape, and armed robbery. Misdemeanors are somewhat less serious crimes. Shoplifting, public drunkenness, and mildly resisting arrest are examples of misdemeanors.

The general distinction between felonies and misdemeanors is based upon the potential sentence for the crime. Offenses punishable by a prison sentence of more than one year are considered felonies. Misdemeanors are punishable by sentences of a year or less, and incarceration is in a county or municipal jail rather than a state prison. Those convicted of felonies may also lose other significant rights, including the right to vote or to serve on a jury.

The same basic action may be a misdemeanor or a felony, depending on the circumstances. For example, petty theft involves stealing less than a certain dollar amount and is a misdemeanor. Stealing goods worth more than the statutorily specified dollar amount is grand theft and constitutes a felony. For other crimes, the first offense may be considered a misdemeanor, but subsequent offenses become felonies.

# Arrest and Prosecution

## STOP AND ARREST

The criminal process often commences with a procedure known as **stop and frisk.** This occurs when the police have reason to suspect that you are engaged in a criminal activity and that you may be armed. Such suspicion may arise if you were loitering outside a home or business in a manner to suggest that you might be "casing" the place for a break-in. After the police have stopped you, they may ask you questions. They may also conduct a frisk, which is a patting down of the outside of your clothing. If they feel something that might be a weapon, the police are permitted to reach into your pocket and remove it. If they feel something soft that could not be a dangerous weapon, the police generally cannot search for it. In June 1993, the Supreme Court expanded police authority to allow removal and seizure of a package of drugs felt during a frisk.

Except for the stop-and-frisk rule, the police may not search you, unless you are under arrest or the police have a **search warrant.** The police may ask you to consent to a search, but there is no reason for you to agree. Refusal to cooperate with a stop and frisk, however, may represent independent grounds to arrest you.

The stop and frisk may be followed by an **arrest.** An arrest occurs when a suspect is taken into custody. The police may obtain an arrest warrant in advance, then seek out and arrest the suspect. If a person is caught in the act of committing a crime and the police lack time to obtain a warrant, the police may perform a **warrantless arrest.** A warrantless arrest must be based upon **probable cause.** Probable cause is a concept meaning that the police have a reasonable belief that a specific person has committed a crime. Probable cause is based on more than just a hunch or a stereotype, but involves far less than the evidence required to convict at trial. A tip from an informer is one way of establishing probable cause. Those subjected to warrantless arrest have an opportunity for a prompt hearing on the presence of probable cause.

Warrantless arrests are generally limited to public situations. For the police to seek you out and arrest you in a private place, an arrest warrant is generally required. The police may put you under surveillance at your house and then arrest you without a warrant after you leave home.

If you are arrested, you should be very careful of what you say or do. Don't resist the arrest or fingerprinting, and give the police your name and address. Don't say anything about the arrest to the police until after you have consulted with an attorney. If you are held in jail, you will have an opportunity to call a friend or relative. Inform them of the situation and arrange for legal representation. Be scrupulously honest with your lawyer—confessions to your lawyer cannot be used against you, due to the attorney-client privilege. Have your lawyer present at any police questioning or lineups at which you might be identified by the purported crime victim.

The police may seek to question you immediately after the arrest, before you have an opportunity to consult with an attorney. The U.S. Constitution guarantees you a right against self-incrimination, so that you cannot be forced to testify against yourself, and you need not respond to such questioning. Historically, the police have sometimes used physical or psychological pressure to coerce confessions even from the innocent. To avoid this scenario, the Supreme Court has required that persons in custody be given a set of **Miranda warnings** (named for the case that created the requirement). Police initially carried a "Miranda card" to remind them of the language, but these warnings are now quite well known to police and many ordinary citizens.

---

### MIRANDA WARNINGS

- You have the right to remain silent. Anything you say can be used against you.
- You have the right to a lawyer and to have one present during questioning.
- If you cannot afford a lawyer, one will be appointed for you before questioning commences.

---

If the police fail to provide Miranda warnings, a suspect may still be prosecuted and convicted. The Miranda warnings are required only for use at trial of statements made by the accused.

## SEARCH AND SEIZURE

The Fourth Amendment to the United States Constitution protects the privacy of Americans and restricts the government's ability to conduct searches. The government may search your home if it obtains a *search warrant.* Such a warrant generally must be obtained from a judge. The police go before the court and present evidence of its probable cause to believe that evidence of a crime is present. This warrant must particularly describe the place or person to be searched and the evidence to be seized. With such a warrant, the police may thoroughly search you, your home, your car, your business, or other places.

Under certain defined circumstances, the police may conduct a warrantless search. The stop and frisk is a limited form of such a warrantless search. Some examples of lawful warrantless searches are:

1. When the police are in hot pursuit of a felon trying to escape the scene of a crime.
2. When the police have probable cause to believe that a vehicle contains illegal items, the police may search the vehicle without a warrant.
3. When an item is in plain view of an officer, it may be seized without a warrant.
4. When the police make a proper arrest, they may search the area immediately surrounding the arrested person.

5. When a person consents to the search and seizure.
6. Searches in some special locations, such as at the national border or at an airport.

What if a search is illegal, due to the absence of a warrant or grounds for a warrantless search, and the police then find evidence of a crime? Under the **exclusionary rule,** evidence from the illegal search cannot be introduced at the criminal trial.

# Pretrial Procedures

After the arrest, the accused typically is **booked,** fingerprinted, and photographed at the local police station. Booking is the official police processing of the arrest. The defendant may be strip-searched.

## HEARING RIGHT

Soon after the booking, the accused has a right to a first appearance before a court. At this point, the judge explains the charges to be brought and the defendant's rights. The court will appoint a lawyer for the defendant if necessary. In a felony case, this appearance is often called a **presentment** or **preliminary arraignment.** This hearing may serve as an **arraignment,** when the defendant is formally advised of the charges and given an opportunity to respond by pleading guilty or not guilty. When the government's case is weak, the judge may dismiss the case in this first appearance.

## RELEASE BEFORE TRIAL

The key aspect of this first-appearance hearing is whether the defendant will be released from custody automatically, or if **bail** will be set. Bail involves the payment of a bond by the defendant in order to secure release from custody. The core function of bail is to ensure that the accused does not go into hiding to avoid trial. In many cases, the defendant may obtain a **release on his or her own recognizance** (without posting a bond). This occurs when the defendant promises to return for trial and convinces the court that he or she is a good risk.

In some cases, even bail may be denied and the defendant held in custody without prospect for release. Bail may be denied for particularly horrendous crimes, if the defendant is considered a threat to the community. Bail may also be denied if the defendant was already on parole or probation and if the defendant presents a particular danger of flight from the jurisdiction before trial.

The next major step in a criminal prosecution is either to present the case to a grand jury for indictment or to hold a preliminary hearing. Both events require a closer investigation of the charges against the defendant. A grand jury is a group of up to twenty-three ordinary citizens who hear testimony and evidence presented only by the prosecution. The grand jury then decides whether to indict the accused and send the defendant to trial, or to ''no bill'' the defendant, releasing the accused from the charges.

At a preliminary hearing, the prosecutor, in the presence of a judge, must present sufficient evidence and witnesses to establish the probable guilt of the defendant. The accused is represented by counsel, who may present witnesses and evidence and may cross-examine prosecution witnesses. The judge decides whether to bind the defendant over for trial. Grand jury indictments are required in federal prosecution of felonies.

If the prosecution proceeds and the defendant maintains innocence, the parties then undergo discovery of evidence. Lawyers may file pretrial motions to the court. For example, the defense may contend that the prosecution's evidence is inadmissible and ask the judge to dismiss the action. If the prosecution prevails, the next step is the criminal trial.

# Trial and Defenses

Defendants have a right to a speedy trial which must quickly follow the indictment or arraignment. Typically, a state might guarantee that the trial begin within sixty days. It is common, however, for defendants to waive their right to be tried so promptly, in order to obtain more time to prepare their defenses.

## THE TRIAL

The Constitution has been interpreted to give the defendant the right to a jury trial for significant crimes (punishable by imprisonment of six months or more). The defendant has a right to a jury of peers, but this does not mean individuals in the same financial or social position as the defendant. A jury of peers simply means that the jury is selected from residents of the accused's community and that no groups have been artificially excluded from serving on the jury. If the crime has received extensive pretrial publicity, the defendant may ask for a **change of venue,** so that the trial can be held in another location where jurors may not be so prejudiced by media coverage of the crime.

Eventually, the criminal case will come to trial. The prosecution will present its evidence. Such evidence may be in the form of eyewitness testimony; namely, individuals who claim to have seen the defendant commit the crime. The prosecution may present documentary evidence of guilt. The prosecution may also present circumstantial evidence, facts that create a strong inference that the defendant must have committed the crime. The defendant has the **presumption of innocence.** This means that the prosecution has the burden of proof to establish guilt beyond a reasonable doubt.

## DEFENSES

Several constitutional protections extend to the trial of the accused. The Fifth Amendment contains a general right to **due process,** which requires procedural fairness, such as an impartial judge. The Sixth Amendment gives the accused a right to confront and cross-examine the witnesses against them. As noted, the defendant has a right to an attorney and the right not to testify. The defendant may seek to exclude some prosecution evidence as inadmissible. The exclusionary rule means that most illegally obtained evidence cannot be introduced against you in trial. This includes evidence from illegal searches and seizures or confessions obtained through coercion or without first giving the accused his or her Miranda warnings.

Criminal defendants may have available other procedural or constitutional defenses. One such defense is known as **entrapment.** Defendants often claim entrapment but seldom succeed. The defense is quite narrow, and the defendant has the burden of proof to demonstrate entrapment. It is not enough to show that government agents suggested the commission of a crime. A police officer offering to sell drugs to a college student is generally not a case of entrapment. Entrapment means that the government somehow induced a person to commit a crime that he or she otherwise would never have considered committing. If the government merely affords a person the opportunity to commit a crime, and the person seizes that opportunity, entrapment is not established.

Entrapment might exist when the government continues at great length in its efforts to catch an individual. Suppose that an undercover agent arrived at your door and offered to sell you a stolen stereo. You declined. The agent then appeared at your door and made the same offer day after day. After you declined to purchase the stereo many times, you finally relented. This degree of government perseverance might constitute entrapment.

The accused may of course maintain that no crime was committed or that he or she is not the guilty party. This defense may involve undermining the testimony of the prosecution witnesses, such as challenging the accuracy of eyewitness testimony. The defendant may also present evidence of his or her innocence. This may consist, for example, of an **alibi,** showing that the defendant was somewhere else at the time of the crime's commission. The defendant may testify but is not required to do so.

Another defense to crime is **self-defense** or the defense of others. It is not unlawful to attack someone in self-defense. To demonstrate self-defense, a defendant must show that he or she had a reasonable fear of an imminent danger of bodily harm from an attacker. This same defense is available if you come to the defense of others endangered by an attack. The force used in self-defense must be reasonable. If the attacker runs away from you, you generally may not pursue him to strike him further. Deadly force (such as a gun or knife) may be used in self-defense only when you are threatened with deadly force. You can also use some force in the defense of your property, but you usually cannot use deadly force in defense of property. Some states have exceptions to this rule. In Texas, you can use deadly force if a person is seeking to enter your property at night.

Another defense is available if the defendant is not responsible for his or her actions. Extreme cases of intoxication may mean that the defendant lacked the state of mind to commit certain crimes. Slight drunkenness is not a defense, though, and some states hold that voluntary intoxication cannot be a defense, no matter how drunk the defendant is. Another such defense is **insanity.** The insanity defense is actually rather narrow, and even a significant psychological problem may not qualify. Standards differ somewhat by state but a common test is that the defendant be so insane as to lack the ability to appreciate the nature of the criminal act or that the conduct was wrongful. Insanity is judged as pertaining to the time of the crime. If the defendant remains insane, a trial cannot proceed, because due process requires that the defendant be able to understand the charges brought. Such a defendant is typically held in an institution until sanity is regained.

Yet another defense is the passage of too much time between the act and the prosecution. The **statute of limitations** is a law that requires that legal proceedings (such as a complaint) commence within a certain period of time. A typical state statute of limitations would be one year for misdemeanors and three years for certain felonies. The statute stops running if the defendant is out of the state during this period or changes his or her identity. For very serious crimes, such as murder, there is no statute of limitations.

# Sentencing

After a person is convicted of a crime, the court metes out some form of sentence. Sentencing has a variety of purposes. Some of the objectives of sentencing are rehabilitation of the offender, incapacitation of the offender so that the crime is not repeated, and deterrence of future crimes by the offender and others.

## Types of Sentences

The law provides for a broad range of sentencing options, depending upon the nature of the crime. The most severe is capital punishment, in which the defendant is executed. Other serious crimes provide for imprisonment for a specified term, often a number of years. Felony sentences are commonly served in state prison, while misdemeanor sentences are typically served in a local jail. In many other cases, the defendant must pay a fine to the state.

A variety of lesser sentences are also available for less serious crimes or first offenders. **Probation** refers to a sentence by which an offender does not go to jail or prison but is released under the supervision of a probation officer. States prohibit probation for certain serious offenses. The offender also agrees to follow certain conditions, such as not carrying a gun, not using illegal drugs, getting a job, and checking in regularly with the probation officer. Probation is for a set period of time, such as one year. If the offender violates the terms of probation during this period, probation may be revoked and he or she may be sent to prison. Revocation of probation requires a hearing to establish the presence of a violation.

In some cases, the convicted criminal may receive a **suspended sentence.** The offender first receives a particular prison sentence (for example, two years in prison), which is then suspended by the judge. The offender is then released without conditions or supervision by a probation officer. In a suspended sentence, the conviction and sentence is a matter of public record and may hamper the job prospects of the convicted. Another procedure is called **deferred sentencing.** After a conviction, the judge will elect to defer sentencing for a period such as a year. If the offender commits no more violations during that year, the judge imposes no sentence at all.

States are increasingly turning to innovative forms of punishment. Many states have **restitution statutes.** Such laws require defendants to pay the victims to compensate them for the losses suffered from the crimes. While conceptually appealing, restitution statutes have limits for the reason that many convicted criminals lack the resources to make restitution. Judges have also turned to public humiliation as a sanction. A convicted criminal may be forced to wear a sign or take out an advertisement in the newspaper confessing his or her guilt. Convicted drunk drivers have been compelled to apply bumper stickers declaring themselves guilty of that crime.

The Eighth Amendment to the Constitution prohibits **cruel and unusual punishment.** This typically concerns punishments such as torture, but courts are extending the amendment to unreasonable prison conditions if the government exhibits "deliberate indifference" to the conditions. A 1993 Supreme Court decision held that being confined to a cell with a smoker could be cruel and unusual punishment if the prisoner could show that the secondhand tobacco smoke presented a serious risk to his or her health.

# Juvenile Justice

The United States provides a justice system for juveniles separate from that for adults. This system tends to be more lenient and often refers to "delinquent acts" rather than crimes. Sentences are also lighter. As juveniles are increasingly committing heinous crimes, the relative lenience of juvenile courts has fallen into some disfavor.

## THE JUVENILE

Each state sets its own age limit for determination of whether an accused person should be tried as an adult or as a juvenile. In most states the age of maturity is eighteen, but a number of states have reduced this age to sixteen or seventeen. Underage individuals are presumptively treated as youths and tried in juvenile court. Most states provide that some juveniles may be tried in an adult court and subjected to the full range of penalties. The juvenile may be transferred to adult court, depending on certain factors. The relevant factors include the seriousness of the crime, the criminal record of the defendant, the age of the defendant, and the likelihood that juvenile status will better enable the rehabilitation of the defendant.

## PRETRIAL

The apprehension of a juvenile is not called an arrest but a *taking into custody*. Juveniles may be taken into custody for the very same criminal acts that would result in the arrest of an adult. Juveniles may also be taken into custody for **status offenses.** Status offenses are not criminal acts proscribed by the legislature but are problems such as repeated truancy at school or habitual disobedience and may apply to those mi-

nors who have run away from home. A single episode of misbehavior does not render a youth a status offender. Consistent misbehavior is required. Juveniles charged with status offenses have basically the same legal protections as those charged with crimes.

As juvenile criminal behavior has grown, status offenses have taken a back seat. Such offenses are still significant, however, as they often reflect an emotionally troubled life that may be amenable to rehabilitation. Various programs, such as youth shelters and counseling, have been established to assist runaways and other troubled youths.

After a juvenile is taken into custody for either a crime or a status offense, the police may choose to file a formal charge, refer the case to social workers, or release the youth to the care of parents. If the police detain the juvenile, a process known as **intake** follows. At this stage the authorities question the juvenile, to assess the seriousness of the problem. Many complaints are eliminated at this stage, and the youth may be referred to a social service agency or have the charges dismissed.

## JUVENILE COURT PROCEDURES

Juveniles in custody must first receive an initial hearing on the validity of their detention. The youth has a right to an attorney and may have one appointed by the court if necessary. Instead of a trial, a juvenile is given an **adjudication hearing.** This functions much like an adult trial, and the juvenile has a constitutional right to due process, including the right to present evidence, cross-examine witnesses, and be represented by an attorney. In contrast to the trial of an adult, a juvenile adjudication hearing is not public.

A juvenile may be found delinquent, rather than guilty. In this event juveniles undergo a **dispositional hearing** in which the judge decides what disposition (sentence) the youth should receive. Juvenile dispositions tend to place more emphasis on rehabilitation and less on deterrence or incarceration as compared to adult sentencing. Probation is a common disposition, and the conditions of probation may be particularly strict, such as a curfew. The juvenile may be sentenced to a juvenile institution for an indeterminate amount of time, up to the maximum statutorily allowed for the violation committed. The youth may instead be sent to a halfway house or foster home for rehabilitation.

Disposition is more limited for status offenders, who have committed no adult crime. Parents may actually take their child to a local prosecutor and ask that a status offender complaint be filed against the juvenile. Such a petition might request that the youth be removed from the home and placed in some sort of government institution or foster home. Many states allow such a ruling for a child who continually refuses to obey the directions of parents or fails to attend school. Such a juvenile might be declared a **person in need of supervision.**

Juveniles have many, but not all, of the constitutional protections afforded adults. The Supreme Court has held that juveniles cannot be found in violation of a criminal act without proof beyond a reasonable doubt, though this does not extend to status offenses. Juveniles also have the right to an attorney and to confront their accusers. Juveniles do not have the right to trial by jury, however. An adult can never be tried for status offenses. Most states permit juveniles to appeal their dispositions, but the Supreme Court has never held that this is constitutionally required.

TOPIC 7

# JURY DUTY

The jury system is central to the American system of justice. Serving on a jury is both a privilege and a responsibility of citizenship. While such service may be a temporary inconvenience, the willingness of citizens to serve is essential to preserve constitutional rights and is reflective of democracy. Community participation in justice is important to public confidence in the system.

## Jury *Venire* and Selection

The process of jury selection can be lengthy and confusing to the ordinary person. While parts of the process may appear arbitrary, they are designed to help select an impartial jury of the defendant's peers.

### JURY *VENIRE*

Jury selection must begin with a pool of possible jurors. This pool of potential jurors is often called a jury *venire*. Choosing the individuals in this pool for any given case requires a list of all possible jurors in the community. There is no such convenient list. In the past, some communities used lists of property taxpayers or telephone book listings. Such lists created a bias toward the wealthier citizens, who are more likely to own property and have more telephone lines. Consequently, exclusive reliance on such lists may violate the constitutional requirement of a **jury of peers.**

A defendant's right to a jury of peers does not mean that the jurors must come from the same walk of life as the defendant. A hot-rodder charged with drunk driving has no right to a jury composed of automobile fanciers. Rather, the term "jury of peers" simply means that no group in the community has been systematically excluded from the jury. The jury pool must represent a "fair cross section" of the community. Suppose that the jury pool was drawn from all those who voted in the last two presidential elections. The hot-rodder might reasonably complain that this unfairly excluded a large number of younger persons in their twenties.

There is no perfect list for a jury *venire*. Many communities still use phone books but supplement them with lists of registered voters, census rolls, and motor vehicle registration lists. Whatever the list used, the jury pool is selected randomly from the list. The *venire* may consist of hundreds of names, depending on the number of trials to be covered and the potential difficulty of finding impartial individuals.

A highly publicized trial may require a larger initial *venire* of potential jurors, because many individuals may already have formed a strong opinion of the case.

If you are in the *venire* of jurors for a given case or cases, you will first receive a card in the mail summoning you to the courthouse. Many people ignore this card—over 50 percent of those summoned to jury duty fail to appear on the designated day and time. It is your civic duty to appear, however, and it is normally a crime if you fail to appear in response to the summons. Failure to appear may result in your arrest, though it is more common for the government to issue a contempt-of-court letter that may result in a fine. Many people on the *venire* will not actually be selected for a jury. One New Jersey study found that 63 percent of those summoned for jury duty never served.

## JURY SELECTION

After responding to your summons to jury duty, you probably will sit in a large courtroom and listen to a judge lecture you on the importance of jury service and your duties. At this point, some jurors will be removed from the pool because of exemptions from jury service. An exemption is a statutory provision declaring that certain groups need not serve on juries, often because their jobs are considered so important that the individuals cannot be taken away from their employment.

Historically, states provided a large number of exemptions from jury service. Even in this century, women were exempted for a variety of reasons, including their duties to home and family. The exemption for women was deemed unconstitutional, but many professional groups are still excluded. A representative list of exemptions might include the clergy, doctors, lawyers, teachers, pharmacists, firefighters, and even embalmers. These professional exemptions do not mean the the individuals *cannot* serve on a jury. The exemptions mean that the professionals are not required to serve.

There is currently a trend toward abolishing all these exemptions. The exclusion of professionals obviously makes the jury less than representative of the community. In some states, even judges serve on juries when summoned. These states still provide some exemption for individuals who would be removed from work necessary for the public health or safety of the community or who can establish some other good cause for being exempted.

States also provide for other exemptions in addition to the named professions. Felons, minors, noncitizens, and those who cannot understand English are typically exempted. Most states also exempt severely disabled individuals. Single parents with minor children or others with special cause may also be excluded. Fear of losing one's job is not a basis for exemption from jury duty.

Suppose that you are summoned for jury duty and have no professional exemption. It also happens that the next month is particularly critical to your business and requires your close attention. You probably can receive a deferral of jury service until a later, more convenient date. Such deferrals are routinely granted.

## VOIR DIRE

Once the exemption process is completed, the court commences *voir dire.* This is a process of questioning jurors to elicit any prejudices that could preclude the individual's impartiality. In some states, the attorneys conduct *voir dire* and question the potential jurors directly. In other states, the attorneys for the parties submit questions to the judge, who does the direct questioning of the *venire.*

*Voir dire* questions might inquire about whether the individual had a strong prejudice against members of a given race or religion. Other questions relate to the facts of the case, such as whether the juror would be willing to consider imposing capital punishment. A common question is whether the potential jurors have read about the case in the papers and formed an opinion about the guilt or innocence of a criminal defendant. Merely reading about a case does not disqualify a juror as biased, but the formation of a strong opinion about guilt will undermine impartiality. The court or lawyers also will ask about education, relevant experiences, family background, and other factors.

If you wish to avoid jury service, you might be tempted to state that you are biased about the case. In addition to being dishonest, this approach might not work. In a Massachusetts case, a doctor openly sought to avoid jury service for financial reasons. He stated that he would be biased in the case. The judge believed that he was lying and ordered the doctor to sit in the courtroom as a spectator for the duration of the trial.

## CHALLENGES

After a juror is questioned, the attorneys may accept him or her or they may attempt to challenge the individual. Such a challenge may prevent the person from serving on the jury. Each side of the case may raise an unlimited number of **challenges for cause.** A challenge for cause involves the attorney asking the judge to excuse the juror because of disqualifying bias or lack of competence for jury service. The judge makes the ultimate decision whether the individual should serve or not.

Each side of the case also gets a limited number of **peremptory challenges.** In capital cases, the defendant may have as many as twenty peremptories, while for misdemeanors peremptories may be limited to four. In a peremptory challenge, an attorney may excuse a prospective juror from service without giving any reason at all. Lawyers typically use peremptory challenges when they have a hunch that a juror will favor the other side but cannot establish this bias sufficiently to convince the judge to accept a challenge for cause.

The theory of jury selection is to find an impartial jury. In reality, each side is seeking to identify and seat jurors who favor its case, even if only subconsciously. Some lawyers hire psychologists for jury selection to help choose favorable jurors. The tobacco industry, for example, has discovered that current smokers tend to be unsympathetic to smokers suing cigarette companies for health harms. It is hoped that the efforts of both sides will balance each other out so that the resulting jury will be reasonably impartial.

Lawyers' use of peremptory challenges is limited by the Constitution. Such challenges cannot be used to exclude a given race or gender from the jury. For example, in a case when an African American is on trial for a crime, there might be only a few African Americans in the jury *venire.* A prosecutor who uses all his or her peremptory challenges against these African Americans, ensuring an all-white jury, violates the Constitution and denies the defendant a jury of peers.

## ALTERNATE JURORS AND JURY SIZE

The *voir dire* and challenge process continues until a full jury can be seated. In complicated cases, *voir dire* can last for months. Most juries consist of twelve persons, though a court usually selects a couple of alternate jurors as well. The alternates sit in the courtroom and observe the case just like the real jurors. Should a juror fall sick during the trial or become disqualified for other reasons, an alternate juror may sit in. This avoids the waste of restarting the trial from the beginning with a new jury.

The twelve-person jury is historically traditional but not constitutionally required. The court has approved six-person juries but has held that five is too few for a criminal action. The reduced number makes it easier and quicker to empanel a jury.

# Trial

Once you are selected for a jury, you sit through the trial in a designated spot in the courtroom. You will likely discover that trials are not as exciting as portrayed on television or in movies. Nevertheless, your close attention is required in order that the parties get a fair verdict.

## TRIAL PROCEDURES

The trial usually will begin with opening arguments from the attorneys for each side in the case. These arguments are not evidence but are persuasive appeals that help you understand the theories of the parties. Each side then will present its evidence in the form of physical exhibits, documents, and witnesses. The witnesses probably will be cross-examined. You must follow this presentation closely and decide which witnesses are believable. It is likely that you will be prohibited from taking notes, so you must struggle to remember key facts. After the evidence, the attorneys will present closing arguments, which are not evidence but which summarize the case and seek to persuade you.

## JURY INSTRUCTIONS

At the end of the trial, the judge will give you instructions to help decide the case. These instructions inform you of the law that should be applied to the facts, based upon the testimony. A judge's instructions might tell you that you have to find certain facts before you may decide the case for a given side.

It is the jury's general responsibility to apply the law, even if you disagree with the law. Some juries have been known to ignore the law, a process known as jury nullification. Such a jury might decide that marijuana should be legal and therefore refuse to convict a person for possession of that drug. Jury nullification is often criticized, but jury deliberations are secret and there is no known way to prevent a jury from nullifying the law and acquitting a defendant. If the jury obviously ignores the law in a civil case, the decision is more likely to be overturned on appeal.

## DELIBERATIONS

Different juries may adopt very different approaches to deliberations. Whatever procedure is chosen, you should speak openly about your views and listen closely to the opinions of fellow jurors. You must decide the case on the evidence presented at trial, not on prejudices or outside sources of information known to you. If you forget something that occurred during the trial, you may ask the judge for information. If you wish to examine an exhibit, it generally will be provided. In contrast, courts commonly deny jury requests for transcripts of trial testimony.

It is expected that there will be disagreement among the jurors. After discussion and give-and-take, the jury is expected to reach a verdict. In criminal cases, the verdict must be unanimous. In civil cases, states provide for verdicts by a **supermajority** of the jury, such as a three-fourths or two-thirds vote. In a criminal case, if you cannot reach a verdict it is called a hung jury, and the judge must declare a **mistrial.** This means that the trial must be conducted again before a new jury. For obvious reasons, courts try to avoid such deadlocks and will urge you to compromise and reach a verdict.

It is very difficult to challenge a jury verdict after the fact. It is important that verdicts have finality and not be subject to constant reopening. Suppose that a juror evinces extreme racial bias toward the defendant during deliberations. Courts are still unsettled about whether evidence of such bias will even be considered. Some judges have refused even to listen to such evidence of bias. This makes it all the more important that unbiased jurors work to ensure a fair result. Courts are more likely to overturn a verdict if a juror lied in *voir dire* about a significant fact such as that he or she has been convicted of a felony. A \$45 million verdict against Lockheed Corporation was overturned because of such a lie.

# Jurors' Rights

Jury service is a duty that may inconvenience you. In the best case you will lose some time at work. In the worst case, you may be penalized or even fired by your employer for losing this time. The law increasingly provides some protections for jurors.

## EMPLOYMENT

In the past under common law, an employer could fire a worker for any reason whatsoever. Today, courts recognize a **wrongful discharge** action that makes it illegal to fire employees for certain public-policy reasons. Courts have consistently found that it is wrongful to fire a person for serving on a jury. The juror will, of course, have to prove that jury service was indeed the cause of the termination. In a 1992 Oklahoma case, the juror successfully proved this point and received \$175,000 in actual damages for being fired and another \$175,000 in punitive damages.

In addition to private wrongful discharge actions, a number of states make it illegal to fire a worker because of jury duty. In Arizona, for example, companies are prohibited from dismissing workers, demoting workers, or taking away seniority rights for time on jury service. This law is punishable by both a fine and imprisonment of the responsible individual.

## PAY

Jurors are paid a *per diem* (an allowance for daily expenses) for their service. The rate of pay for jury service is set by state law and is far below the minimum wage. A common *per diem* is \$5 per day of jury duty. There is momentum to increase the *per diem,* but the most generous states pay only about \$30 per day.

Firms are not necessarily required to pay wages for employees' time spent on jury service. Most cases last only two or three days, however, and companies often pay for this time. When a Los Angeles law firm refused to pay a worker for extended jury duty in 1992, the federal district court reprimanded the firm for evading its civic responsibility. The judge declared that he would ''make them'' pay her.

## SECRECY

Traditionally, the law provides for the **sequestration** of jurors in order to maintain their objectivity. If a trial was receiving great publicity, the jurors would be confined to hotel rooms and denied access to newspapers and television, to prevent them from reading public accounts of their trial. This helped ensure that the jury decided the case only on the facts presented in court.

Today, a more extreme form of sequestration may occur for a different reason. In organized crime prosecutions, jurors have been bribed or threatened by criminals in order to gain an acquittal. In response, the identities of jurors in such trials are kept secret, and the jury may even sit behind a screen. A similar approach may be used in extremely controversial cases, such as certain police-brutality prosecutions. If such a case may produce rioting, jurors may have concern for their safety or fear public blame for bringing in an unpopular verdict. These jurors also may have their identities shielded by the court.

# APPENDIX A

# How to Brief a Case and Selected Cases

## How to Brief a Case

To fully understand the law with respect to business, you need to be able to read and understand court opinions. To make this task easier, you can use a method of case analysis that is called *briefing*. There is a fairly standard procedure that you can follow when you "brief" any court case. You must first read the case opinion carefully. When you feel you understand the case, you can prepare a brief of it.

Although the format of the brief may vary, typically it will present the essentials of the case under headings such as those listed below.

1.  **Citation.** Give the full citation for the case, including the name of the case, the date it was decided, and the court that decided it.
2.  **Facts.** Briefly indicate (a) the reasons for the lawsuit; (b) the identity and arguments of the plaintiff(s) and defendant(s), respectively; and (c) the lower court's decision—if appropriate.
3.  **Issue.** Concisely phrase, in the form of a question, the essential issue before the court. (If more than one issue is involved, you may have two—or even more—questions here.)
4.  **Decision.** Indicate here—with a "yes" or "no," if possible—the court's answer to the question (or questions) in the *Issue* section above.
5.  **Reason.** Summarize as briefly as possible the reasons given by the court for its decision (or decisions) and the case or statutory law relied on by the court in arriving at its decision.

When you prepare your brief, be sure that you include all of the important facts. The basic format is illustrated below in the briefed version of the sample court case that was presented in Chapter 1. We have also annotated the briefed version to indicate the kind of information that is contained in each section.

## Briefed Sample Court Case

### CAMPBELL v. ACUFF-ROSE MUSIC, INC.

Supreme Court of the United States, 1994.
____U.S. ____,
114 S.Ct. 1164,
127 L.Ed.2d 500.

**FACTS** The song "Oh, Pretty Woman" was written in 1964 by Roy Orbison and William Dees. Their ownership rights in the song were transferred to Acuff-Rose Music, Inc.—the current copyright owner and the respondent in this appeal. In 1989, the musical group 2 Live Crew parodied the song without Acuff-Rose's permission. In 1990, after about 250,000 copies of the parody version had been sold, Acuff-Rose sued 2 Live Crew and its record company, alleging copyright infringement. 2 Live Crew claimed that their parodic use of the original song fell within the "fair use" exception to the Copyright Act of 1976. 2 Live Crew contended that the parody commented on and satirized the original work, which is considered a fair use under the act in some circumstances. The district court found for 2 Live Crew, holding that the parody version was a fair use. Acuff-Rose appealed. The court of appeals reversed, holding that 2 Live Crew's parody carried with it a presumption of unfair use because of its intrinsically commercial nature. 2 Live Crew appealed to the United States Supreme Court.

**ISSUE** Could 2 Live Crew's parody version of "Oh, Pretty Woman" be considered a fair use of the original copyrighted song under the Copyright Act of 1976?

**DECISION** Yes. The Supreme Court reversed the appellate court's decision and remanded the case.

**REASON** Section 107 of the Copyright Act sets forth a four-factor test to be used when determining whether the unauthorized use of another's copyrighted work is a "fair use." In regard to the first factor (the "purpose and character of the use, including whether such use is of a commercial nature"), the appellate court held that the commercial nature of 2 Live Crew's parody rendered the group's use presumptively unfair. The Supreme Court disagreed, holding that the transformative value of parody must also be considered. On the second factor (the "nature of the copyrighted work"), the Supreme Court affirmed the lower courts' decision that the original version of "Oh, Pretty Woman" warranted copyright protection under the act. On the third factor (the "amount and substantiality of the portion used in relation to the copyrighted work as a whole"), the appellate court held that 2 Live Crew's parody copied the heart, or essence, of the original work and therefore borrowed too much. The Supreme Court, however, stated that a parody must necessarily "conjure up" enough of the original work for the audience to recognize the "critical wit" intended, and this may require copying the heart of the original version. Whether 2 Live Crew copied musical elements to a greater extent than necessary to conjure up the original song was an issue to be decided on remand. On the final factor (the "effect of the use upon the potential market for or value of the copyrighted work"), the Supreme Court held that because the original and parodic versions served different market functions, the parodic version would probably not affect the market for the original.

## REVIEW OF SAMPLE COURT CASE

**CITATION**   The name of the case is *Campbell v. Acuff-Rose Music, Inc.* The petitioners are 2 Live Crew, a musical group of which Campbell is a member, and the group's record company. The respondent is Acuff-Rose Music, Inc. The case was decided by the United States Supreme Court. Although the opinion has not yet been published in the reporter, the first citation is to the *United States Reports.* The first parallel citation is to the *Supreme Court Reporter* and indicates that the case can be found in volume 114 of that reporter, on page 1164. The second parallel citation is to volume 127, page 500, of the *Lawyers' Edition of the Supreme Court Reports.*

**FACTS**   The *Facts* section identifies the parties to the lawsuit—the petitioners and the respondent—and describes the events leading up to the lawsuit and its appeal. Because this is an appeal to the United States Supreme Court, both the district court and the appellate court decisions are included as part of the history of the case. The petitioners' contention on appeal is included in this section as well.

**ISSUE**   The *Issue* section presents the central issue (or issues) to be decided by the court. In this case, the issue before

the Supreme Court was whether 2 Live Crew's parody of "Oh, Pretty Woman" was a fair use of the copyrighted original song. Cases frequently involve more than one issue.

**DECISION**   The *Decision* section, as the term indicates, contains the court's decision on the issue or issues before it. The decision reflects the opinion of the majority of the judges or justices hearing the case. Decisions by appellate courts are frequently phrased in reference to the lower court's decision. That is, the appellate court may "affirm" the lower court's ruling or "reverse" it. In this particular case, the Supreme Court reversed the decision of the lower court (the federal court of appeals) and remanded, or sent back, the case for further proceedings consistent with the Supreme Court's opinion.

**REASON**   The *Reason* section indicates what relevant laws and judicial principles were applied in forming the particular conclusion arrived at in the case at bar ("before the court"). In this case, the relevant law was Section 107 of the Copyright Act of 1976. The Supreme Court held that the court of appeals erred in its application of the fair use exception by applying a presumption to the first and fourth factor of the fair use test. The case was also remanded for further consideration of the third factor.

## SELECTED CASES FOR BRIEFING

Court opinions can run from a few pages to hundreds of pages in length. For reasons of space, only the essential parts of the opinions are presented in the cases that follow. A series of three asterisks indicates that a portion of the text—other than citations and footnotes—has been omitted. Four asterisks indicate the omission of at least one paragraph.

---

### CASE A.1   *Reference: Problem 5–13*

**AUSTIN v. BERRYMAN**
United States Court of Appeals,
Fourth Circuit, 1989.
878 F.2d 786.

*MURNAGHAN,* Circuit Judge:

We have before us for *en banc* [by the whole court] reconsideration an appeal taken from an action successfully brought by Barbara Austin in the United States District Court for the Western District of Virginia against the Virginia Employment Commission, challenging a denial of unemployment compensation benefits. * * * In brief, Austin charged, *inter alia* [among other things], that the denial of her claim for unemployment benefits, based on a Virginia statute specifically precluding such benefits for any individual who voluntarily quits work to join his or her spouse in

a new location, was an unconstitutional infringement upon the incidents of marriage protected by the fourteenth amendment and an unconstitutional burden on her first amendment right to the free exercise of her religion. Her religion happened to command that she follow her spouse wherever he might go and the sincerity of her religious belief was not questioned. The district court found in Austin's favor and awarded injunctive relief and retroactive benefits.

On appeal, Judge Sprouse, writing for a panel majority, found that the denial of benefits did not implicate Austin's Fourteenth Amendment rights, but that it did unconstitutionally burden Austin's right to the free exercise of her religion. The panel also found, however, that any award of retroactive benefits was barred by the Eleventh Amendment. One panel member concurred with the panel majority as to the Fourteenth and Eleventh Amendment issues, but dissented as to the existence of a free exercise violation. The panel opinion now, of course, has been vacated by a grant of rehearing *en banc.*

After careful consideration of the additional arguments proffered by both sides, the Court, *en banc,* is convinced that the panel majority correctly concluded that denying Austin unemployment benefits did not infringe upon fundamental marital rights protected by the Fourteenth Amendment. To this extent, we adopt the majority panel opinion. We also find, however, that the denial of benefits did not unconstitutionally burden Austin's first amendment right to the free exercise of her religion. We are persuaded that the views expressed on the First Amendment, free exercise of religion claim in the opinion dissenting in part from the panel majority are correct, and we hereby adopt that opinion as that of the *en banc* court. As we find that Austin is not entitled to any relief, we need not address whether the Eleventh Amendment bars an award of retroactive benefits.

The decisive consideration, as we see it, is that the proximate cause of Austin's unemployment is geographic distance, not her religious beliefs. There is no conflict between the circumstances of work and Austin's religious precepts. Austin's religious beliefs do not ''require'' her ''to refrain from the work in question.'' Austin is unable to work simply because she is now too far removed from her employer to make it practical. In striking contrast, if one, for genuine religious beliefs, moves to a new residence in order to continue to live with a spouse, and that residence is not geographically so removed as to preclude regular attendance at the worksite, no unemployment, and hence no unemployment benefits, will arise. That amounts to proof that extent of geographical non-propinquity, not religious belief, led to Austin's disqualification for unemployment benefits.

Austin voluntarily decided to quit her job and join her spouse in a new geographic location 150 miles away. Virginia has stated that every individual who follows such a course, no matter what the reason, religious or non-religious, is disqualified for unemployment benefits. To craft judicially a statutory exception only for those individuals who profess Austin's religious convictions, particularly in the absence of a direct conflict between a given employment practice and a religious belief, would, in our view, result in a subsidy to members of a particular religious belief, impermissible under the Establishment Clause.

Accordingly, the judgment of the district court is REVERSED.

---

## CASE A.2        *Reference: Problem 19–12*

### POTTER v. OSTER

Supreme Court of Iowa, 1988.
426 N.W.2d 148.

*NEUMAN,* Justice.

This is a suit in equity brought by the plaintiffs to rescind an installment land contract based on the seller's inability to convey title. The question on appeal is whether, in an era of declining land values, returning the parties to the status quo works an inequitable result. We think not. Accordingly, we affirm the district court judgment for rescission and restitution.

The facts are largely undisputed. Because the case was tried in equity, our review is *de novo.* We give weight to the findings of the trial court, particularly where the credibility of witnesses is concerned, but we are not bound thereby.

The parties, though sharing a common interest in agribusiness, present a study in contrasts. We think the disparity in their background and experience is notable insofar as it bears on the equities of the transaction in issue. Plaintiff Charles Potter is a farm laborer and his wife, Sue, is a homemaker and substitute teacher. They have lived all their lives within a few miles of the real estate in question. Defendant Merrill Oster is an agricultural journalist and recognized specialist in land investment strategies. He owns Oster Communications, a multimillion dollar publishing concern devoted to furnishing farmers the latest in commodity market analysis and advice on an array of farm issues.

In May 1978, Oster contracted with Florence Stark to purchase her 160-acre farm in Howard County, Iowa, for $260,000 on a ten-year contract at seven percent interest. Oster then sold the homestead and nine acres to Charles and Sue Potter for $70,000. Potters paid $18,850 down and executed a ten-year installment contract for the balance at 8.5% interest. Oster then executed a contract with Robert Bishop for the sale of the remaining 151 acres as part of a package deal that included the sale of seventeen farms for a sum exceeding $5.9 million.

These back-to-back contracts collapsed like dominoes in March 1985 when Bishop failed to pay Oster and Oster failed to pay Stark the installments due on their respective contracts. Stark commenced forfeiture proceedings [proceedings to retake the property because Oster failed to perform a legal obligation—payment under the contract—and thus forfeited his right to the land]. Potters had paid every installment when due under their contract with Oster and had included Stark as a joint payee [one of two or more payees—persons to whom checks or notes are payable; see Chapter 25] with Oster on their March 1, 1985, payment. But they were financially unable to exercise their right to advance the sums due on the entire 160 acres in order to preserve their interest in the nine acres and homestead. As a result, their interest in the real estate was forfeited along with Oster's and Bishop's and they were forced to move from their home in August 1985.

Potters then sued Oster to rescind their contract with him, claiming restitution damages for all consideration paid. * * *

Trial testimony * * * revealed that the market value of the property had decreased markedly since its purchase. Expert appraisers valued the homestead and nine acres between $27,500 and $35,000. Oster himself placed a $28,000 value on the property; Potter $39,000. Evidence was also received placing the reasonable rental value of the property at $150 per month, or a total of $10,800 for the six-year Potter occupancy.

The district court concluded the Potters were entitled to rescission of the contract and return of the consideration paid including principal and interest, cost of improvements, closing expenses, and taxes for a total of $65,169.37. From this the court deducted $10,800 for six years' rental, bringing the final judgment to $54,369.37.

On appeal, Oster challenges the judgment. * * * [H]e claims Potters had an adequate remedy at law for damages which should have been measured by the actual economic loss sustained * * * .

* * * *

Rescission is a restitutionary remedy which attempts to restore the parties to their positions at the time the contract was executed. The remedy calls for a return of the land to the seller, with the buyer given judgment for payments made under the contract plus the value of improvements, less reasonable rental value for the period during which the buyer was in possession. The remedy has long been available in Iowa to buyers under land contracts when the seller has no title to convey.

Rescission is considered an extraordinary remedy, however, and is ordinarily not available to a litigant as a matter of right but only when, in the discretion of the court, it is necessary to obtain equity. Our cases have established three requirements that must be met before rescission will be granted. First, the injured party must not be in default. Second, the breach must be substantial and go to the heart of the contract. Third, remedies at law must be inadequate.

The first two tests are easily met in the present case. Potters are entirely without fault in this transaction. They tendered their 1985 installment payment to Oster before the forfeiture, and no additional payments were due until 1986. On the question of materiality, Oster's loss of equitable title [ownership rights protected in equity] to the homestead by forfeiture caused not only substantial, but total breach of his obligation to insure peaceful possession [an implied promise made by a landowner, when selling or renting land, that the buyer or tenant will not be evicted or disturbed by the landowner or a person having a lien or superior title] and convey marketable title under the Oster-Potter contract.

Only the third test—the inadequacy of damages at law—is contested by Oster on appeal. * * *

Restoring the status quo is the goal of the restitutionary remedy of rescission. Here, the district court accomplished the goal by awarding Potters a sum representing all they had paid under the contract rendered worthless by Oster's default. Oster contends that in an era of declining land values, such a remedy goes beyond achieving the status quo and results in a windfall to the Potters. Unwilling to disgorge the benefits he has received under the unfulfilled contract, Oster would have the court shift the "entrepreneural risk" [the risk assumed by one who initiates, and provides or controls the management of, a business enterprise] of market loss to the Potters by limiting their recovery to the difference between the property's market value at breach ($35,000) and the contract balance ($27,900). In other words, Oster claims the court should have awarded * * * damages. * * *

* * * *

* * * [L]egal remedies are considered inadequate when the damages cannot be measured with sufficient certainty. Contrary to Oster's assertion that Potters' compensation should be limited to the difference between the property's fair market value and contract balance at time of breach, * * * damages are correctly calculated as the difference between contract price and market value at the time for performance. Since the time of performance in this case would have been March 1990, the market value of the homestead and acreage cannot be predicted with any certainty, thus rendering such a formulation inadequate.

Most importantly, the fair market value of the homestead at the time of forfeiture is an incorrect measure of the benefit Potters lost. It fails to account for the special value Potters placed on the property's location and residential features that uniquely suited their family. For precisely this reason, remedies at law are presumed inadequate for breach of a real estate contract. Oster has failed to overcome that presumption here. His characterization of the transaction as a mere market loss for Potters, compensable by a sum which would enable them to make a nominal down payment on an equivalent homestead, has no legal or factual support in this record.

* * *

* * * *

In summary, we find no error in the trial court's conclusion that Potters were entitled to rescission of the contract and return of all benefits allowed thereunder, less the value of reasonable rental for the period of occupancy * * * .

AFFIRMED.

---

### CASE A.3   *Reference: Problem 25–12*

## BERNAL v. RICHARD WOLF MEDICAL INSTRUMENTS CORP.

California Court of Appeal, Fourth District, 1990.
221 Cal.App.3d 1326,
272 Cal.Rptr. 41.

*TAYLOR,* Associate Justice.

Plaintiffs Morris and Rosie Bernal appeal from a judgment for Richard Wolf Medical Instruments Corporation ("Wolf") in their action for personal injuries. During Morris' knee surgery, arthroscopic scissors distributed and warranted by Wolf broke, causing the injury. Plaintiffs' case was predicated, in part, on a strict products liability theory for an allegedly defectively designed instrument * * * . On appeal, they raise instructional error. We reverse.

## I.

In March 1980, Wolf sold a pair of arthroscopic scissors to Mercy Hospital. In November 1984, Morris Bernal underwent arthroscopic knee surgery at Mercy.

During the surgical procedure, a scissor blade broke off inside the knee joint, "floated away," and it became imperative to open up the entire knee joint to find it. As a result * * * , Bernal developed sympathetic dystrophy [a deterioration in the nervous tissue]. His condition will continue to deteriorate and he will probably require a future total knee replacement. Medical testimony indicated Bernal's problems were proximately caused by complications arising from the failure of the scissors during surgery.

Bernal and his wife sued Wolf on several theories, including strict products liability based on design defect * * * .

Bernal's experts testified at trial the scissors broke due to a condition known as "stress corrosion cracking," resulting from a combination of design considerations. The experts did not testify to a "defect" as such, nor did they testify that a reasonable alternative design was possible. * * *

In instructing the jury on Bernal's burden of proof with respect to the alleged design defect, the court gave the version submitted by Wolf, which read in toto as follows: "With respect to the existence of a defect in the design of the scissors, plaintiff must show by a preponderance of the evidence that a reasonable alternative design was possible, which would have avoided the breakage complained of."

Bernal contends this instruction is erroneous, in that it impermissibly places the burden on him to prove a safer alternative design. He further contends, although Wolf's manager testified the company warranted the scissors to be completely free of defects in material and workmanship, the trial judge refused to give any of Bernal's proffered jury instructions on warranty.

## II.

In a case of strict products liability based on a design defect, does the plaintiff have the burden of proving a reasonable alternative design was feasible? We conclude one does not.

We begin with *Baker v. Chrysler Corp.* There the court stated: "Requiring an injured plaintiff who seeks damages against a manufacturer on the basis of strict liability in tort for a defective design to show that alternative designs for the product could reasonably have been developed does not enlarge plaintiff's burden of proof. An injured plaintiff has always had the burden to prove the existence of the defect. The reasonableness of alternative designs, where a design defect is claimed, is part of that burden." Thus, held the court, the burden was upon the injured plaintiff to establish that reasonable alternative designs are possible.

Two years later, however, our [California] Supreme Court decided *Barker v. Lull Engineering Co.* There, the Court articulated a two-pronged definition of a design defect. The tests subsequently have become known as the "consumer expectation" test, and the "risk-benefit" test. The court stated: "[A] product may be found defective in design . . . under either of two alternative tests. First a product may be found defective in design if the plaintiff establishes that the product failed to perform as safely as an ordinary consumer would expect when used in an intended or reasonably foreseeable manner. Second, a product may alternatively be found defective in design if the plaintiff demonstrates that the product's design proximately caused his injury and the defendant fails to establish, in light of the relevant factors, that, on balance, the benefits of the challenged design outweigh the risk of danger inherent in such design."

Noting that past authorities had generally not devoted much attention to the appropriate allocation of the burden of proof, the [California] Supreme Court remarked that the "burden is particularly significant [in that] one of the principal purposes behind the strict product liability doctrine is to relieve an injured plaintiff of many of the onerous evidentiary burdens inherent in a negligence cause of action. Because most of the evidentiary matters which may be relevant to the determination of the adequacy of a product's design under the 'risk benefit' standard—e.g., the feasibility and cost of alternative designs—are similar to issues typically presented in a negligent design case and involve technical matters peculiarly within the knowledge of the manufacturer, we conclude that once the plaintiff * * * [shows] that the injury was proximately caused by the product's design, the burden should appropriately shift to the defendant to prove, in light of the relevant factors, that the product is not defective." * * *

* * * *

* * * [T]here is no question Bernal presented a *prima facie* case that the design of the scissors was a proximate cause of their failure during the surgical procedure, causing disability and the need for future surgery. That is all he had to prove. At that point, Wolf had the burden of proof to show that, on balance, the benefits of the design of the product as a whole outweigh the danger inherent in such design considering, among other enumerated "relevant factors," the feasibility of a safer alternate design. We hold it was error to instruct the jury in the context of design defect that "plaintiff must show by preponderance of the evidence that a reasonable alternative design was possible, which would have avoided the breakage complained of."

Wolf complains to so hold renders it an insurer of its surgical instruments. Not so. Strict liability does not equate with absolute liability. Under the risk-benefit test, the defendant has the burden, and thus the opportunity, to highlight all of the benefits of its product's design before the jury. This would, of course, involve technical information peculiarly within its knowledge, and certainly more readily available to it. Among other things, the defense may show any alternate design would entail unreasonable costs, be uneconomic or impractical, interfere with the product's performance, or create other or increased risks. The case before us is a prime example. Here, the defense produced strong evidence the surgical instrument was made with the best steel available and was reasonably safe for its intended use, but had inherent dangers no human skill or knowledge has yet been able to eliminate. But for the erroneous burden of proof instruction, we would not hesitate to affirm the jury's verdict on this record.

\* \* \* \*

Judgment reversed and remanded for retrial on the [issue] of strict liability \* \* \* . Costs awarded to appellant.

---

CASE A.4     *Reference: Problem 30–8*

## MELLON BANK, N.A. v. SECURITIES SETTLEMENT CORP.

United States District Court,
District of New Jersey, 1989.
710 F.Supp. 991.

*CLARKSON S. FISHER,* District Judge.

Before the court are the motions of plaintiff, Mellon Bank ("Mellon"), and defendant, Securities Settlement Corporation ("SSC"), for summary judgment. At oral argument, the parties agreed that the facts are not in dispute. The transaction underlying this case is relatively simple. SSC performed clearing services in connection with securities transactions in the accounts of one of its customers, Kobrin Securities ("Kobrin"). One of Kobrin's clients was another entity, Barrett Consultants ("Barrett"), to whom SSC sent monthly statements regarding Barrett's account with Kobrin. On the morning of June 4, 1985, SSC, at Kobrin's request, instructed Mellon to wire transfer $113,080.50 to Barrett's account with the Franklin State Bank ("FSB"). Within several hours after Mellon had sent the wire, SSC learned that Kobrin was incapable of paying the securities' purchase price. Although SSC instructed Mellon to cancel the wire transfer, the money went through to Barrett's account. Mellon filed the instant complaint in October of 1987 in the Superior Court of New Jersey, Law Division, Somerset County, seeking reimbursement for the funds it had sent to FSB. SSC removed the case to this court in November of the same year.

\* \* \* \*

The threshold issue is whether Pennsylvania's version of the U.C.C. applies to this action. [Mellon and SSC agreed that Pennsylvania law governed their rights and liabilities.] SSC has cited several cases for the proposition that the U.C.C. does not govern wire transfers and contends that this case must be decided without reference to the statute. Mellon counters that the U.C.C. has been applied by analogy in other jurisdictions and urges the court to do the same. Unfortunately neither party has cited, nor has the court found, decisions from the Pennsylvania state courts which address this question.

There are merits to both positions. On one hand it might be noted that the U.C.C. covers only "items," which 13 Pa.C.S.A. [Pennsylvania Consolidated Statutes Annotated] section 4104 [Pennsylvania's version of UCC 4–104] defines as "any instrument for the payment of money even though it is not negotiable." With this definition as a starting point, it might be added that an instrument is a signed writing which expresses an agreement regarding rights, while the instant case involves an unsigned and electronically transmitted instruction. It could be asserted that this difference is not merely semantic; it illustrates that the U.C.C. was designed to address paper transactions rather than high-speed financial distributions. According to this argument Pennsylvania's trial courts would not adjudicate this case under 13 Pa.C.S.A. section 4101 *et seq.*

On the other hand, a "check is no more than an order on the bank to pay a stated amount ... from the maker's account." Although checks are negotiable instruments, it could be argued that Thomas's definition exactly fits a wire transfer, which is nothing more than an order directing the bank to pay money from one account to another. Moreover, it could be argued that the total exclusion of the U.C.C. from this case would leave the court with little current law upon which to base its decision.

Thus the court must \* \* \* attempt to predict what Pennsylvania's highest court would do if confronted with this situation. \* \* \* The court concludes that it should follow those decisions which have applied the common law while at the same time borrowing appropriate rules from the governing version of the U.C.C.

\* \* \* \*

SSC had a right to stop the \* \* \* wire transfer, and Mellon was under a corresponding duty to use ordinary care in handling SSC's request. \* \* \* Before the court can determine \* \* \* whether Mellon actually used ordinary care, it must examine the wire transfer at issue here.

The transfer was made under BankWire, a system maintained by Mellon and roughly 100 other banks. BankWire procedure requires a customer's authorized representative to instruct Mellon to transfer money from the customer's account to the recipient's account in another bank. After receiving and verifying an instruction, Mellon personnel would when necessary select a "correspondent" bank. The correspondent bank would then serve as a conduit for the transfer to the recipient's bank.

This process does not transmit the funds themselves; rather, upon making the transfer Mellon would debit the customer for the the amount of the transfer, and credit the correspondent bank's account with Mellon. \* \* \* BankWire funds become available on the day following the transfer.

Because BankWire funds are not immediately obtainable, a cancellation does not require the bank to recapture the wired funds. Essentially, a BankWire cancellation requires two steps. First, Mellon sends a cancellation notice to the "correspondent" bank, which in turn instructs the recipient bank to disregard the transfer. Second, Mellon reverses the credit/debit notation which it made upon receiving the transfer order; the customer's account is recredited and the correspondent bank's account is debited, thereby returning the balances to their pre-transfer sums. * * *

* * * *

SSC instructed Mellon to cancel the wire on the same day it learned that the funds were not covered. * * * Within several hours * * * Mellon sent a notice to MHT [the correspondent bank] instructing them to cancel the transaction * * *. Shortly after this message was sent Mellon reversed its account entries; it restored the transferred amount to SSC's account, and debited MHT's account with Mellon to the same amount.

Mellon's notice contained two errors. First, it referred to "YR BK WIRE," i.e., a wire transfer sent by MHT rather than one received by it. Second, the notice gave a transaction number of "184B." Transaction numbers are assigned by BankWire to each transfer request. The wire's true number was "06040184B."

* * * SSC heard nothing from Mellon regarding the transfer. Mellon, however, heard from MHT on several occasions. On June 6, 1985, MHT telephoned Mellon to inform the bank that MHT had not received the June 4, 1985 wire. * * * The next day MHT again contacted Mellon and informed the bank that MHT had no record of receiving a wire transfer denominated by [the transaction number] 184B.

Mellon replied to neither of these correspondences. * * *

On July 12, 1985, MHT wired Mellon that it intended to credit FSB with $113,080.50. In the same communication MHT asked Mellon to wire them in return should Mellon not want the transaction to be completed. MHT also asked

that Mellon credit MHT's account with $113,080.50. Four days later Mellon wired MHT that cancellation instructions had already been issued by Mellon on June 4, 1985. Mellon's wire contained, for the first time, the correct transaction number. Two days after this, on July 18, 1985, MHT requested that FSB authorize a reversal of the June 4 transfer. The next day FSB informed MHT that Barrett had already withdrawn the money.

No reasonable fact finder could conclude that Mellon acted with ordinary care regarding the cancellation. Mellon incorrectly identified the transaction to be cancelled, both by omitting five digits from the transaction number and by indicating that it sought to cancel a wire sent by MHT. The latter error might be considered inconsequential; after all, MHT did respond to Mellon within forty-eight hours to ask about Mellon's wire. But the inaccurate transaction number persisted throughout MHT's attempts to comply with Mellon's instructions; this error tainted such attempts for over one month.

Mellon's error easily ranks with those considered sufficient to constitute a breach of a bank's duty of ordinary care. The record demonstrates that Mellon inaccurately carried out SSC's instructions and that, even though it was twice given notice of MHT's corresponding inability to cancel the wire, Mellon failed to take prompt remedial action. Indeed, the court notes that Mellon's failures transgressed its own internal guidelines.

* * * *

Upon examining the record and the parties' arguments, the court concludes that no reasonable finder of fact could grant Mellon the relief it seeks. Rather, it is SSC who is entitled to judgment as a matter of law. Summary judgment is granted for SSC against all Mellon's claims.

---

## CASE A.5     *Reference: Problem 32–11*

### ALLISON-BRISTOW COMMUNITY SCHOOL DISTRICT v. IOWA CIVIL RIGHTS COMMISSION

Supreme Court of Iowa, 1990.
461 N.W.2d 456.

*SCHULTZ*, Justice.

In this appeal the issue is whether back pay and interest awarded to an employee in a civil rights action qualifies as personal earnings which are exempt from garnishment by a judgment creditor under Iowa Code section 642.21 (1989). The district court held that back pay and interest on the award were not exempt under section 642.21 and could be garnished by a judgment creditor. We hold that the exemption applies to the back pay, but not to the interest.

In 1981, Bernard W. Rowland filed a civil rights complaint against his employer for unlawful discrimination in terminating his employment. The Civil Rights Commission held in favor of Rowland and ordered the employer to pay

him $65,377, less appropriate deductions for federal and state income taxes and social security. It further ordered that attorney fees and interest be paid by the employer. On April 26, 1989, following appeals, the employer filed a satisfaction of judgment and deposited money for payment of the judgment with the clerk of the district court. It is agreed by the parties that the tax withholdings amounted to $19,838 and that the net back-pay award plus interest amounted to $80,248.

In independent actions, Willow Tree Investment Co. (Willow Tree) obtained judgments against Rowland in state and federal courts. It caused a writ of execution to be issued and garnished the clerk of court for the funds held on behalf of Rowland for back pay and interest. On June 9, 1989, Rowland received notice of the garnishment and promptly resisted, claiming that the funds deposited for back pay and interest were personal earnings which fell within the exemption contained in section 642.21. The district court allowed the garnishment.

* * * *

I. Earnings. Throughout this appeal the underlying issue is whether the civil rights award of back pay qualifies as earnings that fall within the exemption in section 642.21. This section defines "earnings" as "compensation paid or payable for personal services, whether denominated as wages, salary, commission, bonus or otherwise. . . ." The district court relied upon federal cases interpreting the federal Consumer Credit Protection Act and upon language in *MidAmerica Savings Bank v. Miehe* in concluding that the purpose of this legislation is to facilitate an employee's payment of living expenses and support. We agree with this broad assertion of purpose, but cannot agree with the district court's next conclusion.

The district court concluded that the legislature did not intend an amount subsequently received for back pay to be exempt earnings. It reasoned that the back pay was received too late to allow an employee to apply it toward day-to-day living expenses incurred during the time period when the back wages were earned. This conclusion ignores the fact that Rowland had living expenses during the period he was wrongfully unemployed. Exemption laws are to be liberally construed to allow debtors and their families assurance that necessary living expenses can be covered. Rowland should be in a position to use the judgment in his favor to replenish the source from which his living expenses were paid during the period he was deprived of earnings. In other words, a judgment creditor should not gain an advantage caused by the wrongful acts of an employer.

Willow Tree urges that the underlying intent of the exemption section is to provide a continuing means of support for a debtor. Willow Tree emphasizes that the Supreme Court found that the legislative intent behind passage of the federal Consumer Credit Protection Act was to prevent personal bankruptcy filings, to preserve a debtor's employment, and to provide an ongoing means of support for a debtor and his family. We concede that one of the purposes of the federal Act is to ensure a continued means of support for the debtor. In this case, however, the exemption is derived from the additional protection given the debtor under state law. Our state law determines the amount of the exemption on the basis of an individual's expected annual income. This method of annual calculation is less attuned to provide a continued means of support for a debtor than the federal Act, which calculates the amount of disposable income that can be garnished on a weekly basis.

\* \* \* Consideration of the relevant Iowa legislation as a whole demands a broader view than the trial court's narrow focus upon an exemption that is conditioned only on the payment of current living expenses. We believe the more appropriate focus should be upon the true nature of the award in question to determine if it falls within the term "earnings" as defined in section 642.21. A civil rights award is unlike a damage award in a typical contract or tort action. The underlying purpose of allowing damages in a civil rights award is compensation for the injury sustained. In civil rights actions, the legislature gave the courts power to provide a wide variety of relief, most of which is equitable in nature.

In unfair employment practices remedial action includes "[h]iring, reinstatement or upgrading of employees with or without pay. . . ." Although part of a civil rights award may be compensation, the real purpose behind a civil rights award is to make the person whole for an injury suffered as a result of unlawful employment discrimination.

In this case, the award not only allowed back pay, but also required the employer to pay the tax withholdings to place the employee in the same position he would have occupied if the wages were received during the period of wrongful discharge. Under these circumstances, we conclude that the judgment entered in Rowland's favor for back pay is an award of earnings paid for personal services as defined in subsection 642.21(3)(a).

Willow Tree \* \* \* claims that Rowland's award of back wages was extinguished and replaced by a judgment debt. Thus, it urges that the back-pay award lost its character as wages and may be garnished as any other judgment. It cites *Stephen O. Cook v. Valentine W. Holbrook* for the proposition that a claim for wages merges into a judgment and becomes a separate and distinct debt losing its character as wages. It also argues that our language in *Chader v. Wilkins* supports the proposition that a judgment is a debt regardless of the nature of the original cause of action.

We cannot agree that the entry of a judgment for back pay resulted in Rowland's losing the exemption provided in section 642.21. *Cook* is distinguishable from this case because the creditor sought to garnish a fund arising from a judgment that was held by an attorney. Likewise, our decision in *Chader* is not controlling. The language in *Chader* does not persuade us to determine that a judgment extinguishes the entire character of the original claim. More important, we believe that stronger authority can be found in those cases holding that an employee's wages remain exempt when he sues an employer and recovers a judgment. We believe that these cases are more consistent with the purposes of Iowa's exemption and civil rights statutes.

\* \* \* \*

Willow Tree also urges that time has destroyed the exempt character of the wages. It cites our decision in *Miehe* for authority that the exemption only lasts for a ninety-day period after the wages are paid if the wages can be traced to a checking or savings account in a financial institution. In this case, the funds have not been transferred to Rowland nor has he exercised any control over the funds. He has not been permitted "a reasonable opportunity to negotiate the paycheck [earnings represented by the judgment] and spend the fund." Under these circumstances it would be premature to establish a ninety-day limit as we did in *Miehe*.

II. Interest. We address Rowland's claim that he is entitled to an exemption in the interest due on the judgment for back-pay wages. He urges that the interest should be construed as "earnings" for the purposes of section 642.21. We do not agree. Interest is allowed for the use of money or as damages for its detention. We hold that the interest is not exempt under section 642.21.

III. Conclusion. In summary, we hold that the amount of Rowland's judgment against his employer for back pay is exempt earnings under section 642.21, but that the amount awarded for interest on the judgment is not exempt. We re-mand for the district court to determine the amount of the exemption and render judgment accordingly.

AFFIRMED IN PART AND REVERSED IN PART.

---

CASE A.6     *Reference: Problem 35–12*

## GREEN v. SHELL OIL CO.

Court of Appeals of Michigan, 1989.
181 Mich.App. 439,
450 N.W.2d 50.

*FITZGERALD*, Justice.

\* \* \* \*

At approximately 6:00 P.M. on December 21, 1981, plaintiff drove into a Shell service station owned and operated by defendant Lanford and leased from defendant Shell Oil Company. Plaintiff filled his gas tank and, as he walked from the self-service island to the station's office to pay for the gasoline, was struck by a slow-moving vehicle plaintiff al-leges was driven by Monica Gottwald. Plaintiff slapped the hood of the vehicle with his hand and yelled for Gottwald to stop and to be more careful. Immediately thereafter, Leslie Salgado, an occupant of the Gottwald vehicle and employee of the station, exited from the vehicle and began striking plaintiff. An unidentified station attendant joined Salgado in his attack on plaintiff.

On January 2, 1982, plaintiff filed a complaint in Oak-land Circuit Court against defendants and Salgado, as well as others no longer parties to the instant action, alleging [among other things] vicarious liability [indirect liability] of defendants for \* \* \* assault and battery and negligence by defendants in failing to provide a safe place for doing business. The case was remanded to district court after mediation.

Defendants moved for and were granted summary dis-position. The district court held that defendants could not be held liable for an intentional tort committed by the service station attendant. The court also held that the attendant owed no duty to stop an assault by a third party. \* \* \*

Plaintiff appealed \* \* \* to circuit court. The circuit court reversed the district court's grant of summary dispo-sition \* \* \*.

\* \* \* \*

We believe that \* \* \* defendant Lanford's employ-ees were in a position to control the unruly situation, to eject the instigator from the premises and to refrain from increasing plaintiff's injuries. On these facts, a jury could find that de-fendant Lanford failed to exercise reasonable care for his invitees' protection.

The question \* \* \* becomes whether Shell Oil had apparent authority over the service station so as to make it liable for the assault on plaintiff. In *Johnston v. American Oil Co.,* the plaintiff's decedent was shot during an alter-cation with the proprietor of a Standard service station, who refused to serve him and his companions. The trial court granted defendant American Oil Company's summary judg-ment motion based on the proprietor's status as an inde-pendent contractor. The plaintiff had pointed to the service station's use of American Oil's trademark and its sale of supplies and products obtained from American Oil. On ap-peal, the panel concluded:

> American Oil's national advertising campaign promot-ing the Standard Oil name and products, including the slogans "As you travel ask us" and "You expect more from Standard and you get it," would seem to raise a sufficient question of fact as to the existence of agency by estoppel or by apparent authority to defeat the grant-ing of summary judgment.

\* \* \* \*

We believe the trial court herein likewise erred in grant-ing the motion for summary judgment. The question, of course, is not whether Murphy is, in fact, an agent of American Oil, the question is whether plaintiff has raised a material issue of fact that requires further proofs before the finding of fact. Here plaintiff has carried that burden.

In his affidavit [a written or printed statement confirmed by oath or affirmation], plaintiff stated:

> I always assumed that a Shell gas station was operated by Shell Oil. I cannot state whether I ever actually con-sidered whether the operators of gas stations have an ownership interest in the business or not, but it was my belief at the time of the assault upon me, and prior, that Shell Oil either owned the facilities and operated them directly, or exercised active control over the operations of the gas station so as to ensure uniform standards of quality, reliability and conduct of the employees at the stations.

According to defendants, Shell Oil exercised no control over the hiring, firing and supervision of the service station employees and had no authority over the supervision, man-agement and control of the station. In addition, defendant Lanford was not required to purchase any parts from Shell Oil. As defendants state on appeal, "the most that can be said is that '[Wayne Lanford] displayed [Shell's] brand signs, that he honored [Shell's] credit cards, [and that Shell's] agents from time to time made suggestions as to operation of the station.' "

In light of the foregoing, we cannot say with any degree of certainty that further factual development of plaintiff's theory of apparent authority would be futile. Accordingly, we believe that plaintiff should be given the opportunity to show that Shell Oil had apparent authority over defendant Lanford's employees.

Defendants also argue that they cannot be held vicariously liable for the attendant's participation in the assault. We agree.

An employer is liable for the intentional tort of his employee if the tort is committed in the course and within the scope of the employment. An employer is not liable if the employee's tortious act is committed while the employee is working for the employer but the act is outside his authority, "as where he steps aside from his employment to gratify some personal animosity or to accomplish some purpose of his own."

An employer's liability may also be based upon a finding that the employee acted within the scope or apparent scope of his employment. Generally, the trier of fact determines whether an employee was acting within the scope or apparent scope of his employment. Summary disposition is appropriate, however, where it is apparent that the employee is acting to accomplish a purpose of his own.

Plaintiff testified at a deposition that Salgado struck him on the left side of the head. Plaintiff fell to the ground, dazed by the blow. The next thing he remembered was being kicked, while laying on the ground, by a man in a brown uniform, allegedly the unidentified station attendant. On this testimony, we conclude that the attendant's violent conduct was engaged in for the purpose of assisting Salgado and not for any purpose in furtherance of the employer's business interests. This is not a situation where the employee was attempting to collect plaintiff's payment on behalf of his employer. Nor is it a situation where the attendant's conduct can be reasonably construed as an attempt to end the altercation or eject plaintiff from the employer's establishment in order to restore order. Accordingly, summary disposition on plaintiff's vicarious liability claim was appropriate. The attendant's action could only be construed as an attempt to accomplish his own purpose, not to further his employer's business interests.

\* \* \* \*

We affirm in part, reverse in part and remand.

---

## CASE A.7   *Reference: Problem 36–10*

### JOHNSTON v. DEL MAR DISTRIBUTING CO.

Court of Appeals of Texas—Corpus Christi, 1989.
776 S.W.2d 768.

*BENAVIDES,* Justice.

Nancy Johnston, appellant, brought suit against her employer, Del Mar Distributing Co., Inc., alleging that her employment had been wrongfully terminated. Del Mar filed a motion for summary judgment in the trial court alleging that appellant's pleadings failed to state a cause of action. After a hearing on the motion, the trial court agreed with Del Mar and granted its motion for summary judgment.

\* \* \* \*

In her petition, appellant alleged that she was employed by Del Mar during the summer of 1987. As a part of her duties, she was required to prepare shipping documents for goods being sent from Del Mar's warehouse located in Corpus Christi, Texas to other cities in Texas. One day, Del Mar instructed appellant to package a semi-automatic weapon (for delivery to a grocery store in Brownsville, Texas) and to label the contents of the package as "fishing gear." Ultimately, the package was to be given to United Parcel Service for shipping. Appellant was required to sign her name to the shipping documents; therefore, she was concerned that her actions might be in violation of some firearm regulation or a regulation of the United Postal Service. Accordingly, she sought the advice of the United States Treasury Department Bureau of Alcohol, Tobacco & Firearms \* \* \*. A few days after she contacted the Bureau, appellant was fired. Appellant brought suit for wrongful termination alleging that

her employment was terminated solely in retaliation for contacting the Bureau.

\* \* \* \*

Del Mar asserted in its motion that, notwithstanding the above described facts, appellant's cause of action was barred by the employment-at-will doctrine. Specifically, Del Mar asserted that since appellant's employment was for an indefinite amount of time, she was an employee-at-will and it had the absolute right to terminate her employment for any reason or no reason at all.

It is well-settled that Texas adheres to the traditional employment-at-will doctrine. The Texas Supreme Court [has] held that absent a specific contractual provision to the contrary, either the employer or the employee may terminate their relationship at any time, for any reason.

Today, the absolute employment-at-will doctrine is increasingly seen as a "relic of early industrial times" and a "harsh anachronism." Accordingly, our Legislature has enacted some exceptions to this doctrine \* \* \*.

Recently, the Texas Supreme Court, recognizing the need to amend the employment-at-will doctrine, invoked its judicial authority to create a very narrow common law exception to the doctrine. In [*Sabine Pilot Service, Inc. v. Hauck*] the Texas Supreme Court was faced with a narrow issue for consideration, i.e., whether an allegation by an employee that he or she was discharged for refusing to perform an illegal act stated a cause of action. The Court held that

public policy, as expressed in the laws of this state and the United States which carry criminal penalties, requires a very narrow exception to the employment-at-will doctrine \* \* \* [t]hat narrow exception covers only the discharge of an employee for the sole reason that the employee refused to perform an illegal act.

Justice Kilgarlin noted in his concurring opinion to *Sabine Pilot* that it is against public policy to allow an employer "to require an employee to break a law or face termination. . . ." He elaborated that to hold otherwise "would promote a thorough disrespect for the laws and legal institutions of our society."

\* \* \* \*

On appeal, appellant alleges that her petition did state a cause of action pursuant to the public policy exception announced in *Sabine Pilot*. In her brief, appellant contends that since Texas law currently provides that an employee has a cause of action when she is fired for refusing to perform an illegal act, it necessarily follows that an employee states a cause of action where she alleges that she is fired for simply inquiring into whether or not she is committing illegal acts. To hold otherwise, she argues, would have a chilling [inhibiting, discouraging] effect on the public policy exception announced in *Sabine Pilot*. We agree.

It is implicit that in order to refuse to do an illegal act, an employee must either know or suspect that the requested act is illegal. In some cases it will be patently obvious that the act is illegal (murder, robbery, theft, etc.); however, in other cases it may not be so apparent. Since ignorance of the law is no defense to a criminal prosecution, it is reasonable to expect that if an employee has a good faith belief that a required act might be illegal, she will try to find out whether the act is in fact illegal prior to deciding what course of action

to take. If an employer is allowed to terminate the employee at this point, the public policy exception announced in *Sabine Pilot* would have little or no effect. To hold otherwise would force an employee, who suspects that a requested act might be illegal, to (1) subject herself to possible discharge if she attempts to find out if the act is in fact illegal; or (2) remain ignorant, perform the act and, if it turns out to be illegal, face possible criminal sanctions.

We hold that since the law recognizes that it is against public policy to allow an employer to coerce its employee to commit a criminal act in furtherance of its own interest, then it is necessarily inferred that the same public policy prohibits the discharge of an employee who in good faith attempts to find out if the act is illegal. It is important to note that we are not creating a new exception to the employment-at-will doctrine. Rather, we are merely enforcing the narrow public policy exception which was created in *Sabine Pilot*.

\* \* \* \*

Furthermore, it is the opinion of this Court that the question of whether or not the requested act was in fact illegal is irrelevant to the determination of this case. We hold that where a plaintiff's employment is terminated for attempting to find out from a regulatory agency if a requested act is illegal, it is not necessary to prove that the requested act was in fact illegal. A plaintiff must, however, establish that she had a good faith belief that the requested act might be illegal, and that such belief was reasonable. \* \* \*

\* \* \* \*

The judgment of the trial court is reversed and remanded for trial.

---

## CASE A.8      *Reference: Problem 42–12*

### MASCHMEIER v. SOUTHSIDE PRESS, LTD.

Court of Appeals of Iowa, 1989.
435 N.W.2d 377.

*HABHAB*, Judge.

Defendant Kenneth E. Maschmeier and Charlotte A. Maschmeier created a corporation, Southside Press, Ltd., that did business at 1220 Second Avenue North in Council Bluffs. This building is owned by Kenneth and Charlotte and was leased by them to the corporation.

Kenneth and Charlotte are the majority shareholders, with each having 1300 shares. They are the only officers and directors of the corporation.

They gifted to their two sons [Marty and Larry] each 1200 shares of stock. All the parties were employed by Southside Press until the summer of 1985 when, because of family disagreements, Marty and Larry were terminated as employees. \* \* \*

The parents on August 2, 1985, created a new corporation, Southside Press of the Midlands, Ltd. They are its only officers and directors. As individuals they terminated

the lease of their building \* \* \* with Southside and leased the same premises to Midlands. In addition, Kenneth, as president of Southside, entered into a lease with himself as president of Midlands whereby the printing equipment and two of the vehicles were leased to Midlands for $22,372 per year for five years, with an option to buy such assets at the end of the lease term at their fair market value but not to exceed $20,000. In addition, the inventory and two other vehicles owned by Southside were sold by it to Midlands. Notwithstanding the fact that a substantial part of the assets of Southside had been disposed of, the parents still received an annual salary from it of more than $20,000.

After Marty and Larry's employment with Southside had terminated, each obtained employment with other printing companies in the same metropolitan area. The family disagreement continued. All stockholders were employed by companies that were competitive to Southside. Ultimately, the parents, as majority shareholders, offered to buy the sons' shares of stock for $20 per share. Their sons felt that this amount was inadequate. Thus, this lawsuit.

In 1985, Southside Press had gross sales of more than $600,000. The trial court found that in 1985 the corporate assets had a fair market value of $160,745. Shareholders' equity was found to be $236,502.92, and divided by the number of shares equals $47.30 per share. The court found that the majority shareholders had been abusive and oppressive to the minority shareholders by wasting the corporate assets and leaving Southside Press only a shell of a corporation. The court ordered the majority shareholders to pay $47.30 per share to the sons, or $56,760 to each son, plus interest at the maximum legal rate from the date of the filing of the petition.

\* \* \* \*

\* \* \* [D]efendants state that the shares were valued at $20 pursuant to the corporate bylaws and should be enforced as an agreement of the shareholders. \* \* \*

\* \* \* \*

Whenever a situation exists which is contrary to the principles of equity and which can be redressed within the scope of judicial action, a court of equity will devise a remedy to meet the situation though no similar relief has been granted before. The district court has the power to liquidate a corporation under [Iowa Code] section 496A.94(1). This statute also allows the district court to fashion other equitable relief.

It is contended that, in order for the trial court to have properly invoked the powers under section 496A.94(1), it had to find either the majority shareholders were oppressive in their conduct towards the minority shareholders, or that the majority shareholders misapplied or wasted corporate assets.

\* \* \* The alleged oppressive conduct by those in control of a close corporation must be analyzed in terms of "fiduciary duties" owed by majority shareholders to the minority shareholders and "reasonable expectations" held by minority shareholders in committing capital and labor to the particular enterprise, in light of the predicament in which minority shareholders in a close corporation can be placed by a "freeze-out" situation.

\* \* \* The trial court found \* \* \* here [that] the majority shareholders attempted to "freeze out" or "squeeze out" the minority shareholders by terminating their employment and not permitting them to participate in the business.

\* \* \* \*

We concur with the trial court's findings that the majority shareholders acted oppressively toward the minority shareholders and wasted corporate assets. In this respect, we further determine that the trial court properly invoked Iowa Code section 496A.94 when it fashioned the remedy requiring the majority shareholders to purchase the shares of the minority.

But that does not resolve the problem[.] \* \* \* The appellant challenges the method fashioned by the trial court in fixing the value of the stock and payment thereof by asserting it should be governed by the bylaws.

The articles of incorporation of Southside vested in the directors of the corporation the "authority to make provisions in the Bylaws of the corporation restricting the transfer of shares of this corporation." This board of directors did when they adopted the following bylaw that relates to restrictions on the transferability of stock. \* \* \*

\* \* \* \*

Section 3 [of the corporate bylaws] is a restriction on stock transfer. If a shareholder intends to sell his stock, he must first offer it to the corporation at a price "agreed upon by the shareholders at each annual meeting." The shareholders must agree on the value of the stock and if they are unable to do so, each has a right to select an appraiser and the appraisers shall appoint another and in this instance the five appraisers are to act as a Board of Appraisers to value the stock.

\* \* \* Since none of the shareholders requested appraisers, we deem this, as the trial court did, to be a waiver. We concur with this statement from the trial court's ruling: "All parties have left the Court with the burden of evaluating the corporate stock."

\* \* \* \*

We agree with the defendants that a contractual formula price is enforceable even if the formula price is less than its fair market value. But here the parties were unable to agree to a price, i.e., at the last meeting of the stockholders. Thus the trial court was called upon to do so.

Courts have generally held that no one factor governs the valuation of shares; but that all factors, such as market value, asset value, future earning prospects, should be considered. In this case, the parties relied rather heavily on what is referred to in the record as book value (shareholders' equity) in arriving at stock value. The trial court likewise used shareholder equity but adjusted that amount by the present day fair market value of corporate assets.

\* \* \* \*

We determine that under the circumstances here the valuation per share as fixed by the trial court and the method it employed in arriving at value is fair and reasonable. However, we further conclude that the amount Larry and Marty are to receive must be reduced by the total amount of loans made to them as they appear on the corporate books.

\* \* \* \*

We affirm and modify.

---

## CASE A.9    *Reference: Problem 46–10*

### ROBERTS v. WALMART STORES, INC.

United States District Court,
Eastern District of Missouri, 1990.
736 F.Supp. 1527.

*LIMBAUGH,* District Judge.

Plaintiffs are black citizens of the United States. Defendant is a retail department store. On December 5, 1989 plaintiffs were customers at a store operated by defendant in St. Charles, Missouri. During this visit plaintiffs purchased several items and presented defendant with a check in payment for the merchandise. Defendant recorded the race of plaintiffs on the check. Plaintiffs, upon becoming aware that their race was being recorded on the check, returned the merchandise and retrieved the check. Plaintiffs then filed a two-count amended complaint against defendant alleging that defendant's practice of recording the race of black citizens who pay for merchandise by check violates the Thirteenth Amendment. * * *

The Thirteenth Amendment is implicated when it is alleged that a private individual or entity deliberately acted in a way to segregate, humiliate or belittle a person of the black race in a way that prevented such a person from freely exercising a right guaranteed to all citizens. * * * Plaintiffs may not maintain a cause of action against defendant, a private corporation, directly under the Thirteenth Amendment. Instead, plaintiffs must base their claims on one of the implementing statutes of the Thirteenth Amendment. * * *

* * * *

Defendant asserts that its recording the race of the plaintiffs on the check is post-formation conduct which is no longer actionable. * * * After Patterson the resolution of this civil rights claim turns on an interpretation of the Missouri Commercial Code to determine whether the contract was formed at the time the alleged violation occurred. The court does not possess enough information about the retail transaction to ascertain whether a contract was already formed at the time defendant recorded the race of plaintiffs on the check. Therefore, defendant's motion to dismiss plaintiffs'' claim * * * is denied.

* * * *

First, defendant asserts that plaintiffs have failed to plead that blacks were treated any differently than whites.

Although plaintiffs did not plead that whites purchasing merchandise by check do not have their race recorded on their check, plaintiffs' complaint should not be dismissed unless it appears that plaintiffs could "prove no set of facts in support of the claim which would entitle them to relief." * * *

Second, defendant asserts that plaintiffs failed to plead a cause of action[.] * * * [N]o civil rights violation occurred because defendant did not refuse to sell plaintiffs the merchandise due to their race. * * * Although defendant was willing to consummate the retail transaction with plaintiffs, defendant is not absolved from liability * * * if defendant's motives in recording the race of plaintiffs was infected with racial discrimination. * * *

* * * *

There is no authority for plaintiffs' argument that payment by check, absent an agreement by the seller to hold the check for a period of time before presentment to the drawee, constitutes an extension of credit rather than a cash transaction. * * *

* * * *

Defendant seeks for the Court to require plaintiffs to file a second amended complaint because "plaintiffs' amended complaint is so vague and ambiguous that defendant cannot reasonably be required to frame a responsive pleading." * * * The Court has reviewed plaintiffs' amended complaint and concludes that plaintiffs' allegations are clear and plain and are undoubtedly sufficient to satisfy the requirements of notice pleading * * * .

[The district court granted defendant's motion to dismiss in part and denied defendant's motion to dismiss in part.]

---

CASE A.10     *Reference: Problem 50–13*

## STRANG v. HOLLOWELL

Court of Appeals of North Carolina, 1990.
387 S.E.2d 664.

[*WELLS*, Judge.]

On 2 January 1987 plaintiff met with defendants Hollowell and Jones in Cary, North Carolina to negotiate a consignment agreement for the sale of plaintiff's 1974 Pantera automobile which had an estimated value of $23,000 to $25,000. A written consignment contract was executed between plaintiff and Hollowell Auto Sales. Defendant Jones, then employed by Hollowell Auto Sales, signed the contract on behalf of Hollowell Auto Sales. Plaintiff gave defendants the keys to his automobile and they transported it by flatbed trailer to the Hollowell Auto Sales lot in Morehead City. Defendants Jones and Hollowell were unable to sell the Pantera and it was returned to plaintiff in August 1987. At that time plaintiff discovered that the automobile had been damaged to an extent which reduced its value to between $10,000 and $12,000.

On 23 December 1987 plaintiff sued defendants Jones and Hollowell for negligence in their bailment of his automobile. Plaintiff was unaware that Hollowell Auto Sales was a trade name for Solar Center, Inc., whose principal place of business is in Carteret County. Plaintiff was under the impression that Hollowell Auto Sales was a sole proprietorship operated by defendant Hollowell. On motion of defendant Hollowell in open court, defendant Solar Center, Inc. was added as an additional party prior to trial.

Defendant Jones did not file an answer to plaintiff's complaint and default judgment was subsequently entered against him. At a non-jury trial, judgment in the amount of $11,000 was entered against defendants Jones and Hollowell, jointly and severally. Defendant Gene Hollowell appeals.

* * * *

The only issue presented in this appeal is whether defendant Hollowell can be held individually liable for plaintiff's damages. Defendant contends that he was acting as an agent of Hollowell Auto Sales and therefore cannot be held personally liable. Defendant further asserts that, regardless of the fact that plaintiff was unaware that Hollowell Auto

Sales was a trade name for Solar Center, Inc., defendant is nevertheless shielded from individual liability because Solar Center, Inc. fulfilled its legal obligation to disclose its relationship with Hollowell Auto Sales by filing an assumed name certificate in [the appropriate county office]. For the following reasons, we disagree.

When plaintiff gave possession of his automobile to defendant under the consignment contract a bailment for the mutual benefit of bailor and bailee was created. This bailment continued until the automobile was returned to plaintiff in August 1987. Defendant was therefore a bailee of plaintiff's automobile while it was in his custody in Morehead City. A bailee is obligated to exercise due care to protect the subject of the bailment from negligent loss, damage, or destruction. His liability depends on the presence or absence of ordinary negligence. While this obligation arises from the relationship created by the contract of bailment, breach of this contractual duty results in a tort. It is well settled that one is personally liable for all torts committed by him, including negligence, notwithstanding that he may have acted as agent for another or as an officer for a corporation. Furthermore, the potential for corporate liability, in addition to individual liability, does not shield the individual tortfeasor from liability. Rather, it provides the injured party a choice as to which party to hold liable for the tort.

Here there is no dispute that plaintiff's automobile was returned to him in a damaged condition. Defendant does not except to the trial court's findings and conclusions that a bailment was created between plaintiff and defendant and that "defendants were negligent in their care and control of the vehicle while it was in their possession." We therefore hold that the trial court correctly ruled that by failing to exercise due care and allowing the automobile to be damaged while in his custody, defendant committed a tort for which he can be held individually liable.

Because the resolution of this case is in tort for negligence, rather than in contract for breach, we need not reach the issue of whether defendant had sufficiently disclosed his agency with Hollowell Auto Sales or with Solar Center, Inc. However, we note that our Supreme Court has said that use of a trade name is not sufficient as a matter of law to disclose the identity of the principal and the fact of agency.

Likewise, the existence of means by which the fact of agency might be discovered is also insufficient to disclose agency.

\*   \*   \*   \*

Affirmed.

---

## CASE A.11    *Reference: Problem 56–9*

## TRANS-ORIENT MARINE CORP. v. STAR TRADING & MARINE, INC.

United States District Court,
Southern District of New York, 1990.
731 F.Supp. 619.

*WILLIAM C. CONNER*, District Judge:

Defendant Republic of the Sudan moves this Court to dismiss the complaint for failure to state a claim or for summary judgment. It claims that the new Republic of the Sudan, as successor state, is not liable for the alleged breach of a five-year exclusive agency contract entered into by the prior sovereign state of Sudan. Defendant further asserts that a fundamental change in circumstances relieves it of any prior contractual obligations.

### FACTS

Plaintiff's cause of action for breach of contract arises from an alleged five-year exclusive agency agreement to represent the Sudan in the United States P.L. 480 program [an agricultural trade development and assistance program]. The alleged October 14, 1983 agreement was effective from October 1, 1984 through September 30, 1989. In April 1985, a military coup deposed the then head of state, declaring a state of emergency and suspending the constitution. A twelve-month transitional military regime followed, which was then replaced by a civilian coalition government. The name of the state was changed from the Sudan to the Republic of Sudan. In June 1989, there was another military coup in which the present military regime overthrew the former civilian administration and suspended the constitution. Both parties agree that the Republic of the Sudan is a foreign sovereign state.

On January 3 and 4, 1985, the then Sudanese government sent letters advising plaintiff that a new agent, CIDCO, had been appointed to handle the contracts under P.L. 480 and that CIDCO would select the shipping agent. This alleged termination of the then-executory contract did not provide the one-year termination notice required under the original contract. Since January 1985, the Sudan has awarded CIDCO a continuing series of contracts to handle the wheat and wheat flour transportation under P.L. 480, in alleged violation of plaintiff's exclusive agency contract. No additional facts are relevant to the present motion.

### DISCUSSION

The present Sudanese government asserts that it is not liable for the contractual obligations of the prior sovereign, pointing to the two military coups of 1985 and 1989 to sustain its position that both the 1985 military regime and the present administration are successor states and that there has been a fundamental change in circumstances. Plaintiff contends that neither the 1985 regime nor the present regime is a successor state but that they represent mere changes in government which do not relieve the present regime from the prior government's contractual obligations. Plaintiff further argues that even if either regime is a successor state, they have ratified the prior government's contract. For the following reasons, summary judgment is denied.

Whether a new administration may terminate the executory portions of its predecessor's contracts is based on the succession of state theory. International law sharply distinguishes the succession of state, which may create a discontinuity of statehood, from a succession of government, which leaves statehood unaffected. It is generally accepted that a change in government, regime or ideology has no effect on that state's international rights and obligations because the state continues to exist despite the change. * * *

However, where one sovereign succeeds another, and a new state is created, the rights and obligations of the successor state are affected. The rule with regard to contracts with private foreign individuals involves a balancing of competing interests. While the successor state is permitted to terminate existing contracts originally executed by the former sovereign and the private party, the successor state is liable to that party only for any amount due him as of the date of the change of sovereignty. But if the contract is totally executory, the successor state is released from the contract.

The Restatement of Foreign Relations Law describes a successor state to include: a state that wholly absorbs another state, that takes over part of the territory of another state, that becomes independent of another state of which it had formed a part, or that arises because of the dismemberment of the state of which it had been a part.

Careful study of defendant's submission reveals that the state of Sudan has not (1) wholly absorbed or been wholly absorbed by another state; (2) partly taken over or been partly taken over by another state; (3) become independent from another state of which it had formed a part; or (4) arisen out of dismemberment of a state of which it had been a part since the date of plaintiff's contract. Under the Restatement's definition, the state of Sudan has remained the same entity since its independence in 1956. Defendant's own exhibit in support of its motion substantiates that only a change in government was effected by the two military coups * * *.

Accordingly, the only changes in the Sudan since its independence in 1956 have been in the government, with seven distinct successive administrations. But there has been only one state.

Defendant unpersuasively emphasizes various aspects of the relevant transitions to reflect the creation of a new state: that the transitions resulted by way of military coups as opposed to routine, constitutional processes, the re-naming of the nation, the suspension of the constitution, the closing of the borders and the declaration of a state of emergency. Treatises, as well as applicable case law, demonstrate that such features do not effect a succession of state. * * *

Furthermore, the Restatement's comparative chart in a Recognition of States section illustrates that a change in government by armed force or fraud, as well as institution of another regime following a civil war, leaves "no question of the existence of the state." It offers as contemporary examples of mere changes in government: Pinochet's 1973 ouster of Allende in Chile, Franco's 1936–39 takeover of Spain, and the Communist revolution in China.

The seminal decision on the distinction between a succession of state versus a change in government is the U. S. Supreme Court decision in *The Sapphire.* In *The Sapphire,* the Supreme Court considered whether a lawsuit begun by the French Emperor, Napoleon III, was abated by the overthrow of the Emperor during the course of litigation. In holding that the action was not extinguished, the Supreme Court stated that, "on the [Emperor's] deposition the sovereignty does not change, but merely the person or persons in whom it resides. . . . A change in such representative works no change in the national sovereignty or its rights."

* * * *

* * * In *United States v. National City Bank of New York,* the district court held the post-revolutionary State of Russia liable on the treasury notes of the pre-revolutionary state. Similarly, in *Jackson v. People's Republic of China,* the district court determined that the People's Republic, as successor government to the Imperial Chinese Government, was successor to its obligations, specifically, payment of principal due on the prior government-issued bonds. The law is clear that the obligations of a state are unaffected by a mere change in government. It is of no consequence that the Sudan allegedly breached an executory contract. The distinction between executed and executory contracts only applies where there has been a succession of state. The military coups of 1985 and 1989 did not effect a succession of state of the Sudan but merely changed the state's governing body, leaving the state's obligations undisturbed.

Defendant's alternative claim that a fundamental change of circumstances has occurred since October, 1983 relieving it of any prior contractual obligations is unsubstantiated. Defendant presents no explanation as to what "circumstances constituted an essential basis of the consent of the parties to be bound by the agreement" or what changes have "radically transform[ed] the extent of obligations still to be performed under the agreement." Having failed to demonstrate a fundamental change in circumstances, the present government is therefore contractually obligated to plaintiff under the October 14, 1983 five-year extension of agency contract if its predecessor indeed breached that agreement.

CONCLUSION

For the reasons discussed above, summary judgment is denied. Plaintiff is directed to brief the additional grounds for dismissal or summary judgment raised in defendant's motion papers by March 19, 1990. Defendant shall reply by March 26, 1990.

SO ORDERED.

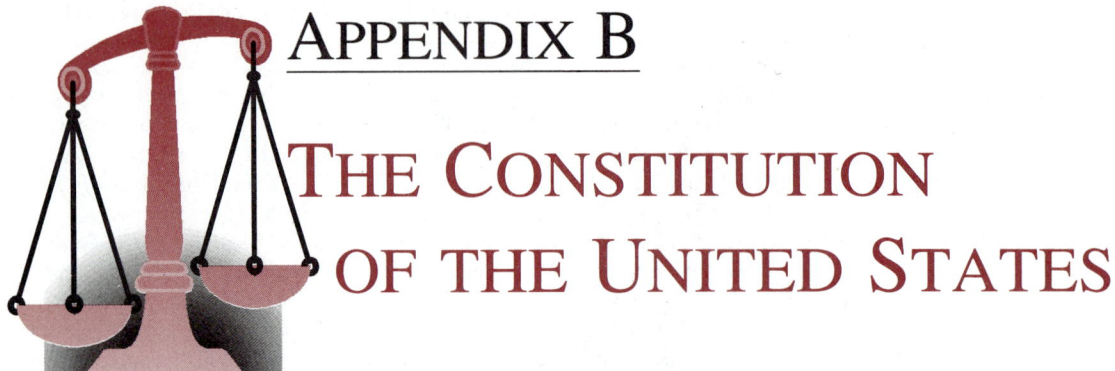

# APPENDIX B

# THE CONSTITUTION OF THE UNITED STATES

### PREAMBLE

We the People of the United States, in Order to form a more perfect Union, establish Justice, insure domestic Tranquility, provide for the common defence, promote the general Welfare, and secure the Blessings of Liberty to ourselves and our Posterity, do ordain and establish this Constitution for the United States of America.

### ARTICLE I

**Section 1.** All legislative Powers herein granted shall be vested in a Congress of the United States, which shall consist of a Senate and House of Representatives.

**Section 2.** The House of Representatives shall be composed of Members chosen every second Year by the People of the several States, and the Electors in each State shall have the Qualifications requisite for Electors of the most numerous Branch of the State Legislature.

No Person shall be a Representative who shall not have attained to the Age of twenty five Years, and been seven Years a Citizen of the United States, and who shall not, when elected, be an Inhabitant of that State in which he shall be chosen.

Representatives and direct Taxes shall be apportioned among the several States which may be included within this Union, according to their respective Numbers, which shall be determined by adding to the whole Number of free Persons, including those bound to Service for a Term of Years, and excluding Indians not taxed, three fifths of all other Persons. The actual Enumeration shall be made within three Years after the first Meeting of the Congress of the United States, and within every subsequent Term of ten Years, in such Manner as they shall by Law direct. The Number of Representatives shall not exceed one for every thirty Thousand, but each State shall have at Least one Representative; and until such enumeration shall be made, the State of New Hampshire shall be entitled to chuse three, Massachusetts eight, Rhode Island and Providence Plantations one, Connecticut five, New York six, New Jersey four, Pennsylvania eight, Delaware one, Maryland six, Virginia ten, North Carolina five, South Carolina five, and Georgia three.

When vacancies happen in the Representation from any State, the Executive Authority thereof shall issue Writs of Election to fill such Vacancies.

The House of Representatives shall chuse their Speaker and other Officers; and shall have the sole Power of Impeachment.

**Section 3.** The Senate of the United States shall be composed of two Senators from each State, chosen by the Legislature thereof, for six Years; and each Senator shall have one Vote.

Immediately after they shall be assembled in Consequence of the first Election, they shall be divided as equally as may be into three Classes. The Seats of the Senators of the first Class shall be vacated at the Expiration of the second Year, of the second Class at the Expiration of the fourth Year, and of the third Class at the Expiration of the sixth Year, so that one third may be chosen every second Year; and if Vacancies happen by Resignation, or otherwise, during the Recess of the Legislature of any State, the Executive thereof may make temporary Appointments until the next Meeting of the Legislature, which shall then fill such Vacancies.

No Person shall be a Senator who shall not have attained to the Age of thirty Years, and been nine Years a Citizen of the United States, and who shall not, when elected, be an Inhabitant of that State for which he shall be chosen.

The Vice President of the United States shall be President of the Senate, but shall have no Vote, unless they be equally divided.

The Senate shall chuse their other Officers, and also a President pro tempore, in the Absence of the Vice President, or when he shall exercise the Office of President of the United States.

The Senate shall have the sole Power to try all Impeachments. When sitting for that Purpose, they shall be on Oath or Affirmation. When the President of the United States is tried, the Chief Justice shall preside: And no Person shall be convicted without the Concurrence of two thirds of the Members present.

Judgment in Cases of Impeachment shall not extend further than to removal from Office, and disqualification to hold and enjoy any Office of honor, Trust, or Profit under the United States: but the Party convicted shall nevertheless be liable and subject to Indictment, Trial, Judgment, and Punishment, according to Law.

**Section 4.** The Times, Places and Manner of holding Elections for Senators and Representatives, shall be prescribed in each State by the Legislature thereof; but the Congress may at any time by Law make or alter such Regulations, except as to the Places of chusing Senators.

The Congress shall assemble at least once in every Year, and such Meeting shall be on the first Monday in December, unless they shall by Law appoint a different Day.

**Section 5.** Each House shall be the Judge of the Elections, Returns, and Qualifications of its own Members, and a Majority of each shall constitute a Quorum to do Business; but a smaller Number may adjourn from day to day, and may be authorized to compel the Attendance of absent Members, in such Manner, and under such Penalties as each House may provide.

Each House may determine the Rules of its Proceedings, punish its Members for disorderly Behavior, and, with the Concurrence of two thirds, expel a Member.

Each House shall keep a Journal of its Proceedings, and from time to time publish the same, excepting such Parts as may in their Judgment require Secrecy; and the Yeas and Nays of the Members of either House on any question shall, at the Desire of one fifth of those Present, be entered on the Journal.

Neither House, during the Session of Congress, shall, without the Consent of the other, adjourn for more than three days, nor to any other Place than that in which the two Houses shall be sitting.

**Section 6.** The Senators and Representatives shall receive a Compensation for their Services, to be ascertained by Law, and paid out of the Treasury of the United States. They shall in all Cases, except Treason, Felony and Breach of the Peace, be privileged from Arrest during their Attendance at the Session of their respective Houses, and in going to and returning from the same; and for any Speech or Debate in either House, they shall not be questioned in any other Place.

No Senator or Representative shall, during the Time for which he was elected, be appointed to any civil Office under the Authority of the United States, which shall have been created, or the Emoluments whereof shall have been increased during such time; and no Person holding any Office under the United States, shall be a Member of either House during his Continuance in Office.

**Section 7.** All Bills for raising Revenue shall originate in the House of Representatives; but the Senate may propose or concur with Amendments as on other Bills.

Every Bill which shall have passed the House of Representatives and the Senate, shall, before it become a Law, be presented to the President of the United States; If he approve he shall sign it, but if not he shall return it, with his Objections to the House in which it shall have originated, who shall enter the Objections at large on their Journal, and proceed to reconsider it. If after such Reconsideration two thirds of that House shall agree to pass the Bill, it shall be sent together with the Objections, to the other House, by which it shall likewise be reconsidered, and if approved by two thirds of that House, it shall become a Law. But in all such Cases the Votes of both Houses shall be determined by Yeas and Nays, and the Names of the Persons voting for and against the Bill shall be entered on the Journal of each House respectively. If any Bill shall not be returned by the President within ten Days (Sundays excepted) after it shall have been presented to him, the Same shall be a Law, in like Manner as if he had signed it, unless the Congress by their Adjournment prevent its Return in which Case it shall not be a Law.

Every Order, Resolution, or Vote, to which the Concurrence of the Senate and House of Representatives may be necessary (except on a question of Adjournment) shall be presented to the President of the United States; and before the Same shall take Effect, shall be approved by him, or being disapproved by him, shall be repassed by two thirds of the Senate and House of Representatives, according to the Rules and Limitations prescribed in the Case of a Bill.

**Section 8.** The Congress shall have Power To lay and collect Taxes, Duties, Imposts and Excises, to pay the Debts and provide for the common Defence and general Welfare of the United States; but all Duties, Imposts and Excises shall be uniform throughout the United States;

To borrow Money on the credit of the United States;

To regulate Commerce with foreign Nations, and among the several States, and with the Indian Tribes;

To establish an uniform Rule of Naturalization, and uniform Laws on the subject of Bankruptcies throughout the United States;

To coin Money, regulate the Value thereof, and of foreign Coin, and fix the Standard of Weights and Measures;

To provide for the Punishment of counterfeiting the Securities and current Coin of the United States;

To establish Post Offices and post Roads;

To promote the Progress of Science and useful Arts, by securing for limited Times to Authors and Inventors the exclusive Right to their respective Writings and Discoveries;

To constitute Tribunals inferior to the supreme Court;

To define and punish Piracies and Felonies committed on the high Seas, and Offenses against the Law of Nations;

To declare War, grant Letters of Marque and Reprisal, and make Rules concerning Captures on Land and Water;

To raise and support Armies, but no Appropriation of Money to that Use shall be for a longer Term than two Years;

To provide and maintain a Navy;

To make Rules for the Government and Regulation of the land and naval Forces;

To provide for calling forth the Militia to execute the Laws of the Union, suppress Insurrections and repel Invasions;

To provide for organizing, arming, and disciplining, the Militia, and for governing such Part of them as may be employed in the Service of the United States, reserving to the States respectively, the Appointment of the Officers, and the Authority of training the Militia according to the discipline prescribed by Congress;

To exercise exclusive Legislation in all Cases whatsoever, over such District (not exceeding ten Miles square) as may, by Cession of particular States, and the Acceptance of Congress, become the Seat of the Government of the United States, and to exercise like Authority over all Places purchased by the Consent of the Legislature of the State in which the Same shall be, for the Erection of Forts, Magazines, Arsenals, dock-Yards, and other needful Buildings;—And

To make all Laws which shall be necessary and proper for carrying into Execution the foregoing Powers, and all other Powers vested by this Constitution in the Government of the United States, or in any Department or Officer thereof.

**Section 9.**   The Migration or Importation of such Persons as any of the States now existing shall think proper to admit, shall not be prohibited by the Congress prior to the Year one thousand eight hundred and eight, but a Tax or duty may be imposed on such Importation, not exceeding ten dollars for each Person.

The privilege of the Writ of Habeas Corpus shall not be suspended, unless when in Cases of Rebellion or Invasion the public Safety may require it.

No Bill of Attainder or ex post facto Law shall be passed.

No Capitation, or other direct, Tax shall be laid, unless in Proportion to the Census or Enumeration herein before directed to be taken.

No Tax or Duty shall be laid on Articles exported from any State.

No Preference shall be given by any Regulation of Commerce or Revenue to the Ports of one State over those of another: nor shall Vessels bound to, or from, one State be obliged to enter, clear, or pay Duties in another.

No Money shall be drawn from the Treasury, but in Consequence of Appropriations made by Law; and a regular Statement and Account of the Receipts and Expenditures of all public Money shall be published from time to time.

No Title of Nobility shall be granted by the United States: And no Person holding any Office of Profit or Trust under them, shall, without the Consent of the Congress, accept of any present, Emolument, Office, or Title, of any kind whatever, from any King, Prince, or foreign State.

**Section 10.**   No State shall enter into any Treaty, Alliance, or Confederation; grant Letters of Marque and Reprisal; coin Money; emit Bills of Credit; make any Thing but gold and silver Coin a Tender in Payment of Debts; pass any Bill of Attainder, ex post facto Law, or Law impairing the Obligation of Contracts, or grant any Title of Nobility.

No State shall, without the Consent of the Congress, lay any Imposts or Duties on Imports or Exports, except what may be absolutely necessary for executing its inspection Laws: and the net Produce of all Duties and Imposts, laid by any State on Imports or Exports, shall be for the Use of the Treasury of the United States; and all such Laws shall be subject to the Revision and Controul of the Congress.

No State shall, without the Consent of Congress, lay any Duty of Tonnage, keep Troops, or Ships of War in time of Peace, enter into any Agreement or Compact with another State, or with a foreign Power, or engage in War, unless actually invaded, or in such imminent Danger as will not admit of delay.

### ARTICLE II

**Section 1.**   The executive Power shall be vested in a President of the United States of America. He shall hold his Office during the Term of four Years, and, together with the Vice President, chosen for the same Term, be elected, as follows:

Each State shall appoint, in such Manner as the Legislature thereof may direct, a Number of Electors, equal to the whole Number of Senators and Representatives to which the State may be entitled in the Congress; but no Senator or Representative, or Person holding an Office of Trust or Profit under the United States, shall be appointed an Elector.

The Electors shall meet in their respective States, and vote by Ballot for two Persons, of whom one at least shall not be an Inhabitant of the same State with themselves. And they shall make a List of all the Persons voted for, and of the Number of Votes for each; which List they shall sign and certify, and transmit sealed to the Seat of the Government of the United States, directed to the President of the Senate. The President of the Senate shall, in the Presence of the Senate and House of Representatives, open all the Certificates, and the Votes shall then be counted. The Person having the greatest Number of Votes shall be the President, if such Number be a Majority of the whole Number of Electors appointed; and if there be more than one who have such Majority, and have an equal Number of Votes, then the House of Representatives shall immediately chuse by Ballot one of them for President; and if no Person have a Majority, then from the five highest on the List the said House shall in like Manner chuse the President. But in chusing the President, the Votes shall be taken by States, the Representation from each State having one Vote; A quorum for this Purpose shall consist of a Member or Members from two thirds of the States, and a Majority of all the States shall be necessary to a Choice. In every Case, after the Choice of the President, the Person having the greater Number of Votes of the Electors shall be the Vice President. But if there should remain two or more who have equal Votes, the Senate shall chuse from them by Ballot the Vice President.

The Congress may determine the Time of chusing the Electors, and the Day on which they shall give their Votes; which Day shall be the same throughout the United States.

No person except a natural born Citizen, or a Citizen of the United States, at the time of the Adoption of this Constitution, shall be eligible to the Office of President; neither shall any Person be eligible to that Office who shall not have attained to the Age of thirty five Years, and been fourteen Years a Resident within the United States.

In Case of the Removal of the President from Office, or of his Death, Resignation or Inability to discharge the Powers and Duties of the said Office, the same shall devolve on the Vice President, and the Congress may by Law provide for the Case of Removal, Death, Resignation or Inability, both of the President and Vice President, declaring what Officer shall then act as President, and such Officer shall act accordingly, until the Disability be removed, or a President shall be elected.

The President shall, at stated Times, receive for his Services, a Compensation, which shall neither be increased nor diminished during the Period for which he shall have been elected, and he shall not receive within that Period any other Emolument from the United States, or any of them.

Before he enter on the Execution of his Office, he shall take the following Oath or Affirmation: ''I do solemnly swear (or affirm) that I will faithfully execute the Office of President of the United States, and will to the best of my Ability, preserve, protect and defend the Constitution of the United States.''

**Section 2.** The President shall be Commander in Chief of the Army and Navy of the United States, and of the Militia of the several States, when called into the actual Service of the United States; he may require the Opinion, in writing, of the principal Officer in each of the executive Departments, upon any Subject relating to the Duties of their respective Offices, and he shall have Power to grant Reprieves and Pardons for Offenses against the United States, except in Cases of Impeachment.

He shall have Power, by and with the Advice and Consent of the Senate to make Treaties, provided two thirds of the Senators present concur; and he shall nominate, and by and with the Advice and Consent of the Senate, shall appoint Ambassadors, other public Ministers and Consuls, Judges of the supreme Court, and all other Officers of the United States, whose Appointments are not herein otherwise provided for, and which shall be established by Law; but the Congress may by Law vest the Appointment of such inferior Officers, as they think proper, in the President alone, in the Courts of Law, or in the Heads of Departments.

The President shall have Power to fill up all Vacancies that may happen during the Recess of the Senate, by granting Commissions which shall expire at the End of their next Session.

**Section 3.** He shall from time to time give to the Congress Information of the State of the Union, and recommend to their Consideration such Measures as he shall judge necessary and expedient; he may, on extraordinary Occasions, convene both Houses, or either of them, and in Case of Disagreement between them, with Respect to the Time of Adjournment, he may adjourn them to such Time as he shall think proper; he shall receive Ambassadors and other public Ministers; he shall take Care that the Laws be faithfully executed, and shall Commission all the Officers of the United States.

**Section 4.** The President, Vice President and all civil Officers of the United States, shall be removed from Office on Impeachment for, and Conviction of, Treason, Bribery, or other high Crimes and Misdemeanors.

### ARTICLE III

**Section 1.** The judicial Power of the United States, shall be vested in one supreme Court, and in such inferior Courts as the Congress may from time to time ordain and establish. The Judges, both of the supreme and inferior Courts, shall hold their Offices during good Behaviour, and shall, at stated Times, receive for their Services a Compensation, which shall not be diminished during their Continuance in Office.

**Section 2.** The judicial Power shall extend to all Cases, in Law and Equity, arising under this Constitution, the Laws of the United States, and Treaties made, or which shall be made, under their Authority;—to all Cases affecting Ambassadors, other public Ministers and Consuls;—to all Cases of admiralty and maritime Jurisdiction;—to Controversies to which the United States shall be a Party;—to Controversies between two or more States;—between a State and Citizens of another State;—between Citizens of different States;—between Citizens of the same State claiming Lands under Grants of different States, and between a State, or the Citizens thereof, and foreign States, Citizens or Subjects.

In all Cases affecting Ambassadors, other public Ministers and Consuls, and those in which a State shall be a Party, the supreme Court shall have original Jurisdiction. In all the other Cases before mentioned, the supreme Court shall have appellate Jurisdiction, both as to Law and Fact, with such Exceptions, and under such Regulations as the Congress shall make.

The Trial of all Crimes, except in Cases of Impeachment, shall be by Jury; and such Trial shall be held in the State where the said Crimes shall have been committed; but when not committed within any State, the Trial shall be at such Place or Places as the Congress may by Law have directed.

**Section 3.** Treason against the United States, shall consist only in levying War against them, or, in adhering to their Enemies, giving them Aid and Comfort. No Person shall be convicted of Treason unless on the Testimony of two Witnesses to the same overt Act, or on Confession in open Court.

The Congress shall have Power to declare the Punishment of Treason, but no Attainder of Treason shall work Corruption of Blood, or Forfeiture except during the Life of the Person attainted.

### ARTICLE IV

**Section 1.** Full Faith and Credit shall be given in each State to the public Acts, Records, and judicial Proceedings of every other State. And the Congress may by general Laws prescribe the Manner in which such Acts, Records and Proceedings shall be proved, and the Effect thereof.

**Section 2.** The Citizens of each State shall be entitled to all Privileges and Immunities of Citizens in the several States.

A Person charged in any State with Treason, Felony, or other Crime, who shall flee from Justice, and be found in another State, shall on Demand of the executive Authority of the State from which he fled, be delivered up, to be removed to the State having Jurisdiction of the Crime.

No Person held to Service or Labour in one State, under the Laws thereof, escaping into another, shall, in Consequence of any Law or Regulation therein, be discharged from such Service or Labour, but shall be delivered up on Claim of the Party to whom such Service or Labour may be due.

**Section 3.** New States may be admitted by the Congress into this Union; but no new State shall be formed or erected within the Jurisdiction of any other State; nor any State be formed by the Junction of two or more States, or Parts of States, without the Consent of the Legislatures of the States concerned as well as of the Congress.

The Congress shall have Power to dispose of and make all needful Rules and Regulations respecting the Territory or other Property belonging to the United States; and nothing in this Constitution shall be so construed as to Prejudice any Claims of the United States, or of any particular State.

**Section 4.** The United States shall guarantee to every State in this Union a Republican Form of Government, and shall protect each of them against Invasion; and on Application of the Legislature, or of the Executive (when the Legislature cannot be convened) against domestic Violence.

### ARTICLE V

The Congress, whenever two thirds of both Houses shall deem it necessary, shall propose Amendments to this Constitution, or, on the Application of the Legislatures of two thirds of the several States, shall call a Convention for proposing Amendments, which, in either Case, shall be valid to all Intents and Purposes, as part of this Constitution, when ratified by the Legislatures of three fourths of the several States, or by Conventions in three fourths thereof, as the one or the other Mode of Ratification may be proposed by the Congress; Provided that no Amendment which may be made prior to the Year One thousand eight hundred and eight shall in any Manner affect the first and fourth Clauses in the Ninth Section of the first Article; and that no State, without its Consent, shall be deprived of its equal Suffrage in the Senate.

### ARTICLE VI

All Debts contracted and Engagements entered into, before the Adoption of this Constitution shall be as valid against the United States under this Constitution, as under the Confederation.

This Constitution, and the Laws of the United States which shall be made in Pursuance thereof; and all Treaties made, or which shall be made, under the Authority of the United States, shall be the supreme Law of the Land; and the Judges in every State shall be bound thereby, any Thing in the Constitution or Laws of any State to the Contrary notwithstanding.

The Senators and Representatives before mentioned, and the Members of the several State Legislatures, and all executive and judicial Officers, both of the United States and of the several States, shall be bound by Oath or Affirmation, to support this Constitution; but no religious Test shall ever be required as a Qualification to any Office or public Trust under the United States.

### ARTICLE VII

The Ratification of the Conventions of nine States shall be sufficient for the Establishment of this Constitution between the States so ratifying the Same.

### AMENDMENT I [1791]

Congress shall make no law respecting an establishment of religion, or prohibiting the free exercise thereof; or abridging the freedom of speech, or of the press; or the right of the people peaceably to assembly, and to petition the Government for a redress of grievances.

### AMENDMENT II [1791]

A well regulated Militia, being necessary to the security of a free State, the right of the people to keep and bear Arms, shall not be infringed.

### AMENDMENT III [1791]

No Soldier shall, in time of peace be quartered in any house, without the consent of the Owner, nor in time of war, but in a manner to be prescribed by law.

### AMENDMENT IV [1791]

The right of the people to be secure in their persons, houses, papers, and effects, against unreasonable searches and seizures, shall not be violated, and no Warrants shall issue, but upon probable cause, supported by Oath or affirmation, and particularly describing the place to be searched, and the persons or things to be seized.

### AMENDMENT V [1791]

No person shall be held to answer for a capital, or otherwise infamous crime, unless on a presentment or indictment of a Grand Jury, except in cases arising in the land or naval forces, or in the Militia, when in actual service in time of War or public danger; nor shall any person be subject for the same offence to be twice put in jeopardy of life or limb; nor shall be compelled in any criminal case to be a witness against himself, nor be deprived of life, liberty, or property, without due process of law; nor shall private property be taken for public use, without just compensation.

### AMENDMENT VI [1791]

In all criminal prosecutions, the accused shall enjoy the right to a speedy and public trial, by an impartial jury of the State and district wherein the crime shall have been committed, which district shall have been previously ascertained by law, and to be informed of the nature and cause of the accusation; to be confronted with the witnesses against him;

to have compulsory process for obtaining witnesses in his favor, and to have the Assistance of Counsel for his defence.

## AMENDMENT VII [1791]

In Suits at common law, where the value in controversy shall exceed twenty dollars, the right of trial by jury shall be preserved, and no fact tried by jury, shall be otherwise re-examined in any Court of the United States, than according to the rules of the common law.

## AMENDMENT VIII [1791]

Excessive bail shall not be required, nor excessive fines imposed, nor cruel and unusual punishments inflicted.

## AMENDMENT IX [1791]

The enumeration in the Constitution, of certain rights, shall not be construed to deny or disparage others retained by the people.

## AMENDMENT X [1791]

The powers not delegated to the United States by the Constitution, nor prohibited by it to the States, are reserved to the States respectively, or to the people.

## AMENDMENT XI [1798]

The Judicial power of the United States shall not be construed to extend to any suit in law or equity, commenced or prosecuted against one of the United States by Citizens of another State, or by Citizens or Subjects of any Foreign State.

## AMENDMENT XII [1804]

The Electors shall meet in their respective states, and vote by ballot for President and Vice-President, one of whom, at least, shall not be an inhabitant of the same state with themselves; they shall name in their ballots the person voted for as President, and in distinct ballots the person voted for as Vice-President, and they shall make distinct lists of all persons voted for as President, and of all persons voted for as Vice-President, and of the number of votes for each, which lists they shall sign and certify, and transmit sealed to the seat of the government of the United States, directed to the President of the Senate;—The President of the Senate shall, in the presence of the Senate and House of Representatives, open all the certificates and the votes shall then be counted;—The person having the greatest number of votes for President, shall be the President, if such number be a majority of the whole number of Electors appointed; and if no person have such majority, then from the persons having the highest numbers not exceeding three on the list of those voted for as President, the House of Representatives shall choose immediately, by ballot, the President. But in choosing the President, the votes shall be taken by states, the representation from each state having one vote; a quorum for this purpose shall consist of a member or members from two-thirds of the states, and a majority of all states shall be necessary to a choice. And if the House of Representatives shall not choose a President whenever the right of choice shall devolve upon them, before the fourth day of March next following, then

the Vice-President shall act as President, as in the case of the death or other constitutional disability of the President.—The person having the greatest number of votes as Vice-President, shall be the Vice-President, if such number be a majority of the whole number of Electors appointed, and if no person have a majority, then from the two highest numbers on the list, the Senate shall choose the Vice-President; a quorum for the purpose shall consist of two-thirds of the whole number of Senators, and a majority of the whole number shall be necessary to a choice. But no person constitutionally ineligible to the office of President shall be eligible to that of Vice-President of the United States.

## AMENDMENT XIII [1865]

**Section 1.** Neither slavery nor involuntary servitude, except as a punishment for crime whereof the party shall have been duly convicted, shall exist within the United States, or any place subject to their jurisdiction.

**Section 2.** Congress shall have power to enforce this article by appropriate legislation.

## AMENDMENT XIV [1868]

**Section 1.** All persons born or naturalized in the United States, and subject to the jurisdiction thereof, are citizens of the United States and of the State wherein they reside. No State shall make or enforce any law which shall abridge the privileges or immunities of citizens of the United States; nor shall any State deprive any person of life, liberty, or property, without due process of law; nor deny to any person within its jurisdiction the equal protection of the laws.

**Section 2.** Representatives shall be apportioned among the several States according to their respective numbers, counting the whole number of persons in each State, excluding Indians not taxed. But when the right to vote at any election for the choice of electors for President and Vice President of the United States, Representatives in Congress, the Executive and Judicial officers of a State, or the members of the Legislature thereof, is denied to any of the male inhabitants of such State, being twenty-one years of age, and citizens of the United States, or in any way abridged, except for participation in rebellion, or other crime, the basis of representation therein shall be reduced in the proportion which the number of such male citizens shall bear to the whole number of male citizens twenty-one years of age in such State.

**Section 3.** No person shall be a Senator or Representative in Congress, or elector of President and Vice President, or hold any office, civil or military, under the United States, or under any State, who having previously taken an oath, as a member of Congress, or as an officer of the United States, or as a member of any State legislature, or as an executive or judicial officer of any State, to support the Constitution of the United States, shall have engaged in insurrection or rebellion against the same, or given aid or comfort to the enemies thereof. But Congress may by a vote of two-thirds of each House, remove such disability.

**Section 4.** The validity of the public debt of the United States, authorized by law, including debts incurred for payment of pensions and bounties for services in suppressing insurrection or rebellion, shall not be questioned. But neither the United States nor any State shall assume or pay any debt or obligation incurred in aid of insurrection or rebellion against the United States, or any claim for the loss or emancipation of any slave; but all such debts, obligations and claims shall be held illegal and void.

**Section 5.** The Congress shall have power to enforce, by appropriate legislation, the provisions of this article.

### AMENDMENT XV [1870]

**Section 1.** The right of citizens of the United States to vote shall not be denied or abridged by the United States or by any State on account of race, color, or previous condition of servitude.

**Section 2.** The Congress shall have power to enforce this article by appropriate legislation.

### AMENDMENT XVI [1913]

The Congress shall have power to lay and collect taxes on incomes, from whatever source derived, without apportionment among the several States, and without regard to any census or enumeration.

### AMENDMENT XVII [1913]

**Section 1.** The Senate of the United States shall be composed of two Senators from each State, elected by the people thereof, for six years; and each Senator shall have one vote. The electors in each State shall have the qualifications requisite for electors of the most numerous branch of the State legislatures.

**Section 2.** When vacancies happen in the representation of any State in the Senate, the executive authority of such State shall issue writs of election to fill such vacancies: *Provided*, That the legislature of any State may empower the executive thereof to make temporary appointments until the people fill the vacancies by election as the legislature may direct.

**Section 3.** This amendment shall not be so construed as to affect the election or term of any Senator chosen before it becomes valid as part of the Constitution.

### AMENDMENT XVIII [1919]

**Section 1.** After one year from the ratification of this article the manufacture, sale, or transportation of intoxicating liquors within, the importation thereof into, or the exportation thereof from the United States and all territory subject to the jurisdiction thereof for beverage purposes is hereby prohibited.

**Section 2.** The Congress and the several States shall have concurrent power to enforce this article by appropriate legislation.

**Section 3.** This article shall be inoperative unless it shall have been ratified as an amendment to the Constitution by the legislatures of the several States, as provided in the Constitution, within seven years from the date of the submission hereof to the States by the Congress.

### AMENDMENT XIX [1920]

**Section 1.** The right of citizens of the United States to vote shall not be denied or abridged by the United States or by any State on account of sex.

**Section 2.** Congress shall have power to enforce this article by appropriate legislation.

### AMENDMENT XX [1933]

**Section 1.** The terms of the President and Vice President shall end at noon on the 20th day of January, and the terms of Senators and Representatives at noon on the 3d day of January, of the years in which such terms would have ended if this article had not been ratified; and the terms of their successors shall then begin.

**Section 2.** The Congress shall assemble at least once in every year, and such meeting shall begin at noon on the 3d day of January, unless they shall by law appoint a different day.

**Section 3.** If, at the time fixed for the beginning of the term of the President, the President elect shall have died, the Vice President elect shall become President. If the President shall not have been chosen before the time fixed for the beginning of his term, or if the President elect shall have failed to qualify, then the Vice President elect shall act as President until a President shall have qualified; and the Congress may by law provide for the case wherein neither a President elect nor a Vice President elect shall have qualified, declaring who shall then act as President, or the manner in which one who is to act shall be selected, and such person shall act accordingly until a President or Vice President shall have qualified.

**Section 4.** The Congress may by law provide for the case of the death of any of the persons from whom the House of Representatives may choose a President whenever the right of choice shall have devolved upon them, and for the case of the death of any of the persons from whom the Senate may choose a Vice President whenever the right of choice shall have devolved upon them.

**Section 5.** Sections 1 and 2 shall take effect on the 15th day of October following the ratification of this article.

**Section 6.** This article shall be inoperative unless it shall have been ratified as an amendment to the Constitution by the legislatures of three-fourths of the several States within seven years from the date of its submission.

### AMENDMENT XXI [1933]

**Section 1.** The eighteenth article of amendment to the Constitution of the United States is hereby repealed.

**Section 2.** The transportation or importation into any State, Territory, or possession of the United States for delivery or use therein of intoxicating liquors, in violation of the laws thereof, is hereby prohibited.

**Section 3.** This article shall be inoperative unless it shall have been ratified as an amendment to the Constitution by conventions in the several States, as provided in the Constitution, within seven years from the date of the submission hereof to the States by the Congress.

### AMENDMENT XXII [1951]

**Section 1.** No person shall be elected to the office of the President more than twice, and no person who has held the office of President, or acted as President, for more than two years of a term to which some other person was elected President shall be elected to the office of President more than once. But this Article shall not apply to any person holding the office of President when this Article was proposed by the Congress, and shall not prevent any person who may be holding the office of President, or acting as President, during the term within which this Article becomes operative from holding the office of President or acting as President during the remainder of such term.

**Section 2.** This article shall be inoperative unless it shall have been ratified as an amendment to the Constitution by the legislatures of three-fourths of the several States within seven years from the date of its submission to the States by the Congress.

### AMENDMENT XXIII [1961]

**Section 1.** The District constituting the seat of Government of the United States shall appoint in such manner as the Congress may direct:

A number of electors of President and Vice President equal to the whole number of Senators and Representatives in Congress to which the District would be entitled if it were a State, but in no event more than the least populous state; they shall be in addition to those appointed by the states, but they shall be considered, for the purposes of the election of President and Vice President, to be electors appointed by a state; and they shall meet in the District and perform such duties as provided by the twelfth article of amendment.

**Section 2.** The Congress shall have power to enforce this article by appropriate legislation.

### AMENDMENT XXIV [1964]

**Section 1.** The right of citizens of the United States to vote in any primary or other election for President or Vice President, for electors for President or Vice President, or for Senator or Representative in Congress, shall not be denied or abridged by the United States, or any State by reason of failure to pay any poll tax or other tax.

**Section 2.** The Congress shall have power to enforce this article by appropriate legislation.

### AMENDMENT XXV [1967]

**Section 1.** In case of the removal of the President from office or of his death or resignation, the Vice President shall become President.

**Section 2.** Whenever there is a vacancy in the office of the Vice President, the President shall nominate a Vice President who shall take office upon confirmation by a majority vote of both Houses of Congress.

**Section 3.** Whenever the President transmits to the President pro tempore of the Senate and the Speaker of the House of Representatives his written declaration that he is unable to discharge the powers and duties of his office, and until he transmits to them a written declaration to the contrary, such powers and duties shall be discharged by the Vice President as Acting President.

**Section 4.** Whenever the Vice President and a majority of either the principal officers of the executive departments or of such other body as Congress may by law provide, transmit to the President pro tempore of the Senate and the Speaker of the House of Representatives their written declaration that the President is unable to discharge the powers and duties of his office, the Vice President shall immediately assume the powers and duties of the office as Acting President.

Thereafter, when the President transmits to the President pro tempore of the Senate and the Speaker of the House of Representatives his written declaration that no inability exists, he shall resume the powers and duties of his office unless the Vice President and a majority of either the principal officers of the executive department or of such other body as Congress may by law provide, transmit within four days to the President pro tempore of the Senate and the Speaker of the House of Representatives their written declaration and the President is unable to discharge the powers and duties of his office. Thereupon Congress shall decide the issue, assembling within forty-eight hours for that purpose if not in session. If the Congress, within twenty-one days after receipt of the latter written declaration, or, if Congress is not in session, within twenty-one days after Congress is required to assemble, determines by two-thirds vote of both Houses that the President is unable to discharge the powers and duties of his office, the Vice President shall continue to discharge the same as Acting President; otherwise, the President shall resume the powers and duties of his office.

### AMENDMENT XXVI [1971]

**Section 1.** The right of citizens of the United States, who are eighteen years of age or older, to vote shall not be denied or abridged by the United States or by any State on account of age.

**Section 2.** The Congress shall have power to enforce this article by appropriate legislation.

### AMENDMENT XXVII [1992]

No law, varying the compensation for the services of the Senators and Representatives, shall take effect, until an election of Representatives shall have intervened.

# APPENDIX C

# THE UNIFORM COMMERCIAL CODE

(Adopted in fifty-two jurisdictions; all fifty States, although Louisiana has adopted only Articles 1, 3, 4, 7, 8, and 9; the District of Columbia; and the Virgin Islands.)

The Code consists of the following articles:

Art.

1. General Provisions
2. Sales
2A. Leases
3. Commercial Paper
4. Bank Deposits and Collections
4A. Funds Transfers
5. Letters of Credit
6. Bulk Transfers (including Alternative B)
7. Warehouse Receipts, Bills of Lading and Other Documents of Title
8. Investment Securities
9. Secured Transactions: Sales of Accounts and Chattel Paper
10. Effective Date and Repealer
11. Effective Date and Transition Provisions

## Article 1
## GENERAL PROVISIONS

### Part 1   Short Title, Construction, Application and Subject Matter of the Act

#### § 1—101.  Short Title.

This Act shall be known and may be cited as Uniform Commercial Code.

#### § 1—102.  Purposes; Rules of Construction; Variation by Agreement.

(1) This Act shall be liberally construed and applied to promote its underlying purposes and policies.

Copyright ©1994 by the American Law Institute and the National Conference of Commissioners on Uniform State Laws. Reproduced with permission.

(2) Underlying purposes and policies of this Act are

(a) to simplify, clarify and modernize the law governing commercial transactions;

(b) to permit the continued expansion of commercial practices through custom, usage and agreement of the parties;

(c) to make uniform the law among the various jurisdictions.

(3) The effect of provisions of this Act may be varied by agreement, except as otherwise provided in this Act and except that the obligations of good faith, diligence, reasonableness and care prescribed by this Act may not be disclaimed by agreement but the parties may by agreement determine the standards by which the performance of such obligations is to be measured if such standards are not manifestly unreasonable.

(4) The presence in certain provisions of this Act of the words "unless otherwise agreed" or words of similar import does not imply that the effect of other provisions may not be varied by agreement under subsection (3).

(5) In this Act unless the context otherwise requires

(a) words in the singular number include the plural, and in the plural include the singular;

(b) words of the masculine gender include the feminine and the neuter, and when the sense so indicates words of the neuter gender may refer to any gender.

#### § 1—103.  Supplementary General Principles of Law Applicable.

Unless displaced by the particular provisions of this Act, the principles of law and equity, including the law merchant and the law relative to capacity to contract, principal and agent, estoppel, fraud, misrepresentation, duress, coercion, mistake, bankruptcy, or other validating or invalidating cause shall supplement its provisions.

#### § 1—104.  Construction Against Implicit Repeal.

This Act being a general act intended as a unified coverage of its subject matter, no part of it shall be deemed to be impliedly repealed by subsequent legislation if such construction can reasonably be avoided.

**§ 1—105. Territorial Application of the Act; Parties' Power to Choose Applicable Law.**

(1) Except as provided hereafter in this section, when a transaction bears a reasonable relation to this state and also to another state or nation the parties may agree that the law either of this state or of such other state or nation shall govern their rights and duties. Failing such agreement this Act applies to transactions bearing an appropriate relation to this state.

(2) Where one of the following provisions of this Act specifies the applicable law, that provision governs and a contrary agreement is effective only to the extent permitted by the law (including the conflict of laws rules) so specified:

> Rights of creditors against sold goods. Section 2—402.
>
> Applicability of the Article on Leases. Sections 2A—105 and 2A—106.
>
> Applicability of the Article on Bank Deposits and Collections. Section 4—102.
>
> Governing law in the Article on Funds Transfers. Section 4A—507.
>
> Bulk sales subject to the Article on Bulk Sales. Section 6—103.
>
> Applicability of the Article on Investment Securities. Section 8—106.
>
> Perfection provisions of the Article on Secured Transactions. Section 9—103.

**§ 1—106. Remedies to Be Liberally Administered.**

(1) The remedies provided by this Act shall be liberally administered to the end that the aggrieved party may be put in as good a position as if the other party had fully performed but neither consequential or special nor penal damages may be had except as specifically provided in this Act or by other rule of law.

(2) Any right or obligation declared by this Act is enforceable by action unless the provision declaring it specifies a different and limited effect.

**§ 1—107. Waiver or Renunciation of Claim or Right After Breach.**

Any claim or right arising out of an alleged breach can be discharged in whole or in part without consideration by a written waiver or renunciation signed and delivered by the aggrieved party.

**§ 1—108. Severability.**

If any provision or clause of this Act or application thereof to any person or circumstances is held invalid, such invalidity shall not affect other provisions or applications of the Act which can be given effect without the invalid provision or application, and to this end the provisions of this Act are declared to be severable.

**§ 1—109. Section Captions.**

Section captions are parts of this Act.

**Part 2  General Definitions and Principles of Interpretation**

**§ 1—201. General Definitions.**

Subject to additional definitions contained in the subsequent Articles of this Act which are applicable to specific Articles or Parts thereof, and unless the context otherwise requires, in this Act:

(1) "Action" in the sense of a judicial proceeding includes recoupment, counterclaim, set-off, suit in equity and any other proceedings in which rights are determined.

(2) "Aggrieved party" means a party entitled to resort to a remedy.

(3) "Agreement" means the bargain of the parties in fact as found in their language or by implication from other circumstances including course of dealing or usage of trade or course of performance as provided in this Act (Sections 1—205 and 2—208). Whether an agreement has legal consequences is determined by the provisions of this Act, if applicable; otherwise by the law of contracts (Section 1—103). (Compare "Contract".)

(4) "Bank" means any person engaged in the business of banking.

(5) "Bearer" means the person in possession of an instrument, document of title, or certificated security payable to bearer or indorsed in blank.

(6) "Bill of lading" means a document evidencing the receipt of goods for shipment issued by a person engaged in the business of transporting or forwarding goods, and includes an airbill. "Airbill" means a document serving for air transportation as a bill of lading does for marine or rail transportation, and includes an air consignment note or air waybill.

(7) "Branch" includes a separately incorporated foreign branch of a bank.

(8) "Burden of establishing" a fact means the burden of persuading the triers of fact that the existence of the fact is more probable than its non-existence.

(9) "Buyer in ordinary course of business" means a person who in good faith and without knowledge that the sale to him is in violation of the ownership rights or security interest of a third party in the goods buys in ordinary course from a person in the business of selling goods of that kind but does not include a pawnbroker. All persons who sell minerals or the like (including oil and gas) at wellhead or minehead shall be deemed to be persons in the business of selling goods of that kind. "Buying" may be for cash or by exchange of other property or on secured or unsecured credit and includes receiving goods or documents of title under a pre-existing contract for sale but does not include a transfer in bulk or as security for or in total or partial satisfaction of a money debt.

(10) "Conspicuous": A term or clause is conspicuous when it is so written that a reasonable person against whom it is to operate ought to have noticed it. A printed heading in capitals (as: NON-NEGOTIABLE BILL OF LADING) is

conspicuous. Language in the body of a form is "conspicuous" if it is in larger or other contrasting type or color. But in a telegram any stated term is "conspicuous". Whether a term or clause is "conspicuous" or not is for decision by the court.

(11) "Contract" means the total legal obligation which results from the parties' agreement as affected by this Act and any other applicable rules of law. (Compare "Agreement".)

(12) "Creditor" includes a general creditor, a secured creditor, a lien creditor and any representative of creditors, including an assignee for the benefit of creditors, a trustee in bankruptcy, a receiver in equity and an executor or administrator of an insolvent debtor's or assignor's estate.

(13) "Defendant" includes a person in the position of defendant in a cross-action or counterclaim.

(14) "Delivery" with respect to instruments, documents of title, chattel paper, or certificated securities means voluntary transfer of possession.

(15) "Document of title" includes bill of lading, dock warrant, dock receipt, warehouse receipt or order for the delivery of goods, and also any other document which in the regular course of business or financing is treated as adequately evidencing that the person in possession of it is entitled to receive, hold and dispose of the document and the goods it covers. To be a document of title a document must purport to be issued by or addressed to a bailee and purport to cover goods in the bailee's possession which are either identified or are fungible portions of an identified mass.

(16) "Fault" means wrongful act, omission or breach.

(17) "Fungible" with respect to goods or securities means goods or securities of which any unit is, by nature or usage of trade, the equivalent of any other like unit. Goods which are not fungible shall be deemed fungible for the purposes of this Act to the extent that under a particular agreement or document unlike units are treated as equivalents.

(18) "Genuine" means free of forgery or counterfeiting.

(19) "Good faith" means honesty in fact in the conduct or transaction concerned.

(20) "Holder" with respect to a negotiable instrument, means the person in possession if the instrument is payable to bearer or, in the cases of an instrument payable to an identified person, if the identified person is in possession. "Holder" with respect to a document of title means the person in possession if the goods are deliverable to bearer or to the order of the person in possession.

(21) To "honor" is to pay or to accept and pay, or where a credit so engages to purchase or discount a draft complying with the terms of the credit.

(22) "Insolvency proceedings" includes any assignment for the benefit of creditors or other proceedings intended to liquidate or rehabilitate the estate of the person involved.

(23) A person is "insolvent" who either has ceased to pay his debts in the ordinary course of business or cannot pay his debts as they become due or is insolvent within the meaning of the federal bankruptcy law.

(24) "Money" means a medium of exchange authorized or adopted by a domestic or foreign government and includes a monetary unit of account established by an intergovernmental organization or by agreement between two or more nations.

(25) A person has "notice" of a fact when

(a) he has actual knowledge of it; or

(b) he has received a notice or notification of it; or

(c) from all the facts and circumstances known to him at the time in question he has reason to know that it exists.

A person "knows" or has "knowledge" of a fact when he has actual knowledge of it. "Discover" or "learn" or a word or phrase of similar import refers to knowledge rather than to reason to know. The time and circumstances under which a notice or notification may cease to be effective are not determined by this Act.

(26) A person "notifies" or "gives" a notice or notification to another by taking such steps as may be reasonably required to inform the other in ordinary course whether or not such other actually comes to know of it. A person "receives" a notice or notification when

(a) it comes to his attention; or

(b) it is duly delivered at the place of business through which the contract was made or at any other place held out by him as the place for receipt of such communications.

(27) Notice, knowledge or a notice or notification received by an organization is effective for a particular transaction from the time when it is brought to the attention of the individual conducting that transaction, and in any event from the time when it would have been brought to his attention if the organization had exercised due diligence. An organization exercises due diligence if it maintains reasonable routines for communicating significant information to the person conducting the transaction and there is reasonable compliance with the routines. Due diligence does not require an individual acting for the organization to communicate information unless such communication is part of his regular duties or unless he has reason to know of the transaction and that the transaction would be materially affected by the information.

(28) "Organization" includes a corporation, government or governmental subdivision or agency, business trust, estate, trust, partnership or association, two or more persons having a joint or common interest, or any other legal or commercial entity.

(29) "Party", as distinct from "third party", means a person who has engaged in a transaction or made an agreement within this Act.

(30) "Person" includes an individual or an organization (See Section 1—102).

(31) "Presumption" or "presumed" means that the trier of fact must find the existence of the fact presumed unless and

until evidence is introduced which would support a finding of its non-existence.

(32) "Purchase" includes taking by sale, discount, negotiation, mortgage, pledge, lien, issue or re-issue, gift or any other voluntary transaction creating an interest in property.

(33) "Purchaser" means a person who takes by purchase.

(34) "Remedy" means any remedial right to which an aggrieved party is entitled with or without resort to a tribunal.

(35) "Representative" includes an agent, an officer of a corporation or association, and a trustee, executor or administrator of an estate, or any other person empowered to act for another.

(36) "Rights" includes remedies.

(37) "Security interest" means an interest in personal property or fixtures which secures payment or performance of an obligation. The retention or reservation of title by a seller of goods notwithstanding shipment or delivery to the buyer (Section 2—401) is limited in effect to a reservation of a "security interest". The term also includes any interest of a buyer of accounts or chattel paper which is subject to Article 9. The special property interest of a buyer of goods on identification of those goods to a contract for sale under Section 2—401 is not a "security interest", but a buyer may also acquire a "security interest" by complying with Article 9. Unless a consignment is intended as security, reservation of title thereunder is not a "security interest," but a consignment is in any event subject to the provisions on consignment sales (Section 2—326).

Whether a transaction creates a lease or security interest is determined by the facts of each case; however, a transaction creates a security interest if the consideration the lessee is to pay the lessor for the right to possession and use of the goods is an obligation for the term of the lease not subject to termination by the lessee, and

(a) the original term of the lease is equal to or greater than the remaining economic life of the goods,

(b) the lessee is bound to renew the lease for the remaining economic life of the goods or is bound to become the owner of the goods,

(c) the lessee has an option to renew the lease for the remaining economic life of the goods for no additional consideration or nominal additional consideration upon compliance with the lease agreement, or

(d) the lessee has an option to become the owner of the goods for no additional consideration or nominal additional consideration upon compliance with the lease agreement.

A transaction does not create a security interest merely because it provides that

(a) the present value of the consideration the lessee is obligated to pay the lessor for the right to possession and use of the goods is substantially equal to or is greater than the fair market value of the goods at the time the lease is entered into,

(b) the lessee assumes risk of loss of the goods, or agrees to pay taxes, insurance, filing, recording, or registration fees, or service or maintenance costs with respect to the goods,

(c) the lessee has an option to renew the lease or to become the owner of the goods,

(d) the lessee has an option to renew the lease for a fixed rent that is equal to or greater than the reasonably predictable fair market rent for the use of the goods for the term of the renewal at the time the option is to be performed, or

(e) the lessee has an option to become the owner of the goods for a fixed price that is equal to or greater than the reasonably predictable fair market value of the goods at the time the option is to be performed.

For purposes of this subsection (37):

(x) Additional consideration is not nominal if (i) when the option to renew the lease is granted to the lessee the rent is stated to be the fair market rent for the use of the goods for the term of the renewal determined at the time the option is to be performed, or (ii) when the option to become the owner of the goods is granted to the lessee the price is stated to be the fair market value of the goods determined at the time the option is to be performed. Additional consideration is nominal if it is less than the lessee's reasonably predictable cost of performing under the lease agreement if the option is not exercised;

(y) "Reasonably predictable" and "remaining economic life of the goods" are to be determined with reference to the facts and circumstances at the time the transaction is entered into; and

(z) "Present value" means the amount as of a date certain of one or more sums payable in the future, discounted to the date certain. The discount is determined by the interest rate specified by the parties if the rate is not manifestly unreasonable at the time the transaction is entered into; otherwise, the discount is determined by a commercially reasonable rate that takes into account the facts and circumstances of each case at the time the transaction was entered into.

(38) "Send" in connection with any writing or notice means to deposit in the mail or deliver for transmission by any other usual means of communication with postage or cost of transmission provided for and properly addressed and in the case of an instrument to an address specified thereon or otherwise agreed, or if there be none to any address reasonable under the circumstances. The receipt of any writing or notice within the time at which it would have arrived if properly sent has the effect of a proper sending.

(39) "Signed" includes any symbol executed or adopted by a party with present intention to authenticate a writing.

(40) "Surety" includes guarantor.

(41) "Telegram" includes a message transmitted by radio, teletype, cable, any mechanical method of transmission, or the like.

(42) ''Term'' means that portion of an agreement which relates to a particular matter.

(43) ''Unauthorized'' signature means one made without actual, implied or apparent authority and includes a forgery.

(44) ''Value''. Except as otherwise provided with respect to negotiable instruments and bank collections (Sections 3—303, 4—208 and 4—209) a person gives ''value'' for rights if he acquires them

> (a) in return for a binding commitment to extend credit or for the extension of immediately available credit whether or not drawn upon and whether or not a charge-back is provided for in the event of difficulties in collection; or

> (b) as security for or in total or partial satisfaction of a pre-existing claim; or

> (c) by accepting delivery pursuant to a preexisting contract for purchase; or

> (d) generally, in return for any consideration sufficient to support a simple contract.

(45) ''Warehouse receipt'' means a receipt issued by a person engaged in the business of storing goods for hire.

(46) ''Written'' or ''writing'' includes printing, typewriting or any other intentional reduction to tangible form.

### § 1—202. Prima Facie Evidence by Third Party Documents.

A document in due form purporting to be a bill of lading, policy or certificate of insurance, official weigher's or inspector's certificate, consular invoice, or any other document authorized or required by the contract to be issued by a third party shall be prima facie evidence of its own authenticity and genuineness and of the facts stated in the document by the third party.

### § 1—203. Obligation of Good Faith.

Every contract or duty within this Act imposes an obligation of good faith in its performance or enforcement.

### § 1—204. Time; Reasonable Time; ''Seasonably''.

(1) Whenever this Act requires any action to be taken within a reasonable time, any time which is not manifestly unreasonable may be fixed by agreement.

(2) What is a reasonable time for taking any action depends on the nature, purpose and circumstances of such action.

(3) An action is taken ''seasonably'' when it is taken at or within the time agreed or if no time is agreed at or within a reasonable time.

### § 1—205. Course of Dealing and Usage of Trade.

(1) A course of dealing is a sequence of previous conduct between the parties to a particular transaction which is fairly to be regarded as establishing a common basis of understanding for interpreting their expressions and other conduct.

(2) A usage of trade is any practice or method of dealing having such regularity of observance in a place, vocation or trade as to justify an expectation that it will be observed with respect to the transaction in question. The existence and scope of such a usage are to be proved as facts. If it is established that such a usage is embodied in a written trade code or similar writing the interpretation of the writing is for the court.

(3) A course of dealing between parties and any usage of trade in the vocation or trade in which they are engaged or of which they are or should be aware give particular meaning to and supplement or qualify terms of an agreement.

(4) The express terms of an agreement and an applicable course of dealing or usage of trade shall be construed wherever reasonable as consistent with each other; but when such construction is unreasonable express terms control both course of dealing and usage of trade and course of dealing controls usage trade.

(5) An applicable usage of trade in the place where any part of performance is to occur shall be used in interpreting the agreement as to that part of the performance.

(6) Evidence of a relevant usage of trade offered by one party is not admissible unless and until he has given the other party such notice as the court finds sufficient to prevent unfair surprise to the latter.

### § 1—206. Statute of Frauds for Kinds of Personal Property Not Otherwise Covered.

(1) Except in the cases described in subsection (2) of this section a contract for the sale of personal property is not enforceable by way of action or defense beyond five thousand dollars in amount or value of remedy unless there is some writing which indicates that a contract for sale has been made between the parties at a defined or stated price, reasonably identifies the subject matter, and is signed by the party against whom enforcement is sought or by his authorized agent.

(2) Subsection (1) of this section does not apply to contracts for the sale of goods (Section 2—201) nor of securities (Section 8—319) nor to security agreements (Section 9—203).

### § 1—207. Performance or Acceptance Under Reservation of Rights.

(1) A party who with explicit reservation of rights performs or promises performance or assents to performance in a manner demanded or offered by the other party does not thereby prejudice the rights reserved. Such words as ''without prejudice'', ''under protest'' or the like are sufficient.

(2) Subsection (1) does not apply to an accord and satisfaction.

### § 1—208. Option to Accelerate at Will.

A term providing that one party or his successor in interest may accelerate payment or performance or require collateral or additional collateral ''at will'' or ''when he deems himself insecure'' or in words of similar import shall be construed to mean that he shall have power to do so only if he in good faith believes that the prospect of payment or performance is impaired. The burden of establishing lack of good faith is on the party against whom the power has been exercised.

### § 1—209. Subordinated Obligations.

An obligation may be issued as subordinated to payment of another obligation of the person obligated, or a creditor may subordinate his right to payment of an obligation by agreement with either the person obligated or another creditor of the person obligated. Such a subordination does not create a security interest as against either the common debtor or a subordinated creditor. This section shall be construed as declaring the law as it existed prior to the enactment of this section and not as modifying it. Added 1966.

Note: *This new section is proposed as an optional provision to make it clear that a subordination agreement does not create a security interest unless so intended.*

# Article 2
# SALES

## Part 1   Short Title, General Construction and Subject Matter

### § 2—101. Short Title.

This Article shall be known and may be cited as Uniform Commercial Code—Sales.

### § 2—102. Scope; Certain Security and Other Transactions Excluded From This Article.

Unless the context otherwise requires, this Article applies to transactions in goods; it does not apply to any transaction which although in the form of an unconditional contract to sell or present sale is intended to operate only as a security transaction nor does this Article impair or repeal any statute regulating sales to consumers, farmers or other specified classes of buyers.

### § 2—103. Definitions and Index of Definitions.

(1)   In this Article unless the context otherwise requires

(a) ''Buyer'' means a person who buys or contracts to buy goods.

(b) ''Good faith'' in the case of a merchant means honesty in fact and the observance of reasonable commercial standards of fair dealing in the trade.

(c) ''Receipt'' of goods means taking physical possession of them.

(d) ''Seller'' means a person who sells or contracts to sell goods.

(2)   Other definitions applying to this Article or to specified Parts thereof, and the sections in which they appear are:
''Acceptance''. Section 2—606.
''Banker's credit''. Section 2—325.
''Between merchants''. Section 2—104.
''Cancellation''. Section 2—106(4).
''Commercial unit''. Section 2—105.
''Confirmed credit''. Section 2—325.
''Conforming to contract''. Section 2—106.
''Contract for sale''. Section 2—106.
''Cover''. Section 2—712.
''Entrusting''. Section 2—403.
''Financing agency''. Section 2—104.
''Future goods''. Section 2—105.
''Goods''. Section 2—105.
''Identification''. Section 2—501.
''Installment contract''. Section 2—612.
''Letter of Credit''. Section 2—325.
''Lot''. Section 2—105.
''Merchant''. Section 2—104.
''Overseas''. Section 2—323.
''Person in position of seller''. Section 2—707.
''Present sale''. Section 2—106.
''Sale''. Section 2—106.
''Sale on approval''. Section 2—326.
''Sale or return''. Section 2—326.
''Termination''. Section 2—106.

(3)   The following definitions in other Articles apply to this Article:
''Check''. Section 3—104.
''Consignee''. Section 7—102.
''Consignor''. Section 7—102.
''Consumer goods''. Section 9—109.
''Dishonor''. Section 3—507.
''Draft''. Section 3—104.

(4)   In addition Article 1 contains general definitions and principles of construction and interpretation applicable throughout this Article.

### § 2—104. Definitions: ''Merchant''; ''Between Merchants''; ''Financing Agency''.

(1)   ''Merchant'' means a person who deals in goods of the kind or otherwise by his occupation holds himself out as having knowledge or skill peculiar to the practices or goods involved in the transaction or to whom such knowledge or skill may be attributed by his employment of an agent or broker or other intermediary who by his occupation holds himself out as having such knowledge or skill.

(2)   ''Financing agency'' means a bank, finance company or other person who in the ordinary course of business makes advances against goods or documents of title or who by arrangement with either the seller or the buyer intervenes in ordinary course to make or collect payment due or claimed under the contract for sale, as by purchasing or paying the seller's draft or making advances against it or by merely taking it for collection whether or not documents of title accompany the draft. ''Financing agency'' includes also a bank or other person who similarly intervenes between persons who are in the position of seller and buyer in respect to the goods (Section 2—707).

(3)   ''Between merchants'' means in any transaction with respect to which both parties are chargeable with the knowledge or skill of merchants.

### § 2—105. Definitions: Transferability; ''Goods''; ''Future'' Goods; ''Lot''; ''Commercial Unit''.

(1)   ''Goods'' means all things (including specially manufactured goods) which are movable at the time of identifi-

cation to the contract for sale other than the money in which the price is to be paid, investment securities (Article 8) and things in action. ''Goods'' also includes the unborn young of animals and growing crops and other identified things attached to realty as described in the section on goods to be severed from realty (Section 2—107).

(2) Goods must be both existing and identified before any interest in them can pass. Goods which are not both existing and identified are ''future'' goods. A purported present sale of future goods or of any interest therein operates as a contract to sell.

(3) There may be a sale of a part interest in existing identified goods.

(4) An undivided share in an identified bulk of fungible goods is sufficiently identified to be sold although the quantity of the bulk is not determined. Any agreed proportion of such a bulk or any quantity thereof agreed upon by number, weight or other measure may to the extent of the seller's interest in the bulk be sold to the buyer who then becomes an owner in common.

(5) ''Lot'' means a parcel or a single article which is the subject matter of a separate sale or delivery, whether or not it is sufficient to perform the contract.

(6) ''Commercial unit'' means such a unit of goods as by commercial usage is a single whole for purposes of sale and division of which materially impairs its character or value on the market or in use. A commercial unit may be a single article (as a machine) or a set of articles (as a suite of furniture or an assortment of sizes) or a quantity (as a bale, gross, or carload) or any other unit treated in use or in the relevant market as a single whole.

### § 2—106. Definitions: ''Contract''; ''Agreement''; ''Contract for Sale''; ''Sale''; ''Present Sale''; ''Conforming'' to Contract; ''Termination''; ''Cancellation''.

(1) In this Article unless the context otherwise requires ''contract'' and ''agreement'' are limited to those relating to the present or future sale of goods. ''Contract for sale'' includes both a present sale of goods and a contract to sell goods at a future time. A ''sale'' consists in the passing of title from the seller to the buyer for a price (Section 2—401). A ''present sale'' means a sale which is accomplished by the making of the contract.

(2) Goods or conduct including any part of a performance are ''conforming'' or conform to the contract when they are in accordance with the obligations under the contract.

(3) ''Termination'' occurs when either party pursuant to a power created by agreement or law puts an end to the contract otherwise than for its breach. On ''termination'' all obligations which are still executory on both sides are discharged but any right based on prior breach or performance survives.

(4) ''Cancellation'' occurs when either party puts an end to the contract for breach by the other and its effect is the same as that of ''termination'' except that the cancelling party also retains any remedy for breach of the whole contract or any unperformed balance.

### § 2—107. Goods to Be Severed From Realty: Recording.

(1) A contract for the sale of minerals or the like (including oil and gas) or a structure or its materials to be removed from realty is a contract for the sale of goods within this Article if they are to be severed by the seller but until severance a purported present sale thereof which is not effective as a transfer of an interest in land is effective only as a contract to sell.

(2) A contract for the sale apart from the land of growing crops or other things attached to realty and capable of severance without material harm thereto but not described in subsection (1) or of timber to be cut is a contract for the sale of goods within this Article whether the subject matter is to be severed by the buyer or by the seller even though it forms part of the realty at the time of contracting, and the parties can by identification effect a present sale before severance.

(3) The provisions of this section are subject to any third party rights provided by the law relating to realty records, and the contract for sale may be executed and recorded as a document transferring an interest in land and shall then constitute notice to third parties of the buyer's rights under the contract for sale.

## Part 2 Form, Formation and Readjustment of Contract

### § 2—201. Formal Requirements; Statute of Frauds.

(1) Except as otherwise provided in this section a contract for the sale of goods for the price of $500 or more is not enforceable by way of action or defense unless there is some writing sufficient to indicate that a contract for sale has been made between the parties and signed by the party against whom enforcement is sought or by his authorized agent or broker. A writing is not insufficient because it omits or incorrectly states a term agreed upon but the contract is not enforceable under this paragraph beyond the quantity of goods shown in such writing.

(2) Between merchants if within a reasonable time a writing in confirmation of the contract and sufficient against the sender is received and the party receiving it has reason to know its contents, its satisfies the requirements of subsection (1) against such party unless written notice of objection to its contents is given within ten days after it is received.

(3) A contract which does not satisfy the requirements of subsection (1) but which is valid in other respects is enforceable

  (a) if the goods are to be specially manufactured for the buyer and are not suitable for sale to others in the ordinary course of the seller's business and the seller, before notice of repudiation is received and under circumstances which reasonably indicate that the goods are for the buyer, has made either a substantial beginning of their manufacture or commitments for their procurement; or

(b) if the party against whom enforcement is sought admits in his pleading, testimony or otherwise in court that a contract for sale was made, but the contract is not enforceable under this provision beyond the quantity of goods admitted; or

(c) with respect to goods for which payment has been made and accepted or which have been received and accepted (Sec. 2—606).

### § 2—202. Final Written Expression: Parol or Extrinsic Evidence.

Terms with respect to which the confirmatory memoranda of the parties agree or which are otherwise set forth in a writing intended by the parties as a final expression of their agreement with respect to such terms as are included therein may not be contradicted by evidence of any prior agreement or of a contemporaneous oral agreement but may be explained or supplemented

(a) by course of dealing or usage of trade (Section 1—205) or by course of performance (Section 2—208); and

(b) by evidence of consistent additional terms unless the court finds the writing to have been intended also as a complete and exclusive statement of the terms of the agreement.

### § 2—203. Seals Inoperative.

The affixing of a seal to a writing evidencing a contract for sale or an offer to buy or sell goods does not constitute the writing a sealed instrument and the law with respect to sealed instruments does not apply to such a contract or offer.

### § 2—204. Formation in General.

(1) A contract for sale of goods may be made in any manner suffcent to show agreement, including conduct by both parties which recognizes the existence of such a contract.

(2) An agreement sufficient to constitute a contract for sale may be found even though the moment of its making is undetermined.

(3) Even though one or more terms are left open a contract for sale does not fail for indefiniteness if the parties have intended to make a contract and there is a reasonably certain basis for giving an appropriate remedy.

### § 2—205. Firm Offers.

An offer by a merchant to buy or sell goods in a signed writing which by its terms gives assurance that it will be held open is not revocable, for lack of consideration, during the time stated or if no time is stated for a reasonable time, but in no event may such period of irrevocability exceed three months; but any such term of assurance on a form supplied by the offeree must be separately signed by the offeror.

### § 2—206. Offer and Acceptance in Formation of Contract.

(1) Unless other unambiguously indicated by the language or circumstances

(a) an offer to make a contract shall be construed as inviting acceptance in any manner and by any medium reasonable in the circumstances;

(b) an order or other offer to buy goods for prompt or current shipment shall be construed as inviting acceptance either by a prompt promise to ship or by the prompt or current shipment of conforming or nonconforming goods, but such a shipment of non-conforming goods does not constitute an acceptance if the seller seasonably notifies the buyer that the shipment is offered only as an accommodation to the buyer.

(2) Where the beginning of a requested performance is a reasonable mode of acceptance an offeror who is not notified of acceptance within a reasonable time may treat the offer as having lapsed before acceptance.

### § 2—207. Additional Terms in Acceptance or Confirmation.

(1) A definite and seasonable expression of acceptance or a written confirmation which is sent within a reasonable time operates as an acceptance even though it states terms additional to or different from those offered or agreed upon, unless acceptance is expressly made conditional on assent to the additional or different terms.

(2) The additional terms are to be construed as proposals for addition to the contract. Between merchants such terms become part of the contract unless:

(a) the offer expressly limits acceptance to the terms of the offer;

(b) they materially alter it; or

(c) notification of objection to them has already been given or is given within a reasonable time after notice of them is received.

(3) Conduct by both parties which recognizes the existence of a contract is sufficient to establish a contract for sale although the writings of the parties do not otherwise establish a contract. In such case the terms of the particular contract consist of those terms on which the writings of the parties agree, together with any supplementary terms incorporated under any other provisions of this Act.

### § 2—208. Course of Performance or Practical Construction.

(1) Where the contract for sale involves repeated occasions for performance by either party with knowledge of the nature of the performance and opportunity for objection to it by the other, any course of performance accepted or acquiesced in without objection shall be relevant to determine the meaning of the agreement.

(2) The express terms of the agreement and any such course of performance, as well as any course of dealing and usage of trade, shall be construed whenever reasonable as consistent with each other; but when such construction is unreasonable, express terms shall control course of performance and course of performance shall control both course of dealing and usage of trade (Section 1—205).

(3) Subject to the provisions of the next section on modification and waiver, such course of performance shall be relevant to show a waiver or modification of any term inconsistent with such course of performance.

### § 2—209. Modification, Rescission and Waiver.

(1) An agreement modifying a contract within this Article needs no consideration to be binding.

(2) A signed agreement which excludes modification or rescission except by a signed writing cannot be otherwise modified or rescinded, but except as between merchants such a requirement on a form supplied by the merchant must be separately signed by the other party.

(3) The requirements of the statute of frauds section of this Article (Section 2—201) must be satisfied if the contract as modified is within its provisions.

(4) Although an attempt at modification or rescission does not satisfy the requirements of subsection (2) or (3) it can operate as a waiver.

(5) A party who has made a waiver affecting an executory portion of the contract may retract the waiver by reasonable notification received by the other party that strict performance will be required of any term waived, unless the retraction would be unjust in view of a material change of position in reliance on the waiver.

### § 2—210. Delegation of Performance; Assignment of Rights.

(1) A party may perform his duty through a delegate unless otherwise agreed or unless the other party has a substantial interest in having his original promisor perform or control the acts required by the contract. No delegation of performance relieves the party delegating of any duty to perform or any liability for breach.

(2) Unless otherwise agreed all rights of either seller or buyer can be assigned except where the assignment would materially change the duty of the other party, or increase materially the burden or risk imposed on him by his contract, or impair materially his chance of obtaining return performance. A right to damages for breach of the whole contract or a right arising out of the assignor's due performance of his entire obligation can be assigned despite agreement otherwise.

(3) Unless the circumstances indicate the contrary a prohibition of assignment of ''the contract'' is to be construed as barring only the delegation to the assignee of the assignor's performance.

(4) An assignment of ''the contract'' or of ''all my rights under the contract'' or an assignment in similar general terms is an assignment of rights and unless the language or the circumstances (as in an assignment for security) indicate the contrary, it is a delegation of performance of the duties of the assignor and its acceptance by the assignee constitutes a promise by him to perform those duties. This promise is enforceable by either the assignor or the other party to the original contract.

(5) The other party may treat any assignment which delegates performance as creating reasonable grounds for insecurity and may without prejudice to his rights against the assignor demand assurances from the assignee (Section 2—609).

## Part 3 General Obligation and Construction of Contract

### § 2—301. General Obligations of Parties.

The obligation of the seller is to transfer and deliver and that of the buyer is to accept and pay in accordance with the contract.

### § 2—302. Unconscionable Contract or Clause.

(1) If the court as a matter of law finds the contract or any clause of the contract to have been unconscionable at the time it was made the court may refuse to enforce the contract, or it may enforce the remainder of the contract without the unconscionable clause, or it may so limit the application of any unconscionable clause as to avoid any unconscionable result.

(2) When it is claimed or appears to the court that the contract or any clause thereof may be unconscionable the parties shall be afforded a reasonable opportunity to present evidence as to its commercial setting, purpose and effect to aid the court in making the determination.

### § 2—303. Allocations or Division of Risks.

Where this Article allocates a risk or a burden as between the parties ''unless otherwise agreed'', the agreement may not only shift the allocation but may also divide the risk or burden.

### § 2—304. Price Payable in Money, Goods, Realty, or Otherwise.

(1) The price can be made payable in money or otherwise. If it is payable in whole or in part in goods each party is a seller of the goods which he is to transfer.

(2) Even though all or part of the price is payable in an interest in realty the transfer of the goods and the seller's obligations with reference to them are subject to this Article, but not the transfer of the interest in realty or the transferor's obligations in connection therewith.

### § 2—305. Open Price Term.

(1) The parties if they so intend can conclude a contract for sale even though the price is not settled. In such a case the price is a reasonable price at the time for delivery if

(a) nothing is said as to price; or

(b) the price is left to be agreed by the parties and they fail to agree; or

(c) the price is to be fixed in terms of some agreed market or other standard as set or recorded by a third person or agency and it is not so set or recorded.

(2) A price to be fixed by the seller or by the buyer means a price for him to fix in good faith.

(3) When a price left to be fixed otherwise than by agreement of the parties fails to be fixed through fault of one party the other may at his option treat the contract as cancelled or himself fix a reasonable price.

(4) Where, however, the parties intend not to be bound unless the price be fixed or agreed and it is not fixed or agreed there is no contract. In such a case the buyer must return any goods already received or if unable so to do must pay their reasonable value at the time of delivery and the seller must return any portion of the price paid on account.

### § 2—306. Output, Requirements and Exclusive Dealings.

(1) A term which measures the quantity by the output of the seller or the requirements of the buyer means such actual output or requirements as may occur in good faith, except that no quantity unreasonably disproportionate to any stated estimate or in the absence of a stated estimate to any normal or otherwise comparable prior output or requirements may be tendered or demanded.

(2) A lawful agreement by either the seller or the buyer for exclusive dealing in the kind of goods concerned imposes unless otherwise agreed an obligation by the seller to use best efforts to supply the goods and by the buyer to use best efforts to promote their sale.

### § 2—307. Delivery in Single Lot or Several Lots.

Unless otherwise agreed all goods called for by a contract for sale must be tendered in a single delivery and payment is due only on such tender but where the circumstances give either party the right to make or demand delivery in lots the price if it can be apportioned may be demanded for each lot.

### § 2—308. Absence of Specified Place for Delivery.

Unless otherwise agreed

(a) the place for delivery of goods is the seller's place of business or if he has none his residence; but

(b) in a contract for sale of identified goods which to the knowledge of the parties at the time of contracting are in some other place, that place is the place for their delivery; and

(c) documents of title may be delivered through customary banking channels.

### § 2—309. Absence of Specific Time Provisions; Notice of Termination.

(1) The time for shipment or delivery or any other action under a contract if not provided in this Article or agreed upon shall be a reasonable time.

(2) Where the contract provides for successive performances but is indefinite in duration it is valid for a reasonable time but unless otherwise agreed may be terminated at any time by either party.

(3) Termination of a contract by one party except on the happening of an agreed event requires that reasonable notification be received by the other party and an agreement

dispensing with notification is invalid if its operation would be unconscionable.

### § 2—310. Open Time for Payment or Running of Credit; Authority to Ship Under Reservation.

Unless otherwise agreed

(a) payment is due at the time and place at which the buyer is to receive the goods even though the place of shipment is the place of delivery; and

(b) if the seller is authorized to send the goods he may ship them under reservation, and may tender the documents of title, but the buyer may inspect the goods after their arrival before payment is due unless such inspection is inconsistent with the terms of the contract (Section 2—513); and

(c) if delivery is authorized and made by way of documents of title otherwise than by subsection (b) then payment is due at the time and place at which the buyer is to receive the documents regardless of where the goods are to be received; and

(d) where the seller is required or authorized to ship the goods on credit the credit period runs from the time of shipment but post-dating the invoice or delaying its dispatch will correspondingly delay the starting of the credit period.

### § 2—311. Options and Cooperation Respecting Performance.

(1) An agreement for sale which is otherwise sufficiently definite (subsection (3) of Section 2—204) to be a contract is not made invalid by the fact that it leaves particulars of performance to be specified by one of the parties. Any such specification must be made in good faith and within limits set by commercial reasonableness.

(2) Unless otherwise agreed specifications relating to assortment of the goods are at the buyer's option and except as otherwise provided in subsections (1)(c) and (3) of Section 2—319 specifications or arrangements relating to shipment are at the seller's option.

(3) Where such specification would materially affect the other party's performance but is not seasonably made or where one party's cooperation is necessary to the agreed performance of the other but is not seasonably forthcoming, the other party in addition to all other remedies

> (a) is excused for any resulting delay in his own performance; and

> (b) may also either proceed to perform in any reasonable manner or after the time for a material part of his own performance treat the failure to specify or to cooperate as a breach by failure to deliver or accept the goods.

### § 2—312. Warranty of Title and Against Infringement; Buyer's Obligation Against Infringement.

(1) Subject to subsection (2) there is in a contract for sale a warranty by the seller that

> (a) the title conveyed shall be good, and its transfer rightful; and

(b) the goods shall be delivered free from any security interest or other lien or encumbrance of which the buyer at the time of contracting has no knowledge.

(2) A warranty under subsection (1) will be excluded or modified only by specific language or by circumstances which give the buyer reason to know that the person selling does not claim title in himself or that he is purporting to sell only such right or title as he or a third person may have.

(3) Unless otherwise agreed a seller who is a merchant regularly dealing in goods of the kind warrants that the goods shall be delivered free of the rightful claim of any third person by way of infringement or the like but a buyer who furnishes specifications to the seller must hold the seller harmless against any such claim which arises out of compliance with the specifications.

## § 2—313. Express Warranties by Affirmation, Promise, Description, Sample.

(1) Express warranties by the seller are created as follows:

(a) Any affirmation of fact or promise made by the seller to the buyer which relates to the goods and becomes part of the basis of the bargain creates an express warranty that the goods shall conform to the affirmation or promise.

(b) Any description of the goods which is made part of the basis of the bargain creates an express warranty that the goods shall conform to the description.

(c) Any sample or model which is made part of the basis of the bargain creates an express warranty that the whole of the goods shall conform to the sample or model.

(2) It is not necessary to the creation of an express warranty that the seller use formal words such as ''warrant'' or ''guarantee'' or that he have a specific intention to make a warranty, but an affirmation merely of the value of the goods or a statement purporting to be merely the seller's opinion or commendation of the goods does not create a warranty.

## § 2—314. Implied Warranty: Merchantability; Usage of Trade.

(1) Unless excluded or modified (Section 2—316), a warranty that the goods shall be merchantable is implied in a contract for their sale if the seller is a merchant with respect to goods of that kind. Under this section the serving for value of food or drink to be consumed either on the premises or elsewhere is a sale.

(2) Goods to be merchantable must be at least such as

(a) pass without objection in the trade under the contract description; and

(b) in the case of fungible goods, are of fair average quality within the description; and

(c) are fit for the ordinary purposes for which such goods are used; and

(d) run, within the variations permitted by the agreement, of even kind, quality and quantity within each unit and among all units involved; and

(e) are adequately contained, packaged, and labeled as the agreement may require; and

(f) conform to the promises or affirmations of fact made on the container or label if any.

(3) Unless excluded or modified (Section 2—316) other implied warranties may arise from course of dealing or usage of trade.

## § 2—315. Implied Warranty: Fitness for Particular Purpose.

Where the seller at the time of contracting has reason to know any particular purpose for which the goods are required and that the buyer is relying on the seller's skill or judgment to select or furnish suitable goods, there is unless excluded or modified under the next section an implied warranty that the goods shall be fit for such purpose.

## § 2—316. Exclusion or Modification of Warranties.

(1) Words or conduct relevant to the creation of an express warranty and words or conduct tending to negate or limit warranty shall be construed wherever reasonable as consistent with each other; but subject to the provisions of this Article on parol or extrinsic evidence (Section 2—202) negation or limitation is inoperative to the extent that such construction is unreasonable.

(2) Subject to subsection (3), to exclude or modify the implied warranty of merchantability or any part of it the language must mention merchantability and in case of a writing must be conspicuous, and to exclude or modify any implied warranty of fitness the exclusion must be by a writing and conspicuous. Language to exclude all implied warranties of fitness is sufficient if it states, for example, that ''There are no warranties which extend beyond the description on the face hereof.''

(3) Notwithstanding subsection (2)

(a) unless the circumstances indicate otherwise, all implied warranties are excluded by expressions like ''as is'', ''with all faults'' or other language which in common understanding calls the buyer's attention to the exclusion of warranties and makes plain that there is no implied warranty; and

(b) when the buyer before entering into the contract has examined the goods or the sample or model as fully as he desired or has refused to examine the goods there is no implied warranty with regard to defects which an examination ought in the circumstances to have revealed to him; and

(c) an implied warranty can also be excluded or modified by course of dealing or course of performance or usage of trade.

(4) Remedies for breach of warranty can be limited in accordance with the provisions of this Article on liquidation or limitation of damages and on contractual modification of remedy (Sections 2—718 and 2—719).

## § 2—317. Cumulation and Conflict of Warranties Express or Implied.

Warranties whether express or implied shall be construed as consistent with each other and as cumulative, but if such construction is unreasonable the intention of the parties shall determine which warranty is dominant. In ascertaining that intention the following rules apply:

(a) Exact or technical specifications displace an inconsistent sample or model or general language of description.

(b) A sample from an existing bulk displaces inconsistent general language of description.

(c) Express warranties displace inconsistent implied warranties other than an implied warranty of fitness for a particular purpose.

## § 2—318. Third Party Beneficiaries of Warranties Express or Implied.

Note: If this Act is introduced in the Congress of the United States this section should be omitted. (States to select one alternative.)

### Alternative A

A seller's warranty whether express or implied extends to any natural person who is in the family or household of his buyer or who is a guest in his home if it is reasonable to expect that such person may use, consume or be affected by the goods and who is injured in person by breach of the warranty. A seller may not exclude or limit the operation of this section.

### Alternative B

A seller's warranty whether express or implied extends to any natural person who may reasonably be expected to use, consume or be affected by the goods and who is injured in person by breach of the warranty. A seller may not exclude or limit the operation of this section.

### Alternative C

A seller's warranty whether express or implied extends to any person who may reasonably be expected to use, consume or be affected by the goods and who is injured by breach of the warranty. A seller may not exclude or limit the operation of this section with respect to injury to the person of an individual to whom the warranty extends. As amended 1966.

## § 2—319. F.O.B. and F.A.S. Terms.

(1) Unless otherwise agreed the term F.O.B. (which means "free on board") at a named place, even though used only in connection with the stated price, is a delivery term under which

(a) when the term is F.O.B. the place of shipment, the seller must at that place ship the goods in the manner provided in this Article (Section 2—504) and bear the expense and risk of putting them into the possession of the carrier; or

(b) when the term is F.O.B. the place of destination, the seller must at his own expense and risk transport the goods to that place and there tender delivery of them in the manner provided in this Article (Section 2—503);

(c) when under either (a) or (b) the term is also F.O.B. vessel, car or other vehicle, the seller must in addition at his own expense and risk load the goods on board. If the term is F.O.B. vessel the buyer must name the vessel and

in an appropriate case the seller must comply with the provisions of this Article on the form of bill of lading (Section 2—323).

(2) Unless otherwise agreed the term F.A.S. vessel (which means "free alongside") at a named port, even though used only in connection with the stated price, is a delivery term under which the seller must

(a) at his own expense and risk deliver the goods alongside the vessel in the manner usual in that port or on a dock designated and provided by the buyer; and

(b) obtain and tender a receipt for the goods in exchange for which the carrier is under a duty to issue a bill of lading.

(3) Unless otherwise agreed in any case falling within subsection (1)(a) or (c) or subsection (2) the buyer must seasonably give any needed instructions for making delivery, including when the term is F.A.S. or F.O.B. the loading berth of the vessel and in an appropriate case its name and sailing date. The seller may treat the failure of needed instructions as a failure of cooperation under this Article (Section 2—311). He may also at his option move the goods in any reasonable manner preparatory to delivery or shipment.

(4) Under the term F.O.B. vessel or F.A.S. unless otherwise agreed the buyer must make payment against tender of the required documents and the seller may not tender nor the buyer demand delivery of the goods in substitution for the documents.

## § 2—320. C.I.F. and C. & F. Terms.

(1) The term C.I.F. means that the price includes in a lump sum the cost of the goods and the insurance and freight to the named destination. The term C. & F. or C.F. means that the price so includes cost and freight to the named destination.

(2) Unless otherwise agreed and even though used only in connection with the stated price and destination, the term C.I.F. destination or its equivalent requires the seller at his own expense and risk to

(a) put the goods into the possession of a carrier at the port for shipment and obtain a negotiable bill or bills of lading covering the entire transportation to the named destination; and

(b) load the goods and obtain a receipt from the carrier (which may be contained in the bill of lading) showing that the freight has been paid or provided for; and

(c) obtain a policy or certificate of insurance, including any war risk insurance, of a kind and on terms then current at the port of shipment in the usual amount, in the currency of the contract, shown to cover the same goods covered by the bill of lading and providing for payment of loss to the order of the buyer or for the account of whom it may concern; but the seller may add to the price the amount of the premium for any such war risk insurance; and

(d) prepare an invoice of the goods and procure any other documents required to effect shipment or to comply with the contract; and

(e) forward and tender with commercial promptness all the documents in due form and with any indorsement necessary to perfect the buyer's rights.

(3) Unless otherwise agreed the term C. & F. or its equivalent has the same effect and imposes upon the seller the same obligations and risks as a C.I.F. term except the obligation as to insurance.

(4) Under the term C.I.F. or C. & F. unless otherwise agreed the buyer must make payment against tender of the required documents and the seller may not tender nor the buyer demand delivery of the goods in substitution for the documents.

### § 2—321. C.I.F. or C. & F.: "Net Landed Weights"; "Payment on Arrival"; Warranty of Condition on Arrival.

Under a contract containing a term C.I.F. or C. & F.

(1) Where the price is based on or is to be adjusted according to "net landed weights", "delivered weights", "out turn" quantity or quality or the like, unless otherwise agreed the seller must reasonably estimate the price. The payment due on tender of the documents called for by the contract is the amount so estimated, but after final adjustment of the price a settlement must be made with commercial promptness.

(2) An agreement described in subsection (1) or any warranty of quality or condition of the goods on arrival places upon the seller the risk of ordinary deterioration, shrinkage and the like in transportation but has no effect on the place or time of identification to the contract for sale or delivery or on the passing of the risk of loss.

(3) Unless otherwise agreed where the contract provides for payment on or after arrival of the goods the seller must before payment allow such preliminary inspection as is feasible; but if the goods are lost delivery of the documents and payment are due when the goods should have arrived.

### § 2—322. Delivery "Ex-Ship".

(1) Unless otherwise agreed a term for delivery of goods "ex-ship" (which means from the carrying vessel) or in equivalent language is not restricted to a particular ship and requires delivery from a ship which has reached a place at the named port of destination where goods of the kind are usually discharged.

(2) Under such a term unless otherwise agreed

(a) the seller must discharge all liens arising out of the carriage and furnish the buyer with a direction which puts the carrier under a duty to deliver the goods; and

(b) the risk of loss does not pass to the buyer until the goods leave the ship's tackle or are otherwise properly unloaded.

### § 2—323. Form of Bill of Lading Required in Overseas Shipment; "Overseas".

(1) Where the contract contemplates overseas shipment and contains a term C.I.F. or C. & F. or F.O.B. vessel, the seller unless otherwise agreed must obtain a negotiable bill of lading stating that the goods have been loaded on board or, in the case of a term C.I.F. or C. & F., received for shipment.

(2) Where in a case within subsection (1) a bill of lading has been issued in a set of parts, unless otherwise agreed if the documents are not to be sent from abroad the buyer may demand tender of the full set; otherwise only one part of the bill of lading need be tendered. Even if the agreement expressly requires a full set

(a) due tender of a single part is acceptable within the provisions of this Article on cure of improper delivery (subsection (1) of Section 2—508); and

(b) even though the full set is demanded, if the documents are sent from abroad the person tendering an incomplete set may nevertheless require payment upon furnishing an indemnity which the buyer in good faith deems adequate.

(3) A shipment by water or by air or a contract contemplating such shipment is "overseas" insofar as by usage of trade or agreement it is subject to the commercial, financing or shipping practices characteristic of international deep water commerce.

### § 2—324. "No Arrival, No Sale" Term.

Under a term "no arrival, no sale" or terms of like meaning, unless otherwise agreed,

(a) the seller must properly ship conforming goods and if they arrive by any means he must tender them on arrival but he assumes no obligation that the goods will arrive unless he has caused the non-arrival; and

(b) where without fault of the seller the goods are in part lost or have so deteriorated as no longer to conform to the contract or arrive after the contract time, the buyer may proceed as if there had been casualty to identified goods (Section 2—613).

### § 2—325. "Letter of Credit" Term; "Confirmed Credit".

(1) Failure of the buyer seasonably to furnish an agreed letter of credit is a breach of the contract for sale.

(2) The delivery to seller of a proper letter of credit suspends the buyer's obligation to pay. If the letter of credit is dishonored, the seller may on seasonable notification to the buyer require payment directly from him.

(3) Unless otherwise agreed the term "letter of credit" or "banker's credit" in a contract for sale means an irrevocable credit issued by a financing agency of good repute and, where the shipment is overseas, of good international repute. The term "confirmed credit" means that the credit must also carry the direct obligation of such an agency which does business in the seller's financial market.

### § 2—326. Sale on Approval and Sale or Return; Consignment Sales and Rights of Creditors.

(1) Unless otherwise agreed, if delivered goods may be returned by the buyer even though they conform to the contract, the transaction is

(a) a "sale on approval" if the goods are delivered primarily for use, and

(b) a "sale or return" if the goods are delivered primarily for resale.

(2) Except as provided in subsection (3), goods held on approval are not subject to the claims of the buyer's creditors until acceptance; goods held on sale or return are subject to such claims while in the buyer's possession.

(3) Where goods are delivered to a person for sale and such person maintains a place of business at which he deals in goods of the kind involved, under a name other than the name of the person making delivery, then with respect to claims of creditors of the person conducting the business the goods are deemed to be on sale or return. The provisions of this subsection are applicable even though an agreement purports to reserve title to the person making delivery until payment or resale or uses such words as "on consignment" or "on memorandum". However, this subsection is not applicable if the person making delivery

    (a) complies with an applicable law providing for a consignor's interest or the like to be evidenced by a sign, or

    (b) establishes that the person conducting the business is generally known by his creditors to be substantially engaged in selling the goods of others, or

    (c) complies with the filing provisions of the Article on Secured Transactions (Article 9).

(4) Any "or return" term of a contract for sale is to be treated as a separate contract for sale within the statute of frauds section of this Article (Section 2—201) and as contradicting the sale aspect of the contract within the provisions of this Article on parol or extrinsic evidence (Section 2—202).

### § 2—327. Special Incidents of Sale on Approval and Sale or Return.

(1) Under a sale on approval unless otherwise agreed

    (a) although the goods are identified to the contract the risk of loss and the title do not pass to the buyer until acceptance; and

    (b) use of the goods consistent with the purpose of trial is not acceptance but failure seasonably to notify the seller of election to return the goods is acceptance, and if the goods conform to the contract acceptance of any part is acceptance of the whole; and

    (c) after due notification of election to return, the return is at the seller's risk and expense but a merchant buyer must follow any reasonable instructions.

(2) Under a sale or return unless otherwise agreed

    (a) the option to return extends to the whole or any commercial unit of the goods while in substantially their original condition, but must be exercised seasonably; and

    (b) the return is at the buyer's risk and expense.

### § 2—328. Sale by Auction.

(1) In a sale by auction if goods are put up in lots each lot is the subject of a separate sale.

(2) A sale by auction is complete when the auctioneer so announces by the fall of the hammer or in other customary manner. Where a bid is made while the hammer is falling in acceptance of a prior bid the auctioneer may in his discretion reopen the bidding or declare the goods sold under the bid on which the hammer was falling.

(3) Such a sale is with reserve unless the goods are in explicit terms put up without reserve. In an auction with reserve the auctioneer may withdraw the goods at any time until he announces completion of the sale. In an auction without reserve, after the auctioneer calls for bids on an article or lot, that article or lot cannot be withdrawn unless no bid is made within a reasonable time. In either case a bidder may retract his bid until the auctioneer's announcement of completion of the sale, but a bidder's retraction does not revive any previous bid.

(4) If the auctioneer knowingly receives a bid on the seller's behalf or the seller makes or procures such as bid, and notice has not been given that liberty for such bidding is reserved, the buyer may at his option avoid the sale or take the goods at the price of the last good faith bid prior to the completion of the sale. This subsection shall not apply to any bid at a forced sale.

## Part 4  Title, Creditors and Good Faith Purchasers

### § 2—401. Passing of Title; Reservation for Security; Limited Application of This Section.

Each provision of this Article with regard to the rights, obligations and remedies of the seller, the buyer, purchasers or other third parties applies irrespective of title to the goods except where the provision refers to such title. Insofar as situations are not covered by the other provisions of this Article and matters concerning title became material the following rules apply:

(1) Title to goods cannot pass under a contract for sale prior to their identification to the contract (Section 2—501), and unless otherwise explicitly agreed the buyer acquires by their identification a special property as limited by this Act. Any retention or reservation by the seller of the title (property) in goods shipped or delivered to the buyer is limited in effect to a reservation of a security interest. Subject to these provisions and to the provisions of the Article on Secured Transactions (Article 9), title to goods passes from the seller to the buyer in any manner and on any conditions explicitly agreed on by the parties.

(2) Unless otherwise explicitly agreed title passes to the buyer at the time and place at which the seller completes his performance with reference to the physical delivery of the goods, despite any reservation of a security interest and even though a document of title is to be delivered at a different time or place; and in particular and despite any reservation of a security interest by the bill of lading

    (a) if the contract requires or authorizes the seller to send the goods to the buyer but does not require him to deliver them at destination, title passes to the buyer at the time and place of shipment; but

(b) if the contract requires delivery at destination, title passes on tender there.

(3) Unless otherwise explicitly agreed where delivery is to be made without moving the goods,

(a) if the seller is to deliver a document of title, title passes at the time when and the place where he delivers such documents; or

(b) if the goods are at the time of contracting already identified and no documents are to be delivered, title passes at the time and place of contracting.

(4) A rejection or other refusal by the buyer to receive or retain the goods, whether or not justified, or a justified revocation of acceptance revests title to the goods in the seller. Such revesting occurs by operation of law and is not a "sale".

### § 2—402. Rights of Seller's Creditors Against Sold Goods.

(1) Except as provided in subsections (2) and (3), rights of unsecured creditors of the seller with respect to goods which have been identified to a contract for sale are subject to the buyer's rights to recover the goods under this Article (Sections 2—502 and 2—716).

(2) A creditor of the seller may treat a sale or an identification of goods to a contract for sale as void if as against him a retention of possession by the seller is fraudulent under any rule of law of the state where the goods are situated, except that retention of possession in good faith and current course of trade by a merchant-seller for a commercially reasonable time after a sale or identification is not fraudulent.

(3) Nothing in this Article shall be deemed to impair the rights of creditors of the seller

(a) under the provisions of the Article on Secured Trans-actions (Article 9); or

(b) where identification to the contract or delivery is made not in current course of trade but in satisfaction of or as security for a pre-existing claim for money, security or the like and is made under circumstances which under any rule of law of the state where the goods are situated would apart from this Article constitute the transaction a fraudulent transfer or voidable preference.

### § 2—403. Power to Transfer; Good Faith Purchase of Goods; "Entrusting".

(1) A purchaser of goods acquires all title which his transferor had or had power to transfer except that a purchaser of a limited interest acquires rights only to the extent of the interest purchased. A person with voidable title has power to transfer a good title to a good faith purchaser for value. When goods have been delivered under a transaction of purchase the purchaser has such power even though

(a) the transferor was deceived as to the identity of the purchaser, or

(b) the delivery was in exchange for a check which is later dishonored, or

(c) it was agreed that the transaction was to be a "cash sale", or

(d) the delivery was procured through fraud punishable as larcenous under the criminal law.

(2) Any entrusting of possession of goods to a merchant who deals in goods of that kind gives him power to transfer all rights of the entruster to a buyer in ordinary course of business.

(3) "Entrusting" includes any delivery and any acquiescence in retention of possession regardless of any condition expressed between the parties to the delivery or acquiescence and regardless of whether the procurement of the entrusting or the possessor's disposition of the goods have been such as to be larcenous under the criminal law.

(4) The rights of other purchasers of goods and of lien creditors are governed by the Articles on Secured Transactions (Article 9), Bulk Transfers (Article 6) and Documents of Title (Article 7).

## Part 5   Performance

### § 2—501. Insurable Interest in Goods; Manner of Identification of Goods.

(1) The buyer obtains a special property and an insurable interest in goods by identification of existing goods as goods to which the contract refers even though the goods so identified are non-conforming and he has an option to return or reject them. Such identification can be made at any time and in any manner explicitly agreed to by the parties. In the absence of explicit agreement identification occurs

(a) when the contract is made if it is for the sale of goods already existing and identified;

(b) if the contract is for the sale of future goods other than those described in paragraph (c), when goods are shipped, marked or otherwise designated by the seller as goods to which the contract refers;

(c) when the crops are planted or otherwise become growing crops or the young are conceived if the contract is for the sale of unborn young to be born within twelve months after contracting or for the sale of crops to be harvested within twelve months or the next normal harvest season after contracting whichever is longer.

(2) The seller retains an insurable interest in goods so long as title to or any security interest in the goods remains in him and where the identification is by the seller alone he may until default or insolvency or notification to the buyer that the identification is final substitute other goods for those identified.

(3) Nothing in this section impairs any insurable interest recognized under any other statute or rule of law.

### § 2—502. Buyer's Right to Goods on Seller's Insolvency.

(1) Subject to subsection (2) and even though the goods have

not been shipped a buyer who has paid a part or all of the price of goods in which he has a special property under the provisions of the immediately preceding section may on making and keeping good a tender of any unpaid portion of their price recover them from the seller if the seller becomes insolvent within ten days after receipt of the first installment on their price.

(2) If the identification creating his special property has been made by the buyer he acquires the right to recover the goods only if they conform to the contract for sale.

### § 2—503. Manner of Seller's Tender of Delivery.

(1) Tender of delivery requires that the seller put and hold conforming goods at the buyer's disposition and give the buyer any notification reasonably necessary to enable him to take delivery. The manner, time and place for tender are determined by the agreement and this Article, and in particular

    (a) tender must be at a reasonable hour, and if it is of goods they must be kept available for the period reasonably necessary to enable the buyer to take possession; but

    (b) unless otherwise agreed the buyer must furnish facilities reasonably suited to the receipt of the goods.

(2) Where the case is within the next section respecting shipment tender requires that the seller comply with its provisions.

(3) Where the seller is required to deliver at a particular destination tender requires that he comply with subsection (1) and also in any appropriate case tender documents as described in subsections (4) and (5) of this section.

(4) Where goods are in the possession of a bailee and are to be delivered without being moved

    (a) tender requires that the seller either tender a negotiable document of title covering such goods or procure acknowledgment by the bailee of the buyer's right to possession of the goods; but

    (b) tender to the buyer of a non-negotiable document of title or of a written direction to the bailee to deliver is sufficient tender unless the buyer seasonably objects, and receipt by the bailee of notification of the buyer's rights fixes those rights as against the bailee and all third persons; but risk of loss of the goods and of any failure by the bailee to honor the non-negotiable document of title or to obey the direction remains on the seller until the buyer has had a reasonable time to present the document or direction, and a refusal by the bailee to honor the document or to obey the direction defeats the tender.

(5) Where the contract requires the seller to deliver documents

    (a) he must tender all such documents in correct form, except as provided in this Article with respect to bills of lading in a set (subsection (2) of Section 2—323); and

    (b) tender through customary banking channels is suf-

ficient and dishonor of a draft accompanying the documents constitutes non-acceptance or rejection.

### § 2—504. Shipment by Seller.

Where the seller is required or authorized to send the goods to the buyer and the contract does not require him to deliver them at a particular destination, then unless otherwise agreed he must

(a) put the goods in the possession of such a carrier and make such a contract for their transportation as may be reasonable having regard to the nature of the goods and other circumstances of the case; and

(b) obtain and promptly deliver or tender in due form any document necessary to enable the buyer to obtain possession of the goods or otherwise required by the agreement or by usage of trade; and

(c) promptly notify the buyer of the shipment.

Failure to notify the buyer under paragraph (c) or to make a proper contract under paragraph (a) is a ground for rejection only if material delay or loss ensues.

### § 2—505. Seller's Shipment under Reservation.

(1) Where the seller has identified goods to the contract by or before shipment:

    (a) his procurement of a negotiable bill of lading to his own order or otherwise reserves in him a security interest in the goods. His procurement of the bill to the order of a financing agency or of the buyer indicates in addition only the seller's expectation of transferring that interest to the person named.

    (b) a non-negotiable bill of lading to himself or his nominee reserves possession of the goods as security but except in a case of conditional delivery (subsection (2) of Section 2—507) a non-negotiable bill of lading naming the buyer as consignee reserves no security interest even though the seller retains possession of the bill of lading.

(2) When shipment by the seller with reservation of a security interest is in violation of the contract for sale it constitutes an improper contract for transportation within the preceding section but impairs neither the rights given to the buyer by shipment and identification of the goods to the contract nor the seller's powers as a holder of a negotiable document.

### § 2—506. Rights of Financing Agency.

(1) A financing agency by paying or purchasing for value a draft which relates to a shipment of goods acquires to the extent of the payment or purchase and in addition to its own rights under the draft and any document of title securing it any rights of the shipper in the goods including the right to stop delivery and the shipper's right to have the draft honored by the buyer.

(2) The right to reimbursement of a financing agency which has in good faith honored or purchased the draft under commitment to or authority from the buyer is not impaired by

subsequent discovery of defects with reference to any relevant document which was apparently regular on its face.

### § 2—507. Effect of Seller's Tender; Delivery on Condition.

(1) Tender of delivery is a condition to the buyer's duty to accept the goods and, unless otherwise agreed, to his duty to pay for them. Tender entitles the seller to acceptance of the goods and to payment according to the contract.

(2) Where payment is due and demanded on the delivery to the buyer of goods or documents of title, his right as against the seller to retain or dispose of them is conditional upon his making the payment due.

### § 2—508. Cure by Seller of Improper Tender or Delivery; Replacement.

(1) Where any tender or delivery by the seller is rejected because non-conforming and the time for performance has not yet expired, the seller may seasonably notify the buyer of his intention to cure and may then within the contract time make a conforming delivery.

(2) Where the buyer rejects a non-conforming tender which the seller had reasonable grounds to believe would be acceptable with or without money allowance the seller may if he seasonably notifies the buyer have a further reasonable time to substitute a conforming tender.

### § 2—509. Risk of Loss in the Absence of Breach.

(1) Where the contract requires or authorizes the seller to ship the goods by carrier

    (a) if it does not require him to deliver them at a particular destination, the risk of loss passes to the buyer when the goods are duly delivered to the carrier even though the shipment is under reservation (Section 2—505); but

    (b) if it does require him to deliver them at a particular destination and the goods are there duly tendered while in the possession of the carrier, the risk of loss passes to the buyer when the goods are there duly so tendered as to enable the buyer to take delivery.

(2) Where the goods are held by a bailee to be delivered without being moved, the risk of loss passes to the buyer

    (a) on his receipt of a negotiable document of title covering the goods; or

    (b) on acknowledgment by the bailee of the buyer's right to possession of the goods; or

    (c) after his receipt of a non-negotiable document of title or other written direction to deliver, as provided in subsection (4)(b) of Section 2—503.

(3) In any case not within subsection (1) or (2), the risk of loss passes to the buyer on his receipt of the goods if the seller is a merchant; otherwise the risk passes to the buyer on tender of delivery.

(4) The provisions of this section are subject to contrary agreement of the parties and to the provisions of this Article on sale on approval (Section 2—327) and on effect of breach on risk of loss (Section 2—510).

### § 2—510. Effect of Breach on Risk of Loss.

(1) Where a tender or delivery of goods so fails to conform to the contract as to give a right of rejection the risk of their loss remains on the seller until cure or acceptance.

(2) Where the buyer rightfully revokes acceptance he may to the extent of any deficiency in his effective insurance coverage treat the risk of loss as having rested on the seller from the beginning.

(3) Where the buyer as to conforming goods already identified to the contract for sale repudiates or is otherwise in breach before risk of their loss has passed to him, the seller may to the extent of any deficiency in his effective insurance coverage treat the risk of loss as resting on the buyer for a commercially reasonable time.

### § 2—511. Tender of Payment by Buyer; Payment by Check.

(1) Unless otherwise agreed tender of payment is a condition to the seller's duty to tender and complete any delivery.

(2) Tender of payment is sufficient when made by any means or in any manner current in the ordinary course of business unless the seller demands payment in legal tender and gives any extension of time reasonably necessary to procure it.

(3) Subject to the provisions of this Act on the effect of an instrument on an obligation (Section 3—802), payment by check is conditional and is defeated as between the parties by dishonor of the check on due presentment.

### § 2—512. Payment by Buyer Before Inspection.

(1) Where the contract requires payment before inspection non-conformity of the goods does not excuse the buyer from so making payment unless

    (a) the non-conformity appears without inspection; or

    (b) despite tender of the required documents the circumstances would justify injunction against honor under the provisions of this Act (Section 5—114).

(2) Payment pursuant to subsection (1) does not constitute an acceptance of goods or impair the buyer's right to inspect or any of his remedies.

### § 2—513. Buyer's Right to Inspection of Goods.

(1) Unless otherwise agreed and subject to subsection (3), where goods are tendered or delivered or identified to the contract for sale, the buyer has a right before payment or acceptance to inspect them at any reasonable place and time and in any reasonable manner. When the seller is required or authorized to send the goods to the buyer, the inspection may be after their arrival.

(2) Expenses of inspection must be borne by the buyer but may be recovered from the seller if the goods do not conform and are rejected.

(3) Unless otherwise agreed and subject to the provisions of this Article on C.I.F. contracts (subsection (3) of Section 2—321), the buyer is not entitled to inspect the goods before payment of the price when the contract provides

    (a) for delivery ''C.O.D.'' or on other like terms; or

(b) for payment against documents of title, except where such payment is due only after the goods are to become available for inspection.

(4) A place or method of inspection fixed by the parties is presumed to be exclusive but unless otherwise expressly agreed it does not postpone identification or shift the place for delivery or for passing the risk of loss. If compliance becomes impossible, inspection shall be as provided in this section unless the place or method fixed was clearly intended as an indispensable condition failure of which avoids the contract.

### § 2—514. When Documents Deliverable on Acceptance; When on Payment.

Unless otherwise agreed documents against which a draft is drawn are to be delivered to the drawee on acceptance of the draft if it is payable more than three days after presentment; otherwise, only on payment.

### § 2—515. Preserving Evidence of Goods in Dispute.

In furtherance of the adjustment of any claim or dispute

(a) either party on reasonable notification to the other and for the purpose of ascertaining the facts and preserving evidence has the right to inspect, test and sample the goods including such of them as may be in the possession or control of the other; and

(b) the parties may agree to a third party inspection or survey to determine the conformity or condition of the goods and may agree that the findings shall be binding upon them in any subsequent litigation or adjustment.

## Part 6   Breach, Repudiation and Excuse

### § 2—601. Buyer's Rights on Improper Delivery.

Subject to the provisions of this Article on breach in installment contracts (Section 2—612) and unless otherwise agreed under the sections on contractual limitations of remedy (Sections 2—718 and 2—719), if the goods or the tender of delivery fail in any respect to conform to the contract, the buyer may

(a) reject the whole; or

(b) accept the whole; or

(c) accept any commercial unit or units and reject the rest.

### § 2—602. Manner and Effect of Rightful Rejection.

(1) Rejection of goods must be within a reasonable time after their delivery or tender. It is ineffective unless the buyer seasonably notifies the seller.

(2) Subject to the provisions of the two following sections on rejected goods (Sections 2—603 and 2—604),

(a) after rejection any exercise of ownership by the buyer with respect to any commercial unit is wrongful as against the seller; and

(b) if the buyer has before rejection taken physical possession of goods in which he does not have a security interest under the provisions of this Article (subsection

(3) of Section 2—711), he is under a duty after rejection to hold them with reasonable care at the seller's disposition for a time sufficient to permit the seller to remove them; but

(c) the buyer has no further obligations with regard to goods rightfully rejected.

(3) The seller's rights with respect to goods wrongfully rejected are governed by the provisions of this Article on Seller's remedies in general (Section 2—703).

### § 2—603. Merchant Buyer's Duties as to Rightfully Rejected Goods.

(1) Subject to any security interest in the buyer (subsection (3) of Section 2—711), when the seller has no agent or place of business at the market of rejection a merchant buyer is under a duty after rejection of goods in his possession or control to follow any reasonable instructions received from the seller with respect to the goods and in the absence of such instructions to make reasonable efforts to sell them for the seller's account if they are perishable or threaten to decline in value speedily. Instructions are not reasonable if on demand indemnity for expenses is not forthcoming.

(2) When the buyer sells goods under subsection (1), he is entitled to reimbursement from the seller or out of the proceeds for reasonable expenses of caring for and selling them, and if the expenses include no selling commission then to such commission as is usual in the trade or if there is none to a reasonable sum not exceeding ten per cent on the gross proceeds.

(3) In complying with this section the buyer is held only to good faith and good faith conduct hereunder is neither acceptance nor conversion nor the basis of an action for damages.

### § 2—604. Buyer's Options as to Salvage of Rightfully Rejected Goods.

Subject to the provisions of the immediately preceding section on perishables if the seller gives no instructions within a reasonable time after notification of rejection the buyer may store the rejected goods for the seller's account or reship them to him or resell them for the seller's account with reimbursement as provided in the preceding section. Such action is not acceptance or conversion.

### § 2—605. Waiver of Buyer's Objections by Failure to Particularize.

(1) The buyer's failure to state in connection with rejection a particular defect which is ascertainable by reasonable inspection precludes him from relying on the unstated defect to justify rejection or to establish breach

(a) where the seller could have cured it if stated seasonably; or

(b) between merchants when the seller has after rejection made a request in writing for a full and final written statement of all defects on which the buyer proposes to rely.

(2) Payment against documents made without reservation of rights precludes recovery of the payment for defects apparent on the face of the documents.

## § 2—606. What Constitutes Acceptance of Goods.

(1) Acceptance of goods occurs when the buyer

(a) after a reasonable opportunity to inspect the goods signifies to the seller that the goods are conforming or that he will take or retain them in spite of their nonconformity; or

(b) fails to make an effective rejection (subsection (1) of Section 2—602), but such acceptance does not occur until the buyer has had a reasonable opportunity to inspect them; or

(c) does any act inconsistent with the seller's ownership; but if such act is wrongful as against the seller it is an acceptance only if ratified by him.

(2) Acceptance of a part of any commercial unit is acceptance of that entire unit.

## § 2—607. Effect of Acceptance; Notice of Breach; Burden of Establishing Breach After Acceptance; Notice of Claim or Litigation to Person Answerable Over.

(1) The buyer must pay at the contract rate for any goods accepted.

(2) Acceptance of goods by the buyer precludes rejection of the goods accepted and if made with knowledge of a nonconformity cannot be revoked because of it unless the acceptance was on the reasonable assumption that the non-conformity would be seasonably cured but acceptance does not of itself impair any other remedy provided by this Article for non-conformity.

(3) Where a tender has been accepted

(a) the buyer must within a reasonable time after he discovers or should have discovered any breach notify the seller of breach or be barred from any remedy; and

(b) if the claim is one for infringement or the like (subsection (3) of Section 2—312) and the buyer is sued as a result of such a breach he must so notify the seller within a reasonable time after he receives notice of the litigation or be barred from any remedy over for liability established by the litigation.

(4) The burden is on the buyer to establish any breach with respect to the goods accepted.

(5) Where the buyer is sued for breach of a warranty or other obligation for which his seller is answerable over

(a) he may give his seller written notice of the litigation. If the notice states that the seller may come in and defend and that if the seller does not do so he will be bound in any action against him by his buyer by any determination of fact common to the two litigations, then unless the seller after seasonable receipt of the notice does come in and defend he is so bound.

(b) if the claim is one for infringement or the like (subsection (3) of Section 2—312) the original seller may demand in writing that his buyer turn over to him control of the litigation including settlement or else be barred from any remedy over and if he also agrees to bear all expense and to satisfy any adverse judgment, then unless the buyer after seasonable receipt of the demand does turn over control the buyer is so barred.

(6) The provisions of subsections (3), (4) and (5) apply to any obligation of a buyer to hold the seller harmless against infringement or the like (subsection (3) of Section 2—312).

## § 2—608. Revocation of Acceptance in Whole or in Part.

(1) The buyer may revoke his acceptance of a lot or commercial unit whose non-conformity substantially impairs its value to him if he has accepted it

(a) on the reasonable assumption that its nonconformity would be cured and it has not been seasonably cured; or

(b) without discovery of such non-conformity if his acceptance was reasonably induced either by the difficulty of discovery before acceptance or by the seller's assurances.

(2) Revocation of acceptance must occur within a reasonable time after the buyer discovers or should have discovered the ground for it and before any substantial change in condition of the goods which is not caused by their own defects. It is not effective until the buyer notifies the seller of it.

(3) A buyer who so revokes has the same rights and duties with regard to the goods involved as if he had rejected them.

## § 2—609. Right to Adequate Assurance of Performance.

(1) A contract for sale imposes an obligation on each party that the other's expectation of receiving due performance will not be impaired. When reasonable grounds for insecurity arise with respect to the performance of either party the other may in writing demand adequate assurance of due performance and until he receives such assurance may if commercially reasonable suspend any performance for which he has not already received the agreed return.

(2) Between merchants the reasonableness of grounds for insecurity and the adequacy of any assurance offered shall be determined according to commercial standards.

(3) Acceptance of any improper delivery or payment does not prejudice the party's right to demand adequate assurance of future performance.

(4) After receipt of a justified demand failure to provide within a reasonable time not exceeding thirty days such assurance of due performance as is adequate under the circumstances of the particular case is a repudiation of the contract.

## § 2—610. Anticipatory Repudiation.

When either party repudiates the contract with respect to a performance not yet due the loss of which will substantially impair the value of the contract to the other, the aggrieved party may

(a) for a commercially reasonable time await performance by the repudiating party; or

(b) resort to any remedy for breach (Section 2—703 or Section 2—711), even though he has notified the repudiating party that he would await the latter's performance and has urged retraction; and

(c) in either case suspend his own performance or proceed in accordance with the provisions of this Article on the seller's right to identify goods to the contract notwithstanding breach or to salvage unfinished goods (Section 2—704).

### § 2—611. Retraction of Anticipatory Repudiation.

(1) Until the repudiating party's next performance is due he can retract his repudiation unless the aggrieved party has since the repudiation cancelled or materially changed his position or otherwise indicated that he considers the repudiation final.

(2) Retraction may be by any method which clearly indicates to the aggrieved party that the repudiating party intends to perform, but must include any assurance justifiably demanded under the provisions of this Article (Section 2—609).

(3) Retraction reinstates the repudiating party's rights under the contract with due excuse and allowance to the aggrieved party for any delay occasioned by the repudiation.

### § 2—612. "Installment Contract"; Breach.

(1) An "installment contract" is one which requires or authorizes the delivery of goods in separate lots to be separately accepted, even though the contract contains a clause "each delivery is a separate contract" or its equivalent.

(2) The buyer may reject any installment which is non-conforming if the non-conformity substantially impairs the value of that installment and cannot be cured or if the non-conformity is a defect in the required documents; but if the non-conformity does not fall within subsection (3) and the seller gives adequate assurance of its cure the buyer must accept that installment.

(3) Whenever non-conformity or default with respect to one or more installments substantially impairs the value of the whole contract there is a breach of the whole. But the aggrieved party reinstates the contract if he accepts a non-conforming installment without seasonably notifying of cancellation or if he brings an action with respect only to past installments or demands performance as to future installments.

### § 2—613. Casualty to Identified Goods.

Where the contract requires for its performance goods identified when the contract is made, and the goods suffer casualty without fault of either party before the risk of loss passes to the buyer, or in a proper case under a "no arrival, no sale" term (Section 2—324) then

(a) if the loss is total the contract is avoided; and

(b) if the loss is partial or the goods have so deteriorated as no longer to conform to the contract the buyer may nevertheless demand inspection and at his option either treat the contract as voided or accept the goods with due allowance from the contract price for the deterioration or the deficiency in quantity but without further right against the seller.

### § 2—614. Substituted Performance.

(1) Where without fault of either party the agreed berthing, loading, or unloading facilities fail or an agreed type of carrier becomes unavailable or the agreed manner of delivery otherwise becomes commercially impracticable but a commercially reasonable substitute is available, such substitute performance must be tendered and accepted.

(2) If the agreed means or manner of payment fails because of domestic or foreign governmental regulation, the seller may withhold or stop delivery unless the buyer provides a means or manner of payment which is commercially a substantial equivalent. If delivery has already been taken, payment by the means or in the manner provided by the regulation discharges the buyer's obligation unless the regulation is discriminatory, oppressive or predatory.

### § 2—615. Excuse by Failure of Presupposed Conditions.

Except so far as a seller may have assumed a greater obligation and subject to the preceding section on substituted performance:

(a) Delay in delivery or non-delivery in whole or in part by a seller who complies with paragraphs (b) and (c) is not a breach of his duty under a contract for sale if performance as agreed has been made impracticable by the occurrence of a contingency the nonoccurrence of which was a basic assumption on which the contract was made or by compliance in good faith with any applicable foreign or domestic governmental regulation or order whether or not it later proves to be invalid.

(b) Where the causes mentioned in paragraph (a) affect only a part of the seller's capacity to perform, he must allocate production and deliveries among his customers but may at his option include regular customers not then under contract as well as his own requirements for further manufacture. He may so allocate in any manner which is fair and reasonable.

(c) The seller must notify the buyer seasonably that there will be delay or non-delivery and, when allocation is required under paragraph (b), of the estimated quota thus made available for the buyer.

### § 2—616. Procedure on Notice Claiming Excuse.

(1) Where the buyer receives notification of a material or indefinite delay or an allocation justified under the preceding section he may by written notification to the seller as to any delivery concerned, and where the prospective deficiency substantially impairs the value of the whole contract under the provisions of this Article relating to breach of installment contracts (Section 2—612), then also as to the whole,

(a) terminate and thereby discharge any unexecuted portion of the contract; or

(b) modify the contract by agreeing to take his available quota in substitution.

(2) If after receipt of such notification from the seller the buyer fails so to modify the contract within a reasonable time not exceeding thirty days the contract lapses with respect to any deliveries affected.

(3) The provisions of this section may not be negated by agreement except in so far as the seller has assumed a greater obligation under the preceding section.

## Part 7    Remedies

### § 2—701. Remedies for Breach of Collateral Contracts Not Impaired.

Remedies for breach of any obligation or promise collateral or ancillary to a contract for sale are not impaired by the provisions of this Article.

### § 2—702. Seller's Remedies on Discovery of Buyer's Insolvency.

(1) Where the seller discovers the buyer to be insolvent he may refuse delivery except for cash including payment for all goods theretofore delivered under the contract, and stop delivery under this Article (Section 2—705).

(2) Where the seller discovers that the buyer has received goods on credit while insolvent he may reclaim the goods upon demand made within ten days after the receipt, but if misrepresentation of solvency has been made to the particular seller in writing within three months before delivery the ten day limitation does not apply. Except as provided in this subsection the seller may not base a right to reclaim goods on the buyer's fraudulent or innocent misrepresentation of solvency or of intent to pay.

(3) The seller's right to reclaim under subsection (2) is subject to the rights of a buyer in ordinary course or other good faith purchaser under this Article (Section 2—403). Successful reclamation of goods excludes all other remedies with respect to them.

### § 2—703. Seller's Remedies in General.

Where the buyer wrongfully rejects or revokes acceptance of goods or fails to make a payment due on or before delivery or repudiates with respect to a part or the whole, then with respect to any goods directly affected and, if the breach is of the whole contract (Section 2—612), then also with respect to the whole undelivered balance, the aggrieved seller may

(a) withhold delivery of such goods;

(b) stop delivery by any bailee as hereafter provided (Section 2—705);

(c) proceed under the next section respecting goods still unidentified to the contract;

(d) resell and recover damages as hereafter provided (Section 2—706);

(e) recover damages for non-acceptance (Section 2—708) or in a proper case the price (Section 2—709);

(f) cancel.

### § 2—704. Seller's Right to Identify Goods to the Contract Notwithstanding Breach or to Salvage Unfinished Goods.

(1) An aggrieved seller under the preceding section may

(a) identify to the contract conforming goods not already identified if at the time he learned of the breach they are in his possession or control;

(b) treat as the subject of resale goods which have demonstrably been intended for the particular contract even though those goods are unfinished.

(2) Where the goods are unfinished an aggrieved seller may in the exercise of reasonable commercial judgment for the purposes of avoiding loss and of effective realization either complete the manufacture and wholly identify the goods to the contract or cease manufacture and resell for scrap or salvage value or proceed in any other reasonable manner.

### § 2—705. Seller's Stoppage of Delivery in Transit or Otherwise.

(1) The seller may stop delivery of goods in the possession of a carrier or other bailee when he discovers the buyer to be insolvent (Section 2—702) and may stop delivery of carload, truckload, planeload or larger shipments of express or freight when the buyer repudiates or fails to make a payment due before delivery or if for any other reason the seller has a right to withhold or reclaim the goods.

(2) As against such buyer the seller may stop delivery until

(a) receipt of the goods by the buyer; or

(b) acknowledgment to the buyer by any bailee of the goods except a carrier that the bailee holds the goods for the buyer; or

(c) such acknowledgment to the buyer by a carrier by reshipment or as warehouseman; or

(d) negotiation to the buyer of any negotiable document of title covering the goods.

(3) (a) To stop delivery the seller must so notify as to enable the bailee by reasonable diligence to prevent delivery of the goods.

(b) After such notification the bailee must hold and deliver the goods according to the directions of the seller but the seller is liable to the bailee for any ensuing charges or damages.

(c) If a negotiable document of title has been issued for goods the bailee is not obliged to obey a notification to stop until surrender of the document.

(d) A carrier who has issued a non-negotiable bill of lading is not obliged to obey a notification to stop received from a person other than the consignor.

## § 2—706. Seller's Resale Including Contract for Resale.

(1) Under the conditions stated in Section 2—703 on seller's remedies, the seller may resell the goods concerned or the undelivered balance thereof. Where the resale is made in good faith and in a commercially reasonable manner the seller may recover the difference between the resale price and the contract price together with any incidental damages allowed under the provisions of this Article (Section 2—710), but less expenses saved in consequence of the buyer's breach.

(2) Except as otherwise provided in subsection (3) or unless otherwise agreed resale may be at public or private sale including sale by way of one or more contracts to sell or of identification to an existing contract of the seller. Sale may be as a unit or in parcels and at any time and place and on any terms but every aspect of the sale including the method, manner, time, place and terms must be commercially reasonable. The resale must be reasonably identified as referring to the broken contract, but it is not necessary that the goods be in existence or that any or all of them have been identified to the contract before the breach.

(3) Where the resale is at private sale the seller must give the buyer reasonable notification of his intention to resell.

(4) Where the resale is at public sale

   (a) only identified goods can be sold except where there is a recognized market for a public sale of futures in goods of the kind; and

   (b) it must be made at a usual place or market for public sale if one is reasonably available and except in the case of goods which are perishable or threaten to decline in value speedily the seller must give the buyer reasonable notice of the time and place of the resale; and

   (c) if the goods are not to be within the view of those attending the sale the notification of sale must state the place where the goods are located and provide for their reasonable inspection by prospective bidders; and

   (d) the seller may buy.

(5) A purchaser who buys in good faith at a resale takes the goods free of any rights of the original buyer even though the seller fails to comply with one or more of the requirements of this section.

(6) The seller is not accountable to the buyer for any profit made on any resale. A person in the position of a seller (Section 2—707) or a buyer who has rightfully rejected or justifiably revoked acceptance must account for any excess over the amount of his security interest, as hereinafter defined (subsection (3) of Section 2—711).

## § 2—707. "Person in the Position of a Seller".

(1) A "person in the position of a seller" includes as against a principal an agent who has paid or become responsible for the price of goods on behalf of his principal or anyone who otherwise holds a security interest or other right in goods similar to that of a seller.

(2) A person in the position of a seller may as provided in this Article withhold or stop delivery (Section 2—705) and resell (Section 2—706) and recover incidental damages (Section 2—710).

## § 2—708. Seller's Damages for Non-Acceptance or Repudiation.

(1) Subject to subsection (2) and to the provisions of this Article with respect to proof of market price (Section 2—723), the measure of damages for non-acceptance or repudiation by the buyer is the difference between the market price at the time and place for tender and the unpaid contract price together with any incidental damages provided in this Article (Section 2—710), but less expenses saved in consequence of the buyer's breach.

(2) If the measure of damages provided in subsection (1) is inadequate to put the seller in as good a position as performance would have done then the measure of damages is the profit (including reasonable overhead) which the seller would have made from full performance by the buyer, together with any incidental damages provided in this Article (Section 2—710), due allowance for costs reasonably incurred and due credit for payments or proceeds of resale.

## § 2—709. Action for the Price.

(1) When the buyer fails to pay the price as it becomes due the seller may recover, together with any incidental damages under the next section, the price

   (a) of goods accepted or of conforming goods lost or damaged within a commercially reasonable time after risk of their loss has passed to the buyer; and

   (b) of goods identified to the contract if the seller is unable after reasonable effort to resell them at a reasonable price or the circumstances reasonably indicate that such effort will be unavailing.

(2) Where the seller sues for the price he must hold for the buyer any goods which have been identified to the contract and are still in his control except that if resale becomes possible he may resell them at any time prior to the collection of the judgment. The net proceeds of any such resale must be credited to the buyer and payment of the judgment entitles him to any goods not resold.

(3) After the buyer has wrongfully rejected or revoked acceptance of the goods or has failed to make a payment due or has repudiated (Section 2—610), a seller who is held not entitled to the price under this section shall nevertheless be awarded damages for non-acceptance under the preceding section.

## § 2—710. Seller's Incidental Damages.

Incidental damages to an aggrieved seller include any commercially reasonable charges, expenses or commissions incurred in stopping delivery, in the transportation, care and custody of goods after the buyer's breach, in connection with return or resale of the goods or otherwise resulting from the breach.

## § 2—711. Buyer's Remedies in General; Buyer's Security Interest in Rejected Goods.

(1) Where the seller fails to make delivery or repudiates or the buyer rightfully rejects or justifiably revokes acceptance then with respect to any goods involved, and with respect to the whole if the breach goes to the whole contract (Section 2—612), the buyer may cancel and whether or not he has done so may in addition to recovering so much of the price as has been paid

(a) "cover" and have damages under the next section as to all the goods affected whether or not they have been identified to the contract; or

(b) recover damages for non-delivery as provided in this Article (Section 2—713).

(2) Where the seller fails to deliver or repudiates the buyer may also

(a) if the goods have been identified recover them as provided in this Article (Section 2—502); or

(b) in a proper case obtain specific performance or replevy the goods as provided in this Article (Section 2—716).

(3) On rightful rejection or justifiable revocation of acceptance a buyer has a security interest in goods in his possession or control for any payments made on their price and any expenses reasonably incurred in their inspection, receipt, transportation, care and custody and may hold such goods and resell them in like manner as an aggrieved seller (Section 2—706).

## § 2—712. "Cover"; Buyer's Procurement of Substitute Goods.

(1) After a breach within the preceding section the buyer may "cover" by making in good faith and without unreasonable delay any reasonable purchase of or contract to purchase goods in substitution for those due from the seller.

(2) The buyer may recover from the seller as damages the difference between the cost of cover and the contract price together with any incidental or consequential damages as hereinafter defined (Section 2—715), but less expenses saved in consequence of the seller's breach.

(3) Failure of the buyer to effect cover within this section does not bar him from any other remedy.

## § 2—713. Buyer's Damages for Non-Delivery or Repudiation.

(1) Subject to the provisions of this Article with respect to proof of market price (Section 2—723), the measure of damages for non-delivery or repudiation by the seller is the difference between the market price at the time when the buyer learned of the breach and the contract price together with any incidental and consequential damages provided in this Article (Section 2—715), but less expenses saved in consequence of the seller's breach.

(2) Market price is to be determined as of the place for tender or, in cases of rejection after arrival or revocation of acceptance, as of the place of arrival.

## § 2—714. Buyer's Damages for Breach in Regard to Accepted Goods.

(1) Where the buyer has accepted goods and given notification (subsection (3) of Section 2—607) he may recover as damages for any non-conformity of tender the loss resulting in the ordinary course of events from the seller's breach as determined in any manner which is reasonable.

(2) The measure of damages for breach of warranty is the difference at the time and place of acceptance between the value of the goods accepted and the value they would have had if they had been as warranted, unless special circumstances show proximate damages of a different amount.

(3) In a proper case any incidental and consequential damages under the next section may also be recovered.

## § 2—715. Buyer's Incidental and Consequential Damages.

(1) Incidental damages resulting from the seller's breach include expenses reasonably incurred in inspection, receipt, transportation and care and custody of goods rightfully rejected, any commercially reasonable charges, expenses or commissions in connection with effecting cover and any other reasonable expense incident to the delay or other breach.

(2) Consequential damages resulting from the seller's breach include

(a) any loss resulting from general or particular requirements and needs of which the seller at the time of contracting had reason to know and which could not reasonably be prevented by cover or otherwise; and

(b) injury to person or property proximately resulting from any breach of warranty.

## § 2—716. Buyer's Right to Specific Performance or Replevin.

(1) Specific performance may be decreed where the goods are unique or in other proper circumstances.

(2) The decree for specific performance may include such terms and conditions as to payment of the price, damages, or other relief as the court may deem just.

(3) The buyer has a right of replevin for goods identified to the contract if after reasonable effort he is unable to effect cover for such goods or the circumstances reasonably indicate that such effort will be unavailing or if the goods have been shipped under reservation and satisfaction of the security interest in them has been made or tendered.

## § 2—717. Deduction of Damages From the Price.

The buyer on notifying the seller of his intention to do so may deduct all or any part of the damages resulting from any breach of the contract from any part of the price still due under the same contract.

## § 2—718. Liquidation or Limitation of Damages; Deposits.

(1) Damages for breach by either party may be liquidated in the agreement but only at an amount which is reasonable in the light of the anticipated or actual harm caused by the breach, the difficulties of proof of loss, and the inconvenience or nonfeasibility of otherwise obtaining an adequate remedy. A term fixing unreasonably large liquidated damages is void as a penalty.

(2) Where the seller justifiably withholds delivery of goods because of the buyer's breach, the buyer is entitled to restitution of any amount by which the sum of his payments exceeds

(a) the amount to which the seller is entitled by virtue of terms liquidating the seller's damages in accordance with subsection (1), or

(b) in the absence of such terms, twenty per cent of the value of the total performance for which the buyer is obligated under the contract or $500, whichever is smaller.

(3) The buyer's right to restitution under subsection (2) is subject to offset to the extent that the seller establishes

(a) a right to recover damages under the provisions of this Article other than subsection (1), and

(b) the amount or value of any benefits received by the buyer directly or indirectly by reason of the contract.

(4) Where a seller has received payment in goods their reasonable value or the proceeds of their resale shall be treated as payments for the purposes of subsection (2); but if the seller has notice of the buyer's breach before reselling goods received in part performance, his resale is subject to the conditions laid down in this Article on resale by an aggrieved seller (Section 2—706).

## § 2—719. Contractual Modification or Limitation of Remedy.

(1) Subject to the provisions of subsections (2) and (3) of this section and of the preceding section on liquidation and limitation of damages,

(a) the agreement may provide for remedies in addition to or in substitution for those provided in this Article and may limit or alter the measure of damages recoverable under this Article, as by limiting the buyer's remedies to return of the goods and repayment of the price or to repair and replacement of non-conforming goods or parts; and

(b) resort to a remedy as provided is optional unless the remedy is expressly agreed to be exclusive, in which case it is the sole remedy.

(2) Where circumstances cause an exclusive or limited remedy to fail of its essential purpose, remedy may be had as provided in this Act.

(3) Consequential damages may be limited or excluded unless the limitation or exclusion is unconscionable. Limitation of consequential damages for injury to the person in the case of consumer goods is prima facie unconscionable but limitation of damages where the loss is commercial is not.

## § 2—720. Effect of "Cancellation" or "Rescission" on Claims for Antecedent Breach.

Unless the contrary intention clearly appears, expressions of "cancellation" or "rescission" of the contract or the like shall not be construed as a renunciation or discharge of any claim in damages for an antecedent breach.

## § 2—721. Remedies for Fraud.

Remedies for material misrepresentation or fraud include all remedies available under this Article for non-fraudulent breach. Neither rescission or a claim for rescission of the contract for sale nor rejection or return of the goods shall bar or be deemed inconsistent with a claim for damages or other remedy.

## § 2—722. Who Can Sue Third Parties for Injury to Goods.

Where a third party so deals with goods which have been identified to a contract for sale as to cause actionable injury to a party to that contract

(a) a right of action against the third party is in either party to the contract for sale who has title to or a security interest or a special property or an insurable interest in the goods; and if the goods have been destroyed or converted a right of action is also in the party who either bore the risk of loss under the contract for sale or has since the injury assumed that risk as against the other;

(b) if at the time of the injury the party plaintiff did not bear the risk of loss as against the other party to the contract for sale and there is no arrangement between them for disposition of the recovery, his suit or settlement is, subject to his own interest, as a fiduciary for the other party to the contract;

(c) either party may with the consent of the other sue for the benefit of whom it may concern.

## § 2—723. Proof of Market Price: Time and Place.

(1) If an action based on anticipatory repudiation comes to trial before the time for performance with respect to some or all of the goods, any damages based on market price (Section 2—708 or Section 2—713) shall be determined according to the price of such goods prevailing at the time when the aggrieved party learned of the repudiation.

(2) If evidence of a price prevailing at the times or places described in this Article is not readily available the price prevailing within any reasonable time before or after the time described or at any other place which in commercial judgment or under usage of trade would serve as a reasonable substitute for the one described may be used, making any proper allowance for the cost of transporting the goods to or from such other place.

(3) Evidence of a relevant price prevailing at a time or place other than the one described in this Article offered by one party is not admissible unless and until he has given the other

party such notice as the court finds sufficient to prevent unfair surprise.

### § 2—724. Admissibility of Market Quotations.

Whenever the prevailing price or value of any goods regularly bought and sold in any established commodity market is in issue, reports in official publications or trade journals or in newspapers or periodicals of general circulation published as the reports of such market shall be admissible in evidence. The circumstances of the preparation of such a report may be shown to affect its weight but not its admissibility.

### § 2—725. Statute of Limitations in Contracts for Sale.

(1) An action for breach of any contract for sale must be commenced within four years after the cause of action has accrued. By the original agreement the parties may reduce the period of limitation to not less than one year but may not extend it.

(2) A cause of action accrues when the breach occurs, regardless of the aggrieved party's lack of knowledge of the breach. A breach of warranty occurs when tender of delivery is made, except that where a warranty explicitly extends to future performance of the goods and discovery of the breach must await the time of such performance the cause of action accrues when the breach is or should have been discovered.

(3) Where an action commenced within the time limited by subsection (1) is so terminated as to leave available a remedy by another action for the same breach such other action may be commenced after the expiration of the time limited and within six months after the termination of the first action unless the termination resulted from voluntary discontinuance or from dismissal for failure or neglect to prosecute.

(4) This section does not alter the law on tolling of the statute of limitations nor does it apply to causes of action which have accrued before this Act becomes effective.

# Article 2A
# LEASES

## Part 1  General Provisions

### § 2A—101. Short Title.

This Article shall be known and may be cited as the Uniform Commercial Code—Leases.

### § 2A—102. Scope.

This Article applies to any transaction, regardless of form, that creates a lease.

### § 2A—103. Definitions and Index of Definitions.

(1) In this Article unless the context otherwise requires:

(a) "Buyer in ordinary course of business" means a person who in good faith and without knowledge that the sale to him [or her] is in violation of the ownership rights or security interest or leasehold interest of a third party in the goods buys in ordinary course from a person in the business of selling goods of that kind but does not include a pawnbroker. "Buying" may be for cash or by exchange of other property or on secured or unsecured credit and includes receiving goods or documents of title under a pre-existing contract for sale but does not include a transfer in bulk or as security for or in total or partial satisfaction of a money debt.

(b) "Cancellation" occurs when either party puts an end to the lease contract for default by the other party.

(c) "Commercial unit" means such a unit of goods as by commercial usage is a single whole for purposes of lease and division of which materially impairs its character or value on the market or in use. A commercial unit may be a single article, as a machine, or a set of articles, as a suite of furniture or a line of machinery, or a quantity, as a gross or carload, or any other unit treated in use or in the relevant market as a single whole.

(d) "Conforming" goods or performance under a lease contract means goods or performance that are in accordance with the obligations under the lease contract.

(e) "Consumer lease" means a lease that a lessor regularly engaged in the business of leasing or selling makes to a lessee, except an organization, who takes under the lease primarily for a personal, family, or household purpose, if the total payments to be made under the lease contract, excluding payments for options to renew or buy, do not exceed $25,000.

(f) "Fault" means wrongful act, omission, breach, or default.

(g) "Finance lease" means a lease in which (i) the lessor does not select, manufacture or supply the goods, (ii) the lessor acquires the goods or the right to possession and use of the goods in connection with the lease, and (iii) either the lessee receives a copy of the contract evidencing the lessor's purchase of the goods on or before signing the lease contract, or the lessee's approval of the contract evidencing the lessor's purchase of the goods is a condition to effectiveness of the lease contract.

(h) "Goods" means all things that are movable at the time of identification to the lease contract, or are fixtures (Section 2A—309), but the term does not include money, documents, instruments, accounts, chattel paper, general intangibles, or minerals or the like, including oil and gas, before extraction. The term also includes the unborn young of animals.

(i) "Installment lease contract" means a lease contract that authorizes or requires the delivery of goods in separate lots to be separately accepted, even though the lease contract contains a clause "each delivery is a separate lease" or its equivalent.

(j) "Lease" means a transfer of the right to possession and use of goods for a term in return for consideration, but a sale, including a sale on approval or a sale or return, or retention or creation of a security interest is not a lease. Unless the context clearly indicates otherwise, the term includes a sublease.

(k) ''Lease agreement'' means the bargain, with respect to the lease, of the lessor and the lessee in fact as found in their language or by implication from other circumstances including course of dealing or usage of trade or course of performance as provided in this Article. Unless the context clearly indicates otherwise, the term includes a sublease agreement.

(l) ''Lease contract'' means the total legal obligation that results from the lease agreement as affected by this Article and any other applicable rules of law. Unless the context clearly indicates otherwise, the term includes a sublease contract.

(m) ''Leasehold interest'' means the interest of the lessor or the lessee under a lease contract.

(n) ''Lessee'' means a person who acquires the right to possession and use of goods under a lease. Unless the context clearly indicates otherwise, the term includes a sublessee.

(o) ''Lessee in ordinary course of business'' means a person who in good faith and without knowledge that the lease to him [or her] is in violation of the ownership rights or security interest or leasehold interest of a third party in the goods, leases in ordinary course from a person in the business of selling or leasing goods of that kind but does not include a pawnbroker. ''Leasing'' may be for cash or by exchange of other property or on secured or unsecured credit and includes receiving goods or documents of title under a pre-existing lease contract but does not include a transfer in bulk or as security for or in total or partial satisfaction of a money debt.

(p) ''Lessor'' means a person who transfers the right to possession and use of goods under a lease. Unless the context clearly indicates otherwise, the term includes a sublessor.

(q) ''Lessor's residual interest'' means the lessor's interest in the goods after expiration, termination, or cancellation of the lease contract.

(r) ''Lien'' means a charge against or interest in goods to secure payment of a debt or performance of an obligation, but the term does not include a security interest.

(s) ''Lot'' means a parcel or a single article that is the subject matter of a separate lease or delivery, whether or not it is sufficient to perform the lease contract.

(t) ''Merchant lessee'' means a lessee that is a merchant with respect to goods of the kind subject to the lease.

(u) ''Present value'' means the amount as of a date certain of one or more sums payable in the future, discounted to the date certain. The discount is determined by the interest rate specified by the parties if the rate was not manifestly unreasonable at the time the transaction was entered into; otherwise, the discount is determined by a commercially reasonable rate that takes into account the facts and circumstances of each case at the time the transaction was entered into.

(v) ''Purchase'' includes taking by sale, lease, mortgage, security interest, pledge, gift, or any other voluntary transaction creating an interest in goods.

(w) ''Sublease'' means a lease of goods the right to possession and use of which was acquired by the lessor as a lessee under an existing lease.

(x) ''Supplier'' means a person from whom a lessor buys or leases goods to be leased under a finance lease.

(y) ''Supply contract'' means a contract under which a lessor buys or leases goods to be leased.

(z) ''Termination'' occurs when either party pursuant to a power created by agreement or law puts an end to the lease contract otherwise than for default.

(2) Other definitions applying to this Article and the sections in which they appear are:

''Accessions''. Section 2A—310(1).
''Construction mortgage''. Section 2A—309(1)(d).
''Encumbrance''. Section 2A—309(1)(e).
''Fixtures''. Section 2A—309(1)(a).
''Fixture filing''. Section 2A—309(1)(b).
''Purchase money lease''. Section 2A—309(1)(c).

(3) The following definitions in other Articles apply to this Article:

''Accounts''. Section 9—106.
''Between merchants''. Section 2—104(3).
''Buyer''. Section 2—103(1)(a).
''Chattel paper''. Section 9—105(1)(b).
''Consumer goods''. Section 9—109(1).
''Documents''. Section 9—105(1)(f).
''Entrusting''. Section 2—403(3).
''General intangibles''. Section 9—106.
''Good faith''. Section 2—103(1)(b).
''Instruments''. Section 9—105(1)(i).
''Merchant''. Section 2—104(1).
''Mortgage''. Section 9—105(1)(j).
''Pursuant to commitment''. Section 9—105(1)(k).
''Receipt''. Section 2—103(1)(c).
''Sale''. Section 2—106(1).
''Sale on Approval''. Section 2—326.
''Sale or Return''. Section 2—326.
''Seller''. Section 2—103(1)(d).

(4) In addition Article 1 contains general definitions and principles of construction and interpretation applicable throughout this Article.

### § 2A—104. Leases Subject to Other Statutes.

(1) A lease, although subject to this Article, is also subject to any applicable:

(a) statute of the United States;

(b) certificate of title statute of this State: (list any certificate of title statutes covering automobiles, trailers, mobile homes, boats, farm tractors, and the like);

(c) certificate of title statute of another jurisdiction (Section 2A—105); or

(d) consumer protection statute of this State.

(2) In case of conflict between the provisions of this Article, other than Sections 2A—105, 2A—304(3) and 2A—305(3), and any statute referred to in subsection (1), the provisions of that statute control.

(3) Failure to comply with any applicable statute has only the effect specified therein.

### § 2A—105. Territorial Application of Article to Goods Covered by Certificate of Title.

Subject to the provisions of Sections 2A—304(3) and 2A—305(3), with respect to goods covered by a certificate of title issued under a statute of this State or of another jurisdiction, compliance and the effect of compliance or noncompliance with a certificate of title statute are governed by the law (including the conflict of laws rules) of the jurisdiction issuing the certificate until the earlier of (a) surrender of the certificate, or (b) four months after the goods are removed from that jurisdiction and thereafter until a new certificate of title is issued by another jurisdiction.

### § 2A—106. Limitation on Power of Parties to Consumer Lease to Choose Applicable Law and Judicial Forum.

(1) If the law chosen by the parties to a consumer lease is that of a jurisdiction other than a jurisdiction in which the lessee resides at the time the lease agreement becomes enforceable or within 30 days thereafter or in which the goods are to be used, the choice is not enforceable.

(2) If the judicial forum chosen by the parties to a consumer lease is a forum that would not otherwise have jurisdiction over the lessee, the choice is not enforceable.

### § 2A—107. Waiver or Renunciation of Claim or Right After Default.

Any claim or right arising out of an alleged default or breach of warranty may be discharged in whole or in part without consideration by a written waiver or renunciation signed and delivered by the aggrieved party.

### § 2A—108. Unconscionability.

(1) If the court as a matter of law finds a lease contract or any clause of a lease contract to have been unconscionable at the time it was made the court may refuse to enforce the lease contract, or it may enforce the remainder of the lease contract without the unconscionable clause, or it may so limit the application of any unconscionable clause as to avoid any unconscionable result.

(2) With respect to a consumer lease, if the court as a matter of law finds that a lease contract or any clause of a lease contract has been induced by unconscionable conduct or that unconscionable conduct has occurred in the collection of a claim arising from a lease contract, the court may grant appropriate relief.

(3) Before making a finding of unconscionability under subsection (1) or (2), the court, on its own motion or that of a party, shall afford the parties a reasonable opportunity to present evidence as to the setting, purpose, and effect of the lease contract or clause thereof, or of the conduct.

(4) In an action in which the lessee claims unconscionability with respect to a consumer lease:

(a) If the court finds unconscionability under subsection (1) or (2), the court shall award reasonable attorney's fees to the lessee.

(b) If the court does not find unconscionability and the lessee claiming unconscionability has brought or maintained an action he [or she] knew to be groundless, the court shall award reasonable attorney's fees to the party against whom the claim is made.

(c) In determining attorney's fees, the amount of the recovery on behalf of the claimant under subsections (1) and (2) is not controlling.

### § 2A—109. Option to Accelerate at Will.

(1) A term providing that one party or his [or her] successor in interest may accelerate payment or performance or require collateral or additional collateral "at will" or "when he [or she] deems himself [or herself] insecure" or in words of similar import must be construed to mean that he [or she] has power to do so only if he [or she] in good faith believes that the prospect of payment or performance is impaired.

(2) With respect to a consumer lease, the burden of establishing good faith under subsection (1) is on the party who exercised the power; otherwise the burden of establishing lack of good faith is on the party against whom the power has been exercised.

## Part 2   Formation and Construction of Lease Contract

### § 2A—201. Statute of Frauds.

(1) A lease contract is not enforceable by way of action or defense unless:

(a) the total payments to be made under the lease contract, excluding payments for options to renew or buy, are less than $1,000; or

(b) there is a writing, signed by the party against whom enforcement is sought or by that party's authorized agent, sufficient to indicate that a lease contract has been made between the parties and to describe the goods leased and the lease term.

(2) Any description of leased goods or of the lease term is sufficient and satisfies subsection (1)(b), whether or not it is specific, if it reasonably identifies what is described.

(3) A writing is not insufficient because it omits or incorrectly states a term agreed upon, but the lease contract is not enforceable under subsection (1)(b) beyond the lease term and the quantity of goods shown in this writing.

(4) A lease contract that does not satisfy the requirements of subsection (1), but which is valid in other respects, is enforceable:

(a) if the goods are to be specially manufactured or obtained for the lessee and are not suitable for lease or sale to others in the ordinary course of the lessor's business, and the lessor, before notice of repudiation is received and under circumstances that reasonably indicate that the goods are for the lessee, has made either a substantial beginning of their manufacture or commitments for their procurement;

(b) if the party against whom enforcement is sought admits in that party's pleading, testimony or otherwise in court that a lease contract was made, but the lease contract is not enforceable under this provision beyond the quantity of goods admitted; or

(c) with respect to goods that have been received and accepted by the lessee.

(5) The lease term under a lease contract referred to in subsection (4) is:

(a) if there is a writing signed by the party against whom enforcement is sought or by that party's authorized agent specifying the lease term, the term so specified;

(b) if the party against whom enforcement is sought admits in that party's pleading, testimony, or otherwise in court a lease term, the term so admitted; or

(c) a reasonable lease term.

### § 2A—202. Final Written Expression: Parol or Extrinsic Evidence.

Terms with respect to which the confirmatory memoranda of the parties agree or which are otherwise set forth in a writing intended by the parties as a final expression of their agreement with respect to such terms as are included therein may not be contradicted by evidence of any prior agreement or of a contemporaneous oral agreement but may be explained or supplemented:

(a) by course of dealing or usage of trade or by course of performance; and

(b) by evidence of consistent additional terms unless the court finds the writing to have been intended also as a complete and exclusive statement of the terms of the agreement.

### § 2A—203. Seals Inoperative.

The affixing of a seal to a writing evidencing a lease contract or an offer to enter into a lease contract does not render the writing a sealed instrument and the law with respect to sealed instruments does not apply to the lease contract or offer.

### § 2A—204. Formation in General.

(1) A lease contract may be made in any manner sufficient to show agreement, including conduct by both parties which recognizes the existence of a lease contract.

(2) An agreement sufficient to constitute a lease contract may be found although the moment of its making is undetermined.

(3) Although one or more terms are left open, a lease contract does not fail for indefiniteness if the parties have intended to make a lease contract and there is a reasonably certain basis for giving an appropriate remedy.

### § 2A—205. Firm Offers.

An offer by a merchant to lease goods to or from another person in a signed writing that by its terms gives assurance it will be held open is not revocable, for lack of consideration, during the time stated or, if no time is stated, for a reasonable time, but in no event may the period of irrevocability exceed 3 months. Any such term of assurance on a form supplied by the offeree must be separately signed by the offeror.

### § 2A—206. Offer and Acceptance in Formation of Lease Contract.

(1) Unless otherwise unambiguously indicated by the language or circumstances, an offer to make a lease contract must be construed as inviting acceptance in any manner and by any medium reasonable in the circumstances.

(2) If the beginning of a requested performance is a reasonable mode of acceptance, an offeror who is not notified of acceptance within a reasonable time may treat the offer as having lapsed before acceptance.

### § 2A—207. Course of Performance or Practical Construction.

(1) If a lease contract involves repeated occasions for performance by either party with knowledge of the nature of the performance and opportunity for objection to it by the other, any course of performance accepted or acquiesced in without objection is relevant to determine the meaning of the lease agreement.

(2) The express terms of a lease agreement and any course of performance, as well as any course of dealing and usage of trade, must be construed whenever reasonable as consistent with each other; but if that construction is unreasonable, express terms control course of performance, course of performance controls both course of dealing and usage of trade, and course of dealing controls usage of trade.

(3) Subject to the provisions of Section 2A—208 on modification and waiver, course of performance is relevant to show a waiver or modification of any term inconsistent with the course of performance.

### § 2A—208. Modification, Rescission and Waiver.

(1) An agreement modifying a lease contract needs no consideration to be binding.

(2) A signed lease agreement that excludes modification or rescission except by a signed writing may not be otherwise modified or rescinded, but, except as between merchants, such a requirement on a form supplied by a merchant must be separately signed by the other party.

(3) Although an attempt at modification or rescission does not satisfy the requirements of subsection (2), it may operate as a waiver.

(4) A party who has made a waiver affecting an executory portion of a lease contract may retract the waiver by reasonable notification received by the other party that strict performance will be required of any term waived, unless the retraction would be unjust in view of a material change of position in reliance on the waiver.

## § 2A—209. Lessee under Finance Lease as Beneficiary of Supply Contract.

(1) The benefit of the supplier's promises to the lessor under the supply contract and of all warranties, whether express or implied, under the supply contract, extends to the lessee to the extent of the lessee's leasehold interest under a finance lease related to the supply contract, but subject to the terms of the supply contract and all of the supplier's defenses or claims arising therefrom.

(2) The extension of the benefit of the supplier's promises to the lessee does not: (a) modify the rights and obligations of the parties to the supply contract, whether arising therefrom or otherwise, or (b) impose any duty or liability under the supply contract on the lessee.

(3) Any modification or rescission of the supply contract by the supplier and the lessor is effective against the lessee unless, prior to the modification or rescission, the supplier has received notice that the lessee has entered into a finance lease related to the supply contract. If the supply contract is modified or rescinded after the lessee enters the finance lease, the lessee has a cause of action against the lessor, and against the supplier if the supplier has notice of the lessee's entering the finance lease when the supply contract is modified or rescinded. The lessee's recovery from such action shall put the lessee in as good a position as if the modification or rescission had not occurred.

## § 2A—210. Express Warranties.

(1) Express warranties by the lessor are created as follows:

(a) Any affirmation of fact or promise made by the lessor to the lessee which relates to the goods and becomes part of the basis of the bargain creates an express warranty that the goods will conform to the affirmation or promise.

(b) Any description of the goods which is made part of the basis of the bargain creates an express warranty that the goods will conform to the description.

(c) Any sample or model that is made part of the basis of the bargain creates an express warranty that the whole of the goods will conform to the sample or model.

(2) It is not necessary to the creation of an express warranty that the lessor use formal words, such as ''warrant'' or ''guarantee,'' or that the lessor have a specific intention to make a warranty, but an affirmation merely of the value of the goods or a statement purporting to be merely the lessor's opinion or commendation of the goods does not create a warranty.

## § 2A—211. Warranties Against Interference and Against Infringement; Lessee's Obligation Against Infringement.

(1) There is in a lease contract a warranty that for the lease term no person holds a claim to or interest in the goods that arose from an act or omission of the lessor, other than a claim by way of infringement or the like, which will interfere with the lessee's enjoyment of its leasehold interest.

(2) Except in a finance lease there is in a lease contract by a lessor who is a merchant regularly dealing in goods of the kind a warranty that the goods are delivered free of the rightful claim of any person by way of infringement or the like.

(3) A lessee who furnishes specifications to a lessor or a supplier shall hold the lessor and the supplier harmless against any claim by way of infringement or the like that arises out of compliance with the specifications.

## § 2A—212. Implied Warranty of Merchantability.

(1) Except in a finance lease, a warranty that the goods will be merchantable is implied in a lease contract if the lessor is a merchant with respect to goods of that kind.

(2) Goods to be merchantable must be at least such as

(a) pass without objection in the trade under the description in the lease agreement;

(b) in the case of fungible goods, are of fair average quality within the description;

(c) are fit for the ordinary purposes for which goods of that type are used;

(d) run, within the variation permitted by the lease agreement, of even kind, quality, and quantity within each unit and among all units involved;

(e) are adequately contained, packaged, and labeled as the lease agreement may require; and

(f) conform to any promises or affirmations of fact made on the container or label.

(3) Other implied warranties may arise from course of dealing or usage of trade.

## § 2A—213. Implied Warranty of Fitness for Particular Purpose.

Except in a finance of lease, if the lessor at the time the lease contract is made has reason to know of any particular purpose for which the goods are required and that the lessee is relying on the lessor's skill or judgment to select or furnish suitable goods, there is in the lease contract an implied warranty that the goods will be fit for that purpose.

## § 2A—214. Exclusion or Modification of Warranties.

(1) Words or conduct relevant to the creation of an express warranty and words or conduct tending to negate or limit a warranty must be construed wherever reasonable as consistent with each other; but, subject to the provisions of Section 2A—202 on parol or extrinsic evidence, negation or limitation is inoperative to the extent that the construction is unreasonable.

(2) Subject to subsection (3), to exclude or modify the implied warranty of merchantability or any part of it the language must mention ''merchantability'', be by a writing, and be conspicuous. Subject to subsection (3), to exclude or modify any implied warranty of fitness the exclusion must be by a writing and be conspicuous. Language to exclude all implied warranties of fitness is sufficient if it is conspicuous and states, for example, ''There is no warranty that the goods will be fit for a particular purpose''.

(3) Notwithstanding subsection (2), but subject to subsection (4),

(a) unless the circumstances indicate otherwise, all implied warranties are excluded by expressions like ''as is'' or ''with all faults'' or by other language that in common understanding calls the lessee's attention to the exclusion of warranties and makes plain that there is no implied warranty, and is conspicuous;

(b) if the lessee before entering into the lease contract has examined the goods or the sample or model as fully as desired or has refused to examine the goods, there is no implied warranty with regard to defects that an examination ought in the circumstances to have revealed; and

(c) an implied warranty may also be excluded or modified by course of dealing, course of performance, or usage of trade.

(4) To exclude or modify a warranty against interference or against infringement (Section 2A—211) or any part of it, the language must be specific, be by a writing, and be conspicuous, unless the circumstances, including course of performance, course of dealing, or usage of trade, give the lessee reason to know that the goods are being leased subject to a claim or interest of any person.

## § 2A—215. Cumulation and Conflict of Warranties Express or Implied.

Warranties, whether express or implied, must be construed as consistent with each other and as cumulative, but if that construction is unreasonable, the intention of the parties determines which warranty is dominant. In ascertaining that intention the following rules apply:

(a) Exact or technical specifications displace an inconsistent sample or model or general language of description.

(b) A sample from an existing bulk displaces inconsistent general language of description.

(c) Express warranties displace inconsistent implied warranties other than an implied warranty of fitness for a particular purpose.

## § 2A—216. Third-Party Beneficiaries of Express and Implied Warranties.

### Alternative A

A warranty to or for the benefit of a lessee under this Article, whether express or implied, extends to any natural person who is in the family or household of the lessee or who is a guest in the lessee's home if it is reasonable to expect that such person may use, consume, or be affected by the goods and who is injured in person by breach of the warranty. This section does not displace principles of law and equity that extend a warranty to or for the benefit of a lessee to other persons. The operation of this section may not be excluded, modified, or limited, but an exclusion, modification, or limitation of the warranty, including any with respect to rights

and remedies, effective against the lessee is also effective against any beneficiary designated under this section.

### Alternative B

A warranty to or for the benefit of a lessee under this Article, whether express or implied, extends to any natural person who may reasonably be expected to use, consume, or be affected by the goods and who is injured in person by breach of the warranty. This section does not displace principles of law and equity that extend a warranty to or for the benefit of a lessee to other persons. The operation of this section may not be excluded, modified, or limited, but an exclusion, modification, or limitation of the warranty, including any with respect to rights and remedies, effective against the lessee is also effective against the beneficiary designated under this section.

### Alternative C

A warranty to or for the benefit of a lessee under this Article, whether express or implied, extends to any person who may reasonably be expected to use, consume, or be affected by the goods and who is injured by breach of the warranty. The operation of this section may not be excluded, modified, or limited with respect to injury to the person of an individual to whom the warranty extends, but an exclusion, modification, or limitation of the warranty, including any with respect to rights and remedies, effective against the lessee is also effective against the beneficiary designated under this section.

## § 2A—217. Identification.

Identification of goods as goods to which a lease contract refers may be made at any time and in any manner explicitly agreed to by the parties. In the absence of explicit agreement, identification occurs:

(a) when the lease contract is made if the lease contract is for a lease of goods that are existing and identified;

(b) when the goods are shipped, marked, or otherwise designated by the lessor as goods to which the lease contract refers, if the lease contract is for a lease of goods that are not existing and identified; or

(c) when the young are conceived, if the lease contract is for a lease of unborn young of animals.

## § 2A—218. Insurance and Proceeds.

(1) A lessee obtains an insurable interest when existing goods are identified to the lease contract even though the goods identified are nonconforming and the lessee has an option to reject them.

(2) If a lessee has an insurable interest only by reason of the lessor's identification of the goods, the lessor, until default or insolvency or notification to the lessee that identification is final, may substitute other goods for those identified.

(3) Notwithstanding a lessee's insurable interest under subsections (1) and (2), the lessor retains an insurable interest until an option to buy has been exercised by the lessee and risk of loss has passed to the lessee.

(4) Nothing in this section impairs any insurable interest recognized under any other statute or rule of law.

(5) The parties by agreement may determine that one or more parties have an obligation to obtain and pay for insurance covering the goods and by agreement may determine the beneficiary of the proceeds of the insurance.

### § 2A—219. Risk of Loss.

(1) Except in the case of a finance lease, risk of loss is retained by the lessor and does not pass to the lessee. In the case of a finance lease, risk of loss passes to the lessee.

(2) Subject to the provisions of this Article on the effect of default on risk of loss (Section 2A—220), if risk of loss is to pass to the lessee and the time of passage is not stated, the following rules apply:

> (a) If the lease contract requires or authorizes the goods to be shipped by carrier.
>
>> (i) and it does not require delivery at a particular destination, the risk of loss passes to the lessee when the goods are duly delivered to the carrier; but
>>
>> (ii) if it does require delivery at a particular destination and the goods are there duly tendered while in the possession of the carrier, the risk of loss passes to the lessee when the goods are there duly so tendered as to enable the lessee to take delivery.
>
> (b) If the goods are held by a bailee to be delivered without being moved, the risk of loss passes to the lessee on acknowledgment by the bailee of the lessee's right to possession of the goods.
>
> (c) In any case not within subsection (a) or (b), the risk of loss passes to the lessee on the lessee's receipt of the goods if the lessor, or, in the case of a finance lease, the supplier, is a merchant; otherwise the risk passes to the lessee on tender of delivery.

### § 2A—220. Effect of Default on Risk of Loss.

(1) Where risk of loss is to pass to the lessee and the time of passage is not stated:

> (a) If a tender or delivery of goods so fails to conform to the lease contract as to give a right of rejection, the risk of their loss remains with the lessor, or, in the case of a finance lease, the supplier, until cure or acceptance.
>
> (b) If the lessee rightfully revokes acceptance, he [or she], to the extent of any deficiency in his [or her] effective insurance coverage, may treat the risk of loss as having remained with the lessor from the beginning.

(2) Whether or not risk of loss is to pass to the lessee, if the lessee as to conforming goods already identified to a lease contract repudiates or is otherwise in default under the lease contract, the lessor, or, in the case of a finance lease, the supplier, to the extent of any deficiency in his [or her] effective insurance coverage may treat the risk of loss as resting on the lessee for a commercially reasonable time.

### § 2A—221. Casualty to Identified Goods.

If a lease contract requires goods identified when the lease contract is made, and the goods suffer casualty without fault of the lessee, the lessor or the supplier before delivery, or the goods suffer casualty before risk of loss passes to the lessee pursuant to the lease agreement or Section 2A—219, then:

(a) if the loss is total, the lease contract is avoided; and

(b) if the loss is partial or the goods have so deteriorated as to no longer conform to the lease contract, the lessee may nevertheless demand inspection and at his [or her] option either treat the lease contract as avoided or, except in a finance lease that is not a consumer lease, accept the goods with due allowance from the rent payable for the balance of the lease term for the deterioration or the deficiency in quantity but without further right against the lessor.

## Part 3 Effect Of Lease Contract

### § 2A—301. Enforceability of Lease Contract.

Except as otherwise provided in this Article, a lease contract is effective and enforceable according to its terms between the parties, against purchasers of the goods and against creditors of the parties.

### § 2A—302. Title to and Possession of Goods.

Except as otherwise provided in this Article, each provision of this Article applies whether the lessor or a third party has title to the goods, and whether the lessor, the lessee, or a third party has possession of the goods, notwithstanding any statute or rule of law that possession or the absence of possession is fraudulent.

### § 2A—303. Alienability of Party's Interest Under Lease Contract or of Lessor's Residual Interest in Goods; Delegation of Performance; Assignment of Rights.

(1) Any interest of a party under a lease contract and the lessor's residual interest in the goods may be transferred unless

> (a) the transfer is voluntary and the lease contract prohibits the transfer; or
>
> (b) the transfer materially changes the duty of or materially increases the burden or risk imposed on the other party to the lease contract, and within a reasonable time after notice of the transfer the other party demands that the transferee comply with subsection (2) and the transferee fails to comply.

(2) Within a reasonable time after demand pursuant to subsection (1)(b), the transferee shall:

> (a) cure or provide adequate assurance that he [or she] will promptly cure any default other than one arising from the transfer;
>
> (b) compensate or provide adequate assurance that he [or she] will promptly compensate the other party to the lease contract and any other person holding an interest in the lease contract, except the party whose interest is being transferred, for any loss to that party resulting from the transfer;

(c) provide adequate assurance of future due performance under the lease contract; and

(d) assume the lease contract.

(3) Demand pursuant to subsection (1)(b) is without prejudice to the other party's rights against the transferee and the party whose interest is transferred.

(4) An assignment of "the lease" or of "all my rights under the lease" or an assignment in similar general terms is a transfer of rights, and unless the language or the circumstances, as in an assignment for security, indicate the contrary, the assignment is a delegation of duties by the assignor to the assignee and acceptance by the assignee constitutes a promise by him [or her] to perform those duties. This promise is enforceable by either the assignor or the other party to the lease contract.

(5) Unless otherwise agreed by the lessor and the lessee, no delegation of performance relieves the assignor as against the other party of any duty to perform or any liability for default.

(6) A right to damages for default with respect to the whole lease contract or a right arising out of the assignor's due performance of his [or her] entire obligation can be assigned despite agreement otherwise.

(7) To prohibit the transfer of an interest of a party under a lease contract, the language of prohibition must be specific, by a writing, and conspicuous.

### § 2A—304. Subsequent Lease of Goods by Lessor.

(1) Subject to the provisions of Section 2A—303, a subsequent lessee from a lessor of goods under an existing lease contract obtains, to the extent of the leasehold interest transferred, the leasehold interest in the goods that the lessor had or had power to transfer, and except as provided in subsection (2) and Section 2A—527(4), takes subject to the existing lease contract. A lessor with voidable title has power to transfer a good leasehold interest to a good faith subsequent lessee for value, but only to the extent set forth in the preceding sentence. When goods have been delivered under a transaction of purchase the lessor has that power even though:

(a) the lessor's transferor was deceived as to the identity of the lessor;

(b) the delivery was in exchange for a check which is later dishonored;

(c) it was agreed that the transaction was to be a "cash sale"; or

(d) the delivery was procured through fraud punishable as larcenous under the criminal law.

(2) A subsequent lessee in the ordinary course of business from a lessor who is a merchant dealing in goods of that kind to whom the goods were entrusted by the existing lessee before the interest of the subsequent lessee became enforceable against the lessor obtains, to the extent of the leasehold interest transferred, all of the lessor's and the existing lessee's rights to the goods, and takes free of the existing lease contract.

(3) A subsequent lessee from the lessor of goods that are subject to an existing lease contract and are covered by a certificate of title issued under a statute of this State or of another jurisdiction takes no greater rights than those provided both by this section and by the certificate of title statute.

### § 2A—305. Sale or Sublease of Goods by Lessee.

(1) Subject to the provisions of Section 2A—303, a buyer or sublessee from the lessee of goods under an existing lease contract obtains, to the extent of the interest transferred, the leasehold interest in the goods that the lessee had or had power to transfer, and except as provided in subsection (2) and Section 2A—511(4), takes subject to the existing lease contract. A lessee with a voidable leasehold interest has power to transfer a good leasehold interest to a good faith buyer for value or a good faith sublessee for value, but only to the extent set forth in the preceding sentence. When goods have been delivered under a transaction of lease the lessee has that power even though:

(a) the lessor was deceived as to the identity of the lessee;

(b) the delivery was in exchange for a check which is later dishonored; or

(c) the delivery was procured through fraud punishable as larcenous under the criminal law.

(2) A buyer in the ordinary course of business or a sublessee in the ordinary course of business from a lessee who is a merchant dealing in goods of that kind to whom the goods were entrusted by the lessor obtains, to the extent of the interest transferred, all of the lessor's and lessee's rights to the goods, and takes free of the existing lease contract.

(3) A buyer or sublessee from the lessee of goods that are subject to an existing lease contract and are covered by a certificate of title issued under a statute of this State or of another jurisdiction takes no greater rights than those provided both by this section and by the certificate of title statute.

### § 2A—306. Priority of Certain Liens Arising by Operation of Law.

If a person in the ordinary course of his [or her] business furnishes services or materials with respect to goods subject to a lease contract, a lien upon those goods in the possession of that person given by statute or rule of law for those materials or services takes priority over any interest of the lessor or lessee under the lease contract or this Article unless the lien is created by statute and the statute provides otherwise or unless the lien is created by rule of law and the rule of law provides otherwise.

### § 2A—307. Priority of Liens Arising by Attachment or Levy on, Security Interests in, and Other Claims to Goods.

(1) Except as otherwise provided in Section 2A—306, a creditor of a lessee takes subject to the lease contract.

(2) Except as otherwise provided in subsections (3) and (4) of this section and in Sections 2A—306 and 2A—308, a creditor of a lessor takes subject to the lease contract:

(a) unless the creditor holds a lien that attached to the

goods before the lease contract became enforceable, or

(b) unless the creditor holds a security interest in the goods that under the Article on Secured Transactions (Article 9) would have priority over any other security interest in the goods perfected by a filing covering the goods and made at the time the lease contract became enforceable, whether or not any other security interest existed.

(3) A lessee in the ordinary course of business takes the leasehold interest free of a security interest in the goods created by the lessor even though the security interest is perfected and the lessee knows of its existence.

(4) A lessee other than a lessee in the ordinary course of business takes the leasehold interest free of a security interest to the extent that it secures future advances made after the secured party acquires knowledge of the lease or more than 45 days after the lease contract becomes enforceable, whichever first occurs, unless the future advances are made pursuant to a commitment entered into without knowledge of the lease and before the expiration of the 45-day period.

## § 2A—308. Special Rights of Creditors.

(1) A creditor of a lessor in possession of goods subject to a lease contract may treat the lease contract as void if as against the creditor retention of possession by the lessor is fraudulent under any statute or rule of law, but retention of possession in good faith and current course of trade by the lessor for a commercially reasonable time after the lease contract becomes enforceable is not fraudulent.

(2) Nothing in this Article impairs the rights of creditors of a lessor if the lease contract (a) becomes enforceable, not in current course of trade but in satisfaction of or as security for a pre-existing claim for money, security, or the like, and (b) is made under circumstances which under any statute or rule of law apart from this Article would constitute the transaction a fraudulent transfer or voidable preference.

(3) A creditor of a seller may treat a sale or an identification of goods to a contract for sale as void if as against the creditor retention of possession by the seller is fraudulent under any statute or rule of law, but retention of possession of the goods pursuant to a lease contract entered into by the seller as lessee and the buyer as lessor in connection with the sale or identification of the goods is not fraudulent if the buyer bought for value and in good faith.

## § 2A—309. Lessor's and Lessee's Rights When Goods Become Fixtures.

(1) In this section:

(a) goods are "fixtures" when they become so related to particular real estate that an interest in them arises under real estate law;

(b) a "fixture filing" is the filing, in the office where a mortgage on the real estate would be recorded or registered, of a financing statement concerning goods that are or are to become fixtures and conforming to the requirements of subsection (5) of Section 9—402;

(c) a lease is a "purchase money lease" unless the lessee has possession or use of the goods or the right to possession or use of the goods before the lease agreement is enforceable;

(d) a mortgage is a "construction mortgage" to the extent it secures an obligation incurred for the construction of an improvement on land including the acquisition cost of the land, if the recorded writing so indicates; and

(e) "encumbrance" includes real estate mortgages and other liens on real estate and all other rights in real estate that are not ownership interests.

(2) Under this Article a lease may be of goods that are fixtures or may continue in goods that become fixtures, but no lease exists under this Article of ordinary building materials incorporated into an improvement on land.

(3) This Article does not prevent creation of a lease of fixtures pursuant to real estate law.

(4) The perfected interest of a lessor of fixtures has priority over a conflicting interest of an encumbrancer or owner of the real estate if:

(a) the lease is a purchase money lease, the conflicting interest of the encumbrancer or owner arises before the goods become fixtures, the interest of the lessor is perfected by a fixture filing before the goods become fixtures or within ten days thereafter, and the lessee has an interest of record in the real estate or is in possession of the real estate; or

(b) the interest of the lessor is perfected by a fixture filing before the interest of the encumbrancer or owner is of record, the lessor's interest has priority over any conflicting interest of a predecessor in title of the encumbrancer or owner, and the lessee has an interest of record in the real estate or is in possession of the real estate.

(5) The interest of a lessor of fixtures, whether or not perfected, has priority over the conflicting interest of an encumbrancer or owner of the real estate if:

(a) the fixtures are readily removable factory or office machines, readily removable equipment that is not primarily used or leased for use in the operation of the real estate, or readily removable replacements of domestic appliances that are goods subject to a consumer lease, and before the goods become fixtures the lease contract is enforceable; or

(b) the conflicting interest is a lien on the real estate obtained by legal or equitable proceedings after the lease contract is enforceable; or

(c) the encumbrancer or owner has consented in writing to the lease or has disclaimed an interest in the goods as fixtures; or

(d) the lessee has a right to remove the goods as against the encumbrancer or owner. If the lessee's right to remove terminates, the priority of the interest of the lessor continues for a reasonable time.

(6) Notwithstanding paragraph (a) of subsection (4) but oth-

erwise subject to subsections (4) and (5), the interest of a lessor of fixtures is subordinate to the conflicting interest of an encumbrancer of the real estate under a construction mortgage recorded before the goods become fixtures if the goods become fixtures before the completion of the construction. To the extent given to refinance a construction mortgage, the conflicting interest of an encumbrancer of the real estate under a mortgage has this priority to the same extent as the encumbrancer of the real estate under the construction mortgage.

(7) In cases not within the preceding subsections, priority between the interest of a lessor of fixtures and the conflicting interest of an encumbrancer or owner of the real estate who is not the lessee is determined by the priority rules governing conflicting interests in real estate.

(8) If the interest of a lessor has priority over all conflicting interests of all owners and encumbrancers of the real estate, the lessor or the lessee may (a) on default, expiration, termination, or cancellation of the lease agreement by the other party but subject to the provisions of the lease agreement and this Article, or (b) if necessary to enforce his [or her] other rights and remedies under this Article, remove the goods from the real estate, free and clear of all conflicting interests of all owners and encumbrancers of the real estate, but he [or she] must reimburse any encumbrancer or owner of the real estate who is not the lessee and who has not otherwise agreed for the cost of repair of any physical injury, but not for any diminution in value of the real estate caused by the absence of the goods removed or by any necessity of replacing them. A person entitled to reimbursement may refuse permission to remove until the party seeking removal gives adequate security for the performance of this obligation.

(9) Even though the lease agreement does not create a security interest, the interest of a lessor of fixtures is perfected by filing a financing statement as a fixture filing for leased goods that are or are to become fixtures in accordance with the relevant provisions of the Article on Secured Transactions (Article 9).

### § 2A—310. Lessor's and Lessee's Rights When Goods Become Accessions.

(1) Goods are ''accessions'' when they are installed in or affixed to other goods.

(2) The interest of a lessor or a lessee under a lease contract entered into before the goods became accessions is superior to all interests in the whole except as stated in subsection (4).

(3) The interest of a lessor or a lessee under a lease contract entered into at the time or after the goods became accessions is superior to all subsequently acquired interests in the whole except as stated in subsection (4) but is subordinate to interests in the whole existing at the time the lease contract was made unless the holders of such interests in the whole have in writing consented to the lease or disclaimed an interest in the goods as part of the whole.

(4) The interest of a lessor or a lessee under a lease contract described in subsection (2) or (3) is subordinate to the interest of

(a) a buyer in the ordinary course of business or a lessee in the ordinary course of business of any interest in the whole acquired after the goods became accessions; or

(b) a creditor with a security interest in the whole perfected before the lease contract was made to the extent that the creditor makes subsequent advances without knowledge of the lease contract.

(5) When under subsections (2) or (3) and (4) a lessor or a lessee of accessions holds an interest that is superior to all interests in the whole, the lessor or the lessee may (a) on default, expiration, termination, or cancellation of the lease contract by the other party but subject to the provisions of the lease contract and this Article, or (b) if necessary to enforce his [or her] other rights and remedies under this Article, remove the goods from the whole, free and clear of all interests in the whole, but he [or she] must reimburse any holder of an interest in the whole who is not the lessee and who has not otherwise agreed for the cost of repair of any physical injury but not for any diminution in value of the whole caused by the absence of the goods removed or by any necessity for replacing them. A person entitled to reimbursement may refuse permission to remove until the party seeking removal gives adequate security for the performance of this obligation.

## Part 4 Performance Of Lease Contract: Repudiated, Substituted And Excused

### § 2A—401. Insecurity: Adequate Assurance of Performance.

(1) A lease contract imposes an obligation on each party that the other's expectation of receiving due performance will not be impaired.

(2) If reasonable grounds for insecurity arise with respect to the performance of either party, the insecure party may demand in writing adequate assurance of due performance. Until the insecure party receives that assurance, if commercially reasonable the insecure party may suspend any performance for which he [or she] has not already received the agreed return.

(3) A repudiation of the lease contract occurs if assurance of due performance adequate under the circumstances of the particular case is not provided to the insecure party within a reasonable time, not to exceed 30 days after receipt of a demand by the other party.

(4) Between merchants, the reasonableness of grounds for insecurity and the adequacy of any assurance offered must be determined according to commercial standards.

(5) Acceptance of any nonconforming delivery or payment does not prejudice the aggrieved party's right to demand adequate assurance of future performance.

### § 2A—402. Anticipatory Repudiation.

If either party repudiates a lease contract with respect to a performance not yet due under the lease contract, the loss of which performance will substantially impair the value of the lease contract to the other, the aggrieved party may:

(a) for a commercially reasonable time, await retraction of repudiation and performance by the repudiating party;

(b) make demand pursuant to Section 2A—401 and await assurance of future performance adequate under the circumstances of the particular case; or

(c) resort to any right or remedy upon default under the lease contract or this Article, even though the aggrieved party has notified the repudiating party that the aggrieved party would await the repudiating party's performance and assurance and has urged retraction. In addition, whether or not the aggrieved party is pursuing one of the foregoing remedies, the aggrieved party may suspend performance or, if the aggrieved party is the lessor, proceed in accordance with the provisions of this Article on the lessor's right to identify goods to the lease contract notwithstanding default or to salvage unfinished goods (Section 2A—524).

### § 2A—403. Retraction of Anticipatory Repudiation.

(1) Until the repudiating party's next performance is due, the repudiating party can retract the repudiation unless, since the repudiation, the aggrieved party has cancelled the lease contract or materially changed the aggrieved party's position or otherwise indicated that the aggrieved party considers the repudiation final.

(2) Retraction may be by any method that clearly indicates to the aggrieved party that the repudiating party intends to perform under the lease contract and includes any assurance demanded under Section 2A—401.

(3) Retraction reinstates a repudiating party's rights under a lease contract with due excuse and allowance to the aggrieved party for any delay occasioned by the repudiation.

### § 2A—404. Substituted Performance.

(1) If without fault of the lessee, the lessor and the supplier, the agreed berthing, loading, or unloading facilities fail or the agreed type of carrier becomes unavailable or the agreed manner of delivery otherwise becomes commercially impracticable, but a commercially reasonable substitute is available, the substitute performance must be tendered and accepted.

(2) If the agreed means or manner of payment fails because of domestic or foreign governmental regulation:

   (a) the lessor may withhold or stop delivery or cause the supplier to withhold or stop delivery unless the lessee provides a means or manner of payment that is commercially a substantial equivalent; and

   (b) if delivery has already been taken, payment by the means or in the manner provided by the regulation discharges the lessee's obligation unless the regulation is discriminatory, oppressive, or predatory.

### § 2A—405. Excused Performance.

Subject to Section 2A—404 on substituted performance, the following rules apply:

(a) Delay in delivery or nondelivery in whole or in part by a lessor or a supplier who complies with paragraphs (b) and (c) is not a default under the lease contract if performance as agreed has been made impracticable by the occurrence of a contingency the nonoccurrence of which was a basic assumption on which the lease contract was made or by compliance in good faith with any applicable foreign or domestic governmental regulation or order, whether or not the regulation or order later proves to be invalid.

(b) If the causes mentioned in paragraph (a) affect only part of the lessor's or the supplier's capacity to perform, he [or she] shall allocate production and deliveries among his [or her] customers but at his [or her] option may include regular customers not then under contract for sale or lease as well as his [or her] own requirements for further manufacture. He [or she] may so allocate in any manner that is fair and reasonable.

(c) The lessor seasonably shall notify the lessee and in the case of a finance lease the supplier seasonably shall notify the lessor and the lessee, if known, that there will be delay or nondelivery and, if allocation is required under paragraph (b), of the estimated quota thus made available for the lessee.

### § 2A—406. Procedure on Excused Performance.

(1) If the lessee receives notification of a material or indefinite delay or an allocation justified under Section 2A—405, the lessee may by written notification to the lessor as to any goods involved, and with respect to all of the goods if under an installment lease contract the value of the whole lease contract is substantially impaired (Section 2A—510):

   (a) terminate the lease contract (Section 2A—505(2)); or

   (b) except in a finance lease that is not a consumer lease, modify the lease contract by accepting the available quota in substitution, with due allowance from the rent payable for the balance of the lease term for the deficiency but without further right against the lessor.

(2) If, after receipt of a notification from the lessor under Section 2A—405, the lessee fails so to modify the lease agreement within a reasonable time not exceeding 30 days, the lease contract lapses with respect to any deliveries affected.

### § 2A—407. Irrevocable Promises: Finance Leases.

(1) In the case of a finance lease that is not a consumer lease the lessee's promises under the lease contract become irrevocable and independent upon the lessee's acceptance of the goods.

(2) A promise that has become irrevocable and independent under subsection (1):

   (a) is effective and enforceable between the parties or against third parties including assignees of the parties, and

   (b) is not subject to cancellation, termination, modification, repudiation, excuse, or substitution without the consent of the party to whom the promise runs.

## Part 5 Default
## A. In General

### § 2A—501. Default: Procedure.

(1) Whether the lessor or the lessee is in default under a lease contract is determined by the lease agreement and this Article.

(2) If the lessor or the lessee is in default under the lease contract, the party seeking enforcement has rights and remedies as provided in this Article and, except as limited by this Article, as provided in the lease agreement.

(3) If the lessor or the lessee is in default under the lease contract, the party seeking enforcement may reduce the party's claim to judgment, or otherwise enforce the lease contract by self-help or any available judicial procedure or nonjudicial procedure, including administrative proceeding, arbitration, or the like, in accordance with this Article.

(4) Except as otherwise provided in this Article or the lease agreement, the rights and remedies referred to in subsections (2) and (3) are cumulative.

(5) If the lease agreement covers both real property and goods, the party seeking enforcement may proceed under this Part as to the goods, or under other applicable law as to both the real property and the goods in accordance with his [or her] rights and remedies in respect of the real property, in which case this Part does not apply.

### § 2A—502. Notice After Default.

Except as otherwise provided in this Article or the lease agreement, the lessor or lessee in default under the lease contract is not entitled to notice of default or notice of enforcement from the other party to the lease agreement.

### § 2A—503. Modification or Impairment of Rights and Remedies.

(1) Except as otherwise provided in this Article, the lease agreement may include rights and remedies for default in addition to or in substitution for those provided in this Article and may limit or alter the measure of damages recoverable under this Article.

(2) Resort to a remedy provided under this Article or in the lease agreement is optional unless the remedy is expressly agreed to be exclusive. If circumstances cause an exclusive or limited remedy to fail of its essential purpose, or provision for an exclusive remedy is unconscionable, remedy may be had as provided in this Article.

(3) Consequential damages may be liquidated under Section 2A—504, or may otherwise be limited, altered, or excluded unless the limitation, alteration, or exclusion is unconscionable. Limitation of consequential damages for injury to the person in the case of consumer goods is prima facie unconscionable but limitation of damages where the loss is commercial is not.

(4) Rights and remedies on default by the lessor or the lessee with respect to any obligation or promise collateral or ancillary to the lease contract are not impaired by this Article.

### § 2A—504. Liquidation of Damages.

(1) Damages payable by either party for default, or any other act or omission, including indemnity for loss or diminution of anticipated tax benefits or loss or damage to lessor's residual interest, may be liquidated in the lease agreement but only at an amount or by a formula that is reasonable in light of the then anticipated harm caused by the default or other act or omission.

(2) If the lease agreement provides for liquidation of damages, and such provision does not comply with subsection (1), or such provision is an exclusive or limited remedy that circumstances cause to fail of its essential purpose, remedy may be had as provided in this Article.

(3) If the lessor justifiably withholds or stops delivery of goods because of the lessee's default or insolvency (Section 2A—525 or 2A—526), the lessee is entitled to restitution of any amount by which the sum of his [or her] payments exceeds:

    (a) the amount to which the lessor is entitled by virtue of terms liquidating the lessor's damages in accordance with subsection (1); or

    (b) in the absence of those terms, 20 percent of the then present value of the total rent the lessee was obligated to pay for the balance of the lease term, or, in the case of a consumer lease, the lesser of such amount or $500.

(4) A lessee's right to restitution under subsection (3) is subject to offset to the extent the lessor establishes:

    (a) a right to recover damages under the provisions of this Article other than subsection (1); and

    (b) the amount or value of any benefits received by the lessee directly or indirectly by reason of the lease contract.

### § 2A—505. Cancellation and Termination and Effect of Cancellation, Termination, Rescission, or Fraud on Rights and Remedies.

(1) On cancellation of the lease contract, all obligations that are still executory on both sides are discharged, but any right based on prior default or performance survives, and the cancelling party also retains any remedy for default of the whole lease contract or any unperformed balance.

(2) On termination of the lease contract, all obligations that are still executory on both sides are discharged but any right based on prior default or performance survives.

(3) Unless the contrary intention clearly appears, expressions of ''cancellation,'' ''rescission,'' or the like of the lease contract may not be construed as a renunciation or discharge of any claim in damages for an antecedent default.

(4) Rights and remedies for material misrepresentation or fraud include all rights and remedies available under this Article for default.

(5) Neither rescission nor a claim for rescission of the lease contract nor rejection or return of the goods may bar or be deemed inconsistent with a claim for damages or other right or remedy.

## § 2A—506. Statute of Limitations.

(1) An action for default under a lease contract, including breach of warranty or indemnity, must be commenced within 4 years after the cause of action accrued. By the original lease contract the parties may reduce the period of limitation to not less than one year.

(2) A cause of action for default accrues when the act or omission on which the default or breach of warranty is based is or should have been discovered by the aggrieved party, or when the default occurs, whichever is later. A cause of action for indemnity accrues when the act or omission on which the claim for indemnity is based is or should have been discovered by the indemnified party, whichever is later.

(3) If an action commenced within the time limited by subsection (1) is so terminated as to leave available a remedy by another action for the same default or breach of warranty or indemnity, the other action may be commenced after the expiration of the time limited and within 6 months after the termination of the first action unless the termination resulted from voluntary discontinuance or from dismissal for failure or neglect to prosecute.

(4) This section does not alter the law on tolling of the statute of limitations nor does it apply to causes of action that have accrued before this Article becomes effective.

## § 2A—507. Proof of Market Rent: Time and Place.

(1) Damages based on market rent (Section 2A—519 or 2A—528) are determined according to the rent for the use of the goods concerned for a lease term identical to the remaining lease term of the original lease agreement and prevailing at the time of the default.

(2) If evidence of rent for the use of the goods concerned for a lease term identical to the remaining lease term of the original lease agreement and prevailing at the times or places described in this Article is not readily available, the rent prevailing within any reasonable time before or after the time described or at any other place or for a different lease term which in commercial judgment or under usage of trade would serve as a reasonable substitute for the one described may be used, making any proper allowance for the difference, including the cost of transporting the goods to or from the other place.

(3) Evidence of a relevant rent prevailing at a time or place or for a lease term other than the one described in this Article offered by one party is not admissible unless and until he [or she] has given the other party notice the court finds sufficient to prevent unfair surprise.

(4) If the prevailing rent or value of any goods regularly leased in any established market is in issue, reports in official publications or trade journals or in newspapers or periodicals of general circulation published as the reports of that market are admissible in evidence. The circumstances of the preparation of the report may be shown to affect its weight but not its admissibility.

## B. Default by Lessor

## § 2A—508. Lessee's Remedies.

(1) If a lessor fails to deliver the goods in conformity to the lease contract (Section 2A—509) or repudiates the lease contract (Section 2A—402), or a lessee rightfully rejects the goods (Section 2A—509) or justifiably revokes acceptance of the goods (Section 2A—517), then with respect to any goods involved, and with respect to all of the goods if under an installment lease contract the value of the whole lease contract is substantially impaired (Section 2A—510), the lessor is in default under the lease contract and the lessee may:

(a) cancel the lease contract (Section 2A—505(1));

(b) recover so much of the rent and security as has been paid, but in the case of an installment lease contract the recovery is that which is just under the circumstances;

(c) cover and recover damages as to all goods affected whether or not they have been identified to the lease contract (Sections 2A—518 and 2A—520), or recover damages for nondelivery (Sections 2A—519 and 2A—520).

(2) If a lessor fails to deliver the goods in conformity to the lease contract or repudiates the lease contract, the lessee may also:

(a) if the goods have been identified, recover them (Section 2A—522); or

(b) in a proper case, obtain specific performance or replevy the goods (Section 2A—521).

(3) If a lessor is otherwise in default under a lease contract, the lessee may exercise the rights and remedies provided in the lease contract and this Article.

(4) If a lessor has breached a warranty, whether express or implied, the lessee may recover damages (Section 2A—519(4)).

(5) On rightful rejection or justifiable revocation of acceptance, a lessee has a security interest in goods in the lessee's possession or control for any rent and security that has been paid and any expenses reasonably incurred in their inspection, receipt, transportation, and care and custody and may hold those goods and dispose of them in good faith and in a commercially reasonable manner, subject to the provisions of Section 2A—527(5).

(6) Subject to the provisions of Section 2A—407, a lessee, on notifying the lessor of the lessee's intention to do so, may deduct all or any part of the damages resulting from any default under the lease contract from any part of the rent still due under the same lease contract.

## § 2A—509. Lessee's Rights on Improper Delivery; Rightful Rejection.

(1) Subject to the provisions of Section 2A—510 on default in installment lease contracts, if the goods or the tender or delivery fail in any respect to conform to the lease contract, the lessee may reject or accept the goods or accept any commercial unit or units and reject the rest of the goods.

(2) Rejection of goods is ineffective unless it is within a reasonable time after tender or delivery of the goods and the lessee seasonably notifies the lessor.

### § 2A—510. Installment Lease Contracts: Rejection and Default.

(1) Under an installment lease contract a lessee may reject any delivery that is nonconforming if the nonconformity substantially impairs the value of that delivery and cannot be cured or the nonconformity is a defect in the required documents; but if the nonconformity does not fall within subsection (2) and the lessor or the supplier gives adequate assurance of its cure, the lessee must accept that delivery.

(2) Whenever nonconformity or default with respect to one or more deliveries substantially impairs the value of the installment lease contract as a whole there is a default with respect to the whole. But, the aggrieved party reinstates the installment lease contract as a whole if the aggrieved party accepts a nonconforming delivery without seasonably notifying of cancellation or brings an action with respect only to past deliveries or demands performance as to future deliveries.

### § 2A—511. Merchant Lessee's Duties as to Rightfully Rejected Goods.

(1) Subject to any security interest of a lessee (Section 2A—508(5)), if a lessor or a supplier has no agent or place of business at the market of rejection, a merchant lessee, after rejection of goods in his [or her] possession or control, shall follow any reasonable instructions received from the lessor or the supplier with respect to the goods. In the absence of those instructions, a merchant lessee shall make reasonable efforts to sell, lease, or otherwise dispose of the goods for the lessor's account if they threaten to decline in value speedily. Instructions are not reasonable if on demand indemnity for expenses is not forthcoming.

(2) If a merchant lessee (subsection (1)) or any other lessee (Section 2A—512) disposes of goods, he [or she] is entitled to reimbursement either from the lessor or the supplier or out of the proceeds for reasonable expenses of caring for and disposing of the goods and, if the expenses include no disposition commission, to such commission as is usual in the trade, or if there is none, to a reasonable sum not exceeding 10 percent of the gross proceeds.

(3) In complying with this section or Section 2A—512, the lessee is held only to good faith. Good faith conduct hereunder is neither acceptance or conversion nor the basis of an action for damages.

(4) A purchaser who purchases in good faith from a lessee pursuant to this section or Section 2A—512 takes the goods free of any rights of the lessor and the supplier even though the lessee fails to comply with one or more of the requirements of this Article.

### § 2A—512. Lessee's Duties as to Rightfully Rejected Goods.

(1) Except as otherwise provided with respect to goods that threaten to decline in value speedily (Section 2A—511) and

subject to any security interest of a lessee (Section 2A—508(5)):

(a) the lessee, after rejection of goods in the lessee's possession, shall hold them with reasonable care at the lessor's or the supplier's disposition for a reasonable time after the lessee's seasonable notification of rejection;

(b) if the lessor or the supplier gives no instructions within a reasonable time after notification of rejection, the lessee may store the rejected goods for the lessor's or the supplier's account or ship them to the lessor or the supplier or dispose of them for the lessor's or the supplier's account with reimbursement in the manner provided in Section 2A—511; but

(c) the lessee has no further obligations with regard to goods rightfully rejected.

(2) Action by the lessee pursuant to subsection (1) is not acceptance or conversion.

### § 2A—513. Cure by Lessor of Improper Tender or Delivery; Replacement.

(1) If any tender or delivery by the lessor or the supplier is rejected because nonconforming and the time for performance has not yet expired, the lessor or the supplier may seasonably notify the lessee of the lessor's or the supplier's intention to cure and may then make a conforming delivery within the time provided in the lease contract.

(2) If the lessee rejects a nonconforming tender that the lessor or the supplier had reasonable grounds to believe would be acceptable with or without money allowance, the lessor or the supplier may have a further reasonable time to substitute a conforming tender if he [or she] seasonably notifies the lessee.

### § 2A—514. Waiver of Lessee's Objections.

(1) In rejecting goods, a lessee's failure to state a particular defect that is ascertainable by reasonable inspection precludes the lessee from relying on the defect to justify rejection or to establish default:

(a) if, stated seasonably, the lessor or the supplier could have cured it (Section 2A—513); or

(b) between merchants if the lessor or the supplier after rejection has made a request in writing for a full and final written statement of all defects on which the lessee proposes to rely.

(2) A lessee's failure to reserve rights when paying rent or other consideration against documents precludes recovery of the payment for defects apparent on the face of the documents.

### § 2A—515. Acceptance of Goods.

(1) Acceptance of goods occurs after the lessee has had a reasonable opportunity to inspect the goods and

(a) the lessee signifies or acts with respect to the goods in a manner that signifies to the lessor or the supplier that the goods are conforming or that the lessee will take or retain them in spite of their nonconformity; or

(b) the lessee fails to make an effective rejection of the goods (Section 2A—509(2)).

(2) Acceptance of a part of any commercial unit is acceptance of that entire unit.

### § 2A—516. Effect of Acceptance of Goods; Notice of Default; Burden of Establishing Default after Acceptance; Notice of Claim or Litigation to Person Answerable Over.

(1) A lessee must pay rent for any goods accepted in accordance with the lease contract, with due allowance for goods rightfully rejected or not delivered.

(2) A lessee's acceptance of goods precludes rejection of the goods accepted. In the case of a finance lease, if made with knowledge of a nonconformity, acceptance cannot be revoked because of it. In any other case, if made with knowledge of a nonconformity, acceptance cannot be revoked because of it unless the acceptance was on the reasonable assumption that the nonconformity would be seasonably cured. Acceptance does not of itself impair any other remedy provided by this Article or the lease agreement for nonconformity.

(3) If a tender has been accepted:

(a) within a reasonable time after the lessee discovers or should have discovered any default, the lessee shall notify the lessor and the supplier, or be barred from any remedy.

(b) except in the case of a consumer lease, within a reasonable time after the lessee receives notice of litigation for infringement or the like (Section 2A—211) the lessee shall notify the lessor or be barred from any remedy over for liability established by the litigation; and

(c) the burden is on the lessee to establish any default.

(4) If a lessee is sued for breach of a warranty or other obligation for which a lessor or a supplier is answerable over:

(a) The lessee may give the lessor or the supplier written notice of the litigation. If the notice states that the lessor or the supplier may come in and defend and that if the lessor or the supplier does not do so he [or she] will be bound in any action against him [or her] by the lessee by any determination of fact common to the two litigations, then unless the lessor or the supplier after seasonable receipt of the notice does come in and defend he [or she] is so bound.

(b) The lessor or the supplier may demand in writing that the lessee turn over control of the litigation including settlement if the claim is one for infringement or the like (Section 2A—211) or else be barred from any remedy over. If the demand states that the lessor or the supplier agrees to bear all expense and to satisfy any adverse judgment, then unless the lessee after seasonable receipt of the demand does turn over control the lessee is so barred.

(5) The provisions of subsections (3) and (4) apply to any obligation of a lessee to hold the lessor or the supplier harmless against infringement or the like (Section 2A—211).

### § 2A—517. Revocation of Acceptance of Goods.

(1) A lessee may revoke acceptance of a lot or commercial unit whose nonconformity substantially impairs its value to the lessee if he [or she] has accepted it:

(a) except in the case of a finance lease, on the reasonable assumption that its nonconformity would be cured and it has not been seasonably cured; or

(b) without discovery of the nonconformity if the lessee's acceptance was reasonably induced either by the lessor's assurances or, except in the case of a finance lease, by the difficulty or discovery before acceptance.

(2) Revocation of acceptance must occur within a reasonable time after the lessee discovers or should have discovered the ground for it and before any substantial change in condition of the goods which is not caused by the nonconformity. Revocation is not effective until the lessee notifies the lessor.

(3) A lessee who so revokes has the same rights and duties with regard to the goods involved as if the lessee had rejected them.

### § 2A—518. Cover; Substitute Goods.

(1) After default by a lessor under the lease contract (Section 2A—508(1)), the lessee may cover by making in good faith and without unreasonable delay any purchase or lease of or contract to purchase or lease goods in substitution for those due from the lessor.

(2) Except as otherwise provided with respect to damages liquidated in the lease agreement (Section 2A—504) or determined by agreement of the parties (Section 1—102(3)), if a lessee's cover is by lease agreement substantially similar to the original lease agreement and the lease agreement is made in good faith and in a commercially reasonable manner, the lessee may recover from the lessor as damages (a) the present value, as of the date of default, of the difference between the total rent for the lease term of the new lease agreement and the total rent for the remaining lease term of the original lease agreement and (b) any incidental or consequential damages less expenses saved in consequence of the lessor's default.

(3) If a lessee's cover does not qualify for treatment under subsection (2), the lessee may recover from the lessor as if the lessee had elected not to cover and Section 2A—519 governs.

### § 2A—519. Lessee's Damages for Non-Delivery, Repudiation, Default and Breach of Warranty in Regard to Accepted Goods.

(1) If a lessee elects not to cover or a lessee elects to cover and the cover does not qualify for treatment under Section 2A—518(2), the measure of damages for non-delivery or repudiation by the lessor or for rejection or revocation of acceptance by the lessee is the present value as of the date of the default of the difference between the then market rent and the original rent, computed for the remaining lease term of the original lease agreement together with incidental and

consequential damages, less expenses saved in consequence of the lessor's default.

(2) Market rent is to be determined as of the place for tender or, in cases of rejection after arrival or revocation of acceptance, as of the place of arrival.

(3) If the lessee has accepted goods and given notification (Section 2A—516(3)), the measure of damages for nonconforming tender or delivery by a lessor is the loss resulting in the ordinary course of events from the lessor's default as determined in any manner that is reasonable together with incidental and consequential damages, less expenses saved in consequence of the lessor's default.

(4) The measure of damages for breach of warranty is the present value at the time and place of acceptance of the difference between the value of the use of the goods accepted and the value if they had been as warranted for the lease term, unless special circumstances show proximate damages of a different amount, together with incidental and consequential damages, less expenses saved in consequence of the lessor's default or breach of warranty.

### § 2A—520. Lessee's Incidental and Consequential Damages.

(1) Incidental damages resulting from a lessor's default include expenses reasonably incurred in inspection, receipt, transportation, and care and custody of goods rightfully rejected or goods the acceptance of which is justifiably revoked, any commercially reasonable charges, expenses or commissions in connection with effecting cover, and any other reasonable expense incident to the default.

(2) Consequential damages resulting from a lessor's default include:

(a) any loss resulting from general or particular requirements and needs of which the lessor at the time of contracting had reason to know and which could not reasonably be prevented by cover or otherwise; and

(b) injury to person or property proximately resulting from any breach of warranty.

### § 2A—521. Lessee's Right to Specific Performance or Replevin.

(1) Specific performance may be decreed if the goods are unique or in other proper circumstances.

(2) A decree for specific performance may include any terms and conditions as to payment of the rent, damages, or other relief that the court deems just.

(3) A lessee has a right of replevin, detinue, sequestration, claim and delivery, or the like for goods identified to the lease contract if after reasonable effort the lessee is unable to effect cover for those goods or the circumstances reasonably indicate that the effort will be unavailing.

### § 2A—522. Lessee's Right to Goods on Lessor's Insolvency.

(1) Subject to subsection (2) and even though the goods have not been shipped, a lessee who has paid a part or all of the rent and security for goods identified to a lease contract (Section 2A—217) on making and keeping good a tender of any unpaid portion of the rent and security due under the lease contract may recover the goods identified from the lessor if the lessor becomes insolvent within 10 days after receipt of the first installment of rent and security.

(2) A lessee acquires the right to recover goods identified to a lease contract only if they conform to the lease contract.

## C. Default by Lessee

### § 2A—523. Lessor's Remedies.

(1) If a lessee wrongfully rejects or revokes acceptance of goods or fails to make a payment when due or repudiates with respect to a part or the whole, then, with respect to any goods involved, and with respect to all of the goods if under an installment lease contract the value of the whole lease contract is substantially impaired (Section 2A—510), the lessee is in default under the lease contract and the lessor may:

(a) cancel the lease contract (Section 2A—505(1));

(b) proceed respecting goods not identified to the lease contract (Section 2A—524);

(c) withhold delivery of the goods and take possession of goods previously delivered (Section 2A—525);

(d) stop delivery of the goods by any bailee (Section 2A—526);

(e) dispose of the goods and recover damages (Section 2A—527), or retain the goods and recover damages (Section 2A—528), or in a proper case recover rent (Section 2A—529).

(2) If a lessee is otherwise in default under a lease contract, the lessor may exercise the rights and remedies provided in the lease contract and this Article.

### § 2A—524. Lessor's Right to Identify Goods to Lease Contract.

(1) A lessor aggrieved under Section 2A—523(1) may:

(a) identify to the lease contract conforming goods not already identified if at the time the lessor learned of the default they were in the lessor's or the supplier's possession or control; and

(b) dispose of goods (Section 2A—527(1)) that demonstrably have been intended for the particular lease contract even though those goods are unfinished.

(2) If the goods are unfinished, in the exercise of reasonable commercial judgment for the purposes of avoiding loss and of effective realization, an aggrieved lessor or the supplier may either complete manufacture and wholly identify the goods to the lease contract or cease manufacture and lease, sell, or otherwise dispose of the goods for scrap or salvage value or proceed in any other reasonable manner.

### § 2A—525. Lessor's Right to Possession of Goods.

(1) If a lessor discovers the lessee to be insolvent, the lessor may refuse to deliver the goods.

(2) The lessor has on default by the lessee under the lease contract the right to take possession of the goods. If the lease contract so provides, the lessor may require the lessee to assemble the goods and make them available to the lessor at a place to be designated by the lessor which is reasonably convenient to both parties. Without removal, the lessor may render unusable any goods employed in trade or business, and may dispose of goods on the lessee's premises (Section 2A—527).

(3) The lessor may proceed under subsection (2) without judicial process if that can be done without breach of the peace or the lessor may proceed by action.

### § 2A—526. Lessor's Stoppage of Delivery in Transit or Otherwise.

(1) A lessor may stop delivery of goods in the possession of a carrier or other bailee if the lessor discovers the lessee to be insolvent and may stop delivery of carload, truckload, planeload, or larger shipments of express or freight if the lessee repudiates or fails to make a payment due before delivery, whether for rent, security or otherwise under the lease contract, or for any other reason the lessor has a right to withhold or take possession of the goods.

(2) In pursuing its remedies under subsection (1) the lessor may stop delivery until

    (a) receipt of the goods by the lessee;

    (b) acknowledgment to the lessee by any bailee of the goods, except a carrier, that the bailee holds the goods for the lessee; or

    (c) such an acknowledgment to the lessee by a carrier via reshipment or as warehouseman.

(3) (a) To stop delivery, a lessor shall so notify as to enable the bailee by reasonable diligence to prevent delivery of the goods.

    (b) After notification, the bailee shall hold and deliver the goods according to the directions of the lessor, but the lessor is liable to the bailee for any ensuing charges or damages.

    (c) A carrier who has issued a nonnegotiable bill of lading is not obliged to obey a notification to stop received from a person other than the consignor.

### § 2A—527. Lessor's Rights to Dispose of Goods.

(1) After a default by a lessee under the lease contract (Section 2A—523(1)) or after the lessor refuses to deliver or take possession of goods (Section 2A—525 or 2A—526), the lessor may dispose of the goods concerned or the undelivered balance thereof in good faith and without unreasonable delay by lease, sale or otherwise.

(2) If the disposition is by lease contract substantially similar to the original lease contract and the lease contract is made in good faith and in a commercially reasonable manner, the lessor may recover from the lessee as damages (a) accrued and unpaid rent as of the date of default, (b) the present value as of the date of default of the difference between the total rent for the remaining lease term of the original lease contract

and the total rent for the lease term of the new lease contract, and (c) any incidental damages allowed under Section 2A—530, less expenses saved in consequence of the lessee's default.

(3) If the lessor's disposition is by lease contract that for any reason does not qualify for treatment under subsection (2), or is by sale or otherwise, the lessor may recover from the lessee as if the lessor had elected not to dispose of the goods and Section 2A—528 governs.

(4) A subsequent buyer or lessee who buys or leases from the lessor in good faith for value as a result of a disposition under this section takes the goods free of the original lease contract and any rights of the original lessee even though the lessor fails to comply with one or more of the requirements of this Article.

(5) The lessor is not accountable to the lessee for any profit made on any disposition. A lessee who has rightfully rejected or justifiably revoked acceptance shall account to the lessor for any excess over the amount of the lessee's security interest (Section 2A—508(5)).

### § 2A—528. Lessor's Damages for Non-Acceptance or Repudiation.

(1) Except as otherwise provided with respect to damages liquidated in the lease agreement (Section 2A—504) or determined by agreement of the parties (Section 1—102(3)), if a lessor elects to retain the goods or a lessor elects to dispose of the goods and disposition is by lease agreement that for any reason does not qualify for treatment under Section 2A—527(2), or is by sale or otherwise, the lessor may recover from the lessee as damages for non-acceptance or repudiation by the lessee (a) accrued and unpaid rent as of the date of default, (b) the present value as of the date of default of the difference between the total rent for the remaining lease term of the original lease agreement and the market rent at the time and place for tender computed for the same lease term, and (c) any incidental damages allowed under Section 2A—530, less expenses saved in consequence of the lessee's default.

(2) If the measure of damages provided in subsection (1) is inadequate to put a lessor in as good a position as performance would have, the measure of damages is the profit, including reasonable overhead, the lessor would have made from full performance by the lessee, together with any incidental damages allowed under Section 2A—530, due allowance for costs reasonably incurred and due credit for payments or proceeds of disposition.

### § 2A—529. Lessor's Action for the Rent.

(1) After default by the lessee under the lease contract (Section 2A—523(1)), if the lessor complies with subsection (2), the lessor may recover from the lessee as damages:

    (a) for goods accepted by the lessee and for conforming goods lost or damaged within a commercially reasonable time after risk of loss passes to the lessee (Section 2A—219), (i) accrued and unpaid rent as of the date of default, (ii) the present value as of the date of default of the rent for the remaining lease term of the lease agreement, and (iii) any incidental damages allowed under Section 2A—530, less expenses saved in consequence of the lessee's default; and

(b) for goods identified to the lease contract if the lessor is unable after reasonable effort to dispose of them at a reasonable price or the circumstances reasonably indicate that effort will be unavailing, (i) accrued and unpaid rent as of the date of default, (ii) the present value as of the date of default of the rent for the remaining lease term of the lease agreement, and (iii) any incidental damages allowed under Section 2A—530, less expenses saved in consequence of the lessee's default.

(2) Except as provided in subsection (3), the lessor shall hold for the lessee for the remaining lease term of the lease agreement any goods that have been identified to the lease contract and are in the lessor's control.

(3) The lessor may dispose of the goods at any time before collection of the judgment for damages obtained pursuant to subsection (1) and the lessor may proceed against the lessee for damages pursuant to Section 2A—527 or Section 2A—528.

(4) Payment of the judgment for damages obtained pursuant to subsection (1) entitles the lessee to use and possession of the goods not then disposed of for the remaining lease term of the lease agreement.

(5) After a lessee has wrongfully rejected or revoked acceptance of goods, has failed to pay rent then due, or has repudiated (Section 2A—402), a lessor who is held not entitled to rent under this section must nevertheless be awarded damages for non-acceptance under Sections 2A—527 and 2A—528.

### § 2A—530. Lessor's Incidental Damages.

Incidental damages to an aggrieved lessor include any commercially reasonable charges, expenses, or commissions incurred in stopping delivery, in the transportation, care and custody of goods after the lessee's default, in connection with return or disposition of the goods, or otherwise resulting from the default.

### § 2A—531. Standing to Sue Third Parties for Injury to Goods.

(1) If a third party so deals with goods that have been identified to a lease contract as to cause actionable injury to a party to the lease contract (a) the lessor has a right of action against the third party, and (b) the lessee also has a right of action against the third party if the lessee:

(i) has a security interest in the goods;

(ii) has an insurable interest in the goods; or

(iii) bears the risk of loss under the lease contract or has since the injury assumed that risk as against the lessor and the goods have been converted or destroyed.

(2) If at the time of the injury the party plaintiff did not bear the risk of loss as against the other party to the lease contract and there is no arrangement between them for disposition of the recovery, his [or her] suit or settlement, subject to his [or her] own interest, is as a fiduciary for the other party to the lease contract.

(3) Either party with the consent of the other may sue for the benefit of whom it may concern.

## Article 3
# COMMERCIAL PAPER

### Part 1 Short Title, Form and Interpretation

### § 3—101. Short Title.

This Article shall be known and may be cited as Uniform Commercial Code—Commercial Paper.

### § 3—102. Definitions and Index of Definitions.

(1) In this Article unless the context otherwise requires

(a) ''Issue'' means the first delivery of an instrument to a holder or a remitter.

(b) An ''order'' is a direction to pay and must be more than an authorization or request. It must identify the person to pay with reasonable certainty. It may be addressed to one or more such persons jointly or in the alternative but not in succession.

(c) A ''promise'' is an undertaking to pay and must be more than an acknowledgment of an obligation.

(d) ''Secondary party'' means a drawer or indorser.

(e) ''Instrument'' means a negotiable instrument.

(2) Other definitions applying to this Article and the sections in which they appear are:

''Acceptance''. Section 3—410.
''Accommodation party''. Section 3—415.
''Alteration''. Section 3—407.
''Certificate of deposit''. Section 3—104.
''Certification''. Section 3—411.
''Check''. Section 3—104.
''Definite time''. Section 3—109.
''Dishonor''. Section 3—507.
''Draft''. Section 3—104.
''Holder in due course''. Section 3—302.
''Negotiation''. Section 3—202.
''Note''. Section 3—104.
''Notice of dishonor''. Section 3—508.
''On demand''. Section 3—108.
''Presentment''. Section 3—504.
''Protest''. Section 3—509.
''Restrictive Indorsement''. Section 3—205.
''Signature''. Section 3—401.

(3) The following definitions in other Articles apply to this Article:

''Account''. Section 4—104.
''Banking Day''. Section 4—104.
''Clearing House''. Section 4—104.
''Collecting Bank''. Section 4—105.
''Customer''. Section 4—104.
''Depositary Bank''. Section 4—105.

"Documentary Draft". Section 4—104.

"Intermediary Bank". Section 4—105.

"Item". Section 4—104.

"Midnight deadline". Section 4—104.

"Payor Bank". Section 4—105.

(4) In addition Article 1 contains general definitions and principles of construction and interpretation applicable throughout this Article.

### § 3—103. Limitations on Scope of Article.

(1) This Article does not apply to money, documents of title or investment securities.

(2) The provisions of this Article are subject to the provisions of the Article on Bank Deposits and Collections (Article 4) and Secured Transactions (Article 9).

### § 3—104. Form of Negotiable Instruments; "Draft"; "Check"; "Certificate of Deposit"; "Note".

(1) Any writing to be a negotiable instrument within this Article must

(a) be signed by the maker or drawer; and

(b) contain an unconditional promise or order to pay a sum certain in money and no other promise, order, obligation or power given by the maker or drawer except as authorized by this Article; and

(c) be payable on demand or at a definite time; and

(d) be payable to order or to bearer.

(2) A writing which complies with the requirements of this section is

(a) a "draft" ("bill of exchange") if it is an order;

(b) a "check" if it is a draft drawn on a bank and payable on demand;

(c) a "certificate of deposit" if it is an acknowledgment by a bank of receipt of money with an engagement to repay it;

(d) a "note" if it is a promise other than a certificate of deposit.

(3) As used in other Articles of this Act, and as the context may require, the terms "draft", "check", "certificate of deposit" and "note" may refer to instruments which are not negotiable within this Article as well as to instruments which are so negotiable.

### § 3—105. When Promise or Order Unconditional.

(1) A promise or order otherwise unconditional is not made conditional by the fact that the instrument

(a) is subject to implied or constructive conditions; or

(b) states its consideration, whether performed or promised, or the transaction which gave rise to the instrument, or that the promise or order is made or the instrument matures in accordance with or "as per" such transaction; or

(c) refers to or states that it arises out of a separate agreement or refers to a separate agreement for rights as to prepayment or acceleration; or

(d) states that it is drawn under a letter of credit; or

(e) states that it is secured, whether by mortgage, reservation of title or otherwise; or

(f) indicates a particular account to be debited or any other fund or source from which reimbursement is expected; or

(g) is limited to payment out of a particular fund or the proceeds of a particular source, if the instrument is issued by a government or governmental agency or unit; or

(h) is limited to payment out of the entire assets of a partnership, unincorporated association, trust or estate by or on behalf of which the instrument is issued.

(2) A promise or order is not unconditional if the instrument

(a) states that it is subject to or governed by any other agreement; or

(b) states that it is to be paid only out of a particular fund or source except as provided in this section.

### § 3—106. Sum Certain.

(1) The sum payable is a sum certain even though it is to be paid

(a) with stated interest or by stated installments; or

(b) with stated different rates of interest before and after default or a specified date; or

(c) with a stated discount or addition if paid before or after the date fixed for payment; or

(d) with exchange or less exchange, whether at a fixed rate or at the current rate; or

(e) with costs of collection or an attorney's fee or both upon default.

(2) Nothing in this section shall validate any term which is otherwise illegal.

### § 3—107. Money.

(1) An instrument is payable in money if the medium of exchange in which it is payable is money at the time the instrument is made. An instrument payable in "currency" or "current funds" is payable in money.

(2) A promise or order to pay a sum stated in a foreign currency is for a sum certain in money and, unless a different medium of payment is specified in the instrument, may be satisfied by payment of that number of dollars which the stated foreign currency will purchase at the buying sight rate for that currency on the day on which the instrument is payable or, if payable on demand, on the day of demand. If such an instrument specifies a foreign currency as the medium of payment the instrument is payable in that currency.

### § 3—108. Payable on Demand.

Instruments payable on demand include those payable at sight or on presentation and those in which no time for payment is stated.

## § 3—109. Definite Time.

(1) An instrument is payable at a definite time if by its terms it is payable

(a) on or before a stated date or at a fixed period after a stated date; or

(b) at a fixed period after sight; or

(c) at a definite time subject to any acceleration; or

(d) at a definite time subject to extension at the option of the holder, or to extension to a further definite time at the option of the maker or acceptor or automatically upon or after a specified act or event.

(2) An instrument which by its terms is otherwise payable only upon an act or event uncertain as to time of occurrence is not payable at a definite time even though the act or event has occurred.

## § 3—110. Payable to Order.

(1) An instrument is payable to order when by its terms it is payable to the order or assigns of any person therein specified with reasonable certainty, or to him or his order, or when it is conspicuously designated on its face as "exchange" or the like and names a payee. It may be payable to the order of

(a) the maker or drawer; or

(b) the drawee; or

(c) a payee who is not maker, drawer or drawee; or

(d) two or more payees together or in the alternative; or

(e) an estate, trust or fund, in which case it is payable to the order of the representative of such estate, trust or fund or his successors; or

(f) an office, or an officer by his title as such in which case it is payable to the principal but the incumbent of the office or his successors may act as if he or they were the holder; or

(g) a partnership or unincorporated association, in which case it is payable to the partnership or association and may be indorsed or transferred by any person thereto authorized.

(2) An instrument not payable to order is not made so payable by such words as "payable upon return of this instrument properly indorsed."

(3) An instrument made payable both to order and to bearer is payable to order unless the bearer words are handwritten or typewritten.

## § 3—111. Payable to Bearer.

An instrument is payable to bearer when by its terms it is payable to

(a) bearer or the order of bearer; or

(b) a specified person or bearer; or

(c) "cash" or the order of "cash", or any other indication which does not purport to designate a specific payee.

## § 3—112. Terms and Omissions Not Affecting Negotiability.

(1) The negotiability of an instrument is not affected by

(a) the omission of a statement of any consideration or of the place where the instrument is drawn or payable; or

(b) a statement that collateral has been given to secure obligations either on the instrument or otherwise of an obligor on the instrument or that in case of default on those obligations the holder may realize on or dispose of the collateral; or

(c) a promise or power to maintain or protect collateral or to give additional collateral; or

(d) a term authorizing a confession of judgment on the instrument if it is not paid when due; or

(e) a term purporting to waive the benefit of any law intended for the advantage or protection of any obligor; or

(f) a term in a draft providing that the payee by indorsing or cashing it acknowledges full satisfaction of an obligation of the drawer; or

(g) a statement in a draft drawn in a set of parts (Section 3—801) to the effect that the order is effective only if no other part has been honored.

(2) Nothing in this section shall validate any term which is otherwise illegal.

## § 3—113. Seal.

An instrument otherwise negotiable is within this Article even though it is under a seal.

## § 3—114. Date, Antedating, Postdating.

(1) The negotiability of an instrument is not affected by the fact that it is undated, antedated or postdated.

(2) Where an instrument is antedated or postdated the time when it is payable is determined by the stated date if the instrument is payable on demand or at a fixed period after date.

(3) Where the instrument or any signature thereon is dated, the date is presumed to be correct.

## § 3—115. Incomplete Instruments.

(1) When a paper whose contents at the time of signing show that it is intended to become an instrument is signed while still incomplete in any necessary respect it cannot be enforced until completed, but when it is completed in accordance with authority given it is effective as completed.

(2) If the completion is unauthorized the rules as to material alteration apply (Section 3—407), even though the paper was not delivered by the maker or drawer; but the burden of establishing that any completion is unauthorized is on the party so asserting.

## § 3—116. Instruments Payable to Two or More Persons.

An instrument payable to the order of two or more persons

(a) if in the alternative is payable to any one of them and may be negotiated, discharged or enforced by any of them who has possession of it;

(b) if not in the alternative is payable to all of them and may be negotiated, discharged or enforced only by all of them.

### § 3—117. Instruments Payable With Words of Description.

An instrument made payable to a named person with the addition of words describing him

(a) as agent or officer of a specified person is payable to his principal but the agent or officer may act as if he were the holder;

(b) as any other fiduciary for a specified person or purpose is payable to the payee and may be negotiated, discharged or enforced by him;

(c) in any other manner is payable to the payee unconditionally and the additional words are without effect on subsequent parties.

### § 3—118. Ambiguous Terms and Rules of Construction.

The following rules apply to every instrument:

(a) Where there is doubt whether the instrument is a draft or a note the holder may treat it as either. A draft drawn on the drawer is effective as a note.

(b) Handwritten terms control typewritten and printed terms, and typewritten control printed.

(c) Words control figures except that if the words are ambiguous figures control.

(d) Unless otherwise specified a provision for interest means interest at the judgment rate at the place of payment from the date of the instrument, or if it is undated from the date of issue.

(e) Unless the instrument otherwise specifies two or more persons who sign as maker, acceptor or drawer or indorser and as a part of the same transaction are jointly and severally liable even though the instrument contains such words as ''I promise to pay.''

(f) Unless otherwise specified consent to extension authorizes a single extension for not longer than the original period. A consent to extension, expressed in the instrument, is binding on secondary parties and accommodation makers. A holder may not exercise his option to extend an instrument over the objection of a maker or acceptor or other party who in accordance with Section 3—604 tenders full payment when the instrument is due.

### § 3—119. Other Writings Affecting Instrument.

(1) As between the obligor and his immediate obligee or any transferee the terms of an instrument may be modified or affected by any other written agreement executed as a part of the same transaction, except that a holder in due course is not affected by any limitation of his rights arising out of the separate written agreement if he had no notice of the limitation when he took the instrument.

(2) A separate agreement does not affect the negotiability of an instrument.

### § 3—120. Instruments ''Payable Through'' Bank.

An instrument which states that it is ''payable through'' a bank or the like designates that bank as a collecting bank to make presentment but does not of itself authorize the bank to pay the instrument.

### § 3—121. Instruments Payable at Bank.

Note: If this Act is introduced in the Congress of the United States this section should be omitted.

(States to select either alternative)

**Alternative A—**

A note or acceptance which states that it is payable at a bank is the equivalent of a draft drawn on the bank payable when it falls due out of any funds of the maker or acceptor in current account or otherwise available for such payment.

**Alternative B—**

A note or acceptance which states that it is payable at a bank is not of itself an order or authorization to the bank to pay it.

### § 3—122. Accrual of Cause of Action.

(1) A cause of action against a maker or an acceptor accrues

(a) in the case of a time instrument on the day after maturity;

(b) in the case of a demand instrument upon its date or, if no date is stated, on the date of issue.

(2) A cause of action against the obligor of a demand or time certificate of deposit accrues upon demand, but demand on a time certificate may not be made until on or after the date of maturity.

(3) A cause of action against a drawer of a draft or an indorser of any instrument accrues upon demand following dishonor of the instrument. Notice of dishonor is a demand.

(4) Unless an instrument provides otherwise, interest runs at the rate provided by law for a judgment

(a) in the case of a maker, acceptor or other primary obligor of a demand instrument, from the date of demand;

(b) in all other cases from the date of accrual of the cause of action.

## Part 2 Transfer and Negotiation

### § 3—201. Transfer: Right to Indorsement.

(1) Transfer of an instrument vests in the transferee such rights as the transferor has therein, except that a transferee who has himself been a party to any fraud or illegality affecting the instrument or who as a prior holder had notice of a defense or claim against it cannot improve his position by taking from a later holder in due course.

(2) A transfer of a security interest in an instrument vests the foregoing rights in the transferee to the extent of the interest transferred.

(3) Unless otherwise agreed any transfer for value of an instrument not then payable to bearer gives the transferee the

specifically enforceable right to have the unqualified indorsement of the transferor. Negotiation takes effect only when the indorsement is made and until that time there is no presumption that the transferee is the owner.

### § 3—202. Negotiation.

(1) Negotiation is the transfer of an instrument in such form that the transferee becomes a holder. If the instrument is payable to order it is negotiated by delivery with any necessary indorsement; if payable to bearer it is negotiated by delivery.

(2) An indorsement must be written by or on behalf of the holder and on the instrument or on a paper so firmly affixed thereto as to become a part thereof.

(3) An indorsement is effective for negotiation only when it conveys the entire instrument or any unpaid residue. If it purports to be of less it operates only as a partial assignment.

(4) Words of assignment, condition, waiver, guaranty, limitation or disclaimer of liability and the like accompanying an indorsement do not affect its character as an indorsement.

### § 3—203. Wrong or Misspelled Name.

Where an instrument is made payable to a person under a misspelled name or one other than his own he may indorse in that name or his own or both; but signature in both names may be required by a person paying or giving value for the instrument.

### § 3—204. Special Indorsement; Blank Indorsement.

(1) A special indorsement specifies the person to whom or to whose order it makes the instrument payable. Any instrument specially indorsed becomes payable to the order of the special indorsee and may be further negotiated only by his indorsement.

(2) An indorsement in blank specifies no particular indorsee and may consist of a mere signature. An instrument payable to order and indorsed in blank becomes payable to bearer and may be negotiated by delivery alone until specially indorsed.

(3) The holder may convert a blank indorsement into a special indorsement by writing over the signature of the indorser in blank any contract consistent with the character of the indorsement.

### § 3—205. Restrictive Indorsements.

An indorsement is restrictive which either

(a) is conditional; or

(b) purports to prohibit further transfer of the instrument; or

(c) includes the words ''for collection'', ''for deposit'', ''pay any bank'', or like terms signifying a purpose of deposit or collection; or

(d) otherwise states that it is for the benefit or use of the indorser or of another person.

### § 3—206. Effect of Restrictive Indorsement.

(1) No restrictive indorsement prevents further transfer or negotiation of the instrument.

(2) An intermediary bank, or a payor bank which is not the depositary bank, is neither given notice nor otherwise affected by a restrictive indorsement of any person except the bank's immediate transferor or the person presenting for payment.

(3) Except for an intermediary bank, any transferee under an indorsement which is conditional or includes the words ''for collection'', ''for deposit'', ''pay any bank'', or like terms (subparagraphs (a) and (c) of Section 3—205) must pay or apply any value given by him for or on the security of the instrument consistently with the indorsement and to the extent that he does so he becomes a holder for value. In addition such transferee is a holder in due course if he otherwise complies with the requirements of Section 3—302 on what constitutes a holder in due course.

(4) The first taker under an indorsement for the benefit of the indorser or another person (subparagraph (d) of Section 3—205) must pay or apply any value given by him for or on the security of the instrument consistently with the indorsement and to the extent that he does so he becomes a holder for value. In addition such taker is a holder in due course if he otherwise complies with the requirements of Section 3—302 on what constitutes a holder in due course. A later holder for value is neither given notice nor otherwise affected by such restrictive indorsement unless he has knowledge that a fiduciary or other person has negotiated the instrument in any transaction for his own benefit or otherwise in breach of duty (subsection (2) of Section 3—304).

### § 3—207. Negotiation Effective Although It May Be Rescinded.

(1) Negotiation is effective to transfer the instrument although the negotiation is

    (a) made by an infant, a corporation exceeding its powers, or any other person without capacity; or

    (b) obtained by fraud, duress or mistake of any kind; or

    (c) part of an illegal transaction; or

    (d) made in breach of duty.

(2) Except as against a subsequent holder in due course such negotiation is in an appropriate case subject to rescission, the declaration of a constructive trust or any other remedy permitted by law.

### § 3—208. Reacquisition.

Where an instrument is returned to or reacquired by a prior party he may cancel any indorsement which is not necessary to his title and reissue or further negotiate the instrument, but any intervening party is discharged as against the reacquiring party and subsequent holders not in due course and if his indorsement has been cancelled is discharged as against subsequent holders in due course as well.

## Part 3   Rights of a Holder

### § 3—301. Rights of a Holder.

The holder of an instrument whether or not he is the owner may transfer or negotiate it and, except as otherwise provided in Section 3—603 on payment or satisfaction, discharge it or enforce payment in his own name.

### § 3—302. Holder in Due Course.

(1) A holder in due course is a holder who takes the instrument

    (a) for value; and

    (b) in good faith; and

    (c) without notice that it is overdue or has been dishonored or of any defense against or claim to it on the part of any person.

(2) A payee may be a holder in due course.

(3) A holder does not become a holder in due course of an instrument:

    (a) by purchase of it at judicial sale or by taking it under legal process; or

    (b) by acquiring it in taking over an estate; or

    (c) by purchasing it as part of a bulk transaction not in regular course of business of the transferor.

(4) A purchaser of a limited interest can be a holder in due course only to the extent of the interest purchased.

### § 3—303. Taking for Value.

A holder takes the instrument for value

(a) to the extent that the agreed consideration has been performed or that he acquires a security interest in or a lien on the instrument otherwise than by legal process; or

(b) when he takes the instrument in payment of or as security for an antecedent claim against any person whether or not the claim is due; or

(c) when he gives a negotiable instrument for it or makes an irrevocable commitment to a third person.

### § 3—304. Notice to Purchaser.

(1) The purchaser has notice of a claim or defense if

    (a) the instrument is so incomplete, bears such visible evidence of forgery or alteration, or is otherwise so irregular as to call into question its validity, terms or ownership or to create an ambiguity as to the party to pay; or

    (b) the purchaser has notice that the obligation of any party is voidable in whole or in part, or that all parties have been discharged.

(2) The purchaser has notice of a claim against the instrument when he has knowledge that a fiduciary has negotiated the instrument in payment of or as security for his own debt or in any transaction for his own benefit or otherwise in breach of duty.

(3) The purchaser has notice that an instrument is overdue if he has reason to know

    (a) that any part of the principal amount is overdue or that there is an uncured default in payment of another instrument of the same series; or

(b) that acceleration of the instrument has been made; or

(c) that he is taking a demand instrument after demand has been made or more than a reasonable length of time after its issue. A reasonable time for a check drawn and payable within the states and territories of the United States and the District of Columbia is presumed to be thirty days.

(4) Knowledge of the following facts does not of itself give the purchaser notice of a defense or claim

    (a) that the instrument is antedated or postdated;

    (b) that it was issued or negotiated in return for an executory promise or accompanied by a separate agreement, unless the purchaser has notice that a defense or claim has arisen from the terms thereof;

    (c) that any party has signed for accommodation;

    (d) that an incomplete instrument has been completed, unless the purchaser has notice of any improper completion;

    (e) that any person negotiating the instrument is or was a fiduciary;

    (f) that there has been default in payment of interest on the instrument or in payment of any other instrument, except one of the same series.

(5) The filing or recording of a document does not of itself constitute notice within the provisions of this Article to a person who would otherwise be a holder in due course.

(6) To be effective notice must be received at such time and in such manner as to give a reasonable opportunity to act on it.

### § 3—305. Rights of a Holder in Due Course.

To the extent that a holder is a holder in due course he takes the instrument free from

(1) all claims to it on the part of any person; and

(2) all defenses of any party to the instrument with whom the holder has not dealt except

    (a) infancy, to the extent that it is a defense to a simple contract; and

    (b) such other incapacity, or duress, or illegality of the transaction, as renders the obligation of the party a nullity; and

    (c) such misrepresentation as has induced the party to sign the instrument with neither knowledge nor reasonable opportunity to obtain knowledge of its character or its essential terms; and

    (d) discharge in insolvency proceedings; and

    (e) any other discharge of which the holder has notice when he takes the instrument.

### § 3—306. Rights of One Not Holder in Due Course.

Unless he has the rights of a holder in due course any person takes the instrument subject to

(a) all valid claims to it on the part of any person; and

(b) all defenses of any party which would be available in an action on a simple contract; and

(c) the defenses of want or failure of consideration, non-performance of any condition precedent, non-delivery, or delivery for a special purpose (Section 3—408); and

(d) the defense that he or a person through whom he holds the instrument acquired it by theft, or that payment or satisfaction to such holder would be inconsistent with the terms of a restrictive indorsement. The claim of any third person to the instrument is not otherwise available as a defense to any party liable thereon unless the third person himself defends the action for such party.

### § 3—307. Burden of Establishing Signatures, Defenses and Due Course.

(1) Unless specifically denied in the pleadings each signature on an instrument is admitted. When the effectiveness of a signature is put in issue

(a) the burden of establishing it is on the party claiming under the signature; but

(b) the signature is presumed to be genuine or authorized except where the action is to enforce the obligation of a purported signer who has died or become incompetent before proof is required.

(2) When signatures are admitted or established, production of the instrument entitles a holder to recover on it unless the defendant establishes a defense.

(3) After it is shown that a defense exists a person claiming the rights of a holder in due course has the burden of establishing that he or some person under whom he claims is in all respects a holder in due course.

## Part 4 Liability of Parties

### § 3—401. Signature.

(1) No person is liable on an instrument unless his signature appears thereon.

(2) A signature is made by use of any name, including any trade or assumed name, upon an instrument, or by any word or mark used in lieu of a written signature.

### § 3—402. Signature in Ambiguous Capacity.

Unless the instrument clearly indicates that a signature is made in some other capacity it is an indorsement.

### § 3—403. Signature by Authorized Representative.

(1) A signature may be made by an agent or other representative, and his authority to make it may be established as in other cases of representation. No particular form of appointment is necessary to establish such authority.

(2) An authorized representative who signs his own name to an instrument

(a) is personally obligated if the instrument neither names the person represented nor shows that the representative signed in a representative capacity;

(b) except as otherwise established between the immediate parties, is personally obligated if the instrument names the person represented but does not show that the representative signed in a representative capacity, or if the instrument does not name the person represented but does show that the representative signed in a representative capacity.

(3) Except as otherwise established the name of an organization preceded or followed by the name and office of an authorized individual is a signature made in a representative capacity.

### § 3—404. Unauthorized Signatures.

(1) Any unauthorized signature is wholly inoperative as that of the person whose name is signed unless he ratifies it or is precluded from denying it; but it operates as the signature of the unauthorized signer in favor of any person who in good faith pays the instrument or takes it for value.

(2) Any unauthorized signature may be ratified for all purposes of this Article. Such ratification does not of itself affect any rights of the person ratifying against the actual signer.

### § 3—405. Impostors; Signature in Name of Payee.

(1) An indorsement by any person in the name of a named payee is effective if

(a) an impostor by use of the mails or otherwise has induced the maker or drawer to issue the instrument to him or his confederate in the name of the payee; or

(b) a person signing as or on behalf of a maker or drawer intends the payee to have no interest in the instrument; or

(c) an agent or employee of the maker or drawer has supplied him with the name of the payee intending the latter to have no such interest.

(2) Nothing in this section shall affect the criminal or civil liability of the person so indorsing.

### § 3—406. Negligence Contributing to Alteration or Unauthorized Signature.

Any person who by his negligence substantially contributes to a material alteration of the instrument or to the making of an unauthorized signature is precluded from asserting the alteration or lack of authority against a holder in due course or against a drawee or other payor who pays the instrument in good faith and in accordance with the reasonable commercial standards of the drawee's or payor's business.

### § 3—407. Alteration.

(1) Any alteration of an instrument is material which changes the contract of any party thereto in any respect, including any such change in

(a) the number or relations of the parties; or

(b) an incomplete instrument, by completing it otherwise than as authorized; or

(c) the writing as signed, by adding to it or by removing any part of it.

(2) As against any person other than a subsequent holder in due course

(a) alteration by the holder which is both fraudulent and material discharges any party whose contract is thereby changed unless that party assents or is precluded from asserting the defense;

(b) no other alteration discharges any party and the instrument may be enforced according to its original tenor, or as to incomplete instruments according to the authority given.

(3) A subsequent holder in due course may in all cases enforce the instrument according to its original tenor, and when an incomplete instrument has been completed, he may enforce it as completed.

### § 3—408. Consideration.

Want or failure of consideration is a defense as against any person not having the rights of a holder in due course (Section 3—305), except that no consideration is necessary for an instrument or obligation thereon given in payment of or as security for an antecedent obligation of any kind. Nothing in this section shall be taken to displace any statute outside this Act under which a promise is enforceable notwithstanding lack or failure of consideration. Partial failure of consideration is a defense pro tanto whether or not the failure is in an ascertained or liquidated amount.

### § 3—409. Draft Not an Assignment.

(1) A check or other draft does not of itself operate as an assignment of any funds in the hands of the drawee available for its payment, and the drawee is not liable on the instrument until he accepts it.

(2) Nothing in this section shall affect any liability in contract, tort or otherwise arising from any letter of credit or other obligation or representation which is not an acceptance.

### § 3—410. Definition and Operation of Acceptance.

(1) Acceptance is the drawee's signed engagement to honor the draft as presented. It must be written on the draft, and may consist of his signature alone. It becomes operative when completed by delivery or notification.

(2) A draft may be accepted although it has not been signed by the drawer or is otherwise incomplete or is overdue or has been dishonored.

(3) Where the draft is payable at a fixed period after sight and the acceptor fails to date his acceptance the holder may complete it by supplying a date in good faith.

### § 3—411. Certification of a Check.

(1) Certification of a check is acceptance. Where a holder procures certification the drawer and all prior indorsers are discharged.

(2) Unless otherwise agreed a bank has no obligation to certify a check.

(3) A bank may certify a check before returning it for lack of proper indorsement. If it does so the drawer is discharged.

### § 3—412. Acceptance Varying Draft.

(1) Where the drawee's proffered acceptance in any manner varies the draft as presented the holder may refuse the acceptance and treat the draft as dishonored in which case the drawee is entitled to have his acceptance cancelled.

(2) The terms of the draft are not varied by an acceptance to pay at any particular bank or place in the United States, unless the acceptance states that the draft is to be paid only at such bank or place.

(3) Where the holder assents to an acceptance varying the terms of the draft each drawer and indorser who does not affirmatively assent is discharged.

### § 3—413. Contract of Maker, Drawer and Acceptor.

(1) The maker or acceptor engages that he will pay the instrument according to its tenor at the time of his engagement or as completed pursuant to Section 3—115 on incomplete instruments.

(2) The drawer engages that upon dishonor of the draft and any necessary notice of dishonor or protest he will pay the amount of the draft to the holder or to any indorser who takes it up. The drawer may disclaim this liability by drawing without recourse.

(3) By making, drawing or accepting the party admits as against all subsequent parties including the drawee the existence of the payee and his then capacity to indorse.

### § 3—414. Contract of Indorser; Order of Liability.

(1) Unless the indorsement otherwise specifies (as by such words as "without recourse") every indorser engages that upon dishonor and any necessary notice of dishonor and protest he will pay the instrument according to its tenor at the time of his indorsement to the holder or to any subsequent indorser who takes it up, even though the indorser who takes it up was not obligated to do so.

(2) Unless they otherwise agree indorsers are liable to one another in the order in which they indorse, which is presumed to be the order in which their signatures appear on the instrument.

### § 3—415. Contract of Accommodation Party.

(1) An accommodation party is one who signs the instrument in any capacity for the purpose of lending his name to another party to it.

(2) When the instrument has been taken for value before it is due the accommodation party is liable in the capacity in which he has signed even though the taker knows of the accommodation.

(3) As against a holder in due course and without notice of the accommodation oral proof of the accommodation is not admissible to give the accommodation party the benefit of discharges dependent on his character as such. In other cases the accommodation character may be shown by oral proof.

(4) An indorsement which shows that it is not in the chain of title is notice of its accommodation character.

(5) An accommodation party is not liable to the party accommodated, and if he pays the instrument has a right of recourse on the instrument against such party.

### § 3—416.  Contract of Guarantor.

(1) "Payment guaranteed" or equivalent words added to a signature mean that the signer engages that if the instrument is not paid when due he will pay it according to its tenor without resort by the holder to any other party.

(2) "Collection guaranteed" or equivalent words added to a signature mean that the signer engages that if the instrument is not paid when due he will pay it according to its tenor, but only after the holder has reduced his claim against the maker or acceptor to judgment and execution has been returned unsatisfied, or after the maker or acceptor has become insolvent or it is otherwise apparent that it is useless to proceed against him.

(3) Words of guaranty which do not otherwise specify guarantee payment.

(4) No words of guaranty added to the signature of a sole maker or acceptor affect his liability on the instrument. Such words added to the signature of one of two or more makers or acceptors create a presumption that the signature is for the accommodation of the others.

(5) When words of guaranty are used presentment, notice of dishonor and protest are not necessary to charge the user.

(6) Any guaranty written on the instrument is enforcible notwithstanding any statute of frauds.

### § 3—417.  Warranties on Presentment and Transfer.

(1) Any person who obtains payment or acceptance and any prior transferor warrants to a person who in good faith pays or accepts that

(a) he has a good title to the instrument or is authorized to obtain payment or acceptance on behalf of one who has a good title; and

(b) he has no knowledge that the signature of the maker or drawer is unauthorized, except that this warranty is not given by a holder in due course acting in good faith

(i) to a maker with respect to the maker's own signature; or

(ii) to a drawer with respect to the drawer's own signature, whether or not the drawer is also the drawee; or

(iii) to an acceptor of a draft if the holder in due course took the draft after the acceptance or obtained the acceptance without knowledge that the drawer's signature was unauthorized; and

(c) the instrument has not been materially altered, except that this warranty is not given by a holder in due course acting in good faith .

(i) to the maker of a note; or

(ii) to the drawer of a draft whether or not the drawer is also the drawee; or

(iii) to the acceptor of a draft with respect to an alteration made prior to the acceptance if the holder in due course took the draft after the acceptance, even though the acceptance provided "payable as originally drawn" or equivalent terms; or

(iv) to the acceptor of a draft with respect to an alteration made after the acceptance.

(2) Any person who transfers an instrument and receives consideration warrants to his transferee and if the transfer is by indorsement to any subsequent holder who takes the instrument in good faith that

(a) he has a good title to the instrument or is authorized to obtain payment or acceptance on behalf of one who has a good title and the transfer is otherwise rightful; and

(b) all signatures are genuine or authorized; and

(c) the instrument has not been materially altered; and

(d) no defense of any party is good against him; and

(e) he has no knowledge of any insolvency proceeding instituted with respect to the maker or acceptor or the drawer of an unaccepted instrument.

(3) By transferring "without recourse" the transferor limits the obligation stated in subsection (2)(d) to a warranty that he has no knowledge of such a defense.

(4) A selling agent or broker who does not disclose the fact that he is acting only as such gives the warranties provided in this section, but if he makes such disclosure warrants only his good faith and authority.

### § 3—418.  Finality of Payment or Acceptance.

Except for recovery of bank payments as provided in the Article on Bank Deposits and Collections (Article 4) and except for liability for breach of warranty on presentment under the preceding section, payment or acceptance of any instrument is final in favor of a holder in due course, or a person who has in good faith changed his position in reliance on the payment.

### § 3—419.  Conversion of Instrument; Innocent Representative.

(1) An instrument is converted when

(a) a drawee to whom it is delivered for acceptance refuses to return it on demand; or

(b) any person to whom it is delivered for payment refuses on demand either to pay or to return it; or

(c) it is paid on a forged indorsement.

(2) In an action against a drawee under subsection (1) the measure of the drawee's liability is the face amount of the instrument. In any other action under subsection (1) the measure of liability is presumed to be the face amount of the instrument.

(3) Subject to the provisions of this Act concerning restrictive indorsements a representative, including a depositary or collecting bank, who has in good faith and in accordance with the reasonable commercial standards applicable to the

business of such representative dealt with an instrument or its proceeds on behalf of one who was not the true owner is not liable in conversion or otherwise to the true owner beyond the amount of any proceeds remaining in his hands.

(4) An intermediary bank or payor bank which is not a depositary bank is not liable in conversion solely by reason of the fact that proceeds of an item indorsed restrictively (Sections 3—205 and 3—206) are not paid or applied consistently with the restrictive indorsement of an indorser other than its immediate transferor.

## Part 5   Presentment, Notice of Dishonor and Protest

### § 3—501.  When Presentment, Notice of Dishonor, and Protest Necessary or Permissible.

(1) Unless excused (Section 3—511) presentment is necessary to charge secondary parties as follows:

(a) presentment for acceptance is necessary to charge the drawer and indorsers of a draft where the draft so provides, or is payable elsewhere than at the residence or place of business of the drawee, or its date of payment depends upon such presentment. The holder may at his option present for acceptance any other draft payable at a stated date;

(b) presentment for payment is necessary to charge any indorser;

(c) in the case of any drawer, the acceptor of a draft payable at a bank or the maker of a note payable at a bank, presentment for payment is necessary, but failure to make presentment discharges such drawer, acceptor or maker only as stated in Section 3—502(1)(b).

(2) Unless excused (Section 3—511)

(a) notice of any dishonor is necessary to charge any indorser;

(b) in the case of any drawer, the acceptor of a draft payable at a bank or the maker of a note payable at a bank, notice of any dishonor is necessary, but failure to give such notice discharges such drawer, acceptor or maker only as stated in Section 3—502(1)(b).

(3) Unless excused (Section 3—511) protest of any dishonor is necessary to charge the drawer and indorsers of any draft which on its face appears to be drawn or payable outside of the states, territories, dependencies, and possessions of the United States, the District of Columbia and the Commonwealth of Puerto Rico. The holder may at his option make protest of any dishonor of any other instrument and in the case of a foreign draft may on insolvency of the acceptor before maturity make protest for better security.

(4) Notwithstanding any provision of this section, neither presentment nor notice of dishonor nor protest is necessary to charge an indorser who has indorsed an instrument after maturity.

### § 3—502.  Unexcused Delay; Discharge.

(1) Where without excuse any necessary presentment or notice of dishonor is delayed beyond the time when it is due

(a) any indorser is discharged; and

(b) any drawer or the acceptor of a draft payable at a bank or the maker of a note payable at a bank who because the drawee or payor bank becomes insolvent during the delay is deprived of funds maintained with the drawee or payor bank to cover the instrument may discharge his liability by written assignment to the holder of his rights against the drawee or payor bank in respect of such funds, but such drawer, acceptor or maker is not otherwise discharged.

(2) Where without excuse a necessary protest is delayed beyond the time when it is due any drawer or indorser is discharged.

### § 3—503.  Time of Presentment.

(1) Unless a different time is expressed in the instrument the time for any presentment is determined as follows:

(a) where an instrument is payable at or a fixed period after a stated date any presentment for acceptance must be made on or before the date it is payable;

(b) where an instrument is payable after sight it must either be presented for acceptance or negotiated within a reasonable time after date or issue whichever is later;

(c) where an instrument shows the date on which it is payable presentment for payment is due on that date;

(d) where an instrument is accelerated presentment for payment is due within a reasonable time after the acceleration;

(e) with respect to the liability of any secondary party presentment for acceptance or payment of any other instrument is due within a reasonable time after such party becomes liable thereon.

(2) A reasonable time for presentment is determined by the nature of the instrument, any usage of banking or trade and the facts of the particular case. In the case of an uncertified check which is drawn and payable within the United States and which is not a draft drawn by a bank the following are presumed to be reasonable periods within which to present for payment or to initiate bank collection:

(a) with respect to the liability of the drawer, thirty days after date or issue whichever is later; and

(b) with respect to the liability of an indorser, seven days after his indorsement.

(3) Where any presentment is due on a day which is not a full business day for either the person making presentment or the party to pay or accept, presentment is due on the next following day which is a full business day for both parties.

(4) Presentment to be sufficient must be made at a reasonable hour, and if at a bank during its banking day.

### § 3—504.  How Presentment Made.

(1) Presentment is a demand for acceptance or payment made

upon the maker, acceptor, drawee or other payor by or on behalf of the holder.

(2) Presentment may be made

(a) by mail, in which event the time of presentment is determined by the time of receipt of the mail; or

(b) through a clearing house; or

(c) at the place of acceptance or payment specified in the instrument or if there be none at the place of business or residence of the party to accept or pay. If neither the party to accept or pay nor anyone authorized to act for him is present or accessible at such place presentment is excused.

(3) It may be made

(a) to any one of two or more makers, acceptors, drawees or other payors; or

(b) to any person who has authority to make or refuse the acceptance or payment.

(4) A draft accepted or a note made payable at a bank in the United States must be presented at such bank.

(5) In the cases described in Section 4—210 presentment may be made in the manner and with the result stated in that section.

### § 3—505. Rights of Party to Whom Presentment Is Made.

(1) The party to whom presentment is made may without dishonor require

(a) exhibition of the instrument; and

(b) reasonable identification of the person making presentment and evidence of his authority to make it if made for another; and

(c) that the instrument be produced for acceptance or payment at a place specified in it, or if there be none at any place reasonable in the circumstances; and

(d) a signed receipt on the instrument for any partial or full payment and its surrender upon full payment.

(2) Failure to comply with any such requirement invalidates the presentment but the person presenting has a reasonable time in which to comply and the time for acceptance or payment runs from the time of compliance.

### § 3—506. Time Allowed for Acceptance or Payment.

(1) Acceptance may be deferred without dishonor until the close of the next business day following presentment. The holder may also in a good faith effort to obtain acceptance and without either dishonor of the instrument or discharge of secondary parties allow postponement of acceptance for an additional business day.

(2) Except as a longer time is allowed in the case of documentary drafts drawn under a letter of credit, and unless an earlier time is agreed to by the party to pay, payment of an instrument may be deferred without dishonor pending reasonable examination to determine whether it is properly payable, but payment must be made in any event before the close of business on the day of presentment.

### § 3—507. Dishonor; Holder's Right of Recourse; Term Allowing Re-Presentment.

(1) An instrument is dishonored when

(a) a necessary or optional presentment is duly made and due acceptance or payment is refused or cannot be obtained within the prescribed time or in case of bank collections the instrument is seasonably returned by the midnight deadline (Section 4—301); or

(b) presentment is excused and the instrument is not duly accepted or paid.

(2) Subject to any necessary notice of dishonor and protest, the holder has upon dishonor an immediate right of recourse against the drawers and indorsers.

(3) Return of an instrument for lack of proper indorsement is not dishonor.

(4) A term in a draft or an indorsement thereof allowing a stated time for re-presentment in the event of any dishonor of the draft by nonacceptance if a time draft or by nonpayment if a sight draft gives the holder as against any secondary party bound by the term an option to waive the dishonor without affecting the liability of the secondary party and he may present again up to the end of the stated time.

### § 3—508. Notice of Dishonor.

(1) Notice of dishonor may be given to any person who may be liable on the instrument by or on behalf of the holder or any party who has himself received notice, or any other party who can be compelled to pay the instrument. In addition an agent or bank in whose hands the instrument is dishonored may give notice to his principal or customer or to another agent or bank from which the instrument was received.

(2) Any necessary notice must be given by a bank before its midnight deadline and by any other person before midnight of the third business day after dishonor or receipt of notice of dishonor.

(3) Notice may be given in any reasonable manner. It may be oral or written and in any terms which identify the instrument and state that it has been dishonored. A misdescription which does not mislead the party notified does not vitiate the notice. Sending the instrument bearing a stamp, ticket or writing stating that acceptance or payment has been refused or sending a notice of debit with respect to the instrument is sufficient.

(4) Written notice is given when sent although it is not received.

(5) Notice to one partner is notice to each although the firm has been dissolved.

(6) When any party is in insolvency proceedings instituted after the issue of the instrument notice may be given either to the party or to the representative of his estate.

(7) When any party is dead or incompetent notice may be sent to his last known address or given to his personal representative.

(8) Notice operates for the benefit of all parties who have rights on the instrument against the party notified.

## § 3—509. Protest; Noting for Protest.

(1) A protest is a certificate of dishonor made under the hand and seal of a United States consul or vice consul or a notary public or other person authorized to certify dishonor by the law of the place where dishonor occurs. It may be made upon information satisfactory to such person.

(2) The protest must identify the instrument and certify either that due presentment has been made or the reason why it is excused and that the instrument has been dishonored by non-acceptance or nonpayment.

(3) The protest may also certify that notice of dishonor has been given to all parties or to specified parties.

(4) Subject to subsection (5) any necessary protest is due by the time that notice of dishonor is due.

(5) If, before protest is due, an instrument has been noted for protest by the officer to make protest, the protest may be made at any time thereafter as of the date of the noting.

## § 3—510. Evidence of Dishonor and Notice of Dishonor.

The following are admissible as evidence and create a presumption of dishonor and of any notice of dishonor therein shown:

(a) a document regular in form as provided in the preceding section which purports to be a protest;

(b) the purported stamp or writing of the drawee, payor bank or presenting bank on the instrument or accompanying it stating that acceptance or payment has been refused for reasons consistent with dishonor;

(c) any book or record of the drawee, payor bank, or any collecting bank kept in the usual course of business which shows dishonor, even though there is no evidence of who made the entry.

## § 3—511. Waived or Excused Presentment, Protest or Notice of Dishonor or Delay Therein.

(1) Delay in presentment, protest or notice of dishonor is excused when the party is without notice that it is due or when the delay is caused by circumstances beyond his control and he exercises reasonable diligence after the cause of the delay ceases to operate.

(2) Presentment or notice or protest as the case may be is entirely excused when

    (a) the party to be charged has waived it expressly or by implication either before or after it is due; or

    (b) such party has himself dishonored the instrument or has countermanded payment or otherwise has no reason to expect or right to require that the instrument be accepted or paid; or

    (c) by reasonable diligence the presentment or protest cannot be made or the notice given.

(3) Presentment is also entirely excused when

    (a) the maker, acceptor or drawee of any instrument ex-

cept a documentary draft is dead or in insolvency proceedings instituted after the issue of the instrument; or

    (b) acceptance or payment is refused but not for want of proper presentment.

(4) Where a draft has been dishonored by nonacceptance a later presentment for payment and any notice of dishonor and protest for nonpayment are excused unless in the meantime the instrument has been accepted.

(5) A waiver of protest is also a waiver of presentment and of notice of dishonor even though protest is not required.

(6) Where a waiver of presentment or notice or protest is embodied in the instrument itself it is binding upon all parties; but where it is written above the signature of an indorser it binds him only.

## Part 6 Discharge

### § 3—601. Discharge of Parties.

(1) The extent of the discharge of any party from liability on an instrument is governed by the sections on

    (a) payment or satisfaction (Section 3—603); or

    (b) tender of payment (Section 3—604); or

    (c) cancellation or renunciation (Section 3—605); or

    (d) impairment of right of recourse or of collateral (Section 3—606); or

    (e) reacquisition of the instrument by a prior party (Section 3—208); or

    (f) fraudulent and material alteration (Section 3—407); or

    (g) certification of a check (Section 3—411); or

    (h) acceptance varying a draft (Section 3—412); or

    (i) unexcused delay in presentment or notice of dishonor or protest (Section 3—502).

(2) Any party is also discharged from his liability on an instrument to another party by any other act or agreement with such party which would discharge his simple contract for the payment of money.

(3) The liability of all parties is discharged when any party who has himself no right of action or recourse on the instrument

    (a) reacquires the instrument in his own right; or

    (b) is discharged under any provision of this Article, except as otherwise provided with respect to discharge for impairment of recourse or of collateral (Section 3—606).

### § 3—602. Effect of Discharge Against Holder in Due Course.

No discharge of any party provided by this Article is effective against a subsequent holder in due course unless he has notice thereof when he takes the instrument.

### § 3—603. Payment or Satisfaction.

(1) The liability of any party is discharged to the extent of

his payment or satisfaction to the holder even though it is made with knowledge of a claim of another person to the instrument unless prior to such payment or satisfaction the person making the claim either supplies indemnity deemed adequate by the party seeking the discharge or enjoins payment or satisfaction by order of a court of competent jurisdiction in an action in which the adverse claimant and the holder are parties. This subsection does not, however, result in the discharge of the liability

(a) of a party who in bad faith pays or satisfies a holder who acquired the instrument by theft or who (unless having the rights of a holder in due course) holds through one who so acquired it; or

(b) of a party (other than an intermediary bank or a payor bank which is not a depositary bank) who pays or satisfies the holder of an instrument which has been restrictively indorsed in a manner not consistent with the terms of such restrictive indorsement.

(2) Payment or satisfaction may be made with the consent of the holder by any person including a stranger to the instrument. Surrender of the instrument to such a person gives him the rights of a transferee (Section 3—201).

### § 3—604. Tender of Payment.

(1) Any party making tender of full payment to a holder when or after it is due is discharged to the extent of all subsequent liability for interest, costs and attorney's fees.

(2) The holder's refusal of such tender wholly discharges any party who has a right of recourse against the party making the tender.

(3) Where the maker or acceptor of an instrument payable otherwise than on demand is able and ready to pay at every place of payment specified in the instrument when it is due, it is equivalent to tender.

### § 3—605. Cancellation and Renunciation.

(1) The holder of an instrument may even without consideration discharge any party

(a) in any manner apparent on the face of the instrument or the indorsement, as by intentionally cancelling the instrument or the party's signature by destruction or mutilation, or by striking out the party's signature; or

(b) by renouncing his rights by a writing signed and delivered or by surrender of the instrument to the party to be discharged.

(2) Neither cancellation nor renunciation without surrender of the instrument affects the title thereto.

### § 3—606. Impairment of Recourse or of Collateral.

(1) The holder discharges any party to the instrument to the extent that without such party's consent the holder

(a) without express reservation of rights releases or agrees not to sue any person against whom the party has to the knowledge of the holder a right of recourse or agrees to suspend the right to enforce against such person the instrument or collateral or otherwise discharges such per-

son, except that failure or delay in effecting any required presentment, protest or notice of dishonor with respect to any such person does not discharge any party as to whom presentment, protest or notice of dishonor is effective or unnecessary; or

(b) unjustifiably impairs any collateral for the instrument given by or on behalf of the party or any person against whom he has a right of recourse.

(2) By express reservation of rights against a party with a right of recourse the holder preserves

(a) all his rights against such party as of the time when the instrument was originally due; and

(b) the right of the party to pay the instrument as of that time; and

(c) all rights of such party to recourse against others.

## Part 7   Advice of International Sight Draft

### § 3—701. Letter of Advice of International Sight Draft.

(1) A "letter of advice" is a drawer's communication to the drawee that a described draft has been drawn.

(2) Unless otherwise agreed when a bank receives from another bank a letter of advice of an international sight draft the drawee bank may immediately debit the drawer's account and stop the running of interest pro tanto. Such a debit and any resulting credit to any account covering outstanding drafts leaves in the drawer full power to stop payment or otherwise dispose of the amount and creates no trust or interest in favor of the holder.

(3) Unless otherwise agreed and except where a draft is drawn under a credit issued by the drawee, the drawee of an international sight draft owes the drawer no duty to pay an unadvised draft but if it does so and the draft is genuine, may appropriately debit the drawer's account.

## Part 8   Miscellaneous

### § 3—801. Drafts in a Set.

(1) Where a draft is drawn in a set of parts, each of which is numbered and expressed to be an order only if no other part has been honored, the whole of the parts constitutes one draft but a taker of any part may become a holder in due course of the draft.

(2) Any person who negotiates, indorses or accepts a single part of a draft drawn in a set thereby becomes liable to any holder in due course of that part as if it were the whole set, but as between different holders in due course to whom different parts have been negotiated the holder whose title first accrues has all rights to the draft and its proceeds.

(3) As against the drawee the first presented part of a draft drawn in a set is the part entitled to payment, or if a time

draft to acceptance and payment. Acceptance of any subsequently presented part renders the drawee liable thereon under subsection (2). With respect both to a holder and to the drawer payment of a subsequently presented part of a draft payable at sight has the same effect as payment of a check notwithstanding an effective stop order (Section 4—407).

(4) Except as otherwise provided in this section, where any part of a draft in a set is discharged by payment or otherwise the whole draft is discharged.

### § 3—802. Effect of Instrument on Obligation for Which It Is Given.

(1) Unless otherwise agreed where an instrument is taken for an underlying obligation

(a) the obligation is pro tanto discharged if a bank is drawer, maker or acceptor of the instrument and there is no recourse on the instrument against the underlying obligor; and

(b) in any other case the obligation is suspended pro tanto until the instrument is due or if it is payable on demand until its presentment. If the instrument is dishonored action may be maintained on either the instrument or the obligation; discharge of the underlying obligor on the instrument also discharges him on the obligation.

(2) The taking in good faith of a check which is not postdated does not of itself so extend the time on the original obligation as to discharge a surety.

### § 3—803. Notice to Third Party.

Where a defendant is sued for breach of an obligation for which a third person is answerable over under this Article he may give the third person written notice of the litigation, and the person notified may then give similar notice to any other person who is answerable over to him under this Article. If the notice states that the person notified may come in and defend and that if the person notified does not do so he will in any action against him by the person giving the notice be bound by any determination of fact common to the two litigations, then unless after seasonable receipt of the notice the person notified does come in and defend he is so bound.

### § 3—804. Lost, Destroyed or Stolen Instruments.

The owner of an instrument which is lost, whether by destruction, theft or otherwise, may maintain an action in his own name and recover from any party liable thereon upon due proof of his ownership, the facts which prevent his production of the instrument and its terms. The court may require security indemnifying the defendant against loss by reason of further claims on the instrument.

### § 3—805. Instruments Not Payable to Order or to Bearer.

This Article applies to any instrument whose terms do not preclude transfer and which is otherwise negotiable within this Article but which is not payable to order or to bearer, except that there can be no holder in due course of such an instrument.

## Revised Article 3
# NEGOTIABLE INSTRUMENTS

## Part 1  General Provisions and Definitions

### § 3—101. Short Title.

This Article may be cited as Uniform Commercial Code— Negotiable Instruments.

### § 3—102. Subject Matter.

(a) This Article applies to negotiable instruments. It does not apply to money, to payment orders governed by Article 4A, or to securities governed by Article 8.

(b) If there is conflict between this Article and Article 4 or 9, Articles 4 and 9 govern.

(c) Regulations of the Board of Governors of the Federal Reserve System and operating circulars of the Federal Reserve Banks supersede any inconsistent provision of this Article to the extent of the inconsistency.

### § 3—103. Definitions.

(a) In this Article:

(1) ''Acceptor'' means a drawee who has accepted a draft.

(2) ''Drawee'' means a person ordered in a draft to make payment.

(3) ''Drawer'' means a person who signs or is identified in a draft as a person ordering payment.

(4) ''Good faith'' means honesty in fact and the observance of reasonable commercial standards of fair dealing.

(5) ''Maker'' means a person who signs or is identified in a note as a person undertaking to pay.

(6) ''Order'' means a written instruction to pay money signed by the person giving the instruction. The instruction may be addressed to any person, including the person giving the instruction, or to one or more persons jointly or in the alternative but not in succession. An authorization to pay is not an order unless the person authorized to pay is also instructed to pay.

(7) ''Ordinary care'' in the case of a person engaged in business means observance of reasonable commercial standards, prevailing in the area in which the person is located, with respect to the business in which the person is engaged. In the case of a bank that takes an instrument for processing for collection or payment by automated means, reasonable commercial standards do not require the bank to examine the instrument if the failure to examine does not violate the bank's prescribed procedures and the bank's procedures do not vary unreasonably from general banking usage not disapproved by this Article or Article 4.

(8) ''Party'' means a party to an instrument.

(9) ''Promise'' means a written undertaking to pay money signed by the person undertaking to pay. An acknowledgment of an obligation by the obligor is not a

promise unless the obligor also undertakes to pay the obligation.

(10) "Prove" with respect to a fact means to meet the burden of establishing the fact (Section 1—201(8)).

(11) "Remitter" means a person who purchases an instrument from its issuer if the instrument is payable to an identified person other than the purchaser.

(b);(c) [Other definitions' section references deleted.]

(d) In addition, Article 1 contains general definitions and principles of construction and interpretation applicable throughout this Article.

## § 3—104. Negotiable Instrument.

(a) Except as provided in subsections (c) and (d), "negotiable instrument" means an unconditional promise or order to pay a fixed amount of money, with or without interest or other charges described in the promise or order, if it:

(1) is payable to bearer or to order at the time it is issued or first comes into possession of a holder;

(2) is payable on demand or at a definite time; and

(3) does not state any other undertaking or instruction by the person promising or ordering payment to do any act in addition to the payment of money, but the promise or order may contain (i) an undertaking or power to give, maintain, or protect collateral to secure payment, (ii) an authorization or power to the holder to confess judgment or realize on or dispose of collateral, or (iii) a waiver of the benefit of any law intended for the advantage or protection of an obligor.

(b) "Instrument" means a negotiable instrument.

(c) An order that meets all of the requirements of subsection (a), except paragraph (1), and otherwise falls within the definition of "check" in subsection (f) is a negotiable instrument and a check.

(d) A promise or order other than a check is not an instrument if, at the time it is issued or first comes into possession of a holder, it contains a conspicuous statement, however expressed, to the effect that the promise or order is not negotiable or is not an instrument governed by this Article.

(e) An instrument is a "note" if it is a promise and is a "draft" if it is an order. If an instrument falls within the definition of both "note" and "draft," a person entitled to enforce the instrument may treat it as either.

(f) "Check" means (i) a draft, other than a documentary draft, payable on demand and drawn on a bank or (ii) a cashier's check or teller's check. An instrument may be a check even though it is described on its face by another term, such as "money order."

(g) "Cashier's check" means a draft with respect to which the drawer and drawee are the same bank or branches of the same bank.

(h) "Teller's check" means a draft drawn by a bank (i) on another bank, or (ii) payable at or through a bank.

(i) "Traveler's check" means an instrument that (i) is payable on demand, (ii) is drawn on or payable at or through a bank, (iii) is designated by the term "traveler's check" or by a substantially similar term, and (iv) requires, as a condition to payment, a countersignature by a person whose specimen signature appears on the instrument.

(j) "Certificate of deposit" means an instrument containing an acknowledgment by a bank that a sum of money has been received by the bank and a promise by the bank to repay the sum of money. A certificate of deposit is a note of the bank.

## § 3—105. Issue of Instrument.

(a) "Issue" means the first delivery of an instrument by the maker or drawer, whether to a holder or nonholder, for the purpose of giving rights on the instrument to any person.

(b) An unissued instrument, or an unissued incomplete instrument that is completed, is binding on the maker or drawer, but nonissuance is a defense. An instrument that is conditionally issued or is issued for a special purpose is binding on the maker or drawer, but failure of the condition or special purpose to be fulfilled is a defense.

(c) "Issuer" applies to issued and unissued instruments and means a maker or drawer of an instrument.

## § 3—106. Unconditional Promise or Order.

(a) Except as provided in this section, for the purposes of Section 3—104(a), a promise or order is unconditional unless it states (i) an express condition to payment, (ii) that the promise or order is subject to or governed by another writing, or (iii) that rights or obligations with respect to the promise or order are stated in another writing. A reference to another writing does not of itself make the promise or order conditional.

(b) A promise or order is not made conditional (i) by a reference to another writing for a statement of rights with respect to collateral, prepayment, or acceleration, or (ii) because payment is limited to resort to a particular fund or source.

(c) If a promise or order requires, as a condition to payment, a countersignature by a person whose specimen signature appears on the promise or order, the condition does not make the promise or order conditional for the purposes of Section 3—104(a). If the person whose specimen signature appears on an instrument fails to countersign the instrument, the failure to countersign is a defense to the obligation of the issuer, but the failure does not prevent a transferee of the instrument from becoming a holder of the instrument.

(d) If a promise or order at the time it is issued or first comes into possession of a holder contains a statement, required by applicable statutory or administrative law, to the effect that the rights of a holder or transferee are subject to claims or defenses that the issuer could assert against the original payee, the promise or order is not thereby made conditional for the purposes of Section 3—104(a); but if the promise or order is an instrument, there cannot be a holder in due course of the instrument.

### § 3—107. Instrument Payable in Foreign Money.

Unless the instrument otherwise provides, an instrument that states the amount payable in foreign money may be paid in the foreign money or in an equivalent amount in dollars calculated by using the current bank-offered spot rate at the place of payment for the purchase of dollars on the day on which the instrument is paid.

### § 3—108. Payable on Demand or at Definite Time.

(a)  A promise or order is "payable on demand" if it (i) states that it is payable on demand or at sight, or otherwise indicates that it is payable at the will of the holder, or (ii) does not state any time of payment.

(b)  A promise or order is "payable at a definite time" if it is payable on elapse of a definite period of time after sight or acceptance or at a fixed date or dates or at a time or times readily ascertainable at the time the promise or order is issued, subject to rights of (i) prepayment, (ii) acceleration, (iii) extension at the option of the holder, or (iv) extension to a further definite time at the option of the maker or acceptor or automatically upon or after a specified act or event.

(c)  If an instrument, payable at a fixed date, is also payable upon demand made before the fixed date, the instrument is payable on demand until the fixed date and, if demand for payment is not made before that date, becomes payable at a definite time on the fixed date.

### § 3—109. Payable to Bearer or to Order.

(a)  A promise or order is payable to bearer if it:

(1)  states that it is payable to bearer or to the order of bearer or otherwise indicates that the person in possession of the promise or order is entitled to payment;

(2)  does not state a payee; or

(3)  states that it is payable to or to the order of cash or otherwise indicates that it is not payable to an identified person.

(b)  A promise or order that is not payable to bearer is payable to order if it is payable (i) to the order of an identified person or (ii) to an identified person or order. A promise or order that is payable to order is payable to the identified person.

(c)  An instrument payable to bearer may become payable to an identified person if it is specially indorsed pursuant to Section 3—205(a). An instrument payable to an identified person may become payable to bearer if it is indorsed in blank pursuant to Section 3—205(b).

### § 3—110. Identification of Person to Whom Instrument Is Payable.

(a)  The person to whom an instrument is initially payable is determined by the intent of the person, whether or not authorized, signing as, or in the name or behalf of, the issuer of the instrument. The instrument is payable to the person intended by the signer even if that person is identified in the instrument by a name or other identification that is not that of the intended person. If more than one person signs in the name or behalf of the issuer of an instrument and all the signers do not intend the same person as payee, the instrument is payable to any person intended by one or more of the signers.

(b)  If the signature of the issuer of an instrument is made by automated means, such as a check-writing machine, the payee of the instrument is determined by the intent of the person who supplied the name or identification of the payee, whether or not authorized to do so.

(c)  A person to whom an instrument is payable may be identified in any way, including by name, identifying number, office, or account number. For the purpose of determining the holder of an instrument, the following rules apply:

(1)  If an instrument is payable to an account and the account is identified only by number, the instrument is payable to the person to whom the account is payable. If an instrument is payable to an account identified by number and by the name of a person, the instrument is payable to the named person, whether or not that person is the owner of the account identified by number.

(2)  If an instrument is payable to:

(i)  a trust, an estate, or a person described as trustee or representative of a trust or estate, the instrument is payable to the trustee, the representative, or a successor of either, whether or not the beneficiary or estate is also named;

(ii)  a person described as agent or similar representative of a named or identified person, the instrument is payable to the represented person, the representative, or a successor of the representative;

(iii)  a fund or organization that is not a legal entity, the instrument is payable to a representative of the members of the fund or organization; or

(iv)  an office or to a person described as holding an office, the instrument is payable to the named person, the incumbent of the office, or a successor to the incumbent.

(d)  If an instrument is payable to two or more persons alternatively, it is payable to any of them and may be negotiated, discharged, or enforced by any or all of them in possession of the instrument. If an instrument is payable to two or more persons not alternatively, it is payable to all of them and may be negotiated, discharged, or enforced only by all of them. If an instrument payable to two or more persons is ambiguous as to whether it is payable to the persons alternatively, the instrument is payable to the persons alternatively.

### § 3—111. Place of Payment.

Except as otherwise provided for items in Article 4, an instrument is payable at the place of payment stated in the instrument. If no place of payment is stated, an instrument is payable at the address of the drawee or maker stated in the instrument. If no address is stated, the place of payment is the place of business of the drawee or maker. If a drawee or maker has more than one place of business, the place of payment is any place of business of the drawee or maker chosen by the person entitled to enforce the instrument. If the drawee or maker has no place of business, the place of payment is the residence of the drawee or maker.

### § 3—112. Interest.

(a) Unless otherwise provided in the instrument, (i) an instrument is not payable with interest, and (ii) interest on an interest-bearing instrument is payable from the date of the instrument.

(b) Interest may be stated in an instrument as a fixed or variable amount of money or it may be expressed as a fixed or variable rate or rates. The amount or rate of interest may be stated or described in the instrument in any manner and may require reference to information not contained in the instrument. If an instrument provides for interest, but the amount of interest payable cannot be ascertained from the description, interest is payable at the judgment rate in effect at the place of payment of the instrument and at the time interest first accrues.

### § 3—113. Date of Instrument.

(a) An instrument may be antedated or postdated. The date stated determines the time of payment if the instrument is payable at a fixed period after date. Except as provided in Section 4—401(c), an instrument payable on demand is not payable before the date of the instrument.

(b) If an instrument is undated, its date is the date of its issue or, in the case of an unissued instrument, the date it first comes into possession of a holder.

### § 3—114. Contradictory Terms of Instrument.

If an instrument contains contradictory terms, typewritten terms prevail over printed terms, handwritten terms prevail over both, and words prevail over numbers.

### § 3—115. Incomplete Instrument.

(a) ''Incomplete instrument'' means a signed writing, whether or not issued by the signer, the contents of which show at the time of signing that it is incomplete but that the signer intended it to be completed by the addition of words or numbers.

(b) Subject to subsection (c), if an incomplete instrument is an instrument under Section 3—104, it may be enforced according to its terms if it is not completed, or according to its terms as augmented by completion. If an incomplete instrument is not an instrument under Section 3—104, but, after completion, the requirements of Section 3—104 are met, the instrument may be enforced according to its terms as augmented by completion.

(c) If words or numbers are added to an incomplete instrument without authority of the signer, there is an alteration of the incomplete instrument under Section 3—407.

(d) The burden of establishing that words or numbers were added to an incomplete instrument without authority of the signer is on the person asserting the lack of authority.

### § 3—116. Joint and Several Liability; Contribution.

(a) Except as otherwise provided in the instrument, two or more persons who have the same liability on an instrument as makers, drawers, acceptors, indorsers who indorse as joint payees, or anomalous indorsers are jointly and severally liable in the capacity in which they sign.

(b) Except as provided in Section 3—419(e) or by agreement of the affected parties, a party having joint and several liability who pays the instrument is entitled to receive from any party having the same joint and several liability contribution in accordance with applicable law.

(c) Discharge of one party having joint and several liability by a person entitled to enforce the instrument does not affect the right under subsection (b) of a party having the same joint and several liability to receive contribution from the party discharged.

### § 3—117. Other Agreements Affecting Instrument.

Subject to applicable law regarding exclusion of proof of contemporaneous or previous agreements, the obligation of a party to an instrument to pay the instrument may be modified, supplemented, or nullified by a separate agreement of the obligor and a person entitled to enforce the instrument, if the instrument is issued or the obligation is incurred in reliance on the agreement or as part of the same transaction giving rise to the agreement. To the extent an obligation is modified, supplemented, or nullified by an agreement under this section, the agreement is a defense to the obligation.

### § 3—118. Statute of Limitations.

(a) Except as provided in subsection (e), an action to enforce the obligation of a party to pay a note payable at a definite time must be commenced within six years after the due date or dates stated in the note or, if a due date is accelerated, within six years after the accelerated due date.

(b) Except as provided in subsection (d) or (e), if demand for payment is made to the maker of a note payable on demand, an action to enforce the obligation of a party to pay the note must be commenced within six years after the demand. If no demand for payment is made to the maker, an action to enforce the note is barred if neither principal nor interest on the note has been paid for a continuous period of 10 years.

(c) Except as provided in subsection (d), an action to enforce the obligation of a party to an unaccepted draft to pay the draft must be commenced within three years after dishonor of the draft or 10 years after the date of the draft, whichever period expires first.

(d) An action to enforce the obligation of the acceptor of a certified check or the issuer of a teller's check, cashier's check, or traveler's check must be commenced within three years after demand for payment is made to the acceptor or issuer, as the case may be.

(e) An action to enforce the obligation of a party to a certificate of deposit to pay the instrument must be commenced within six years after demand for payment is made to the maker, but if the instrument states a due date and the maker is not required to pay before that date, the six-year period begins when a demand for payment is in effect and the due date has passed.

(f) An action to enforce the obligation of a party to pay an accepted draft, other than a certified check, must be commenced (i) within six years after the due date or dates stated in the draft or acceptance if the obligation of the acceptor is payable at a definite time, or (ii) within six years after the date of the acceptance if the obligation of the acceptor is payable on demand.

(g) Unless governed by other law regarding claims for indemnity or contribution, an action (i) for conversion of an instrument, for money had and received, or like action based on conversion, (ii) for breach of warranty, or (iii) to enforce an obligation, duty, or right arising under this Article and not governed by this section must be commenced within three years after the [cause of action] accrues.

### § 3—119. Notice of Right to Defend Action.

In an action for breach of an obligation for which a third person is answerable over pursuant to this Article or Article 4, the defendant may give the third person written notice of the litigation, and the person notified may then give similar notice to any other person who is answerable over. If the notice states (i) that the person notified may come in and defend and (ii) that failure to do so will bind the person notified in an action later brought by the person giving the notice as to any determination of fact common to the two litigations, the person notified is so bound unless after seasonable receipt of the notice the person notified does come in and defend.

## Part 2 Negotiation, Transfer, and Indorsement

### § 3—201. Negotiation.

(a) ''Negotiation'' means a transfer of possession, whether voluntary or involuntary, of an instrument by a person other than the issuer to a person who thereby becomes its holder.

(b) Except for negotiation by a remitter, if an instrument is payable to an identified person, negotiation requires transfer of possession of the instrument and its indorsement by the holder. If an instrument is payable to bearer, it may be negotiated by transfer of possession alone.

### § 3—202. Negotiation Subject to Rescission.

(a) Negotiation is effective even if obtained (i) from an infant, a corporation exceeding its powers, or a person without capacity, (ii) by fraud, duress, or mistake, or (iii) in breach of duty or as part of an illegal transaction.

(b) To the extent permitted by other law, negotiation may be rescinded or may be subject to other remedies, but those remedies may not be asserted against a subsequent holder in due course or a person paying the instrument in good faith and without knowledge of facts that are a basis for rescission or other remedy.

### § 3—203. Transfer of Instrument; Rights Acquired by Transfer.

(a) An instrument is transferred when it is delivered by a person other than its issuer for the purpose of giving to the person receiving delivery the right to enforce the instrument.

(b) Transfer of an instrument, whether or not the transfer is a negotiation, vests in the transferee any right of the transferor to enforce the instrument, including any right as a holder in due course, but the transferee cannot acquire rights of a holder in due course by a transfer, directly or indirectly, from a holder in due course if the transferee engaged in fraud or illegality affecting the instrument.

(c) Unless otherwise agreed, if an instrument is transferred for value and the transferee does not become a holder because of lack of indorsement by the transferor, the transferee has a specifically enforceable right to the unqualified indorsement of the transferor, but negotiation of the instrument does not occur until the indorsement is made.

(d) If a transferor purports to transfer less than the entire instrument, negotiation of the instrument does not occur. The transferee obtains no rights under this Article and has only the rights of a partial assignee.

### § 3—204. Indorsement.

(a) ''Indorsement'' means a signature, other than that of a signer as maker, drawer, or acceptor, that alone or accompanied by other words is made on an instrument for the purpose of (i) negotiating the instrument, (ii) restricting payment of the instrument, or (iii) incurring indorser's liability on the instrument, but regardless of the intent of the signer, a signature and its accompanying words is an indorsement unless the accompanying words, terms of the instrument, place of the signature, or other circumstances unambiguously indicate that the signature was made for a purpose other than indorsement. For the purpose of determining whether a signature is made on an instrument, a paper affixed to the instrument is a part of the instrument.

(b) ''Indorser'' means a person who makes an indorsement.

(c) For the purpose of determining whether the transferee of an instrument is a holder, an indorsement that transfers a security interest in the instrument is effective as an unqualified indorsement of the instrument.

(d) If an instrument is payable to a holder under a name that is not the name of the holder, indorsement may be made by the holder in the name stated in the instrument or in the holder's name or both, but signature in both names may be required by a person paying or taking the instrument for value or collection.

### § 3—205. Special Indorsement; Blank Indorsement; Anomalous Indorsement.

(a) If an indorsement is made by the holder of an instrument, whether payable to an identified person or payable to bearer, and the indorsement identifies a person to whom it makes the instrument payable, it is a ''special indorsement.'' When specially indorsed, an instrument becomes payable to the identified person and may be negotiated only by the indorsement of that person. The principles stated in Section 3—110 apply to special indorsements.

(b) If an indorsement is made by the holder of an instrument and it is not a special indorsement, it is a ''blank indorsement.'' When indorsed in blank, an instrument becomes payable to bearer and may be negotiated by transfer of possession alone until specially indorsed.

(c) The holder may convert a blank indorsement that consists only of a signature into a special indorsement by writing, above the signature of the indorser, words identifying the person to whom the instrument is made payable.

(d) ''Anomalous indorsement'' means an indorsement made by a person who is not the holder of the instrument. An anomalous indorsement does not affect the manner in which the instrument may be negotiated.

### § 3—206. Restrictive Indorsement.

(a) An indorsement limiting payment to a particular person or otherwise prohibiting further transfer or negotiation of the instrument is not effective to prevent further transfer or negotiation of the instrument.

(b) An indorsement stating a condition to the right of the indorsee to receive payment does not affect the right of the indorsee to enforce the instrument. A person paying the instrument or taking it for value or collection may disregard the condition, and the rights and liabilities of that person are not affected by whether the condition has been fulfilled.

(c) If an instrument bears an indorsement (i) described in Section 4—201(b), or (ii) in blank or to a particular bank using the words ''for deposit,'' ''for collection,'' or other words indicating a purpose of having the instrument collected by a bank for the indorser or for a particular account, the following rules apply:

(1) A person, other than a bank, who purchases the instrument when so indorsed converts the instrument unless the amount paid for the instrument is received by the indorser or applied consistently with the indorsement.

(2) A depositary bank that purchases the instrument or takes it for collection when so indorsed converts the instrument unless the amount paid by the bank with respect to the instrument is received by the indorser or applied consistently with the indorsement.

(3) A payor bank that is also the depositary bank or that takes the instrument for immediate payment over the counter from a person other than a collecting bank converts the instrument unless the proceeds of the instrument are received by the indorser or applied consistently with the indorsement.

(4) Except as otherwise provided in paragraph (3), a payor bank or intermediary bank may disregard the indorsement and is not liable if the proceeds of the instrument are not received by the indorser or applied consistently with the indorsement.

(d) Except for an indorsement covered by subsection (c), if an instrument bears an indorsement using words to the effect that payment is to be made to the indorsee as agent, trustee, or other fiduciary for the benefit of the indorser or another person, the following rules apply:

(1) Unless there is notice of breach of fiduciary duty as provided in Section 3—307, a person who purchases the instrument from the indorsee or takes the instrument from the indorsee for collection or payment may pay the proceeds of payment or the value given for the instrument to the indorsee without regard to whether the indorsee violates a fiduciary duty to the indorser.

(2) A subsequent transferee of the instrument or person who pays the instrument is neither given notice nor otherwise affected by the restriction in the indorsement unless the transferee or payor knows that the fiduciary dealt with the instrument or its proceeds in breach of fiduciary duty.

(e) The presence on an instrument of an indorsement to which this section applies does not prevent a purchaser of the instrument from becoming a holder in due course of the instrument unless the purchaser is a converter under subsection (c) or has notice or knowledge of breach of fiduciary duty as stated in subsection (d).

(f) In an action to enforce the obligation of a party to pay the instrument, the obligor has a defense if payment would violate an indorsement to which this section applies and the payment is not permitted by this section.

### § 3—207. Reacquisition.

Reacquisition of an instrument occurs if it is transferred to a former holder, by negotiation or otherwise. A former holder who reacquires the instrument may cancel indorsements made after the reacquirer first became a holder of the instrument. If the cancellation causes the instrument to be payable to the reacquirer or to bearer, the reacquirer may negotiate the instrument. An indorser whose indorsement is canceled is discharged, and the discharge is effective against any subsequent holder.

## Part 3  Enforcement of Instruments

### § 3—301. Person Entitled to Enforce Instrument.

''Person entitled to enforce'' an instrument means (i) the holder of the instrument, (ii) a nonholder in possession of the instrument who has the rights of a holder, or (iii) a person not in possession of the instrument who is entitled to enforce the instrument pursuant to Section 3—309 or 3—418(d). A person may be a person entitled to enforce the instrument even though the person is not the owner of the instrument or is in wrongful possession of the instrument.

### § 3—302. Holder in Due Course.

(a) Subject to subsection (c) and Section 3—106(d), ''holder in due course'' means the holder of an instrument if:

(1) the instrument when issued or negotiated to the holder does not bear such apparent evidence of forgery

or alteration or is not otherwise so irregular or incomplete as to call into question its authenticity; and

(2) the holder took the instrument (i) for value, (ii) in good faith, (iii) without notice that the instrument is overdue or has been dishonored or that there is an uncured default with respect to payment of another instrument issued as part of the same series, (iv) without notice that the instrument contains an unauthorized signature or has been altered, (v) without notice of any claim to the instrument described in Section 3—306, and (vi) without notice that any party has a defense or claim in recoupment described in Section 3—305(a).

(b) Notice of discharge of a party, other than discharge in an insolvency proceeding, is not notice of a defense under subsection (a), but discharge is effective against a person who became a holder in due course with notice of the discharge. Public filing or recording of a document does not of itself constitute notice of a defense, claim in recoupment, or claim to the instrument.

(c) Except to the extent a transferor or predecessor in interest has rights as a holder in due course, a person does not acquire rights of a holder in due course of an instrument taken (i) by legal process or by purchase in an execution, bankruptcy, or creditor's sale or similar proceeding, (ii) by purchase as part of a bulk transaction not in ordinary course of business of the transferor, or (iii) as the successor in interest to an estate or other organization.

(d) If, under Section 3—303(a)(1), the promise of performance that is the consideration for an instrument has been partially performed, the holder may assert rights as a holder in due course of the instrument only to the fraction of the amount payable under the instrument equal to the value of the partial performance divided by the value of the promised performance.

(e) If (i) the person entitled to enforce an instrument has only a security interest in the instrument and (ii) the person obliged to pay the instrument has a defense, claim in recoupment, or claim to the instrument that may be asserted against the person who granted the security interest, the person entitled to enforce the instrument may assert rights as a holder in due course only to an amount payable under the instrument which, at the time of enforcement of the instrument, does not exceed the amount of the unpaid obligation secured.

(f) To be effective, notice must be received at a time and in a manner that gives a reasonable opportunity to act on it.

(g) This section is subject to any law limiting status as a holder in due course in particular classes of transactions.

### § 3—303. Value and Consideration.

(a) An instrument is issued or transferred for value if:

(1) the instrument is issued or transferred for a promise of performance, to the extent the promise has been performed;

(2) the transferee acquires a security interest or other lien in the instrument other than a lien obtained by judicial proceeding;

(3) the instrument is issued or transferred as payment of, or as security for, an antecedent claim against any person, whether or not the claim is due;

(4) the instrument is issued or transferred in exchange for a negotiable instrument; or

(5) the instrument is issued or transferred in exchange for the incurring of an irrevocable obligation to a third party by the person taking the instrument.

(b) ''Consideration'' means any consideration sufficient to support a simple contract. The drawer or maker of an instrument has a defense if the instrument is issued without consideration. If an instrument is issued for a promise of performance, the issuer has a defense to the extent performance of the promise is due and the promise has not been performed. If an instrument is issued for value as stated in subsection (a), the instrument is also issued for consideration.

### § 3—304. Overdue Instrument.

(a) An instrument payable on demand becomes overdue at the earliest of the following times:

(1) on the day after the day demand for payment is duly made;

(2) if the instrument is a check, 90 days after its date; or

(3) if the instrument is not a check, when the instrument has been outstanding for a period of time after its date which is unreasonably long under the circumstances of the particular case in light of the nature of the instrument and usage of the trade.

(b) With respect to an instrument payable at a definite time the following rules apply:

(1) If the principal is payable in installments and a due date has not been accelerated, the instrument becomes overdue upon default under the instrument for nonpayment of an installment, and the instrument remains overdue until the default is cured.

(2) If the principal is not payable in installments and the due date has not been accelerated, the instrument becomes overdue on the day after the due date.

(3) If a due date with respect to principal has been accelerated, the instrument becomes overdue on the day after the accelerated due date.

(c) Unless the due date of principal has been accelerated, an instrument does not become overdue if there is default in payment of interest but no default in payment of principal.

### § 3—305. Defenses and Claims in Recoupment.

(a) Except as stated in subsection (b), the right to enforce the obligation of a party to pay an instrument is subject to the following:

(1) a defense of the obligor based on (i) infancy of the obligor to the extent it is a defense to a simple contract, (ii) duress, lack of legal capacity, or illegality of the transaction which, under other law, nullifies the obligation of the obligor, (iii) fraud that induced the obligor to sign the instrument with neither knowledge nor reasonable

opportunity to learn of its character or its essential terms, or (iv) discharge of the obligor in insolvency proceedings;

(2) a defense of the obligor stated in another section of this Article or a defense of the obligor that would be available if the person entitled to enforce the instrument were enforcing a right to payment under a simple contract; and

(3) a claim in recoupment of the obligor against the original payee of the instrument if the claim arose from the transaction that gave rise to the instrument; but the claim of the obligor may be asserted against a transferee of the instrument only to reduce the amount owing on the instrument at the time the action is brought.

(b) The right of a holder in due course to enforce the obligation of a party to pay the instrument is subject to defenses of the obligor stated in subsection (a)(1), but is not subject to defenses of the obligor stated in subsection (a)(2) or claims in recoupment stated in subsection (a)(3) against a person other than the holder.

(c) Except as stated in subsection (d), in an action to enforce the obligation of a party to pay the instrument, the obligor may not assert against the person entitled to enforce the instrument a defense, claim in recoupment, or claim to the instrument (Section 3—306) of another person, but the other person's claim to the instrument may be asserted by the obligor if the other person is joined in the action and personally asserts the claim against the person entitled to enforce the instrument. An obligor is not obliged to pay the instrument if the person seeking enforcement of the instrument does not have rights of a holder in due course and the obligor proves that the instrument is a lost or stolen instrument.

(d) In an action to enforce the obligation of an accommodation party to pay an instrument, the accommodation party may assert against the person entitled to enforce the instrument any defense or claim in recoupment under subsection (a) that the accommodated party could assert against the person entitled to enforce the instrument, except the defenses of discharge in insolvency proceedings, infancy, and lack of legal capacity.

### § 3—306. Claims to an Instrument.

A person taking an instrument, other than a person having rights of a holder in due course, is subject to a claim of a property or possessory right in the instrument or its proceeds, including a claim to rescind a negotiation and to recover the instrument or its proceeds. A person having rights of a holder in due course takes free of the claim to the instrument.

### § 3—307. Notice of Breach of Fiduciary Duty.

(a) In this section:

(1) ''Fiduciary'' means an agent, trustee, partner, corporate officer or director, or other representative owing a fiduciary duty with respect to an instrument.

(2) ''Represented person'' means the principal, beneficiary, partnership, corporation, or other person to whom the duty stated in paragraph (1) is owed.

(b) If (i) an instrument is taken from a fiduciary for payment or collection or for value, (ii) the taker has knowledge of the fiduciary status of the fiduciary, and (iii) the represented person makes a claim to the instrument or its proceeds on the basis that the transaction of the fiduciary is a breach of fiduciary duty, the following rules apply:

(1) Notice of breach of fiduciary duty by the fiduciary is notice of the claim of the represented person.

(2) In the case of an instrument payable to the represented person or the fiduciary as such, the taker has notice of the breach of fiduciary duty if the instrument is (i) taken in payment of or as security for a debt known by the taker to be the personal debt of the fiduciary, (ii) taken in a transaction known by the taker to be for the personal benefit of the fiduciary, or (iii) deposited to an account other than an account of the fiduciary, as such, or an account of the represented person.

(3) If an instrument is issued by the represented person or the fiduciary as such, and made payable to the fiduciary personally, the taker does not have notice of the breach of fiduciary duty unless the taker knows of the breach of fiduciary duty.

(4) If an instrument is issued by the represented person or the fiduciary as such, to the taker as payee, the taker has notice of the breach of fiduciary duty if the instrument is (i) taken in payment of or as security for a debt known by the taker to be the personal debt of the fiduciary, (ii) taken in a transaction known by the taker to be for the personal benefit of the fiduciary, or (iii) deposited to an account other than an account of the fiduciary, as such, or an account of the represented person.

### § 3—308. Proof of Signatures and Status as Holder in Due Course.

(a) In an action with respect to an instrument, the authenticity of, and authority to make, each signature on the instrument is admitted unless specifically denied in the pleadings. If the validity of a signature is denied in the pleadings, the burden of establishing validity is on the person claiming validity, but the signature is presumed to be authentic and authorized unless the action is to enforce the liability of the purported signer and the signer is dead or incompetent at the time of trial of the issue of validity of the signature. If an action to enforce the instrument is brought against a person as the undisclosed principal of a person who signed the instrument as a party to the instrument, the plaintiff has the burden of establishing that the defendant is liable on the instrument as a represented person under Section 3—402(a).

(b) If the validity of signatures is admitted or proved and there is compliance with subsection (a), a plaintiff producing the instrument is entitled to payment if the plaintiff proves entitlement to enforce the instrument under Section 3—301, unless the defendant proves a defense or claim in recoupment. If a defense or claim in recoupment is proved, the right to payment of the plaintiff is subject to the defense or claim, except to the extent the plaintiff proves that the plaintiff has rights of a holder in due course which are not subject to the defense or claim.

## § 3—309. Enforcement of Lost, Destroyed, or Stolen Instrument.

(a) A person not in possession of an instrument is entitled to enforce the instrument if (i) the person was in possession of the instrument and entitled to enforce it when loss of possession occurred, (ii) the loss of possession was not the result of a transfer by the person or a lawful seizure, and (iii) the person cannot reasonably obtain possession of the instrument because the instrument was destroyed, its whereabouts cannot be determined, or it is in the wrongful possession of an unknown person or a person that cannot be found or is not amenable to service of process.

(b) A person seeking enforcement of an instrument under subsection (a) must prove the terms of the instrument and the person's right to enforce the instrument. If that proof is made, Section 3—308 applies to the case as if the person seeking enforcement had produced the instrument. The court may not enter judgment in favor of the person seeking enforcement unless it finds that the person required to pay the instrument is adequately protected against loss that might occur by reason of a claim by another person to enforce the instrument. Adequate protection may be provided by any reasonable means.

## § 3—310. Effect of Instrument on Obligation for Which Taken.

(a) Unless otherwise agreed, if a certified check, cashier's check, or teller's check is taken for an obligation, the obligation is discharged to the same extent discharge would result if an amount of money equal to the amount of the instrument were taken in payment of the obligation. Discharge of the obligation does not affect any liability that the obligor may have as an indorser of the instrument.

(b) Unless otherwise agreed and except as provided in subsection (a), if a note or an uncertified check is taken for an obligation, the obligation is suspended to the same extent the obligation would be discharged if an amount of money equal to the amount of the instrument were taken, and the following rules apply:

(1) In the case of an uncertified check, suspension of the obligation continues until dishonor of the check or until it is paid or certified. Payment or certification of the check results in discharge of the obligation to the extent of the amount of the check.

(2) In the case of a note, suspension of the obligation continues until dishonor of the note or until it is paid. Payment of the note results in discharge of the obligation to the extent of the payment.

(3) Except as provided in paragraph (4), if the check or note is dishonored and the obligee of the obligation for which the instrument was taken is the person entitled to enforce the instrument, the obligee may enforce either the instrument or the obligation. In the case of an instrument of a third person which is negotiated to the obligee

by the obligor, discharge of the obligor on the instrument also discharges the obligation.

(4) If the person entitled to enforce the instrument taken for an obligation is a person other than the obligee, the obligee may not enforce the obligation to the extent the obligation is suspended. If the obligee is the person entitled to enforce the instrument but no longer has possession of it because it was lost, stolen, or destroyed, the obligation may not be enforced to the extent of the amount payable on the instrument, and to that extent the obligee's rights against the obligor are limited to enforcement of the instrument.

(c) If an instrument other than one described in subsection (a) or (b) is taken for an obligation, the effect is (i) that stated in subsection (a) if the instrument is one on which a bank is liable as maker or acceptor, or (ii) that stated in subsection (b) in any other case.

## § 3—311. Accord and Satisfaction by Use of Instrument.

(a) If a person against whom a claim is asserted proves that (i) that person in good faith tendered an instrument to the claimant as full satisfaction of the claim, (ii) the amount of the claim was unliquidated or subject to a bona fide dispute, and (iii) the claimant obtained payment of the instrument, the following subsections apply.

(b) Unless subsection (c) applies, the claim is discharged if the person against whom the claim is asserted proves that the instrument or an accompanying written communication contained a conspicuous statement to the effect that the instrument was tendered as full satisfaction of the claim.

(c) Subject to subsection (d), a claim is not discharged under subsection (b) if either of the following applies:

(1) The claimant, if an organization, proves that (i) within a reasonable time before the tender, the claimant sent a conspicuous statement to the person against whom the claim is asserted that communications concerning disputed debts, including an instrument tendered as full satisfaction of a debt, are to be sent to a designated person, office, or place, and (ii) the instrument or accompanying communication was not received by that designated person, office, or place.

(2) The claimant, whether or not an organization, proves that within 90 days after payment of the instrument, the claimant tendered repayment of the amount of the instrument to the person against whom the claim is asserted. This paragraph does not apply if the claimant is an organization that sent a statement complying with paragraph (1)(i).

(d) A claim is discharged if the person against whom the claim is asserted proves that within a reasonable time before collection of the instrument was initiated, the claimant, or an agent of the claimant having direct responsibility with respect to the disputed obligation, knew that the instrument was tendered in full satisfaction of the claim.

## § 3—312. Lost, Destroyed, or Stolen Cashier's Check, Teller's Check, or Certified Check.

(a) In this section:

(1) ''Check'' means a cashier's check, teller's check, or certified check.

(2) ''Claimant'' means a person who claims the right to receive the amount of a cashier's check, teller's check, or certified check that was lost, destroyed, or stolen.

(3) ''Declaration of loss'' means a written statement, made under penalty of perjury, to the effect that (i) the declarer lost possession of a check, (ii) the declarer is the drawer or payee of the check, in the case of a certified check, or the remitter or payee of the check, in the case of a cashier's check or teller's check, (iii) the loss of possession was not the result of a transfer by the declarer or a lawful seizure, and (iv) the declarer cannot reasonably obtain possession of the check because the check was destroyed, its whereabouts cannot be determined, or it is in the wrongful possession of an unknown person or a person that cannot be found or is not amenable to service of process.

(4) ''Obligated bank'' means the issuer of a cashier's check or teller's check or the acceptor of a certified check.

(b) A claimant may assert a claim to the amount of a check by a communication to the obligated bank describing the check with reasonable certainty and requesting payment of the amount of the check, if (i) the claimant is the drawer or payee of a certified check or the remitter or payee of a cashier's check or teller's check, (ii) the communication contains or is accompanied by a declaration of loss of the claimant with respect to the check, (iii) the communication is received at a time and in a manner affording the bank a reasonable time to act on it before the check is paid, and (iv) the claimant provides reasonable identification if requested by the obligated bank. Delivery of a declaration of loss is a warranty of the truth of the statements made in the declaration. If a claim is asserted in compliance with this subsection, the following rules apply:

(1) The claim becomes enforceable at the later of (i) the time the claim is asserted, or (ii) the 90th day following the date of the check, in the case of a cashier's check or teller's check, or the 90th day following the date of the acceptance, in the case of a certified check.

(2) Until the claim becomes enforceable, it has no legal effect and the obligated bank may pay the check or, in the case of a teller's check, may permit the drawee to pay the check. Payment to a person entitled to enforce the check discharges all liability of the obligated bank with respect to the check.

(3) If the claim becomes enforceable before the check is presented for payment, the obligated bank is not obliged to pay the check.

(4) When the claim becomes enforceable, the obligated bank becomes obliged to pay the amount of the check to the claimant if payment of the check has not been made to a person entitled to enforce the check. Subject to Section 4—302(a)(1), payment to the claimant discharges all liability of the obligated bank with respect to the check.

(c) If the obligated bank pays the amount of a check to a claimant under subsection (b)(4) and the check is presented for payment by a person having rights of a holder in due course, the claimant is obliged to (i) refund the payment to the obligated bank if the check is paid, or (ii) pay the amount of the check to the person having rights of a holder in due course if the check is dishonored.

(d) If a claimant has the right to assert a claim under subsection (b) and is also a person entitled to enforce a cashier's check, teller's check, or certified check which is lost, destroyed, or stolen, the claimant may assert rights with respect to the check either under this section or Section 3—309.

## Part 4 Liability of Parties

### § 3—401. Signature.

(a) A person is not liable on an instrument unless (i) the person signed the instrument, or (ii) the person is represented by an agent or representative who signed the instrument and the signature is binding on the represented person under Section 3—402.

(b) A signature may be made (i) manually or by means of a device or machine, and (ii) by the use of any name, including a trade or assumed name, or by a word, mark, or symbol executed or adopted by a person with present intention to authenticate a writing.

### § 3—402. Signature by Representative.

(a) If a person acting, or purporting to act, as a representative signs an instrument by signing either the name of the represented person or the name of the signer, the represented person is bound by the signature to the same extent the represented person would be bound if the signature were on a simple contract. If the represented person is bound, the signature of the representative is the ''authorized signature of the represented person'' and the represented person is liable on the instrument, whether or not identified in the instrument.

(b) If a representative signs the name of the representative to an instrument and the signature is an authorized signature of the represented person, the following rules apply:

(1) If the form of the signature shows unambiguously that the signature is made on behalf of the represented person who is identified in the instrument, the representative is not liable on the instrument.

(2) Subject to subsection (c), if (i) the form of the signature does not show unambiguously that the signature is made in a representative capacity or (ii) the represented person is not identified in the instrument, the representative is liable on the instrument to a holder in due course that took the instrument without notice that the representative was not intended to be liable on the instrument. With respect to any other person, the representative is liable on the instrument unless the representative proves

that the original parties did not intend the representative to be liable on the instrument.

(c) If a representative signs the name of the representative as drawer of a check without indication of the representative status and the check is payable from an account of the represented person who is identified on the check, the signer is not liable on the check if the signature is an authorized signature of the represented person.

### § 3—403. Unauthorized Signature.

(a) Unless otherwise provided in this Article or Article 4, an unauthorized signature is ineffective except as the signature of the unauthorized signer in favor of a person who in good faith pays the instrument or takes it for value. An unauthorized signature may be ratified for all purposes of this Article.

(b) If the signature of more than one person is required to constitute the authorized signature of an organization, the signature of the organization is unauthorized if one of the required signatures is lacking.

(c) The civil or criminal liability of a person who makes an unauthorized signature is not affected by any provision of this Article which makes the unauthorized signature effective for the purposes of this Article.

### § 3—404. Impostors; Fictitious Payees.

(a) If an impostor, by use of the mails or otherwise, induces the issuer of an instrument to issue the instrument to the impostor, or to a person acting in concert with the impostor, by impersonating the payee of the instrument or a person authorized to act for the payee, an indorsement of the instrument by any person in the name of the payee is effective as the indorsement of the payee in favor of a person who, in good faith, pays the instrument or takes it for value or for collection.

(b) If (i) a person whose intent determines to whom an instrument is payable (Section 3—110(a) or (b)) does not intend the person identified as payee to have any interest in the instrument, or (ii) the person identified as payee of an instrument is a fictitious person, the following rules apply until the instrument is negotiated by special indorsement:

(1) Any person in possession of the instrument is its holder.

(2) An indorsement by any person in the name of the payee stated in the instrument is effective as the indorsement of the payee in favor of a person who, in good faith, pays the instrument or takes it for value or for collection.

(c) Under subsection (a) or (b), an indorsement is made in the name of a payee if (i) it is made in a name substantially similar to that of the payee or (ii) the instrument, whether or not indorsed, is deposited in a depositary bank to an account in a name substantially similar to that of the payee.

(d) With respect to an instrument to which subsection (a) or (b) applies, if a person paying the instrument or taking it for value or for collection fails to exercise ordinary care in paying or taking the instrument and that failure substantially contributes to loss resulting from payment of the instrument, the

person bearing the loss may recover from the person failing to exercise ordinary care to the extent the failure to exercise ordinary care contributed to the loss.

### § 3—405. Employer's Responsibility for Fraudulent Indorsement by Employee.

(a) In this section:

(1) "Employee" includes an independent contractor and employee of an independent contractor retained by the employer.

(2) "Fraudulent indorsement" means (i) in the case of an instrument payable to the employer, a forged indorsement purporting to be that of the employer, or (ii) in the case of an instrument with respect to which the employer is the issuer, a forged indorsement purporting to be that of the person identified as payee.

(3) "Responsibility" with respect to instruments means authority (i) to sign or indorse instruments on behalf of the employer, (ii) to process instruments received by the employer for bookkeeping purposes, for deposit to an account, or for other disposition, (iii) to prepare or process instruments for issue in the name of the employer, (iv) to supply information determining the names or addresses of payees of instruments to be issued in the name of the employer, (v) to control the disposition of instruments to be issued in the name of the employer, or (vi) to act otherwise with respect to instruments in a responsible capacity. "Responsibility" does not include authority that merely allows an employee to have access to instruments or blank or incomplete instrument forms that are being stored or transported or are part of incoming or outgoing mail, or similar access.

(b) For the purpose of determining the rights and liabilities of a person who, in good faith, pays an instrument or takes it for value or for collection, if an employer entrusted an employee with responsibility with respect to the instrument and the employee or a person acting in concert with the employee makes a fraudulent indorsement of the instrument, the indorsement is effective as the indorsement of the person to whom the instrument is payable if it is made in the name of that person. If the person paying the instrument or taking it for value or for collection fails to exercise ordinary care in paying or taking the instrument and that failure substantially contributes to loss resulting from the fraud, the person bearing the loss may recover from the person failing to exercise ordinary care to the extent the failure to exercise ordinary care contributed to the loss.

(c) Under subsection (b), an indorsement is made in the name of the person to whom an instrument is payable if (i) it is made in a name substantially similar to the name of that person or (ii) the instrument, whether or not indorsed, is deposited in a depositary bank to an account in a name substantially similar to the name of that person.

### § 3—406. Negligence Contributing to Forged Signature or Alteration of Instrument.

(a) A person whose failure to exercise ordinary care substantially contributes to an alteration of an instrument or to the making of a forged signature on an instrument is precluded from asserting the alteration or the forgery against a person who, in good faith, pays the instrument or takes it for value or for collection.

(b) Under subsection (a), if the person asserting the preclusion fails to exercise ordinary care in paying or taking the instrument and that failure substantially contributes to loss, the loss is allocated between the person precluded and the person asserting the preclusion according to the extent to which the failure of each to exercise ordinary care contributed to the loss.

(c) Under subsection (a), the burden of proving failure to exercise ordinary care is on the person asserting the preclusion. Under subsection (b), the burden of proving failure to exercise ordinary care is on the person precluded.

### § 3—407. Alteration.

(a) "Alteration" means (i) an unauthorized change in an instrument that purports to modify in any respect the obligation of a party, or (ii) an unauthorized addition of words or numbers or other change to an incomplete instrument relating to the obligation of a party.

(b) Except as provided in subsection (c), an alteration fraudulently made discharges a party whose obligation is affected by the alteration unless that party assents or is precluded from asserting the alteration. No other alteration discharges a party, and the instrument may be enforced according to its original terms.

(c) A payor bank or drawee paying a fraudulently altered instrument or a person taking it for value, in good faith and without notice of the alteration, may enforce rights with respect to the instrument (i) according to its original terms, or (ii) in the case of an incomplete instrument altered by unauthorized completion, according to its terms as completed.

### § 3—408. Drawee Not Liable on Unaccepted Draft.

A check or other draft does not of itself operate as an assignment of funds in the hands of the drawee available for its payment, and the drawee is not liable on the instrument until the drawee accepts it.

### § 3—409. Acceptance of Draft; Certified Check.

(a) "Acceptance" means the drawee's signed agreement to pay a draft as presented. It must be written on the draft and may consist of the drawee's signature alone. Acceptance may be made at any time and becomes effective when notification pursuant to instructions is given or the accepted draft is delivered for the purpose of giving rights on the acceptance to any person.

(b) A draft may be accepted although it has not been signed by the drawer, is otherwise incomplete, is overdue, or has been dishonored.

(c) If a draft is payable at a fixed period after sight and the acceptor fails to date the acceptance, the holder may complete the acceptance by supplying a date in good faith.

(d) "Certified check" means a check accepted by the bank on which it is drawn. Acceptance may be made as stated in subsection (a) or by a writing on the check which indicates that the check is certified. The drawee of a check has no obligation to certify the check, and refusal to certify is not dishonor of the check.

### § 3—410. Acceptance Varying Draft.

(a) If the terms of a drawee's acceptance vary from the terms of the draft as presented, the holder may refuse the acceptance and treat the draft as dishonored. In that case, the drawee may cancel the acceptance.

(b) The terms of a draft are not varied by an acceptance to pay at a particular bank or place in the United States, unless the acceptance states that the draft is to be paid only at that bank or place.

(c) If the holder assents to an acceptance varying the terms of a draft, the obligation of each drawer and indorser that does not expressly assent to the acceptance is discharged.

### § 3—411. Refusal to Pay Cashier's Checks, Teller's Checks, and Certified Checks.

(a) In this section, "obligated bank" means the acceptor of a certified check or the issuer of a cashier's check or teller's check bought from the issuer.

(b) If the obligated bank wrongfully (i) refuses to pay a cashier's check or certified check, (ii) stops payment of a teller's check, or (iii) refuses to pay a dishonored teller's check, the person asserting the right to enforce the check is entitled to compensation for expenses and loss of interest resulting from the nonpayment and may recover consequential damages if the obligated bank refuses to pay after receiving notice of particular circumstances giving rise to the damages.

(c) Expenses or consequential damages under subsection (b) are not recoverable if the refusal of the obligated bank to pay occurs because (i) the bank suspends payments, (ii) the obligated bank asserts a claim or defense of the bank that it has reasonable grounds to believe is available against the person entitled to enforce the instrument, (iii) the obligated bank has a reasonable doubt whether the person demanding payment is the person entitled to enforce the instrument, or (iv) payment is prohibited by law.

### § 3—412. Obligation of Issuer of Note or Cashier's Check.

The issuer of a note or cashier's check or other draft drawn on the drawer is obliged to pay the instrument (i) according to its terms at the time it was issued or, if not issued, at the time it first came into possession of a holder, or (ii) if the issuer signed an incomplete instrument, according to its terms when completed, to the extent stated in Sections 3—115 and 3—407. The obligation is owed to a person entitled to enforce the instrument or to an indorser who paid the instrument under Section 3—415.

## § 3—413. Obligation of Acceptor.

(a) The acceptor of a draft is obliged to pay the draft (i) according to its terms at the time it was accepted, even though the acceptance states that the draft is payable ''as originally drawn'' or equivalent terms, (ii) if the acceptance varies the terms of the draft, according to the terms of the draft as varied, or (iii) if the acceptance is of a draft that is an incomplete instrument, according to its terms when completed, to the extent stated in Sections 3—115 and 3—407. The obligation is owed to a person entitled to enforce the draft or to the drawer or an indorser who paid the draft under Section 3—414 or 3—415.

(b) If the certification of a check or other acceptance of a draft states the amount certified or accepted, the obligation of the acceptor is that amount. If (i) the certification or acceptance does not state an amount, (ii) the amount of the instrument is subsequently raised, and (iii) the instrument is then negotiated to a holder in due course, the obligation of the acceptor is the amount of the instrument at the time it was taken by the holder in due course.

## § 3—414. Obligation of Drawer.

(a) This section does not apply to cashier's checks or other drafts drawn on the drawer.

(b) If an unaccepted draft is dishonored, the drawer is obliged to pay the draft (i) according to its terms at the time it was issued or, if not issued, at the time it first came into possession of a holder, or (ii) if the drawer signed an incomplete instrument, according to its terms when completed, to the extent stated in Sections 3—115 and 3—407. The obligation is owed to a person entitled to enforce the draft or to an indorser who paid the draft under Section 3—415.

(c) If a draft is accepted by a bank, the drawer is discharged, regardless of when or by whom acceptance was obtained.

(d) If a draft is accepted and the acceptor is not a bank, the obligation of the drawer to pay the draft if the draft is dishonored by the acceptor is the same as the obligation of an indorser under Section 3—415(a) and (c).

(e) If a draft states that it is drawn ''without recourse'' or otherwise disclaims liability of the drawer to pay the draft, the drawer is not liable under subsection (b) to pay the draft if the draft is not a check. A disclaimer of the liability stated in subsection (b) is not effective if the draft is a check.

(f) If (i) a check is not presented for payment or given to a depositary bank for collection within 30 days after its date, (ii) the drawee suspends payments after expiration of the 30-day period without paying the check, and (iii) because of the suspension of payments, the drawer is deprived of funds maintained with the drawee to cover payment of the check, the drawer to the extent deprived of funds may discharge its obligation to pay the check by assigning to the person entitled to enforce the check the rights of the drawer against the drawee with respect to the funds.

## § 3—415. Obligation of Indorser.

(a) Subject to subsections (b), (c), and (d) and to Section 3—419(d), if an instrument is dishonored, an indorser is obliged to pay the amount due on the instrument (i) according to the terms of the instrument at the time it was indorsed, or (ii) if the indorser indorsed an incomplete instrument, according to its terms when completed, to the extent stated in Sections 3—115 and 3—407. The obligation of the indorser is owed to a person entitled to enforce the instrument or to a subsequent indorser who paid the instrument under this section.

(b) If an indorsement states that it is made ''without recourse'' or otherwise disclaims liability of the indorser, the indorser is not liable under subsection (a) to pay the instrument.

(c) If notice of dishonor of an instrument is required by Section 3—503 and notice of dishonor complying with that section is not given to an indorser, the liability of the indorser under subsection (a) is discharged.

(d) If a draft is accepted by a bank after an indorsement is made, the liability of the indorser under subsection (a) is discharged.

(e) If an indorser of a check is liable under subsection (a) and the check is not presented for payment, or given to a depositary bank for collection, within 30 days after the day the indorsement was made, the liability of the indorser under subsection (a) is discharged.

## § 3—416. Transfer Warranties.

(a) A person who transfers an instrument for consideration warrants to the transferee and, if the transfer is by indorsement, to any subsequent transferee that:

> (1) the warrantor is a person entitled to enforce the instrument;

> (2) all signatures on the instrument are authentic and authorized;

> (3) the instrument has not been altered;

> (4) the instrument is not subject to a defense or claim in recoupment of any party which can be asserted against the warrantor; and

> (5) the warrantor has no knowledge of any insolvency proceeding commenced with respect to the maker or acceptor or, in the case of an unaccepted draft, the drawer.

(b) A person to whom the warranties under subsection (a) are made and who took the instrument in good faith may recover from the warrantor as damages for breach of warranty an amount equal to the loss suffered as a result of the breach, but not more than the amount of the instrument plus expenses and loss of interest incurred as a result of the breach.

(c) The warranties stated in subsection (a) cannot be disclaimed with respect to checks. Unless notice of a claim for breach of warranty is given to the warrantor within 30 days after the claimant has reason to know of the breach and the identity of the warrantor, the liability of the warrantor under subsection (b) is discharged to the extent of any loss caused by the delay in giving notice of the claim.

(d) A [cause of action] for breach of warranty under this

section accrues when the claimant has reason to know of the breach.

## § 3—417. Presentment Warranties.

(a) If an unaccepted draft is presented to the drawee for payment or acceptance and the drawee pays or accepts the draft, (i) the person obtaining payment or acceptance, at the time of presentment, and (ii) a previous transferor of the draft, at the time of transfer, warrant to the drawee making payment or accepting the draft in good faith that:

(1) the warrantor is, or was, at the time the warrantor transferred the draft, a person entitled to enforce the draft or authorized to obtain payment or acceptance of the draft on behalf of a person entitled to enforce the draft;

(2) the draft has not been altered; and

(3) the warrantor has no knowledge that the signature of the drawer of the draft is unauthorized.

(b) A drawee making payment may recover from any warrantor damages for breach of warranty equal to the amount paid by the drawee less the amount the drawee received or is entitled to receive from the drawer because of the payment. In addition, the drawee is entitled to compensation for expenses and loss of interest resulting from the breach. The right of the drawee to recover damages under this subsection is not affected by any failure of the drawee to exercise ordinary care in making payment. If the drawee accepts the draft, breach of warranty is a defense to the obligation of the acceptor. If the acceptor makes payment with respect to the draft, the acceptor is entitled to recover from any warrantor for breach of warranty the amounts stated in this subsection.

(c) If a drawee asserts a claim for breach of warranty under subsection (a) based on an unauthorized indorsement of the draft or an alteration of the draft, the warrantor may defend by proving that the indorsement is effective under Section 3—404 or 3—405 or the drawer is precluded under Section 3—406 or 4—406 from asserting against the drawee the unauthorized indorsement or alteration.

(d) If (i) a dishonored draft is presented for payment to the drawer or an indorser or (ii) any other instrument is presented for payment to a party obliged to pay the instrument, and (iii) payment is received, the following rules apply:

(1) The person obtaining payment and a prior transferor of the instrument warrant to the person making payment in good faith that the warrantor is, or was, at the time the warrantor transferred the instrument, a person entitled to enforce the instrument or authorized to obtain payment on behalf of a person entitled to enforce the instrument.

(2) The person making payment may recover from any warrantor for breach of warranty an amount equal to the amount paid plus expenses and loss of interest resulting from the breach.

(e) The warranties stated in subsections (a) and (d) cannot be disclaimed with respect to checks. Unless notice of a claim for breach of warranty is given to the warrantor within 30 days after the claimant has reason to know of the breach and

the identity of the warrantor, the liability of the warrantor under subsection (b) or (d) is discharged to the extent of any loss caused by the delay in giving notice of the claim.

(f) A [cause of action] for breach of warranty under this section accrues when the claimant has reason to know of the breach.

## § 3—418. Payment or Acceptance by Mistake.

(a) Except as provided in subsection (c), if the drawee of a draft pays or accepts the draft and the drawee acted on the mistaken belief that (i) payment of the draft had not been stopped pursuant to Section 4—403 or (ii) the signature of the drawer of the draft was authorized, the drawee may recover the amount of the draft from the person to whom or for whose benefit payment was made or, in the case of acceptance, may revoke the acceptance. Rights of the drawee under this subsection are not affected by failure of the drawee to exercise ordinary care in paying or accepting the draft.

(b) Except as provided in subsection (c), if an instrument has been paid or accepted by mistake and the case is not covered by subsection (a), the person paying or accepting may, to the extent permitted by the law governing mistake and restitution, (i) recover the payment from the person to whom or for whose benefit payment was made or (ii) in the case of acceptance, may revoke the acceptance.

(c) The remedies provided by subsection (a) or (b) may not be asserted against a person who took the instrument in good faith and for value or who in good faith changed position in reliance on the payment or acceptance. This subsection does not limit remedies provided by Section 3—417 or 4—407.

(d) Notwithstanding Section 4—215, if an instrument is paid or accepted by mistake and the payor or acceptor recovers payment or revokes acceptance under subsection (a) or (b), the instrument is deemed not to have been paid or accepted and is treated as dishonored, and the person from whom payment is recovered has rights as a person entitled to enforce the dishonored instrument.

## § 3—419. Instruments Signed for Accommodation.

(a) If an instrument is issued for value given for the benefit of a party to the instrument ("accommodated party") and another party to the instrument ("accommodation party") signs the instrument for the purpose of incurring liability on the instrument without being a direct beneficiary of the value given for the instrument, the instrument is signed by the accommodation party "for accommodation."

(b) An accommodation party may sign the instrument as maker, drawer, acceptor, or indorser and, subject to subsection (d), is obliged to pay the instrument in the capacity in which the accommodation party signs. The obligation of an accommodation party may be enforced notwithstanding any statute of frauds and whether or not the accommodation party receives consideration for the accommodation.

(c) A person signing an instrument is presumed to be an accommodation party and there is notice that the instrument is signed for accommodation if the signature is an anomalous indorsement or is accompanied by words indicating that the signer is acting as surety or guarantor with respect to the obligation of another party to the instrument. Except as provided in Section 3—605, the obligation of an accommodation party to pay the instrument is not affected by the fact that the person enforcing the obligation had notice when the instrument was taken by that person that the accommodation party signed the instrument for accommodation.

(d) If the signature of a party to an instrument is accompanied by words indicating unambiguously that the party is guaranteeing collection rather than payment of the obligation of another party to the instrument, the signer is obliged to pay the amount due on the instrument to a person entitled to enforce the instrument only if (i) execution of judgment against the other party has been returned unsatisfied, (ii) the other party is insolvent or in an insolvency proceeding, (iii) the other party cannot be served with process, or (iv) it is otherwise apparent that payment cannot be obtained from the other party.

(e) An accommodation party who pays the instrument is entitled to reimbursement from the accommodated party and is entitled to enforce the instrument against the accommodated party. An accommodated party who pays the instrument has no right of recourse against, and is not entitled to contribution from, an accommodation party.

### § 3—420. Conversion of Instrument.

(a) The law applicable to conversion of personal property applies to instruments. An instrument is also converted if it is taken by transfer, other than a negotiation, from a person not entitled to enforce the instrument or a bank makes or obtains payment with respect to the instrument for a person not entitled to enforce the instrument or receive payment. An action for conversion of an instrument may not be brought by (i) the issuer or acceptor of the instrument or (ii) a payee or indorsee who did not receive delivery of the instrument either directly or through delivery to an agent or a co-payee.

(b) In an action under subsection (a), the measure of liability is presumed to be the amount payable on the instrument, but recovery may not exceed the amount of the plaintiff's interest in the instrument.

(c) A representative, other than a depositary bank, who has in good faith dealt with an instrument or its proceeds on behalf of one who was not the person entitled to enforce the instrument is not liable in conversion to that person beyond the amount of any proceeds that it has not paid out.

## Part 5  Dishonor

### § 3—501. Presentment.

(a) "Presentment" means a demand made by or on behalf of a person entitled to enforce an instrument (i) to pay the instrument made to the drawee or a party obliged to pay the instrument or, in the case of a note or accepted draft payable at a bank, to the bank, or (ii) to accept a draft made to the drawee.

(b) The following rules are subject to Article 4, agreement of the parties, and clearing-house rules and the like:

(1) Presentment may be made at the place of payment of the instrument and must be made at the place of payment if the instrument is payable at a bank in the United States; may be made by any commercially reasonable means, including an oral, written, or electronic communication; is effective when the demand for payment or acceptance is received by the person to whom presentment is made; and is effective if made to any one of two or more makers, acceptors, drawees, or other payors.

(2) Upon demand of the person to whom presentment is made, the person making presentment must (i) exhibit the instrument, (ii) give reasonable identification and, if presentment is made on behalf of another person, reasonable evidence of authority to do so, and ( . . . ) sign a receipt on the instrument for any payment made or surrender the instrument if full payment is made.

(3) Without dishonoring the instrument, the party to whom presentment is made may (i) return the instrument for lack of a necessary indorsement, or (ii) refuse payment or acceptance for failure of the presentment to comply with the terms of the instrument, an agreement of the parties, or other applicable law or rule.

(4) The party to whom presentment is made may treat presentment as occurring on the next business day after the day of presentment if the party to whom presentment is made has established a cut-off hour not earlier than 2 P.M. for the receipt and processing of instruments presented for payment or acceptance and presentment is made after the cut-off hour.

### § 3—502. Dishonor.

(a) Dishonor of a note is governed by the following rules:

(1) If the note is payable on demand, the note is dishonored if presentment is duly made to the maker and the note is not paid on the day of presentment.

(2) If the note is not payable on demand and is payable at or through a bank or the terms of the note require presentment, the note is dishonored if presentment is duly made and the note is not paid on the day it becomes payable or the day of presentment, whichever is later.

(3) If the note is not payable on demand and paragraph (2) does not apply, the note is dishonored if it is not paid on the day it becomes payable.

(b) Dishonor of an unaccepted draft other than a documentary draft is governed by the following rules:

(1) If a check is duly presented for payment to the payor bank otherwise than for immediate payment over the counter, the check is dishonored if the payor bank makes timely return of the check or sends timely notice of dishonor or nonpayment under Section 4—301 or 4—302, or becomes accountable for the amount of the check under Section 4—302.

(2) If a draft is payable on demand and paragraph (1) does not apply, the draft is dishonored if presentment for payment is duly made to the drawee and the draft is not paid on the day of presentment.

(3) If a draft is payable on a date stated in the draft, the draft is dishonored if (i) presentment for payment is duly made to the drawee and payment is not made on the day the draft becomes payable or the day of presentment, whichever is later, or (ii) presentment for acceptance is duly made before the day the draft becomes payable and the draft is not accepted on the day of presentment.

(4) If a draft is payable on elapse of a period of time after sight or acceptance, the draft is dishonored if presentment for acceptance is duly made and the draft is not accepted on the day of presentment.

(c) Dishonor of an unaccepted documentary draft occurs according to the rules stated in subsection (b)(2), (3), and (4), except that payment or acceptance may be delayed without dishonor until no later than the close of the third business day of the drawee following the day on which payment or acceptance is required by those paragraphs.

(d) Dishonor of an accepted draft is governed by the following rules:

(1) If the draft is payable on demand, the draft is dishonored if presentment for payment is duly made to the acceptor and the draft is not paid on the day of presentment.

(2) If the draft is not payable on demand, the draft is dishonored if presentment for payment is duly made to the acceptor and payment is not made on the day it becomes payable or the day of presentment, whichever is later.

(e) In any case in which presentment is otherwise required for dishonor under this section and presentment is excused under Section 3—504, dishonor occurs without presentment if the instrument is not duly accepted or paid.

(f) If a draft is dishonored because timely acceptance of the draft was not made and the person entitled to demand acceptance consents to a late acceptance, from the time of acceptance the draft is treated as never having been dishonored.

### § 3—503. Notice of Dishonor.

(a) The obligation of an indorser stated in Section 3—415(a) and the obligation of a drawer stated in Section 3—414(d) may not be enforced unless (i) the indorser or drawer is given notice of dishonor of the instrument complying with this section or (ii) notice of dishonor is excused under Section 3—504(b).

(b) Notice of dishonor may be given by any person; may be given by any commercially reasonable means, including an oral, written, or electronic communication; and is sufficient if it reasonably identifies the instrument and indicates that the instrument has been dishonored or has not been paid or accepted. Return of an instrument given to a bank for collection is sufficient notice of dishonor.

(c) Subject to Section 3—504(c), with respect to an instrument taken for collection by a collecting bank, notice of dishonor must be given (i) by the bank before midnight of the next banking day following the banking day on which the bank receives notice of dishonor of the instrument, or (ii) by any other person within 30 days following the day on which the person receives notice of dishonor. With respect to any other instrument, notice of dishonor must be given within 30 days following the day on which dishonor occurs.

### § 3—504. Excused Presentment and Notice of Dishonor.

(a) Presentment for payment or acceptance of an instrument is excused if (i) the person entitled to present the instrument cannot with reasonable diligence make presentment, (ii) the maker or acceptor has repudiated an obligation to pay the instrument or is dead or in insolvency proceedings, (iii) by the terms of the instrument presentment is not necessary to enforce the obligation of indorsers or the drawer, (iv) the drawer or indorser whose obligation is being enforced has waived presentment or otherwise has no reason to expect or right to require that the instrument be paid or accepted, or (v) the drawer instructed the drawee not to pay or accept the draft or the drawee was not obligated to the drawer to pay the draft.

(b) Notice of dishonor is excused if (i) by the terms of the instrument notice of dishonor is not necessary to enforce the obligation of a party to pay the instrument, or (ii) the party whose obligation is being enforced waived notice of dishonor. A waiver of presentment is also a waiver of notice of dishonor.

(c) Delay in giving notice of dishonor is excused if the delay was caused by circumstances beyond the control of the person giving the notice and the person giving the notice exercised reasonable diligence after the cause of the delay ceased to operate.

### § 3—505. Evidence of Dishonor.

(a) The following are admissible as evidence and create a presumption of dishonor and of any notice of dishonor stated:

(1) a document regular in form as provided in subsection (b) which purports to be a protest;

(2) a purported stamp or writing of the drawee, payor bank, or presenting bank on or accompanying the instrument stating that acceptance or payment has been refused unless reasons for the refusal are stated and the reasons are not consistent with dishonor;

(3) a book or record of the drawee, payor bank, or collecting bank, kept in the usual course of business which shows dishonor, even if there is no evidence of who made the entry.

(b) A protest is a certificate of dishonor made by a United States consul or vice consul, or a notary public or other person authorized to administer oaths by the law of the place where dishonor occurs. It may be made upon information satisfactory to that person. The protest must identify the instrument and certify either that presentment has been made or, if not made, the reason why it was not made, and that the instrument has been dishonored by nonacceptance or nonpayment. The protest may also certify that notice of dishonor has been given to some or all parties.

## Part 6  Discharge and Payment

### § 3—601. Discharge and Effect of Discharge.

(a) The obligation of a party to pay the instrument is discharged as stated in this Article or by an act or agreement with the party which would discharge an obligation to pay money under a simple contract.

(b) Discharge of the obligation of a party is not effective against a person acquiring rights of a holder in due course of the instrument without notice of the discharge.

### § 3—602. Payment.

(a) Subject to subsection (b), an instrument is paid to the extent payment is made (i) by or on behalf of a party obliged to pay the instrument, and (ii) to a person entitled to enforce the instrument. To the extent of the payment, the obligation of the party obliged to pay the instrument is discharged even though payment is made with knowledge of a claim to the instrument under Section 3—306 by another person.

(b) The obligation of a party to pay the instrument is not discharged under subsection (a) if:

(1) a claim to the instrument under Section 3—306 is enforceable against the party receiving payment and (i) payment is made with knowledge by the payor that payment is prohibited by injunction or similar process of a court of competent jurisdiction, or (ii) in the case of an instrument other than a cashier's check, teller's check, or certified check, the party making payment accepted, from the person having a claim to the instrument, indemnity against loss resulting from refusal to pay the person entitled to enforce the instrument; or

(2) the person making payment knows that the instrument is a stolen instrument and pays a person it knows is in wrongful possession of the instrument.

### § 3—603. Tender of Payment.

(a) If tender of payment of an obligation to pay an instrument is made to a person entitled to enforce the instrument, the effect of tender is governed by principles of law applicable to tender of payment under a simple contract.

(b) If tender of payment of an obligation to pay an instrument is made to a person entitled to enforce the instrument and the tender is refused, there is discharge, to the extent of the amount of the tender, of the obligation of an indorser or accommodation party having a right of recourse with respect to the obligation to which the tender relates.

(c) If tender of payment of an amount due on an instrument is made to a person entitled to enforce the instrument, the

obligation of the obligor to pay interest after the due date on the amount tendered is discharged. If presentment is required with respect to an instrument and the obligor is able and ready to pay on the due date at every place of payment stated in the instrument, the obligor is deemed to have made tender of payment on the due date to the person entitled to enforce the instrument.

### § 3—604. Discharge by Cancellation or Renunciation.

(a) A person entitled to enforce an instrument, with or without consideration, may discharge the obligation of a party to pay the instrument (i) by an intentional voluntary act, such as surrender of the instrument to the party, destruction, mutilation, or cancellation of the instrument, cancellation or striking out of the party's signature, or the addition of words to the instrument indicating discharge, or (ii) by agreeing not to sue or otherwise renouncing rights against the party by a signed writing.

(b) Cancellation or striking out of an indorsement pursuant to subsection (a) does not affect the status and rights of a party derived from the indorsement.

### § 3—605. Discharge of Indorsers and Accommodation Parties.

(a) In this section, the term "indorser" includes a drawer having the obligation described in Section 3—414(d).

(b) Discharge, under Section 3—604, of the obligation of a party to pay an instrument does not discharge the obligation of an indorser or accommodation party having a right of recourse against the discharged party.

(c) If a person entitled to enforce an instrument agrees, with or without consideration, to an extension of the due date of the obligation of a party to pay the instrument, the extension discharges an indorser or accommodation party having a right of recourse against the party whose obligation is extended to the extent the indorser or accommodation party proves that the extension caused loss to the indorser or accommodation party with respect to the right of recourse.

(d) If a person entitled to enforce an instrument agrees, with or without consideration, to a material modification of the obligation of a party other than an extension of the due date, the modification discharges the obligation of an indorser or accommodation party having a right of recourse against the person whose obligation is modified to the extent the modification causes loss to the indorser or accommodation party with respect to the right of recourse. The loss suffered by the indorser or accommodation party as a result of the modification is equal to the amount of the right of recourse unless the person enforcing the instrument proves that no loss was caused by the modification or that the loss caused by the modification was an amount less than the amount of the right of recourse.

(e) If the obligation of a party to pay an instrument is secured by an interest in collateral and a person entitled to enforce the instrument impairs the value of the interest in collateral, the obligation of an indorser or accommodation party having a right of recourse against the obligor is discharged to the extent of the impairment. The value of an interest in collateral is impaired to the extent (i) the value of the interest is reduced to an amount less than the amount of the right of recourse of the party asserting discharge, or (ii) the reduction in value of the interest causes an increase in the amount by which the amount of the right of recourse exceeds the value of the interest. The burden of proving impairment is on the party asserting discharge.

(f) If the obligation of a party is secured by an interest in collateral not provided by an accommodation party and a person entitled to enforce the instrument impairs the value of the interest in collateral, the obligation of any party who is jointly and severally liable with respect to the secured obligation is discharged to the extent the impairment causes the party asserting discharge to pay more than that party would have been obliged to pay, taking into account rights of contribution, if impairment had not occurred. If the party asserting discharge is an accommodation party not entitled to discharge under subsection (e), the party is deemed to have a right to contribution based on joint and several liability rather than a right to reimbursement. The burden of proving impairment is on the party asserting discharge.

(g) Under subsection (e) or (f), impairing value of an interest in collateral includes (i) failure to obtain or maintain perfection or recordation of the interest in collateral, (ii) release of collateral without substitution of collateral of equal value, (iii) failure to perform a duty to preserve the value of collateral owed, under Article 9 or other law, to a debtor or surety or other person secondarily liable, or (iv) failure to comply with applicable law in disposing of collateral.

(h) An accommodation party is not discharged under subsection (c), (d), or (e) unless the person entitled to enforce the instrument knows of the accommodation or has notice under Section 3—419(c) that the instrument was signed for accommodation.

(i) A party is not discharged under this section if (i) the party asserting discharge consents to the event or conduct that is the basis of the discharge, or (ii) the instrument or a separate agreement of the party provides for waiver of discharge under this section either specifically or by general language indicating that parties waive defenses based on suretyship or impairment of collateral.

## ADDENDUM TO REVISED ARTICLE 3
### Notes to Legislative Counsel

1. If revised Article 3 is adopted in your state, the reference in Section 2—511 to Section 3—802 should be changed to Section 3—310.

2. If revised Article 3 is adopted in your state and the Uniform Fiduciaries Act is also in effect in your state, you may want to consider amending Uniform Fiduciaries Act § 9 to conform to Section 3—307(b)(2)(iii) and (4)(iii). See Official Comment 3 to Section 3—307.

# Article 4
# BANK DEPOSITS AND COLLECTIONS

## Part 1    General Provisions and Definitions

### § 4—101. Short Title.

This Article shall be known and may be cited as Uniform Commercial Code—Bank Deposits and Collections.

### § 4—102. Applicability.

(1) To the extent that items within this Article are also within the scope of Articles 3 and 8, they are subject to the provisions of those Articles. In the event of conflict the provisions of this Article govern those of Article 3 but the provisions of Article 8 govern those of this Article.

(2) The liability of a bank for action or non-action with respect to any item handled by it for purposes of presentment, payment or collection is governed by the law of the place where the bank is located. In the case of action or non-action by or at a branch or separate office of a bank, its liability is governed by the law of the place where the branch or separate office is located.

### § 4—103. Variation by Agreement; Measure of Damages; Certain Action Constituting Ordinary Care.

(1) The effect of the provisions of this Article may be varied by agreement except that no agreement can disclaim a bank's responsibility for its own lack of good faith or failure to exercise ordinary care or can limit the measure of damages for such lack or failure; but the parties may by agreement determine the standards by which such responsibility is to be measured if such standards are not manifestly unreasonable.

(2) Federal Reserve regulations and operating letters, clearing house rules, and the like, have the effect of agreements under subsection (1), whether or not specifically assented to by all parties interested in items handled.

(3) Action or nonaction approved by this Article or pursuant to Federal Reserve regulations or operating letters constitutes the exercise of ordinary care and, in the absence of special instructions, action or nonaction consistent with clearing house rules and the like or with a general banking usage not disapproved by this Article, prima facie constitutes the exercise of ordinary care.

(4) The specification or approval of certain procedures by this Article does not constitute disapproval of other procedures which may be reasonable under the circumstances.

(5) The measure of damages for failure to exercise ordinary care in handling an item is the amount of the item reduced by an amount which could not have been realized by the use of ordinary care, and where there is bad faith it includes other damages, if any, suffered by the party as a proximate consequence.

### § 4—104. Definitions and Index of Definitions.

(1) In this Article unless the context otherwise requires

(a) ''Account'' means any account with a bank and includes a checking, time, interest or savings account;

(b) ''Afternoon'' means the period of a day between noon and midnight;

(c) ''Banking day'' means that part of any day on which a bank is open to the public for carrying on substantially all of its banking functions;

(d) ''Clearing house'' means any association of banks or other payors regularly clearing items;

(e) ''Customer'' means any person having an account with a bank or for whom a bank has agreed to collect items and includes a bank carrying an account with another bank;

(f) ''Documentary draft'' means any negotiable or non-negotiable draft with accompanying documents, securities or other papers to be delivered against honor of the draft;

(g) ''Item'' means any instrument for the payment of money even though it is not negotiable but does not include money;

(h) ''Midnight deadline'' with respect to a bank is midnight on its next banking day following the banking day on which it receives the relevant item or notice or from which the time for taking action commences to run, whichever is later;

(i) ''Properly payable'' includes the availability of funds for payment at the time of decision to pay or dishonor;

(j) ''Settle'' means to pay in cash, by clearing house settlement, in a charge or credit or by remittance, or otherwise as instructed. A settlement may be either provisional or final;

(k) ''Suspends payments'' with respect to a bank means that it has been closed by order of the supervisory authorities, that a public officer has been appointed to take it over or that it ceases or refuses to make payments in the ordinary course of business.

(2) Other definitions applying to this Article and the sections in which they appear are:

    ''Collecting bank'' Section 4—105.
    ''Depositary bank'' Section 4—105.
    ''Intermediary bank'' Section 4—105.
    ''Payor bank'' Section 4—105.
    ''Presenting bank'' Section 4—105.
    ''Remitting bank'' Section 4—105.

(3) The following definitions in other Articles apply to this Article:

    ''Acceptance'' Section 3—410.
    ''Certificate of deposit'' Section 3—104.
    ''Certification'' Section 3—411.
    ''Check'' Section 3—104.
    ''Draft'' Section 3—104.
    ''Holder in due course'' Section 3—302.
    ''Notice of dishonor'' Section 3—508.
    ''Presentment'' Section 3—504.

    ''Protest'' Section 3—509.
    ''Secondary party'' Section 3—102.

(4) In addition Article 1 contains general definitions and principles of construction and interpretation applicable throughout this Article.

**§ 4—105. ''Depositary Bank''; ''Intermediary Bank''; ''Collecting Bank''; ''Payor Bank''; ''Presenting Bank''; ''Remitting Bank''.**

In this Article unless the context otherwise requires:

(a) ''Depositary bank'' means the first bank to which an item is transferred for collection even though it is also the payor bank;

(b) ''Payor bank'' means a bank by which an item is payable as drawn or accepted;

(c) ''Intermediary bank'' means any bank to which an item is transferred in course of collection except the depositary or payor bank;

(d) ''Collecting bank'' means any bank handling the item for collection except the payor bank;

(e) ''Presenting bank'' means any bank presenting an item except a payor bank;

(f) ''Remitting bank'' means any payor or intermediary bank remitting for an item.

**§ 4—106. Separate Office of a Bank.**

A branch or separate office of a bank [maintaining its own deposit ledgers] is a separate bank for the purpose of computing the time within which and determining the place at or to which action may be taken or notices or orders shall be given under this Article and under Article 3.

Note: *The brackets are to make it optional with the several states whether to require a branch to maintain its own deposit ledgers in order to be considered to be a separate bank for certain purposes under Article 4. In some states ''maintaining its own deposit ledgers'' is a satisfactory test. In others branch banking practices are such that this test would not be suitable.*

**§ 4—107. Time of Receipt of Items.**

(1) For the purpose of allowing time to process items, prove balances and make the necessary entries on its books to determine its position for the day, a bank may fix an afternoon hour of 2 P.M. or later as a cut-off hour for the handling of money and items and the making of entries on its books.

(2) Any item or deposit of money received on any day after a cut-off hour so fixed or after the close of the banking day may be treated as being received at the opening of the next banking day.

**§ 4—108. Delays.**

(1) Unless otherwise instructed, a collecting bank in a good faith effort to secure payment may, in the case of specific items and with or without the approval of any person involved, waive, modify or extend time limits imposed or permitted by this Act for a period not in excess of an additional

banking day without discharge of secondary parties and without liability to its transferor or any prior party.

(2) Delay by a collecting bank or payor bank beyond time limits prescribed or permitted by this Act or by instructions is excused if caused by interruption of communication facilities, suspension of payments by another bank, war, emergency conditions or other circumstances beyond the control of the bank provided it exercises such diligence as the circumstances require.

### § 4—109. Process of Posting.

The ''process of posting'' means the usual procedure followed by a payor bank in determining to pay an item and in recording the payment including one or more of the following or other steps as determined by the bank:

(a) verification of any signature;

(b) ascertaining that sufficient funds are available;

(c) affixing a ''paid'' or other stamp;

(d) entering a charge or entry to a customer's account;

(e) correcting or reversing an entry or erroneous action with respect to the item.

## Part 2  Collection of Items: Depositary and Collecting Banks

### § 4—201. Presumption and Duration of Agency Status of Collecting Banks and Provisional Status of Credits; Applicability of Article; Item Indorsed ''Pay Any Bank''.

(1) Unless a contrary intent clearly appears and prior to the time that a settlement given by a collecting bank for an item is or becomes final (subsection (3) of Section 4—211 and Sections 4—212 and 4—213) the bank is an agent or subagent of the owner of the item and any settlement given for the item is provisional. This provision applies regardless of the form of indorsement or lack of indorsement and even though credit given for the item is subject to immediate withdrawal as of right or is in fact withdrawn; but the continuance of ownership of an item by its owner and any rights of the owner to proceeds of the item are subject to rights of a collecting bank such as those resulting from outstanding advances on the item and valid rights of setoff. When an item is handled by banks for purposes of presentment, payment and collection, the relevant provisions of this Article apply even though action of parties clearly establishes that a particular bank has purchased the item and is the owner of it.

(2) After an item has been indorsed with the words ''pay any bank'' or the like, only a bank may acquire the rights of a holder

(a) until the item has been returned to the customer initiating collection; or

(b) until the item has been specially indorsed by a bank to a person who is not a bank.

### § 4—202. Responsibility for Collection; When Action Seasonable.

(1) A collecting bank must use ordinary care in

(a) presenting an item or sending it for presentment; and

(b) sending notice of dishonor or non-payment or returning an item other than a documentary draft to the bank's transferor [or directly to the depositary bank under subsection (2) of Section 4—212] *(see note to Section 4—212)* after learning that the item has not been paid or accepted as the case may be; and

(c) settling for an item when the bank receives final settlement; and

(d) making or providing for any necessary protest; and

(e) notifying its transferor of any loss or delay in transit within a reasonable time after discovery thereof.

(2) A collecting bank taking proper action before its midnight deadline following receipt of an item, notice or payment acts seasonably; taking proper action within a reasonably longer time may be seasonable but the bank has the burden of so establishing.

(3) Subject to subsection (1)(a), a bank is not liable for the insolvency, neglect, misconduct, mistake or default of another bank or person or for loss or destruction of an item in transit or in the possession of others.

### § 4—203. Effect of Instructions.

Subject to the provisions of Article 3 concerning conversion of instruments (Section 3—419) and the provisions of both Article 3 and this Article concerning restrictive indorsements only a collecting bank's transferor can give instructions which affect the bank or constitute notice to it and a collecting bank is not liable to prior parties for any action taken pursuant to such instructions or in accordance with any agreement with its transferor.

### § 4—204. Methods of Sending and Presenting; Sending Direct to Payor Bank.

(1) A collecting bank must send items by reasonably prompt method taking into consideration any relevant instructions, the nature of the item, the number of such items on hand, and the cost of collection involved and the method generally used by it or others to present such items.

(2) A collecting bank may send

(a) any item direct to the payor bank;

(b) any item to any non-bank payor if authorized by its transferor; and

(c) any item other than documentary drafts to any non-bank payor, if authorized by Federal Reserve regulation or operating letter, clearing house rule or the like.

(3) Presentment may be made by a presenting bank at a place where the payor bank has requested that presentment be made.

## § 4—205. Supplying Missing Indorsement; No Notice from Prior Indorsement.

(1) A depository bank which has taken an item for collection may supply any indorsement of the customer which is necessary to title unless the item contains the words "payee's indorsement required" or the like. In the absence of such a requirement a statement placed on the item by the depositary bank to the effect that the item was deposited by a customer or credited to his account is effective as the customer's indorsement.

(2) An intermediary bank, or payor bank which is not a depository bank, is neither given notice nor otherwise affected by a restrictive indorsement of any person except the bank's immediate transferor.

## § 4—206. Transfer Between Banks.

Any agreed method which identifies the transferor bank is sufficient for the item's further transfer to another bank.

## § 4—207. Warranties of Customer and Collecting Bank on Transfer or Presentment of Items; Time for Claims.

(1) Each customer or collecting bank who obtains payment or acceptance of an item and each prior customer and collecting bank warrants to the payor bank or other payor who in good faith pays or accepts the item that

(a) he has a good title to the item or is authorized to obtain payment or acceptance on behalf of one who has a good title; and

(b) he has no knowledge that the signature of the maker or drawer is unauthorized, except that this warranty is not given by any customer or collecting bank that is a holder in due course and acts in good faith

(i) to a maker with respect to the maker's own signature; or

(ii) to a drawer with respect to the drawer's own signature, whether or not the drawer is also the drawee; or

(iii) to an acceptor of an item if the holder in due course took the item after the acceptance or obtained the acceptance without knowledge that the drawer's signature was unauthorized; and

(c) the item has not been materially altered, except that this warranty is not given by any customer or collecting bank that is a holder in due course and acts in good faith

(i) to the maker of a note; or

(ii) to the drawer of a draft whether or not the drawer is also the drawee; or

(iii) to the acceptor of an item with respect to an alteration made prior to the acceptance if the holder in due course took the item after the acceptance, even though the acceptance provided "payable as originally drawn" or equivalent terms; or

(iv) to the acceptor of an item with respect to an alteration made after the acceptance.

(2) Each customer and collecting bank who transfers an item and receives a settlement or other consideration for it warrants to his transferee and to any subsequent collecting bank who takes the item in good faith that

(a) he has a good title to the item or is authorized to obtain payment or acceptance on behalf of one who has a good title and the transfer is otherwise rightful; and

(b) all signatures are genuine or authorized; and

(c) the item has not been materially altered; and

(d) no defense of any party is good against him; and

(e) he has no knowledge of any insolvency proceeding instituted with respect to the maker or acceptor or the drawer of an unaccepted item.

In addition each customer and collecting bank so transferring an item and receiving a settlement or other consideration engages that upon dishonor and any necessary notice of dishonor and protest he will take up the item.

(3) The warranties and the engagement to honor set forth in the two preceding subsections arise notwithstanding the absence of indorsement or words of guaranty or warranty in the transfer or presentment and a collecting bank remains liable for their breach despite remittance to its transferor. Damages for breach of such warranties or engagement to honor shall not exceed the consideration received by the customer or collecting bank responsible plus finance charges and expenses related to the item, if any.

(4) Unless a claim for breach of warranty under this section is made within a reasonable time after the person claiming learns of the breach, the person liable is discharged to the extent of any loss caused by the delay in making claim.

## § 4—208. Security Interest of Collecting Bank in Items, Accompanying Documents and Proceeds.

(1) A bank has a security interest in an item and any accompanying documents or the proceeds of either

(a) in case of an item deposited in an account to the extent to which credit given for the item has been withdrawn or applied;

(b) in case of an item for which it has given credit available for withdrawal as of right, to the extent of the credit given whether or not the credit is drawn upon and whether or not there is a right of charge-back; or

(c) if it makes an advance on or against the item.

(2) When credit which has been given for several items received at one time or pursuant to a single agreement is withdrawn or applied in part the security interest remains upon all the items, any accompanying documents or the proceeds of either. For the purpose of this section, credits first given are first withdrawn.

(3) Receipt by a collecting bank of a final settlement for an item is a realization on its security interest in the item, accompanying documents and proceeds. To the extent and so long as the bank does not receive final settlement for the item or give up possession of the item or accompanying documents

for purposes other than collection, the security interest continues and is subject to the provisions of Article 9 except that

(a) no security agreement is necessary to make the security interest enforceable (subsection (1)(a) of Section 9—203); and

(b) no filing is required to perfect the security interest; and

(c) the security interest has priority over conflicting perfected security interests in the item, accompanying documents or proceeds.

### § 4—209. When Bank Gives Value for Purposes of Holder in Due Course.

For purposes of determining its status as a holder in due course, the bank has given value to the extent that it has a security interest in an item provided that the bank otherwise complies with the requirements of Section 3—302 on what constitutes a holder in due course.

### § 4—210. Presentment by Notice of Item Not Payable by, Through or at a Bank; Liability of Secondary Parties.

(1) Unless otherwise instructed, a collecting bank may present an item not payable by, through or at a bank by sending to the party to accept or pay a written notice that the bank holds the item for acceptance or payment. The notice must be sent in time to be received on or before the day when presentment is due and the bank must meet any requirement of the party to accept or pay under Section 3—505 by the close of the bank's next banking day after it knows of the requirement.

(2) Where presentment is made by notice and neither honor nor request for compliance with a requirement under Section 3—505 is received by the close of business on the day after maturity or in the case of demand items by the close of business on the third banking day after notice was sent, the presenting bank may treat the item as dishonored and charge any secondary party by sending him notice of the facts.

### § 4—211. Media of Remittance; Provisional and Final Settlement in Remittance Cases.

(1) A collecting bank may take in settlement of an item

(a) a check of the remitting bank or of another bank on any bank except the remitting bank; or

(b) a cashier's check or similar primary obligation of a remitting bank which is a member of or clears through a member of the same clearing house or group as the collecting bank; or

(c) appropriate authority to charge an account of the remitting bank or of another bank with the collecting bank; or

(d) if the item is drawn upon or payable by a person other than a bank, a cashier's check, certified check or other bank check or obligation.

(2) If before its midnight deadline the collecting bank properly dishonors a remittance check or authorization to charge on itself or presents or forwards for collection a remittance instrument of or on another bank which is of a kind approved by subsection (1) or has not been authorized by it, the collecting bank is not liable to prior parties in the event of the dishonor of such check, instrument or authorization.

(3) A settlement for an item by means of a remittance instrument or authorization to charge is or becomes a final settlement as to both the person making and the person receiving the settlement

(a) if the remittance instrument or authorization to charge is of a kind approved by subsection (1) or has not been authorized by the person receiving the settlement and in either case the person receiving the settlement acts seasonably before its midnight deadline in presenting, forwarding for collection or paying the instrument or authorization,—at the time the remittance instrument or authorization is finally paid by the payor by which it is payable;

(b) if the person receiving the settlement has authorized remittance by a non-bank check or obligation or by a cashier's check or similar primary obligation of or a check upon the payor or other remitting bank which is not of a kind approved by subsection (1)(b),—at the time of the receipt of such remittance check or obligation; or

(c) if in a case not covered by sub-paragraphs (a) or (b) the person receiving the settlement fails to seasonably present, forward for collection, pay or return a remittance instrument or authorization to it to charge before its midnight deadline,—at such midnight deadline.

### § 4—212. Right of Charge-Back or Refund.

(1) If a collecting bank has made provisional settlement with its customer for an item and itself fails by reason of dishonor, suspension of payments by a bank or otherwise to receive a settlement for the item which is or becomes final, the bank may revoke the settlement given by it, charge back the amount of any credit given for the item to its customer's account or obtain refund from its customer whether or not it is able to return the items if by its midnight deadline or within a longer reasonable time after it learns the facts it returns the item or sends notification of the facts. These rights to revoke, charge-back and obtain refund terminate if and when a settlement for the item received by the bank is or becomes final (subsection (3) of Section 4—211 and subsections (2) and (3) of Section 4—213).

[(2) Within the time and manner prescribed by this section and Section 4—301, an intermediary or payor bank, as the case may be, may return an unpaid item directly to the depositary bank and may send for collection a draft on the depositary bank and obtain reimbursement. In such case, if the depositary bank has received provisional settlement for the item, it must reimburse the bank drawing the draft and any provisional credits for the item between banks shall become and remain final.]

Note: *Direct returns is recognized as an innovation that is not yet established bank practice, and therefore, Paragraph 2 has been bracketed. Some lawyers have doubts whether it should be included in legislation or left to development by agreement.*

(3) A depositary bank which is also the payor may charge-back the amount of an item to its customer's account or obtain refund in accordance with the section governing return of an item received by a payor bank for credit on its books (Section 4—301).

(4) The right to charge-back is not affected by

(a) prior use of the credit given for the item; or

(b) failure by any bank to exercise ordinary care with respect to the item but any bank so failing remains liable.

(5) A failure to charge-back or claim refund does not affect other rights of the bank against the customer or any other party.

(6) If credit is given in dollars as the equivalent of the value of an item payable in a foreign currency the dollar amount of any charge-back or refund shall be calculated on the basis of the buying sight rate for the foreign currency prevailing on the day when the person entitled to the charge-back or refund learns that it will not receive payment in ordinary course.

### § 4—213. Final Payment of Item by Payor Bank; When Provisional Debits and Credits Become Final; When Certain Credits Become Available for Withdrawal.

(1) An item is finally paid by a payor bank when the bank has done any of the following, whichever happens first:

(a) paid the item in cash; or

(b) settled for the item without reserving a right to revoke the settlement and without having such right under statute, clearing house rule or agreement; or

(c) completed the process of posting the item to the indicated account of the drawer, maker or other person to be charged therewith; or

(d) made a provisional settlement for the item and failed to revoke the settlement in the time and manner permitted by statute, clearing house rule or agreement.

Upon a final payment under subparagraphs (b), (c) or (d) the payor bank shall be accountable for the amount of the item.

(2) If provisional settlement for an item between the presenting and payor banks is made through a clearing house or by debits or credits in an account between them, then to the extent that provisional debits or credits for the item are entered in accounts between the presenting and payor banks or between the presenting and successive prior collecting banks seriatim, they become final upon final payment of the item by the payor bank.

(3) If a collecting bank receives a settlement for an item which is or becomes final (subsection (3) of Section 4—211, subsection (2) of Section 4—213) the bank is accountable to its customer for the amount of the item and any provisional credit given for the item in an account with its customer becomes final.

(4) Subject to any right of the bank to apply the credit to an obligation of the customer, credit given by a bank for an item in an account with its customer becomes available for withdrawal as of right

(a) in any case where the bank has received a provisional settlement for the item,—when such settlement becomes final and the bank has had a reasonable time to learn that the settlement is final;

(b) in any case where the bank is both a depositary bank and a payor bank and the item is finally paid,—at the opening of the bank's second banking day following receipt of the item.

(5) A deposit of money in a bank is final when made but, subject to any right of the bank to apply the deposit to an obligation of the customer, the deposit becomes available for withdrawal as of right at the opening of the bank's next banking day following receipt of the deposit.

### § 4—214. Insolvency and Preference.

(1) Any item in or coming into the possession of a payor or collecting bank which suspends payment and which item is not finally paid shall be returned by the receiver, trustee or agent in charge of the closed bank to the presenting bank or the closed bank's customer.

(2) If a payor bank finally pays an item and suspends payments without making a settlement for the item with its customer or the presenting bank which settlement is or becomes final, the owner of the item has a preferred claim against the payor bank.

(3) If a payor bank gives or a collecting bank gives or receives a provisional settlement for an item and thereafter suspends payments, the suspension does not prevent or interfere with the settlement becoming final if such finality occurs automatically upon the lapse of certain time or the happening of certain events (subsection (3) of Section 4—211, subsections (1)(d), (2) and (3) of Section 4—213).

(4) If a collecting bank receives from subsequent parties settlement for an item which settlement is or becomes final and suspends payments without making a settlement for the item with its customer which is or becomes final, the owner of the item has a preferred claim against such collecting bank.

## Part 3   Collection of Items: Payor Banks

### § 4—301. Deferred Posting; Recovery of Payment by Return of Items; Time of Dishonor.

(1) Where an authorized settlement for a demand item (other than a documentary draft) received by a payor bank otherwise than for immediate payment over the counter has been made before midnight of the banking day of receipt the payor bank may revoke the settlement and recover any payment if before it has made final payment (subsection (1) of Section 4—213) and before its midnight deadline it

(a) returns the item; or

(b) sends written notice of dishonor or nonpayment if

the item is held for protest or is otherwise unavailable for return.

(2) If a demand item is received by a payor bank for credit on its books it may return such item or send notice of dishonor and may revoke any credit given or recover the amount thereof withdrawn by its customer, if it acts within the time limit and in the manner specified in the preceding subsection.

(3) Unless previous notice of dishonor has been sent an item is dishonored at the time when for purposes of dishonor it is returned or notice sent in accordance with this section.

(4) An item is returned:

(a) as to an item received through a clearing house, when it is delivered to the presenting or last collecting bank or to the clearing house or is sent or delivered in accordance with its rules; or

(b) in all other cases, when it is sent or delivered to the bank's customer or transferor or pursuant to his instructions.

### § 4—302. Payor Bank's Responsibility for Late Return of Item.

In the absence of a valid defense such as breach of a presentment warranty (subsection (1) of Section 4— 207), settlement effected or the like, if an item is presented on and received by a payor bank the bank is accountable for the amount of

(a) a demand item other than a documentary draft whether properly payable or not if the bank, in any case where it is not also the depositary bank, retains the item beyond midnight of the banking day of receipt without settling for it or, regardless of whether it is also the depositary bank, does not pay or return the item or send notice of dishonor until after its midnight deadline; or

(b) any other properly payable item unless within the time allowed for acceptance or payment of that item the bank either accepts or pays the item or returns it and accompanying documents.

### § 4—303. When Items Subject to Notice, Stop-Order, Legal Process or Setoff; Order in Which Items May Be Charged or Certified.

(1) Any knowledge, notice or stop-order received by, legal process served upon or setoff exercised by a payor bank, whether or not effective under other rules of law to terminate, suspend or modify the bank's right or duty to pay an item or to charge its customer's account for the item, comes too late to so terminate, suspend or modify such right or duty if the knowledge, notice, stop-order or legal process is received or served and a reasonable time for the bank to act thereon expires or the setoff is exercised after the bank has done any of the following:

(a) accepted or certified the item;

(b) paid the item in cash;

(c) settled for the item without reserving a right to revoke

the settlement and without having such right under statute, clearing house rule or agreement;

(d) completed the process of posting the item to the indicated account of the drawer, maker or other person to be charged therewith or otherwise has evidenced by examination of such indicated account and by action its decision to pay the item; or

(e) become accountable for the amount of the item under subsection (1)(d) of Section 4—213 and Section 4—302 dealing with the payor bank's responsibility for late return of items.

(2) Subject to the provisions of subsection (1) items may be accepted, paid, certified or charged to the indicated account of its customer in any order convenient to the bank.

## Part 4 Relationship Between Payor Bank and Its Customer

### § 4—401. When Bank May Charge Customer's Account.

(1) As against its customer, a bank may charge against his account any item which is otherwise properly payable from that account even though the charge creates an overdraft.

(2) A bank which in good faith makes payment to a holder may charge the indicated account of its customer according to

(a) the original tenor of his altered item; or

(b) the tenor of his completed item, even though the bank knows the item has been completed unless the bank has notice that the completion was improper.

### § 4—402. Bank's Liability to Customer for Wrongful Dishonor.

A payor bank is liable to its customer for damages proximately caused by the wrongful dishonor of an item. When the dishonor occurs through mistake liability is limited to actual damages proved. If so proximately caused and proved damages may include damages for an arrest or prosecution of the customer or other consequential damages. Whether any consequential damages are proximately caused by the wrongful dishonor is a question of fact to be determined in each case.

### § 4—403. Customer's Right to Stop Payment; Burden of Proof of Loss.

(1) A customer may by order to his bank stop payment of any item payable for his account but the order must be received at such time and in such manner as to afford the bank a reasonable opportunity to act on it prior to any action by the bank with respect to the item described in Section 4—303.

(2) An oral order is binding upon the bank only for fourteen calendar days unless confirmed in writing within that period. A written order is effective for only six months unless renewed in writing.

(3) The burden of establishing the fact and amount of loss resulting from the payment of an item contrary to a binding stop payment order is on the customer.

### § 4—404. Bank Not Obligated to Pay Check More Than Six Months Old.

A bank is under no obligation to a customer having a checking account to pay a check, other than a certified check, which is presented more than six months after its date, but it may charge its customer's account for a payment made thereafter in good faith.

### § 4—405. Death or Incompetence of Customer.

(1) A payor or collecting bank's authority to accept, pay or collect an item or to account for proceeds of its collection if otherwise effective is not rendered ineffective by incompetence of a customer of either bank existing at the time the item is issued or its collection is undertaken if the bank does not know of an adjudication of incompetence. Neither death nor incompetence of a customer revokes such authority to accept, pay, collect or account until the bank knows of the fact of death or of an adjudication of incompetence and has reasonable opportunity to act on it.

(2) Even with knowledge a bank may for 10 days after the date of death pay or certify checks drawn on or prior to that date unless ordered to stop payment by a person claiming an interest in the account.

### § 4—406. Customer's Duty to Discover and Report Unauthorized Signature or Alteration.

(1) When a bank sends to its customer a statement of account accompanied by items paid in good faith in support of the debit entries or holds the statement and items pursuant to a request or instructions of its customer or otherwise in a reasonable manner makes the statement and items available to the customer, the customer must exercise reasonable care and promptness to examine the statement and items to discover his unauthorized signature or any alteration on an item and must notify the bank promptly after discovery thereof.

(2) If the bank establishes that the customer failed with respect to an item to comply with the duties imposed on the customer by subsection (1) the customer is precluded from asserting against the bank

    (a) his unauthorized signature or any alteration on the item if the bank also establishes that it suffered a loss by reason of such failure; and

    (b) an unauthorized signature or alteration by the same wrongdoer on any other item paid in good faith by the bank after the first item and statement was available to the customer for a reasonable period not exceeding fourteen calendar days and before the bank receives notification from the customer of any such unauthorized signature or alteration.

(3) The preclusion under subsection (2) does not apply if the customer establishes lack of ordinary care on the part of the bank in paying the item(s).

(4) Without regard to care or lack of care of either the customer or the bank a customer who does not within one year from the time the statement and items are made available to the customer (subsection (1)) discover and report his unauthorized signature or any alteration on the face or back of the item or does not within three years from that time discover and report any unauthorized indorsement is precluded from asserting against the bank such unauthorized signature or indorsement or such alteration.

(5) If under this section a payor bank has a valid defense against a claim of a customer upon or resulting from payment of an item and waives or fails upon request to assert the defense the bank may not assert against any collecting bank or other prior party presenting or transferring the item a claim based upon the unauthorized signature or alteration giving rise to the customer's claim.

### § 4—407. Payor Bank's Right to Subrogation on Improper Payment.

If a payor bank has paid an item over the stop payment order of the drawer or maker or otherwise under circumstances giving a basis for objection by the drawer or maker, to prevent unjust enrichment and only to the extent necessary to prevent loss to the bank by reason of its payment of the item, the payor bank shall be subrogated to the rights

    (a) of any holder in due course on the item against the drawer or maker; and

    (b) of the payee or any other holder of the item against the drawer or maker either on the item or under the transaction out of which the item arose; and

    (c) of the drawer or maker against the payee or any other holder of the item with respect to the transaction out of which the item arose.

## Part 5    Collection of Documentary Drafts

### § 4—501. Handling of Documentary Drafts; Duty to Send for Presentment and to Notify Customer of Dishonor.

A bank which takes a documentary draft for collection must present or send the draft and accompanying documents for presentment and upon learning that the draft has not been paid or accepted in due course must seasonably notify its customer of such fact even though it may have discounted or bought the draft or extended credit available for withdrawal as of right.

### § 4—502. Presentment of "On Arrival" Drafts.

When a draft or the relevant instructions require presentment "on arrival", "when goods arrive" or the like, the collecting bank need not present until in its judgment a reasonable time for arrival of the goods has expired. Refusal to pay or accept because the goods have not arrived is not dishonor; the bank must notify its transferor of such refusal but need not present the draft again until it is instructed to do so or learns of the arrival of the goods.

**§ 4—503. Responsibility of Presenting Bank for Documents and Goods; Report of Reasons for Dishonor; Referee in Case of Need.**

Unless otherwise instructed and except as provided in Article 5 a bank presenting a documentary draft

(a) must deliver the documents to the drawee on acceptance of the draft if it is payable more than three days after presentment; otherwise, only on payment; and

(b) upon dishonor, either in the case of presentment for acceptance or presentment for payment, may seek and follow instructions from any referee in case of need designated in the draft or if the presenting bank does not choose to utilize his services it must use diligence and good faith to ascertain the reason for dishonor, must notify its transferor of the dishonor and of the results of its effort to ascertain the reasons therefor and must request instructions.

But the presenting bank is under no obligation with respect to goods represented by the documents except to follow any reasonable instructions seasonably received; it has a right to reimbursement for any expense incurred in following instructions and to prepayment of or indemnity for such expenses.

**§ 4—504. Privilege of Presenting Bank to Deal With Goods; Security Interest for Expenses.**

(1) A presenting bank which, following the dishonor of a documentary draft, has seasonably requested instructions but does not receive them within a reasonable time may store, sell, or otherwise deal with the goods in any reasonable manner.

(2) For its reasonable expenses incurred by action under subsection (1) the presenting bank has a lien upon the goods or their proceeds, which may be foreclosed in the same manner as an unpaid seller's lien.

# Revised Article 4
# BANK DEPOSITS AND COLLECTIONS

## Part 1   General Provisions and Definitions

**§ 4—101. Short Title.**

This Article may be cited as Uniform Commercial Code— Bank Deposits and Collections.

**§ 4—102. Applicability.**

(a) To the extent that items within this Article are also within Articles 3 and 8, they are subject to those Articles. If there is conflict, this Article governs Article 3, but Article 8 governs this Article.

(b) The liability of a bank for action or non-action with respect to an item handled by it for purposes of presentment, payment, or collection is governed by the law of the place where the bank is located. In the case of action or non-action by or at a branch or separate office of a bank, its liability is governed by the law of the place where the branch or separate office is located.

**§ 4—103. Variation by Agreement; Measure of Damages; Action Constituting Ordinary Care.**

(a) The effect of the provisions of this Article may be varied by agreement, but the parties to the agreement cannot disclaim a bank's responsibility for its lack of good faith or failure to exercise ordinary care or limit the measure of damages for the lack or failure. However, the parties may determine by agreement the standards by which the bank's responsibility is to be measured if those standards are not manifestly unreasonable.

(b) Federal Reserve regulations and operating circulars, clearing-house rules, and the like have the effect of agreements under subsection (a), whether or not specifically assented to by all parties interested in items handled.

(c) Action or non-action approved by this Article or pursuant to Federal Reserve regulations or operating circulars is the exercise of ordinary care and, in the absence of special instructions, action or non-action consistent with clearing-house rules and the like or with a general banking usage not disapproved by this Article, is prima facie the exercise of ordinary care.

(d) The specification or approval of certain procedures by this Article is not disapproval of other procedures that may be reasonable under the circumstances.

(e) The measure of damages for failure to exercise ordinary care in handling an item is the amount of the item reduced by an amount that could not have been realized by the exercise of ordinary care. If there is also bad faith it includes any other damages the party suffered as a proximate consequence.

**§ 4—104. Definitions and Index of Definitions.**

(a) In this Article, unless the context otherwise requires:

(1) ''Account'' means any deposit or credit account with a bank, including a demand, time, savings, passbook, share draft, or like account, other than an account evidenced by a certificate of deposit;

(2) ''Afternoon'' means the period of a day between noon and midnight;

(3) ''Banking day'' means the part of a day on which a bank is open to the public for carrying on substantially all of its banking functions;

(4) ''Clearing house'' means an association of banks or other payors regularly clearing items;

(5) ''Customer'' means a person having an account with a bank or for whom a bank has agreed to collect items, including a bank that maintains an account at another bank;

(6) ''Documentary draft'' means a draft to be presented for acceptance or payment if specified documents, certificated securities (Section 8—102) or instructions for uncertificated securities (Section 8—308), or other certificates, statements, or the like are to be received by the

drawee or other payor before acceptance or payment of the draft;

(7) "Draft" means a draft as defined in Section 3—104 or an item, other than an instrument, that is an order;

(8) "Drawee" means a person ordered in a draft to make payment;

(9) "Item" means an instrument or a promise or order to pay money handled by a bank for collection or payment. The term does not include a payment order governed by Article 4A or a credit or debit card slip;

(10) "Midnight deadline" with respect to a bank is midnight on its next banking day following the banking day on which it receives the relevant item or notice or from which the time for taking action commences to run, whichever is later;

(11) "Settle" means to pay in cash, by clearing-house settlement, in a charge or credit or by remittance, or otherwise as agreed. A settlement may be either provisional or final;

(12) "Suspends payments" with respect to a bank means that it has been closed by order of the supervisory authorities, that a public officer has been appointed to take it over, or that it ceases or refuses to make payments in the ordinary course of business.

(b);(c) [Other definitions' section references deleted.]

(d) In addition, Article 1 contains general definitions and principles of construction and interpretation applicable throughout this Article.

### § 4—105. "Bank"; "Depositary Bank"; "Payor Bank"; "Intermediary Bank"; "Collecting Bank"; "Presenting Bank".

In this Article:

(1) "Bank" means a person engaged in the business of banking, including a savings bank, savings and loan association, credit union, or trust company;

(2) "Depositary bank" means the first bank to take an item even though it is also the payor bank, unless the item is presented for immediate payment over the counter;

(3) "Payor bank" means a bank that is the drawee of a draft;

(4) "Intermediary bank" means a bank to which an item is transferred in course of collection except the depositary or payor bank;

(5) "Collecting bank" means a bank handling an item for collection except the payor bank;

(6) "Presenting bank" means a bank presenting an item except a payor bank.

### § 4—106. Payable Through or Payable at Bank: Collecting Bank.

(a) If an item states that it is "payable through" a bank identified in the item, (i) the item designates the bank as a collecting bank and does not by itself authorize the bank to

pay the item, and (ii) the item may be presented for payment only by or through the bank.

### Alternative A

(b) If an item states that it is "payable at" a bank identified in the item, the item is equivalent to a draft drawn on the bank.

### Alternative B

(b) If an item states that it is "payable at" a bank identified in the item, (i) the item designates the bank as a collecting bank and does not by itself authorize the bank to pay the item, and (ii) the item may be presented for payment only by or through the bank.

(c) If a draft names a nonbank drawee and it is unclear whether a bank named in the draft is a co-drawee or a collecting bank, the bank is a collecting bank.

### § 4—107. Separate Office of Bank.

A branch or separate office of a bank is a separate bank for the purpose of computing the time within which and determining the place at or to which action may be taken or notices or orders shall be given under this Article and under Article 3.

### § 4—108. Time of Receipt of Items.

(a) For the purpose of allowing time to process items, prove balances, and make the necessary entries on its books to determine its position for the day, a bank may fix an afternoon hour of 2 P.M. or later as a cutoff hour for the handling of money and items and the making of entries on its books.

(b) An item or deposit of money received on any day after a cutoff hour so fixed or after the close of the banking day may be treated as being received at the opening of the next banking day.

### § 4—109. Delays.

(a) Unless otherwise instructed, a collecting bank in a good faith effort to secure payment of a specific item drawn on a payor other than a bank, and with or without the approval of any person involved, may waive, modify, or extend time limits imposed or permitted by this [act] for a period not exceeding two additional banking days without discharge of drawers or indorsers or liability to its transferor or a prior party.

(b) Delay by a collecting bank or payor bank beyond time limits prescribed or permitted by this [act] or by instructions is excused if (i) the delay is caused by interruption of communication or computer facilities, suspension of payments by another bank, war, emergency conditions, failure of equipment, or other circumstances beyond the control of the bank, and (ii) the bank exercises such diligence as the circumstances require.

### § 4—110. Electronic Presentment.

(a) "Agreement for electronic presentment" means an agreement, clearing-house rule, or Federal Reserve regulation or operating circular, providing that presentment of an item may be made by transmission of an image of an item or information describing the item (''presentment notice'') rather than delivery of the item itself. The agreement may provide for procedures governing retention, presentment, payment, dishonor, and other matters concerning items subject to the agreement.

(b) Presentment of an item pursuant to an agreement for presentment is made when the presentment notice is received.

(c) If presentment is made by presentment notice, a reference to ''item'' or ''check'' in this Article means the presentment notice unless the context otherwise indicates.

### § 4—111. Statute of Limitations.

An action to enforce an obligation, duty, or right arising under this Article must be commenced within three years after the [cause of action] accrues.

## Part 2  Collection of Items: Depositary and Collecting Banks

### § 4—201. Status of Collecting Bank As Agent and Provisional Status of Credits; Applicability of Article; Item Indorsed ''Pay Any Bank''.

(a) Unless a contrary intent clearly appears and before the time that a settlement given by a collecting bank for an item is or becomes final, the bank, with respect to an item, is an agent or sub-agent of the owner of the item and any settlement given for the item is provisional. This provision applies regardless of the form of indorsement or lack of indorsement and even though credit given for the item is subject to immediate withdrawal as of right or is in fact withdrawn; but the continuance of ownership of an item by its owner and any rights of the owner to proceeds of the item are subject to rights of a collecting bank, such as those resulting from outstanding advances on the item and rights of recoupment or setoff. If an item is handled by banks for purposes of presentment, payment, collection, or return, the relevant provisions of this Article apply even though action of the parties clearly establishes that a particular bank has purchased the item and is the owner of it.

(b) After an item has been indorsed with the words ''pay any bank'' or the like, only a bank may acquire the rights of a holder until the item has been:

(1) returned to the customer initiating collection; or

(2) specially indorsed by a bank to a person who is not a bank.

### § 4—202. Responsibility for Collection or Return; When Action Timely.

(a) A collecting bank must exercise ordinary care in:

(1) presenting an item or sending it for presentment;

(2) sending notice of dishonor or nonpayment or returning an item other than a documentary draft to the bank's transferor after learning that the item has not been paid or accepted, as the case may be;

(3) settling for an item when the bank receives final settlement; and

(4) notifying its transferor of any loss or delay in transit within a reasonable time after discovery thereof.

(b) A collecting bank exercises ordinary care under subsection (a) by taking proper action before its midnight deadline following receipt of an item, notice, or settlement. Taking proper action within a reasonably longer time may constitute the exercise of ordinary care, but the bank has the burden of establishing timeliness.

(c) Subject to subsection (a)(1), a bank is not liable for the insolvency, neglect, misconduct, mistake, or default of another bank or person or for loss or destruction of an item in the possession of others or in transit.

### § 4—203. Effect of Instructions.

Subject to Article 3 concerning conversion of instruments (Section 3—420) and restrictive indorsements (Section 3—206), only a collecting bank's transferor can give instructions that affect the bank or constitute notice to it, and a collecting bank is not liable to prior parties for any action taken pursuant to the instructions or in accordance with any agreement with its transferor.

### § 4—204. Methods of Sending and Presenting; Sending Directly to Payor Bank.

(a) A collecting bank shall send items by a reasonably prompt method, taking into consideration relevant instructions, the nature of the item, the number of those items on hand, the cost of collection involved, and the method generally used by it or others to present those items.

(b) A collecting bank may send:

(1) an item directly to the payor bank;

(2) an item to a nonbank payor if authorized by its transferor; and

(3) an item other than documentary drafts to a nonbank payor, if authorized by Federal Reserve regulation or operating circular, clearing-house rule, or the like.

(c) Presentment may be made by a presenting bank at a place where the payor bank or other payor has requested that presentment be made.

### § 4—205. Depositary Bank Holder of Unindorsed Item.

If a customer delivers an item to a depositary bank for collection:

(1) the depositary bank becomes a holder of the item at the time it receives the item for collection if the customer at the time of delivery was a holder of the item, whether or not the customer indorses the item, and, if the bank satisfies the other requirements of Section 3—302, it is a holder in due course; and

(2) the depositary bank warrants to collecting banks, the payor bank or other payor, and the drawer that the amount of the item was paid to the customer or deposited to the customer's account.

## § 4—206.  Transfer Between Banks.

Any agreed method that identifies the transferor bank is sufficient for the item's further transfer to another bank.

## § 4—207.  Transfer Warranties.

(a)  A customer or collecting bank that transfers an item and receives a settlement or other consideration warrants to the transferee and to any subsequent collecting bank that:

(1)  the warrantor is a person entitled to enforce the item;

(2)  all signatures on the item are authentic and authorized;

(3)  the item has not been altered;

(4)  the item is not subject to a defense or claim in recoupment (Section 3—305(a)) of any party that can be asserted against the warrantor; and

(5)  the warrantor has no knowledge of any insolvency proceeding commenced with respect to the maker or acceptor or, in the case of an unaccepted draft, the drawer.

(b)  If an item is dishonored, a customer or collecting bank transferring the item and receiving settlement or other consideration is obliged to pay the amount due on the item (i) according to the terms of the item at the time it was transferred, or (ii) if the transfer was of an incomplete item, according to its terms when completed as stated in Sections 3—115 and 3—407. The obligation of a transferor is owed to the transferee and to any subsequent collecting bank that takes the item in good faith. A transferor cannot disclaim its obligation under this subsection by an indorsement stating that it is made ''without recourse'' or otherwise disclaiming liability.

(c)  A person to whom the warranties under subsection (a) are made and who took the item in good faith may recover from the warrantor as damages for breach of warranty an amount equal to the loss suffered as a result of the breach, but not more than the amount of the item plus expenses and loss of interest incurred as a result of the breach.

(d)  The warranties stated in subsection (a) cannot be disclaimed with respect to checks. Unless notice of a claim for breach of warranty is given to the warrantor within 30 days after the claimant has reason to know of the breach and the identity of the warrantor, the warrantor is discharged to the extent of any loss caused by the delay in giving notice of the claim.

(e)  A cause of action for breach of warranty under this section accrues when the claimant has reason to know of the breach.

## § 4—208.  Presentment Warranties.

(a)  If an unaccepted draft is presented to the drawee for payment or acceptance and the drawee pays or accepts the draft, (i) the person obtaining payment or acceptance, at the time of presentment, and (ii) a previous transferor of the draft, at the time of transfer, warrant to the drawee that pays or accepts the draft in good faith that:

(1)  the warrantor is, or was, at the time the warrantor transferred the draft, a person entitled to enforce the draft

or authorized to obtain payment or acceptance of the draft on behalf of a person entitled to enforce the draft;

(2)  the draft has not been altered; and

(3)  the warrantor has no knowledge that the signature of the purported drawer of the draft is unauthorized.

(b)  A drawee making payment may recover from a warrantor damages for breach of warranty equal to the amount paid by the drawee less the amount the drawee received or is entitled to receive from the drawer because of the payment. In addition, the drawee is entitled to compensation for expenses and loss of interest resulting from the breach. The right of the drawee to recover damages under this subsection is not affected by any failure of the drawee to exercise ordinary care in making payment. If the drawee accepts the draft (i) breach of warranty is a defense to the obligation of the acceptor, and (ii) if the acceptor makes payment with respect to the draft, the acceptor is entitled to recover from a warrantor for breach of warranty the amounts stated in this subsection.

(c)  If a drawee asserts a claim for breach of warranty under subsection (a) based on an unauthorized indorsement of the draft or an alteration of the draft, the warrantor may defend by proving that the indorsement is effective under Section 3—404 or 3—405 or the drawer is precluded under Section 3—406 or 4—406 from asserting against the drawee the unauthorized indorsement or alteration.

(d)  If (i) a dishonored draft is presented for payment to the drawer or an indorser or (ii) any other item is presented for payment to a party obliged to pay the item, and the item is paid, the person obtaining payment and a prior transferor of the item warrant to the person making payment in good faith that the warrantor is, or was, at the time the warrantor transferred the item, a person entitled to enforce the item or authorized to obtain payment on behalf of a person entitled to enforce the item. The person making payment may recover from any warrantor for breach of warranty an amount equal to the amount paid plus expenses and loss of interest resulting from the breach.

(e)  The warranties stated in subsections (a) and (d) cannot be disclaimed with respect to checks. Unless notice of a claim for breach of warranty is given to the warrantor within 30 days after the claimant has reason to know of the breach and the identity of the warrantor, the warrantor is discharged to the extent of any loss caused by the delay in giving notice of the claim.

(f)  A cause of action for breach of warranty under this section accrues when the claimant has reason to know of the breach.

## § 4—209.  Encoding and Retention Warranties.

(a)  A person who encodes information on or with respect to an item after issue warrants to any subsequent collecting bank and to the payor bank or other payor that the information is correctly encoded. If the customer of a depositary bank encodes, that bank also makes the warranty.

(b)  A person who undertakes to retain an item pursuant to an agreement for electronic presentment warrants to any subsequent collecting bank and to the payor bank or other payor that retention and presentment of the item comply with the agreement. If a customer of a depositary bank undertakes to retain an item, that bank also makes this warranty.

(c) A person to whom warranties are made under this section and who took the item in good faith may recover from the warrantor as damages for breach of warranty an amount equal to the loss suffered as a result of the breach, plus expenses and loss of interest incurred as a result of the breach.

### § 4—210. Security Interest of Collecting Bank in Items, Accompanying Documents and Proceeds.

(a) A collecting bank has a security interest in an item and any accompanying documents or the proceeds of either:

(1) in case of an item deposited in an account, to the extent to which credit given for the item has been withdrawn or applied;

(2) in case of an item for which it has given credit available for withdrawal as of right, to the extent of the credit given, whether or not the credit is drawn upon or there is a right of charge-back; or

(3) if it makes an advance on or against the item.

(b) If credit given for several items received at one time or pursuant to a single agreement is withdrawn or applied in part, the security interest remains upon all the items, any accompanying documents or the proceeds of either. For the purpose of this section, credits first given are first withdrawn.

(c) Receipt by a collecting bank of a final settlement for an item is a realization on its security interest in the item, accompanying documents, and proceeds. So long as the bank does not receive final settlement for the item or give up possession of the item or accompanying documents for purposes other than collection, the security interest continues to that extent and is subject to Article 9, but:

(1) no security agreement is necessary to make the security interest enforceable (Section 9—203(1)(a));

(2) no filing is required to perfect the security interest; and

(3) the security interest has priority over conflicting perfected security interests in the item, accompanying documents, or proceeds.

### § 4—211. When Bank Gives Value for Purposes of Holder in Due Course.

For purposes of determining its status as a holder in due course, a bank has given value to the extent it has a security interest in an item, if the bank otherwise complies with the requirements of Section 3—302 on what constitutes a holder in due course.

### § 4—212. Presentment by Notice of Item Not Payable by, Through, or at Bank; Liability of Drawer or Indorser.

(a) Unless otherwise instructed, a collecting bank may present an item not payable by, through, or at a bank by sending to the party to accept or pay a written notice that the bank holds the item for acceptance or payment. The notice must be sent in time to be received on or before the day when presentment is due and the bank must meet any requirement of the party to accept or pay under Section 3—501 by the close of the bank's next banking day after it knows of the requirement.

(b) If presentment is made by notice and payment, acceptance, or request for compliance with a requirement under Section 3—501 is not received by the close of business on the day after maturity or, in the case of demand items, by the close of business on the third banking day after notice was sent, the presenting bank may treat the item as dishonored and charge any drawer or indorser by sending it notice of the facts.

### § 4—213. Medium and Time of Settlement by Bank.

(a) With respect to settlement by a bank, the medium and time of settlement may be prescribed by Federal Reserve regulations or circulars, clearing-house rules, and the like, or agreement. In the absence of such prescription:

(1) the medium of settlement is cash or credit to an account in a Federal Reserve bank of or specified by the person to receive settlement; and

(2) the time of settlement is:

(i) with respect to tender of settlement by cash, a cashier's check, or teller's check, when the cash or check is sent or delivered;

(ii) with respect to tender of settlement by credit in an account in a Federal Reserve Bank, when the credit is made;

(iii) with respect to tender of settlement by a credit or debit to an account in a bank, when the credit or debit is made or, in the case of tender of settlement by authority to charge an account, when the authority is sent or delivered; or

(iv) with respect to tender of settlement by a funds transfer, when payment is made pursuant to Section 4A—406(a) to the person receiving settlement.

(b) If the tender of settlement is not by a medium authorized by subsection (a) or the time of settlement is not fixed by subsection (a), no settlement occurs until the tender of settlement is accepted by the person receiving settlement.

(c) If settlement for an item is made by cashier's check or teller's check and the person receiving settlement, before its midnight deadline:

(1) presents or forwards the check for collection, settlement is final when the check is finally paid; or

(2) fails to present or forward the check for collection, settlement is final at the midnight deadline of the person receiving settlement.

(d) If settlement for an item is made by giving authority to charge the account of the bank giving settlement in the bank receiving settlement, settlement is final when the charge is made by the bank receiving settlement if there are funds available in the account for the amount of the item.

### § 4—214. Right of Charge-Back or Refund; Liability of Collecting Bank: Return of Item.

(a) If a collecting bank has made provisional settlement with its customer for an item and fails by reason of dishonor, suspension of payments by a bank, or otherwise to receive settlement for the item which is or becomes final, the bank may revoke the settlement given by it, charge back the amount of any credit given for the item to its customer's account, or obtain refund from its customer, whether or not it is able to return the item, if by its midnight deadline or within a longer reasonable time after it learns the facts it returns the item or sends notification of the facts. If the return or notice is delayed beyond the bank's midnight deadline or a longer reasonable time after it learns the facts, the bank may revoke the settlement, charge back the credit, or obtain refund from its customer, but it is liable for any loss resulting from the delay. These rights to revoke, charge back, and obtain refund terminate if and when a settlement for the item received by the bank is or becomes final.

(b) A collecting bank returns an item when it is sent or delivered to the bank's customer or transferor or pursuant to its instructions.

(c) A depositary bank that is also the payor may charge back the amount of an item to its customer's account or obtain refund in accordance with the section governing return of an item received by a payor bank for credit on its books (Section 4—301).

(d) The right to charge back is not affected by:

(1) previous use of a credit given for the item; or

(2) failure by any bank to exercise ordinary care with respect to the item, but a bank so failing remains liable.

(e) A failure to charge back or claim refund does not affect other rights of the bank against the customer or any other party.

(f) If credit is given in dollars as the equivalent of the value of an item payable in foreign money, the dollar amount of any charge-back or refund must be calculated on the basis of the bank-offered spot rate for the foreign money prevailing on the day when the person entitled to the charge-back or refund learns that it will not receive payment in ordinary course.

### § 4—215. Final Payment of Item by Payor Bank; When Provisional Debits and Credits Become Final; When Certain Credits Become Available for Withdrawal.

(a) An item is finally paid by a payor bank when the bank has first done any of the following:

(1) paid the item in cash;

(2) settled for the item without having a right to revoke the settlement under statute, clearing-house rule, or agreement; or

(3) made a provisional settlement for the item and failed to revoke the settlement in the time and manner permitted by statute, clearing-house rule, or agreement.

(b) If provisional settlement for an item does not become final, the item is not finally paid.

(c) If provisional settlement for an item between the presenting and payor banks is made through a clearing house or by debits or credits in an account between them, then to the extent that provisional debits or credits for the item are entered in accounts between the presenting and payor banks or between the presenting and successive prior collecting banks seriatim, they become final upon final payment of the item by the payor bank.

(d) If a collecting bank receives a settlement for an item which is or becomes final, the bank is accountable to its customer for the amount of the item and any provisional credit given for the item in an account with its customer becomes final.

(e) Subject to (i) applicable law stating a time for availability of funds and (ii) any right of the bank to apply the credit to an obligation of the customer, credit given by a bank for an item in a customer's account becomes available for withdrawal as of right:

(1) if the bank has received a provisional settlement for the item, when the settlement becomes final and the bank has had a reasonable time to receive return of the item and the item has not been received within that time;

(2) if the bank is both the depositary bank and the payor bank, and the item is finally paid, at the opening of the bank's second banking day following receipt of the item.

(f) Subject to applicable law stating a time for availability of funds and any right of a bank to apply a deposit to an obligation of the depositor, a deposit of money becomes available for withdrawal as of right at the opening of the bank's next banking day after receipt of the deposit.

### § 4—216. Insolvency and Preference.

(a) If an item is in or comes into the possession of a payor or collecting bank that suspends payment and the item has not been finally paid, the item must be returned by the receiver, trustee, or agent in charge of the closed bank to the presenting bank or the closed bank's customer.

(b) If a payor bank finally pays an item and suspends payments without making a settlement for the item with its customer or the presenting bank which settlement is or becomes final, the owner of the item has a preferred claim against the payor bank.

(c) If a payor bank gives or a collecting bank gives or receives a provisional settlement for an item and thereafter suspends payments, the suspension does not prevent or interfere with the settlement's becoming final if the finality occurs automatically upon the lapse of certain time or the happening of certain events.

(d) If a collecting bank receives from subsequent parties settlement for an item, which settlement is or becomes final and the bank suspends payments without making a settlement for the item with its customer which settlement is or becomes final, the owner of the item has a preferred claim against the collecting bank.

## Part 3 Collection of Items: Payor Banks

### § 4—301. Deferred Posting; Recovery of Payment by Return of Items; Time of Dishonor; Return of Items by Payor Bank.

(a) If a payor bank settles for a demand item other than a documentary draft presented otherwise than for immediate payment over the counter before midnight of the banking day of receipt, the payor bank may revoke the settlement and recover the settlement if, before it has made final payment and before its midnight deadline, it

(1) returns the item; or

(2) sends written notice of dishonor or nonpayment if the item is unavailable for return.

(b) If a demand item is received by a payor bank for credit on its books, it may return the item or send notice of dishonor and may revoke any credit given or recover the amount thereof withdrawn by its customer, if it acts within the time limit and in the manner specified in subsection (a).

(c) Unless previous notice of dishonor has been sent, an item is dishonored at the time when for purposes of dishonor it is returned or notice sent in accordance with this section.

(d) An item is returned:

(1) as to an item presented through a clearing house, when it is delivered to the presenting or last collecting bank or to the clearing house or is sent or delivered in accordance with clearing-house rules; or

(2) in all other cases, when it is sent or delivered to the bank's customer or transferor or pursuant to instructions.

### § 4—302. Payor Bank's Responsibility for Late Return of Item.

(a) If an item is presented to and received by a payor bank, the bank is accountable for the amount of:

(1) a demand item, other than a documentary draft, whether properly payable or not, if the bank, in any case in which it is not also the depositary bank, retains the item beyond midnight of the banking day of receipt without settling for it or, whether or not it is also the depositary bank, does not pay or return the item or send notice of dishonor until after its midnight deadline; or

(2) any other properly payable item unless, within the time allowed for acceptance or payment of that item, the bank either accepts or pays the item or returns it and accompanying documents.

(b) The liability of a payor bank to pay an item pursuant to subsection (a) is subject to defenses based on breach of a presentment warranty (Section 4—208) or proof that the person seeking enforcement of the liability presented or transferred the item for the purpose of defrauding the payor bank.

### § 4—303. When Items Subject to Notice, Stop-Payment Order, Legal Process, or Setoff; Order in Which Items May Be Charged or Certified.

(a) Any knowledge, notice, or stop-payment order received by, legal process served upon, or setoff exercised by a payor bank comes too late to terminate, suspend, or modify the bank's right or duty to pay an item or to charge its customer's account for the item if the knowledge, notice, stop-payment order, or legal process is received or served and a reasonable time for the bank to act thereon expires or the setoff is exercised after the earliest of the following:

(1) the bank accepts or certifies the item;

(2) the bank pays the item in cash;

(3) the bank settles for the item without having a right to revoke the settlement under statute, clearing-house rule, or agreement;

(4) the bank becomes accountable for the amount of the item under Section 4—302 dealing with the payor bank's responsibility for late return of items; or

(5) with respect to checks, a cutoff hour no earlier than one hour after the opening of the next banking day after the banking day on which the bank received the check and no later than the close of that next banking day or, if no cutoff hour is fixed, the close of the next banking day after the banking day on which the bank received the check.

(b) Subject to subsection (a), items may be accepted, paid, certified, or charged to the indicated account of its customer in any order.

## Part 4 Relationship Between Payor Bank and its Customer

### § 4—401. When Bank May Charge Customer's Account.

(a) A bank may charge against the account of a customer an item that is properly payable from the account even though the charge creates an overdraft. An item is properly payable if it is authorized by the customer and is in accordance with any agreement between the customer and bank.

(b) A customer is not liable for the amount of an overdraft if the customer neither signed the item nor benefited from the proceeds of the item.

(c) A bank may charge against the account of a customer a check that is otherwise properly payable from the account, even though payment was made before the date of the check, unless the customer has given notice to the bank of the post-dating describing the check with reasonable certainty. The notice is effective for the period stated in Section 4—403(b) for stop-payment orders, and must be received at such time and in such manner as to afford the bank a reasonable opportunity to act on it before the bank takes any action with respect to the check described in Section 4—303. If a bank charges against the account of a customer a check before the date stated in the notice of postdating, the bank is liable for damages for the loss resulting from its act. The loss may include damages for dishonor of subsequent items under Section 4—402.

(d) A bank that in good faith makes payment to a holder may charge the indicated account of its customer according to:

(1) the original terms of the altered item; or

(2) the terms of the completed item, even though the bank knows the item has been completed unless the bank has notice that the completion was improper.

### § 4—402. Bank's Liability to Customer for Wrongful Dishonor; Time of Determining Insufficiency of Account.

(a) Except as otherwise provided in this Article, a payor bank wrongfully dishonors an item if it dishonors an item that is properly payable, but a bank may dishonor an item that would create an overdraft unless it has agreed to pay the overdraft.

(b) A payor bank is liable to its customer for damages proximately caused by the wrongful dishonor of an item. Liability is limited to actual damages proved and may include damages for an arrest or prosecution of the customer or other consequential damages. Whether any consequential damages are proximately caused by the wrongful dishonor is a question of fact to be determined in each case.

(c) A payor bank's determination of the customer's account balance on which a decision to dishonor for insufficiency of available funds is based may be made at any time between the time the item is received by the payor bank and the time that the payor bank returns the item or gives notice in lieu of return, and no more than one determination need be made. If, at the election of the payor bank, a subsequent balance determination is made for the purpose of reevaluating the bank's decision to dishonor the item, the account balance at that time is determinative of whether a dishonor for insufficiency of available funds is wrongful.

### § 4—403. Customer's Right to Stop Payment; Burden of Proof of Loss.

(a) A customer or any person authorized to draw on the account if there is more than one person may stop payment of any item drawn on the customer's account or close the account by an order to the bank describing the item or account with reasonable certainty received at a time and in a manner that affords the bank a reasonable opportunity to act on it before any action by the bank with respect to the item described in Section 4—303. If the signature of more than one person is required to draw on an account, any of these persons may stop payment or close the account.

(b) A stop-payment order is effective for six months, but it lapses after 14 calendar days if the original order was oral and was not confirmed in writing within that period. A stop-payment order may be renewed for additional six-month periods by a writing given to the bank within a period during which the stop-payment order is effective.

(c) The burden of establishing the fact and amount of loss resulting from the payment of an item contrary to a stop-payment order or order to close an account is on the customer. The loss from payment of an item contrary to a stop-payment order may include damages for dishonor of subsequent items under Section 4—402.

### § 4—404. Bank Not Obliged to Pay Check More Than Six Months Old.

A bank is under no obligation to a customer having a checking account to pay a check, other than a certified check, which is presented more than six months after its date, but it may charge its customer's account for a payment made thereafter in good faith.

### § 4—405. Death or Incompetence of Customer.

(a) A payor or collecting bank's authority to accept, pay, or collect an item or to account for proceeds of its collection, if otherwise effective, is not rendered ineffective by incompetence of a customer of either bank existing at the time the item is issued or its collection is undertaken if the bank does not know of an adjudication of incompetence. Neither death nor incompetence of a customer revokes the authority to accept, pay, collect, or account until the bank knows of the fact of death or of an adjudication of incompetence and has reasonable opportunity to act on it.

(b) Even with knowledge, a bank may for 10 days after the date of death pay or certify checks drawn on or before the date unless ordered to stop payment by a person claiming an interest in the account.

### § 4—406. Customer's Duty to Discover and Report Unauthorized Signature or Alteration.

(a) A bank that sends or makes available to a customer a statement of account showing payment of items for the account shall either return or make available to the customer the items paid or provide information in the statement of account sufficient to allow the customer reasonably to identify the items paid. The statement of account provides sufficient information if the item is described by item number, amount, and date of payment.

(b) If the items are not returned to the customer, the person retaining the items shall either retain the items or, if the items are destroyed, maintain the capacity to furnish legible copies of the items until the expiration of seven years after receipt of the items. A customer may request an item from the bank that paid the item, and that bank must provide in a reasonable time either the item or, if the item has been destroyed or is not otherwise obtainable, a legible copy of the item.

(c) If a bank sends or makes available a statement of account or items pursuant to subsection (a), the customer must exercise reasonable promptness in examining the statement or the items to determine whether any payment was not authorized because of an alteration of an item or because a purported signature by or on behalf of the customer was not authorized. If, based on the statement or items provided, the customer should reasonably have discovered the unauthorized payment, the customer must promptly notify the bank of the relevant facts.

(d) If the bank proves that the customer failed, with respect to an item, to comply with the duties imposed on the customer by subsection (c), the customer is precluded from asserting against the bank:

(1) the customer's unauthorized signature or any alteration on the item, if the bank also proves that it suffered a loss by reason of the failure; and

(2) the customer's unauthorized signature or alteration by the same wrongdoer on any other item paid in good faith by the bank if the payment was made before the bank received notice from the customer of the unauthorized signature or alteration and after the customer had been afforded a reasonable period of time, not exceeding 30 days, in which to examine the item or statement of account and notify the bank.

(e) If subsection (d) applies and the customer proves that the bank failed to exercise ordinary care in paying the item and that the failure substantially contributed to loss, the loss is allocated between the customer precluded and the bank asserting the preclusion according to the extent to which the failure of the customer to comply with subsection (c) and the failure of the bank to exercise ordinary care contributed to the loss. If the customer proves that the bank did not pay the item in good faith, the preclusion under subsection (d) does not apply.

(f) Without regard to care or lack of care of either the customer or the bank, a customer who does not within one year after the statement or items are made available to the customer (subsection (a)) discover and report the customer's unauthorized signature on or any alteration on the item is precluded from asserting against the bank the unauthorized signature or alteration. If there is a preclusion under this subsection, the payor bank may not recover for breach or warranty under Section 4—208 with respect to the unauthorized signature or alteration to which the preclusion applies.

### § 4—407. Payor Bank's Right to Subrogation on Improper Payment.

If a payor has paid an item over the order of the drawer or maker to stop payment, or after an account has been closed, or otherwise under circumstances giving a basis for objection by the drawer or maker, to prevent unjust enrichment and only to the extent necessary to prevent loss to the bank by reason of its payment of the item, the payor bank is subrogated to the rights

(1) of any holder in due course on the item against the drawer or maker;

(2) of the payee or any other holder of the item against the drawer or maker either on the item or under the transaction out of which the item arose; and

(3) of the drawer or maker against the payee or any other holder of the item with respect to the transaction out of which the item arose.

## Part 5    Collection of Documentary Drafts

### § 4—501. Handling of Documentary Drafts; Duty to Send for Presentment and to Notify Customer of Dishonor.

A bank that takes a documentary draft for collection shall present or send the draft and accompanying documents for presentment and, upon learning that the draft has not been paid or accepted in due course, shall seasonably notify its customer of the fact even though it may have discounted or bought the draft or extended credit available for withdrawal as of right.

### § 4—502. Presentment of "On Arrival" Drafts.

If a draft or the relevant instructions require presentment "on arrival", "when goods arrive" or the like, the collecting bank need not present until in its judgment a reasonable time for arrival of the goods has expired. Refusal to pay or accept because the goods have not arrived is not dishonor; the bank must notify its transferor of the refusal but need not present the draft again until it is instructed to do so or learns of the arrival of the goods.

### § 4—503. Responsibility of Presenting Bank for Documents and Goods; Report of Reasons for Dishonor; Referee in Case of Need.

Unless otherwise instructed and except as provided in Article 5, a bank presenting a documentary draft:

(1) must deliver the documents to the drawee on acceptance of the draft if it is payable more than three days after presentment, otherwise, only on payment; and

(2) upon dishonor, either in the case of presentment for acceptance or presentment for payment, may seek and follow instructions from any referee in case of need designated in the draft or, if the presenting bank does not choose to utilize the referee's services, it must use diligence and good faith to ascertain the reason for dishonor, must notify its transferor of the dishonor and of the results of its effort to ascertain the reasons therefor, and must request instructions.

However, the presenting bank is under no obligation with respect to goods represented by the documents except to follow any reasonable instructions seasonably received; it has a right to reimbursement for any expense incurred in following instructions and to prepayment of or indemnity for those expenses.

### § 4—504. Privilege of Presenting Bank to Deal With Goods; Security Interest for Expenses.

(a) A presenting bank that, following the dishonor of a documentary draft, has seasonably requested instructions but does not receive them within a reasonable time may store, sell, or otherwise deal with the goods in any reasonable manner.

(b) For its reasonable expenses incurred by action under subsection (a) the presenting bank has a lien upon the goods or their proceeds, which may be foreclosed in the same manner as an unpaid seller's lien.

# Article 4A
# FUNDS TRANSFERS*

## Part 1   Subject Matter and Definitions

### § 4A—101.   Short Title.

This Article may be cited as Uniform Commercial Code—Funds Transfers.

### § 4A—102.   Subject Matter.

Except as otherwise provided in Section 4A—108, this Article applies to funds transfers defined in Section 4A—104.

### § 4A—103.   Payment Order—Definitions.

(a) In this Article:

(1) "Payment order" means an instruction of a sender to a receiving bank, transmitted orally, electronically, or in writing, to pay, or to cause another bank to pay, a fixed or determinable amount of money to a beneficiary if:

(i) the instruction does not state a condition to payment to the beneficiary other than time of payment,

(ii) the receiving bank is to be reimbursed by debiting an account of, or otherwise receiving payment from, the sender, and

(iii) the instruction is transmitted by the sender directly to the receiving bank or to an agent, funds-transfer system, or communication system for transmittal to the receiving bank.

(2) "Beneficiary" means the person to be paid by the beneficiary's bank.

(3) "Beneficiary's bank" means the bank identified in a payment order in which an account of the beneficiary is to be credited pursuant to the order or which otherwise is to make payment to the beneficiary if the order does not provide for payment to an account.

(4) "Receiving bank" means the bank to which the sender's instruction is addressed.

(5) "Sender" means the person giving the instruction to the receiving bank.

(b) If an instruction complying with subsection (a)(1) is to make more than one payment to a beneficiary, the instruction is a separate payment order with respect to each payment.

(c) A payment order is issued when it is sent to the receiving bank.

### § 4A—104.   Funds Transfer—Definitions.

In this Article:

(a) "Funds transfer" means the series of transactions, beginning with the originator's payment order, made for the purpose of making payment to the beneficiary of the order. The term includes any payment order issued by the originator's bank or an intermediary bank intended to carry out the originator's payment order. A funds transfer is completed by acceptance by the beneficiary's bank of a payment order for the benefit of the beneficiary of the originator's payment order.

(b) "Intermediary bank" means a receiving bank other than the originator's bank or the beneficiary's bank.

(c) "Originator" means the sender of the first payment order in a funds transfer.

(d) "Originator's bank" means (i) the receiving bank to which the payment order of the originator is issued if the originator is not a bank, or (ii) the originator if the originator is a bank.

### § 4A—105.   Other Definitions.

(a) In this Article:

(1) "Authorized account" means a deposit account of a customer in a bank designated by the customer as a source of payment of payment orders issued by the customer to the bank. If a customer does not so designate an account, any account of the customer is an authorized account if payment of a payment order from that account is not inconsistent with a restriction on the use of that account.

(2) "Bank" means a person engaged in the business of banking and includes a savings bank, savings and loan association, credit union, and trust company. A branch or separate office of a bank is a separate bank for purposes of this Article.

(3) "Customer" means a person, including a bank, having an account with a bank or from whom a bank has agreed to receive payment orders.

(4) "Funds-transfer business day" of a receiving bank means the part of a day during which the receiving bank is open for the receipt, processing, and transmittal of payment orders and cancellations and amendments of payment orders.

(5) "Funds-transfer system" means a wire transfer network, automated clearing house, or other communication system of a clearing house or other association of banks through which a payment order by a bank may be transmitted to the bank to which the order is addressed.

(6) "Good faith" means honesty in fact and the observance of reasonable commercial standards of fair dealing.

(7) "Prove" with respect to a fact means to meet the burden of establishing the fact (Section 1— 201(8)).

(b) Other definitions applying to this Article and the sections in which they appear are:

| | |
|---|---|
| "Acceptance" | Section 4A—209 |
| "Beneficiary" | Section 4A—103 |
| "Beneficiary's bank" | Section 4A—103 |
| "Executed" | Section 4A—301 |
| "Execution date" | Section 4A—301 |
| "Funds transfer" | Section 4A—104 |
| "Funds-transfer system rule" | Section 4A—501 |

---

*Approved in substance by the National Conference of Commissioners on Uniform State Laws and The American Law Institute.

"Intermediary bank" Section 4A—104

"Originator" Section 4A—104

"Originator's bank" Section 4A—104

"Payment by beneficiary's bank to beneficiary" Section 4A—405

"Payment by originator to beneficiary" Section 4A—406

"Payment by sender to receiving bank" Section 4A—403

"Payment date" Section 4A—401

"Payment order" Section 4A—103

"Receiving bank" Section 4A—103

"Security procedure" Section 4A—201

"Sender" Section 4A—103

(c) The following definitions in Article 4 apply to this Article:

"Clearing house" Section 4—104

"Item" Section 4—104

"Suspends payments" Section 4—104

(d) In addition, Article 1 contains general definitions and principles of construction and interpretation applicable throughout this Article.

### § 4A—106. Time Payment Order Is Received.

(a) The time of receipt of a payment order or communication cancelling or amending a payment order is determined by the rules applicable to receipt of a notice stated in Section 1—201(27). A receiving bank may fix a cut-off time or times on a funds-transfer business day for the receipt and processing of payment orders and communications cancelling or amending payment orders. Different cut-off times may apply to payment orders, cancellations, or amendments, or to different categories of payment orders, cancellations, or amendments. A cut-off time may apply to senders generally or different cut-off times may apply to different senders or categories of payment orders. If a payment order or communicaion cancelling or amending a payment order is received after the close of a funds-transfer business day or after the appropriate cut-off time on a funds-transfer business day, the receiving bank may treat the payment order or communication as received at the opening of the next funds-transfer business day.

(b) If this Article refers to an execution date or payment date or states a day on which a receiving bank is required to take action, and the date or day does not fall on a funds-transfer business day, the next day that is a funds-transfer business day is treated as the date or day stated, unless the contrary is stated in this Article.

### § 4A—107. Federal Reserve Regulations and Operating Circulars.

Regulations of the Board of Governors of the Federal Reserve System and operating circulars of the Federal Reserve Banks supersede any inconsistent provision of this Article to the extent of the inconsistency.

### § 4A—108. Exclusion of Consumer Transactions Governed by Federal Law.

This Article does not apply to a funds transfer any part of which is governed by the Electronic Fund Transfer Act of 1978 (Title XX, Public Law 95—630, 92 Stat. 3728, 15 U.S.C. § 1693 et seq.) as amended from time to time.

## Part 2 Issue and Acceptance of Payment Order

### § 4A—201. Security Procedure.

"Security procedure" means a procedure established by agreement of a customer and a receiving bank for the purpose of (i) verifying that a payment order or communication amending or cancelling a payment order is that of the customer, or (ii) detecting error in the transmission or the content of the payment order or communication. A security procedure may require the use of algorithms or other codes, identifying words or numbers, encryption, callback procedures, or similar security devices. Comparison of a signature on a payment order or communication with an authorized specimen signature of the customer is not by itself a security procedure.

### § 4A—202. Authorized and Verified Payment Orders.

(a) A payment order received by the receiving bank is the authorized order of the person identified as sender if that person authorized the order or is otherwise bound by it under the law of agency.

(b) If a bank and its customer have agreed that the authenticity of payment orders issued to the bank in the name of the customer as sender will be verified pursuant to a security procedure, a payment order received by the receiving bank is effective as the order of the customer, whether or not authorized, if (i) the security procedure is a commercially reasonable method of providing security against unauthorized payment orders, and (ii) the bank proves that it accepted the payment order in good faith and in compliance with the security procedure and any written agreement or instruction of the customer restricting acceptance of payment orders issued in the name of the customer. The bank is not required to follow an instruction that violates a written agreement with the customer or notice of which is not received at a time and in a manner affording the bank a reasonable opportunity to act on it before the payment order is accepted.

(c) Commercial reasonableness of a security procedure is a question of law to be determined by considering the wishes of the customer expressed to the bank, the circumstances of the customer known to the bank, including the size, type, and frequency of payment orders normally issued by the customer to the bank, alternative security procedures offered to the customer, and security procedures in general use by customers and receiving banks similarly situated. A security procedure is deemed to be commercially reasonable if (i) the security procedure was chosen by the customer after the bank offered, and the customer refused, a security procedure that was commercially reasonable for that customer, and (ii) the customer expressly agreed in writing to be bound by any payment order, whether or not authorized, issued in its name and accepted by the bank in compliance with the security procedure chosen by the customer.

(d) The term ''sender'' in this Article includes the customer in whose name a payment order is issued if the order is the authorized order of the customer under subsection (a), or it is effective as the order of the customer under subsection (b).

(e) This section applies to amendments and cancellations of payment orders to the same extent it applies to payment orders.

(f) Except as provided in this section and in Section 4A—203(a)(1), rights and obligations arising under this section or Section 4A—203 may not be varied by agreement.

## § 4A—203. Unenforceability of Certain Verified Payment Orders.

(a) If an accepted payment order is not, under Section 4A—202(a), an authorized order of a customer identified as sender, but is effective as an order of the customer pursuant to Section 4A—202(b), the following rules apply:

(1) By express written agreement, the receiving bank may limit the extent to which it is entitled to enforce or retain payment of the payment order.

(2) The receiving bank is not entitled to enforce or retain payment of the payment order if the customer proves that the order was not caused, directly or indirectly, by a person (i) entrusted at any time with duties to act for the customer with respect to payment orders or the security procedure, or (ii) who obtained access to transmitting facilities of the customer or who obtained, from a source controlled by the customer and without authority of the receiving bank, information facilitating breach of the security procedure, regardless of how the information was obtained or whether the customer was at fault. Information includes any access device, computer software, or the like.

(b) This section applies to amendments of payment orders to the same extent it applies to payment orders.

## § 4A—204. Refund of Payment and Duty of Customer to Report with Respect to Unauthorized Payment Order.

(a) If a receiving bank accepts a payment order issued in the name of its customer as sender which is (i) not authorized and not effective as the order of the customer under Section 4A—202, or (ii) not enforceable, in whole or in part, against the customer under Section 4A—203, the bank shall refund any payment of the payment order received from the customer to the extent the bank is not entitled to enforce payment and shall pay interest on the refundable amount calculated from the date the bank received payment to the date of the refund. However, the customer is not entitled to interest from the bank on the amount to be refunded if the customer fails to exercise ordinary care to determine that the order was not authorized by the customer and to notify the bank of the

relevant facts within a reasonable time not exceeding 90 days after the date the customer received notification from the bank that the order was accepted or that the customer's account was debited with respect to the order. The bank is not entitled to any recovery from the customer on account of a failure by the customer to give notification as stated in this section.

(b) Reasonable time under subsection (a) may be fixed by agreement as stated in Section 1—204(1), but the obligation of a receiving bank to refund payment as stated in subsection (a) may not otherwise be varied by agreement.

## § 4A—205. Erroneous Payment Orders.

(a) If an accepted payment order was transmitted pursuant to a security procedure for the detection of error and the payment order (i) erroneously instructed payment to a beneficiary not intended by the sender, (ii) erroneously instructed payment in an amount greater than the amount intended by the sender, or (iii) was an erroneously transmitted duplicate of a payment order previously sent by the sender, the following rules apply:

(1) If the sender proves that the sender or a person acting on behalf of the sender pursuant to Section 4A—206 complied with the security procedure and that the error would have been detected if the receiving bank had also complied, the sender is not obliged to pay the order to the extent stated in paragraphs (2) and (3).

(2) If the funds transfer is completed on the basis of an erroneous payment order described in clause (i) or (iii) of subsection (a), the sender is not obliged to pay the order and the receiving bank is entitled to recover from the beneficiary any amount paid to the beneficiary to the extent allowed by the law governing mistake and restitution.

(3) If the funds transfer is completed on the basis of a payment order described in clause (ii) of subsection (a), the sender is not obliged to pay the order to the extent the amount received by the beneficiary is greater than the amount intended by the sender. In that case, the receiving bank is entitled to recover from the beneficiary the excess amount received to the extent allowed by the law governing mistake and restitution.

(b) If (i) the sender of an erroneous payment order described in subsection (a) is not obliged to pay all or part of the order, and (ii) the sender receives notification from the receiving bank that the order was accepted by the bank or that the sender's account was debited with respect to the order, the sender has a duty to exercise ordinary care, on the basis of information available to the sender, to discover the error with respect to the order and to advise the bank of the relevant facts within a reasonable time, not exceeding 90 days, after the bank's notification was received by the sender. If the bank proves that the sender failed to perform that duty, the sender is liable to the bank for the loss the bank proves it incurred as a result of the failure, but the liability of the sender may not exceed the amount of the sender's order.

(c) This section applies to amendments to payment orders to the same extent it applies to payment orders.

## § 4A—206. Transmission of Payment Order through Funds-Transfer or Other Communication System.

(a) If a payment order addressed to a receiving bank is transmitted to a funds-transfer system or other thirdparty communication system for transmittal to the bank, the system is deemed to be an agent of the sender for the purpose of transmitting the payment order to the bank. If there is a discrepancy between the terms of the payment order transmitted to the system and the terms of the payment order transmitted by the system to the bank, the terms of the payment order of the sender are those transmitted by the system. This section does not apply to a funds-transfer system of the Federal Reserve Banks.

(b) This section applies to cancellations and amendments to payment orders to the same extent it applies to payment orders.

## § 4A—207. Misdescription of Beneficiary.

(a) Subject to subsection (b), if, in a payment order received by the beneficiary's bank, the name, bank account number, or other identification of the beneficiary refers to a nonexistent or unidentifiable person or account, no person has rights as a beneficiary of the order and acceptance of the order cannot occur.

(b) If a payment order received by the beneficiary's bank identifies the beneficiary both by name and by an identifying or bank account number and the name and number identify different persons, the following rules apply:

(1) Except as otherwise provided in subsection (c), if the beneficiary's bank does not know that the name and number refer to different persons, it may rely on the number as the proper identification of the beneficiary of the order. The beneficiary's bank need not determine whether the name and number refer to the same person.

(2) If the beneficiary's bank pays the person identified by name or knows that the name and number identify different persons, no person has rights as beneficiary except the person paid by the beneficiary's bank if that person was entitled to receive payment from the originator of the funds transfer. If no person has rights as beneficiary, acceptance of the order cannot occur.

(c) If (i) a payment order described in subsection (b) is accepted, (ii) the originator's payment order described the beneficiary inconsistently by name and number, and (iii) the beneficiary's bank pays the person identified by number as permitted by subsection (b)(1), the following rules apply:

(1) If the originator is a bank, the originator is obliged to pay its order.

(2) If the originator is not a bank and proves that the person identified by number was not entitled to receive payment from the originator, the originator is not obliged to pay its order unless the originator's bank proves that the originator, before acceptance of the originator's order, had notice that payment of a payment order issued by the originator might be made by the beneficiary's bank on the basis of an identifying or bank account number even if it identifies a person different from the named beneficiary. Proof of notice may be made by any admissible evidence. The originator's bank satisfies the burden of proof if it proves that the originator, before the payment order was accepted, signed a writing stating the information to which the notice relates.

(d) In a case governed by subsection (b)(1), if the beneficiary's bank rightfully pays the person identified by number and that person was not entitled to receive payment from the originator, the amount paid may be recovered from that person to the extent allowed by the law governing mistake and restitution as follows:

(1) If the originator is obliged to pay its payment order as stated in subsection (c), the originator has the right to recover.

(2) If the originator is not a bank and is not obliged to pay its payment order, the originator's bank has the right to recover.

## § 4A—208. Misdescription of Intermediary Bank or Beneficiary's Bank.

(a) This subsection applies to a payment order identifying an intermediary bank or the beneficiary's bank only by an identifying number.

(1) The receiving bank may rely on the number as the proper identification of the intermediary or beneficiary's bank and need not determine whether the number identifies a bank.

(2) The sender is obliged to compensate the receiving bank for any loss and expenses incurred by the receiving bank as a result of its reliance on the number in executing or attempting to execute the order.

(b) This subsection applies to a payment order identifying an intermediary bank or the beneficiary's bank both by name and an identifying number if the name and number identify different persons.

(1) If the sender is a bank, the receiving bank may rely on the number as the proper identification of the intermediary or beneficiary's bank if the receiving bank, when it executes the sender's order, does not know that the name and number identify different persons. The receiving bank need not determine whether the name and number refer to the same person or whether the number refers to a bank. The sender is obliged to compensate the receiving bank for any loss and expenses incurred by the receiving bank as a result of its reliance on the number in executing or attempting to execute the order.

(2) If the sender is not a bank and the receiving bank proves that the sender, before the payment order was accepted, had notice that the receiving bank might rely on the number as the proper identification of the intermediary or beneficiary's bank even if it identifies a person different from the bank identified by name, the rights and obligations of the sender and the receiving bank are governed by subsection (b)(1), as though the sender were a bank. Proof of notice may be made by any admissible

evidence. The receiving bank satisfies the burden of proof if it proves that the sender, before the payment order was accepted, signed a writing stating the information to which the notice relates.

(3) Regardless of whether the sender is a bank, the receiving bank may rely on the name as the proper identification of the intermediary or beneficiary's bank if the receiving bank, at the time it executes the sender's order, does not know that the name and number identify different persons. The receiving bank need not determine whether the name and number refer to the same person.

(4) If the receiving bank knows that the name and number identify different persons, reliance on either the name or the number in executing the sender's payment order is a breach of the obligation stated in Section 4A—302(a)(1).

### § 4A—209. Acceptance of Payment Order.

(a) Subject to subsection (d), a receiving bank other than the beneficiary's bank accepts a payment order when it executes the order.

(b) Subject to subsections (c) and (d), a beneficiary's bank accepts a payment order at the earliest of the following times:

(1) When the bank (i) pays the beneficiary as stated in Section 4A—405(a) or 4A—405(b), or (ii) notifies the beneficiary of receipt of the order or that the account of the beneficiary has been credited with respect to the order unless the notice indicates that the bank is rejecting the order or that funds with respect to the order may not be withdrawn or used until receipt of payment from the sender of the order;

(2) When the bank receives payment of the entire amount of the sender's order pursuant to Section 4A—403(a)(1) or 4A—403(a)(2); or

(3) The opening of the next funds-transfer business day of the bank following the payment date of the order if, at that time, the amount of the sender's order is fully covered by a withdrawable credit balance in an authorized account of the sender or the bank has otherwise received full payment from the sender, unless the order was rejected before that time or is rejected within (i) one hour after that time, or (ii) one hour after the opening of the next business day of the sender following the payment date if that time is later. If notice of rejection is received by the sender after the payment date and the authorized account of the sender does not bear interest, the bank is obliged to pay interest to the sender on the amount of the order for the number of days elapsing after the payment date to the day the sender receives notice or learns that the order was not accepted, counting that day as an elapsed day. If the withdrawable credit balance during that period falls below the amount of the order, the amount of interest payable is reduced accordingly.

(c) Acceptance of a payment order cannot occur before the order is received by the receiving bank. Acceptance does not occur under subsection (b)(2) or (b)(3) if the beneficiary of the payment order does not have an account with the receiving

bank, the account has been closed, or the receiving bank is not permitted by law to receive credits for the beneficiary's account.

(d) A payment order issued to the originator's bank cannot be accepted until the payment date if the bank is the beneficiary's bank, or the execution date if the bank is not the beneficiary's bank. If the originator's bank executes the originator's payment order before the execution date or pays the beneficiary of the originator's payment order before the payment date and the payment order is subsequently cancelled pursuant to Section 4A—211(b), the bank may recover from the beneficiary any payment received to the extent allowed by the law governing mistake and restitution.

### § 4A—210. Rejection of Payment Order.

(a) A payment order is rejected by the receiving bank by a notice of rejection transmitted to the sender orally, electronically, or in writing. A notice of rejection need not use any particular words and is sufficient if it indicates that the receiving bank is rejecting the order or will not execute or pay the order. Rejection is effective when the notice is given if transmission is by a means that is reasonable in the circumstances. If notice of rejection is given by a means that is not reasonable, rejection is effective when the notice is received. If an agreement of the sender and receiving bank establishes the means to be used to reject a payment order, (i) any means complying with the agreement is reasonable and (ii) any means not complying is not reasonable unless no significant delay in receipt of the notice resulted from the use of the noncomplying means.

(b) This subsection applies if a receiving bank other than the beneficiary's bank fails to execute a payment order despite the existence on the execution date of a withdrawable credit balance in an authorized account of the sender sufficient to cover the order. If the sender does not receive notice of rejection of the order on the execution date and the authorized account of the sender does not bear interest, the bank is obliged to pay interest to the sender on the amount of the order for the number of days elapsing after the execution date to the earlier of the day the order is cancelled pursuant to Section 4A—211(d) or the day the sender receives notice or learns that the order was not executed, counting the final day of the period as an elapsed day. If the withdrawable credit balance during that period falls below the amount of the order, the amount of interest is reduced accordingly.

(c) If a receiving bank suspends payments, all unaccepted payment orders issued to it are are deemed rejected at the time the bank suspends payments.

(d) Acceptance of a payment order precludes a later rejection of the order. Rejection of a payment order precludes a later acceptance of the order.

### § 4A—211. Cancellation and Amendment of Payment Order.

(a) A communication of the sender of a payment order cancelling or amending the order may be transmitted to the receiving bank orally, electronically, or in writing. If a security procedure is in effect between the sender and the receiving bank, the communication is not effective to cancel or amend the order unless the communication is verified pursuant to the security procedure or the bank agrees to the cancellation or amendment.

(b) Subject to subsection (a), a communication by the sender cancelling or amending a payment order is effective to cancel or amend the order if notice of the communication is received at a time and in a manner affording the receiving bank a reasonable opportunity to act on the communication before the bank accepts the payment order.

(c) After a payment order has been accepted, cancellation or amendment of the order is not effective unless the receiving bank agrees or a funds-transfer system rule allows cancellation or amendment without agreement of the bank.

(1) With respect to a payment order accepted by a receiving bank other than the beneficiary's bank, cancellation or amendment is not effective unless a conforming cancellation or amendment of the payment order issued by the receiving bank is also made.

(2) With respect to a payment order accepted by the beneficiary's bank, cancellation or amendment is not effective unless the order was issued in execution of an unauthorized payment order, or because of a mistake by a sender in the funds transfer which resulted in the issuance of a payment order (i) that is a duplicate of a payment order previously issued by the sender, (ii) that orders payment to a beneficiary not entitled to receive payment from the originator, or (iii) that orders payment in an amount greater than the amount the beneficiary was entitled to receive from the originator. If the payment order is cancelled or amended, the beneficiary's bank is entitled to recover from the beneficiary any amount paid to the beneficiary to the extent allowed by the law governing mistake and restitution.

(d) An unaccepted payment order is cancelled by operation of law at the close of the fifth funds-transfer business day of the receiving bank after the execution date or payment date of the order.

(e) A cancelled payment order cannot be accepted. If an accepted payment order is cancelled, the acceptance is nullified and no person has any right or obligation based on the acceptance. Amendment of a payment order is deemed to be cancellation of the original order at the time of amendment and issue of a new payment order in the amended form at the same time.

(f) Unless otherwise provided in an agreement of the parties or in a funds-transfer system rule, if the receiving bank, after accepting a payment order, agrees to cancellation or amendment of the order by the sender or is bound by a funds-transfer system rule allowing cancellation or amendment without the bank's agreement, the sender, whether or not cancellation or amendment is effective, is liable to the bank for any loss and expenses, including reasonable attorney's fees, incurred by the bank as a result of the cancellation or amendment or attempted cancellation or amendment.

(g) A payment order is not revoked by the death or legal incapacity of the sender unless the receiving bank knows of the death or of an adjudication of incapacity by a court of competent jurisdiction and has reasonable opportunity to act before acceptance of the order.

(h) A funds-transfer system rule is not effective to the extent it conflicts with subsection (c)(2).

### § 4A—212. Liability and Duty of Receiving Bank Regarding Unaccepted Payment Order.

If a receiving bank fails to accept a payment order that it is obliged by express agreement to accept, the bank is liable for breach of the agreement to the extent provided in the agreement or in this Article, but does not otherwise have any duty to accept a payment order or, before acceptance, to take any action, or refrain from taking action, with respect to the order except as provided in this Article or by express agreement. Liability based on acceptance arises only when acceptance occurs as stated in Section 4A—209, and liability is limited to that provided in this Article. A receiving bank is not the agent of the sender or beneficiary of the payment order it accepts, or of any other party to the funds transfer, and the bank owes no duty to any party to the funds transfer except as provided in this Article or by express agreement.

## Part 3 Execution of Sender's Payment Order by Receiving Bank

### § 4A—301. Execution and Execution Date.

(a) A payment order is "executed" by the receiving bank when it issues a payment order intended to carry out the payment order received by the bank. A payment order received by the beneficiary's bank can be accepted but cannot be executed.

(b) "Execution date" of a payment order means the day on which the receiving bank may properly issue a payment order in execution of the sender's order. The execution date may be determined by instruction of the sender but cannot be earlier than the day the order is received and, unless otherwise determined, is the day the order is received. If the sender's instruction states a payment date, the execution date is the payment date or an earlier date on which execution is reasonably necessary to allow payment to the beneficiary on the payment date.

### § 4A—302. Obligations of Receiving Bank in Execution of Payment Order.

(a) Except as provided in subsections (b) through (d), if the receiving bank accepts a payment order pursuant to Section 4A—209(a), the bank has the following obligations in executing the order:

(1) The receiving bank is obliged to issue, on the execution date, a payment order complying with the sender's order and to follow the sender's instructions concerning (i) any intermediary bank or funds-transfer system to be used in carrying out the funds transfer, or (ii) the means by which payment orders are to be transmitted in the

funds transfer. If the originator's bank issues a payment order to an intermediary bank, the originator's bank is obliged to instruct the intermediary bank according to the instruction of the originator. An intermediary bank in the funds transfer is similarly bound by an instruction given to it by the sender of the payment order it accepts.

(2) If the sender's instruction states that the funds transfer is to be carried out telephonically or by wire transfer or otherwise indicates that the funds transfer is to be carried out by the most expeditious means, the receiving bank is obliged to transmit its payment order by the most expeditious available means, and to instruct any intermediary bank accordingly. If a sender's instruction states a payment date, the receiving bank is obliged to transmit its payment order at a time and by means reasonably necessary to allow payment to the beneficiary on the payment date or as soon thereafter as is feasible.

(b) Unless otherwise instructed, a receiving bank executing a payment order may (i) use any funds-transfer system if use of that system is reasonable in the circumstances, and (ii) issue a payment order to the beneficiary's bank or to an intermediary bank through which a payment order conforming to the sender's order can expeditiously be issued to the beneficiary's bank if the receiving bank exercises ordinary care in the selection of the intermediary bank. A receiving bank is not required to follow an instruction of the sender designating a funds-transfer system to be used in carrying out the funds transfer if the receiving bank, in good faith, determines that it is not feasible to follow the instruction or that following the instruction would unduly delay completion of the funds transfer.

(c) Unless subsection (a)(2) applies or the receiving bank is otherwise instructed, the bank may execute a payment order by transmitting its payment order by first class mail or by any means reasonable in the circumstances. If the receiving bank is instructed to execute the sender's order by transmitting its payment order by a particular means, the receiving bank may issue its payment order by the means stated or by any means as expeditious as the means stated.

(d) Unless instructed by the sender, (i) the receiving bank may not obtain payment of its charges for services and expenses in connection with the execution of the sender's order by issuing a payment order in an amount equal to the amount of the sender's order less the amount of the charges, and (ii) may not instruct a subsequent receiving bank to obtain payment of its charges in the same manner.

### § 4A—303. Erroneous Execution of Payment Order.

(a) A receiving bank that (i) executes the payment order of the sender by issuing a payment order in an amount greater than the amount of the sender's order, or (ii) issues a payment order in execution of the sender's order and then issues a duplicate order, is entitled to payment of the amount of the sender's order under Section 4A—402(c) if that subsection is otherwise satisfied. The bank is entitled to recover from the beneficiary of the erroneous order the excess payment received to the extent allowed by the law governing mistake and restitution.

(b) A receiving bank that executes the payment order of the sender by issuing a payment order in an amount less than the amount of the sender's order is entitled to payment of the amount of the sender's order under Section 4A—402(c) if (i) that subsection is otherwise satisfied and (ii) the bank corrects its mistake by issuing an additional payment order for the benefit of the beneficiary of the sender's order. If the error is not corrected, the issuer of the erroneous order is entitled to receive or retain payment from the sender of the order it accepted only to the extent of the amount of the erroneous order. This subsection does not apply if the receiving bank executes the sender's payment order by issuing a payment order in an amount less than the amount of the sender's order for the purpose of obtaining payment of its charges for services and expenses pursuant to instruction of the sender.

(c) If a receiving bank executes the payment order of the sender by issuing a payment order to a beneficiary different from the beneficiary of the sender's order and the funds transfer is completed on the basis of that error, the sender of the payment order that was erroneously executed and all previous senders in the funds transfer are not obliged to pay the payment orders they issued. The issuer of the erroneous order is entitled to recover from the beneficiary of the order the payment received to the extent allowed by the law governing mistake and restitution.

### § 4A—304. Duty of Sender to Report Erroneously Executed Payment Order.

If the sender of a payment order that is erroneously executed as stated in Section 4A—303 receives notification from the receiving bank that the order was executed or that the sender's account was debited with respect to the order, the sender has a duty to exercise ordinary care to determine, on the basis of information available to the sender, that the order was erroneously executed and to notify the bank of the relevant facts within a reasonable time not exceeding 90 days after the notification from the bank was received by the sender. If the sender fails to perform that duty, the bank is not obliged to pay interest on any amount refundable to the sender under Section 4A—402(d) for the period before the bank learns of the execution error. The bank is not entitled to any recovery from the sender on account of a failure by the sender to perform the duty stated in this section.

### § 4A—305. Liability for Late or Improper Execution or Failure to Execute Payment Order.

(a) If a funds transfer is completed but execution of a payment order by the receiving bank in breach of Section 4A—302 results in delay in payment to the beneficiary, the bank is obliged to pay interest to either the originator or the beneficiary of the funds transfer for the period of delay caused by the improper execution. Except as provided in subsection (c), additional damages are not recoverable.

(b) If execution of a payment order by a receiving bank in breach of Section 4A—302 results in (i) noncompletion of the funds transfer, (ii) failure to use an intermediary bank designated by the originator, or (iii) issuance of a payment order that does not comply with the terms of the payment order of the originator, the bank is liable to the originator for its expenses in the funds transfer and for incidental expenses and interest losses, to the extent not covered by subsection (a), resulting from the improper execution. Except as provided in subsection (c), additional damages are not recoverable.

(c) In addition to the amounts payable under subsections (a) and (b), damages, including consequential damages, are recoverable to the extent provided in an express written agreement of the receiving bank.

(d) If a receiving bank fails to execute a payment order it was obliged by express agreement to execute, the receiving bank is liable to the sender for its expenses in the transaction and for incidental expenses and interest losses resulting from the failure to execute. Additional damages, including consequential damages, are recoverable to the extent provided in an express written agreement of the receiving bank, but are not otherwise recoverable.

(e) Reasonable attorney's fees are recoverable if demand for compensation under subsection (a) or (b) is made and refused before an action is brought on the claim. If a claim is made for breach of an agreement under subsection (d) and the agreement does not provide for damages, reasonable attorney's fees are recoverable if demand for compensation under subsection (d) is made and refused before an action is brought on the claim.

(f) Except as stated in this section, the liability of a receiving bank under subsections (a) and (b) may not be varied by agreement.

## Part 4  Payment

### § 4A—401.  Payment Date.

"Payment date" of a payment order means the day on which the amount of the order is payable to the beneficiary by the beneficiary's bank. The payment date may be determined by instruction of the sender but cannot be earlier than the day the order is received by the beneficiary's bank and, unless otherwise determined, is the day the order is received by the beneficiary's bank.

### § 4A—402.  Obligation of Sender to Pay Receiving Bank.

(a) This section is subject to Sections 4A—205 and 4A—207.

(b) With respect to a payment order issued to the beneficiary's bank, acceptance of the order by the bank obliges the sender to pay the bank the amount of the order, but payment is not due until the payment date of the order.

(c) This subsection is subject to subsection (e) and to Section 4A—303. With respect to a payment order issued to a receiving bank other than the beneficiary's bank, acceptance of the order by the receiving bank obliges the sender to pay the bank the amount of the sender's order. Payment by the sender is not due until the execution date of the sender's order. The obligation of that sender to pay its payment order is excused if the funds transfer is not completed by acceptance by the beneficiary's bank of a payment order instructing payment to the beneficiary of that sender's payment order.

(d) If the sender of a payment order pays the order and was not obliged to pay all or part of the amount paid, the bank receiving payment is obliged to refund payment to the extent the sender was not obliged to pay. Except as provided in Sections 4A—204 and 4A—304, interest is payable on the refundable amount from the date of payment.

(e) If a funds transfer is not completed as stated in subsection (c) and an intermediary bank is obliged to refund payment as stated in subsection (d) but is unable to do so because not permitted by applicable law or because the bank suspends payments, a sender in the funds transfer that executed a payment order in compliance with an instruction, as stated in Section 4A—302(a)(1), to route the funds transfer through that intermediary bank is entitled to receive or retain payment from the sender of the payment order that it accepted. The first sender in the funds transfer that issued an instruction requiring routing through that intermediary bank is subrogated to the right of the bank that paid the intermediary bank to refund as stated in subsection (d).

(f) The right of the sender of a payment order to be excused from the obligation to pay the order as stated in subsection (c) or to receive refund under subsection (d) may not be varied by agreement.

### § 4A—403.  Payment by Sender to Receiving Bank.

(a) Payment of the sender's obligation under Section 4A—402 to pay the receiving bank occurs as follows:

(1) If the sender is a bank, payment occurs when the receiving bank receives final settlement of the obligation through a Federal Reserve Bank or through a funds-transfer system.

(2) If the sender is a bank and the sender (i) credited an account of the receiving bank with the sender, or (ii) caused an account of the receiving bank in another bank to be credited, payment occurs when the credit is withdrawn or, if not withdrawn, at midnight of the day on which the credit is withdrawable and the receiving bank learns of that fact.

(3) If the receiving bank debits an account of the sender with the receiving bank, payment occurs when the debit is made to the extent the debit is covered by a withdrawable credit balance in the account.

(b) If the sender and receiving bank are members of a funds-transfer system that nets obligations multilaterally among participants, the receiving bank receives final settlement when settlement is complete in accordance with the rules of the system. The obligation of the sender to pay the amount of a payment order transmitted through the funds-transfer system may be satisfied, to the extent permitted by the rules of the system, by setting off and applying against the sender's obligation the right of the sender to receive payment from the receiving bank of the amount of any other payment order transmitted to the sender by the receiving bank through the funds-transfer system. The aggregate balance of obligations owed by each sender to each receiving bank in the funds-transfer system may be satisfied, to the extent permitted by the rules of the system, by setting off and applying against that balance the aggregate balance of obligations owed to the sender by other members of the system. The aggregate balance is determined after the right of setoff stated in the second sentence of this subsection has been exercised.

(c) If two banks transmit payment orders to each other under an agreement that settlement of the obligations of each bank to the other under Section 4A—402 will be made at the end of the day or other period, the total amount owed with respect to all orders transmitted by one bank shall be set off against the total amount owed with respect to all orders transmitted by the other bank. To the extent of the setoff, each bank has made payment to the other.

(d) In a case not covered by subsection (a), the time when payment of the sender's obligation under Section 4A—402(b) or 4A—402(c) occurs is governed by applicable principles of law that determine when an obligation is satisfied.

### § 4A—404. Obligation of Beneficiary's Bank to Pay and Give Notice to Beneficiary.

(a) Subject to Sections 4A—211(e), 4A—405(d), and 4A—405(e), if a beneficiary's bank accepts a payment order, the bank is obliged to pay the amount of the order to the beneficiary of the order. Payment is due on the payment date of the order, but if acceptance occurs on the payment date after the close of the funds-transfer business day of the bank, payment is due on the next funds-transfer business day. If the bank refuses to pay after demand by the beneficiary and receipt of notice of particular circumstances that will give rise to consequential damages as a result of nonpayment, the beneficiary may recover damages resulting from the refusal to pay to the extent the bank had notice of the damages, unless the bank proves that it did not pay because of a reasonable doubt concerning the right of the beneficiary to payment.

(b) If a payment order accepted by the beneficiary's bank instructs payment to an account of the beneficiary, the bank is obliged to notify the beneficiary of receipt of the order before midnight of the next funds-transfer business day following the payment date. If the payment order does not instruct payment to an account of the beneficiary, the bank is required to notify the beneficiary only if notice is required by the order. Notice may be given by first class mail or any other means reasonable in the circumstances. If the bank fails to give the required notice, the bank is obliged to pay interest to the beneficiary on the amount of the payment order from the day notice should have been given until the day the beneficiary learned of receipt of the payment order by the bank. No other damages are recoverable. Reasonable attorney's

fees are also recoverable if demand for interest is made and refused before an action is brought on the claim.

(c) The right of a beneficiary to receive payment and damages as stated in subsection (a) may not be varied by agreement or a funds-transfer system rule. The right of a beneficiary to be notified as stated in subsection (b) may be varied by agreement of the beneficiary or by a funds-transfer system rule if the beneficiary is notified of the rule before initiation of the funds transfer.

### § 4A—405. Payment by Beneficiary's Bank to Beneficiary.

(a) If the beneficiary's bank credits an account of the beneficiary of a payment order, payment of the bank's obligation under Section 4A—404(a) occurs when and to the extent (i) the beneficiary is notified of the right to withdraw the credit, (ii) the bank lawfully applies the credit to a debt of the beneficiary, or (iii) funds with respect to the order are otherwise made available to the beneficiary by the bank.

(b) If the beneficiary's bank does not credit an account of the beneficiary of a payment order, the time when payment of the bank's obligation under Section 4A—404(a) occurs is governed by principles of law that determine when an obligation is satisfied.

(c) Except as stated in subsections (d) and (e), if the beneficiary's bank pays the beneficiary of a payment order under a condition to payment or agreement of the beneficiary giving the bank the right to recover payment from the beneficiary if the bank does not receive payment of the order, the condition to payment or agreement is not enforceable.

(d) A funds-transfer system rule may provide that payments made to beneficiaries of funds transfers made through the system are provisional until receipt of payment by the beneficiary's bank of the payment order it accepted. A beneficiary's bank that makes a payment that is provisional under the rule is entitled to refund from the beneficiary if (i) the rule requires that both the beneficiary and the originator be given notice of the provisional nature of the payment before the funds transfer is initiated, (ii) the beneficiary, the beneficiary's bank, and the originator's bank agreed to be bound by the rule, and (iii) the beneficiary's bank did not receive payment of the payment order that it accepted. If the beneficiary is obliged to refund payment to the beneficiary's bank, acceptance of the payment order by the beneficiary's bank is nullified and no payment by the originator of the funds transfer to the beneficiary occurs under Section 4A—406.

(e) This subsection applies to a funds transfer that includes a payment order transmitted over a funds-transfer system that (i) nets obligations multilaterally among participants, and (ii) has in effect a loss-sharing agreement among participants for the purpose of providing funds necessary to complete settlement of the obligations of one or more participants that do not meet their settlement obligations. If the beneficiary's bank in the funds transfer accepts a payment order and the system fails to complete settlement pursuant to its rules with respect to any payment order in the funds transfer, (i) the acceptance by the beneficiary's bank is nullified and no person has any right or obligation based on the acceptance, (ii) the beneficiary's bank is entitled to recover payment from the beneficiary, (iii) no payment by the originator to the beneficiary occurs under Section 4A—406, and (iv) subject to Section 4A—402(e), each sender in the funds transfer is excused from its obligation to pay its payment order under Section 4A—402(c) because the funds transfer has not been completed.

### § 4A—406. Payment by Originator to Beneficiary; Discharge of Underlying Obligation.

(a) Subject to Sections 4A—211(e), 4A—405(d), and 4A—405(e), the originator of a funds transfer pays the beneficiary of the originator's payment order (i) at the time a payment order for the benefit of the beneficiary is accepted by the beneficiary's bank in the funds transfer and (ii) in an amount equal to the amount of the order accepted by the beneficiary's bank, but not more than the amount of the originator's order.

(b) If payment under subsection (a) is made to satisfy an obligation, the obligation is discharged to the same extent discharge would result from payment to the beneficiary of the same amount in money, unless (i) the payment under subsection (a) was made by a means prohibited by the contract of the beneficiary with respect to the obligation, (ii) the beneficiary, within a reasonable time after receiving notice of receipt of the order by the beneficiary's bank, notified the originator of the beneficiary's refusal of the payment, (iii) funds with respect to the order were not withdrawn by the beneficiary or applied to a debt of the beneficiary, and (iv) the beneficiary would suffer a loss that could reasonably have been avoided if payment had been made by a means complying with the contract. If payment by the originator does not result in discharge under this section, the originator is subrogated to the rights of the beneficiary to receive payment from the beneficiary's bank under Section 4A—404(a).

(c) For the purpose of determining whether discharge of an obligation occurs under subsection (b), if the beneficiary's bank accepts a payment order in an amount equal to the amount of the originator's payment order less charges of one or more receiving banks in the funds transfer, payment to the beneficiary is deemed to be in the amount of the originator's order unless upon demand by the beneficiary the originator does not pay the beneficiary the amount of the deducted charges.

(d) Rights of the originator or of the beneficiary of a funds transfer under this section may be varied only by agreement of the originator and the beneficiary.

## Part 5    Miscellaneous Provisions

### § 4A—501. Variation by Agreement and Effect of Funds-Transfer System Rule.

(a) Except as otherwise provided in this Article, the rights and obligations of a party to a funds transfer may be varied by agreement of the affected party.

(b) "Funds-transfer system rule" means a rule of an association of banks (i) governing transmission of payment orders by means of a funds-transfer system of the association or rights and obligations with respect to those orders, or (ii) to the extent the rule governs rights and obligations between banks that are parties to a funds transfer in which a Federal Reserve Bank, acting as an intermediary bank, sends a payment order to the beneficiary's bank. Except as otherwise provided in this Article, a funds-transfer system rule governing rights and obligations between participating banks using the system may be effective even if the rule conflicts with this Article and indirectly affects another party to the funds transfer who does not consent to the rule. A funds-transfer system rule may also govern rights and obligations of parties other than participating banks using the system to the extent stated in Sections 4A—404(c), 4A—405(d), and 4A—507(c).

### § 4A—502. Creditor Process Served on Receiving Bank; Setoff by Beneficiary's Bank.

(a) As used in this section, "creditor process" means levy, attachment, garnishment, notice of lien, sequestration, or similar process issued by or on behalf of a creditor or other claimant with respect to an account.

(b) This subsection applies to creditor process with respect to an authorized account of the sender of a payment order if the creditor process is served on the receiving bank. For the purpose of determining rights with respect to the creditor process, if the receiving bank accepts the payment order the balance in the authorized account is deemed to be reduced by the amount of the payment order to the extent the bank did not otherwise receive payment of the order, unless the creditor process is served at a time and in a manner affording the bank a reasonable opportunity to act on it before the bank accepts the payment order.

(c) If a beneficiary's bank has received a payment order for payment to the beneficiary's account in the bank, the following rules apply:

(1) The bank may credit the beneficiary's account. The amount credited may be set off against an obligation owed by the beneficiary to the bank or may be applied to satisfy creditor process served on the bank with respect to the account.

(2) The bank may credit the beneficiary's account and allow withdrawal of the amount credited unless creditor process with respect to the account is served at a time and in a manner affording the bank a reasonable opportunity to act to prevent withdrawal.

(3) If creditor process with respect to the beneficiary's account has been served and the bank has had a reasonable opportunity to act on it, the bank may not reject the payment order except for a reason unrelated to the service of process.

(d) Creditor process with respect to a payment by the originator to the beneficiary pursuant to a funds transfer may be served only on the beneficiary's bank with respect to the debt owed by that bank to the beneficiary. Any other bank served with the creditor process is not obliged to act with respect to the process.

## § 4A—503. Injunction or Restraining Order with Respect to Funds Transfer.

For proper cause and in compliance with applicable law, a court may restrain (i) a person from issuing a payment order to initiate a funds transfer, (ii) an originator's bank from executing the payment order of the originator, or (iii) the beneficiary's bank from releasing funds to the beneficiary or the beneficiary from withdrawing the funds. A court may not otherwise restrain a person from issuing a payment order, paying or receiving payment of a payment order, or otherwise acting with respect to a funds transfer.

## § 4A—504. Order in Which Items and Payment Orders May Be Charged to Account; Order of Withdrawals from Account.

(a)  If a receiving bank has received more than one payment order of the sender or one or more payment orders and other items that are payable from the sender's account, the bank may charge the sender's account with respect to the various orders and items in any sequence.

(b)  In determining whether a credit to an account has been withdrawn by the holder of the account or applied to a debt of the holder of the account, credits first made to the account are first withdrawn or applied.

## § 4A—505. Preclusion of Objection to Debit of Customer's Account.

If a receiving bank has received payment from its customer with respect to a payment order issued in the name of the customer as sender and accepted by the bank, and the customer received notification reasonably identifying the order, the customer is precluded from asserting that the bank is not entitled to retain the payment unless the customer notifies the bank of the customer's objection to the payment within one year after the notification was received by the customer.

## § 4A—506. Rate of Interest.

(a)  If, under this Article, a receiving bank is obliged to pay interest with respect to a payment order issued to the bank, the amount payable may be determined (i) by agreement of the sender and receiving bank, or (ii) by a funds-transfer system rule if the payment order is transmitted through a funds-transfer system.

(b)  If the amount of interest is not determined by an agreement or rule as stated in subsection (a), the amount is calculated by multiplying the applicable Federal Funds rate by the amount on which interest is payable, and then multiplying the product by the number of days for which interest is payable. The applicable Federal Funds rate is the average of the Federal Funds rates published by the Federal Reserve Bank of New York for each of the days for which interest is payable divided by 360. The Federal Funds rate for any day on which

a published rate is not available is the same as the published rate for the next preceding day for which there is a published rate. If a receiving bank that accepted a payment order is required to refund payment to the sender of the order because the funds transfer was not completed, but the failure to complete was not due to any fault by the bank, the interest payable is reduced by a percentage equal to the reserve requirement on deposits of the receiving bank.

## § 4A—507. Choice of Law.

(a)  The following rules apply unless the affected parties otherwise agree or subsection (c) applies:

(1)  The rights and obligations between the sender of a payment order and the receiving bank are governed by the law of the jurisdiction in which the receiving bank is located.

(2)  The rights and obligations between the beneficiary's bank and the beneficiary are governed by the law of the jurisdiction in which the beneficiary's bank is located.

(3)  The issue of when payment is made pursuant to a funds transfer by the originator to the beneficiary is governed by the law of the jurisdiction in which the beneficiary's bank is located.

(b)  If the parties described in each paragraph of subsection (a) have made an agreement selecting the law of a particular jurisdiction to govern rights and obligations between each other, the law of that jurisdiction governs those rights and obligations, whether or not the payment order or the funds transfer bears a reasonable relation to that jurisdiction.

(c)  A funds-transfer system rule may select the law of a particular jurisdiction to govern (i) rights and obligations between participating banks with respect to payment orders transmitted or processed through the system, or (ii) the rights and obligations of some or all parties to a funds transfer any part of which is carried out by means of the system. A choice of law made pursuant to clause (i) is binding on participating banks. A choice of law made pursuant to clause (ii) is binding on the originator, other sender, or a receiving bank having notice that the funds-transfer system might be used in the funds transfer and of the choice of law by the system when the originator, other sender, or receiving bank issued or accepted a payment order. The beneficiary of a funds transfer is bound by the choice of law if, when the funds transfer is initiated, the beneficiary has notice that the funds-transfer system might be used in the funds transfer and of the choice of law by the sytem. The law of a jurisdiction selected pursuant to this subsection may govern, whether or not that law bears a reasonable relation to the matter in issue.

(d)  In the event of inconsistency between an agreement under subsection (b) and a choice-of-law rule under subsection (c), the agreement under subsection (b) prevails.

(e)  If a funds transfer is made by use of more than one funds-transfer system and there is inconsistency between choice-of-law rules of the systems, the matter in issue is governed by the law of the selected jurisdiction that has the most significant relationship to the matter in issue.

# Article 5
# LETTERS OF CREDIT

## § 5—101. Short Title.

This Article shall be known and may be cited as Uniform Commercial Code—Letters of Credit.

## § 5—102. Scope.

(1) This Article applies

(a) to a credit issued by a bank if the credit requires a documentary draft or a documentary demand for payment; and

(b) to a credit issued by a person other than a bank if the credit requires that the draft or demand for payment be accompanied by a document of title; and

(c) to a credit issued by a bank or other person if the credit is not within subparagraphs (a) or (b) but conspicuously states that it is a letter of credit or is conspicuously so entitled.

(2) Unless the engagement meets the requirements of subsection (1), this Article does not apply to engagements to make advances or to honor drafts or demands for payment, to authorities to pay or purchase, to guarantees or to general agreements.

(3) This Article deals with some but not all of the rules and concepts of letters of credit as such rules or concepts have developed prior to this act or may hereafter develop. The fact that this Article states a rule does not by itself require, imply or negate application of the same or a converse rule to a situation not provided for or to a person not specified by this Article.

## § 5—103. Definitions.

(1) In this Article unless the context otherwise requires

(a) "Credit" or "letter of credit" means an engagement by a bank or other person made at the request of a customer and of a kind within the scope of this Article (Section 5—102) that the issuer will honor drafts or other demands for payment upon compliance with the conditions specified in the credit. A credit may be either revocable or irrevocable. The engagement may be either an agreement to honor or a statement that the bank or other person is authorized to honor.

(b) A "documentary draft" or a "documentary demand for payment" is one honor of which is conditioned upon the presentation of a document or documents. "Document" means any paper including document of title, security, invoice, certificate, notice of default and the like.

(c) An "issuer" is a bank or other person issuing a credit.

(d) A "beneficiary" of a credit is a person who is entitled under its terms to draw or demand payment.

(e) An "advising bank" is a bank which gives notification of the issuance of a credit by another bank.

(f) A "confirming bank" is a bank which engages either that it will itself honor a credit already issued by another bank or that such a credit will be honored by the issuer or a third bank.

(g) A "customer" is a buyer or other person who causes an issuer to issue a credit. The term also includes a bank which procures issuance or confirmation on behalf of that bank's customer.

(2) Other definitions applying to this Article and the sections in which they appear are:

"Notation of Credit". Section 5—108.
"Presenter". Section 5—112(3).

(3) Definitions in other Articles applying to this Article and the sections in which they appear are:

"Accept" or "Acceptance". Section 3—410.
"Contract for sale". Section 2—106.
"Draft". Section 3—104.
"Holder in due course". Section 3—302.
"Midnight deadline". Section 4—104.
"Security". Section 8—102.

(4) In addition, Article 1 contains general definitions and principles of construction and interpretation applicable throughout this Article.

## § 5—104. Formal Requirements; Signing.

(1) Except as otherwise required in subsection (1)(c) of Section 5—102 on scope, no particular form of phrasing is required for a credit. A credit must be in writing and signed by the issuer and a confirmation must be in writing and signed by the confirming bank. A modification of the terms of a credit or confirmation must be signed by the issuer or confirming bank.

(2) A telegram may be a sufficient signed writing if it identifies its sender by an authorized authentication. The authentication may be in code and the authorized naming of the issuer in an advice of credit is a sufficient signing.

## § 5—105. Consideration.

No consideration is necessary to establish a credit or to enlarge or otherwise modify its terms.

## § 5—106. Time and Effect of Establishment of Credit.

(1) Unless otherwise agreed a credit is established

(a) as regards the customer as soon as a letter of credit is sent to him or the letter of credit or an authorized written advice of its issuance is sent to the beneficiary; and

(b) as regards the beneficiary when he receives a letter of credit or an authorized written advice of its issuance.

(2) Unless otherwise agreed once an irrevocable credit is established as regards the customer it can be modified or revoked only with the consent of the customer and once it is established as regards the beneficiary it can be modified or revoked only with his consent.

(3) Unless otherwise agreed after a revocable credit is established it may be modified or revoked by the issuer without notice to or consent from the customer or beneficiary.

(4) Notwithstanding any modification or revocation of a revocable credit any person authorized to honor or negotiate

under the terms of the original credit is entitled to reimbursement for or honor of any draft or demand for payment duly honored or negotiated before receipt of notice of the modification or revocation and the issuer in turn is entitled to reimbursement from its customer.

### § 5—107. Advice of Credit; Confirmation; Error in Statement of Terms.

(1) Unless otherwise specified an advising bank by advising a credit issued by another bank does not assume any obligation to honor drafts drawn or demands for payment made under the credit but it does assume obligation for the accuracy of its own statement.

(2) A confirming bank by confirming a credit becomes directly obligated on the credit to the extent of its confirmation as though it were its issuer and acquires the rights of an issuer.

(3) Even though an advising bank incorrectly advises the terms of a credit it has been authorized to advise the credit is established as against the issuer to the extent of its original terms.

(4) Unless otherwise specified the customer bears as against the issuer all risks of transmission and reasonable translation or interpretation of any message relating to a credit.

### § 5—108. "Notation Credit"; Exhaustion of Credit.

(1) A credit which specifies that any person purchasing or paying drafts drawn or demands for payment made under it must note the amount of the draft or demand on the letter or advice of credit is a "notation credit".

(2) Under a notation credit

(a) a person paying the beneficiary or purchasing a draft or demand for payment from him acquires a right to honor only if the appropriate notation is made and by transferring or forwarding for honor the documents under the credit such a person warrants to the issuer that the notation has been made; and

(b) unless the credit or a signed statement that an appropriate notation has been made accompanies the draft or demand for payment the issuer may delay honor until evidence of notation has been procured which is satisfactory to it but its obligation and that of its customer continue for a reasonable time not exceeding thirty days to obtain such evidence.

(3) If the credit is not a notation credit

(a) the issuer may honor complying drafts or demands for payment presented to it in the order in which they are presented and is discharged pro tanto by honor of any such draft or demand;

(b) as between competing good faith purchasers of complying drafts or demands the person first purchasing his priority over a subsequent purchaser even though the later purchased draft or demand has been first honored.

### § 5—109. Issuer's Obligation to Its Customer.

(1) An issuer's obligation to its customer includes good faith and observance of any general banking usage but unless otherwise agreed does not include liability or responsibility

(a) for performance of the underlying contract for sale or other transaction between the customer and the beneficiary; or

(b) for any act or omission of any person other than itself or its own branch or for loss or destruction of a draft, demand or document in transit or in the possession of others; or

(c) based on knowledge or lack of knowledge of any usage of any particular trade.

(2) An issuer must examine documents with care so as to ascertain that on their face they appear to comply with the terms of the credit but unless otherwise agreed assumes no liability or responsibility for the genuineness, falsification or effect of any document which appears on such examination to be regular on its face.

(3) A non-bank issuer is not bound by any banking usage of which it has no knowledge.

### § 5—110. Availability of Credit in Portions; Presenter's Reservation of Lien or Claim.

(1) Unless otherwise specified a credit may be used in portions in the discretion of the beneficiary.

(2) Unless otherwise specified a person by presenting a documentary draft or demand for payment under a credit relinquishes upon its honor all claims to the documents and a person by transferring such draft or demand or causing such presentment authorizes such relinquishment. An explicit reservation of claim makes the draft or demand noncomplying.

### § 5—111. Warranties on Transfer and Presentment.

(1) Unless otherwise agreed the beneficiary by transferring or presenting a documentary draft or demand for payment warrants to all interested parties that the necessary conditions of the credit have been complied with. This is in addition to any warranties arising under Articles 3, 4, 7 and 8.

(2) Unless otherwise agreed a negotiating, advising, confirming, collecting or issuing bank presenting or transferring a draft or demand for payment under a credit warrants only the matters warranted by a collecting bank under Article 4 and any such bank transferring a document warrants only the matters warranted by an intermediary under Articles 7 and 8.

### § 5—112. Time Allowed for Honor or Rejection; Withholding Honor or Rejection by Consent; "Presenter".

(1) A bank to which a documentary draft or demand for payment is presented under a credit may without dishonor of the draft, demand or credit

(a) defer honor until the close of the third banking day following receipt of the documents; and

(b) further defer honor if the presenter has expressly or impliedly consented thereto.

Failure to honor within the time here specified constitutes dishonor of the draft or demand and of the credit [except as otherwise provided in subsection (4) of Section 5—114 on conditional payment].

Note: *The bracketed language in the last sentence of subsection (1) should be included only if the optional provisions of Section 5—114(4) and (5) are included.*

(2) Upon dishonor the bank may unless otherwise instructed fulfill its duty to return the draft or demand and the documents by holding them at the disposal of the presenter and sending him an advice to that effect.

(3) "Presenter" means any person presenting a draft or demand for payment for honor under a credit even though that person is a confirming bank or other correspondent which is acting under an issuer's authorization.

## § 5—113. Indemnities.

(1) A bank seeking to obtain (whether for itself or another) honor, negotiation or reimbursement under a credit may give an indemnity to induce such honor, negotiation or reimbursement.

(2) An indemnity agreement inducing honor, negotiation or reimbursement

(a) unless otherwise explicitly agreed applies to defects in the documents but not in the goods; and

(b) unless a longer time is explicitly agreed expires at the end of ten business days following receipt of the documents by the ultimate customer unless notice of objection is sent before such expiration date. The ultimate customer may send notice of objection to the person from whom he received the documents and any bank receiving such notice is under a duty to send notice to its transferor before its midnight deadline.

## § 5—114. Issuer's Duty and Privilege to Honor; Right to Reimbursement.

(1) An issuer must honor a draft or demand for payment which complies with the terms of the relevant credit regardless of whether the goods or documents conform to the underlying contract for sale or other contract between the customer and the beneficiary. The issuer is not excused from honor of such a draft or demand by reason of an additional general term that all documents must be satisfactory to the issuer, but an issuer may require that specified documents must be satisfactory to it.

(2) Unless otherwise agreed when documents appear on their face to comply with the terms of a credit but a required document does not in fact conform to the warranties made on negotiation or transfer of a document of title (Section 7—507) or of a certificated security (Section 8—306) or is forged or fraudulent or there is fraud in the transaction:

(a) the issuer must honor the draft or demand for payment if honor is demanded by a negotiating bank or other holder of the draft or demand which has taken the draft or demand under the credit and under circumstances which would make it a holder in due course (Section 3—302)

and in an appropriate case would make it a person to whom a document of title has been duly negotiated (Section 7—502) or a bona fide purchaser of a certificated security (Section 8—302); and

(b) in all other cases as against its customer, an issuer acting in good faith may honor the draft or demand for payment despite notification from the customer of fraud, forgery or other defect not apparent on the face of the documents but a court of appropriate jurisdiction may enjoin such honor.

(3) Unless otherwise agreed an issuer which has duly honored a draft or demand for payment is entitled to immediate reimbursement of any payment made under the credit and to be put in effectively available funds not later than the day before maturity of any acceptance made under the credit.

[(4) When a credit provides for payment by the issuer on receipt of notice that the required documents are in the possession of a correspondent or other agent of the issuer

(a) any payment made on receipt of such notice is conditional; and

(b) the issuer may reject documents which do not comply with the credit if it does so within three banking days following its receipt of the documents; and

(c) in the event of such rejection, the issuer is entitled by charge back or otherwise to return of the payment made.]

[(5) In the case covered by subsection (4) failure to reject documents within the time specified in sub-paragraph (b) constitutes acceptance of the documents and makes the payment final in favor of the beneficiary.]

Note: *Subsections (4) and (5) are bracketed as optional. If they are included the bracketed language in the last sentence of Section 5—112(1) should also be included.*

## § 5—115. Remedy for Improper Dishonor or Anticipatory Repudiation.

(1) When an issuer wrongfully dishonors a draft or demand for payment presented under a credit the person entitled to honor has with respect to any documents the rights of a person in the position of a seller (Section 2—707) and may recover from the issuer the face amount of the draft or demand together with incidental damages under Section 2—710 on seller's incidental damages and interest but less any amount realized by resale or other use or disposition of the subject matter of the transaction. In the event no resale or other utilization is made the documents, goods or other subject matter involved in the transaction must be turned over to the issuer on payment of judgment.

(2) When an issuer wrongfully cancels or otherwise repudiates a credit before presentment of a draft or demand for payment drawn under it the beneficiary has the rights of a seller after anticipatory repudiation by the buyer under Section 2—610 if he learns of the repudiation in time reasonably to avoid procurement of the required documents. Otherwise the beneficiary has an immediate right of action for wrongful dishonor.

## § 5—116. Transfer and Assignment.

(1) The right to draw under a credit can be transferred or assigned only when the credit is expressly designated as transferable or assignable.

(2) Even through the credit specifically states that it is nontransferable or nonassignable the beneficiary may before performance of the conditions of the credit assign his right to proceeds. Such an assignment is an assignment of an account under Article 9 on Secured Transactions and is governed by that Article except that

> (a) the assignment is ineffective until the letter of credit or advice of credit is delivered to the assignee which delivery constitutes perfection of the security interest under Article 9; and

> (b) the issuer may honor drafts or demands for payment drawn under the credit until it receives a notification of the assignment signed by the beneficiary which reasonably identifies the credit involved in the assignment and contains a request to pay the assignee; and

> (c) after what reasonably appears to be such a notification has been received the issuer may without dishonor refuse to accept or pay even to a person otherwise entitled to honor until the letter of credit or advice of credit is exhibited to the issuer.

(3) Except where the beneficiary has effectively assigned his right to draw or his right to proceeds, nothing in this section limits his right to transfer or negotiate drafts or demands drawn under the credit.

## § 5—117. Insolvency of Bank Holding Funds for Documentary Credit.

(1) Where an issuer or an advising or confirming bank or a bank which has for a customer procured issuance of a credit by another bank becomes insolvent before final payment under the credit and the credit is one to which this Article is made applicable by paragraphs (a) or (b) of Section 5—102(1) on scope, the receipt or allocation of funds or collateral to secure or meet obligations under the credit shall have the following results:

> (a) to the extent of any funds or collateral turned over after or before the insolvency as indemnity against or specifically for the purpose of payment of drafts or demands for payment drawn under the designated credit, the drafts or demands are entitled to payment in preference over depositors or other general creditors of the issuer or bank; and

> (b) on expiration of the credit or surrender of the beneficiary's rights under it unused any person who has given such funds or collateral is similarly entitled to return thereof; and

> (c) a charge to a general or current account with a bank if specifically consented to for the purpose of indemnity against or payment of drafts or demands for payment drawn under the designated credit falls under the same rules as if the funds had been drawn out in cash and then turned over with specific instructions.

(2) After honor or reimbursement under this section the customer or other person for whose account the insolvent bank has acted is entitled to receive the documents involved.

# Article 6
# BULK TRANSFERS

## § 6—101. Short Title.

This Article shall be known and may be cited as Uniform Commercial Code—Bulk Transfers.

## § 6—102. "Bulk Transfers"; Transfers of Equipment; Enterprises Subject to This Article; Bulk Transfers Subject to This Article.

(1) A "bulk transfer" is any transfer in bulk and not in the ordinary course of the transferor's business of a major part of the materials, supplies, merchandise or other inventory (Section 9—109) of an enterprise subject to this Article.

(2) A transfer of a substantial part of the equipment (Section 9—109) of such an enterprise is a bulk transfer if it is made in connection with a bulk transfer of inventory, but not otherwise.

(3) The enterprises subject to this Article are all those whose principal business is the sale of merchandise from stock, including those who manufacture what they sell.

(4) Except as limited by the following section all bulk transfers of goods located within this state are subject to this Article.

## § 6—103. Transfers Excepted From This Article.

The following transfers are not subject to this Article:

(1) Those made to give security for the performance of an obligation;

(2) General assignments for the benefit of all the creditors of the transferor, and subsequent transfers by the assignee thereunder;

(3) Transfers in settlement or realization of a lien or other security interests;

(4) Sales by executors, administrators, receivers, trustees in bankruptcy, or any public officer under judicial process;

(5) Sales made in the course of judicial or administrative proceedings for the dissolution or reorganization of a corporation and of which notice is sent to the creditors of the corporation pursuant to order of the court or administrative agency;

(6) Transfers to a person maintaining a known place of business in this State who becomes bound to pay the debts of the transferor in full and gives public notice of that fact, and who is solvent after becoming so bound;

(7) A transfer to a new business enterprise organized to take over and continue the business, if public notice of the transaction is given and the new enterprise assumes the debts of the transferor and he receives nothing from the transaction except an interest in the new enterprise junior to the claims of creditors;

(8) Transfers of property which is exempt from execution.

Public notice under subsection (6) or subsection (7) may be given by publishing once a week for two consecutive weeks in a newspaper of general circulation where the transferor had its principal place of business in this state an advertisement including the names and addresses of the transferor and transferee and the effective date of the transfer.

### § 6—104. Schedule of Property, List of Creditors.

(1) Except as provided with respect to auction sales (Section 6—108), a bulk transfer subject to this Article is ineffective against any creditor of the transferor unless:

(a) The transferee requires the transferor to furnish a list of his existing creditors prepared as stated in this section; and

(b) The parties prepare a schedule of the property transferred sufficient to identify it; and

(c) The transferee preserves the list and schedule for six months next following the transfer and permits inspection of either or both and copying therefrom at all reasonable hours by any creditor of the transferor, or files the list and schedule in (a public office to be here identified).

(2) The list of creditors must be signed and sworn to or affirmed by the transferor or his agent. It must contain the names and business addresses of all creditors of the transferor, with the amounts when known, and also the names of all persons who are known to the transferor to assert claims against him even though such claims are disputed. If the transferor is the obligor of an outstanding issue of bonds, debentures or the like as to which there is an indenture trustee, the list of creditors need include only the name and address of the indenture trustee and the aggregate outstanding principal amount of the issue.

(3) Responsibility for the completeness and accuracy of the list of creditors rests on the transferor, and the transfer is not rendered ineffective by errors or omissions therein unless the transferee is shown to have had knowledge.

### § 6—105. Notice to Creditors.

In addition to the requirements of the preceding section, any bulk transfer subject to this Article except one made by auction sale (Section 6—108) is ineffective against any creditor of the transferor unless at least ten days before he takes possession of the goods or pays for them, whichever happens first, the transferee gives notice of the transfer in the manner and to the persons hereafter provided (Section 6—107).

### [§ 6—106. Application of the Proceeds.

In addition to the requirements of the two preceding sections:
(1) Upon every bulk transfer subject to this Article for which new consideration becomes payable except those made by sale at auction it is the duty of the transferee to assure that such consideration is applied so far as necessary to pay those debts of the transferor which are either shown on the list furnished by the transferor (Section 6—104) or filed in writing in the place stated in the notice (Section 6—107) within thirty days after the mailing of such notice. This duty of the transferee runs to all the holders of such debts, and may be enforced by any of them for the benefit of all.

(2) If any of said debts are in dispute the necessary sum may be withheld from distribution until the dispute is settled or adjudicated.

(3) If the consideration payable is not enough to pay all of the said debts in full distribution shall be made pro rata.]

Note: *This section is bracketed to indicate division of opinion as to whether or not it is a wise provision, and to suggest that this is a point on which State enactments may differ without serious damage to the principle of uniformity. In any State where this section is omitted, the following parts of sections, also bracketed in the text, should also be omitted, namely:*
Section 6—107(2)(e).
    6—108(3)(c).
    6—109(2).
   *In any State where this section is enacted, these other provisions should be also.*

### Optional Subsection (4)

[(4) The transferee may within ten days after he takes possession of the goods pay the consideration into the (specify court) in the county where the transferor had its principal place of business in this state and thereafter may discharge his duty under this section by giving notice by registered or certified mail to all the persons to whom the duty runs that the consideration has been paid into that court and that they should file their claims there. On motion of any interested party, the court may order the distribution of the consideration to the persons entitled to it.]

Note: *Optional subsection (4) is recommended for those states which do not have a general statute providing for payment of money into court.*

### § 6—107. The Notice.

(1) The notice to creditors (Section 6—105) shall state:

(a) that a bulk transfer is about to be made; and

(b) the names and business addresses of the transferor and transferee, and all other business names and addresses used by the transferor within three years last past so far as known to the transferee; and

(c) whether or not all the debts of the transferor are to be paid in full as they fall due as a result of the transaction, and if so, the address to which creditors should send their bills.

(2) If the debts of the transferor are not to be paid in full as they fall due or if the transferee is in doubt on that point then the notice shall state further:

(a) the location and general description of the property to be transferred and the estimated total of the transferor's debts;

(b) the address where the schedule of property and list of creditors (Section 6—104) may be inspected;

(c) whether the transfer is to pay existing debts and if so the amount of such debts and to whom owing;

(d) whether the transfer is for new consideration and if so the amount of such consideration and the time and place of payment; [and]

[(e) if for new consideration the time and place where creditors of the transferor are to file their claims.]

(3) The notice in any case shall be delivered personally or sent by registered or certified mail to all the persons shown on the list of creditors furnished by the transferor (Section 6—104) and to all other persons who are known to the transferee to hold or assert claims against the transferor.

### § 6—108. Auction Sales; "Auctioneer".

(1) A bulk transfer is subject to this Article even though it is by sale at auction, but only in the manner and with the results stated in this section.

(2) The transferor shall furnish a list of his creditors and assist in the preparation of a schedule of the property to be sold, both prepared as before stated (Section 6—104).

(3) The person or persons other than the transferor who direct, control or are responsible for the auction are collectively called the "auctioneer". The auctioneer shall:

(a) receive and retain the list of creditors and prepare and retain the schedule of property for the period stated in this Article (Section 6—104);

(b) give notice of the auction personally or by registered or certified mail at least ten days before it occurs to all persons shown on the list of creditors and to all other persons who are known to him to hold or assert claims against the transferor; [and]

[(c) assure that the net proceeds of the auction are applied as provided in this Article (Section 6—106).]

(4) Failure of the auctioneer to perform any of these duties does not affect the validity of the sale or the title of the purchasers, but if the auctioneer knows that the auction constitutes a bulk transfer such failure renders the auctioneer liable to the creditors of the transferor as a class for the sums owing to them from the transferor up to but not exceeding the net proceeds of the auction. If the auctioneer consists of several persons their liability is joint and several.

### § 6—109. What Creditors Protected; [Credit for Payment to Particular Creditors].

(1) The creditors of the transferor mentioned in this Article are those holding claims based on transactions or events occurring before the bulk transfer, but creditors who become such after notice to creditors is given (Sections 6—105 and 6—107) are not entitled to notice.

[(2) Against the aggregate obligation imposed by the provisions of this Article concerning the application of the proceeds (Section 6—106 and subsection (3)(c) of 6—108) the transferee or auctioneer is entitled to credit for sums paid to particular creditors of the transferor, not exceeding the sums believed in good faith at the time of the payment to be properly payable to such creditors.]

### § 6—110. Subsequent Transfers.

When the title of a transferee to property is subject to a defect by reason of his noncompliance with the requirements of this Article, then:

(1) a purchaser of any of such property from such transferee who pays no value or who takes with notice of such noncompliance takes subject to such defect, but

(2) a purchaser for value in good faith and without such notice takes free of such defect.

### § 6—111. Limitation of Actions and Levies.

No action under this Article shall be brought nor levy made more than six months after the date on which the transferee took possession of the goods unless the transfer has been concealed. If the transfer has been concealed, actions may be brought or levies made within six months after its discovery.

Note to Article 6: *Section 6—106 is bracketed to indicate division of opinion as to whether or not it is a wise provision, and to suggest that this is a point on which State enactments may differ without serious damage to the principle of uniformity.*

*In any State where Section 6—106 is not enacted, the following parts of sections, also bracketed in the text, should also be omitted, namely:*
*Sec. 6—107(2)(e).*
    *6—108(3)(c).*
    *6—109(2).*
*In any State where Section 6—106 is enacted, these other provisions should be also.*

# Article 6
## Alternative B*

### § 6—101. Short Title.

This Article shall be known and may be cited as Uniform Commercial Code—Bulk Sales.

### § 6—102. Definitions and Index of Definitions.

(1) In this Article, unless the context otherwise requires:

(a) "Assets" means the inventory that is the subject of a bulk sale and any tangible and intangible personal property used or held for use primarily in, or arising from, the seller's business and sold in connection with that inventory, but the term does not include:

(i) fixtures (Section 9—313(1)(a)) other than readily removable factory and office machines;

(ii) the lessee's interest in a lease of real property; or

(iii) property to the extent it is generally exempt from creditor process under nonbankruptcy law.

---

* Approved in substance by the National Conference of Commissioners on Uniform State Laws and The American Law Institute. States have the choice of adopting this alternative to the existing Article 6 or repealing Article 6 entirely (Alternative A).

(b) ''Auctioneer'' means a person whom the seller engages to direct, conduct, control, or be responsible for a sale by auction.

(c) ''Bulk sale'' means:

(i) in the case of a sale by auction or a sale or series of sales conducted by a liquidator on the seller's behalf, a sale or series of sales not in the ordinary course of the seller's business of more than half of the seller's inventory, as measured by value on the date of the bulk-sale agreement, if on that date the auctioneer or liquidator has notice, or after reasonable inquiry would have had notice, that the seller will not continue to operate the same or a similar kind of business after the sale or series of sales; and

(ii) in all other cases, a sale not in the ordinary course of the seller's business of more than half the seller's inventory, as measured by value on the date of the bulk-sale agreement, if on that date the buyer has notice, or after reasonable inquiry would have had notice, that the seller will not continue to operate the same or a similar kind of business after the sale.

(d) ''Claim'' means a right to payment from the seller, whether or not the right is reduced to judgment, liquidated, fixed, matured, disputed, secured, legal, or equitable. The term includes costs of collection and attorney's fees only to the extent that the laws of this state permit the holder of the claim to recover them in an action against the obligor.

(e) ''Claimant'' means a person holding a claim incurred in the seller's business other than:

(i) an unsecured and unmatured claim for employment compensation and benefits, including commissions and vacation, severance, and sick-leave pay;

(ii) a claim for injury to an individual or to property, or for breach of warranty, unless:

(A) a right of action for the claim has accrued;

(B) the claim has been asserted against the seller; and

(C) the seller knows the identity of the person asserting the claim and the basis upon which the person has asserted it; and

(States to Select One Alternative)

*Alternative A*

[(iii) a claim for taxes owing to a governmental unit.]

*Alternative B*

[(iii) a claim for taxes owing to a governmental unit, if:

(A) a statute governing the enforcement of the claim permits or requires notice of the bulk sale to be given to the governmental unit in a manner other than by compliance with the requirements of this Article; and

(B) notice is given in accordance with the statute.]

(f) ''Creditor'' means a claimant or other person holding a claim.

(g)(i) ''Date of the bulk sale'' means:

(A) if the sale is by auction or is conducted by a liquidator on the seller's behalf, the date on which more than ten percent of the net proceeds is paid to or for the benefit of the seller; and

(B) in all other cases, the later of the date on which:

(I) more than ten percent of the net contract price is paid to or for the benefit of the seller; or

(II) more than ten percent of the assets, as measured by value, are transferred to the buyer.

(ii) For purposes of this subsection:

(A) delivery of a negotiable instrument (Section 3—104(1)) to or for the benefit of the seller in exchange for assets constitutes payment of the contract price pro tanto;

(B) to the extent that the contract price is deposited in an escrow, the contract price is paid to or for the benefit of the seller when the seller acquires the unconditional right to receive the deposit or when the deposit is delivered to the seller or for the benefit of the seller, whichever is earlier; and

(C) an asset is transferred when a person holding an unsecured claim can no longer obtain through judicial proceedings rights to the asset that are superior to those of the buyer arising as a result of the bulk sale. A person holding an unsecured claim can obtain those superior rights to a tangible asset at least until the buyer has an unconditional right, under the bulk-sale agreement, to possess the asset, and a person holding an unsecured claim can obtain those superior rights to an intangible asset at least until the buyer has an unconditional right, under the bulk-sale agreement, to use the asset.

(h) ''Date of the bulk-sale agreement'' means:

(i) in the case of a sale by auction or conducted by a liquidator (subsection (c)(i)), the date on which the seller engages the auctioneer or liquidator; and

(ii) in all other cases, the date on which a bulk-sale agreement becomes enforceable between the buyer and the seller.

(i) ''Debt'' means liability on a claim.

(j) ''Liquidator'' means a person who is regularly engaged in the business of disposing of assets for businesses contemplating liquidation or dissolution.

(k) "Net contract price" means the new consideration the buyer is obligated to pay for the assets less:

(i) the amount of any proceeds of the sale of an asset, to the extent the proceeds are applied in partial or total satisfaction of a debt secured by the asset; and

(ii) the amount of any debt to the extent it is secured by a security interest or lien that is enforceable against the asset before and after it has been sold to a buyer. If a debt is secured by an asset and other property of the seller, the amount of the debt secured by a security interest or lien that is enforceable against the asset is determined by multiplying the debt by a fraction, the numerator of which is the value of the new consideration for the asset on the date of the bulk sale and the denominator of which is the value of all property securing the debt on the date of the bulk sale.

(l) "Net proceeds" means the new consideration received for assets sold at a sale by auction or a sale conducted by a liquidator on the seller's behalf less:

(i) commissions and reasonable expenses of the sale;

(ii) the amount of any proceeds of the sale of an asset, to the extent the proceeds are applied in partial or total satisfaction of a debt secured by the asset; and

(iii) the amount of any debt to the extent it is secured by a security interest or lien that is enforceable against the asset before and after it has been sold to a buyer. If a debt is secured by an asset and other property of the seller, the amount of the debt secured by a security interest or lien that is enforceable against the asset is determined by multiplying the debt by a fraction, the numerator of which is the value of the new consideration for the asset on the date of the bulk sale and the denominator of which is the value of all property securing the debt on the date of the bulk sale.

(m) A sale is "in the ordinary course of the seller's business" if the sale comports with usual or customary practices in the kind of business in which the seller is engaged or with the seller's own usual or customary practices.

(n) "United States" includes its territories and possessions and the Commonwealth of Puerto Rico.

(o) "Value" means fair market value.

(p) "Verified" means signed and sworn to or affirmed.

(2) The following definitions in other Articles apply to this Article:

| | | |
|---|---|---|
| (a) | "Buyer." | Section 2—103(1)(a). |
| (b) | "Equipment." | Section 9—109(2). |
| (c) | "Inventory." | Section 9—109(4). |
| (d) | "Sale." | Section 2—106(1). |
| (e) | "Seller." | Section 2—103(1)(d). |

(3) In addition, Article 1 contains general definitions and principles of construction and interpretation applicable throughout this Article.

## § 6—103. Applicability of Article.

(1) Except as otherwise provided in subsection (3), this Article applies to a bulk sale if:

(a) the seller's principal business is the sale of inventory from stock; and

(b) on the date of the bulk-sale agreement the seller is located in this state or, if the seller is located in a jurisdiction that is not a part of the United States, the seller's major executive office in the United States is in this state.

(2) A seller is deemed to be located at his [or her] place of business. If a seller has more than one place of business, the seller is deemed located at his [or her] chief executive office.

(3) This Article does not apply to:

(a) a transfer made to secure payment or performance of an obligation;

(b) a transfer of collateral to a secured party pursuant to Section 9—503;

(c) a sale of collateral pursuant to Section 9—504;

(d) retention of collateral pursuant to Section 9—505;

(e) a sale of an asset encumbered by a security interest or lien if (i) all the proceeds of the sale are applied in partial or total satisfaction of the debt secured by the security interest or lien or (ii) the security interest or lien is enforceable against the asset after it has been sold to the buyer and the net contract price is zero;

(f) a general assignment for the benefit of creditors or to a subsequent transfer by the assignee;

(g) a sale by an executor, administrator, receiver, trustee in bankruptcy, or any public officer under judicial process;

(h) a sale made in the course of judicial or administrative proceedings for the dissolution or reorganization of an organization;

(i) a sale to a buyer whose principal place of business is in the United States and who:

(i) not earlier than 21 days before the date of the bulk sale, (A) obtains from the seller a verified and dated list of claimants of whom the seller has notice three days before the seller sends or delivers the list to the buyer or (B) conducts a reasonable inquiry to discover the claimants;

(ii) assumes in full the debts owed to claimants of whom the buyer has knowledge on the date the buyer receives the list of claimants from the seller or on the date the buyer completes the reasonable inquiry, as the case may be;

(iii) is not insolvent after the assumption; and

(iv) gives written notice of the assumption not later than 30 days after the date of the bulk sale by sending or delivering a notice to the claimants identified in subparagraph (ii) or by filing a notice in the office of the [Secretary of State];

(j) a sale to a buyer whose principal place of business is in the United States and who:

(i) assumes in full the debts that were incurred in the seller's business before the date of the bulk sale;

(ii) is not insolvent after the assumption; and

(iii) gives written notice of the assumption not later than 30 days after the date of the bulk sale by sending or delivering a notice to each creditor whose debt is assumed or by filing a notice in the office of the [Secretary of State];

(k) a sale to a new organization that is organized to take over and continue the business of the seller and that has its principal place of business in the United States if:

(i) the buyer assumes in full the debts that were incurred in the seller's business before the date of the bulk sale;

(ii) the seller receives nothing from the sale except an interest in the new organization that is subordinate to the claims against the organization arising from the assumption; and

(iii) the buyer gives written notice of the assumption not later than 30 days after the date of the bulk sale by sending or delivering a notice to each creditor whose debt is assumed or by filing a notice in the office of the [Secretary of State];

(l) a sale of assets having:

(i) a value, net of liens and security interests, of less than $10,000. If a debt is secured by assets and other property of the seller, the net value of the assets is determined by subtracting from their value an amount equal to the product of the debt multiplied by a fraction, the numerator of which is the value of the assets on the date of the bulk sale and the denominator of which is the value of all property securing the debt on the date of the bulk sale; or

(ii) a value of more than $25,000,000 on the date of the bulk-sale agreement; or

(m) a sale required by, and made pursuant to, statute.

(4) The notice under subsection (3)(i)(iv) must state: (i) that a sale that may constitute a bulk sale has been or will be made; (ii) the date or prospective date of the bulk sale; (iii) the individual, partnership, or corporate names and the addresses of the seller and buyer; (iv) the address to which inquiries about the sale may be made, if different from the seller's address; and (v) that the buyer has assumed or will assume in full the debts owed to claimants of whom the buyer has knowledge on the date the buyer receives the list of claimants from the seller or completes a reasonable inquiry to discover the claimants.

(5) The notice under subsections (3)(j)(iii) and (3)(k)(iii) must state: (i) that a sale that may constitute a bulk sale has been or will be made; (ii) the date or prospective date of the bulk sale; (iii) the individual, partnership, or corporate names and the addresses of the seller and buyer; (iv) the address to which inquiries about the sale may be made, if different from the seller's address; and (v) that the buyer has assumed or will assume the debts that were incurred in the seller's business before the date of the bulk sale.

(6) For purposes of subsection (3)(l), the value of assets is presumed to be equal to the price the buyer agrees to pay for the assets. However, in a sale by auction or a sale conducted by a liquidator on the seller's behalf, the value of assets is presumed to be the amount the auctioneer or liquidator reasonably estimates the assets will bring at auction or upon liquidation.

### § 6—104. Obligations of Buyer.

(1) In a bulk sale as defined in Section 6—102(1)(c)(ii) the buyer shall:

(a) obtain from the seller a list of all business names and addresses used by the seller within three years before the date the list is sent or delivered to the buyer;

(b) unless excused under subsection (2), obtain from the seller a verified and dated list of claimants of whom the seller has notice three days before the seller sends or delivers the list to the buyer and including, to the extent known by the seller, the address of and the amount claimed by each claimant;

(c) obtain from the seller or prepare a schedule of distribution (Section 6—106(1));

(d) give notice of the bulk sale in accordance with Section 6—105;

(e) unless excused under Section 6—106(4), distribute the net contract price in accordance with the undertakings of the buyer in the schedule of distribution; and

(f) unless excused under subsection (2), make available the list of claimants (subsection (1)(b)) by:

(i) promptly sending or delivering a copy of the list without charge to any claimant whose written request is received by the buyer no later than six months after the date of the bulk sale;

(ii) permitting any claimant to inspect and copy the list at any reasonable hour upon request received by the buyer no later than six months after the date of the bulk sale; or

(iii) filing a copy of the list in the office of the [Secretary of State] no later than the time for giving a notice of the bulk sale (Section 6—105(5)). A list filed in accordance with this subparagraph must state the individual, partnership, or corporate name and a mailing address of the seller.

(2) A buyer who gives notice in accordance with Section 6—105(2) is excused from complying with the requirements of subsections (1)(b) and (1)(f).

### § 6—105. Notice to Claimants.

(1) Except as otherwise provided in subsection (2), to comply with Section 6—104(1)(d) the buyer shall send or deliver a written notice of the bulk sale to each claimant on the list

of claimants (Section 6—104(1)(b)) and to any other claimant of which the buyer has knowledge at the time the notice of the bulk sale is sent or delivered.

(2)  A buyer may comply with Section 6—104(1)(d) by filing a written notice of the bulk sale in the office of the [Secretary of State] if:

(a)  on the date of the bulk-sale agreement the seller has 200 or more claimants, exclusive of claimants holding secured or matured claims for employment compensation and benefits, including commissions and vacation, severance, and sick-leave pay; or

(b)  the buyer has received a verified statement from the seller stating that, as of the date of the bulk-sale agreement, the number of claimants, exclusive of claimants holding secured or matured claims for employment compensation and benefits, including commissions and vacation, severance, and sick-leave pay, is 200 or more.

(3)  The written notice of the bulk sale must be accompanied by a copy of the schedule of distribution (Section 6—106(1)) and state at least:

(a)  that the seller and buyer have entered into an agreement for a sale that may constitute a bulk sale under the laws of the State of _____ ;

(b)  the date of the agreement;

(c)  the date on or after which more than ten percent of the assets were or will be transferred;

(d)  the date on or after which more than ten percent of the net contract price was or will be paid, if the date is not stated in the schedule of distribution;

(e)  the name and a mailing address of the seller;

(f)  any other business name and address listed by the seller pursuant to Section 6—104(1)(a);

(g)  the name of the buyer and an address of the buyer from which information concerning the sale can be obtained;

(h)  a statement indicating the type of assets or describing the assets item by item;

(i)  the manner in which the buyer will make available the list of claimants (Section 6—104(1)(f)), if applicable; and

(j)  if the sale is in total or partial satisfaction of an antecedent debt owed by the seller, the amount of the debt to be satisfied and the name of the person to whom it is owed.

(4)  For purposes of subsections (3)(e) and (3)(g), the name of a person is the person's individual, partnership, or corporate name.

(5)  The buyer shall give notice of the bulk sale not less than 45 days before the date of the bulk sale and, if the buyer gives notice in accordance with subsection (1), not more than 30 days after obtaining the list of claimants.

(6)  A written notice substantially complying with the requirements of subsection (3) is effective even though it contains minor errors that are not seriously misleading.

(7)  A form substantially as follows is sufficient to comply with subsection (3):

*Notice of Sale*

(1)  _____ , whose address is _____ , is described in this notice as the ''seller.''

(2)  _____ , whose address is _____ , is described in this notice as the ''buyer.''

(3)  The seller has disclosed to the buyer that within the past three years the seller has used other business names, operated at other addresses, or both, as follows: _____ .

(4)  The seller and the buyer have entered into an agreement dated _____ , for a sale that may constitute a bulk sale under the laws of the State of _____ .

(5)  The date on or after which more than ten percent of the assets that are the subject of the sale were or will be transferred is _____ , and [if not stated in the schedule of distribution] the date on or after which more than ten percent of the net contract price was or will be paid is _____ .

(6)  The following assets are the subject of the sale: _____ .

(7)  [If applicable] The buyer will make available to claimants of the seller a list of the seller's claimants in the following manner: _____ .

(8)  [If applicable] The sale is to satisfy $_____ of an antecedent debt owed by the seller to _____ .

(9)  A copy of the schedule of distribution of the net contract price accompanies this notice.

*[End of Notice]*

### § 6—106.  Schedule of Distribution.

(1)  The seller and buyer shall agree on how the net contract price is to be distributed and set forth their agreement in a written schedule of distribution.

(2)  The schedule of distribution may provide for distribution to any person at any time, including distribution of the entire net contract price to the seller.

(3)  The buyer's undertakings in the schedule of distribution run only to the seller. However, a buyer who fails to distribute the net contract price in accordance with the buyer's undertakings in the schedule of distribution is liable to a creditor only as provided in Section 6—107(1).

(4)  If the buyer undertakes in the schedule of distribution to distribute any part of the net contract price to a person other than the seller, and, after the buyer has given notice in accordance with Section 6—105, some or all of the anticipated net contract price is or becomes unavailable for distribution as a consequence of the buyer's or seller's having complied with an order of court, legal process, statute, or rule of law, the buyer is excused from any obligation arising under this Article or under any contract with the seller to distribute the

net contract price in accordance with the buyer's undertakings in the schedule if the buyer:

(a) distributes the net contract price remaining available in accordance with any priorities for payment stated in the schedule of distribution and, to the extent that the price is insufficient to pay all the debts having a given priority, distributes the price pro rata among those debts shown in the schedule as having the same priority;

(b) distributes the net contract price remaining available in accordance with an order of court;

(c) commences a proceeding for interpleader in a court of competent jurisdiction and is discharged from the proceeding; or

(d) reaches a new agreement with the seller for the distribution of the net contract price remaining available, sets forth the new agreement in an amended schedule of distribution, gives notice of the amended schedule, and distributes the net contract price remaining available in accordance with the buyer's undertakings in the amended schedule.

(5) The notice under subsection (4)(d) must identify the buyer and the seller, state the filing number, if any, of the original notice, set forth the amended schedule, and be given in accordance with subsection (1) or (2) of Section 6—105, whichever is applicable, at least 14 days before the buyer distributes any part of the net contract price remaining available.

(6) If the seller undertakes in the schedule of distribution to distribute any part of the net contract price, and, after the buyer has given notice in accordance with Section 6—105, some or all of the anticipated net contract price is or becomes unavailable for distribution as a consequence of the buyer's or seller's having complied with an order of court, legal process, statute, or rule of law, the seller and any person in control of the seller are excused from any obligation arising under this Article or under any agreement with the buyer to distribute the net contract price in accordance with the seller's undertakings in the schedule if the seller:

(a) distributes the net contract price remaining available in accordance with any priorities for payment stated in the schedule of distribution and, to the extent that the price is insufficient to pay all the debts having a given priority, distributes the price pro rata among those debts shown in the schedule as having the same priority;

(b) distributes the net contract price remaining available in accordance with an order of court;

(c) commences a proceeding for interpleader in a court of competent jurisdiction and is discharged from the proceeding; or

(d) prepares a written amended schedule of distribution of the net contract price remaining available for distribution, gives notice of the amended schedule, and distributes the net contract price remaining available in accordance with the amended schedule.

(7) The notice under subsection (6)(d) must identify the buyer and the seller, state the filing number, if any, of the original notice, set forth the amended schedule, and be given in accordance with subsection (1) or (2) of Section 6—105, whichever is applicable, at least 14 days before the seller distributes any part of the net contract price remaining available.

### § 6—107. Liability for Noncompliance.

(1) Except as provided in subsection (3), and subject to the limitation in subsection (4):

(a) a buyer who fails to comply with the requirements of Section 6—104(1)(e) with respect to a creditor is liable to the creditor for damages in the amount of the claim, reduced by any amount that the creditor would not have realized if the buyer had complied; and

(b) a buyer who fails to comply with the requirements of any other subsection of Section 6—104 with respect to a claimant is liable to the claimant for damages in the amount of the claim, reduced by any amount that the claimant would not have realized if the buyer had complied.

(2) In an action under subsection (1), the creditor has the burden of establishing the validity and amount of the claim, and the buyer has the burden of establishing the amount that the creditor would not have realized if the buyer had complied.

(3) A buyer who:

(a) made a good faith and commercially reasonable effort to comply with the requirements of Section 6—104(1) or to exclude the sale from the application of this Article under Section 6—103(3); or

(b) on or after the date of the bulk-sale agreement, but before the date of the bulk sale, held a good faith and commercially reasonable belief that this Article does not apply to the particular sale

is not liable to creditors for failure to comply with the requirements of Section 6—104. The buyer has the burden of establishing the good faith and commercial reasonableness of the effort or belief.

(4) In a single bulk sale the cumulative liability of the buyer for failure to comply with the requirements of Section 6—104(1) may not exceed an amount equal to:

(a) if the assets consist only of inventory and equipment, twice the net contract price, less the amount of any part of the net contract price paid to or applied for the benefit of the seller or a creditor; or

(b) if the assets include property other than inventory and equipment, twice the net value of the inventory and equipment less the amount of the portion of any part of the net contract price paid to or applied for the benefit of the seller or a creditor which is allocable to the inventory and equipment.

(5) For the purposes of subsection (4)(b), the "net value" of an asset is the value of the asset less (i) the amount of any

proceeds of the sale of an asset, to the extent the proceeds are applied in partial or total satisfaction of a debt secured by the asset and (ii) the amount of any debt to the extent it is secured by a security interest or lien that is enforceable against the asset before and after it has been sold to a buyer. If a debt is secured by an asset and other property of the seller, the amount of the debt secured by a security interest or lien that is enforceable against the asset is determined by multiplying the debt by a fraction, the numerator of which is the value of the asset on the date of the bulk sale and the denominator of which is the value of all property securing the debt on the date of the bulk sale. The portion of a part of the net contract price paid to or applied for the benefit of the seller or a creditor that is ''allocable to the inventory and equipment'' is the portion that bears the same ratio to that part of the net contract price as the net value of the inventory and equipment bears to the net value of all of the assets.

(6) A payment made by the buyer to a person to whom the buyer is, or believes he [or she] is, liable under subsection (1) reduces pro tanto the buyer's cumulative liability under subsection (4).

(7) No action may be brought under subsection (1)(b) by or on behalf of a claimant whose claim is unliquidated or contingent.

(8) A buyer's failure to comply with the requirements of Section 6—104(1) does not (i) impair the buyer's rights in or title to the assets, (ii) render the sale ineffective, void, or voidable, (iii) entitle a creditor to more than a single satisfaction of his [or her] claim, or (iv) create liability other than as provided in this Article.

(9) Payment of the buyer's liability under subsection (1) discharges pro tanto the seller's debt to the creditor.

(10) Unless otherwise agreed, a buyer has an immediate right of reimbursement from the seller for any amount paid to a creditor in partial or total satisfaction of the buyer's liability under subsection (1).

(11) If the seller is an organization, a person who is in direct or indirect control of the seller, and who knowingly, intentionally, and without legal justification fails, or causes the seller to fail, to distribute the net contract price in accordance with the schedule of distribution is liable to any creditor to whom the seller undertook to make payment under the schedule for damages caused by the failure.

### § 6—108. Bulk Sales by Auction; Bulk Sales Conducted by Liquidator.

(1) Sections 6—104, 6—105, 6—106, and 6—107 apply to a bulk sale by auction and a bulk sale conducted by a liquidator on the seller's behalf with the following modifications:

(a) ''buyer'' refers to auctioneer or liquidator, as the case may be;

(b) ''net contract price'' refers to net proceeds of the auction or net proceeds of the sale, as the case may be;

(c) the written notice required under Section 6—105(3)

must be accompanied by a copy of the schedule of distribution (Section 6—106(1)) and state at least:

(i) that the seller and the auctioneer or liquidator have entered into an agreement for auction or liquidation services that may constitute an agreement to make a bulk sale under the laws of the State of _____ ;

(ii) the date of the agreement;

(iii) the date on or after which the auction began or will begin or the date on or after which the liquidator began or will begin to sell assets on the seller's behalf;

(iv) the date on or after which more than ten percent of the net proceeds of the sale were or will be paid, if the date is not stated in the schedule of distribution;

(v) the name and a mailing address of the seller;

(vi) any other business name and address listed by the seller pursuant to Section 6—104(1)(a);

(vii) the name of the auctioneer or liquidator and an address of the auctioneer or liquidator from which information concerning the sale can be obtained;

(viii) a statement indicating the type of assets or describing the assets item by item;

(ix) the manner in which the auctioneer or liquidator will make available the list of claimants (Section 6—104(1)(f)), if applicable; and

(x) if the sale is in total or partial satisfaction of an antecedent debt owed by the seller, the amount of the debt to be satisfied and the name of the person to whom it is owed; and

(d) in a single bulk sale the cumulative liability of the auctioneer or liquidator for failure to comply with the requirements of this section may not exceed the amount of the net proceeds of the sale allocable to inventory and equipment sold less the amount of the portion of any part of the net proceeds paid to or applied for the benefit of a creditor which is allocable to the inventory and equipment.

(2) A payment made by the auctioneer or liquidator to a person to whom the auctioneer or liquidator is, or believes he [or she] is, liable under this section reduces pro tanto the auctioneer's or liquidator's cumulative liability under subsection (1)(d).

(3) A form substantially as follows is sufficient to comply with subsection (1)(c):

*Notice of Sale*

(1) _____ , whose address is _____ , is described in this notice as the ''seller.''

(2) _____ , whose address is _____ , is described in this notice as the ''auctioneer'' or ''liquidator.''

(3) The seller has disclosed to the auctioneer or liquidator that within the past three years the seller has used other business names, operated at other addresses, or both, as follows: _____ .

(4) The seller and the auctioneer or liquidator have entered into an agreement dated ___ for auction or liquidation services that may constitute an agreement to make a bulk sale under the laws of the State of _____ .

(5) The date on or after which the auction began or will begin or the date on or after which the liquidator began or will begin to sell assets on the seller's behalf is _____ , and [if not stated in the schedule of distribution] the date on or after which more than ten percent of the net proceeds of the sale were or will be paid is _____ .

(6) The following assets are the subject of the sale: _____ .

(7) [If applicable] The auctioneer or liquidator will make available to claimants of the seller a list of the seller's claimants in the following manner: _____ .

(8) [If applicable] The sale is to satisfy $_____ of an antecedent debt owed by the seller to _____ .

(9) A copy of the schedule of distribution of the net proceeds accompanies this notice.

[End of Notice]

(4) A person who buys at a bulk sale by auction or conducted by a liquidator need not comply with the requirements of Section 6—104(1) and is not liable for the failure of an auctioneer or liquidator to comply with the requirements of this section.

### § 6—109. What Constitutes Filing; Duties of Filing Officer; Information from Filing Officer.

(1) Presentation of a notice or list of claimants for filing and tender of the filing fee or acceptance of the notice or list by the filing officer constitutes filing under this Article.

(2) The filing officer shall:

(a) mark each notice or list with a file number and with the date and hour of filing;

(b) hold the notice or list or a copy for public inspection;

(c) index the notice or list according to each name given for the seller and for the buyer; and

(d) note in the index the file number and the addresses of the seller and buyer given in the notice or list.

(3) If the person filing a notice or list furnishes the filing officer with a copy, the filing officer upon request shall note upon the copy the file number and date and hour of the filing of the original and send or deliver the copy to the person.

(4) The fee for filing and indexing and for stamping a copy furnished by the person filing to show the date and place of filing is $_____ for the first page and $_____ for each additional page. The fee for indexing each name beyond the first two is $_____ .

(5) Upon request of any person, the filing officer shall issue a certificate showing whether any notice or list with respect to a particular seller or buyer is on file on the date and hour stated in the certificate. If a notice or list is on file, the certificate must give the date and hour of filing of each notice or list and the name and address of each seller, buyer, auctioneer, or liquidator. The fee for the certificate is $_____ if the request for the certificate is in the standard form prescribed by the [Secretary of State] and otherwise is $_____ . Upon request of any person, the filing officer shall furnish a copy of any filed notice or list for a fee of $_____ .

(6) The filing officer shall keep each notice or list for two years after it is filed.

### § 6—110. Limitation of Actions.

(1) Except as provided in subsection (2), an action under this Article against a buyer, auctioneer, or liquidator must be commenced within one year after the date of the bulk sale.

(2) If the buyer, auctioneer, or liquidator conceals the fact that the sale has occurred, the limitation is tolled and an action under this Article may be commenced within the earlier of (i) one year after the person bringing the action discovers that the sale has occurred or (ii) one year after the person bringing the action should have discovered that the sale has occurred, but no later than two years after the date of the bulk sale. Complete noncompliance with the requirements of this Article does not of itself constitute concealment.

(3) An action under Section 6—107(11) must be commenced within one year after the alleged violation occurs.

# Article 7

# Warehouse Receipts, Bills of Lading and Other Documents of Title

## Part 1   General

### § 7—101. Short Title.

This Article shall be known and may be cited as Uniform Commercial Code—Documents of Title.

### § 7—102. Definitions and Index of Definitions.

(1) In this Article, unless the context otherwise requires:

(a) "Bailee" means the person who by a warehouse receipt, bill of lading or other document of title acknowledges possession of goods and contracts to deliver them.

(b) "Consignee" means the person named in a bill to whom or to whose order the bill promises delivery.

(c) "Consignor" means the person named in a bill as the person from whom the goods have been received for shipment.

(d) "Delivery order" means a written order to deliver goods directed to a warehouseman, carrier or other person who in the ordinary course of business issues warehouse receipts or bills of lading.

(e) "Document" means document of title as defined in the general definitions in Article 1 (Section 1—201).

(f) "Goods" means all things which are treated as movable for the purposes of a contract of storage or transportation.

(g) "Issuer" means a bailee who issues a document except that in relation to an unaccepted delivery order it means the person who orders the possessor of goods to deliver. Issuer includes any person for whom an agent or employee purports to act in issuing a document if the agent or employee has real or apparent authority to issue documents, notwithstanding that the issuer received no goods or that the goods were misdescribed or that in any other respect the agent or employee violated his instructions.

(h) ''Warehouseman'' is a person engaged in the business of storing goods for hire.

(2) Other definitions applying to this Article or to specified Parts thereof, and the sections in which they appear are: ''Duly negotiate''. Section 7—501.

''Person entitled under the document''. Section 7—403(4).

(3) Definitions in other Articles applying to this Article and the sections in which they appear are:

''Contract for sale''. Section 2—106.

''Overseas''. Section 2—323.

''Receipt'' of goods. Section 2—103.

(4) In addition Article 1 contains general definitions and principles of construction and interpretation applicable throughout this Article.

### § 7—103. Relation of Article to Treaty, Statute, Tariff, Classification or Regulation.

To the extent that any treaty or statute of the United States, regulatory statute of this State or tariff, classification or regulation filed or issued pursuant thereto is applicable, the provisions of this Article are subject thereto.

### § 7—104. Negotiable and Nonnegotiable Warehouse Receipt, Bill of Lading or Other Document of Title.

(1) A warehouse receipt, bill of lading or other document of title is negotiable

(a) if by its terms the goods are to be delivered to bearer or to the order of a named person; or

(b) where recognized in overseas trade, if it runs to a named person or assigns.

(2) Any other document is nonnegotiable. A bill of lading in which it is stated that the goods are consigned to a named person is not made negotiable by a provision that the goods are to be delivered only against a written order signed by the same or another named person.

### § 7—105. Construction Against Negative Implication.

The omission from either Part 2 or Part 3 of this Article of a provision corresponding to a provision made in the other Part does not imply that a corresponding rule of law is not applicable.

## Part 2  Warehouse Receipts: Special Provisions

### § 7—201. Who May Issue a Warehouse Receipt; Storage Under Government Bond.

(1) A warehouse receipt may be issued by any warehouseman.

(2) Where goods including distilled spirits and agricultural commodities are stored under a statute requiring a bond against withdrawal or a license for the issuance of receipts in the nature of warehouse receipts, a receipt issued for the goods has like effect as a warehouse receipt even though issued by a person who is the owner of the goods and is not a warehouseman.

### § 7—202. Form of Warehouse Receipt; Essential Terms; Optional Terms.

(1) A warehouse receipt need not be in any particular form.

(2) Unless a warehouse receipt embodies within its written or printed terms each of the following, the warehouseman is liable for damages caused by the omission to a person injured thereby:

(a) the location of the warehouse where the goods are stored;

(b) the date of issue of the receipt;

(c) the consecutive number of the receipt;

(d) a statement whether the goods received will be delivered to the bearer, to a specified person, or to a specified person or his order;

(e) the rate of storage and handling charges, except that where goods are stored under a field warehousing arrangement a statement of that fact is sufficient on a non-negotiable receipt;

(f) a description of the goods or of the packages containing them;

(g) the signature of the warehouseman, which may be made by his authorized agent;

(h) if the receipt is issued for goods of which the warehouseman is owner, either solely or jointly or in common with others, the fact of such ownership; and

(i) a statement of the amount of advances made and of liabilities incurred for which the warehouseman claims a lien or security interest (Section 7—209). If the precise amount of such advances made or of such liabilities incurred is, at the time of the issue of the receipt, unknown to the warehouseman or to his agent who issues it, a statement of the fact that advances have been made or liabilities incurred and the purpose thereof is sufficient.

(3) A warehouseman may insert in his receipt any other terms which are not contrary to the provisions of this Act and do not impair his obligation of delivery (Section 7—403) or his duty of care (Section 7—204). Any contrary provisions shall be ineffective.

### § 7—203. Liability for Nonreceipt or Misdescription.

A party to or purchaser for value in good faith of a document of title other than a bill of lading relying in either case upon the description therein of the goods may recover from the issuer damages caused by the nonreceipt or misdescription of the goods, except to the extent that the document conspicuously indicates that the issuer does not know whether any part or all of the goods in fact were received or conform to the description, as where the description is in terms of marks or labels or kind, quantity or condition, or the receipt or description is qualified by "contents, condition and quality unknown", "said to contain" or the like, if such indication be true, or the party or purchaser otherwise has notice.

### § 7—204. Duty of Care; Contractual Limitation of Warehouseman's Liability.

(1) A warehouseman is liable for damages for loss of or injury to the goods caused by his failure to exercise such care in regard to them as a reasonably careful man would exercise under like circumstances but unless otherwise agreed he is not liable for damages which could not have been avoided by the exercise of such care.

(2) Damages may be limited by a term in the warehouse receipt or storage agreement limiting the amount of liability in case of loss or damage, and setting forth a specific liability per article or item, or value per unit of weight, beyond which the warehouseman shall not be liable; provided, however, that such liability may on written request of the bailor at the time of signing such storage agreement or within a reasonable time after receipt of the warehouse receipt be increased on part or all of the goods thereunder, in which event increased rates may be charged based on such increased valuation, but that no such increase shall be permitted contrary to a lawful limitation of liability contained in the warehouseman's tariff, if any. No such limitation is effective with respect to the warehouseman's liability for conversion to his own use.

(3) Reasonable provisions as to the time and manner of presenting claims and instituting actions based on the bailment may be included in the warehouse receipt or tariff.

(4) This section does not impair or repeal . . .

Note: *Insert in subsection (4) a reference to any statute which imposes a higher responsibility upon the warehouseman or invalidates contractual limitations which would be permissible under this Article.*

### § 7—205. Title Under Warehouse Receipt Defeated in Certain Cases.

A buyer in the ordinary course of business of fungible goods sold and delivered by a warehouseman who is also in the business of buying and selling such goods takes free of any claim under a warehouse receipt even though it has been duly negotiated.

### § 7—206. Termination of Storage at Warehouseman's Option.

(1) A warehouseman may on notifying the person on whose account the goods are held and any other person known to claim an interest in the goods require payment of any charges and removal of the goods from the warehouse at the termination of the period of storage fixed by the document, or, if no period is fixed, within a stated period not less than thirty days after the notification. If the goods are not removed before the date specified in the notification, the warehouseman may sell them in accordance with the provisions of the section on enforcement of a warehouseman's lien (Section 7—210).

(2) If a warehouseman in good faith believes that the goods are about to deteriorate or decline in value to less than the amount of his lien within the time prescribed in subsection (1) for notification, advertisement and sale, the warehouseman may specify in the notification any reasonable shorter time for removal of the goods and in case the goods are not removed, may sell them at public sale held not less than one week after a single advertisement or posting.

(3) If as a result of a quality or condition of the goods of which the warehouseman had no notice at the time of deposit the goods are a hazard to other property or to the warehouse or to persons, the warehouseman may sell the goods at public or private sale without advertisement on reasonable notification to all persons known to claim an interest in the goods. If the warehouseman after a reasonable effort is unable to sell the goods he may dispose of them in any lawful manner and shall incur no liability by reason of such disposition.

(4) The warehouseman must deliver the goods to any person entitled to them under this Article upon due demand made at any time prior to sale or other disposition under this section.

(5) The warehouseman may satisfy his lien from the proceeds of any sale or disposition under this section but must hold the balance for delivery on the demand of any person to whom he would have been bound to deliver the goods.

### § 7—207. Goods Must Be Kept Separate; Fungible Goods.

(1) Unless the warehouse receipt otherwise provides, a warehouseman must keep separate the goods covered by each receipt so as to permit at all times identification and delivery of those goods except that different lots of fungible goods may be commingled.

(2) Fungible goods so commingled are owned in common by the persons entitled thereto and the warehouseman is severally liable to each owner for that owner's share. Where because of overissue a mass of fungible goods is insufficient to meet all the receipts which the warehouseman has issued against it, the persons entitled include all holders to whom overissued receipts have been duly negotiated.

### § 7—208. Altered Warehouse Receipts.

Where a blank in a negotiable warehouse receipt has been filled in without authority, a purchaser for value and without notice of the want of authority may treat the insertion as authorized. Any other unauthorized alteration leaves any receipt enforceable against the issuer according to its original tenor.

### § 7—209. Lien of Warehouseman.

(1) A warehouseman has a lien against the bailor on the goods covered by a warehouse receipt or on the proceeds thereof in his possession for charges for storage or transportation (including demurrage and terminal charges), insurance, labor, or charges present or future in relation to the goods, and for expenses necessary for preservation of the goods or reasonably incurred in their sale pursuant to law. If the person on whose account the goods are held is liable

for like charges or expenses in relation to other goods whenever deposited and it is stated in the receipt that a lien is claimed for charges and expenses in relation to other goods, the warehouseman also has a lien against him for such charges and expenses whether or not the other goods have been delivered by the warehouseman. But against a person to whom a negotiable warehouse receipt is duly negotiated a warehouseman's lien is limited to charges in an amount or at a rate specified on the receipt or if no charges are so specified then to a reasonable charge for storage of the goods covered by the receipt subsequent to the date of the receipt.

(2) The warehouseman may also reserve a security interest against the bailor for a maximum amount specified on the receipt for charges other than those specified in subsection (1), such as for money advanced and interest. Such a security interest is governed by the Article on Secured Transactions (Article 9).

(3)(a) A warehouseman's lien for charges and expenses under subsection (1) or a security interest under subsection (2) is also effective against any person who so entrusted the bailor with possession of the goods that a pledge of them by him to a good faith purchaser for value would have been valid but is not effective against a person as to whom the document confers no right in the goods covered by it under Section 7—503.

(b) A warehouseman's lien on household goods for charges and expenses in relation to the goods under subsection (1) is also effective against all persons if the depositor was the legal possessor of the goods at the time of deposit. ''Household goods'' means furniture, furnishings and personal effects used by the depositor in a dwelling.

(4) A warehouseman loses his lien on any goods which he voluntarily delivers or which he unjustifiably refuses to deliver.

### § 7—210. Enforcement of Warehouseman's Lien.

(1) Except as provided in subsection (2), a warehouseman's lien may be enforced by public or private sale of the goods in bloc or in parcels, at any time or place and on any terms which are commercially reasonable, after notifying all persons known to claim an interest in the goods. Such notification must include a statement of the amount due, the nature of the proposed sale and the time and place of any public sale. The fact that a better price could have been obtained by a sale at a different time or in a different method from that selected by the warehouseman is not of itself sufficient to establish that the sale was not made in a commercially reasonable manner. If the warehouseman either sells the goods in the usual manner in any recognized market therefor, or if he sells at the price current in such market at the time of his sale, or if he has otherwise sold in conformity with commercially reasonable practices among dealers in the type of goods sold, he has sold in a commercially reasonable manner. A sale of more goods than apparently necessary to be offered to ensure satisfaction of the obligation is not commercially reasonable except in cases covered by the preceding sentence.

(2) A warehouseman's lien on goods other than goods stored by a merchant in the course of his business may be enforced only as follows:

(a) All persons known to claim an interest in the goods must be notified.

(b) The notification must be delivered in person or sent by registered or certified letter to the last known address of any person to be notified.

(c) The notification must include an itemized statement of the claim, a description of the goods subject to the lien, a demand for payment within a specified time not less than ten days after receipt of the notification, and a conspicuous statement that unless the claim is paid within the time the goods will be advertised for sale and sold by auction at a specified time and place.

(d) The sale must conform to the terms of the notification.

(e) The sale must be held at the nearest suitable place to that where the goods are held or stored.

(f) After the expiration of the time given in the notification, an advertisement of the sale must be published once a week for two weeks consecutively in a newspaper of general circulation where the sale is to be held. The advertisement must include a description of the goods, the name of the person on whose account they are being held, and the time and place of the sale. The sale must take place at least fifteen days after the first publication. If there is no newspaper of general circulation where the sale is to be held, the advertisement must be posted at least ten days before the sale in not less than six conspicuous places in the neighborhood of the proposed sale.

(3) Before any sale pursuant to this section any person claiming a right in the goods may pay the amount necessary to satisfy the lien and the reasonable expenses incurred under this section. In that event the goods must not be sold, but must be retained by the warehouseman subject to the terms of the receipt and this Article.

(4) The warehouseman may buy at any public sale pursuant to this section.

(5) A purchaser in good faith of goods sold to enforce a warehouseman's lien takes the goods free of any rights of persons against whom the lien was valid, despite noncompliance by the warehouseman with the requirements of this section.

(6) The warehouseman may satisfy his lien from the proceeds of any sale pursuant to this section but must hold the balance, if any, for delivery on demand to any person to whom he would have been bound to deliver the goods.

(7) The rights provided by this section shall be in addition to all other rights allowed by law to a creditor against his debtor.

(8) Where a lien is on goods stored by a merchant in the course of his business the lien may be enforced in accordance with either subsection (1) or (2).

(9) The warehouseman is liable for damages caused by failure to comply with the requirements for sale under this section and in case of willful violation is liable for conversion.

## Part 3   Bills of Lading: Special Provisions

### § 7—301. Liability for Nonreceipt or Misdescription; "Said to Contain"; "Shipper's Load and Count"; Improper Handling.

(1) A consignee of a nonnegotiable bill who has given value in good faith or a holder to whom a negotiable bill has been duly negotiated relying in either case upon the description therein of the goods, or upon the date therein shown, may recover from the issuer damages caused by the misdating of the bill or the nonreceipt or misdescription of the goods, except to the extent that the document indicates that the issuer does not know whether any part of all of the goods in fact were received or conform to the description, as where the description is in terms of marks or labels or kind, quantity, or condition or the receipt or description is qualified by "contents or condition of contents of packages unknown", "said to contain", "shipper's weight, load and count" or the like, if such indication be true.

(2) When goods are loaded by an issuer who is a common carrier, the issuer must count the packages of goods if package freight and ascertain the kind and quantity if bulk freight. In such cases "shipper's weight, load and count" or other words indicating that the description was made by the shipper are ineffective except as to freight concealed by packages.

(3) When bulk freight is loaded by a shipper who makes available to the issuer adequate facilities for weighing such freight, an issuer who is a common carrier must ascertain the kind and quantity within a reasonable time after receiving the written request of the shipper to do so. In such cases "shipper's weight" or other words of like purport are ineffective.

(4) The issuer may by inserting in the bill the words "shipper's weight, load and count" or other words of like purport indicate that the goods were loaded by the shipper; and if such statement be true the issuer shall not be liable for damages caused by the improper loading. But their omission does not imply liability for such damages.

(5) The shipper shall be deemed to have guaranteed to the issuer the accuracy at the time of shipment of the description, marks, labels, number, kind, quantity, condition and weight, as furnished by him; and the shipper shall indemnify the issuer against damage caused by inaccuracies in such particulars. The right of the issuer to such indemnity shall in no way limit his responsibility and liability under the contract of carriage to any person other than the shipper.

### § 7—302. Through Bills of Lading and Similar Documents.

(1) The issuer of a through bill of lading or other document embodying an undertaking to be performed in part by persons acting as its agents or by connecting carriers is liable to anyone entitled to recover on the document for any breach by such other persons or by a connecting carrier of its obligation under the document but to the extent that the bill covers an undertaking to be performed overseas or in territory not contiguous to the continental United States or an undertaking including matters other than transportation this liability may be varied by agreement of the parties.

(2) Where goods covered by a through bill of lading or other document embodying an undertaking to be performed in part by persons other than the issuer are received by any such person, he is subject with respect to his own performance while the goods are in his possession to the obligation of the issuer. His obligation is discharged by delivery of the goods to another such person pursuant to the document, and does not include liability for breach by any other such persons or by the issuer.

(3) The issuer of such through bill of lading or other document shall be entitled to recover from the connecting carrier or such other person in possession of the goods when the breach of the obligation under the document occurred, the amount it may be required to pay to anyone entitled to recover on the document therefor, as may be evidenced by any receipt, judgment, or transcript thereof, and the amount of any expense reasonably incurred by it in defending any action brought by anyone entitled to recover on the document therefor.

### § 7—303. Diversion; Reconsignment; Change of Instructions.

(1) Unless the bill of lading otherwise provides, the carrier may deliver the goods to a person or destination other than that stated in the bill or may otherwise dispose of the goods on instructions from

  (a) the holder of a negotiable bill; or

  (b) the consignor on a nonnegotiable bill notwithstanding contrary instructions from the consignee; or

  (c) the consignee on a nonnegotiable bill in the absence of contrary instructions from the consignor, if the goods have arrived at the billed destination or if the consignee is in possession of the bill; or

  (d) the consignee on a nonnegotiable bill if he is entitled as against the consignor to dispose of them.

(2) Unless such instructions are noted on a negotiable bill of lading, a person to whom the bill is duly negotiated can hold the bailee according to the original terms.

### § 7—304. Bills of Lading in a Set.

(1) Except where customary in overseas transportation, a bill of lading must not be issued in a set of parts. The issuer is liable for damages caused by violation of this subsection.

(2) Where a bill of lading is lawfully drawn in a set of parts, each of which is numbered and expressed to be valid only if the goods have not been delivered against any other part, the whole of the parts constitute one bill.

(3) Where a bill of lading is lawfully issued in a set of parts and different parts are negotiated to different persons, the title of the holder to whom the first due negotiation is made prevails as to both the document and the goods even though any later holder may have received the goods from the carrier in good faith and discharged the carrier's obligation by surrender of his part.

(4) Any person who negotiates or transfers a single part of a bill of lading drawn in a set is liable to holders of that part as if it were the whole set.

(5) The bailee is obliged to deliver in accordance with Part 4 of this Article against the first presented part of a bill of lading lawfully drawn in a set. Such delivery discharges the bailee's obligation on the whole bill.

### § 7—305. Destination Bills.

(1) Instead of issuing a bill of lading to the consignor at the place of shipment a carrier may at the request of the consignor procure the bill to be issued at destination or at any other place designated in the request.

(2) Upon request of anyone entitled as against the carrier to control the goods while in transit and on surrender of any outstanding bill of lading or other receipt covering such goods, the issuer may procure a substitute bill to be issued at any place designated in the request.

### § 7—306. Altered Bills of Lading.

An unauthorized alteration or filling in of a blank in a bill of lading leaves the bill enforceable according to its original tenor.

### § 7—307. Lien of Carrier.

(1) A carrier has a lien on the goods covered by a bill of lading for charges subsequent to the date of its receipt of the goods for storage or transportation (including demurrage and terminal charges) and for expenses necessary for preservation of the goods incident to their transportation or reasonably incurred in their sale pursuant to law. But against a purchaser for value of a negotiable bill of lading a carrier's lien is limited to charges stated in the bill or the applicable tariffs, or if no charges are stated then to a reasonable charge.

(2) A lien for charges and expenses under subsection (1) on goods which the carrier was required by law to receive for transportation is effective against the consignor or any person entitled to the goods unless the carrier had notice that the consignor lacked authority to subject the goods to such charges and expenses. Any other lien under subsection (1) is effective against the consignor and any person who permitted the bailor to have control or possession of the goods unless the carrier had notice that the bailor lacked such authority.

(3) A carrier loses his lien on any goods which he voluntarily delivers or which he unjustifiably refuses to deliver.

### § 7—308. Enforcement of Carrier's Lien.

(1) A carrier's lien may be enforced by public or private sale of the goods, in bloc or in parcels, at any time or place and on any terms which are commercially reasonable, after notifying all persons known to claim an interest in the goods. Such notification must include a statement of the amount due, the nature of the proposed sale and the time and place of any public sale. The fact that a better price could have been obtained by a sale at a different time or in a different method from that selected by the carrier is not of itself sufficient to establish that the sale was not made in a commercially reasonable manner. If the carrier either sells the goods in the usual manner in any recognized market therefor or if he sells at the price current in such market at the time of his sale or if he has otherwise sold in conformity with commercially reasonable practices among dealers in the type of goods sold he has sold in a commercially reasonable manner. A sale of more goods than apparently necessary to be offered to ensure satisfaction of the obligation is not commercially reasonable except in cases covered by the preceding sentence.

(2) Before any sale pursuant to this section any person claiming a right in the goods may pay the amount necessary to satisfy the lien and the reasonable expenses incurred under this section. In that event the goods must not be sold, but must be retained by the carrier subject to the terms of the bill and this Article.

(3) The carrier may buy at any public sale pursuant to this section.

(4) A purchaser in good faith of goods sold to enforce a carrier's lien takes the goods free of any rights of persons against whom the lien was valid, despite noncompliance by the carrier with the requirements of this section.

(5) The carrier may satisfy his lien from the proceeds of any sale pursuant to this section but must hold the balance, if any, for delivery on demand to any person to whom he would have been bound to deliver the goods.

(6) The rights provided by this section shall be in addition to all other rights allowed by law to a creditor against his debtor.

(7) A carrier's lien may be enforced in accordance with either subsection (1) or the procedure set forth in subsection (2) of Section 7—210.

(8) The carrier is liable for damages caused by failure to comply with the requirements for sale under this section and in case of willful violation is liable for conversion.

### § 7—309. Duty of Care; Contractual Limitation of Carrier's Liability.

(1) A carrier who issues a bill of lading whether negotiable or nonnegotiable must exercise the degree of care in relation to the goods which a reasonably careful man would exercise under like circumstances. This subsection does not repeal or change any law or rule of law which imposes liability upon a common carrier for damages not caused by its negligence.

(2) Damages may be limited by a provision that the carrier's liability shall not exceed a value stated in the document if

the carrier's rates are dependent upon value and the consignor by the carrier's tariff is afforded an opportunity to declare a higher value or a value as lawfully provided in the tariff, or where no tariff is filed he is otherwise advised of such opportunity; but no such limitation is effective with respect to the carrier's liability for conversion to its own use.

(3)  Reasonable provisions as to the time and manner of presenting claims and instituting actions based on the shipment may be included in a bill of lading or tariff.

## Part 4   Warehouse Receipts and Bills of Lading: General Obligations

### § 7—401. Irregularities in Issue of Receipt or Bill or Conduct of Issuer.

The obligations imposed by this Article on an issuer apply to a document of title regardless of the fact that

(a)  the document may not comply with the requirements of this Article or of any other law or regulation regarding its issue, form or content; or

(b)  the issuer may have violated laws regulating the conduct of his business; or

(c)  the goods covered by the document were owned by the bailee at the time the document was issued; or

(d)  the person issuing the document does not come within the definition of warehouseman if it purports to be a warehouse receipt.

### § 7—402. Duplicate Receipt or Bill; Overissue.

Neither a duplicate nor any other document of title purporting to cover goods already represented by an outstanding document of the same issuer confers any right in the goods, except as provided in the case of bills in a set, overissue of documents for fungible goods and substitutes for lost, stolen or destroyed documents. But the issuer is liable for damages caused by his overissue or failure to identify a duplicate document as such by conspicuous notation on its face.

### § 7—403. Obligation of Warehouseman or Carrier to Deliver; Excuse.

(1)  The bailee must deliver the goods to a person entitled under the document who complies with subsections (2) and (3), unless and to the extent that the bailee establishes any of the following:

(a)  delivery of the goods to a person whose receipt was rightful as against the claimant;

(b)  damage to or delay, loss or destruction of the goods for which the bailee is not liable [, but the burden of establishing negligence in such cases is on the person entitled under the document];

Note: *The brackets in (1)(b) indicate that State enactments may differ on this point without serious damage to the principle of uniformity.*

(c)  previous sale or other disposition of the goods in lawful enforcement of a lien or on warehouseman's lawful termination of storage;

(d)  the exercise by a seller of his right to stop delivery pursuant to the provisions of the Article on Sales (Section 2—705);

(e)  a diversion, reconsignment or other disposition pursuant to the provisions of this Article (Section 7—303) or tariff regulating such right;

(f)  release, satisfaction or any other fact affording a personal defense against the claimant;

(g)  any other lawful excuse.

(2)  A person claiming goods covered by a document of title must satisfy the bailee's lien where the bailee so requests or where the bailee is prohibited by law from delivering the goods until the charges are paid.

(3)  Unless the person claiming is one against whom the document confers no right under Sec. 7—503(1), he must surrender for cancellation or notation of partial deliveries any outstanding negotiable document covering the goods, and the bailee must cancel the document or conspicuously note the partial delivery thereon or be liable to any person to whom the document is duly negotiated.

(4)  ''Person entitled under the document'' means holder in the case of a negotiable document, or the person to whom delivery is to be made by the terms of or pursuant to written instructions under a nonnegotiable document.

### § 7—404. No Liability for Good Faith Delivery Pursuant to Receipt or Bill.

A bailee who in good faith including observance of reasonable commercial standards has received goods and delivered or otherwise disposed of them according to the terms of the document of title or pursuant to this Article is not liable therefor. This rule applies even though the person from whom he received the goods had no authority to procure the document or to dispose of the goods and even though the person to whom he delivered the goods had no authority to receive them.

## Part 5   Warehouse Receipts and Bills of Lading: Negotiation and Transfer

### § 7—501. Form of Negotiation and Requirements of ''Due Negotiation''.

(1)  A negotiable document of title running to the order of a named person is negotiated by his indorsement and delivery. After his indorsement in blank or to bearer any person can negotiate it by delivery alone.

(2)(a)  A negotiable document of title is also negotiated by delivery alone when by its original terms it runs to bearer.

(b)  When a document running to the order of a named person is delivered to him the effect is the same as if the document had been negotiated.

(3)  Negotiation of a negotiable document of title after it has been indorsed to a specified person requires indorsement by the special indorsee as well as delivery.

(4) A negotiable document of title is "duly negotiated" when it is negotiated in the manner stated in this section to a holder who purchases it in good faith without notice of any defense against or claim to it on the part of any person and for value, unless it is established that the negotiation is not in the regular course of business or financing or involves receiving the document in settlement or payment of a money obligation.

(5) Indorsement of a nonnegotiable document neither makes it negotiable nor adds to the transferee's rights.

(6) The naming in a negotiable bill of a person to be notified of the arrival of the goods does not limit the negotiability of the bill nor constitute notice to a purchaser thereof of any interest of such person in the goods.

## § 7—502. Rights Acquired by Due Negotiation.

(1) Subject to the following section and to the provisions of Section 7—205 on fungible goods, a holder to whom a negotiable document of title has been duly negotiated acquires thereby:

    (a) title to the document;

    (b) title to the goods;

    (c) all rights accruing under the law of agency or estoppel, including rights to goods delivered to the bailee after the document was issued; and

    (d) the direct obligation of the issuer to hold or deliver the goods according to the terms of the document free of any defense or claim by him except those arising under the terms of the document or under this Article. In the case of a delivery order the bailee's obligation accrues only upon acceptance and the obligation acquired by the holder is that the issuer and any indorser will procure the acceptance of the bailee.

(2) Subject to the following section, title and rights so acquired are not defeated by any stoppage of the goods represented by the document or by surrender of such goods by the bailee, and are not impaired even though the negotiation or any prior negotiation constituted a breach of duty or even though any person has been deprived of possession of the document by misrepresentation, fraud, accident, mistake, duress, loss, theft or conversion, or even though a previous sale or other transfer of the goods or document has been made to a third person.

## § 7—503. Document of Title to Goods Defeated in Certain Cases.

(1) A document of title confers no right in goods against a person who before issuance of the document had a legal interest or a perfected security interest in them and who neither

    (a) delivered or entrusted them or any document of title covering them to the bailor or his nominee with actual or apparent authority to ship, store or sell or with power to obtain delivery under this Article (Section 7—403) or with power of disposition under this Act (Sections 2—403 and 9—307) or other statute or rule of law; nor

    (b) acquiesced in the procurement by the bailor or his nominee of any document of title.

(2) Title to goods based upon an unaccepted delivery order is subject to the rights of anyone to whom a negotiable warehouse receipt or bill of lading covering the goods has been duly negotiated. Such a title may be defeated under the next section to the same extent as the rights of the issuer or a transferee from the issuer.

(3) Title to goods based upon a bill of lading issued to a freight forwarder is subject to the rights of anyone to whom a bill issued by the freight forwarder is duly negotiated; but delivery by the carrier in accordance with Part 4 of this Article pursuant to its own bill of lading discharges the carrier's obligation to deliver.

## § 7—504. Rights Acquired in the Absence of Due Negotiation; Effect of Diversion; Seller's Stoppage of Delivery.

(1) A transferee of a document, whether negotiable or nonnegotiable, to whom the document has been delivered but not duly negotiated, acquires the title and rights which his transferor had or had actual authority to convey.

(2) In the case of a nonnegotiable document, until but not after the bailee receives notification of the transfer, the rights of the transferee may be defeated

    (a) by those creditors of the transferor who could treat the sale as void under Section 2—402; or

    (b) by a buyer from the transferor in ordinary course of business if the bailee has delivered the goods to the buyer or received notification of his rights; or

    (c) as against the bailee by good faith dealings of the bailee with the transferor.

(3) A diversion or other change of shipping instructions by the consignor in a nonnegotiable bill of lading which causes the bailee not to deliver to the consignee defeats the consignee's title to the goods if they have been delivered to a buyer in ordinary course of business and in any event defeats the consignee's rights against the bailee.

(4) Delivery pursuant to a nonnegotiable document may be stopped by a seller under Section 2—705, and subject to the requirement of due notification there provided. A bailee honoring the seller's instructions is entitled to be indemnified by the seller against any resulting loss or expense.

## § 7—505. Indorser Not a Guarantor for Other Parties.

The indorsement of a document of title issued by a bailee does not make the indorser liable for any default by the bailee or by previous indorsers.

## § 7—506. Delivery Without Indorsement: Right to Compel Indorsement.

The transferee of a negotiable document of title has a specifically enforceable right to have his transferor supply any necessary indorsement but the transfer becomes a negotiation only as of the time the indorsement is supplied.

### § 7—507. Warranties on Negotiation or Transfer of Receipt or Bill.

Where a person negotiates or transfers a document of title for value otherwise than as a mere intermediary under the next following section, then unless otherwise agreed he warrants to his immediate purchaser only in addition to any warranty made in selling the goods

(a) that the document is genuine; and

(b) that he has no knowledge of any fact which would impair its validity or worth; and

(c) that his negotiation or transfer is rightful and fully effective with respect to the title to the document and the goods it represents.

### § 7—508. Warranties of Collecting Bank as to Documents.

A collecting bank or other intermediary known to be entrusted with documents on behalf of another or with collection of a draft or other claim against delivery of documents warrants by such delivery of the documents only its own good faith and authority. This rule applies even though the intermediary has purchased or made advances against the claim or draft to be collected.

### § 7—509. Receipt or Bill: When Adequate Compliance With Commercial Contract.

The question whether a document is adequate to fulfill the obligations of a contract for sale or the conditions of a credit is governed by the Articles on Sales (Article 2) and on Letters of Credit (Article 5).

## Part 6   Warehouse Receipts and Bills of Lading: Miscellaneous Provisions

### § 7—601. Lost and Missing Documents.

(1) If a document has been lost, stolen or destroyed, a court may order delivery of the goods or issuance of a substitute document and the bailee may without liability to any person comply with such order. If the document was negotiable the claimant must post security approved by the court to indemnify any person who may suffer loss as a result of non-surrender of the document. If the document was not negotiable, such security may be required at the discretion of the court. The court may also in its discretion order payment of the bailee's reasonable costs and counsel fees.

(2) A bailee who without court order delivers goods to a person claiming under a missing negotiable document is liable to any person injured thereby, and if the delivery is not in good faith becomes liable for conversion. Delivery in good faith is not conversion if made in accordance with a filed classification or tariff or, where no classification or tariff is filed, if the claimant posts security with the bailee in an amount at least double the value of the goods at the time of posting to indemnify any person injured by the delivery who files a notice of claim within one year after the delivery.

### § 7—602. Attachment of Goods Covered by a Negotiable Document.

Except where the document was originally issued upon delivery of the goods by a person who had no power to dispose of them, no lien attaches by virtue of any judicial process to goods in the possession of a bailee for which a negotiable document of title is outstanding unless the document be first surrendered to the bailee or its negotiation enjoined, and the bailee shall not be compelled to deliver the goods pursuant to process until the document is surrendered to him or impounded by the court. One who purchases the document for value without notice of the process or injunction takes free of the lien imposed by judicial process.

### § 7—603. Conflicting Claims; Interpleader.

If more than one person claims title or possession of the goods, the bailee is excused from delivery until he has had a reasonable time to ascertain the validity of the adverse claims or to bring an action to compel all claimants to interplead and may compel such interpleader, either in defending an action for nondelivery of the goods, or by original action, whichever is appropriate.

## Article 8
# INVESTMENT SECURITIES

## Part 1   Short Title and General Matters

### § 8—101. Short Title.

This Article shall be known and may be cited as Uniform Commercial Code—Investment Securities.

### § 8—102. Definitions and Index of Definitions.

(1) In this Article, unless the context otherwise requires:

(a) A "certificated security" is a share, participation, or other interest in property of or an enterprise of the issuer or an obligation of the issuer which is

(i) represented by an instrument issued in bearer or registered form;

(ii) of a type commonly dealt in on securities exchanges or markets or commonly recognized in any area in which it is issued or dealt in as a medium for investment; and

(iii) either one of a class or series or by its terms divisible into a class or series of shares, participations, interests, or obligations.

(b) An "uncertificated security" is a share, participation, or other interest in property or an enterprise of the issuer or an obligation of the issuer which is

(i) not represented by an instrument and the transfer of which is registered upon books maintained for that purpose by or on behalf of the issuer;

(ii) of a type commonly dealt in on securities exchanges or markets; and

(iii) either one of a class or series or by its terms divisible into a class or series of shares, participations, interests, or obligations.

(c) A "security" is either a certificated or an uncertificated security. If a security is certificated, the terms "security" and "certificated security" may mean either the intangible interest, the instrument representing that interest, or both, as the context requires. A writing that is a certificated security is governed by this Article and not by Article 3, even though it also meets the requirements of that Article. This Article does not apply to money. If a certificated security has been retained by or surrendered to the issuer or its transfer agent for reasons other than registration of transfer, other temporary purpose, payment, exchange, or acquisition by the issuer, that security shall be treated as an uncertificated security for purposes of this Article.

(d) A certificated security is in "registered form" if

(i) it specifies a person entitled to the security or the rights it represents; and

(ii) its transfer may be registered upon books maintained for that purpose by or on behalf of the issuer, or the security so states.

(e) A certificated security is in "bearer form" if it runs to bearer according to its terms and not by reason of any indorsement.

(2) A "subsequent purchaser" is a person who takes other than by original issue.

(3) A "clearing corporation" is a corporation registered as a "clearing agency" under the federal securities laws or a corporation:

(a) at least 90 percent of whose capital stock is held by or for one or more organizations, none of which, other than a national securities exchange or association, holds in excess of 20 percent of the capital stock of the corporation, and each of which is

(i) subject to supervision or regulation pursuant to the provisions of federal or state banking laws or state insurance laws,

(ii) a broker or dealer or investment company registered under the federal securities laws, or

(iii) a national securities exchange or association registered under the federal securities laws; and

(b) any remaining capital stock of which is held by individuals who have purchased it at or prior to the time of their taking office as directors of the corporation and who have purchased only so much of the capital stock as is necessary to permit them to qualify as directors.

(4) A "custodian bank" is a bank or trust company that is supervised and examined by state or federal authority having supervision over banks and is acting as custodian for a clearing corporation.

(5) Other definitions applying to this Article or to specified Parts thereof and the sections in which they appear are:

"Adverse claim". Section 8—302.
"Bona fide purchaser". Section 8—302.
"Broker". Section 8—303.
"Debtor". Section 9—105.
"Financial intermediary". Section 8—313.
"Guarantee of the signature". Section 8—402.
"Initial transaction statement". Section 8—408.
"Instruction". Section 8—308.
"Intermediary bank". Section 4—105.
"Issuer". Section 8—201.
"Overissue". Section 8—104.
"Secured Party". Section 9—105.
"Security Agreement". Section 9—105.

(6) In addition, Article 1 contains general definitions and principles of construction and interpretation applicable throughout this Article.

Amended in 1962, 1973 and 1977.

### § 8—103. Issuer's Lien.

A lien upon a security in favor of an issuer thereof is valid against a purchaser only if:

(a) the security is certificated and the right of the issuer to the lien is noted conspicuously thereon; or

(b) the security is uncertificated and a notation of the right of the issuer to the lien is contained in the initial transaction statement sent to the purchaser or, if his interest is transferred to him other than by registration of transfer, pledge, or release, the initial transaction statement sent to the registered owner or the registered pledgee.

Amended in 1977.

### § 8—104. Effect of Overissue; "Overissue".

(1) The provisions of this Article which validate a security or compel its issue or reissue do not apply to the extent that validation, issue, or reissue would result in overissue; but if:

(a) an identical security which does not constitute an overissue is reasonably available for purchase, the person entitled to issue or validation may compel the issuer to purchase the security for him and either to deliver a certificated security or to register the transfer of an uncertificated security to him, against surrender of any certificated security he holds; or

(b) a security is not so available for purchase, the person entitled to issue or validation may recover from the issuer the price he or the last purchaser for value paid for it with interest from the date of his demand.

(2) "Overissue" means the issue of securities in excess of the amount the issuer has corporate power to issue.

Amended in 1977.

## § 8—105. Certificated Securities Negotiable; Statements and Instructions Not Negotiable; Presumptions.

(1) Certificated securities governed by this Article are negotiable instruments.

(2) Statements (Section 8—408), notices, or the like, sent by the issuer of uncertificated securities and instructions (Section 8—308) are neither negotiable instruments nor certificated securities.

(3) In any action on a security:

(a) unless specifically denied in the pleadings, each signature on a certificated security, in a necessary indorsement, on an initial transaction statement, or on an instruction, is admitted;

(b) if the effectiveness of a signature is put in issue, the burden of establishing it is on the party claiming under the signature, but the signature is presumed to be genuine or authorized;

(c) if signatures on a certificated security are admitted or established, production of the security entitles a holder to recover on it unless the defendant establishes a defense or a defect going to the validity of the security;

(d) if signatures on an initial transaction statement are admitted or established, the facts stated in the statement are presumed to be true as of the time of its issuance; and

(e) after it is shown that a defense or defect exists, the plaintiff has the burden of establishing that he or some person under whom he claims is a person against whom the defense or defect is ineffective (Section 8—202).

Amended in 1977.

## § 8—106. Applicability.

The law (including the conflict of laws rules) of the jurisdiction of organization of the issuer governs the validity of a security, the effectiveness of registration by the issuer, and the rights and duties of the issuer with respect to:

(a) registration of transfer of a certificated security;

(b) registration of transfer, pledge, or release of an uncertificated security; and

(c) sending of statements of uncertificated securities.

Amended in 1977.

## § 8—107. Securities Transferable; Action for Price.

(1) Unless otherwise agreed and subject to any applicable law or regulation respecting short sales, a person obligated to transfer securities may transfer any certificated security of the specified issue in bearer form or registered in the name of the transferee, or indorsed to him or in blank, or he may transfer an equivalent uncertificated security to the transferee or a person designated by the transferee.

(2) If the buyer fails to pay the price as it comes due under a contract of sale, the seller may recover the price of:

(a) certificated securities accepted by the buyer;

(b) uncertificated securities that have been transferred to the buyer or a person designated by the buyer; and

(c) other securities if efforts at their resale would be unduly burdensome or if there is no readily available market for their resale.

Amended in 1977.

## § 8—108. Registration of Pledge and Release of Uncertificated Securities.

A security interest in an uncertificated security may be evidenced by the registration of pledge to the secured party or a person designated by him. There can be no more than one registered pledge of an uncertificated security at any time. The registered owner of an uncertificated security is the person in whose name the security is registered, even if the security is subject to a registered pledge. The rights of a registered pledgee of an uncertificated security under this Article are terminated by the registration of release.

Added in 1977.

## Part 2 Issue—Issuer

### § 8—201. "Issuer."

(1) With respect to obligations on or defenses to a security, "issuer" includes a person who:

(a) places or authorizes the placing of his name on a certificated security (otherwise than as authenticating trustee, registrar, transfer agent, or the like) to evidence that it represents a share, participation, or other interest in his property or in an enterprise, or to evidence his duty to perform an obligation represented by the certificated security;

(b) creates shares, participations, or other interests in his property or in an enterprise or undertakes obligations, which shares, participations, interests, or obligations are uncertificated securities;

(c) directly or indirectly creates fractional interests in his rights or property, which fractional interests are represented by certificated securities; or

(d) becomes responsible for or in place of any other person described as an issuer in this section.

(2) With respect to obligations on or defenses to a security, a guarantor is an issuer to the extent of his guaranty, whether or not his obligation is noted on a certificated security or on statements of uncertificated securities sent pursuant to Section 8—408.

(3) With respect to registration of transfer, pledge, or release (Part 4 of this Article), "issuer" means a person on whose behalf transfer books are maintained.

Amended in 1977.

## § 8—202. Issuer's Responsibility and Defenses; Notice of Defect or Defense.

(1) Even against a purchaser for value and without notice, the terms of a security include:

(a) if the security is certificated, those stated on the security;

(b) if the security is uncertificated, those contained in the initial transaction statement sent to such purchaser or, if his interest is transferred to him other than by registration of transfer, pledge, or release, the initial transaction statement sent to the registered owner or registered pledgee; and

(c) those made part of the security by reference, on the certificated security or in the initial transaction statement, to another instrument, indenture, or document or to a constitution, statute, ordinance, rule, regulation, order or the like, to the extent that the terms referred to do not conflict with the terms stated on the certificated security or contained in the statement. A reference under this paragraph does not of itself charge a purchaser for value with notice of a defect going to the validity of the security, even though the certificated security or statement expressly states that a person accepting it admits notice.

(2) A certificated security in the hands of a purchaser for value or an uncertificated security as to which an initial transaction statement has been sent to a purchaser for value, other than a security issued by a government or governmental agency or unit, even though issued with a defect going to its validity, is valid with respect to the purchaser if he is without notice of the particular defect unless the defect involves a violation of constitutional provisions, in which case the security is valid with respect to a subsequent purchaser for value and without notice of the defect. This subsection applies to an issuer that is a government or governmental agency or unit only if either there has been substantial compliance with the legal requirements governing the issue or the issuer has received a substantial consideration for the issue as a whole or for the particular security and a stated purpose of the issue is one for which the issuer has power to borrow money or issue the security.

(3) Except as provided in the case of certain unauthorized signatures (Section 8—205), lack of genuineness of a certificated security or an initial transaction statement is a complete defense, even against a purchaser for value and without notice.

(4) All other defenses of the issuer of a certificated or uncertificated security, including nondelivery and conditional delivery of a certificated security, are ineffective against a purchaser for value who has taken without notice of the particular defense.

(5) Nothing in this section shall be construed to affect the right of a party to a ''when, as and if issued'' or a ''when distributed'' contract to cancel the contract in the event of a material change in the character of the security that is the subject of the contract or in the plan or arrangement pursuant to which the security is to be issued or distributed.

Amended in 1977.

### § 8—203. Staleness as Notice of Defects or Defenses.

(1) After an act or event creating a right to immediate performance of the principal obligation represented by a certificated security or that sets a date on or after which the security is to be presented or surrendered for redemption or exchange, a purchaser is charged with notice of any defect in its issue or defense of the issuer if:

(a) the act or event is one requiring the payment of money, the delivery of certificated securities, the registration of transfer of uncertificated securities, or any of these on presentation or surrender of the certificated security, the funds or securities are available on the date set for payment or exchange, and he takes the security more than one year after that date; and

(b) the act or event is not covered by paragraph (a) and he takes the security more than 2 years after the date set for surrender or presentation or the date on which performance became due.

(2) A call that has been revoked is not within subsection (1).

Amended in 1977.

### § 8—204. Effect of Issuer's Restrictions on Transfer.

A restriction on transfer of a security imposed by the issuer, even if otherwise lawful, is ineffective against any person without actual knowledge of it unless:

(a) the security is certificated and the restriction is noted conspicuously thereon; or

(b) the security is uncertificated and a notation of the restriction is contained in the initial transaction statement sent to the person or, if his interest is transferred to him other than by registration of transfer, pledge, or release, the initial transaction statement sent to the registered owner or the registered pledgee.

Amended in 1977.

### § 8—205. Effect of Unauthorized Signature on Certificated Security or Initial Transaction Statement.

An unauthorized signature placed on a certificated security prior to or in the course of issue or placed on an initial transaction statement is ineffective, but the signature is effective in favor of a purchaser for value of the certificated security or a purchaser for value of an uncertificated security to whom the initial transaction statement has been sent, if the purchaser is without notice of the lack of authority and the signing has been done by:

(a) an authenticating trustee, registrar, transfer agent, or other person entrusted by the issuer with the signing of the security, of similar securities, or of initial transaction statements or the immediate preparation for signing of any of them; or

(b) an employee of the issuer, or of any of the foregoing, entrusted with responsible handling of the security or initial transaction statement.

Amended in 1977.

## § 8—206. Completion or Alteration of Certificated Security or Initial Transaction Statement.

(1) If a certificated security contains the signatures necessary to its issue or transfer but is incomplete in any other respect:

(a) any person may complete it by filling in the blanks as authorized; and

(b) even though the blanks are incorrectly filled in, the security as completed is enforceable by a purchaser who took it for value and without notice of the incorrectness.

(2) A complete certificated security that has been improperly altered, even though fraudulently, remains enforceable, but only according to its original terms.

(3) If an initial transaction statement contains the signatures necessary to its validity, but is incomplete in any other respect:

(a) any person may complete it by filling in the blanks as authorized; and

(b) even though the blanks are incorrectly filled in, the statement as completed is effective in favor of the person to whom it is sent if he purchased the security referred to therein for value and without notice of the incorrectness.

(4) A complete initial transaction statement that has been improperly altered, even though fraudulently, is effective in favor of a purchaser to whom it has been sent, but only according to its original terms.

Amended in 1977.

## § 8—207. Rights and Duties of Issuer With Respect to Registered Owners and Registered Pledgees.

(1) Prior to due presentment for registration of transfer of a certificated security in registered form, the issuer or indenture trustee may treat the registered owner as the person exclusively entitled to vote, to receive notifications, and otherwise to exercise all the rights and powers of an owner.

(2) Subject to the provisions of subsections (3), (4), and (6), the issuer or indenture trustee may treat the registered owner of an uncertificated security as the person exclusively entitled to vote, to receive notifications, and otherwise to exercise all the rights and powers of an owner.

(3) The registered owner of an uncertificated security that is subject to a registered pledge is not entitled to registration of transfer prior to the due presentment to the issuer of a release instruction. The exercise of conversion rights with respect to a convertible uncertificated security is a transfer within the meaning of this section.

(4) Upon due presentment of a transfer instruction from the registered pledgee of an uncertificated security, the issuer shall:

(a) register the transfer of the security to the new owner free of pledge, if the instruction specifies a new owner (who may be the registered pledgee) and does not specify a pledgee;

(b) register the transfer of the security to the new owner subject to the interest of the existing pledgee, if the instruction specifies a new owner and the existing pledgee; or

(c) register the release of the security from the existing pledge and register the pledge of the security to the other pledgee, if the instruction specifies the existing owner and another pledgee.

(5) Continuity of perfection of a security interest is not broken by registration of transfer under subsection (4)(b) or by registration of release and pledge under subsection (4)(c), if the security interest is assigned.

(6) If an uncertificated security is subject to a registered pledge:

(a) any uncertificated securities issued in exchange for or distributed with respect to the pledged security shall be registered subject to the pledge;

(b) any certificated securities issued in exchange for or distributed with respect to the pledged security shall be delivered to the registered pledgee; and

(c) any money paid in exchange for or in redemption of part or all of the security shall be paid to the registered pledgee.

(7) Nothing in this Article shall be construed to affect the liability of the registered owner of a security for calls, assessments, or the like.

Amended in 1977.

## § 8—208. Effect of Signature of Authenticating Trustee, Registrar, or Transfer Agent.

(1) A person placing his signature upon a certificated security or an initial transaction statement as authenticating trustee, registrar, transfer agent, or the like, warrants to a purchaser for value of the certificated security or a purchaser for value of an uncertificated security to whom the initial transaction statement has been sent, if the purchaser is without notice of the particular defect, that:

(a) the certificated security or initial transaction statement is genuine;

(b) his own participation in the issue or registration of the transfer, pledge, or release of the security is within his capacity and within the scope of the authority received by him from the issuer; and

(c) he has reasonable grounds to believe the security is in the form and within the amount the issuer is authorized to issue.

(2) Unless otherwise agreed, a person by so placing his signature does not assume responsibility for the validity of the security in other respects.

Amended in 1962 and 1977.

# Part 3   Transfer

## § 8—301. Rights Acquired by Purchaser.

(1) Upon transfer of a security to a purchaser (Section 8—313), the purchaser acquires the rights in the security which

his transferor had or had actual authority to convey unless the purchaser's rights are limited by Section 8—302(4).

(2) A transferee of a limited interest acquires rights only to the extent of the interest transferred. The creation or release of a security interest in a security is the transfer of a limited interest in that security.

Amended in 1977.

### § 8—302. "Bona Fide Purchaser"; "Adverse Claim"; Title Acquired by Bona Fide Purchaser.

(1) A "bona fide purchaser" is a purchaser for value in good faith and without notice of any adverse claim:

    (a) who takes delivery of a certificated security in bearer form or in registered form, issued or indorsed to him or in blank;

    (b) to whom the transfer, pledge, or release of an uncertificated security is registered on the books of the issuer; or

    (c) to whom a security is transferred under the provisions of paragraph (c), (d)(i), or (g) of Section 8—313(1).

(2) "Adverse claim" includes a claim that a transfer was or would be wrongful or that a particular adverse person is the owner of or has an interest in the security.

(3) A bona fide purchaser in addition to acquiring the rights of a purchaser (Section 8—301) also acquires his interest in the security free of any adverse claim.

(4) Notwithstanding Section 8—301(1), the transferee of a particular certificated security who has been a party to any fraud or illegality affecting the security, or who as a prior holder of that certificated security had notice of an adverse claim, cannot improve his position by taking from a bona fide purchaser.

Amended in 1977.

### § 8—303. "Broker".

"Broker" means a person engaged for all or part of his time in the business of buying and selling securities, who in the transaction concerned acts for, buys a security from, or sells a security to, a customer. Nothing in this Article determines the capacity in which a person acts for purposes of any other statute or rule to which the person is subject.

### § 8—304. Notice to Purchaser of Adverse Claims.

(1) A purchaser (including a broker for the seller or buyer, but excluding an intermediary bank) of a certificated security is charged with notice of adverse claims if:

    (a) the security, whether in bearer or registered form, has been indorsed "for collection" or "for surrender" or for some other purpose not involving transfer; or

    (b) the security is in bearer form and has on it an unambiguous statement that it is the property of a person other than the transferor. The mere writing of a name on a security is not such a statement.

(2) A purchaser (including a broker for the seller or buyer, but excluding an intermediary bank) to whom the transfer, pledge, or release of an uncertificated security is registered is charged with notice of adverse claims as to which the issuer has a duty under Section 8—403(4) at the time of registration and which are noted in the initial transaction statement sent to the purchaser or, if his interest is transferred to him other than by registration of transfer, pledge, or release, the initial transaction statement sent to the registered owner or the registered pledgee.

(3) The fact that the purchaser (including a broker for the seller or buyer) of a certificated or uncertificated security has notice that the security is held for a third person or is registered in the name of or indorsed by a fiduciary does not create a duty of inquiry into the rightfulness of the transfer or constitute constructive notice of adverse claims. However, if the purchaser (excluding an intermediary bank) has knowledge that the proceeds are being used or that the transaction is for the individual benefit of the fiduciary or otherwise in breach of duty, the purchaser is charged with notice of adverse claims.

Amended in 1977.

### § 8—305. Staleness as Notice of Adverse Claims.

An act or event that creates a right to immediate performance of the principal obligation represented by a certificated security or sets a date on or after which a certificated security is to be presented or surrendered for redemption or exchange does not itself constitute any notice of adverse claims except in the case of a transfer:

(a) after one year from any date set for presentment or surrender for redemption or exchange; or

(b) after 6 months from any date set for payment of money against presentation or surrender of the security if funds are available for payment on that date.

Amended in 1977.

### § 8—306. Warranties on Presentment and Transfer of Certificated Securities; Warranties of Originators of Instructions.

(1) A person who presents a certificated security for registration of transfer or for payment or exchange warrants to the issuer that he is entitled to the registration, payment, or exchange. But, a purchaser for value and without notice of adverse claims who receives a new, reissued, or re-registered certificated security on registration of transfer or receives an initial transaction statement confirming the registration of transfer of an equivalent uncertificated security to him warrants only that he has no knowledge of any unauthorized signature (Section 8—311) in a necessary indorsement.

(2) A person by transferring a certificated security to a purchaser for value warrants only that:

    (a) his transfer is effective and rightful;

    (b) the security is genuine and has not been materially altered; and

    (c) he knows of no fact which might impair the validity of the security.

(3) If a certificated security is delivered by an intermediary known to be entrusted with delivery of the security on behalf of another or with collection of a draft or other claim against delivery, the intermediary by delivery warrants only his own good faith and authority, even though he has purchased or made advances against the claim to be collected against the delivery.

(4) A pledgee or other holder for security who redelivers a certificated security received, or after payment and on order of the debtor delivers that security to a third person, makes only the warranties of an intermediary under subsection (3).

(5) A person who originates an instruction warrants to the issuer that:

    (a) he is an appropriate person to originate the instruction; and

    (b) at the time the instruction is presented to the issuer he will be entitled to the registration of transfer, pledge, or release.

(6) A person who originates an instruction warrants to any person specially guaranteeing his signature (subsection 8—312(3)) that:

    (a) he is an appropriate person to originate the instruction; and

    (b) at the time the instruction is presented to the issuer

        (i) he will be entitled to the registration of transfer, pledge, or release; and

        (ii) the transfer, pledge, or release requested in the instruction will be registered by the issuer free from all liens, security interests, restrictions, and claims other than those specified in the instruction.

(7) A person who originates an instruction warrants to a purchaser for value and to any person guaranteeing the instruction (Section 8—312(6)) that:

    (a) he is an appropriate person to originate the instruction;

    (b) the uncertificated security referred to therein is valid; and

    (c) at the time the instruction is presented to the issuer

        (i) the transferor will be entitled to the registration of transfer, pledge, or release;

        (ii) the transfer, pledge, or release requested in the instruction will be registered by the issuer free from all liens, security interests, restrictions, and claims other than those specified in the instruction; and

        (iii) the requested transfer, pledge, or release will be rightful.

(8) If a secured party is the registered pledgee or the registered owner of an uncertificated security, a person who originates an instruction of release or transfer to the debtor or, after payment and on order of the debtor, a transfer instruction to a third person, warrants to the debtor or the third person only that he is an appropriate person to originate the instruction and, at the time the instruction is presented to the issuer, the transferor will be entitled to the registration of release or transfer. If a transfer instruction to a third person who is a purchaser for value is originated on order of the debtor, the debtor makes to the purchaser the warranties of paragraphs (b), (c)(ii) and (c)(iii) of subsection (7).

(9) A person who transfers an uncertificated security to a purchaser for value and does not originate an instruction in connection with the transfer warrants only that:

    (a) his transfer is effective and rightful; and

    (b) the uncertificated security is valid.

(10) A broker gives to his customer and to the issuer and a purchaser the applicable warranties provided in this section and has the rights and privileges of a purchaser under this section. The warranties of and in favor of the broker, acting as an agent are in addition to applicable warranties given by and in favor of his customer.

Amended in 1962 and 1977.

### § 8—307. Effect of Delivery Without Indorsement; Right to Compel Indorsement.

If a certificated security in registered form has been delivered to a purchaser without a necessary indorsement he may become a bona fide purchaser only as of the time the indorsement is supplied; but against the transferor, the transfer is complete upon delivery and the purchaser has a specifically enforceable right to have any necessary indorsement supplied.

Amended in 1977.

### § 8—308. Indorsements; Instructions.

(1) An indorsement of a certificated security in registered form is made when an appropriate person signs on it or on a separate document an assignment or transfer of the security or a power to assign or transfer it or his signature is written without more upon the back of the security.

(2) An indorsement may be in blank or special. An indorsement in blank includes an indorsement to bearer. A special indorsement specifies to whom the security is to be transferred, or who has power to transfer it. A holder may convert a blank indorsement into a special indorsement.

(3) An indorsement purporting to be only of part of a certificated security representing units intended by the issuer to be separately transferable is effective to the extent of the indorsement.

(4) An ''instruction'' is an order to the issuer of an uncertificated security requesting that the transfer, pledge, or release from pledge of the uncertificated security specified therein be registered.

(5) An instruction originated by an appropriate person is:

    (a) a writing signed by an appropriate person; or

    (b) a communication to the issuer in any form agreed upon in a writing signed by the issuer and an appropriate person.

If an instruction has been originated by an appropriate person but is incomplete in any other respect, any person may complete it as authorized and the issuer may rely on it as completed even though it has been completed incorrectly.

(6) "An appropriate person" in subsection (1) means the person specified by the certificated security or by special indorsement to be entitled to the security.

(7) "An appropriate person" in subsection (5) means:

(a) for an instruction to transfer or pledge an uncertificated security which is then not subject to a registered pledge, the registered owner; or

(b) for an instruction to transfer or release an uncertificated security which is then subject to a registered pledge, the registered pledgee.

(8) In addition to the persons designated in subsections (6) and (7), "an appropriate person" in subsections (1) and (5) includes:

(a) if the person designated is described as a fiduciary but is no longer serving in the described capacity, either that person or his successor;

(b) if the persons designated are described as more than one person as fiduciaries and one or more are no longer serving in the described capacity, the remaining fiduciary or fiduciaries, whether or not a successor has been appointed or qualified;

(c) if the person designated is an individual and is without capacity to act by virtue of death, incompetence, infancy, or otherwise, his executor, administrator, guardian, or like fiduciary;

(d) if the persons designated are described as more than one person as tenants by the entirety or with right of survivorship and by reason of death all cannot sign, the survivor or survivors;

(e) a person having power to sign under applicable law or controlling instrument; and

(f) to the extent that the person designated or any of the foregoing persons may act through an agent, his authorized agent.

(9) Unless otherwise agreed, the indorser of a certificated security by his indorsement or the originator of an instruction by his origination assumes no obligation that the security will be honored by the issuer but only the obligations provided in Section 8—306.

(10) Whether the person signing is appropriate is determined as of the date of signing and an indorsement made by or an instruction originated by him does not become unauthorized for the purposes of this Article by virtue of any subsequent change of circumstances.

(11) Failure of a fiduciary to comply with a controlling instrument or with the law of the state having jurisdiction of the fiduciary relationship, including any law requiring the fiduciary to obtain court approval of the transfer, pledge, or release, does not render his indorsement or an instruction originated by him unauthorized for the purposes of this Article.

Amended in 1962 and 1977.

### § 8—309. Effect of Indorsement Without Delivery.

An indorsement of a certificated security, whether special or in blank, does not constitute a transfer until delivery of the certificated security on which it appears or, if the indorsement is on a separate document, until delivery of both the document and the certificated security.

Amended in 1977.

### § 8—310. Indorsement of Certificated Security in Bearer Form.

An indorsement of a certificated security in bearer form may give notice of adverse claims (Section 8—304) but does not otherwise affect any right to registration the holder possesses.

Amended in 1977.

### § 8—311. Effect of Unauthorized Indorsement or Instruction.

Unless the owner or pledgee has ratified an unauthorized indorsement or instruction or is otherwise precluded from asserting its ineffectiveness:

(a) he may assert its ineffectiveness against the issuer or any purchaser, other than a purchaser for value and without notice of adverse claims, who has in good faith received a new, reissued, or re-registered certificated security on registration of transfer or received an initial transaction statement confirming the registration of transfer, pledge, or release of an equivalent uncertificated security to him; and

(b) an issuer who registers the transfer of a certificated security upon the unauthorized indorsement or who registers the transfer, pledge, or release of an uncertificated security upon the unauthorized instruction is subject to liability for improper registration (Section 8—404).

Amended in 1977.

### § 8—312. Effect of Guaranteeing Signature, Indorsement or Instruction.

(1) Any person guaranteeing a signature of an indorser of a certificated security warrants that at the time of signing:

(a) the signature was genuine;

(b) the signer was an appropriate person to indorse (Section 8—308); and

(c) the signer had legal capacity to sign.

(2) Any person guaranteeing a signature of the originator of an instruction warrants that at the time of signing:

(a) the signature was genuine;

(b) the signer was an appropriate person to originate the instruction (Section 8—308) if the person specified in the instruction as the registered owner or registered pledgee of the uncertificated security was, in fact, the registered owner or registered pledgee of the security, as to which fact the signature guarantor makes no warranty;

(c) the signer had legal capacity to sign; and

(d) the taxpayer identification number, if any, appearing on the instruction as that of the registered owner or registered pledgee was the taxpayer identification number of the signer or of the owner or pledgee for whom the signer was acting.

(3) Any person specially guaranteeing the signature of the originator of an instruction makes not only the warranties of a signature guarantor (subsection (2)) but also warrants that at the time the instruction is presented to the issuer:

(a) the person specified in the instruction as the registered owner or registered pledgee of the uncertificated security will be the registered owner or registered pledgee; and

(b) the transfer, pledge, or release of the uncertificated security requested in the instruction will be registered by the issuer free from all liens, security interests, restrictions, and claims other than those specified in the instruction.

(4) The guarantor under subsections (1) and (2) or the special guarantor under subsection (3) does not otherwise warrant the rightfulness of the particular transfer, pledge, or release.

(5) Any person guaranteeing an indorsement of a certificated security makes not only the warranties of a signature guarantor under subsection (1) but also warrants the rightfulness of the particular transfer in all respects.

(6) Any person guaranteeing an instruction requesting the transfer, pledge, or release of an uncertificated security makes not only the warranties of a special signature guarantor under subsection (3) but also warrants the rightfulness of the particular transfer, pledge, or release in all respects.

(7) No issuer may require a special guarantee of signature (subsection (3)), a guarantee of indorsement (subsection (5)), or a guarantee of instruction (subsection (6)) as a condition to registration of transfer, pledge, or release.

(8) The foregoing warranties are made to any person taking or dealing with the security in reliance on the guarantee, and the guarantor is liable to the person for any loss resulting from breach of the warranties.

Amended in 1977.

### § 8—313. When Transfer to Purchaser Occurs; Financial Intermediary as Bona Fide Purchaser; "Financial Intermediary".

(1) Transfer of a security or a limited interest (including a security interest) therein to a purchaser occurs only:

(a) at the time he or a person designated by him acquires possession of a certificated security;

(b) at the time the transfer, pledge, or release of an uncertificated security is registered to him or a person designated by him;

(c) at the time his financial intermediary acquires possession of a certificated security specially indorsed to or issued in the name of the purchaser;

(d) at the time a financial intermediary, not a clearing corporation, sends him confirmation of the purchase and also by book entry or otherwise identifies as belonging to the purchaser

(i) a specific certificated security in the financial intermediary's possession;

(ii) a quantity of securities that constitute or are part of a fungible bulk of certificated securities in the financial intermediary's possession or of uncertificated securities registered in the name of the financial intermediary; or

(iii) a quantity of securities that constitute or are part of a fungible bulk of securities shown on the account of the financial intermediary on the books of another financial intermediary;

(e) with respect to an identified certificated security to be delivered while still in the possession of a third person, not a financial intermediary, at the time that person acknowledges that he holds for the purchaser;

(f) with respect to a specific uncertificated security the pledge or transfer of which has been registered to a third person, not a financial intermediary, at the time that person acknowledges that he holds for the purchaser;

(g) at the time appropriate entries to the account of the purchaser or a person designated by him on the books of a clearing corporation are made under Section 8—320;

(h) with respect to the transfer of a security interest where the debtor has signed a security agreement containing a description of the security, at the time a written notification, which, in the case of the creation of the security interest, is signed by the debtor (which may be a copy of the security agreement) or which, in the case of the release or assignment of the security interest created pursuant to this paragraph, is signed by the secured party, is received by

(i) a financial intermediary on whose books the interest of the transferor in the security appears;

(ii) a third person, not a financial intermediary, in possession of the security, if it is certificated;

(iii) a third person, not a financial intermediary, who is the registered owner of the security, if it is uncertificated and not subject to a registered pledge; or

(iv) a third person, not a financial intermediary, who is the registered pledgee of the security, if it is uncertificated and subject to a registered pledge;

(i) with respect to the transfer of a security interest where the transferor has signed a security agreement containing a description of the security, at the time new value is given by the secured party; or

(j) with respect to the transfer of a security interest where the secured party is a financial intermediary and the security has already been transferred to the financial intermediary under paragraphs (a), (b), (c), (d), or (g), at the time the transferor has signed a security agreement containing a description of the security and value is given by the secured party.

(2) The purchaser is the owner of a security held for him by a financial intermediary, but cannot be a bona fide purchaser

of a security so held except in the circumstances specified in paragraphs (c), (d)(i), and (g) of subsection (1). If a security so held is part of a fungible bulk, as in the circumstances specified in paragraphs (d)(ii) and (d)(iii) of subsection (1), the purchaser is the owner of a proportionate property interest in the fungible bulk.

(3) Notice of an adverse claim received by the financial intermediary or by the purchaser after the financial intermediary takes delivery of a certificated security as a holder for value or after the transfer, pledge, or release of an uncertificated security has been registered free of the claim to a financial intermediary who has given value is not effective either as to the financial intermediary or as to the purchaser. However, as between the financial intermediary and the purchaser the purchaser may demand transfer of an equivalent security as to which no notice of adverse claim has been received.

(4) A ''financial intermediary'' is a bank, broker, clearing corporation, or other person (or the nominee of any of them) which in the ordinary course of its business maintains security accounts for its customers and is acting in that capacity. A financial intermediary may have a security interest in securities held in account for its customer.

Amended in 1962 and 1977.

### § 8—314.  Duty to Transfer, When Completed.

(1)  Unless otherwise agreed, if a sale of a security is made on an exchange or otherwise through brokers:

(a)  the selling customer fulfills his duty to transfer at the time he:

(i)  places a certificated security in the possession of the selling broker or a person designated by the broker;

(ii)  causes an uncertificated security to be registered in the name of the selling broker or a person designated by the broker;

(iii)  if requested, causes an acknowledgment to be made to the selling broker that a certificated or uncertificated security is held for the broker; or

(iv)  places in the possession of the selling broker or of a person designated by the broker a transfer instruction for an uncertificated security, providing the issuer does not refuse to register the requested transfer if the instruction is presented to the issuer for registration within 30 days thereafter; and

(b)  the selling broker, including a correspondent broker acting for a selling customer, fulfills his duty to transfer at the time he:

(i)  places a certificated security in the possession of the buying broker or a person designated by the buying broker;

(ii)  causes an uncertificated security to be registered in the name of the buying broker or a person designated by the buying broker;

(iii)  places in the possession of the buying broker or of a person designated by the buying broker a transfer instruction for an uncertificated security, providing the issuer does not refuse to register the requested transfer if the instruction is presented to the issuer for registration within 30 days thereafter; or

(iv)  effects clearance of the sale in accordance with the rules of the exchange on which the transaction took place.

(2)  Except as provided in this section or unless otherwise agreed, a transferor's duty to transfer a security under a contract of purchase is not fulfilled until he:

(a)  places a certificated security in form to be negotiated by the purchaser in the possession of the purchaser or of a person designated by the purchaser;

(b)  causes an uncertificated security to be registered in the name of the purchaser or a person designated by the purchaser; or

(c)  if the purchaser requests, causes an acknowledgment to be made to the purchaser that a certificated or uncertificated security is held for the purchaser.

(3)  Unless made on an exchange, a sale to a broker purchasing for his own account is within subsection (2) and not within subsection (1).

Amended in 1977.

### § 8—315.  Action Against Transferee Based Upon Wrongful Transfer.

(1)  Any person against whom the transfer of a security is wrongful for any reason, including his incapacity, as against anyone except a bona fide purchaser, may:

(a)  reclaim possession of the certificated security wrongfully transferred;

(b)  obtain possession of any new certificated security representing all or part of the same rights;

(c)  compel the origination of an instruction to transfer to him or a person designated by him an uncertificated security constituting all or part of the same rights; or

(d)  have damages.

(2)  If the transfer is wrongful because of an unauthorized indorsement of a certificated security, the owner may also reclaim or obtain possession of the security or a new certificated security, even from a bona fide purchaser, if the ineffectiveness of the purported indorsement can be asserted against him under the provisions of this Article on unauthorized indorsements (Section 8—311).

(3)  The right to obtain or reclaim possession of a certificated security or to compel the origination of a transfer instruction may be specifically enforced and the transfer of a certificated or uncertificated security enjoined and a certificated security impounded pending the litigation.

Amended in 1977.

### § 8—316. Purchaser's Right to Requisites for Registration of Transfer, Pledge, or Release on Books.

Unless otherwise agreed, the transferor of a certificated security or the transferor, pledgor, or pledgee of an uncertificated security on due demand must supply his purchaser with any proof of his authority to transfer, pledge, or release or with any other requisite necessary to obtain registration of the transfer, pledge, or release of the security; but if the transfer, pledge, or release is not for value, a transferor, pledgor, or pledgee need not do so unless the purchaser furnishes the necessary expenses. Failure within a reasonable time to comply with a demand made gives the purchaser the right to reject or rescind the transfer, pledge, or release.

Amended in 1977.

### § 8—317. Creditors' Rights.

(1) Subject to the exceptions in subsections (3) and (4), no attachment or levy upon a certificated security or any share or other interest represented thereby which is outstanding is valid until the security is actually seized by the officer making the attachment or levy, but a certificated security which has been surrendered to the issuer may be reached by a creditor by legal process at the issuer's chief executive office in the United States.

(2) An uncertificated security registered in the name of the debtor may not be reached by a creditor except by legal process at the issuer's chief executive office in the United States.

(3) The interest of a debtor in a certificated security that is in the possession of a secured party not a financial intermediary or in an uncertificated security registered in the name of a secured party not a financial intermediary (or in the name of a nominee of the secured party) may be reached by a creditor by legal process upon the secured party.

(4) The interest of a debtor in a certificated security that is in the possession of or registered in the name of a financial intermediary or in an uncertificated security registered in the name of a financial intermediary may be reached by a creditor by legal process upon the financial intermediary on whose books the interest of the debtor appears.

(5) Unless otherwise provided by law, a creditor's lien upon the interest of a debtor in a security obtained pursuant to subsection (3) or (4) is not a restraint on the transfer of the security, free of the lien, to a third party for new value; but in the event of a transfer, the lien applies to the proceeds of the transfer in the hands of the secured party or financial intermediary, subject to any claims having priority.

(6) A creditor whose debtor is the owner of a security is entitled to aid from courts of appropriate jurisdiction, by injunction or otherwise, in reaching the security or in satisfying the claim by means allowed at law or in equity in regard to property that cannot readily be reached by ordinary legal process.

Amended in 1977.

### § 8—318. No Conversion by Good Faith Conduct.

An agent or bailee who in good faith (including observance of reasonable commercial standards if he is in the business of buying, selling, or otherwise dealing with securities) has received certificated securities and sold, pledged, or delivered them or has sold or caused the transfer or pledge of uncertificated securities over which he had control according to the instructions of his principal, is not liable for conversion or for participation in breach of fiduciary duty although the principal had no right so to deal with the securities.

Amended in 1977.

### § 8—319. Statute of Frauds.

A contract for the sale of securities is not enforceable by way of action or defense unless:

(a) there is some writing signed by the party against whom enforcement is sought or by his authorized agent or broker, sufficient to indicate that a contract has been made for sale of a stated quantity of described securities at a defined or stated price;

(b) delivery of a certificated security or transfer instruction has been accepted, or transfer of an uncertificated security has been registered and the transferee has failed to send written objection to the issuer within 10 days after receipt of the initial transaction statement confirming the registration, or payment has been made, but the contract is enforceable under this provision only to the extent of the delivery, registration, or payment;

(c) within a reasonable time a writing in confirmation of the sale or purchase and sufficient against the sender under paragraph (a) has been received by the party against whom enforcement is sought and he has failed to send written objection to its contents within 10 days after its receipt; or

(d) the party against whom enforcement is sought admits in his pleading, testimony, or otherwise in court that a contract was made for the sale of a stated quantity of described securities at a defined or stated price.

Amended in 1977.

### § 8—320. Transfer or Pledge Within Central Depository System.

(1) In addition to other methods, a transfer, pledge, or release of a security or any interest therein may be effected by the making of appropriate entries on the books of a clearing corporation reducing the account of the transferor, pledgor, or pledgee and increasing the account of the transferee, pledgee, or pledgor by the amount of the obligation or the number of shares or rights transferred, pledged, or released, if the security is shown on the account of a transferor, pledgor, or pledgee on the books of the clearing corporation; is subject to the control of the clearing corporation; and

    (a) if certificated,

        (i) is in the custody of the clearing corporation, another clearing corporation, a custodian bank, or a nominee of any of them; and

(ii) is in bearer form or indorsed in blank by an appropriate person or registered in the name of the clearing corporation, a custodian bank, or a nominee of any of them; or

(b) if uncertificated, is registered in the name of the clearing corporation, another clearing corporation, a custodian bank, or a nominee of any of them.

(2) Under this section entries may be made with respect to like securities or interests therein as a part of a fungible bulk and may refer merely to a quantity of a particular security without reference to the name of the registered owner, certificate or bond number, or the like, and, in appropriate cases, may be on a net basis taking into account other transfers, pledges, or releases of the same security.

(3) A transfer under this section is effective (Section 8—313) and the purchaser acquires the rights of the transferor (Section 8—301). A pledge or release under this section is the transfer of a limited interest. If a pledge or the creation of a security interest is intended, the security interest is perfected at the time when both value is given by the pledgee and the appropriate entries are made (Section 8—321). A transferee or pledgee under this section may be a bona fide purchaser (Section 8—302).

(4) A transfer or pledge under this section is not a registration of transfer under Part 4.

(5) That entries made on the books of the clearing corporation as provided in subsection (1) are not appropriate does not affect the validity or effect of the entries or the liabilities or obligations of the clearing corporation to any person adversely affected thereby.

Added in 1962; amended in 1977.

### § 8—321. Enforceability, Attachment, Perfection and Termination of Security Interests.

(1) A security interest in a security is enforceable and can attach only if it is transferred to the secured party or a person designated by him pursuant to a provision of Section 8—313(1).

(2) A security interest so transferred pursuant to agreement by a transferor who has rights in the security to a transferee who has given value is a perfected security interest, but a security interest that has been transferred solely under paragraph (i) of Section 8—313(1) becomes unperfected after 21 days unless, within that time, the requirements for transfer under any other provision of Section 8—313(1) are satisfied.

(3) A security interest in a security is subject to the provisions of Article 9, but:

(a) no filing is required to perfect the security interest; and

(b) no written security agreement signed by the debtor is necessary to make the security interest enforceable, except as provided in paragraph (h), (i), or (j) of Section 8—313(1). The secured party has the rights and duties provided under Section 9—207, to the extent they are

applicable, whether or not the security is certificated, and, if certificated, whether or not it is in his possession.

(4) Unless otherwise agreed, a security interest in a security is terminated by transfer to the debtor or a person designated by him pursuant to a provision of Section 8—313(1). If a security is thus transferred, the security interest, if not terminated, becomes unperfected unless the security is certificated and is delivered to the debtor for the purpose of ultimate sale or exchange or presentation, collection, renewal, or registration of transfer. In that case, the security interest becomes unperfected after 21 days unless, within that time, the security (or securities for which it has been exchanged) is transferred to the secured party or a person designated by him pursuant to a provision of Section 8—313(1).

Added in 1977.

## Part 4 Registration

### § 8—401. Duty of Issuer to Register Transfer, Pledge, or Release.

(1) If a certificated security in registered form is presented to the issuer with a request to register transfer or an instruction is presented to the issuer with a request to register transfer, pledge, or release, the issuer shall register the transfer, pledge, or release as requested if:

(a) the security is indorsed or the instruction was originated by the appropriate person or persons (Section 8—308);

(b) reasonable assurance is given that those indorsements or instructions are genuine and effective (Section 8—402);

(c) the issuer has no duty as to adverse claims or has discharged the duty (Section 8—403);

(d) any applicable law relating to the collection of taxes has been complied with; and

(e) the transfer, pledge, or release is in fact rightful or is to a bona fide purchaser.

(2) If an issuer is under a duty to register a transfer, pledge, or release of a security, the issuer is also liable to the person presenting a certificated security or an instruction for registration or his principal for loss resulting from any unreasonable delay in registration or from failure or refusal to register the transfer, pledge, or release.

Amended in 1977.

### § 8—402. Assurance that Indorsements and Instructions Are Effective.

(1) The issuer may require the following assurance that each necessary indorsement of a certificated security or each instruction (Section 8—308) is genuine and effective:

(a) in all cases, a guarantee of the signature (Section 8—312(1) or (2)) of the person indorsing a certificated security or originating an instruction including, in the case of an instruction, a warranty of the taxpayer identification number or, in the absence thereof, other reasonable assurance of identity;

(b) if the indorsement is made or the instruction is originated by an agent, appropriate assurance of authority to sign;

(c) if the indorsement is made or the instruction is originated by a fiduciary, appropriate evidence of appointment or incumbency;

(d) if there is more than one fiduciary, reasonable assurance that all who are required to sign have done so; and

(e) if the indorsement is made or the instruction is originated by a person not covered by any of the foregoing, assurance appropriate to the case corresponding as nearly as may be to the foregoing.

(2) A "guarantee of the signature" in subsection (1) means a guarantee signed by or on behalf of a person reasonably believed by the issuer to be responsible. The issuer may adopt standards with respect to responsibility if they are not manifestly unreasonable.

(3) "Appropriate evidence of appointment or incumbency" in subsection (1) means:

(a) in the case of a fiduciary appointed or qualified by a court, a certificate issued by or under the direction or supervision of that court or an officer thereof and dated within 60 days before the date of presentation for transfer, pledge, or release; or

(b) in any other case, a copy of a document showing the appointment or a certificate issued by or on behalf of a person reasonably believed by the issuer to be responsible or, in the absence of that document or certificate, other evidence reasonably deemed by the issuer to be appropriate. The issuer may adopt standards with respect to the evidence if they are not manifestly unreasonable. The issuer is not charged with notice of the contents of any document obtained pursuant to this paragraph (b) except to the extent that the contents relate directly to the appointment or incumbency.

(4) The issuer may elect to require reasonable assurance beyond that specified in this section, but if it does so and, for a purpose other than that specified in subsection (3)(b), both requires and obtains a copy of a will, trust, indenture, articles of co-partnership, by-laws, or other controlling instrument, it is charged with notice of all matters contained therein affecting the transfer, pledge, or release.

Amended in 1977.

## § 8—403. Issuer's Duty as to Adverse Claims.

(1) An issuer to whom a certificated security is presented for registration shall inquire into adverse claims if:

(a) a written notification of an adverse claim is received at a time and in a manner affording the issuer a reasonable opportunity to act on it prior to the issuance of a new, reissued, or re-registered certificated security, and the notification identifies the claimant, the registered owner, and the issue of which the security is a part, and provides an address for communications directed to the claimant; or

(b) the issuer is charged with notice of an adverse claim from a controlling instrument it has elected to require under Section 8—402(4).

(2) The issuer may discharge any duty of inquiry by any reasonable means, including notifying an adverse claimant by registered or certified mail at the address furnished by him or, if there be no such address, at his residence or regular place of business that the certificated security has been presented for registration of transfer by a named person, and that the transfer will be registered unless within 30 days from the date of mailing the notification, either:

(a) an appropriate restraining order, injunction, or other process issues from a court of competent jurisdiction; or

(b) there is filed with the issuer an indemnity bond, sufficient in the issuer's judgment to protect the issuer and any transfer agent, registrar, or other agent of the issuer involved from any loss it or they may suffer by complying with the adverse claim.

(3) Unless an issuer is charged with notice of an adverse claim from a controlling instrument which it has elected to require under Section 8—402(4) or receives notification of an adverse claim under subsection (1), if a certificated security presented for registration is indorsed by the appropriate person or persons the issuer is under no duty to inquire into adverse claims. In particular:

(a) an issuer registering a certificated security in the name of a person who is a fiduciary or who is described as a fiduciary is not bound to inquire into the existence, extent, or correct description of the fiduciary relationship; and thereafter the issuer may assume without inquiry that the newly registered owner continues to be the fiduciary until the issuer receives written notice that the fiduciary is no longer acting as such with respect to the particular security;

(b) an issuer registering transfer on an indorsement by a fiduciary is not bound to inquire whether the transfer is made in compliance with a controlling instrument or with the law of the state having jurisdiction of the fiduciary relationship, including any law requiring the fiduciary to obtain court approval of the transfer; and

(c) the issuer is not charged with notice of the contents of any court record or file or other recorded or unrecorded document even though the document is in its possession and even though the transfer is made on the indorsement of a fiduciary to the fiduciary himself or to his nominee.

(4) An issuer is under no duty as to adverse claims with respect to an uncertificated security except:

(a) claims embodied in a restraining order, injunction, or other legal process served upon the issuer if the process was served at a time and in a manner affording the issuer a reasonable opportunity to act on it in accordance with the requirements of subsection (5);

(b) claims of which the issuer has received a written notification from the registered owner or the registered pledgee if the notification was received at a time and in a manner affording the issuer a reasonable opportunity to act on it in accordance with the requirements of subsection (5);

(c) claims (including restrictions on transfer not imposed by the issuer) to which the registration of transfer to the present registered owner was subject and were so noted in the initial transaction statement sent to him; and

(d) claims as to which an issuer is charged with notice from a controlling instrument it has elected to require under Section 8—402(4).

(5) If the issuer of an uncertificated security is under a duty as to an adverse claim, he discharges that duty by:

(a) including a notation of the claim in any statements sent with respect to the security under Sections 8—408(3), (6), and (7); and

(b) refusing to register the transfer or pledge of the security unless the nature of the claim does not preclude transfer or pledge subject thereto.

(6) If the transfer or pledge of the security is registered subject to an adverse claim, a notation of the claim must be included in the initial transaction statement and all subsequent statements sent to the transferee and pledgee under Section 8—408.

(7) Notwithstanding subsections (4) and (5), if an uncertificated security was subject to a registered pledge at the time the issuer first came under a duty as to a particular adverse claim, the issuer has no duty as to that claim if transfer of the security is requested by the registered pledgee or an appropriate person acting for the registered pledgee unless:

(a) the claim was embodied in legal process which expressly provides otherwise;

(b) the claim was asserted in a written notification from the registered pledgee;

(c) the claim was one as to which the issuer was charged with notice from a controlling instrument it required under Section 8—402(4) in connection with the pledgee's request for transfer; or

(d) the transfer requested is to the registered owner.

Amended in 1977.

### § 8—404. Liability and Non-Liability for Registration.

(1) Except as provided in any law relating to the collection of taxes, the issuer is not liable to the owner, pledgee, or any other person suffering loss as a result of the registration of a transfer, pledge, or release of a security if:

(a) there were on or with a certificated security the necessary indorsements or the issuer had received an instruction originated by an appropriate person (Section 8—308); and

(b) the issuer had no duty as to adverse claims or has discharged the duty (Section 8—403).

(2) If an issuer has registered a transfer of a certificated

security to a person not entitled to it, the issuer on demand shall deliver a like security to the true owner unless:

(a) the registration was pursuant to subsection (1);

(b) the owner is precluded from asserting any claim for registering the transfer under Section 8—405(1); or

(c) the delivery would result in overissue, in which case the issuer's liability is governed by Section 8—104.

(3) If an issuer has improperly registered a transfer, pledge, or release of an uncertificated security, the issuer on demand from the injured party shall restore the records as to the injured party to the condition that would have obtained if the improper registration had not been made unless:

(a) the registration was pursuant to subsection (1); or

(b) the registration would result in overissue, in which case the issuer's liability is governed by Section 8—104.

Amended in 1977.

### § 8—405. Lost, Destroyed, and Stolen Certificated Securities.

(1) If a certificated security has been lost, apparently destroyed, or wrongfully taken, and the owner fails to notify the issuer of that fact within a reasonable time after he has notice of it and the issuer registers a transfer of the security before receiving notification, the owner is precluded from asserting against the issuer any claim for registering the transfer under Section 8—404 or any claim to a new security under this section.

(2) If the owner of a certificated security claims that the security has been lost, destroyed, or wrongfully taken, the issuer shall issue a new certificated security or, at the option of the issuer, an equivalent uncertificated security in place of the original security if the owner:

(a) so requests before the issuer has notice that the security has been acquired by a bona fide purchaser;

(b) files with the issuer a sufficient indemnity bond; and

(c) satisfies any other reasonable requirements imposed by the issuer.

(3) If, after the issue of a new certificated or uncertificated security, a bona fide purchaser of the original certificated security presents it for registration of transfer, the issuer shall register the transfer unless registration would result in overissue, in which event the issuer's liability is governed by Section 8—104. In addition to any rights on the indemnity bond, the issuer may recover the new certificated security from the person to whom it was issued or any person taking under him except a bona fide purchaser or may cancel the uncertificated security unless a bona fide purchaser or any person taking under a bona fide purchaser is then the registered owner or registered pledgee thereof.

Amended in 1977.

### § 8—406. Duty of Authenticating Trustee, Transfer Agent, or Registrar.

(1) If a person acts as authenticating trustee, transfer agent, registrar, or other agent for an issuer in the registration of

transfers of its certificated securities or in the registration of transfers, pledges, and releases of its uncertificated securities, in the issue of new securities, or in the cancellation of surrendered securities:

(a) he is under a duty to the issuer to exercise good faith and due diligence in performing his functions; and

(b) with regard to the particular functions he performs, he has the same obligation to the holder or owner of a certificated security or to the owner or pledgee of an uncertificated security and has the same rights and privileges as the issuer has in regard to those functions.

(2) Notice to an authenticating trustee, transfer agent, registrar or other agent is notice to the issuer with respect to the functions performed by the agent.

Amended in 1977.

### § 8—407. Exchangeability of Securities.

(1) No issuer is subject to the requirements of this section unless it regularly maintains a system for issuing the class of securities involved under which both certificated and uncertificated securities are regularly issued to the category of owners, which includes the person in whose name the new security is to be registered.

(2) Upon surrender of a certificated security with all necessary·indorsements and presentation of a written request by the person surrendering the security, the issuer, if he has no duty as to adverse claims or has discharged the duty (Section 8—403), shall issue to the person or a person designated by him an equivalent uncertificated security subject to all liens, restrictions, and claims that were noted on the certificated security.

(3) Upon receipt of a transfer instruction originated by an appropriate person who so requests, the issuer of an uncertificated security shall cancel the uncertificated security and issue an equivalent certificated security on which must be noted conspicuously any liens and restrictions of the issuer and any adverse claims (as to which the issuer has a duty under Section 8—403(4)) to which the uncertificated security was subject. The certificated security shall be registered in the name of and delivered to:

(a) the registered owner, if the uncertificated security was not subject to a registered pledge; or

(b) the registered pledgee, if the uncertificated security was subject to a registered pledge.

Added in 1977.

### § 8—408. Statements of Uncertificated Securities.

(1) Within 2 business days after the transfer of an uncertificated security has been registered, the issuer shall send to the new registered owner and, if the security has been transferred subject to a registered pledge, to the registered pledgee a written statement containing:

(a) a description of the issue of which the uncertificated security is a part;

(b) the number of shares or units transferred;

(c) the name and address and any taxpayer identification number of the new registered owner and, if the security has been transferred subject to a registered pledge, the name and address and any taxpayer identification number of the registered pledgee;

(d) a notation of any liens and restrictions of the issuer and any adverse claims (as to which the issuer has a duty under Section 8—403(4)) to which the uncertificated security is or may be subject at the time of registration or a statement that there are none of those liens, restrictions, or adverse claims; and

(e) the date the transfer was registered.

(2) Within 2 business days after the pledge of an uncertificated security has been registered, the issuer shall send to the registered owner and the registered pledgee a written statement containing:

(a) a description of the issue of which the uncertificated security is a part;

(b) the number of shares or units pledged;

(c) the name and address and any taxpayer identification number of the registered owner and the registered pledgee;

(d) a notation of any liens and restrictions of the issuer and any adverse claims (as to which the issuer has a duty under Section 8—403(4)) to which the uncertificated security is or may be subject at the time of registration or a statement that there are none of those liens, restrictions, or adverse claims; and

(e) the date the pledge was registered.

(3) Within 2 business days after the release from pledge of an uncertificated security has been registered, the issuer shall send to the registered owner and the pledgee whose interest was released a written statement containing:

(a) a description of the issue of which the uncertificated security is a part;

(b) the number of shares or units released from pledge;

(c) the name and address and any taxpayer identification number of the registered owner and the pledgee whose interest was released;

(d) a notation of any liens and restrictions of the issuer and any adverse claims (as to which the issuer has a duty under Section 8—403(4)) to which the uncertificated security is or may be subject at the time of registration or a statement that there are none of those liens, restrictions, or adverse claims; and

(e) the date the release was registered.

(4) An "initial transaction statement" is the statement sent to:

(a) the new registered owner and, if applicable, to the registered pledgee pursuant to subsection (1);

(b) the registered pledgee pursuant to subsection (2); or

(c) the registered owner pursuant to subsection (3).

Each initial transaction statement shall be signed by or on behalf of the issuer and must be identified as "Initial Transaction Statement".

(5) Within 2 business days after the transfer of an uncertificated security has been registered, the issuer shall send to the former registered owner and the former registered pledgee, if any, a written statement containing:

(a) a description of the issue of which the uncertificated security is a part;

(b) the number of shares or units transferred;

(c) the name and address and any taxpayer identification number of the former registered owner and of any former registered pledgee; and

(d) the date the transfer was registered.

(6) At periodic intervals no less frequent than annually and at any time upon the reasonable written request of the registered owner, the issuer shall send to the registered owner of each uncertificated security a dated written statement containing:

(a) a description of the issue of which the uncertificated security is a part;

(b) the name and address and any taxpayer identification number of the registered owner;

(c) the number of shares or units of the uncertificated security registered in the name of the registered owner on the date of the statement;

(d) the name and address and any taxpayer identification number of any registered pledgee and the number of shares or units subject to the pledge; and

(e) a notation of any liens and restrictions of the issuer and any adverse claims (as to which the issuer has a duty under Section 8—403(4)) to which the uncertificated security is or may be subject or a statement that there are none of those liens, restrictions, or adverse claims.

(7) At periodic intervals no less frequent than annually and at any time upon the reasonable written request of the registered pledgee, the issuer shall send to the registered pledgee of each uncertificated security a dated written statement containing:

(a) a description of the issue of which the uncertificated security is a part;

(b) the name and address and any taxpayer identification number of the registered owner;

(c) the name and address and any taxpayer identification number of the registered pledgee;

(d) the number of shares or units subject to the pledge; and

(e) a notation of any liens and restrictions of the issuer and any adverse claims (as to which the issuer has a duty under Section 8—403(4)) to which the uncertificated security is or may be subject or a statement that there are none of those liens, restrictions, or adverse claims.

(8) If the issuer sends the statements described in subsections (6) and (7) at periodic intervals no less frequent than quarterly, the issuer is not obliged to send additional statements upon request unless the owner or pledgee requesting them pays to the issuer the reasonable cost of furnishing them.

(9) Each statement sent pursuant to this section must bear a conspicuous legend reading substantially as follows: "This statement is merely a record of the rights of the addressee as of the time of its issuance. Delivery of this statement, of itself, confers no rights on the recipient. This statement is neither a negotiable instrument nor a security."

Added in 1977.

# Article 9
# SECURED TRANSACTIONS; SALES OF ACCOUNTS AND CHATTEL PAPER

Note: *The adoption of this Article should be accompanied by the repeal of existing statutes dealing with conditional sales, trust receipts, factor's liens where the factor is given a nonpossessory lien, chattel mortgages, crop mortgages, mortgages on railroad equipment, assignment of accounts and generally statutes regulating security interests in personal property.*

*Where the state has a retail installment selling act or small loan act, that legislation should be carefully examined to determine what changes in those acts are needed to conform them to this Article. This Article primarily sets out rules defining rights of a secured party against persons dealing with the debtor; it does not prescribe regulations and controls which may be necessary to curb abuses arising in the small loan business or in the financing of consumer purchases on credit. Accordingly there is no intention to repeal existing regulatory acts in those fields by enactment or re-enactment of Article 9. See Section 9—203(4) and the Note thereto.*

## Part 1  Short Title, Applicability and Definitions

### § 9—101. Short Title.

This Article shall be known and may be cited as Uniform Commercial Code—Secured Transactions.

### § 9—102. Policy and Subject Matter of Article.

(1) Except as otherwise provided in Section 9—104 on excluded transactions, this Article applies

(a) to any transaction (regardless of its form) which is intended to create a security interest in personal property or fixtures including goods, documents, instruments, general intangibles, chattel paper or accounts; and also

(b) to any sale of accounts or chattel paper.

(2) This Article applies to security interests created by contract including pledge, assignment, chattel mortgage, chattel trust, trust deed, factor's lien, equipment trust, conditional sale, trust receipt, other lien or title retention contract and lease or consignment intended as security. This Article does not apply to statutory liens except as provided in Section 9—310.

(3) The application of this Article to a security interest in a secured obligation is not affected by the fact that the obligation is itself secured by a transaction or interest to which this Article does not apply.

### § 9—103. Perfection of Security Interest in Multiple State Transactions.

(1) Documents, instruments and ordinary goods.

(a) This subsection applies to documents and instruments and to goods other than those covered by a certificate of title described in subsection (2), mobile goods described in subsection (3), and minerals described in subsection (5).

(b) Except as otherwise provided in this subsection, perfection and the effect of perfection or non-perfection of a security interest in collateral are governed by the law of the jurisdiction where the collateral is when the last event occurs on which is based the assertion that the security interest is perfected or unperfected.

(c) If the parties to a transaction creating a purchase money security interest in goods in one jurisdiction understand at the time that the security interest attaches that the goods will be kept in another jurisdiction, then the law of the other jurisdiction governs the perfection and the effect of perfection or non-perfection of the security interest from the time it attaches until thirty days after the debtor receives possession of the goods and thereafter if the goods are taken to the other jurisdiction before the end of the thirty-day period.

(d) When collateral is brought into and kept in this state while subject to a security interest perfected under the law of the jurisdiction from which the collateral was removed, the security interest remains perfected, but if action is required by Part 3 of this Article to perfect the security interest,

(i) if the action is not taken before the expiration of the period of perfection in the other jurisdiction or the end of four months after the collateral is brought into this state, whichever period first expires, the security interest becomes unperfected at the end of that period and is thereafter deemed to have been unperfected as against a person who became a purchaser after removal;

(ii) if the action is taken before the expiration of the period specified in subparagraph (i), the security interest continues perfected thereafter;

(iii) for the purpose of priority over a buyer of consumer goods (subsection (2) of Section 9—307), the period of the effectiveness of a filing in the jurisdiction from which the collateral is removed is governed by the rules with respect to perfection in subparagraphs (i) and (ii).

(2) Certificate of title.

(a) This subsection applies to goods covered by a certificate of title issued under a statute of this state or of another jurisdiction under the law of which indication of a security interest on the certificate is required as a condition of perfection.

(b) Except as otherwise provided in this subsection, perfection and the effect of perfection or non-perfection of the security interest are governed by the law (including the conflict of laws rules) of the jurisdiction issuing the certificate until four months after the goods are removed from that jurisdiction and thereafter until the goods are registered in another jurisdiction, but in any event not beyond surrender of the certificate. After the expiration of that period, the goods are not covered by the certificate of title within the meaning of this section.

(c) Except with respect to the rights of a buyer described in the next paragraph, a security interest, perfected in another jurisdiction otherwise than by notation on a certificate of title, in goods brought into this state and thereafter covered by a certificate of title issued by this state is subject to the rules stated in paragraph (d) of subsection (1).

(d) If goods are brought into this state while a security interest therein is perfected in any manner under the law of the jurisdiction from which the goods are removed and a certificate of title is issued by this state and the certificate does not show that the goods are subject to the security interest or that they may be subject to security interests not shown on the certificate, the security interest is subordinate to the rights of a buyer of the goods who is not in the business of selling goods of that kind to the extent that he gives value and receives delivery of the goods after issuance of the certificate and without knowledge of the security interest.

(3) Accounts, general intangibles and mobile goods.

(a) This subsection applies to accounts (other than an account described in subsection (5) on minerals) and general intangibles (other than uncertificated securities) and to goods which are mobile and which are of a type normally used in more than one jurisdiction, such as motor vehicles, trailers, rolling stock, airplanes, shipping containers, road building and construction machinery and commercial harvesting machinery and the like, if the goods are equipment or are inventory leased or held for lease by the debtor to others, and are not covered by a certificate of title described in subsection (2).

(b) The law (including the conflict of laws rules) of the jurisdiction in which the debtor is located governs the perfection and the effect of perfection or non-perfection of the security interest.

(c) If, however, the debtor is located in a jurisdiction which is not a part of the United States, and which does not provide for perfection of the security interest by filing or recording in that jurisdiction, the law of the jurisdiction in the United States in which the debtor has its major executive office in the United States governs the perfection and the effect of perfection or non-perfection of the security interest through filing. In the alternative, if the debtor is located in a jurisdiction which is not a part of the United States or Canada and the collateral is accounts or general intangibles for money due or to become due, the security interest may be perfected by notification to the account debtor. As used in this paragraph, ''United States'' includes its territories and possessions and the Commonwealth of Puerto Rico.

(d) A debtor shall be deemed located at his place of business if he has one, at his chief executive office if he has more than one place of business, otherwise at his residence. If, however, the debtor is a foreign air carrier under the Federal Aviation Act of 1958, as amended, it shall be deemed located at the designated office of the agent upon whom service of process may be made on behalf of the foreign air carrier.

(e) A security interest perfected under the law of the jurisdiction of the location of the debtor is perfected until the expiration of four months after a change of the debtor's location to another jurisdiction, or until perfection would have ceased by the law of the first jurisdiction, whichever period first expires. Unless perfected in the new jurisdiction before the end of that period, it becomes unperfected thereafter and is deemed to have been unperfected as against a person who became a purchaser after the change.

(4) Chattel paper.

The rules stated for goods in subsection (1) apply to a possessory security interest in chattel paper. The rules stated for accounts in subsection (3) apply to a nonpossessory security interest in chattel paper, but the security interest may not be perfected by notification to the account debtor.

(5) Minerals.

Perfection and the effect of perfection or non-perfection of a security interest which is created by a debtor who has an interest in minerals or the like (including oil and gas) before extraction and which attaches thereto as extracted, or which attaches to an account resulting from the sale thereof at the wellhead or minehead are governed by the law (including the conflict of laws rules) of the jurisdiction wherein the wellhead or minehead is located.

(6) Uncertificated securities.

The law (including the conflict of laws rules) of the jurisdiction of organization of the issuer governs the perfection and the effect of perfection or non-perfection of a security interest in uncertificated securities.

Amended in 1972 and 1977.

### § 9—104. Transactions Excluded From Article.

This Article does not apply

(a) to a security interest subject to any statute of the United States, to the extent that such statute governs the rights of parties to and third parties affected by transactions in particular types of property; or

(b) to a landlord's lien; or

(c) to a lien given by statute or other rule of law for services or materials except as provided in Section 9—310 on priority of such liens; or

(d) to a transfer of a claim for wages, salary or other compensation of an employee; or

(e) to a transfer by a government or governmental subdivision or agency; or

(f) to a sale of accounts or chattel paper as part of a sale of the business out of which they arose, or an assignment of accounts or chattel paper which is for the purpose of collection only, or a transfer of a right to payment under a contract to an assignee who is also to do the performance under the contract or a transfer of a single account to an assignee in whole or partial satisfaction of a preexisting indebtedness; or

(g) to a transfer of an interest in or claim in or under any policy of insurance, except as provided with respect to proceeds (Section 9—306) and priorities in proceeds (Section 9—312); or

(h) to a right represented by a judgment (other than a judgment taken on a right to payment which was collateral); or

(i) to any right of set-off; or

(j) except to the extent that provision is made for fixtures in Section 9—313, to the creation or transfer of an interest in or lien on real estate, including a lease or rents thereunder; or

(k) to a transfer in whole or in part of any claim arising out of tort; or

(*l*) to a transfer of an interest in any deposit account (subsection (1) of Section 9—105), except as provided with respect to proceeds (Section 9—306) and priorities in proceeds (Section 9—312).

### § 9—105. Definitions and Index of Definitions.

(1) In this Article unless the context otherwise requires:

(a) ''Account debtor'' means the person who is obligated on an account, chattel paper or general intangible;

(b) ''Chattel paper'' means a writing or writings which evidence both a monetary obligation and a security interest in or a lease of specific goods, but a charter or other contract involving the use or hire of a vessel is not chattel paper. When a transaction is evidenced both by such a security agreement or a lease and by an instrument or a series of instruments, the group of writings taken together constitutes chattel paper;

(c) ''Collateral'' means the property subject to a security interest, and includes accounts and chattel paper which have been sold;

(d) ''Debtor'' means the person who owes payment or other performance of the obligation secured, whether or not he owns or has rights in the collateral, and includes the seller of accounts or chattel paper. Where the debtor and the owner of the collateral are not the same person, the term ''debtor'' means the owner of the collateral in any provision of the Article dealing with the collateral, the obligor in any provision dealing with the obligation, and may include both where the context so requires;

(e) ''Deposit account'' means a demand, time, savings, passbook or like account maintained with a bank, savings and loan association, credit union or like organization, other than an account evidenced by a certificate of deposit;

(f) ''Document'' means document of title as defined in the general definitions of Article 1 (Section 1—201), and a receipt of the kind described in subsection (2) of Section 7—201;

(g) ''Encumbrance'' includes real estate mortgages and other liens on real estate and all other rights in real estate that are not ownership interests;

(h) ''Goods'' includes all things which are movable at the time the security interest attaches or which are fixtures (Section 9—313), but does not include money, documents, instruments, accounts, chattel paper, general intangibles, or minerals or the like (including oil and gas) before extraction. ''Goods'' also includes standing timber which is to be cut and removed under a conveyance or contract for sale, the unborn young of animals, and growing crops;

(i) ''Instrument'' means a negotiable instrument (defined in Section 3—104), or a certificated security (defined in Section 8—102) or any other writing which evidences a right to the payment of money and is not itself a security agreement or lease and is of a type which is in ordinary course of business transferred by delivery with any necessary indorsement or assignment;

(j) ''Mortgage'' means a consensual interest created by a real estate mortgage, a trust deed on real estate, or the like;

(k) An advance is made ''pursuant to commitment'' if the secured party has bound himself to make it, whether or not a subsequent event of default or other event not within his control has relieved or may relieve him from his obligation;

(l) ''Security agreement'' means an agreement which creates or provides for a security interest;

(m) ''Secured party'' means a lender, seller or other person in whose favor there is a security interest, including a person to whom accounts or chattel paper have been sold. When the holders of obligations issued under an indenture of trust, equipment trust agreement or the like are represented by a trustee or other person, the representative is the secured party;

(n) ''Transmitting utility'' means any person primarily engaged in the railroad, street railway or trolley bus business, the electric or electronics communications transmission business, the transmission of goods by pipeline, or the transmission or the production and transmission of electricity, steam, gas or water, or the provision of sewer service.

(2) Other definitions applying to this Article and the sections in which they appear are:

> ''Account''. Section 9—106.
> ''Attach''. Section 9—203.
> ''Construction mortgage''. Section 9—313(1).
> ''Consumer goods''. Section 9—109(1).
> ''Equipment''. Section 9—109(2).
> ''Farm products''. Section 9—109(3).
> ''Fixture''. Section 9—313(1).
> ''Fixture filing''. Section 9—313(1).
> ''General intangibles''. Section 9—106.
> ''Inventory''. Section 9—109(4).
> ''Lien creditor''. Section 9—301(3).
> ''Proceeds''. Section 9—306(1).
> ''Purchase money security interest''. Section 9—107.
> ''United States''. Section 9—103.

(3) The following definitions in other Articles apply to this Article:

> ''Check''. Section 3—104.
> ''Contract for sale''. Section 2—106.
> ''Holder in due course''. Section 3—302.
> ''Note''. Section 3—104.
> ''Sale''. Section 2—106.

(4) In addition Article 1 contains general definitions and principles of construction and interpretation applicable throughout this Article.

### § 9—106. Definitions: ''Account''; ''General Intangibles''.

''Account'' means any right to payment for goods sold or leased or for services rendered which is not evidenced by an instrument or chattel paper, whether or not it has been earned by performance. ''General intangibles'' means any personal property (including things in action) other than goods, accounts, chattel paper, documents, instruments, and money. All rights to payment earned or unearned under a charter or other contract involving the use or hire of a vessel and all rights incident to the charter or contract are accounts.

### § 9—107. Definitions: ''Purchase Money Security Interest''.

A security interest is a ''purchase money security interest'' to the extent that it is

(a) taken or retained by the seller of the collateral to secure all or part of its price; or

(b) taken by a person who by making advances or incurring an obligation gives value to enable the debtor to acquire rights in or the use of collateral if such value is in fact so used.

### § 9—108. When After-Acquired Collateral Not Security for Antecedent Debt.

Where a secured party makes an advance, incurs an obligation, releases a perfected security interest, or otherwise gives new value which is to be secured in whole or in part by after-acquired property his security interest in the after-acquired collateral shall be deemed to be taken for new value and not as security for an antecedent debt if the debtor acquires his rights in such collateral either in the ordinary course of his business or under a contract of purchase made pursuant to the security agreement within a reasonable time after new value is given.

### § 9—109. Classification of Goods; "Consumer Goods"; "Equipment"; "Farm Products"; "Inventory".

Goods are

(1) "consumer goods" if they are used or bought for use primarily for personal, family or household purposes;

(2) "equipment" if they are used or bought for use primarily in business (including farming or a profession) or by a debtor who is a non-profit organization or a governmental subdivision or agency or if the goods are not included in the definitions of inventory, farm products or consumer goods;

(3) "farm products" if they are crops or livestock or supplies used or produced in farming operations or if they are products of crops or livestock in their unmanufactured states (such as ginned cotton, wool-clip, maple syrup, milk and eggs), and if they are in the possession of a debtor engaged in raising, fattening, grazing or other farming operations. If goods are farm products they are neither equipment nor inventory;

(4) "inventory" if they are held by a person who holds them for sale or lease or to be furnished under contracts of service or if he has so furnished them, or if they are raw materials, work in process or materials used or consumed in a business. Inventory of a person is not to be classified as his equipment.

### § 9—110. Sufficiency of Description.

For purposes of this Article any description of personal property or real estate is sufficient whether or not it is specific if it reasonably identifies what is described.

### § 9—111. Applicability of Bulk Transfer Laws.

The creation of a security interest is not a bulk transfer under Article 6 (see Section 6—103).

### § 9—112. Where Collateral Is Not Owned by Debtor.

Unless otherwise agreed, when a secured party knows that collateral is owned by a person who is not the debtor, the owner of the collateral is entitled to receive from the secured party any surplus under Section 9—502(2) or under Section 9—504(1), and is not liable for the debt or for any deficiency after resale, and he has the same right as the debtor

(a) to receive statements under Section 9—208;

(b) to receive notice of and to object to a secured party's proposal to retain the collateral in satisfaction of the indebtedness under Section 9—505;

(c) to redeem the collateral under Section 9—506;

(d) to obtain injunctive or other relief under Section 9—507(1); and

(e) to recover losses caused to him under Section 9—208(2).

### § 9—113. Security Interests Arising Under Article on Sales or Under Article on Leases.

A security interest arising solely under the Article on Sales (Article 2) or the Article on Leases is subject to the provisions of this Article except that to the extent that and so long as the debtor does not have or does not lawfully obtain possession of the goods

(a) no security agreement is necessary to make the security interest enforceable; and

(b) no filing is required to perfect the security interest; and

(c) the rights of the secured party on default by the debtor are governed (i) by the Article on Sales (Article 2) in the case of a security interest arising solely under such Article or (ii) by the Article on Leases (Article 2A) in the case of a security interest arising solely under such Article.

### § 9—114. Consignment.

(1) A person who delivers goods under a consignment which is not a security interest and who would be required to file under this Article by paragraph (3)(c) of Section 2—326 has priority over a secured party who is or becomes a creditor of the consignee and who would have a perfected security interest in the goods if they were the property of the consignee, and also has priority with respect to identifiable cash proceeds received on or before delivery of the goods to a buyer, if

(a) the consignor complies with the filing provision of the Article on Sales with respect to consignments (paragraph (3)(c) of Section 2—326) before the consignee receives possession of the goods; and

(b) the consignor gives notification in writing to the holder of the security interest if the holder has filed a financing statement covering the same types of goods before the date of the filing made by the consignor; and

(c) the holder of the security interest receives the notification within five years before the consignee receives possession of the goods; and

(d) the notification states that the consignor expects to deliver goods on consignment to the consignee, describing the goods by item or type.

(2) In the case of a consignment which is not a security interest and in which the requirements of the preceding subsection have not been met, a person who delivers goods to another is subordinate to a person who would have a perfected security interest in the goods if they were the property of the debtor.

## Part 2  Validity of Security Agreement and Rights of Parties Thereto

### § 9—201. General Validity of Security Agreement.

Except as otherwise provided by this Act a security agreement is effective according to its terms between the parties, against purchasers of the collateral and against creditors. Nothing in this Article validates any charge or practice illegal under any statute or regulation thereunder governing usury, small loans, retail installment sales, or the like, or extends the application of any such statute or regulation to any transaction not otherwise subject thereto.

### § 9—202. Title to Collateral Immaterial.

Each provision of this Article with regard to rights, obligations and remedies applies whether title to collateral is in the secured party or in the debtor.

### § 9—203. Attachment and Enforceability of Security Interest; Proceeds; Formal Requisites.

(1) Subject to the provisions of Section 4—208 on the security interest of a collecting bank, Section 8—321 on security interests in securities and Section 9—113 on a security interest arising under the Article on Sales, a security interest is not enforceable against the debtor or third parties with respect to the collateral and does not attach unless:

> (a) the collateral is in the possession of the secured party pursuant to agreement, or the debtor has signed a security agreement which contains a description of the collateral and in addition, when the security interest covers crops growing or to be grown or timber to be cut, a description of the land concerned;
>
> (b) value has been given; and
>
> (c) the debtor has rights in the collateral.

(2) A security interest attaches when it becomes enforceable against the debtor with respect to the collateral. Attachment occurs as soon as all of the events specified in subsection (1) have taken place unless explicit agreement postpones the time of attaching.

(3) Unless otherwise agreed a security agreement gives the secured party the rights to proceeds provided by Section 9—306.

(4) A transaction, although subject to this Article, is also subject to . . . . . . . .*, and in the case of conflict between the provisions of this Article and any such statute, the provisions of such statute control. Failure to comply with any applicable statute has only the effect which is specified therein.

Note: *At * in subsection (4) insert reference to any local statute regulating small loans, retail installment sales and the like.*

*The foregoing subsection (4) is designed to make it clear that certain transactions, although subject to this Article, must also comply with other applicable legislation.*

*This Article is designed to regulate all the "security" aspects of transactions within its scope. There is, however, much regulatory legislation, particularly in the consumer field, which supplements this Article and should not be repealed by its enactment. Examples are small loan acts, retail installment selling acts and the like. Such acts may provide for licensing and rate regulation and may prescribe particular forms of contract. Such provisions should remain in force despite the enactment of this Article. On the other hand if a retail installment selling act contains provisions on filing, rights on default, etc., such provisions should be repealed as inconsistent with this Article except that inconsistent provisions as to deficiencies, penalties, etc., in the Uniform Consumer Credit Code and other recent related legislation should remain because those statutes were drafted after the substantial enactment of the Article and with the intention of modifying certain provisions of this Article as to consumer credit.*

### § 9—204. After-Acquired Property; Future Advances.

(1) Except as provided in subsection (2), a security agreement may provide that any or all obligations covered by the security agreement are to be secured by after-acquired collateral.

(2) No security interest attaches under an after-acquired property clause to consumer goods other than accessions (Section 9—314) when given as additional security unless the debtor acquires rights in them within ten days after the secured party gives value.

(3) Obligations covered by a security agreement may include future advances or other value whether or not the advances or value are given pursuant to commitment (subsection (1) of Section 9—105).

### § 9—205. Use or Disposition of Collateral Without Accounting Permissible.

A security interest is not invalid or fraudulent against creditors by reason of liberty in the debtor to use, commingle or dispose of all or part of the collateral (including returned or repossessed goods) or to collect or compromise accounts or chattel paper, or to accept the return of goods or make repossessions, or to use, commingle or dispose of proceeds, or by reason of the failure of the secured party to require the debtor to account for proceeds or replace collateral. This section does not relax the requirements of possession where perfection of a security interest depends upon possession of the collateral by the secured party or by a bailee.

### § 9—206. Agreement Not to Assert Defenses Against Assignee; Modification of Sales Warranties Where Security Agreement Exists.

(1) Subject to any statute or decision which establishes a different rule for buyers or lessees of consumer goods, an agreement by a buyer or lessee that he will not assert against an assignee any claim or defense which he may have against the seller or lessor is enforceable by an assignee who takes his assignment for value, in good faith and without notice of a claim or defense, except as to defenses of a type which may be asserted against a holder in due course of a negotiable instrument under the Article on Commercial Paper (Article 3). A buyer who as part of one transaction signs both a negotiable instrument and a security agreement makes such an agreement.

(2) When a seller retains a purchase money security interest in goods the Article on Sales (Article 2) governs the sale and any disclaimer, limitation or modification of the seller's warranties.

### § 9—207. Rights and Duties When Collateral is in Secured Party's Possession.

(1) A secured party must use reasonable care in the custody and preservation of collateral in his possession. In the case of an instrument or chattel paper reasonable care includes

taking necessary steps to preserve rights against prior parties unless otherwise agreed.

(2) Unless otherwise agreed, when collateral is in the secured party's possession

(a) reasonable expenses (including the cost of any insurance and payment of taxes or other charges) incurred in the custody, preservation, use or operation of the collateral are chargeable to the debtor and are secured by the collateral;

(b) the risk of accidental loss or damage is on the debtor to the extent of any deficiency in any effective insurance coverage;

(c) the secured party may hold as additional security any increase or profits (except money) received from the collateral, but money so received, unless remitted to the debtor, shall be applied in reduction of the secured obligation;

(d) the secured party must keep the collateral identifiable but fungible collateral may be commingled;

(e) the secured party may repledge the collateral upon terms which do not impair the debtor's right to redeem it.

(3) A secured party is liable for any loss caused by his failure to meet any obligation imposed by the preceding subsections but does not lose his security interest.

(4) A secured party may use or operate the collateral for the purpose of preserving the collateral or its value or pursuant to the order of a court of appropriate jurisdiction or, except in the case of consumer goods, in the manner and to the extent provided in the security agreement.

### § 9—208. Request for Statement of Account or List of Collateral.

(1) A debtor may sign a statement indicating what he believes to be the aggregate amount of unpaid indebtedness as of a specified date and may send it to the secured party with a request that the statement be approved or corrected and returned to the debtor. When the security agreement or any other record kept by the secured party identifies the collateral a debtor may similarly request the secured party to approve or correct a list of the collateral.

(2) The secured party must comply with such a request within two weeks after receipt by sending a written correction or approval. If the secured party claims a security interest in all of a particular type of collateral owned by the debtor he may indicate that fact in his reply and need not approve or correct an itemized list of such collateral. If the secured party without reasonable excuse fails to comply he is liable for any loss caused to the debtor thereby; and if the debtor has properly included in his request a good faith statement of the obligation or a list of the collateral or both the secured party may claim a security interest only as shown in the statement against persons misled by his failure to comply. If he no longer has an interest in the obligation or collateral at the time the request is received he must disclose the name and address of any successor in interest known to him and he is liable for any loss caused to the debtor as a result of failure to disclose. A successor in interest is not subject to this section until a request is received by him.

(3) A debtor is entitled to such a statement once every six months without charge. The secured party may require payment of a charge not exceeding $10 for each additional statement furnished.

## Part 3 Rights of Third Parties; Perfected and Unperfected Security Interests; Rules of Priority

### § 9—301. Persons Who Take Priority Over Unperfected Security Interests; Rights of "Lien Creditor".

(1) Except as otherwise provided in subsection (2), an unperfected security interest is subordinate to the rights of

(a) persons entitled to priority under Section 9—312;

(b) a person who becomes a lien creditor before the security interest is perfected;

(c) in the case of goods, instruments, documents, and chattel paper, a person who is not a secured party and who is a transferee in bulk or other buyer not in ordinary course of business or is a buyer of farm products in ordinary course of business, to the extent that he gives value and receives delivery of the collateral without knowledge of the security interest and before it is perfected;

(d) in the case of accounts and general intangibles, a person who is not a secured party and who is a transferee to the extent that he gives value without knowledge of the security interest and before it is perfected.

(2) If the secured party files with respect to a purchase money security interest before or within ten days after the debtor receives possession of the collateral, he takes priority over the rights of a transferee in bulk or of a lien creditor which arise between the time the security interest attaches and the time of filing.

(3) A "lien creditor" means a creditor who has acquired a lien on the property involved by attachment, levy or the like and includes an assignee for benefit of creditors from the time of assignment, and a trustee in bankruptcy from the date of the filing of the petition or a receiver in equity from the time of appointment.

(4) A person who becomes a lien creditor while a security interest is perfected takes subject to the security interest only to the extent that it secures advances made before he becomes a lien creditor or within 45 days thereafter or made without knowledge of the lien or pursuant to a commitment entered into without knowledge of the lien.

### § 9—302. When Filing Is Required to Perfect Security Interest; Security Interests to Which Filing Provisions of This Article Do Not Apply.

(1) A financing statement must be filed to perfect all security interests except the following:

(a) a security interest in collateral in possession of the secured party under Section 9—305;

(b) a security interest temporarily perfected in instruments or documents without delivery under Section 9—304 or in proceeds for a 10 day period under Section 9—306;

(c) a security interest created by an assignment of a beneficial interest in a trust or a decedent's estate;

(d) a purchase money security interest in consumer goods; but filing is required for a motor vehicle required to be registered; and fixture filing is required for priority over conflicting interests in fixtures to the extent provided in Section 9—313;

(e) an assignment of accounts which does not alone or in conjunction with other assignments to the same assignee transfer a significant part of the outstanding accounts of the assignor;

(f) a security interest of a collecting bank (Section 4—208) or in securities (Section 8—321) or arising under the Article on Sales (see Section 9—113) or covered in subsection (3) of this section;

(g) an assignment for the benefit of all the creditors of the transferor, and subsequent transfers by the assignee thereunder.

(2) If a secured party assigns a perfected security interest, no filing under this Article is required in order to continue the perfected status of the security interest against creditors of and transferees from the original debtor.

(3) The filing of a financing statement otherwise required by this Article is not necessary or effective to perfect a security interest in property subject to

(a) a statute or treaty of the United States which provides for a national or international registration or a national or international certificate of title or which specifies a place of filing different from that specified in this Article for filing of the security interest; or

(b) the following statutes of this state; [list any certificate of title statute covering automobiles, trailers, mobile homes, boats, farm tractors, or the like, and any central filing statute.]; but during any period in which collateral is inventory held for sale by a person who is in the business of selling goods of that kind, the filing provisions of this Article (Part 4) apply to a security interest in that collateral created by him as debtor; or

(c) a certificate of title statute of another jurisdiction under the law of which indication of a security interest on the certificate is required as a condition of perfection (subsection (2) of Section 9—103).

(4) Compliance with a statute or treaty described in subsection (3) is equivalent to the filing of a financing statement under this Article, and a security interest in property subject to the statute or treaty can be perfected only by compliance therewith except as provided in Section 9—103 on multiple state transactions. Duration and renewal of perfection of a

security interest perfected by compliance with the statute or treaty are governed by the provisions of the statute or treaty; in other respects the security interest is subject to this Article.

Amended in 1972 and 1977.

### § 9—303. When Security Interest Is Perfected; Continuity of Perfection.

(1) A security interest is perfected when it has attached and when all of the applicable steps required for perfection have been taken. Such steps are specified in Sections 9—302, 9—304, 9—305 and 9—306. If such steps are taken before the security interest attaches, it is perfected at the time when it attaches.

(2) If a security interest is originally perfected in any way permitted under this Article and is subsequently perfected in some other way under this Article, without an intermediate period when it was unperfected, the security interest shall be deemed to be perfected continuously for the purposes of this Article.

### § 9—304. Perfection of Security Interest in Instruments, Documents, and Goods Covered by Documents; Perfection by Permissive Filing; Temporary Perfection Without Filing or Transfer of Possession.

(1) A security interest in chattel paper or negotiable documents may be perfected by filing. A security interest in money or instruments (other than certificated securities or instruments which constitute part of chattel paper) can be perfected only by the secured party's taking possession, except as provided in subsections (4) and (5) of this section and subsections (2) and (3) of Section 9—306 on proceeds.

(2) During the period that goods are in the possession of the issuer of a negotiable document therefor, a security interest in the goods is perfected by perfecting a security interest in the document, and any security interest in the goods otherwise perfected during such period is subject thereto.

(3) A security interest in goods in the possession of a bailee other than one who has issued a negotiable document therefor is perfected by issuance of a document in the name of the secured party or by the bailee's receipt of notification of the secured party's interest or by filing as to the goods.

(4) A security interest in instruments (other than certificated securities) or negotiable documents is perfected without filing or the taking of possession for a period of 21 days from the time it attaches to the extent that it arises for new value given under a written security agreement.

(5) A security interest remains perfected for a period of 21 days without filing where a secured party having a perfected security interest in an instrument (other than a certificated security), a negotiable document or goods in possession of a bailee other than one who has issued a negotiable document therefor

(a) makes available to the debtor the goods or documents representing the goods for the purpose of ultimate sale or exchange or for the purpose of loading, unloading, storing, shipping, transshipping, manufacturing, processing or otherwise dealing with them in a manner preliminary to their sale or exchange, but priority between conflicting security interests in the goods is subject to subsection (3) of Section 9—312; or

(b) delivers the instrument to the debtor for the purpose of ultimate sale or exchange or of presentation, collection, renewal or registration of transfer.

(6) After the 21 day period in subsections (4) and (5) perfection depends upon compliance with applicable provisions of this Article.

### § 9—305. When Possession by Secured Party Perfects Security Interest Without Filing.

A security interest in letters of credit and advices of credit (subsection (2)(a) of Section 5—116), goods, instruments (other than certificated securities), money, negotiable documents, or chattel paper may be perfected by the secured party's taking possession of the collateral. If such collateral other than goods covered by a negotiable document is held by a bailee, the secured party is deemed to have possession from the time the bailee receives notification of the secured party's interest. A security interest is perfected by possession from the time possession is taken without a relation back and continues only so long as possession is retained, unless otherwise specified in this Article. The security interest may be otherwise perfected as provided in this Article before or after the period of possession by the secured party.

### § 9—306. "Proceeds"; Secured Party's Rights on Disposition of Collateral.

(1) "Proceeds" includes whatever is received upon the sale, exchange, collection or other disposition of collateral or proceeds. Insurance payable by reason of loss or damage to the collateral is proceeds, except to the extent that it is payable to a person other than a party to the security agreement. Money, checks, deposit accounts, and the like are "cash proceeds". All other proceeds are "noncash proceeds".

(2) Except where this Article otherwise provides, a security interest continues in collateral notwithstanding sale, exchange or other disposition thereof unless the disposition was authorized by the secured party in the security agreement or otherwise, and also continues in any identifiable proceeds including collections received by the debtor.

(3) The security interest in proceeds is a continuously perfected security interest if the interest in the original collateral was perfected but it ceases to be a perfected security interest and becomes unperfected ten days after receipt of the proceeds by the debtor unless

(a) a filed financing statement covers the original collateral and the proceeds are collateral in which a security interest may be perfected by filing in the office or offices where the financing statement has been filed and, if the proceeds are acquired with cash proceeds, the description of collateral in the financing statement indicates the types of property constituting the proceeds; or

(b) a filed financing statement covers the original collateral and the proceeds are identifiable cash proceeds; or

(c) the security interest in the proceeds is perfected before the expiration of the ten day period.

Except as provided in this section, a security interest in proceeds can be perfected only by the methods or under the circumstances permitted in this Article for original collateral of the same type.

(4) In the event of insolvency proceedings instituted by or against a debtor, a secured party with a perfected security interest in proceeds has a perfected security interest only in the following proceeds:

(a) in identifiable noncash proceeds and in separate deposit accounts containing only proceeds;

(b) in identifiable cash proceeds in the form of money which is neither commingled with other money nor deposited in a deposit account prior to the insolvency proceedings;

(c) in identifiable cash proceeds in the form of checks and the like which are not deposited in a deposit account prior to the insolvency proceedings; and

(d) in all cash and deposit accounts of the debtor in which proceeds have been commingled with other funds, but the perfected security interest under this paragraph (d) is

(i) subject to any right to set-off; and

(ii) limited to an amount not greater than the amount of any cash proceeds received by the debtor within ten days before the institution of the insolvency proceedings less the sum of (I) the payments to the secured party on account of cash proceeds received by the debtor during such period and (II) the cash proceeds received by the debtor during such period to which the secured party is entitled under paragraphs (a) through (c) of this subsection (4).

(5) If a sale of goods results in an account or chattel paper which is transferred by the seller to a secured party, and if the goods are returned to or are repossessed by the seller or the secured party, the following rules determine priorities:

(a) If the goods were collateral at the time of sale, for an indebtedness of the seller which is still unpaid, the original security interest attaches again to the goods and continues as a perfected security interest if it was perfected at the time when the goods were sold. If the security interest was originally perfected by a filing which is still effective, nothing further is required to continue the perfected status; in any other case, the secured party must take possession of the returned or repossessed goods or must file.

(b) An unpaid transferee of the chattel paper has a security interest in the goods against the transferor. Such security interest is prior to a security interest asserted under paragraph (a) to the extent that the transferee of the chattel paper was entitled to priority under Section 9—308.

(c) An unpaid transferee of the account has a security interest in the goods against the transferor. Such security interest is subordinate to a security interest asserted under paragraph (a).

(d) A security interest of an unpaid transferee asserted under paragraph (b) or (c) must be perfected for protection against creditors of the transferor and purchasers of the returned or repossessed goods.

## § 9—307. Protection of Buyers of Goods.

(1) A buyer in ordinary course of business (subsection (9) of Section 1—201) other than a person buying farm products from a person engaged in farming operations takes free of a security interest created by his seller even though the security interest is perfected and even though the buyer knows of its existence [subject to the Food Security Act of 1985 (7 U.S.C. Section 1631)].

(2) In the case of consumer goods, a buyer takes free of a security interest even though perfected if he buys without knowledge of the security interest, for value and for his own personal, family or household purposes unless prior to the purchase the secured party has filed a financing statement covering such goods.

(3) A buyer other than a buyer in ordinary course of business (subsection (1) of this section) takes free of a security interest to the extent that it secures future advances made after the secured party acquires knowledge of the purchase, or more than 45 days after the purchase, whichever first occurs, unless made pursuant to a commitment entered into without knowledge of the purchase and before the expiration of the 45 day period.

## § 9—308. Purchase of Chattel Paper and Instruments.

A purchaser of chattel paper or an instrument who gives new value and takes possession of it in the ordinary course of his business has priority over a security interest in the chattel paper or instrument

(a) which is perfected under Section 9—304 (permissive filing and temporary perfection) or under Section 9—306 (perfection as to proceeds) if he acts without knowledge that the specific paper or instrument is subject to a security interest; or

(b) which is claimed merely as proceeds of inventory subject to a security interest (Section 9—306) even though he knows that the specific paper or instrument is subject to the security interest.

## § 9—309. Protection of Purchasers of Instruments, Documents and Securities.

Nothing in this Article limits the rights of a holder in due course of a negotiable instrument (Section 3—302) or a holder to whom a negotiable document of title has been duly negotiated (Section 7—501) or a bona fide purchaser of a security (Section 8—302) and the holders or purchasers take priority over an earlier security interest even though perfected. Filing under this Article does not constitute notice of the security interest to such holders or purchasers.

## § 9—310. Priority of Certain Liens Arising by Operation of Law.

When a person in the ordinary course of his business furnishes services or materials with respect to goods subject to a security interest, a lien upon goods in the possession of such person given by statute or rule of law for such materials or services takes priority over a perfected security interest unless the lien is statutory and the statute expressly provides otherwise.

## § 9—311. Alienability of Debtor's Rights: Judicial Process.

The debtor's rights in collateral may be voluntarily or involuntarily transferred (by way of sale, creation of a security interest, attachment, levy, garnishment or other judicial process) notwithstanding a provision in the security agreement prohibiting any transfer or making the transfer constitute a default.

## § 9—312. Priorities Among Conflicting Security Interests in the Same Collateral.

(1) The rules of priority stated in other sections of this Part and in the following sections shall govern when applicable: Section 4—208 with respect to the security interests of collecting banks in items being collected, accompanying documents and proceeds; Section 9—103 on security interests related to other jurisdictions; Section 9—114 on consignments.

(2) A perfected security interest in crops for new value given to enable the debtor to produce the crops during the production season and given not more than three months before the crops become growing crops by planting or otherwise takes priority over an earlier perfected security interest to the extent that such earlier interest secures obligations due more than six months before the crops become growing crops by planting or otherwise, even though the person giving new value had knowledge of the earlier security interest.

(3) A perfected purchase money security interest in inventory has priority over a conflicting security interest in the same inventory and also has priority in identifiable cash proceeds received on or before the delivery of the inventory to a buyer if

(a) the purchase money security interest is perfected at the time the debtor receives possession of the inventory; and

(b) the purchase money secured party gives notification in writing to the holder of the conflicting security interest if the holder had filed a financing statement covering the same types of inventory (i) before the date of the filing made by the purchase money secured party, or (ii) before the beginning of the 21 day period where the purchase money security interest is temporarily perfected without filing or possession (subsection (5) of Section 9—304); and

(c) the holder of the conflicting security interest receives the notification within five years before the debtor receives possession of the inventory; and

(d) the notification states that the person giving the notice has or expects to acquire a purchase money security interest in inventory of the debtor, describing such inventory by item or type.

(4) A purchase money security interest in collateral other than inventory has priority over a conflicting security interest in the same collateral or its proceeds if the purchase money security interest is perfected at the time the debtor receives possession of the collateral or within ten days thereafter.

(5) In all cases not governed by other rules stated in this section (including cases of purchase money security interests which do not qualify for the special priorities set forth in subsections (3) and (4) of this section), priority between conflicting security interests in the same collateral shall be determined according to the following rules:

(a) Conflicting security interests rank according to priority in time of filing or perfection. Priority dates from the time a filing is first made covering the collateral or the time the security interest is first perfected, whichever is earlier, provided that there is no period thereafter when there is neither filing nor perfection.

(b) So long as conflicting security interests are unperfected, the first to attach has priority.

(6) For the purposes of subsection (5) a date of filing or perfection as to collateral is also a date of filing or perfection as to proceeds.

(7) If future advances are made while a security interest is perfected by filing, the taking of possession, or under Section 8—321 on securities, the security interest has the same priority for the purposes of subsection (5) with respect to the future advances as it does with respect to the first advance. If a commitment is made before or while the security interest is so perfected, the security interest has the same priority with respect to advances made pursuant thereto. In other cases a perfected security interest has priority from the date the advance is made.

## § 9—313. Priority of Security Interests in Fixtures.

(1) In this section and in the provisions of Part 4 of this Article referring to fixture filing, unless the context otherwise requires

(a) goods are "fixtures" when they become so related to particular real estate that an interest in them arises under real estate law

(b) a "fixture filing" is the filing in the office where a mortgage on the real estate would be filed or recorded of a financing statement covering goods which are or are to become fixtures and conforming to the requirements of subsection (5) of Section 9—402

(c) a mortgage is a "construction mortgage" to the extent that it secures an obligation incurred for the construction of an improvement on land including the acquisition cost of the land, if the recorded writing so indicates.

(2) A security interest under this Article may be created in goods which are fixtures or may continue in goods which become fixtures, but no security interest exists under this Article in ordinary building materials incorporated into an improvement on land.

(3) This Article does not prevent creation of an encumbrance upon fixtures pursuant to real estate law.

(4) A perfected security interest in fixtures has priority over the conflicting interest of an encumbrancer or owner of the real estate where

(a) the security interest is a purchase money security interest, the interest of the encumbrancer or owner arises before the goods become fixtures, the security interest is perfected by a fixture filing before the goods become fixtures or within ten days thereafter, and the debtor has an interest of record in the real estate or is in possession of the real estate; or

(b) the security interest is perfected by a fixture filing before the interest of the encumbrancer or owner is of record, the security interest has priority over any conflicting interest of a predecessor in title of the encumbrancer or owner, and the debtor has an interest of record in the real estate or is in possession of the real estate; or

(c) the fixtures are readily removable factory or office machines or readily removable replacements of domestic appliances which are consumer goods, and before the goods become fixtures the security interest is perfected by any method permitted by this Article; or

(d) the conflicting interest is a lien on the real estate obtained by legal or equitable proceedings after the security interest was perfected by any method permitted by this Article.

(5) A security interest in fixtures, whether or not perfected, has priority over the conflicting interest of an encumbrancer or owner of the real estate where

(a) the encumbrancer or owner has consented in writing to the security interest or has disclaimed an interest in the goods as fixtures; or

(b) the debtor has a right to remove the goods as against the encumbrancer or owner. If the debtor's right terminates, the priority of the security interest continues for a reasonable time.

(6) Notwithstanding paragraph (a) of subsection (4) but otherwise subject to subsections (4) and (5), a security interest in fixtures is subordinate to a construction mortgage recorded before the goods become fixtures if the goods become fixtures before the completion of the construction. To the extent that it is given to refinance a construction mortgage, a mortgage has this priority to the same extent as the construction mortgage.

(7) In cases not within the preceding subsections, a security interest in fixtures is subordinate to the conflicting interest of an encumbrancer or owner of the related real estate who is not the debtor.

(8) When the secured party has priority over all owners and

encumbrancers of the real estate, he may, on default, subject to the provisions of Part 5, remove his collateral from the real estate but he must reimburse any encumbrancer or owner of the real estate who is not the debtor and who has not otherwise agreed for the cost of repair of any physical injury, but not for any diminution in value of the real estate caused by the absence of the goods removed or by any necessity of replacing them. A person entitled to reimbursement may refuse permission to remove until the secured party gives adequate security for the performance of this obligation.

### § 9—314. Accessions.

(1) A security interest in goods which attaches before they are installed in or affixed to other goods takes priority as to the goods installed or affixed (called in this section "accessions") over the claims of all persons to the whole except as stated in subsection (3) and subject to Section 9—315(1).

(2) A security interest which attaches to goods after they become part of a whole is valid against all persons subsequently acquiring interests in the whole except as stated in subsection (3) but is invalid against any person with an interest in the whole at the time the security interest attaches to the goods who has not in writing consented to the security interest or disclaimed an interest in the goods as part of the whole.

(3) The security interests described in subsections (1) and (2) do not take priority over

(a) a subsequent purchaser for value of any interest in the whole; or

(b) a creditor with a lien on the whole subsequently obtained by judicial proceedings; or

(c) a creditor with a prior perfected security interest in the whole to the extent that he makes subsequent advances

if the subsequent purchase is made, the lien by judicial proceedings obtained or the subsequent advance under the prior perfected security interest is made or contracted for without knowledge of the security interest and before it is perfected. A purchaser of the whole at a foreclosure sale other than the holder of a perfected security interest purchasing at his own foreclosure sale is a subsequent purchaser within this section.

(4) When under subsections (1) or (2) and (3) a secured party has an interest in accessions which has priority over the claims of all persons who have interests in the whole, he may on default subject to the provisions of Part 5 remove his collateral from the whole but he must reimburse any encumbrancer or owner of the whole who is not the debtor and who has not otherwise agreed for the cost of repair of any physical injury but not for any diminution in value of the whole caused by the absence of the goods removed or by any necessity for replacing them. A person entitled to reimbursement may refuse permission to remove until the secured party gives adequate security for the performance of this obligation.

### § 9—315. Priority When Goods Are Commingled or Processed.

(1) If a security interest in goods was perfected and subsequently the goods or a part thereof have become part of a product or mass, the security interest continues in the product or mass if

(a) the goods are so manufactured, processed, assembled or commingled that their identity is lost in the product or mass; or

(b) a financing statement covering the original goods also covers the product into which the goods have been manufactured, processed or assembled.

In a case to which paragraph (b) applies, no separate security interest in that part of the original goods which has been manufactured, processed or assembled into the product may be claimed under Section 9—314.

(2) When under subsection (1) more than one security interest attaches to the product or mass, they rank equally according to the ratio that the cost of the goods to which each interest originally attached bears to the cost of the total product or mass.

### § 9—316. Priority Subject to Subordination.

Nothing in this Article prevents subordination by agreement by any person entitled to priority.

### § 9—317. Secured Party Not Obligated on Contract of Debtor.

The mere existence of a security interest or authority given to the debtor to dispose of or use collateral does not impose contract or tort liability upon the secured party for the debtor's acts or omissions.

### § 9—318. Defenses Against Assignee; Modification of Contract After Notification of Assignment; Term Prohibiting Assignment Ineffective; Identification and Proof of Assignment.

(1) Unless an account debtor has made an enforceable agreement not to assert defenses or claims arising out of a sale as provided in Section 9—206 the rights of an assignee are subject to

(a) all the terms of the contract between the account debtor and assignor and any defense or claim arising therefrom; and

(b) any other defense or claim of the account debtor against the assignor which accrues before the account debtor receives notification of the assignment.

(2) So far as the right to payment or a part thereof under an assigned contract has not been fully earned by performance, and notwithstanding notification of the assignment, any modification of or substitution for the contract made in good faith and in accordance with reasonable commercial standards is effective against an assignee unless the account debtor has otherwise agreed but the assignee acquires corresponding rights under the modified or substituted contract. The assignment may provide that such modification or substitution is a breach by the assignor.

(3) The account debtor is authorized to pay the assignor until the account debtor receives notification that the amount due or to become due has been assigned and that payment is to

be made to the assignee. A notification which does not reasonably identify the rights assigned is ineffective. If requested by the account debtor, the assignee must seasonably furnish reasonable proof that the assignment has been made and unless he does so the account debtor may pay the assignor.

(4) A term in any contract between an account debtor and an assignor is ineffective if it prohibits assignment of an account or prohibits creation of a security interest in a general intangible for money due or to become due or requires the account debtor's consent to such assignment or security interest.

## Part 4  Filing

### § 9—401. Place of Filing; Erroneous Filing; Removal of Collateral.

*First Alternative Subsection (1)*

(1) The proper place to file in order to perfect a security interest is as follows:

    (a) when the collateral is timber to be cut or is minerals or the like (including oil and gas) or accounts subject to subsection (5) of Section 9—103, or when the financing statement is filed as a fixture filing (Section 9—313) and the collateral is goods which are or are to become fixtures, then in the office where a mortgage on the real estate would be filed or recorded;

    (b) in all other cases, in the office of the [Secretary of State].

*Second Alternative Subsection (1)*

(1) The proper place to file in order to perfect a security interest is as follows:

    (a) when the collateral is equipment used in farming operations, or farm products, or accounts or general intangibles arising from or relating to the sale of farm products by a farmer, or consumer goods, then in the office of the . . . . . . . . in the county of the debtor's residence or if the debtor is not a resident of this state then in the office of the . . . . . . . . in the county where the goods are kept, and in addition when the collateral is crops growing or to be grown in the office of the . . . . . . . . in the county where the land is located;

    (b) when the collateral is timber to be cut or is minerals or the like (including oil and gas) or accounts subject to subsection (5) of Section 9—103, or when the financing statement is filed as a fixture filing (Section 9—313) and the collateral is goods which are or are to become fixtures, then in the office where a mortgage on the real estate would be filed or recorded;

    (c) in all other cases, in the office of the [Secretary of State].

*Third Alternative Subsection (1)*

(1) The proper place to file in order to perfect a security interest is as follows:

    (a) when the collateral is equipment used in farming operations, or farm products, or accounts or general intan-

gibles arising from or relating to the sale of farm products by a farmer, or consumer goods, then in the office of the . . . . . . . . in the county of the debtor's residence or if the debtor is not a resident of this state then in the office of the . . . . . . . . in the county where the goods are kept, and in addition when the collateral is crops growing or to be grown in the office of the . . . . . . . . in the county where the land is located;

    (b) when the collateral is timber to be cut or is minerals or the like (including oil and gas) or accounts subject to subsection (5) of Section 9—103, or when the financing statement is filed as a fixture filing (Section 9—313) and the collateral is goods which are or are to become fixtures, then in the office where a mortgage on the real estate would be filed or recorded;

    (c) in all other cases, in the office of the [Secretary of State] and in addition, if the debtor has a place of business in only one county of this state, also in the office of . . . . . . . . of such county, or, if the debtor has no place of business in this state, but resides in the state, also in the office of . . . . . . . . of the county which he resides.

Note: *One of the three alternatives should be selected as subsection (1).*

(2) A filing which is made in good faith in an improper place or not in all of the places required by this section is nevertheless effective with regard to any collateral as to which the filing complied with the requirements of this Article and is also effective with regard to collateral covered by the financing statement against any person who has knowledge of the contents of such financing statement.

(3) A filing which is made in the proper place in this state continues effective even though the debtor's residence or place of business or the location of the collateral or its use, whichever controlled the original filing, is thereafter changed.

*Alternative Subsection (3)*

[(3) A filing which is made in the proper county continues effective for four months after a change to another county of the debtor's residence or place of business or the location of the collateral, whichever controlled the original filing. It becomes ineffective thereafter unless a copy of the financing statement signed by the secured party is filed in the new county within said period. The security interest may also be perfected in the new county after the expiration of the four-month period; in such case perfection dates from the time of perfection in the new county. A change in the use of the collateral does not impair the effectiveness of the original filing.]

(4) The rules stated in Section 9—103 determine whether filing is necessary in this state.

(5) Notwithstanding the preceding subsections, and subject to subsection (3) of Section 9—302, the proper place to file in order to perfect a security interest in collateral, including fixtures, of a transmitting utility is the office of the [Secretary of State]. This filing constitutes a fixture filing (Section 9—

313) as to the collateral described therein which is or is to become fixtures.

(6) For the purposes of this section, the residence of an organization is its place of business if it has one or its chief executive office if it has more than one place of business.

Note: *Subsection (6) should be used only if the state chooses the Second or Third Alternative Subsection (1).*

### § 9—402. Formal Requisites of Financing Statement; Amendments; Mortgage as Financing Statement.

(1) A financing statement is sufficient if it gives the names of the debtor and the secured party, is signed by the debtor, gives an address of the secured party from which information concerning the security interest may be obtained, gives a mailing address of the debtor and contains a statement indicating the types, or describing the items, of collateral. A financing statement may be filed before a security agreement is made or a security interest otherwise attaches. When the financing statement covers crops growing or to be grown, the statement must also contain a description of the real estate concerned. When the financing statement covers timber to be cut or covers minerals or the like (including oil and gas) or accounts subject to subsection (5) of Section 9—103, or when the financing statement is filed as a fixture filing (Section 9—313) and the collateral is goods which are or are to become fixtures, the statement must also comply with subsection (5). A copy of the security agreement is sufficient as a financing statement if it contains the above information and is signed by the debtor. A carbon, photographic or other reproduction of a security agreement or a financing statement is sufficient as a financing statement if the security agreement so provides or if the original has been filed in this state.

(2) A financing statement which otherwise complies with subsection (1) is sufficient when it is signed by the secured party instead of the debtor if it is filed to perfect a security interest in

(a) collateral already subject to a security interest in another jurisdiction when it is brought into this state, or when the debtor's location is changed to this state. Such a financing statement must state that the collateral was brought into this state or that the debtor's location was changed to this state under such circumstances; or

(b) proceeds under Section 9—306 if the security interest in the original collateral was perfected. Such a financing statement must describe the original collateral; or

(c) collateral as to which the filing has lapsed; or

(d) collateral acquired after a change of name, identity or corporate structure of the debtor (subsection (7)).

(3) A form substantially as follows is sufficient to comply with subsection (1):

Name of debtor (or assignor) .............................
Address ...............................................
Name of secured party (or assignee) .....................
Address ...............................................

1. This financing statement covers the following types (or items) of property:
(Describe) .............................................
2. (If collateral is crops) The above described crops are growing or are to be grown on:
(Describe Real Estate) .................................
3. (If applicable) The above goods are to become fixtures on *
*Where appropriate substitute either ''The above timber is standing on . . . .'' or ''The above minerals or the like (including oil and gas) or accounts will be financed at the wellhead or minehead of the well or mine located on . . . .''
(Describe Real Estate) .................................
and this financing statement is to be filed [for record] in the real estate records. (If the debtor does not have an interest of record) The name of a record owner is ......
4. (If products of collateral are claimed) Products of the collateral are also covered.

(use ............................................
whichever Signature of Debtor (or Assignor)

is ............................................
applicable) Signature of Secured Party
(or Assignee)

(4) A financing statement may be amended by filing a writing signed by both the debtor and the secured party. An amendment does not extend the period of effectiveness of a financing statement. If any amendment adds collateral, it is effective as to the added collateral only from the filing date of the amendment. In this Article, unless the context otherwise requires, the term ''financing statement'' means the original financing statement and any amendments.

(5) A financing statement covering timber to be cut or covering minerals or the like (including oil and gas) or accounts subject to subsection (5) of Section 9—103, or a financing statement filed as a fixture filing (Section 9—313) where the debtor is not a transmitting utility, must show that it covers this type of collateral, must recite that it is to be filed [for record] in the real estate records, and the financing statement must contain a description of the real estate [sufficient if it were contained in a mortgage of the real estate to give constructive notice of the mortgage under the law of this state]. If the debtor does not have an interest of record in the real estate, the financing statement must show the name of a record owner.

(6) A mortgage is effective as a financing statement filed as a fixture filing from the date of its recording if

(a) the goods are described in the mortgage by item or type; and

(b) the goods are or are to become fixtures related to the real estate described in the mortgage; and

(c) the mortgage complies with the requirements for a financing statement in this section other than a recital that it is to be filed in the real estate records; and

(d) the mortgage is duly recorded.

No fee with reference to the financing statement is required other than the regular recording and satisfaction fees with respect to the mortgage.

(7) A financing statement sufficiently shows the name of the debtor if it gives the individual, partnership or corporate name of the debtor, whether or not it adds other trade names or names of partners. Where the debtor so changes his name or in the case of an organization its name, identity or corporate structure that a filed financing statement becomes seriously misleading, the filing is not effective to perfect a security interest in collateral acquired by the debtor more than four months after the change, unless a new appropriate financing statement is filed before the expiration of that time. A filed financing statement remains effective with respect to collateral transferred by the debtor even though the secured party knows of or consents to the transfer.

(8) A financing statement substantially complying with the requirements of this section is effective even though it contains minor errors which are not seriously misleading.

Note: *Language in brackets is optional.*

Note: *Where the state has any special recording system for real estate other than the usual grantor-grantee index (as, for instance, a tract system or a title registration or Torrens system) local adaptations of subsection (5) and Section 9—403(7) may be necessary. See Mass.Gen.Laws Chapter 106, Section 9—409.*

### § 9—403. What Constitutes Filing; Duration of Filing; Effect of Lapsed Filing; Duties of Filing Officer.

(1) Presentation for filing of a financing statement and tender of the filing fee or acceptance of the statement by the filing officer constitutes filing under this Article.

(2) Except as provided in subsection (6) a filed financing statement is effective for a period of five years from the date of filing. The effectiveness of a filed financing statement lapses on the expiration of the five year period unless a continuation statement is filed prior to the lapse. If a security interest perfected by filing exists at the time insolvency proceedings are commenced by or against the debtor, the security interest remains perfected until termination of the insolvency proceedings and thereafter for a period of sixty days or until expiration of the five year period, whichever occurs later. Upon lapse the security interest becomes unperfected, unless it is perfected without filing. If the security interest becomes unperfected upon lapse, it is deemed to have been unperfected as against a person who became a purchaser or lien creditor before lapse.

(3) A continuation statement may be filed by the secured party within six months prior to the expiration of the five year period specified in subsection (2). Any such continuation statement must be signed by the secured party, identify the original statement by file number and state that the original statement is still effective. A continuation statement signed by a person other than the secured party of record must be accompanied by a separate written statement of assignment signed by the secured party of record and complying with

subsection (2) of Section 9—405, including payment of the required fee. Upon timely filing of the continuation statement, the effectiveness of the original statement is continued for five years after the last date to which the filing was effective whereupon it lapses in the same manner as provided in subsection (2) unless another continuation statement is filed prior to such lapse. Succeeding continuation statements may be filed in the same manner to continue the effectiveness of the original statement. Unless a statute on disposition of public records provides otherwise, the filing officer may remove a lapsed statement from the files and destroy it immediately if he has retained a microfilm or other photographic record, or in other cases after one year after the lapse. The filing officer shall so arrange matters by physical annexation of financing statements to continuation statements or other related filings, or by other means, that if he physically destroys the financing statements of a period more than five years past, those which have been continued by a continuation statement or which are still effective under subsection (6) shall be retained.

(4) Except as provided in subsection (7) a filing officer shall mark each statement with a file number and with the date and hour of filing and shall hold the statement or a microfilm or other photographic copy thereof for public inspection. In addition the filing officer shall index the statement according to the name of the debtor and shall note in the index the file number and the address of the debtor given in the statement.

(5) The uniform fee for filing and indexing and for stamping a copy furnished by the secured party to show the date and place of filing for an original financing statement or for a continuation statement shall be $. . . . . . . if the statement is in the standard form prescribed by the [Secretary of State] and otherwise shall be $. . . . . . ., plus in each case, if the financing statement is subject to subsection (5) of Section 9—402, $. . . . . . . The uniform fee for each name more than one required to be indexed shall be $. . . . . . . The secured party may at his option show a trade name for any person and an extra uniform indexing fee of $. . . . . . . shall be paid with respect thereto.

(6) If the debtor is a transmitting utility (subsection (5) of Section 9—401) and a filed financing statement so states, it is effective until a termination statement is filed. A real estate mortgage which is effective as a fixture filing under subsection (6) of Section 9—402 remains effective as a fixture filing until the mortgage is released or satisfied of record or its effectiveness otherwise terminates as to the real estate.

(7) When a financing statement covers timber to be cut or covers minerals or the like (including oil and gas) or accounts subject to subsection (5) of Section 9—103, or is filed as a fixture filing, [it shall be filed for record and] the filing officer shall index it under the names of the debtor and any owner of record shown on the financing statement in the same fashion as if they were the mortgagors in a mortgage of the real estate described, and, to the extent that the law of this state provides for indexing of mortgages under the name of the mortgagee, under the name of the secured party as if he were the mortgagee thereunder, or where indexing is by description

in the same fashion as if the financing statement were a mortgage of the real estate described.

Note: *In states in which writings will not appear in the real estate records and indices unless actually recorded the bracketed language in subsection (7) should be used.*

### § 9—404. Termination Statement.

(1) If a financing statement covering consumer goods is filed on or after . . . . . . . ., then within one month or within ten days following written demand by the debtor after there is no outstanding secured obligation and no commitment to make advances, incur obligations or otherwise give value, the secured party must file with each filing officer with whom the financing statement was filed, a termination statement to the effect that he no longer claims a security interest under the financing statement, which shall be identified by file number. In other cases whenever there is no outstanding secured obligation and no commitment to make advances, incur obligations or otherwise give value, the secured party must on written demand by the debtor send the debtor, for each filing officer with whom the financing statement was filed, a termination statement to the effect that he no longer claims a security interest under the financing statement, which shall be identified by file number. A termination statement signed by a person other than the secured party of record must be accompanied by a separate written statement of assignment signed by the secured party of record complying with subsection (2) of Section 9—405, including payment of the required fee. If the affected secured party fails to file such a termination statement as required by this subsection, or to send such a termination statement within ten days after proper demand therefor, he shall be liable to the debtor for one hundred dollars, and in addition for any loss caused to the debtor by such failure.

(2) On presentation to the filing officer of such a termination statement he must note it in the index. If he has received the termination statement in duplicate, he shall return one copy of the termination statement to the secured party stamped to show the time of receipt thereof. If the filing officer has a microfilm or other photographic record of the financing statement, and of any related continuation statement, statement of assignment and statement of release, he may remove the originals from the files at any time after receipt of the termination statement, or if he has no such record, he may remove them from the files at any time after one year after receipt of the termination statement.

(3) If the termination statement is in the standard form prescribed by the [Secretary of State], the uniform fee for filing and indexing the termination statement shall be $. . . . . . . ., and otherwise shall be $. . . . . . . ., plus in each case an additional fee of $. . . . . . . for each name more than one against which the termination statement is required to be indexed.

Note: *The date to be inserted should be the effective date of the revised Article 9.*

### § 9—405. Assignment of Security Interest; Duties of Filing Officer; Fees.

(1) A financing statement may disclose an assignment of a security interest in the collateral described in the financing statement by indication in the financing statement of the name and address of the assignee or by an assignment itself or a copy thereof on the face or back of the statement. On presentation to the filing officer of such a financing statement the filing officer shall mark the same as provided in Section 9—403(4). The uniform fee for filing, indexing and furnishing filing data for a financing statement so indicating an assignment shall be $. . . . . . . . if the statement is in the standard form prescribed by the [Secretary of State] and otherwise shall be $. . . . . . . ., plus in each case an additional fee of $. . . . . . . for each name more than one against which the financing statement is required to be indexed.

(2) A secured party may assign of record all or part of his rights under a financing statement by the filing in the place where the original financing statement was filed of a separate written statement of assignment signed by the secured party of record and setting forth the name of the secured party of record and the debtor, the file number and the date of filing of the financing statement and the name and address of the assignee and containing a description of the collateral assigned. A copy of the assignment is sufficient as a separate statement if it complies with the preceding sentence. On presentation to the filing officer of such a separate statement, the filing officer shall mark such separate statement with the date and hour of the filing. He shall note the assignment on the index of the financing statement, or in the case of a fixture filing, or a filing covering timber to be cut, or covering minerals or the like (including oil and gas) or accounts subject to subsection (5) of Section 9—103, he shall index the assignment under the name of the assignor as grantor and, to the extent that the law of this state provides for indexing the assignment of a mortgage under the name of the assignee, he shall index the assignment of the financing statement under the name of the assignee. The uniform fee for filing, indexing and furnishing filing data about such a separate statement of assignment shall be $. . . . . if the statement is in the standard form prescribed by the [Secretary of State] and otherwise shall be $. . . . ., plus in each case an additional fee of $. . . . . for each name more than one against which the statement of assignment is required to be indexed. Notwithstanding the provisions of this subsection, an assignment of record of a security interest in a fixture contained in a mortgage effective as a fixture filing (subsection (6) of Section 9—402) may be made only by an assignment of the mortgage in the manner provided by the law of this state other than this Act.

(3) After the disclosure or filing of an assignment under this section, the assignee is the secured party of record.

### § 9—406. Release of Collateral; Duties of Filing Officer; Fees.

A secured party of record may by his signed statement release all or a part of any collateral described in a filed financing statement. The statement of release is sufficient if it contains a description of the collateral being released, the name and address of the debtor, the name and address of the secured party, and the file number of the financing statement. A statement of release signed by a person other than the secured party of record must be accompanied by a separate written statement of assignment signed by the secured party of record and complying with subsection (2) of Section 9—405, including payment of the required fee. Upon presentation of such a statement of release to the filing officer he shall mark the statement with the hour and date of filing and shall note the same upon the margin of the index of the filing of the financing statement. The uniform fee for filing and noting such a statement of release shall be $. . . . . . if the statement is in the standard form prescribed by the [Secretary of State] and otherwise shall be $. . . . . ., plus in each case an additional fee of $. . . . . . for each name more than one against which the statement of release is required to be indexed.

### § 9—407. Information From Filing Officer.

[(1) If the person filing any financing statement, termination statement, statement of assignment, or statement of release, furnishes the filing officer a copy thereof, the filing officer shall upon request note upon the copy the file number and date and hour of the filing of the original and deliver or send the copy to such person.]

[(2) Upon request of any person, the filing officer shall issue his certificate showing whether there is on file on the date and hour stated therein, any presently effective financing statement naming a particular debtor and any statement of assignment thereof and if there is, giving the date and hour of filing of each such statement and the names and addresses of each secured party therein. The uniform fee for such a certificate shall be $. . . . . . if the request for the certificate is in the standard form prescribed by the [Secretary of State] and otherwise shall be $. . . . . . . Upon request the filing officer shall furnish a copy of any filed financing statement or statement of assignment for a uniform fee of $. . . . . . per page.]

Note: *This section is proposed as an optional provision to require filing officers to furnish certificates. Local law and practices should be consulted with regard to the advisability of adoption.*

### § 9—408. Financing Statements Covering Consigned or Leased Goods.

A consignor or lessor of goods may file a financing statement using the terms "consignor," "consignee," "lessor," "lessee" or the like instead of the terms specified in Section 9—402. The provisions of this Part shall apply as appropriate to such a financing statement but its filing shall not of itself be a factor in determining whether or not the consignment or lease is intended as security (Section 1—201(37)). However, if it is determined for other reasons that the consignment or lease is so intended, a security interest of the consignor or lessor which attaches to the consigned or leased goods is perfected by such filing.

## Part 5 Default

### § 9—501. Default; Procedure When Security Agreement Covers Both Real and Personal Property.

(1) When a debtor is in default under a security agreement, a secured party has the rights and remedies provided in this Part and except as limited by subsection (3) those provided in the security agreement. He may reduce his claim to judgment, foreclose or otherwise enforce the security interest by any available judicial procedure. If the collateral is documents the secured party may proceed either as to the documents or as to the goods covered thereby. A secured party in possession has the rights, remedies and duties provided in Section 9—207. The rights and remedies referred to in this subsection are cumulative.

(2) After default, the debtor has the rights and remedies provided in this Part, those provided in the security agreement and those provided in Section 9—207.

(3) To the extent that they give rights to the debtor and impose duties on the secured party, the rules stated in the subsections referred to below may not be waived or varied except as provided with respect to compulsory disposition of collateral (subsection (3) of Section 9—504 and Section 9—505) and with respect to redemption of collateral (Section 9—506) but the parties may by agreement determine the standards by which the fulfillment of these rights and duties is to be measured if such standards are not manifestly unreasonable:

(a) subsection (2) of Section 9—502 and subsection (2) of Section 9—504 insofar as they require accounting for surplus proceeds of collateral;

(b) subsection (3) of Section 9—504 and subsection (1) of Section 9—505 which deal with disposition of collateral;

(c) subsection (2) of Section 9—505 which deals with acceptance of collateral as discharge of obligation;

(d) Section 9—506 which deals with redemption of collateral; and

(e) subsection (1) of Section 9—507 which deals with the secured party's liability for failure to comply with this Part.

(4) If the security agreement covers both real and personal property, the secured party may proceed under this Part as to the personal property or he may proceed as to both the real and the personal property in accordance with his rights and remedies in respect of the real property in which case the provisions of this Part do not apply.

(5) When a secured party has reduced his claim to judgment the lien of any levy which may be made upon his collateral by virtue of any execution based upon the judgment shall relate back to the date of the perfection of the security interest in such collateral. A judicial sale, pursuant to such execution, is a foreclosure of the security interest by judicial procedure within the meaning of this section, and the secured party may purchase at the sale and thereafter hold the collateral free of any other requirements of this Article.

## § 9—502. Collection Rights of Secured Party.

(1) When so agreed and in any event on default the secured party is entitled to notify an account debtor or the obligor on an instrument to make payment to him whether or not the assignor was theretofore making collections on the collateral, and also to take control of any proceeds to which he is entitled under Section 9—306.

(2) A secured party who by agreement is entitled to charge back uncollected collateral or otherwise to full or limited recourse against the debtor and who undertakes to collect from the account debtors or obligors must proceed in a commercially reasonable manner and may deduct his reasonable expenses of realization from the collections. If the security agreement secures an indebtedness, the secured party must account to the debtor for any surplus, and unless otherwise agreed, the debtor is liable for any deficiency. But, if the underlying transaction was a sale of accounts or chattel paper, the debtor is entitled to any surplus or is liable for any deficiency only if the security agreement so provides.

## § 9—503. Secured Party's Right to Take Possession After Default.

Unless otherwise agreed a secured party has on default the right to take possession of the collateral. In taking possession a secured party may proceed without judicial process if this can be done without breach of the peace or may proceed by action. If the security agreement so provides the secured party may require the debtor to assemble the collateral and make it available to the secured party at a place to be designated by the secured party which is reasonably convenient to both parties. Without removal a secured party may render equipment unusable, and may dispose of collateral on the debtor's premises under Section 9—504.

## § 9—504. Secured Party's Right to Dispose of Collateral After Default; Effect of Disposition.

(1) A secured party after default may sell, lease or otherwise dispose of any or all of the collateral in its then condition or following any commercially reasonable preparation or processing. Any sale of goods is subject to the Article on Sales (Article 2). The proceeds of disposition shall be applied in the order following to

(a) the reasonable expenses of retaking, holding, preparing for sale or lease, selling, leasing and the like and, to the extent provided for in the agreement and not prohibited by law, the reasonable attorneys' fees and legal expenses incurred by the secured party;

(b) the satisfaction of indebtedness secured by the security interest under which the disposition is made;

(c) the satisfaction of indebtedness secured by any subordinate security interest in the collateral if written notification of demand therefor is received before distribution of the proceeds is completed. If requested by the secured party, the holder of a subordinate security interest must seasonably furnish reasonable proof of his interest, and unless he does so, the secured party need not comply with his demand.

(2) If the security interest secures an indebtedness, the secured party must account to the debtor for any surplus, and, unless otherwise agreed, the debtor is liable for any deficiency. But if the underlying transaction was a sale of accounts or chattel paper, the debtor is entitled to any surplus or is liable for any deficiency only if the security agreement so provides.

(3) Disposition of the collateral may be by public or private proceedings and may be made by way of one or more contracts. Sale or other disposition may be as a unit or in parcels and at any time and place and on any terms but every aspect of the disposition including the method, manner, time, place and terms must be commercially reasonable. Unless collateral is perishable or threatens to decline speedily in value or is of a type customarily sold on a recognized market, reasonable notification of the time and place of any public sale or reasonable notification of the time after which any private sale or other intended disposition is to be made shall be sent by the secured party to the debtor, if he has not signed after default a statement renouncing or modifying his right to notification of sale. In the case of consumer goods no other notification need be sent. In other cases notification shall be sent to any other secured party from whom the secured party has received (before sending his notification to the debtor or before the debtor's renunciation of his rights) written notice of a claim of an interest in the collateral. The secured party may buy at any public sale and if the collateral is of a type customarily sold in a recognized market or is of a type which is the subject of widely distributed standard price quotations he may buy at private sale.

(4) When collateral is disposed of by a secured party after default, the disposition transfers to a purchaser for value all of the debtor's rights therein, discharges the security interest under which it is made and any security interest or lien subordinate thereto. The purchaser takes free of all such rights and interests even though the secured party fails to comply with the requirements of this Part or of any judicial proceedings

(a) in the case of a public sale, if the purchaser has no knowledge of any defects in the sale and if he does not buy in collusion with the secured party, other bidders or the person conducting the sale; or

(b) in any other case, if the purchaser acts in good faith.

(5) A person who is liable to a secured party under a guaranty, indorsement, repurchase agreement or the like and who receives a transfer of collateral from the secured party or is subrogated to his rights has thereafter the rights and duties of the secured party. Such a transfer of collateral is not a sale or disposition of the collateral under this Article.

## § 9—505. Compulsory Disposition of Collateral; Acceptance of the Collateral as Discharge of Obligation.

(1) If the debtor has paid sixty per cent of the cash price in the case of a purchase money security interest in consumer goods or sixty per cent of the loan in the case of another

security interest in consumer goods, and has not signed after default a statement renouncing or modifying his rights under this Part a secured party who has taken possession of collateral must dispose of it under Section 9—504 and if he fails to do so within ninety days after he takes possession the debtor at his option may recover in conversion or under Section 9—507(1) on secured party's liability.

(2) In any other case involving consumer goods or any other collateral a secured party in possession may, after default, propose to retain the collateral in satisfaction of the obligation. Written notice of such proposal shall be sent to the debtor if he has not signed after default a statement renouncing or modifying his rights under this subsection. In the case of consumer goods no other notice need be given. In other cases notice shall be sent to any other secured party from whom the secured party has received (before sending his notice to the debtor or before the debtor's renunciation of his rights) written notice of a claim of an interest in the collateral. If the secured party receives objection in writing from a person entitled to receive notification within twenty-one days after the notice was sent, the secured party must dispose of the collateral under Section 9—504. In the absence of such written objection the secured party may retain the collateral in satisfaction of the debtor's obligation. Amended in 1972.

### § 9—506. Debtor's Right to Redeem Collateral.

At any time before the secured party has disposed of collateral or entered into a contract for its disposition under Section 9—504 or before the obligation has been discharged under Section 9—505(2) the debtor or any other secured party may unless otherwise agreed in writing after default redeem the collateral by tendering fulfillment of all obligations secured by the collateral as well as the expenses reasonably incurred by the secured party in retaking, holding and preparing the collateral for disposition, in arranging for the sale, and to the extent provided in the agreement and not prohibited by law, his reasonable attorneys' fees and legal expenses.

### § 9—507. Secured Party's Liability for Failure to Comply With This Part.

(1) If it is established that the secured party is not proceeding in accordance with the provisions of this Part disposition may be ordered or restrained on appropriate terms and conditions. If the disposition has occurred the debtor or any person entitled to notification or whose security interest has been made known to the secured party prior to the disposition has a right to recover from the secured party any loss caused by a failure to comply with the provisions of this Part. If the collateral is consumer goods, the debtor has a right to recover in any event an amount not less than the credit service charge plus ten per cent of the principal amount of the debt or the time price differential plus 10 per cent of the cash price.

(2) The fact that a better price could have been obtained by a sale at a different time or in a different method from that selected by the secured party is not of itself sufficient to establish that the sale was not made in a commercially reasonable manner. If the secured party either sells the collateral in the usual manner in any recognized market therefor or if he sells at the price current in such market at the time of his sale or if he has otherwise sold in conformity with reasonable commercial practices among dealers in the type of property sold he has sold in a commercially reasonable manner. The principles stated in the two preceding sentences with respect to sales also apply as may be appropriate to other types of disposition. A disposition which has been approved in any judicial proceeding or by any bona fide creditors' committee or representative of creditors shall conclusively be deemed to be commercially reasonable, but this sentence does not indicate that any such approval must be obtained in any case nor does it indicate that any disposition not so approved is not commercially reasonable.

## Article 10
# EFFECTIVE DATE AND REPEALER

### § 10—101. Effective Date.

This Act shall become effective at midnight on December 31st following its enactment. It applies to transactions entered into and events occurring after that date.

### § 10—102. Specific Repealer; Provision for Transition.

(1) The following acts and all other acts and parts of acts inconsistent herewith are hereby repealed:
(Here should follow the acts to be specifically repealed including the following:

> Uniform Negotiable Instruments Act
> Uniform Warehouse Receipts Act
> Uniform Sales Act
> Uniform Bills of Lading Act
> Uniform Stock Transfer Act
> Uniform Conditional Sales Act
> Uniform Trust Receipts Act
>> Also any acts regulating:
> Bank collections
> Bulk sales
> Chattel mortgages
> Conditional sales
> Factor's lien acts
> Farm storage of grain and similar acts
> Assignment of accounts receivable)

(2) Transactions validly entered into before the effective date specified in Section 10—101 and the rights, duties and interests flowing from them remain valid thereafter and may be terminated, completed, consummated or enforced as required or permitted by any statute or other law amended or repealed by this Act as though such repeal or amendment had not occurred.

Note: *Subsection (1) should be separately prepared for each state. The foregoing is a list of statutes to be checked.*

### § 10—103. General Repealer.

Except as provided in the following section, all acts and parts of acts inconsistent with this Act are hereby repealed.

## § 10—104. Laws Not Repealed.

(1) The Article on Documents of Title (Article 7) does not repeal or modify any laws prescribing the form or contents of documents of title or the services or facilities to be afforded by bailees, or otherwise regulating bailees' businesses in respects not specifically dealt with herein; but the fact that such laws are violated does not affect the status of a document of title which otherwise complies with the definition of a document of title (Section 1—201).

[(2) This Act does not repeal ...........*, cited as the Uniform Act for the Simplification of Fiduciary Security Transfers, and if in any respect there is any inconsistency between that Act and the Article of this Act on investment securities (Article 8) the provisions of the former Act shall control.]

Note: *At * in subsection (2) insert the statutory reference to the Uniform Act for the Simplification of Fiduciary Security Transfers if such Act has previously been enacted. If it has not been enacted, omit subsection (2).*

# Article 11
# (REPORTERS' DRAFT) EFFECTIVE DATE AND TRANSITION PROVISIONS

This material has been numbered Article 11 to distinguish it from Article 10, the transition provision of the 1962 Code, which may still remain in effect in some states to cover transition problems from pre-Code law to the original Uniform Commercial Code. Adaptation may be necessary in particular states. The terms ''[old Code]'' and ''[new Code]'' and ''[old U.C.C.]'' and ''[new U.C.C.]'' are used herein, and should be suitably changed in each state.

Note: *This draft was prepared by the Reporters and has not been passed upon by the Review Committee, the Permanent Editorial Board, the American Law Institute, or the National Conference of Commissioners on Uniform State Laws. It is submitted as a working draft which may be adapted as appropriate in each state.*

## § 11—101. Effective Date.

This Act shall become effective at 12:01 A.M. on ————, 19 ——— .

## § 11—102. Preservation of Old Transition Provision.

The provisions of [here insert reference to the original transition provision in the particular state] shall continue to apply to [the new U.C.C.] and for this purpose the [old U.C.C. and new U.C.C.] shall be considered one continuous statute.

## § 11—103. Transition to [New Code]—General Rule.

Transactions validly entered into after [effective date of old U.C.C.] and before [effective date of new U.C.C.], and which were subject to the provisions of [old U.C.C.] and which would be subject to this Act as amended if they had been entered into after the effective date of [new U.C.C.] and the rights, duties and interests flowing from such transactions remain valid after the latter date and may be terminated, completed, consummated or enforced as required or permitted by the [new U.C.C.]. Security interests arising out of such transactions which are perfected when [new U.C.C.] becomes effective shall remain perfected until they lapse as provided in [new U.C.C.], and may be continued as permitted by [new U.C.C.], except as stated in Section 11—105.

## § 11—104. Transition Provision on Change of Requirement of Filing.

A security interest for the perfection of which filing or the taking of possession was required under [old U.C.C.] and which attached prior to the effective date of [new U.C.C.] but was not perfected shall be deemed perfected on the effective date of [new U.C.C.] if [new U.C.C.] permits perfection without filing or authorizes filing in the office or offices where a prior ineffective filing was made.

## § 11—105. Transition Provision on Change of Place of Filing.

(1) A financing statement or continuation statement filed prior to [effective date of new U.C.C.] which shall not have lapsed prior to [the effective date of new U.C.C.] shall remain effective for the period provided in the [old Code], but not less than five years after the filing.

(2) With respect to any collateral acquired by the debtor subsequent to the effective date of [new U.C.C.], any effective financing statement or continuation statement described in this section shall apply only if the filing or filings are in the office or offices that would be appropriate to perfect the security interests in the new collateral under [new U.C.C.].

(3) The effectiveness of any financing statement or continuation statement filed prior to [effective date of new U.C.C.] may be continued by a continuation statement as permitted by [new U.C.C.], except that if [new U.C.C.] requires a filing in an office where there was no previous financing statement, a new financing statement conforming to Section 11—106 shall be filed in that office.

(4) If the record of a mortgage of real estate would have been effective as a fixture filing of goods described therein if [new U.C.C.] had been in effect on the date of recording the mortgage, the mortgage shall be deemed effective as a fixture filing as to such goods under subsection (6) of Section 9—402 of the [new U.C.C.] on the effective date of [new U.C.C.].

## § 11—106. Required Refilings.

(1) If a security interest is perfected or has priority when this Act takes effect as to all persons or as to certain persons without any filing or recording, and if the filing of a financing statement would be required for the perfection or priority of the security interest against those persons under [new U.C.C.], the perfection and priority rights of the security interest continue until 3 years after the effective date of [new U.C.C.]. The perfection will then lapse unless a financing statement is filed as provided in subsection (4) or unless the security interest is perfected otherwise than by filing.

(2) If a security interest is perfected when [new U.C.C.] takes effect under a law other than [U.C.C.] which requires no further filing, refiling or recording to continue its perfection, perfection continues until and will lapse 3 years after [new U.C.C.] takes effect, unless a financing statement is filed as provided in subsection (4) or unless the security interest is perfected otherwise than by filing, or unless under subsection (3) of Section 9—302 the other law continues to govern filing.

(3) If a security interest is perfected by a filing, refiling or recording under a law repealed by this Act which required further filing, refiling or recording to continue its perfection, perfection continues and will lapse on the date provided by the law so repealed for such further filing, refiling or recording unless a financing statement is filed as provided in subsection (4) or unless the security interest is perfected otherwise than by filing.

(4) A financing statement may be filed within six months before the perfection of a security interest would otherwise lapse. Any such financing statement may be signed by either the debtor or the secured party. It must identify the security agreement, statement or notice (however denominated in any statute or other law repealed or modified by this Act), state the office where and the date when the last filing, refiling or recording, if any, was made with respect thereto, and the filing number, if any, or book and page, if any, of recording and further state that the security agreement, statement or notice, however denominated, in another filing office under the [U.C.C.] or under any statute or other law repealed or modified by this Act is still effective. Section 9—401 and Section 9—103 determine the proper place to file such a financing statement. Except as specified in this subsection, the provisions of Section 9—403(3) for continuation statements apply to such a financing statement.

§ 11—107. **Transition Provisions as to Priorities.**

Except as otherwise provided in [Article 11], [old U.C.C.] shall apply to any questions of priority if the positions of the parties were fixed prior to the effective date of [new U.C.C.]. In other cases questions of priority shall be determined by [new U.C.C.].

§ 11—108. **Presumption that Rule of Law Continues Unchanged.**

Unless a change in law has clearly been made, the provisions of [new U.C.C.] shall be deemed declaratory of the meaning of the [old U.C.C.].

# OFFICIAL TEXT—UCC—1994

The preceding articles and sections constitute the official text of the Uniform Commercial Code as of 1994.

# APPENDIX D

# UNITED NATIONS CONVENTION ON CONTRACTS FOR THE INTERNATIONAL SALE OF GOODS (EXCERPTS)

## Part I.  SPHERE OF APPLICATION AND GENERAL PROVISIONS

\* \* \* \*

### Chapter II—General Provisions

\* \* \* \*

#### Article 8

(1) For the purposes of this Convention statements made by and other conduct of a party are to be interpreted according to his intent where the other party knew or could not have been unaware what that intent was.

(2) If the preceding paragraph is not applicable, statements made by and other conduct of a party are to be interpreted according to the understanding that a reasonable person of the same kind as the other party would have had in the same circumstances.

(3) In determining the intent of a party or the understanding a reasonable person would have had, due consideration is to be given to all relevant circumstances of the case including the negotiations, any practices which the parties have established between themselves, usages and any subsequent conduct of the parties.

#### Article 9

(1) The parties are bound by any usage to which they have agreed and by any practices which they have established between themselves.

(2) The parties are considered, unless otherwise agreed, to have impliedly made applicable to their contract or its formation a usage of which the parties knew or ought to have

known and which in international trade is widely known to, and regularly observed by, parties to contracts of the type involved in the particular trade concerned.

\* \* \* \*

#### Article 11

A contract of sale need not be concluded in or evidenced by writing and is not subject to any other requirement as to form. It may be proved by any means, including witnesses.

\* \* \* \*

## Part II.  FORMATION OF THE CONTRACT

#### Article 14

(1) A proposal for concluding a contract addressed to one or more specific persons constitutes an offer if it is sufficiently definite and indicates the intention of the offeror to be bound in case of acceptance. A proposal is sufficiently definite if it indicates the goods and expressly or implicitly fixes or makes provision for determining the quantity and the price.

(2) A proposal other than one addressed to one or more specific persons is to be considered merely as an invitation to make offers, unless the contrary is clearly indicated by the person making the proposal.

#### Article 15

(1) An offer becomes effective when it reaches the offeree.

(2) An offer, even if it is irrevocable, may be withdrawn if the withdrawal reaches the offeree before or at the same time as the offer.

### Article 16

(1) Until a contract is concluded an offer may be revoked if the revocation reaches the offeree before he has dispatched an acceptance.

(2) However, an offer cannot be revoked:

(a) If it indicates, whether by stating a fixed time for acceptance or otherwise, that it is irrevocable; or

(b) If it was reasonable for the offeree to rely on the offer as being irrevocable and the offeree has acted in reliance on the offer.

### Article 17

An offer, even if it is irrevocable, is terminated when a rejection reaches the offeror.

### Article 18

(1) A statement made by or other conduct of the offeree indicating assent to an offer is an acceptance. Silence or inactivity does not in itself amount to acceptance.

(2) An acceptance of an offer becomes effective at the moment the indication of assent reaches the offeror. An acceptance is not effective if the indication of assent does not reach the offeror within the time he has fixed or, if no time is fixed, within a reasonable time, due account being taken of the circumstances of the transaction, including the rapidity of the means of communication employed by the offeror. An oral offer must be accepted immediately unless the circumstances indicate otherwise.

(3) However, if, by virtue of the offer or as a result of practices which the parties have established between themselves or of usage, the offeree may indicate assent by performing an act, such as one relating to the dispatch of the goods or payment of the price, without notice to the offeror, the acceptance is effective at the moment the act is performed, provided that the act is performed within the period of time laid down in the preceding paragraph.

### Article 19

(1) A reply to an offer which purports to be an acceptance but contains additions, limitations or other modifications is a rejection of the offer and constitutes a counter-offer.

(2) However, a reply to an offer which purports to be an acceptance but contains additional or different terms which do not materially alter the terms of the offer constitutes an acceptance, unless the offeror, without undue delay, objects orally to the discrepancy or dispatches a notice to that effect. If he does not so object, the terms of the contract are the terms of the offer with the modifications contained in the acceptance.

(3) Additional or different terms relating, among other things, to the price, payment, quality and quantity of the goods, place and time of delivery, extent of one party's liability to the other or the settlement of disputes are considered to alter the terms of the offer materially.

\*    \*    \*    \*

### Article 22

An acceptance may be withdrawn if the withdrawal reaches the offeror before or at the same time as the acceptance would have become effective.

\*    \*    \*    \*

## Part III.    SALE OF GOODS

## Chapter I—General Provisions

### Article 25

A breach of contract committed by one of the parties is fundamental if it results in such detriment to the other party as substantially to deprive him of what he is entitled to expect under the contract, unless the party in breach did not foresee and a reasonable person of the same kind in the same circumstances would not have foreseen such a result.

\*    \*    \*    \*

### Article 28

If, in accordance with the provisions of this Convention, one party is entitled to require performance of any obligation by the other party, a court is not bound to enter a judgment for specific performance unless the court would do so under its own law in respect of similar contracts of sale not governed by this Convention.

### Article 29

(1) A contract may be modified or terminated by the mere agreement of the parties.

(2) A contract in writing which contains a provision requiring any modification or termination by agreement to be in writing may not be otherwise modified or terminated by agreement. However, a party may be precluded by his conduct from asserting such a provision to the extent that the other party has relied on that conduct.

## Chapter II—Obligations of the Seller
\*    \*    \*    \*

**Section II.   Conformity of the Goods and Third Party Claims**

### Article 35

(1) The seller must deliver goods which are of the quantity, quality and description required by the contract and which are contained or packaged in the manner required by the contract.

(2) Except where the parties have agreed otherwise, the goods do not conform with the contract unless they:

(a) Are fit for the purposes for which goods of the same description would ordinarily be used;

(b) Are fit for any particular purpose expressly or impliedly made known to the seller at the time of the conclusion of the contract, except where the circumstances show that the buyer did not rely, or that it was unreasonable for him to rely, on the seller's skill and judgment;

(c) Possess the qualities of goods which the seller has held out to the buyer as a sample or model;

(d) Are contained or packaged in the manner usual for such goods or, where there is no such manner, in a manner adequate to preserve and protect the goods.

(3) The seller is not liable under subparagraphs (a) to (d) of the preceding paragraph for any lack of conformity of the goods if at the time of the conclusion of the contract the buyer knew or could not have been unaware of such lack of conformity.

\* \* \* \*

### Article 64

(1) The seller may declare the contract avoided:

(a) If the failure by the buyer to perform any of his obligations under the contract or this Convention amounts to a fundamental breach of contract; or

(b) If the buyer does not, within the additional period of time fixed by the seller in accordance with paragraph (1) of article 63, perform his obligation to pay the price or take delivery of the goods, or if he declares that he will not do so within the period so fixed.

(2) However, in cases where the buyer has paid the price, the seller loses the right to declare the contract avoided unless he does so:

(a) In respect of late performance by the buyer, before the seller has become aware that performance has been rendered; or

(b) In respect of any breach other than late performance by the buyer, within a reasonable time:

(i) After the seller knew or ought to have known of the breach; or

(ii) After the expiration of any additional period of time fixed by the seller in accordance with paragraph (1) of article 63, or after the buyer has declared that he will not perform his obligations within such an additional period.

\* \* \* \*

## Chapter IV—Passing of Risk
\* \* \* \*

### Article 67

(1) If the contract of sale involves carriage of the goods and the seller is not bound to hand them over at a particular place, the risk passes to the buyer when the goods are handed over to the first carrier for transmission to the buyer in accordance with the contract of sale. If the seller is bound to hand the goods over to a carrier at a particular place, the risk does not pass to the buyer until the goods are handed over to the carrier at that place. The fact that the seller is authorized to retain documents controlling the disposition of the goods does not affect the passage of the risk.

(2) Nevertheless, the risk does not pass to the buyer until the goods are clearly identified to the contract, whether by markings on the goods, by shipping documents, by notice given to the buyer or otherwise.

\* \* \* \*

## Chapter V—Provisions Common to the Obligations of the Seller and of the Buyer

### Section I. Anticipatory Breach and Instalment Contracts

### Article 71

(1) A party may suspend the performance of his obligations if, after the conclusion of the contract, it becomes apparent that the other party will not perform a substantial part of his obligations as a result of:

(a) A serious deficiency in his ability to perform or in his creditworthiness; or

(b) His conduct in preparing to perform or in performing the contract.

(2) If the seller has already dispatched the goods before the grounds described in the preceding paragraph become evident, he may prevent the handing over of the goods to the buyer even though the buyer holds a document which entitles him to obtain them. The present paragraph relates only to the rights in the goods as between the buyer and the seller.

(3) A party suspending performance, whether before or after dispatch of the goods, must immediately give notice of the suspension to the other party and must continue with performance if the other party provides adequate assurance of his performance.

### Article 72

(1) If prior to the date for performance of the contract it is clear that one of the parties will commit a fundamental breach of contract, the other party may declare the contract avoided.

(2) If time allows, the party intending to declare the contract avoided must give reasonable notice to the other party in order to permit him to provide adequate assurance of his performance.

(3) The requirements of the preceding paragraph do not apply if the other party has declared that he will not perform his obligations.

### Article 73

(1) In the case of a contract for delivery of goods by instalments, if the failure of one party to perform any of his obligations in respect of any instalment constitutes a fundamental breach of contract with respect to that instalment, the other party may declare the contract avoided with respect to that instalment.

(2) If one party's failure to perform any of his obligations in respect of any instalment gives the other party good grounds to conclude that a fundamental breach of contract will occur with respect to future instalments, he may declare the contract avoided for the future, provided that he does so within a reasonable time.

(3) A buyer who declares the contract avoided in respect of any delivery may, at the same time, declare it avoided in respect of deliveries already made or of future deliveries if, by reason of their interdependence, those deliveries could not be used for the purpose contemplated by the parties at the time of the conclusion of the contract.

## Section II. Damages

### Article 74

Damages for breach of contract by one party consist of a sum equal to the loss, including loss of profit, suffered by the other party as a consequence of the breach. Such damages may not exceed the loss which the party in breach foresaw or ought to have foreseen at the time of the conclusion of the contract, in the light of the facts and matters of which he then knew or ought to have known, as a possible consequence of the breach of contract.

### Article 75

If the contract is avoided and if, in a reasonable manner and within a reasonable time after avoidance, the buyer has bought goods in replacement or the seller has resold the goods, the party claiming damages may recover the difference between the contract price and the price in the substitute transaction as well as any further damages recoverable under article 74.

### Article 76

(1) If the contract is avoided and there is a current price for the goods, the party claiming damages may, if he has not made a purchase or resale under article 75, recover the difference between the price fixed by the contract and the current price at the time of avoidance as well as any further damages recoverable under article 74. If, however, the party claiming damages has avoided the contract after taking over the goods, the current price at the time of such taking over shall be applied instead of the current price at the time of avoidance.

(2) For the purposes of the preceding paragraph, the current price is the price prevailing at the place where delivery of the goods should have been made or, if there is no current price at that place, the price at such other place as serves as a reasonable substitute, making due allowance for differences in the cost of transporting the goods.

### Article 77

A party who relies on a breach of contract must take such measures as are reasonable in the circumstances to mitigate the loss, including loss of profit, resulting from the breach. If he fails to take such measures, the party in breach may claim a reduction in the damages in the amount by which the loss should have been mitigated.

# APPENDIX E

# THE UNIFORM PARTNERSHIP ACT

(Adopted in forty-nine states [all of the states except Louisiana], the District of Columbia, the Virgin Islands, and Guam. The adoptions by Alabama and Nebraska do not follow the official text in every respect, but are substantially similar, with local variations.)

The Act consists of 7 Parts as follows:

    I. Preliminary Provisions

    II. Nature of Partnership

    III. Relations of Partners to Persons Dealing with the Partnership

    IV. Relations of Partners to One Another

    V. Property Rights of a Partner

    VI. Dissolution and Winding Up

    VII. Miscellaneous Provisions

An Act to make uniform the Law of Partnerships

Be it enacted, etc.:

## Part I    Preliminary Provisions

### Sec. 1.  Name of Act

This act may be cited as Uniform Partnership Act.

### Sec. 2.  Definition of Terms

In this act, "Court" includes every court and judge having jurisdiction in the case.

"Business" includes every trade, occupation, or profession.

"Person" includes individuals, partnerships, corporations, and other associations.

"Bankrupt" includes bankrupt under the Federal Bankruptcy Act or insolvent under any state insolvent act.

"Conveyance" includes every assignment, lease, mortgage, or encumbrance.

"Real property" includes land and any interest or estate in land.

### Sec. 3.  Interpretation of Knowledge and Notice

(1)  A person has "knowledge" of a fact within the meaning of this act not only when he has actual knowledge thereof, but also when he has knowledge of such other facts as in the circumstances shows bad faith.

(2)  A person has "notice" of a fact within the meaning of this act when the person who claims the benefit of the notice:

    (a)  States the fact to such person, or

    (b)  Delivers through the mail, or by other means of communication, a written statement of the fact to such person or to a proper person at his place of business or residence.

### Sec. 4.  Rules of Construction

(1)  The rule that statutes in derogation of the common law are to be strictly construed shall have no application to this act.

(2)  The law of estoppel shall apply under this act.

(3)  The law of agency shall apply under this act.

(4)  This act shall be so interpreted and construed as to effect its general purpose to make uniform the law of those states which enact it.

(5)  This act shall not be construed so as to impair the obligations of any contract existing when the act goes into effect, nor to affect any action or proceedings begun or right accrued before this act takes effect.

### Sec. 5.  Rules for Cases Not Provided for in This Act.

In any case not provided for in this act the rules of law and equity, including the law merchant, shall govern.

## Part II    Nature of Partnership

### Sec. 6.  Partnership Defined

(1)  A partnership is an association of two or more persons to carry on as co-owners a business for profit.

(2)  But any association formed under any other statute of this state, or any statute adopted by authority, other than the authority of this state, is not a partnership under this act, unless such association would have been a partnership in this state prior to the adoption of this act; but this act shall apply to limited partnerships except in so far as the statutes relating to such partnerships are inconsistent herewith.

### Sec. 7.  Rules for Determining the Existence of a Partnership

In determining whether a partnership exists, these rules shall apply:

(1) Except as provided by Section 16 persons who are not partners as to each other are not partners as to third persons.

(2) Joint tenancy, tenancy in common, tenancy by the entireties, joint property, common property, or part ownership does not of itself establish a partnership, whether such co-owners do or do not share any profits made by the use of the property.

(3) The sharing of gross returns does not of itself establish a partnership, whether or not the persons sharing them have a joint or common right or interest in any property from which the returns are derived.

(4) The receipt by a person of a share of the profits of a business is prima facie evidence that he is a partner in the business, but no such inference shall be drawn if such profits were received in payment:

> (a) As a debt by installments or otherwise,
>
> (b) As wages of an employee or rent to a landlord,
>
> (c) As an annuity to a widow or representative of a deceased partner,
>
> (d) As interest on a loan, though the amount of payment vary with the profits of the business,
>
> (e) As the consideration for the sale of a good-will of a business or other property by installments or otherwise.

### Sec. 8. Partnership Property

(1) All property originally brought into the partnership stock or subsequently acquired by purchase or otherwise, on account of the partnership, is partnership property.

(2) Unless the contrary intention appears, property acquired with partnership funds is partnership property.

(3) Any estate in real property may be acquired in the partnership name. Title so acquired can be conveyed only in the partnership name.

(4) A conveyance to a partnership in the partnership name, though without words of inheritance, passes the entire estate of the grantor unless a contrary intent appears.

## Part III   Relations of Partners to Persons Dealing with the Partnership

### Sec. 9. Partner Agent of Partnership as to Partnership Business

(1) Every partner is an agent of the partnership for the purpose of its business, and the act of every partner, including the execution in the partnership name of any instrument, for apparently carrying on in the usual way the business of the partnership of which he is a member binds the partnership, unless the partner so acting has in fact no authority to act for the partnership in the particular matter, and the person with whom he is dealing has knowledge of the fact that he has no such authority.

(2) An act of a partner which is not apparently for the carrying on of the business of the partnership in the usual way does not bind the partnership unless authorized by the other partners.

(3) Unless authorized by the other partners or unless they have abandoned the business, one or more but less than all the partners have no authority to:

> (a) Assign the partnership property in trust for creditors or on the assignee's promise to pay the debts of the partnership,
>
> (b) Dispose of the good-will of the business,
>
> (c) Do any other act which would make it impossible to carry on the ordinary business of a partnership,
>
> (d) Confess a judgment,
>
> (e) Submit a partnership claim or liability to arbitration or reference.

(4) No act of a partner in contravention of a restriction on authority shall bind the partnership to persons having knowledge of the restriction.

### Sec. 10. Conveyance of Real Property of the Partnership

(1) Where title to real property is in the partnership name, any partner may convey title to such property by a conveyance executed in the partnership name; but the partnership may recover such property unless the partner's act binds the partnership under the provisions of paragraph (1) of section 9, or unless such property has been conveyed by the grantee or a person claiming through such grantee to a holder for value without knowledge that the partner, in making the conveyance, has exceeded his authority.

(2) Where title to real property is in the name of the partnership, a conveyance executed by a partner, in his own name, passes the equitable interest of the partnership, provided the act is one within the authority of the partner under the provisions of paragraph (1) of section 9.

(3) Where title to real property is in the name of one or more but not all the partners, and the record does not disclose the right of the partnership, the partners in whose name the title stands may convey title to such property, but the partnership may recover such property if the partners' act does not bind the partnership under the provisions of paragraph (1) of section 9, unless the purchaser or his assignee, is a holder for value, without knowledge.

(4) Where the title to real property is in the name of one or more or all the partners, or in a third person in trust for the partnership, a conveyance executed by a partner in the partnership name, or in his own name, passes the equitable interest of the partnership, provided the act is one within the authority of the partner under the provisions of paragraph (1) of section 9.

(5) Where the title to real property is in the names of all the partners a conveyance executed by all the partners passes all their rights in such property.

### Sec. 11. Partnership Bound by Admission of Partner

An admission or representation made by any partner concerning partnership affairs within the scope of his authority as conferred by this act is evidence against the partnership.

### Sec. 12. Partnership Charged with Knowledge of or Notice to Partner

Notice to any partner of any matter relating to partnership affairs, and the knowledge of the partner acting in the particular matter, acquired while a partner or then present to his mind, and the knowledge of any other partner who reasonably could and should have communicated it to the acting partner, operate as notice to or knowledge of the partnership, except in the case of a fraud on the partnership committed by or with the consent of that partner.

### Sec. 13. Partnership Bound by Partner's Wrongful Act

Where, by any wrongful act or omission of any partner acting in the ordinary course of the business of the partnership or with the authority of his co-partners, loss or injury is caused to any person, not being a partner in the partnership, or any penalty is incurred, the partnership is liable therefor to the same extent as the partner so acting or omitting to act.

### Sec. 14. Partnership Bound by Partner's Breach of Trust

The partnership is bound to make good the loss:

(a) Where one partner acting within the scope of his apparent authority receives money or property of a third person and misapplies it; and

(b) Where the partnership in the course of its business receives money or property of a third person and the money or property so received is misapplied by any partner while it is in the custody of the partnership.

### Sec. 15. Nature of Partner's Liability

All partners are liable

(a) Jointly and severally for everything chargeable to the partnership under sections 13 and 14.

(b) Jointly for all other debts and obligations of the partnership; but any partner may enter into a separate obligation to perform a partnership contract.

### Sec. 16. Partner by Estoppel

(1) When a person, by words spoken or written or by conduct, represents himself, or consents to another representing him to any one, as a partner in an existing partnership or with one or more persons not actual partners, he is liable to any such person to whom such representation has been made, who has, on the faith of such representation, given credit to the actual or apparent partnership, and if he has made such representation or consented to its being made in a public manner he is liable to such person, whether the representation has or has not been made or communicated to such person so giving credit by or with the knowledge of the apparent partner making the representation or consenting to its being made.

(a) When a partnership liability results, he is liable as though he were an actual member of the partnership.

(b) When no partnership liability results, he is liable jointly with the other persons, if any, so consenting to the contract or representation as to incur liability, otherwise separately.

(2) When a person has been thus represented to be a partner in an existing partnership, or with one or more persons not actual partners, he is an agent of the persons consenting to such representation to bind them to the same extent and in the same manner as though he were a partner in fact, with respect to persons who rely upon the representation. Where all the members of the existing partnership consent to the representation, a partnership act or obligation results; but in all other cases it is the joint act or obligation of the person acting and the persons consenting to the representation.

### Sec. 17. Liability of Incoming Partner

A person admitted as a partner into an existing partnership is liable for all the obligations of the partnership arising before his admission as though he had been a partner when such obligations were incurred, except that this liability shall be satisfied only out of partnership property.

## Part IV  Relations of Partners to One Another

### Sec. 18. Rules Determining Rights and Duties of Partners

The rights and duties of the partners in relation to the partnership shall be determined, subject to any agreement between them, by the following rules:

(a) Each partner shall be repaid his contributions, whether by way of capital or advances to the partnership property and share equally in the profits and surplus remaining after all liabilities, including those to partners, are satisfied; and must contribute towards the losses, whether of capital or otherwise, sustained by the partnership according to his share in the profits.

(b) The partnership must indemnify every partner in respect of payments made and personal liabilities reasonably incurred by him in the ordinary and proper conduct of its business, or for the preservation of its business or property.

(c) A partner, who in aid of the partnership makes any payment or advance beyond the amount of capital which he agreed to contribute, shall be paid interest from the date of the payment or advance.

(d) A partner shall receive interest on the capital contributed by him only from the date when repayment should be made.

(e) All partners have equal rights in the management and conduct of the partnership business.

(f) No partner is entitled to remuneration for acting in the partnership business, except that a surviving partner is entitled to reasonable compensation for his services in winding up the partnership affairs.

(g) No person can become a member of a partnership without the consent of all the partners.

(h) Any difference arising as to ordinary matters connected with the partnership business may be decided by a majority of the partners; but no act in contravention of any agreement between the partners may be done rightfully without the consent of all the partners.

### Sec. 19. Partnership Books

The partnership books shall be kept, subject to any agreement between the partners, at the principal place of business of the partnership, and every partner shall at all times have access to and may inspect and copy any of them.

### Sec. 20. Duty of Partners to Render Information

Partners shall render on demand true and full information of all things affecting the partnership to any partner or the legal representative of any deceased partner or partner under legal disability.

### Sec. 21. Partner Accountable as a Fiduciary

(1) Every partner must account to the partnership for any benefit, and hold as trustee for it any profits derived by him without the consent of the other partners from any transaction connected with the formation, conduct, or liquidation of the partnership or from any use by him of its property.

(2) This section applies also to the representatives of a deceased partner engaged in the liquidation of the affairs of the partnership as the personal representatives of the last surviving partner.

### Sec. 22. Right to an Account

Any partner shall have the right to a formal account as to partnership affairs:

(a) If he is wrongfully excluded from the partnership business or possession of its property by his co-partners,

(b) If the right exists under the terms of any agreement,

(c) As provided by section 21,

(d) Whenever other circumstances render it just and reasonable.

### Sec. 23. Continuation of Partnership beyond Fixed Term

(1) When a partnership for a fixed term or particular undertaking is continued after the termination of such term or particular undertaking without any express agreement, the rights and duties of the partners remain the same as they were at such termination, so far as is consistent with a partnership at will.

(2) A continuation of the business by the partners or such of them as habitually acted therein during the term, without any settlement or liquidation of the partnership affairs, is prima facie evidence of a continuation of the partnership.

## Part V    Property Rights of a Partner

### Sec. 24. Extent of Property Rights of a Partner

The property rights of a partner are (1) his rights in specific partnership property, (2) his interest in the partnership, and (3) his right to participate in the management.

### Sec. 25. Nature of a Partner's Right in Specific Partnership Property

(1) A partner is co-owner with his partners of specific partnership property holding as a tenant in partnership.

(2) The incidents of this tenancy are such that:

(a) A partner, subject to the provisions of this act and to any agreement between the partners, has an equal right with his partners to possess specific partnership property for partnership purposes; but he has no right to possess such property for any other purpose without the consent of his partners.

(b) A partner's right in specific partnership property is not assignable except in connection with the assignment of rights of all the partners in the same property.

(c) A partner's right in specific partnership property is not subject to attachment or execution, except on a claim against the partnership. When partnership property is attached for a partnership debt the partners, or any of them, or the representatives of a deceased partner, cannot claim any right under the homestead or exemption laws.

(d) On the death of a partner his right in specific partnership property vests in the surviving partner or partners, except where the deceased was the last surviving partner, when his right in such property vests in his legal representative. Such surviving partner or partners, or the legal representative of the last surviving partner, has no right to possess the partnership property for any but a partnership purpose.

(e) A partner's right in specific partnership property is not subject to dower, curtesy, or allowances to widows, heirs, or next of kin.

### Sec. 26. Nature of Partner's Interest in the Partnership

A partner's interest in the partnership is his share of the profits and surplus, and the same is personal property.

### Sec. 27. Assignment of Partner's Interest

(1) A conveyance by a partner of his interest in the partnership does not of itself dissolve the partnership, nor, as against the other partners in the absence of agreement, entitle the assignee, during the continuance of the partnership, to interfere in the management or administration of the partnership business or affairs, or to require any information or account of partnership transactions, or to inspect the partnership books; but it merely entitles the assignee to receive in accordance with his contract the profits to which the assigning partner would otherwise be entitled.

(2) In case of a dissolution of the partnership, the assignee is entitled to receive his assignor's interest and may require an account from the date only of the last account agreed to by all the partners.

### Sec. 28. Partner's Interest Subject to Charging Order

(1) On due application to a competent court by any judgment creditor of a partner, the court which entered the judgment,

order, or decree, or any other court, may charge the interest of the debtor partner with payment of the unsatisfied amount of such judgment debt with interest thereon; and may then or later appoint a receiver of his share of the profits, and of any other money due or to fall due to him in respect of the partnership, and make all other orders, directions, accounts and inquiries which the debtor partner might have made, or which the circumstances of the case may require.

(2) The interest charged may be redeemed at any time before foreclosure, or in case of a sale being directed by the court may be purchased without thereby causing a dissolution:

(a) With separate property, by any one or more of the partners, or

(b) With partnership property, by any one or more of the partners with the consent of all the partners whose interests are not so charged or sold.

(3) Nothing in this act shall be held to deprive a partner of his right, if any, under the exemption laws, as regards his interest in the partnership.

## Part VI   Dissolution and Winding up

### Sec. 29.  Dissolution Defined

The dissolution of a partnership is the change in the relation of the partners caused by any partner ceasing to be associated in the carrying on as distinguished from the winding up of the business.

### Sec. 30.  Partnership not Terminated by Dissolution

On dissolution the partnership is not terminated, but continues until the winding up of partnership affairs is completed.

### Sec. 31.  Causes of Dissolution

Dissolution is caused:

(1) Without violation of the agreement between the partners,

(a) By the termination of the definite term or particular undertaking specified in the agreement,

(b) By the express will of any partner when no definite term or particular undertaking is specified,

(c) By the express will of all the partners who have not assigned their interests or suffered them to be charged for their separate debts, either before or after the termination of any specified term or particular undertaking,

(d) By the expulsion of any partner from the business bona fide in accordance with such a power conferred by the agreement between the partners;

(2) In contravention of the agreement between the partners, where the circumstances do not permit a dissolution under any other provision of this section, by the express will of any partner at any time;

(3) By any event which makes it unlawful for the business of the partnership to be carried on or for the members to carry it on in partnership;

(4) By the death of any partner;

(5) By the bankruptcy of any partner or the partnership;

(6) By decree of court under section 32.

### Sec. 32.  Dissolution by Decree of Court

(1) On application by or for a partner the court shall decree a dissolution whenever:

(a) A partner has been declared a lunatic in any judicial proceeding or is shown to be of unsound mind,

(b) A partner becomes in any other way incapable of performing his part of the partnership contract,

(c) A partner has been guilty of such conduct as tends to affect prejudicially the carrying on of the business,

(d) A partner wilfully or persistently commits a breach of the partnership agreement, or otherwise so conducts himself in matters relating to the partnership business that it is not reasonably practicable to carry on the business in partnership with him,

(e) The business of the partnership can only be carried on at a loss,

(f) Other circumstances render a dissolution equitable.

(2) On the application of the purchaser of a partner's interest under sections 28 or 29 [should read 27 or 28];

(a) After the termination of the specified term or particular undertaking,

(b) At any time if the partnership was a partnership at will when the interest was assigned or when the charging order was issued.

### Sec. 33.  General Effect of Dissolution on Authority of Partner

Except so far as may be necessary to wind up partnership affairs or to complete transactions begun but not then finished, dissolution terminates all authority of any partner to act for the partnership,

(1) With respect to the partners,

(a) When the dissolution is not by the act, bankruptcy or death of a partner; or

(b) When the dissolution is by such act, bankruptcy or death of a partner, in cases where section 34 so requires.

(2) With respect to persons not partners, as declared in section 35.

### Sec. 34.  Rights of Partner to Contribution from Copartners after Dissolution

Where the dissolution is caused by the act, death or bankruptcy of a partner, each partner is liable to his copartners for his share of any liability created by any partner acting for the partnership as if the partnership had not been dissolved unless

(a) The dissolution being by act of any partner, the partner acting for the partnership had knowledge of the dissolution, or

(b) The dissolution being by the death or bankruptcy of a partner, the partner acting for the partnership had knowledge or notice of the death or bankruptcy.

## Sec. 35. Power of Partner to Bind Partnership to Third Persons after Dissolution

(1) After dissolution a partner can bind the partnership except as provided in Paragraph (3).

(a) By any act appropriate for winding up partnership affairs or completing transactions unfinished at dissolution;

(b) By any transaction which would bind the partnership if dissolution had not taken place, provided the other party to the transaction

(I) Had extended credit to the partnership prior to dissolution and had no knowledge or notice of the dissolution; or

(II) Though he had not so extended credit, had nevertheless known of the partnership prior to dissolution, and, having no knowledge or notice of dissolution, the fact of dissolution had not been advertised in a newspaper of general circulation in the place (or in each place if more than one) at which the partnership business was regularly carried on.

(2) The liability of a partner under paragraph (1b) shall be satisfied out of partnership assets alone when such partner had been prior to dissolution

(a) Unknown as a partner to the person with whom the contract is made; and

(b) So far unknown and inactive in partnership affairs that the business reputation of the partnership could not be said to have been in any degree due to his connection with it.

(3) The partnership is in no case bound by any act of a partner after dissolution

(a) Where the partnership is dissolved because it is unlawful to carry on the business, unless the act is appropriate for winding up partnership affairs; or

(b) Where the partner has become bankrupt; or

(c) Where the partner has no authority to wind up partnership affairs; except by a transaction with one who

(I) Had extended credit to the partnership prior to dissolution and had no knowledge or notice of his want of authority; or

(II) Had not extended credit to the partnership prior to dissolution, and, having no knowledge or notice of his want of authority, the fact of his want of authority has not been advertised in the manner provided for advertising the fact of dissolution in paragraph (1bII).

(4) Nothing in this section shall affect the liability under Section 16 of any person who after dissolution represents himself or consents to another representing him as a partner in a partnership engaged in carrying on business.

## Sec. 36. Effect of Dissolution on Partner's Existing Liability

(1) The dissolution of the partnership does not of itself discharge the existing liability of any partner.

(2) A partner is discharged from any existing liability upon dissolution of the partnership by an agreement to that effect between himself, the partnership creditor and the person or partnership continuing the business; and such agreement may be inferred from the course of dealing between the creditor having knowledge of the dissolution and the person or partnership continuing the business.

(3) Where a person agrees to assume the existing obligations of a dissolved partnership, the partners whose obligations have been assumed shall be discharged from any liability to any creditor of the partnership who, knowing of the agreement, consents to a material alteration in the nature or time of payment of such obligations.

(4) The individual property of a deceased partner shall be liable for all obligations of the partnership incurred while he was a partner but subject to the prior payment of his separate debts.

## Sec. 37. Right to Wind Up

Unless otherwise agreed the partners who have not wrongfully dissolved the partnership or the legal representative of the last surviving partner, not bankrupt, has the right to wind up the partnership affairs; provided, however, that any partner, his legal representative or his assignee, upon cause shown, may obtain winding up by the court.

## Sec. 38. Rights of Partners to Application of Partnership Property

(1) When dissolution is caused in any way, except in contravention of the partnership agreement, each partner, as against his co-partners and all persons claiming through them in respect of their interests in the partnership, unless otherwise agreed, may have the partnership property applied to discharge its liabilities, and the surplus applied to pay in cash the net amount owing to the respective partners. But if dissolution is caused by expulsion of a partner, bona fide under the partnership agreement and if the expelled partner is discharged from all partnership liabilities, either by payment or agreement under section 36(2), he shall receive in cash only the net amount due him from the partnership.

(2) When dissolution is caused in contravention of the partnership agreement the rights of the partners shall be as follows:

(a) Each partner who has not caused dissolution wrongfully shall have,

(I) All the rights specified in paragraph (1) of this section, and

(II) The right, as against each partner who has caused the dissolution wrongfully, to damages for breach of the agreement.

(b) The partners who have not caused the dissolution wrongfully, if they all desire to continue the business in the same name, either by themselves or jointly with others, may do so, during the agreed term for the partnership and for that purpose may possess the partnership property, provided they secure the payment by bond approved by the court, or pay to any partner who has caused the dissolution wrongfully, the value of his interest in the partnership at the dissolution, less any damages recoverable under clause (2a II) of the section, and in like manner indemnify him against all present or future partnership liabilities.

(c) A partner who has caused the dissolution wrongfully shall have:

(I) If the business is not continued under the provisions of paragraph (2b) all the rights of a partner under paragraph (1), subject to clause (2a II), of this section,

(II) If the business is continued under paragraph (2b) of this section the right as against his co-partners and all claiming through them in respect of their interests in the partnership, to have the value of his interest in the partnership, less any damages caused to his co-partners by the dissolution, ascertained and paid to him in cash, or the payment secured by bond approved by the court, and to be released from all existing liabilities of the partnership; but in ascertaining the value of the partner's interest the value of the good-will of the business shall not be considered.

### Sec. 39. Rights Where Partnership Is Dissolved for Fraud or Misrepresentation

Where a partnership contract is rescinded on the ground of the fraud or misrepresentation of one of the parties thereto, the party entitled to rescind is, without prejudice to any other right, entitled,

(a) To a lien on, or right of retention of, the surplus of the partnership property after satisfying the partnership liabilities to third persons for any sum of money paid by him for the purchase of an interest in the partnership and for any capital or advances contributed by him; and

(b) To stand, after all liabilities to third persons have been satisfied, in the place of the creditors of the partnership for any payments made by him in respect of the partnership liabilities; and

(c) To be indemnified by the person guilty of the fraud or making the representation against all debts and liabilities of the partnership.

### Sec. 40. Rules for Distribution

In settling accounts between the partners after dissolution, the following rules shall be observed, subject to any agreement to the contrary:

(a) The assets of the partnership are:

(I) The partnership property,

(II) The contributions of the partners necessary for the payment of all the liabilities specified in clause (b) of this paragraph.

(b) The liabilities of the partnership shall rank in order of payment, as follows:

(I) Those owing to creditors other than partners,

(II) Those owing to partners other than for capital and profits,

(III) Those owing to partners in respect of capital,

(IV) Those owing to partners in respect of profits.

(c) The assets shall be applied in the order of their declaration in clause (a) of this paragraph to the satisfaction of the liabilities.

(d) The partners shall contribute, as provided by section 18(a) the amount necessary to satisfy the liabilities; but if any, but not all, of the partners are insolvent, or, not being subject to process, refuse to contribute, the other partners shall contribute their share of the liabilities, and, in the relative proportions in which they share the profits, the additional amount necessary to pay the liabilities.

(e) An assignee for the benefit of creditors or any person appointed by the court shall have the right to enforce the contributions specified in clause (d) of this paragraph.

(f) Any partner or his legal representative shall have the right to enforce the contributions specified in clause (d) of this paragraph, to the extent of the amount which he has paid in excess of his share of the liability.

(g) The individual property of a deceased partner shall be liable for the contributions specified in clause (d) of this paragraph.

(h) When partnership property and the individual properties of the partners are in possession of a court for distribution, partnership creditors shall have priority on partnership property and separate creditors on individual property, saving the rights of lien or secured creditors as heretofore.

(i) Where a partner has become bankrupt or his estate is insolvent the claims against his separate property shall rank in the following order:

(I) Those owing to separate creditors,

(II) Those owing to partnership creditors,

(III) Those owing to partners by way of contribution.

### Sec. 41. Liability of Persons Continuing the Business in Certain Cases

(1) When any new partner is admitted into an existing partnership, or when any partner retires and assigns (or the representative of the deceased partner assigns) his rights in partnership property to two or more of the partners, or to one or more of the partners and one or more third persons, if the business is continued without liquidation of the partnership affairs, creditors of the first or dissolved partnership are also creditors of the partnership so continuing the business.

(2) When all but one partner retire and assign (or the representative of a deceased partner assigns) their rights in partnership property to the remaining partner, who continues the business without liquidation of partnership affairs, either alone or with others, creditors of the dissolved partnership

are also creditors of the person or partnership so continuing the business.

(3) When any partner retires or dies and the business of the dissolved partnership is continued as set forth in paragraphs (1) and (2) of this section, with the consent of the retired partners or the representative of the deceased partner, but without any assignment of his right in partnership property, rights of creditors of the dissolved partnership and of the creditors of the person or partnership continuing the business shall be as if such assignment had been made.

(4) When all the partners or their representatives assign their rights in partnership property to one or more third persons who promise to pay the debts and who continue the business of the dissolved partnership, creditors of the dissolved partnership are also creditors of the person or partnership continuing the business.

(5) When any partner wrongfully causes a dissolution and the remaining partners continue the business under the provisions of section 38(2b), either alone or with others, and without liquidation of the partnership affairs, creditors of the dissolved partnership are also creditors of the person or partnership continuing the business.

(6) When a partner is expelled and the remaining partners continue the business either alone or with others, without liquidation of the partnership affairs, creditors of the dissolved partnership are also creditors of the person or partnership continuing the business.

(7) The liability of a third person becoming a partner in the partnership continuing the business, under this section, to the creditors of the dissolved partnership shall be satisfied out of partnership property only.

(8) When the business of a partnership after dissolution is continued under any conditions set forth in this section the creditors of the dissolved partnership, as against the separate creditors of the retiring or deceased partner or the representative of the deceased partner, have a prior right to any claim of the retired partner or the representative of the deceased partner against the person or partnership continuing the business, on account of the retired or deceased partner's interest in the dissolved partnership or on account of any consideration promised for such interest or for his right in partnership property.

(9) Nothing in this section shall be held to modify any right of creditors to set aside any assignment on the ground of fraud.

(10) The use by the person or partnership continuing the business of the partnership name, or the name of a deceased partner as part thereof, shall not of itself make the individual property of the deceased partner liable for any debts contracted by such person or partnership.

## Sec. 42. Rights of Retiring or Estate of Deceased Partner When the Business Is Continued

When any partner retires or dies, and the business is continued under any of the conditions set forth in section 41 (1, 2, 3, 5, 6), or section 38(2b) without any settlement of accounts as between him or his estate and the person or partnership continuing the business, unless otherwise agreed, he or his legal representative as against such persons or partnership may have the value of his interest at the date of dissolution ascertained, and shall receive as an ordinary creditor an amount equal to the value of his interest in the dissolved partnership with interest, or, at his option or at the option of his legal representative, in lieu of interest, the profits attributable to the use of his right in the property of the dissolved partnership; provided that the creditors of the dissolved partnership as against the separate creditors, or the representative of the retired or deceased partner, shall have priority on any claim arising under this section, as provided by section 41(8) of this act.

## Sec. 43. Accrual of Actions

The right to an account of his interest shall accrue to any partner, or his legal representative, as against the winding up partners or the surviving partners or the person or partnership continuing the business, at the date of dissolution, in the absence of any agreement to the contrary.

## Part VII  Miscellaneous Provisions

### Sec. 44. When Act Takes Effect

This act shall take effect on the ___ day of ___ one thousand nine hundred and ___.

### Sec. 45. Legislation Repealed

All acts or parts of acts inconsistent with this act are hereby repealed.

# APPENDIX F

# THE REVISED UNIFORM PARTNERSHIP ACT (EXCERPTS)

## Article 2.

## GENERAL PROVISIONS

\* \* \* \*

### § 201. Partnership as Entity.

A partnership is an entity.

\* \* \* \*

### § 203. Partnership Property.

Property transferred to or otherwise acquired by a partnership is property of the partnership and not of the partners individually.

### § 204. When Property is Partnership Property.

(a) Property is partnership property if acquired in the name of:

(1) the partnership; or

(2) one or more partners with an indication in the instrument transferring title to the property of the person's capacity as a partner or of the existence of a partnership but without an indication of the name of the partnership.

(b) Property is acquired in the name of the partnership by a transfer to:

(1) the partnership in its name; or

(2) one or more partners in their capacity as partners in the partnership, if the name of the partnership is indicated in the instrument transferring title to the property.

(c) Property is presumed to be partnership property if purchased with partnership assets, even if not acquired in the name of the partnership or of one or more partners with an indication in the instrument transferring title to the property of the person's capacity as a partner or of the existence of a partnership.

(d) Property acquired in the name of one or more of the partners, without an indication in the instrument transferring title to the property of the person's capacity as a partner or of the existence of a partnership and without use of partnership assets, is presumed to be separate property, even if used for partnership purposes.

## Article 3.

## RELATIONS OF PARTNERS TO PERSONS DEALING WITH PARTNERSHIP

\* \* \* \*

### § 302. Transfer of Partnership Property.

(a) Subject to the effect of a statement of partnership authority under Section 303:

(1) Partnership property held in the name of the partnership may be transferred by an instrument of transfer executed by a partner in the partnership name.

(2) Partnership property held in the name of one or more partners with an indication in the instrument transferring the property to them of their capacity as partners or of the existence of a partnership, but without an indication of the name of the partnership, may be transferred by an instrument of transfer executed by the persons in whose name the property is held.

(3) A partnership may recover property transferred under this subsection if it proves that execution of the instrument of transfer did not bind the partnership under Section 301, unless the property was transferred by the initial transferee or a person claiming through the initial transferee to a subsequent transferee who gave value without having notice that the person who executed the instrument of initial transfer lacked authority to bind the partnership.

(b) Partnership property held in the name of one or more persons other than the partnership, without an indication in the instrument transferring the property to them of their capacity as partners or of the existence of a partnership, may be transferred free of claims of the partnership or the partners by the persons in whose name the property is held to a transferee who gives value without having notice that it is partnership property.

(c) If a person holds all of the partners' interests in the partnership, all of the partnership property vests in that person. The person may execute a document in the name of the partnership to evidence vesting of the property in that person and may file or record the document.

\* \* \* \*

### § 306. Partner's Liability.

All partners are liable jointly and severally for all obligations of the partnership unless otherwise agreed by the claimant or provided by law.

### § 307. Actions by and Against Partnership and Partners.

(a) A partnership may sue and be sued in the name of the partnership.

(b) An action may be brought against the partnership and any or all of the partners in the same action or in separate actions.

(c) A judgment against a partnership is not by itself a judgment against a partner. A judgment against a partnership may not be satisfied from a partner's assets unless there is also a judgment against the partner.

(d) A judgment creditor of a partner may not levy execution against the assets of the partner to satisfy a judgment based on a claim against the partnership unless:

(1) a judgment based on the same claim has been obtained against the partnership and a writ of execution on the judgment has been returned unsatisfied in whole or in part;

(2) an involuntary case under Title 11 of the United States Code has been commenced against the partnership and has not been dismissed within 60 days after commencement, or the partnership has commenced a voluntary case under Title 11 of the United States Code and the case has not been dismissed;

(3) the partner has agreed that the creditor need not exhaust partnership assets;

(4) a court grants permission to the judgment creditor to levy execution against the assets of a partner based on a finding that partnership assets subject to execution are clearly insufficient to satisfy the judgment, that exhaustion of partnership assets is excessively burdensome, or that the grant of permission is an appropriate exercise of the court's equitable powers; or

(5) liability is imposed on the partner by law or contract independent of the existence of the partnership.

(e) This section applies to any partnership liability or obligation resulting from a representation by a partner or purported partner under Section 308.

\* \* \* \*

## Article 5.
## TRANSFEREES AND CREDITORS OF PARTNER

### § 501. Partner's Interest in Partnership Property not Transferable.

A partner is not a co-owner of partnership property and has no interest in partnership property which can be transferred, either voluntarily or involuntarily.

\* \* \* \*

## Article 6.
## PARTNER'S DISSOCIATION

### § 601. Events Causing Partner's Dissociation.

A partner is dissociated from a partnership upon:

(1) receipt by the partnership of notice of the partner's express will to withdraw as a partner or upon any later date specified in the notice;

(2) an event agreed to in the partnership agreement as causing the partner's dissociation;

(3) the partner's expulsion pursuant to the partnership agreement;

(4) the partner's expulsion by the unanimous vote of the other partners if:

(i) it is unlawful to carry on the partnership business with that partner;

(ii) there has been a transfer of all or substantially all of that partner's transferable interest in the partnership, other than a transfer for security purposes, or a court order charging the partner's interest, which has not been foreclosed;

(iii) within 90 days after the partnership notifies a corporate partner that it will be expelled because it has filed a certificate of dissolution or the equivalent, its charter has been revoked, or its right to conduct business has been suspended by the jurisdiction of its incorporation, there is no revocation of the certificate of dissolution or no reinstatement of its charter or its right to conduct business; or

(iv) a partnership that is a partner has been dissolved and its business is being wound up;

(5) on application by the partnership or another partner, the partner's expulsion by judicial determination because:

(i) the partner engaged in wrongful conduct that adversely and materially affected the partnership business;

(ii) the partner willfully or persistently committed a material breach of the partnership agreement or of a duty owed to the partnership or the other partners under Section 404; or

(iii) the partner engaged in conduct relating to the partnership business which makes it not reasonably practicable to carry on the business in partnership with the partner;

(6) the partner's:

(i) becoming a debtor in bankruptcy;

(ii) executing an assignment for the benefit of creditors;

(iii) seeking, consenting to, or acquiescing in the appointment of a trustee, receiver, or liquidator of that partner or of all or substantially all of that partner's property; or

(iv) failing, within 90 days after the appointment, to have vacated or stayed the appointment of a trustee, receiver, or liquidator of the partner or of all or substantially all of the partner's property obtained without the partner's consent or acquiescence, or failing within 90 days after the expiration of a stay to have the appointment vacated;

(7) in the case of a partner who is an individual:

(i) the partner's death;

(ii) the appointment of a guardian or general conservator for the partner; or

(iii) a judicial determination that the partner has otherwise become incapable of performing the partner's duties under the partnership agreement;

(8) in the case of a partner that is a trust or is acting as a partner by virtue of being a trustee of a trust, distribution of the trust's entire transferable interest in the partnership, but not merely by reason of the substitution of a successor trustee;

(9) in the case of a partner that is an estate or is acting as a partner by virtue of being a personal representative of an estate, distribution of the estate's entire transferable interest in the partnership, but not merely by reason of the substitution of a successor personal representative; or

(10) termination of a partner who is not an individual, partnership, corporation, trust, or estate.

\* \* \* \*

# Article 7.
# PARTNER'S DISSOCIATION WHEN BUSINESS NOT WOUND UP

### § 701. Purchase of Dissociated Partner's Interest.

(a) If a partner is dissociated from a partnership without resulting in a dissolution and winding up of the partnership business under Section 801, the partnership shall cause the dissociated partner's interest in the partnership to be purchased for a buyout price determined pursuant to subsection (b).

(b) The buyout price of a dissociated partner's interest is the amount that would have been distributable to the dissociating partner under Section 808(b) if, on the date of dissociation, the assets of the partnership were sold at a price equal to the greater of the liquidation value or the value based on a sale of the entire business as a going concern without the dissociated partner and the partnership were wound up as of that date. In either case, the selling price of the partnership assets must be determined on the basis of the amount that would be paid by a willing buyer to a willing seller, neither being under any compulsion to buy or sell, and with knowledge of all relevant facts. Interest must be paid from the date of dissociation to the date of payment.

(c) Damages for wrongful dissociation under Section 602(b), and all other amounts owing, whether or not presently due, from the dissociated partner to the partnership, must be offset against the buyout price. Interest must be paid from the date the amount owed becomes due to the date of payment.

(d) A partnership shall indemnify a dissociated partner against all partnership liabilities incurred before the dissociation, except liabilities then unknown to the partnership, and against all partnership liabilities incurred after the dissociation, except liabilities incurred by an act of the dissociated partner under Section 702. For purposes of this subsection, a liability not known to a partner other than the dissociated partner is not known to the partnership.

(e) If no agreement for the purchase of a dissociated partner's interest is reached within 120 days after a written demand for payment, the partnership shall pay, or cause to be paid, in cash to the dissociated partner the amount the partnership estimates to be the buyout price and accrued interest, reduced by any offsets and accrued interest under subsection (c).

(f) If a deferred payment is authorized under subsection (h), the partnership may tender a written offer to pay the amount it estimates to be the buyout price and accrued interest, reduced by any offsets under subsection (c), stating the time of payment, the amount and type of security for payment, and the other terms and conditions of the obligation.

(g) The payment or tender required by subsection (e) or (f) must be accompanied by the following:

(1) a statement of partnership assets and liabilities as of the date of dissociation;

(2) the latest available partnership balance sheet and income statement, if any;

(3) an explanation of how the estimated amount of the payment was calculated; and

(4) written notice that the payment is in full satisfaction of the obligation to purchase unless, within 120 days after the written notice, the dissociated partner commences an action to determine the buyout price, any offsets under subsection (c), or other terms of the obligation to purchase.

(h) A partner who wrongfully dissociates before the expiration of a definite term or the completion of a particular undertaking is not entitled to payment of any portion of the buyout price until the expiration of the term or completion of the undertaking, unless the partner establishes to the satisfaction of the court that earlier payment will not cause undue hardship to the business of the partnership. A deferred payment must be adequately secured and bear interest.

(i) A dissociated partner may maintain an action against the partnership, pursuant to Section 406(b)(2)(ii), to determine the buyout price of that partner's interest, any offsets under subsection (c), or other terms of the obligation to purchase. The action must be commenced within 120 days after the partnership has tendered payment or an offer to pay or within one year after written demand for payment if no payment or offer to pay is tendered. The court shall determine the buyout price of the dissociated partner's interest, any offset due under subsection (c), and accrued interest, and enter judgment for any additional payment or refund. If deferred payment is authorized under subsection (h), the court shall also determine the security for payment and other terms of the obligation to purchase. The court may assess reasonable attorney's fees and the fees and expenses of appraisers or other experts for a party to the action, in amounts the court finds equitable, against a party that the court finds acted arbitrarily, vexatiously, or not in good faith. The finding may be based on the partnership's failure to tender payment or an offer to pay or to comply with subsection (g).

# APPENDIX G

# REVISED UNIFORM LIMITED PARTNERSHIP ACT, 1976, WITH 1985 AMENDMENTS

## Article 1
## GENERAL PROVISIONS

### Section 101. Definitions.

As used in this [Act], unless the context otherwise requires:

(1) "Certificate of limited partnership" means the certificate referred to in Section 201, and the certificate as amended or restated.

(2) "Contribution" means any cash, property, services rendered, or a promissory note or other binding obligation to contribute cash or property or to perform services, which a partner contributes to a limited partnership in his capacity as a partner.

(3) "Event of withdrawal of a general partner" means an event that causes a person to cease to be a general partner as provided in Section 402.

(4) "Foreign limited partnership" means a partnership formed under the laws of any state other than this State and having as partners one or more general partners and one or more limited partners.

(5) "General partner" means a person who has been admitted to a limited partnership as a general partner in accordance with the partnership agreement and named in the certificate of limited partnership as a general partner.

(6) "Limited partner" means a person who has been admitted to a limited partnership as a limited partner in accordance with the partnership agreement.

(7) "Limited partnership" and "domestic limited partnership" mean a partnership formed by two or more persons under the laws of this State and having one or more general partners and one or more limited partners.

(8) "Partner" means a limited or general partner.

(9) "Partnership agreement" means any valid agreement, written or oral, of the partners as to the affairs of a limited partnership and the conduct of its business.

(10) "Partnership interest" means a partner's share of the profits and losses of a limited partnership and the right to receive distributions of partnership assets.

(11) "Person" means a natural person, partnership, limited partnership (domestic or foreign), trust, estate, association, or corporation.

(12) "State" means a state, territory, or possession of the United States, the District of Columbia, or the Commonwealth of Puerto Rico.

### Section 102. Name.

The name of each limited partnership as set forth in its certificate of limited partnership:

(1) shall contain without abbreviation the words "limited partnership";

(2) may not contain the name of a limited partner unless (i) it is also the name of a general partner or the corporate name of a corporate general partner, or (ii) the business of the limited partnership had been carried on under that name before the admission of that limited partner;

(3) may not be the same as, or deceptively similar to, the name of any corporation or limited partnership organized under the laws of this State or licensed or registered as a foreign corporation or limited partnership in this State; and

(4) may not contain the following words [here insert prohibited words].

### Section 103. Reservation of Name.

(a) The exclusive right to the use of a name may be reserved by:

(1) any person intending to organize a limited partnership under this [Act] and to adopt that name;

(2) any domestic limited partnership or any foreign limited partnership registered in this State which, in either case, intends to adopt that name;

(3) any foreign limited partnership intending to register in this State and adopt that name; and

(4) any person intending to organize a foreign limited partnership and intending to have it register in this State and adopt that name.

(b) The reservation shall be made by filing with the Secretary of State an application, executed by the applicant, to reserve a specified name. If the Secretary of State finds that the name is available for use by a domestic or foreign limited partnership, he [or she] shall reserve the name for the exclusive use of the applicant for a period of 120 days. Once having so reserved a name, the same applicant may not again reserve the same name until more than 60 days after the expiration of the last 120-day period for which that applicant reserved that name. The right to the exclusive use of a reserved name may be transferred to any other person by filing in the office of the Secretary of State a notice of the transfer, executed by the applicant for whom the name was reserved and specifying the name and address of the transferee.

### Section 104.  Specified Office and Agent.

Each limited partnership shall continuously maintain in this State:

(1)  an office, which may but need not be a place of its business in this State, at which shall be kept the records required by Section 105 to be maintained; and

(2)  an agent for service of process on the limited partnership, which agent must be an individual resident of this State, a domestic corporation, or a foreign corporation authorized to do business in this State.

### Section 105.  Records to Be Kept.

(a)  Each limited partnership shall keep at the office referred to in Section 104(1) the following:

(1)  a current list of the full name and last known business address of each partner, separately identifying the general partners (in alphabetical order) and the limited partners (in alphabetical order);

(2)  a copy of the certificate of limited partnership and all certificates of amendment thereto, together with executed copies of any powers of attorney pursuant to which any certificate has been executed;

(3)  copies of the limited partnership's federal, state and local income tax returns and reports, if any, for the three most recent years;

(4)  copies of any then effective written partnership agreements and of any financial statements of the limited partnership for the three most recent years; and

(5)  unless contained in a written partnership agreement, a writing setting out:

(i)  the amount of cash and a description and statement of the agreed value of the other property or services contributed by each partner and which each partner has agreed to contribute;

(ii)  the times at which or events on the happening of which any additional contributions agreed to be made by each partner are to be made;

(iii)  any right of a partner to receive, or of a general partner to make, distributions to a partner which include a return of all or any part of the partner's contribution; and

(iv)  any events upon the happening of which the limited partnership is to be dissolved and its affairs wound up.

(b) Records kept under this section are subject to inspection and copying at the reasonable request and at the expense of any partner during ordinary business hours.

### Section 106.  Nature of Business.

A limited partnership may carry on any business that a partnership without limited partners may carry on except [here designate prohibited activities].

### Section 107.  Business Transactions of Partners with Partnership.

Except as provided in the partnership agreement, a partner may lend money to and transact other business with the limited partnership and, subject to other applicable law, has the same rights and obligations with respect thereto as a person who is not a partner.

## Article 2
# FORMATION; CERTIFICATE OF LIMITED PARTNERSHIP

### Section 201.  Certificate of Limited Partnership.

(a)  In order to form a limited partnership, a certificate of limited partnership must be executed and filed in the office of the Secretary of State. The certificate shall set forth:

(1)  the name of the limited partnership;

(2)  the address of the office and the name and address of the agent for service of process required to be maintained by Section 104;

(3)  the name and the business address of each general partner;

(4)  the latest date upon which the limited partnership is to dissolve; and

(5)  any other matters the general partners determine to include therein.

(b)  A limited partnership is formed at the time of the filing of the certificate of limited partnership in the office of the Secretary of State or at any later time specified in the certificate of limited partnership if, in either case, there has been substantial compliance with the requirements of this section.

### Section 202.  Amendment to Certificate.

(a)  A certificate of limited partnership is amended by filing a certificate of amendment thereto in the office of the Secretary of State. The certificate shall set forth:

(1)  the name of the limited partnership;

(2)  the date of filing the certificate; and

(3)  the amendment to the certificate.

(b) Within 30 days after the happening of any of the following events, an amendment to a certificate of limited partnership reflecting the occurrence of the event or events shall be filed:

(1) the admission of a new general partner;

(2) the withdrawal of a general partner; or

(3) the continuation of the business under Section 801 after an event of withdrawal of a general partner.

(c) A general partner who becomes aware that any statement in a certificate of limited partnership was false when made or that any arrangements or other facts described have changed, making the certificate inaccurate in any respect, shall promptly amend the certificate.

(d) A certificate of limited partnership may be amended at any time for any other proper purpose the general partners determine.

(e) No person has any liability because an amendment to a certificate of limited partnership has not been filed to reflect the occurrence of any event referred to in subsection (b) of this section if the amendment is filed within the 30-day period specified in subsection (b).

(f) A restated certificate of limited partnership may be executed and filed in the same manner as a certificate of amendment.

## Section 203. Cancellation of Certificate.

A certificate of limited partnership shall be cancelled upon the dissolution and the commencement of winding up of the partnership or at any other time there are no limited partners. A certificate of cancellation shall be filed in the office of the Secretary of State and set forth:

(1) the name of the limited partnership;

(2) the date of filing of its certificate of limited partnership;

(3) the reason for filing the certificate of cancellation;

(4) the effective date (which shall be a date certain) of cancellation if it is not to be effective upon the filing of the certificate; and

(5) any other information the general partners filing the certificate determine.

## Section 204. Execution of Certificates.

(a) Each certificate required by this Article to be filed in the office of the Secretary of State shall be executed in the following manner:

(1) an original certificate of limited partnership must be signed by all general partners;

(2) a certificate of amendment must be signed by at least one general partner and by each other general partner designated in the certificate as a new general partner; and

(3) a certificate of cancellation must be signed by all general partners.

(b) Any person may sign a certificate by an attorney-in-fact, but a power of attorney to sign a certificate relating to the admission of a general partner must specifically describe the admission.

(c) The execution of a certificate by a general partner constitutes an affirmation under the penalties of perjury that the facts stated therein are true.

## Section 205. Execution by Judicial Act.

If a person required by Section 204 to execute any certificate fails or refuses to do so, any other person who is adversely affected by the failure or refusal may petition the [designate the appropriate court] to direct the execution of the certificate. If the court finds that it is proper for the certificate to be executed and that any person so designated has failed or refused to execute the certificate, it shall order the Secretary of State to record an appropriate certificate.

## Section 206. Filing in Office of Secretary of State.

(a) Two signed copies of the certificate of limited partnership and of any certificates of amendment or cancellation (or of any judicial decree of amendment or cancellation) shall be delivered to the Secretary of State. A person who executes a certificate as an agent or fiduciary need not exhibit evidence of his [or her] authority as a prerequisite to filing. Unless the Secretary of State finds that any certificate does not conform to law, upon receipt of all filing fees required by law he [or she] shall:

(1) endorse on each duplicate original the word "Filed" and the day, month, and year of the filing thereof;

(2) file one duplicate original in his [or her] office; and

(3) return the other duplicate original to the person who filed it or his [or her] representative.

(b) Upon the filing of a certificate of amendment (or judicial decree of amendment) in the office of the Secretary of State, the certificate of limited partnership shall be amended as set forth therein, and upon the effective date of a certificate of cancellation (or a judicial decree thereof), the certificate of limited partnership is cancelled.

## Section 207. Liability for False Statement in Certificate.

If any certificate of limited partnership or certificate of amendment or cancellation contains a false statement, one who suffers loss by reliance on the statement may recover damages for the loss from:

(1) any person who executes the certificate, or causes another to execute it on his behalf, and knew, and any general partner who knew or should have known, the statement to be false at the time the certificate was executed; and

(2) any general partner who thereafter knows or should have known that any arrangement or other fact described in the certificate has changed, making the statement inaccurate in any respect within a sufficient time before the statement was relied upon reasonably to have enabled that general partner to cancel or amend the certificate, or to file a petition for its cancellation or amendment under Section 205.

### Section 208. Scope of Notice.

The fact that a certificate of limited partnership is on file in the office of the Secretary of State is notice that the partnership is a limited partnership and the persons designated therein as general partners are general partners, but it is not notice of any other fact.

### Section 209. Delivery of Certificates to Limited Partners.

Upon the return by the Secretary of State pursuant to Section 206 of a certificate marked ''Filed,'' the general partners shall promptly deliver or mail a copy of the certificate of limited partnership and each certificate of amendment or cancellation to each limited partner unless the partnership agreement provides otherwise.

# Article 3
# LIMITED PARTNERS

### Section 301. Admission of Additional Limited Partners.

(a) A person becomes a limited partner on the later of:

(1) the date the original certificate of limited partnership is filed; or

(2) the date stated in the records of the limited partnership as the date that person becomes a limited partner.

(b) After the filing of a limited partnership's original certificate of limited partnership, a person may be admitted as an additional limited partner:

(1) in the case of a person acquiring a partnership interest directly from the limited partnership, upon compliance with the partnership agreement or, if the partnership agreement does not so provide, upon the written consent of all partners; and

(2) in the case of an assignee of a partnership interest of a partner who has the power, as provided in Section 704, to grant the assignee the right to become a limited partner, upon the exercise of that power and compliance with any conditions limiting the grant or exercise of the power.

### Section 302. Voting.

Subject to Section 303, the partnership agreement may grant to all or a specified group of the limited partners the right to vote (on a per capita or other basis) upon any matter.

### Section 303. Liability to Third Parties.

(a) Except as provided in subsection (d), a limited partner is not liable for the obligations of a limited partnership unless he [or she] is also a general partner or, in addition to the exercise of his [or her] rights and powers as a limited partner, he [or she] participates in the control of the business. However, if the limited partner participates in the control of the business, he [or she] is liable only to persons who transact business with the limited partnership reasonably believing, based upon the limited partner's conduct, that the limited partner is a general partner.

(b) A limited partner does not participate in the control of the business within the meaning of subsection (a) solely by doing one or more of the following:

(1) being a contractor for or an agent or employee of the limited partnership or of a general partner or being an officer, director, or shareholder of a general partner that is a corporation;

(2) consulting with and advising a general partner with respect to the business of the limited partnership;

(3) acting as surety for the limited partnership or guaranteeing or assuming one or more specific obligations of the limited partnership;

(4) taking any action required or permitted by law to bring or pursue a derivative action in the right of the limited partnership;

(5) requesting or attending a meeting of partners;

(6) proposing, approving, or disapproving, by voting or otherwise, one or more of the following matters:

(i) the dissolution and winding up of the limited partnership;

(ii) the sale, exchange, lease, mortgage, pledge, or other transfer of all or substantially all of the assets of the limited partnership;

(iii) the incurrence of indebtedness by the limited partnership other than in the ordinary course of its business;

(iv) a change in the nature of the business;

(v) the admission or removal of a general partner;

(vi) the admission or removal of a limited partner;

(vii) a transaction involving an actual or potential conflict of interest between a general partner and the limited partnership or the limited partners;

(viii) an amendment to the partnership agreement or certificate of limited partnership; or

(ix) matters related to the business of the limited partnership not otherwise enumerated in this subsection (b), which the partnership agreement states in writing may be subject to the approval or disapproval of limited partners;

(7) winding up the limited partnership pursuant to Section 803; or

(8) exercising any right or power permitted to limited partners under this [Act] and not specifically enumerated in this subsection (b).

(c) The enumeration in subsection (b) does not mean that the possession or exercise of any other powers by a limited partner constitutes participation by him [or her] in the business of the limited partnership.

(d) A limited partner who knowingly permits his [or her] name to be used in the name of the limited partnership, except under circumstances permitted by Section 102(2), is liable to creditors who extend credit to the limited partnership without actual knowledge that the limited partner is not a general partner.

### Section 304. Person Erroneously Believing Himself [or Herself] Limited Partner.

(a) Except as provided in subsection (b), a person who makes a contribution to a business enterprise and erroneously but in good faith believes that he [or she] has become a limited partner in the enterprise is not a general partner in the enterprise and is not bound by its obligations by reason of making the contribution, receiving distributions from the enterprise, or exercising any rights of a limited partner, if, on ascertaining the mistake, he [or she]:

(1) causes an appropriate certificate of limited partnership or a certificate of amendment to be executed and filed; or

(2) withdraws from future equity participation in the enterprise by executing and filing in the office of the Secretary of State a certificate declaring withdrawal under this section.

(b) A person who makes a contribution of the kind described in subsection (a) is liable as a general partner to any third party who transacts business with the enterprise (i) before the person withdraws and an appropriate certificate is filed to show withdrawal, or (ii) before an appropriate certificate is filed to show that he [or she] is not a general partner, but in either case only if the third party actually believed in good faith that the person was a general partner at the time of the transaction.

### Section 305. Information.

Each limited partner has the right to:

(1) inspect and copy any of the partnership records required to be maintained by Section 105; and

(2) obtain from the general partners from time to time upon reasonable demand (i) true and full information regarding the state of the business and financial condition of the limited partnership, (ii) promptly after becoming available, a copy of the limited partnership's federal, state, and local income tax returns for each year, and (iii) other information regarding the affairs of the limited partnership as is just and reasonable.

## Article 4
# GENERAL PARTNERS

### Section 401. Admission of Additional General Partners.

After the filing of a limited partnership's original certificate of limited partnership, additional general partners may be admitted as provided in writing in the partnership agreement or, if the partnership agreement does not provide in writing for the admission of additional general partners, with the written consent of all partners.

### Section 402. Events of Withdrawal.

Except as approved by the specific written consent of all partners at the time, a person ceases to be a general partner of a limited partnership upon the happening of any of the following events:

(1) the general partner withdraws from the limited partnership as provided in Section 602;

(2) the general partner ceases to be a member of the limited partnership as provided in Section 702;

(3) the general partner is removed as a general partner in accordance with the partnership agreement;

(4) unless otherwise provided in writing in the partnership agreement, the general partner: (i) makes an assignment for the benefit of creditors; (ii) files a voluntary petition in bankruptcy; (iii) is adjudicated a bankrupt or insolvent; (iv) files a petition or answer seeking for himself [or herself] any reorganization, arrangement, composition, readjustment, liquidation, dissolution, or similar relief under any statute, law, or regulation; (v) files an answer or other pleading admitting or failing to contest the material allegations of a petition filed against him [or her] in any proceeding of this nature; or (vi) seeks, consents to, or acquiesces in the appointment of a trustee, receiver, or liquidator of the general partner or of all or any substantial part of his [or her] properties;

(5) unless otherwise provided in writing in the partnership agreement, [120] days after the commencement of any proceeding against the general partner seeking reorganization, arrangement, composition, readjustment, liquidation, dissolution, or similar relief under any statute, law, or regulation, the proceeding has not been dismissed, or if within [90] days after the appointment without his [or her] consent or acquiescence of a trustee, receiver, or liquidator of the general partner or of all or any substantial part of his [or her] properties, the appointment is not vacated or stayed or within [90] days after the expiration of any such stay, the appointment is not vacated;

(6) in the case of a general partner who is a natural person,

(i) his [or her] death; or

(ii) the entry of an order by a court of competent jurisdiction adjudicating him [or her] incompetent to manage his [or her] person or his [or her] estate;

(7) in the case of a general partner who is acting as a general partner by virtue of being a trustee of a trust, the termination of the trust (but not merely the substitution of a new trustee);

(8) in the case of a general partner that is a separate partnership, the dissolution and commencement of winding up of the separate partnership;

(9) in the case of a general partner that is a corporation, the filing of a certificate of dissolution, or its equivalent, for the corporation or the revocation of its charter; or

(10) in the case of an estate, the distribution by the fiduciary of the estate's entire interest in the partnership.

### Section 403. General Powers and Liabilities.

(a) Except as provided in this [Act] or in the partnership agreement, a general partner of a limited partnership has the rights and powers and is subject to the restrictions of a partner in a partnership without limited partners.

(b) Except as provided in this [Act], a general partner of a limited partnership has the liabilities of a partner in a partnership without limited partners to persons other than the partnership and the other partners. Except as provided in this [Act] or in the partnership agreement, a general partner of a limited partnership has the liabilities of a partner in a partnership without limited partners to the partnership and to the other partners.

### Section 404.  Contributions by General Partner.

A general partner of a limited partnership may make contributions to the partnership and share in the profits and losses of, and in distributions from, the limited partnership as a general partner. A general partner also may make contributions to and share in profits, losses, and distributions as a limited partner. A person who is both a general partner and a limited partner has the rights and powers, and is subject to the restrictions and liabilities, of a general partner and, except as provided in the partnership agreement, also has the powers, and is subject to the restrictions, of a limited partner to the extent of his [or her] participation in the partnership as a limited partner.

### Section 405.  Voting.

The partnership agreement may grant to all or certain identified general partners the right to vote (on a per capita or any other basis), separately or with all or any class of the limited partners, on any matter.

## Article 5
## FINANCE

### Section 501.  Form of Contribution.

The contribution of a partner may be in cash, property, or services rendered, or a promissory note or other obligation to contribute cash or property or to perform services.

### Section 502.  Liability for Contribution.

(a) A promise by a limited partner to contribute to the limited partnership is not enforceable unless set out in a writing signed by the limited partner.

(b) Except as provided in the partnership agreement, a partner is obligated to the limited partnership to perform any enforceable promise to contribute cash or property or to perform services, even if he [or she] is unable to perform because of death, disability, or any other reason. If a partner does not make the required contribution of property or services, he [or she] is obligated at the option of the limited partnership to contribute cash equal to that portion of the value, as stated in the partnership records required to be kept pursuant to Section 105, of the stated contribution which has not been made.

(c) Unless otherwise provided in the partnership agreement, the obligation of a partner to make a contribution or return money or other property paid or distributed in violation of this [Act] may be compromised only by consent of all partners. Notwithstanding the compromise, a creditor of a limited partnership who extends credit, or, otherwise acts in reliance on that obligation after the partner signs a writing which reflects the obligation and before the amendment or cancellation thereof to reflect the compromise may enforce the original obligation.

### Section 503.  Sharing of Profits and Losses.

The profits and losses of a limited partnership shall be allocated among the partners, and among classes of partners, in the manner provided in writing in the partnership agreement. If the partnership agreement does not so provide in writing, profits and losses shall be allocated on the basis of the value, as stated in the partnership records required to be kept pursuant to Section 105, of the contributions made by each partner to the extent they have been received by the partnership and have not been returned.

### Section 504.  Sharing of Distributions.

Distributions of cash or other assets of a limited partnership shall be allocated among the partners and among classes of partners in the manner provided in writing in the partnership agreement. If the partnership agreement does not so provide in writing, distributions shall be made on the basis of the value, as stated in the partnership records required to be kept pursuant to Section 105, of the contributions made by each partner to the extent they have been received by the partnership and have not been returned.

## Article 6
## DISTRIBUTIONS
## AND WITHDRAWAL

### Section 601.  Interim Distributions.

Except as provided in this Article, a partner is entitled to receive distributions from a limited partnership before his [or her] withdrawal from the limited partnership and before the dissolution and winding up thereof to the extent and at the times or upon the happening of the events specified in the partnership agreement.

### Section 602.  Withdrawal of General Partner.

A general partner may withdraw from a limited partnership at any time by giving written notice to the other partners, but if the withdrawal violates the partnership agreement, the limited partnership may recover from the withdrawing general partner damages for breach of the partnership agreement and offset the damages against the amount otherwise distributable to him [or her].

### Section 603.  Withdrawal of Limited Partner.

A limited partner may withdraw from a limited partnership at the time or upon the happening of events specified in writing in the partnership agreement. If the agreement does not specify in writing the time or the events upon the happening of which a limited partner may withdraw or a definite time for the dissolution and winding up of the limited partnership, a limited partner may withdraw upon not less than six months' prior written notice to each general partner at his [or her] address on the books of the limited partnership at its office in this State.

### Section 604. Distribution Upon Withdrawal.

Except as provided in this Article, upon withdrawal any withdrawing partner is entitled to receive any distribution to which he [or she] is entitled under the partnership agreement and, if not otherwise provided in the agreement, he [or she] is entitled to receive, within a reasonable time after withdrawal, the fair value of his [or her] interest in the limited partnership as of the date of withdrawal based upon his [or her] right to share in distributions from the limited partnership.

### Section 605. Distribution in Kind.

Except as provided in writing in the partnership agreement, a partner, regardless of the nature of his [or her] contribution, has no right to demand and receive any distribution from a limited partnership in any form other than cash. Except as provided in writing in the partnership agreement, a partner may not be compelled to accept a distribution of any asset in kind from a limited partnership to the extent that the percentage of the asset distributed to him [or her] exceeds a percentage of that asset which is equal to the percentage in which he [or she] shares in distributions from the limited partnership.

### Section 606. Right to Distribution.

At the time a partner becomes entitled to receive a distribution, he [or she] has the status of, and is entitled to all remedies available to, a creditor of the limited partnership with respect to the distribution.

### Section 607. Limitations on Distribution.

A partner may not receive a distribution from a limited partnership to the extent that, after giving effect to the distribution, all liabilities of the limited partnership, other than liabilities to partners on account of their partnership interests, exceed the fair value of the partnership assets.

### Section 608. Liability Upon Return of Contribution.

(a) If a partner has received the return of any part of his [or her] contribution without violation of the partnership agreement or this [Act], he [or she] is liable to the limited partnership for a period of one year thereafter for the amount of the returned contribution, but only to the extent necessary to discharge the limited partnership's liabilities to creditors who extended credit to the limited partnership during the period the contribution was held by the partnership.

(b) If a partner has received the return of any part of his [or her] contribution in violation of the partnership agreement or this [Act], he [or she] is liable to the limited partnership for a period of six years thereafter for the amount of the contribution wrongfully returned.

(c) A partner receives a return of his [or her] contribution to the extent that a distribution to him [or her] reduces his [or her] share of the fair value of the net assets of the limited partnership below the value, as set forth in the partnership records required to be kept pursuant to Section 105, of his [or her] contribution which has not been distributed to him [or her].

## Article 7
## ASSIGNMENT OF PARTNERSHIP INTERESTS

### Section 701. Nature of Partnership Interest.

A partnership interest is personal property.

### Section 702. Assignment of Partnership Interest.

Except as provided in the partnership agreement, a partnership interest is assignable in whole or in part. An assignment of a partnership interest does not dissolve a limited partnership or entitle the assignee to become or to exercise any rights of a partner. An assignment entitles the assignee to receive, to the extent assigned, only the distribution to which the assignor would be entitled. Except as provided in the partnership agreement, a partner ceases to be a partner upon assignment of all his [or her] partnership interest.

### Section 703. Rights of Creditor.

On application to a court of competent jurisdiction by any judgment creditor of a partner, the court may charge the partnership interest of the partner with payment of the unsatisfied amount of the judgment with interest. To the extent so charged, the judgment creditor has only the rights of an assignee of the partnership interest. This [Act] does not deprive any partner of the benefit of any exemption laws applicable to his [or her] partnership interest.

### Section 704. Right of Assignee to Become Limited Partner.

(a) An assignee of a partnership interest, including an assignee of a general partner, may become a limited partner if and to the extent that (i) the assignor gives the assignee that right in accordance with authority described in the partnership agreement, or (ii) all other partners consent.

(b) An assignee who has become a limited partner has, to the extent assigned, the rights and powers, and is subject to the restrictions and liabilities, of a limited partner under the partnership agreement and this [Act]. An assignee who becomes a limited partner also is liable for the obligations of his [or her] assignor to make and return contributions as provided in Articles 5 and 6. However, the assignee is not obligated for liabilities unknown to the assignee at the time he [or she] became a limited partner.

(c) If an assignee of a partnership interest becomes a limited partner, the assignor is not released from his [or her] liability to the limited partnership under Sections 207 and 502.

### Section 705. Power of Estate of Deceased or Incompetent Partner.

If a partner who is an individual dies or a court of competent jurisdiction adjudges him [or her] to be incompetent to manage his [or her] person or his [or her] property, the partner's executor, administrator, guardian, conservator, or other legal representative may exercise all of the partner's rights for the purpose of settling his [or her] estate or administering his [or her] property, including any power the partner had to give an assignee the right to become a limited partner. If a partner is a corporation, trust, or other entity and is dissolved or terminated, the powers of that partner may be exercised by its legal representative or successor.

# Article 8
## DISSOLUTION

### Section 801. Nonjudicial Dissolution.

A limited partnership is dissolved and its affairs shall be wound up upon the happening of the first to occur of the following:

(1) at the time specified in the certificate of limited partnership;

(2) upon the happening of events specified in writing in the partnership agreement;

(3) written consent of all partners;

(4) an event of withdrawal of a general partner unless at the time there is at least one other general partner and the written provisions of the partnership agreement permit the business of the limited partnership to be carried on by the remaining general partner and that partner does so, but the limited partnership is not dissolved and is not required to be wound up by reason of any event of withdrawal if, within 90 days after the withdrawal, all partners agree in writing to continue the business of the limited partnership and to the appointment of one or more additional general partners if necessary or desired; or

(5) entry of a decree of judicial dissolution under Section 802.

### Section 802. Judicial Dissolution.

On application by or for a partner the [designate the appropriate court] court may decree dissolution of a limited partnership whenever it is not reasonably practicable to carry on the business in conformity with the partnership agreement.

### Section 803. Winding Up.

Except as provided in the partnership agreement, the general partners who have not wrongfully dissolved a limited partnership or, if none, the limited partners, may wind up the limited partnership's affairs; but the [designate the appropriate court] court may wind up the limited partnership's affairs upon application of any partner, his [or her] legal representative, or assignee.

### Section 804. Distribution of Assets.

Upon the winding up of a limited partnership, the assets shall be distributed as follows:

(1) to creditors, including partners who are creditors, to the extent permitted by law, in satisfaction of liabilities of the limited partnership other than liabilities for distributions to partners under Section 601 or 604;

(2) except as provided in the partnership agreement, to partners and former partners in satisfaction of liabilities for distributions under Section 601 or 604; and

(3) except as provided in the partnership agreement, to partners first for the return of their contributions and secondly respecting their partnership interests, in the proportions in which the partners share in distributions.

# Article 9
## FOREIGN LIMITED PARTNERSHIPS

### Section 901. Law Governing.

Subject to the Constitution of this State, (i) the laws of the state under which a foreign limited partnership is organized govern its organization and internal affairs and the liability of its limited partners, and (ii) a foreign limited partnership may not be denied registration by reason of any difference between those laws and the laws of this State.

### Section 902. Registration.

Before transacting business in this State, a foreign limited partnership shall register with the Secretary of State. In order to register, a foreign limited partnership shall submit to the Secretary of State, in duplicate, an application for registration as a foreign limited partnership, signed and sworn to by a general partner and setting forth:

(1) the name of the foreign limited partnership and, if different, the name under which it proposes to register and transact business in this State;

(2) the State and date of its formation;

(3) the name and address of any agent for service of process on the foreign limited partnership whom the foreign limited partnership elects to appoint; the agent must be an individual resident of this State, a domestic corporation, or a foreign corporation having a place of business in, and authorized to do business in, this State;

(4) a statement that the Secretary of State is appointed the agent of the foreign limited partnership for service of process if no agent has been appointed under paragraph (3) or, if appointed, the agent's authority has been revoked or if the agent cannot be found or served with the exercise of reasonable diligence;

(5) the address of the office required to be maintained in the state of its organization by the laws of that state or, if not so required, of the principal office of the foreign limited partnership;

(6) the name and business address of each general partner; and

(7) the address of the office at which is kept a list of the names and addresses of the limited partners and their capital contributions, together with an undertaking by the foreign limited partnership to keep those records until the foreign limited partnership's registration in this State is cancelled or withdrawn.

### Section 903. Issuance of Registration.

(a) If the Secretary of State finds that an application for

registration conforms to law and all requisite fees have been paid, he [or she] shall:

(1) endorse on the application the word "Filed", and the month, day, and year of the filing thereof;

(2) file in his [or her] office a duplicate original of the application; and

(3) issue a certificate of registration to transact business in this State.

(b) The certificate of registration, together with a duplicate original of the application, shall be returned to the person who filed the application or his [or her] representative.

### Section 904. Name.

A foreign limited partnership may register with the Secretary of State under any name, whether or not it is the name under which it is registered in its state of organization, that includes without abbreviation the words "limited partnership" and that could be registered by a domestic limited partnership.

### Section 905. Changes and Amendments.

If any statement in the application for registration of a foreign limited partnership was false when made or any arrangements or other facts described have changed, making the application inaccurate in any respect, the foreign limited partnership shall promptly file in the office of the Secretary of State a certificate, signed and sworn to by a general partner, correcting such statement.

### Section 906. Cancellation of Registration.

A foreign limited partnership may cancel its registration by filing with the Secretary of State a certificate of cancellation signed and sworn to by a general partner. A cancellation does not terminate the authority of the Secretary of State to accept service of process on the foreign limited partnership with respect to [claims for relief] [causes of action] arising out of the transactions of business in this State.

### Section 907. Transaction of Business Without Registration.

(a) A foreign limited partnership transacting business in this State may not maintain any action, suit, or proceeding in any court of this State until it has registered in this State.

(b) The failure of a foreign limited partnership to register in this State does not impair the validity of any contract or act of the foreign limited partnership or prevent the foreign limited partnership from defending any action, suit, or proceeding in any court of this State.

(c) A limited partner of a foreign limited partnership is not liable as a general partner of the foreign limited partnership solely by reason of having transacted business in this State without registration.

(d) A foreign limited partnership, by transacting business in this State without registration, appoints the Secretary of State as its agent for service of process with respect to [claims for relief] [causes of action] arising out of the transaction of business in this State.

### Section 908. Action by [Appropriate Official].

The [designate the appropriate official] may bring an action to restrain a foreign limited partnership from transacting business in this State in violation of this Article.

## Article 10
# DERIVATIVE ACTIONS

### Section 1001. Right of Action.

A limited partner may bring an action in the right of a limited partnership to recover a judgment in its favor if general partners with authority to do so have refused to bring the action or if an effort to cause those general partners to bring the action is not likely to succeed.

### Section 1002. Proper Plaintiff.

In a derivative action, the plaintiff must be a partner at the time of bringing the action and (i) must have been a partner at the time of the transaction of which he [or she] complains or (ii) his [or her] status as a partner must have devolved upon him by operation of law or pursuant to the terms of the partnership agreement from a person who was a partner at the time of the transaction.

### Section 1003. Pleading.

In a derivative action, the complaint shall set forth with particularity the effort of the plaintiff to secure initiation of the action by a general partner or the reasons for not making the effort.

### Section 1004. Expenses.

If a derivative action is successful, in whole or in part, or if anything is received by the plaintiff as a result of a judgment, compromise, or settlement of an action or claim, the court may award the plaintiff reasonable expenses, including reasonable attorney's fees, and shall direct him [or her] to remit to the limited partnership the remainder of those proceeds received by him [or her].

## Article 11
# MISCELLANEOUS

### Section 1101. Construction and Application.

This [Act] shall be so applied and construed to effectuate its general purpose to make uniform the law with respect to the subject of this [Act] among states enacting it.

### Section 1102. Short Title.

This [Act] may be cited as the Uniform Limited Partnership Act.

### Section 1103. Severability.

If any provision of this [Act] or its application to any person or circumstance is held invalid, the invalidity does not affect other provisions or applications of the [Act] which can be given effect without the invalid provision or application, and to this end the provisions of this [Act] are severable.

## Section 1104. Effective Date, Extended Effective Date, and Repeal.

Except as set forth below, the effective date of this [Act] is _____and the following acts [list existing limited partnership acts] are hereby repealed:

(1) The existing provisions for execution and filing of certificates of limited partnerships and amendments thereunder and cancellations thereof continue in effect until [specify time required to create central filing system], the extended effective date, and Sections 102, 103, 104, 105, 201, 202, 203, 204 and 206 are not effective until the extended effective date.

(2) Section 402, specifying the conditions under which a general partner ceases to be a member of a limited partnership, is not effective until the extended effective date, and the applicable provisions of existing law continue to govern until the extended effective date.

(3) Sections 501, 502 and 608 apply only to contributions and distributions made after the effective date of this [Act].

(4) Section 704 applies only to assignments made after the effective date of this [Act].

(5) Article 9, dealing with registration of foreign limited partnerships, is not effective until the extended effective date.

(6) Unless otherwise agreed by the partners, the applicable provisions of existing law governing allocation of profits and losses (rather than the provisions of Section 503), distributions to a withdrawing partner (rather than the provisions of Section 604), and distributions of assets upon the winding up of a limited partnership (rather than the provisions of Section 804) govern limited partnerships formed before the effective date of this [Act].

## Section 1105. Rules for Cases Not Provided For in This [Act].

In any case not provided for in this [Act] the provisions of the Uniform Partnership Act govern.

## Section 1106. Savings Clause.

The repeal of any statutory provision by this [Act] does not impair, or otherwise affect, the organization or the continued existence of a limited partnership existing at the effective date of this [Act], nor does the repeal of any existing statutory provision by this [Act] impair any contract or affect any right accrued before the effective date of this [Act].

# APPENDIX H

# THE REVISED MODEL BUSINESS CORPORATION ACT

---

## Chapter 1.
## GENERAL PROVISIONS

### Subchapter A. Short Title and Reservation of Power

#### § 1.01 Short Title

This Act shall be known and may be cited as the ''[name of state] Business Corporation Act.''

#### § 1.02 Reservation of Power to Amend or Repeal

The [name of state legislature] has power to amend or repeal all or part of this Act at any time and all domestic and foreign corporations subject to this Act are governed by the amendment or repeal.

### Subchapter B. Filing Documents

#### § 1.20 Filing Requirements

(a) A document must satisfy the requirements of this section, and of any other section that adds to or varies these requirements, to be entitled to filing by the secretary of state.

(b) This Act must require or permit filing the document in the office of the secretary of state.

(c) The document must contain the information required by this Act. It may contain other information as well.

(d) The document must be typewritten or printed.

(e) The document must be in the English language. A corporate name need not be in English if written in English letters or Arabic or Roman numerals, and the certificate of existence required of foreign corporations need not be in English if accompanied by a reasonably authenticated English translation.

(f) The document must be executed:

(1) by the chairman of the board of directors of a domestic or foreign corporation, by its president, or by another of its officers;

(2) if directors have not been selected or the corporation has not been formed, by an incorporator; or

(3) if the corporation is in the hands of a receiver, trustee, or other court-appointed fiduciary, by that fiduciary.

(g) The person executing the document shall sign it and state beneath or opposite his signature his name and the capacity in which he signs. The document may but need not contain: (1) the corporate seal, (2) an attestation by the secretary or an assistant secretary, (3) an acknowledgement, verification, or proof.

(h) If the secretary of state has prescribed a mandatory form for the document under section 1.21, the document must be in or on the prescribed form.

(i) The document must be delivered to the office of the secretary of state for filing and must be accompanied by one exact or conformed copy (except as provided in sections 5.03 and 15.09), the correct filing fee, and any franchise tax, license fee, or penalty required by this Act or other law.

#### § 1.21 Forms

(a) The secretary of state may prescribe and furnish on request forms for: (1) an application for a certificate of existence, (2) a foreign corporation's application for a certificate of authority to transact business in this state, (3) a foreign corporation's application for a certificate of withdrawal, and (4) the annual report. If the secretary of state so requires, use of these forms is mandatory.

(b) The secretary of state may prescribe and furnish on request forms for other documents required or permitted to be filed by this Act but their use is not mandatory.

#### § 1.22 Filing, Service, and Copying Fees

(a) The secretary of state shall collect the following fees when the documents described in this subsection are delivered to him for filing:

| Document | Fee |
|---|---|
| (1) Articles of incorporation | $_____. |
| (2) Application for use of indistinguishable name | $_____. |
| (3) Application for reserved name | $_____. |
| (4) Notice of transfer of reserved name | $_____. |

(5) Application for registered name     $_____.

(6) Application for renewal of registered name     $_____.

(7) Corporation's statement of change of registered agent or registered office or both     $_____.

(8) Agent's statement of change of registered office for each affected corporation not to exceed a total of     $_____.

(9) Agent's statement of resignation     No fee.

(10) Amendment of articles of incorporation     $_____.

(11) Restatement of articles of incorporation with amendment of articles     $_____.

(12) Articles of merger or share exchange     $_____.

(13) Articles of dissolution     $_____.

(14) Articles of revocation of dissolution     $_____.

(15) Certificate of administrative dissolution     No fee.

(16) Application for reinstatement following administrative dissolution     $_____.

(17) Certificate of reinstatement     No fee.

(18) Certificate of judicial dissolution     No fee.

(19) Application for certificate of authority     No fee.

(20) Application for amended certificate of authority     $_____.

(21) Application for certificate of withdrawal     $_____.

(22) Certificate of revocation of authority to transact business     No fee.

(23) Annual report     $_____.

(24) Articles of correction     $_____.

(25) Application for certificate of existence or authorization     $_____.

(26) Any other document required or permitted to be filed by this Act.     $_____.

(b) The secretary of state shall collect a fee of $_____ each time process is served on him under this Act. The party to a proceeding causing service of process is entitled to recover this fee as costs if he prevails in the proceeding.

(c) The secretary of state shall collect the following fees for copying and certifying the copy of any filed document relating to a domestic or foreign corporation:

(1) $_____ a page for copying; and

(2) $_____ for the certificate.

### § 1.23 Effective Time and Date of Document

(a) Except as provided in subsection (b) and section 1.24(c), a document accepted for filing is effective:

(1) at the time of filing on the date it is filed, as evidenced by the secretary of state's date and time endorsement on the original document; or

(2) at the time specified in the document as its effective time on the date it is filed.

(b) A document may specify a delayed effective time and date, and if it does so the document becomes effective at the time and date specified. If a delayed effective date but no time is specified, the document is effective at the close of business on that date. A delayed effective date for a document may not be later than the 90th day after the date it is filed.

### § 1.24 Correcting Filed Document

(a) A domestic or foreign corporation may correct a document filed by the secretary of state if the document (1) contains an incorrect statement or (2) was defectively executed, attested, sealed, verified, or acknowledged.

(b) A document is corrected:

(1) by preparing articles of correction that (i) describe the document (including its filing date) or attach a copy of it to the articles, (ii) specify the incorrect statement and the reason it is incorrect or the manner in which the execution was defective, and (iii) correct the incorrect statement or defective execution; and

(2) by delivering the articles to the secretary of state for filing.

(c) Articles of correction are effective on the effective date of the document they correct except as to persons relying on the uncorrected document and adversely affected by the correction. As to those persons, articles of correction are effective when filed.

### § 1.25 Filing Duty of Secretary of State

(a) If a document delivered to the office of the secretary of state for filing satisfies the requirements of section 1.20, the secretary of state shall file it.

(b) The secretary of state files a document by stamping or otherwise endorsing "Filed," together with his name and official title and the date and time of receipt, on both the original and the document copy and on the receipt for the filing fee. After filing a document, except as provided in sections 5.03 and 15.10, the secretary of state shall deliver the document copy, with the filing fee receipt (or acknowledgement of receipt if no fee is required) attached, to the domestic or foreign corporation or its representative.

(c) If the secretary of state refuses to file a document, he shall return it to the domestic or foreign corporation or its representative within five days after the document was delivered, together with a brief, written explanation of the reason for his refusal.

(d) The secretary of state's duty to file documents under this section is ministerial. His filing or refusing to file a document does not:

(1) affect the validity or invalidity of the document in whole or part;

(2) relate to the correctness or incorrectness of information contained in the document;

(3) create a presumption that the document is valid or invalid or that information contained in the document is correct or incorrect.

## § 1.26 Appeal From Secretary of State's Refusal to File Document

(a) If the secretary of state refuses to file a document delivered to his office for filing, the domestic or foreign corporation may appeal the refusal to the [name or describe] court [of the county where the corporation's principal office (or, if none in this state, its registered office) is or will be located] [of _____ county]. The appeal is commenced by petitioning the court to compel filing the document and by attaching to the petition the document and the secretary of state's explanation of his refusal to file.

(b) The court may summarily order the secretary of state to file the document or take other action the court considers appropriate.

(c) The court's final decision may be appealed as in other civil proceedings.

## § 1.27 Evidentiary Effect of Copy of Filed Document

A certificate attached to a copy of the document filed by the secretary of state, bearing his signature (which may be in facsimile) and the seal of this state, is conclusive evidence that the original document is on file with the secretary of state.

## § 1.28 Certificate of Existence

(a) Anyone may apply to the secretary of state to furnish a certificate of existence for a domestic corporation or a certificate of authorization for a foreign corporation.

(b) A certificate of existence or authorization sets forth:

(1) the domestic corporation's corporate name or the foreign corporation's corporate name used in this state;

(2) that (i) the domestic corporation is duly incorporated under the law of this state, the date of its incorporation, and the period of its duration if less than perpetual; or (ii) that the foreign corporation is authorized to transact business in this state;

(3) that all fees, taxes, and penalties owed to this state have been paid, if (i) payment is reflected in the records of the secretary of state and (ii) nonpayment affects the existence or authorization of the domestic or foreign corporation;

(4) that its most recent annual report required by section 16.22 has been delivered to the secretary of state;

(5) that articles of dissolution have not been filed; and

(6) other facts of record in the office of the secretary of state that may be requested by the applicant.

(c) Subject to any qualification stated in the certificate, a certificate of existence or authorization issued by the secretary of state may be relied upon as conclusive evidence that the domestic or foreign corporation is in existence or is authorized to transact business in this state.

## § 1.29 Penalty for Signing False Document

(a) A person commits an offense if he signs a document he knows is false in any material respect with intent that the document be delivered to the secretary of state for filing.

(b) An offense under this section is a [_____] misdemeanor [punishable by a fine of not to exceed $_____].

## Subchapter C. Secretary of State

### § 1.30 Powers

The secretary of state has the power reasonably necessary to perform the duties required of him by this Act.

## Subchapter D. Definitions

### § 1.40 Act Definitions

In this Act:

(1) "Articles of incorporation" include amended and restated articles of incorporation and articles of merger.

(2) "Authorized shares" means the shares of all classes a domestic or foreign corporation is authorized to issue.

(3) "Conspicuous" means so written that a reasonable person against whom the writing is to operate should have noticed it. For example, printing in italics or boldface or contrasting color, or typing in capitals or underlined, is conspicuous.

(4) "Corporation" or "domestic corporation" means a corporation for profit, which is not a foreign corporation, incorporated under or subject to the provisions of this Act.

(5) "Deliver" includes mail.

(6) "Distribution" means a direct or indirect transfer of money or other property (except its own shares) or incurrence of indebtedness by a corporation to or for the benefit of its shareholders in respect of any of its shares. A distribution may be in the form of a declaration or payment of a dividend; a purchase, redemption, or other acquisition of shares; a distribution of indebtedness; or otherwise.

(7) "Effective date of notice" is defined in section 1.41.

(8) "Employee" includes an officer but not a director. A director may accept duties that make him also an employee.

(9) "Entity" includes corporation and foreign corporation; not-for-profit corporation; profit and not-for-profit unincorporated association; business trust, estate, partnership, trust, and two or more persons having a joint or common economic interest; and state, United States, and foreign government.

(10) "Foreign corporation" means a corporation for profit incorporated under a law other than the law of this state.

(11) "Governmental subdivision" includes authority, county, district, and municipality.

(12) "Includes" denotes a partial definition.

(13) "Individual" includes the estate of an incompetent or deceased individual.

(14) "Means" denotes an exhaustive definition.

(15) "Notice" is defined in section 1.41.

(16) "Person" includes individual and entity.

(17) "Principal office" means the office (in or out of this state) so designated in the annual report where the principal executive offices of a domestic or foreign corporation are located.

(18) "Proceeding" includes civil suit and criminal, administrative, and investigatory action.

(19) "Record date" means the date established under chapter 6 or 7 on which a corporation determines the identity of its shareholders and their shareholdings for purposes of this Act. The determinations shall be made as of the close of business on the record date unless another time for doing so is specified when the record date is fixed.

(20) "Secretary" means the corporate officer to whom the board of directors has delegated responsibility under section 8.40(c) for custody of the minutes of the meetings of the board of directors and of the shareholders and for authenticating records of the corporation.

(21) "Share" means the unit into which the proprietary interests in a corporation are divided.

(22) "Shareholder" means the person in whose name shares are registered in the records of a corporation or the beneficial owner of shares to the extent of the rights granted by a nominee certificate on file with a corporation.

(23) "State," when referring to a part of the United States, includes a state and commonwealth (and their agencies and governmental subdivisions) and a territory, and insular possession (and their agencies and governmental subdivisions) of the United States.

(24) "Subscriber" means a person who subscribes for shares in a corporation, whether before or after incorporation.

(25) "United States" includes district, authority, bureau, commission, department, and any other agency of the United States.

(26) "Voting group" means all shares of one or more classes or series that under the articles of incorporation or this Act are entitled to vote and be counted together collectively on a matter at a meeting of shareholders. All shares entitled by the articles of incorporation or this Act to vote generally on the matter are for that purpose a single voting group.

### § 1.41 Notice

(a) Notice under this Act shall be in writing unless oral notice is reasonable under the circumstances.

(b) Notice may be communicated in person; by telephone, telegraph, teletype, or other form of wire or wireless communication; or by mail or private carrier. If these forms of personal notice are impracticable, notice may be communicated by a newspaper of general circulation in the area where published; or by radio, television, or other form of public broadcast communication.

(c) Written notice by a domestic or foreign corporation to its shareholder, if in a comprehensible form, is effective when mailed, if mailed postpaid and correctly addressed to the shareholder's address shown in the corporation's current record of shareholders.

(d) Written notice to a domestic or foreign corporation (authorized to transact business in this state) may be addressed to its registered agent at its registered office or to the corporation or its secretary at its principal office shown in its most recent annual report or, in the case of a foreign corporation that has not yet delivered an annual report, in its application for a certificate of authority.

(e) Except as provided in subsections (c) and (d), written notice, if in a comprehensible form, is effective at the earliest of the following:

(1) when received;

(2) five days after its deposit in the United States Mail, as evidenced by the postmark, if mailed postpaid and correctly addressed;

(3) on the date shown on the return receipt, if sent by registered or certified mail, return receipt requested, and the receipt is signed by or on behalf of the addressee.

(f) Oral notice is effective when communicated if communicated in a comprehensible manner.

(g) If this Act prescribes notice requirements for particular circumstances, those requirements govern. If articles of incorporation or bylaws prescribe notice requirements, not inconsistent with this section or other provisions of this Act, those requirements govern.

### § 1.42 Number of Shareholders

(a) For purposes of this Act, the following identified as a shareholder in a corporation's current record of shareholders constitutes one shareholder:

(1) three or fewer co-owners;

(2) a corporation, partnership, trust, estate, or other entity;

(3) the trustees, guardians, custodians, or other fiduciaries of a single trust, estate, or account.

(b) For purposes of this Act, shareholdings registered in substantially similar names constitute one shareholder if it is reasonable to believe that the names represent the same person.

# Chapter 2.
# INCORPORATION

### § 2.01 Incorporators

One or more persons may act as the incorporator or incorporators of a corporation by delivering articles of incorporation to the secretary of state for filing.

## § 2.02 Articles of Incorporation

(a) The articles of incorporation must set forth:

(1) a corporate name for the corporation that satisfies the requirements of section 4.01;

(2) the number of shares the corporation is authorized to issue;

(3) the street address of the corporation's initial registered office and the name of its initial registered agent at that office; and

(4) the name and address of each incorporator.

(b) The articles of incorporation may set forth:

(1) the names and addresses of the individuals who are to serve as the initial directors;

(2) provisions not inconsistent with law regarding:

(i) the purpose or purposes for which the corporation is organized;

(ii) managing the business and regulating the affairs of the corporation;

(iii) defining, limiting, and regulating the powers of the corporation, its board of directors, and shareholders;

(iv) a par value for authorized shares or classes of shares;

(v) the imposition of personal liability on shareholders for the debts of the corporation to a specified extent and upon specified conditions;

(3) any provision that under this Act is required or permitted to be set forth in the bylaws; and

(4) a provision eliminating or limiting the liability of a director to the corporation or its shareholders for money damages for any action taken, or any failure to take any action, as a director, except liability for (A) the amount of a financial benefit received by a director to which he is not entitled; (B) an intentional infliction of harm on the corporation or the shareholders; (C) a violation of section 8.33; or (D) an intentional violation of criminal law.

(c) The articles of incorporation need not set forth any of the corporate powers enumerated in this Act.

## § 2.03 Incorporation

(a) Unless a delayed effective date is specified, the corporate existence begins when the articles of incorporation are filed.

(b) The secretary of state's filing of the articles of incorporation is conclusive proof that the incorporators satisfied all conditions precedent to incorporation except in a proceeding by the state to cancel or revoke the incorporation or involuntarily dissolve the corporation.

## § 2.04 Liability for Preincorporation Transactions

All persons purporting to act as or on behalf of a corporation, knowing there was no incorporation under this Act, are jointly and severally liable for all liabilities created while so acting.

## § 2.05 Organization of Corporation

(a) After incorporation:

(1) if initial directors are named in the articles of incorporation, the initial directors shall hold an organizational meeting, at the call of a majority of the directors, to complete the organization of the corporation by appointing officers, adopting bylaws, and carrying on any other business brought before the meeting;

(2) if initial directors are not named in the articles, the incorporator or incorporators shall hold an organizational meeting at the call of a majority of the incorporators:

(i) to elect directors and complete the organization of the corporation; or

(ii) to elect a board of directors who shall complete the organization of the corporation.

(b) Action required or permitted by this Act to be taken by incorporators at an organizational meeting may be taken without a meeting if the action taken is evidenced by one or more written consents describing the action taken and signed by each incorporator.

(c) An organizational meeting may be held in or out of this state.

## § 2.06 Bylaws

(a) The incorporators or board of directors of a corporation shall adopt initial bylaws for the corporation.

(b) The bylaws of a corporation may contain any provision for managing the business and regulating the affairs of the corporation that is not inconsistent with law or the articles of incorporation.

## § 2.07 Emergency Bylaws

(a) Unless the articles of incorporation provide otherwise, the board of directors of a corporation may adopt bylaws to be effective only in an emergency defined in subsection (d). The emergency bylaws, which are subject to amendment or repeal by the shareholders, may make all provisions necessary for managing the corporation during the emergency, including:

(1) procedures for calling a meeting of the board of directors;

(2) quorum requirements for the meeting; and

(3) designation of additional or substitute directors.

(b) All provisions of the regular bylaws consistent with the emergency bylaws remain effective during the emergency. The emergency bylaws are not effective after the emergency ends.

(c) Corporate action taken in good faith in accordance with the emergency bylaws:

(1) binds the corporation; and

(2) may not be used to impose liability on a corporate director, officer, employee, or agent.

(d) An emergency exists for purposes of this section if a

quorum of the corporation's directors cannot readily be assembled because of some catastrophic event.

# Chapter 3.
# PURPOSES AND POWERS

## § 3.01 Purposes

(a) Every corporation incorporated under this Act has the purpose of engaging in any lawful business unless a more limited purpose is set forth in the articles of incorporation.

(b) A corporation engaging in a business that is subject to regulation under another statute of this state may incorporate under this Act only if permitted by, and subject to all limitations of, the other statute.

## § 3.02 General Powers

Unless its articles of incorporation provide otherwise, every corporation has perpetual duration and succession in its corporate name and has the same powers as an individual to do all things necessary or convenient to carry out its business and affairs, including without limitation power:

(1) to sue and be sued, complain and defend in its corporate name;

(2) to have a corporate seal, which may be altered at will, and to use it, or a facsimile of it, by impressing or affixing it or in any other manner reproducing it;

(3) to make and amend bylaws, not inconsistent with its articles of incorporation or with the laws of this state, for managing the business and regulating the affairs of the corporation;

(4) to purchase, receive, lease, or otherwise acquire, and own, hold, improve, use, and otherwise deal with, real or personal property, or any legal or equitable interest in property, wherever located;

(5) to sell, convey, mortgage, pledge, lease, exchange, and otherwise dispose of all or any part of its property;

(6) to purchase, receive, subscribe for, or otherwise acquire; own, hold, vote, use, sell, mortgage, lend, pledge, or otherwise dispose of; and deal in and with shares or other interests in, or obligations of, any other entity;

(7) to make contracts and guarantees, incur liabilities, borrow money, issue its notes, bonds, and other obligations (which may be convertible into or include the option to purchase other securities of the corporation), and secure any of its obligations by mortgage or pledge of any of its property, franchises, or income;

(8) to lend money, invest and reinvest its funds, and receive and hold real and personal property as security for repayment;

(9) to be a promoter, partner, member, associate, or manager of any partnership, joint venture, trust, or other entity;

(10) to conduct its business, locate offices, and exercise the powers granted by this Act within or without this state;

(11) to elect directors and appoint officers, employees, and agents of the corporation, define their duties, fix their compensation, and lend them money and credit;

(12) to pay pensions and establish pension plans, pension trusts, profit sharing plans, share bonus plans, share option plans, and benefit or incentive plans for any or all of its current or former directors, officers, employees, and agents;

(13) to make donations for the public welfare or for charitable, scientific, or educational purposes;

(14) to transact any lawful business that will aid governmental policy;

(15) to make payments or donations, or do any other act, not inconsistent with law, that furthers the business and affairs of the corporation.

## § 3.03 Emergency Powers

(a) In anticipation of or during an emergency defined in subsection (d), the board of directors of a corporation may:

(1) modify lines of succession to accommodate the incapacity of any director, officer, employee, or agent; and

(2) relocate the principal office, designate alternative principal offices or regional offices, or authorize the officers to do so.

(b) During an emergency defined in subsection (d), unless emergency bylaws provide otherwise:

(1) notice of a meeting of the board of directors need be given only to those directors whom it is practicable to reach and may be given in any practicable manner, including by publication and radio; and

(2) one or more officers of the corporation present at a meeting of the board of directors may be deemed to be directors for the meeting, in order of rank and within the same rank in order of seniority, as necessary to achieve a quorum.

(c) Corporate action taken in good faith during an emergency under this section to further the ordinary business affairs of the corporation:

(1) binds the corporation; and

(2) may not be used to impose liability on a corporate director, officer, employee, or agent.

(d) An emergency exists for purposes of this section if a quorum of the corporation's directors cannot readily be assembled because of some catastrophic event.

## § 3.04 Ultra Vires

(a) Except as provided in subsection (b), the validity of corporate action may not be challenged on the ground that the corporation lacks or lacked power to act.

(b) A corporation's power to act may be challenged:

(1) in a proceeding by a shareholder against the corporation to enjoin the act;

(2) in a proceeding by the corporation, directly, derivatively, or through a receiver, trustee, or other legal rep-

resentative, against an incumbent or former director, officer, employee, or agent of the corporation; or

(3) in a proceeding by the Attorney General under section 14.30.

(c) In a shareholder's proceeding under subsection (b)(1) to enjoin an unauthorized corporate act, the court may enjoin or set aside the act, if equitable and if all affected persons are parties to the proceeding, and may award damages for loss (other than anticipated profits) suffered by the corporation or another party because of enjoining the unauthorized act.

# Chapter 4.
# NAME

### § 4.01  Corporate Name

(a)  A corporate name:

(1)  must contain the word "corporation," "incorporated," "company," or "limited," or the abbreviation "corp.," "inc.," "co.," or "ltd.," or words or abbreviations of like import in another language; and

(2)  may not contain language stating or implying that the corporation is organized for a purpose other than that permitted by section 3.01 and its articles of incorporation.

(b)  Except as authorized by subsections (c) and (d), a corporate name must be distinguishable upon the records of the secretary of state from:

(1)  the corporate name of a corporation incorporated or authorized to transact business in this state;

(2)  a corporate name reserved or registered under section 4.02 or 4.03;

(3)  the fictitious name adopted by a foreign corporation authorized to transact business in this state because its real name is unavailable; and

(4)  the corporate name of a not-for-profit corporation incorporated or authorized to transact business in this state.

(c)  A corporation may apply to the secretary of state for authorization to use a name that is not distinguishable upon his records from one or more of the names described in subsection (b). The secretary of state shall authorize use of the name applied for if:

(1)  the other corporation consents to the use in writing and submits an undertaking in form satisfactory to the secretary of state to change its name to a name that is distinguishable upon the records of the secretary of state from the name of the applying corporation; or

(2)  the applicant delivers to the secretary of state a certified copy of the final judgment of a court of competent jurisdiction establishing the applicant's right to use the name applied for in this state.

(d)  A corporation may use the name (including the fictitious name) of another domestic or foreign corporation that is used in this state if the other corporation is incorporated or authorized to transact business in this state and the proposed user corporation:

(1)  has merged with the other corporation;

(2)  has been formed by reorganization of the other corporation; or

(3)  has acquired all or substantially all of the assets, including the corporate name, of the other corporation.

(e)  This Act does not control the use of fictitious names.

### § 4.02  Reserved Name

(a)  A person may reserve the exclusive use of a corporate name, including a fictitious name for a foreign corporation whose corporate name is not available, by delivering an application to the secretary of state for filing. The application must set forth the name and address of the applicant and the name proposed to be reserved. If the secretary of state finds that the corporate name applied for is available, he shall reserve the name for the applicant's exclusive use for a nonrenewable 120-day period.

(b)  The owner of a reserved corporate name may transfer the reservation to another person by delivering to the secretary of state a signed notice of the transfer that states the name and address of the transferee.

### § 4.03  Registered Name

(a)  A foreign corporation may register its corporate name, or its corporate name with any addition required by section 15.06, if the name is distinguishable upon the records of the secretary of state from the corporate names that are not available under section 4.01(b)(3).

(b)  A foreign corporation registers its corporate name, or its corporate name with any addition required by section 15.06, by delivering to the secretary of state for filing an application:

(1)  setting forth its corporate name, or its corporate name with any addition required by section 15.06, the state or country and date of its incorporation, and a brief description of the nature of the business in which it is engaged; and

(2)  accompanied by a certificate of existence (or a document of similar import) from the state or country of incorporation.

(c)  The name is registered for the applicant's exclusive use upon the effective date of the application.

(d)  A foreign corporation whose registration is effective may renew it for successive years by delivering to the secretary of state for filing a renewal application, which complies with the requirements of subsection (b), between October 1 and December 31 of the preceding year. The renewal application renews the registration for the following calendar year.

(e)  A foreign corporation whose registration is effective may thereafter qualify as a foreign corporation under that name or consent in writing to the use of that name by a corporation thereafter incorporated under this Act or by another foreign corporation thereafter authorized to transact business in this state. The registration terminates when the domestic corporation is incorporated or the foreign corporation qualifies or consents to the qualification of another foreign corporation under the registered name.

# Chapter 5.
# OFFICE AND AGENT

### § 5.01   Registered Office and Registered Agent

Each corporation must continuously maintain in this state:

(1) a registered office that may be the same as any of its places of business; and

(2) a registered agent, who may be:

(i) an individual who resides in this state and whose business office is identical with the registered office;

(ii) a domestic corporation or not-for-profit domestic corporation whose business office is identical with the registered office; or

(iii) a foreign corporation or not-for-profit foreign corporation authorized to transact business in this state whose business office is identical with the registered office.

### § 5.02   Change of Registered Office or Registered Agent

(a) A corporation may change its registered office or registered agent by delivering to the secretary of state for filing a statement of change that sets forth:

(1) the name of the corporation;

(2) the street address of its current registered office;

(3) if the current registered office is to be changed, the street address of the new registered office;

(4) the name of its current registered agent;

(5) if the current registered agent is to be changed, the name of the new registered agent and the new agent's written consent (either on the statement or attached to it) to the appointment; and

(6) that after the change or changes are made, the street addresses of its registered office and the business office of its registered agent will be identical.

(b) If a registered agent changes the street address of his business office, he may change the street address of the registered office of any corporation for which he is the registered agent by notifying the corporation in writing of the change and signing (either manually or in facsimile) and delivering to the secretary of state for filing a statement that complies with the requirements of subsection (a) and recites that the corporation has been notified of the change.

### § 5.03   Resignation of Registered Agent

(a) A registered agent may resign his agency appointment by signing and delivering to the secretary of state for filing the signed original and two exact or conformed copies of a statement of resignation. The statement may include a statement that the registered office is also discontinued.

(b) After filing the statement the secretary of state shall mail one copy to the registered office (if not discontinued) and the other copy to the corporation at its principal office.

(c) The agency appointment is terminated, and the registered office discontinued if so provided, on the 31st day after the date on which the statement was filed.

### § 5.04   Service on Corporation

(a) A corporation's registered agent is the corporation's agent for service of process, notice, or demand required or permitted by law to be served on the corporation.

(b) If a corporation has no registered agent, or the agent cannot with reasonable diligence be served, the corporation may be served by registered or certified mail, return receipt requested, addressed to the secretary of the corporation at its principal office. Service is perfected under this subsection at the earliest of:

(1) the date the corporation receives the mail;

(2) the date shown on the return receipt, if signed on behalf of the corporation; or

(3) five days after its deposit in the United States Mail, if mailed postpaid and correctly addressed.

(c) This section does not prescribe the only means, or necessarily the required means, of serving a corporation.

# Chapter 6.
# SHARES AND DISTRIBUTIONS

## Subchapter A.   Shares

### § 6.01   Authorized Shares

(a) The articles of incorporation must prescribe the classes of shares and the number of shares of each class that the corporation is authorized to issue. If more than one class of shares is authorized, the articles of incorporation must prescribe a distinguishing designation for each class, and prior to the issuance of shares of a class the preferences, limitations, and relative rights of that class must be described in the articles of incorporation. All shares of a class must have preferences, limitations, and relative rights identical with those of other shares of the same class except to the extent otherwise permitted by section 6.02.

(b) The articles of incorporation must authorize (1) one or more classes of shares that together have unlimited voting rights, and (2) one or more classes of shares (which may be the same class or classes as those with voting rights) that together are entitled to receive the net assets of the corporation upon dissolution.

(c) The articles of incorporation may authorize one or more classes of shares that:

(1) have special, conditional, or limited voting rights, or no right to vote, except to the extent prohibited by this Act;

(2) are redeemable or convertible as specified in the articles of incorporation (i) at the option of the corporation,

the shareholder, or another person or upon the occurrence of a designated event; (ii) for cash, indebtedness, securities, or other property; (iii) in a designated amount or in an amount determined in accordance with a designated formula or by reference to extrinsic data or events;

(3) entitle the holders to distributions calculated in any manner, including dividends that may be cumulative, noncumulative, or partially cumulative;

(4) have preference over any other class of shares with respect to distributions, including dividends and distributions upon the dissolution of the corporation.

(d) The description of the designations, preferences, limitations, and relative rights of share classes in subsection (c) is not exhaustive.

### § 6.02 Terms of Class or Series Determined by Board of Directors

(a) If the articles of incorporation so provide, the board of directors may determine, in whole or part, the preferences, limitations, and relative rights (within the limits set forth in section 6.01) of (1) any class of shares before the issuance of any shares of that class or (2) one or more series within a class before the issuance of any shares of that series.

(b) Each series of a class must be given a distinguishing designation.

(c) All shares of a series must have preferences, limitations, and relative rights identical with those of other shares of the same series and, except to the extent otherwise provided in the description of the series, of those of other series of the same class.

(d) Before issuing any shares of a class or series created under this section, the corporation must deliver to the secretary of state for filing articles of amendment, which are effective without shareholder action, that set forth:

(1) the name of the corporation;

(2) the text of the amendment determining the terms of the class or series of shares;

(3) the date it was adopted; and

(4) a statement that the amendment was duly adopted by the board of directors.

### § 6.03 Issued and Outstanding Shares

(a) A corporation may issue the number of shares of each class or series authorized by the articles of incorporation. Shares that are issued are outstanding shares until they are reacquired, redeemed, converted, or cancelled.

(b) The reacquisition, redemption, or conversion of outstanding shares is subject to the limitations of subsection (c) of this section and to section 6.40.

(c) At all times that shares of the corporation are outstanding, one or more shares that together have unlimited voting rights and one or more shares that together are entitled to receive the net assets of the corporation upon dissolution must be outstanding.

### § 6.04 Fractional Shares

(a) A corporation may:

(1) issue fractions of a share or pay in money the value of fractions of a share;

(2) arrange for disposition of fractional shares by the shareholders;

(3) issue scrip in registered or bearer form entitling the holder to receive a full share upon surrendering enough scrip to equal a full share.

(b) Each certificate representing scrip must be conspicuously labeled ''scrip'' and must contain the information required by section 6.25(b).

(c) The holder of a fractional share is entitled to exercise the rights of a shareholder, including the right to vote, to receive dividends, and to participate in the assets of the corporation upon liquidation. The holder of scrip is not entitled to any of these rights unless the scrip provides for them.

(d) The board of directors may authorize the issuance of scrip subject to any condition considered desirable, including:

(1) that the scrip will become void if not exchanged for full shares before a specified date; and

(2) that the shares for which the scrip is exchangeable may be sold and the proceeds paid to the scripholders.

## Subchapter B. Issuance of Shares

### § 6.20 Subscription for Shares before Incorporation

(a) A subscription for shares entered into before incorporation is irrevocable for six months unless the subscription agreement provides a longer or shorter period or all the subscribers agree to revocation.

(b) The board of directors may determine the payment terms of subscriptions for shares that were entered into before incorporation, unless the subscription agreement specifies them. A call for payment by the board of directors must be uniform so far as practicable as to all shares of the same class or series, unless the subscription agreement specifies otherwise.

(c) Shares issued pursuant to subscriptions entered into before incorporation are fully paid and nonassessable when the corporation receives the consideration specified in the subscription agreement.

(d) If a subscriber defaults in payment of money or property under a subscription agreement entered into before incorporation, the corporation may collect the amount owed as any other debt. Alternatively, unless the subscription agreement provides otherwise, the corporation may rescind the agreement and may sell the shares if the debt remains unpaid more than 20 days after the corporation sends written demand for payment to the subscriber.

(e) A subscription agreement entered into after incorporation is a contract between the subscriber and the corporation subject to section 6.21.

## § 6.21 Issuance of Shares

(a) The powers granted in this section to the board of directors may be reserved to the shareholders by the articles of incorporation.

(b) The board of directors may authorize shares to be issued for consideration consisting of any tangible or intangible property or benefit to the corporation, including cash, promissory notes, services performed, contracts for services to be performed, or other securities of the corporation.

(c) Before the corporation issues shares, the board of directors must determine that the consideration received or to be received for shares to be issued is adequate. That determination by the board of directors is conclusive insofar as the adequacy of consideration for the issuance of shares relates to whether the shares are validly issued, fully paid, and nonassessable.

(d) When the corporation receives the consideration for which the board of directors authorized the issuance of shares, the shares issued therefor are fully paid and nonassessable.

(e) The corporation may place in escrow shares issued for a contract for future services or benefits or a promissory note, or make other arrangements to restrict the transfer of the shares, and may credit distributions in respect of the shares against their purchase price, until the services are performed, the note is paid, or the benefits received. If the services are not performed, the note is not paid, or the benefits are not received, the shares escrowed or restricted and the distributions credited may be cancelled in whole or part.

## § 6.22 Liability of Shareholders

(a) A purchaser from a corporation of its own shares is not liable to the corporation or its creditors with respect to the shares except to pay the consideration for which the shares were authorized to be issued (section 6.21) or specified in the subscription agreement (section 6.20).

(b) Unless otherwise provided in the articles of incorporation, a shareholder of a corporation is not personally liable for the acts or debts of the corporation except that he may become personally liable by reason of his own acts or conduct.

## § 6.23 Share Dividends

(a) Unless the articles of incorporation provide otherwise, shares may be issued pro rata and without consideration to the corporation's shareholders or to the shareholders of one or more classes or series. An issuance of shares under this subsection is a share dividend.

(b) Shares of one class or series may not be issued as a share dividend in respect of shares of another class or series unless (1) the articles of incorporation so authorize, (2) a majority of the votes entitled to be cast by the class or series to be issued approve the issue, or (3) there are no outstanding shares of the class or series to be issued.

(c) If the board of directors does not fix the record date for determining shareholders entitled to a share dividend, it is the date the board of directors authorizes the share dividend.

## § 6.24 Share Options

A corporation may issue rights, options, or warrants for the purchase of shares of the corporation. The board of directors shall determine the terms upon which the rights, options, or warrants are issued, their form and content, and the consideration for which the shares are to be issued.

## § 6.25 Form and Content of Certificates

(a) Shares may but need not be represented by certificates. Unless this Act or another statute expressly provides otherwise, the rights and obligations of shareholders are identical whether or not their shares are represented by certificates.

(b) At a minimum each share certificate must state on its face:

(1) the name of the issuing corporation and that it is organized under the law of this state;

(2) the name of the person to whom issued; and

(3) the number and class of shares and the designation of the series, if any, the certificate represents.

(c) If the issuing corporation is authorized to issue different classes of shares or different series within a class, the designations, relative rights, preferences, and limitations applicable to each class and the variations in rights, preferences, and limitations determined for each series (and the authority of the board of directors to determine variations for future series) must be summarized on the front or back of each certificate. Alternatively, each certificate may state conspicuously on its front or back that the corporation will furnish the shareholder this information on request in writing and without charge.

(d) Each share certificate (1) must be signed (either manually or in facsimile) by two officers designated in the bylaws or by the board of directors and (2) may bear the corporate seal or its facsimile.

(e) If the person who signed (either manually or in facsimile) a share certificate no longer holds office when the certificate is issued, the certificate is nevertheless valid.

## § 6.26 Shares without Certificates

(a) Unless the articles of incorporation or bylaws provide otherwise, the board of directors of a corporation may authorize the issue of some or all of the shares of any or all of its classes or series without certificates. The authorization does not affect shares already represented by certificates until they are surrendered to the corporation.

(b) Within a reasonable time after the issue or transfer of shares without certificates, the corporation shall send the shareholder a written statement of the information required on certificates by section 6.25(b) and (c), and, if applicable, section 6.27.

## § 6.27 Restriction on Transfer or Registration of Shares and Other Securities

(a) The articles of incorporation, bylaws, an agreement among shareholders, or an agreement between shareholders and the corporation may impose restrictions on the transfer or registration of transfer of shares of the corporation. A restriction does not affect shares issued before the restriction was adopted unless the holders of the shares are parties to the restriction agreement or voted in favor of the restriction.

(b) A restriction on the transfer or registration of transfer of shares is valid and enforceable against the holder or a transferee of the holder if the restriction is authorized by this section and its existence is noted conspicuously on the front or back of the certificate or is contained in the information statement required by section 6.26(b). Unless so noted, a restriction is not enforceable against a person without knowledge of the restriction.

(c) A restriction on the transfer or registration of transfer of shares is authorized:

(1) to maintain the corporation's status when it is dependent on the number or identity of its shareholders;

(2) to preserve exemptions under federal or state securities law;

(3) for any other reasonable purpose.

(d) A restriction on the transfer or registration of transfer of shares may:

(1) obligate the shareholder first to offer the corporation or other persons (separately, consecutively, or simultaneously) an opportunity to acquire the restricted shares;

(2) obligate the corporate or other persons (separately, consecutively, or simultaneously) to acquire the restricted shares;

(3) require the corporation, the holders of any class of its shares, or another person to approve the transfer of the restricted shares, if the requirement is not manifestly unreasonable;

(4) prohibit the transfer of the restricted shares to designated persons or classes of persons, if the prohibition is not manifestly unreasonable.

(e) For purposes of this section, "shares" includes a security convertible into or carrying a right to subscribe for or acquire shares.

### § 6.28 Expense of Issue

A corporation may pay the expenses of selling or underwriting its shares, and of organizing or reorganizing the corporation, from the consideration received for shares.

## Subchapter C. Subsequent Acquisition of Shares by Shareholders and Corporation

### § 6.30 Shareholders' Preemptive Rights

(a) The shareholders of a corporation do not have a preemptive right to acquire the corporation's unissued shares except to the extent the articles of incorporation so provide.

(b) A statement included in the articles of incorporation that "the corporation elects to have preemptive rights" (or words of similar import) means that the following principles apply except to the extent the articles of incorporation expressly provide otherwise:

(1) The shareholders of the corporation have a preemptive right, granted on uniform terms and conditions prescribed by the board of directors to provide a fair and reasonable opportunity to exercise the right, to acquire proportional amounts of the corporation's unissued shares upon the decision of the board of directors to issue them.

(2) A shareholder may waive his preemptive right. A waiver evidenced by a writing is irrevocable even though it is not supported by consideration.

(3) There is no preemptive right with respect to:

(i) shares issued as compensation to directors, officers, agents, or employees of the corporation, its subsidiaries or affiliates;

(ii) shares issued to satisfy conversion or option rights created to provide compensation to directors, officers, agents, or employees of the corporation, its subsidiaries or affiliates;

(iii) shares authorized in articles of incorporation that are issued within six months from the effective date of incorporation;

(iv) shares sold otherwise than for money.

(4) Holders of shares of any class without general voting rights but with preferential rights to distributions or assets have no preemptive rights with respect to shares of any class.

(5) Holders of shares of any class with general voting rights but without preferential rights to distributions or assets have no preemptive rights with respect to shares of any class with preferential rights to distributions or assets unless the shares with preferential rights are convertible into or carry a right to subscribe for or acquire shares without preferential rights.

(6) Shares subject to preemptive rights that are not acquired by shareholders may be issued to any person for a period of one year after being offered to shareholders at a consideration set by the board of directors that is not lower than the consideration set for the exercise of preemptive rights. An offer at a lower consideration or after the expiration of one year is subject to the shareholders' preemptive rights.

(c) For purposes of this section, "shares" includes a security convertible into or carrying a right to subscribe for or acquire shares.

### § 6.31 Corporation's Acquisition of Its Own Shares

(a) A corporation may acquire its own shares and shares so acquired constitute authorized but unissued shares.

(b) If the articles of incorporation prohibit the reissue of acquired shares, the number of authorized shares is reduced by the number of shares acquired, effective upon amendment of the articles of incorporation.

(c) Articles of amendment may be adopted by the board of directors without shareholder action, shall be delivered to the secretary of state for filing, and shall set forth:

(1) the name of the corporation;

(2) the reduction in the number of authorized shares, itemized by class and series; and

(3) the total number of authorized shares, itemized by class and series, remaining after reduction of the shares.

## Subchapter D. Distributions

### § 6.40 Distributions to Shareholders

(a) A board of directors may authorize and the corporation may make distributions to its shareholders subject to restriction by the articles of incorporation and the limitation in subsection (c).

(b) If the board of directors does not fix the record date for determining shareholders entitled to a distribution (other than one involving a purchase, redemption, or other acquisition of the corporation's shares), it is the date the board of directors authorizes the distribution.

(c) No distribution may be made if, after giving it effect:

(1) the corporation would not be able to pay its debts as they become due in the usual course of business; or

(2) the corporation's total assets would be less than the sum of its total liabilities plus (unless the articles of incorporation permit otherwise) the amount that would be needed, if the corporation were to be dissolved at the time of the distribution, to satisfy the preferential rights upon dissolution of shareholders whose preferential rights are superior to those receiving the distribution.

(d) The board of directors may base a determination that a distribution is not prohibited under subsection (c) either on financial statements prepared on the basis of accounting practices and principles that are reasonable in the circumstances or on a fair valuation or other method that is reasonable in the circumstances.

(e) Except as provided in subsection (g), the effect of a distribution under subsection (c) is measured:

(1) in the case of distribution by purchase, redemption, or other acquisition of the corporation's shares, as of the earlier of (i) the date money or other property is transferred or debt incurred by the corporation or (ii) the date the shareholder ceases to be a shareholder with respect to the acquired shares;

(2) in the case of any other distribution of indebtedness, as of the date the indebtedness is distributed;

(3) in all other cases, as of (i) the date the distribution is authorized if the payment occurs within 120 days after the date of authorization or (ii) the date the payment is made if it occurs more than 120 days after the date of authorization.

(f) A corporation's indebtedness to a shareholder incurred by reason of a distribution made in accordance with this section is at parity with the corporation's indebtedness to its general, unsecured creditors except to the extent subordinated by agreement.

(g) Indebtedness of a corporation, including indebtedness issued as a distribution, is not considered a liability for purposes of determinations under subsection (c) if its terms provide that payment of principal and interest are made only if and to the extent that payment of a distribution to shareholders could then be made under this section. If the indebtedness is issued as a distribution, each payment of principal or interest is treated as a distribution, the effect of which is measured on the date the payment is actually made.

# Chapter 7.
# SHAREHOLDERS

## Subchapter A. Meetings

### § 7.01 Annual Meeting

(a) A corporation shall hold annually at a time stated in or fixed in accordance with the bylaws a meeting of shareholders.

(b) Annual shareholders' meetings may be held in or out of this state at the place stated in or fixed in accordance with the bylaws. If no place is stated in or fixed in accordance with the bylaws, annual meetings shall be held at the corporation's principal office.

(c) The failure to hold an annual meeting at the time stated in or fixed in accordance with a corporation's bylaws does not affect the validity of any corporate action.

### § 7.02 Special Meeting

(a) A corporation shall hold a special meeting of shareholders:

(1) on call of its board of directors or the person or persons authorized to do so by the articles of incorporation or bylaws; or

(2) if the holders of at least 10 percent of all the votes entitled to be cast on any issue proposed to be considered at the proposed special meeting sign, date, and deliver to the corporation's secretary one or more written demands for the meeting describing the purpose or purposes for which it is to be held.

(b) If not otherwise fixed under sections 7.03 or 7.07, the record date for determining shareholders entitled to demand a special meeting is the date the first shareholder signs the demand.

(c) Special shareholders' meetings may be held in or out of this state at the place stated in or fixed in accordance with the bylaws. If no place is stated or fixed in accordance with the bylaws, special meetings shall be held at the corporation's principal office.

(d) Only business within the purpose or purposes described in the meeting notice required by section 7.05(c) may be conducted at a special shareholders' meeting.

## § 7.03 Court-Ordered Meeting

(a) The [name or describe] court of the county where a corporation's principal office (or, if none in this state, its registered office) is located may summarily order a meeting to be held:

(1) on application of any shareholder of the corporation entitled to participate in an annual meeting if an annual meeting was not held within the earlier of 6 months after the end of the corporation's fiscal year or 15 months after its last annual meeting; or

(2) on application of a shareholder who signed a demand for a special meeting valid under section 7.02 if:

(i) notice of the special meeting was not given within 30 days after the date the demand was delivered to the corporation's secretary; or

(ii) the special meeting was not held in accordance with the notice.

(b) The court may fix the time and place of the meeting, determine the shares entitled to participate in the meeting, specify a record date for determining shareholders entitled to notice of and to vote at the meeting, prescribe the form and content of the meeting notice, fix the quorum required for specific matters to be considered at the meeting (or direct that the votes represented at the meeting constitute a quorum for action on those matters), and enter other orders necessary to accomplish the purpose or purposes of the meeting.

## § 7.04 Action without Meeting

(a) Action required or permitted by this Act to be taken at a shareholders' meeting may be taken without a meeting if the action is taken by all the shareholders entitled to vote on the action. The action must be evidenced by one or more written consents describing the action taken, signed by all the shareholders entitled to vote on the action, and delivered to the corporation for inclusion in the minutes or filing with the corporate records.

(b) If not otherwise determined under sections 7.03 or 7.07, the record date for determining shareholders entitled to take action without a meeting is the date the first shareholder signs the consent under subsection (a).

(c) A consent signed under this section has the effect of a meeting vote and may be described as such in any document.

(d) If this Act requires that notice of proposed action be given to nonvoting shareholders and the action is to be taken by unanimous consent of the voting shareholders, the corporation must give its nonvoting shareholders written notice of the proposed action at least 10 days before the action is taken. The notice must contain or be accompanied by the same material that, under this Act, would have been required to be sent to nonvoting shareholders in a notice of meeting at which the proposed action would have been submitted to the shareholders for action.

## § 7.05 Notice of Meeting

(a) A corporation shall notify shareholders of the date, time, and place of each annual and special shareholders' meeting no fewer than 10 nor more than 60 days before the meeting date. Unless this Act or the articles of incorporation require otherwise, the corporation is required to give notice only to shareholders entitled to vote at the meeting.

(b) Unless this Act or the articles of incorporation require otherwise, notice of an annual meeting need not include a description of the purpose or purposes for which the meeting is called.

(c) Notice of a special meeting must include a description of the purpose or purposes for which the meeting is called.

(d) If not otherwise fixed under sections 7.03 or 7.07, the record date for determining shareholders entitled to notice of and to vote at an annual or special shareholders' meeting is the day before the first notice is delivered to shareholders.

(e) Unless the bylaws require otherwise, if an annual or special shareholders' meeting is adjourned to a different date, time, or place, notice need not be given of the new date, time, or place if the new date, time, or place is announced at the meeting before adjournment. If a new record date for the adjourned meeting is or must be fixed under section 7.07, however, notice of the adjourned meeting must be given under this section to persons who are shareholders as of the new record date.

## § 7.06 Waiver of Notice

(a) A shareholder may waive any notice required by this Act, the articles of incorporation, or bylaws before or after the date and time stated in the notice. The waiver must be in writing, be signed by the shareholder entitled to the notice, and be delivered to the corporation for inclusion in the minutes or filing with the corporate records.

(b) A shareholder's attendance at a meeting:

(1) waives objection to lack of notice or defective notice of the meeting, unless the shareholder at the beginning of the meeting objects to holding the meeting or transacting business at the meeting;

(2) waives objection to consideration of a particular matter at the meeting that is not within the purpose or purposes described in the meeting notice, unless the shareholder objects to considering the matter when it is presented.

## § 7.07 Record Date

(a) The bylaws may fix or provide the manner of fixing the record date for one or more voting groups in order to determine the shareholders entitled to notice of a shareholders' meeting, to demand a special meeting, to vote, or to take any other action. If the bylaws do not fix or provide for fixing a record date, the board of directors of the corporation may fix a future date as the record date.

(b) A record date fixed under this section may not be more than 70 days before the meeting or action requiring a determination of shareholders.

(c) A determination of shareholders entitled to notice of or to vote at a shareholders' meeting is effective for any adjournment of the meeting unless the board of directors fixes a new record date, which it must do if the meeting is adjourned to a date more than 120 days after the date fixed for the original meeting.

(d) If a court orders a meeting adjourned to a date more than 120 days after the date fixed for the original meeting, it may provide that the original record date continues in effect or it may fix a new record date.

## Subchapter B. Voting

### § 7.20 Shareholders' List for Meeting

(a) After fixing a record date for a meeting, a corporation shall prepare an alphabetical list of the names of all its shareholders who are entitled to notice of a shareholders' meeting. The list must be arranged by voting group (and within each voting group by class or series of shares) and show the address of and number of shares held by each shareholder.

(b) The shareholders' list must be available for inspection by any shareholder, beginning two business days after notice of the meeting is given for which the list was prepared and continuing through the meeting, at the corporation's principal office or at a place identified in the meeting notice in the city where the meeting will be held. A shareholder, his agent, or attorney is entitled on written demand to inspect and, subject to the requirements of section 16.02(c), to copy the list, during regular business hours and at his expense, during the period it is available for inspection.

(c) The corporation shall make the shareholders' list available at the meeting, and any shareholder, his agent, or attorney is entitled to inspect the list at any time during the meeting or any adjournment.

(d) If the corporation refuses to allow a shareholder, his agent, or attorney to inspect the shareholders' list before or at the meeting (or copy the list as permitted by subsection (b)), the [name or describe] court of the county where a corporation's principal office (or, if none in this state, its registered office) is located, on application of the shareholder, may summarily order the inspection or copying at the corporation's expense and may postpone the meeting for which the list was prepared until the inspection or copying is complete.

(e) Refusal or failure to prepare or make available the shareholders' list does not affect the validity of action taken at the meeting.

### § 7.21 Voting Entitlement of Shares

(a) Except as provided in subsections (b) and (c) or unless the articles of incorporation provide otherwise, each outstanding share, regardless of class, is entitled to one vote on each matter voted on at a shareholders' meeting. Only shares are entitled to vote.

(b) Absent special circumstances, the shares of a corporation are not entitled to vote if they are owned, directly or indirectly, by a second corporation, domestic or foreign, and the first corporation owns, directly or indirectly, a majority of the shares entitled to vote for directors of the second corporation.

(c) Subsection (b) does not limit the power of a corporation to vote any shares, including its own shares, held by it in a fiduciary capacity.

(d) Redeemable shares are not entitled to vote after notice of redemption is mailed to the holders and a sum sufficient to redeem the shares has been deposited with a bank, trust company, or other financial institution under an irrevocable obligation to pay the holders the redemption price on surrender of the shares.

### § 7.22 Proxies

(a) A shareholder may vote his shares in person or by proxy.

(b) A shareholder may appoint a proxy to vote or otherwise act for him by signing an appointment form, either personally or by his attorney-in-fact.

(c) An appointment of a proxy is effective when received by the secretary or other officer or agent authorized to tabulate votes. An appointment is valid for 11 months unless a longer period is expressly provided in the appointment form.

(d) An appointment of a proxy is revocable by the shareholder unless the appointment form conspicuously states that it is irrevocable and the appointment is coupled with an interest. Appointments coupled with an interest include the appointment of:

> (1) a pledgee;

> (2) a person who purchased or agreed to purchase the shares;

> (3) a creditor of the corporation who extended it credit under terms requiring the appointment;

> (4) an employee of the corporation whose employment contract requires the appointment; or

> (5) a party to a voting agreement created under section 7.31.

(e) The death or incapacity of the shareholder appointing a proxy does not affect the right of the corporation to accept the proxy's authority unless notice of the death or incapacity is received by the secretary or other officer or agent authorized to tabulate votes before the proxy exercises his authority under the appointment.

(f) An appointment made irrevocable under subsection (d) is revoked when the interest with which it is coupled is extinguished.

(g) A transferee for value of shares subject to an irrevocable appointment may revoke the appointment if he did not know of its existence when he acquired the shares and the existence of the irrevocable appointment was not noted conspicuously on the certificate representing the shares or on the information statement for shares without certificates.

(h) Subject to section 7.24 and to any express limitation on the proxy's authority appearing on the face of the appointment form, a corporation is entitled to accept the proxy's vote or other action as that of the shareholder making the appointment.

## § 7.23 Shares Held by Nominees

(a) A corporation may establish a procedure by which the beneficial owner of shares that are registered in the name of a nominee is recognized by the corporation as the shareholder. The extent of this recognition may be determined in the procedure.

(b) The procedure may set forth:

(1) the types of nominees to which it applies;

(2) the rights or privileges that the corporation recognizes in a beneficial owner;

(3) the manner in which the procedure is selected by the nominee;

(4) the information that must be provided when the procedure is selected;

(5) the period for which selection of the procedure is effective; and

(6) other aspects of the rights and duties created.

## § 7.24 Corporation's Acceptance of Votes

(a) If the name signed on a vote, consent, waiver, or proxy appointment corresponds to the name of a shareholder, the corporation if acting in good faith is entitled to accept the vote, consent, waiver, or proxy appointment and give it effect as the act of the shareholder.

(b) If the name signed on a vote, consent, waiver, or proxy appointment does not correspond to the name of its shareholder, the corporation if acting in good faith is nevertheless entitled to accept the vote, consent, waiver, or proxy appointment and give it effect as the act of the shareholder if:

(1) the shareholder is an entity and the name signed purports to be that of an officer or agent of the entity;

(2) the name signed purports to be that of an administrator, executor, guardian, or conservator representing the shareholder and, if the corporation requests, evidence of fiduciary status acceptable to the corporation has been presented with respect to the vote, consent, waiver, or proxy appointment;

(3) the name signed purports to be that of a receiver or trustee in bankruptcy of the shareholder and, if the corporation requests, evidence of this status acceptable to the corporation has been presented with respect to the vote, consent, waiver, or proxy appointment;

(4) the name signed purports to be that of a pledgee, beneficial owner, or attorney-in-fact of the shareholder and, if the corporation requests, evidence acceptable to the corporation of the signatory's authority to sign for the shareholder has been presented with respect to the vote, consent, waiver, or proxy appointment;

(5) two or more persons are the shareholder as co-tenants or fiduciaries and the name signed purports to be the name of at least one of the coowners and the person signing appears to be acting on behalf of all the coowners.

(c) The corporation is entitled to reject a vote, consent, waiver, or proxy appointment if the secretary or other officer or agent authorized to tabulate votes, acting in good faith, has reasonable basis for doubt about the validity of the signature on it or about the signatory's authority to sign for the shareholder.

(d) The corporation and its officer or agent who accepts or rejects a vote, consent, waiver, or proxy appointment in good faith and in accordance with the standards of this section are not liable in damages to the shareholder for the consequences of the acceptance or rejection.

(e) Corporate action based on the acceptance or rejection of a vote, consent, waiver, or proxy appointment under this section is valid unless a court of competent jurisdiction determines otherwise.

## § 7.25 Quorum and Voting Requirements for Voting Groups

(a) Shares entitled to vote as a separate voting group may take action on a matter at a meeting only if a quorum of those shares exists with respect to that matter. Unless the articles of incorporation or this Act provide otherwise, a majority of the votes entitled to be cast on the matter by the voting group constitutes a quorum of that voting group for action on that matter.

(b) Once a share is represented for any purpose at a meeting, it is deemed present for quorum purposes for the remainder of the meeting and for any adjournment of that meeting unless a new record date is or must be set for that adjourned meeting.

(c) If a quorum exists, action on a matter (other than the election of directors) by a voting group is approved if the votes cast within the voting group favoring the action exceed the votes cast opposing the action, unless the articles of incorporation or this Act require a greater number of affirmative votes.

(d) An amendment of articles of incorporation adding, changing, or deleting a quorum or voting requirement for a voting group greater than specified in subsection (b) or (c) is governed by section 7.27.

(e) The election of directors is governed by section 7.28.

## § 7.26 Action by Single and Multiple Voting Groups

(a) If the articles of incorporation or this Act provide for voting by a single voting group on a matter, action on that matter is taken when voted upon by that voting group as provided in section 7.25.

(b) If the articles of incorporation or this Act provide for voting by two or more voting groups on a matter, action on that matter is taken only when voted upon by each of those voting groups counted separately as provided in section 7.25. Action may be taken by one voting group on a matter even though no action is taken by another voting group entitled to vote on the matter.

## § 7.27 Greater Quorum or Voting Requirements

(a) The articles of incorporation may provide for a greater quorum or voting requirement for shareholders (or voting groups of shareholders) than is provided for by this Act.

(b) An amendment to the articles of incorporation that adds, changes, or deletes a greater quorum or voting requirement must meet the same quorum requirement and be adopted by the same vote and voting groups required to take action under the quorum and voting requirements then in effect or proposed to be adopted, whichever is greater.

### § 7.28 Voting for Directors; Cumulative Voting

(a) Unless otherwise provided in the articles of incorporation, directors are elected by a plurality of the votes cast by the shares entitled to vote in the election at a meeting at which a quorum is present.

(b) Shareholders do not have a right to cumulate their votes for directors unless the articles of incorporation so provide.

(c) A statement included in the articles of incorporation that "[all] [a designated voting group of] shareholders are entitled to cumulate their votes for directors" (or words of similar import) means that the shareholders designated are entitled to multiply the number of votes they are entitled to cast by the number of directors for whom they are entitled to vote and cast the product for a single candidate or distribute the product among two or more candidates.

(d) Shares otherwise entitled to vote cumulatively may not be voted cumulatively at a particular meeting unless:

(1) the meeting notice or proxy statement accompanying the notice states conspicuously that cumulative voting is authorized; or

(2) a shareholder who has the right to cumulate his votes gives notice to the corporation not less than 48 hours before the time set for the meeting of his intent to cumulate his votes during the meeting, and if one shareholder gives this notice all other shareholders in the same voting group participating in the election are entitled to cumulate their votes without giving further notice.

## Subchapter C. Voting Trusts and Agreements

### § 7.30 Voting Trusts

(a) One or more shareholders may create a voting trust, conferring on a trustee the right to vote or otherwise act for them, by signing an agreement setting out the provisions of the trust (which may include anything consistent with its purpose) and transferring their shares to the trustee. When a voting trust agreement is signed, the trustee shall prepare a list of the names and addresses of all owners of beneficial interests in the trust, together with the number and class of shares each transferred to the trust, and deliver copies of the list and agreement to the corporation's principal office.

(b) A voting trust becomes effective on the date the first shares subject to the trust are registered in the trustee's name. A voting trust is valid for not more than 10 years after its effective date unless extended under subsection (c).

(c) All or some of the parties to a voting trust may extend it for additional terms of not more than 10 years each by signing an extension agreement and obtaining the voting trustee's written consent to the extension. An extension is valid for 10 years from the date the first shareholder signs the extension agreement. The voting trustee must deliver copies of the extension agreement and list of beneficial owners to the corporation's principal office. An extension agreement binds only those parties signing it.

### § 7.31 Voting Agreements

(a) Two or more shareholders may provide for the manner in which they will vote their shares by signing an agreement for that purpose. A voting agreement created under this section is not subject to the provisions of section 7.30.

(b) A voting agreement created under this section is specifically enforceable.

### § 7.32 Shareholder Agreements

(a) An agreement among the shareholders of a corporation that complies with this section is effective among the shareholders and the corporation even though it is inconsistent with one or more other provisions of this Act in that it:

(1) eliminates the board of directors or restricts the discretion or powers of the board of directors;

(2) governs the authorization or making of distributions whether or not in proportion to ownership of shares, subject to the limitations in section 6.40;

(3) establishes who shall be directors or officers of the corporation, or their terms of office or manner of selection or removal;

(4) governs, in general or in regard to specific matters, the exercise or division of voting power by or between the shareholders and directors or by or among any of them, including use of weighted voting rights or director proxies;

(5) establishes the terms and conditions of any agreement for the transfer or use of property or the provision of services between the corporation and any shareholder, director, officer or employee of the corporation or among any of them;

(6) transfers to one or more shareholders or other persons all or part of the authority to exercise the corporate powers or to manage the business and affairs of the corporation, including the resolution of any issue about which there exists a deadlock among directors or shareholders;

(7) requires dissolution of the corporation at the request of one or more of the shareholders or upon the occurrence of a specified event or contingency; or

(8) otherwise governs the exercise of the corporate powers or the management of the business and affairs of the corporation or the relationship among the shareholders, the directors and the corporation, or among any of them, and is not contrary to public policy.

(b) An agreement authorized by this section shall be:

(1) set forth (A) in the articles of incorporation or bylaws and approved by all persons who are shareholders at the time of the agreement or (B) in a written agreement that

is signed by all persons who are shareholders at the time of the agreement and is made known to the corporation;

(2) subject to amendment only by all persons who are shareholders at the time of the amendment, unless the agreement provides otherwise; and

(3) valid for 10 years, unless the agreement provides otherwise.

(c) The existence of an agreement authorized by this section shall be noted conspicuously on the front or back of each certificate for outstanding shares or on the information statement required by section 6.26(b). If at the time of the agreement the corporation has shares outstanding represented by certificates, the corporation shall recall the outstanding certificates and issue substitute certificates that comply with this subsection. The failure to note the existence of the agreement on the certificate or information statement shall not affect the validity of the agreement or any action taken pursuant to it. Any purchaser of shares who, at the time of purchase, did not have knowledge of the existence of the agreement shall be entitled to rescission of the purchase. A purchaser shall be deemed to have knowledge of the existence of the agreement if its existence is noted on the certificate or information statement for the shares in compliance with this subsection and, if the shares are not represented by a certificate, the information statement is delivered to the purchaser at or prior to the time of purchase of the shares. An action to enforce the right of rescission authorized by this subsection must be commenced within the earlier of 90 days after discovery of the existence of the agreement or two years after the time of purchase of the shares.

(d) An agreement authorized by this section shall cease to be effective when shares of the corporation are listed on a national securities exchange or regularly traded in a market maintained by one or more members of a national or affiliated securities association. If the agreement ceases to be effective for any reason, the board of directors may, if the agreement is contained or referred to in the corporation's articles of incorporation or bylaws, adopt an amendment to the articles of incorporation or bylaws, without shareholder action, to delete the agreement and any references to it.

(e) An agreement authorized by this section that limits the discretion or powers of the board of directors shall relieve the directors of, and impose upon the person or persons in whom such discretion or powers are vested, liability for acts or omissions imposed by law on directors to the extent that the discretion or powers of the directors are limited by the agreement.

(f) The existence or performance of an agreement authorized by this section shall not be a ground for imposing personal liability on any shareholder for the acts or debts of the corporation even if the agreement or its performance treats the corporation as if it were a partnership or results in failure to observe the corporate formalities otherwise applicable to the matters governed by the agreement.

(g) Incorporators or subscribers for shares may act as shareholders with respect to an agreement authorized by this section if no shares have been issued when the agreement is made.

## Subchapter D. Derivative Proceedings

### § 7.40  Subchapter Definitions

In this subchapter:

(1) "Derivative proceeding" means a civil suit in the right of a domestic corporation or, to the extent provided in section 7.47, in the right of a foreign corporation.

(2) "Shareholder" includes a beneficial owner whose shares are held in a voting trust or held by a nominee on the beneficial owner's behalf.

### § 7.41  Standing

A shareholder may not commence or maintain a derivative proceeding unless the shareholder:

(1) was a shareholder of the corporation at the time of the act or omission complained of or became a shareholder through transfer by operation of law from one who was a shareholder at that time; and

(2) fairly and adequately represents the interests of the corporation in enforcing the right of the corporation.

### § 7.42  Demand

No shareholder may commence a derivative proceeding until:

(1) a written demand has been made upon the corporation to take suitable action; and

(2) 90 days have expired from the date the demand was made unless the shareholder has earlier been notified that the demand has been rejected by the corporation or unless irreparable injury to the corporation would result by waiting for the expiration of the 90 day period.

### § 7.43  Stay of Proceedings

If the corporation commences an inquiry into the allegations made in the demand or complaint, the court may stay any derivative proceeding for such period as the court deems appropriate.

### § 7.44  Dismissal

(a) A derivative proceeding shall be dismissed by the court on motion by the corporation if one of the groups specified in subsections (b) or (f) has determined in good faith after conducting a reasonable inquiry upon which its conclusions are based that the maintenance of the derivative proceeding is not in the best interests of the corporation.

(b) Unless a panel is appointed pursuant to subsection (f), the determination in subsection (a) shall be made by:

(1) a majority vote of independent directors present at a meeting of the board of directors if the independent directors constitute a quorum; or

(2) a majority vote of a committee consisting of two or more independent directors appointed by majority vote of independent directors present at a meeting of the board of directors, whether or not such independent directors constituted a quorum.

(c) None of the following shall by itself cause a director to be considered not independent for purposes of this section:

(1) the nomination or election of the director by persons who are defendants in the derivative proceeding or against whom action is demanded;

(2) the naming of the director as a defendant in the derivative proceeding or as a person against whom action is demanded; or

(3) the approval by the director of the act being challenged in the derivative proceeding or demand if the act resulted in no personal benefit to the director.

(d) If a derivative proceeding is commenced after a determination has been made rejecting a demand by a shareholder, the complaint shall allege with particularity facts establishing either (1) that a majority of the board of directors did not consist of independent directors at the time the determination was made or (2) that the requirements of subsection (a) have not been met.

(e) If a majority of the board of directors does not consist of independent directors at the time the determination is made, the corporation shall have the burden of proving that the requirements of subsection (a) have been met. If a majority of the board of directors consists of independent directors at the time the determination is made, the plaintiff shall have the burden of proving that the requirements of subsection (a) have not been met.

(f) The court may appoint a panel of one or more independent persons upon motion by the corporation to make a determination whether the maintenance of the derivative proceeding is in the best interests of the corporation. In such case, the plaintiff hall have the burden of proving that the requirements of subsection (a) have not been met.

### § 7.45 **Discontinuance or Settlement**

A derivative proceeding may not be discontinued or settled without the court's approval. If the court determines that a proposed discontinuance or settlement will substantially affect the interests of the corporation's shareholders or a class of shareholders, the court shall direct that notice be given to the shareholders affected.

### § 7.46 **Payment of Expenses**

On termination of the derivative proceeding the court may:

(1) order the corporation to pay the plaintiff's reasonable expenses (including counsel fees) incurred in the proceeding if it finds that the proceeding has resulted in a substantial benefit to the corporation;

(2) order the plaintiff to pay any defendant's reasonable expenses (including counsel fees) incurred in defending the proceeding if it finds that the proceeding was commenced or maintained without reasonable cause or for an improper purpose; or

(3) order a party to pay an opposing party's reasonable expenses (including counsel fees) incurred because of the filing of a pleading, motion or other paper, if it finds that the pleading, motion or other paper was not well grounded in fact, after reasonable inquiry, or warranted by existing law or a good faith argument for the extension, modification or reversal of existing law and was interposed for an improper purpose, such as to harass or to cause unnecessary delay or needless increase in the cost of litigation.

### § 7.47 **Applicability to Foreign Corporations**

In any derivative proceeding in the right of a foreign corporation, the matters covered by this subchapter shall be governed by the laws of the jurisdiction of incorporation of the foreign corporation except for sections 7.43, 7.45 and 7.46.

# Chapter 8.
# DIRECTORS AND OFFICERS

## Subchapter A. **Board of Directors**

### § 8.01 **Requirement for and Duties of Board of Directors**

(a) Except as provided in subsection (c), each corporation must have a board of directors.

(b) All corporate powers shall be exercised by or under the authority of, and the business and affairs of the corporation managed under the direction of, its board of directors, subject to any limitation set forth in the articles of incorporation.

(c) A corporation having 50 or fewer shareholders may dispense with or limit the authority of a board of directors by describing in its articles of incorporation who will perform some or all of the duties of a board of directors.

### § 8.02 **Qualifications of Directors**

The articles of incorporation or bylaws may prescribe qualifications for directors. A director need not be a resident of this state or a shareholder of the corporation unless the articles of incorporation or bylaws so prescribe.

### § 8.03 **Number and Election of Directors**

(a) A board of directors must consist of one or more individuals, with the number specified in or fixed in accordance with the articles of incorporation or bylaws.

(b) If a board of directors has power to fix or change the number of directors, the board may increase or decrease by 30 percent or less the number of directors last approved by the shareholders, but only the shareholders may increase or decrease by more than 30 percent the number of directors last approved by the shareholders.

(c) The articles of incorporation or bylaws may establish a variable range for the size of the board of directors by fixing a minimum and maximum number of directors. If a variable range is established, the number of directors may be fixed or changed from time to time, within the minimum and maximum, by the shareholders or the board of directors. After shares are issued, only the shareholders may change the range for the size of the board or change from a fixed to a variable-range size board or vice versa.

(d) Directors are elected at the first annual shareholders' meeting and at each annual meeting thereafter unless their terms are staggered under section 8.06.

## § 8.04 Election of Directors by Certain Classes of Shareholders

If the articles of incorporation authorize dividing the shares into classes, the articles may also authorize the election of all or a specified number of directors by the holders of one or more authorized classes of shares. Each class (or classes) of shares entitled to elect one or more directors is a separate voting group for purposes of the election of directors.

## § 8.05 Terms of Directors Generally

(a) The terms of the initial directors of a corporation expire at the first shareholders' meeting at which directors are elected.

(b) The terms of all other directors expire at the next annual shareholders' meeting following their election unless their terms are staggered under section 8.06.

(c) A decrease in the number of directors does not shorten an incumbent director's term.

(d) The term of a director elected to fill a vacancy expires at the next shareholders' meeting at which directors are elected.

(e) Despite the expiration of a director's term, he continues to serve until his successor is elected and qualifies or until there is a decrease in the number of directors.

## § 8.06 Staggered Terms for Directors

If there are nine or more directors, the articles of incorporation may provide for staggering their terms by dividing the total number of directors into two or three groups, with each group containing one-half or one-third of the total, as near as may be. In that event, the terms of directors in the first group expire at the first annual shareholders' meeting after their election, the terms of the second group expire at the second annual shareholders' meeting after their election, and the terms of the third group, if any, expire at the third annual shareholders' meeting after their election. At each annual shareholders' meeting held thereafter, directors shall be chosen for a term of two years or three years, as the case may be, to succeed those whose terms expire.

## § 8.07 Resignation of Directors

(a) A director may resign at any time by delivering written notice to the board of directors, its chairman, or to the corporation.

(b) A resignation is effective when the notice is delivered unless the notice specifies a later effective date.

## § 8.08 Removal of Directors by Shareholders

(a) The shareholders may remove one or more directors with or without cause unless the articles of incorporation provide that directors may be removed only for cause.

(b) If a director is elected by a voting group of shareholders, only the shareholders of that voting group may participate in the vote to remove him.

(c) If cumulative voting is authorized, a director may not be removed if the number of votes sufficient to elect him under cumulative voting is voted against his removal. If cumulative voting is not authorized, a director may be removed only if the number of votes cast to remove him exceeds the number of votes cast not to remove him.

(d) A director may be removed by the shareholders only at a meeting called for the purpose of removing him and the meeting notice must state that the purpose, or one of the purposes, of the meeting is removal of the director.

## § 8.09 Removal of Directors by Judicial Proceeding

(a) The [name or describe] court of the county where a corporation's principal office (or, if none in this state, its registered office) is located may remove a director of the corporation from office in a proceeding commenced either by the corporation or by its shareholders holding at least 10 percent of the outstanding shares of any class if the court finds that (1) the director engaged in fraudulent or dishonest conduct, or gross abuse of authority or discretion, with respect to the corporation and (2) removal is in the best interest of the corporation.

(b) The court that removes a director may bar the director from reelection for a period prescribed by the court.

(c) If shareholders commence a proceeding under subsection (a), they shall make the corporation a party defendant.

## § 8.10 Vacancy on Board

(a) Unless the articles of incorporation provide otherwise, if a vacancy occurs on a board of directors, including a vacancy resulting from an increase in the number of directors:

(1) the shareholders may fill the vacancy;

(2) the board of directors may fill the vacancy; or

(3) if the directors remaining in office constitute fewer than a quorum of the board, they may fill the vacancy by the affirmative vote of a majority of all the directors remaining in office.

(b) If the vacant office was held by a director elected by a voting group of shareholders, only the holders of shares of that voting group are entitled to vote to fill the vacancy if it is filled by the shareholders.

(c) A vacancy that will occur at a specific later date (by reason of a resignation effective at a later date under section 8.07(b) or otherwise) may be filled before the vacancy occurs but the new director may not take office until the vacancy occurs.

## § 8.11 Compensation of Directors

Unless the articles of incorporation or bylaws provide otherwise, the board of directors may fix the compensation of directors.

## Subchapter B. Meetings and Action of the Board

### § 8.20 Meetings

(a) The board of directors may hold regular or special meetings in or out of this state.

(b) Unless the articles of incorporation or bylaws provide otherwise, the board of directors may permit any or all directors to participate in a regular or special meeting by, or conduct the meeting through the use of, any means of communication by which all directors participating may simultaneously hear each other during the meeting. A director participating in a meeting by this means is deemed to be present in person at the meeting.

### § 8.21 Action without Meeting

(a) Unless the articles of incorporation or bylaws provide otherwise, action required or permitted by this Act to be taken at a board of directors' meeting may be taken without a meeting if the action is taken by all members of the board. The action must be evidenced by one or more written consents describing the action taken, signed by each director, and included in the minutes or filed with the corporate records reflecting the action taken.

(b) Action taken under this section is effective when the last director signs the consent, unless the consent specifies a different effective date.

(c) A consent signed under this section has the effect of a meeting vote and may be described as such in any document.

### § 8.22 Notice of Meeting

(a) Unless the articles of incorporation or bylaws provide otherwise, regular meetings of the board of directors may be held without notice of the date, time, place, or purpose of the meeting.

(b) Unless the articles of incorporation or bylaws provide for a longer or shorter period, special meetings of the board of directors must be preceded by at least two days' notice of the date, time, and place of the meeting. The notice need not describe the purpose of the special meeting unless required by the articles of incorporation or bylaws.

### § 8.23 Waiver of Notice

(a) A director may waive any notice required by this Act, the articles of incorporation, or bylaws before or after the date and time stated in the notice. Except as provided by subsection (b), the waiver must be in writing, signed by the director entitled to the notice, and filed with the minutes or corporate records.

(b) A director's attendance at or participation in a meeting waives any required notice to him of the meeting unless the director at the beginning of the meeting (or promptly upon his arrival) objects to holding the meeting or transacting business at the meeting and does not thereafter vote for or assent to action taken at the meeting.

### § 8.24 Quorum and Voting

(a) Unless the articles of incorporation or bylaws require a greater number, a quorum of a board of directors consists of:

(1) a majority of the fixed number of directors if the corporation has a fixed board size; or

(2) a majority of the number of directors prescribed, or if no number is prescribed the number in office immediately before the meeting begins, if the corporation has a variable-range size board.

(b) The articles of incorporation or bylaws may authorize a quorum of a board of directors to consist of no fewer than one-third of the fixed or prescribed number of directors determined under subsection (a).

(c) If a quorum is present when a vote is taken, the affirmative vote of a majority of directors present is the act of the board of directors unless the articles of incorporation or bylaws require the vote of a greater number of directors.

(d) A director who is present at a meeting of the board of directors or a committee of the board of directors when corporate action is taken is deemed to have assented to the action taken unless: (1) he objects at the beginning of the meeting (or promptly upon his arrival) to holding it or transacting business at the meeting; (2) his dissent or abstention from the action taken is entered in the minutes of the meeting; or (3) he delivers written notice of his dissent or abstention to the presiding officer of the meeting before its adjournment or to the corporation immediately after adjournment of the meeting. The right of dissent or abstention is not available to a director who votes in favor of the action taken.

### § 8.25 Committees

(a) Unless the articles of incorporation or bylaws provide otherwise, a board of directors may create one or more committees and appoint members of the board of directors to serve on them. Each committee may have two or more members, who serve at the pleasure of the board of directors.

(b) The creation of a committee and appointment of members to it must be approved by the greater of (1) a majority of all the directors in office when the action is taken or (2) the number of directors required by the articles of incorporation or bylaws to take action under section 8.24.

(c) Sections 8.20 through 8.24, which govern meetings, action without meetings, notice and waiver of notice, and quorum and voting requirements of the board of directors, apply to committees and their members as well.

(d) To the extent specified by the board of directors or in the articles of incorporation or bylaws, each committee may exercise the authority of the board of directors under section 8.01.

(e) A committee may not, however:

(1) authorize distributions;

(2) approve or propose to shareholders action that this Act requires to be approved by shareholders;

(3) fill vacancies on the board of directors or on any of its committees;

(4) amend articles of incorporation pursuant to section 10.02;

(5) adopt, amend, or repeal bylaws;

(6) approve a plan of merger not requiring shareholder approval;

(7) authorize or approve reacquisition of shares, except according to a formula or method prescribed by the board of directors; or

(8) authorize or approve the issuance or sale or contract for sale of shares, or determine the designation and relative rights, preferences, and limitations of a class or series of shares, except that the board of directors may authorize a committee (or a senior executive officer of the corporation) to do so within limits specifically prescribed by the board of directors.

(f) The creation of, delegation of authority to, or action by a committee does not alone constitute compliance by a director with the standards of conduct described in section 8.30.

## Subchapter C.  Standards of Conduct

### § 8.30  General Standards for Directors

(a) A director shall discharge his duties as a director, including his duties as a member of a committee:

(1) in good faith;

(2) with the care an ordinarily prudent person in a like position would exercise under similar circumstances; and

(3) in a manner he reasonably believes to be in the best interests of the corporation.

(b) In discharging his duties a director is entitled to rely on information, opinions, reports, or statements, including financial statements and other financial data, if prepared or presented by:

(1) one or more officers or employees of the corporation whom the director reasonably believes to be reliable and competent in the matters presented;

(2) legal counsel, public accountants, or other persons as to matters the director reasonably believes are within the person's professional or expert competence; or

(3) a committee of the board of directors of which he is not a member if the director reasonably believes the committee merits confidence.

(c) A director is not acting in good faith if he has knowledge concerning the matter in question that makes reliance otherwise permitted by subsection (b) unwarranted.

(d) A director is not liable for any action taken as a director, or any failure to take any action, if he performed the duties of his office in compliance with this section.

### § 8.33  Liability for Unlawful Distributions

(a) A director who votes for or assents to a distribution made in violation of section 6.40 or the articles of incorporation is personally liable to the corporation for the amount of the distribution that exceeds what could have been distributed without violating section 6.40 or the articles of incorporation if it is established that he did not perform his duties in compliance with section 8.30. In any proceeding commenced under this section, a director has all of the defenses ordinarily available to a director.

(b) A director held liable under subsection (a) for an unlawful distribution is entitled to contribution:

(1) from every other director who could be held liable under subsection (a) for the unlawful distribution; and

(2) from each shareholder for the amount the shareholder accepted knowing the distribution was made in violation of section 6.40 or the articles of incorporation.

(c) A proceeding under this section is barred unless it is commenced within two years after the date on which the effect of the distribution was measured under section 6.40(e) or (g).

## Subchapter D.  Officers

### § 8.40  Required Officers

(a) A corporation has the officers described in its bylaws or appointed by the board of directors in accordance with the bylaws.

(b) A duly appointed officer may appoint one or more officers or assistant officers if authorized by the bylaws or the board of directors.

(c) The bylaws or the board of directors shall delegate to one of the officers responsibility for preparing minutes of the directors' and shareholders' meetings and for authenticating records of the corporation.

(d) The same individual may simultaneously hold more than one office in a corporation.

### § 8.41  Duties of Officers

Each officer has the authority and shall perform the duties set forth in the bylaws or, to the extent consistent with the bylaws, the duties prescribed by the board of directors or by direction of an officer authorized by the board of directors to prescribe the duties of other officers.

### § 8.42  Standards of Conduct for Officers

(a) An officer with discretionary authority shall discharge his duties under that authority:

(1) in good faith;

(2) with the care an ordinarily prudent person in a like position would exercise under similar circumstances; and

(3) in a manner he reasonably believes to be in the best interests of the corporation.

(b) In discharging his duties an officer is entitled to rely on information, opinions, reports, or statements, including financial statements and other financial data, if prepared or presented by:

(1) one or more officers or employees of the corporation whom the officer reasonably believes to be reliable and competent in the matters presented; or

(2) legal counsel, public accountants, or other persons as to matters the officer reasonably believes are within the person's professional or expert competence.

(c) An officer is not acting in good faith if he has knowledge concerning the matter in question that makes reliance otherwise permitted by subsection (b) unwarranted.

(d) An officer is not liable for any action taken as an officer, or any failure to take any action, if he performed the duties of his office in compliance with this section.

### § 8.43 Resignation and Removal of Officers

(a) An officer may resign at any time by delivering notice to the corporation. A resignation is effective when the notice is delivered unless the notice specifies a later effective date. If a resignation is made effective at a later date and the corporation accepts the future effective date, its board of directors may fill the pending vacancy before the effective date if the board of directors provides that the successor does not take office until the effective date.

(b) A board of directors may remove any officer at any time with or without cause.

### § 8.44 Contract Rights of Officers

(a) The appointment of an officer does not itself create contract rights.

(b) An officer's removal does not affect the officer's contract rights, if any, with the corporation. An officer's resignation does not affect the corporation's contract rights, if any, with the officer.

## Subchapter E. Indemnification

### § 8.50 Subchapter Definitions

In this subchapter:

(1) "Corporation" includes any domestic or foreign predecessor entity of a corporation in a merger or other transaction in which the predecessor's existence ceased upon consummation of the transaction.

(2) "Director" means an individual who is or was a director of a corporation or an individual who, while a director of a corporation, is or was serving at the corporation's request as a director, officer, partner, trustee, employee, or agent of another foreign or domestic corporation, partnership, joint venture, trust, employee benefit plan, or other enterprise. A director is considered to be serving an employee benefit plan at the corporation's request if his duties to the corporation also impose duties on, or otherwise involve services by, him to the plan or to participants in or beneficiaries of the plan. "Director" includes, unless the context requires otherwise, the estate or personal representative of a director.

(3) "Expenses" include counsel fees.

(4) "Liability" means the obligation to pay a judgment, settlement, penalty, fine (including an excise tax assessed with respect to an employee benefit plan), or reasonable expenses incurred with respect to a proceeding.

(5) "Official capacity" means: (i) when used with respect to a director, the office of director in a corporation; and (ii) when used with respect to an individual other than a director, as contemplated in section 8.56, the office in a corporation held by the officer or the employment or agency relationship undertaken by the employee or agent on behalf of the corporation. "Official capacity" does not include service for any other foreign or domestic corporation or any partnership, joint venture, trust, employee benefit plan, or other enterprise.

(6) "Party" includes an individual who was, is, or is threatened to be made a named defendant or respondent in a proceeding.

(7) "Proceeding" means any threatened, pending, or completed action, suit, or proceeding, whether civil, criminal, administrative, or investigative and whether formal or informal.

### § 8.51 Authority to Indemnify

(a) Except as provided in subsection (d), a corporation may indemnify an individual made a party to a proceeding because he is or was a director against liability incurred in the proceeding if:

(1) he conducted himself in good faith; and

(2) he reasonably believed:

(i) in the case of conduct in his official capacity with the corporation, that his conduct was in its best interests; and

(ii) in all other cases, that his conduct was at least not opposed to its best interests; and

(3) in the case of any criminal proceeding, he had no reasonable cause to believe his conduct was unlawful.

(b) A director's conduct with respect to an employee benefit plan for a purpose he reasonably believed to be in the interests of the participants in and beneficiaries of the plan is conduct that satisfies the requirement of subsection (a)(2)(ii).

(c) The termination of a proceeding by judgment, order, settlement, conviction, or upon a plea of nolo contendere or its equivalent is not, of itself, determinative that the director did not meet the standard of conduct described in this section.

(d) A corporation may not indemnify a director under this section:

(1) in connection with a proceeding by or in the right of the corporation in which the director was adjudged liable to the corporation; or

(2) in connection with any other proceeding charging improper personal benefit to him, whether or not involving action in his official capacity, in which he was ad-

judged liable on the basis that personal benefit was improperly received by him.

(e) Indemnification permitted under this section in connection with a proceeding by or in the right of the corporation is limited to reasonable expenses incurred in connection with the proceeding.

## § 8.52 Mandatory Indemnification

Unless limited by its articles of incorporation, a corporation shall indemnify a director who was wholly successful, on the merits or otherwise, in the defense of any proceeding to which he was a party because he is or was a director of the corporation against reasonable expenses incurred by him in connection with the proceeding.

## § 8.53 Advance for Expenses

(a) A corporation may pay for or reimburse the reasonable expenses incurred by a director who is a party to a proceeding in advance of final disposition of the proceeding if:

(1) the director furnishes the corporation a written affirmation of his good faith belief that he has met the standard of conduct described in section 8.51;

(2) the director furnishes the corporation a written undertaking, executed personally or on his behalf, to repay the advance if it is ultimately determined that he did not meet the standard of conduct; and

(3) a determination is made that the facts then known to those making the determination would not preclude indemnification under this subchapter.

(b) The undertaking required by subsection (a)(2) must be an unlimited general obligation of the director but need not be secured and may be accepted without reference to financial ability to make repayment.

(c) Determinations and authorizations of payments under this section shall be made in the manner specified in section 8.55.

## § 8.54 Court-Ordered Indemnification

Unless a corporation's articles of incorporation provide otherwise, a director of the corporation who is a party to a proceeding may apply for indemnification to the court conducting the proceeding or to another court of competent jurisdiction. On receipt of an application, the court after giving any notice the court considers necessary may order indemnification if it determines:

(1) the director is entitled to mandatory indemnification under section 8.52, in which case the court shall also order the corporation to pay the director's reasonable expenses incurred to obtain court-ordered indemnification; or

(2) the director is fairly and reasonably entitled to indemnification in view of all the relevant circumstances, whether or not he met the standard of conduct set forth in section 8.51 or was adjudged liable as described in section 8.51(d), but if he was adjudged so liable his indemnification is limited to reasonable expenses incurred.

## § 8.55 Determination and Authorization of Indemnification

(a) A corporation may not indemnify a director under section 8.51 unless authorized in the specific case after a determination has been made that indemnification of the director is permissible in the circumstances because he has met the standard of conduct set forth in section 8.51.

(b) The determination shall be made:

(1) by the board of directors by majority vote of a quorum consisting of directors not at the time parties to the proceeding;

(2) if a quorum cannot be obtained under subdivision (1), by majority vote of a committee duly designated by the board of directors (in which designation directors who are parties may participate), consisting solely of two or more directors not at the time parties to the proceeding;

(3) by special legal counsel:

(i) selected by the board of directors or its committee in the manner prescribed in subdivision (1) or (2); or

(ii) if a quorum of the board of directors cannot be obtained under subdivision (1) and a committee cannot be designated under subdivision (2), selected by majority vote of the full board of directors (in which selection directors who are parties may participate); or

(4) by the shareholders, but shares owned by or voted under the control of directors who are at the time parties to the proceeding may not be voted on the determination.

(c) Authorization of indemnification and evaluation as to reasonableness of expenses shall be made in the same manner as the determination that indemnification is permissible, except that if the determination is made by special legal counsel, authorization of indemnification and evaluation as to reasonableness of expenses shall be made by those entitled under subsection (b)(3) to select counsel.

## § 8.56 Indemnification of Officers, Employees, and Agents

Unless a corporation's articles of incorporation provide otherwise:

(1) an officer of the corporation who is not a director is entitled to mandatory indemnification under section 8.52, and is entitled to apply for court-ordered indemnification under section 8.54, in each case to the same extent as a director;

(2) the corporation may indemnify and advance expenses under this subchapter to an officer, employee, or agent of the corporation who is not a director to the same extent as to a director; and

(3) a corporation may also indemnify and advance expenses to an officer, employee, or agent who is not a director to the extent, consistent with public policy, that may be provided by its articles of incorporation, bylaws,

general or specific action of its board of directors, or contract.

### § 8.57 Insurance

A corporation may purchase and maintain insurance on behalf of an individual who is or was a director, officer, employee, or agent of the corporation, or who, while a director, officer, employee, or agent of the corporation, is or was serving at the request of the corporation as a director, officer, partner, trustee, employee, or agent of another foreign or domestic corporation, partnership, joint venture, trust, employee benefit plan, or other enterprise, against liability asserted against or incurred by him in that capacity or arising from his status as a director, officer, employee, or agent, whether or not the corporation would have power to indemnify him against the same liability under section 8.51 or 8.52.

### § 8.58 Application of Subchapter

(a) A provision treating a corporation's indemnification of or advance for expenses to directors that is contained in its articles of incorporation, bylaws, a resolution of its shareholders or board of directors, or in a contract or otherwise, is valid only if and to the extent the provision is consistent with this subchapter. If articles of incorporation limit indemnification or advance for expenses, indemnification and advance for expenses are valid only to the extent consistent with the articles.

(b) This subchapter does not limit a corporation's power to pay or reimburse expenses incurred by a director in connection with his appearance as a witness in a proceeding at a time when he has not been made a named defendant or respondent to the proceeding.

## Subchapter F. Directors' Conflicting Interest Transactions

### § 8.60 Subchapter Definitions

In this subchapter:

(1) "Conflicting interest" with respect to a corporation means the interest a director of the corporation has respecting a transaction effected or proposed to be effected by the corporation (or by a subsidiary of the corporation or any other entity in which the corporation has a controlling interest) if

(i) whether or not the transaction is brought before the board of directors of the corporation for action, the director knows at the time of commitment that he or a related person is a party to the transaction or has a beneficial financial interest in or so closely linked to the transaction and of such financial significance to the director or a related person that the interest would reasonably be expected to exert an influence on the director's judgment if he were called upon to vote on the transaction; or

(ii) the transaction is brought (or is of such character and significance to the corporation that it would in the normal course be brought) before the board of directors of the corporation for action, and the director

knows at the time of commitment that any of the following persons is either a party to the transaction or has a beneficial financial interest in or so closely linked to the transaction and of such financial significance to the person that the interest would reasonably be expected to exert an influence on the director's judgment if he were called upon to vote on the transaction: (A) an entity (other than the corporation) of which the director is a director, general partner, agent, or employee; (B) a person that controls one or more of the entities specified in subclause (A) or an entity that is controlled by, or is under common control with, one or more of the entities specified in subclause (A); or (C) an individual who is a general partner, principal, or employer of the director.

(2) "Director's conflicting interest transaction" with respect to a corporation means a transaction effected or proposed to be effected by the corporation (or by a subsidiary of the corporation or any other entity in which the corporation has a controlling interest) respecting which a director of the corporation has a conflicting interest.

(3) "Related person" of a director means (i) the spouse (or a parent or sibling thereof) of the director, or a child, grandchild, sibling, parent (or spouse of any thereof) of the director, or an individual having the same home as the director, or a trust or estate of which an individual specified in this clause (i) is a substantial beneficiary; or (ii) a trust, estate, incompetent, conservatee, or minor of which the director is a fiduciary.

(4) "Required disclosure" means disclosure by the director who has a conflicting interest of (i) the existence and nature of his conflicting interest, and (ii) all facts known to him respecting the subject matter of the transaction that an ordinarily prudent person would reasonably believe to be material to a judgment about whether or not to proceed with the transaction.

(5) "Time of commitment" respecting a transaction means the time when the transaction is consummated or, if made pursuant to contract, the time when the corporation (or its subsidiary or the entity in which it has a controlling interest) becomes contractually obligated so that its unilateral withdrawal from the transaction would entail significant loss, liability, or other damage.

### § 8.61 Judicial Action

(a) A transaction effected or proposed to be effected by a corporation (or by a subsidiary of the corporation or any other entity in which the corporation has a controlling interest) that is not a director's conflicting interest transaction may not be enjoined, set aside, or give rise to an award of damages or other sanctions, in a proceeding by a shareholder or by or in the right of the corporation, because a director of the corporation, or any person with whom or which he has a personal, economic, or other association, has an interest in the transaction.

(b) A director's conflicting interest transaction may not be enjoined, set aside, or give rise to an award of damages or other sanctions, in a proceeding by a shareholder or by or in the right of the corporation, because the director, or any person with whom or which he has a personal, economic, or other association, has an interest in the transaction, if:

(1) directors' action respecting the transaction was at any time taken in compliance with section 8.62;

(2) shareholders' action respecting the transaction was at any time taken in compliance with section 8.63; or

(3) the transaction, judged according to the circumstances at the time of commitment, is established to have been fair to the corporation.

### § 8.62  Directors' Action

(a) Directors' action respecting a transaction is effective for purposes of section 8.61(b)(1) if the transaction received the affirmative vote of a majority (but no fewer than two) of those qualified directors on the board of directors or on a duly empowered committee of the board who voted on the transaction after either required disclosure to them (to the extent the information was not known by them) or compliance with subsection (b); provided that action by a committee is so effective only if:

(1) all its members are qualified directors; and

(2) its members are either all the qualified directors on the board or are appointed by the affirmative vote of a majority of the qualified directors on the board.

(b) If a director has a conflicting interest respecting a transaction, but neither he nor a related person of the director specified in section 8.60(3)(i) is a party to the transaction, and if the director has a duty under law or professional canon, or a duty of confidentiality to another person, respecting information relating to the transaction such that the director may not make the disclosure described in section 8.60(4)(ii), then disclosure is sufficient for purposes of subsection (a) if the director (1) discloses to the directors voting on the transaction the existence and nature of his conflicting interest and informs them of the character and limitations imposed by that duty before their vote on the transaction, and (2) plays no part, directly or indirectly, in their deliberations or vote.

(c) A majority (but no fewer than two) of all the qualified directors on the board of directors, or on the committee, constitutes a quorum for purposes of action that complies with this section. Directors' action that otherwise complies with this section is not affected by the presence or vote of a director who is not a qualified director.

(d) For purposes of this section, "qualified director" means, with respect to a director's conflicting interest transaction, any director who does not have either (1) a conflicting interest respecting the transaction, or (2) a familial, financial, professional, or employment relationship with a second director who does have a conflicting interest respecting the transaction, which relationship would, in the circumstances, reasonably be expected to exert an influence on the first director's judgment when voting on the transaction.

### § 8.63  Shareholders' Action

(a) Shareholders' action respecting a transaction is effective for purposes of section 8.61(b)(2) if a majority of the votes entitled to be cast by the holders of all qualified shares were cast in favor of the transaction after (1) notice to shareholders describing the director's conflicting interest transaction, (2) provision of the information referred to in subsection (d), and (3) required disclosure to the shareholders who voted on the transaction (to the extent the information was not known by them).

(b) For purposes of this section, "qualified shares" means any shares entitled to vote with respect to the director's conflicting interest transaction except shares that, to the knowledge, before the vote, of the secretary (or other officer or agent of the corporation authorized to tabulate votes), are beneficially owned (or the voting of which is controlled) by a director who has a conflicting interest respecting the transaction or by a related person of the director, or both.

(c) A majority of the votes entitled to be cast by the holders of all qualified shares constitutes a quorum for purposes of action that complies with this section. Subject to the provisions of subsections (d) and (e), shareholders' action that otherwise complies with this section is not affected by the presence of holders, or the voting, of shares that are not qualified shares.

(d) For purposes of compliance with subsection (a), a director who has a conflicting interest respecting the transaction shall, before the shareholders' vote, inform the secretary (or other office or agent of the corporation authorized to tabulate votes) of the number, and the identity of persons holding or controlling the vote, of all shares that the director knows are beneficially owned (or the voting of which is controlled) by the director or by a related person of the director, or both.

(e) If a shareholders' vote does not comply with subsection (a) solely because of a failure of a director to comply with subsection (d), and if the director establishes that his failure did not determine and was not intended by him to influence the outcome of the vote, the court may, with or without further proceedings respecting section 8.61(b)(3), take such action respecting the transaction and the director, and give such effect, if any, to the shareholders' vote, as it considers appropriate in the circumstances.

# Chapter 9.
# [RESERVED]

# Chapter 10.
# AMENDMENT OF ARTICLES OF INCORPORATION AND BYLAWS

## Subchapter A.  Amendment of Articles of Incorporation

### § 10.01  Authority to Amend

(a) A corporation may amend its articles of incorporation at any time to add or change a provision that is required or permitted in the articles of incorporation or to delete a provision not required in the articles of incorporation. Whether a provision is required or permitted in the articles of incorporation is determined as of the effective date of the amendment.

(b) A shareholder of the corporation does not have a vested property right resulting from any provision in the articles of incorporation, including provisions relating to management, control, capital structure, dividend entitlement, or purpose or duration of the corporation.

## § 10.02 Amendment by Board of Directors

Unless the articles of incorporation provide otherwise, a corporation's board of directors may adopt one or more amendments to the corporation's articles of incorporation without shareholder action:

(1) to extend the duration of the corporation if it was incorporated at a time when limited duration was required by law;

(2) to delete the names and addresses of the initial directors;

(3) to delete the name and address of the initial registered agent or registered office, if a statement of change is on file with the secretary of state;

(4) to change each issued and unissued authorized share of an outstanding class into a greater number of whole shares if the corporation has only shares of that class outstanding;

(5) to change the corporate name by substituting the word "corporation," "incorporated," "company," "limited," or the abbreviation "corp.," "inc.," "co.," or "ltd.," for a similar word or abbreviation in the name, or by adding, deleting, or changing a geographical attribution for the name; or

(6) to make any other change expressly permitted by this Act to be made without shareholder action.

## § 10.03 Amendment by Board of Directors and Shareholders

(a) A corporation's board of directors may propose one or more amendments to the articles of incorporation for submission to the shareholders.

(b) For the amendment to be adopted:

(1) the board of directors must recommend the amendment to the shareholders unless the board of directors determines that because of conflict of interest or other special circumstances it should make no recommendation and communicates the basis for its determination to the shareholders with the amendment; and

(2) the shareholders entitled to vote on the amendment must approve the amendment as provided in subsection (e).

(c) The board of directors may condition its submission of the proposed amendment on any basis.

(d) The corporation shall notify each shareholder, whether or not entitled to vote, of the proposed shareholders' meeting in accordance with section 7.05. The notice of meeting must also state that the purpose, or one of the purposes, of the meeting is to consider the proposed amendment and contain or be accompanied by a copy or summary of the amendment.

(e) Unless this Act, the articles of incorporation, or the board of directors (acting pursuant to subsection (c)) require a greater vote or a vote by voting groups, the amendment to be adopted must be approved by:

(1) a majority of the votes entitled to be cast on the amendment by any voting group with respect to which the amendment would create dissenters' rights; and

(2) the votes required by sections 7.25 and 7.26 by every other voting group entitled to vote on the amendment.

## § 10.04 Voting on Amendments by Voting Groups

(a) The holders of the outstanding shares of a class are entitled to vote as a separate voting group (if shareholder voting is otherwise required by this Act) on a proposed amendment if the amendment would:

(1) increase or decrease the aggregate number of authorized shares of the class;

(2) effect an exchange or reclassification of all or part of the shares of the class into shares of another class;

(3) effect an exchange or reclassification, or create the right of exchange, of all or part of the shares of another class into shares of the class;

(4) change the designation, rights, preferences, or limitations of all or part of the shares of the class;

(5) change the shares of all or part of the class into a different number of shares of the same class;

(6) create a new class of shares having rights or preferences with respect to distributions or to dissolution that are prior, superior, or substantially equal to the shares of the class;

(7) increase the rights, preferences, or number of authorized shares of any class that, after giving effect to the amendment, have rights or preferences with respect to distributions or to dissolution that are prior, superior, or substantially equal to the shares of the class;

(8) limit or deny an existing preemptive right of all or part of the shares of the class; or

(9) cancel or otherwise affect rights to distributions or dividends that have accumulated but not yet been declared on all or part of the shares of the class.

(b) If a proposed amendment would affect a series of a class of shares in one or more of the ways described in subsection (a), the shares of that series are entitled to vote as a separate voting group on the proposed amendment.

(c) If a proposed amendment that entitles two or more series of shares to vote as separate voting groups under this section would affect those two or more series in the same or a substantially similar way, the shares of all the series so affected must vote together as a single voting group on the proposed amendment.

(d)  A class or series of shares is entitled to the voting rights granted by this section although the articles of incorporation provide that the shares are nonvoting shares.

### § 10.05  Amendment before Issuance of Shares

If a corporation has not yet issued shares, its incorporators or board of directors may adopt one or more amendments to the corporation's articles of incorporation.

### § 10.06  Articles of Amendment

A corporation amending its articles of incorporation shall deliver to the secretary of state for filing articles of amendment setting forth:

(1)  the name of the corporation;

(2)  the text of each amendment adopted;

(3)  if an amendment provides for an exchange, reclassification, or cancellation of issued shares, provisions for implementing the amendment if not contained in the amendment itself;

(4)  the date of each amendment's adoption;

(5)  if an amendment was adopted by the incorporators or board of directors without shareholder action, a statement to that effect and that shareholder action was not required;

(6)  if an amendment was approved by the shareholders:

(i)  the designation, number of outstanding shares, number of votes entitled to be cast by each voting group entitled to vote separately on the amendment, and number of votes of each voting group indisputably represented at the meeting;

(ii)  either the total number of votes cast for and against the amendment by each voting group entitled to vote separately on the amendment or the total number of undisputed votes cast for the amendment by each voting group and a statement that the number cast for the amendment by each voting group was sufficient for approval by that voting group.

### § 10.07  Restated Articles of Incorporation

(a)  A corporation's board of directors may restate its articles of incorporation at any time with or without shareholder action.

(b)  The restatement may include one or more amendments to the articles. If the restatement includes an amendment requiring shareholder approval, it must be adopted as provided in section 10.03.

(c)  If the board of directors submits a restatement for shareholder action, the corporation shall notify each shareholder, whether or not entitled to vote, of the proposed shareholders' meeting in accordance with section 7.05. The notice must also state that the purpose, or one of the purposes, of the meeting is to consider the proposed restatement and contain or be accompanied by a copy of the restatement that identifies any amendment or other change it would make in the articles.

(d)  A corporation restating its articles of incorporation shall deliver to the secretary of state for filing articles of restatement setting forth the name of the corporation and the text of the restated articles of incorporation together with a certificate setting forth:

(1)  whether the restatement contains an amendment to the articles requiring shareholder approval and, if it does not, that the board of directors adopted the restatement; or

(2)  if the restatement contains an amendment to the articles requiring shareholder approval, the information required by section 10.06.

(e)  Duly adopted restated articles of incorporation supersede the original articles of incorporation and all amendments to them.

(f)  The secretary of state may certify restated articles of incorporation, as the articles of incorporation currently in effect, without including the certificate information required by subsection (d).

### § 10.08  Amendment Pursuant to Reorganization

(a)  A corporation's articles of incorporation may be amended without action by the board of directors or shareholders to carry out a plan of reorganization ordered or decreed by a court of competent jurisdiction under federal statute if the articles of incorporation after amendment contain only provisions required or permitted by section 2.02.

(b)  The individual or individuals designated by the court shall deliver to the secretary of state for filing articles of amendment setting forth:

(1)  the name of the corporation;

(2)  the text of each amendment approved by the court;

(3)  the date of the court's order or decree approving the articles of amendment;

(4)  the title of the reorganization proceeding in which the order or decree was entered; and

(5)  a statement that the court had jurisdiction of the proceeding under federal statute.

(c)  Shareholders of a corporation undergoing reorganization do not have dissenters' rights except as and to the extent provided in the reorganization plan.

(d)  This section does not apply after entry of a final decree in the reorganization proceeding even though the court retains jurisdiction of the proceeding for limited purposes unrelated to consummation of the reorganization plan.

### § 10.09  Effect of Amendment

An amendment to articles of incorporation does not affect a cause of action existing against or in favor of the corporation, a proceeding to which the corporation is a party, or the existing rights of persons other than shareholders of the corporation. An amendment changing a corporation's name does not abate a proceeding brought by or against the corporation in its former name.

## Subchapter B.  Amendment of Bylaws

### § 10.20  Amendment by Board of Directors or Shareholders

(a)  A corporation's board of directors may amend or repeal the corporation's bylaws unless:

(1)  the articles of incorporation or this Act reserve this power exclusively to the shareholders in whole or part; or

(2)  the shareholders in amending or repealing a particular bylaw provide expressly that the board of directors may not amend or repeal that bylaw.

(b)  A corporation's shareholders may amend or repeal the corporation's bylaws even though the bylaws may also be amended or repealed by its board of directors.

### § 10.21  Bylaw Increasing Quorum or Voting Requirement for Shareholders

(a)  If expressly authorized by the articles of incorporation, the shareholders may adopt or amend a bylaw that fixes a greater quorum or voting requirement for shareholders (or voting groups of shareholders) than is required by this Act. The adoption or amendment of a bylaw that adds, changes, or deletes a greater quorum or voting requirement for shareholders must meet the same quorum requirement and be adopted by the same vote and voting groups required to take action under the quorum and voting requirement then in effect or proposed to be adopted, whichever is greater.

(b)  A bylaw that fixes a greater quorum or voting requirement for shareholders under subsection (a) may not be adopted, amended, or repealed by the board of directors.

### § 10.22  Bylaw Increasing Quorum or Voting Requirement for Directors

(a)  A bylaw that fixes a greater quorum or voting requirement for the board of directors may be amended or repealed:

(1)  if originally adopted by the shareholders, only by the shareholders;

(2)  if originally adopted by the board of directors, either by the shareholders or by the board of directors.

(b)  A bylaw adopted or amended by the shareholders that fixes a greater quorum or voting requirement for the board of directors may provide that it may be amended or repealed only by a specified vote of either the shareholders or the board of directors.

(c)  Action by the board of directors under subsection (a)(2) to adopt or amend a bylaw that changes the quorum or voting requirement for the board of directors must meet the same quorum requirement and be adopted by the same vote required to take action under the quorum and voting requirement then in effect or proposed to be adopted, whichever is greater.

## Chapter 11.
## MERGER AND SHARE EXCHANGE

### § 11.01

(a)  One or more corporations may merge into another corporation if the board of directors of each corporation adopts and its shareholders (if required by section 11.03) approve a plan of merger.

(b)  The plan of merger must set forth:

(1)  the name of each corporation planning to merge and the name of the surviving corporation into which each other corporation plans to merge;

(2)  the terms and conditions of the merger; and

(3)  the manner and basis of converting the shares of each corporation into shares, obligations, or other securities of the surviving or any other corporation or into cash or other property in whole or part.

(c)  The plan of merger may set forth:

(1)  amendments to the articles of incorporation of the surviving corporation; and

(2)  other provisions relating to the merger.

### § 11.02  Share Exchange

(a)  A corporation may acquire all of the outstanding shares of one or more classes or series of another corporation if the board of directors of each corporation adopts and its shareholders (if required by section 11.03) approve the exchange.

(b)  The plan of exchange must set forth:

(1)  the name of the corporation whose shares will be acquired and the name of the acquiring corporation;

(2)  the terms and conditions of the exchange;

(3)  the manner and basis of exchanging the shares to be acquired for shares, obligations, or other securities of the acquiring or any other corporation or for cash or other property in whole or part.

(c)  The plan of exchange may set forth other provisions relating to the exchange.

(d)  This section does not limit the power of a corporation to acquire all or part of the shares of one or more classes or series of another corporation through a voluntary exchange or otherwise.

### § 11.03  Action on Plan

(a)  After adopting a plan of merger or share exchange, the board of directors of each corporation party to the merger, and the board of directors of the corporation whose shares will be acquired in the share exchange, shall submit the plan of merger (except as provided in subsection (g)) or share exchange for approval by its shareholders.

(b)  For a plan of merger or share exchange to be approved:

(1)  the board of directors must recommend the plan of merger or share exchange to the shareholders, unless the board of directors determines that because of conflict of interest or other special circumstances it should make no

recommendation and communicates the basis for its determination to the shareholders with the plan; and

(2) the shareholders entitled to vote must approve the plan.

(c) The board of directors may condition its submission of the proposed merger or share exchange on any basis.

(d) The corporation shall notify each shareholder, whether or not entitled to vote, of the proposed shareholders' meeting in accordance with section 7.05. The notice must also state that the purpose, or one of the purposes, of the meeting is to consider the plan of merger or share exchange and contain or be accompanied by a copy or summary of the plan.

(e) Unless this Act, the articles of incorporation, or the board of directors (acting pursuant to subsection (c)) require a greater vote or a vote by voting groups, the plan of merger or share exchange to be authorized must be approved by each voting group entitled to vote separately on the plan by a majority of all the votes entitled to be cast on the plan by that voting group.

(f) Separate voting by voting groups is required:

(1) on a plan of merger if the plan contains a provision that, if contained in a proposed amendment to articles of incorporation, would require action by one or more separate voting groups on the proposed amendment under section 10.04;

(2) on a plan of share exchange by each class or series of shares included in the exchange, with each class or series constituting a separate voting group.

(g) Action by the shareholders of the surviving corporation on a plan of merger is not required if:

(1) the articles of incorporation of the surviving corporation will not differ (except for amendments enumerated in section 10.02) from its articles before the merger;

(2) each shareholder of the surviving corporation whose shares were outstanding immediately before the effective date of the merger will hold the same number of shares, with identical designations, preferences, limitations, and relative rights, immediately after;

(3) the number of voting shares outstanding immediately after the merger, plus the number of voting shares issuable as a result of the merger (either by the conversion of securities issued pursuant to the merger or the exercise of rights and warrants issued pursuant to the merger), will not exceed by more than 20 percent the total number of voting shares of the surviving corporation outstanding immediately before the merger; and

(4) the number of participating shares outstanding immediately after the merger, plus the number of participating shares issuable as a result of the merger (either by the conversion of securities issued pursuant to the merger or the exercise of rights and warrants issued pursuant to the merger), will not exceed by more than 20 percent the total number of participating shares outstanding immediately before the merger.

(h) As used in subsection (g):

(1) ''Participating shares'' means shares that entitle their holders to participate without limitation in distributions.

(2) ''Voting shares'' means shares that entitle their holders to vote unconditionally in elections of directors.

(i) After a merger or share exchange is authorized, and at any time before articles of merger or share exchange are filed, the planned merger or share exchange may be abandoned (subject to any contractual rights), without further shareholder action, in accordance with the procedure set forth in the plan of merger or share exchange or, if none is set forth, in the manner determined by the board of directors.

## § 11.04 Merger of Subsidiary

(a) A parent corporation owning at least 90 percent of the outstanding shares of each class of a subsidiary corporation may merge the subsidiary into itself without approval of the shareholders of the parent or subsidiary.

(b) The board of directors of the parent shall adopt a plan of merger that sets forth:

(1) the names of the parent and subsidiary; and

(2) the manner and basis of converting the shares of the subsidiary into shares, obligations, or other securities of the parent or any other corporation or into cash or other property in whole or part.

(c) The parent shall mail a copy or summary of the plan of merger to each shareholder of the subsidiary who does not waive the mailing requirement in writing.

(d) The parent may not deliver articles of merger to the secretary of state for filing until at least 30 days after the date it mailed a copy of the plan of merger to each shareholder of the subsidiary who did not waive the mailing requirement.

(e) Articles of merger under this section may not contain amendments to the articles of incorporation of the parent corporation (except for amendments enumerated in section 10.02).

## § 11.05 Articles of Merger or Share Exchange

(a) After a plan of merger or share exchange is approved by the shareholders, or adopted by the board of directors if shareholder approval is not required, the surviving or acquiring corporation shall deliver to the secretary of state for filing articles of merger or share exchange setting forth:

(1) the plan of merger or share exchange;

(2) if shareholder approval was not required, a statement to that effect;

(3) if approval of the shareholders of one or more corporations party to the merger or share exchange was required:

(i) the designation, number of outstanding shares, and number of votes entitled to be cast by each voting group entitled to vote separately on the plan as to each corporation; and

(ii) either the total number of votes cast for and against the plan by each voting group entitled to vote separately on the plan or the total number of undisputed votes cast for the plan separately by each voting group and a statement that the number cast for the plan by each voting group was sufficient for approval by that voting group.

(b) Unless a delayed effective date is specified, a merger or share exchange takes effect when the articles of merger or share exchange are filed.

### § 11.06 Effect of Merger or Share Exchange

(a) When a merger takes effect:

(1) every other corporation party to the merger merges into the surviving corporation and the separate existence of every corporation except the surviving corporation ceases;

(2) the title to all real estate and other property owned by each corporation party to the merger is vested in the surviving corporation without reversion or impairment;

(3) the surviving corporation has all liabilities of each corporation party to the merger;

(4) a proceeding pending against any corporation party to the merger may be continued as if the merger did not occur or the surviving corporation may be substituted in the proceeding for the corporation whose existence ceased;

(5) the articles of incorporation of the surviving corporation are amended to the extent provided in the plan of merger; and

(6) the shares of each corporation party to the merger that are to be converted into shares, obligations, or other securities of the surviving or any other corporation or into cash or other property are converted and the former holders of the shares are entitled only to the rights provided in the articles of merger or to their rights under chapter 13.

(b) When a share exchange takes effect, the shares of each acquired corporation are exchanged as provided in the plan, and the former holders of the shares are entitled only to the exchange rights provided in the articles of share exchange or to their rights under chapter 13.

### § 11.07 Merger of Share Exchange with Foreign Corporation

(a) One or more foreign corporations may merge or enter into a share exchange with one or more domestic corporations if:

(1) in a merger, the merger is permitted by the law of the state or country under whose law each foreign corporation is incorporated and each foreign corporation complies with that law in effecting the merger;

(2) in a share exchange, the corporation whose shares will be acquired is a domestic corporation, whether or not a share exchange is permitted by the law of the state or country under whose law the acquiring corporation is incorporated;

(3) the foreign corporation complies with section 11.05 if it is the surviving corporation of the merger or acquiring corporation of the share exchange; and

(4) each domestic corporation complies with the applicable provisions of sections 11.01 through 11.04 and, if it is the surviving corporation of the merger or acquiring corporation of the share exchange, with section 11.05.

(b) Upon the merger or share exchange taking effect, the surviving foreign corporation of a merger and the acquiring foreign corporation of a share exchange is deemed:

(1) to appoint the secretary of state as its agent for service of process in a proceeding to enforce any obligation or the rights of dissenting shareholders of each domestic corporation party to the merger or share exchange; and

(2) to agree that it will promptly pay to the dissenting shareholders of each domestic corporation party to the merger or share exchange the amount, if any, to which they are entitled under chapter 13.

(c) This section does not limit the power of a foreign corporation to acquire all or part of the shares of one or more classes or series of a domestic corporation through a voluntary exchange or otherwise.

## Chapter 12.
## SALE OF ASSETS

### § 12.01 Sale of Assets in Regular Course of Business and Mortgage of Assets

(a) A corporation may, on the terms and conditions and for the consideration determined by the board of directors:

(1) sell, lease, exchange, or otherwise dispose of all, or substantially all, of its property in the usual and regular course of business;

(2) mortgage, pledge, dedicate to the repayment of indebtedness (whether with or without recourse), or otherwise encumber any or all of its property whether or not in the usual and regular course of business; or

(3) transfer any or all of its property to a corporation all the shares of which are owned by the corporation.

(b) Unless the articles of incorporation require it, approval by the shareholders of a transaction described in subsection (a) is not required.

### § 12.02 Sale of Assets Other Than in Regular Course of Business

(a) A corporation may sell, lease, exchange, or otherwise dispose of all, or substantially all, of its property (with or without the good will), otherwise than in the usual and regular course of business, on the terms and conditions and for the consideration determined by the corporation's board of directors, if the board of directors proposes and its shareholders approve the proposed transaction.

(b) For a transaction to be authorized:

(1) the board of directors must recommend the proposed transaction to the shareholders unless the board of directors determines that because of conflict of interest or other special circumstances it should make no recommendation and communicates the basis for its determination to the shareholders with the submission of the proposed transaction; and

(2) the shareholders entitled to vote must approve the transaction.

(c) The board of directors may condition its submission of the proposed transaction on any basis.

(d) The corporation shall notify each shareholder, whether or not entitled to vote, of the proposed shareholders' meeting in accordance with section 7.05. The notice must also state that the purpose, or one of the purposes, of the meeting is to consider the sale, lease, exchange, or other disposition of all, or substantially all, the property of the corporation and contain or be accompanied by a description of the transaction.

(e) Unless the articles of incorporation or the board of directors (acting pursuant to subsection (c)) require a greater vote or a vote by voting groups, the transaction to be authorized must be approved by a majority of all the votes entitled to be cast on the transaction.

(f) After a sale, lease, exchange, or other disposition of property is authorized, the transaction may be abandoned (subject to any contractual rights) without further shareholder action.

(g) A transaction that constitutes a distribution is governed by section 6.40 and not by this section.

# Chapter 13.
# DISSENTERS' RIGHTS

## Subchapter A. Right to Dissent and Obtain Payment for Shares

### § 13.01 Definitions

In this chapter:

(1) "Corporation" means the issuer of the shares held by a dissenter before the corporate action, or the surviving or acquiring corporation by merger or share exchange of that issuer.

(2) "Dissenter" means a shareholder who is entitled to dissent from corporate action under section 13.02 and who exercises that right when and in the manner required by sections 13.20 through 13.28.

(3) "Fair value," with respect to a dissenter's shares, means the value of the shares immediately before the effectuation of the corporate action to which the dissenter objects, excluding any appreciation or depreciation in anticipation of the corporate action unless exclusion would be inequitable.

(4) "Interest" means interest from the effective date of the corporate action until the date of payment, at the average rate currently paid by the corporation on its prin-

cipal bank loans or, if none, at a rate that is fair and equitable under all the circumstances.

(5) "Record shareholder" means the person in whose name shares are registered in the records of a corporation or the beneficial owner of shares to the extent of the rights granted by a nominee certificate on file with a corporation.

(6) "Beneficial shareholder" means the person who is a beneficial owner of shares held in a voting trust or by a nominee as the record shareholder.

(7) "Shareholder" means the record shareholder or the beneficial shareholder.

### § 13.02 Right to Dissent

(a) A shareholder is entitled to dissent from, and obtain payment of the fair value of his shares in the event of, any of the following corporate actions:

(1) consummation of a plan of merger to which the corporation is a party (i) if shareholder approval is required for the merger by section 11.03 or the articles of incorporation and the shareholder is entitled to vote on the merger or (ii) if the corporation is a subsidiary that is merged with its parent under section 11.04;

(2) consummation of a plan of share exchange to which the corporation is a party as the corporation whose shares will be acquired, if the shareholder is entitled to vote on the plan;

(3) consummation of a sale or exchange of all, or substantially all, of the property of the corporation other than in the usual and regular course of business, if the shareholder is entitled to vote on the sale or exchange, including a sale in dissolution, but not including a sale pursuant to court order or a sale for cash pursuant to a plan by which all or substantially all of the net proceeds of the sale will be distributed to the shareholders within one year after the date of sale;

(4) an amendment of the articles of incorporation that materially and adversely affects rights in respect of a dissenter's shares because it:

(i) alters or abolishes a preferential right of the shares;

(ii) creates, alters, or abolishes a right in respect of redemption, including a provision respecting a sinking fund for the redemption or repurchase, of the shares;

(iii) alters or abolishes a preemptive right of the holder of the shares to acquire shares or other securities;

(iv) excludes or limits the right of the shares to vote on any matter, or to cumulate votes, other than a limitation by dilution through issuance of shares or other securities with similar voting rights; or

(v) reduces the number of shares owned by the shareholder to a fraction of a share if the fractional share so created is to be acquired for cash under section 6.04; or

(5) any corporate action taken pursuant to a shareholder vote to the extent the articles of incorporation, bylaws, or a resolution of the board of directors provides that voting or nonvoting shareholders are entitled to dissent and obtain payment for their shares.

(b) A shareholder entitled to dissent and obtain payment for his shares under this chapter may not challenge the corporate action creating his entitlement unless the action is unlawful or fraudulent with respect to the shareholder or the corporation.

### § 13.03 Dissent by Nominees and Beneficial Owners

(a) A record shareholder may assert dissenters' rights as to fewer than all the shares registered in his name only if he dissents with respect to all shares beneficially owned by any one person and notifies the corporation in writing of the name and address of each person on whose behalf he asserts dissenters' rights. The rights of a partial dissenter under this subsection are determined as if the shares as to which he dissents and his other shares were registered in the names of different shareholders.

(b) A beneficial shareholder may assert dissenters' rights as to shares held on his behalf only if:

(1) he submits to the corporation the record shareholder's written consent to the dissent not later than the time the beneficial shareholder asserts dissenters' rights; and

(2) he does so with respect to all shares of which he is the beneficial shareholder or over which he has power to direct the vote.

## Subchapter B. Procedure for Exercise of Dissenters' Rights

### § 13.20 Notice of Dissenters' Rights

(a) If proposed corporate action creating dissenters' rights under section 13.02 is submitted to a vote at a shareholders' meeting, the meeting notice must state that shareholders are or may be entitled to assert dissenters' rights under this chapter and be accompanied by a copy of this chapter.

(b) If corporate action creating dissenters' rights under section 13.02 is taken without a vote of shareholders, the corporation shall notify in writing all shareholders entitled to assert dissenters' rights that the action was taken and send them the dissenters' notice described in section 13.22.

### § 13.21 Notice of Intent to Demand Payment

(a) If proposed corporate action creating dissenters' rights under section 13.02 is submitted to a vote at a shareholders' meeting, a shareholder who wishes to assert dissenters' rights (1) must deliver to the corporation before the vote is taken written notice of his intent to demand payment for his shares if the proposed action is effectuated and (2) must not vote his shares in favor of the proposed action.

(b) A shareholder who does not satisfy the requirements of subsection (a) is not entitled to payment for his shares under this chapter.

### § 13.22 Dissenters' Notice

(a) If proposed corporate action creating dissenters' right under section 13.02 is authorized at a shareholders' meeting, the corporation shall deliver a written dissenters' notice to all shareholders who satisfied the requirements of section 13.21.

(b) The dissenters' notice must be sent no later than 10 days after the corporate action was taken, and must:

(1) state where the payment demand must be sent and where and when certificates for certificated shares must be deposited;

(2) inform holders of uncertificated shares to what extent transfer of the shares will be restricted after the payment demand is received;

(3) supply a form for demanding payment that includes the date of the first announcement to news media or to shareholders of the terms of the proposed corporate action and requires that the person asserting dissenters' rights certify whether or not he acquired beneficial ownership of the shares before that date;

(4) set a date by which the corporation must receive the payment demand, which date may not be fewer than 30 nor more than 60 days after the date the subsection (a) notice is delivered; and

(5) be accompanied by a copy of this chapter.

### § 13.23 Duty to Demand Payment

(a) A shareholder sent a dissenters' notice described in section 13.22 must demand payment, certify whether he acquired beneficial ownership of the shares before the date required to be set forth in the dissenter's notice pursuant to section 13.22(b)(3), and deposit his certificates in accordance with the terms of the notice.

(b) The shareholder who demands payment and deposits his shares under section (a) retains all other rights of a shareholder until these rights are cancelled or modified by the taking of the proposed corporate action.

(c) A shareholder who does not demand payment or deposit his share certificates where required, each by the date set in the dissenters' notice, is not entitled to payment for his shares under this chapter.

### § 13.24 Share Restrictions

(a) The corporation may restrict the transfer of uncertificated shares from the date the demand for their payment is received until the proposed corporate action is taken or the restrictions released under section 13.26.

(b) The person for whom dissenters' rights are asserted as to uncertificated shares retains all other rights of a shareholder until these rights are cancelled or modified by the taking of the proposed corporate action.

### § 13.25 Payment

(a) Except as provided in section 13.27, as soon as the proposed corporate action is taken, or upon receipt of a payment demand, the corporation shall pay each dissenter who complied with section 13.23 the amount the corporation estimates to be the fair value of his shares, plus accrued interest.

(b) The payment must be accompanied by:

(1) the corporation's balance sheet as of the end of a fiscal year ending not more than 16 months before the date of payment, an income statement for that year, a statement of changes in shareholders' equity for that year, and the latest available interim financial statements, if any;

(2) a statement of the corporation's estimate of the fair value of the shares;

(3) an explanation of how the interest was calculated;

(4) a statement of the dissenter's right to demand payment under section 13.28; and

(5) a copy of this chapter.

### § 13.26 Failure to Take Action

(a) If the corporation does not take the proposed action within 60 days after the date set for demanding payment and depositing share certificates, the corporation shall return the deposited certificates and release the transfer restrictions imposed on uncertificated shares.

(b) If after returning deposited certificates and releasing transfer restrictions, the corporation takes the proposed action, it must send a new dissenters' notice under section 13.22 and repeat the payment demand procedure.

### § 13.27 After-Acquired Shares

(a) A corporation may elect to withhold payment required by section 13.25 from a dissenter unless he was the beneficial owner of the shares before the date set forth in the dissenters' notice as the date of the first announcement to news media or to shareholders of the terms of the proposed corporate action.

(b) To the extent the corporation elects to withhold payment under subsection (a), after taking the proposed corporate action, it shall estimate the fair value of the shares, plus accrued interest, and shall pay this amount to each dissenter who agrees to accept it in full satisfaction of his demand. The corporation shall send with its offer a statement of its estimate of the fair value of the shares, an explanation of how the interest was calculated, and a statement of the dissenter's right to demand payment under section 13.28.

### § 13.28 Procedure If Shareholder Dissatisfied with Payment or Offer

(a) A dissenter may notify the corporation in writing of his own estimate of the fair value of his shares and amount of interest due, and demand payment of his estimate (less any payment under section 13.25), or reject the corporation's offer under section 13.27 and demand payment of the fair value of his shares and interest due, if:

(1) the dissenter believes that the amount paid under section 13.25 or offered under section 13.27 is less than the fair value of his shares or that the interest due is incorrectly calculated;

(2) the corporation fails to make payment under section 13.25 within 60 days after the date set for demanding payment; or

(3) the corporation, having failed to take the proposed action, does not return the deposited certificates or release the transfer restrictions imposed on uncertificated shares within 60 days after the date set for demanding payment.

(b) A dissenter waives his right to demand payment under this section unless he notifies the corporation of his demand in writing under subsection (a) within 30 days after the corporation made or offered payment for his shares.

## Subchapter C. Judicial Appraisal of Shares

### § 13.30 Court Action

(a) If a demand for payment under section 13.28 remains unsettled, the corporation shall commence a proceeding within 60 days after receiving the payment demand and petition the court to determine the fair value of the shares and accrued interest. If the corporation does not commence the proceeding within the 60-day period, it shall pay each dissenter whose demand remains unsettled the amount demanded.

(b) The corporation shall commence the proceeding in the [name or describe] court of the county where a corporation's principal office (or, if none in this state, its registered office) is located. If the corporation is a foreign corporation without a registered office in this state, it shall commence the proceeding in the county in this state where the registered office of the domestic corporation merged with or whose shares were acquired by the foreign corporation was located.

(c) The corporation shall make all dissenters (whether or not residents of this state) whose demands remain unsettled parties to the proceeding as in an action against their shares and all parties must be served with a copy of the petition. Non-residents may be served by registered or certified mail or by publication as provided by law.

(d) The jurisdiction of the court in which the proceeding is commenced under subsection (b) is plenary and exclusive. The court may appoint one or more persons as appraisers to receive evidence and recommend decision on the question of fair value. The appraisers have the powers described in the order appointing them, or in any amendment to it. The dissenters are entitled to the same discovery rights as parties in other civil proceedings.

(e) Each dissenter made a party to the proceeding is entitled to judgment (1) for the amount, if any, by which the court finds the fair value of his shares, plus interest, exceeds the amount paid by the corporation or (2) for the fair value, plus accrued interest, of his after-acquired shares for which the corporation elected to withhold payment under section 13.27.

### § 13.31 Court Costs and Counsel Fees

(a) The court in an appraisal proceeding commenced under section 13.30 shall determine all costs of the proceeding, including the reasonable compensation and expenses of appraisers appointed by the court. The court shall assess the costs against the corporation, except that the court may assess costs against all or some of the dissenters, in amounts the court finds equitable, to the extent the court finds dissenters acted arbitrarily, vexatiously, or not in good faith in demanding payment under section 13.28.

(b) The court may also assess the fees and expenses of counsel and experts for the respective parties, in amounts the court finds equitable:

(1) against the corporation and in favor of any or all dissenters if the court finds the corporation did not substantially comply with the requirements of sections 13.20 through 13.28; or

(2) against either the corporation or a dissenter, in favor of any other party, if the court finds that the party against whom the fees and expenses are assessed acted arbitrarily, vexatiously, or not in good faith with respect to the rights provided by this chapter.

(c) If the court finds that the services of counsel for any dissenter were of substantial benefit to other dissenters similarly situated, and that the fees for those services should not be assessed against the corporation, the court may award to these counsel reasonable fees to be paid out of the amounts awarded the dissenters who were benefited.

# Chapter 14.
# DISSOLUTION

## Subchapter A. Voluntary Dissolution

### § 14.01 Dissolution by Incorporators or Initial Directors

A majority of the incorporators or initial directors of a corporation that has not issued shares or has not commenced business may dissolve the corporation by delivering to the secretary of state for filing articles of dissolution that set forth:

(1) the name of the corporation;

(2) the date of its incorporation;

(3) either (i) that none of the corporation's shares has been issued or (ii) that the corporation has not commenced business;

(4) that no debt of the corporation remains unpaid;

(5) that the net assets of the corporation remaining after winding up have been distributed to the shareholders, if shares were issued; and

(6) that a majority of the incorporators or initial directors authorized the dissolution.

### § 14.02 Dissolution by Board of Directors and Shareholders

(a) A corporation's board of directors may propose dissolution for submission to the shareholders.

(b) For a proposal to dissolve to be adopted:

(1) the board of directors must recommend dissolution to the shareholders unless the board of directors determines that because of conflict of interest or other special circumstances it should make no recommendation and communicates the basis for its determination to the shareholders; and

(2) the shareholders entitled to vote must approve the proposal to dissolve as provided in subsection (e).

(c) The board of directors may condition its submission of the proposal for dissolution on any basis.

(d) The corporation shall notify each shareholder, whether or not entitled to vote, of the proposed shareholders' meeting in accordance with section 7.05. The notice must also state that the purpose, or one of the purposes, of the meeting is to consider dissolving the corporation.

(e) Unless the articles of incorporation or the board of directors (acting pursuant to subsection (c)) require a greater vote or a vote by voting groups, the proposal to dissolve to be adopted must be approved by a majority of all the votes entitled to be cast on that proposal.

### § 14.03 Articles of Dissolution

(a) At any time after dissolution is authorized, the corporation may dissolve by delivering to the secretary of state for filing articles of dissolution setting forth:

(1) the name of the corporation;

(2) the date dissolution was authorized;

(3) if dissolution was approved by the shareholders;

(i) the number of votes entitled to be cast on the proposal to dissolve; and

(ii) either the total number of votes cast for and against dissolution or the total number of undisputed votes cast for dissolution and a statement that the number cast for dissolution was sufficient for approval.

(4) If voting by voting groups is required, the information required by subparagraph (3) shall be separately provided for each voting group entitled to vote separately on the plan to dissolve.

(b) A corporation is dissolved upon the effective date of its articles of dissolution.

### § 14.04 Revocation of Dissolution

(a) A corporation may revoke its dissolution within 120 days of its effective date.

(b) Revocation of dissolution must be authorized in the same manner as the dissolution was authorized unless that authorization permitted revocation by action by the board of directors alone, in which event the board of directors may revoke the dissolution without shareholder action.

(c) After the revocation of dissolution is authorized, the corporation may revoke the dissolution by delivering to the secretary of state for filing articles of revocation of dissolution, together with a copy of its articles of dissolution, that set forth:

(1) the name of the corporation;

(2) the effective date of the dissolution that was revoked;

(3) the date that the revocation of dissolution was authorized;

(4) if the corporation's board of directors (or incorporators) revoked the dissolution, a statement to that effect;

(5) if the corporation's board of directors revoked a dissolution authorized by the shareholders, a statement that revocation was permitted by action by the board of directors alone pursuant to that authorization; and

(6) if shareholder action was required to revoke the dissolution, the information required by section 14.03(3) or (4).

(d) Unless a delayed effective date is specified, revocation of dissolution is effective when articles of revocation of dissolution are filed.

(e) When the revocation of dissolution is effective, it relates back to and takes effect as of the effective date of the dissolution and the corporation resumes carrying on its business as if dissolution had never occurred.

## § 14.05 Effect of Dissolution

(a) A dissolved corporation continues its corporate existence but may not carry on any business except that appropriate to wind up and liquidate its business and affairs, including:

(1) collecting its assets;

(2) disposing of its properties that will not be distributed in kind to its shareholders;

(3) discharging or making provision for discharging its liabilities;

(4) distributing its remaining property among its shareholders according to their interests; and

(5) doing every other act necessary to wind up and liquidate its business and affairs.

(b) Dissolution of a corporation does not:

(1) transfer title to the corporation's property;

(2) prevent transfer of its shares or securities, although the authorization to dissolve may provide for closing the corporation's share transfer records;

(3) subject its directors or officers to standards of conduct different from those prescribed in chapter 8;

(4) change quorum or voting requirements for its board of directors or shareholders; change provisions for selection, resignation, or removal of its directors or officers or both; or change provisions for amending its bylaws;

(5) prevent commencement of a proceeding by or against the corporation in its corporate name;

(6) abate or suspend a proceeding pending by or against the corporation on the effective date of dissolution; or

(7) terminate the authority of the registered agent of the corporation.

## § 14.06 Known Claims against Dissolved Corporation

(a) A dissolved corporation may dispose of the known claims against it by following the procedure described in this section.

(b) The dissolved corporation shall notify its known claimants in writing of the dissolution at any time after its effective date. The written notice must:

(1) describe information that must be included in a claim;

(2) provide a mailing address where a claim may be sent;

(3) state the deadline, which may not be fewer than 120 days from the effective date of the written notice, by which the dissolved corporation must receive the claim; and

(4) state that the claim will be barred if not received by the deadline.

(c) A claim against the dissolved corporation is barred:

(1) if a claimant who was given written notice under subsection (b) does not deliver the claim to the dissolved corporation by the deadline;

(2) if a claimant whose claim was rejected by the dissolved corporation does not commence a proceeding to enforce the claim within 90 days from the effective date of the rejection notice.

(d) For purposes of this section, "claim" does not include a contingent liability or a claim based on an event occurring after the effective date of dissolution.

## § 14.07 Unknown Claims against Dissolved Corporation

(a) A dissolved corporation may also publish notice of its dissolution and request that persons with claims against the corporation present them in accordance with the notice.

(b) The notice must:

(1) be published one time in a newspaper of general circulation in the county where the dissolved corporation's principal office (or, if none in this state, its registered office) is or was last located;

(2) describe the information that must be included in a claim and provide a mailing address where the claim may be sent; and

(3) state that a claim against the corporation will be barred unless a proceeding to enforce the claim is commenced within five years after the publication of the notice.

(c) If the dissolved corporation publishes a newspaper notice in accordance with subsection (b), the claim of each of the following claimants is barred unless the claimant commences a proceeding to enforce the claim against the dissolved corporation within five years after the publication date of the newspaper notice:

(1) a claimant who did not receive written notice under section 14.06;

(2) a claimant whose claim was timely sent to the dissolved corporation but not acted on;

(3) a claimant whose claim is contingent or based on an event occurring after the effective date of dissolution.

(d) A claim may be enforced under this section:

(1) against the dissolved corporation, to the extent of its undistributed assets; or

(2) if the assets have been distributed in liquidation, against a shareholder of the dissolved corporation to the extent of his pro rata share of the claim or the corporate assets distributed to him in liquidation, whichever is less, but a shareholder's total liability for all claims under this section may not exceed the total amount of assets distributed to him.

## Subchapter B. Administrative Dissolution

### § 14.20 Grounds for Administrative Dissolution

The secretary of state may commence a proceeding under section 14.21 to administratively dissolve a corporation if:

(1) the corporation does not pay within 60 days after they are due any franchise taxes or penalties imposed by this Act or other law;

(2) the corporation does not deliver its annual report to the secretary of state within 60 days after it is due;

(3) the corporation is without a registered agent or registered office in this state for 60 days or more;

(4) the corporation does not notify the secretary of state within 60 days that its registered agent or registered office has been changed, that its registered agent has resigned, or that its registered office has been discontinued; or

(5) the corporation's period of duration stated in its articles of incorporation expires.

### § 14.21 Procedure for and Effect of Administrative Dissolution

(a) If the secretary of state determines that one or more grounds exist under section 14.20 for dissolving a corporation, he shall serve the corporation with written notice of his determination under section 5.04.

(b) If the corporation does not correct each ground for dissolution or demonstrate to the reasonable satisfaction of the secretary of state that each ground determined by the secretary of state does not exist within 60 days after service of the notice is perfected under section 5.04, the secretary of state shall administratively dissolve the corporation by signing a certificate of dissolution that recites the ground or grounds for dissolution and its effective date. The secretary of state shall file the original of the certificate and serve a copy on the corporation under section 5.04.

(c) A corporation administratively dissolved continues its corporate existence but may not carry on any business except that necessary to wind up and liquidate its business and affairs under section 14.05 and notify claimants under sections 14.06 and 14.07.

(d) The administrative dissolution of a corporation does not terminate the authority of its registered agent.

### § 14.22 Reinstatement Following Administrative Dissolution

(a) A corporation administratively dissolved under section 14.21 may apply to the secretary of state for reinstatement within two years after the effective date of dissolution. The application must:

(1) recite the name of the corporation and the effective date of its administrative dissolution;

(2) state that the ground or grounds for dissolution either did not exist or have been eliminated;

(3) state that the corporation's name satisfies the requirements of section 4.01; and

(4) contain a certificate from the [taxing authority] reciting that all taxes owed by the corporation have been paid.

(b) If the secretary of state determines that the application contains the information required by subsection (a) and that the information is correct, he shall cancel the certificate of dissolution and prepare a certificate of reinstatement that recites his determination and the effective date of reinstatement, file the original of the certificate, and serve a copy on the corporation under section 5.04.

(c) When the reinstatement is effective, it relates back to and takes effect as of the effective date of the administrative dissolution and the corporation resumes carrying on its business as if the administrative dissolution had never occurred.

### § 14.23 Appeal from Denial of Reinstatement

(a) If the secretary of state denies a corporation's application for reinstatement following administrative dissolution, he shall serve the corporation under section 5.04 with a written notice that explains the reason or reasons for denial.

(b) The corporation may appeal the denial of reinstatement to the [name or describe] court within 30 days after service of the notice of denial is perfected. The corporation appeals by petitioning the court to set aside the dissolution and attaching to the petition copies of the secretary of state's certificate of dissolution, the corporation's application for reinstatement, and the secretary of state's notice of denial.

(c) The court may summarily order the secretary of state to reinstate the dissolved corporation or may take other action the court considers appropriate.

(d) The court's final decision may be appealed as in other civil proceedings.

## Subchapter C. Judicial Dissolution

### § 14.30 Grounds for Judicial Dissolution

The [name or describe court or courts] may dissolve a corporation:

(1) in a proceeding by the attorney general if it is established that:

(i) the corporation obtained its articles of incorporation through fraud; or

(ii) the corporation has continued to exceed or abuse the authority conferred upon it by law;

(2) in a proceeding by a shareholder if it is established that:

(i) the directors are deadlocked in the management of the corporate affairs, the shareholders are unable to break the deadlock, and irreparable injury to the corporation is threatened or being suffered, or the business and affairs of the corporation can no longer be conducted to the advantage of the shareholders generally, because of the deadlock;

(ii) the directors or those in control of the corporation have acted, are acting, or will act in a manner that is illegal, oppressive, or fraudulent;

(iii) the shareholders are deadlocked in voting power and have failed, for a period that includes at least two consecutive annual meeting dates, to elect successors to directors whose terms have expired; or

(iv) the corporate assets are being misapplied or wasted;

(3) in a proceeding by a creditor if it is established that:

(i) the creditor's claim has been reduced to judgment, the execution on the judgment returned unsatisfied, and the corporation is insolvent; or

(ii) the corporation has admitted in writing that the creditor's claim is due and owing and the corporation is insolvent; or

(4) in a proceeding by the corporation to have its voluntary dissolution continued under court supervision.

### § 14.31 Procedure for Judicial Dissolution

(a) Venue for a proceeding by the attorney general to dissolve a corporation lies in [name the county or counties]. Venue for a proceeding brought by any other party named in section 14.30 lies in the county where a corporation's principal office (or, if none in this state, its registered office) is or was last located.

(b) It is not necessary to make shareholders parties to a proceeding to dissolve a corporation unless relief is sought against them individually.

(c) A court in a proceeding brought to dissolve a corporation may issue injunctions, appoint a receiver or custodian pendente lite with all powers and duties the court directs, take other action required to preserve the corporate assets wherever located, and carry on the business of the corporation until a full hearing can be held.

### § 14.32 Receivership or Custodianship

(a) A court in a judicial proceeding brought to dissolve a corporation may appoint one or more receivers to wind up and liquidate, or one or more custodians to manage, the business and affairs of the corporation. The court shall hold a hearing, after notifying all parties to the proceeding and any interested persons designated by the court, before appointing a receiver or custodian. The court appointing a receiver or custodian has exclusive jurisdiction over the corporation and all its property wherever located.

(b) The court may appoint an individual or a domestic or foreign corporation (authorized to transact business in this state) as a receiver or custodian. The court may require the receiver or custodian to post bond, with or without sureties, in an amount the court directs.

(c) The court shall describe the powers and duties of the receiver or custodian in its appointing order, which may be amended from time to time. Among other powers:

(1) the receiver (i) may dispose of all or any part of the assets of the corporation wherever located, at a public or private sale, if authorized by the court; and (ii) may sue and defend in his own name as receiver of the corporation in all courts of this state;

(2) the custodian may exercise all of the powers of the corporation, through or in place of its board of directors or officers, to the extent necessary to manage the affairs of the corporation in the best interests of its shareholders and creditors.

(d) The court during a receivership may redesignate the receiver a custodian, and during a custodianship may redesignate the custodian a receiver, if doing so is in the best interests of the corporation, its shareholders, and creditors.

(e) The court from time to time during the receivership or custodianship may order compensation paid and expense disbursements or reimbursements made to the receiver or custodian and his counsel from the assets of the corporation or proceeds from the sale of the assets.

### § 14.33 Decree of Dissolution

(a) If after a hearing the court determines that one or more grounds for judicial dissolution described in section 14.30 exist, it may enter a decree dissolving the corporation and specifying the effective date of the dissolution, and the clerk of the court shall deliver a certified copy of the decree to the secretary of state, who shall file it.

(b) After entering the decree of dissolution, the court shall direct the winding up and liquidation of the corporation's business and affairs in accordance with section 14.05 and the notification of claimants in accordance with sections 14.06 and 14.07.

## Subchapter D. Miscellaneous

### § 14.40 Deposit with State Treasurer

Assets of a dissolved corporation that should be transferred to a creditor, claimant, or shareholder of the corporation who cannot be found or who is not competent to receive them shall be reduced to cash and deposited with the state treasurer or other appropriate state official for safekeeping. When the creditor, claimant, or shareholder furnishes satisfactory proof of entitlement to the amount deposited, the state treasurer or other appropriate state official shall pay him or his representative that amount.

# [Chapter 15. FOREIGN CORPORATIONS. OMITTED.]

# Chapter 16.
# RECORDS AND REPORTS

## Subchapter A. Records

### § 16.01 Corporate Records

(a) A corporation shall keep as permanent records minutes of all meetings of its shareholders and board of directors, a record of all actions taken by the shareholders or board of directors without a meeting, and a record of all actions taken by a committee of the board of directors in place of the board of directors on behalf of the corporation.

(b) A corporation shall maintain appropriate accounting records.

(c) A corporation or its agent shall maintain a record of its shareholders, in a form that permits preparation of a list of the names and addresses of all shareholders, in alphabetical order by class of shares showing the number and class of shares held by each.

(d) A corporation shall maintain its records in written form or in another form capable of conversion into written form within a reasonable time.

(e) A corporation shall keep a copy of the following records at its principal office:

(1) its articles or restated articles of incorporation and all amendments to them currently in effect;

(2) its bylaws or restated bylaws and all amendments to them currently in effect;

(3) resolutions adopted by its board of directors creating one or more classes or series of shares, and fixing their relative rights, preferences, and limitations, if shares issued pursuant to those resolutions are outstanding;

(4) the minutes of all shareholders' meetings, and records of all action taken by shareholders without a meeting, for the past three years;

(5) all written communications to shareholders generally within the past three years, including the financial statements furnished for the past three years under section 16.20;

(6) a list of the names and business addresses of its current directors and officers; and

(7) its most recent annual report delivered to the secretary of state under section 16.22.

### § 16.02 Inspection of Records by Shareholders

(a) Subject to section 16.03(c), a shareholder of a corporation is entitled to inspect and copy, during regular business hours at the corporation's principal office, any of the records of the corporation described in section 16.01(e) if he gives the corporation written notice of his demand at least five business days before the date on which he wishes to inspect and copy.

(b) A shareholder of a corporation is entitled to inspect and copy, during regular business hours at a reasonable location specified by the corporation, any of the following records of the corporation if the shareholder meets the requirements of subsection (c) and gives the corporation written notice of his demand at least five business days before the date on which he wishes to inspect and copy:

(1) excerpts from minutes of any meeting of the board of directors, records of any action of a committee of the board of directors while acting in place of the board of directors on behalf of the corporation, minutes of any meeting of the shareholders, and records of action taken by the shareholders or board of directors without a meeting, to the extent not subject to inspection under section 16.02(a);

(2) accounting records of the corporation; and

(3) the record of shareholders.

(c) A shareholder may inspect and copy the records identified in subsection (b) only if:

(1) his demand is made in good faith and for a proper purpose;

(2) he describes with reasonable particularity his purpose and the records he desires to inspect; and

(3) the records are directly connected with his purpose.

(d) The right of inspection granted by this section may not be abolished or limited by a corporation's articles of incorporation or bylaws.

(e) This section does not affect:

(1) the right of a shareholder to inspect records under section 7.20 or, if the shareholder is in litigation with the corporation, to the same extent as any other litigant;

(2) the power of a court, independently of this Act, to compel the production of corporate records for examination.

(f) For purposes of this section, ''shareholder'' includes a beneficial owner whose shares are held in a voting trust or by a nominee on his behalf.

### § 16.03 Scope of Inspection Right

(a) A shareholder's agent or attorney has the same inspection and copying rights as the shareholder he represents.

(b) The right to copy records under section 16.02 includes, if reasonable, the right to receive copies made by photographic, xerographic, or other means.

(c) The corporation may impose a reasonable charge, covering the costs of labor and material, for copies of any documents provided to the shareholder. The charge may not exceed the estimated cost of production or reproduction of the records.

(d) The corporation may comply with a shareholder's demand to inspect the record of shareholders under section 16.02(b)(3) by providing him with a list of its shareholders that was compiled no earlier than the date of the shareholder's demand.

### § 16.04 Court-Ordered Inspection

(a) If a corporation does not allow a shareholder who complies with section 16.02(a) to inspect and copy any records required by that subsection to be available for inspection, the [name or describe court] of the county where the corporation's principal office (or, if none in this state, its registered office) is located may summarily order inspection and copying of the records demanded at the corporation's expense upon application of the shareholder.

(b) If a corporation does not within a reasonable time allow a shareholder to inspect and copy any other record, the shareholder who complies with section 16.02(b) and (c) may apply to the [name or describe court] in the county where the corporation's principal office (or, if none in this state, its registered office) is located for an order to permit inspection and copying of the records demanded. The court shall dispose of an application under this subsection on an expedited basis.

(c) If the court orders inspection and copying of the records demanded, it shall also order the corporation to pay the shareholder's costs (including reasonable counsel fees) incurred to obtain the order unless the corporation proves that it refused inspection in good faith because it had a reasonable basis for doubt about the right of the shareholder to inspect the records demanded.

(d) If the court orders inspection and copying of the records demanded, it may impose reasonable restrictions on the use or distribution of the records by the demanding shareholder.

## Subchapter B. Reports

### § 16.20 Financial Statements for Shareholders

(a) A corporation shall furnish its shareholders annual financial statements, which may be consolidated or combined statements of the corporation and one or more of its subsidiaries, as appropriate, that include a balance sheet as of the end of the fiscal year, an income statement for that year, and a statement of changes in shareholders' equity for the year unless that information appears elsewhere in the financial statements. If financial statements are prepared for the corporation on the basis of generally accepted accounting principles, the annual financial statements must also be prepared on that basis.

(b) If the annual financial statements are reported upon by a public accountant, his report must accompany them. If not, the statements must be accompanied by a statement of the president or the person responsible for the corporation's accounting records:

(1) stating his reasonable belief whether the statements were prepared on the basis of generally accepted accounting principles and, if not, describing the basis of preparation; and

(2) describing any respects in which the statements were not prepared on a basis of accounting consistent with the statements prepared for the preceding year.

(c) A corporation shall mail the annual financial statements to each shareholder within 120 days after the close of each fiscal year. Thereafter, on written request from a shareholder who was not mailed the statements, the corporation shall mail him the latest financial statements.

### § 16.21 Other Reports to Shareholders

(a) If a corporation indemnifies or advances expenses to a director under section 8.51, 8.52, 8.53, or 8.54 in connection with a proceeding by or in the right of the corporation, the corporation shall report the indemnification or advance in writing to the shareholders with or before the notice of the next shareholders' meeting.

(b) If a corporation issues or authorizes the issuance of shares for promissory notes or for promises to render services in the future, the corporation shall report in writing to the shareholders the number of shares authorized or issued, and the consideration received by the corporation, with or before the notice of the next shareholders' meeting.

### § 16.22 Annual Report for Secretary of State

(a) Each domestic corporation, and each foreign corporation authorized to transact business in this state, shall deliver to the secretary of state for filing an annual report that sets forth:

(1) the name of the corporation and the state or country under whose law it is incorporated;

(2) the address of its registered office and the name of its registered agent at that office in this state;

(3) the address of its principal office;

(4) the names and business addresses of its directors and principal officers;

(5) a brief description of the nature of its business;

(6) the total number of authorized shares, itemized by class and series, if any, within each class; and

(7) the total number of issued and outstanding shares, itemized by class and series, if any, within each class.

(b) Information in the annual report must be current as of the date the annual report is executed on behalf of the corporation.

(c) The first annual report must be delivered to the secretary of state between January 1 and April 1 of the year following the calendar year in which a domestic corporation was incorporated or a foreign corporation was authorized to transact business. Subsequent annual reports must be delivered to the secretary of state between January 1 and April 1 of the following calendar years.

(d) If an annual report does not contain the information required by this section, the secretary of state shall promptly notify the reporting domestic or foreign corporation in writing and return the report to it for correction. If the report is corrected to contain the information required by this section and delivered to the secretary of state within 30 days after the effective date of notice, it is deemed to be timely filed.

## Chapter 17.
# TRANSITION PROVISIONS

### § 17.01 Application to Existing Domestic Corporations

This Act applies to all domestic corporations in existence on its effective date that were incorporated under any general statute of this state providing for incorporation of corporations for profit if power to amend or repeal the statute under which the corporation was incorporated was reserved.

## § 17.02 Application to Qualified Foreign Corporations

A foreign corporation authorized to transact business in this state on the effective date of this Act is subject to this Act but is not required to obtain a new certificate of authority to transact business under this Act.

## § 17.03 Saving Provision

(a) Except as provided in subsection (b), the repeal of a statute by this Act does not affect:

(1) the operation of the statute or any action taken under it before its repeal;

(2) any ratification, right, remedy, privilege, obligation, or liability acquired, accrued, or incurred under the statute before its repeal;

(3) any violation of the statute, or any penalty, forfeiture, or punishment incurred because of the violation, before its repeal;

(4) any proceeding, reorganization, or dissolution commenced under the statute before its repeal, and the proceeding, reorganization, or dissolution may be completed in accordance with the statute as if it had not been repealed.

(b) If a penalty or punishment imposed for violation of a statute repealed by this Act is reduced by this Act, the penalty or punishment if not already imposed shall be imposed in accordance with this Act.

## § 17.04 Severability

If any provision of this Act or its application to any person or circumstance is held invalid by a court of competent jurisdiction, the invalidity does not affect other provisions or applications of the Act that can be given effect without the invalid provision or application, and to this end the provisions of the Act are severable.

## § 17.05 Repeal

The following laws and parts of laws are repealed: [to be inserted].

## § 17.06 Effective Date

This Act takes effect _____ .

# APPENDIX I

# SECURITIES ACT OF 1933 (EXCERPTS)

## Definitions

**Section 2.** When used in this title, unless the context requires—

(1) The term ''security'' means any note, stock, treasury stock, bond, debenture, evidence of indebtedness, certificate of interest or participation in any profit-sharing agreement, collateral-trust certificate, preorganization certificate or subscription, transferable share, investment contract, voting-trust certificate, certificate of deposit for a security, fractional undivided interest in oil, gas, or other mineral rights, any put, call, straddle, option, or privilege on any security, certificate of deposit, or group or index of securities (including any interest therein or based on the value thereof), or any put, call, straddle, option, or privilege entered into on a national securities exchange relating to foreign currency, or, in general, any interest or participation in, temporary or interim certificate for, receipt for, guarantee of, or warrant or right to subscribe to or purchase, any of the foregoing.

## Exempted Securities

**Section 3.** (a) Except as hereinafter expressly provided the provisions of this title shall not apply to any of the following classes of securities:

\* \* \* \*

(2) Any security issued or guaranteed by the United States or any territory thereof, or by the District of Columbia, or by any State of the United States, or by any political subdivision of a State or Territory, or by any public instrumentality of one or more States or Territories, or by any person controlled or supervised by and acting as an instrumentality of the Government of the United States pursuant to authority granted by the Congress of the United States; or any certificate of deposit for any of the foregoing; or any security issued or guaranteed by any bank; or any security issued by or representing an interest in or a direct obligation of a Federal Reserve Bank. \* \* \*

(3) Any note, draft, bill of exchange, or banker's acceptance which arises out of a current transaction or the proceeds of which have been or are to be used for current transactions, and which has a maturity at the time of issuance of not exceeding nine months, exclusive of days of grace, or any renewal thereof the maturity of which is likewise limited;

(4) Any security issued by a person organized and operated exclusively for religious, educational, benevolent, fraternal, charitable, or reformatory purposes and not for pecuniary profit, and no part of the net earnings of which inures to the benefit of any person, private stockholder, or individual;

\* \* \* \*

(11) Any security which is a part of an issue offered and sold only to persons resident within a single State or Territory, where the issuer of such security is a person resident and doing business within, or, if a corporation, incorporated by and doing business within, such State or Territory.

(b) The Commission may from time to time by its rules and regulations and subject to such terms and conditions as may be described therein, add any class of securities to the securities exempted as provided in this section, if it finds that the enforcement of this title with respect to such securities is not necessary in the public interest and for the protection of investors by reason of the small amount involved or the limited character of the public offering; but no issue of securities shall be exempted under this subsection where the aggregate amount at which such issue is offered to the public exceeds $5,000,000.

## Exempted Transactions

**Section 4.** The provisions of section 5 shall not apply to—

(1) transactions by any person other than an issuer, underwriter, or dealer.

(2) transactions by an issuer not involving any public offering.

(3) transactions by a dealer (including an underwriter no longer acting as an underwriter in respect of the security involved in such transactions), except—

(A)  transactions taking place prior to the expiration of forty days after the first date upon which the security was bona fide offered to the public by the issuer or by or through an underwriter.

(B) transactions in a security as to which a registration statement has been filed taking place prior to the expiration of forty days after the effective date of such registration statement or prior to the expiration of forty days after the first date upon which the security was bona fide offered to the public by the issuer or by or through an underwriter after such effective date, whichever is later (excluding in the computation of such forty days any time during which a stop order issued under section 8 is in effect as to the security), or such shorter period as the Commission may specify by rules and regulations or order, and

(C) transactions as to the securities constituting the whole or a part of an unsold allotment to or subscription by such dealer as a participant in the distribution of such securities by the issuer or by or through an underwriter.

With respect to transactions referred to in clause (B), if securities of the issuer have not previously been sold pursuant to an earlier effective registration statement the applicable period, instead of forty days, shall be ninety days, or such shorter period as the Commission may specify by rules and regulations or order.

(4) brokers' transactions, executed upon customers' orders on any exchange or in the over-the-counter market but not the solicitation of such orders.

    \*   \*   \*   \*

(6) transactions involving offers or sales by an issuer solely to one or more accredited investors, if the aggregate offering price of an issue of securities offered in reliance on this paragraph does not exceed the amount allowed under Section 3(b) of this title, if there is no advertising or public solicitation in connection with the transaction by the issuer or anyone acting on the issuer's behalf, and if the issuer files such notice with the Commission as the Commission shall prescribe.

## Prohibitions Relating to Interstate Commerce and the Mails

**Section 5.** (a) Unless a registration statement is in effect as to a security, it shall be unlawful for any person, directly or indirectly—

(1) to make use of any means or instruments of transportation or communication in interstate commerce or of the mails to sell such security through the use or medium of any prospectus or otherwise; or

(2) to carry or cause to be carried through the mails or in interstate commerce, by any means or instruments of transportation, any such security for the purpose of sale or for delivery after sale.

(b) It shall be unlawful for any person, directly or indirectly—

(1) to make use of any means or instruments of transportation or communication in interstate commerce or of the mails to carry or transmit any prospectus relating to any security with respect to which a registration statement has been filed under this title, unless such prospectus meets the requirements of section 10, or

(2) to carry or to cause to be carried through the mails or in interstate commerce any such security for the purpose of sale or for delivery after sale, unless accompanied or preceded by a prospectus that meets the requirements of subsection (a) of section 10.

(c) It shall be unlawful for any person, directly, or indirectly, to make use of any means or instruments of transportation or communication in interstate commerce or of the mails to offer to sell or offer to buy through the use or medium of any prospectus or otherwise any security, unless a registration statement has been filed as to such security, or while the registration statement is the subject of a refusal order or stop order or (prior to the effective date of the registration statement) any public proceeding of examination under section 8.

# APPENDIX J

# SECURITIES EXCHANGE ACT OF 1934 (EXCERPTS)

## Definitions and Application of Title

**Section 3.** (a) When used in this title, unless the context otherwise requires—

    \*   \*   \*   \*

(4) The term "broker" means any person engaged in the business of effecting transactions in securities for the account of others, but does not include a bank.

(5) The term "dealer" means any person engaged in the business of buying and selling securities for his own account, through a broker or otherwise, but does not include a bank, or any person insofar as he buys or sells securities for his own account, either individually or in some fiduciary capacity, but not as part of a regular business.

    \*   \*   \*   \*

(7) The term "director" means any director of a corporation or any person performing similar functions with respect to any organization, whether incorporated or unincorporated.

(8) The term "issuer" means any person who issues or proposes to issue any security; except that with respect to certificates of deposit for securities, voting-trust certificates, or collateral-trust certificates, or with respect to certificates of interest or shares in an unincorporated investment trust not having a board of directors or the fixed, restricted management, or unit type, the term "issuer" means the person or persons performing the acts and assuming the duties of depositor or manager pursuant to the provisions of the trust or other agreement or instrument under which such securities are issued; and except that with respect to equipment-trust certificates or like securities, the term "issuer" means the person by whom the equipment or property is, or is to be, used.

(9) The term "person" means a natural person, company, government, or political subdivision, agency, or instrumentality of a government.

## Regulation of the Use of Manipulative and Deceptive Devices

**Section 10.** It shall be unlawful for any person, directly or indirectly, by the use of any means or instrumentality of interstate commerce or of the mails, or of any facility of any national securities exchange—

(a) To effect a short sale, or to use or employ any stop-loss order in connection with the purchase or sale, of any security registered on a national securities exchange, in contravention of such rules and regulations as the Commission may prescribe as necessary or appropriate in the public interest or for the protection of investors.

(b) To use or employ, in connection with the purchase or sale of any security registered on a national securities exchange or any security not so registered, any manipulative or deceptive device or contrivance in contravention of such rules and regulations as the Commission may prescribe as necessary or appropriate in the public interest or for the protection of investors.

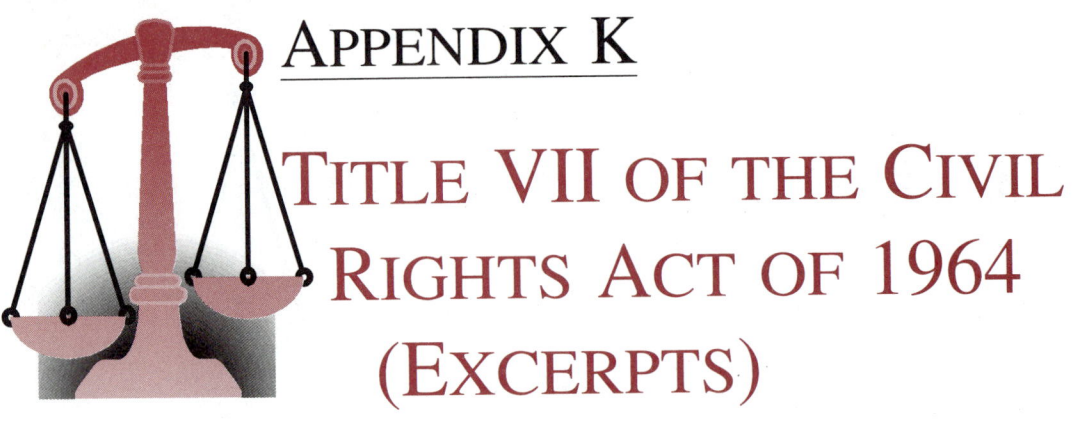

# APPENDIX K

# TITLE VII OF THE CIVIL RIGHTS ACT OF 1964 (EXCERPTS)

**Section 703. Unlawful Employment Practices.** (a) It shall be an unlawful employment practice for an employer—

(1) to fail or refuse to hire or to discharge any individual, or otherwise to discriminate against any individual with respect to his compensation, terms, conditions, or privileges of employment, because of such individual's race, color, religion, sex, or national origin; or

(2) to limit, segregate, or classify his employees or applicants for employment in any way which would deprive or tend to deprive any individual of employment opportunities or otherwise adversely affect his status as an employee, because of such individual's race, color, religion, sex, or national origin.

(b) It shall be an unlawful employment practice for an employment agency to fail or refuse to refer for employment, or otherwise to discriminate against, any individual because of his race, color, religion, sex, or national origin, or to classify or refer for employment any individual on the basis or his race, color, religion, sex, or national origin.

(c) It shall be an unlawful employment practice for a labor organization—

(1) to exclude or to expel from its membership, or otherwise to discriminate against, any individual because of his race, color, religion, sex, or national origin;

(2) to limit, segregate, or classify its membership or applicants for membership, or to classify or fail or refuse to refer for employment any individual, in any way which would deprive or tend to deprive any individual of employment opportunities, or would limit such employment opportunities or otherwise adversely affect his status as an employee or as an applicant for employment, because of such individual's race, color, religion, sex, or national origin; or

(3) to cause or attempt to cause an employer to discriminate against an individual in violation of this section.

(d) It shall be an unlawful employment practice for any employer, labor organization, or joint labor-management committee controlling apprenticeship or other training or retraining, including on-the-job training programs to discriminate against any individual because of his race, color, religion, sex, or national origin in admission to, or employment in, any program established to provide apprenticeship or other training.

(e) Notwithstanding any other provision of this subchapter—

(1) it shall not be an unlawful employment practice for an employer to hire and employ employees, for an employment agency to classify, or refer for employment any individual, for a labor organization to classify its membership or to classify or refer for employment any individual, or for an employer, labor organization, or joint labor-management committee controlling apprenticeship or other training or retraining programs to admit or employ any individual in any such program, on the basis of his religion, sex, or national origin in those certain instances where religion, sex, or national origin is a bona fide occupational qualification reasonably necessary to the normal operation of that particular business or enterprise, and

(2) it shall not be an unlawful employment practice for a school, college, university, or other educational institution or institution of learning to hire and employ employees of a particular religion if such school, college, university, or other educational institution or institution of learning is, in whole or in substantial part, owned, supported, controlled, or managed by a particular religion or by a particular religious corporation, association, or society, or if the curriculum of such school, college, university, or other educational institution or institution of learning is directed toward the propagation of a particular religion.

(f) As used in this subchapter, the phrase "unlawful employment practice" shall not be deemed to include any action or measure taken by an employer, labor organization, joint labor-management committee, or employment agency with respect to an individual who is a member of the Communist Party of the United States or of any other organization required to register as a Communist-action or Communist-front organization. * * *

(g) Notwithstanding any other provision of this subchapter, it shall not be an unlawful employment practice for an employer to fail or refuse to hire and employ any individual for any position, for an employer to discharge any individual from any position, or for an employment agency to fail or refuse to refer any individual for employment in any position, or for a labor organization to fail or refuse to refer any individual for employment in any position, if—

(1) the occupancy of such position, or access to the premises in or upon which any part of the duties of such position is performed or is to be performed, is subject to any requirement imposed in the interest of the national security of the United States *   *   * and

(2) such individual has not fulfilled or has ceased to fulfill that requirement.

(h) Notwithstanding any other provision of this subchapter, it shall not be an unlawful employment practice for an employer to apply different standards of compensation, or different terms, conditions, or privileges of employment pursuant to a bona fide seniority or merit system, or a system which measures earnings by quantity or quality of production or to employees who work in different locations, provided that such differences are not the result of an intention to discriminate because of race, color, religion, sex, or national origin, nor shall it be an unlawful employment practice for an employer to give and act upon the results of any professionally developed ability test provided that such test, its administration or action upon the results is not designed, intended or used to discriminate because of race, color, religion, sex, or national origin. *   *   *

(j) Nothing contained in this subchapter shall be interpreted to require any employer, employment agency, labor organization, or joint labor-management committee subject to this subchapter to grant preferential treatment to any individual or to any group because of the race, color, religion, sex, or national origin of such individual or group on account of an imbalance which may exist with respect to the total number or percentage of persons of any race, color, religion, sex, or national origin employed by any employer, referred or classified for employment by any employment agency or labor organization, or admitted to, or employed in, any appren-

ticeship or other training program, in comparison with the total number or percentage of persons of such race, color, religion, sex, or national origin in any community, State, section, or other area, or in the available work force in any community, State, section, or other area.

*   *   *   *

**Section 704. Other Unlawful Employment Practices.** (a) It shall be an unlawful employment practice for an employer to discriminate against any of his employees or applicants for employment, for an employment agency, or joint labor-management committee controlling apprenticeship or other training or retraining, including on-the-job training programs, to discriminate against any individual, or for a labor organization to discriminate against any member thereof or applicant for membership, because he has opposed any practice made an unlawful employment practice by this subchapter, or because he has made a charge, testified, assisted, or participated in any manner in an investigation, proceeding, or hearing under this subchapter.

(b) It shall be an unlawful employment practice for an employer, labor organization, employment agency, or joint labor-management committee controlling apprenticeship or other training or retraining, including on-the-job training programs, to print or publish or cause to be printed or published any notice or advertisement relating to employment by such an employer or membership or any classification or referral for employment by such a labor organization, or relating to any classification or referral for employment by such an employment agency, or relating to admission to, or employment in, any program established to provide apprenticeship or other training by such a joint-labor-management committee, indicating any preference, limitation, specification, or discrimination, based on race, color, religion, sex, or national origin, except that such a notice or advertisement may indicate a preference, limitation, specification, or discrimination based on religion, sex or national origin when religion, sex, or national origin is a bona fide occupational qualification for employment.

# APPENDIX L

# AMERICANS WITH DISABILITIES ACT OF 1990 (EXCERPTS)

## Title I—EMPLOYMENT

### Sec. 101. Definitions.

As used in this title: * * *

(8) **Qualified individual with a disability.**—The term ''qualified individual with a disability'' means an individual with a disability who, with or without reasonable accommodation, can perform the essential functions of the employment position that such individual holds or desires. For the purposes of this title, consideration shall be given to the employer's judgment as to what functions of a job are essential, and if an employer has prepared a written description before advertising or interviewing applicants for the job, this description shall be considered evidence of the essential functions of the job.

(9) **Reasonable accommodation.**—The term ''reasonable accommodation'' may include—

(A) making existing facilities used by employees readily accessible to and usable by individuals with disabilities; and

(B) job restructuring, part-time or modified work schedules, reassignment to a vacant position, acquisition or modification of equipment or devices, appropriate adjustment or modifications of examinations, training materials or policies, the provision of qualified readers or interpreters, and other similar accommodations for individuals with disabilities.

(10) **Undue Hardship.**—

(A) **In general.**—The term ''undue hardship'' means an action requiring significant difficulty or expense, when considered in light of the factors set forth in subparagraph (B).

(B) **Factors to be considered.**—In determining whether an accommodation would impose an undue hardship on a covered entity, factors to be considered include—

(i) the nature and cost of accommodation needed under this Act;

(ii) the overall financial resources of the facility or facilities involved in the provision of the reasonable accommodation; the number of persons employed at such facility; the effect on expenses and resources, or the impact otherwise of such accommodation upon the operation of the facility;

(iii) the overall financial resources of the covered entity; the overall size of the business of a covered entity with respect to the number of its employees; the number, type, and location of its facilities; and

(iv) the type of operation or operations of the covered entity, including the composition, structure, and functions of the workforce of such entity; the geographic separateness, administrative, or fiscal relationship of the facility or facilities in question to the covered entity.

### Sec. 102. Discrimination.

(a) **General Rule.**—No covered entity shall discriminate against a qualified individual with a disability because of the disability of such individual in regard to job application procedures, the hiring, advancement, or discharge of employees, employee compensation, job training, and other terms, conditions, and privileges of employment.

(b) **Construction.**—As used in subsection (a), the term ''discriminate'' includes—

(1) limiting, segregating, or classifying a job applicant or employee in a way that adversely affects the opportunities or status of such applicant or employee because of the disability of such applicant or employee;

(2) participating in a contractual or other arrangement or relationship that has the effect of subjecting a covered entity's qualified applicant or employee with a disability to the discrimination prohibited by this title (such relationship includes a relationship with an employment or referral agency, labor union, an organization providing fringe benefits to an employee of the covered entity, or an organization providing training and apprenticeship programs);

(3) utilizing standards, criteria, or methods of administration—

(A) that have the effect of discrimination on the basis of disability; or

(B) that perpetuate the discrimination of others who are subject to common administrative control;

(4) excluding or otherwise denying equal jobs or benefits to a qualified individual because of the known disability of an individual with whom the qualified individual is known to have a relationship or association;

(5)

(A) not making reasonable accommodations to the known physical or mental limitations of an otherwise qualified individual with a disability who is an applicant or employee, unless such covered entity can demonstrate that the accommodation would impose an undue hardship on the operation of the business of such covered entity; or

(B) denying employment opportunities to a job applicant or employee who is an otherwise qualified individual with a disability, if such denial is based on the need of such covered entity to make reasonable accommodation to the physical or mental impairments of the employee or applicant;

(6) using qualification standards, employment tests or other selection criteria that screen out or tend to screen out an individual with a disability or a class of individuals with disabilities unless the standard, test or other selection criteria, as used by the covered entity, is shown to be job-related for the position in question and is consistent with business necessity; and

(7) failing to select and administer tests concerning employment in the most effective manner to ensure that, when such test is administered to a job applicant or employee who has a disability that impairs sensory, manual, or speaking skills, such test results accurately reflect the skills, aptitude, or whatever other factor of such applicant or employee that such test purports to measure, rather than reflecting the impaired sensory, manual, or speaking skills of such employee or applicant (except where such skills are the factors that the test purports to measure). *   *   *

### Sec. 104. Illegal Use of Drugs and Alcohol. *   *   *

(b) **Rules of Construction.**—Nothing in subsection (a) shall be construed to exclude as a qualified individual with a disability an individual who—

(1) has successfully completed a supervised drug rehabilitation program and is no longer engaging in the illegal use of drugs, or has otherwise been rehabilitated successfully and is no longer engaging in such use;

(2) is participating in a supervised rehabilitation program and is no longer engaging in such use; or

(3) is erroneously regarded as engaging in such use, but is not engaging in such use; except that it shall not be a violation of this Act for a covered entity to adopt or administer reasonable policies or procedures, including but not limited to drug testing, designed to ensure that an individual described in paragraph (1) or (2) is no longer engaging in the illegal use of drugs. *   *   *

### Sec. 107. Enforcement.

(a) **Powers, Remedies, and Procedures.**—The powers, remedies, and procedures set forth in sections 705, 706, 707, 709, and 710 of the Civil Rights Act of 1964 (42 U.S.C. 2000e-4, 2000e-5, 2000e-6, 2000e-8, and 2000e-9) shall be the powers, remedies, and procedures this title provides to the Commission, to the Attorney General, or to any person alleging discrimination on the basis of disability in violation of any provision of this Act, or regulations promulgated under section 106, concerning employment.

(b) **Coordination.**—The agencies with enforcement authority for actions which allege employment discrimination under this title and under the Rehabilitation Act of 1973 shall develop procedures to ensure that administrative complaints filed under this title and under the Rehabilitation Act of 1973 are dealt with in a manner that avoids duplication of effort and prevents imposition of inconsistent or conflicting standards for the same requirements under this title and the Rehabilitation Act of 1973. The Commission, the Attorney General, and the Office of Federal Contract Compliance Programs shall establish such coordinating mechanisms (similar to provisions contained in the joint regulations promulgated by the Commission and the Attorney General at part 42 of title 28 and part 1691 of title 29, Code of Federal Regulations, and the Memorandum of Understanding between the Commission and the Office of Federal Contract Compliance Programs dated January 16, 1981 (46 Fed. Reg. 7435, January 23, 1981)) in regulations implementing this title and Rehabilitation Act of 1973 not later than 18 months after the date of enactment of this Act.

### Sec. 108. Effective Date.

This title shall become effective 24 months after the date of enactment.

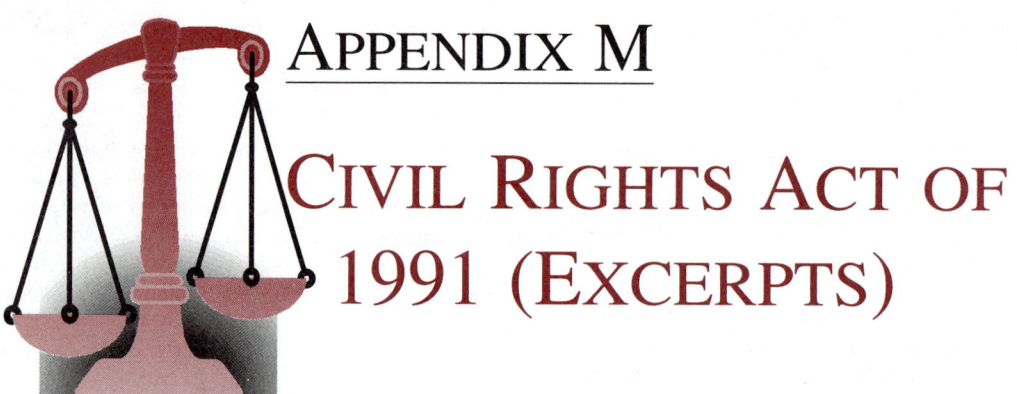

# APPENDIX M

# CIVIL RIGHTS ACT OF 1991 (EXCERPTS)

## Section 3. Purposes.

The purposes of this Act are—

(1) to provide appropriate remedies for intentional discrimination and unlawful harassment in the workplace;

(2) to codify the concepts of "business necessity" and "job related" enunciated by the Supreme Court in *Griggs v. Duke Power Co.*, 401 U.S. 424 (1971), and in the other Supreme Court decisions prior to *Wards Cove Packing Co. v. Atonio*, 490 U.S. 642 (1989);

(3) to confirm statutory authority and provide statutory guidelines for the adjudication of disparate impact suits under title VII of the Civil Rights Act of 1964 (42 U.S.C. 2000e *et seq.*); and

(4) to respond to recent decisions of the Supreme Court by expanding the scope of relevant civil rights statutes in order to provide adequate protection to victims of discrimination.

## Section 101. Prohibition against All Racial Discrimination in the Making and Enforcement of Contracts.

Section 1977 of the Revised Statutes (42 U.S.C. 1981) is amended * * * by adding at the end the following new subsections:

(b) For purposes of this section, the term "make and enforce contracts" includes the making, performance, modification, and termination of contracts, and the enjoyment of all benefits, privileges, terms, and conditions of the contractual relationship.

(c) The rights protected by this section are protected against impairment by nongovernmental discrimination and impairment under color of State law.

## Section 102. Damages in Cases of Intentional Discrimination.

The Revised Statutes are amended by inserting after section 1977 (42 U.S.C.1981) the following new section:

## Section 1977A. Damages in Cases of Intentional Discrimination in Employment.

(a) Right of Recovery.—

(1) Civil Rights.—In an action brought by a complaining party under section 706 or 717 of the Civil Rights Act of 1964 (42 U.S.C. 2000e-5) against a respondent who engaged in unlawful intentional discrimination (not an employment practice that is unlawful because of its disparate impact) prohibited under section 703, 704, or 717 of the Act (42 U.S.C. 2000e-2 or 2000e-3), and provided that the complaining party cannot recover under section 1977 of the Revised Statutes (42 U.S.C.1981), the complaining party may recover compensatory and punitive damages as allowed in subsection (b), in addition to any relief authorized by section 706(g) of the Civil Rights Act of 1964, from the respondent.

* * * *

(b) Compensatory and Punitive Damages.—

(1) Determination of Punitive Damages.—A complaining party may recover punitive damages under this section against a respondent (other than a government, government agency or political subdivision) if the complaining party demonstrates that the respondent engaged in a discriminatory practice or discriminatory practices with malice or with reckless indifference to the federally protected rights of an aggrieved individual.

(2) Exclusions from Compensatory Damages.—Compensatory damages awarded under this section shall not include backpay, interest on backpay, or any other type of relief authorized under section 706(g) of the Civil Rights Act of 1964.

(3) Limitations.—The sum of the amount of compensatory damages awarded under this section for future pecuniary losses, emotional pain, suffering, inconvenience, mental anguish, loss of enjoyment of life, and other nonpecuniary losses, and the amount of punitive damages awarded under this section, shall not exceed, for each complaining party—

(A) in the case of a respondent who has more than 14 and fewer than 101 employees in each of 20 or more calendar weeks in the current or preceding calendar year, $50,000;

(B) in the case of a respondent who has more than 100 and fewer than 201 employees in each of 20 or more calendar weeks in the current or preceding calendar year, $100,000; and

(C) in the case of a respondent who has more than 200 and fewer than 501 employees in each of 20 or more calendar weeks in the current or preceding calendar year, $200,000; and

(D) in the case of a respondent who has more than 500 employees in each of 20 or more calendar weeks in the current or preceding calendar year, $300,000.

\* \* \* \*

## Section 105. Burden of Proof in Disparate Impact Cases.

(a) Section 703 of the Civil Rights Act of 1964 (42 U.S.C. 2000e-2) is amended by adding at the end the following new [subsections to 703(k)(1)]—

(A) An unlawful employment practice based on disparate impact is established under this title only if—

(i) a complaining party demonstrates that a respondent uses a particular employment practice that causes a disparate impact on the basis of race, color, religion, sex, or national origin and the respondent fails to demonstrate that the challenged practice is job related for the position in question and consistent with business necessity; or

(ii) the complaining party makes the demonstration described in subparagraph (C) with respect to an alternative employment practice and the respondent refuses to adopt such alternative employment practice.

\* \* \* \*

(C) The demonstration referred to by subparagraph (A)(ii) shall be in accordance with the law as it existed on June 4, 1989, with respect to the concept of "alternative employment practice."

\* \* \* \*

## Section 107. Clarifying Prohibition against Impermissible Consideration of Race, Color, Religion, Sex, or National Origin in Employment Practices.

(a) In General.—Section 703 of the Civil Rights Act of 1964 (42 U.S.C. 2000e-2) (as amended by sections 105 and 106) is further amended by adding at the end the following new subsection:

(m) Except as otherwise provided in this title, an unlawful employment practice is established when the complaining party demonstrates that race, color, religion, sex, or national origin was a motivating factor for any employment practice, even though other factors also motivated the practice.

\* \* \* \*

## Section 109. Protection of Extraterritorial Employment.

(a) Definition of Employee.—Section 701(f) of the Civil Rights Act of 1964 (42 U.S.C. 2000e(f)) and section 101(4) of the Americans with Disabilities Act of 1990 (42 U.S.C. 12111(4)) are each amended by adding at the end the following: "With respect to employment in a foreign country, such term includes an individual who is a citizen of the United States."

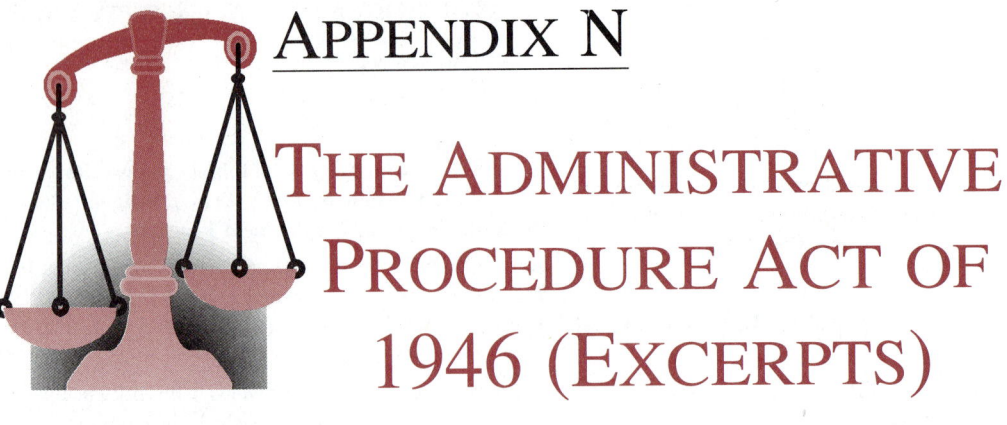

# APPENDIX N

# THE ADMINISTRATIVE PROCEDURE ACT OF 1946 (EXCERPTS)

## Section 551. Definitions

For the purpose of this subchapter—

\* \* \* \*

(4) ''rule'' means the whole or a part of an agency statement of general or particular applicability and future effect designed to implement, interpret, or prescribe law or policy or describing the organization, procedure, or practice requirements of an agency and includes the approval or prescription for the future of rates, wages, corporate or financial structures or reorganizations thereof, prices, facilities, appliances, services or allowances therefor or of valuations, costs, or accounting, or practices bearing on any of the foregoing[.]

\* \* \* \*

## Section 552. Public Information; Agency Rules, Opinions, Orders, Records, and Proceedings

(a) Each agency shall make available to the public information as follows:

(1) Each agency shall separately state and currently publish in the Federal Register for the guidance of the public—

(A) descriptions of its central and field organization and the established places at which, the employees \* \* \* from whom, and the methods whereby, the public may obtain information, make submittals or requests, or obtain decisions;

\* \* \* \*

(C) rules of procedure, descriptions of forms available or the places at which forms may be obtained, and instructions as to the scope and contents of all papers, reports, or examinations;

(D) substantive rules of general applicability adopted as authorized by law, and statements of general policy or interpretations of general applicability formulated and adopted by the agency[.] \* \* \*

\* \* \* \*

## Section 552b. Open Meetings

\* \* \* \*

(j) Each agency subject to the requirements of this section shall annually report to Congress regarding its compliance with such requirements, including a tabulation of the total number of agency meetings open to the public, the total number of meetings closed to the public, the reasons for closing such meetings, and a description of any litigation brought against the agency under this section, including any costs assessed against the agency in such litigation \* \* \*

\* \* \* \*

## Section 553. Rule Making

\* \* \* \*

(b) General notice of proposed rule making shall be published in the Federal Register, unless persons subject thereto are named and either personally served or otherwise have actual notice thereof in accordance with law. \* \* \*

(c) After notice required by this section, the agency shall give interested persons an opportunity to participate in the rule making through submission of written data, views, or arguments with or without opportunity for oral presentation. \* \* \*

\* \* \* \*

## Section 554. Adjudications

\* \* \* \*

(b) Persons entitled to notice of an agency hearing shall be timely informed of—

(1) the time, place, and nature of the hearing;

(2) the legal authority and jurisdiction under which the hearing is to be held; and

(3) the matters of fact and law asserted.

\* \* \* \*

(c) The agency shall give all interested parties opportunity for—

(1) the submission and consideration of facts, arguments, offers of settlement, or proposals of adjustment when

time, the nature of the proceeding, and the public interest permit; and

(2) to the extent that the parties are unable so to determine a controversy by consent, hearing and decision on notice * * *.

* * * *

## Section 555. Ancillary Matters

* * * *

(c) Process, requirement of a report, inspection, or other investigative act or demand may not be issued, made, or enforced except as authorized by law. A person compelled to submit data or evidence is entitled to retain or, on payment of lawfully prescribed costs, procure a copy or transcript thereof, except that in a nonpublic investigatory proceeding the witness may for good cause be limited to inspection of the official transcript of his testimony.

* * * *

(e) Prompt notice shall be given of the denial in whole or in part of a written application, petition, or other request of an interested person made in connection with any agency proceeding. * * *

## Section 556. Hearings; Presiding Employees; Powers and Duties; Burden of Proof; Evidence; Record as Basis of Decision

* * * *

(b) There shall preside at the taking of evidence—

(1) the agency;

(2) one or more members of the body which comprises the agency; or

(3) one or more administrative law judges * * *.

* * * *

(c) Subject to published rules of the agency and within its powers, employees presiding at hearings may—

(1) administer oaths and affirmations;

(2) issue subpoenas authorized by law;

(3) rule on offers of proof and receive relevant evidence;

(4) take depositions or have depositions taken when the ends of justice would be served;

(5) regulate the course of the hearing;

(6) hold conferences for the settlement or simplification of the issues by consent of the parties or by the use of alternative means of dispute resolution as provided in subchapter IV of this chapter;

(7) inform the parties as to the availability of one or more alternative means of dispute resolution, and encourage use of such methods;

* * * *

(9) dispose of procedural requests or similar matters;

(10) make or recommend decisions in accordance with * * * this title; and

(11) take other action authorized by agency rule consistent with this subchapter.

* * * *

## Section 702. Right of Review

A person suffering legal wrong because of agency action * * * is entitled to judicial review thereof. An action in a court of the United States seeking relief other than money damages and stating a claim that an agency or an officer or employee thereof acted or failed to act in an official capacity or under color of legal authority shall not be dismissed nor relief therein be denied on the ground that it is against the United States or that the United States is an indispensable party. The United States may be named as a defendant in any such action, and a judgment or decree may be entered against the United States: Provided, [t]hat any mandatory or injunctive decree shall specify the [f]ederal officer or officers (by name or by title), and their successors in office, personally responsible for compliance. * * *

* * * *

## Section 704. Actions Reviewable

Agency action made reviewable by statute and final agency action for which there is no other adequate remedy in a court are subject to judicial review. A preliminary, procedural, or intermediate agency action or ruling not directly reviewable is subject to review on the review of the final agency action.

# APPENDIX O

# THE GENERAL AGREEMENT ON TARIFFS AND TRADE OF 1994 (EXCERPTS)

## Part I

## FINAL ACT EMBODYING THE RESULTS OF THE URUGUAY ROUND OF MULTILATERAL TRADE NEGOTIATIONS

**1.** Having met in order to conclude the Uruguay Round of Multilateral Trade Negotiations, the representatives of the Governments and of the European Communities, members of the Trade Negotiations Committee * * *, *agree* that the Agreement Establishing the Multilateral Trade Organization and the Ministerial Decisions and Declarations * * * embody the results of their negotiations and form an integral part of this Final Act.

*   *   *   *

## Part II

## AGREEMENT ESTABLISHING THE MULTILATERAL TRADE ORGANIZATION

The *Parties* to this Agreement,

*Recognizing* that their relations in the field of trade and economic endeavour should be conducted with a view to raising standards of living, ensuring full employment and a large and steadily growing volume of real income and effective demand, and expanding the production and trade in good and services, while allowing for the optimal use of the world's resources in accordance with the objective of sustainable development, seeking both to protect and preserve the environment and enhance the means for doing so in a manner consistent with their respective needs and concerns at different levels of economic development,

*Recognizing* further that there is need for positive efforts designed to ensure that developing countries * * * secure a share in the growth in international trade commensurate with the needs of their economic development,

*Being desirous* of contributing to these objectives by entering into reciprocal and mutually advantageous arrangements directed to the substantial reduction of tariffs and other barriers to trade and to the elimination of discriminatory treatment in international trade relations,

*Resolved*, therefore, to develop an integrated, more viable and durable multilateral trading system encompassing the General Agreement on Tariffs and Trade, the results of the past trade liberalization efforts, and all of the results of the Uruguay Round of multilateral trade negotiations,

*Determined* to preserve the basic principles and to further the objectives underlying this multilateral trading system,

*Agree* as follows:
*   *   *   *

The Multilateral Trade Organization [MTO] * * * is hereby established.

*   *   *   *

[The] MTO shall facilitate the implementation, administration, operation, and further the objectives, of this Agreement and of the Multilateral Trade Agreements, and shall also provide the framework for the implementation, administration and operation of the Plurilateral Trade Agreements.

*   *   *   *

[Except] as otherwise provided for under this Agreement or the Multilateral Trade Agreements, the MTO shall be guided by the decisions, procedures and customary practices followed by the contracting parties of the GATT 1947 and the bodies established in the framework of the GATT 1947.

*   *   *   *

# AGREEMENT ON AGRICULTURE

\* \* \* \*

**2.** In accordance with the Mid-Term Review Agreement that government measures of assistance, whether direct or indirect, to encourage agricultural and rural development are an integral part of the development programmes of developing countries, investment subsidies which are generally available to agriculture in developing country Members and agricultural input subsidies generally available to low-income or resource poor producers in developing country Members shall be exempt from domestic support reduction commitments that would otherwise be applicable to such measures, as shall domestic support to producers in developing country Members to encourage diversification from growing illicit narcotic crops. \* \* \*

\* \* \* \*

# AGREEMENT ON TEXTILES AND CLOTHING

\* \* \* \*

**1.** Members agree that circumvention by transshipment, rerouting, false declaration concerning country or place of origin, and falsification of official documents, frustrates the implementation of this Agreement to integrate the textiles and clothing sector into the GATT 1994. Accordingly, Members should establish the necessary legal provisions and/or administrative procedures to address and take action against such circumvention. Members further agree that, consistent with their domestic laws and procedures, they will cooperate fully to address problems arising from circumvention.

\* \* \* \*

**2.** Safeguard action may be taken \* \* \* when, on the basis of a determination by a Member, it is demonstrated that a particular product is being imported into its territory in such increased quantities as to cause serious damage, or actual threat thereof, to the domestic industry producing like and/ or directly competitive products. Serious damage or actual threat thereof must demonstrably be caused by such increased quantities in total imports of that product and not by such other factors as technological changes or changes in consumer preference.

\* \* \* \*

# AGREEMENT ON TECHNICAL BARRIERS TO TRADE

\* \* \* \*

**2.2** Members shall ensure that technical regulations are not prepared, adopted or applied with a view to or with the effect of creating unnecessary obstacles to international trade. For this purpose, technical regulations shall not be more trade-restrictive than necessary to fulfil a legitimate objective, taking account of the risks non-fulfilment would create. Such legitimate objectives [include] national security requirements; the prevention of deceptive practices; protection of human health or safety, animal or plant life or health, or the environment. In assessing such risks, relevant elements of consideration [include] \* \* \* available scientific and technical information, related processing technology or intended end uses of products.

\* \* \* \*

# AGREEMENT ON IMPLEMENTATION OF ARTICLE VI OF GATT 1994

\* \* \* \*

**2.1** For the purpose of this Agreement a product is to be considered as being dumped, i.e., introduced into the commerce of another country at less than its normal value, if the export price of the product exported from one country to another is less than the comparable price, in the ordinary course of trade, for the like product when destined for consumption in the exporting country.

\* \* \* \*

**3.5** It must be demonstrated that the dumped imports are \* \* \* causing injury within the meaning of this Agreement. The demonstration of a causal relationship between the dumped imports and the injury to the domestic industry shall be based on an examination of all relevant evidence before the authorities. The authorities shall also examine any known factors other than the dumped imports which at the same time are injuring the domestic industry, and the injuries caused by these other factors must not be attributed to the dumped imports. Factors which may be relevant in this respect include \* \* \* the volume and prices of imports not sold at dumping prices, contraction in demand or changes in the patterns of consumption, trade restrictive practices of and competition between the foreign and domestic producers, developments in technology and the export performance and productivity of the domestic industry.

\* \* \* \*

**9.2** When an anti-dumping duty is imposed in respect of any product, such anti-dumping duty shall be collected in the appropriate amounts in each case, on a non-discriminatory basis on imports of such product from all sources found to be dumped and causing injury, except as to imports from those sources from which price undertakings under the terms of this Agreement have been accepted. The authorities shall name the supplier or suppliers of the product concerned. If, however, several suppliers from the same country are involved, and it is impracticable to name all of these suppliers, the authorities may name the supplying country concerned. If several suppliers from more than one country are involved, the authorities may name either all the suppliers involved, or, if this is impracticable, all the supplying countries involved.

\* \* \* \*

# AGREEMENT ON PRESHIPMENT INSPECTION

\* \* \* \*

**12.** User Members shall ensure that preshipment inspection entities do not request exporters to provide information regarding:

(a) manufacturing data related to patented, licensed or undisclosed processes, or to processes for which a patent is pending;

(b) unpublished technical data other than necessary to demonstrate compliance with technical regulations or standards;

(c) internal pricing, including manufacturing costs;

(d) profit levels;

(e) the terms of contracts between exporters and their suppliers unless it is not otherwise possible for the entity to conduct the inspection in question. In such cases, the entity shall only request the information necessary for this purpose.

\* \* \* \*

# AGREEMENT ON SUBSIDIES AND COUNTERVAILING MEASURES

\* \* \* \*

**3.1** Except as provided in the Agreement on Agriculture, the following subsidies \* \* \* shall be prohibited:

(a) subsidies contingent, in law or in fact, whether solely or as one of several other conditions, upon export performance \* \* \*;

(b) subsidies contingent, whether solely or as one of several other conditions, upon the use of domestic over imported goods.

\* \* \* \*

# AGREEMENT ON SAFEGUARDS

\* \* \* \*

**2.** A Member may apply a safeguard measure to a product only if that Member has determined \* \* \* that such product is being imported into its territory in such increased quantities, absolute or relative to domestic production, and under such conditions as to cause or threaten to cause serious injury to the domestic industry that produces like or directly competitive products.

\* \* \* \*

**8.** Safeguard measures shall be applied only to the extent as may be necessary to prevent or remedy serious injury and to facilitate adjustment. \* \* \*

\* \* \* \*

**12.** The total period of application of a safeguard measure including the period of application of any provisional measure, the period of initial application and any extension thereof, shall not exceed eight years.

\* \* \* \*

**19.** Safeguard measures shall not be applied against a product originating in a developing country Member as long as its share of imports of the product concerned in the importing Member does not exceed 3 [percent], provided that, developing country Members with less than 3 [percent] import share collectively account for not more than 9 [percent] of total imports of the product concerned.

\* \* \* \*

# GENERAL AGREEMENT ON TRADE IN SERVICES

\* \* \* \*

**1.** With respect to any measure covered by this Agreement, each Member shall accord immediately and unconditionally to services and service suppliers of any other Member, treatment no less favourable than that it accords to like services and service suppliers of any other country.

\* \* \* \*

# AGREEMENT ON TRADE-RELATED ASPECTS OF INTELLECTUAL PROPERTY RIGHTS, INCLUDING TRADE IN COUNTERFEIT GOODS

\* \* \* \*

**1.** Members shall ensure that enforcement procedures \* \* \* are available under their national laws so as to permit effective action against any act of infringement of intellectual property rights covered by this Agreement, including expeditious remedies to prevent infringements and remedies which constitute a deterrent to further infringements. These procedures shall be applied in such a manner as to avoid the creation of barriers to legitimate trade and to provide for safeguards against their abuse.

**2.** Procedures concerning the enforcement of intellectual property rights shall be fair and equitable. They shall not be unnecessarily complicated or costly, or entail unreasonable time-limits or unwarranted delays.

\* \* \* \*

# UNDERSTANDING ON RULES AND PROCEDURES GOVERNING THE SETTLEMENT OF DISPUTES

\* \* \* \*

**2.1** The Dispute Settlement Body (DSB) \* \* \* shall administer these rules and procedures and \* \* \* the consultation and dispute settlement provisions of the covered agreements. \* \* \*

# APPENDIX P

# THE NORTH AMERICAN FREE TRADE AGREEMENT OF 1993 (EXCERPTS)

## Part One: GENERAL PART

### Chapter One: Objectives

#### Article 101: Establishment of the Free Trade Area

The Parties to this Agreement * * * hereby establish a free trade area.

#### Article 102: Objectives

**1.** The objectives of this Agreement * * * are to: (a) eliminate barriers to trade in, and facilitate the cross-border movement of, goods and services between the territories of the Parties; (b) promote conditions of fair competition in the free trade area; (c) increase substantially investment opportunities in the territories of the Parties; (d) provide adequate and effective protection and enforcement of intellectual property rights in each Party's territory; (e) create effective procedures for the implementation and application of this Agreement, for its joint administration and for the resolution of disputes; and (f) establish a framework for further trilateral, regional and multilateral cooperation to expand and enhance the benefits of this Agreement.

* * * *

## Part Two: TRADE IN GOODS

### Chapter Three: National Treatment and Market Access for Goods

* * * *

#### Article 301: National Treatment

**1.** Each Party shall accord national treatment to the goods of another Party in accordance with Article III of the General Agreement on Tariffs and Trade (GATT) * * * .

**2.** [N]ational treatment shall mean, with respect to a state or province, treatment no less favorable than the most favorable treatment accorded by such state or province to any like, directly competitive or substitutable goods, as the case may be, of the Party of which it forms a part.

* * * *

#### Article 302: Tariff Elimination

**1.** Except as otherwise provided in this Agreement, no Party may increase any existing customs duty, or adopt any customs duty, on an originating good.

**2.** [E]ach Party shall progressively eliminate its customs duties on originating goods in accordance with its Schedule * * * .

* * * *

#### Article 316: Consultations and Committee on Trade in Goods

**1.** The Parties hereby establish a Committee on Trade in Goods, comprising representatives of each Party.

* * * *

**3.** The Parties shall convene at least once each year a meeting of their officials responsible for customs, immigration, inspection of food and agricultural products, border inspection facilities, and regulation of transportation for the purpose of addressing issues related to movement of goods through the Parties' ports of entry.

* * * *

## Part Three: TECHNICAL BARRIERS TO TRADE

### Chapter Nine: Standards-Related Measures

* * * *

#### Article 904: Basic Rights and Obligations

Right to Take Standards-Related Measures

**1.** Each Party may * * * adopt, maintain or apply any standards-related measure, including any such measure relating to safety, the protection of human, animal or plant life or health, the environment or consumers, and any measure to ensure its enforcement or implementation. Such measures include those to prohibit the importation of a good of another Party or the provision of a service by a service provider of another Party that fails to comply with the applicable requirements of those measures or to complete the Party's approval procedures.

\* \* \* \*

Unnecessary Obstacles

**4.** No Party may prepare, adopt, maintain or apply any standards-related measure with a view to or with the effect of creating an unnecessary obstacle to trade between the Parties. An unnecessary obstacle to trade shall not be deemed to be created where: (a) the demonstrable purpose of the measure is to achieve a legitimate objective; and (b) the measure does not operate to exclude goods of another Party that meet that legitimate objective.

\* \* \* \*

### Article 913: Committee on Standards-Related Measures

**1.** The Parties hereby establish a Committee on Standards-Related Measures, comprising representatives of each Party.

**2.** The Committee's functions shall include: (a) monitoring the implementation and administration of this Chapter * * * ; (b) facilitating the process by which the Parties make compatible their standards-related measures; (c) providing a forum for the Parties to consult on issues relating to standards-related measures * * * ; (d) enhancing cooperation on the development, application and enforcement of standards-related measures; and (e) considering nongovernmental, regional and multilateral developments regarding standards-related measures, including under the GATT.

\* \* \* \*

## Part Five: INVESTMENT, SERVICES AND RELATED MATTERS

### Chapter Eleven: Investment

SECTION A—INVESTMENT

\* \* \* \*

### Article 1102: National Treatment

\* \* \* \*

**2.** Each Party shall accord to investments of investors of another Party treatment no less favorable than that it accords, in like circumstances, to investments of its own investors with respect to the establishment, acquisition, expansion, management, conduct, operation, and sale or other disposition of investments.

\* \* \* \*

**4.** For greater certainty, no Party may: (a) impose on an investor of another Party a requirement that a minimum level of equity in an enterprise in the territory of the Party be held by its nationals, other than nominal qualifying shares for directors or incorporators of corporations; or (b) require an investor of another Party, by reason of its nationality, to sell or otherwise dispose of an investment in the territory of the Party.

\* \* \* \*

## Part Six: INTELLECTUAL PROPERTY

### Chapter Seventeen: Intellectual Property

### Article 1701: Nature and Scope of Obligations

**1.** Each Party shall provide in its territory to the nationals of another Party adequate and effective protection and enforcement of intellectual property rights, while ensuring that measures to enforce intellectual property rights do not themselves become barriers to legitimate trade.

\* \* \* \*

### Article 1705: Copyright

\* \* \* \*

**2.** Each Party shall provide to authors and their successors in interest those rights enumerated in the Berne Convention in respect of works covered by paragraph 1, including the right to authorize or prohibit: (a) the importation into the Party's territory of copies of the work made without the right holder's authorization; (b) the first public distribution of the original and each copy of the work by sale, rental or otherwise; (c) the communication of a work to the public; and (d) the commercial rental of the original or a copy of a computer program. Subparagraph (d) shall not apply where the copy of the computer program is not itself an essential object of the rental. Each Party shall provide that putting the original or a copy of a computer program on the market with the right holder's consent shall not exhaust the rental right.

\* \* \* \*

**4.** Each Party shall provide that, where the term of protection of a work, other than a photographic work or a work of applied art, is to be calculated on a basis other than the life of a natural person, the term shall be not less than 50 years from the end of the calendar year of the first authorized publication of the work or, failing such authorized publication within 50 years from the making of the work, 50 years from the end of the calendar year of making.

**5.** Each Party shall confine limitations or exceptions to the rights provided for in this Article to certain special cases that do not conflict with a normal exploitation of the work and do not unreasonably prejudice the legitimate interests of the right holder.

\* \* \* \*

## Article 1706: Sound Recordings

**1.** Each Party shall provide to the producer of a sound recording the right to authorize or prohibit: (a) the direct or indirect reproduction of the sound recording; (b) the importation into the Party's territory of copies of the sound recording made without the producer's authorization; (c) the first public distribution of the original and each copy of the sound recording by sale, rental or otherwise; and (d) the commercial rental of the original or a copy of the sound recording, except where expressly otherwise provided in a contract between the producer of the sound recording and the authors of the works fixed therein. Each Party shall provide that putting the original or a copy of a sound recording on the market with the right holder's consent shall not exhaust the rental right.

\* \* \* \*

## Article 1708: Trademarks

\* \* \* \*

**4.** Each Party shall provide a system for the registration of trademarks, which shall include: (a) examination of applications; (b) notice to be given to an applicant of the reasons for the refusal to register a trademark; (c) a reasonable opportunity for the applicant to respond to the notice; (d) publication of each trademark either before or promptly after it is registered; and (e) a reasonable opportunity for interested persons to petition to cancel the registration of a trademark. A Party may provide for a reasonable opportunity for interested persons to oppose the registration of a trademark.

\* \* \* \*

**7.** Each Party shall provide that the initial registration of a trademark be for a term of at least 10 years and that the registration be indefinitely renewable for terms of not less than 10 years when conditions for renewal have been met.

\* \* \* \*

## Article 1709: Patents

**1.** Subject to paragraphs 2 and 3, each Party shall make patents available for any inventions, whether products or processes, in all fields of technology, provided that such inventions are new, result from an inventive step and are capable of industrial application. For purposes of this Article, a Party may deem the terms ''inventive step'' and ''capable of industrial application'' to be synonymous with the terms ''non-obvious'' and ''useful,'' respectively.

\* \* \* \*

## Article 1711: Trade Secrets

**1.** Each Party shall provide the legal means for any person to prevent trade secrets from being disclosed to, acquired by, or used by others without the consent of the person lawfully in control of the information in a manner contrary to honest commercial practices, in so far as: (a) the information is secret in the sense that it is not, as a body or in the precise configuration and assembly of its components, generally known among or readily accessible to persons that normally deal with the kind of information in question; (b) the information has actual or potential commercial value because it is secret; and (c) the person lawfully in control of the information has taken reasonable steps under the circumstances to keep it secret.

\* \* \* \*

## Article 1714: Enforcement of Intellectual Property Rights: General Provisions

\* \* \* \*

**3.** Each Party shall provide that decisions on the merits of a case in judicial and administrative enforcement proceedings shall: (a) preferably be in writing and preferably state the reasons on which the decisions are based; (b) be made available at least to the parties in a proceeding without undue delay; and (c) be based only on evidence in respect of which such parties were offered the opportunity to be heard.

**4.** Each Party shall ensure that parties in a proceeding have an opportunity to have final administrative decisions reviewed by a judicial authority of that Party and, subject to jurisdictional provisions in its domestic laws concerning the importance of a case, to have reviewed at least the legal aspects of initial judicial decisions on the merits of a case. Notwithstanding the above, no Party shall be required to provide for judicial review of acquittals in criminal cases.

\* \* \* \*

## Article 1717: Criminal Procedures and Penalties

**1.** Each Party shall provide criminal procedures and penalties to be applied at least in cases of willful trademark counterfeiting or copyright piracy on a commercial scale. Each Party shall provide that penalties available include imprisonment or monetary fines, or both, sufficient to provide a deterrent, consistent with the level of penalties applied for crimes of a corresponding gravity.

**2.** Each Party shall provide that, in appropriate cases, its judicial authorities may order the seizure, forfeiture and destruction of infringing goods and of any materials and implements the predominant use of which has been in the commission of the offense.

# APPENDIX Q

# A GUIDE TO RESEARCH IN BUSINESS LAW— INCLUDING USING THE INTERNET

A business student who wishes to do research on legal topics can consult many sources. Depending on the focus of the research, different types of sources should be consulted. For example, if the researcher only wants a general overview of the law, he or she could look at a secondary legal source— such as a legal encyclopedia, a *Restatement of the Law,* or a treatise. If the student wants to consult a primary source of law, such as an actual court case, then he or she might look at a judicial reporter. Other primary sources include constitutions, statutes, and regulations. If a researcher wants to look at commentaries on the status of the law today, there is a plethora of law reviews and topical legal journals that provide scholarly articles on current issues of legal interest.

Any person undertaking legal research will want to become familiar with the ''finding tools'' of legal research— computer data bases, law digests, looseleaf services, bar association publications, weekly bulletins, and so on—that are available today. These services and publications not only assist the researcher in locating legal documents but also keep the student abreast of recent legal developments.

The summary below explains how these and other legal research tools can be used to assist the business student in learning more about the topics discussed in this text.

## COMPUTERIZED RESEARCH ASSISTANCE

The days of the hunched-over law clerk searching through copious volumes of dusty tomes filled with ancient cases are not completely over, but, as could be expected, computers have streamlined legal research techniques. Today, there are a number of data bases—collections of information useful to anyone doing legal research—that can be accessed through several high-speed data-delivery systems. The two major legal research systems are LEXIS and WESTLAW.

LEXIS and WESTLAW allow for access to the full text of cases, statutes, and regulations—both state and federal— with a minimum of physical effort and time delay. Both

systems are kept extremely current, and often the latest cases can be retrieved through these systems before they are available in the printed reporters. The systems also include specialized libraries of materials on specific topics, such as criminal law, legal ethics, and other topics, which can provide assistance to the student researcher.

## DOING LEGAL RESEARCH USING THE INTERNET

When you do legal research, you do not necessarily have to go to a law library. Neither do you necessarily have to subscribe to the two specialized legal research electronic systems, WESTLAW and LEXIS. Rather, if you have a computer and a modem, you may be able to access sources for legal research from the Internet.

### WHAT THE INTERNET IS AND IS NOT

The Internet is a loosely configured web of over 25,000 educational, corporate, and research computer networks around the world. It started in 1969 when the Defense Department wanted to put together a research and development communications network that was designed to survey nuclear war.

There is no central computer on the Internet. Rather, with each message that you send there is an address code that allows any computer in the Internet to forward it toward its destination.

There is no governing body for the Internet. The closest thing that resembles one is the Internet Society in Reston, Virginia, which is a volunteer organization of individuals and corporate members. The Internet Society promotes ''Net'' use and oversees new communications developments.

### GETTING ON THE INTERNET

There are basically two ways to get on the Internet: through your college or university or through a commercial service.

**USING YOUR COLLEGE OR UNIVERSITY GATEWAY** If you are enrolled in a college or university, it is probably connected directly to the Internet and pays thousands of dollars a year for this hookup. One of the uses of a college Internet subscription is typically electronic mail, otherwise known as E-mail, or e-mail. Faculty, administrators, and students can get an **"address"** and a **"password."** The address is just like a mailbox at which you receive electronic information. Addresses differ depending on the *gateway* that leads you from your computer through another computer to the person or address you want to reach.

You can get your address now by looking at a copy of the handout that your college or university gives new users. Then you can start playing with E-mail. One of the first things to do is to roam through the user-friendly **gopher** family of software. The way you do this is as follows:

- Open your connection the way you would to send or receive E-mail.
- Type **"gopher."**
- Hit return (or enter).
- Now you will see a first-level menu of choices. Pick one by moving the arrow up or down to the item you want to open or type the letter where your cursor is blinking.
- When you are done playing, type **"Q"** and it will **Quit.**

You may want to contact the so-called "mother of all gophers" site at the University of Minnesota. You do this in the following way:

- Type **"gopher."**
- Then type **"consultant@micro.umn.edu."**

**ACCESSING THE INTERNET VIA COMMERCIAL SERVICES** Virtually anybody can sign up for commercial on-line service and be able to access the electronic mail (E-mail) part of the Internet. These services include Delphi, America On-Line, CompuServe, Prodigy, and others. There is a monthly service charge and then a per-minute usage fee for each of the services.

Alternatively, you can subscribe to a gateway company, such as *The World* in Boston, which charges $20 a month per phone for direct access to the Internet.

## HARDWARE AND SOFTWARE

Virtually any computer will work as long as you have a modem attached to it. The faster the modem, usually the better off you are. Many modems sold today have a 14,400 bps speed, and some are being sold with higher speeds.

The communications software that you purchase for accessing the Internet will determine how easy it is for you to use it. For those using IBM and compatibles running Windows, there is *WinGopher,* a graphical interface for the Internet. Additional programs include *NetCruiser* by NetCom and *TCP/Connect II* and *WorldLink* by InterCon. For those using Macintosh systems, the latter two are available as well as a version of *WinGopher* for Macintosh.

By the time you read this, there will undoubtedly be even more "user-friendly" communications software systems for accessing the Internet, including those directly provided by Delphi and other on-line services.

## WHAT TO EXPECT IN THE AREA OF LEGAL RESEARCH MATERIALS

Do not expect a library at your fingertips. Rather, think of C-Span that you can watch on cable TV—a lot of raw data. You can, for example, browse through the entire Americans with Disabilities Act of 1990 as well as many other acts. Additionally, you can "chat" with other people because there are **bulletin board services (BBSs)** for every conceivable subject matter, many of which are law related. Nolo Press, which publishes numerous legal materials, may already have its *Nolo News* on line through the Internet.

You can also obtain blank forms, such as simple contracts and tax forms. The forms usually do not come with documentation, however.

## RAW DATA AVAILABLE

Virtually all United States Supreme Court decisions, the texts of treaties, such as the North American Free Trade Agreement (NAFTA), and many state statutes, such as all of those from California, are available through the Internet.

The White House press releases are available on a daily basis. You are allowed to search through them for a particular topic, such as gun control.

All information from the Patent office, such as *Patent Office Publications*, is starting to become available on line.

**GETTING INFORMATION ON THE SUPREME COURT** The United States Supreme Court now makes available its decisions in electronic format within minutes of their releases. By using the service, you can read the majority and dissenting opinions on cases that interest you. To produce Supreme Court rulings, go to the University of Maryland gopher at:

**info.umde.edu**

and choose **Educational Resources/United States/ Supreme Court.**

**GETTING INFORMATION ON THE UNITED STATES CODE** If you want information on the U.S.C, you can go to the Cleveland State University gopher at:

**gopher.law.csuohio.edu**

## HYPERNET SEARCHING

Through the Internet, you can access Cornell University Law School's computer. Using a "hypertext" research tool, you can pull up a document and then click on a phrase or word. Within seconds you will be linked to other relevant information sources on the Internet.

## INDEPENDENT BULLETIN BOARD SERVICES (BBSs)

There are thousands of independent bulletin board services that are operating either from someone's home or from an office. Many local BBSs are connected to other BBSs nationwide. Local BBSs are generally listed in the classified ad section of newspapers or in computer magazines.

If you are in the state of Washington, for example, there is a BBS that allows you to access all of the laws of the state of Washington. FedWorld is a BBS that offers connections to numerous government-run BBSs. They in turn provide government documents. You can reach FedWorld through the Internet.

One BBS gives information and discussions of mediation and dispute resolution; it is Conflict-Net. Its BBS direct phone number is 415–322–0162. Its Internet address is **telnet ipc.apc.org.**

## OBTAINING THE *LEGAL LIST*

There is a 70- to 100-page listing of where to find law on the Internet. It gives you complete instructions on how to access different sources (if you are familiar with the Internet). The following are two ways to obtain this legal list through commercial services:

- **On-Line America:** Type "**goLEGAL.**" Ask for file NN94INT.TXT.
- **CompuServe:** Go to "**LAWSIG, LIBRARY.**" Ask for **NN94INT.TXT**.

The following is a way to obtain a general listing of law-related gophers throughout the world:

- Type **riceinfo.rice.edu**.
- Then choose **law-gophers.** This will provide you with a list of gophers from around the world that provide law-related information and indicate how you can access them. This is one way to find out about the laws in any of the fifty states or in foreign countries. It also allows you to access gophers set up by law schools from around the world.

## THE WORLD-WIDE WEB

There is something called a "distributed hypermedia" feature on the Internet called the World-Wide Web. What you do is click on words within a document and the World-Wide Web will take you to other documents around the world. The two main entries into the World-Wide Web are:

- **O'Reilly's Global Network Navigator**—It gives you the Declaration of Independence, the U.S. Constitution, and jumping-off points to most of the legal information in the Web. This includes the law libraries at Cornell, Columbia University, Indiana University, and Washington and Lee University.
- **Cornell Law School's Legal Information Institute**—allows you to access Supreme Court decisions

a couple of days after they have been handed down and then allows you to get into the World-Wide Web.

## CHOOSING A PASSWORD

It is important that you choose a password that cannot be easily discovered by others. Otherwise, others may get into your electronic mail, and you will end up with a huge phone bill. Here are some rules for choosing and keeping secret your password:

- Do not use any words that are in any dictionary.
- Use at least eight characters.
- Do not use obvious passwords, such as sports teams or your birthday.
- Mix up numbers, special characters, and letters. Mix with upper- and lowercase.
- Never write your password in any place where people can find it.
- Change passwords frequently.
- Do not "lend" your password to anyone else.
- Do not tell your password to someone over the phone.

# LEGAL ENCYCLOPEDIAS

Legal encyclopedias cover topics of law in a general manner. They explain subjects, define terms, and offer historical as well as current coverage. They are also helpful in finding primary sources of authority. The two major legal encyclopedias are *Corpus Juris Secundum* (C.J.S.), published by West Publishing Company, and *American Jurisprudence 2d* (Am.Jur.2d)—"2d" means second edition—published by the Lawyers Co-Operative Publishing Company. Each of these encyclopedias divides the law into more than four hundred topics. Although legal discussions in these encyclopedias give broad statements of accepted law, because the discussions are extensively footnoted, the encyclopedias are valuable sources for research.

Some states also have encyclopedias, such as *Texas Jurisprudence 3d*. A less technical reference is *The Guide to American Law: Everyone's Legal Encyclopedia,* which is published by West Publishing Company.

# RESTATEMENTS OF THE LAW

The *Restatements of the Law* are compilations of the common law covering various legal areas. There are *Restatements* of the law of agency, conflict of laws, contracts, judgments, property, restitution, security, torts, trusts, foreign relations law, and landlord-tenant law. A student wishing more information on the law of contracts, for example, might consult the *Restatement (Second) of Contracts.* (The word "second" in parentheses means second edition.) Similarly, if a student is interested in studying the law of agency in more detail, he or she could look at the *Restatement (Second) of Agency.* The title of each *Restatement* follows this same format. The *Restatements* include a summary of the "black letter" law on a particular topic, an explanatory comment on the general principles underlying that law, and examples of particular cases and variations on the general proposition.

# TREATISES

Treatises are like encyclopedias; they are written by specialists on certain subjects. Longer treatises are frequently published in multiple volumes. There are treatises for virtually all of the major topics of law. When updated, treatises are usually accurate explanations of the law in a particular area, and, at the same time, they are usually easy to read and a good source to which to turn when beginning one's legal research. For example, *Prosser and Keeton on Torts* would assist a student in researching those topics introduced in Chapters 6, 7, and 8 of this text. *Collier on Bankruptcy* outlines the law presented in Chapter 33 of this text.

# DIGESTS OF CASE LAW

Digests are indexes to American case law. There are digests for both the federal and state court systems. Digests consist primarily of case summaries, which are arranged topically, from each jurisdiction. The advantage of a digest is that researchers can review cases from, for example, all appellate courts for a ten-year period. The American Digest System is the master index giving access to all cases published in the National Reporter System. The American Digest System includes the *Decennial Digest Series,* which is published every ten years, and the *General Digest Series* that is issued periodically between publications of the *Decennial Digest Series.*

There are also a number of subject-matter digests and jurisdictional digests, which are simply extractions of digested cases from the master index. When one is researching a relatively narrow legal topic such as patent law, which was presented in Chapter 8 of this text, the *U.S. Patents Quarterly Digest* would be a promising source of information.

# JUDICIAL REPORTERS

Judicial reporters are volumes for various jurisdictions that contain reported appellate decisions and opinions. As discussed in Chapter 1 of this text, there are reporters published by jurisdiction (for example, the *Federal Reporter* includes all cases from the federal courts of appeals, and the *Federal Supplement* contains cases selected for publication from the U.S. district courts and other federal courts), and there are also reporters that cover specific geographical regions (for example, the *Southern Reporter* covers state appellate cases for the states of Louisiana, Mississippi, Alabama, and Florida). In these reporters, cases are reported chronologically, according to the date of the decision.

In addition to general reporters, some subject reporters are also published. For example, a student who wishes to learn more about bankruptcy and reorganization (discussed in Chapter 33 of the text) would be able to find cases on that subject in the *American Bankruptcy Reports.*

# ANNOTATED STATUTES

The *United States Code* (U.S.C.) contains the text of the U.S. Constitution and current federal legislation. There are two annotated versions of the U.S. Code: the *United States Code Annotated* (U.S.C.A.) and the *United States Code Service* (U.S.C.S.). The textual arrangement in these annotated volumes is identical to that found in the official U.S. Code. Unlike the U.S. Code itself, however, as explained in Chapter 1, these annotated volumes provide summaries of cases that have interpreted the statutory sections. If there are numerous case annotations, an outline of the annotations is also provided to make the research easier.

# LOOSELEAF SERVICES

Looseleaf services collect legal source material in certain subject areas and are kept current by frequent supplementation (often, once a week). They offer another practical means of access to the law in particular areas of interest. Two of the primary publishers of looseleaf services are the Bureau of National Affairs (BNA) and the Commerce Clearing House (CCH). The *BNA Corporate Practice Series* would be useful for a researcher who wants to study those topics introduced in Unit Eight of this text (on business organizations). The *BNA International Trade Reporter* would supplement the materials presented in this text on international law both in Unit Three covering sales contracts and in Chapter 56. The *CCH Employment Practices Guide* would be useful in researching employment and labor relations law (introduced in Chapters 36 and 37). The *CCH Congressional Index* would assist research on administrative law (discussed in Chapter 45). This two-volume set indexes bills, committee reports, and hearings. It also includes sections on pending bills, bill status tables, members of Congress and their voting records, and so on. A final example of a looseleaf service is the *CCH Secured Transactions Guide,* which would help expand the student's knowledge of the concepts presented in Chapter 31 (on secured transactions).

# LAW REVIEWS

Law reviews are scholarly publications edited by law students or legal associations. Law reviews are published periodically (some once a year, others two or more times a year) and cover a broad range of legal topics. The contents of most law reviews include (1) commentaries about the law, usually written by law professors, judges, or practicing attorneys; (2) reviews of books recently written about the law; (3) comments by a student writer explaining the meaning of five or six recent cases; and (4) student notes on specific topics of law. Almost every accredited law school publishes a law review. A scholarly article or review can be found on virtually every topic of law in some issue of a law review, and depending on the topics covered in a particular review, it may assist the researcher in finding further information on any of the subjects presented in this book. The *Harvard Law Review* is one of the most prestigious law reviews. There are many more of equal quality.

# TOPICAL LAW JOURNALS

In addition to the general law reviews, many law schools also publish law journals on specific topics. The contents of the journals are similar to those of the law reviews—scholarly articles, book reviews, case comments, and student notes—but the range of topics is limited to a specified area. The list of topical journals is quite extensive, and there is likely to be an individual journal on almost every topic covered in this text.

For instance, *Environmental Law* focuses on the impact of various laws on the environment; this journal would therefore assist the student in obtaining a more comprehensive understanding of Chapter 47 of this text (on environmental law). The *Antitrust Law Journal* would offer further detail on the materials presented in Chapter 48 (on antitrust). The *Journal of Products Liability* focuses on the materials presented in Chapter 25 (on product liability). A number of law journals focus specifically on international law. Students interested in researching topics in this area might consult the *American Journal of Comparative Law,* the *American Journal of International Law,* or a number of other topical journals on this subject published by law schools.

# WEEKLY NEWSLETTERS/BULLETINS

To keep abreast of recent developments in the judicial and executive branches of the government, one should consult the following weekly publications:

1. *United States Law Week*—This is a weekly looseleaf service published in two volumes. The first volume is designed specifically to provide coverage of the United States Supreme Court. The second volume covers topics of general law; the items presented concern legal developments that, although they are unrelated to the Supreme Court, are of national significance.

2. *United States Supreme Court Bulletin*—This is a weekly looseleaf set designed specifically to provide coverage of the United States Supreme Court. This set contains a copy of the Supreme Court opinions rendered during the current term. In addition, there are sections that provide subject access to everything on the court's docket and a copy of the docket. Other sections include rules of the Supreme Court and a tentative calendar for arguments before the Court.

3. *Weekly Compilation of Presidential Documents*—This weekly publication includes executive orders, proclamations, reorganization plans, speeches, and press conferences. All official presidential documents, except executive agreements, are included. Everything found in this compilation is arranged in chronological order. A student wishing to learn more about administrative law (covered in Chapter 45 of this text) would find this publication useful.

# BAR ASSOCIATION PUBLICATIONS

Bar associations also issue legal materials of various kinds, including newletters and periodicals, that may be useful for the researcher. The *American Bar Association Journal* and the *National Bar Journal,* for example, both contain reports on association activities, articles on legal topics, and notices of recent developments in the law. Additionally, many of the specialized sections of the bar publish their own quarterly newsletters, such as the *American Patent Law Association Quarterly Journal,* which provides the members of the section with an update of the most recent developments in this area of the law.

# FORM BOOKS

If a business student had to draft a contract or some other document, or wanted to see the ''typical language'' found in a legal instrument, he or she would want to look at one of the many form books available. These books frequently offer instructions on how to fill in the sample forms included in the books. An example of a form book is *American Jurisprudence Legal Forms 2d,* a twenty-volume set that contains legal forms of every kind for a commercial transaction. The *American Jurisprudence Pleading and Practice Forms,* in contrast, provides forms that are essential to litigation.

# LIST OF SELECTED RESEARCH SOURCES

Administrative Law Bulletin
American Bankruptcy Law Journal
American Business Law Journal
American Civil Law Journal
American Journal of Comparative Law
American Journal of Criminal Law
American Journal of International Law
American Journal of Tax Policy
American Journal of Trial Advocacy
American Judicature Society Journal
American Jurisprudence Forms Proof of Facts
American Jurisprudence Legal Forms 2d
American Jurisprudence Pleading and Practice Forms
American Lawyer
American Patent Law Association Quarterly Journal
American Society of International Law Proceedings
Annals of Air and Space Law
Annual Review of Banking Law
Annual Survey of Bankruptcy Law
Antitrust Law Journal
Arbitration Law
Banking Law Journal
Bender's Uniform Commercial Code Service
BNA Antitrust and Trade Regulation Reporter

BNA Collective Bargaining and Negotiations and Contracts

BNA Corporate Practice Series

BNA International Trade Report

BNA Labor Relations Reporter

BNA Media Law Reporter

BNA Patent, Trademark and Copyright Reporter

BNA Securities Regulations and Law Reporter

BNA United States Law Week

Boston University International Law Journal

Business Law Journal

CCH Bankruptcy Law Reporter

CCH Congressional Index

CCH Consumer Products Safety and Health Guide

CCH Contract Cases

CCH Copyright Law Reporter

CCH Employment Practices Decisions

CCH Labor Law Reporter

CCH Products Liability Reporter

CCH Secured Transactions Guide

Chicago Legal Forum

Clearinghouse for Civil Rights Research

Code of Federal Regulations

Computer Law Journal

Congressional Information Service Index

Congressional Record

Criminal Law Bulletin

Decennial Digest

Environmental Law

Federal Register

Federal Reporter

Federal Rules Decisions

Federal Rules of Civil Procedure

Federal Supplement

Federal Trade Commission Reports

General Digest

George Washington Journal of International Law and Economics

Harvard Environmental Law Review

Harvard International Law Journal

Harvard Journal of Law and Public Policy

Index to Legal Periodicals

Insurance Law Journal

Intellectual Property Journal

International and Comparative Law Bulletin

International Journal of Medicine and Law

International Journal of Politics

International Journal of the Sociology of Law

International Law Reporter

International Review of Law and Economics

International Social Science Journal

International Trade Reporter

Journal of Contemporary Law

Journal of Corporate Taxation

Journal of Energy and Natural Resources Law

Journal of Law and Commerce

Journal of Law and Economics

Journal of Law and Politics

Journal of Law and Technology

Journal of Products Liability

Journal of Real Estate Taxation

Journal of the American Medical Association

Law and Contemporary Problems

Legal Times of Washington

Loyola Entertainment Law Journal

Maryland Journal of International Law and Trade

Media Law Reporter

Mediation Quarterly

Moore's Federal Practice

National Bar Journal

New Republic

North Atlantic Regional Business Law Review

Northwestern Journal of International Law and Business

Notre Dame Journal of Law, Ethics and Public Policy

Patent and Trademark Review

Performing Arts Review

Prentice Hall: Securities Regulation

Quarterly Journal of Economics

Real Estate Law Journal

Real Property Probate and Trust Journal

Restatement (Second) of Agency

Restatement (Second) of Contracts

Restatement (Second) of Torts

Restatement (Second) of Trusts

Restatement of Property

Review of Litigation

Rutgers Journal of Computers, Technology and the Law

Shepard's Acts and Cases by Popular Names Citations

Social Sciences and Humanities Index

Stanford Environmental Law Journal

Stanford Journal of International Law

Student Lawyer

Supreme Court Bulletin

Supreme Court Reporter

Texas International Law Journal

Trademark Law Handbook

U.S. Attorney General Opinions

U.S. Code Annotated

U.S. Code Congressional and Administrative News

U.S. Code Service

U.S. Patents Quarterly Digest

U.S. Statutes at Large

Uniform Commercial Code Series (Callaghan)

Virginia Journal of International Law

Wall Street Journal

West's Bankruptcy Reporter

Women's Law Journal

Yale Journal of International Law

Yale Journal of World Public Order

Yearbook of Law—Computers and Technology

# Appendix R

# Spanish Equivalents for Important Legal Terms in English

**Abandoned property:** bienes abandonados

**Acceptance:** aceptación; consentimiento; acuerdo

**Acceptor:** aceptante

**Accession:** toma de posesión; aumento; accesión

**Accommodation indorser:** avalista de favor

**Accommodation party:** firmante de favor

**Accord:** acuerdo; convenio; arregio

**Accord and satisfaction:** transacción ejecutada

**Act of state doctrine:** doctrina de acto de gobierno

**Administrative law:** derecho administrativo

**Administrative process:** procedimiento o metódo administrativo

**Administrator:** administrador (-a)

**Adverse possession:** posesión de hecho susceptible de proscripción adquisitiva

**Affirmative action:** acción afirmativa

**Affirmative defense:** defensa afirmativa

**After-acquired property:** bienes adquiridos con posterioridad a un hecho dado

**Agency:** mandato; agencia

**Agent:** mandatorio; agente; representante

**Agreement:** convenio; acuerdo; contrato

**Alien corporation:** empresa extranjera

**Allonge:** hojas adicionales de endosos

**Answer:** contestación de la demande; alegato

**Anticipatory repudiation:** anuncio previo de las partes de su imposibilidad de cumplir con el contrato

**Appeal:** apelación; recurso de apelación

**Appellate jurisdiction:** jurisdicción de apelaciones

**Appraisal right:** derecho de valuación

**Arbitration:** arbitraje

**Arson:** incendio intencional

**Articles of partnership:** contrato social

**Artisan's lien:** derecho de retención que ejerce al artesano

**Assault:** asalto; ataque; agresión

**Assignment of rights:** transmisión; transferencia; cesión

**Assumption of risk:** no resarcimiento por exposición voluntaria al peligro

**Attachment:** auto judicial que autoriza el embargo; embargo

**Bailee:** depositario

**Bailment:** depósito; constitución en depósito

**Bailor:** depositante

**Bankruptcy trustee:** síndico de la quiebra

**Battery:** agresión; física

**Bearer:** portador; tenedor

**Bearer instrument:** documento al portador

**Bequest or legacy:** legado (de bienes muebles)

**Bilateral contract:** contrato bilateral

**Bill of lading:** conocimiento de embarque; carta de porte

**Bill of Rights:** declaración de derechos

**Binder:** póliza de seguro provisoria; recibo de pago a cuenta del precio

**Blank indorsement:** endoso en blanco

**Blue sky laws:** leyes reguladoras del comercio bursátil

**Bond:** título de crédito; garantía; caución

**Bond indenture:** contrato de emisión de bonos; contrato del ampréstito

**Breach of contract:** incumplimiento de contrato

**Brief:** escrito; resumen; informe

**Burglary:** violación de domicilio

**Business judgment rule:** regla de juicio comercial

**Business tort:** agravio comercial

**Case law:** ley de casos; derecho casuístico

**Cashier's check:** cheque de caja

**Causation in fact:** causalidad en realidad

**Cease-and-desist order:** orden para cesar y desistir

**Certificate of deposit:** certificado de depósito

**Certified check:** cheque certificado

**Charitable trust:** fideicomiso para fines benéficos

**Chattel:** bien mueble

**Check:** cheque

**Chose in action:** derecho inmaterial; derecho de acción

**Civil law:** derecho civil

**Close corporation:** sociedad de un solo accionista o de un grupo restringido de accionistas

**Closed shop:** taller agremiado (emplea solamente a miembros de un gremio)

**Closing argument:** argumento al final

**Codicil:** codicilo

**Collateral:** guarantía; bien objeto de la guarantía real

**Comity:** cortesía; cortesía entre naciones

**Commercial paper:** instrumentos negociables; documentos a valores comerciales

**Common law:** derecho consuetudinario; derecho común; ley común

**Common stock:** acción ordinaria

**Comparative negligence:** negligencia comparada

**Compensatory damages:** daños y perjuicios reales o compensatorios

**Concurrent conditions:** condiciones concurrentes

**Concurrent jurisdiction:** competencia concurrente de varios tribunales para entender en una misma causa

**Concurring opinion:** opinión concurrente

**Condition:** condición

**Condition precedent:** condición suspensiva

**Condition subsequent:** condición resolutoria

**Confiscation:** confiscación

**Confusion:** confusión; fusión

**Conglomerate merger:** fusión de firmas que operan en distintos mercados

**Consent decree:** acuerdo entre las partes aprobado por un tribunal

**Consequential damages:** daños y perjuicios indirectos

**Consideration:** consideración; motivo; contraprestación

**Consolidation:** consolidación

**Constructive delivery:** entrega simbólica

**Constructive trust:** fideicomiso creado por aplicación de la ley

**Consumer protection law:** ley para proteger el consumidor

**Contract:** contrato

**Contract under seal:** contrato formal o sellado

**Contributory negligence:** negligencia de la parte actora

**Conversion:** usurpación; conversión de valores

**Copyright:** derecho de autor

**Corporation:** sociedad anónima; corporación; persona jurídica

**Co-sureties:** cogarantes

**Counterclaim:** reconvención; contrademanda

**Counteroffer:** contraoferta

**Course of dealing:** curso de transacciones

**Course of performance:** curso de cumplimiento

**Covenant:** pacto; garantía; contrato

**Covenant not to sue:** pacto or contrato a no demandar

**Covenant of quiet enjoyment:** garantía del uso y goce pacífico del inmueble

**Creditors' composition agreement:** concordato preventivo

**Crime:** crimen; delito; contravención

**Criminal law:** derecho penal

**Cross-examination:** contrainterrogatorio

**Cure:** cura; cuidado; derecho de remediar un vicio contractual

**Customs receipts:** recibos de derechos aduaneros

**Damages:** daños; indemnización por daños y perjuicios

**Debit card:** tarjeta de dé bito

**Debtor:** deudor

**Debt securities:** seguridades de deuda

**Deceptive advertising:** publicidad engañosa

**Deed:** escritura; título; acta translativa de domino

**Defamation:** difamación

**Delegation of duties:** delegación de obligaciones

**Demand deposit:** depósito a la vista

**Depositions:** declaración de un testigo fuera del tribunal

**Devise:** legado; deposición testamentaria (bienes inmuebles)

**Directed verdict:** veredicto según orden del juez y sin participación activa del jurado

**Direct examination:** interrogatorio directo; primer interrogatorio

**Disaffirmance:** repudiación; renuncia; anulación

**Discharge:** descargo; liberación; cumplimiento

**Disclosed principal:** mandante revelado

**Discovery:** descubrimiento; producción de la prueba

**Dissenting opinion:** opinión disidente

**Dissolution:** disolución; terminación

**Diversity of citizenship:** competencia de los tribunales federales para entender en causas cuyas partes intervinientes son cuidadanos de distintos estados

**Divestiture:** extinción premature de derechos reales

**Dividend:** dividendo

**Docket:** orden del día; lista de causas pendientes

**Domestic corporation:** sociedad local

**Draft:** orden de pago; letrade cambio

**Drawee:** girado; beneficiario

**Drawer:** librador

**Duress:** coacción; violencia

**Easement:** servidumbre

**Embezzlement:** desfalco; malversación

**Eminent domain:** poder de expropiación

**Employment discrimination:** discriminación en el empleo

**Entrepreneur:** empresario

**Environmental law:** ley ambiental

**Equal dignity rule:** regla de dignidad egual

**Equity security:** tipo de participación en una sociedad

**Estate:** propiedad; patrimonio; derecho

**Estop:** impedir; prevenir

**Ethical issue:** cuestión ética

**Exclusive jurisdiction:** competencia exclusiva

**Exculpatory clause:** cláusula eximente

**Executed contract:** contrato ejecutado

**Execution:** ejecución; cumplimiento

**Executor:** albacea

**Executory contract:** contrato aún no completamente consumado

**Executory interest:** derecho futuro
**Express contract:** contrato expreso
**Expropriation:** expropriación

**Federal question:** caso federal
**Fee simple:** pleno dominio; dominio absoluto
**Fee simple absolute:** dominio absoluto
**Fee simple defeasible:** dominio sujeta a una condición resolutoria
**Felony:** crimen; delito grave
**Fictitious payee:** beneficiario ficticio
**Fiduciary:** fiduciaro
**Firm offer:** oferta en firme
**Fixture:** inmueble por destino, incorporación a anexación
**Floating lien:** gravamen continuado
**Foreign corporation:** sociedad extranjera; U.S. sociedad constituída en otro estado
**Forgery:** falso; falsificación
**Formal contract:** contrato formal
**Franchise:** privilegio; franquicia; concesión
**Franchisee:** persona que recibe una concesión
**Franchisor:** persona que vende una concesión
**Fraud:** fraude; dolo; engaño
**Future interest:** bien futuro

**Garnishment:** embargo de derechos
**General partner:** socio comanditario
**General warranty deed:** escritura translativa de domino con garantía de título
**Gift:** donación
**Gift** *causa mortis:* donación por causa de muerte
**Gift** *inter vivos:* donación entre vivos
**Good faith:** buena fe
**Good faith purchaser:** comprador de buena fe

**Holder:** tenedor por contraprestación
**Holder in due course:** tenedor legítimo
**Holographic will:** testamento ológrafo

**Homestead exemption laws:** leyes que exceptúan las casas de familia de ejecución por duedas generales
**Horizontal merger:** fusión horizontal

**Identification:** identificación
**Implied-in-fact contract:** contrato implícito en realidad
**Implied warranty:** guarantía implícita
**Implied warranty of merchantability:** garantía implícita de vendibilidad
**Impossibility of performance:** imposibilidad de cumplir un contrato
**Imposter:** imposter
**Incidental beneficiary:** beneficiario incidental; beneficiario secundario
**Incidental damages:** daños incidentales
**Indictment:** auto de acusación; acusación
**Indorsee:** endorsatario
**Indorsement:** endoso
**Indorser:** endosante
**Informal contract:** contrato no formal; contrato verbal
**Information:** acusación hecha por el ministerio público
**Injunction:** mandamiento; orden de no innovar
**Innkeeper's lien:** derecho de retención que ejerce el posadero
**Installment contract:** contrato de pago en cuotas
**Insurable interest:** interés asegurable
**Intended beneficiary:** beneficiario destinado
**Intentional tort:** agravio; cuasi-delito intenciónal
**International law:** derecho internaciónal
**Interrogatories:** preguntas escritas sometidas por una parte a la otra o a un testigo
**Inter vivos** trust: fideicomiso entre vivos
**Intestacy laws:** leyes de la condición de morir intestado
**Intestate:** intestado
**Investment company:** compañia de inversiones
**Issue:** emisión

**Joint tenancy:** derechos conjuntos en un bien inmueble en favor del beneficiario sobreviviente
**Judgment** *n.o.v.*: juicio no obstante veredicto
**Judgment rate of interest:** interés de juicio
**Judicial process:** acto de procedimiento; proceso jurídico
**Judicial review:** revisión judicial
**Jurisdiction:** jurisdicción

**Larceny:** robo; hurto
**Law:** derecho; ley; jurisprudencia
**Lease:** contrato de locación; contrato de alquiler
**Leasehold estate:** bienes forales
**Legal rate of interest:** interés legal
**Legatee:** legatario
**Letter of credit:** carta de crédito
**Levy:** embargo; comiso
**Libel:** libelo; difamación escrita
**Life estate:** usufructo
**Limited partner:** comanditario
**Limited partnership:** sociedad en comandita
**Liquidation:** liquidación; realización
**Lost property:** objetos perdidos

**Majority opinion:** opinión de la mayoría
**Maker:** persona que realiza u ordena; librador
**Mechanic's lien:** gravamen de constructor
**Mediation:** mediación; intervención
**Merger:** fusión
**Mirror image rule:** fallo de reflejo
**Misdemeanor:** infracción; contravención
**Mislaid property:** bienes extraviados
**Mitigation of damages:** reducción de daños
**Mortgage:** hypoteca
**Motion to dismiss:** excepción parentoria
**Mutual fund:** fondo mutual

**Negotiable instrument:** instrumento negociable
**Negotiation:** negociación
**Nominal damages:** daños y perjuicios nominales

**Novation:** novación
**Nuncupative will:** testamento nuncupativo

**Objective theory of contracts:** teoria objetiva de contratos
**Offer:** oferta
**Offeree:** persona que recibe una oferta
**Offeror:** oferente
**Order instrument:** instrumento o documento a la orden
**Original jurisdiction:** jurisdicción de primera instancia
**Output contract:** contrato de producción

**Parol evidence rule:** regla relativa a la prueba oral
**Partially disclosed principal:** mandante revelado en parte
**Partnership:** sociedad colectiva; asociación; asociación de participación
**Past consideration:** causa o contraprestación anterior
**Patent:** patente; privilegio
**Pattern or practice:** muestra o práctica
**Payee:** beneficiario de un pago
**Penalty:** pena; penalidad
*Per capita:* por cabeza
**Perfection:** perfeción
**Performance:** cumplimiento; ejecución
**Personal defenses:** excepciones personales
**Personal property:** bienes muebles
*Per stirpes:* por estirpe
**Plea bargaining:** regateo por un alegato
**Pleadings:** alegatos
**Pledge:** prenda
**Police powers:** poders de policia y de prevención del crimen
**Policy:** póliza
**Positive law:** derecho positivo; ley positiva
**Possibility of reverter:** posibilidad de reversión
**Precedent:** precedente
**Preemptive right:** derecho de prelación
**Preferred stock:** acciones preferidas
**Premium:** recompensa; prima

**Presentment warranty:** garantía de presentación
**Price discrimination:** discriminación en los precios
**Principal:** mandante; principal
**Privity:** nexo jurídico
**Privity of contract:** relación contractual
**Probable cause:** causa probable
**Probate:** verificación; verificación del testamento
**Probate court:** tribunal de sucesiones y tutelas
**Proceeds:** resultados; ingresos
**Profit:** beneficio; utilidad; lucro
**Promise:** promesa
**Promisee:** beneficiario de una promesa
**Promisor:** promtente
**Promissory estoppel:** impedimento promisorio
**Promissory note:** pagaré; nota de pago
**Promoter:** promotor; fundador
**Proximate cause:** causa inmediata o próxima
**Proxy:** apoderado; poder
**Punitive, or exemplary, damages:** daños y perjuicios punitivos o ejemplares

**Qualified indorsement:** endoso con reservas
**Quasi contract:** contrato tácito o implícito
**Quitclaim deed:** acto de transferencia de una propiedad por finiquito, pero sin ninguna garantía sobre la validez del título transferido

**Ratification:** ratificación
**Real property:** bienes inmuebles
**Reasonable doubt:** duda razonable
**Rebuttal:** refutación
**Recognizance:** promesa; compromiso; reconocimiento
**Recording statutes:** leyes estatales sobre registros oficiales
**Redress:** reporacíon
**Reformation:** rectificación; reforma; corrección
**Rejoinder:** dúplica; contrarréplica
**Release:** liberación; renuncia a un derecho
**Remainder:** substitución; reversión

**Remedy:** recurso; remedio; reparación
**Replevin:** acción reivindicatoria; reivindicación
**Reply:** réplica
**Requirements contract:** contrato de suministro
**Rescission:** rescisión
*Res judicata:* cosa juzgada; res judicata
*Respondeat superior:* responsabilidad del mandante o del maestro
**Restitution:** restitución
**Restrictive indorsement:** endoso restrictivo
**Resulting trust:** fideicomiso implícito
**Reversion:** reversión; sustitución
**Revocation:** revocación; derogación
**Right of contribution:** derecho de contribución
**Right of reimbursement:** derecho de reembolso
**Right of subrogation:** derecho de subrogación
**Right-to-work law:** ley de libertad de trabajo
**Robbery:** robo
**Rule 10b-5:** Regla 10b-5

**Sale:** venta; contrato de compreventa
**Sale on approval:** venta a ensayo; venta sujeta a la aprobación del comprador
**Sale or return:** venta con derecho de devolución
**Sales contract:** contrato de compraventa; boleto de compraventa
**Satisfaction:** satisfacción; pago
*Scienter:* a sabiendas
**S corporation:** S corporación
**Secured party:** acreedor garantizado
**Secured transaction:** transacción garantizada
**Securities:** volares; titulos; seguridades
**Security agreement:** convenio de seguridad
**Security interest:** interés en un bien dado en garantía que permite a quien lo detenta venderlo en caso de incumplimiento

**Service mark:** marca de identificación de servicios

**Shareholder's derivative suit:** acción judicial entablada por un accionista en nombre de la sociedad

**Signature:** firma; rúbrica

**Slander:** difamación oral; calumnia

**Sovereign immunity:** immunidad soberana

**Special indorsement:** endoso especial; endoso a la orden de una person en particular

**Specific performance:** ejecución precisa, según los términos del contrato

**Spendthrift trust:** fideicomiso para pródigos

**Stale check:** cheque vencido

*Stare decisis:* acatar las decisiones, observar los precedentes

**Statutory law:** derecho estatutario; derecho legislado; derecho escrito

**Stock:** acciones

**Stock warrant:** certificado para la compra de acciones

**Stop-payment order:** orden de suspensión del pago de un cheque dada por el librador del mismo

**Strict liability:** responsabilidad uncondicional

**Summary judgment:** fallo sumario

**Tangible property:** bienes corpóreos

**Tenancy at will:** inguilino por tiempo indeterminado (según la voluntad del propietario)

**Tenancy by sufferance:** posesión por tolerancia

**Tenancy by the entirety:** locación conyugal conjunta

**Tenancy for years:** inguilino por un término fijo

**Tenancy in common:** specie de copropiedad indivisa

**Tender:** oferta de pago; oferta de ejecución

**Testamentary trust:** fideicomiso testamentario

**Testator:** testador (-a)

**Third party beneficiary contract:** contrato para el beneficio del tercero-beneficiario

**Tort:** agravio; cuasi-delito

**Totten trust:** fideicomiso creado por un depósito bancario

**Trade acceptance:** letra de cambio aceptada

**Trademark:** marca registrada

**Trade name:** nombre comercial; razón social

**Traveler's check:** cheque del viajero

**Trespass to land:** ingreso no authorizado a las tierras de otro

**Trespass to personal property:** violación de los derechos posesorios de un tercero con respecto a bienes muebles

**Trust:** fideicomiso; trust

*Ultra vires:* ultra vires; fuera de la facultad (de una sociedad anónima)

**Unanimous opinion:** opinión unámine

**Unconscionable contract or clause:** contrato leonino; cláusula leonino

**Underwriter:** subscriptor; asegurador

**Unenforceable contract:** contrato que no se puede hacer cumplir

**Unilateral contract:** contrato unilateral

**Union shop:** taller agremiado; empresa en la que todos los empleados son miembros del gremio o sindicato

**Universal defenses:** defensas legitimas o legales

**Usage of trade:** uso comercial

**Usury:** usura

**Valid contract:** contrato válido

**Venue:** lugar; sede del proceso

**Vertical merger:** fusión vertical de empresas

**Voidable contract:** contrato anulable

**Void contract:** contrato nulo; contrato inválido, sin fuerza legal

*Voir dire:* examen preliminar de un testigo a jurado por el tribunal para determinar su competencia

**Voting trust:** fideicomiso para ejercer el derecho de voto

**Waiver:** renuncia; abandono

**Warranty of habitability:** garantía de habitabilidad

**Watered stock:** acciones diluídos; capital inflado

**White-collar crime:** crimen administrativo

**Writ of attachment:** mandamiento de ejecución; mandamiento de embargo

**Writ of *certiorari*:** auto de avocación; auto de certiorari

**Writ of execution:** auto ejecutivo; mandamiento de ejecución

**Writ of mandamus:** auto de mandamus; mandamiento; orden judicial

# GLOSSARY

## A

**Abandoned property** Property with which the owner has voluntarily parted, with no intention of recovering it.

**Abandonment** In landlord-tenant law, a tenant's departure from leased premises completely, with no intention of returning before the end of the lease term.

*Abus de droit* A doctrine developed in the French courts. The doctrine modified employment at will and protected workers exercising their rights from wrongful discharge and other employer abuses.

**Acceleration clause** A clause in an installment contract that provides for all future payments to become due immediately upon the failure to tender timely payments or upon the occurrence of a specified event.

**Acceptance** (1) In contract law, the offeree's notification to the offeror that the offeree agrees to be bound by the terms of the offeror's proposal. Although historically the terms of acceptance had to be the mirror image of the terms of the offer, the UCC provides that even modified terms of the offer in a definite expression of acceptance constitute a contract. (2) In commercial paper law, the drawee's signed agreement to pay a draft when presented.

**Acceptor** The person (the drawee) who accepts a draft and who engages to be primarily responsible for its payment.

**Accession** The changing (for example, through manufacturing) of one good into a new good (for example, flour into bread); the right, upon payment for the original materials, to keep an article manufactured out of goods that were innocently converted.

**Accommodation party** A person who signs an instrument for the purpose of lending his or her credit to another party on the instrument.

**Accord and satisfaction** An agreement and payment (or other performance) between two parties, one of whom has a right of action against the other. After the agreement has been made and payment or other performance has been tendered, the "accord and satisfaction" is complete.

**Accredited investors** In the context of securities offerings, "sophisticated" investors, such as banks, insurance companies, investment companies, the issuer's executive officers and directors, and persons whose income or net worth exceeds certain limits.

**Acquittal** A certification or declaration following a trial that the individual accused of a crime is innocent, or free from guilt, and is thus absolved of the charges.

**Act of state doctrine** A doctrine that provides that the judicial branch of one country will not examine the validity of public acts committed by a recognized foreign government within its own territory.

**Actionable** Capable of serving as the basis of a lawsuit. An actionable claim can be pursued in a lawsuit or other court action.

**Actual malice** Real and demonstrable evil intent. In a defamation suit, a statement made about a public figure normally must be made with actual malice (with either knowledge of its falsity or a reckless disregard of the truth) for liability to be incurred.

*Actus reus* A guilty (prohibited) act. The commission of a prohibited act is one of the two essential elements required for criminal liability, the other element being the intent to commit a crime.

**Adequate protection doctrine** In bankruptcy law, a doctrine that protects secured creditors from losing their security as a result of an automatic stay on legal proceedings by creditors against the debtor once the debtor petitions for bankruptcy relief. In certain circumstances, the bankruptcy court may provide adequate protection by requiring the debtor or trustee to pay the creditor or provide additional guaranties to protect the creditor against the losses suffered by the creditor as a result of the stay.

**Adhesion contract** A "standard form" contract, such as that between a large retailer and a consumer, in which the stronger party dictates the terms.

**Adjudication** The act of rendering a judicial decision. In administrative process, the proceeding in which an administrative law judge hears and decides on issues that arise when an administrative agency charges a person or a firm with violating a law or regulation enforced by the agency.

**Administrative agency** A federal or state government agency established to perform a specific function. Administrative agencies are authorized by legislative acts to make and enforce rules relating to the purpose for which they were established.

**Administrative law** A body of law created by administrative agencies—such as the Securities and Exchange Commission and the Federal Trade

Commission—in the form of rules, regulations, orders, and decisions in order to carry out their duties and responsibilities. This law can initially be enforced by these agencies outside the judicial process.

**Administrative law judge (ALJ)** One who presides over an administrative agency hearing and who has the power to administer oaths, take testimony, rule on questions of evidence, and make determinations of fact.

**Administrative process** The procedure used by administrative agencies in the administration of law.

**Administrator** One who is appointed by a court to handle the probate (disposition) of a person's estate if that person dies intestate (without a will).

**Adverse possession** The acquisition of title to real property by occupying it openly, without the consent of the owner, for a period of time specified by state statutes. The occupation must be actual, open, notorious, exclusive, and in opposition to all others, including the owner.

**Affidavit** A written or printed voluntary statement of facts, confirmed by the oath or affirmation of the party making it and made before a person having the authority to administer the oath or affirmation.

**Affirmative action** Job-hiring policies that give special consideration or compensatory treatment to minority groups in an effort to overcome present effects of past discrimination.

**Affirmative defense** A response to a plaintiff's claim that does not deny the plaintiff's facts but attacks the plaintiff's legal right to bring an action. An example is the running of the statute of limitations.

**After-acquired evidence** A type of evidence submitted in support of an affirmative defense in employment discrimination cases. Evidence that, prior to the employer's discriminatory act, the employee engaged in misconduct sufficient to warrant dismissal had the employer known of it earlier.

**After-acquired property** Property of the debtor that is acquired after a secured creditor's interest in the debtor's property has been created.

**Age of majority** The age at which an individual is considered legally capable of conducting himself or herself responsibly. A person of this age is entitled to the full rights of citizenship, including the right to vote at elections. In contract law, one who is no longer an infant and can no longer disaffirm a contract.

**Agency** A relationship between two persons in which, by agreement or otherwise, one is bound by the words and acts of the other. The former is a principal; the latter is an agent.

**Agent** A person authorized by another to act for or in place of him or her.

**Aggressor** The acquiring corporation in a takeover attempt.

**Agreement** A meeting of two or more minds. Often used as a synonym for contract.

**Alien corporation** A designation in the United States for a corporation formed in another country but doing business in the United States.

**Allonge** A piece of paper firmly attached to a negotiable instrument, upon which transferees can make indorsements if there is no room left on the instrument itself.

**Alterations** In the context of leaseholds, improvements or changes made that materially affect the condition of the property. Thus, for example, erecting additional structures probably would (and painting interior walls would not) be considered making alterations.

**Alternative dispute resolution (ADR)** The resolution of disputes in ways other than those involved in the traditional judicial process. Mediation and arbitration are forms of ADR.

**Amend** To change and improve through a formal procedure.

**American Arbitration Association (AAA)** The major organization offering arbitration services in the United States.

**Analogy** In logical reasoning, an assumption that if two things are similar in some respects, they will be similar in other respects also. Often used in legal reasoning to infer the appropriate application of legal principles in a case being decided by referring to previous cases involving different facts but considered to come within the policy underlying the rule.

**Annuity** An insurance policy that pays the insured fixed, periodic payments for life or for a term of years, as stipulated in the policy, after the insured reaches a specified age.

**Answer** Procedurally, a defendant's response to the complaint.

**Antecedent claim** A preexisting claim. In negotiable instruments law, taking an instrument in satisfaction of an antecedent claim is taking the instrument for value—that is, for valid consideration.

**Anticipatory repudiation** An assertion or action by a party indicating that he or she will not perform an obligation that the party is contractually obligated to perform at a future time.

**Antitrust law** The body of federal and state laws and statutes protecting trade and commerce from unlawful restraints, price discrimination, price fixing, and monopolies. The principal federal antitrust statutes are the Sherman Act (1890), the Clayton Act (1914), and the Federal Trade Commission Act (1914).

**Apparent authority** Authority that is only apparent, not real. In agency law, a person may be deemed to have had the power to act as an agent for another party if the other party's manifestations to a third party led the third party to believe that an agency existed when, in fact, it did not.

**Appellant** The party who takes an appeal from one court to another; sometimes referred to as the petitioner.

**Appellee** The party against whom an appeal is taken—that is, the party who opposes setting aside or reversing the judgment; sometimes referred to as the respondent.

**Appraisal right**   A dissenting shareholder's right, if he or she objects to an extraordinary transaction of the corporation (such as a merger or consolidation), to have his or her shares appraised and to be paid the fair market value of his or her shares by the corporation.

**Appropriation**   In tort law, the act of making a thing one's own or exercising or making use of an object to subserve one's own interest. When the act is wrongful, a tort is committed.

**Arbitrary and capricious test**   The court reviewing an informal administrative agency action applies this test to determine whether or not that action was in clear error. The court gives wide discretion to the expertise of the agency and decides if the agency had sufficient factual information upon which to base its action. If no clear error was made, then the agency's action stands.

**Arbitration**   The settling of a dispute by submitting it to a disinterested third party (other than a court), who renders a legally binding decision.

**Arbitration clause**   A clause in a contract that provides that, in case of a dispute, the parties will determine their rights by arbitration rather than through the judicial system.

**Arraignment**   A court proceeding in which an individual is formally charged with the criminal offense stated in the information or indictment and enters a plea (guilty, not guilty, or *nolo contendere*) in response.

**Arson**   The malicious burning of another's dwelling. Some statutes have expanded this to include any real property regardless of ownership and the destruction of property by other means—for example, by explosion.

**Articles of incorporation**   The document filed with the appropriate governmental agency, usually the secretary of state, when a business is incorporated; state statutes usually prescribe what kind of information must be contained in the articles of incorporation.

**Articles of partnership**   A written agreement that sets forth each partner's rights in, and obligations to, the partnership.

**Artisan's lien**   A possessory lien given to a person who has made improvements and added value to another person's personal property as security for payment for services performed.

**Assault**   Any word or action intended to make another person fearful of immediate physical harm; a reasonably believable threat.

**Assignment**   The act of transferring to another all or part of one's rights arising under a contract.

**Assumption of risk**   A doctrine whereby a plaintiff may not recover for injuries or damages suffered from risks he or she knows of and assents to. A defense against negligence that can be used when the plaintiff has knowledge of and appreciates a danger and voluntarily exposes himself or herself to the danger.

**Attachment**   (1) In a secured transaction, the process by which a security interest in the property of another becomes enforceable. (2) The legal process of seizing another's property in accordance with a writ or judicial order for the purpose of securing satisfaction of a judgment yet to be rendered.

**Attempted monopolization**   Any actions by a firm to eliminate competition and gain monopoly power.

**Attractive nuisance doctrine**   A common law doctrine under which a landowner or landlord may be held liable for injuries incurred by children who are lured onto the property by something dangerous and enticing thereon.

**Automated teller machine (ATM)**   An electronic customer-bank communication terminal that, when activated by an access card and a personal identification number, can conduct routine banking transactions.

**Automatic stay**   A suspension of all judicial proceedings upon the occurrence of an independent event. Under the Bankruptcy Code, the moment a petition to commence bankruptcy proceedings is filed, all litigation by creditors against a debtor and the debtor's property is suspended.

**Award**   As a noun, the decision rendered by an arbitrator or other extrajudicial decider of a controversy. As a verb, to give or assign by sentence, judicial determination, or otherwise after a careful weighing of evidence, as when a jury awards damages.

# B

**Bail**   An amount of money set by the court that must be paid by a criminal defendant to the court before the defendant will be released from custody. Bail is set to assure that an individual accused of a crime will appear for further criminal proceedings. If the accused provides bail, whether in cash or in a surety bond, then he or she is released from jail in exchange.

**Bailee**   One to whom goods are entrusted by a bailor.

**Bailee's lien**   A possessory lien, or claim, that a bailee entitled to compensation can place on the bailed property to ensure that he or she will be paid for the services provided. The lien is effective as long as the bailee retains possession of the bailed goods and has not agreed to extend credit to the bailor. Sometimes referred to as an artisan's lien.

**Bailment**   An agreement in which goods or personal property of one person (a bailor) are entrusted to another (a bailee), who is obligated to return the bailed property to the bailor or dispose of it as directed.

**Bailor**   One who entrusts goods to a bailee.

**Bait-and-switch advertising**   Advertising a product at a very attractive price (the ''bait'') and then informing the consumer, once he or she is in the store, that the advertised product is either not available or is of poor quality; the customer is then urged to purchase (''switched'' to) a more expensive item.

**Banker's acceptance**   A negotiable instrument that is commonly used in international trade. A banker's acceptance is drawn by a creditor against the debtor, who pays the draft at maturity. The drawer creates a draft without designating a payee. The draft can pass through many parties' hands before a bank (drawee) accepts it, transforming the draft into a banker's acceptance. Acceptances can be purchased and sold in a way similar to securities.

**Battery** The unprivileged, intentional touching of another.

**Bearer** A person in the possession of an instrument payable to bearer or indorsed in blank.

**Bearer instrument** In the law of commercial paper, any instrument that runs to the bearer, including instruments payable to the bearer or to "cash."

**Bequest** A gift by will of personal property (from the verb to bequeath).

**Beyond a reasonable doubt** The standard used to determine the guilt or innocence of a person criminally charged. To be guilty of a crime, one must be proved guilty "beyond and to the exclusion of every reasonable doubt." A reasonable doubt is one that would cause a prudent person to hesitate before acting in matters important to him or her.

**Bilateral contract** A contract that includes the exchange of a promise for a promise.

**Bill of Rights** The first ten amendments to the Constitution.

**Bill of lading** A document that serves both as evidence of the receipt of goods for shipment and as documentary evidence of title to the goods.

**Binder** A written, temporary insurance policy.

**Blank indorsement** An indorsement made by the mere writing of the indorser's name on the back of an instrument. Such indorsement causes an instrument, otherwise payable to order, to become payable to bearer and negotiated only by delivery.

**Blue laws** State or local laws that make the performance of commercial activities on Sunday illegal.

**Blue sky laws** State laws that regulate the offer and sale of securities.

**Bona fide occupational qualification (BFOQ)** Under Title VII of the Civil Rights Act of 1964, identifiable characteristics reasonably necessary to the normal operation of a particular business. These characteristics can include gender, national origin, and religion, but not race.

**Bond** A certificate that evidences a corporate debt. It is a security that involves no ownership interest in the issuing corporation.

**Bond indenture** A contract between the issuer of a bond and the bondholder.

**Bounty payment** A reward (payment) given to a person or persons who perform a certain service—such as informing legal authorities of illegal actions.

**Breach** To violate a law, by an act or an omission, or to break a legal obligation that one owes to another person or to society.

**Breach of contract** Failure, without legal excuse, of a promisor to perform the obligations of a contract.

**Brief** A written summary or statement prepared by one side in a lawsuit to explain its case to the judge; a typical brief has a facts summary, a law summary, and an argument about how the law applies to the facts.

**Burglary** The unlawful entry into a building with the intent to commit a felony. (Some state statutes expand this to include the intent to commit any crime.)

**Business ethics** Ethics in a business context; a consensus of what constitutes right or wrong behavior in the world of business and the application of moral principles to situations that arise in a business setting.

**Business invitees** Those people, such as customers or clients, who are invited onto business premises by the owner of those premises for business purposes.

**Business judgment rule** A rule that immunizes corporate management from liability for actions that are undertaken in good faith, when the actions are within both the power of the corporation and the authority of management to make.

**Business necessity defense** A showing that an employment practice that discriminates against members of a protected class is related to job performance.

**Business tort** A tort occurring within the business context; typical business torts are wrongful interference with the business or contractual relationships of others and unfair competition.

**Business trust** A voluntary form of business organization in which investors (trust beneficiaries) transfer cash or property to trustees in exchange for trust certificates that represent their investment shares. Management of the business and trust property is handled by the trustees for the use and benefit of the investors. The certificate holders have limited liability (are not responsible for the debts and obligations incurred by the trust) and share in the trust's profits.

**Buy-sell agreement** A buy-out agreement. In the context of partnerships, an express agreement made at the time of partnership formation for one or more of the partners to buy out the other or others should the situation warrant—and thus provide for the smooth dissolution of the partnership.

**Bylaws** A set of governing rules or regulations adopted by a corporation or other association.

**Bystander** A spectator, witness, or person standing nearby when an event occurred and who did not engage in the business or act leading to the event.

# C

**Cause of action** A situation or set of facts that entitles a party to sustain a legal action against another and gives the party the right to seek a judicial remedy on his or her behalf.

**Case law** Rules of law announced in court decisions. Case law includes the aggregate of reported cases that interpret judicial precedents, statutes, regulations, and constitutional provisions.

**Cash surrender value** The amount that the insurer has agreed to pay to the insured if a life insurance policy is canceled before the insured's death.

**Cashier's check** A draft drawn by a bank on itself.

**Categorical imperative**  A concept developed by the philosopher Immanual Kant as an ethical guideline for behavior. In deciding whether an action is right or wrong, or desirable or undesirable, a person should evaluate the action in terms of what would happen if everybody else in the same situation, or category, acted the same way.

**Causation in fact**  An act or omission without which an event would not have occurred.

**Cause of action**  A situation or set of facts that entitles a party to sustain a legal action against another and gives the party the right to seek a judicial remedy on his or her behalf.

**Cease-and-desist order**  An administrative or judicial order prohibiting a person or business firm from conducting activities that an agency or court has deemed illegal.

**Certificate of deposit (CD)**  An instrument evidencing a promissory acknowledgment by a bank of a receipt of money with an engagement to repay it.

**Certificate of incorporation**  The primary document that evidences corporate existence (referred to as articles of incorporation in some states).

**Certificate of limited partnership**  A certificate that is required for the establishment of a limited partnership. The certificate must be filed with the designated state official (usually the secretary of state).

**Certification mark**  A mark used by one or more persons, other than the owner, to certify the region, materials, mode of manufacture, quality, or accuracy of the owner's goods or services. When used by members of a cooperative, association, or other organization, such a mark is referred to as a collective mark. Examples of certification marks include the ''Good Housekeeping Seal of Approval'' and ''UL Tested.''

**Certified check**  A check drawn by an individual on his or her own account but bearing a guaranty (acceptance) by a bank that the bank will pay the check regardless of whether the drawer's account contains adequate funds at the time the check is presented.

**Chancellor**  An advisor to the king at the time of the early King's Courts of England. Individuals petitioned the king for relief when they could not obtain an adequate remedy in a court of law, and these petitions were decided by the chancellor.

**Charging order**  In partnership law, an order granted by a court to a judgment creditor that entitles the creditor to attach profits or assets of a partner upon dissolution of the partnership.

**Charitable trust**  A trust in which the property held by a trustee must be used for a charitable purpose, such as the advancement of health, education, or religion.

**Chattel**  A tangible piece of personal property or an intangible right therein.

**Chattel paper**  Any writing or writings that show both a debt and the fact that the debt is secured by personal property. In many instances, chattel paper consists of a negotiable instrument coupled with a security agreement.

**Check**  A draft drawn by a drawer ordering the drawee bank or financial institution to pay a certain amount of money to the holder on demand.

**Checks and balances**  The national government is composed of three separate branches: the executive, the legislative, and the judicial. Each branch of the government exercises a check upon the actions of the others.

**Choice-of-language clause**  A clause in a contract designating the official language by which the contract will be interpreted in the event of a future disagreement over the contract's terms.

**Choice-of-law clause**  A clause in a contract designating the law that will govern the contract. For example, two contracting parties from different countries may choose the law of a third country to govern their agreement.

**Citation**  A citation indicates where a particular constitutional provision, statute, reported case, or article may be found; also an order for a defendant to appear in court or indicating that a person has violated a legal rule.

**Civil law**  The branch of law dealing with the definition and enforcement of all private or public rights, as opposed to criminal matters.

**Civil law system**  A system of law derived from that of the Roman Empire and based on a code rather than case law; the predominant system of law in the nations of continental Europe and the nations that were once their colonies. In the United States, Louisiana is the only state that has a civil law system.

**Close corporation**  A corporation whose shareholders are limited to a small group of persons, often including only family members. The rights of shareholders of a close corporation usually are restricted regarding the transfer of shares to others.

**Closed shop**  A firm that requires union membership by its workers as a condition of employment. The closed shop was made illegal by the Taft-Hartley Act of 1947.

**Closing**  The final step in the sale of real estate—also called settlement or closing escrow. The escrow agent coordinates the closing with the recording of deeds, the obtaining of title insurance, and other concurrent closing activities. Several costs must be paid, in cash, at the time of closing, and they can range from several hundred to several thousand dollars, depending on the amount of the mortgage loan and other conditions of sale.

**Closing argument**  An argument made after the plaintiff and defendant have rested their cases. Closing arguments are made prior to the jury charges.

**Codicil**  A written supplement or modification to a will. Codicils must be executed with the same formalities as a will.

**Collateral**  In a broad sense, any property used as security for a loan. Under the UCC, property of a debtor in which a creditor has an interest or a right.

**Collateral promise**  A secondary promise that is ancillary to a principal transaction or primary contractual relationship, such as a promise made by one person to pay the debts or discharge the duties of another if the latter fails to perform. A collateral promise normally must be in writing to be enforceable.

**Collecting bank** Any bank handling an item for collection, except the payor bank.

**Collective bargaining** The process by which labor and management negotiate the terms and conditions of employment, including such things as hours and workplace conditions.

**Collective mark** A mark used by members of a cooperative, association, or other organization to certify the region, materials, mode of manufacture, quality, or accuracy of the specific goods or services. Examples of collective marks include the labor union marks found on tags of certain products and the credits of movies, which indicate the various associations and organizations that participated in the making of the movies.

**Comity** A deference by which one nation gives effect to the laws and judicial decrees of another nation. This recognition is based primarily upon respect.

**Comment period** A period of time following an administrative agency's publication of a notice of a proposed rule during which private parties may comment in writing on the agency proposal in an effort to influence agency policy. The agency takes any comments received into consideration when drafting the final version of the regulation.

**Commerce clause** The provision in Article I, Section 8, of the U.S. Constitution that gives Congress exclusive powers over interstate commerce.

**Commercial impracticability** A doctrine under which a seller may be excused from performing a contract when (1) a contingency occurs, (2) the contingency's occurrence makes performance impracticable, and (3) the nonoccurrence of the contingency was a basic assumption on which the contract was made. Despite the fact that UCC 2–615 expressly frees only sellers under this doctrine, courts have not distinguished between buyers and sellers in applying it.

**Commercial paper** Under UCC Article 3, negotiable instruments (signed writings that contain an unconditional promise or order to pay an exact sum of money, either when demanded or at an exact future time), including drafts, promissory notes, certificates of deposit, and checks.

**Commingle** To put funds or goods together into one mass so that the funds or goods are so mixed that they no longer have separate identities.

**Common areas** In landlord-tenant law, the portion of the premises over which the landlord retains control and maintenance responsibilities. Common areas may include stairs, lobbies, garages, hallways, and other areas in common use.

**Common law** That body of law developed from custom or judicial decisions in English and U.S. courts, not attributable to a legislature.

**Common stock** Shares of ownership in a corporation that are lowest in priority with respect to payment of dividends and distribution of the corporation's assets upon dissolution.

**Community property** A form of concurrent ownership of property in which each spouse owns an undivided one-half interest in property. This type of ownership applies to most property acquired by the husband or wife during the course of marriage. It generally does not apply to property acquired prior to the marriage or to property acquired by gift or inheritance during the marriage. After a divorce, community property is divided equally in some states and according to the discretion of the court in other states.

**Comparative negligence** A theory in tort law under which the liability for injuries resulting from negligent acts is shared by all persons who were guilty of negligence (including the injured party), on the basis of each person's proportionate carelessness.

**Compensatory damages** A money award equivalent to the actual value of injuries or damages sustained by the aggrieved party.

**Complaint** The pleading made by a plaintiff or a charge made by the state alleging wrongdoing on the part of the defendant.

**Computer crime** Any wrongful act that is directed against computers and computer parts, or wrongful use or abuse of computers or software.

**Conciliation** A form of alternative dispute resolution in which the parties reach an agreement themselves with the help of a neutral third party, called a conciliator, who facilitates the negotiations.

**Concurrent conditions** Conditions that must occur or be performed at the same time; they are mutually dependent. No obligations arise until these conditions are simultaneously performed.

**Concurrent jurisdiction** Jurisdiction that exists when two different courts have the power to hear a case. For example, some cases can be heard in a federal or state court.

**Concurrent ownership** Joint ownership.

**Condition** A qualification, provision, or clause in a contractual agreement, the occurrence of which creates, suspends, or terminates the obligations of the contracting parties.

**Condition precedent** In a contractual agreement, a condition that must be met before the other party's obligations arise.

**Condition subsequent** A condition in a contract that, if not met, discharges an existing obligation of the other party.

**Confession of judgment** A judgment entered against a debtor by a creditor, with the debtor's permission and for an agreed sum, without the use of legal proceedings.

**Confiscation** A government's taking of privately owned business or personal property without a proper public purpose or an award of just compensation.

**Conforming goods** Goods that conform to contract specifications.

**Confusion**  The mixing together of goods belonging to two or more owners so that the independent goods cannot be identified.

**Conglomerate merger**  A merger between firms that do not compete with each other because they are in different markets (as opposed to horizontal and vertical mergers).

**Consent**  Voluntary agreement to a proposition or an act of another. A concurrence of wills.

**Consequential damages**  Special damages that compensate for a loss that is not direct or immediate (for example, lost profits). The special damages must have been reasonably foreseeable at the time the breach or injury occurred in order for the plaintiff to collect them.

**Consideration**  That which motivates the exchange of promises or performance in a contractual agreement. The consideration, which must be present to make the contract legally binding, must result in a detriment to the promisee (something of legal value, legally sufficient, and bargained for) or a benefit to the promisor.

**Consignment**  A transaction in which an owner of goods (the consignor) delivers the goods to another (the consignee) for the consignee to sell. The consignee pays the consignor for the goods when the consignee sells the goods.

**Consolidation**  A contractual and statutory process whereby two or more corporations join to become a completely new corporation. The original corporations cease to exist, and the new corporation acquires all their assets and liabilities.

**Constructive delivery**  An act equivalent to the actual, physical delivery of property that cannot be physically delivered because of difficulty or impossibility; to illustrate, the transfer of a key to a safe constructively delivers the contents of the safe.

**Constructive eviction**  Depriving a person of the possession of rental property that he or she leases by rendering the premises unfit or unsuitable for occupancy.

**Constructive trust**  A trust created by operation of law against one who wrongfully has obtained or holds a legal right to property that the person should not, in equity and good conscience, hold and enjoy.

**Consumer law**  Statutes, agency rules, and judicial decisions protecting consumers of goods and services from dangerous manufacturing techniques, mislabeling, unfair credit practices, deceptive advertising, and so on. Consumer laws provide remedies and protections that are not ordinarily available to merchants or to businesses.

**Consumer-debtors**  Debtors whose debts are primarily consumer debts—that is, debts for purchases that are primarily for household or personal use.

**Continuation statement**  A statement that, if filed within six months prior to the expiration date of the original financing statement, continues the effectiveness of the original statement for another five years. The effectiveness of a financing statement can be continued in the same manner indefinitely.

**Contract**  A set of promises constituting an agreement between parties, giving each a legal duty to the other and also the right to seek a remedy for the breach of the promises/duties owed to each. The elements of an enforceable contract are competent parties, a proper or legal purpose, consideration (an exchange of promises/duties), and mutuality of agreement and of obligation.

**Contract under seal**  A formal agreement in which the seal is a substitute for consideration. A court will not invalidate a contract under seal for lack of consideration.

**Contractual capacity**  The threshold mental capacity required by the law for a party who enters into a contract to be bound by that contract.

**Contributory negligence**  A theory in tort law under which a complaining party's own negligence contributed to or caused his or her injuries. Contributory negligence is an absolute bar to recovery in a minority of jurisdictions.

**Conversion**  The wrongful taking or retaining possession of personal property that belongs to another.

**Conveyance**  The transfer of a title to land from one person to another by deed; a document (such as a deed or a mortgage) by which an interest in land is transferred from one person to another.

**Conviction**  The outcome of a criminal trial in which the defendant has been found guilty of the crime charged and on which sentencing, or punishment, is based.

**Cooperative**  An association that is organized to provide an economic service to its members (or shareholders). An incorporated cooperative is a nonprofit corporation. It will make distributions of dividends, or profits, to its owners on the basis of their transactions with the cooperative rather than on the basis of the amount of capital they contributed. Examples of cooperatives are consumer purchasing cooperatives, credit cooperatives, and farmers' cooperatives.

**Copyright**  The exclusive right of ''authors'' to publish, print, or sell an intellectual production for a statutory period of time. A copyright has the same monopolistic nature as a patent or trademark, but it differs in that it applies exclusively to works of art, literature, and other works of authorship (including computer programs).

**Corporate charter**  The document issued by a state official (usually the secretary of state) granting a corporation legal existence and the right to function.

**Corporation**  A legal entity created under the authority of the laws of a state or the federal government. The entity is distinct from its shareholders/owners.

**Cosign**  The act of signing a document (such as a note promising to pay another in return for a loan or other benefit) jointly with another person and thereby assuming liability for performing what was promised in the document.

**Cost-benefit analysis**  A way to reach decisions in which the costs of a given action are compared with the benefits of the action.

**Co-surety**   A joint surety. One who assumes liability jointly with another surety for the payment of an obligation.

**Counteradvertising**   New advertising that is undertaken pursuant to a Federal Trade Commission order for the purpose of correcting earlier false claims that were made about a product.

**Counterclaim**   A claim made by a defendant in a civil lawsuit that in effect sues the plaintiff; it can be based on entirely different grounds than those given in the plaintiff's complaint.

**Counteroffer**   An offeree's response to an offer in which the offeree rejects the original offer and at the same time makes a new offer.

**Course of dealing**   A sequence of previous conduct between the parties to a particular transaction that establishes a common basis for their understanding.

**Course of performance**   The conduct that occurs under the terms of a particular agreement; such conduct indicates what the parties to an agreement intended it to mean.

**Court of equity**   A court that decides controversies and administers justice according to the rules, principles, and precedents of equity.

**Court of law**   A court in which the only remedies that could be granted were things of value, such as money damages. In the early English King's Court, courts of law were distinct from courts of equity.

**Covenant not to compete**   A contractual promise to refrain from competing with another party for a certain period of time (not excessive in duration) and within a reasonable geographic area. Although covenants not to compete restrain trade, they are commonly found in partnership agreements, business sale agreements, and employment contracts. If they are ancillary to such agreements, covenants not to compete will normally be enforced by the courts unless the time period or geographic area is deemed unreasonable.

**Covenant not to sue**   An agreement to substitute a contractual obligation for some other type of action.

**Covenant running with the land**   An executory promise made between a grantor and a grantee to which they and subsequent owners of the land are bound.

**Cover**   Under the UCC, a remedy of the buyer that allows the buyer, on the seller's breach, to purchase the goods from another seller and substitute them for the goods due under the contract. If the cost of cover exceeds the cost of the contract goods, the breaching seller will be liable to the buyer for the difference.

**Cram-down provision**   A provision of the Bankruptcy Code that allows a court to confirm a debtor's Chapter 11 reorganization plan even though only one class of creditors has accepted it. To exercise the court's right under this provision, the court must demonstrate that the plan does not discriminate unfairly against any creditors and is fair and equitable.

**Crashworthiness doctrine**   A doctrine that imposes liability for defects in the design or construction of motor vehicles that increase the extent of injuries to passengers if an accident occurs. The doctrine holds even when the defects do not actually cause the accident.

**Creditors' composition agreement**   An agreement formed between a debtor and his or her creditors in which the creditors agree to accept a lesser sum than that owed by the debtor in full satisfaction of the debt.

**Crime**   A broad term for violations of law that are punishable by the state and are codified by legislatures. The objective of criminal law is to protect the public.

**Criminal law**   Law that governs and defines those actions that are crimes and that subject the convicted offender to punishment imposed by the government.

**Cross-examination**   The questioning of an opposing witness during the trial.

**Cure**   The right of a party who tenders nonconforming performance to correct his or her performance within the contract period [UCC 3–508].

# D

**Damages**   Money sought as a remedy for a breach of contract or for a tortious act.

**Debtor**   A person who owes a sum of money or other obligations to another.

**Debtor in possession (DIP)**   In Chapter 11 bankruptcy proceedings, a debtor who is allowed, for the benefit of all concerned, to continue in possession of the estate in bankruptcy (the business) and to continue business operations.

**Deed**   A document by which title to property (usually real property) is passed.

**Defalcation**   The misuse of funds.

**Defamation**   Anything published or publicly spoken that causes injury to another's good name, reputation, or character.

**Default**   The failure to observe a promise or discharge an obligation. The term is commonly used to mean the failure to pay a debt when it is due.

**Default judgment**   A judgment entered by a clerk or court against a party who has failed to appear in court to answer or defend against a claim that has been brought against him or her by another party.

**Defendant**   One against whom a lawsuit is brought; the accused person in a criminal proceeding.

**Defense**   That which a defendant offers and alleges in an action or suit as a reason why the plaintiff should not recover or establish what he or she seeks.

**Deficiency judgment**   A judgment against a debtor for the amount of a debt remaining unpaid after collateral has been repossessed and sold or after foreclosure proceedings.

**Delegation**   The transfer of a contractual duty to a third party. The party delegating the duty (the delegator) to the third party (the delegatee) is still obliged to perform on the contract should the delegatee fail to perform.

**Delegation doctrine**   A doctrine based on Article I, Section 8, of the U.S. Constitution, which has been construed to allow Congress to delegate some of its power to make and implement laws to administrative agencies. The delegation is considered to be proper as long as Congress sets standards outlining the scope of the agency's authority.

**Delivery order**   A written order to deliver goods directed to a warehouser, carrier, or other person who, in the ordinary course of business, issues warehouse receipts or bills of lading [UCC 7–102(1)(d)].

**Demand deposit**   Funds (accepted by a bank) subject to immediate withdrawal, in contrast to a time deposit, which requires that a depositor wait a specific time before withdrawing or pay a penalty for early withdrawal.

**Depositary bank**   The first bank to which an item is transferred for collection, even though it may also be the payor bank.

**Deposition**   A generic term that refers to any evidence verified by oath. As a legal term, it is often limited to the testimony of a witness taken under oath before a trial, with the opportunity of cross-examination.

**Destination contract**   A contract for the sale of goods in which the seller assumes liability for any losses or damage to the goods until they are tendered at the destination specified in the contract.

**Devise**   To make a gift of real property by will.

**Direct examination**   The examination of a witness by the attorney who calls the witness to the stand to testify on behalf of the attorney's client.

**Disaffirmance**   The repudiation of an obligation.

**Discharge**   The termination of one's obligation. In contract law, discharge occurs when the parties have fully performed their contractual obligations or when events, conduct of the parties, or operation of the law releases the parties from further performance.

**Discharge in bankruptcy**   The release of a debtor from all debts that are provable, except those specifically excepted from discharge by statute.

**Disclosed principal**   A principal whose identity and existence as a principal is known by a third person at the time a transaction is conducted by an agent.

**Discovery**   A method by which opposing parties may obtain information from each other to prepare for trial. Generally governed by rules of procedure, but may be controlled by the court.

**Disparagement of property**   Economically injurious falsehoods made about another's product or property. A general term for torts that are more specifically referred to as slander of quality or slander of title.

**Disparate-impact discrimination**   In an employment context, discrimination that results from certain employer practices or procedures that, although not discriminatory on their face, have a discriminatory effect. For example, a requirement that all employees have high school diplomas is not necessarily discriminatory, but it may have the effect of discriminating against minority groups.

**Disparate-treatment discrimination**   In an employment context, intentional discrimination against indi-

viduals on the basis of color, gender, national origin, race, or religion.

**Dissolution**   The formal disbanding of a partnership or a corporation. It can take place by (1) agreement of the parties or the shareholders and board of directors, (2) the death of a partner, (3) the expiration of a time period stated in a partnership agreement or a certificate of incorporation, or (4) court order.

**Distribution agreement**   A contract between a seller and a distributor of the seller's products setting out the terms and conditions of the distributorship.

**Diversity of citizenship**   Under Article III, Section 2, of the Constitution, a basis for federal court jurisdiction over a lawsuit between citizens of different states.

**Divestiture**   The act of selling one or more of a company's parts, such as a subsidiary or plant; often mandated by the courts in merger or monopolization cases.

**Dividend**   A distribution to corporate shareholders, disbursed in proportion to the number of shares held.

**Docket**   The list of cases entered on a court's calendar and thus scheduled to be heard by the court.

**Document of title**   Paper exchanged in the regular course of business that evidences the right to possession of goods (for example, a bill of lading or warehouse receipt).

**Domestic corporation**   In a given state, a corporation that does business in, and is organized under the laws of, that state.

**Double jeopardy**   Jeopardy is the risk of conviction or punishment. A second prosecution for the same criminal offense (again placing a person in jeopardy) violates the Fifth Amendment of the U.S. Constitution.

**Draft**   Any instrument drawn on a drawee (such as a bank) that orders the drawee to pay a certain sum of money.

**Dram shop acts**   State statutes that impose liability on the owners of bars and taverns, as well as those who serve alcoholic drinks to the public, for injuries resulting from accidents caused by intoxicated persons when the sellers or servers of alcoholic drinks contributed to the intoxication.

**Drawee**   The person who is ordered to pay a draft or check. With a check, a financial institution is always the drawee.

**Drawer**   A person who initiates a draft (including a check), thereby ordering the drawee to pay.

**Due diligence**   A required standard of care that certain professionals, such as accountants, must meet to avoid liability for securities violations. Under securities law, an accountant will be deemed to have exercised due diligence if he or she followed generally accepted accounting principles and generally accepted auditing standards and had, ''after reasonable investigation, reasonable grounds to believe and did believe, at the time such part of the registration statement became effective, that the statements therein were true and that there was no omission of a material fact required to be stated therein or necessary to make the statements therein not misleading.''

**Due negotiation**   The transfer of a document of title in such form that the transferee becomes a holder [UCC 7–501].

**Due process clause**   The provisions of the Fifth and Fourteenth Amendments to the Constitution provide that no person shall be deprived of life, liberty, or property without due process of law (fair and just reason and procedure). Similar clauses are found in most state constitutions.

**Dumping**   Selling goods in a foreign country at a price below the price charged for the same goods in the domestic market.

**Duress**   Unlawful pressure brought to bear on a person, overcoming that person's free will and causing him or her to do (or refrain from doing) what he or she otherwise would not (or would) have done.

**Duty of care**   The duty of all persons, as established by tort law, to exercise a reasonable amount of care in their dealings with others. Failure to exercise due care, which is normally determined by the ''reasonable person standard,'' constitutes the tort of negligence.

# E

**Easement**   A nonpossessory right to use another's property in a manner established by either express or implied agreement.

**Eighty-day cooling-off period**   A provision of the Taft-Hartley Act that allows federal courts to issue injunctions against strikes that might create a national emergency.

**Ejectment**   The eviction of a tenant from leased premises. A remedy at common law to which the landlord can resort when a tenant fails to pay rent for leased premises. To obtain possession of the premises, the landlord must appear in court and show that the defaulting tenant is in wrongful possession.

**Electronic fund transfer (EFT)**   A transfer of funds with the use of an electronic terminal, a telephone, a computer, or magnetic tape.

**Electronic fund transfer system (EFTS)**   A system used to transfer funds electronically.

**Embezzlement**   The fraudulent appropriation of money or other property by a person to whom the money or property has been entrusted.

**Eminent domain**   The power of a government to take land for public use from private citizens for just compensation.

**Employment-at-will doctrine**   A common law doctrine under which employer-employee contracts are considered to be ''at will''—that is, either party may terminate an employment contract at any time and for any reason, unless the contract specifies otherwise. Although several states still adhere to the employment-at-will doctrine, exceptions are frequently made on the basis of an implied employment contract or public policy.

**Employment discrimination**   Treating employees or job applicants unequally on the basis of race, sex, nationality, religion, or age; prohibited by Title VII of the Civil Rights Act of 1964 as amended.

**Enabling legislation**   Statutes enacted by Congress that authorize the creation of an administrative agency and specify the name, composition, and powers of the agency being created.

**Endowment insurance**   A type of insurance that combines life insurance with an investment so that if the insured outlives the policy, the face value is paid to him or her; if the insured does not outlive the policy, the face value is paid to his or her beneficiary.

**Entrapment**   In criminal law, a defense in which the defendant claims that he or she was induced by a public official—usually an undercover agent or police officer—to commit a crime that he or she would otherwise not have committed.

**Entrepreneur**   One who initiates and assumes the financial risks of a new enterprise and who undertakes to provide or control its management.

**Entrustment**   The transfer of goods to a merchant who deals in goods of that kind and who may transfer those goods and all rights to them to a buyer in the ordinary course of business [UCC 2–403(2)].

**Environmental impact statement (EIS)**   A statement required by the National Environmental Policy Act for any major federal action that will significantly affect the quality of the environment. The statement must analyze the action's impact on the environment and alternative actions that might be taken.

**Environmental law**   All statutory, regulatory, and common law relating to the protection of the environment.

**Equal dignity rule**   In most states, a rule stating that express authority given to an agent must be in writing if the contract to be made on behalf of the principal is required to be in writing.

**Equal protection clause**   The clause in the Fourteenth Amendment to the Constitution that guarantees that no state will ''deny to any person within its jurisdiction the equal protection of the laws.'' This clause mandates that the state governments treat similarly situated individuals in a similar manner.

**Equitable maxims**   Propositions, general statements, or principles of law that are frequently involved in equity jurisdiction.

**Equitable servitudes**   Restrictions on the use of land that are enforceable in a court of equity.

**Equity of redemption**   The right of a mortgagor who has breached the mortgage agreement to redeem or purchase the property prior to foreclosure proceedings.

**Escheat**   The transfer of property to the state when the owner of the property dies without heirs.

**Escrow account**   An account that is generally held in the name of the depositor and escrow agent; the funds in the account are paid to a third person only upon fulfillment of the escrow condition.

**Establishment clause**   The clause in the First Amendment to the Constitution that prohibits Congress from creating any law ''respecting an establishment of religion.''

**Estop**    To bar, impede, or preclude.

**Estray statutes**    Statutes dealing with finders' rights in property when the true owners are unknown.

**Ethics**    Moral principles and values applied to social behavior.

**Eviction**    Depriving a person of the possession of land or rental property that he or she owns or leases.

*Ex parte* **contact**    Communication with an administrative agency that are not placed in the record.

**Exclusionary rule**    In criminal procedure, a rule under which any evidence that is obtained in violation of the accused's constitutional rights guaranteed by the Fourth, Fifth, and Sixth Amendments, as well as any evidence derived from illegally obtained evidence, will not be admissible in court.

**Exclusive distributorship**    A distributorship in which the seller and distributor of the seller's products agree that the distributor has the exclusive right to distribute the seller's products in a certain geographic area.

**Exclusive jurisdiction**    Jurisdiction that exists when a case can be heard only in a particular court.

**Exclusive-dealing contract**    An agreement under which a producer of goods agrees to sell its goods exclusively through one distributor.

**Exculpatory clause**    A clause that releases a party (to a contract) from liability for his or her wrongful acts.

**Executed contract**    A contract that has been completely performed by both parties.

**Execution**    An action to carry into effect the directions in a decree or judgment; otherwise stated, an official carrying out of a court's order or judgment.

**Executive agency**    An administrative agency (or subagency) within a cabinet department of the executive branch of the government.

**Executor**    A person appointed by a testator to see that his or her will is administered appropriately.

**Executory contract**    A contract that has not as yet been fully performed.

**Executory interest**    A future interest, held by a person other than the grantor, that either cuts short or begins some time after the natural termination of the preceding estate.

**Export**    To sell products to buyers located in other countries.

**Express authority**    Authority expressly given by one party to another. In agency law, an agent has express authority to act for a principal if both parties agree, orally or in writing, that an agency relationship exists in which the agent had the power (authority) to act in the place of, and on behalf of, the principal.

**Express contract**    A contract that is oral and/or written (as opposed to an implied contract).

**Express warranty**    A promise, ancillary to an underlying sales agreement, that is included in the written or oral terms of the sales agreement under which the promisor assures the quality, description, or performance of the goods.

**Expropriation**    The seizure by a government of privately owned business or personal property for a proper public purpose and with just compensation.

**Extension clause**    A clause in a time instrument extending the instrument's date of maturity. An extension clause is the reverse of an acceleration clause.

# F

**Federal Reserve System**    A network of twelve central banks headed by a board of governors, with the advice of the Federal Advisory Council and the Federal Open Market Committee, to give the United States an elastic currency, supervise and regulate banking activities, and facilitate the flow and discounting of commercial paper. All national banks and state-chartered banks that voluntarily join the system are members.

**Federal Rules of Civil Procedure (FRCP)**    The rules controlling all procedural matters in civil trials brought before the federal district courts.

**Federal question**    A question that pertains to the U.S. Constitution, acts of Congress, or treaties. A federal question provides jurisdiction for federal courts. This jurisdiction arises from Article III, Section 2, of the Constitution.

**Federal system**    A system of government in which power is divided by a written constitution between a central government and regional, or subdivisional, governments. Each level must have some domain in which its policies are dominant and some genuine political or constitutional guarantee of its authority.

**Federalism**    A system of government in which power is divided by a written constitution between a central government and regional, or subdivisional, governments. Each level must have some domain in which its policies are dominant and some genuine political or constitutional guarantee of its authority. The United States has a federal government in which power is shared between the central government and the state governments.

**Fee simple**    A form of property ownership entitling the property owner to use, possess, or dispose of the property as he or she chooses during his or her lifetime. Upon death, the interest in the property descends to the owner's heirs.

**Fee simple absolute**    An estate or interest in land with no time, disposition, or descendibility limitations.

**Fee simple defeasible**    An estate that can be taken away (by the prior grantor) upon the occurrence or nonoccurrence of a specified event.

**Felony**    A crime—such as arson, murder, rape, or robbery—that carries the most severe sanctions, usually ranging from one year in a state or federal prison to the forfeiture of one's life.

**Fictitious payee**    A payee on a negotiable instrument whom the maker or drawer does not intend to have an interest in the instrument. Indorsements by fictitious payees are not forgeries under negotiable instruments law.

**Fiduciary**  As a noun, a person having a duty created by his or her undertaking to act primarily for another's benefit in matters connected with the undertaking. As an adjective, a relationship founded upon trust and confidence.

**Fiduciary relationship**  A relationship founded upon trust and confidence.

**Final order**  The final decision of an administrative agency on an issue. If no appeal is taken, or if the case is not reviewed or considered anew by the agency commission, the administrative law judge's initial order becomes the final order of the agency.

**Financial institutions**  Organizations authorized to do business under state or federal laws relating to financial institutions. For example, under the Electronic Fund Transfer Act, financial institutions include banks, savings and loan associations, credit unions, and any other business entities that directly or indirectly hold accounts belonging to consumers.

**Financing statement**  A document prepared by a secured creditor, and filed with the appropriate state or local official, to give notice to the public that the creditor claims an interest in collateral belonging to a certain named debtor. The financing statement must be signed by the debtor, contain the addresses of both the debtor and creditor, and describe the collateral by type or item.

**Firm offer**  An offer (by a merchant) that is irrevocable without consideration for a period of time (not longer than three months). A firm offer by a merchant must be in writing and must be signed by the offeror.

**Fixture**  A thing that was once personal property but that has become attached to real property in such a way that it takes on the characteristics of real property and becomes part of that real property.

**Float time**  The time between the issuance of a check and the deduction of the amount of the check from the drawer's account.

**Floating lien**  A security interest retained in collateral even when the collateral changes in character, classification, or location.

**Force majeure clause**  A clause in a contract stipulating that certain unforeseen events—such as war, political upheavals, acts of God, or other events—will excuse a party from liability for nonperformance of contractual obligations.

**Foreign corporation**  In a given state, a corporation that does business in the state without being incorporated therein.

**Forfeiture**  The termination of a lease, according to its terms or the terms of a statute, when one of the parties fails to fulfill a condition under the lease and thereby breaches it.

**Forgery**  The false or unauthorized signature of a document, or the false making of a document, with the intent to defraud.

**Formal contract**  An agreement or contract that by law requires for its validity a specific form, such as executed under seal.

**Formal rulemaking**  Agency rulemaking that is much more extensive than informal rulemaking and in which a public hearing is conducted in the manner of a trial. After the hearing is concluded, the agency is required to prepare a formal written statement describing its findings based on the evidence presented by both sides. Also referred to as rulemaking-on-a-record.

**Forum**  A jurisdiction, court, or place in which disputes are litigated and legal remedies are sought.

**Forum-selection clause**  A clause in a contract designating the forum (the nation, state, or jurisdiction) in which a dispute will be litigated.

**Franchise**  A written agreement whereby an owner of a trademark, trade name, or copyright licenses another to use that trademark, trade name, or copyright, under specified conditions or limitations, in the selling of goods and services.

**Franchisee**  One receiving a license to use another's (the franchisor's) trademark, trade name, or copyright in the sale of goods and services.

**Franchisor**  One licensing another (the franchisee) to use his or her trademark, trade name, or copyright in the sale of goods or services.

**Fraud**  Any misrepresentation, either by misstatement or omission of a material fact, knowingly made with the intention of deceiving another and on which a reasonable person would and does rely to his or her detriment.

**Free exercise clause**  The clause in the First Amendment to the Constitution that prohibits Congress from making any law "prohibiting the free exercise" of religion.

**Frustration of purpose**  A court-created doctrine under which a party to a contract will be relieved of his or her duty to perform when the objective purpose for performance no longer exists (due to reasons beyond that party's control).

**Fungible goods**  Goods that are alike by physical nature, by agreement, or by trade usage. Examples of fungible goods are wheat, oil, and wine that are identical in type and quality.

**Future interest**  An interest in real property that is not at present possessory but will or may be possessory in the future. Remainders and reversions are future interests.

# G

**Garnishment**  A legal process whereby a creditor appropriates the debtor's property or wages that are in the hands of a third party.

**General partner**  In a limited partnership, a partner who assumes responsibility for the management of the partnership and liability for all partnership debts.

**Generally accepted accounting principles (GAAP)**  The conventions, rules, and procedures necessary to define accepted accounting practices at a particular time. The source of the principles is the Federal Accounting Standards Board.

**Generally accepted auditing standards (GAAS)** Standards concerning an auditor's professional qualities and the judgment exercised by him or her in the performance of an examination and report. The source of the standards is the American Institute of Certified Public Accountants.

**Genuineness of assent** Knowing and voluntary assent to the terms of a contract. If a contract is formed as a result of a mistake, misrepresentation, undue influence, or duress, genuineness of assent is lacking, and the contract will be voidable.

**Gift** Any voluntary transfer of property made without consideration, past or present.

**Gift *causa mortis*** A gift made in contemplation of death. If the donor does not die of that ailment, the gift is revoked.

**Gift *inter vivos*** A gift made during one's lifetime and not in contemplation of imminent death, in contrast to a gift causa mortis.

**Good Samaritan statutes** State statutes that provide that persons who provide emergency services to, or rescue, others in peril—unless they do so recklessly, thus causing further harm—cannot be sued for negligence.

**Good faith purchaser** A purchaser who buys without notice of any circumstance that would put a person of ordinary prudence on inquiry as to whether the seller has valid title to the goods being sold.

**Grant deed** A deed that simply recites words of consideration and conveyance. Under statute, a grant deed may impliedly warrant that at least the grantor has not conveyed the property's title to someone else.

**Group boycott** The boycott of a particular person or firm by a group of competitors; prohibited under the Sherman Act.

**Guarantor** One who agrees to satisfy the debt of another (the debtor) only if and when the debtor fails to pay the debt. A guarantor's liability is thus secondary.

# H

**Hearsay** An oral or written statement made out of court that is later offered in court by a witness (not the person who made the statement) to prove the truth of the matter asserted in the statement. Hearsay is generally inadmissible as evidence.

**Herfindahl-Hirschman Index (HHI)** An index of market power used to calculate whether a merger of two corporations will result in monopoly power and thus violate antitrust laws.

**Holder** A person "who is in possession of a document of title or negotiable instrument or a certificated investment security drawn, issued, or indorsed to him or his order or to bearer or in blank" [UCC 1–201(20)].

**Holder in due course** Any holder who acquires a negotiable instrument for value; in good faith; and without notice that the instrument is overdue, that it

has been dishonored, or that any defense or claim to it exists on the part of any person.

**Holographic will** A will written entirely in the signer's handwriting and usually not witnessed.

**Homestead exemption** A law allowing an owner to designate his or her house and adjoining land as a homestead and thus exempt it from liability for his or her general debt.

**Horizontal merger** A merger between two businesses or persons competing in the marketplace.

**Horizontal restraint** Any agreement that in some way restrains competition between rival firms competing in the same market. Price fixing and horizontal market division are examples of horizontal restraints on competition.

**Hot-cargo agreement** An agreement in which employers voluntarily agree with unions not to handle, use, or deal in non-union-produced goods of other employers. A type of secondary boycott explicitly prohibited by the Landrum-Griffin Act of 1959.

**Hung jury** A jury whose members are so irreconcilably divided in their opinions that they cannot come to a verdict by the requisite number of jurors. The judge in this situation may order a new trial.

**Hybrid rulemaking** A set of loosely defined procedures for agency rulemaking that incorporate advantages of both the formal and informal procedures. As with formal rulemaking, there is an opportunity for direct participation through a public hearing, but the right of interested parties to cross-examine witnesses is much more restricted.

# I

**Identification** Proof that a thing is what it is purported or represented to be. In the sale of goods, the express designation of the goods provided for in the contract.

**Implied authority** Authority that is created not by an explicit oral or written agreement but by implication. In agency law, implied authority (of the agent) can be conferred by custom, inferred from the position the agent occupies, or implied by virtue of being reasonably necessary to carry out express authority.

**Implied warranty** A warranty that the law implies through either the situation of the parties or the nature of the transaction.

**Implied warranty of fitness for a particular purpose** A presumed promise made by a merchant seller of goods that the goods are fit for the particular purpose for which the buyer will use the goods. The seller must know the buyer's purpose and know that the buyer is relying on the seller's skill and judgment to select suitable goods.

**Implied warranty of habitability** A presumed promise by the landlord that rented residential premises are fit for human habitation—that is, free of violations of building and sanitary codes.

**Implied warranty of merchantability** A presumed promise by a merchant seller of goods that the goods are reasonably fit for the general purpose for which they are sold, are properly packaged and labeled, and are of proper quality.

**Implied-in-fact contract** A contract formed in whole or in part from the conduct of the parties (as opposed to an express contract).

**Impossibility of performance** A doctrine under which a party to a contract is relieved of his or her duty to perform when performance becomes impossible or totally impracticable (through no fault of either party).

**Imposter** One who, with the intent to deceive, pretends to be somebody else.

*In pari delicto* At equal fault.

*In personam jurisdiction* Court jurisdiction over the ''person'' involved in a legal action.

*In rem* **jurisdiction** Court jurisdiction over a defendant's property.

**Incidental beneficiary** A third party who incidentally benefits from a contract but whose benefit was not the reason the contract was formed; an incidental beneficiary has no rights in a contract and cannot sue the promisor if the contract is breached.

**Incidental damages** Damages resulting from a breach of contract, including all reasonable expenses incurred because of the breach.

**Incoterms** International shipping terms, such as FOB (free on board), that define the responsibilities of buyers and sellers, including when risk of loss passes from one party to the other.

**Independent contractor** One who works for, and receives payment from, an employer but whose working conditions and methods are not controlled by the employer. An independent contractor is not an employee but may be an agent.

**Independent regulatory agency** An administrative agency that is not considered part of the government's executive branch and is not subject to the authority of the president. Agency officials cannot be removed without cause.

**Indictment** A charge or written accusation, issued by a grand jury, that a named person has committed a crime.

**Indorsee** The one to whom a negotiable instrument is transferred by indorsement.

**Indorsement** A signature placed on an instrument or a document of title for the purpose of transferring one's ownership in the instrument or document of title.

**Indorser** One who, being the payee or holder of a negotiable instrument, signs his or her name on the back of it.

**Informal contract** A contract that does not require a specified form or formality for its validity.

**Informal rulemaking** A procedure in agency rulemaking that requires (1) notice; (2) opportunity for comment; and (3) a general statement of the basis for, and purpose of, the proposed rule. Also referred to as notice-and-comment rulemaking.

**Information** A formal accusation or complaint (without an indictment) issued in certain types of actions by a prosecuting attorney or other law officer, such as a magistrate. The types of actions are set forth in the rules of states or in the Federal Rules of Criminal Procedure.

**Information return** A tax return submitted by a partnership that only reports the income earned by the business. The partnership as an entity does not pay taxes on the income received by the partnership. A partner's profit from the partnership (whether distributed or not) is taxed as individual income to the individual partner.

**Initial order** In the context of administrative law, an agency's disposition in a matter other than a rulemaking. An administrative law judge's initial order becomes final unless it is appealed.

**Injunction** A court decree ordering a person to do, or refrain from doing, a certain act or activity.

**Innkeeper's lien** A possessory or statutory lien allowing the innkeeper to take the personal property of a guest, brought into the hotel, as security for nonpayment of the guest's bill (debt).

**Innocent misrepresentation** A false statement of fact or an act made in good faith that deceives and causes harm or injury to another.

**Insider** A corporate director or officer, or other employee or agent, with access to confidential information and a duty not to disclose that information in violation of insider-trading laws.

**Insider trading** Purchasing or selling securities on the basis of information that has not been made available to the public.

**Insolvent** A term describing a person whose liabilities exceed the value of owned assets or a person who ''either has ceased to pay his debts in the ordinary course of business or cannot pay his debts as they come due'' [UCC 1–201(23)].

**Installment contract** A contract in which payments due are made periodically. Also may allow for delivery of goods in separate lots with payment made for each.

**Insurable interest** An interest either in a person's life or well-being or in property that is sufficiently substantial that insuring against injury to the person or damage to the property does not amount to a mere wagering (betting) contract.

**Insurance** A contract in which, for a stipulated consideration, one party agrees to compensate the other for loss on a specific subject by a specified peril.

**Integrated contract** A written contract that constitutes the final expression of the parties' agreement. If a contract is integrated, evidence extraneous to the contract that contradicts or alters the meaning of the contract in any way is inadmissible.

**Intellectual property** Property resulting from intellectual, creative processes—the products of an individual's mind.

**Intended beneficiary** A third party for whose benefit a contract is formed; intended beneficiaries can sue the promisor if such a contract is breached.

**Intentional tort** A wrongful act knowingly committed.

*Inter vivos* **trust** A trust created by the grantor (settlor) and effective during the grantor's lifetime (that is, a trust not established by a will).

**Intermediary bank** Any bank to which an item is transferred in the course of collection, except the depositary or payor bank.

**International law** The law that governs relations among nations. International customs and treaties are generally considered to be two of the most important sources of international law.

**International organization** In international law, a term that generally refers to an organization composed mainly of nations and usually established by treaty. The United States is a member of more than one hundred multilateral and bilateral organizations, including at least twenty through the United Nations.

**Interpretative rules** Administrative agency rules that are simply statements and opinions issued by an agency explaining how the agency interprets and intends to apply the statutes it enforces. Such rules are not automatically binding on private individuals or organizations.

**Interrogatories** A series of written questions for which written answers are prepared and then signed under oath by a party to a lawsuit (the plaintiff or the defendant).

**Intestacy laws** State laws determining the division and descent of the property of one who dies intestate (without a will).

**Intestate** One who has died without having created a valid will.

**Investment company** A company that acts on behalf of many smaller shareholders/owners by buying a large portfolio of securities and managing that portfolio professionally.

**Invitee** A person who, either expressly or impliedly, is privileged to enter upon another's land. The inviter owes the invitee (for example, a customer in a store) the duty to exercise reasonable care to protect the invitee from harm.

**Issue** The first transfer, or delivery, of an instrument to a holder.

# J

**Joint and several liability** A doctrine under which a plaintiff may sue, and collect a judgment from, any of several jointly liable defendants, regardless of that particular defendant's degree of fault. In partnership law, joint and several liability means a third party may sue one or more of the partners separately or all of them together, at his or her option. This is true even if the partner did not participate in, ratify, or know about whatever it was that gave rise to the cause of action.

**Joint liability** Shared liability. In partnership law, partners incur joint liability for partnership obligations and debts. For example, if a third party sues a partner on a partnership debt, the partner has the right to insist that the other partners be sued with him or her.

**Joint stock company** A hybrid form of business organization that combines characteristics of a corporation (shareholder-owners, management by directors and officers of the company, and perpetual existence) and a partnership (it is formed by agreement, not statute; property is usually held in the names of the members; and the shareholders have personal liability for business debts). Usually, the joint stock company is regarded as a partnership for tax and other legally related purposes.

**Joint tenancy** The ownership interest of two or more co-owners of property whereby each owns an undivided portion of the property. Upon the death of one of the joint tenants, his or her interest automatically passes to the others and cannot be transferred by the will of the deceased.

**Joint venture** A joint undertaking of a specific commercial enterprise by an association of persons. A joint venture is normally not a legal entity and is treated like a partnership for federal income tax purposes.

**Judgment *n.o.v.*** A judgment notwithstanding the verdict; may be entered by the court for the plaintiff (or the defendant) after there has been a jury verdict for the defendant (or the plaintiff).

**Judgment rate of interest** A rate of interest fixed by statute that is applied to a monetary judgment from the moment the judgment is awarded by a court until the judgment is paid or terminated.

**Judicial process** The procedures relating to, or connected with, the administration of justice through the judicial system.

**Judicial review** The authority of a court to reexamine a previously considered dispute; the process by which a court decides on the constitutionality of legislative acts.

**Jurisdiction** The authority of a court to hear and decide a specific action.

**Jurisprudence** The science or philosophy of law.

**Justiciable controversy** Appropriate for court review. A justiciable controversy is one that is not hypothetical or academic but real and substantial.

# K

**Keogh plan** A tax-deferred pension or profit-sharing retirement plan for self-employed taxpayers. The taxpayer funds the plan each year with tax-deductible contributions, which are capped at a certain amount. Also known as a H.R. 10 plan.

# L

**Laches** The equitable doctrine that bars a party's right to legal action if the party has neglected for an unreasonable length of time to act upon his or her rights.

**Landlord's lien** A landlord's remedy for a tenant's

failure to pay rent. When permitted under a statute or the lease agreement, the landlord may take and keep or sell whatever of the defaulting tenant's property is on the leased premises.

**Larceny** The act of taking another person's personal property unlawfully. Some states classify larceny as either grand or petit, depending on the property's value.

**Law** A body of rules of conduct with legal force and effect, prescribed by the controlling authority (the government) of a society.

**Lease** A transfer by the landlord/lessor of real or personal property to the tenant/lessee for a period of time for consideration (usually the payment of rent). Upon termination of the lease, the property reverts to the lessor.

**Lease agreement** An agreement between a landlord and tenant setting forth the terms of the lease.

**Leasehold estate** An estate in realty held by a tenant under a lease. In every leasehold estate, the tenant has a qualified right to possess and/or use the land.

**Legacy** A gift of personal property under a will.

**Legal rate of interest** A rate of interest fixed by statute as either the maximum rate of interest allowed by law or a rate of interest applied when the parties to a contract intend, but do not fix, an interest rate in the contract. In the latter case, the rate is frequently the same as the statutory maximum rate permitted.

**Legal realism** A school of legal thought of the 1920s and 1930s that challenged many existing jurisprudential assumptions, particularly the assumption that subjective elements played no part in judicial reasoning. The legal realists, as the term implies, generally advocated a less abstract and more realistic approach to the law, an approach that would take into account customary practices and the circumstances in which transactions take place. The school left a lasting imprint on American jurisprudence.

**Legal reasoning** The process of reasoning by which a judge harmonizes his or her decision with the judicial decisions of previous cases.

**Legatee** A person who inherits personal property under a will.

**Legislative rules** Administrative agency rules that carry the same weight as congressionally enacted statutes.

**Lessee** A person who pays for the use or possession of another's property.

**Lessor** A property owner who allows others to use his or her property in exchange for the payment of rent.

**Letter of credit** A written instrument, usually issued by a bank on behalf of a customer or other person, in which the issuer promises to honor drafts or other demands for payment by third persons in accordance with the terms of the instrument.

**Leveraged buy-out (LBO)** A corporate takeover financed by loans secured by the acquired corporation's assets or by the issuance of corporate bonds, resulting in a high debt load for the corporation.

**Levy** The obtaining of money by legal process through the seizure and sale of property, usually done after a writ of execution has been issued.

**Liability** Any actual or potential legal obligation, duty, debt, or responsibility.

**License** A revocable privilege to use another's intellectual property or to enter onto another's real property.

**Licensee** One who receives a license to use, or enter onto, another's property.

**Lien** An encumbrance upon a property to satisfy or protect a claim for payment of a debt.

**Lien creditor** One whose claim is secured by a lien on particular property, as distinguished from a general creditor, who has no such security.

**Life estate** An interest in land that exists only for the duration of the life of some person, usually the holder of the estate.

**Limited liability company (LLC)** A hybrid form of business organization or enterprise authorized by a state in which its members have limited liability and taxes on profits are passed through that entity to its members.

**Limited partner** In a limited partnership, a partner who contributes capital to the partnership but has no right to participate in the management and operation of the business. The limited partner assumes no liability for partnership debts beyond the capital contributed.

**Limited partnership** A partnership consisting of one or more general partners (who manage the business and are liable to the full extent of their personal assets for debts of the partnership) and of one or more limited partners (who contribute only assets and are liable only up to the amount contributed by them).

**Limited-payment life** A type of life insurance for which premiums are payable for a definite period, after which the policy is fully paid.

**Liquidated damages** An amount, stipulated in the contract, that the parties to a contract believe to be a reasonable estimation of the damages that will occur in the event of a breach.

**Liquidation** The sale of the assets of a business or an individual for cash and the distribution of the cash received to creditors, with the balance going to the owner(s).

**Litigant** A party to a lawsuit.

**Long arm statute** A state statute that permits a state to obtain jurisdiction over nonresident individuals and corporations. Individuals or corporations, however, must have certain "minimum contacts" with that state for the statute to apply.

**Lost property** Property with which the owner has involuntarily parted and then cannot find or recover.

# M

**Magistrate's court** A court of limited jurisdiction that is presided over by a public official (magistrate) with certain judicial authority, such as the power to set bail.

**Mailbox rule** A rule providing that an acceptance of an offer becomes effective upon dispatch (upon being placed in a mailbox), if mail is, expressly or impliedly, an authorized means of communication of acceptance to the offeror.

**Maker** One who issues a promissory note or certificate of deposit (that is, one who promises to pay a certain sum to the holder of the note or CD).

**Malpractice** Professional misconduct or the lack of the requisite degree of skill as a professional or the negligence—the failure to exercise due care—on the part of a professional, such as a physician, is commonly referred to as malpractice.

**Marine insurance** Insurance protecting shippers and vessel owners from losses or damages sustained by a vessel or its cargo during the transport of goods or materials by water.

**Market concentration** A situation that exists when a small number of firms share the market for a particular good or service. For example, if the four largest grocery stores in Chicago accounted for 80 percent of all retail food sales, the market clearly would be concentrated in those four firms.

**Market power** The power of a firm to control the market for its product. A monopoly has the greatest degree of market power.

**Market-share liability** A method of sharing liability among several firms that manufactured or marketed a particular product that may have caused plaintiff's injury. This form of liability sharing is used when the true source of the product is unidentifiable. Each firm's liability is proportionate to its respective share of the relevant market for the product. Market-share liability applies only if the injuring product is fungible, the true manufacturer is unidentifiable, and the unknown character of the manufacturer is not the plaintiff's fault.

**Market share test** The primary measure of monopoly power. A firm's market share is the percentage of a market that the firm controls.

**Marketable title** Title to real estate that is reasonably free from encumbrances, defects in the chain of title, and other events that affect title, such as adverse possession.

**Marshalling assets** The arrangement or ranking of assets in a certain order toward the payment of debts. In equity, when two creditors have recourse to the same property of the debtor, but one has recourse to other property of the debtor, that creditor must resort first to those assets of the debtor not available to the other creditor.

**Mask work** A series of images related to the pattern formed by the many layers of a semiconductor chip product.

**Mechanic's lien** A statutory lien upon the real property of another, created to ensure priority of payment for work performed and materials furnished in erecting or repairing a building or other structure.

**Mediation** A method of settling disputes outside of court by using the services of a neutral third party, who acts as a communicating agent between the parties; a method of dispute settlement that is less formal than arbitration.

*Mens rea* Mental state, or intent. A wrongful mental state is as necessary as a wrongful act to establish criminal liability. What constitutes a mental state varies according to the wrongful action. Thus, for murder, the mens rea is the intent to take life; for theft, the mens rea must involve both the knowledge that the property belongs to another and the intent to deprive the owner of it.

**Merger** A contractual process by which one corporation (the surviving corporation) acquires all the assets and liabilities of another corporation (the merged corporation). The shareholders of the merged corporation receive either payment for their shares or shares in the surviving corporation.

**Mini-trial** A private proceeding that assists disputing parties in determining whether to take their case to court. During the proceeding, each party's attorney briefly argues the party's case before the other party and (usually) a neutral third party, who acts as an adviser. If the parties fail to reach an agreement, the adviser renders an opinion as to how a court would likely decide the issue.

**Minimum wage** The lowest wage, either by government regulation or union contract, that an employer may pay an hourly worker.

**Mirror image rule** A common law rule that requires, for a valid contractual agreement, that the terms of the offeree's acceptance adhere exactly to the terms of the offeror's offer.

**Misdemeanor** A lesser crime than a felony, punishable by a fine or imprisonment for up to one year in other than a state or federal penitentiary.

**Mislaid property** Property that the owner has voluntarily parted with and then cannot find or recover.

**Mitigation of damages** The rule requiring the party suing to have done whatever was reasonable to minimize the damages caused by the defendant.

**Money laundering** Falsely reporting income that has been obtained through criminal activity as income obtained through a legitimate business enterprise—in effect, ''laundering'' the ''dirty money.''

**Monopolization** The possession of monopoly power in the relevant market and the willful acquisition or maintenance of the power, as distinguished from growth or development as a consequence of a superior product, business acumen, or historic accident. A violation of Section 2 of the Sherman Act requires that both of these elements be established.

**Monopoly** A term generally used to describe a market for which there is a single seller.

**Monopoly power** An extreme amount of market power.

**Mortgage** A written instrument giving a creditor (the mortgagee) an interest (lien) in the debtor's (mortgagor's) property as security for a debt.

**Mortgagee**   The creditor who takes the security interest under the mortgage agreement.

**Mortgagor**   The debtor who pledges collateral in a mortgage agreement.

**Most-favored-nation status**   A status granted in an international treaty by a provision stating that the citizens of the contracting nations may enjoy the privileges accorded by either party to citizens of the most favored nations. Generally, most-favored-nation clauses are designed to establish equality of international treatment in regard to imports or exports.

**Motion for a directed verdict**   In a jury trial, a motion for the judge to take the decision out of the hands of the jury and direct a verdict for the moving party on the grounds that the other party has not produced sufficient evidence to support his or her claim.

**Motion for judgment on the pleadings**   A motion, which can be brought by either party to a lawsuit after the pleadings are closed, for the court to decide the issue without proceeding to trial. This motion may be used when only questions of law are at issue.

**Motion to dismiss**   A pleading in which a defendant admits the facts as alleged by the plaintiff but asserts that the plaintiff's claim fails to state a cause of action (that is, has no basis in law) or that there are other grounds on which a suit should be dismissed. Also called a demurrer.

**Multiple product order**   An order issued by the Federal Trade Commission to a firm that has engaged in deceptive advertising by which the firm is required to cease and desist from false advertising not only in regard to the product that was the subject of the action but also in regard to all the firm's other products.

**Mutual assent**   The element of agreement in the formation of a contract. The manifestation of contract parties' mutual assent to the same bargain is required to establish a contract.

**Mutual fund**   A specific type of investment company that continually buys or sells to investors shares of ownership in a portfolio.

**Mutual rescission**   An agreement between the parties to cancel their contract, releasing the parties from further obligations under the contract. The object of the agreement is to restore the parties to the positions they would have occupied had no contract ever been formed. See also Rescission.

# N

**National law**   Law that pertains to a particular nation (as opposed to international law).

**Natural law school**   The oldest and one of the most significant schools of legal thought. Adherents of the natural law school believe that government and the legal system should reflect universal moral and ethical principles that are inherent in human nature.

**Necessaries**   Necessities required for life, such as food, shelter, clothing, and medical attention; normally, necessaries are also considered to include items or services appropriate to an individual's circumstances and condition in life.

**Negligence**   The failure to exercise the standard of care that a reasonable person would exercise in similar circumstances.

**Negligence per se**   An action or failure to act in violation of a statutory requirement.

**Negligent misrepresentation**   Any manifestation through words or conduct that amounts to an untrue statement of fact made in circumstances in which a reasonable and prudent person would not have done (or failed to do) that which led to the misrepresentation. A representation made with an honest belief in its truth may still be negligent due to (1) a lack of reasonable care in ascertaining the facts, (2) the manner of expression, or (3) the absence of the skill or competence required by a particular business or profession.

**Negotiable instrument**   A written and signed unconditional promise or order to pay a specified sum of money on demand or at a definite time to order (to a specific person or entity) or to bearer.

**Negotiated rulemaking**   Administrative agency rulemaking allowing parties interested in or affected by a new rule to negotiate with the agency in the rule's drafting. Notice of a negotiated rulemaking is published in the *Federal Register*. Interested and affected parties apply to members of a negotiating committee, which is presided over by a neutral third party.

**Negotiation**   The transferring of a negotiable instrument to another in such form that the transferee becomes a holder.

**No par shares**   Corporate shares that have no face value—that is, no specific dollar amount is printed on their face.

*Nolo contendere*   Latin for ''I will not contest it.'' A criminal defendant's plea in which he or she chooses not to challenge, or contest, the charges brought by the government. Although the defendant may still be sentenced or fined, the plea neither admits nor denies guilt.

**Nominal damages**   A small monetary award (often one dollar) granted to a plaintiff when no actual damage was suffered.

**Notary public**   A person authorized by a state government or the federal government to administer oaths and to attest to the authenticity of signatures.

**Notice of Proposed Rulemaking**   A notice published (in the Federal Register) by an administrative agency describing a proposed rule. The notice must give the time and place for which agency proceedings on the proposed rule will be held, a description of the nature of the proceedings, the legal authority for the proceedings (which is usually the agency's enabling legislation), and the terms of the proposed rule or the subject matter of the proposed rule.

**Novation**   The substitution, by agreement, of a new contract for an old one, with the rights under the old one being terminated. Typically, there is a substitution of a new person who is responsible for the contract and the removal of the original party's rights and duties under the contract.

**Nuisance**   An act that interferes unlawfully with a person's possession or ability to use his or her property.

**Nuncupative will**   An oral will (often called a death-bed will) made before witnesses; usually limited to transfers of personal property.

# O

**Objective theory of contracts**   The view taken by American law that contracting parties shall only be bound by terms that can actually be inferred from promises made. Contract law does not examine a contracting party's subjective intent or underlying motive.

**Offer**   An offeror's proposal to do something, which creates in the offeree accepting the offer a legal power to bind the offeror to the terms of the proposal by accepting the offer.

**Offeree**   A person to whom an offer is made.

**Offeror**   A person who makes an offer.

**Omnibus, or other-driver, clause**   A provision in an automobile insurance policy that protects the vehicle owner who has taken out the insurance policy and anyone who drives the vehicle with the owner's permission.

**Opening statement**   A statement made to the jury at the beginning of the trial by a party's attorney, prior to the presentation of evidence. The attorney briefly outlines the evidence that will be offered and the legal theory that will be pursued.

**Opinion**   A statement by the court expressing the reasons for its decision in a case.

**Option contract**   A contract under which the offeror cannot revoke his or her offer for a stipulated time period, and the offeree can accept or reject the offer during this period without fear of the offer's being made to another person. The offeree must give consideration for the option (the irrevocable offer) to be enforceable.

**Order for relief**   A court's grant of assistance to a complainant. In the context of bankruptcy, relief consists of discharging a complainant's debts.

**Order instrument**   A negotiable instrument that is payable to the order of a specific person.

**Output contract**   A binding agreement in which a seller agrees to deliver/sell the seller's entire output of a good (an unspecified amount at the time of agreement) to a buyer, and the buyer agrees to buy all the goods supplied.

**Overdraft**   A check written on a checking account in which there are insufficient funds to cover the check.

# P

**Par-value shares**   Corporate shares that have a specific face value, or formal cash-in value, written on them, such as one penny or one dollar.

**Parol evidence rule**   A substantive rule of contracts under which a court will not receive into evidence prior statements or contemporaneous oral statements that contradict a written agreement when the court finds that the written agreement was intended by the parties to be a final, complete, and unambiguous expression of their agreement.

**Partially disclosed principal**   A principal whose identity is unknown by a third person, but the third person knows that the agent is or may be acting for a principal at the time the contract is made.

**Partnership**   An association of two or more persons to carry on, as co-owners, a business for profit.

**Partnership by estoppel**   A judicially created partnership that may, at the court's discretion, be imposed for purposes of fairness. The court can prevent those who present themselves as partners (but who are not) from escaping liability if a third person relies on an alleged partnership in good faith and is harmed as a result.

**Past consideration**   An act done before the contract is made, which ordinarily, by itself, cannot be consideration for a later promise to pay for the act.

**Patent**   A government grant that gives an inventor the exclusive right or privilege to make, use, or sell his or her invention for a limited time period. The word patent usually refers to some invention and designates either the instrument by which patent rights are evidenced or the patent itself.

**Payee**   A person to whom an instrument is made payable.

**Payor bank**   A bank on which an item is payable as drawn (or is payable as accepted).

**Penalty**   A sum inserted into a contract, not as a measure of compensation for its breach but rather as punishment for a default. The agreement as to the amount will not be enforced, and recovery will be limited to actual damages.

*Per capita*   A Latin term meaning per person. In the law governing estate distribution, a method of distributing the property of an intestate's estate by which all the heirs receive equal shares.

*Per se violation*   A type of anticompetitive agreement—such as a price-fixing agreement—that is considered to be so injurious to the public that there is no need to determine whether it actually injures market competition; rather, it is in itself (per se) a violation of the Sherman Act.

*Per stirpes*   A Latin term meaning by the roots. In the law governing estate distribution, a method of distributing an intestate's estate in which a class or group of distributees take the share to which their deceased ancestor would have been entitled.

**Perfect tender rule**   A common law rule under which a seller was required to deliver to the buyer goods that conformed perfectly to the requirements stipulated in the sales contract. A tender of nonconforming goods would automatically constitute a breach of contract. Under the UCC, the rule has been greatly modified.

**Perfection**   The method by which a secured party obtains a priority by notice that his or her security interest in the debtor's collateral is effective against the debtor's subsequent creditors. Usually accomplished by filing a financing statement at a location set out in the state statute.

**Performance**   In contract law, the fulfillment of one's duties arising under a contract with another; the normal way of discharging one's contractual obligations.

**Periodic tenancy**   A lease interest in land for an indefinite period involving payment of rent at fixed intervals, such as week to week, month to month, or year to year.

**Personal defenses**   Defenses that can be used to avoid payment to an ordinary holder of a negotiable instrument. Personal defenses cannot be used to avoid payment to a holder in due course (HDC) or (under the shelter principle) to a holder through an HDC.

**Personal identification number (PIN)**   A number given to the holder of an access card that is used to conduct financial transactions in electronic fund transfer systems. Typically, the card will not provide access to a system without the number, which is meant to be kept secret to inhibit unauthorized use of the card.

**Personal property**   Property that is movable; any property that is not real property.

**Personalty**   Personal property.

**Petition in bankruptcy**   An application to a bankruptcy court for relief in bankruptcy; filing for bankruptcy. The official forms required for a petition in bankruptcy must be completed accurately, sworn to under oath, and signed by the debtor.

**Petitioner**   The party who presents a petition to a court, initiates an equity proceeding, or appeals from a judgment.

**Petty offense**   In criminal law, the least serious kind of wrong, such as a traffic or building-code violation.

**Plaintiff**   One who initiates a lawsuit.

**Plea bargaining**   The process by which the accused and the prosecutor in a criminal case work out a mutually satisfactory disposition of the case, subject to court approval. Usually involves the defendant's pleading guilty to a lesser offense in return for a lighter sentence.

**Pleadings**   Statements by the plaintiff and the defendant that detail the facts, charges, and defenses. Modern rules simplify common law pleading, often requiring only the complaint, an answer, and sometimes a reply to the answer.

**Pledge**   The bailment of personal property to a creditor as security for the payment of a debt.

**Point-of-sale system**   An electronic customer-merchant-bank communication terminal that, when activated by an access card and a personal identification number, can debit the customer's account to cover a purchase from the merchant.

**Police powers**   Powers possessed by states as part of their inherent sovereignty. These powers may be exercised to protect or promote public health, safety, or morals, or the general welfare.

**Policy**   In insurance law, the contract of indemnity against a contingent loss between the insurer and the insured.

**Positive law**   The objective laws legally created by a society, as opposed to natural law or the unwritten laws arising from social customs; also called black-letter law.

**Positivist school**   A school of legal thought that holds that there can be no higher law than a nation's positive law—law created by a particular society at a particular point in time. In contrast to the natural law school, the positivist school maintains that there are no ''natural'' rights; rights come into existence only when there is a sovereign power (government) to confer and enforce those rights.

**Potentially responsible party (PRP)**   A liable party under the Comprehensive Environmental Response, Compensation, and Liability Act (CERCLA), or Superfund. A person who generated the hazardous waste, transported the hazardous waste, owned or operated a waste site at the time of disposal, or currently owns or operates a site may be responsible for some or all of the clean-up costs involved in removing the hazardous chemicals.

**Power of attorney**   A document or instrument authorizing another to act as one's agent or attorney.

**Preauthorized transfer**   A transaction authorized in advance to recur at substantially regular intervals. The terms and procedure for preauthorized electronic fund transfers through certain financial institutions are subject to the Electronic Fund Transfer Act.

**Precedent**   A court decision that furnishes an example or authority for deciding subsequent cases in which identical or similar facts are presented.

**Predatory pricing**   The pricing of a product below cost with the intent to drive competitors out of the market.

**Preemption**   A doctrine under which certain federal laws preempt, or take precedence over, state or local laws.

**Preemptive rights**   Rights held by shareholders that entitle them to purchase newly issued shares of a corporation's stock, equal in percentage to shares presently held, before the stock is offered to any outside buyers. Preemptive rights enable shareholders to maintain their proportionate ownership and voice in the corporation.

**Preference**   In bankruptcy proceedings, the debtor's favoring of one creditor over others by making payments or transferring property to that creditor at the expense of the rights of other creditors in the bankruptcy estate. The bankruptcy trustee is allowed to recover payments made both voluntarily and involuntarily to one creditor in preference over another.

**Preferred stock**   Classes of stock that have priority over common stock both as to payment of dividends and distribution of assets upon the corporation's dissolution.

**Preliminary hearing**   An initial hearing used in

many felony cases to establish whether or not it is proper to detain the defendant. A magistrate reviews the evidence and decides if there is probable cause to believe that the defendant committed the crime charged.

**Premium** In insurance law, the price for insurance protection for a specified period of time.

**Preponderance of the evidence** The standard of proof generally used in civil trials requiring that the existence of a fact in issue be more probable than not—that is, it must be shown that the fact is more likely to exist than to not exist.

**Presentment warranty** An implied warranty, made by any person who seeks payment or acceptance of a negotiable instrument to any person who in good faith pays or accepts the instrument, that the party presenting the instrument has good title to the instrument or is authorized to obtain payment or acceptance on behalf of a person who has good title, has no knowledge that the signature of the maker or the drawer is unauthorized, and has no knowledge that the instrument has been materially altered [UCC 3–417(1), 3–418].

**Pretrial conference** A conference, scheduled before the trial begins, between the judge and the attorneys litigating the suit. The parties may settle the dispute, clarify the issues, schedule discovery, and so on during the conference.

**Pretrial motion** A written or oral application to a court for a ruling or order, made before trial.

**Price discrimination** Setting prices in such a way that two competing buyers pay two different prices for an identical product or service.

**Price fixing agreement** Fixing—by means of an anticompetitive agreement between competitors—the prices of products or services.

**Prima facie case** A case in which the plaintiff has produced sufficient evidence of his or her conclusion that the case can go to a jury; a case in which the evidence compels the plaintiff's conclusion if the defendant produces no evidence to rebut it.

**Principal** In agency law, a person who, by agreement or otherwise, authorizes an agent to act on his or her behalf in such a way that the acts of the agent become binding on the principal.

**Private law** Law governing the behavior of individual members of society as that behavior affects other individuals. Examples of private law are contract law and tort law.

**Privatization** The replacement of government-paid-for products and services by private firms.

**Privilege** In tort law, the ability to act contrary to another person's right without that person's having legal redress for such acts. Privilege is usually raised as a defense.

**Privileges and immunities clause** Special rights and exceptions provided by law. Article IV, Section 2, of the Constitution requires states not to discriminate against one another's citizens. A resident of one state cannot be treated as an alien when in another state; he or she may not be denied such privileges and immunities as legal protection, access to courts, travel rights, or property rights.

**Privity of contract** The relationship that exists between the promisor and the promisee of a contract.

**Probable cause** Reasonable grounds to believe the existence of facts warranting certain actions, such as the search or arrest of a person.

**Probate** The process of proving and validating a will and the settling of all matters pertaining to administration, guardianship, and like matters.

**Probate court** A court having jurisdiction over proceedings concerning the settlement of a person's estate.

**Procedural law** Rules that define the manner in which the rights and duties of individuals may be enforced.

**Procedural rule** A rule that describes an agency's methods of operation and establishes procedures for dealing with the agency.

**Proceeds** In secured transactions law, whatever is received when the collateral is sold, exchanged, collected, or otherwise disposed of, such as insurance payments for destroyed or lost collateral. Money, checks, and the like are cash proceeds, whereas all other proceeds received are noncash proceeds.

**Product liability** The legal liability of manufacturers and sellers to buyers, users, and sometimes bystanders for injuries or damages suffered because of defects in goods purchased. Liability arises when a product has a defective condition that makes it unreasonably dangerous to the user or consumer.

**Product misuse** A defense against product liability that may be raised when the plaintiff used a product in a manner not intended by the manufacturer. If the misuse is reasonably foreseeable, the seller will not escape liability unless measures were taken to guard against the harm that could result from the misuse.

**Profit** In real property law, the right to enter upon and remove things from the property of another (for example, the right to enter onto a person's land and remove sand and gravel therefrom).

**Promise** A declaration that binds the person who makes it (promisor) to do or not to do a certain act. The person to whom the promise is made (promisee) has a right to expect or demand the performance of some particular thing.

**Promisee** A person to whom a promise is made.

**Promisor** A person who makes a promise.

**Promissory estoppel** A doctrine that applies when a promisor reasonably expects a promise to induce definite and substantial action or forbearance by the promisee, and that does induce such action or forbearance in reliance thereon; such a promise is binding if injustice can be avoided only by enforcing the promise. See also Estoppel.

**Promissory note** A written instrument signed by a maker unconditionally promising to pay a certain sum in money to a payee or a holder on demand or on a specified date.

**Promoter**   An entrepreneur who participates in the organization of a corporation in its formative stage, usually by issuing a prospectus, procuring subscriptions to the stock, making contract purchases, securing a charter, and the like.

**Property**   The legally protected rights and interests a person has in anything with an ascertainable value that is subject to ownership. See also Personal property; Real property.

**Prospectus**   A document that contains all material facts about a company and its operations so that those who wish to purchase stock (invest) in the corporation have the basis for making an informed decision.

**Protected class**   A class of persons with identifiable characteristics who historically have been victimized by discriminatory treatment for certain purposes. Depending on the context, these characteristics include age, color, gender, national origin, race, and religion.

**Proximate cause**   The "next" or "substantial" cause; in tort law, a concept used to determine whether a plaintiff's injury was the natural and continuous result of a defendant's negligent act. If the negligent act of a defendant was the sole cause or a substantial cause of injuries to a plaintiff, the defendant will be liable.

**Proxy**   In corporation law, a written agreement between a stockholder and another under which the stockholder authorizes the other to vote the stockholder's shares in a certain manner.

**Public figures**   Individuals who are thrust into the public limelight. Public figures include government officials and politicians, movie stars, well-known businesspersons, and generally anybody who becomes known to the public because of his or her position or activities.

**Public law**   Law governing the relationships between individuals and their government. Examples of public law are administrative law, constitutional law, and criminal law.

**Public policy**   What the government decides to do or not to do.

**Public prosecutor**   An individual, acting as a trial lawyer, who initiates and conducts criminal cases in the government's name and on behalf of the people.

**Puffery**   A salesperson's often exaggerated claims concerning the quality of the goods offered for sale. Such claims involve opinions rather than facts and are not considered to be legally binding promises or warranties.

**Punitive damages**   Compensation in excess of actual or consequential damages. They are awarded in order to punish the wrongdoer and usually will be awarded only in cases involving willful or malicious misconduct.

**Purchase-money security interest**   A security interest to the extent that it is (1) taken or retained by a seller of the collateral to secure all or part of the price of the collateral or (2) taken by a creditor who, by making advances or incurring an obligation, gives value to enable the debtor to acquire rights in, or use of, the collateral, if such value is in fact so used.

# Q

**Qualified indorsement**   An indorsement on a negotiable instrument by which the indorser disclaims to subsequent holders secondary liability on the instrument; the most common qualified indorsement is "without recourse."

*Quantum meruit*   Literally, "as much as he deserves"—an expression describing the extent of liability on a contract implied in law (quasi contract). An equitable doctrine based on the concept that one who benefits from another's labor and materials should not be unjustly enriched thereby but should be required to pay a reasonable amount for the benefits received, even absent a contract.

**Quasi contract**   An obligation or contract imposed by law, in the absence of agreement, to prevent unjust enrichment. Sometimes referred to as an implied-in-law contract (a legal fiction) to distinguish it from an implied-in-fact contract.

*Quasi in rem* **jurisdiction**   Court's jurisdiction over a person based on a claim against the person's interest in property located within the court's jurisdiction.

**Questions of fact**   In lawsuits, issues involving factual disputes that can be decided by a jury.

**Questions of law**   In lawsuits, issues involving the application or interpretation of law; therefore, the judge, and not the jury, decides the issues.

**Quitclaim deed**   A deed intended to pass any title, interest, or claim that the grantor may have in the premises but not professing that such title is valid and not containing any warranty or covenants of title.

**Quorum**   The number of members of a decision-making body that must be present before business may be transacted.

**Quota**   An assigned import limit on goods.

# R

**Ratification**   The approval or validation of a previous action. In contract law, the confirmation of a voidable act (that is, an act that without ratification would not be an enforceable contractual obligation). In agency law, the confirmation by one person of an act or contract performed or entered into on his or her behalf by another, who assumed, without authority, to act as his or her agent.

**Reaffirmation agreement**   An agreement between a debtor and a creditor in which the debtor reaffirms, or promises to pay, a debt dischargeable in bankruptcy. To be enforceable, the agreement must be made prior to the discharge of the debt by the bankruptcy court.

**Real property**   Immovable property consisting of land and buildings thereupon, as opposed to personal property, which can be moved. In the absence of a contract, real property includes things growing on the land before they are severed (such as timber), as well as fixtures.

**Reasonable person standard**  The standard of behavior expected of a hypothetical "reasonable person." The standard against which negligence is measured and that must be observed to avoid liability for negligence.

**Rebuttal**  The refutation of evidence introduced by an adverse party's attorney.

**Receiver**  A court-appointed person who receives, preserves, and manages a business or other property that is involved in bankruptcy proceedings.

**Recording statutes**  Statutes requiring that deeds, mortgages, and other real property transactions be recorded so as to provide notice to future purchasers, creditors, and encumbrancers of an existing claim on the property.

**Red herring**  A preliminary prospectus that can be distributed to potential investors after the registration statement (for a securities offering) has been filed with the Securities and Exchange Commission. The name derives from the red legend printed across the prospectus stating that the registration has been filed but has not become effective.

**Reformation**  A court-ordered correction of a written contract so that it reflects the true intentions of the parties.

**Regulation E**  A set of rules issued by the Federal Reserve System's board of governors under the authority of the Electronic Fund Transfer Act to protect users of electronic fund transfer systems.

**Regulation Z**  A set of rules promulgated by the Federal Reserve System's board of governors to implement the provisions of the Truth-in-Lending Act.

**Rejoinder**  The defendant's answer to the plaintiff's rebuttal.

**Release**  The relinquishment, concession, or giving up of a right, claim, or privilege, by the person in whom it exists or to whom it accrues, to the person against whom it might have been enforced or demanded.

**Relevant evidence**  Evidence tending to make a fact at issue in the case more or less probable than it would be without the evidence. Only relevant evidence is admissible in court.

**Remainder**  A future interest in property, held by a person other than the grantor, that occurs at the natural termination of the preceding estate.

**Remedy**  The relief given to innocent parties, by law or by contract, to enforce a right or to prevent or compensate for the violation of a right.

**Remedy at law**  A remedy available in a court of law. Money damages are awarded as a remedy at law.

**Remedy in equity**  A remedy allowed by courts in situations where remedies at law are not appropriate. Remedies in equity are based on settled rules of fairness, justice, and honesty.

**Remitter**  A person who sends money, or remits payment.

**Rent escalation**  An increase in rent during a lease term according to a lease clause.

**Repair-and-deduct statutes**  Statutes providing that a tenant may pay for repairs and deduct the cost of the repairs from the rent, as a remedy for a landlord's failure to maintain leased premises.

**Replevin**  An action brought to recover the possession of personal property unlawfully held by another.

**Reply**  Procedurally, a plaintiff's response to a defendant's answer.

**Requirements contract**  An agreement under which a promisor promises to supply the promisee with all the goods and/or services the promisee might require from period to period.

*Res ipsa loquitur*  A doctrine under which negligence may be inferred simply because an event occurred, if it is the type of event that would not occur absent negligence. Literally, the term means the thing speaks for itself.

**Resale price maintenance agreement**  An agreement between a manufacturer and a retailer in which the manufacturer specifies the minimum retail price of its products. Resale price maintenance agreements are illegal per se under the Sherman Act.

**Rescission**  A remedy whereby a contract is terminated and the parties are returned to the positions they occupied before the contract was made; may be effected through the mutual consent of the parties, by their conduct, or by the decree of a court of equity.

*Respondeat superior*  In Latin, "Let the master respond." A principle of law whereby a principal or an employer is held liable for the wrongful acts committed by agents or employees while acting within the scope of their agency or employment.

**Respondent**  In equity practice, the party who answers a bill or other proceeding. In appellate practice, the party against whom an appeal is taken (sometimes referred to as the appellee).

**Restitution**  An equitable remedy under which a person is restored to his or her original position prior to loss or injury, or placed in the position he or she would have been in had the breach not occurred.

**Restraint on trade**  Any conspiracy or combination that unlawfully eliminates competition or facilitates the creation of a monopoly or monopoly pricing.

**Restrictive indorsement**  Any indorsement of a negotiable instrument that purports to condition or prohibit further transfer of the instrument. As against payor and intermediary banks, such indorsements are usually ineffective.

**Resulting trust**  A trust implied in law from the intentions of the parties to a given transaction. A trust in which a party holds legal title for the benefit of another, although without expressed intent to do so, because the presumption of such intent arises by operation of law.

**Retained earnings**  The portion of a corporation's profits that has not been paid out as dividends to shareholders.

**Retaliatory eviction**  The eviction of a tenant because of the tenant's complaints, participation in a tenant's union, or similar activity with which the landlord does not agree.

**Reversionary interest**   A future residuary interest retained in property by the grantor. For example, a landowner who conveys property to another for life creates retains a future interest in the property. When the person holding the life estate dies, the property will revert to the grantor (unless the grantor has transferred the future interest to another party).

**Revocation**   In contract law, the withdrawal of an offer by an offeror; unless the offer is irrevocable, it can be revoked at any time prior to acceptance without liability.

**Right of contribution**   The right of a co-surety who pays more than his or her proportionate share upon a debtor's default to recover the excess paid from other co-sureties.

**Right of entry**   The right to peaceably take or resume possession of real property.

**Right of first refusal**   The right to purchase personal or real property—such as corporate shares or real estate—before the property is offered for sale to others.

**Right of reimbursement**   The legal right of a person to be restored, repaid, or indemnified for costs, expenses, or losses incurred or expended on behalf of another.

**Right of subrogation**   The right of a person to stand in the place of (be substituted for) another, giving the substituted party the same legal rights that the original party had.

**Right-to-work laws**   State laws generally providing that employees are not to be required to join a union as a condition of receiving or retaining employment.

**Risk**   A specified contingency or peril.

**Risk management**   Planning that is undertaken to protect one's interest should some event threaten to undermine its security. In the context of insurance, transferring certain risks from the insured to the insurance company.

**Robbery**   Theft from a person, accompanied by force or fear of force.

**Rule 10b-5**   A rule of the Securities and Exchange Commission that makes it unlawful, in connection with the purchase or sale of any security, to make any untrue statement of a material fact or to omit a material fact if such omission causes the statement to be misleading.

**Rule of reason**   A test by which a court balances the reasons (such as economic efficiency) for an agreement against its potentially anticompetitive effects. In antitrust litigation, many practices are analyzed under the rule of reason.

**Rulemaking**   The actions undertaken by administrative agencies when formally adopting new regulations or amending old ones. Under the Administrative Procedures Act, rulemaking includes notifying the public of proposed rules or changes and receiving and considering the public's comments.

**Rulemaking record**   Agency rulemaking that is much more extensive than informal rulemaking and in which a public hearing is conducted in the manner of a trial. After the hearing is concluded, the agency is required to prepare a formal written statement describing its findings based on the evidence presented by both sides. Also referred to as formal rulemaking.

**Rules of evidence**   Rules governing the admissibility of evidence in trial courts.

# S

**S corporation**   A close business corporation that has met certain requirements as set out by the Internal Revenue Code and thus qualifies for special income-tax treatment. Essentially, an S corporation is taxed the same as a partnership, but its owners enjoy the privilege of limited liability.

**Sale**   The passing of title to property from the seller to the buyer for a price.

**Sale on approval**   A type of conditional sale that becomes absolute only when the buyer approves, or is satisfied with, the good(s) sold. Besides express approval of goods, approval may be inferred if the buyer keeps the goods beyond a reasonable time or uses the goods in any way that is inconsistent with the seller's ownership.

**Sale or return**   A type of conditional sale wherein title and possession pass from the seller to the buyer; however, the buyer retains the option to rescind or return the goods during a specified period even though the goods conform to the contract.

*Scienter*   Knowledge by the misrepresenting party that material facts have been falsely represented or omitted with an intent to deceive.

**Secondary boycott**   A union's refusal to work for, purchase from, or handle the products of a secondary employer, with whom the union has no dispute, with the object of forcing that employer to stop doing business with the primary employer, with whom the union has a labor dispute.

**Secured party**   A lender, seller, or any other person in whose favor there is a security interest, including a person to whom accounts or chattel paper has been sold.

**Secured transaction**   Any transaction, regardless of its form, that is intended to create a security interest in personal property or fixtures, including goods, documents, and other intangibles.

**Securities and Exchange Commission (SEC)**   The federal administrative agency created by the Securities Exchange Act of 1934 to regulate and supervise the trading of securities, investigate securities fraud, and enforce federal securities laws.

**Securities**   Stock certificates, bonds, notes, debentures, warrants, or other documents given as evidence of an ownership interest in the corporation or as a promise of repayment by the corporation.

**Security agreement**   The agreement that creates or provides for a security interest between the debtor and a secured party.

**Security interest** Every interest "in personal property or fixtures [emphasis added] that secures payment or performance of an obligation" [UCC 1–201(37)].

**Self-defense** The legally recognized privilege to protect one's self or property against injury by another. The privilege of self-defense only protects acts that are reasonably necessary to protect one's self or property.

**Seniority system** In regard to employment relationships, a system in which those who have worked longest for the company are first in line for promotions, salary increases, and other benefits; they are also the last to be laid off if the work force must be reduced.

**Sentence** The punishment, or penalty, ordered by the court to be inflicted on the person convicted of a crime.

**Service mark** A mark used in the sale or the advertising of services, such as to distinguish the services of one person from the services of others. Titles, character names, and other distinctive features of radio and television programs may be registered as service marks.

**Sexual harassment** In the employment context, hiring or granting of job promotions or other benefits in return for sexual favors or language or conduct that is so sexually offensive that it creates a hostile working environment.

**Sham transaction** A false transaction without substance that is undertaken with the intent to defraud a creditor or the government. An example of a sham transaction is the sale of assets to a friend or relative for the purpose of concealing assets from creditors or a bankruptcy court.

**Shareholder's derivative suit** A suit brought by a shareholder to enforce a corporate cause of action against a third person.

**Shari'a** Civil law principles of some Middle Eastern countries that are based on the Islamic directives that follow the teachings of the prophet Mohammed.

**Shelter principle** The principle that the holder of a negotiable instrument who cannot qualify as a holder in due course (HDC), but who derives his or her title through an HDC, acquires the rights of an HDC.

**Sheriff's deed** The deed given to the purchaser of property at a sheriff's sale as part of the foreclosure process against the owner of the property.

**Shipment contract** A contract for the sale of goods in which the buyer assumes liability for any losses or damage to the goods on the seller's delivery of the goods to a carrier.

**Short-form merger** A merger between a subsidiary corporation and a parent corporation that owns at least 90 percent of the outstanding shares of each class of stock issued by the subsidiary corporation. Short-form mergers can be accomplished without the approval of the shareholders of either corporation.

**Signature** The name or mark of a person, written by that person or at his or her direction. In commercial law, any name, word, or mark used with the intention to authenticate a writing constitutes a signature.

**Slander of quality** Publication of false information about another's product, alleging it is not what its seller claims; also referred to as trade libel.

**Slander of title** The publication of a statement that denies or casts doubt upon another's legal ownership of any property, causing financial loss to that property's owner.

**Small claims courts** Special courts in which parties may litigate small claims (usually, claims involving $2,500 or less). Attorneys are not required in small claims courts, and in many states, attorneys are not allowed to represent the parties.

**Sole proprietorship** The simplest form of business, in which the owner is the business; thus, anyone who does business without creating a formal business entity has a sole proprietorship. The owner of a sole proprietorship reports business income on his or her personal income tax return and is legally responsible for all debts and obligations incurred by the business.

**Sovereign immunity** A doctrine that immunizes foreign nations from the jurisdiction of U.S. courts when certain conditions are satisfied.

**Special indorsement** An indorsement on an instrument that specifies to whom or to whose order the instrument is payable.

**Special warranty deed** A deed in which the grantor only covenants to warrant and defend the title against claims and demands of the grantor and all persons claiming by, through, and under the grantor.

**Specific performance** An equitable remedy requiring exactly the performance that was specified in a contract. Usually granted only when money damages would be an inadequate remedy and the subject matter of the contract is unique (for example, real property).

**Spendthrift trust** A trust created to protect the beneficiary from spending all the money to which he or she is entitled. Only a certain portion of the total amount is given to the beneficiary at any one time, and most states prohibit creditors from attaching assets of the trust.

**Stale check** A check, other than a certified check, that is presented for payment more than six months after its date.

**Standard of review** The test that a court applies when reviewing the actions of an administrative agency.

**Standing** The requirement that an individual must have a sufficient stake in a controversy before he or she can bring a lawsuit. The plaintiff must demonstrate that he or she either has been injured or threatened with injury.

**Stare decisis** A flexible doctrine of the courts, recognizing the value of following prior decisions (precedents) in cases similar to the one before the court; the courts' practice of being consistent with prior decisions based on similar facts.

**Statute** A written law enacted by the legislature under constitutional authority declaring something, prohibiting something, or commanding that something be so.

**Statute of Frauds** A state statute under which certain types of contracts must be in writing to be enforceable.

**Statute of limitations** A statute of the federal government or state government setting the maximum time period during which certain actions can be brought or rights enforced. After the time period set out in the applicable statute of limitations has run, no legal action can be brought.

**Statute of repose** Basically, a statute of limitations that is not dependent upon the happening of a cause of action. Statutes of repose generally begin to run at an earlier date and run for a longer period of time than statutes of limitations.

**Statutory law** Laws enacted by a legislative body (as opposed to constitutional law, administrative law, or case law).

**Statutory period of redemption** A time period (usually set by state statute) during which the property subject to a defaulted mortgage, land contract, or other contract can be redeemed by the debtor after foreclosure or judicial sale.

**Stock** In corporation law, an equity or ownership interest in a corporation, measured in units of shares.

**Stock certificate** A certificate issued by a corporation evidencing the ownership of a specified number of shares at a specified value.

**Stock warrant** A certificate commonly attached to preferred stock and bonds that grants the owner the right to buy a given number of shares of stock, usually within a set time period.

**Stop-payment order** An order by the drawer of a draft or check directing the drawer's bank not to pay the check.

**Strict liability** Liability regardless of fault. In tort law, strict liability is imposed on a merchant who introduces into commerce a good that is unreasonably dangerous when in a defective condition.

**Sublease** A lease executed by the lessee of real estate to a third person, conveying the same interest that the lessee enjoys, but for a shorter term than that held by the lessee (as compared with an assignment of a lease, in which the lessee transfers the entire unexpired term of the leasehold to a third party).

**Subpoena** A document commanding a person to appear at a certain time and place to give testimony concerning a certain matter.

**Substantial evidence test** The test applied by a court reviewing an administrative agency's informal action. The court determines whether the agency acted unreasonably and overturns the agency's findings only if unsupported by a substantial body of evidence.

**Substantive law** Law that defines the rights and duties of individuals with respect to each other, as opposed to procedural law, which defines the manner in which these rights and duties may be enforced.

**Summary judgment** A judgment entered by a trial court prior to trial that is based on the valid assertion by one of the parties that there are no disputed issues of fact that would necessitate a trial.

**Summary jury trial** A relatively recent method of settling disputes in which a trial is held but the jury's verdict is not binding. The verdict only acts as a guide to both sides in reaching an agreement during the mandatory negotiations that immediately follow the trial. If a settlement is not reached, both sides have the right to a full trial later.

**Summons** A document informing a person that a legal action has been commenced against him or her and that he or she must appear in court on a certain date to answer the plaintiff's complaint. The document is delivered by a sheriff or other official.

**Supremacy clause** The clause in Article VI of the Constitution that provides that the Constitution, laws, and treaties of the United States are ''the supreme Law of the Land.'' Under this clause, state laws that directly conflict with federal law will be rendered invalid.

**Surety** One who agrees to be primarily responsible for the debt of another, such as a cosigner on a note.

**Suretyship** A contract in which a third party to a debtor-creditor relationship (the surety) promises that the third party will be primarily responsible for the debtor's obligation.

**Surviving corporation** The remaining, or continuing, corporation following a merger. The surviving corporation is vested with the merged corporation's legal rights and obligations.

**Syllogism** A form of deductive reasoning consisting of a major premise, a minor premise, and a conclusion.

**Symbolic speech** Nonverbal conduct that expresses opinions or thoughts about a subject. Symbolic speech is protected under the First Amendment's guarantee of freedom of speech.

**Syndicate** An investment group of persons or firms brought together for the purpose of financing a project that they would not or could not undertake independently.

# T

**Target corporation** The acquired corporation in a corporate takeover; a corporation to whose shareholders a tender offer is submitted.

**Tariff** An import tax on goods.

**Technology licensing** Allowing another to use and profit from intellectual property (patents, copyrights, trademarks, innovative products or processes, and so on) for consideration. In the context of international business transactions, technology licensing sometimes is an attractive alternative to the establishment of foreign production facilities.

**Teller's check** A negotiable instrument drawn by a bank on another bank or drawn by a bank and *payable at* or *payable through* a bank.

**Tenancy at sufferance** Tenancy by one who, after rightfully being in possession of leased premises, continues (wrongfully) to occupy the property after the lease has been terminated. The tenant has no estate in the land and occupies it only because the person entitled to evict has not done so.

**Tenancy at will** The right of a tenant to remain in possession of land with permission of the landlord until either the tenant or the landlord chooses to terminate the tenancy.

**Tenancy by the entirety** The joint ownership of property by husband and wife. Neither party can alienate or encumber the property without the consent of the other. The property is inherited by the survivor of the two, and dissolution of marriage transforms a tenancy by the entirety into a tenancy in common.

**Tenancy for years** A nonfreehold estate/lease for a specified period of time, after which the interest reverts to the grantor.

**Tenancy in common** Co-ownership of property in which each party owns an undivided interest that passes to his or her heirs at death.

**Tender** A timely offer or expression of willingness to pay a debt or perform an obligation.

**Tender offer** An offer to purchase shares made by one company directly to the shareholders of another company; often referred to more simply as a "takeover bid."

**Term insurance** A type of life insurance policy for which premiums are paid for a specified term. Payment on the policy is due only if death occurs within the term period. Premiums are less expensive than for whole life or limited-payment life, and there is usually no cash surrender value.

**Testamentary trust** A trust that is created by will and therefore does not take effect until the death of the testator.

**Testate** The condition of having died with a valid will.

**Testator** One who makes and executes a will.

**Third party beneficiary contract** A contract between two or more parties, the performance of which is intended to benefit a third party directly, thus giving the third party a right to file suit for breach of contract by either of the original contracting parties.

**Tippee** A person who receives inside information.

**Title insurance** Insurance commonly purchased by a purchaser of real property to protect against loss in the event that the title to the property is not free from liens or superior ownership claims.

**Tombstone ad** An advertisement, in a format resembling a tombstone, of a securities offering. The ad informs potential investors of where and how they may obtain a prospectus.

**Tort** Civil (as opposed to criminal) wrongs not arising from a breach of contract. A breach of a legal duty owed by the defendant to the plaintiff; the breach must be the proximate cause of the harm done to the plaintiff.

**Tortfeasor** One who commits a tort.

**Totten trust** A trust created by the deposit of a person's own money in his or her own name as a trustee for another. It is a tentative trust, revocable at will until the depositor dies or completes the gift in his or her lifetime by some unequivocal act or declaration.

**Toxic tort** Failure to use or to clean up properly or where prohibited to use toxic chemicals that cause harm to a person or society.

**Trade acceptance** A draft drawn by the seller of goods on the purchaser and accepted by the purchaser's written promise to pay the draft. Once accepted, the purchaser becomes primarily liable to pay the draft.

**Trade fixture** The personal property of a commercial tenant that has been installed or affixed to real property for a business purpose. When the lease ends, the tenant can remove the fixture but must repair any damage to the real property caused by the fixture's removal.

**Trade libel** The publication of false information about another's product, alleging it is not what its seller claims; also referred to as slander of quality.

**Trade name** A name used in commercial activity to designate a particular business, a place at which a business is located, or a class of goods. Trade names can be exclusive or nonexclusive. Examples of trade names are Sears, Safeway, and Firestone.

**Trade secrets** Information or processes that give a business an advantage over competitors who do not know the information or processes.

**Trademark** A word or symbol that has become sufficiently associated with a good (at common law) or has been registered with a government agency. Once a trademark is established, the owner has exclusive use of it and has the right to bring a legal action against those who infringe upon the protection given the trademark.

**Tradeoff** A desired result that one must sacrifice (trade off) to obtain another desired result.

**Transfer warranties** Warranties (guaranties) made by the indorser and transferor of a negotiable instrument to all subsequent transferees and holders who take the instrument in good faith that (1) the transferor has good title to the instrument or is otherwise authorized to obtain payment or acceptance on behalf of one who does have good title; (2) all signatures are genuine or authorized; (3) the instrument has not been materially altered; (4) no defense of any party is good against the transferor; and (5) the transferor has no knowledge of any insolvency proceedings against the maker, the acceptor, or the drawer of an unaccepted instrument.

**Traveler's check** An instrument purchased from a bank, express company, or the like, in various denominations, that can be used as cash upon a second signature by the purchaser. It has the characteristics of a cashier's check.

**Treasure trove** Money or coin, gold, silver, or bullion found hidden in the earth or other private place, the owner of which is unknown; literally, treasure found.

**Treaty** An agreement, or compact, formed between two independent nations.

**Treble damages** Damages consisting of single damages determined by a jury and tripled in amount in certain cases as required by statute.

**Trespass to land**   At common law, the intentional or unintentional passing over another person's land un-invited, regardless of whether any physical damage is done to the land. Today a majority of courts find tres-pass only in cases of intentional intrusion, negligence, or some ''abnormally dangerous activity'' on the part of the defendant.

**Trespass to personal property**   Any wrongful transgression or offense against the personal property of another.

**Trespasser**   One who commits the tort of trespass in one of its forms.

**Trial Court**   A court in which most cases usually begin and in which questions of fact are examined.

**Trust**   (1) A form of business organization somewhat similar to a corporation. Originally, the trust was a device by which several corporations that were en-gaged in the same general line of business combined for their mutual advantage to eliminate competition and control the market for their products. The term trust derived from the transfer of the voting power of the corporations' shareholders to the committee or board that controlled the organization. (2) An arrangement in which title to property is held by one person (a trustee) for the benefit of another (a beneficiary).

**Trust indorsement**   An indorsement for the benefit of the indorser or a third person; also known as an agency indorsement. The indorsement results in legal title vesting in the original indorsee.

**Trustee**   One who holds title to property for the use or benefit of another (the beneficiary).

**Tying arrangement**   An agreement between a buyer and a seller under which the buyer of a specific product or service is obligated to purchase additional products or services from the seller.

**Type I error**   An error made as a result of a decision or an action.

**Type II error**   An error made as a result of the failure to make a decision or take action.

## U

*Ultra vires*   A Latin term meaning beyond the powers. Activities of a corporation's managers that are outside the scope of the power granted them by the corpora-tion's charter or the laws of the state of incorporation are ultra vires acts.

**Unconscionability**   A doctrine under which courts may deny enforcement of a contract or clause on the basis of public policy, when one party, as a result of his or her disproportionate bargaining power, is forced to accept terms that are unfairly burdensome and that unfairly benefit the dominating party.

**Unconscionable contract or clause**   A contract or clause that is void on the basis of public policy because one party, as a result of his or her disproportionate bargaining power, is forced to accept terms that are unfairly burdensome and that unfairly benefit the dom-

inating party.

**Underwriter**   In insurance law, the one assuming a risk in return for the payment of a premium; the insurer. In securities law, any person, banker, or syndicate that guarantees a definite sum of money to a business or government in return for the issue of stock or bonds, usually for resale purposes.

**Undisclosed principal**   A principal whose identity is unknown by a third person, and the third person has no knowledge that the agent is acting in an agency capacity at the time the contract is made.

**Unenforceable contract**   A valid contract having no legal effect or force in a court action.

**Unilateral contract**   A contract that includes the exchange of a promise for an act.

**Union shop**   A place of employment in which all workers, once employed, must become union members within a specified period of time as a condition of their continued employment.

**Unitary system**   A centralized governmental system in which local or subdivisional governments exercise only those powers given to them by the central government.

**U.S. trustee**   A government official who performs ap-pointing and other administrative tasks that a bank-ruptcy judge would otherwise have to perform.

**Universal defenses**   Defenses that can be used to avoid payment to all holders of a negotiable instrument, including a holder in due course (HDC) or (under the shelter principle) a holder through an HDC. Also called real defenses.

**Universal life**   A type of insurance that combines some aspects of term insurance with some aspects of whole life insurance.

**Unlawful detainer**   The unjustifiable retention of the possession of real property by one whose right to pos-session has terminated—as when a tenant holds over after the end of the lease term in spite of the landlord's demand for possession.

**Unreasonably dangerous product**   In product lia-bility, a product that is defective to the point of threat-ening a consumer's health and safety. A product will be considered unreasonably dangerous if it is danger-ous beyond the expectation of the ordinary consumer or if a less dangerous alternative was economically feasible for the manufacturer, but the manufacturer failed to produce it.

**Usage of trade**   Any practice or method of dealing having such regularity of observance in a place, vo-cation, or trade as to justify an expectation that it will be observed with respect to the transaction in question.

**Usury**   Charging an illegal rate of interest.

**Utilitarianism**   An approach to ethical reasoning in which ethically correct behavior is not related to any absolute ethical or moral values but to an evaluation of the consequences of a given action on those who will be affected by it. In utilitarian reasoning, a ''good'' decision is one that results in the greatest good for the greatest number of people affected by the decision.

# V

**Valid contract** A properly constituted contract having legal strength or force.

**Validation notice** An initial notice to a debtor from a collection agency informing the debtor that he or she has thirty days to challenge the debt and request verification.

**Venue** The geographical district in which an action is tried and from which the jury is selected.

**Verdict** A formal decision made by a jury.

**Vertical merger** A combining of two firms, one of which purchases goods for resale from the other. If a producer or wholesaler acquires a retailer, it is a forward vertical merger. If a retailer or distributor acquires its producer, it is a backward vertical merger.

**Vertical restraint** Any agreement restraining competition that is made between firms at different levels in the same chain of production or distribution of an item.

**Vertically integrated firm** A firm that carries out two or more functional phases (manufacture, distribution, retailing, etc.) of a product.

**Vesting** The creation of an absolute or unconditional right or power.

**Vicarious liability** Legal responsibility placed on one person for the acts of another.

**Void contract** A contract having no legal force or binding effect.

**Voidable contract** A contract that may be legally annulled at the option of one of the parties.

*Voir dire* From the French, meaning "to speak the truth." A phrase denoting the preliminary questions that attorneys for the plaintiff and the defendant ask prospective jurors to determine whether potential jury members are biased or have any connection with a party to the action or with a prospective witness.

**Voting trust** The transfer of title by stockholders of shares of a corporation to a trustee who is authorized to vote the shares on their behalf.

# W

**Waiver** An intentional, knowing relinquishment of a legal right.

**Warehouse receipt** A document of title issued by a bailee-warehouser to cover the goods stored in the warehouse.

**Warranty deed** A deed under which the grantor guarantees to the grantee that the grantor has title to the property conveyed in the deed, that there are no encumbrances on the property other than what the grantor has represented, and that the grantee will enjoy quiet possession.

**Waste** The abuse or destructive use of real property by one who is in rightful possession of the property but who does not have title to it. Waste does not include ordinary depreciation due to age and normal use.

**Watered stock** Stock issued by a corporation as if fully paid for, when in fact less than par value has been paid.

**Wetlands** Areas of land designated by government agencies (such as the Army Corps of Engineers or the Environmental Protection Agency) as protected areas that suppose wildlife and that therefore cannot be filled in or dredged by private contractors or parties.

**Whistleblowing** Telling the government or the press that one's employer is engaged in some unsafe or illegal activity.

**White-collar crime** Nonviolent crime committed by corporations and individuals. Embezzlement and commercial bribery are two examples of white-collar crime.

**Whole life** A life insurance policy in which the insured pays a level premium for his or her entire life and in which there is a constantly accumulating cash value that can be withdrawn or borrowed against by the borrower. Sometimes referred to as straight life insurance.

**Will** An instrument directing what is to be done with the testator's property upon his or her death, made by the testator and revocable during his or her lifetime. No interests pass until the testator dies.

**Winding up** The second of two stages involved in the dissolution of a partnership or corporation. Once the firm is dissolved, it continues to exist legally until the process of winding up all business affairs (collecting and distributing the firm's assets) is complete.

**Workers' compensation laws** State statutes establishing an administrative procedure for compensating workers' injuries that arise out of, or in the course of, their employment, regardless of fault. Instead of suing the employer, an injured worker files a claim with the administrative agency or board that administers the local workers' compensation claims.

**Working papers** The various documents used and developed by an accountant during an audit. Working papers include notes, computations, memoranda, copies, and other papers that make up the work product of an accountant's services to a client.

**Workout** A common law or bankruptcy out-of-court negotiation with creditors in which a debtor enters into an agreement with a creditor or creditors for a payment or plan to discharge the debtor's debt(s).

**Writ of attachment** A writ employed to enforce obedience to an order or judgment of the court. The writ may take the form of taking or seizing property to bring it under the control of the court.

**Writ of *certiorari*** A writ from a higher court asking the lower court for the record of a case.

**Writ of execution** A writ that puts in force a court's decree or judgment.

**Wrongful discharge** An employer's termination of an employee's employment in violation of common law principles or statutory law that protects a specific class of employees.

# TABLE OF CASES

The principal cases are in bold type. Cases cited or discussed are in roman type. Cases that can also be retrieved on West's LEGAL CLERK Research Software System are indicated by a colored dot. To determine which of the three versions of LEGAL CLERK a particular case appears on, please turn to the text page cited and refer to the color-coded computer symbol printed with the case citation.

A red computer symbol indicates that the case appears on *Uniform Commercial Code/Article 2—Sales (Version 1.0)*. A blue computer symbol indicates that the case is on *Government Regulation and the Legal Environment of Business (Version 1.0)*. A tan computer symbol identifies the case as appearing on *Contracts (Version 1.0)*.

## A

AB&B, Inc. v. Banfi Products, Inc., 765
Abyaneh v. Merchants Bank, North, 581
Action Printing Co. v. Beede, 360
Adams v. Adams, 289–290
Adams v. George W. Cochran & Co., 719–720
Adams v. Lindsell, 244
**Advent Systems, Ltd. v. Unisys Corp., 367–368**
Agins v. Tiburon, 1020
Agis v. Howard Johnson Co., 704
**Alabama Power Co. v. Dunaway, 1037–1038**
Aldana v. Colonial Palms Plaza, Ltd., 325
Ali v. Playgirl, Inc., 133
Allegheny, County of v. American Civil Liberties Union, 96
Allen v. Weyerhaeuser, Inc., 339
Allison v. Nationwide Mutual Insurance Co., 1071
Allison-Bristow Community School District v. Iowa Civil Rights Commission, 630
Allstate Insurance Co. v. Winnebago County Fair Association, Inc., 1004–1005
Alm v. Aluminum Co. of America, 477–478
**Alpo Petfoods, Inc. v. Ralston Purina Co., 136–137**
**Alsatel-Société Alsacienne et Lorraine de Télécommunications et d'Electronique v. S.A. Novasam, 204–205**
Aluminum Co. of America, United States v., 953
**Amalgamated Clothing and Textile Workers Union v. Wal-Mart Stores, Inc., 832–833**

Amberboy v. Société de Banque Privée, 510
American Academic Suppliers, Inc. v. Beckley-Cardy, Inc., 962
**American Dental Association v. Martin, 897–898**
American Dredging Co. v. Plaza Petroleum, Inc., 366
American Federal Bank, FSB v. Parker, 528
**American Federation of Government Employees, AFL-CIO, Local 2391 v. Martin, 707–708**
American Geophysical Union v. Texaco, Inc., 155
American Tobacco Co., United States v., 327
Ann M. v. Pacific Plaza Shopping Center, 1041
**Anspec Co. v. Johnson Controls, Inc., 937–938**
Antares Aircraft, L.P. v. Federal Republic of Nigeria, 1132
Apfelblat v. National Bank of Wyandotte-Taylor, 273
Apple Computer, Inc. v. Franklin Computer Corp., 153
Apple Computer, Inc. v. Microsoft Corp., 153
Argentina, Republic of v. Weltover, Inc., 1129
● Arizona v. Maricopa County Medical Society, 962–963
Arkansas v. Oklahoma, 965
Armory v. Delamirie, 981
● Armster v. United States District Court for the Central District of California, 82–83
Arnold, Schwinn & Co., United States v., 950
Artukovich & Sons, Inc. v. Reliance Truck Co., 228
● Aspen Skiing Co. v. Aspen Highlands Skiing Corp., 963
Atari Games Corp. v. Nintendo of America, Inc., 162
Atlantic Cleaners & Dyers, Inc. v. United States, 946
Atlantic Richfield Co. v. Razumic, 764–765
Augustine v. Marriott Hotel, 1049
Austin v. Berryman, 104
**Austin v. Michigan Chamber of Commerce, 95–96**
● Austin Instrument, Inc. v. Loral Corp., 290
Autry v. Republic Productions, 337
Aymes v. Bonelli, 672
● Azar v. Lehigh Corp., 142

## B

Baby M, In re, 5, 294
Badger v. Linscott, 800
**BAII Banking Corp. v. UPG, Inc., 418–419**
**Baker, In re, 641–642**
Ballinger v. Palm Springs Aerial Tramway, 108
**Balvik v. Sylvester, 856–857**
**Banque Worms v. Davis Construction Co., 598–599**
Barber v. United States National Bank, 568
Barclays Bank of New York, N.A., State v., 510
● Barnes v. Treece, 246

Basic Books, Inc. v. Kinko's Graphics Corp., 154

Batson v. Kentucky, 74, 83

Baughn v. Honda Motor Co., 39

**Baxter International, Inc. v. Morris, 295–296**

Bazak International Corp. v. Mast Industries, 307

**Beasley v. Medin, 218–219**

**Beck Oil Co. v. Texaco Refining & Marketing, Inc., 762–763**

Bell v. Town of Wells, 1048

**Bellsouth Advertising & Publishing Corp. v. Donnelley Information Publishing, Inc., 150–151**

**Bennett v. Shinoda Floral, Inc., 254–255**

Berkowitz v. Baron, 1111–1112

Bernal v. Richard Wolf Medical Instruments Corp., 478

● Berthiaume v. Minnesota Mutual Life Insurance Co., 1070

Bethlehem Steel Corp. v. Ernst & Whinney, 1103

**Bias v. Advantage International, Inc., 666–667**

Bickford v. Mattocks, 977

Bidlack v. Wheelabrator Corp., 311

**Big Knob Volunteer Fire Co. v. Lowe & Moyer Garage, Inc., 603–604**

● Bigelow-Sanford, Inc. v. Gunny Corp., 443

Bily v. Arthur Young & Co., 1103

**Bisbey v. D.C. National Bank, 575–576**

Blackmon v. Hindrew, 526

Blettell, Estate of v. Snider, 986–987

Blinder, Robinson & Co. v. Alzado, 800

**Bloom v. Weiser, 674–675**

Bloomingdale Partners, In re, 943

Blue Chip Stamps v. Manor Drug Stores, 1106

Board of Trade of San Francisco v. Swiss Credit Bank, 428

Board of Trustees of State University of New York v. Fox, 93

Board of Trustees of University of Alabama v. Calhoun, 1093

● **Bobby Floars Toyota, Inc. v. Smith, 267–268**

Boender v. Chicago North Clubhouse Association, Inc., 609

**Bolan v. Bolan, 1076–1077**

Bower v. AT&T Technologies, Inc., 361

**Boyd, Payne, Gates & Farthing, P.C. v. Payne, Gates, Farthing & Radd, P.C., 810–811**

Bradley v. Pizzaco of Nebraska, Inc., 726

Bradley v. Wingnut Films, Ltd., 109

Bray, In re, 652

**Bray v. Kate, 116**

**Breeling v. Churchill, 1022–1023**

Brind v. International Trust Co., 979

Britt, State v., 188

Britton v. Turner, 222

Broadway Management Corp. v. Briggs, 509

**Brockwell v. Lake Gaston Sales and Service, 993–994**

Brooke Group, Ltd. v. Brown & Williamson Tobacco Corp., 955

Brown v. Board of Education of Topeka, 5

Brown Shoe v. United States, 957

Brown University, United States v., 967, 968

Browning-Ferris Industries of Vermont, Inc. v. Kelco Disposal, Inc., 472

● Bunny Bear, Inc. v. Peterson, 904

**Burack v. I. Burack, Inc., 858–859**

Burchett v. Allied Concord Financial Corp., 520

**Burger King Corp. v. Weaver, 760–761**

Burke v. Burke, 1094

Burnell v. General Telephone Co. of Illinois, Inc., 39

● Butkovich & Sons, Inc. v. State Bank of St. Charles, 339

Butler v. Frontier Telephone Co., 971

# C

● Calcote v. Citizens & Southern National Bank, 613

Callis v. Colonial Properties, Inc., 1045

Calvert Cliffs Coordinating Committee v. Atomic Energy Commission, 929

**Campbell v. Acuff-Rose Music, Inc., 20–22**

**Campbell v. Bic Corp., 35**

**Campbell Soup Co. v. Wentz, 287** , 382

**Cancik, Estate of, 1073–1074**

Canter's Pharmacy, Inc. v. Elizabeth Associates, 799–800

Caribbean Marine Services Co. v. Baldrige, 905

Carnival Leisure Industries, Ltd. v. Aubin, 311

Carola v. Grogan, 799

● Carpenter v. Alberto Culver Co., 461

Carpenter v. Mason, 352

Carroll Air Systems, Inc. v. Greenbaum, 122

● Carson v. Here's Johnny Portable Toilets, 133

Casey v. Kastel, 662

Casino Marketing Group, Inc., State v., 910

**Cates v. International Telephone and Telegraph Corp., 776–777**

Causby, United States v., 971

**Central Bank Denver, N.A. v. First Interstate Bank of Denver, N.A., 1107–1108**

Central Bank of Denver, N.A. v. Mehaffy, Rider, Windholz & Wilson, 1103–1104

Central Hudson Gas & Electric Corp. v. Public Service Commission of New York, 93

Central Properties, Inc. v. Robbinson, 246

Cerezo v. Babson Brothers Co., 621

**Chabad House-Lubavitch of Palm Beach County, Inc. v. Banks, 80**

Chabal v. Reagan, 904

**Chafetz v. United Parcel Service, Inc., 308–310**

Chang v. First Colonial Savings Bank, 247

Charles of the Ritz Distributing Corp. v. Federal Trade Commission, 907

Charrier v. Bell, 986

Charter Township of Ypsilanti v. General Motors Corp., 209

Chemical Dynamics, Inc. v. Newfeld, 844

**Chemical Waste Management, Inc. v. Hunt, 87–88**

Chestman, United States v., 878

Chiarella v. United States, 873, 882

Chicago v. Matchmaker Real Estate Sales Center, Inc., 672

Chicago Board of Trade v. United States, 947

Chicago Professional Sports Limited Partnership v. National Basketball Association, 950

Chocolate Manufacturers Association v. Block, 891

**Chosnyka v. Meyer, 241**

Christian Methodist Episcopal Church v. S&S Construction Co., 700

**Chrysler Credit Corp. v. Keeling, 618–619**

Chrysler Motors Corp. v. International Union, Allied Industrial Workers of America, 34

CIBA-Geigy Corp. v. Environmental Protection Agency, 942

● Cidis v. White, 274

**Cincinnati, City of v. Discovery Network, Inc., 93–94**

Cipollone v. Liggett Group, Inc., 89

City of (see name of city)

● Clement v. Prestwich, 325

**Clyburn v. Allstate Insurance Co., 1060,** 1131

CMI Corp. v. Leemar Steel Co., 427

● **Coca-Cola Co., The v. The Koke Co. of America, 145–146**

Cohen v. Cowles Media Co., 229

Coker International, Inc. v. Burlington Industries, Inc., 339

Coleman v. Charlesworth, 765

Colgate & Co., United States v., 952

● Colorado Carpet Installation, Inc. v. Palermo, 393

**Colorado-Kansas Grain Co. v. Reifschneider, 368–369**

Columbus-America Discovery Group, Inc. v. Atlantic Mutual Insurance Co., 982

Columbus-America Discovery Group, Inc. v. Unidentified, Wrecked and Abandoned Sailing Vessel, 982

Commerce Properties, Inc. v. Linthicum, 1045

Commonwealth v. _____ (see opposing party)

**Compaq Computer Corp. v. Horton, 837–838**

Computer Associates International v. Altai, Inc., 153

● **Computer Network, Ltd. v. Purcell Tire & Rubber Co., 216–217**

Congregation Lubavitch v. City of Cincinnati, 96

Connecticut National Bank and Trust Co. v. Chadwick, 1094

Consolidated Edison Co. v. Public Service Commission, 94

Continental Forest Products v. White Lumber Sales, Inc., 416

● Continental T.V., Inc. v. GTE Sylvania, Inc., 950, **951–952**

Cook v. Rhode Island Department of Mental Health, 729

Cooper v. French, 1049

Coopers & Lybrand v. Fox, 823

Corning Glass Works v. Brennan, 739

**Council 4, AFSCME, State v., 57–58**

County of (see name of county)

Cozzi v. North Palos Elementary School District No. 117, 40

Crane Ice Cream Co. v. Terminal Freezing & Heating Co., 318

Credit Alliance Corp. v. Arthur Andersen & Co., 1101, 1112

**Crews v. W.A. Brown & Son, Inc., 454**

● Crisan, In re Estate of, 228

Crocker v. Winthrop Laboratories, Division of Sterling Drug, Inc., 466

Cross v. Midtown Club, Inc., 822

Crothers by Crothers v. Cohen, 461

**Cubby, Inc. v. Compuserve, Inc., 135–136**

● Cudahy Foods Co. v. Holloway, 393

**Cumis Insurance Society, Inc. v. Girard Bank, 556–557**

**Curde v. Tri-City Bank & Trust Company, 571–572**

Currey, In re, 652

Cusack, United States v., 172

## D

Daniels v. Essex Group, Inc., 725

David Tunick, Inc. v. Kornfeld, 415

Davidow v. Inwood North Professional Group-Phase I, 1044

**Davis v. Celotex Corp., 852–853**

Davis v. Davis, 1048

**Dawkins and Co. v. L&L Planting Co., 378**

DBI Services, Inc. v. Amerada Hess Corp., 142

Defeo v. Amfarms Associates, 244

Deffenbaugh Industries v. Angus, 720

● Delta Junction, City of v. Mack Trucks, Inc., 695, 883

Dempsey v. Rosenthal, 461

Department of Energy, Ohio v., 941

Diamond v. Diehr and Lutton, 148

● **Diamond v. Oreamuno, 869–870**

Diaz v. Pan American World Airways, Inc., 735

Dickinson v. Dodds, 246

**Dirks v. SEC, 871–873**

DMI Furniture, Inc. v. Brown, Kraft & Co., 1112

Dodge v. Ford Motor Co., 837

**Dodson v. Shrader, 263–264**

Dolan v. City of Tigard, 1024, 1048

Donahue v. Fair Employment and Housing Commission, 104

**Dougherty, Paul S., III, In the matter of the amended administrative penalty order issued to, 171–172**

Douglas v. Aztec Petroleum Corp., 672

Drs. Laves, Sarewitz and Walko v. Briggs, 229

Duggin v. Adams, 142

● **Dun & Bradstreet, Inc. v. Greenmoss Builders, Inc., 138–139**

Dunay v. Ladenburg, Thalmann & Co., 784

● Dunn v. General Equities of Iowa, Ltd., 355

## E

E. I. du Pont de Nemours & Co., United States v., 957

**E. I. du Pont de Nemours & Co. v. Christopher, 156–157**

● Eames v. James, 246

Eastern Railroad Presidents Conference v. Noerr Motor Freight, Inc., 961

Eastman Kodak Co. v. Image Technical Services, Inc., 963

**Eckert International, Inc. v. Government of the Sovereign Democratic Republic of Fiji, 1118**

EEOC (see Equal Employment Opportunity Commission)

Eifler v. Shurgard Capital Management Corp., 1005

Electrical Workers Local 1245 v. Skinner, 707

Electromation, Inc., 745

Ellison v. Brady, 725

Elsken v. Network Multi-Family Security Corp., 355

**Elsner v. Albrecht, 914–915**

●**Embs v. Pepsi-Cola Bottling Co. of Lexington, Kentucky, Inc., 474–475**

**Employment Division, Department of Human Resources of the State of Oregon v. Smith, 97**

Engel Industries, Inc. v. First American Bank, N.A., 480

Ensley Branch, N.A.A.C.P. v. City of Birmingham, 101

Environmental Protection Agency v. National Crushed Stone Association, 942

Epps v. St. Mary's Hospital of Athens, Inc., 709

Equal Employment Opportunity Commission v. AIC Security, 743

Equal Employment Opportunity Commission v. Arabian American Oil Co., 1125

Ernst & Ernst v. Hochfelder, 877–878, 1106

**Escott v. BarChris Construction Corp., 862–863, 1105**

Estate of (see name of party)

Eustler v. First National Bank, Pawhuska, 535

Evergreen Amusement Corp. v. Milstead, 252

**Executive Coach Builders v. Bush & Cook Leasing, Inc., 408–409**

## F

●Faherty v. Faherty, 62

**Fairchild Publications Division of Capital Cities Media, Inc. v. Rosston, Kremer & Slawter, Inc., 681–682**

Fairmount Glass Works v. Grunden-Martin Woodenware Co., 232

Faith v. Singleton, 1093

Faretta v. California, 63

Farmers Bank of Greenwood v. Perry, 1005

Farmers Cooperative Elevator Co. v. Union State Bank, 655

Federal Baseball Club of Baltimore, Inc. v. National League of Professional Baseball Clubs, 960

**Federal Deposit Insurance Corp. v. Culver, 521–522**

Federal Deposit Insurance Corp. v. W. Hugh Meyer & Associates, Inc., 613

Federal Deposit Insurance Corp. v. Woodside Construction, Inc., 585

Federal Trade Commission v. Indiana Federation of Dentists, 963

●**Federal Trade Commission v. Procter & Gamble Co., 958–959**

**Feist & Feist Realty Corp. v. Dockside Urban Renewal Corp., 242–243**

Feist Publications, Inc. v. Rural Telephone Service Co., 150

**Felton Investment Group v. Taurman, 789–790**

Fidelity & Casualty Co. v. First City Bank of Dallas, 545

**Filanto, S.P.A. v. Chilewich International Corp., 386–387**

●Fineman v. Citicorp USA, Inc., 260

Fink v. Cox, 248

Firelock, Inc. v. District Court, 20th Judicial District, 62

**First American Bank and Trust v. Rishoi, 555–556**

First Fidelity Bank, N.A. v. Government of Antigua & Barbuda, 664

**First Florida Bank, N.A. v. Max Mitchell & Co., 1101–1102**

First National Bank of Boston v. Bellotti, 94

First Virginia Bank-Colonial v. Masri, M.D., 582

**Firstier Bank, N.A. v. Triplett, 542–543**

Fish, In re, 613

Fitzner Pontiac-Buick-Cadillac, Inc. v. Smith, 461

**Fitzpatrick v. Madonna, 469–470**

Fleet Factors Corp., United States v., 934

**Fletcher v. Kidder, Peabody & Co., 56–57**

Fletcher v. Rylands, 123

Flowers Baking Co. v. R-P Packaging, Inc., 393

FMC Corp. v. Boesky, 878–879

Foakes v. Beer, 251

Foltz v. U.S. News & World Report, Inc., 878

**Fong Fung-Ying and Attorney General, 200**

**Fortino v. Quasar Co., A Division of Matsushita Electric Corp. of America, 1125–1126**

●Foster & Marshall, Inc. v. Pfister, 290

Foucart v. Paul, 986

Frazee v. Illinois Department of Employment Security, 96

●Freeman v. Garcia, 1004

**Fudge v. Penthouse International, Ltd., 108–109**

Fulton National Bank v. Delco Corp., 489

## G

Gaillard v. Natomas Co., 859

**Gainesville Radiology Group v. Hummel, 78–79**

Galatia Community State Bank v. Kindy, 510

Garavalia v. Heat Controller, Inc., 462

Garrett v. Mazda Motors of America, 483

●Gates v. Arizona Brewing Co., 61–62

Gault, In re, 176

Geary v. United States Steel Corp., 39

General Electric, United States v., 704

**General Motors Acceptance Corp. v. Abington Casualty Insurance Co., 507–508**

**General Motors Acceptance Corp. v. Daniels, 626–627**

Gerber v. City National Bank of Florida, 567–568

Gibbons v. Ogden, 85

Gibbs v. American Savings & Loan, 247

Giberson v. Ford Motor Co., 474

Gibson v. Cranage, 331

Gilbert Family Partnership v. Nido Corp., 1105

Giles v. Pick Hotels Corp., 126

Gilmer v. Interstate/Johnson Lane Corp., 55

Gladney v. Paul Revere Life Insurance Co., 1070

**Glenn v. Hoteltron Systems, Inc., 839–840**

Gooden v. Day's Inn, 1005

Gordonsville Industries, Inc. v. American Artos Corp., 394

**Goss v. Trinity Savings & Loan Association, 496–497**

Grand Jury No. 86–3 (Will Roberts Corp.), In re, 802

**Graves v. Kelley, 974–975**

Gray v. Great American Reserve Insurance Co., 1070

Gray v. Martino, 259

• Graybar Electric Co. v. Shook, 411

Green v. Shell Oil Co., 696

• **Greenman v. Yuba Power Products, Inc., 467–468**

**Greenwood Trust Co. v. Commonwealth of Massachusetts, 89–90**

• Griggs v. Duke Power Co., 740

Grimes v. Ohio Edison Co., 844–845

Grinnell Corp., United States v., 952

Gruenemeier v. Seven-Up Co., 40

Guilford Yacht Association, Inc. v. Northeast Dredging, Inc., 252

Gull Air, Inc., In re, 652

Guth v. Loft, Inc., 880

# H

H. C. Blackwell Co. v. Kenworth Truck Co., 764

• H. R. Moch Co. v. Rensselaer Water Co., 325

H. Rosenblum, Inc. v. Adler, 1111

**Hadley v. Baxendale , 342, 343–344**

• Halbman v. Lemke, 273–274

Hallmark Cards, Inc. v. Peevy, 630

• Hamaker v. Kenwel-Jackson Machine Co., 859

**Hamer v. Sidway, 249–250**

**Hapag-Lloyd, A.G. v. Marine Indemnity Insurance Co. of America, 437–438**

Harless v. First National Bank in Fairmont, 703

**Harmer v. Virginia Electric and Power Co., 730**

Harmony Unlimited, Inc. v. Chivetta, 629–630

Harris v. City of Zion, Lake County, Illinois, 96

**Harris v. Forklift Systems, Inc., 723–724**

Harris v. Looney, 823

Harris v. New York, 183

Harris v. U.S. Trustee, 652

Harris Corp. v. National Iranian Radio and Television, 1128–1129

Hartman v. Walkertown Shopping Center, Inc., 115

Harwood Pharmacal Co. v. National Broadcasting Co., 136

**Hawaii Corp., The, In re, 1098–1100**

Hawkins v. McGee, 231, 341

• **Haydocy Pontiac, Inc. v. Lee, 265–266**

Hayes International Corp., United States v., 172

Hazen Paper Co. v. Biggins, 40

Healy v. Brewster, 252

• **Heart of Atlanta Motel v. United States, 86–87**

• **Heggblade-Marguleas-Tenneco, Inc. v. Sunshine Biscuit, Inc., 380–381**

• Helvey v. Wabash County REMC, 393

**Henery v. Robinson, 421–422**

Henningsen v. Bloomfield Motors, Inc., 482

Herman & MacLean v. Huddleston, 1106

Hermitage Methodist Homes of Virginia, Inc. v. Dominion Trust Co., 1094

Herrin v. Sutherland, 971

Hershberger, State v., 103

Hessenthaler v. Farzin, 307

Hicklin v. Orbeck, 99

Hicks v. Flanagan, 1024

**Hill v. Zimmerer, 754–755**

Hirsch v. S. C. Johnson & Son, Inc., 133

Hochster v. De La Tour, 332

Hodgdon v. Mt. Mansfield Co., 733

• **Hoffman v. Red Owl Stores, Inc., 256–257**

**Hoffman Homes, Inc. v. Administrator, United States Environmental Protection Agency, 931–932**

Holland v. Illinois, 74

Holly v. First National Bank, 252

**Holly Hill Acres, Ltd. v. Charter Bank of Gainesville, 494–495**

Hotchkiss v. National City Bank of New York, 231

**Humana Health Care Plans v. Snyder-Gilbert, 1057–1058**

• Hunter v. Hayes, 260

**Husker News Co. v. South Ottumwa Savings Bank, 535–536**

# I

ICC Industries, Inc. v. United States, 1128

Illinois v. Perkins, 188

In re (see name of party)

• **Industrial Lift Truck Service Corp. v. Mitsubishi International Corp., 224–225**

Inniss v. Methot Buick-Opel, Inc., 428

Insurance Commissioner v. Equitable Life Assurance Society, 1131

International Business Machines Corp. v. United States, 956

International Shoe Co. v. Washington, 42, 804

International Technical Instruments, Inc. v. Engineering Measurements Co., 442

**Intertherm, Inc. v. Olympic Homes Systems, Inc., 817–818**

Isaacs v. Huntington Memorial Hospital, 1040

Ismael v. Goodman Toyota, 462

• Iverson v. Scholl, Inc., 274

# J

J.E.B. v. Alabama ex rel. T.B., 74, 83

Jackson v. Anchor Packing Co., 471

Jackson v. McCleod, 740

**Jacobs & Young, Inc. v. Kent, 330–331**

**Jacobson v. United States, 180**

James Daniel Good Real Property, United States v., 176

**Jason's Foods, Inc. v. Peter Eckrich & Sons, Inc.,** 401–402

Jensen v. Ray Kim Ford, Inc., 923

**Joe Morgan, Inc., In re, 515–516**

**Joel v. Morison, 686–687**

● **Johns-Manville Corp., In re,** 643–644

Johnson, Texas v., 93

Johnson v. Calvert, 294

Johnson v. Honeywell Information Systems, Inc., 736

Johnson v. Johnson, 1046

**Johnson v. State, 166–167**

**Johnson v. Town of Trail Creek, 622–623**

Johnston v. Del Mar Distributing Co., 720

Jones v. Bank of Nevada, 613

● **Jones v. Star Credit Corp.,** 298, **382–383**

Jones v. United States, 177

Jordon v. K-Mart Corp., 478

Judd v. Citibank, 586

Just for Kids, Inc., In re, 595

### K

K & M Contracting, Inc. v. Citizens National Bank, 537

Kahr v. Markland, 412

Kahriger, United States v., 91

Kampman v. Pittsburgh Contracting and Engineering Co., 304

**Katco v. Briney, 178–179**

Kaufman v. Jaffe, 284

Kayser-Roth Corp., United States v., 937

Kelley v. EPA, 935

Kelly-Springfield Tire Co., Matter of Establishment Inspection of, 711

Kemp v. Beneke, 483

**Kendall Yacht Corp. v. United California Bank, 552–553**

**Kenrich Petrochemicals, Inc. v. National Labor Relations Board, 717–718**

Kerr Steamship Co. v. Radio Corp. of America, 355

Kesterson v. Cronan, 987

Khan v. Shiley, Inc., 283, 466

Khoury, People v., 187

Kid Gloves, Inc. v. First National Bank of Jefferson Parrish, 546

Kirkland v. Todd, 630

**Kirsch v. Prince George's County, 1018–1019**

Klas v. Van Wagoner, 290

Klein v. Pyrodyne Corp., 127

Klim v. Jones, 619

Kling, Estate of, 1093

**Klos v. Molenda, 1016–1017**

Kloster-Madsen, Inc. v. Tafi's, Inc., 629

**Knight Communications, Inc. v. Boatmen's National Bank of St. Louis, 559–560**

**Kotovsky v. Ski Liberty Operating Corp., 297**

**Kraft, Inc. v. Federal Trade Commission, 909–910**

**Kruser v. Bank of America NT & SA, 577–579**

Kumar Corp. v. Nopal Lines, Ltd., 411–412

● Kveragas v. Scottish Inns, Inc., 126–127

### L

L.M.T. Steel Products, Inc. v. Peirson, 671

Labine v. Vincent, 1083

Laird v. Scribner Cooperative, Inc., 462

LaJaunie v. DaGrossa, 311

Lamb v. Phillip Morris, Inc., 1129

Lanci v. Metropolitan Insurance Co., 289

● Landrine v. Mego Corp., 39–40

● **Lane v. Honeycutt, 406–408**

Lange v. United States, 252

Larese v. Creamland Dairies, Inc., 765

● Lawrence v. Fox, 321

**Lawrence Paper Co. v. Rosen & Co., 234–235**

**Lawson v. Rogers, 774–775**

**Lazar, In re, 638–639**

Lazar v. Thermal Equipment Corp., 695

Leasefirst v. Hartford Rexall Drugs, 14

Ledford, In re, 784

● **Lefkowitz v. Great Minneapolis Surplus Store, Inc., 232–234**

Lehmann v. Toys 'Я' Us, 725

**Lenkin v. Beckman, 791–792**

Lessin, Ohio v., 76–77

Levinson v. American Thermex, Inc., 630

Levondosky v. Marina Associates, 462

**Libera, United States v., 874–875**

Libra Bank Ltd. v. Banco Nacional de Costa Rica, S.A., 1116, 1128

**Liddle v. Salem School District No. 600, 989–990**

**Light v. Sheets, 1032–1033**

Lindeman v. Eli Lilly and Co., 461

Little Rock & Fort Smith Railway Co. v. Eubanks, 296

Liviola, United States v., 172

Locke v. Arabi Grain & Elevator Co., 412

● Loeb & Co. v. Schreiner, 393

**Loral Fairchild Corp. v. Victor Co. of Japan, Ltd., 42, 805–806**

Lotus Development Corp. v. Paperback Software International, Ltd., 153

Louisiana-Pacific Corp. v. Asarco, Inc., 942

**Lowther v. Riggleman, 793–794**

Lucas v. Hamm, 321

● **Lucy v. Zehmer, 270–271**

Ludvigson, State v., 188

Lumley v. Gye, 129

Lupofresh, Inc. v. Pabst Brewing Co., 442

Lynch v. Donnelly, 96

Lysaght v. State of New Jersey, 910

### M

Macklowe v. 42nd Street Development Corp., 800

Mackowick v. Westinghouse Electric Corp., 478

● **MacPherson v. Buick Motor Co., 464–465**

● Maine v. Taylor, 103

Mandeville Island Farms, Inc. v. American Crystal Sugar Co., 946

Mann v. Helmsley-Spear, Inc., 311

Mannington Mills, Inc. v. Congoleum Corp., 1128

Marbury v. Madison, 51, 85

**Maresco v. Evans Chemetics, Division of W.R. Grace & Co., 728–729**

● Maricopa County Medical Society, Arizona v., 962–963

Marine Midland Bank-New York v. Graybar Electric Co., 509

**Marsh v. Oregon Natural Resources Council, 899–900 , 929**

● **Marshall v. Barlow's, Inc., 98, 712, 894**

Marston Enterprises, Inc. v. Seattle-First National Bank, 545–546

Martin v. Martin's News Service, Inc., 859

● Martin v. New York State Department of Mental Hygiene, 82

**Martin Rispens & Son v. Hall Farms, Inc., 448–449**

Maryland Bank and Trust Co., United States v., 934

Maschmeier v. Southside Press, Ltd., 845

Massengil v. Indiana National Bank, 614

Master Distributors Inc. v. Pako Corp., 145

**Matsushita Electric Industrial Co. v. Zenith Radio Corp., 1124**

Matter of (see name of party)

**MBank of El Paso v. Sanchez, 688–689**

McCall v. Owens, 653

McCarthy v. United States, 986

McCarthy, Kenney & Reidy, P.C. v. First National Bank of Boston, 545

McConnell v. Commonwealth Pictures Corp., 294

McCormick Piano & Organ Co. v. Geiger, 924

McCune v. Neitzel, 109

McGowan v. Maryland, 96

McGowan v. McGowan, 1046

McGuire v. Radisson Hotels International, Inc., 883

**McKennon v. Nashville Banner Publishing Co., 736**

McLain v. Real Estate Board of New Orleans, Inc., 85

McLamb, United States v., 935

**McLanahan v. Farmers Insurance Co. of Washington, 327–328**

McLaughlin v. Pannell Kerr Forster, 844

Meads v. Citicorp Credit Services, Inc., 126

Mehl v. Mehl, 783

● Meinhard-Commercial Corp. v. Hargo Woolen Mills, 411

Mellon Bank, N.A. v. Securities Settlement Corp., 582

**Metropolitan Creditors Service of Sacramento v. Sadri, 292–293**

Metropolitan Life Insurance Co. v. Reeves, 986

Metz v. Transit Mix, Inc., 727

● **Michael v. First Chicago Corp., 983–984**

**Midwest Environmental Consulting & Remediation Services, Inc. v. Peoples Bank of Bloomington, 616–618**

Midwest Management Corp. v. Stephens, 844

**Miller v. Payco-General American Credits, Inc., 918–919**

Mineral Park Land Co. v. Howard, 335

Minnick v. Mississippi, 183

**Miranda v. Arizona, 182–183 , 188**

**Missouri Pacific Railway Co. v. Elmore & Stahl, 1001–1002**

M&M Wholesale Florist, Inc. v. Emmons, 823

M'Naghten's Case, 177

Mogilevsky v. Superior Court, 744

Moldea v. New York Times Co., 109

Monetti, S.P.A. v. Anchor Hocking Corp., 394

Money Mart Check Cashing Center, Inc. v. Epicycle Corp., 527–528

**Moore v. Puget Sound Plywood, Inc., 457**

Moore v. Regents of the University of California, 1047

**Moores v. Greenberg, 1097–1098**

Morgan, United States v., 950

**Morris v. Mack's Used Cars, 921–922**

Moser v. Federal Communications Commission, 910

● Motor Vehicle Manufacturers Association v. State Farm Mutual Automobile Insurance Co., 904

Motor Vehicle Manufacturers Association of the United States v. State, 62

**Motorists Mutual Insurance Co. v. Richmond, 1055–1056**

**Mueller v. Soffer, 995–996**

Multimedia Publishing of South Carolina, Inc. v. Mullins, 845

Muniz, Pennsylvania v., 183

Murphy v. Canion, 785

Musick, Peeler & Garrett v. Employers Insurance of Wausau, 867

Myers v. Putzmeister, Inc., 859

## N

National Bank v. Quinn, 567

National Bank of Joliet v. Bergeron Cadillac, Inc., 630

National Labor Relations Board v. Bildisco and Bildisco, 645

National Organization for Women, Inc. v. Joseph Scheidler, 140

National Pawn Brokers Unlimited v. Osterman, Inc., 655

● National Society of Professional Engineers v. United States, 948–949

● NCAA v. Board of Regents of the University of Oklahoma, 962

NCH Corp. v. Broyles, 672

**Neptune Research & Development, Inc. v. Teknics Industrial Systems, Inc., 424–425**

New England Mutual Life Insurance Co. v. Johnson, 1071

New Era Publications International, ApS v. Carol Publishing Group, 162

● **New Jersey Mortgage & Investment Corp. v. Berenyi, 524–525**

New York, State of v. Shore Realty Corp., 937

New York v. Burger, 904

New York v. Quarles, 183

**New York Life Insurance Co. v. Johnson, 1061–1062**

New York Times Co. v. Sullivan, 111
Nicol v. Imagematrix, Inc., 722
Niehaus v. Delaware Valley Medical Center, 742
Niemiec v. Kellmark Corp., 312
Nike, Inc. v. ''Just Did It'' Enterprises, 161–162
Nilsson v. Continental Machine Manufacturing Co., 859
Nixon, United States v., 52
NLO, Inc., In re, 59
**Nollan v. California Coastal Commission, 1020–1021,** 1048
Nordlinger v. Hahn, 104
**North Charleston, City of v. Claxton, 973**

## O

O'Brien v. O'Brien, 1046
O'Driscoll v. Hercules, Inc., 740
**Oestman v. National Farmers Union Insurance Co., 661–662**
Ognibene v. Citibank, N.A., 582
Ohio v. Department of Energy, 940
**Ohio v. Lessin, 76–77**
● O'Keefe v. Lee Calan Imports, Inc., 246
Oklahoma, Arkansas v., 965
Oklahoma Press Publishing Co. v. Walling, 894
**Old Island Fumigation, Inc. v. Barbee, 124**
Oliker v. Gershunoff, 799
Olsen v. Hawkins, 269
Omoruyi, United States v., 83
O'Neill v. Commissioner of Internal Revenue, 1090
O'Neill v. Williams, 1024
● Ontai v. Straub Clinic and Hospital, Inc., 478
Orders Distributing Co. v. Newsome Carpets & Wallcovering, 784
Original Appalachian Artworks, Inc. v. Topps Chewing Gum, Inc., 161
**Orr v. Orr, 321–322**
Ort v. Fowler, 583
Ortelere v. Teachers' Retirement Board, 271
Osborne v. Ohio, 92
Otto, People v., 709
Overton v. Reilly, 733
● Owens v. Haas, 325
Owens-Corning Fiberglas, In re, 145

## P

Pacific Mutual Life Insurance Co. v. Haslip, 472, 1130
Palmer v. BRG of Georgia, Inc., 963
**Palsgraf v. Long Island Railroad Co., 117–118**
Pando by Pando v. Fernandez, 311
Paramount Communications, Inc. v. QVC Network, Inc., 848, 881
● Park, United States v., 171
Parker v. Brown, 961
Parker v. Domino's Pizza, Inc., 884
**Parker v. Twentieth Century-Fox Film Corp., 345–346**
Parra v. Tarasco, Inc., 127

Parrett v. Platte Valley State Bank & Trust Co., 568
**Partipilo v. Hallman, 222–223**
Patterson v. Rohm Gesellschaft, 478
Pedraza v. Shell Oil Co., 711
**Pedro v. Pedro, 842–843**
Peel v. Attorney Registration and Disciplinary Commission, 103
Peerless Glass Co. v. Pacific Crockery Co., 276
Pell v. Victor J. Andrew High School, 40
Pennfield Corp. v. Meadow Valley Electric, Inc., 471
Pennsylvania v. Monnick, 183
Pennsylvania Department of Public Welfare v. Davenport, 652
People v. _____ (see opposing party)
**Peoples Restaurant v. Sabo, 70**
Perez v. Van Groningen & Sons, Inc., 695
Perez-Medina v. First Team Auction, Inc., 412
Perkins, Illinois v., 188
Peterson v. Fortier, 765
● **Pfizer, Inc., In re, 907–908**
**Phoenix v. Garbage Services Co., 939–940**
Piazza v. Major League Baseball, 960
**Piper, In re Estate of, 977–978**
**Pitman v. Flanagan Lumber Co., 797–798**
Pittsburgh Testing Laboratory v. Farnsworth & Chambers, Inc., 252
Plessy v. Ferguson, 5
Port Ship Service, Inc. v. Norton, Lilly & Co., 695–696
Porter v. Citibank, N.A., 581
Potter v. Oster, 356
Powell v. H.E.F. Partnership, 1112
Powers v. Ohio, 74
**Prince v. Atlanta Coca-Cola Bottling Co., 997–998**
**Product Liability (Case VI ZR 103/89), Re, 198**
Professional Real Estate Investors Inc. v. Columbia Pictures Industries, Inc., 961
**Providence & Worcester Railroad Co. v. Sargent & Greenleaf, Inc., 372–373**
Provident Mutual Life Insurance Co. v. Tachtronic Instruments, Inc., 1044
Pym v. Campbell, 308

## Q

Qualitex Co. v. Jacobsen Products Co., 145
Quality Inns International, Inc. v. McDonald's Corp., 162
Quantum Development Corp., In re, 507
Quarles, New York v., 183
**Quick v. Peoples Bank of Cullman County, 140–141**

## R

R.A.V. v. City of St. Paul, Minnesota, 93
**Racicky v. Simon, 349–350**
Racquemore v. State, 188
Radtke v. Everett, 723
**Raffles v. Wichelhaus, 278**
Ramirez v. Bureau of State Lottery, 509–510
**Ramsey v. Gordon, 669–670**

Raritan River Steel Co. v. Cherry, Bekaert & Holland, 1102

Raymond Motor Transportation, Inc. v. Rice, 87

• REA Express, Inc. v. Brennan, 719

Read v. South Carolina National Bank, 568

**Red River Commodities, Inc. v. Eidsness, 677–678**

Reese v. United States, 732

Regents of the University of California v. Bakke, 742

Regional Properties, Inc. v. Financial & Real Estate Consulting Co., 228

Reliance Cooperage Corp. v. Treat, 332

Reliance Electric Co. v. Emerson Electric Co., 879

Republic of Argentina v. Weltover, Inc., 1129

Republic National Bank of Miami, United States v., 176

Resolution Trust Corporation v. 1601 Partners, Ltd., 510

• Rheinberg-Kellerei GMBH v. Vineyard Wine Co., 427

Rhodes v. Inland-Rome, Inc., 103–104

Rhodes v. Wilkins, 306

Rice v. Branigar Organization, Inc., 924

Richelman v. Kewanee Machinery & Conveyor Co., 477

**Richmond, In re, 633–634**

Ricketts v. Scothorn, 256

Riley v. Kingsley Underwriting Agencies, Ltd., 394

Ringling Bros.-Barnum and Bailey Combined Shows v. Ringling, 807

Ritz-Craft Corp. v. Stanford Management Group, 394

Rivendell Forest Products, Ltd. v. Georgia-Pacific Corp., 260

**Roberts v. National Liberty Group of Companies, 1063–1064**

Roberts v. Walmart Stores, Inc., 924

Robertson v. Estate of Zimmerman, 986

Robertson v. Levy, 804

Robertson v. Methow Valley Citizens' Council, 929

Robinson v. Jacksonville Shipyards, Inc., 92

**Robotham v. State, 101–102**

• Rose v. Sheehan Buick, Inc., 274

**Rosenberg v. Son, Inc., 319–320**

Rosenfeld v. Southern Pacific Co., 735

**Rosiny v. Schmidt, 808–809**

• Ross Cattle Co. v. Lewis, 427

Roth v. Ray-Stel's Hair Stylists, Inc., 461

Rowland v. Magna Millikin Bank of Decatur, N.A., 924

Roxberry v. Robertson and Penn, Inc., 720

Royal Bed and Spring Co. v. Famossul Industria e Comercio de Moveis Ltda., 393–394

**Royal Jones & Associates, Inc. v. First Thermal Systems, Inc., 432**

Rushing Construction Co. v. MCM Ventures, II, Inc., 1044–1045

• Rutyna v. Collection Accounts Terminal, Inc., 924

Ruzicka v. Conde Nast Publications, Inc., 260

Ryan v. Weiner, 355–356

Rybicki, United States v., 187

Rylands v. Fletcher, 123

## S

Safeway Stores v. Suburban Foods, 148

Saldana v. State, 187

Salinas, City of v. Souza & McCue Construction Co., 283

Samuel Nichols, Inc. v. Molway, 228–229

Sanchez, United States v., 91

Sanders v. Putman, 1094

**Sandsend Financial Consultants, Ltd. v. Federal Home Loan Bank Board, 894–895**

Sandusky Land, Ltd. v. Uniplan Groups, Inc., 1105

Santiago v. Sherwin-Williams Co., 471

Save the Bay Committee, Inc. v. Mayor of City of Savannah, 926

SCFC ILC, Inc. v. Visa U.S.A., Inc., 957

Schaefers v. Apel, 1024

• Schmalz v. Hardy Salt Co., 289

**Schreier, United States v., 29**

• Schrier v. Home Indemnity Co., 411

**Schroyer v. McNeal, 120–121**

**Schwadel v. Uchitel, 850–851**

Schwartzman v. Schwartzman Packing Co., 837

Schwartzreich v. Bauman-Basch, Inc., 252

• Scott v. Fox Brothers Enterprises, Inc., 325

**SDR Associates v. ARG Enterprises, Inc., 1031–1032**

Seagate Technology, Inc. v. International Business Machines Corp., 163

Seaver v. Ransom, 321

SEC (see Securities and Exchange Commission)

Securities and Exchange Commission v. Cherif, 878

Securities and Exchange Commission v. Gotchey, 879

Securities and Exchange Commission v. Musella, 882

Securities and Exchange Commission v. Peters, 879

**Securities and Exchange Commission v. Texas Gulf Sulphur Co., 870–871**

• Securities and Exchange Commission v. W. J. Howey Co., 861, 878

Sedima, S.P.R.L. v. Imrex Co., 140

Sega Enterprises, Ltd. v. Accolade, Inc., 162

Senn v. Scudieri, 745

• Servbest Foods, Inc. v. Emessee Industries, Inc., 442–443

**Sessa v. Riegle, 446–447**

Shawmut Worcester County Bank v. First American Bank & Trust, 581–582

• **Shearson/American Express, Inc. v. McMahon, 54–55**

Shell Oil Co. v. Pedraza, 711

Shelley v. Kraemer, 1022

Sherwood v. Walker, 279

Sho-Pro of Indiana, Inc. v. Brown, 481

Shore Realty Corp., State of New York v., 937

• Sierra Club v. Costle, 904

Sierra Club v. Morton, 44, 91

Silicone Gel Breast Implants Product Liability Litigation, In re, 847

Simmons v. Yelverton, 1004

Simpson v. James, 1112

Sindell v. Abbott Laboratories, 471

Singleton v. Commissioner of Internal Revenue, 51

Skandinavia, Inc. v. Cormier, 822

Slutsky, United States v., 98

**Smart v. Woo, 979–980**
**Smith v. Buege, 316–317**
Smith v. California, 135
Smith v. Cutter Biological, Inc., 471
Smith v. Van Gorkom, 827, 880
• Socony-Vacuum Oil Co., United States v., 948
**Sony Corp. v. Universal City Studios, 151–152**
Sonzinsky v. United States, 91
**Soroka v. Dayton Hudson Corp., 709–710**
Soundgarden v. Eikenberry, 93
• South Carolina Recycling and Disposal, Inc., United States v., 942
Southern Life and Health Insurance Co. v. Tumer, 472
Southwestern Bell Telephone Co. v. United Video Cablevision of St. Louis, Inc., 355
**Spectrum Sports, Inc. v. McQuillan, 954–955**
**Spinnaker Software Corp. v. Nicholson, 849–850**
Spirn v. Joseph, 1044
St. Mary's Honor Center v. Hicks, 740
Stacy v. Williams, 339
Stambovsky v. Ackley, 355
Stanard v. Urban, 1025
Standard Oil Co. of California v. United States, 955
Stanley v. Brooks, 696
**Staples v. Bangor Hydro-Electric Co., 110–111**
Star Chevrolet Co. v. Green, 274
State v. _____ (see opposing party)
State Farm Mutual Automobile Insurance Company v. Partridge, 1063
Steinmeyer v. Schroeppel, 358
**Steinroe Income Trust v. Continental Bank, N.A., 540–541**
Stephens Industries, Inc. v. Haskins & Sells, 1111
• **Sterling v. Velsicol Chemical Corp., 926–927**
Sterling Mirror of Maryland, Inc. v. Gordon, 967
Stern Electronics, Inc. v. Kaufman, 153
**Stevenson v. TRW, Inc., 916–918**
Stewart & Stevenson Services, Inc. v. Kratochvil, 1004
Strang v. Hollowell, 1005
• Strother v. Strother, 783–784
Summers v. State Farm Mutual Automobile Insurance Co., 735
**Summit Health, Ltd. v. Pinhas, 946–947**
Sun Maid Raisin Growers v. Victor Packing Co., 338–339
• Sun Savings and Loan Association v. Dierdorff, 142
Supreme Court of New Hampshire v. Piper, 99
Sutton v. Smith, 62
Sutton's Steel & Supply, Inc. v. Van Stavern, 695
Swartzbauer v. Lead Industry Association, 471
**Syrovy v. Alpine Resources, Inc. 335–336**

**T**

T&E Industries, Inc. v. Safety Light Corp., 940
Tafflin v. Levitt, 140
• Taylor, Maine v., 103
Taylor v. Caldwell, 358
Taylor Bay Protective Association v. Environmental Protection Agency, 942

• **Texaco, Inc. v. Pennzoil Co., 129–131,** 236
Texas v. Johnson, 93
**Texas Department of Human Services v. Green, 705–706**
Texas Trading & Milling Corp. v. Federal Republic of Nigeria, 1129
**Theis v. duPont Glore Forgan Inc., 679–680**
• Thomas v. Review Board of the Indiana Employment Security Division, 102–103
**Thompson, In re Estate of, 1080–1081**
Thompson Crane & Trucking Co. v. Eyman, 286
• Thompson Medical Co. v. Federal Trade Commission, 923–924
Thorne v. C&S Sales Group, 800
Tin Cup Pass Limited Partnership v. Daniels, 822–823
Tinker v. Des Moines School District, 93
Toibb v. Radloff, 643
**Tongish v. Thomas, 436–437**
Toomer v. Witsell, 99
**Topjian Plumbing and Heating, Inc. v. Bruce Topjian, Inc., 620–621**
Toro Co. v. Krouse, Kern & Co., 1112
Totten, In the Matter of, 1089
Toyota Motor Sales U.S.A., Inc. v. Superior Court, 698
Tracey Service Co., In re, 652
Trail Leasing, Inc. v. Drovers First American Bank, 528
Transamerica Commercial Finance Corp. v. Naef, 966
Trans-Orient Marine Corp. v. Star Trading & Marine, Inc., 1129
Travco Corp. v. Citizens Federal Savings & Loan Association, 545
Trimble v. Gordon, 1083, 1132
Turner v. General Motors Corp., 475
• **Tuttle v. Buck, 132–133**
TXO Production Corp. v. The Alliance Resources Corp., 472

**U**

Ultramares Corp. v. Touche, 1100
**United Automobile Workers v. Johnson Controls, Inc., 31–33,** 735
United Mine Workers of America v. Pennington, 961
United States v. _____ (see opposing party)
United States Trust Co. of New York v. McSweeney, 567
United States Trustee v. Harris, 652
United Tote, Inc., United States v., 957
UWM Post, The v. Board of Regents of the University of Wisconsin System, 93

**V**

Valerino v. Little, 844
Vanguard Insurance Co. v. Clarke, 1063
**Veco Corp. v. Babcock, 828–829**
Vermont Yankee Nuclear Power Corp. v. Natural Resources Defense Council, Inc., 904
Versaggi, People v., 158
• Vertac Chemical Corp., United States v., 943

Vesely v. Security First National Bank of Sheboygan Trust Department, 528

- Vokes v. Arthur Murray, Inc., 281–282
- Vuitton et Fils, S.A. v. Crown Handbags, 146–147

# W

W.C.M. Window Co. v. Bernardi, 802

W. S. Kirkpatrick & Co. v. Environmental Tectonics Corp., International, 1116–1117

Wabash Independent Oil Co. v. King & Wills Insurance Agency, 663–664

Wackenhut Corp. v. Lippert, 1049

Wagner v. City of Globe, 704

Waldrep v. Nosrat, 290

Walker, In re, 614

Walker v. Crigler, 1027–1028

Ward v. K-Mart Corp., 127

Warner v. Texas & Pacific Railroad Co., 302

Watertown Federal Savings and Loan v. Spanks, 507

Waterville Industries, Inc. v. Finance Authority of Maine, 935

Weber v. Rivera, 347

- Webster v. Blue Ship Tea Room, Inc., 451–452
- Webster Street Partnership, Ltd. v. Sheridan, 274

Wegner v. Milwaukee Mutual Insurance Co., 1024

Weichert v. Ryan, 229

Weinsaft, In re Estate of, 259–260

Welansky, Commonwealth v., 167

Weller v. Spring Creek Resort, Inc., 221–222

We're Associates Co. v. Cohen, Stracher & Bloom, P.C., 822

Whatley, In re, 609–610

Whelan Associates, Inc. v. Jaslow Dental Laboratory, Inc., 153

Whitaker v. Associated Credit Services, Inc., 276–277

White v. Randolph, 1083–1084

White v. Samsung Electronics America, Inc., 133–134

Wickard v. Filburn, 85

Wiegert, In the Matter of, 613–614

Wilk v. American Medical Association, 949–950

Wilkin v. 1st Source Bank, 279–280

Williams v. Burrus, 788

- Williams v. Walker-Thomas Furniture Co., 359
- Wilson Floors Co. v. Sciota Park, Ltd., 304

Wineworths Group, Ltd. v. Comité Interprofessionel du Vin de Champagne, 201–202

Winters v. Houston Chronicle Publishing, 719

Wishing Well Club, Inc. v. Akron, 292

Witlin, Estate of v. Rio Hondo Associates, 778–779

Wood v. Board of County Commissioners of Fremont County, 1007–1008

# X

Xieng v. Peoples National Bank of Washington, 23, 737–738

# Y

Yellow Freight Systems, Inc. v. Reich, 745

- Yommer v. McKenzie, 126

Young v. Hessel Tractor & Equipment Co., 443

# Z

- Zauderer v. Office of Disciplinary Counsel, 103

Zeigler v. Cardona, 1087–1088

Ziluck, In re, 591–592

Zorach v. Clauson, 96

# INDEX

## A

*A.G. (Aktiengesellschaft),* 437n, 1120

AAA (American Arbitration Association), 58–59, 1127

ABA. *See* American Bar Association

Abandoned property, 982, 985

Abandonment, termination of lease by, 1042

Abatement, 1074

Abbreviations, 13, 19

Abnormally dangerous activities, 123–124

Absolute defense, 111

Absolute guaranty, 625–626

Absolute privilege, 111

Abstract, 79

*Abus de droit,* 199

Academic degree, as personal property, 1046

Acceleration clause, 498

Acceptance:
  banker's, 489
  in contracts. *See* Contract(s), acceptance in; Sales contract(s), acceptance in
  of deposits, by bank, 562–566
  of gift, 978–980
  of goods, 420, 437–439
  partial, 422
  trade, 489, 531
    *illustrated,* 490

Accepted goods, 420, 437–439

Acceptor, 530

Access card, 570

Accession, acquisition of personal property by, 980, 984

Accidental death benefits, 1068

Accommodation indorser, 533

Accommodation maker, 533

Accommodation parties, 533

Accommodations, reasonable, ADA requirements and, 729–731, 732–734, 743

Accord, satisfaction and, 253–254, 258, 333–334, 337

Account:
  checking. *See* Check(s)
  escrow, 1014, 1032

Account party, 425

Accountants:
  communications of, with clients, 894, 1110
  duty of care of, 1096–1097
  liability of, 1095–1112
    under Securities Act of 1933, 1104–1105, 1108, 1109
    under Securities Exchange Act of 1934, 1105–1108, 1109
    *summarized,* 1109–1110
  negligence of, 1096–1098, 1109
  working papers of, 1108, 1110

Accounting:
  agent's duty of, 667–668
  partner's right to, 773–775

Accredited investors, 865

Acquired immune deficiency syndrome. *See* AIDS

Acquiring corporation, 851

Acquittal, 186

Act:
  of commission, 165
  criminal, 165–166, 171n, 803
  of God, 392
  guilty, 165
  of maker of will, revocation of will by, 1078, 1080–1081, 1082
  of omission, 165
  of parties, agency termination by, 690–691, 693
  of partner, dissolution of partnership by, 787
  of subagent, principal's liability for, 690
  *ultra vires,* 803–804, 856

Act of state doctrine, 1116–1117

Action, cause of, 33, 107, 456

Actionable behavior, 107

Actual authority, 692–693

Actual delivery, 990

Actual fraud, 1098

Actual malice, 111

Actual notice, 790

*Actus reus,* 165

ADA. *See* Americans with Disabilities Act

ADEA. *See* Age Discrimination in Employment Act

Adequate protection doctrine, 635

Adhesion contracts, 251, 286, 288, 297–298, 300

Adjudication, by administrative agencies, 887

Administration, estate, 1075, 1091

Administrative agencies:
  adjudication by, 887
  controls over, 900–901
  creation of, 8, 886–887
  enforcement by, 887, 893–895
  executive, 887
  functions of, 8, 889–890
  independent regulatory, 887
    *summarized,* 889
  investigation by, 893–895
  judicial review of, 896–900
  letter requesting information from, *illustrated,* 902
  parallel, supremacy clause and, 901–903
  powers of, 887–889
  procedures of, 889–896
  prosecution by, 895
  public accountability and, 901
  rulemaking by, 887, 890–893
  state, 901–903
  subagencies and, *summarized,* 888
  types of, 887

Administrative law, 2, 8–9, 886
  how to find, 13

Administrative law judge (ALJ), 896, 909, 965

Administrative Procedure Act (APA)(1946), 890, 891, 893, 894, 896, 897, 898, 900, 903

Administrative process, 889–896. *See also* Administrative agencies

Administrator, 1073

Admission(s), 379
  as exception to Statute of Frauds, 302, 306
  request for, 72
Adoption:
  of corporate bylaws, 815
  of preincorporation contract, 811
ADR. See Alternative dispute resolution
Adversarial system of justice, 63
Adverse possession, 1009, 1016–1017
Advertising:
  bait-and-switch, 908
  constitutional protection and, 93–94, 802
  consumer protection and, 906–910
  contractual offers and, 232–234
  counteradvertising and, 909
  deceptive, 907–908, 909–910
  fax, 910
  tombstone, 862
  unfair, 907–908
Advising bank, 425
Affidavit, 620
Affiliate, 866–867
Affirmation:
  of fact, 446, 459
  of judgment, 45–46, 79
Affirmative action, 31, 731, 734–735
Affirmative defense, 69
Affirmative duty, 558
After-acquired property, 600
Age. See also Children; Infancy; Minor(s)
  discrimination based on, 33, 55, 660, 727–729
  electronic, copyright infringement in, 153–154
  employment discrimination based on, 33, 1134
  of majority, 262
  misrepresentation of, 264, 272
    insurance and, 1065
Age Discrimination in Employment Act (ADEA)(1967), 33, 55, 660, 721, 727
  foreign countries and, 1125, 1134
Agency(ies):
  administrative. See Administrative agencies
  executive, 887
  independent regulatory, 9, 887
    summarized, 889
Agency indorsements, 505
Agency relationships, 657–700. See also Agent(s)

ambassadors and, 664
corporate directors and, 824
corporate officers and executives and, 826
defined, 658–659
employer-employee, 659, 685–688
employer-independent contractor, 659–662, 688–689
exclusive, 668
Focus on Ethics feature on, 697–700
formation of, 662–664, 675, 677–678, 699–700
  summarized, 665
franchises and, 883–884
insurance company and, 1053, 1056
interest coupled with, 691
international business transactions and, 1119
liability in, 673–690
partners and, 779
termination of, 690–693
  summarized, 693
Agent(s). See also Agency relationship(s)
  authority of,
    ambassadors and, 664
    scope of, 673–680, 684, 692–693
  authorized, 534
  bankruptcy of, agency termination and, 692, 693
  corporate officers and executives as, 826
  crimes of, 803
    principal's liability for, 690
  death of, agency termination and, 692, 693
  defined, 533
  duties of, 664–668, 697
  emergency powers of, 678
  escrow, 1014, 1032
  foreign, 1119
  gratuitous, 683n
  insanity of, agency termination and, 692, 693
  insurance, 1053, 1056
  misrepresentation by, 684–685
  negotiable instruments and, 508
  principal's rights and remedies against, 669
  real estate, 1014
  registered, of corporation, 815
  remedies of, 668–669
  rights of, 668–669
  signature of, 533–534, 584–585
  torts of, 803

principal's liability for, 683–688
  unauthorized, 534
  warranties of, 683
Aggregate theory of partnership, 769
Aggressor, 846, 853
Agreed consideration, 512n
Agreement(s):
  agency formation by, 662–663
  to agree, contractual offer versus, 235–236
  arbitration, 53, 57
  bailment, 991
  bilateral, 1114
  buy-sell, 794
  collective bargaining, 645
  compromise, 333
  contractual. See Contract(s), agreement in
  creditors' composition, 623, 624
  discharge of contract by, 326, 333–334, 337
  dissolution of partnership by, 787
  distribution, 1119
  fair trade, 952
  family settlement, 1075
  franchise, 757–763
  hot-cargo, 718
  international, 1114
  lease, 383, 385
  listing, 1014
  multilateral, 1114
  mutual, 691, 693
  obstructing the legal process, 298, 300
  of parties, 415
  partnership, 769
    illustrated, 770–771
  prenuptial, 306
  price-fixing, 948, 952, 967–968
  reaffirmation, 633n, 642–643
  resale price maintenance, 952
  retainer, 66
  sales, tie-in, 956
  security. See Security agreement
  settlement, 333
  shareholder, 807–809
  stock-subscription, 840
  substituted. See Novation
  surrender by, 1042
  truncation, 566
  voting, shareholder, 835, 841
Agricultural associations, exemption of, from antitrust laws, 960
AIDS, 729, 731
Air pollution, 929–931

Air rights, as real property, 971
*Aktiengesellschaft (A.G.),* 437n, 1120
Alcoholic, contractual capacity and, 269n
ALI. *See* American Law Institute
Alien(s):
  contractual capacity and, 271
  enemy, 271
Alien corporation, 804, 812
Alienation, restraints against, 316
ALJ (administrative law judge), 896, 909, 965
Allonge, 502
Alteration:
  of check, 561–562
  of contract, 334, 337
  leased premises and, 1030
  material, 522–523, 525
Alternative dispute resolution (ADR), 52–61
  court-mandated, 59
Ambassadors, apparent agency authority of, 664
Ambiguous terms, 308
Amendment:
  of articles of incorporation, 847
  of financing statement, 606
  to U.S. Constitution. *See* Bill of Rights; specific amendments
American Arbitration Association (AAA), 58–59, 1127
American Bar Association (ABA), 7, 1074–1075
  Corporation, Banking, and Business Law Section of, Committee on Corporate Laws of, 806
  Model Rules of Professional Conduct of, 1097
American Institute of Certified Public Accountants, 1096
American law, sources of, 2, 7–9
  *summarized,* 8
American Law Institute (ALI), 8, 107n, 165n, 214
Americans with Disabilities Act (ADA)(1990), 708, 721, 729–731, 732, 743
  foreign countries and, 1125, 1134n
Analogy, reasoning by, 6
Analysis, cost-benefit, 28
ANCOM (Andean Common Market), 1114
Andean Common Market (ANCOM), 1114
Annulment, revocation of will by, 1081, 1082

Answer, 66, 69, 73
Antecedent claim, 513
Anti-assignment clauses, 315–316
Anticipatory repudiation:
  of a contract, 332
  sales, 422–425
Antidumping duty, 1121
Antilapse clauses, 1059
Antitrust law, 755–756, 887, 944–963. *See also* Clayton Act; Sherman Antitrust Act
  enforcement of, 959–960
  ethics and, 967–968
  exclusionary practices and, 955–956
  exemptions from, 960–961
  franchising and, 761n
  international business transactions and, 960, 1123–1124
  mergers and, 956–959
APA. *See* Administrative Procedure Act
Apparent authority of agent, 675, 677–678, 684, 693, 699–700
  ambassadors and, 664
Appeal:
  court procedures for, 79–81
  criminal, 196
  notice of, 79
Appearance, initial, in criminal process, 185
Appellant, 79
  *defined,* 19
Appellate courts, 14
  federal, 47–49
  state, 44–46, 47
Appellate jurisdiction, 43, 51
Appellate procedures, 79–81
Appellee, 79
  *defined,* 19
Appraisal clause, 1059
Appropriation, 133–134
Approval, sale on, 402, 991
Arbitrary and capricious test, 898
Arbitration:
  agreements providing for, 53, 57, 1059, 1126, 1127
  award under, 53
    setting aside of, 57
  clause requiring, 53, 1059, 1126, 1127
  international, 57, 1126, 1127
  as means of dispute resolution, alternative, 52–59, 60
  international, 57, 1126, 1127
  public policy and, 55, 57
  services providing, 58–59
  statutes and, 53

Argentina:
  corporate law in, 202–203
  liability of limited partners in, 798
  limited liability companies (LLC) in, 759
  privatization in, 206
Argument, closing, 75, 77
Aristotle, 2
Army Corps of Engineers, 931
Arraignment, 185
Arrest, 183, 185
Arson, 168–169, 173
Articles:
  of Confederation, 84
  of dissolution, 855
  of incorporation, 803, 813–815
    amendment of, 847
    *illustrated,* 814
  of merger, 847
  of partnership, 769
Artisan's lien, 113, 615, 624
ASEAN (Association of Southeast Asian Nations), 1114
Assault, 5, 106–107, 114
Assent:
  conditioned, 375
  in contracts. *See* Contract(s), assent to
  manifest, 322, 323
  offeror's, 375
Asset(s):
  of corporation, purchase of, 851–853
  marshaling of, 768
  partnership, distribution of, 792–794
Assignee, 314, 500
Assignment(s):
  for benefit of creditors, 623–624
  consideration and, 315
  *defined,* 314
  gratuitous, 315
  of insurance, 1065
  of lease, 1039
  of negotiable instruments, 500
  notice of, 317
  novation versus, 318–320
  of rights, 313
    all, 318
    not subject to, 315, 323
    third party, *summarized,* 323
  of security interest, 606
  Statute of Frauds and, 314–315
Assignor, 314
Association of Southeast Asian Nations (ASEAN), 1114
Assumption of risk, 119–121, 122, 476

Assurance, perfect tender rule and, 417–419

ATMs. *See* Automated teller machines

Atomic Energy Act (1954), 928, 940

Attachment, 590, 593, 619–621, 624
  prejudgment, 616
  writ of, 620–621

Attempted monopolization, 953–955

Attorney(s). *See also* Lawyers
  attorney-client privilege, 894
  consulting with, 65
  duty of care of, 1097–1098
  -in-fact, 674n
  fees of, 65, 66
  liability of, 1095–1112
    *summarized,* 1109–1110
  negligence of, 1096–1098, 1109
  power of, 674
    *illustrated,* 676
  right to, during criminal procedures, 92, 181

Attractive nuisance doctrine, 1036

Auctions, contractual offers and, 234–235

Auditor, liability of, 1100–1103, 1109

Austria, membership in European Union and, 204

Authority:
  actual, 692–693
  of agent, 534, 673–680, 684, 692–693
    ambassadors and, 664
    apparent, 675, 677–678, 684, 693, 699–700
    principal's obligation to third party and, 673–680
    *summarized,* 684
  certificate of, 804
  express, 244, 673–675, 684
  implied, 675, 684, 782
  of partners, 782

Authorized agent, 534

Automated teller machines (ATMs), 570, 585, 586
  nonproprietary, 566

Automatic stay, 635, 648

Automobile(s):
  crashworthiness doctrine and, 475
  insurance and, 1067–1068
  lemon laws and, 421n, 440

Automobile Dealers' Day in Court Act (Automobile Dealers'

Franchise Act)(1956), 756, 762

Automobile Dealers' Franchise Act (Automobile Dealers' Day in Court Act)(1956), 756, 762

Avoidance, principal's right of, 669

Award, arbitration, 53
  setting aside of, 57


**B**

Baby-boomer generation, 744

Bad faith, of arbitrator, 57

Bail, 185
  excessive, constitutional provision against, 92, 181

Bailed property, bailee's right to use, 992

Bailee, 400, 414, 988
  bailment for sole benefit of, 991, 996
  bailor and, bailment for mutual benefit of, 991, 996, 1000
  care required of, *illustrated,* 992
  duties of, 994–996
  lien of, 618, 993
  rights of, 992–994
    *summarized,* 1003

Bailment(s), 125, 988–1005
  agreement creating, 991
  *defined,* 988
  elements of, 989–991
  ethics and, 1049
  implied warranty of merchantability and, 997
  involuntary, 990n
  mutual-benefit, 991, 996, 1000
  ordinary, 991
  Statute of Frauds and, 991
  termination of, 999
  voluntary, 990n

Bailor, 988
  bailee and, bailment for mutual benefit of, 991, 996, 1000
  bailment for sole benefit of, 991
  duties and rights of, 996–998
    *summarized,* 1003

Bait-and-switch advertising, 908

Balance sheet insolvency, 632n

Bangladesh, child labor in, 210

Bank(s). *See also* Check(s)
  advising, 425
  certification by, 531, 550n
  collecting, 563, 564
  collection process of, 563–566
  customer of. *See* Customer of bank
  *defined,* 548

depository, 563–564

depository, 563n

draft of, 489n

electronic fund transfers and. *See* Electronic fund transfer(s)

Export-Import, 1121

*Focus on Ethics* feature on, 583–586

as HDC, 514

intermediary, 563, 564

letter of credit issued by, 425

liability of,
  electronic fund transfers and, 575–576, 580
  for wrongful payment, 554, 563

negligence of, 559–560, 563

paying, 425

payor, 563

relationship of, with customer, 551

statements of, examination of, 558–559, 563

World, 191

Banker's acceptance, 489

Bankruptcy, 631–652. *See also* Bankruptcy Code

adequate protection concept in, 635

of agent, agency termination and, 692, 693

of assignor, assignment revocation by, 315

automatic stay in, 635, 648

Chapter 7 liquidations in, 632–643, 650, 768

Chapter 11 reorganization in, 632, 643–648, 650
  revision of, *Emerging Trends* feature on, 646–647

Chapter 12 family-farmer plans, 649–650

Chapter 13 individuals' repayment plans, 632, 648–649, 650

collective bargaining agreements and, 645

constitutional provision for, 631

creditors' committees and, 645

discharge in, 334, 337, 640–642, 649
  liability on negotiable instrument and, 523, 525
  *Emerging Trends* feature on, 646–647

estate in, property of, 635

exemptions in, 636

family-farmer plans in, 649–650

*Focus on Ethics* feature on, 655–656
forms of relief in, comparison of, *summarized*, 650
fraud in, 169, 173, 638–639
involuntary, 635
ordinary, 632
of partner, dissolution of partnership by, 787
partnerships and, 768
petition for, 632–635
plan in, 645, 647–648
preferences in, 637–638
of principal, agency termination and, 692, 693
straight, 632
trustee in, 632, 637–639
   powers of, 637
voluntary, 632–634
Bankruptcy Code, 410, 631–650, 656. *See also* Bankruptcy
chapters of, 632
   comparison of, *summarized*, 650
   cram-down provisions of, 647–648
Bankruptcy judge, 636
Bankruptcy Reform Act (1978). *See* Bankruptcy Code
*Bankruptcy Reporter* (Bankr.)(West), 14
Bargain, basis of, 446–447
Bargained-for exchange, 248, 258
Bargaining:
   collective, 645, 716
   plea, 181
Baseball, exemption of, from antitrust laws, 960
Basis of the bargain, 446–447
Battery, 106–107, 114
Battle of the forms, 372
Bearer, 499, 501
   payment to order of, 498–499, 501
Bearer instruments, 499, 501
Bearer paper:
   conversion of, to order paper, 502
      *illustrated*, 503
   negotiation of, 502
Behavior:
   actionable, 107
   predatory, competition versus, 131
Belgium:
   European Union membership and, 204
   limited liability companies (LLC)

in, 759
Ben & Jerry's Homemade, Inc., 211
Beneficiary:
   creditor, 321, 323
   donee, 321, 323
   intended, 320–324
   of letter of credit, 425
   third party. *See* Third party beneficiaries
Bentham, Jeremy, 28
Bequest, 1073, 1082
Berne Convention, 155–156
Better Business Bureaus, 909, 911
Beyond a reasonable doubt, 75, 186
BFOQ (*bona fide* occupational qualification), 735
Bilateral contract, 219, 226, 243–245, 1114
Bilateral mistakes, 275, 288
Bill(s):
   of exchange, 487
      *illustrated*, 489
   of lading, 397, 425
      *defined*, 999
      *illustrated*, 398
   through, 1002
Bill of Rights, 802
   business and, 91–99
   corporations and, 802
   protections guaranteed by, 181
      *summarized*, 92
Bill of Rights of 1689, 192
Bills of Exchange Act (1882), 486
Blackstone, Sir William, 3
Blank indorsements, 503, 506
Blue laws, 96, 293
Blue sky laws, 877
*Blue Sky Reporter* (Commerce Clearing House), 877n
Board of directors. *See* Directors, corporate
Body tissue, as personal property, 1047
*Bona fide* occupational qualification (BFOQ), 735
*Bona fide* purchaser, 637, 645, 835n
Bonaparte, Napoleon, 192
Bond(s), 860
   callable, 818
   convertible, 818
   corporate, types of, *summarized*, 818
   debenture, 818
   mortgage, 818
   stocks versus, 819

Books. *See* Record(s), business
''Bootlegging,'' 971
Borrowed servants, 687
Bounty payments, 875
Boycott:
   consumer, 211–212
   group, 948
   secondary, 718
Bradley, Michael, 646
Brandeis, Louis D., 947
Brazil:
   intellectual property protection in, 201
   limited liability companies (LLC) in, 759
   torts in, 197
Breach:
   of contract. *See* Contract(s), breach of; Sales contract(s), breach of
   of duty of care, 115–117
   of peace, 653
   of warranty, 438–439
      liability on negotiable instrument and, 523, 525
      recovery for, 471, 474
Bribery:
   commercial, 169, 173
   of foreign officials, 38, 169, 173, 191, 1127, 1133–1134
   gifts versus, 191
   of public officials, 169, 173
Brief, 79
Broker:
   insurance, 1053, 1056
   real estate, 1014
Building permits, 1019–1021
Bulk transfers, 405–406
Burden of proof, 75
Burglary, 168, 173
Business:
   Bill of Rights and, 91–99
   crimes affecting, 167–176
      *Emerging Trends* feature on, 174–175
      *summarized*, 173
   ethics and. *See* Business ethics
   international. *See* International business transactions
   liability insurance for, 1068–1069
   regulation of. *See* Government regulation
   women in, international business transactions and, 191
   wrongful entry into, 132–133
Business ethics, 24–40. *See also* Ethics

behavioral obstacles and, 28–30
complexity of, 25
consequences and, 27
corporate structure and, 30
criminal penalties and, 36–37
decision making and, 26
*defined,* 25
duty and, 27
*Emerging Trends* feature on, 36–37
employment relationships and, 31–34
management and, 30, 34–38
nature of, 24–26
standards of, 26–28
trade-offs and, 25–26
Business impracticality, dissolution of partnership and, 789
Business invitees, 115
Business judgment rule, 829, 831
Business law, ethics and, 26–27
Business necessity defense, 735
Business organization(s), 747–884
business trusts as, 755–756
cooperative as, 756
corporations as, 750. *See also* Corporation(s)
*Focus on Ethics* feature on, 880–884
franchises as, 756–757, 760–763, 883–884
investment groups as, 755
joint stock companies as, 755
joint ventures as, 753–755
limited liability company (LLC) as, 756, 780n
partnerships as, 749–750. *See also* Partnership(s)
shareholder form of, 801
sole proprietorships as, 748–749
syndicates as, 755
taxation of. *See* Taxation
Business relationship(s), wrongful interference with, 131
Business torts, 128–142
appropriation as, 133–134
defamation as, 134–136
*defined,* 128
disparagement of property as, 136–139
wrongful entry into business as, 132–133
wrongful interference as. *See* Wrongful interference
Business trust, 755–756
Buyer(s). *See also* Purchaser
breach of sales contract by, 404
of chattel paper, security interests and, 604–605

examination of goods by, 456
of farm products, security interests and, 597, 604
of letter of credit, 425
merchant, 434
of negotiable instruments, security interests and, 604–605
as nonmerchant, acceptance and, 372, 375
obligations of, 419–422
*summarized,* 423
in the ordinary course of business, 408, 430, 602–604
remedies of, 433–439
rights of, 420
secured party versus, 602–606
"Buyers Guide," 912
Buy-sell agreement, 794
Bylaws, corporate, 803
adoption of, 815
Bystanders, strict liability and, 474–475

# C

C.&F. (cost, insurance, and freight), 400
C.I.F. (cost, insurance, and freight), 400
C.O.D. (collect on delivery) shipment, 420
Cable Communications Policy Act (1984), 160
Callable bonds, 818
Callable preferred stock, 819
Canada:
jury selection in, 79
legal system in, 90
NAFTA and, 1122–1123
preemption of local regulations in, 90
*voir dire* in, 79
Cancellation. *See also* Rescission
of contract, 284
by buyer, 435
insurance, 1059–1060
by seller, 433
discharge of liability on negotiable instrument by, 525, 542–543
of lease, 1034
Capacity. *See also* Incapacity; Incompetence; Insanity; Mental incompetence
contractual. *See* Contract(s), capacity in
partnerships and, 767–768, 772
testamentary, 1075–1077
Capital, need for, 752–753, 813

Capper-Volstead Act (1922), 960
Care:
bailee and, 992
due, efficiency versus, 584
duty of, 827, 831, 880–881, 994–995, 1096–1098
breach of, 115–117
ordinary, 559
reasonable, 1036
bailments and, 991, 992
of collateral, 606–607
Carrier:
common, bailments and, 1000–1002
connecting, bailments and, 1002
substitution of, 415
Carrier cases, 397, 400, 415
Case(s):
carrier, 397, 400, 415
citations to. *See* Citations
court, sample, 19–22
criminal, steps in, *summarized,* 184
diethylstilbestrol (DES), 471
of first impression, 5
noncarrier, 414
*prima facie,* 123, 725–726, 727, 735
remanding of, 45, 80
ripeness of, 897
United States Supreme Court review of, 50–51
Case digests, 16
Case law, 6
how to analyze, 16–22
how to find, 13–16
old, 16
reading and understanding of, 16–22
Case titles, 16
Cash surrender value, 1059
Cashier's check, 488, 489, 548, 550–551, 555–556
*illustrated,* 549
Catalogues, contractual offers and, 232
Categorical imperative, 27
Causation, 117–119, 466
Cause:
of action, 33, 456
challenge for, 73
good, 645
probable, 98, 107, 175–176, 181, 183, 185
proximate, 117–118, 579, 997
removal of corporate director for, 825, 830
without, 830
*Caveat emptor,* 444, 906, 1015

CCPA (Consumer Credit Protection Act)(1968), 569, 622n, 913
CD. *See* Certificate, of deposit
Cease-and-desist order, 717, 896, 909
CERCLA (Comprehensive Environmental Response, Compensation, and Liability Act)(Superfund)(1980), 934–935, 937–940, 964–965
Certificate:
  of authority, 804
  of deposit (CD), 487, 488, 491
    *illustrated,* 491
  of dissolution, 855n
  of incorporation, 815
  of limited partnership, 796
  stock, 835
    *illustrated,* 820, 868
  voting trust, 835
Certification of check, by bank, 531, 550n
Certification marks, 147
Certified check, 549–551
  *illustrated,* 550
*Certiorari:*
  denial of, 711n
  writ of, 50–51, 81
Chain-style business franchise, 757
Challenge to juror, 73
Chancellor, 10
Chancery, courts of, 10
Chapters, bankruptcy. *See* Bankruptcy; Bankruptcy Code
Charge(s):
  to jury, 75
  late, 1034
Charging order, 775–776
Charitable corporation, 806
Charitable subscriptions, 257–259
Charitable trusts, 1089
Charter, corporate, 811, 812–813, 815
Chattel, 970, 984
Chattel paper, 596
  buyers of, security interests and, 605–606
  *defined,* 589
Check(s), 487, 488–490, 547–568
  altered, payment on, 561–562
  cashier's, 488, 489, 548, 550–551, 555–556
    *illustrated,* 549
  certification of, 531, 550n
  certified, 549–551
    *illustrated,* 550
  clearance of, 564–565, 566
    *illustrated,* 565
  collection process for, 563–566

*defined,* 547–548
deposits of, 514
  acceptance of, 562–566
  destroyed, 550–551
  dishonor of, 551, 563
  honoring of, 551–562
    *summarized,* 563
  lost, 550–551
  overdrafts and, 551–553, 563
  poorly filled-out, *illustrated,* 562
  postdated, 553, 563
  remitter of, 548
  stale, 553, 563
  stolen, 550–551
  stop-payment order on, 553–556, 563
    *illustrated,* 554
  teller's, 488, 489, 548, 550–551, 555–556
  traveler's, 488, 490, 548–549
    *illustrated,* 549
  truncation and, 558, 566n
  withdrawals of, 514
  wrongful payment on, 554, 563
Checks and balances system, 49, 85
Child labor, 715
Child Protection and Toy Safety Act (1969), 920
Children. *See also* Age; Infancy; Minor(s)
  born after execution of will, 1081, 1082
  illegitimate, inheritance laws and, 1131–1132
  labor and, 715
  surviving, intestacy laws and, 1082–1083
Chile, limited liability companies (LLC) in, 759
China:
  contract law in, 196
  lawyers in, 194
CHIPS (New York Clearing House Interbank Payments Systems), 579
Choice-of-language clause, 391
Choice-of-law clause, 391, 1127
Choice-of-Law Convention, 391
*Chusik Hoesa,* 203
CIBN (United Nations Convention on International Bills of Exchange and International Promissory Notes), 497
Cicero, 3
Circulars, contractual offers and, 232
CISG. *See* United Nations Convention for International

Sale of Goods
Citation(s), 8n, 13, 16
  case, how to read, 17–18
  *defined,* 14
  parallel, 14
Citizenship, diversity of, 49
Civil law, criminal law versus, 9–10, 11, 164
Civil law legal systems, 192–194
Civil Rights Act (1866), 727
Civil Rights Act (1964), 86, 96, 191
  Title VII of, 721, 722–727, 737
    foreign countries and, 1125, 1134n
Civil Rights Act (1968) (Fair Housing Act), 1022
Civil Rights Act (1991), 726–727
  foreign countries and, 1125
Civil War, 944, 945
CLA (Consumer Leasing Act)(1988), 915
Claim(s):
  antecedent, 513
  to negotiable instrument, HDC status and, 517–518, 519
  notice of, 438
  preexisting, 513
  settlement of, consideration and, 253–256, 258
Class, protected, 721
  illegal contracts and, 299, 301
Clayton Act (1914), 294n, 852, 944, 955–959, 960
Clean Air Act (1963) and amendments, 928, 929–931
Clean Water Act (1972), 931, 940, 965–966
Clear and convincing evidence, 75
Clearinghouse rule, 566
Clerical error, 308
Clients:
  professionals' communication with, 894, 1110
  professionals' liability to, 1109
Clinton, William, 715n, 935
Close corporations, 806–809, 812
Closed shop, 718
Closely held corporation, 806
Closing, of sale of real property, 1015
Closing arguments, 75, 77
COBRA (Consolidated Omnibus Budget Reconciliation Act)(1985), 714–715
Coca-Cola Company, 209
*Code of Federal Regulations* (C.F.R.), 13
*Code Napoleon,* 192, 193, 194, 199

Codicil, 1078, 1082
Codified law, 192–194
Coinsurance clause, 1058
Collateral, 491
  after-acquired property as, 600
  debtor's rights in, 592
  *defined,* 589
  description of, 595, 608–611
  disposition of, proceeds from, 599–600
  disputed claims to, 601–606
    *summarized,* 605
  inventory as, 597, 602
  moved to another jurisdiction, 597–598
  perfection of security interest and, 595, 596, 597
  reasonable care of, 606–607
  redemption of, 612
  release of, 606
  repossession of, 611
  retention of, by secured party, 608
  secured party's right to take possession of, 608
  types of, perfection of security interest and, *illustrated,* 596, 597
  value of, impairment of, 543–544
Collateral heirs, 1083
Collateral note, 491
Collateral promises, 302, 303–306
Collect on delivery (C.O.D.), 420
Collecting bank, 563, 564
Collection:
  of checks, by banks, 563–566
  indorsement for, 505
Collective bargaining, 645, 716
Collective marks, 147–148
Collision insurance, 1067
Color(s):
  discrimination based on, 722, 1022, 1027
  international business transactions and, 190
Comity, principle of, 1116
Comment period, 890–891
Commerce clause, 85–88
Commercial bribery, 169, 173
Commercial fund transfers, 569, 579–580
Commercial impracticability, 335–336, 337, 416–417
Commercial paper, 486–568
  *defined,* 486
  *Focus on Ethics* feature on, 583–586
Commercial property, 1036–1038
Commercial speech, 93–94, 802

Commercial unit, 421
Commercially reasonable time, 404
Commingled interests, 816
Commission, sin of, 26
Common areas, 1030, 1038
Common carriers, bailments and, 1000–1002
Common law, 2
  *defined,* 4
  environmental protection and, 925–927
  present day, 6
  as source of law, 8
  tradition of, 4–7
Common law legal systems, 192, 194
Common Market, 204
Common stock, 819, 821
Communication:
  of acceptance, 243–245, 372
  accountant-client, 894, 1110
  attorney-client, 894, 1110
  confidential, 894, 1110
  *ex-parte,* 891, 896
  international business transactions and, 190
  of offer, 236
  privacy rights and, 708–709
  privileged, 111, 894, 1110
Community, corporation's duty to, 209
Community property, 974, 976, 984, 1046
Comparative fault, 476–477
Comparative law, 189–212
Comparative legal systems, 191–195
Comparative negligence, 121, 122
Compelling or overriding interest, 100
Compensation:
  bailee's right of, 992–993, 1003
  of corporate directors, 825, 831
  just, 92, 970, 1006, 1018
  of partner, 773
  principal's duty of, 668
  unemployment, 714
  workers', 713, 1069
Compensatory damages, 341, 348, 472, 727, 731
Competence, degrees of. *See also* Capacity
Competition:
  covenant in restraint of, 294–296, 300
  predatory behavior versus, 131
  simulated, 132
  social responsibility and, 211
Compilations of facts,

copyrightability, 149–151
Complaint, 66, 73
  *illustrated,* 67
Complete defense, 522
Complete dominion and control, 977
Complete performance, 329, 337
Comprehensive Environmental Response, Compensation, and Liability Act (CERCLA) (Superfund) (1980), 934–935, 937–940, 964–965
Comprehensive insurance, 1067
Compromise agreement, 333
Computer(s):
  crime and, 29, 158–159
  defamation by, 134–136
  electronic copying and, 154, 1046
  privacy rights and, 159
  software for. *See* Computer software
Computer software. *See also* Intellectual property
  copyright protection for, 152, 155, 1046
  patents for, 148–149
  piracy of, 158
Computer Software Copyright Act (1980), 152
Conciliation, as means of alternative dispute resolution, 52, 60
Concurrent causation doctrine, 1063
Concurrent conditions, 327, 328
Concurrent jurisdiction, 49–50, 51
Concurrent ownership, 974–976, 984
Concurring opinion, 19
Condition(s), 326–329, 337
  concurrent, 327, 328
  constructive, 329
  *defined,* 327
  disclosure of, under EFTA, 572–573, 574, 580
  express, 327, 328–329
  implied, 327, 328–329
  orally agreed-upon, 308
  precedent, 327–328
  subsequent, 327, 328
Conditional guaranty, 626
Conditional indorsements, 505, 506
Conditioned assent, 375
Conduct, pattern of, 353
Confederal form of government, 84
Confederation, Articles of, 84
Conference(s). *See also* Meeting(s)
  international, 1114–1115

pretrial, 72, 73. *See also* Meeting(s)

Confession of judgment, 773

Confidentiality:
accountant-client communications and, 1110
attorney-client communications and, 894, 1110
professional-client communications and, 1110

Confirmation, written, between merchants, 377

Confiscation, 1116
of real property, through zoning laws, 1018

Conflicts of interest, 298, 829

Conforming goods, 413, 414, 415

Confusion, acquisition of personal property by, 980–981, 984

Conglomerate mergers, 957

Connecting carriers, bailments and, 1002

Consensual lien, 615

Consent:
as defense to criminal liability, 177
as defense against tort, 107

Consequential damages, 341, 342–344, 348, 441

Consideration(s):
in contracts. *See* Contract(s), consideration in; Sales contract(s), consideration in settlement, 65
statement of, 493

Consignee, 403

Consignment, 403

Consignor, 403

Consolidated Omnibus Budget Reconciliation Act (COBRA) (1985), 714–715

Consolidations, 847–851
*illustrated,* 847

Constitution, U.S.:
amendments to. *See* Bill of Rights; specific amendments
bankruptcy provision of, 631
boundaries of federal judicial power established by, 49
commerce clause of, 85–88
comparison of, to other constitutions, 192
Congress empowered to create administrative agencies by, 889
constitutional law based upon, 2
cross-examination of opposing witnesses guaranteed by, 92, 181

cruel and unusual punishment prohibited by, 92, 181
double jeopardy prohibited by, 92, 181, 196
due process clause of, 91, 92, 99–100, 181, 472, 620, 802, 970
eminent domain laws and, 1017
equal protection clause of, 100–102
excessive bails and fines prohibited by, 92, 181, 472
export taxes prohibited by, 1121
federal courts authorized by, 41
federal question defined by, 49
freedom of contract protected by, 217
freedom of speech guaranteed by, 92–96
garnishment of wages under, 919
government's authority to regulate business under, 84–104
intellectual property protection and, 143
involuntary servitude prohibited by, 350n
lifetime appointments of federal judiciary under, 47
privilege against self-incrimination under, 92, 98, 181, 802, 894n
privileges and immunities clause of, 99, 802
protections guaranteed by, 181
*summarized,* 92
right to attorney during criminal procedures guaranteed by, 92, 181
right to jury trial guaranteed by, 72, 92, 181
spending power under, 91
supremacy clause of, 89–90, 901–903
as supreme law of the land, 7, 8
taxing power under, 90–91
treaties and, 1114
United States Supreme Court created by, 47
unreasonable searches and seizures prohibited by, 92, 98, 181, 707, 711, 802, 893–894

Constitutional Convention, 85

Constitutional law, 2, 7, 8

Constitutions, as foundation for legal systems, 191–192

Construction, rules of, 381–382

Construction contracts:

breach of, measure of damages for, *illustrated,* 342
specific performance and, 350n

Constructive conditions, 329

Constructive delivery, 976, 990

Constructive eviction, 1029

Constructive fraud, 1098

Constructive notice, 693, 1013

Constructive trusts, 669, 1087–1088, 1089

Consumer(s):
boycotts by, 211–212
buyers of consumer goods from, security interests and, 604–605
credit protection and, 913–920, 966
credit sales transactions and, 440, 493–494, 526–527
as debtors, special protection for, 628, 632
fund transfers by, 569, 571–579
health and safety protection for, 920
laws protecting, 906–924
sales transactions of, 459
welfare of, 34–35

Consumer Credit Protection Act (CCPA)(1968), 569, 622n, 913

Consumer goods, security interests and, 597, 604–605, 608–609

Consumer Leasing Act (CLA)(1988), 915

Consumer Product Safety Act (1972), 920

Consumer Product Safety Commission (CPSC), 920

Consumer-debtors, 628, 632

Contingent fees, 65

Contingent liability on negotiable instrument, 531

Continuation statement, 598

Continuing guaranty, 625

Contract(s), 213–362
acceptance in, 219
authorized means of, 244–245
communication of, 243–245
*defined,* 239
international business transactions and, 196
mailbox rule and, 244, 245
mirror image rule and, 238, 239, 372, 387–388
mode and timeliness of, 243–245
silence as, 242–243
unequivocal, 239–241
adhesion, 251, 286, 288, 297–298, 300

adoption of, 811
agreement in, 230–247
alteration of, 334, 337
anticipatory repudiation of, 332
arbitration clause in, 53
assent to, 219, 275–290
  mutual, 230–231
basic requirements of, 219
bilateral, 219, 226, 243–245
breach of, 12
  *defined,* 340
  deliberate, 341n
  liability on negotiable
    instrument and, 523, 525
  material, 329, 331–332, 337
  minor, 332
  nondeliberate, 341n
  professional's liability for,
    1095–1096, 1109
  remedies for, 429–443
    *summarized,* 441
  waiver of, 353
cancellation of, 284, 433, 435,
  1059–1060
capacity in, 219, 261–274
  alcoholics and, 269n
  aliens and, 271
  *defined,* 261
  incapacity and, 272
  intoxicated persons and,
    269–271, 272
  mentally incompetent persons
    and, 271, 272
  minors and, 262–269, 272
classification of, 219–226
  *summarized,* 226
clear, specific wording in, 331
for commission of a tort, 298,
  300
to commit a crime, 294, 300
consideration in, 219, 248–260
  adequacy of, 250–251, 258
  agreed, 512n
  assignments and, 315
  *defined,* 248, 258
  failure of, liability on
    negotiable instrument and,
    523–524, 525
  lack of, liability on negotiable
    instrument and, 523–524,
    525
  legal sufficiency of, 249–250,
    258
  moral obligations and, 252
  past, 253, 258
  preexisting duty rule and,
    251–252, 258
  problems concerning, 253–259
    *summarized,* 258

transfer warranties and, 538,
  539
without, enforceability of,
  256–259
construction,
  breach of, measure of damages
    for, *illustrated,* 342
  specific performance and, 350n
contrary to public policy,
  294–298, 300
contrary to statute, 291–299, 300
creation of easement or profit by,
  1009
*defined,* 216
destination, 397, 400, 415
disaffirmance of, 262–267, 269,
  271, 272
discharge of, 326
  by accord and satisfaction,
    333–334, 337
  by agreement, 326, 333–334,
    337
  by commercial impracticability,
    335–336, 337
  by frustration of purpose, 335,
    336
  by impossibility of
    performance, 335, 337
  by novation, 333, 337
  by operation of law, 326,
    334–337
  by performance, 326, 329–333,
    337
  by rescission, 333, 337
  *summarized,* 337
discriminatory, 298, 300
divisible, 299
duration of, 370
elements of, 219
employment, implied, 703,
  741–742
errors in, 308
exclusive-dealing, 955–956
executed, 225, 226, 333
executory, 225, 226, 333
express, 220–222, 226
*Focus on Ethics* feature on,
  357–362
form of, 219. *See also* Statute of
  Frauds
formal, 225, 226
freedom from, 218
freedom of, 217–218, 357–358
illegal, withdrawal from, 299
implied, 220–222, 703, 741–742
  in fact, 220–221, 226
  in law. *See* Quasi contracts
incapacity and, 272
incomplete, 308

indivisible, 299
informal, 225, 226
injuring public service, 298, 300
installment, 416
insurance. *See* Insurance, contract
  for
integrated, 308
interests in land and, 301, 302
international. *See* International
  business transactions
interpretation of, 226–227
law governing, 10, 215–216
  versus sales law, *illustrated,*
    379
legality of, 219
limitation of remedies and, 353
modification of, good faith and,
  377
national laws of, comparison of,
  195–197
nonvoidable, 268
objective theory of, 216–217
offer in, 219
  acceptance of. *See* Contract(s),
    acceptance in
  advertisements, catalogues,
    price lists, circulars and,
    232–234
  agreement to agree versus,
    235–236
  auctions and, 234–235
  communication of, 236
  counteroffer and, 238, 240
  *defined,* 231
  definiteness of, 236
  intention and, 231–234
  international business
    transactions and, 196
  irrevocable, 237, 240, 388
  mirror image rule and, 238,
    239, 372, 387–388
  preliminary negotiations
    versus, 232
  rejection of, 238, 240
  requirements of, 231–236
  revocation of, 220, 236–237,
    240
  termination of, 236–239
  methods of, *summarized,* 240
  terms of. *See* Term(s)
ongoing, duration of, 370
option, 237, 240
  merchant's firm offer versus,
    371n
oral,
  enforcement of. *See* Statute of
    Frauds
  ethics and, 359
output, 370–371

for personal services, 315, 317, 318, 323
  specific performance and, 350
plain meaning rule and, 226–227
preincorporation, 811
price-fixing, 1123
principal's liability for, 680–683, 684
privity of, 313, 453, 463, 464–465, 1100
proposed, supervening illegality of, offer termination and, 239, 240
quasi. *See* Quasi contracts
ratification of, 262, 267–268, 269, 272, 678–680, 811
repudiation of, 332, 417, 435–437
requirements, 370
requirements of, 219
rescission of, 252, 284, 333, 337
for sale of goods. *See* Sales contract(s)
for sale of real property, 1013–1016
under seal, 225
severable, 299
shipment, 397, 400, 415
simple, 225
"standard-form," 288
subject to orally agreed-upon conditions, 308
subsequently modified, 308
termination of. *See* Contract(s), discharge of
terms of. *See* Term(s)
third parties and. *See* Third parties; Third party beneficiaries
tie-in, 1123
types of, 219–226
  *summarized,* 226
unconscionable, 251, 296, 300, 382–383, 385
unenforceable, 226
unilateral, 219–220, 226
valid, 225–226
void, 226, 261, 272, 308
voidable, 226, 261, 272, 308, 673
withdrawal from, 299
wording in, 331
writing requirements for. *See* Statute of Frauds
Contractor, independent. *See* Independent contractor
Contractual relationship, wrongful interference with, 129–131
Contribution(s):
  political, 94–96, 803n

right of,
  partner's, 793
  surety's or guaranty's, 627–628
Contributory negligence, 121, 122
Conversion, 113–114, 981
  bailment and, 995
  of order paper to bearer paper and vice versa, 502
    *illustrated,* 503
Convertible bonds, 818
Convertible preferred stock, 819, 820
Conveyance of real property, 1007, 1011–1017
Conviction, 186
"Cooling-off" period, for door-to-door sales, 333n, 348n, 911
Cooperation:
  perfect tender rule and, 417–419
  principal's duty of, 668
Cooperative, 756
Copyright(s), 19, 143, 149–156
  third party infringement claims and, 445, 458
Copyright Act (1976), 149, 151, 152
Corporate charter, 811, 812–813, 815
"Corporate veil, piercing of," 750, 802, 816
Corporation(s), 750, 801–879
  acquiring, 851
  adoption of preincorporation contract by, 811
  alien, 803, 812
  Bill of Rights and, 802
  bonds of, 818
  bylaws of, 803
  capital structure of, 813
  characteristics of, 802
  charitable, 806
  charter of, 811, 812–813, 815
  classification of, 804–811
    *summarized,* 812
  close, 806–809, 812
  closely held, 806
  consolidation of, 847–851
  crime and, 36–37, 170–177, 175, 803
  *de facto,* 816
  *de jure,* 815–816
  *defined,* 632n
  directors of. *See* Directors, corporate
  dissolution of, 854–857
    shareholders' rights and, 838–839
  dividends of, 836–837
  domestic, 804, 812

duration of, 813
duty of,
  to community, 209
  to shareholders, 208
  to society, 209–210
  to stakeholders, 208–209
earnings of, 802, 836
eleemosynary, 806
entity of, disregarding, 816–818
  by estoppel, 816
ethics and, 30, 34–38
family, 806
financing of, 818–821
first organizational meeting of, 815
foreign, 804, 812
formation of, 811–815. *See also* Incorporation
global responsibilities of, 210
insolvency of, 836
internal organization of, 813–814
jurisdiction of courts over, 42
as legal person, 802, 894n
liability of,
  for crimes, 170, 803
  for torts, 803
liquidation of, 854, 857–858
management of, 807
merger of. *See* Merger(s)
minimum-contacts requirement for jurisdiction over, 42
name of, 813
national laws regarding, comparison of, 202–203
nature of, 802–803, 813
nonprofit, 806, 812
not-for-profit, 806
officers of. *See* Officers, corporate
organization of, 813–814
as partner, 772
partnerships and sole proprietorships compared to, 750–753
as person, 802, 894n
"piercing veil of," 750, 802, 816
political contributions and, 94–96, 803n
powers of, 803–804
principal office of, 815
private, 806, 812
privately held, 806
privatization and, 205–206
privilege against self-incrimination and, 98, 802, 894n
professional, 809–811, 812
profits of, 802, 836

promotional activities and, 811–812
public, 806, 812
purchase of assets of, 851–853
purpose of, 813
registered agent of, 815
registered office of, 815
retained earnings of, 802, 836
S, 750, 753, 758, 809, 812
shareholders of. *See* Shareholder(s)
social responsibility and, *Focus on Ethics* feature on, 208–212
stock of. *See* Stock(s)
surplus of, 836
surviving, 847
target, 846, 853
taxation of, 750, 751, 752, 802
termination of, 854–858
*ultra vires* acts and, 803–804, 856
Corporations commissioner, 877
Cost, insurance, and freight (C.I.F. or C.&F.), 400
Cost-benefit analysis, 28
Co-sureties, 627
Counteradvertising, 909
Counterclaim, 66, 69
Counterfeit Access Device and Computer Fraud and Abuse Act (1984), 159, 160
Counteroffer, 238, 240
Course of performance, 308
Course of dealing:
  implied warranty arising from, 452, 458
  parol evidence and, 308, 380, 384
Course of performance:
  implied warranty arising from, 452, 458
  parol evidence and, 308, 381, 384
Court(s). *See also* Alternative dispute resolution (ADR)
  alternative dispute resolution (ADR) mandated by, 59
  appellate, 14
    federal, 47–49
    state, 44–46, 47
  case in, sample of, 16–22
  of chancery, 10
  decisions of, 19. *See also* Judgment(s)
    federal, 14, 16, 17–18
    state, 14, 17
  domestic relations, 44
  early English, 4, 10, 18

of equity, 10, 11
European, of Justice, 204
federal, 46–52. *See also* United States Supreme
  authority of from U.S. Constitution, 41
  decisions of, 14, 16, 17–18
  jurisdiction of, 49–52, 85
jurisdiction of. *See* Jurisdiction
king's, 4, 8, 10, 486
of law, 10
magistrate's, 185
municipal, 44
opinions of. *See* Court(s), decisions of
probate, 43, 1073
procedures in. *See* Court procedures
rent-a-judge, 59–60
reviewing, 14
small claims, 44
state, 44–46
  decisions of, 14, 17
  *illustrated*, 45
  trial, 14
  federal, 46–47, 48
  state, 44, 47
United States, of Appeals, 47
United States, of Federal Claims, 46, 47
United States Bankruptcy, 46, 47, 631
United States Claims, 46n
United States district, 46–47, 48, 631
United States Supreme,
  appeals to from highest state courts, 44, 46
  created by U.S. Constitution, 47
  decisions of, 14, 16, 17
  as highest court in federal court system, 47
  how cases reach, 50–51
  jurisdiction of, 47, 49
  justices of, 19
    legal philosophy of, 3
    lifetime appointments of justices of, 47
    power of judicial review established by, 51–52
    as supreme law of the land, 41
United States Tax, 46, 47
United States territorial, 41
venue and, 43
Court procedures, 63–83
  for appeal, 79–81
  comparative legal systems and, 194

posttrial, 77–79
  *summarized*, 81
pretrial, 66–74
  *summarized*, 73
rules of, 64–65
during trial, 74–77
  *summarized*, 77
Covenant(s):
  not to compete, 294–296, 300
  not to sue, 253, 255–256, 258
  of quiet enjoyment, 1029
  restrictive, 294, 300, 1022–1023
  running with the land, 1021
Cover, buyer's right of, 435
CPSC (Consumer Product Safety Commission), 920
Cram-down provisions of Bankruptcy Code, 647–648
Crashworthiness doctrine, 475
Credit:
  consumer protection and, 913–920, 966
  letter of, 425
    *illustrated*, 426
  line of, 600
  sales transactions and, 440, 493–494, 526–527
Credit cards, lost or stolen, 916
Creditor(s). *See also* Secured party
  assignment for benefit of, 623–624
  committees of, 645
  composition agreements of, 623, 624
  duties of, 606–607
  information requested by, 606
  laws assisting, 615–624
  lien, 601, 637
  meeting of, 636
  remedies of, 607–612, 615–524
    *summarized*, 624
  rights of, 606–607, 1065
  *Focus on Ethics* feature on, 653–656
  secured. *See* Secured party
  unsecured, 640
Creditor beneficiary, 321, 323
Crime(s). *See also* Criminal law
  of agent, principal's liability for, 690
  classification of, 165
  computer, 29, 158–159
  contract to commit, 294, 300
  corporations and, 36–37, 170–177, 175, 803
  criminal act and, 165–166, 171n
    *defined*, 164
  financial, 158
  on leased premises, 1040–1041

RICO and, 173, 175–176
of third parties, injuries caused by, 1038
white-collar, 167–176
*Emerging Trends* feature on, 174–175
*summarized,* 173
Crime Control Act (1973), 160
Criminal act, 165–166, 171n
Criminal law, 164–188. *See also* Crime(s)
civil law versus, 9–10, 11, 164
corporate penalties under, 36–37
essentials of liability under, 165–167
intent and, 166, 171n
nature of, 164–165
negligence and, 166, 167
procedures in, 181–186
*summarized,* 184
purpose and knowledge in, 166–167
Criminal procedures, 181–186
*summarized,* 184
Cross-examination, 75, 77
Crown jewel defense, 855
Cruel and unusual punishment, constitutional provision against, 92, 181
Cuba, limited liability companies (LLC) in, 759
Cumulative convertible preferred stock, 820
Cumulative preferred stock, 819, 820
Cumulative voting, 830n, 834–835, 841
results of, *illustrated,* 835
Cure, 415–416
*Curia regis,* 4
Customer of bank:
affirmative duty of, 558
death or incompetence of, 553, 563, 692n
liability of,
for unauthorized electronic fund transfers, 577–578, 580
for wrongful stop-payment order, 554–555, 563
negligence of, 558–562, 563
relationship of, with bank, 551
Customer restrictions, antitrust law and, 950
Customs, international, 1114

**D**

Damage(s), 11, 106, 340–347
buyer's right to recover, 435–439

compensatory, 341, 348, 472, 727, 731
consequential, 341, 342–344, 348, 441
construction contracts and, 342
for emotional distress, 109
exemplary, 284
incidental, 341, 431
limitation of, 439
liquidated, 348, 439
penalties versus, 346–347
mitigation of, 344–346
nominal, 341, 344, 348
punitive, 284, 341, 344, 348, 727, 731
*Emerging Trends* feature on, 472–473
as requirement, in tort law, 119
seller's right to recover, 433
special, 342
*summarized,* 348
tenant's lawsuit for, 1034
treble, 575
types of, 341–344, 348
Dangerous conditions, 687
Dangerous products, 464, 468–469
Data, theft of, 159
Davis-Bacon Act (1931), 702
*De facto* corporations, 816
*De jure* corporations, 815–816
Deadly force, 178–179
Death:
of agent, agency termination and, 692, 693
of assignor, assignment revocation by, 315
of bank customer, 553, 563, 692n
of essential party, impossibility of performance and, 335
of offeror or offeree, offer termination and, 239, 240
of partner, 776
dissolution of partnership by, 787
of principal, agency termination and, 692, 693
Debenture bonds, 818
Debit card, 570
Debt(s):
collection of, 918–919, 922, 966–967
of estate, 306
liquidation of, 254
preexisting, 638
promise to pay, statute of limitations and, 256, 258
reaffirmation of, 642–643
status of, debtor's request for, 607

unliquidated, 254
Debt securities, 818
Debtor(s):
collateral of,
debtor's rights to, 592
priority of creditors' claims to, *summarized,* 605
consumer, 628, 632
default of, 607–612
*defined,* 589
duties of, 606–607
name of, filing of financing statement under, 595
in possession (DIP), 644–645
property of, liens on, 638
protection for, 628
rights of, 592, 606–607, 628
Deceit, 114. *See also* Fraud; Misrepresentation
intention and, 283–284, 288
obtaining goods through, 168, 173
Deceptive advertising, 907–908, 909–910
Decision making, ethics and, 26
Decisions, court. *See* Court(s), decisions of
Declaration of revocation of will, 1080
Deductive reasoning, 5
Deed(s):
creation of easement or profit by, 1009
grant, 1012
quitclaim, 1011, 1013
sheriff's, 1012
signed, sealed, and delivered, 1013n
warranty, 1011
*illustrated,* 1012
Defalcation, 1096
Defamation, 109–111, 114
in business, 134–136
by computer, 134–136
Defamatory speech, 92
Default, secured transactions and, 607–612
Default judgment, 66
Defendant:
criminal, rights of, 92, 181–186
*defined,* 5, 19
Defense(s), 11
absolute, 111
affirmative, 69
to assault, 107
to battery, 107
complete, 522
against corporate takeovers, *summarized,* 855

to criminal liability, 176–181
to defamation, 111
against employment discrimination claims, 735–736
of guarantor, 627
against holders of negotiable instruments, 520–526
  summarized, 525
to liability, 1105
limited, 511
to negligence, 119–121, 122, 466, 1096
against negotiable instrument, HDC status and, 517–518, 519
of others, as defense against tort, 107
partial, 522
against payment under insurance contract, 1061–1064
personal, 511, 523–526
of property, as defense against tort, 107
real, 511, 520–523, 525
self,
  as defense to criminal liability, 178–179
  as defense against tort, 107
to strict liability, 475–477
of surety, 627
against third party beneficiaries, 322n
universal, 511, 520–523, 525
waiver of, 440
to wrongful interference, 131–132
Defense Products Act (1950), 960
Deferred posting of checks, 564
Deficiency judgment, 611, 623, 922
Definiteness of terms, 236
Delegatee, 317
Delegation(s), 313
  duties, not subject to, 317–318, 323
  third party rights and, summarized, 323
Delegation doctrine, 889
Delegator, 317
Delivery:
  actual, 990
  collect on (C.O.D.), 420
  constructive, 976, 990
  ex-ship, 400
  of gift, 976–977
  without movement of goods, 397, 400–402
  place of, 414–415
  of possession, 990

seller's right to withhold, 429–430
tender of, 414, 456
time for, 370
Delivery order, 999
Demand, payment on, 497, 501
Demand deposit, 488
Demand instruments, 487, 488
  overdue, HDC status and, 516, 517, 519
Demurrer, 66
Denmark, membership in European Union and, 204
Department of. See United States Department of
Deposit(s):
  certificate of (CD). See Certificate, of deposit
  of checks, 514
    acceptance of, 562–566
    direct, 570
    indorsement for, 505, 506
    security, 1034
Depositary bank, 563–564
"Deposited acceptance rule," 244
Depositions, 71–72, 73
Depository bank, 563n
DES (diethylstilbestrol) cases, 471
Descendants, lineal, 1083
Destination contracts, 397, 400, 415
Destruction:
  of check, 550–551
  of identified goods, 417
  of leased premises, 1042–1043
  of subject matter,
    impossibility of performance and, 335
    offer termination by, 238, 239, 240
  of will, 1078, 1082
Destructive computer programming, 158
Determinable fee, 1007
Detrimental reliance, 237–238, 256–257, 258, 322, 323. See also Promissory estoppel
Devise, 1073, 1082
Diethylstilbestrol (DES) cases, 471
Difficulties, unforeseen, consideration and, 251–252
Digests, case, 16
Digital audiotape (DAT), copyright infringement and, 152
DIP (debtor in possession), 644–645
Direct collection, 606
Direct deposits, 570
Direct examination, 75, 77

Direct exporting, 1119
Directed verdict, 75
Directors, corporate:
  agency and, 824
  compensation of, 825, 831
  duties of, 827–829, 831, 854, 880–881
  election of, 825, 831
  failure of, to declare a dividend, 836–837
  indemnification of, 826
  insider trading and, 828, 867, 869–873, 882
  liability of, 829–830, 831
    for crimes, 170–173, 175
  management responsibilities of, 826–827, 831
  meeting of, 825, 831
  mismanagement and, 827, 831
  negligence and, 827
  pervasiveness of control of, 172–173, 175
  qualifications of, 825, 831
  removal of, for cause, 825, 830
  rights of, 825–826, 831
  role of, 824–830
    summarized, 831
  trustees versus, 824
Disability:
  defined, 729
  discrimination based on, 729–731, 732–734, 743
Disaffirmance:
  by intoxicated persons, 269, 272
  by mentally incompetent persons, 271, 272
  by minors, 262–267, 272
Discharge:
  in bankruptcy, 334, 337, 640–642, 649
    liability on negotiable instrument and, 523, 525
  of contract. See Contract(s), discharge of
  from liability on negotiable instrument, 525, 541–544
  by payment or cancellation, 525
  wrongful, 33, 703
Disclaimer of warranty, 445–446, 455–456, 458
Disclosed principal, 680–682
Disclosure:
  Federal Reserve Board Regulation Z and, 913
  of interest, 829
  under Rule 10b-5, 870–871
  seller's duty of, 1015–1016
  of terms and condition, under EFTA, 572–573, 574, 580

Discovery, 66, 71–72, 73
Discrimination:
  employment. *See* Employment
    discrimination
  price, 33, 955
  reverse, 734, 742–743
Discriminatory contracts, 298, 300
Dishonor:
  of negotiable instrument,
    532–533, 540, 551, 563
    HDC status and, 517, 519
  wrongful, of check, 551, 563
Dismissals, 69–71
Disparagement of property,
    136–139
Disparate-impact discrimination,
    725–726
Disparate-treatment discrimination,
    725
Dissenting opinion, 19
Dissolution:
  articles of, 855
  certificate of, 855n
  of corporation, 854–857
    shareholders' rights and,
      838–839
  involuntary, 856–857
  of limited partnership, 798
  notice of, 790
  of partnership, 786, 787–790
  voluntary, 854–856
Distress, emotional, intentional
    infliction of, 107–109, 114
Distribution:
  agreement for, 1119
  order of, intestacy laws and,
    1082–1086
  *per capita,* 1084, 1086
    *illustrated,* 1085
  *per stirpes,* 1084
    *illustrated,* 1085
  of property, in bankruptcy, 640
Distributorship, 757
Diversification merger, 957
Diversity of citizenship, 49
Divestiture, 959
Dividends, 836–837
Divisible contracts, 299
Divorce, revocation of will by,
    1081, 1082
Document(s):
  face of, 227
  facsimile (fax) copies of, 307
  notarization of, 674
  request for, 72
  of title, 414, 420, 596
    negotiability of, 999–1000
    UCC and, 999
Documentation. *See* Record(s)

DOJ. *See* United States Department
    of Justice
Domestic corporation, 804, 812
Domestic relations courts, 44
Dominion and control, 977
Donative intent, 977–978
Donee, 976
Donee beneficiary, 321, 323
Donor, 976
Door-to-door sales, 333n, 348n,
    911
Double indemnity, 1068
Double jeopardy, 92, 181, 186
Double-taxation, 780, 802
Dow Chemical Company, 210
Draft(s), 487, 488–490
  bank, 489n
  dishonor of, 540
  sight, 489
  time, 489
Dram shop acts, 122, 745
Drawee, 488
  *defined,* 548
  drawer's signature and, 534n
Drawer, 488
  *defined,* 530, 548
  signature of, 534n
    forged, 556–561
Drinking water, 932–933
Drugs:
  abuse of, 733–734
  testing for, 706–708, 745
Due care, efficiency versus, 584
Due diligence standard, 1104–1105
Due negotiation, 1000
Due process:
  procedural, 100
  substantive, 99–100
Due process clause, 91, 92,
    99–100, 181, 472, 620, 802,
    970
Dumping, 1121
Durable power of attorney, 674
Duration:
  of contract, 370
  of corporation, 813
  of partnership, 769, 772, 795
Duress:
  contract illegal through, 299, 301
  as defense to criminal liability,
    178
  economic, 286, 288
  extreme, 523
  genuineness of assent and,
    285–286, 288
  liability on negotiable instrument
    and, 523, 525, 526
  ordinary, 525, 526
Duty(ies). *See also* Obligation(s)

affirmative, 558
  of agent, 664–668, 697
  assignment of, 315
  of bailee, 994–996
    *summarized,* 1003
  of bailor, 996–998
    *summarized,* 1003
  of bank customer, 558
  of care, 114–115, 827, 831,
    880–881, 1096–1098
    breach of, 115–117
    *summarized,* 1003
  of corporate directors, 827–829,
    831, 854, 880–881
  of corporate officers, 827–829,
    831, 880–881
  of corporations. *See*
    Corporation(s), duty of
  of creditor, 606–607
  of debtor, 606–607
  delegation of. *See* Delegation(s)
  ethics and, 27
  fiduciary. *See* Fiduciary
    relationships
  insurance contracts and, 1061
  among joint venturers, 753–755
  of landlords, 1029
  of landowners, 115–116
  of loyalty, 827–829, 831, 880
  of minors, 262–264, 272
  not subject to delegation,
    317–318, 323
  of offeree, to reject offer,
    242–243
  of partners, 778–779, 781–782,
    880–881
  preexisting, consideration and,
    251–252, 258
  of principal, 664–665, 668,
    697–698
  of professionals, 116–117
  rescue and, 117
  return of bailed property and,
    995
  of seller, 1015–1016
  of shareholders, majority,
    841–843, 881–882
  statutory, product liability and,
    466
  of tenants, 1030
  of trustee, 1090
  to warn, 117


**E**

Earnest money, 1014
Earnings, retained, 802, 836. *See
    also* Income; Profit(s)
Easements, 1009–1010

EC (European Community), 1114, 1122. *See also* European Union

ECOA (Equal Credit Opportunity Act) (1974), 915, 966

Economic duress, 286, 288

ECPA (Electronic Communications Privacy Act) (1986), 160, 708–709

ECSC (European Coal and Steel Community), 1122

EEC (European Economic Community), 1122

EEOC. *See* Equal Employment Opportunity Commission

Effective financing statement (EFS), 604

EFS (effective financing statement), 604

EFT. *See* Electronic fund transfer(s)

EFTA. *See* Electronic Fund Transfer Act

EFTS (electronic fund transfer systems). *See* Electronic fund transfer(s)

Egypt:
  employment law in, 199
  government regulation in, 203–204
  privatization and, 206
  torts in, 197

Eighth Amendment, 92, 181, 472

EIS (environmental impact statement), 928–929

Ejectment, 1035

Election. *See also* Voting
  of corporate directors, 825, 831
  of remedies, 352–353

Electronic age, copyright infringement in, 153–154

Electronic Communications Privacy Act (ECPA) (1986), 160, 708–709

Electronic fund transfer(s) (EFT), 569–582
  commercial, 569, 579–580
  consumer, 569, 571–579
  direct deposits and withdrawals by, 570
  ethics and, 585–586
  preauthorized, 573, 580
  reversibility and, 573, 575
  stopping payment and, 573, 575
  types of, 570–571
  unauthorized, 576–579, 580

Electronic Fund Transfer Act (EFTA)(1978), 160, 569, 571–580

summarized, 580

Electronic fund transfer systems (EFTS). *See* Electronic fund transfer(s)

Eleemosynary corporation, 806

Emancipation of minors, 266

Embezzlement, 168, 173, 1096

Emergency powers of agent, 678

Eminent domain, 1006, 1017–1018

Emotional distress, intentional infliction of, 107–109, 114

Employee(s). *See also* Employment
  AIDS testing and, 708
  dangerous, 731
  with disability, 729–731, 743
    *Emerging Trends* feature on, 732–734
  discrimination and. *See* Employment discrimination
  drug testing and, 706–708, 745
  drug use and, 733–734
  electronic communications and, 709
  family and medical leave for, 715, 744
  fatigued, 745
  health insurance and, 714–715
  health and safety protection for, 711–713, 745
  independent contractor versus, 659–660, 699
  intentional torts of, employer's liability for, 687–688
  key, 715
  labor relations and, 716–718
    *Focus on Ethics* feature on, 741–746
  lie-detector tests and, 706
  misconduct of, employment discrimination claim and, 735–736
  negligence of, employer's liability for, 685–687
  performance monitoring and, 708–709, 745
  preemployment physicals and, 731
  preemployment screening procedures and, 709–710, 745
  privacy rights of, 706–710, 745–746
  retirement and security income for, 713–714
  ''spies'' and, 745–746
  status as, IRS factors for determining, 660, 699
  telephone conversations of, 708–709

unemployment compensation and, 714

workers' compensation and, 713

Employee Polygraph Protection Act (1988), 706

Employee Retirement Income Security Act (ERISA) (1974), 714

Employer(s). *See also* Employment
  liability of, 685–688, 709, 726–727
  obligations of, under COBRA, 714–715

Employer-employee relationships, 659, 685–688

Employer-independent contractor relationships, 659–662, 688–689
  ethics and, 661–662

Employment, 702–720. *See also* Employee(s); Employer(s)
  accommodations for disabled workers and, 729–731, 743
    *Emerging Trends* feature on, 732–734
  affirmative action and, 731, 734–735
  at will, 198–200, 702, 703–704, 741–742
  contract of, implied, 703, 741–742
  discrimination and. *See* Employment discrimination
  employee privacy rights and, 706–710, 745–746
  ethics and, 30–34
  health and safety in, 711–713, 745
  labor relations and, 716–718
    *Focus on Ethics* feature on, 741–746
  national laws of, comparison of, 198–200
  preemployment screening procedures and, 709–710, 745
  privacy rights and, 34
  safety and, 172–173, 731
  whistleblowing and, 30, 175, 703, 704–706, 742
  at will, 198–200, 702, 703–704, 741–742

Employment discrimination, 31–34, 721–740, 742–744
  based on age, 33, 55, 660, 727–729, 1134
  based on disability, 729–731, 732–734, 743
  based on gender, 722–725

based on pregnancy, 722
based on race, color, or national
    origin, 55, 722
based on religion, 722
defenses to claims of, 735–736
disparate-impact, 725–726
disparate-treatment, 725
intentional, unintentional versus,
    725–726
international business
    transactions and, 1125–1126,
    1134
reverse, 734, 742–743
unintentional, intentional versus,
    725–726
Employment-at-will, 702, 703–704,
    741–742
national laws regarding,
    comparison of, 198–200
Enabling legislation, 8, 887
Encoding warranties, 565–566
Encyclopedias, legal, 16
Endangered Species Act (1973),
    928, 929
Endorsement. *See* Indorsement(s)
Endowment insurance, 1064–1065
Enemy aliens, 271
Enforcement:
    by administrative agencies, 887,
        893–895
    of antitrust laws, 959–960
    of arbitration agreements, 53
    of contracts, 226
    of judgment, 81
    of promises without
        consideration, 256–259
    of security agreements, 590–592
England. *See also* United Kingdom
    jury selection in, 79
    liability of accountants to third
        parties in, 1102
    standards of proximate cause in,
        118
    Statute of Frauds and, 388
    *voir dire* in, 79
    waiver of protection-sale
        protections in, 610
    warranty of habitability in, 1032
    whistleblowing in, 706
Entrapment, as defense to criminal
    liability, 179–180
Entrepreneur, 748
Entrustment rule, 408–409
Environmental impact statement
    (EIS), 928–929
Environmental law, 925–943
    air pollution and, 929–931
    common law and, 925–927
    ethics and, 964–966

federal regulation and, 927–941
    major statutes regarding,
        *summarized,* 928
noise pollution and, 933
oil pollution and, 933
radiation and, 940–941
state and local regulation and,
    941
toxic chemicals and, 936–940
water pollution and, 931–933,
    965–966
Environmental Protection Agency
    (EPA), 8, 886, 889, 895, 898,
    901, 929, 930, 931, 932–933,
    934, 935, 936, 937, 940, 965
EPA. *See* Environmental Protection
    Agency
Equal Credit Opportunity Act
    (ECOA) (1974), 915, 966
Equal dignity rule, 662n, 673–674
Equal Employment Opportunity
    Commission (EEOC), 33, 96,
    722, 723, 725, 731, 732, 733,
    744, 886, 889, 1134n
Equal protection clause, 100–102
Equitable insolvency, 632n
Equitable interest, 830
Equitable maxims, 11
Equitable relief, 11
Equitable remedies, 352
Equitable servitudes, 1022–1023
Equity:
    courts of, 10, 11
    law versus, 12–13
    of redemption, 623
    remedies in. *See* Remedy(ies), in
        equity
Equity securities, 818
ERISA (Employee Retirement
    Income Security Act) (1974),
    714
Error(s). *See also* Mistake(s)
    clerical, 308
    in contract, 308
    scrivener's, 276
    Type I and Type II, 26
    typographic, 308
Escheat, 1072
Escrow account, 1014, 1032
Escrow agent, 1014, 1032
Establishment clause, 96
Estate(s):
    administration of, 1091
        summary procedures in, 1075
    debts of, 306
    leasehold, 1010–1011, 1026
    life, 1008
    privity of, 1021
    in property, in bankruptcy, 635

*pur autre vie,* 1008n
    taxation of, 1092
Estoppel:
    agency formation by, 663–664,
        675, 677–678, 699–700
    corporation by, 816
    minor's misrepresentation of age
        and, 264
    partnership by, 772
    promissory, 237–238, 240,
        256–257, 258, 302, 307
        ethics and, 360–361
Estray statutes, 981–982
Ethical standards. *See* Ethics
Ethics. *See also* Business ethics
    agency relationships and,
        697–700
    antitrust law and, 967–968
    bailments and, 1049
    bankruptcy and, 655–656
    business organizations and,
        880–884
    business. *See* Business ethics
    consequences and, 27
    contract law and, *Focus on
        Ethics* feature on, 357–362
    corporate structure and, 30
    creditors' rights and, 653–656
    criminal penalties and, 36–37
    deadly force and, 179
    duty and, 27, 117
    electronic fund transfers and,
        585–586
    *Emerging Trends* feature on,
        36–37
    employee relations and, 741–746
    employer-independent contractor
        relationships and, 661–662
    employment and, 741–746
    environmental law and, 964–966
    freedom of contract and,
        357–358
    garnishment and, 623
    government regulation and,
        964–968
    illegality versus, 27, 34
    institutionalization of, 36–37
    insurance and, 1130–1131
    international business
        transactions and, 190–191
    international codes of, 37
    international law and, 1132
    investing and, 212
    Kantian, 27
    landlord-tenant relationships and,
        1049–1050
    law and, 26–27
    management and, 30, 34–38
    outcome-based, 28

professional-client
communications and, 1110
property and, 1046–1050
public welfare offenses and, 172
religion and, 27
social responsibility and, *Focus on Ethics* feature on, 208–212
sovereign immunity and, 1132–1133
utilitarian, 28
EU. *See* European Union
Euratom (European Atomic Energy Community), 1122
Europe:
civil law in, bailments and, 998
intellectual property protection in, 201
piercing the corporate veil in, 818
rights of illegitimate children in, 1084
shareholder form of business organization developed in, 801
European Atomic Energy Community (Euratom), 1122
European Coal and Steel Community (ECSC), 1122
European Community (EC), 1114, 1122. *See also* European Union
European Court of Justice, 204
European Economic Community (EEC), 1122
European Union (EU), 204–205, 1114, 1122
advertising regulation in, 908
intellectual property protection in, 201
liability for hazardous waste disposal in, 939–940
product liability in, 470
regulation of mergers in, 959
Eviction, 1029
constructive, 1029
partial, 1029
retaliatory, 1029
Evidence:
appellate procedure and, 79–80
clear and convincing, 75
extrinsic, 227
preponderance of, 75
*prima facie*, 440, 1096
relevant, 74
rules of, 74
*Ex relatione*, 74n
Examination(s):
of bank statements, 558–559, 563

preemployment physical, 731
request for, 72
of title, 1014–1015
of witnesses, 75, 77
constitutional right of, 92, 181
Excessive bails and fines, constitutional provision against, 92, 181, 472
Exchange:
bargained-for, 248, 258
bill of, 487
*illustrated*, 489
Exchange tender offer, 848
Exclusionary rule, 181
Exclusive agency, 668
Exclusive distributorship, 1119
Exclusive jurisdiction, 49–50, 51
Exclusive-dealing contracts, 955–956
Exculpatory clauses, 296–297, 300, 353, 993, 1038
Executed contracts, 225, 226, 333
Execution, 607
fraud in, 520–522, 525
writ of, 616, 619, 621, 624
Executive agencies, 887
Executive committee, 826
Executive controls, 900
Executor, 1073
Executory contracts, 225, 226, 333
Executory interest, 1008–1009
Executory promise, 512
Exemplary damages, 284
Exempted rulemaking, 890
Exemption(s):
from antitrust laws, 960–961
bankruptcy, 636
homestead, 628
private placement, 865
from securities registration, 864
*illustrated*, 866
transaction, 864–867
*Ex-parte* communications, 891, 896
Expedited Funds Availability Act (1987), 566
Export Administration Act (1979), 1121
Export Trading Company Act (1982), 1121
Export-Import Bank, 1121
Exporting, 1119
control of, 1121
Express authority, 673–675, 684
Express authorization, 244
Express bailment agreement, 991
Express conditions, 327, 328–329
Express contract, 220–222, 226
Express powers, 803
Express ratification, 267, 679

Express trusts, 1086–1087, 1089
Express warranties, 446–449, 455, 458, 459, 922
Expressions of opinion, 231
Expropriation, 1116
Extension clause, 498
Extreme duress, 523, 525
Extrinsic evidence, 227
*Exxon Valdez*, 933

**F**

F.A.S. (free alongside), 400
F.O.B. (free on board), 400
Face of the instrument, 227
Facsimile copies, 307
Fact(s):
affirmation of, 446, 459
causation in, 117
compilations of, copyrightability, 149–151
honesty in, 518
justifiable ignorance of, 299, 301
material, 275–276, 277–278, 288, 854
mistake of, 177
question of, 45, 70
statement of, 112, 281
Fair Credit Billing Act (1974), 915–916
Fair Credit Reporting Act (FCRA) (1970), 160, 916–918
Fair Debt Collection Practices Act (FDCPA)(1977), 918–919, 966
Fair Housing Act (Civil Rights Act)(1968), 1022
Fair Labor Standards Act (Wage-Hour Law) (FLSA) (1938), 715–716
Fair Packaging and Labeling Act (1966), 911
Fair trade agreements, 952
''Fair use'' doctrine, 151, 153
Fair value, 1121
of land, 1018
of shareholder's shares, 848
Faith:
bad, 57
good, 645
HDC concept and, 583–584
False Claims Act (1863), 704n, 742n
False Claims Reform Act (1986), 704, 742
False imprisonment, 107, 114
False pretenses, obtaining goods by, 168, 173
Family corporation, 806

Family Educational Rights and Privacy Act (1974), 160
Family farmer:
  bankruptcy plans and, 649–650
  *defined,* 649
Family Farmer Bankruptcy Act, 649
Family and Medical Leave Act (FMLA) (1993), 715, 744
Family settlement agreements, 1075
Farm products, buyers of, security interests and, 597, 604
Farmers, *defined,* 635n
FASB (Financial Accounting Standards Board), 1096
Fault, comparative, 476–477
Fax advertising, 910
Fax copies, 307
FCC (Federal Communications Commission), 9, 889, 910, 961
FCPA (Foreign Corrupt Practices Act) (1977), 38, 169, 191, 1127, 1133
FCRA (Fair Credit Reporting Act) (1970), 160, 916–918
FDA (Food and Drug Administration), 2, 8, 473, 920, 929
FDCPA (Fair Debt Collection Practices Act) (1977), 918–919, 966
Federal Arbitration Act (1925), 53
Federal Aviation Act, 596
"Federal Box," 913
Federal Bureau of Investigation, 902
Federal Cigarette Labeling and Advertising Act (1965), 89
Federal Communications Commission (FCC), 9, 889, 910, 961
Federal courts. *See* Court(s), federal
Federal Deposit Insurance Corporation, 585
Federal Elections Campaign Act (1974), 803n
Federal Food, Drug, and Cosmetic Act (FFDCA) (1938), 466, 920
Federal Hazardous Substances Act (1960), 920
Federal Insecticide, Fungicide, and Rodenticide Act (FIFRA) (1947), 928, 936
Federal Insurance Contributions Act (FICA), 713
Federal legal systems, 191–192

Federal Maritime Commission, 961
Federal questions, 49
*Federal Register,* 890, 891, 893
  *illustrated,* 892
*Federal Reporter* (F. or F.2d or F.3d) (West), 14
Federal Reserve System, 887, 889
  Board of Governors of (Fed), 566, 889
    EFTA and, 571
    Regulation E of, 571
    Regulation Z of, 911, 913
  clearance of checks by, 564–565, 566
  wire transfer network of (Fedwire), 579
Federal Rules of Civil Procedure (FRCP), 64, 71
*Federal Supplement* (F.Supp.) (West), 14
Federal Trade Commission (FTC), 8, 9, 232, 886, 887, 889, 895, 906–907, 911, 913, 914, 918
  antitrust laws enforced by, 959–960
  appeals from, 47
  consumer credit sales and, 440, 493–494, 526–527
  deceptive advertising and, 909–910
  door-to-door sales and, 348n
  franchise regulations of, 757
  funeral-home trade regulated by, 912
  "Guides on Bait Advertising" of, 908
  HDC rights limited by, 493–494, 526–527, 628
  interlocking directorates and, 959
  Magnuson-Moss Warranty Act enforced by, 459
  "Mail Order Rule" of 1975 of, 912
  "Mail or Telephone Order Merchandise Rule" of 1933 of, 912
  merger guidelines of, 956–957
  Rule 433 of, 493–494, 526–527, 628
  "Used Motor Vehicle Regulation Rule" of, 912
  used-car business regulated by, 912
Federal Trade Commission Act (1914), 8, 294n, 887, 906, 944, 959, 1123
Federal Unemployment Tax Act (1935), 714
Federal Water Pollution Control

Act (FWPCA) (1948), 928, 931, 933
Federalism, 85
Fedwire, 579
Fee simple, 973–974, 984
  absolute, 1007
  defeasible, 1007
Felonies, 165
FFDCA (Federal Food, Drug, and Cosmetic Act)(1938), 466, 920
FICA (Federal Insurance Contributions Act), 713
Fictitious payee rule, 537–538
Fiduciary relationship(s):
  agency and, 659, 880–881
  corporate directors and, 828, 831, 854, 880–881
  corporate officers and, 828, 831, 880–881
  between majority and minority shareholders, 842
  partners and, 778–779
FIFRA (Federal Insecticide, Fungicide, and Rodenticide Act) (1947), 928, 936
Fifth Amendment, 91, 92, 98, 99, 100, 181, 182, 186, 706, 802, 894, 970, 1018, 1048
Filing:
  of bankruptcy petition, 632–635
  of bankruptcy plan, 645, 648
  perfection of security interest by, 595–596
*Filius nullius,* 1131
Final order, 896
Financial Accounting Standards Board (FASB), 1096
Financial crimes, 158
Financial institutions, EFTA definition of, 571. *See also* Bank(s)
Financial statements:
  reasonably foreseeable users of, 1102–1103, 1109
  unaudited, 1096–1097
Financing:
  corporate, 818–821
  of real property, 1015
Financing statement, 595
  amendment of, 606
  effective (EFS), 604
  *illustrated,* 594
Fines, excessive, constitutional provision against, 92, 181, 472
Finland, membership in European Union and, 204
Fire insurance, 1066–1067
  *summarized,* 1066
First Amendment, 91, 92, 93, 94, 100, 109, 706, 802, 948

First refusal, right of, 838

First-money-in, first-money-out rule, 514

Fish and Wildlife Coordination Act (1958), 929

Fisheries, exemption of, from antitrust laws, 960

Fisheries Cooperative Marketing Act (1976), 960

Fitness, implied warranty of, 452, 455, 458
bailments and, 997

Fixed amount of money, negotiable instruments and, 495–497, 501

Fixed fees, 65

Fixed-income securities, 818

Fixture(s), 1030
*defined,* 972
as real property, 972–973
security interests in, 597
trade, 973

Flammable Fabrics Act (1953), 466, 911, 920

Float time, 569

Floating-lien concept, 600–601

FLSA (Fair Labor Standards Act) (Wage-Hour Law) (1938), 715–716

FMLA (Family and Medical Leave Act) (1993), 715, 733

FOIA (Freedom of Information Act) (1966), 160, 901, 902

Food and Drug Administration (FDA), 2, 8, 473, 920, 929

Force(s):
deadly, 178–179
justifiable use of, 178–179
superseding intervening, 119

*Force majeure* clause, 391–392

Foreclosure, mortgage, 623, 624

Foreign agent, 1119

Foreign corporation, 804, 812

Foreign Corrupt Practices Act (FCPA) (1977), 38, 169, 191, 1127, 1133

Foreign distributor, 1119

Foreign officials, bribery of, 38, 169, 173, 191, 1127, 1133–1134

Foreign Sovereign Immunities Act (FSIA), 1117, 1133

Foreign trade. *See* International business transactions

Foreseeability:
of consequential damages, 441
of risk, 118–119, 1036, 1040–1041
users of financial statements and,

1102–1103, 1109

Forfeiture:
of property, under RICO, 175–176
termination of lease by, 1042

Forgery, 167, 173
of drawer's signature, 556–561
of indorsement, 518, 561
international law and, 557
of maker's or drawer's signature, 518, 520, 525

Form(s):
battle of, 372
of contracts, 219. *See also* Statute of Frauds

Formal contracts, 225, 226

Formal rulemaking, 890, 891

Forum-selection clause, 391, 1127

Fourteenth Amendment, 91, 92, 98–99, 100, 181, 620, 802, 970, 1018, 1132

Fourth Amendment, 91, 92, 98, 181, 183, 706, 707, 711, 893–894

France:
celebrity appropriation in, 134
constitution of, 192
employment law in, 199
European Union membership and, 204
forged negotiable instruments in, 557
intellectual property protection in, 201–202
limited liability companies (LLC) in, 759
Napoleonic Code of, 192, 193, 194, 199
objective theory of contract in, 217
privatization and, 206
promissory estoppel in, 257
standards of proximate cause in, 118
Statute of Frauds and, 388
wrongful interference with a contractual relationship in, 131

Franchise(s), 756–757, 760–763
agency law and, 883–884
agreement creating, 757–763
chain-style, 757
*defined,* 756
distributorship as, 757
government regulation of, 757–758
international business transactions and, 1119, 1120

manufacturing or process plant, 757
termination of, 761–763
types of, 757

Franchisee, 756

Franchisor, 756

Fraud, 112, 114. *See also* Deceit; Misrepresentation
actual, 1098
bankruptcy, 169, 173
constructive, 1098
contract illegal through, 299, 301
elements of, 280–284, 288
in the execution, 520–522, 525
in the inducement, 524, 525
mail, 169, 173
obtaining goods through, 168, 173
professional's liability for, 1098–1100, 1109

Fraudulent misrepresentation. *See* Misrepresentation, fraudulent

Fraudulent transfers, bankruptcy and, 638–639

FRCP (Federal Rules of Civil Procedure), 64, 71

Free alongside (F.A.S.), 400

Free exercise clause, 96

Free on board (F.O.B.), 400

Freedom:
from contract, 218
of contract, 217–218, 357–358
of religion, 92, 96–97
of speech, 92–96, 109

Freedom of Information Act (FOIA) (1966), 160, 901, 902

Friedman, Milton, 208

Frozen embryos, as personal property, 1047–1048

Frustration of purpose, 335, 336

FSIA (Foreign Sovereign Immunities Act), 1117, 1133

FTC. *See* Federal Trade Commission

Full competence, 262

Full disclosure, 285

Full warranty, 459

Fund, mutual, 876

Fundamental right, 100

Funeral-home trade, FTC regulation of, 912

Fungible goods, 396, 471, 980
bailment of, 991

Fur Products Labeling Act (1951), 910

Future advances, security interests and, 600

Future goods, 395

Future interests, 1008–1009
FWPCA (Federal Water Pollution Control Act) (1948), 928, 931, 933

## G

GAAP (generally accepted accounting principles), 1096, 1105
GAAS (generally accepted auditing standards), 1096, 1105
Gambling, 292–293, 300
  liability on negotiable instrument and, 524
Garnishment, 621–623, 624, 919, 922
GATT (General Agreement on Tariffs and Trade), 1122
Gender:
  discrimination based on, 722–725, 1027
    international business transactions and, 191
  sexual harassment and, 33–34, 723–725, 743–744
  insurance rates and, 1131
General Agreement on Tariffs and Trade (GATT), 1122
General Assembly of the United Nations, 1114
General devise, 1073, 1082
General jurisdiction, 43, 44
General partner, 794
General partnerships, 749
  limited partnership versus, 795
General power of attorney, *illustrated*, 676
General warrant, 98
Generally accepted accounting principles (GAAP), 1096, 1105
Generally accepted auditing standards (GAAS), 1096, 1105
Genuineness of assent, 219, 275–290
  *summarized*, 288
Germany:
  Commercial Code of 1900 in, 192, 194196
  constitution of, 192
  contract assignment in, 317
  European Union membership and, 204
  government regulation in, 203
  impossibility of performance in, 336
  insider trading in, 875

intellectual property protection in, 201
labor policy in, 1134
limited liability companies (LLC) in, 759
piercing the corporate veil in, 818
specific performance in, 441
takings law in, 1021
unconscionability in, 287
*Gesellschaft mit beschranker Haftung* (GmbH), 759
Gift(s):
  acceptance of, 978–980
  acquisition of personal property by, 976–980, 984
  bribery versus, 191
  *causa mortis,* 978–980
  delivery of, 976–978
  donee beneficiary and, 321, 323
  *inter vivos,* 978
  testamentary, 976
  by will, 1073–1074, 1082
GmbH *(Gesellschaft mit beschranker Haftung),* 759
Golden parachute, 855
Good cause, 645
Good faith, 645
  contract modification and, 377
  *defined,* 514, 519
  HDC concept and, 583–584
  legal reasoning and, 6
  limitations and, 371
  sales contracts and, 413–414
  taking in, HDC status and, 514–516, 518, 519
Good faith purchaser:
  *defined,* 406
  in international art world, 407
  minor's duty of restitution and, 263n
  UCC on, 263n
Good Samaritan statutes, 123
Good title, 445, 458
Goods. *See also* Product(s)
  acceptance of, 420
    revocation of, 420–422
  accepted, 437–439
  buyer's examination of, 456
  buyer's rights in, 434–435
  conforming, 413, 414, 415
  consumer, security interests and, 597, 604–605, 608–609
  contracts for sale of. *See* Sales contract(s)
  *defined,* 366
  delivery of. *See* Delivery
  dumping of, 1121

fungible, 396, 471, 980
  bailment of, 991
future, 395
identification of, 395–396
identified, 405, 415
  buyer's right, to recover, 434
  destruction of, 417
leased, 383, 385, 475
nonconforming, 372, 437–438
obtaining by false pretenses, 168, 173
real property versus, 365, 366
rejection of, 434
security interest in, 435
seller's rights in, 430–431
services versus, 366–368
sold, 409–410
specially manufactured, 379
stolen, 168, 173
in transit, 430
unsolicited, 912
Government:
  confederal form of, 84
  constitutional powers of, 85–91
  police powers of, 87, 1018
  regulation by. *See* Government regulation
Government regulation, 84–104, 885–968
  antitrust law and, 755–756, 761n
  constitutional authority for, 889
  environment and. *See* Environmental law
  *Focus on Ethics* feature on, 964–968
  of franchising, 757–758
  international business transactions and, 1120–1123
  investing in foreign countries and, 1120–1123
  of investment companies, 876–877
  land-use, 1048–1049
  local, preemption of, 89, 90
  by national government, 85–87
  national laws on, comparison of, 203–204
  of securities. *See* Securities, regulation of
  by states, 87–88, 757, 877
Government-in-the-Sunshine Act (1976), 901
Grace period, 1059
Grand jury, 52, 72, 92, 181
Grandchildren, distribution to under intestacy laws, 1084–1086
Grant deed, 1012

Grantee, 1011
Grantor, 1011
Gratuitous agent, 683n
Gratuitous assignments, 315
Great Britain, abandoned property in, 982. *See also* England
Greece, membership in European Union and, 204
Green Century Funds, 212
Greenmail, 855
Group boycott, 948
Guarantor, 304, 625
  defenses of, 627
  rights of, 627–628
Guaranty, 624, 625–627
  parties to, *illustrated,* 625
"Guides on Bait Advertising," 908
Guilty act, 165
Gulf Cooperation Council, protection of intellectual property in, 201

# H

H.B. Fuller Company, 33
Habitability, 1030
  warranty of, 1015, 1032
"Hacking," 29, 159
Hague Convention on the Law Applicable to Contracts for the International Sale of Goods, 391
Hand, Learned, 953n
Handwritten statement, 492
Harassment:
  hostile-environment, 723
  *quid pro quo,* 723
  sexual, 33–34, 722–725, 743–744
Hazardous Substances Labeling Act, 466
Hazardous wastes, 936–940
HDC. *See* Holder in due course
Headnotes, 16
Health insurance, 714–715, 733
Health protection:
  for consumers, 920
  for employees, 711–713, 745
Hearing(s):
  administrative agency, 896
  arbitration, 53
  pretrial, 72, 73
Hearsay, 74
Heirs, collateral, 1083
Herbicides, 936
Herfindahl-Hirschman Index (HHI), 957
HHI (Herfindahl-Hirschman Index), 957

Holder, 493. *See also* Holder in due course
  defenses against, 520–526
    *summarized,* 525
  *defined,* 500, 511–512, 519, 548
  HDC versus, 511–512
  through an HDC, 518, 520
  payee as, 548
Holder in due course (HDC), 494. *See also* Holder
  commercial bank as, 514
  defenses against, 520–526
    *summarized,* 525
  *defined,* 512
  good faith and, 583–584
  holder through, 518, 520
  holder versus, 511–512
  requirements for status of, 512–518
    *summarized,* 519
  rights of, limitation of, 493–494, 526–527, 628
Holmes, Oliver Wendell, Jr., 3
Holographic will, 1077, 1082
Homeowners' insurance, 1067
Homestead exemption, 628
Honesty, in fact, 518
Hong Kong, employment law in, 199
Horizontal market division, 948
Horizontal mergers, 956–957
Horizontal restraints, 948–950
Hostile-environment harassment, 723
Hot-cargo agreements, 718
Hourly fees, 65
HUD (United States Department of Housing and Urban Development), 912
Hung jury, 186
Hybrid rulemaking, 890, 891

# I

ICC (Interstate Commerce Commission), 887, 889, 961, 1001n
Identification:
  of goods, 395–396
  of subject matter, 288
Identified goods, 405, 414
  buyer's right to recover, 434
  destruction of, 417
Identified person, 499
Illegal dividends, 836
Illegality:
  dissolution of partnership by, 787–788

effect of, 298–299, 300
  ethics versus, 27, 34
  leases and, 1027–1028
  liability on negotiable instrument and, 523, 524–525
  supervening, offer termination and, 239, 240
Illegitimacy, inheritance laws and, 1131–1132
Illusory promise, 253
Immigration Act (1990), 716
Immigration and Nationality Act (1952), 716n
Immunity, as defense to criminal liability, 181
Impairment of collateral or recourse, 543–544
Implication, creation of easement or profit by, 1009
Implied authority, 675, 684, 782
Implied bailment agreement, 991
Implied conditions, 327, 328–329
Implied contract, 220–222, 703, 741–742
Implied powers, 803
Implied ratification, 267, 679
Implied trusts, 1087–1089
Implied warranty. *See* Warranty(ies), implied
Implied-in-fact contract, 220–221, 226
Imports, control of, 1121–1122
Impossibility:
  agency termination and, 692, 693
  of performance,
    contract discharge by, 335, 337
    ethics and, 358
    temporary, 336–337
Imposter, 536–537
Imposter rule, 537
Imprisonment, false, 107, 114
Improper incorporation, 815–816
*In pari delicto,* 298
*In personam* jurisdiction, 42, 51
*In rem* jurisdiction, 42, 51
Incapacity. *See also* Capacity; Incompetence; Insanity; Mental incompetence
  contractual, legal effect of, *summarized,* 272
  of essential party, impossibility of performance and, 335
  of partner, dissolution of partnership and, 788–789
Incidental beneficiaries, 320, 322–324
Incidental damages, 341, 431
Income. *See also* Earnings; Profit(s)

retirement and security, 713–714
of trust, 1090–1091
Incompetence. *See also* Capacity;
Incapacity
of bank customer, 553, 563, 692n
of offeror or offeree, offer
termination and, 239, 240
Incomplete contracts, 308
Incomplete instruments, HDC
status and, 517–518, 519
Incontestability clause, 1058
Incorporation. *See also*
Corporation(s), formation of
articles of, 803, 813–815, 847
*illustrated,* 814
certificate of, 815
improper, 815–816
preincorporation contracts and,
811
procedures for, 812–815
Incorporators, 813, 815
Incoterms, 405
Indemnification:
of corporate officers and
directors, 826
principal's duty of, 668
principal's right to, 670
Indenture, 1107n
Indenture trustee, 1107n
Independent contractor:
*defined,* 659
employee versus, 659–660, 699
ethics and, 661–662
torts of, principal's liability for,
688–689
Independent regulatory agencies, 9,
887
*summarized,* 889
India:
contract law in, 196–197
government regulation in, 203
privatization and, 206
Indictment, 185
Indirect collection, 606
Indirect exporting, 1119
Indivisible contracts, 299
Indorsee, 502
Indorsement(s). *See also*
Signature(s)
agency, 505
by agents, 508
blank, 503, 506
for collection, 505
conditional, 505, 506
consequences of, *summarized,*
506
correction of name and, 507
*defined,* 499
for deposit, 505, 506

forged, 518, 561
multiple payees and, 507–508
on negotiable instruments,
502–508
*summarized,* 506
problems with, 507–508
prohibiting further indorsement,
505, 506
by public officials, 508
qualified, 504, 506
restrictive, 504–507
special, 503–504, 506
transfer by, 538
trust, 505–507
types of, 503–507
*summarized,* 506
unauthorized,
fictitious payee rule and,
537–538
imposter rule and, 536–537
unqualified, 504
Indorser, 502
accommodation, 533
qualified, 530n
signature liability of, 492, 506
transfer warranty liability and,
539
unqualified, 531
Infancy, as defense to criminal
liability, 176. *See also* Age;
Children; Minor(s)
Informal contracts, 225, 226
Informal rulemaking, 890–891
Information:
from administrative agency, letter
requesting, *illustrated,* 902
creditors' request for, 606
in criminal process, 185
Information return, 749, 769
Infringement:
copyright, 19, 151–152, 153–154
patent, 148
trademark, 146–147
warranty against, 445, 458
Inheritance. *See also* Intestacy
laws; Will(s)
acquisition of personal property
by, 980, 984
illegitimacy and, 1131–1132
transfer by, 1016
Initial appearance in criminal
process, 185
Initial order, 896
Injunction, 12
negative, 350n
Injunctive relief, 926
Injury(ies):
leased premises and, 1035–1039
legally recognizable, 119

as requirement,
in fraud, 284, 288
in tort law, 119
Inland marine insurance policy,
1068
Innkeeper(s):
bailments and, 1002
lien of, 615, 619, 624
Innocent misrepresentation, 284,
288
by agent, 685
Insanity. *See also* Capacity;
Incapacity; Incompetence;
Mental incompetence
of agent, agency termination and,
692, 693
as defense to criminal liability,
177
of partner, dissolution of
partnership and, 788
of principal, agency termination
and, 692, 693
Insider, 170, 410, 638
Insider trading, 170, 173, 861,
869–875, 882–883
corporate officers and directors
and, 828, 867, 869–873, 882
outsiders and, 873–874
reporting of, 875
sanctions and, 875
Insider Trading Sanctions Act
(1985), 875
Insider Trading and Securities
Fraud Enforcement Act
(1988), 875
Insolvency, 410
balance sheet, 632n
of corporation, 836
equitable, 632n
of partner, 793n
presumption of, 638
under UCC, 430
Inspection:
of business records,
director's right of, 825–826
partner's right of, 773
shareholder's right of, 807n,
837–838
buyer's right of, 420
OSHA, 711
Installment contracts, 416
Instrument. *See* Negotiable
instrument(s)
Insurable interest, 405, 1053,
1055–1056
Insurance, 1052–1071
assignment of, 1065
automobile, 1067–1068
business liability, 1068–1069

claims and, 1130–1131
classifications of, 1053
  *summarized,* 1054–1055
contract for, 1053, 1056–1064
  agents versus brokers and,
    1053, 1056
  application for, 1056
  cancellation of, 1059–1060
  cash surrender value of, 1059
  defenses against payment
    under, 1061–1064
  duties under, 1061
  effective date of, 1056–1058
  multiple insurance coverage
    and, 1059
  provisions and clauses of,
    1058–1059
  rights under, 1061, 1065
  termination of, 1065
*defined,* 1052
ethics and, 1130–1131
exemption of, from antitrust
  laws, 960
fire, 1065–1067
  *summarized,* 1066
gender-based rates and, 1131
health, 714–715, 733
homeowners', 1067
key-person, 1053
liability. *See* Liability insurance
life, 1053, 1064–1065
malpractice, 1069
marine, 1068
minor's liability for, 266–267
moral hazard and, 1130
policy for. *See* Insurance,
  contract for
premium for, 1053
property, 1053, 1055–1056
terminology of, 1053
title, 1015
types of, 1064–1069
underwriter of, 1053
workers' compensation, 1069
Insured, 1053
Insurer, 1053
Intangible property, 971, 984, 989,
  1046
  perfection of security interest
    and, 596
Integrated contract, 308
Intellectual property, 143–157,
  1046
  national laws regarding,
    comparison of, 200–202
Intended beneficiaries, 320–324
Intent, intention:
  contractual offer and, 231–234
  criminal law and, 166, 171n

to deceive, 283–284, 288, 1106
donative, 977–978
fixtures and, 972–973
monopolization and, 953
statements of, 231
torts and. *See* Intentional torts
trademark law and, 147
Intentional discrimination,
  unintentional versus, 725–726
Intentional infliction of emotional
  distress, 107–109, 114
Intentional interference, with
  contractual relationship,
  129–131
Intentional torts:
  of employee, employer's liability
    for, 687–688
  against persons, 106–112
    *summarized,* 114
  against property, 112–114
    *summarized,* 114
  *summarized,* 114
*Inter vivos* trusts, 1075,
  1086–1087, 1089
Interest(s):
  agency coupled with, 691
  commingled, 816
  compelling or overriding, 100
  conflict of, 298, 829
  equitable, 830
  executory, 1008–1009
  full disclosure of, 829
  future, 1008–1009
  insurable, 405, 1053, 1055–1056
  judgment rate of, 292, 495
  landlord's, transfer of, 1039
  legal rate of, 292, 300, 495
  nonpossessory, 1009–1011
  ownership, 830, 1006–1011
  partner's,
    in partnership, 773, 775–776
    transfer of, dissolution of
      partnership by, 787
  prejudgment rate of, 292
  protected, 105
  reversionary, 1008, 1027
  security. *See* Security interest
  sufficient, 405
  tenant's, transfer of, 1039
Interlocking directorates, antitrust
  law and, 959
Intermediary bank, 563, 564
Internal Revenue Code:
  liability of accountants under,
    1095, 1108, 1110
  Subchapter S of, 809
Internal Revenue Service (IRS),
  286, 570, 742, 758, 769, 901,
  1092

factors of, for determining
  employee status, 660, 699
private-letter ruling of, 780
International agreements, 1114
International business transactions,
  1113–1129. *See also*
  International law
acceptance in, 196
agency relationships with foreign
  firms and, 1119
antitrust laws and, 960,
  1123–1124
arbitration agreements and, 57
comparative law and, 189–212
computer-related theft and, 28
contracts for, disputes regarding,
  1126–1127
copyright law and, 155–156
discrimination laws and,
  1125–1126, 1134
distributorships and, 1119
ethics and, 37, 38
expansion of opportunities for,
  205–206
exporting and, 1119
franchising and, 1119, 1120
good faith purchaser and, 407
government regulation of,
  1120–1123
import control and, 1121–1122
letters of credit and, 425–426
manufacturing abroad and, 1119
parol evidence in, 310
patent law and, 149, 1125
purchase orders for, *illustrated,*
  389–390
remedies for breach in, 440–441
restraint of trade and, 1123
revocation of acceptance in, 422
risk of loss and, 404–405
special contract provisions for,
  391–392
United States laws and, 1134
International Chamber of
  Commerce, 1126
International conferences,
  1114–1115
International contracts. *See*
  International business
  transactions
International Convention for the
  Protection of Industrial
  Property, 1125n
International Court of Justice,
  Statute of, 1114
International customs, 1114
International Franchise Association,
  37
International law, 189, 1113–1118.

*See also* International business transactions; United Nations Convention for International Sale of Goods
  act of state doctrine and, 1116–1117
  comity, principle of, and, 1116
  *defined,* 1113–1114
  electronic fund transfers and, 576
  enforcement of attachments and, 621
  ethics and, 1132
  forged negotiable instruments and, 557
  fraudulent transfers and, 639
  national law versus, 1114
  nature and sources of, 1113–1115
  negotiable instruments and, 497
  notice of claims under, 438
  principles and doctrines of, 1115–1118
  sovereign immunity and, 1116, 1117–1118, 1132–1133
International organizations, 1114–1115
  multilateral, *summarized,* 1115
International purchase order, *illustrated,* 389–390
International Trade Administration (ITA), 1121, 1122
International Trade Commission (ITC), 1121–1122
Interpretative rules, 893
Interrogatories, 71, 72, 73
Interstate commerce, 85, 945
Interstate Commerce Act (1887), 944, 964
Interstate Commerce Commission (ICC), 887, 889, 961, 1001n
Interstate Land Sales Full Disclosure Act (1968), 912
Interstate Oil Compact (1935), 960
Intestacy laws, 1072, 1081–1086
  order of distribution under, 1082–1086
  surviving spouse and children and, 1082–1084
Intoxication:
  contractual capacity and, 269–271, 272
  as defense to criminal liability, 176–177
  involuntary, 176–177
  voluntary, 177
Intrastate commerce, 85
Invasion of privacy, 111–112, 114. *See also* Privacy
Inventory, as collateral, 597, 602

Investment companies, regulation of, 876–877
Investment Company Act (1940), 876
Investment Company Act Amendments (1970), 876
Investment group, 755
Investments:
  ethics and, 212
  in foreign nations, 1120–1123
Investor(s):
  accredited, 865
  protection of. *See* Securities, regulation of
Invitations to negotiate, 232
Invitee, 115, 1035
Involuntary bailment, 990n
Involuntary dissolution, 856–857
Involuntary intoxication, 176–177
Involuntary servitude, 350n
Ireland, membership in European Union and, 204
Irregular instruments, HDC status and, 518, 519
Irresistible-impulse test of insanity, 177
Irrevocable offer, 237, 240, 388
IRS. *See* Internal Revenue Service
Israel, entrapment defense in, 180
Issue, 488
Issuer, 425
ITA (International Trade Administration), 1121, 1122
Italy:
  European Union membership and, 204
  limited liability companies (LLC) in, 759
ITC (International Trade Commission), 1121–1122

**J**

Japan:
  Commercial Code of 1890 in, 192
  franchise termination in, 763
  intellectual property protection in, 200–201
  manufacturing plants in United States established by, 1119
  partnership law in, 779
  sexual harassment in, 724
Johnson & Johnson Company, Tylenol crisis and, 36
Joint adventure, 753
Joint liability, 779, 781–782
Joint and several liability, 782
Joint stock company, 755, 801

Joint tenancy, 974–975, 984
Joint ventures, 753–755
  antitrust law and, 950
  international business transactions and, 1120
Judge(s). *See also* Justice(s)
  administrative law (ALJ), 896, 909, 965
  bankruptcy, 636
  comparative legal systems and, 194
  *defined,* 19
  federal, lifetime appointments of, 47
  rent-a-, 59–60
Judgment(s):
  affirmation of, 45–46, 79
  before trial, 69–71, 73
  business, 829, 831
  confession of, 773
  default, 66
  deficiency, 611, 623, 922
  enforcement of, 81
  as a matter of law, 75
  *n.o.v.,* 79, 81
  partners and, 768
  partnerships and, 768
  on the pleadings, 69–70, 73
  reversal of, 45, 79–80
  summary, 70–71, 73
Judgment rate of interest, 292, 495
Judicial decree, dissolution of partnership by, 788–790
Judicial lien, 615, 619
Judicial remedies, 334
Judicial review, 51–52
  of administrative agency orders, 896–900
Jurisdiction:
  appellate, 43, 51
  concurrent versus exclusive, 49–50, 51
  *defined,* 41–42
  exclusive versus concurrent, 49–50, 51
  of federal courts, 47, 49–52, 85
  general, 43, 44
  *in personam,* 42, 51
  *in rem,* 42, 51
  limited, 43, 44
  minimum-contacts requirement and, 804–805
  movement of collateral and, 597–598
  original, 43, 51
  *quasi in rem,* 42
  Sherman Antitrust Act and, 945–947
  subject matter, 42–43, 51

*summarized*, 51
of United States Supreme Court,
    47, 49
Jurisprudence, 3
Jurisprudential thought, schools of,
    3–4
Jury:
    grand, 52, 72, 92, 181
    hung, 186
    instructions to, 75–77
    petit, 72
    selection of, 72–74, 79
    trial by, 72, 92, 181
    verdict of, 77, 186
Just compensation, 92, 970, 1006,
    1018
Justice(s). *See also* Judge(s)
    adversarial system of, 63
    *defined*, 19
    Department of. *See* United States
        Department of Justice
    European Court of, 204
    legal philosophy of, 3
    privatization of, 59–61
    of United States Supreme Court,
        19
    lifetime appointments of, 47
Justiciable controversy, 43–44, 897
Justifiable ignorance of the facts,
    299, 301
Justifiable reliance, 256, 284, 288,
    307
Justifiable use of force, as defense
    to criminal liability, 178–179


**K**

Kant, Immanuel, 27
Kasten, Robert W., Jr., 473
Keogh plan, 749
Key employee, 715
Key-person insurance, 1053
King's courts, 4, 8, 10, 486
Koenig, Thomas, 472
Korea:
    corporate law in, 203
    partnership law in, 779


**L**

L.S. (*locus sigilli*), 225
Labeling and packaging laws,
    910–911
Labor:
    child, 715
    employment and, laws regarding,
        701–746
    exemption of, from antitrust
        laws, 960

Labor-Management Relations Act
    (Taft-Hartley Act) (1947), 718
Labor-Management Reporting and
    Disclosure Act (Landrum-
    Griffin Act) (1959), 718
Laches, doctrine of, 11
Land. *See also* Real property
    covenant running with, 1021
    interests in, Statute of Frauds
        and, 301
    owners of, duties of, 115–116
    as real property, 971
    request for entry upon, 72
    sale of, contract for,
        damages for breach of, 341
        specific performance and, 350
    trespass to, 112–113, 114
Landlord(s):
    duties of, 1029
    failure of, to maintain leased
        property, 1032–1034
    interest of, transfer of, 1039
    liability of, 1036–1038
        *Emerging Trends* feature on,
            1040–1041
    lien of, 1035
    remedies of, 1034–1035
Landlord-tenant relationships,
    1026–1045. *See also*
    Landlord(s); Lease(s); Leased
    premises; Tenant(s)
    creation of, 1026–1028
    *Emerging Trends* feature on,
        1040–1041
    ethics and, 1049–1050
    liability for injuries on premises
        and, 1035–1039
    rights and duties in, 1028–1035
    transfer of rights to leased
        property in, 1039
Landrum-Griffin Act (Labor-
    Management Reporting and
    Disclosure Act)(1959), 718
Land-use regulations, 1048–1049
Language:
    choice of, international business
        transactions and, 391
    computer software copyright
        protection and, 152, 155,
        1046
    international business
        transactions and, 190, 391
Lapse of time:
    agency termination by, 690, 693
    offer termination by, 238, 239,
        240
Lapsed legacy, 1074
Larceny, 168, 173
Last clear chance, 121

Late charges, 1034
Law(s). *See also* Legal systems;
    Statute(s)
    administrative. *See*
        Administrative law
    agency. *See* Agency relationships
    American. *See* American law
    antitrust. *See* Antitrust law
    blue, 96, 293
    blue sky, 877
    business, 26–27
    case. *See* Case law
    choice-of clause, 1127
    civil versus criminal, 9–10, 11,
        164
    classifications of, 9–10
    codified, 192–194
    common. *See* Common law
    comparative, 189–212
    constitutional, 2, 7, 8
    consumer, 906–924
    contract. *See* Contract(s)
    copyright. *See* Copyright(s)
    courts of, 10
    creditor assistance provided by,
        615–624
    criminal. *See* Criminal law
    debtor assistance provided by,
        628
    employee and labor, 701–746
    environmental. *See*
        Environmental law
    equity versus, 12–13
    ethics and, 26–27
    franchising, 756
    inheritance. *See* Inheritance
    international. *See* International
        law
    intestacy. *See* Intestacy laws
    labeling, 910–911
    labor and employment, 701–746
    lemon, 421n, 440
    misrepresentation of, 282
    mistake of, 177
    national, 189
        comparison of, 195–204
        international versus, 1114
    natural, 3
    nature of, 3
    operation of. *See* Operation of
        law
    packaging, 910–911
    patent, 148–149
    positive, 3
    private versus public, 9, 10
    procedural versus substantive, 9,
        10
    public versus private, 9, 10
    question of, 45, 70

remedies at. *See* Remedy(ies), at law

Restatements of, 6. *See also* specific Restatements

right-to-work, 718

Sabbath, 293, 300

statutory. *See* Statutory law

substantive versus procedural, 9, 10

Sunday closing, 96, 293, 300

tort. *See* Tort(s)

trademark, 143, 144–147, 148

uniform, 7. *See also* specific uniform laws

warranty. *See* Warranty(ies)

workers' compensation, 713

zoning, 1018–1021

Law Merchant *(Lex Mercatoria),* 364, 486

Lawsuit:
 comparative legal systems and, 194–195
 covenant not to bring, 253, 255–256, 258
 derivative, shareholder's, 829, 839–840
 landlord's, for unpaid rent, 1035
 parties to, 19
 stages in, *illustrated,* 64
 standing to bring, 43–44, 91, 313, 897
 tenant's, for damages, 1034

Lawyer(s). *See also* Attorney(s)
 comparative legal systems and, 194–195
 numbers of, by country, 195

Lawyers Cooperative Publishing Company, 16

*Lawyers' Edition of the Supreme Court Reports* (L.Ed. or L.Ed.2d.), 14, 16

LBOs (leveraged buy-outs), 854

Lease(s), 1026–1028. *See also* Landlord-tenant relationships; Leased premises
 agreement to form, 383, 385
 assignment of, 316, 323, 1039
 cancellation of, 1034
 form of, 1027
 of goods, 383, 385, 475
 maintenance obligations under, 1031–1032
 renewal of, 1043
 termination of, 1034, 1042–1043

Leased premises. *See also* Landlord-tenant relationships; Lease(s)
 abandonment of, 1042
 alteration of, 1030

crimes on, 1040–1041
 defects on, 1036
 destruction of, 1042–1043
 injuries on, liability for, 1035–1039
 maintenance of, 1030–1034
 release of, 1042
 repairs and, 1038
 rights to, transfer of, 1039
 surrender of, 1042
 use of, 1029–1030

Leased property. *See* Leased premises

Leasehold estates, 1010–1011, 1026. *See also* Lease(s)

Legacy, 1073
 lapsed, 1074

Legal capacity. *See* Capacity

Legal encyclopedias, 16

Legal fees, 65, 66

Legal malpractice, 117

Legal process, agreement obstructing, 298, 300

Legal rate of interest, 292, 300, 495

Legal realism, 4

Legal reasoning:
 *defined,* 5
 *stare decisis* and, 5–6

Legal systems. *See also* Law(s)
 comparative, 191–195
 civil law, 192–194
 common law, 192, 194
 constitutional foundations of, 191–192
 forgery in, 557
 judges in, 194
 lawyers in, 194
 litigation in, 194–195
 procedures in, 194
 *summarized,* 194
 federal, 191–192

Legally recognizable injury, 119

Legatee, 1074

Legislation, enabling, 887. *See also* Law(s); Statute(s)

Legislative controls, 900–901

Legislative rules, 889, 893

Lemon laws, 421n, 440

Lessee, 383, 1026

Lessor, 383, 1026

Letter of credit, 425
 *illustrated,* 426

Leveraged buy-outs (LBOs), 854

Levi Strauss & Company, 209, 210

Levy, 607–608

*Lex Mercatoria* (Law Merchant), 364, 486

Liability(ies). *See also* Liability

insurance
 of accountants, 1095–1112
 *summarized,* 1109–1110
 agency relationships and, 673–690
 of attorneys, 1095–1112
 *summarized,* 1109–1110
 of auditors, 1100–1103, 1109
 of bailee, 993–994
 of bank, 554, 563, 575–576, 579
 of bank customer, 554–555, 563, 578–579, 580
 civil, under RICO, 139–141
 CERCLA and, 934, 937–940
 contingent, 531
 of corporate directors and officers, 829–830, 831
 of corporate promoters, 811–812
 criminal, 165–167, 1108
 of corporate officers and directors, 170–173, 175
 of corporation, 170
 defenses to, 176–182
 defenses to, 1105
 of delegatee, 318
 discharge from, 541–544
 of employer, 685–688, 709, 726–727
 without fault. *See* Strict liability
 of indorser, 492, 506
 for injuries on leased premises, 1035–1039
 insurance contracts, parties to and, 1065, 1066
 joint, 779, 781–782
 joint and several, 782
 among joint venturers, 753–755
 of landlord, 1036–1038
 *Emerging Trends* feature on, 1040–1041
 of lenders, under CERCLA, 934
 limitation of. *See* Limitation(s)
 market-share, 471
 of minors, 266–267, 268–269, 272
 of parents, 269
 of partners, 750, 751, 768, 779, 780, 781–782, 795
 incoming, 782
 limited, 796, 798
 of partnerships, 768
 primary, 530–531
 of principal, 680–690
 product. *See* Product liability
 of professionals, 1095–1112
 *summarized,* 1109–1110
 to reasonably foreseeable users, 1102–1103
 RICO and, 139–141

secondary, 531–532, 550n, 625
of shareholders, 750, 751, 752,
    840–841
    of professional corporation,
        810
sharing of, 471
signature, 529–538
of social hosts, 122
of sole proprietorships, 749, 750,
    751
strict. *See* Strict liability
of tenants, 1038–1039
of trustees, 938–939
vicarious, 685
of warehouse companies, 1002
warranty, 538–541
    of bailor, 997
Liability insurance:
    automobile, 1067
    business, 1068–1069
    for corporate directors and
        officers, 826
    homeowners' policies and, 1067
    for injuries on insured's property,
        1067
    malpractice, 1069
    product, 1069
Libel, 92, 109, 114
    trade, 136
License, 1010
    professional, as personal
        property, 1046–1047
Licensee, 1035–1036
Licensing:
    international business
        transactions and, 1119–1120
    technology, 1119–1120
Licensing statutes, 293–294, 300
Lie-detector tests, 706
Lien(s):
    artisan's, 113, 615, 624
    bailee's, 618, 993
    consensual, 615
    on debtor's property, 638
    *defined*, 433, 615
    floating, 600–601
    innkeeper's, 615, 619, 624
    judicial, 615, 619
    landlord's, 1035
    mechanic's, 615, 616–618, 624
    possessory, 618, 993, 1003
    seller's, 433
    statutory, 615
    storage, 618
    warranty against, 445, 458
Lien creditor, 601, 637
Life estate, 1008
Life insurance, 1053, 1064–1065

Limitation(s):
    of damages, 439
    good faith, 371
    of HDC rights, 493–494,
        526–527, 628
    on investigative powers, 894–895
    of liability,
        bailee's right to, 993–994
        landlord's, *Emerging Trends*
            feature on, 1040–1041
    quasi contracts and, 223–225
    on recovery, strict product
        liability and, 471, 474
    of remedies, 353, 439–440
    on rights of property owners,
        1017–1023
    statute of. *See* Statute of
        limitations
    subject matter jurisdiction and,
        42–43
Limitation-of-liability clause, 353
Limited competence, 262
Limited defenses, 511
Limited guaranty, 625
Limited jurisdiction, 43, 44
Limited liability company (LLC),
    756, 780n
    *Emerging Trends* feature on,
        758–759
Limited liability partnerships
    (LLPs), Emerging Trends
    feature on, 780–781
Limited partner. *See* Partner(s),
    limited
Limited partnership. *See*
    Partnership(s), limited
Limited warranty, 459
Limited-payment insurance, 1064
Line of credit, 600
Lineal descendants, 1083
Liquidated damages, 346–347, 348,
    439
Liquidation:
    Chapter 7. *See* Bankruptcy,
        Chapter 7 liquidations in
    of corporation, 854, 857–858
    of debt, 254
Listing agreement, 1014
Litigant, 43
Litigation, comparative legal
    systems and, 194–195
LLC. *See* Limited liability
    company
LLPs (limited liability
    partnerships), *Emerging
    Trends* feature on, 780–781
Loan(s). *See also* Usury
    guarantor on, 304

minor's liability for, 266–267
mortgage, 314
Lobster trap defense, 855
*Locus sigilli* (L.S.), 225
Logical thought progression, 5–6
Long arm statutes, 42
"Look and feel" protection, 155
Loss, proof of, 1066
Lost property, 981–982, 985
    checks as, 550–551
Low Level Radioactive Waste
    Policy Act (1980), 928, 940
Loyalty:
    duty of, 667, 827–829, 831, 880
Lucid interval, 271
Luxembourg, membership in
    European Union and, 204

### M

Magistrate, 185
Magistrate's court, 185
Magna Carta, 192
Magnuson-Moss Warranty Act
    (1975), 455, 459, 922
Mail fraud, 169, 173
"Mail Order Rule" of 1975, 912
"Mail or Telephone Order
    Merchandise Rule" of 1933,
    912
Mailbox rule, 244, 245
Mail-order sales, 911–912
Main purpose rule, 304–305, 625
Maintenance of leased premises,
    1030–1034
Majority, age of, 262
Majority opinion, 19
Majority shareholders, duties of,
    841–843, 881–882
Maker, 490
    accommodation, 533
    *defined*, 530
    revocation of will by act of,
        1078, 1080–1081
Malice, actual, 111
Malpractice, 116–117, 810, 1097
Malpractice insurance, 1069
Management:
    of corporations, 826–827, 831
        close, 807
    ethics and, 30, 34–38
    of partnerships, 773, 795
        limited, 773n, 795, 796–798
    risk, 1052
    styles of, international business
        transactions and, 190
Manifest assent, 322, 323
Manufacturing abroad, 1119

Manufacturing franchise, 757
Marine insurance, 1068
Marine Protection, Research, and
    Sanctuaries Act (Ocean
    Dumping Act) (1972), 928,
    933
Marital property, 1046–1047
Market concentration, 956
Market power, 945
Marketability, negotiable
    instruments and, 492
Marketable title, 1014–1015
Market-share liability, 471
Market-share test, 953
Marriage:
    promises made in consideration
        of, 302, 306
    property of, 1046–1047
    revocation of will by, 1081, 1082
Marshaling assets, 768
Master-servant relationships, 659
Material alteration, 522–523, 525
Material breach of contract, 329,
    331–332, 337
Material fact, 275–276, 277–278,
    288, 854
Maurois, Andre, 846
MBCA. *See* Model Business
    Corporation Act
McCarran-Ferguson Act (1945),
    960
McDonald's Corporation, 211
Mechanic's lien, 615, 616–618,
    624
Mediation, as means of alternative
    dispute resolution, 52–53, 60
Medical malpractice, 117
Medicare, 713
Meeting(s). *See also* Conference(s)
    corporate, first, 815
    of corporate directors, 825, 831
    creditors', 636
    shareholders', 830, 832, 841
*Mens rea,* 166
Mental incapacity. *See* Mental
    incompetence
Mental incompetence. *See also*
    Capacity; Incapacity;
    Incompetence; Insanity
    contractual capacity and, 271,
        272
    liability on negotiable instrument
        and, 523, 525
    of offeror or offeree, offer
        termination and, 239, 240
Merchant(s):
    *defined,* 368–369, 445n
    firm offer of, 371, 377, 384

option contract versus, 371n
    implied warranty of
        merchantability and,
        450–452, 455–456, 458
    rules between, 375
    sales contracts between, 307
Merchant buyer, 434
Merchantability, implied warranty
    of, 366–367, 450–452,
    455–456, 458, 997
    bailments and, 997
Merger(s), 846–851
    antitrust law and, 956–959
    articles of, 847
    conglomerate, 957
    diversification, 957
    horizontal, 956–957
    *illustrated,* 847
    parent-subsidiary, 848
    product-extension, 957–959
    release of leased property and,
        1042
    short-form, 848
    vertical, 957
Merger Treaty, 1122
Mexico:
    commercial code of, 197
    contract law in, 197
    employment law in, 199
    government regulation in, 204
    intellectual property protection
        in, 201
    limited liability companies (LLC)
        in, 759
    NAFTA and, 1122–1123
    standards of proximate cause in,
        118
Miami International Arbitration and
    Mediation Institute, 1127
Mill, John Stuart, 28
Mini-trial, 59, 60
Minimum contacts, jurisdiction
    over foreign corporations and,
    42, 804–805
Minimum wage, 716
Minor(s). *See also* Age; Children;
    Infancy
    contractual capacity of, 262–269,
        272
    emancipation of, 266
    status as, liability on negotiable
        instrument and, 523, 525
    torts of, 268–269
Minority shareholders, majority
    shareholders versus, 841–843,
    881–882
*Miranda* rule, 181–183
Mirror image rule, 238, 239, 372,

387–388
Misappropriation theory, 873–874
Misdemeanor, 165
Mislaid property, 981, 985
Misrepresentation. *See also* Deceit;
    Fraud
    of age, 264, 272
    by agent, 684–685
    fraudulent, 112, 114, 280–284,
        288
        by agent, 684–685
    genuineness of assent and,
        280–284, 288
    innocent, 284, 288
        by agent, 685
    of law, 282
    negligent, 285, 288
    nonfraudulent, 284–285, 288
    product liability and, 466
    silence as, 282–283
Mistake(s), 275–280, 288. *See also*
    Error(s)
    bilateral, 275, 288
    as defense to criminal liability,
        177
    electronic fund transfers and,
        575, 580
    ethics and, 358
    of fact, 177
        material, 277–278, 288
    of law, 177
    mutual, 275, 277–280, 288
    unilateral, 275–277; 288
    in value, 278–280, 288
Misuse of product, 476
Mitigation of damages, 344–346
*M'Naghten* test of insanity, 177
Model Business Corporation Act
    (MBCA), 7, 801
    Statutory Close Corporation
        Supplement to, 806, 856
Model Law on International Credit
    Transfers, 576
Model Penal Code, 165, 167, 170,
    177, 179
Model Rules of Professional
    Conduct, 1097
Model State Administrative
    Procedure Act, 903
Money:
    earnest, 1014
    first-in, first-money-out rule and,
        514
    fixed amount of, 495–497, 501
    laundering of, 169–170, 173
    payment in, 495, 497, 501
    sum certain in, 495n
Monopolization, 952–955

attempted, 953–955
Monopoly, 945
Monopoly power, 945, 953
Moral hazard, 1130
Moral obligations, consideration
    and, 252
Mortgage, 314, 1015
    assignment of, 316, 323
    foreclosure and, 623, 624
    negotiable instrument secured by,
        494–495
Mortgage bonds, 818
Mortgage note, 491
Mortgagee, 623, 1015
Mortgagor, 623, 1015
Most-favored-nation status, 1122
Motion(s):
    for directed verdict, 75
    to dismiss, 66, 69, 73
    for judgment *n.o.v.,* 79, 81
    for judgment on the pleadings,
        69–70, 73
    for new trial, 77–79, 81
    posttrial, 77–79
        *summarized,* 81
    pretrial, 69, 73
    for summary judgment, 70–71,
        73
Motor vehicles:
    crashworthiness doctrine and,
        475
    insurance for, 1067–1068
    lemon laws and, 421n, 440
Multilateral agreement, 1114
Multiple insurance coverage, 1059
Multiple payees, indorsement by,
    507–508
Multiple product orders, 909
Municipal courts, 44
Mutual agreement, 691, 693
Mutual assent, 230–231
Mutual fund, 876
Mutual mistakes, 272, 277–280,
    288
Mutual rescission, 333, 337, 347n
Mutual-benefit bailment, 991, 996,
    1000

**N**

N.A. (National Association), 1101n
NAFTA (North American Free
    Trade Agreement), 201, 1114,
    1122–1123
Name(s):
    corporate, 813
    correction of, on indorsement,
        507

of debtor, financing statement
    filed under, 595
Napoleonic Code, 192, 193, 194,
    199
NASD (National Association of
    Securities Dealers), 867
National Association (N.A.), 1101n
National Association of Securities
    Dealers (NASD), 867
National Conference of
    Commissioners (NCC) on
    Uniform State Law(s), 7, 8,
    364, 405, 410n, 486, 550n,
    757, 758, 766, 922, 1026,
    1074–1075
National Cooperative Production
    Amendments (1993), 961
National Cooperative Research Act
    (1984), 961
National Environmental Policy Act
    (NEPA)(1969), 928–929
National Hispanic Business
    Agenda, 209
National Institute for Occupational
    Safety and Health, 711
National Labor Relations Act
    (NLRA)(Wagner Act)(1935),
    716, 744
National Labor Relations Board
    (NLRB), 89, 716–718, 744,
    886, 889
National law(s), 189
    comparison of, 195–204
    international versus, 1114
National origin, discrimination
    based on, 722, 1022, 1027
National Reporter System (West),
    14, 16
    *illustrated,* 15
National Trust & Savings
    Association (NT & SA), 577n
Natural law school, 3
Navigable waters, 931–932
NCC. *See* National Conference of
    Commissioners (NCC) on
    Uniform State Law(s)
Necessaries, 266, 271, 272
Necessity, creation of easement or
    profit by, 1009
Negative injunctions, 350n
Negligence, 114–123
    of accountant, 1096–1098, 1109
    of attorney, 1096–1098, 1109
    bailees and, 995
    of bank, 559–560, 563
    of bank customer, 558–562, 563
    causation and, 117–119
    comparative, 121, 122

contributory, 121, 122
corporate officers and directors
    and, 827
criminal law and, 166, 167
defenses to, 119–121, 122, 466,
    1096
*defined,* 122, 464
elements of, 114–115, 122
of employee, employer's liability
    for, 685–687
environmental protection and,
    926–927
foreseeability and, 118–119
*per se,* 122, 466
presumption of, 995–996
product liability and, 464–466
    strict liability compared with,
        476
of professional, 1096–1098, 1109
*summarized,* 122
superseding intervening force
    and, 119
warehouse companies and, 1002
Negligent misrepresentation, 285,
    288
Negotiable bill of lading,
    *illustrated,* 398
Negotiable document of title, 414,
    999–1000
Negotiable instrument(s):
    assignment of, 316, 323, 500
    bearer instruments as, 499, 501
    bills of exchange as, 487, 489
    buyers of, security interests and,
        604–605
    cancellation of, 542–543
    certificates of deposit (CDs) as,
        487, 488, 491
    characteristics of, *summarized,*
        488
    checks as. *See* Check(s)
    claims to, HDC status and,
        517–518, 519
    consumer credit sales
        transactions and, 440
    defenses against, HDC status
        and, 517–518, 519
    demand instruments as, 487, 488
    dishonor of, 532–533, 540, 551,
        563
    dishonored, HDC status and, 517,
        519
    drafts as. *See* Draft(s)
    fixed amount of money to be
        paid for, 495, 501
    *Focus on Ethics* feature on,
        583–586
    function of, 487

holder of. *See* Holder; Holder in due course
incomplete,
   HDC status and, 517–518, 519
   unauthorized completion of, 525
indorsements on, 502–508. *See also* Indorsement(s)
   consequences of, *summarized,* 506
   problems with, 507–508
   *summarized,* 506
   types of, 503–507
   *summarized,* 506
international law for, 497
irregular, HDC status and, 518, 519
liability on,
   discharge from, 541–544
   signature, 529–538
   warranty, 538–541
marketability of, 491
negotiability of,
   factors not affecting, 500
   requirements for, 491–499
   *summarized,* 501
negotiation of, 500–502
nondelivery of, 525, 526
nonnegotiable instruments versus, 487
notes as. *See* Note(s)
order instruments as, 493, 499, 501
overdue, HDC status and, 516–517, 519
payable at a definite time, 497–498, 501
payable on demand, 497, 501
payable in money, 495, 497, 501
payment on from a particular fund, 494
perfection of security interest and, 596
presentment of, proper, 532
reacquisition of, 543
references of, to other agreements, 493–494
secured by a mortgage, 494–495
signatures on, 492, 506, 529–538
sum certain in money to be paid for, 495n
time instruments as, 487, 488
trade acceptances as, 489, 490
transfer of, 500–502, 538–539
types of, 487–491
   *summarized,* 488
as value, 513–514
writing requirement for,

491–492, 501
Negotiated rulemaking, 890, 891, 893
Negotiated Rulemaking Act (1990), 891
Negotiation(s):
   due, 1000
   as means of alternative dispute resolution, 52, 60
   of negotiable instruments, 500–502
   preliminary, offer versus, 232
NEPA (National Environmental Policy Act) (1969), 928–929
Net profits, 836
Netherlands:
   European Union membership and, 204
   torts in, 197
New York Clearing House Interbank Payments Systems (CHIPS), 579
New Zealand, emotional distress damages in, 109
Nigeria, corporate law in, 202
Ninth Amendment, 91, 92, 706
Nixon, Richard, 52
NLRA (National Labor Relations Act) (Wagner Act) (1935), 716, 744
NLRB (National Labor Relations Board), 89, 716–718, 744, 886, 889
No competence, 262
Noerr-Pennington doctrine, 961
No-fault insurance, 1068
Noise Control Act (1972), 928, 933
Noise pollution, 933
*Nolo contendere* plea, 185, 826
Nominal damages, 341, 344, 348
Noncarrier cases, 414
Nonconforming goods, 372, 437–438
Nondelivery:
   buyer's right to recover damages for, 435–437
   of negotiable instrument, 526
Nonfraudulent misrepresentation, 284–285, 288
Nonindorser, transfer warranty liability and, 539
Nonmerchants, 372, 375
Nonnegotiable instruments, 487
Nonnegotiable warehouse receipt, *illustrated,* 399
Nonnotification, 606
Nonowners, sales by, 406–410
Nonpossessory interests,

1009–1011
Nonprofit corporation, 806, 812
Nonproprietary ATMs, 566
Nonvoidable contracts, 268
No-par shares, 840
Norris-LaGuardia Act (1932), 716
North American Free Trade Agreement (NAFTA), 201, 1114, 1122–1123
Norway, membership in European Union and, 204
Notary public, 674
Note(s), 487, 488
   collateral, 491
   mortgage, 491
   promissory, 490–491
Not-for-profit corporation, 806
Notice:
   actual, 790
   agency termination and, 692–693
   of appeal, 79
   of assignment, 317
   of claims, under international law, 438
   constructive, 693, 1013
   copyright law and, 156
   of dangerous conditions, 687
   of dishonor of negotiable instrument, 533
   of dissolution, 790
   equitable servitudes and, 1022–1023
   of proposed rulemaking, 890
   of revocation,
      of acceptance, 422
      of assignment, 315
   of shareholders' meeting, 830, 832, 841
   of stopping of delivery of goods in transit, 430
   taking without, HDC status and, 516–518, 519
   termination by, 1042
   timely, 430
   validation, 918
Notice-and-comment rulemaking, 890
Notice-race statute, 1012
Notification:
   agent's duty of, 667
   chattel paper and, 606
Novation, 318–320, 333, 337, 811
NRC (Nuclear Regulatory Commission), 889, 902, 929, 940
NT & SA (National Trust & Savings Association), 577n

Nuclear Regulatory Commission (NRC), 889, 902, 929, 940
Nuclear Waste Policy Act (1982), 928, 940
Nuisance, 925–926, 1030
Nuncupative will, 1077, 1078, 1082

# O

OASDI (Old Age, Survivors, and Disability Insurance), 713
Obedience, agent's duty of, 667
Objective impossibility of performance, 335
Objective theory of contracts, 216–217
Objects, request for, 72
Obligation(s). *See also* Duty(ies)
  of buyer, 419–422
    *summarized,* 423
  moral, consideration and, 252
  primary, Statute of Frauds and, 303–304
  secondary, Statute of Frauds and, 303–304
  of seller, 414–419
    *summarized,* 423
  voidable, HDC status and, 518
Obligor, 314
Occupancy clause, 1066
Occupational Safety and Health Act (1970), 172–173, 711
Occupational Safety and Health Administration (OSHA), 711, 887
Occupational Safety and Health Review Commission, 711
Occurrence of specific event, agency termination by, 691, 693
Ocean dumping, 933
Ocean Dumping Act (Marine Protection, Research, and Sanctuaries Act) (1972), 928, 933
Ocean marine insurance policy, 1068
Offenses:
  petty, 165
  public welfare, 172
Offer:
  contractual. *See* Contract(s), offer in; Sales contract(s), offer in
  tender, 830, 853–854
Offeree, 219, 231
  counteroffer by, 238, 240
  death or incompetence of, 239, 240

duty of, to reject offer, 242–243
  rejection of offer by, 238, 240
Offeror, 219, 231
  assent of, 375
  death or incompetence of, 239, 240
  revocation of offer by, 236–237, 240
Office of Federal Contract Compliance Programs, 731
Office of Interstate Land Sales Registration, 913
Officers, corporate:
  criminal acts of, 803
  duties of, 827–829, 831, 880–881
  indemnification of, 826
  insider trading and, 828, 867, 869–873, 882
  liability of, 829–830, 831
    for crimes, 170–173, 175
  mismanagement and, 827, 831
  negligence and, 827
  pervasiveness of control of, 172–173, 175
  "responsible corporate officer doctrine" and, 170–172
  role of, 824–830
    *summarized,* 831
  torts of, 803
Official, public:
  bribery of, 169, 173
  negotiable instruments and, 508
Oil marketing, exemption of, from antitrust laws, 960
Oil pollution, 933
Oil Pollution Act (1990), 928, 933
Old Age, Survivors, and Disability Insurance (OASDI), 713
Older Workers Benefit Protection Act (1990), 33
Olographic will, 1077
Omission, sin of, 26
Omnibus clause, 1068
Omnibus Trade and Competitiveness Act (1988), 1127n
One-year rule, under Statute of Frauds, 301–303
  *illustrated,* 303
Open delivery term, 370
Open payment term, 370
Open price term, 370
Open terms, 369–370
Opening statements, 74–75, 77
Operation of law:
  agency formation by, 664
  agency termination and, 692, 693
  contract discharge by, 326, 334–337

offer termination by, 238–239, 240
  partnership dissolution by, 787–788
  will revocation by, 1081
Opinion(s):
  of courts. *See* Court(s), decisions of
  expressions of, 231
  statement of, 112, 281, 447–449, 458
Option(s):
  to purchase, 991
  sales contracts and, 370
Option contract, 237, 240
  merchant's firm offer versus, 371n
Oral contract. *See* Contract(s), oral
Oral will, 1077
Order(s):
  of administrative agencies, 896
  cease-and-desist, 717, 896, 909
  charging, 775–776
  delivery, 999
  of distribution, intestacy laws and, 1082–1086
  final, 896
  initial, 896
  to pay, 487, 488–490
  purchase,
    *illustrated,* 373–374
    international, *illustrated,* 389–390
  for relief, 633
  stop-payment, 553–556, 563
    *illustrated,* 554
    under EFTA, 573, 575
  unconditional, to pay, 492–495, 501
Order instruments, 493, 499, 501
Order paper:
  conversion of to bearer paper, 502
    *illustrated,* 503
  negotiation of, 502
Ordinance, 7
Ordinary bailments, 991
Ordinary care, 559
Organizations, international, 1114–1115
  multilateral, *summarized,* 1115
Organized Crime Control Act (1970), 139
Original jurisdiction, 43, 51
OSHA (Occupational Safety and Health Administration), 711, 887
OTC (over the counter), 861
Outcome-based ethics, 28

Output contract, 370–371
Outsiders, under Rule 10b-5 and, 873–874
Over the counter (OTC), 861
Overdrafts, 551–553, 563
Overdue instruments, HDC status and, 516–517, 519
Overlapping warranties, 453
Ownership. *See* Property, ownership of; Title
Ownership interest, 830, 1006–1011

## P

P.A. (professional association), 809
P.C. (professional corporation), 809–811, 812
Packaging laws, 910–911
Pac-man defense, 846, 855
Panama, limited liability companies (LLC) in, 759
Parallel citation, 14
Parents, liability for minor's torts and, 269
Parent-subsidiary merger, 848
Paris Convention, 1125
Parol evidence rule, 291, 307–310
  sales contracts and, 379–382, 384
Partial acceptance, 422
Partial defense, 522
Partial eviction, 1029
Partial performance, 302, 306, 379
Partially disclosed principal, 680–682
Participating preferred stock, 819
Partition, 974
Partner(s):
  acts of, dissolution of partnership by, 787
  as agent, 779
  authority of, 782
  bankruptcy of, 768
    dissolution of partnership by, 787
  compensation of, 773
  corporation as, 772
  death of, 776
    dissolution of partnership by, 787
  duties of, 778–779, 781–782, 880–881
  general, 794
  improper conduct of, dissolution of partnership and, 789
  incapacity of, dissolution of partnership and, 788–789
  incoming, liability of, 782
  insanity of, dissolution of

partnership and, 788
  insolvency of, 793n
  interest of, in partnership, 773, 775–776
  judgments and, 768
  legal capacity of, 767–768, 772
  liability of, 750, 751, 768, 779, 780, 781–782, 795
  limited, 794
    liabilities of, 796, 798
    management of partnership and, 796–798
    management rights of, 773n, 795
    rights of, 796
  management rights of, 773, 795
  new, admission of, dissolution of partnership by, 787
  powers of, 778–779, 781–782, 787
  remedies of, 774n
  rights among, 773–777, 793
  at will, 769, 772, 787
Partnership(s), 749–750, 766–800
  aggregate theory of, 769
  agreement to form. *See* Agreement(s), partnership
  articles of, 769
  assets of, distribution of, 792–794
  bankruptcy of, 768
  buy-sell agreements and, 794
  corporations and sole proprietorships compared to, 751–753
  *defined,* 767
  dissolution of, 786, 787–790
  duration of, 769, 772, 795
  by estoppel, 772
  formation of, 769–772, 795
  general, 749
    limited partnership versus, 795
  judgments and, 768
  legal capacity of, 767–768, 772
  liability of, 768
  limited, 749–750, 794–798
    certificate of, 796
    dissolution of, 798
    formation of, 795, 796
    general partnership versus, 795
    management of, 773n, 795
  management of, 773, 795
  nature of, 767–769
  operation of, 772–779, 781–782
  privilege against self-incrimination and, 98
  property of, 776–777
  special, 794
  taxation and, 749, 751, 752, 769,

780
  tenants in, 768, 776
  for a term, 769
  termination of, 786–794
  at will, 769, 772, 787
  winding up of, 790–792
Par-value shares, 840
Passage of title. *See* Title, passage of
Passwords, protection of computer data with, 159
Past consideration, 253, 258
Patent(s), 143, 148–149, 1125
  third party infringement claims and, 445, 458
Pattern of conduct, 353
Pay-by-telephone systems, 570–571
Payee(s), 488
  *defined,* 548
  fictitious, 537–538
  as holder, 548
  multiple, 507–508
Paying bank, 425
Payment(s):
  on altered check, 561–562
  bounty, 875
  buyer's obligation of, 420
  at a definite time, 497–498, 501
  on demand, 497, 501
  discharge by, 541–542
  on forged indorsement, 561
  on forged signature of drawer, 556–561
  insurance contract and, 1061–1064
  in money, 495, 497, 501
  to order of bearer, 498–499, 501
  previous, discharge of liability by, 525
  stopping of, 553–556, 563
    under EFTA, 573, 575
  tender of, 541–542
  wrongful, 554, 563
Payor bank, 563
Peace, breach of, 653
Penalties, liquidated damages versus, 346–347
People's Republic of China. *See* China
*Per capita* distribution, 1084, 1086
  *illustrated,* 1085
*Per se* violations, 947, 948, 952, 956, 1123
*Per stirpes* distribution, 1084
  *illustrated,* 1085
Peremptory challenge, 73
Perfect tender rule, 414–419
Perfection, of security interest. *See* Security interest, perfection of

Performance:
  agent's duty of, 665–667
  complete, 329, 337
  contract discharge by, 225, 226,
    326, 329–333, 337
  cooperation regarding, 370
  course of, 308, 381
    implied warranty arising from,
      452, 458
  duty of, assignment of, 315
  impossibility of,
    contract discharge by, 335, 337
    ethics and, 358
    temporary, 336–337
  impracticability of, 335–336, 337
  monitoring of, 708–709, 745
  partial, 302, 306, 379
  personal, contract for, 315, 317,
    318, 323
    specific performance and, 350
  routine and nonpersonal, 318
  of sales contract, 413–425
  to satisfaction of another, 331
  specific. See Specific
    performance
  substantial, 329–331, 337
  suspension of, 336–337, 422
  time for, 332–333
  uncertain, consideration and, 253,
    258
Periodic tenancy, 1010, 1042
Permanence, negotiable instruments
  and, 492
Permit, building, 1019–1021
Person:
  corporation as, 802, 894n
  identified, 499
  intentional torts against, 106–112
  jurisdiction of courts over, 42, 51
Personal defenses, 511, 523–526
Personal identification number
  (PIN), 570, 586, 587
Personal property:
  abandoned, 982, 985
  bailed. See also Bailment(s)
    bailee's duty to return, 995
    bailee's right to use, 992
  bailment of. See Bailment(s)
  conversion of, 113–114, 981, 995
  defined, 112, 970, 984
  intangible. See Intangible
    property
  lost, 981–982, 985
    checks as, 550–551
  mislaid, 981, 985
  nature of, 971, 984
  ownership of, acquisition of,
    976–981, 984
  rights in, 1046–1048

  summarized, 984–985
  tangible. See Tangible property
  trespass to, 112, 113, 114
Personal recognizance, 185
Personal representative, 1073, 1091
Personal services, contract for, 315,
  317, 318, 323
  specific performance and, 350
Personalty. See Personal property
Pervasiveness of control, 172–173,
  175
Pesticides, 936
Petit jury, 72
Petition for bankruptcy, 632–635
Petitioner, 79
  defined, 19
Petroleum Marketing Practices Act
  (PMPA) (1979), 756–757, 762
Petty offenses, 165
Photocopies and copyright law,
  153–154
Physical possession, 1029
"Piercing the corporate veil," 750,
  802, 816
PIN (personal identification
  number), 570, 586, 587
Place of delivery, 414–415
Plain meaning rule, 226–227
Plaintiff, 5, 19
Plant life, as real property, 972
Plato, 2
Plea, nolo contendere, 185, 826
Plea bargaining, 181
Pleadings, 66–69, 73
Pledge, 593
PMPA (Petroleum Marketing
  Practices Act) (1979),
  756–757, 762
PMSI (purchase-money security
  interest), 592–593, 602,
  604–605, 608
Point-of-sale systems, 570
Poison pill defense, 846, 855
Poland, employment law in, 199
Police powers, 87, 1018
Political contributions, 94–96, 803n
Political speech, 94–96, 802
Pollution:
  air, 929–931
  noise, 933
  oil, 933
  water, 931–933, 965–966
Portability, negotiable instruments
  and, 492
Portugal:
  European Union membership
    and, 204
  limited liability companies (LLC)
    in, 759

Positive law, 3
Positivist school, 3
Possession:
  acquisition of personal property
    by, 976, 984
  adverse, 1009, 1016–1017
  bailee's right of, 992, 1003
  debtor in, 644–645
  delivery of, 990
  landlord's duty to deliver, 1029
  landlord's recovery of, 1035
  perfection of security interest by,
    593
  physical, 1029
  retention of, 1029
  tenant's legal right to, 1029
Possessory lien, 618, 993, 1003
Postal Reorganization Act (1970),
  912
Postdated checks, 553, 563
Posting of checks, 564
Potentially responsible parties
  (PRPs), 934, 937
Pound, Roscoe, 214
Power(s):
  of administrative agencies,
    887–889
  of agent, 678
  of attorney, 674
    illustrated, 676
  of avoidance, 637
  of bankruptcy trustee, 637
  constitutional, of government,
    85–91
  of corporation, 803–804
  emergency, of agent, 678
  express, 803
  federal judicial, 49, 51–52
  of government, 85–91. See also
    Government regulation
  implied, 803
  investigative, administrative
    agencies, 893–895
  market, 945
  monopoly, 945, 953
  of partners, 778–779, 781–782,
    787
  police, 87, 1018
  regulatory. See Government
    regulation
  separation of, 85
  of shareholders, 830, 841
  sovereign, 84
  spending, 91
  taxing, 90–91
  of trustee, 1090
    in bankruptcy, 637
Preauthorized transfers, 573, 580
Precedent, 4

Predatory behavior, competition versus, 131
Predatory pricing, 952
Preemployment physicals, 731
Preemployment screening procedures, 709–710, 745
Preemption, 89, 90
Preemptive rights, 835–836, 841
Preexisting claim, 513
Preexisting debt, 638
Preexisting duty, 251–252, 258
Preferred stock, 819, 820, 821
Pregnancy, discrimination based on, 722
Pregnancy Discrimination Act (1978), 722
Preincorporation contract, 811
Prejudgment attachment, 616
Prejudgment rate of interest, 292
Prejudgment remedy, 620
Preliminary negotiations, offer versus, 232
Premises, leased. *See* Leased premises
Prenuptial agreements, 306
Preponderance of evidence, 75
Prescription, creation of easement or profit by, 1009–1010
Presentment, proper, of negotiable instrument, 532
Presentment warranties, 539–641
Presumption:
   of insolvency, 638
   rebuttable, 641
Pretrial conference, 72, 73
Pretrial motions, 69, 73
Pretrial procedures, 66–74
   *summarized,* 73
Pretrial prosecution, 185
Preventive measures, ethics and, 37
Price(s):
   control of, franchising and, 761
   fixing of. *See* Price fixing
   predatory pricing and, 952
   purchase, seller's right to recover, 431–432
Price discrimination, 955
   in employment, 33
Price fixing, 1123
   agreement of, 948, 952, 967–968
Price lists, contractual offers and, 232
Price term, necessity of, 388
*Prima facie* case, 123, 725–726, 727, 735
*Prima facie* evidence, 440, 1096
Primary liability on negotiable instrument, 530–531
Primary obligation, Statute of

Frauds and, 303–304
Principal, 658. *See also* Agency relationships
   agent's authority to bind, *summarized,* 684
   agent's rights and remedies against, 669–670
   bankruptcy of, agency termination and, 692, 693
   death of, agency termination and, 692, 693
   *defined,* 533
   disclosed, 680–682
   duties of, 664–665, 668, 697–698
   insanity of, agency termination and, 692, 693
   liability of, 680–690
   partially disclosed, 680–682
   remedies of, 668–670
   rights of, 668–670
   tortious conduct of, 683
   of trust, 1090–1091
   undisclosed, 680, 682–683, 690
Principal-agent relationships. *See* Agency relationships
Prior dealing, 308
Prior similar incidents rule, 1038, 1040
Privacy:
   right to, 91
      computers and, 159
      employees and, 706–710, 745–746
      employment and, 33
      invasion of, 111–112, 114
      telephone and, 708–709
Privacy Act (1974), 159, 160, 902
Private corporation, 806, 812
Private franchise. *See* Franchise(s)
Private law, 9, 10
Private placement exemption, 865
Private retirement plans, 714
Private-letter ruling, 780
Privately held corporation, 806
Privatization, 205–206
   of justice, 59–61
Privilege:
   accountant-client communications and, 894, 1110
   attorney-client communications and, 894, 1110
   professional-client communications and, 1110
   publication and, 110
Privileged speech, 111
Privileges and immunities clause, 99, 802
Privity:

of contract, 313, 453, 463, 464–465, 1100
of estate, 1021
*Pro se* representation, 63, 1057n
Probable cause, 98, 107, 175–176, 181, 183, 185
Probate, nonprobate versus, 1074–1075
Probate courts, 43, 1073
Procedural due process, 100
Procedural law, 9, 10
Procedural rules, 893
Proceeds, from disposition of collateral, 599–600, 611
Process server, 66
Processing-plant franchise, 757
Procter & Gamble, 212
Product(s). *See also* Goods
   farm, buyers of, security interests and, 597, 604
   liability and. *See* Product liability
   misuse of, 476
   unreasonably dangerous, 464, 468–469
Product liability, 463–484
   insurance for, 1069
   misrepresentation and, 466
   negligence and, 464–466
      strict liability compared with, 476
   privity of contract and, 463, 464–465
   strict, 125, 466–471, 474–477
      bystanders and, 474–475
      defenses to, 475–477
      leased goods and, 475
      limitations on recovery and, 471, 474
      negligence compared with, 476
      requirements of, 468–471
      sharing of, 471
      unreasonably dangerous products and, 464, 468–469
   warranties and, 463–464
Product Liability Fairness Act, 473
Product-extension merger, 957–959
Production, acquisition of personal property by, 976, 984
Professional(s)
   client communications and, 1110
   duty of, 116–117, 1096–1098
   liability of, 1095–1112
      *summarized,* 1109–1110
   license of, as personal property, 1046–1047
   malpractice insurance for, 1069
   negligence of, 1097
Professional association (P.A.), 809

Professional corporation (P.C.), 809–811, 812

Profit(s). *See also* Earnings; Income
  corporate, 802, 836
  net, 836
  as nonpossessory interest in real property, 972, 1009–1011
  short-swing, 875

Promise(s), 215
  collateral, 302, 303–306
  without consideration, enforceability of, 256–259
  in consideration of marriage, 302, 306
  of debt repayment, statute of limitations and, 256, 258
  executory, 512
  illusory, 253
  to pay, 256, 258, 487, 488, 490–491, 492–495, 501
  to ship, 371–372
  unconditional, to pay, 492–495, 501

Promisee, 215
  legal sufficiency of consideration and, 249, 258

Promisor, 215
  legal sufficiency of consideration and, 249, 258

Promissory estoppel, 237–238, 240, 256–257, 258, 302, 307
  ethics and, 360–361

Promissory note, 490–491

Promoters, corporate, 811–812

Prompt shipment, 371–372

Proof:
  burden of, 75
  of loss, 1066

Proper presentment, 532

Property, 969–1050
  after-acquired, 600
  of bankruptcy estate, 635
  community, 974, 976, 984, 1046
  confiscation of, 1116
  debtor's, liens on, 638
  defense of, as defense against tort, 107
  *defined*, 970
  disparagement of, 136–139
  distribution of, in bankruptcy, 640
  expropriation of, 1116
  *Focus on Ethics* feature on, 1046–1050
  forfeiture of, 175–176
  insurance coverage for, 1053, 1055–1056
  intangible. *See* Intangible property

intellectual. *See* Intellectual property

intentional torts against, 112–114
  *summarized*, 114

jurisdiction over, 42, 51

leased. *See* Leased premises

marital, 1046–1047

ownership of, 973–981, 984
  acquisition of, 976–981, 984
  concurrent, 974–976, 984
  limitations on, 1017–1023

partner's rights and, 775–777

partnership, 776–777

personal. *See* Personal property

real. *See* Real property

tangible. *See* Tangible property

taxes on, 1034

theft of, computer crimes and, 158, 971

unreasonable search and seizure of, 92, 98, 181

Prosecution:
  by administrative agencies, 895
  immunity from, 181
  pretrial, 185

Prospectus, 811
  red herring, 862

Protected class, 721
  illegal contracts and, 299, 301

Protected expression, 149

Protected interests, 105

Protection, adequate, doctrine of, 635

Proximate cause, 117–118, 579, 997

Proxy, 832–833, 841

Proxy statements, 875–874

PRPs (potentially responsible parties), 934, 937

Public accountability, of administrative agencies, 901

Public corporation, 806, 812

Public figures, defamation and, 111

Public law, 9, 10

Public officials:
  bribery of, 169, 173
  negotiable instruments and, 508

Public policy:
  arbitrability and, 55, 57
  contracts contrary to, 294–298, 300
  exception to employment-at-will doctrine based upon, 703–704
  international enforcement of arbitration agreements and, 57

Public prosecutor, 185

Public service, contracts injuring, 298, 300

Public welfare offenses, 172

Publication:
  privileged, 110
  as requirement for tort of defamation, 110–111
  of will, 1078

Puffery, 112, 281, 448–449, 907

Puffing. *See* Puffery

Punitive damages, 284, 341, 344, 348, 727, 731
  *Emerging Trends* feature on, 472–473

Purchase:
  acquisition of personal property by, 976, 984
  of assets of corporation, 851–853
  option to, 991

Purchase order:
  *illustrated*, 373–374
  international, *illustrated*, 389–390

Purchase price, seller's right to recover, 431–432

Purchaser. *See also* Buyer(s)
  *bona fide*, 637, 645, 835n
  good faith. *See* Good faith purchaser
  of securities, accountants' liability to, 1104

Purchase-money security interest (PMSI), 592–593, 602, 604–605, 608

Pure Food and Drugs Act (1906), 920

Pure notice statute, 1012

Purpose achieved, agency termination by, 690, 693

## Q

Qualified indorsements, 504, 506

Qualified indorser, 531n

Qualified privilege, 111

Quality, slander of, 136–137

Quality control:
  franchising and, 761
  labor laws and, 744–745

*Quantum meruit*, 222, 252, 351–352

Quasi contracts, 222–225, 226
  liability for necessaries under, 272
  recovery based on, 351, 352, 361

*Quasi in rem* jurisdiction, 42

Question(s):
  of fact, 45, 70
  federal, 49

of law, 45, 70
*Quid pro quo* harassment, 723
Quiet enjoyment, covenant of, 1029
Quitclaim deed, 1011, 1013
Quorum, 825
Quotas, 1121

# R

Race, discrimination based on, 55, 722, 1022, 1027
Race statute, 1012
Racketeer Influenced and Corrupt Organizations Act (RICO) (1970), 128, 139–141
  criminal violations under, 173, 175–176
Radiation, 940–941
Ratification:
  agency formation by, 663
  of contract,
    by intoxicated person, 269, 272
    by mentally incompetent person, 271, 272
    by minor, 262, 267–268, 272
    preincorporation, 811
    by principal, 678–680
  express, 267, 679
  implied, 267, 679
  requirements for, *summarized,* 679
Rational-basis test, 99, 100, 101–102
RCRA (Resource Conservation and Recovery Act)(1976), 928, 936–937, 940
Reacquisition, discharge by, 543
Reaffirmation:
  agreement of, 633n, 642–643
  of debt, in bankruptcy, 642–643
Real defenses, 511, 520–523, 525
Real estate. *See* Real property
Real estate agent or broker, 1014
Real Estate Settlement Procedures Act (1976), 912–913, 1015
Real property, 1006–1025
  commercial, 1036–1038
  conveyance of, 1007, 1011–1017
  *defined,* 112, 970
  financing of, 1015
  goods versus, 365, 366
  interests in, Statute of Frauds and, 301, 302
  land-use regulations and, 1048–1049
  leased. *See* Leased premises
  nature of, 971–973
  nonpossessory interests in,

1009–1011
  nuisance and, 925–926
  ownership interests in, 1006–1011
    limitations on, 1017–1023
  rights to, limitations on, 1017–1023
  sale or transfer of, 341–342, 350, 912–913, 1007, 1011–1017
    contracts for, 1013–1016
    under seal, 225n
    Statute of Frauds and, 301, 302
  zoning laws and, 1018–1021
Realty. *See* Real property
Reasonable accommodations:
  *Emerging Trends* feature on, 732–734
  undue hardship versus, 729–730, 732–734
Reasonable belief, 178
Reasonable care, 1036
  of collateral, 606–607
Reasonable person standard, 106, 115, 322–323, 725, 743–744
Reasonable time, 332, 400, 517
  commercially, 404
Reasonably foreseeable users of financial statements, 1102–1103, 1109
Reasoning:
  by analogy, 6
  deductive, 5
  legal, 5–6
  Rebuttable presumption, 641
Rebuttal, 75, 77
Receipt, warehouse, 999
  *illustrated,* 399
Receiver, 644, 858
Recklessness, criminal law and, 166, 167
Record(s):
  business,
    director's right to inspect, 825–826
    partner's right to inspect, 773
    shareholder's right to inspect, 807n, 837–838
  of electronic fund transactions, 573, 580
  rulemaking, 891
Recording statutes, 1012
Recourse, impairment of, 543–544
Recross-examination, 75, 77
Red herring prospectus, 862
Redeemable preferred stock, 819
Redemption:
  equity of, 623
  right of, 612
  statutory period of, 623

Redirect examination, 75, 77
Referendum, 7
Reformation, 351, 352
Refusal:
  to deal, 952
  first, right of, 838
Registration statement, 861–863
Regulation, by government. *See* Government regulation
Regulation A, of SEC, 864
Regulation CC, 566
Regulation D, of SEC, 864–867
Regulation DD, 566
Regulation E, of Federal Reserve Board, 571
Regulation M, 915
Regulation Z, of Federal Reserve Board, 911, 913
Regulatory agencies. *See* Government regulation
Regulatory Flexibility Act (1980), 901
Rehabilitation Act (1973), 731, 732
Reimbursement:
  principal's duty of, 668
  surety's or guaranty's right of, 627
Rejection:
  of goods, 434
  of offer, 238, 240
Rejoinder, 75, 77
Release, 253, 254–255, 258
  of collateral, 606
  of corporate promoter, 811
  termination of lease by, 1042
Relevant evidence, 74
Reliance:
  detrimental. *See* Detrimental reliance
  justifiable, 256, 284, 288, 307
Religion:
  discrimination based on, 722, 1022, 1027
  ethics and, 27
  freedom of, 92, 96–97
Remainder, 1008
Remedy(ies), 429–443. *See also* Right(s)
  of agent, 668–669
  under Americans with Disabilities Act, 731
  of buyer, 433–439
  contractual provisions affecting, 439–440
  creditor's, 607–612, 615–524
    *summarized,* 624
  of customer of buyer, 438–439
  damages as. *See* Damage(s)
  *defined,* 10, 340

election of, 352–353
equitable, *summarized,* 352
in equity, 340
    remedies at law versus, 10–13
international business
        transactions and, 440–441
judicial, 334
landlord, 1034–1035
at law, 340
    remedies in equity versus,
        10–13
limitation of, 353, 439–440
of partner, 774n
prejudgment, 620
of principal, 668–670
quasi-contractual recovery as,
        351, 352, 361
reformation as, 351, 352
of secured party, 607–612
    *summarized,* 611
of seller, 429–433
    *summarized,* 441
of tenant, 1032–1034
under Title VII of the Civil
        Rights Act of 1964,
        726–727
Remitter, 548
Renewal of lease, 1043
Rent, 1034–1035
    withholding of, 1032–1033
Rent escalation clause, 1034
''Rent strike'' statutes, 1032
Rent-a-judge courts, 59–60
Repair-and-deduct statutes,
        1033–1034
Repairs, leased premises and, 1038
Replevin:
    buyer's right of, 434–435
    *defined,* 434
Reply, 66, 69
*Reports,* 14
Repose, statutes of, 474
Repossession:
    of collateral, 611
    ''self-help,'' 653, 689n
Repudiation:
    of contract, 417
        anticipatory, 332
        buyer's right to recover
            damages for, 435–437
    sales contract, anticipatory,
        422–425
Requests, discovery process and,
        72
Requirements contract, 370
*Res ipsa loquitur,* 121–122
Resale price maintenance
        agreements, 952
Resales, of securities, 866–867

Rescission, 12, 282, 444. *See also*
        Cancellation
    of contract, 252
    contract discharge by, 333, 337
    door-to-door sales and, 333n,
        348n, 911
    mutual, 333, 337, 347n
    of reaffirmation agreement, 643
    restitution and, 347–350, 352
    unilateral, 347n
Rescue, duty and, 117
Residuary clause, 1073, 1082
Residuum, 1073
Resource Conservation and
        Recovery Act (RCRA)(1976),
        928, 936–937, 940
*Respondeat superior,* 685–688,
        690, 699, 700, 803, 1027
Respondent, 79
    *defined,* 19
''Responsible corporate officer
        doctrine,'' 170–172
Restatement rule, 1101–1102, 1109
Restatements of the Law:
    of Agency (Second), 658
        as authoritative summary of the
            law of agency, 659n
        scope of employment under,
            685
    of Contracts, 6
    of Contracts (Second), 6,
        214–215, 264, 307, 321,
        327n, 328
    of Torts, 156
    of Torts, (Second) 107n, 1101,
        1103
        strict liability and, 464,
            467–468, 475
    of Trusts, 1090n, 1091n
Restitution:
    *in specie,* 348
    intoxicated persons and, 269, 272
    mentally incompetent persons
        and, 272
    minor's duty of, 262–264, 272
    rescission and, 347–350, 352
    restoration versus, 263n
Restoration, 263n
Restraints on trade, 948–950. *See
        also* Antitrust law
    *defined,* 944
    international, 1123
    vertical, 948, 950–952
Restricted stock certificate, 868
Restrictive covenant, 294, 300,
        1022–1023
Restrictive indorsements, 504–507
Resulting trusts, 1088–1089
Retained earnings, 802, 836

Retainer agreement, 66
Retaliatory eviction, 1029
Retention warranties, 565–566
Retirement and security income,
        713–714
Return, sale or, 402–404
Revenue Act (1971), 1121
Reverse discrimination, 734,
        742–743
Reversibility, of electronic fund
        transfers, 573, 575
Reversionary interest, 1008, 1027
Review:
    judicial, 51–52, 896–900
    standards of, 899–900
Reviewing court, 14
Revised Model Business
        Corporation Act (RMBCA),
        801, 802, 804, 807, 813, 814,
        815, 816, 818, 825, 826, 827,
        829, 830, 832, 834, 835, 836,
        837, 838, 839n, 840, 848, 849,
        850, 852, 855, 856
Revised Uniform Limited
        Partnership Act (RULPA),
        795, 796, 797, 798
Revised Uniform Partnership Act
        (RUPA), 766, 768n, 769n,
        772, 776n, 778n, 779n, 782n,
        787n, 792n, 794n
Revised Uniform Principal and
        Income Act, 1090n, 1091n
Revocation:
    of acceptance, 420–422
    declaration of, 1080
    of discharge, in bankruptcy, 642
    of gratuitous assignment, 315
    of offer, 220, 236–237, 240
    of will, 1078, 1080–1081, 1082
Revolutionary War, 84, 801
RICO. *See* Racketeer Influenced
        and Corrupt Organizations Act
Right(s). *See also* Remedy(ies)
    abuse of, 199
    of agent, 668–669
    air, as real property, 971
    appraisal, 848–850
    assignment of. *See* Assignment(s)
    to attorney in criminal
        procedures, 92, 181
    of bailee, 992–994
        *summarized,* 1003
    of bailor, 996
        *summarized,* 1003
    Bill of. *See* Bill of Rights
    of buyer, 420
    of contribution, 627–628, 793
    of corporate directors, 825–826,
        831

of creditors, 606–607, 1065
*Focus on Ethics* feature on,
653–656
of criminal defendant, 92,
181–186
of debtors, 592, 606–607, 628
of employees, 706–710, 718,
745–746
of entry, 1035
of first refusal, 838
fundamental, 100
of guarantor, 627–628
of HDC, limitation of, 493–494,
526–527, 628
of intended beneficiary, 322
insurance contracts and, 1061,
1064
of joint tenant, 974–975
among joint venturers, 753–755
to jury trial, 72, 92, 181
to leased property, transfer of,
1039
of minors, 262–267, 272
*Miranda,* 181–183
not subject to assignment, 315,
323
of ownership. *See* Property,
ownership of; Real property,
ownership interests in; Title
among partners, 773–777, 793
limited, 796
in personal property, 1046–1048
preemptive, 835–836
of principal, 668–670
privacy. *See* Privacy, right to
of redemption, 612
of reimbursement, 627
of secured party, 607–612
of seller, 415–416
of shareholders, 807n, 835–840,
841
of subrogation, 627
subsurface, as real property,
971–972
of surety, 627–628
survivorship, 974–975
of tenants, 1029–1030
of third parties, 313–325
*summarized,* 323
voidable, 637
under a will, 1081
to work, 718
Right to Financial Privacy Act
(1978), 160
Right-to-work laws, 718
Ripeness, 897
Risk:
assumption of, 119–121, 122,
476

*defined,* 1052
foreseeable, 1036, 1040–1041
of loss, 397, 400–406
international sales contracts
and, 404–405
shipper and, 1001
management of, 1052
pooling of, 1052–1053
Rivers and Harbors Appropriations
Act (1899), 928, 931
RMBCA. *See* Revised Model
Business Corporation Act
Robbery, 168, 173
Robinson-Patman Act (1936), 955
Rosenzweig, Michael, 636
Rule(s):
of evidence, 74
interpretative, 893
legislative, 889, 893
procedural, 893
of reason, 947
Rulemaking:
by administrative agencies, 887,
890–893
exempted, 890
formal, 890, 891
hybrid, 890, 891
informal, 890–891
negotiated, 890, 891, 893
notice-and-comment, 890
Rulemaking record, 891
RULPA (Revised Uniform Limited
Partnership Act), 795, 796,
797, 798
RUPA. *See* Revised Uniform
Partnership Act
Rustad, Michael, 472

**S**

S corporation, 750, 753, 758, 809,
812
S.A. (*sociedad
anonima*)(Argentina), 202
S.A. (*societe anonyme*)(Europe),
1120
S.C. (service corporation), 809
Sabbath laws, 293, 300
Safe Drinking Water Act (1974),
928, 932
Safety protection:
for consumers, 920
in workplace, 172–173, 711–713,
731, 745
principal's duty to provide, 668
Sale(s):
on approval, 402, 991
consumer, 459
consumer credit and, 440,

493–494, 526–527
consumer protection laws and,
911–913
*defined,* 366
door-to-door, 333n, 348n, 911
of goods. *See* Sales contract(s)
of land, 341–342, 350
mail-order, 911–912
by nonowners, 406–410
of real property. *See* Real
property, sale or transfer of
or return, 402–404
"short," 875n
telephone, 911–912
warranties of. *See* Warranty(ies)
Sales contract(s):
acceptance in, 371–376, 384
communication of, 372
means of, 371
anticipatory repudiation of,
422–425
battle of the forms and, 372
breach of,
buyer's, 404
damages for, 341
remedies for, 429–443
*summarized,* 441
risk of loss and, 404
seller's, 404
buyer's obligations and, 419–422
*summarized,* 423
buyer's right to cancel, 435
cancellation of, 433, 435
consideration in, 376–377, 384
preexisting duty and, 252n
formation of, 369–383
*summarized,* 384–385
time of, 388, 391
good faith and, 413–414
insurable interest and, 405
law of, *illustrated,* 215
versus contract law, illustrated,
379
merchants and, 307, 371, 375,
377, 384. *See also*
Merchant(s)
mirror image rule and, 238n,
372, 387–388
nonowners and, 406–410
offer in, 369–371, 384
merchant's firm, 371, 377, 384
mirror image rule and, 238n,
372, 387–388
options and, 370
parol evidence and, 379–382,
384
passage of title and, 395–397
*summarized,* 403
performance of, 413–425

repudiation of, 422–425, 435–437

risk of loss and, 397, 400–406

rules of construction and, 381–382

for sale on approval, 402, 991

for sale or return, 402–404

seller's obligations and, 414–419
  summarized, 423

seller's right to cancel, 433

Statute of Frauds and, 302, 306, 307, 377–379, 384

terms of. See Term(s)

unconscionability and, 382–383, 385

Sales warranties. See Warranty(ies)

''Sandwich'' generation, 744

Satisfaction:
  accord and, 253–254, 258, 333–334, 337
  of another, performance and, 331

Saudi Arabia:
  contract law in, 196
  intellectual property protection in, 201
  respondeat superior in, 687

Schools of jurisprudential thought, 3–4

Scienter, 283, 285, 1106

Scorched earth defense, 855

Screening procedures, preemployment, 709–710, 745

Scrivener's error, 276

Seal, contract under, 225

Search warrant, 98, 181, 183, 185, 893–894

Searches and seizures, unreasonable, constitutional prohibition of, 92, 98, 181, 707, 711, 802, 893–894

SEC. See Securities and Exchange Commission

Second Amendment, 92

Secondary boycotts, 718

Secondary liability:
  guaranty and, 625
  on negotiable instrument, 531–532, 550n

Secondary obligation, Statute of Frauds and, 303–304

Secured creditor. See Secured party

Secured party. See also Creditor(s)
  buyer versus, 602–606
  defined, 589
  remedies of, upon debtor's default, 607–612
    summarized, 611
  rights of, in collateral, 607–612
    summarized, 611

value given by, 592

Secured transactions, 588–614
  concept and terminology of, illustrated, 589
  default and, 607–612

Securities:
  debt, 818
  defined, 818
  equity, 818
  exempt, 864
  fixed-income, 818
  purchasers of, accountants' liability to, 1104
  registration of, 861–863
    exemptions from, 864
    illustrated, 866
  regulation of,
    by federal government, 860–877
    by state government, 877
  resales of, 866–867
  traded over the counter (OTC), 861

Securities Act (1933), 860, 861–867, 877, 913
  liability of accountants under, 1104–1105, 1108, 1109
  registration of securities under, 861–864

Securities Act Amendments (1975), 876

Securities and Exchange Commission (SEC), 9, 860–861, 886, 887, 889, 1104, 1105
  Regulation A of, 864
  Regulation D of, 864–867
  Rule 10b-5 of, 867, 869–874, 877, 1106–1108
    Section 16(b) of Securities Exchange Act and, illustrated, 876
  Rule 14a-8 of, 832

Securities Enforcement Remedies Act (1990), 861

Securities Exchange Act (1934), 860–861, 866, 867, 869–876, 877
  liability of accountants under, 1104, 1105–1108, 1109
  Section 10(b) of, 867, 869–874, 1106–1108, 1109
  Section 14(a) of, 875–876
  Section 16(b) of, 875
    SEC Rule 10b-5 and, illustrated, 876

Security agreement:
  defined, 589
  illustrated, 590

Security deposits, 1034

Security interest, 405, 491n
  assignment of, 606
  collateral and. See Collateral
  conflicting claims and, 601–606
    summarized, 605
  creation of, 589–592
  defined, 589
  in goods, buyer's right to, 435
  perfection of, 593–599
    automatic, 593, 604
    effective time of, 598–599
    exceptions to, 596–597
    by filing, 595–596
    methods of, illustrated, 596, 597
  purchase-money (PMSI), 592–593, 602, 604–605, 608
  scope of, 599–601

Self-defense:
  as defense to criminal liability, 178–179
  as defense against tort, 107

''Self-help'' repossession, 653, 689n

Self-incrimination, privilege against, 92, 98, 181, 802, 894n

Self-tender, 854

Seller's talk, 112, 281, 448

Seller:
  breach of sales contract by, 404
  duties of, 414–419
    to disclose, 1015–1016
    summarized, 423
  of letter of credit, 425
  lien of, 433
  as nonmerchant, acceptance and, 372, 375
  remedies of, 429–433
    summarized, 441
  retention of sold goods by, 409–410
  rights of, 415–416

''Selling short,'' 875n

Seniority system, 735

Sentencing, 186

Separation of powers, 85

Servants, borrowed, 687

Service corporation (S.C.), 809

Service marks, 143, 147

Services:
  goods versus, 366–368
  personal, contract for, 315, 317, 318, 323
  theft of, 159, 917

Servitude, equitable, 1022–1023

Settlement:
  agreement of, 333

of claims, consideration and, 253–256, 258

considerations regarding, 65

Seventh Amendment, 72, 92

Severable contracts, 299

Sex:

employment discrimination based on, 722–725, 1027

international business transactions and, 191

sexual harassment and, 33–34, 723–725, 743–744

insurance rates and, 1131

Sham transactions, 410

Share(s). *See also* Stock(s)

no-par, 840

par-value, 840

transfer of, 807–809, 838

valuation of, 838, 849–850

Shareholder(s):

agreement of, 807–909

voting, 835, 841

approval of, for merger, consolidation, or dissolution, 850–851

consolidations and, 848–851

corporation's duty to, 208

derivative suit of, 829, 839–840

liability of, 750, 751, 752, 810, 840–841

majority, duties of, 841–843, 881–882

meetings of, 830, 832, 841

mergers and, 848–851

minority, majority shareholders versus, 841–843, 881–882

powers of, 830, 841

of professional corporation, liability of, 810

proposals and, 832–833

rights of, 807n, 835–840, 841, 848–850

role of, 830, 832–843

*summarized,* 841

voting by, 834–835, 841

Shareholder voting agreements, 835, 841

*Shari'a,* 194

Shark repellant defense, 855

Shelter principle, 512n, 520

Sheriff's deed, 1012

Sherman Antitrust Act (1890), 294n, 756, 944, 945–947, 959, 964

extraterritorial effect of, 1123

Section 1 of, 945, 947–952, 956, 967

Section 2 of, 945, 952–955

Shipment:

C.O.D. (collect on delivery), 420

promise of, 371–372

prompt, 371–372

Shipment contracts, 397, 400, 415

Shipper, risk of loss and, 1001

''Short sale,'' 875n

Short-form merger, 848

Short-swing profits, 875

Sight draft, 489

Signature(s). *See also* Indorsement(s)

of agent, 533–534, 584–585

*defined,* 530

drawer's, drawee and, 534n

forged, 518, 556–561

of incorporators, 813, 815

liability and, 492, 506

merchant's firm offer and, 371, 377

on negotiable instrument, 492, 501, 506, 529–539

of testator on will, 1077

unauthorized, 534–536

Silence:

acceptance by, 242–243

as misrepresentation, 282–283

Simple contracts, 225

Simulated competition, 132

Single European Act, 1122

Sixth Amendment, 92, 181

Slander, 92, 109, 114

of quality, 136–137

of title, 136, 138–139

Small Business Administration Act (1958), 960

Small claims courts, 44

Smokeless Tobacco Health Education Act (1986), 911

Social hosts, 122

Social responsibility, *Focus on Ethics* feature on, 208–212

Social Security, 659, 713, 714

Social Security Act (1935), 713

Social Security Administration, 713, 901

*Sociedad anonima* (S.A.)(Argentina), 202

*Societe anonyme* (S.A.)(Europe), 1120

Society, corporation's duty to, 209–210

Software. *See* Computer software

Sold goods, 409–410

Soldiers' and Sailors' Civil Relief Act (1940), 337n

Sole proprietorships, 748–749

corporations and partnerships compared to, 751–753

privilege against self-

incrimination and, 98

Sovereign immunity, doctrine of, 1116, 1117–1118, 1132–1133

Sovereign power, 84

Spain:

Commercial Code of 1885 in, 192

European Union membership and, 204

torts in, 197

Special damages, 342

Special indorsements, 503–504, 506

Special partnerships, 794

Special warranty deed, 1011

Specially manufactured goods, 379

Specific devise, 1073, 1082

Specific performance, 11–12, 306, 341, 350, 352, 441

buyer's right to obtain, 434

Speech:

commercial, 93–94, 802

defamatory, 92

freedom of, 92–96, 109

political, 94–96, 802

privileged, 111

symbolic, 93

unprotected, 92–94

Spendthrift trust, 1089

Spouse, surviving, intestacy laws and, 1082–1083

Stakeholder(s), corporation's duty to, 208–209

Stale checks, 553, 563

Standard(s):

ethical. *See* Ethics

of reasonable care, bailments and, 991, 992

of review, 898–900

''Standard-form contracts,'' 288

Standing to sue, 43–44, 91, 313, 897

*Stare decisis,* doctrine of, 4–6, 8, 16, 192

State(s):

administrative agencies of, 901–903

bankruptcy exemptions of, 636n

chartering of corporations by, 812–813

consumer protection laws of, 921–922

courts of. *See* Court(s), state

employment discrimination laws of, 737–738

environmental regulation by, 941

inheritance taxes of, 1092

of mind, 166–167, 171n

police powers of, 87, 1018

regulatory powers of, 87–88, 757, 877
whistleblower laws of, 704
workers' compensation laws of, 713
zoning laws of, 1018–1021
Statement(s):
bank, examination of, 558–559, 563
of consideration, 493
continuation, 598
environmental impact (EIS), 928–929
of fact, 112, 281
financial,
reasonably foreseeable users of, 1102–1103, 1109
unaudited, 1096–1097
financing, 595
amendment of, 606
effective (EFS), 604
*illustrated,* 594
handwritten, 492
of intention, 231
opening, 74–75, 77
of opinion, 112, 281, 447–449, 458
proxy, 874–875
registration, 861–863
termination, 607
of value, 447–449
*Status quo,* 12
Statute(s), 7
accountants' potential liability under, 1104–1108, 1109
arbitration, 53
assignments prohibited by, 315, 323
building construction and maintenance, 1030–1031
close corporation, 806–807
contracts contrary to, 291–299, 300
dram shop, 122, 745
estray, 981–982
federal environmental,
*summarized,* 928
of Frauds. *See* Statute of Frauds
Good Samaritan, 123
insurance contracts and, 1058
licensing, 293–294, 300
of limitations. *See* Statute of limitations
limited liability company (LLC), 758–759
limited liability partnership, 780
long arm, 42
notice-race, 1012
product liability, 466

pure notice, 1012
race, 1012
recording, 1012
"rent strike," 1032
repair-and-deduct, 1033–1034
of repose, 474
whistleblower, 704–706, 742
workers' compensation, 713
Statute of Frauds, 291, 299, 301–307
agency formation and, 662n
applicability of, 302
assignments and, 314–315
bailments and, 991
CISG and, 388
equitable servitudes and, 1022–1023
estate debts and, 306
ethics and, 359–360
exceptions to, 302, 304–305, 306–307, 625
guaranty contract under, 625
history of, 299, 301
main purpose rule and, 304–305, 625
merchants and, 368n
one-year rule under, 301–303
parol evidence rule and, 308
provisions of, *summarized,* 302
quasi-contractual recovery and, 351
release of leased property and, 1042
rescission agreements and, 333
sales contracts and, 377–379, 384
surrender of leased property and, 1042
UCC and, 302, 306, 307, 388
writing requirements under, 302, 307
Statute of limitations, 11
contract discharge by, 334, 337
as defense to criminal liability, 181
promises to pay debts barred by, 256, 258
strict liability and, 471, 474
warranties and, 456–457
Statutory citations, 18
Statutory law, 2, 6, 7–9
how to find, 13
Statutory lien, 615
Statutory period of redemption, 623
Stock(s), 818–821, 860. *See also* Share(s)
bonds versus, 819
certificate of. *See* Stock certificate
common, 819, 821

with preferences, 821
preferred, 819, 820, 821
purchase of, 853–854
types of, *summarized,* 819
watered, 840–841
Stock certificate, 820, 835
*illustrated,* 820, 868
Stock subscriptions, 840
Stock warrants, 836
Stock-subscription agreement, 840
Stolen goods, receipt of, 168, 173
Stop-payment order, 553–556, 563
under EFTA, 573, 575
*illustrated,* 554
Storage lien, 618
Strict liability, 105, 123–125
common carriers and, 1000
environmental protection and, 926–927
innkeepers and, 1002
product liability and, 125, 466–471, 474–477. *See also* Product liability
Subagent, acts of, principal's liability for, 690
Subchapter S Revision Act (1982), 809
Subject matter:
destruction of,
impossibility of performance and, 335
offer termination by, 238, 239, 240
identity of, 288
jurisdiction over, 42–43, 51
value of, 288
Subleases, 1039
Subpoena, 893
Subrogation, surety's or guaranty's right of, 627
Subscriptions:
charitable, 257–259
stock, 840
Substance abuse, 733–734
Substantial evidence test, 898
Substantial performance, 329–331, 337
Substantive due process, 99–100
Substantive law, 9, 10
Substituted agreement. *See* Novation
Subsurface rights, as real property, 971–972
Sufferance, tenancy at, 1011
Sufficient interest, 405
Sum certain in money, 495n
Summary judgment, 70–71, 73
Summary jury trial (SJT), 59, 60
Summary procedures, in estate

administration, 1075
Summons, 66, 73
  *illustrated,* 68
Sunday closing laws, 96, 293, 300
"Super-discharge," 649
Superfund (Comprehensive
  Environmental Response,
  Compensation, and Liability
  Act) (CERCLA) (1980),
  934–935, 937–940, 964–965
Superfund Amendments and
  Reauthorization Act (1986),
  937
Superseding intervening force, 119
Supervening illegality, offer
  termination and, 239, 240
Supremacy clause, 89–90, 901–903
*Supreme Court Reporter*
  (S.Ct.)(West), 14, 16
Surety(ies):
  co-, 627
  defenses of, 627
  rights of, 627–628
Suretyship, 624–625
  parties to, *illustrated,* 625
Surplus, 836
Surrender by agreement, 1042
Surviving corporation, 847
Suspension of performance,
  336–337, 422
Sweden:
  European Union membership
    and, 204
  lawyers in, 194
Switzerland, limited liability
  companies (LLC) in, 759
Syllogism, 5
Symbolic speech, 93
Syndicate, 755

## T

Taft-Hartley Act (Labor-
  Management Relations Act)
  (1947), 718
Taiwan:
  employment law in, 199
  government regulation in, 203
Taking, of real property, through
  zoning laws, 1018
Tangible property, 971, 984, 989
  perfection of security interest
    and, 597
Target corporation, 846, 853
Tariffs, 1121
Tax Reform Act (1976), 160
Taxation:
  of corporations, 802
    S, 750, 753, 758

double-, 780, 802
estate, 1092
of exports, constitutional
  prohibition of, 1121
government's power to levy and,
  90–91
on imports, 1121
information return and, 749, 769
inheritance, 1092
Keogh plan and, 749
leased property and, 1034
limited liability company (LLC)
  and, 758–759
limited liability partnerships and,
  780
partnerships and, 749, 751, 752,
  769, 780
S corporations and, 750, 753,
  758
Social Security, 659, 713
of sole proprietorships, 751, 752
TCPA (Telephone Consumer
  Protection Act)(1991), 910
Technology licensing, 1119–1120
Telemarketing, 910
Telephone, privacy and, 708–709
Telephone Consumer Protection
  Act (TCPA)(1991), 910
Telephone sales, 911–912
Teller's check, 488, 489, 548,
  550–551, 555–556
Temporary impossibility, 336–337
Tenancy:
  in common, 975, 984
  by the entirety, 974, 975, 984
  joint, 974–975, 984
  in partnership, 768, 776
  periodic, 1010, 1042
  at sufferance, 1011
  at will, 1010
  for years, 1010
Tenant(s):
  failure of, to pay rent, 1034–1035
  interest of, transfer of, 1039
  liability of, 1038–1039
  remedies of, 1032–1034
  rights of, 1029–1030
Tender, 329
  of delivery, 414, 456
  of payment, 541–542
  self-, 854
Tender offer, 830, 853–854
Tentative trust, 1089
Tenth Amendment, 7, 92
Term(s):
  addition of, 240n
  ambiguous, 308
  consistent additional, 380
  contract, 397, 400

definiteness of, 236
disclosure of, under EFTA,
  572–573, 574, 580
incoterms as, 405
of offer, 231
open, 369–370
open delivery, 370
open price, 370
partnership for, 769
price, necessity of, 388
Term insurance, 1064
Termination:
  of agency relationship, 690–693
    *summarized,* 693
  of bailments, 999
  of contract. See Contract(s),
    discharge of
  of corporation, 854–858
  of easement, 1010
  of franchise, 761–763
  of insurance contract, 1065
  of lease, 1034, 1042–1043
  by notice, 1042
  of offer, 236–239
    methods of, *summarized,* 240
  of partnership, 786–794
  of profit, 1010
  of trust, 1091
Termination statement, 607
Territorial restrictions, antitrust law
  and, 950
Testamentary capacity, 1075–1077
Testamentary disposition, 1072
Testamentary gift, 976
Testamentary trusts, 1087, 1089
Testator, 1073
Theft:
  of check, 550–551
  computer-related, 158, 971
  of services, 159, 971
Third Amendment, 91, 92, 706
Third parties. See also Third party
  beneficiaries
  accountants' liability to,
    1100–1103, 1109
  apparent authority of agent and,
    675, 677–678, 684
  attorneys' liability to,
    1103–1104, 1109
  auditors' liability to, 1100–1103,
    1109
  crimes of, injuries caused by,
    1038
  as good faith purchasers, 263n
  notice to, of agency termination,
    692–693
  rights of, 313–325
    *summarized,* 323
  warranties and, 445, 453–454

Third party beneficiaries, 313, 320–324. *See also* Third parties
  defenses against, 322n
  incidental, 320, 322–324
  intended, 320–322
  rights of, 322
   *summarized*, 323
Thirteenth Amendment, 350n
Through bill of lading, 1002
Tie-in contracts, 1123
Tie-in sales agreement, 956
TILA. *See* Truth-in-Lending Act
Time:
  for acceptance of offer, 243–245
  commercially reasonable, 404
  for contract formation, 388, 391
  definite, payment at, 497–498, 501
  for delivery, 370
  employee compensation and, 716
  examination of bank statements and, 558–559, 563
  float, 569
  lapse of,
   agency termination by, 690, 693
   offer termination by, 238, 239, 240
  perceptions of, international business transactions and, 190
  of perfection of security interest, 598–599
  for performance, 332–333
  reasonable, 332, 400, 517
  commercially, 404
Time draft, 489
Time instruments, 487, 488
  overdue, HDC status and, 516–517, 519
Time insurance policy, 1068
Tippee, 873, 882
Tipper/tippee theory, 873, 882
TISA (Truth-In-Savings Act)(1991), 566
Title:
  document of, 414, 420, 596
   negotiability of, 999–1000
   UCC and, 999
  examination of, 1014–1015
  good, 445, 458
  marketable, 1014–1015
  passage of, in sales contracts, 395–397
   *summarized*, 403
  slander of, 136, 138–139
  void, 406
  voidable, 406

  warranty of, 445–446, 458
Title insurance, 1015
Tombstone ad, 862
Tort(s), 5, 105–127
  of agent, principal's liability for, 683–688
  business. *See* Business torts
  causation and, 117–119
  contract for commission of, 298, 300
  corporations and, 803
  damages and, 119
  defenses to. *See* Defense(s)
  of employee, employer's liability and, 687–688
  exception to employment-at-will doctrine based upon, 704
  of independent contractor, principal's liability for, 688–689
  injury requirement for, 119
  intentional. *See* Intentional torts
  law of, basis of, 106
  of minor, 268–269
  national laws of, comparison of, 197–198
  *per se*, 109–110
  of principal, 683
  strict liability and. *See* Strict liability
  toxic, 926–927
Tortfeasor, 106, 687
Totality of the circumstances rule, 1038, 1040
Totten trust, 1089–1090
Toxic chemicals, 936–940
Toxic substances, 936
Toxic Substances Control Act (1976), 928, 936
Toxic torts, 926–927
Toxic waste, 964–965
Trade:
  foreign. *See* International business transactions
  restraints on. *See* Restraints on trade
  usage of. *See* Usage of trade
Trade acceptance, 489, 531
  *illustrated*, 490
Trade associations, 948–950
Trade fixtures, 973
Trade libel, 136
Trade names, 148
Trade secrets, 156–157
Trade-off(s):
  business ethics and, 25–26
  *defined*, 25
Trademark(s), 143, 144–147, 148
  third party infringement claims

  and, 445, 458
Trademark Revision Act (1988), 147
Trading, insider. *See* Insider trading
Trading with the Enemy Act (1917), 1121
Transfer(s):
  bulk, 405–406
  fraudulent, 638–639
  fund. *See* Electronic fund transfer(s)
  by indorsement, 538
  by inheritance, 1016
  of negotiable instruments, 500–502, 538–541
  of partner's interest, dissolution of partnership by, 787
  preauthorized, 573, 580
  of real property. *See* Real property, transfer of ownership of
  of rights to leased property, 1039
  of shares, 807–809, 838
  wire. *See* Electronic fund transfer(s)
Transfer warranty, 504, 538–539
Traveler's check, 488, 490, 548–549
  *illustrated*, 549
Treasure trove, 982
Treaty:
  *defined*, 1114
  of Rome, 204, 1122
Treble damages, 575
Trespass:
  to land, 112–113, 114
  to personal property, 112, 113, 114
  to personalty, 113
Trespasser, 1036
Trial:
  criminal, 185–186
   lie-detector tests and, 706
  jury,
   right to, 72, 92, 181
   summary (SJT), 59, 60
  mini-, 59, 60
  new, motion for, 77–79, 81
Trial courts, 14
  federal, 46–47, 48
  state, 44, 47
Trial procedures, *summarized*, 77
Truncation, 558, 566n
Truncation agreement, 566
Trust(s), 1072, 1086–1091
  allocation between principal and income under, 1090–1091
  arrangement of, *illustrated*, 1086
  business, 755–756

charitable, 1089
constructive, 669, 1087–1088, 1089
*defined,* 1089
express, 1086–1087, 1089
implied, 1087–1089
income from, 1090–1091
*inter vivos,* 1075, 1086–1087, 1089
principal of, 1090–1091
resulting, 1088–1089
spendthrift, 1089
*summarized,* 1089
tentative, 1089
termination of, 1091
testamentary, 1087, 1089
Totten, 1089–1090
trustee and, 1072, 1090–1091
voting, 835, 841
Trust indorsements, 505–507
Trustee(s), 1072, 1090–1091
in bankruptcy. *See* Bankruptcy, trustee in
corporate directors and, 824
duties of, 1090
indenture, 1107n
liability of, 938–939
powers of, 1090
United States, 637
Truth, as defense against defamation, 111
Truth-in-Lending Act (TILA) (1968), 628, 912, 913–915, 916, 919
Truth-in-Lending Simplification and Reform Act (1980), 913n
Truth-In-Savings Act (TISA)(1991), 566
Truth-in-securities bill, 860
Tunisia, definition of tort in, 197
Turkey, limited liability companies (LLC) in, 759
Twenty-seventh Amendment, 91n
Tying arrangement, 956
Type I and Type II errors, 26
Typographic error, 306

# U

UCC. *See* Uniform Commercial Code
UCCC (Uniform Consumer Credit Code) (1968), 911, 922
unconscionability under, 298
UFTA (Uniform Fraudulent Transfer Act), 410
ULPA (Uniform Limited Partnership Act), 794, 796
*Ultra vires* doctrine, 803–804, 856

*Ultramares* rule, 1100–1102, 1109
Unanimous opinion, 19
Unanimous verdict, 186
Unaudited financial statements, 1096–1097
Unauthorized agent, 534
Unauthorized indorsements, 536–538
Unauthorized signatures, 534–536
Unauthorized transfers, 576–579, 580
Uncertain performance, consideration and, 253, 258
Unconditionality, of promise or order to pay, 493–495, 501
Unconscionability, 297–298, 300
contracts and, 251, 296, 300, 382–383, 385
ethics and, 358–359
genuineness of assent and, 286, 288
leases and, 1028
warranty disclaimers and, 456
Unconscionable contract, 251, 296, 300, 382–383, 385
Underwriter, 1053
Undisclosed principal, 680, 682–683, 690
Undue hardship, reasonable accommodation versus, 729–730, 732–734
Undue influence:
contract illegal through, 299, 301
genuineness of assent and, 285, 288
liability on negotiable instrument and, 526
wills and, 1078
Unemployment compensation, 714
Unenforceable contract, 226
Unfair advertising, 907–908
Unforeseen difficulties, consideration and, 251–252
Uniform Bills of Lading Act, 7
Uniform Commercial Code (UCC), 7, 8
addition of contract terms and, 240n
Article 2 of, 215, 365–369, 757
leases and, 383, 385
similarity of, to CISG, 1114–1115
Article 2A of, 997
Article 3 of, 365, 583
checks governed by, 547
revision and, 486–487
Article 4 of, 365, 583
checks governed by, 547
revision and, 486, 487

Article 4A of, 569
Article 6 of, 365n, 405–406
Article 7 of, 365, 999
Article 8 of, 365n, 596
Article 9 of, 365, 588, 589–592, 604, 618, 619, 653, 654
attachment under, 619
bulk transfers under, 405–406
buyer's obligations under, 419–422
*summarized,* 423
CISG versus, 387–388, 391
on commercial paper and banking, 485–587
common carriers, liability of, under, 1001
consumer protection provisions of, 911, 922
contract under seal and, 225n
documents of title and, 999
election of remedies under, 352–353
on electronic fund transfers, 569
entrustment rule and, 408
good faith and, 413–414
limitations and, 371
good faith purchasers and, 263n
history of, 364
implied warranty of merchantability under, bailments and, 997
insolvency under, 430
insurable interest under, 405
international business transactions and, 196, 1114–1115
limitations under,
good faith, 371
of remedies, 353
liquidated damages under, 346
merchant defined by, 368–369, 445n
mirror image rule and, 238n, 387–388
parol evidence rule and, 308
passage of title under, 395–397
*summarized,* 403
preexisting duty and, 252n
priority of liens under, 618
remedies under, for breach of contract, 429–443
election of, 352–353
limitation of, 353
*summarized,* 441
risk of loss under, 397, 400–406
on secured transactions, 588, 589–592
seller's obligations under, 414–419

*summarized,* 423

Statute of Frauds and, 302, 306, 307, 388

statute of limitations and, 334, 456–457

sufficiency of the writing under, 307

unconscionability under, 286, 298

waiver or renunciation by aggrieved party and, 254n

warranties under, 444–462

*summarized,* 458

Uniform Commercial Credit Code, 440

Uniform Consumer Credit Code (UCCC) (1968), 911, 922

unconscionability under, 298

Uniform Fraudulent Transfer Act (UFTA), 410

Uniform laws, 7. *See also* specific uniform laws

Uniform Limited Partnership Act (ULPA), 794, 796

Uniform Negotiable Instruments Law (1896), 7, 364, 486

Uniform Partnership Act (UPA), 7, 766, 767, 768, 769n, 772, 773, 774, 775, 776, 778, 779, 781, 782, 786, 787, 788, 791, 792, 795

Uniform Prenuptial Agreements Act (UPAA), 7, 306

Uniform Principal and Income Act, 1090n

Uniform Probate Code (UPC), 7, 1075, 1077, 1078, 1081, 1083, 1086, 1091

Uniform Residential Landlord and Tenant Act (URLTA), 1026, 1027, 1028, 1029, 1034

Uniform Sales Act (1906), 7, 364

Uniform Securities Act, 877

Uniform Status of Children of Assisted Conception Act, 7

Uniform Stock Transfer Act, 7

Uniform Surrogacy Act, 7

Uniform Trade Secrets Act, 156

Uniform Warehouse Receipts Act, 7

Unilateral contract, 219–220, 226

Unilateral mistakes, 275–277, 288

Unilateral rescission, 347n

Uninsured motorist coverage, 1068

Unintentional discrimination, intentional versus, 725–726

Union shop, 718

Unions, 716–718

United Kingdom. *See also* England

constitution of, 192

European Union membership and, 204

false statements on insurance applications in, 1062

warranties and puffing in, 449

United Nations:

Commission on International Trade Law of, 1114

Economic and Social Council of, 37

forged negotiable instruments and, 557

General Assembly of, 1114

United Nations Commission on International Trade Law, 576

United Nations Convention on International Bills of Exchange and International Promissory Notes (CIBN), 497

United Nations Convention on Contracts for International Sale of Goods (CISG), 195, 310, 360, 385–387, 1114–1115

notice of claims under, 438

remedies for breach under, 440–441

risk of loss under, 404–405

UCC versus, 387–388, 391

warranties under, 459–460

United Nations Convention on the Recognition and Enforcement of Foreign Arbitral Awards, 1126–1127

arbitration agreements and, 57

United States Army Corps of Engineers, 931

United States Bankruptcy Court, 46, 47

United States Claims Court, 46n

*United States Code* (U.S.C.), 8n, 13

Title 11 of, 631–632

*United States Code Annotated* (U.S.C.A.)(West), 13

United States Constitution. *See* Constitution, U.S.

United States Court of Federal Claims, 46, 47

United States Department of Agriculture, 604n

United States Department of Commerce, 1122

United States Department of Defense, 929

United States Department of Energy, 940–941

United States Department of Health

and Human Services, 711, 888, 911

United States Department of Housing and Urban Development (HUD), 912

United States Department of the Interior, 929

United States Department of Justice, 704, 711, 852, 861, 888, 914, 960

enforcement of antitrust laws by, 959–960, 967–968

merger guidelines of, 956–957

United States Department of Labor, 707, 711, 716, 731, 745, 887, 888, 929

United States Department of Transportation, 707

United States district courts, 46–47, 48, 631

*United States Statutes at Large,* 13

*United States Reports* (U.S.), 14, 16

United States Sentencing Commission, 173

United States Sentencing Guidelines, 36–37, 174

United States Supreme Court. *See* Court(s), United States Supreme

United States Tax Court, 46, 47

United States Trustee, 637

Universal Copyright Convention, 156

Universal defenses, 511, 520–523, 525

Universal life insurance, 1065

Unjust enrichment, 222, 226

Unlawful detainer, 1035

Unlimited guaranty, 625

Unliquidated debt, 254

Unprotected speech, 92–94

Unqualified indorsements, 504

Unqualified indorser, 531

Unreasonably dangerous products, 464, 468–469

Unsecured creditors, 640

Unsolicited merchandise, 912

UPA. *See* Uniform Partnership Act

UPAA (Uniform Prenuptial Agreements Act), 7, 306

UPC (Uniform Probate Code), 7, 1075, 1077, 1078, 1081, 1083, 1086, 1091

URLTA. *See* Uniform Residential Landlord and Tenant Act

Uruguay, definition of tort in, 197

Uruguay Round, 1122

Usage of trade:
  implied warranty arising from, 452, 458
  parol evidence and, 308, 380, 384
  ''Used Motor Vehicle Regulation Rule,'' 912
Used-car business, FTC regulation of, 912
Usury, 292, 300
Utilitarian ethics, 28
Utilitarianism, 28

## V

Valid contracts, 225–226
Validation notice, 918
Value:
  cash surrender, 1059
  of collateral, impairment of, 543–544
  fair, 1121
    of land, 1018
    of shareholder's shares, 848
  given by secured party, 592
  impairment of, 543–544
  of letter of credit, 425
  mistake in, 278–280, 288
  negotiable instrument as, 513–514
  statement of, 447–449
  of subject matter, 288
  taking for, HDC status and, 512–514, 519
    illustrated, 513
Vandalism, 158
Variance, zoning, 1019
Vegetation, as real property, 972
Venue, 43
Verdict:
  directed, 75
  jury, 77, 186
  unanimous, 186
Vertical mergers, 957
Vertical restraints, 948, 950–952
Vertically integrated firms, 950
Vesting, 322
Vicarious liability, 685
Vietnam War, 3, 93
Void contract, 226, 261, 272, 308
Void title, 406
Voidable contract, 226, 261, 272, 308, 673
Voidable obligations, HDC status and, 518
Voidable rights, 637
Voidable title, 406
*Voir dire,* 73, 78, 79
Voluntary bailment, 990n

Voluntary dissolution, 854–856
Voluntary intoxication, 177
Voting. *See also* Election
  by corporate directors, 825
  cumulative, 830n, 834–835, 841
    results of, *illustrated,* 835
  by shareholders, 834–835, 841
Voting lists, 834, 841
Voting trust, 835, 841
Voting trust certificate, 835
Voyage insurance policy, 1068

## W

Wage(s):
  garnishment of, 919, 922
  minimum, 716
Wage-Hour Law (Fair Labor Standards Act)(FLSA) (1938), 715–716
Wagner Act (National Labor Relations Act)(NLRA) (1935), 716, 744
Waiver, 33
  of breach, 353
  of defenses, 440
Wal-Mart, 210
Walsh-Healy Act (1936), 702
War, agency termination and, 692, 693
Warehouse companies, 1002
Warehouse receipt, 999
  *illustrated,* 399
Warrant(s):line general, 98
  search, 98, 181, 183, 185, 893–894
  stock, 836
Warranty(ies), 444–462
  of agent, 683
  breach of,
    buyer's customer's right to recover damages for, 438–439
    buyer's right to recover damages for, 438
    liability on negotiable instrument and, 523, 525
    recovery for, 471, 474
  *defined,* 435n
  disclaimers of, 445–446, 455–456, 458
  encoding, 565–566
  express, 446–449, 455, 458, 459, 922
  full, 459
  of habitability, 1015, 1032
  implied, 450–452, 455–456, 458
    arising from course of dealing or trade usage, 452, 458

  of fitness for a particular purpose, 452, 455, 458
    leased goods and, 475
  of habitability, 1015, 1032
  of merchantability, 366–367, 450–452, 455–456, 458, 997
  international business transactions and, 459–460
  against liens, 445, 458
  limited, 459
  overlapping, 453
  presentment, 539–541
  product liability and, 463–464
  retention, 565–566
  statute of limitations and, 456–457
  *summarized,* 458
  third parties and, 445, 453–454
  of title, 445–446, 458
  transfer, 504, 538–539
  unconscionability and, 456
Warranty Act. *See* Magnuson-Moss Warranty Act
Warranty deed, 1011
  *illustrated,* 1012
Warranty liability:
  of bailor, 997
  on negotiable instrument, 538–541
Washington International Center, 189–190
Waste, tenant's duty not to commit, 1030
Water(s):
  drinking, 932–933
  navigable, 931–932
Water pollution, 931–933, 965–966
Water Quality Act (1987), 931
Watered stock, 840–841
Webb-Pomerane Act (1918), 960
Welfare, consumer, 33–34
West Publishing Company, 13, 14
Wetlands, 931
Whistleblower Protection Act (1989), 704
Whistleblowing, 30, 175
  *defined,* 703
  statutory protection for, 704–706, 742
White knight defense, 846, 855
White-collar crimes, 167–176
  *Emerging Trends* feature on, 174–175
  crimes, *summarized,* 173
Whole life insurance, 1064
Will(s), 1072–1081. *See also* Inheritance
  codicil to, 1080, 1082

creation of easement or profit by, 1009
*defined,* 1072
destruction of, 1078, 1082
formal requirements of, 1077–1078
gifts by, 1073–1074, 1082
holographic, 1077, 1082
*illustrated,* 1079
intestacy laws and, 1072, 1081–1086
nuncupative, 1077, 1078, 1082
olographic, 1077
oral, 1077
partnership at, 769, 772, 787
personal property acquired by, 980, 984
probate of, nonprobate versus, 1074–1075
publication of, 1078
revocation of, 1078, 1080–1081, 1082
rights under, 1081
signature requirement for, 1077
*summarized,* 1082
tenancy at, 1010
testamentary capacity and, 1075–1077
testamentary trusts and, 1087
undue influence and, 1078
witness requirement for, 1077–1078
William the Conqueror, 4
Winding up of partnership, 790–792
Wire and Mail Fraud Act (WMFA) (1988), 169
Wire transfer. *See* Electronic fund transfer(s)
Withdrawal:
 check and, 514
 direct, 570
 of partner, dissolution of partnership by, 787
Witness(es):
 examination of, 75, 77
 opposing, constitutional right of cross-examination of, 92, 181
 to will, 1077–1078
WMFA (Wire and Mail Fraud Act) (1988), 169
Women, in business, international business transactions and, 191
Wool Products Labeling Act (1939), 910–911
Workers' compensation, 713, 1069
Working papers, 1108, 1110
Workouts, 643
Workplace, health and safety in, 172–173, 711–713, 731, 745
 principal's duty to provide, 668
World Bank, 191
World Trade Organization (WTO), 1122
World War II, 3
Writ:
 of attachment, 620–621
 of *certiorari,* 50–51, 81
 of execution, 616, 619, 621, 624
Wrongful discharge, 33, 703
Wrongful entry into business, 132–133
Wrongful interference:
 with business relationship, 131
 with contractual relationship, 129–131
 defenses to, 131–132
Wrongful payment, 554, 563
WTO (World Trade Organization), 1122

# Y

*Year Books,* 4
Years, tenancy for, 1010

# Z

Zoning laws, 1018–1021
Zoning variance, 1019